Peterson's Sports Scholarships & College Athletic Programs

5th Edition

PETERSON'S

A ⓝelnet. COMPANY

About Peterson's, a Nelnet company

Peterson's (www.petersons.com) is a leading provider of education information and advice, with books and online resources focusing on education search, test preparation, and financial aid. Its Web site offers searchable databases and interactive tools for contacting educational institutions, online practice tests and instruction, and planning tools for securing financial aid. Peterson's serves 110 million education consumers annually.

For more information, contact Peterson's, 2000 Lenox Drive, Lawrenceville, NJ 08648; 800-338-3282; or find us on the World Wide Web at www.petersons.com/about.

Editor: Joe Krasowski; Production Editor: Craig Heinz; Copy Editor: Sally Ross; Research Project Manager: Daniel Margolin; Programmer: Phyllis Johnson; Manufacturing Manager: Ivona Skibicki; Composition Manager: Linda M. Williams; Interior Design: Christina Chattin.

ISSN 1069-1383
ISBN-13: 978-0-7689-1524-2
ISBN-10: 0-7689-1524-4

Printed in the United States of America

10 9 8 7 6 5 4 3   08 07 06

Fifth Edition

Contents

Foreword

Maintaining a competitive athletic program at an institution of higher learning is a difficult balancing act. As early as 1906, Palmer Pierce, the first president of the National Collegiate Athletic Association (NCAA), recognized the precarious nature of intercollegiate athletics and warned against the dangers of professionalism, recruiting abuses, and the corrosion of academic values in the pursuit of victory on the playing field. William Preston Few, President of Duke University, also asserted during that time, "There is good in intercollegiate athletics, when properly conducted. They have made considerable contributions to American college life and deserve to be saved from the perils that threaten them and the evils that now actually beset them."

Are the Awards Worth the Risks?

Although the potential for conflict between the academic mission of a university and the goals of its athletic department is not a new phenomenon, the conflict has intensified over the past century as the financial stakes of college athletics have risen exponentially. The revenue produced by winning athletic programs has reached unprecedented levels—both for individuals and for institutions. While this increased revenue is not inherently corrosive of academic values, recent scandals in a variety of schools around the country certainly illustrate the dangers that can accompany the pursuit of victory to the exclusion of all else.

Given this potential danger, what is the justification for maintaining a competitive athletic program on campus?

Why accept the very real risks often associated with such an endeavor? The answer is quite simple—the potential benefits are many and well worth the risk. As theologian and author Michael Novak once said, "Were I the president of a new state university or private college . . . I would strongly urge the development of a high-level athletic program within the realistic means of the school. The costs are great, but so are the returns—the rejoicing of the human spirit, the unifying of many."

Are the Awards Worth Saving?

The clichés about the value of athletics are true and enduring. Athletics confer many gifts, including self-discipline, teamwork, perseverance, effort in the face of adversity, development of a healthy lifestyle, and the creation of a sense of common purpose and community. From ancient Greece to the modern world, the conviction has persisted that athletics can play an important role in physical, intellectual, and emotional development.

President Few was right. For all their potential problems, college athletics are worth saving. And it is incumbent upon those of us responsible for the maintenance of athletic programs to continue the balancing act to ensure that all the richness of sport in an educational setting—the traditions, the rivalries, the opportunities for personal growth—are preserved for our current student-athletes, for their children, and for their children's children.

Joseph Alleva
Director of Athletics, Duke University

A Note from the Peterson's Editors

Over the years, athletic scholarships have opened up opportunities for countless students interested in attending college. Scholarships allow athletically gifted students to defray many of the costs of a college education while participating in a sport they love, at a higher level of competition. When viewed with the proper perspective, athletic scholarships can greatly enhance the college experience.

Because the overwhelming majority of student-athletes will not make professional careers out of the sports they pursue in college, it is essential that anyone who is considering accepting an athletic scholarship also thinks seriously about how to secure the skills needed to earn a living in a field other than athletics once college is over.

That is why Peterson's is publishing this guide. There are four introductory sections that provide important information to help you win a sports scholarship and succeed as a student-athlete. However, these sections offer more than just the tricks-of-the-trade when it comes to winning a sports scholarship—they also offer real insight from coaches and athletic directors into what qualities they look for when recruiting prospective student-athletes.

THE RECRUITING PROCESS goes beyond the technical aspects of recruiting and includes tips on how to handle the campus visit and succeed as a nonscholarship athlete. Through the words of several athletic directors at major institutions, this section also discusses the importance of maintaining balance and discipline in athletics, in the classroom, and in life.

COACH'S FORUM provides real insight from college coaches into how they recruit and what they look for in the perfect student-athlete.

The **NCAA GUIDE FOR THE COLLEGE-BOUND STUDENT-ATHLETE** informs prospective student-athletes about eligibility requirements and the role of the Initial-Eligibility Clearinghouse.

Finally, the **How To Use This Guide** article explains the criteria used to select the programs included in this guide, data collection procedures, and how to search for a specific athletic program.

If participating in intercollegiate athletics is a dream of yours, follow that dream. However, remember that college is more than just an avenue to playing the sport you love. It is also about creating a well-rounded, intelligent, and civically responsible individual.

Peterson's publishes a full line of resources to help guide you through the college search and selection and financial aid processes. Peterson's publications can be found at your local bookstore, library, and high school guidance office or online at www.petersons.com.

The editors at Peterson's wish you the best of luck in your search for the right athletic program and scholarship opportunity for you!

the *Recruiting* Process

Finding Your Perfect Fit in College Athletics

Edgar Johnson
Director of Athletics, University of Delaware

The decision about which type of college or university to attend is based on more than the strength of the academic environment, the richness of the academic traditions, and the academic challenges an institution offers. It is also based on myriad other nonacademic factors.

Does the School Fit?

The quality of the campus experience, the attractiveness of residence life facilities, the availability of recreational facilities, the amount of participation in intercollegiate athletics, and the opportunities to study abroad and participate in undergraduate research all can contribute to your decision on what college or university to attend. For sure, your decision will need to be based on personal likes, dislikes, talents, and ambitions. If you wish to participate in college athletics, it is imperative that you pick an institution that is the right fit for you—both academically and athletically.

Where Can I Succeed?

One of the most important decisions is to decide at what level you can or want to participate. The NCAA comprises three Divisions—I, II, and III— each of which presents diverse athletic challenges and various levels of scholarship support.

- Division I institutions are the most highly competitive and offer the greatest amount of athletic scholarship aid.
- Division II athletic programs are somewhat less competitive and less recognizable, especially by the national media, and generally award about half the number of athletic scholarships that Division I institutions do.
- Division III institutions provide competitive opportunities but are not permitted to offer athletic scholarships.

However, financial aid based on academic merit and the student's financial need is available.

In addition to athletic scholarships, all NCAA member institutions are permitted to award merit- and need-based financial aid to recruited student-athletes. The combination of a partial athletic scholarship and other forms of financial aid is commonly offered to student-athletes. Athletic scholarships are awarded solely on athletic ability and may come attached with stringent obligations that interfere with student-athletes' academic or nonacademic interests. That is why student-athletes need to be both organized and disciplined in order to achieve both academic and athletic success.

College Is Much More Than Athletics

Academics are emphasized in all three NCAA divisions and are measured by retention and graduation rates. For Division I and II prospective student-athletes, the satisfactory completion of initial-eligibility requirements and certification as a qualifier by the NCAA Clearinghouse is mandatory to establish eligibility prior to being eligible for financial aid, practice, and competition during the first academic year in residence. (See "NCAA Initial-Eligibility Clearinghouse" on page 27.) Every high school guidance counselor has the required forms that must be sent to the National Clearinghouse for initial eligibility certification. But keep in mind that the prospective student-athlete must assume responsibility for the timely completion of the initial eligibility certification process.

How Do I Decide?

There are many colleges and universities that sponsor highly competitive intercollegiate athletics programs. If participation on a varsity team is an important requisite of the collegiate experience, you should choose an institution where there is a strong possibility that you will have opportunities to compete. Most prospective students are not blue-chip athletes and may not be highly recruited. Therefore, it is important to know if you may walk on or try out for a varsity team before the choice of a university or college is finalized. If you are not a recruited athlete, it is always best to meet with the coach and discuss your interest in competing and provide information on your competitive background. It is also important to ask about the team's tryout policy and how successful previous walk-ons have been in the specific sports program in which you are interested. The more you know about the coach, the team, and its policies the less stressful the tryout experience will be and the more certain you'll find the right fit.

If your talent, ability, and commitment allow you to compete at the Division I level, you owe it to yourself to pursue that opportunity. However, if your talent and/or commitment are not compatible with Division I competition, don't despair. Division II and III athletic programs are just as challenging and fulfilling and offer many of the same competitive and championship opportunities.

Whether you are a blue-chip athlete or a walk-on, the best athletic experience comes from participation in intercollegiate athletics—regardless of the level. The benefits are lifelong. Commit yourself to having a great academic experience and prepare yourself for the next forty or more years of your professional life. But also enjoy the experience that intercollegiate athletics provide for you over the next four years. There is nothing quite so challenging and rewarding. It will change your life forever.

You Can't Take the Student Out of the Student Athlete

John P. Hardt
Director of Athletics and Recreation, Bucknell University

As a prospective student athlete, you have many decisions to make when it comes to choosing a college. As you can plainly see by the size of this reference guide, your options are plentiful. With guidance from your parents, coaches, and teachers, you should gather as much information as you can about the colleges that interest you and carefully weigh the programs they offer against your own interests.

The prioritization of the factors upon which you will ultimately base your decision will be uniquely yours. Level of competition (Division I, II, III, or NAIA), cost, financial aid, school size, geography, and facilities are all important factors to consider. While each of these is vitally important, allow me to suggest that you make an institution's ability to provide a quality balance of athletics and academics a key component of your search. Even if you are part of the extremely small percentage of young athletes with professional sports aspirations, you will be well served to consider your educational progression when making your college choice.

As director of athletics and recreation at Bucknell University, I have seen first-hand the benefits of a university mission that stresses a balance among academics and extracurricular activities. Bucknell has an undergraduate enrollment of 3,350, and nearly 800 of these students, or about 25 percent, are varsity athletes. More than 2,500 students participate in athletics, either at the varsity, club, or intramural level.

Over the past thirty years, Bucknell has been a model of success not only on the athletic fields but also for producing high-quality scholars. Since 1970, Bucknell has ranked third among all Division I institutions, with 107 Academic All-America selections, and recently Bucknell was awarded the prestigious Academic Achievement Award from the NCAA for leading the nation, with a perfect 100 percent student-athlete graduation rate. In addition, Bucknell has captured the Patriot League Presidents' Cup signifying overall athletic excellence, ten times in thirteen years.

Achievements like these do not happen by accident. Bucknell, like many schools at all levels across the nation, provides a structure that allows its student-athletes to excel both in the classroom and on the athletic fields. If academics is high on your priority list during your college search, do some investigation on what types of academic support is available for student-athletes at your schools of interest.

Students Are Priorities

First and foremost, the welfare of the student-athlete is the number one priority in all of Bucknell's athletics planning. Practices and games are scheduled in such a way as to minimize missed class time. An academic enhancement program is in place to monitor and counsel student-athletes who are having difficulties with their studies. A Sideline Coaches Program allows members of the faculty and staff to spend behind-the-scenes time with a team, fostering positive relationships between the athletics program and the academic and administrative community. A new faculty mentoring program is in the works that will assign faculty members to each varsity program to act as liaisons between student-athletes and their professors and deans. All of these initiatives are designed to keep the lines of communications open between student-athletes, coaches, and faculty members.

I understand the significant role athletics play in a well-rounded education, and these programs are good examples of the type of support that institutions like Bucknell have in place to ensure that mission.

Athletics promote many specific learning outcomes: discipline, teamwork, performance under pressure, concentration, preparation (both mental and physical) for an all-consuming event, time management and prioritization, awareness of the implications of choices made (sometimes through the immediate feedback of wins and losses or playing vs. riding the bench), resilience, perseverance, and sportsmanship. As the late commissioner of Major League Baseball and Yale University President A. Bartlett Giamatti said, "Athletics teaches lessons valuable to the individual by stretching the human spirit in ways that nothing else can."

The student-athlete experience that we promote at Bucknell is far from what you may read about in your daily newspaper. Social misconduct on the part of coaches and student-athletes, zero-percent graduation rates, and charges of academic fraud do exist in college athletics. What those negative headlines have masked, however, is the fact that many institutions—more than likely the vast majority of schools at all levels of college athletics—are conducting their business aboveboard while providing their student-athletes quality educations. With some research on your part, they are easy to find. Yes, winning games is extremely important at schools like Bucknell but not at the expense of the overall mission. With a little legwork on your part, you can find a college that matches your needs both athletically and academically.

Not a Blue-Chip Recruit? Why Not Walk On?

Receiving an athletic scholarship today is not as easy at it was 25 years ago. In fact, the number of scholarships has decreased in many sports and competition is fierce for the few scholarships that are available. However, even if you are not offered an athletic scholarship, you do have options. You can do exactly what thousands of other student-athletes are doing at every level of competition and in every sport—become a walk-on.

"Walking on" provides non-recruited high school athletes the opportunity to play a sport for a particular school. Simply stated, walking on means trying out for a team. As a "walk-on," you'll receive many of the same benefits as recruited players, you just won't be rewarded with a scholarship for your on-field efforts. Not only is the ability to walk on a benefit to student-athletes, it also a major benefit to college coaches. For example, an athlete may be quite talented, but not good enough to earn a scholarship. The limited number of scholarships available to college athletic programs makes accepting walk-ons an important part of an athletic program.

Also, college coaches tend to be territorial in their recruiting. Although they may search the entire nation, particularly if they have a major college program, they usually maintain most of their contacts with high schools and junior colleges within their immediate regions, their own states, and four or five adjacent states. This is an important consideration for potential walk-ons. Just because you weren't recruited by a particular school isn't necessarily an indictment of your athletic ability. It could simply mean that the school made a mistake in its evaluation or simply didn't have the resources to recruit in your area.

If participating in collegiate sports has always been your dream, but you haven't had college coaches beating down your door with full athletic scholarship offers, don't become discouraged. Here are some tips to help you land a spot on a team as a walk-on:

- **Evaluate your talents objectively.** Don't over-evaluate your ability. This could result in unattainable expectations and disappointment.

- **Do your homework.** Find out if the program(s) you are considering have a history of playing walk-ons.

- **Make sure the school offers your desired major.** The college search and selection process, whether scholarship or non-scholarship, must be the same.

- **Contact the coach of each school you are considering.** Determine your opportunity to play. Make sure the coach wants you to walk on. Do not try to walk on at a school after a coach has shown little or no interest in you.

- **Once you have decided on a school, call the college coach and get your name on the roster.** You will receive the summer mailings and, in effect, become a full-fledged member of the team. In fact, by the time the team members discover your walk-on status, you will already be well accepted by them.

Note: If you are not awarded an athletic scholarship during your first year as a student-athlete, there may still be good news on the horizon. Many walk-ons are rewarded for their hard work and dedication with an athletic scholarship in subsequent years.

Although walking on may not seem as glamorous as being a highly recruited superstar who is courted by every college in the country, if your goal is to compete in collegiate athletics, it may be your best—and only—option.

Coach's Forum

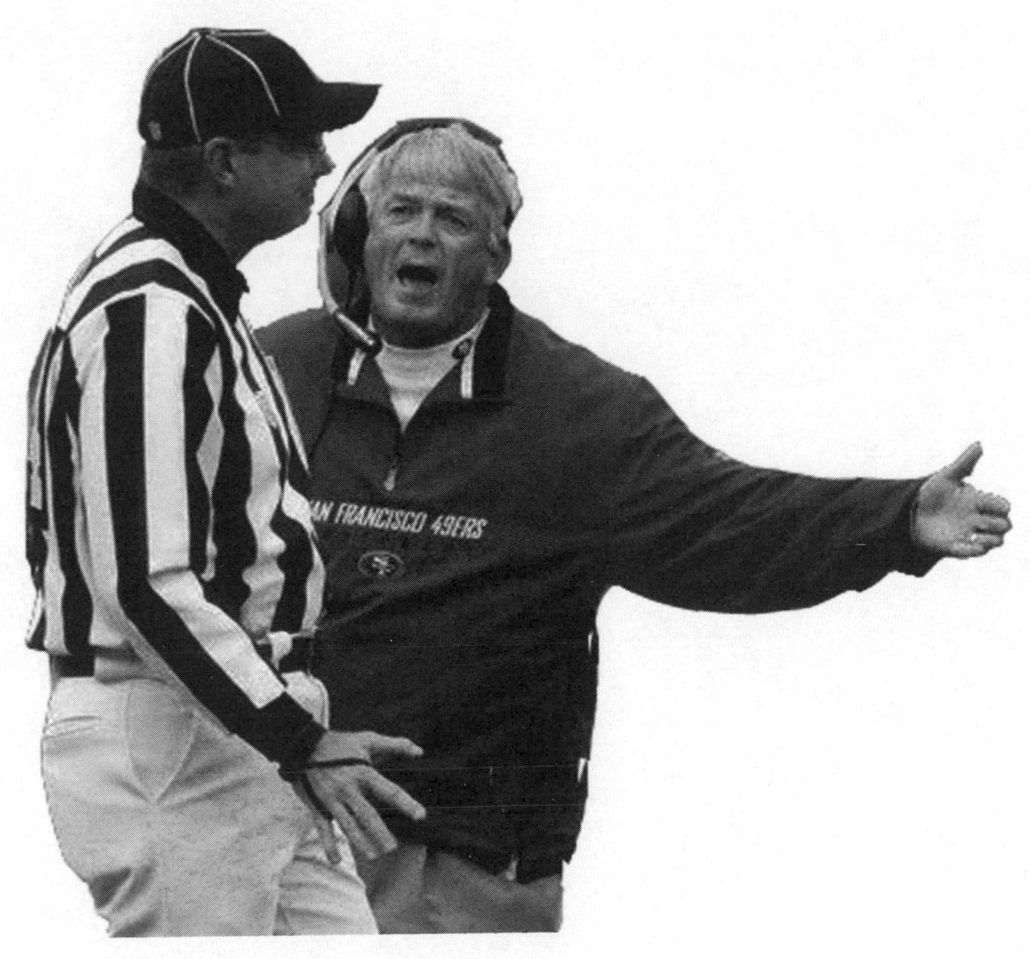

Coach's Forum

A coach is the best source for information about a sports program at a particular college or university. This article gives insight from actual coaches into what they really look for when recruiting prospective student-athletes.

Andy Talley
Head Football Coach
Villanova University

Villanova Football has a proud history. Over the past nineteen years, the program has won four league championships and has made six NCAA playoff appearances. In 1997, the team was ranked number one in the country for seven weeks. In 2002, Villanova played in the national semifinals and was named the East Coast Athletic Conference Team of the Year.

In addition to its winning tradition, the program is proud of the many great individuals who have gone on to succeed in the NFL, including Oakland Raiders Hall-of-Fame defensive end Howie Long, Philadelphia Eagles running back Brian Westbrook, and Atlanta Falcons wide receiver Brian Finneran.

Although Villanova is extremely proud of the accomplishments of these players, the program would not be as successful as it is without the contribution of every student-athlete who works tirelessly to succeed both academically and athletically.

Admissions

Admission standards at Villanova University are very competitive, and recruited athletes can sometimes be given special academic consideration. That is not to say that prospective student-athletes are not required to meet certain academic standards. Assuredly, one's SAT scores, classroom work, GPA, and the strength of the high school curriculum play important roles in Villanova's decision to accept or reject a prospective student-athlete. However, student-athletes are also considered based on their performance in athletics—a factor that often carries equal weight as academics when it comes to an admissions decision.

Recruiting

Because of its high academic standards, it is imperative that Villanova recruits nationally. During the recruiting process, we look for students who carry a strong B average in their high school course work and at least a 1000 SAT score. Just as important, however, is someone who possesses great character and a strong desire to succeed.

After extensive junior recruiting, calling recruiting services' lists, and writing and talking to high school coaches, we prepare our follow-up list. Once we have personally visited with a player and have evaluated his film, we invite him to campus. The campus visit is critical for us because we want to find out how a player will fit into our setting from an academic, social, and athletic perspective. It is after the campus visit when we usually make our decision on whether or not to offer the student an athletic scholarship.

College Search Advice

Potential college football players should start their search immediately following the fall football season of their junior year. It is important that players evaluate themselves honestly when it comes to determining the level at which they are able to compete. After a frank discussion with your high school coach, you will have a better understanding of what level matches your ability. Don't make the mistake of narrowing your choices to only those schools that match your athletic ability. It is important to determine where you will be able to succeed academically as well. You don't want to have to stop playing football because you are struggling or even failing to fulfill your academic requirements.

Once you have an idea of which schools match both your athletic and academic needs, start planning ahead. If you want to get the attention of college coaches and win an athletic scholarship you must not only perform athletically, you must also bring your athletic ability to the attention of prospective college coaches. A videotape of your high school highlights is a great way to bring attention to your ability. In fact, creating both a highlight tape along with two game films is advisable.

If a college invites you for a visit, take your parents or guardians. They can provide some valuable insight. Be sociable and respectful toward everyone you meet. Be on time for all meetings and get all of your questions answered. Since you only have five official visits to determine whether a particular college is the right fit, find out as much as you can during each visit—don't let them go to waste. Talk to the academic adviser and professors on the campus. It is important to understand the academic expectations of the university. Also, talk to players about academic advisement and tutorial help. When talking to players and coaches, try to get a true evaluation of the position for which you are being recruited and find out how many players are already in the program or are being recruited to play the same position. This should play a role in your ultimate decision to compete athletically at a particular institution.

Deciding on a college or university to attend as a student-athlete is a major life decision. Choose an institution for the right reasons—not just because you are impressed by the recruiter but rather because the institution and athletic program offer everything you want. Consult with your parents and coaches to help you reach the proper decision. When you finally make your decision, you should understand the commitment you have made not only to the institution and athletic program but also to yourself and to your future.

Although athletics is an important factor in the development of a well-rounded person, at Villanova, we constantly emphasize, both before and during a prospective student-athlete's visit, that academics come first. Moreover, student-athletes also need to understand that we are not just giving them a scholarship based on their athletic ability, they will have to earn it both on the field and in the classroom.

Becky Burleigh
Women's Head Soccer Coach
University of Florida

The University of Florida's (UF) soccer program has taken the express route to elite status. UF stunned the soccer community in 1998 by claiming its first NCAA championship in just its fourth season. In addition to winning an NCAA title, UF has also made two College Cup (Final Four) appearances, won six Southeastern Conference Tournament titles, and appeared in seven NCAA tournaments—all in just nine years of existence.

I joined the program in 1994 and coached the first UF women's soccer team in 1995. The following year was the first time we went undefeated in both the Southeast Conference and tournament competition. We did this again from 1998 to 2000. In 1998, I became the second woman coach to lead a team to the national semifinals and the first to win an NCAA title. In 2001, UF made its second College Cup appearance, losing in overtime to eventual champion Santa Clara University.

Prominent UF alumnae include two current U.S. National Team members, forward Abby Wambach and defender Heather Mitts. Former UF forward Danielle Fotopoulos holds the NCAA Division I scoring record. Fotopoulos was also a member of the 1999 U.S. World Cup championship team. The program also boasts two former NCAA Student-Athlete of the Year award winners, Erin Baxter in 1998 and Sarah Yohe in 1999. Both Baxter and Yohe, along with teammates Wambach, Mitts, Fotopoulos, Meri Flaherty, and Karyn Hall all participated in the WUSA, the women's U.S. professional soccer league.

Admissions

All students at the University of Florida are measured by a competitive standard that varies from year to year based on the level of the pool of applicants. Any student, including a student-athlete, who does not meet that year's standard has the option of having his or her application reviewed by an admissions committee composed of university faculty and administrators. The 2003 GPA range was between 3.7 and 4.2; SAT scores were between 1200 and 1370; and ACT scores were between 26 and 30.

Recruiting

Every coach looks for different attributes in the student-athletes they recruit. At the University of Florida, we emphasize finding players who possess a "specialty," as opposed to being average at a variety of skills. We want student-athletes who are the best in the area, the state, or the country in any particular skill. That might mean they are the fastest or the strongest, the best with the ball at their feet, students of the game, or the most competitive. Intangibles such as leadership, desire, and work ethic play a large role in our recruitment process, as do other factors including character, academic success, and coachability. Much of this information is garnered from coaches (both high school and club), teachers, guidance counselors, family, and friends.

In order to locate a potential recruit, we attend a variety of tournaments—both high school and club. We also use Olympic Development Program (ODP) events and All-Star events to try to locate that special student-athlete. We

Questions to Ask When Considering an Athletic Program

Here are some of the key questions prospective student-athletes should ask when considering a college or university athletic program.

The Institution

- How large is the student body?
- Does the institution offer what you want: major, academic and housing facilities, type of environment, and student services?
- Does the school have character and spirit?
- What is the social climate like at the school?

Location

- How far from home is the school?
- What are the surroundings of the university like?
- Is the campus safe?
- Is the school in an area you wish to live? (urban, rural, suburban)

Academics

- What percentage of student-athletes graduate within four years?
- What is the graduation rate and grade point average of athletes in your particular sport? Do they major in a variety of fields?
- What academic support services are available for student athletes? (academic advising, preferred scheduling, tutoring, study table, etc.) Are these services available to both scholarship and non-scholarship athletes?

Athletics

- What is the athletic tradition of the institution? How successful is the program? Is the program a consistent winner? Is it in a rebuilding mode?
- What is the reputation of the head coach and does he or she have job security?
- What is the reputation of the assistant coaching staff and how long has it been together?
- What are the facilities like? (stadium, strength-training program, medical facilities, etc.)

- To which athletic association, division, and/or conference does the team in your sport belong? How competitive is this group considered nationally?
- What is the process for qualifying for the team?
- How soon can you expect to play?
- Can you participate in two or more sports?
- How much time per week can you expect to practice during the season? Out of season? How long is the season? Will it be possible for you to manage athletics and keep up with studies in your planned major?
- How much travel is involved? Does the institution pay for all traveling expenses or is the team required to raise money?
- What coaching methods are used and what is the coach's philosophy? Is specific behavior, dress, or diet required of team members? Are there specific weight restrictions?
- How much media exposure does the program receive?
- What are the current players like?
- What is the school's red-shirt policy?
- Does the program have a history of NCAA infractions? Is the program currently or has it ever been under investigation or on probation?

Athletic Scholarships

- What types of athletic scholarships are offered? What does a full scholarship cover? Is summer school education part of the scholarship offer? What does a partial scholarship cover? If tuition and housing expenses increase, does the amount of the scholarship also increase?
- How many scholarships are awarded in your sport?
- What are the criteria for renewing a scholarship? (Most athletic scholarships are awarded for one academic year at a time and are renewed if the college's criteria are met.)
- What happens in cases of injury? Would the scholarship be withdrawn or not renewed? (NCAA rules do not permit colleges to promise that scholarships will be continued despite injuries, but you can find out what has happened in past cases.)
- What is the college's general policy regarding withdrawal of scholarships due to poor grades or disciplinary infractions?

---

attempt to recruit our state and home area first, then our region and beyond. Players and parents should realize that only two coaches from an institution can recruit at any one time, so it is imperative for the student-athlete to keep coaches of schools in which they have interest up to date with schedules of upcoming events. An effective and easy way to maintain communication is through e-mail, although coaches can only answer them after September 1 of your junior year.

Balancing Athletics and Academics

At UF, we talk about the three S's—school, soccer, and social life. There is plenty of time for all three, but balance and priority are keys. College is a whole new experience, and students are confronted with a variety of choices throughout their college career. The importance of balancing athletics and academics and setting priorities cannot be underestimated.

Student-athletes face the burden of managing their time wisely, since travel, practice, and games take up a significant portion of their time. For example, when playing on the road, our players leave on Thursday night and don't return until Sunday evening. However, there is plenty of down time for them to study, so we insist that study materials be brought along on all away games. To meet the demands of athletics and academics, student-athletes need to be creative. Many of our players submit their course work via the internet, take one-on-one proctored tests, and complete much of their course work while traveling.

Student-athletes who struggle academically often feel overwhelmed in all areas of their collegiate life, including their sport. Therefore, learning how to balance both academics and athletics is an important priority.

College Search Advice

The most important piece of advice for a prospective student-athlete is to take an active role in your recruitment! Don't wait for the phone to ring or coaches to come calling. Once you enter high school, use every available resource to research colleges and universities. The Internet (www.petersons.com) provides access to every school in America (and beyond). If you live near a university (even if you are not interested in attending it), watch the team practice and/or play. You may be inspired by a visiting team, and you may also gain more understanding of where your skill level fits in among other schools. If your family takes vacations, check out neighboring universities. You can take as many unofficial (meaning you pay the costs to visit) visits to institutions as you like. Try to meet with the coach or an assistant, but if they are unavailable, contact the admissions department and schedule a tour or interview. When visiting a college campus, go prepared with a list of questions, ask for a tour of the campus and its facilities, and try to meet some members of the team so that you can ask them questions as well.

In addition to meeting coaches and players, a meeting with an academic contact in your proposed field of study is usually easy to arrange and can give you great insight into the academic part of the institution.

If you are unable to attend a college in person or get a coach to see you play, videotapes are a good way to at least get your foot in the door and could possibly lead to the coach attending an upcoming event. As a general rule, make your tape, DVD, or streaming video of good quality, representative of your play, and of a highlight nature.

When narrowing your college choices, a good rule of thumb is to ask yourself whether you would be happy at a given institution, regardless of whether or not you would be playing your sport. Other ways to narrow down a list of schools might be based on size, geography, and academic programs offered.

Whatever your ultimate decision might be, participation in collegiate athletics is an experience that will add excitement now and help to mold your future, because collegiate athletics prepares you for life. It teaches you how to perform under pressure, handle highs and lows, and develop good work habits, while leaving an indelible imprint on your future.

Fran Dunphy
Men's Head Basketball Coach
University of Pennsylvania

I have always held the student part of student-athlete in very high regard. Teenagers come to college campuses every year with hopes of becoming a special part of a team, winning a conference championship, and/or earning individual star honors. However, it is the education one receives that is just as meaningful as anything else that happens during one's college career.

The University of Pennsylvania is an Ivy League school located in Philadelphia, Pennsylvania. None of the eight schools that make up the Ivy League offer athletic scholarships. Financial aid comes to need-based applicants only and is never based on academic or athletic merit. When recruiting at the Ivy League level, we look for the same qualities that every other NCAA Division I program looks for—initially. However, unlike other schools, Ivy League schools need to be a little more creative. We have to find the student-athlete who is not only strong enough academically to be admitted into our institutions but who can also flourish among the best college students in the country. Restrictions academically, as far as admissions are concerned, and financially, as far as the cost of an Ivy League education is concerned, are the main hurdles to becoming an Ivy League student-athlete.

Recruiting

We don't like to use the term "difficult" when discussing the admissions criteria at Ivy League schools, rather, we prefer to use the term "unique." Coaches at Ivy League institutions have to do much more homework and touch bases with many more prospective students than coaches at most Division I programs.

Creativity in recruiting high-quality student-athletes is one of the best tools an Ivy League coach can have. Finding players who are good athletes, good students, and have the financial means to attend an Ivy League institution like Penn is the main obstacle we face. These recruits have to understand the discipline it takes to be successful at both their academics and athletics. But it is the business of educating these student-athletes on a daily basis that keeps me coming to work every morning.

What I initially look for in a student-athlete is size, speed, agility, and a good skill set. After that, I look at a player's knowledge of the game and how he uses that knowledge on the basketball court. Next, it's important that everyone on a team perform a role. Determining how a potential student-athlete will fit into that role is critical. Finally, I want to know how he's going to react when the game is on the line. Does he want the ball? Is he looking for the better player on the court to get the ball to? Does he see the play before it happens? Exhibiting a thorough understanding of the game is what excites most coaches about certain student-athletes.

College Search Advice

In order for recruited student-athletes to make the best decision on where to attend college, there is a specific process they should go through. Determine how good you really are—not how good you think you are—before applying to schools and calling coaches. Is it important for you to play right away, or would it be acceptable if you were a role player on the team? If you choose to play for a nationally ranked program, are you assured of playing time? Who else is currently playing at your position? Look at the environment of the school, the quality of the education it offers, the people you will be hanging around with, and ask yourself, "Do I fit in? Is it important that my family and friends can come and watch me play? Do I think I can make an impact on the athletic program and the campus? How will participating in college athletics at this particular school affect my future once my playing days are over?"

College is very different from high school. Time management becomes your best friend. But so do your teammates, roommates, coaches, and professors. College is an exciting time in every student's life, and to be an athlete during that time is even more exhilarating. Take advantage of every opportunity afforded to you and be prepared to work harder than you ever have before. In the end,

every experience, grade, shot, and friend you make will last a lifetime.

Greg Strobel
Head Wrestling Coach
Lehigh University

Lehigh's wrestling program dates back to 1909 and is one of the top wrestling programs in the nation. Lehigh is a small private school but regularly competes against the Big 10 and Big 12 programs. The wrestling program ranks fifth in producing NCAA champions, eighth in producing All-Americans, and has won thirty-one Eastern Intercollegiate Wrestling Association (EIWA) championships. Lehigh has placed as high as second in the NCAA Championship tournament and in the top ten three of the past four years. While at Lehigh, I have coached two NCAA Championship teams. As a former Olympic Coach (1996 and 2000), I have had the opportunity to coach international teams including the Pan Am and World teams for eighteen years.

Admissions

Lehigh University is a private Pennsylvania school ranked in the top 15 percent of all universities. Last year's freshman class had an average SAT score of 1294. Although Lehigh is very selective in its admissions process, recruited athletes do get some special consideration. However, we do not have slots that guarantee the acceptance of a limited number of below-average students.

Recruiting

We use a "shot-gun" approach to recruiting prospects we do not already know. The process begins with a form letter and questionnaire sent to all state placers in several key wrestling states (Pennsylvania, New Jersey, New York, Ohio, Illinois, California, Florida). A prospective student-athlete who fills out the questionnaire and returns it indicates an interest in our program and gives us the opportunity to screen for academic and athletic ability.

Most of the top recruits are well known by the top schools. We use the national ranking services to identify these athletes and use our network of loyal alumni who scour the newspapers for the best wrestlers from the seven key states. These wrestlers are contacted by letter during their junior year and then by telephone after July 1 prior to their senior year.

What to Do on Your Campus Visit

The following tips provide you with the necessary information to help make your recruiting visit as enjoyable and stress-free as possible. By following these eight tips, you'll be well on your way to competing at the college or university level of your choice:

1. Plan your trip in advance and consider the following details:
   - Date, time, and location of the visit
   - Travel expenses
   - What to bring
2. Plan a meeting with the chairperson of your top choice of study.
3. Ask questions about the admissions procedures and arrange to meet with a representative from the Admissions Office.
4. Visit the campus during a typical day and attend a class and a team practice.
5. Visit with some of the players. Talk with freshmen and sophomores to get their perspective on what the first-year experience is like.
6. Have plenty of questions prepared. Refer to "Questions to Ask When Considering an Athletic Program" on page 13 or a list of questions you should ask during your visit.
7. Be observant and take notes about what you saw as soon as your visit is over, so the details are fresh in your mind. Your notes might include information about facilities, equipment, the appearance of the campus, policies, deadlines, the student body, and your potential teammates.
8. Write a thank you note to the coach as soon as you return home from your visit.

Athletes should not wait for coaches to contact them. Coaches are extremely busy during the season, and, although we recruit diligently, we may overlook potentially good candidates. I know that if an athlete contacts me, he is interested in advancing his career at Lehigh. This piques my interest in him. Once we have identified qualified student-athletes, it is important to develop a relationship to determine if the athlete is a good fit for our program. During our conversations with prospective wrestlers, we try to assess their character, work ethic, goals, dedication, responsibility, and respect as well as their athletic ability.

College athletics is quite different from high school athletics, just as college academics differs from high school academics. Personal responsibility is the key. Students need to be self-directed and be able to balance the rigors of college life. I tell my athletes they should try to be the best student and the best athlete they can be. We have done very well attracting athletes who believe in this philosophy.

College Search Advice

Athletes who are thinking about competing in college should start as early as possible to prepare themselves for the academic and athletic requirements they will face. Honors classes, core curriculum, good study habits, GPA, and work ethic are a few of the necessary attributes. I believe kids should start thinking about their possibilities while in junior high. High academic achievement will expand their options; they should narrow their options during their junior year. We see more and more student-athletes with a fairly narrow list by the start of their senior year, and most are opting for an early decision. I recommend an early decision only when the student-athlete is certain of his choice. Research is important. Student-athletes should find out what graduates from a particular school are doing for a living, if the coach stays in contact with former team members, and how loyal the alumni are.

Athletes should visit campuses unofficially during the summer of their junior year and schedule an official visit for the fall. During an official visit, a prospective student-athlete should try to determine what it would be like to be a student-athlete at that school. Go to classes, meet professors, check out the social scene, and watch the team practice and/or compete. Attending summer camp is another great way to check out the school and the team. (More than half of our team attended our summer wrestling camp.)

There are three major factors to consider when choosing a college: academic interest, athletic program, and affordability. I always ask student-athletes what other schools they are looking at. The answer tells me what their priorities are. If they name high academic schools without quality wrestling programs, I know they are not very interested in wrestling. If they name schools with good wrestling programs but lower academic standards, I know they are only interested in wrestling. I am looking for student-athletes who want the best of both worlds.

Most student-athletes are looking for athletic scholarships, but in many cases they should be looking for affordability and need-based aid. Not all schools offer scholarships, and all sports do not have the same number of scholarships to offer. NCAA rules limit wrestling programs to 9.9 full-ride scholarships that can be divided into partial-aid packages. Most of our student-athletes are on need-based aid packages. The student-athlete and the coach should make the financial issues clear at the beginning of the recruiting process.

Going to college and competing in intercollegiate athletics is a major step in one's life. The choices you make will affect you for the rest of your life. Do your research. Narrow your choices. Settle only for what you want.

Steve Swanson
Women's Head Soccer Coach
University of Virginia

Over the past fifteen years, I have coached women's soccer at the collegiate level for three different schools—Dartmouth College, Stanford University, and now at the University of Virginia. Although our sport is getting more attention, attracts more fans, and becomes increasingly more competitive, my overriding philosophy will never change. The more I coach, the more I realize how important it is, for the player's sake, to keep things simple.

Recruiting

Like soccer, recruiting is a fairly simple process. Coaches gather information on student-athletes whom they feel can help their programs. Concurrently, they try to educate these student-athletes on the benefits of both their school and their soccer program, hoping they will choose to attend the school and play for them. Conversely, student-athletes gather information on the school and athletic programs in which they are interested and find the school/athletic program that meets their needs. Recruiting is truly about coaches and prospective student-athletes gathering and sharing information. Why then do more and more student-athletes find the recruiting process overwhelming? Why are there so many rules associated with college recruiting? Why is there so much pressure on coaches and student-athletes? Why do so many student-athletes verbally commit to a program before they even make an official visit? The short and simple answer to these questions is—winning.

College athletics is big business, and winning is a large part of this business. Increased revenue for athletic departments, media attention, polls, rankings, and coaching salaries are just a few of the reasons why there is a greater emphasis on winning. It inevitably follows that in

order to win at the collegiate level, a coach must be able to recruit well. Add to this the possibility of student-athletes earning scholarships for their education, and you have a simple process that gets much more complex and pressurized for both sides.

To make this simple for the student-athlete, I am going to highlight what I feel are the most important aspects of the recruiting process. If student-athletes follow these steps toward recruiting, they will be on their way to a more enjoyable, positive, and less stressful journey.

I can't stress enough that you must take ownership of the recruiting process. It is your college experience, not your parents', your club coaches', your high school coaches', or your siblings'. The more you take ownership of the process, the more likely you will find a program and school that fits your needs. Of course, you should seek guidance from your parents, coaches, and other people you trust, but in the end, the choice is yours.

Most college coaches look for student-athletes who are responsible, enthusiastic, persistent, disciplined, and motivated. These are the kinds of qualities that are going to allow any student to successfully manage the demands of getting an undergraduate degree and playing a college sport. The first opportunity for them to find out if you have these qualities is through the recruiting process. Not only should you have the right attitude during the process, but you should also demand it in the coaches who are recruiting you.

If you embrace the recruiting process and tackle it the same way you do your sport, the chances of selecting the right program will increase immensely.

Prioritize Your Needs

One of the first questions I ask any student-athlete is: "What are your needs and which schools have the best chance of fulfilling them?" Amazingly, many student-athletes have a hard time answering this question. Many have never even taken the time to think about their needs. This is the single most important part of the process from your perspective. If you don't know what your needs are, you will seldom find a school that is right for you. Or you will select a school based on something as minor as the school's colors. If you know what your needs are, you will find a school that meets those needs—or at least the majority of them.

College Search Advice

As competition escalates in college athletics, many student-athletes do not believe they have control over the recruiting process. They find that weekly phone calls, instant messaging, e-mails, letters, and earlier offers make the process stressful. Prospective student-athletes feel pressured to make decisions early, especially if their teammates and others are committing to schools early. Inevitably, student-athletes are making decisions about college (one could argue one of the most significant times in their life) with less and less information. The process is controlling them instead of the student-athletes controlling the process. Once you have prioritized your needs,

you are on your way to gaining control of the recruiting process. You must begin to research schools and programs that fit your needs.

When deciding on a school, look closely at the quality of its academic programs. Find out the credentials of the faculty, see what the course offerings are, and talk to someone in the department you are interested in.

Also, you must investigate the quality of the school's athletic program. Contact the coach; get feedback from

National Letter of Intent

The Collegiate Commissioners Association (CCA) administers the National Letter of Intent program. Started in 1964 with seven conferences and eight independent institutions, the program now includes more than 500 institutions from over 50 leagues.

By signing a National Letter of Intent, a prospective student-athlete agrees to attend the designated college or university for one academic year. Pursuant to the terms of the National Letter of Intent program, participating institutions agree to provide financial aid for one academic year to the student-athlete, provided he or she is admitted to the institution and is eligible for financial aid under NCAA rules. An important provision of the National Letter of Intent program is a recruiting prohibition applied after a prospective student-athlete signs a Letter of Intent. This prohibition requires participating institutions to cease recruitment of a prospective student-athlete once a National Letter of Intent is signed with another institution.

The National Letter of Intent has many advantages to both prospective student-athletes and participating educational institutions.
- Once a National Letter of Intent is signed, prospective student-athletes are no longer subject to further recruiting contacts and calls.
- Student-athletes are assured of an athletic scholarship for one full academic year. (If not for the National Letter of Intent program, a student could find his or her scholarship taken by a more highly recruited student only weeks or days before classes begin.)
- Institutions can be certain that once the student-athlete has signed a Letter of Intent, there is no need to continue recruiting for that position. (Without the program, last-minute changes by student-athletes could open scholarships and positions on teams.)
- By emphasizing student-athletes' commitments to educational institutions, not particular coaches or teams, the program focuses university athletics on educational objectives. The program promotes student-athletes' academic objectives and helps to sustain the amateur nature of college sports.

There are restrictions on signing a National Letter of Intent that may affect your eligibility. These restrictions are contained in the letter of intent. Read it carefully. If you have questions about the National Letter of Intent signing dates, refer to the chart below. If you have questions about signing restrictions, contact the conference office of the college you are interested in attending.

Do not sign any institutional or conference letter of intent (or financial aid agreement) before the National Letter of Intent signing date. If you have questions about the National Letter of Intent program, please call the National Letter of Intent office at 205-458-3000 or visit its Web site at www.national-letter.org.

Signing Dates for the 2005-2006 Academic Year

Sport	Initial Signing Date	Final Signing Date
Basketball (Early Period)	November 10, 2004	November 17, 2004
Basketball (Late Period)	April 13, 2005	May 18, 2005
Football (Mid-year junior college transfer)	December 15, 2004	January 15, 2005
Football (Regular Period)	February 2, 2005	April 1, 2005
Field Hockey, Soccer, Men's Water Polo*	February 2, 2005	August 1, 2005
All Other Sports (Early Period)	November 10, 2004	November 17, 2004
All Other Sports (Late Period)	April 13, 2005	August 1, 2005

*These sports do not have an early signing period.

players about the program; find out how quickly you might play, if at all; try to determine the coach's philosophy; and learn as much as you can about NCAA rules and what you can and cannot do during the recruiting process. Following these steps will help you plan ahead and provide you with an organized way of gathering information on the schools/programs in which you are interested.

By taking control of the recruiting process, prioritizing your needs, and creating an organized plan, you will make the recruiting process less stressful, more productive, and rewarding.

NCAA Guide
for the
College-bound
Student Athelete

Academic-Eligibility Requirements for Prospective Student Athletes

Division I 2005 through 2007

If you enroll in a Division I college between 2005 and 2007 and want to participate in athletics or receive an athletic scholarship, you must meet the following academic standards:

- Graduate from high school
- Complete the 14 core courses listed below
- Present a minimum required grade-point-average (GPA) in your core courses
- Achieve a combined SAT or ACT sum score that matches your core-course GPA in the GPA and test score index

To qualify for NCAA athletics, you must complete the following 14 required core courses:

- 4 years of English
- 2 years of mathematics (Algebra I or higher level)
- 2 years of natural or physical science (including 1 year of lab science if offered by your high school)
- 1 extra year of English, mathematics, or natural/physical science
- 2 years of social science
- 3 years of extra core courses (from any category above or foreign language, nondoctrinal religion, or philosophy)

Note: Computer science courses can be used only if your high school grants graduation credit in mathematics or natural/physical science and the courses appear on the core-course list as math or science.

You will be a nonqualifier if you do not meet the academic requirements listed above. As a nonqualifier you:

- May not participate in athletic competition or practice during your first year in college;
- May receive financial aid based only on need, (not athletics-based financial aid) in your first year in college; and
- May play only three seasons (to earn a fourth season you must graduate before your fifth year of college).

The NCAA

The National Collegiate Athletic Association, also known as the NCAA or "the Association," is the organization through which many of the nation's colleges and universities speak and act on athletics matters at the national level. It is a nonprofit, voluntary association of more than 1,260 schools, conferences, organizations and individuals devoted to the sound administration of intercollegiate athletics. Its mission is to protect the best interests of student-athletes.

In 1973, the Association's membership was divided into three legislative and competitive Divisions I, II, and III. The three divisions currently have 1,006 active members (325 in Division I, 270 in Division II, and 411 in Division III). The most notable difference among the three divisions is that institutions in Divisions I and II may offer athletics scholarships, while Division III schools do not offer athletics scholarships. You may contact the NCAA at:

NCAA NCAA Membership Services
P.O. Box 6222
Indianapolis, IN 46202-6222
Telephone: 317-917-6222
Fax: 317-917-6622
Web site: www.ncaa.org

23

Division I 2008 and Later

If you enroll in a Division I college in 2008 or later and want to participate in athletics or receive an athletic scholarship, you must meet all NCAA requirements for 2005–2007 and have completed two additional core courses (new total of 16), as shown below:

The 16 required core courses are:

- 4 years of English
- 3 years of mathematics (Algebra I or higher level)
- 2 years of natural or physical science (including 1 year of lab science if offered by your high school)
- 1 extra year of English, mathematics, or natural/ physical science
- 2 years of social science
- 4 years of extra courses (from any category above, or foreign language, nondoctrinal religion, or philosophy)

Division II 2005 and Later

If you enroll in a Division II college in 2005 or later and want to participate in athletics or receive an athletics scholarship, you must meet the following academic standards:

- Graduate from high school
- Complete the 14 core courses listed below
- Present a 2.000 grade-point-average (GPA) in your core courses
- Achieve a combined SAT score of 820 or a sum score of 68 on the ACT

The 14 required core courses include:

- 3 years of English
- 2 years of mathematics (Algebra I or higher level)

Core GPA and Test Score Index—Division I

Core GPA	SAT	ACT
3.550 & above	400	37
3.525	410	38
3.500	420	39
3.475	430	40
3.450	440	41
3.425	450	41
3.400	460	42
3.375	470	42
3.350	480	43
3.325	490	44
3.300	500	44
3.275	510	45
3.250	520	46
3.225	530	46
3.200	540	47
3.175	550	47
3.150	560	48
3.125	570	49
3.100	580	49
3.075	590	50
3.050	600	50
3.025	610	51
3.000	620	52
2.975	630	52
2.950	640	53
2.925	650	53
2.900	660	54
2.875	670	55

Core GPA	SAT	ACT
2.850	680	56
2.825	690	56
2.800	700	57
2.775	710	58
2.750	720	59
2.725	730	59
2.700	730	60
2.675	740–750	61
2.650	760	62
2.625	770	63
2.600	780	64
2.575	790	65
2.550	800	66
2.525	810	67
2.500	820	68
2.475	830	69
2.450	840–850	70
2.425	860	70
2.400	860	71
2.375	870	72
2.350	880	73
2.325	890	74
2.300	900	75
2.275	910	76
2.250	920	77
2.225	930	78
2.200	940	79
Note: Chart assumes 14 core-course schedule		

- 2 years of natural or physical science (including 1 year of lab science if offered by your high school)
- 2 extra years of English, mathematics, or natural/physical science
- 2 years of social science
- 3 years of additional courses (from any category above or foreign language, nondoctrinal religion, or philosophy

Note: Computer science courses can be used only if your high school grants graduation credit in mathematics or natural/physical science and the courses appear on the core-course list as math or science.

You will be a partial qualifier if you do not meet the academic requirements listed above but have graduated from high school and do meet one of the following:

- The specified minimum SAT or ACT score
- Completion of the required 14 core courses with a 2.000 GPA in your core-courses

As a partial qualifier, you:

- May practice with your team at its home facility;
- May receive an athletic scholarship during your first year;
- May not compete during your freshman year; and
- May compete in the four seasons remaining.

If you have not graduated from high school or have not presented the core-course GPA, SAT, or ACT scores required for a qualifier, you will be considered a nonqualifier. As a nonqualifier, you:

- May not participate in athletic competition or practice during your first year in college;
- May receive financial aid based only on need (not athletics-based financial aid) in your first year in college; and
- May play in four seasons.

Reprinted by permission from the NCAA, "NCAA Guide for the College-Bound Student Athlete," 2004–05.

Division III

Contact your Division III college regarding its policies on financial aid, practice, and competition.

Each NCAA member institution has its own admission requirements. Remember, meeting the NCAA academic rules does not guarantee your admission into a college. You must still apply for admission.

ACT and SAT Tests

You must achieve the required score on an SAT or ACT test before your full-time college enrollment. You must do this whether you are a citizen of the U.S. or of a foreign country. You must take the national test given on one of the dates shown below.

Note: No campus or state tests, like those given in Colorado and Illinois, may substitute for the national SAT or ACT.

National Testing Dates

SAT	ACT
October 9, 2004	September 25, 2004
November 6, 2004	October 23, 2004
December 4, 2004	December 11, 2004
January 22, 2005	February 12, 2005
March 12, 2005	April 19, 2005
May 7, 2005	June 11, 2005
June 4, 2005	

Academic-Eligibility Waivers

If you don't meet the academic requirements to be a qualifier, a waiver of the requirements may be filed on your behalf. This waiver can be filed only by an NCAA school. Contact the NCAA or the college you will attend for information about the waiver process.

NCAA Initial-Eligibility Clearinghouse

NCAA member institutions agree that it is important for all high school students to meet minimum academic standards to practice or compete in college athletics. The clearinghouse evaluates student courses, grades, and test scores to determine whether students meet prescribed minimum academic requirements. The NCAA membership is committed to academic success and graduation of its student-athletes. This is a primary guiding principle of the Association.

NCAA Initial Eligibility and Admission

Admission to an NCAA college or university is not the same as NCAA initial eligibility. Each institution decides which students to admit, based on its admissions criteria. Keep in mind that if a student-athlete meets NCAA initial-eligibility standards, that student still may not be admitted to the institution. Likewise, a student-athlete who gains admission to a college or university may not meet NCAA initial-eligibility standards.

Note: The clearinghouse certifies your eligibility to compete as a student-athlete, but your college must accept you as a student.

The clearinghouse evaluates your academic record to determine if you are eligible to participate at a Division I or II college as a freshman student-athlete. (The clearinghouse is not the NCAA, but an organization that performs services relative to initial eligibility for the NCAA.) You must register with the clearinghouse so that your high-school transcripts and SAT or ACT test scores may be evaluated. To register with the clearinghouse, contact:

NCAA Initial-Eligibility Clearinghouse
P.O. Box 4043
Iowa City, Iowa 52243-4043
Telephone: 877-262-1492
   319-337-1492 (International)
   877-861-3003 (24-hour response line)
Fax: 319-337-1556
www.ncaaclearinghouse.net

Clearinghouse Registration

To register with the clearinghouse, you must complete and sign the Student Release Form (SRF) and send it to the clearinghouse along with a $30 registration fee. This SRF does two things:

- It authorizes each high school you've attended to send the clearinghouse your transcript, test scores, proof of graduation, and other necessary academic information.
- It authorizes the clearinghouse to send your academic information to all colleges that request your eligibility status.

The preferred method is to register online. Go online to www.ncaaclearinghouse.net. Select "Prospective Student-Athletes" and click on "Domestic Student Release Form" or "Foreign Student Release Form." Complete the SRF form online, and include your credit or debit card information to pay the fee. Then follow instructions to complete the transaction. Print both Copy 1 and Copy 2 of the transcript release form, sign them, and give both to your high school counselor. You can print out additional copies of the completed form for your records.

If you elect to register by paper application, type or clearly print your information on a paper copy of the SRF. You can download the form at www.ncaaclearinghouse.net. Fax one signed copy of the SRF to the clearinghouse with your credit or debit card information or send the SRF by U.S. mail with a check or money order for $30. Give Copies 1 and 2 of the transcript release form to your high school counselor. Keep a copy for your own records.

When completing the SRF sections, please follow the step-by-step instructions outlined below.

Section I: Student Information
Enter all information accurately, including your Social Security number (SSN) and date of birth. This information must match exactly other data the clearinghouse receives for you (like high school transcripts and requests from colleges seeking your eligibility status).

Frequently Asked Questions

Q: *Do I have to register with the clearinghouse?*

A: Yes. If you want to participate in Division I or II athletics as a freshman, you must register with the clearinghouse.

Q: *Is clearinghouse certification the same as college admission?*

A: No. Initial-eligibility certification from the clearinghouse does not guarantee your admission to any Division I or II college. You must apply for college admission separately. The clearinghouse only determines whether you meet NCAA requirements as a freshman student-athlete in a Division I or II college to be able to compete, practice, and receive an athletic scholarship.

Q: *May I send my academic information directly to the clearinghouse?*

A: No. Transcripts must come to the clearinghouse by mail directly from the high school—not from you. Give Copies 1 and 2 of the transcript release form to your counselor at the high school from which you will be graduating. The clearinghouse will not accept faxed transcripts.

Q: *Who may see my academic information?*

A: The clearinghouse will provide eligibility information only to colleges that request your academic information. If no NCAA member institution requests your eligibility status, the clearinghouse may not process an eligibility-status certification.

Q: *When is the best time for me to register with the clearinghouse?*

A: Register after your junior year in high school. If you do not submit all required documents, your file will be incomplete and will be discarded after three years. After that time you will need to reregister and pay your fee again.

Q: *Is there a registration deadline?*

A: No. However, you must be certified as a qualifier before you can receive an athletic scholarship or practice or compete at a Division I or II college.

Q: *What if I have attended more than one high school?*

A: If you have attended multiple high schools since ninth grade, the clearinghouse must receive an official transcript for each school. Transcripts can come directly from each school, or from the high school from which you are graduating. Check with your high school counselor.

Q: *How may I arrange for the testing agency to send my scores directly to the clearinghouse?*

A: When you register to take the ACT or the SAT, mark code 9999 so that the testing agency will send your scores to the clearinghouse. The clearinghouse may also take your scores from your official transcript.

Section II: High School You Now Attend

Enter the name, address, and code number of the high school you now attend, along with your expected date of high school graduation. Get your high school code from your counselor or use the code look-up at www.ncaaclearinghouse.net. Click on "Prospective Student-Athletes" then "List of Approved Core Courses."

Section III: Schools You Previously Attended

If you have attended more than one school, including summer school, complete Section III. List in chronological order all schools you previously attended, starting with the most recent. If you attended ninth grade in a junior-high school located in the same school system where you later attended high school, do not list the ninth-grade school. If you need to list more schools than space allows, use a separate sheet of paper.

Special Instructions for Web Users: If you need to enter more than six high schools, contact the clearinghouse at 877-262-1492. Or, once you've registered with the clearinghouse, select "Prospective Student-Athletes" then "Registered Student Login," then add information for the additional schools on your record.

Section IV: Personal Identification Number (PIN)

Create a personal identification number (PIN) of four digits (numbers between 0 and 9) that you can easily remember. Do not choose a PIN that might be easily guessed like your birthday or street address. Record your PIN in a safe place.

Checking Your File Status

Once you have submitted your SRF and PIN, you may check your status in one of three ways:

- Visit www.ncaaclearinghouse.net, click on "Prospective Student-Athletes" then "Registered Student Login" and enter your SSN and PIN.
- Call the clearinghouse's 24-hour, toll-free number at 877-861-3003 from a touch-tone phone. You will be asked to enter your SSN and PIN.
- Call the clearinghouse customer service line at 877-262-1492.

If you have forgotten your PIN, simply fax or mail your new PIN to the clearinghouse along with your name, address, SSN, date of birth, and signature.

Section V: Clearinghouse Communication Method

The clearinghouse may communicate with you by e-mail or U.S. mail. This will include most correspondence and certification reports. E-mail correspondence will require that you have submitted a valid e-mail address in Section I of your SRF. You will need to indicate the option you prefer. We encourage you to select the e-mail option. E-mail will enable you to receive correspondence from the clearinghouse up to two weeks earlier than regular mail. You may change your communication option or update your e-mail address at www.ncaaclearinghouse.net or by writing or faxing the clearinghouse.

Section VI: Pay Your Fee

Your form will be eligible for processing only with payment of a $30 application fee (or submission of a fee waiver if you have been granted a waiver). You may pay by debit or credit card, or by check or money order. Do not send cash. If you send your form by fax, you must pay by debit or credit card.

You are eligible for a waiver of the registration fee only if you have already received a waiver of the ACT or SAT fee. Your SRF fee waiver section or the proper SRF must then be completed by an authorized high school official and include the school seal. If you registered online, an authorized high school official may validate the waiver online by following procedures on the clearinghouse Web site. If you have not yet been granted a fee waiver by ACT or SAT, you are not yet eligible for a waiver of the registration fee.

Section VII: Authorization Signature

Carefully examine the entire SRF to make sure you have completed it correctly, included your fee payment autho-rization, and signed it. If you are younger than 18 years old, your parent or legal guardian must also sign.

If you complete your SRF on the Web, you will be asked to verify your signature by checking a box to verify your identity. A similar check box and name field is also included for your parent or guardian who must provide a signature if you are younger than 18.

Section VIII: SRF Completion by Your High School

Your high school will complete your registration by sending Copy 1, along with your high school transcript, to the clearinghouse. After graduation, but before your high school closes for the summer, your high school must send Copy 2 to the clearinghouse, along with a copy of your final transcript confirming your high school gradua-tion.

If you have any questions while registered with the clearinghouse, you can submit them by e-mail at www. ncaaclearinghouse.net. Go to the "Prospective Student-Athlete" page, select "Registered Student Login," input your SSN and PIN, click on "Contact Clearinghouse," and type in your questions. You will receive a response within two working days.

Reprinted by permission from the NCAA, "NCAA Guide for the College-Bound Student-Athlete," 2004–05.

How to Use This Guide

Profiles of College Athletic Programs

The **PROFILES OF COLLEGE ATHLETIC PRO-GRAMS** section is arranged alphabetically by university or college name. The profiles themselves are divided into two sections—general institution data and athletic program data. The data is provided in capsule form for quick review and comparison. The following breakdown of the profile format explains the data elements in detail. Any item that does not apply to a particular institution or for which no information was supplied is omitted from that institution's profile.

School: The first section of each profile lists the institution's official name, nickname, primary division affiliation, primary athletic conference(s)/association(s) affiliation, and Web site. Keep in mind that sports at a particular institution can be played under the governance of different associations or divisions or can change affiliations. For example, basketball at a specific college could play under NCAA I; football under NCAA III; and soccer under NAIA. Also, not every sport or institution is affiliated with an athletic association. If an institution is not affiliated with a conference or association, the term "independent" is used. Be sure to contact institutions directly about this information if it plays a role in your final decision about any college or university of interest to you.

Institutional control: Private institutions are designated as *independent* (nonprofit), *proprietary* (profit-making), or *independent* with a specific religious denomination or affiliation. Nondenominational or interdenominational religious orientation is possible and would be indicated. Public institutions are designated by the source of funding. Designations include *federal, state, province, commonwealth* (Puerto Rico), *territory* (U.S. territories), *county, district* (an educational administrative unit often having boundaries different from units of local government), *city, state* and *local* (local may refer to county, district, or city), or state-supported (funded primarily by the state but administratively autonomous).

Religious affiliation is also noted here.

Founding date: If the year an institution was chartered differs from the year when instruction actually began, the earlier date is given.

System or administrative affiliation: Any coordinate institutions or system affiliations are indicated. An institution that has separate colleges or campuses for men and women but shares facilities and courses is termed a coordinate institution. A formal administrative grouping of institutions, either private or public, of which the college is a part, or the name of a single institution with which the college is administratively affiliated, is a system.

Student body: An institution is *coed* (coeducational—admits men and women), *primarily* (80 percent or more) *women, primarily men, women only,* or *men only.*

Setting: Institutions are designated as *urban* (located within a major city), *suburban* (a residential area within commuting distance of a major city), *small-town* (a small but compactly settled area not within commuting distance of a major city), or *rural* (a remote and sparsely populated area). The phrase *easy access to . . .* indicates that the campus is within an hour's drive of the nearest major metropolitan area that has a population greater than 500,000.

Undergraduate students: This category provides the number of full-time and part-time students enrolled in undergraduate degree programs as of fall 2003. The percentage of full-time undergraduates and the percentage of men and women are given.

Entrance level: This category is reported by each institution and provides a classification of a particular institution's entrance level difficulty. Classifications are as follows: *most difficult, very difficult, moderately difficult, minimally difficult,* and *noncompetitive.*

Percent of applicants admitted: This refers to the percentage of applicants who were granted admission to the institution.

Freshmen: Admission figures are given for the number of students who applied for fall 2003 admission, the number of those who were accepted, and the number who enrolled. Freshmen statistics include the percentage of freshmen who took the SAT I and received verbal and math scores above 500, above 600, and above 700.

Tuition and fees: Costs are given for the 2004–05 academic year or for the 2003–04 academic year if

2004–05 figures were not yet available. Annual expenses may be expressed as a comprehensive fee (including full-time tuition, mandatory fees, and college room and board) or as separate figures for full-time tuition, fees, room and board, or room only. For public institutions where tuition differs according to residence, separate figures are given for area or state residents and for nonresidents.

Financial Aid: Information presented represents aid awarded to all incoming freshmen for the 2003–04 academic year. Figures are given for: *average need-based gift aid, average non-need based aid,* and *average aid to full-time undergraduates.*

Athletic Department: This information was gathered and provided by College Coaches Online (www. collegecoachesonline.com). College Coaches Online is a database of more than 15,000 current college coaches. It allows users to find the names, addresses, e-mail addresses, and phone numbers of these coaches. Information includes the telephone number, e-mail address, and fax number of the school's Director of Athletics (if available) along with the telephone number and e-mail address of the Sports Information Director (if available).

Men's and Women's Coaches: This section lists coaches' telephone numbers and e-mail addresses for all sports gathered by College Coaches Online. If a particular sport, coach's name, telephone number, or e-mail address is not included in the College Coaches Online database, it is omitted from the profile.

Indexes

The Indexes are divided into three categories: **Geographic Listing of College Athletic Programs, College Athletic Programs by Sport,** and **College Athletic Programs by Division.**

The **Geographic Listing of College Athletic Programs** is arranged by state and then alphabetically by institution name. The **College Athletic Programs by Sport** is divided into 18 categories, including:

- Baseball
- Basketball
- Cheerleading
- Cross-Country
- Diving
- Field Hockey
- Football
- Golf

- Gymnastics
- Ice Hockey
- Lacrosse
- Soccer
- Softball
- Swimming
- Tennis
- Track and Field
- Volleyball
- Wrestling

Each school is followed by the designation of *women (w), men (m),* or *men and women (m/w),* to indicate whether the sport is offered to men, to women, or to both men and women. The **College Athletic Programs by Division** is divided into four categories: *NCAA Division I, NCAA Division II, NCAA Division III,* and *NAIA.* Within the division categories, the colleges are organized alphabetically by college name, then alphabetically by institution name. In all indexes, the page number appears to the right following the institution name.

Data Collection Procedures

The data collection efforts were conducted by two different organizations: The general institution data contained in the **PROFILES OF COLLEGE ATHLETIC PROGRAMS** and **INDEXES** were researched between fall 2003 and spring 2004 through *Peterson's Annual Survey of Undergraduate Institutions,* while the athletic program data were gathered in fall 2003 and winter 2004 by College Coaches Online and provided to Peterson's for use in this guide.

The general institution data included in this edition have been submitted by officials (usually admissions and financial aid officers, registrars, or institutional research personnel) at the colleges. In addition, many of the institutions that submitted data were contacted directly by the Peterson's research staff to verify unusual figures, resolve discrepancies, or obtain additional data. All usable information received in time for publication has been included. The omission of any particular item from the profiles signifies that the information is either not applicable to that institution or not available.

The athletic program data provided to Peterson's is identical to the current data found on the College Coaches Online Web site (www.collegecoachesonline.com). The data was updated and verified between fall 2003 and winter 2004 by visiting more than 1,300 NCAA and NAIA college and university athletic Web sites. Each institution's Sports Information Director or assistant was asked to visit and verify the accuracy of the data found on College Coaches Online.

Because of Peterson's comprehensive editorial review and because all general institution data comes directly from college officials, we believe that the information gathered through *Peterson's Annual Survey of Undergraduate Institutions* and presented in this guide is accurate. However, Peterson's did not use the same comprehensive editorial review of the athletic program data gathered by College Coaches Online and therefore cannot verify the complete accuracy of the athletic program data. Therefore, we suggest you verify this information with a specific college or university.

Criteria for Inclusion in This Book

To be included in this guide, an institution must have full accreditation or be a candidate for accreditation (preaccreditation) status by an institutional or specialized accrediting body recognized by the U.S. Department of Education or the Council for Higher Education Accredi-

tation (CHEA). Institutional accrediting bodies, which review each institution as a whole, include the six regional associations of schools and colleges (Middle States, New England, North Central, Northwest, Southern, and Western), each of which is responsible for a specific portion of the United States and its territories. Other institutional accrediting bodies are national in scope and accredit specific kinds of institutions (e.g., bible colleges, independent colleges, and rabbinical and Talmudic schools.) Program registration by the New York State Board of Regents is considered to be the equivalent of institutional accreditation, since the board requires that all programs offered by an institution meet its standards before recognition is granted. There are recognized specialized or professional accrediting bodies in more than forty different fields, each of which is authorized to accredit institutions or specific programs in its particular field. For specialized institutions that offer programs in one field only, we designate this to be the equivalent of institutional accreditation. A full explanation of the accrediting process and complete information on recognized, institutional (regional and national), and specialized accrediting bodies can be found online at www.chea.org or at www.ed.gov/admins/finaid/accred/index.html.

profiles
of
College
Athletic
Programs

ABILENE CHRISTIAN UNIVERSITY
Abilene, Texas

Wildcats ◆ NCAA II ◆ Lone Star Conference ◆ http://www.acu.edu/

Independent religious comprehensive, founded 1906, affiliated with Church of Christ
Coed, 4,111 undergraduate students, 94% full-time, 56% women, 44% men
Urban 208-acre campus
Moderately difficult entrance level, 53% of applicants were admitted

Freshmen *Admission:* 4,011 applied, 2,117 were accepted, 949 enrolled. *Test scores:* SAT verbal scores over 500: 71%; SAT math scores over 500: 72%; SAT verbal scores over 600: 27%; SAT math scores over 600: 30%; SAT verbal scores over 700: 5%; SAT math scores over 700: 5%.
Tuition and fees (2003–04): $13,290 (full-time). *Room and board:* $5080 (room only: $2160).
Financial Aid (All incoming freshmen): *Average need-based gift aid:* $7717. *Average non-need based aid:* $4233. *Average aid to full-time undergraduates:* $9677.
Athletic Department: *Director of Athletics:* Wally Bullington; Phone: 325-674-4865; Fax: 325-674-6831; E-mail: fwb90a@acu.edu. *Sports Information Director:* Lance Fleming; Phone: 325-674-2693; E-mail: flemingl@acu.edu.

MEN'S COACHES
Baseball: Britt Bonneau; Phone: 915-674-2325; E-mail: bonneaub@acu.edu.
Basketball: Klint Pleasant; Phone: 915-674-2913; E-mail: klint.pleasant@acu.edu.
Cross Country: Jon Murray; Phone: 915-674-2711; E-mail: murrayj@acu.edu.
Football: Gary Gaines; Phone: 915-674-2353; E-mail: gainesg@acu.edu.
Golf: Mike Campbell; Phone: 915-674-2331; E-mail: mike.campbell@acu.edu.
Tennis: Hutton Jones; Phone: 915-674-2591; E-mail: jonesh@acu.edu.
Track and Field: Jon Murray; Phone: 915-674-2711; E-mail: murrayj@acu.edu.

WOMEN'S COACHES
Basketball: Shawna Lavender; Phone: 915-674-2841; E-mail: lavenders@acu.edu.
Cross Country: Jon Murray; Phone: 915-674-2711; E-mail: murrayj@acu.edu.
Softball: Chantiel Wilson; Phone: 915-674-2735; E-mail: chantiel.wilson@acu.edu.
Tennis: Hutton Jones; Phone: 915-674-2591; E-mail: jonesh@acu.edu.
Track and Field: Jon Murray; Phone: 915-674-2711; E-mail: murrayj@acu.edu.
Volleyball: Brek Horn; Phone: 915-674-2590; E-mail: hornb@acu.edu.

ADAMS STATE COLLEGE
Alamosa, Colorado

Grizzlies ◆ NCAA II ◆ Rocky Mountain Athletic Conference ◆ http://www.adams.edu/

State-supported comprehensive, founded 1921, part of State Colleges in Colorado
Coed, 2,423 undergraduate students, 67% full-time, 58% women, 42% men
Small-town 90-acre campus
Moderately difficult entrance level, 7% of applicants were admitted

Freshmen *Admission:* 1,903 applied, 1,418 were accepted, 461 enrolled. *Test scores:* SAT verbal scores over 500: 51%; SAT math scores over 500: 48%; SAT verbal scores over 600: 11%; SAT math scores over 600: 14%; SAT verbal scores over 700: 1%.
Tuition and fees (2003–04): $2492 (resident), $8122 (nonresident). *Room and board:* $5730 (room only: $2880).
Financial Aid (All incoming freshmen): *Average need-based gift aid:* $4485. *Average non-need based aid:* $2223. *Average aid to full-time undergraduates:* $4805.

Athletic Department: *Director of Athletics:* Jeff Geiser; Phone: 970-587-7402; Fax: 970-587-7276; E-mail: jpgeiser@adams.edu. *Sports Information Director:* Chris Day; Phone: 970-587-7825; E-mail: cldday@adams.edu.

MEN'S COACHES
Basketball: Larry Mortensen; Phone: 970-587-7274; E-mail: lsmorten@adams.edu.
Cross Country: Damon Martin; Phone: 970-587-7266; E-mail: ddmartin@adams.edu.
Football: Wayne McGinn; Phone: 970-674-7283; E-mail: rwmcginn@adams.edu.
Golf: Cole Wasinger; Phone: 970 873 1995; E-mail: adamsstategolf@hotmail.com.
Track and Field: Damon Martin; Phone: 970-587-7266; E-mail: ddmartin@adams.edu.
Wrestling: Jason Ramsetter; Phone: 970-589-7271; E-mail: rljehlic@adams.edu.

WOMEN'S COACHES
Basketball: Jeff Storm; Phone: 970-589-7251; E-mail: jdstorm@adams.edu.
Cross Country: Damon Martin; Phone: 970-587-7266; E-mail: ddmartin@adams.edu.
Soccer: Dale Roden; Phone: 970-589-7254; E-mail: ldroden@adams.edu.
Softball: Penny Graves; Phone: 970-589-7842; E-mail: pdgraves@adams.edu.
Track and Field: Damon Martin; Phone: 970-587-7266; E-mail: ddmartin@adams.edu.
Volleyball: Katie Moskowitz; Phone: 970-589-7404; E-mail: kmmoskow@adams.edu.

ADELPHI UNIVERSITY
Garden City, New York

Panthers ◆ NCAA II ◆ Atlantic Soccer Conference; New York Collegiate Athletic Conference ◆ http://www.adelphi.edu/

Independent university, founded 1896
Coed, 4,157 undergraduate students, 82% full-time, 71% women, 29% men
Suburban 75-acre campus with easy access to New York City
Moderately difficult entrance level, 68% of applicants were admitted

Freshmen *Admission:* 4,379 applied, 3,089 were accepted, 792 enrolled. *Test scores:* SAT verbal scores over 500: 69%; SAT math scores over 500: 78%; SAT verbal scores over 600: 24%; SAT math scores over 600: 27%; SAT verbal scores over 700: 3%; SAT math scores over 700: 4%.
Tuition and fees (2003–04): $17,800 (full-time). *Room and board:* $8500.
Financial Aid (All incoming freshmen): *Average need-based gift aid:* $5256. *Average non-need based aid:* $8982. *Average aid to full-time undergraduates:* $13,500.
Athletic Department: *Director of Athletics:* Robert Hartwell; Phone: 516-877-4231; Fax: 516-877-4237; E-mail: hartwell@adelphi.edu. *Sports Information Director:* Suzette Thweatt-McQueen; Phone: 516-877-4236; E-mail: thweatt@adelphi.edu.

MEN'S COACHES
Baseball: Dom Scala; Phone: 516-877-4240; E-mail: dscala1045@aol.com.
Basketball: James Cosgrove; Phone: 516-877-4246; E-mail: cosgrove@adelphi.edu.
Cheerleading: Alex Campbell; Phone: 516-877-4240.
Cross Country: Mike Belfiore; Phone: 516-877-4243; E-mail: belfiore@adelphi.edu.
Golf: Walter Ostroske; Phone: 516-877-4240.
Lacrosse: Sandy Kapatos; Phone: 516-877-4244; E-mail: kapatos@adelphi.edu.
Soccer: Robert Montgomery; Phone: 516-877-4234; E-mail: montgome@adelphi.edu.
Swimming: Linda Jelovich; Phone: 516-877-4247; E-mail: jelovic2@adelphi.edu.
Tennis: William Klocke; Phone: 516-877-4240; E-mail: williamklocke@adelphi.edu.
Track and Field: Mike Belfiore; Phone: 516-877-4243; E-mail: belfiore@adelphi.edu.

Adelphi University *(continued)*
WOMEN'S COACHES
Basketball: Kelley Watts; Phone: 516-877-4246; E-mail: watts@adelphi.edu.
Cheerleading: Alex Campbell; Phone: 516-877-4240.
Cross Country: Mike Belfiore; Phone: 516-877-4243; E-mail: belfiore@adelphi.edu.
Lacrosse: Jill Lessne; Phone: 516-877-4240; E-mail: jilllax@aol.com.
Soccer: Rich Ilsley; Phone: 516-877-4233; E-mail: ilsley@adelphi.edu.
Swimming: Linda Jelovich; Phone: 516-877-4247; E-mail: jelovic2@adelphi.edu.
Tennis: William Klocke; Phone: 516-877-4240; E-mail: williamklocke@adelphi.edu.
Volleyball: Joe Chojnacki; Phone: 516-877-4240; E-mail: joechoj@aol.com.

ADRIAN COLLEGE
Adrian, Michigan
Bulldogs ◆ NCAA III ◆ Michigan Intercollegiate Conference
◆ http://www.adrian.edu/

Independent religious 4-year, founded 1859, affiliated with United Methodist Church
Coed, 1,028 undergraduate students, 96% full-time, 56% women, 44% men
Small-town 100-acre campus with easy access to Detroit and Toledo
Moderately difficult entrance level, 85% of applicants were admitted

Freshmen *Admission:* 1,300 applied, 1,143 were accepted, 307 enrolled.
Tuition and fees (2003–04): $16,570 (full-time). *Room and board:* $5760 (room only: $2460).
Financial Aid (All incoming freshmen): *Average need-based gift aid:* $10,344. *Average non-need based aid:* $7004. *Average aid to full-time undergraduates:* $16,684.
Athletic Department: *Director of Athletics:* Henry Mensing; Phone: 517-264-3972; Fax: 517-264-3802; E-mail: hmensing@adrian.edu. *Sports Information Director:* Aaron Klotz; Phone: 517-264-3976; E-mail: gklotz@adrian.edu.

MEN'S COACHES
Baseball: Craig Rainey; Phone: 517-264-3977; E-mail: crainey@adrian.edu.
Basketball: Buck Riley; Phone: 517-264-3978; E-mail: mriley@adrian.edu.
Cross Country: Riki Carson; Phone: 517-264-3992; E-mail: rcarson@adrian.edu.
Football: Jim Lyall; Phone: 517-264-3995; E-mail: jlyall@adrian.edu.
Golf: Buck Riley; Phone: 517-264-3978; E-mail: mriley@adrian.edu.
Soccer: Jeff Rosenbrook; Phone: 517-264-3990; E-mail: jrosenbrook@adrian.edu.
Tennis: Phone: 517-264-3972.
Track and Field: Riki Carson; Phone: 517-264-3992; E-mail: rcarson@adrian.edu.

WOMEN'S COACHES
Basketball: Kathy Morris; Phone: 517-264-3975; E-mail: kmorris@adrian.edu.
Cross Country: Riki Carson; Phone: 517-264-3992; E-mail: rcarson@adrian.edu.
Golf: Cyndi Beaubien; Phone: 517-265-5161; E-mail: cbeaubien@adrian.edu.
Soccer: Rick Gutierrez; Phone: 517-264-3990; E-mail: rgutierrez@adrian.edu.
Softball: Molly Moore; Phone: 517-264-3998; E-mail: mmoore@adrian.edu.
Tennis: Karen Caine; Phone: 517-265-5161.
Track and Field: Riki Carson; Phone: 517-264-3992; E-mail: rcarson@adrian.edu.
Volleyball: Michael Watkins; Phone: 517-264-3975; E-mail: mwatkins@adrian.edu.

AGNES SCOTT COLLEGE
Decatur, Georgia
Scotties ◆ NCAA III ◆ Independent
◆ http://www.agnesscott.edu/

Independent religious comprehensive, founded 1889, affiliated with Presbyterian Church (U.S.A.)
Women only, 898 undergraduate students, 95% full-time, 100% women
Urban 100-acre campus with easy access to Atlanta
Very difficult entrance level, 66% of applicants were admitted

Freshmen *Admission:* 782 applied, 514 were accepted, 213 enrolled.
Test scores: SAT verbal scores over 500: 91%; SAT math scores over 500: 84%; SAT verbal scores over 600: 62%; SAT math scores over 600: 44%; SAT verbal scores over 700: 16%; SAT math scores over 700: 4%.
Tuition and fees (2003–04): $20,470 (full-time). *Room and board:* $7760.
Financial Aid (All incoming freshmen): *Average need-based gift aid:* $16,564. *Average non-need based aid:* $9407. *Average aid to full-time undergraduates:* $21,564.
Athletic Department: *Director of Athletics:* Joeleen Akin; Phone: 404-471-6170; Fax: 404-471-6099; E-mail: jakin@agnesscott.edu. *Sports Information Director:* Jon McLamb; Phone: 404-471-6491; E-mail: jmclamb@agnesscott.edu.

WOMEN'S COACHES
Basketball: Joeleen Akin; Phone: 404-471-6170; E-mail: jakin@agnesscott.edu.
Cross Country: John Roberts; Phone: 404-471-6475; E-mail: jroberts@agnesscott.edu.
Soccer: Joe Bergin; Phone: 404-471-6941; E-mail: jbergin@agnesscott.edu.
Softball: James Hilleary; Phone: 404-471-6358; E-mail: jhilleary@agnesscott.edu.
Swimming: Kevin Kohler; Phone: 404-471-5493; E-mail: kkohler@agnesscott.edu.
Tennis: Jon McLamb; Phone: 404-471-6491; E-mail: jmclamb@agnesscott.edu.
Volleyball: James Hilleary; Phone: 404-471-6358; E-mail: jhilleary@agnesscott.edu.

ALABAMA AGRICULTURAL AND MECHANICAL UNIVERSITY
Huntsville, Alabama
Bulldogs ◆ NCAA I ◆ Southwestern Athletic Conference
◆ http://www.aamu.edu/

State-supported university, founded 1875
Coed, 5,326 undergraduate students, 93% full-time, 53% women, 47% men
Suburban 2,001-acre campus
Minimally difficult entrance level, 47% of applicants were admitted

Freshmen *Admission:* 8,295 applied, 3,697 were accepted, 1,301 enrolled.
Tuition and fees (2004–05): $3872 (resident), $6704 (nonresident). *Room and board:* $4500 (room only: $2600).
Financial Aid (All incoming freshmen): *Average need-based gift aid:* $2804. *Average non-need based aid:* $2625. *Average aid to full-time undergraduates:* $7284.
Athletic Department: *Director of Athletics:* James Martin; Phone: 256-372-4001; Fax: 256-372-5951. *Sports Information Director:* Rickey Hazel; Phone: 256-372-4005; E-mail: sportsinfo@aamu.edu.

MEN'S COACHES
Baseball: Thomas Wesley; Phone: 256-372-4004; E-mail: baseball@aamu.edu.
Basketball: Vann Pettaway; Phone: 256-372-4009; E-mail: lvpettaway@aamu.edu.
Cross Country: Kim Seals; Phone: 256-372-4013; E-mail: kcabell@aamu.edu.
Football: Anthony Jones; Phone: 256-372-5360; E-mail: ajones@aamu.edu.
Golf: Josh Oliver; Phone: 256-372-4000.

Soccer: Salah Yousif; Phone: 256-372-4788; E-mail: syousif@aamu.edu.

Tennis: Thomas Colvin; Phone: 256-372-5317; E-mail: tc@aamu.edu.

Track and Field: Kim Seals; Phone: 256-372-4013; E-mail: kcabell@aamu.edu.

WOMEN'S COACHES

Basketball: Altherias Warmley; Phone: 256-372-4008; E-mail: awormley@aamu.edu.

Cross Country: Kim Seals; Phone: 256-372-4013; E-mail: kcabell@aamu.edu.

Golf: Rodney Whittle; Phone: 256-372-8260; E-mail: rwhittle@aamu.edu.

Soccer: Frank Davies; Phone: 256-372-8265; E-mail: frank_davies@aamu.edu.

Softball: Phone: 256-372-4703.

Tennis: Thomas Colvin; Phone: 256-372-5317; E-mail: tc@aamu.edu.

Track and Field: Kim Seals; Phone: 256-372-4013; E-mail: kcabell@aamu.edu.

Volleyball: Betty Austin; Phone: 256-372-4267; E-mail: baustin@aamu.edu.

ALABAMA STATE UNIVERSITY
Montgomery, Alabama

Hornets ◆ NCAA I ◆ Southwestern Athletic Conference ◆ http://www.alasu.edu/

State-supported comprehensive, founded 1867, part of Alabama Commission on Higher Education
Coed, 5,020 undergraduate students, 85% full-time, 59% women, 41% men
Urban 172-acre campus
Minimally difficult entrance level, 37% of applicants were admitted

Freshmen *Admission:* 11,462 applied, 4,267 were accepted, 1,249 enrolled. *Test scores:* SAT verbal scores over 500: 13%; SAT math scores over 500: 9%; SAT verbal scores over 600: 1%; SAT math scores over 600: 1%.
Tuition and fees (2003–04): $3600 (resident), $7200 (nonresident). *Room and board:* $3700 (room only: $1980).
Financial Aid (All incoming freshmen): *Average need-based gift aid:* $3414. *Average non-need based aid:* $3723. *Average aid to full-time undergraduates:* $6578.
Athletic Department: *Director of Athletics:* Robert Spivery; Phone: 334-229-4507; Fax: 334-229-4992.

MEN'S COACHES

Baseball: Larry Watkins; Phone: 334-229-4228.
Basketball: Rob Spivery; Phone: 334-229-4509.
Cross Country: Horace Crump; Phone: 334-229-4583.
Football: L.C. Cole; Phone: 334-229-4444.
Golf: Henry Duncombe; Phone: 334-229-4507.
Tennis: Bernard Sewell; Phone: 334-229-4581.
Track and Field: Horace Crump; Phone: 334-229-4583.

WOMEN'S COACHES

Basketball: Freda Freeman-Jackson; Phone: 334-229-4515.
Cross Country: Horace Crump; Phone: 334-229-4583.
Golf: Henry Duncombe; Phone: 334-229-4507.
Softball: Jennifer Collins; Phone: 334-229-4507.
Tennis: Bernard Sewell; Phone: 334-229-4581.
Track and Field: Horace Crump; Phone: 334-229-4583.
Volleyball: Sonja Price; Phone: 334-229-4516.

ALBANY STATE UNIVERSITY
Albany, Georgia

Golden Rams ◆ NCAA II ◆ Southern Intercollegiate Athletic Conference ◆ http://www.asurams.edu/

State-supported comprehensive, founded 1903, part of University System of Georgia
Coed, 3,169 undergraduate students, 83% full-time, 66% women, 34% men
Urban 144-acre campus
Minimally difficult entrance level, 2% of applicants were admitted

Freshmen *Admission:* 2,751 applied, 652 were accepted, 466 enrolled. *Test scores:* SAT verbal scores over 500: 18%; SAT math scores over 500: 18%; SAT verbal scores over 600: 2%; SAT math scores over 600: 1%; SAT verbal scores over 700: %.
Tuition and fees (2003–04): $2774 (resident), $9410 (nonresident). *Room and board:* $3760 (room only: $1770).
Financial Aid (All incoming freshmen): *Average aid to full-time undergraduates:* $6698.
Athletic Department: *Director of Athletics:* John Davis; Phone: 229-430-4754; Fax: 229-430-1774; E-mail: jidavis@asurams.edu. *Sports Information Director:* Edythe Bradley; Phone: 229-430-4673; E-mail: ebradley@asurams.edu.

MEN'S COACHES

Baseball: Edward Taylor; Phone: 229-430-1829; E-mail: eltaylor@asurams.edu.
Basketball: John Davis; Phone: 229-430-4754; E-mail: jidavis@asurams.edu.
Cheerleading: Michelle Clarke; Phone: 229-430-4754; E-mail: mclarke@asurams.edu.
Cross Country: Willie Laster; Phone: 229-430-4761; E-mail: wlaster@asurams.edu.
Football: Mike White; Phone: 229-430-4768; E-mail: jmswhite@asurams.edu.
Track and Field: Willie Laster; Phone: 229-430-4761; E-mail: wlaster@asurams.edu.

WOMEN'S COACHES

Basketball: Robert Skinner; Phone: 229-430-3817; E-mail: rskinner@asurams.edu.
Cheerleading: Michelle Clarke; Phone: 229-430-4754; E-mail: mclarke@asurams.edu.
Cross Country: Willie Laster; Phone: 229-430-4761; E-mail: wlaster@asurams.edu.
Softball: Robert Skinner; Phone: 229-430-3817; E-mail: rskinner@asurams.edu.
Tennis: Lonnie White; Phone: 229-430-4754.
Track and Field: Willie Laster; Phone: 229-430-4761; E-mail: wlaster@asurams.edu.
Volleyball: Robert Skinner; Phone: 229-430-3817; E-mail: rskinner@asurams.edu.

ALBERTSON COLLEGE OF IDAHO
Caldwell, Idaho

Coyotes ◆ NAIA ◆ Cascade Collegiate Conference ◆ http://www.albertson.edu/

Independent comprehensive, founded 1891
Coed, 821 undergraduate students, 96% full-time, 54% women, 46% men
Suburban 50-acre campus
Moderately difficult entrance level, 80% of applicants were admitted

Freshmen *Admission:* 643 applied, 507 were accepted, 182 enrolled. *Test scores:* SAT verbal scores over 500: 82%; SAT math scores over 500: 80%; SAT verbal scores over 600: 33%; SAT math scores over 600: 39%; SAT verbal scores over 700: 6%; SAT math scores over 700: 4%.
Tuition and fees (2003–04): $14,400 (full-time). *Room and board:* $5050 (room only: $2450).
Financial Aid (All incoming freshmen): *Average need-based gift aid:* $3851. *Average non-need based aid:* $5234. *Average aid to full-time undergraduates:* $15,138.

Albertson College of Idaho (*continued*)

Athletic Department: *Director of Athletics:* Marty Holly; Phone: 208-459-5850; Fax: 208-459-5854; E-mail: mholly@albertson.edu. *Sports Information Director:* Mike Safford Jr.; Phone: 208-459-5681; E-mail: msafford@albertson.edu.

MEN'S COACHES

Baseball: Shawn Humberger; Phone: 208-459-5861; E-mail: shumberger@albertson.edu.

Basketball: Mark Owen; Phone: 208-459-5864; E-mail: msafford@albertson.edu.

Cross Country: Patrick McCurry; Phone: 208-459-5085; E-mail: pmccurry@albertson.edu.

Golf: Garry Matlock; Phone: 208-459-5019; E-mail: gmatlock@albertson.edu.

Soccer: John Calpin; Phone: 208-459-5857; E-mail: jcaplin@albertson.edu.

Swimming: Mike Shines; Phone: 208-459-5874; E-mail: mshines@albertson.edu.

Track and Field: Patrick McCurry; Phone: 208-459-5085; E-mail: pmccurry@albertson.edu.

WOMEN'S COACHES

Basketball: Reagan Rossi; Phone: 208-459-5855; E-mail: rrossi@albertson.edu.

Cross Country: Patrick McCurry; Phone: 208-459-5085; E-mail: pmccurry@albertson.edu.

Golf: Garry Matlock; Phone: 208-459-5019; E-mail: gmatlock@albertson.edu.

Soccer: Aisha Reed; Phone: 208-459-5867; E-mail: areed@albertson.edu.

Softball: Kelly Gibbons; Phone: 208-459-5113; E-mail: kgibbons@albertson.edu.

Swimming: Mike Shines; Phone: 208-459-5874; E-mail: mshines@albertson.edu.

Tennis: Cisco Limbago; Phone: 208-459-5856; E-mail: climbago@albertson.edu.

Track and Field: Patrick McCurry; Phone: 208-459-5085; E-mail: pmccurry@albertson.edu.

Volleyball: Liz Mendiola; Phone: 208-459-5858; E-mail: lmendiola@albertson.edu.

ALBERTUS MAGNUS COLLEGE
New Haven, Connecticut

Falcons ◆ NCAA III ◆ Great Northeast Athletic Conference ◆ http://www.albertus.edu/

Independent Roman Catholic comprehensive, founded 1925
Coed, 1,806 undergraduate students, 94% full-time, 69% women, 31% men
Suburban 55-acre campus with easy access to New York City and Hartford
Moderately difficult entrance level, 78% of applicants were admitted

Freshmen *Admission:* 532 applied, 419 were accepted, 229 enrolled. *Test scores:* SAT verbal scores over 500: 30%; SAT math scores over 500: 29%; SAT verbal scores over 600: 5%; SAT math scores over 600: 8%; SAT math scores over 700: 1%.
Tuition and fees (2003–04): $16,808 (full-time). *Room and board:* $7330.
Financial Aid (All incoming freshmen): *Average need-based gift aid:* $8700. *Average non-need based aid:* $6000. *Average aid to full-time undergraduates:* $11,500.
Athletic Department: *Director of Athletics:* Jay Moran; Phone: 203-773-8578; Fax: 203-773-7533; E-mail: jmoran@albertus.edu. *Sports Information Director:* Jennifer Pacelli; Phone: 203-773-8579; E-mail: jpacelli@albertus.edu.

MEN'S COACHES

Baseball: Joe Tonelli; Phone: 203-773-8578; E-mail: athletics@albertus.edu.

Basketball: Bob McMahon; Phone: 203-773-8575; E-mail: athletics@albertus.edu.

Cross Country: Jennifer Pacelli; Phone: 203-773-8579; E-mail: jpacelli@albertus.edu.

Soccer: George Bedocs; Phone: 203-773-8936; E-mail: gbedocs@snet.net.

Tennis: Ron Waite; Phone: 203-773-8575; E-mail: athletics@albertus.edu.

WOMEN'S COACHES

Basketball: Ed Panzo; Phone: 203-773-8575; E-mail: athletics@albertus.edu.

Cross Country: Jennifer Pacelli; Phone: 203-773-8579; E-mail: jpacelli@albertus.edu.

Softball: Ed Panzo; Phone: 203-773-8575; E-mail: athletics@albertus.edu.

Tennis: Betsy Fehy; Phone: 203-773-8575; E-mail: athletics@albertus.edu.

Volleyball: Stacy Shannon; Phone: 203-773-8575; E-mail: athletics@albertus.edu.

ALBION COLLEGE
Albion, Michigan

Britons ◆ NCAA III ◆ Michigan Intercollegiate Conference ◆ http://www.albion.edu/

Independent Methodist 4-year, founded 1835
Coed, 1,732 undergraduate students, 98% full-time, 57% women, 43% men
Small-town 565-acre campus with easy access to Detroit
Moderately difficult entrance level, 82% of applicants were admitted

Freshmen *Admission:* 1,534 applied, 1,332 were accepted, 487 enrolled. *Test scores:* SAT verbal scores over 500: 84%; SAT math scores over 500: 86%; SAT verbal scores over 600: 46%; SAT math scores over 600: 44%; SAT verbal scores over 700: 7%; SAT math scores over 700: 9%.
Tuition and fees (2003–04): $21,948 (full-time). *Room and board:* $6262 (room only: $3062).
Financial Aid (All incoming freshmen): *Average need-based gift aid:* $16,321. *Average non-need based aid:* $12,065. *Average aid to full-time undergraduates:* $19,184.
Athletic Department: *Director of Athletics:* Peter Hart; Phone: 517-629-0281; Fax: 517-629-1648. *Sports Information Director:* Bobby Lee; Phone: 517-629-0434; E-mail: blee@albion.edu.

MEN'S COACHES

Baseball: Scott Carden; Phone: 517-629-0517; E-mail: scarden@albion.edu.

Basketball: Mike Turner; Phone: 517-629-0457; E-mail: mturner@albion.edu.

Cheerleading: Jaime Walls; Phone: 517-629-0281; E-mail: jcarter@albion.edu.

Cross Country: Hayden Smith; Phone: 517-629-0514; E-mail: hsmith@albion.edu.

Diving: Keith Havens; Phone: 517-629-0282; E-mail: khavens@albion.edu.

Football: Craig Rundle; Phone: 517-629-0459; E-mail: crundle@albion.edu.

Golf: Mike Turner; Phone: 517-629-0457; E-mail: mturner@albion.edu.

Soccer: Jerry Block; Phone: 517-629-0506; E-mail: jblock@albion.edu.

Swimming: Keith Havens; Phone: 517-629-0282; E-mail: khavens@albion.edu.

Tennis: Scott Frew; Phone: 517-629-0739; E-mail: sfrew@albion.edu.

Track and Field: Hayden Smith; Phone: 517-629-0514; E-mail: hsmith@albion.edu.

WOMEN'S COACHES

Basketball: Doreen Belkowski; Phone: 517-629-0516; E-mail: dbelkowski@albion.edu.

Cheerleading: Jaime Walls; Phone: 517-629-0281; E-mail: jcarter@albion.edu.

Cross Country: Hayden Smith; Phone: 517-629-0514; E-mail: hsmith@albion.edu.

Diving: Keith Havens; Phone: 517-629-0282; E-mail: khavens@albion.edu.

Golf: Nicole Hilderley; Phone: 517-629-0515; E-mail: bhilderley@tds.net.

Soccer: Lisa Rochek; Phone: 517-629-0521; E-mail: lroschek@albion.edu.

Softball: Julie Liljeberg; Phone: 517-629-0515; E-mail: jliljeberg@albion.edu.

Swimming: Keith Havens; Phone: 517-629-0282; E-mail: khavens@albion.edu.

Tennis: Scott Frew; Phone: 517-629-0739; E-mail: sfrew@albion.edu.
Track and Field: Hayden Smith; Phone: 517-629-0514; E-mail: hsmith@albion.edu.
Volleyball: Russell Frey; Phone: 517-629-0738; E-mail: rfrey@albion.edu.

ALBRIGHT COLLEGE
Reading, Pennsylvania

Lions ◆ NCAA III ◆ Commonwealth Conference ◆ http://www.albright.edu/

Independent religious comprehensive, founded 1856, affiliated with United Methodist Church
Coed, 2,046 undergraduate students, 97% full-time, 56% women, 44% men
Suburban 118-acre campus with easy access to Philadelphia
Moderately difficult entrance level, 70% of applicants were admitted

Freshmen *Admission:* 2,967 applied, 2,137 were accepted, 456 enrolled. *Test scores:* SAT verbal scores over 500: 56%; SAT math scores over 500: 56%; SAT verbal scores over 600: 16%; SAT math scores over 600: 18%; SAT verbal scores over 700: 1%; SAT math scores over 700: 2%.
Tuition and fees (2004–05): $24,580 (full-time). *Room and board:* $7510 (room only: $4275).
Financial Aid (All incoming freshmen): *Average need-based gift aid:* $14,389. *Average non-need based aid:* $14,639. *Average aid to full-time undergraduates:* $18,066.
Athletic Department: *Director of Athletics:* Steve George; Phone: 610-921-7535; Fax: 610-921-7566; E-mail: sgeorge@alb.edu. *Sports Information Director:* Jeff Feiler; Phone: 610-921-7678; E-mail: jfeiler@alb.edu.

MEN'S COACHES
Baseball: Jeff Feiler; Phone: 610-921-7678; E-mail: jfeiler@alb.edu.
Basketball: Rick Ferry; Phone: 610-921-7825; E-mail: rferry@alb.edu.
Cheerleading: Claudia Schadler-Duong; Phone: 610-921-2381; E-mail: albrightcheer@aol.com.
Cross Country: Dan Scott; Phone: 610-921-7830; E-mail: athletics@alb.edu.
Football: E.J. Sandusky; Phone: 610-921-7840; E-mail: ejsandusky@alb.edu.
Golf: Ray Mest; Phone: 610-921-7850; E-mail: raym@alb.edu.
Soccer: Tommy Greenawalt; Phone: 610-921-7535; E-mail: athletics@alb.edu.
Swimming: John Stuhltrager; Phone: 610-921-7837; E-mail: jstuhltrager@alb.edu.
Tennis: Dale Yoder; Phone: 610-921-7820; E-mail: dyoder@alb.edu.
Track and Field: Dan Scott; Phone: 610-921-7830; E-mail: athletics@alb.edu.
Wrestling: Joe Reilly; Phone: 610-921-7535; E-mail: athletics@alb.edu.

WOMEN'S COACHES
Basketball: Rick Ferry; Phone: 610-921-7825; E-mail: rferry@alb.edu.
Cheerleading: Claudia Schadler-Duong; Phone: 610-921-2381; E-mail: albrightcheer@aol.com.
Cross Country: John Saldibar; Phone: 610-921-7830; E-mail: athletics@alb.edu.
Field Hockey: Amy Lincoln; Phone: 610-921-7207; E-mail: alincoln@alb.edu.
Soccer: Tommy Greenawalt; Phone: 610-921-7535; E-mail: athletics@alb.edu.
Softball: Angela Nunan; Phone: 610-921-7535; E-mail: anunan@alb.edu.
Swimming: John Stuhltrager; Phone: 610-921-7837; E-mail: jstuhltrager@alb.edu.
Tennis: Paul McDonough; Phone: 610-921-7535; E-mail: athletics@alb.edu.
Track and Field: John Saldibar; Phone: 610-921-7830; E-mail: athletics@alb.edu.
Volleyball: Angela Pierce; Phone: 610-921-7535; E-mail: angelap@alb.edu.

ALCORN STATE UNIVERSITY
Alcorn State, Mississippi

Braves ◆ NCAA I ◆ Southwestern Athletic Conference ◆ http://www.alcorn.edu/

State-supported comprehensive, founded 1871, part of Mississippi Institutions of Higher Learning
Coed, 2,662 undergraduate students, 89% full-time, 61% women, 39% men
Rural 1,756-acre campus
Minimally difficult entrance level, 22% of applicants were admitted

Freshmen *Admission:* 4,619 applied, 1,008 were accepted, 483 enrolled.
Tuition and fees (2003–04): $4440 (resident), $8946 (nonresident). *Room and board:* $3821 (room only: $2164).
Financial Aid (All incoming freshmen): *Average need-based gift aid:* $4200. *Average non-need based aid:* $2300. *Average aid to full-time undergraduates:* $6600.
Athletic Department: *Director of Athletics:* Robert Raines; Phone: 601-877-6500; Fax: 601-877-3821. *Sports Information Director:* Tyrone Broxton; Phone: 601-877-6466.

MEN'S COACHES
Baseball: Willie McGowan; Phone: 601-877-6279.
Basketball: Samuel West; Phone: 601-877-6274.
Cross Country: Alisha Shields-Gadson; Phone: 601-877-6503.
Football: Johnny Thomas; Phone: 601-877-6503.
Golf: Ocie Brown; Phone: 601-877-6278.
Tennis: Tony Dodgen; Phone: 601-877-6277.
Track and Field: Alisha Shields-Gadson; Phone: 601-877-6503.

WOMEN'S COACHES
Basketball: Shirley Walker; Phone: 601-877-6467.
Cross Country: Alisha Shields-Gadson; Phone: 601-877-6503.
Golf: Ocie Brown; Phone: 601-877-6278.
Softball: Millicent Sylvan; Phone: 601-877-6275.
Tennis: Tony Dodgen; Phone: 601-877-6277.
Track and Field: Alisha Shields-Gadson; Phone: 601-877-6503.
Volleyball: Millicent Sylvan; Phone: 601-877-6275.

ALDERSON-BROADDUS COLLEGE
Philippi, West Virginia

Battlers ◆ NCAA II ◆ West Virginia Intercollegiate Athletic Conference ◆ http://www.ab.edu/

Independent religious comprehensive, founded 1871, affiliated with American Baptist Churches in the U.S.A.
Coed, 674 undergraduate students, 90% full-time, 70% women, 30% men
Rural 170-acre campus
Moderately difficult entrance level, 63% of applicants were admitted

Freshmen *Admission:* 864 applied, 551 were accepted, 129 enrolled. *Test scores:* SAT verbal scores over 500: 42%; SAT math scores over 500: 63%; SAT verbal scores over 600: 9%; SAT math scores over 600: 13%; SAT math scores over 700: 2%.
Tuition and fees (2004–05): $17,116 (full-time). *Room and board:* $5534.
Financial Aid (All incoming freshmen): *Average need-based gift aid:* $4310. *Average non-need based aid:* $17,868. *Average aid to full-time undergraduates:* $16,422.
Athletic Department: *Director of Athletics:* J.D. Long; Phone: 304-457-6266; Fax: 304-457-6291; E-mail: lonjd@mail.ab.edu. *Sports Information Director:* Michelle Odai; Phone: 304-457-6390; E-mail: odaiml@mail.ab.edu.

MEN'S COACHES
Baseball: Kit Laird; Phone: 304-457-6265; E-mail: lairdje@mail.ab.edu.
Basketball: Greg Zimmerman; Phone: 304-457-6284; E-mail: zimmermang@mail.ab.edu.
Cross Country: Jim Seaton; Phone: 304-457-6279; E-mail: seatonjr@mail.ab.edu.
Soccer: Dan Kelly; Phone: 304-457-6263; E-mail: kellydp@mail.ab.edu.
Track and Field: Jim Seaton; Phone: 304-457-6279; E-mail: seatonjr@mail.ab.edu.

Alderson-Broaddus College *(continued)*

WOMEN'S COACHES

Basketball: Laurie Herrington-Arnet; Phone: 304-457-6332; E-mail: herrington-arnettl@mail.ab.edu.
Cross Country: Jim Seaton; Phone: 304-457-6279; E-mail: seatonjr@mail.ab.edu.
Softball: J.D. Long; Phone: 304-457-6266; E-mail: longjd@mail.ab.edu.
Track and Field: Jim Seaton; Phone: 304-457-6279; E-mail: seatonjr@mail.ab.edu.
Volleyball: J.D. Long; Phone: 304-457-6266; E-mail: longjd@mail.ab.edu.

ALFRED UNIVERSITY
Alfred, New York

Saxons ◆ NCAA III ◆ Empire 8 Conference
◆ http://www.alfred.edu/

Independent university, founded 1836
Coed, 2,055 undergraduate students, 95% full-time, 52% women, 48% men
Rural 232-acre campus with easy access to Rochester
Moderately difficult entrance level, 6% of applicants were admitted

Freshmen *Admission:* 2,169 applied, 1,493 were accepted, 474 enrolled. *Test scores:* SAT verbal scores over 500: 80%; SAT math scores over 500: 78%; SAT verbal scores over 600: 32%; SAT math scores over 600: 30%; SAT verbal scores over 700: 6%; SAT math scores over 700: 5%.
Tuition and fees (2003–04): $19,278 (full-time). *Room and board:* $9012 (room only: $4696).
Financial Aid (All incoming freshmen): *Average need-based gift aid:* $15,180. *Average non-need based aid:* $6678. *Average aid to full-time undergraduates:* $19,226.
Athletic Department: *Director of Athletics:* Jim Moretti; Phone: 607-871-2193; Fax: 607-871-2874; E-mail: moretti@alfred.edu. *Sports Information Director:* Mark Whitehouse; Phone: 607-871-2904; E-mail: whitehouse@alfred.edu.

MEN'S COACHES

Basketball: Jay Murphy; Phone: 607-871-2900; E-mail: fmurphy@alfred.edu.
Cheerleading: Phone: 607-871-2193; E-mail: cheer@alfred.edu.
Cross Country: Andrew Weishaar; Phone: 607-871-2626; E-mail: weishaara@alfred.edu.
Diving: Brian Striker; Phone: 607-871-2893; E-mail: striker@alfred.edu.
Football: Dave Murray; Phone: 607-871-2193; E-mail: murrayd@alfred.edu.
Lacrosse: Preston Chapman; Phone: 607-871-2890; E-mail: chapman@alfred.edu.
Soccer: Ken Hassler; Phone: 607-871-2899; E-mail: fhassler@alfred.edu.
Swimming: Brian Striker; Phone: 607-871-2893; E-mail: striker@alfred.edu.
Tennis: Brian Friedland; Phone: 607-871-3089; E-mail: bfriedland@hotmail.com.
Track and Field: Andrew Weishaar; Phone: 607-871-2626; E-mail: weishaara@alfred.edu.

WOMEN'S COACHES

Basketball: Michele Finn; Phone: 607-871-2898; E-mail: finnma@alfred.edu.
Cheerleading: Phone: 607-871-2193; E-mail: cheer@alfred.edu.
Cross Country: Andrew Weishaar; Phone: 607-871-2626; E-mail: weishaara@alfred.edu.
Diving: Brian Striker; Phone: 607-871-2893; E-mail: striker@alfred.edu.
Lacrosse: Anne Windover; Phone: 416-871-2628; E-mail: windovera@alfred.edu.
Soccer: Jamie McLaughlin; Phone: 607-871-2896; E-mail: mclaugj@alfred.edu.
Softball: Jamie McLaughlin; Phone: 607-871-2896; E-mail: mclaugj@alfred.edu.
Swimming: Brian Striker; Phone: 607-871-2893; E-mail: striker@alfred.edu.
Tennis: Brian Friedland; Phone: 607-871-3089; E-mail: bfriedland@hotmail.com.

Track and Field: Andrew Weishaar; Phone: 607-871-2626; E-mail: weishaara@alfred.edu.
Volleyball: Steve Brzezinski; Phone: 607-871-2193; E-mail: brzezinski@alfred.edu.

ALICE LLOYD COLLEGE
Pippa Passes, Kentucky

Eagles ◆ NAIA ◆ Appalachian Conference
◆ http://www.alc.edu/

Independent 4-year, founded 1923
Coed, 617 undergraduate students, 96% full-time, 54% women, 46% men
Rural 175-acre campus
Moderately difficult entrance level, 56% of applicants were admitted

Freshmen *Admission:* 870 applied, 503 were accepted, 204 enrolled. *Test scores:* SAT verbal scores over 500: 60%; SAT math scores over 500: 30%; SAT verbal scores over 600: 40%; SAT math scores over 600: 10%.
Tuition and fees (2004–05): $1040 (full-time). *Room and board:* $3600 (room only: $1650).
Financial Aid (All incoming freshmen): *Average need-based gift aid:* $6654. *Average non-need based aid:* $6360. *Average aid to full-time undergraduates:* $8281.
Athletic Department: *Director of Athletics:* Gary Gibson; Phone: 606-368-6119; Fax: 606-368-6217; E-mail: garygibson@alc.edu. *Sports Information Director:* Stephanie Damron; Phone: 606-368-2083; E-mail: stephaniedamron@alc.edu.

MEN'S COACHES

Baseball: Scott Cornett; Phone: 606-368-6120; E-mail: scottcornett@alc.edu.
Basketball: Gary Gibson; Phone: 606-368-6119; E-mail: garygibson@alc.edu.
Cross Country: Kevin Slone; Phone: 606-368-6127; E-mail: kevinslone@alc.edu.

WOMEN'S COACHES

Basketball: Tim Rice; Phone: 606-368-6127; E-mail: timrice@alc.edu.
Cross Country: Kevin Slone; Phone: 606-368-6127; E-mail: kevinslone@alc.edu.
Softball: Tim Rice; Phone: 606-368-6127; E-mail: timrice@alc.edu.

ALLEGHENY COLLEGE
Meadville, Pennsylvania

Gators ◆ NCAA III ◆ North Coast Athletic Conference
◆ http://www.allegheny.edu/

Independent 4-year, founded 1815
Coed, 1,849 undergraduate students, 98% full-time, 52% women, 48% men
Small-town 254-acre campus
Very difficult entrance level, 8% of applicants were admitted

Freshmen *Admission:* 2,438 applied, 2,002 were accepted, 481 enrolled. *Test scores:* SAT verbal scores over 500: 89%; SAT math scores over 500: 93%; SAT verbal scores over 600: 53%; SAT math scores over 600: 52%; SAT verbal scores over 700: 9%; SAT math scores over 700: 9%.
Tuition and fees (2003–04): $24,400 (full-time). *Room and board:* $5880 (room only: $3000).
Financial Aid (All incoming freshmen): *Average need-based gift aid:* $15,172. *Average non-need based aid:* $9601. *Average aid to full-time undergraduates:* $20,797.
Athletic Department: *Director of Athletics:* Larry Lee; Phone: 814-332-2824; Fax: 814-332-1217; E-mail: larry.lee@allegheny.edu. *Sports Information Director:* Ken Baker; Phone: 814-332-5952; E-mail: kbaker@allegheny.edu.

MEN'S COACHES

Baseball: Mike Ferris; Phone: 814-332-2830; E-mail: michael.ferris@allegheny.edu.

Basketball: Rob Clune; Phone: 814-332-2819; E-mail: robert.clune@allegheny.edu.
Cheerleading: Keri Fadden; Phone: 814-332-2824; E-mail: kfadden@allegheny.edu.
Cross Country: Bill Ross; Phone: 814-332-2827; E-mail: william.ross@allegheny.edu.
Diving: Tom Erdos; Phone: 814-332-2808; E-mail: thomas.erdos@allegheny.edu.
Football: Mark Matlak; Phone: 814-332-2826; E-mail: mark.matlak@allegheny.edu.
Golf: Jeff Groff; Phone: 814-332-2811; E-mail: jeff.groff@allegheny.edu.
Soccer: Angelo Panzetta; Phone: 814-332-5208; E-mail: angelo.panzetta@allegheny.edu.
Swimming: Tom Erdos; Phone: 814-332-2808; E-mail: thomas.erdos@allegheny.edu.
Tennis: Jared Luteran; Phone: 814-332-2809; E-mail: jared.luteran@allegheny.edu.
Track and Field: Bill Ross; Phone: 814-332-2827; E-mail: william.ross@allegheny.edu.

WOMEN'S COACHES
Basketball: Jennifer Riemer; Phone: 814-332-2807; E-mail: jennifer.reimer@allegheny.edu.
Cheerleading: Keri Fadden; Phone: 814-332-2824; E-mail: kfadden@allegheny.edu.
Cross Country: Bill Ross; Phone: 814-332-2827; E-mail: william.ross@allegheny.edu.
Diving: Tom Erdos; Phone: 814-332-2808; E-mail: thomas.erdos@allegheny.edu.
Lacrosse: Paul Bonus; Phone: 814-332-2828; E-mail: paul.bonus@allegheny.edu.
Soccer: Paul Bonus; Phone: 814-332-2811; E-mail: paul.bonus@allegheny.edu.
Softball: Sandra Sanford; Phone: 814-332-2807; E-mail: sandra.sanford@allegheny.edu.
Swimming: Tom Erdos; Phone: 814-332-2808; E-mail: thomas.erdos@allegheny.edu.
Tennis: Jared Luteran; Phone: 814-332-2809; E-mail: jared.luteran@allegheny.edu.
Track and Field: Bill Ross; Phone: 814-332-2827; E-mail: william.ross@allegheny.edu.
Volleyball: Bridget Sheehan; Phone: 814-332-2822; E-mail: bridget.sheehan@allegheny.edu.

ALLEN UNIVERSITY
Columbia, South Carolina
Yellow Jackets ◆ NAIA ◆ Eastern Intercollegiate Conference ◆ http://www.allenuniversity.edu/

Independent African Methodist Episcopal 4-year, founded 1870
Coed, 565 undergraduate students, 98% full-time, 38% women, 62% men
Suburban campus
Minimally difficult entrance level, 61% of applicants were admitted

Freshmen *Admission:* 784 applied, 479 were accepted, 145 enrolled.
Tuition and fees (2003–04): $7808 (full-time). *Room and board:* $2105.
Financial Aid (All incoming freshmen): *Average need-based gift aid:* $2213. *Average aid to full-time undergraduates:* $7025.
Athletic Department: *Director of Athletics:* Ronald Sims; Phone: 803-376-5807; Fax: 803-376-5701; E-mail: rsims@allenuniversity.edu. *Sports Information Director:* Carlton Green; Phone: 803-376-5729; E-mail: cgreen6655@aol.com.

MEN'S COACHES
Baseball: Phone: 803-376-5729.
Basketball: Phone: 803-376-5729.
Cross Country: Phone: 803-376-5729.
Football: Sherman Simmons; Phone: 803-376-5770; E-mail: ssimmons@allenuniversity.edu.
Tennis: Phone: 803-376-5729.
Track and Field: Phone: 803-376-5729.

WOMEN'S COACHES
Basketball: Phone: 803-376-5729.
Cross Country: Phone: 803-376-5729.
Softball: Phone: 803-376-5729.
Tennis: Phone: 803-376-5729.
Track and Field: Phone: 803-376-5729.
Volleyball: Phone: 803-376-5729.

ALLIANT INTERNATIONAL UNIVERSITY
San Diego, California
NAIA ◆ Independent ◆ http://www.alliant.edu/

Independent university, founded 1952, part of Alliant International University
Coed, 420 undergraduate students, 87% full-time, 55% women, 45% men
Suburban 60-acre campus
Moderately difficult entrance level, 65% of applicants were admitted

Freshmen *Admission:* 376 applied, 226 were accepted, 71 enrolled.
Tuition and fees (2004–05): $19,360 (full-time). *Room and board:* $7430.
Financial Aid (All incoming freshmen): *Average non-need based aid:* $2000. *Average aid to full-time undergraduates:* $21,250.
Athletic Department: *Director of Athletics:* Dan Kettlehake; Phone: 858-635-4630; Fax: 858-635-4648; E-mail: dkettlehake@alliant.edu.

MEN'S COACHES
Cross Country: Ben Nichols; Phone: 858-635-4647; E-mail: bnichols@alliant.edu.
Soccer: Lance Thompson; Phone: 858-635-4648; E-mail: lthompson@alliant.edu.
Tennis: Ashish Selarka; Phone: 858-635-4644; E-mail: aselarka@alliant.edu.
Track and Field: Ben Nichols; Phone: 858-635-4647; E-mail: bnichols@alliant.edu.

WOMEN'S COACHES
Cross Country: Ben Nichols; Phone: 858-635-4647; E-mail: bnichols@alliant.edu.
Soccer: Lance Thompson; Phone: 858-635-4648; E-mail: lthompson@alliant.edu.
Tennis: Ashish Selarka; Phone: 858-635-4644; E-mail: aselarka@alliant.edu.
Track and Field: Ben Nichols; Phone: 858-635-4647; E-mail: bnichols@alliant.edu.
Volleyball: Allen Allen; Phone: 858-635-4649; E-mail: aallen@alliant.edu.

ALMA COLLEGE
Alma, Michigan
Scotts ◆ NCAA III ◆ Michigan Intercollegiate Conference ◆ http://www.alma.edu/

Independent Presbyterian 4-year, founded 1886
Coed, 1,291 undergraduate students, 97% full-time, 58% women, 42% men
Small-town 125-acre campus
Moderately difficult entrance level, 75% of applicants were admitted

Freshmen *Admission:* 1,497 applied, 1,155 were accepted, 322 enrolled.
Tuition and fees (2003–04): $18,854 (full-time). *Room and board:* $6712 (room only: $3324).
Financial Aid (All incoming freshmen): *Average need-based gift aid:* $14,573. *Average non-need based aid:* $12,904. *Average aid to full-time undergraduates:* $17,417.
Athletic Department: *Director of Athletics:* Jim Cole; Phone: 989-463-7281; Fax: 989-463-7018; E-mail: cole@alma.edu. *Sports Information Director:* Aaron Brock; Phone: 989-463-7019; E-mail: brock@alma.edu.

MEN'S COACHES
Baseball: John Leister; Phone: 989-463-7265; E-mail: leister@alma.edu.
Basketball: Ed Kohtala; Phone: 989-463-7106; E-mail: kohtala@alma.edu.
Cheerleading: Amy Klopf; Phone: 989-463-7279; E-mail: abklopf@yahoo.com.

Tennis: Phone: 803-376-5729.
Track and Field: Phone: 803-376-5729.
Volleyball: Phone: 803-376-5729.

Alma College *(continued)*

Cross Country: Dan Gibson; Phone: 989-463-7074; E-mail: gibsond@alma.edu.
Diving: Greg Baadte; Phone: 989-463-7323; E-mail: baadte@alma.edu.
Football: Jim Cole; Phone: 989-463-7281; E-mail: cole@alma.edu.
Golf: Mark Starkweather; Phone: 989-463-7276; E-mail: starkweather@alma.edu.
Soccer: Jeff Bateson; Phone: 989-463-7352; E-mail: bateson@alma.edu.
Swimming: Greg Baadte; Phone: 989-463-7323; E-mail: baadte@alma.edu.
Tennis: Brandan Snook; Phone: 989-463-7276; E-mail: snook@alma.edu.
Track and Field: Matt Chovanec; Phone: 989-463-7074; E-mail: mchovanec@alma.edu.

WOMEN'S COACHES

Basketball: Charlie Goffnet; Phone: 989-463-7781; E-mail: goffnett@alma.edu.
Cheerleading: Amy Klopf; Phone: 989-463-7279; E-mail: abklopf@yahoo.com.
Cross Country: Dan Gibson; Phone: 989-463-7074; E-mail: gibsond@alma.edu.
Diving: Greg Baadte; Phone: 989-463-7323; E-mail: baadte@alma.edu.
Golf: Charlie Goffnet; Phone: 989-463-7781; E-mail: goffnett@alma.edu.
Soccer: Chi Ly; Phone: 989-463-7089; E-mail: ly@alma.edu.
Softball: Denny Griffin; Phone: 989-463-7988; E-mail: griffin@alma.edu.
Swimming: Greg Baadte; Phone: 989-463-7323; E-mail: baadte@alma.edu.
Tennis: Chi Ly; Phone: 989-463-7089; E-mail: ly@alma.edu.
Track and Field: Dan Gibson; Phone: 989-463-7074; E-mail: gibsond@alma.edu.
Volleyball: Steve Humm; Phone: 989-463-7088; E-mail: humm@alma.edu.

ALVERNIA COLLEGE
Reading, Pennsylvania

Crusaders ◆ NCAA III ◆ Pennsylvania Athletic Conference ◆ http://www.alvernia.edu/

Independent Roman Catholic comprehensive, founded 1958
Coed, 1,848 undergraduate students, 75% full-time, 67% women, 33% men
Suburban 85-acre campus with easy access to Philadelphia
Moderately difficult entrance level, 84% of applicants were admitted

Freshmen *Admission:* 692 applied, 556 were accepted, 292 enrolled. *Test scores:* SAT verbal scores over 500: 32%; SAT math scores over 500: 33%; SAT verbal scores over 600: 7%; SAT math scores over 600: 6%; SAT verbal scores over 700: %.
Tuition and fees (2003–04): $16,362 (full-time). *Room and board:* $6950 (room only: $3490).
Financial Aid (All incoming freshmen): *Average need-based gift aid:* $9768. *Average non-need based aid:* $10,371. *Average aid to full-time undergraduates:* $13,704.
Athletic Department: *Director of Athletics:* John McCloskey; Phone: 610-796-8374; Fax: 610-796-8349; E-mail: john.mccloskey@alvernia.edu. *Sports Information Director:* Jon King; Phone: 610-796-8261; E-mail: jon.king@alvernia.edu.

MEN'S COACHES

Baseball: Yogi Lutz; Phone: 610-796-8476; E-mail: yogiball@enter.net.
Basketball: Jack McCloskey; Phone: 610-796-8244; E-mail: jack.mccloskey@alvernia.edu.
Cross Country: Joe McCool; Phone: 610-796-8473.
Golf: Jon King; Phone: 610-796-8261; E-mail: jon.king@alvernia.edu.
Soccer: Travis Berger; Phone: 610-796-8208; E-mail: bergertab@aol.com.
Tennis: Chris Emkey; Phone: 610-796-8276; E-mail: christopher.emkey@alvernia.edu.

WOMEN'S COACHES

Basketball: Kevin Calabria; Phone: 610-796-8315; E-mail: kevin.calabria@alvernia.edu.
Cross Country: Joe McCool; Phone: 610-796-8473.

Field Hockey: Laura Gingrich; Phone: 610-796-8273; E-mail: laura.gingrich@alvernia.edu.
Lacrosse: Jennifer Gossert; Phone: 610-796-8273; E-mail: jennifer.gossert@alvernia.edu.
Soccer: Laura Witman; Phone: 610-796-8309; E-mail: laura.witman@alvernia.edu.
Softball: Craig Wojswillo; Phone: 610-796-8473; E-mail: craig.wojszwillo@alvernia.edu.
Tennis: Chris Emkey; Phone: 610-796-8276; E-mail: christopher.emkey@alvernia.edu.
Volleyball: Bob Shuman; Phone: 610-796-8315; E-mail: robert.shuman@alvernia.edu.

ALVERNO COLLEGE
Milwaukee, Wisconsin

Inferno ◆ NCAA III ◆ Independent ◆ http://www.alverno.edu/

Independent Roman Catholic comprehensive, founded 1887
Women only, 1,951 undergraduate students, 62% full-time, 99% women, 1% men
Suburban 46-acre campus
Moderately difficult entrance level, 56% of applicants were admitted

Freshmen *Admission:* 811 applied, 455 were accepted, 279 enrolled.
Tuition and fees (2003–04): $13,638 (full-time). *Room and board:* $5260.
Athletic Department: *Director of Athletics:* Sue Hansen; Phone: 414-382-6323; Fax: 414-382-6316; E-mail: sue.hansen@alverno.edu. *Sports Information Director:* Heather Burtman; Phone: 414-382-6456; E-mail: heather.burtman@alverno.edu.

WOMEN'S COACHES

Basketball: Sue Hansen; Phone: 414-382-6323; E-mail: sue.hansen@alverno.edu.
Cheerleading: Brooke Wegner; Phone: 414-382-6324; E-mail: brooke.wegner@alverno.edu.
Cross Country: Ben Van Male; Phone: 414-382-6456; E-mail: benvanmale@alverno.edu.
Soccer: Katie Klugiewicz; Phone: 414-382-6456; E-mail: katie.klugiewicz@alverno.edu.
Softball: Heather Burtman; Phone: 414-382-6456; E-mail: heather.burtman@alverno.edu.
Volleyball: Kay Wolfestetter; Phone: 414-382-6444; E-mail: kay.wolferstetter@alverno.edu.

AMERICAN INTERNATIONAL COLLEGE
Springfield, Massachusetts

Yellow Jackets ◆ NCAA II ◆ Atlantic Hockey Conference; Northeast-10 Conference ◆ http://www.aic.edu/

Independent comprehensive, founded 1885
Coed, 1,188 undergraduate students, 85% full-time, 53% women, 47% men
Urban 58-acre campus
Moderately difficult entrance level, 77% of applicants were admitted

Freshmen *Admission:* 1,347 applied, 1,031 were accepted, 331 enrolled. *Test scores:* SAT verbal scores over 500: 51%; SAT math scores over 500: 52%; SAT verbal scores over 600: 4%; SAT math scores over 600: 3%.
Tuition and fees (2004–05): $17,800 (full-time). *Room and board:* $8500 (room only: $4232).
Financial Aid (All incoming freshmen): *Average need-based gift aid:* $10,474. *Average non-need based aid:* $6250. *Average aid to full-time undergraduates:* $18,364.
Athletic Department: *Director of Athletics:* Robert Burke; Phone: 413-205-3532; Fax: 413-205-3803; E-mail: burkeath@aol.com. *Sports Information Director:* George Sylvester; Phone: 413-205-3572; E-mail: sid@acad.aic.edu.

MEN'S COACHES

Baseball: Nick Callini; Phone: 413-205-3078; E-mail: jacketsbaseball@hotmail.com.
Basketball: Art Luptowski; Phone: 413-205-3538.
Football: Art Wilkins; Phone: 413-205-3545.
Golf: Gary Wright; Phone: 413-205-3522; E-mail: gwright@acad.aic.edu.
Ice Hockey: Gary Wright; Phone: 413-205-3522; E-mail: gwright@acad.aic.edu.
Lacrosse: Justin Mickiewicz; Phone: 413-205-3566; E-mail: jmickiewicz@grsd.org.
Soccer: Fred Balbino; Phone: 413-205-3595; E-mail: fred.balbino@the-spa.com.
Tennis: Adam Feldman; Phone: 413-205-3540; E-mail: adfeld@hotmail.com.
Wrestling: Shirzad Ahmadi; Phone: 413-205-3553; E-mail: aicwr@aol.com.

WOMEN'S COACHES

Basketball: Peter Cinella; Phone: 413-205-3924; E-mail: pcinella@acad.aic.edu.
Field Hockey: Alison Pratt; Phone: 413-205-3921; E-mail: apratt@acad.aic.edu.
Lacrosse: Alison Pratt; Phone: 413-205-3921; E-mail: apratt@acad.aic.edu.
Soccer: Ciro Vivano; Phone: 413-205-3922; E-mail: cv1257@aol.com.
Softball: Judy Groff; Phone: 413-205-3919; E-mail: jgroff@acad.aic.edu.
Tennis: Sandra Robinson; Phone: 413-205-3920; E-mail: srobinso@acad.aic.edu.
Volleyball: Alex Temkin; Phone: 413-205-3553; E-mail: atemkin@aicvolleyball.com.

AMERICAN UNIVERSITY
Washington, District of Columbia

Eagles ◆ NCAA I ◆ Patriot League Conference ◆ http://www.american.edu/

Independent Methodist university, founded 1893
Coed, 5,752 undergraduate students, 94% full-time, 62% women, 38% men
Suburban 84-acre campus
Very difficult entrance level, 52% of applicants were admitted

Freshmen *Admission:* 10,282 applied, 6,107 were accepted, 1,238 enrolled. *Test scores:* SAT verbal scores over 500: 96%; SAT math scores over 500: 95%; SAT verbal scores over 600: 64%; SAT math scores over 600: 54%; SAT verbal scores over 700: 17%; SAT math scores over 700: 10%.
Tuition and fees (2004–05): $26,307 (full-time). *Room and board:* $10,260.
Financial Aid (All incoming freshmen): *Average need-based gift aid:* $12,968. *Average non-need based aid:* $14,590. *Average aid to full-time undergraduates:* $23,430.
Athletic Department: *Director of Athletics:* Joni Comstock; Phone: 202-885-3001; Fax: 202-885-3029; E-mail: comstock@american.edu.
Sports Information Director: Shaun May; Phone: 202-885-3030; E-mail: smay@american.edu.

MEN'S COACHES

Basketball: Jeff Jones; Phone: 202-885-3010; E-mail: mensbasketball@american.edu.
Cheerleading: Meagan Breen; Phone: 202-885-3025; E-mail: mbreen@american.edu.
Cross Country: Matt Centrowitz; Phone: 202-885-3026; E-mail: mattc@american.edu.
Diving: Mark Davin; Phone: 202-885-3080; E-mail: markdavin@american.edu.
Golf: Josh Cupp; Phone: 202-885-3077; E-mail: jcupp@american.edu.
Soccer: Todd West; Phone: 202-885-3014; E-mail: twest@american.edu.
Swimming: Mark Davin; Phone: 202-885-3080; E-mail: markdavin@american.edu.
Tennis: Martin Blackman; Phone: 202-885-3017; E-mail: martinb@american.edu.
Track and Field: Matt Centrowitz; Phone: 202-885-3026; E-mail: mattc@american.edu.

Wrestling: Mark Cody; Phone: 202-885-3066; E-mail: mcody@american.edu.

WOMEN'S COACHES

Basketball: Shann Hart; Phone: 202-885-3019; E-mail: hart@american.edu.
Cheerleading: Meagan Breen; Phone: 202-885-3025; E-mail: mbreen@american.edu.
Cross Country: Matt Centrowitz; Phone: 202-885-3026; E-mail: mattc@american.edu.
Diving: Mark Davin; Phone: 202-885-3080; E-mail: markdavin@american.edu.
Field Hockey: Steve Jennings; Phone: 202-885-3018; E-mail: sjennin@american.edu.
Lacrosse: Ashley Flanigan; Phone: 202-885-3072; E-mail: ashley@american.edu.
Soccer: Mike Brady; Phone: 202-885-3047; E-mail: mbrady@american.edu.
Swimming: Mark Davin; Phone: 202-885-3080; E-mail: markdavin@american.edu.
Tennis: Carol Daniels; Phone: 202-885-3049; E-mail: cdaniel@american.edu.
Track and Field: Matt Centrowitz; Phone: 202-885-3026; E-mail: mattc@american.edu.
Volleyball: Barry Goldberg; Phone: 202-885-3031; E-mail: barryg@american.edu.

AMHERST COLLEGE
Amherst, Massachusetts

(M) Lord Jeffs (W) Lady Jeffs ◆ NCAA III ◆ New England Small College Conference ◆ http://www.amherst.edu/

Independent 4-year, founded 1821
Coed, 1,623 undergraduate students, 100% full-time, 49% women, 51% men
Small-town 1,000-acre campus
Most difficult entrance level, 2% of applicants were admitted

Freshmen *Admission:* 5,631 applied, 1,001 were accepted, 413 enrolled. *Test scores:* SAT verbal scores over 500: 100%; SAT math scores over 500: 100%; SAT verbal scores over 600: 93%; SAT math scores over 600: 93%; SAT verbal scores over 700: 64%; SAT math scores over 700: 65%.
Tuition and fees (2003–04): $29,730 (full-time). *Room and board:* $7740 (room only: $4150).
Financial Aid (All incoming freshmen): *Average need-based gift aid:* $21,798. *Average aid to full-time undergraduates:* $23,487.
Athletic Department: *Director of Athletics:* Peter Gooding; Phone: 413-542-2274; Fax: 413-542-2026; E-mail: pjgooding@amherst.edu.
Sports Information Director: Kevin Graber; Phone: 413-542-2390; E-mail: kegraber@amherst.edu.

MEN'S COACHES

Baseball: Bill Thurston; Phone: 413-542-2284.
Basketball: Dave Hixon; Phone: 413-542-2069; E-mail: ddhixon@amherst.edu.
Cross Country: Erik Nedeau; Phone: 413-542-8117; E-mail: elnedeau@amherst.edu.
Diving: Derek Chicarillo; Phone: 413-542-2366; E-mail: dmchicarilli@amherst.edu.
Football: E.J. Mills; Phone: 413-542-8197; E-mail: ejmills@amherst.edu.
Golf: Jack Arena; Phone: 413-542-7950; E-mail: jaarena@amherst.edu.
Ice Hockey: Jack Arena; Phone: 413-542-7950; E-mail: jaarena@amherst.edu.
Lacrosse: Tom Carmean; Phone: 413-542-2113; E-mail: thcarmean@amherst.edu.
Soccer: Milton Gooding; Phone: 413-542-8223; E-mail: mpgooding@amherst.edu.
Swimming: Nick Nichols; Phone: 413-542-2366; E-mail: nnichols@amherst.edu.
Tennis: Peter Robson; Phone: 413-542-5757; E-mail: phrobson@amherst.edu.
Track and Field: Erik Nedeau; Phone: 413-542-8117; E-mail: elnedeau@amherst.edu.

WOMEN'S COACHES

Basketball: Billy McBride; Phone: 413-542-7947; E-mail: btmcbride@amherst.edu.

Amherst College *(continued)*

Cross Country: Erik Nedeau; Phone: 413-542-8117; E-mail: elnedeau@ amherst.edu.

Diving: Derek Chicarillo; Phone: 413-542-2366; E-mail: dmchicarilli@ amherst.edu.

Field Hockey: Carol Kneer; Phone: 413-542-8376; E-mail: crknerr@ amherst.edu.

Golf: Michele Morgan; Phone: 413-542-2362; E-mail: mcmorgan@ amherst.edu.

Lacrosse: Christine Paradis; Phone: 413-542-8136; E-mail: cyparadis@ amherst.edu.

Soccer: Michele Morgan; Phone: 413-542-2392; E-mail: mcmorgan@ amherst.edu.

Softball: Sue Everden; Phone: 413-542-7939; E-mail: sjeverden@ amherst.edu.

Swimming: Nick Nichols; Phone: 413-542-2366; E-mail: nnichols@ amherst.edu.

Tennis: Jackie Bagwell; Phone: 413-542-2316; E-mail: jkbagwell@ amherst.edu.

Track and Field: Erik Nedeau; Phone: 413-542-8117; E-mail: elnedeau@ amherst.edu.

Volleyball: Sue Everden; Phone: 413-542-7939; E-mail: sjeverden@ amherst.edu.

ANDERSON COLLEGE
Anderson, South Carolina

Trojans ◆ NCAA II ◆ Carolinas-Virginia Athletics Conference ◆ http://www.ac.edu/

Independent Baptist 4-year, founded 1911
Coed, 1,664 undergraduate students, 75% full-time, 63% women, 37% men
Suburban 44-acre campus
Moderately difficult entrance level, 74% of applicants were admitted

Freshmen *Admission:* 822 applied, 647 were accepted, 344 enrolled. *Test scores:* SAT verbal scores over 500: 52%; SAT math scores over 500: 56%; SAT verbal scores over 600: 12%; SAT math scores over 600: 14%; SAT verbal scores over 700: 1%; SAT math scores over 700: 1%.
Tuition and fees (2004–05): $14,225 (full-time). *Room and board:* $5765 (room only: $2910).
Financial Aid (All incoming freshmen): *Average need-based gift aid:* $7784. *Average non-need based aid:* $5181. *Average aid to full-time undergraduates:* $15,426.
Athletic Department: *Director of Athletics:* Bobby Beville; Phone: 864-231-2029; Fax: 864-231-5601; E-mail: bbeville@ac.edu. *Sports Information Director:* Cobb Oxford; Phone: 864-231-2097; E-mail: coxford@ac.edu.

MEN'S COACHES
Baseball: Joe Miller; Phone: 864-231-2013; E-mail: jmiller@ac.edu.
Basketball: Doug Novak; Phone: 864-231-2022; E-mail: dnovak@ac. edu.
Cross Country: Leroy Thomas; Phone: 864-231-2088; E-mail: lthomas@ ac.edu.
Golf: Danny Neal; Phone: 864-231-5610; E-mail: dneal@ac.edu.
Soccer: Rob Miller; Phone: 864-231-2024; E-mail: rmiller@ac.edu.
Tennis: Brett Simpson; Phone: 864-231-2098; E-mail: bsimpson@ac. edu.
Track and Field: Leroy Thomas; Phone: 864-231-2088; E-mail: lthomas@ac.edu.
Wrestling: Dock Kelly; Phone: 864-231-5752; E-mail: dkelly@ac.edu.

WOMEN'S COACHES
Basketball: Kevin Pederson; Phone: 864-231-2011; E-mail: kpederson@ ac.edu.
Cross Country: Leroy Thomas; Phone: 864-231-2088; E-mail: lthomas@ ac.edu.
Golf: Danny Neal; Phone: 864-231-5610; E-mail: dneal@ac.edu.
Soccer: Bailey Woods; Phone: 864-231-2012; E-mail: bwoods@ac.edu.
Softball: Christine Yon; Phone: 864-231-2109; E-mail: cyon@ac.edu.
Tennis: Brett Simpson; Phone: 864-231-2098; E-mail: bsimpson@ac. edu.
Track and Field: Leroy Thomas; Phone: 864-231-2088; E-mail: lthomas@ac.edu.
Volleyball: Jennifer Bell; Phone: 864-231-5679; E-mail: jbell@ac.edu.

ANDERSON UNIVERSITY
Anderson, Indiana

Ravens ◆ NCAA III ◆ Heartland Collegiate Conference ◆ http://www.anderson.edu/

Independent religious comprehensive, founded 1917, affiliated with Church of God
Coed, 2,121 undergraduate students, 92% full-time, 58% women, 42% men
Suburban 100-acre campus with easy access to Indianapolis
Moderately difficult entrance level, 7% of applicants were admitted

Freshmen *Admission:* 2,083 applied, 1,502 were accepted, 598 enrolled. *Test scores:* SAT verbal scores over 500: 58%; SAT math scores over 500: 58%; SAT verbal scores over 600: 18%; SAT math scores over 600: 17%; SAT verbal scores over 700: 4%; SAT math scores over 700: 2%.
Tuition and fees (2003–04): $17,050 (full-time). *Room and board:* $5560 (room only: $3330).
Financial Aid (All incoming freshmen): *Average need-based gift aid:* $10,048. *Average non-need based aid:* $8127. *Average aid to full-time undergraduates:* $15,628.
Athletic Department: *Director of Athletics:* Mike Zapolski; Phone: 765-649-4483; Fax: 765-641-3857; E-mail: mjzapolski@anderson.edu. *Sports Information Director:* Justin Bates; Phone: 765-641-4479; E-mail: jbbates@anderson.edu.

MEN'S COACHES
Baseball: Don Brandon; Phone: 765-641-4488; E-mail: dbrandon@ anderson.edu.
Basketball: Dennis Lehnus; Phone: 765-641-4480; E-mail: dolehnus@ anderson.edu.
Cheerleading: Aurora Doster; Phone: 765-635-4495; E-mail: brentandaurora@yahoo.com.
Cross Country: Larry Maddox; Phone: 765-641-4485; E-mail: lcfmaddox@anderson.edu.
Football: Jeff Judge; Phone: 765-641-4469; E-mail: jpjudge@anderson. edu.
Golf: Paul Gray; Phone: 765-641-4489; E-mail: phgray@anderson.edu.
Soccer: Scott Fridley; Phone: 765-641-4499; E-mail: stfridley@ anderson.edu.
Tennis: Galen Scott; Phone: 765-641-4464.
Track and Field: Larry Maddox; Phone: 765-641-4485; E-mail: lcfmaddox@anderson.edu.

WOMEN'S COACHES
Basketball: Marcie Taylor; Phone: 765-641-4495; E-mail: mjtaylor@ anderson.edu.
Cheerleading: Aurora Doster; Phone: 765-635-4495; E-mail: brentandaurora@yahoo.com.
Cross Country: Larry Maddox; Phone: 765-641-4485; E-mail: lcfmaddox@anderson.edu.
Golf: Marcie Taylor; Phone: 765-641-4495; E-mail: mjtaylor@ anderson.edu.
Soccer: Scott Fridley; Phone: 765-641-4499; E-mail: stfridley@ anderson.edu.
Softball: Larry Holloway; Phone: 765-533-2371; E-mail: lwholloway@ anderson.edu.
Tennis: Sue Hammel; Phone: 765-642-6448.
Track and Field: Larry Maddox; Phone: 765-641-4485; E-mail: lcfmaddox@anderson.edu.
Volleyball: Tami Miller; Phone: 765-641-4476; E-mail: trmiller@ anderson.edu.

ANGELO STATE UNIVERSITY
San Angelo, Texas

(M)Rams; (W)Rambelles ◆ NCAA II ◆ Lone Star Conference ◆ http://www.angelo.edu/

State-supported comprehensive, founded 1928, part of Texas State University System
Coed, 5,618 undergraduate students, 81% full-time, 56% women, 44% men
Urban 268-acre campus
Moderately difficult entrance level, 99% of applicants were admitted

Freshmen *Admission:* 2,146 applied, 2,126 were accepted, 1,148 enrolled. *Test scores:* SAT verbal scores over 500: 42%; SAT math scores over 500: 43%; SAT verbal scores over 600: 11%; SAT math scores over 600: 11%; SAT verbal scores over 700: 1%; SAT math scores over 700: 1%.
Tuition and fees (2003–04): $2930 (resident), $8594 (nonresident). *Room and board:* $4646 (room only: $3024).
Financial Aid (All incoming freshmen): *Average need-based gift aid:* $2062. *Average non-need based aid:* $1593. *Average aid to full-time undergraduates:* $4283.
Athletic Department: *Director of Athletics:* Kathleen Brasfield; Phone: 915-942-2264; Fax: 915-942-2277; E-mail: kathleen.brasfield@angelo.edu. *Sports Information Director:* M.L. Stark Hinkle; Phone: 915-942-2264; E-mail: ml.hinkle@angelo.edu.

MEN'S COACHES
Baseball: Kevin Brooks; Phone: 325-942-2264.
Basketball: Joe Esposito; Phone: 325-942-2264; E-mail: joe.esposito@angelo.edu.
Cheerleading: Phone: 325-942-2264; E-mail: cheerleader@angelo.edu.
Cross Country: James Reid Jr.; Phone: 325-942-2091; E-mail: james.reid@angelo.edu.
Football: Jerry Vandergriff; Phone: 325-942-2091; E-mail: jerry.vandergriff@angelo.edu.
Track and Field: James Reid Jr.; Phone: 325-942-2091; E-mail: james.reid@angelo.edu.

WOMEN'S COACHES
Basketball: Sally Wailing-Brooks; Phone: 325-942-2264; E-mail: sally.brooks@angelo.edu.
Cheerleading: Phone: 325-942-2264; E-mail: cheerleader@angelo.edu.
Cross Country: James Reid Jr.; Phone: 325-942-2091; E-mail: james.reid@angelo.edu.
Soccer: Tom Brown Jr.; Phone: 325-942-2264; E-mail: tom.brown@angelo.edu.
Softball: Dana Jenkins; Phone: 325-942-2264.
Track and Field: James Reid Jr.; Phone: 325-942-2091; E-mail: james.reid@angelo.edu.
Volleyball: Kathleen Brasfield; Phone: 325-942-2264; E-mail: kathleen.brasfield@angelo.edu.

ANNA MARIA COLLEGE
Paxton, Massachusetts

Amcats ◆ NCAA III ◆ Commonwealth Coast Conference ◆ http://www.annamaria.edu/

Independent Roman Catholic comprehensive, founded 1946
Coed, 731 undergraduate students, 75% full-time, 66% women, 34% men
Rural 180-acre campus with easy access to Boston
Moderately difficult entrance level, 86% of applicants were admitted

Freshmen *Admission:* 568 applied, 500 were accepted, 159 enrolled. *Test scores:* SAT verbal scores over 500: 36%; SAT math scores over 500: 31%; SAT verbal scores over 600: 6%; SAT math scores over 600: 8%.
Tuition and fees (2003–04): $19,145 (full-time). *Room and board:* $6995.
Financial Aid (All incoming freshmen): *Average need-based gift aid:* $10,252. *Average non-need based aid:* $10,385. *Average aid to full-time undergraduates:* $15,423.
Athletic Department: *Director of Athletics:* Len Smith; Phone: 508-849-3447; Fax: 508-849-3449; E-mail: lsmith@annamaria.edu. *Sports Information Director:* David Gentleman; Phone: 508-849-3252; E-mail: dgentleman@annamaria.edu.

MEN'S COACHES
Baseball: Mike Wilson; Phone: 508-753-2288; E-mail: mwilson@annamaria.edu.
Basketball: Dave Shea; Phone: 508-849-3499; E-mail: dshea@annamaria.edu.
Cheerleading: Emily English; Phone: 508-849-3446.
Cross Country: John Patraitis; Phone: 508-849-3446; E-mail: jpatraitis@aol.com.
Golf: David Shea; Phone: 508-849-3499; E-mail: dshea@annamaria.edu.
Soccer: David Gentleman; Phone: 508-849-3252; E-mail: dgentleman@annamaria.edu.

WOMEN'S COACHES
Basketball: Jim Gately; Phone: 508-849-3446.
Cheerleading: Emily English; Phone: 508-849-3446.
Field Hockey: Sharon Zenevitch; Phone: 508-849-3288; E-mail: szenevitch@annamaria.edu.
Soccer: Kelly Parent; Phone: 508-849-3446.
Softball: Phone: 508-849-3446.
Volleyball: Bethany Quinton; Phone: 508-849-3446.

APPALACHIAN STATE UNIVERSITY
Boone, North Carolina

Mountaineers ◆ NCAA I ◆ Northern Pacific Field Hockey Conference; Southern Conference ◆ http://www.appstate.edu/

State-supported comprehensive, founded 1899, part of University of North Carolina System
Coed, 12,934 undergraduate students, 91% full-time, 51% women, 49% men
Small-town 340-acre campus
Moderately difficult entrance level, 62% of applicants were admitted

Freshmen *Admission:* 9,598 applied, 6,293 were accepted, 2,473 enrolled. *Test scores:* SAT verbal scores over 500: 75%; SAT math scores over 500: 78%; SAT verbal scores over 600: 24%; SAT math scores over 600: 26%; SAT verbal scores over 700: 3%; SAT math scores over 700: 2%.
Tuition and fees (2003–04): $2927 (resident), $12,294 (nonresident). *Room and board:* $4435 (room only: $2770).
Financial Aid (All incoming freshmen): *Average need-based gift aid:* $3780. *Average non-need based aid:* $2316. *Average aid to full-time undergraduates:* $5581.
Athletic Department: *Director of Athletics:* Roachel Laney; Phone: 828-262-4010; Fax: 828-262-2556; E-mail: laneyrj@appstate.edu. *Sports Information Director:* Kelby Siler; Phone: 828-262-2268; E-mail: silerkj@appstate.edu.

MEN'S COACHES
Baseball: Troy Heustess; Phone: 828-262-6097; E-mail: heustsswt@appstate.edu.
Basketball: Houston Fancher; Phone: 828-262-3081; E-mail: fancherjh@appstate.edu.
Cheerleading: Christy Welch; Phone: 828-262-7162; E-mail: cwelch97@yahoo.com.
Cross Country: Mike Curcio; Phone: 828-262-6559; E-mail: curciom@appstate.edu.
Football: Jerry Moore; Phone: 828-262-2501; E-mail: watsnda@appstate.edu.
Golf: Bill Dicus; Phone: 828-262-2497; E-mail: dicuswa@appstate.edu.
Soccer: Paul Stahlschmidt; Phone: 828-262-6965; E-mail: stahlschmidt@appstate.edu.
Tennis: Bob Lake; Phone: 828-262-3068; E-mail: lakers@appstate.edu.
Track and Field: John Weaver; Phone: 828-262-3074; E-mail: weaverjt@appstate.edu.
Wrestling: Paul Mance; Phone: 828-262-3082; E-mail: mancepe@appstate.edu.

WOMEN'S COACHES
Basketball: Adrienne Shuler; Phone: 828-262-3081; E-mail: shulerad@appstate.edu.
Cheerleading: Christy Welch; Phone: 828-262-7162; E-mail: cwelch97@yahoo.com.
Cross Country: Mike Curcio; Phone: 828-262-6559; E-mail: curciom@appstate.edu.
Field Hockey: Mandy Latz; Phone: 828-262-3080; E-mail: latzao@appstate.edu.

Appalachian State University *(continued)*

Golf: Bill Dicus; Phone: 828-262-2497; E-mail: dicuswa@appstate.edu.
Soccer: Ben Popoola; Phone: 828-262-2563; E-mail: popoolabo@appstate.edu.
Softball: Willie Rucker; Phone: 828-262-6748; E-mail: ruckerwl@appstate.edu.
Tennis: Colin Crothers; Phone: 828-262-6598; E-mail: crotherscp@appstate.edu.
Track and Field: John Weaver; Phone: 828-262-3074; E-mail: weaverjt@appstate.edu.
Volleyball: Chad Callihan; Phone: 828-262-2844; E-mail: callihancm@appstate.edu.

AQUINAS COLLEGE
Grand Rapids, Michigan

Saints ◆ NAIA ◆ Wolverine-Hoosier Conference ◆ http://www.aquinas.edu/

Independent Roman Catholic comprehensive, founded 1886
Coed, 1,828 undergraduate students, 81% full-time, 66% women, 34% men
Suburban 107-acre campus with easy access to Detroit
Moderately difficult entrance level, 79% of applicants were admitted

Freshmen *Admission:* 1,361 applied, 1,078 were accepted, 284 enrolled.
Tuition and fees (2003–04): $16,400 (full-time). *Room and board:* $5494 (room only: $2510).
Financial Aid (All incoming freshmen): *Average need-based gift aid:* $13,754. *Average non-need based aid:* $9767. *Average aid to full-time undergraduates:* $16,001.
Athletic Department: *Director of Athletics:* Terry Bocian; Phone: 616-632-2475; Fax: 616-732-4548; E-mail: bociater@aquinas.edu. *Sports Information Director:* Damon Bouwkamp; Phone: 616-632-2482; E-mail: bouwkdam@aquinas.edu.

MEN'S COACHES
Baseball: Doug Greenslate; Phone: 616-632-2874; E-mail: greendou@aquinas.edu.
Basketball: Dave Hammer; Phone: 616-632-2478; E-mail: hammedav@aquinas.edu.
Cheerleading: Emma Powell; Phone: 616-632-2874; E-mail: epowell@alam.org.
Cross Country: Mike Wojciakowski; Phone: 616-632-2876; E-mail: wooddav@aquinas.edu.
Golf: Tom Gunn; Phone: 616-632-2874; E-mail: athletics@aquinas.edu.
Soccer: Abraham Shearer; Phone: 616-632-2874; E-mail: shearabr@aquinas.edu.
Tennis: Jerry Hendrick; Phone: 616-632-2874; E-mail: athletics@aquinas.edu.
Track and Field: Mike Wojciakowski; Phone: 616-632-2876; E-mail: wooddav@aquinas.edu.

WOMEN'S COACHES
Basketball: Linda Nash; Phone: 616-632-2473; E-mail: nashlin@aquinas.edu.
Cheerleading: Emma Powell; Phone: 616-632-2874; E-mail: epowell@alam.org.
Cross Country: Jenny Ziegler; Phone: 616-632-2876; E-mail: wooddav@aquinas.edu.
Golf: Dan Pupel; Phone: 616-632-2874; E-mail: athletics@aquinas.edu.
Soccer: Meghan Luckett; Phone: 616-632-2874; E-mail: luckemeg@aquinas.edu.
Softball: Ray Sheler; Phone: 616-632-2874; E-mail: rovarn22@yahoo.com.
Tennis: Gerry Adams; Phone: 616-632-2874; E-mail: athletics@aquinas.edu.
Track and Field: Jenny Ziegler; Phone: 616-632-2876; E-mail: wooddav@aquinas.edu.
Volleyball: Jan Nevelle; Phone: 616-632-2874; E-mail: neveljan@aquinas.edu.

ARCADIA UNIVERSITY
Glenside, Pennsylvania

Scarlet Knights ◆ NCAA III ◆ Pennsylvania Athletic Conference ◆ http://www.arcadia.edu/

Independent religious comprehensive, founded 1853, affiliated with Presbyterian Church (U.S.A.)
Coed, 1,840 undergraduate students, 85% full-time, 74% women, 26% men
Suburban 60-acre campus with easy access to Philadelphia
Moderately difficult entrance level, 70% of applicants were admitted

Freshmen *Admission:* 2,691 applied, 2,014 were accepted, 507 enrolled. *Test scores:* SAT verbal scores over 500: 69%; SAT math scores over 500: 65%; SAT verbal scores over 600: 26%; SAT math scores over 600: 22%; SAT verbal scores over 700: 1%; SAT math scores over 700: 2%.
Tuition and fees (2004–05): $22,720 (full-time). *Room and board:* $8960.
Financial Aid (All incoming freshmen): *Average need-based gift aid:* $8013. *Average non-need based aid:* $7234. *Average aid to full-time undergraduates:* $18,085.
Athletic Department: *Director of Athletics:* Shirley Liddle; Phone: 215-572-2955; Fax: 215-572-2159; E-mail: liddle@arcadia.edu. *Sports Information Director:* Tom Carlin; Phone: 215-572-2955; E-mail: carlin@arcadia.edu.

MEN'S COACHES
Baseball: Stan Exeter; Phone: 215-572-4028; E-mail: exeter@arcadia.edu.
Basketball: Pat Dorney; Phone: 215-572-2976; E-mail: dorneyp@arcadia.edu.
Cross Country: Richard Smith; Phone: 215-572-2976; E-mail: smith2@arcadia.edu.
Golf: Carol Gallagher; Phone: 215-572-2976; E-mail: carolagallagher@aol.com.
Soccer: Tom Carlin; Phone: 215-572-2982; E-mail: carlin@arcadia.edu.
Swimming: Larry Davis; Phone: 215-572-2951; E-mail: daviss@arcadia.edu.
Tennis: Tom McGovern; Phone: 215-572-2978.

WOMEN'S COACHES
Basketball: Valerie Ridge; Phone: 215-572-2978; E-mail: ridge@arcadia.edu.
Cross Country: Richard Smith; Phone: 215-572-2976; E-mail: smith2@arcadia.edu.
Field Hockey: Laura-Ann Lane; Phone: 215-572-4018; E-mail: lanel@arcadia.edu.
Golf: Carol Gallagher; Phone: 215-572-2976; E-mail: carolagallagher@aol.com.
Lacrosse: Cindy Joseph; Phone: 215-572-4018; E-mail: josephl@arcadia.edu.
Soccer: Rick Brownell; Phone: 215-572-2982; E-mail: brownelr@arcadia.edu.
Softball: Linda Detra; Phone: 215-572-2996; E-mail: detra@arcadia.edu.
Swimming: Larry Davis; Phone: 215-572-2951; E-mail: daviss@arcadia.edu.
Tennis: Tom McGovern; Phone: 215-572-2978.
Volleyball: Anthony Carpenter; Phone: 215-572-4018; E-mail: carpenter@arcadia.edu.

ARIZONA STATE UNIVERSITY
Tempe, Arizona

Sun Devils ◆ NCAA I ◆ Pacific-10 Conference ◆ http://www.asu.edu/

State-supported university, founded 1885, part of Arizona State University
Coed, 38,627 undergraduate students, 80% full-time, 52% women, 48% men
Suburban 814-acre campus with easy access to Phoenix
Moderately difficult entrance level, 9% of applicants were admitted

Freshmen *Admission:* 19,785 applied, 17,490 were accepted, 7,126 enrolled. *Test scores:* SAT verbal scores over 500: 70%; SAT math scores

over 500: 73%; SAT verbal scores over 600: 26%; SAT math scores over 600: 32%; SAT verbal scores over 700: 5%; SAT math scores over 700: 6%.
Tuition and fees (2003–04): $3595 (resident), $12,115 (nonresident). *Room and board:* $6453 (room only: $4101).
Financial Aid (All incoming freshmen): *Average need-based gift aid:* $4570. *Average non-need based aid:* $3687. *Average aid to full-time undergraduates:* $6264.
Athletic Department: *Director of Athletics:* Gene Smith; Phone: 480-965-9743; Fax: 480-965-1829. *Sports Information Director:* Mark Brand; Phone: 480-965-6592; E-mail: mark.brand@asu.edu.

MEN'S COACHES
Baseball: Pat Murphy; Phone: 480-965-3677.
Basketball: Rob Evans; Phone: 480-965-8182; E-mail: rob.evans@asu.edu.
Cross Country: Greg Kraft; Phone: 480-965-5660; E-mail: gregory.kraft@asu.edu.
Diving: Mark Bradshaw; Phone: 480-965-3636; E-mail: mark.bradshaw@asu.edu.
Football: Dirk Koetter; Phone: 480-965-5053; E-mail: victoria.gaytan@asu.edu.
Golf: Randy Lein; Phone: 480-965-3262; E-mail: coach.lein@asu.edu.
Swimming: Michael Chasson; Phone: 480-965-2974; E-mail: michael.chasson@asu.edu.
Tennis: Lou Belken; Phone: 480-965-3666; E-mail: lou.belken@asu.edu.
Track and Field: Greg Kraft; Phone: 480-965-5660; E-mail: gregory.kraft@asu.edu.
Wrestling: Thom Ortiz; Phone: 480-965-3828.

WOMEN'S COACHES
Basketball: Charli Turner Thorne; Phone: 480-965-6387; E-mail: asuhoop@asu.edu.
Cross Country: Greg Kraft; Phone: 480-965-5660; E-mail: gregory.kraft@asu.edu.
Diving: Mark Bradshaw; Phone: 480-965-3636; E-mail: mark.bradshaw@asu.edu.
Golf: Melissa McNamara; Phone: 480-965-7081; E-mail: melissa.mcnamara@asu.edu.
Gymnastics: John Spini; Phone: 480-965-7843; E-mail: spini@asu.edu.
Soccer: Ray Leone; Phone: 480-965-1715; E-mail: ray.leone@asu.edu.
Softball: Linda Wells; Phone: 480-965-3973; E-mail: ica-softball@asu.edu.
Swimming: Michael Chasson; Phone: 480-965-2974; E-mail: michael.chasson@asu.edu.
Tennis: Sheila McInerney; Phone: 480-965-4333; E-mail: wtennis@asu.edu.
Track and Field: Greg Kraft; Phone: 480-965-5660; E-mail: gregory.kraft@asu.edu.
Volleyball: Brad Saindon; Phone: 480-965-2035.

ARKANSAS STATE UNIVERSITY
Jonesboro, Arkansas
Indians ◆ NCAA I ◆ Sun Belt Conference ◆ http://www.astate.edu/

State-supported comprehensive, founded 1909, part of Arkansas State University System
Coed, 9,413 undergraduate students, 79% full-time, 59% women, 41% men
Small-town 942-acre campus with easy access to Memphis
Moderately difficult entrance level, 68% of applicants were admitted

Freshmen *Admission:* 3,088 applied, 2,039 were accepted, 1,525 enrolled.
Tuition and fees (2003–04): $4810 (resident), $10,720 (nonresident). *Room and board:* $3640.
Financial Aid (All incoming freshmen): *Average need-based gift aid:* $2450. *Average non-need based aid:* $1500. *Average aid to full-time undergraduates:* $2900.
Athletic Department: *Director of Athletics:* Dean Lee; Phone: 870-972-3880; Fax: 870-972-3886; E-mail: deanlee@astate.edu. *Sports Information Director:* Gina Bowman; Phone: 870-972-2541; E-mail: gbowman@astate.edu.

MEN'S COACHES
Baseball: Keith Kessinger; Phone: 870-972-2700; E-mail: kkessinger@astate.edu.

Basketball: Dickey Nutt; Phone: 870-972-2077; E-mail: dnutt@astate.edu.
Cheerleading: Martha McFerron; Phone: 870-935-5730; E-mail: asuspirit@aol.com.
Cross Country: Jay Flanagan; Phone: 870-972-3350; E-mail: jflanaga@astate.edu.
Football: Steve Roberts; Phone: 870-972-2082; E-mail: sroberts@astate.edu.
Golf: Neil Abel; Phone: 870-972-3411; E-mail: neila@astate.edu.
Track and Field: Jay Flanagan; Phone: 870-972-3350; E-mail: jflanaga@astate.edu.

WOMEN'S COACHES
Basketball: Bryan Boyer; Phone: 870-972-2303; E-mail: brianb@astate.edu.
Cheerleading: Martha McFerron; Phone: 870-935-5730; E-mail: asuspirit@aol.com.
Cross Country: Jay Flanagan; Phone: 870-972-3350; E-mail: jflanaga@astate.edu.
Golf: Chris Adams; Phone: 870-972-2777; E-mail: cadams@astate.edu.
Soccer: Jason Wharton; Phone: 870-910-3930; E-mail: jwharton@astate.edu.
Tennis: Marcia Williams; Phone: 870-972-3876; E-mail: mgwillia@astate.edu.
Track and Field: Jay Flanagan; Phone: 870-972-3350; E-mail: jflanaga@astate.edu.
Volleyball: Craig Cummings; Phone: 870-972-3876; E-mail: ccummings@astate.edu.

ARKANSAS TECH UNIVERSITY
Russellville, Arkansas
Wonder Boys; Golden Suns ◆ NCAA II ◆ Gulf South Conference ◆ http://www.atu.edu/

State-supported comprehensive, founded 1909
Coed, 5,889 undergraduate students, 87% full-time, 53% women, 47% men
Small-town 516-acre campus
Moderately difficult entrance level, 6% of applicants were admitted

Freshmen *Admission:* 2,990 applied, 1,683 were accepted, 1,507 enrolled. *Test scores:* SAT verbal scores over 500: 54%; SAT math scores over 500: 54%; SAT verbal scores over 600: 27%; SAT math scores over 600: 18%; SAT math scores over 700: 9%.
Tuition and fees (2003–04): $3820 (resident), $7360 (nonresident). *Room and board:* $3725 (room only: $2016).
Financial Aid (All incoming freshmen): *Average need-based gift aid:* $1968. *Average non-need based aid:* $4148. *Average aid to full-time undergraduates:* $3110.
Athletic Department: *Director of Athletics:* Steve Mullins; Phone: 479-968-0245; Fax: 479-964-0829; E-mail: steve.mullins@mail.atu.edu. *Sports Information Director:* Larry Smith; Phone: 479-968-0645; E-mail: larry.smith@mail.atu.edu.

MEN'S COACHES
Baseball: Billy Goss; Phone: 501-968-0648; E-mail: billy.goss@mail.atu.edu.
Basketball: Rick McCormick; Phone: 501-968-0365; E-mail: rick.mccormick@mail.atu.edu.
Cheerleading: Stephanie Hailey; Phone: 501-968-0249; E-mail: stephanie.hailey@mail.atu.edu.
Football: Steve Mullins; Phone: 501-968-0245; E-mail: steve.mullins@mail.atu.edu.
Golf: Dave Falconer; Phone: 501-968-0212; E-mail: david.falconer@mail.atu.edu.

WOMEN'S COACHES
Basketball: Carin Pinion-McNabb; Phone: 501-968-0285; E-mail: carin.pinion@mail.atu.edu.
Cheerleading: Stephanie Hailey; Phone: 501-968-0249; E-mail: stephanie.hailey@mail.atu.edu.
Cross Country: Tom Aspel; Phone: 501-968-0213; E-mail: tom.aspel@mail.atu.edu.
Golf: Roy McSpadden; Phone: 501-968-4888; E-mail: roymac@cox-internet.com.
Softball: Kristie Betancur; Phone: 501-964-3231; E-mail: kristie.betancur@mail.atu.edu.

Arkansas Tech University (*continued*)

Tennis: Shery Forrest; Phone: 501-498-6071; E-mail: shery.forrest@mail.atu.edu.
Volleyball: Amanda Thiessen; Phone: 501-968-0513; E-mail: amanda.wilson@mail.atu.edu.

ARMSTRONG ATLANTIC STATE UNIVERSITY
Savannah, Georgia

Pirates ◆ NCAA II ◆ Peach Belt Conference
◆ http://www.armstrong.edu/

State-supported comprehensive, founded 1935, part of University System of Georgia
Coed, 5,743 undergraduate students, 60% full-time, 68% women, 32% men
Suburban 250-acre campus
Minimally difficult entrance level, 7% of applicants were admitted

Freshmen *Admission:* 1,685 applied, 1,099 were accepted, 847 enrolled. *Test scores:* SAT verbal scores over 500: 60%; SAT math scores over 500: 49%; SAT verbal scores over 600: 16%; SAT math scores over 600: 12%; SAT verbal scores over 700: 1%; SAT math scores over 700: 1%.
Tuition and fees (2003–04): $2602 (resident), $9238 (nonresident). *Room only:* $4500.
Financial Aid (All incoming freshmen): *Average need-based gift aid:* $1500. *Average non-need based aid:* $1000. *Average aid to full-time undergraduates:* $5110.
Athletic Department: *Director of Athletics:* Eddie Aenchbacher; Phone: 912-921-5854; Fax: 912-921-5571; E-mail: aenchbed@mail.armstrong.edu. *Sports Information Director:* Chad Jackson; Phone: 912-921-3255; E-mail: jacksoch@mail.armstrong.edu.

MEN'S COACHES
Baseball: Joe Roberts; Phone: 912-921-5686.
Basketball: Jeff Burkhamer; Phone: 912-927-5683; E-mail: burkhaje@mail.armstrong.edu.
Cheerleading: Michalle Quarles; Phone: 912-352-4535.
Golf: Michael Butler; Phone: 912-927-5844; E-mail: mbutler01@aol.com.
Tennis: Simon Earnshaw; Phone: 912-927-5842; E-mail: earnshsi@mail.armstrong.edu.

WOMEN'S COACHES
Basketball: Roger Hodge; Phone: 912-927-5861; E-mail: hodgerog@mail.armstrong.edu.
Cheerleading: Michalle Quarles; Phone: 912-352-4535.
Softball: Marty McDanial; Phone: 912-927-2391; E-mail: mcdanima@mail.armstrong.edu.
Tennis: Simon Earnshaw; Phone: 912-927-5842; E-mail: earnshsi@mail.armstrong.edu.
Volleyball: Alan Segal; Phone: 912-927-3785; E-mail: segalala@mail.armstrong.edu.

ASBURY COLLEGE
Wilmore, Kentucky

Eagles ◆ NAIA ◆ Kentucky Intercollegiate Conference
◆ http://www.asbury.edu/

Independent nondenominational comprehensive, founded 1890
Coed, 1,191 undergraduate students, 96% full-time, 58% women, 42% men
Small-town 400-acre campus with easy access to Lexington
Moderately difficult entrance level, 72% of applicants were admitted

Freshmen *Admission:* 820 applied, 598 were accepted, 258 enrolled. *Test scores:* SAT verbal scores over 500: 86%; SAT math scores over 500: 71%; SAT verbal scores over 600: 47%; SAT math scores over 600: 37%; SAT verbal scores over 700: 14%; SAT math scores over 700: 6%.

Tuition and fees (2004–05): $17,808 (full-time). *Room and board:* $4498 (room only: $2560).
Financial Aid (All incoming freshmen): *Average need-based gift aid:* $7119. *Average non-need based aid:* $7451. *Average aid to full-time undergraduates:* $12,565.
Athletic Department: *Director of Athletics:* David Baillie; Phone: 859-858-3511; Fax: 859-858-3921; E-mail: david.baillie@asbury.edu. *Sports Information Director:* Gwen Kirby; Phone: 859-858-3511; E-mail: gwen.birby@asbury.edu.

MEN'S COACHES
Basketball: Jim Aller; Phone: 859-858-3511; E-mail: jaller@asbury.edu.
Cross Country: Ray VanArragon; Phone: 859-858-3511; E-mail: raymond.vanarragon@asbury.edu.
Soccer: Josh Oakley; Phone: 859-858-3511; E-mail: joakley@asbury.edu.
Swimming: Conrhod Zonio; Phone: 859-858-3511; E-mail: conrhod.zonio@asbury.edu.
Tennis: Ron Harper; Phone: 859-858-3511; E-mail: ron.harper@asbury.edu.

WOMEN'S COACHES
Basketball: Debi Powell; Phone: 859-858-3511; E-mail: dpowell@asbury.edu.
Cross Country: Ray VanArragon; Phone: 859-858-3511; E-mail: raymond.vanarragon@asbury.edu.
Soccer: Paul Nesselroade; Phone: 859-858-3511; E-mail: paul.nesselroade@asbury.edu.
Swimming: Conrhod Zonio; Phone: 859-858-3511; E-mail: conrhod.zonio@asbury.edu.
Tennis: Tom Harper; Phone: 859-858-3511; E-mail: tom.harper@asbury.edu.
Volleyball: Craig Mosqueda; Phone: 859-858-3511; E-mail: cmosqueda@asbury.edu.

ASHLAND UNIVERSITY
Ashland, Ohio

Eagles ◆ NCAA II ◆ Great Lakes Intercollegiate Conference
◆ http://www.ashland.edu/

Independent religious comprehensive, founded 1878, affiliated with Brethren Church
Coed, 2,782 undergraduate students, 86% full-time, 61% women, 39% men
Small-town 98-acre campus with easy access to Cleveland
Moderately difficult entrance level, 83% of applicants were admitted

Freshmen *Admission:* 2,102 applied, 1,811 were accepted, 610 enrolled. *Test scores:* SAT verbal scores over 500: 61%; SAT math scores over 500: 59%; SAT verbal scores over 600: 21%; SAT math scores over 600: 19%; SAT verbal scores over 700: 1%; SAT math scores over 700: 3%.
Tuition and fees (2004–05): $18,858 (full-time). *Room and board:* $6964 (room only: $3740).
Financial Aid (All incoming freshmen): *Average need-based gift aid:* $12,451. *Average non-need based aid:* $7356. *Average aid to full-time undergraduates:* $17,172.
Athletic Department: *Director of Athletics:* Bill Goldberg; Phone: 419-289-5441; Fax: 419-289-5468. *Sports Information Director:* Al King; Phone: 419-289-5441.

MEN'S COACHES
Baseball: John Schaly; Phone: 419-289-5444; E-mail: jschaly@ashland.edu.
Basketball: Roger Lyons; Phone: 419-289-5443; E-mail: rlyons1@ashland.edu.
Cheerleading: Vicki Wirick; Phone: 419-289-5063.
Cross Country: Bill Gallagher; Phone: 419-289-5459; E-mail: autrack@hotmail.com.
Football: Lee Owens; Phone: 419-289-5447; E-mail: football@ashland.edu.
Golf: Ben Cavey; Phone: 419-289-5441.
Soccer: John Hall; Phone: 419-289-5466; E-mail: soccer@ashland.edu.
Swimming: Paul Graham; Phone: 419-289-5445; E-mail: pgraham@ashland.edu.
Track and Field: Bill Gallagher; Phone: 419-289-5459; E-mail: autrack@hotmail.com.

Wrestling: Ray Kowatch; Phone: 419-289-5456; E-mail: rkowatch@ashland.edu.

WOMEN'S COACHES

Basketball: Sue Ramsey; Phone: 419-289-5469; E-mail: sramsey@ashland.edu.
Cheerleading: Vicki Wirick; Phone: 419-289-5063.
Cross Country: Bill Gallagher; Phone: 419-289-5459; E-mail: autrack@hotmail.com.
Golf: Steve Paramore; Phone: 419-289-5454.
Soccer: John Hall; Phone: 419-289-5466; E-mail: soccer@ashland.edu.
Softball: Sheila Gulas; Phone: 419-289-5453; E-mail: sgulas@ashland.edu.
Swimming: Paul Graham; Phone: 419-289-5445; E-mail: pgraham@ashland.edu.
Tennis: Carl Leedy; Phone: 419-289-5441.
Track and Field: Bill Gallagher; Phone: 419-289-5459; E-mail: autrack@hotmail.com.
Volleyball: Connie Surowicz; Phone: 419-289-5454.

ASSUMPTION COLLEGE
Worcester, Massachusetts

Greyhounds ◆ NCAA II ◆ Eastern College Athletic Conference; Northeast-10 Conference ◆ http://www.assumption.edu/

Independent Roman Catholic comprehensive, founded 1904
Coed, 2,133 undergraduate students, 99% full-time, 62% women, 38% men
Suburban 145-acre campus with easy access to Boston
Moderately difficult entrance level, 72% of applicants were admitted

Freshmen *Admission:* 2,901 applied, 2,279 were accepted, 640 enrolled. *Test scores:* SAT verbal scores over 500: 74%; SAT math scores over 500: 74%; SAT verbal scores over 600: 21%; SAT math scores over 600: 22%; SAT verbal scores over 700: 1%; SAT math scores over 700: 1%.
Tuition and fees (2003–04): $21,165 (full-time). *Room and board:* $5090 (room only: $3120).
Financial Aid (All incoming freshmen): *Average need-based gift aid:* $11,168. *Average non-need based aid:* $8440. *Average aid to full-time undergraduates:* $15,166.
Athletic Department: *Director of Athletics:* Ted Paulauskas; Phone: 508-767-7279; Fax: 508-798-2568; E-mail: teddyp@assumption.edu. *Sports Information Director:* Steve Morris; Phone: 508-767-7240; E-mail: merc@assumption.edu.

MEN'S COACHES

Baseball: Jim Vail; Phone: 508-767-7232; E-mail: baseball@assumption.edu.
Basketball: Tom Ackerman; Phone: 508-767-7330; E-mail: tackerma@assumption.edu.
Cross Country: Mark Perrone; Phone: 508-767-7233; E-mail: mperrone@assumption.edu.
Football: Sean Mahoney; Phone: 508-767-7454; E-mail: smahoney@assumption.edu.
Golf: Tim Bibaud; Phone: 508-767-7411; E-mail: tbeebs@aol.com.
Ice Hockey: Keith Hughes; Phone: 508-767-7179; E-mail: ihockey@assumption.edu.
Lacrosse: Chris Widelo; Phone: 508-767-7179; E-mail: mlax@assumption.edu.
Soccer: Bryan Laut; Phone: 508-767-7236; E-mail: msoccer@assumption.edu.
Tennis: John Ippolito; Phone: 508-767-7411; E-mail: accoach@lycos.com.
Track and Field: Mark Perrone; Phone: 508-767-7233; E-mail: mperrone@assumption.edu.

WOMEN'S COACHES

Basketball: Kerry Phayre; Phone: 508-767-7282; E-mail: kphayre@assumption.edu.
Cross Country: Mark Perrone; Phone: 508-767-7233; E-mail: mperrone@assumption.edu.
Field Hockey: Deb Draper; Phone: 508-767-7233; E-mail: ddraper@assumption.edu.
Lacrosse: Deb Draper; Phone: 508-767-7233; E-mail: ddraper@assumption.edu.

Soccer: Neil Stafford; Phone: 508-767-7236; E-mail: wsoccer@assumption.edu.
Softball: Ralph Delucia; Phone: 508-767-7298; E-mail: softball@assumption.edu.
Tennis: Jordana Ruggeri; Phone: 508-767-7411; E-mail: wtennis@assumption.edu.
Track and Field: Mark Perrone; Phone: 508-767-7233; E-mail: mperrone@assumption.edu.
Volleyball: Mindy Plog; Phone: 508-767-7411; E-mail: volleyball@assumption.edu.

ATHENS STATE UNIVERSITY
Athens, Alabama

Bears ◆ NAIA ◆ Independent ◆ http://www.athens.edu/

State-supported upper-level, founded 1822, part of The Alabama College System
Coed, 2,537 undergraduate students, 40% full-time, 68% women, 32% men
Small-town 45-acre campus
Noncompetitive entrance level, 87% of applicants were admitted

Freshmen *Admission:* 582 applied, 508 were accepted.
Tuition and fees (2003–04): $3570 (resident), $6720 (nonresident). *Room only:* $900.
Athletic Department: *Director of Athletics:* Harold Murrell; Phone: 256-233-8279; Fax: 256-233-8164; E-mail: murreh@athens.edu.

MEN'S COACHES

Basketball: Harold Murrell; Phone: 256-233-8279; E-mail: murreh@athens.edu.

WOMEN'S COACHES

Softball: Larry Keenum; Phone: 256-233-8127; E-mail: l.keenum@athens.edu.

ATLANTA CHRISTIAN COLLEGE
East Point, Georgia

Chargers ◆ NAIA ◆ Independent ◆ http://www.acc.edu/

Independent Christian 4-year, founded 1937
Coed, 394 undergraduate students
Suburban 52-acre campus with easy access to Atlanta
Moderately difficult entrance level, 36% of applicants were admitted

Freshmen *Admission:* 737 applied, 265 were accepted.
Tuition and fees (2003–04): $10,800 (full-time). *Room and board:* $4150.
Athletic Department: *Director of Athletics:* Joe Griffin; Phone: 404-669-2052; Fax: 404-460-2411; E-mail: jgriffin@acc.edu. *Sports Information Director:* Alan Wilson; E-mail: awilson@acc.edu.

MEN'S COACHES

Baseball: Alan Wilson; Phone: 404-669-2059; E-mail: awilson@acc.edu.
Basketball: Joe Griffin; Phone: 404-669-2052; E-mail: jgriffin@acc.edu.
Golf: Joe Griffin; Phone: 404-669-2052; E-mail: jgriffin@acc.edu.
Soccer: Randy Douglas; Phone: 404-460-2410; E-mail: rdouglas@acc.edu.

WOMEN'S COACHES

Basketball: Alan Wilson; Phone: 404-669-2059; E-mail: awilson@acc.edu.
Soccer: Randy Douglas; Phone: 404-460-2410; E-mail: rdouglas@acc.edu.

AUBURN UNIVERSITY
Auburn University, Alabama

Tigers ◆ NCAA I ◆ Southeastern Conference ◆ http://www.auburn.edu/

State-supported university, founded 1856
Coed, 19,251 undergraduate students, 91% full-time, 48% women, 52% men
Small-town 1,875-acre campus with easy access to Atlanta and Birmingham
Moderately difficult entrance level, 76% of applicants were admitted

Freshmen *Admission:* 12,439 applied, 9,653 were accepted, 3,706 enrolled. *Test scores:* SAT verbal scores over 500: 79%; SAT math scores over 500: 84%; SAT verbal scores over 600: 27%; SAT math scores over 600: 37%; SAT verbal scores over 700: 5%; SAT math scores over 700: 7%.
Tuition and fees (2003–04): $4426 (resident), $12,886 (nonresident). *Room and board:* $5970 (room only: $2500).
Financial Aid (All incoming freshmen): *Average need-based gift aid:* $3113. *Average non-need based aid:* $3385. *Average aid to full-time undergraduates:* $5709.
Athletic Department: *Director of Athletics:* David Housel; Phone: 334-844-4750; Fax: 334-844-9778; E-mail: houseda@auburn.edu. *Sports Information Director:* Meredith Jenkins; Phone: 334-844-9800; E-mail: heinsml@auburn.edu.

MEN'S COACHES
Baseball: Steve Renfroe; Phone: 334-844-4975; E-mail: renfrsw@auburn.edu.
Basketball: Cliff Ellis; Phone: 334-844-9750.
Cheerleading: Susan Nunnelly; Phone: 334-844-4750.
Cross Country: Ralph Spry; Phone: 334-844-9790; E-mail: spryral@auburn.edu.
Diving: Jeff Shaffer; Phone: 334-844-9753; E-mail: shaffjs@auburn.edu.
Football: Tommy Tuberville; Phone: 334-844-4750; E-mail: tuberth@auburn.edu.
Golf: Mike Griffin; Phone: 334-844-9750; E-mail: griffgm@auburn.edu.
Swimming: David Marsh; Phone: 334-844-9746; E-mail: marshdw@auburn.edu.
Tennis: Eric Shore; Phone: 334-844-9750; E-mail: shoreej@auburn.edu.
Track and Field: Ralph Spry; Phone: 334-844-9750; E-mail: spryral@auburn.edu.

WOMEN'S COACHES
Basketball: Joe Ciampi; Phone: 334-844-9750; E-mail: ciampjr@auburn.edu.
Cheerleading: Susan Nunnelly; Phone: 334-844-4750.
Cross Country: Ralph Spry; Phone: 334-844-9790; E-mail: spryral@auburn.edu.
Diving: Jeff Shaffer; Phone: 334-844-9753; E-mail: shaffjs@auburn.edu.
Golf: Kim Evans; Phone: 334-844-9766; E-mail: evanski@auburn.edu.
Gymnastics: Jeff Thompson; Phone: 334-844-5046; E-mail: thompj9@auburn.edu.
Soccer: Karen Hoppa; Phone: 334-844-9773; E-mail: richtka@auburn.edu.
Softball: Tina Deese; Phone: 334-844-9781; E-mail: deeseti@auburn.edu.
Swimming: David Marsh; Phone: 334-844-9746; E-mail: marshdw@auburn.edu.
Tennis: Troy Porco; Phone: 334-844-9739; E-mail: porcots@auburn.edu.
Track and Field: Ralph Spry; Phone: 334-844-9750; E-mail: spryral@auburn.edu.
Volleyball: Laura Farina; Phone: 334-844-9794; E-mail: farinla@auburn.edu.

AUBURN UNIVERSITY MONTGOMERY
Montgomery, Alabama

Senators ◆ NAIA ◆ Georgia Alabama Carolina Conference ◆ http://www.aum.edu/

State-supported comprehensive, founded 1967, part of Auburn University
Coed, 4,492 undergraduate students, 63% full-time, 64% women, 36% men
Suburban 500-acre campus
Moderately difficult entrance level, 99% of applicants were admitted

Freshmen *Admission:* 962 applied, 954 were accepted, 906 enrolled.
Tuition and fees (2003–04): $4130 (resident), $11,930 (nonresident). *Room and board:* $4890 (room only: $2400).
Financial Aid (All incoming freshmen): *Average aid to full-time undergraduates:* $4795.
Athletic Department: *Director of Athletics:* Bill Elder; Phone: 334-244-3540; Fax: 334-244-3886; E-mail: welder@mail.aum.edu. *Sports Information Director:* Travis Jarome; Phone: 334-244-3832; E-mail: tjarome@mail.aum.edu.

MEN'S COACHES
Baseball: Q. V. Lowe; Phone: 334-244-3236.
Basketball: Larry Chapman; Phone: 334-244-3542; E-mail: lchapman@mail.aum.edu.
Soccer: Brett Teach; Phone: 334-244-3617; E-mail: bteach1@mail.aum.edu.
Tennis: Anuk Christiansz; Phone: 334-244-3448; E-mail: achrist1@mail.aum.edu.

WOMEN'S COACHES
Basketball: Stephen Crotz; Phone: 334-244-3366; E-mail: scrotz@mail.aum.edu.
Soccer: Brett Teach; Phone: 334-244-3617; E-mail: bteach1@mail.aum.edu.
Tennis: Anuk Christiansz; Phone: 334-244-3448; E-mail: achrist1@mail.aum.edu.

AUGSBURG COLLEGE
Minneapolis, Minnesota

Auggies ◆ NCAA III ◆ Minnesota Intercollegiate Athletic Conference ◆ http://www.augsburg.edu/

Independent Lutheran comprehensive, founded 1869
Coed, 2,861 undergraduate students, 81% full-time, 58% women, 42% men
Urban 23-acre campus
Moderately difficult entrance level, 79% of applicants were admitted

Freshmen *Admission:* 935 applied, 765 were accepted, 377 enrolled. *Test scores:* SAT verbal scores over 500: 82%; SAT math scores over 500: 85%; SAT verbal scores over 600: 39%; SAT math scores over 600: 30%; SAT verbal scores over 700: 4%; SAT math scores over 700: 5%.
Tuition and fees (2003–04): $19,398 (full-time). *Room and board:* $5900 (room only: $3010).
Financial Aid (All incoming freshmen): *Average need-based gift aid:* $10,790. *Average non-need based aid:* $15,769. *Average aid to full-time undergraduates:* $14,339.
Athletic Department: *Director of Athletics:* Paul Grauer; Phone: 612-330-1243; Fax: 612-330-1372; E-mail: grauerp@augsburg.edu. *Sports Information Director:* Don Stoner; Phone: 612-330-1677; E-mail: stoner@augsburg.edu.

MEN'S COACHES
Baseball: Keith Bateman; Phone: 612-330-1395; E-mail: batemank@augsburg.edu.
Basketball: Brian Ammann; Phone: 612-330-1238; E-mail: ammann@augsburg.edu.
Cheerleading: Kelly Langums; Phone: 612-330-1105; E-mail: spiritteams@aol.com.
Cross Country: Dennis Barker; Phone: 612-330-1435; E-mail: barkerd@augsburg.edu.

Diving: Charlie King; Phone: 612-330-1249; E-mail: charlesgking@hotmail.com.
Football: Jack Osberg; Phone: 612-330-1235; E-mail: osbergj@augsburg.edu.
Golf: Brian Ammann; Phone: 612-330-1238; E-mail: ammann@augsburg.edu.
Ice Hockey: Mike Schwartz; Phone: 612-330-1163; E-mail: schwartm@augsburg.edu.
Soccer: Mike Navarre; Phone: 612-330-1623; E-mail: navarre@augsburg.edu.
Swimming: Charlie King; Phone: 612-330-1249; E-mail: charlesgking@hotmail.com.
Track and Field: Dennis Barker; Phone: 612-330-1435; E-mail: barkerd@augsburg.edu.
Wrestling: Jeff Swensen; Phone: 612-330-1241; E-mail: swensonj@augsburg.edu.

WOMEN'S COACHES

Basketball: Dave Johnson; Phone: 612-330-1239; E-mail: johnso98@augsburg.edu.
Cheerleading: Kelly Langums; Phone: 612-330-1105; E-mail: spiritteams@aol.com.
Cross Country: Dennis Barker; Phone: 612-330-1435; E-mail: barkerd@augsburg.edu.
Diving: Charlie King; Phone: 612-330-1249; E-mail: charlesgking@hotmail.com.
Golf: Tom Nygaard; Phone: 612-330-1249; E-mail: tnygaard@threeriversparkdistrict.org.
Soccer: Mike Navarre; Phone: 612-330-1623; E-mail: navarre@augsburg.edu.
Softball: Carol Enke; Phone: 612-330-1250; E-mail: enke@augsburg.edu.
Swimming: Charlie King; Phone: 612-330-1249; E-mail: charlesgking@hotmail.com.
Track and Field: Dennis Barker; Phone: 612-330-1435; E-mail: barkerd@augsburg.edu.
Volleyball: Cathy Skinner; Phone: 612-330-1541; E-mail: skinnerc@augsburg.edu.

AUGUSTANA COLLEGE
Rock Island, Illinois

Vikings ◆ NCAA III ◆ College Conference of Illinois and Wisconsin Conference ◆ http://www.augustana.edu/

Independent religious 4-year, founded 1860, affiliated with Evangelical Lutheran Church in America
Coed, 2,309 undergraduate students, 99% full-time, 58% women, 42% men
Suburban 115-acre campus
Moderately difficult entrance level, 68% of applicants were admitted

Freshmen *Admission:* 3,021 applied, 2,060 were accepted, 614 enrolled.
Tuition and fees (2003–04): $20,829 (full-time). *Room and board:* $5781 (room only: $2928).
Financial Aid (All incoming freshmen): *Average need-based gift aid:* $11,801. *Average non-need based aid:* $7644. *Average aid to full-time undergraduates:* $15,925.
Athletic Department: *Director of Athletics:* Greg Wallace; Phone: 309-794-7521; Fax: 309-794-7525; E-mail: pewallace@augustana.edu. *Sports Information Director:* Dave Wrath; Phone: 309-794-7521; E-mail: pewrath@augustana.edu.

MEN'S COACHES

Baseball: Greg Wallace; Phone: 309-794-7521; E-mail: pewallace@augustana.edu.
Basketball: Grey Giovanine; Phone: 309-794-7254.
Cheerleading: Linda Prebyl; Phone: 309-794-7521; E-mail: peprebyl@augustana.edu.
Cross Country: Paul Olsen; Phone: 309-794-7257; E-mail: enolsen@augustana.edu.
Diving: Gary Ackerson; Phone: 309-794-7519; E-mail: peackerson@augustana.edu.
Football: Jim Barnes; Phone: 309-794-7326.
Golf: Grey Giovanne; Phone: 309-794-7254.
Soccer: Scott Mejia; Phone: 309-794-7398; E-mail: pemejia@augustana.edu.

Swimming: Gary Ackerson; Phone: 309-794-7519; E-mail: peackerson@augustana.edu.
Tennis: Brad Dietzel; Phone: 309-794-7521; E-mail: pedietzel@augustana.edu.
Track and Field: Paul Olsen; Phone: 309-794-7257; E-mail: enolsen@augustana.edu.
Track and Field: Paul Olsen; Phone: 309-794-7257; E-mail: enolsen@augustana.edu.
Wrestling: Pat Marsh; Phone: 309-794-7392; E-mail: pemarsh@augustana.edu.

WOMEN'S COACHES

Basketball: James Black; Phone: 309-794-7523; E-mail: peblack@augustana.edu.
Cheerleading: Linda Prebyl; Phone: 309-794-7521; E-mail: peprebyl@augustana.edu.
Cross Country: Fred Whiteside; Phone: 309-794-7524; E-mail: pewhiteside@augustana.edu.
Diving: Gary Ackerson; Phone: 309-794-7519; E-mail: peackerson@augustana.edu.
Golf: Ron Standley; Phone: 309-794-7486; E-mail: pestandley@augustana.edu.
Soccer: Scott Mejia; Phone: 309-794-7398; E-mail: pemejia@augustana.edu.
Softball: Kris Kistler; Phone: 309-794-7529; E-mail: pekistler@augustana.edu.
Swimming: Gary Ackerson; Phone: 309-794-7519; E-mail: peackerson@augustana.edu.
Tennis: Brad Dietzel; Phone: 309-794-7521; E-mail: pedietzel@augustana.edu.
Track and Field: Fred Whiteside; Phone: 309-794-7524; E-mail: pewhiteside@augustana.edu.
Volleyball: Betsy Knott; Phone: 309-794-7432; E-mail: peknott@augustana.edu.

AUGUSTANA COLLEGE
Sioux Falls, South Dakota

Vikings ◆ NCAA II ◆ North Central Intercollegiate Conference ◆ http://www.augie.edu/

Independent religious comprehensive, founded 1860, affiliated with Evangelical Lutheran Church in America
Coed, 1,810 undergraduate students, 93% full-time, 63% women, 37% men
Urban 100-acre campus
Moderately difficult entrance level, 8% of applicants were admitted

Freshmen *Admission:* 1,692 applied, 1,338 were accepted, 438 enrolled. *Test scores:* SAT verbal scores over 500: 88%; SAT math scores over 500: 88%; SAT verbal scores over 600: 57%; SAT math scores over 600: 46%; SAT verbal scores over 700: 19%; SAT math scores over 700: 15%.
Tuition and fees (2003–04): $16,972 (full-time). *Room and board:* $5026 (room only: $2600).
Financial Aid (All incoming freshmen): *Average need-based gift aid:* $11,424. *Average non-need based aid:* $8020. *Average aid to full-time undergraduates:* $15,870.
Athletic Department: *Director of Athletics:* Bill Gross; Phone: 605-274-4315; Fax: 605-274-5298; E-mail: bill_gross@augie.edu. *Sports Information Director:* Kevin Ludwig; Phone: 605-274-4335; E-mail: kevin_ludwig@augie.edu.

MEN'S COACHES

Baseball: Jeff Holm; Phone: 605-274-5541; E-mail: jeff_holm@augie.edu.
Basketball: Tom Billeter; Phone: 605-274-4317; E-mail: tom_billeter@augie.edu.
Cross Country: Tracy Hellman; Phone: 605-274-5528; E-mail: tracy_hellman@augie.edu.
Football: Jim Heinitz; Phone: 605-274-4338; E-mail: jim_heinitz@augie.edu.
Golf: Denny Cadwell; Phone: 605-274-4848; E-mail: dcazzies@aol.com.
Tennis: Aaron Boyd; Phone: 605-373-1123; E-mail: mcenroe44@aol.com.
Track and Field: Tracy Hellman; Phone: 605-274-4323; E-mail: tracy_hellman@augie.edu.

Augustana College *(continued)*

Wrestling: Jason Reitmeier; Phone: 605-274-4321; E-mail: jason_reitmeier@augie.edu.

WOMEN'S COACHES

Basketball: Dave Krauth; Phone: 605-274-5531; E-mail: dave_krauth@augie.edu.
Cross Country: Tracy Hellman; Phone: 605-274-5528; E-mail: tracy_hellman@augie.edu.
Golf: Peggy Kirby; Phone: 605-929-6113.
Soccer: Steve Burckhalter; Phone: 605-274-5468; E-mail: steve_burckhalter@augie.edu.
Softball: Jenny Hill; Phone: 605-274-5527.
Tennis: Aaron Boyd; Phone: 605-373-1123; E-mail: mcenroe44@aol.com.
Track and Field: Tracy Hellman; Phone: 605-274-4323; E-mail: tracy_hellman@augie.edu.
Volleyball: Kim Sudbeck; Phone: 605-274-5539.

AUGUSTA STATE UNIVERSITY
Augusta, Georgia

Jaguars ◆ NCAA II ◆ Peach Belt Conference ◆ http://www.aug.edu/

State-supported comprehensive, founded 1925, part of University System of Georgia
Coed, 5,257 undergraduate students, 67% full-time, 64% women, 36% men
Urban 72-acre campus
Minimally difficult entrance level, 7% of applicants were admitted

Freshmen *Admission:* 1,714 applied, 1,106 were accepted, 917 enrolled. *Test scores:* SAT verbal scores over 500: 45%; SAT math scores over 500: 45%; SAT verbal scores over 600: 10%; SAT math scores over 600: 10%; SAT verbal scores over 700: %; SAT math scores over 700: 1%.
Tuition and fees (2003–04): $2592 (resident), $9226 (nonresident).
Financial Aid (All incoming freshmen): *Average need-based gift aid:* $4033. *Average non-need based aid:* $3996. *Average aid to full-time undergraduates:* $4381.
Athletic Department: *Director of Athletics:* Clint Bryant; Phone: 706-737-1626; Fax: 706-737-1782; E-mail: cbryant@aug.edu. *Sports Information Director:* Joey Warren; Phone: 706-737-7925; E-mail: jwarren3@aug.edu.

MEN'S COACHES

Baseball: Skip Fite; Phone: 706-731-7917; E-mail: sfite@aug.edu.
Basketball: Gary Tuell; Phone: 706-667-4765; E-mail: gtuell@aug.edu.
Cheerleading: Frank Rodriguez; Phone: 706-667-1626; E-mail: ciscolive22@aol.com.
Golf: Josh Gregory; Phone: 706-731-7992; E-mail: jgregor2@aug.edu.
Tennis: Michael McGrath; Phone: 706-667-4349; E-mail: mmcgrath@aug.edu.

WOMEN'S COACHES

Basketball: Greg Wilson; Phone: 706-731-7915; E-mail: gwilson@aug.edu.
Cheerleading: Frank Rodriguez; Phone: 706-667-1626; E-mail: ciscolive22@aol.com.
Cross Country: Buck Harris; Phone: 706-731-7914; E-mail: bharris@aug.edu.
Golf: Trelle Kite; Phone: 706-729-2079; E-mail: tkite@aug.edu.
Softball: Melissa Mullins; Phone: 706-731-7916; E-mail: mmullins@aug.edu.
Tennis: Michael McGrath; Phone: 706-667-4349; E-mail: mmcgrath@aug.edu.
Volleyball: Tess Gresham; Phone: 706-667-4766; E-mail: tgresha4@aug.edu.

AURORA UNIVERSITY
Aurora, Illinois

Spartans ◆ NCAA III ◆ Illini-Badger Football Conference; Northern Illinois-Iowa Conference ◆ http://www.aurora.edu/

Independent comprehensive, founded 1893
Coed, 1,646 undergraduate students, 87% full-time, 64% women, 36% men
Suburban 26-acre campus with easy access to Chicago
Moderately difficult entrance level, 60% of applicants were admitted

Freshmen *Admission:* 1,485 applied, 834 were accepted, 333 enrolled. *Test scores:* SAT verbal scores over 500: 38%; SAT math scores over 500: 57%.
Tuition and fees (2004–05): $14,750 (full-time). *Room and board:* $6614 (room only: $2968).
Financial Aid (All incoming freshmen): *Average need-based gift aid:* $5699. *Average non-need based aid:* $8660. *Average aid to full-time undergraduates:* $15,733.
Athletic Department: *Director of Athletics:* Mark Walsh; Phone: 630-844-5111; Fax: 630-844-7809; E-mail: mwalsh@aurora.edu. *Sports Information Director:* Brian Kipley; Phone: 630-844-7575; E-mail: bkipley@aurora.edu.

MEN'S COACHES

Baseball: Shaun Neitzel; Phone: 630-844-6515; E-mail: sneitzel@aurora.edu.
Basketball: James Lancaster; Phone: 630-844-5144; E-mail: jlancast@aurora.edu.
Cheerleading: Michelle Neitzel; Phone: 630-844-5469; E-mail: mneitzel@aurora.edu.
Cross Country: James Kluckhohn; Phone: 630-844-5473; E-mail: jkluckho@aurora.edu.
Football: Jim Scott; Phone: 630-844-5115; E-mail: jscott@aurora.edu.
Golf: John Donofrio; Phone: 630-844-3855; E-mail: donofrio@aurora.edu.
Soccer: Pete Watkins; Phone: 630-844-5268; E-mail: pwatkins@aurora.edu.
Tennis: Jessi Laffey; Phone: 630-844-5152; E-mail: jlaffey@aurora.edu.
Track and Field: James Kluckhohn; Phone: 630-844-5473; E-mail: jkluckho@aurora.edu.

WOMEN'S COACHES

Basketball: Jennifer Buckley; Phone: 630-844-5112; E-mail: jbuckley@aurora.edu.
Cheerleading: Michelle Neitzel; Phone: 630-844-5469; E-mail: mneitzel@aurora.edu.
Cross Country: James Kluckhohn; Phone: 630-844-5473; E-mail: jkluckho@aurora.edu.
Soccer: Kanute Drugan; Phone: 630-844-4207; E-mail: kdrugan@aurora.edu.
Softball: Mike McKenzie; Phone: 630-844-4939; E-mail: mmckenzi@aurora.edu.
Tennis: Jessi Laffey; Phone: 630-844-5152; E-mail: jlaffey@aurora.edu.
Track and Field: James Kluckhohn; Phone: 630-844-5473; E-mail: jkluckho@aurora.edu.
Volleyball: Jerry Angle; Phone: 630-844-5261; E-mail: jangle@aurora.edu.

AUSTIN COLLEGE
Sherman, Texas

Kangaroos ◆ NCAA III ◆ American Southwest Conference ◆ http://www.austincollege.edu/

Independent Presbyterian comprehensive, founded 1849
Coed, 1,294 undergraduate students, 99% full-time, 56% women, 44% men
Suburban 60-acre campus with easy access to Dallas–Fort Worth
Very difficult entrance level, 66% of applicants were admitted

Freshmen *Admission:* 1,328 applied, 960 were accepted, 338 enrolled. *Test scores:* SAT verbal scores over 500: 94%; SAT math scores over 500: 93%; SAT verbal scores over 600: 62%; SAT math scores over 600: 63%; SAT verbal scores over 700: 15%; SAT math scores over 700: 10%.

Tuition and fees (2004–05): $19,165 (full-time). *Room and board:* $7089 (room only: $3255).
Financial Aid (All incoming freshmen): *Average need-based gift aid:* $12,476. *Average non-need based aid:* $7477. *Average aid to full-time undergraduates:* $17,854.
Athletic Department: *Director of Athletics:* Tim Millerick; Phone: 903-813-2228; Fax: 903-813-3196. *Sports Information Director:* Chuck Sadowski; Phone: 903-813-2499; E-mail: csadowski@austincollege.edu.

MEN'S COACHES
Baseball: Bruce Mauppin; Phone: 903-813-2516; E-mail: bmauppin@austincollege.edu.
Basketball: Chris Destreich; Phone: 903-813-2318; E-mail: coestreich@austincollege.edu.
Cheerleading: Tracy May; Phone: 903-813-2516.
Diving: Philip Wiggins; Phone: 903-813-2319; E-mail: pwiggins@austincollege.edu.
Football: Davis Norman; Phone: 903-813-2401; E-mail: dnorman@austincollege.edu.
Golf: Keith Strickland; Phone: 903-813-2499.
Soccer: Ryan Shea; Phone: 903-813-2400; E-mail: rshea@austincollege.edu.
Swimming: Philip Wiggins; Phone: 903-813-2319; E-mail: pwiggins@austincollege.edu.
Tennis: Ed Garza; Phone: 903-813-2515; E-mail: egarza@austincollege.edu.

WOMEN'S COACHES
Basketball: Debra Hunter; Phone: 903-813-2516; E-mail: dhunter@austincollege.edu.
Cheerleading: Tracy May; Phone: 903-813-2516.
Diving: Philip Wiggins; Phone: 903-813-2319; E-mail: pwiggins@austincollege.edu.
Soccer: Paul Burns; Phone: 903-813-2516; E-mail: pburns@austincollege.edu.
Swimming: Philip Wiggins; Phone: 903-813-2319; E-mail: pwiggins@austincollege.edu.
Tennis: Ed Garza; Phone: 903-813-2515; E-mail: egarza@austincollege.edu.
Volleyball: Ed Garza; Phone: 903-813-2516; E-mail: egarza@austincollege.edu.

AUSTIN PEAY STATE UNIVERSITY
Clarksville, Tennessee
Governors ◆ NCAA I ◆ Ohio Valley Conference; Pioneer Football League Conference ◆ http://www.apsu.edu/

State-supported comprehensive, founded 1927, part of Tennessee Board of Regents
Coed, 7,188 undergraduate students, 73% full-time, 63% women, 37% men
Suburban 200-acre campus with easy access to Nashville
Moderately difficult entrance level, 93% of applicants were admitted

Freshmen *Admission:* 2,207 applied, 2,064 were accepted, 1,191 enrolled. *Test scores:* SAT verbal scores over 500: 38%; SAT math scores over 500: 30%; SAT verbal scores over 600: 11%; SAT math scores over 600: 7%; SAT verbal scores over 700: 1%.
Tuition and fees (2003–04): $4004 (resident), $11,936 (nonresident). *Room and board:* $4096 (room only: $2450).
Financial Aid (All incoming freshmen): *Average need-based gift aid:* $3452. *Average non-need based aid:* $2260. *Average aid to full-time undergraduates:* $4576.
Athletic Department: *Director of Athletics:* Dave Loos; Phone: 931-221-7904; Fax: 931-221-7830; E-mail: loosd@apsu.edu. *Sports Information Director:* Brad Kirtley; Phone: 931-221-7561; E-mail: kirtleyb@apsu.edu.

MEN'S COACHES
Baseball: Gary McClure; Phone: 931-221-6266; E-mail: mcclureg@apsu.edu.
Basketball: Dave Loos; Phone: 931-221-7904; E-mail: loosd@apsu.edu.
Cheerleading: Stacy Blackston; Phone: 931-221-7904; E-mail: sgblackston@yahoo.com.
Cross Country: Yvonne Lowe; Phone: 931-221-7211; E-mail: lowey@apsu.edu.

Football: Carroll McCray; Phone: 931-221-7991; E-mail: mccrayc@apsu.edu.
Golf: Mark Leroux; Phone: 931-221-7647; E-mail: lerouxm@apsu.edu.
Tennis: Brian Surface; Phone: 931-221-6101; E-mail: bsurface22@hotmail.com.

WOMEN'S COACHES
Basketball: Andy Blackston; Phone: 931-221-7202; E-mail: blackstona@apsu.edu.
Cheerleading: Stacy Blackston; Phone: 931-221-7904; E-mail: sgblackston@yahoo.com.
Cross Country: Yvonne Lowe; Phone: 931-221-7211; E-mail: lowey@apsu.edu.
Golf: Mark Leroux; Phone: 931-221-7647; E-mail: lerouxm@apsu.edu.
Soccer: Kelly Poole; Phone: 931-221-7972; E-mail: poolek@apsu.edu.
Softball: Tara McCoy; Phone: 931-221-6190; E-mail: mccoyt@apsu.edu.
Tennis: Brian Surface; Phone: 931-221-6101; E-mail: bsurface22@hotmail.com.
Track and Field: Yvonne Lowe; Phone: 931-221-7211; E-mail: lowey@apsu.edu.
Volleyball: Cheryl Holt; Phone: 931-221-7203; E-mail: holtca@apsu.edu.

AVERETT UNIVERSITY
Danville, Virginia
Cougars ◆ NCAA III ◆ USA South Athletic Conference ◆ http://www.averett.edu/

Independent religious comprehensive, founded 1859, affiliated with Baptist General Association of Virginia
Coed, 2,087 undergraduate students, 61% full-time, 58% women, 42% men
Small-town 19-acre campus with easy access to Greensboro and Raleigh
Moderately difficult entrance level, 87% of applicants were admitted

Freshmen *Admission:* 778 applied, 694 were accepted, 230 enrolled. *Test scores:* SAT verbal scores over 500: 39%; SAT math scores over 500: 34%; SAT verbal scores over 600: 10%; SAT math scores over 600: 7%; SAT verbal scores over 700: 1%.
Tuition and fees (2003–04): $17,600 (full-time). *Room and board:* $6020 (room only: $4460).
Financial Aid (All incoming freshmen): *Average need-based gift aid:* $8902. *Average non-need based aid:* $8012. *Average aid to full-time undergraduates:* $11,668.
Athletic Department: *Director of Athletics:* Vesa Hiltunen; Phone: 434-791-5700; Fax: 434-791-5740; E-mail: vesa.hiltunen@averett.edu. *Sports Information Director:* Sam Ferguson; Phone: 434-791-5700; E-mail: sam.ferguson@averett.edu.

MEN'S COACHES
Baseball: Ed Fulton; Phone: 434-791-5030; E-mail: ed.fulton@averett.edu.
Basketball: Kirk Chandler; Phone: 434-791-5689; E-mail: kirk.chandler@averett.edu.
Cheerleading: Rebecca Clark; Phone: 434-791-5762; E-mail: rclark@averett.edu.
Cross Country: David Pavord; Phone: 434-791-2472.
Football: Mike Dunlevy; Phone: 434-791-4991; E-mail: mike.dunlevy@averett.edu.
Golf: Jim Gourlay; Phone: 434-791-5749; E-mail: jim.gourlay@averett.edu.
Soccer: Jim Gourlay; Phone: 434-791-5749; E-mail: jim.gourlay@averett.edu.
Tennis: Vesa Hiltunen; Phone: 434-791-5701; E-mail: vesa.hiltunen@averett.edu.

WOMEN'S COACHES
Basketball: Kathy Bocock; Phone: 434-791-5688; E-mail: kathy.bocock@averett.edu.
Cheerleading: Rebecca Clark; Phone: 434-791-5762; E-mail: rclark@averett.edu.
Cross Country: David Pavord; Phone: 434-791-2472.
Soccer: Kelly Gregory; Phone: 434-791-5869; E-mail: kelly.gregory@averett.edu.
Softball: Kathy Bocock; Phone: 434-791-5688; E-mail: kathy.bocock@averett.edu.

Averett University *(continued)*

Tennis: Darnay Miller; Phone: 434-791-5737; E-mail: darnay.miller@averett.edu.
Volleyball: Darnay Miller; Phone: 434-791-5737; E-mail: darnay.miller@averett.edu.

AVILA UNIVERSITY
Kansas City, Missouri

Eagles ◆ NAIA ◆ Heart of America Conference ◆ http://www.avila.edu/

Independent Roman Catholic comprehensive, founded 1916
Coed, 1,160 undergraduate students, 76% full-time, 62% women, 38% men
Suburban 50-acre campus
Minimally difficult entrance level, 39% of applicants were admitted

Freshmen *Admission:* 936 applied, 395 were accepted, 152 enrolled. *Test scores:* SAT verbal scores over 500: 37%; SAT math scores over 500: 50%; SAT verbal scores over 600: 12%; SAT math scores over 600: 12%.
Tuition and fees (2004–05): $15,870 (full-time). *Room and board:* $5400.
Financial Aid (All incoming freshmen): *Average non-need based aid:* $7000.
Athletic Department: *Director of Athletics:* Mike Sharpe; Phone: 816-501-3756; E-mail: sharpemr@mail.avila.edu. *Sports Information Director:* Greg Mittelsteadt; Phone: 816-501-3740; E-mail: mittelsteadtgt@mail.avila.edu.

MEN'S COACHES
Baseball: Ryan Howard; Phone: 816-501-3789; E-mail: howardrt@mail.avila.edu.
Basketball: Nick Totta; Phone: 816-501-3743; E-mail: tottanl@mail.avila.edu.
Football: Tim Johnson; Phone: 816-501-2486; E-mail: johnsontg@mail.avila.edu.
Soccer: Patrick Phillips; Phone: 816-501-2417; E-mail: phillipsrp@mail.avila.edu.
Volleyball: Brett Talcott; Phone: 816-501-2472; E-mail: talcottbc@mail.avila.edu.

WOMEN'S COACHES
Basketball: Greg Mittelsteadt; Phone: 816-501-3740; E-mail: mittelsteadtgt@mail.avila.edu.
Golf: Jerry Krause; Phone: 816-501-2489; E-mail: jerrylkrause@compuserve.com.
Soccer: Paul McNally; Phone: 816-501-2475; E-mail: mcnallypk@mail.avila.edu.
Softball: Steve Keel; Phone: 816-501-2418; E-mail: keelsc@mail.avila.edu.
Volleyball: Brett Talcott; Phone: 816-501-2472; E-mail: talcottbc@mail.avila.edu.

AZUSA PACIFIC UNIVERSITY
Azusa, California

Cougars ◆ NAIA ◆ Golden State Conference ◆ http://www.apu.edu/

Independent nondenominational comprehensive, founded 1899
Coed, 4,373 undergraduate students, 96% full-time, 64% women, 36% men
Small-town 60-acre campus with easy access to Los Angeles
Moderately difficult entrance level, 81% of applicants were admitted

Freshmen *Admission:* 2,472 applied, 2,042 were accepted, 912 enrolled. *Test scores:* SAT verbal scores over 500: 67%; SAT math scores over 500: 68%; SAT verbal scores over 600: 24%; SAT math scores over 600: 28%; SAT verbal scores over 700: 3%; SAT math scores over 700: 3%.
Tuition and fees (2003–04): $19,024 (full-time). *Room and board:* $5696 (room only: $3150).
Financial Aid (All incoming freshmen): *Average need-based gift aid:* $9368. *Average non-need based aid:* $4975. *Average aid to full-time undergraduates:* $12,352.

Athletic Department: *Director of Athletics:* Bill Odell; Phone: 626-815-5081; Fax: 626-815-5084; E-mail: bodell@apu.edu. *Sports Information Director:* Gary Pine; Phone: 626-815-5085; E-mail: gpine@apu.edu.

MEN'S COACHES
Baseball: Paul Svagdis; Phone: 626-815-6000; E-mail: psvagdis@apu.edu.
Basketball: Bill Odell; Phone: 626-815-5081; E-mail: bodell@apu.edu.
Cheerleading: Lyndsey Shervik; Phone: 626-815-6000; E-mail: shervikl@hotmail.com.
Cross Country: Bill Reeves; Phone: 626-815-3856; E-mail: breeves@apu.edu.
Football: Peter Shinnick; Phone: 626-815-6000; E-mail: pshinnick@apu.edu.
Soccer: Phil Wolf; Phone: 626-815-6000; E-mail: pwolf@apu.edu.
Tennis: Mark Bohren; Phone: 626-815-6000; E-mail: slehman@apu.edu.
Track and Field: Kevin Reid; Phone: 626-815-6000; E-mail: kreid@apu.edu.

WOMEN'S COACHES
Basketball: Danelle Liles; Phone: 626-815-6000; E-mail: dliles@apu.edu.
Cheerleading: Lyndsey Shervik; Phone: 626-815-6000; E-mail: shervikl@hotmail.com.
Cross Country: Bill Reeves; Phone: 626-815-3856; E-mail: breeves@apu.edu.
Soccer: Jason Surrell; Phone: 626-815-6000; E-mail: jsurrell@apu.edu.
Softball: Sharon Lehman; Phone: 626-815-6000; E-mail: slehman@apu.edu.
Tennis: Mark Bohren; Phone: 626-815-6000; E-mail: slehman@apu.edu.
Track and Field: Mike Barnett; Phone: 626-815-6000; E-mail: mbarnett@apu.edu.
Volleyball: Gerry Gregory; Phone: 626-815-6000; E-mail: ggregory@apu.edu.

BABSON COLLEGE
Wellesley, Massachusetts

Beavers ◆ NCAA III ◆ New England Women's & Men's Athletics Conference ◆ http://www.babson.edu/

Independent comprehensive, founded 1919
Coed, 1,717 undergraduate students, 100% full-time, 40% women, 60% men
Suburban 370-acre campus with easy access to Boston
Very difficult entrance level, 3% of applicants were admitted

Freshmen *Admission:* 2,991 applied, 1,110 were accepted, 395 enrolled. *Test scores:* SAT verbal scores over 500: 98%; SAT math scores over 500: 100%; SAT verbal scores over 600: 54%; SAT math scores over 600: 83%; SAT verbal scores over 700: 7%; SAT math scores over 700: 19%.
Tuition and fees (2003–04): $27,248 (full-time). *Room and board:* $9978 (room only: $6438).
Financial Aid (All incoming freshmen): *Average need-based gift aid:* $18,147. *Average non-need based aid:* $8750. *Average aid to full-time undergraduates:* $22,477.
Athletic Department: *Director of Athletics:* Frank Millerick; Phone: 781-239-4528; Fax: 781-239-5218; E-mail: millerick@babson.edu. *Sports Information Director:* Chris Buck; Phone: 781-239-4553; E-mail: cbuck@babson.edu.

MEN'S COACHES
Baseball: Matt Noone; Phone: 781-239-5823; E-mail: mnoone@babson.edu.
Basketball: Stephen Brennan; Phone: 781-239-4945; E-mail: brennanst@babson.edu.
Cross Country: Matt Taylor; Phone: 781-239-5822; E-mail: mtaylor1@babson.edu.
Diving: Rick Echlov; Phone: 781-239-5726; E-mail: echlov@babson.edu.
Golf: Mike Vassalotti; Phone: 781-239-4250.
Ice Hockey: Paul Donato; Phone: 781-239-6091; E-mail: donato@babson.edu.
Lacrosse: Jim Castrataro; Phone: 781-239-5730; E-mail: castrataro@babson.edu.

Soccer: Jon Anderson; Phone: 781-239-4251; E-mail: andersonj@babson.edu.
Swimming: Rick Echlov; Phone: 781-239-5726; E-mail: echlov@babson.edu.
Tennis: Jim Berrigan; Phone: 781-239-5220; E-mail: jberrigan@babson.edu.
Track and Field: Matt Taylor; Phone: 781-239-5822; E-mail: mtaylor1@babson.edu.

WOMEN'S COACHES

Basketball: Judy Blinstrub; Phone: 781-239-4418; E-mail: blinstrub@babson.edu.
Cross Country: Matt Taylor; Phone: 781-239-5822; E-mail: mtaylor1@babson.edu.
Diving: Rick Echlov; Phone: 781-239-5726; E-mail: echlov@babson.edu.
Field Hockey: Laurie Magoon; Phone: 781-239-4593; E-mail: lmagoon@babson.edu.
Lacrosse: Kully Hagerman; Phone: 781-239-5826; E-mail: khagerman@babson.edu.
Softball: Dave Canan; Phone: 781-239-4619; E-mail: dcanan@babson.edu.
Swimming: Rick Echlov; Phone: 781-239-5726; E-mail: echlov@babson.edu.
Tennis: Jim Berrigan; Phone: 781-239-5220; E-mail: jberrigan@babson.edu.
Track and Field: Matt Taylor; Phone: 781-239-5822; E-mail: mtaylor1@babson.edu.
Volleyball: Bob Bennett; Phone: 781-239-6672; E-mail: hching@babson.edu.

BACONE COLLEGE
Muskogee, Oklahoma

Warriors ◆ NAIA ◆ Central States Football Conference; Red River Conference ◆ http://www.bacone.edu/

Independent religious 4-year, founded 1880, affiliated with American Baptist Churches in the U.S.A.
Coed, 914 undergraduate students, 76% full-time, 54% women, 46% men
Small-town 220-acre campus with easy access to Tulsa
Minimally difficult entrance level, 62% of applicants were admitted

Freshmen *Admission:* 819 applied, 479 were accepted, 231 enrolled. *Test scores:* SAT verbal scores over 500: 41%; SAT math scores over 500: 24%; SAT verbal scores over 600: 6%.
Tuition and fees (2004–05): $8530 (full-time). *Room and board:* $5700 (room only: $3000).
Athletic Department: *Director of Athletics:* David Ross; Phone: 918-781-7285; Fax: 918-781-7416; E-mail: rossd@bacone.edu. *Sports Information Director:* Dawn Reed; Phone: 918-781-7359; E-mail: reedd@bacone.edu.

MEN'S COACHES

Baseball: Matt Cloud; Phone: 918-781-7237; E-mail: cloudm@bacone.edu.
Basketball: Alan Foster; Phone: 918-781-7212; E-mail: fostera@bacone.edu.
Cheerleading: Karmen Hall; Phone: 918-781-7265; E-mail: hallk@bacone.edu.
Cross Country: Kevin Gordon; Phone: 918-781-7364; E-mail: gordonk@bacone.edu.
Football: David Ross; Phone: 918-781-7285; E-mail: rossd@bacone.edu.
Golf: Alan Foster; Phone: 918-781-7212; E-mail: fostera@bacone.edu.
Soccer: Derek Larkin; Phone: 918-781-7267; E-mail: larkind@bacone.edu.
Track and Field: Kevin Gordon; Phone: 918-781-7364; E-mail: gordonk@bacone.edu.
Wrestling: Kenard Booker; Phone: 918-781-7369; E-mail: bookerk@bacone.edu.

WOMEN'S COACHES

Cheerleading: Karmen Hall; Phone: 918-781-7265; E-mail: hallk@bacone.edu.
Cross Country: Kevin Gordon; Phone: 918-781-7364; E-mail: gordonk@bacone.edu.
Soccer: Derek Larkin; Phone: 918-781-7267; E-mail: larkind@bacone.edu.

Softball: Dawn Reed; Phone: 918-781-7359; E-mail: reedd@bacone.edu.
Track and Field: Kevin Gordon; Phone: 918-781-7364; E-mail: gordonk@bacone.edu.
Volleyball: Ann Mesman; Phone: 918-781-7243; E-mail: mesmana@bacone.edu.

BAKER UNIVERSITY
Baldwin City, Kansas

Wildcats ◆ NAIA ◆ Heart of America Conference ◆ http://www.bakeru.edu/

Independent United Methodist comprehensive, founded 1858
Coed, 1,015 undergraduate students, 95% full-time, 57% women, 43% men
Small-town 26-acre campus with easy access to Kansas City
Moderately difficult entrance level, 82% of applicants were admitted

Freshmen *Admission:* 945 applied, 771 were accepted, 226 enrolled. *Test scores:* SAT verbal scores over 500: 61%; SAT math scores over 500: 67%; SAT verbal scores over 600: 19%; SAT math scores over 600: 20%; SAT verbal scores over 700: 2%.
Tuition and fees (2003–04): $14,560 (full-time). *Room and board:* $5300 (room only: $2400).
Financial Aid (All incoming freshmen): *Average need-based gift aid:* $6338. *Average non-need based aid:* $5000. *Average aid to full-time undergraduates:* $15,987.
Athletic Department: *Director of Athletics:* Dan Harris; Phone: 785-594-8474; E-mail: dan.harris@bakeru.edu. *Sports Information Director:* Matt Hallauer; Phone: 785-594-8343; E-mail: matt.hallauer@bakeru.edu.

MEN'S COACHES

Baseball: Philip Hannon; Phone: 785-594-8493; E-mail: phil.hannon@bakeru.edu.
Basketball: Rick Weaver; Phone: 785-594-8422; E-mail: rick.weaver@bakeru.edu.
Cheerleading: Courtney Williams; Phone: 785-594-4556; E-mail: courtney.williams@bakeru.edu.
Cross Country: Rob Mallinder; Phone: 785-594-8580; E-mail: rob.mallinder@bakeru.edu.
Football: John Frangoulis; Phone: 785-594-8462; E-mail: john.frangoulis@bakeru.edu.
Golf: Rick Weaver; Phone: 785-594-8422; E-mail: rick.weaver@bakeru.edu.
Soccer: Ron Pulvers; Phone: 785-594-4551; E-mail: ron.pulvers@bakeru.edu.
Tennis: Regan Dodd; Phone: 785-594-4557; E-mail: regan.dodd@bakeru.edu.
Track and Field: Rob Mallinder; Phone: 785-594-8580; E-mail: rob.mallinder@bakeru.edu.

WOMEN'S COACHES

Basketball: Susan Decker; Phone: 785-594-4542; E-mail: susan.decker@bakeru.edu.
Cheerleading: Courtney Williams; Phone: 785-594-4556; E-mail: courtney.williams@bakeru.edu.
Cross Country: Rob Mallinder; Phone: 785-594-8580; E-mail: rob.mallinder@bakeru.edu.
Golf: Karen Exon; Phone: 785-594-8489; E-mail: karen.exon@bakeru.edu.
Soccer: Nate Houser; Phone: 785-594-4444; E-mail: nate.houser@bakeru.edu.
Softball: Jennifer Wright; Phone: 785-594-4567; E-mail: jennifer.wright@bakeru.edu.
Tennis: Regan Dodd; Phone: 785-594-4557; E-mail: regan.dodd@bakeru.edu.
Track and Field: Rob Mallinder; Phone: 785-594-8580; E-mail: rob.mallinder@bakeru.edu.

BALDWIN-WALLACE COLLEGE
Berea, Ohio

Yellow Jackets ◆ NCAA III ◆ Ohio Athletic Conference
◆ http://www.bw.edu/

Independent Methodist comprehensive, founded 1845
Coed, 3,862 undergraduate students, 79% full-time, 61% women, 39% men
Suburban 100-acre campus with easy access to Cleveland
Moderately difficult entrance level, 78% of applicants were admitted

Freshmen *Admission:* 2,211 applied, 1,820 were accepted, 702 enrolled. *Test scores:* SAT verbal scores over 500: 76%; SAT math scores over 500: 75%; SAT verbal scores over 600: 33%; SAT math scores over 600: 31%; SAT verbal scores over 700: 5%; SAT math scores over 700: 6%.
Tuition and fees (2003–04): $18,478 (full-time). *Room and board:* $5402 (room only: $3042).
Financial Aid (All incoming freshmen): *Average need-based gift aid:* $12,226. *Average non-need based aid:* $8525. *Average aid to full-time undergraduates:* $16,774.
Athletic Department: *Director of Athletics:* Steve Bankson; Phone: 440-826-2184; Fax: 440-826-2192; E-mail: sbankson@bw.edu. *Sports Information Director:* Kevin Ruple; Phone: 440-826-2327; E-mail: kruple@bw.edu.

MEN'S COACHES
Baseball: Bob Fisher; Phone: 440-826-2182; E-mail: rfisher@bw.edu.
Basketball: Steve Bankson; Phone: 440-826-2039; E-mail: sbankson@bw.edu.
Cheerleading: Laura Truman; Phone: 440-826-2182; E-mail: l35a42@aol.com.
Cross Country: Bill Taraschke; Phone: 440-826-3322; E-mail: wtarasch@bw.edu.
Football: John Snell; Phone: 440-826-2069; E-mail: jsnell@bw.edu.
Golf: Chris Kibler; Phone: 440-826-2183; E-mail: ckibler@bw.edu.
Soccer: Reid Ayers; Phone: 440-826-3839; E-mail: rayers@bw.edu.
Swimming: Michael Gallagher; Phone: 440-826-2387; E-mail: mgallagh@bw.edu.
Tennis: Brian Rector; Phone: 440-826-2184; E-mail: rectobr@stratos.net.
Track and Field: Bill Taraschke; Phone: 440-826-3322; E-mail: wtarasch@bw.edu.
Wrestling: Rich Fleming; Phone: 440-826-3258; E-mail: rfleming@bw.edu.

WOMEN'S COACHES
Basketball: Cheri Harrer; Phone: 440-826-3299; E-mail: charrer@bw.edu.
Cheerleading: Laura Truman; Phone: 440-826-2182; E-mail: l35a42@aol.com.
Cross Country: Bill Taraschke; Phone: 440-826-3322; E-mail: wtarasch@bw.edu.
Golf: Jim Meyer; Phone: 440-826-3433; E-mail: jimeyer@bw.edu.
Soccer: Reid Ayers; Phone: 440-826-3853; E-mail: rayers@bw.edu.
Softball: Joe Yocabet; Phone: 440-826-3398.
Swimming: Michael Gallagher; Phone: 440-826-2387; E-mail: mgallagh@bw.edu.
Tennis: Jack Bethlenfalvy; Phone: 440-826-2184; E-mail: jbethlen@bw.edu.
Track and Field: Bill Taraschke; Phone: 440-826-3322; E-mail: wtarasch@bw.edu.
Volleyball: Vicki Brault; Phone: 440-826-3254; E-mail: vbrault@bw.edu.

BALL STATE UNIVERSITY
Muncie, Indiana

Cardinals ◆ NCAA I ◆ Mid-American Conference; Midwestern Intercollegiate Volleyball Conference ◆ http://www.bsu.edu/

State-supported university, founded 1918
Coed, 17,641 undergraduate students, 93% full-time, 53% women, 47% men
Suburban 955-acre campus with easy access to Indianapolis
Moderately difficult entrance level, 71% of applicants were admitted

Freshmen *Admission:* 10,695 applied, 8,117 were accepted, 3,987 enrolled. *Test scores:* SAT verbal scores over 500: 59%; SAT math scores over 500: 60%; SAT verbal scores over 600: 18%; SAT math scores over 600: 18%; SAT verbal scores over 700: 2%; SAT math scores over 700: 2%.
Tuition and fees (2003–04): $5930 (resident), $14,348 (nonresident). *Room and board:* $5880.
Financial Aid (All incoming freshmen): *Average need-based gift aid:* $4669. *Average non-need based aid:* $2764. *Average aid to full-time undergraduates:* $6616.
Athletic Department: *Director of Athletics:* Bubba Cunningham; Phone: 765-285-1671; Fax: 765-285-5123; E-mail: bcunningham@bsu.edu. *Sports Information Director:* Kathy Muffenbier; Phone: 765-285-8242; E-mail: kmuffenb@bsu.edu.

MEN'S COACHES
Baseball: Greg Beals; Phone: 765-285-8226; E-mail: gdbeals@bsu.edu.
Basketball: Tim Buckley; Phone: 765-285-8141; E-mail: tbuckley@bsu.edu.
Cheerleading: Wendy Richards; Phone: 765-741-9433; E-mail: wrichards@varsityspirit.com.
Cross Country: B.J. McKay; Phone: 765-285-5448.
Diving: Kami Abrell; Phone: 765-285-8909.
Football: Brady Hoke; Phone: 765-285-8251.
Golf: Mike Fleck; Phone: 765-285-8391; E-mail: mfleck@bsu.edu.
Swimming: Bob Thomas; Phone: 765-285-8909; E-mail: bthomas3@bsu.edu.
Tennis: Bill Richards; Phone: 765-285-8906; E-mail: brichard@bsu.edu.
Track and Field: Jermaine Jones; Phone: 765-285-5448; E-mail: jejones2@bsu.edu.
Volleyball: Joel Walton; Phone: 765-285-1744; E-mail: jwalton@bsu.edu.

WOMEN'S COACHES
Basketball: Tracy Roller; Phone: 765-285-8225; E-mail: troller@bsu.edu.
Cheerleading: Wendy Richards; Phone: 765-741-9433; E-mail: wrichards@varsityspirit.com.
Cross Country: Sue Parks; Phone: 765-285-5168; E-mail: sparks@bsu.edu.
Diving: Kami Abrell; Phone: 765-285-8909.
Field Hockey: Annette Payne; Phone: 765-285-5165; E-mail: apayne@bsu.edu.
Golf: Shelly Sanders; Phone: 765-285-4086; E-mail: ssanders@bsu.edu.
Gymnastics: Mary Roth; Phone: 765-285-1221; E-mail: mroth@bsu.edu.
Soccer: Ron Rainey; Phone: 765-285-2478; E-mail: rrainey@bsu.edu.
Softball: Terri Laux; Phone: 765-285-5137; E-mail: tlaux@bsu.edu.
Swimming: Laura Seibold-Caudill; Phone: 765-285-5173; E-mail: lseibold@bsu.edu.
Tennis: Kathy Bull; Phone: 765-285-5174; E-mail: kbull@bsu.edu.
Track and Field: Sue Parks; Phone: 765-285-5168; E-mail: sparks@bsu.edu.
Volleyball: Randy Litchfield; Phone: 765-285-1465; E-mail: rlitchfi@bsu.edu.

BAPTIST BIBLE COLLEGE OF PENNSYLVANIA
Clarks Summit, Pennsylvania

Defenders ◆ NCAA III ◆ Independent ◆ http://www.bbc.edu/

Independent Baptist comprehensive, founded 1932
Coed, 734 undergraduate students, 93% full-time, 56% women, 44% men
Suburban 124-acre campus
Minimally difficult entrance level, 88% of applicants were admitted

Freshmen *Admission:* 352 applied, 306 were accepted, 153 enrolled. *Test scores:* SAT verbal scores over 500: 55%; SAT math scores over 500: 45%; SAT verbal scores over 600: 20%; SAT math scores over 600: 14%; SAT verbal scores over 700: 5%; SAT math scores over 700: 1%.
Tuition and fees (2003–04): $11,700 (full-time). *Room and board:* $4982.
Financial Aid (All incoming freshmen): *Average aid to full-time undergraduates:* $5629.
Athletic Department: *Director of Athletics:* James Huckaby; Phone: 570-585-9256; Fax: 570-586-9336; E-mail: jhuckaby@bbc.edu. *Sports Information Director:* Kristi Parker; Phone: 570-585-9323; E-mail: kparker@bbc.edu.

MEN'S COACHES
Basketball: Mike Show; Phone: 570-585-9384; E-mail: mshow@bbc.edu.
Cheerleading: Kristi Parker; Phone: 570-585-9323; E-mail: kparker@bbc.edu.
Cross Country: Tom Williams; Phone: 570-585-9245; E-mail: twilliams@bbc.edu.
Soccer: Roger Jacobs; Phone: 570-585-9325; E-mail: rjacobs@bbc.edu.
Track and Field: Tom Williams; Phone: 570-585-9245; E-mail: twilliams@bbc.edu.
Volleyball: Dave Schumaker; Phone: 570-585-9323; E-mail: dshumaker@bbc.edu.
Wrestling: Chris Davis; Phone: 570-585-9239; E-mail: cdavis@bbc.edu.

WOMEN'S COACHES
Basketball: Sherrie Halloway; Phone: 570-585-9238; E-mail: sholloway@bbc.edu.
Cheerleading: Kristi Parker; Phone: 570-585-9323; E-mail: kparker@bbc.edu.
Cross Country: Tom Williams; Phone: 570-585-9245; E-mail: twilliams@bbc.edu.
Soccer: Chris Davis; Phone: 570-585-9239; E-mail: cdavis@bbc.edu.
Softball: Bill Higey; Phone: 570-585-9304; E-mail: bhigley@bbc.edu.
Track and Field: Tom Williams; Phone: 570-585-9245; E-mail: twilliams@bbc.edu.
Volleyball: Dave Schumaker; Phone: 570-585-9323; E-mail: dshumaker@bbc.edu.

BARBER-SCOTIA COLLEGE
Concord, North Carolina

Sabers ◆ NAIA ◆ Eastern Intercollegiate Conference ◆ http://www.b-sc.edu/

Independent religious 4-year, founded 1867, affiliated with Presbyterian Church (U.S.A.)
Coed, 742 undergraduate students, 99% full-time, 43% women, 57% men
Small-town 23-acre campus with easy access to Charlotte
Minimally difficult entrance level, 66% of applicants were admitted

Freshmen *Admission:* 1,502 applied, 1,058 were accepted, 294 enrolled.
Tuition and fees (2004–05): $10,618 (full-time). *Room and board:* $4452.
Athletic Department: *Director of Athletics:* James Stinson; Phone: 704-789-2960; Fax: 704-789-2911; E-mail: jstinson@b-sc.edu.

MEN'S COACHES
Baseball: Phone: 704-789-2960.
Basketball: James Stinson; Phone: 704-789-2960; E-mail: jstinson@b-sc.edu.
Cross Country: Donnel Dunning; Phone: 704-789-2930.
Track and Field: Donnel Dunning; Phone: 704-789-2930.

WOMEN'S COACHES
Basketball: Hythia Evans; Phone: 704-789-2930.
Cross Country: Donnel Dunning; Phone: 704-789-2930.
Softball: Reginald Isley; Phone: 704-789-2621.
Track and Field: Donnel Dunning; Phone: 704-789-2930.
Volleyball: Reginald Isley; Phone: 704-789-2621.

BARD COLLEGE
Annandale-on-Hudson, New York

Raptors ◆ NCAA III ◆ Eastern College Athletic Conference ◆ http://www.bard.edu/

Independent comprehensive, founded 1860
Coed, 1,382 undergraduate students, 96% full-time, 58% women, 42% men
Rural 600-acre campus
Very difficult entrance level, 4% of applicants were admitted

Freshmen *Admission:* 3,367 applied, 1,310 were accepted, 382 enrolled. *Test scores:* SAT verbal scores over 500: 100%; SAT math scores over 500: 99%; SAT verbal scores over 600: 88%; SAT math scores over 600: 68%; SAT verbal scores over 700: 31%; SAT math scores over 700: 15%.
Tuition and fees (2003–04): $29,038 (full-time). *Room and board:* $8544 (room only: $4282).
Financial Aid (All incoming freshmen): *Average need-based gift aid:* $20,311. *Average non-need based aid:* $13,095. *Average aid to full-time undergraduates:* $23,503.
Athletic Department: *Director of Athletics:* Kristen Hall; Phone: 845-758-7528; Fax: 845-758-7647; E-mail: hall@bard.edu. *Sports Information Director:* Scott Swere; Phone: 845-758-7530; E-mail: swere@bard.edu.

MEN'S COACHES
Basketball: Chris Wood; Phone: 845-758-7334; E-mail: wood@bard.edu.
Cross Country: Fred Pavlich; Phone: 845-758-7531; E-mail: fpavlich@bard.edu.
Soccer: Scott Swere; Phone: 845-758-7530; E-mail: swere@bard.edu.
Tennis: Fred Feldman; Phone: 845-758-7531; E-mail: feldman@bard.edu.
Volleyball: Owen Roberts; Phone: 845-758-7531; E-mail: roberts@bard.edu.

WOMEN'S COACHES
Basketball: Sara Heller; Phone: 845-758-7531; E-mail: sheller@bard.edu.
Cross Country: Fred Pavlich; Phone: 845-758-7531; E-mail: fpavlich@bard.edu.
Soccer: Jason Pavlich; Phone: 845-758-7531; E-mail: pavlich@bard.edu.
Tennis: Fred Feldman; Phone: 845-758-7531; E-mail: feldman@bard.edu.
Volleyball: Owen Roberts; Phone: 845-758-7531; E-mail: roberts@bard.edu.

BARRY UNIVERSITY
Miami Shores, Florida

Buccaneers ◆ NCAA II ◆ Sunshine State Conference ◆ http://www.barry.edu/

Independent Roman Catholic university, founded 1940
Coed, 5,893 undergraduate students, 74% full-time, 67% women, 33% men
Suburban 122-acre campus with easy access to Miami
Moderately difficult entrance level, 69% of applicants were admitted

Freshmen *Admission:* 3,186 applied, 2,236 were accepted, 518 enrolled. *Test scores:* SAT verbal scores over 500: 43%; SAT math scores over 500: 36%; SAT verbal scores over 600: 8%; SAT math scores over 600: 9%.
Tuition and fees (2004–05): $21,350 (full-time). *Room and board:* $7400.
Financial Aid (All incoming freshmen): *Average need-based gift aid:* $10,016. *Average non-need based aid:* $6123. *Average aid to full-time undergraduates:* $19,310.

Barry University *(continued)*

Athletic Department: *Director of Athletics:* Michael Covone; Phone: 305-899-3551; Fax: 305-899-3556; E-mail: mcovone@mail.barry.edu. *Sports Information Director:* Dennis Jezek; Phone: 305-899-3897; E-mail: djezek@mail.barry.edu.

MEN'S COACHES

Baseball: Juan Ranero; Phone: 305-889-3558; E-mail: jranero@mail.barry.edu.
Basketball: Cesar Odio; Phone: 305-899-3557; E-mail: codio@mail.barry.edu.
Cheerleading: Keith Smith; Phone: 305-889-3553; E-mail: bksmith@mail.barry.edu.
Golf: Jimmy Stobs; Phone: 305-889-3061; E-mail: jstobs@mail.barry.edu.
Soccer: Steve McCrath; Phone: 305-899-3560; E-mail: smccrath@mail.barry.edu.
Tennis: George Samuel; Phone: 305-899-3495; E-mail: gsamuel@mail.barry.edu.

WOMEN'S COACHES

Basketball: Nicci Hays; Phone: 305-899-3562; E-mail: nhays@mail.barry.edu.
Cheerleading: Keith Smith; Phone: 305-889-3553; E-mail: bksmith@mail.barry.edu.
Golf: Roger White; Phone: 305-899-3552; E-mail: rwhite@mail.barry.edu.
Soccer: Kyllene Carter Weiss; Phone: 305-899-3372; E-mail: kweiss@mail.barry.edu.
Softball: Shelly Lis; Phone: 305-889-3564; E-mail: slis@mail.barry.edu.
Tennis: George Samuel; Phone: 305-899-3495; E-mail: gsamuel@mail.barry.edu.
Volleyball: Dave Nichols; Phone: 305-889-3563; E-mail: dnichols@mail.barry.edu.

BARTON COLLEGE
Wilson, North Carolina

Bulldogs ◆ NCAA II ◆ Carolinas-Virginia Athletics Conference ◆ http://www.barton.edu/

Independent religious 4-year, founded 1902, affiliated with Christian Church (Disciples of Christ)
Coed, 1,188 undergraduate students, 80% full-time, 71% women, 29% men
Small-town 62-acre campus with easy access to Raleigh-Durham, NC
Minimally difficult entrance level, 71% of applicants were admitted

Freshmen *Admission:* 930 applied, 692 were accepted, 249 enrolled. *Test scores:* SAT verbal scores over 500: 40%; SAT math scores over 500: 44%; SAT verbal scores over 600: 5%; SAT math scores over 600: 9%; SAT math scores over 700: 2%.
Tuition and fees (2003–04): $14,278 (full-time). *Room and board:* $5036 (room only: $2408).
Financial Aid (All incoming freshmen): *Average need-based gift aid:* $4740. *Average non-need based aid:* $2761. *Average aid to full-time undergraduates:* $13,195.
Athletic Department: *Director of Athletics:* Gary Hall; Phone: 252-399-6514; Fax: 252-399-6516; E-mail: ghall@barton.edu. *Sports Information Director:* John Hackney; Phone: 252-399-6514.

MEN'S COACHES

Baseball: Todd Wilkinson; Phone: 252-399-6552; E-mail: twilkinson@barton.edu.
Basketball: Ron Lievense; Phone: 252-399-6524; E-mail: rlievens@barton.edu.
Cheerleading: Cathy Whitley; Phone: 252-399-6519; E-mail: cwhitley@barton.edu.
Cross Country: Sheryl Neff; Phone: 252-399-6515; E-mail: sneff@barton.edu.
Golf: John Hackney; Phone: 252-399-6515; E-mail: jhackney@barton.edu.
Soccer: Gary Hall; Phone: 252-399-6517; E-mail: ghall@barton.edu.
Tennis: Marc Walters; Phone: 252-399-6485; E-mail: mwalters@barton.edu.

WOMEN'S COACHES

Basketball: Wendee Saintsing; Phone: 252-399-6519; E-mail: wsaintsi@barton.edu.
Cheerleading: Cathy Whitley; Phone: 252-399-6519; E-mail: cwhitley@barton.edu.
Cross Country: Sheryl Neff; Phone: 252-399-6515; E-mail: sneff@barton.edu.
Soccer: Stacey Tant; Phone: 252-399-6518; E-mail: stant@barton.edu.
Softball: Sheryl Neff; Phone: 252-399-6536; E-mail: sneff@barton.edu.
Tennis: Marc Walters; Phone: 252-399-6485; E-mail: mwalters@barton.edu.
Volleyball: Wendee Saintsing; Phone: 252-399-6519; E-mail: wsaintsi@barton.edu.

BATES COLLEGE
Lewiston, Maine

Bobcats ◆ NCAA III ◆ New England Small College Conference ◆ http://www.bates.edu/

Independent 4-year, founded 1855
Coed, 1,746 undergraduate students, 100% full-time, 52% women, 48% men
Small-town 109-acre campus
Most difficult entrance level, 3% of applicants were admitted

Freshmen *Admission:* 4,089 applied, 1,254 were accepted, 487 enrolled. *Test scores:* SAT verbal scores over 500: 99%; SAT math scores over 500: 100%; SAT verbal scores over 600: 92%; SAT math scores over 600: 93%; SAT verbal scores over 700: 29%; SAT math scores over 700: 34%.
Tuition and fees (2004–05): Comprehensive fee (includes tuition, fees, and room and board): $37,500.
Financial Aid (All incoming freshmen): *Average need-based gift aid:* $22,873. *Average aid to full-time undergraduates:* $25,606.
Athletic Department: *Director of Athletics:* Suzanne Coffey; Phone: 207-786-6341; Fax: 207-786-8232; E-mail: scoffey@bates.edu. *Sports Information Director:* Aaron Todd; Phone: 207-786-6411; E-mail: atodd@bates.edu.

MEN'S COACHES

Baseball: Craig Vandersea; Phone: 207-786-6063; E-mail: cvanders@bates.edu.
Basketball: Joe Reilly; Phone: 207-786-6343; E-mail: jreilly2@bates.edu.
Cross Country: Al Fereshetian; Phone: 207-786-6360; E-mail: afereshe@bates.edu.
Diving: Dana Mulholland; Phone: 207-786-6351; E-mail: dmulholl@bates.edu.
Football: Mark Harriman; Phone: 207-786-6344; E-mail: mharrima@bates.edu.
Lacrosse: Peter Lasagna; Phone: 207-786-8263; E-mail: plasagna@bates.edu.
Soccer: George Purgavie; Phone: 207-786-6357; E-mail: gpurgavi@bates.edu.
Swimming: Dana Mulholland; Phone: 207-786-6351; E-mail: dmulholl@bates.edu.
Tennis: Paul Gastonguay; Phone: 207-786-6442; E-mail: pgastong@bates.edu.
Track and Field: Al Fereshetian; Phone: 207-786-6360; E-mail: afereshe@bates.edu.

WOMEN'S COACHES

Basketball: James Murphy; Phone: 207-786-6369; E-mail: jmurphy@bates.edu.
Cross Country: Carolyn Court; Phone: 207-786-6356; E-mail: ccourt@bates.edu.
Diving: Dana Mulholland; Phone: 207-786-6351; E-mail: dmulholl@bates.edu.
Field Hockey: Wynn Hohlt; Phone: 207-786-6350; E-mail: whohlt@bates.edu.
Lacrosse: Wynn Hohlt; Phone: 207-786-6350; E-mail: whohlt@bates.edu.
Soccer: Jim Murphy; Phone: 207-786-6369; E-mail: afereshe@bates.edu.
Softball: Gwen Lexow; Phone: 207-786-6362; E-mail: glexow@bates.edu.
Swimming: Dana Mulholland; Phone: 207-786-6351; E-mail: dmulholl@bates.edu.
Tennis: Paul Gastonguay; Phone: 207-786-6442; E-mail: pgastong@bates.edu.

Track and Field: Carolyn Court; Phone: 207-786-6356; E-mail: ccourt@
bates.edu.
Volleyball: Jen Bowman; Phone: 207-786-8389; E-mail: jbowman@
bates.edu.

BAYLOR UNIVERSITY
Waco, Texas

Bears ◆ NCAA I ◆ Big 12 Conference
◆ http://www.baylor.edu/

Independent Baptist university, founded 1845
Coed, 11,712 undergraduate students, 96% full-time, 58% women,
42% men
Urban 432-acre campus with easy access to Dallas–Fort Worth
Moderately difficult entrance level, 82% of applicants were admitted

Freshmen *Admission:* 8,931 applied, 7,341 were accepted, 2,678 enrolled. *Test scores:* SAT verbal scores over 500: 88%; SAT math scores
over 500: 92%; SAT verbal scores over 600: 43%; SAT math scores
over 600: 51%; SAT verbal scores over 700: 9%; SAT math scores
over 700: 10%.
Tuition and fees (2003–04): $18,430 (full-time). *Room and board:* $5434
(room only: $2728).
Financial Aid (All incoming freshmen): *Average need-based gift aid:* $9948.
Average non-need based aid: $6361. *Average aid to full-time under-
graduates:* $14,384.
Athletic Department: *Director of Athletics:* Ian McCaw; Phone: 254-710-
2816; Fax: 254-710-2823; E-mail: ian_mccaw@baylor.edu. *Sports Information Director:* Heath Nielsen; Phone: 254-710-3538; E-mail:
heath_nielsen@baylor.edu.

MEN'S COACHES

Baseball: Steve Smith; Phone: 254-710-3097; E-mail: steve_smith@
baylor.edu.
Basketball: Scott Drew; Phone: 254-710-3096; E-mail: scott_drew@
baylor.edu.
Cross Country: Todd Harbour; Phone: 254-710-3053; E-mail:
todd_harbour@baylor.edu.
Football: Guy Morriss; Phone: 254-710-3058; E-mail: guy_morriss@
baylor.edu.
Golf: Greg Priest; Phone: 254-710-3093; E-mail: greg_priest@baylor.
edu.
Tennis: Matt Knoll; Phone: 254-710-3484; E-mail: matt_knoll@baylor.
edu.
Track and Field: Clyde Hart; Phone: 254-710-3032.

WOMEN'S COACHES

Basketball: Kim Mulkey-Robertson; Phone: 254-710-3949; E-mail:
kim_mulkey-robertson@baylor.edu.
Cross Country: Todd Harbour; Phone: 254-710-3053; E-mail:
todd_harbour@baylor.edu.
Golf: Sylvia Ferdon; Phone: 254-710-3079; E-mail: sylvia_ferdon@
baylor.edu.
Soccer: George Van Linder; Phone: 254-710-3090; E-mail:
george_vanlinder@baylor.edu.
Softball: Glenn Moore; Phone: 254-710-3055; E-mail: glenn_moore@
baylor.edu.
Tennis: Joey Scrivano; Phone: 254-710-1323; E-mail: joey_scrivano@
baylor.edu.
Track and Field: Clyde Hart; Phone: 254-710-3032.
Volleyball: Brian Hosfeld; Phone: 254-710-3034; E-mail:
brian_hosfeld@baylor.edu.

BAY PATH COLLEGE
Longmeadow, Massachusetts

Wildcats ◆ NCAA III ◆ North Atlantic Conference ◆ http://
www.baypath.edu/

Independent comprehensive, founded 1897
Women only, 1,242 undergraduate students, 82% full-time, 100%
women, 100% men
Suburban 48-acre campus with easy access to Boston
Moderately difficult entrance level, 82% of applicants were admitted

Freshmen *Admission:* 476 applied, 389 were accepted, 263 enrolled.
Test scores: SAT verbal scores over 500: 57%; SAT math scores over
500: 45%; SAT verbal scores over 600: 11%; SAT math scores over
600: 8%.
Tuition and fees (2003–04): $16,890 (full-time). *Room and board:* $8020.
Financial Aid (All incoming freshmen): *Average need-based gift aid:* $8566.
Average non-need based aid: $11,440. *Average aid to full-time under-
graduates:* $12,520.
Athletic Department: *Director of Athletics:* Steve Smith; Phone: 413-565-
1244; Fax: 413-565-1103; E-mail: ssmith@baypath.edu.

WOMEN'S COACHES

Basketball: Dusty Hoyt; Phone: 413-565-1244.
Cross Country: Brad Klinedinst; Phone: 413-565-1244.
Soccer: Todd Ditmar; Phone: 413-565-1244.
Softball: Steven Smith; Phone: 413-565-1244; E-mail: ssmith@baypath.
edu.
Volleyball: Sara May; Phone: 413-565-1244.

BELHAVEN COLLEGE
Jackson, Mississippi

Blazers ◆ NAIA ◆ Gulf Coast Conference
◆ http://www.belhaven.edu/

Independent Presbyterian comprehensive, founded 1883
Coed, 2,023 undergraduate students, 94% full-time, 66% women,
34% men
Urban 42-acre campus
Moderately difficult entrance level, 51% of applicants were admitted

Freshmen *Admission:* 595 applied, 333 were accepted, 206 enrolled.
Test scores: SAT verbal scores over 500: 78%; SAT math scores over
500: 65%; SAT verbal scores over 600: 45%; SAT math scores over
600: 36%; SAT verbal scores over 700: 20%; SAT math scores over
700: 7%.
Tuition and fees (2004–05): $13,440 (full-time). *Room and board:* $5240.
Financial Aid (All incoming freshmen): *Average need-based gift aid:* $6540.
Average non-need based aid: $5737. *Average aid to full-time under-
graduates:* $11,861.
Athletic Department: *Director of Athletics:* Dale Hatcher; Phone: 601-
968-5936; Fax: 601-965-7025; E-mail: dhatcher@belhaven.edu. *Sports
Information Director:* Michael Dukes; Phone: 601-968-8765; E-mail:
mdukes@belhaven.edu.

MEN'S COACHES

Baseball: Denson Hill; Phone: 601-968-8898; E-mail: hdenson@
belhaven.edu.
Basketball: Dale Hatcher; Phone: 601-968-5936; E-mail: dhatcher@
belhaven.edu.
Cheerleading: Lisa Hubbard; Phone: 601-968-8892; E-mail:
hubbardjlac@aol.com.
Cross Country: Christie Barber; Phone: 601-968-8765; E-mail: cbarber@
belhaven.edu.
Football: Scott Highsmith; Phone: 601-965-7024; E-mail: shighsmith@
belhaven.edu.
Golf: Phone: 601-968-5956.
Soccer: Phil Moyer; Phone: 601-965-7013; E-mail: pmoyer@belhaven.
edu.
Tennis: Judy Chance; Phone: 601-968-8842; E-mail: jchance@belhaven.
edu.

WOMEN'S COACHES

Basketball: Billy Evans; Phone: 601-968-8812; E-mail: bevans@
belhaven.edu.

Belhaven College *(continued)*

Cheerleading: Lisa Hubbard; Phone: 601-968-8892; E-mail: hubbardjlac@aol.com.

Cross Country: Christie Barber; Phone: 601-968-8765; E-mail: cbarber@belhaven.edu.

Golf: Phone: 601-968-5956.

Soccer: Corey Rose; Phone: 601-968-8708; E-mail: crose@belhaven.edu.

Softball: Andrea Roberts; Phone: 601-968-8768; E-mail: aroberts@belhaven.edu.

Tennis: Judy Chance; Phone: 601-968-8842; E-mail: jchance@belhaven.edu.

Volleyball: Julie Langford; Phone: 601-968-8891; E-mail: jlangford@belhaven.edu.

BELLARMINE UNIVERSITY
Louisville, Kentucky

Knights ◆ NCAA II ◆ Great Lakes Valley Conference ◆ http://www.bellarmine.edu/

Independent Roman Catholic comprehensive, founded 1950
Coed, 2,561 undergraduate students, 62% full-time, 60% women, 40% men
Suburban 120-acre campus
Moderately difficult entrance level, 82% of applicants were admitted

Freshmen *Admission:* 1,485 applied, 1,212 were accepted, 453 enrolled. *Test scores:* SAT verbal scores over 500: 79%; SAT math scores over 500: 74%; SAT verbal scores over 600: 33%; SAT math scores over 600: 28%; SAT verbal scores over 700: 2%; SAT math scores over 700: 4%.
Tuition and fees (2004–05): $19,950 (full-time). *Room and board:* $5780 (room only: $3290).
Financial Aid (All incoming freshmen): *Average aid to full-time undergraduates:* $13,762.
Athletic Department: *Director of Athletics:* Rick Bagby; Phone: 502-452-8380; Fax: 502-452-8450; E-mail: rbagby@bellarmine.edu. *Sports Information Director:* Shannon Potee; Phone: 502-452-8034; E-mail: spotee@bellarmine.edu.

MEN'S COACHES
Baseball: Scott Wiegandt; Phone: 502-452-8496; E-mail: swiegandt@bellarmine.edu.

Basketball: Chris Pullem; Phone: 502-452-8383; E-mail: ipatrick@bellarmine.edu.

Cheerleading: T.J. Johnson; Phone: 502-452-8380; E-mail: bellarminesid@bellarmine.edu.

Cross Country: John Wellerding; Phone: 502-452-8380; E-mail: jwellerding@bellarmine.edu.

Golf: Ernie Denham; Phone: 502-452-8380; E-mail: edenham@bellarmine.edu.

Soccer: Tim Chastonay; Phone: 502-452-8043; E-mail: tchastonay@bellarmine.edu.

Tennis: Greg Stephenson; Phone: 502-452-8312.

Track and Field: Jim Vargo; Phone: 502-452-8042; E-mail: jvargo@bellarmine.edu.

WOMEN'S COACHES
Basketball: Dave Smith; Phone: 502-452-8382; E-mail: dsmith@bellarmine.edu.

Cheerleading: T.J. Johnson; Phone: 502-452-8380; E-mail: bellarminesid@bellarmine.edu.

Cross Country: John Wellerding; Phone: 502-452-8380; E-mail: jwellerding@bellarmine.edu.

Field Hockey: Dan Hubbuch; Phone: 502-452-8380.

Golf: Shannon Main; Phone: 502-452-8380; E-mail: smain@bellarmine.edu.

Soccer: Tim Chastonay; Phone: 502-452-8043; E-mail: tchastonay@bellarmine.edu.

Softball: Renee Hicks; Phone: 502-452-8380.

Tennis: Greg Stephenson; Phone: 502-452-8312.

Track and Field: Jim Vargo; Phone: 502-452-8042; E-mail: jvargo@bellarmine.edu.

Volleyball: Dee Dee Olmstead; Phone: 502-452-8380.

BELLEVUE UNIVERSITY
Bellevue, Nebraska

Bruins ◆ NAIA ◆ Midlands Collegiate Conference ◆ http://www.bellevue.edu/

Independent comprehensive, founded 1965
Coed, 3,933 undergraduate students, 68% full-time, 50% women, 50% men
Suburban 35-acre campus with easy access to Omaha
Noncompetitive entrance level

Freshmen *Admission:* 327 enrolled.
Tuition and fees (2004–05): $4740 (full-time).
Financial Aid (All incoming freshmen): *Average need-based gift aid:* $303. *Average non-need based aid:* $1344.
Athletic Department: *Director of Athletics:* Jerry Mosser; Phone: 402-293-3784; Fax: 402-293-2086; E-mail: mosser@bellevue.edu. *Sports Information Director:* Brian Dunn; Phone: 402-293-2073; E-mail: bdunn@bellevue.edu.

MEN'S COACHES
Baseball: Mike Evans; Phone: 402-293-3782; E-mail: mevans@bellevue.edu.

Basketball: Todd Eisner; Phone: 402-293-2024; E-mail: eisner@bellevue.edu.

Soccer: Aaron Champenoy; Phone: 402-293-2094; E-mail: champenoy@bellevue.edu.

WOMEN'S COACHES
Soccer: Dan Harvey; Phone: 402-293-3741; E-mail: harvey@bellevue.edu.

Softball: Ed Lehotak; Phone: 402-293-2095; E-mail: lehotak@bellevue.edu.

Volleyball: Deb Grafentin; Phone: 402-293-3783; E-mail: deb@bellevue.edu.

BELMONT ABBEY COLLEGE
Belmont, North Carolina

Crusaders ◆ NCAA II ◆ Carolinas-Virginia Athletics Conference ◆ http://www.belmontabbeycollege.edu/

Independent Roman Catholic 4-year, founded 1876
Coed, 863 undergraduate students, 89% full-time, 60% women, 40% men
Small-town 650-acre campus with easy access to Charlotte
Moderately difficult entrance level, 71% of applicants were admitted

Freshmen *Admission:* 811 applied, 558 were accepted, 147 enrolled. *Test scores:* SAT verbal scores over 500: 50%; SAT math scores over 500: 43%; SAT verbal scores over 600: 13%; SAT math scores over 600: 13%; SAT verbal scores over 700: 1%; SAT math scores over 700: 1%.
Tuition and fees (2004–05): $15,778 (full-time). *Room and board:* $8100 (room only: $4556).
Financial Aid (All incoming freshmen): *Average need-based gift aid:* $11,408. *Average non-need based aid:* $9240. *Average aid to full-time undergraduates:* $13,265.
Athletic Department: *Director of Athletics:* Eliane Kebbe; Phone: 704-825-6802; Fax: 704-825-6570; E-mail: elianekebbe@bac.edu. *Sports Information Director:* Matt Kline; Phone: 704-825-6541; E-mail: mattkline@bac.edu.

MEN'S COACHES
Baseball: Kermit Smith; Phone: 704-825-6804; E-mail: kermitsmith@bac.edu.

Basketball: Dip Metress; Phone: 704-825-6800; E-mail: darrenmetress@bac.edu.

Cross Country: Paul Shanley; Phone: 704-825-6217; E-mail: paulshanley@bac.edu.

Golf: Doug Ehman; Phone: 704-825-0540; E-mail: dougehmann@bac.edu.

Soccer: Charles Marrow; Phone: 704-825-6806; E-mail: charlesmorrow@bac.edu.

Tennis: Matt Kline; Phone: 704-825-6541; E-mail: mattkline@bac.edu.

WOMEN'S COACHES
Basketball: Missy Tiber; Phone: 704-825-6805; E-mail: missytiber@bac.edu.

Cross Country: Paul Shanley; Phone: 704-825-6217; E-mail: paulshanley@bac.edu.
Soccer: Scot Wieland; Phone: 704-825-6243; E-mail: scotwieland@bac.edu.
Softball: Lee Swanson; Phone: 704-825-6801; E-mail: leeswanson@bac.edu.
Tennis: Matt Kline; Phone: 704-825-6217; E-mail: mattkline@bac.edu.
Volleyball: Lee Swanson; Phone: 704-825-6801; E-mail: leeswanson@bac.edu.

BELMONT UNIVERSITY
Nashville, Tennessee

Bruins ◆ NCAA I ◆ Atlantic Sun Conference ◆ http://www.belmont.edu/

Independent Baptist comprehensive, founded 1951
Coed, 2,989 undergraduate students, 89% full-time, 61% women, 39% men
Urban 34-acre campus
Moderately difficult entrance level, 8% of applicants were admitted

Freshmen *Admission:* 1,607 applied, 1,207 were accepted, 603 enrolled. *Test scores:* SAT verbal scores over 500: 86%; SAT math scores over 500: 83%; SAT verbal scores over 600: 34%; SAT math scores over 600: 37%; SAT verbal scores over 700: 2%; SAT math scores over 700: 6%.
Tuition and fees (2003–04): $15,954 (full-time). *Room and board:* $6032 (room only: $2850).
Financial Aid (All incoming freshmen): *Average need-based gift aid:* $2314. *Average non-need based aid:* $5266. *Average aid to full-time undergraduates:* $2545.
Athletic Department: *Director of Athletics:* Mike Strickland; Phone: 615-460-5547; Fax: 615-460-5584; E-mail: stricklandm@mail.belmont.edu. *Sports Information Director:* Matt Wilson; Phone: 615-460-6698; E-mail: wilsonm@mail.belmont.edu.

MEN'S COACHES
Baseball: Dave Jarvis; Phone: 615-460-6166; E-mail: jarvisd@mail.belmont.edu.
Basketball: Rick Byrd; Phone: 615-460-6263; E-mail: byrdr@mail.belmont.edu.
Cheerleading: Lindsey Tonkin; Phone: 615-791-1541; E-mail: tonka08@aol.com.
Cross Country: Jeff Langdon; Phone: 615-460-6046; E-mail: langdonje@mail.belmont.edu.
Golf: Carroll Clark; Phone: 615-790-7600; E-mail: clarkcb@mail.belmont.edu.
Soccer: Earle Davidson; Phone: 615-460-6134; E-mail: davidsone@mail.belmont.edu.
Tennis: Jim Madrigal; Phone: 615-460-6014; E-mail: madrigalj@mail.belmont.edu.
Track and Field: Jeff Langdon; Phone: 615-460-6046; E-mail: langdonje@mail.belmont.edu.

WOMEN'S COACHES
Basketball: Tony Cross; Phone: 615-460-6264; E-mail: crosst@mail.belmont.edu.
Cheerleading: Lindsey Tonkin; Phone: 615-791-1541; E-mail: tonka08@aol.com.
Cross Country: Seth Sheridan; Phone: 615-460-6163; E-mail: sheridans@mail.belmont.edu.
Golf: Lissa Horton; Phone: 615-790-7600; E-mail: hortonl@mail.belmont.edu.
Soccer: Chris Bosworth; Phone: 615-460-6013; E-mail: bosworthc@mail.belmont.edu.
Softball: Jose Garcia; Phone: 615-460-5624; E-mail: garciaj@mail.belmont.edu.
Tennis: Mark Srouji; Phone: 615-460-6014; E-mail: sroujim@mail.belmont.edu.
Track and Field: Seth Sheridan; Phone: 615-460-6163; E-mail: sheridans@mail.belmont.edu.
Volleyball: Deane Webb; Phone: 615-460-5986; E-mail: webbd@mail.belmont.edu.

BELOIT COLLEGE
Beloit, Wisconsin

Buccaneers ◆ NCAA III ◆ Midwest Conference ◆ http://www.beloit.edu/

Independent 4-year, founded 1846
Coed, 1,332 undergraduate students, 92% full-time, 61% women, 39% men
Small-town 65-acre campus with easy access to Chicago and Milwaukee
Very difficult entrance level, 62% of applicants were admitted

Freshmen *Admission:* 1,901 applied, 1,321 were accepted, 346 enrolled. *Test scores:* SAT verbal scores over 500: 95%; SAT math scores over 500: 91%; SAT verbal scores over 600: 70%; SAT math scores over 600: 53%; SAT verbal scores over 700: 22%; SAT math scores over 700: 11%.
Tuition and fees (2003–04): $24,386 (full-time). *Room and board:* $5478 (room only: $2672).
Financial Aid (All incoming freshmen): *Average need-based gift aid:* $14,347. *Average non-need based aid:* $8566. *Average aid to full-time undergraduates:* $18,345.
Athletic Department: *Director of Athletics:* Dave DeGeorge; Phone: 608-363-2234; Fax: 608-363-2044; E-mail: degeored@beloit.edu. *Sports Information Director:* Keith Domke; Phone: 608-363-2229; E-mail: bucsid@beloit.edu.

MEN'S COACHES
Baseball: Dave DeGeorge; Phone: 608-363-2039; E-mail: degeorge@beloit.edu.
Basketball: Cecil Youngblood; Phone: 608-363-2237; E-mail: youngblc@beloit.edu.
Cross Country: Dave Eckburg; Phone: 608-363-2235; E-mail: blieseb@beloit.edu.
Football: Ed DeGeorge; Phone: 608-363-2234; E-mail: degeored@beloit.edu.
Golf: Cecil Youngblood; Phone: 608-363-2237; E-mail: youngblc@beloit.edu.
Soccer: Tim Schmiechen; Phone: 608-363-2259; E-mail: schmiech@beloit.edu.
Swimming: Kevin Schober; Phone: 608-363-2477; E-mail: kevinschober@hotmail.com.
Tennis: Tim Schmiechen; Phone: 608-363-2259; E-mail: schmiech@beloit.edu.
Track and Field: Brian Bliese; Phone: 608-363-2235; E-mail: blieseb@beloit.edu.

WOMEN'S COACHES
Basketball: Michelle Broderick; Phone: 608-363-2398; E-mail: broderic@beloit.edu.
Cross Country: Dave Eckburg; Phone: 608-363-2235; E-mail: blieseb@beloit.edu.
Golf: Cecil Youngblood; Phone: 608-363-2237; E-mail: youngblc@beloit.edu.
Soccer: Robyn Serge; Phone: 608-363-2398; E-mail: rserge5@aol.com.
Softball: Maureen Boyle; Phone: 608-363-2236; E-mail: boylem@beloit.edu.
Swimming: Kevin Schober; Phone: 608-363-2477; E-mail: kevinschober@hotmail.com.
Tennis: Bob Hodge; Phone: 608-363-2334; E-mail: hodgeb@beloit.edu.
Track and Field: Brian Bliese; Phone: 608-363-2235; E-mail: blieseb@beloit.edu.
Volleyball: Maureen Boyle; Phone: 608-363-2236; E-mail: boylem@beloit.edu.

BEMIDJI STATE UNIVERSITY
Bemidji, Minnesota

Beavers ◆ NCAA II ◆ College Hockey America Conference; Northern Sun Intercollegiate Conference; Western Collegiate Hockey Conference ◆ http://www.bemidjistate.edu/

State-supported comprehensive, founded 1919, part of Minnesota State Colleges and Universities System
Coed, 4,660 undergraduate students, 74% full-time, 53% women, 47% men
Small-town 89-acre campus
Moderately difficult entrance level, 73% of applicants were admitted

Freshmen *Admission:* 1,542 applied, 1,134 were accepted, 692 enrolled.
Tuition and fees (2003–04): $5048 (resident), $9910 (nonresident). *Room and board:* $4597 (room only: $2448).
Financial Aid (All incoming freshmen): *Average need-based gift aid:* $4106. *Average non-need based aid:* $5062. *Average aid to full-time undergraduates:* $6360.
Athletic Department: *Director of Athletics:* Rick Goeb; Phone: 218-755-4022; Fax: 218-755-3898; E-mail: rgoeb@bemidjistate.edu. *Sports Information Director:* Andy Bartlett; Phone: 218-755-4603; E-mail: jbartlett@bemidjistate.edu.

MEN'S COACHES
Baseball: Chris Brown; Phone: 218-755-4620; E-mail: cdbrown@bemidjistate.edu.
Basketball: Jeff Guiot; Phone: 218-755-2774; E-mail: jguiot@bemidjistate.edu.
Football: Jeff Tesch; Phone: 218-755-2772; E-mail: jtesch@bemidjistate.edu.
Golf: Donald Niskanen; Phone: 218-755-4619; E-mail: nisky@paulbunyan.net.
Ice Hockey: Tom Serratore; Phone: 218-755-2879; E-mail: tserratore@bemidjistate.edu.
Track and Field: Craig Hougen; Phone: 218-755-2883; E-mail: chougen@bemidjistate.edu.

WOMEN'S COACHES
Basketball: Mike Power; Phone: 218-755-3783; E-mail: mpower@bemidjistate.edu.
Cross Country: Craig Hougen; Phone: 218-755-2883; E-mail: chougen@bemidjistate.edu.
Golf: Bob Kobilka; Phone: 218-755-4619.
Soccer: Jim Stone; Phone: 218-755-3784; E-mail: jstone@bemidjistate.edu.
Softball: Amanda Went; Phone: 218-755-4251; E-mail: awent@bemidjistate.edu.
Tennis: Kari Wood; Phone: 218-755-4619; E-mail: kwood@bemidjistate.edu.
Track and Field: Craig Hougen; Phone: 218-755-2883; E-mail: chougen@bemidjistate.edu.
Volleyball: Kim Falkenhagen; Phone: 218-755-3785; E-mail: kfalkenhagen@bemidjistate.edu.

BENEDICT COLLEGE
Columbia, South Carolina

Tigers ◆ NCAA II ◆ Southern Intercollegiate Athletic Conference ◆ http://www.benedict.edu/

Independent Baptist 4-year, founded 1870
Coed, 3,005 undergraduate students, 95% full-time, 50% women, 50% men
Urban 20-acre campus
Minimally difficult entrance level, 73% of applicants were admitted

Freshmen *Admission:* 4,039 applied, 2,867 were accepted, 643 enrolled.
Test scores: SAT verbal scores over 500: 10%; SAT math scores over 500: 13%; SAT verbal scores over 600: 3%; SAT math scores over 600: 5%; SAT verbal scores over 700: 1%; SAT math scores over 700: 2%.
Tuition and fees (2003–04): $11,586 (full-time). *Room and board:* $5434.
Athletic Department: *Director of Athletics:* Willie Washington; Phone: 803-733-7418; Fax: 803-733-7423. *Sports Information Director:* Derrick Johnson; Phone: 803-733-7421.

MEN'S COACHES
Baseball: Derrick Johnson; Phone: 803-231-2164.
Basketball: Fred Watson; Phone: 803-253-5346.
Cheerleading: Teri Mills; Phone: 803-253-5155.
Cross Country: Erica Hepburn; Phone: 803-733-7419.
Football: John Hendrick; Phone: 803-255-1734.
Golf: Herman Belton; Phone: 803-806-3257.
Tennis: Larry Scheper; Phone: 803-253-5075.
Track and Field: Gary Reynolds; Phone: 803-255-1735.

WOMEN'S COACHES
Basketball: Maurice Bailey; Phone: 803-806-3224.
Cheerleading: Teri Mills; Phone: 803-253-5155.
Cross Country: Erica Hepburn; Phone: 803-733-7419.
Golf: Herman Belton; Phone: 803-806-3257.
Softball: Gwendolyn Rouse; Phone: 803-733-7420.
Tennis: Larry Scheper; Phone: 803-253-5075.
Track and Field: Gary Reynolds; Phone: 803-255-1735.
Volleyball: Gwendolyn Rouse; Phone: 803-733-7420.

BENEDICTINE COLLEGE
Atchison, Kansas

Ravens ◆ NAIA ◆ Heart of America Conference ◆ http://www.benedictine.edu/

Independent Roman Catholic comprehensive, founded 1859
Coed, 1,271 undergraduate students, 77% full-time, 52% women, 48% men
Small-town 225-acre campus with easy access to Kansas City
Moderately difficult entrance level, 94% of applicants were admitted

Freshmen *Admission:* 580 applied, 556 were accepted, 253 enrolled.
Test scores: SAT verbal scores over 500: 68%; SAT math scores over 500: 64%; SAT verbal scores over 600: 16%; SAT math scores over 600: 19%; SAT verbal scores over 700: 3%; SAT math scores over 700: 3%.
Tuition and fees (2003–04): $14,613 (full-time). *Room and board:* $5920 (room only: $2560).
Financial Aid (All incoming freshmen): *Average need-based gift aid:* $8078. *Average non-need based aid:* $5405. *Average aid to full-time undergraduates:* $13,908.
Athletic Department: *Director of Athletics:* Larry Wilcox; Phone: 913-367-5340; Fax: 913-367-2564; E-mail: lwilcox@benedictine.edu. *Sports Information Director:* Jim Schneiderhahn; Phone: 913-367-5340; E-mail: jims@benedictine.edu.

MEN'S COACHES
Baseball: Dan Griggs; Phone: 913-367-5340; E-mail: dgriggs@benedictine.edu.
Basketball: Joe Brickner; Phone: 913-367-5340; E-mail: brickner@benedictine.edu.
Cheerleading: Dianne Dickenson; Phone: 913-360-5340; E-mail: dianned@benedictine.edu.
Cross Country: Rex Lane; Phone: 913-367-5340; E-mail: rlane@benedictine.edu.
Football: Larry Wilcox; Phone: 913-367-5340; E-mail: lwilcox@benedictine.edu.
Golf: Jim Schneiderhahn; Phone: 913-367-5340; E-mail: jims@benedictine.edu.
Soccer: Dan Leahy; Phone: 913-367-5340; E-mail: dleahy@benedictine.edu.
Tennis: Mike King; Phone: 913-367-5340; E-mail: mking@benedictine.edu.
Track and Field: Myles Bacon; Phone: 913-360-7369; E-mail: mking@benedictine.edu.

WOMEN'S COACHES
Basketball: Chad Folsom; Phone: 913-360-5340; E-mail: cfolsom@benedictine.edu.
Cheerleading: Dianne Dickenson; Phone: 913-360-5340; E-mail: dianned@benedictine.edu.
Cross Country: Rex Lane; Phone: 913-367-5340; E-mail: rlane@benedictine.edu.
Golf: Jim Schneiderhahn; Phone: 913-367-5340; E-mail: jims@benedictine.edu.
Soccer: Jim Schneiderhahn; Phone: 913-367-5340; E-mail: jims@benedictine.edu.

Softball: Tim Crowley; Phone: 913-360-5340; E-mail: tcrowley@ benedictine.edu.
Tennis: Mike King; Phone: 913-367-5340; E-mail: mking@benedictine. edu.
Track and Field: Myles Bacon; Phone: 913-360-7369; E-mail: mking@ benedictine.edu.
Volleyball: Chad McDole; Phone: 913-367-5340; E-mail: cmcdole@ benedictine.edu.

BENEDICTINE UNIVERSITY
Lisle, Illinois

Eagles ◆ NCAA III ◆ Illini-Badger Football Conference; Northern Illinois-Iowa Conference ◆ http://www.ben.edu/

Independent Roman Catholic comprehensive, founded 1887
Coed, 2,114 undergraduate students, 70% full-time, 63% women, 37% men
Suburban 108-acre campus with easy access to Chicago
Moderately difficult entrance level

Freshmen *Admission:* 303 enrolled.
Tuition and fees (2004–05): $17,470 (full-time). *Room and board:* $6370.
Financial Aid (All incoming freshmen): *Average need-based gift aid:* $5697. *Average non-need based aid:* $6715. *Average aid to full-time undergraduates:* $13,399.
Athletic Department: *Director of Athletics:* Lynn O'Linski; Phone: 630-829-6150; Fax: 630-960-0899; E-mail: lolinski@ben.edu. *Sports Information Director:* Jill Redmond; Phone: 630-829-6164; E-mail: jredmond@ben.edu.

MEN'S COACHES
Baseball: John Ostrowski; Phone: 630-829-6147; E-mail: jostrowski@ ben.edu.
Basketball: Keith Bunkerburg; Phone: 630-829-6146; E-mail: kbunkenburg@ben.edu.
Cross Country: Jon Wolcott; Phone: 630-829-6163; E-mail: jwolcott@ ben.edu.
Football: Tom Mitchell; Phone: 630-829-6153; E-mail: tmitchell@ben. edu.
Golf: Keith Bunkerburg; Phone: 630-829-6146; E-mail: kbunkenburg@ ben.edu.
Soccer: Derek Niepomnik; Phone: 630-829-6165; E-mail: dniepomnik@ben.edu.
Swimming: Tim Keeley; Phone: 630-829-6151; E-mail: tkeeley@ben. edu.

WOMEN'S COACHES
Basketball: Chris Hitchcock; Phone: 630-829-6142; E-mail: chitchcock@ben.edu.
Cross Country: Jon Wolcott; Phone: 630-829-6163; E-mail: jwolcott@ ben.edu.
Golf: Keith Bunkerburg; Phone: 630-829-6146; E-mail: kbunkenburg@ ben.edu.
Soccer: Brenton Joseph; Phone: 630-829-6165; E-mail: bjoseph@ben. edu.
Softball: Kate Keller; Phone: 630-829-6149; E-mail: kkeller@ben.edu.
Swimming: Tim Keeley; Phone: 630-829-6151; E-mail: tkeeley@ben. edu.
Tennis: Kate Keller; Phone: 630-829-6149; E-mail: kkeller@ben.edu.
Track and Field: Jon Wolcott; Phone: 630-829-6163; E-mail: jwolcott@ ben.edu.
Volleyball: Karen Seremet Kunka; Phone: 630-829-6154; E-mail: kseremet@ben.edu.

BENNETT COLLEGE
Greensboro, North Carolina

Belles ◆ NCAA III ◆ Independent ◆ http://www.bennett.edu/

Independent United Methodist 4-year, founded 1873
Women only, 486 undergraduate students, 99% full-time, 100% women, 100% men
Urban 55-acre campus
Moderately difficult entrance level, 10% of applicants were admitted

Freshmen *Admission:* 1,554 applied, 154 were accepted, 142 enrolled. *Test scores:* SAT verbal scores over 500: 10%; SAT math scores over 500: 8%; SAT math scores over 600: 2%.

Tuition and fees (2003–04): $10,978 (full-time). *Room and board:* $5072 (room only: $2526).
Financial Aid (All incoming freshmen): *Average aid to full-time undergraduates:* $10,475.
Athletic Department: *Director of Athletics:* Angie Abraham; Phone: 336-517-2256; Fax: 336-378-0511; E-mail: aabraham@bennett.edu. *Sports Information Director:* Angie Abraham; Phone: 336-517-2256; E-mail: aabraham@bennett.edu.

WOMEN'S COACHES
Basketball: Angie Abraham; Phone: 336-517-2256; E-mail: aabraham@ bennett.edu.
Softball: Loris Boyd-Groover; Phone: 336-517-2256.
Tennis: Loris Boyd-Groover; Phone: 336-517-2256.
Track and Field: Carl Bibbs; Phone: 336-517-2256.
Volleyball: Joyce Spruill; Phone: 336-517-2255; E-mail: jspruill@ bennett.edu.

BENTLEY COLLEGE
Waltham, Massachusetts

Falcons ◆ NCAA II ◆ Atlantic Hockey Conference; Northeast-10 Conference ◆ http://www.bentley.edu/

Independent comprehensive, founded 1917
Coed, 4,344 undergraduate students, 91% full-time, 43% women, 57% men
Suburban 143-acre campus with easy access to Boston
Moderately difficult entrance level, 44% of applicants were admitted

Freshmen *Admission:* 5,474 applied, 2,529 were accepted, 955 enrolled. *Test scores:* SAT verbal scores over 500: 88%; SAT math scores over 500: 98%; SAT verbal scores over 600: 36%; SAT math scores over 600: 63%; SAT verbal scores over 700: 3%; SAT math scores over 700: 11%.
Tuition and fees (2003–04): $24,324 (full-time). *Room and board:* $9580 (room only: $5570).
Financial Aid (All incoming freshmen): *Average need-based gift aid:* $14,594. *Average non-need based aid:* $11,058. *Average aid to full-time undergraduates:* $22,260.
Athletic Department: *Director of Athletics:* Bob Defelice; Phone: 781-891-2256; Fax: 781-891-2648; E-mail: rdefelice@bentley.edu. *Sports Information Director:* Dick Lipe; Phone: 781-891-2334; E-mail: rlipe@ bentley.edu.

MEN'S COACHES
Baseball: Bob Defelice; Phone: 781-891-2332; E-mail: rdefelice@ bentley.edu.
Basketball: Jay Lawson; Phone: 781-891-2993; E-mail: jlawson@ bentley.edu.
Cheerleading: Christine Palumbo; Phone: 781-891-2256.
Cross Country: Ed Lyons; Phone: 781-891-2995; E-mail: elyons@bentley. edu.
Diving: Rick Danehy; Phone: 781-891-3415.
Football: Peter Yetten; Phone: 781-891-2338; E-mail: tboerman@ bentley.edu.
Golf: Don Moorhead; Phone: 781-891-2333; E-mail: dmoorhead@ bentley.edu.
Ice Hockey: Ryan Soderquist; Phone: 781-891-2492; E-mail: rsoderquist@bentley.edu.
Lacrosse: Jim Murphy; Phone: 781-891-2339; E-mail: jmurphy4@ bentley.edu.
Soccer: Peter Simonini; Phone: 781-891-2336; E-mail: psimonini@ bentley.edu.
Swimming: Mary Kay Samko; Phone: 781-891-3415; E-mail: msamko@ bentley.edu.
Tennis: Cory Tusler; Phone: 781-891-2337; E-mail: ctusler@bentley. edu.
Track and Field: Ed Lyons; Phone: 781-891-2995; E-mail: elyons@ bentley.edu.

WOMEN'S COACHES
Basketball: Barbara Stevens; Phone: 781-891-2996; E-mail: bstevens@ bentley.edu.
Cheerleading: Christine Palumbo; Phone: 781-891-2256.
Cross Country: Ed Lyons; Phone: 781-891-2995; E-mail: elyons@bentley. edu.
Diving: Rick Danehy; Phone: 781-891-3415.

Bentley College *(continued)*

Field Hockey: Kelly McGowan; Phone: 781-891-2335; E-mail: kwest@bentley.edu.

Lacrosse: Ben Saraydarian; Phone: 781-891-2324; E-mail: bsaraydarian@bentley.edu.

Soccer: Lauren Lukis; Phone: 781-891-2451; E-mail: llukis@bentley.edu.

Softball: Dawn MacMillan; Phone: 781-891-2449; E-mail: dmacmillan@bentley.edu.

Swimming: Mary Kay Samko; Phone: 781-891-3415; E-mail: msamko@bentley.edu.

Tennis: Alex Wong; Phone: 781-891-2761; E-mail: awong1@bentley.edu.

Track and Field: Ed Lyons; Phone: 781-891-2995; E-mail: elyons@bentley.edu.

Volleyball: Sandy Hoffman; Phone: 781-891-2780; E-mail: shoffman@bentley.edu.

BEREA COLLEGE
Berea, Kentucky

Mountaineers ◆ NAIA ◆ Kentucky Intercollegiate Conference ◆ http://www.berea.edu/

Independent 4-year, founded 1855
Coed, 1,560 undergraduate students, 97% full-time, 60% women, 40% men
Small-town 140-acre campus
Very difficult entrance level, 2% of applicants were admitted

Freshmen *Admission:* 2,119 applied, 530 were accepted, 396 enrolled. *Test scores:* SAT verbal scores over 500: 71%; SAT math scores over 500: 72%; SAT verbal scores over 600: 30%; SAT math scores over 600: 25%; SAT verbal scores over 700: 6%; SAT math scores over 700: 1%.
Tuition and fees (2003–04): $507 (full-time). *Room and board:* $4523 (room only: $2415).
Financial Aid (All incoming freshmen): *Average need-based gift aid:* $25,485. *Average aid to full-time undergraduates:* $26,605.
Athletic Department: *Director of Athletics:* Joan Weston; Phone: 859-985-3568; Fax: 859-985-3919; E-mail: joan_weston@berea.edu.

MEN'S COACHES
Baseball: Todd Morris; Phone: 859-985-3423.
Basketball: John Mills; Phone: 859-985-3482.
Cross Country: Mike Johnson; Phone: 859-985-3578; E-mail: mike_johnson@berea.edu.
Golf: Roland Wierwille; Phone: 859-985-3424; E-mail: coach_wierville@berea.edu.
Soccer: David Vaughn; Phone: 859-985-8604.
Swimming: Mike Johnson; Phone: 859-985-3578; E-mail: mike_johnson@berea.edu.
Tennis: Allen Jackson; Phone: 859-985-3423.
Track and Field: Mike Johnson; Phone: 859-985-3578; E-mail: mike_johnson@berea.edu.

WOMEN'S COACHES
Basketball: Bunky Harkleroad; Phone: 859-985-3423; E-mail: bunky_harkleroad@berea.edu.
Cross Country: Mike Johnson; Phone: 859-985-3578; E-mail: mike_johnson@berea.edu.
Soccer: Francis O'Hara; Phone: 859-985-4510; E-mail: francis_o'hara@berea.edu.
Softball: Scott Buchanan; Phone: 859-985-3602; E-mail: sbuchanan@iclub.org.
Swimming: Mike Johnson; Phone: 859-985-3578; E-mail: mike_johnson@berea.edu.
Tennis: Allen Jackson; Phone: 859-985-3423; E-mail: joan_weston@berea.edu.
Track and Field: Kelly Ambrose; Phone: 859-985-3433; E-mail: kelly_ambrose@berea.edu.
Volleyball: Jason Montgomery; Phone: 859-985-3423; E-mail: jason_montgomery@berea.edu.

BERNARD M. BARUCH COLLEGE OF THE CITY UNIVERSITY OF NEW YORK
New York, New York

Bearcats ◆ NCAA III ◆ CUNY Athletic Conference ◆ http://www.baruch.cuny.edu/

State and locally supported comprehensive, founded 1919, part of City University of New York System
Coed, 12,462 undergraduate students, 72% full-time, 57% women, 43% men
Urban campus
Very difficult entrance level, 38% of applicants were admitted

Freshmen *Admission:* 9,446 applied, 3,425 were accepted, 1,674 enrolled. *Test scores:* SAT verbal scores over 500: 61%; SAT math scores over 500: 86%; SAT verbal scores over 600: 18%; SAT math scores over 600: 40%; SAT verbal scores over 700: 2%; SAT math scores over 700: 7%.
Tuition and fees (2004–05): $4300 (resident), $8940 (nonresident).
Financial Aid (All incoming freshmen): *Average need-based gift aid:* $4800. *Average non-need based aid:* $1600. *Average aid to full-time undergraduates:* $5380.
Athletic Department: *Director of Athletics:* William Eng; Phone: 646-312-5046; Fax: 646-312-5041; E-mail: william_eng@baruch.cuny.edu. *Sports Information Director:* John Neves; Phone: 646-312-5048; E-mail: sid@baruch.cuny.edu.

MEN'S COACHES
Baseball: Miguel Iglesias; Phone: 646-312-5052; E-mail: iglesiam@etechinsights.com.
Basketball: Ray Rankis; Phone: 646-312-5045; E-mail: ray_rankis@baruch.cuny.edu.
Diving: Pushaen Gunasinghe; Phone: 646-312-5060; E-mail: puahaentri@aol.com.
Soccer: Ranford Champagnie; Phone: 646-312-5040.
Swimming: Pushaen Gunasinghe; Phone: 646-312-5060; E-mail: puahaentri@aol.com.
Tennis: Florin Giuglescu; Phone: 646-312-5040; E-mail: fgiuglescu@aol.com.
Volleyball: Justin Stack; Phone: 646-312-5040; E-mail: just3cdk@aol.com.

WOMEN'S COACHES
Basketball: Robert Dinardo; Phone: 646-312-5040; E-mail: bdteach4@aol.com.
Cross Country: Bill Eng; Phone: 646-312-5046; E-mail: william_eng@baruch.cuny.edu.
Diving: Pushaen Gunasinghe; Phone: 646-312-5060; E-mail: puahaentri@aol.com.
Softball: Jose Negroni; Phone: 646-312-5040; E-mail: coachjose23@aol.com.
Swimming: Pushaen Gunasinghe; Phone: 646-312-5060; E-mail: puahaentri@aol.com.
Tennis: Florin Giuglescu; Phone: 646-312-5040; E-mail: fgiuglescu@aol.com.
Volleyball: Krishna Dass; Phone: 646-312-5053; E-mail: krishna_dass@baruch.cuny.edu.

BERRY COLLEGE
Mount Berry, Georgia

Vikings ◆ NAIA ◆ TranSouth Conference ◆ http://www.berry.edu/

Independent interdenominational comprehensive, founded 1902
Coed, 1,895 undergraduate students, 98% full-time, 63% women, 37% men
Suburban 28,000-acre campus with easy access to Atlanta
Moderately difficult entrance level, 82% of applicants were admitted

Freshmen *Admission:* 1,846 applied, 1,531 were accepted, 505 enrolled. *Test scores:* SAT verbal scores over 500: 89%; SAT math scores over 500: 84%; SAT verbal scores over 600: 49%; SAT math scores over 600: 39%; SAT verbal scores over 700: 8%; SAT math scores over 700: 6%.

Tuition and fees (2003–04): $15,220 (full-time). *Room and board:* $6190 (room only: $3470).
Financial Aid (All incoming freshmen): *Average need-based gift aid:* $11,255. *Average non-need based aid:* $11,958. *Average aid to full-time undergraduates:* $13,919.
Athletic Department: *Director of Athletics:* Todd Brooks; Phone: 706-236-1721; Fax: 706-236-5497; E-mail: tbrooks@berry.edu. *Sports Information Director:* Jeff Gable; Phone: 706-290-2146.

MEN'S COACHES

Baseball: David Beasley; Phone: 706-236-1743; E-mail: dbeasley@berry.edu.
Basketball: Jeff Haarlow; Phone: 706-236-1733; E-mail: jhaarlow@berry.edu.
Cross Country: Paul Deaton; Phone: 706-236-2147; E-mail: pdeaton@berry.edu.
Golf: Brian Farrer; Phone: 706-238-5904.
Soccer: Richard Vardy; Phone: 706-236-1728; E-mail: rvardy@berry.edu.
Tennis: Clay Hightower; Phone: 706-236-1746; E-mail: chightower@berry.edu.

WOMEN'S COACHES

Basketball: Jim Izard; Phone: 706-236-2240; E-mail: jizard@berry.edu.
Cross Country: Paul Deaton; Phone: 706-236-2147; E-mail: pdeaton@berry.edu.
Golf: Brian Farrer; Phone: 706-238-5904.
Soccer: Lorenzo Canalis; Phone: 706-236-1734; E-mail: lcanalis@berry.edu.
Tennis: Clay Hightower; Phone: 706-236-1746; E-mail: chightower@berry.edu.

BETHANY COLLEGE
Lindsborg, Kansas

Swedes ◆ NAIA ◆ Kansas Collegiate Conference ◆ http://www.bethanylb.edu/

Independent Lutheran 4-year, founded 1881
Coed, 631 undergraduate students, 92% full-time, 44% women, 56% men
Small-town 80-acre campus
Moderately difficult entrance level, 66% of applicants were admitted

Freshmen *Admission:* 775 applied, 548 were accepted, 172 enrolled. *Test scores:* SAT verbal scores over 500: 30%; SAT math scores over 500: 50%; SAT verbal scores over 600: 1%; SAT math scores over 600: 7%.
Tuition and fees (2004–05): $14,800 (full-time). *Room and board:* $5150 (room only: $2800).
Financial Aid (All incoming freshmen): *Average need-based gift aid:* $4640. *Average non-need based aid:* $2333. *Average aid to full-time undergraduates:* $15,277.
Athletic Department: *Director of Athletics:* Jon Daniels; Phone: 785-227-3380; Fax: 785-227-2021; E-mail: danielsj@bethanylb.edu. *Sports Information Director:* John Pearson; Phone: 785-227-3380; E-mail: pearsonj@bethanylb.edu.

MEN'S COACHES

Baseball: Matt Tramel; Phone: 785-227-3380; E-mail: tramelm@bethanylb.edu.
Basketball: Clair Oleen.
Cheerleading: Vicki Cornett; Phone: 785-227-3380; E-mail: cornettv@bethanylb.edu.
Cross Country: Joe Wilkerson; Phone: 785-227-3380; E-mail: wilkersonj@bethanylb.edu.
Football: Ted Kessinger; Phone: 785-227-3380; E-mail: rothgebc@bethanylb.edu.
Golf: Jon Daniels; Phone: 785-227-3380; E-mail: danielsj@bethanylb.edu.
Soccer: Bobby Peterson; Phone: 785-227-3380; E-mail: petersonb@bethanylb.edu.
Tennis: Vic Bateman; Phone: 785-227-3380; E-mail: batemanv@bethanylb.edu.
Track and Field: Joe Wilkerson; Phone: 785-227-3380; E-mail: wilkersonj@bethanylb.edu.

WOMEN'S COACHES

Basketball: Trent May; Phone: 785-227-3380; E-mail: mayt@bethanylb.edu.

Cheerleading: Vicki Cornett; Phone: 785-227-3380; E-mail: cornettv@bethanylb.edu.
Cross Country: Joe Wilkerson; Phone: 785-227-3380; E-mail: wilkersonj@bethanylb.edu.
Soccer: Bobby Peterson; Phone: 785-227-3380; E-mail: petersonb@bethanylb.edu.
Softball: Janice Fiene; Phone: 785-227-3380; E-mail: fienej@bethanylb.edu.
Tennis: Vic Bateman; Phone: 785-227-3380; E-mail: batemanv@bethanylb.edu.
Track and Field: Joe Wilkerson; Phone: 785-227-3380; E-mail: wilkersonj@bethanylb.edu.
Volleyball: Tom Bosley; Phone: 785-227-3380; E-mail: bosleyt@bethanylb.edu.

BETHANY COLLEGE
Bethany, West Virginia

Bison ◆ NCAA III ◆ Presidents' Athletic Conference ◆ http://www.bethanywv.edu/

Independent religious 4-year, founded 1840, affiliated with Christian Church (Disciples of Christ)
Coed, 900 undergraduate students, 98% full-time, 51% women, 49% men
Rural 1,600-acre campus with easy access to Pittsburgh
Moderately difficult entrance level, 67% of applicants were admitted

Freshmen *Admission:* 957 applied, 703 were accepted, 271 enrolled. *Test scores:* SAT verbal scores over 500: 53%; SAT math scores over 500: 50%; SAT verbal scores over 600: 14%; SAT math scores over 600: 14%; SAT verbal scores over 700: 1%; SAT math scores over 700: 1%.
Tuition and fees (2003–04): $13,535 (full-time). *Room and board:* $6300 (room only: $3200).
Financial Aid (All incoming freshmen): *Average aid to full-time undergraduates:* $11,000.
Athletic Department: *Director of Athletics:* Jan Forsty; Phone: 304-829-7251; Fax: 304-829-7290; E-mail: jforsty@bethanywv.edu. *Sports Information Director:* Kirk Reed; Phone: 304-829-7292; E-mail: kreed@bethanywv.edu.

MEN'S COACHES

Baseball: Rick Carver; Phone: 304-829-7246; E-mail: rcarver@bethanywv.edu.
Basketball: Aaron Huffman; Phone: 304-829-7269; E-mail: ahuffman@bethanywv.edu.
Cross Country: John McGowan; Phone: 304-829-7254; E-mail: jmcgowan@bethanywv.edu.
Diving: John McGowan; Phone: 304-829-7254; E-mail: jmcgowan@bethanywv.edu.
Football: Chris Snyder; Phone: 304-829-7242; E-mail: csnyder@bethanywv.edu.
Soccer: Kosmas Mouratidis; Phone: 304-829-7238; E-mail: kmouratidis@bethanywv.edu.
Swimming: John McGowan; Phone: 304-829-7254; E-mail: jmcgowan@bethanywv.edu.
Tennis: Aaron Huffman; Phone: 304-829-7269; E-mail: ahuffman@bethanywv.edu.
Track and Field: Don Burns; Phone: 304-829-7252; E-mail: dburns@bethanywv.edu.

WOMEN'S COACHES

Basketball: Jina Derubbo; Phone: 304-829-7267; E-mail: jsderubbo@bethanywv.edu.
Cross Country: John McGowan; Phone: 304-829-7254; E-mail: jmcgowan@bethanywv.edu.
Diving: John McGowan; Phone: 304-829-7254; E-mail: jmcgowan@bethanywv.edu.
Soccer: Frankie Taal; Phone: 304-829-7031; E-mail: ftaal@bethanywv.edu.
Softball: Jan Frosty; Phone: 304-829-7271; E-mail: jforsty@bethanywv.edu.
Swimming: John McGowan; Phone: 304-829-7254; E-mail: jmcgowan@bethanywv.edu.
Tennis: Jina Derubbo; Phone: 304-829-7267; E-mail: jsderubbo@bethanywv.edu.

Bethany College *(continued)*

Track and Field: Don Burns; Phone: 304-829-7252; E-mail: dburns@bethanywv.edu.
Volleyball: Jan Frosty; Phone: 304-829-7271; E-mail: jforsty@bethanywv.edu.

BETHANY COLLEGE OF THE ASSEMBLIES OF GOD
Scotts Valley, California

Bruins ◆ NAIA ◆ California Pacific Conference ◆ http://www.bethany.edu/

Independent Assemblies of God comprehensive, founded 1919
Coed, 504 undergraduate students, 74% full-time, 38% women, 62% men
Small-town 40-acre campus with easy access to San Francisco and San Jose
Minimally difficult entrance level, 74% of applicants were admitted

Freshmen *Admission:* 208 applied, 154 were accepted, 84 enrolled. *Test scores:* SAT verbal scores over 500: 53%; SAT math scores over 500: 50%; SAT verbal scores over 600: 24%; SAT math scores over 600: 21%; SAT verbal scores over 700: 5%; SAT math scores over 700: 5%.
Tuition and fees (2003–04): $12,580 (full-time). *Room and board:* $5380 (room only: $2520).
Financial Aid (All incoming freshmen): *Average need-based gift aid:* $7000. *Average non-need based aid:* $14,500. *Average aid to full-time undergraduates:* $8300.
Athletic Department: *Director of Athletics:* Sheldon Parkinson; Phone: 831-438-3800; Fax: 831-438-6202; E-mail: sparkinson@fc.bethany.edu.

MEN'S COACHES
Baseball: Giuseppe Chiaramonte; Phone: 831-438-3800.
Basketball: Alan Wilson; Phone: 831-438-3800.
Golf: Dale Kassler; Phone: 831-438-3800.
Soccer: Jeff Biacher; Phone: 831-438-3800.
WOMEN'S COACHES
Basketball: Dan Mooney; Phone: 831-438-3800.
Golf: Dale Kassler; Phone: 831-438-3800.
Soccer: Greg Olson; Phone: 831-438-3800.
Softball: Russ Rogers; Phone: 831-438-3800.
Volleyball: Andy Mandon; Phone: 831-438-3800.

BETHEL COLLEGE
Mishawaka, Indiana

Pilots ◆ NAIA ◆ Mid-Central Conference ◆ http://www.bethelcollege.edu/

Independent religious comprehensive, founded 1947, affiliated with Missionary Church
Coed, 1,740 undergraduate students, 74% full-time, 63% women, 37% men
Suburban 70-acre campus
Minimally difficult entrance level, 66% of applicants were admitted

Freshmen *Admission:* 684 applied, 445 were accepted, 306 enrolled. *Test scores:* SAT verbal scores over 500: 64%; SAT math scores over 500: 66%; SAT verbal scores over 600: 22%; SAT math scores over 600: 25%; SAT verbal scores over 700: 2%; SAT math scores over 700: 2%.
Tuition and fees (2003–04): $14,530 (full-time). *Room and board:* $4680.
Financial Aid (All incoming freshmen): *Average need-based gift aid:* $3388. *Average non-need based aid:* $2820. *Average aid to full-time undergraduates:* $12,049.
Athletic Department: *Director of Athletics:* Mike Lightfoot; Phone: 574-257-3345; Fax: 574-257-3385; E-mail: lightfm@bethelcollege.edu. *Sports Information Director:* Pete Morey; Phone: 574-257-2676; E-mail: moreyp@bethelcollege.edu.

MEN'S COACHES
Baseball: Seth Zartman; Phone: 574-257-3287.
Basketball: Mike Lightfoot; Phone: 574-257-3345; E-mail: lightfm@bethelcollege.edu.
Cheerleading: Kristin Levan; Phone: 574-257-3343.
Cross Country: Don Hendricks; Phone: 574-257-2598.
Golf: Chris Hess; Phone: 574-257-3371.
Soccer: Pablo Rodriguez; Phone: 574-257-3438; E-mail: rodrigp@bethelcollege.edu.
Tennis: John Natali; Phone: 574-257-3514; E-mail: natalij@bethelcollege.edu.
Track and Field: Tony Natali; Phone: 574-257-3478.
Wrestling: Tony Holt; Phone: 574-257-3205.
WOMEN'S COACHES
Basketball: Jody Martinez; Phone: 574-257-3447; E-mail: martinj@bethelcollege.edu.
Cheerleading: Kristin Levan; Phone: 574-257-3343.
Cross Country: Don Hendricks; Phone: 574-257-2598.
Soccer: Pete Morey; Phone: 574-257-2676; E-mail: moreyp@bethelcollege.edu.
Softball: Adam Roorbach; Phone: 574-257-3418; E-mail: roorbaa@bethelcollege.edu.
Tennis: John Natali; Phone: 574-257-3514; E-mail: natalij@bethelcollege.edu.
Track and Field: Tony Natali; Phone: 574-257-3478.
Volleyball: Julia Reininga; Phone: 574-257-2573; E-mail: reininj@bethelcollege.edu.

BETHEL COLLEGE
North Newton, Kansas

Threshers ◆ NAIA ◆ Kansas Collegiate Conference ◆ http://www.bethelks.edu/

Independent religious 4-year, founded 1887, affiliated with Mennonite Church USA
Coed, 470 undergraduate students, 93% full-time, 53% women, 47% men
Small-town 60-acre campus with easy access to Wichita
Moderately difficult entrance level, 70% of applicants were admitted

Freshmen *Admission:* 527 applied, 378 were accepted, 98 enrolled. *Test scores:* SAT verbal scores over 500: 56%; SAT math scores over 500: 67%; SAT verbal scores over 600: 22%; SAT math scores over 700: 22%.
Tuition and fees (2003–04): $13,900 (full-time). *Room and board:* $5900.
Financial Aid (All incoming freshmen): *Average need-based gift aid:* $3847. *Average non-need based aid:* $6892. *Average aid to full-time undergraduates:* $14,258.
Athletic Department: *Director of Athletics:* Diane Flickner; Phone: 316-284-5279; Fax: 316-284-5830; E-mail: flickner@bethelks.edu. *Sports Information Director:* Troy Fowler; Phone: 316-284-5263; E-mail: troyf@bethelks.edu.

MEN'S COACHES
Basketball: Gary Chupp; Phone: 316-284-5278; E-mail: gchupp@bethelks.edu.
Cross Country: Tracy Tuttle; Phone: 316-284-5821; E-mail: ttuttle@bethelks.edu.
Football: Michael Moore; Phone: 316-284-5382; E-mail: mmoore@bethelks.edu.
Golf: Gregg Dick; Phone: 316-284-5277; E-mail: greggd@bethelks.edu.
Soccer: Gerry Sieber; Phone: 316-284-5297; E-mail: gsieber@bethelks.edu.
Tennis: Angela Brodhagen; Phone: 316-284-5299; E-mail: abrodhagen@bethelks.edu.
Track and Field: Tracy Tuttle; Phone: 316-284-5821; E-mail: ttuttle@bethelks.edu.
WOMEN'S COACHES
Basketball: DeAnn Huxman; Phone: 316-284-5311; E-mail: dhuxman@bethelks.edu.
Cross Country: Tracy Tuttle; Phone: 316-284-5821; E-mail: ttuttle@bethelks.edu.
Golf: Gregg Dick; Phone: 316-284-5277; E-mail: greggd@bethelks.edu.
Soccer: Troy Fowler; Phone: 316-284-5263; E-mail: troyf@bethelks.edu.

Tennis: Angela Brodhagen; Phone: 316-284-5299; E-mail: abrodhagen@bethelks.edu.
Track and Field: Tracy Tuttle; Phone: 316-284-5821; E-mail: ttuttle@bethelks.edu.
Volleyball: Beverly Mayer; Phone: 316-284-5298; E-mail: bmayer@bethelks.edu.

BETHEL COLLEGE
McKenzie, Tennessee

Wildcats ◆ NAIA ◆ Kentucky Intercollegiate Conference ◆ http://www.bethel-college.edu/

Independent Cumberland Presbyterian comprehensive, founded 1842
Coed, 1,149 undergraduate students, 83% full-time, 56% women, 44% men
Small-town 100-acre campus
Minimally difficult entrance level, 48% of applicants were admitted

Freshmen *Admission:* 492 applied, 264 were accepted, 132 enrolled. *Test scores:* SAT verbal scores over 500: 27%; SAT math scores over 500: 54%.
Tuition and fees (2003–04): $9630 (full-time). *Room and board:* $5080.
Financial Aid (All incoming freshmen): *Average need-based gift aid:* $3542. *Average non-need based aid:* $1000. *Average aid to full-time undergraduates:* $9042.
Athletic Department: *Director of Athletics:* Jeff Britt; Phone: 731-352-4203; Fax: 731-352-4238; E-mail: brittj@bethel-college.edu. *Sports Information Director:* Matt Floyd; Phone: 731-352-4231; E-mail: floydm@bethel-college.edu.

MEN'S COACHES
Baseball: Glenn Hayes; Phone: 731-352-4206; E-mail: athletics@bethel-college.edu.
Basketball: Jeff Britt; Phone: 731-352-4203; E-mail: brittj@bethel-college.edu.
Cheerleading: Audra Henderson; Phone: 731-352-4219; E-mail: hendersona@bethel-college.edu.
Cross Country: Rusty Thompson; Phone: 731-352-4266; E-mail: thompsonr@bethel-college.edu.
Football: Dino Kaklis; Phone: 731-352-4213; E-mail: kaklisd@bethel-college.edu.
Golf: Jerry Wilcoxson; Phone: 731-352-4201; E-mail: wilcoxsonj@bethel-college.edu.
Soccer: Kerry Brimmo; Phone: 731-352-4252; E-mail: brimmok@bethel-college.edu.
Tennis: Matt Floyd; Phone: 731-352-4231; E-mail: floydm@bethel-college.edu.
Track and Field: Steve Hookfin; Phone: 731-352-4211; E-mail: hookfins@bethel-college.edu.

WOMEN'S COACHES
Basketball: Larry Eddings; Phone: 731-352-4204; E-mail: eddingsl@bethel-college.edu.
Cheerleading: Audra Henderson; Phone: 731-352-4219; E-mail: hendersona@bethel-college.edu.
Cross Country: Rusty Thompson; Phone: 731-352-4266; E-mail: thompsonr@bethel-college.edu.
Golf: Catherine Hester; Phone: 731-352-4246; E-mail: hesterc@bethel-college.edu.
Soccer: Misty Aird; Phone: 731-352-4229; E-mail: airdm@bethel-college.edu.
Softball: Teresa Woods; Phone: 731-352-4015; E-mail: woodst@bethel-college.edu.
Tennis: Matt Floyd; Phone: 731-352-4231; E-mail: floydm@bethel-college.edu.
Track and Field: Steve Hookfin; Phone: 731-352-4211; E-mail: hookfins@bethel-college.edu.
Volleyball: Malissa Vaughn; Phone: 731-352-4228; E-mail: vaughnm@bethel-college.edu.

BETHEL UNIVERSITY
St. Paul, Minnesota

Royals ◆ NCAA III ◆ Minnesota Intercollegiate Athletic Conference ◆ http://www.bethel.edu/

Independent religious comprehensive, founded 1871, affiliated with Baptist General Conference
Coed, 2,911 undergraduate students, 89% full-time, 61% women, 39% men
Suburban 231-acre campus with easy access to Twin Cities
Moderately difficult entrance level, 92% of applicants were admitted

Freshmen *Admission:* 1,512 applied, 1,370 were accepted, 658 enrolled. *Test scores:* SAT verbal scores over 500: 80%; SAT math scores over 500: 83%; SAT verbal scores over 600: 46%; SAT math scores over 600: 48%; SAT verbal scores over 700: 17%; SAT math scores over 700: 10%.
Tuition and fees (2004–05): $19,990 (full-time). *Room and board:* $6570 (room only: $3900).
Financial Aid (All incoming freshmen): *Average need-based gift aid:* $10,068. *Average non-need based aid:* $3281. *Average aid to full-time undergraduates:* $15,437.
Athletic Department: *Director of Athletics:* Dave Klostreich; Phone: 651-638-6396; Fax: 651-635-8645; E-mail: d-klostreich@bethel.edu. *Sports Information Director:* Greg Peterson; Phone: 651-638-6394; E-mail: g-peterson2@bethel.edu.

MEN'S COACHES
Baseball: Greg Indlecoffer; Phone: 651-638-6143; E-mail: g-indlecoffer@bethel.edu.
Basketball: Bob Bjorklund; Phone: 651-638-6395; E-mail: robert-bjorklund@bethel.edu.
Cross Country: Jim Timp; Phone: 651-638-6399; E-mail: jttimp@hotmail.com.
Football: Steve Johnson; Phone: 651-638-6398; E-mail: johstea@bethel.edu.
Golf: Bill Schulenberg; Phone: 651-638-6154; E-mail: bschules@juno.com.
Ice Hockey: Peter Aus; Phone: 651-638-6471; E-mail: p-aus@bethel.edu.
Soccer: Chad Osgood; Phone: 651-638-6535; E-mail: chad-osgood@bethel.edu.
Tennis: Dan Morton; Phone: 651-638-6565; E-mail: dmorton@wans.net.
Track and Field: Mike Goldman; Phone: 651-638-6399; E-mail: m-goldman@bethel.edu.

WOMEN'S COACHES
Basketball: Jon Herbrechtsmeyer; Phone: 651-638-6032; E-mail: jherbrec@bethel.edu.
Cross Country: Suzanne Ray; Phone: 651-635-8508; E-mail: suzanne-ray@bethel.edu.
Soccer: Scott Krohn; Phone: 651-638-8522; E-mail: scott.krohn@moundsviewschools.org.
Softball: Darin Thompson; Phone: 651-638-6401; E-mail: thodar@bethel.edu.
Tennis: Dan Morton; Phone: 651-638-6565; E-mail: dmorton@wans.net.
Track and Field: Suzanne Ray; Phone: 651-635-8505; E-mail: suzanne-ray@bethel.edu.
Volleyball: Gretchen Hunt; Phone: 651-638-6790; E-mail: gretchen-hansen@bethel.edu.

BETHUNE-COOKMAN COLLEGE
Daytona Beach, Florida

Wildcats ◆ NCAA I ◆ Mid-Eastern Athletic Conference ◆ http://www.bethune.cookman.edu/

Independent Methodist 4-year, founded 1904
Coed, 2,794 undergraduate students, 94% full-time, 59% women, 41% men
Urban 60-acre campus with easy access to Orlando
Minimally difficult entrance level, 63% of applicants were admitted

Freshmen *Admission:* 4,024 applied, 2,681 were accepted, 832 enrolled. *Test scores:* SAT verbal scores over 500: 13%; SAT math scores over 500: 10%; SAT verbal scores over 600: 1%; SAT math scores over 600: 1%.

Bethune-Cookman College *(continued)*

Tuition and fees (2003–04): $10,106 (full-time). *Room and board:* $6374.
Financial Aid (All incoming freshmen): *Average need-based gift aid:* $7240. *Average non-need based aid:* $7155. *Average aid to full-time undergraduates:* $14,690.
Athletic Department: *Director of Athletics:* Lynn Thompson; Phone: 386-481-2216; Fax: 386-481-2251; E-mail: thompsol@cookman.edu. *Sports Information Director:* Opio Mashariki; Phone: 386-481-2206; E-mail: mashario@cookman.edu.

MEN'S COACHES
Baseball: Mervyl Melendez; Phone: 386-481-2224.
Basketball: Clifford Reed; Phone: 386-481-2214; E-mail: reedcl@cookman.edu.
Cheerleading: Sheila Jackson; Phone: 386-481-2629; E-mail: jacksosh@cookman.edu.
Football: Alvin Wyatt; Phone: 386-481-2200; E-mail: wyattc@cookman.edu.
Golf: Gary Freeman; Phone: 386-481-2214.
Tennis: Trey Bogue; Phone: 386-481-2204; E-mail: boguet@cookman.edu.

WOMEN'S COACHES
Basketball: Sandra Booker; Phone: 386-481-2217; E-mail: bookers@cookman.edu.
Cheerleading: Sheila Jackson; Phone: 386-481-2629; E-mail: jacksosh@cookman.edu.
Golf: Gary Freeman; Phone: 386-481-2247; E-mail: freemang@cookman.edu.
Softball: Laura Watten; Phone: 386-481-2245; E-mail: wattenl@cookman.edu.
Tennis: Trey Bogue; Phone: 386-481-2204; E-mail: boguet@cookman.edu.
Track and Field: Walter McCoy; Phone: 386-481-2225; E-mail: mccoym@cookman.edu.
Volleyball: Paula Thompson; Phone: 386-481-2226; E-mail: thompspa@cookman.edu.

BIOLA UNIVERSITY
La Mirada, California

Eagles ◆ NAIA ◆ Golden State Conference ◆ http://www.biola.edu/

Independent interdenominational university, founded 1908
Coed, 3,232 undergraduate students, 90% full-time, 63% women, 37% men
Suburban 95-acre campus with easy access to Los Angeles
Moderately difficult entrance level, 78% of applicants were admitted

Freshmen *Admission:* 1,901 applied, 1,483 were accepted, 814 enrolled. *Test scores:* SAT verbal scores over 500: 78%; SAT math scores over 500: 73%; SAT verbal scores over 600: 37%; SAT math scores over 600: 32%; SAT verbal scores over 700: 7%; SAT math scores over 700: 6%.
Tuition and fees (2003–04): $19,564 (full-time). *Room and board:* $5967 (room only: $3207).
Financial Aid (All incoming freshmen): *Average aid to full-time undergraduates:* $15,325.
Athletic Department: *Director of Athletics:* Dave Holmquist; Phone: 562-906-4522; Fax: 562-903-4890; E-mail: david.holmquist@bubbs.biola.edu. *Sports Information Director:* Ken Carlson; Phone: 562-903-4889; E-mail: ken.carlson@biola.edu.

MEN'S COACHES
Basketball: Dave Holmquist; Phone: 562-906-4522; E-mail: david.holmquist@bubbs.biola.edu.
Cross Country: Leroy Neal; Phone: 562-944-0351; E-mail: leroy.neal@bubbs.biola.edu.
Soccer: Bryan Kuderman; Phone: 562-944-0351; E-mail: bu.men.soccer@biola.edu.
Swimming: Phone: 562-944-0351.
Track and Field: Leroy Neal; Phone: 562-944-0351; E-mail: leroy.neal@bubbs.biola.edu.

WOMEN'S COACHES
Basketball: Tom Pryor; Phone: 562-944-0351.
Cross Country: Leroy Neal; Phone: 562-944-0351; E-mail: leroy.neal@bubbs.biola.edu.

Soccer: Michael Silzer; Phone: 562-944-0351; E-mail: bu.women.soccer@biola.edu.
Softball: Jessica Logsdon; Phone: 562-944-0351.
Swimming: Phone: 562-944-0351.
Tennis: Dee Henry; Phone: 562-944-0351; E-mail: dee.henry@bubbs.biola.edu.
Track and Field: Leroy Neal; Phone: 562-944-0351; E-mail: leroy.neal@bubbs.biola.edu.
Volleyball: Aaron Seltzer; Phone: 562-944-0351; E-mail: bu.volleyball@biola.edu.

BIRMINGHAM-SOUTHERN COLLEGE
Birmingham, Alabama

Panthers ◆ NCAA I ◆ Big South Conference ◆ http://www.bsc.edu/

Independent Methodist comprehensive, founded 1856
Coed, 1,303 undergraduate students, 98% full-time, 58% women, 42% men
Urban 196-acre campus
Moderately difficult entrance level, 87% of applicants were admitted

Freshmen *Admission:* 1,080 applied, 956 were accepted, 356 enrolled. *Test scores:* SAT verbal scores over 500: 92%; SAT math scores over 500: 88%; SAT verbal scores over 600: 59%; SAT math scores over 600: 52%; SAT verbal scores over 700: 15%; SAT math scores over 700: 13%.
Tuition and fees (2003–04): $18,930 (full-time). *Room and board:* $6104 (room only: $3444).
Financial Aid (All incoming freshmen): *Average need-based gift aid:* $7192. *Average non-need based aid:* $10,438. *Average aid to full-time undergraduates:* $14,913.
Athletic Department: *Director of Athletics:* Joe Dean; Phone: 205-226-4938; Fax: 205-226-3049; E-mail: jdean@bsc.edu. *Sports Information Director:* Jason Falls; Phone: 205-226-4905; E-mail: jfalls@bsc.edu.

MEN'S COACHES
Baseball: Brian Shoop; Phone: 205-226-4797; E-mail: bshoop@bsc.edu.
Basketball: Duane Reboul; Phone: 205-226-4889; E-mail: dreboul@bsc.edu.
Cross Country: Elisa Bragga; Phone: 205-226-7780; E-mail: ebragga@bsc.edu.
Golf: Tom Miller; Phone: 205-226-7763; E-mail: tmiller@bsc.edu.
Soccer: Preston Goldfarb; Phone: 205-226-4895; E-mail: pgoldfar@bsc.edu.
Tennis: Michael Metz; Phone: 205-226-4996; E-mail: mmetz@bsc.edu.

WOMEN'S COACHES
Basketball: Janine Hoffman; Phone: 205-226-7733; E-mail: jhoffman@bsc.edu.
Cross Country: Elisa Bragga; Phone: 205-226-7780; E-mail: ebragga@bsc.edu.
Golf: Tom Miller; Phone: 205-226-7763; E-mail: tmiller@bsc.edu.
Soccer: Keidane McAlpine; Phone: 205-226-7731; E-mail: kmcalpin@bsc.edu.
Softball: Tyra Perry; Phone: 205-226-7741; E-mail: tperry@bsc.edu.
Tennis: Ann Dielen; Phone: 205-226-4891; E-mail: adielen@bsc.edu.
Volleyball: Tonya Charland; Phone: 205-226-4944; E-mail: tlarson@bsc.edu.

BLACKBURN COLLEGE
Carlinville, Illinois

Beavers ◆ NCAA III ◆ St. Louis Athletic Conference ◆ http://www.blackburn.edu/

Independent Presbyterian 4-year, founded 1837
Coed, 615 undergraduate students, 97% full-time, 58% women, 42% men
Small-town 80-acre campus with easy access to St. Louis
Moderately difficult entrance level, 51% of applicants were admitted

Freshmen *Admission:* 792 applied, 442 were accepted, 176 enrolled.

Tuition and fees (2004–05): $12,360 (full-time). *Room and board:* $3580 (room only: $1680).
Financial Aid (All incoming freshmen): *Average need-based gift aid:* $8105. *Average non-need based aid:* $3400. *Average aid to full-time undergraduates:* $9662.
Athletic Department: *Director of Athletics:* Joe Ramsey; Phone: 217-854-3231; Fax: 217-854-5520; E-mail: jrams@mail.blackburn.edu.

MEN'S COACHES
Baseball: Mike Neal; Phone: 217-854-3231; E-mail: mneal@mail.blackburn.edu.
Basketball: David Kaneshiro; Phone: 217-854-3231; E-mail: dkane@mail.blackburn.edu.
Cross Country: Amber Daulbaugh; Phone: 217-854-3231; E-mail: adaul@mail.blackburn.edu.
Football: Skip Mathieson; Phone: 217-854-3231; E-mail: smath@mail.blackburn.edu.
Golf: Rusty Ingram; Phone: 217-854-3231; E-mail: ringr@mail.blackburn.edu.
Soccer: Gene Baker; Phone: 217-854-3231; E-mail: gbake@mail.blackburn.edu.

WOMEN'S COACHES
Basketball: Amber Daulbaugh; Phone: 217-854-3231; E-mail: adaul@mail.blackburn.edu.
Cross Country: Amber Daulbaugh; Phone: 217-854-3231; E-mail: adaul@mail.blackburn.edu.
Soccer: Gene Baker; Phone: 217-854-3231; E-mail: gbake@mail.blackburn.edu.
Softball: Kris Hoff; Phone: 217-854-3231; E-mail: khoff@mail.blackburn.edu.
Tennis: David Kaneshiro; Phone: 217-854-3231; E-mail: dkane@mail.blackburn.edu.
Volleyball: Jane Thomas; Phone: 217-854-3231; E-mail: jthom@mail.blackburn.edu.

BLACK HILLS STATE UNIVERSITY
Spearfish, South Dakota
Yellow Jackets ◆ NAIA ◆ Dakota Conference ◆ http://www.bhsu.edu/

State-supported comprehensive, founded 1883, part of South Dakota University System
Coed, 3,671 undergraduate students, 73% full-time, 64% women, 36% men
Small-town 123-acre campus
Minimally difficult entrance level, 99% of applicants were admitted

Freshmen *Admission:* 1,299 applied, 1,288 were accepted, 707 enrolled.
Tuition and fees (2003–04): $5504 (resident), $10,529 (nonresident). *Room and board:* $3196 (room only: $1716).
Athletic Department: *Director of Athletics:* Steve Meeker; Phone: 605-642-6882; Fax: 605-642-6539; E-mail: stevemeeker@bhsu.edu.

MEN'S COACHES
Basketball: Mike Kruszynski; Phone: 605-642-6607; E-mail: michaelkruszynski@bhsu.edu.
Cross Country: Scott Walkinshaw; Phone: 605-642-6486; E-mail: scottwalkinshaw@bhsu.edu.
Football: John Scott; Phone: 605-642-6036; E-mail: johnscott@bhsu.edu.
Track and Field: Scott Walkinshaw; Phone: 605-642-6486; E-mail: scottwalkinshaw@bhsu.edu.

WOMEN'S COACHES
Basketball: Mark Nore; Phone: 605-642-6886; E-mail: marknore@bhsu.edu.
Cross Country: Scott Walkinshaw; Phone: 605-642-6486; E-mail: scottwalkinshaw@bhsu.edu.
Track and Field: Scott Walkinshaw; Phone: 605-642-6486; E-mail: scottwalkinshaw@bhsu.edu.
Volleyball: Jkett Albers; Phone: 605-642-6885; E-mail: jhettalbers@bhsu.edu.

BLOOMFIELD COLLEGE
Bloomfield, New Jersey
Deacons ◆ NCAA II ◆ Central Atlantic Collegiate Conference ◆ http://www.bloomfield.edu/

Independent religious 4-year, founded 1868, affiliated with Presbyterian Church (U.S.A.)
Coed, 2,083 undergraduate students
Suburban 12-acre campus with easy access to New York City
Minimally difficult entrance level, 6% of applicants were admitted

Freshmen *Admission:* 1,712 applied, 959 were accepted. *Test scores:* SAT verbal scores over 500: 12%; SAT math scores over 500: 14%; SAT verbal scores over 600: 3%; SAT math scores over 600: 3%; SAT verbal scores over 700: 1%; SAT math scores over 700: 1%.
Tuition and fees (2004–05): $13,900 (full-time). *Room and board:* $6750 (room only: $3375).
Financial Aid (All incoming freshmen): *Average aid to full-time undergraduates:* $10,609.
Athletic Department: *Director of Athletics:* Sheila Wooten; Phone: 973-748-9000; Fax: 979-259-1085. *Sports Information Director:* Nancy D'Uva; Phone: 973-748-9000; E-mail: nancy_d'uva@bloomfield.edu.

MEN'S COACHES
Baseball: Matt Belford; Phone: 973-748-9000; E-mail: matthew_belford@bloomfield.edu.
Basketball: Gerald Homes; Phone: 973-748-9000; E-mail: gerald_holmes@bloomfield.edu.
Cross Country: Michael Grant; Phone: 973-748-9000.
Soccer: Raymond Brown; Phone: 973-748-9000.

WOMEN'S COACHES
Basketball: Jerry Wimberly; Phone: 973-748-9000; E-mail: jerry_wimberly@bloomfield.edu.
Soccer: Jose Monroy; Phone: 973-748-9000; E-mail: jose_monroy@bloomfield.edu.
Softball: Anthony Nesto; Phone: 973-748-9000; E-mail: anthony_nesto@bloomfield.edu.
Volleyball: Stephen Fenton; Phone: 973-748-9000; E-mail: stephen_fenton@bloomfield.edu.

BLOOMSBURG UNIVERSITY OF PENNSYLVANIA
Bloomsburg, Pennsylvania
Huskies ◆ NCAA II ◆ Pennsylvania State Athletic Conference ◆ http://www.bloomu.edu/

State-supported comprehensive, founded 1839, part of Pennsylvania State System of Higher Education
Coed, 7,520 undergraduate students, 93% full-time, 61% women, 39% men
Small-town 282-acre campus
Moderately difficult entrance level, 67% of applicants were admitted

Freshmen *Admission:* 7,274 applied, 5,123 were accepted, 1,671 enrolled. *Test scores:* SAT verbal scores over 500: 55%; SAT math scores over 500: 60%; SAT verbal scores over 600: 9%; SAT math scores over 600: 12%; SAT verbal scores over 700: %; SAT math scores over 700: 1%.
Tuition and fees (2003–04): $5844 (resident), $12,742 (nonresident). *Room and board:* $5000.
Financial Aid (All incoming freshmen): *Average need-based gift aid:* $3824. *Average aid to full-time undergraduates:* $11,145.
Athletic Department: *Director of Athletics:* Mary Gardner; Phone: 570-389-4050; Fax: 570-389-2099; E-mail: mgardner@bloomu.edu. *Sports Information Director:* Tom McGuire; Phone: 570-389-4413; E-mail: tmcguire@bloomu.edu.

MEN'S COACHES
Baseball: Matt Haney; Phone: 570-389-4375; E-mail: mhaney@bloomu.edu.
Basketball: Terry Conrad; Phone: 570-389-4370; E-mail: tconrad@bloomu.edu.
Cross Country: Karen Brandt; Phone: 570-389-5123; E-mail: kbrandt@bloomu.edu.

Bloomsburg University of Pennsylvania *(continued)*

Football: Danny Hale; Phone: 570-389-4359; E-mail: dhale@bloomu.edu.

Soccer: Paul Payne; Phone: 570-389-4381; E-mail: ppayne@bloomu.edu.

Swimming: R.J. Wotyak; Phone: 570-389-4155; E-mail: rwojtyla@bloomu.edu.

Tennis: Marty Coyne; Phone: 570-389-4939; E-mail: mcoyne@bloomu.edu.

Track and Field: Karen Brandt; Phone: 570-389-5123; E-mail: kbrandt@bloomu.edu.

Wrestling: Dan Wirnsberger; Phone: 570-389-4282; E-mail: dwirnsbe@bloomu.edu.

WOMEN'S COACHES

Basketball: Monica Starrett; Phone: 570-389-4683; E-mail: mstarret@bloomu.edu.

Cross Country: Karen Brandt; Phone: 570-389-5123; E-mail: kbrandt@bloomu.edu.

Field Hockey: Jan Hutchinson; Phone: 570-389-4380; E-mail: jhutchin@bloomu.edu.

Lacrosse: Kathy Frick; Phone: 570-389-4972; E-mail: kfrick@bloomu.edu.

Soccer: Sandy Dickson; Phone: 570-389-4162; E-mail: sdickson@bloomu.edu.

Softball: Jan Hutchinson; Phone: 570-389-4380; E-mail: jhutchin@bloomu.edu.

Swimming: Dave Rider; Phone: 570-389-4362; E-mail: rider@planetx.bloomu.edu.

Tennis: Marty Coyne; Phone: 570-389-4939; E-mail: mcoyne@bloomu.edu.

Track and Field: Karen Brandt; Phone: 570-389-5123; E-mail: kbrandt@bloomu.edu.

BLUEFIELD COLLEGE
Bluefield, Virginia

Rams ◆ NAIA ◆ Appalachian Conference
◆ http://www.bluefield.edu/

Independent Southern Baptist 4-year, founded 1922
Coed, 731 undergraduate students, 90% full-time, 53% women, 47% men
Small-town 85-acre campus
Moderately difficult entrance level, 64% of applicants were admitted

Freshmen *Admission:* 415 applied, 278 were accepted, 88 enrolled. *Test scores:* SAT verbal scores over 500: 31%; SAT math scores over 500: 31%; SAT verbal scores over 600: 7%; SAT math scores over 600: 7%; SAT verbal scores over 700: 2%.
Tuition and fees (2003–04): $10,165 (full-time). *Room and board:* $5410 (room only: $2090).
Financial Aid (All incoming freshmen): *Average need-based gift aid:* $7192. *Average non-need based aid:* $4764. *Average aid to full-time undergraduates:* $9153.
Athletic Department: *Director of Athletics:* Scott Bryan; Phone: 276-326-4252; Fax: 276-326-4386; E-mail: sbryan@bluefield.edu. *Sports Information Director:* Jason Massey; Phone: 276-326-4274; E-mail: jmassey@mail.bluefield.edu.

MEN'S COACHES

Baseball: Billy Berry; Phone: 276-326-4545; E-mail: wberry@bluefield.edu.

Basketball: Tommy Brown; Phone: 276-326-4251; E-mail: tbrown@bluefield.edu.

Golf: Mike Meade; Phone: 276-326-4477; E-mail: mmeade@bluefield.edu.

Soccer: Jeremy Schwartz; Phone: 276-326-4349; E-mail: jschwartz@bluefield.edu.

WOMEN'S COACHES

Basketball: Cheryl Fielitz; Phone: 276-326-4281; E-mail: cfielitz@bluefield.edu.

Soccer: Jeremy Schwartz; Phone: 276-326-4349; E-mail: jschwartz@bluefield.edu.

Softball: Steve Gore; Phone: 276-326-4402.

Volleyball: Cynthia Huff-Gore; Phone: 276-326-4402; E-mail: chuffgore@bluefield.edu.

BLUEFIELD STATE COLLEGE
Bluefield, West Virginia

Big Blues ◆ NCAA II ◆ West Virginia Intercollegiate Athletic Conference ◆ http://www.bluefieldstate.edu/

State-supported 4-year, founded 1895, part of Higher Education Policy Commission System
Coed, 3,511 undergraduate students, 68% full-time, 63% women, 37% men
Small-town 45-acre campus
Noncompetitive entrance level, 99% of applicants were admitted

Freshmen *Admission:* 1,359 applied, 1,315 were accepted, 664 enrolled. *Test scores:* SAT verbal scores over 500: 28%; SAT math scores over 500: 33%; SAT math scores over 600: 3%.
Tuition and fees (2003–04): $2806 (resident), $6894 (nonresident).
Financial Aid (All incoming freshmen): *Average need-based gift aid:* $3000. *Average non-need based aid:* $1400. *Average aid to full-time undergraduates:* $5000.
Athletic Department: *Director of Athletics:* Terry Brown; Phone: 304-327-4191; Fax: 304-327-4179; E-mail: tbrown@bluefieldstate.edu. *Sports Information Director:* Mike Proffitt; Phone: 304-327-4594.

MEN'S COACHES

Baseball: Geoff Hunter; Phone: 304-327-4084; E-mail: ghunter@bluefield.wvnet.edu.

Basketball: Charlie Puckett; Phone: 304-327-4207; E-mail: cpuckett@bluefieldstate.edu.

Cheerleading: Phone: 304-327-4208.

Cross Country: Gary Brown; Phone: 304-327-4190; E-mail: gbrown@bluefieldstate.edu.

Golf: Charles Puckett; Phone: 304-327-4207; E-mail: cpuckett@bluefieldstate.edu.

Tennis: Todd Buckingham; Phone: 304-327-4594.

WOMEN'S COACHES

Basketball: Gary Brown; Phone: 304-327-4190; E-mail: gbrown@bluefieldstate.edu.

Cheerleading: Phone: 304-327-4208.

Cross Country: Gary Brown; Phone: 304-327-4190; E-mail: gbrown@bluefieldstate.edu.

Softball: Todd Buckingham; Phone: 304-327-4594.

Tennis: Todd Buckingham; Phone: 304-327-4594.

BLUE MOUNTAIN COLLEGE
Blue Mountain, Mississippi

Toppers ◆ NAIA ◆ TranSouth Conference
◆ http://www.bmc.edu/

Independent Southern Baptist 4-year, founded 1873
Women only, 431 undergraduate students, 77% full-time, 82% women, 18% men
Rural 44-acre campus with easy access to Memphis
Minimally difficult entrance level, 6% of applicants were admitted

Freshmen *Admission:* 129 applied, 83 were accepted, 61 enrolled.
Tuition and fees (2003–04): $6800 (full-time). *Room and board:* $3526 (room only: $1300).
Financial Aid (All incoming freshmen): *Average need-based gift aid:* $2898. *Average non-need based aid:* $5915.
Athletic Department: *Director of Athletics:* Johnnie Armstrong; Phone: 662-685-4771; Fax: 626-685-4776; E-mail: johnniea1@hotmail.com.

WOMEN'S COACHES

Basketball: Jack Moser; Phone: 626-685-4771; E-mail: jmoser@bmc.edu.

Tennis: Bill Dowdy; Phone: 626-685-4771; E-mail: dowdy@bmc.edu.

BLUFFTON COLLEGE
Bluffton, Ohio

Beavers ◆ NCAA III ◆ Heartland Collegiate Conference ◆ http://www.bluffton.edu/

Independent Mennonite comprehensive, founded 1899
Coed, 1,056 undergraduate students, 92% full-time, 60% women, 40% men
Small-town 65-acre campus with easy access to Toledo
Moderately difficult entrance level, 74% of applicants were admitted

Freshmen *Admission:* 901 applied, 691 were accepted, 236 enrolled. *Test scores:* SAT verbal scores over 500: 59%; SAT math scores over 500: 63%; SAT verbal scores over 600: 27%; SAT math scores over 600: 17%; SAT verbal scores over 700: 3%; SAT math scores over 700: 3%.
Tuition and fees (2004–05): $18,350 (full-time). *Room and board:* $6270 (room only: $2868).
Financial Aid (All incoming freshmen): *Average need-based gift aid:* $12,061. *Average non-need based aid:* $7323. *Average aid to full-time undergraduates:* $16,665.
Athletic Department: *Director of Athletics:* Phil Talavinia; Phone: 419-358-3227; Fax: 419-358-3070; E-mail: talaviniap@bluffton.edu. *Sports Information Director:* Ben Risinger; Phone: 419-358-3070; E-mail: risingerb@bluffton.edu.

MEN'S COACHES
Baseball: James Grandey; Phone: 419-358-3292; E-mail: grandeyj@bluffton.edu.
Basketball: Guy Neal; Phone: 419-358-3222; E-mail: nealg@bluffton.edu.
Cross Country: Phone: 419-358-3898.
Football: Greg Brooks; Phone: 419-358-3225; E-mail: brooksg@bluffton.edu.
Golf: Allen Curtiss; Phone: 419-358-3226; E-mail: curtissc@bluffton.edu.
Soccer: Steve Smucker; Phone: 419-358-3010; E-mail: smuckers@bluffton.edu.
Tennis: Blake Kindle; Phone: 419-358-3424; E-mail: kindleb@bluffton.edu.
Track and Field: Nate Smith; Phone: 419-358-3031; E-mail: smithn@bluffton.edu.

WOMEN'S COACHES
Basketball: Amanda Curtis; Phone: 419-358-3224; E-mail: curtisa@bluffton.edu.
Cross Country: Phone: 419-358-3898.
Golf: Laura Goins; Phone: 419-358-3354; E-mail: goinsl@bluffton.edu.
Soccer: Steve Smucker; Phone: 419-358-3010; E-mail: smuckers@bluffton.edu.
Softball: Holly Spann; Phone: 419-358-3376; E-mail: spannh@bluffton.edu.
Tennis: Nate Smith; Phone: 419-358-3031; E-mail: smithn@bluffton.edu.
Track and Field: Nate Smith; Phone: 419-358-3031; E-mail: smithn@bluffton.edu.
Volleyball: Sara Wakefield; Phone: 419-358-3223; E-mail: wakefields@bluffton.edu.

BOISE STATE UNIVERSITY
Boise, Idaho

Broncos ◆ NCAA I ◆ Pacific-10 Conference; Western Athletic Conference ◆ http://www.boisestate.edu/

State-supported comprehensive, founded 1932, part of Idaho System of Higher Education
Coed, 16,551 undergraduate students, 63% full-time, 54% women, 46% men
Urban 130-acre campus
Minimally difficult entrance level, 92% of applicants were admitted

Freshmen *Admission:* 3,900 applied, 3,602 were accepted, 2,137 enrolled.
Tuition and fees (2003–04): $3251 (resident), $9971 (nonresident). *Room and board:* $4426.

Financial Aid (All incoming freshmen): *Average need-based gift aid:* $3234. *Average non-need based aid:* $1070. *Average aid to full-time undergraduates:* $6165.
Athletic Department: *Director of Athletics:* Gene Bleymaier; Phone: 208-426-1826; Fax: 208-426-3361; E-mail: gbleyma@boisestate.edu. *Sports Information Director:* Lori Hays; Phone: 208-426-3438; E-mail: lhays@boisestate.edu.

MEN'S COACHES
Basketball: Gregg Graham; Phone: 208-426-4214; E-mail: ggraham@boisestate.edu.
Cheerleading: Julie Stevens; Phone: 208-426-4355; E-mail: jstevens@boisestate.edu.
Cross Country: Mike Maynard; Phone: 208-426-3657; E-mail: maynard@boisestate.edu.
Football: Dan Hawkins; Phone: 208-426-1281; E-mail: dhawkins@boisestate.edu.
Golf: Mike Young; Phone: 208-426-3747; E-mail: myoung@boisestate.edu.
Tennis: Greg Patton; Phone: 208-426-5706; E-mail: gpatton@boisestate.edu.
Track and Field: Mike Maynard; Phone: 208-426-3657; E-mail: maynard@boisestate.edu.
Wrestling: Gregg Randall; Phone: 208-426-1889; E-mail: grandall@boisestate.edu.

WOMEN'S COACHES
Basketball: Jen Warden; Phone: 208-426-1952; E-mail: jwarden@boisestate.edu.
Cheerleading: Julie Stevens; Phone: 208-426-4355; E-mail: jstevens@boisestate.edu.
Cross Country: Mike Maynard; Phone: 208-426-3657; E-mail: maynard@boisestate.edu.
Golf: Lisa Wasinger; Phone: 208-426-3167; E-mail: lwasinger@boisestate.edu.
Gymnastics: Sam Sandmire; Phone: 208-426-1657; E-mail: ssandmi@boisestate.edu.
Soccer: Steve Lucas; Phone: 208-426-5425; E-mail: slucas@boisestate.edu.
Tennis: Mark Tichenor; Phone: 208-426-5709; E-mail: mtichenor@boisestate.edu.
Track and Field: Mike Maynard; Phone: 208-426-3657; E-mail: maynard@boisestate.edu.
Volleyball: Scott Sandel; Phone: 208-426-1656; E-mail: ssandel@boisestate.edu.

BOSTON COLLEGE
Chestnut Hill, Massachusetts

Eagles ◆ NCAA I ◆ Big East Conference; Hockey East Conference ◆ http://www.bc.edu/

Independent Roman Catholic (Jesuit) university, founded 1863
Coed, 8,851 undergraduate students, 100% full-time, 52% women, 48% men
Suburban 240-acre campus with easy access to Boston
Very difficult entrance level, 3% of applicants were admitted

Freshmen *Admission:* 22,424 applied, 6,896 were accepted, 1,839 enrolled. *Test scores:* SAT verbal scores over 500: 96%; SAT math scores over 500: 98%; SAT verbal scores over 600: 79%; SAT math scores over 600: 87%; SAT verbal scores over 700: 23%; SAT math scores over 700: 36%.
Tuition and fees (2003–04): $27,542 (full-time). *Room and board:* $9300 (room only: $5650).
Financial Aid (All incoming freshmen): *Average need-based gift aid:* $17,386. *Average non-need based aid:* $5193. *Average aid to full-time undergraduates:* $22,072.
Athletic Department: *Director of Athletics:* Gene Defilippo; Phone: 617-552-4681; Fax: 617-552-2080; E-mail: eugene.defilippo.2@bc.edu. *Sports Information Director:* Richard Kelley; Phone: 617-552-3039; E-mail: richard.kelley.1@bc.edu.

MEN'S COACHES
Baseball: Peter Hughes; Phone: 617-552-3092; E-mail: peter.hughes.1@bc.edu.
Basketball: Al Skinner; Phone: 617-552-3006; E-mail: mens.basketball@bc.edu.

Boston College (continued)

Cheerleading: Erika Beam; Phone: 617-552-3005; E-mail: erika.beam.1@bc.edu.
Cross Country: Randy Thomas; Phone: 617-552-3008; E-mail: cross.country@bc.edu.
Diving: Deanna Zechmann; Phone: 617-552-3037; E-mail: swimming.diving@bc.edu.
Football: Tom O'Brien; Phone: 617-552-3010; E-mail: bc.football@bc.edu.
Golf: Trevor Drum; Phone: 617-552-1643; E-mail: trevor.drum.1@bc.edu.
Ice Hockey: Jerry York; Phone: 617-552-3028; E-mail: mens.icehockey@bc.edu.
Soccer: Ed Kelly; Phone: 617-552-4084; E-mail: mens.soccer@bc.edu.
Swimming: Tom Groden; Phone: 617-552-3037; E-mail: thomas.groden.1@bc.edu.
Tennis: Scott Wilkens; Phone: 617-552-3169; E-mail: scott.wilkins.1@bc.edu.
Track and Field: Randy Thomas; Phone: 617-552-3008; E-mail: track.field@bc.edu.

WOMEN'S COACHES

Basketball: Cathy Inglese; Phone: 617-552-4530; E-mail: womens.basketball@bc.edu.
Cheerleading: Erika Beam; Phone: 617-552-3005; E-mail: erika.beam.1@bc.edu.
Cross Country: Randy Thomas; Phone: 617-552-3008; E-mail: cross.country@bc.edu.
Diving: Deanna Zechmann; Phone: 617-552-3037; E-mail: swimming.diving@bc.edu.
Field Hockey: Sherren Granese; Phone: 617-552-3410; E-mail: field.hockey@bc.edu.
Golf: Frank Kolarik; Phone: 617-552-8759; E-mail: francis.kolarik.1@bc.edu.
Lacrosse: Shari Krasnoo; Phone: 617-552-8959; E-mail: shari.krasnoo.1@bc.edu.
Soccer: Alison Foley; Phone: 617-552-3214; E-mail: alison.foley.1@bc.edu.
Softball: Jennifer Finley; Phone: 617-552-3107; E-mail: jennifer.finley.1@bc.edu.
Swimming: Tom Groden; Phone: 617-552-3037; E-mail: thomas.groden.1@bc.edu.
Tennis: Nigel Bentley; Phone: 617-552-3171; E-mail: nigel.bentley.1@bc.edu.
Track and Field: Randy Thomas; Phone: 617-552-3008; E-mail: track.field@bc.edu.
Volleyball: Andrea Leonard; Phone: 617-552-8520; E-mail: andrea.leonard.1@bc.edu.

BOSTON UNIVERSITY
Boston, Massachusetts

Terriers ◆ NCAA I ◆ America East Conference; Hockey East Conference ◆ http://www.bu.edu/

Independent university, founded 1839
Coed, 17,681 undergraduate students, 92% full-time, 59% women, 41% men
Urban 132-acre campus
Very difficult entrance level, 5% of applicants were admitted

Freshmen *Admission:* 29,356 applied, 15,191 were accepted, 3,961 enrolled. *Test scores:* SAT verbal scores over 500: 100%; SAT math scores over 500: 100%; SAT verbal scores over 600: 78%; SAT math scores over 600: 85%; SAT verbal scores over 700: 21%; SAT math scores over 700: 25%.
Tuition and fees (2003–04): $28,906 (full-time). *Room and board:* $9288 (room only: $5930).
Financial Aid (All incoming freshmen): *Average need-based gift aid:* $17,289. *Average non-need based aid:* $11,902. *Average aid to full-time undergraduates:* $24,669.
Athletic Department: *Director of Athletics:* Gary Strickler; Phone: 617-353-1905; Fax: 617-353-5286; E-mail: gskrinar@bu.edu. *Sports Information Director:* Ed Carpenter; Phone: 617-353-2872; E-mail: busid@bu.edu.

MEN'S COACHES

Basketball: Dennis Wolff; Phone: 617-353-5864; E-mail: djwolff@bu.edu.

Cross Country: Bruce Lehane; Phone: 617-353-6092; E-mail: lehane@bu.edu.
Diving: Agnes Miller; Phone: 617-353-4633; E-mail: agmiller@bu.edu.
Golf: Gary Skrinar; Phone: 617-353-2717; E-mail: gskrinar@bu.edu.
Ice Hockey: Jack Parker; Phone: 617-353-4639.
Soccer: Neil Roberts; Phone: 617-353-2766; E-mail: neilrob@bu.edu.
Swimming: Reagh Wetmore; Phone: 617-353-4633; E-mail: rwetmore@bu.edu.
Tennis: Jeremy Taylor; Phone: 617-353-2846; E-mail: taylorj@bu.edu.
Track and Field: Pete Schuderi; Phone: 617-353-2911; E-mail: pschuder@bu.edu.
Wrestling: Carl Adams; Phone: 617-353-2757; E-mail: cadams@bu.edu.

WOMEN'S COACHES

Basketball: Margaret McKeon; Phone: 617-353-4669; E-mail: mckeon@bu.edu.
Cross Country: Bruce Lehane; Phone: 617-353-6092; E-mail: lehane@bu.edu.
Diving: Agnes Miller; Phone: 617-353-4633; E-mail: agmiller@bu.edu.
Field Hockey: Sally Starr; Phone: 617-353-3039; E-mail: sfstarr@bu.edu.
Golf: Cammy Landry; Phone: 617-353-7761; E-mail: cammyl@hotmail.com.
Lacrosse: Liza Shoemaker; Phone: 617-353-8457; E-mail: lizas@bu.edu.
Soccer: Nancy Feldman; Phone: 617-353-8456; E-mail: buwosoc@bu.edu.
Softball: Amy Hayes; Phone: 617-353-5409; E-mail: amyhayes@bu.edu.
Swimming: Reagh Wetmore; Phone: 617-353-4633; E-mail: rwetmore@bu.edu.
Tennis: Lesley Sheehan; Phone: 617-353-3235; E-mail: lsheehan@bu.edu.
Track and Field: Lesley Lehane; Phone: 617-353-6092; E-mail: lehane@bu.edu.

BOWDOIN COLLEGE
Brunswick, Maine

Polar Bears ◆ NCAA III ◆ New England Small College Conference ◆ http://www.bowdoin.edu/

Independent 4-year, founded 1794
Coed, 1,647 undergraduate students, 100% full-time, 49% women, 51% men
Small-town 200-acre campus with easy access to Portland
Most difficult entrance level, 2% of applicants were admitted

Freshmen *Admission:* 4,719 applied, 1,154 were accepted, 465 enrolled. *Test scores:* SAT verbal scores over 500: 99%; SAT math scores over 500: 99%; SAT verbal scores over 600: 92%; SAT math scores over 600: 91%; SAT verbal scores over 700: 47%; SAT math scores over 700: 40%.
Tuition and fees (2003–04): $30,120 (full-time). *Room and board:* $7670 (room only: $3450).
Financial Aid (All incoming freshmen): *Average need-based gift aid:* $23,916. *Average non-need based aid:* $1000. *Average aid to full-time undergraduates:* $27,162.
Athletic Department: *Director of Athletics:* Jeff Ward; Phone: 207-725-3016; Fax: 207-725-3019; E-mail: jward2@bowdoin.edu. *Sports Information Director:* James Caton; Phone: 207-725-3254; E-mail: jcaton@bowdoin.edu.

MEN'S COACHES

Baseball: Michael Connolly; Phone: 207-725-3751; E-mail: mconnoll@bowdoin.edu.
Basketball: Tim Gilbride; Phone: 207-725-3352; E-mail: tgilbrid@bowdoin.edu.
Cross Country: Peter Slovenski; Phone: 207-725-3010; E-mail: pslovens@bowdoin.edu.
Diving: Harvey Wheeler; Phone: 207-725-3527.
Football: David Caputi; Phone: 207-725-3746; E-mail: dcaputi@bowdoin.edu.
Golf: Tomas Fortson; Phone: 207-725-3984; E-mail: tfortson@bowdoin.edu.
Ice Hockey: Terry Meagher; Phone: 207-725-3328; E-mail: tmeagher@bowdoin.edu.
Lacrosse: Tom Mccabe; Phone: 207-725-3351; E-mail: tmccabe@bowdoin.edu.
Soccer: Brian Ainscough; Phone: 207-725-3665; E-mail: bainscou@bowdoin.edu.

Swimming: Brad Burnham; Phone: 207-725-3527; E-mail: bburnham@bowdoin.edu.
Tennis: Jane Patterson; Phone: 207-725-3310; E-mail: jpaterso@bowdoin.edu.
Track and Field: Peter Slovenski; Phone: 207-725-3010; E-mail: pslovens@bowdoin.edu.

WOMEN'S COACHES
Basketball: Stephanie Pemper; Phone: 207-725-3649; E-mail: spemper@bowdoin.edu.
Cross Country: Peter Slovenski; Phone: 207-725-3010; E-mail: pslovens@bowdoin.edu.
Diving: Harvey Wheeler; Phone: 207-725-3527.
Field Hockey: Nicola Pearson; Phone: 207-725-3329; E-mail: npearson@bowdoin.edu.
Lacrosse: Elizabeth Grote; Phone: 207-725-4148; E-mail: egrote@bowdoin.edu.
Soccer: John Cullen; Phone: 207-725-3721; E-mail: jcullen@bowdoin.edu.
Softball: Dawn Strout; Phone: 207-725-3945; E-mail: dstrout@bowdoin.edu.
Swimming: Brad Burnham; Phone: 207-725-3527; E-mail: bburnham@bowdoin.edu.
Tennis: Jane Patterson; Phone: 207-725-3310; E-mail: jpaterso@bowdoin.edu.
Track and Field: Peter Slovenski; Phone: 207-725-3010; E-mail: pslovens@bowdoin.edu.
Volleyball: Kellie Bearman; Phone: 207-725-3371; E-mail: kbearman@bowdoin.edu.

BOWIE STATE UNIVERSITY
Bowie, Maryland

Bulldogs ◆ NCAA II ◆ Central Intercollegiate Athletic Conference ◆ http://www.bowiestate.edu/

State-supported comprehensive, founded 1865, part of University System of Maryland
Coed, 3,988 undergraduate students, 78% full-time, 63% women, 37% men
Small-town 312-acre campus with easy access to Baltimore and Washington, DC
Minimally difficult entrance level, 46% of applicants were admitted

Freshmen *Admission:* 3,537 applied, 1,704 were accepted, 771 enrolled. *Test scores:* SAT verbal scores over 500: 19%; SAT math scores over 500: 18%; SAT verbal scores over 600: 2%; SAT math scores over 600: 3%.
Tuition and fees (2003–04): $4722 (resident), $12,065 (nonresident). *Room and board:* $6020 (room only: $4337).
Financial Aid (All incoming freshmen): *Average need-based gift aid:* $4776. *Average non-need based aid:* $3224. *Average aid to full-time undergraduates:* $7061.
Athletic Department: *Director of Athletics:* Renardo Hall; Phone: 301-860-3393; Fax: 301-860-3585; E-mail: rhall@bowiestate.edu.

MEN'S COACHES
Basketball: Luke D'Alessio; Phone: 301-860-3576.
Cheerleading: Tonja Thomas; Phone: 301-860-3572; E-mail: goldengirls66@hotmail.com.
Cross Country: Marc Harrison; Phone: 301-860-3575; E-mail: mharrison@bowiestate.edu.
Football: Henry Frazier; Phone: 301-860-3578; E-mail: hfrazier@bowiestate.edu.
Track and Field: Marc Harrison; Phone: 301-860-3575; E-mail: mharrison@bowiestate.edu.

WOMEN'S COACHES
Basketball: Russell Davis; Phone: 301-860-3573.
Cheerleading: Tonja Thomas; Phone: 301-860-3572; E-mail: goldengirls66@hotmail.com.
Cross Country: Marc Harrison; Phone: 301-860-3575; E-mail: mharrison@bowiestate.edu.
Softball: Ken Scott; Phone: 301-860-3571.
Tennis: Monique Graves; Phone: 301-860-3571.
Track and Field: Marc Harrison; Phone: 301-860-3575; E-mail: mharrison@bowiestate.edu.
Volleyball: Melody Webb; Phone: 301-860-3583.

BOWLING GREEN STATE UNIVERSITY
Bowling Green, Ohio

Falcons ◆ NCAA I ◆ Central Collegiate Hockey Conference; Mid-American Conference ◆ http://www.bgsu.edu/

State-supported university, founded 1910
Coed, 15,481 undergraduate students, 93% full-time, 56% women, 44% men
Small-town 1,230-acre campus with easy access to Toledo
Moderately difficult entrance level, 89% of applicants were admitted

Freshmen *Admission:* 10,281 applied, 9,283 were accepted, 3,541 enrolled. *Test scores:* SAT verbal scores over 500: 53%; SAT math scores over 500: 53%; SAT verbal scores over 600: 16%; SAT math scores over 600: 17%; SAT verbal scores over 700: 3%; SAT math scores over 700: 3%.
Tuition and fees (2003–04): $7144 (resident), $14,104 (nonresident). *Room and board:* $5892 (room only: $3642).
Financial Aid (All incoming freshmen): *Average need-based gift aid:* $3295. *Average non-need based aid:* $2653. *Average aid to full-time undergraduates:* $7701.
Athletic Department: *Director of Athletics:* Paul Krebs; Phone: 419-372-2401; Fax: 419-372-6969; E-mail: pkrebs@bgnet.bgsu.edu. *Sports Information Director:* J.D. Campbell; Phone: 419-372-2401; E-mail: jdcampb@bgnet.bgsu.edu.

MEN'S COACHES
Baseball: Dan Schmitz; Phone: 419-372-2401; E-mail: danjs@bgnet.bgsu.edu.
Basketball: Dan Dakich; Phone: 419-372-2255.
Cross Country: Cami Wells; Phone: 419-372-2401; E-mail: clwells@bgnet.bgsu.edu.
Football: Gregg Brandon; Phone: 419-372-2401; E-mail: greggb@bgnet.bgsu.edu.
Golf: Garry Winger; Phone: 419-372-2401; E-mail: gwinger@bgnet.bgsu.edu.
Ice Hockey: Scott Palugh; Phone: 419-372-2964; E-mail: spaluch@bgnet.bgsu.edu.
Soccer: Mel Mahler; Phone: 419-372-2964; E-mail: soccer@bgnet.bgsu.edu.

WOMEN'S COACHES
Basketball: Curt Miller; Phone: 419-372-2401; E-mail: millerc@bgnet.bgsu.edu.
Cross Country: Cami Wells; Phone: 419-372-2401; E-mail: clwells@bgnet.bgsu.edu.
Diving: Jane Wobser; Phone: 419-372-2060.
Golf: Kurt Thomas; Phone: 419-372-2401; E-mail: kurttom@bgnet.bgsu.edu.
Gymnastics: Dan Connelly; Phone: 419-372-2401; E-mail: cdan@bgnet.bgsu.edu.
Soccer: Andy Richards; Phone: 419-372-2401; E-mail: arich@bgnet.bgsu.edu.
Softball: Leigh Ross-Shaw; Phone: 419-372-2401; E-mail: rleigh@bgnet.bgsu.edu.
Swimming: Keri Buff; Phone: 419-372-2060.
Tennis: Penny Dean; Phone: 419-372-2401; E-mail: jdean@bgnet.bgsu.edu.
Track and Field: Scott Sehmann; Phone: 419-372-2401; E-mail: sehmans@bgnet.bgsu.edu.
Volleyball: Denise Van Dewalle; Phone: 419-372-2401; E-mail: denisev@bgnet.bgsu.edu.

BRADLEY UNIVERSITY
Peoria, Illinois

Braves ◆ NCAA I ◆ Missouri Valley Conference ◆ http://www.bradley.edu/

Independent comprehensive, founded 1897
Coed, 5,305 undergraduate students, 93% full-time, 54% women, 46% men
Urban 75-acre campus with easy access to Chicago and St. Louis
Moderately difficult entrance level, 66% of applicants were admitted

Freshmen *Admission:* 5,207 applied, 3,570 were accepted, 1,105 enrolled. *Test scores:* SAT verbal scores over 500: 81%; SAT math scores over 500: 82%; SAT verbal scores over 600: 40%; SAT math scores over 600: 46%; SAT verbal scores over 700: 4%; SAT math scores over 700: 8%.
Tuition and fees (2003–04): $16,930 (full-time). *Room and board:* $5980 (room only: $3400).
Financial Aid (All incoming freshmen): *Average need-based gift aid:* $8907. *Average non-need based aid:* $9614. *Average aid to full-time undergraduates:* $11,545.
Athletic Department: *Director of Athletics:* Ken Kavanagh; Phone: 309-677-2670; Fax: 309-677-3626; E-mail: kavanagh@bradley.edu. *Sports Information Director:* Bobby Parker; Phone: 309-677-2624; E-mail: bparker@bumail.bradley.edu.

MEN'S COACHES
Baseball: Dewey Kalmer; Phone: 309-677-2684; E-mail: dvk@bradley.edu.
Basketball: Jim Les; Phone: 309-677-2668; E-mail: jles@bradley.edu.
Cheerleading: Katie Kuhns; Phone: 309-677-3266.
Cross Country: David Beachem; Phone: 309-677-2643; E-mail: djb@bradley.edu.
Golf: Dave Schliepsiek; Phone: 309-677-4410; E-mail: dschliep@bradley.edu.
Soccer: Jim Derose; Phone: 309-677-2674; E-mail: derose@bradley.edu.
Tennis: Drew Barrett; Phone: 309-677-4567; E-mail: barrett@bradley.edu.

WOMEN'S COACHES
Basketball: Paula Buscher; Phone: 309-677-2666; E-mail: rrunyon@bradley.edu.
Cheerleading: Katie Kuhns; Phone: 309-677-3266.
Cross Country: David Beachem; Phone: 309-677-2643; E-mail: djb@bradley.edu.
Golf: Bo Ryan; Phone: 309-677-2627; E-mail: rryan@bradley.edu.
Golf: Bo Ryan; Phone: 309-677-2627; E-mail: rryan@bradley.edu.
Softball: Venus Taylor; Phone: 309-677-2692; E-mail: vtaylor@bradley.edu.
Tennis: Sheryl Sattler; Phone: 309-677-2675; E-mail: sattler@bradley.edu.
Track and Field: David Beachem; Phone: 309-677-2643; E-mail: djb@bradley.edu.
Volleyball: Scott Luster; Phone: 309-677-2649; E-mail: luster@bradley.edu.

BRANDEIS UNIVERSITY
Waltham, Massachusetts

Judges ◆ NCAA III ◆ University Athletic Conference ◆ http://www.brandeis.edu/

Independent university, founded 1948
Coed, 3,175 undergraduate students, 99% full-time, 56% women, 44% men
Suburban 235-acre campus with easy access to Boston
Most difficult entrance level, 40% of applicants were admitted

Freshmen *Admission:* 5,770 applied, 2,524 were accepted, 824 enrolled. *Test scores:* SAT verbal scores over 500: 100%; SAT math scores over 500: 98%; SAT verbal scores over 600: 87%; SAT math scores over 600: 83%; SAT verbal scores over 700: 33%; SAT math scores over 700: 31%.
Tuition and fees (2003–04): $29,875 (full-time). *Room and board:* $8323 (room only: $4675).

Financial Aid (All incoming freshmen): *Average need-based gift aid:* $18,208. *Average non-need based aid:* $14,182. *Average aid to full-time undergraduates:* $22,569.
Athletic Department: *Director of Athletics:* Jeff Cohen; Phone: 781-736-3632; Fax: 781-736-3656; E-mail: cohenjef@brandeis.edu. *Sports Information Director:* Adam Levin; Phone: 781-736-3631; E-mail: aslevin@brandeis.edu.

MEN'S COACHES
Baseball: Pete Varney; Phone: 781-736-3639; E-mail: varney@brandeis.edu.
Basketball: Brian Meehan; Phone: 781-736-3634.
Cheerleading: Lauren Belden; Phone: 781-736-3630.
Cross Country: Jean Cann; Phone: 781-736-3654; E-mail: jeancann@brandeis.edu.
Diving: Jim Brainerd; Phone: 781-736-3651.
Golf: Bill Shipman; Phone: 781-736-3650; E-mail: shipman@brandeis.edu.
Soccer: Mike Coven; Phone: 781-736-3638.
Swimming: James Zotz; Phone: 781-736-3649; E-mail: zotz@brandeis.edu.
Tennis: Rocky Jarvis; Phone: 781-736-3648; E-mail: jarvis@brandeis.edu.
Track and Field: Jean Cann; Phone: 781-736-3654; E-mail: jeancann@brandeis.edu.

WOMEN'S COACHES
Basketball: Carol Simon; Phone: 781-736-3646; E-mail: csimon@brandeis.edu.
Cheerleading: Lauren Belden; Phone: 781-736-3630.
Cross Country: Jean Cann; Phone: 781-736-3654; E-mail: jeancann@brandeis.edu.
Diving: Jim Brainerd; Phone: 781-736-3651.
Soccer: Denise Dallamora; Phone: 781-736-3644; E-mail: dallamora@brandeis.edu.
Softball: Mary Sullivan; Phone: 781-736-3643; E-mail: sullivan@brandeis.edu.
Swimming: James Zotz; Phone: 781-736-3649; E-mail: zotz@brandeis.edu.
Tennis: Rocky Jarvis; Phone: 781-736-3648; E-mail: jarvis@brandeis.edu.
Track and Field: Jean Cann; Phone: 781-736-3654; E-mail: jeancann@brandeis.edu.
Volleyball: Sheryl Sousa; Phone: 781-736-3663; E-mail: sousa@brandeis.edu.

BRENAU UNIVERSITY
Gainesville, Georgia

Golden Tigers ◆ NAIA ◆ Georgia Alabama Carolina Conference ◆ http://www.brenau.edu/

Independent comprehensive, founded 1878
Women only, 586 undergraduate students, 92% full-time, 100% women, 100% men
Small-town 57-acre campus with easy access to Atlanta
Moderately difficult entrance level, 74% of applicants were admitted

Freshmen *Admission:* 333 applied, 247 were accepted, 121 enrolled. *Test scores:* SAT verbal scores over 500: 51%; SAT math scores over 500: 43%; SAT verbal scores over 600: 17%; SAT math scores over 600: 9%; SAT verbal scores over 700: 2%.
Tuition and fees (2004–05): Comprehensive fee (includes tuition, fees, and room and board): $22,670.
Financial Aid (All incoming freshmen): *Average need-based gift aid:* $13,726. *Average non-need based aid:* $7661. *Average aid to full-time undergraduates:* $15,407.
Athletic Department: *Director of Athletics:* Bill Rogers; Phone: 770-534-6230; Fax: 770-534-6221.

WOMEN'S COACHES
Soccer: Mike Lochstampfor; Phone: 770-534-6231.
Tennis: Bill Rogers; Phone: 770-534-6230.
Volleyball: Scott Haney; Phone: 770-534-6230; E-mail: shaney@lib.brenau.edu.

BRESCIA UNIVERSITY
Owensboro, Kentucky

Bearcats ◆ NAIA ◆ Kentucky Intercollegiate Conference ◆ http://www.brescia.edu/

Independent Roman Catholic comprehensive, founded 1950
Coed
Urban 9-acre campus
Moderately difficult entrance level, 73% of applicants were admitted

Freshmen *Admission:* 264 applied, 210 were accepted.
Tuition and fees (2003–04): $10,820 (full-time). *Room and board:* $4800 (room only: $3600).
Financial Aid (All incoming freshmen): *Average need-based gift aid:* $4965. *Average non-need based aid:* $8729. *Average aid to full-time undergraduates:* $5516.
Athletic Department: *Director of Athletics:* John Reilly; Phone: 270-686-4292; E-mail: johnr@brescia.edu. *Sports Information Director:* Jason Vittone; Phone: 270-686-4207; E-mail: jasonv@brescia.edu.

MEN'S COACHES
Baseball: Jason Vittone; Phone: 270-686-4207; E-mail: jasonv@brescia.edu.
Basketball: John Reilly; Phone: 270-686-4292; E-mail: johnr@brescia.edu.
Golf: Marty Rowe; Phone: 270-686-4317; E-mail: martyr@brescia.edu.
Soccer: Bill Ashby; Phone: 270-686-4341; E-mail: billa@brescia.edu.

WOMEN'S COACHES
Basketball: Marty Rowe; Phone: 270-686-4317; E-mail: martyr@brescia.edu.
Golf: Marty Rowe; Phone: 270-686-4317; E-mail: martyr@brescia.edu.
Soccer: Bill Ashby; Phone: 270-686-4341; E-mail: billa@brescia.edu.
Softball: Brad Huskisson; Phone: 270-686-4330; E-mail: bradh1@brescia.edu.
Tennis: Phone: 270-686-4330.
Volleyball: Serena Springer; Phone: 270-686-4330; E-mail: springer71@adelphia.net.

BREVARD COLLEGE
Brevard, North Carolina

Tornados ◆ NAIA ◆ Appalachian Conference ◆ http://www.brevard.edu/

Independent United Methodist 4-year, founded 1853
Coed, 604 undergraduate students, 94% full-time, 46% women, 54% men
Small-town 120-acre campus
Minimally difficult entrance level, 82% of applicants were admitted

Freshmen *Admission:* 534 applied, 436 were accepted, 157 enrolled. *Test scores:* SAT verbal scores over 500: 49%; SAT math scores over 500: 41%; SAT verbal scores over 600: 11%; SAT math scores over 600: 8%; SAT verbal scores over 700: 3%.
Tuition and fees (2003–04): $13,680 (full-time). *Room and board:* $5510.
Financial Aid (All incoming freshmen): *Average need-based gift aid:* $9940. *Average non-need based aid:* $2445. *Average aid to full-time undergraduates:* $12,150.
Athletic Department: *Director of Athletics:* Gill Payne; Phone: 828-883-8230; Fax: 828-884-3790; E-mail: gpayne@brevard.edu. *Sports Information Director:* Kelly Jones; Phone: 828-883-8288; E-mail: jonesk@brevard.edu.

MEN'S COACHES
Baseball: Gill Payne; Phone: 828-884-8230; E-mail: gpayne@brevard.edu.
Basketball: Mike Jones; Phone: 828-884-8267; E-mail: jonesms@brevard.edu.
Cheerleading: Kristen Weaver; Phone: 828-884-8230; E-mail: weaverkm@brevard.edu.
Cross Country: Thomas Cason; Phone: 828-884-8228; E-mail: casonwt@brevard.edu.
Golf: Phone: 828-884-8230.
Soccer: Michael Louter; Phone: 828-884-8394; E-mail: loutermj@brevard.edu.
Track and Field: Thomas Cason; Phone: 828-884-8228; E-mail: casonwt@brevard.edu.

WOMEN'S COACHES
Basketball: Tammy George; Phone: 828-884-8241; E-mail: georgetl@brevard.edu.
Cheerleading: Kristen Weaver; Phone: 828-884-8230; E-mail: weaverkm@brevard.edu.
Cross Country: Thomas Cason; Phone: 828-884-8228; E-mail: casonwt@brevard.edu.
Soccer: Thorsten Path; Phone: 828-884-8222; E-mail: paththor@brevard.edu.
Softball: Kelly Jones; Phone: 828-884-8288; E-mail: jonesk@brevard.edu.
Track and Field: Thomas Cason; Phone: 828-884-8228; E-mail: casonwt@brevard.edu.
Volleyball: Brenda Skeffington; Phone: 828-884-8203; E-mail: skeffib@brevard.edu.

BREWTON-PARKER COLLEGE
Mt. Vernon, Georgia

NAIA ◆ Georgia Alabama Carolina Conference ◆ http://www.bpc.edu/

Independent Southern Baptist 4-year, founded 1904
Coed, 1,109 undergraduate students, 79% full-time, 65% women, 35% men
Rural 280-acre campus
Minimally difficult entrance level, 97% of applicants were admitted

Freshmen *Admission:* 522 applied, 500 were accepted, 282 enrolled. *Test scores:* SAT verbal scores over 500: 41%; SAT math scores over 500: 33%; SAT verbal scores over 600: 11%; SAT math scores over 600: 7%; SAT verbal scores over 700: 2%.
Tuition and fees (2004–05): $11,070 (full-time). *Room and board:* $4450 (room only: $2150).
Financial Aid (All incoming freshmen): *Average need-based gift aid:* $6270. *Average non-need based aid:* $6655. *Average aid to full-time undergraduates:* $7827.
Athletic Department: *Director of Athletics:* Steve Barker; Phone: 912-583-3178; Fax: 912-583-4352; E-mail: sbarker@bpc.edu. *Sports Information Director:* Bill Glass; Phone: 912-583-3180; E-mail: bglass@bpc.edu.

MEN'S COACHES
Baseball: Chad Parker; Phone: 912-583-3274; E-mail: cparker@bpc.edu.
Basketball: Steve Barker; Phone: 912-583-3178; E-mail: sbarker@bpc.edu.
Soccer: Ben Moore; Phone: 912-583-3181; E-mail: bmoore@bpc.edu.

WOMEN'S COACHES
Basketball: Sheila Simmons; Phone: 912-583-3176; E-mail: ssimmons@bpc.edu.
Soccer: Bill Glass; Phone: 912-583-3180; E-mail: bglass@bpc.edu.
Softball: Jason Bryant; Phone: 912-583-3182; E-mail: jbryant@bpc.edu.
Volleyball: Jason Bryant; Phone: 912-583-3182; E-mail: jbryant@bpc.edu.

BRIAR CLIFF UNIVERSITY
Sioux City, Iowa

Chargers ◆ NAIA ◆ Great Plains Conference ◆ http://www.briarcliff.edu/

Independent Roman Catholic comprehensive, founded 1930
Coed, 1,063 undergraduate students, 83% full-time, 60% women, 40% men
Suburban 70-acre campus
Moderately difficult entrance level, 77% of applicants were admitted

Freshmen *Admission:* 1,297 applied, 1,040 were accepted, 258 enrolled. *Test scores:* SAT verbal scores over 600: 50%; SAT math scores over 600: 50%.

Briar Cliff University *(continued)*

Tuition and fees (2003–04): $16,350 (full-time). *Room and board:* $5310 (room only: $2655).

Financial Aid (All incoming freshmen): *Average need-based gift aid:* $4980. *Average non-need based aid:* $3700. *Average aid to full-time undergraduates:* $16,410.

Athletic Department: *Director of Athletics:* Dick Strittmatter; Phone: 712-279-1617; Fax: 712-279-5592; E-mail: strittmatterd@briarcliff.edu. *Sports Information Director:* Jared Bodammer; Phone: 712-279-1653; E-mail: bodammerj@briarcliff.edu.

MEN'S COACHES

Baseball: Boyd Pitkin; Phone: 712-279-5553; E-mail: pitkin@briarcliff.edu.

Basketball: Mike Beard; Phone: 712-279-5441; E-mail: beardm@briarcliff.edu.

Cross Country: Brian Betzold; Phone: 712-279-5593; E-mail: betzoldb@briarcliff.edu.

Football: Dick Strittmatter; Phone: 712-279-1617; E-mail: strittmatterd@briarcliff.edu.

Golf: Brian Eben; Phone: 712-279-1634; E-mail: ebenb@briarcliff.edu.

Soccer: Tim Mann; Phone: 712-279-1656; E-mail: mannt@briarcliff.edu.

Track and Field: Brian Betzold; Phone: 712-279-5593; E-mail: betzoldb@briarcliff.edu.

Wrestling: Andy Krueger; Phone: 712-279-1716.

WOMEN'S COACHES

Basketball: Pam Gohl; Phone: 712-279-5493; E-mail: hupkeh@briarcliff.edu.

Cross Country: Brian Betzold; Phone: 712-279-5593; E-mail: betzoldb@briarcliff.edu.

Golf: Emily Beswick; Phone: 712-279-1775; E-mail: beswicke@briarcliff.edu.

Soccer: Jared Bodammer; Phone: 712-279-1653; E-mail: bodammerj@briarcliff.edu.

Softball: Heather Hupke; Phone: 712-279-1686; E-mail: hupkeh@briarcliff.edu.

Track and Field: Brian Betzold; Phone: 712-279-5593; E-mail: betzoldb@briarcliff.edu.

Volleyball: Mary Schroeder; Phone: 712-279-5262; E-mail: schrodm@briarcliff.edu.

BRIDGEWATER COLLEGE
Bridgewater, Virginia

Eagles ◆ NCAA III ◆ Old Dominion Conference ◆ http://www.bridgewater.edu/

Independent religious 4-year, founded 1880, affiliated with Church of the Brethren

Coed, 1,403 undergraduate students, 98% full-time, 55% women, 45% men

Small-town 190-acre campus

Moderately difficult entrance level, 85% of applicants were admitted

Freshmen *Admission:* 1,388 applied, 1,221 were accepted, 391 enrolled. *Test scores:* SAT verbal scores over 500: 53%; SAT math scores over 500: 56%; SAT verbal scores over 600: 14%; SAT math scores over 600: 16%; SAT verbal scores over 700: 2%; SAT math scores over 700: 1%.

Tuition and fees (2004–05): $17,990 (full-time). *Room and board:* $8480 (room only: $4245).

Financial Aid (All incoming freshmen): *Average need-based gift aid:* $12,450. *Average non-need based aid:* $6097. *Average aid to full-time undergraduates:* $15,840.

Athletic Department: *Director of Athletics:* Curt Kendall; Phone: 540-828-5407; Fax: 540-828-5484; E-mail: ckendall@bridgewater.edu. *Sports Information Director:* Steve Cox; Phone: 540-828-5360; E-mail: scox@bridgewater.edu.

MEN'S COACHES

Baseball: Curt Kendall; Phone: 540-828-5407; E-mail: ckendall@bridgewater.edu.

Basketball: Bill Leatherman; Phone: 540-828-5403; E-mail: bleather@bridgewater.edu.

Cheerleading: Maria Dove; Phone: 540-828-9883; E-mail: mdove1999@aol.com.

Cross Country: Lori Shrock; Phone: 540-828-5712; E-mail: lschrock@bridgewater.edu.

Football: Mike Clark; Phone: 540-828-5406; E-mail: mclark@bridgewater.edu.

Golf: Leroy Williams; Phone: 540-828-5626; E-mail: lwilliam@bridgewater.edu.

Soccer: Mike Brizendine; Phone: 540-828-5756; E-mail: mbrizend@bridgewater.edu.

Tennis: Steve Watson; Phone: 540-828-5345; E-mail: swatson@bridgewater.edu.

Track and Field: Shane Stevens; Phone: 540-828-5465; E-mail: sstevens@bridgewater.edu.

WOMEN'S COACHES

Basketball: Jean Willi; Phone: 540-828-5400; E-mail: jwilli@bridgewater.edu.

Cheerleading: Maria Dove; Phone: 540-828-9883; E-mail: mdove1999@aol.com.

Cross Country: Lori Shrock; Phone: 540-828-5682; E-mail: lschrock@bridgewater.edu.

Field Hockey: Ally Kenyon; Phone: 540-828-5784; E-mail: akenyon@bridgewater.edu.

Lacrosse: Amy Hamilton; Phone: 540-828-5777; E-mail: ahamilto@bridgewater.edu.

Soccer: Mike Brizendine; Phone: 540-828-5756; E-mail: mbrizend@bridgewater.edu.

Softball: Donnie Fulk; Phone: 540-828-5390; E-mail: dfulk@bridgewater.edu.

Tennis: Mimi Knight; Phone: 540-828-5402; E-mail: tbricker@bridgewater.edu.

Track and Field: Shane Stevens; Phone: 540-828-5465; E-mail: sstevens@bridgewater.edu.

Volleyball: Mary Frances Heishman; Phone: 540-828-5405; E-mail: mheishma@bridgewater.edu.

BRIDGEWATER STATE COLLEGE
Bridgewater, Massachusetts

Bears ◆ NCAA III ◆ Little East Conference; Massachusetts State College Athletic Conference; New England Football Conference; New England Women's Lacrosse Conference ◆ http://www.bridgew.edu/

State-supported comprehensive, founded 1840, part of Massachusetts Public Higher Education System

Coed, 7,597 undergraduate students, 82% full-time, 61% women, 39% men

Suburban 235-acre campus with easy access to Boston

Moderately difficult entrance level, 69% of applicants were admitted

Freshmen *Admission:* 5,540 applied, 4,005 were accepted, 1,304 enrolled. *Test scores:* SAT verbal scores over 500: 56%; SAT math scores over 500: 56%; SAT verbal scores over 600: 10%; SAT math scores over 600: 11%; SAT verbal scores over 700: 1%; SAT math scores over 700: %.

Tuition and fees (2004–05): $4560 (resident), $10,700 (nonresident). *Room and board:* $5922 (room only: $3552).

Financial Aid (All incoming freshmen): *Average need-based gift aid:* $3396. *Average non-need based aid:* $3876. *Average aid to full-time undergraduates:* $6230.

Athletic Department: *Director of Athletics:* John Harper; Phone: 978-531-1353; Fax: 978-531-5353; E-mail: jharper@bridgew.edu. *Sports Information Director:* Mike Holbrook; Phone: 978-531-2656; E-mail: mholbrook@bridgew.edu.

MEN'S COACHES

Baseball: Rick Smith; Phone: 508-531-1352; E-mail: mdcabinetry@msn.com.

Basketball: Joe Farroba; Phone: 508-531-1352; E-mail: bridgew_hoops@bridgew.edu.

Cross Country: Ed Delgado; Phone: 508-531-1352; E-mail: edelgado110hh@aol.com.

Diving: Rob Ferreira; Phone: 508-531-1352; E-mail: rferreira25@hotmail.com.

Football: Peter Mazzaferro; Phone: 508-531-2073; E-mail: pmazzaferro@bridgew.edu.

Soccer: Brendan Adams; Phone: 508-531-1352; E-mail: kbadams@bridgew.edu.

Swimming: Brett Oteri; Phone: 508-531-1352; E-mail: boteri@bridgew.edu.
Tennis: Mike Bradley; Phone: 508-531-1352; E-mail: mjbradley@bridgew.edu.
Track and Field: Ed Delgado; Phone: 508-531-1352; E-mail: edelgado110hh@aol.com.
Wrestling: Mike Kenney; Phone: 508-531-1352; E-mail: m1kenney@bridgew.edu.

WOMEN'S COACHES
Basketball: Bridgett Casey; Phone: 508-531-1352; E-mail: bcasey@bridgew.edu.
Cross Country: Ed Delgado; Phone: 508-531-1352; E-mail: edelgado110hh@aol.com.
Diving: Rob Ferreira; Phone: 508-531-1352; E-mail: rferreira25@hotmail.com.
Field Hockey: Courtney Evans; Phone: 508-531-1352; E-mail: cpevans@bridgew.edu.
Lacrosse: Josh Hexter; Phone: 508-588-5388; E-mail: jhexter@bridgew.edu.
Soccer: Andrea Zeigler; Phone: 508-531-1352; E-mail: andreazeigler@comcast.net.
Softball: Janet Maguire; Phone: 508-531-1352; E-mail: jmaguire@bridgew.edu.
Swimming: Brett Oteri; Phone: 508-531-1352; E-mail: boteri@bridgew.edu.
Tennis: Charles Robinson; Phone: 508-531-1352; E-mail: crobinson@bridgew.edu.
Track and Field: Ed Delgado; Phone: 508-531-1352; E-mail: edelgado110hh@aol.com.
Volleyball: Ken Duarte; Phone: 508-531-1352; E-mail: kduarte@bridgew.edu.

BRIGHAM YOUNG UNIVERSITY
Provo, Utah
Cougars ◆ NCAA I ◆ Mountain West Conference ◆ http://www.byu.edu/

Independent religious university, founded 1875, affiliated with The Church of Jesus Christ of Latter-day Saints, part of Church Education System (CES) of The Church of Jesus Christ of Latter-day Saints
Coed, 29,932 undergraduate students, 89% full-time, 49% women, 51% men
Suburban 557-acre campus with easy access to Salt Lake City
Moderately difficult entrance level, 79% of applicants were admitted

Freshmen *Admission:* 9,300 applied, 7,227 were accepted, 5,331 enrolled. *Test scores:* SAT verbal scores over 500: 91%; SAT math scores over 500: 94%; SAT verbal scores over 600: 54%; SAT math scores over 600: 60%; SAT verbal scores over 700: 14%; SAT math scores over 700: 17%.
Tuition and fees (2003–04): $3150 (full-time). *Room and board:* $5354.
Financial Aid (All incoming freshmen): *Average need-based gift aid:* $1644. *Average non-need based aid:* $2878. *Average aid to full-time undergraduates:* $2434.
Athletic Department: *Director of Athletics:* Val Hale; Phone: 801-422-8704; Fax: 801-378-5981; E-mail: val_hale@byu.edu. *Sports Information Director:* Norma Collett; Phone: 801-422-4908; E-mail: norma_collett@byu.edu.

MEN'S COACHES
Baseball: Vance Law; Phone: 801-378-5049; E-mail: val4@email.byu.edu.
Basketball: Steve Cleveland; Phone: 801-378-3612; E-mail: steve_cleveland@byu.edu.
Cheerleading: Nate Felt; Phone: 801-422-8014; E-mail: stancafelt@hotmail.com.
Cross Country: Ed Eyestone; Phone: 801-422-3329.
Diving: Keith Russell; Phone: 801-422-4874; E-mail: keith_russell@byu.edu.
Football: Gary Crowton; Phone: 801-422-2916; E-mail: football@byucougars.com.
Golf: Bruce Brockbank; Phone: 801-422-7304; E-mail: brb3@email.byu.edu.
Swimming: Tim Powers; Phone: 801-422-2143; E-mail: timothy_powers@byu.edu.

Tennis: Brad Pearce; Phone: 801-422-3679; E-mail: jho3@email.byu.edu.
Track and Field: Mark Robison; Phone: 801-422-3830; E-mail: mark_robison@byu.edu.
Volleyball: Tom Peterson; Phone: 801-422-8291; E-mail: tom_peterson@byu.edu.

WOMEN'S COACHES
Basketball: Jeff Judkins; Phone: 801-422-1265; E-mail: jeff_judkins@byu.edu.
Cheerleading: Nate Felt; Phone: 801-422-8014; E-mail: stancafelt@hotmail.com.
Cross Country: Patrick Shane; Phone: 801-422-7922; E-mail: pes4@email.byu.edu.
Diving: Keith Russell; Phone: 801-422-4874; E-mail: keith_russell@byu.edu.
Golf: Sue Nyhus; Phone: 801-422-9787; E-mail: sbn5@email.byu.edu.
Gymnastics: Brad Cattermole; Phone: 801-422-4769; E-mail: bc29@email.byu.edu.
Soccer: Jennifer Rockwood; Phone: 801-422-8732; E-mail: jrockwood@byu.edu.
Softball: Gordon Eakin; Phone: 801-422-1158; E-mail: ge7@email.byu.edu.
Swimming: Stan Crump; Phone: 801-422-2396; E-mail: timothy_powers@byu.edu.
Tennis: Craig Manning; Phone: 801-422-8729; E-mail: craig_manning@byu.edu.
Track and Field: Craig Poole; Phone: 801-422-7508; E-mail: mark_robison@byu.edu.
Volleyball: Karen Lamb; Phone: 801-422-2808; E-mail: kl6@email.byu.edu.

BRIGHAM YOUNG UNIVERSITY–HAWAII
Laie, Hawaii
Seasiders ◆ NCAA II ◆ Pacific West Conference ◆ http://www.byuh.edu/

Independent Latter-day Saints 4-year, founded 1955
Coed, 2,703 undergraduate students, 90% full-time, 54% women, 46% men
Small-town 60-acre campus with easy access to Honolulu
Moderately difficult entrance level, 3% of applicants were admitted

Freshmen *Admission:* 2,989 applied, 860 were accepted, 262 enrolled.
Tuition and fees (2003–04): $2580 (full-time). *Room and board:* $4660 (room only: $2000).
Financial Aid (All incoming freshmen): *Average need-based gift aid:* $3000. *Average non-need based aid:* $1245. *Average aid to full-time undergraduates:* $2200.
Athletic Department: *Director of Athletics:* Ken Wagner; Phone: 808-293-3764; Fax: 808-293-3763; E-mail: wagnerk@byuh.edu. *Sports Information Director:* Scott Lowe; Phone: 808-293-3764; E-mail: lowes@byuh.edu.

MEN'S COACHES
Basketball: Ken Wagner; Phone: 808-293-3764; E-mail: wagnerk@byuh.edu.
Cheerleading: Berenice Elkington; Phone: 808-293-3764.
Cross Country: Norman Kaluhiokalani; Phone: 808-293-3752; E-mail: kaluhion@byuh.edu.
Tennis: David Porter; Phone: 808-293-3755; E-mail: porterd@byuh.edu.

WOMEN'S COACHES
Cheerleading: Berenice Elkington; Phone: 808-293-3764.
Cross Country: Norman Kaluhiokalani; Phone: 808-293-3752; E-mail: kaluhion@byuh.edu.
Softball: Jackson Mapu; Phone: 808-293-3423; E-mail: mapuj@byuh.edu.
Volleyball: Wilfred Navalta; Phone: 808-293-3756; E-mail: navaltaw@byuh.edu.

BROOKLYN COLLEGE OF THE CITY UNIVERSITY OF NEW YORK
Brooklyn, New York

Bridges ◆ NCAA III ◆ CUNY Athletic Conference ◆ http://www.brooklyn.cuny.edu/

State and locally supported comprehensive, founded 1930, part of City University of New York System
Coed, 10,960 undergraduate students, 70% full-time, 60% women, 40% men
Urban 26-acre campus
Moderately difficult entrance level, 39% of applicants were admitted

Freshmen *Admission:* 7,128 applied, 2,595 were accepted, 1,349 enrolled. *Test scores:* SAT verbal scores over 500: 56%; SAT math scores over 500: 67%; SAT verbal scores over 600: 16%; SAT math scores over 600: 21%; SAT verbal scores over 700: 3%; SAT math scores over 700: 3%.
Tuition and fees (2004–05): $4353 (resident), $8993 (nonresident).
Financial Aid (All incoming freshmen): *Average need-based gift aid:* $3300. *Average non-need based aid:* $4000. *Average aid to full-time undergraduates:* $5400.
Athletic Department: *Director of Athletics:* Bruce Filosa; Phone: 718-951-5366; Fax: 718-951-4882; E-mail: bfilosa@brooklyn.cuny.edu. *Sports Information Director:* Alex Lang; Phone: 718-951-5366; E-mail: alang@brooklyn.cuny.edu.

MEN'S COACHES
Basketball: Steve Podias; Phone: 718-951-5366.
Cross Country: Ricardo Haughton; Phone: 718-951-5366.
Soccer: Antonio Supendia; Phone: 718-951-5366.
Tennis: Frank Davis; Phone: 718-951-5366.
Track and Field: Ricardo Haughton; Phone: 718-951-5366.
Volleyball: Andrew Woolward; Phone: 718-951-5366.

WOMEN'S COACHES
Basketball: Alex Lang; Phone: 718-951-5366; E-mail: alang@brooklyn.cuny.edu.
Cross Country: Ricardo Haughton; Phone: 718-951-5366.
Softball: Jaclyn Apicello; Phone: 718-951-5366.
Tennis: Maria Bucca; Phone: 718-951-5366.
Track and Field: Ricardo Haughton; Phone: 718-951-5366.
Volleyball: Danielle Madden; Phone: 718-951-5366.

BROWN UNIVERSITY
Providence, Rhode Island

Bears ◆ NCAA I ◆ Ivy League Conference; Ivy League Conference ◆ http://www.brown.edu/

Independent university, founded 1764
Coed, 5,906 undergraduate students, 96% full-time, 55% women, 45% men
Urban 140-acre campus with easy access to Boston
Most difficult entrance level, 18% of applicants were admitted

Freshmen *Admission:* 15,157 applied, 2,442 were accepted, 1,393 enrolled. *Test scores:* SAT verbal scores over 500: 98%; SAT math scores over 500: 99%; SAT verbal scores over 600: 87%; SAT math scores over 600: 91%; SAT verbal scores over 700: 51%; SAT math scores over 700: 55%.
Tuition and fees (2003–04): $29,846 (full-time). *Room and board:* $8096 (room only: $5030).
Financial Aid (All incoming freshmen): *Average need-based gift aid:* $22,313. *Average aid to full-time undergraduates:* $24,635.
Athletic Department: *Director of Athletics:* David Roach; Phone: 401-863-2972; Fax: 401-863-1436; E-mail: david_roach@brown.edu. *Sports Information Director:* Christopher Humm; Phone: 401-863-1095; E-mail: christopher_humm@brown.edu.

MEN'S COACHES
Baseball: Marek Drabinski; Phone: 401-863-3090; E-mail: alice_watson@brown.edu.
Basketball: Glen Miller; Phone: 401-863-1226; E-mail: glen_miller@brown.edu.
Cheerleading: Kent Stetson; Phone: 401-863-3090.
Cross Country: Robert Johnson; Phone: 401-863-2400; E-mail: brown_track@brown.edu.
Diving: Peter Brown; Phone: 401-863-1919; E-mail: peter_brown@brown.edu.
Football: Phil Estes; Phone: 401-863-2424; E-mail: francis_sheehan@brown.edu.
Golf: Ed Hanley; Phone: 401-863-2603; E-mail: michael_harbour@brown.edu.
Ice Hockey: Roger Grillo; Phone: 401-863-1915; E-mail: roger_grillo@brown.edu.
Lacrosse: Scott Nelson; Phone: 401-863-3780; E-mail: scott_nelson@brown.edu.
Soccer: Mike Noonan; Phone: 401-863-2349; E-mail: michael_noonan@brown.edu.
Swimming: Peter Brown; Phone: 401-863-1919; E-mail: peter_brown@brown.edu.
Tennis: Jay Harris; Phone: 401-863-3637; E-mail: jay_harris@brown.edu.
Track and Field: Robert Johnson; Phone: 401-863-2400; E-mail: brown_track@brown.edu.
Wrestling: Dave Amato; Phone: 401-863-3089; E-mail: david_amato@brown.edu.

WOMEN'S COACHES
Basketball: Jean Burr; Phone: 401-863-2383; E-mail: jean_burr@brown.edu.
Cheerleading: Kent Stetson; Phone: 401-863-3090.
Cross Country: Robert Johnson; Phone: 401-863-2400; E-mail: brown_track@brown.edu.
Diving: Peter Brown; Phone: 401-863-1919; E-mail: peter_brown@brown.edu.
Field Hockey: Carolyn Norris; Phone: 401-863-3052; E-mail: carolan_norris@brown.edu.
Golf: Mike Harbour; Phone: 401-863-2603; E-mail: michael_harbour@brown.edu.
Gymnastics: Sara Carver Milne; Phone: 401-863-1950; E-mail: sara_carver@brown.edu.
Lacrosse: Theresa Ingram; Phone: 401-863-9378; E-mail: theresa_ingram@brown.edu.
Soccer: Phil Pincince; Phone: 401-863-1952; E-mail: phil_pincince@brown.edu.
Softball: Pam McCreesh; Phone: 401-863-7583; E-mail: pam_mccreesh@brown.edu.
Swimming: Peter Brown; Phone: 401-863-1919; E-mail: peter_brown@brown.edu.
Tennis: Norma Taylor; Phone: 401-863-2104; E-mail: norma_taylor@brown.edu.
Track and Field: Robert Johnson; Phone: 401-863-2400; E-mail: brown_track@brown.edu.
Volleyball: Diane Short; Phone: 401-863-7418; E-mail: diane_short@brown.edu.

BRYAN COLLEGE
Dayton, Tennessee

Lions ◆ NAIA ◆ Appalachian Conference ◆ http://www.bryan.edu/

Independent interdenominational 4-year, founded 1930
Coed, 557 undergraduate students
Small-town 100-acre campus
Moderately difficult entrance level, 35% of applicants were admitted

Freshmen *Admission:* 539 applied, 186 were accepted. *Test scores:* SAT verbal scores over 500: 76%; SAT math scores over 500: 68%; SAT verbal scores over 600: 31%; SAT math scores over 600: 23%; SAT verbal scores over 700: 11%; SAT math scores over 700: 6%.
Tuition and fees (2003–04): $13,500 (full-time). *Room and board:* $4400.
Financial Aid (All incoming freshmen): *Average need-based gift aid:* $3813. *Average non-need based aid:* $4766. *Average aid to full-time undergraduates:* $9150.
Athletic Department: *Director of Athletics:* Sandy Zensen; Phone: 423-775-7255; Fax: 423-775-7485; E-mail: zensensa@bryan.edu.

MEN'S COACHES
Baseball: Preston Douglas; Phone: 423-775-7569; E-mail: douglapr@bryan.edu.

Basketball: Morris Michalski; Phone: 423-775-7310; E-mail: michalmo@bryan.edu.
Soccer: Sandy Zensen; Phone: 423-775-7255; E-mail: zensensa@bryan.edu.

WOMEN'S COACHES
Basketball: Matt Bollant; Phone: 423-775-7255.
Soccer: Marc Neddo; Phone: 423-775-7235; E-mail: neddoma@bryan.edu.
Volleyball: Jerri Morgan; Phone: 423-775-7263; E-mail: morganje@bryan.edu.

BRYANT COLLEGE
Smithfield, Rhode Island

Bulldogs ◆ NCAA II ◆ Northeast-10 Conference ◆ http://www.bryant.edu/

Independent comprehensive, founded 1863
Coed, 2,976 undergraduate students, 92% full-time, 41% women, 59% men
Suburban 392-acre campus with easy access to Boston and Providence
Moderately difficult entrance level, 5% of applicants were admitted

---

Freshmen *Admission:* 3,910 applied, 2,320 were accepted, 778 enrolled. *Test scores:* SAT verbal scores over 500: 74%; SAT math scores over 500: 86%; SAT verbal scores over 600: 15%; SAT math scores over 600: 30%; SAT verbal scores over 700: 1%; SAT math scores over 700: 3%.
Tuition and fees (2004–05): $23,580 (full-time). *Room and board:* $8974 (room only: $5148).
Financial Aid (All incoming freshmen): *Average need-based gift aid:* $9199. *Average non-need based aid:* $7660. *Average aid to full-time undergraduates:* $15,609.
Athletic Department: *Director of Athletics:* Dan Gavitt; Phone: 401-232-6070; Fax: 401-232-6076; E-mail: dgavitt@bryant.edu. *Sports Information Director:* Jason Sullivan; Phone: 401-232-6072; E-mail: jsulliva@bryant.edu.

MEN'S COACHES
Baseball: Jon Siogren; Phone: 401-232-6397; E-mail: jsjogren@bryant.edu.
Basketball: Max Good; Phone: 401-232-6077; E-mail: mgood@bryant.edu.
Cheerleading: Jessica Fiore; Phone: 401-232-6070; E-mail: fiorejess@yahoo.com.
Cross Country: Amy Laughlin; Phone: 401-232-6526; E-mail: laughlin@bryant.edu.
Football: Marty Fine; Phone: 401-232-6399.
Golf: Archie Boulet; Phone: 401-232-6222.
Lacrosse: Rory Whipple; Phone: 401-232-6974; E-mail: rwhipple@bryant.edu.
Soccer: Seamus Purcell; Phone: 401-232-6718; E-mail: spurcell@bryant.edu.
Tennis: Larry Sack; Phone: 401-232-6354.
Track and Field: Amy Laughlin; Phone: 401-232-6526; E-mail: laughlin@bryant.edu.

WOMEN'S COACHES
Basketball: Mary Burke; Phone: 401-232-6075; E-mail: mlburke@bryant.edu.
Cheerleading: Jessica Fiore; Phone: 401-232-6070; E-mail: fiorejess@yahoo.com.
Cross Country: Amy Laughlin; Phone: 401-232-6526; E-mail: laughlin@bryant.edu.
Field Hockey: Coni Fichera; Phone: 401-232-6975; E-mail: cfichera@bryant.edu.
Golf: Kris Kennedy; Phone: 401-232-6316; E-mail: kkennedy@bryant.edu.
Lacrosse: Conie Fichera; Phone: 401-232-6975; E-mail: cfichera@bryant.edu.
Soccer: Chris Flint; Phone: 401-232-6511; E-mail: cflint@bryant.edu.
Softball: Lisa Ann Wallace; Phone: 401-232-6074; E-mail: lwallace@bryant.edu.
Tennis: Barbara Cilli; Phone: 401-232-6468; E-mail: bcilli@bryant.edu.
Track and Field: Amy Laughlin; Phone: 401-232-6526; E-mail: laughlin@bryant.edu.
Volleyball: Theresa Garlacy; Phone: 401-232-6360; E-mail: tgarlac@bryant.edu.

BRYN MAWR COLLEGE
Bryn Mawr, Pennsylvania

Mawrters ◆ NCAA III ◆ Centennial Conference ◆ http://www.brynmawr.edu/

Independent university, founded 1885
Women only, 1,334 undergraduate students, 96% full-time, 98% women, 2% men
Suburban 135-acre campus with easy access to Philadelphia
Most difficult entrance level, 51% of applicants were admitted

---

Freshmen *Admission:* 1,748 applied, 899 were accepted, 352 enrolled. *Test scores:* SAT verbal scores over 500: 98%; SAT math scores over 500: 99%; SAT verbal scores over 600: 82%; SAT math scores over 600: 68%; SAT verbal scores over 700: 38%; SAT math scores over 700: 15%.
Tuition and fees (2003–04): $27,520 (full-time). *Room and board:* $9370 (room only: $5400).
Financial Aid (All incoming freshmen): *Average need-based gift aid:* $21,413. *Average aid to full-time undergraduates:* $25,888.
Athletic Department: *Director of Athletics:* Amy Campbell; Phone: 610-526-7364; Fax: 610-526-7347; E-mail: acampbel@brynmawr.edu. *Sports Information Director:* Danya Pilgrim; Phone: 610-526-7308; E-mail: dpilgrim@brynmawr.edu.

WOMEN'S COACHES
Basketball: Rebecca Cusumano-Seidel; Phone: 610-526-7344; E-mail: rcusuman@brynmawr.edu.
Cross Country: Dan Talbot; Phone: 610-526-7306; E-mail: dtalbot@brynmawr.edu.
Field Hockey: Danya Pilgrim; Phone: 610-526-7308; E-mail: dpilgrim@brynmawr.edu.
Lacrosse: Katie Tarr; Phone: 610-526-7305; E-mail: ktarr@brynmawr.edu.
Soccer: Amy Nakamoto; Phone: 610-526-7345; E-mail: anakamot@brynmawr.edu.
Swimming: Judy Wolfe; Phone: 610-526-7349; E-mail: jwolfe@brynmawr.edu.
Tennis: Judy Law; Phone: 610-526-7309; E-mail: jlaw@brynmawr.edu.
Track and Field: Dan Talbot; Phone: 610-526-7306; E-mail: dtalbot@brynmawr.edu.
Volleyball: Joan Braid; Phone: 610-526-6579; E-mail: jbraid@brynmawr.edu.

BUCKNELL UNIVERSITY
Lewisburg, Pennsylvania

Bison ◆ NCAA I ◆ Big South Conference; Patriot League Conference ◆ http://www.bucknell.edu/

Independent comprehensive, founded 1846
Coed, 3,486 undergraduate students, 99% full-time, 50% women, 50% men
Small-town 445-acre campus
Very difficult entrance level, 37% of applicants were admitted

---

Freshmen *Admission:* 7,706 applied, 2,961 were accepted, 906 enrolled. *Test scores:* SAT verbal scores over 500: 99%; SAT math scores over 500: 100%; SAT verbal scores over 600: 77%; SAT math scores over 600: 88%; SAT verbal scores over 700: 15%; SAT math scores over 700: 29%.
Tuition and fees (2003–04): $28,960 (full-time). *Room and board:* $6302 (room only: $3365).
Financial Aid (All incoming freshmen): *Average need-based gift aid:* $17,500. *Average non-need based aid:* $3250. *Average aid to full-time undergraduates:* $21,500.
Athletic Department: *Director of Athletics:* John Hardt; Phone: 570-577-1232; E-mail: jhardt@bucknell.edu. *Sports Information Director:* Joe Terry; Phone: 570-577-1227; E-mail: terry@bucknell.edu.

MEN'S COACHES
Baseball: Gene Depew; Phone: 570-577-3593; E-mail: depew@bucknell.edu.
Basketball: Pat Flannery; Phone: 570-577-1267; E-mail: flannery@bucknell.edu.

Bucknell University *(continued)*

Cheerleading: Heather Walters; Phone: 570-577-1232; E-mail: hwalters@bucknell.edu.
Cross Country: Kevin Donner; Phone: 570-577-1482; E-mail: kdonner@bucknell.edu.
Diving: Errol Carter; Phone: 570-577-1530; E-mail: ecarter@bucknell.edu.
Football: Tim Landis; Phone: 570-577-1134; E-mail: tlandis@bucknell.edu.
Golf: Jim Cotner; Phone: 570-577-3075; E-mail: jcotner@bucknell.edu.
Lacrosse: Sid Jamieson; Phone: 570-577-3059; E-mail: jamieson@bucknell.edu.
Soccer: Brenden Nash; Phone: 570-577-3083; E-mail: bnash@bucknell.edu.
Swimming: Jerry Foley; Phone: 570-577-1530; E-mail: foley@bucknell.edu.
Tennis: Rebecca Helt; Phone: 570-577-3598; E-mail: helt@bucknell.edu.
Track and Field: Kevin Donner; Phone: 570-577-1482; E-mail: kdonner@bucknell.edu.

WOMEN'S COACHES
Basketball: Kathy Fedorjaka; Phone: 570-577-3919; E-mail: fedorjka@bucknell.edu.
Cheerleading: Heather Walters; Phone: 570-577-1232; E-mail: hwalters@bucknell.edu.
Cross Country: Kevin Donner; Phone: 570-577-1482; E-mail: kdonner@bucknell.edu.
Diving: Errol Carter; Phone: 570-577-1530; E-mail: ecarter@bucknell.edu.
Field Hockey: Heather Lewis; Phone: 570-577-1927; E-mail: hlewis@bucknell.edu.
Golf: Kevin Jamieson; Phone: 570-577-8193; E-mail: kjamieso@bucknell.edu.
Lacrosse: Randall Flynn; Phone: 570-577-3717; E-mail: rflynn@bucknell.edu.
Soccer: Chrissy Findlay; Phone: 570-577-1772; E-mail: cfindlay@bucknell.edu.
Softball: Janelle Brenemain; Phone: 570-577-3553; E-mail: jbrenema@bucknell.edu.
Swimming: Jerry Foley; Phone: 570-577-1530; E-mail: foley@bucknell.edu.
Tennis: Rebecca Helt; Phone: 570-577-3598; E-mail: helt@bucknell.edu.
Volleyball: Cindy Opalski; Phone: 570-577-3048; E-mail: copalski@bucknell.edu.

BUENA VISTA UNIVERSITY
Storm Lake, Iowa

Beavers ◆ NCAA III ◆ Iowa Athletic Conference ◆ http://www.bvu.edu/

Independent religious comprehensive, founded 1891, affiliated with Presbyterian Church (U.S.A.)
Coed, 1,288 undergraduate students, 98% full-time, 53% women, 47% men
Small-town 60-acre campus
Moderately difficult entrance level, 85% of applicants were admitted

Freshmen *Admission:* 1,333 applied, 1,125 were accepted, 378 enrolled.
Tuition and fees (2003–04): $19,862 (full-time). *Room and board:* $5544.
Financial Aid (All incoming freshmen): *Average need-based gift aid:* $13,367. *Average non-need based aid:* $11,472. *Average aid to full-time undergraduates:* $19,418.
Athletic Department: *Director of Athletics:* Jan Travis; Phone: 712-749-2016; Fax: 712-749-1460; E-mail: travisj@bvu.edu. *Sports Information Director:* Paul Misner; Phone: 712-749-2633; E-mail: misnerp@bvu.edu.

MEN'S COACHES
Baseball: Steve Eddie; Phone: 712-749-2298; E-mail: eddies@bvu.edu.
Basketball: Brian Van Haaften; Phone: 712-749-2252; E-mail: vanhaaften@bvu.edu.
Cross Country: Brett Carney; Phone: 712-749-2265; E-mail: carney@bvu.edu.
Diving: Deb Blanchard; Phone: 712-749-2031; E-mail: blanchard@bvu.edu.
Football: Steve Osterberger; Phone: 712-749-2259; E-mail: osterbergers@bvu.edu.
Golf: Jim Nurse; Phone: 712-749-2077; E-mail: nursej@bvu.edu.
Soccer: Matt Klosterman; Phone: 712-749-2266; E-mail: klostermanm@bvu.edu.
Swimming: Deb Blanchard; Phone: 712-749-2031; E-mail: blanchard@bvu.edu.
Tennis: John Johnson; Phone: 712-749-2253.
Track and Field: Brett Carney; Phone: 712-749-2265; E-mail: carney@bvu.edu.
Wrestling: Mark Schwab; Phone: 712-749-2657; E-mail: baxtera@bvu.edu.

WOMEN'S COACHES
Basketball: Janet Berry; Phone: 712-749-2137; E-mail: berry@bvu.edu.
Cross Country: Brett Carney; Phone: 712-749-2265; E-mail: carney@bvu.edu.
Diving: Deb Blanchard; Phone: 712-749-2031; E-mail: blanchard@bvu.edu.
Golf: Tom Bohnenkamp; Phone: 712-749-2253; E-mail: tombgolf@aurelia.k12.ia.us.
Soccer: Matt Klosterman; Phone: 712-749-2266; E-mail: klostermanm@bvu.edu.
Softball: Marge Willadsen; Phone: 712-749-2254; E-mail: willadsen@bvu.edu.
Swimming: Deb Blanchard; Phone: 712-749-2031; E-mail: blanchard@bvu.edu.
Tennis: John Johnson; Phone: 712-749-2253.
Track and Field: Brett Carney; Phone: 712-749-2265; E-mail: carney@bvu.edu.
Volleyball: Amy Sander; Phone: 712-749-2135; E-mail: sander@bvu.edu.

BUFFALO STATE COLLEGE, STATE UNIVERSITY OF NEW YORK
Buffalo, New York

Bengals ◆ NCAA III ◆ SUNY Athletic Conference ◆ http://www.buffalostate.edu/

State-supported comprehensive, founded 1867
Coed, 9,003 undergraduate students, 86% full-time, 60% women, 40% men
Urban 115-acre campus
Moderately difficult entrance level, 48% of applicants were admitted

Freshmen *Admission:* 7,820 applied, 4,118 were accepted, 1,365 enrolled. *Test scores:* SAT verbal scores over 500: 48%; SAT math scores over 500: 50%; SAT verbal scores over 600: 8%; SAT math scores over 600: 10%; SAT verbal scores over 700: 1%; SAT math scores over 700: 1%.
Tuition and fees (2003–04): $5059 (resident), $11,009 (nonresident). *Room and board:* $5866 (room only: $3734).
Financial Aid (All incoming freshmen): *Average need-based gift aid:* $2071. *Average non-need based aid:* $1638. *Average aid to full-time undergraduates:* $3937.
Athletic Department: *Director of Athletics:* Jerry Boyes; Phone: 716-878-6534; Fax: 716-878-3401; E-mail: boyesjs@buffalostate.edu. *Sports Information Director:* Jeff Ventura; Phone: 716-878-6030; E-mail: venturjm@buffalostate.edu.

MEN'S COACHES
Basketball: Dick Bihr; Phone: 716-878-6519; E-mail: bihrrj@bscmail.buffalostate.edu.
Cheerleading: Ali Farmer; Phone: 716-878-5420.
Cross Country: James Ramos; Phone: 716-878-5413; E-mail: ramos573@aol.com.
Diving: Mike Switalski; Phone: 716-878-3576; E-mail: switalmf@bscmail.buffalostate.edu.
Football: Bob Swank; Phone: 716-878-3634; E-mail: swankbe@bscmail.buffalostate.edu.
Ice Hockey: James Fowler; Phone: 716-878-6516; E-mail: fowlerjc@bscmail.buffalostate.edu.
Soccer: Rudy Pompert; Phone: 716-878-6631; E-mail: pomperra@buffalostate.edu.

Swimming: Mike Switalski; Phone: 716-878-3576; E-mail: switalmf@bscmail.buffalostate.edu.

Track and Field: Eugene Lewis; Phone: 716-878-3721; E-mail: lewiser@bscmail.buffalostate.edu.

WOMEN'S COACHES

Basketball: Jerome Moss; Phone: 716-878-3587; E-mail: mossj@buffalostate.edu.

Cheerleading: Ali Farmer; Phone: 716-878-5420.

Cross Country: James Ramos; Phone: 716-878-5413; E-mail: ramos573@aol.com.

Diving: Mike Switalski; Phone: 716-878-3576; E-mail: switalmf@bscmail.buffalostate.edu.

Lacrosse: Megan Stevens; Phone: 716-878-6526; E-mail: stevenma@bscmail.buffalostate.edu.

Soccer: Nick DeMarsh; Phone: 716-878-3816; E-mail: demarsna@buffalostate.edu.

Softball: Sandra Hollander; Phone: 716-878-5425; E-mail: hollansl@buffalostate.edu.

Swimming: Mike Switalski; Phone: 716-878-3576; E-mail: switalmf@bscmail.buffalostate.edu.

Track and Field: Eugene Lewis; Phone: 716-878-3721; E-mail: lewiser@bscmail.buffalostate.edu.

Volleyball: Adrienne Turley; Phone: 716-878-6509; E-mail: turleyaa@buffalostate.edu.

BUTLER UNIVERSITY
Indianapolis, Indiana

Bulldogs ◆ NCAA I ◆ Great Western Lacrosse Conference; Horizon League Conference; Pioneer Football League Conference ◆ http://www.butler.edu/

Independent comprehensive, founded 1855
Coed, 3,657 undergraduate students, 98% full-time, 63% women, 37% men
Urban 290-acre campus
Moderately difficult entrance level, 70% of applicants were admitted

Freshmen *Admission:* 4,329 applied, 3,350 were accepted, 976 enrolled. *Test scores:* SAT verbal scores over 500: 88%; SAT math scores over 500: 88%; SAT verbal scores over 600: 45%; SAT math scores over 600: 52%; SAT verbal scores over 700: 8%; SAT math scores over 700: 9%.
Tuition and fees (2003–04): $21,210 (full-time). *Room and board:* $7040 (room only: $3240).
Financial Aid (All incoming freshmen): *Average need-based gift aid:* $12,500. *Average non-need based aid:* $8300. *Average aid to full-time undergraduates:* $17,307.
Athletic Department: *Director of Athletics:* John Parry; Phone: 317-940-9878; Fax: 317-940-9808; E-mail: jparry@butler.edu. *Sports Information Director:* Jim McGrath; Phone: 317-940-9414; E-mail: jmcgrath@butler.edu.

MEN'S COACHES

Baseball: Steve Farley; Phone: 317-940-9721; E-mail: sfarley@butler.edu.

Basketball: Todd Lickliter; Phone: 317-940-9377; E-mail: tlicklit@butler.edu.

Cross Country: Joe Franklin; Phone: 317-940-9921; E-mail: jbfrankl@butler.edu.

Diving: Nicole Ellis; Phone: 317-940-9908; E-mail: nellis@butler.edu.

Football: Kit Cartwright; Phone: 317-940-9476; E-mail: ncartwri@butler.edu.

Golf: Ben Weaver; Phone: 317-297-3366; E-mail: baweaver@butler.edu.

Lacrosse: Craig Kahoun; Phone: 317-940-9316; E-mail: cekahoun@butler.edu.

Soccer: Joe Sochacki; Phone: 317-940-9922; E-mail: jsochack@butler.edu.

Swimming: Nicole Ellis; Phone: 317-940-9908; E-mail: nellis@butler.edu.

Tennis: Jason Suscha; Phone: 317-940-9253; E-mail: jsuscha@butler.edu.

Track and Field: Joe Franklin; Phone: 317-940-9921; E-mail: jbfrankl@butler.edu.

WOMEN'S COACHES

Basketball: Beth Couture; Phone: 317-940-9277; E-mail: bcouture@butler.edu.

Cross Country: Joe Franklin; Phone: 317-940-9921; E-mail: jbfrankl@butler.edu.

Diving: Nicole Ellis; Phone: 317-940-9908; E-mail: nellis@butler.edu.

Golf: Steve Jones; Phone: 317-940-9375; E-mail: spjones@butler.edu.

Soccer: Woody Sherwood; Phone: 317-940-6496; E-mail: jsherwoo@butler.edu.

Softball: Tom Spencer; Phone: 317-940-9618; E-mail: tspencer@butler.edu.

Swimming: Nicole Ellis; Phone: 317-940-9908; E-mail: nellis@butler.edu.

Tennis: Jason Suscha; Phone: 317-940-9253; E-mail: jsuscha@butler.edu.

Track and Field: Joe Franklin; Phone: 317-940-9921; E-mail: jbfrankl@butler.edu.

Volleyball: Sharon Clark; Phone: 317-940-9211; E-mail: sclark@butler.edu.

CABRINI COLLEGE
Radnor, Pennsylvania

Cavaliers ◆ NCAA III ◆ Pennsylvania Athletic Conference ◆ http://www.cabrini.edu/

Independent Roman Catholic comprehensive, founded 1957
Coed, 1,715 undergraduate students, 83% full-time, 64% women, 36% men
Suburban 112-acre campus with easy access to Philadelphia
Minimally difficult entrance level, 83% of applicants were admitted

Freshmen *Admission:* 2,302 applied, 1,910 were accepted, 403 enrolled. *Test scores:* SAT verbal scores over 500: 47%; SAT math scores over 500: 42%; SAT verbal scores over 600: 8%; SAT math scores over 600: 8%; SAT verbal scores over 700: 1%; SAT math scores over 700: 2%.
Tuition and fees (2003–04): $20,420 (full-time). *Room and board:* $8550.
Financial Aid (All incoming freshmen): *Average need-based gift aid:* $4820. *Average non-need based aid:* $6619. *Average aid to full-time undergraduates:* $12,222.
Athletic Department: *Director of Athletics:* Leslie Danehy; Phone: 610-902-8571; Fax: 610-902-8385; E-mail: ldanehy@cabrini.edu. *Sports Information Director:* Bob Macartney; Phone: 610-902-8259; E-mail: bob.macartney@cabrini.edu.

MEN'S COACHES

Basketball: John Dzik; Phone: 610-902-8386; E-mail: jdzik@cabrini.edu.

Cross Country: Tom O'Hora; Phone: 610-902-8387; E-mail: tohora@cabrini.edu.

Golf: Tony Verde; Phone: 610-902-8530; E-mail: tverde@cabrini.edu.

Lacrosse: Steve Colfer; Phone: 610-902-8557; E-mail: scolfer@cabrini.edu.

Soccer: Doug Meder; Phone: 610-902-8387; E-mail: coachmeder@aol.com.

Tennis: Rich Aldrete; Phone: 610-902-8387; E-mail: rdaldrete@aol.com.

Track and Field: Tom O'Hora; Phone: 610-902-8387; E-mail: tohora@cabrini.edu.

WOMEN'S COACHES

Basketball: Darlene Hilebrand; Phone: 610-902-8387; E-mail: darlene.m.hildebrand@cabrini.edu.

Cross Country: Tom O'Hora; Phone: 610-902-8387; E-mail: tohora@cabrini.edu.

Field Hockey: Jackie Neary; Phone: 610-902-8387; E-mail: jackie.neary@cabrini.edu.

Lacrosse: Jackie Neary; Phone: 610-902-8387; E-mail: jackie.neary@cabrini.edu.

Soccer: Ken Prothero; Phone: 610-902-8387; E-mail: kprothero@juno.com.

Softball: Karen Pelkey; Phone: 610-902-8387; E-mail: kpelkey@cabrini.edu.

Tennis: Phone: 610-902-8387.

Track and Field: Tom O'Hora; Phone: 610-902-8387; E-mail: tohora@cabrini.edu.

Volleyball: Tricia Arnold; Phone: 610-902-3906; E-mail: arnoldtri@cabrini.edu.

CALDWELL COLLEGE
Caldwell, New Jersey

Cougars ◆ NCAA II ◆ Central Atlantic Collegiate Conference
◆ http://www.caldwell.edu/

Independent Roman Catholic comprehensive, founded 1939
Coed, 1,836 undergraduate students, 59% full-time, 69% women,
31% men
Suburban 100-acre campus with easy access to New York City
Moderately difficult entrance level, 71% of applicants were admitted

Freshmen *Admission:* 1,164 applied, 806 were accepted, 283 enrolled.
Test scores: SAT verbal scores over 500: 31%; SAT math scores over
500: 27%; SAT verbal scores over 600: 4%; SAT math scores over
600: 4%.
Tuition and fees (2003–04): $17,060 (full-time). *Room and board:* $7000.
Financial Aid (All incoming freshmen): *Average need-based gift aid:* $7525.
Average aid to full-time undergraduates: $10,332.
Athletic Department: *Director of Athletics:* Mark Corino; Phone: 973-
618-3412; Fax: 973-618-3370; E-mail: mcorino@caldwell.edu. *Sports
Information Director:* Michael Lamberti; Phone: 973-618-3567;
E-mail: mlamberti@caldwell.edu.
MEN'S COACHES
Baseball: Chris Reardon; Phone: 973-618-3462; E-mail: creardon@
caldwell.edu.
Basketball: Mark Corino; Phone: 973-618-3412; E-mail: mcorino@
caldwell.edu.
Football: Ray DiNino; Phone: 973-618-3404; E-mail: rdinino@caldwell.
edu.
Soccer: Jamie Nash; Phone: 973-618-3573; E-mail: jnash@caldwell.
edu.
Tennis: Bob Reich; Phone: 973-618-3659; E-mail: breich@caldwell.edu.
WOMEN'S COACHES
Basketball: Nicole Durnien-Amato; Phone: 973-618-3361; E-mail:
ndurnien@caldwell.edu.
Cross Country: John Tosato; Phone: 973-618-3468; E-mail: jtosato@
caldwell.edu.
Soccer: Brian Davies; Phone: 973-618-3648; E-mail: bdavies@caldwell.
edu.
Softball: Dean Johnson; Phone: 973-618-3321; E-mail: djohnson@
caldwell.edu.
Tennis: Tim Nellegar; Phone: 973-618-3404; E-mail: tnellegar@
caldwell.edu.

CALIFORNIA BAPTIST UNIVERSITY
Riverside, California

Lancers ◆ NAIA ◆ Golden State Conference ◆ http://
www.calbaptist.edu/

Independent Southern Baptist comprehensive, founded 1950
Coed, 1,753 undergraduate students, 82% full-time, 66% women,
34% men
Suburban 82-acre campus with easy access to Los Angeles
Minimally difficult entrance level, 82% of applicants were admitted

Freshmen *Admission:* 705 applied, 594 were accepted, 221 enrolled.
Test scores: SAT verbal scores over 500: 53%; SAT math scores over
500: 56%; SAT verbal scores over 600: 18%; SAT math scores over
600: 10%; SAT verbal scores over 700: 1%.
Tuition and fees (2004–05): $15,940 (full-time). *Room and board:* $6310
(room only): $2640).
Financial Aid (All incoming freshmen): *Average need-based gift aid:* $6590.
Average non-need based aid: $3400. *Average aid to full-time under-
graduates:* $9840.
Athletic Department: *Director of Athletics:* Doug Huckaby; Phone: 909-
343-4381; Fax: 909-689-4754; E-mail: dhuckaby@calbaptist.edu.
Sports Information Director: Roger Horne; Phone: 909-343-4297;
E-mail: rhorne@calbaptist.edu.
MEN'S COACHES
Baseball: Gary Adcock; Phone: 909-343-4382; E-mail: gadcock@
calbaptist.edu.
Basketball: Tim Collins; Phone: 909-343-4453; E-mail: tcollins@
calbaptist.edu.

Cross Country: Bill Donald; Phone: 909-343-4296; E-mail: bdonald@
calbaptist.edu.
Diving: Rick Rowland; Phone: 909-343-4522; E-mail: rrowland@
calbaptist.edu.
Soccer: Shayon Jalayer; Phone: 909-343-4445; E-mail:
shayon_jalayer@hotmail.com.
Swimming: Rick Rowland; Phone: 909-343-4522; E-mail: rrowland@
calbaptist.edu.
Volleyball: Ryan McGuyre; Phone: 909-343-4596; E-mail: rmcguyre@
calbaptist.edu.
WOMEN'S COACHES
Basketball: Eric Spencer; Phone: 909-343-4320; E-mail: gadcock@
calbaptist.edu.
Cross Country: Bill Donald; Phone: 909-343-4296; E-mail: bdonald@
calbaptist.edu.
Diving: Rick Rowland; Phone: 909-343-4522; E-mail: rrowland@
calbaptist.edu.
Soccer: Colleen Kelly; Phone: 909-343-5020; E-mail: ckelly@calbaptist.
edu.
Softball: Mike Smith; Phone: 909-343-4452; E-mail: msmith@
calbaptist.edu.
Swimming: Rick Rowland; Phone: 909-343-4522; E-mail: rrowland@
calbaptist.edu.
Volleyball: Ryan McGuyre; Phone: 909-343-4596; E-mail: rmcguyre@
calbaptist.edu.

CALIFORNIA INSTITUTE OF TECHNOLOGY
Pasadena, California

Beavers ◆ NCAA III ◆ Southern California Athletic
Conference ◆ http://www.caltech.edu/

Independent university, founded 1891
Coed, 891 undergraduate students, 100% full-time, 33% women,
67% men
Suburban 124-acre campus with easy access to Los Angeles
Most difficult entrance level, 14% of applicants were admitted

Freshmen *Admission:* 3,071 applied, 520 were accepted, 191 enrolled.
Test scores: SAT verbal scores over 500: 99%; SAT verbal scores over
600: 94%; SAT math scores over 600: 100%; SAT verbal scores over
700: 77%; SAT math scores over 700: 96%.
Tuition and fees (2004–05): $25,551 (full-time). *Room and board:* $8013.
Financial Aid (All incoming freshmen): *Average need-based gift aid:*
$23,278. *Average non-need based aid:* $25,272. *Average aid to full-
time undergraduates:* $23,545.
Athletic Department: *Director of Athletics:* Tim Downes; Phone: 626-
395-6148; Fax: 626-584-0589; E-mail: tdownes@studaff.caltech.edu.
Sports Information Director: Michael Rupp; Phone: 626-395-3260;
E-mail: mrupp@studaff.caltech.edu.
MEN'S COACHES
Baseball: John D'Auria; Phone: 626-395-3263; E-mail: jdauria@
studaff.caltech.edu.
Basketball: Roy Dow; Phone: 626-395-3264; E-mail: rhdow@studaff.
caltech.edu.
Cross Country: Scott Jung; Phone: 626-395-3260; E-mail: scott@admis-
sions.caltech.edu.
Diving: Clint Dodd; Phone: 626-395-6853; E-mail: clinton@studaff.
caltech.edu.
Golf: John Suarez; Phone: 626-395-3255; E-mail: jsuarez@studaff.
caltech.edu.
Soccer: Rolando Uribe; Phone: 626-395-3266; E-mail: ruribe@studaff.
caltech.edu.
Swimming: Clint Dodd; Phone: 626-395-6853; E-mail: clinton@studaff.
caltech.edu.
Tennis: Mandy Gamble; Phone: 626-395-3265; E-mail: mgamble@
studaff.caltech.edu.
Track and Field: Julie Levesque; Phone: 626-395-3260; E-mail: jtingle@
studaff.caltech.edu.
WOMEN'S COACHES
Basketball: Sandra Marbut; Phone: 626-395-3674; E-mail: smarbut@
caltech.edu.
Cross Country: Scott Jung; Phone: 626-395-3260; E-mail: scott@admis-
sions.caltech.edu.

Diving: Clint Dodd; Phone: 626-395-6853; E-mail: clinton@studaff.caltech.edu.
Swimming: Clint Dodd; Phone: 626-395-6853; E-mail: clinton@studaff.caltech.edu.
Tennis: Mandy Gamble; Phone: 626-395-3265; E-mail: mgamble@studaff.caltech.edu.
Track and Field: Julie Levesque; Phone: 626-395-3260; E-mail: jtingle@studaff.caltech.edu.
Volleyball: Brent Reger; Phone: 626-395-3262; E-mail: breger@studaff.caltech.edu.

CALIFORNIA LUTHERAN UNIVERSITY
Thousand Oaks, California

Kingsmen, (W) Regals ◆ NCAA III ◆ Southern California Athletic Conference ◆ http://www.clunet.edu/

Independent Lutheran comprehensive, founded 1959
Coed, 1,920 undergraduate students, 89% full-time, 56% women, 44% men
Suburban 290-acre campus with easy access to Los Angeles
Moderately difficult entrance level, 73% of applicants were admitted

Freshmen *Admission:* 1,217 applied, 941 were accepted, 336 enrolled. *Test scores:* SAT verbal scores over 500: 77%; SAT math scores over 500: 77%; SAT verbal scores over 600: 30%; SAT math scores over 600: 24%; SAT verbal scores over 700: 3%; SAT math scores over 700: 2%.
Tuition and fees (2003–04): $20,400 (full-time). *Room and board:* $7200 (room only: $3550).
Financial Aid (All incoming freshmen): *Average need-based gift aid:* $12,740. *Average non-need based aid:* $3000. *Average aid to full-time undergraduates:* $17,000.
Athletic Department: *Director of Athletics:* Bruce Bryde; Phone: 805-493-3402; Fax: 805-493-3860; E-mail: bryde@clunet.edu. *Sports Information Director:* Scott Flanders; Phone: 805-493-3153; E-mail: flanders@clunet.edu.

MEN'S COACHES
Baseball: Marty Slimak; Phone: 805-493-3398; E-mail: slimak@clunet.edu.
Basketball: Rich Rider; Phone: 805-493-3404; E-mail: rider@clunet.edu.
Cross Country: Scott Fickerson; Phone: 805-493-3862; E-mail: sfickers@clunet.edu.
Football: Scott Squires; Phone: 805-493-3399; E-mail: squires@clunet.edu.
Golf: Jeff Lindgren; Phone: 805-493-3539; E-mail: jklindgren@aol.com.
Soccer: Dan Kuntz; Phone: 805-493-3855; E-mail: kuntz@clunet.edu.
Tennis: Mike Gennette; Phone: 805-493-3262; E-mail: gennette@clunet.edu.
Track and Field: Scott Fickerson; Phone: 805-493-3862; E-mail: sfickers@clunet.edu.

WOMEN'S COACHES
Basketball: Kristy Hopkins; Phone: 805-493-3711; E-mail: khopkins@clunet.edu.
Cross Country: Scott Fickerson; Phone: 805-493-3862; E-mail: sfickers@clunet.edu.
Soccer: Dan Kuntz; Phone: 805-493-3855; E-mail: kuntz@clunet.edu.
Softball: Debby Day; Phone: 805-493-3408; E-mail: dday@clunet.edu.
Tennis: Nancy Garrison; Phone: 805-493-3833; E-mail: garrison@clunet.edu.
Track and Field: Scott Fickerson; Phone: 805-493-3862; E-mail: sfickers@clunet.edu.
Volleyball: Greg Gibbins; Phone: 805-493-3832; E-mail: ggibbon@clunet.edu.

CALIFORNIA MARITIME ACADEMY
Vallejo, California

Keel Haulers ◆ NAIA ◆ California Pacific Conference ◆ http://www.csum.edu/

State-supported 4-year, founded 1929, part of California State University System
Coed, primarily men, 670 undergraduate students
Suburban 64-acre campus with easy access to San Francisco
Moderately difficult entrance level, 61% of applicants were admitted

Freshmen *Admission:* 831 applied, 505 were accepted.
Tuition and fees (2003–04): $2396 (resident), $10,856 (nonresident). *Room and board:* $6750 (room only: $3130).
Financial Aid (All incoming freshmen): *Average aid to full-time undergraduates:* $19,329.
Athletic Department: *Director of Athletics:* Pat Hollister; Phone: 707-654-1052; Fax: 707-654-1056; E-mail: phollister@csum.edu.

MEN'S COACHES
Basketball: Dan Dion; Phone: 707-654-1057.
Golf: Bob Stewart; Phone: 707-654-1357.
Soccer: Teale Matterson; Phone: 510-524-2800; E-mail: tealesoccer@aol.com.

WOMEN'S COACHES
Volleyball: Manny Johnson; Phone: 707-654-1058.

CALIFORNIA POLYTECHNIC STATE UNIVERSITY, SAN LUIS OBISPO
San Luis Obispo, California

Mustangs ◆ NCAA I ◆ Big West Conference; Pacific-10 Conference ◆ http://www.calpoly.edu/

State-supported comprehensive, founded 1901, part of California State University System
Coed, 17,257 undergraduate students, 95% full-time, 44% women, 56% men
Small-town 6,000-acre campus
Moderately difficult entrance level, 38% of applicants were admitted

Freshmen *Admission:* 20,827 applied, 7,989 were accepted, 2,828 enrolled. *Test scores:* SAT verbal scores over 500: 87%; SAT math scores over 500: 94%; SAT verbal scores over 600: 37%; SAT math scores over 600: 62%; SAT verbal scores over 700: 4%; SAT math scores over 700: 14%.
Tuition and fees (2004–05): $3459 (resident), $10,227 (nonresident). *Room and board:* $7479 (room only: $4221).
Financial Aid (All incoming freshmen): *Average need-based gift aid:* $1205. *Average aid to full-time undergraduates:* $6063.
Athletic Department: *Director of Athletics:* John McCutcheon; Phone: 805-756-2924; Fax: 805-756-2650; E-mail: jmccutch@calpoly.edu. *Sports Information Director:* Brian Thurmond; Phone: 805-756-2410; E-mail: bthurmon@calpoly.edu.

MEN'S COACHES
Baseball: Larry Lee; Phone: 805-756-6367; E-mail: llee@calpoly.edu.
Basketball: Kevin Bromley; Phone: 805-756-6559.
Cheerleading: Chris Baker; Phone: 805-756-7188; E-mail: baker@calpoly.edu.
Cross Country: Mark Conover; Phone: 805-756-2235; E-mail: mconover@calpoly.edu.
Diving: Rich Firman; Phone: 805-756-5714; E-mail: rfirman@calpoly.edu.
Football: Rick Ellerson; Phone: 805-756-5166.
Golf: Scott Cartwright; Phone: 805-756-5156; E-mail: slopga@aol.com.
Soccer: Wolfgang Gartner; Phone: 805-756-7070; E-mail: wgartner@calpoly.edu.
Swimming: Rich Firman; Phone: 805-756-5714; E-mail: rfirman@calpoly.edu.
Tennis: Trevor Kronemann; Phone: 805-756-2777; E-mail: tkronema@calpoly.edu.

California Polytechnic State University, San Luis Obispo *(continued)*

Track and Field: Terry Crawford; Phone: 805-756-1130; E-mail: tcrawfor@calpoly.edu.
Wrestling: John Azevedo; Phone: 805-756-5131; E-mail: jvazeved@calpoly.edu.

WOMEN'S COACHES
Basketball: Faith Mimnaugh; Phone: 805-756-1159; E-mail: fmimnaug@calpoly.edu.
Cheerleading: Chris Baker; Phone: 805-756-7188; E-mail: baker@calpoly.edu.
Cross Country: Mark Conover; Phone: 805-756-2235; E-mail: mconover@calpoly.edu.
Diving: Rich Firman; Phone: 805-756-5714; E-mail: rfirman@calpoly.edu.
Golf: Thomas Moos; Phone: 805-756-7295; E-mail: tmoos@calpoly.edu.
Soccer: Alex Crozier; Phone: 805-756-2590; E-mail: acrozier@calpoly.edu.
Softball: Lisa Boyer; Phone: 805-756-1539; E-mail: lboyer@calpoly.edu.
Swimming: Rich Firman; Phone: 805-756-5714; E-mail: rfirman@calpoly.edu.
Tennis: Hugh Bream; Phone: 805-756-2768; E-mail: hcbream@aol.com.
Track and Field: Terry Crawford; Phone: 805-756-1130; E-mail: tcrawfor@calpoly.edu.
Volleyball: Steve Schlick; Phone: 805-756-2850; E-mail: sschlick@calpoly.edu.

CALIFORNIA STATE POLYTECHNIC UNIVERSITY, POMONA
Pomona, California

Broncos ◆ NCAA II ◆ California Collegiate Athletic Conference ◆ http://www.csupomona.edu/

State-supported comprehensive, founded 1938, part of California State University System
Coed, 17,650 undergraduate students, 83% full-time, 43% women, 57% men
Urban 1,400-acre campus with easy access to Los Angeles
Moderately difficult entrance level, 31% of applicants were admitted

Freshmen *Admission:* 11,040 applied, 3,345 were accepted, 2,284 enrolled. *Test scores:* SAT verbal scores over 500: 54%; SAT math scores over 500: 64%; SAT verbal scores over 600: 12%; SAT math scores over 600: 26%; SAT verbal scores over 700: 1%; SAT math scores over 700: 3%.
Tuition and fees (2004–05): $2046 (resident), $10,506 (nonresident). *Room and board:* $6747.
Financial Aid (All incoming freshmen): *Average need-based gift aid:* $5049. *Average non-need based aid:* $1449. *Average aid to full-time undergraduates:* $7332.
Athletic Department: *Director of Athletics:* Glenn Shenker; Phone: 909-869-4631; Fax: 909-869-2814; E-mail: grshenker@csupomona.edu. *Sports Information Director:* Paul Helms; Phone: 909-869-2812; E-mail: phelms@csupomona.edu.

MEN'S COACHES
Baseball: Mike Ashman; Phone: 909-869-2829; E-mail: mdashman@csupomona.edu.
Basketball: Greg Kamansky; Phone: 909-869-2833; E-mail: glkamansky@csupomona.edu.
Cross Country: Jim Sackett; Phone: 909-869-2831; E-mail: jsackett@csupomona.edu.
Soccer: Paul Caligiuri; Phone: 909-869-2821; E-mail: pdcaligiuri@csupomona.edu.
Tennis: Sandy Kriezel; Phone: 909-869-2830; E-mail: sskriezel@csupomona.edu.
Track and Field: Jim Sackett; Phone: 909-869-2831; E-mail: jsackett@csupomona.edu.

WOMEN'S COACHES
Basketball: Paul Thomas; Phone: 909-869-2824; E-mail: pbthomas@csupomona.edu.
Cross Country: Jim Sackett; Phone: 909-869-2831; E-mail: jsackett@csupomona.edu.
Soccer: Paul Caligiuri; Phone: 909-869-2810; E-mail: pdcaligiuri@csupomona.edu.
Tennis: Sandy Kriezel; Phone: 909-869-2830; E-mail: sskriezel@csupomona.edu.
Track and Field: Jim Sackett; Phone: 909-869-2831; E-mail: jsackett@csupomona.edu.
Volleyball: Rosie Wegrich; Phone: 909-869-2822; E-mail: rwegrich@csupomona.edu.

CALIFORNIA STATE UNIVERSITY, BAKERSFIELD
Bakersfield, California

Roadrunners ◆ NCAA II ◆ California Collegiate Athletic Conference; Pacific-10 Conference ◆ http://www.csubak.edu/

State-supported comprehensive, founded 1970, part of California State University System
Coed, 5,882 undergraduate students
Urban 575-acre campus
Moderately difficult entrance level, 63% of applicants were admitted

Freshmen *Admission:* 1,935 applied, 1,223 were accepted.
Tuition and fees (2003–04): $2427 (resident), $8067 (nonresident). *Room and board:* $4900.
Financial Aid (All incoming freshmen): *Average need-based gift aid:* $5332. *Average non-need based aid:* $1980. *Average aid to full-time undergraduates:* $6094.
Athletic Department: *Director of Athletics:* Rudy Carvajal; Phone: 661-664-2200; Fax: 661-664-2376; E-mail: rcarvajal@csub.edu. *Sports Information Director:* Kevin Gilmore; Phone: 661-664-6071; E-mail: kgilmore@csub.edu.

MEN'S COACHES
Basketball: Henry Clark; Phone: 661-664-2190; E-mail: hclark@csubak.edu.
Cheerleading: Crystal Lei; Phone: 661-664-2188.
Golf: Dave Barber; Phone: 661-664-6222.
Soccer: Simon Tobin; Phone: 661-664-2428; E-mail: stobin@csubak.edu.
Swimming: Bob Steele; Phone: 661-664-2327; E-mail: bsteele@csubak.edu.
Track and Field: Alan Collatz; Phone: 661-664-3476; E-mail: acollatz@csub.edu.
Wrestling: T.J. Kerr; Phone: 661-664-2343; E-mail: tkerr@csubak.edu.

WOMEN'S COACHES
Basketball: Tim LaKose; Phone: 661-664-2425; E-mail: tlakose@csub.edu.
Cheerleading: Crystal Lei; Phone: 661-664-2188.
Cross Country: Cregg Weinmann; Phone: 661-664-2499; E-mail: cweinmann@csubak.edu.
Soccer: Simon Tobin; Phone: 661-664-2428; E-mail: stobin@csubak.edu.
Softball: Kathy Welter; Phone: 661-664-3056; E-mail: kwelter@csubak.edu.
Swimming: Pat Skehan; Phone: 661-664-2071; E-mail: pskehan@csubak.edu.
Tennis: Robert Limpias; Phone: 661-664-3081; E-mail: rlimpias@csub.edu.
Track and Field: Alan Collatz; Phone: 661-664-3476; E-mail: acollatz@csub.edu.
Volleyball: John Price; Phone: 661-664-2269; E-mail: jprice@csubak.edu.

CALIFORNIA STATE UNIVERSITY, CHICO

Chico, California

Wildcats ◆ NCAA II ◆ California Collegiate Athletic Conference ◆ http://www.csuchico.edu/

State-supported comprehensive, founded 1887, part of California State University System
Coed, 13,903 undergraduate students, 90% full-time, 54% women, 46% men
Small-town 119-acre campus
Moderately difficult entrance level, 71% of applicants were admitted

Freshmen *Admission:* 9,157 applied, 6,718 were accepted, 2,001 enrolled. *Test scores:* SAT verbal scores over 500: 60%; SAT math scores over 500: 65%; SAT verbal scores over 600: 15%; SAT math scores over 600: 17%; SAT verbal scores over 700: 1%; SAT math scores over 700: 1%.
Tuition and fees (2003–04): $2796 (resident), $13,302 (nonresident). *Room and board:* $7245 (room only: $4910).
Athletic Department: *Director of Athletics:* Anita Barker; Phone: 530-898-6470; Fax: 530-898-4699; E-mail: abarker@csuchico.edu. *Sports Information Director:* Teresa Clements; Phone: 530-898-4658; E-mail: tclements@csuchico.edu.

MEN'S COACHES

Baseball: Lindsay Meggs; Phone: 530-898-4374; E-mail: lmeggs@csuchico.edu.
Basketball: Prescott Smith; Phone: 530-898-5160; E-mail: plsmith@csuchico.edu.
Cheerleading: Cheri Furniss; Phone: 530-898-5298; E-mail: cfurniss@csuchico.edu.
Cross Country: Gary Towne; Phone: 530-898-4955; E-mail: gtowne@csuchico.edu.
Golf: Keith Thomas; Phone: 530-898-5708; E-mail: kthomas@csuchico.edu.
Soccer: Mike O'Malley; Phone: 530-898-6810; E-mail: momalley@csuchico.edu.
Track and Field: Kirk Freitas; Phone: 530-898-5150; E-mail: kfreitas@csuchico.edu.

WOMEN'S COACHES

Basketball: Lynne Deyoung; Phone: 530-898-5123; E-mail: lrdeyoung@csuchico.edu.
Cheerleading: Cheri Furniss; Phone: 530-898-5298; E-mail: cfurniss@csuchico.edu.
Cross Country: Gary Towne; Phone: 530-898-4955; E-mail: gtowne@csuchico.edu.
Golf: Keith Thomas; Phone: 530-898-5708; E-mail: kthomas@csuchico.edu.
Soccer: Kim Sutton; Phone: 530-898-6085; E-mail: ktsutton@csuchico.edu.
Softball: Teri Rupe; Phone: 530-898-4685; E-mail: trupe@csuchico.edu.
Track and Field: Oliver Hanf; Phone: 530-898-5735; E-mail: ohanf@csuchico.edu.
Volleyball: Cody Hein; Phone: 530-898-6180; E-mail: cbhein@csuchico.edu.

CALIFORNIA STATE UNIVERSITY, DOMINGUEZ HILLS

Carson, California

Toros ◆ NCAA II ◆ California Collegiate Athletic Conference ◆ http://www.csudh.edu/

State-supported comprehensive, founded 1960, part of California State University System
Coed, 8,134 undergraduate students, 62% full-time, 69% women, 31% men
Urban 350-acre campus with easy access to Los Angeles
Moderately difficult entrance level, 4% of applicants were admitted

Freshmen *Admission:* 1,937 applied, 920 were accepted, 693 enrolled.
Tuition and fees (2004–05): $2478 (resident), $10,938 (nonresident). *Room only:* $5022.

Financial Aid (All incoming freshmen): *Average need-based gift aid:* $5453. *Average non-need based aid:* $2773. *Average aid to full-time undergraduates:* $6999.
Athletic Department: *Director of Athletics:* Ron Prettyman; Phone: 303-243-3893; Fax: 310-217-6975; E-mail: rprettyman@csudh.edu. *Sports Information Director:* Patrick Guillen; Phone: 303-243-3764; E-mail: pguillen@csudh.edu.

MEN'S COACHES

Baseball: George Wing; Phone: 310-243-3765; E-mail: gwing@csudh.edu.
Basketball: Larry Hauser; Phone: 310-243-3891; E-mail: lhauser@csudh.edu.
Golf: Dr. John Johnson; Phone: 310-243-3555; E-mail: jjohnson@csudh.edu.
Soccer: Joe Flanagan; Phone: 310-243-2221; E-mail: jflanagan@csudh.edu.

WOMEN'S COACHES

Basketball: Van Girard; Phone: 310-243-2211; E-mail: vgirard@csudh.edu.
Cross Country: Warren Edmondson; Phone: 310-243-3878; E-mail: wedmonson@csudh.edu.
Soccer: Joe Flanagan; Phone: 310-243-2221; E-mail: jflanagan@csudh.edu.
Softball: Jim Maier; Phone: 310-243-3889; E-mail: jmaier@csudh.edu.
Track and Field: Warren Edmondson; Phone: 310-243-3878; E-mail: wedmonson@csudh.edu.
Volleyball: Ali Wood; Phone: 310-243-2222; E-mail: awood@csudh.edu.

CALIFORNIA STATE UNIVERSITY, FRESNO

Fresno, California

Bulldogs ◆ NCAA I ◆ Pacific-10 Conference; Western Athletic Conference ◆ http://www.csufresno.edu/

State-supported comprehensive, founded 1911, part of California State University System
Coed, 18,574 undergraduate students, 77% full-time, 58% women, 42% men
Urban 1,410-acre campus
Moderately difficult entrance level, 68% of applicants were admitted

Freshmen *Admission:* 10,374 applied, 7,247 were accepted, 2,590 enrolled. *Test scores:* SAT verbal scores over 500: 37%; SAT math scores over 500: 45%; SAT verbal scores over 600: 9%; SAT math scores over 600: 11%; SAT verbal scores over 700: 1%; SAT math scores over 700: 1%.
Tuition and fees (2004–05): $2414 (resident), $13,288 (nonresident). *Room and board:* $7073.
Financial Aid (All incoming freshmen): *Average need-based gift aid:* $3285. *Average non-need based aid:* $1766. *Average aid to full-time undergraduates:* $7533.
Athletic Department: *Director of Athletics:* Scott Johnson; Phone: 559-278-3178; Fax: 559-278-6611; E-mail: athleticdirector@csufresno.edu. *Sports Information Director:* Steve Weakland; Phone: 559-278-2509; E-mail: sweaklan@csufresno.edu.

MEN'S COACHES

Baseball: Mike Batesole; Phone: 559-278-2178; E-mail: mcurtis@csufresno.edu.
Basketball: Ray Lopes; Phone: 559-278-2748; E-mail: rlopes@csufresno.edu.
Football: Pat Hill; Phone: 559-278-3015; E-mail: phill@csufresno.edu.
Golf: Mike Watney; Phone: 559-278-2345; E-mail: mikewat@csufresno.edu.
Soccer: Jeremy Proud; Phone: 559-278-4226.
Tennis: Brad Dancer; Phone: 559-278-4032; E-mail: dancerbrad@aol.com.
Track and Field: Bob Fraley; Phone: 559-278-4097; E-mail: liederrun4fun@netscape.net.
Wrestling: Dennis Deliddo; Phone: 559-278-4804; E-mail: dennisd@csufresno.edu.

WOMEN'S COACHES

Basketball: Stacy Johnson-Klein; Phone: 559-278-2236; E-mail: sjohnson-klein@csufresno.edu.

California State University, Fresno *(continued)*

Cross Country: Shannon Lieder; Phone: 559-278-4097.
Diving: Robb Pendergrass; Phone: 559-278-4698; E-mail: rpendergrass@csufresno.edu.
Soccer: Stacey Welp; Phone: 559-278-8101; E-mail: stacyw@csufresno.edu.
Softball: Margie Wright; Phone: 559-278-4453; E-mail: hildaf@csufresno.edu.
Swimming: Tom Milich; Phone: 559-278-4698.
Tennis: Simon Thibodeau; Phone: 559-278-4422; E-mail: epper3210@cs.com.
Track and Field: Bob Fraley; Phone: 559-278-4907; E-mail: liederrun4fun@netscape.net.
Volleyball: Linda Vivas; Phone: 559-278-2837; E-mail: lindyv@csufresno.edu.

CALIFORNIA STATE UNIVERSITY, FULLERTON
Fullerton, California

Titans ◆ NCAA I ◆ Big West Conference; Pacific-10 Conference ◆ http://www.fullerton.edu/

State-supported comprehensive, founded 1957, part of California State University System
Coed, 26,896 undergraduate students, 69% full-time, 60% women, 40% men
Urban 225-acre campus with easy access to Los Angeles
Moderately difficult entrance level, 6% of applicants were admitted

Freshmen *Admission:* 17,723 applied, 11,751 were accepted, 3,271 enrolled. *Test scores:* SAT verbal scores over 500: 41%; SAT math scores over 500: 51%; SAT verbal scores over 600: 8%; SAT math scores over 600: 14%; SAT math scores over 700: 1%.
Tuition and fees (2003–04): $2516 (resident), $10,976 (nonresident). *Room only:* $4127.
Financial Aid (All incoming freshmen): *Average need-based gift aid:* $6404. *Average non-need based aid:* $3123. *Average aid to full-time undergraduates:* $6592.
Athletic Department: *Director of Athletics:* Brian Quinn; Phone: 714-278-2777; Fax: 714-278-5396; E-mail: bquinn@fullerton.edu. *Sports Information Director:* Mel Franks; Phone: 714-278-3970; E-mail: mfranks@fullerton.edu.

MEN'S COACHES
Baseball: George Horton; Phone: 714-278-3789; E-mail: csufbaseball@fullerton.edu.
Basketball: Robert Burton; Phone: 714-278-3711; E-mail: rburton@fullerton.edu.
Cross Country: John Elders; Phone: 714-278-3490; E-mail: jelders@fullerton.edu.
Soccer: Al Mistri; Phone: 714-278-5414; E-mail: amistri@fullerton.edu.
Track and Field: John Elders; Phone: 714-278-3490; E-mail: jelders@fullerton.edu.
Wrestling: Dan Hicks; Phone: 714-278-2138; E-mail: dhicks@fullerton.edu.

WOMEN'S COACHES
Basketball: Maryalyce Jeremiah; Phone: 714-278-3604; E-mail: mjeremiah@fullerton.edu.
Cross Country: John Elders; Phone: 714-278-3490; E-mail: jelders@fullerton.edu.
Gymnastics: Julie Knight; Phone: 714-278-3842; E-mail: jknight@fullerton.edu.
Soccer: Ali Khosroshahin; Phone: 714-278-5657; E-mail: alik@fullerton.edu.
Softball: Michelle Gromacki; Phone: 714-278-3495; E-mail: mgromacki@fullerton.edu.
Tennis: Bill Reynolds; Phone: 714-278-3053; E-mail: wreynolds@fullerton.edu.
Track and Field: John Elders; Phone: 714-278-3490; E-mail: jelders@fullerton.edu.
Volleyball: Carolyn Zimmerman; Phone: 714-278-3052; E-mail: czimmerman@fullerton.edu.

CALIFORNIA STATE UNIVERSITY, HAYWARD
Hayward, California

Pioneers ◆ NCAA III ◆ California Pacific Conference; Independent ◆ http://www.csuhayward.edu/

State-supported comprehensive, founded 1957, part of California State University System
Coed, 9,380 undergraduate students, 79% full-time, 63% women, 37% men
Suburban 343-acre campus with easy access to San Francisco
Moderately difficult entrance level, 47% of applicants were admitted

Freshmen *Admission:* 4,665 applied, 2,177 were accepted, 682 enrolled. *Test scores:* SAT verbal scores over 500: 36%; SAT math scores over 500: 43%; SAT verbal scores over 600: 9%; SAT math scores over 600: 9%; SAT verbal scores over 700: 1%; SAT math scores over 700: 1%.
Tuition and fees (2004–05): $2418 (resident), $10,878 (nonresident). *Room only:* $3705.
Financial Aid (All incoming freshmen): *Average need-based gift aid:* $6494. *Average aid to full-time undergraduates:* $6918.
Athletic Department: *Director of Athletics:* Debby DeAngelis; Phone: 510-885-3038; Fax: 510-885-2282; E-mail: ddeangel@csuhayward.edu. *Sports Information Director:* Marty Valdez; Phone: 510-885-3528; E-mail: mvaldez@csuhayward.edu.

MEN'S COACHES
Baseball: Dirk Morrison; Phone: 510-885-3046; E-mail: dmorriso@csuhayward.edu.
Basketball: .
Basketball: Will Biggs; Phone: 510-885-3037; E-mail: wbiggs@csuhayward.edu.
Cheerleading: Beth Milan; Phone: 925-785-4181.
Cross Country: Greg Ryan; Phone: 510-885-3093; E-mail: gryan@csuhayward.edu.
Golf: Tim Tierney; Phone: 510-885-3036; E-mail: ttierney@csuhayward.edu.
Soccer: Jair Fory; Phone: 510-885-4756; E-mail: jfory@csuhayward.edu.

WOMEN'S COACHES
Basketball: Sara Judd; Phone: 510-885-3066; E-mail: sjudd@csuhayward.edu.
Cheerleading: Beth Milan; Phone: 925-785-4181.
Cross Country: Greg Ryan; Phone: 510-885-3093; E-mail: gryan@csuhayward.edu.
Golf: Tim Tierney; Phone: 510-885-3036; E-mail: ttierney@csuhayward.edu.
Soccer: Amy Foreman; Phone: 510-885-4190; E-mail: aforeman@csuhayward.edu.
Softball: Cara Holt; Phone: 510-885-3045.
Swimming: Anthony Garcia; Phone: 510-885-3044; E-mail: agarcia@csuhayward.edu.
Volleyball: Jim Spagle; Phone: 510-885-4805; E-mail: jspagle@csuhayward.edu.

CALIFORNIA STATE UNIVERSITY, LONG BEACH
Long Beach, California

49ers; Dirtbags ◆ NCAA I ◆ Big West Conference ◆ http://www.csulb.edu/

State-supported comprehensive, founded 1949, part of California State University System
Coed, 28,067 undergraduate students, 77% full-time, 60% women, 40% men
Suburban 320-acre campus with easy access to Los Angeles
Moderately difficult entrance level, 5% of applicants were admitted

Freshmen *Admission:* 27,869 applied, 13,751 were accepted, 3,516 enrolled. *Test scores:* SAT verbal scores over 500: 49%; SAT math scores over 500: 63%; SAT verbal scores over 600: 12%; SAT math scores over 600: 20%; SAT verbal scores over 700: 1%; SAT math scores over 700: 2%.

Tuition and fees (2004–05): $2362 (resident), $10,822 (nonresident). *Room and board:* $5800.
Financial Aid (All incoming freshmen): *Average need-based gift aid:* $3500. *Average non-need based aid:* $1698. *Average aid to full-time undergraduates:* $7125.
Athletic Department: *Director of Athletics:* Bill Shumard; Phone: 562-985-7976; Fax: 562-985-8197; E-mail: bshumard@csulb.edu. *Sports Information Director:* Steve Janisch; Phone: 562-985-7797; E-mail: sjanisch@csulb.edu.

MEN'S COACHES
Baseball: Mike Weathers; Phone: 562-985-7548; E-mail: sweathe2@csulb.edu.
Basketball: Larry Reynolds; Phone: 562-985-7975; E-mail: lreynold@csulb.edu.
Cross Country: Andy Sythe; Phone: 562-985-4666; E-mail: asythe@csulb.edu.
Golf: Bob Livingstone; Phone: 562-985-4050; E-mail: boblivy@csulb.edu.
Track and Field: Andy Sythe; Phone: 562-985-4666; E-mail: asythe@csulb.edu.
Volleyball: Alan Knipe; Phone: 562-985-1798; E-mail: aknipe@csulb.edu.

WOMEN'S COACHES
Basketball: Mary Hegarty; Phone: 562-985-7975; E-mail: mhegarty@csulb.edu.
Cross Country: Andy Sythe; Phone: 562-985-4666; E-mail: asythe@csulb.edu.
Golf: Sue Ewart; Phone: 562-985-5475; E-mail: sewart@csulb.edu.
Soccer: Pete Reynaud; Phone: 562-985-1858; E-mail: preynaud@csulb.edu.
Softball: Pete Manarino; Phone: 562-985-8364; E-mail: pmanarin@csulb.edu.
Tennis: Jenny Hilt; Phone: 562-985-4336; E-mail: jhilt@csulb.edu.
Track and Field: Andy Sythe; Phone: 562-985-4666; E-mail: asythe@csulb.edu.
Volleyball: Brian Gimmillaro; Phone: 562-985-8366.

CALIFORNIA STATE UNIVERSITY, LOS ANGELES
Los Angeles, California
Golden Eagles ◆ NCAA II ◆ California Collegiate Athletic Conference ◆ http://www.calstatela.edu/

State-supported comprehensive, founded 1947, part of California State University System
Coed, 14,421 undergraduate students
Urban 173-acre campus
Moderately difficult entrance level, 54% of applicants were admitted

Freshmen *Admission:* 12,198 applied, 6,642 were accepted.
Tuition and fees (2003–04): $2440 (resident), $11,648 (nonresident). *Room only:* $3338.
Financial Aid (All incoming freshmen): *Average need-based gift aid:* $6791. *Average aid to full-time undergraduates:* $7482.
Athletic Department: *Director of Athletics:* Carol Dunn; Phone: 323-343-3080; Fax: 323-343-6535; E-mail: cdunn@cslanet.calstatela.edu. *Sports Information Director:* Chris Hughes; Phone: 323-343-5308; E-mail: chughes3@calstatela.edu.

MEN'S COACHES
Baseball: John Herbold; Phone: 323-343-3093; E-mail: jherbol@cslanet.calstatela.edu.
Basketball: Dave Yanai; Phone: 323-343-3090; E-mail: dyanai@calstatela.edu.
Cheerleading: Christy Bolingbroke; Phone: 323-343-3080; E-mail: csula_cheer@hotmail.com.
Soccer: Chris Chamides; Phone: 323-343-3089; E-mail: cchamid@calstatela.edu.
Tennis: Tina Karnasky; Phone: 323-343-3094; E-mail: tkarwas@calstatela.edu.
Track and Field: Christopher Asher; Phone: 323-343-6413; E-mail: casher@calstatela.edu.

WOMEN'S COACHES
Basketball: Marcia Murota; Phone: 323-343-3091; E-mail: mmurota@calstatela.edu.

Cheerleading: Christy Bolingbroke; Phone: 323-343-3080; E-mail: csula_cheer@hotmail.com.
Cross Country: Christopher Asher; Phone: 323-343-6413; E-mail: casher@calstatela.edu.
Soccer: Chris Chamides; Phone: 323-343-3089; E-mail: cchamid@calstatela.edu.
Tennis: Tina Karnasky; Phone: 323-343-3094; E-mail: tkarwas@calstatela.edu.
Track and Field: Christopher Asher; Phone: 323-343-6413; E-mail: casher@calstatela.edu.
Volleyball: Bill Lawler; Phone: 323-343-3087; E-mail: blawler@calstatela.edu.

CALIFORNIA STATE UNIVERSITY, MONTEREY BAY
Seaside, California
Otters ◆ NAIA ◆ California Pacific Conference ◆ http://csumb.edu/

State-supported comprehensive, founded 1994, part of California State University
Coed, 2,753 undergraduate students, 97% full-time, 58% women, 42% men
1,500-acre campus with easy access to San Jose
Minimally difficult entrance level, 15% of applicants were admitted

Freshmen *Admission:* 3,023 applied, 2,508 were accepted, 565 enrolled.
Tuition and fees (2003–04): $2474 (resident), $11,498 (nonresident). *Room and board:* $6190 (room only: $3990).
Financial Aid (All incoming freshmen): *Average aid to full-time undergraduates:* $6514.
Athletic Department: *Director of Athletics:* Bill Trumbo; Phone: 831-582-4270; Fax: 831-582-4023; E-mail: bill_trumbo@csumb.edu. *Sports Information Director:* Sarah Bernson; Phone: 831-582-4783; E-mail: sarah_bernson@csumb.edu.

MEN'S COACHES
Basketball: Bill Trumbo; Phone: 831-582-4504; E-mail: mensbasketball@csumb.edu.
Cross Country: Yi Mao; Phone: 831-582-3015; E-mail: yi_mao@csumb.edu.
Golf: Bill Paulson; Phone: 831-582-4258; E-mail: bill_paulson@csumb.edu.
Soccer: Artie Cairel; Phone: 831-582-4536; E-mail: artie_cairel@csumb.edu.

WOMEN'S COACHES
Basketball: Amber Magner; Phone: 831-582-4505; E-mail: mensbasketball@csumb.edu.
Cross Country: Yi Mao; Phone: 831-582-3015; E-mail: yi_mao@csumb.edu.
Golf: Marcia Juergens; Phone: 831-582-4258; E-mail: marcia_juergens@csumb.edu.
Soccer: Heidi Covington; Phone: 831-582-4685; E-mail: womens_soccercoach@csumb.edu.
Volleyball: Jerry Gregg; Phone: 831-582-4509; E-mail: volleyball@csumb.edu.

CALIFORNIA STATE UNIVERSITY, NORTHRIDGE
Northridge, California
Matadors ◆ NCAA I ◆ Big West Conference ◆ http://www.csun.edu/

State-supported comprehensive, founded 1958, part of California State University System
Coed, 24,462 undergraduate students, 75% full-time, 59% women, 41% men
Urban 353-acre campus with easy access to Los Angeles
Moderately difficult entrance level, 82% of applicants were admitted

Freshmen *Admission:* 10,600 applied, 8,788 were accepted, 3,298 enrolled.

California State University, Northridge *(continued)*

Tuition and fees (2003–04): $2444 (resident), $11,468 (nonresident). *Room and board:* $6400.
Financial Aid (All incoming freshmen): *Average need-based gift aid:* $6000. *Average non-need based aid:* $2900. *Average aid to full-time undergraduates:* $10,674.
Athletic Department: *Director of Athletics:* Richard Dull; Phone: 818-677-3208; Fax: 818-677-4762; E-mail: richard.dull@csun.edu. *Sports Information Director:* Ryan Finney; Phone: 818-677-2313; E-mail: ryan.finney@csun.edu.

MEN'S COACHES
Baseball: Steve Rousey; Phone: 818-677-7055; E-mail: stephen.rousey@csun.edu.
Basketball: Bobby Braswell; Phone: 818-677-3231; E-mail: bobby.braswell@csun.edu.
Cross Country: Don Strametz; Phone: 818-677-3608; E-mail: don.strametz@mail.csun.edu.
Diving: Roland King; Phone: 818-677-4732; E-mail: roland.king@csun.edu.
Golf: Jim Bracken; Phone: 818-677-3228; E-mail: jbb51213@csun.edu.
Soccer: Terry Davila; Phone: 818-677-2379; E-mail: terry.davila@csun.edu.
Swimming: Barry Schreifels; Phone: 818-677-3239; E-mail: rbs45306@csun.edu.
Track and Field: Don Strametz; Phone: 818-677-3608; E-mail: don.strametz@mail.csun.edu.
Volleyball: Jeff Campbell; Phone: 818-677-4512; E-mail: jeff.campbell@csun.edu.

WOMEN'S COACHES
Basketball: Tammy Holder; Phone: 818-677-3995; E-mail: tammyh@csun.edu.
Cross Country: Don Strametz; Phone: 818-677-3608; E-mail: don.strametz@mail.csun.edu.
Diving: Roland King; Phone: 818-677-4732; E-mail: roland.king@csun.edu.
Golf: Bonnie Murphy; Phone: 818-677-7006; E-mail: bonniejm@msn.com.
Soccer: Mac Thompson; Phone: 818-677-2946.
Softball: Barbara Jordan; Phone: 818-677-3854; E-mail: bj18ngu@earthlink.net.
Swimming: Barry Schreifels; Phone: 818-677-3239; E-mail: rbs45306@csun.edu.
Tennis: Gary Victor; Phone: 818-677-4731; E-mail: gary.victor@csun.edu.
Track and Field: Don Strametz; Phone: 818-677-3608; E-mail: don.strametz@mail.csun.edu.
Volleyball: Jeff Stork; Phone: 818-677-4104; E-mail: jeff.stork@csun.edu.

CALIFORNIA STATE UNIVERSITY, SACRAMENTO
Sacramento, California

Hornets ◆ NCAA I ◆ Big Sky Conference; Pacific Coast Softball Conference ◆ http://www.csus.edu/

State-supported comprehensive, founded 1947, part of California State University System
Coed, 22,562 undergraduate students, 76% full-time, 58% women, 42% men
Urban 300-acre campus
Moderately difficult entrance level, 51% of applicants were admitted

Freshmen *Admission:* 11,214 applied, 5,864 were accepted, 2,446 enrolled. *Test scores:* SAT verbal scores over 500: 40%; SAT math scores over 500: 49%; SAT verbal scores over 600: 9%; SAT math scores over 600: 11%; SAT verbal scores over 700: 1%; SAT math scores over 700: 1%.
Tuition and fees (2003–04): $2513 (resident), $11,440 (nonresident). *Room and board:* $6523.
Financial Aid (All incoming freshmen): *Average need-based gift aid:* $1738. *Average non-need based aid:* $4512. *Average aid to full-time undergraduates:* $7109.

Athletic Department: *Director of Athletics:* Terry Wanless; Phone: 916-278-6348; Fax: 916-278-5429; E-mail: sacad@csus.edu. *Sports Information Director:* Brian Berger; Phone: 916-278-4313; E-mail: bwberger@csus.edu.

MEN'S COACHES
Baseball: John Smith; Phone: 916-278-7225; E-mail: jsmith@csus.edu.
Basketball: Jerome Jenkins; Phone: 916-278-5345; E-mail: jjenkins@csus.edu.
Cheerleading: Laurie Harris; Phone: 916-983-3099; E-mail: lharris@uca.com.
Cross Country: Kathleen Raske; Phone: 916-278-7052; E-mail: raskek@csus.edu.
Football: Steve Mooshagian; Phone: 916-278-7053; E-mail: mshagian@saclink.csus.edu.
Golf: Rene Mondine; Phone: 916-278-5284; E-mail: rmondine@csus.edu.
Soccer: Michael Linenberger; Phone: 916-278-6769; E-mail: bergs@csus.edu.
Tennis: Sherif Zaher; Phone: 916-278-5276; E-mail: szaher@csus.edu.
Track and Field: Kathleen Raske; Phone: 916-278-7052; E-mail: raskek@csus.edu.

WOMEN'S COACHES
Basketball: Dan Muscatell; Phone: 916-278-4479; E-mail: dmuscatell@csus.edu.
Cheerleading: Laurie Harris; Phone: 916-983-3099; E-mail: lharris@uca.com.
Cross Country: Kathleen Raske; Phone: 916-278-7052; E-mail: raskek@csus.edu.
Golf: Rene Mondine; Phone: 916-278-5284; E-mail: rmondine@csus.edu.
Gymnastics: Kim Hughes; Phone: 916-278-5361; E-mail: kwhughes@csus.edu.
Soccer: Karen Hanks; Phone: 916-278-5281; E-mail: khanks@csus.edu.
Softball: Kathy Strahan; Phone: 916-278-5376; E-mail: kstrahan@csus.edu.
Tennis: Bill Campbell; Phone: 916-859-5910; E-mail: williamc@sparetimeinc.com.
Track and Field: Kathleen Raske; Phone: 916-278-7052; E-mail: raskek@csus.edu.
Volleyball: Debby Colberg; Phone: 916-278-6427; E-mail: dcolberg@csus.edu.

CALIFORNIA STATE UNIVERSITY, SAN BERNARDINO
San Bernardino, California

Coyotes ◆ NCAA II ◆ California Collegiate Athletic Conference ◆ http://www.csusb.edu/

State-supported comprehensive, founded 1965, part of California State University System
Coed, 12,119 undergraduate students, 82% full-time, 65% women, 35% men
Suburban 430-acre campus with easy access to Los Angeles
Moderately difficult entrance level, 56% of applicants were admitted

Freshmen *Admission:* 6,463 applied, 3,948 were accepted, 1,383 enrolled. *Test scores:* SAT verbal scores over 500: 24%; SAT math scores over 500: 30%; SAT verbal scores over 600: 4%; SAT math scores over 600: 6%; SAT verbal scores over 700: %.
Tuition and fees (2003–04): $1932 (resident), $8700 (nonresident). *Room and board:* $5383 (room only: $4205).
Athletic Department: *Director of Athletics:* Nancy Sinpson; Phone: 909-880-5011; Fax: 909-880-5984; E-mail: nsimpson@csusb.edu. *Sports Information Director:* Mike Murphy; Phone: 909-880-5012; E-mail: michaelj@csusb.edu.

MEN'S COACHES
Baseball: Don Parnell; Phone: 909-880-5021; E-mail: dparnell@csusb.edu.
Basketball: Jeff Oliver; Phone: 909-880-5015; E-mail: joliver@csusb.edu.
Cheerleading: SuzAnne McDonald; Phone: 909-880-5011.
Golf: Greg Price; Phone: 909-880-5354; E-mail: gprice@csusb.edu.
Soccer: Christian Johnson; Phone: 909-880-5017; E-mail: johnsonc@csusb.edu.

WOMEN'S COACHES

Basketball: Kevin Becker; Phone: 909-880-5014; E-mail: kbecker@csusb.edu.
Cheerleading: SuzAnne McDonald; Phone: 909-880-5011.
Cross Country: Tom Burleson; Phone: 909-880-5055; E-mail: burleson@csusb.edu.
Soccer: Christian Johnson; Phone: 909-880-5017; E-mail: johnsonc@csusb.edu.
Softball: Dawn Castaneda; Phone: 909-880-5022; E-mail: dcastane@csusb.edu.
Tennis: Tom Starzyk; Phone: 909-880-7233; E-mail: tstarzyk@csusb.edu.
Volleyball: Kim Cherniss; Phone: 909-880-5050; E-mail: kcyotevb@csusb.edu.

CALIFORNIA STATE UNIVERSITY, SAN MARCOS
San Marcos, California

Cougars ◆ NAIA ◆ Independent ◆ http://www.csusm.edu/

State-supported comprehensive, founded 1990, part of California State University System
Coed, 6,407 undergraduate students, 70% full-time, 60% women, 40% men
Suburban 304-acre campus with easy access to San Diego
Moderately difficult entrance level, 73% of applicants were admitted

Freshmen *Admission:* 4,317 applied, 3,166 were accepted, 890 enrolled. *Test scores:* SAT verbal scores over 500: 45%; SAT math scores over 500: 52%; SAT verbal scores over 600: 9%; SAT math scores over 600: 11%; SAT verbal scores over 700: 1%; SAT math scores over 700: %.
Tuition and fees (2003–04): $2414 (resident), $9182 (nonresident). *Room only:* $7470.
Financial Aid (All incoming freshmen): *Average aid to full-time undergraduates:* $5213.
Athletic Department: *Director of Athletics:* Debbie Dale; Phone: 760-750-7102; Fax: 760-750-3660; E-mail: ddale@mailhost1.csusm.edu. *Sports Information Director:* Paige Jennings; Phone: 760-750-4058; E-mail: pjenning@csusm.edu.

MEN'S COACHES

Cross Country: Steve Scott; Phone: 760-750-7105; E-mail: sscott@csusm.edu.
Golf: Fred Hanover; Phone: 760-750-7110; E-mail: fhanover@mailhost1.csusm.edu.
Track and Field: Steve Scott; Phone: 760-750-7105; E-mail: sscott@csusm.edu.

WOMEN'S COACHES

Cross Country: Steve Scott; Phone: 760-750-7105; E-mail: sscott@csusm.edu.
Golf: Dan Anderson; Phone: 760-750-7110; E-mail: danderson@csusm.edu.
Track and Field: Steve Scott; Phone: 760-750-7105; E-mail: sscott@csusm.edu.

CALIFORNIA STATE UNIVERSITY, STANISLAUS
Turlock, California

Warriors ◆ NCAA II ◆ California Collegiate Athletic Conference ◆ http://www.csustan.edu/

State-supported comprehensive, founded 1957, part of California State University System
Coed, 6,154 undergraduate students, 68% full-time, 66% women, 34% men
Small-town 220-acre campus
Moderately difficult entrance level, 60% of applicants were admitted

Freshmen *Admission:* 2,687 applied, 1,733 were accepted, 670 enrolled. *Test scores:* SAT verbal scores over 500: 56%; SAT math scores over

500: 58%; SAT verbal scores over 600: 10%; SAT math scores over 600: 12%; SAT verbal scores over 700: 1%; SAT math scores over 700: 1%.
Tuition and fees (2003–04): $2503 (resident), $10,963 (nonresident). *Room and board:* $7242 (room only: $4322).
Financial Aid (All incoming freshmen): *Average need-based gift aid:* $3471. *Average non-need based aid:* $1264. *Average aid to full-time undergraduates:* $6739.
Athletic Department: *Director of Athletics:* Milton Richards; Phone: 209-667-3016; Fax: 209-667-3313; E-mail: mrichards@csustan.edu. *Sports Information Director:* Hung Tsai; E-mail: htsai@csustan.edu.

MEN'S COACHES

Baseball: Kenny Leonesio; Phone: 209-667-3272; E-mail: kleonesio@csustan.edu.
Basketball: Keith Larsen; Phone: 209-667-3528; E-mail: klarsen@menlo.edu.
Cross Country: Kim Duyst; Phone: 209-667-3312; E-mail: kduyst@csustan.edu.
Golf: Jim Hanny; Phone: 209-667-3639; E-mail: jhanny@stan.csustan.edu.
Soccer: Eric Mild; Phone: 209-667-7059; E-mail: emild@csustan.edu.
Track and Field: Kim Duyst; Phone: 209-667-3312; E-mail: kduyst@csustan.edu.

WOMEN'S COACHES

Basketball: Sharon Turner-Dean; Phone: 209-667-3424; E-mail: sturner-dean@csustan.edu.
Cross Country: Kim Duyst; Phone: 209-667-3312; E-mail: kduyst@csustan.edu.
Soccer: Nicole Van Dyke; Phone: 209-667-3802; E-mail: nvandyke@stan.csustan.edu.
Softball: Jan Schefkowitz; Phone: 209-667-3105; E-mail: jschefkowitz@csustan.edu.
Track and Field: Kim Duyst; Phone: 209-667-3312; E-mail: kduyst@csustan.edu.
Volleyball: Cindy Nikkel; Phone: 209-667-3803; E-mail: cnikkel@csustan.edu.

CALIFORNIA UNIVERSITY OF PENNSYLVANIA
California, Pennsylvania

Vulcans ◆ NCAA II ◆ Pennsylvania State Athletic Conference ◆ http://www.cup.edu/

State-supported comprehensive, founded 1852, part of Pennsylvania State System of Higher Education
Coed, 5,392 undergraduate students, 87% full-time, 53% women, 47% men
Small-town 148-acre campus with easy access to Pittsburgh
Moderately difficult entrance level, 74% of applicants were admitted

Freshmen *Admission:* 2,721 applied, 2,038 were accepted, 996 enrolled. *Test scores:* SAT verbal scores over 500: 43%; SAT math scores over 500: 36%; SAT verbal scores over 600: 8%; SAT math scores over 600: 8%; SAT verbal scores over 700: 1%; SAT math scores over 700: 1%.
Tuition and fees (2003–04): $6008 (resident), $8358 (nonresident). *Room and board:* $5378 (room only: $2766).
Athletic Department: *Director of Athletics:* Thomas Pucci; Phone: 724-938-4351; Fax: 724-938-5849; E-mail: pucci@cup.edu. *Sports Information Director:* Dave Smith; Phone: 724-938-4552; E-mail: smith_dw@cup.edu.

MEN'S COACHES

Baseball: Mike Conte; Phone: 724-938-5837; E-mail: conte@cup.edu.
Basketball: Bill Brown; Phone: 724-938-4360; E-mail: brown@cup.edu.
Cheerleading: Lisa Smith; Phone: 724-938-5837; E-mail: conte_m@cup.edu.
Cross Country: Ray Kuhles; Phone: 724-938-5828; E-mail: kuhles@cup.edu.
Football: John Luckhardt; Phone: 724-938-4019; E-mail: luckhardt@cup.edu.
Soccer: Dennis Laskey; Phone: 724-938-5793; E-mail: laskey@cup.edu.
Track and Field: Ray Kuhles; Phone: 724-938-5828; E-mail: kuhles@cup.edu.

California University of Pennsylvania *(continued)*

WOMEN'S COACHES

Basketball: Darcie Vincent; Phone: 724-938-4554; E-mail: vincent@cup.edu.

Cheerleading: Lisa Smith; Phone: 724-938-5837; E-mail: conte_m@cup.edu.

Cross Country: Ray Kuhles; Phone: 724-938-5828; E-mail: kuhles@cup.edu.

Soccer: Dennis Laskey; Phone: 724-938-4351; E-mail: laskey@cup.edu.

Softball: Rick Bertagrollli; Phone: 724-938-5794; E-mail: bertagnolli@cup.edu.

Swimming: Edward Denny; Phone: 724-938-4328; E-mail: denny@cup.edu.

Tennis: Pablo Montana; Phone: 724-938-4237; E-mail: montana@cup.edu.

Track and Field: Ray Kuhles; Phone: 724-938-5828; E-mail: kuhles@cup.edu.

Volleyball: Melissa Meyers; Phone: 724-938-5876; E-mail: myers_m@cup.edu.

CALUMET COLLEGE OF SAINT JOSEPH
Whiting, Indiana

Crimson Wave ◆ NAIA ◆ Chicagoland Collegiate Conference ◆ http://www.ccsj.edu/

Independent Roman Catholic comprehensive, founded 1951
Coed, 1,214 undergraduate students, 37% full-time, 59% women, 41% men
Urban 25-acre campus with easy access to Chicago
Minimally difficult entrance level, 68% of applicants were admitted

Freshmen *Admission:* 160 applied, 117 were accepted, 108 enrolled. *Test scores:* SAT verbal scores over 500: 17%; SAT math scores over 500: 21%; SAT verbal scores over 600: 4%; SAT math scores over 600: 4%.
Tuition and fees (2003–04): $9000 (full-time).
Athletic Department: *Director of Athletics:* Andy Juscik; Phone: 219-473-4327; Fax: 219-473-4259.

MEN'S COACHES

Baseball: Frank Eccles; Phone: 219-473-4241.

Basketball: Nathan Pomeday; Phone: 219-473-4214.

Volleyball: Brian Erminger; Phone: 219-473-4323.

WOMEN'S COACHES

Basketball: Andy Juscik; Phone: 219-473-4327.

Soccer: Greg Erminger; Phone: 219-473-4323.

Softball: Phone: 219-473-4327.

Volleyball: John Steinhilber; Phone: 219-473-4327.

CALVIN COLLEGE
Grand Rapids, Michigan

Knights ◆ NCAA III ◆ Michigan Intercollegiate Conference ◆ http://www.calvin.edu/

Independent religious comprehensive, founded 1876, affiliated with Christian Reformed Church
Coed, 4,289 undergraduate students, 95% full-time, 56% women, 44% men
Suburban 370-acre campus
Moderately difficult entrance level, 98% of applicants were admitted

Freshmen *Admission:* 1,933 applied, 1,906 were accepted, 1,042 enrolled. *Test scores:* SAT verbal scores over 500: 87%; SAT math scores over 500: 90%; SAT verbal scores over 600: 53%; SAT math scores over 600: 52%; SAT verbal scores over 700: 16%; SAT math scores over 700: 14%.
Tuition and fees (2003–04): $16,775 (full-time). *Room and board:* $5840 (room only: $3180).

Financial Aid (All incoming freshmen): *Average need-based gift aid:* $8912. *Average non-need based aid:* $4839. *Average aid to full-time undergraduates:* $12,583.
Athletic Department: *Director of Athletics:* Kevin Vande Streek; Phone: 616-526-6176; Fax: 616-526-8551; E-mail: kvstreek@calvin.edu. *Sports Information Director:* Jeffrey Febus; Phone: 616-526-6169; E-mail: jfebus@calvin.edu.

MEN'S COACHES

Baseball: Jeff Pettinga; Phone: 616-957-6176; E-mail: pett@calvin.edu.

Basketball: Kevin Vande Streek; Phone: 616-957-6704; E-mail: kvstreek@calvin.edu.

Cross Country: Brian Diemer; Phone: 616-957-6031; E-mail: bkchase@aol.com.

Diving: Dan Gelderloos; Phone: 616-957-6703; E-mail: dgelderl@calvin.edu.

Golf: Jim Timmer; Phone: 616-957-6037; E-mail: jtimmer@calvin.edu.

Soccer: Chris Hughes; Phone: 616-957-6606; E-mail: crh4@calvin.edu.

Swimming: Dan Gelderloos; Phone: 616-957-6703; E-mail: dgelderl@calvin.edu.

Tennis: John Ross; Phone: 616-957-6176; E-mail: jr23@calvin.edu.

Track and Field: Jong II Kim; Phone: 616-957-6176; E-mail: jikim@calvin.edu.

WOMEN'S COACHES

Basketball: John Ross; Phone: 616-957-6030; E-mail: jr23@calvin.edu.

Cross Country: Nancy Meyer; Phone: 616-957-6224; E-mail: meyn@calvin.edu.

Diving: Dan Gelderloos; Phone: 616-957-6703; E-mail: dgelderl@calvin.edu.

Golf: Jerry Bergsma; Phone: 616-957-6020; E-mail: jbergsma@calvin.edu.

Soccer: Mark Recker; Phone: 616-957-6176; E-mail: mark.recker@pinerest.org.

Softball: Amber Warners; Phone: 616-957-6222; E-mail: awarners@calvin.edu.

Swimming: Dan Gelderloos; Phone: 616-957-6703; E-mail: dgelderl@calvin.edu.

Tennis: Jerry Bergsma; Phone: 616-957-8611; E-mail: jbergsma@calvin.edu.

Track and Field: Jong-II Kim; Phone: 616-957-6224; E-mail: jikim@calvin.edu.

Volleyball: Amber Warners; Phone: 616-957-6181; E-mail: awarners@calvin.edu.

CAMERON UNIVERSITY
Lawton, Oklahoma

Aggies ◆ NCAA II ◆ Lone Star Conference ◆ http://www.cameron.edu/

State-supported comprehensive, founded 1908, part of Oklahoma State Regents for Higher Education
Coed, 5,193 undergraduate students, 60% full-time, 57% women, 43% men
Small-town 160-acre campus
Minimally difficult entrance level, 100% of applicants were admitted

Freshmen *Admission:* 888 applied, 888 were accepted, 888 enrolled.
Tuition and fees (2004–05): $2943 (resident), $6843 (nonresident). *Room and board:* $2854.
Athletic Department: *Director of Athletics:* Sam Carroll; Phone: 580-581-2460; Fax: 580-581-5537; E-mail: samc@cameron.edu. *Sports Information Director:* Steve Doughty; Phone: 580-581-2303; E-mail: steved@cameron.edu.

MEN'S COACHES

Baseball: Todd Holland; Phone: 580-581-2479; E-mail: tholland@cameron.edu.

Basketball: Garreite Mantle; Phone: 580-581-2405; E-mail: garrette@cameron.edu.

Golf: Jerry Hinciar; Phone: 580-581-2468; E-mail: jerryh@cameron.edu.

Tennis: James Helvey; Phone: 580-581-2354; E-mail: jameshel@cameron.edu.

WOMEN'S COACHES

Basketball: Dick Halterman; Phone: 580-581-2529; E-mail: dickh@cameron.edu.

Softball: Gladys Crawford; Phone: 580-581-2528; E-mail: gcrawfor@cameron.edu.
Tennis: James Helvey; Phone: 580-581-2460; E-mail: jameshel@cameron.edu.
Volleyball: Kim Vinson; Phone: 580-581-2462; E-mail: kimv@cameron.edu.

CAMPBELLSVILLE UNIVERSITY
Campbellsville, Kentucky

Tigers ◆ NAIA ◆ Mid-South Conference
◆ http://www.campbellsville.edu/

Independent religious comprehensive, founded 1906, affiliated with Kentucky Baptist Convention
Coed, 1,721 undergraduate students, 68% full-time, 56% women, 44% men
Small-town 80-acre campus
Moderately difficult entrance level, 77% of applicants were admitted

Freshmen *Admission:* 1,053 applied, 839 were accepted, 365 enrolled. *Test scores:* SAT verbal scores over 500: 51%; SAT math scores over 500: 48%; SAT verbal scores over 600: 16%; SAT math scores over 600: 12%; SAT math scores over 700: 3%.
Tuition and fees (2003–04): $12,824 (full-time). *Room and board:* $4976 (room only: $2290).
Financial Aid (All incoming freshmen): *Average need-based gift aid:* $10,022. *Average non-need based aid:* $7840. *Average aid to full-time undergraduates:* $13,328.
Athletic Department: *Director of Athletics:* Rusty Hollingsworth; Phone: 270-789-5257; E-mail: rhollingsworth@campbellsville.edu. *Sports Information Director:* Bryan Blair; Phone: 270-789-5276; E-mail: bfblair@campbellsville.edu.

MEN'S COACHES
Baseball: Beauford Sanders; Phone: 270-789-5056; E-mail: bwsanders@campbellsville.edu.
Basketball: Keith Adkins; Phone: 270-789-5259; E-mail: ckadkins@campbellsville.edu.
Cheerleading: Amanda Day; Phone: 270-789-5547.
Cross Country: Paul Bodenhamer; Phone: 270-789-5437; E-mail: phbodenhamer@campbellsville.edu.
Football: Mark Peach; Phone: 270-789-5262; E-mail: mapeach@campbellsville.edu.
Golf: P.J. Throckmorton; Phone: 270-789-5179.
Soccer: Adam Preston; Phone: 270-789-5140.
Tennis: Leigh Sullivan; Phone: 270-789-5156; E-mail: ljsullivan@campbellsville.edu.
Track and Field: David Pool; Phone: 270-789-5517; E-mail: dapool@campbellsville.edu.

WOMEN'S COACHES
Basketball: Donna Wise; Phone: 270-789-5261; E-mail: dwise@campbellsville.edu.
Cheerleading: Amanda Day; Phone: 270-789-5547.
Cross Country: Paul Bodenhamer; Phone: 270-789-5437; E-mail: phbodenhamer@campbellsville.edu.
Golf: P.J. Throckmorton; Phone: 270-789-5179.
Soccer: Abbie Whitley; Phone: 270-789-5072; E-mail: awhitley@campbellsville.edu.
Softball: Shannon Wathen; Phone: 270-789-5261; E-mail: slwathen@campbellsville.edu.
Tennis: Leigh Sullivan; Phone: 270-789-5156; E-mail: ljsullivan@campbellsville.edu.
Track and Field: David Pool; Phone: 270-789-5517; E-mail: dapool@campbellsville.edu.
Volleyball: Billy Gregory; Phone: 270-789-5179; E-mail: wrgregory@campbellsville.edu.

CAMPBELL UNIVERSITY
Buies Creek, North Carolina

Fighting Camels ◆ NCAA I ◆ Atlantic Sun Conference; Colonial Athletic Conference ◆ http://www.campbell.edu/

Independent religious university, founded 1887, affiliated with North Carolina Baptist State Convention
Coed, 2,535 undergraduate students, 94% full-time, 55% women, 45% men
Rural 850-acre campus with easy access to Raleigh
Moderately difficult entrance level, 58% of applicants were admitted

Freshmen *Admission:* 1,780 applied, 1,032 were accepted, 679 enrolled. *Test scores:* SAT verbal scores over 500: 77%; SAT math scores over 500: 76%; SAT verbal scores over 600: 31%; SAT math scores over 600: 30%; SAT verbal scores over 700: 3%; SAT math scores over 700: 2%.
Tuition and fees (2003–04): $13,512 (full-time). *Room and board:* $4756.
Financial Aid (All incoming freshmen): *Average need-based gift aid:* $4877. *Average non-need based aid:* $9999. *Average aid to full-time undergraduates:* $17,770.
Athletic Department: *Director of Athletics:* Stan Williamson; Phone: 910-893-1326; Fax: 910-893-1330; E-mail: williamson@mailcenter.campbell.edu. *Sports Information Director:* Stan Cole; Phone: 910-893-1331; E-mail: cole@mailcenter.campbell.edu.

MEN'S COACHES
Baseball: Chip Smith; Phone: 910-893-1354; E-mail: csmith@mailcenter.campbell.edu.
Basketball: Robbie Laing; Phone: 910-893-1335; E-mail: laingr@mailcenter.campbell.edu.
Cheerleading: Sarah Rapalje; Phone: 910-893-1844; E-mail: rapaljes@mailcenter.campbell.edu.
Cross Country: Ken Frenette; Phone: 910-893-1356; E-mail: frenette@mailcenter.campbell.edu.
Golf: John Crooks; Phone: 910-893-1370; E-mail: crooks@mailcenter.campbell.edu.
Soccer: Doug Hess; Phone: 910-893-1333; E-mail: hess@mailcenter.campbell.edu.
Tennis: David Johnson; Phone: 910-893-1351; E-mail: johnsond@mailcenter.campbell.edu.
Track and Field: Ken Frenette; Phone: 910-893-1356; E-mail: frenette@mailcenter.campbell.edu.
Wrestling: Dave Auble; Phone: 910-893-1358; E-mail: auble@mailcenter.campbell.edu.

WOMEN'S COACHES
Basketball: Wanda Watkins; Phone: 910-893-1346; E-mail: watkins@mailcenter.campbell.edu.
Cheerleading: Sarah Rapalje; Phone: 910-893-1844; E-mail: rapaljes@mailcenter.campbell.edu.
Cross Country: Ken Frenette; Phone: 910-893-1356; E-mail: frenette@mailcenter.campbell.edu.
Golf: John Crooks; Phone: 910-893-1370; E-mail: crooks@mailcenter.campbell.edu.
Soccer: Pat Ferguson; Phone: 910-893-1324; E-mail: ferguson@mailcenter.campbell.edu.
Softball: Drew Peterson; Phone: 910-893-1355; E-mail: peterson@mailcenter.campbell.edu.
Swimming: Phone: 910-893-1354.
Tennis: David Johnson; Phone: 910-893-1351; E-mail: johnsond@mailcenter.campbell.edu.
Track and Field: Ken Frenette; Phone: 910-893-1356; E-mail: frenette@mailcenter.campbell.edu.
Volleyball: Malinda Ashcraft; Phone: 910-893-1343; E-mail: ashcraft@mailcenter.campbell.edu.

CANISIUS COLLEGE
Buffalo, New York

Golden Griffins ◆ NCAA I ◆ Atlantic Hockey Conference; Metro Atlantic Athletic Conference
◆ http://www.canisius.edu/

Independent Roman Catholic (Jesuit) comprehensive, founded 1870
Coed, 3,535 undergraduate students, 88% full-time, 55% women, 45% men
Urban 36-acre campus
Moderately difficult entrance level, 82% of applicants were admitted

Freshmen *Admission:* 3,437 applied, 2,868 were accepted, 836 enrolled. *Test scores:* SAT verbal scores over 500: 77%; SAT math scores over 500: 78%; SAT verbal scores over 600: 27%; SAT math scores over 600: 32%; SAT verbal scores over 700: 4%; SAT math scores over 700: 4%.
Tuition and fees (2003–04): $20,193 (full-time). *Room and board:* $7970 (room only: $3430).
Financial Aid (All incoming freshmen): *Average need-based gift aid:* $12,653. *Average non-need based aid:* $9283. *Average aid to full-time undergraduates:* $18,278.
Athletic Department: *Director of Athletics:* Tim Dillon; Phone: 716-888-2972; Fax: 716-888-2980; E-mail: dillont@canisius.edu. *Sports Information Director:* Marc Gignac; Phone: 716-888-2978; E-mail: gignacm@canisius.edu.

MEN'S COACHES
Baseball: Mark Notaro; Phone: 716888-888-3251; E-mail: notaro1@canisius.edu.
Basketball: Mike MacDonald; Phone: 716888-888-2904; E-mail: macdonam@canisius.edu.
Cross Country: Peter Osmond; Phone: 716888-888-3761; E-mail: osmondp@canisius.edu.
Diving: Kristine Mincher; Phone: 716888-888-2963; E-mail: mincherk@canisius.edu.
Golf: Todd Hummel; Phone: 716888-888-3763; E-mail: hummelt@canisius.edu.
Ice Hockey: Brian Cavanaugh; Phone: 716888-888-2957; E-mail: cavanaub@canisius.edu.
Lacrosse: Randy Mearns; Phone: 716888-888-2967; E-mail: mearnsr@canisius.edu.
Soccer: Jim Hesch; Phone: 716888-888-2897; E-mail: heschj@canisius.edu.
Swimming: Jason Morini; Phone: 716888-888-2963; E-mail: morinij@canisius.edu.

WOMEN'S COACHES
Basketball: Mike Decillis; Phone: 716888-888-2976; E-mail: decillim@canisius.edu.
Cross Country: Peter Osmond; Phone: 716888-888-3761; E-mail: osmondp@canisius.edu.
Diving: Kristine Mincher; Phone: 716888-888-2963; E-mail: mincherk@canisius.edu.
Lacrosse: Scott Teeter; Phone: 716-741-3764; E-mail: teeters@canisius.edu.
Soccer: Meagan Dougherty; Phone: 716888-888-2899; E-mail: dougherm@canisius.edu.
Softball: Mike Rappl; Phone: 716888-888-2975; E-mail: rappl@canisius.edu.
Swimming: Jason Morini; Phone: 716888-888-2963; E-mail: morinij@canisius.edu.
Volleyball: Cathy Hummel; Phone: 716888-888-2891; E-mail: hummelc@canisius.edu.

CAPITAL UNIVERSITY
Columbus, Ohio

Crusaders ◆ NCAA III ◆ Ohio Athletic Conference ◆ http://www.capital.edu/

Independent religious comprehensive, founded 1830, affiliated with Evangelical Lutheran Church in America
Coed, 2,830 undergraduate students, 76% full-time, 64% women, 36% men
Suburban 48-acre campus
Moderately difficult entrance level, 81% of applicants were admitted

Freshmen *Admission:* 2,216 applied, 1,871 were accepted, 577 enrolled. *Test scores:* SAT verbal scores over 500: 70%; SAT math scores over 500: 72%; SAT verbal scores over 600: 28%; SAT math scores over 600: 27%; SAT verbal scores over 700: 4%; SAT math scores over 700: 5%.
Tuition and fees (2003–04): $20,500 (full-time). *Room and board:* $6050.
Financial Aid (All incoming freshmen): *Average need-based gift aid:* $11,268. *Average non-need based aid:* $8777. *Average aid to full-time undergraduates:* $17,774.
Athletic Department: *Director of Athletics:* Roger Welsh; Phone: 614-236-6528; Fax: 614-236-6178. *Sports Information Director:* Leonard Reich; Phone: 614-236-6174; E-mail: lreich@capital.edu.

MEN'S COACHES
Baseball: Greg Weynich; Phone: 614-236-6203; E-mail: gregweyrich@aol.com.
Basketball: Damon Goodwin; Phone: 614-236-6913; E-mail: dgoodwin@capital.edu.
Cheerleading: Amber Jones; Phone: 614-236-6911; E-mail: beramj@netscape.net.
Cross Country: Damon Goodwin; Phone: 614-236-6913; E-mail: dgoodwin@capital.edu.
Football: Jim Collins; Phone: 614-236-6184; E-mail: jcollins@capital.edu.
Golf: Jim Collins; Phone: 614-236-6184; E-mail: jcollins@capital.edu.
Soccer: Dwight Burgess; Phone: 614-236-6375; E-mail: dburgess@capital.edu.
Tennis: Shaun Stamps; Phone: 614-236-6554; E-mail: sstamps@capital.edu.
Track and Field: Fred Barends; Phone: 614-236-6919; E-mail: fbarends@capital.edu.

WOMEN'S COACHES
Basketball: Dixie Jeffers; Phone: 614-236-6551; E-mail: djeffers@capital.edu.
Cheerleading: Amber Jones; Phone: 614-236-6911; E-mail: beramj@netscape.net.
Cross Country: Damon Goodwin; Phone: 614-236-6913; E-mail: dgoodwin@capital.edu.
Golf: Pam Briggs; Phone: 614-236-6918; E-mail: pbriggs@capital.edu.
Soccer: Dwight Burgess; Phone: 614-236-6375; E-mail: dburgess@capital.edu.
Softball: Nanette Payne; Phone: 614-236-6487; E-mail: npayne@capital.edu.
Tennis: Shaun Stamps; Phone: 614-236-6554; E-mail: sstamps@capital.edu.
Track and Field: Fred Barends; Phone: 614-236-6919; E-mail: fbarends@capital.edu.
Volleyball: Pam Briggs; Phone: 614-236-6918; E-mail: pbriggs@capital.edu.

CARDINAL STRITCH UNIVERSITY
Milwaukee, Wisconsin

NAIA ◆ Chicagoland Collegiate Conference
◆ http://www.stritch.edu/

Independent Roman Catholic comprehensive, founded 1937
Coed, 3,251 undergraduate students, 90% full-time, 68% women, 32% men
Suburban 40-acre campus
Moderately difficult entrance level, 96% of applicants were admitted

Freshmen *Admission:* 617 applied, 572 were accepted, 241 enrolled. *Test scores:* SAT verbal scores over 500: 50%; SAT math scores over 500: 60%; SAT verbal scores over 600: 30%.

Tuition and fees (2003–04): $14,540 (full-time). *Room and board:* $5160.
Financial Aid (All incoming freshmen): *Average need-based gift aid:* $7783. *Average non-need based aid:* $8323. *Average aid to full-time undergraduates:* $9467.
Athletic Department: *Director of Athletics:* Denny Fox; Phone: 414-410-4121; Fax: 414-410-4127; E-mail: dlfox@stritch.edu. *Sports Information Director:* John Pfaffl; Phone: 414-410-4123; E-mail: jppfaffl@stritch.edu.

MEN'S COACHES

Baseball: Michael Zolecki; Phone: 414-410-4519; E-mail: mjzolecki@stritch.edu.
Basketball: Denny Fox; Phone: 414-410-4121; E-mail: dlfox@stritch.edu.
Cross Country: John Pfaffl; Phone: 414-410-4123; E-mail: jppfaffl@stritch.edu.
Soccer: Patrick Clemens; Phone: 414-410-4125; E-mail: pjclemens@stritch.edu.
Volleyball: Mac Milleur; Phone: 414-410-4174; E-mail: mbmilleur@stritch.edu.

WOMEN'S COACHES

Basketball: Richard Panella; Phone: 414-410-4122; E-mail: rapanella@stritch.edu.
Cross Country: John Pfaffl; Phone: 414-410-4123; E-mail: jppfaffl@stritch.edu.
Soccer: Patrick Clemens; Phone: 414-410-4125; E-mail: pjclemens@stritch.edu.
Softball: Richard Panella; Phone: 414-410-4122; E-mail: rapanella@stritch.edu.
Volleyball: Martin Dobson; Phone: 414-410-4518; E-mail: mvdobson@stritch.edu.

CARLETON COLLEGE
Northfield, Minnesota

Knights ◆ NCAA III ◆ Minnesota Intercollegiate Athletic Conference ◆ http://www.carleton.edu/

Independent 4-year, founded 1866
Coed, 1,943 undergraduate students, 99% full-time, 52% women, 48% men
Small-town 955-acre campus with easy access to Minneapolis–St. Paul
Very difficult entrance level, 3% of applicants were admitted

Freshmen *Admission:* 4,737 applied, 1,414 were accepted, 488 enrolled. *Test scores:* SAT verbal scores over 500: 100%; SAT math scores over 500: 100%; SAT verbal scores over 600: 91%; SAT math scores over 600: 92%; SAT verbal scores over 700: 52%; SAT math scores over 700: 44%.
Tuition and fees (2003–04): $28,527 (full-time). *Room and board:* $5868 (room only: $2547).
Financial Aid (All incoming freshmen): *Average need-based gift aid:* $17,394. *Average non-need based aid:* $3109. *Average aid to full-time undergraduates:* $22,267.
Athletic Department: *Director of Athletics:* Leon Lunder; Phone: 507-646-4056; Fax: 507-646-5550; E-mail: llunder@carleton.edu. *Sports Information Director:* Eric Sieger; Phone: 507-646-4185; E-mail: esieger@carleton.edu.

MEN'S COACHES

Baseball: Bill Nelson; Phone: 507-646-4051; E-mail: bnelson@carleton.edu.
Basketball: Guy Kalland; Phone: 507-646-4055; E-mail: gkalland@carleton.edu.
Cross Country: Bill Terriquez; Phone: 507-646-4053; E-mail: wterriqu@carleton.edu.
Diving: Andy Clark; Phone: 507-646-4584; E-mail: aclark@carleton.edu.
Football: Chris Brann; Phone: 507-646-4054.
Golf: Phil Zrimsek; Phone: 507-646-7114; E-mail: pzrimsek@rconnect.com.
Soccer: Bob Carlson; Phone: 507-646-5840; E-mail: rcarlson@carleton.edu.
Swimming: Andy Clark; Phone: 507-646-4584; E-mail: aclark@carleton.edu.
Tennis: Sarah Hurst; Phone: 507-646-4482; E-mail: shurst@carleton.edu.

Track and Field: Dave Ricks; Phone: 507-646-7808; E-mail: daricks@carleton.edu.

WOMEN'S COACHES

Basketball: Tammy Metcalf-Filzen; Phone: 507-646-4058; E-mail: tmetcalf@carleton.edu.
Cross Country: Donna Ricks; Phone: 507-646-4485; E-mail: dricks@carleton.edu.
Diving: Andy Clark; Phone: 507-646-4584; E-mail: aclark@carleton.edu.
Golf: Eric Sieger; Phone: 507-646-4185; E-mail: esieger@carleton.edu.
Soccer: Karen Parker; Phone: 507-646-4484; E-mail: knparker@carleton.edu.
Softball: Amy Tenute; Phone: 507-646-5898; E-mail: atenute@carleton.edu.
Swimming: Andy Clark; Phone: 507-646-4584; E-mail: aclark@carleton.edu.
Tennis: Sarah Hurst; Phone: 507-646-4482; E-mail: shurst@carleton.edu.
Track and Field: Donna Ricks; Phone: 507-646-4485; E-mail: dricks@carleton.edu.
Volleyball: Heidi Luehmann; Phone: 507-646-4447; E-mail: hjaynes@carleton.edu.

CARLOW COLLEGE
Pittsburgh, Pennsylvania

Celtics ◆ NAIA ◆ American Mideast Conference ◆ http://www.carlow.edu/

Independent Roman Catholic comprehensive, founded 1929
Coed, primarily women, 1,824 undergraduate students
Urban 14-acre campus
Moderately difficult entrance level

Freshmen *Test scores:* SAT verbal scores over 500: 53%; SAT math scores over 500: 44%; SAT verbal scores over 600: 16%; SAT math scores over 600: 11%; SAT verbal scores over 700: 2%; SAT math scores over 700: 1%.
Tuition and fees (2003–04): $15,264 (full-time). *Room and board:* $6110.
Athletic Department: *Director of Athletics:* George Sliman; Phone: 412-578-8826; Fax: 412-578-8704; E-mail: gsliman@carlow.edu. *Sports Information Director:* Sarah Wivell; Phone: 412-578-6022; E-mail: swivell@carlow.edu.

WOMEN'S COACHES

Basketball: John Brown; Phone: 412-578-6345; E-mail: jjbrown@carlow.edu.
Soccer: Edward Child; Phone: 412-578-6345; E-mail: echild@carlow.edu.
Softball: Dan Richtar; Phone: 412-578-6345; E-mail: drichtar@carlow.edu.
Tennis: Tom Merchant; Phone: 412-578-6345.
Volleyball: Julie Gaul; Phone: 412-578-6345; E-mail: jgaul@carlow.edu.

CARNEGIE MELLON UNIVERSITY
Pittsburgh, Pennsylvania

Tartans ◆ NCAA III ◆ University Athletic Conference ◆ http://www.cmu.edu/

Independent university, founded 1900
Coed, 5,484 undergraduate students, 95% full-time, 40% women, 60% men
Urban 103-acre campus
Very difficult entrance level, 34% of applicants were admitted

Freshmen *Admission:* 14,467 applied, 5,561 were accepted, 1,341 enrolled. *Test scores:* SAT verbal scores over 500: 97%; SAT math scores over 500: 100%; SAT verbal scores over 600: 78%; SAT math scores over 600: 97%; SAT verbal scores over 700: 30%; SAT math scores over 700: 66%.
Tuition and fees (2003–04): $29,410 (full-time). *Room and board:* $8155 (room only: $4705).

Carnegie Mellon University *(continued)*

Financial Aid (All incoming freshmen): *Average need-based gift aid:* $16,116. *Average non-need based aid:* $9831. *Average aid to full-time undergraduates:* $22,085.
Athletic Department: *Director of Athletics:* John Harvey; Phone: 412-268-8054; Fax: 412-268-3099; E-mail: jh8d@andrew.cmu.edu. *Sports Information Director:* Bethany McClam; Phone: 412-268-3087; E-mail: bmcclam@andrew.cmu.edu.

MEN'S COACHES

Basketball: Tony Wingen; Phone: 412-268-2218; E-mail: aw30@andrew.cmu.edu.
Cheerleading: Dan Barnett; Phone: 412-268-2000; E-mail: dbarnett@andrew.cmu.edu.
Cross Country: Dario Donatelli; Phone: 412-268-2220; E-mail: dd7s@andrew.cmu.edu.
Diving: Patti McClure; Phone: 412-268-2346.
Football: Rich Lackner; Phone: 412-268-2216; E-mail: rl2n@andrew.cmu.edu.
Golf: Rich Erdelyi; Phone: 412-268-2219; E-mail: rerdelyi@andrew.cmu.edu.
Soccer: Nick Gaudioso; Phone: 412-268-2217; E-mail: ng0p@andrew.cmu.edu.
Swimming: Dave Belowich; Phone: 412-268-2346; E-mail: david2@andrew.cmu.edu.
Tennis: Andrew Girard; Phone: 412-268-5179; E-mail: agirard@andrew.cmu.edu.
Track and Field: Dario Donatelli; Phone: 412-268-2220; E-mail: dd7s@andrew.cmu.edu.

WOMEN'S COACHES

Basketball: Gerri Seidl; Phone: 412-268-3306; E-mail: gs2n@andrew.cmu.edu.
Cheerleading: Dan Barnett; Phone: 412-268-2000; E-mail: dbarnett@andrew.cmu.edu.
Cross Country: Dario Donatelli; Phone: 412-268-2220; E-mail: dd7s@andrew.cmu.edu.
Diving: Patti McClure; Phone: 412-268-2346.
Golf: Rich Erdelyi; Phone: 412-268-2219; E-mail: rerdelyi@andrew.cmu.edu.
Soccer: Heather Kendra; Phone: 412-268-2187; E-mail: hkendra@andrew.cmu.edu.
Swimming: Dave Belowich; Phone: 412-268-2346; E-mail: david2@andrew.cmu.edu.
Tennis: Andrew Girard; Phone: 412-268-5179; E-mail: agirard@andrew.cmu.edu.
Track and Field: Dario Donatelli; Phone: 412-268-2220; E-mail: dd7s@andrew.cmu.edu.
Volleyball: Julie Webb; Phone: 412-268-2193; E-mail: jwebb@andrew.cmu.edu.

CARROLL COLLEGE
Helena, Montana

Fighting Saints ◆ NAIA ◆ Frontier Conference ◆ http://www.carroll.edu/

Independent Roman Catholic 4-year, founded 1909
Coed, 1,411 undergraduate students, 87% full-time, 58% women, 42% men
Small-town 64-acre campus
Moderately difficult entrance level, 79% of applicants were admitted

Freshmen *Admission:* 899 applied, 742 were accepted, 310 enrolled. *Test scores:* SAT verbal scores over 500: 74%; SAT math scores over 500: 76%; SAT verbal scores over 600: 27%; SAT math scores over 600: 23%; SAT verbal scores over 700: 7%; SAT math scores over 700: 4%.
Tuition and fees (2003–04): $14,666 (full-time). *Room and board:* $5810 (room only: $2720).
Financial Aid (All incoming freshmen): *Average need-based gift aid:* $9017. *Average non-need based aid:* $5722. *Average aid to full-time undergraduates:* $14,377.
Athletic Department: *Director of Athletics:* Bruce Parker; Phone: 406-447-5479; Fax: 406-447-4955; E-mail: bparker@carroll.edu. *Sports Information Director:* Brandon Veltri; Phone: 406-447-4486; E-mail: bveltri@carroll.edu.

MEN'S COACHES

Basketball: Gary Turcott; Phone: 406-447-4486; E-mail: gturcott@carroll.edu.
Football: Mike Van Diest; Phone: 406-447-4485; E-mail: mvandies@carroll.edu.
Golf: Bill Lannan; Phone: 406-442-4022; E-mail: theholeone@aol.com.

WOMEN'S COACHES

Basketball: Shawn Nelson; Phone: 406-447-4489; E-mail: snelson@carroll.edu.
Golf: Bill Lannan; Phone: 406-442-4022; E-mail: theholeone@aol.com.
Soccer: Mark Hiemenz; Phone: 406-447-5518; E-mail: mhiemenz@carroll.edu.
Volleyball: Amy Heuiser; Phone: 406-447-4487; E-mail: aheuiser@carroll.edu.

CARROLL COLLEGE
Waukesha, Wisconsin

Pioneers ◆ NCAA III ◆ Midwest Conference ◆ http://www.cc.edu/

Independent Presbyterian comprehensive, founded 1846
Coed, 2,699 undergraduate students, 76% full-time, 67% women, 33% men
Suburban 52-acre campus with easy access to Milwaukee
Moderately difficult entrance level, 69% of applicants were admitted

Freshmen *Admission:* 2,064 applied, 1,607 were accepted, 513 enrolled.
Tuition and fees (2004–05): $18,170 (full-time). *Room and board:* $5600 (room only: $3030).
Financial Aid (All incoming freshmen): *Average need-based gift aid:* $11,414. *Average non-need based aid:* $7148. *Average aid to full-time undergraduates:* $14,036.
Athletic Department: *Director of Athletics:* Kris Jacobsen; Phone: 262-524-7319; Fax: 262-524-7376; E-mail: kjacobse@cc.edu. *Sports Information Director:* Rick Mobley; Phone: 262-524-7106; E-mail: rmobley@cc.edu.

MEN'S COACHES

Baseball: Steve Dannhoff; Phone: 262-524-7105; E-mail: sdannhof@cc.edu.
Basketball: David Schultz; Phone: 262-524-7322; E-mail: daschult@cc.edu.
Cheerleading: Julie Rapps; Phone: 262-524-7278; E-mail: jrapps@cc.edu.
Cross Country: Shawn Thielitz; Phone: 262-524-7317; E-mail: sthielit@cc.edu.
Football: Jeff Voris; Phone: 262-650-4885; E-mail: jvoris@cc.edu.
Golf: Warren Garstecki; Phone: 262-524-7321; E-mail: wgarstec@cc.edu.
Soccer: Rick Mobley; Phone: 262-524-7106; E-mail: rmobley@cc.edu.
Tennis: Greg Rabidoux; Phone: 262-527-1211; E-mail: grabido@cc.edu.
Track and Field: Shawn Thielitz; Phone: 262-524-7317; E-mail: sthielit@cc.edu.

WOMEN'S COACHES

Basketball: Kris Jacobsen; Phone: 262-524-7319; E-mail: kjacobse@cc.edu.
Cheerleading: Julie Rapps; Phone: 262-524-7278; E-mail: jrapps@cc.edu.
Cross Country: Shawn Thielitz; Phone: 262-524-7317; E-mail: sthielit@cc.edu.
Golf: Warren Garstecki; Phone: 262-524-7321; E-mail: wgarstec@cc.edu.
Soccer: Jason Bretzmann; Phone: 262-951-3027; E-mail: jbretzma@cc.edu.
Softball: Melinda Barth; Phone: 262-524-4830; E-mail: mbarth@cc.edu.
Tennis: Al Pruefer; Phone: 262-527-1211; E-mail: apruefer@cc.edu.
Track and Field: Shawn Thielitz; Phone: 262-524-7317; E-mail: sthielit@cc.edu.
Volleyball: Anne Slattery; Phone: 262-524-7321; E-mail: aslatter@cc.edu.

CARSON-NEWMAN COLLEGE
Jefferson City, Tennessee

Eagles ◆ NCAA II ◆ South Atlantic Conference ◆ http://www.cn.edu/

Independent Southern Baptist comprehensive, founded 1851
Coed, 1,942 undergraduate students, 92% full-time, 55% women, 45% men
Small-town 90-acre campus with easy access to Knoxville
Moderately difficult entrance level, 84% of applicants were admitted

Freshmen *Admission:* 1,124 applied, 992 were accepted, 367 enrolled.
Tuition and fees (2004–05): $14,420 (full-time). *Room and board:* $4930 (room only: $1850).
Financial Aid (All incoming freshmen): *Average need-based gift aid:* $8721. *Average non-need based aid:* $4730. *Average aid to full-time undergraduates:* $12,542.
Athletic Department: *Director of Athletics:* David Barger; Phone: 865-471-2102; Fax: 865-471-3514; E-mail: dbarger@cn.edu. *Sports Information Director:* Marlin Curnett; Phone: 865-471-2106; E-mail: mcurnutt@cn.edu.

MEN'S COACHES
Baseball: Brent Achord; Phone: 865-471-3465; E-mail: bachord@cn.edu.
Basketball: Dale Clayton; Phone: 865-471-3367; E-mail: dclayton@cn.edu.
Cross Country: B. Whitney Lee; Phone: 865-471-3454; E-mail: blee@cn.edu.
Football: Ken Sparks; Phone: 865-471-3466; E-mail: ksparks@cn.edu.
Golf: John Minor; Phone: 865-471-3370; E-mail: jminor@cn.edu.
Soccer: Allen Vital; Phone: 865-471-3520; E-mail: avital@cn.edu.
Tennis: Jean Love; Phone: 865-471-3244; E-mail: jlove@cn.edu.
Track and Field: David Needs; Phone: 865-471-3360; E-mail: dneeds@cn.edu.
Wrestling: Don Elia; Phone: 865-471-3247; E-mail: delia@cn.edu.

WOMEN'S COACHES
Basketball: Dean Walsh; Phone: 865-471-3511; E-mail: dwalsh@cn.edu.
Cross Country: B. Whitney Lee; Phone: 865-471-3454; E-mail: blee@cn.edu.
Soccer: Philip McNamara; Phone: 865-471-3395; E-mail: pmcnamara@cn.edu.
Softball: Vickee Kazee-Hollifield; Phone: 865-471-3424.
Tennis: Jean Love; Phone: 865-471-3244; E-mail: jlove@cn.edu.
Track and Field: David Needs; Phone: 865-471-3360; E-mail: dneeds@cn.edu.
Volleyball: Perry Robinson; Phone: 865-471-4216; E-mail: probinson@cn.edu.

CARTHAGE COLLEGE
Kenosha, Wisconsin

Redmen ◆ NCAA III ◆ College Conference of Illinois and Wisconsin Conference ◆ http://www.carthage.edu/

Independent religious comprehensive, founded 1847, affiliated with Evangelical Lutheran Church in America
Coed, 2,508 undergraduate students, 78% full-time, 58% women, 42% men
Suburban 72-acre campus with easy access to Chicago and Milwaukee
Moderately difficult entrance level, 71% of applicants were admitted

Freshmen *Admission:* 3,346 applied, 2,449 were accepted, 582 enrolled. *Test scores:* SAT verbal scores over 500: 77%; SAT math scores over 500: 77%; SAT verbal scores over 600: 37%; SAT math scores over 600: 54%; SAT verbal scores over 700: 2%; SAT math scores over 700: 10%.
Tuition and fees (2004–05): $21,250 (full-time). *Room and board:* $6250.
Financial Aid (All incoming freshmen): *Average need-based gift aid:* $4093. *Average non-need based aid:* $7319. *Average aid to full-time undergraduates:* $7070.
Athletic Department: *Director of Athletics:* Robert Bonn; Phone: 262-551-5931; Fax: 262-551-5995; E-mail: rbonn@carthage.edu. *Sports Information Director:* Steve Marovich; Phone: 262-551-5740; E-mail: carthagesid@carthage.edu.

MEN'S COACHES
Baseball: Augie Schmidt; Phone: 262-551-5935; E-mail: aschmidt@carthage.edu.
Basketball: Bosko Djurickovic; Phone: 262-551-6627; E-mail: bosko@carthage.edu.
Cheerleading: Amy Carter; Phone: 262-260-2040; E-mail: acarter@scj.com.
Cross Country: Brett Witt; Phone: 262-551-6184; E-mail: bwitt@carthage.edu.
Football: Tim Rucks; Phone: 262-551-5929; E-mail: trucks@carthage.edu.
Golf: Dave Roehl; Phone: 262-551-5491; E-mail: droehl@carthage.edu.
Soccer: Steve Domin; Phone: 262-551-5930; E-mail: sdomin@carthage.edu.
Swimming: Gregg Earhart; Phone: 262-551-6192; E-mail: gearhart@carthage.edu.
Tennis: Brady Lindsley; Phone: 262-551-5932; E-mail: blindsley@carthage.edu.
Track and Field: Steve Ray; Phone: 262-551-5928; E-mail: sray@carthage.edu.

WOMEN'S COACHES
Basketball: Tim Bernero; Phone: 262-551-5713; E-mail: tbernero@carthage.edu.
Cheerleading: Amy Carter; Phone: 262-260-2040; E-mail: acarter@scj.com.
Cross Country: Stephanie Ulicny; Phone: 262-551-5927; E-mail: sulicny@carthage.edu.
Golf: Brian Mosher; Phone: 262-551-5934; E-mail: bmosher@carthage.edu.
Soccer: Steve Domin; Phone: 262-551-5930; E-mail: sdomin@carthage.edu.
Softball: Amy Gillmore; Phone: 262-551-5511; E-mail: agillmore@carthage.edu.
Swimming: Susan Nutty; Phone: 262-551-6631; E-mail: smn@carthage.edu.
Tennis: Brady Lindsley; Phone: 262-551-5932; E-mail: blindsley@carthage.edu.
Track and Field: Steve Ray; Phone: 262-551-5928; E-mail: sray@carthage.edu.
Volleyball: Leanne Ullmer; Phone: 262-551-6681; E-mail: lulmer@carthage.edu.

CASCADE COLLEGE
Portland, Oregon

Thunderbirds ◆ NAIA ◆ Cascade Collegiate Conference ◆ http://www.cascade.edu/

Independent religious 4-year, founded 1994, affiliated with Church of Christ
Coed, 280 undergraduate students, 94% full-time, 51% women, 49% men
Urban 13-acre campus
Noncompetitive entrance level, 100% of applicants were admitted

Freshmen *Admission:* 232 applied, 232 were accepted, 74 enrolled. *Test scores:* SAT verbal scores over 500: 65%; SAT math scores over 500: 46%; SAT verbal scores over 600: 19%; SAT math scores over 600: 8%; SAT verbal scores over 700: 2%.
Tuition and fees (2004–05): $11,190 (full-time). *Room and board:* $5800.
Financial Aid (All incoming freshmen): *Average need-based gift aid:* $1441. *Average non-need based aid:* $1599. *Average aid to full-time undergraduates:* $10,383.
Athletic Department: *Director of Athletics:* Gerry Nixon; Phone: 503-257-1259; Fax: 503-257-1270; E-mail: gnixon@cascade.edu.

MEN'S COACHES
Basketball: Matthew Greenleaf; Phone: 503-257-1259; E-mail: mgreenleaf@cascade.edu.
Cheerleading: Phone: 503-257-1371; E-mail: athletics@cascade.edu.
Cross Country: Shilah Merrill; Phone: 503-257-1259; E-mail: smerrill@cascade.edu.
Soccer: Micah Saxman; Phone: 503-257-1259; E-mail: msaxman@cascade.edu.
Track and Field: Shilah Merrill; Phone: 503-257-1259; E-mail: smerrill@cascade.edu.

Cascade College *(continued)*

WOMEN'S COACHES

Basketball: Cody Harrod; Phone: 503-257-1371; E-mail: charrod@cascade.edu.
Cheerleading: Phone: 503-257-1371; E-mail: athletics@cascade.edu.
Cross Country: Shilah Merrill; Phone: 503-257-1259; E-mail: smerrill@cascade.edu.
Soccer: Don Miller; Phone: 503-257-1259; E-mail: dmiller@cascade.edu.
Track and Field: Shilah Merrill; Phone: 503-257-1259; E-mail: smerrill@cascade.edu.
Volleyball: Angela Stewart; Phone: 503-257-1259; E-mail: astewart@cascade.edu.

CASE WESTERN RESERVE UNIVERSITY
Cleveland, Ohio

Spartans ◆ NCAA III ◆ University Athletic Conference ◆ http://www.case.edu/

Independent university, founded 1826
Coed, 3,587 undergraduate students, 92% full-time, 39% women, 61% men
Urban 150-acre campus
Very difficult entrance level, 74% of applicants were admitted

Freshmen *Admission:* 4,680 applied, 3,525 were accepted, 878 enrolled. *Test scores:* SAT verbal scores over 500: 94%; SAT math scores over 500: 99%; SAT verbal scores over 600: 73%; SAT math scores over 600: 84%; SAT verbal scores over 700: 29%; SAT math scores over 700: 44%.
Tuition and fees (2003–04): $24,342 (full-time). *Room and board:* $7660 (room only: $4770).
Financial Aid (All incoming freshmen): *Average need-based gift aid:* $16,412. *Average non-need based aid:* $9112. *Average aid to full-time undergraduates:* $23,458.
Athletic Department: *Director of Athletics:* Kristin Hughes; Phone: 216-368-5165; Fax: 216-368-5475; E-mail: kristin.hughes@case.edu. *Sports Information Director:* Creg Jantz; Phone: 216-368-6517; E-mail: creg.jantz@case.edu.

MEN'S COACHES

Baseball: Jerry Seimon; Phone: 216-368-5379; E-mail: jerry.seimon@case.edu.
Basketball: Sean McDonnell; Phone: 216-368-2865; E-mail: sean.mcdonnell@case.edu.
Cheerleading: Jackie King; Phone: 216-368-2420.
Cross Country: Kathy Lanese; Phone: 216-368-5280; E-mail: kathy.lanese@case.edu.
Diving: Chris Conlon; Phone: 216-368-2894; E-mail: christopher.conlon@case.edu.
Football: Joe Perella; Phone: 216-368-2864; E-mail: joe.perella@case.edu.
Soccer: Mike Pilger; Phone: 216-368-5236; E-mail: michael.pilger@case.edu.
Swimming: Chris Conlon; Phone: 216-368-2894; E-mail: christopher.conlon@case.edu.
Tennis: Nancy Rahn; Phone: 216-368-2421; E-mail: nancy.rahn@case.edu.
Track and Field: Dennis Harris; Phone: 216-368-2419; E-mail: dennis.harris@case.edu.
Wrestling: Bob Del Rosa; Phone: 216-368-5166; E-mail: robert.delrosa@case.edu.

WOMEN'S COACHES

Basketball: Kristin Hughes; Phone: 216-368-5165; E-mail: kristin.hughes@case.edu.
Cheerleading: Jackie King; Phone: 216-368-2420.
Cross Country: Kathy Lanese; Phone: 216-368-5280; E-mail: kathy.lanese@case.edu.
Diving: Chris Conlon; Phone: 216-368-2894; E-mail: christopher.conlon@case.edu.
Soccer: Emily Donovan; Phone: 216-368-2192; E-mail: emily.donovan@case.edu.
Softball: Jennie Amodio; Phone: 216-368-0322; E-mail: jennie.amodio@case.edu.
Swimming: Chris Conlon; Phone: 216-368-2894; E-mail: christopher.conlon@case.edu.
Tennis: Nancy Rahn; Phone: 216-368-2421; E-mail: nancy.rahn@case.edu.
Track and Field: Dennis Harris; Phone: 216-368-2419; E-mail: dennis.harris@case.edu.
Volleyball: Nelson Wittenmyer; Phone: 216-368-0364; E-mail: nelson.wittenmeyer@case.edu.

CASTLETON STATE COLLEGE
Castleton, Vermont

Spartans ◆ NCAA III ◆ North Atlantic Conference ◆ http://www.castleton.edu/

State-supported comprehensive, founded 1787, part of Vermont State Colleges System
Coed, 1,699 undergraduate students, 88% full-time, 59% women, 41% men
Rural 160-acre campus
Moderately difficult entrance level, 77% of applicants were admitted

Freshmen *Admission:* 1,434 applied, 1,139 were accepted, 410 enrolled. *Test scores:* SAT verbal scores over 500: 41%; SAT math scores over 500: 40%; SAT verbal scores over 600: 9%; SAT math scores over 600: 9%; SAT math scores over 700: 1%.
Tuition and fees (2004–05): $6146 (resident), $13,086 (nonresident). *Room and board:* $6454.
Athletic Department: *Director of Athletics:* Deanna Tyson; Phone: 802-468-1365; Fax: 802-468-2189; E-mail: deanna.tyson@castleton.edu.

MEN'S COACHES

Baseball: Ted Shipley; Phone: 802-468-1485; E-mail: ted.shipley@castleton.edu.
Basketball: Ted Shipley; Phone: 802-468-1485; E-mail: ted.shipley@castleton.edu.
Cross Country: John Klein; Phone: 802-468-1282; E-mail: john.klein@castleton.edu.
Ice Hockey: Greg Stone; Phone: 802-468-1249; E-mail: gregory.stone@castleton.edu.
Lacrosse: Dan Seamon; Phone: 802-468-1250; E-mail: dan.seaman@castleton.edu.
Soccer: Chris O'Brien; Phone: 802-468-1110; E-mail: msoccer@castleton.edu.
Tennis: Bruce Moreton; Phone: 802-468-1110; E-mail: tim.barrett@castleton.edu.

WOMEN'S COACHES

Basketball: Tim Barrett; Phone: 802-468-1468; E-mail: tim.barrett@castleton.edu.
Cross Country: John Klein; Phone: 802-468-1282; E-mail: john.klein@castleton.edu.
Field Hockey: Brooke Wright; Phone: 802-468-6075; E-mail: fieldhockey@castleton.edu.
Lacrosse: Miche Chamberlain; Phone: 802-773-6066; E-mail: deanna.tyson@castleton.edu.
Soccer: Al Alvine; Phone: 802-468-1110; E-mail: wsoccer@castleton.edu.
Softball: Eric Ramsey; Phone: 802-468-1110; E-mail: softball@castleton.edu.
Tennis: Paul Cohen; Phone: 802-468-1453; E-mail: paul.cohen@castleton.edu.

CATAWBA COLLEGE
Salisbury, North Carolina

Indians ◆ NCAA II ◆ Deep South Lacrosse Conference; South Atlantic Conference ◆ http://www.catawba.edu/

Independent religious comprehensive, founded 1851, affiliated with United Church of Christ
Coed, 1,452 undergraduate students, 96% full-time, 55% women, 45% men
Small-town 210-acre campus with easy access to Charlotte
Moderately difficult entrance level, 57% of applicants were admitted

Freshmen *Admission:* 933 applied, 597 were accepted, 252 enrolled. *Test scores:* SAT verbal scores over 500: 55%; SAT math scores over

500: 66%; SAT verbal scores over 600: 14%; SAT math scores over 600: 19%; SAT verbal scores over 700: 2%; SAT math scores over 700: 1%.
Tuition and fees (2003–04): $16,400 (full-time). *Room and board:* $5600.
Financial Aid (All incoming freshmen): *Average need-based gift aid:* $7458. *Average non-need based aid:* $7554. *Average aid to full-time undergraduates:* $7458.
Athletic Department: *Director of Athletics:* Dennis Davidson; Phone: 704-637-4474; Fax: 704-637-5705. *Sports Information Director:* Jim Lewis; Phone: 704-637-4720; E-mail: jdlewis@catawba.edu.
MEN'S COACHES
Baseball: Jim Gantt; Phone: 704-637-4469; E-mail: jimgantt@catawba.edu.
Basketball: Jim Baker; Phone: 704-637-4473; E-mail: jwbaker@catawba.edu.
Cheerleading: Patricia Williams; Phone: 704-637-4474.
Cross Country: Bill Haggerty; Phone: 704-637-4473; E-mail: bhaggert@catawba.edu.
Football: Chip Hester; Phone: 704-637-4724; E-mail: lbhester@catawba.edu.
Golf: Sam Gealy; Phone: 704-637-4236; E-mail: sgealy@catawba.edu.
Lacrosse: Peter Bourque; Phone: 704-637-4485; E-mail: pbourque@catawba.edu.
Soccer: Craig Turnbull; Phone: 704-637-4348; E-mail: cturnbul@catawba.edu.
Tennis: Jack Thompson; Phone: 704-637-4467; E-mail: jvthomps@catawba.edu.
WOMEN'S COACHES
Basketball: Angie Morton; Phone: 704-637-4471; E-mail: acmorton@catawba.edu.
Cheerleading: Patricia Williams; Phone: 704-637-4474.
Cross Country: Bill Haggerty; Phone: 704-637-4473; E-mail: bhaggert@catawba.edu.
Field Hockey: Catherine Howard; Phone: 704-637-4281; E-mail: cahoward@catawba.edu.
Golf: Sam Gealy; Phone: 704-637-4236; E-mail: sgealy@catawba.edu.
Soccer: John Cullen; Phone: 704-637-4324; E-mail: jmcullen@catawba.edu.
Softball: Nan Whitley; Phone: 704-637-4359; E-mail: nwhitley@catawba.edu.
Swimming: Betsy Graham; Phone: 704-637-4762; E-mail: ebgraham@catawba.edu.
Tennis: Jack Thompson; Phone: 704-637-4467; E-mail: jvthomps@catawba.edu.
Volleyball: Ginger Ashley; Phone: 704-637-4480; E-mail: gcashley@catawba.edu.

THE CATHOLIC UNIVERSITY OF AMERICA
Washington, District of Columbia
Cardinals ◆ NCAA III ◆ Capital Athletic Conference; Old Dominion Conference ◆ http://www.cua.edu/

Independent religious university, founded 1887, affiliated with Roman Catholic Church
Coed, 2,759 undergraduate students, 90% full-time, 56% women, 44% men
Urban 144-acre campus
Moderately difficult entrance level, 79% of applicants were admitted

Freshmen *Admission:* 2,748 applied, 2,251 were accepted, 673 enrolled. *Test scores:* SAT verbal scores over 500: 87%; SAT math scores over 500: 86%; SAT verbal scores over 600: 46%; SAT math scores over 600: 44%; SAT verbal scores over 700: 8%; SAT math scores over 700: 4%.
Tuition and fees (2004–05): $24,750 (full-time). *Room and board:* $9498 (room only: $5428).
Financial Aid (All incoming freshmen): *Average need-based gift aid:* $3783. *Average non-need based aid:* $9144. *Average aid to full-time undergraduates:* $14,369.
Athletic Department: *Director of Athletics:* Robert Talbot; Phone: 202-319-5286; Fax: 202-319-6199; E-mail: talbot@cua.edu. *Sports Information Director:* Chris Panter; Phone: 202-319-5610; E-mail: panter@cua.edu.

MEN'S COACHES
Baseball: Ross Natoli; Phone: 202-319-5286; E-mail: natoli@cua.edu.
Basketball: Mike Lonergan; Phone: 202-319-6046; E-mail: lonergan@cua.edu.
Cheerleading: Kim Parrott; Phone: 202-319-5286; E-mail: cuacheercoach@yahoo.com.
Cross Country: Mark Robinson; Phone: 202-319-5286; E-mail: mrobinson@nw.org.
Football: Tom Mullholland; Phone: 202-319-6045; E-mail: mulholland31@yahoo.com.
Lacrosse: Brooks Singer; Phone: 202-319-5286; E-mail: culacrosse@aol.com.
Soccer: Scott Racek; Phone: 202-319-5286; E-mail: racek@cua.edu.
Swimming: Tom Calomeris; Phone: 202-319-5286; E-mail: cua-athletics@cua.edu.
Track and Field: Jerry McGee; Phone: 202-319-5286; E-mail: mcgeej@cua.edu.
WOMEN'S COACHES
Basketball: Maggie Lonergan; Phone: 202-319-5286; E-mail: lonergam@cua.edu.
Cheerleading: Kim Parrott; Phone: 202-319-5286; E-mail: cuacheercoach@yahoo.com.
Cross Country: Joe Fisher; Phone: 202-319-5286; E-mail: jfisher974@aol.com.
Field Hockey: Gia Fenoglio Cillizza; Phone: 202-319-5286; E-mail: gcillizza@njdc.com.
Lacrosse: Kristine Manning; Phone: 202-319-5286; E-mail: manningk@cua.edu.
Soccer: Scott Racek; Phone: 202-319-5286; E-mail: racek@cua.edu.
Softball: Bruce McConkey; Phone: 202-319-5286; E-mail: cua-athletics@cua.edu.
Swimming: Tom Calomeris; Phone: 202-319-5286; E-mail: cua-athletics@cua.edu.
Tennis: Dana Dowd; Phone: 202-319-5286; E-mail: cua-athletics@cua.edu.
Track and Field: Joe Fisher; Phone: 202-319-5286; E-mail: jfisher974@aol.com.
Volleyball: Nagy Abdelrazek; Phone: 202-319-5286; E-mail: abdelrazek@cua.edu.

CAZENOVIA COLLEGE
Cazenovia, New York
Wildcats ◆ NCAA III ◆ Eastern College Athletic Conference ◆ http://www.cazenovia.edu/

Independent 4-year, founded 1824
Coed, 997 undergraduate students, 80% full-time, 75% women, 25% men
Small-town 40-acre campus with easy access to Syracuse
Minimally difficult entrance level, 81% of applicants were admitted

Freshmen *Admission:* 1,053 applied, 889 were accepted, 273 enrolled. *Test scores:* SAT math scores over 500: 41%; SAT math scores over 600: 5%.
Tuition and fees (2003–04): $16,970 (full-time). *Room and board:* $6960 (room only: $3740).
Financial Aid (All incoming freshmen): *Average need-based gift aid:* $12,000. *Average non-need based aid:* $3650. *Average aid to full-time undergraduates:* $14,561.
Athletic Department: *Director of Athletics:* NA; Fax: 315-655-1099. *Sports Information Director:* Todd Widrick; Phone: 315-655-7241; E-mail: twidrick@cazenovia.edu.
MEN'S COACHES
Baseball: Peter Liddell; Phone: 315-655-7141; E-mail: pliddell@cazenovia.edu.
Basketball: Todd Widrick; Phone: 315-655-7241; E-mail: twidrick@cazenovia.edu.
Cheerleading: Heather Joncas; Phone: 315-655-7142; E-mail: hjoncas@cazenovia.edu.
Cross Country: Dave Oja; Phone: 315-655-7141; E-mail: daveoja@a-znet.com.
Golf: Todd Widrick; Phone: 315-655-7241; E-mail: twidrick@cazenovia.edu.
Lacrosse: Rob Kenna; Phone: 315-655-7265; E-mail: skempton@cazenovia.edu.

Cazenovia College (*continued*)

Soccer: Jan Holmblad; Phone: 315-655-7142; E-mail: jhholmblad@cazenovia.edu.

WOMEN'S COACHES

Basketball: Bill Motto; Phone: 315-655-7142; E-mail: wmotto@cazenovia.edu.
Cheerleading: Heather Joncas; Phone: 315-655-7142; E-mail: hjoncas@cazenovia.edu.
Cross Country: Dave Oja; Phone: 315-655-7141; E-mail: daveoja@a-znet.com.
Lacrosse: Jeff Shultis; Phone: 315-655-7327; E-mail: jmshultis@cazenovia.edu.
Soccer: Jeff Shultis; Phone: 315-655-7142; E-mail: jmshultis@cazenovia.edu.
Softball: Donna Formica; Phone: 315-655-7142; E-mail: jtodd@cazenovia.edu.
Volleyball: Wayne Mandel; Phone: 315-655-7142; E-mail: wmandel@cazenovia.edu.

CEDAR CREST COLLEGE
Allentown, Pennsylvania

Falcons ◆ NCAA III ◆ Pennsylvania Athletic Conference ◆ http://www.cedarcrest.edu/

Independent religious comprehensive, founded 1867, affiliated with United Church of Christ
Women only, 1,725 undergraduate students, 51% full-time, 95% women, 5% men
Suburban 84-acre campus with easy access to Philadelphia
Moderately difficult entrance level, 73% of applicants were admitted

Freshmen *Admission:* 1,317 applied, 957 were accepted, 306 enrolled. *Test scores:* SAT verbal scores over 500: 75%; SAT math scores over 500: 68%; SAT verbal scores over 600: 28%; SAT math scores over 600: 25%; SAT verbal scores over 700: 4%; SAT math scores over 700: 1%.
Tuition and fees (2004–05): $21,900 (full-time). *Room and board:* $7595.
Financial Aid (All incoming freshmen): *Average need-based gift aid:* $13,216. *Average non-need based aid:* $12,039. *Average aid to full-time undergraduates:* $17,109.
Athletic Department: *Director of Athletics:* Kelly McCloskey; Phone: 610-606-4666; E-mail: kmcclosk@cedarcrest.edu. *Sports Information Director:* Beth Oudin; Phone: 610-606-4666.

WOMEN'S COACHES

Basketball: Chris Heery; Phone: 610-606-4666; E-mail: heeryc@nwlehighsd.org.
Cross Country: Dan Donohue; Phone: 610-606-4666; E-mail: djdonohu@cedarcrest.edu.
Field Hockey: Kerry Ashbury; Phone: 610-606-4666; E-mail: klasbury@cedarcrest.edu.
Lacrosse: Kelly McCloskey; Phone: 610-606-4666; E-mail: kmcclosk@cedarcrest.edu.
Soccer: Brian Exton; Phone: 610-606-4666; E-mail: bjexton@cedarcrest.edu.
Softball: Kristy Gestl; Phone: 610-606-4666; E-mail: softball@cedarcrest.edu.
Tennis: Daniel Watts; Phone: 610-606-4666; E-mail: tennis@cedarcrest.edu.
Volleyball: Patrick Morgan; Phone: 610-606-4666; E-mail: vball@cedarcrest.edu.

CEDARVILLE UNIVERSITY
Cedarville, Ohio

Yellow Jackets ◆ NAIA ◆ American Mideast Conference ◆ http://www.cedarville.edu/

Independent Baptist comprehensive, founded 1887
Coed, 2,996 undergraduate students, 94% full-time, 54% women, 46% men
Rural 400-acre campus with easy access to Columbus and Dayton
Moderately difficult entrance level, 81% of applicants were admitted

Freshmen *Admission:* 2,174 applied, 1,762 were accepted, 787 enrolled. *Test scores:* SAT verbal scores over 500: 91%; SAT math scores over 500: 86%; SAT verbal scores over 600: 49%; SAT math scores over 600: 45%; SAT verbal scores over 700: 12%; SAT math scores over 700: 8%.
Tuition and fees (2003–04): $14,944 (full-time). *Room and board:* $5010 (room only: $2684).
Financial Aid (All incoming freshmen): *Average need-based gift aid:* $1051. *Average non-need based aid:* $5856. *Average aid to full-time undergraduates:* $12,611.
Athletic Department: *Director of Athletics:* Pete Reese; Phone: 937-766-7759; Fax: 937-766-5556; E-mail: reeser@cedarville.edu. *Sports Information Director:* Mark Womack; Phone: 937-766-7766; E-mail: womackm@cedarville.edu.

MEN'S COACHES

Baseball: Greg Hughes; Phone: 937-766-3246; E-mail: hughesg@cedarville.edu.
Basketball: Ray Slagle; Phone: 937-766-7644; E-mail: slaglew@cedarville.edu.
Cheerleading: Dawn Scott; Phone: 937-766-4477; E-mail: scottd@cedarville.edu.
Cross Country: Paul Orchard; Phone: 937-766-7762; E-mail: orchardp@cedarville.edu.
Golf: Ryan Bowen; Phone: 937-766-7758; E-mail: bowenr@cedarville.edu.
Soccer: Ben Belleman; Phone: 937-766-3247; E-mail: belleman@cedarville.edu.
Tennis: Alan Edlund; Phone: 937-766-3477; E-mail: edlunda@cedarville.edu.
Track and Field: Jeff Bolender; Phone: 937-766-4136; E-mail: bolender@cedarville.edu.

WOMEN'S COACHES

Basketball: Kirk Martin; Phone: 937-766-4127; E-mail: martink@cedarville.edu.
Cheerleading: Dawn Scott; Phone: 937-766-4477; E-mail: scottd@cedarville.edu.
Cross Country: Elvin King; Phone: 937-766-7758; E-mail: kinge@cedarville.edu.
Soccer: John McGillivray; Phone: 937-766-7757; E-mail: mcgilliv@cedarville.edu.
Softball: Sue Carpenter; Phone: 937-766-4973; E-mail: carpents@cedarville.edu.
Tennis: Pam Johnson; Phone: 937-766-7765; E-mail: johnsonp@cedarville.edu.
Track and Field: Jeff Bolender; Phone: 937-766-4136; E-mail: bolender@cedarville.edu.
Volleyball: Teresa Clark; Phone: 937-766-7763; E-mail: clarkt@cedarville.edu.

CENTENARY COLLEGE
Hackettstown, New Jersey

Cyclones ◆ NCAA III ◆ Skyline Conference ◆ http://www.centenarycollege.edu/

Independent religious comprehensive, founded 1867, affiliated with United Methodist Church
Coed, 1,759 undergraduate students, 82% full-time, 67% women, 33% men
Suburban 42-acre campus with easy access to New York City
Moderately difficult entrance level, 70% of applicants were admitted

Freshmen *Admission:* 737 applied, 540 were accepted, 350 enrolled. *Test scores:* SAT verbal scores over 500: 33%; SAT math scores over 500: 27%; SAT verbal scores over 600: 6%; SAT math scores over 600: 8%; SAT verbal scores over 700: 1%; SAT math scores over 700: 1%.
Tuition and fees (2003–04): $17,700 (full-time). *Room and board:* $7150.
Financial Aid (All incoming freshmen): *Average need-based gift aid:* $10,938. *Average non-need based aid:* $10,038. *Average aid to full-time undergraduates:* $12,845.
Athletic Department: *Director of Athletics:* Diane Finnan; Phone: 908-852-1400; Fax: 908-813-8295; E-mail: finnand@centenarycollege.edu. *Sports Information Director:* Josh Huber; Phone: 908-852-1400.

MEN'S COACHES

Baseball: Dave Sawicki; Phone: 908-852-1400; E-mail: sawickid@centenarycollege.edu.
Basketball: Abe Kasbo; Phone: 908-852-1400.

Cross Country: Doug Fink; Phone: 908-852-1400; E-mail: finkd@centenarycollege.edu.
Golf: Lou Paterno; Phone: 908-852-1400.
Lacrosse: Dave Carty; Phone: 908-852-1400; E-mail: cartyd@centenarycollege.edu.
Soccer: Stewart Smith; Phone: 908-852-1400.
Wrestling: Doug Fink; Phone: 908-852-1400; E-mail: finkd@centenarycollege.edu.

WOMEN'S COACHES

Basketball: Rachel Hartung; Phone: 908-852-1400.
Cross Country: Doug Fink; Phone: 908-852-1400; E-mail: finkd@centenarycollege.edu.
Golf: Lou Paterno; Phone: 908-852-1400.
Lacrosse: Debbie Tait; Phone: 908-852-1400.
Soccer: Kevin Davies; Phone: 908-852-1400.
Softball: Billie Jo Blackwell; Phone: 908-852-1400.
Volleyball: Kathy Fink; Phone: 908-852-1400.

CENTENARY COLLEGE OF LOUISIANA
Shreveport, Louisiana

Gents ◆ NCAA I ◆ Mid-Continent Conference ◆ http://www.centenary.edu/

Independent United Methodist comprehensive, founded 1825
Coed, 845 undergraduate students, 97% full-time, 59% women, 41% men
Suburban 65-acre campus
Moderately difficult entrance level, 71% of applicants were admitted

Freshmen *Admission:* 802 applied, 594 were accepted, 197 enrolled. *Test scores:* SAT verbal scores over 500: 84%; SAT math scores over 500: 80%; SAT verbal scores over 600: 46%; SAT math scores over 600: 41%; SAT verbal scores over 700: 6%; SAT math scores over 700: 5%.
Tuition and fees (2003–04): $17,250 (full-time). *Room and board:* $5850 (room only: $2900).
Financial Aid (All incoming freshmen): *Average need-based gift aid:* $10,841. *Average non-need based aid:* $8429. *Average aid to full-time undergraduates:* $13,278.
Athletic Department: *Director of Athletics:* Taylor Moore; Phone: 318-869-5275; Fax: 318-869-5145; E-mail: tfmoore@centenary.edu. *Sports Information Director:* David Pratt; Phone: 318-869-5092; E-mail: dpratt@centenary.edu.

MEN'S COACHES

Baseball: Ed McCann; Phone: 318-869-5095; E-mail: emccann@centenary.edu.
Basketball: Kevin Johnson; Phone: 318-869-5089; E-mail: kjohnson@centenary.edu.
Cheerleading: Penny Pate; Phone: 318-869-7251.
Cross Country: Julie Cavalier; Phone: 318-869-7311; E-mail: cavali7@aol.com.
Golf: Martin Stewart; Phone: 318-869-5150; E-mail: mlsgolf01@aol.com.
Soccer: Eric Mayo; Phone: 318-869-5165; E-mail: emayo@centenary.edu.
Swimming: Butch Jordan; Phone: 318-869-5275; E-mail: bjcosst@aol.com.
Tennis: Larry Jacobs; Phone: 318-869-5285; E-mail: ljacobs@centenary.edu.

WOMEN'S COACHES

Basketball: David Winkler; Phone: 318-869-5758; E-mail: dwinkler@centenary.edu.
Cheerleading: Penny Pate; Phone: 318-869-7251.
Cross Country: Julie Cavalier; Phone: 318-869-7311; E-mail: cavali7@aol.com.
Golf: Ken Dupree; Phone: 318-869-7314; E-mail: kdupree@centenary.edu.
Gymnastics: Bill Hardy; Phone: 318-869-3547; E-mail: gohardinc@aol.com.
Soccer: Chase Wooten; Phone: 318-869-5165; E-mail: cwooten@centenary.edu.
Softball: Mark Montgomery; Phone: 318-869-5094; E-mail: mmontgom@centenary.edu.

Swimming: Butch Jordan; Phone: 318-869-5275; E-mail: bjcosst@aol.com.
Tennis: Larry Jacobs; Phone: 318-869-5285; E-mail: ljacobs@centenary.edu.
Volleyball: Jenny Hazelwood; Phone: 318-869-5717; E-mail: jhazelwo@centenary.edu.

CENTRAL CHRISTIAN COLLEGE OF KANSAS
McPherson, Kansas

Tigers ◆ NAIA ◆ Midlands Collegiate Conference ◆ http://www.centralchristian.edu/

Independent Free Methodist 4-year, founded 1884
Coed, 320 undergraduate students
Small-town 16-acre campus
Moderately difficult entrance level, 98% of applicants were admitted

Freshmen *Admission:* 363 applied, 354 were accepted.
Tuition and fees (2004–05): $13,125 (full-time). *Room and board:* $4100 (room only: $1900).
Financial Aid (All incoming freshmen): *Average need-based gift aid:* $3278. *Average non-need based aid:* $4580. *Average aid to full-time undergraduates:* $9840.
Athletic Department: *Director of Athletics:* Jerry Malone; Phone: 620-241-0723; Fax: 620-241-3529; E-mail: jerry.malone@centralchristian.edu. *Sports Information Director:* Matt Ball; Phone: 620-241-0723; E-mail: matt.ball@centralchristian.edu.

MEN'S COACHES

Baseball: Jared Hamilton; Phone: 620-241-0723; E-mail: jared.hamilton@centralchristian.edu.
Basketball: Justin Gillette; Phone: 620-241-0723; E-mail: justin.gillette@centralchristian.edu.
Cheerleading: Rochelle Wissehr; Phone: 620-241-0723; E-mail: rochelle.wissehr@centralchristian.edu.
Cross Country: Don Mason; Phone: 620-241-0723; E-mail: don.mason@centralchristian.edu.
Golf: Roy Milam; Phone: 620-241-0723; E-mail: roy.milam@centralchristian.edu.
Soccer: Matt Ball; Phone: 620-241-0723; E-mail: matt.ball@centralchristian.edu.
Tennis: Shana Leck; Phone: 620-241-0723; E-mail: shana.leck@centralchristian.edu.

WOMEN'S COACHES

Basketball: Bryan Minnich; Phone: 620-241-0723; E-mail: bryan.minnich@centralchristian.edu.
Cheerleading: Rochelle Wissehr; Phone: 620-241-0723; E-mail: rochelle.wissehr@centralchristian.edu.
Cross Country: Don Mason; Phone: 620-241-0723; E-mail: don.mason@centralchristian.edu.
Golf: Roy Milam; Phone: 620-241-0723; E-mail: roy.milam@centralchristian.edu.
Soccer: Mike Reimer; Phone: 620-241-0723; E-mail: mike.reimer@centralchristian.edu.
Softball: Tana Rangel; Phone: 620-241-0723; E-mail: tana.rangel@centralchristian.edu.
Tennis: Shana Leck; Phone: 620-241-0723; E-mail: shana.leck@centralchristian.edu.
Volleyball: Gordon Reimer; Phone: 620-241-0723; E-mail: gordon.reimer@centralchristian.edu.

CENTRAL COLLEGE
Pella, Iowa

Dutch ◆ NCAA III ◆ Iowa Athletic Conference ◆ http://www.central.edu/

Independent religious 4-year, founded 1853, affiliated with Reformed Church in America
Coed, 1,698 undergraduate students, 97% full-time, 57% women, 43% men
Small-town 133-acre campus with easy access to Des Moines
Moderately difficult entrance level, 78% of applicants were admitted

Freshmen *Admission:* 1,865 applied, 1,549 were accepted, 417 enrolled.

Central College (continued)

Tuition and fees (2003–04): $17,753 (full-time). *Room and board:* $6145 (room only: $3132).
Financial Aid (All incoming freshmen): *Average need-based gift aid:* $14,991. *Average non-need based aid:* $8395. *Average aid to full-time undergraduates:* $15,561.
Athletic Department: *Director of Athletics:* Al Dorenkamp; Phone: 641-628-5310; Fax: 641-628-5356; E-mail: dorenkampa@central.edu. *Sports Information Director:* Abby Gonzales; Phone: 641-628-5278; E-mail: sportsinfo@central.edu.

MEN'S COACHES

Baseball: Adam Stevens; Phone: 641-628-5396; E-mail: stevensa@central.edu.
Basketball: Mike Boschee; Phone: 641-628-5225; E-mail: boscheem@central.edu.
Cheerleading: Teresa Van Vark; Phone: 641-628-5240; E-mail: vanvarkt@central.edu.
Cross Country: Jeff Bovee; Phone: 641-628-5178; E-mail: boveej@central.edu.
Football: Jeff McMartin; Phone: 641-628-7609; E-mail: mcmartinj@central.edu.
Golf: Charlie Estabrook; Phone: 641-628-7694; E-mail: estabrookc@central.edu.
Soccer: Gary Laodlaw; Phone: 641-628-5789; E-mail: laidlawg@central.edu.
Tennis: Doug Stursha; Phone: 641-628-5194; E-mail: stursmad@central.edu.
Track and Field: Kevin Sanger; Phone: 641-628-7603; E-mail: sangerk@central.edu.
Wrestling: Matt Diehl; Phone: 641-628-5230; E-mail: diehlm@central.edu.

WOMEN'S COACHES

Basketball: Mick Angel; Phone: 641-628-7652; E-mail: angelm@central.edu.
Cheerleading: Teresa Van Vark; Phone: 641-628-5240; E-mail: vanvarkt@central.edu.
Cross Country: Jeff Bovee; Phone: 641-628-5178; E-mail: boveej@central.edu.
Golf: Greg Hoekstra; Phone: 641-628-5226; E-mail: gwhoekstra@pella.com.
Soccer: Phone: 641-628-7609; E-mail: ellisc@central.edu.
Softball: George Wares; Phone: 641-628-5195; E-mail: waresg@central.edu.
Tennis: Doug Stursha; Phone: 641-628-5194; E-mail: stursmad@central.edu.
Track and Field: Kevin Sanger; Phone: 641-628-7603; E-mail: sangerk@central.edu.
Volleyball: Kent Clayberg; Phone: 641-628-5139; E-mail: claybergm@central.edu.

CENTRAL CONNECTICUT STATE UNIVERSITY
New Britain, Connecticut

Blue Devils ◆ NCAA I ◆ Northeast Conference ◆ http://www.ccsu.edu/

State-supported comprehensive, founded 1849, part of Connecticut State University System
Coed, 9,401 undergraduate students, 72% full-time, 51% women, 49% men
Suburban 294-acre campus
Moderately difficult entrance level, 57% of applicants were admitted

Freshmen *Admission:* 5,503 applied, 3,024 were accepted, 1,203 enrolled. *Test scores:* SAT verbal scores over 500: 62%; SAT math scores over 500: 59%; SAT verbal scores over 600: 13%; SAT math scores over 600: 12%; SAT verbal scores over 700: 1%; SAT math scores over 700: 1%.
Tuition and fees (2003–04): $5384 (resident), $11,306 (nonresident). *Room and board:* $6706 (room only: $3826).
Financial Aid (All incoming freshmen): *Average need-based gift aid:* $4670. *Average non-need based aid:* $1908. *Average aid to full-time undergraduates:* $5609.

Athletic Department: *Director of Athletics:* Charles Jones; Phone: 860-832-3038; Fax: 860-832-3754; E-mail: jonesc@ccsu.edu. *Sports Information Director:* Thomas Pincince; Phone: 860-832-3039; E-mail: pincincet@ccsu.edu.

MEN'S COACHES

Baseball: Charlie Hickey; Phone: 860-832-3074; E-mail: hickeyc@ccsu.edu.
Basketball: Howie Dickenman; Phone: 860-832-3053.
Cheerleading: Angela Shaw; Phone: 860-832-3040.
Cross Country: George Kawecki; Phone: 860-832-3055; E-mail: kawecki@ccsu.edu.
Football: Paul Schudel; Phone: 860-832-3064; E-mail: schudelp@ccsu.edu.
Golf: Ed Batogowski; Phone: 860-832-3043; E-mail: batogowskie@ccsu.edu.
Soccer: Shawn Green; Phone: 860-832-3051; E-mail: greens@ccsu.edu.
Track and Field: George Kawecki; Phone: 860-832-3054; E-mail: kawecki@ccsu.edu.

WOMEN'S COACHES

Basketball: Yvette Harris; Phone: 860-832-3782; E-mail: harrisy@ccsu.edu.
Cheerleading: Angela Shaw; Phone: 860-832-3040.
Cross Country: George Kawecki; Phone: 860-832-3055; E-mail: kawecki@ccsu.edu.
Diving: Dave Maliar; Phone: 860-832-3073.
Golf: Dennis Coscina; Phone: 860-832-3268; E-mail: tdddg@aol.com.
Lacrosse: Kristen Mullady; Phone: 860-832-3069; E-mail: mulladyk@ccsu.edu.
Soccer: Mick D'Arcy; Phone: 860-832-3092; E-mail: darcym@ccsu.edu.
Softball: Mandy Roczniak; Phone: 860-832-3050; E-mail: roczniaka@ccsu.edu.
Swimming: Bill Ball; Phone: 860-832-3073; E-mail: ballb@ccsu.edu.
Track and Field: George Kawecki; Phone: 860-832-3055; E-mail: kawecki@ccsu.edu.
Volleyball: Linda Sagnelli; Phone: 860-832-3056; E-mail: sagnellil@ccsu.edu.

CENTRAL METHODIST COLLEGE
Fayette, Missouri

Eagles ◆ NAIA ◆ Heart of America Conference ◆ http://www.cmc.edu/

Independent Methodist comprehensive, founded 1854
Coed, 850 undergraduate students, 93% full-time, 52% women, 48% men
Small-town 80-acre campus
Moderately difficult entrance level, 70% of applicants were admitted

Freshmen *Admission:* 1,033 applied, 756 were accepted, 224 enrolled.
Tuition and fees (2003–04): $13,760 (full-time). *Room and board:* $4920 (room only: $2420).
Financial Aid (All incoming freshmen): *Average need-based gift aid:* $3476. *Average non-need based aid:* $5347. *Average aid to full-time undergraduates:* $10,131.
Athletic Department: *Director of Athletics:* Larry Anderson; Phone: 660-248-6347; Fax: 660-248-1632; E-mail: landerso@cmc.edu. *Sports Information Director:* Denise Guttery; Phone: 660-248-6350; E-mail: dguttery@cmc.edu.

MEN'S COACHES

Baseball: Jim Dapkus; Phone: 660-248-6352; E-mail: jdapkus@cmc.edu.
Basketball: Jeff Sherman; Phone: 660-248-6355; E-mail: jsherm01@cmc.edu.
Cheerleading: Sherry Wells; Phone: 660-248-6346; E-mail: dthompso@cmc.edu.
Cross Country: Gary Stoner; Phone: 660-248-6312; E-mail: gstoner@cmc.edu.
Football: Merle Masonholder; Phone: 660-248-6209; E-mail: mmasonho@cmc.edu.
Golf: Doug Fessler; Phone: 660-248-6358; E-mail: dfessler@cmc.edu.
Soccer: Moz Rahmatpanah; Phone: 660-248-6564; E-mail: mrahmatp@cmc.edu.
Track and Field: Gary Stoner; Phone: 660-248-6312; E-mail: gstoner@cmc.edu.

WOMEN'S COACHES

Basketball: Doug Fessler; Phone: 660-248-6358; E-mail: dfessler@cmc.edu.
Cheerleading: Sherry Wells; Phone: 660-248-6346; E-mail: dthompso@cmc.edu.
Cross Country: Gary Stoner; Phone: 660-248-6312; E-mail: gstoner@cmc.edu.
Golf: Doug Fessler; Phone: 660-248-6358; E-mail: dfessler@cmc.edu.
Soccer: Pat Reardon; Phone: 660-248-6348; E-mail: preardon@cmc.edu.
Softball: Pat Reardon; Phone: 660-248-6348; E-mail: preardon@cmc.edu.
Track and Field: Gary Stoner; Phone: 660-248-6312; E-mail: gstoner@cmc.edu.
Volleyball: Dominique Savage; Phone: 660-248-6353; E-mail: dsavage@cmc.edu.

CENTRAL MICHIGAN UNIVERSITY
Mount Pleasant, Michigan

Chippewas ◆ NCAA I ◆ Mid-American Conference ◆ http://www.cmich.edu/

State-supported university, founded 1892
Coed, 19,642 undergraduate students, 87% full-time, 59% women, 41% men
Small-town 854-acre campus
Moderately difficult entrance level, 67% of applicants were admitted

Freshmen *Admission:* 13,489 applied, 9,490 were accepted, 3,680 enrolled. *Test scores:* SAT verbal scores over 500: 59%; SAT math scores over 500: 66%; SAT verbal scores over 600: 25%; SAT math scores over 600: 23%; SAT verbal scores over 700: 3%; SAT math scores over 700: 2%.
Tuition and fees (2003–04): $5218 (resident), $12,148 (nonresident). *Room and board:* $5924 (room only: $2962).
Financial Aid (All incoming freshmen): *Average need-based gift aid:* $3929. *Average non-need based aid:* $3202. *Average aid to full-time undergraduates:* $8123.
Athletic Department: *Director of Athletics:* Herb Deromedi; Phone: 989-774-3046; Fax: 989-774-5391; E-mail: herb.deromedi@cmich.edu. *Sports Information Director:* Fred Stabley; Phone: 989-774-3277; E-mail: frederick.stabley@cmich.edu.

MEN'S COACHES

Baseball: Steve Jaksa; Phone: 989-774-4392; E-mail: jaksa1sp@cmich.edu.
Basketball: Jay Smith; Phone: 989-774-4302; E-mail: jay.s.smith@cmich.edu.
Cheerleading: Jennifer Elmquist; Phone: 989-430-6794.
Cross Country: Craig Fuller; Phone: 989-774-7315; E-mail: craig.fuller@cmich.edu.
Football: Brian Kelly; Phone: 989-774-3896.
Track and Field: Jim Knapp; Phone: 989-774-3729; E-mail: jim.a.knapp@cmich.edu.
Wrestling: Tom Borrelli; Phone: 989-774-3856; E-mail: borre1tr@cmich.edu.

WOMEN'S COACHES

Basketball: Eileen Kleinfelter; Phone: 989-774-1140; E-mail: eileen.kleinfelter@cmich.edu.
Cheerleading: Jennifer Elmquist; Phone: 989-430-6794.
Cross Country: Karen Lutzke; Phone: 989-774-1447; E-mail: lutzk1ka@cmich.edu.
Field Hockey: Cristy Freese; Phone: 989-774-6672; E-mail: frees1c@cmich.edu.
Gymnastics: Jerry Reighard; Phone: 989-774-6696; E-mail: jerry.reighard@cmich.edu.
Soccer: Mark Salisbury; Phone: 989-774-1123; E-mail: salis1mh@cmich.edu.
Softball: Margo Jonker; Phone: 989-774-6688; E-mail: margo.jonker@cmich.edu.
Track and Field: Karen Lutze; Phone: 989-774-1447; E-mail: lutzk1ka@cmich.edu.
Volleyball: Elaine Piha; Phone: 989-774-2370; E-mail: piha1ea@cmich.edu.

CENTRAL MISSOURI STATE UNIVERSITY
Warrensburg, Missouri

(M) Mules, (W) Jennies ◆ NCAA II ◆ Mid-America Intercollegiate Conference ◆ http://www.cmsu.edu/

State-supported comprehensive, founded 1871
Coed, 8,707 undergraduate students, 82% full-time, 54% women, 46% men
Small-town 1,561-acre campus with easy access to Kansas City
Moderately difficult entrance level, 76% of applicants were admitted

Freshmen *Admission:* 3,544 applied, 2,709 were accepted, 1,438 enrolled.
Tuition and fees (2003–04): $5340 (resident), $9960 (nonresident). *Room and board:* $4796 (room only: $2998).
Financial Aid (All incoming freshmen): *Average need-based gift aid:* $3754. *Average non-need based aid:* $2644. *Average aid to full-time undergraduates:* $5692.
Athletic Department: *Director of Athletics:* Jerry Hughes; Phone: 660-543-4521; Fax: 660-543-8034; E-mail: hughes@cmsu1.cmsu.edu. *Sports Information Director:* Joe Moore; Phone: 660-543-4312; E-mail: jhmoore@cmsu1.cmsu.edu.

MEN'S COACHES

Baseball: Darin Hendrickson; Phone: 660-543-4800; E-mail: cmsubb@iland.net.
Basketball: KimAnderson; Phone: 660-543-4251; E-mail: kanderson@cmsu1.cmsu.edu.
Cheerleading: Anne Best; Phone: 660-543-4250; E-mail: aeb53690@cmsu2.cmsu.edu.
Cross Country: Kirk Pederson; Phone: 660-543-8309; E-mail: pedersen@cmsu1.cmsu.edu.
Football: Willie Fritz; Phone: 660-543-4252; E-mail: wfritz@cmsu1.cmsu.edu.
Golf: Tim Poe; Phone: 660-543-4182.
Track and Field: Kirk Pederson; Phone: 660-543-8309; E-mail: pedersen@cmsu1.cmsu.edu.
Wrestling: Robin Ersland; Phone: 660-543-8511; E-mail: ersland@cmsu1.cmsu.edu.

WOMEN'S COACHES

Basketball: Scott Ballard; Phone: 660-543-4253; E-mail: ballard@cmsu1.cmsu.edu.
Cheerleading: Anne Best; Phone: 660-543-4250; E-mail: aeb53690@cmsu2.cmsu.edu.
Cross Country: Kirk Pederson; Phone: 660-543-8309; E-mail: pedersen@cmsu1.cmsu.edu.
Soccer: Geoff VanDeusen; Phone: 660-543-4187; E-mail: gvandeusen@cmsu1.cmsu.edu.
Softball: Rhesa Sumrell; Phone: 660-543-4139; E-mail: sumrell@cmsu1.cmsu.edu.
Track and Field: Kirk Pederson; Phone: 660-543-8309; E-mail: pedersen@cmsu1.cmsu.edu.
Volleyball: Peggy Martin; Phone: 660-543-4011; E-mail: pmartin@cmsu1.cmsu.edu.

CENTRAL WASHINGTON UNIVERSITY
Ellensburg, Washington

Wildcats ◆ NCAA II ◆ Great Northwest Athletic Conference ◆ http://www.cwu.edu/

State-supported comprehensive, founded 1891
Coed, 9,296 undergraduate students, 88% full-time, 52% women, 48% men
Small-town 380-acre campus
Moderately difficult entrance level, 80% of applicants were admitted

Freshmen *Admission:* 3,905 applied, 3,261 were accepted, 1,336 enrolled. *Test scores:* SAT verbal scores over 500: 46%; SAT math scores over 500: 49%; SAT verbal scores over 600: 12%; SAT math scores over 600: 12%; SAT verbal scores over 700: 1%; SAT math scores over 700: 1%.

Central Washington University (continued)

Tuition and fees (2003–04): $4023 (resident), $11,799 (nonresident). *Room and board:* $5745 (room only: $3000).
Financial Aid (All incoming freshmen): *Average need-based gift aid:* $5045. *Average non-need based aid:* $3087. *Average aid to full-time undergraduates:* $4414.
Athletic Department: *Director of Athletics:* Jack Bishop; Phone: 509-963-1914; Fax: 509-963-2390; E-mail: bishopj@cwu.edu. *Sports Information Director:* Jonathan Gordon; Phone: 509-963-1485; E-mail: gordonj@cwu.edu.

MEN'S COACHES

Baseball: Desi Storcy; Phone: 509-963-3018; E-mail: storeyd@cwu.edu.
Basketball: Greg Sparling; Phone: 509-963-1926; E-mail: sparling@cwu.edu.
Cheerleading: Kathey Hatfield; Phone: 509-962-2717; E-mail: katheyhatfield@yahoo.com.
Cross Country: Kevin Adkisson; Phone: 509-963-1956; E-mail: adkisson@cwu.edu.
Football: John Zamberlin; Phone: 509-963-1910; E-mail: zamberlj@cwu.edu.
Swimming: Jesse Weston; Phone: 509-963-3010; E-mail: westonjes@cwu.edu.
Track and Field: Kevin Adkisson; Phone: 509-963-1956; E-mail: adkisson@cwu.edu.
Wrestling: Jeremy Zender; Phone: 509-963-1907; E-mail: zenderj@cwu.edu.

WOMEN'S COACHES

Basketball: Jeff Whitney; Phone: 509-963-1934; E-mail: whitneyj@cwu.edu.
Cheerleading: Kathey Hatfield; Phone: 509-962-2717; E-mail: katheyhatfield@yahoo.com.
Cross Country: Kevin Adkisson; Phone: 509-963-1956; E-mail: adkisson@cwu.edu.
Soccer: Michael Farrand; Phone: 509-963-1939; E-mail: farrandm@cwu.edu.
Softball: Gary Frederick; Phone: 509-963-1904; E-mail: frederic@cwu.edu.
Swimming: Jesse Weston; Phone: 509-963-3010; E-mail: westonjes@cwu.edu.
Track and Field: Kevin Adkisson; Phone: 509-963-1956; E-mail: adkisson@cwu.edu.
Volleyball: Mario Andaya; Phone: 509-963-1983; E-mail: andayam@cwu.edu.

CENTRE COLLEGE
Danville, Kentucky

Colonels ◆ NCAA III ◆ Southern Collegiate Athletic Conference ◆ http://www.centre.edu/

Independent religious 4-year, founded 1819, affiliated with Presbyterian Church (U.S.A.)
Coed, 1,062 undergraduate students, 100% full-time, 52% women, 48% men
Small-town 100-acre campus
Very difficult entrance level, 74% of applicants were admitted

Freshmen *Admission:* 1,409 applied, 1,063 were accepted, 272 enrolled. *Test scores:* SAT verbal scores over 500: 97%; SAT math scores over 500: 91%; SAT verbal scores over 600: 62%; SAT math scores over 600: 56%; SAT verbal scores over 700: 20%; SAT math scores over 700: 12%.
Tuition and fees (2003–04): $20,400 (full-time). *Room and board:* $6900 (room only: $3500).
Financial Aid (All incoming freshmen): *Average need-based gift aid:* $15,177. *Average non-need based aid:* $8487. *Average aid to full-time undergraduates:* $17,222.
Athletic Department: *Director of Athletics:* Brian Chafin; Phone: 859-238-5485; Fax: 859-236-6081; E-mail: chafin@centre.edu. *Sports Information Director:* Ed Rall; Phone: 859-238-5489; E-mail: rall@centre.edu.

MEN'S COACHES

Baseball: Ed Rall; Phone: 859-238-5489; E-mail: rall@centre.edu.
Basketball: Greg Mason; Phone: 859-238-5491; E-mail: masong@centre.edu.
Cheerleading: Teresa Lyons; Phone: 859-238-5485.
Cross Country: Lisa Owens; Phone: 859-238-5494; E-mail: lowens@centre.edu.
Diving: Dean Brownley; Phone: 859-238-5540; E-mail: brownley@centre.edu.
Football: Andy Frye; Phone: 859-238-5496; E-mail: frye@centre.edu.
Golf: Greg Mason; Phone: 859-238-5491; E-mail: masong@cente.edu.
Soccer: Jeb Burch; Phone: 859-238-5253; E-mail: burchj@centre.edu.
Swimming: Dean Brownley; Phone: 859-238-5540; E-mail: brownley@centre.edu.
Tennis: Matt Vonderbrink; Phone: 859-238-5490; E-mail: vndrbrnk@centre.edu.
Track and Field: Lisa Owens; Phone: 859-238-5494; E-mail: lowens@centre.edu.

WOMEN'S COACHES

Basketball: Jennifer Ruff; Phone: 859-238-8753; E-mail: ruff@centre.edu.
Cheerleading: Teresa Lyons; Phone: 859-238-5485.
Cross Country: Lisa Owens; Phone: 859-238-5494; E-mail: lowens@centre.edu.
Diving: Dean Brownley; Phone: 859-238-5540; E-mail: brownley@centre.edu.
Field Hockey: Tom Hobbs; Phone: 859-238-8746; E-mail: hobbs@centre.edu.
Golf: Jennifer Ruff; Phone: 859-238-8753; E-mail: ruff@centre.edu.
Soccer: Gina Nicoletti; Phone: 859-238-5493; E-mail: gina@centre.edu.
Softball: Wendie Austin-Robinson; Phone: 859-238-8756; E-mail: austin@centre.edu.
Swimming: Dean Brownley; Phone: 859-238-5540; E-mail: brownley@centre.edu.
Tennis: Matt Vonderbrink; Phone: 859-238-5490; E-mail: vndrbrnk@centre.edu.
Track and Field: Lisa Owens; Phone: 859-238-5494; E-mail: lowens@centre.edu.
Volleyball: Stephanie Dragan; Phone: 859-238-5475; E-mail: dragan@centre.edu.

CHADRON STATE COLLEGE
Chadron, Nebraska

Eagles ◆ NCAA II ◆ Rocky Mountain Athletic Conference ◆ http://www.csc.edu/

State-supported comprehensive, founded 1911, part of Nebraska State College System
Coed, 2,294 undergraduate students, 77% full-time, 60% women, 40% men
Small-town 281-acre campus
Noncompetitive entrance level

Freshmen *Admission:* 503 enrolled. *Test scores:* SAT math scores over 500: 43%; SAT math scores over 600: 29%.
Tuition and fees (2003–04): $3241 (resident), $5851 (nonresident). *Room and board:* $3862 (room only: $1778).
Financial Aid (All incoming freshmen): *Average need-based gift aid:* $1842. *Average aid to full-time undergraduates:* $2406.
Athletic Department: *Director of Athletics:* Brad Smith; Phone: 308-432-6345; Fax: 308-432-6466; E-mail: bsmith@csc.edu. *Sports Information Director:* Con Marshall; Phone: 308-432-6212; E-mail: cmarshall@csc.edu.

MEN'S COACHES

Basketball: Dan Beebe; Phone: 308-432-6348; E-mail: dbeebe@csc.edu.
Cheerleading: Laure Sinn; Phone: 308-432-6455; E-mail: lsinn@csc.edu.
Football: Brad Smith; Phone: 308-432-6345; E-mail: bsmith@csc.edu.
Track and Field: John Reiners; Phone: 308-432-6425; E-mail: jreiners@csc.edu.
Wrestling: Scott Ritzen; Phone: 308-432-6343; E-mail: sritzen@csc.edu.

WOMEN'S COACHES

Basketball: Tom Anderson; Phone: 308-432-6339; E-mail: tandersen@csc.edu.
Cheerleading: Laure Sinn; Phone: 308-432-6455; E-mail: lsinn@csc.edu.
Golf: Gary Benson; Phone: 308-432-6288; E-mail: gbenson@csc.edu.
Track and Field: John Reiners; Phone: 308-432-6425; E-mail: jreiners@csc.edu.
Volleyball: Dawn Brammer; Phone: 308-432-6346; E-mail: dbrammer@csc.edu.

CHAMINADE UNIVERSITY OF HONOLULU

Honolulu, Hawaii

Silverswords ◆ NCAA II ◆ Pacific West Conference ◆ http://www.chaminade.edu/

Independent Roman Catholic comprehensive, founded 1955
Coed, 1,063 undergraduate students, 97% full-time, 68% women, 32% men
Urban 62-acre campus
Moderately difficult entrance level, 95% of applicants were admitted

Freshmen *Admission:* 830 applied, 799 were accepted, 254 enrolled. *Test scores:* SAT verbal scores over 500: 38%; SAT math scores over 500: 44%; SAT verbal scores over 600: 9%; SAT math scores over 600: 11%; SAT math scores over 700: 1%.
Tuition and fees (2003–04): $13,500 (full-time). *Room and board:* $7930 (room only: $4150).
Financial Aid (All incoming freshmen): *Average need-based gift aid:* $9575. *Average non-need based aid:* $4765. *Average aid to full-time undergraduates:* $12,278.
Athletic Department: *Director of Athletics:* Aaron Griess; Phone: 808-739-4696; Fax: 808-739-4695; E-mail: agriess@chaminade.edu. *Sports Information Director:* Matt Mahar; Phone: 808-735-4748; E-mail: mmahar@chaminade.edu.

MEN'S COACHES

Basketball: Aaron Griess; Phone: 808-735-4790; E-mail: agriess@chaminade.edu.
Cross Country: James Oshira; Phone: 808-735-4836; E-mail: joshiro@chaminade.edu.
Tennis: Dennis Conroy; Phone: 808-735-4790; E-mail: dconroy@chaminade.edu.

WOMEN'S COACHES

Cross Country: James OShira; Phone: 808-735-4836; E-mail: joshiro@chaminade.edu.
Softball: Walter Kaaihili; Phone: 808-735-4790; E-mail: wkaaihil@chaminade.edu.
Tennis: Dennis Conroy; Phone: 808-735-4790; E-mail: dconroy@chaminade.edu.
Volleyball: Glennie Adams; Phone: 808-735-4778; E-mail: gadams@chaminade.edu.

CHAPMAN UNIVERSITY

Orange, California

Panthers ◆ NCAA III ◆ Independent ◆ http://www.chapman.edu/

Independent religious comprehensive, founded 1861, affiliated with Christian Church (Disciples of Christ)
Coed, 3,443 undergraduate students, 95% full-time, 57% women, 43% men
Suburban 45-acre campus with easy access to Los Angeles
Moderately difficult entrance level, 62% of applicants were admitted

Freshmen *Admission:* 3,084 applied, 1,902 were accepted, 850 enrolled. *Test scores:* SAT verbal scores over 500: 94%; SAT math scores over 500: 95%; SAT verbal scores over 600: 43%; SAT math scores over 600: 45%; SAT verbal scores over 700: 7%; SAT math scores over 700: 5%.
Tuition and fees (2004–05): $26,150 (full-time). *Room and board:* $9082.
Financial Aid (All incoming freshmen): *Average need-based gift aid:* $16,443. *Average non-need based aid:* $12,296. *Average aid to full-time undergraduates:* $19,142.
Athletic Department: *Director of Athletics:* David Currey; Phone: 714-997-6691; Fax: 714-997-6010; E-mail: dcurrey@chapman.edu. *Sports Information Director:* Doug Aiken; Phone: 714-997-6900; E-mail: daiken@chapman.edu.

MEN'S COACHES

Baseball: Tom Tereschuk; Phone: 714-997-6662; E-mail: teres@chapman.edu.
Basketball: Mike Bokosky; Phone: 714-532-6083.
Cross Country: Anna Wlodarczyk; Phone: 714-997-6939; E-mail: awlodarc@chapman.edu.
Football: KenVisser; Phone: 714-744-7675; E-mail: visser@chapman.edu.
Golf: Brian Wood; Phone: 714-997-6651; E-mail: bwood@chapman.edu.
Lacrosse: Whit Judd; Phone: 714-997-6514; E-mail: chapmanlax@yahoo.com.
Soccer: Eddie Carrillo; Phone: 714-997-6502; E-mail: carrillo@chapman.edu.
Swimming: Dennis Ploessel; Phone: 714-532-6034; E-mail: dploesse@chapman.edu.
Tennis: Will Marino; Phone: 714-997-6654; E-mail: wmarino@chapman.edu.

WOMEN'S COACHES

Basketball: Carol Jue; Phone: 714-997-6510; E-mail: jue@chapman.edu.
Cross Country: Anna Wlodarczyk; Phone: 714-997-6939; E-mail: awlodarc@chapman.edu.
Soccer: Craig Bennett; Phone: 714-628-7279; E-mail: cbennett@chapman.edu.
Softball: Janet Lloyd; Phone: 714-997-6518; E-mail: jlloyd@chapman.edu.
Swimming: Dennis Ploessel; Phone: 714-532-6034; E-mail: dploesse@chapman.edu.
Tennis: Will Marino; Phone: 714-997-6654; E-mail: wmarino@chapman.edu.
Track and Field: Anna Wlodarczyk; Phone: 714-997-6939; E-mail: awlodarc@chapman.edu.
Volleyball: Mary Cahill; Phone: 714-997-6669; E-mail: cahill@chapman.edu.

CHARLESTON SOUTHERN UNIVERSITY

Charleston, South Carolina

Buccaneers ◆ NCAA I ◆ Big South Conference ◆ http://www.charlestonsouthern.edu/

Independent Baptist comprehensive, founded 1964
Coed, 2,676 undergraduate students, 79% full-time, 62% women, 38% men
Suburban 500-acre campus
Moderately difficult entrance level, 79% of applicants were admitted

Freshmen *Admission:* 2,111 applied, 1,688 were accepted, 440 enrolled. *Test scores:* SAT verbal scores over 500: 47%; SAT math scores over 500: 44%; SAT verbal scores over 600: 9%; SAT math scores over 600: 12%; SAT verbal scores over 700: 1%; SAT math scores over 700: 1%.
Tuition and fees (2003–04): $14,456 (full-time). *Room and board:* $5544.
Financial Aid (All incoming freshmen): *Average need-based gift aid:* $8130. *Average non-need based aid:* $6589. *Average aid to full-time undergraduates:* $10,828.
Athletic Department: *Director of Athletics:* Hank Small; Phone: 843-863-7080; Fax: 843-863-7695; E-mail: hsmall@csuniv.edu. *Sports Information Director:* David Shelton; Phone: 843-863-7688; E-mail: dshelton@csuniv.edu.

MEN'S COACHES

Baseball: Gary Murphy; Phone: 843-863-7591; E-mail: gmurphy@csuniv.edu.
Basketball: Jim Platt; Phone: 843-863-7690; E-mail: jplatt@csuniv.edu.
Cheerleading: Deborah Collins; Phone: 843-871-8978; E-mail: debbcsu7@cs.com.
Cross Country: Travis Alexander; Phone: 843-863-7671; E-mail: talexand@csuniv.edu.
Football: Jay Mills; Phone: 843-863-7119; E-mail: jmills@csuniv.edu.
Golf: Howard Vroon; Phone: 843-863-7122; E-mail: hvroon@csuniv.edu.
Tennis: Randy Bloemendaal; Phone: 843-863-7145; E-mail: rbloemendaal@csuniv.edu.
Track and Field: Tim Langford; Phone: 843-863-7174; E-mail: tlangford@csuniv.edu.

WOMEN'S COACHES

Basketball: Stephanie Yelton; Phone: 843-863-7684; E-mail: syelton@csuniv.edu.

Charleston Southern University *(continued)*
Cheerleading: Deborah Collins; Phone: 843-871-8978; E-mail: debbcsu7@cs.com.
Cross Country: Travis Alexander; Phone: 843-863-7671; E-mail: talexand@csuniv.edu.
Golf: Howard Vroon; Phone: 843-863-7122; E-mail: hvroon@csuniv.edu.
Soccer: Eric Terrill; Phone: 843-863-7931; E-mail: eterrill@csuniv.edu.
Softball: Joyce Wellhoefer; Phone: 843-863-7686; E-mail: jwellhoe@csuniv.edu.
Tennis: Randy Bloemendaal; Phone: 843-863-7145; E-mail: rbloemendaal@csuniv.edu.
Track and Field: Tosha Ansley; Phone: 843-863-7111; E-mail: tansley@csuniv.edu.
Volleyball: Danyel Bellush; Phone: 843-863-7680; E-mail: dlonigro@csuniv.edu.

CHATHAM COLLEGE
Pittsburgh, Pennsylvania

Cougars ◆ NCAA III ◆ Atlantic Women's Colleges Conference ◆ http://www.chatham.edu/

Independent comprehensive, founded 1869
Women only, 704 undergraduate students, 58% full-time, 95% women, 5% men
Urban 32-acre campus
Moderately difficult entrance level, 61% of applicants were admitted

Freshmen *Admission:* 243 applied, 149 were accepted, 78 enrolled. *Test scores:* SAT verbal scores over 500: 74%; SAT math scores over 500: 41%; SAT verbal scores over 600: 34%; SAT math scores over 600: 13%; SAT verbal scores over 700: 3%; SAT math scores over 700: 1%.
Tuition and fees (2003–04): $20,552 (full-time). *Room and board:* $6714 (room only: $3514).
Financial Aid (All incoming freshmen): *Average need-based gift aid:* $9427. *Average non-need based aid:* $6732. *Average aid to full-time undergraduates:* $20,984.
Athletic Department: *Director of Athletics:* Amy Buxbaum; Phone: 412-365-1650; Fax: 412-365-1724; E-mail: abuxbaum@chatham.edu. *Sports Information Director:* Ron Giles; Phone: 412-365-1269; E-mail: rgiles@chatham.edu.

WOMEN'S COACHES
Basketball: Amy Blackmond; Phone: 412-365-1650; E-mail: abuxbaum@chatham.edu.
Soccer: Richardo Iribarren; Phone: 412-365-1650; E-mail: riribarren@chatham.edu.
Softball: Phil Mastrean; Phone: 412-365-1650; E-mail: pmastrean@chatham.edu.
Swimming: Kara Cotter; Phone: 365-1650; E-mail: kcotter@chatham.edu.
Tennis: Danni Piccolo; Phone: 365-1650; E-mail: dpiccolo@chatham.edu.
Volleyball: Greg Lockley; Phone: 365-1650; E-mail: glockley@chatham.edu.

CHESTNUT HILL COLLEGE
Philadelphia, Pennsylvania

Griffins ◆ NCAA III ◆ Atlantic Women's Colleges Conference; Eastern College Athletic Conference ◆ http://www.chc.edu/

Independent Roman Catholic comprehensive, founded 1924
Coed, primarily women, 906 undergraduate students, 71% full-time, 81% women, 19% men
Suburban 45-acre campus
Moderately difficult entrance level, 75% of applicants were admitted

Freshmen *Admission:* 973 applied, 751 were accepted, 203 enrolled. *Test scores:* SAT verbal scores over 500: 42%; SAT math scores over

500: 34%; SAT verbal scores over 600: 9%; SAT math scores over 600: 5%; SAT verbal scores over 700: 1%.
Tuition and fees (2004–05): $20,345 (full-time). *Room and board:* $7500.
Financial Aid (All incoming freshmen): *Average need-based gift aid:* $8125. *Average non-need based aid:* $6050. *Average aid to full-time undergraduates:* $14,050.
Athletic Department: *Director of Athletics:* Janice Kuklick; Phone: 215-248-7060; Fax: 215-248-7047; E-mail: jkuklick@chc.edu.

MEN'S COACHES
Basketball: Paul Rieser; Phone: 215-248-7091.
Tennis: Roger Mallery; Phone: 215-242-7715.

WOMEN'S COACHES
Basketball: Paul Rieser; Phone: 215-248-7091.
Field Hockey: Janice Kuklick; Phone: 215-248-7060; E-mail: jkuklick@chc.edu.
Lacrosse: Janice Kuklick; Phone: 215-248-7060; E-mail: jkuklick@chc.edu.
Soccer: Shawn Ferris; Phone: 215-242-7715.
Softball: Valerie Brennan; Phone: 215-248-7060.
Tennis: Roger Mallery; Phone: 215-242-7715.
Volleyball: Nora Dollarton; Phone: 215-248-7060.

CHEYNEY UNIVERSITY OF PENNSYLVANIA
Cheyney, Pennsylvania

Wolves ◆ NCAA II ◆ Pennsylvania State Athletic Conference ◆ http://www.cheyney.edu/

State-supported comprehensive, founded 1837, part of Pennsylvania State System of Higher Education
Coed, 1,251 undergraduate students, 94% full-time, 55% women, 45% men
Suburban 275-acre campus with easy access to Philadelphia
Minimally difficult entrance level, 62% of applicants were admitted

Freshmen *Admission:* 2,146 applied, 1,336 were accepted, 382 enrolled.
Tuition and fees (2003–04): $5353 (resident), $12,251 (nonresident). *Room and board:* $5383 (room only: $2944).
Financial Aid (All incoming freshmen): *Average need-based gift aid:* $1876. *Average non-need based aid:* $7000. *Average aid to full-time undergraduates:* $10,675.

MEN'S COACHES
Basketball: Robert Marshall; Phone: 610-399-2267.
Cross Country: Jewel Lyons; Phone: 610-399-2777.
Football: John Parker; Phone: 610-399-2309.
Track and Field: Jewel Lyons; Phone: 610-399-2777.

WOMEN'S COACHES
Basketball: Tara Owens; Phone: 610-399-2601.
Cross Country: Jewel Lyons; Phone: 610-399-2777.
Track and Field: Jewel Lyons; Phone: 610-399-2777.
Volleyball: Milton Colston; Phone: 610-399-2777.

CHICAGO STATE UNIVERSITY
Chicago, Illinois

Cougars ◆ NCAA I ◆ Mid-Continent Conference ◆ http://www.csu.edu/

State-supported comprehensive, founded 1867
Coed, 4,904 undergraduate students, 65% full-time, 73% women, 27% men
Urban 161-acre campus
Moderately difficult entrance level, 4% of applicants were admitted

Freshmen *Admission:* 2,425 applied, 1,019 were accepted, 542 enrolled.
Tuition and fees (2004–05): $6143 (resident), $10,973 (nonresident). *Room and board:* $6032.
Financial Aid (All incoming freshmen): *Average aid to full-time undergraduates:* $2045.

Athletic Department: *Director of Athletics:* Albert Avant; Phone: 773-995-2995; Fax: 773-995-3656; E-mail: aavant@csu.edu. *Sports Information Director:* Ben Greenberg; Phone: 773-995-2217; E-mail: bgreen21@csu.edu.

MEN'S COACHES

Baseball: Terrence Jackson; Phone: 773-995-3659; E-mail: t-jackson2@csu.edu.
Basketball: Kevin Jones; Phone: 773-995-3657; E-mail: k-jones40@csu.edu.
Cross Country: Sudie Davis; Phone: 773-995-2230; E-mail: s-davis@csu.edu.
Golf: Charlie Hayes; Phone: 773-995-2376; E-mail: c-hayes1@csu.edu.
Tennis: Titania Harris; Phone: 773-995-3642; E-mail: t-harris4@csu.edu.
Track and Field: Sudie Davis; Phone: 773-995-2230; E-mail: s-davis@csu.edu.

WOMEN'S COACHES

Basketball: Angela Jackson; Phone: 773-995-2289; E-mail: ay-jackson@csu.edu.
Cross Country: Mamie Rallins; Phone: 773-995-3637; E-mail: ma-rallins@csu.edu.
Golf: Loritz Clark; Phone: 773-995-3697; E-mail: l-clark@csu.edu.
Tennis: Titania Harris; Phone: 773-995-3642; E-mail: t-harris4@csu.edu.
Track and Field: Mamie Rallins; Phone: 773-995-3637; E-mail: ma-rallins@csu.edu.
Volleyball: Heidi Cartisser; Phone: 773-995-2459; E-mail: h-cartisser@csu.edu.

CHOWAN COLLEGE
Murfreesboro, North Carolina

Braves ◆ NCAA III ◆ USA South Athletic Conference ◆ http://www.chowan.edu/

Independent Baptist 4-year, founded 1848
Coed, 790 undergraduate students, 95% full-time, 43% women, 57% men
Rural 300-acre campus with easy access to Norfolk and Hampton Roads
Minimally difficult entrance level, 66% of applicants were admitted

Freshmen *Admission:* 1,464 applied, 979 were accepted, 254 enrolled. *Test scores:* SAT verbal scores over 500: 20%; SAT math scores over 500: 21%; SAT verbal scores over 600: 2%; SAT math scores over 600: 2%.
Tuition and fees (2004–05): $14,100 (full-time). *Room and board:* $6100 (room only: $2900).
Financial Aid (All incoming freshmen): *Average need-based gift aid:* $8092. *Average non-need based aid:* $12,010. *Average aid to full-time undergraduates:* $10,619.
Athletic Department: *Director of Athletics:* Debbie Warren; Phone: 252-398-6468; Fax: 252-398-1390; E-mail: warred@chowan.edu. *Sports Information Director:* Meredith Davies-Long; Phone: 252-398-6286; E-mail: longm@chowan.edu.

MEN'S COACHES

Baseball: Steve Flack; Phone: 252-398-6228; E-mail: flacks@chowan.edu.
Basketball: Jim Tribbett; Phone: 252-398-6244; E-mail: tribbj@chowan.edu.
Cheerleading: Meaghan Howard; Phone: 252-398-6432; E-mail: howarm@chowan.edu.
Football: Steve Gill; Phone: 252-398-6434; E-mail: gills@chowan.edu.
Golf: Chris Howard; Phone: 252-398-6454; E-mail: howarc@chowan.edu.
Soccer: Nate Wiley; Phone: 252-398-6378; E-mail: wileyn@chowan.edu.

WOMEN'S COACHES

Basketball: Scott Groniger; Phone: 252-398-6433; E-mail: gronis@chowan.edu.
Cheerleading: Meaghan Howard; Phone: 252-398-6432; E-mail: howarm@chowan.edu.
Cross Country: Ellen Groniger; Phone: 252-398-6433; E-mail: gronis@chowan.edu.
Soccer: Stuart Horne; Phone: 252-398-6324; E-mail: hornej@chowan.edu.

Softball: Meredith Davies-Long; Phone: 252-398-6286; E-mail: longm@chowan.edu.
Volleyball: Meaghan Howard; Phone: 252-398-6432; E-mail: howarm@chowan.edu.

CHRISTIAN BROTHERS UNIVERSITY
Memphis, Tennessee

Buccaneers ◆ NCAA II ◆ Gulf South Conference ◆ http://www.cbu.edu/

Independent Roman Catholic comprehensive, founded 1871
Coed, 1,582 undergraduate students, 76% full-time, 57% women, 43% men
Urban 70-acre campus
Moderately difficult entrance level, 87% of applicants were admitted

Freshmen *Admission:* 879 applied, 749 were accepted, 281 enrolled. *Test scores:* SAT verbal scores over 500: 70%; SAT math scores over 500: 71%; SAT verbal scores over 600: 24%; SAT math scores over 600: 30%; SAT verbal scores over 700: 3%; SAT math scores over 700: 4%.
Tuition and fees (2003–04): $17,190 (full-time). *Room and board:* $5100 (room only: $2300).
Financial Aid (All incoming freshmen): *Average need-based gift aid:* $6081. *Average non-need based aid:* $9629. *Average aid to full-time undergraduates:* $14,203.
Athletic Department: *Director of Athletics:* Joseph Nadicksbernd; Phone: 901-321-3000; Fax: 901-321-3570; E-mail: jpnadick@cbu.edu. *Sports Information Director:* Justin Maskus; Phone: 901-321-3378; E-mail: jmaskus@cbu.edu.

MEN'S COACHES

Baseball: Phil Goodwin; Phone: 901-321-3375; E-mail: pgoodwin@cbu.edu.
Basketball: Mike Nienaber; Phone: 901-321-3372; E-mail: mnienabe@cbu.edu.
Cross Country: Seamus Loftus; Phone: 901-321-3361; E-mail: sloftus@cbu.edu.
Golf: Anna Massa; Phone: 901-681-0501; E-mail: amassa@cbu.edu.
Soccer: Seamus Loftus; Phone: 901-321-3361; E-mail: sloftus@cbu.edu.
Tennis: Seamus Loftus; Phone: 901-321-3361; E-mail: sloftus@cbu.edu.

WOMEN'S COACHES

Basketball: Todd Schaefer; Phone: 901-321-4116; E-mail: tschaefe@cbu.edu.
Cross Country: Seamus Loftus; Phone: 901-321-3361; E-mail: sloftus@cbu.edu.
Soccer: Seamus Loftus; Phone: 901-321-3361; E-mail: sloftus@cbu.edu.
Softball: Donna Crone; Phone: 901-321-3478; E-mail: dcrone@cbu.edu.
Tennis: Seamus Loftus; Phone: 901-321-3361; E-mail: sloftus@cbu.edu.
Volleyball: In-Sik Hwang; Phone: 901-321-3371; E-mail: hwang@cbu.edu.

CHRISTIAN HERITAGE COLLEGE
El Cajon, California

Hawks ◆ NAIA ◆ Golden State Conference ◆ http://www.christianheritage.edu/

Independent nondenominational 4-year, founded 1970
Coed, 524 undergraduate students, 89% full-time, 62% women, 38% men
Suburban 55-acre campus with easy access to San Diego
Moderately difficult entrance level, 7% of applicants were admitted

Freshmen *Admission:* 208 applied, 147 were accepted, 90 enrolled. *Test scores:* SAT verbal scores over 500: 52%; SAT math scores over 500: 42%; SAT verbal scores over 600: 7%; SAT math scores over 600: 17%; SAT verbal scores over 700: 2%.
Tuition and fees (2003–04): $14,000 (full-time). *Room and board:* $5990.
Financial Aid (All incoming freshmen): *Average need-based gift aid:* $6399. *Average non-need based aid:* $2712. *Average aid to full-time undergraduates:* $10,668.

Christian Heritage College *(continued)*

Athletic Department: *Director of Athletics:* Kelvin Starr; Phone: 619-590-1731; Fax: 619-590-1734; E-mail: kstarr@christianheritage.edu. *Sports Information Director:* Jackie Armstrong; Phone: 619-590-1788; E-mail: jarmstrong@christianheritage.edu.

MEN'S COACHES

Basketball: Kelvin Starr; Phone: 619-590-1731; E-mail: kstarr@christianheritage.edu.
Cross Country: Chad Bickley; Phone: 619-590-1730; E-mail: cbickley@christianheritage.edu.
Soccer: Kevin Elwell; Phone: 619-441-2200; E-mail: kelwell@christianheritage.edu.

WOMEN'S COACHES

Basketball: Will Cunningham; Phone: 619-441-2200; E-mail: wcunningham@christianheritage.edu.
Cross Country: Chad Bickley; Phone: 619-590-1730; E-mail: cbickley@christianheritage.edu.
Soccer: Kevin Elwell; Phone: 619-441-2200; E-mail: kelwell@christianheritage.edu.
Volleyball: Danielle Demko; Phone: 619-441-2200; E-mail: ddemko@christianheritage.edu.

CHRISTOPHER NEWPORT UNIVERSITY
Newport News, Virginia

Captains ◆ NCAA III ◆ USA South Athletic Conference
◆ http://www.cnu.edu/

State-supported comprehensive, founded 1960
Coed, 4,680 undergraduate students, 87% full-time, 56% women, 44% men
Suburban 175-acre campus with easy access to Norfolk
Moderately difficult entrance level, 58% of applicants were admitted

Freshmen *Admission:* 4,794 applied, 2,787 were accepted, 1,210 enrolled. *Test scores:* SAT verbal scores over 500: 91%; SAT math scores over 500: 88%; SAT verbal scores over 600: 33%; SAT math scores over 600: 30%; SAT verbal scores over 700: 4%; SAT math scores over 700: 3%.
Tuition and fees (2003–04): $4600 (resident), $12,300 (nonresident). *Room and board:* $6700 (room only: $4400).
Financial Aid (All incoming freshmen): *Average need-based gift aid:* $3156. *Average non-need based aid:* $1444. *Average aid to full-time undergraduates:* $4499.
Athletic Department: *Director of Athletics:* C.J. Woollum; Phone: 757-594-7217; Fax: 757-594-7839; E-mail: cjwoollu@cnu.edu. *Sports Information Director:* Wayne Block; Phone: 757-594-7382; E-mail: wblock@cnu.edu.

MEN'S COACHES

Baseball: John Harvell; Phone: 757-594-7054; E-mail: jharvell@cnu.edu.
Basketball: C.J. Woollum; Phone: 757-594-7217; E-mail: cjwoollu@cnu.edu.
Cheerleading: Leeann Teasdale; Phone: 757-594-7025; E-mail: cheergymelite@aol.com.
Cross Country: Keith Maurer; Phone: 757-594-7213; E-mail: coachkwm@aol.com.
Football: Matt Kelchner; Phone: 757-594-7584; E-mail: kelchner@cnu.edu.
Golf: Chad Wilson; Phone: 757-594-7978; E-mail: golf@cnu.edu.
Soccer: Steve Shaw; Phone: 757-594-7383; E-mail: sshaw@cnu.edu.
Tennis: Rush Cole; Phone: 757-594-7372; E-mail: rucole@cnu.edu.
Track and Field: Vince Brown; Phone: 757-594-7289; E-mail: vbrown@cnu.edu.

WOMEN'S COACHES

Basketball: Carolyn Hunter; Phone: 757-594-7103; E-mail: chunter@cnu.edu.
Cheerleading: Leeann Teasdale; Phone: 757-594-7025; E-mail: cheergymelite@aol.com.
Cross Country: Keith Maurer; Phone: 757-594-7213; E-mail: coachkwm@aol.com.
Field Hockey: Carrie Moura; Phone: 757-594-7920; E-mail: cmoura@cnu.edu.

Lacrosse: Kwame Lloyd; Phone: 757-594-7381; E-mail: klloyd@cnu.edu.
Soccer: Kwane Lloyd; Phone: 757-594-7381; E-mail: klloyd@cnu.edu.
Softball: Keith Parr; Phone: 757-594-7849; E-mail: joykeith1@juno.com.
Tennis: Jerry Nuttycombe; Phone: 757-594-8751; E-mail: jnutty@cnu.edu.
Track and Field: Vince Brown; Phone: 757-594-7289; E-mail: vbrown@cnu.edu.
Volleyball: Lindsay Sheppard; Phone: 757-594-7890.

THE CITADEL, THE MILITARY COLLEGE OF SOUTH CAROLINA
Charleston, South Carolina

Bulldogs ◆ NCAA I ◆ Southern Conference
◆ http://www.citadel.edu/

State-supported comprehensive, founded 1842
Coed, primarily men, 2,150 undergraduate students, 95% full-time, 8% women, 92% men
Urban 130-acre campus
Moderately difficult entrance level, 3% of applicants were admitted

Freshmen *Admission:* 1,919 applied, 588 were accepted, 553 enrolled. *Test scores:* SAT verbal scores over 500: 77%; SAT math scores over 500: 80%; SAT verbal scores over 600: 26%; SAT math scores over 600: 30%; SAT verbal scores over 700: 3%; SAT math scores over 700: 3%.
Tuition and fees (2003–04): $5897 (resident), $14,308 (nonresident). *Room and board:* $4778.
Financial Aid (All incoming freshmen): *Average need-based gift aid:* $3742. *Average non-need based aid:* $7258. *Average aid to full-time undergraduates:* $5798.
Athletic Department: *Director of Athletics:* Les Robinson; Phone: 843-953-5030; Fax: 843-953-6727; E-mail: les.robinson@citadel.edu. *Sports Information Director:* Mike Hayden; Phone: 843-953-5353; E-mail: mike.hayden@citadel.edu.

MEN'S COACHES

Baseball: Pat Dennis; Phone: 843-953-5901; E-mail: pat.dennis@citadel.edu.
Basketball: Pat Dennis; Phone: 843-953-5903; E-mail: pat.dennis@citadel.edu.
Cheerleading: Brittany Meyers; Phone: 843-953-1411; E-mail: brittany.meyers@citadel.edu.
Cross Country: Jody Huddleston; Phone: 843-953-5900; E-mail: huddlestonj@citadel.edu.
Football: Ellis Johnson; Phone: 843-953-5123; E-mail: ellis.johnson@citadel.edu.
Golf: Kim Lewellen; Phone: 843-953-6703; E-mail: lewellenjk@bellsouth.net.
Tennis: Toby Simpson; Phone: 843-953-4845; E-mail: toby.simpson@citadel.edu.
Track and Field: Jody Huddleston; Phone: 843-953-5900; E-mail: huddlestonj@citadel.edu.
Wrestling: Rob Hjerling; Phone: 843-953-4865; E-mail: robert.hjerling@citadel.edu.

WOMEN'S COACHES

Cheerleading: Brittany Meyers; Phone: 843-953-1411; E-mail: brittany.meyers@citadel.edu.
Cross Country: Jody Huddleston; Phone: 843-953-5900; E-mail: huddlestonj@citadel.edu.
Golf: Kim Lewellen; Phone: 843-953-6703; E-mail: lewellenjk@bellsouth.net.
Soccer: Megan Hjerling; Phone: 843-953-5844; E-mail: megan.hoban@citadel.edu.
Track and Field: Jody Huddleston; Phone: 843-953-5900; E-mail: huddlestonj@citadel.edu.
Volleyball: Wendy Anderson; Phone: 843-953-7034; E-mail: wendy.anderson@citadel.edu.

CITY COLLEGE OF THE CITY UNIVERSITY OF NEW YORK
New York, New York

Beavers ◆ NCAA III ◆ CUNY Athletic Conference; Knickerbocker Lacrosse Conference
◆ http://www.ccny.cuny.edu/

State and locally supported university, founded 1847, part of City University of New York System
Coed, 8,838 undergraduate students, 67% full-time, 49% women, 51% men
Urban 35-acre campus
Moderately difficult entrance level, 38% of applicants were admitted

Freshmen *Admission:* 6,584 applied, 2,329 were accepted, 1,173 enrolled. *Test scores:* SAT verbal scores over 500: 37%; SAT math scores over 500: 50%; SAT verbal scores over 600: 11%; SAT math scores over 600: 20%; SAT verbal scores over 700: 2%; SAT math scores over 700: 4%.
Tuition and fees (2003–04): $4339 (resident), $8899 (nonresident).
Athletic Department: *Director of Athletics:* Robert Coleman; Phone: 212-650-7550; Fax: 212-650-8230; E-mail: rcoleman@ccny.cuny.edu. *Sports Information Director:* Karina Jorge; Phone: 212-650-7524; E-mail: kjorge@ccny.cuny.edu.

MEN'S COACHES
Basketball: Andre Stampfel; Phone: 212-650-7557; E-mail: astampfel@ccny.cuny.edu.
Lacrosse: Phone: 212-650-8228; E-mail: fuzzard40@aol.com.
Soccer: Osborne Carter; Phone: 212-650-8228; E-mail: osborne.carter@njecpo.org.
Tennis: Esu Ma'at; Phone: 212-650-8228; E-mail: esumaat1@yahoo.com.
Track and Field: Leroy Solomon; Phone: 212-650-8228; E-mail: lemanstc@aol.com.
Volleyball: Robert Pichardo; Phone: 212-650-7549; E-mail: acevedopichardo@msn.com.

WOMEN'S COACHES
Basketball: Gerald Davis; Phone: 212-650-7524.
Soccer: Dragos Herinean; Phone: 212-650-8228; E-mail: dragos22@hotmail.com.
Tennis: Esu Ma'at; Phone: 212-650-8228; E-mail: esumaat1@yahoo.com.
Track and Field: Leroy Solomon; Phone: 212-650-8228; E-mail: lemanstc@aol.com.
Volleyball: Robert Pichardo; Phone: 212-650-7549; E-mail: acevedopichardo@msn.com.

CLAFLIN UNIVERSITY
Orangeburg, South Carolina

Panthers ◆ NAIA ◆ Eastern Intercollegiate Conference
◆ http://www.claflin.edu/

Independent United Methodist 4-year, founded 1869
Coed, 1,546 undergraduate students, 95% full-time, 68% women, 32% men
Small-town 32-acre campus with easy access to Columbia
Minimally difficult entrance level, 5% of applicants were admitted

Freshmen *Admission:* 1,714 applied, 869 were accepted, 350 enrolled. *Test scores:* SAT verbal scores over 500: 34%; SAT math scores over 500: 40%; SAT verbal scores over 600: 8%; SAT math scores over 600: 10%; SAT verbal scores over 700: 1%; SAT math scores over 700: 1%.
Tuition and fees (2003–04): $9654 (full-time). *Room and board:* $5184 (room only): $2348).
Financial Aid (All incoming freshmen): *Average aid to full-time undergraduates:* $9000.
Athletic Department: *Director of Athletics:* Leroy Durant; Phone: 803-535-5341; Fax: 803-535-5610.

MEN'S COACHES
Baseball: Brian Newsome; Phone: 803-535-5295; E-mail: bnewsome@claflin.edu.

Basketball: Ron Woodard; Phone: 803-535-5360; E-mail: rwoodard@claflin.edu.
Cheerleading: Stephanie Smith; Phone: 803-535-5362.
Cross Country: Jeffrey Hughes; Phone: 803-535-5368; E-mail: jhughes@claflin.edu.
Track and Field: Jeffrey Hughes; Phone: 803-535-5368; E-mail: jhughes@claflin.edu.

WOMEN'S COACHES
Basketball: Miriam Samuels; Phone: 803-535-5449; E-mail: msamuels@claflin.edu.
Cheerleading: Stephanie Smith; Phone: 803-535-5362.
Cross Country: Jeffrey Hughes; Phone: 803-535-5368; E-mail: jhughes@claflin.edu.
Softball: Hampton Jordan; Phone: 803-535-5591; E-mail: hjordan@claflin.edu.
Track and Field: Jeffrey Hughes; Phone: 803-535-5368; E-mail: jhughes@claflin.edu.
Volleyball: Vernell Keitt; Phone: 803-535-5367.

CLAREMONT McKENNA COLLEGE
Claremont, California

(M) Stags, (W) Athenas ◆ NCAA III ◆ Southern California Athletic Conference ◆ http://www.claremontmckenna.edu/

Independent 4-year, founded 1946, part of The Claremont Colleges Consortium
Coed, 1,050 undergraduate students, 100% full-time, 45% women, 55% men
Small-town 50-acre campus with easy access to Los Angeles
Very difficult entrance level, 3% of applicants were admitted

Freshmen *Admission:* 2,892 applied, 842 were accepted, 284 enrolled. *Test scores:* SAT verbal scores over 500: 100%; SAT math scores over 500: 100%; SAT verbal scores over 600: 93%; SAT math scores over 600: 95%; SAT verbal scores over 700: 46%; SAT math scores over 700: 51%.
Tuition and fees (2003–04): $27,700 (full-time). *Room and board:* $9180 (room only): $4590).
Financial Aid (All incoming freshmen): *Average need-based gift aid:* $21,194. *Average non-need based aid:* $4784. *Average aid to full-time undergraduates:* $24,119.
Athletic Department: *Director of Athletics:* Mike Sutton; Phone: 909-607-3562; Fax: 909-621-8848; E-mail: michael.sutton@claremontmckenna.edu. *Sports Information Director:* Kelly Beck; Phone: 909-607-2904; E-mail: kelly.beck@claremontmckenna.edu.

MEN'S COACHES
Baseball: Randy Town; Phone: 909-607-3796; E-mail: randy.town@claremontmckenna.edu.
Basketball: Ken Scalmanini; Phone: 909-607-7153; E-mail: kenneth.scalmanini@claremontmckenna.edu.
Cross Country: John Goldhammer; Phone: 909-607-3564; E-mail: john.goldhammer@claremontmckenna.edu.
Diving: Gurgen Militosyan; Phone: 909-607-9338.
Football: Rick Candaele; Phone: 909-607-1768; E-mail: richard.candaele@claremontmckenna.edu.
Golf: Bim Jollymour; Phone: 909-607-9204; E-mail: bimj@aol.com.
Soccer: Dan Calichman; Phone: 909-607-7471; E-mail: daniel.calichman@claremontmckenna.edu.
Swimming: Charlie Griffiths; Phone: 909-607-9338; E-mail: charles.griffiths@claremontmckenna.edu.
Tennis: Paul Settles; Phone: 909-607-3563; E-mail: paul.settles@claremontmckenna.edu.
Track and Field: John Goldhammer; Phone: 909-607-3564; E-mail: john.goldhammer@claremontmckenna.edu.

WOMEN'S COACHES
Basketball: Jodie Burton; Phone: 909-607-3139; E-mail: jodie.burton@claremontmckenna.edu.
Cross Country: John Goldhammer; Phone: 909-607-3564; E-mail: john.goldhammer@claremontmckenna.edu.
Diving: Gurgen Militosyan; Phone: 909-607-9338.
Lacrosse: Lauren Uhr; Phone: 909-607-9204; E-mail: lauren.uhr@claremontmckenna.edu.
Soccer: Jennifer Clark; Phone: 909-607-9069; E-mail: jennifer.clark@claremontmckenna.edu.

Claremont McKenna College (*continued*)

Softball: Andrea Kenney; Phone: 909-607-8613; E-mail: andrea.kenney@claremontmckenna.edu.
Swimming: Charlie Griffiths; Phone: 909-607-9338; E-mail: charles.griffiths@claremontmckenna.edu.
Tennis: Maxanne Retzlaff; Phone: 909-607-4237; E-mail: maxanne.retzlaff@claremontmckenna.edu.
Track and Field: John Goldhammer; Phone: 909-607-3564; E-mail: john.goldhammer@claremontmckenna.edu.
Volleyball: Dianna Turner; Phone: 909-607-9204; E-mail: dianna.turner@claremontmckenna.edu.

CLARION UNIVERSITY OF PENNSYLVANIA
Clarion, Pennsylvania

Golden Eagles ◆ NCAA II ◆ Pennsylvania State Athletic Conference ◆ http://www.clarion.edu/

State-supported comprehensive, founded 1867, part of Pennsylvania State System of Higher Education
Coed, 5,943 undergraduate students, 89% full-time, 62% women, 38% men
Rural 100-acre campus
Minimally difficult entrance level, 76% of applicants were admitted

Freshmen *Admission:* 3,447 applied, 2,673 were accepted, 1,315 enrolled. *Test scores:* SAT verbal scores over 500: 37%; SAT math scores over 500: 35%; SAT verbal scores over 600: 6%; SAT math scores over 600: 6%; SAT verbal scores over 700: 1%.
Tuition and fees (2003–04): $5998 (resident), $9448 (nonresident). *Room and board:* $4560 (room only: $2994).
Financial Aid (All incoming freshmen): *Average need-based gift aid:* $3410. *Average non-need based aid:* $1363. *Average aid to full-time undergraduates:* $5456.
Athletic Department: *Director of Athletics:* Bob Carlson; Phone: 814-393-1997; Fax: 814-393-2063; E-mail: rcarlson@clarion.edu. *Sports Information Director:* Rich Herman; Phone: 814-393-2334; E-mail: rherman@clarion.edu.

MEN'S COACHES
Baseball: Scott Feldman; Phone: 814-393-1651; E-mail: sfeldman@clarion.edu.
Basketball: Ron Righter; Phone: 814-393-2510; E-mail: rrighter@clarion.edu.
Cheerleading: Jamie Bero; Phone: 814-393-2312; E-mail: jbero@clarion.edu.
Cross Country: Pat Mooney; Phone: 814-393-2081; E-mail: pmooney@clarion.edu.
Diving: Mark Van Dyke; Phone: 814-393-2457; E-mail: mvandyke@clarion.edu.
Football: Malen Luke; Phone: 814-393-2258; E-mail: mluke@clarion.edu.
Golf: Al LeFevre; Phone: 814-226-1884; E-mail: alefevre@clarion.edu.
Swimming: Mark Van Dyke; Phone: 814-393-2457; E-mail: mvandyke@clarion.edu.
Track and Field: Pat Mooney; Phone: 814-393-2081; E-mail: pmooney@clarion.edu.
Wrestling: Ken Nellis; Phone: 814-393-2455; E-mail: knellis@clarion.edu.

WOMEN'S COACHES
Basketball: Gie Parsons; Phone: 814-393-2200; E-mail: mparsons@clarion.edu.
Cheerleading: Jamie Bero; Phone: 814-393-2312; E-mail: jbero@clarion.edu.
Cross Country: Pat Mooney; Phone: 814-393-2081; E-mail: pmooney@clarion.edu.
Diving: Mark Van Dyke; Phone: 814-393-2457; E-mail: mvandyke@clarion.edu.
Soccer: Nina Alonzo; Phone: 814-393-2376; E-mail: calonzo@clarion.edu.
Softball: Natalie Martin; Phone: 814-393-2118.
Swimming: Mark Van Dyke; Phone: 814-393-2457; E-mail: mvandyke@clarion.edu.
Tennis: Lori Sabatose; Phone: 814-393-1667; E-mail: lsabatose@mail.clarion.edu.

Track and Field: Pat Mooney; Phone: 814-393-2081; E-mail: pmooney@clarion.edu.
Volleyball: Tracey Fluharty; Phone: 814-393-1987; E-mail: tfluharty@clarion.edu.

CLARK ATLANTA UNIVERSITY
Atlanta, Georgia

Panthers ◆ NCAA II ◆ Southern Intercollegiate Athletic Conference ◆ http://www.cau.edu/

Independent United Methodist university, founded 1865
Coed, 3,920 undergraduate students, 97% full-time, 71% women, 29% men
Urban 113-acre campus with easy access to Atlanta
Moderately difficult entrance level, 51% of applicants were admitted

Freshmen *Admission:* 6,939 applied, 3,664 were accepted, 953 enrolled. *Test scores:* SAT verbal scores over 500: 61%; SAT math scores over 500: 54%; SAT verbal scores over 600: 42%; SAT math scores over 600: 41%; SAT math scores over 700: 1%.
Tuition and fees (2003–04): $12,862 (full-time). *Room and board:* $6438 (room only: $3778).
Financial Aid (All incoming freshmen): *Average need-based gift aid:* $3014. *Average aid to full-time undergraduates:* $4915.
Athletic Department: *Director of Athletics:* Brenda Edmond; Phone: 404-880-6116; Fax: 404-880-8102; E-mail: bedmond2@cau.edu. *Sports Information Director:* Lawanda Pearson; Phone: 404-880-6685; E-mail: lpearson@cau.edu.

MEN'S COACHES
Baseball: Chris Atwell; Phone: 404-880-8215; E-mail: catwell@cau.edu.
Basketball: Anthony Witherspoon; Phone: 404-880-8129.
Cheerleading: Billette Owens-Ashford; Phone: 404-880-8123.
Cross Country: Pamela Page; Phone: 404-880-6051; E-mail: ppage@cau.edu.
Football: Tracey Ham; Phone: 404-880-6037; E-mail: tham@cau.edu.
Tennis: Larry Nolley; Phone: 404-880-6188.
Track and Field: Pamela Page; Phone: 404-880-6051; E-mail: ppage@cau.edu.

WOMEN'S COACHES
Basketball: Vanessa White; Phone: 404-880-8127; E-mail: vwhite@cau.edu.
Cheerleading: Billette Owens-Ashford; Phone: 404-880-8123.
Cross Country: Pamela Page; Phone: 404-880-6051; E-mail: ppage@cau.edu.
Softball: Lawanda Pearson; Phone: 404-880-6685; E-mail: lpearson@cau.edu.
Tennis: Larry Nolley; Phone: 404-880-8129; E-mail: lnolley@cau.edu.
Track and Field: Pamela Page; Phone: 404-880-6051; E-mail: ppage@cau.edu.
Volleyball: Tamica Jones; Phone: 404-880-8123; E-mail: tjones@cau.edu.

CLARKE COLLEGE
Dubuque, Iowa

Crusaders ◆ NCAA III ◆ Midwestern Intercollegiate Volleyball Conference; Northern Illinois-Iowa Conference ◆ http://www.clarke.edu/

Independent Roman Catholic comprehensive, founded 1843
Coed, 1,005 undergraduate students, 80% full-time, 70% women, 30% men
Urban 55-acre campus
Moderately difficult entrance level, 57% of applicants were admitted

Freshmen *Admission:* 704 applied, 391 were accepted, 171 enrolled.
Tuition and fees (2003–04): $17,090 (full-time). *Room and board:* $6075 (room only: $2970).
Financial Aid (All incoming freshmen): *Average need-based gift aid:* $13,890. *Average non-need based aid:* $11,526. *Average aid to full-time undergraduates:* $17,349.

Athletic Department: *Director of Athletics:* Curt Long; Phone: 563-588-6462; Fax: 563-588-6666; E-mail: curt.long@clarke.edu. *Sports Information Director:* Jerry Hanson; Phone: 563-588-6360; E-mail: jerry.hanson@clarke.edu.

MEN'S COACHES

Baseball: Eric Frese; Phone: 563-588-6601; E-mail: eric.frese@clarke.edu.
Basketball: Jon Davison; Phone: 563-588-6344; E-mail: jon.davison@clarke.edu.
Cross Country: Joe Wagner; Phone: 563-588-6619; E-mail: joe.wagner@clarke.edu.
Golf: Jon Davison; Phone: 563-588-6344; E-mail: jon.davison@clarke.edu.
Soccer: Pat Herbst; Phone: 563-588-6760; E-mail: pat.herbst@clarke.edu.
Tennis: Rick Arrington; Phone: 563-588-6386; E-mail: rick.arrington@clarke.edu.
Volleyball: Joe Fleckenstein; Phone: 563-588-6619; E-mail: joe.fleckenstein@clarke.edu.

WOMEN'S COACHES

Basketball: Joan Steffen; Phone: 563-588-6570; E-mail: joan.steffen@clarke.edu.
Cross Country: Joe Wagner; Phone: 563-588-6619; E-mail: joe.wagner@clarke.edu.
Golf: Casey Kohr; Phone: 563-588-6341; E-mail: casey.kohr@clarke.edu.
Soccer: Pat Herbst; Phone: 563-588-6760; E-mail: pat.herbst@clarke.edu.
Softball: Cara Clark; Phone: 563-588-6619; E-mail: cara.clark@clarke.edu.
Tennis: Rick Arrington; Phone: 563-588-6386; E-mail: rick.arrington@clarke.edu.
Volleyball: Peg Harbaugh; Phone: 563-588-6619; E-mail: peg.harbaugh@clarke.edu.

CLARKSON UNIVERSITY
Potsdam, New York

Golden Knights ◆ NCAA III ◆ Eastern College Athletic Conference; Upstate Collegiate Athletic Conference ◆ http://www.clarkson.edu/

Independent university, founded 1896
Coed, 2,723 undergraduate students, 99% full-time, 24% women, 76% men
Small-town 640-acre campus
Very difficult entrance level, 81% of applicants were admitted

Freshmen *Admission:* 2,698 applied, 2,189 were accepted, 721 enrolled. *Test scores:* SAT verbal scores over 500: 84%; SAT math scores over 500: 96%; SAT verbal scores over 600: 34%; SAT math scores over 600: 61%; SAT verbal scores over 700: 5%; SAT math scores over 700: 13%.
Tuition and fees (2004–05): $24,140 (full-time). *Room and board:* $9068 (room only: $4728).
Financial Aid (All incoming freshmen): *Average need-based gift aid:* $8393. *Average non-need based aid:* $7633. *Average aid to full-time undergraduates:* $17,110.
Athletic Department: *Director of Athletics:* Sean Frazier; Phone: 315-268-6622; Fax: 315-268-7613. *Sports Information Director:* Gary Mikel; Phone: 315-268-6673; E-mail: mikelg@clarkson.edu.

MEN'S COACHES

Baseball: Jim Kane; Phone: 315-268-3759; E-mail: jkanebas@clarkson.edu.
Basketball: Tobin Anderson; Phone: 315-268-3766; E-mail: tobina@clarkson.edu.
Cross Country: Jim Kane; Phone: 315-268-6622; E-mail: jkanebas@clarkson.edu.
Golf: Bill Bergan; Phone: 315-268-3767; E-mail: lacrosse@clarkson.edu.
Ice Hockey: George Roll; Phone: 315-268-3874; E-mail: groll@clarkson.edu.
Lacrosse: Bill Bergan; Phone: 315-268-3767; E-mail: lacrosse@clarkson.edu.
Soccer: Will Steinrotter; Phone: 315-268-7983; E-mail: mnsoccer@clarkson.edu.

Swimming: Mick Maguire; Phone: 315-268-7931; E-mail: maguirem@clarkson.edu.
Tennis: Tobin Anderson; Phone: 315-268-3766; E-mail: tobina@clarkson.edu.

WOMEN'S COACHES

Basketball: Ann Parks; Phone: 315-268-3757; E-mail: parksam@clarkson.edu.
Cross Country: Jim Kane; Phone: 315-268-6622; E-mail: jkanebas@clarkson.edu.
Lacrosse: Chapel Love; Phone: 315-268-4448; E-mail: clove@clarkson.edu.
Soccer: Laurel Kane; Phone: 315-268-6594; E-mail: lstewart@clarkson.edu.
Swimming: Mick Maguire; Phone: 315-268-7931; E-mail: maguirem@clarkson.edu.
Tennis: Ann Parks; Phone: 315-268-3757; E-mail: parksam@clarkson.edu.
Volleyball: Laura Mandell; Phone: 315-268-4294; E-mail: lmandell@clarkson.edu.

CLARK UNIVERSITY
Worcester, Massachusetts

Cougars ◆ NCAA III ◆ New England Women's & Men's Athletics Conference ◆ http://www.clarku.edu/

Independent university, founded 1887
Coed, 2,190 undergraduate students, 91% full-time, 61% women, 39% men
Urban 50-acre campus with easy access to Boston
Moderately difficult entrance level, 56% of applicants were admitted

Freshmen *Admission:* 3,950 applied, 2,488 were accepted, 541 enrolled. *Test scores:* SAT verbal scores over 500: 88%; SAT math scores over 500: 91%; SAT verbal scores over 600: 49%; SAT math scores over 600: 55%; SAT verbal scores over 700: 8%; SAT math scores over 700: 10%.
Tuition and fees (2003–04): $26,965 (full-time). *Room and board:* $5150 (room only: $3150).
Financial Aid (All incoming freshmen): *Average need-based gift aid:* $18,012. *Average non-need based aid:* $12,056. *Average aid to full-time undergraduates:* $23,136.
Athletic Department: *Director of Athletics:* Linda Moulton; Phone: 508-793-7160; Fax: 508-793-7627; E-mail: lmoulton@clarku.edu. *Sports Information Director:* Joe Brady; Phone: 508-793-7164; E-mail: jbrady@clarku.edu.

MEN'S COACHES

Baseball: Jason Falcon; Phone: 508-421-3832; E-mail: jfalcon@clarku.edu.
Basketball: Paul Phillips; Phone: 508-793-7430; E-mail: pphillips@clarku.edu.
Cross Country: Chris D'Aniello; Phone: 508-793-7516; E-mail: cdaniello@clarku.edu.
Diving: Paul Phillips; Phone: 508-793-7170; E-mail: pephillips@clarku.edu.
Lacrosse: Evan Davis; Phone: 508-793-7729; E-mail: rdavis@clarku.edu.
Soccer: David Kulik; Phone: 508-793-7636; E-mail: dkulik@clarku.edu.
Swimming: Paul Phillips; Phone: 508-793-7170; E-mail: pephillips@clarku.edu.
Tennis: Barry Ndinya; Phone: 508-793-7516; E-mail: bndinya@clarku.edu.

WOMEN'S COACHES

Basketball: Pat Glispin; Phone: 508-793-7628; E-mail: pglispin@clarku.edu.
Cross Country: Chris D'Aniello; Phone: 508-793-7516; E-mail: cdaniello@clarku.edu.
Diving: Paul Phillips; Phone: 508-793-7170; E-mail: pephillips@clarku.edu.
Field Hockey: Linda Wage; Phone: 508-793-7637; E-mail: lwage@clarku.edu.
Soccer: Joe Brady; Phone: 508-793-7164; E-mail: jbrady@clarku.edu.
Softball: Linda Wage; Phone: 508-793-7637; E-mail: lwage@clarku.edu.
Swimming: Paul Phillips; Phone: 508-793-7170; E-mail: pephillips@clarku.edu.

Clark University *(continued)*

Tennis: Barry Ndinya; Phone: 508-793-7516; E-mail: bndinya@clarku. edu.
Volleyball: Karen Chambers Farrell; Phone: 508-421-3796; E-mail: kcfarrell@clarku.edu.

CLAYTON COLLEGE & STATE UNIVERSITY
Morrow, Georgia

Lakers ◆ NCAA II ◆ Peach Belt Conference ◆ http://www.clayton.edu/

State-supported 4-year, founded 1969, part of University System of Georgia
Coed, 5,661 undergraduate students, 47% full-time, 69% women, 31% men
Suburban 163-acre campus with easy access to Atlanta
Minimally difficult entrance level

Freshmen *Admission:* 617 enrolled.
Tuition and fees (2003–04): $2702 (resident), $9306 (nonresident).
Athletic Department: *Director of Athletics:* Mason Barfield; Phone: 770-961-3465; Fax: 770-960-5127; E-mail: masonbarfield@mail.clayton. edu. *Sports Information Director:* Gid Rowell; Phone: 770-960-4319; E-mail: gidrowell@mail.clayton.edu.

MEN'S COACHES
Basketball: Gordon Gibbons; Phone: 770-961-3654; E-mail: gordongibbons@mail.clayton.edu.
Cheerleading: Monique Holland; Phone: 770-961-3454; E-mail: moniqueholland@mail.clayton.edu.
Cross Country: Mike Mead; Phone: 770-961-2076; E-mail: mikemead@ mail.clayton.edu.
Golf: Bob Hill; Phone: 770-961-3742; E-mail: roberthill@mail.clayton. edu.
Soccer: John Rootes; Phone: 770-960-2077; E-mail: johnrootes@mail. clayton.edu.
Track and Field: Mike Mead; Phone: 770-961-2076; E-mail: mikemead@ mail.clayton.edu.

WOMEN'S COACHES
Basketball: A.C. McCullers; Phone: 770-961-3669; E-mail: acmccullers@mail.clayton.edu.
Cheerleading: Monique Holland; Phone: 770-961-3454; E-mail: moniqueholland@mail.clayton.edu.
Cross Country: Mike Mead; Phone: 770-961-2076; E-mail: mikemead@ mail.clayton.edu.
Soccer: T.O. Totty; Phone: 770-960-4261; E-mail: tottytotty@mail. clayton.edu.
Tennis: Elizabeth Nieto; Phone: 770-960-4318; E-mail: elizabethnieto@ mail.clayton.edu.
Track and Field: Mike Mead; Phone: 770-961-2076; E-mail: mikemead@ mail.clayton.edu.

CLEMSON UNIVERSITY
Clemson, South Carolina

Tigers ◆ NCAA I ◆ Atlantic Coast Conference ◆ http://www.clemson.edu/

State-supported university, founded 1889
Coed, 13,813 undergraduate students, 93% full-time, 45% women, 55% men
Small-town 1,400-acre campus
Moderately difficult entrance level, 52% of applicants were admitted

Freshmen *Admission:* 11,315 applied, 5,864 were accepted, 2,753 enrolled. *Test scores:* SAT verbal scores over 500: 91%; SAT math scores over 500: 95%; SAT verbal scores over 600: 47%; SAT math scores over 600: 63%; SAT verbal scores over 700: 7%; SAT math scores over 700: 13%.
Tuition and fees (2003–04): $6934 (resident), $14,532 (nonresident). *Room and board:* $5038 (room only: $2894).

Financial Aid (All incoming freshmen): *Average need-based gift aid:* $3331. *Average non-need based aid:* $6495. *Average aid to full-time undergraduates:* $9405.
Athletic Department: *Director of Athletics:* Terry Don Phillips; Phone: 864-656-1935; Fax: 864-656-0299; E-mail: pterry@clemson.edu. *Sports Information Director:* Tim Bourret; Phone: 864-656-1926; E-mail: btimoth@clemson.edu.

MEN'S COACHES
Baseball: Jack Leggett; Phone: 864-656-1947; E-mail: leggetj@clemson. edu.
Basketball: Oliver Purnell; Phone: 864-656-1954; E-mail: opurnel@ clemson.edu.
Cheerleading: Katie Mang; Phone: 864-654-9398; E-mail: kmang@ clemson.edu.
Diving: Leslie Hasselbach; Phone: 864-656-1925; E-mail: lhassel@ clemson.edu.
Football: Tommy Bowden; Phone: 864-656-2796; E-mail: tbowden@ clemson.edu.
Golf: Larry Penley; Phone: 864-656-1930; E-mail: plarry@clemson.edu.
Soccer: Trevor Adair; Phone: 864-656-1945; E-mail: amcmaho@ clemson.edu.
Swimming: Christopher Ip; Phone: 864-656-2215; E-mail: cip@clemson. edu.
Tennis: Chuck Kriese; Phone: 864-656-2252; E-mail: kriesec@clemson. edu.
Track and Field: Bob Pollack; Phone: 864-656-2269; E-mail: pollocr@ clemson.edu.

WOMEN'S COACHES
Basketball: Jim Davis; Phone: 864-656-1919; E-mail: dj@clemson.edu.
Cheerleading: Katie Mang; Phone: 864-654-9398; E-mail: kmang@ clemson.edu.
Diving: Leslie Hasselbach; Phone: 864-656-1925; E-mail: lhassel@ clemson.edu.
Soccer: Todd Bramble; Phone: 864-656-1944; E-mail: tbrambl@ clemson.edu.
Swimming: Christopher Ip; Phone: 864-656-2215; E-mail: cip@clemson. edu.
Tennis: Nancy Harris; Phone: 864-656-1323; E-mail: nh@clemson.edu.
Track and Field: Marcia Fletcher Noad; Phone: 864-656-1941; E-mail: marciaf@clemson.edu.
Volleyball: Jolene Jordan-Hoover; Phone: 864-656-1931; E-mail: hjolene@clemson.edu.

CLEVELAND STATE UNIVERSITY
Cleveland, Ohio

Vikings ◆ NCAA I ◆ Horizon League Conference ◆ http://www.csuohio.edu/

State-supported university, founded 1964
Coed, 10,054 undergraduate students, 69% full-time, 54% women, 46% men
Urban 70-acre campus with easy access to Akron
Noncompetitive entrance level, 79% of applicants were admitted

Freshmen *Admission:* 2,813 applied, 2,205 were accepted, 987 enrolled. *Test scores:* SAT verbal scores over 500: 39%; SAT math scores over 500: 39%; SAT verbal scores over 600: 9%; SAT math scores over 600: 11%; SAT verbal scores over 700: 1%; SAT math scores over 700: 2%.
Tuition and fees (2003–04): $6072 (resident), $11,940 (nonresident). *Room and board:* $7805 (room only: $5316).
Financial Aid (All incoming freshmen): *Average need-based gift aid:* $4912. *Average non-need based aid:* $7282. *Average aid to full-time undergraduates:* $6543.
Athletic Department: *Director of Athletics:* Lee Reed; Phone: 216-687-4808; Fax: 216-687-9242; E-mail: l.e.reed@csuohio.edu. *Sports Information Director:* Brian McCann; Phone: 216-687-5115; E-mail: b.mccann66@csuohio.edu.

MEN'S COACHES
Baseball: Jay Murphy; Phone: 216-687-4822; E-mail: j.murphy@ csuohio.edu.
Basketball: Mike Garland; Phone: 216-687-4817; E-mail: m.q.garland@ csuohio.edu.
Cheerleading: Beneatha Barkley; Phone: 216-687-5119; E-mail: bcbdance@aol.com.

Diving: Rich Karban; Phone: 216-687-4813; E-mail: rkarban@comcast. net.
Golf: Tom Porten; Phone: 216-687-2390; E-mail: t.porten@csuohio.edu.
Soccer: Pete Curtis; Phone: 216-687-4810; E-mail: p.curtis@csuohio. edu.
Swimming: Wally Morton; Phone: 216-687-4809; E-mail: g.morton@ csuohio.edu.
Tennis: Brian Etzkin; Phone: 216-687-4811; E-mail: b.etzkin@csuohio. edu.
Wrestling: Jack Effner; Phone: 216-687-4805; E-mail: j.effner@csuohio. edu.

WOMEN'S COACHES
Basketball: Kate Peterson; Phone: 216-687-5289; E-mail: k.l. peterson48@csuohio.edu.
Cheerleading: Beneatha Barkley; Phone: 216-687-5119; E-mail: bcbdance@aol.com.
Cross Country: Aaron Rood; Phone: 216-687-7256; E-mail: aaronrood@ hotmail.com.
Diving: Rich Karban; Phone: 216-687-4813; E-mail: rkarban@comcast. net.
Golf: Tom Porten; Phone: 216-687-2390; E-mail: t.porten@csuohio.edu.
Softball: Julie Jones; Phone: 216-687-5110; E-mail: j.a.jones@csuohio. edu.
Swimming: Mike Lehto; Phone: 216-687-4813; E-mail: m.lehto@ csuohio.edu.
Tennis: Brian Etzkin; Phone: 216-687-4811; E-mail: b.etzkin@csuohio. edu.
Volleyball: Chuck Voss; Phone: 216-687-5112; E-mail: m.lehto@ csuohio.edu.

COASTAL CAROLINA UNIVERSITY
Conway, South Carolina
Chants ◆ NCAA I ◆ Big South Conference ◆ http://www.coastal.edu/

State-supported comprehensive, founded 1954
Coed, 5,610 undergraduate students, 88% full-time, 52% women, 48% men
Suburban 244-acre campus
Moderately difficult entrance level, 69% of applicants were admitted

Freshmen *Admission:* 4,527 applied, 3,208 were accepted, 1,272 enrolled. *Test scores:* SAT verbal scores over 500: 56%; SAT math scores over 500: 68%; SAT verbal scores over 600: 12%; SAT math scores over 600: 18%; SAT verbal scores over 700: 1%; SAT math scores over 700: 1%.
Tuition and fees (2003–04): $5270 (resident), $12,950 (nonresident). *Room and board:* $5770 (room only: $3700).
Financial Aid (All incoming freshmen): *Average need-based gift aid:* $3160. *Average non-need based aid:* $6087. *Average aid to full-time undergraduates:* $6625.
Athletic Department: *Director of Athletics:* Warren Koegel; Phone: 843-349-2146; Fax: 843-349-2893; E-mail: wkoegel@coastal.edu. *Sports Information Director:* John Martin; Phone: 843-349-2822; E-mail: jamartin@coastal.edu.

MEN'S COACHES
Baseball: Gary Gilmore; Phone: 843-349-2816; E-mail: baseball@ coastal.edu.
Basketball: Pete Strickland; Phone: 843-349-2818; E-mail: pstrickl@ coastal.edu.
Cheerleading: Gina Simeone; Phone: 843-349-2820; E-mail: ginasimeone14@yahoo.com.
Cross Country: Andrew Allden; Phone: 843-349-2907; E-mail: allden@ coastal.edu.
Football: David Bennett; Phone: 843-234-3487; E-mail: dbennett@ coastal.edu.
Golf: Allen Terrell; Phone: 843-349-2902; E-mail: aterrell@coastal.edu.
Soccer: Shaun Docking; Phone: 843-349-2803; E-mail: sdocking@ coastal.edu.
Tennis: Jody Davis; Phone: 843-349-2832; E-mail: jody@coastal.edu.
Track and Field: Andrew Allden; Phone: 843-349-2907; E-mail: allden@ coastal.edu.

WOMEN'S COACHES
Basketball: Alan Leforce; Phone: 843-349-2931; E-mail: mkost@ coastal.edu.

Cheerleading: Gina Simeone; Phone: 843-349-2820; E-mail: ginasimeone14@yahoo.com.
Cross Country: Alan Connie; Phone: 843-349-2904; E-mail: aconnie@ coastal.edu.
Golf: Brian Ashley; Phone: 843-349-2850; E-mail: bashley@coastal.edu.
Soccer: Karrie Miller; Phone: 843-349-2859; E-mail: kmiller@coastal. edu.
Softball: Jess Dannelly; Phone: 843-349-2827; E-mail: jess@coastal.edu.
Tennis: Jody Davis; Phone: 843-349-2832; E-mail: jody@coastal.edu.
Track and Field: Alan Connie; Phone: 843-349-2904; E-mail: aconnie@ coastal.edu.
Volleyball: Kristen Bauer; Phone: 843-349-2814; E-mail: kbauer@ coastal.edu.

COE COLLEGE
Cedar Rapids, Iowa
Kohawks ◆ NCAA III ◆ Iowa Athletic Conference ◆ http://www.coe.edu/

Independent religious comprehensive, founded 1851, affiliated with Presbyterian Church
Coed, 1,290 undergraduate students, 91% full-time, 56% women, 44% men
Urban 53-acre campus
Moderately difficult entrance level, 60% of applicants were admitted

Freshmen *Admission:* 1,336 applied, 943 were accepted, 322 enrolled. *Test scores:* SAT verbal scores over 500: 81%; SAT math scores over 500: 78%; SAT verbal scores over 600: 42%; SAT math scores over 600: 42%; SAT verbal scores over 700: 3%; SAT math scores over 700: 9%.
Tuition and fees (2003–04): $21,605 (full-time). *Room and board:* $5780 (room only: $2720).
Financial Aid (All incoming freshmen): *Average need-based gift aid:* $14,651. *Average non-need based aid:* $9396. *Average aid to full-time undergraduates:* $19,879.
Athletic Department: *Director of Athletics:* John Chandler; Phone: 319-399-8622; Fax: 319-399-8721; E-mail: jchandle@coe.edu. *Sports Information Director:* Bryan Boettcher; Phone: 319-399-8570; E-mail: sid@coe.edu.

MEN'S COACHES
Baseball: Steve Cook; Phone: 319-399-8849; E-mail: scook@coe.edu.
Basketball: Brent Brase; Phone: 319-399-8625; E-mail: bbrase@coe.edu.
Cross Country: Elaine Rydze; Phone: 319-399-8620; E-mail: erydze@coe. edu.
Diving: Bobby Kelly; Phone: 319-399-8659; E-mail: rkelley@coe.edu.
Football: Erik Raeburn; Phone: 319-399-8567; E-mail: eraeburn@coe. edu.
Golf: Bill Fletcher; Phone: 319-399-8599; E-mail: o-athletics@coe.edu.
Soccer: Brad Stiles; Phone: 319-399-8852; E-mail: coachstiles@webtv. net.
Swimming: Bobby Kelly; Phone: 319-399-8659; E-mail: rkelley@coe. edu.
Tennis: Eric Rodgers; Phone: 319-399-8799; E-mail: erodgers@coe.edu.
Track and Field: Paul Wagner; Phone: 319-399-8550; E-mail: pwagner@ coe.edu.
Wrestling: John Oostendrop; Phone: 319-399-8234; E-mail: joostend@ coe.edu.

WOMEN'S COACHES
Basketball: Melissa Bruner; Phone: 319-399-8808; E-mail: mbruner@ coe.edu.
Cross Country: Elaine Rydze; Phone: 319-399-8620; E-mail: erydze@coe. edu.
Diving: Bobby Kelly; Phone: 319-399-8659; E-mail: rkelley@coe.edu.
Golf: Mary Meisterling; Phone: 319-399-8599; E-mail: mmeiste102@ aol.com.
Soccer: Mickey Wu; Phone: 319-399-8727; E-mail: mwu@coe.edu.
Softball: Bob Timmons; Phone: 319-399-8859; E-mail: btimmons@coe. edu.
Swimming: Bobby Kelly; Phone: 319-399-8659; E-mail: rkelley@coe. edu.
Tennis: Eric Rodgers; Phone: 319-399-8799; E-mail: erodgers@coe.edu.
Track and Field: Paul Wagner; Phone: 319-399-8550; E-mail: pwagner@ coe.edu.
Volleyball: Heather Nail; Phone: 319-399-8233; E-mail: hnail@coe.edu.

COKER COLLEGE
Hartsville, South Carolina

Cobras ◆ NCAA II ◆ Carolinas-Virginia Athletics Conference ◆ http://www.coker.edu/

Independent 4-year, founded 1908
Coed, 482 undergraduate students, 98% full-time, 58% women, 42% men
Small-town 30-acre campus with easy access to Charlotte
Moderately difficult entrance level, 93% of applicants were admitted

Freshmen *Admission:* 654 applied, 619 were accepted, 148 enrolled. *Test scores:* SAT verbal scores over 500: 48%; SAT math scores over 500: 52%; SAT verbal scores over 600: 11%; SAT math scores over 600: 11%; SAT math scores over 700: 1%.
Tuition and fees (2003–04): $16,165 (full-time). *Room and board:* $5326 (room only: $2846).
Financial Aid (All incoming freshmen): *Average need-based gift aid:* $4975. *Average non-need based aid:* $5583. *Average aid to full-time undergraduates:* $16,979.
Athletic Department: *Director of Athletics:* Tim Griggs♂; Phone: 843-383-8071; Fax: 843-383-8167; E-mail: tgriggs@coker.edu. *Sports Information Director:* Paul Lyon; Phone: 843-383-8068; E-mail: plyon@coker.edu.

MEN'S COACHES
Baseball: Dave Schmotzer; Phone: 843-383-8105.
Basketball: Dan Schmotzer; Phone: 843-383-8072.
Cross Country: Ley Fletcher; Phone: 843-383-8190; E-mail: lfletcher@pascal.coker.edu.
Golf: John Handrigan; Phone: 843-383-8393; E-mail: jhandrigan@coker.edu.
Soccer: Chris Ayer; Phone: 843-383-8168; E-mail: cayer@coker.edu.
Tennis: John Blackburn; Phone: 843-383-8076; E-mail: jblackburn@coker.edu.

WOMEN'S COACHES
Basketball: Katie Pate; Phone: 843-383-8075; E-mail: kpate@pascal.coker.edu.
Cross Country: Ley Fletcher; Phone: 843-383-8190; E-mail: lfletcher@pascal.coker.edu.
Soccer: Chris Ayer; Phone: 843-383-8168; E-mail: cayer@coker.edu.
Softball: Dave Hanna; Phone: 843-383-8164.
Tennis: John Blackburn; Phone: 843-383-8076; E-mail: jblackburn@coker.edu.
Volleyball: Cindy Robarge; Phone: 843-383-8070; E-mail: crobarge@pascal.coker.edu.

COLBY COLLEGE
Waterville, Maine

White Mules ◆ NCAA III ◆ New England Small College Conference ◆ http://www.colby.edu/

Independent 4-year, founded 1813
Coed, 1,768 undergraduate students, 100% full-time, 54% women, 46% men
Small-town 714-acre campus
Most difficult entrance level, 3% of applicants were admitted

Freshmen *Admission:* 4,126 applied, 1,388 were accepted, 474 enrolled. *Test scores:* SAT verbal scores over 500: 98%; SAT math scores over 500: 99%; SAT verbal scores over 600: 88%; SAT math scores over 600: 89%; SAT verbal scores over 700: 34%; SAT math scores over 700: 37%.
Tuition and fees (2004–05): Comprehensive fee (includes tuition, fees, and room and board): $37,570.
Financial Aid (All incoming freshmen): *Average need-based gift aid:* $25,937. *Average aid to full-time undergraduates:* $25,468.
Athletic Department: *Director of Athletics:* Marcella Zalot; Phone: 207-872-3467; Fax: 207-872-3420; E-mail: mkzalot@colby.edu. *Sports Information Director:* William Sodoma; Phone: 207-872-3769; E-mail: wcsodoma@colby.edu.

MEN'S COACHES
Baseball: Tom Dexter; Phone: 207-872-3369; E-mail: tadexter@colby.edu.

Basketball: Richard Whitmore; Phone: 207-872-3367; E-mail: rlwhitmo@colby.edu.
Cross Country: Todd Coffin; Phone: 207-872-3373; E-mail: tcoffin@colby.edu.
Diving: Tom Burton; Phone: 207-872-3370; E-mail: tkburton@colby.edu.
Football: Ed Mestieri; Phone: 207-872-3366; E-mail: ejmestie@colby.edu.
Golf: Jim Tortorella; Phone: 207-872-3368; E-mail: jtortor@colby.edu.
Ice Hockey: Jim Tortorella; Phone: 207-872-3368; E-mail: jtortor@colby.edu.
Lacrosse: Rob Quinn; Phone: 207-872-3092; E-mail: rpquinn@colby.edu.
Soccer: Mark Serjewian; Phone: 207-872-3106; E-mail: mrserdje@colby.edu.
Swimming: Tom Burton; Phone: 207-872-3370; E-mail: tkburton@colby.edu.
Tennis: Michael Morgan; Phone: 207-872-3550; E-mail: mmorgan@colby.edu.
Track and Field: Todd Coffin; Phone: 207-872-3373; E-mail: tcoffin@colby.edu.

WOMEN'S COACHES
Basketball: Tricia O'Brien; Phone: 207-872-3375; E-mail: pmobrien@colby.edu.
Cross Country: Debra Aitken; Phone: 207-872-3363; E-mail: daaitken@colby.edu.
Diving: Tom Burton; Phone: 207-872-3370; E-mail: tkburton@colby.edu.
Field Hockey: Heidi Godomsky; Phone: 207-872-3372; E-mail: hmgodoms@colby.edu.
Lacrosse: Heidi Godomsky; Phone: 207-872-3372; E-mail: hmgodoms@colby.edu.
Soccer: Jennifer Holsten; Phone: 207-872-3079; E-mail: jholsten@colby.edu.
Softball: Dick Bailey; Phone: 207-872-3767; E-mail: rwbailey@colby.edu.
Swimming: Tom Burton; Phone: 207-872-3370; E-mail: tkburton@colby.edu.
Tennis: Michael Morgan; Phone: 207-872-3550; E-mail: mmorgan@colby.edu.
Track and Field: Debra Aitken; Phone: 207-872-3363; E-mail: daaitken@colby.edu.
Volleyball: Candice Parent; Phone: 207-872-3545; E-mail: cbparent@colby.edu.

COLBY-SAWYER COLLEGE
New London, New Hampshire

Chargers ◆ NCAA III ◆ Commonwealth Coast Conference ◆ http://www.colby-sawyer.edu/

Independent 4-year, founded 1837
Coed, 986 undergraduate students, 97% full-time, 65% women, 35% men
Small-town 200-acre campus
Moderately difficult entrance level, 73% of applicants were admitted

Freshmen *Admission:* 1,434 applied, 1,178 were accepted, 305 enrolled. *Test scores:* SAT verbal scores over 500: 59%; SAT math scores over 500: 46%; SAT verbal scores over 600: 12%; SAT math scores over 600: 10%; SAT verbal scores over 700: 1%; SAT math scores over 700: %.
Tuition and fees (2004–05): $23,310 (full-time). *Room and board:* $8950 (room only: $4980).
Financial Aid (All incoming freshmen): *Average need-based gift aid:* $11,235. *Average non-need based aid:* $3826. *Average aid to full-time undergraduates:* $13,813.
Athletic Department: *Director of Athletics:* Debi Field McGrath; Phone: 603-526-3609; Fax: 603-526-3435; E-mail: dmcgrath@colby-sawyer.edu. *Sports Information Director:* Adam Kamras; Phone: 603-526-3783; E-mail: akamras@colby-sawyer.edu.

MEN'S COACHES
Baseball: Jim Broughton; Phone: 603-526-3607; E-mail: jbroughton@colby-sawyer.edu.
Basketball: Bill Foti; Phone: 603-526-3613; E-mail: wfoti@colby-sawyer.edu.

Cheerleading: Phone: 603-526-3775.
Diving: Ron Keenhold; Phone: 603-526-3436.
Soccer: Peter Steese; Phone: 603-526-3611; E-mail: psteese@colby-sawyer.edu.
Swimming: Rick Goerlitz; Phone: 603-526-3436; E-mail: rgoerlitz@colby-sawyer.edu.
Tennis: Rick Ellis; Phone: 603-526-3708; E-mail: rellis@colby-sawyer.edu.
Track and Field: Peter Steese; Phone: 603-526-3611; E-mail: psteese@colby-sawyer.edu.

WOMEN'S COACHES
Basketball: George Martin; Phone: 603-526-3604; E-mail: gmartin@colby-sawyer.edu.
Cheerleading: Phone: 603-526-3775.
Diving: Ron Keenhold; Phone: 603-526-3436.
Lacrosse: Paul Stinson; Phone: 603-526-3605; E-mail: pstinson@colby-sawyer.edu.
Soccer: Paul Stinson; Phone: 603-526-3605; E-mail: pstinson@colby-sawyer.edu.
Swimming: Rick Goerlitz; Phone: 603-526-3436; E-mail: rgoerlitz@colby-sawyer.edu.
Tennis: Phone: 603-526-3606.
Track and Field: Peter Steese; Phone: 603-526-3611; E-mail: psteese@colby-sawyer.edu.
Volleyball: Chad Braegelmann; Phone: 603-526-3894; E-mail: cbraegelmann@colby-sawyer.edu.

COLGATE UNIVERSITY
Hamilton, New York

Red Raiders ◆ NCAA I ◆ Eastern College Athletic Conference; Patriot League Conference
◆ http://www.colgate.edu/

Independent comprehensive, founded 1819
Coed, 2,796 undergraduate students, 99% full-time, 50% women, 50% men
Rural 515-acre campus
Very difficult entrance level, 31% of applicants were admitted

Freshmen *Admission:* 6,789 applied, 2,126 were accepted, 725 enrolled. *Test scores:* SAT verbal scores over 500: 98%; SAT math scores over 500: 99%; SAT verbal scores over 600: 82%; SAT math scores over 600: 90%; SAT verbal scores over 700: 33%; SAT math scores over 700: 40%.
Tuition and fees (2003–04): $29,940 (full-time). *Room and board:* $7155 (room only: $3455).
Financial Aid (All incoming freshmen): *Average need-based gift aid:* $23,783. *Average aid to full-time undergraduates:* $26,802.
Athletic Department: *Director of Athletics:* Don Vaughan; Phone: 315-228-7611; Fax: 315-228-7008; E-mail: dvaughan@mail.colgate.edu.
Sports Information Director: Bob Cornell; Phone: 315-228-7616; E-mail: rcornell@mail.colgate.edu.

MEN'S COACHES
Basketball: Emmett Davis; Phone: 315-228-7571; E-mail: epdavis@mail.colgate.edu.
Cheerleading: Jill Strand; Phone: 315-228-7928; E-mail: jstrand@mail.colgate.edu.
Cross Country: Arthur McKinnon; Phone: 315-228-7585; E-mail: amckinnon@mail.colgate.edu.
Diving: Matt Leone; Phone: 315-228-7604; E-mail: mleone@mail.colgate.edu.
Football: Dick Biddie; Phone: 315-228-7603; E-mail: rbiddle@mail.colgate.edu.
Golf: Braden Houston; Phone: 315-228-7060; E-mail: bhouston@mail.colgate.edu.
Ice Hockey: Stan Moore; Phone: 315-228-7572; E-mail: sbmoore@mail.colgate.edu.
Lacrosse: Jim Nagle; Phone: 315-228-7716; E-mail: jnagle@mail.colgate.edu.
Soccer: Mike Doherty; Phone: 315-228-7574; E-mail: mdoherty@mail.colgate.edu.
Swimming: Steve Jungbluth; Phone: 315-228-7614; E-mail: sjungbluth@mail.colgate.edu.
Tennis: Edward Wheeler; Phone: 315-228-7584; E-mail: ewheeler@mail.colgate.edu.

Track and Field: Arthur McKinnon; Phone: 315-228-7585; E-mail: amckinnon@mail.colgate.edu.
WOMEN'S COACHES
Basketball: Beth Combs; Phone: 315-228-7129; E-mail: espycher@mail.colgate.edu.
Cheerleading: Jill Strand; Phone: 315-228-7928; E-mail: jstrand@mail.colgate.edu.
Cross Country: Laura Crain; Phone: 315-228-7866; E-mail: lnardelli@mail.colgate.edu.
Diving: Matt Leone; Phone: 315-228-7604; E-mail: mleone@mail.colgate.edu.
Field Hockey: Cathy Foto; Phone: 315-228-7582; E-mail: cfoto@mail.colgate.edu.
Lacrosse: Katrina Silva; Phone: 315-228-7065; E-mail: ksilva@mail.colgate.edu.
Soccer: Kathy Brawn; Phone: 315-228-7762; E-mail: kbrawn@mail.colgate.edu.
Softball: Vickie Sax; Phone: 315-228-7118; E-mail: vsax@mail.colgate.edu.
Swimming: Steve Jungbluth; Phone: 315-228-7614; E-mail: sjungbluth@mail.colgate.edu.
Tennis: Edward Wheeler; Phone: 315-228-7584; E-mail: ewheeler@mail.colgate.edu.
Track and Field: Laura Crain; Phone: 315-228-7866; E-mail: lnardelli@mail.colgate.edu.
Volleyball: Jenna Panatier; Phone: 315-228-7969; E-mail: jpanatier@mail.colgate.edu.

COLLEGE MISERICORDIA
Dallas, Pennsylvania

Cougars ◆ NCAA III ◆ Pennsylvania Athletic Conference
◆ http://www.misericordia.edu/

Independent Roman Catholic comprehensive, founded 1924
Coed, 2,360 undergraduate students, 59% full-time, 78% women, 22% men
Small-town 100-acre campus
Moderately difficult entrance level, 75% of applicants were admitted

Freshmen *Admission:* 1,037 applied, 799 were accepted, 329 enrolled. *Test scores:* SAT verbal scores over 500: 57%; SAT math scores over 500: 59%; SAT verbal scores over 600: 12%; SAT math scores over 600: 12%; SAT verbal scores over 700: 1%; SAT math scores over 700: 1%.
Tuition and fees (2003–04): $17,970 (full-time). *Room and board:* $7500 (room only: $4300).
Financial Aid (All incoming freshmen): *Average need-based gift aid:* $9782. *Average non-need based aid:* $5883. *Average aid to full-time undergraduates:* $13,898.
Athletic Department: *Director of Athletics:* Michael Mould; Phone: 570-674-6294; Fax: 570-675-2441; E-mail: mmould@misericordia.edu.
Sports Information Director: Scott Crispell; Phone: 570-674-6398; E-mail: scrispel@misericordia.edu.

MEN'S COACHES
Baseball: Chuck Edkins; Phone: 570-674-6397; E-mail: cedkins@misericordia.edu.
Basketball: Dave Martin; Phone: 570-674-6317; E-mail: dmartin@misericordia.edu.
Cheerleading: Tara Coletti; Phone: 570-674-6294; E-mail: coachcoletti@netscape.net.
Cross Country: Frank Kinkead; Phone: 570-674-3365; E-mail: fkinkead@misericordia.edu.
Golf: Arnie Garinger; Phone: 570-674-6294; E-mail: frismond@misericordia.edu.
Lacrosse: Jim Ricardo; Phone: 570-674-3366; E-mail: jricardo@misericordia.edu.
Soccer: Chuck Edkins; Phone: 570-674-6397; E-mail: cedkins@misericordia.edu.
Swimming: Nancy Edkins; Phone: 570-674-6446; E-mail: nedkins@misericordia.edu.
Track and Field: Frank Kinkead; Phone: 570-674-3365; E-mail: fkinkead@misericordia.edu.
WOMEN'S COACHES
Basketball: Christine Lardon; Phone: 570-674-6447; E-mail: clardon@misericordia.edu.

College Misericordia (continued)

Cheerleading: Tara Coletti; Phone: 570-674-6294; E-mail: coachcoletti@netscape.net.
Cross Country: Frank Kinkead; Phone: 570-674-3365; E-mail: fkinkead@misericordia.edu.
Field Hockey: Robyn Fedor; Phone: 570-674-6491; E-mail: rfedor@misericordia.edu.
Lacrosse: Robyn Fedor; Phone: 570-674-6491; E-mail: rfedor@misericordia.edu.
Soccer: Mark Stauffer; Phone: 570-674-6492; E-mail: mstauffe@misericordia.edu.
Softball: Charlotte Slocum; Phone: 570-674-6276; E-mail: cslocum@misericordia.edu.
Swimming: Nancy Edkins; Phone: 570-674-6446; E-mail: nedkins@misericordia.edu.
Tennis: Phone: 570-674-6294.
Track and Field: Frank Kinkead; Phone: 570-674-3365; E-mail: fkinkead@misericordia.edu.
Volleyball: Phone: 570-674-6294.

COLLEGE OF CHARLESTON
Charleston, South Carolina

Cougars ◆ NCAA I ◆ Southern Conference; Southern Intercollegiate Athletic Conference ◆ http://www.cofc.edu/

State-supported comprehensive, founded 1770
Coed, 9,824 undergraduate students, 91% full-time, 63% women, 37% men
Urban 52-acre campus
Moderately difficult entrance level, 59% of applicants were admitted

Freshmen *Admission:* 7,606 applied, 4,560 were accepted, 1,874 enrolled. *Test scores:* SAT verbal scores over 500: 97%; SAT math scores over 500: 98%; SAT verbal scores over 600: 55%; SAT math scores over 600: 54%; SAT verbal scores over 700: 8%; SAT math scores over 700: 6%.
Tuition and fees (2003–04): $5770 (resident), $13,032 (nonresident). *Room and board:* $6117 (room only: $4057).
Financial Aid (All incoming freshmen): *Average need-based gift aid:* $3132. *Average non-need based aid:* $9748. *Average aid to full-time undergraduates:* $8261.
Athletic Department: *Director of Athletics:* Jerry Baker; Phone: 843-953-8251; Fax: 843-953-8296; E-mail: bakerj@cofc.edu. *Sports Information Director:* Tony Ciuffo; Phone: 843-953-6720; E-mail: ciuffo@cofc.edu.
MEN'S COACHES
Baseball: John Pawlowski; Phone: 843-953-5916; E-mail: pawlowskij@cofc.edu.
Basketball: Tom Herrion; Phone: 843-953-5556; E-mail: herriont@cofc.edu.
Cheerleading: Charlie Thiel; Phone: 843-953-5556.
Cross Country: Amy Schuckert; Phone: 843-953-5556; E-mail: schuckerta@cofc.edu.
Diving: Mike Diamond; Phone: 843-953-5960.
Golf: Mark Steelman; Phone: 843-953-6578; E-mail: steelmanm@cofc.edu.
Soccer: Ralph Lundy; Phone: 843-953-8253; E-mail: lundyr@cofc.edu.
Swimming: Bruce Zimmerman; Phone: 843-953-5960; E-mail: zimmermanb@cofc.edu.
Tennis: Phil Whitesell; Phone: 843-953-5466; E-mail: whitesellp@cofc.edu.
WOMEN'S COACHES
Basketball: Nancy Wilson; Phone: 843-953-6536; E-mail: wilsonn@cofc.edu.
Cheerleading: Charlie Thiel; Phone: 843-953-5556.
Cross Country: Amy Schuckert; Phone: 843-953-5556; E-mail: schuckerta@cofc.edu.
Diving: Mike Diamond; Phone: 843-953-5960.
Golf: Jamie Futrell; Phone: 843-953-5642; E-mail: futrellj@cofc.edu.
Soccer: Kevin Dempsey; Phone: 843-953-5583; E-mail: dempseyk@cofc.edu.
Softball: Chandelle Schulte; Phone: 843-953-6316; E-mail: schultec@cofc.edu.

Swimming: Bruce Zimmerman; Phone: 843-953-5960; E-mail: zimmermanb@cofc.edu.
Tennis: Angelo Anastopoulo; Phone: 843-953-5466; E-mail: anastopa@cofc.edu.
Track and Field: Amy Schuckert; Phone: 843-953-5556; E-mail: schuckerta@cofc.edu.
Volleyball: Sherry Dunbar; Phone: 843-953-8246; E-mail: dunbars@cofc.edu.

COLLEGE OF MOUNT ST. JOSEPH
Cincinnati, Ohio

Lions ◆ NCAA III ◆ Heartland Collegiate Conference ◆ http://www.msj.edu/

Independent Roman Catholic comprehensive, founded 1920
Coed, 1,876 undergraduate students, 68% full-time, 69% women, 31% men
Suburban 88-acre campus
Moderately difficult entrance level, 76% of applicants were admitted

Freshmen *Admission:* 863 applied, 655 were accepted, 309 enrolled. *Test scores:* SAT verbal scores over 500: 52%; SAT math scores over 500: 56%; SAT verbal scores over 600: 13%; SAT math scores over 600: 14%; SAT verbal scores over 700: 1%; SAT math scores over 700: 2%.
Tuition and fees (2004–05): $18,440 (full-time). *Room and board:* $5845 (room only: $2875).
Financial Aid (All incoming freshmen): *Average need-based gift aid:* $8000. *Average non-need based aid:* $3800. *Average aid to full-time undergraduates:* $13,000.
Athletic Department: *Director of Athletics:* Steve Radcliffe; Phone: 513-244-4381; Fax: 513-244-4928; E-mail: steve_radcliffe@mail.msj.edu. *Sports Information Director:* Dane Neumeister; Phone: 513-244-4927.
MEN'S COACHES
Baseball: Chuck Murray; Phone: 513-244-4402.
Basketball: Larry Cox; Phone: 513-244-4929; E-mail: larry_cox@mail.msj.edu.
Cheerleading: Lindsay Simpson; Phone: 513-244-4311.
Cross Country: Bryan Hagopian; Phone: 513-244-4842.
Football: Rod Huber; Phone: 513-244-4896.
Golf: Rick Stalder; Phone: 513-244-4842.
Tennis: Mark Resler; Phone: 513-244-3276.
Track and Field: Bryan Hagopian; Phone: 513-244-4842.
Wrestling: Tom Wynn; Phone: 513-244-4474.
WOMEN'S COACHES
Basketball: Melissia Patterson; Phone: 513-244-4590; E-mail: melissia_patterson@mail.msj.edu.
Cheerleading: Lindsay Simpson; Phone: 513-244-4311.
Cross Country: Bryan Hagopian; Phone: 513-244-4842.
Golf: Phone: 513-244-4842.
Soccer: Sam Pogoni; Phone: 513-244-4842.
Softball: Beth Goderwis; Phone: 513-244-4853.
Tennis: Linda Lupp; Phone: 513-244-3276.
Track and Field: Bryan Hagopian; Phone: 513-244-4842.
Volleyball: Michele Benoit; Phone: 513-244-4316; E-mail: michele_benoit@mail.msj.edu.

COLLEGE OF MOUNT SAINT VINCENT
Riverdale, New York

Dolphins ◆ NCAA III ◆ Skyline Conference ◆ http://www.mountsaintvincent.edu/

Independent comprehensive, founded 1911
Coed, 1,281 undergraduate students, 87% full-time, 79% women, 21% men
Suburban 70-acre campus with easy access to New York City
Moderately difficult entrance level, 8% of applicants were admitted

Freshmen *Admission:* 1,609 applied, 1,202 were accepted, 336 enrolled. *Test scores:* SAT verbal scores over 500: 44%; SAT math scores over

500: 40%; SAT verbal scores over 600: 10%; SAT math scores over 600: 5%; SAT verbal scores over 700: 1%.
Tuition and fees (2003–04): $19,050 (full-time). *Room and board:* $7800.
Financial Aid (All incoming freshmen): *Average aid to full-time undergraduates:* $16,000.
Athletic Department: *Director of Athletics:* Chuck Mancuso; Phone: 718-405-3410; Fax: 718-405-3765. *Sports Information Director:* Joseph DeBenedictis; Phone: 718-405-3410.

MEN'S COACHES

Basketball: Dave Genovese; Phone: 718-405-3410.
Cross Country: Tina Fahan; Phone: 718-405-3410; E-mail: tfahan@cmsv.edu.
Lacrosse: Pat Yannarelli; Phone: 718-405-3410.
Soccer: Steve Iallonardo; Phone: 718-405-3410.
Tennis: John Rabsatt; Phone: 718-405-3410.
Volleyball: Patrick Dietz; Phone: 718-405-3410.

WOMEN'S COACHES

Basketball: Andrew Francis; Phone: 718-405-3410.
Cross Country: Tina Fahan; Phone: 718-405-3410; E-mail: tfahan@cmsv.edu.
Lacrosse: Michael Spinner; Phone: 718-405-3410.
Soccer: Cathy Ingram; Phone: 718-405-3410.
Softball: Mary Marra; Phone: 718-405-3410.
Swimming: Phone: 718-405-3410.
Tennis: Sam Manardi; Phone: 718-405-3410.
Track and Field: Lonnie Evans; Phone: 718-405-3410.
Volleyball: Francisco Martinez; Phone: 718-405-3410.

THE COLLEGE OF NEW JERSEY
Ewing, New Jersey

Lions ◆ NCAA III ◆ New Jersey Athletic Conference ◆ http://www.tcnj.edu/

State-supported comprehensive, founded 1855
Coed, 5,938 undergraduate students, 95% full-time, 60% women, 40% men
Suburban 255-acre campus with easy access to Philadelphia
Very difficult entrance level, 49% of applicants were admitted

Freshmen *Admission:* 6,373 applied, 3,070 were accepted, 1,178 enrolled. *Test scores:* SAT verbal scores over 500: 92%; SAT math scores over 500: 96%; SAT verbal scores over 600: 67%; SAT math scores over 600: 78%; SAT verbal scores over 700: 16%; SAT math scores over 700: 25%.
Tuition and fees (2003–04): $8206 (resident), $12,781 (nonresident). *Room and board:* $7744 (room only: $5565).
Financial Aid (All incoming freshmen): *Average need-based gift aid:* $6668. *Average non-need based aid:* $4951. *Average aid to full-time undergraduates:* $8241.
Athletic Department: *Director of Athletics:* Kevin McHugh; Phone: 609-771-2231; Fax: 609-637-5133; E-mail: mchughk@tcnj.edu. *Sports Information Director:* Ann King; Phone: 609-771-2517; E-mail: aking@tcnj.edu.

MEN'S COACHES

Baseball: Rick Dell; Phone: 609-771-2374; E-mail: rdell@tcnj.edu.
Basketball: John Castaldo; Phone: 609-771-2446; E-mail: castaldo@tcnj.edu.
Cross Country: Steve Dolan; Phone: 609-771-2975; E-mail: trackxc@tcnj.edu.
Diving: Brian Bishop; Phone: 609-771-3250; E-mail: bbishop@tcnj.edu.
Football: Eric Hamilton; Phone: 609-771-2340; E-mail: hamilton@tcnj.edu.
Golf: Charlie Gallagher; Phone: 609-771-2951; E-mail: gallaghe@tcnj.edu.
Soccer: George Nazario; Phone: 609-771-2444; E-mail: nazariog@tcnj.edu.
Swimming: Brian Bishop; Phone: 609-771-3250; E-mail: bbishop@tcnj.edu.
Tennis: Scott Dicheck; Phone: 609-771-3021; E-mail: dicheck@tcnj.edu.
Track and Field: Steve Dolan; Phone: 609-771-2975; E-mail: trackxc@tcnj.edu.
Wrestling: David Icenhower; Phone: 609-771-2227; E-mail: icenhowe@tcnj.edu.

WOMEN'S COACHES

Basketball: Dawn Henderson; Phone: 609-771-3030; E-mail: dhenders@tcnj.edu.

Cross Country: Steve Dolan; Phone: 609-771-2975; E-mail: trackxc@tcnj.edu.
Field Hockey: Sharon Pfluger; Phone: 609-771-2243; E-mail: spfluger@tcnj.edu.
Lacrosse: Sharon Pfluger; Phone: 609-771-2243; E-mail: spfluger@tcnj.edu.
Soccer: Joe Russo; Phone: 609-771-3155; E-mail: jrusso@tcnj.edu.
Softball: Sally Miller; Phone: 609-771-2365; E-mail: millers@tcnj.edu.
Swimming: Jennifer Harnett; Phone: 609-771-2383; E-mail: harnett@tcnj.edu.
Tennis: Scott Dicheck; Phone: 609-771-3021; E-mail: dicheck@tcnj.edu.
Track and Field: Steve Dolan; Phone: 609-771-2975; E-mail: trackxc@tcnj.edu.

THE COLLEGE OF NEW ROCHELLE
New Rochelle, New York

Blue Angels ◆ NCAA III ◆ New York Women's Athletic Conference ◆ http://cnr.edu/

Independent comprehensive, founded 1904
Coed, primarily women, 967 undergraduate students, 64% full-time, 94% women, 6% men
Suburban 20-acre campus with easy access to New York City
Moderately difficult entrance level, 6% of applicants were admitted

Freshmen *Admission:* 1,210 applied, 619 were accepted, 117 enrolled. *Test scores:* SAT verbal scores over 500: 47%; SAT math scores over 500: 33%; SAT verbal scores over 600: 12%; SAT math scores over 600: 8%; SAT verbal scores over 700: 2%.
Tuition and fees (2004–05): $19,350 (full-time). *Room and board:* $7400.
Financial Aid (All incoming freshmen): *Average need-based gift aid:* $9051. *Average non-need based aid:* $8475. *Average aid to full-time undergraduates:* $15,741.
Athletic Department: *Director of Athletics:* Harold Crocker; Phone: 914-654-5315; Fax: 914-654-5828; E-mail: hcrocker@cnr.edu. *Sports Information Director:* Harold Crocker; Phone: 914-654-5315; E-mail: hcrocker@cnr.edu.

WOMEN'S COACHES

Basketball: Kathryn Murray; Phone: 914-654-5315.
Cross Country: Jill Vollweiler; Phone: 914-654-5315.
Softball: Bob D'Avanzo; Phone: 914-654-5315.
Swimming: Tony Salvarrey; Phone: 914-654-5315; E-mail: tsalvarrey@cnr.edu.
Tennis: Rick Tovar; Phone: 914-654-5315.
Volleyball: Susan Kimmel; Phone: 914-654-5315; E-mail: skimmel@cnr.edu.

COLLEGE OF NOTRE DAME OF MARYLAND
Baltimore, Maryland

Gators ◆ NCAA III ◆ Atlantic Women's Colleges Conference ◆ http://www.ndm.edu/

Independent Roman Catholic comprehensive, founded 1873
Women only, 1,582 undergraduate students, 39% full-time, 94% women, 6% men
Suburban 58-acre campus
Moderately difficult entrance level, 73% of applicants were admitted

Freshmen *Admission:* 397 applied, 288 were accepted, 170 enrolled. *Test scores:* SAT verbal scores over 500: 58%; SAT math scores over 500: 54%; SAT verbal scores over 600: 18%; SAT math scores over 600: 15%; SAT verbal scores over 700: 4%; SAT math scores over 700: 1%.
Tuition and fees (2004–05): $20,300 (full-time). *Room and board:* $7800.
Financial Aid (All incoming freshmen): *Average need-based gift aid:* $15,600. *Average non-need based aid:* $9202. *Average aid to full-time undergraduates:* $20,796.
Athletic Department: *Director of Athletics:* Scot Reisinger; Phone: 410-532-3588; Fax: 410-532-5796; E-mail: sreisinger@ndm.edu. *Sports Information Director:* Ryan Eigenbrode; Phone: 410-532-5378; E-mail: reigenbrode@ndm.edu.

College of Notre Dame of Maryland *(continued)*
WOMEN'S COACHES
Basketball: Scot Reisinger; Phone: 410-532-3588; E-mail: sreisinger@ndm.edu.
Field Hockey: Ashley Hohnstine; Phone: 410-532-3589; E-mail: ahohnstine@ndm.edu.
Lacrosse: Melissa Falen; Phone: 410-532-3585; E-mail: mfalen@ndm.edu.
Soccer: Jay Golomb; Phone: 410-532-5388; E-mail: jkgsoccer@comcast.net.
Swimming: Curt Jordan; Phone: 410-532-3588; E-mail: curt.jordan@carefirst.com.
Tennis: Cathy Fisher; Phone: 410-532-3588; E-mail: cfisher@ndm.edu.
Volleyball: Don Metil; Phone: 410-532-3588; E-mail: dmetil@ndm.edu.

COLLEGE OF SAINT BENEDICT
Saint Joseph, Minnesota

Blazers ◆ NCAA III ◆ Minnesota Intercollegiate Athletic Conference ◆ http://www.csbsju.edu/

Independent Roman Catholic 4-year, founded 1887
Coed, primarily women, 2,054 undergraduate students, 97% full-time, 100% women, 100% men
Small-town 315-acre campus with easy access to Minneapolis–St. Paul
Moderately difficult entrance level, 90% of applicants were admitted

Freshmen *Admission:* 1,174 applied, 1,057 were accepted, 502 enrolled. *Test scores:* SAT verbal scores over 500: 78%; SAT math scores over 500: 80%; SAT verbal scores over 600: 39%; SAT math scores over 600: 40%; SAT verbal scores over 700: 8%; SAT math scores over 700: 6%.
Tuition and fees (2003–04): $20,685 (full-time). *Room and board:* $5987 (room only: $3169).
Financial Aid (All incoming freshmen): *Average need-based gift aid:* $12,163. *Average non-need based aid:* $5518. *Average aid to full-time undergraduates:* $17,823.
Athletic Department: *Director of Athletics:* Carol Howe-Veenstra; Phone: 320-363-5201; Fax: 320-363-6098; E-mail: choweveenstr@csbsju.edu. *Sports Information Director:* Mike Durbin; Phone: 320-363-5073; E-mail: mdurbin@csbsju.edu.
WOMEN'S COACHES
Basketball: Mike Durbin; Phone: 320-363-5073; E-mail: mdurbin@csbsju.edu.
Cross Country: Robin Balder-Lanoue; Phone: 320-363-5514; E-mail: rbalderlano@csbsju.edu.
Diving: Bill Saxton; Phone: 320-363-3352; E-mail: wsaxton@csbsju.edu.
Golf: Theresa Solarz; Phone: 320-363-5301; E-mail: tsolarz@csbsju.edu.
Soccer: Kate Hand; Phone: 320-363-5873; E-mail: khand@csbsju.edu.
Softball: Denny Johnson; Phone: 320-363-5983; E-mail: djohnson@csbsju.edu.
Swimming: Bill Saxton; Phone: 320-363-3352; E-mail: wsaxton@csbsju.edu.
Tennis: Janna Lafountaine; Phone: 320-363-5567; E-mail: jlafountain@csbsju.edu.
Track and Field: Robin Balder-Lanoue; Phone: 320-363-5514; E-mail: rbalderlano@csbsju.edu.
Volleyball: Michele Swanson Blaeser; Phone: 320-363-5286; E-mail: mblaeser@csbsju.edu.

COLLEGE OF ST. CATHERINE
St. Paul, Minnesota

Wildcats ◆ NCAA III ◆ Minnesota Intercollegiate Athletic Conference ◆ http://www.stkate.edu/

Independent Roman Catholic comprehensive, founded 1905
Women only, 3,681 undergraduate students, 65% full-time, 97% women, 3% men
Urban 110-acre campus with easy access to Minneapolis
Moderately difficult entrance level, 7% of applicants were admitted

Freshmen *Admission:* 1,170 applied, 904 were accepted, 407 enrolled. *Test scores:* SAT verbal scores over 500: 87%; SAT math scores over

500: 75%; SAT verbal scores over 600: 59%; SAT math scores over 600: 47%; SAT verbal scores over 700: 9%; SAT math scores over 700: 22%.
Tuition and fees (2003–04): $19,770 (full-time). *Room and board:* $5460 (room only: $3060).
Financial Aid (All incoming freshmen): *Average need-based gift aid:* $7658. *Average non-need based aid:* $16,970. *Average aid to full-time undergraduates:* $19,926.
Athletic Department: *Director of Athletics:* Sheila Brown; Phone: 651-690-8771; Fax: 651-690-8790; E-mail: sfbrown@stkate.edu. *Sports Information Director:* Eric Stacey; Phone: 651-690-8778; E-mail: emstacey@stkate.edu.

WOMEN'S COACHES
Basketball: Tim Kjar; Phone: 651-690-8780; E-mail: tckjar@stkate.edu.
Cross Country: Jason Altman; Phone: 651-690-6994; E-mail: jraltman@stkate.edu.
Soccer: Jeremy Driver; Phone: 651-690-6984; E-mail: jbdriver@stkate.edu.
Softball: Madge Makowske; Phone: 651-690-8779; E-mail: mmakowske@stkate.edu.
Swimming: Nicole Roberts; Phone: 651-690-8774; E-mail: nmroberts@stkate.edu.
Tennis: Eric Stacey; Phone: 651-690-6992; E-mail: emstacey@stkate.edu.
Track and Field: Jason Altman; Phone: 651-690-6994; E-mail: jraltman@stkate.edu.
Volleyball: Nicole Hess; Phone: 651-690-6082; E-mail: nmhess@stkate.edu.

COLLEGE OF SAINT ELIZABETH
Morristown, New Jersey

Eagles ◆ NCAA III ◆ Independent ◆ http://www.cse.edu/

Independent Roman Catholic comprehensive, founded 1899
Women only, 1,276 undergraduate students, 56% full-time, 93% women, 7% men
Suburban 188-acre campus with easy access to New York City
Moderately difficult entrance level, 81% of applicants were admitted

Freshmen *Admission:* 456 applied, 369 were accepted, 151 enrolled. *Test scores:* SAT verbal scores over 500: 34%; SAT math scores over 500: 39%; SAT verbal scores over 600: 8%; SAT math scores over 600: 9%; SAT verbal scores over 700: 2%; SAT math scores over 700: 3%.
Tuition and fees (2003–04): $17,450 (full-time). *Room and board:* $8130.
Financial Aid (All incoming freshmen): *Average need-based gift aid:* $14,620. *Average non-need based aid:* $11,531. *Average aid to full-time undergraduates:* $16,732.
Athletic Department: *Director of Athletics:* Carol Kashow; Phone: 973-290-4207; Fax: 973-290-4217; E-mail: ckashow@cse.edu. *Sports Information Director:* Donna Lindemeyer; Phone: 973-290-4442; E-mail: dlindemeyer@cse.edu.

WOMEN'S COACHES
Basketball: Bill Errickson; Phone: 973-290-4207.
Soccer: Michael Kovacs; Phone: 973-290-4207.
Softball: Erin Layton; Phone: 973-290-4205.
Swimming: Jill Kopicki; Phone: 973-290-4207; E-mail: mmorlando@cse.edu.
Tennis: Janette Fassel; Phone: 973-290-4207.
Volleyball: John Ciaccio; Phone: 973-290-4205.

COLLEGE OF ST. JOSEPH
Rutland, Vermont

Fighting Saints ◆ NAIA ◆ Sunrise Conference ◆ http://www.csj.edu/

Independent Roman Catholic comprehensive, founded 1950
Coed, 309 undergraduate students, 68% full-time, 61% women, 39% men
Small-town 90-acre campus
Minimally difficult entrance level, 81% of applicants were admitted

Freshmen *Admission:* 141 applied, 114 were accepted, 39 enrolled. *Test scores:* SAT verbal scores over 500: 35%; SAT math scores over 500: 27%; SAT verbal scores over 600: 4%; SAT math scores over 600: 6%.
Tuition and fees (2003–04): $12,700 (full-time). *Room and board:* $6400 (room only: $3100).
Financial Aid (All incoming freshmen): *Average need-based gift aid:* $8089. *Average non-need based aid:* $4111. *Average aid to full-time undergraduates:* $11,461.
Athletic Department: *Director of Athletics:* Kevin Knauer; Phone: 802-773-5900; E-mail: kknauer@csj.edu.

MEN'S COACHES
Basketball: Jeff White; Phone: 802-773-5900; E-mail: jwhite@csj.edu.
Soccer: Ray Fish; Phone: 802-773-5900; E-mail: rfish@csj.edu.

WOMEN'S COACHES
Basketball: JoJo Valente; Phone: 802-773-5900; E-mail: jvalente@csj.edu.
Soccer: Kevin Knauer; Phone: 802-773-5900; E-mail: kknauer@csj.edu.
Softball: Kevin Knauer; Phone: 802-773-5900; E-mail: kknauer@csj.edu.

COLLEGE OF SAINT MARY
Omaha, Nebraska

Flames ◆ NAIA ◆ Midlands Collegiate Conference ◆ http://www.csm.edu/

Independent Roman Catholic 4-year, founded 1923
Women only, 915 undergraduate students, 66% full-time, 99% women, 1% men
Suburban 25-acre campus
Minimally difficult entrance level, 70% of applicants were admitted

Freshmen *Admission:* 218 applied, 153 were accepted, 78 enrolled.
Tuition and fees (2004–05): $16,877 (full-time). *Room and board:* $5700.
Financial Aid (All incoming freshmen): *Average need-based gift aid:* $9341. *Average non-need based aid:* $6862. *Average aid to full-time undergraduates:* $13,754.
Athletic Department: *Director of Athletics:* Leigh Officer; Phone: 402-399-2332; Fax: 402-399-2381; E-mail: officer@csm.edu. *Sports Information Director:* Lee O'Donnell; Phone: 402-399-2359; E-mail: lodonnell@csm.edu.

WOMEN'S COACHES
Basketball: Angie Kristensen; Phone: 402-399-6271; E-mail: akristensen@csm.edu.
Cross Country: Scott Stanley; Phone: 402-399-2358; E-mail: sstanley@csm.edu.
Golf: Pat O'Hara; Phone: 402-289-0900; E-mail: pohara@csm.edu.
Soccer: John Carlson; Phone: 402-399-2382; E-mail: jpcarlson@csm.edu.
Softball: Darren Petersen; Phone: 402-399-2352; E-mail: dpetersen@csm.edu.
Volleyball: Trish Siedlik; Phone: 402-399-2607; E-mail: tsiedlik@csm.edu.

THE COLLEGE OF SAINT ROSE
Albany, New York

Golden Knights ◆ NCAA II ◆ Northeast-10 Conference ◆ http://www.strose.edu/

Independent comprehensive, founded 1920
Coed, 2,898 undergraduate students, 88% full-time, 74% women, 26% men
Urban 28-acre campus
Moderately difficult entrance level, 70% of applicants were admitted

Freshmen *Admission:* 1,917 applied, 1,414 were accepted, 535 enrolled. *Test scores:* SAT verbal scores over 500: 64%; SAT math scores over 500: 36%; SAT verbal scores over 600: 16%; SAT math scores over 600: 3%; SAT verbal scores over 700: 1%.
Tuition and fees (2003–04): $15,638 (full-time). *Room and board:* $7226 (room only: $3374).
Financial Aid (All incoming freshmen): *Average need-based gift aid:* $3496. *Average non-need based aid:* $1875. *Average aid to full-time undergraduates:* $7565.
Athletic Department: *Director of Athletics:* Catherine Cummings Haker; Phone: 518-454-5282; Fax: 518-458-5457. *Sports Information Director:* David Alexander; Phone: 518-454-5282.

MEN'S COACHES
Baseball: Bob Bellizzi; Phone: 518-454-2041; E-mail: bellizzr@strose.edu.
Basketball: Brian Beaury; Phone: 518-458-5490.
Cross Country: Andrew Rickert; Phone: 518-454-2063.
Diving: Keith Murray; Phone: 518-458-5405.
Golf: Gerald Fitzgerald; Phone: 518-458-5405.
Soccer: Jeremy Bogan; Phone: 518-454-5150.
Swimming: Keith Murray; Phone: 518-458-5405.

WOMEN'S COACHES
Basketball: Karen Haag; Phone: 518-454-2064.
Cross Country: Andrew Rickert; Phone: 518-454-2063.
Diving: Keith Murray; Phone: 518-458-5405.
Soccer: Laurie Gutheil; Phone: 518-454-2042.
Softball: Phone: 518-458-2063.
Swimming: Keith Murray; Phone: 518-458-5405.
Volleyball: Brian Goodale; Phone: 518-454-2063.

THE COLLEGE OF ST. SCHOLASTICA
Duluth, Minnesota

Saints ◆ NCAA III ◆ Independent; Northern Collegiate Hockey Conference ◆ http://www.css.edu/

Independent religious comprehensive, founded 1912, affiliated with Roman Catholic Church
Coed, 2,308 undergraduate students, 89% full-time, 70% women, 30% men
Suburban 186-acre campus
Moderately difficult entrance level, 85% of applicants were admitted

Freshmen *Admission:* 1,206 applied, 1,062 were accepted, 437 enrolled. *Test scores:* SAT verbal scores over 500: 79%; SAT math scores over 500: 71%; SAT verbal scores over 600: 33%; SAT math scores over 600: 29%; SAT verbal scores over 700: 4%; SAT math scores over 700: 4%.
Tuition and fees (2003–04): $19,302 (full-time). *Room and board:* $5668 (room only: $3228).
Financial Aid (All incoming freshmen): *Average need-based gift aid:* $5060. *Average non-need based aid:* $7958. *Average aid to full-time undergraduates:* $16,351.
Athletic Department: *Director of Athletics:* Dana Moore; Phone: 218-723-6721; Fax: 218-723-5958; E-mail: dmoore@css.edu. *Sports Information Director:* Jen Walter; Phone: 218-723-6422; E-mail: jwalter@css.edu.

MEN'S COACHES
Baseball: John Baggs; Phone: 218-723-6298; E-mail: jbaggs@css.edu.
Basketball: David Stariger; Phone: 218-723-6609; E-mail: dstanige@css.edu.

The College of St. Scholastica *(continued)*

Cross Country: Steve Pfingsten; Phone: 218-723-6001; E-mail: spfingst@css.edu.
Ice Hockey: Cory Borys; Phone: 218-723-6610; E-mail: cborys@css.edu.
Soccer: Nic Bacigalupo; Phone: 218-723-6603; E-mail: nbacigal@css.edu.
Tennis: Wells Patten; Phone: 218-723-7050; E-mail: rpatten@css.edu.

WOMEN'S COACHES

Basketball: Stacy Deadrick; Phone: 218-723-6299; E-mail: sdeadric@css.edu.
Cross Country: Steve Pfingsten; Phone: 218-723-6001; E-mail: spfingst@css.edu.
Soccer: Dave Reyelts; Phone: 218-723-6603; E-mail: dreyelts@css.edu.
Softball: Jen Walter; Phone: 218-723-6422; E-mail: jwalter@css.edu.
Tennis: Wells Patten; Phone: 218-723-7050; E-mail: rpatten@css.edu.
Track and Field: Steve Pfingsten; Phone: 218-723-6001; E-mail: spfingst@css.edu.
Volleyball: Dana Moore; Phone: 218-723-6721; E-mail: dmoore@css.edu.

COLLEGE OF SANTA FE
Santa Fe, New Mexico

Knights ◆ NAIA ◆ Independent ◆ http://www.csf.edu/

Independent comprehensive, founded 1947
Coed, 1,389 undergraduate students, 49% full-time, 60% women, 40% men
Suburban 100-acre campus with easy access to Albuquerque
Moderately difficult entrance level, 79% of applicants were admitted

Freshmen *Admission:* 503 applied, 407 were accepted, 163 enrolled. *Test scores:* SAT verbal scores over 500: 83%; SAT math scores over 500: 66%; SAT verbal scores over 600: 45%; SAT math scores over 600: 17%; SAT verbal scores over 700: 10%; SAT math scores over 700: 3%.
Tuition and fees (2003–04): $19,505 (full-time). *Room and board:* $5788 (room only: $2724).
Financial Aid (All incoming freshmen): *Average need-based gift aid:* $9023. *Average non-need based aid:* $4044. *Average aid to full-time undergraduates:* $17,508.
Athletic Department: *Director of Athletics:* Marga Matakovich; Phone: 505-473-6373; E-mail: mmatakov@csf.edu.

MEN'S COACHES

Tennis: Doug MacCurdy; Phone: 505-473-6545; E-mail: dmaccurdy@csf.edu.

WOMEN'S COACHES

Tennis: Doug MacCurdy; Phone: 505-473-6545; E-mail: dmaccurdy@csf.edu.

COLLEGE OF STATEN ISLAND OF THE CITY UNIVERSITY OF NEW YORK
Staten Island, New York

Dolphins ◆ NCAA III ◆ CUNY Athletic Conference ◆ http://www.csi.cuny.edu/

State and locally supported comprehensive, founded 1955, part of City University of New York System
Coed, 11,101 undergraduate students, 65% full-time, 59% women, 41% men
Urban 204-acre campus with easy access to New York City
Moderately difficult entrance level, 100% of applicants were admitted

Freshmen *Admission:* 6,487 applied, 6,487 were accepted, 2,127 enrolled. *Test scores:* SAT verbal scores over 500: 53%; SAT math scores over 500: 56%; SAT verbal scores over 600: 12%; SAT math scores over 600: 13%; SAT verbal scores over 700: 2%; SAT math scores over 700: 1%.

Tuition and fees (2003–04): $4308 (resident), $8948 (nonresident).
Financial Aid (All incoming freshmen): *Average need-based gift aid:* $4878. *Average aid to full-time undergraduates:* $5130.
Athletic Department: *Director of Athletics:* Harold Merritt; Phone: 718-982-3160; E-mail: merritt@postbox.csi.cuny.edu. *Sports Information Director:* Jason Fein; Phone: 718-982-3149; E-mail: fein@postbox.csi.cuny.edu.

MEN'S COACHES

Baseball: Bill Cali; Phone: 718-982-3171; E-mail: fein@postbox.csi.cuny.edu.
Basketball: Tony Petosa; Phone: 718-982-3166; E-mail: fein@postbox.csi.cuny.edu.
Cheerleading: Knight; Phone: 718-982-3163; E-mail: jfknight0426@juno.com.
Soccer: Marc D'Orazio; Phone: 718-982-3151; E-mail: fein@postbox.csi.cuny.edu.
Swimming: Oleg Soloviev; Phone: 718-982-3245; E-mail: fein@postbox.csi.cuny.edu.
Tennis: Bruce Knittle; Phone: 718-982-3165; E-mail: fein@postbox.csi.cuny.edu.

WOMEN'S COACHES

Basketball: Marguerite Gualtieri; Phone: 718-982-3164; E-mail: fein@postbox.csi.cuny.edu.
Cheerleading: Knight; Phone: 718-982-3163; E-mail: jfknight0426@juno.com.
Softball: Stella Porto; Phone: 718-982-3163; E-mail: fein@postbox.csi.cuny.edu.
Swimming: Oleg Soloviev; Phone: 718-982-3245; E-mail: fein@postbox.csi.cuny.edu.
Tennis: Bruce Knittle; Phone: 718-982-3165; E-mail: fein@postbox.csi.cuny.edu.
Volleyball: Jason Fein; Phone: 718-982-3163; E-mail: fein@postbox.csi.cuny.edu.

COLLEGE OF THE HOLY CROSS
Worcester, Massachusetts

Crusaders ◆ NCAA I ◆ Atlantic Hockey Conference; Big South Conference; Patriot League Conference ◆ http://www.holycross.edu/

Independent Roman Catholic (Jesuit) 4-year, founded 1843
Coed, 2,773 undergraduate students, 99% full-time, 54% women, 46% men
Suburban 174-acre campus with easy access to Boston
Very difficult entrance level, 40% of applicants were admitted

Freshmen *Admission:* 5,035 applied, 2,131 were accepted, 698 enrolled. *Test scores:* SAT verbal scores over 500: 98%; SAT math scores over 500: 98%; SAT verbal scores over 600: 71%; SAT math scores over 600: 79%; SAT verbal scores over 700: 19%; SAT math scores over 700: 14%.
Tuition and fees (2003–04): $28,011 (full-time). *Room and board:* $8440 (room only: $4220).
Financial Aid (All incoming freshmen): *Average need-based gift aid:* $16,254. *Average non-need based aid:* $15,228. *Average aid to full-time undergraduates:* $22,257.
Athletic Department: *Director of Athletics:* Richard Regan; Phone: 508-793-2582; Fax: 508-793-3863; E-mail: rregan@holycross.edu. *Sports Information Director:* Larry Napolitano; Phone: 508-793-3941; E-mail: lnapolit@holycross.edu.

MEN'S COACHES

Baseball: Fran O'Brien; Phone: 508-793-2326; E-mail: fobrien@holycross.edu.
Basketball: Ralph Willard; Phone: 508-793-2555; E-mail: rwillard@holycross.edu.
Cheerleading: Laura Turner; Phone: 508-793-2326; E-mail: lturner@holycross.edu.
Cross Country: Jim Kavanagh; Phone: 508-793-2571; E-mail: jkavanag@holycross.edu.
Diving: Wilson Aybar; Phone: 508-793-3430; E-mail: waybar@holycross.edu.
Football: Tom Gilmore; Phone: 508-793-2311; E-mail: lhenness@holycross.edu.
Golf: Bob Molt; Phone: 508-793-2571; E-mail: rmolt@holycross.edu.

Ice Hockey: Paul Pearl; Phone: 508-793-2326; E-mail: ppearl@holycross.edu.
Lacrosse: Mike McCaffrey; Phone: 508-793-2674; E-mail: mmccaffr@holycross.edu.
Soccer: Elvis Comrie; Phone: 508-793-2726; E-mail: ecomrie@holycross.edu.
Swimming: Barry Parenteau; Phone: 508-793-3430; E-mail: bparente@holycross.edu.
Tennis: Mike Lucas; Phone: 508-793-3071; E-mail: mlucas@holycross.edu.
Track and Field: Jim Kavanagh; Phone: 508-793-2571; E-mail: jkavanag@holycross.edu.

WOMEN'S COACHES

Basketball: Bill Gibbons; Phone: 508-793-3429; E-mail: bgibbons@holycross.edu.
Cheerleading: Laura Turner; Phone: 508-793-2326; E-mail: lturner@holycross.edu.
Cross Country: Egetta Alfonso; Phone: 508-793-2315; E-mail: ealfonso@holycross.edu.
Diving: Wilson Aybar; Phone: 508-793-3430; E-mail: waybar@holycross.edu.
Field Hockey: Meg Galligan; Phone: 508-793-2319; E-mail: mgalliga@holycross.edu.
Golf: Bob Molt; Phone: 508-793-2571; E-mail: rmolt@holycross.edu.
Lacrosse: Stephanie Pavlick; Phone: 508-793-3682; E-mail: spavlick@holycross.edu.
Soccer: Mary Curtis; Phone: 508-793-3624; E-mail: mcurtis@holycross.edu.
Softball: Bob Neville; Phone: 508-793-3627; E-mail: bneville@holycross.edu.
Swimming: Barry Parenteau; Phone: 508-793-3430; E-mail: bparente@holycross.edu.
Tennis: Mike Lucas; Phone: 508-793-3626; E-mail: mlucas@holycross.edu.
Track and Field: Egetta Alfonso; Phone: 508-793-2315; E-mail: ealfonso@holycross.edu.
Volleyball: Chris Ridolfi; Phone: 508-793-3623; E-mail: cridolfi@holycross.edu.

COLLEGE OF THE OZARKS
Point Lookout, Missouri

Bobcats ◆ NAIA ◆ Midlands Collegiate Conference ◆ http://www.cofo.edu/

Independent Presbyterian 4-year, founded 1906
Coed, 1,348 undergraduate students, 95% full-time, 56% women, 44% men
Small-town 1,000-acre campus
Moderately difficult entrance level, 1% of applicants were admitted

Freshmen *Admission:* 2,076 applied, 290 were accepted, 254 enrolled.
Tuition and fees (2004–05): $250 (full-time). *Room and board:* $3550 (room only: $1800).
Financial Aid (All incoming freshmen): *Average need-based gift aid:* $7716. *Average non-need based aid:* $12,422. *Average aid to full-time undergraduates:* $12,422.
Athletic Department: *Director of Athletics:* Al Waller; Phone: 417-334-6411; Fax: 417-348-1432; E-mail: waller@cofo.edu. *Sports Information Director:* Candace Sullinger; Phone: 417-334-6411; E-mail: sullinge@cofo.edu.

MEN'S COACHES
Baseball: Patrick McGaha; Phone: 417-334-6411.
Basketball: Steve Shepherd; Phone: 417-334-6411.
Cheerleading: Carissa Cox; Phone: 417-334-6411.

WOMEN'S COACHES
Basketball: George Wilson; Phone: 417-334-6411.
Cheerleading: Carissa Cox; Phone: 417-334-6411.
Volleyball: Don Hoeck; Phone: 417-334-6411.

COLLEGE OF THE SOUTHWEST
Hobbs, New Mexico

Mustangs ◆ NAIA ◆ Red River Conference
◆ http://www.csw.edu/

Independent comprehensive, founded 1962
Coed, 696 undergraduate students, 68% full-time, 66% women, 34% men
Small-town 162-acre campus
Moderately difficult entrance level, 1% of applicants were admitted

Freshmen *Admission:* 592 applied, 93 were accepted, 64 enrolled. *Test scores:* SAT verbal scores over 500: 20%; SAT math scores over 500: 36%.
Tuition and fees (2004–05): $8415 (full-time). *Room and board:* $4600.
Financial Aid (All incoming freshmen): *Average need-based gift aid:* $2453. *Average non-need based aid:* $2075. *Average aid to full-time undergraduates:* $6344.
Athletic Department: *Director of Athletics:* Bert Luallen; Phone: 505-392-6561; Fax: 505-392-6006; E-mail: bluallen@csw.edu.

MEN'S COACHES
Baseball: JimMarshall; Phone: 505-392-6561.
Golf: Ross Funk; Phone: 505-392-6561; E-mail: rfunk@csw.edu.
Soccer: Phone: 505-392-6561.

WOMEN'S COACHES
Golf: Ross Funk; Phone: 505-392-6561; E-mail: rfunk@csw.edu.
Soccer: Rob Fulton; Phone: 505-392-6561; E-mail: rfulton@csw.edu.
Volleyball: Bert Luallen; Phone: 505-392-6561; E-mail: bluallen@csw.edu.

THE COLLEGE OF WILLIAM AND MARY
Williamsburg, Virginia

Tribe ◆ NCAA I ◆ Atlantic 10 Conference; Colonial Athletic Conference ◆ http://www.wm.edu/

State-supported university, founded 1693
Coed, 5,748 undergraduate students, 99% full-time, 56% women, 44% men
Small-town 1,200-acre campus with easy access to Richmond
Very difficult entrance level, 42% of applicants were admitted

Freshmen *Admission:* 10,161 applied, 3,488 were accepted, 1,326 enrolled. *Test scores:* SAT verbal scores over 500: 99%; SAT math scores over 500: 100%; SAT verbal scores over 600: 88%; SAT math scores over 600: 86%; SAT verbal scores over 700: 43%; SAT math scores over 700: 35%.
Tuition and fees (2003–04): $6430 (resident), $21,130 (nonresident). *Room and board:* $5794 (room only: $3428).
Financial Aid (All incoming freshmen): *Average need-based gift aid:* $6978. *Average non-need based aid:* $5405. *Average aid to full-time undergraduates:* $8251.
Athletic Department: *Director of Athletics:* Terry Driscoll; Phone: 757-221-3332; Fax: 757-221-2989. *Sports Information Director:* Pete Clawson; Phone: 757-221-3369; E-mail: pmclaw@wm.edu.

MEN'S COACHES
Baseball: Jim Farr; Phone: 757-221-3399; E-mail: jafarr@wm.edu.
Basketball: Tony Shaver; Phone: 757-221-3339; E-mail: tlshav@wm.edu.
Cheerleading: Heather Ursu; Phone: 757-221-3353.
Cross Country: Alex Gibby; Phone: 757-221-3398; E-mail: amgibb@wm.edu.
Diving: Robert McNamee; Phone: 757-221-3393.
Football: Jimmye Laycock; Phone: 757-221-3334.
Golf: Jay Albaugh; Phone: 757-221-3046; E-mail: jaalba@wm.edu.
Soccer: Chris Norris; Phone: 757-221-3321; E-mail: cmnorr@wm.edu.
Swimming: Gregg Sarbak; Phone: 757-221-3393; E-mail: gdsarb@wm.edu.
Tennis: Peter Daub; Phone: 757-221-3383; E-mail: pbdaub@wm.edu.
Track and Field: Dan Stimson; Phone: 757-221-3397; E-mail: dgstim@wm.edu.

The College of William and Mary *(continued)*

WOMEN'S COACHES

Basketball: Debbie Taylor; Phone: 757-221-3391; E-mail: dltay2@wm.edu.

Cheerleading: Heather Ursu; Phone: 757-221-3353.

Cross Country: Pat Van Rossum; Phone: 757-221-3396; E-mail: rpvanx@wm.edu.

Diving: Robert McNamee; Phone: 757-221-3393.

Field Hockey: Peel Hawthorne; Phone: 757-221-3390; E-mail: pshawt@wm.edu.

Golf: Jay Albaugh; Phone: 757-221-3046; E-mail: jaalba@wm.edu.

Gymnastics: Mary Lewis; Phone: 757-221-3411; E-mail: mklewi@wm.edu.

Lacrosse: Tara Brown; Phone: 757-221-3389; E-mail: txkell@wm.edu.

Soccer: John Daly; Phone: 757-221-3387; E-mail: jbdaly@wm.edu.

Swimming: Gregg Sarbak; Phone: 757-221-3393; E-mail: gdsarb@wm.edu.

Tennis: Kevin Epley; Phone: 757-221-3384; E-mail: epper3210@cs.com.

Track and Field: Dan Stimson; Phone: 757-221-3397; E-mail: dgstim@wm.edu.

Volleyball: Debbie Hill; Phone: 757-221-3395; E-mail: cdhill@wm.edu.

THE COLLEGE OF WOOSTER
Wooster, Ohio

Fighting Scots ◆ NCAA III ◆ North Coast Athletic Conference ◆ http://www.wooster.edu/

Independent religious 4-year, founded 1866, affiliated with Presbyterian Church (U.S.A.)
Coed, 1,871 undergraduate students, 98% full-time, 53% women, 47% men
Small-town 240-acre campus with easy access to Cleveland
Moderately difficult entrance level, 6% of applicants were admitted

Freshmen *Admission:* 2,560 applied, 1,780 were accepted, 552 enrolled. *Test scores:* SAT verbal scores over 500: 90%; SAT math scores over 500: 91%; SAT verbal scores over 600: 53%; SAT math scores over 600: 53%; SAT verbal scores over 700: 14%; SAT math scores over 700: 9%.
Tuition and fees (2003–04): $25,040 (full-time). *Room and board:* $6260 (room only: $2850).
Financial Aid (All incoming freshmen): *Average need-based gift aid:* $15,668. *Average non-need based aid:* $11,355. *Average aid to full-time undergraduates:* $21,412.

MEN'S COACHES

Baseball: Tim Pettorini; Phone: 330-263-2180; E-mail: tpettorini@wooster.edu.

Basketball: Steve Moore; Phone: 330-263-2176; E-mail: smoore@wooster.edu.

Cross Country: Dennis Rice; Phone: 330-263-2175; E-mail: drice@wooster.edu.

Football: Mike Schmitz; Phone: 330-263-2177; E-mail: mschmitz@wooster.edu.

Golf: Rich Danch; Phone: 330-263-2170; E-mail: rdanch@wooster.edu.

Lacrosse: Jason Tarnon; Phone: 330-263-2179; E-mail: jtarnow@wooster.edu.

Soccer: Graham Ford; Phone: 330-263-2348; E-mail: gford@wooster.edu.

Swimming: Keith Beckett; Phone: 330-263-2178; E-mail: kbeckett@wooster.edu.

Tennis: Hayden Schilling; Phone: 330-263-2452; E-mail: hschilling@wooster.edu.

Track and Field: Dennis Rice; Phone: 330-263-2175; E-mail: drice@wooster.edu.

WOMEN'S COACHES

Basketball: Lisa Campanell Komara; Phone: 330-263-2174; E-mail: lcampanell@wooster.edu.

Cross Country: Dennis Rice; Phone: 330-263-2175; E-mail: drice@wooster.edu.

Field Hockey: Brenda Meese; Phone: 330-263-2173; E-mail: bmeese@wooster.edu.

Lacrosse: Alison Share; Phone: 330-263-2182; E-mail: ashare@wooster.edu.

Soccer: David Brown; Phone: 330-263-2503; E-mail: dvbrown@wooster.edu.

Softball: Lori Jefferes; Phone: 330-263-2679; E-mail: ljefferes@wooster.edu.

Swimming: Keith Beckett; Phone: 330-263-2178; E-mail: kbeckett@wooster.edu.

Tennis: Lauren Cline; Phone: 330-263-2518; E-mail: dcline@wooster.edu.

Track and Field: Dennis Rice; Phone: 330-263-2175; E-mail: drice@wooster.edu.

Volleyball: Terri Mason; Phone: 330-263-2172; E-mail: tmason@wooster.edu.

COLORADO CHRISTIAN UNIVERSITY
Lakewood, Colorado

Cougars ◆ NCAA II ◆ Rocky Mountain Athletic Conference ◆ http://www.ccu.edu/

Independent interdenominational comprehensive, founded 1914
Coed, 1,462 undergraduate students, 78% full-time, 60% women, 40% men
Suburban 26-acre campus with easy access to Denver
Moderately difficult entrance level, 73% of applicants were admitted

Freshmen *Admission:* 920 applied, 702 were accepted, 265 enrolled. *Test scores:* SAT verbal scores over 500: 82%; SAT math scores over 500: 69%; SAT verbal scores over 600: 35%; SAT math scores over 600: 29%; SAT verbal scores over 700: 10%; SAT math scores over 700: 4%.
Tuition and fees (2004–05): $15,140 (full-time). *Room and board:* $6042 (room only: $3452).
Financial Aid (All incoming freshmen): *Average need-based gift aid:* $7355. *Average non-need based aid:* $15,070. *Average aid to full-time undergraduates:* $9712.
Athletic Department: *Director of Athletics:* Douglas Yager; Phone: 303-963-3187; Fax: 303-963-3181; E-mail: dyager@ccu.edu. *Sports Information Director:* Aimee Davison; Phone: 303-963-3185; E-mail: aduffy@ccu.edu.

MEN'S COACHES

Basketball: Brannon Hays; Phone: 303-963-3191; E-mail: bhays@ccu.edu.

Cross Country: Jaimie Cartwright; Phone: 303-963-3180; E-mail: jcartwright@ccu.edu.

Golf: Mike Sims; Phone: 303-963-3183; E-mail: psims@ccu.edu.

Soccer: Brian Todd; Phone: 303-963-3186; E-mail: btodd@ccu.edu.

Tennis: Keplin Crabb; Phone: 303-963-3193; E-mail: kcrabb@ccu.edu.

WOMEN'S COACHES

Basketball: Kristen Buckley; Phone: 303-963-3188; E-mail: kbuckley@ccu.edu.

Cross Country: Jaimie Cartwright; Phone: 303-963-3180; E-mail: jcartwright@ccu.edu.

Soccer: Tammy Wishard; Phone: 303-963-3196; E-mail: tawishard@ccu.edu.

Tennis: Keplin Crabb; Phone: 303-963-3193; E-mail: kcrabb@ccu.edu.

Volleyball: Natalie Alred; Phone: 303-963-3184; E-mail: nalred@ccu.edu.

THE COLORADO COLLEGE
Colorado Springs, Colorado

Tigers ◆ NCAA III ◆ Independent; Western Collegiate Hockey Conference ◆ http://www.coloradocollege.edu/

Independent comprehensive, founded 1874
Coed, 1,941 undergraduate students, 99% full-time, 54% women, 46% men
Urban 90-acre campus with easy access to Denver
Very difficult entrance level, 49% of applicants were admitted

Freshmen *Admission:* 3,533 applied, 1,975 were accepted, 524 enrolled. *Test scores:* SAT verbal scores over 500: 96%; SAT math scores over

500: 97%; SAT verbal scores over 600: 70%; SAT math scores over 600: 70%; SAT verbal scores over 700: 22%; SAT math scores over 700: 16%.
Tuition and fees (2003–04): $27,635 (full-time). *Room and board:* $6840 (room only: $3664).
Financial Aid (All incoming freshmen): *Average need-based gift aid:* $20,035. *Average non-need based aid:* $12,279. *Average aid to full-time undergraduates:* $22,299.
Athletic Department: *Director of Athletics:* Julie Soriero; Phone: 719-389-6475; Fax: 719-389-6873; E-mail: jsoriero@coloradocollege.edu. *Sports Information Director:* Dave Moross; Phone: 719-389-6755; E-mail: dmoross@coloradocollege.edu.

MEN'S COACHES
Basketball: Mike McCubbin; Phone: 719-389-6482; E-mail: mmccubbin@coloradocollege.edu.
Cross Country: Ted Castaneda; Phone: 719-389-6483; E-mail: tcastaneda@coloradocollege.edu.
Diving: Ellen Walker; Phone: 719-389-6486; E-mail: athletics@coloradocollege.edu.
Football: Bob Bodor; Phone: 719-389-6314; E-mail: bbodor@coloradocollege.edu.
Ice Hockey: Scott Owens; Phone: 719-389-6480; E-mail: sowens@coloradocollege.edu.
Lacrosse: David Zazzaro; Phone: 719-389-6808; E-mail: dzazzaro@coloradocollege.edu.
Soccer: Horst Richardson; Phone: 719-389-6517; E-mail: hrichardson@coloradocollege.edu.
Swimming: Brian Pearson; Phone: 719-389-6486; E-mail: bpearson@coloradocollege.edu.
Tennis: Dave Adams; Phone: 719-389-6481; E-mail: dadams@cmsd.k12.co.us.
Track and Field: Ted Castaneda; Phone: 719-389-6483; E-mail: tcastaneda@coloradocollege.edu.

WOMEN'S COACHES
Basketball: Kelly Mahlum; Phone: 719-389-6478; E-mail: kmahlum@coloradocollege.edu.
Cross Country: Ted Castaneda; Phone: 719-389-6483; E-mail: tcastaneda@coloradocollege.edu.
Diving: Ellen Walker; Phone: 719-389-6486; E-mail: athletics@coloradocollege.edu.
Lacrosse: Susan Stuart; Phone: 719-389-6497; E-mail: sstuart@coloradocollege.edu.
Soccer: Erik Oman; Phone: 719-389-6492; E-mail: eoman@coloradocollege.edu.
Softball: Lisa Reimer; Phone: 719-389-6749; E-mail: sstuart@coloradocollege.edu.
Swimming: Brian Pearson; Phone: 719-389-6486; E-mail: bpearson@coloradocollege.edu.
Tennis: Dave Adams; Phone: 719-389-6481; E-mail: dadams@cmsd.k12.co.us.
Track and Field: Ted Castaneda; Phone: 719-389-6483; E-mail: tcastaneda@coloradocollege.edu.
Volleyball: Rick Swan; Phone: 719-389-6485; E-mail: rswan@coloradocollege.edu.

COLORADO SCHOOL OF MINES
Golden, Colorado
Orediggers ◆ NCAA II ◆ Rocky Mountain Athletic Conference ◆ http://www.mines.edu/

State-supported university, founded 1874
Coed, 2,664 undergraduate students, 97% full-time, 23% women, 77% men
Small-town 373-acre campus with easy access to Denver
Very difficult entrance level, 78% of applicants were admitted

Freshmen *Admission:* 3,049 applied, 2,422 were accepted, 668 enrolled. *Test scores:* SAT verbal scores over 500: 90%; SAT math scores over 500: 98%; SAT verbal scores over 600: 52%; SAT math scores over 600: 79%; SAT verbal scores over 700: 11%; SAT math scores over 700: 25%.
Tuition and fees (2004–05): $6433 (resident), $19,763 (nonresident). *Room and board:* $6100 (room only: $3200).
Financial Aid (All incoming freshmen): *Average need-based gift aid:* $6900. *Average non-need based aid:* $4910. *Average aid to full-time undergraduates:* $13,100.

Athletic Department: *Director of Athletics:* Marv Kay; Phone: 303-273-3363; Fax: 303-273-3362; E-mail: mkay@mines.edu. *Sports Information Director:* Greg Murphy; Phone: 303-273-3095; E-mail: gjmurphy@mines.edu.

MEN'S COACHES
Baseball: Mike Mulvaney; Phone: 303-273-3367; E-mail: mmulvane@mines.edu.
Basketball: Pryor Orser; Phone: 303-273-3364; E-mail: porser@mines.edu.
Cheerleading: Alicia Jessop; Phone: 303-324-1676; E-mail: ajessop@mines.edu.
Cross Country: Oscar Boes; Phone: 303-273-3882; E-mail: aboes@mines.edu.
Football: Bob Stitt; Phone: 303-273-3365; E-mail: bstitt@mines.edu.
Golf: Bob Writz; Phone: 303-273-3368; E-mail: writz@mho.net.
Soccer: Frank Kohlenstein; Phone: 303-273-3369; E-mail: fkohlens@mines.edu.
Swimming: Dave Hughes; Phone: 303-273-3370; E-mail: dhughes@mines.edu.
Tennis: Steve Wimberly; Phone: 303-384-2295; E-mail: swimberl@mines.edu.
Track and Field: Scott Van Sickle; Phone: 303-273-3368; E-mail: sv_001@hotmail.com.
Wrestling: Steve Kimpel; Phone: 303-273-3352; E-mail: skimpel@mines.edu.

WOMEN'S COACHES
Basketball: Paula Krueger; Phone: 303-273-3366; E-mail: pkrueger@mines.edu.
Cheerleading: Alicia Jessop; Phone: 303-324-1676; E-mail: ajessop@mines.edu.
Cross Country: Oscar Boes; Phone: 303-273-3882; E-mail: aboes@mines.edu.
Softball: Mark Roberts; Phone: 303-384-2296; E-mail: coachrbrts@aol.com.
Swimming: Dave Hughes; Phone: 303-273-3370; E-mail: dhughes@mines.edu.
Track and Field: Scott Van Sickle; Phone: 303-273-3368; E-mail: sv_001@hotmail.com.
Volleyball: Shelly Johnson; Phone: 303-273-3371; E-mail: shjohnso@mines.edu.

COLORADO STATE UNIVERSITY
Fort Collins, Colorado
Rams ◆ NCAA I ◆ Mountain West Conference ◆ http://www.colostate.edu/

State-supported university, founded 1870, part of Colorado State University System
Coed, 21,689 undergraduate students, 88% full-time, 51% women, 49% men
Urban 666-acre campus with easy access to Denver
Moderately difficult entrance level, 76% of applicants were admitted

Freshmen *Admission:* 12,027 applied, 9,520 were accepted, 3,802 enrolled. *Test scores:* SAT verbal scores over 500: 77%; SAT math scores over 500: 79%; SAT verbal scores over 600: 27%; SAT math scores over 600: 33%; SAT verbal scores over 700: 3%; SAT math scores over 700: 3%.
Tuition and fees (2003–04): $3744 (resident), $14,216 (nonresident). *Room and board:* $6045.
Financial Aid (All incoming freshmen): *Average need-based gift aid:* $4618. *Average non-need based aid:* $896. *Average aid to full-time undergraduates:* $6485.
Athletic Department: *Director of Athletics:* Mark Driscoll; Phone: 970-491-3350; E-mail: jkietz@lamar.colostate.edu. *Sports Information Director:* Gary Ozzello; Phone: 970-491-5067; E-mail: ramsid@lamar.colostate.edu.

MEN'S COACHES
Basketball: Chris Denker; Phone: 970-491-6569; E-mail: chris.denker@colostate.edu.
Cheerleading: Brenda Bockelman; Phone: 970-491-5725.
Cross Country: Del Hessel; Phone: 970-491-5434; E-mail: bedard@lamar.colostate.edu.
Football: Sonny Lubick; Phone: 970-491-6131; E-mail: lkrier@lamar.colostate.edu.

Colorado State University (continued)

Golf: Jamie Bermel; Phone: 970-491-2946; E-mail: jbermel@lamar. colostate.edu.

Track and Field: Del Hessel; Phone: 970-491-5434; E-mail: bedard@ lamar.colostate.edu.

WOMEN'S COACHES

Basketball: Chris Denker; Phone: 970-491-6569; E-mail: chris.denker@ colostate.edu.

Cheerleading: Brenda Bockelman; Phone: 970-491-5725.

Cross Country: Del Hessel; Phone: 970-491-5434; E-mail: bedard@lamar. colostate.edu.

Diving: Morry Arbini; Phone: 970-491-6026; E-mail: jmattos@lamar. colostate.edu.

Golf: Angie Hopkins; Phone: 970-491-3589.

Softball: Mary Yori; Phone: 970-491-6000; E-mail: yori@lamar. colostate.edu.

Swimming: John Mattos; Phone: 970-491-6026; E-mail: jmattos@ colostate.edu.

Tennis: Jon Messick; Phone: 970-491-1311; E-mail: jmessick@lamar. colostate.edu.

Track and Field: Del Hessel; Phone: 970-491-5434; E-mail: bedard@ lamar.colostate.edu.

Volleyball: Tom Hilbert; Phone: 970-491-6582; E-mail: thilbert@lamar. colostate.edu.

COLORADO STATE UNIVERSITY-PUEBLO
Pueblo, Colorado

Thunderwolves ◆ NCAA II ◆ Rocky Mountain Athletic Conference ◆ http://www.colostate-pueblo.edu/

State-supported comprehensive, founded 1933, part of Colorado State University System
Coed, 6,078 undergraduate students, 55% full-time, 60% women, 40% men
Suburban 275-acre campus with easy access to Colorado Springs
Moderately difficult entrance level, 93% of applicants were admitted

Freshmen *Admission:* 1,665 applied, 1,587 were accepted, 637 enrolled. *Test scores:* SAT verbal scores over 500: 51%; SAT math scores over 500: 49%; SAT verbal scores over 600: 7%; SAT math scores over 600: 11%; SAT verbal scores over 700: 2%.
Tuition and fees (2003–04): $2930 (resident), $12,920 (nonresident). *Room and board:* $5742 (room only: $2794).
Financial Aid (All incoming freshmen): *Average need-based gift aid:* $4139. *Average non-need based aid:* $4422. *Average aid to full-time undergraduates:* $5151.
Athletic Department: *Director of Athletics:* Joe Folda; Phone: 719-549-2713; Fax: 719-549-2768; E-mail: joe.folda@colostate-pueblo.edu. *Sports Information Director:* Matt Hildner; Phone: 719-549-2022; E-mail: matthew.hildner@colostate-pueblo.edu.

MEN'S COACHES

Baseball: Stan Sanchez; Phone: 719-549-2065; E-mail: stan.sanchez@ colostate-pueblo.edu.

Basketball: Joe Folda; Phone: 719-549-2713; E-mail: joe.folda@ colostate-pueblo.edu.

Golf: Dave Lewis; Phone: 719-547-2280; E-mail: dlewis@fone.net.

Soccer: Roy Stanley; Phone: 719-549-2793; E-mail: roy.stanley@ colostate-pueblo.edu.

Tennis: Bob Scott; Phone: 719-549-2740; E-mail: robert.scott@ colostate-pueblo.edu.

WOMEN'S COACHES

Basketball: Misty Murphy; Phone: 719-549-2382; E-mail: misty. murphy@colostate-pueblo.edu.

Soccer: Roy Stanley; Phone: 719-549-2793; E-mail: roy.stanley@ colostate-pueblo.edu.

Softball: Shane Showalter; Phone: 719-549-2767; E-mail: thomas. showalter@colostate-pueblo.edu.

Tennis: Bob Scott; Phone: 719-549-2740; E-mail: robert.scott@ colostate-pueblo.edu.

Volleyball: Tom Shoji; Phone: 719-549-2794; E-mail: thomas.shoji@ colostate-pueblo.edu.

COLUMBIA COLLEGE
Columbia, Missouri

Cougars ◆ NAIA ◆ American Midwest Conference ◆ http://www.ccis.edu/

Independent religious comprehensive, founded 1851, affiliated with Christian Church (Disciples of Christ)
Coed, 916 undergraduate students, 75% full-time, 62% women, 38% men
Small-town 29-acre campus
Minimally difficult entrance level, 55% of applicants were admitted

Freshmen *Admission:* 891 applied, 524 were accepted, 157 enrolled.
Tuition and fees (2004–05): $11,589 (full-time). *Room and board:* $4913 (room only: $3090).
Financial Aid (All incoming freshmen): *Average need-based gift aid:* $3140. *Average non-need based aid:* $7680. *Average aid to full-time undergraduates:* $7267.
Athletic Department: *Director of Athletics:* Bob Burchard; Phone: 573-875-7410; Fax: 573-875-7415; E-mail: rpburchard@ccis.edu. *Sports Information Director:* Amber Cox; Phone: 573-875-7419; E-mail: alcox@email.ccis.edu.

MEN'S COACHES

Basketball: Bob Burchard; Phone: 573-875-7410; E-mail: rpburchard@ ccis.edu.

Soccer: John Klein; Phone: 573-875-7413; E-mail: jdklein@ccis.edu.

WOMEN'S COACHES

Basketball: Mike Davis; Phone: 573-875-7417; E-mail: mbdavis@ccis. edu.

Softball: Wendy Spratt; Phone: 573-875-7414; E-mail: wsspratt@ccis. edu.

Volleyball: Melinda Wrye-Washington; Phone: 573-875-7409; E-mail: mwwashington@ccis.edu.

COLUMBIA UNIVERSITY
New York, New York

Bears ◆ NCAA I ◆ Ivy League Conference
◆ http://www.college.columbia.edu/

Independent 4-year, founded 1754, part of Columbia University
Coed, 4,181 undergraduate students, 100% full-time, 51% women, 49% men
Urban 35-acre campus
Most difficult entrance level, 1% of applicants were admitted

Freshmen *Admission:* 14,648 applied, 1,643 were accepted, 1,010 enrolled. *Test scores:* SAT verbal scores over 500: 99%; SAT math scores over 500: 100%; SAT verbal scores over 600: 89%; SAT math scores over 600: 93%; SAT verbal scores over 700: 60%; SAT math scores over 700: 59%.
Tuition and fees (2003–04): $29,788 (full-time). *Room and board:* $8802 (room only: $5136).
Financial Aid (All incoming freshmen): *Average need-based gift aid:* $25,694. *Average aid to full-time undergraduates:* $28,684.
Athletic Department: *Director of Athletics:* John Reeves; Phone: 212-854-2537; Fax: 212-854-8168; E-mail: jar14@columbia.edu. *Sports Information Director:* Thad Dohm; Phone: 212-854-7064; E-mail: td2035@ columbia.edu.

MEN'S COACHES

Baseball: Paul Fernandes; Phone: 212-854-7772; E-mail: pef1@ columbia.edu.

Basketball: Joseph Jones; Phone: 212-854-3419; E-mail: jj2119@ columbia.edu.

Cheerleading: Melissa Signor; Phone: 212-854-2538; E-mail: columbiacheer@hotmail.com.

Cross Country: Willy Wood; Phone: 212-854-3436; E-mail: waw8@ columbia.edu.

Diving: Gordon Spencer; Phone: 212-854-6922; E-mail: gs19@ columbia.edu.

Football: Bob Shoop; Phone: 212-854-7061; E-mail: rs2241@columbia. edu.

Golf: Al Carlson; Phone: 212-854-7147; E-mail: agc1@columbia.edu.

Soccer: Dieter Ficken; Phone: 212-854-5436; E-mail: dwf1@columbia.edu.
Swimming: Jim Bolster; Phone: 212-854-7059; E-mail: jbb2@columbia.edu.
Tennis: Bid Goswami; Phone: 212-854-4696; E-mail: bkg1@columbia.edu.
Track and Field: Willy Wood; Phone: 212-854-3436; E-mail: waw8@columbia.edu.
Wrestling: Brendan Buckley; Phone: 212-854-3435; E-mail: lem2@columbia.edu.

WOMEN'S COACHES

Basketball: Jay Butler; Phone: 212-854-8861; E-mail: jjb48@columbia.edu.
Cheerleading: Melissa Signor; Phone: 212-854-2538; E-mail: columbiacheer@hotmail.com.
Cross Country: Willy Wood; Phone: 212-854-3436; E-mail: waw8@columbia.edu.
Diving: Gordon Spencer; Phone: 212-854-6922; E-mail: gs19@columbia.edu.
Field Hockey: Susan Eicher; Phone: 212-854-9361; E-mail: sfe7@columbia.edu.
Lacrosse: Kerri Whitaker; Phone: 212-854-3115; E-mail: kw2020@columbia.edu.
Soccer: Kevin McCarthy; Phone: 212-854-4559; E-mail: kjm28@columbia.edu.
Softball: Kayla Noonan; Phone: 212-854-2805; E-mail: kn239@columbia.edu.
Swimming: Diana Caskey; Phone: 212-854-8865; E-mail: dbc3@columbia.edu.
Tennis: Rob Kresberg; Phone: 212-854-7296; E-mail: rbk14@columbia.edu.
Track and Field: Willy Wood; Phone: 212-854-3436; E-mail: waw8@columbia.edu.
Volleyball: Monica Holmes; Phone: 212-854-8864; E-mail: mh2269@columbia.edu.

COLUMBIA COLLEGE
Columbia, South Carolina

Fighting Koalas ◆ NAIA ◆ Independent
◆ http://www.columbiacollegesc.edu/

Independent United Methodist comprehensive, founded 1854
Women only, 1,187 undergraduate students, 78% full-time, 97% women, 3% men
Suburban 33-acre campus
Moderately difficult entrance level, 86% of applicants were admitted

Freshmen *Admission:* 960 applied, 824 were accepted, 180 enrolled. *Test scores:* SAT verbal scores over 500: 39%; SAT math scores over 500: 35%; SAT verbal scores over 600: 8%; SAT math scores over 600: 5%; SAT math scores over 700: 1%.
Tuition and fees (2003–04): $17,280 (full-time). *Room and board:* $5245 (room only: $2830).
Financial Aid (All incoming freshmen): *Average need-based gift aid:* $7456. *Average non-need based aid:* $7256. *Average aid to full-time undergraduates:* $17,398.
Athletic Department: *Director of Athletics:* Ana Oliver; Phone: 803-786-3723; Fax: 803-786-3868; E-mail: aoliver@colacoll.edu. *Sports Information Director:* James Morrison; Phone: 803-786-3846; E-mail: jmorrison@colacoll.edu.

WOMEN'S COACHES

Soccer: Patrick Faulds; Phone: 803-786-3897; E-mail: pfaulds@colacoll.edu.
Tennis: James Morrison; Phone: 803-786-3846; E-mail: jmorrison@colacoll.edu.
Volleyball: Lyndsay Wheeler; Phone: 803-786-3060; E-mail: lwheeler@colacoll.edu.

COLUMBIA UNION COLLEGE
Takoma Park, Maryland

Pioneers ◆ NCAA II ◆ Independent ◆ http://www.cuc.edu/

Independent Seventh-day Adventist comprehensive, founded 1904
Coed, 1,159 undergraduate students, 66% full-time, 64% women, 36% men
Suburban 19-acre campus with easy access to Washington, DC
Minimally difficult entrance level, 50% of applicants were admitted

Freshmen *Admission:* 851 applied, 460 were accepted, 187 enrolled. *Test scores:* SAT verbal scores over 500: 29%; SAT math scores over 500: 24%; SAT verbal scores over 600: 10%; SAT math scores over 600: 3%; SAT verbal scores over 700: 1%; SAT math scores over 700: 1%.
Tuition and fees (2003–04): $15,248 (full-time). *Room and board:* $5295.
Athletic Department: *Director of Athletics:* Al Bacchus; Phone: 301-891-4481; Fax: 301-891-4552; E-mail: esimmons@cuc.edu. *Sports Information Director:* Donna Polk; Phone: 301-891-4176; E-mail: athletic@cuc.edu.

MEN'S COACHES

Baseball: Rhett Ross; Phone: 301-891-4026; E-mail: baseball@cuc.edu.
Basketball: Calvin Dunbar; Phone: 301-891-4024; E-mail: mensbb@cuc.edu.
Cross Country: Calvin Dunbar; Phone: 301-891-4024; E-mail: track@cuc.edu@cuc.edu.
Soccer: Anthony Ogunsanya; Phone: 301-891-4553; E-mail: msoccer@cuc.edu.
Track and Field: Calvin Dunbar; Phone: 301-891-4024; E-mail: track@cuc.edu@cuc.edu.

WOMEN'S COACHES

Basketball: Donna Polk; Phone: 301-891-4176; E-mail: womensbb@cuc.edu@cuc.edu.
Cross Country: Calvin Dunbar; Phone: 301-891-4024; E-mail: track@cuc.edu@cuc.edu.
Soccer: Juan Torres; Phone: 301-891-4553; E-mail: wsoccer@cuc.edu.
Softball: Ed Hendrickson; Phone: 301-891-4540; E-mail: softball@cuc.edu.
Track and Field: Calvin Dunbar; Phone: 301-891-4024; E-mail: track@cuc.edu@cuc.edu.

COLUMBUS STATE UNIVERSITY
Columbus, Georgia

Cougars ◆ NCAA II ◆ Peach Belt Conference ◆ http://www.colstate.edu/

State-supported comprehensive, founded 1958, part of University System of Georgia
Coed, 5,994 undergraduate students, 66% full-time, 62% women, 38% men
Suburban 132-acre campus with easy access to Atlanta
Minimally difficult entrance level, 72% of applicants were admitted

Freshmen *Admission:* 2,637 applied, 1,859 were accepted, 1,157 enrolled. *Test scores:* SAT verbal scores over 500: 42%; SAT math scores over 500: 38%; SAT verbal scores over 600: 10%; SAT math scores over 600: 8%; SAT verbal scores over 700: 1%.
Tuition and fees (2003–04): $2676 (resident), $9312 (nonresident). *Room and board:* $5270 (room only: $2900).
Financial Aid (All incoming freshmen): *Average need-based gift aid:* $2738. *Average non-need based aid:* $1596. *Average aid to full-time undergraduates:* $3921.
Athletic Department: *Director of Athletics:* Herbert Greene; Phone: 706-565-3531; Fax: 706-569-3435; E-mail: greene_herbert@colstate.edu. *Sports Information Director:* Mike Peacock; Phone: 706-569-3434; E-mail: peacock_mike@colstate.edu.

MEN'S COACHES

Baseball: Greg Appleton; Phone: 706-568-2444; E-mail: appleton_greg@colstate.edu.
Basketball: Herbert Greene; Phone: 706-565-3531; E-mail: greene_herbert@colstate.edu.
Cheerleading: Jimbo Davis; Phone: 706-568-2317; E-mail: davis_james@colstate.edu.

Columbus State University *(continued)*

Cross Country: J.D. Evilsizer; Phone: 334-297-1646; E-mail: jdevilsizer@aol.com.
Golf: Mark Immelman; Phone: 706-565-4329; E-mail: immelman_mark@colstate.edu.
Tennis: Evan Isaacs; Phone: 706-569-3042; E-mail: isaacs_evan@colstate.edu.

WOMEN'S COACHES

Basketball: Jay Sparks; Phone: 706-565-3669; E-mail: sparks_jay@colstate.edu.
Cheerleading: Jimbo Davis; Phone: 706-568-2317; E-mail: davis_james@colstate.edu.
Cross Country: J.D. Evilsizer; Phone: 334-297-1646; E-mail: jdevilsizer@aol.com.
Soccer: Jay Entlich; Phone: 706-464-6341; E-mail: jentlich@hotmail.com.
Softball: Tiffany Tootle; Phone: 706-569-3102; E-mail: tootle_tiffany@colstate.edu.
Tennis: Evan Isaacs; Phone: 706-565-4331; E-mail: isaacs_evan@colstate.edu.

CONCORD COLLEGE
Athens, West Virginia

Mountain Lions ◆ NCAA II ◆ West Virginia Intercollegiate Athletic Conference ◆ http://www.concord.edu/

State-supported 4-year, founded 1872, part of State College System of West Virginia
Coed, 2,933 undergraduate students
Rural 100-acre campus
Minimally difficult entrance level, 6% of applicants were admitted

Freshmen *Admission:* 2,121 applied, 1,334 were accepted. *Test scores:* SAT verbal scores over 500: 50%; SAT math scores over 500: 48%; SAT verbal scores over 600: 17%; SAT math scores over 600: 19%; SAT verbal scores over 700: 1%; SAT math scores over 700: 3%.
Tuition and fees (2003–04): $3198 (resident), $7278 (nonresident). *Room and board:* $4938 (room only: $2284).
Financial Aid (All incoming freshmen): *Average need-based gift aid:* $2921. *Average non-need based aid:* $4171. *Average aid to full-time undergraduates:* $6676.
Athletic Department: *Director of Athletics:* Steve Lee; Phone: 304-384-5331; Fax: 304-384-5117; E-mail: slee@concord.edu. *Sports Information Director:* Ernie Horn; Phone: 304-384-6259; E-mail: ehorn@concord.edu.

MEN'S COACHES

Baseball: Kevin Garrett; Phone: 304-384-5340; E-mail: coachgarrett@concord.edu.
Basketball: Steve Cox; Phone: 304-384-5330; E-mail: coxs@concord.edu.
Cheerleading: Lisa Blankenship; Phone: 304-384-5347.
Cross Country: Mike Cox; Phone: 304-384-6238; E-mail: coxm@concord.edu.
Football: Greg Quick; Phone: 304-384-5953; E-mail: coachquick@concord.edu.
Golf: Kevin O'Sullivan; Phone: 304-384-6248; E-mail: golf@concord.edu.
Soccer: Steve Barrett; Phone: 304-384-5131; E-mail: barretts@concord.edu.
Tennis: Joe Blankenship; Phone: 304-384-5295; E-mail: ace10spro@yahoo.com.
Track and Field: Mike Cox; Phone: 304-384-5347; E-mail: coxm@concord.edu.

WOMEN'S COACHES

Basketball: Kenny Osborne; Phone: 304-384-5344; E-mail: coachosborne@concord.edu.
Cheerleading: Lisa Blankenship; Phone: 304-384-5347.
Cross Country: Mike Cox; Phone: 304-384-6238; E-mail: coxm@concord.edu.
Soccer: Steve Barrett; Phone: 304-384-5131; E-mail: barretts@concord.edu.
Softball: Pat Hardin; Phone: 304-384-5342; E-mail: hardinp@concord.edu.

Tennis: Joe Blankenship; Phone: 304-384-5295; E-mail: ace10spro@yahoo.com.
Track and Field: Mike Cox; Phone: 304-384-6238; E-mail: coxm@concord.edu.
Volleyball: Pat Hardin; Phone: 304-384-5342; E-mail: hardinp@concord.edu.

CONCORDIA COLLEGE
Moorhead, Minnesota

Cobbers ◆ NCAA III ◆ Minnesota Intercollegiate Athletic Conference ◆ http://www.concordiacollege.edu/

Independent religious 4-year, founded 1891, affiliated with Evangelical Lutheran Church in America
Coed, 2,856 undergraduate students, 97% full-time, 63% women, 37% men
Suburban 120-acre campus
Moderately difficult entrance level, 85% of applicants were admitted

Freshmen *Admission:* 2,444 applied, 2,098 were accepted, 783 enrolled. *Test scores:* SAT verbal scores over 500: 85%; SAT math scores over 500: 83%; SAT verbal scores over 600: 42%; SAT math scores over 600: 36%; SAT verbal scores over 700: 5%; SAT math scores over 700: 4%.
Tuition and fees (2003–04): $16,560 (full-time). *Room and board:* $4540 (room only: $2040).
Financial Aid (All incoming freshmen): *Average need-based gift aid:* $8625. *Average aid to full-time undergraduates:* $12,095.
Athletic Department: *Director of Athletics:* Bob Nick; Phone: 218-299-4438; Fax: 218-299-4189; E-mail: nick@cord.edu. *Sports Information Director:* Jim Cella; Phone: 218-299-3194; E-mail: cella@cord.edu.

MEN'S COACHES

Baseball: Don Burgau; Phone: 218-299-3209; E-mail: bburgau@cord.edu.
Basketball: Duane Siverson; Phone: 218-299-4160; E-mail: dsiverso@cord.edu.
Cross Country: Garrick Larson; Phone: 218-299-4304; E-mail: gzlarson@cord.edu.
Football: Terry Horan; Phone: 218-299-3499; E-mail: horant@cord.edu.
Golf: Troy Odegaard; Phone: 218-299-4921; E-mail: odegaard@cord.edu.
Ice Hockey: Steve Baumgartner; Phone: 218-299-4166; E-mail: baumgart@cord.edu.
Soccer: Jim Cella; Phone: 218-299-3194; E-mail: cella@cord.edu.
Tennis: Bob Nick; Phone: 218-299-4438; E-mail: nick@cord.edu.
Track and Field: Garrick Larson; Phone: 218-299-4304; E-mail: gzlarson@cord.edu.
Wrestling: Doug Perry; Phone: 218-299-4436; E-mail: perry@cord.edu.

WOMEN'S COACHES

Basketball: Bob Kohler; Phone: 218-299-4439; E-mail: kohler@cord.edu.
Cross Country: Marv Roeske; Phone: 218-299-4163; E-mail: roeske@cord.edu.
Diving: Patrick Anderson; Phone: 218-299-4468.
Golf: Duane Siverson; Phone: 218-299-4160; E-mail: dsiverso@cord.edu.
Soccer: Dan Weiler; Phone: 218-299-4941; E-mail: weiler@cord.edu.
Softball: Steve Baumgartner; Phone: 218-299-4166; E-mail: baumgart@cord.edu.
Swimming: Julie Lucier; Phone: 218-299-4468; E-mail: jlucier@cord.edu.
Tennis: Bob Nick; Phone: 218-299-4438; E-mail: nick@cord.edu.
Track and Field: Marv Roeske; Phone: 218-299-4163; E-mail: roeske@cord.edu.
Volleyball: Tim Mosser; Phone: 218-299-3520; E-mail: mosser@cord.edu.

CONCORDIA COLLEGE
Bronxville, New York

Clippers ◆ NCAA II ◆ New York Collegiate Athletic Conference ◆ http://www.concordia-ny.edu/

Independent Lutheran 4-year, founded 1881, part of Concordia University System
Coed, 666 undergraduate students, 87% full-time, 60% women, 40% men
Suburban 33-acre campus with easy access to New York City
Moderately difficult entrance level, 69% of applicants were admitted

Freshmen *Admission:* 658 applied, 485 were accepted, 137 enrolled. *Test scores:* SAT verbal scores over 500: 39%; SAT math scores over 500: 39%; SAT verbal scores over 600: 9%; SAT math scores over 600: 8%; SAT verbal scores over 700: 1%; SAT math scores over 700: 1%.
Tuition and fees (2004–05): $18,700 (full-time). *Room and board:* $7600.
Athletic Department: *Director of Athletics:* Ivan Marquez; Phone: 914-337-9300; Fax: 914-395-4515; E-mail: ism@concordia-ny.edu. *Sports Information Director:* Kris Zeiter; Phone: 914-337-9300; E-mail: kmz@concordia-ny.edu.

MEN'S COACHES
Baseball: Bob Greiner; Phone: 914-337-9300; E-mail: rlg@concordia-ny.edu.
Basketball: John Dwinell; Phone: 914-337-9300; E-mail: jsd@concordia-ny.edu.
Cross Country: Mike Cavanaugh; Phone: 914-337-9300.
Soccer: Laurence Pitturo; Phone: 914-337-9300.
Tennis: Neil Tarangioli; Phone: 914-337-9300; E-mail: njt@concordia-ny.edu.

WOMEN'S COACHES
Basketball: Monge Codio; Phone: 914-337-9300; E-mail: codio5210@aol.com.
Cross Country: Mike Cavanaugh; Phone: 914-337-9300.
Soccer: Alex Sanchez; Phone: 914-337-9300.
Softball: Kathy Laoutaris; Phone: 914-337-9300; E-mail: kml@concordia-ny.edu.
Tennis: Kela Simunyola; Phone: 914-337-9300; E-mail: tms@concordia-ny.edu.
Volleyball: Kris Zeiter; Phone: 914-337-9300; E-mail: kmz@concordia-ny.edu.

CONCORDIA UNIVERSITY
Irvine, California

Eagles ◆ NAIA ◆ Golden State Conference ◆ http://www.cui.edu/

Independent religious comprehensive, founded 1972, affiliated with Lutheran Church–Missouri Synod, part of The Ten-campus Concordia University System
Coed, 1,337 undergraduate students, 92% full-time, 65% women, 35% men
Suburban 70-acre campus with easy access to Los Angeles
Moderately difficult entrance level, 33% of applicants were admitted

Freshmen *Admission:* 986 applied, 270 were accepted, 261 enrolled. *Test scores:* SAT verbal scores over 500: 66%; SAT math scores over 500: 68%; SAT verbal scores over 600: 23%; SAT math scores over 600: 22%; SAT verbal scores over 700: 3%; SAT math scores over 700: 3%.
Tuition and fees (2004–05): $18,800 (full-time). *Room and board:* $6670 (room only: $4000).
Financial Aid (All incoming freshmen): *Average need-based gift aid:* $6974. *Average non-need based aid:* $6147. *Average aid to full-time undergraduates:* $14,511.
Athletic Department: *Director of Athletics:* Jody Wise; Phone: 949-854-8002; Fax: 949-854-6771. *Sports Information Director:* Nick Askew; Phone: 949-854-8002.

MEN'S COACHES
Baseball: Jackie Schniepp; Phone: 949-854-8002.
Basketball: Phone: 949-854-8002.
Cross Country: Martin Gonzalez; Phone: 949-854-8002.

Soccer: Don Ebert; Phone: 949-854-8002.
Track and Field: Martin Gonzalez; Phone: 949-854-8002.

WOMEN'S COACHES
Basketball: Greg Dinneen; Phone: 949-854-8002.
Cross Country: Martin Gonzalez; Phone: 949-854-8002.
Soccer: Don Ebert; Phone: 949-854-8002.
Softball: Frank Rizzo; Phone: 949-854-8002.
Track and Field: Martin Gonzalez; Phone: 949-854-8002.
Volleyball: Jennifer Kelly; Phone: 949-854-8002.

CONCORDIA UNIVERSITY
River Forest, Illinois

Cougars ◆ NCAA III ◆ Illini-Badger Football Conference; Northern Illinois-Iowa Conference ◆ http://www.curf.edu/

Independent religious comprehensive, founded 1864, affiliated with Lutheran Church–Missouri Synod, part of Concordia University System
Coed, 1,203 undergraduate students, 83% full-time, 63% women, 37% men
Suburban 40-acre campus with easy access to Chicago
Moderately difficult entrance level, 21% of applicants were admitted

Freshmen *Admission:* 1,094 applied, 228 were accepted, 227 enrolled.
Tuition and fees (2003–04): $18,200 (full-time). *Room and board:* $5400.
Financial Aid (All incoming freshmen): *Average need-based gift aid:* $5563. *Average non-need based aid:* $6783. *Average aid to full-time undergraduates:* $11,205.
Athletic Department: *Director of Athletics:* Brian Miller; Phone: 708-209-3117; Fax: 708-209-3154; E-mail: crfmillerbj@curf.edu. *Sports Information Director:* Jim Egan; Phone: 708-209-3541; E-mail: crfeganjj@curf.edu.

MEN'S COACHES
Baseball: Spiro Lempesis; Phone: 708-209-3125; E-mail: crflempess@curf.edu.
Basketball: Brian Miller; Phone: 708-209-3117; E-mail: crfmillerbj@curf.edu.
Cheerleading: Lauren Wellen; Phone: 708-209-3151; E-mail: crfwellenla@curf.edu.
Cross Country: David Risch; Phone: 708-209-3649; E-mail: crfrischda@curf.edu.
Football: Jeff Hynes; Phone: 708-209-3332; E-mail: crfhynesj@curf.edu.
Soccer: George Mihalopoulos; Phone: 708-209-3569; E-mail: crfmihalog@curf.edu.
Tennis: Jill Beilke; Phone: 708-209-3124; E-mail: crfbeilkeja@curf.edu.
Track and Field: David Risch; Phone: 708-209-3649; E-mail: crfrischda@curf.edu.

WOMEN'S COACHES
Basketball: Tamlyn Tills; Phone: 708-209-3106; E-mail: crftillstg@curf.edu.
Cheerleading: Lauren Wellen; Phone: 708-209-3151; E-mail: crfwellenla@curf.edu.
Cross Country: David Risch; Phone: 708-209-3649; E-mail: crfrischda@curf.edu.
Soccer: George Mihalopoulos; Phone: 708-209-3569; E-mail: crfmihalog@curf.edu.
Softball: Kathy Gebhardt; Phone: 708-209-3008; E-mail: crfgebharkk@curf.edu.
Tennis: Jill Beilke; Phone: 708-209-3124; E-mail: crfbeilkeja@curf.edu.
Track and Field: David Risch; Phone: 708-209-3649; E-mail: crfrischda@curf.edu.
Volleyball: Kathy Gebhardt; Phone: 708-209-3008; E-mail: crfgebharkk@curf.edu.

CONCORDIA UNIVERSITY
Ann Arbor, Michigan

Cardinals ◆ NAIA ◆ Wolverine-Hoosier Conference ◆ http://www.cuaa.edu/

Independent religious comprehensive, founded 1963, affiliated with Lutheran Church–Missouri Synod, part of Concordia University System
Coed, 438 undergraduate students, 86% full-time, 57% women, 43% men
Suburban 234-acre campus with easy access to Detroit
Moderately difficult entrance level, 74% of applicants were admitted

Freshmen *Admission:* 320 applied, 241 were accepted, 72 enrolled. *Test scores:* SAT verbal scores over 500: 100%; SAT math scores over 500: 33%; SAT verbal scores over 600: 33%.
Tuition and fees (2003–04): $17,250 (full-time). *Room and board:* $6745.
Financial Aid (All incoming freshmen): *Average need-based gift aid:* $9768. *Average non-need based aid:* $7755. *Average aid to full-time undergraduates:* $14,900.
Athletic Department: *Director of Athletics:* Karl Kling; Phone: 734-995-7343; Fax: 734-995-4883; E-mail: klingk@cuaa.edu. *Sports Information Director:* Tony Baldwin; Phone: 734-995-7344; E-mail: baldwa@cuaa.edu.

MEN'S COACHES
Baseball: Karl Kling; Phone: 734-995-7343; E-mail: klingk@cuaa.edu.
Basketball: Ben Limback; Phone: 734-995-7436; E-mail: limbab@cuaa.edu.
Soccer: Piotr Westwalewicz; Phone: 734-995-4607; E-mail: westp@cuaa.edu.

WOMEN'S COACHES
Basketball: Greg Rehberg; Phone: 734-995-7443; E-mail: rehbeg@cuaa.edu.
Soccer: Piotr Westwalewicz; Phone: 734-995-4607; E-mail: westp@cuaa.edu.
Softball: Jennifer Teague; Phone: 734-995-7345; E-mail: teaguj@cuaa.edu.
Volleyball: Irick Gardner; Phone: 734-995-4607; E-mail: gardni@cuaa.edu.

CONCORDIA UNIVERSITY
Seward, Nebraska

Bulldogs ◆ NAIA ◆ Great Plains Conference ◆ http://www.cune.edu/

Independent religious comprehensive, founded 1894, affiliated with Lutheran Church–Missouri Synod, part of Concordia University System
Coed, 1,202 undergraduate students, 93% full-time, 57% women, 43% men
Small-town 120-acre campus with easy access to Omaha
Moderately difficult entrance level, 86% of applicants were admitted

Freshmen *Admission:* 728 applied, 646 were accepted, 222 enrolled. *Test scores:* SAT verbal scores over 500: 72%; SAT math scores over 500: 64%; SAT verbal scores over 600: 24%; SAT math scores over 600: 31%; SAT verbal scores over 700: 10%; SAT math scores over 700: 10%.
Tuition and fees (2003–04): $16,000 (full-time). *Room and board:* $4480 (room only: $1980).
Financial Aid (All incoming freshmen): *Average need-based gift aid:* $3963. *Average non-need based aid:* $5652. *Average aid to full-time undergraduates:* $14,550.
Athletic Department: *Director of Athletics:* Grant Schmidt; Phone: 402-643-7328; Fax: 402-643-3966; E-mail: gschmidt@seward.cune.edu. *Sports Information Director:* Lowell Erickson; Phone: 402-643-7392; E-mail: lerickson@seward.cune.edu.

MEN'S COACHES
Baseball: Jeremy Geidel; Phone: 402-643-7328; E-mail: jgeidel@seward.cune.edu.
Basketball: Grant Schmidt; Phone: 402-643-7328; E-mail: gschmidt@seward.cune.edu.

Cross Country: Kregg Einspahr; Phone: 402-643-7328; E-mail: keinspahr@seward.cune.edu.
Football: Courtney Meyer; Phone: 402-643-7328; E-mail: cmeyer@seward.cune.edu.
Golf: Carl Everts; Phone: 402-643-7328; E-mail: ceverts@seward.cune.edu.
Soccer: William Schranz; Phone: 402-643-7328; E-mail: wschranz@seward.cune.edu.
Tennis: Mark Lemke; Phone: 402-643-7206; E-mail: mlemke@seward.cune.edu.
Track and Field: Kregg Einspahr; Phone: 402-643-7328; E-mail: keinspahr@seward.cune.edu.

WOMEN'S COACHES
Basketball: Todd Voss; Phone: 402-643-7328; E-mail: tvoss@seward.cune.edu.
Cross Country: Kregg Einspahr; Phone: 402-643-7328; E-mail: keinspahr@seward.cune.edu.
Golf: Carl Everts; Phone: 402-643-7328; E-mail: ceverts@seward.cune.edu.
Soccer: William Schranz; Phone: 402-643-7328; E-mail: wschranz@seward.cune.edu.
Softball: Frank Greene; Phone: 402-643-7430; E-mail: fgreene@seward.cune.edu.
Tennis: Mark Lemke; Phone: 402-643-7206; E-mail: mlemke@seward.cune.edu.
Track and Field: Kregg Einspahr; Phone: 402-643-7328; E-mail: keinspahr@seward.cune.edu.
Volleyball: Randy Krieger; Phone: 402-643-7328; E-mail: rkrieger@seward.cune.edu.

CONCORDIA UNIVERSITY
Portland, Oregon

Cavaliers ◆ NAIA ◆ Cascade Collegiate Conference ◆ http://www.cu-portland.edu/

Independent religious comprehensive, founded 1905, affiliated with Lutheran Church–Missouri Synod, part of Concordia University System
Coed, 905 undergraduate students, 82% full-time, 62% women, 38% men
Urban 13-acre campus
Moderately difficult entrance level, 71% of applicants were admitted

Freshmen *Admission:* 631 applied, 452 were accepted, 128 enrolled. *Test scores:* SAT verbal scores over 500: 59%; SAT math scores over 500: 57%; SAT verbal scores over 600: 14%; SAT math scores over 600: 16%; SAT verbal scores over 700: 3%; SAT math scores over 700: %.
Tuition and fees (2003–04): $17,490 (full-time). *Room and board:* $5050.
Financial Aid (All incoming freshmen): *Average need-based gift aid:* $9500. *Average non-need based aid:* $5000. *Average aid to full-time undergraduates:* $12,000.
Athletic Department: *Director of Athletics:* Joel Schuldheisz; Phone: 503-280-8516; Fax: 503-280-8591; E-mail: jschuldheisz@cu-portland.edu. *Sports Information Director:* Grant Landy; Phone: 503-280-8141; E-mail: glandy@cu-portland.edu.

MEN'S COACHES
Baseball: Rob Vance; Phone: 503-280-8691; E-mail: rvance@cu-portland.edu.
Basketball: Brad Barbarick; Phone: 503-280-8598; E-mail: bbarbarick@cu-portland.edu.
Golf: Thomas Meier; Phone: 503-280-8678; E-mail: tmeier@cu-portland.edu.
Soccer: Dan Birkey; Phone: 503-280-8551; E-mail: dbirkey@cu-portland.edu.

WOMEN'S COACHES
Basketball: Jeffrey Stanek; Phone: 503-280-8547; E-mail: jstanek@cu-portland.edu.
Golf: Thomas Meier; Phone: 503-280-8678; E-mail: tmeier@cu-portland.edu.
Soccer: Grant Landy; Phone: 503-280-8141; E-mail: glandy@cu-portland.edu.
Softball: Carrie Kosderka-Farrell; Phone: 503-280-8616; E-mail: ckosderka@cu-portland.edu.
Volleyball: Christopher Duenow; Phone: 503-280-8689; E-mail: cduenow@cu-portland.edu.

CONCORDIA UNIVERSITY AT AUSTIN

Austin, Texas

Tornados ◆ NCAA III ◆ American Southwest Conference ◆ http://www.concordia.edu/

Independent religious comprehensive, founded 1926, affiliated with Lutheran Church–Missouri Synod, part of Concordia University System
Coed, 1,031 undergraduate students, 69% full-time, 56% women, 44% men
Urban 20-acre campus with easy access to San Antonio
Moderately difficult entrance level, 76% of applicants were admitted

Freshmen *Admission:* 523 applied, 396 were accepted, 170 enrolled. *Test scores:* SAT verbal scores over 500: 47%; SAT math scores over 500: 53%; SAT verbal scores over 600: 7%; SAT math scores over 600: 14%; SAT verbal scores over 700: 1%; SAT math scores over 700: 2%.
Tuition and fees (2003–04): $14,410 (full-time). *Room and board:* $6150 (room only: $3590).
Financial Aid (All incoming freshmen): *Average need-based gift aid:* $11,343. *Average non-need based aid:* $6376. *Average aid to full-time undergraduates:* $12,476.
Athletic Department: *Director of Athletics:* Linda Lowery; Phone: 512-486-1162; Fax: 512-302-4365; E-mail: linda.lowery@concordia.edu. *Sports Information Director:* Jeanette McKinney; Phone: 512-486-1165; E-mail: jeanette.lowery@concordia.edu.

MEN'S COACHES
Baseball: Mike Gardner; Phone: 512-486-1160; E-mail: jeffrey.meyer@concordia.edu.
Basketball: Jim Jost; Phone: 512-486-1161; E-mail: jim.jost@concordia.edu.
Cross Country: Alex Aldaco; Phone: 512-486-1266; E-mail: alex.aldaco@concordia.edu.
Golf: Linda Lowery; Phone: 512-486-1162; E-mail: linda.lowery@concordia.edu.
Soccer: Paul Muller; Phone: 512-486-1263; E-mail: paul.muller@concordia.edu.
Tennis: Lincoln Ward; Phone: 512-486-1275; E-mail: lincoln.ward@concordia.edu.

WOMEN'S COACHES
Basketball: Linda Sharp; Phone: 512-486-1163; E-mail: linda.sharp@concordia.edu.
Cross Country: Alex Aldaco; Phone: 512-486-1266; E-mail: alex.aldaco@concordia.edu.
Golf: Linda Lowery; Phone: 512-486-1162; E-mail: linda.lowery@concordia.edu.
Softball: Craig Potts; Phone: 512-486-1264; E-mail: craig.potts@concordia.edu.
Tennis: Lincoln Ward; Phone: 512-486-1275; E-mail: lincoln.ward@concordia.edu.
Volleyball: Latonya Whybrew; Phone: 512-486-1265; E-mail: latonya.whybrew@concordia.edu.

CONCORDIA UNIVERSITY, ST. PAUL

St. Paul, Minnesota

Golden Bears ◆ NCAA II ◆ Northern Sun Intercollegiate Conference ◆ http://www.csp.edu/

Independent religious comprehensive, founded 1893, affiliated with Lutheran Church–Missouri Synod, part of Concordia University System
Coed, 1,741 undergraduate students, 86% full-time, 59% women, 41% men
Urban 37-acre campus
Minimally difficult entrance level, 63% of applicants were admitted

Freshmen *Admission:* 728 applied, 465 were accepted, 167 enrolled. *Test scores:* SAT verbal scores over 500: 63%; SAT math scores over 500: 63%; SAT verbal scores over 600: 27%; SAT math scores over 600: 27%; SAT verbal scores over 700: 9%; SAT math scores over 700: 9%.
Tuition and fees (2004–05): $19,928 (full-time). *Room and board:* $6156.
Financial Aid (All incoming freshmen): *Average need-based gift aid:* $10,627. *Average non-need based aid:* $6097. *Average aid to full-time undergraduates:* $14,775.
Athletic Department: *Director of Athletics:* David Herbster; Phone: 651-641-8700; Fax: 651-641-8787; E-mail: herbster@csp.edu. *Sports Information Director:* Jen Foley; Phone: 651-641-8893; E-mail: foley@csp.edu.

MEN'S COACHES
Baseball: Mark McKenzie; Phone: 651-603-6208; E-mail: mckenzie@csp.edu.
Basketball: Ryan Freeberg; Phone: 651-603-6250; E-mail: freeberg@csp.edu.
Cross Country: Jonathan Breithbarth; Phone: 651-641-8796; E-mail: breitbarth@csp.edu.
Football: Shannon Currier; Phone: 651-603-6181; E-mail: currier@csp.edu.
Track and Field: Mark McConeghey; Phone: 651-641-8784; E-mail: mcconeghey@csp.edu.

WOMEN'S COACHES
Basketball: Paul Fessler; Phone: 651-603-6167; E-mail: fessler@csp.edu.
Cross Country: Jonathan Breithbarth; Phone: 651-641-8796; E-mail: breitbarth@csp.edu.
Soccer: Scott Zachmann; Phone: 651-641-8726; E-mail: zachmann@csp.edu.
Softball: Tom Rubbelke; Phone: 651-641-8886; E-mail: rubbelke@csp.edu.
Track and Field: Mark McConeghey; Phone: 651-641-8784; E-mail: mcconeghey@csp.edu.
Volleyball: Brady Starkey; Phone: 651-641-6173; E-mail: starkey@csp.edu.

CONCORDIA UNIVERSITY WISCONSIN

Mequon, Wisconsin

Falcons ◆ NCAA III ◆ Illini-Badger Football Conference; Lake Michigan Conference ◆ http://www.cuw.edu/

Independent religious comprehensive, founded 1881, affiliated with Lutheran Church–Missouri Synod
Coed, 3,990 undergraduate students, 54% full-time, 63% women, 37% men
Suburban 155-acre campus with easy access to Milwaukee
Moderately difficult entrance level, 76% of applicants were admitted

Freshmen *Admission:* 1,276 applied, 1,024 were accepted, 362 enrolled.
Tuition and fees (2003–04): $15,575 (full-time). *Room and board:* $5790.
Financial Aid (All incoming freshmen): *Average need-based gift aid:* $11,000. *Average non-need based aid:* $4000. *Average aid to full-time undergraduates:* $15,000.
Athletic Department: *Director of Athletics:* Rob Barnhill; Phone: 262-243-4404; Fax: 262-243-4475; E-mail: rob.barnhill@cuw.edu. *Sports Information Director:* Rick Riehl; Phone: 262-243-4544; E-mail: rick.riehl@cuw.edu.

MEN'S COACHES
Baseball: Val Keiper; Phone: 262-243-4266; E-mail: val.keiper@cuw.edu.
Basketball: Pete Gnan; Phone: 262-243-4381.
Cheerleading: Stephanie Barnhill; Phone: 262-243-4570; E-mail: stephanie.barnhill@cuw.edu.
Cross Country: Paul Paynter; Phone: 262-243-4484; E-mail: paul.paynter@cuw.edu.
Football: Jeff Gabrielson; Phone: 262-243-4224; E-mail: jeff.gabrielsen@cuw.edu.
Golf: Cary Stelmachowicz; Phone: 262-243-4210; E-mail: cary.stelmachowicz@cuw.edu.
Soccer: Tom Saleska; Phone: 262-243-4258; E-mail: tom.saleska@cuw.edu.
Tennis: Tom Weber; Phone: 262-243-4467; E-mail: thomas.weber@cuw.edu.

Concordia University Wisconsin *(continued)*

Track and Field: Paul Paynter; Phone: 262-243-4484; E-mail: paul.paynter@cuw.edu.
Wrestling: Bret Corner; Phone: 262-243-4486; E-mail: bret.corner@cuw.edu.

WOMEN'S COACHES

Basketball: Chuck Oliver; Phone: 262-243-4525; E-mail: chuck.oliver@cuw.edu.
Cheerleading: Stephanie Barnhill; Phone: 262-243-4570; E-mail: stephanie.barnhill@cuw.edu.
Cross Country: Paul Paynter; Phone: 262-243-4484; E-mail: paul.paynter@cuw.edu.
Golf: Ken Gaschk; Phone: 262-243-4305.
Soccer: Ryan Middendorf; Phone: 262-243-4385.
Softball: Steve Crook; Phone: 262-243-4419; E-mail: steve.crook@cuw.edu.
Tennis: Crystal Welter; Phone: 262-243-4385.
Track and Field: Paul Paynter; Phone: 262-243-4484; E-mail: paul.paynter@cuw.edu.
Volleyball: Joseph Cawley; Phone: 262-243-4559.

CONNECTICUT COLLEGE
New London, Connecticut

Camels ◆ NCAA III ◆ New England Small College Conference ◆ http://www.connecticutcollege.edu/

Independent comprehensive, founded 1911
Coed, 1,837 undergraduate students, 95% full-time, 59% women, 41% men
Suburban 702-acre campus
Very difficult entrance level, 4% of applicants were admitted

Freshmen *Admission:* 4,396 applied, 1,536 were accepted, 511 enrolled. *Test scores:* SAT verbal scores over 500: 98%; SAT math scores over 500: 99%; SAT verbal scores over 600: 83%; SAT math scores over 600: 84%; SAT verbal scores over 700: 20%; SAT math scores over 700: 17%.
Tuition and fees (2004–05): Comprehensive fee (includes tuition, fees, and room and board): $37,900.
Financial Aid (All incoming freshmen): *Average need-based gift aid:* $21,077. *Average aid to full-time undergraduates:* $22,748.
Athletic Department: *Director of Athletics:* Fran Shields; Phone: 860-439-2570; Fax: 860-439-2516; E-mail: fjshi@conncoll.edu. *Sports Information Director:* Will Tomasian; Phone: 860-439-2501; E-mail: wgtom@conncoll.edu.

MEN'S COACHES

Basketball: Tom Satran; Phone: 860-439-2565; E-mail: tsat@conncoll.edu.
Cross Country: Jim Butler; Phone: 860-439-5445; E-mail: jsbut@conncoll.edu.
Diving: Nora Kelly; Phone: 860-439-2507; E-mail: njkel@conncoll.edu.
Ice Hockey: Jim Ward; Phone: 860-439-5237; E-mail: jbwar2@conncoll.edu.
Lacrosse: Dave Campbell; Phone: 860-439-2564; E-mail: djcam@conncoll.edu.
Soccer: Bill Lessig; Phone: 860-439-2554; E-mail: wrles@conncoll.edu.
Swimming: Marc Benvenuti; Phone: 860-439-2507; E-mail: mdben2@conncoll.edu.
Tennis: Paul Huch; Phone: 860-439-2568; E-mail: mdben2@conncoll.edu.
Track and Field: William Wuyke; Phone: 860-439-2555; E-mail: wcwuy@conncoll.edu.

WOMEN'S COACHES

Basketball: Laura Hungerford; Phone: 860-439-2781; E-mail: lehun@conncoll.edu.
Cross Country: Ned Bishop; Phone: 860-439-2566; E-mail: nbis@conncoll.edu.
Diving: Nora Kelly; Phone: 860-439-2507; E-mail: njkel@conncoll.edu.
Field Hockey: Debbie Lavigne; Phone: 860-439-2876; E-mail: dblav@conncoll.edu.
Lacrosse: Anne Crosby; Phone: 860-439-2563; E-mail: amcro2@conncoll.edu.
Soccer: Ken Kline; Phone: 860-439-2567; E-mail: kakli@conncoll.edu.

Swimming: Marc Benvenuti; Phone: 860-439-2507; E-mail: mdben2@conncoll.edu.
Tennis: Paul Huch; Phone: 860-439-2568; E-mail: mdben2@conncoll.edu.
Track and Field: William Wuyke; Phone: 860-439-2555; E-mail: wcwuy@conncoll.edu.
Volleyball: Joshua Edmed; Phone: 860-439-2704; E-mail: jaedm@conncoll.edu.

CONVERSE COLLEGE
Spartanburg, South Carolina

All Stars ◆ NCAA II ◆ Independent
◆ http://www.converse.edu/

Independent comprehensive, founded 1889
Women only, 701 undergraduate students, 84% full-time, 100% women, 100% men
Urban 70-acre campus
Moderately difficult entrance level, 69% of applicants were admitted

Freshmen *Admission:* 508 applied, 349 were accepted, 179 enrolled. *Test scores:* SAT verbal scores over 500: 80%; SAT math scores over 500: 72%; SAT verbal scores over 600: 32%; SAT math scores over 600: 27%; SAT verbal scores over 700: 6%; SAT math scores over 700: 4%.
Tuition and fees (2003–04): $18,915 (full-time). *Room and board:* $5795.
Financial Aid (All incoming freshmen): *Average need-based gift aid:* $15,866. *Average non-need based aid:* $17,061. *Average aid to full-time undergraduates:* $18,039.
Athletic Department: *Director of Athletics:* Margaret Moore; Phone: 864-577-2057; Fax: 864-577-2054; E-mail: margaret.moore@converse.edu. *Sports Information Director:* Tatum Clowney; Phone: 864-577-2062; E-mail: tatum.clowney@converse.edu.

WOMEN'S COACHES

Basketball: Beth Coil; Phone: 864-577-2055; E-mail: coordinatorbeth.coil@converse.edu.
Cheerleading: Nikeshia Jackson; Phone: 864-577-2050; E-mail: nikeshia.jackson@converse.edu.
Cross Country: Robin Tarpinian; Phone: 864-577-2050; E-mail: robin.tarpinian@converse.edu.
Soccer: Shannon Rossley; Phone: 864-577-2062; E-mail: shannon.rossley@converse.edu.
Tennis: Jeffrey Batkin; Phone: 864-577-2050; E-mail: jeffery.batkin@converse.edu.
Volleyball: Tara Brooks; Phone: 864-577-2061; E-mail: tara.brooks@converse.edu.

COPPIN STATE UNIVERSITY
Baltimore, Maryland

Eagles ◆ NCAA I ◆ Mid-Eastern Athletic Conference ◆ http://www.coppin.edu/

State-supported comprehensive, founded 1900, part of University System of Maryland
Coed, 3,092 undergraduate students
Urban 33-acre campus
Moderately difficult entrance level, 47% of applicants were admitted

Freshmen *Admission:* 2,270 applied, 1,078 were accepted.
Tuition and fees (2003–04): $4384 (resident), $10,206 (nonresident). *Room and board:* $5952 (room only: $3694).
Financial Aid (All incoming freshmen): *Average need-based gift aid:* $4188. *Average non-need based aid:* $4510. *Average aid to full-time undergraduates:* $6130.
Athletic Department: *Director of Athletics:* Ron Mitchell; Phone: 410-951-3723; Fax: 410-951-3717; E-mail: rmitchell@coppin.edu. *Sports Information Director:* Kevin Paige; Phone: 410-951-3744; E-mail: kpaige@coppin.edu.

MEN'S COACHES

Baseball: Guy Robertson; Phone: 410-951-3740; E-mail: grobertson@coppin.edu.

Basketball: Ron Mitchell; Phone: 410-383-3723; E-mail: rmitchell@coppin.edu.
Cheerleading: Monique Lemar; Phone: 410-951-3737.
Cross Country: Carl Hicks; Phone: 410-951-3722; E-mail: chicks@coppin.edu.
Tennis: Brendon Travis; Phone: 410-951-3743; E-mail: btravis@coppin.edu.
Track and Field: Carl Hicks; Phone: 410-383-5695; E-mail: chicks@coppin.edu.

WOMEN'S COACHES
Basketball: Derek Brown; Phone: 410-951-3733; E-mail: dbrown@coppin.edu.
Cheerleading: Monique Lemar; Phone: 410-951-3737.
Cross Country: Patrick Bailey; Phone: 410-951-3732; E-mail: pbailey@coppin.edu.
Softball: Marcie Hickey; Phone: 410-951-3721; E-mail: mhickey@coppin.edu.
Tennis: Brendon Travis; Phone: 410-951-3743; E-mail: btravis@coppin.edu.
Track and Field: Patrick Bailey; Phone: 410-951-6399; E-mail: pbailey@coppin.edu.
Volleyball: China Jude; Phone: 410-951-3724; E-mail: cjude@coppin.edu.

CORNELL COLLEGE
Mount Vernon, Iowa
Rams ◆ NCAA III ◆ Iowa Athletic Conference ◆ http://www.cornellcollege.edu/

Independent Methodist 4-year, founded 1853
Coed, 1,117 undergraduate students, 99% full-time, 59% women, 41% men
Small-town 129-acre campus
Moderately difficult entrance level, 65% of applicants were admitted

Freshmen Admission: 1,555 applied, 1,067 were accepted, 367 enrolled. Test scores: SAT verbal scores over 500: 94%; SAT math scores over 500: 91%; SAT verbal scores over 600: 59%; SAT math scores over 600: 54%; SAT verbal scores over 700: 17%; SAT math scores over 700: 16%.
Tuition and fees (2003–04): $21,790 (full-time). Room and board: $6035 (room only: $2825).
Financial Aid (All incoming freshmen): Average need-based gift aid: $17,235. Average non-need based aid: $13,796. Average aid to full-time undergraduates: $21,330.
Athletic Department: Director of Athletics: Tina Hill; Phone: 319-895-4257; Fax: 319-895-5895; E-mail: thill@cornellcollege.edu. Sports Information Director: Darren Miller; Phone: 319-895-4483; E-mail: sid@cornellcollege.edu.

MEN'S COACHES
Baseball: Frank Fishler; Phone: 319-895-4117; E-mail: ffishler@mid-land.k12.ia.us.
Basketball: Ed Timm; Phone: 319-895-4268; E-mail: etimm@cornellcollege.edu.
Cheerleading: Krystal Wright; Phone: 319-895-4257; E-mail: kwright@cornellcollege.edu.
Cross Country: Lonnie Speidel; Phone: 319-895-4398; E-mail: lspeidel@cornellcollege.edu.
Football: Ray Reasland; Phone: 319-895-4230; E-mail: rreasland@cornellcollege.edu.
Golf: Jim Dickerson; Phone: 319-895-4448; E-mail: lyra-jim@soli.inav.net.
Soccer: Curt Lewis; Phone: 319-895-4257; E-mail: curtsoccer@hotmail.com.
Tennis: Rusty Graff; Phone: 319-895-4257; E-mail: rgraff@cornellcollege.edu.
Track and Field: Lonnie Speidel; Phone: 319-895-4257; E-mail: lspeidel@cornellcollege.edu.
Wrestling: Drew Pariano; Phone: 319-895-4338; E-mail: dpariano@cornellcollege.edu.

WOMEN'S COACHES
Basketball: Nicole Kotrba; Phone: 319-895-4265; E-mail: nkotrba@cornellcollege.edu.
Cheerleading: Krystal Wright; Phone: 319-895-4257; E-mail: kwright@cornellcollege.edu.

Cross Country: Lonnie Speidel; Phone: 319-895-4398; E-mail: lspeidel@cornellcollege.edu.
Golf: Jim Dickerson; Phone: 319-895-4448; E-mail: lyra-jim@soli.inav.net.
Soccer: Steve Robertson; Phone: 319-895-4150; E-mail: srobertson@cornellcollege.edu.
Softball: Lori Moss; Phone: 319-895-4257; E-mail: lmoss@cornellcollege.edu.
Track and Field: Lonnie Speidel; Phone: 319-895-4398; E-mail: lspeidel@cornellcollege.edu.
Volleyball: Jeff Meeker; Phone: 319-895-4398; E-mail: jmeeker@cornellcollege.edu.

CORNELL UNIVERSITY
Ithaca, New York
Big Red ◆ NCAA I ◆ Ivy League Conference ◆ http://www.cornell.edu/

Independent university, founded 1865
Coed, 13,655 undergraduate students, 100% full-time, 50% women, 50% men
Small-town 745-acre campus with easy access to Syracuse
Most difficult entrance level, 31% of applicants were admitted

Freshmen Admission: 20,441 applied, 6,334 were accepted, 3,135 enrolled. Test scores: SAT verbal scores over 500: 98%; SAT math scores over 500: 98%; SAT verbal scores over 600: 85%; SAT math scores over 600: 91%; SAT verbal scores over 700: 37%; SAT math scores over 700: 58%.
Tuition and fees (2003–04): $28,754 (full-time). Room and board: $9580 (room only: $5675).
Financial Aid (All incoming freshmen): Average need-based gift aid: $19,100. Average aid to full-time undergraduates: $24,800.
Athletic Department: Director of Athletics: Andy Noel; Phone: 607-255-8832; Fax: 607-255-9791; E-mail: jan16@cornell.edu. Sports Information Director: Laura Strange; Phone: 607-255-5627; E-mail: lls15@cornell.edu.

MEN'S COACHES
Baseball: Tom Ford; Phone: 607-255-6604; E-mail: twf2@cornell.edu.
Basketball: Steve Donahue; Phone: 607-255-1316; E-mail: scd25@cornell.edu.
Cross Country: Nathan Taylor; Phone: 607-255-7494; E-mail: rnt2@cornell.edu.
Diving: Joe Lucia; Phone: 607-255-7255; E-mail: jjl15@cornell.edu.
Football: Jim Knowles; Phone: 607-255-4391.
Golf: Matt Baughan; Phone: 607-257-3661; E-mail: jmb72@cornell.edu.
Ice Hockey: Mike Schafer; Phone: 607-255-6674; E-mail: mcs14@cornell.edu.
Lacrosse: Jeff Tambroni; Phone: 607-255-4718; E-mail: jjt11@cornell.edu.
Soccer: Bryan Scales; Phone: 607-255-1312; E-mail: bs38@cornell.edu.
Swimming: Joe Lucia; Phone: 607-255-7255; E-mail: jjl15@cornell.edu.
Tennis: Barry Schoonmaker; Phone: 607-255-0082; E-mail: bs40@cornell.edu.
Track and Field: Nathan Taylor; Phone: 607-255-7494; E-mail: rnt2@cornell.edu.
Wrestling: Rob Koll; Phone: 607-255-7307; E-mail: rk45@cornell.edu.

WOMEN'S COACHES
Basketball: Dayna Smith; Phone: 607-255-3720; E-mail: dms931@cornell.edu.
Cross Country: Lou Duesing; Phone: 607-255-3475; E-mail: ld22@cornell.edu.
Diving: John Holohan; Phone: 607-255-8794; E-mail: jdh58@cornell.edu.
Field Hockey: Donna Hornibrook; Phone: 607-255-5520; E-mail: djh57@cornell.edu.
Gymnastics: Paul Beckwith; Phone: 607-255-7024; E-mail: pab12@cornell.edu.
Lacrosse: Jennifer Graap; Phone: 607-255-4979; E-mail: jlg42@cornell.edu.
Soccer: Berhane Andeberhan; Phone: 607-255-4762; E-mail: ba22@cornell.edu.
Softball: Dick Blood; Phone: 607-255-8500; E-mail: rb53@cornell.edu.

Cornell University *(continued)*

Swimming: John Holohan; Phone: 607-255-8794; E-mail: jdh58@cornell.edu.
Tennis: Tom Brownlie; Phone: 607-255-0040; E-mail: tb22@cornell.edu.
Track and Field: Lou Duesing; Phone: 607-255-3475; E-mail: ld22@cornell.edu.
Volleyball: Christie Roes; Phone: 607-255-3813; E-mail: cj32@cornell.edu.

CORNERSTONE UNIVERSITY
Grand Rapids, Michigan

Golden Eagles ◆ NAIA ◆ Wolverine-Hoosier Conference ◆ http://www.cornerstone.edu/

Independent nondenominational comprehensive, founded 1941
Coed, 2,074 undergraduate students, 76% full-time, 62% women, 38% men
Suburban 132-acre campus
Moderately difficult entrance level, 73% of applicants were admitted

Freshmen *Admission:* 1,285 applied, 973 were accepted, 359 enrolled.
Tuition and fees (2003–04): $14,420 (full-time). *Room and board:* $5426 (room only: $2476).
Financial Aid (All incoming freshmen): *Average need-based gift aid:* $7568. *Average non-need based aid:* $4180. *Average aid to full-time undergraduates:* $12,746.
Athletic Department: *Director of Athletics:* Dave Grube; Phone: 616-222-1412; Fax: 616-222-1542; E-mail: dave_grube@cornerstone.edu. *Sports Information Director:* Carla Fles; Phone: 616-222-1425; E-mail: carla_fles@cornerstone.edu.

MEN'S COACHES
Basketball: Kim Elders; Phone: 616-831-7006; E-mail: kelders@cornerstone.edu.
Cross Country: Rod Wortley; Phone: 616-831-7006; E-mail: rwortley@cornerstone.edu.
Golf: Steve Thomas; Phone: 616-222-1425; E-mail: sthomas@gazellesports.com.
Soccer: Mark Bell; Phone: 616-831-7006; E-mail: mbell@cornerstone.edu.
Track and Field: Rod Wortley; Phone: 616-831-7006; E-mail: rwortley@cornerstone.edu.

WOMEN'S COACHES
Basketball: Carla Fles; Phone: 616-831-7006; E-mail: carla_a_sterk@cornerstone.edu.
Cross Country: Rod Wortley; Phone: 616-831-7006; E-mail: rwortley@cornerstone.edu.
Soccer: Randy Strawer; Phone: 616-222-1413; E-mail: randy_strawser@cornerstone.edu.
Softball: Kim Zainea; Phone: 616-831-7006; E-mail: kfordyce@cornerstone.edu.
Track and Field: Rod Wortley; Phone: 616-831-7006; E-mail: rwortley@cornerstone.edu.
Volleyball: Steve Burmaster; Phone: 616-831-7006; E-mail: steve_burmaster@cornerstone.edu.

COVENANT COLLEGE
Lookout Mountain, Georgia

Scots ◆ NAIA ◆ Appalachian Conference ◆ http://www.covenant.edu/

Independent religious comprehensive, founded 1955, affiliated with Presbyterian Church in America
Coed, 1,198 undergraduate students, 98% full-time, 59% women, 41% men
Suburban 250-acre campus
Moderately difficult entrance level, 58% of applicants were admitted

Freshmen *Admission:* 715 applied, 433 were accepted, 243 enrolled.
Test scores: SAT verbal scores over 500: 86%; SAT math scores over

500: 81%; SAT verbal scores over 600: 58%; SAT math scores over 600: 49%; SAT verbal scores over 700: 16%; SAT math scores over 700: 10%.
Tuition and fees (2003–04): $18,230 (full-time). *Room and board:* $5600.
Financial Aid (All incoming freshmen): *Average need-based gift aid:* $7396. *Average non-need based aid:* $5565. *Average aid to full-time undergraduates:* $14,597.
Athletic Department: *Director of Athletics:* Brian Crossman; Phone: 706-419-1513; Fax: 706-419-1660; E-mail: crossman@covenant.edu. *Sports Information Director:* Roy Heintz; Phone: 706-419-1514; E-mail: heintz@covenant.edu.

MEN'S COACHES
Basketball: Lance Richardson; Phone: 706-419-4516; E-mail: lrichardson@covenant.edu.
Cross Country: David Taylor; Phone: 706-419-1506; E-mail: dtaylor@covenant.edu.
Soccer: Brian Crossman; Phone: 706-419-1513; E-mail: crossman@covenant.edu.

WOMEN'S COACHES
Basketball: Roy Heintz; Phone: 706-419-1514; E-mail: heintz@covenant.edu.
Cross Country: David Taylor; Phone: 706-419-1506; E-mail: dtaylor@covenant.edu.
Soccer: Mark Duble; Phone: 706-419-1508; E-mail: mduble@covenant.edu.
Volleyball: Will Stern; Phone: 706-419-1512; E-mail: stern@covenant.edu.

CREIGHTON UNIVERSITY
Omaha, Nebraska

Bluejays ◆ NCAA I ◆ Missouri Valley Conference ◆ http://www.creighton.edu/

Independent Roman Catholic (Jesuit) university, founded 1878
Coed, 3,736 undergraduate students, 92% full-time, 61% women, 39% men
Urban 110-acre campus
Moderately difficult entrance level, 86% of applicants were admitted

Freshmen *Admission:* 3,199 applied, 2,813 were accepted, 933 enrolled.
Test scores: SAT verbal scores over 500: 86%; SAT math scores over 500: 89%; SAT verbal scores over 600: 47%; SAT math scores over 600: 52%; SAT verbal scores over 700: 10%; SAT math scores over 700: 10%.
Tuition and fees (2003–04): $19,922 (full-time). *Room and board:* $6826 (room only: $3870).
Financial Aid (All incoming freshmen): *Average need-based gift aid:* $11,404. *Average non-need based aid:* $8716. *Average aid to full-time undergraduates:* $18,136.
Athletic Department: *Director of Athletics:* Bruce Rasmussen; Phone: 402-280-2720; Fax: 402-280-5596; E-mail: bdrass@creighton.edu. *Sports Information Director:* Matthew Beltz; Phone: 402-280-5801; E-mail: mbeltz@creighton.edu.

MEN'S COACHES
Baseball: Ed Servais; Phone: 402-280-2483; E-mail: eservais@creighton.edu.
Basketball: Dana Altman; Phone: 402-280-1795.
Cheerleading: Judy Streitz; Phone: 402-280-2563; E-mail: jstreitz@creighton.edu.
Cross Country: John Wissler; Phone: 402-280-3611.
Golf: Debbie Conry; Phone: 402-280-1722; E-mail: dmcbluejaygolf@aol.com.
Soccer: Bob Warming; Phone: 402-280-5785; E-mail: warming@creighton.edu.
Tennis: Tom Lilly; Phone: 402-280-2490; E-mail: tomlilly@creighton.edu.

WOMEN'S COACHES
Basketball: Jim Flanery; Phone: 402-280-4741; E-mail: flan@creighton.edu.
Cheerleading: Judy Streitz; Phone: 402-280-2563; E-mail: jstreitz@creighton.edu.
Cross Country: John Wissler; Phone: 402-280-3611.
Golf: Debbie Conry; Phone: 402-280-1722; E-mail: dmcbluejaygolf@aol.com.

Soccer: Bruce Erickson; Phone: 402-280-5553; E-mail: erickson@creighton.edu.
Softball: Brent Vigness; Phone: 402-280-2949; E-mail: bvigness@creighton.edu.
Tennis: Tom Lilly; Phone: 402-280-2490; E-mail: tomlilly@creighton.edu.
Volleyball: Kirsten Bernthal Booth; Phone: 402-280-5794; E-mail: kbb49780@creighton.edu.

CROWN COLLEGE
St. Bonifacius, Minnesota

Storm ◆ NAIA ◆ Upper Midwest Athletic Conference ◆ http://www.crown.edu/

Independent religious comprehensive, founded 1916, affiliated with The Christian and Missionary Alliance
Coed, 986 undergraduate students, 76% full-time, 57% women, 43% men
Suburban 215-acre campus with easy access to Minneapolis–St. Paul
Minimally difficult entrance level, 82% of applicants were admitted

Freshmen *Admission:* 473 applied, 388 were accepted, 118 enrolled. *Test scores:* SAT verbal scores over 500: 55%; SAT math scores over 500: 72%; SAT verbal scores over 600: 9%; SAT math scores over 600: 45%.
Tuition and fees (2003–04): $13,168 (full-time). *Room and board:* $5552 (room only: $2528).
Financial Aid (All incoming freshmen): *Average need-based gift aid:* $4488. *Average non-need based aid:* $1975. *Average aid to full-time undergraduates:* $9452.
Athletic Department: *Director of Athletics:* Matt Darr; Phone: 952-446-4325; Fax: 952-446-4104; E-mail: darrm@crown.edu. *Sports Information Director:* Elizabeth Manninen; Phone: 952-446-4119; E-mail: mannine@crown.edu.

MEN'S COACHES
Baseball: Kelly Spann; Phone: 952-446-4146; E-mail: spannk@crown.edu.
Basketball: Don Rekoske; Phone: 952-446-4170; E-mail: rekosked@crown.edu.
Cross Country: Scott Stinson; Phone: 952-446-4117; E-mail: stinsons@crown.edu.
Football: John Auer; Phone: 952-446-4235; E-mail: auerj@crown.edu.
Golf: Don Rekoske; Phone: 952-446-4170; E-mail: rekosked@crown.edu.
Soccer: Rob Michels; Phone: 952-446-4188; E-mail: michelsr@crown.edu.

WOMEN'S COACHES
Basketball: Elizabeth Manninen; Phone: 952-446-4119; E-mail: mannine@crown.edu.
Cross Country: Scott Stinson; Phone: 952-446-4117; E-mail: stinsons@crown.edu.
Soccer: Owen Clarke; Phone: 952-446-4179; E-mail: darrm@crown.edu.
Softball: Gayle Grant; Phone: 952-446-4321; E-mail: grantg@crown.edu.
Volleyball: April Fisk; Phone: 952-446-4179; E-mail: fiska@crown.edu.

CULVER-STOCKTON COLLEGE
Canton, Missouri

Wildcats ◆ NAIA ◆ Heart of America Conference ◆ http://www.culver.edu/

Independent religious 4-year, founded 1853, affiliated with Christian Church (Disciples of Christ)
Coed, 835 undergraduate students, 92% full-time, 57% women, 43% men
Rural 143-acre campus
Moderately difficult entrance level, 72% of applicants were admitted

Freshmen *Admission:* 1,018 applied, 729 were accepted, 219 enrolled.

Tuition and fees (2003–04): $12,400 (full-time). *Room and board:* $5450 (room only: $2525).
Financial Aid (All incoming freshmen): *Average need-based gift aid:* $8922. *Average non-need based aid:* $8562. *Average aid to full-time undergraduates:* $11,637.
Athletic Department: *Director of Athletics:* Rodney Walton; Phone: 217-231-6424; Fax: 217-231-6442; E-mail: rwalton@culver.edu. *Sports Information Director:* John Schild; Phone: 217-231-6532; E-mail: jschild@culver.edu.

MEN'S COACHES
Baseball: Doug Bletcher; Phone: 217-231-6374; E-mail: dbletcher@culver.edu.
Basketball: Steve Hill; Phone: 217-231-6393; E-mail: shill@culver.edu.
Cheerleading: Kelly Hentzen; Phone: 217-231-6544; E-mail: khentzen@culver.edu.
Football: Shawn Mennenga; Phone: 217-231-6390; E-mail: smennenga@culver.edu.
Golf: Bill Schneider; Phone: 217-231-6391; E-mail: wschneider@culver.edu.
Soccer: Tom Baker; Phone: 217-231-6359; E-mail: tbaker@culver.edu.

WOMEN'S COACHES
Basketball: Dan Chapla; Phone: 217-231-6311; E-mail: dchapla@culver.edu.
Cheerleading: Kelly Hentzen; Phone: 217-231-6544; E-mail: khentzen@culver.edu.
Golf: John Duncanson; Phone: 217-231-6483; E-mail: jduncanson@culver.edu.
Soccer: Matt Longo; Phone: 217-653-0404; E-mail: soccer@rnet.com.
Softball: Gretta Melsted; Phone: 217-231-6392.
Volleyball: Barb Crist; Phone: 217-231-6379; E-mail: barbcrist@yahoo.com.

CUMBERLAND COLLEGE
Williamsburg, Kentucky

Patriots ◆ NAIA ◆ Mid-South Conference ◆ http://www.cumberlandcollege.edu/

Independent Kentucky Baptist comprehensive, founded 1889
Coed, 1,604 undergraduate students, 84% full-time, 53% women, 47% men
Rural 50-acre campus with easy access to Knoxville
Moderately difficult entrance level, 72% of applicants were admitted

Freshmen *Admission:* 1,105 applied, 791 were accepted, 414 enrolled. *Test scores:* SAT verbal scores over 500: 54%; SAT math scores over 500: 47%; SAT verbal scores over 600: 14%; SAT math scores over 600: 13%; SAT verbal scores over 700: 1%; SAT math scores over 700: 2%.
Tuition and fees (2004–05): $11,858 (full-time). *Room and board:* $5126.
Financial Aid (All incoming freshmen): *Average need-based gift aid:* $5023. *Average non-need based aid:* $5311. *Average aid to full-time undergraduates:* $13,557.
Athletic Department: *Director of Athletics:* Randy Vernon; Phone: 606-539-4389; Fax: 606-539-4467. *Sports Information Director:* Jennifer Wake; Phone: 606-539-4389.

MEN'S COACHES
Baseball: Terry Stigall; Phone: 606-539-4387.
Basketball: Don Butcher; Phone: 606-539-4361.
Cross Country: Floyd Stroud; Phone: 606-539-4139.
Football: Chuck King; Phone: 606-539-4423.
Golf: Bill Sergent; Phone: 606-539-4364.
Soccer: Rob Miller; Phone: 606-539-4386.
Swimming: Lance Huber; Phone: 606-539-4485.
Tennis: Chin Trek Tan; Phone: 606-539-4457.
Track and Field: Floyd Stroud; Phone: 606-539-4139.
Wrestling: Jess Wilder; Phone: 606-539-4389.

WOMEN'S COACHES
Basketball: Melissa Irvin; Phone: 606-539-4478.
Cross Country: Floyd Stroud; Phone: 606-539-4139.
Golf: Bill Sergent; Phone: 606-539-4364.
Soccer: Tim Wolz; Phone: 606-539-4044.
Softball: Angie Dean; Phone: 606-539-4178.
Swimming: Lance Huber; Phone: 606-539-4485.
Tennis: Chin Trek Tan; Phone: 606-539-4457.

Cumberland College (*continued*)
Track and Field: Floyd Stroud; Phone: 606-539-4139.
Volleyball: Jon Campbell; Phone: 606-539-4155.

CUMBERLAND UNIVERSITY
Lebanon, Tennessee

Bulldogs ◆ NAIA ◆ TranSouth Conference
◆ http://www.cumberland.edu/

Independent comprehensive, founded 1842
Coed, 921 undergraduate students, 84% full-time, 57% women, 43% men
Small-town 44-acre campus with easy access to Nashville
Moderately difficult entrance level, 61% of applicants were admitted

Freshmen *Admission:* 532 applied, 353 were accepted, 210 enrolled. *Test scores:* SAT verbal scores over 500: 40%; SAT math scores over 500: 35%; SAT verbal scores over 600: 10%; SAT math scores over 600: 10%.
Tuition and fees (2003–04): $12,230 (full-time). *Room and board:* $4480.
Financial Aid (All incoming freshmen): *Average aid to full-time undergraduates:* $10,192.
Athletic Department: *Director of Athletics:* Pat Lawson; Phone: 615-444-2562; Fax: 615-444-2569; E-mail: plawson@cumberland.edu. *Sports Information Director:* Pat Lawson; Phone: 615-444-2562; E-mail: plawson@cumberland.edu.

MEN'S COACHES
Baseball: Woody Hunt; Phone: 615-444-2562; E-mail: whunt@cumberland.edu.
Basketball: Lonnie Thompson; Phone: 615-444-2562; E-mail: lthompson@cumberland.edu.
Cross Country: Gary Robinson; Phone: 615-444-2562; E-mail: grobinson@cumberland.edu.
Football: Herschel Moore; Phone: 615-444-2562; E-mail: athletics@cumberland.edu.
Golf: Phone: 615-444-2562.
Soccer: Bryan Johnson; Phone: 615-444-2562; E-mail: bjohnson@cumberland.edu.
Tennis: Bill Riddle; Phone: 615-444-2562; E-mail: athletics@cumberland.edu.
Wrestling: Jarad Swint; Phone: 615-444-2562; E-mail: jswint@cumberland.edu.

WOMEN'S COACHES
Basketball: Clint Mason; Phone: 615-444-2562; E-mail: cmason@cumberland.edu.
Cross Country: Gary Robinson; Phone: 615-444-2562; E-mail: grobinson@cumberland.edu.
Soccer: Bryan Johnson; Phone: 615-444-2562; E-mail: bjohnson@cumberland.edu.
Softball: Junior Hawkins; Phone: 615-444-2562; E-mail: jhawkins@cumberland.edu.
Tennis: Bill Riddle; Phone: 615-444-2562; E-mail: athletics@cumberland.edu.
Volleyball: Dwayne Deering; Phone: 615-444-2562; E-mail: ddeering@cumberland.edu.

CURRY COLLEGE
Milton, Massachusetts

Colonels ◆ NCAA III ◆ Commonwealth Coast Conference; New England Football Conference ◆ http://www.curry.edu/

Independent comprehensive, founded 1879
Coed, 2,501 undergraduate students, 67% full-time, 55% women, 45% men
Suburban 131-acre campus with easy access to Boston
Moderately difficult entrance level, 7% of applicants were admitted

Freshmen *Admission:* 2,311 applied, 1,593 were accepted, 473 enrolled. *Test scores:* SAT verbal scores over 500: 30%; SAT math scores over 500: 20%; SAT verbal scores over 600: 7%; SAT math scores over 600: 3%; SAT verbal scores over 700: 1%; SAT math scores over 700: 1%.
Tuition and fees (2004–05): $22,340 (full-time). *Room and board:* $8180 (room only: $4620).
Financial Aid (All incoming freshmen): *Average need-based gift aid:* $10,478. *Average non-need based aid:* $7000. *Average aid to full-time undergraduates:* $14,659.
Athletic Department: *Director of Athletics:* Steve Nelson; Phone: 617-333-2109; Fax: 617-333-2027; E-mail: snelson@curry.edu. *Sports Information Director:* Ken Golner; Phone: 617-333-2324; E-mail: kgolner@curry.edu.

MEN'S COACHES
Baseball: Dave Perdios; Phone: 617-333-2055; E-mail: dperdios@curry.edu.
Basketball: Malcolm Wynn; Phone: 617-333-2200; E-mail: mwynn0403@curry.edu.
Cheerleading: Cristyn DeMerchant; Phone: 617-333-2919; E-mail: cdemerch0903@curry.edu.
Football: Steve Nelson; Phone: 617-333-2109; E-mail: snelson@curry.edu.
Ice Hockey: Rob Davies; Phone: 617-696-9275; E-mail: rdavies@curry.edu.
Lacrosse: Neal Anderson; Phone: 617-333-2052; E-mail: nanderso1002@curry.edu.
Soccer: Morten Jorgensen; Phone: 617-333-2093; E-mail: mjorgens0802@curry.edu.
Tennis: John Ritucci; Phone: 617-333-2217; E-mail: jritucci0703@curry.edu.

WOMEN'S COACHES
Basketball: Diana Cutaia; Phone: 617-333-2205; E-mail: dcutaia0903@curry.edu.
Cheerleading: Cristyn DeMerchant; Phone: 617-333-2919; E-mail: cdemerch0903@curry.edu.
Cross Country: Emer Molloy; Phone: 617-333-2217; E-mail: emolloy0603@curry.edu.
Lacrosse: Caitlin Roberts; Phone: 617-333-2943; E-mail: cmrobert@curry.edu.
Soccer: Danielle Ferrara Toomey; Phone: 617-333-2377; E-mail: dferrara@curry.edu.
Softball: Lou Bello; Phone: 617-333-2352; E-mail: bweckwor@curry.edu.
Tennis: Paul Dorsey; Phone: 617-333-2217.

DAEMEN COLLEGE
Amherst, New York

Wildcats ◆ NAIA ◆ American Mideast Conference ◆ http://www.daemen.edu/

Independent comprehensive, founded 1947
Coed, 1,761 undergraduate students, 80% full-time, 76% women, 24% men
Suburban 35-acre campus with easy access to Buffalo
Moderately difficult entrance level, 7% of applicants were admitted

Freshmen *Admission:* 1,800 applied, 1,252 were accepted, 355 enrolled. *Test scores:* SAT verbal scores over 500: 54%; SAT math scores over 500: 57%; SAT verbal scores over 600: 9%; SAT math scores over 600: 9%.
Tuition and fees (2003–04): $15,120 (full-time). *Room and board:* $7000.
Financial Aid (All incoming freshmen): *Average need-based gift aid:* $7234. *Average non-need based aid:* $5823. *Average aid to full-time undergraduates:* $13,903.
Athletic Department: *Director of Athletics:* Don Silveri; Phone: 716-839-8380; Fax: 716-839-8516; E-mail: dsilveri@daemen.edu. *Sports Information Director:* Dave Skolen; Phone: 716-839-8336; E-mail: dskolen@daemen.edu.

MEN'S COACHES
Basketball: Don Silveri; Phone: 719-839-8380; E-mail: dsilveri@daemen.edu.
Cross Country: Jeff Gruendike; Phone: 719-839-8346; E-mail: jgruendi@daemen.edu.
Golf: Don Silveri; Phone: 719-839-8380; E-mail: dsilveri@daemen.edu.
Soccer: Randy Pawlik; Phone: 719-839-8346; E-mail: rpawlik@daemen.edu.

WOMEN'S COACHES

Basketball: Dave Skolen; Phone: 719-839-8336; E-mail: dskolen@daemen.edu.

Cross Country: Jeff Gruendike; Phone: 719-839-8346; E-mail: jgruendi@daemen.edu.

Soccer: Mike DiNunzio; Phone: 719-839-8346; E-mail: mdinunzi@daemen.edu.

Volleyball: Katie Schrantz; Phone: 719-839-8346; E-mail: jessanderson12@yahoo.com.

DAKOTA STATE UNIVERSITY
Madison, South Dakota

Trojans ◆ NAIA ◆ Dakota Conference
◆ http://www.dsu.edu/

State-supported comprehensive, founded 1881
Coed, 2,098 undergraduate students, 60% full-time, 53% women, 47% men
Rural 40-acre campus with easy access to Sioux Falls
Minimally difficult entrance level, 93% of applicants were admitted

Freshmen *Admission:* 525 applied, 487 were accepted, 320 enrolled.
Tuition and fees (2003–04): $4378 (resident), $9090 (nonresident). *Room and board:* $3089.
Financial Aid (All incoming freshmen): *Average non-need based aid:* $3715. *Average aid to full-time undergraduates:* $6179.
Athletic Department: *Director of Athletics:* Thomas Gioglio; Phone: 605-256-5229; Fax: 605-256-5138; E-mail: tom.gioglio@dsu.edu. *Sports Information Director:* Nick Huntimer; Phone: 605-256-5229; E-mail: huntimn@pluto.dsu.edu.

MEN'S COACHES

Baseball: Patrick Dolan; Phone: 605-256-5232; E-mail: patrick.dolan@dsu.edu.

Basketball: Tim Schuring; Phone: 605-256-5234; E-mail: tim.schuring@dsu.edu.

Cheerleading: Andrea Lindberg; Phone: 605-256-5229; E-mail: lindbera@pluto.dsu.edu.

Cross Country: Buzz Stevenson; Phone: 605-256-5236; E-mail: buzz.stevenson@dsu.edu.

Football: Gene Wockenfuss; Phone: 605-256-5656; E-mail: gene.wockenfuss@dsu.edu.

Golf: Wade Kooiman; Phone: 605-256-7392; E-mail: wade.kooiman@dsu.edu.

Track and Field: Buzz Stevenson; Phone: 605-256-5236; E-mail: buzz.stevenson@dsu.edu.

WOMEN'S COACHES

Basketball: Jeff Dittman; Phone: 605-256-5246; E-mail: jeff.dittman@dsu.edu.

Cheerleading: Andrea Lindberg; Phone: 605-256-5229; E-mail: lindbera@pluto.dsu.edu.

Cross Country: Buzz Stevenson; Phone: 605-256-5236; E-mail: buzz.stevenson@dsu.edu.

Golf: Wade Kooiman; Phone: 605-256-7392; E-mail: wade.kooiman@dsu.edu.

Softball: Mikki Cochrane; Phone: 605-256-5846; E-mail: mikki.cochrane@dsu.edu.

Track and Field: Buzz Stevenson; Phone: 605-256-5236; E-mail: buzz.stevenson@dsu.edu.

Volleyball: Cindy Henning; Phone: 605-256-5689; E-mail: cindy.henning@dsu.edu.

DAKOTA WESLEYAN UNIVERSITY
Mitchell, South Dakota

Tigers ◆ NAIA ◆ Great Plains Conference
◆ http://www.dwu.edu/

Independent United Methodist comprehensive, founded 1885
Coed, 738 undergraduate students, 90% full-time, 58% women, 42% men
Small-town 50-acre campus
Moderately difficult entrance level, 75% of applicants were admitted

Freshmen *Admission:* 543 applied, 418 were accepted, 162 enrolled.

Tuition and fees (2004–05): $14,558 (full-time). *Room and board:* $4262 (room only: $1802).
Financial Aid (All incoming freshmen): *Average need-based gift aid:* $4442. *Average non-need based aid:* $6792. *Average aid to full-time undergraduates:* $11,145.
Athletic Department: *Director of Athletics:* Scott Gines; Phone: 605-995-2146; Fax: 605-995-2150; E-mail: scgines@dwu.edu. *Sports Information Director:* Darrell Orand; Phone: 605-995-2854; E-mail: daorand@dwu.edu.

MEN'S COACHES

Baseball: Adam Neisius; Phone: 605-995-2853; E-mail: adneisiu@dwu.edu.

Basketball: Doug Martin; Phone: 605-995-2875; E-mail: domartin@dwu.edu.

Cross Country: Paul Ekern; Phone: 605-995-2858; E-mail: paekern@dwu.edu.

Football: Tony Harprer; Phone: 605-995-2852; E-mail: toharper@dwu.edu.

Golf: Christopher Gomez; Phone: 605-995-2179; E-mail: chgomez@dwu.edu.

Track and Field: Leslie Hardesty; Phone: 605-995-2954; E-mail: lehardes@dwu.edu.

Wrestling: Bill Rincker; Phone: 605-995-2149.

WOMEN'S COACHES

Basketball: Kevin Lein; Phone: 605-995-2634; E-mail: kelein@dwu.edu.

Cross Country: Paul Ekern; Phone: 605-995-2858; E-mail: paekern@dwu.edu.

Golf: Christopher Gomez; Phone: 605-995-2179; E-mail: chgomez@dwu.edu.

Softball: Kevin Lein; Phone: 605-995-2634; E-mail: kelein@dwu.edu.

Track and Field: Leslie Hardesty; Phone: 605-995-2954; E-mail: lehardes@dwu.edu.

Volleyball: Kylee Johnson; Phone: 605-995-2855; E-mail: kyjohnso@dwu.edu.

DALLAS BAPTIST UNIVERSITY
Dallas, Texas

Patriots ◆ NCAA II ◆ Heartland Conference; Independent
◆ http://www.dbu.edu/

Independent religious comprehensive, founded 1965, affiliated with Baptist General Convention of Texas
Coed, 3,444 undergraduate students, 55% full-time, 60% women, 40% men
Urban 293-acre campus
Moderately difficult entrance level, 70% of applicants were admitted

Freshmen *Admission:* 740 applied, 505 were accepted, 298 enrolled. *Test scores:* SAT verbal scores over 500: 75%; SAT math scores over 500: 75%; SAT verbal scores over 600: 26%; SAT math scores over 600: 24%; SAT verbal scores over 700: 3%; SAT math scores over 700: 3%.
Tuition and fees (2003–04): $11,010 (full-time). *Room and board:* $4290 (room only: $1790).
Financial Aid (All incoming freshmen): *Average need-based gift aid:* $2360. *Average non-need based aid:* $9526. *Average aid to full-time undergraduates:* $9520.
Athletic Department: *Director of Athletics:* Fax: 214-333-5306. *Sports Information Director:* E-mail: sports@dbu.edu.

MEN'S COACHES

Baseball: Mike Bard; Phone: 214-333-5324.

Cross Country: Denny Giles; Phone: 214-333-5324; E-mail: dennyg@dbu.edu.

Soccer: David Grannis; Phone: 214-333-5324; E-mail: sports@dbu.edu.

Tennis: Clare Heineman; Phone: 214-333-5324; E-mail: sports@dbu.edu.

Track and Field: Denny Giles; Phone: 214-333-5324; E-mail: dennyg@dbu.edu.

Volleyball: Rob Heineman; Phone: 214-333-5324; E-mail: safesetz@yahoo.com.

WOMEN'S COACHES

Cross Country: Denny Giles; Phone: 214-333-5324; E-mail: dennyg@dbu.edu.

Soccer: David Grannis; Phone: 214-333-5324; E-mail: sports@dbu.edu.

Dallas Baptist University *(continued)*

Tennis: Clare Heineman; Phone: 214-333-5324; E-mail: sports@dbu.edu.

Track and Field: Denny Giles; Phone: 214-333-5324; E-mail: dennyg@dbu.edu.

Volleyball: Cathy Ray; Phone: 214-333-5324; E-mail: sports@dbu.edu.

DANA COLLEGE
Blair, Nebraska

Vikings ◆ NAIA ◆ Great Plains Conference
◆ http://www.dana.edu/

Independent religious 4-year, founded 1884, affiliated with Evangelical Lutheran Church in America
Coed, 581 undergraduate students, 97% full-time, 41% women, 59% men
Small-town 150-acre campus with easy access to Omaha
Moderately difficult entrance level, 98% of applicants were admitted

Freshmen *Admission:* 583 applied, 572 were accepted, 164 enrolled. *Test scores:* SAT verbal scores over 500: 71%; SAT math scores over 500: 59%; SAT verbal scores over 600: 30%; SAT math scores over 600: 18%; SAT verbal scores over 700: 12%.
Tuition and fees (2003–04): $15,750 (full-time). *Room and board:* $4880 (room only: $1900).
Financial Aid (All incoming freshmen): *Average need-based gift aid:* $4141. *Average non-need based aid:* $5477. *Average aid to full-time undergraduates:* $15,504.
Athletic Department: *Director of Athletics:* Jim Krueger; Phone: 402-426-7296; Fax: 402-426-7299; E-mail: jkrueger@acad2.dana.edu. *Sports Information Director:* Kristen Gay; Phone: 402-426-7367.

MEN'S COACHES
Baseball: Chad Gorman; Phone: 402-426-7913; E-mail: cgorman@acad2.dana.edu.
Basketball: Chris Fear; Phone: 402-426-7294; E-mail: cfear@acad2.dana.edu.
Cross Country: Bob Spangler; Phone: 402-426-7292; E-mail: rspangle@acad2.dana.edu.
Football: Bill Danenhauer; Phone: 402-426-7292.
Soccer: Shad Beam; Phone: 402-426-7389; E-mail: sbeam@acad2.dana.edu.
Track and Field: Allen Friesen; Phone: 402-426-7392; E-mail: afriesen@acad2.dana.edu.
Wrestling: Steve Costanzo; Phone: 402-426-7288; E-mail: scostanz@acad2.dana.edu.

WOMEN'S COACHES
Basketball: Brenda Mechels; Phone: 402-426-7283; E-mail: bmechels@acad2.dana.edu.
Cross Country: Bob Spangler; Phone: 402-426-7292; E-mail: rspangle@acad2.dana.edu.
Soccer: Kristen Gay; Phone: 402-426-7367; E-mail: kgay@acad2.dana.edu.
Softball: Marcy Roff; Phone: 402-426-7376; E-mail: mroff@acad2.dana.edu.
Track and Field: Allen Friesen; Phone: 402-426-7392; E-mail: afriesen@acad2.dana.edu.
Volleyball: Laurel Derry; Phone: 402-426-7298; E-mail: lderry@acad2.dana.edu.

DANIEL WEBSTER COLLEGE
Nashua, New Hampshire

Eagles ◆ NCAA III ◆ Great Northeast Athletic Conference
◆ http://www.dwc.edu/

Independent 4-year, founded 1965
Coed, 1,050 undergraduate students, 78% full-time, 27% women, 73% men
Suburban 50-acre campus with easy access to Boston
Moderately difficult entrance level, 79% of applicants were admitted

Freshmen *Admission:* 642 applied, 506 were accepted, 141 enrolled. *Test scores:* SAT verbal scores over 500: 69%; SAT math scores over 500: 74%; SAT verbal scores over 600: 18%; SAT math scores over 600: 30%; SAT verbal scores over 700: 3%; SAT math scores over 700: 2%.
Tuition and fees (2004–05): $21,630 (full-time). *Room and board:* $8170 (room only: $4110).
Financial Aid (All incoming freshmen): *Average need-based gift aid:* $6160. *Average non-need based aid:* $5400. *Average aid to full-time undergraduates:* $16,101.
Athletic Department: *Director of Athletics:* John Griffith; Phone: 603-577-6498; Fax: 603-577-6597; E-mail: griffith@dwc.edu. *Sports Information Director:* Greg Andruskevich; Phone: 603-577-6496; E-mail: andruskevich@dwc.edu.

MEN'S COACHES
Baseball: Jim Cardello; Phone: 603-577-6497; E-mail: jcardello@adelphia.net.
Basketball: Chad Davis; Phone: 603-577-6493; E-mail: davis@dwc.edu.
Cross Country: Josh Rogers; Phone: 603-577-6496.
Lacrosse: Rick McKenzie; Phone: 603-577-6491; E-mail: mckenzie@dwc.edu.
Soccer: Donovan Breunig; Phone: 603-577-6497; E-mail: breunig@dwc.edu.

WOMEN'S COACHES
Basketball: Cori Hughes; Phone: 603-577-6495; E-mail: huhughes@dwc.edu.
Cross Country: Josh Rogers; Phone: 603-577-6496.
Soccer: Cori Hughes; Phone: 603-577-6495; E-mail: hughes@dwc.edu.
Softball: Cori Hughes; Phone: 603-577-6495; E-mail: huhughes@dwc.edu.
Volleyball: Staci Branon; Phone: 603-577-6491.

DARTMOUTH COLLEGE
Hanover, New Hampshire

Big Green ◆ NCAA I ◆ Ivy League Conference ◆ http://www.dartmouth.edu/

Independent university, founded 1769
Coed, 4,098 undergraduate students, 99% full-time, 49% women, 51% men
Small-town 265-acre campus
Most difficult entrance level, 17% of applicants were admitted

Freshmen *Admission:* 11,855 applied, 2,155 were accepted, 1,077 enrolled. *Test scores:* SAT verbal scores over 500: 100%; SAT math scores over 500: 99%; SAT verbal scores over 600: 92%; SAT math scores over 600: 92%; SAT verbal scores over 700: 62%; SAT math scores over 700: 63%.
Tuition and fees (2003–04): $29,256 (full-time). *Room and board:* $8739 (room only: $5175).
Financial Aid (All incoming freshmen): *Average need-based gift aid:* $23,278. *Average non-need based aid:* $300. *Average aid to full-time undergraduates:* $26,516.
Athletic Department: *Director of Athletics:* Josie Harper; Phone: 603-646-2465; Fax: 603-646-3348. *Sports Information Director:* Kathy Slattery; Phone: 603-646-2468; E-mail: kathleen.r.slattery@dartmouth.edu.

MEN'S COACHES
Baseball: Bob Whalen; Phone: 603-646-2477; E-mail: robert.d.whalen@dartmouth.edu.
Basketball: Dave Faucher; Phone: 603-646-2401; E-mail: david.g.faucher@dartmouth.edu.
Cheerleading: Phone: 603-646-2254; E-mail: dartmouth.football.cheerleading@dartmouth.edu.
Cross Country: Barry Harwick; Phone: 603-646-2540; E-mail: barry.harwick@dartmouth.edu.
Diving: Chris Hamilton; Phone: 603-646-2254; E-mail: christopher.w.hamilton@dartmouth.edu.
Football: John Lyons; Phone: 603-646-2467; E-mail: john.j.lyons@dartmouth.edu.
Golf: Jason Calhoun; Phone: 603-646-1315; E-mail: jason.m.calhoun@dartmouth.edu.
Ice Hockey: Bob Gaudet; Phone: 603-646-2469; E-mail: robert.j.gaudet@dartmouth.edu.
Lacrosse: Bill Wilson; Phone: 603-646-3135; E-mail: william.w.wilson.jr@dartmouth.edu.

Soccer: Jeff Cook; Phone: 603-646-3082; E-mail: jeffrey.j.cook@dartmouth.edu.

Swimming: Jim Wilson; Phone: 603-646-3433; E-mail: a.james.wilson@dartmouth.edu.

Tennis: Chuck Kinyon; Phone: 603-646-3819; E-mail: charles.m.kinyon@dartmouth.edu.

Track and Field: Barry Harwick; Phone: 603-646-2540; E-mail: barry.harwick@dartmouth.edu.

WOMEN'S COACHES

Basketball: Chris Wielgus; Phone: 603-646-3194; E-mail: christina.h.wielgus@dartmouth.edu.

Cheerleading: Phone: 603-646-2254; E-mail: dartmouth.football.cheerleading@dartmouth.edu.

Cross Country: Maribel Sanchez; Phone: 603-646-2571; E-mail: maribel.s.souther@dartmouth.edu.

Diving: Chris Hamilton; Phone: 603-646-2254; E-mail: christopher.w.hamilton@dartmouth.edu.

Field Hockey: Amy Fowler; Phone: 603-646-2498; E-mail: amy.r.fowler@dartmouth.edu.

Golf: Kevin Gibson; Phone: 603-646-1315; E-mail: kevin.r.gibson@dartmouth.edu.

Lacrosse: Amy Patton; Phone: 603-646-3955; E-mail: amy.r.patton@dartmouth.edu.

Soccer: Ben Landis; Phone: 603-646-2178; E-mail: benjamin.w.landis@dartmouth.edu.

Softball: Jen Goodwin; Phone: 603-646-3111; E-mail: jeanette.goodwin@dartmouth.edu.

Swimming: Joann Brislin; Phone: 603-646-2219; E-mail: joann.a.brislin@dartmouth.edu.

Tennis: Bob Dallis; Phone: 603-646-3494; E-mail: robert.dallis@dartmouth.edu.

Track and Field: Sandra Ford-Centonze; Phone: 603-646-3570; E-mail: sandra.ford-centonze@dartmouth.edu.

Volleyball: Ann Marie Larese; Phone: 603-646-3529; E-mail: ann.marie.larese@dartmouth.edu.

DAVENPORT UNIVERSITY
Grand Rapids, Michigan

Panthers ◆ NAIA ◆ Independent
◆ http://www.davenport.edu/

Independent comprehensive, founded 1866, part of Davenport University
Coed, 1,751 undergraduate students, 37% full-time, 63% women, 37% men
Urban campus
Noncompetitive entrance level, 60% of applicants were admitted

Freshmen *Admission:* 452 applied, 295 were accepted, 156 enrolled.
Tuition and fees (2003–04): $10,270 (full-time). *Room only:* $3400.
Athletic Department: *Director of Athletics:* Paul Lowden; Phone: 616-451-3511; Fax: 616-732-1185; E-mail: paul.lowden@davenport.edu.

MEN'S COACHES

Basketball: Corey McNeal; Phone: 616-451-3511; E-mail: corey.mcneal@davenport.edu.

Golf: Dan Strock; Phone: 616-451-3511.

Soccer: Steve Coleman; Phone: 616-451-3511.

WOMEN'S COACHES

Basketball: Mark Youngs; Phone: 616-451-3511; E-mail: mark.youngs@davenport.edu.

Golf: Dan Strock; Phone: 616-451-3511.

Soccer: Steve Coleman; Phone: 616-451-3511.

DAVIDSON COLLEGE
Davidson, North Carolina

Wildcats ◆ NCAA I ◆ Colonial Athletic Conference; Northern Pacific Field Hockey Conference; Pioneer Football League Conference; Southern Conference ◆ http://www.davidson.edu/

Independent Presbyterian 4-year, founded 1837
Coed, 1,712 undergraduate students, 100% full-time, 50% women, 50% men
Small-town 556-acre campus with easy access to Charlotte
Very difficult entrance level, 3% of applicants were admitted

Freshmen *Admission:* 3,927 applied, 1,249 were accepted, 490 enrolled. *Test scores:* SAT verbal scores over 500: 99%; SAT math scores over 500: 100%; SAT verbal scores over 600: 87%; SAT math scores over 600: 91%; SAT verbal scores over 700: 38%; SAT math scores over 700: 39%.
Tuition and fees (2003–04): $25,903 (full-time). *Room and board:* $7371 (room only: $3892).
Financial Aid (All incoming freshmen): *Average need-based gift aid:* $15,593. *Average non-need based aid:* $7558. *Average aid to full-time undergraduates:* $17,782.
Athletic Department: *Director of Athletics:* Jim Murphy; Phone: 704-894-2373; Fax: 704-894-2556; E-mail: jamurphy@davidson.edu. *Sports Information Director:* Rick Bender; Phone: 704-894-2123; E-mail: ribender@davidson.edu.

MEN'S COACHES

Baseball: Dick Cooke; Phone: 704-894-2368; E-mail: dicooke@davidson.edu.

Basketball: Bob McKillop; Phone: 704-894-2384; E-mail: bomckillop@davidson.edu.

Cheerleading: Jeanette Scire; Phone: 704-894-2378; E-mail: jescire@davidson.edu.

Cross Country: Gary Andrew; Phone: 704-894-2367; E-mail: gaandrew@davidson.edu.

Diving: Ted Hautau; Phone: 704-894-2944; E-mail: tehautau@davidson.edu.

Football: Mike Toop; Phone: 704-894-2380; E-mail: mitoop@davidson.edu.

Golf: Tim Straub; Phone: 704-894-2585; E-mail: tistraub@davidson.edu.

Soccer: Matt Spear; Phone: 704-894-2345; E-mail: maspear@davidson.edu.

Swimming: Tim Kelly; Phone: 704-894-2812; E-mail: tikelly@davidson.edu.

Tennis: Jeff Frank; Phone: 704-894-2438; E-mail: jefrank@davidson.edu.

Track and Field: Gary Andrew; Phone: 704-894-2367; E-mail: gaandrew@davidson.edu.

Wrestling: T.J. Jaworsky; Phone: 704-894-2805; E-mail: tjjaworsky@davidson.edu.

WOMEN'S COACHES

Basketball: Annete Watts; Phone: 704-894-2819; E-mail: anwatts@davidson.edu.

Cheerleading: Jeanette Scire; Phone: 704-894-2378; E-mail: jescire@davidson.edu.

Cross Country: Jennifer Straub; Phone: 704-894-2808; E-mail: jestraub@davidson.edu.

Diving: Ted Hautau; Phone: 704-894-2944; E-mail: tehautau@davidson.edu.

Field Hockey: Lisa Thompson; Phone: 704-894-2121; E-mail: lithompsonn@davidson.edu.

Lacrosse: Mary Schwartz; Phone: 704-894-2525; E-mail: maschwartz@davidson.edu.

Soccer: Kevin Hundley; Phone: 704-894-2818; E-mail: kehundley@davidson.edu.

Swimming: Tim Kelly; Phone: 704-894-2812; E-mail: tikelly@davidson.edu.

Tennis: Caroline Price; Phone: 704-894-2437; E-mail: caprice@davidson.edu.

Track and Field: Jennifer Straub; Phone: 704-894-2808; E-mail: jestraub@davidson.edu.

Volleyball: Tim Cowie; Phone: 704-894-2633; E-mail: ticowie@davidson.edu.

DAVIS & ELKINS COLLEGE
Elkins, West Virginia

Senators ◆ NCAA II ◆ West Virginia Intercollegiate Athletic Conference ◆ http://www.davisandelkins.edu/

Independent Presbyterian 4-year, founded 1904
Coed, 624 undergraduate students, 91% full-time, 60% women, 40% men
Small-town 170-acre campus
Minimally difficult entrance level, 70% of applicants were admitted

Freshmen *Admission:* 691 applied, 484 were accepted, 116 enrolled. *Test scores:* SAT verbal scores over 500: 43%; SAT math scores over 500: 37%; SAT verbal scores over 600: 13%; SAT math scores over 600: 12%; SAT verbal scores over 700: 3%.
Tuition and fees (2004–05): $14,668 (full-time). *Room and board:* $5926.
Financial Aid (All incoming freshmen): *Average need-based gift aid:* $4636. *Average non-need based aid:* $10,878. *Average aid to full-time undergraduates:* $12,038.
Athletic Department: *Director of Athletics:* Ralph Hill; Phone: 304-637-1252; Fax: 304-637-1414; E-mail: hill@davisandelkins.edu. *Sports Information Director:* Rob Bratton; Phone: 304-637-1426; E-mail: brattonr@davisandelkins.edu.

MEN'S COACHES
Baseball: Ryan Brisbin; Phone: 304-637-1342; E-mail: brisbinr@davisandelkins.edu.
Basketball: Amrit Rayfield; Phone: 304-637-1398; E-mail: raya@davisandelkins.edu.
Cross Country: Will Shaw; Phone: 304-637-1923; E-mail: wsh@davisandelkins.edu.
Golf: Chris Gow; Phone: 304-637-1402; E-mail: mulligan@meer.net.
Soccer: Mark Stollsteimer; Phone: 304-637-1388; E-mail: stolli@davisandelkins.edu.
Tennis: Lee Underwood; Phone: 304-637-1403; E-mail: leeunderwood2000@yahoo.com.

WOMEN'S COACHES
Basketball: Jay Dailer; Phone: 304-637-1387; E-mail: dailerj@davisandelkins.edu.
Cross Country: Will Shaw; Phone: 304-637-1923; E-mail: wsh@davisandelkins.edu.
Soccer: Greg Mitchell; Phone: 304-637-1435; E-mail: mitchelg@davisandelkins.edu.
Softball: Anthony Bates; Phone: 304-637-1397; E-mail: chubate@hotmail.com.
Tennis: Lee Underwood; Phone: 304-637-1403; E-mail: leeunderwood2000@yahoo.com.
Volleyball: Wayne Hart; Phone: 304-637-1923.

DEFIANCE COLLEGE
Defiance, Ohio

Yellow Jackets ◆ NCAA III ◆ Heartland Collegiate Conference ◆ http://www.defiance.edu/

Independent religious comprehensive, founded 1850, affiliated with United Church of Christ
Coed, 938 undergraduate students, 76% full-time, 57% women, 43% men
Small-town 150-acre campus with easy access to Toledo
Moderately difficult entrance level, 72% of applicants were admitted

Freshmen *Admission:* 796 applied, 597 were accepted, 216 enrolled. *Test scores:* SAT verbal scores over 500: 53%; SAT math scores over 500: 47%; SAT verbal scores over 600: 18%; SAT math scores over 600: 15%; SAT math scores over 700: 5%.
Tuition and fees (2003–04): $17,365 (full-time). *Room and board:* $5250 (room only: $2650).
Financial Aid (All incoming freshmen): *Average non-need based aid:* $6536. *Average aid to full-time undergraduates:* $12,984.
Athletic Department: *Director of Athletics:* Dick Kaiser; Phone: 419-783-2343; Fax: 419-783-2369; E-mail: dkaiser@defiance.edu. *Sports Information Director:* Nate Jorgensen; Phone: 419-783-2566; E-mail: njorgensen@defiance.edu.

MEN'S COACHES
Baseball: Jonathan Miller; Phone: 419-783-2341; E-mail: cdonsbach@defiance.edu.
Basketball: Jonathan Miller; Phone: 419-783-2346; E-mail: jmiller@defiance.edu.
Cross Country: Matt Lydum; Phone: 419-783-2385; E-mail: mlydum@defiance.edu.
Football: Jonathan Miller; Phone: 419-783-2378; E-mail: rtaylor@defiance.edu.
Golf: J.D. Despain; Phone: 419-783-2342; E-mail: bosshog68@hotmail.com.
Soccer: Brian Kelley; Phone: 419-783-2588; E-mail: bkelley@defiance.edu.
Tennis: Brad Harsha; Phone: 419-783-2365; E-mail: bharsha@defiance.edu.
Track and Field: Matt Lydum; Phone: 419-783-2385; E-mail: mlydum@defiance.edu.

WOMEN'S COACHES
Basketball: Tom Barnes; Phone: 419-783-2391; E-mail: tbarnes@defiance.edu.
Cross Country: Matt Lydum; Phone: 419-783-2385; E-mail: mlydum@defiance.edu.
Golf: Dave Plant; Phone: 419-783-2342; E-mail: dplant@defiance.edu.
Soccer: Brian Kelley; Phone: 419-783-2588; E-mail: bkelley@defiance.edu.
Softball: Kary Kankey; Phone: 419-783-2379; E-mail: kkankey@defiance.edu.
Tennis: greg Reineke; Phone: 419-783-2342; E-mail: greineke@defiance.edu.
Track and Field: Matt Lydum; Phone: 419-783-2385; E-mail: mlydum@defiance.edu.
Volleyball: David Kwan; Phone: 419-783-2326; E-mail: dkwan@defiance.edu.

DELAWARE STATE UNIVERSITY
Dover, Delaware

Hornets ◆ NCAA I ◆ Mid-Eastern Athletic Conference ◆ http://www.desu.edu/

State-supported comprehensive, founded 1891, part of Delaware Higher Education Commission
Coed, 2,992 undergraduate students, 85% full-time, 58% women, 42% men
Small-town 400-acre campus
Moderately difficult entrance level, 46% of applicants were admitted

Freshmen *Admission:* 3,204 applied, 1,601 were accepted, 618 enrolled. *Test scores:* SAT verbal scores over 500: 13%; SAT math scores over 500: 14%; SAT verbal scores over 600: 2%; SAT math scores over 600: 2%.
Tuition and fees (2003–04): $4296 (resident), $9276 (nonresident). *Room and board:* $6344 (room only: $4004).
Financial Aid (All incoming freshmen): *Average non-need based aid:* $6597. *Average aid to full-time undergraduates:* $6389.
Athletic Department: *Director of Athletics:* Hallie Gregory; Phone: 302-857-6030; Fax: 302-857-6034; E-mail: hgregory@desu.edu. *Sports Information Director:* Dennis Jones; Phone: 302-857-6068; E-mail: djones@desu.edu.

MEN'S COACHES
Baseball: J.P. Blandin; Phone: 302-857-6035; E-mail: dsubaseball@hotmail.com.
Basketball: Greg Jackson; Phone: 302-857-7559.
Cheerleading: Anita Brinkley; Phone: 302-857-6039; E-mail: abrinkle@dsc.edu.
Cross Country: Duane Henry; Phone: 302-857-6040; E-mail: dhenry@dsc.edu.
Football: Al Lavan; Phone: 302-857-6048; E-mail: bblackna@dsc.edu.
Tennis: Alex Becton; Phone: 302-857-7440; E-mail: aalbecton@aol.com.
Track and Field: Duane Henry; Phone: 302-857-6040; E-mail: dhenry@dsc.edu.
Wrestling: Darren Archangelo; Phone: 302-857-7443; E-mail: darrenarchangelo@yahoo.com.

WOMEN'S COACHES
Basketball: Ed Davis; Phone: 302-857-6041; E-mail: edavis@dsc.edu.

Cheerleading: Anita Brinkley; Phone: 302-857-6039; E-mail: abrinkle@dsc.edu.
Cross Country: Connie Hayes; Phone: 302-857-6039; E-mail: chayes@dsc.edu.
Soccer: Duane Henry; Phone: 302-857-6040; E-mail: dehenry@dsc.edu.
Softball: Jeff Savage; Phone: 302-857-7740; E-mail: jsavage@dsc.edu.
Tennis: Alex Becton; Phone: 302-857-7440; E-mail: aalbecton@aol.com.
Track and Field: Connie Hayes; Phone: 302-857-6039; E-mail: chayes@dsc.edu.
Volleyball: Jane Hicks; Phone: 302-857-6033; E-mail: jfhicks@dsc.edu.

DELAWARE VALLEY COLLEGE
Doylestown, Pennsylvania

Aggies ◆ NCAA III ◆ Middle Atlantic Conference ◆ http://www.devalcol.edu/

Independent comprehensive, founded 1896
Coed, 1,958 undergraduate students, 74% full-time, 51% women, 49% men
Suburban 600-acre campus with easy access to Philadelphia
Moderately difficult entrance level, 82% of applicants were admitted

Freshmen *Admission:* 1,556 applied, 1,283 were accepted, 440 enrolled. *Test scores:* SAT verbal scores over 500: 46%; SAT math scores over 500: 48%; SAT verbal scores over 600: 11%; SAT math scores over 600: 9%; SAT verbal scores over 700: 1%.
Tuition and fees (2003–04): $19,304 (full-time). *Room and board:* $7372 (room only): $3342).
Financial Aid (All incoming freshmen): *Average need-based gift aid:* $11,773. *Average non-need based aid:* $8432. *Average aid to full-time undergraduates:* $15,196.
Athletic Department: *Director of Athletics:* Frank Wolfgang; Phone: 215-489-2268; Fax: 215-230-2963; E-mail: wolfganf@devalcol.edu. *Sports Information Director:* Matt Levy; Phone: 215-489-2937; E-mail: levym@devalcol.edu.

MEN'S COACHES
Baseball: Bob Altieri; Phone: 215-489-2379; E-mail: altierir@devalcol.edu.
Basketball: Denny Surovec; Phone: 215-489-2380; E-mail: surovecd@devalcol.edu.
Cheerleading: Maureen Doyle; Phone: 215-489-2925; E-mail: doylem@devalcol.edu.
Cross Country: Ed Andrewevich; Phone: 215-489-4982; E-mail: andrewle@devalcol.edu.
Football: G.A. Mangus; Phone: 215-489-2439; E-mail: mangusg@devalcol.edu.
Golf: Doug Linde; Phone: 215-489-2260; E-mail: linded@devalcol.edu.
Soccer: Kalman Csapo; Phone: 215-489-4983; E-mail: csapok@devalcol.edu.
Track and Field: Ed Andrewevich; Phone: 215-489-4982; E-mail: andrewle@devalcol.edu.
Wrestling: Brandon Totten; Phone: 215-489-2356; E-mail: tottenb@devalcol.edu.

WOMEN'S COACHES
Basketball: Laura Hogan; Phone: 215-489-2381; E-mail: hoganl@devalcol.edu.
Cheerleading: Maureen Doyle; Phone: 215-489-2925; E-mail: doylem@devalcol.edu.
Cross Country: Ed Andrewevich; Phone: 215-489-4982; E-mail: andrewle@devalcol.edu.
Field Hockey: Jennifer Wolfgang; Phone: 215-489-2300; E-mail: wolfganj@devalcol.edu.
Soccer: Kevin Doherty; Phone: 215-489-2934; E-mail: dohertyk@devalcol.edu.
Softball: Richard Matarese; Phone: 215-489-2358; E-mail: mataresr@devalcol.edu.
Track and Field: Ed Andrewevich; Phone: 215-489-4982; E-mail: andrewle@devalcol.edu.
Volleyball: Shawn Rush; Phone: 215-489-2925; E-mail: rushs@devalcol.edu.

DELTA STATE UNIVERSITY
Cleveland, Mississippi

Statesmen ◆ NCAA II ◆ Gulf South Conference ◆ http://www.deltastate.edu/

State-supported comprehensive, founded 1924, part of Mississippi Institutions of Higher Learning
Coed, 3,156 undergraduate students, 81% full-time, 62% women, 38% men
Small-town 332-acre campus
Minimally difficult entrance level, 26% of applicants were admitted

Freshmen *Admission:* 1,289 applied, 330 were accepted, 330 enrolled.
Tuition and fees (2003–04): $3772 (resident), $8389 (nonresident). *Room and board:* $3270.
Athletic Department: *Director of Athletics:* Brad Teague; Phone: 662-846-4300; Fax: 662-846-4297; E-mail: bteague@deltastate.edu. *Sports Information Director:* Paul Smith; Phone: 662-846-4284.

MEN'S COACHES
Baseball: Mike Kinnison; Phone: 662-846-4291; E-mail: mkinnisn@deltastate.edu.
Basketball: Steve Rives; Phone: 662-846-4461; E-mail: srives@deltastate.edu.
Cheerleading: Kim Logan; Phone: 662-846-4300; E-mail: klogan@deltastate.edu.
Diving: Chrissy Young; Phone: 662-846-4730.
Football: Rick Rhoades; Phone: 662-846-4292; E-mail: rrhoades@deltastate.edu.
Golf: Sam Dunning; Phone: 662-846-3456; E-mail: sd2@deltastate.edu.
Soccer: JimAllen; Phone: 662-846-4300; E-mail: gfckfrogs@yahoo.com.
Swimming: Ronnie Mayers; Phone: 662-846-4730; E-mail: rmayers@deltastate.edu.
Tennis: Asa Atkinson; Phone: 662-846-6740; E-mail: asa@tecinfo.com.

WOMEN'S COACHES
Basketball: Sandra Rushing; Phone: 662-846-4465; E-mail: srushing@deltastate.edu.
Cheerleading: Kim Logan; Phone: 662-846-4300; E-mail: klogan@deltastate.edu.
Cross Country: Doug Pinkerton; Phone: 662-846-4569; E-mail: dpinkrtn@deltastate.edu.
Diving: Chrissy Young; Phone: 662-846-4730.
Soccer: JimAllen; Phone: 662-846-4300; E-mail: gfckfrogs@yahoo.com.
Softball: David Kuhn; Phone: 662-846-4288; E-mail: dkuhn@deltastate.edu.
Swimming: Ronnie Mayers; Phone: 662-846-4730; E-mail: rmayers@deltastate.edu.

DENISON UNIVERSITY
Granville, Ohio

Big Red ◆ NCAA III ◆ North Coast Athletic Conference ◆ http://www.denison.edu/

Independent 4-year, founded 1831
Coed, 2,232 undergraduate students, 95% full-time, 56% women, 44% men
Small-town 1,200-acre campus with easy access to Columbus
Moderately difficult entrance level, 60% of applicants were admitted

Freshmen *Admission:* 3,141 applied, 2,125 were accepted, 629 enrolled. *Test scores:* SAT verbal scores over 500: 97%; SAT math scores over 500: 96%; SAT verbal scores over 600: 57%; SAT math scores over 600: 59%; SAT verbal scores over 700: 12%; SAT math scores over 700: 11%.
Tuition and fees (2003–04): $25,760 (full-time). *Room and board:* $7290 (room only): $3980).
Financial Aid (All incoming freshmen): *Average need-based gift aid:* $16,913. *Average non-need based aid:* $11,031. *Average aid to full-time undergraduates:* $22,501.
Athletic Department: *Director of Athletics:* Larry Scheiderer; Phone: 740-587-6428; Fax: 740-587-6362; E-mail: scheiderer@denison.edu. *Sports Information Director:* Craig Hicks; Phone: 740-587-6546; E-mail: hicksc@denison.edu.

Denison University (*continued*)

MEN'S COACHES

Baseball: Barry Craddock; Phone: 740-587-6714; E-mail: craddock@denison.edu.
Basketball: Bob Ghiloni; Phone: 740-587-6586; E-mail: ghiloni@denison.edu.
Cheerleading: Simone Roberts; Phone: 740-587-6580.
Cross Country: Phil Torrens; Phone: 740-587-6661; E-mail: sarahtorrens@ecr.net.
Diving: Anne Gillie; Phone: 740-587-6236; E-mail: gilliea@denison.edu.
Football: Nick Fletcher; Phone: 740-587-6585; E-mail: fletchern@denison.edu.
Golf: Kyle Pottkotter; Phone: 740-587-6778; E-mail: pottkotterk@denison.edu.
Lacrosse: Mike Caravana; Phone: 740-587-6590; E-mail: caravana@denison.edu.
Soccer: Rob Russo; Phone: 740-587-5735; E-mail: russo@denison.edu.
Swimming: Gregg Parini; Phone: 740-587-6678; E-mail: parini@denison.edu.
Tennis: Peter Burling; Phone: 740-587-6689; E-mail: burling@denison.edu.
Track and Field: Pam Fanaritis; Phone: 740-587-6661; E-mail: fanaritis@denison.edu.

WOMEN'S COACHES

Basketball: Sara Lee; Phone: 740-587-6290; E-mail: lees@denison.edu.
Cheerleading: Simone Roberts; Phone: 740-587-6580.
Cross Country: Phil Torrens; Phone: 740-587-6661; E-mail: sarahtorrens@ecr.net.
Diving: Anne Gillie; Phone: 740-587-6236; E-mail: gilliea@denison.edu.
Field Hockey: P.J. Soteriades; Phone: 740-587-6584; E-mail: soteriades@denison.edu.
Lacrosse: Stephani Brzezowski; Phone: 740-587-5664; E-mail: brzezowski@denison.edu.
Soccer: Gail Murphy; Phone: 740-587-5728; E-mail: murphyg@denison.edu.
Softball: Holly Bruder; Phone: 740-587-6784; E-mail: bruderh@denison.edu.
Swimming: Gregg Parini; Phone: 740-587-6678; E-mail: parini@denison.edu.
Tennis: Peter Burling; Phone: 740-587-6689; E-mail: burling@denison.edu.
Track and Field: Pam Fanaritis; Phone: 740-587-6661; E-mail: fanaritis@denison.edu.
Volleyball: Sara Lee; Phone: 740-587-6290; E-mail: lees@denison.edu.

DEPAUL UNIVERSITY
Chicago, Illinois

Blue Demons ◆ NCAA I ◆ Conference USA Conference ◆ http://www.depaul.edu/

Independent Roman Catholic university, founded 1898
Coed, 14,585 undergraduate students, 74% full-time, 58% women, 42% men
Urban 36-acre campus
Moderately difficult entrance level, 73% of applicants were admitted

Freshmen *Admission:* 9,463 applied, 6,903 were accepted, 2,261 enrolled. *Test scores:* SAT verbal scores over 500: 78%; SAT math scores over 500: 75%; SAT verbal scores over 600: 34%; SAT math scores over 600: 28%; SAT verbal scores over 700: 5%; SAT math scores over 700: 4%.
Tuition and fees (2003–04): $18,790 (full-time). *Room and board:* $8790 (room only: $5970).
Financial Aid (All incoming freshmen): *Average need-based gift aid:* $10,925. *Average non-need based aid:* $7425. *Average aid to full-time undergraduates:* $15,552.
Athletic Department: *Director of Athletics:* Jean Lenti Ponsetto; Phone: 773-325-7503; Fax: 773-325-7529; E-mail: jlentipo@depaul.edu. *Sports Information Director:* Greg Greenwell; Phone: 773-325-7546; E-mail: ggreenwe@depaul.edu.

MEN'S COACHES

Basketball: Dave Leitao; Phone: 773-325-7521; E-mail: ljepsen@depaul.edu.
Cheerleading: Phone: 773-325-7526; E-mail: cheer@depaul.edu.
Cross Country: Gordon Thomson; Phone: 773-325-1452; E-mail: gthomson@depaul.edu.
Golf: Betty Kaufman; Phone: 773-325-7520; E-mail: ekaufman@depaul.edu.
Soccer: Craig Blazer; Phone: 773-325-7231; E-mail: cblazer@depaul.edu.
Tennis: Mark Adrizzone; Phone: 773-325-7232; E-mail: mardizzo@depaul.edu.
Track and Field: Gordon Thomson; Phone: 773-325-1452; E-mail: gthomson@depaul.edu.

WOMEN'S COACHES

Basketball: Doug Bruno; Phone: 773-325-7507; E-mail: dbruno@depaul.edu.
Cheerleading: Phone: 773-325-7526; E-mail: cheer@depaul.edu.
Cross Country: Gordon Thomson; Phone: 773-325-1452; E-mail: gthomson@depaul.edu.
Soccer: John Wilson; Phone: 773-325-2075; E-mail: jwilso13@depaul.edu.
Softball: Eugene Lenti; Phone: 773-325-7253; E-mail: elenti@depaul.edu.
Tennis: Mark Aroizzone; Phone: 773-325-7232; E-mail: mardizzo@depaul.edu.
Track and Field: Gordon Thomson; Phone: 773-325-1452; E-mail: gthomson@depaul.edu.
Volleyball: Dawn Dockstader; Phone: 773-325-7250; E-mail: ddockstader@depaul.edu.

DEPAUW UNIVERSITY
Greencastle, Indiana

Tigers ◆ NCAA III ◆ Southern Collegiate Athletic Conference ◆ http://www.depauw.edu/

Independent religious 4-year, founded 1837, affiliated with United Methodist Church
Coed, 2,365 undergraduate students, 98% full-time, 55% women, 45% men
Small-town 655-acre campus with easy access to Indianapolis
Moderately difficult entrance level, 62% of applicants were admitted

Freshmen *Admission:* 3,651 applied, 2,296 were accepted, 581 enrolled. *Test scores:* SAT verbal scores over 500: 95%; SAT math scores over 500: 95%; SAT verbal scores over 600: 54%; SAT math scores over 600: 62%; SAT verbal scores over 700: 13%; SAT math scores over 700: 12%.
Tuition and fees (2003–04): $24,450 (full-time). *Room and board:* $7050 (room only: $3650).
Financial Aid (All incoming freshmen): *Average need-based gift aid:* $19,012. *Average non-need based aid:* $11,856. *Average aid to full-time undergraduates:* $22,191.
Athletic Department: *Director of Athletics:* Page Cotton; Phone: 765-658-4938; Fax: 765-658-4964; E-mail: pagecotton@depauw.edu. *Sports Information Director:* Bill Wagner; Phone: 765-658-4630; E-mail: bwagner@depauw.edu.

MEN'S COACHES

Baseball: Matt Walker; Phone: 765-658-4939; E-mail: mwalker@depauw.edu.
Basketball: Bill Fenlon; Phone: 765-658-4940; E-mail: bfenlon@depauw.edu.
Cheerleading: John Carter; Phone: 765-658-4800; E-mail: jcarter@depauw.edu.
Cross Country: Kori Stoffregen; Phone: 765-658-4945; E-mail: kstoffregen@depauw.edu.
Diving: Adam Cohen; Phone: 765-658-4119; E-mail: acohen@depauw.edu.
Football: Bill Lynch; Phone: 765-658-4908; E-mail: blynch@depauw.edu.
Golf: Vince Lazar; Phone: 765-658-4921; E-mail: vlazar@depauw.edu.
Soccer: Page Cotton; Phone: 765-658-4938; E-mail: pagecotton@depauw.edu.
Swimming: Adam Cohen; Phone: 765-658-4119; E-mail: acohen@depauw.edu.
Tennis: Tom Cath; Phone: 765-658-4280; E-mail: tcath@depauw.edu.
Track and Field: Kori Stoffregen; Phone: 765-658-4945; E-mail: kstoffregen@depauw.edu.

WOMEN'S COACHES

Basketball: Kris Huffman; Phone: 765-658-4960; E-mail: khuffman@depauw.edu.
Cheerleading: John Carter; Phone: 765-658-4800; E-mail: jcarter@depauw.edu.
Cross Country: Kori Stoffregen; Phone: 765-658-4945; E-mail: kstoffregen@depauw.edu.
Diving: Mary Bretscher; Phone: 765-658-4946; E-mail: mbretscher@depauw.edu.
Field Hockey: Carla Lane; Phone: 765-658-4931; E-mail: cgasbarra@depauw.edu.
Golf: Vince Lazar; Phone: 765-658-4921; E-mail: vlazar@depauw.edu.
Soccer: John Carter; Phone: 765-658-4961; E-mail: jcarter@depauw.edu.
Softball: Bonnie Skrenta; Phone: 765-658-4967; E-mail: bskrenta@depauw.edu.
Swimming: Mary Bretscher; Phone: 765-658-4946; E-mail: mbretscher@depauw.edu.
Tennis: Scott Riggle; Phone: 765-658-4935; E-mail: sriggle@depauw.edu.
Track and Field: Kori Stoffregen; Phone: 765-658-4945; E-mail: kstoffregen@depauw.edu.
Volleyball: Deb Zellers; Phone: 765-658-4969; E-mail: dzellers@depauw.edu.

DESALES UNIVERSITY
Center Valley, Pennsylvania

Bulldogs ◆ NCAA III ◆ Freedom Conference ◆ http://www.desales.edu/

Independent Roman Catholic comprehensive, founded 1964
Coed, 2,167 undergraduate students, 74% full-time, 57% women, 43% men
Suburban 350-acre campus with easy access to Philadelphia and New York City
Moderately difficult entrance level, 76% of applicants were admitted

Freshmen *Admission:* 1,678 applied, 1,284 were accepted, 395 enrolled. *Test scores:* SAT verbal scores over 500: 69%; SAT math scores over 500: 70%; SAT verbal scores over 600: 24%; SAT math scores over 600: 24%; SAT verbal scores over 700: 3%; SAT math scores over 700: 2%.
Tuition and fees (2003–04): $18,390 (full-time). *Room and board:* $7080.
Financial Aid (All incoming freshmen): *Average need-based gift aid:* $10,062. *Average non-need based aid:* $5145. *Average aid to full-time undergraduates:* $12,656.
Athletic Department: *Director of Athletics:* Scott Coval; Phone: 610-282-1100; Fax: 610-282-2279; E-mail: scott.coval@desales.edu. *Sports Information Director:* B.J. Spigelmyer; Phone: 610-282-1100; E-mail: william.spigelmyer@desales.edu.

MEN'S COACHES

Baseball: Tim Neiman; Phone: 610-282-1100; E-mail: timothy.neiman@desales.edu.
Basketball: Scott Coval; Phone: 610-282-1100; E-mail: scott.coval@desales.edu.
Cheerleading: Kristy Frederick; Phone: 610-282-1100; E-mail: kfred@rcn.com.
Cross Country: Al Weiner; Phone: 610-282-1100; E-mail: alan.weiner@desales.edu.
Golf: Scott Coval; Phone: 610-282-1100; E-mail: scott.coval@desales.edu.
Lacrosse: Donovan Quill; Phone: 610-282-1100; E-mail: donovan.quill@desales.edu.
Soccer: George Crampton; Phone: 610-282-1100; E-mail: george.crampton@desales.edu.
Tennis: Al Senavitis; Phone: 610-282-1100.
Track and Field: Al Weiner; Phone: 610-282-1100; E-mail: alan.weiner@desales.edu.

WOMEN'S COACHES

Basketball: Fred Richter; Phone: 610-282-1100; E-mail: fmr24esu@aol.com.
Cheerleading: Kristy Frederick; Phone: 610-282-1100; E-mail: kfred@rcn.com.
Cross Country: Gordon Hornig; Phone: 610-282-1100; E-mail: g.k.hornig@att.net.

Soccer: David Yob; Phone: 610-282-1100; E-mail: acwsocyob@msn.com.
Softball: Rachel Turoscy; Phone: 610-282-1100; E-mail: rachel.turoscy@desales.edu.
Tennis: Al Senavitis; Phone: 610-282-1100.
Track and Field: Gordon Hornig; Phone: 610-282-1100; E-mail: g.k.hornig@att.net.
Volleyball: Helen Deegan; Phone: 610-282-1100; E-mail: helen.deegan@desales.edu.

DICKINSON COLLEGE
Carlisle, Pennsylvania

Red Devils ◆ NCAA III ◆ Centennial Conference ◆ http://www.dickinson.edu/

Independent 4-year, founded 1773
Coed, 2,276 undergraduate students, 98% full-time, 56% women, 44% men
Suburban 115-acre campus with easy access to Harrisburg
Very difficult entrance level, 49% of applicants were admitted

Freshmen *Admission:* 4,633 applied, 2,394 were accepted, 624 enrolled. *Test scores:* SAT verbal scores over 500: 99%; SAT math scores over 500: 98%; SAT verbal scores over 600: 73%; SAT math scores over 600: 74%; SAT verbal scores over 700: 14%; SAT math scores over 700: 18%.
Tuition and fees (2004–05): $30,300 (full-time). *Room and board:* $7600 (room only: $3920).
Financial Aid (All incoming freshmen): *Average need-based gift aid:* $19,821. *Average non-need based aid:* $10,943. *Average aid to full-time undergraduates:* $23,101.
Athletic Department: *Director of Athletics:* Leslie Poolman; Phone: 717-245-1320; Fax: 717-245-1441; E-mail: poolman@dickinson.edu. *Sports Information Director:* Charlie McGuire; Phone: 717-245-1652; E-mail: mcguire@dickinson.edu.

MEN'S COACHES

Baseball: Russell Wrenn; Phone: 717-245-1320; E-mail: wrennr@dickinson.edu.
Basketball: Dennis Csensits; Phone: 717-245-1650; E-mail: csensitd@dickinson.edu.
Cross Country: Don Nichter; Phone: 717-245-1365; E-mail: nichter@dickinson.edu.
Football: Darwin Breaux; Phone: 717-245-1644; E-mail: breaux@dickinson.edu.
Golf: Darwin Breaux; Phone: 717-245-1644; E-mail: breaux@dickinson.edu.
Lacrosse: Dave Webster; Phone: 717-245-1595; E-mail: websterd@dickinson.edu.
Soccer: Mark Brown; Phone: 717-245-1693; E-mail: brownma@dickinson.edu.
Swimming: Paul Richards; Phone: 717-245-1523; E-mail: richards@dickinson.edu.
Tennis: Jonathan Birbeck; Phone: 717-240-6219; E-mail: reddeviltennis@aol.com.
Track and Field: John Hartpence; Phone: 717-245-1919; E-mail: hartpenj@dickinson.edu.

WOMEN'S COACHES

Basketball: Dina Henry; Phone: 717-245-1625; E-mail: henryd@dickinson.edu.
Cross Country: Don Nichter; Phone: 717-245-1365; E-mail: nichter@dickinson.edu.
Field Hockey: Allison Risser; Phone: 717-245-1526; E-mail: risser@dickinson.edu.
Golf: Dean Walen; Phone: 717-245-1693; E-mail: walend@dickinson.edu.
Lacrosse: Kasey Ryan; Phone: 717-245-1662; E-mail: ryank@dickinson.edu.
Soccer: Shellee Copley; Phone: 717-245-1981; E-mail: copley@dickinson.edu.
Softball: Matt Richwine; Phone: 717-245-1733; E-mail: richwinm@dickinson.edu.
Swimming: Paul Richards; Phone: 717-245-1523; E-mail: richards@dickinson.edu.
Tennis: Becky Cecere; Phone: 717-245-1693; E-mail: cecere@dickinson.edu.

Dickinson College (*continued*)

Track and Field: John Hartpence; Phone: 717-245-1919; E-mail: hartpenj@dickinson.edu.
Volleyball: Mike Beachy; Phone: 717-245-1331; E-mail: beachym@dickinson.edu.

DICKINSON STATE UNIVERSITY
Dickinson, North Dakota

Blue Hawks ◆ NAIA ◆ Dakota Conference
◆ http://www.dsu.nodak.edu/

State-supported 4-year, founded 1918, part of North Dakota University System
Coed, 2,461 undergraduate students, 70% full-time, 57% women, 43% men
Small-town 100-acre campus
Noncompetitive entrance level, 99% of applicants were admitted

Freshmen *Admission:* 717 applied, 712 were accepted, 684 enrolled. *Test scores:* SAT verbal scores over 500: 43%; SAT math scores over 500: 91%; SAT verbal scores over 600: 12%; SAT math scores over 600: 36%; SAT verbal scores over 700: 6%; SAT math scores over 700: 18%.
Tuition and fees (2003–04): $3139 (resident), $7406 (nonresident). *Room and board:* $3350 (room only: $1200).
Athletic Department: *Director of Athletics:* Roger Ternes; Phone: 701-483-2159; Fax: 701-483-0501; E-mail: roger.ternes@dickinsonstate.edu. *Sports Information Director:* Duane Monlux; Phone: 701-483-2716; E-mail: duane.d.monlux@dickinsonstate.edu.

MEN'S COACHES
Baseball: Duane Monlux; Phone: 701-483-2716; E-mail: duane.d.monlux@dickinsonstate.edu.
Basketball: Scott Berry; Phone: 701-483-2473; E-mail: scott.berry@dickinsonstate.edu.
Cross Country: Thadd O'Donnell; Phone: 701-483-2568; E-mail: thadd.odonnell@dickinsonstate.edu.
Football: Hank Biesiot; Phone: 701-483-2735; E-mail: henry.biesiot@dickinsonstate.edu.
Golf: Tim Damiel; Phone: 701-483-2100; E-mail: tim.daniel@dickinsonstate.edu.
Track and Field: Pete Stanton; Phone: 701-483-2386; E-mail: p.stanton@dickinsonstate.edu.
Wrestling: Thadd O'Donnell; Phone: 701-483-2568; E-mail: thadd.odonnell@dickinsonstate.edu.

WOMEN'S COACHES
Basketball: Tara Kreklau; Phone: 701-483-2102; E-mail: tara.kreklau@dickinsonstate.edu.
Cross Country: Thadd O'Donnell; Phone: 701-483-2568; E-mail: thadd.odonnell@dickinsonstate.edu.
Golf: Tim Damiel; Phone: 701-483-2100; E-mail: tim.daniel@dickinsonstate.edu.
Softball: Guy Fridley; Phone: 701-483-2173; E-mail: guy.fridley@dickinsonstate.edu.
Track and Field: Pete Stanton; Phone: 701-483-2386; E-mail: p.stanton@dickinsonstate.edu.
Volleyball: David Moody; Phone: 701-483-2120; E-mail: david.moody@dickinsonstate.edu.

DILLARD UNIVERSITY
New Orleans, Louisiana

NAIA ◆ Gulf Coast Conference ◆ http://www.dillard.edu/

Independent interdenominational 4-year, founded 1869
Coed, 2,312 undergraduate students, 90% full-time, 78% women, 22% men
Urban 55-acre campus
Moderately difficult entrance level, 58% of applicants were admitted

Freshmen *Admission:* 3,372 applied, 2,155 were accepted, 609 enrolled. *Test scores:* SAT verbal scores over 500: 30%; SAT math scores over 500: 30%; SAT verbal scores over 600: 10%; SAT math scores over 600: 6%; SAT verbal scores over 700: 2%; SAT math scores over 700: 1%.
Tuition and fees (2003–04): $10,865 (full-time). *Room and board:* $6440.
Financial Aid (All incoming freshmen): *Average need-based gift aid:* $3822. *Average non-need based aid:* $4009. *Average aid to full-time undergraduates:* $13,692.
Athletic Department: *Director of Athletics:* Clifford Barthe; Phone: 504-816-4004; Fax: 504-816-4365.

MEN'S COACHES
Basketball: Marco Borne; Phone: 504-816-4004.
Cross Country: Terrence Saulney; Phone: 504-816-4004.
Tennis: James Branch; Phone: 504-816-4004.

WOMEN'S COACHES
Cross Country: Mark Cook; Phone: 504-816-4004.
Tennis: James Branch; Phone: 504-816-4004.
Volleyball: Javonne Butler; Phone: 504-816-4004.

DOANE COLLEGE
Crete, Nebraska

Tigers ◆ NAIA ◆ Great Plains Conference
◆ http://www.doane.edu/

Independent religious comprehensive, founded 1872, affiliated with United Church of Christ
Coed, 1,610 undergraduate students, 85% full-time, 56% women, 44% men
Small-town 300-acre campus with easy access to Omaha
Moderately difficult entrance level, 79% of applicants were admitted

Freshmen *Admission:* 1,097 applied, 922 were accepted, 291 enrolled.
Tuition and fees (2004–05): $15,970 (full-time). *Room and board:* $4720.
Financial Aid (All incoming freshmen): *Average need-based gift aid:* $9680. *Average non-need based aid:* $7538. *Average aid to full-time undergraduates:* $12,638.
Athletic Department: *Director of Athletics:* Fran Schwenk; Phone: 402-826-8201; Fax: 402-826-8647; E-mail: fschwenk@doane.edu. *Sports Information Director:* Rick Schmuecker; Phone: 402-826-8248; E-mail: athletics@doane.edu.

MEN'S COACHES
Baseball: Jack Hudkins; Phone: 402-826-8646.
Basketball: Ian Brown; Phone: 402-826-6717.
Cross Country: Ed Fye; Phone: 402-826-8300; E-mail: efye@doane.edu.
Football: Fran Schwenk; Phone: 402-826-8201; E-mail: fschwenk@doane.edu.
Golf: Scott Johnson; Phone: 402-826-6717.
Soccer: Eliot Siegman; Phone: 402-826-8622; E-mail: esiegman@aol.com.
Tennis: Pee Fiumefreddo; Phone: 402-826-8227; E-mail: pfiumefreddo@doane.edu.
Track and Field: Ed Fye; Phone: 402-826-8300; E-mail: efye@doane.edu.

WOMEN'S COACHES
Basketball: Tracee Fairbanks; Phone: 402-826-8636; E-mail: tfairbanks@doane.edu.
Cross Country: Ed Fye; Phone: 402-826-8300; E-mail: efye@doane.edu.
Golf: Scott Johnson; Phone: 402-826-6717.
Soccer: Eliot Siegman; Phone: 402-826-8622; E-mail: esiegman@aol.com.
Softball: Barry Mosley; Phone: 402-826-6735; E-mail: bmosley@doane.edu.
Tennis: Pee Fiumefreddo; Phone: 402-826-8227; E-mail: pfiumefreddo@doane.edu.
Track and Field: Ed Fye; Phone: 402-826-8300; E-mail: efye@doane.edu.
Volleyball: Cindy Meyer; Phone: 402-826-8202; E-mail: cmeyer@doane.edu.

DOMINICAN COLLEGE
Orangeburg, New York

Chargers ◆ NCAA II ◆ Central Atlantic Collegiate Conference ◆ http://www.dc.edu/

Independent comprehensive, founded 1952
Coed, 1,303 undergraduate students, 71% full-time, 67% women, 33% men
Suburban 26-acre campus with easy access to New York City
Moderately difficult entrance level, 86% of applicants were admitted

---

Freshmen *Admission:* 847 applied, 743 were accepted, 257 enrolled. *Test scores:* SAT verbal scores over 500: 28%; SAT math scores over 500: 28%; SAT verbal scores over 600: 4%; SAT math scores over 600: 4%.
Tuition and fees (2003–04): $16,650 (full-time). *Room and board:* $8160.
Financial Aid (All incoming freshmen): *Average need-based gift aid:* $10,277. *Average non-need based aid:* $13,508. *Average aid to full-time undergraduates:* $13,323.
Athletic Department: *Director of Athletics:* Joseph Clinton; Phone: 845-398-3009; Fax: 845-398-3042; E-mail: joseph.clinton@dc.edu. *Sports Information Director:* Kelly-Ann DiGiulio; Phone: 845-398-3009; E-mail: kellyann.digiulio@dc.edu.

MEN'S COACHES
Baseball: Rick Gianetti; Phone: 845-398-3009; E-mail: rskip14@aol.com.
Basketball: Joe Clinton; Phone: 845-398-3009; E-mail: joseph.clinton@dc.edu.
Cross Country: Tom Riley; Phone: 845-398-3009.
Golf: Jim Gallagher; Phone: 845-398-3009; E-mail: jgallag489@aol.com.
Lacrosse: Dale Aberling; Phone: 845-398-3009; E-mail: dale.abeling@dc.edu.
Soccer: Michael Swanwick; Phone: 845-398-3009; E-mail: michael.swanwick@dc.edu.

WOMEN'S COACHES
Basketball: John Burke; Phone: 845-398-3008; E-mail: john.burke@dc.edu.
Cross Country: Virginia Capicchioni; Phone: 845-398-3009; E-mail: mtag88@aol.com.
Lacrosse: Virginia Capicchioni; Phone: 845-398-3009; E-mail: mtag88@aol.com.
Soccer: Phil Fluhr; Phone: 845-398-3008; E-mail: phil.fluhr@dc.edu.
Softball: Rick Krasny; Phone: 845-398-3008; E-mail: fpitchcoachrick@aol.com.
Volleyball: Jessica Gallaway; Phone: 845-398-3008; E-mail: mddusty@aol.com.

DOMINICAN UNIVERSITY
River Forest, Illinois

Stars ◆ NCAA III ◆ Northern Illinois-Iowa Conference ◆ http://www.dom.edu/

Independent Roman Catholic comprehensive, founded 1901
Coed, 1,211 undergraduate students, 83% full-time, 69% women, 31% men
Suburban 30-acre campus with easy access to Chicago
Moderately difficult entrance level, 85% of applicants were admitted

---

Freshmen *Admission:* 665 applied, 548 were accepted, 241 enrolled.
Tuition and fees (2004–05): $19,000 (full-time). *Room and board:* $5890.
Financial Aid (All incoming freshmen): *Average need-based gift aid:* $10,721. *Average non-need based aid:* $8812. *Average aid to full-time undergraduates:* $12,904.
Athletic Department: *Director of Athletics:* Barb Bolich; Phone: 708-524-6556; Fax: 708-488-5095; E-mail: bbolich@dom.edu. *Sports Information Director:* Ken Trendel; Phone: 708-524-6232; E-mail: ktrendel@dom.edu.

MEN'S COACHES
Baseball: Terry Casey; Phone: 708-524-6796; E-mail: tcasey@dom.edu.
Basketball: Mark White; Phone: 708-524-6518; E-mail: mkwhite@dom.edu.
Cross Country: Wesley Wheeler; Phone: 708-524-6551.

Soccer: Erick Baumann; Phone: 708-524-5054; E-mail: ebauman@dom.edu.
Tennis: Robert Neuman; Phone: 708-524-6545.

WOMEN'S COACHES
Basketball: Larry Lanciotti; Phone: 708-524-6453; E-mail: llanciot@dom.edu.
Cross Country: Wesley Wheeler; Phone: 708-524-6551; E-mail: wwheeler@dom.edu.
Soccer: Joanna Fulton; Phone: 708-524-6547; E-mail: jfulton@dom.edu.
Softball: Michele Oswald; Phone: 708-524-6237; E-mail: moswald@dom.edu.
Tennis: Robert Neuman; Phone: 708-524-6545.
Volleyball: Meghan Maxwell; Phone: 708-524-6516; E-mail: mmaxwell@dom.edu.

DOMINICAN UNIVERSITY OF CALIFORNIA
San Rafael, California

Penguins ◆ NAIA ◆ California Pacific Conference ◆ http://www.dominican.edu/

Independent religious comprehensive, founded 1890, affiliated with Roman Catholic Church
Coed, 1,124 undergraduate students, 76% full-time, 75% women, 25% men
Suburban 80-acre campus with easy access to San Francisco
Moderately difficult entrance level, 55% of applicants were admitted

---

Freshmen *Admission:* 1,792 applied, 980 were accepted, 245 enrolled. *Test scores:* SAT verbal scores over 500: 64%; SAT math scores over 500: 57%; SAT verbal scores over 600: 20%; SAT math scores over 600: 17%; SAT verbal scores over 700: 4%; SAT math scores over 700: 2%.
Tuition and fees (2003–04): $22,650 (full-time). *Room and board:* $9420.
Financial Aid (All incoming freshmen): *Average need-based gift aid:* $17,984. *Average non-need based aid:* $12,009. *Average aid to full-time undergraduates:* $21,822.
Athletic Department: *Director of Athletics:* Ian McGregor; Phone: 415-458-3758; Fax: 415-485-9746; E-mail: mcgregor@dominican.edu. *Sports Information Director:* Bill Treseler; Phone: 415-482-3526; E-mail: btreseler@dominican.edu.

MEN'S COACHES
Basketball: Bill Treseler; Phone: 415-454-3526; E-mail: btreseler@dominican.edu.
Cheerleading: Carol Harbers; Phone: 415-482-3500; E-mail: harbers@dominican.edu.
Soccer: John Brooks; Phone: 415-482-3505; E-mail: jbrooks@dominican.edu.
Tennis: Steve Tourdo; Phone: 415-454-1209; E-mail: stourdo@dominican.edu.

WOMEN'S COACHES
Basketball: Scott Davis; Phone: 415-482-3506; E-mail: sdavis@dominican.edu.
Cheerleading: Carol Harbers; Phone: 415-482-3500; E-mail: harbers@dominican.edu.
Soccer: Ralph Montes; Phone: 415-482-3505.
Softball: Kirstin Jensen; Phone: 415-257-1306; E-mail: kjensen@dominican.edu.
Tennis: Anne Zarranondia; Phone: 415-482-3500; E-mail: btreseler@dominican.edu.
Volleyball: Roger Goodwin; Phone: 415-257-1304; E-mail: rgoodwin@dominican.edu.

DORDT COLLEGE
Sioux Center, Iowa

Defenders ◆ NAIA ◆ Great Plains Conference ◆ http://www.dordt.edu/

Independent Christian Reformed comprehensive, founded 1955
Coed, 1,287 undergraduate students, 96% full-time, 54% women, 46% men
Small-town 100-acre campus
Moderately difficult entrance level, 92% of applicants were admitted

Freshmen *Admission:* 780 applied, 717 were accepted, 351 enrolled. *Test scores:* SAT verbal scores over 500: 95%; SAT math scores over 500: 95%; SAT verbal scores over 600: 57%; SAT math scores over 600: 58%; SAT verbal scores over 700: 24%; SAT math scores over 700: 25%.
Tuition and fees (2003–04): $15,770 (full-time). *Room and board:* $4400 (room only: $2310).
Financial Aid (All incoming freshmen): *Average need-based gift aid:* $9147. *Average non-need based aid:* $7655. *Average aid to full-time undergraduates:* $14,845.
Athletic Department: *Director of Athletics:* Rick Vander Berg; Phone: 712-722-6305; Fax: 712-722-6303; E-mail: rickvb@dordt.edu. *Sports Information Director:* Mike Byker; Phone: 712-722-6301; E-mail: mbyker@dordt.edu.

MEN'S COACHES
Baseball: Jeff Schouten; Phone: 712-722-6300; E-mail: jschoute@dordt.edu.
Basketball: Greg Van Soelen; Phone: 712-722-6095; E-mail: gregvs@dordt.edu.
Cross Country: Ross Goheen; Phone: 712-722-6311; E-mail: rgoheen@dordt.edu.
Golf: Mark Christians; Phone: 712-722-6262; E-mail: mark@dordt.edu.
Soccer: Craig Stiemsma; Phone: 712-722-6738; E-mail: craigs@dordt.edu.
Tennis: Len Rhoda; Phone: 712-722-6234; E-mail: lrhoda@dordt.edu.
Track and Field: Syne Altena; Phone: 712-722-6235; E-mail: saltena@dordt.edu.

WOMEN'S COACHES
Basketball: Glenn Bouma; Phone: 712-722-6310; E-mail: gbouma@dordt.edu.
Cross Country: Ross Goheen; Phone: 712-722-6311; E-mail: rgoheen@dordt.edu.
Soccer: William Elgersma; Phone: 712-722-6486; E-mail: welgersm@dordt.edu.
Softball: Donald Draayer; Phone: 712-722-6079; E-mail: don@dordt.edu.
Tennis: Rudy Folkerts; Phone: 712-722-6300; E-mail: rfolkert@dordt.edu.
Track and Field: Syne Altena; Phone: 712-722-6235; E-mail: saltena@dordt.edu.
Volleyball: Tom Van Den Bosch; Phone: 712-722-6092; E-mail: tomvb@dordt.edu.

DOWLING COLLEGE
Oakdale, New York

Golden Lions ◆ NCAA II ◆ New York Collegiate Athletic Conference ◆ http://www.dowling.edu/

Independent comprehensive, founded 1955
Coed, 3,095 undergraduate students, 69% full-time, 61% women, 39% men
Suburban 157-acre campus with easy access to New York City
Moderately difficult entrance level, 97% of applicants were admitted

Freshmen *Admission:* 2,465 applied, 2,384 were accepted, 487 enrolled. *Test scores:* SAT verbal scores over 500: 53%; SAT math scores over 500: 43%; SAT verbal scores over 600: 8%; SAT math scores over 600: 11%; SAT verbal scores over 700: 1%; SAT math scores over 700: 1%.
Tuition and fees (2004–05): $15,330 (full-time). *Room only:* $5300.
Financial Aid (All incoming freshmen): *Average need-based gift aid:* $5400. *Average non-need based aid:* $5095. *Average aid to full-time undergraduates:* $10,411.

Athletic Department: *Director of Athletics:* Robert Dranoff; Phone: 631-244-3019; Fax: 631-244-3317; E-mail: dranoffr@dowling.edu. *Sports Information Director:* Chris Celano; Phone: 631-244-3019; E-mail: celanoc@dowling.edu.

MEN'S COACHES
Baseball: Carmen Carcone; Phone: 631-244-3019; E-mail: carconec@dowling.edu.
Basketball: Mike Voyack; Phone: 631-244-3038; E-mail: voyackm@dowling.edu.
Cheerleading: Jen Vullo; Phone: 631-244-3019.
Golf: Jeff Dimarco; Phone: 631-244-3019; E-mail: dimarcoj@dowling.edu.
Lacrosse: Tim Boyle; Phone: 631-244-3314; E-mail: boylet@dowling.edu.
Soccer: John DiRico; Phone: 631-244-3315; E-mail: diricoj@dowling.edu.
Tennis: Craig Schwartz; Phone: 631-244-3019; E-mail: schwartzc@dowling.edu.

WOMEN'S COACHES
Basketball: Fran Arato; Phone: 631-244-3294; E-mail: aratof@dowling.edu.
Cheerleading: Jen Vullo; Phone: 631-244-3019.
Cross Country: Tracy DiMarco; Phone: 631-244-3019; E-mail: dimarcot@dowling.edu.
Softball: Jim Kiernan; Phone: 631-244-3019; E-mail: kiernanj@dowling.edu.
Tennis: Lorraine Bouklas; Phone: 631-244-3019; E-mail: bouklasl@dowling.edu.
Volleyball: Alex Koszalka; Phone: 631-244-3019; E-mail: koszalka@dowling.edu.

DRAKE UNIVERSITY
Des Moines, Iowa

Bulldogs ◆ NCAA I ◆ Missouri Valley Conference; Pioneer Football League Conference ◆ http://www.drake.edu/

Independent university, founded 1881
Coed, 3,434 undergraduate students, 92% full-time, 59% women, 41% men
Suburban 120-acre campus
Moderately difficult entrance level, 82% of applicants were admitted

Freshmen *Admission:* 3,174 applied, 2,647 were accepted, 815 enrolled. *Test scores:* SAT verbal scores over 500: 87%; SAT math scores over 500: 87%; SAT verbal scores over 600: 46%; SAT math scores over 600: 52%; SAT verbal scores over 700: 7%; SAT math scores over 700: 12%.
Tuition and fees (2003–04): $19,420 (full-time). *Room and board:* $5700 (room only: $2760).
Financial Aid (All incoming freshmen): *Average need-based gift aid:* $12,101. *Average non-need based aid:* $9376. *Average aid to full-time undergraduates:* $15,961.
Athletic Department: *Director of Athletics:* Dave Blank; Phone: 515-271-2889; Fax: 515-271-3791; E-mail: dave.blank@drake.edu. *Sports Information Director:* Mike Mahon; Phone: 515-271-3012; E-mail: mike.mahon@drake.edu.

MEN'S COACHES
Basketball: Tom Davis; Phone: 515-271-3894; E-mail: tom.davis@drake.edu.
Cheerleading: Tabbi Ireland; Phone: 515-963-7812.
Cross Country: Dan Hostager; Phone: 515-271-4138; E-mail: dan.hostager@drake.edu.
Football: Rob Ash; Phone: 515-271-2104; E-mail: rob.ash@drake.edu.
Golf: Scott Bohlender; Phone: 515-271-1926; E-mail: scott.bohlender@drake.edu.
Soccer: Sean Holmes; Phone: 515-271-2716; E-mail: sean.holmes@drake.edu.
Tennis: Jay Udwadia; Phone: 515-271-4916; E-mail: david.paschal@drake.edu.
Track and Field: Natasha Kaiser-Brown; Phone: 515-271-4138; E-mail: natasha.kaiser-brown@drake.edu.

WOMEN'S COACHES
Basketball: Amy Stephens; Phone: 515-271-2165; E-mail: amy.stephens@drake.edu.
Cheerleading: Tabbi Ireland; Phone: 515-963-7812.

Cross Country: Dan Hostager; Phone: 515-271-4138; E-mail: dan. hostager@drake.edu.

Soccer: Corbin Stone; Phone: 515-271-2173; E-mail: corbin.stone@ drake.edu.

Softball: Rich Calvert; Phone: 515-271-3282; E-mail: rich.calvert@ drake.edu.

Tennis: Ryun Ferrell; Phone: 515-271-2726; E-mail: ryun.ferrell@drake. edu.

Track and Field: Natasha Kaiser-Brown; Phone: 515-271-2748; E-mail: natasha.kaiser-brown@drake.edu.

Volleyball: Randy Dolson; Phone: 515-271-2760; E-mail: randy. dolson@drake.edu.

DREW UNIVERSITY
Madison, New Jersey

Rangers ◆ NCAA III ◆ Freedom Conference ◆ http://www.drew.edu/

Independent religious university, founded 1867, affiliated with United Methodist Church
Coed, 1,606 undergraduate students, 96% full-time, 61% women, 39% men
Suburban 186-acre campus with easy access to New York City
Moderately difficult entrance level, 65% of applicants were admitted

Freshmen *Admission:* 2,746 applied, 1,894 were accepted, 421 enrolled. *Test scores:* SAT verbal scores over 500: 95%; SAT math scores over 500: 90%; SAT verbal scores over 600: 57%; SAT math scores over 600: 53%; SAT verbal scores over 700: 18%; SAT math scores over 700: 9%.
Tuition and fees (2003–04): $27,906 (full-time). *Room and board:* $7644 (room only: $4840).
Athletic Department: *Director of Athletics:* Connee Zotos; Phone: 973-408-3648; Fax: 973-408-3014; E-mail: czotos@drew.edu. *Sports Information Director:* Jennifer Brauner; Phone: 973-408-3574; E-mail: jbrauner@drew.edu.

MEN'S COACHES
Baseball: Vince Masco; Phone: 973-408-3443; E-mail: vmasco@drew. edu.
Basketball: Walter Townes; Phone: 973-408-3719.
Cross Country: David Hagan; Phone: 973-408-3441; E-mail: dhagan@ drew.edu.
Lacrosse: Tom Leanos; Phone: 973-408-3573; E-mail: tleanos@drew. edu.
Soccer: Lenny Armuth; Phone: 973-408-3135; E-mail: larmuth@drew. edu.
Swimming: Rebecca Mitchell; Phone: 973-408-3094; E-mail: rvmitche@ drew.edu.
Tennis: Ira Miller; Phone: 973-408-3115; E-mail: imiller@drew.edu.

WOMEN'S COACHES
Basketball: Anne Jones; Phone: 973-408-3616; E-mail: ajones@drew. edu.
Cross Country: David Hagan; Phone: 973-408-3441; E-mail: dhagan@ drew.edu.
Field Hockey: Kelly Ford; Phone: 973-408-3021.
Lacrosse: Kim Christos; Phone: 973-408-3087; E-mail: kchristos@drew. edu.
Soccer: Christa Racine; Phone: 973-408-3650; E-mail: cracine@drew. edu.
Softball: Tammy Evans; Phone: 973-408-3017; E-mail: tlevans@drew. edu.
Swimming: Rebecca Mitchell; Phone: 973-408-3094; E-mail: rvmitche@ drew.edu.
Tennis: Ira Miller; Phone: 973-408-3115; E-mail: imiller@drew.edu.

DREXEL UNIVERSITY
Philadelphia, Pennsylvania

Dragons ◆ NCAA I ◆ Colonial Athletic Conference ◆ http://www.drexel.edu/

Independent university, founded 1891
Coed, 11,613 undergraduate students, 81% full-time, 40% women, 60% men
Urban 42-acre campus
Moderately difficult entrance level, 73% of applicants were admitted

Freshmen *Admission:* 10,390 applied, 7,285 were accepted, 2,097 enrolled. *Test scores:* SAT verbal scores over 500: 90%; SAT math scores over 500: 96%; SAT verbal scores over 600: 43%; SAT math scores over 600: 61%; SAT verbal scores over 700: 7%; SAT math scores over 700: 13%.
Tuition and fees (2003–04): $21,305 (full-time). *Room and board:* $9600 (room only: $5700).
Financial Aid (All incoming freshmen): *Average need-based gift aid:* $4603. *Average non-need based aid:* $7045. *Average aid to full-time undergraduates:* $10,728.
Athletic Department: *Director of Athletics:* Eric Zillmer; Phone: 215-895-1977; Fax: 215-895-2037; E-mail: sports@drexel.edu. *Sports Information Director:* Aimee Cicero; Phone: 215-895-1570; E-mail: afc24@ drexel.edu.

MEN'S COACHES
Basketball: James Flint; Phone: 215-895-1367; E-mail: flint@drexel.edu.
Cheerleading: Sophia Avanzato; Phone: 215-895-1400.
Diving: Larry May; Phone: 215-895-2029; E-mail: larrymay@comcast. net.
Golf: Mike Dynda; Phone: 215-895-6083; E-mail: golfcoach@drexel. edu.
Lacrosse: Chris Bates; Phone: 215-895-1859; E-mail: bates@drexel.edu.
Soccer: Lew Meehl; Phone: 215-895-1936; E-mail: meehl@drexel.edu.
Swimming: Bruce Bronsdon; Phone: 215-895-2028; E-mail: swim@ drexel.edu.
Tennis: Whitney Thain; Phone: 215-895-2032; E-mail: tennis@drexel. edu.
Wrestling: Jack Childs; Phone: 215-895-1592; E-mail: childsjp@drexel. edu.

WOMEN'S COACHES
Basketball: Denise Dillom; Phone: 215-895-1967; E-mail: denisedillon@ drexel.edu.
Cheerleading: Sophia Avanzato; Phone: 215-895-1400.
Diving: Larry May; Phone: 215-895-2029; E-mail: larrymay@comcast. net.
Field Hockey: Denise Zelenak; Phone: 215-895-1789; E-mail: fieldhockey@drexel.edu.
Lacrosse: Anne Marie Vesco; Phone: 215-895-1885; E-mail: av47@ drexel.edu.
Soccer: Ray Goon; Phone: 215-895-1595; E-mail: goonrw@drexel.edu.
Softball: Terry Deturo; Phone: 215-895-1837; E-mail: terry.deturo@ drexel.edu.
Swimming: Bruce Bronsdon; Phone: 215-895-2028; E-mail: swim@ drexel.edu.
Tennis: Whitney Thain; Phone: 215-895-2032; E-mail: tennis@drexel. edu.

DRURY UNIVERSITY
Springfield, Missouri

Panthers ◆ NCAA II ◆ Heartland Conference; Missouri Valley Conference ◆ http://www.drury.edu/

Independent comprehensive, founded 1873
Coed, 1,541 undergraduate students, 97% full-time, 56% women, 44% men
Urban 80-acre campus
Moderately difficult entrance level, 76% of applicants were admitted

Freshmen *Admission:* 1,128 applied, 865 were accepted, 365 enrolled. *Test scores:* SAT verbal scores over 500: 85%; SAT math scores over 500: 90%; SAT verbal scores over 600: 50%; SAT math scores over 600: 54%; SAT verbal scores over 700: 18%; SAT math scores over 700: 11%.

Drury University *(continued)*

Tuition and fees (2004–05): $13,904 (full-time). *Room and board:* $5128.
Financial Aid (All incoming freshmen): *Average need-based gift aid:* $6084. *Average non-need based aid:* $2885. *Average aid to full-time under-graduates:* $7147.
Athletic Department: *Director of Athletics:* Edsel Matthews; Phone: 417-873-7294; Fax: 417-873-7510; E-mail: ematthews@drury.edu. *Sports Information Director:* Dan Cashel; Phone: 417-873-7222; E-mail: dcashel@drury.edu.

MEN'S COACHES

Basketball: Gary Stanfield; Phone: 417-873-7265; E-mail: gstanfie@drury.edu.
Cheerleading: Cremin Mosley; Phone: 417-873-7265; E-mail: cmosley@drury.edu.
Cross Country: Jon Van Arkel; Phone: 417-873-7567; E-mail: xcntry@drury.edu.
Diving: Richard Hackett; Phone: 417-873-7422; E-mail: breynold@drury.edu.
Golf: Brent Milleson; Phone: 417-873-6879; E-mail: bmilleso@drury.edu.
Soccer: Marshall Ray; Phone: 417-873-7830; E-mail: mray1@drury.edu.
Swimming: Brian Reynolds; Phone: 417-873-7293; E-mail: breynold@drury.edu.
Tennis: Amine Boustani; Phone: 417-873-7439; E-mail: aboustan@drury.edu.

WOMEN'S COACHES

Basketball: Nyla Milleson; Phone: 417-873-7853; E-mail: nmilleso@drury.edu.
Cheerleading: Cremin Mosley; Phone: 417-873-7265; E-mail: cmosley@drury.edu.
Cross Country: Jon Van Arkel; Phone: 417-873-7567; E-mail: xcntry@drury.edu.
Diving: Richard Hackett; Phone: 417-873-7422; E-mail: breynold@drury.edu.
Golf: Lisa Tinkler; Phone: 417-873-7576; E-mail: ltinkler@drury.edu.
Soccer: Chris Baker; Phone: 417-873-7477; E-mail: cbaker1@drury.edu.
Swimming: Brian Reynolds; Phone: 417-873-7293; E-mail: breynold@drury.edu.
Tennis: Kim Swearengin; Phone: 417-873-6847; E-mail: kadamson@drury.edu.
Volleyball: Lawrence Anderson; Phone: 417-873-7252; E-mail: landerso@drury.edu.

DUKE UNIVERSITY
Durham, North Carolina

Blue Devils ◆ NCAA I ◆ Atlantic Coast Conference ◆ http://www.duke.edu/

Independent religious university, founded 1838, affiliated with United Methodist Church
Coed, 6,248 undergraduate students, 99% full-time, 49% women, 51% men
Suburban 8,500-acre campus
Most difficult entrance level, 23% of applicants were admitted

Freshmen *Admission:* 16,729 applied, 3,873 were accepted, 1,619 en-rolled. *Test scores:* SAT verbal scores over 500: 99%; SAT math scores over 500: 100%; SAT verbal scores over 600: 91%; SAT math scores over 600: 94%; SAT verbal scores over 700: 51%; SAT math scores over 700: 66%.
Tuition and fees (2003–04): $29,345 (full-time). *Room and board:* $8210 (room only: $4430).
Financial Aid (All incoming freshmen): *Average need-based gift aid:* $21,432. *Average non-need based aid:* $7030. *Average aid to full-time undergraduates:* $25,832.
Athletic Department: *Director of Athletics:* Joe Alleva; Phone: 919-684-5700; Fax: 919-684-7866; E-mail: alleva@duaa.duke.edu. *Sports Information Director:* Jon Jackson; Phone: 919-684-2633; E-mail: sid@duaa.duke.edu.

MEN'S COACHES

Baseball: Bill Hillier; Phone: 919-684-2358; E-mail: bhillsr@duaa.duke.edu.
Basketball: Mike Krzyzewski; Phone: 919-613-7500; E-mail: gbbrown@duaa.duke.edu.
Cheerleading: Teresa Ward; Phone: 919-489-3223; E-mail: teresaward@duaa.duke.edu.
Cross Country: Norm Ogilvie; Phone: 919-681-6355; E-mail: no@duaa.duke.edu.
Diving: Andy Scott; Phone: 919-684-5945.
Diving: Andy Scott; Phone: 919-684-5945; E-mail: andy.scott@duaa.duke.edu.
Football: Ted Roof; Phone: 919-684-2635; E-mail: troof@duaa.duke.edu.
Golf: Rod Myers; Phone: 919-681-2494; E-mail: rwmyers@duaa.duke.edu.
Lacrosse: Mike Pressler; Phone: 919-684-4427; E-mail: jalberic@duaa.duke.edu.
Soccer: John Rennie; Phone: 919-668-5734; E-mail: john.rennie@duaa.duke.edu.
Swimming: Bob Thompson; Phone: 919-684-5945.
Tennis: Jay Lapidus; Phone: 919-684-2120; E-mail: jaylapidus@hotmail.com.
Track and Field: Norm Ogilvie; Phone: 919-661-6355; E-mail: no@duaa.duke.edu.
Wrestling: Clar Anderson; Phone: 919-681-0249; E-mail: coach.anderson@duaa.duke.edu.

WOMEN'S COACHES

Basketball: Gail Goestenkors; Phone: 919-613-7565; E-mail: gag@duaa.duke.edu.
Cheerleading: Teresa Ward; Phone: 919-489-3223; E-mail: teresaward@duaa.duke.edu.
Cross Country: Jan Ogilvie; Phone: 919-661-6355; E-mail: jso1@duaa.duke.edu.
Diving: Andy Scott; Phone: 919-684-5945; E-mail: andy.scott@duaa.duke.edu.
Field Hockey: Beth Bozman; Phone: 919-684-4116; E-mail: bozman@duaa.duke.edu.
Golf: Dan Brooks; Phone: 919-681-2628; E-mail: dsb5@duaa.duke.edu.
Lacrosse: Kerstin Kimel; Phone: 919-684-4166; E-mail: kmkimel@duaa.duke.edu.
Soccer: Robbie Church; Phone: 919-668-5749; E-mail: church@duaa.duke.edu.
Swimming: Bob Thompson; Phone: 919-684-5945.
Tennis: Jamie Ashworth; Phone: 919-668-0345; E-mail: jeaduke10s@duaa.duke.edu.
Track and Field: Jan Ogilvie; Phone: 919-681-6355; E-mail: no@duaa.duke.edu.
Volleyball: Jolene Nagel; Phone: 919-684-4834; E-mail: jnagel@duaa.duke.edu.

DUQUESNE UNIVERSITY
Pittsburgh, Pennsylvania

Dukes ◆ NCAA I ◆ Atlantic 10 Conference; Metro Atlantic Athletic Conference ◆ http://www.duq.edu/

Independent Roman Catholic university, founded 1878
Coed, 5,724 undergraduate students, 94% full-time, 59% women, 41% men
Urban 43-acre campus
Moderately difficult entrance level, 81% of applicants were admitted

Freshmen *Admission:* 3,894 applied, 3,280 were accepted, 1,492 en-rolled. *Test scores:* SAT verbal scores over 500: 79%; SAT math scores over 500: 79%; SAT verbal scores over 600: 30%; SAT math scores over 600: 33%; SAT verbal scores over 700: 3%; SAT math scores over 700: 3%.
Tuition and fees (2003–04): $19,425 (full-time). *Room and board:* $7482 (room only: $4082).
Financial Aid (All incoming freshmen): *Average need-based gift aid:* $13,142. *Average non-need based aid:* $7957. *Average aid to full-time undergraduates:* $16,069.
Athletic Department: *Director of Athletics:* Brian Colleary; Phone: 412-396-5589; Fax: 412-396-6210; E-mail: colleary@duq.edu. *Sports Information Director:* Dave Saba; Phone: 412-396-5861; E-mail: saba@duq.edu.

MEN'S COACHES

Baseball: Mike Wilson; Phone: 412-396-5245; E-mail: wilson@duq.edu.

Basketball: Danny Nee; Phone: 412-396-6567; E-mail: nee@duq.edu.
Cheerleading: Veronica Rose; Phone: 412-396-6565; E-mail: duathletics@duq.edu.
Cross Country: Jim Lear; Phone: 412-396-6565; E-mail: jlear7074@yahoo.com.
Football: Gregg Gattuso; Phone: 412-396-1157; E-mail: gattuso@duq.edu.
Golf: Nellie King; Phone: 412-396-6565; E-mail: sinker2@aol.com.
Soccer: Wade Jean; Phone: 412-396-5242; E-mail: jean@duq.edu.
Swimming: Dave Sheets; Phone: 412-396-1866; E-mail: sheets@duq.edu.
Tennis: Whitney Snyder; Phone: 412-396-6565; E-mail: duathletics@duq.edu.
Track and Field: Bryan Delsite; Phone: 412-396-5238; E-mail: delsite@duq.edu.
Wrestling: John Hartupee; Phone: 412-396-5463; E-mail: hartupeej@duq.edu.

WOMEN'S COACHES

Basketball: Dan Durkin; Phone: 412-396-5126; E-mail: durkin@duq.edu.
Cheerleading: Veronica Rose; Phone: 412-396-6565; E-mail: duathletics@duq.edu.
Cross Country: Bryan Delsite; Phone: 412-396-5238; E-mail: delsite@duq.edu.
Lacrosse: Kim Eldridge; Phone: 412-396-4744; E-mail: eldridge@duq.edu.
Soccer: James Walker; Phone: 412-396-5241; E-mail: walkerj58@duq.edu.
Swimming: Dave Sheets; Phone: 412-396-1866; E-mail: sheets@duq.edu.
Tennis: Joe Camillo; Phone: 412-396-5239; E-mail: camillo@stargate.duq.edu.
Track and Field: Bryan Delsite; Phone: 412-396-5238; E-mail: delsite@duq.edu.
Volleyball: Steve Opperman; Phone: 412-396-5247; E-mail: opperman@duq.edu.

D'YOUVILLE COLLEGE
Buffalo, New York

Spartans ◆ NCAA III ◆ Independent ◆ http://www.dyc.edu/

Independent comprehensive, founded 1908
Coed, 976 undergraduate students, 80% full-time, 75% women, 25% men
Urban 7-acre campus
Moderately difficult entrance level, 69% of applicants were admitted

Freshmen Admission: 860 applied, 597 were accepted, 139 enrolled. Test scores: SAT verbal scores over 500: 39%; SAT math scores over 500: 51%; SAT verbal scores over 600: 5%; SAT math scores over 600: 8%.
Tuition and fees (2003–04): $14,160 (full-time). Room and board: $6960.
Financial Aid (All incoming freshmen): Average need-based gift aid: $10,144. Average non-need based aid: $6457. Average aid to full-time undergraduates: $14,081.
Athletic Department: Director of Athletics: Brian Miller; Phone: 716-881-7789; Fax: 716-881-7788; E-mail: millerb@dyc.edu. Sports Information Director: Ellie Hanover; Phone: 716-881-7789; E-mail: hanovere@dyc.edu.

MEN'S COACHES
Baseball: Mike Webster; Phone: 716-881-7676.
Basketball: Brian Miller; Phone: 716-881-7689; E-mail: millerb@dyc.edu.
Soccer: Josh Dannecker; Phone: 716-655-5256.
Volleyball: John Hutton; Phone: 716-881-7789; E-mail: huttonj@dyc.edu.

WOMEN'S COACHES
Basketball: Mark Herr; Phone: 716-283-8320.
Cross Country: Brian Miller; Phone: 716-881-7789; E-mail: millerb@dyc.edu.
Soccer: Amanda Slater; Phone: 716-913-8429.
Softball: Ellie Hanover; Phone: 716-881-7789; E-mail: hanovere@dyc.edu.
Volleyball: John Hutton; Phone: 716-881-7789; E-mail: huttonj@dyc.edu.

EARLHAM COLLEGE
Richmond, Indiana

Quakers ◆ NCAA III ◆ North Coast Athletic Conference ◆ http://www.earlham.edu/

Independent religious comprehensive, founded 1847, affiliated with Society of Friends
Coed, 1,170 undergraduate students, 97% full-time, 56% women, 44% men
Small-town 800-acre campus with easy access to Cincinnati, Indianapolis, and Dayton
Moderately difficult entrance level, 68% of applicants were admitted

Freshmen Admission: 1,410 applied, 1,088 were accepted, 348 enrolled. Test scores: SAT verbal scores over 500: 90%; SAT math scores over 500: 89%; SAT verbal scores over 600: 63%; SAT math scores over 600: 45%; SAT verbal scores over 700: 25%; SAT math scores over 700: 14%.
Tuition and fees (2003–04): $24,560 (full-time). Room and board: $5416 (room only: $2650).
Financial Aid (All incoming freshmen): Average need-based gift aid: $12,713. Average non-need based aid: $6779. Average aid to full-time undergraduates: $21,442.
Athletic Department: Director of Athletics: Frank Carr; Phone: 765-983-1483; Fax: 765-983-1446; E-mail: carrfr@earlham.edu. Sports Information Director: Jonathan Mires; Phone: 765-983-1795; E-mail: miresjo@earlham.edu.

MEN'S COACHES
Baseball: Tom Parkevich; Phone: 765-983-1237; E-mail: parketh@earlham.edu.
Basketball: Jeff Justus; Phone: 765-983-1845; E-mail: justuje@earlham.edu.
Cross Country: Pat Thomas; Phone: 765-983-1494; E-mail: thomapa@earlham.edu.
Football: Lawrence Livingston; Phone: 765-983-1233; E-mail: livinla@earlham.edu.
Soccer: Roy Messer; Phone: 765-983-1485; E-mail: messero@earlham.edu.
Tennis: Brandon Padgett; Phone: 765-983-1484; E-mail: padgebr@earlham.edu.
Track and Field: Nick Johnson; Phone: 765-983-1837; E-mail: johnsni@earlham.edu.

WOMEN'S COACHES
Basketball: Jeannine Ruh; Phone: 765-983-1486; E-mail: ruhje@earlham.edu.
Cross Country: Pat Thomas; Phone: 765-983-1494; E-mail: thomapa@earlham.edu.
Field Hockey: Jill Butcher; Phone: 765-983-1481; E-mail: butchji@earlham.edu.
Lacrosse: Jill Butcher; Phone: 765-983-1481; E-mail: butchji@earlham.edu.
Soccer: Jim Watts; Phone: 765-983-1447; E-mail: wattsja@earlham.edu.
Tennis: Brandon Padgett; Phone: 765-983-1484; E-mail: padgebr@earlham.edu.
Track and Field: Nick Johnson; Phone: 765-983-1837; E-mail: johnsni@earlham.edu.
Volleyball: Sarah Edwards; Phone: 765-983-1794; E-mail: edwarsa@earlham.edu.

EAST CAROLINA UNIVERSITY
Greenville, North Carolina

Pirates ◆ NCAA I ◆ Conference USA Conference ◆ http://www.ecu.edu/

State-supported university, founded 1907, part of The University of North Carolina
Coed, 16,935 undergraduate students, 91% full-time, 59% women, 41% men
Urban 1,000-acre campus
Moderately difficult entrance level, 73% of applicants were admitted

Freshmen Admission: 11,005 applied, 8,423 were accepted, 3,534 enrolled. Test scores: SAT verbal scores over 500: 60%; SAT math scores

East Carolina University (continued)

over 500: 68%; SAT verbal scores over 600: 14%; SAT math scores over 600: 16%; SAT verbal scores over 700: 1%; SAT math scores over 700: 1%.
Tuition and fees (2003–04): $3131 (resident), $13,270 (nonresident). *Room and board:* $5540 (room only: $2640).
Financial Aid (All incoming freshmen): *Average need-based gift aid:* $3584. *Average non-need based aid:* $6315.
Athletic Department: *Director of Athletics:* Nick Floyd; Phone: 252-328-4503; Fax: 252-328-4537; E-mail: brittli@mail.ecu.edu. *Sports Information Director:* Craig Wells; Phone: 252-328-4522; E-mail: wellscr@mail.ecu.edu.

MEN'S COACHES

Baseball: Randy Mazey; Phone: 252-328-4604; E-mail: mazeyr@mail.ecu.edu.
Basketball: Bill Herrion; Phone: 252-328-4592.
Cheerleading: Susie Hetzler Glynn; Phone: 252-328-4510; E-mail: glynns@mail.ecu.edu.
Cross Country: Len Klepack; Phone: 252-328-4605; E-mail: klepackl@mail.ecu.edu.
Diving: Rich MacDonald; Phone: 252-328-4608; E-mail: macdonaldr@mail.ecu.edu.
Football: John Thompson; Phone: 252-328-4568; E-mail: pricej@mail.ecu.edu.
Golf: Kevin Williams; Phone: 252-328-4606; E-mail: williamsk@mail.ecu.edu.
Soccer: Michael Benn; Phone: 252-328-4626; E-mail: bennm@mail.ecu.edu.
Swimming: Rick Kobe; Phone: 252-328-4608; E-mail: kober@mail.ecu.edu.
Tennis: Tom Morris; Phone: 252-328-4609; E-mail: morrist@mail.ecu.edu.
Track and Field: Bill Carson; Phone: 252-328-4610; E-mail: carsonw@mail.ecu.edu.

WOMEN'S COACHES

Basketball: Sharon Baldwin; Phone: 252-328-4586; E-mail: baldwins@mail.ecu.edu.
Cheerleading: Susie Hetzler Glynn; Phone: 252-328-4510; E-mail: glynns@mail.ecu.edu.
Cross Country: Len Klepack; Phone: 252-328-4605; E-mail: klepackl@mail.ecu.edu.
Diving: Rich MacDonald; Phone: 252-328-4608; E-mail: macdonaldr@mail.ecu.edu.
Golf: Kevin Williams; Phone: 252-328-4606; E-mail: williamsk@mail.ecu.edu.
Soccer: Rob Donnenwirth; Phone: 252-328-4672; E-mail: donnenwirthr@mail.ecu.edu.
Softball: Tracy Kee; Phone: 252-328-4607; E-mail: keet@mail.ecu.edu.
Swimming: Rick Kobe; Phone: 252-328-4608; E-mail: kober@mail.ecu.edu.
Tennis: Tom Morris; Phone: 252-328-4609; E-mail: morrist@mail.ecu.edu.
Track and Field: Matt Munson; Phone: 252-328-4611; E-mail: munsonm@mail.ecu.edu.
Volleyball: Colleen Munson; Phone: 252-328-4612; E-mail: munsonc@mail.ecu.edu.

EAST CENTRAL UNIVERSITY
Ada, Oklahoma

Tigers ◆ NCAA II ◆ Lone Star Conference ◆ http://www.ecok.edu/

State-supported comprehensive, founded 1909, part of Oklahoma State Regents for Higher Education
Coed, 3,685 undergraduate students, 86% full-time, 59% women, 41% men
Small-town 140-acre campus with easy access to Oklahoma City
Moderately difficult entrance level

Freshmen *Admission:* 704 enrolled.
Tuition and fees (2003–04): $3458 (resident), $7358 (nonresident). *Room and board:* $2774 (room only: $960).
Financial Aid (All incoming freshmen): *Average need-based gift aid:* $3569. *Average non-need based aid:* $1589. *Average aid to full-time undergraduates:* $6896.

Athletic Department: *Director of Athletics:* Fax: 580-332-4036. *Sports Information Director:* Zac Underwood; Phone: 580-332-8000; E-mail: zunderwood@mailclerk.ecok.edu.

MEN'S COACHES

Baseball: Ron Hill; Phone: 580-436-4940; E-mail: rhill@mailclerk.ecok.edu.
Basketball: Wayne Cobb; Phone: 580-310-5566.
Cheerleading: Teryl Rayburn; Phone: 580-310-5468.
Cross Country: Susan Payne; Phone: 580-310-5521; E-mail: spayne@mailclerk.ecok.edu.
Football: Dennis Darnell; Phone: 580-310-5362; E-mail: ddarnell@mailclerk.ecok.edu.
Golf: Nic Bailey; Phone: 580-310-5617.
Tennis: Charlie Hibbard; Phone: 580-310-5523.

WOMEN'S COACHES

Basketball: Kent Franz; Phone: 580-310-5568; E-mail: kfranz@mailclerk.ecok.edu.
Cheerleading: Teryl Rayburn; Phone: 580-310-5468.
Cross Country: Susan Payne; Phone: 580-310-5521; E-mail: spayne@mailclerk.ecok.edu.
Soccer: Heather Beam; Phone: 580-310-5747; E-mail: hbeam@mailclerk.ecok.edu.
Softball: Ron Miller; Phone: 580-310-5363; E-mail: rmiller@mailclerk.ecok.edu.
Tennis: Charlie Hibbard; Phone: 580-310-5523.

EASTERN CONNECTICUT STATE UNIVERSITY
Willimantic, Connecticut

Warriors ◆ NCAA III ◆ Little East Conference ◆ http://www.easternct.edu/

State-supported comprehensive, founded 1889, part of Connecticut State University System
Coed, 4,716 undergraduate students, 77% full-time, 57% women, 43% men
Small-town 179-acre campus
Moderately difficult entrance level, 57% of applicants were admitted

Freshmen *Admission:* 3,116 applied, 1,822 were accepted, 783 enrolled. *Test scores:* SAT verbal scores over 500: 59%; SAT math scores over 500: 61%; SAT verbal scores over 600: 11%; SAT math scores over 600: 13%; SAT verbal scores over 700: 1%; SAT math scores over 700: 1%.
Tuition and fees (2004–05): $6122 (resident), $12,856 (nonresident). *Room and board:* $7266 (room only: $3950).
Athletic Department: *Director of Athletics:* Joyce Wong; Phone: 860-465-5169; Fax: 860-465-4696; E-mail: wongi@easternct.edu. *Sports Information Director:* Bob Molta; Phone: 860-465-5172; E-mail: molta@easternct.edu.

MEN'S COACHES

Baseball: Bill Holowaty; Phone: 860-465-5185; E-mail: holowatyb@easternct.edu.
Basketball: William Geitner; Phone: 860-465-5332; E-mail: geitnerw@easternct.edu.
Cross Country: Frank Poulin; Phone: 860-465-4341; E-mail: poulinf@easternct.edu.
Lacrosse: Jon Basti; Phone: 860-465-5178; E-mail: bastij@easternct.edu.
Soccer: Frantz Innocent; Phone: 860-465-4334; E-mail: innocentf@easternct.edu.
Track and Field: Frank Poulin; Phone: 860-465-4341; E-mail: poulinf@easternct.edu.

WOMEN'S COACHES

Basketball: Denise Bierly; Phone: 860-465-4586; E-mail: bierlyd@easternct.edu.
Cross Country: Frank Poulin; Phone: 860-465-4341; E-mail: poulinf@easternct.edu.
Field Hockey: Kathy Railey; Phone: 860-465-4333; E-mail: raileyk@easternct.edu.
Lacrosse: Kathy Railey; Phone: 860-465-4333; E-mail: raileyk@easternct.edu.
Soccer: Chris D'Ambrosio; Phone: 860-465-0175; E-mail: cdambo@aol.com.

Softball: Diana Pepin; Phone: 860-465-5182; E-mail: pepind@easternct.edu.
Swimming: Maureen Fahey; Phone: 860-917-5933; E-mail: faheym@easternct.edu.
Track and Field: Frank Poulin; Phone: 860-465-4341; E-mail: poulinf@easternct.edu.
Volleyball: Joe Ward; Phone: 860-465-0176; E-mail: wardj@easternct.edu.

EASTERN ILLINOIS UNIVERSITY
Charleston, Illinois

Panthers ◆ NCAA I ◆ Missouri Valley Conference; Ohio Valley Conference ◆ http://www.eiu.edu/

State-supported comprehensive, founded 1895
Coed, 9,845 undergraduate students, 90% full-time, 58% women, 42% men
Small-town 320-acre campus
Moderately difficult entrance level, 76% of applicants were admitted

Freshmen *Admission:* 8,103 applied, 6,313 were accepted, 1,918 enrolled.
Tuition and fees (2003–04): $4982 (resident), $12,107 (nonresident). *Room and board:* $6210.
Financial Aid (All incoming freshmen): *Average need-based gift aid:* $2470. *Average non-need based aid:* $5185. *Average aid to full-time undergraduates:* $8044.
Athletic Department: *Director of Athletics:* Rich McDuffie; Phone: 217-581-2319; Fax: 217-581-7001; E-mail: ramcduffie@eiu.edu. *Sports Information Director:* David Kidwell; Phone: 217-581-7480; E-mail: dakidwell@eiu.edu.

MEN'S COACHES
Baseball: Jim Schmitz; Phone: 217-581-2522; E-mail: csjrs@eiu.edu.
Basketball: Rick Samuels; Phone: 217-581-2511; E-mail: cfrs1@eiu.edu.
Cheerleading: Tom Leong; Phone: 217-581-9113; E-mail: tomeiu@hotmail.com.
Cross Country: John McInerney; Phone: 217-581-6647; E-mail: cfjpm1@eiu.edu.
Football: Bob Spoo; Phone: 217-581-7762; E-mail: cfras2@eiu.edu.
Golf: Mike Moncel; Phone: 217-581-6007; E-mail: mlmoncel@eiu.edu.
Soccer: Adam Howarth; Phone: 217-581-6442; E-mail: ahowarth@eiu.edu.
Swimming: Ray Padovan; Phone: 217-581-2612; E-mail: cfrfp@eiu.edu.
Tennis: Brian Holzgrafe; Phone: 217-581-3326; E-mail: bmholzgrafe@hotmail.com.
Track and Field: Tom Akers; Phone: 217-581-2625; E-mail: cstla@eiu.edu.
Wrestling: Ralph McCausland; Phone: 217-581-6039; E-mail: cfrem1@eiu.edu.

WOMEN'S COACHES
Basketball: Linda Wunder; Phone: 217-581-6008; E-mail: cflw@eiu.edu.
Cheerleading: Tom Leong; Phone: 217-581-9113; E-mail: tomeiu@hotmail.com.
Cross Country: John McInerney; Phone: 217-581-6647; E-mail: cfjpm1@eiu.edu.
Golf: Jay Albaugh; Phone: 217-581-6007; E-mail: csjaa2@eiu.edu.
Soccer: Steve Ballard; Phone: 217-581-7062; E-mail: cfsjb@eiu.edu.
Softball: Lloydene Searle; Phone: 217-581-2093; E-mail: csls@eiu.edu.
Swimming: Ray Padovan; Phone: 217-581-2612; E-mail: cfrfp@eiu.edu.
Tennis: Brian Holzgrafe; Phone: 217-581-3326; E-mail: bmholzgrafe@hotmail.com.
Track and Field: Mary Wallace; Phone: 217-581-7144; E-mail: cfmew@eiu.edu.
Volleyball: Brenda Winkeler; Phone: 217-581-2924; E-mail: bkwinkeler@eiu.edu.

EASTERN KENTUCKY UNIVERSITY
Richmond, Kentucky

Colonels ◆ NCAA I ◆ Ohio Valley Conference ◆ http://www.eku.edu/

State-supported comprehensive, founded 1906, part of Kentucky Council on Post Secondary Education
Coed, 13,567 undergraduate students, 77% full-time, 61% women, 39% men
Small-town 500-acre campus with easy access to Lexington
Noncompetitive entrance level, 76% of applicants were admitted

Freshmen *Admission:* 5,513 applied, 4,211 were accepted, 2,561 enrolled. *Test scores:* SAT verbal scores over 500: 47%; SAT math scores over 500: 44%; SAT verbal scores over 600: 15%; SAT math scores over 600: 12%; SAT verbal scores over 700: 1%; SAT math scores over 700: 1%.
Tuition and fees (2004–05): $3298 (resident), $8990 (nonresident). *Room and board:* $5450 (room only: $2730).
Financial Aid (All incoming freshmen): *Average need-based gift aid:* $3998. *Average non-need based aid:* $1783. *Average aid to full-time undergraduates:* $5774.
Athletic Department: *Director of Athletics:* John Shafer; Phone: 859-622-2120; Fax: 859-622-5108; E-mail: john.shafer@eku.edu. *Sports Information Director:* Ryan Simmons; Phone: 859-622-1253.

MEN'S COACHES
Baseball: Elvis Domniguez; Phone: 859-622-2128.
Basketball: Travis Ford; Phone: 859-622-6501; E-mail: travis.ford@eku.edu.
Cheerleading: Daniel Quick; Phone: 859-622-3654; E-mail: quickdaniel@hotmail.com.
Cross Country: Rick Erdmann; Phone: 859-622-2126; E-mail: rick.erdmann@eku.edu.
Football: Danny Hope; Phone: 859-622-2146.
Golf: Pat Stephens; Phone: 859-622-1000.
Tennis: Rob Oertell; Phone: 859-622-2133.
Track and Field: Rick Erdmann; Phone: 859-622-2126; E-mail: rick.erdmann@eku.edu.

WOMEN'S COACHES
Basketball: Larry Inman; Phone: 859-622-2127; E-mail: larry.inman@eku.edu.
Cheerleading: Daniel Quick; Phone: 859-622-3654; E-mail: quickdaniel@hotmail.com.
Cross Country: Rick Erdmann; Phone: 859-622-2126; E-mail: rick.erdmann@eku.edu.
Golf: Joni Stephens; Phone: 859-622-1000; E-mail: joni.stephens@eku.edu.
Softball: Jane Worthington; Phone: 859-622-1246; E-mail: jane.worthington@eku.edu.
Tennis: Rob Oertell; Phone: 859-622-2133.
Track and Field: Rick Erdmann; Phone: 859-622-2126; E-mail: rick.erdmann@eku.edu.
Volleyball: Lori Duncan; Phone: 859-622-2141; E-mail: lori.duncan@eku.edu.

EASTERN MENNONITE UNIVERSITY
Harrisonburg, Virginia

Royals ◆ NCAA III ◆ Old Dominion Conference ◆ http://www.emu.edu/

Independent Mennonite comprehensive, founded 1917
Coed, 965 undergraduate students, 96% full-time, 60% women, 40% men
Small-town 93-acre campus
Moderately difficult entrance level, 83% of applicants were admitted

Freshmen *Admission:* 605 applied, 498 were accepted, 196 enrolled. *Test scores:* SAT verbal scores over 500: 68%; SAT math scores over 500: 59%; SAT verbal scores over 600: 32%; SAT math scores over 600: 32%; SAT verbal scores over 700: 5%; SAT math scores over 700: 13%.

Eastern Mennonite University *(continued)*

Tuition and fees (2003–04): $17,350 (full-time). *Room and board:* $5640 (room only: $2900).
Financial Aid (All incoming freshmen): *Average need-based gift aid:* $9700. *Average non-need based aid:* $7200. *Average aid to full-time undergraduates:* $13,900.
Athletic Department: *Director of Athletics:* Larry Martin; Phone: 540-432-4646; Fax: 540-432-4444; E-mail: larry.martin@emu.edu. *Sports Information Director:* Seth McGuffin; Phone: 540-432-4441; E-mail: seth.mcguffin@emu.edu.

MEN'S COACHES

Baseball: Rob Roeschley; Phone: 540-432-4333; E-mail: roeschrd@emu.edu.
Basketball: Kirby Dean; Phone: 540-432-4337; E-mail: kirby.dean@emu.edu.
Cross Country: Lester Zook; Phone: 540-432-4439; E-mail: zooklr@emu.edu.
Soccer: Roger Mast; Phone: 540-432-4437; E-mail: mastre@emu.edu.
Tennis: Harlan De Brun; Phone: 540-432-4567; E-mail: debrunh@emu.edu.
Track and Field: Paul Johnson; Phone: 540-432-4133; E-mail: johnsonp@emu.edu.
Volleyball: Jason Axford; Phone: 540-432-4331; E-mail: jason.axford@emu.edu.

WOMEN'S COACHES

Basketball: Richard McElwee; Phone: 540-432-4328; E-mail: richard.mcelwee@emu.edu.
Cross Country: Lester Zook; Phone: 540-432-4439; E-mail: zooklr@emu.edu.
Field Hockey: Brenda Bechler; Phone: 540-432-4438; E-mail: brenda.bechler@emu.edu.
Soccer: Greg Steffen; Phone: 540-432-4489.
Softball: J.D. McCurdy; Phone: 540-432-4481; E-mail: jd.mccurdy@emu.edu.
Tennis: Harlan De Brun; Phone: 540-432-4567; E-mail: debrunh@emu.edu.
Track and Field: Paul Johnson; Phone: 540-432-4432; E-mail: johnsonp@emu.edu.
Volleyball: Ruth-Anne Wildeman; Phone: 540-432-4436; E-mail: widemanr@emu.edu.

EASTERN MICHIGAN UNIVERSITY
Ypsilanti, Michigan

Eagles ◆ NCAA I ◆ Mid-American Conference;
Mid-Continent Conference ◆ http://www.emich.edu/

State-supported comprehensive, founded 1849
Coed, 19,577 undergraduate students, 69% full-time, 61% women, 39% men
Suburban 460-acre campus with easy access to Detroit
Moderately difficult entrance level, 75% of applicants were admitted

Freshmen *Admission:* 9,044 applied, 7,139 were accepted, 2,577 enrolled. *Test scores:* SAT verbal scores over 500: 56%; SAT math scores over 500: 54%; SAT verbal scores over 600: 16%; SAT math scores over 600: 20%; SAT verbal scores over 700: 2%; SAT math scores over 700: 3%.
Tuition and fees (2003–04): $5627 (resident), $15,045 (nonresident). *Room and board:* $5850 (room only: $2748).
Financial Aid (All incoming freshmen): *Average need-based gift aid:* $4103. *Average non-need based aid:* $2050. *Average aid to full-time undergraduates:* $10,754.
Athletic Department: *Director of Athletics:* David Diles; Phone: 734-487-1050; E-mail: david.diles@emich.edu. *Sports Information Director:* Jim Streeter; Phone: 734-487-0317; E-mail: jim.streeter@emich.edu.

MEN'S COACHES

Baseball: Roger Coryell; Phone: 734-487-0315; E-mail: roger.coryell@emich.edu.
Basketball: Jim Boone; Phone: 734-487-0214.
Cheerleading: Mindy Gentz; Phone: 248-982-4308; E-mail: mindy_gentz@yahoo.com.
Cross Country: Brad Fairchild; Phone: 734-487-0236; E-mail: brad.fairchild@emich.edu.

Diving: Buck Smith; Phone: 734-487-3079; E-mail: buck.smith@emich.edu.
Football: Jeff Genyk; Phone: 734-487-2160.
Golf: Bruce Cunningham; Phone: 734-487-6703; E-mail: bruce.cunningham@emich.edu.
Swimming: Peter Linn; Phone: 734-487-0463; E-mail: peter.linn@emich.edu.
Track and Field: Brad Fairchild; Phone: 734-487-0236; E-mail: brad.fairchild@emich.edu.
Wrestling: Charles Branch; Phone: 734-487-0395; E-mail: charles.branch@emich.edu.

WOMEN'S COACHES

Basketball: Suzy Merchant; Phone: 734-487-0481.
Cheerleading: Mindy Gentz; Phone: 248-982-4308; E-mail: mindy_gentz@yahoo.com.
Cross Country: Bob Maybouer; Phone: 734-487-0262; E-mail: rmaybouer@emich.edu.
Diving: Buck Smith; Phone: 734-487-3079; E-mail: buck.smith@emich.edu.
Golf: Scott King; Phone: 734-487-6435; E-mail: sking5@emich.edu.
Gymnastics: Steve Wilce; Phone: 734-487-1082; E-mail: steve.wilce@emich.edu.
Soccer: Scott Hall; Phone: 734-487-2144; E-mail: scott.hall@emich.edu.
Softball: Karen Baird; Phone: 734-487-1031; E-mail: kbaird3@emich.edu.
Swimming: Sam Jalet; Phone: 734-487-0288; E-mail: sam.jalet@emich.edu.
Tennis: Tim Gray; Phone: 734-487-2244; E-mail: tgray3@emich.edu.
Track and Field: Bob Maybouer; Phone: 734-487-0262; E-mail: rmaybouer@emich.edu.
Volleyball: Kim Berrington; Phone: 734-487-0291; E-mail: kim.berrington@emich.edu.

EASTERN NAZARENE COLLEGE
Quincy, Massachusetts

Crusaders ◆ NCAA III ◆ Commonwealth Coast Conference
◆ http://www.enc.edu/

Independent religious comprehensive, founded 1918, affiliated with Church of the Nazarene
Coed, 1,069 undergraduate students, 98% full-time, 61% women, 39% men
Suburban 15-acre campus with easy access to Boston
Moderately difficult entrance level, 66% of applicants were admitted

Freshmen *Admission:* 552 applied, 342 were accepted, 202 enrolled. *Test scores:* SAT verbal scores over 500: 88%; SAT math scores over 500: 82%; SAT verbal scores over 600: 48%; SAT math scores over 600: 39%; SAT verbal scores over 700: 22%; SAT math scores over 700: 20%.
Tuition and fees (2003–04): $16,608 (full-time). *Room and board:* $5638.
Financial Aid (All incoming freshmen): *Average need-based gift aid:* $2469. *Average non-need based aid:* $5099. *Average aid to full-time undergraduates:* $8844.
Athletic Department: *Director of Athletics:* Nancy Detwiler; Phone: 617-745-3638; Fax: 617-745-3938; E-mail: detwilen@enc.edu. *Sports Information Director:* Carolyn Morse; Phone: 617-745-3639; E-mail: morsec@enc.edu.

MEN'S COACHES

Baseball: Todd Reid; Phone: 617-745-3648; E-mail: reidt@enc.edu.
Basketball: Corey Zink; Phone: 617-745-3637; E-mail: zinkc@enc.edu.
Cross Country: Ed Gardner; Phone: 617-774-3844; E-mail: gardnere@enc.edu.
Soccer: Christian Huizenga; Phone: 617-745-3641; E-mail: huizengc@enc.edu.
Tennis: Cristian Popa; Phone: 617-745-3598; E-mail: popac@enc.edu.

WOMEN'S COACHES

Basketball: Ken Hardee; Phone: 617-745-3598; E-mail: hardeek@enc.edu.
Cross Country: Ed Gardner; Phone: 617-774-3844; E-mail: gardnere@enc.edu.
Soccer: Chris McClain; Phone: 617-745-3593; E-mail: mclainc@enc.edu.

Softball: Steve Wolf; Phone: 617-745-3597; E-mail: wolfs@enc.edu.
Volleyball: Derek Schmidt; Phone: 617-745-3647; E-mail: schmittd@enc.edu.

EASTERN NEW MEXICO UNIVERSITY
Portales, New Mexico

Greyhounds ◆ NCAA II ◆ Lone Star Conference ◆ http://www.enmu.edu/

State-supported comprehensive, founded 1934, part of Eastern New Mexico University System
Coed, 3,015 undergraduate students, 81% full-time, 58% women, 42% men
Rural 240-acre campus
Minimally difficult entrance level, 74% of applicants were admitted

Freshmen *Admission:* 1,810 applied, 1,342 were accepted, 558 enrolled. *Test scores:* SAT verbal scores over 500: 40%; SAT math scores over 500: 37%; SAT verbal scores over 600: 11%; SAT math scores over 600: 6%; SAT verbal scores over 700: 3%.
Tuition and fees (2003–04): $2472 (resident), $8028 (nonresident). *Room and board:* $4290 (room only: $1990).
Athletic Department: *Director of Athletics:* Mike Maguire; Phone: 505-562-2153; Fax: 505-562-2822; E-mail: michael.maguire@enmu.edu. *Sports Information Director:* Robert McKinney; Phone: 505-562-4309; E-mail: mckinner@enmu.edu.

MEN'S COACHES
Baseball: Phil Clabaugh; Phone: 505-562-2889; E-mail: phillip.clabaugh@enmu.edu.
Basketball: Shawn Scanlan; Phone: 505-562-2433; E-mail: shawn.scanlan@enmu.edu.
Cheerleading: Amy King; Phone: 505-359-3391; E-mail: cheerenmu@yahoo.com.
Cross Country: Greg Lasage; Phone: 505-562-2976; E-mail: greg.lasage@enmu.edu.
Football: Bud Elliot; Phone: 505-562-2239; E-mail: bud.elliott@enmu.edu.

WOMEN'S COACHES
Basketball: Dan Buzard; Phone: 505-562-2233; E-mail: dan.buzard@enmu.edu.
Cheerleading: Amy King; Phone: 505-359-3391; E-mail: cheerenmu@yahoo.com.
Cross Country: Greg Lasage; Phone: 505-562-2976; E-mail: greg.lasage@enmu.edu.
Softball: Kevin Blaskowski; Phone: 505-562-4349; E-mail: kevin.blaskowski@enmu.edu.
Tennis: Christne Blaeser; Phone: 505-562-2882; E-mail: christine.blaeser@enmu.edu.
Volleyball: Mike Maguire; Phone: 505-562-2153; E-mail: michael.maguire@enmu.edu.

EASTERN OREGON UNIVERSITY
La Grande, Oregon

Mountaineers ◆ NAIA ◆ Cascade Collegiate Conference ◆ http://www.eou.edu/

State-supported comprehensive, founded 1929, part of Oregon University System
Coed, 3,041 undergraduate students, 64% full-time, 58% women, 42% men
Rural 121-acre campus
Moderately difficult entrance level, 102% of applicants were admitted

Freshmen *Admission:* 714 applied, 709 were accepted, 339 enrolled. *Test scores:* SAT verbal scores over 500: 50%; SAT math scores over 500: 49%; SAT verbal scores over 600: 14%; SAT math scores over 600: 14%; SAT verbal scores over 700: 2%; SAT math scores over 700: 2%.

Tuition and fees (2004–05): $5517 (resident), $5517 (nonresident). *Room and board:* $6100 (room only: $3250).
Financial Aid (All incoming freshmen): *Average need-based gift aid:* $3205. *Average non-need based aid:* $707. *Average aid to full-time undergraduates:* $7558.
Athletic Department: *Director of Athletics:* Robert Cashell; Phone: 541-962-3364; Fax: 541-962-3498; E-mail: rob.cashell@eou.edu. *Sports Information Director:* Sam Ghrist; Phone: 541-962-3499; E-mail: sam.ghrist@eou.edu.

MEN'S COACHES
Baseball: Wes McAllster; Phone: 541-962-3110; E-mail: wmcallas@eou.edu.
Basketball: Art Furman; Phone: 541-962-3569; E-mail: afurman@eou.edu.
Cheerleading: Cynthia Chandler; Phone: 541-962-3364; E-mail: cindyk@eoni.com.
Cross Country: Ben Welch; Phone: 541-962-3851; E-mail: bwelch@eou.edu.
Football: Jim Fenwick; Phone: 541-962-3382; E-mail: jim.fenwick@eou.edu.
Track and Field: Ben Welch; Phone: 541-962-3851; E-mail: bwelch@eou.edu.

WOMEN'S COACHES
Basketball: Anji Weissenfluh; Phone: 541-962-3743; E-mail: aweissen@eou.edu.
Cheerleading: Cynthia Chandler; Phone: 541-962-3364; E-mail: cindyk@eoni.com.
Cross Country: Ben Welch; Phone: 541-962-3851; E-mail: bwelch@eou.edu.
Soccer: Colleen Fagan; Phone: 541-962-3850; E-mail: colleen.e.fagan@dfw.state.or.us.
Softball: Anji Weissenfluh; Phone: 541-962-3743; E-mail: aweissen@eou.edu.
Track and Field: Ben Welch; Phone: 541-962-3851; E-mail: bwelch@eou.edu.
Volleyball: Ryan Platt; Phone: 541-962-3687; E-mail: rplatt@eou.edu.

EASTERN UNIVERSITY
St. Davids, Pennsylvania

Eagles ◆ NCAA III ◆ Pennsylvania Athletic Conference ◆ http://www.eastern.edu/

Independent American Baptist Churches in the USA comprehensive, founded 1952
Coed, 2,200 undergraduate students, 88% full-time, 66% women, 34% men
Small-town 107-acre campus with easy access to Philadelphia
Moderately difficult entrance level, 72% of applicants were admitted

Freshmen *Admission:* 1,193 applied, 929 were accepted, 415 enrolled. *Test scores:* SAT verbal scores over 500: 78%; SAT math scores over 500: 68%; SAT verbal scores over 600: 30%; SAT math scores over 600: 27%; SAT verbal scores over 700: 8%; SAT math scores over 700: 4%.
Tuition and fees (2004–05): $17,700 (full-time). *Room and board:* $7600 (room only: $4150).
Financial Aid (All incoming freshmen): *Average need-based gift aid:* $10,180. *Average non-need based aid:* $13,323. *Average aid to full-time undergraduates:* $12,782.
Athletic Department: *Director of Athletics:* Harry Gutelius; Phone: 610-341-1785; Fax: 610-341-1317; E-mail: hguteliu@eastern.edu. *Sports Information Director:* Mark Birtwistle; Phone: 610-341-1784; E-mail: mbirtwis@eastern.edu.

MEN'S COACHES
Baseball: Brian Burke; Phone: 610-341-1784; E-mail: bburke@eastern.edu.
Basketball: Matt Nadelhoffer; Phone: 610-341-1784; E-mail: mnadelho@eastern.edu.
Cheerleading: Rebecca Nadelhoffer; Phone: 610-341-1454; E-mail: rnadelho@eastern.edu.
Golf: Derek Ritchie; Phone: 610-341-1955; E-mail: dritchie@eastern.edu.
Soccer: Mark Wagner; Phone: 610-341-1784; E-mail: mwagner@eastern.edu.

Eastern University *(continued)*

Tennis: Gershwin Sandburg; Phone: 610-341-1784; E-mail: gsandbur@eastern.edu.

WOMEN'S COACHES

Basketball: Dave Storm; Phone: 610-341-1784; E-mail: dstorm@eastern.edu.
Cheerleading: Rebecca Nadelhoffer; Phone: 610-341-1454; E-mail: rnadelho@eastern.edu.
Field Hockey: Beth Petitte; Phone: 610-341-1784; E-mail: bpetitte@eastern.edu.
Lacrosse: Carolyn Urban; Phone: 610-341-1784; E-mail: curban@eastern.edu.
Soccer: Dan Mouw; Phone: 610-341-1784; E-mail: dmouw@eastern.edu.
Softball: Mark Ambler; Phone: 610-341-1784; E-mail: mambler@eastern.edu.
Tennis: Gershwin Sandburg; Phone: 610-341-1784; E-mail: gsandbur@eastern.edu.
Volleyball: Mark Birtwistle; Phone: 610-341-1784; E-mail: mbirtwis@eastern.edu.

EASTERN WASHINGTON UNIVERSITY
Cheney, Washington

Eagles ◆ NCAA I ◆ Big Sky Conference ◆ http://www.ewu.edu/

State-supported comprehensive, founded 1882
Coed, 9,067 undergraduate students, 85% full-time, 58% women, 42% men
Small-town 335-acre campus
Moderately difficult entrance level, 79% of applicants were admitted

Freshmen *Admission:* 3,585 applied, 2,913 were accepted, 1,393 enrolled. *Test scores:* SAT verbal scores over 500: 50%; SAT math scores over 500: 51%; SAT verbal scores over 600: 16%; SAT math scores over 600: 16%; SAT verbal scores over 700: 1%; SAT math scores over 700: 1%.
Tuition and fees (2003–04): $3812 (resident), $12,668 (nonresident). *Room and board:* $5200.
Financial Aid (All incoming freshmen): *Average need-based gift aid:* $4094. *Average non-need based aid:* $3011. *Average aid to full-time undergraduates:* $13,293.
Athletic Department: *Director of Athletics:* Scott Barnes; Phone: 509-359-2461; Fax: 509-359-2828; E-mail: scott.barnes@mail.ewu.edu. *Sports Information Director:* Dave Cook; Phone: 509-359-6334; E-mail: dcook@mailserver.ewu.edu.

MEN'S COACHES

Basketball: Ray Giacoletti; Phone: 509-359-2497.
Cheerleading: Michelle Wilson; Phone: 509-359-2463.
Cross Country: Stan Kerr; Phone: 509-359-2376; E-mail: skerr@mailserver.ewu.edu.
Football: Paul Wulff; Phone: 509-359-6696; E-mail: paul.wulff@mail.ewu.edu.
Golf: Marc Hughes; Phone: 509-359-2462; E-mail: mthughes@centurytel.net.
Tennis: Sunya Herold; Phone: 509-359-2515; E-mail: sherold@mailserver.ewu.edu.
Track and Field: Stan Kerr; Phone: 509-359-2376; E-mail: skerr@mailserver.ewu.edu.

WOMEN'S COACHES

Basketball: Wendy Schuller; Phone: 509-359-2318; E-mail: wendy.schuller@mail.ewu.edu.
Cheerleading: Michelle Wilson; Phone: 509-359-2463.
Cross Country: Marcia Mecklenburg; Phone: 509-359-2426; E-mail: mmecklenburg@mailserver.ewu.edu.
Golf: Marc Hughes; Phone: 509-359-2462; E-mail: mthughes@centurytel.net.
Soccer: George Hageage; Phone: 509-359-7949; E-mail: george.hageage@mail.ewu.edu.
Tennis: Sunya Herold; Phone: 509-359-2515; E-mail: sherold@mailserver.ewu.edu.

Track and Field: Marcia Mecklenburg; Phone: 509-359-2426; E-mail: mmecklenburg@mailserver.ewu.edu.
Volleyball: Wade Benson; Phone: 509-359-7020; E-mail: wade.benson@mailserver.ewu.edu.

EAST STROUDSBURG UNIVERSITY OF PENNSYLVANIA
East Stroudsburg, Pennsylvania

Warriors ◆ NCAA II ◆ Pennsylvania State Athletic Conference ◆ http://www.esu.edu/

State-supported comprehensive, founded 1893, part of Pennsylvania State System of Higher Education
Coed, 5,121 undergraduate students, 91% full-time, 58% women, 42% men
Small-town 213-acre campus
Moderately difficult entrance level, 66% of applicants were admitted

Freshmen *Admission:* 4,370 applied, 3,067 were accepted, 1,084 enrolled. *Test scores:* SAT verbal scores over 500: 42%; SAT math scores over 500: 46%; SAT verbal scores over 600: 6%; SAT math scores over 600: 8%.
Tuition and fees (2003–04): $5979 (resident), $12,877 (nonresident). *Room and board:* $4464 (room only: $2868).
Financial Aid (All incoming freshmen): *Average need-based gift aid:* $2892. *Average non-need based aid:* $5513. *Average aid to full-time undergraduates:* $3859.
Athletic Department: *Director of Athletics:* Carey Snyder; Phone: 570-422-3034; Fax: 570-422-3063; E-mail: carey.snyder@po-box.esu.edu. *Sports Information Director:* Chris Myers; Phone: 570-422-3312; E-mail: cmyers@po-box.esu.edu.

MEN'S COACHES

Baseball: Roger Barren; Phone: 570-422-3263; E-mail: roger.barren@po-box.esu.edu.
Basketball: Jeff Wilson; Phone: 570-422-3339.
Cross Country: Joe Koch; Phone: 570-422-3054; E-mail: joe.koch@po-box.esu.edu.
Football: Dennis Douds; Phone: 570-422-3322; E-mail: denny.douds@po-box.esu.edu.
Soccer: Derek Arneaud; Phone: 570-422-3648; E-mail: derek.arneaud@po-box.esu.edu.
Tennis: Al McCormick; Phone: 570-422-3901; E-mail: acormick@po-box.esu.edu.
Track and Field: Joe Koch; Phone: 570-422-3054; E-mail: joe.koch@po-box.esu.edu.
Volleyball: Peter Viteritti; Phone: 570-422-3642; E-mail: pviteritti@po-box.esu.edu.
Wrestling: Angelo Borzio; Phone: 570-422-3313; E-mail: aborzio@esu.edu.

WOMEN'S COACHES

Basketball: Juliene Simpson; Phone: 570-422-3107; E-mail: jsimpson@po-box.esu.edu.
Cross Country: Joe Koch; Phone: 570-422-3054; E-mail: joe.koch@po-box.esu.edu.
Field Hockey: Sandy Miller; Phone: 570-422-3101; E-mail: sandy.miller@po-box.esu.edu.
Lacrosse: Sandy Miller; Phone: 570-422-3101; E-mail: sandy.miller@po-box.esu.edu.
Soccer: Derek Arneaud; Phone: 570-422-3648; E-mail: derek.arneaud@po-box.esu.edu.
Softball: Jamie Brown; Phone: 570-422-3122; E-mail: jamieb@po-box.esu.edu.
Swimming: Lisa Pizzuto; Phone: 570-422-3873; E-mail: lpizzuto@po-box.esu.edu.
Tennis: Al McCormick; Phone: 570-422-3901; E-mail: acormick@po-box.esu.edu.
Track and Field: Joe Koch; Phone: 570-422-3054; E-mail: joe.koch@po-box.esu.edu.
Volleyball: Peter Viteritti; Phone: 570-422-3672; E-mail: pviteritti@po-box.esu.edu.

EAST TENNESSEE STATE UNIVERSITY
Johnson City, Tennessee

Buccaneers ◆ NCAA I ◆ Southern Conference ◆ http://www.etsu.edu/

State-supported university, founded 1911, part of State University and Community College System of Tennessee, Tennessee Board of Regents
Coed, 9,550 undergraduate students, 83% full-time, 58% women, 42% men
Small-town 366-acre campus
Moderately difficult entrance level, 82% of applicants were admitted

Freshmen *Admission:* 3,825 applied, 3,132 were accepted, 1,615 enrolled. *Test scores:* SAT verbal scores over 500: 59%; SAT math scores over 500: 57%; SAT verbal scores over 600: 19%; SAT math scores over 600: 18%; SAT verbal scores over 700: 2%; SAT math scores over 700: 2%.
Tuition and fees (2003–04): $3839 (resident), $11,771 (nonresident). *Room and board:* $4658 (room only: $2000).
Financial Aid (All incoming freshmen): *Average need-based gift aid:* $2946. *Average non-need based aid:* $2488. *Average aid to full-time undergraduates:* $4792.
Athletic Department: *Director of Athletics:* Dave Mullins; Phone: 423-439-4646; Fax: 423-439-5294. *Sports Information Director:* Michael White; Phone: 423-439-4220; E-mail: whitem@mail.etsu.edu.

MEN'S COACHES
Baseball: Tony Skole; Phone: 423-439-4496; E-mail: skole@mail.etsu.edu.
Basketball: Murray Bartow; Phone: 423-439-4207; E-mail: bartow@etsu.edu.
Cheerleading: Renee Hathaway; Phone: 423-439-4343.
Cross Country: Dave Walker; Phone: 423-439-8478.
Football: Paul Hamilton; Phone: 423-439-4261; E-mail: hamiltop@etsu.edu.
Golf: Fred Warren; Phone: 423-439-5589; E-mail: warrenf@mail.etsu.edu.
Tennis: Yaser Zaatini; Phone: 423-439-5262; E-mail: yabysdad@hotmail.com.
Track and Field: Dave Walker; Phone: 423-439-8478.

WOMEN'S COACHES
Basketball: Karen Kemp; Phone: 423-439-6995; E-mail: kempk@mail.etsu.edu.
Cheerleading: Renee Hathaway; Phone: 423-439-4343.
Cross Country: Dave Walker; Phone: 423-439-8478.
Golf: Stephanie Reynolds; Phone: 423-439-7425; E-mail: etsugolf1@yahoo.com.
Soccer: Heather Henson; Phone: 423-439-4294; E-mail: hensonha@mail.etsu.edu.
Softball: Amy Fuller; Phone: 423-439-4279; E-mail: fullera@mail.etsu.edu.
Tennis: Steve Brooks; Phone: 423-439-8441; E-mail: etsutennis@hotmail.com.
Track and Field: Dave Walker; Phone: 423-439-8478.
Volleyball: Lindsey Devine; Phone: 423-439-4259; E-mail: devine@etsu.edu.

EAST TEXAS BAPTIST UNIVERSITY
Marshall, Texas

Tigers ◆ NCAA III ◆ American Southwest Conference ◆ http://www.etbu.edu/

Independent Baptist 4-year, founded 1912
Coed, 1,354 undergraduate students, 88% full-time, 51% women, 49% men
Small-town 200-acre campus
Moderately difficult entrance level, 51% of applicants were admitted

Freshmen *Admission:* 742 applied, 407 were accepted, 248 enrolled.
Tuition and fees (2003–04): $10,290 (full-time). *Room and board:* $3624 (room only: $1470).

Financial Aid (All incoming freshmen): *Average need-based gift aid:* $5523. *Average non-need based aid:* $3749. *Average aid to full-time undergraduates:* $10,210.
Athletic Department: *Director of Athletics:* Kent Reeves; Phone: 903-923-2228; Fax: 903-935-0162. *Sports Information Director:* David Weaver; Phone: 903-923-2228.

MEN'S COACHES
Baseball: Robert Riggs; Phone: 903-923-2228.
Basketball: Bert West; Phone: 903-923-2228.
Cross Country: Bert West; Phone: 903-923-2228.
Football: Ralph Harris; Phone: 903-923-2228.
Soccer: Jose Alonzo; Phone: 903-923-2228.

WOMEN'S COACHES
Basketball: Tracy Stellato; Phone: 903-923-2228.
Cross Country: Bert West; Phone: 903-923-2228.
Soccer: Jose Alonzo; Phone: 903-923-2228.
Softball: Kent Reeves; Phone: 903-923-2228.
Volleyball: Suzanne Wingrove; Phone: 903-923-2228.

ECKERD COLLEGE
St. Petersburg, Florida

Triton ◆ NCAA II ◆ Sunshine State Conference ◆ http://www.eckerd.edu/

Independent Presbyterian 4-year, founded 1958
Coed, 1,631 undergraduate students, 98% full-time, 55% women, 45% men
Suburban 267-acre campus with easy access to Tampa
Moderately difficult entrance level, 7% of applicants were admitted

Freshmen *Admission:* 2,046 applied, 1,569 were accepted, 433 enrolled. *Test scores:* SAT verbal scores over 500: 79%; SAT math scores over 500: 77%; SAT verbal scores over 600: 35%; SAT math scores over 600: 33%; SAT verbal scores over 700: 7%; SAT math scores over 700: 4%.
Tuition and fees (2003–04): $22,774 (full-time). *Room and board:* $5970 (room only: $2812).
Financial Aid (All incoming freshmen): *Average aid to full-time undergraduates:* $17,208.
Athletic Department: *Director of Athletics:* Bob Fortosis; Phone: 727-864-8252; Fax: 727-864-8968; E-mail: fortoscr@eckerd.edu. *Sports Information Director:* Kathrine Turnbow; Phone: 727-864-8242; E-mail: turnboka@eckerd.edu.

MEN'S COACHES
Baseball: Bill Mathews; Phone: 727-864-8253; E-mail: coachb29@aol.com.
Basketball: Tom Ryan; Phone: 727-864-8305; E-mail: ryantj@eckerd.edu.
Golf: Bill Buttner; Phone: 727-864-8251; E-mail: wabuttner@aol.com.
Soccer: Phone: 727-864-7697; E-mail: menssoccer@eckerd.edu.
Tennis: Scott Dei; Phone: 727-864-8251; E-mail: ectennis@eckerd.edu.

WOMEN'S COACHES
Basketball: Brian Schultes; Phone: 727-864-8586; E-mail: shultebf@eckerd.edu.
Cross Country: Phone: 727-864-8251; E-mail: rayrunner@yahoo.com.
Soccer: Joe McCauley; Phone: 727-864-8254.
Softball: Jana Fields; Phone: 727-864-8723; E-mail: jana_fields@hotmail.com.
Tennis: Scott Dei; Phone: 727-864-8251; E-mail: ectennis@eckerd.edu.
Volleyball: Andrew Joseph; Phone: 727-864-8251; E-mail: josephaj@eckerd.edu.

EDGEWOOD COLLEGE
Madison, Wisconsin

Eagles ◆ NCAA III ◆ Lake Michigan Conference ◆ http://www.edgewood.edu/

Independent Roman Catholic comprehensive, founded 1927
Coed, 1,909 undergraduate students, 76% full-time, 73% women, 27% men
Urban 55-acre campus
Moderately difficult entrance level, 78% of applicants were admitted

Freshmen *Admission:* 1,060 applied, 852 were accepted, 314 enrolled. *Test scores:* SAT verbal scores over 500: 60%; SAT math scores over 500: 80%; SAT verbal scores over 600: 20%; SAT math scores over 600: 20%.
Tuition and fees (2003–04): $15,100 (full-time). *Room and board:* $5350 (room only: $2708).
Financial Aid (All incoming freshmen): *Average non-need based aid:* $9669. *Average aid to full-time undergraduates:* $11,283.
Athletic Department: *Director of Athletics:* Steven Larson; Phone: 608-663-3249; Fax: 608-663-6703; E-mail: glarson@edgewood.edu. *Sports Information Director:* Clare Hunter; Phone: 608-663-8352; E-mail: chunter@edgewood.edu.

MEN'S COACHES
Baseball: Al Brisack; Phone: 608-663-3289; E-mail: abrisack@edgewood.edu.
Basketball: Steven Larson; Phone: 608-663-3249; E-mail: glarson@edgewood.edu.
Cross Country: Al Brisack; Phone: 608-663-3289; E-mail: abrisack@edgewood.edu.
Golf: Gary Oftedahl; Phone: 608-663-2895; E-mail: goftedahl@edgewood.edu.
Soccer: Tim Alexander; Phone: 608-663-3280; E-mail: talexander@edgewood.edu.

WOMEN'S COACHES
Basketball: Clare Hunter; Phone: 608-663-8352; E-mail: chunter@edgewood.edu.
Cross Country: Al Brisack; Phone: 608-663-3289; E-mail: abrisack@edgewood.edu.
Golf: Clare Hunter; Phone: 608-663-8352; E-mail: chunter@edgewood.edu.
Soccer: Tim Alexander; Phone: 608-663-3280; E-mail: talexander@edgewood.edu.
Softball: J.P. Richard; Phone: 608-663-3249; E-mail: jprichards55@hotmail.com.
Tennis: Andy Berens; Phone: 608-663-3249; E-mail: teixeira@charter.net.
Volleyball: Cindy Hanson; Phone: 608-663-3249; E-mail: chanson@swatsports.org.

EDINBORO UNIVERSITY OF PENNSYLVANIA
Edinboro, Pennsylvania

Fighting Scots ◆ NCAA II ◆ Pennsylvania State Athletic Conference ◆ http://www.edinboro.edu/

State-supported comprehensive, founded 1857, part of Pennsylvania State System of Higher Education
Coed, 7,029 undergraduate students, 89% full-time, 58% women, 42% men
Small-town 585-acre campus
Moderately difficult entrance level, 66% of applicants were admitted

Freshmen *Admission:* 3,950 applied, 2,710 were accepted, 1,455 enrolled. *Test scores:* SAT verbal scores over 500: 39%; SAT math scores over 500: 38%; SAT verbal scores over 600: 8%; SAT math scores over 600: 7%; SAT verbal scores over 700: 1%.
Tuition and fees (2003–04): $5764 (resident), $8064 (nonresident). *Room and board:* $5086 (room only: $3120).
Financial Aid (All incoming freshmen): *Average need-based gift aid:* $1500. *Average non-need based aid:* $2000. *Average aid to full-time undergraduates:* $5658.

Athletic Department: *Director of Athletics:* Bruce Baumgartner; Phone: 814-732-2776; Fax: 814-732-2910; E-mail: bbaumgartner@edinboro.edu. *Sports Information Director:* Bob Shreve; Phone: 814-732-2776; E-mail: rshreve@edinboro.edu.

MEN'S COACHES
Basketball: Greg Walcavich; Phone: 814-732-2776; E-mail: gwalcavich@edinboro.edu.
Cheerleading: Christine Beddick; Phone: 814-732-2776; E-mail: cbeddick@edinboro.edu.
Cross Country: Doug Watts; Phone: 814-732-2776; E-mail: dwatts@edinboro.edu.
Football: Lou Tepper; Phone: 814-732-2776; E-mail: ltepper@edinboro.edu.
Swimming: Chris Rhodes; Phone: 814-732-2776; E-mail: crhodes@edinboro.edu.
Track and Field: Doug Watts; Phone: 814-732-2776; E-mail: dwatts@edinboro.edu.
Wrestling: Tim Flynn; Phone: 814-732-2776; E-mail: tflynn@edinboro.edu.

WOMEN'S COACHES
Basketball: Stan Swank; Phone: 814-732-2776; E-mail: sswank@edinboro.edu.
Cheerleading: Christine Beddick; Phone: 814-732-2776; E-mail: cbeddick@edinboro.edu.
Cross Country: Doug Watts; Phone: 814-732-2776; E-mail: dwatts@edinboro.edu.
Soccer: Gary Kagiavas; Phone: 814-732-2776; E-mail: gkagiavas@edinboro.edu.
Softball: Dan Gierlak; Phone: 814-732-2776; E-mail: dgierlak@edinboro.edu.
Swimming: Chris Rhodes; Phone: 814-732-2776; E-mail: crhodes@edinboro.edu.
Track and Field: Doug Watts; Phone: 814-732-2776; E-mail: dwatts@edinboro.edu.
Volleyball: Lynn Theehs; Phone: 814-732-2776; E-mail: ltheehs@edinboro.edu.

EDWARD WATERS COLLEGE
Jacksonville, Florida

Tigers ◆ NAIA ◆ Eastern Intercollegiate Conference; Independent ◆ http://www.ewc.edu/

Independent African Methodist Episcopal 4-year, founded 1866
Coed, 1,320 undergraduate students, 97% full-time, 49% women, 51% men
Urban 20-acre campus
Noncompetitive entrance level

Freshmen *Admission:* 552 enrolled.
Tuition and fees (2003–04): $7567 (full-time). *Room and board:* $5469 (room only: $2576).
Financial Aid (All incoming freshmen): *Average need-based gift aid:* $4835. *Average non-need based aid:* $1488. *Average aid to full-time undergraduates:* $4835.
Athletic Department: *Director of Athletics:* James Day; Phone: 904-470-8275; Fax: 904-470-8041. *Sports Information Director:* Henry Smith; Phone: 904-470-8255.

MEN'S COACHES
Baseball: Alton Burden; Phone: 904-470-8281.
Basketball: Buster Harvey; Phone: 904-470-8281.
Football: Lamonte Massie; Phone: 904-470-8281; E-mail: ljmassie@ewc.edu.
Golf: Phone: 904-470-8281.
Track and Field: Phone: 904-470-8281.

WOMEN'S COACHES
Basketball: Regina Mosley; Phone: 904-470-8281.
Golf: Phone: 904-470-8281.
Softball: Valerie Crimes; Phone: 904-470-8281.
Track and Field: Phone: 904-470-8281.

ELIZABETH CITY STATE UNIVERSITY
Elizabeth City, North Carolina

Vikings ◆ NCAA II ◆ Central Intercollegiate Athletic Conference ◆ http://www.ecsu.edu/

State-supported comprehensive, founded 1891, part of University of North Carolina System
Coed, 2,282 undergraduate students, 84% full-time, 63% women, 37% men
Small-town 125-acre campus with easy access to Norfolk
Moderately difficult entrance level, 72% of applicants were admitted

Freshmen *Admission:* 1,383 applied, 1,046 were accepted, 464 enrolled. *Test scores:* SAT verbal scores over 500: 10%; SAT math scores over 500: 10%; SAT verbal scores over 600: 2%; SAT math scores over 600: 1%.
Tuition and fees (2003–04): $2643 (resident), $10,514 (nonresident). *Room and board:* $4608.
Athletic Department: *Director of Athletics:* Edward McLean; Phone: 252-335-3396; Fax: 252-335-3627; E-mail: emclean@mail.ecsu.edu. *Sports Information Director:* April Emory; Phone: 252-335-3278; E-mail: aemory@mail.ecsu.edu.

MEN'S COACHES
Baseball: Terrance Whittle; Phone: 252-335-3392; E-mail: tmwhittle@mail.ecsu.edu.
Basketball: Shawn Walker; Phone: 252-335-3673; E-mail: swalker@mail.ecsu.edu.
Cross Country: Shawn Walker; Phone: 252-335-3673; E-mail: swalker@mail.ecsu.edu.
Football: Waverly Tillar; Phone: 252-335-3628; E-mail: twaverly@mail.ecsu.edu.
Golf: Lavern Jones; Phone: 252-335-3236; E-mail: ljones@mail.ecsu.edu.

WOMEN'S COACHES
Basketball: Fred Batchelor; Phone: 252-335-3403; E-mail: fmbatchelor@mail.ecsu.edu.
Cross Country: Shawn Walker; Phone: 252-335-3673; E-mail: swalker@mail.ecsu.edu.
Softball: Janie Cofield; Phone: 252-335-3393.
Tennis: Eugene O'Neil; Phone: 252-335-3344; E-mail: eoneal@mail.ecsu.edu.
Track and Field: Cybthia Williams; Phone: 252-335-3383.
Volleyball: Revonda Whitley; Phone: 252-335-3387; E-mail: rrwhitley@mail.ecsu.edu.

ELIZABETHTOWN COLLEGE
Elizabethtown, Pennsylvania

Blue Jays ◆ NCAA III ◆ Commonwealth Conference ◆ http://www.etown.edu/

Independent religious comprehensive, founded 1899, affiliated with Church of the Brethren
Coed, 1,975 undergraduate students, 90% full-time, 65% women, 35% men
Small-town 185-acre campus with easy access to Baltimore and Philadelphia
Moderately difficult entrance level, 83% of applicants were admitted

Freshmen *Admission:* 2,541 applied, 1,780 were accepted, 496 enrolled. *Test scores:* SAT verbal scores over 500: 77%; SAT math scores over 500: 80%; SAT verbal scores over 600: 28%; SAT math scores over 600: 32%; SAT verbal scores over 700: 4%; SAT math scores over 700: 4%.
Tuition and fees (2003–04): $22,500 (full-time). *Room and board:* $6300 (room only: $3150).
Financial Aid (All incoming freshmen): *Average need-based gift aid:* $12,322. *Average non-need based aid:* $13,779. *Average aid to full-time undergraduates:* $15,322.
Athletic Department: *Director of Athletics:* Nancy Latimore; Phone: 717-361-1407; Fax: 717-361-1488; E-mail: latimonj@etown.edu. *Sports Information Director:* Ian Showalter; Phone: 717-361-1311; E-mail: showalih@etown.edu.

MEN'S COACHES
Baseball: Matt Jones; Phone: 717-361-1463; E-mail: jonesms@etown.edu.
Basketball: Bob Schlosser; Phone: 717-361-1141; E-mail: schlosra@etown.edu.
Cross Country: Chris Straub; Phone: 717-361-1140; E-mail: straubce@etown.edu.
Golf: Keith Marks; Phone: 717-361-1130; E-mail: markskm@etown.edu.
Lacrosse: Chuck Maloy; Phone: 717-361-1980; E-mail: maloyc@etown.edu.
Soccer: Skip Roderick; Phone: 717-361-1144; E-mail: roderiad@etown.edu.
Swimming: Mike Guinivan; Phone: 717-361-1274; E-mail: guinivmr@etown.edu.
Tennis: Matt Helsel; Phone: 717-361-1475; E-mail: etowntennis@comcast.net.
Track and Field: Chris Straub; Phone: 717-361-1140; E-mail: straubce@etown.edu.
Wrestling: Eric Walker; Phone: 717-361-1137; E-mail: walkered@etown.edu.

WOMEN'S COACHES
Basketball: Yvonne Kauffman; Phone: 717-361-1138; E-mail: kauffmye@etown.edu.
Cross Country: Mike Dager; Phone: 717-361-1140; E-mail: dagerm@etown.edu.
Field Hockey: Aimee Seward; Phone: 717-361-1981; E-mail: sewarda@etown.edu.
Lacrosse: Aimee Seward; Phone: 717-361-1981; E-mail: sewarda@etown.edu.
Soccer: Barry Dohner; Phone: 717-361-1462; E-mail: dohnerbm@etown.edu.
Softball: Kathy Staib; Phone: 717-361-1533.
Swimming: Mike Guinivan; Phone: 717-361-1274; E-mail: guinivmr@etown.edu.
Tennis: Matt Helsel; Phone: 717-361-1475; E-mail: etowntennis@comcast.net.
Track and Field: Chris Straub; Phone: 717-361-1140; E-mail: straubce@etown.edu.
Volleyball: Randall Kreider; Phone: 717-361-1472; E-mail: randall.kreider@att.net.

ELMHURST COLLEGE
Elmhurst, Illinois

Blue Jays ◆ NCAA III ◆ College Conference of Illinois and Wisconsin Conference ◆ http://www.elmhurst.edu/

Independent religious comprehensive, founded 1871, affiliated with United Church of Christ
Coed, 2,396 undergraduate students, 86% full-time, 66% women, 34% men
Suburban 38-acre campus with easy access to Chicago
Moderately difficult entrance level, 64% of applicants were admitted

Freshmen *Admission:* 1,511 applied, 1,100 were accepted, 366 enrolled.
Tuition and fees (2003–04): $18,600 (full-time). *Room and board:* $6030 (room only: $3460).
Financial Aid (All incoming freshmen): *Average need-based gift aid:* $11,209. *Average non-need based aid:* $7540. *Average aid to full-time undergraduates:* $15,023.
Athletic Department: *Director of Athletics:* Paul Krohn; Phone: 630-617-3146; Fax: 630-617-3726; E-mail: paulk@elmhurst.edu.

MEN'S COACHES
Baseball: Clark Jones; Phone: 630-617-3143; E-mail: clarkj@elmhurst.edu.
Basketball: Mark Scherer; Phone: 630-617-3147; E-mail: marks@elmhurst.edu.
Cheerleading: Cheryl Leoni; Phone: 630-617-3189; E-mail: cheryll@elmhurst.edu.
Cross Country: Greg Huffaker; Phone: 630-617-3151; E-mail: gregh@elmhurst.edu.
Football: Paul Krohn; Phone: 630-617-3146; E-mail: paulk@elmhurst.edu.
Golf: David Ditomasso; Phone: 630-617-3470; E-mail: davidd@elmhurst.edu.

Elmhurst College *(continued)*

Tennis: John Baines; Phone: 630-617-3775; E-mail: jbaines@elmhurst.edu.

Track and Field: Greg Huffaker; Phone: 630-617-3151; E-mail: gregh@elmhurst.edu.

Wrestling: Steve Marianetti; Phone: 630-617-3774; E-mail: stevem@elmhurst.edu.

WOMEN'S COACHES

Cheerleading: Cheryl Leoni; Phone: 630-617-3189; E-mail: cheryll@elmhurst.edu.

Cross Country: Erik Guta; Phone: 630-617-3151; E-mail: guta@elmhurst.edu.

Golf: Mark Scherer; Phone: 630-617-3147; E-mail: marks@elmhurst.edu.

Soccer: David Ditomasso; Phone: 630-617-3470; E-mail: davidd@elmhurst.edu.

Softball: Lori Brown; Phone: 630-617-6140; E-mail: lorib@elmhurst.edu.

Tennis: Hope Samper; Phone: 630-617-3144; E-mail: hopes@elmhurst.edu.

Track and Field: Erik Guta; Phone: 630-617-3151; E-mail: guta@elmhurst.edu.

Volleyball: Julie Hall; Phone: 630-617-3145; E-mail: julieh@elmhurst.edu.

ELMIRA COLLEGE
Elmira, New York

Soaring Eagles ◆ NCAA III ◆ Empire 8 Conference ◆ http://www.elmira.edu/

Independent 4-year, founded 1855
Coed, 1,533 undergraduate students, 82% full-time, 72% women, 28% men
Small-town 42-acre campus
Moderately difficult entrance level, 7% of applicants were admitted

Freshmen *Admission:* 1,895 applied, 1,274 were accepted, 339 enrolled. *Test scores:* SAT verbal scores over 500: 74%; SAT math scores over 500: 70%; SAT verbal scores over 600: 25%; SAT math scores over 600: 23%; SAT verbal scores over 700: 4%; SAT math scores over 700: 4%.
Tuition and fees (2004–05): $27,030 (full-time). *Room and board:* $8330.
Financial Aid (All incoming freshmen): *Average need-based gift aid:* $15,702. *Average non-need based aid:* $13,516. *Average aid to full-time undergraduates:* $20,772.
Athletic Department: *Director of Athletics:* Patricia Thompson; Phone: 607-735-1730; Fax: 607-735-1717; E-mail: pthompson@elmira.edu. *Sports Information Director:* Matt Donohue; Phone: 607-735-1976; E-mail: mdonohue@elmira.edu.

MEN'S COACHES

Basketball: Pat Donnelly; Phone: 607-735-1967; E-mail: pdonnelly@elmira.edu.

Cheerleading: Elvis Moya; Phone: 607-735-1872; E-mail: emoya@elmira.edu.

Golf: Aaron Saul; Phone: 607-735-1969; E-mail: asaul@elmira.edu.

Ice Hockey: Tim Ceglarski; Phone: 607-735-1970; E-mail: tceglarski@elmira.edu.

Lacrosse: Peter Lawrence; Phone: 607-735-1805; E-mail: plawrence@elmira.edu.

Soccer: Matt Tantalo; Phone: 607-735-1980; E-mail: mtantalo@elmira.edu.

Tennis: Phil Levkanich; Phone: 607-735-8786; E-mail: ecathletics@elmira.edu.

WOMEN'S COACHES

Basketball: Matt Donahue; Phone: 607-735-1976; E-mail: mdonohue@elmira.edu.

Cheerleading: Elvis Moya; Phone: 607-735-1872; E-mail: emoya@elmira.edu.

Field Hockey: Bern Macca; Phone: 607-735-1858; E-mail: bmacca@elmira.edu.

Golf: Paul Nemetz-Carlson; Phone: 607-735-1837; E-mail: pnemetz-carlson@elmira.edu.

Lacrosse: Bern Macca; Phone: 607-275-3253; E-mail: bmacca@elmira.edu.

Soccer: Franco Bari; Phone: 607-735-1973; E-mail: fbari@elmira.edu.

Softball: Rhonda Faunce; Phone: 607-735-1732; E-mail: rfaunce@elmira.edu.

Tennis: Phil Levkanich; Phone: 607-735-8786; E-mail: ecathletics@elmira.edu.

Volleyball: Rhonda Faunce; Phone: 607-735-1732; E-mail: rfaunce@elmira.edu.

ELMS COLLEGE
Chicopee, Massachusetts

Blazers ◆ NCAA III ◆ North Atlantic Conference ◆ http://www.elms.edu/

Independent Roman Catholic comprehensive, founded 1928
Coed, primarily women, 830 undergraduate students, 69% full-time, 80% women, 20% men
Suburban 32-acre campus
Moderately difficult entrance level, 81% of applicants were admitted

Freshmen *Admission:* 420 applied, 376 were accepted, 153 enrolled. *Test scores:* SAT verbal scores over 500: 50%; SAT math scores over 500: 41%; SAT verbal scores over 600: 7%; SAT math scores over 600: 5%.
Tuition and fees (2004–05): $19,970 (full-time). *Room and board:* $7750.
Financial Aid (All incoming freshmen): *Average need-based gift aid:* $11,832. *Average non-need based aid:* $11,191. *Average aid to full-time undergraduates:* $16,425.
Athletic Department: *Director of Athletics:* Louise McCleary; Phone: 413-265-2395; Fax: 413-592-7074; E-mail: mcclearyl@elms.edu. *Sports Information Director:* Justin Mokerzecki; Phone: 413-265-2440; E-mail: mokerzeckij@elms.edu.

MEN'S COACHES

Basketball: Ed Silva; Phone: 413-594-2328; E-mail: silvae@elms.edu.

Cross Country: Carl Fetteroll; Phone: 413-594-2452; E-mail: fetterollc@elms.edu.

Golf: Don Lapierre; Phone: 413-594-2433; E-mail: lapierred@elms.edu.

Soccer: John Amaral; Phone: 413-594-2348; E-mail: amaralj@elms.edu.

Swimming: Rob Kane; Phone: 413-594-2439; E-mail: kaner@elms.edu.

Volleyball: Fito Ramos; Phone: 413-594-2761; E-mail: ramosf@elms.edu.

WOMEN'S COACHES

Basketball: Laura Habacker; Phone: 413-594-2342; E-mail: habackerl@elms.edu.

Cross Country: Carl Fetterol; Phone: 413-594-2452; E-mail: fetterollc@elms.edu.

Field Hockey: Katie Grabiec; Phone: 413-594-2338; E-mail: grabieck@elms.edu.

Lacrosse: Katie Grabiec; Phone: 413-594-2338; E-mail: grabieck@elms.edu.

Soccer: Jessica Moore; Phone: 413-594-2406; E-mail: moorej@elms.edu.

Softball: Cheryl Condon; Phone: 413-594-2212; E-mail: condonc@elms.edu.

Swimming: Rob Kane; Phone: 413-594-2439; E-mail: kaner@elms.edu.

Volleyball: Fito Ramos; Phone: 413-594-2761; E-mail: ramosf@elms.edu.

ELON UNIVERSITY
Elon, North Carolina

Phoenix ◆ NCAA I ◆ Southern Conference ◆ http://www.elon.edu/

Independent religious comprehensive, founded 1889, affiliated with United Church of Christ
Coed, 4,431 undergraduate students, 97% full-time, 62% women, 38% men
Suburban 580-acre campus with easy access to Raleigh
Moderately difficult entrance level, 43% of applicants were admitted

Freshmen *Admission:* 7,052 applied, 3,205 were accepted, 1,227 enrolled. *Test scores:* SAT verbal scores over 500: 89%; SAT math scores

over 500: 92%; SAT verbal scores over 600: 37%; SAT math scores over 600: 43%; SAT verbal scores over 700: 4%; SAT math scores over 700: 5%.
Tuition and fees (2003–04): $16,570 (full-time). *Room and board:* $5670 (room only: $2770).
Financial Aid (All incoming freshmen): *Average need-based gift aid:* $6776. *Average non-need based aid:* $3974. *Average aid to full-time undergraduates:* $11,543.
Athletic Department: *Director of Athletics:* Al White; Phone: 336-278-6705; Fax: 336-278-6767; E-mail: whitea@elon.edu. *Sports Information Director:* Matt Eviston; Phone: 336-278-6711; E-mail: meviston@elon.edu.

MEN'S COACHES
Baseball: Mike Kennedy; Phone: 336-278-6741; E-mail: kennedy@elon.edu.
Basketball: Ernie Nestor; Phone: 336-278-6730; E-mail: enestor@elon.edu.
Cheerleading: Sandra Bays; Phone: 336-278-6760; E-mail: sbays@elon.edu.
Cross Country: Bill Morningstar; Phone: 336-278-6740; E-mail: mornings@elon.edu.
Football: Paul Hamilton; Phone: 336-278-6721; E-mail: phamilton@elon.edu.
Golf: Bill Morningstar; Phone: 336-278-6740; E-mail: mornings@elon.edu.
Soccer: Mike Reilly; Phone: 336-278-6746; E-mail: reillym@elon.edu.
Tennis: Tom Parham; Phone: 336-278-6737; E-mail: tparham@elon.edu.

WOMEN'S COACHES
Basketball: Brenda Paul; Phone: 336-278-6733; E-mail: paulbren@elon.edu.
Cheerleading: Sandra Bays; Phone: 336-278-6760; E-mail: sbays@elon.edu.
Cross Country: Jackie Sgambati; Phone: 336-278-6739; E-mail: jsgambati@elon.edu.
Golf: Chris Dockrill; Phone: 336-278-6842; E-mail: cdockrill@elon.edu.
Soccer: Paul Webster; Phone: 336-278-6745; E-mail: websterp@elon.edu.
Softball: Patti Raduenz; Phone: 336-278-6744; E-mail: praduenz@elon.edu.
Tennis: Tom Parham; Phone: 336-278-6737; E-mail: tparham@elon.edu.
Track and Field: Jackie Sgambati; Phone: 336-278-6739; E-mail: jsgambati@elon.edu.
Volleyball: Mary Tendler; Phone: 336-278-6743; E-mail: mtendler@elon.edu.

EMBRY-RIDDLE AERONAUTICAL UNIVERSITY
Prescott, Arizona

Eagles ◆ NAIA ◆ Florida Sun Conference
◆ http://www.embryriddle.edu/

Independent comprehensive, founded 1978
Coed, primarily men, 1,631 undergraduate students, 87% full-time, 16% women, 84% men
Small-town 547-acre campus
Moderately difficult entrance level, 80% of applicants were admitted

Freshmen *Admission:* 1,250 applied, 1,001 were accepted, 304 enrolled. *Test scores:* SAT verbal scores over 500: 70%; SAT math scores over 500: 80%; SAT verbal scores over 600: 32%; SAT math scores over 600: 44%; SAT verbal scores over 700: 4%; SAT math scores over 700: 7%.
Tuition and fees (2004–05): $22,180 (full-time). *Room and board:* $6206 (room only: $3370).
Financial Aid (All incoming freshmen): *Average need-based gift aid:* $4363. *Average non-need based aid:* $5410. *Average aid to full-time undergraduates:* $13,483.
Athletic Department: *Director of Athletics:* Steve Ridder; Phone: 386-323-5025; Fax: 386-323-5002; E-mail: steven.ridder@erau.edu. *Sports Information Director:* Jamie Joss; Phone: 386-323-5006; E-mail: jamie.joss@erau.edu.

MEN'S COACHES
Soccer: Chuck Cone; Phone: 928-777-3894; E-mail: conec@erau.edu.
Wrestling: John Petty; Phone: 928-777-3853; E-mail: pettycd1@erau.edu.

WOMEN'S COACHES
Soccer: Dan Blank; Phone: 386-323-5012; E-mail: daniel.blank@erau.edu.
Volleyball: Katrina Meyer; Phone: 928-777-6654; E-mail: mccorc82@erau.edu.

EMBRY-RIDDLE AERONAUTICAL UNIVERSITY
Daytona Beach, Florida

Eagles ◆ NAIA ◆ Florida Sun Conference
◆ http://www.embryriddle.edu/

Independent comprehensive, founded 1926
Coed, primarily men, 4,518 undergraduate students, 92% full-time, 18% women, 82% men
Urban 178-acre campus with easy access to Orlando
Moderately difficult entrance level, 82% of applicants were admitted

Freshmen *Admission:* 3,073 applied, 2,507 were accepted, 1,017 enrolled. *Test scores:* SAT verbal scores over 500: 72%; SAT math scores over 500: 82%; SAT verbal scores over 600: 27%; SAT math scores over 600: 40%; SAT verbal scores over 700: 2%; SAT math scores over 700: 5%.
Tuition and fees (2004–05): $22,190 (full-time). *Room and board:* $6630 (room only: $3600).
Financial Aid (All incoming freshmen): *Average need-based gift aid:* $3823. *Average non-need based aid:* $4567. *Average aid to full-time undergraduates:* $13,641.
Athletic Department: *Director of Athletics:* Steve Ridder; Phone: 386-323-5025; Fax: 386-323-5002; E-mail: steven.ridder@erau.edu. *Sports Information Director:* Jamie Joss; Phone: 386-323-5006; E-mail: jamie.joss@erau.edu.

MEN'S COACHES
Baseball: Greg Guilliams; Phone: 386-323-5010; E-mail: gregory.guilliams@erau.edu.
Basketball: Steve Ridder; Phone: 386-323-5025; E-mail: steven.ridder@erau.edu.
Cheerleading: Carrie Rosolino; Phone: 386-323-5018; E-mail: carrie.rosolino@erau.edu.
Cross Country: Mike Rosolino; Phone: 386-323-5008; E-mail: michael.rosolino@erau.edu.
Golf: Maria Lopez; Phone: 386-323-5013; E-mail: maria.lopez@erau.edu.
Soccer: David Gregson; Phone: 386-323-5014; E-mail: david.gregson@erau.edu.
Tennis: Scott Linn; Phone: 386-323-5009; E-mail: scott.linn@erau.edu.

WOMEN'S COACHES
Cheerleading: Carrie Rosolino; Phone: 386-323-5018; E-mail: carrie.rosolino@erau.edu.
Cross Country: Mike Rosolino; Phone: 386-323-5008; E-mail: michael.rosolino@erau.edu.
Golf: Maria Lopez; Phone: 386-323-5013; E-mail: maria.lopez@erau.edu.
Tennis: Scott Linn; Phone: 386-323-5009; E-mail: scott.linn@erau.edu.
Volleyball: Trina Keeton; Phone: 386-323-5005; E-mail: trina.keeton@erau.edu.

EMERSON COLLEGE
Boston, Massachusetts

Lions ◆ NCAA II ◆ Great Northeast Athletic Conference;
New England Women's Lacrosse Conference
◆ http://www.emerson.edu/

Independent comprehensive, founded 1880
Coed, 3,401 undergraduate students, 87% full-time, 61% women,
39% men
Urban campus
Very difficult entrance level, 46% of applicants were admitted

Freshmen *Admission:* 4,321 applied, 2,090 were accepted, 701 enrolled.
Test scores: SAT verbal scores over 500: 98%; SAT math scores over
500: 94%; SAT verbal scores over 600: 64%; SAT math scores over
600: 46%; SAT verbal scores over 700: 13%; SAT math scores over
700: 6%.
Tuition and fees (2003–04): $22,693 (full-time). *Room and board:* $9828
(room only: $5850).
Financial Aid (All incoming freshmen): *Average need-based gift aid:* $9798.
Average non-need based aid: $11,409. *Average aid to full-time under-
graduates:* $11,209.
Athletic Department: *Director of Athletics:* Rudy Keeling; Phone: 617-
824-8691; Fax: 617-824-8529; E-mail: rudy_keeling@emerson.edu.
Sports Information Director: Roger Crosley; Phone: 617-824-8458;
E-mail: roger_crosley@emerson.edu.

MEN'S COACHES
Baseball: Mitch Lebowitz; Phone: 617-824-8930; E-mail:
mitchell_lebowitz@emerson.edu.
Basketball: Hank Smith; Phone: 617-824-8123; E-mail: henry_smith@
emerson.edu.
Cross Country: John Furey; Phone: 617-375-5600; E-mail: john_furey@
emerson.edu.
Lacrosse: Phone: 617-824-8930; E-mail: stanford_nance@emerson.edu.
Soccer: Jared Scarpaci; Phone: 617-824-8930; E-mail: jared_scarpaci@
emerson.edu.
Tennis: Keith Warner; Phone: 617-824-8906; E-mail: keith_warner@
emerson.edu.

WOMEN'S COACHES
Basketball: Melissa Hart; Phone: 617-824-8122; E-mail: melissa_hart@
emerson.edu.
Cross Country: John Furey; Phone: 617-375-5600; E-mail: jfurey@
fitcorp.com.
Lacrosse: Phone: 617-824-8930; E-mail: stanford_nance@emerson.edu.
Soccer: Kristin Parnell; Phone: 617-824-8905; E-mail: kristin_parnell@
emerson.edu.
Softball: Phil McElroy; Phone: 617-646-7503; E-mail: philip_mcelroy@
emerson.edu.
Tennis: gary Chafetz; Phone: 617-824-8930; E-mail: chafet@aol.com.
Volleyball: Chrissy Horan; Phone: 617-824-8471; E-mail:
christine_horan@emerson.edu.

EMMANUEL COLLEGE
Franklin Springs, Georgia

Lions ◆ NAIA ◆ Georgia Alabama Carolina Conference
◆ http://www.emmanuelcollege.edu/

Independent religious 4-year, founded 1919, affiliated with
Pentecostal Holiness Church
Coed, 742 undergraduate students, 86% full-time, 57% women,
43% men
Rural 90-acre campus with easy access to Atlanta
Minimally difficult entrance level, 51% of applicants were admitted

Freshmen *Admission:* 672 applied, 331 were accepted, 192 enrolled.
Tuition and fees (2003–04): $9004 (full-time). *Room and board:* $4136
(room only: $1950).
Financial Aid (All incoming freshmen): *Average need-based gift aid:* $3057.
Average non-need based aid: $3996. *Average aid to full-time under-
graduates:* $8817.
Athletic Department: *Director of Athletics:* Mike Bona; Phone: 706-245-
7226; Fax: 706-245-4424.

MEN'S COACHES
Baseball: Ryan Gray; Phone: 706-245-2859.
Basketball: Jerry Boone; Phone: 706-245-7226.
Soccer: Jimmy Stephens; Phone: 706-245-7226; E-mail: jstephens@
eclions.net.
Tennis: Mark Goodwin; Phone: 706-245-7226.

WOMEN'S COACHES
Basketball: Arlon Beadles; Phone: 706-245-7226; E-mail: abeadles@
eclions.net.
Soccer: Jimmy Stephens; Phone: 706-245-7226; E-mail: jstephens@
eclions.net.
Softball: Ricky Sanders; Phone: 706-245-7226; E-mail: rsanders@
emmanuelcollege.edu.
Tennis: Mark Goodwin; Phone: 706-245-7226.

EMMANUEL COLLEGE
Boston, Massachusetts

Saints ◆ NCAA III ◆ Great Northeast Athletic Conference
◆ http://www.emmanuel.edu/

Independent Roman Catholic comprehensive, founded 1919
Coed, 1,628 undergraduate students, 74% full-time, 77% women,
23% men
Urban 16-acre campus
Moderately difficult entrance level, 2% of applicants were admitted

Freshmen *Admission:* 2,318 applied, 406 were accepted, 406 enrolled.
Test scores: SAT verbal scores over 500: 69%; SAT math scores over
500: 56%; SAT verbal scores over 600: 22%; SAT math scores over
600: 17%; SAT verbal scores over 700: 2%; SAT math scores over
700: 1%.
Tuition and fees (2004–05): $20,500 (full-time). *Room and board:* $9000.
Financial Aid (All incoming freshmen): *Average need-based gift aid:*
$10,945. *Average non-need based aid:* $14,180. *Average aid to full-
time undergraduates:* $15,439.
Athletic Department: *Director of Athletics:* Pam Roecker; Phone: 617-
735-9985; Fax: 617-735-9885; E-mail: roeckerp@emmanuel.edu.
Sports Information Director: Alexis Mastronardi; Phone: 617-735-
9986; E-mail: mastronardi@emmanuel.edu.

MEN'S COACHES
Basketball: Lance Tucker; Phone: 617-735-9849; E-mail: tuckerl@
emmanuel.edu.
Cross Country: Tony Darocha; Phone: 617-735-9863; E-mail: darochat@
emmanuel.edu.
Soccer: Julio Avila; Phone: 617-735-9985; E-mail: avila@emmanuel.
edu.
Track and Field: Tony Darocha; Phone: 617-735-9863; E-mail:
darochat@emmanuel.edu.
Volleyball: Doug Porrell; Phone: 617-735-9985.

WOMEN'S COACHES
Basketball: Andy Yosinoff; Phone: 617-735-9985; E-mail: yosinoff@
emmanuel.edu.
Cross Country: Tony Darocha; Phone: 617-735-9863; E-mail: darochat@
emmanuel.edu.
Soccer: Wayne Currie; Phone: 617-735-9864; E-mail: currie@
emmanuel.edu.
Softball: Virginia Snyder-Cardozo; Phone: 617-735-9985; E-mail:
cardozv@emmanuel.edu.
Tennis: Rob Miller; Phone: 617-735-9985; E-mail: millerr@emmanuel.
edu.
Track and Field: Tony Darocha; Phone: 617-735-9863; E-mail:
darochat@emmanuel.edu.
Volleyball: Joe Seid; Phone: 617-735-9864; E-mail: seidj@emmanuel.
edu.

EMORY & HENRY COLLEGE
Emory, Virginia

Wasps ◆ NCAA III ◆ Old Dominion Conference ◆ http://www.ehc.edu/

Independent United Methodist comprehensive, founded 1836
Coed, 886 undergraduate students, 97% full-time, 51% women, 49% men
Rural 331-acre campus
Moderately difficult entrance level, 79% of applicants were admitted

Freshmen *Admission:* 916 applied, 746 were accepted, 224 enrolled. *Test scores:* SAT verbal scores over 500: 65%; SAT math scores over 500: 64%; SAT verbal scores over 600: 29%; SAT math scores over 600: 21%; SAT verbal scores over 700: 2%; SAT math scores over 700: 3%.
Tuition and fees (2003–04): $15,900 (full-time). *Room and board:* $6050 (room only: $2930).
Financial Aid (All incoming freshmen): *Average need-based gift aid:* $11,400. *Average non-need based aid:* $7898. *Average aid to full-time undergraduates:* $13,231.
Athletic Department: *Director of Athletics:* Lou Wacker; Phone: 276-944-6234; Fax: 276-944-6738; E-mail: lawacker@ehc.edu. *Sports Information Director:* Nathan Graybeal; Phone: 276-944-6830; E-mail: ngraybea@ehc.edu.
MEN'S COACHES
Baseball: Dewey Lusk; Phone: 276-944-6855; E-mail: dglusk@ehc.edu.
Basketball: Bob Johnson; Phone: 276-944-6236; E-mail: rjjohnso@ehc.edu.
Cheerleading: Nickie Asher; Phone: 276-944-4121.
Cross Country: Cindy Dimarino; Phone: 276-944-6659.
Football: Lou Wacker; Phone: 276-944-6234; E-mail: lawacker@ehc.edu.
Golf: Lou Wacker; Phone: 276-944-6234; E-mail: lawacker@ehc.edu.
Soccer: Craig Appleby; Phone: 276-944-6831; E-mail: cappleby@ehc.edu.
Tennis: Jim Barker; Phone: 276-944-6845; E-mail: jbarker@ehc.edu.
WOMEN'S COACHES
Basketball: Joy Scruggs; Phone: 276-944-6238; E-mail: jscruggs@ehc.edu.
Cheerleading: Nickie Asher; Phone: 276-944-4121.
Cross Country: Cindy Dimarino; Phone: 276-944-6659.
Soccer: Jimi Meyer; Phone: 276-944-6696; E-mail: jmeyer@ehc.edu.
Softball: Shannon Farley; Phone: 276-944-6885; E-mail: spfarley@ehc.edu.
Tennis: Beverly Hatch; Phone: 276-944-6148; E-mail: bshatch@ehc.edu.
Volleyball: Cassie Poschyla; Phone: 276-944-6885; E-mail: cpochyla@ehc.edu.

EMORY UNIVERSITY
Atlanta, Georgia

Eagles ◆ NCAA III ◆ University Athletic Conference ◆ http://www.emory.edu/

Independent Methodist university, founded 1836
Coed, 6,297 undergraduate students, 98% full-time, 56% women, 44% men
Suburban 631-acre campus
Most difficult entrance level, 41% of applicants were admitted

Freshmen *Admission:* 10,372 applied, 4,357 were accepted, 1,606 enrolled. *Test scores:* SAT verbal scores over 500: 100%; SAT math scores over 500: 100%; SAT verbal scores over 600: 90%; SAT math scores over 600: 95%; SAT verbal scores over 700: 40%; SAT math scores over 700: 51%.
Tuition and fees (2003–04): $27,952 (full-time). *Room and board:* $8920 (room only: $5612).
Financial Aid (All incoming freshmen): *Average need-based gift aid:* $19,147. *Average non-need based aid:* $12,428. *Average aid to full-time undergraduates:* $24,007.
Athletic Department: *Director of Athletics:* Chuck Gordon; Phone: 404-727-6547; Fax: 404-727-4989; E-mail: cgordon@emory.edu. *Sports Information Director:* John Arenberg; Phone: 404-727-6553; E-mail: jarenbe@emory.edu.

MEN'S COACHES
Baseball: Mike Twardoski; Phone: 404-727-0877; E-mail: mtwardo@emory.edu.
Basketball: Brett Zuver; Phone: 404-727-4422; E-mail: bzuver@emory.edu.
Cross Country: John Curtin; Phone: 404-727-4098; E-mail: jcurtin@emory.edu.
Diving: Jon Howell; Phone: 404-727-4081; E-mail: jphowel@emory.edu.
Golf: Mike Phillips; Phone: 404-727-4097; E-mail: mphil03@emory.edu.
Soccer: Mike Rubesch; Phone: 404-727-0597; E-mail: mrubesc@emory.edu.
Swimming: Jon Howell; Phone: 404-727-4081; E-mail: jphowel@emory.edu.
Tennis: John Browning; Phone: 404-727-7270; E-mail: jbrow25@emory.edu.
Track and Field: John Curtin; Phone: 404-727-4098; E-mail: jcurtin@emory.edu.
WOMEN'S COACHES
Basketball: Christy Thomaskutty; Phone: 404-712-2454; E-mail: cthomas6@learnlink.emory.edu.
Cross Country: John Curtin; Phone: 404-727-4098; E-mail: jcurtin@emory.edu.
Diving: Jon Howell; Phone: 404-727-4081; E-mail: jphowel@emory.edu.
Soccer: Mike Sabatelle; Phone: 404-727-2839; E-mail: msabate@emory.edu.
Softball: Penny Siqueiros; Phone: 404-727-7311; E-mail: psiquei@emory.edu.
Swimming: Jon Howell; Phone: 404-727-4081; E-mail: jphowel@emory.edu.
Tennis: Amy Smith; Phone: 404-727-6539; E-mail: amy.smith@learnlink.emory.edu.
Track and Field: John Curtin; Phone: 404-727-4098; E-mail: jcurtin@emory.edu.
Volleyball: Jenny McDowell; Phone: 404-727-4693; E-mail: jmcdowe@emory.edu.

EMPORIA STATE UNIVERSITY
Emporia, Kansas

Hornets ◆ NCAA II ◆ Mid-America Intercollegiate Conference ◆ http://www.emporia.edu/

State-supported comprehensive, founded 1863, part of Kansas Board of Regents
Coed, 4,434 undergraduate students, 87% full-time, 61% women, 39% men
Small-town 207-acre campus with easy access to Wichita
Noncompetitive entrance level, 73% of applicants were admitted

Freshmen *Admission:* 1,477 applied, 1,090 were accepted, 817 enrolled.
Tuition and fees (2003–04): $2776 (resident), $8914 (nonresident). *Room and board:* $4222 (room only: $2104).
Financial Aid (All incoming freshmen): *Average need-based gift aid:* $1458. *Average non-need based aid:* $731. *Average aid to full-time undergraduates:* $3878.
Athletic Department: *Director of Athletics:* Kent Weiser; Phone: 620-341-5350; Fax: 620-341-5603; E-mail: weiserke@emporia.edu. *Sports Information Director:* Don Weast; Phone: 620-341-5526; E-mail: weastdon@emporia.edu.

MEN'S COACHES
Baseball: Bob Fornelli; Phone: 620-341-5930; E-mail: fornellb@emporia.edu.
Basketball: David Moe; Phone: 620-341-6226; E-mail: moedavid@emporia.edu.
Cheerleading: Mary Decker; Phone: 620-341-5481; E-mail: deckerma@emporia.edu.
Cross Country: Dave Harris; Phone: 620-341-5938; E-mail: harrisda@emporia.edu.
Football: David Wiemers; Phone: 620-341-5504; E-mail: wiemersd@emporia.edu.
Tennis: Shawn Siegele; Phone: 620-341-5354; E-mail: siegeles@emporia.edu.

Emporia State University *(continued)*

Track and Field: Dave Harris; Phone: 620-341-5938; E-mail: harrisda@emporia.edu.

WOMEN'S COACHES

Basketball: Brandon Schneider; Phone: 620-341-5932; E-mail: schneidb@emporia.edu.

Cheerleading: Mary Decker; Phone: 620-341-5481; E-mail: deckerma@emporia.edu.

Cross Country: Dave Harris; Phone: 620-341-5938; E-mail: harrisda@emporia.edu.

Soccer: Ivan Huntoon; Phone: 620-341-5036; E-mail: huntooni@emporia.edu.

Softball: Stacy Gemeinhardt; Phone: 620-341-6164; E-mail: gemeinhs@emporia.edu.

Tennis: Shawn Siegele; Phone: 620-341-5354; E-mail: siegeles@emporia.edu.

Track and Field: Dave Harris; Phone: 620-341-5938; E-mail: harrisda@emporia.edu.

Volleyball: Maxine Mehus; Phone: 620-341-5931; E-mail: mehusmax@emporia.edu.

ENDICOTT COLLEGE
Beverly, Massachusetts

Gulls ◆ NCAA III ◆ Commonwealth Coast Conference; New England Football Conference ◆ http://www.endicott.edu/

Independent comprehensive, founded 1939
Coed, 1,755 undergraduate students, 92% full-time, 63% women, 37% men
Suburban 240-acre campus with easy access to Boston
Moderately difficult entrance level, 6% of applicants were admitted

Freshmen *Admission:* 2,484 applied, 1,198 were accepted, 457 enrolled. *Test scores:* SAT verbal scores over 500: 64%; SAT math scores over 500: 71%; SAT verbal scores over 600: 10%; SAT math scores over 600: 13%; SAT verbal scores over 700: 1%; SAT math scores over 700: 1%.
Tuition and fees (2003–04): $17,408 (full-time). *Room and board:* $8858 (room only: $6210).
Financial Aid (All incoming freshmen): *Average need-based gift aid:* $5516. *Average non-need based aid:* $5027. *Average aid to full-time undergraduates:* $11,668.
Athletic Department: *Director of Athletics:* Larry Hiser; Phone: 978-232-2304; Fax: 978-232-2600; E-mail: lhiser@endicott.edu. *Sports Information Director:* Jennifer Lucey; Phone: 978-232-2316; E-mail: jlucey@endicott.edu.

MEN'S COACHES

Baseball: Larry Hiser; Phone: 978-232-2304; E-mail: lhiser@endicott.edu.

Basketball: Mike Plansky; Phone: 978-232-2317; E-mail: mplansky@endicott.edu.

Cheerleading: Angela Licciardo; Phone: 978-232-2015; E-mail: alicciar@endicott.edu.

Cross Country: Sean Dunleavy; Phone: 978-232-2447; E-mail: sdunleav@endicott.edu.

Football: James Wells; Phone: 978-232-2324; E-mail: jwells@endicott.edu.

Golf: Mike Bemis; Phone: 978-232-2307; E-mail: mbemis@endicott.edu.

Lacrosse: Sean Quirk; Phone: 978-232-2010; E-mail: squirk@endicott.edu.

Soccer: Steffano Franciosa; Phone: 978-232-2308; E-mail: sfrancio@endicott.edu.

Tennis: Mark Herlihy; Phone: 978-232-2178; E-mail: mherlihy@endicott.edu.

Volleyball: Tim Byram; Phone: 978-232-2443; E-mail: tbyram@endicott.edu.

WOMEN'S COACHES

Basketball: Jennifer Lucey; Phone: 978-232-2316; E-mail: jlucey@endicott.edu.

Cheerleading: Angela Licciardo; Phone: 978-232-2015; E-mail: alicciar@endicott.edu.

Cross Country: Sean Dunleavy; Phone: 978-232-2447; E-mail: sdunleav@endicott.edu.

Field Hockey: Laura O'Neil; Phone: 978-232-2303; E-mail: loneil@endicott.edu.

Golf: Mike Bemis; Phone: 978-232-2307; E-mail: mbemis@endicott.edu.

Lacrosse: Laura O'Neil; Phone: 978-232-2303; E-mail: loneil@endicott.edu.

Soccer: Dina Gentile; Phone: 978-232-2430; E-mail: dgentile@endicott.edu.

Softball: Mark Velleux; Phone: 978-232-2306; E-mail: mveilleu@endicott.edu.

Tennis: Mark Herlihy; Phone: 978-232-2178; E-mail: mherlihy@endicott.edu.

Volleyball: Tim Byram; Phone: 978-232-2443; E-mail: tbyram@endicott.edu.

ERSKINE COLLEGE
Due West, South Carolina

Flying Fleet ◆ NCAA II ◆ Carolinas-Virginia Athletics Conference ◆ http://www.erskine.edu/

Independent religious 4-year, founded 1839, affiliated with Associate Reformed Presbyterian Church
Coed, 589 undergraduate students, 98% full-time, 58% women, 42% men
Rural 85-acre campus
Moderately difficult entrance level, 69% of applicants were admitted

Freshmen *Admission:* 806 applied, 567 were accepted, 176 enrolled. *Test scores:* SAT verbal scores over 500: 77%; SAT math scores over 500: 79%; SAT verbal scores over 600: 32%; SAT math scores over 600: 33%; SAT verbal scores over 700: 10%; SAT math scores over 700: 6%.
Tuition and fees (2003–04): $17,367 (full-time). *Room and board:* $5799.
Financial Aid (All incoming freshmen): *Average need-based gift aid:* $8456. *Average non-need based aid:* $9150. *Average aid to full-time undergraduates:* $16,500.
Athletic Department: *Director of Athletics:* Chip Sherer; Phone: 864-379-8745; Fax: 864-379-2197; E-mail: csherer@erskine.edu. *Sports Information Director:* Thomas Holand; Phone: 864-379-8799; E-mail: tholland@erskine.edu.

MEN'S COACHES

Baseball: Kevin Nichols; Phone: 864-379-8777; E-mail: nichols@erskine.edu.

Basketball: Mark Peeler; Phone: 864-379-8859; E-mail: mlp@erskine.edu.

Cross Country: John Showalter; Phone: 864-379-8868; E-mail: showaltr@erskine.edu.

Soccer: Lance Watkins; Phone: 864-379-8895; E-mail: watkinsl@erskine.edu.

Tennis: Vardon Cox; Phone: 864-379-8846; E-mail: cox@erskine.edu.

WOMEN'S COACHES

Basketball: Maggie Peeler; Phone: 864-379-6689; E-mail: mgpeeler@erskine.edu.

Cross Country: John Showalter; Phone: 864-379-8868; E-mail: showaltr@erskine.edu.

Soccer: Sheri Green; Phone: 864-379-2131.

Softball: Alleen Hawkins; Phone: 864-379-6685; E-mail: hawkins@erskine.edu.

Tennis: Calhoun Parr; Phone: 864-379-8767; E-mail: parr@erskine.edu.

EUREKA COLLEGE
Eureka, Illinois

Red Devils ◆ NCAA III ◆ Illini-Badger Football Conference; Northern Illinois-Iowa Conference ◆ http://www.eureka.edu/

Independent religious 4-year, founded 1855, affiliated with Christian Church (Disciples of Christ)
Coed, 516 undergraduate students, 98% full-time, 56% women, 44% men
Small-town 112-acre campus
Moderately difficult entrance level, 73% of applicants were admitted

Freshmen *Admission:* 635 applied, 474 were accepted, 138 enrolled.

Tuition and fees (2004–05): $13,400 (full-time). *Room and board:* $5880 (room only: $2820).
Financial Aid (All incoming freshmen): *Average need-based gift aid:* $9106. *Average non-need based aid:* $7854. *Average aid to full-time undergraduates:* $14,689.
Athletic Department: *Director of Athletics:* Joe Barth; Phone: 309-467-6373; Fax: 309-467-6402; E-mail: jbarth@eureka.edu. *Sports Information Director:* Shelly Lindsey; Phone: 309-467-6456; E-mail: slindsey@eureka.edu.

MEN'S COACHES
Baseball: Airren Nylin; Phone: 309-467-6376; E-mail: anylin@eureka.edu.
Basketball: Mike DeGeorge; Phone: 309-467-6371; E-mail: mdegeorge@eureka.edu.
Diving: Jennifer Lind; Phone: 309-467-6375; E-mail: jlind@eureka.edu.
Football: Darrell Crouch; Phone: 309-467-6369; E-mail: dcrouch@eureka.edu.
Golf: Joe Barth; Phone: 309-467-6373; E-mail: jbarth@eureka.edu.
Swimming: Jennifer Lind; Phone: 309-467-6375; E-mail: jlind@eureka.edu.
Tennis: Steve Shaw; Phone: 309-467-6370; E-mail: sshaw@eureka.edu.
Track and Field: John Kropke; Phone: 309-467-6369; E-mail: jkropke@eureka.edu.

WOMEN'S COACHES
Basketball: Sandy Schuster; Phone: 309-467-6377; E-mail: sschuster@eureka.edu.
Diving: Jennifer Lind; Phone: 309-467-6375; E-mail: jlind@eureka.edu.
Softball: Karen Sweitzer; Phone: 309-467-6374; E-mail: ksweitzer@eureka.edu.
Swimming: Jennifer Lind; Phone: 309-467-6375; E-mail: jlind@eureka.edu.
Tennis: Steve Shaw; Phone: 309-467-6370; E-mail: sshaw@eureka.edu.
Track and Field: John Kropke; Phone: 309-467-6369; E-mail: jkropke@eureka.edu.
Volleyball: Molly Logan; Phone: 309-467-6865; E-mail: mlogan@eureka.edu.

EVANGEL UNIVERSITY
Springfield, Missouri
Crusaders ◆ NAIA ◆ Heart of America Conference ◆ http://www.evangel.edu/

Independent religious comprehensive, founded 1955, affiliated with Assemblies of God
Coed, 1,811 undergraduate students, 96% full-time, 59% women, 41% men
Urban 80-acre campus
Moderately difficult entrance level, 95% of applicants were admitted

---

Freshmen *Admission:* 862 applied, 696 were accepted, 442 enrolled.
Tuition and fees (2004–05): $11,945 (full-time). *Room and board:* $4360 (room only: $2100).
Financial Aid (All incoming freshmen): *Average need-based gift aid:* $5035. *Average non-need based aid:* $4047. *Average aid to full-time undergraduates:* $7408.
Athletic Department: *Director of Athletics:* David Stair; Phone: 417-865-2815; Fax: 417-865-6906; E-mail: staird@evangel.edu. *Sports Information Director:* David Filmore; Phone: 417-865-2815; E-mail: fillmored@evangel.edu.

MEN'S COACHES
Baseball: Al Poland; Phone: 417-865-2815; E-mail: polanda@evangel.edu.
Basketball: Steve Jenkins; Phone: 417-865-2815; E-mail: jenkinss@evangel.edu.
Cross Country: Lynn Bowen; Phone: 417-865-2815; E-mail: bowenl@evangel.edu.
Football: Scott Metcalf; Phone: 417-865-2815; E-mail: metcalfs@evangel.edu.
Golf: Steve Jenkins; Phone: 417-865-2815; E-mail: jenkinss@evangel.edu.
Track and Field: Keith Hardy; Phone: 417-865-2815; E-mail: hardyk@evangel.edu.

WOMEN'S COACHES
Basketball: Leon Neal; Phone: 417-865-2815; E-mail: neall@evangel.edu.

Cross Country: Lynn Bowen; Phone: 417-865-2815; E-mail: bowenl@evangel.edu.
Golf: Duane Huechteman; Phone: 417-865-2815; E-mail: huechtemand@evangel.edu.
Softball: Jerry Breaux; Phone: 417-865-2815; E-mail: breauxj@evangel.edu.
Tennis: Celeste Jenkins; Phone: 417-865-2815; E-mail: jenkinsc@evangel.edu.
Track and Field: Lynn Bowen; Phone: 417-865-2815; E-mail: bowenl@evangel.edu.
Volleyball: Mary Penrod; Phone: 417-865-2815; E-mail: penrodm@evangel.edu.

THE EVERGREEN STATE COLLEGE
Olympia, Washington
Geoducks ◆ NAIA ◆ Cascade Collegiate Conference ◆ http://www.evergreen.edu/

State-supported comprehensive, founded 1967
Coed, 4,103 undergraduate students, 86% full-time, 56% women, 44% men
Small-town 1,000-acre campus with easy access to Seattle
Moderately difficult entrance level, 92% of applicants were admitted

---

Freshmen *Admission:* 1,521 applied, 1,422 were accepted, 460 enrolled.
Test scores: SAT verbal scores over 500: 88%; SAT math scores over 500: 73%; SAT verbal scores over 600: 52%; SAT math scores over 600: 29%; SAT verbal scores over 700: 12%; SAT math scores over 700: 4%.
Tuition and fees (2003–04): $3804 (resident), $13,485 (nonresident). *Room and board:* $5772 (room only: $3582).
Financial Aid (All incoming freshmen): *Average need-based gift aid:* $4766. *Average non-need based aid:* $3750. *Average aid to full-time undergraduates:* $9500.
Athletic Department: *Director of Athletics:* Dave Weber; Phone: 360-867-6531; Fax: 360-867-6783; E-mail: weberd@evergreen.edu. *Sports Information Director:* James Portune; Phone: 360-867-6537; E-mail: portunej@evergreen.edu.

MEN'S COACHES
Basketball: John Barbee; Phone: 360-867-6725; E-mail: barbiej@evergreen.edu.
Cross Country: Craig Dickson; Phone: 360-867-6741; E-mail: dicksonc@evergreen.edu.
Soccer: Tom Boatright; Phone: 360-867-6770; E-mail: boatys1@attbi.com.

WOMEN'S COACHES
Basketball: Monica Heuer; Phone: 360-867-6858; E-mail: heuerm@evergreen.edu.
Cross Country: Craig Dickson; Phone: 360-867-6741; E-mail: dicksonc@evergreen.edu.
Soccer: Arlene McMahon; Phone: 360-867-6538; E-mail: mcmahona@evergreen.edu.
Volleyball: Bill Lash; Phone: 360-867-6528; E-mail: lashb@evergreen.edu.

FAIRFIELD UNIVERSITY
Fairfield, Connecticut
Stags ◆ NCAA I ◆ Great Western Lacrosse Conference; Metro Atlantic Athletic Conference; Patriot League Conference ◆ http://www.fairfield.edu/

Independent Roman Catholic (Jesuit) comprehensive, founded 1942
Coed, 4,020 undergraduate students, 84% full-time, 58% women, 42% men
Suburban 200-acre campus with easy access to New York City
Moderately difficult entrance level, 52% of applicants were admitted

---

Freshmen *Admission:* 7,655 applied, 3,782 were accepted, 789 enrolled.
Test scores: SAT verbal scores over 500: 94%; SAT math scores over

Fairfield University *(continued)*

500: 96%; SAT verbal scores over 600: 46%; SAT math scores over 600: 57%; SAT verbal scores over 700: 5%; SAT math scores over 700: 7%.
Tuition and fees (2003–04): $26,585 (full-time). *Room and board:* $8920 (room only: $5270).
Financial Aid (All incoming freshmen): *Average need-based gift aid:* $10,639. *Average non-need based aid:* $10,134. *Average aid to full-time undergraduates:* $16,388.
Athletic Department: *Director of Athletics:* Eugene Doris; Phone: 203-254-4000; Fax: 203-254-4117; E-mail: edoris@mail.fairfield.edu. *Sports Information Director:* Allen Gibson; Phone: 203-254-4000; E-mail: agibson@mail.fairfield.edu.

MEN'S COACHES

Baseball: John Slosar; Phone: 203-254-4000; E-mail: jslosar@mail.fairfield.edu.
Basketball: Tim O'Toole; Phone: 203-254-4000; E-mail: sdaly@mail.fairfield.edu.
Cross Country: Andrew Harrington; Phone: 203-254-4000; E-mail: aharrington@mail.fairfield.edu.
Diving: Dan Vener; Phone: 203-254-4000; E-mail: twobunions@aol.com.
Golf: Len Roberto; Phone: 203-254-4000; E-mail: lrobe12568@aol.com.
Lacrosse: Ted Spencer; Phone: 203-254-4000; E-mail: tspencer@mail.fairfield.edu.
Soccer: Carl Rees; Phone: 203-254-4000; E-mail: crees@mail.fairfield.edu.
Swimming: William Farley; Phone: 203-254-4000; E-mail: wfarley@mail.fairfield.edu.
Tennis: Jeffrey Wyshner; Phone: 203-254-4000; E-mail: jwyshner@mail.fairfield.edu.

WOMEN'S COACHES

Basketball: Diane Nolan; Phone: 203-254-4000; E-mail: dmnolan@mail.fairfield.edu.
Cross Country: Andrew Harrington; Phone: 203-254-4000; E-mail: aharrington@mail.fairfield.edu.
Diving: Dan Vener; Phone: 203-254-4000; E-mail: twobunions@aol.com.
Field Hockey: Jackie Leonard; Phone: 203-254-4000; E-mail: jleonard@mail.fairfield.edu.
Golf: Jean Gaston; Phone: 203-254-4000; E-mail: twobunions@aol.com.
Lacrosse: Stacey McCue; Phone: 203-254-4000; E-mail: smccue@mail.fairfield.edu.
Soccer: Maria Piechocki; Phone: 203-254-4000; E-mail: mpiechocki@mail.fairfield.edu.
Softball: Julie Brzezinski; Phone: 203-254-4000; E-mail: jbrzezinski@mail.fairfield.edu.
Swimming: William Farley; Phone: 203-254-4000; E-mail: wfarley@mail.fairfield.edu.
Tennis: Jeffrey Wyshner; Phone: 203-254-4000; E-mail: jwyshner@mail.fairfield.edu.
Volleyball: Jeff Werneke; Phone: 203-254-4000; E-mail: jwerneke@mail.fairfield.edu.

FAIRLEIGH DICKINSON UNIVERSITY, COLLEGE AT FLORHAM

Madison, New Jersey

Devils ◆ NCAA III ◆ Freedom Conference ◆ http://www.fdu.edu/

Independent comprehensive, founded 1942
Coed, 2,645 undergraduate students, 85% full-time, 54% women, 46% men
Suburban 178-acre campus with easy access to New York City
Moderately difficult entrance level, 72% of applicants were admitted

Freshmen *Admission:* 2,884 applied, 2,162 were accepted, 616 enrolled. *Test scores:* SAT verbal scores over 500: 55%; SAT math scores over 500: 59%; SAT verbal scores over 600: 12%; SAT math scores over 600: 14%; SAT verbal scores over 700: 1%; SAT math scores over 700: 1%.

Tuition and fees (2003–04): $21,880 (full-time). *Room and board:* $8250 (room only: $4832).
Financial Aid (All incoming freshmen): *Average need-based gift aid:* $10,244. *Average non-need based aid:* $4450. *Average aid to full-time undergraduates:* $17,474.
Athletic Department: *Director of Athletics:* William Klika; Phone: 973-443-8960; Fax: 973-443-8796; E-mail: klikaad@fdu.edu. *Sports Information Director:* Scott Giglio; Phone: 973-443-8965; E-mail: giglio@fdu.edu.

MEN'S COACHES

Baseball: Doug Radziewicz; Phone: 973-443-8826; E-mail: radz@fdu.edu.
Basketball: Roger Kindel; Phone: 973-443-8964; E-mail: kindel@fdu.edu.
Cheerleading: Dina Marie Occhipinti; Phone: 973-267-8939; E-mail: occhipdi@shu.edu.
Cross Country: Dante Fedeli; Phone: 973-443-8961; E-mail: fedeli@fdu.edu.
Football: Rich Mosca; Phone: 973-443-8913; E-mail: rmosc@hotmail.com.
Golf: Roger Kindel; Phone: 973-443-8964; E-mail: kindel@fdu.edu.
Lacrosse: Pat Scarpello; Phone: 973-443-8963; E-mail: pscarp@fdu.edu.
Soccer: Tom McLoughlin; Phone: 973-443-8827; E-mail: tommcl@fdu.edu.
Swimming: Peter Loftus; Phone: 973-443-8960; E-mail: anyoneat89@aol.com.
Tennis: Nancy Dorn Keeler; Phone: 973-443-8046; E-mail: keeler@fdu.edu.

WOMEN'S COACHES

Basketball: Nancy Dorn Keeler; Phone: 973-443-8046; E-mail: keeler@fdu.edu.
Cheerleading: Dina Marie Occhipinti; Phone: 973-267-8939; E-mail: occhipdi@shu.edu.
Cross Country: Dante Fedeli; Phone: 973-443-8961; E-mail: fedeli@fdu.edu.
Field Hockey: Ann Petracco; Phone: 973-443-8544; E-mail: petracco@fdu.edu.
Golf: Roger Kindel; Phone: 973-443-8964; E-mail: kindel@fdu.edu.
Lacrosse: Adrienne Booth; Phone: 973-443-8829; E-mail: abooth@fdu.edu.
Soccer: Renee Montana; Phone: 973-443-8943; E-mail: montana@fdu.edu.
Softball: Dante Fedeli; Phone: 973-443-8961; E-mail: fedeli@fdu.edu.
Swimming: Peter Loftus; Phone: 973-443-8960; E-mail: anyoneat89@aol.com.
Tennis: Nancy Dorn Keeler; Phone: 973-443-8046; E-mail: keeler@fdu.edu.
Volleyball: Al Campora; Phone: 973-443-8017; E-mail: coachalvb@hotmail.com.

FAIRMONT STATE UNIVERSITY

Fairmont, West Virginia

Falcons ◆ NCAA II ◆ West Virginia Intercollegiate Athletic Conference ◆ http://www.fscwv.edu/

State-supported comprehensive, founded 1865, part of State College System of West Virginia
Coed, 6,813 undergraduate students, 70% full-time, 56% women, 44% men
Small-town 80-acre campus
Minimally difficult entrance level, 96% of applicants were admitted

Freshmen *Admission:* 2,057 applied, 1,986 were accepted, 1,254 enrolled.
Tuition and fees (2003–04): $3130 (resident), $7038 (nonresident). *Room and board:* $5080 (room only: $2410).
Financial Aid (All incoming freshmen): *Average need-based gift aid:* $3547. *Average non-need based aid:* $2649. *Average aid to full-time undergraduates:* $4375.
Athletic Department: *Director of Athletics:* Dave Cooper; Phone: 304-367-4220; Fax: 304-367-0202; E-mail: dcooper@mail.fscwv.edu. *Sports Information Director:* Jim Brinkman; Phone: 304-367-4264; E-mail: jbrinkman@mail.fscwv.edu.

MEN'S COACHES

Baseball: Ray Bonnett; Phone: 304-367-4146; E-mail: rbonnett@mail.fscwv.edu.

Basketball: Butch Haswell; Phone: 304-367-4150; E-mail: ahaswell@mail.fscwv.edu.
Cheerleading: Dee Johnson; Phone: 304-367-4220; E-mail: djcheer@ma.rr.com.
Cross Country: Mary Mlinarcik; Phone: 304-367-4220.
Football: Rusty Elliott; Phone: 304-367-4117; E-mail: jelliott@mail.fscwv.edu.
Golf: Reid Amos; Phone: 304-366-7649; E-mail: ramos@mail.fscwv.edu.
Swimming: Pat Snively; Phone: 304-367-4220; E-mail: swimteam@mail.fscwv.edu.
Tennis: Ken Miller; Phone: 304-367-4220.

WOMEN'S COACHES
Basketball: Steve McDonald; Phone: 304-367-4194; E-mail: smcdonald@mail.fscwv.edu.
Cheerleading: Dee Johnson; Phone: 304-367-4220; E-mail: djcheer@ma.rr.com.
Cross Country: Mary Mlinarcik; Phone: 304-367-4220.
Golf: Brenda Moran; Phone: 304-367-4220.
Softball: Joni Bokanovich; Phone: 304-367-4185; E-mail: rbonnett@mail.fscwv.edu.
Swimming: Pat Snively; Phone: 304-367-4220; E-mail: swimteam@mail.fscwv.edu.
Tennis: Ken Miller; Phone: 304-367-4220.
Volleyball: Larry Hill; Phone: 304-367-4279; E-mail: lhill@mail.fscwv.edu.

FARMINGDALE STATE UNIVERSITY OF NEW YORK
Farmingdale, New York

Rams ◆ NCAA III ◆ Skyline Conference
◆ http://www.farmingdale.edu/

State-supported 4-year, founded 1912, part of State University of New York System
Coed, 5,949 undergraduate students, 61% full-time, 43% women, 57% men
Small-town 380-acre campus with easy access to New York City
Moderately difficult entrance level, 55% of applicants were admitted

Freshmen *Admission:* 3,739 applied, 2,063 were accepted, 876 enrolled. *Test scores:* SAT verbal scores over 500: 36%; SAT math scores over 500: 46%; SAT verbal scores over 600: 4%; SAT math scores over 600: 8%; SAT math scores over 700: 1%.
Tuition and fees (2003–04): $5211 (resident), $11,161 (nonresident). *Room and board:* $7680 (room only: $4300).
Financial Aid (All incoming freshmen): *Average need-based gift aid:* $3851. *Average non-need based aid:* $2443. *Average aid to full-time undergraduates:* $4784.
Athletic Department: *Director of Athletics:* Michael Harrington; Phone: 631-420-2482; Fax: 631-420-2294; E-mail: harrinm@farmingdale.edu. *Sports Information Director:* Deana Ward; Phone: 631-420-2178; E-mail: warddt@farmingdale.edu.

MEN'S COACHES
Baseball: Ken Rocco; Phone: 631-420-2123; E-mail: roccokn@farmingdale.edu.
Basketball: Bill Musto; Phone: 631-420-2253.
Cross Country: Arnold Minkoff; Phone: 631-420-2631; E-mail: minkofa@farmingdale.edu.
Golf: Tom Azzara; Phone: 631-420-2599; E-mail: azzaratf@farmingdale.edu.
Lacrosse: Steve D'Argenio; Phone: 631-420-2606.
Soccer: Chuck Schimpf; Phone: 631-420-2620; E-mail: schimpc@farmingdale.edu.
Track and Field: Arnold Minkoff; Phone: 631-420-2631; E-mail: minkofa@farmingdale.edu.

WOMEN'S COACHES
Basketball: Chris Mooney; Phone: 631-420-2204; E-mail: mooneyc@farmingdale.edu.
Cross Country: Arnold Minkoff; Phone: 631-420-2631; E-mail: minkofa@farmingdale.edu.
Soccer: Ernesto Phan; Phone: 631-420-2383; E-mail: phanae@farmingdale.edu.

Softball: Chris Mooney; Phone: 631-420-2204; E-mail: mooneyc@farmingdale.edu.
Track and Field: Arnold Minkoff; Phone: 631-420-2631; E-mail: minkofa@farmingdale.edu.
Volleyball: Phone: 631-420-2124.

FAULKNER UNIVERSITY
Montgomery, Alabama

Eagles ◆ NAIA ◆ Georgia Alabama Carolina Conference
◆ http://www.faulkner.edu/

Independent religious comprehensive, founded 1942, affiliated with Church of Christ
Coed, 2,303 undergraduate students, 72% full-time, 64% women, 36% men
Urban 75-acre campus
Minimally difficult entrance level, 58% of applicants were admitted

Freshmen *Admission:* 575 applied, 316 were accepted, 314 enrolled. *Test scores:* SAT verbal scores over 500: 64%; SAT math scores over 500: 56%; SAT verbal scores over 600: 22%; SAT math scores over 600: 14%; SAT verbal scores over 700: 2%; SAT math scores over 700: 2%.
Tuition and fees (2004–05): $10,200 (full-time). *Room and board:* $5000 (room only: $2400).
Financial Aid (All incoming freshmen): *Average need-based gift aid:* $2500. *Average non-need based aid:* $1600. *Average aid to full-time undergraduates:* $4600.
Athletic Department: *Director of Athletics:* Jim Sanderson; Phone: 334-386-7148; Fax: 334-386-7277; E-mail: jsanderson@faulkner.edu. *Sports Information Director:* Phone: 334-386-7153; E-mail: damos@faulkner.edu.

MEN'S COACHES
Baseball: Brent Barker; Phone: 334-386-7148; E-mail: bbarker@faulkner.edu.
Basketball: Jim Sanderson; Phone: 334-386-7148; E-mail: jsanderson@faulkner.edu.
Cross Country: Phone: 334-386-7148.

WOMEN'S COACHES
Cross Country: Phone: 334-386-7148.
Softball: Hal Wynn; Phone: 334-386-7285; E-mail: hwynn@faulkner.edu.
Volleyball: Rayla Black; Phone: 334-386-7149; E-mail: rtblack@faulkner.edu.

FAYETTEVILLE STATE UNIVERSITY
Fayetteville, North Carolina

Broncos ◆ NCAA II ◆ Central Intercollegiate Athletic Conference ◆ http://www.uncfsu.edu/

State-supported comprehensive, founded 1867, part of University of North Carolina System
Coed, 4,359 undergraduate students, 81% full-time, 63% women, 37% men
Urban 156-acre campus with easy access to Raleigh
Minimally difficult entrance level, 8% of applicants were admitted

Freshmen *Admission:* 1,914 applied, 1,629 were accepted, 802 enrolled. *Test scores:* SAT verbal scores over 500: 18%; SAT math scores over 500: 17%; SAT verbal scores over 600: 2%; SAT math scores over 600: 2%; SAT verbal scores over 700: 1%.
Tuition and fees (2004–05): $2354 (resident), $11,715 (nonresident). *Room and board:* $4120 (room only: $2320).
Financial Aid (All incoming freshmen): *Average need-based gift aid:* $7803. *Average non-need based aid:* $3350. *Average aid to full-time undergraduates:* $6776.
Athletic Department: *Director of Athletics:* William Carver; Phone: 910-672-1315; Fax: 910-672-1241; E-mail: wcarver@uncfsu.edu. *Sports Information Director:* Marion Crowe; Phone: 910-672-1349; E-mail: mcrowe@uncfsu.edu.

Fayetteville State University *(continued)*

MEN'S COACHES

Basketball: Sam Hanger; Phone: 910-672-1396; E-mail: shanger@uncfsu.edu.
Cheerleading: L Miller; Phone: 910-672-1314; E-mail: lmiller@uncfsu.edu.
Cross Country: David Solomon; Phone: 910-672-1510.
Football: Kenneth Phillips; Phone: 910-672-1648; E-mail: kphillips@uncfsu.edu.
Golf: Raymond McDougal; Phone: 910-672-1511; E-mail: rmcdougal@uncfsu.edu.
Track and Field: Jack Poulus; Phone: 910-672-1937.

WOMEN'S COACHES

Basketball: Eric Tucker; Phone: 910-672-1061; E-mail: etucker@uncfsu.edu.
Cheerleading: L Miller; Phone: 910-672-1314; E-mail: lmiller@uncfsu.edu.
Cross Country: Doris Moncrief; Phone: 910-672-1061; E-mail: dmoncrief@uncfsu.edu.
Softball: Gail Mays; Phone: 910-672-1349.
Tennis: Elorie Hill; Phone: 910-672-1513; E-mail: ehill@uncfsu.edu.
Track and Field: Jack Poulus; Phone: 910-672-1937.
Volleyball: Elorine Hill; Phone: 910-672-1513; E-mail: ehill@uncfsu.edu.

FELICIAN COLLEGE
Lodi, New Jersey

Golden Falcons ◆ NCAA II ◆ Central Atlantic Collegiate
Conference ◆ http://www.felician.edu/

Independent Roman Catholic comprehensive, founded 1942
Coed, 1,416 undergraduate students, 69% full-time, 76% women, 24% men
Suburban 37-acre campus with easy access to New York City
Moderately difficult entrance level, 70% of applicants were admitted

Freshmen *Admission:* 1,115 applied, 805 were accepted, 240 enrolled.
Test scores: SAT verbal scores over 500: 25%; SAT math scores over 500: 29%; SAT verbal scores over 600: 4%; SAT math scores over 600: 5%.
Tuition and fees (2004–05): $17,125 (full-time). *Room and board:* $7500.
Financial Aid (All incoming freshmen): *Average aid to full-time undergraduates:* $11,130.
Athletic Department: *Director of Athletics:* Ben Dinallo; Phone: 201-559-3507; Fax: 201-559-6188.

MEN'S COACHES

Baseball: Christopher Langan; Phone: 201-559-3509; E-mail: svensons@inet.felician.edu.
Basketball: Darryl Jacobs; Phone: 201-559-3508; E-mail: jacobsd@inet.felician.edu.
Cheerleading: Dawn Murray; Phone: 201-559-6144; E-mail: murrayda@inet.felician.edu.
Cross Country: John Brennan; Phone: 201-559-6119.
Soccer: Tony Scoricolla; Phone: 201-559-3595; E-mail: scorciollaa@inet.felician.edu.

WOMEN'S COACHES

Basketball: Ben Dinallo; Phone: 201-559-3507.
Cheerleading: Dawn Murray; Phone: 201-559-6144; E-mail: murrayda@inet.felician.edu.
Cross Country: John Brennan; Phone: 201-559-6119.
Soccer: Erin Fitzgerald; Phone: 201-559-6119.
Softball: Kathy Hill; Phone: 201-559-6114; E-mail: mayk@inet.felician.edu.
Volleyball: George Mon; Phone: 201-559-3599.

FERRIS STATE UNIVERSITY
Big Rapids, Michigan

Bulldogs ◆ NCAA II ◆ Great Lakes Intercollegiate Conference
◆ http://www.ferris.edu/

State-supported comprehensive, founded 1884
Coed, 10,767 undergraduate students, 79% full-time, 47% women, 53% men
Small-town 850-acre campus with easy access to Grand Rapids
Minimally difficult entrance level, 72% of applicants were admitted

Freshmen *Admission:* 12,184 applied, 8,951 were accepted, 2,248 enrolled.
Tuition and fees (2003–04): $6186 (resident), $12,230 (nonresident). *Room and board:* $6326 (room only: $3118).
Financial Aid (All incoming freshmen): *Average need-based gift aid:* $3000. *Average non-need based aid:* $2000. *Average aid to full-time undergraduates:* $7050.
Athletic Department: *Director of Athletics:* Tom Kirinovic; Phone: 231-591-2863; Fax: 231-591-2869; E-mail: kirinovt@ferris.edu. *Sports Information Director:* Joe Gorby; Phone: 231-591-2336; E-mail: gorbyj@ferris.edu.

MEN'S COACHES

Basketball: Bill Sall; Phone: 231-591-2877; E-mail: sallw@ferris.edu.
Cheerleading: Anne Werner; Phone: 231-591-2000; E-mail: anne_e_werner@yahoo.com.
Cross Country: Jeff Kavalunas; Phone: 231-591-2876; E-mail: kavalunj@ferris.edu.
Football: Jeff Pierce; Phone: 231-591-2864; E-mail: piercej@ferris.edu.
Golf: Brad Bedortha; Phone: 231-591-5249; E-mail: bedorthb@ferris.edu.
Ice Hockey: Bob Daniels; Phone: 231-591-2884; E-mail: danielsb@ferris.edu.
Tennis: Kevin Brandalik; Phone: 231-591-3655; E-mail: brandalk@ferris.edu.
Track and Field: Jeff Kavalunas; Phone: 231-591-2876; E-mail: kavalunj@ferris.edu.

WOMEN'S COACHES

Basketball: Tracey Fisk; Phone: 231-591-2878; E-mail: fiskt@ferris.edu.
Cheerleading: Anne Werner; Phone: 231-591-2000; E-mail: anne_e_werner@yahoo.com.
Cross Country: Jeff Kavalunas; Phone: 231-591-2876; E-mail: kavalunj@ferris.edu.
Golf: Brad Bedortha; Phone: 231-591-5249; E-mail: bedorthb@ferris.edu.
Soccer: Melissa Eging; Phone: 231-591-2879; E-mail: egingm@ferris.edu.
Softball: Keri Becker; Phone: 231-591-3512; E-mail: beckerk@ferris.edu.
Tennis: David Ramos; Phone: 231-591-3651; E-mail: ramosd@ferris.edu.
Track and Field: Jeff Kavalunas; Phone: 231-591-2876; E-mail: kavalunj@ferris.edu.
Volleyball: Tia Brandel-Wilhelm; Phone: 231-591-2871; E-mail: brandelt@ferris.edu.

FERRUM COLLEGE
Ferrum, Virginia

Panthers ◆ NCAA III ◆ USA South Athletic Conference
◆ http://www.ferrum.edu/

Independent United Methodist 4-year, founded 1913
Coed, 954 undergraduate students, 100% full-time, 43% women, 57% men
Rural 720-acre campus
Minimally difficult entrance level, 73% of applicants were admitted

Freshmen *Admission:* 1,126 applied, 829 were accepted, 304 enrolled.
Test scores: SAT verbal scores over 500: 27%; SAT math scores over 500: 24%; SAT verbal scores over 600: 5%; SAT math scores over 600: 4%.
Tuition and fees (2004–05): $16,840 (full-time). *Room and board:* $5700.

Financial Aid (All incoming freshmen): *Average need-based gift aid:* $9348. *Average non-need based aid:* $4500. *Average aid to full-time undergraduates:* $11,450.
Athletic Department: *Director of Athletics:* Michael Kinder; Phone: 540-365-4493; Fax: 540-365-4472; E-mail: tkinder@ferrum.edu. *Sports Information Director:* Gary Holden; Phone: 540-365-4306; E-mail: gholden@ferrum.edu.

MEN'S COACHES

Baseball: Abe Naff; Phone: 540-365-4488; E-mail: anaff@ferrum.edu.
Basketball: Ed Wills; Phone: 540-365-4480; E-mail: ewills@ferrum.edu.
Cheerleading: T.J. Agee; Phone: 540-365-5573; E-mail: agee@ferrum.edu.
Cross Country: Ed Wills; Phone: 540-365-4480; E-mail: ewills@ferrum.edu.
Football: Dave Davis; Phone: 540-365-4486; E-mail: ddavis@ferrum.edu.
Golf: Ted Kinder; Phone: 540-365-4493; E-mail: tkinder@ferrum.edu.
Soccer: David Edwards; Phone: 540-365-4490; E-mail: dedwards@ferrum.edu.
Tennis: Gary Holden; Phone: 540-365-4306; E-mail: gholden@ferrum.edu.

WOMEN'S COACHES

Basketball: Donna Doonan; Phone: 540-365-4495; E-mail: ddoonan@ferrum.edu.
Cheerleading: T.J. Agee; Phone: 540-365-5573; E-mail: agee@ferrum.edu.
Cross Country: Ed Wills; Phone: 540-365-4480; E-mail: ewills@ferrum.edu.
Lacrosse: Celia Mosier; Phone: 540-365-5567; E-mail: cmosier@ferrum.edu.
Soccer: Celia Mosier; Phone: 540-365-5567; E-mail: cmosier@ferrum.edu.
Softball: Vickie Van Kleeck; Phone: 540-365-4489; E-mail: vvankleeck@ferrum.edu.
Tennis: David Edwards; Phone: 540-365-4490; E-mail: dedwards@ferrum.edu.
Volleyball: Kelly Caputo; Phone: 540-365-4497; E-mail: kcaputo@ferrum.edu.

FISHER COLLEGE
Boston, Massachusetts

Falcons ◆ NAIA ◆ Sunrise Conference
◆ http://www.fisher.edu/

Independent primarily 2-year, founded 1903
Coed, 556 undergraduate students, 100% full-time, 69% women, 31% men
Urban campus
Minimally difficult entrance level, 6% of applicants were admitted

Freshmen *Admission:* 1,534 applied, 1,006 were accepted, 314 enrolled.
Tuition and fees (2004–05): $17,575 (full-time). *Room and board:* $9975.
Athletic Department: *Director of Athletics:* Scott Dunlin; Phone: 617-236-8877; Fax: 617-236-5473.

MEN'S COACHES

Baseball: Scott Dunlin; Phone: 617-236-8877.
Basketball: James Greer; Phone: 617-236-8877.

WOMEN'S COACHES

Basketball: Troy Smith; Phone: 617-236-8877.
Softball: Phone: 617-236-8877.

FISK UNIVERSITY
Nashville, Tennessee

Bulldogs ◆ NCAA III ◆ Independent ◆ http://www.fisk.edu/

Independent religious comprehensive, founded 1866, affiliated with United Church of Christ
Coed, 850 undergraduate students, 97% full-time, 69% women, 31% men
Urban 40-acre campus
Moderately difficult entrance level, 63% of applicants were admitted

Freshmen *Admission:* 1,122 applied, 743 were accepted, 231 enrolled.
Test scores: SAT verbal scores over 500: 34%; SAT math scores over 500: 29%; SAT verbal scores over 600: 6%; SAT math scores over 600: 7%.
Tuition and fees (2003–04): $11,235 (full-time). *Room and board:* $5770 (room only: $3350).
Financial Aid (All incoming freshmen): *Average need-based gift aid:* $3700. *Average non-need based aid:* $7100. *Average aid to full-time undergraduates:* $12,500.
Athletic Department: *Director of Athletics:* Larry Glover; Phone: 615-329-8782; Fax: 615-329-8715. *Sports Information Director:* Antoine Buchanan; Phone: 615-329-8782.

MEN'S COACHES

Baseball: McKinley Young; Phone: 615-329-8784.
Basketball: Larry Glover; Phone: 615-329-8782.
Cheerleading: Andrea Campbell; Phone: 615-329-8500.
Cross Country: David Rachel; Phone: 615-329-8500.
Golf: Larry Glover; Phone: 615-329-8782.
Soccer: Conrad Hurt; Phone: 615-329-8500.
Tennis: Robert Moore; Phone: 615-329-8500.
Track and Field: David Rachel; Phone: 615-329-8500.

WOMEN'S COACHES

Basketball: Tracye Davis; Phone: 615-329-8500.
Cheerleading: Andrea Campbell; Phone: 615-329-8500.
Cross Country: David Rachel; Phone: 615-329-8500.
Golf: Larry Glover; Phone: 615-329-8782.
Soccer: Conrad Hurt; Phone: 615-329-8500.
Softball: Antoine Buchanan; Phone: 615-329-8500.
Tennis: Robert Moore; Phone: 615-329-8500.
Track and Field: David Rachel; Phone: 615-329-8500.
Volleyball: Shewanna Buchanan; Phone: 615-329-8500.

FITCHBURG STATE COLLEGE
Fitchburg, Massachusetts

Falcons ◆ NCAA III ◆ Little East Conference; Massachusetts State College Athletic Conference; New England Football Conference ◆ http://www.fsc.edu/

State-supported comprehensive, founded 1894, part of Massachusetts Public Higher Education System
Coed, 3,482 undergraduate students, 77% full-time, 55% women, 45% men
Small-town 45-acre campus with easy access to Boston
Moderately difficult entrance level, 57% of applicants were admitted

Freshmen *Admission:* 3,211 applied, 1,960 were accepted, 632 enrolled.
Test scores: SAT verbal scores over 500: 54%; SAT math scores over 500: 55%; SAT verbal scores over 600: 14%; SAT math scores over 600: 11%; SAT verbal scores over 700: 1%.
Tuition and fees (2003–04): $4200 (resident), $10,280 (nonresident). *Room and board:* $5506 (room only: $3276).
Financial Aid (All incoming freshmen): *Average need-based gift aid:* $3765. *Average non-need based aid:* $2190. *Average aid to full-time undergraduates:* $5865.
Athletic Department: *Director of Athletics:* Sue Lauder; Phone: 978-665-3314; Fax: 978-665-3710; E-mail: slauder@fsc.edu. *Sports Information Director:* Rusty Eggen; Phone: 978-665-3343; E-mail: reggen@fsc.edu.

MEN'S COACHES

Baseball: Pete Eqbert; Phone: 978-665-3726; E-mail: pegbert@fsc.edu.
Basketball: Shawn Conrad; Phone: 978-665-4683; E-mail: sdccc419@aol.com.

Fitchburg State College *(continued)*

Cross Country: Jim Jellison; Phone: 978-665-3494; E-mail: jjellison@fsc.com.

Football: Patrick Haverty; Phone: 978-665-4307; E-mail: phaverty@fsc.edu.

Ice Hockey: Dean Fuller; Phone: 978-665-4691; E-mail: fullerd47474@yahoo.com.

Soccer: Helder Botto; Phone: 978-665-4693; E-mail: falconsoccerhb@aol.com.

Track and Field: Jim Jellison; Phone: 978-665-3494; E-mail: jjellison@fsc.com.

WOMEN'S COACHES

Basketball: Walter Paschell; Phone: 978-665-4685; E-mail: dribble25@hotmail.com.

Cross Country: Jim Jellison; Phone: 978-665-3494; E-mail: jjellison@fsc.com.

Field Hockey: Beth Bacher; Phone: 978-665-4689; E-mail: islandsplash@worldnet.att.net.

Soccer: Pam Neff; Phone: 978-665-4695; E-mail: pjneff8@aol.com.

Softball: Michele Daley; Phone: 978-665-4697; E-mail: dales1525@yahoo.com.

Track and Field: Jim Jellison; Phone: 978-665-3494; E-mail: jjellison@fsc.com.

FLAGLER COLLEGE

St. Augustine, Florida

Saints ◆ NAIA ◆ Florida Sun Conference
◆ http://www.flagler.edu/

Independent 4-year, founded 1968
Coed, 2,033 undergraduate students, 98% full-time, 61% women, 39% men
Small-town 36-acre campus with easy access to Jacksonville
Moderately difficult entrance level, 5% of applicants were admitted

Freshmen *Admission:* 1,897 applied, 628 were accepted, 443 enrolled. *Test scores:* SAT verbal scores over 500: 89%; SAT math scores over 500: 87%; SAT verbal scores over 600: 34%; SAT math scores over 600: 28%; SAT verbal scores over 700: 4%; SAT math scores over 700: 2%.
Tuition and fees (2004–05): $8000 (full-time). *Room and board:* $4750.
Financial Aid (All incoming freshmen): *Average need-based gift aid:* $2463. *Average non-need based aid:* $4601. *Average aid to full-time undergraduates:* $6696.
Athletic Department: *Director of Athletics:* Dave Barnett; Phone: 904-819-6252; Fax: 904-810-2369; E-mail: athldept@flagler.edu. *Sports Information Director:* Trevor Doll; Phone: 904-819-6252; E-mail: athldept@flagler.edu.

MEN'S COACHES

Baseball: Dave Barnett; Phone: 904-819-6252; E-mail: athldept@flagler.edu.

Basketball: Bo Clark; Phone: 904-819-6252; E-mail: athldept@flagler.edu.

Cross Country: Dave Williams; Phone: 904-819-6252; E-mail: athldept@flagler.edu.

Golf: Don Robbins; Phone: 904-819-6409; E-mail: golfcoach@flagler.edu.

Soccer: John Lynch; Phone: 904-819-6252; E-mail: athl@flagler.edu.

Tennis: Walter Shinn; Phone: 904-819-6252; E-mail: athl@flagler.edu.

WOMEN'S COACHES

Basketball: Ashley Bland; Phone: 904-819-6307; E-mail: athl@flagler.edu.

Cross Country: Dave Williams; Phone: 904-819-6252; E-mail: athldept@flagler.edu.

Golf: Taylor Mott; Phone: 904-819-6252; E-mail: athl@flagler.edu.

Soccer: Scott Baker; Phone: 904-819-6252; E-mail: athl@flagler.edu.

Tennis: Walter Shinn; Phone: 904-819-6252; E-mail: athl@flagler.edu.

Volleyball: Taylor Mott; Phone: 904-819-6252; E-mail: athl@flagler.edu.

FLORIDA AGRICULTURAL AND MECHANICAL UNIVERSITY

Tallahassee, Florida

Rattlers ◆ NCAA I ◆ Mid-Eastern Athletic Conference
◆ http://www.famu.edu/

State-supported university, founded 1887, part of State University System of Florida
Coed, 11,164 undergraduate students, 89% full-time, 57% women, 43% men
Urban 419-acre campus
Moderately difficult entrance level, 68% of applicants were admitted

Freshmen *Admission:* 5,467 applied, 3,875 were accepted, 2,493 enrolled. *Test scores:* SAT verbal scores over 500: 52%; SAT math scores over 500: 52%; SAT verbal scores over 600: 11%; SAT math scores over 600: 12%; SAT verbal scores over 700: 1%; SAT math scores over 700: 1%.
Tuition and fees (2003–04): $2951 (resident), $13,306 (nonresident). *Room and board:* $5238 (room only: $3278).
Financial Aid (All incoming freshmen): *Average need-based gift aid:* $3043. *Average non-need based aid:* $5272. *Average aid to full-time undergraduates:* $7803.
Athletic Department: *Director of Athletics:* J.R. Lee; Phone: 850-599-3868; Fax: 850-599-3810; E-mail: john.lee@famu.edu. *Sports Information Director:* Alvin Hollins; Phone: 850-599-3200; E-mail: alvin.hollins jr@famu.edu.

MEN'S COACHES

Baseball: Joe Durant; Phone: 850-599-3202; E-mail: joseph.durant@famu.edu.

Basketball: Mike Gillespie; Phone: 850-599-3868; E-mail: michael.gillespie@famu.edu.

Football: Billy Joe; Phone: 850-599-3723; E-mail: william.joe@famu.edu.

Golf: Marvin Green; Phone: 850-599-8813; E-mail: marvin.green@famu.edu.

Swimming: Mark Howell; Phone: 850-412-7860.

Tennis: Carl Goodman; Phone: 850-599-3128; E-mail: carl.goodman@famu.edu.

Track and Field: Rey Robinson; Phone: 850-599-8138; E-mail: reynaud@famu.edu.

WOMEN'S COACHES

Basketball: Debra Clark; Phone: 850-599-2193; E-mail: debra.clark@famu.edu.

Softball: Veronica Wiggins; Phone: 850-599-3239.

Swimming: Mark Howell; Phone: 850-412-7860.

Tennis: James Hargrove; Phone: 850-599-2735.

Track and Field: Donya Andrews; Phone: 850-599-8075; E-mail: donya.andrews-little@famu.edu.

Volleyball: Tony Trifonov; Phone: 850-599-2194; E-mail: tanio@famu.edu.

FLORIDA ATLANTIC UNIVERSITY

Boca Raton, Florida

Owls ◆ NCAA I ◆ Atlantic Sun Conference
◆ http://www.fau.edu/

State-supported university, founded 1961, part of State University System of Florida
Coed, 21,072 undergraduate students, 51% full-time, 61% women, 39% men
Suburban 850-acre campus with easy access to Miami
Moderately difficult entrance level, 70% of applicants were admitted

Freshmen *Admission:* 8,202 applied, 5,915 were accepted, 2,440 enrolled. *Test scores:* SAT verbal scores over 500: 57%; SAT math scores over 500: 59%; SAT verbal scores over 600: 14%; SAT math scores over 600: 15%; SAT verbal scores over 700: 2%; SAT math scores over 700: 1%.
Tuition and fees (2003–04): $2943 (resident), $13,955 (nonresident). *Room and board:* $5600.
Financial Aid (All incoming freshmen): *Average need-based gift aid:* $5557. *Average non-need based aid:* $2260. *Average aid to full-time undergraduates:* $6569.

Athletic Department: *Director of Athletics:* Craig Angelos; Phone: 561-297-3199; Fax: 561-297-3963; E-mail: cangelos@fau.edu. *Sports Information Director:* Katrina McCormick; Phone: 561-297-3163; E-mail: kmccormi@fau.edu.

MEN'S COACHES

Baseball: Kevin Cooney; Phone: 561-297-3956; E-mail: kcooney@fau.edu.

Basketball: Sidney Green; Phone: 561-297-0097; E-mail: sgreen@fau.edu.

Cheerleading: Carrie Noah; Phone: 561-297-0031; E-mail: carrienoah@hotmail.com.

Cross Country: Alex Smolka; Phone: 561-297-3716; E-mail: asmolka@fau.edu.

Diving: Ashleye Henyan; Phone: 561-297-3784.

Football: Howard Schnellenberg; Phone: 561-297-1042; E-mail: howard@fau.edu.

Golf: Matt Anderson; Phone: 561-297-2217; E-mail: manders@fau.edu.

Soccer: Koss Donev; Phone: 561-297-3711; E-mail: donev@fau.edu.

Swimming: Steve Eckelkamp; Phone: 561-297-3784; E-mail: fauswim@fau.edu.

Tennis: Alex Alcantara; Phone: 561-297-2793; E-mail: aalex007@hotmail.com.

WOMEN'S COACHES

Basketball: Chancellor Dugan; Phone: 561-297-3712; E-mail: cdugan@fau.edu.

Cheerleading: Carrie Noah; Phone: 561-297-0031; E-mail: carrienoah@hotmail.com.

Cross Country: Alex Smolka; Phone: 561-297-3716; E-mail: asmolka@fau.edu.

Diving: Ashleye Henyan; Phone: 561-297-3784.

Golf: Joan Joyce; Phone: 561-297-3713; E-mail: jjoyce@fau.edu.

Soccer: Brian Dooley; Phone: 561-297-3743; E-mail: bdooley@fau.edu.

Softball: Joan Joyce; Phone: 561-297-3713; E-mail: jjoyce@fau.edu.

Swimming: Steve Eckelkamp; Phone: 561-297-3784; E-mail: fauswim@fau.edu.

Tennis: Alex Alcantara; Phone: 561-297-2793; E-mail: aalex007@hotmail.com.

Track and Field: Alex Smolka; Phone: 561-297-3716; E-mail: asmolka@fau.edu.

Volleyball: Jody Brown; Phone: 561-297-3595; E-mail: jbrown@fau.edu.

FLORIDA GULF COAST UNIVERSITY
Fort Myers, Florida

Eagles ◆ NCAA II ◆ Independent ◆ http://www.fgcu.edu/

State-supported comprehensive, founded 1991, part of State University System of Florida
Coed, 4,836 undergraduate students, 70% full-time, 63% women, 37% men
Suburban 760-acre campus
Moderately difficult entrance level, 70% of applicants were admitted

Freshmen *Admission:* 2,578 applied, 1,854 were accepted, 880 enrolled. *Test scores:* SAT verbal scores over 500: 60%; SAT math scores over 500: 60%; SAT verbal scores over 600: 13%; SAT math scores over 600: 16%; SAT verbal scores over 700: 1%; SAT math scores over 700: 1%.
Tuition and fees (2003–04): $2921 (resident), $13,271 (nonresident). *Room and board:* $8000 (room only: $4220).
Financial Aid (All incoming freshmen): *Average need-based gift aid:* $3491. *Average non-need based aid:* $3200. *Average aid to full-time undergraduates:* $6061.
Athletic Department: *Director of Athletics:* Carl McAloose; Phone: 239-590-7007; Fax: 239-590-7014; E-mail: cmcaloos@fgcu.edu. *Sports Information Director:* Allison Allie; Phone: 239-590-7075; E-mail: aallie@fgcu.edu.

MEN'S COACHES

Baseball: Dave Tollett; Phone: 239-590-7051; E-mail: dtollett@fgcu.edu.

Basketball: Dave Blaza; Phone: 239-590-7039; E-mail: dblaza@fgcu.edu.

Cheerleading: Anne Francis; Phone: 239-590-7012.

Cross Country: Chris Highfield; Phone: 239-590-7032; E-mail: chighfie@fgcu.edu.

Golf: Jim Suttie; Phone: 239-590-7005; E-mail: jsuttie@fgcu.edu.

Tennis: J. Webb Horton; Phone: 239-590-7009; E-mail: jwhorton@fgcu.edu.

WOMEN'S COACHES

Basketball: Karl Smesko; Phone: 239-590-7038; E-mail: ksmesko@fgcu.edu.

Cheerleading: Anne Francis; Phone: 239-590-7012.

Cross Country: Chris Highfield; Phone: 239-590-7032; E-mail: chighfie@fgcu.edu.

Golf: Holly Vaughn; Phone: 239-590-7004; E-mail: hvaughn@fgcu.edu.

Softball: David Deiros; Phone: 239-590-7052; E-mail: ddeiros@fgcu.edu.

Tennis: Fred Drilling; Phone: 239-590-7008; E-mail: fdrillin@fgcu.edu.

Volleyball: Jaye Flood; Phone: 239-590-7012; E-mail: jflood@fgcu.edu.

FLORIDA INSTITUTE OF TECHNOLOGY
Melbourne, Florida

Panthers ◆ NCAA II ◆ Sunshine State Conference ◆ http://www.fit.edu/

Independent university, founded 1958
Coed, 2,346 undergraduate students, 95% full-time, 30% women, 70% men
Small-town 130-acre campus with easy access to Orlando
Moderately difficult entrance level, 85% of applicants were admitted

Freshmen *Admission:* 2,146 applied, 1,836 were accepted, 551 enrolled. *Test scores:* SAT verbal scores over 500: 77%; SAT math scores over 500: 90%; SAT verbal scores over 600: 34%; SAT math scores over 600: 54%; SAT verbal scores over 700: 4%; SAT math scores over 700: 10%.
Tuition and fees (2003–04): $22,600 (full-time). *Room and board:* $6140 (room only: $3250).
Financial Aid (All incoming freshmen): *Average need-based gift aid:* $15,269. *Average non-need based aid:* $6833. *Average aid to full-time undergraduates:* $20,298.
Athletic Department: *Director of Athletics:* Bill Jurgens; Phone: 321-674-8032; Fax: 321-984-8529; E-mail: bjurgens@fit.edu. *Sports Information Director:* Christa Parulis-Kaye; Phone: 321-674-7484; E-mail: cparulis@fit.edu.

MEN'S COACHES

Baseball: Paul Knight; Phone: 321-674-8193; E-mail: pknight@fit.edu.

Basketball: Kris Olson; Phone: 321-674-7511; E-mail: kolson@fit.edu.

Cheerleading: Beth Callahan; Phone: 321-674-8032; E-mail: nabcallahan@aol.com.

Cross Country: Peter Mazzone; Phone: 321-674-7209; E-mail: pmazzone@fit.edu.

Soccer: Kevin Johnson; Phone: 321-674-8064; E-mail: kjohnson@fit.edu.

WOMEN'S COACHES

Basketball: John Reynolds; Phone: 321-674-7512; E-mail: reynolds@fit.edu.

Cheerleading: Beth Callahan; Phone: 321-674-8032; E-mail: nabcallahan@aol.com.

Cross Country: Peter Mazzone; Phone: 321-674-7209; E-mail: pmazzone@fit.edu.

Softball: Nancy Bottge; Phone: 321-674-7199; E-mail: dugout14@msn.com.

Volleyball: Pat Barrett; Phone: 321-674-7333; E-mail: patbarrett@fit.edu.

FLORIDA INTERNATIONAL UNIVERSITY
Miami, Florida

Golden Panthers ◆ NCAA I ◆ Atlantic Soccer Conference; Sun Belt Conference ◆ http://www.fiu.edu/

State-supported university, founded 1965, part of State University System of Florida
Coed, 27,269 undergraduate students, 60% full-time, 57% women, 43% men
Urban 573-acre campus
Moderately difficult entrance level, 47% of applicants were admitted

Freshmen *Admission:* 8,450 applied, 3,631 were accepted, 3,071 enrolled. *Test scores:* SAT verbal scores over 500: 92%; SAT math scores over 500: 94%; SAT verbal scores over 600: 34%; SAT math scores over 600: 35%; SAT verbal scores over 700: 4%; SAT math scores over 700: 4%.
Tuition and fees (2003–04): $2889 (resident), $13,917 (nonresident). *Room and board:* $8822 (room only: $5442).
Financial Aid (All incoming freshmen): *Average need-based gift aid:* $3281. *Average non-need based aid:* $4269. *Average aid to full-time undergraduates:* $6489.
Athletic Department: *Director of Athletics:* Rick Mello; Phone: 305-348-2756; Fax: 305-348-2963; E-mail: mellor@fiu.edu. *Sports Information Director:* Danny Kambel; Phone: 305-348-2084; E-mail: kambeld@fiu.edu.

MEN'S COACHES
Baseball: Danny Price; Phone: 305-348-3166; E-mail: priced@fiu.edu.
Basketball: Donnie Marsh; Phone: 305-348-6684; E-mail: marshk@fiu.edu.
Cheerleading: Maria George; Phone: 305-348-6203; E-mail: fiucheer@fiu.edu.
Cross Country: Steve Rubin; Phone: 305-348-1044; E-mail: rubins@fiu.edu.
Football: Don Strock; Phone: 305-222-4150; E-mail: football@fiu.edu.
Soccer: Karl Kremser; Phone: 305-348-2124; E-mail: kremserk@fiu.edu.
Track and Field: Steve Rubin; Phone: 305-348-1044; E-mail: rubins@fiu.edu.
Track and Field: Steve Rubin; Phone: 305-348-1044; E-mail: rubins@fiu.edu.

WOMEN'S COACHES
Basketball: Cindy Russo; Phone: 305-348-3160; E-mail: xrussoc@fiu.edu.
Cheerleading: Maria George; Phone: 305-348-6203; E-mail: fiucheer@fiu.edu.
Cross Country: Steve Rubin; Phone: 305-348-1044; E-mail: rubins@fiu.edu.
Diving: KZ Li; Phone: 305-348-3169.
Golf: David Pezzino; Phone: 305-348-2804; E-mail: pezzinod@fiu.edu.
Soccer: Everton Edwards; Phone: 305-348-3411; E-mail: edwardse@fiu.edu.
Softball: Kim Gwydir; Phone: 305-348-6155; E-mail: gwydirk@fiu.edu.
Swimming: Noemi Zaharia; Phone: 305-348-3169; E-mail: zaharian@fiu.edu.
Tennis: Ronni Bernstein; Phone: 305-348-6201; E-mail: bernster@fiu.edu.
Track and Field: Steve Rubin; Phone: 305-348-1044; E-mail: rubins@fiu.edu.
Volleyball: Cookie Stevens; Phone: 305-348-2756; E-mail: stevensd@fiu.edu.

FLORIDA MEMORIAL COLLEGE
Miami-Dade, Florida

Lions ◆ NAIA ◆ Florida Sun Conference ◆ http://www.fmc.edu/

Independent religious 4-year, founded 1879, affiliated with Baptist Church
Coed
Suburban 77-acre campus
Noncompetitive entrance level

Tuition and fees (2003–04): $10,433 (full-time). *Room and board:* $4547 (room only: $2426).
Financial Aid (All incoming freshmen): *Average need-based gift aid:* $3000. *Average aid to full-time undergraduates:* $10,850.
Athletic Department: *Director of Athletics:* Robert Smith; Phone: 305-626-3168; Fax: 305-626-3169; E-mail: resmith@fmc.edu. *Sports Information Director:* Flecia Henderson; Phone: 305-626-3194; E-mail: fhender@fmc.edu.

MEN'S COACHES
Baseball: Robert Smith; Phone: 305-626-3167; E-mail: resmith@fmc.edu.
Basketball: Kenny Bellinger; Phone: 305-626-3165; E-mail: kbelling@fmc.edu.
Cheerleading: Angel Johnson; Phone: 305-626-3166; E-mail: johnson@fmc.edu.
Cross Country: Roosevelt Richardson; Phone: 305-626-3692; E-mail: rrichard@fmc.edu.
Track and Field: Roosevelt Richardson; Phone: 305-626-3692; E-mail: rrichard@fmc.edu.

WOMEN'S COACHES
Basketball: Kenneth Marshall; Phone: 305-626-3167; E-mail: kmarshal@fmc.edu.
Cheerleading: Angel Johnson; Phone: 305-626-3166; E-mail: johnson@fmc.edu.
Cross Country: Roosevelt Richardson; Phone: 305-626-3692; E-mail: rrichard@fmc.edu.
Track and Field: Roosevelt Richardson; Phone: 305-626-3692; E-mail: rrichard@fmc.edu.
Volleyball: Robert Robaina; Phone: 305-626-3692; E-mail: rrobain@fmc.edu.

FLORIDA SOUTHERN COLLEGE
Lakeland, Florida

Moccasins ◆ NCAA II ◆ Sunshine State Conference ◆ http://www.flsouthern.edu/

Independent religious comprehensive, founded 1885, affiliated with United Methodist Church
Coed, 1,841 undergraduate students, 96% full-time, 60% women, 40% men
Suburban 100-acre campus with easy access to Tampa and Orlando
Moderately difficult entrance level, 72% of applicants were admitted

Freshmen *Admission:* 1,735 applied, 1,295 were accepted, 439 enrolled. *Test scores:* SAT verbal scores over 500: 52%; SAT math scores over 500: 58%; SAT verbal scores over 600: 16%; SAT math scores over 600: 15%; SAT verbal scores over 700: 1%; SAT math scores over 700: 2%.
Tuition and fees (2003–04): $17,492 (full-time). *Room and board:* $6050 (room only: $3350).
Financial Aid (All incoming freshmen): *Average need-based gift aid:* $11,998. *Average non-need based aid:* $10,180. *Average aid to full-time undergraduates:* $15,924.
Athletic Department: *Director of Athletics:* Lois Webb; Phone: 863-680-4254; Fax: 863-680-4120; E-mail: lwebb@flsouthern.edu. *Sports Information Director:* Tim Carpenter; Phone: 863-680-3955; E-mail: ffltim@aol.com.

MEN'S COACHES
Baseball: Pete Meyer; Phone: 863-680-4264; E-mail: pmeyer@flsouthern.edu.
Basketball: Tony Longa; Phone: 863-680-4252; E-mail: tlonga@flsouthern.edu.

Cheerleading: Katie McKenzie; Phone: 863-698-9209.
Cross Country: Buck Dawson; Phone: 863-680-5013; E-mail: adawson@flsouthern.edu.
Golf: Doug Gordin; Phone: 863-680-4352; E-mail: dgordin@flsouthern.edu.
Soccer: Kris Paul; Phone: 863-680-4258; E-mail: kpahl@flsouthern.edu.
Swimming: Lee Stauffer; Phone: 863-680-6200; E-mail: lstauffer@flsouthern.edu.
Tennis: Jeff Kutac; Phone: 863-680-4739; E-mail: jkutac@flsouthern.edu.

WOMEN'S COACHES

Basketball: Diane Foli; Phone: 863-680-4250; E-mail: dfoli@flsouthern.edu.
Cheerleading: Katie McKenzie; Phone: 863-698-9209.
Cross Country: Buck Dawson; Phone: 863-680-5013; E-mail: adawson@flsouthern.edu.
Golf: Robbie Davis; Phone: 863-616-6409; E-mail: ldavis@flsouthern.edu.
Soccer: Christine Rizzieri; Phone: 863-616-6455; E-mail: crizzieri@flsouthern.edu.
Softball: Chris Bellotto; Phone: 863-680-4249; E-mail: cbellotto@flsouthern.edu.
Swimming: Lee Stauffer; Phone: 863-680-6200; E-mail: lstauffer@flsouthern.edu.
Tennis: Vicky Martin; Phone: 863-616-6442; E-mail: vmartin@flsouthern.edu.
Volleyball: Jill Stephens; Phone: 863-680-4474; E-mail: jstephens@flsouthern.edu.

FLORIDA STATE UNIVERSITY
Tallahassee, Florida

Seminoles ◆ NCAA I ◆ Atlantic Coast Conference ◆ http://www.fsu.edu/

State-supported university, founded 1851, part of State University System of Florida
Coed, 29,630 undergraduate students, 88% full-time, 57% women, 43% men
Suburban 448-acre campus
Very difficult entrance level, 4% of applicants were admitted

Freshmen *Admission:* 31,264 applied, 13,037 were accepted, 6,081 enrolled. *Test scores:* SAT verbal scores over 500: 87%; SAT math scores over 500: 91%; SAT verbal scores over 600: 40%; SAT math scores over 600: 43%; SAT verbal scores over 700: 5%; SAT math scores over 700: 5%.
Tuition and fees (2003–04): $2860 (resident), $13,888 (nonresident). *Room and board:* $6168 (room only: $3280).
Financial Aid (All incoming freshmen): *Average need-based gift aid:* $3607. *Average non-need based aid:* $1885. *Average aid to full-time undergraduates:* $4147.
Athletic Department: *Director of Athletics:* Dave Hart; Phone: 850-644-1079; Fax: 850-644-7293. *Sports Information Director:* Rob Wilson; Phone: 850-644-1403.

MEN'S COACHES

Baseball: Mike Martin; Phone: 850-644-1073; E-mail: shough@mailer.fsu.edu.
Basketball: Leonard Hamilton; Phone: 850-644-5229.
Cheerleading: Staci Sutton; Phone: 850-644-3017.
Cross Country: Bob Braman; Phone: 850-644-3270; E-mail: rbraman@mailer.fsu.edu.
Diving: Patrick Jeffrey; Phone: 850-644-1734; E-mail: pjeffrey@mailer.fsu.edu.
Football: Bobby Bowden; Phone: 850-644-1465.
Golf: Micky Goetze; Phone: 850-644-7289.
Swimming: Neil Harper; Phone: 850-644-5946; E-mail: nharper@mailer.fsu.edu.
Tennis: Dwayne Hulquist; Phone: 850-644-1738.
Track and Field: Bob Braman; Phone: 850-644-5550; E-mail: rbraman@mailer.fsu.edu.

WOMEN'S COACHES

Basketball: Sue Semrau; Phone: 850-644-3641; E-mail: ssemrau@mailer.fsu.edu.
Cheerleading: Staci Sutton; Phone: 850-644-3017.

Cross Country: Bob Braman; Phone: 850-644-3270; E-mail: rbraman@mailer.fsu.edu.
Diving: Patrick Jeffrey; Phone: 850-644-1734; E-mail: pjeffrey@mailer.fsu.edu.
Golf: Debbie Dillman; Phone: 850-644-7290.
Soccer: Patrick Baker; Phone: 850-644-7724; E-mail: pdbaker@mailer.fsu.edu.
Softball: Joanne Graf; Phone: 850-644-2386; E-mail: jgraf@mailer.fsu.edu.
Swimming: Neil Harper; Phone: 850-644-1890; E-mail: nharper@mailer.fsu.edu.
Tennis: Lise Gregory; Phone: 850-644-1092; E-mail: lgregory@mailer.fsu.edu.
Track and Field: Bob Braman; Phone: 850-645-1250; E-mail: rbraman@mailer.fsu.edu.
Volleyball: Todd Kress; Phone: 850-644-3796.

FONTBONNE UNIVERSITY
St. Louis, Missouri

Griffins ◆ NCAA III ◆ St. Louis Athletic Conference ◆ http://www.fontbonne.edu/

Independent Roman Catholic comprehensive, founded 1917
Coed, 1,767 undergraduate students, 74% full-time, 77% women, 23% men
Suburban 13-acre campus
Moderately difficult entrance level, 83% of applicants were admitted

Freshmen *Admission:* 505 applied, 409 were accepted, 205 enrolled.
Tuition and fees (2004–05): $15,420 (full-time). *Room and board:* $6988.
Financial Aid (All incoming freshmen): *Average aid to full-time undergraduates:* $13,725.
Athletic Department: *Director of Athletics:* lmckinne@fontbonne.edu; Phone: 314-862-1444; Fax: 314-889-4507; E-mail: lmckinne@fontbonne.edu. *Sports Information Director:* Lance Thornhill; Phone: 314-862-1444; E-mail: lthornhi@fontbonne.edu.

MEN'S COACHES

Baseball: Scott Cooper; Phone: 314-889-8064.
Basketball: Lee McKinney; Phone: 314-889-1444; E-mail: lmckinne@fontbonne.edu.
Cheerleading: Gina Cuccio; Phone: 314-889-3456.
Golf: Lance Thornhill; Phone: 314-889-1466; E-mail: lthornhi@fontbonne.edu.
Soccer: Brian Hoener; Phone: 314-889-4534.
Tennis: Keith Quigley; Phone: 314-889-1413.

WOMEN'S COACHES

Basketball: Keith Quigley; Phone: 314-889-1413.
Cheerleading: Gina Cuccio; Phone: 314-889-3456.
Cross Country: Charles Helbling; Phone: 314-889-1466.
Soccer: Mark Giesing; Phone: 314-889-4535; E-mail: mgiesing@fontbonne.edu.
Softball: John Conway; Phone: 314-889-4534; E-mail: jconway@toberson.com.
Tennis: Keith Quigley; Phone: 314-889-1413.
Track and Field: Charles Helbling; Phone: 314-889-1466.
Volleyball: Kim Kutis-Hantak; Phone: 314-889-1413.

FORDHAM UNIVERSITY
New York, New York

Rams ◆ NCAA I ◆ Atlantic 10 Conference; Patriot League Conference ◆ http://www.fordham.edu/

Independent Roman Catholic (Jesuit) university, founded 1841
Coed, 7,403 undergraduate students, 90% full-time, 60% women, 40% men
Urban 85-acre campus
Very difficult entrance level, 57% of applicants were admitted

Freshmen *Admission:* 12,801 applied, 6,862 were accepted, 1,728 enrolled. *Test scores:* SAT verbal scores over 500: 89%; SAT math scores

Fordham University *(continued)*

over 500: 91%; SAT verbal scores over 600: 49%; SAT math scores over 600: 50%; SAT verbal scores over 700: 9%; SAT math scores over 700: 6%.
Tuition and fees (2003–04): $24,720 (full-time). *Room and board:* $9700.
Financial Aid (All incoming freshmen): *Average need-based gift aid:* $14,812. *Average non-need based aid:* $6954. *Average aid to full-time undergraduates:* $17,591.
Athletic Department: *Director of Athletics:* Frank McLaughlin; Phone: 718-817-4300; Fax: 718-817-5588; E-mail: fmclaughlin@fordham.edu. *Sports Information Director:* Joe DiBari; Phone: 718-817-4300; E-mail: dibari@fordham.edu.

MEN'S COACHES
Baseball: Dan Gallagher; Phone: 718-817-4292; E-mail: dgallagher@fordham.edu.
Basketball: Dereck Whittenburg; Phone: 718-817-4245; E-mail: rohill@fordham.edu.
Cross Country: Tom Dewey; Phone: 718-817-4298; E-mail: dewey@fordham.edu.
Diving: Zhihua Hu; Phone: 718-817-4256.
Football: David Clawson; Phone: 718-817-4280; E-mail: dematteo@fordham.edu.
Golf: Paul Dillion; Phone: 718-817-4300; E-mail: diazjr@fordham.edu.
Soccer: Jim McElderry; Phone: 718-817-4269; E-mail: jmcelderry@fordham.edu.
Swimming: Stephen Potsklan; Phone: 718-817-4256; E-mail: potsklan@fordham.edu.
Tennis: Bob Hawthorn; Phone: 718-817-4300.
Track and Field: Tom Dewey; Phone: 718-817-4298; E-mail: dewey@fordham.edu.

WOMEN'S COACHES
Basketball: Jim Lewis; Phone: 718-817-4270; E-mail: lewisiii@fordham.edu.
Cross Country: Tom Dewey; Phone: 718-817-4298; E-mail: dewey@fordham.edu.
Diving: Zhihua Hu; Phone: 718-817-4256.
Soccer: Ness Selmani; Phone: 718-817-4267; E-mail: selmani@fordham.edu.
Softball: Bridget Baxter; Phone: 718-817-4412; E-mail: baxter@fordham.edu.
Swimming: Stephen Potsklan; Phone: 718-817-4256; E-mail: potsklan@fordham.edu.
Tennis: Leslie Allen; Phone: 718-817-4300; E-mail: leallen@fordham.edu.
Track and Field: Tom Dewey; Phone: 718-817-4298; E-mail: dewey@fordham.edu.
Volleyball: Mesan Gamble; Phone: 718-817-4297; E-mail: gamble@fordham.edu.

FORT HAYS STATE UNIVERSITY
Hays, Kansas

Tigers ◆ NCAA II ◆ Rocky Mountain Athletic Conference ◆ http://www.fhsu.edu/

State-supported comprehensive, founded 1902, part of Kansas Board of Regents
Coed, 5,920 undergraduate students, 70% full-time, 54% women, 46% men
Small-town 200-acre campus
Noncompetitive entrance level, 93% of applicants were admitted

Freshmen *Admission:* 1,938 applied, 1,813 were accepted, 904 enrolled.
Tuition and fees (2003–04): $2539 (resident), $8672 (nonresident). *Room and board:* $4843 (room only: $2146).
Financial Aid (All incoming freshmen): *Average need-based gift aid:* $3361. *Average non-need based aid:* $2125. *Average aid to full-time undergraduates:* $5180.
Athletic Department: *Director of Athletics:* Tom Spicer; Phone: 785-628-4353; Fax: 785-628-4383; E-mail: tspicer@fhsu.edu. *Sports Information Director:* Jason McCullough; Phone: 785-628-5903; E-mail: jmccullo@fhsu.edu.

MEN'S COACHES
Baseball: Matt Ranson; Phone: 785-628-4357; E-mail: mranson@fhsu.edu.

Basketball: Mark Johnson; Phone: 785-628-4355; E-mail: mjohnson@fhsu.edu.
Cheerleading: Bridget Ballinger; Phone: 785-628-4361; E-mail: bballing@fhsu.edu.
Cross Country: Jim Krob; Phone: 785-628-4395; E-mail: jkrob@fhsu.edu.
Football: Tim O'Connor; Phone: 785-628-4399; E-mail: toconnor@fhsu.edu.
Golf: Mark Pahls; Phone: 785-628-4429; E-mail: mpahls@fhsu.edu.
Track and Field: Jim Krob; Phone: 785-628-4395; E-mail: jkrob@fhsu.edu.
Wrestling: Cody Bickley; Phone: 785-628-5392; E-mail: cbickley@fhsu.edu.

WOMEN'S COACHES
Basketball: Annette Wiles; Phone: 785-628-4375; E-mail: awiles@fhsu.edu.
Cheerleading: Bridget Ballinger; Phone: 785-628-4361; E-mail: bballing@fhsu.edu.
Cross Country: Jim Krob; Phone: 785-628-4395; E-mail: jkrob@fhsu.edu.
Softball: Ed Wilkerson; Phone: 785-628-5885; E-mail: ewilkers@fhsu.edu.
Tennis: Brian Flax; Phone: 785-628-5854; E-mail: bflax@fhsu.edu.
Track and Field: Jim Krob; Phone: 785-628-4395; E-mail: jkrob@fhsu.edu.
Volleyball: Jesse Mahoney; Phone: 785-628-4392; E-mail: jmahoney@fhsu.edu.

FORT LEWIS COLLEGE
Durango, Colorado

Skyhawks ◆ NCAA II ◆ Rocky Mountain Athletic Conference ◆ http://www.fortlewis.edu/

State-supported 4-year, founded 1911
Coed, 4,182 undergraduate students, 92% full-time, 48% women, 52% men
Small-town 350-acre campus
Moderately difficult entrance level, 75% of applicants were admitted

Freshmen *Admission:* 3,146 applied, 2,440 were accepted, 923 enrolled.
Test scores: SAT verbal scores over 500: 51%; SAT math scores over 500: 54%; SAT math scores over 600: 15%; SAT math scores over 600: 11%; SAT verbal scores over 700: 1%.
Tuition and fees (2003–04): $2788 (resident), $11,328 (nonresident). *Room and board:* $5564 (room only: $3014).
Financial Aid (All incoming freshmen): *Average need-based gift aid:* $3850. *Average non-need based aid:* $1988. *Average aid to full-time undergraduates:* $6484.
Athletic Department: *Director of Athletics:* Dave Preszler; Phone: 970-247-7480; Fax: 970-247-7655; E-mail: preszler_d@fortlewis.edu. *Sports Information Director:* Sarah Meier; Phone: 970-247-7441; E-mail: meier_s@fortlewis.edu.

MEN'S COACHES
Basketball: Bob Hofman; Phone: 970-247-7499; E-mail: hofman_r@fortlewis.edu.
Cross Country: Ken Flint; Phone: 970-247-7485; E-mail: flint_k@fortlewis.edu.
Football: Todd Throckmorton; Phone: 970-247-7095; E-mail: throckmorton@fortlewis.edu.
Golf: Bud Anderson; Phone: 970-247-8674; E-mail: budanderson@hotmail.com.
Soccer: Jeremy Gunn; Phone: 970-247-7461; E-mail: gunn_j@fortlewis.edu.

WOMEN'S COACHES
Basketball: Patty Patton Shearer; Phone: 970-247-7606; E-mail: shearer_p@fortlewis.edu.
Cross Country: Ken Flint; Phone: 970-247-7485; E-mail: flint_k@fortlewis.edu.
Soccer: Jaymee Carozza; Phone: 970-247-7640; E-mail: stone_j@fortlewis.edu.
Softball: Pam Adams; Phone: 970-247-7067; E-mail: adams_p@fortlewis.edu.
Volleyball: Shelly Aaland; Phone: 970-247-7062; E-mail: aaland_m@fortlewis.edu.

FORT VALLEY STATE UNIVERSITY
Fort Valley, Georgia

Wildcats ◆ NCAA II ◆ Southern Intercollegiate Athletic Conference ◆ http://www.fvsu.edu/

State-supported comprehensive, founded 1895, part of University System of Georgia
Coed, 2,291 undergraduate students, 86% full-time, 56% women, 44% men
Small-town 1,365-acre campus
Moderately difficult entrance level, 5% of applicants were admitted

Freshmen *Admission:* 2,484 applied, 1,194 were accepted, 511 enrolled.
Tuition and fees (2003–04): $2782 (resident), $9418 (nonresident). *Room and board:* $4178.
Financial Aid (All incoming freshmen): *Average aid to full-time undergraduates:* $7200.
Athletic Department: *Director of Athletics:* Gwendolyn Reeves; Phone: 478-825-6238; Fax: 478-825-6889; E-mail: reevesg@fvsu.edu. *Sports Information Director:* Russell Boone; Phone: 478-825-6209; E-mail: booner@fvsu.edu.

MEN'S COACHES
Basketball: Michael Moore; Phone: 478-825-6873; E-mail: moorem@fvsu.edu.
Cross Country: Tyree Price; Phone: 478-825-6238; E-mail: tjumper200@hotmail.com.
Football: John Morgan; Phone: 478-827-3054; E-mail: morgan@fvsu.edu.
Tennis: Willie Foster; Phone: 478-825-6629.
Track and Field: Kevin Thomas; Phone: 478-825-6873.

WOMEN'S COACHES
Basketball: Lonnie Bartley; Phone: 478-825-6292; E-mail: bartleyl@fvsu.edu.
Cross Country: Darlene Moore; Phone: 478-825-6873.
Softball: Jimmie Reed; Phone: 478-825-6321.
Tennis: Willie Foster; Phone: 478-825-6629.
Track and Field: Darlene Moore; Phone: 478-825-6873.
Volleyball: Emory Lightfoot; Phone: 478-825-6622.

FRAMINGHAM STATE COLLEGE
Framingham, Massachusetts

Rams ◆ NCAA III ◆ Little East Conference; Massachusetts State College Athletic Conference; New England Football Conference ◆ http://www.framingham.edu/

State-supported comprehensive, founded 1839, part of Massachusetts Public Higher Education System
Coed, 3,892 undergraduate students, 80% full-time, 66% women, 34% men
Suburban 73-acre campus with easy access to Boston
Moderately difficult entrance level, 55% of applicants were admitted

Freshmen *Admission:* 4,214 applied, 2,319 were accepted, 625 enrolled.
Test scores: SAT verbal scores over 500: 69%; SAT math scores over 500: 68%; SAT verbal scores over 600: 16%; SAT math scores over 600: 15%; SAT verbal scores over 700: 1%; SAT math scores over 700: 1%.
Tuition and fees (2003–04): $4324 (resident), $10,404 (nonresident). *Room and board:* $5058.
Financial Aid (All incoming freshmen): *Average need-based gift aid:* $2885. *Average non-need based aid:* $1467. *Average aid to full-time undergraduates:* $6246.
Athletic Department: *Director of Athletics:* Thomas Kelley; Phone: 508-626-4614; Fax: 508-626-4069; E-mail: tomk@frc.mass.edu. *Sports Information Director:* Kathy Lynch; Phone: 508-626-4612; E-mail: klynch@frc.mass.edu.

MEN'S COACHES
Baseball: Michael Sarno; Phone: 508-626-4566; E-mail: msarno@frc.mass.edu.
Basketball: Don Spellman; Phone: 508-626-1220; E-mail: fschoopdfs@aol.com.
Cheerleading: Sue Perriera; Phone: 508-626-1220; E-mail: fsccheerleaders@yahoo.com.
Cross Country: Michele Doody; Phone: 508-626-1220; E-mail: ydoodyrun@aol.com.
Football: Mark Sullivan; Phone: 508-626-4597; E-mail: fscramfootball@aol.com.
Ice Hockey: Chris Googins; Phone: 508-626-1220; E-mail: googinsc@aol.com.
Soccer: Dean Nichols; Phone: 508-626-1220; E-mail: deannichols66@hotmail.com.

WOMEN'S COACHES
Basketball: Ambrose MacNeil; Phone: 508-626-1220.
Cheerleading: Sue Perriera; Phone: 508-626-1220; E-mail: fsccheerleaders@yahoo.com.
Cross Country: Michele Doody; Phone: 508-626-1220; E-mail: ydoodyrun@aol.com.
Field Hockey: Stephanie Bunker; Phone: 508-626-1220; E-mail: sbunker@intral.com.
Soccer: Christa Bebas; Phone: 508-626-1220; E-mail: bebas@rocketmail.com.
Softball: Rich Paulhus; Phone: 508-626-1220; E-mail: thegame13rp@aol.com.
Volleyball: Sean O'Connor; Phone: 508-626-1220.

THE FRANCISCAN UNIVERSITY
Clinton, Iowa

Saints ◆ NAIA ◆ Midwest Classic Conference ◆ http://www.tfu.edu/

Independent Roman Catholic 4-year, founded 1918
Coed, 426 undergraduate students, 88% full-time, 56% women, 44% men
Small-town 24-acre campus with easy access to Chicago
Minimally difficult entrance level, 8% of applicants were admitted

Freshmen *Admission:* 208 applied, 171 were accepted, 54 enrolled.
Tuition and fees (2003–04): $14,180 (full-time). *Room and board:* $5250 (room only: $2500).
Financial Aid (All incoming freshmen): *Average need-based gift aid:* $8062. *Average non-need based aid:* $8512. *Average aid to full-time undergraduates:* $10,642.
Athletic Department: *Director of Athletics:* Meg Schebler; Phone: 563-242-4023; Fax: 563-243-8580; E-mail: megsch@tfu.edu. *Sports Information Director:* Scott Westbrook; Phone: 563-242-4257; E-mail: scowes@tfu.edu.

MEN'S COACHES
Baseball: Desi Druschel; Phone: 563-242-4257; E-mail: desdru@tfu.edu.
Basketball: Andy Eberhart; Phone: 563-242-4257; E-mail: andebe@tfu.edu.
Cross Country: Dan French; Phone: 563-242-4257; E-mail: danfre@tfu.edu.
Golf: Andy Eberhart; Phone: 563-242-4257; E-mail: andebe@tfu.edu.
Soccer: Scott Westbrook; Phone: 563-242-4257; E-mail: scowes@tfu.edu.
Track and Field: Dan French; Phone: 563-242-4257; E-mail: danfre@tfu.edu.

WOMEN'S COACHES
Basketball: Dan French; Phone: 563-242-4257; E-mail: megsch@tfu.edu.
Cross Country: Dan French; Phone: 563-242-4257; E-mail: danfre@tfu.edu.
Soccer: Scott Westbrook; Phone: 563-242-4257; E-mail: scowes@tfu.edu.
Softball: Brandon Eberhart; Phone: 563-242-4257; E-mail: softball@tfu.edu.
Track and Field: Dan French; Phone: 563-242-4257; E-mail: danfre@tfu.edu.
Volleyball: Shelly Mohr; Phone: 563-242-4257; E-mail: shemoh@tfu.edu.

FRANCIS MARION UNIVERSITY
Florence, South Carolina

Patriots ◆ NCAA II ◆ Peach Belt Conference ◆ http://www.fmarion.edu/

State-supported comprehensive, founded 1970
Coed, 3,097 undergraduate students, 93% full-time, 61% women, 39% men
Rural 309-acre campus
Moderately difficult entrance level, 8% of applicants were admitted

Freshmen *Admission:* 2,057 applied, 1,565 were accepted, 764 enrolled. *Test scores:* SAT verbal scores over 500: 35%; SAT math scores over 500: 40%; SAT verbal scores over 600: 6%; SAT math scores over 600: 7%; SAT verbal scores over 700: 1%; SAT math scores over 700: 1%.
Tuition and fees (2003–04): $5082 (resident), $10,029 (nonresident). *Room and board:* $4282 (room only: $2092).
Athletic Department: *Director of Athletics:* Murray Hartzler; Phone: 843-661-1237; Fax: 843-661-1373; E-mail: hartzler@fmarion.edu. *Sports Information Director:* Michael Hawkins; Phone: 843-661-1222; E-mail: hawkins@fmarion.edu.

MEN'S COACHES
Baseball: Art Inabinet; Phone: 843-661-1242; E-mail: ainabinet@fmarion.edu.
Basketball: John Schweitz; Phone: 843-661-1247; E-mail: jschweitz@fmarion.edu.
Cross Country: Mark Bluman; Phone: 843-661-1239; E-mail: mbluman@fmarion.edu.
Golf: Jonathan Burnett; Phone: 843-661-1352; E-mail: jburnett@fmarion.edu.
Soccer: Murray Hartzler; Phone: 843-661-1237; E-mail: mhartzler@fmarion.edu.
Tennis: Garth Thomson; Phone: 843-661-1185; E-mail: gthomson@fmarion.edu.
Track and Field: Mark Bluman; Phone: 843-661-1239; E-mail: mbluman@fmarion.edu.

WOMEN'S COACHES
Basketball: Valecia Tedder; Phone: 843-661-1249; E-mail: vtedder@fmarion.edu.
Cross Country: Mark Bluman; Phone: 843-661-1239; E-mail: mbluman@fmarion.edu.
Soccer: Murray Hartzler; Phone: 843-661-1237; E-mail: mhartzler@fmarion.edu.
Softball: Jack Byerley; Phone: 843-661-1238; E-mail: jbyerley@fmarion.edu.
Tennis: Garth Thomson; Phone: 843-661-1185; E-mail: gthomson@fmarion.edu.
Track and Field: Mark Bluman; Phone: 843-661-1239; E-mail: mbluman@fmarion.edu.
Volleyball: Sony Kirkpatrick; Phone: 843-661-1246; E-mail: ekirkpatrick@fmarion.edu.

FRANKLIN AND MARSHALL COLLEGE
Lancaster, Pennsylvania

Diplomats ◆ NCAA III ◆ Centennial Conference ◆ http://www.fandm.edu/

Independent 4-year, founded 1787
Coed, 1,923 undergraduate students, 98% full-time, 48% women, 52% men
Suburban 125-acre campus with easy access to Philadelphia
Very difficult entrance level, 53% of applicants were admitted

Freshmen *Admission:* 3,616 applied, 2,085 were accepted, 503 enrolled. *Test scores:* SAT verbal scores over 500: 94%; SAT math scores over 500: 97%; SAT verbal scores over 600: 63%; SAT math scores over 600: 69%; SAT verbal scores over 700: 15%; SAT math scores over 700: 21%.
Tuition and fees (2003–04): $28,860 (full-time). *Room and board:* $7070 (room only: $4580).

Financial Aid (All incoming freshmen): *Average need-based gift aid:* $18,551. *Average non-need based aid:* $14,949. *Average aid to full-time undergraduates:* $21,654.
Athletic Department: *Director of Athletics:* Peter Van Buskirk; Phone: 717-291-3819; Fax: 717-358-4440; E-mail: peter.vanbuskirk@fandm.edu. *Sports Information Director:* Edward Haas; Phone: 717-291-3838; E-mail: edward.haas@fandm.edu.

MEN'S COACHES
Baseball: Brett Boretti; Phone: 717-358-4530; E-mail: brett.boretti@fandm.edu.
Basketball: Glenn Robinson; Phone: 717-291-4106; E-mail: glenn.robinson@fandm.edu.
Cross Country: Keith Dieterle; Phone: 717-291-4070; E-mail: kiethdieterle@fandm.edu.
Football: Shawn Halloran; Phone: 717-291-4105; E-mail: shawn.halloran@fandm.edu.
Golf: Glenn Robinson; Phone: 717-291-4106; E-mail: glenn.robinson@fandm.edu.
Lacrosse: Bill Gorrow; Phone: 717-291-3865; E-mail: william.gorrow@fandm.edu.
Soccer: Dan Wagner; Phone: 717-291-4103; E-mail: dan.wagner@fandm.edu.
Swimming: Bob Rueppel; Phone: 717-291-3897; E-mail: bob.rueppel@fandm.edu.
Tennis: Ken Birkett; Phone: 717-291-4243; E-mail: knbirkett@aol.com.
Track and Field: Carl Schnabel; Phone: 717-291-4100; E-mail: carl.schnabel@fandm.edu.
Wrestling: Pete Schuyler; Phone: 717-291-4101; E-mail: peter.schuyler@fandm.edu.

WOMEN'S COACHES
Basketball: Beth Elbon; Phone: 717-291-4108; E-mail: beth.elbon@fandm.edu.
Cross Country: Keith Dieterle; Phone: 717-291-4100; E-mail: kiethdieterle@fandm.edu.
Field Hockey: Melissa Reiss; Phone: 717-291-4090; E-mail: melissa.reiss@fandm.edu.
Golf: Beth Elbon; Phone: 717-291-4108; E-mail: beth.elbon@fandm.edu.
Lacrosse: Anne Phillips; Phone: 717-358-7162; E-mail: anne.phillips@fandm.edu.
Soccer: Steve O'Day; Phone: 717-291-3989; E-mail: steven.oday@fandm.edu.
Softball: Ann Goropoulos; Phone: 717-358-4546; E-mail: ann.goropoulos@fandm.edu.
Swimming: Bob Rueppel; Phone: 717-291-3897; E-mail: bob.rueppel@fandm.edu.
Tennis: Patty Epps; Phone: 717-291-4107; E-mail: patty.epps@fandm.edu.
Track and Field: Carl Schnabel; Phone: 717-291-4100; E-mail: carl.schnabel@fandm.edu.
Volleyball: Mary Kate Boland; Phone: 717-291-4154; E-mail: marykate.boland@fandm.edu.

FRANKLIN COLLEGE
Franklin, Indiana

Grizzlies ◆ NCAA III ◆ Heartland Collegiate Conference ◆ http://www.franklincollege.edu/

Independent religious 4-year, founded 1834, affiliated with American Baptist Churches in the U.S.A.
Coed, 1,038 undergraduate students, 95% full-time, 56% women, 44% men
Small-town 74-acre campus with easy access to Indianapolis
Moderately difficult entrance level, 82% of applicants were admitted

Freshmen *Admission:* 681 applied, 587 were accepted, 277 enrolled. *Test scores:* SAT verbal scores over 500: 53%; SAT math scores over 500: 57%; SAT verbal scores over 600: 14%; SAT math scores over 600: 12%; SAT verbal scores over 700: 2%; SAT math scores over 700: 2%.
Tuition and fees (2003–04): $16,925 (full-time). *Room and board:* $5270 (room only: $3080).
Financial Aid (All incoming freshmen): *Average need-based gift aid:* $10,516. *Average non-need based aid:* $9566. *Average aid to full-time undergraduates:* $12,753.

Athletic Department: *Director of Athletics:* Kerry Prather; Phone: 317-738-8121; Fax: 317-738-8248; E-mail: kprather@franklincollege.edu. *Sports Information Director:* Kevin Elixman; Phone: 317-738-8184; E-mail: kelixman@franklincollege.edu.

MEN'S COACHES
Baseball: Lance Marshall; Phone: 317-738-8136; E-mail: lmarshall@franklincollege.edu.
Basketball: Kerry Prather; Phone: 317-738-8121; E-mail: kprather@franklincollege.edu.
Cheerleading: Christina Merchant; Phone: 317-738-8121; E-mail: cmerchant@franklincollege.edu.
Cross Country: Paul Sargent; Phone: 317-738-8037; E-mail: psargent@franklincollege.edu.
Football: Mike Leonard; Phone: 317-738-8128; E-mail: mleonard@franklincollege.edu.
Golf: Richard Park; Phone: 317-738-8250; E-mail: rpark@franklincollege.edu.
Soccer: Maurice Schilten; Phone: 317-738-8033; E-mail: mschilten@franklincollege.edu.
Tennis: Rusty Hughes; Phone: 317-738-8121; E-mail: rhughes@franklincollege.edu.
Track and Field: Paul Sargent; Phone: 317-738-8037; E-mail: psargent@franklincollege.edu.

WOMEN'S COACHES
Basketball: Mike Jewett; Phone: 317-738-8202; E-mail: mjewett@franklincollege.edu.
Cheerleading: Christina Merchant; Phone: 317-738-8121; E-mail: cmerchant@franklincollege.edu.
Cross Country: Paul Sargent; Phone: 317-738-8037; E-mail: psargent@franklincollege.edu.
Golf: Steve Richards; Phone: 317-738-8121; E-mail: srichards@franklincollege.edu.
Soccer: Maurice Schilten; Phone: 317-738-8033; E-mail: mschilten@franklincollege.edu.
Softball: Jenny Johnson-Kappes; Phone: 317-738-8127; E-mail: vjohnson-kappes@franklincollege.edu.
Tennis: Rusty Hughes; Phone: 317-738-8121; E-mail: rhughes@franklincollege.edu.
Track and Field: Paul Sargent; Phone: 317-738-8037; E-mail: psargent@franklincollege.edu.
Volleyball: Lori Wilkerson; Phone: 317-738-8130; E-mail: lwilkerson@franklincollege.edu.

FRANKLIN PIERCE COLLEGE
Rindge, New Hampshire

Ravens ◆ NCAA II ◆ Northeast-10 Conference ◆ http://www.fpc.edu/

Independent comprehensive, founded 1962
Coed, 1,591 undergraduate students, 99% full-time, 49% women, 51% men
Rural 1,000-acre campus
Moderately difficult entrance level, 87% of applicants were admitted

Freshmen *Admission:* 3,347 applied, 2,895 were accepted, 514 enrolled. *Test scores:* SAT verbal scores over 500: 55%; SAT math scores over 500: 48%; SAT verbal scores over 600: 12%; SAT math scores over 600: 11%; SAT verbal scores over 700: 1%.
Tuition and fees (2004–05): $22,510 (full-time). *Room and board:* $7655 (room only: $4280).
Financial Aid (All incoming freshmen): *Average need-based gift aid:* $11,535. *Average non-need based aid:* $10,060. *Average aid to full-time undergraduates:* $15,585.
Athletic Department: *Director of Athletics:* Bruce Kirsh; Phone: 603-899-4080; Fax: 603-899-4328. *Sports Information Director:* Doug Monson; Phone: 603-899-4222.

MEN'S COACHES
Baseball: Jayson King; Phone: 603-899-4084; E-mail: kingj@fpc.edu.
Basketball: Dave Chadbourne; Phone: 603-899-4011; E-mail: chadbod@fpc.edu.
Cross Country: Ahmad Boura; Phone: 603-899-4355; E-mail: ahmadb@fpc.edu.
Golf: Owen Houghton; Phone: 603-899-4085; E-mail: houghto@fpc.edu.
Ice Hockey: Jay McCormick; Phone: 603-899-4087; E-mail: mccormackj@fpc.edu.
Lacrosse: Jay McCormick; Phone: 603-899-4085; E-mail: mccormackj@fpc.edu.
Soccer: Marco Koolman; Phone: 603-899-4082; E-mail: koolmanm@fpc.edu.
Tennis: Chet Porowski; Phone: 603-899-4085; E-mail: porowsc@fpc.edu.

WOMEN'S COACHES
Basketball: Mark Swasey; Phone: 603-899-4081; E-mail: swaseym@fpc.edu.
Cross Country: Ahmad Boura; Phone: 603-899-4355; E-mail: ahmadb@fpc.edu.
Field Hockey: Judy Heddy; Phone: 603-899-4365; E-mail: heddyj@fpc.edu.
Golf: Dana Hennessy; Phone: 603-899-4085; E-mail: hennesd@fpc.edu.
Lacrosse: Judy Heddy; Phone: 603-899-4365; E-mail: heddyj@fpc.edu.
Soccer: Jeff Bailey; Phone: 603-899-4072; E-mail: baileyj@fpc.edu.
Softball: Dick Hurley; Phone: 603-899-4088; E-mail: hurleyr@fpc.edu.
Tennis: Chet Porowski; Phone: 603-899-4085; E-mail: porowsc@fpc.edu.
Volleyball: Jayson King; Phone: 603-899-4084; E-mail: kingj@fpc.edu.

FREED-HARDEMAN UNIVERSITY
Henderson, Tennessee

Lions ◆ NAIA ◆ TranSouth Conference
◆ http://www.fhu.edu/

Independent religious comprehensive, founded 1869, affiliated with Church of Christ
Coed, 1,447 undergraduate students, 95% full-time, 53% women, 47% men
Small-town 96-acre campus
Moderately difficult entrance level, 99% of applicants were admitted

Freshmen *Admission:* 663 applied, 658 were accepted, 375 enrolled.
Tuition and fees (2003–04): $11,046 (full-time). *Room and board:* $5320 (room only: $2960).
Financial Aid (All incoming freshmen): *Average need-based gift aid:* $5544. *Average non-need based aid:* $9615. *Average aid to full-time undergraduates:* $8529.
Athletic Department: *Director of Athletics:* Charlie Smith; Phone: 731-989-6900; Fax: 731-989-6910; E-mail: csmith@fhu.edu. *Sports Information Director:* Gregg Lee; Phone: 731-989-6907; E-mail: glee@fhu.edu.

MEN'S COACHES
Baseball: Chuck Box; Phone: 731-989-6900; E-mail: cbox@fhu.edu.
Basketball: Mike McCutchen; Phone: 731-989-6900; E-mail: mmccutchen@fhu.edu.
Cheerleading: Melissa Lomoriello; Phone: 731-989-6900; E-mail: mlomoriello@fhu.edu.
Cross Country: Patrick McCarthy; Phone: 731-989-6994; E-mail: pmccarthy@fhu.edu.
Golf: Gregg Lee; Phone: 731-989-6900; E-mail: glee@fhu.edu.
Soccer: Jason Elliott; Phone: 731-989-6900; E-mail: jelliott@fhu.edu.
Tennis: Charlie Smith; Phone: 731-989-6900; E-mail: csmith@fhu.edu.

WOMEN'S COACHES
Basketball: Dale Neal; Phone: 731-989-6900; E-mail: dneal@fhu.edu.
Cheerleading: Melissa Lomoriello; Phone: 731-989-6900; E-mail: mlomoriello@fhu.edu.
Cross Country: Patrick McCarthy; Phone: 731-989-6994; E-mail: pmccarthy@fhu.edu.
Golf: Gregg Lee; Phone: 731-989-6900; E-mail: glee@fhu.edu.
Soccer: Jason Elliott; Phone: 731-989-6900; E-mail: jelliott@fhu.edu.
Softball: Todd Humphry; Phone: 731-989-6900; E-mail: thumphry@fhu.edu.
Tennis: Charlie Smith; Phone: 731-989-6900; E-mail: csmith@fhu.edu.
Volleyball: Todd Humphry; Phone: 731-989-6900; E-mail: thumphry@fhu.edu.

FRESNO PACIFIC UNIVERSITY
Fresno, California

Sunbirds ◆ NAIA ◆ Golden State Conference ◆ http://www.fresno.edu/

Independent religious comprehensive, founded 1944, affiliated with Mennonite Brethren Church
Coed, 1,380 undergraduate students, 74% full-time, 61% women, 39% men
Suburban 42-acre campus
Moderately difficult entrance level, 68% of applicants were admitted

Freshmen *Admission:* 580 applied, 360 were accepted, 191 enrolled. *Test scores:* SAT verbal scores over 500: 57%; SAT math scores over 500: 50%; SAT verbal scores over 600: 17%; SAT math scores over 600: 18%; SAT verbal scores over 700: 2%; SAT math scores over 700: 2%.
Tuition and fees (2003–04): $17,592 (full-time). *Room and board:* $4870 (room only: $2130).
Financial Aid (All incoming freshmen): *Average need-based gift aid:* $8392. *Average non-need based aid:* $2500. *Average aid to full-time undergraduates:* $15,231.
Athletic Department: *Director of Athletics:* Gary Nachtigall; Phone: 559-453-2122; Fax: 559-453-2005; E-mail: gnachtig@fresno.edu. *Sports Information Director:* Ken Isaak; Phone: 559-453-2264; E-mail: kwisaak@fresno.edu.

MEN'S COACHES
Basketball: Mark Yoder; Phone: 559-453-2235; E-mail: myoder@fresno.edu.
Cross Country: Eric Schwab; Phone: 559-453-2260; E-mail: elschwab@fresno.edu.
Soccer: Jaime Ramirez; Phone: 559-453-2085; E-mail: jramirez@fresno.edu.
Track and Field: Eric Schwab; Phone: 559-453-2260; E-mail: elschwab@fresno.edu.

WOMEN'S COACHES
Basketball: Diane Wiese; Phone: 559-453-2253; E-mail: djwestst@fresno.edu.
Cross Country: Eric Schwab; Phone: 559-453-2260; E-mail: elschwab@fresno.edu.
Soccer: Jaime Ramirez; Phone: 559-453-2085; E-mail: jramirez@fresno.edu.
Track and Field: Eric Schwab; Phone: 559-453-2260; E-mail: elschwab@fresno.edu.
Volleyball: Dennis Janzen; Phone: 559-453-2074; E-mail: djanzen@fresno.edu.

FRIENDS UNIVERSITY
Wichita, Kansas

Falcons ◆ NAIA ◆ Kansas Collegiate Conference ◆ http://www.friends.edu/

Independent comprehensive, founded 1898
Coed, 2,629 undergraduate students
Urban 45-acre campus
Moderately difficult entrance level, 90% of applicants were admitted

Freshmen *Admission:* 668 applied, 620 were accepted.
Tuition and fees (2003–04): $13,790 (full-time). *Room and board:* $6464 (room only: $4132).
Financial Aid (All incoming freshmen): *Average need-based gift aid:* $6031. *Average non-need based aid:* $7448. *Average aid to full-time undergraduates:* $8102.
Athletic Department: *Director of Athletics:* Joe Zimmerman; Phone: 316-295-5700; Fax: 316-295-5030; E-mail: zimmerj@friends.edu. *Sports Information Director:* Mark Carvalho; Phone: 316-295-5769; E-mail: baseball@friends.edu.

MEN'S COACHES
Baseball: Mark Carvalho; Phone: 316-295-5769; E-mail: baseball@friends.edu.
Basketball: Dale Faber; Phone: 316-295-5150; E-mail: faberd@friends.edu.

Cross Country: Mike Howe; Phone: 316-295-5620; E-mail: howem@friends.edu.
Football: Monty Lewis; Phone: 316-295-5619.
Golf: Damon DuPont; Phone: 316-295-5700; E-mail: dupond@friends.edu.
Soccer: Bill Shilling; Phone: 316-295-5700.
Tennis: John McKee; Phone: 316-295-5674.
Track and Field: Mike Howe; Phone: 316-295-5620; E-mail: howem@friends.edu.

WOMEN'S COACHES
Basketball: Gayla Soyez; Phone: 316-295-5613; E-mail: soyez@friends.edu.
Cross Country: Mike Howe; Phone: 316-295-5620; E-mail: howem@friends.edu.
Soccer: Erica Shaffer; Phone: 316-295-5700.
Softball: Tina Schremmer; Phone: 316-295-5763; E-mail: schremmer@friends.edu.
Tennis: David Goodman; Phone: 316-295-5413.
Track and Field: Mike Howe; Phone: 316-295-5620; E-mail: howem@friends.edu.
Volleyball: Tina Schremmer; Phone: 316-295-5763; E-mail: schremmer@friends.edu.

FROSTBURG STATE UNIVERSITY
Frostburg, Maryland

Bobcats ◆ NCAA III ◆ Allegheny Mountain Conference ◆ http://www.frostburg.edu/

State-supported comprehensive, founded 1898, part of University System of Maryland
Coed, 4,588 undergraduate students, 93% full-time, 51% women, 49% men
Small-town 260-acre campus with easy access to Baltimore and Washington, DC
Moderately difficult entrance level, 76% of applicants were admitted

Freshmen *Admission:* 3,905 applied, 3,068 were accepted, 990 enrolled. *Test scores:* SAT verbal scores over 500: 55%; SAT math scores over 500: 58%; SAT verbal scores over 600: 13%; SAT math scores over 600: 15%; SAT verbal scores over 700: 1%; SAT math scores over 700: 1%.
Tuition and fees (2004–05): $5830 (resident), $13,374 (nonresident). *Room and board:* $5772 (room only: $2954).
Financial Aid (All incoming freshmen): *Average need-based gift aid:* $4678. *Average non-need based aid:* $2533. *Average aid to full-time undergraduates:* $5969.
Athletic Department: *Director of Athletics:* Ralph Brewer; Phone: 301-687-4471; Fax: 301-687-4780; E-mail: rbrewer@frostburg.edu. *Sports Information Director:* Chris Starke; Phone: 301-687-4371; E-mail: cstarke@frostburg.edu.

MEN'S COACHES
Baseball: Chris McKnight; Phone: 301-687-4273; E-mail: cmcknight@frostburg.edu.
Basketball: Webb Hatch; Phone: 301-687-3093; E-mail: whatch@frostburg.edu.
Cheerleading: Ellie Stevenson; Phone: 301-687-3241; E-mail: estevenson@frostburg.edu.
Cross Country: Randy Lowe; Phone: 301-687-4313; E-mail: rlowe@frostburg.edu.
Diving: Troy Strieby; Phone: 301-687-7021; E-mail: tstrieby@frostburg.edu.
Football: Rubin Stevenson; Phone: 301-687-4086; E-mail: rstevenson@frostburg.edu.
Soccer: Keith Byrnes; Phone: 301-687-3072; E-mail: kbyrnes@mail.frostburg.edu.
Swimming: Troy Strieby; Phone: 301-687-7021; E-mail: tstrieby@frostburg.edu.
Tennis: Stuart Swink; Phone: 301-687-4350; E-mail: sswink@frostburg.edu.
Track and Field: Felix Moreno; Phone: 301-687-3243; E-mail: fmoreno@frostburg.edu.

WOMEN'S COACHES
Basketball: Jody Pepple; Phone: 301-687-4466; E-mail: jpepple@frostburg.edu.

Cheerleading: Ellie Stevenson; Phone: 301-687-3241; E-mail: estevenson@frostburg.edu.
Cross Country: Randy Lowe; Phone: 301-687-4313; E-mail: rlowe@frostburg.edu.
Diving: Troy Strieby; Phone: 301-687-7021; E-mail: tstrieby@frostburg.edu.
Field Hockey: Nicole Bonvouloir; Phone: 301-687-4476; E-mail: nbonvouloir@frostburg.edu.
Lacrosse: Nicole Bonvouloir; Phone: 301-687-4476; E-mail: nbonvouloir@frostburg.edu.
Soccer: Brian Parker; Phone: 301-687-4356; E-mail: bparker@frostburg.edu.
Softball: Chris Starke; Phone: 301-687-4371; E-mail: cstarke@frostburg.edu.
Swimming: Troy Strieby; Phone: 301-687-7021; E-mail: tstrieby@frostburg.edu.
Tennis: Stuart Swink; Phone: 301-687-4350; E-mail: sswink@frostburg.edu.
Track and Field: Felix Moreno; Phone: 301-687-3243; E-mail: fmoreno@frostburg.edu.
Volleyball: Jeff Billington; Phone: 301-687-7014; E-mail: jbillington@frostburg.edu.

FURMAN UNIVERSITY
Greenville, South Carolina
Paladins ◆ NCAA I ◆ Southern Conference ◆ http://www.furman.edu/

Independent comprehensive, founded 1826
Coed, 2,814 undergraduate students, 96% full-time, 57% women, 43% men
Suburban 750-acre campus
Very difficult entrance level, 64% of applicants were admitted

Freshmen *Admission:* 3,773 applied, 2,259 were accepted, 687 enrolled. *Test scores:* SAT verbal scores over 500: 97%; SAT math scores over 500: 97%; SAT verbal scores over 600: 75%; SAT math scores over 600: 74%; SAT verbal scores over 700: 23%; SAT math scores over 700: 19%.
Tuition and fees (2003–04): $22,712 (full-time). *Room and board:* $5968 (room only: $3288).
Financial Aid (All incoming freshmen): *Average need-based gift aid:* $17,574. *Average non-need based aid:* $10,393. *Average aid to full-time undergraduates:* $20,488.
Athletic Department: *Director of Athletics:* Gary Clark; Phone: 864-294-2150; Fax: 864-294-3059; E-mail: gary.clark@furman.edu. *Sports Information Director:* Hunter Reid; Phone: 864-294-2150; E-mail: hunter.reid@furman.edu.

MEN'S COACHES
Baseball: Ron Smith; Phone: 864-294-2146; E-mail: ron.smith@furman.edu.
Basketball: Larry Davis; Phone: 864-294-2170; E-mail: larry.davis@furman.edu.
Cheerleading: Billy Bush; Phone: 864-350-7645; E-mail: ron.smith@furman.edu.
Cross Country: Gene Mullin; Phone: 864-294-3459; E-mail: gene.mullin@furman.edu.
Football: Bobby Lamb; Phone: 864-294-2120; E-mail: bobby.lamb@furman.edu.
Golf: Todd Satterfield; Phone: 864-294-9093; E-mail: todd.satterfield@furman.edu.
Soccer: Doug Allison; Phone: 864-294-2011; E-mail: doog.allison@furman.edu.
Tennis: Paul Scarpa; Phone: 864-294-2039; E-mail: paul.scarpa@furman.edu.
Track and Field: Gene Mullin; Phone: 864-294-3459; E-mail: gene.mullin@furman.edu.

WOMEN'S COACHES
Basketball: Sam Dixon; Phone: 864-294-3429; E-mail: sam.dixon@furman.edu.
Cheerleading: Billy Bush; Phone: 864-350-7645; E-mail: ron.smith@furman.edu.
Cross Country: Gene Mullin; Phone: 864-294-3459; E-mail: gene.mullin@furman.edu.

Golf: Mic Potter; Phone: 864-294-9093; E-mail: mic.potter@furman.edu.
Soccer: Brian Lee; Phone: 864-294-3428; E-mail: brian.lee@furman.edu.
Softball: Bonnie Flynn; Phone: 864-294-3430; E-mail: bonnie.flynn@furman.edu.
Tennis: Debbie Southern; Phone: 864-294-3428; E-mail: debbie.southern@furman.edu.
Track and Field: Gene Mullin; Phone: 864-294-3459; E-mail: gene.mullin@furman.edu.
Volleyball: Michelle Young; Phone: 864-294-3326; E-mail: michelle.young@furman.edu.

GALLAUDET UNIVERSITY
Washington, District of Columbia
Bison ◆ NCAA III ◆ Capital Athletic Conference ◆ http://www.gallaudet.edu/

Independent university, founded 1864
Coed, 1,168 undergraduate students, 96% full-time, 53% women, 47% men
Urban 99-acre campus
Moderately difficult entrance level, 67% of applicants were admitted

Freshmen *Admission:* 603 applied, 426 were accepted, 238 enrolled.
Tuition and fees (2003–04): $9660 (full-time). *Room and board:* $8030.
Financial Aid (All incoming freshmen): *Average need-based gift aid:* $12,417. *Average non-need based aid:* $10,377. *Average aid to full-time undergraduates:* $13,606.
Athletic Department: *Director of Athletics:* James DeStefano; Phone: 202-651-5603; Fax: 202-651-5274; E-mail: james.destefano@gallaudet.edu. *Sports Information Director:* Richard Coco; Phone: 202-651-5602; E-mail: richard.coco@gallaudet.edu.

MEN'S COACHES
Baseball: Kris Gould; Phone: 202-651-5621; E-mail: kris.gould@gallaudet.edu.
Basketball: James Destefano; Phone: 202-651-5603; E-mail: james.destefano@gallaudet.edu.
Cheerleading: Linnae Gallino; Phone: 202-651-5603; E-mail: linnae19@aol.com.
Cross Country: Karen Sanfacon; Phone: 202-651-5621; E-mail: luvrun@wyndtell.com.
Football: James Grayton; Phone: 202-651-5603; E-mail: james.grayton@gallaudet.edu.
Soccer: Maher Eshgi; Phone: 202-651-5603.
Swimming: Rosemary Stifner; Phone: 202-651-5265; E-mail: rosemary.stifter@gallaudet.edu.
Track and Field: Thomas Withrow; Phone: 202-651-5621; E-mail: tewithrow@aol.com.
Wrestling: Marty Willigan; Phone: 202-651-5010; E-mail: martywrestle@aol.com.

WOMEN'S COACHES
Basketball: Kitty Baldridge; Phone: 202-651-5478; E-mail: kathryn.baldridge@gallaudet.edu.
Cheerleading: Linnae Gallino; Phone: 202-651-5603; E-mail: linnae19@aol.com.
Cross Country: Karen Sanfacon; Phone: 202-651-5621; E-mail: luvrun@wyndtell.com.
Soccer: Franklin Torres; Phone: 202-651-5603; E-mail: franklin.torres@gallaudet.edu.
Softball: Sarah Doleac; Phone: 202-651-5603; E-mail: sarah.doleac@galladet.edu.
Swimming: Rosemary Stifner; Phone: 202-651-5265; E-mail: rosemary.stifter@gallaudet.edu.
Tennis: Dyan Kovacs; Phone: 202-651-5603; E-mail: dyan.kovacs@gallaudet.edu.
Track and Field: Thomas Withrow; Phone: 202-651-5621; E-mail: tewithrow@aol.com.
Volleyball: Pat O'Brien; Phone: 202-651-5603; E-mail: vbgally@aol.com.

GANNON UNIVERSITY
Erie, Pennsylvania

Golden Knights ◆ NCAA II ◆ Great Lakes Intercollegiate Conference ◆ http://www.gannon.edu/

Independent Roman Catholic comprehensive, founded 1925
Coed, 2,435 undergraduate students, 88% full-time, 58% women, 42% men
Urban 13-acre campus with easy access to Cleveland
Moderately difficult entrance level, 81% of applicants were admitted

Freshmen *Admission:* 2,227 applied, 1,872 were accepted, 613 enrolled. *Test scores:* SAT verbal scores over 500: 61%; SAT math scores over 500: 66%; SAT verbal scores over 600: 17%; SAT math scores over 600: 21%; SAT verbal scores over 700: 2%; SAT math scores over 700: 1%.
Tuition and fees (2004–05): $17,500 (full-time). *Room and board:* $7070 (room only: $3840).
Financial Aid (All incoming freshmen): *Average need-based gift aid:* $10,488. *Average non-need based aid:* $4651. *Average aid to full-time undergraduates:* $12,406.
Athletic Department: *Director of Athletics:* Gilbert Zimmermann; Phone: 814-871-7772; Fax: 814-871-7575; E-mail: sukitsch002@gannon.edu. *Sports Information Director:* Dan Teliski; Phone: 814-871-7418; E-mail: teliski002@gannon.edu.

MEN'S COACHES
Baseball: Rick Iacobucci; Phone: 814-871-5846; E-mail: iacobucc001@gannon.edu.
Basketball: Jerry Slocum; Phone: 814-871-7417; E-mail: slocum001@gannon.edu.
Cheerleading: Karen Douglas; Phone: 814-871-7416.
Cross Country: John Carrig; Phone: 814-871-5320; E-mail: jcarrig@velocity.net.
Football: Bill Elias; Phone: 814-871-5786; E-mail: elias001@gannon.edu.
Golf: Tom Simmons; Phone: 814-871-5338; E-mail: simmons015@gannon.edu.
Soccer: Rob Van Rheenen; Phone: 814-871-5810; E-mail: vanrheen001@gannon.edu.
Swimming: Don Sherman; Phone: 814-871-7763; E-mail: sherman001@gannon.edu.
Wrestling: Don Henry; Phone: 814-871-7768; E-mail: henry001@gannon.edu.

WOMEN'S COACHES
Basketball: Cleve Wright; Phone: 814-871-7419; E-mail: wright026@gannon.edu.
Cheerleading: Karen Douglas; Phone: 814-871-7416.
Cross Country: John Carrig; Phone: 814-871-5320; E-mail: jcarrig@velocity.net.
Golf: Amy Adams-Gierlak; Phone: 814-796-6792; E-mail: adamsgie001@gannon.edu.
Lacrosse: Steve Wagner; Phone: 814-871-5625; E-mail: wagner014@gannon.edu.
Soccer: Colin Peterson; Phone: 814-871-7410; E-mail: petersen001@gannon.edu.
Softball: Beth Pierce; Phone: 814-871-7311; E-mail: pierce003@gannon.edu.
Swimming: Don Sherman; Phone: 814-871-7763; E-mail: sherman001@gannon.edu.
Volleyball: Michelle Mason; Phone: 814-871-7245; E-mail: mason006@gannon.edu.

GARDNER-WEBB UNIVERSITY
Boiling Springs, North Carolina

Bulldogs ◆ NCAA I ◆ Atlantic Sun Conference; Big South Conference; Northeast Conference ◆ http://www.gardner-webb.edu/

Independent Baptist comprehensive, founded 1905
Coed, 2,682 undergraduate students, 85% full-time, 64% women, 36% men
Small-town 250-acre campus with easy access to Charlotte
Moderately difficult entrance level, 7% of applicants were admitted

Freshmen *Admission:* 1,753 applied, 1,303 were accepted, 369 enrolled. *Test scores:* SAT verbal scores over 500: 55%; SAT math scores over 500: 56%; SAT verbal scores over 600: 17%; SAT math scores over 600: 17%; SAT verbal scores over 700: 4%; SAT math scores over 700: 1%.
Tuition and fees (2003–04): $14,340 (full-time). *Room and board:* $5140 (room only: $2140).
Financial Aid (All incoming freshmen): *Average need-based gift aid:* $7246. *Average non-need based aid:* $6860. *Average aid to full-time undergraduates:* $11,925.
Athletic Department: *Director of Athletics:* Chuck Burch; Phone: 704-406-4342; Fax: 704-406-4739; E-mail: cburch@gardner-webb.edu. *Sports Information Director:* Marc Rabb; Phone: 704-406-4355; E-mail: mrabb@gardner-webb.edu.

MEN'S COACHES
Baseball: Rusty Stroupe; Phone: 704-406-4343; E-mail: rstroupe@gardner-webb.edu.
Basketball: Rick Scruggs; Phone: 704-406-4348; E-mail: rscruggs@gardner-webb.edu.
Cheerleading: Phone: 704-406-4340; E-mail: cheer@gardner-webb.edu.
Cross Country: Brian Baker; Phone: 704-406-3861; E-mail: bbaker@gardner-webb.edu.
Football: Steve Patton; Phone: 704-406-4344; E-mail: spatton@gardner-webb.edu.
Golf: Tee Burton; Phone: 704-406-3986; E-mail: tburton@gardner-webb.edu.
Soccer: Tony Setzer; Phone: 704-406-4350; E-mail: tsetzer@gardner-webb.edu.
Tennis: Mike Griffith; Phone: 704-406-4639; E-mail: mgriffith@gardner-webb.edu.
Track and Field: Brian Baker; Phone: 704-406-3861; E-mail: bbaker@gardner-webb.edu.
Wrestling: Dick Wince; Phone: 704-406-4354; E-mail: rwince@gardner-webb.edu.

WOMEN'S COACHES
Basketball: Barry Street; Phone: 704-406-4352; E-mail: bstreet@gardner-webb.edu.
Cheerleading: Phone: 704-406-4340; E-mail: cheer@gardner-webb.edu.
Cross Country: Brian Baker; Phone: 704-406-3861; E-mail: bbaker@gardner-webb.edu.
Golf: Tee Burton; Phone: 704-406-3986; E-mail: tburton@gardner-webb.edu.
Soccer: Kevin Mounce; Phone: 704-406-4353; E-mail: kmounce@gardner-webb.edu.
Softball: Tom Cole; Phone: 704-406-4351; E-mail: tcole@gardner-webb.edu.
Swimming: Mike Simpson; Phone: 704-406-3860; E-mail: msimpson@gardner-webb.edu.
Tennis: Mike Griffith; Phone: 704-406-4639; E-mail: mgriffith@gardner-webb.edu.
Track and Field: Brian Baker; Phone: 704-406-3861; E-mail: bbaker@gardner-webb.edu.
Volleyball: Cole Tallman; Phone: 704-406-4736; E-mail: ctallman@gardner-webb.edu.

GENEVA COLLEGE
Beaver Falls, Pennsylvania

Golden Tornadoes ◆ NAIA ◆ American Mideast Conference; Mid-States Football Conference ◆ http://www.geneva.edu/

Independent religious comprehensive, founded 1848, affiliated with Reformed Presbyterian Church of North America
Coed, 1,817 undergraduate students
Small-town 55-acre campus with easy access to Pittsburgh
Moderately difficult entrance level, 56% of applicants were admitted

Freshmen *Admission:* 1,790 applied, 1,073 were accepted. *Test scores:* SAT verbal scores over 500: 72%; SAT math scores over 500: 64%; SAT verbal scores over 600: 27%; SAT math scores over 600: 26%; SAT verbal scores over 700: 4%; SAT math scores over 700: 4%.
Tuition and fees (2004–05): $16,590 (full-time). *Room and board:* $6600 (room only: $3440).
Financial Aid (All incoming freshmen): *Average need-based gift aid:* $10,100. *Average non-need based aid:* $9255. *Average aid to full-time undergraduates:* $13,601.
Athletic Department: *Director of Athletics:* Geno DeMarco; Phone: 724-847-6648; Fax: 724-847-5001; E-mail: gdemarco@geneva.edu. *Sports Information Director:* Van Zanic; Phone: 724-847-6886; E-mail: vgzanic@geneva.edu.

MEN'S COACHES
Baseball: Alan Sumner; Phone: 724-847-6650.
Basketball: Jeff Santarsiero; Phone: 724-847-6653; E-mail: jsantars@geneva.edu.
Cross Country: Brett Otte; Phone: 724-847-6761; E-mail: bjotte@geneva.edu.
Football: Eugene DeMarco; Phone: 724-847-6648; E-mail: gdemarco@geneva.edu.
Soccer: David Murray; Phone: 724-847-5226; E-mail: dbmurray@geneva.edu.
Track and Field: Brett Otte; Phone: 724-847-6761; E-mail: bjotte@geneva.edu.

WOMEN'S COACHES
Basketball: Ron Galbreath; Phone: 724-847-6651.
Cross Country: Brett Otte; Phone: 724-847-6761; E-mail: bjotte@geneva.edu.
Soccer: David Murray; Phone: 724-847-5226; E-mail: dbmurray@geneva.edu.
Softball: Van Zanic; Phone: 724-847-6886; E-mail: vgzanic@geneva.edu.
Tennis: Mandee Craft; Phone: 724-847-6650.
Track and Field: Brett Otte; Phone: 724-847-6761; E-mail: bjotte@geneva.edu.
Volleyball: Wendy Smith; Phone: 724-847-6104; E-mail: wbsmith@geneva.edu.

GEORGE FOX UNIVERSITY
Newberg, Oregon

Bruins ◆ NCAA III ◆ Northwest Conference ◆ http://www.georgefox.edu/

Independent Friends university, founded 1891
Coed, 1,717 undergraduate students, 78% full-time, 59% women, 41% men
Small-town 73-acre campus with easy access to Portland
Moderately difficult entrance level, 93% of applicants were admitted

Freshmen *Admission:* 876 applied, 815 were accepted, 337 enrolled. *Test scores:* SAT verbal scores over 500: 74%; SAT math scores over 500: 74%; SAT verbal scores over 600: 36%; SAT math scores over 600: 32%; SAT verbal scores over 700: 6%; SAT math scores over 700: 4%.
Tuition and fees (2003–04): $19,810 (full-time). *Room and board:* $6300 (room only: $3500).
Financial Aid (All incoming freshmen): *Average need-based gift aid:* $11,721. *Average non-need based aid:* $7551. *Average aid to full-time undergraduates:* $15,611.
Athletic Department: *Director of Athletics:* Craig Taylor; Phone: 503-554-2911; Fax: 503-554-3864; E-mail: ctaylor@georgefox.edu. *Sports Information Director:* Blair Cash; Phone: 503-554-2926; E-mail: bcash@georgefox.edu.

MEN'S COACHES
Baseball: Pat Bailey; Phone: 541-554-2914; E-mail: pbailey@georgefox.edu.
Basketball: Mark Sundquist; Phone: 541-554-2918; E-mail: msundquist@georgefox.edu.
Cross Country: Wes Cook; Phone: 541-554-2915; E-mail: wcook@georgefox.edu.
Soccer: Manfred Tschan; Phone: 541-554-2919; E-mail: mtschan@georgefox.edu.
Tennis: Rick Cruz; Phone: 541-554-2923; E-mail: rcruz@georgefox.edu.
Track and Field: Wes Cook; Phone: 541-554-2915; E-mail: wcook@georgefox.edu.

WOMEN'S COACHES
Basketball: Scott Rueck; Phone: 541-554-2920; E-mail: srueck@georgefox.edu.
Cross Country: Wes Cook; Phone: 541-554-2915; E-mail: wcook@georgefox.edu.
Soccer: Andy Hetherington; Phone: 541-554-2923; E-mail: ahetherington@georgefox.edu.
Softball: Bob Steenson; Phone: 541-554-2921; E-mail: bsteenso@georgefox.edu.
Tennis: Rick Cruz; Phone: 541-554-2923; E-mail: rcruz@georgefox.edu.
Track and Field: Wes Cook; Phone: 541-554-2915; E-mail: wcook@georgefox.edu.
Volleyball: Steve Grant; Phone: 541-554-2917; E-mail: sgrant@georgefox.edu.

GEORGE MASON UNIVERSITY
Fairfax, Virginia

Patriots ◆ NCAA I ◆ Colonial Athletic Conference ◆ http://www.gmu.edu/

State-supported university, founded 1957
Coed, 17,102 undergraduate students, 75% full-time, 55% women, 45% men
Suburban 677-acre campus with easy access to Washington, DC
Moderately difficult entrance level, 64% of applicants were admitted

Freshmen *Admission:* 9,768 applied, 6,460 were accepted, 2,251 enrolled. *Test scores:* SAT verbal scores over 500: 74%; SAT math scores over 500: 80%; SAT verbal scores over 600: 27%; SAT math scores over 600: 31%; SAT verbal scores over 700: 3%; SAT math scores over 700: 4%.
Tuition and fees (2003–04): $5112 (resident), $14,952 (nonresident). *Room and board:* $6040 (room only: $3640).
Financial Aid (All incoming freshmen): *Average need-based gift aid:* $5311. *Average non-need based aid:* $5866. *Average aid to full-time undergraduates:* $6966.
Athletic Department: *Director of Athletics:* Thomas O'Connor; Phone: 703-993-3256; Fax: 703-993-3239; E-mail: toconno2@gmu.edu. *Sports Information Director:* Jeff O'Bier; Phone: 703-993-3261; E-mail: jobier@gmu.edu.

MEN'S COACHES
Baseball: Bill Brown; Phone: 703-993-3282; E-mail: wbrown@gmu.edu.
Basketball: Jim Larranaga; Phone: 703-993-3240; E-mail: jlarrana@gmu.edu.
Cheerleading: Robin Burkhart; Phone: 703-993-3292; E-mail: rburkhar@gmu.edu.
Cross Country: Dalton Ebanks; Phone: 703-993-3285; E-mail: debanks@gmu.edu.
Diving: Roland McDonald; Phone: 703-993-3591; E-mail: rmcdona1@gmu.edu.
Golf: Linda Gaudi; Phone: 703-993-3267; E-mail: lgaudi@gmu.edu.
Soccer: Fran O'Leary; Phone: 703-993-3288; E-mail: foleary@gmu.edu.
Swimming: Peter Ward; Phone: 703-993-3930; E-mail: pward2@gmu.edu.
Tennis: Gary Quam; Phone: 703-993-3201; E-mail: gquam@gmu.edu.
Track and Field: Dalton Ebanks; Phone: 703-993-3285; E-mail: debanks@gmu.edu.
Volleyball: Fred Chao; Phone: 703-993-3227; E-mail: fchao@gmu.edu.

George Mason University (continued)

Wrestling: Brian Shaffer; Phone: 703-993-3299; E-mail: bshaffer@gmu. edu.

WOMEN'S COACHES

Basketball: Debbie Taneyhill-Aigner; Phone: 703-993-3275; E-mail: dtaneyhi@gmu.edu.
Cheerleading: Robin Burkhart; Phone: 703-993-3292; E-mail: rburkhar@gmu.edu.
Cross Country: Angie Taylor; Phone: 703-993-3294; E-mail: ataylorc@ gmu.edu.
Diving: Roland McDonald; Phone: 703-993-3591; E-mail: rmcdona1@ gmu.edu.
Lacrosse: Amy Umbach; Phone: 703-993-3219; E-mail: aumbach@gmu. edu.
Soccer: Joe Cicala; Phone: 703-993-3295; E-mail: jcicala@gmu.edu.
Softball: Elizabeth Fulcher; Phone: 703-993-3296; E-mail: efulcher@ gmu.edu.
Swimming: Peter Ward; Phone: 703-993-3930; E-mail: pward2@gmu. edu.
Tennis: JD Almond; Phone: 703-993-3255.
Track and Field: Angie Taylor; Phone: 703-993-3294; E-mail: ataylorc@ gmu.edu.
Volleyball: Pat Kendrick; Phone: 703-993-3298; E-mail: pkendric@gmu. edu.

GEORGETOWN COLLEGE
Georgetown, Kentucky

Tigers ◆ NAIA ◆ Mid-South Conference
◆ http://www.georgetowncollege.edu/

Independent religious comprehensive, founded 1829, affiliated with Baptist Church
Coed, 1,321 undergraduate students, 94% full-time, 57% women, 43% men
Suburban 110-acre campus with easy access to Cincinnati
Moderately difficult entrance level, 75% of applicants were admitted

Freshmen *Admission:* 1,065 applied, 849 were accepted, 368 enrolled. *Test scores:* SAT verbal scores over 500: 60%; SAT math scores over 500: 59%; SAT verbal scores over 600: 20%; SAT math scores over 600: 17%; SAT verbal scores over 700: 8%; SAT math scores over 700: 2%.
Tuition and fees (2003–04): $16,370 (full-time). *Room and board:* $5190 (room only: $2500).
Financial Aid (All incoming freshmen): *Average need-based gift aid:* $8727. *Average non-need based aid:* $6734. *Average aid to full-time undergraduates:* $15,367.
Athletic Department: *Director of Athletics:* Eric Ward; Phone: 502-863-8223; Fax: 502-868-8892; E-mail: eric_ward@georgetowncollege.edu. *Sports Information Director:* Amy Reid; Phone: 502-863-7972; E-mail: amy_reid@georgetowncollege.edu.

MEN'S COACHES

Baseball: Jim Hinerman; Phone: 502-863-8207; E-mail: james_hinerman@georgetowncollege.edu.
Basketball: Happy Osborne; Phone: 502-863-8055; E-mail: happy_osborne@georgetowncollege.edu.
Cheerleading: Brian Harris; Phone: 502-863-1002; E-mail: ckut@ bellsouth.net.
Cross Country: Abe Padilla; Phone: 502-863-7018; E-mail: abe_padilla@ georgetowncollege.edu.
Football: Bill Cronin; Phone: 502-863-8064; E-mail: bill_cronin@ georgetowncollege.edu.
Golf: Flash Williams; Phone: 502-863-8206; E-mail: kyflash@aol.com.
Soccer: Jim Tussey; Phone: 502-863-8122; E-mail: jim_tussey@ georgetowncollege.edu.
Tennis: Kevin Calhoun; Phone: 502-863-7060; E-mail: kevin_calhoun@ georgetowncollege.edu.

WOMEN'S COACHES

Basketball: Susan Johnson; Phone: 502-863-8060; E-mail: susan_johnson@georgetowncollege.edu.
Cheerleading: Brian Harris; Phone: 502-863-1002; E-mail: ckut@ bellsouth.net.
Cross Country: Abe Padilla; Phone: 502-863-7018; E-mail: abe_padilla@ georgetowncollege.edu.

Golf: Flash Williams; Phone: 502-863-8206; E-mail: kyflash@aol.com.
Soccer: Jim Tussey; Phone: 502-863-8122; E-mail: jim_tussey@ georgetowncollege.edu.
Softball: Thomas Thornton; Phone: 502-863-7017; E-mail: thomas_thornton@georgetowncollege.edu.
Tennis: Kevin Calhoun; Phone: 502-863-7060; E-mail: kevin_calhoun@ georgetowncollege.edu.
Volleyball: Donna Hawkins; Phone: 502-863-8061; E-mail: donna_hawkins@georgetowncollege.edu.

GEORGETOWN UNIVERSITY
Washington, District of Columbia

Hoyas ◆ NCAA I ◆ Big East Conference; Patriot League
Conference ◆ http://www.georgetown.edu/

Independent Roman Catholic (Jesuit) university, founded 1789
Coed, 6,550 undergraduate students, 97% full-time, 54% women, 46% men
Urban 110-acre campus
Most difficult entrance level, 23% of applicants were admitted

Freshmen *Admission:* 15,420 applied, 3,505 were accepted, 1,528 enrolled. *Test scores:* SAT verbal scores over 500: 99%; SAT math scores over 500: 99%; SAT verbal scores over 600: 88%; SAT math scores over 600: 91%; SAT verbal scores over 700: 39%; SAT math scores over 700: 43%.
Tuition and fees (2003–04): $28,209 (full-time). *Room and board:* $10,033 (room only: $6653).
Financial Aid (All incoming freshmen): *Average need-based gift aid:* $18,140. *Average non-need based aid:* $3000. *Average aid to full-time undergraduates:* $22,976.
Athletic Department: *Director of Athletics:* Joe Lang; Phone: 202-687-2435; Fax: 202-687-5366; E-mail: langj@georgetown.edu. *Sports Information Director:* Scott Homa; Phone: 202-687-5241; E-mail: homas@georgetown.edu.

MEN'S COACHES

Baseball: Peter Wilk; Phone: 202-687-2462; E-mail: wilkp@ georgetown.edu.
Basketball: Craig Esherick; Phone: 202-687-2374.
Cheerleading: Samantha Hunter; Phone: 202-583-6469.
Cross Country: Ron Helmer; Phone: 202-687-2448; E-mail: helmerr@ georgetown.edu.
Diving: Amy Kress; Phone: 202-687-2407.
Football: Bob Benson; Phone: 202-687-2493; E-mail: bensonr@ georgetown.edu.
Golf: Tom Hunter; Phone: 202-687-2400; E-mail: huntert@georgetown. edu.
Lacrosse: Dave Urich; Phone: 202-687-2460; E-mail: urickd@ georgetown.edu.
Soccer: Keith Tabatznik; Phone: 202-687-2364; E-mail: tabatznk@ georgetown.edu.
Swimming: Bethany Bower; Phone: 202-687-2407; E-mail: bowerb@ georgetown.edu.
Tennis: Rich Bausch; Phone: 202-687-2436; E-mail: bauschr@ georgetown.edu.
Track and Field: Ron Helmer; Phone: 202-687-2448; E-mail: helmerr@ georgetown.edu.

WOMEN'S COACHES

Basketball: Patrick Knapp; Phone: 202-687-2354; E-mail: knappp@ georgetown.edu.
Cheerleading: Samantha Hunter; Phone: 202-583-6469.
Cross Country: Ron Helmer; Phone: 202-687-2448; E-mail: helmerr@ georgetown.edu.
Diving: Amy Kress; Phone: 202-687-2407.
Field Hockey: Laurie Carroll; Phone: 202-687-6499; E-mail: carroll1@ georgetown.edu.
Golf: Leland Beckel; Phone: 202-687-7960; E-mail: flb4@georgetown. edu.
Lacrosse: Kim Simons; Phone: 202-687-6550; E-mail: simonsk@ georgetown.edu.
Soccer: Diane Drake; Phone: 202-687-7344; E-mail: draked@ georgetown.edu.
Swimming: Bethany Bower; Phone: 202-687-2407; E-mail: bowerb@ georgetown.edu.

Tennis: Rich Bausch; Phone: 202-687-2436; E-mail: bauschr@georgetown.edu.
Track and Field: Ron Helmer; Phone: 202-687-2448; E-mail: helmerr@georgetown.edu.
Volleyball: Li Liu; Phone: 202-687-3828; E-mail: liul@georgetown.edu.

THE GEORGE WASHINGTON UNIVERSITY
Washington, District of Columbia

Colonials ◆ NCAA I ◆ Atlantic 10 Conference ◆ http://www.gwu.edu/

Independent university, founded 1821
Coed, 10,436 undergraduate students, 89% full-time, 57% women, 43% men
Urban 36-acre campus
Very difficult entrance level, 4% of applicants were admitted

Freshmen *Admission:* 18,442 applied, 7,103 were accepted, 2,266 enrolled. *Test scores:* SAT verbal scores over 500: 97%; SAT math scores over 500: 98%; SAT verbal scores over 600: 72%; SAT math scores over 600: 73%; SAT verbal scores over 700: 20%; SAT math scores over 700: 18%.
Tuition and fees (2004–05): $30,820 (full-time). *Room and board:* $10,210 (room only: $7210).
Financial Aid (All incoming freshmen): *Average need-based gift aid:* $15,651. *Average non-need based aid:* $13,836. *Average aid to full-time undergraduates:* $26,888.
Athletic Department: *Director of Athletics:* Jack Kvancz; Phone: 202-994-6650; Fax: 202-994-6818; E-mail: jkvancz@gwu.edu. *Sports Information Director:* Brad Bower; Phone: 202-994-0339; E-mail: bbower@gwu.edu.

MEN'S COACHES
Baseball: Tom Walter; Phone: 202-994-7399; E-mail: gwbsbl@gwu.edu.
Basketball: Karl Hobbs; Phone: 202-994-6651; E-mail: khobbs@gwu.edu.
Cross Country: Deb Cane; Phone: 202-994-5972; E-mail: rundeb@gwu.edu.
Diving: Krista Irish; Phone: 202-994-5712; E-mail: kirish@gwu.edu.
Golf: Scott Allen; Phone: 202-994-5969; E-mail: golfscot@gwu.edu.
Soccer: George Lidster; Phone: 202-994-6893; E-mail: gwsoccer@gwu.edu.
Swimming: Dan Rhinehart; Phone: 202-994-5712; E-mail: djrswim@aol.com.
Tennis: Tom Hawkins; Phone: 202-994-6650; E-mail: thawkins@gwu.edu.

WOMEN'S COACHES
Basketball: Joe McKeown; Phone: 202-994-6387.
Cross Country: Deb Cane; Phone: 202-994-5972; E-mail: rundeb@gwu.edu.
Diving: Krista Irish; Phone: 202-994-5712; E-mail: kirish@gwu.edu.
Gymnastics: Margie Cunningham; Phone: 202-994-5718; E-mail: mfcgym@aol.com.
Lacrosse: Jennifer Morris; Phone: 202-994-5891; E-mail: jtmorris@gwu.edu.
Soccer: Tanya Vogel; Phone: 202-994-0152; E-mail: wsoccer@gwu.edu.
Softball: Shaunte' Fremin; Phone: 202-994-2086; E-mail: sfremin@gwu.edu.
Swimming: Dan Rhinehart; Phone: 202-994-5712; E-mail: djrswim@aol.com.
Tennis: Megan Wise; Phone: 202-994-6748; E-mail: gwutennis@gwu.edu.
Volleyball: Jo Coronel; Phone: 202-994-5879; E-mail: jcoronel@gwu.edu.

GEORGIA COLLEGE & STATE UNIVERSITY
Milledgeville, Georgia

Bobcats ◆ NCAA II ◆ Peach Belt Conference ◆ http://www.gcsu.edu/

State-supported comprehensive, founded 1889, part of University System of Georgia
Coed, 4,662 undergraduate students, 86% full-time, 60% women, 40% men
Small-town 590-acre campus
Moderately difficult entrance level, 6% of applicants were admitted

Freshmen *Admission:* 2,547 applied, 1,590 were accepted, 1,031 enrolled. *Test scores:* SAT verbal scores over 500: 79%; SAT math scores over 500: 76%; SAT verbal scores over 600: 21%; SAT math scores over 600: 19%; SAT verbal scores over 700: 2%; SAT math scores over 700: 1%.
Tuition and fees (2003–04): $3596 (resident), $12,602 (nonresident). *Room and board:* $6282.
Athletic Department: *Director of Athletics:* Stan Aldridge; Phone: 478-445-6341; Fax: 478-445-1790; E-mail: stan.aldridge@gcsu.edu. *Sports Information Director:* Brad Muller; Phone: 478-445-1779; E-mail: brad.muller@gcsu.edu.

MEN'S COACHES
Baseball: Steve Mrowka; Phone: 478-445-5319; E-mail: smrowka@gcsu.edu.
Basketball: Terry Sellers; Phone: 478-445-4289; E-mail: tsellers@gcsu.edu.
Cheerleading: Jerry Fly; Phone: 478-445-0939; E-mail: jerry.fly@gcsu.edu.
Cross Country: Joe Samprone; Phone: 478-445-3521; E-mail: samprone@bellsouth.net.
Golf: Jimmy Wilson; Phone: 478-445-0796; E-mail: jimmyewilson@yahoo.com.
Tennis: Steve Barsby; Phone: 478-445-1778; E-mail: steve.barsby@gcsu.edu.

WOMEN'S COACHES
Basketball: John Carrick; Phone: 478-445-1788; E-mail: john.carrick@gcsu.edu.
Cheerleading: Jerry Fly; Phone: 478-445-0939; E-mail: jerry.fly@gcsu.edu.
Cross Country: Joe Samprone; Phone: 478-445-3521; E-mail: samprone@bellsouth.net.
Soccer: Robert Parr; Phone: 478-445-5112; E-mail: robert.parr@gcsu.edu.
Softball: Windy Thees; Phone: 478-445-6870; E-mail: w.thees@gcsu.edu.
Tennis: Steve Barsby; Phone: 478-445-1778; E-mail: steve.barsby@gcsu.edu.

GEORGIA INSTITUTE OF TECHNOLOGY
Atlanta, Georgia

Yellow Jackets ◆ NCAA I ◆ Atlantic Coast Conference ◆ http://www.gatech.edu/

State-supported university, founded 1885, part of University System of Georgia
Coed, 11,257 undergraduate students, 92% full-time, 28% women, 72% men
Urban 400-acre campus
Very difficult entrance level, 62% of applicants were admitted

Freshmen *Admission:* 8,573 applied, 5,386 were accepted, 2,235 enrolled. *Test scores:* SAT verbal scores over 500: 99%; SAT math scores over 500: 100%; SAT verbal scores over 600: 77%; SAT math scores over 600: 95%; SAT verbal scores over 700: 23%; SAT math scores over 700: 50%.
Tuition and fees (2003–04): $4076 (resident), $16,002 (nonresident). *Room and board:* $6264 (room only: $3624).

Georgia Institute of Technology (continued)

Financial Aid (All incoming freshmen): *Average need-based gift aid:* $3489. *Average non-need based aid:* $2188. *Average aid to full-time undergraduates:* $7701.
Athletic Department: *Director of Athletics:* Dave Braine; Phone: 404-894-5411; Fax: 404-894-1248; E-mail: dave.braine@gtaa.gatech.edu. *Sports Information Director:* Allison George; Phone: 404-894-5445; E-mail: ageorge@at.gtaa.gatech.edu.

MEN'S COACHES
Baseball: Danny Hall; Phone: 404-894-5471; E-mail: dhall@gtaa.gatech.edu.
Basketball: Paul Hewitt; Phone: 404-894-5425; E-mail: phewitt@gtaa.gatech.edu.
Cheerleading: Lauren Gryszkiewicz; Phone: 404-385-0403; E-mail: laureng@gtaa.gatech.edu.
Cross Country: Alan Drosky; Phone: 404-894-4420; E-mail: adrosky@gtaa.gatech.edu.
Diving: John Ames; Phone: 404-385-1293; E-mail: john.ames@gtaa.gatech.edu.
Football: Chan Gailey; Phone: 404-894-5420; E-mail: lwatts@gtaa.gatech.edu.
Golf: Bruce Heppler; Phone: 404-894-0961; E-mail: bheppler@gtaa.gatech.edu.
Swimming: Seth Baron; Phone: 404-894-1734; E-mail: sbaron@gtaa.gatech.edu.
Tennis: Kenny Thorne; Phone: 404-894-0459; E-mail: kthorne@gtaa.gatech.edu.
Track and Field: Grover Hinsdale; Phone: 404-894-5488; E-mail: ghinsdale@gtaa.gatech.edu.

WOMEN'S COACHES
Basketball: Machelle Joseph; Phone: 404-894-5406; E-mail: mjoseph@gtaa.gatech.edu.
Cheerleading: Lauren Gryszkiewicz; Phone: 404-385-0403; E-mail: laureng@gtaa.gatech.edu.
Cross Country: Alan Drosky; Phone: 404-894-4420; E-mail: adrosky@gtaa.gatech.edu.
Diving: John Ames; Phone: 404-385-1293; E-mail: john.ames@gtaa.gatech.edu.
Softball: Ehren Earleywine; Phone: 404-894-5415; E-mail: eearleywine@gtaa.gatech.edu.
Swimming: Seth Baron; Phone: 404-894-1734; E-mail: sbaron@gtaa.gatech.edu.
Tennis: Bryan Shelton; Phone: 404-894-0458; E-mail: bshelton@gtaa.gatech.edu.
Track and Field: Alan Drosky; Phone: 404-894-4420; E-mail: adrosky@gtaa.gatech.edu.
Volleyball: Bond Shymansky; Phone: 404-894-5453; E-mail: bond@gtaa.gatech.edu.

GEORGIAN COURT UNIVERSITY
Lakewood, New Jersey
Lions ◆ NCAA II ◆ Central Atlantic Collegiate Conference ◆ http://www.gcorgian.edu/

Independent Roman Catholic comprehensive, founded 1908
Women only, 1,956 undergraduate students, 65% full-time, 90% women, 10% men
Suburban 150-acre campus with easy access to New York City and Philadelphia
Moderately difficult entrance level, 83% of applicants were admitted

Freshmen *Admission:* 378 applied, 324 were accepted, 138 enrolled. *Test scores:* SAT verbal scores over 500: 34%; SAT math scores over 500: 29%; SAT verbal scores over 600: 4%; SAT math scores over 600: 4%.
Tuition and fees (2004–05): $17,924 (full-time). *Room and board:* $7200.
Financial Aid (All incoming freshmen): *Average need-based gift aid:* $11,278. *Average non-need based aid:* $7640. *Average aid to full-time undergraduates:* $12,674.
Athletic Department: *Director of Athletics:* Laura Liesman; Phone: 732-364-2200; Fax: 732-961-9887; E-mail: liesmanl@georgian.edu. *Sports Information Director:* Laura Liesman; Phone: 732-364-2200; E-mail: liesmanl@georgian.edu.

WOMEN'S COACHES
Basketball: Debra Emery; Phone: 732-364-2200; E-mail: emeryd@georgian.edu.
Cross Country: Kerwin Lanz; Phone: 732-364-2200; E-mail: klanz@aol.com.
Soccer: Adam Curtis; Phone: 732-364-2200; E-mail: adamcurtis@comcast.net.
Softball: Melanie Morris; Phone: 732-364-2200; E-mail: morrism@georgian.edu.
Tennis: Gregory Wyzykowski; Phone: 732-364-2200; E-mail: wyzykowskig@georgian.edu.
Volleyball: Jeff Mangold; Phone: 732-364-2200; E-mail: jeffmangold@yahoo.com.

GEORGIA SOUTHERN UNIVERSITY
Statesboro, Georgia
Eagles ◆ NCAA I ◆ Southern Conference ◆ http://www.georgiasouthern.edu/

State-supported comprehensive, founded 1906, part of University System of Georgia
Coed, 13,696 undergraduate students, 89% full-time, 50% women, 50% men
Small-town 634-acre campus
Moderately difficult entrance level, 58% of applicants were admitted

Freshmen *Admission:* 7,921 applied, 4,277 were accepted, 2,764 enrolled. *Test scores:* SAT verbal scores over 500: 66%; SAT math scores over 500: 65%; SAT verbal scores over 600: 14%; SAT math scores over 600: 16%; SAT verbal scores over 700: 1%; SAT math scores over 700: 1%.
Tuition and fees (2003–04): $2912 (resident), $9548 (nonresident). *Room and board:* $5628 (room only: $3428).
Financial Aid (All incoming freshmen): *Average need-based gift aid:* $4801. *Average non-need based aid:* $1307. *Average aid to full-time undergraduates:* $6133.
Athletic Department: *Director of Athletics:* Sam Baker; Phone: 912-681-5047; Fax: 912-681-1269; E-mail: sbaker@gasou.edu. *Sports Information Director:* Tom McClellan; Phone: 912-681-5239; E-mail: tmcclell@gasou.edu.

MEN'S COACHES
Baseball: Rodney Hennon; Phone: 912-681-7360; E-mail: rhennon@www2.gasou.edu.
Basketball: Jeff Price; Phone: 912-681-5376; E-mail: jprice@gasou.edu.
Cheerleading: Barry Munkasy; Phone: 912-681-0985; E-mail: bmunkasy@gasou.edu.
Football: Mike Sewak; Phone: 912-681-5522; E-mail: msewak@gasou.edu.
Golf: Larry Mays; Phone: 912-681-7066; E-mail: lmays@gasou.edu.
Soccer: Kevin Chambers; Phone: 912-681-1204; E-mail: kcham@gasou.edu.
Tennis: Justin Mills; Phone: 912-486-7067; E-mail: jwmiles@gasou.edu.

WOMEN'S COACHES
Basketball: Rusty Cram; Phone: 912-681-0568; E-mail: rcram@gasou.edu.
Cheerleading: Barry Munkasy; Phone: 912-681-0985; E-mail: bmunkasy@gasou.edu.
Cross Country: Todd Lane; Phone: 912-681-0784; E-mail: tlane@gasou.edu.
Diving: Jake Sinclair; Phone: 912-681-5740.
Soccer: Ashley Hart; Phone: 912-681-0270; E-mail: aehart@georgiasouthern.edu.
Softball: Natalie Poole; Phone: 912-871-1501; E-mail: npoole@gasou.edu.
Swimming: Niki Jones; Phone: 912-681-1394; E-mail: njones@gasou.edu.
Tennis: Erica Perkins; Phone: 912-681-0887; E-mail: eperkins@gasou.edu.
Track and Field: Todd Lane; Phone: 912-681-0784; E-mail: tlane@gasou.edu.
Volleyball: Kerry Messersmith; Phone: 912-681-1502; E-mail: kmesser@gasou.edu.

GEORGIA SOUTHWESTERN STATE UNIVERSITY
Americus, Georgia

Hurricanes ◆ NAIA ◆ Georgia Alabama Carolina Conference ◆ http://www.gsw.edu/

State-supported comprehensive, founded 1906, part of University System of Georgia
Coed, 2,094 undergraduate students, 72% full-time, 66% women, 34% men
Small-town 255-acre campus
Moderately difficult entrance level, 79% of applicants were admitted

Freshmen *Admission:* 1,128 applied, 833 were accepted, 386 enrolled. *Test scores:* SAT verbal scores over 500: 47%; SAT math scores over 500: 39%; SAT verbal scores over 600: 8%; SAT math scores over 600: 7%; SAT verbal scores over 700: 1%.
Tuition and fees (2003–04): $2782 (resident), $9418 (nonresident). *Room and board:* $4204 (room only: $2160).
Financial Aid (All incoming freshmen): *Average need-based gift aid:* $3157. *Average non-need based aid:* $3072. *Average aid to full-time undergraduates:* $5552.
Athletic Department: *Director of Athletics:* Randolph Barksdale; Phone: 229-931-2222; Fax: 229-931-2143; E-mail: arb1@canes.gsw.edu. *Sports Information Director:* Michele Haywood; Phone: 229-931-2217; E-mail: mrh@canes.gsw.edu.

MEN'S COACHES
Baseball: Bryan McLain; Phone: 229-268-2843; E-mail: bsm@canes.gsw.edu.
Basketball: Randolph Barksdale; Phone: 229-931-2222; E-mail: arb1@canes.gsw.edu.
Tennis: Brennon Sewell; Phone: 229-268-4056; E-mail: jbs10s@sowega.net.

WOMEN'S COACHES
Basketball: Jennifer Rodkey; Phone: 229-931-2231; E-mail: keyrod20@yahoo.com.
Softball: Eddie Ward; Phone: 229-931-2222; E-mail: draw@sowega.net.
Tennis: Brennon Sewell; Phone: 229-268-4056; E-mail: jbs10s@sowega.net.
Volleyball: Michele Haywood; Phone: 229-931-2217; E-mail: mrh@canes.gsw.edu.

GEORGIA STATE UNIVERSITY
Atlanta, Georgia

Panthers ◆ NCAA I ◆ Atlantic Sun Conference ◆ http://www.gsu.edu/

State-supported university, founded 1913, part of University System of Georgia
Coed, 20,177 undergraduate students, 67% full-time, 61% women, 39% men
Urban 44-acre campus
Moderately difficult entrance level, 58% of applicants were admitted

Freshmen *Admission:* 8,177 applied, 4,563 were accepted, 2,008 enrolled. *Test scores:* SAT verbal scores over 500: 75%; SAT math scores over 500: 75%; SAT verbal scores over 600: 26%; SAT math scores over 600: 27%; SAT verbal scores over 700: 3%; SAT math scores over 700: 4%.
Tuition and fees (2004–05): $4312 (resident), $14,898 (nonresident). *Room and board:* $7118 (room only: $5130).
Financial Aid (All incoming freshmen): *Average need-based gift aid:* $5829. *Average non-need based aid:* $3882. *Average aid to full-time undergraduates:* $5565.
Athletic Department: *Director of Athletics:* Greg Manning; Phone: 404-651-3173; Fax: 404-651-0824; E-mail: athglm@langate.gsu.edu. *Sports Information Director:* Steve Ruthsatz; Phone: 404-651-3168; E-mail: athspr@langate.gsu.edu.

MEN'S COACHES
Baseball: Mike Hurst; Phone: 404-244-5804; E-mail: athdph@langate.gsu.edu.

Basketball: Michael Perry; Phone: 404-651-3182; E-mail: athmap@langate.gsu.edu.
Cheerleading: Nicole Duncan; Phone: 404-651-3987; E-mail: oduncan1913@aol.com.
Cross Country: John Rowland; Phone: 404-651-1704; E-mail: athjwr@langate.gsu.edu.
Golf: Matt Clark; Phone: 404-651-3375; E-mail: mclark@gsu.edu.
Soccer: Kerem Daser; Phone: 404-651-1210; E-mail: athkrd@langate.gsu.edu.
Tennis: Nick Brochu; Phone: 404-651-2962; E-mail: athnbx@langate.gsu.edu.
Track and Field: John Rowland; Phone: 404-651-1704; E-mail: athjwr@langate.gsu.edu.

WOMEN'S COACHES
Basketball: Lea Henry; Phone: 404-651-3190; E-mail: athllh@langate.gsu.edu.
Cheerleading: Nicole Duncan; Phone: 404-651-3987; E-mail: oduncan1913@aol.com.
Cross Country: Jessica Graham; Phone: 404-651-1704; E-mail: musjsg@langate.gsu.edu.
Golf: Cathy Mant; Phone: 404-651-9231; E-mail: athcm@langate.gsu.edu.
Soccer: Domenic Martelli; Phone: 404-651-4631; E-mail: athdam@langate.gsu.edu.
Softball: Bob Heck; Phone: 404-651-4054; E-mail: athreh@langate.gsu.edu.
Tennis: Andy Smith; Phone: 404-651-0456; E-mail: athajs@langate.gsu.edu.
Track and Field: John Rowland; Phone: 404-651-1704; E-mail: athjwr@langate.gsu.edu.
Volleyball: Richard Leonard; Phone: 404-651-3183; E-mail: athrcl@langate.gsu.edu.

GETTYSBURG COLLEGE
Gettysburg, Pennsylvania

Bullets ◆ NCAA III ◆ Centennial Conference ◆ http://www.gettysburg.edu/

Independent religious 4-year, founded 1832, affiliated with Evangelical Lutheran Church in America
Coed, 2,597 undergraduate students, 99% full-time, 52% women, 48% men
Suburban 230-acre campus with easy access to Baltimore and Washington, DC
Most difficult entrance level, 44% of applicants were admitted

Freshmen *Admission:* 5,017 applied, 2,317 were accepted, 695 enrolled. *Test scores:* SAT verbal scores over 500: 100%; SAT math scores over 500: 99%; SAT verbal scores over 600: 66%; SAT math scores over 600: 71%; SAT verbal scores over 700: 10%; SAT math scores over 700: 8%.
Tuition and fees (2003–04): $28,674 (full-time). *Room and board:* $6972 (room only: $3696).
Financial Aid (All incoming freshmen): *Average need-based gift aid:* $18,491. *Average non-need based aid:* $8430. *Average aid to full-time undergraduates:* $23,099.
Athletic Department: *Director of Athletics:* David Wright; Phone: 717-337-6401; Fax: 717-337-6528; E-mail: dwright@gettysburg.edu. *Sports Information Director:* Matt Daskivich; Phone: 717-337-6527; E-mail: mdaskivi@gettysburg.edu.

MEN'S COACHES
Baseball: John Campo; Phone: 717-337-6413; E-mail: jcampo@gettysburg.edu.
Basketball: George Petrie; Phone: 717-337-6406; E-mail: gpetrie@gettysburg.edu.
Cheerleading: Kelly Jones; Phone: 717-337-6438; E-mail: kjones@gettysburg.edu.
Cross Country: Bob Condon; Phone: 717-337-6403; E-mail: bcondon@gettysburg.edu.
Football: Barry Streeter; Phone: 717-337-6414; E-mail: bhstreet@gettysburg.edu.
Golf: George Petrie; Phone: 717-337-6406; E-mail: gpetrie@gettysburg.edu.
Lacrosse: Hank Janczyk; Phone: 717-337-6405; E-mail: hjanczyk@gettysburg.edu.

Gettysburg College *(continued)*

Soccer: Devin O'Neil; Phone: 717-337-6407; E-mail: doneill@gettysburg.edu.
Swimming: Mike Rawleigh; Phone: 717-337-6306; E-mail: mrawleig@gettysburg.edu.
Tennis: Bill Pfitzinger; Phone: 717-337-6532; E-mail: bpfitzin@gettysburg.edu.
Track and Field: Bob Condon; Phone: 717-337-6403; E-mail: bcondon@gettysburg.edu.
Wrestling: Troy Dell; Phone: 717-337-6415; E-mail: tdell@gettysburg.edu.

WOMEN'S COACHES

Basketball: Mike Kirkpatrick; Phone: 717-337-6409; E-mail: mkirkpat@gettysburg.edu.
Cheerleading: Kelly Jones; Phone: 717-337-6438; E-mail: kjones@gettysburg.edu.
Cross Country: Bob Condon; Phone: 717-337-6403; E-mail: bcondon@gettysburg.edu.
Field Hockey: Barb Jordan; Phone: 717-337-6431; E-mail: bjordan@gettysburg.edu.
Golf: Todd Wawrousek; Phone: 717-337-6460; E-mail: twawrous@gettysburg.edu.
Lacrosse: Carol Cantele; Phone: 717-337-6404; E-mail: ccantele@gettysburg.edu.
Soccer: Todd Wawrousek; Phone: 717-337-6460; E-mail: twawrous@gettysburg.edu.
Softball: Mike Kirkpatrick; Phone: 717-337-6409; E-mail: mkirkpat@gettysburg.edu.
Swimming: Mike Rawleigh; Phone: 717-337-6306; E-mail: mrawleig@gettysburg.edu.
Tennis: Bill Pfitzinger; Phone: 717-337-6532; E-mail: bpfitzin@gettysburg.edu.
Track and Field: Bob Condon; Phone: 717-337-6403; E-mail: bcondon@gettysburg.edu.
Volleyball: Kim Kelly; Phone: 717-337-6410; E-mail: kkelly@gettysburg.edu.

GLENVILLE STATE COLLEGE
Glenville, West Virginia

Pioneers ◆ NCAA II ◆ West Virginia Intercollegiate Athletic Conference ◆ http://www.glenville.edu/

State-supported 4-year, founded 1872, part of West Virginia Higher Education Policy Commission
Coed, 1,377 undergraduate students, 88% full-time, 54% women, 46% men
Rural 331-acre campus
Noncompetitive entrance level, 100% of applicants were admitted

Freshmen *Admission:* 777 applied, 777 were accepted, 313 enrolled. *Test scores:* SAT verbal scores over 500: 30%; SAT math scores over 500: 29%; SAT verbal scores over 600: 9%; SAT math scores over 600: 6%; SAT verbal scores over 700: 2%; SAT math scores over 700: 1%.
Tuition and fees (2003–04): $2952 (resident), $7306 (nonresident). *Room and board:* $4860 (room only: $2400).
Financial Aid (All incoming freshmen): *Average need-based gift aid:* $4073. *Average non-need based aid:* $2615. *Average aid to full-time undergraduates:* $7301.
Athletic Department: *Director of Athletics:* Greg Bamberger; Phone: 304-462-4102; Fax: 304-462-5593; E-mail: bamberger@glenville.edu. *Sports Information Director:* Dwaine Osborne; Phone: 304-462-7361.

MEN'S COACHES

Basketball: Chad Hankinson; Phone: 304-462-7361; E-mail: chankinson@glenville.edu.
Cross Country: Sherry Carr Smith; Phone: 304-462-4102; E-mail: slsmith@glenville.edu.
Football: Paul Schaffner; Phone: 304-462-7361; E-mail: shaffner@glenville.edu.
Golf: Rick Simmons; Phone: 304-462-7361.
Track and Field: Sherry Carr Smith; Phone: 304-462-4102; E-mail: slsmith@glenville.edu.

WOMEN'S COACHES

Basketball: Steve Harold; Phone: 304-462-4102; E-mail: harold@glenville.edu.
Cross Country: Sherry Carr Smith; Phone: 304-462-4102; E-mail: slsmith@glenville.edu.
Golf: Rick Simmons; Phone: 304-462-7361.
Softball: Gerald Szabo; Phone: 304-462-4102; E-mail: gszabo@glenville.edu.
Track and Field: Sherry Carr Smith; Phone: 304-462-4102; E-mail: slsmith@glenville.edu.
Volleyball: Gerald Szabo; Phone: 304-462-4102; E-mail: gszabo@glenville.edu.

GOLDEY-BEACOM COLLEGE
Wilmington, Delaware

Lightning ◆ NCAA II ◆ Central Atlantic Collegiate Conference ◆ http://goldey.gbc.edu/

Independent comprehensive, founded 1886
Coed, 1,049 undergraduate students
Suburban 27-acre campus with easy access to Philadelphia
Moderately difficult entrance level, 78% of applicants were admitted

Freshmen *Admission:* 408 applied, 319 were accepted. *Test scores:* SAT verbal scores over 500: 33%; SAT math scores over 500: 32%; SAT verbal scores over 600: 6%; SAT math scores over 600: 6%; SAT verbal scores over 700: 1%; SAT math scores over 700: 2%.
Tuition and fees (2003–04): $11,349 (full-time). *Room only:* $3937.
Athletic Department: *Director of Athletics:* Chris Morgan; Phone: 302-225-6330; Fax: 302-998-6823; E-mail: morganc@gbc.edu. *Sports Information Director:* Lynne Nathan; Phone: 302-225-6217; E-mail: nathanc@gbc.edu.

MEN'S COACHES

Basketball: Chuck Hammond; Phone: 302-225-6352; E-mail: hammond@gbc.edu.
Cross Country: Kelly Parsley; Phone: 302-225-6358; E-mail: parslek@gbc.edu.
Golf: Jim Mahoney; Phone: 302-225-6358; E-mail: mahonej@gbc.edu.
Soccer: Michael Finizio; Phone: 302-225-6355; E-mail: finiziom@gbc.edu.

WOMEN'S COACHES

Basketball: Mary Malone; Phone: 302-225-6334; E-mail: malonem@gbc.edu.
Cross Country: Kelly Parsley; Phone: 302-225-6358; E-mail: parslek@gbc.edu.
Golf: Jim Mahoney; Phone: 302-225-6358; E-mail: mahonej@gbc.edu.
Soccer: Chris Morgan; Phone: 302-225-6330; E-mail: morganc@gbc.edu.
Softball: Mary Pat Kwoka; Phone: 302-225-6224; E-mail: kwokamp@gbc.edu.
Volleyball: Rich Bowers; Phone: 302-225-6213; E-mail: bowersr@gbc.edu.

GONZAGA UNIVERSITY
Spokane, Washington

Bulldogs ◆ NCAA I ◆ West Coast Conference ◆ http://www.gonzaga.edu/

Independent Roman Catholic comprehensive, founded 1887
Coed, 3,981 undergraduate students, 95% full-time, 55% women, 45% men
Urban 94-acre campus
Moderately difficult entrance level, 74% of applicants were admitted

Freshmen *Admission:* 3,713 applied, 2,846 were accepted, 908 enrolled. *Test scores:* SAT verbal scores over 500: 88%; SAT math scores over 500: 89%; SAT verbal scores over 600: 48%; SAT math scores over 600: 50%; SAT verbal scores over 700: 9%; SAT math scores over 700: 9%.
Tuition and fees (2003–04): $20,735 (full-time). *Room and board:* $5960 (room only: $3110).
Financial Aid (All incoming freshmen): *Average need-based gift aid:* $11,652. *Average non-need based aid:* $6044. *Average aid to full-time undergraduates:* $13,016.

Athletic Department: *Director of Athletics:* Mike Roth; Phone: 509-323-3519; Fax: 509-323-5787; E-mail: roth@athletics.gonzaga.edu. *Sports Information Director:* Oliver Pierce; Phone: 509-323-6373; E-mail: pierce@athletics.gonzaga.edu.

MEN'S COACHES

Baseball: Mark Machtolf; Phone: 509-323-4209; E-mail: machtolf@athletics.gonzaga.edu.
Basketball: Mark Few; Phone: 509-323-4218; E-mail: few@athletics.gonzaga.edu.
Cheerleading: Steve Kramer; Phone: 509-323-2290; E-mail: youthrebound@ior.com.
Cross Country: Kevin Swaim; Phone: 509-323-5782; E-mail: swaimguxc@msn.com.
Golf: Robert Gray; Phone: 509-323-4081; E-mail: gray@athletics.gonzaga.edu.
Soccer: Einar Thorarinsson; Phone: 509-323-4076; E-mail: thorarinsson@athletics.gonzaga.edu.
Tennis: John Gant; Phone: 509-323-4206; E-mail: gant@athletics.gonzaga.edu.
Track and Field: Kevin Swaim; Phone: 509-323-5782; E-mail: swaimguxc@msn.com.

WOMEN'S COACHES

Basketball: Kelly Graves; Phone: 509-323-4217; E-mail: graves@athletics.gonzaga.edu.
Cheerleading: Steve Kramer; Phone: 509-323-2290; E-mail: youthrebound@ior.com.
Cross Country: Kevin Swaim; Phone: 509-323-5782; E-mail: swaimguxc@msn.com.
Golf: Robert Gray; Phone: 509-323-4081; E-mail: gray@athletics.gonzaga.edu.
Soccer: Shannon Stiles; Phone: 509-323-4222; E-mail: stiles@athletics.gonzaga.edu.
Tennis: Alisha Woodroof; Phone: 509-323-4074.
Track and Field: Kevin Swaim; Phone: 509-323-5782; E-mail: swaimguxc@msn.com.
Volleyball: Kip Yoshimura; Phone: 509-323-6376; E-mail: yoshimura@athletics.gonzaga.edu.

GORDON COLLEGE
Wenham, Massachusetts

Fighting Scots ◆ NCAA III ◆ Commonwealth Coast Conference ◆ http://www.gordon.edu/

Independent nondenominational comprehensive, founded 1889
Coed, 1,640 undergraduate students, 98% full-time, 65% women, 35% men
Small-town 500-acre campus with easy access to Boston
Moderately difficult entrance level, 78% of applicants were admitted

Freshmen *Admission:* 1,080 applied, 845 were accepted, 427 enrolled. *Test scores:* SAT verbal scores over 500: 96%; SAT math scores over 500: 93%; SAT verbal scores over 600: 62%; SAT math scores over 600: 60%; SAT verbal scores over 700: 15%; SAT math scores over 700: 10%.
Tuition and fees (2003–04): $20,234 (full-time). *Room and board:* $5748 (room only: $3850).
Financial Aid (All incoming freshmen): *Average need-based gift aid:* $10,443. *Average non-need based aid:* $10,204. *Average aid to full-time undergraduates:* $13,852.
Athletic Department: *Director of Athletics:* Joe Hakes; Phone: 978-867-4136; E-mail: jhakes@hope.gordon.edu. *Sports Information Director:* Stephen Leonard; Phone: 978-867-4853; E-mail: sportsinfo@hope.gordon.edu.

MEN'S COACHES

Baseball: Bob Dickerman; Phone: 978-867-4858.
Basketball: Michael Schauer; Phone: 978-867-4327; E-mail: mschauer@hope.gordon.edu.
Cross Country: Stephen Leonard; Phone: 978-867-4853; E-mail: sleonard@hope.gordon.edu.
Lacrosse: Skip Milne; Phone: 978-867-4826.
Soccer: Marc Whitehouse; Phone: 978-867-4336; E-mail: whitehouse@hope.gordon.edu.
Swimming: Frank Giarmona; Phone: 978-867-4116; E-mail: fgiarmona@hope.gordon.edu.
Tennis: Bill Davis; Phone: 978-867-4858.

WOMEN'S COACHES

Basketball: Jeannine Cavallaro; Phone: 978-867-4834; E-mail: jcavallaro@hope.gordon.edu.
Cross Country: Stephen Leonard; Phone: 978-867-4853; E-mail: sleonard@hope.gordon.edu.
Field Hockey: Cory Ward; Phone: 978-867-4338; E-mail: cward@hope.gordon.edu.
Lacrosse: Cory Ward; Phone: 978-867-4338; E-mail: cward@hope.gordon.edu.
Soccer: Rick Burns; Phone: 978-867-4330; E-mail: rburns@hope.gordon.edu.
Softball: Phone: 978-867-4116.
Swimming: Frank Giarmona; Phone: 978-927-4116; E-mail: fgiarmona@hope.gordon.edu.
Tennis: Bill Davis; Phone: 978-867-4858.
Volleyball: Amy Bowen; Phone: 978-867-4324; E-mail: abowen@hope.gordon.edu.

GOSHEN COLLEGE
Goshen, Indiana

Maple Leafs ◆ NAIA ◆ Mid-Central Conference ◆ http://www.goshen.edu/

Independent Mennonite 4-year, founded 1894
Coed, 920 undergraduate students, 86% full-time, 62% women, 38% men
Small-town 135-acre campus
Moderately difficult entrance level, 49% of applicants were admitted

Freshmen *Admission:* 608 applied, 371 were accepted, 182 enrolled. *Test scores:* SAT verbal scores over 500: 78%; SAT math scores over 500: 83%; SAT verbal scores over 600: 49%; SAT math scores over 600: 44%; SAT verbal scores over 700: 18%; SAT math scores over 700: 10%.
Tuition and fees (2003–04): $16,650 (full-time). *Room and board:* $5800 (room only: $3000).
Financial Aid (All incoming freshmen): *Average need-based gift aid:* $10,696. *Average non-need based aid:* $8042. *Average aid to full-time undergraduates:* $15,229.
Athletic Department: *Director of Athletics:* Ken Pletcher; Phone: 574-535-7491; Fax: 574-535-7531; E-mail: kenjp@goshen.edu. *Sports Information Director:* Cory Furman; Phone: 574-535-7497; E-mail: coryf@goshen.edu.

MEN'S COACHES

Baseball: Brent Hoober; Phone: 574-535-7495; E-mail: brentah@goshen.edu.
Basketball: Stan Daugherty; Phone: 574-535-7493; E-mail: stanrd@goshen.edu.
Cross Country: Lyle Miller; Phone: 574-535-7079; E-mail: lylegm@goshen.edu.
Golf: Brent Kaufman; Phone: 574-535-7748; E-mail: brentjk@goshen.edu.
Soccer: Thavisak Mounsithiraj; Phone: 574-535-7253; E-mail: thavisakm@goshen.edu.
Tennis: Stan King; Phone: 574-535-7498; E-mail: stanbk@goshen.edu.
Track and Field: Rick Clark; Phone: 574-535-7079; E-mail: rickvc@goshen.edu.

WOMEN'S COACHES

Basketball: Steve Wiktorowski; Phone: 574-535-7492; E-mail: stevelw@goshen.edu.
Cross Country: Lyle Miller; Phone: 574-535-7079; E-mail: lylegm@goshen.edu.
Soccer: Thavisak Mounsithiraj; Phone: 574-535-7253; E-mail: thavisakm@goshen.edu.
Softball: Marc Green; Phone: 574-535-7233; E-mail: marclg@goshen.edu.
Tennis: Leon Brenneman; Phone: 574-535-7743; E-mail: leonrb@goshen.edu.
Track and Field: Rick Clark; Phone: 574-535-7079; E-mail: rickvc@goshen.edu.
Volleyball: Kent Natziger; Phone: 574-535-7658; E-mail: kentdn@goshen.edu.

GOUCHER COLLEGE
Baltimore, Maryland
Gophers ◆ NCAA III ◆ Capital Athletic Conference ◆ http://
www.goucher.edu/

Independent comprehensive, founded 1885
Coed, 1,310 undergraduate students, 97% full-time, 68% women,
32% men
Suburban 287-acre campus
Moderately difficult entrance level, 62% of applicants were admitted

Freshmen *Admission:* 2,751 applied, 1,779 were accepted, 342 enrolled.
Test scores: SAT verbal scores over 500: 96%; SAT math scores over
500: 91%; SAT verbal scores over 600: 61%; SAT math scores over
600: 51%; SAT verbal scores over 700: 14%; SAT math scores over
700: 8%.
Tuition and fees (2003–04): $24,450 (full-time). *Room and board:* $8350
(room only: $2675).
Financial Aid (All incoming freshmen): *Average need-based gift aid:*
$15,727. *Average non-need based aid:* $10,284. *Average aid to full-
time undergraduates:* $18,565.
Athletic Department: *Director of Athletics:* Geoffrey Miller; Phone: 410-
337-6385; Fax: 410-337-6576; E-mail: gmiller@goucher.edu. *Sports
Information Director:* Mike Sanders; Phone: 410-337-6474; E-mail:
msanders@goucher.edu.

MEN'S COACHES
Basketball: Leonard Trevino; Phone: 410-337-6284; E-mail: ltrevino@
goucher.edu.
Cross Country: John Caslin; Phone: 410-337-6462; E-mail: jcaslin@
goucher.edu.
Lacrosse: Kyle Hannan; Phone: 410-337-6573; E-mail: khannan@
goucher.edu.
Soccer: Gary Dunda; Phone: 410-337-6400; E-mail: gdunda@goucher.
edu.
Swimming: Tom Till; Phone: 410-337-6383; E-mail: ttill@goucher.edu.
Tennis: Rob Hubbard; Phone: 410-337-6542; E-mail: rhubbard@
goucher.edu.
Track and Field: John Caslin; Phone: 410-337-6462; E-mail: jcaslin@
goucher.edu.

WOMEN'S COACHES
Basketball: Charleata Neal; Phone: 410-337-6386; E-mail: cneal@
goucher.edu.
Cross Country: John Caslin; Phone: 410-337-6462; E-mail: jcaslin@
goucher.edu.
Field Hockey: Susan Mackley; Phone: 410-337-6547; E-mail: smackley@
goucher.edu.
Lacrosse: Kara Carlin; Phone: 410-337-6574; E-mail: kacarlin@
goucher.edu.
Soccer: Michele Hoffman; Phone: 410-337-6577; E-mail: mhoffman@
goucher.edu.
Swimming: Tom Till; Phone: 410-337-6388; E-mail: ttill@goucher.edu.
Tennis: Sally Baum; Phone: 410-337-6389; E-mail: sbaum@goucher.
edu.
Track and Field: John Caslin; Phone: 410-337-6462; E-mail: jcaslin@
goucher.edu.
Volleyball: Jeremy Price; Phone: 410-337-6286; E-mail: jprice@goucher.
edu.

GRACE COLLEGE
Winona Lake, Indiana
Lancers ◆ NAIA ◆ Mid-Central Conference
◆ http://www.grace.edu/

Independent religious comprehensive, founded 1948, affiliated with
Fellowship of Grace Brethren Churches
Coed, 1,086 undergraduate students, 88% full-time, 50% women,
50% men
Small-town 160-acre campus
Moderately difficult entrance level, 68% of applicants were admitted

Freshmen *Admission:* 768 applied, 549 were accepted, 181 enrolled.
Test scores: SAT verbal scores over 500: 67%; SAT math scores over

500: 67%; SAT verbal scores over 600: 27%; SAT math scores over
600: 19%; SAT verbal scores over 700: 3%; SAT math scores over
700: 3%.
Tuition and fees (2003–04): $14,070 (full-time). *Room and board:* $5755
(room only: $2865).
Financial Aid (All incoming freshmen): *Average need-based gift aid:* $8344.
Average non-need based aid: $11,021. *Average aid to full-time under-
graduates:* $12,333.
Athletic Department: *Director of Athletics:* Jeff Kowatch; Phone: 574-
372-5100; Fax: 574-372-5677; E-mail: kowatcjl@grace.edu. *Sports
Information Director:* Jason Knavel; Phone: 574-372-5100; E-mail:
knaveljm@grace.edu.

MEN'S COACHES
Baseball: Dennis Boyd; Phone: 574-372-5100; E-mail: doyddw@grace.
edu.
Basketball: Jim Kessler; Phone: 574-372-5100; E-mail: jckessler@grace.
edu.
Cheerleading: Brenda Worrell; Phone: 574-372-5100; E-mail: worrelbs@
grace.edu.
Cross Country: Neal Butler; Phone: 574-372-5100; E-mail: butlernr@
grace.edu.
Golf: Doug Black; Phone: 574-372-5100.
Soccer: Roy Danielson; Phone: 574-372-5100; E-mail: danielrg@grace.
edu.
Tennis: Mike Grill; Phone: 574-372-5100; E-mail: grillem@grace.edu.
Track and Field: Neal Butler; Phone: 574-372-5100; E-mail: butlernr@
grace.edu.

WOMEN'S COACHES
Basketball: Steve Carlson; Phone: 574-372-5100; E-mail: carlsost@
grace.edu.
Cheerleading: Brenda Worrell; Phone: 574-372-5100; E-mail: worrelbs@
grace.edu.
Cross Country: Neal Butler; Phone: 574-372-5100; E-mail: butlernr@
grace.edu.
Soccer: Eric Mikel; Phone: 574-372-5100; E-mail: mikelee@grace.edu.
Softball: Setphen Liebsch; Phone: 574-372-5100; E-mail: liebsch@ligtel.
com.
Tennis: Jason Knavel; Phone: 574-372-5100; E-mail: knaveljm@grace.
edu.
Track and Field: Neal Butler; Phone: 574-372-5100; E-mail: butlernr@
grace.edu.
Volleyball: Karen Peterson; Phone: 574-372-5100; E-mail: peterska@
grace.edu.

GRACELAND UNIVERSITY
Lamoni, Iowa
Yellow Jackets ◆ NAIA ◆ Heart of America Conference
◆ http://www.graceland.edu/

Independent Community of Christ comprehensive, founded 1895
Coed, 2,033 undergraduate students, 66% full-time, 66% women,
34% men
Small-town 169-acre campus with easy access to Des Moines
Moderately difficult entrance level, 57% of applicants were admitted

Freshmen *Admission:* 1,016 applied, 585 were accepted, 254 enrolled.
Test scores: SAT verbal scores over 500: 41%; SAT math scores over
500: 56%; SAT verbal scores over 600: 11%; SAT math scores over
600: 16%; SAT verbal scores over 700: 2%; SAT math scores over
700: 2%.
Tuition and fees (2003–04): $14,800 (full-time). *Room and board:* $4750
(room only: $1770).
Financial Aid (All incoming freshmen): *Average need-based gift aid:*
$11,506. *Average non-need based aid:* $9873. *Average aid to full-time
undergraduates:* $15,583.
Athletic Department: *Director of Athletics:* Dan Hanton; Phone: 641-
784-5341; Fax: 641-784-5472; E-mail: hanton@graceland.edu. *Sports
Information Director:* Amy Woodruff; Phone: 641-784-5318; E-mail:
awoodruf@graceland.edu.

MEN'S COACHES
Baseball: Brady McKillip; Phone: 641-784-5351; E-mail: bmckilli@
graceland.edu.
Basketball: Rich Harrop; Phone: 641-784-5314; E-mail: harrop@
graceland.edu.

Cross Country: Kent Allshouse; Phone: 641-784-5464; E-mail: allshous@graceland.edu.
Football: Chris Welch; Phone: 641-784-5313; E-mail: welch@graceland.edu.
Golf: Kevin Brunner; Phone: 641-784-5175; E-mail: brunner@graceland.edu.
Soccer: Ivan Joseph; Phone: 641-784-5430; E-mail: joseph@graceland.edu.
Tennis: Jerry Hampton; Phone: 641-784-5316; E-mail: hampton@graceland.edu.
Track and Field: Kent Allshouse; Phone: 641-784-5464; E-mail: allshous@graceland.edu.
Volleyball: Stu Sherman; Phone: 641-784-5317; E-mail: ssherman@graceland.edu.

WOMEN'S COACHES
Basketball: Laura Pollard; Phone: 641-784-5304; E-mail: lpollard@graceland.edu.
Cross Country: Kent Allshouse; Phone: 641-784-5464; E-mail: allshous@graceland.edu.
Golf: Kevin Brunner; Phone: 641-784-5175; E-mail: brunner@graceland.edu.
Soccer: Kevin Sherry; Phone: 641-784-5321; E-mail: sherry@graceland.edu.
Softball: Bill Dudek; Phone: 641-784-5319; E-mail: dudek@graceland.edu.
Tennis: Jerry Hampton; Phone: 641-784-5316; E-mail: hampton@graceland.edu.
Track and Field: Kent Allshouse; Phone: 641-784-5464; E-mail: allshous@graceland.edu.
Volleyball: Stew McDole; Phone: 641-784-5315; E-mail: mcdole@graceland.edu.

GRAMBLING STATE UNIVERSITY
Grambling, Louisiana

Tigers ◆ NCAA I ◆ Southwestern Athletic Conference ◆ http://www.gram.edu/

State-supported university, founded 1901, part of University of Louisiana System Board of Supervisors
Coed, 4,175 undergraduate students
Small-town 380-acre campus
Noncompetitive entrance level, 62% of applicants were admitted

Freshmen *Admission:* 2,923 applied, 1,811 were accepted.
Tuition and fees (2003–04): $3182 (resident), $8532 (nonresident). *Room and board:* $3356 (room only: $3356).
Financial Aid (All incoming freshmen): *Average need-based gift aid:* $4000. *Average non-need based aid:* $2826. *Average aid to full-time undergraduates:* $5900.
Athletic Department: *Director of Athletics:* Albert Dennis; Phone: 318-274-2625; Fax: 318-274-2608; E-mail: dennisa@gram.edu. *Sports Information Director:* Roderick Mosley; Phone: 318-274-6281.

MEN'S COACHES
Baseball: Wilbert Ellis; Phone: 318-274-6121; E-mail: ellis@gram.edu.
Basketball: Larry Wright; Phone: 318-274-6204; E-mail: @gram.edu.
Cross Country: Bertram Lovell; Phone: 318-274-6387.
Football: Doug Williams; Phone: 318-274-6539; E-mail: addwilliams@aol.com.
Golf: T. Thomas; Phone: 318-274-6082; E-mail: thomas@gram.edu.
Tennis: Philippe Carter; Phone: 318-274-2608.
Track and Field: Bertram Lovell; Phone: 318-274-6387.

WOMEN'S COACHES
Basketball: Rusty Ponton; Phone: 318-274-6335; E-mail: ponton@gram.edu.
Cross Country: Bertram Lovell; Phone: 318-274-6387.
Golf: T. Thomas; Phone: 318-274-6082; E-mail: thomas@gram.edu.
Softball: Vanessa Johnson; Phone: 318-274-6199; E-mail: johnson@gram.edu.
Tennis: T. Thomas; Phone: 318-274-6082; E-mail: thomas@gram.edu.
Track and Field: Bertram Lovell; Phone: 318-274-6387.
Volleyball: Frederick Payne; Phone: 318-274-3216; E-mail: payne@gram.edu.

GRAND CANYON UNIVERSITY
Phoenix, Arizona

Antelopes ◆ NCAA II ◆ California Collegiate Athletic Conference ◆ http://www.gcu.edu/

Independent Southern Baptist comprehensive, founded 1949
Coed, 1,609 undergraduate students, 82% full-time, 64% women, 36% men
Suburban 90-acre campus
Moderately difficult entrance level, 62% of applicants were admitted

Freshmen *Admission:* 823 applied, 567 were accepted, 371 enrolled.
Tuition and fees (2003–04): $14,500 (full-time). *Room and board:* $7130.
Financial Aid (All incoming freshmen): *Average need-based gift aid:* $2814. *Average non-need based aid:* $4633. *Average aid to full-time undergraduates:* $7818.
Athletic Department: *Director of Athletics:* John Pierson; Phone: 602-589-2834; Fax: 602-589-2529; E-mail: jpierson@grand-canyon.edu. *Sports Information Director:* Rebecca Brutlag; Phone: 602-589-2795; E-mail: rbrutlag@grand-canyon.edu.

MEN'S COACHES
Baseball: Dave Stapleton; Phone: 602-589-2817.
Basketball: Leighton McCrary; Phone: 602-589-2818.
Golf: John Pierson; Phone: 602-589-2834; E-mail: jpierson@grand-canyon.edu.
Soccer: Petar Draskin; Phone: 602-589-2835; E-mail: pdraksin@grand-canyon.edu.

WOMEN'S COACHES
Basketball: Kip Drown; Phone: 602-589-2814; E-mail: kdrown@grand-canyon.edu.
Golf: John Pierson; Phone: 602-589-2834; E-mail: jpierson@grand-canyon.edu.
Soccer: Petar Draskin; Phone: 602-589-2835; E-mail: pdraksin@grand-canyon.edu.
Softball: Ann Pedersen; Phone: 602-589-2884; E-mail: apedersen@grand-canyon.edu.
Tennis: Karla Wojcik; Phone: 602-589-2813.
Volleyball: Kris Naber; Phone: 602-589-2791; E-mail: vball@grand-canyon.edu.

GRAND VALLEY STATE UNIVERSITY
Allendale, Michigan

Lakers ◆ NCAA II ◆ Great Lakes Intercollegiate Conference ◆ http://www.gvsu.edu/

State-supported comprehensive, founded 1960
Coed, 17,807 undergraduate students, 84% full-time, 60% women, 40% men
Small-town 900-acre campus with easy access to Grand Rapids
Moderately difficult entrance level, 70% of applicants were admitted

Freshmen *Admission:* 12,145 applied, 8,861 were accepted, 3,288 enrolled.
Tuition and fees (2003–04): $5648 (resident), $12,216 (nonresident). *Room and board:* $5768.
Financial Aid (All incoming freshmen): *Average need-based gift aid:* $4225. *Average non-need based aid:* $2250. *Average aid to full-time undergraduates:* $6880.
Athletic Department: *Director of Athletics:* Tim Selgo; Phone: 616-331-8800; Fax: 616-331-3232; E-mail: selgot@gvsu.edu. *Sports Information Director:* Tim Nott; Phone: 616-331-3275; E-mail: nottt@gvsu.edu.

MEN'S COACHES
Baseball: Steve Lyon; Phone: 616-331-3584; E-mail: lyons@gvsu.edu.
Basketball: Terri Smith; Phone: 616-331-3205; E-mail: smitht@gvsu.edu.
Cheerleading: Randy Orr; Phone: 616-331-3584; E-mail: gvsucheercoachorr@gvsu.edu.
Cross Country: Jerry Baltes; Phone: 616-331-3360; E-mail: baltesj@gvsu.edu.
Football: Brian Kelly; Phone: 616-331-3178; E-mail: kellyb@gvsu.edu.

Grand Valley State University *(continued)*

Golf: Don Underwood; Phone: 616-331-1000; E-mail: underwod@gvsu.edu.

Swimming: Dewey Newsome; Phone: 616-331-3394; E-mail: newsomed@gvsu.edu.

Tennis: John Black; Phone: 616-331-3378; E-mail: blackjo@gvsu.edu.

Track and Field: Jerry Baltes; Phone: 616-331-3360; E-mail: baltesj@gvsu.edu.

WOMEN'S COACHES

Basketball: Dawn Plitzuweit; Phone: 616-331-3208; E-mail: plitzuwd@gvsu.edu.

Cheerleading: Randy Orr; Phone: 616-331-3584; E-mail: gvsucheercoachorr@gvsu.edu.

Cross Country: Jerry Baltes; Phone: 616-331-3360; E-mail: baltesj@gvsu.edu.

Golf: Lori Stinson; Phone: 616-331-3082; E-mail: stinsonl@gvsu.edu.

Soccer: David DiIanni; Phone: 616-331-3080; E-mail: diiannid@gvsu.edu.

Softball: Doug Woods; Phone: 616-331-3135; E-mail: woodsd@gvsu.edu.

Swimming: Dewey Newsome; Phone: 616-331-3394; E-mail: newsomed@gvsu.edu.

Tennis: John Black; Phone: 616-331-3378; E-mail: blackjo@gvsu.edu.

Track and Field: Jerry Baltes; Phone: 616-331-3360; E-mail: baltesj@gvsu.edu.

Volleyball: Deanne Scanlon; Phone: 616-331-3339; E-mail: scanlond@gvsu.edu.

GRAND VIEW COLLEGE
Des Moines, Iowa

Vikings ◆ NAIA ◆ Midwest Classic Conference ◆ http://www.gvc.edu/

Independent religious 4-year, founded 1896, affiliated with Evangelical Lutheran Church in America
Coed, 1,630 undergraduate students, 73% full-time, 70% women, 30% men
Urban 25-acre campus
Minimally difficult entrance level, 92% of applicants were admitted

Freshmen *Admission:* 438 applied, 414 were accepted, 167 enrolled. *Test scores:* SAT verbal scores over 500: 67%; SAT math scores over 500: 67%; SAT verbal scores over 600: 34%; SAT math scores over 600: 34%.
Tuition and fees (2003–04): $14,740 (full-time). *Room and board:* $5232.
Financial Aid (All incoming freshmen): *Average need-based gift aid:* $9605. *Average non-need based aid:* $9116. *Average aid to full-time undergraduates:* $12,706.
Athletic Department: *Director of Athletics:* Lou Yacinich; Phone: 515-263-2897; Fax: 515-263-2882; E-mail: lyacininch@gvc.edu. *Sports Information Director:* Andy Hamilton; Phone: 515-263-6040; E-mail: ahamilton@gvc.edu.

MEN'S COACHES

Baseball: Lou Yacinich; Phone: 515-263-2897; E-mail: lyacinich@gvc.edu.

Basketball: Denis Schaefer; Phone: 515-263-2896; E-mail: dschaefer@gvc.edu.

Cheerleading: Staci Horton; Phone: 515-263-6047; E-mail: shorton@gvc.edu.

Cross Country: Patrick McDermott; Phone: 515-263-6048; E-mail: pmcdermott@gvc.edu.

Soccer: Blair Reid; Phone: 515-263-2964; E-mail: breid@gvc.edu.

WOMEN'S COACHES

Basketball: Garey Smith; Phone: 515-263-2944; E-mail: gsmith@gvc.edu.

Cheerleading: Staci Horton; Phone: 515-263-6047; E-mail: shorton@gvc.edu.

Cross Country: Patrick McDermott; Phone: 515-263-6048; E-mail: pmcdermott@gvc.edu.

Soccer: Ventsi Stoimirov; Phone: 515-263-6159; E-mail: vstoimirov@gvc.edu.

Softball: Lewis Yancinich Jr.; Phone: 515-263-2965; E-mail: layacinich@gvc.edu.

Volleyball: LeAnn Stefani; Phone: 515-263-2898; E-mail: lstefani@gvc.edu.

GREEN MOUNTAIN COLLEGE
Poultney, Vermont

Eagles ◆ NCAA II ◆ Independent
◆ http://www.greenmtn.edu/

Independent religious 4-year, founded 1834, affiliated with United Methodist Church
Coed, 661 undergraduate students, 95% full-time, 47% women, 53% men
Small-town 155-acre campus
Moderately difficult entrance level, 80% of applicants were admitted

Freshmen *Admission:* 718 applied, 574 were accepted, 182 enrolled. *Test scores:* SAT verbal scores over 500: 49%; SAT math scores over 500: 44%; SAT verbal scores over 600: 17%; SAT math scores over 600: 10%; SAT verbal scores over 700: 2%.
Tuition and fees (2003–04): $20,290 (full-time). *Room and board:* $6300.
Financial Aid (All incoming freshmen): *Average need-based gift aid:* $8413. *Average non-need based aid:* $9101. *Average aid to full-time undergraduates:* $10,983.
Athletic Department: *Director of Athletics:* Chris Gilmore; Phone: 802-287-8238; Fax: 802-287-8099; E-mail: athletic@greenmtn.edu. *Sports Information Director:* Carol Denniston; Phone: 802-287-8378; E-mail: dennistonc@greenmtn.edu.

MEN'S COACHES

Basketball: Jim Graffam; Phone: 802-287-8242; E-mail: graffamj@greenmtn.edu.

Golf: Mike Porrier; Phone: 802-287-8238; E-mail: porrierm@greenmtn.edu.

Lacrosse: William Lowe; Phone: 802-287-8366.

Soccer: Chris Gilmore; Phone: 802-287-8238; E-mail: athletic@greenmtn.edu.

Tennis: Rob Purdy; Phone: 802-287-8238; E-mail: sports@greenmtn.edu.

WOMEN'S COACHES

Basketball: Megan Chawansky; Phone: 802-287-8292; E-mail: chawanskym@greenmtn.edu.

Golf: Mike Porrier; Phone: 802-287-8238; E-mail: porrierm@greenmtn.edu.

Soccer: Rick Stainton; Phone: 802-287-8238.

Softball: Jen Heath; Phone: 802-287-8238; E-mail: daviesb@greenmtn.edu.

Tennis: Rob Purdy; Phone: 802-287-8238; E-mail: sports@greenmtn.edu.

Volleyball: Kip Dalury; Phone: 802-287-8238.

GREENSBORO COLLEGE
Greensboro, North Carolina

Pride ◆ NCAA III ◆ USA·South Athletic Conference ◆ http://www.gborocollege.edu/

Independent United Methodist comprehensive, founded 1838
Coed, 1,176 undergraduate students, 75% full-time, 56% women, 44% men
Urban 75-acre campus with easy access to Charlotte
Moderately difficult entrance level, 70% of applicants were admitted

Freshmen *Admission:* 875 applied, 648 were accepted, 229 enrolled. *Test scores:* SAT verbal scores over 500: 43%; SAT math scores over 500: 45%; SAT verbal scores over 600: 10%; SAT math scores over 600: 9%; SAT verbal scores over 700: 2%.
Tuition and fees (2003–04): $15,720 (full-time). *Room and board:* $6030.
Financial Aid (All incoming freshmen): *Average need-based gift aid:* $4240. *Average non-need based aid:* $3830. *Average aid to full-time undergraduates:* $11,555.
Athletic Department: *Director of Athletics:* Kim Strable; Phone: 336-272-7102; Fax: 336-217-7237; E-mail: strablek@gborocollege.edu. *Sports Information Director:* Bob Lowe; Phone: 336-272-7102; E-mail: blowe@gborocollege.edu.

MEN'S COACHES

Baseball: Ken Carlyle; Phone: 336-272-7102; E-mail: kcarlyle@gborocollege.edu.

Basketball: Lynn Ramage; Phone: 336-272-7102; E-mail: lramage@gborocollege.edu.
Cheerleading: Wanda Lane-Illescas; Phone: 336-272-7102; E-mail: willescas@gborocollege.edu.
Cross Country: Jason Tuggle; Phone: 336-272-7102; E-mail: jtuggle@gborocollege.edu.
Football: Neal Mitchell; Phone: 336-272-7102; E-mail: nmitchell@gborocollege.edu.
Golf: Robert Linville; Phone: 336-272-7102; E-mail: linviller@gborocollege.edu.
Lacrosse: Dan Cetrone; Phone: 336-272-7102; E-mail: dcetrone@gborocollege.edu.
Soccer: Rusty Scarborough; Phone: 336-272-7102; E-mail: rscarborough@gborocollege.edu.
Tennis: Pat Williams; Phone: 336-272-7102; E-mail: pwilliams@gborocollege.edu.

WOMEN'S COACHES
Basketball: Jason Tuggle; Phone: 336-272-7102; E-mail: jtuggle@gborocollege.edu.
Cheerleading: Wanda Lane-Illescas; Phone: 336-272-7102; E-mail: willescas@gborocollege.edu.
Cross Country: Jason Tuggle; Phone: 336-272-7102; E-mail: jtuggle@gborocollege.edu.
Lacrosse: Gregg Gebhard; Phone: 336-282-5141; E-mail: ggebhard@gborocollege.edu.
Soccer: Doug Shank; Phone: 336-272-7102; E-mail: dshank@gborocollege.edu.
Softball: Kama Tucker; Phone: 336-272-7102; E-mail: tuckerk@gborocollege.edu.
Swimming: Kevin Thornton; Phone: 336-272-7102; E-mail: kthornton@gborocollege.edu.
Tennis: Pat Williams; Phone: 336-272-7102; E-mail: pwilliams@gborocollege.edu.
Volleyball: Jean Lojko; Phone: 336-272-7102; E-mail: lojkoj@gborocollege.edu.

GREENVILLE COLLEGE
Greenville, Illinois

Panthers ◆ NCAA III ◆ Illini-Badger Football Conference; St. Louis Athletic Conference ◆ http://www.greenville.edu/

Independent Free Methodist comprehensive, founded 1892
Coed, 1,188 undergraduate students, 95% full-time, 52% women, 48% men
Small-town 12-acre campus with easy access to St. Louis
Moderately difficult entrance level, 94% of applicants were admitted

Freshmen *Admission:* 697 applied, 665 were accepted, 263 enrolled. *Test scores:* SAT verbal scores over 500: 70%; SAT math scores over 500: 67%; SAT verbal scores over 600: 27%; SAT math scores over 600: 22%; SAT verbal scores over 700: 3%.
Tuition and fees (2003–04): $15,776 (full-time). *Room and board:* $5566 (room only: $2634).
Financial Aid (All incoming freshmen): *Average need-based gift aid:* $9739. *Average non-need based aid:* $8334. *Average aid to full-time under-graduates:* $12,863.
Athletic Department: *Director of Athletics:* Douglas Faulkner; Phone: 618-664-6620; Fax: 618-664-1060; E-mail: dfaulkner@greenville.edu. *Sports Information Director:* B.J. Schneck; Phone: 618-664-6621; E-mail: wschneck@greenville.edu.

MEN'S COACHES
Baseball: Lynn Carlson; Phone: 618-664-6623; E-mail: lcarlson@greenville.edu.
Basketball: George Barber; Phone: 618-664-6624; E-mail: gbarber@greenville.edu.
Cross Country: Brian Patton; Phone: 618-664-6627; E-mail: bpatton@greenville.edu.
Football: Scott Kessler; Phone: 618-664-6726; E-mail: scotty.kessler@greenville.edu.
Soccer: Brian McMahon; Phone: 618-664-6637; E-mail: bmcmahon@greenville.edu.
Tennis: Brett Brannon; Phone: 618-664-7103; E-mail: bbrannon@greenville.edu.
Track and Field: Brian Patton; Phone: 618-664-6627; E-mail: bpatton@greenville.edu.

WOMEN'S COACHES
Basketball: Roy Mulholland; Phone: 618-664-6625; E-mail: romulholland@greenville.edu.
Cross Country: Brian Patton; Phone: 618-664-6627; E-mail: bpatton@greenville.edu.
Soccer: Brian McMahon; Phone: 618-664-6637; E-mail: bmcmahon@greenville.edu.
Softball: Brian Reinhard; Phone: 618-664-6835; E-mail: breinhard@greenville.edu.
Tennis: Pam Craig; Phone: 618-664-6639; E-mail: pcraig@greenville.edu.
Track and Field: Brian Patton; Phone: 618-664-6627; E-mail: bpatton@greenville.edu.
Volleyball: Tom Ackerman; Phone: 618-537-3748; E-mail: crossroadsvb9@yahoo.com.

GRINNELL COLLEGE
Grinnell, Iowa

Pioneers ◆ NCAA III ◆ Midwest Conference ◆ http://www.grinnell.edu/

Independent 4-year, founded 1846
Coed, 1,524 undergraduate students, 97% full-time, 55% women, 45% men
Small-town 120-acre campus
Very difficult entrance level, 6% of applicants were admitted

Freshmen *Admission:* 2,284 applied, 1,443 were accepted, 404 enrolled. *Test scores:* SAT verbal scores over 500: 95%; SAT math scores over 500: 97%; SAT verbal scores over 600: 82%; SAT math scores over 600: 85%; SAT verbal scores over 700: 42%; SAT math scores over 700: 43%.
Tuition and fees (2003–04): $24,490 (full-time). *Room and board:* $6570 (room only: $3080).
Financial Aid (All incoming freshmen): *Average need-based gift aid:* $15,876. *Average non-need based aid:* $10,370. *Average aid to full-time undergraduates:* $19,662.
Athletic Department: *Director of Athletics:* Dee Fairchild; Phone: 641-269-3800; Fax: 641-269-3818; E-mail: fairchi@grinnell.edu. *Sports Information Director:* Jenny Wood; Phone: 641-269-3675; E-mail: wood@grinnell.edu.

MEN'S COACHES
Baseball: Tim Hollibaugh; Phone: 641-269-3822; E-mail: hollibau@grinnell.edu.
Basketball: David Arseneault; Phone: 641-269-3830; E-mail: arseneau@grinnell.edu.
Cross Country: Will Freeman; Phone: 641-269-3812; E-mail: freemanw@grinnell.edu.
Diving: Kelly Rose; Phone: 641-269-4848.
Football: Greg Wallace; Phone: 641-269-4219; E-mail: wallaceg@grinnell.edu.
Golf: Greg Wallace; Phone: 641-269-4219; E-mail: wallaceg@grinnell.edu.
Soccer: Jenny Wood; Phone: 641-269-3820; E-mail: wood@grinnell.edu.
Swimming: Erin Hurley; Phone: 641-269-4848; E-mail: hurley@grinnell.edu.
Tennis: Andy Hamilton; Phone: 641-269-3822; E-mail: hamiltoa@grinnell.edu.
Track and Field: Will Freeman; Phone: 641-269-3812; E-mail: freemanw@grinnell.edu.

WOMEN'S COACHES
Basketball: Andy Hamilton; Phone: 641-269-3832; E-mail: hamiltoa@grinnell.edu.
Cross Country: Evelyn Freeman; Phone: 641-269-3810; E-mail: freemane@grinnell.edu.
Diving: Kelly Rose; Phone: 641-269-4848.
Golf: David Arsenault; Phone: 641-269-3830; E-mail: arseneau@grinnell.edu.
Soccer: Heather Benning; Phone: 641-269-4971; E-mail: benning@grinnell.edu.
Softball: Tom Sonnichsen; Phone: 641-269-3814; E-mail: sonnichs@grinnell.edu.
Swimming: Erin Hurley; Phone: 641-269-4848; E-mail: hurley@grinnell.edu.

Grinnell College *(continued)*

Tennis: Barb Waite; Phone: 641-269-3828; E-mail: waiteb@grinnell.edu.

Track and Field: Evelyn Freeman; Phone: 641-269-3810; E-mail: freemane@grinnell.edu.

Volleyball: Tom Sonnichsen; Phone: 641-269-3814; E-mail: sonnichs@grinnell.edu.

GROVE CITY COLLEGE
Grove City, Pennsylvania

Wolverines ◆ NCAA III ◆ Presidents' Athletic Conference ◆ http://www.gcc.edu/

Independent Presbyterian 4-year, founded 1876
Coed, 2,314 undergraduate students, 98% full-time, 50% women, 50% men
Small-town 150-acre campus with easy access to Pittsburgh
Most difficult entrance level, 5% of applicants were admitted

Freshmen *Admission:* 2,199 applied, 893 were accepted, 567 enrolled. *Test scores:* SAT verbal scores over 500: 97%; SAT math scores over 500: 97%; SAT verbal scores over 600: 72%; SAT math scores over 600: 72%; SAT verbal scores over 700: 18%; SAT math scores over 700: 21%.
Tuition and fees (2003–04): $9526 (full-time). *Room and board:* $4852.
Financial Aid (All incoming freshmen): *Average need-based gift aid:* $5014. *Average non-need based aid:* $2537. *Average aid to full-time undergraduates:* $4947.
Athletic Department: *Director of Athletics:* Don Lyle; Phone: 724-458-2122; Fax: 724-458-3855; E-mail: dllyle@gcc.edu. *Sports Information Director:* Ryan Briggs; Phone: 724-458-3365; E-mail: rabriggs@gcc.edu.

MEN'S COACHES
Baseball: Rob Skaricich; Phone: 724-458-3836; E-mail: rwskaricich@gcc.edu.
Basketball: Steve Lamie; Phone: 724-458-3866; E-mail: sslamie@gcc.edu.
Cross Country: Tim Rice; Phone: 724-458-2123; E-mail: thrice@gcc.edu.
Diving: Dave Fritz; Phone: 724-458-2110; E-mail: dcfritz@gcc.edu.
Football: Chris Smith; Phone: 724-458-2126; E-mail: cwsmith@gcc.edu.
Golf: Chris Smith; Phone: 724-458-2126; E-mail: cwsmith@gcc.edu.
Soccer: Donald Lyle; Phone: 724-458-2122; E-mail: dllyle@gcc.edu.
Swimming: Dave Fritz; Phone: 724-458-2110; E-mail: dcfritz@gcc.edu.
Tennis: Joe Walters; Phone: 724-458-2125; E-mail: jdwalters@gcc.edu.
Track and Field: Jim Chinn; Phone: 724-458-2900; E-mail: jhchinn@gcc.edu.

WOMEN'S COACHES
Cross Country: Tim Rice; Phone: 724-458-0212; E-mail: thrice@gcc.edu.
Diving: Cathy Jacobs; Phone: 724-458-2138; E-mail: cejacobs@gcc.edu.
Golf: Chris Smith; Phone: 724-458-2126; E-mail: cwsmith@gcc.edu.
Soccer: Melissa Lamie; Phone: 724-458-2128; E-mail: mdlamie@gcc.edu.
Softball: Michelle Santom; Phone: 724-458-2130; E-mail: mssantom@gcc.edu.
Swimming: Cathy Jacobs; Phone: 724-458-2138; E-mail: cejacobs@gcc.edu.
Tennis: Cathy Jacobs; Phone: 724-458-2138; E-mail: cejacobs@gcc.edu.
Track and Field: Allison Williams; Phone: 724-458-3863; E-mail: mawilliams@gcc.edu.
Volleyball: Susan Roberts; Phone: 724-458-2129; E-mail: skroberts@gcc.edu.

GUILFORD COLLEGE
Greensboro, North Carolina

Quakers ◆ NCAA III ◆ Old Dominion Conference ◆ http://www.guilford.edu/

Independent religious 4-year, founded 1837, affiliated with Society of Friends
Coed, 2,101 undergraduate students, 83% full-time, 61% women, 39% men
Suburban 340-acre campus
Moderately difficult entrance level, 65% of applicants were admitted

Freshmen *Admission:* 1,647 applied, 1,137 were accepted, 334 enrolled. *Test scores:* SAT verbal scores over 500: 81%; SAT math scores over 500: 79%; SAT verbal scores over 600: 44%; SAT math scores over 600: 35%; SAT verbal scores over 700: 13%; SAT math scores over 700: 5%.
Financial Aid (All incoming freshmen): *Average need-based gift aid:* $13,555. *Average non-need based aid:* $6061. *Average aid to full-time undergraduates:* $18,318.
Athletic Department: *Director of Athletics:* Marion Kirby; Phone: 336-316-2190; Fax: 336-316-2953; E-mail: mkirby@guilford.edu. *Sports Information Director:* Dave Walters; Phone: 336-316-2107; E-mail: dwalters@guilford.edu.

MEN'S COACHES
Baseball: Gene Baker; Phone: 336-316-2161; E-mail: gbaker@guilford.edu.
Basketball: Tom Palombo; Phone: 316-2290; E-mail: tpalombo@guilford.edu.
Football: Micke Ketchum; Phone: 316-2159; E-mail: mketchum@guilford.edu.
Golf: Jack Jenson; Phone: 316-2157; E-mail: jjensen@guilford.edu.
Lacrosse: John Burke; Phone: 316-2106; E-mail: jburke@guilford.edu.
Soccer: Liam Beherns; Phone: 316-2343; E-mail: liam.behrens@ymcagreensboro.org.

WOMEN'S COACHES
Basketball: Stephanie Flamini; Phone: 316-2344; E-mail: sflamini@guilford.edu.
Lacrosse: Tara Caminiti-Raggett; Phone: 316-2197; E-mail: tcaminit@guilford.edu.
Soccer: Eric Lewis; Phone: 316-2375; E-mail: tcaminit@guilford.edu.
Softball: Ty Cook; Phone: 316-2247; E-mail: tlc32420@aol.com.
Tennis: Jenni Wolos; Phone: 316-2167; E-mail: jwolos@guilford.edu.
Volleyball: Glenda Dellinger; Phone: 316-2189; E-mail: gparrish@guilford.edu.

GUSTAVUS ADOLPHUS COLLEGE
St. Peter, Minnesota

Gusties ◆ NCAA III ◆ Minnesota Intercollegiate Athletic Conference ◆ http://www.gustavus.edu/

Independent religious 4-year, founded 1862, affiliated with Evangelical Lutheran Church in America
Coed, 2,574 undergraduate students, 98% full-time, 57% women, 43% men
Small-town 330-acre campus with easy access to Minneapolis–St. Paul
Very difficult entrance level, 76% of applicants were admitted

Freshmen *Admission:* 2,317 applied, 1,790 were accepted, 688 enrolled. *Test scores:* SAT verbal scores over 500: 90%; SAT math scores over 500: 94%; SAT verbal scores over 600: 58%; SAT math scores over 600: 63%; SAT verbal scores over 700: 17%; SAT math scores over 700: 14%.
Tuition and fees (2003–04): $21,660 (full-time). *Room and board:* $5460 (room only: $3060).
Financial Aid (All incoming freshmen): *Average need-based gift aid:* $11,430. *Average non-need based aid:* $6386. *Average aid to full-time undergraduates:* $15,604.
Athletic Department: *Director of Athletics:* Al Molde; Phone: 507-933-7622; Fax: 507-933-8412; E-mail: almolde@gustavus.edu. *Sports Information Director:* Tim Kennedy; Phone: 507-933-7647; E-mail: timgasid@gustavus.edu.

MEN'S COACHES
Baseball: Mike Carroll; Phone: 507-933-6297; E-mail: mcarroll@gustavus.edu.
Basketball: Mark Hanson; Phone: 507-933-7037; E-mail: mjh44@gustavus.edu.
Cross Country: Scott Jerome; Phone: 507-933-7632; E-mail: sjerome@gustavus.edu.
Diving: Jon Carlson; Phone: 507-933-7694; E-mail: carlson@gustavus.edu.
Football: Jay Schoenbeck; Phone: 507-933-7611; E-mail: jts@gustavus.edu.
Golf: Scott Moe; Phone: 507-933-7610; E-mail: smoe@gustavus.edu.
Ice Hockey: Brett Peterson; Phone: 507-933-7615; E-mail: bpeters4@gustavus.edu.
Soccer: Larry Zelenz; Phone: 507-933-7699; E-mail: lzelenz@gustavus.edu.
Swimming: Jon Carlson; Phone: 507-933-7694; E-mail: carlson@gustavus.edu.
Tennis: Steve Wilkinson; Phone: 507-933-1614; E-mail: swilkins@gustavus.edu.
Track and Field: Tom Thorkelson; Phone: 507-933-7657; E-mail: tork@gustavus.edu.

WOMEN'S COACHES
Basketball: Mickey Haller; Phone: 507-933-6145; E-mail: mhaller@gustavus.edu.
Cross Country: Scott Jerome; Phone: 507-933-7632; E-mail: sjerome@gustavus.edu.
Diving: Jon Carlson; Phone: 507-933-7694; E-mail: carlson@gustavus.edu.
Golf: Wayne Norman; Phone: 507-933-7620; E-mail: wnorman@gustavus.edu.
Gymnastics: Kris Glidden; Phone: 507-933-6409; E-mail: kglidden@gac.edu.
Soccer: Larry Zelenz; Phone: 507-933-7619; E-mail: lzelenz@gustavus.edu.
Softball: Shanda Ness; Phone: 507-933-6417; E-mail: sness@gustavus.edu.
Swimming: Jon Carlson; Phone: 507-933-7694; E-mail: carlson@gustavus.edu.
Tennis: Jon Carlson; Phone: 507-933-7694; E-mail: carlson@gustavus.edu.
Track and Field: Tom Thorkelson; Phone: 507-933-7657; E-mail: tork@gustavus.edu.
Volleyball: Kari Eckheart; Phone: 507-933-6416; E-mail: keckhear@gustavus.edu.

GWYNEDD-MERCY COLLEGE
Gwynedd Valley, Pennsylvania

Griffins ◆ NCAA III ◆ Pennsylvania Athletic Conference ◆ http://www.gmc.edu/

Independent Roman Catholic comprehensive, founded 1948
Coed, 2,177 undergraduate students, 56% full-time, 77% women, 23% men
Suburban 170-acre campus with easy access to Philadelphia
Moderately difficult entrance level, 6% of applicants were admitted

Freshmen *Admission:* 1,679 applied, 972 were accepted, 247 enrolled. *Test scores:* SAT verbal scores over 500: 45%; SAT math scores over 500: 42%; SAT verbal scores over 600: 7%; SAT math scores over 600: 7%; SAT verbal scores over 700: 1%.
Tuition and fees (2003–04): $16,700 (full-time). *Room and board:* $7300.
Financial Aid (All incoming freshmen): *Average need-based gift aid:* $11,660. *Average non-need based aid:* $6585. *Average aid to full-time undergraduates:* $14,942.
Athletic Department: *Director of Athletics:* Keith Mondillo; Phone: 215-641-5574; Fax: 215-542-4683; E-mail: mondillo.k@gmc.edu. *Sports Information Director:* Paul Murphy; Phone: 215-641-7300; E-mail: murphy.p@gmc.edu.

MEN'S COACHES
Baseball: Paul Murphy; Phone: 215-646-7300; E-mail: murphy.p@gmc.edu.
Basketball: John Baron; Phone: 215-646-7300; E-mail: baron.j@gmc.edu.
Cross Country: Phone: 215-646-7300.

Golf: Russ Jones; Phone: 215-646-7300; E-mail: jones.r@gmc.edu.
Soccer: Dave Bontempo; Phone: 215-646-7300; E-mail: bontempo.d@gmc.edu.
Tennis: Jim Holt; Phone: 215-646-7300; E-mail: holt.j@gmc.edu.
Track and Field: Bill Neely; Phone: 215-646-7300; E-mail: neely.b@gmc.edu.

WOMEN'S COACHES
Basketball: Keith Mondillo; Phone: 215-641-5574; E-mail: mondillo.k@gmc.edu.
Cross Country: Phone: 215-646-7300.
Field Hockey: Sarah Wesner; Phone: 215-646-7300; E-mail: wesner.s@gmc.edu.
Golf: Russ Jones; Phone: 215-646-7300; E-mail: jones.r@gmc.edu.
Lacrosse: Sarah Quintois; Phone: 215-641-5533; E-mail: quintois.s@gmc.edu.
Soccer: Jason Neumann; Phone: 215-646-7300; E-mail: neumann.j@gmc.edu.
Softball: Ray Perri; Phone: 215-646-7300; E-mail: perri.r@gmc.edu.
Track and Field: Bill Neely; Phone: 215-646-7300; E-mail: neely.b@gmc.edu.
Volleyball: Sondra Stoczllo; Phone: 215-646-7300; E-mail: sstoczko@aol.com.

HAMILTON COLLEGE
Clinton, New York

Continentals ◆ NCAA III ◆ New York Collegiate Athletic Conference; Upstate Collegiate Athletic Conference ◆ http://www.hamilton.edu/

Independent 4-year, founded 1812
Coed, 1,797 undergraduate students, 99% full-time, 51% women, 49% men
Small-town 1,200-acre campus
Very difficult entrance level, 3% of applicants were admitted

Freshmen *Admission:* 4,405 applied, 1,457 were accepted, 467 enrolled. *Test scores:* SAT verbal scores over 500: 97%; SAT math scores over 500: 97%; SAT verbal scores over 600: 80%; SAT math scores over 600: 88%; SAT verbal scores over 700: 30%; SAT math scores over 700: 28%.
Tuition and fees (2003–04): $30,200 (full-time). *Room and board:* $7360 (room only: $3800).
Financial Aid (All incoming freshmen): *Average need-based gift aid:* $20,610. *Average non-need based aid:* $10,234. *Average aid to full-time undergraduates:* $22,861.
Athletic Department: *Director of Athletics:* Dave Thompson; Phone: 315-859-4754; Fax: 315-859-4117; E-mail: dthompso@hamilton.edu. *Sports Information Director:* Jim Taylor; Phone: 315-859-4685; E-mail: jtaylor@hamilton.edu.

MEN'S COACHES
Baseball: John Keady; Phone: 315-859-4763; E-mail: jkeady@hamilton.edu.
Basketball: Tom Murphy; Phone: 315-859-4750; E-mail: tmurphy@hamilton.edu.
Cross Country: Brett Hull; Phone: 315-859-4759; E-mail: bhull@hamilton.edu.
Diving: Andrew Hastings; Phone: 315-859-4794.
Football: Pete Alvanos; Phone: 315-859-4757; E-mail: palvanos@hamilton.edu.
Golf: Al Highducheck; Phone: 315-859-4114.
Ice Hockey: Phil Grady; Phone: 315-859-4762; E-mail: pgrady@hamilton.edu.
Lacrosse: Gene McCabe; Phone: 315-859-4531.
Soccer: Perry Nizzi; Phone: 315-859-4756; E-mail: pnizzi@hamilton.edu.
Swimming: T.J. Davis; Phone: 315-859-4794; E-mail: tjdavis@hamilton.edu.
Tennis: Jamie King; Phone: 315-859-4758; E-mail: jking@hamilton.edu.
Track and Field: Brett Hull; Phone: 315-859-4759; E-mail: bhull@hamilton.edu.

WOMEN'S COACHES
Basketball: Julie Diehl; Phone: 315-859-4817; E-mail: jdiehl@hamilton.edu.
Cross Country: Ellen Hull; Phone: 315-859-4759; E-mail: ehull@hamilton.edu.

Hamilton College *(continued)*

Diving: Andrew Hastings; Phone: 315-859-4794.
Field Hockey: Tracy Kelleher; Phone: 315-859-4760.
Lacrosse: Patty Kloidt; Phone: 315-859-4755; E-mail: pkloidt@hamilton.edu.
Soccer: Colette Gilligan; Phone: 315-859-4643; E-mail: cgilliga@hamilton.edu.
Softball: Susan Keller; Phone: 315-859-4806; E-mail: sekeller@hamilton.edu.
Swimming: T.J. Davis; Phone: 315-859-4794; E-mail: tjdavis@hamilton.edu.
Tennis: Jamie King; Phone: 315-859-4758; E-mail: jking@hamilton.edu.
Track and Field: Ellen Hull; Phone: 315-859-4759; E-mail: ehull@hamilton.edu.
Volleyball: Susan Keller; Phone: 315-859-4806; E-mail: sekeller@hamilton.edu.

HAMLINE UNIVERSITY
St. Paul, Minnesota

Pipers ◆ NCAA III ◆ Minnesota Intercollegiate Athletic Conference ◆ http://www.hamline.edu/

Independent religious comprehensive, founded 1854, affiliated with United Methodist Church
Coed, 1,980 undergraduate students, 95% full-time, 63% women, 37% men
Urban 50-acre campus
Moderately difficult entrance level, 7% of applicants were admitted

Freshmen *Admission:* 1,815 applied, 1,353 were accepted, 455 enrolled. *Test scores:* SAT verbal scores over 500: 84%; SAT math scores over 500: 85%; SAT verbal scores over 600: 53%; SAT math scores over 600: 42%; SAT verbal scores over 700: 14%; SAT math scores over 700: 8%.
Tuition and fees (2003–04): $20,832 (full-time). *Room and board:* $6220 (room only: $3208).
Financial Aid (All incoming freshmen): *Average need-based gift aid:* $7334. *Average non-need based aid:* $14,665. *Average aid to full-time undergraduates:* $21,930.
Athletic Department: *Director of Athletics:* Dan O'Brien; Phone: 651-523-3075; E-mail: dobrien@gw.hamline.edu. *Sports Information Director:* Troy Mallat; Phone: 651-523-2786; E-mail: tmallat01@gw.hamline.edu.

MEN'S COACHES
Baseball: Jason Verdugo; Phone: 651-523-2035; E-mail: jverdugo@gw.hamline.edu.
Basketball: Tom Gilles; Phone: 651-523-2242; E-mail: tgilles@gw.hamline.edu.
Cross Country: Paul Schmaedeke; Phone: 651-523-2319; E-mail: pschmaedeke@gw.hamline.edu.
Diving: John Karpe; Phone: 651-523-2275.
Football: Donovon Larson; Phone: 651-523-2595; E-mail: dllarson@gw.hamline.edu.
Ice Hockey: Pat Cullen; Phone: 651-523-2243; E-mail: pcullen@gw.hamline.edu.
Soccer: Andy Coutts; Phone: 651-523-2036; E-mail: acoutts@gw.hamline.edu.
Swimming: Andy Hanson; Phone: 651-523-2275; E-mail: ahanson01@gw.hamline.edu.
Tennis: Dan Haertl; Phone: 651-523-2310; E-mail: dhaertl@gw.hamline.edu.
Track and Field: Paul Schmaedeke; Phone: 651-523-2319; E-mail: pschmaedeke@gw.hamline.edu.

WOMEN'S COACHES
Basketball: Lisa Parsons; Phone: 651-523-2310; E-mail: lparsons@gw.hamline.edu.
Cross Country: Toby Hatlevig; Phone: 651-523-2033; E-mail: thatlevig@gw.hamline.edu.
Diving: John Karpe; Phone: 651-523-2275.
Soccer: Tony Englund; Phone: 651-523-2045; E-mail: aenglundiii01@gw.hamline.edu.
Softball: Janelle Tieken; Phone: 651-523-2304; E-mail: jtieken@gw.hamline.edu.

Swimming: Andy Hanson; Phone: 651-523-2275; E-mail: ahanson01@gw.hamline.edu.
Tennis: Dan Haertl; Phone: 651-523-2310; E-mail: dhaertl@gw.hamline.edu.
Track and Field: Paul Schmaedeke; Phone: 651-523-2372; E-mail: pschmaedeke@gw.hamline.edu.
Volleyball: Gina Rollie; Phone: 651-523-2331; E-mail: grollie01@gw.hamline.edu.

HAMPDEN-SYDNEY COLLEGE
Hampden-Sydney, Virginia

Tigers ◆ NCAA III ◆ Old Dominion Conference ◆ http://www.hsc.edu/

Independent religious 4-year, founded 1776, affiliated with Presbyterian Church (U.S.A.)
Men only, 1,039 undergraduate students, 99% full-time, 99% women, 100% men
Rural 660-acre campus with easy access to Richmond
Moderately difficult entrance level, 71% of applicants were admitted

Freshmen *Admission:* 1,156 applied, 825 were accepted, 306 enrolled. *Test scores:* SAT verbal scores over 500: 80%; SAT math scores over 500: 85%; SAT verbal scores over 600: 34%; SAT math scores over 600: 35%; SAT verbal scores over 700: 7%; SAT math scores over 700: 3%.
Tuition and fees (2003–04): $21,387 (full-time). *Room and board:* $7020 (room only: $2968).
Financial Aid (All incoming freshmen): *Average need-based gift aid:* $13,201. *Average non-need based aid:* $18,554. *Average aid to full-time undergraduates:* $15,481.
Athletic Department: *Director of Athletics:* Joe Bush; Phone: 434-223-6153; Fax: 434-223-6348; E-mail: jbush@hsc.edu. *Sports Information Director:* Donnie Turlington; Phone: 434-223-6156; E-mail: dturlington@hsc.edu.

MEN'S COACHES
Baseball: Jeff Kinne; Phone: 434-223-6981; E-mail: jkinne@hsc.edu.
Basketball: Bubba Smith; Phone: 434-223-6160; E-mail: rsmith@hsc.edu.
Cross Country: Chad Warner; Phone: 434-223-6280; E-mail: cwarner@hsc.edu.
Football: Marty Favret; Phone: 434-223-6256; E-mail: mfavret@hsc.edu.
Golf: Joe Bush; Phone: 434-223-6153; E-mail: jbush@hsc.edu.
Lacrosse: Ray Rostan; Phone: 434-223-6158; E-mail: rrostan@hsc.edu.
Soccer: Bert Molinary; Phone: 434-223-6290; E-mail: bmolinary@hsc.edu.
Tennis: Bert Molinary; Phone: 434-223-6290; E-mail: bmolinary@hsc.edu.

HAMPTON UNIVERSITY
Hampton, Virginia

Pirates ◆ NCAA I ◆ Mid-Eastern Atlantic Conference ◆ http://www.hamptonu.edu/

Independent university, founded 1868
Coed, 4,979 undergraduate students, 90% full-time, 61% women, 39% men
Urban 210-acre campus with easy access to Norfolk
Moderately difficult entrance level, 63% of applicants were admitted

Freshmen *Admission:* 5,696 applied, 3,505 were accepted, 1,050 enrolled. *Test scores:* SAT verbal scores over 500: 66%; SAT math scores over 500: 53%; SAT verbal scores over 600: 19%; SAT math scores over 600: 7%; SAT verbal scores over 700: 1%; SAT math scores over 700: 1%.
Tuition and fees (2003–04): $12,864 (full-time). *Room and board:* $6118.
Financial Aid (All incoming freshmen): *Average need-based gift aid:* $1343. *Average non-need based aid:* $2419. *Average aid to full-time undergraduates:* $3166.

Athletic Department: *Director of Athletics:* Malcolm Avery; Phone: 757-727-5641; Fax: 757-728-6995; E-mail: malcolm.avery@hamptonu.edu. *Sports Information Director:* Jamar Ross; Phone: 757-727-5727; E-mail: jamar.ross@hamptonu.edu.

MEN'S COACHES

Basketball: Bobby Collins; Phone: 757-727-6818; E-mail: bobby.collins@hamptonu.edu.
Cheerleading: Melonne Watkins; Phone: 757-727-5273; E-mail: edwina.simmons@hamptonu.edu.
Cross Country: David Boyd; Phone: 757-727-5721; E-mail: david.boyd@hamptonu.edu.
Football: Joe Taylor; Phone: 757-727-5322; E-mail: joseph.taylor@hamptonu.edu.
Golf: Burl Bowens; Phone: 757-727-5503; E-mail: deanofmen@hamptonu.edu.
Tennis: Robert Screen; Phone: 757-727-5822.
Track and Field: David Boyd; Phone: 757-727-5721; E-mail: david.boyd@hamptonu.edu.

WOMEN'S COACHES

Basketball: Patricia Bibbs; Phone: 757-727-6851; E-mail: patricia.bibbs@hamptonu.edu.
Cheerleading: Melonne Watkins; Phone: 757-727-5273; E-mail: edwina.simmons@hamptonu.edu.
Cross Country: Maurice Pierce; Phone: 757-727-5724; E-mail: maurice.pierce@hamptonu.edu.
Golf: Burl Bowens; Phone: 757-727-5503; E-mail: deanofmen@hamptonu.edu.
Softball: Tiny Laster; Phone: 757-727-5822; E-mail: tiny.laster@hamptonu.edu.
Tennis: Robert Screen; Phone: 757-727-5822; E-mail: robert.screen@hamptonu.edu.
Track and Field: Maurice Pierce; Phone: 757-727-5724; E-mail: maurice.pierce@hamptonu.edu.
Volleyball: Tiny Laster; Phone: 757-727-5822; E-mail: tiny.laster@hamptonu.edu.

HANNIBAL-LAGRANGE COLLEGE
Hannibal, Missouri

Trojans ◆ NAIA ◆ American Midwest Conference ◆ http://www.hlg.edu/

Independent Southern Baptist 4-year, founded 1858
Coed, 1,133 undergraduate students
Small-town 110-acre campus
Moderately difficult entrance level, 94% of applicants were admitted

Freshmen *Admission:* 335 applied, 314 were accepted.
Tuition and fees (2003–04): $10,160 (full-time). *Room and board:* $3780.
Financial Aid (All incoming freshmen): *Average need-based gift aid:* $2877. *Average aid to full-time undergraduates:* $7951.
Athletic Department: *Director of Athletics:* Tom Huffy; Phone: 573-221-3675; Fax: 573-221-9424; E-mail: thufty@hlg.edu. *Sports Information Director:* Jason Durst; Phone: 573-221-3675; E-mail: jwdurst@hlg.edu.

MEN'S COACHES

Baseball: Clay Biggs; Phone: 573-221-3675; E-mail: cbiggs@hlg.edu.
Basketball: Eric Barnes; Phone: 573-221-3675; E-mail: ebarnes@hlg.edu.
Cheerleading: Barb Lemons; Phone: 573-221-3675; E-mail: blemons@hlg.edu.
Cross Country: Clay Biggs; Phone: 573-221-3675; E-mail: cbiggs@hlg.edu.
Golf: Eric Barnes; Phone: 573-221-3675; E-mail: ebarnes@hlg.edu.
Soccer: David Erskine; Phone: 573-221-3675; E-mail: derskine@hlg.edu.

WOMEN'S COACHES

Basketball: Jennifer Durst; Phone: 573-221-3675; E-mail: jdurst@hlg.edu.
Cheerleading: Barb Lemons; Phone: 573-221-3675; E-mail: blemons@hlg.edu.
Cross Country: Clay Biggs; Phone: 573-221-3675; E-mail: cbiggs@hlg.edu.
Soccer: Jason Nichols; Phone: 573-221-3675; E-mail: jnichols@hlg.edu.
Softball: Dan Hurst; Phone: 573-221-3675; E-mail: dhurst@hlg.edu.
Volleyball: Dan Hurst; Phone: 573-221-3675; E-mail: dhurst@hlg.edu.

HANOVER COLLEGE
Hanover, Indiana

Panthers ◆ NCAA III ◆ Heartland Collegiate Conference ◆ http://www.hanover.edu/

Independent Presbyterian 4-year, founded 1827
Coed, 997 undergraduate students, 99% full-time, 54% women, 46% men
Rural 630-acre campus with easy access to Louisville
Moderately difficult entrance level, 72% of applicants were admitted

Freshmen *Admission:* 1,364 applied, 1,073 were accepted, 292 enrolled. *Test scores:* SAT verbal scores over 500: 79%; SAT math scores over 500: 87%; SAT verbal scores over 600: 39%; SAT math scores over 600: 43%; SAT verbal scores over 700: 6%; SAT math scores over 700: 8%.
Tuition and fees (2003–04): $14,700 (full-time). *Room and board:* $5900 (room only: $2800).
Financial Aid (All incoming freshmen): *Average need-based gift aid:* $13,764. *Average non-need based aid:* $15,332. *Average aid to full-time undergraduates:* $15,245.
Athletic Department: *Director of Athletics:* Lynn Hall; Phone: 812-866-7385; Fax: 812-866-6818; E-mail: hall@hanover.edu. *Sports Information Director:* Carter Cloyd; Phone: 812-866-7010; E-mail: cloyd@hanover.edu.

MEN'S COACHES

Baseball: Dick Naylor; Phone: 812-866-7374; E-mail: naylor@hanover.edu.
Basketball: Mike Beitzel; Phone: 812-866-7371; E-mail: beitzel@hanover.edu.
Cross Country: Josh Payne; Phone: 812-866-7383; E-mail: payne@hanover.edu.
Football: Wayne Perry; Phone: 812-866-7376; E-mail: perry@hanover.edu.
Golf: Peter Preocanin; Phone: 812-866-6860; E-mail: preocanin@hanover.edu.
Soccer: Craig Jones; Phone: 812-866-6806; E-mail: jonescr@hanover.edu.
Tennis: Terry Peebles; Phone: 812-866-7377; E-mail: jcouch@hanover.edu.
Track and Field: Josh Payne; Phone: 812-866-7383; E-mail: payne@hanover.edu.

WOMEN'S COACHES

Basketball: Molly Jones; Phone: 812-866-7386; E-mail: jonesm@hanover.edu.
Cross Country: Josh Payne; Phone: 812-866-7383; E-mail: payne@hanover.edu.
Golf: Travis Calvert; Phone: 812-866-6800; E-mail: calvertt@hanover.edu.
Soccer: Yi Lin Liu; Phone: 812-866-7388; E-mail: linliu@hanover.edu.
Softball: Nancy Plantz; Phone: 812-866-6819; E-mail: plantz@hanover.edu.
Tennis: Nancy Plantz; Phone: 812-866-6819; E-mail: plantz@hanover.edu.
Track and Field: Josh Payne; Phone: 812-866-7383; E-mail: payne@hanover.edu.
Volleyball: Peter Preocanin; Phone: 812-866-6860; E-mail: preocanin@hanover.edu.

HARDING UNIVERSITY
Searcy, Arkansas

Bisons ◆ NCAA II ◆ Gulf South Conference ◆ http://www.harding.edu/

Independent religious comprehensive, founded 1924, affiliated with Church of Christ
Coed, 4,036 undergraduate students, 96% full-time, 55% women, 45% men
Small-town 200-acre campus with easy access to Little Rock
Moderately difficult entrance level, 59% of applicants were admitted

Freshmen *Admission:* 1,750 applied, 1,020 were accepted, 971 enrolled. *Test scores:* SAT verbal scores over 500: 75%; SAT math scores over

Harding University *(continued)*

500: 65%; SAT verbal scores over 600: 30%; SAT math scores over 600: 31%; SAT verbal scores over 700: 6%; SAT math scores over 700: 6%.
Tuition and fees (2003–04): $10,120 (full-time). *Room and board:* $4770 (room only: $2240).
Financial Aid (All incoming freshmen): *Average need-based gift aid:* $5828. *Average non-need based aid:* $4118. *Average aid to full-time undergraduates:* $8687.
Athletic Department: *Director of Athletics:* Greg Harnden; Phone: 501-279-4305; Fax: 501-279-4138. *Sports Information Director:* Scott Goode; Phone: 501-279-4760; E-mail: sgoode@harding.edu.

MEN'S COACHES

Baseball: Shane Fullerton; Phone: 501-279-4344; E-mail: sfullerton@harding.edu.
Basketball: Jeff Morgan; Phone: 501-279-4754; E-mail: jrmorgan@harding.edu.
Cheerleading: Kellee Blickenstaff; Phone: 501-279-4305; E-mail: hucheer@cablelynx.com.
Cross Country: Steve Guymon; Phone: 501-279-4360; E-mail: sguymon@harding.edu.
Football: Randy Tribble; Phone: 501-279-4755; E-mail: rtribble@harding.edu.
Golf: Nicky Boyd; Phone: 501-279-4551; E-mail: nboyd@harding.edu.
Soccer: Greg Harris; Phone: 501-279-4911; E-mail: gharris@harding.edu.
Tennis: David Elliot; Phone: 501-279-4758; E-mail: crainwater@harding.edu.
Track and Field: Steve Guymon; Phone: 501-279-4360; E-mail: sguymon@harding.edu.

WOMEN'S COACHES

Basketball: Brad Francis; Phone: 501-279-4249; E-mail: bfrancis@harding.edu.
Cheerleading: Kellee Blickenstaff; Phone: 501-279-4305; E-mail: hucheer@cablelynx.com.
Cross Country: Steve Guymon; Phone: 501-279-4360; E-mail: sguymon@harding.edu.
Soccer: Greg Harris; Phone: 501-279-4911; E-mail: gharris@harding.edu.
Tennis: David Elliot; Phone: 501-279-4758; E-mail: crainwater@harding.edu.
Track and Field: Steve Guymon; Phone: 501-279-4360; E-mail: sguymon@harding.edu.
Volleyball: Keith Giboney; Phone: 501-279-4176; E-mail: kgiboney@harding.edu.

HARDIN-SIMMONS UNIVERSITY
Abilene, Texas

(m)Cowboys (w) Cowgirls; (M)Cowboys (W) Cowgirls ◆ NCAA III ◆ American Southwest Conference ◆ http://www.hsutx.edu/

Independent Baptist comprehensive, founded 1891
Coed, 1,954 undergraduate students, 87% full-time, 54% women, 46% men
Urban 120-acre campus
Moderately difficult entrance level, 54% of applicants were admitted

Freshmen *Admission:* 1,202 applied, 643 were accepted, 444 enrolled. *Test scores:* SAT verbal scores over 500: 61%; SAT math scores over 500: 64%; SAT verbal scores over 600: 17%; SAT math scores over 600: 19%; SAT verbal scores over 700: 1%; SAT math scores over 700: 2%.
Tuition and fees (2004–05): $13,376 (full-time). *Room and board:* $3922 (room only: $1953).
Financial Aid (All incoming freshmen): *Average need-based gift aid:* $4710. *Average non-need based aid:* $2856. *Average aid to full-time undergraduates:* $11,340.
Athletic Department: *Director of Athletics:* John Neese; Phone: 325-670-1273; Fax: 915-670-1572; E-mail: jneese@hsutx.edu. *Sports Information Director:* Chad Grubbs; Phone: 325-670-1473; E-mail: cgrubbs@hsutx.edu.

MEN'S COACHES

Baseball: Steve Coleman; Phone: 915-670-1493; E-mail: scoleman@hsutx.edu.
Basketball: Dylan Howard; Phone: 915-670-1474; E-mail: dhoward@hsutx.edu.
Football: Jimmie Keeling; Phone: 915-670-1471; E-mail: football@hsutx.edu.
Golf: David Sherman; Phone: 915-670-1374; E-mail: dsherman@hsutx.edu.
Soccer: Dan Heger; Phone: 915-670-1469; E-mail: dheger@hsutx.edu.
Tennis: Jimmy Cole; Phone: 915-670-1446; E-mail: jcole@hsutx.edu.

WOMEN'S COACHES

Basketball: Shanna Briggs; Phone: 915-670-1468; E-mail: sbriggs@hsutx.edu.
Golf: David Sherman; Phone: 915-670-1374; E-mail: dsherman@hsutx.edu.
Soccer: Marccus Wood; Phone: 915-670-5834; E-mail: mwood@hsutx.edu.
Softball: Rita Jordan; Phone: 915-671-2126; E-mail: rjordan@hsutx.edu.
Tennis: Jimmy Cole; Phone: 915-670-1446; E-mail: jcole@hsutx.edu.
Volleyball: Hugh Hernesman; Phone: 915-670-1553; E-mail: hsuvolleyball@yahoo.com.

HARRIS-STOWE STATE COLLEGE
St. Louis, Missouri

Hornets ◆ NAIA ◆ American Midwest Conference ◆ http://www.hssc.edu/

State-supported 4-year, founded 1857, part of Missouri Coordinating Board for Higher Education
Coed, 1,911 undergraduate students, 31% full-time, 77% women, 23% men
Urban 22-acre campus
Moderately difficult entrance level, 42% of applicants were admitted

Freshmen *Admission:* 433 applied, 204 were accepted, 128 enrolled.
Tuition and fees (2003–04): $3280 (resident), $6306 (nonresident).
Financial Aid (All incoming freshmen): *Average non-need based aid:* $1383. *Average aid to full-time undergraduates:* $1702.
Athletic Department: *Director of Athletics:* Rich Fanning; Phone: 314-340-3534; Fax: 314-340-5762; E-mail: fanningr@hssc.edu.

MEN'S COACHES

Baseball: Darren Munns; Phone: 314-340-5721; E-mail: munnsd@hssc.edu.
Basketball: George Little; Phone: 314-340-5721; E-mail: glittle0102@aol.com.
Soccer: Jerry Beckerle; Phone: 314-644-2883; E-mail: jbsplace@swbell.net.

WOMEN'S COACHES

Basketball: Darnell Davis; Phone: 314-385-1260; E-mail: djndjd@aol.com.
Soccer: Rock Rone; Phone: 314-340-3530; E-mail: roner@hssc.edu.
Track and Field: Adolph Hoskins; Phone: 314-340-3530.
Volleyball: Jeff Taylor; Phone: 314-868-0392; E-mail: taylorj@hssc.edu.

HARTWICK COLLEGE
Oneonta, New York

Hawks ◆ NCAA III ◆ Atlantic Soccer Conference; Empire 8 Conference ◆ http://www.hartwick.edu/

Independent 4-year, founded 1797
Coed, 1,466 undergraduate students, 96% full-time, 58% women, 42% men
Small-town 425-acre campus with easy access to Albany
Moderately difficult entrance level, 9% of applicants were admitted

Freshmen *Admission:* 1,853 applied, 1,654 were accepted, 447 enrolled. *Test scores:* SAT verbal scores over 500: 82%; SAT math scores over 500: 84%; SAT verbal scores over 600: 29%; SAT math scores over 600: 32%; SAT verbal scores over 700: 3%; SAT math scores over 700: 4%.
Tuition and fees (2004–05): $26,560 (full-time). *Room and board:* $7280 (room only: $3840).

Financial Aid (All incoming freshmen): *Average need-based gift aid:* $10,715. *Average non-need based aid:* $12,479. *Average aid to full-time undergraduates:* $22,000.
Athletic Department: *Director of Athletics:* Betty Powell; Phone: 607-431-4701; Fax: 607-431-4018; E-mail: powellb@hartwick.edu. *Sports Information Director:* Michael Chilson; Phone: 607-431-4703; E-mail: chilsonm@hartwick.edu.

MEN'S COACHES

Baseball: Barry Shelton; Phone: 607-431-4706; E-mail: sheltonb@hartwick.edu.
Basketball: Tim McGraw; Phone: 607-431-4770; E-mail: mcgrawt@hartwick.edu.
Cross Country: Joe Dombrowski; Phone: 607-431-4707; E-mail: dombrowskij@hartwick.edu.
Diving: Gary Zurn; Phone: 607-431-4714; E-mail: zurng@hartwick.edu.
Football: Mark Carr; Phone: 607-431-4729; E-mail: carrm@hartwick.edu.
Golf: Tim McGraw; Phone: 607-431-4770; E-mail: mcgrawt@hartwick.edu.
Lacrosse: Bill Bjorness; Phone: 607-431-4717; E-mail: bjornessw@hartwick.edu.
Soccer: Jim Lennox; Phone: 607-431-4712; E-mail: soccermen@hartwick.edu.
Swimming: Dale Rothenberger; Phone: 607-431-4714; E-mail: rothenberged@hartwick.edu.
Tennis: Andrea Pontius; Phone: 607-431-4704; E-mail: pontiusa@hartwick.edu.
Track and Field: Joe Dombrowski; Phone: 607-431-4707; E-mail: dombrowskij@hartwick.edu.

WOMEN'S COACHES

Basketball: Daphne Thompson; Phone: 607-431-4709; E-mail: thompsond@hartwick.edu.
Cross Country: Joe Dombrowski; Phone: 607-431-4707; E-mail: dombrowskij@hartwick.edu.
Diving: Gary Zurn; Phone: 607-431-4714; E-mail: zurng@hartwick.edu.
Field Hockey: Anna Meyer; Phone: 607-431-4715; E-mail: meyera@hartwick.edu.
Lacrosse: Cathy Knight; Phone: 607-431-4795; E-mail: knightc@hartwick.edu.
Soccer: Ken Kutler; Phone: 607-431-4728; E-mail: soccerwomen@hartwick.edu.
Softball: Jennifer Barnett; Phone: 607-431-4711; E-mail: barnettj@hartwick.edu.
Swimming: Dale Rothenberger; Phone: 607-431-4714; E-mail: rothenberged@hartwick.edu.
Tennis: Andrea Pontius; Phone: 607-431-4704; E-mail: pontiusa@hartwick.edu.
Track and Field: Joe Dombrowski; Phone: 607-431-4707; E-mail: dombrowskij@hartwick.edu.
Volleyball: Louise Lansing; Phone: 607-431-4722; E-mail: lansingl@hartwick.edu.

HARVARD UNIVERSITY
Cambridge, Massachusetts

Crimson ◆ NCAA I ◆ Ivy League Conference ◆ http://www.harvard.edu/

Independent university, founded 1636
Coed, 6,635 undergraduate students, 100% full-time, 47% women, 53% men
Urban 380-acre campus with easy access to Boston
Most difficult entrance level, 1% of applicants were admitted

Freshmen *Admission:* 20,987 applied, 2,095 were accepted, 1,635 enrolled.
Tuition and fees (2003–04): $29,060 (full-time). *Room and board:* $8868.
Financial Aid (All incoming freshmen): *Average need-based gift aid:* $23,762. *Average aid to full-time undergraduates:* $25,702.
Athletic Department: *Director of Athletics:* Bob Scalise; Phone: 617-495-2204; Fax: 617-496-9950; E-mail: scalise@fas.harvard.edu. *Sports Information Director:* John Veneziano; Phone: 617-495-2206; E-mail: jpvenez@fas.harvard.edu.

MEN'S COACHES

Baseball: Joe Walsh; Phone: 617-495-2629; E-mail: walsh2@fas.harvard.edu.

Basketball: Frank Sullivan; Phone: 617-495-4856; E-mail: fsulliv@fas.harvard.edu.
Cross Country: Frank Haggerty; Phone: 617-495-2218; E-mail: fhaggert@fas.harvard.edu.
Diving: Keith Miller; Phone: 617-496-8790; E-mail: kdmiller@fas.harvard.edu.
Football: Tim Murphy; Phone: 617-495-2207; E-mail: tmurphy@fas.harvard.edu.
Golf: Bob Leonard; Phone: 617-495-0686; E-mail: rjlwin@hotmail.com.
Ice Hockey: Mark Mazzoleni; Phone: 617-495-2418; E-mail: mazzolen@fas.harvard.edu.
Lacrosse: Scott Anderson; Phone: 617-495-4890; E-mail: shanders@fas.harvard.edu.
Soccer: John Kerr; Phone: 617-495-4549; E-mail: jkerr@fas.harvard.edu.
Swimming: Tim Murphy; Phone: 617-495-2268; E-mail: tdmurphy@fas.harvard.edu.
Tennis: David Fish; Phone: 617-495-3676; E-mail: fish@fas.harvard.edu.
Track and Field: Frank Haggerty; Phone: 617-495-2218; E-mail: fhaggert@fas.harvard.edu.
Volleyball: Rob Keller; Phone: 617-495-0485.
Wrestling: Jay Weiss; Phone: 617-496-1968; E-mail: jtweiss@fas.harvard.edu.

WOMEN'S COACHES

Basketball: Kathy Delaney-Smith; Phone: 617-495-9321; E-mail: delaneys@fas.harvard.edu.
Cross Country: Frank Haggerty; Phone: 617-495-2218; E-mail: fhaggert@fas.harvard.edu.
Diving: Keith Miller; Phone: 617-496-8790; E-mail: kdmiller@fas.harvard.edu.
Field Hockey: Sue Caples; Phone: 617-495-5262; E-mail: secaples@fas.harvard.edu.
Golf: Warren Smith; Phone: 617-495-0686; E-mail: wjsmith@fas.harvard.edu.
Lacrosse: Carole Kleinfelder; Phone: 617-495-5245; E-mail: kleinfel@fas.harvard.edu.
Soccer: Tim Wheaton; Phone: 617-495-3775; E-mail: twheaton@fas.harvard.edu.
Softball: Jennifer Allard; Phone: 617-495-2405; E-mail: allard@fas.harvard.edu.
Swimming: Stephanie Morowski; Phone: 617-495-1989; E-mail: morawski@fas.harvard.edu.
Tennis: Gordon Graham; Phone: 617-495-3704; E-mail: ggraham@fas.harvard.edu.
Track and Field: Frank Haggerty; Phone: 617-495-2218; E-mail: fhaggert@fas.harvard.edu.
Volleyball: Jennifer Weiss; Phone: 617-496-7390; E-mail: jaweiss@fas.harvard.edu.

HASKELL INDIAN NATIONS UNIVERSITY
Lawrence, Kansas

Fighting Indians ◆ NAIA ◆ Central States Football Conference; Midlands Collegiate Conference ◆ http://www.haskell.edu/

Federally supported 4-year, founded 1884
Coed, 1,028 undergraduate students, 90% full-time, 47% women, 53% men
Suburban 320-acre campus
Minimally difficult entrance level

Freshmen *Admission:* 350 enrolled.
Tuition and fees (2003–04): $210 (resident), $210 (nonresident). *Room and board:* $70.
Athletic Department: *Director of Athletics:* Dwight Pickering; Phone: 785-749-8459; E-mail: dpickering@haskell.edu.

MEN'S COACHES

Basketball: Jaimie Morrison; Phone: 785-749-8459; E-mail: jmorrison@haskell.edu.
Cheerleading: Denise Cesare; Phone: 785-749-8459; E-mail: dcesare@haskell.edu.

Haskell Indian Nations University *(continued)*

Cross Country: Al Gipp; Phone: 785-749-8459; E-mail: agipp@haskell. edu.
Football: Eric Brock; Phone: 785-749-8459; E-mail: ebrock@haskell. edu.
Golf: Phone: 785-749-8459.
Track and Field: Joe Bointy; Phone: 785-749-8459; E-mail: jbointy@ haskell.edu.

WOMEN'S COACHES
Basketball: Phil Homeratha; Phone: 785-749-8459; E-mail: phomeratha@haskell.edu.
Cheerleading: Denise Cesare; Phone: 785-749-8459; E-mail: dcesare@ haskell.edu.
Cross Country: Al Gipp; Phone: 785-749-8459; E-mail: agipp@haskell. edu.
Softball: Phone: 785-749-8459.
Track and Field: Joe Bointy; Phone: 785-749-8459; E-mail: jbointy@ haskell.edu.
Volleyball: Judith Gipp; Phone: 785-749-8459; E-mail: jgipp@haskell. edu.

HASTINGS COLLEGE
Hastings, Nebraska
Broncos ◆ NAIA ◆ Great Plains Conference
◆ http://www.hastings.edu/

Independent Presbyterian comprehensive, founded 1882
Coed, 1,074 undergraduate students, 98% full-time, 48% women, 52% men
Small-town 109-acre campus
Moderately difficult entrance level, 77% of applicants were admitted

Freshmen *Admission:* 1,553 applied, 1,236 were accepted, 339 enrolled. *Test scores:* SAT verbal scores over 500: 85%; SAT math scores over 500: 81%; SAT verbal scores over 600: 41%; SAT math scores over 600: 44%; SAT verbal scores over 700: 16%; SAT math scores over 700: 20%.
Tuition and fees (2003–04): $15,398 (full-time). *Room and board:* $4530 (room only: $1910).
Financial Aid (All incoming freshmen): *Average need-based gift aid:* $8902. *Average non-need based aid:* $6723. *Average aid to full-time undergraduates:* $11,722.
Athletic Department: *Director of Athletics:* Fran Hummel; Phone: 402-461-7331; Fax: 402-461-7489; E-mail: fhummel@hastings.edu. *Sports Information Director:* Troy Katen; Phone: 402-461-7309; E-mail: tkaten@hastings.edu.

MEN'S COACHES
Baseball: Jim Boeve; Phone: 402-461-7395; E-mail: jboeve@hastings. edu.
Basketball: Lance Creech; Phone: 402-461-7336; E-mail: lcreech@ hastings.edu.
Cheerleading: Traci Boeve; Phone: 402-461-7789; E-mail: tboeve@ hastings.edu.
Cross Country: Kendrick Clay; Phone: 402-461-7395; E-mail: kclay@ hastings.edu.
Football: Paul Mierkiewicz; Phone: 402-461-7395; E-mail: pmierkiewicz@hastings.edu.
Golf: Roger Doerr; Phone: 402-461-7395; E-mail: rdoerr@hastings.edu.
Soccer: Chris Kranjc; Phone: 402-461-7395; E-mail: ckranjc@hastings. edu.
Tennis: Paul Spence; Phone: 402-461-7331; E-mail: pspence@hastings. edu.
Track and Field: Kendrick Clay; Phone: 402-461-7395; E-mail: kclay@ hastings.edu.

WOMEN'S COACHES
Basketball: na; Phone: 402-461-7395.
Cheerleading: Traci Boeve; Phone: 402-461-7789; E-mail: tboeve@ hastings.edu.
Cross Country: Kendrick Clay; Phone: 402-461-7395; E-mail: kclay@ hastings.edu.
Golf: Roger Doerr; Phone: 402-461-7395; E-mail: rdoerr@hastings.edu.
Soccer: Phone: 402-461-7395.
Softball: Fran Hummel; Phone: 402-461-7331; E-mail: fhummel@ hastings.edu.

Tennis: Diane Wigert; Phone: 402-461-7331; E-mail: dwigert@hastings. edu.
Track and Field: Kendrick Clay; Phone: 402-461-7395; E-mail: kclay@ hastings.edu.
Volleyball: Fred Aubuchon; Phone: 402-461-7395; E-mail: faubuchon@ hastings.edu.

HAVERFORD COLLEGE
Haverford, Pennsylvania
Fords ◆ NCAA II ◆ Centennial Conference
◆ http://www.haverford.edu/

Independent 4-year, founded 1833
Coed, 1,163 undergraduate students, 100% full-time, 52% women, 48% men
Suburban 200-acre campus with easy access to Philadelphia
Most difficult entrance level, 3% of applicants were admitted

Freshmen *Admission:* 2,973 applied, 878 were accepted, 313 enrolled. *Test scores:* SAT verbal scores over 500: 99%; SAT math scores over 500: 99%; SAT verbal scores over 600: 92%; SAT math scores over 600: 92%; SAT verbal scores over 700: 46%; SAT math scores over 700: 44%.
Tuition and fees (2003–04): $28,880 (full-time). *Room and board:* $9020 (room only: $5050).
Financial Aid (All incoming freshmen): *Average need-based gift aid:* $21,824. *Average aid to full-time undergraduates:* $23,617.
Athletic Department: *Director of Athletics:* Greg Kannerstein; Phone: 610-896-1120; Fax: 610-896-1224; E-mail: gkanners@haverford.edu. *Sports Information Director:* John Douglas; Phone: 610-896-1042; E-mail: jdouglas@haverford.edu.

MEN'S COACHES
Baseball: Dave Beccaria; Phone: 610-896-1172; E-mail: dbeccari@ haverford.edu.
Basketball: Mike Mucci; Phone: 610-896-1315; E-mail: mmucci@ haverford.edu.
Cross Country: Tom Donnelly; Phone: 610-896-1122; E-mail: tdonnell@ haverford.edu.
Lacrosse: Mike Murphy; Phone: 610-896-1343; E-mail: m1murphy@ haverford.edu.
Soccer: Joe Amorim; Phone: 610-896-1123; E-mail: jamorim@ haverford.edu.
Tennis: Sean Sloane; Phone: 610-896-1119; E-mail: ssloane@haverford. edu.
Track and Field: Tom Donnelly; Phone: 610-896-1122; E-mail: tdonnell@haverford.edu.

WOMEN'S COACHES
Basketball: Jim Osborne; Phone: 610-896-1433; E-mail: josborne@ haverford.edu.
Cross Country: Fran Rizzo; Phone: 610-896-4997; E-mail: frizzo@ haverford.edu.
Field Hockey: Maryann Foley-Schiller; Phone: 610-896-1118; E-mail: mschille@haverford.edu.
Lacrosse: Maryann Foley-Schiller; Phone: 610-896-1118; E-mail: mschille@haverford.edu.
Soccer: Wendy Smith; Phone: 610-896-1307; E-mail: w1smith@ haverford.edu.
Softball: John Kelly; Phone: 610-896-4999; E-mail: jkelly@haverford. edu.
Tennis: Ann Koger; Phone: 610-896-1127; E-mail: akoger@haverford. edu.
Track and Field: Fran Rizzo; Phone: 610-896-4997; E-mail: frizzo@ haverford.edu.
Volleyball: Amy Bergin; Phone: 610-896-4211; E-mail: abergin@ haverford.edu.

HAWAI'I PACIFIC UNIVERSITY
Honolulu, Hawaii

Sea Warriors ◆ NCAA II ◆ Pacific West Conference ◆ http://www.hpu.edu/

Independent comprehensive, founded 1965
Coed, 6,735 undergraduate students, 60% full-time, 56% women, 44% men
Urban 140-acre campus
Moderately difficult entrance level, 74% of applicants were admitted

Freshmen *Admission:* 2,710 applied, 2,194 were accepted, 590 enrolled. *Test scores:* SAT verbal scores over 500: 58%; SAT math scores over 500: 55%; SAT verbal scores over 600: 14%; SAT math scores over 600: 18%; SAT verbal scores over 700: 1%; SAT math scores over 700: 2%.
Tuition and fees (2003–04): $10,368 (full-time). *Room and board:* $8770.
Financial Aid (All incoming freshmen): *Average need-based gift aid:* $4035. *Average non-need based aid:* $4144. *Average aid to full-time undergraduates:* $10,032.
Athletic Department: *Director of Athletics:* Russell Dung; Phone: 808-544-0220; Fax: 808-521-7998; E-mail: rdung@hpu.edu. *Sports Information Director:* Jarnett Lono; Phone: 808-544-0223; E-mail: athletics@hpu.edu.

MEN'S COACHES
Baseball: Allan Sato; Phone: 808-543-0821; E-mail: alsato@hpu.edu.
Basketball: Russell Dung; Phone: 808-544-0220; E-mail: rdung@hpu.edu.
Cheerleading: Phone: 808-566-2477; E-mail: cheer@hpu.edu.
Cross Country: Vien Schwinn; Phone: 808-544-0221; E-mail: athletics@hpu.edu.
Tennis: Henry Somerville; Phone: 808-544-0221; E-mail: hpuhenry@yahoo.com.

WOMEN'S COACHES
Cheerleading: Phone: 808-566-2477; E-mail: cheer@hpu.edu.
Cross Country: Vien Schwinn; Phone: 808-544-0221.
Softball: Howard Okita; Phone: 808-236-3534; E-mail: athletics@hpu.edu.
Tennis: Henry Somerville; Phone: 808-544-0221; E-mail: hpuhenry@yahoo.com.
Volleyball: Tita Ahuna; Phone: 808-544-0222; E-mail: tahuna@hpu.edu.

HEIDELBERG COLLEGE
Tiffin, Ohio

The 'Berg ◆ NCAA III ◆ Ohio Athletic Conference ◆ http://www.heidelberg.edu/

Independent religious comprehensive, founded 1850, affiliated with United Church of Christ
Coed, 1,054 undergraduate students, 92% full-time, 52% women, 48% men
Small-town 110-acre campus
Moderately difficult entrance level, 96% of applicants were admitted

Freshmen *Admission:* 1,649 applied, 1,610 were accepted, 319 enrolled. *Test scores:* SAT verbal scores over 500: 45%; SAT math scores over 500: 40%; SAT verbal scores over 600: 15%; SAT math scores over 600: 7%.
Tuition and fees (2004–05): $14,900 (full-time). *Room and board:* $6710.
Financial Aid (All incoming freshmen): *Average need-based gift aid:* $8900. *Average non-need based aid:* $5000. *Average aid to full-time undergraduates:* $14,046.
Athletic Department: *Director of Athletics:* Jerry McDonald; Phone: 419-448-2356; Fax: 419-448-2025; E-mail: jmcdonal@heidelberg.edu. *Sports Information Director:* Aaron Chimenti; Phone: 419-448-2140; E-mail: achiment@heidelberg.edu.

MEN'S COACHES
Baseball: Matt Palm; Phone: 419-448-2009; E-mail: baseball@heidelberg.edu.
Basketball: Duane Sheldon; Phone: 419-448-2006; E-mail: basketball-men@heidelberg.edu.
Cheerleading: Kristin Stiffler; Phone: 419-448-2019; E-mail: athletics@heidelberg.edu.
Cross Country: Bret Kimple; Phone: 419-448-2011; E-mail: xc-men@heidelberg.edu.
Football: Brian Cochran; Phone: 419-448-2052; E-mail: bcochran@heidelberg.edu.
Golf: Kurt Ramler; Phone: 419-448-2382; E-mail: golf@heidelberg.edu.
Soccer: Brian Haley; Phone: 419-448-2119; E-mail: soccer-men@heidelberg.edu.
Tennis: Jerry McDonald; Phone: 419-448-2356; E-mail: tennis-men@heidelberg.edu.
Track and Field: Bret Kimple; Phone: 419-448-2011; E-mail: xc-men@heidelberg.edu.
Wrestling: Jason Miller; Phone: 419-448-2377; E-mail: wrestling@heidelberg.edu.

WOMEN'S COACHES
Basketball: Karen McConnell; Phone: 419-448-2010; E-mail: basketball-women@heidelberg.edu.
Cheerleading: Kristin Stiffler; Phone: 419-448-2019; E-mail: athletics@heidelberg.edu.
Cross Country: Bev Buckley; Phone: 419-448-2378; E-mail: xc-women@heidelberg.edu.
Golf: Eric Slosser; Phone: 419-448-2380; E-mail: athletics@heidelberg.edu.
Soccer: Michele Sandor; Phone: 419-448-2381; E-mail: soccer-women@heidelberg.edu.
Softball: Missy Roggow; Phone: 419-448-2289; E-mail: softball@heidelberg.edu.
Tennis: Pat Ortner; Phone: 419-448-2378; E-mail: tennis-women@heidelberg.edu.
Track and Field: Bev Buckley; Phone: 419-448-2378; E-mail: xc-women@heidelberg.edu.
Volleyball: Jason Miller; Phone: 419-448-2377; E-mail: volleyball@heidelberg.edu.

HENDERSON STATE UNIVERSITY
Arkadelphia, Arkansas

Reddies ◆ NCAA II ◆ Gulf South Conference ◆ http://www.hsu.edu/

State-supported comprehensive, founded 1890
Coed, 3,050 undergraduate students, 90% full-time, 57% women, 43% men
Small-town 139-acre campus with easy access to Little Rock
Moderately difficult entrance level, 7% of applicants were admitted

Freshmen *Admission:* 1,878 applied, 1,189 were accepted, 412 enrolled. *Test scores:* SAT verbal scores over 500: 56%; SAT math scores over 500: 64%; SAT verbal scores over 600: 32%; SAT math scores over 600: 32%.
Tuition and fees (2003–04): $3635 (resident), $7015 (nonresident). *Room and board:* $3984.
Financial Aid (All incoming freshmen): *Average need-based gift aid:* $4400. *Average non-need based aid:* $3900. *Average aid to full-time undergraduates:* $3780.
Athletic Department: *Director of Athletics:* Sam Goodwin; Phone: 870-230-5072; Fax: 870-230-5408; E-mail: goodwis@hsu.edu. *Sports Information Director:* Troy Mitchell; Phone: 870-230-5197; E-mail: mitchet@hsu.edu.

MEN'S COACHES
Baseball: Pete Southall; Phone: 870-230-5071; E-mail: southap@hsu.edu.
Basketball: Joe Redmond; Phone: 870-230-5193; E-mail: redmonj@hsu.edu.
Football: Jesse Branch; Phone: 870-230-5201; E-mail: branchj@hsu.edu.
Golf: Willie Tate; Phone: 870-230-5035; E-mail: tatew@hsu.edu.
Swimming: Coak Matthews; Phone: 870-230-5206; E-mail: matthec@hsu.edu.

WOMEN'S COACHES
Basketball: Jeff Caldwell; Phone: 870-230-5123; E-mail: caldwej@hsu.edu.
Cross Country: Brenda Joiner; Phone: 870-230-5444; E-mail: joinerb@hsu.edu.
Softball: Richie Bruister; Phone: 870-230-5575; E-mail: bruistr@hsu.edu.

Henderson State University *(continued)*
Swimming: Coak Matthews; Phone: 870-230-5206; E-mail: matthec@hsu.edu.
Tennis: Brenda Joiner; Phone: 870-230-5444; E-mail: joinerb@hsu.edu.
Volleyball: Rhonda Thigpen; Phone: 870-230-5194; E-mail: thigper@hsu.edu.

HENDRIX COLLEGE
Conway, Arkansas

Warriors ◆ NCAA III ◆ Southern Collegiate Athletic Conference ◆ http://www.hendrix.edu/

Independent United Methodist comprehensive, founded 1876
Coed, 1,050 undergraduate students, 98% full-time, 57% women, 43% men
Suburban 158-acre campus with easy access to Little Rock
Very difficult entrance level, 81% of applicants were admitted

Freshmen *Admission:* 891 applied, 770 were accepted, 267 enrolled. *Test scores:* SAT verbal scores over 500: 93%; SAT math scores over 500: 92%; SAT verbal scores over 600: 67%; SAT math scores over 600: 61%; SAT verbal scores over 700: 21%; SAT math scores over 700: 15%.
Tuition and fees (2003–04): $15,630 (full-time). *Room and board:* $5340 (room only: $2354).
Financial Aid (All incoming freshmen): *Average need-based gift aid:* $9915. *Average non-need based aid:* $12,994. *Average aid to full-time undergraduates:* $13,344.
Athletic Department: *Director of Athletics:* Danny Powell; Phone: 501-450-1265; Fax: 501-450-3805; E-mail: powell@hendrix.edu. *Sports Information Director:* Will Amerine; Phone: 501-450-1426; E-mail: amerine@hendrix.edu.

MEN'S COACHES
Baseball: Lane Stahl; Phone: 501-450-3898; E-mail: stahl@hendrix.edu.
Basketball: Jason Rhodes; Phone: 501-450-1278; E-mail: rhodes@hendrix.edu.
Cheerleading: Laurie Smith; Phone: 501-450-1391; E-mail: smithl@hendrix.edu.
Cross Country: Larry Rogers; Phone: 501-450-1460; E-mail: rogers@hendrix.edu.
Diving: Mike Bailey; Phone: 501-450-1311.
Golf: Jason Rhodes; Phone: 501-450-1278; E-mail: rhodes@hendrix.edu.
Soccer: Glen Tourville; Phone: 501-450-3818; E-mail: tourville@hendrix.edu.
Swimming: Jim Kelly; Phone: 501-450-1311; E-mail: kelly@hendrix.edu.
Tennis: Harold Henderson; Phone: 501-450-4033; E-mail: henderson@hendrix.edu.
Track and Field: Larry Rogers; Phone: 501-450-1460; E-mail: rogers@hendrix.edu.

WOMEN'S COACHES
Basketball: Chuck Winkelman; Phone: 501-450-1313; E-mail: winkelman@hendrix.edu.
Cheerleading: Laurie Smith; Phone: 501-450-1391; E-mail: smithl@hendrix.edu.
Cross Country: Larry Rogers; Phone: 501-450-1460; E-mail: rogers@hendrix.edu.
Diving: Mike Bailey; Phone: 501-450-1311.
Golf: Jason Rhodes; Phone: 501-450-1278; E-mail: rhodes@hendrix.edu.
Soccer: Glen Tourville; Phone: 501-450-3818; E-mail: tourville@hendrix.edu.
Softball: Amy Weaver; Phone: 501-450-3899; E-mail: weaver@hendrix.edu.
Swimming: Jim Kelly; Phone: 501-450-1311; E-mail: kelly@hendrix.edu.
Tennis: Harold Henderson; Phone: 501-450-4033; E-mail: henderson@hendrix.edu.
Track and Field: Larry Rogers; Phone: 501-450-1460; E-mail: rogers@hendrix.edu.
Volleyball: Mary Ann Schlientz; Phone: 501-450-4576; E-mail: schlientz@hendrix.edu.

HIGH POINT UNIVERSITY
High Point, North Carolina

Panthers ◆ NCAA I ◆ Big South Conference ◆ http://www.highpoint.edu/

Independent United Methodist comprehensive, founded 1924
Coed, 2,684 undergraduate students, 91% full-time, 61% women, 39% men
Suburban 77-acre campus with easy access to Charlotte
Moderately difficult entrance level, 9% of applicants were admitted

Freshmen *Admission:* 1,709 applied, 1,491 were accepted, 550 enrolled. *Test scores:* SAT verbal scores over 500: 56%; SAT math scores over 500: 59%; SAT verbal scores over 600: 16%; SAT math scores over 600: 15%; SAT verbal scores over 700: 2%; SAT math scores over 700: 2%.
Tuition and fees (2004–05): $15,700 (full-time). *Room and board:* $6780 (room only: $2890).
Financial Aid (All incoming freshmen): *Average need-based gift aid:* $5000. *Average non-need based aid:* $5000. *Average aid to full-time undergraduates:* $11,400.
Athletic Department: *Director of Athletics:* Woody Gibson; Phone: 336-841-9105; E-mail: wgibson@highpoint.edu. *Sports Information Director:* Lee Owen; Phone: 336-841-4605; E-mail: lowen@highpoint.edu.

MEN'S COACHES
Baseball: Sal Bando Jr.; Phone: 336-841-9190; E-mail: sbando@highpoint.edu.
Basketball: Bart Lundy; Phone: 336-841-9181; E-mail: blundy@highpoint.edu.
Cheerleading: Jennifer Pfeiffer; Phone: 336-841-4669; E-mail: jpfeiff80@aol.com.
Cross Country: Al Barnes; Phone: 336-841-9272; E-mail: abarnes@highpoint.edu.
Golf: J.B. White; Phone: 336-841-9015; E-mail: jbwhite@highpoint.edu.
Soccer: Peter Broadley; Phone: 336-841-4607; E-mail: pbroadle@highpoint.edu.
Tennis: Jerry Tertzagin; Phone: 336-841-9273; E-mail: gterzagi@highpoint.edu.
Track and Field: Al Barnes; Phone: 336-841-9272; E-mail: abarnes@highpoint.edu.

WOMEN'S COACHES
Basketball: Tooey Loy; Phone: 336-841-4613; E-mail: lloy@highpoint.edu.
Cheerleading: Jennifer Pfeiffer; Phone: 336-841-4669; E-mail: jpfeiff80@aol.com.
Cross Country: Al Barnes; Phone: 336-841-9272; E-mail: abarnes@highpoint.edu.
Golf: Julie Streng; Phone: 336-841-4674; E-mail: jstreng@highpoint.edu.
Soccer: Tracie Foels; Phone: 336-841-4573; E-mail: tfoels@highpoint.edu.
Tennis: Jerry Tertzagin; Phone: 336-841-9273; E-mail: gterzagi@highpoint.edu.
Track and Field: Al Barnes; Phone: 336-841-9272; E-mail: abarnes@highpoint.edu.
Volleyball: Chad Esposito; Phone: 336-841-4629; E-mail: cesposit@highpoint.edu.

HILBERT COLLEGE
Hamburg, New York

Hawks ◆ NCAA III ◆ Eastern College Athletic Conference ◆ http://www.hilbert.edu/

Independent 4-year, founded 1957
Coed, 1,055 undergraduate students, 68% full-time, 63% women, 37% men
Small-town 40-acre campus with easy access to Buffalo
Minimally difficult entrance level, 96% of applicants were admitted

Freshmen *Admission:* 380 applied, 357 were accepted, 164 enrolled. *Test scores:* SAT verbal scores over 500: 34%; SAT math scores over 500: 39%; SAT verbal scores over 600: 4%; SAT math scores over 600: 5%; SAT math scores over 700: 1%.

Tuition and fees (2004–05): $14,000 (full-time). *Room and board:* $5670 (room only: $2200).
Financial Aid (All incoming freshmen): *Average need-based gift aid:* $7691. *Average non-need based aid:* $5191. *Average aid to full-time undergraduates:* $10,659.
Athletic Department: *Director of Athletics:* Richard Walsh; Phone: 716-649-7900; Fax: 716-649-6429; E-mail: rwalsh@hilbert.edu. *Sports Information Director:* Robert DeGrandpre; Phone: 716-649-7900; E-mail: rdegrandpre@hilbert.edu.

MEN'S COACHES

Baseball: Sam Rutkowski; Phone: 716-649-7900; E-mail: sandsrut@aol.com.
Basketball: Rob DeGrandpre; Phone: 716-649-7900; E-mail: rdegrandpre@hilbert.edu.
Cross Country: Dick Barry; Phone: 716-649-7900; E-mail: dicbarry@att.net.
Golf: Phone: 716-649-7900.
Soccer: Kevin Mahoney; Phone: 716-649-7900; E-mail: kevinmahoney973@hotmail.com.
Volleyball: Adam Jolley; Phone: 716-649-7900; E-mail: ajolley@hilbertcollege.com.

WOMEN'S COACHES

Basketball: Andrea Agnello; Phone: 716-649-7900; E-mail: aagnello@hilbert.edu.
Cross Country: Dick Barry; Phone: 716-649-7900; E-mail: dicbarry@att.net.
Soccer: James Ruggiero; Phone: 716-649-7900; E-mail: jruggiero@hilbert.edu.
Softball: Bill Goc; Phone: 716-649-7900; E-mail: bgoc@hilbert.edu.
Volleyball: Adam Jolley; Phone: 716-649-7900; E-mail: ajolley@hilbertcollege.com.

HILLSDALE COLLEGE
Hillsdale, Michigan

Chargers ◆ NCAA II ◆ Great Lakes Intercollegiate Conference ◆ http://www.hillsdale.edu/

Independent 4-year, founded 1844
Coed, 1,230 undergraduate students, 97% full-time, 53% women, 47% men
Small-town 200-acre campus
Very difficult entrance level, 75% of applicants were admitted

Freshmen *Admission:* 1,150 applied, 881 were accepted, 360 enrolled. *Test scores:* SAT verbal scores over 500: 97%; SAT math scores over 500: 93%; SAT verbal scores over 600: 71%; SAT math scores over 600: 62%; SAT verbal scores over 700: 25%; SAT math scores over 700: 14%.
Tuition and fees (2003–04): $16,050 (full-time). *Room and board:* $6400 (room only: $3140).
Financial Aid (All incoming freshmen): *Average need-based gift aid:* $8921. *Average non-need based aid:* $7500. *Average aid to full-time undergraduates:* $11,823.
Athletic Department: *Director of Athletics:* Mike Kovalchik; Phone: 517-437-7364; Fax: 517-437-3923; E-mail: mike.kovalchik@hillsdale.edu. *Sports Information Director:* Dennis Worden; Phone: 517-607-3172; E-mail: dennis.worden@hillsdale.edu.

MEN'S COACHES

Baseball: Paul Noce; Phone: 517-607-7364; E-mail: paul.noce@hillsdale.edu.
Basketball: Ed Douma; Phone: 517-607-3121; E-mail: ed.douma@hillsdale.edu.
Cross Country: Bill Lundberg; Phone: 517-607-3134; E-mail: bill.lundberg@hillsdale.edu.
Football: Keith Otterbein; Phone: 517-607-3138; E-mail: keith.otterbein@hillsdale.edu.
Golf: Sam Hargraves; Phone: 517-607-2316; E-mail: sam.hargraves@hillsdale.edu.
Swimming: Mary Ann Gerzanick; Phone: 517-607-3142; E-mail: maryanne.gerzanick@hillsdale.edu.
Tennis: Sue Abel; Phone: 517-607-3171; E-mail: sue.abel@hillsdale.edu.
Track and Field: Bill Lundberg; Phone: 517-607-3134; E-mail: bill.lundberg@hillsdale.edu.

WOMEN'S COACHES

Basketball: Claudette Charney; Phone: 517-607-3124; E-mail: claudette.charney@hillsdale.edu.

Cross Country: Penny Neer; Phone: 517-607-3155; E-mail: penny.neer@hillsdale.edu.
Softball: Jay Jondro; Phone: 517-607-3191; E-mail: coachjondro@yahoo.com.
Swimming: Mary Ann Gerzanick; Phone: 517-607-3142; E-mail: maryanne.gerzanick@hillsdale.edu.
Tennis: Sue Abel; Phone: 517-607-3137; E-mail: sue.abel@hillsdale.edu.
Track and Field: Penny Neer; Phone: 517-607-3155; E-mail: penny.neer@hillsdale.edu.
Volleyball: Chris Gravel; Phone: 517-607-3126; E-mail: chris.gravel@hillsdale.edu.

HIRAM COLLEGE
Hiram, Ohio

Terriers ◆ NCAA III ◆ North Coast Athletic Conference ◆ http://www.hiram.edu/

Independent religious 4-year, founded 1850, affiliated with Christian Church (Disciples of Christ)
Coed, 1,110 undergraduate students, 80% full-time, 58% women, 42% men
Rural 110-acre campus with easy access to Cleveland
Very difficult entrance level, 80% of applicants were admitted

Freshmen *Admission:* 888 applied, 778 were accepted, 236 enrolled. *Test scores:* SAT verbal scores over 500: 80%; SAT math scores over 500: 71%; SAT verbal scores over 600: 42%; SAT math scores over 600: 32%; SAT verbal scores over 700: 11%; SAT math scores over 700: 3%.
Tuition and fees (2003–04): $21,134 (full-time). *Room and board:* $7100 (room only: $3160).
Financial Aid (All incoming freshmen): *Average need-based gift aid:* $8601. *Average non-need based aid:* $9657. *Average aid to full-time undergraduates:* $17,172.
Athletic Department: *Director of Athletics:* Tom Mulligan; Phone: 330-569-5940; Fax: 330-569-5392; E-mail: mulligante@hiram.edu. *Sports Information Director:* Jason Tirotta; Phone: 330-569-5495; E-mail: tirottaja@hiram.edu.

MEN'S COACHES

Baseball: Howard Jenter; Phone: 330-569-5348; E-mail: jenterhe@hiram.edu.
Basketball: Tim Rice; Phone: 330-569-5346; E-mail: riceth@hiram.edu.
Cross Country: Tom Mulligan; Phone: 330-569-5940; E-mail: mulligante@hiram.edu.
Diving: Jack Groselle; Phone: 330-569-5343; E-mail: grosellejr@hiram.edu.
Football: Mike Meyer; Phone: 330-569-5345; E-mail: meyerme@hiram.edu.
Golf: David Donald; Phone: 330-326-3139; E-mail: donalddj@hiram.edu.
Soccer: Dan Palmer; Phone: 330-569-5344; E-mail: palmerdm@hiram.edu.
Swimming: Jack Groselle; Phone: 330-569-5343; E-mail: grosellejr@hiram.edu.
Tennis: Pete Brann; Phone: 330-569-5341; E-mail: brannpj@hiram.edu.
Track and Field: Mike Lazusky; Phone: 330-569-5446; E-mail: lazuskymj@hiram.edu.

WOMEN'S COACHES

Basketball: Anne Hayman; Phone: 330-569-5352; E-mail: haynamae@hiram.edu.
Cross Country: Tom Mulligan; Phone: 330-569-5940; E-mail: mulligante@hiram.edu.
Diving: Jack Groselle; Phone: 330-569-5343; E-mail: grosellejr@hiram.edu.
Golf: Tim Rice; Phone: 330-326-5346; E-mail: riceth@hiram.edu.
Soccer: Nicole Barbuto; Phone: 330-569-5968; E-mail: barbutona@hiram.edu.
Softball: Susan Woodford; Phone: 330-569-5478; E-mail: woodfordsa@hiram.edu.
Swimming: Jack Groselle; Phone: 330-569-5343; E-mail: grosellejr@hiram.edu.
Tennis: Pete Brann; Phone: 330-569-5341; E-mail: brannpj@hiram.edu.
Track and Field: Mike Lazusky; Phone: 330-569-5446; E-mail: lazuskymj@hiram.edu.
Volleyball: Ellen Dempsey; Phone: 330-569-5350; E-mail: dempseyee@hiram.edu.

HOBART AND WILLIAM SMITH COLLEGES

Geneva, New York

(M) Statesmen (W) Herons ◆ NCAA III ◆ Patriot League Conference; Upstate Collegiate Athletic Conference ◆ http://www.hws.edu/

Independent 4-year, founded 1822
Coed, 1,873 undergraduate students, 100% full-time, 55% women, 45% men
Small-town 200-acre campus with easy access to Rochester and Syracuse
Very difficult entrance level, 56% of applicants were admitted

Freshmen *Admission:* 3,277 applied, 2,045 were accepted, 516 enrolled. *Test scores:* SAT verbal scores over 500: 89%; SAT math scores over 500: 94%; SAT verbal scores over 600: 41%; SAT math scores over 600: 46%; SAT verbal scores over 700: 5%; SAT math scores over 700: 5%.
Tuition and fees (2003–04): $28,948 (full-time). *Room and board:* $7588 (room only: $4000).
Financial Aid (All incoming freshmen): *Average need-based gift aid:* $19,868. *Average non-need based aid:* $17,486. *Average aid to full-time undergraduates:* $22,509.
Athletic Department: *Director of Athletics:* Michael Hanna; Phone: 315-781-3565; Fax: 315-781-3570; E-mail: hanna@hws.edu. *Sports Information Director:* Ken DeBolt; Phone: 315-781-3538; E-mail: debolt@hws.edu.

MEN'S COACHES

Basketball: Rich Roche; Phone: 315-781-3620; E-mail: rroche@hws.edu.
Cross Country: Ron Fleury; Phone: 315-781-3565; E-mail: rfleury@localnet.com.
Football: Mike Cragg; Phone: 315-781-3566; E-mail: cragg@hws.edu.
Golf: Bill Quinn; Phone: 315-781-3565; E-mail: bqbball@yahoo.com.
Ice Hockey: Mark Taylor; Phone: 315-781-3539; E-mail: mtaylor@hws.edu.
Lacrosse: Matt Kerwick; Phone: 315-781-3715; E-mail: kerwick@hws.edu.
Soccer: Shawn Griffin; Phone: 315-781-3625; E-mail: griffin@hws.edu.
Tennis: Carol Weymuller; Phone: 315-781-3645; E-mail: weymuller@hws.edu.

WOMEN'S COACHES

Basketball: Glenn Begley; Phone: 315-781-3932; E-mail: begly@hws.edu.
Cross Country: Jack Warner; Phone: 315-781-3939; E-mail: jwarner@hws.edu.
Diving: Heather Boyum; Phone: 315-781-3567.
Field Hockey: Sally Scatton; Phone: 315-781-3940; E-mail: scatton@hws.edu.
Lacrosse: Pat Genovese; Phone: 315-781-3941; E-mail: genovese@hws.edu.
Soccer: Aliceann Wilber; Phone: 315-781-3933; E-mail: wilber@hws.edu.
Swimming: Kelly Kisner; Phone: 315-781-3567; E-mail: kisner@hws.edu.
Tennis: Chip Fishback; Phone: 315-781-3936; E-mail: fishback@hws.edu.

HOFSTRA UNIVERSITY

Hempstead, New York

Pride ◆ NCAA I ◆ Atlantic 10 Conference; Colonial Athletic Conference ◆ http://www.hofstra.edu/

Independent university, founded 1935
Coed, 9,387 undergraduate students, 89% full-time, 53% women, 47% men
Suburban 240-acre campus with easy access to New York City
Moderately difficult entrance level, 70% of applicants were admitted

Freshmen *Admission:* 11,691 applied, 8,000 were accepted, 1,877 enrolled. *Test scores:* SAT verbal scores over 500: 83%; SAT math scores

over 500: 88%; SAT verbal scores over 600: 29%; SAT math scores over 600: 35%; SAT verbal scores over 700: 2%; SAT math scores over 700: 3%.
Tuition and fees (2003–04): $18,412 (full-time). *Room and board:* $8700 (room only: $5600).
Financial Aid (All incoming freshmen): *Average need-based gift aid:* $8636. *Average non-need based aid:* $7192. *Average aid to full-time undergraduates:* $11,220.
Athletic Department: *Director of Athletics:* Harry Royle; Phone: 516-463-6750; Fax: 516-463-4860; E-mail: hprhhr@hofstra.edu. *Sports Information Director:* Jim Sheehan; Phone: 516-463-6764; E-mail: hprjbs@hofstra.edu.

MEN'S COACHES

Baseball: Chris Dotolo; Phone: 516-463-5065; E-mail: christopher.l.dotolo@hofstra.edu.
Basketball: Tom Pecora; Phone: 516-463-6757; E-mail: thomas.pecora@hofstra.edu.
Cheerleading: Christine Nowierski; Phone: 516-463-6750; E-mail: hucheercoach@aol.com.
Cross Country: James Sewell; Phone: 516-463-6702; E-mail: james.e.sewell@hofstra.edu.
Football: Joe Gardi; Phone: 516-463-5315; E-mail: joseph.gardi@hofstra.edu.
Golf: Robert Schwalb; Phone: 516-463-6821; E-mail: robert.a.schwalb@hofstra.edu.
Lacrosse: John Danowski; Phone: 516-463-6628; E-mail: john.e.danowski@hofstra.edu.
Soccer: Rich Nuttall; Phone: 516-463-6762; E-mail: richard.m.nuttall@hofstra.edu.
Tennis: Bill Gerdts; Phone: 516-463-4968; E-mail: william.e.gerdts@hofstra.edu.
Wrestling: Tom Ryan; Phone: 516-463-6615; E-mail: thomas.s.ryan@hofstra.edu.

WOMEN'S COACHES

Basketball: Felisha Legette-Jack; Phone: 516-463-5069; E-mail: felisha.legette-jack@hofstra.edu.
Cheerleading: Christine Nowierski; Phone: 516-463-6750; E-mail: hucheercoach@aol.com.
Cross Country: James Sewell; Phone: 516-463-6702; E-mail: james.e.sewell@hofstra.edu.
Field Hockey: Kathy De Angelis; Phone: 516-463-3712; E-mail: kathleen.deangelis@hofstra.edu.
Golf: Robert Schwalb; Phone: 516-463-6821; E-mail: robert.a.schwalb@hofstra.edu.
Lacrosse: Shelly Klaes-Bawcombe; Phone: 516-463-6761; E-mail: shelley.c.klaes@hofstra.edu.
Soccer: Joanne Russell; Phone: 516-463-6946; E-mail: joanne.russell@hofstra.edu.
Softball: Bill Edwards; Phone: 516-463-5085; E-mail: william.w.edwards@hofstra.edu.
Tennis: Bill Gerdts; Phone: 516-463-4968; E-mail: william.e.gerdts@hofstra.edu.
Volleyball: Fran Kalafer; Phone: 516-463-6758; E-mail: francine.kalafer@hofstra.edu.

HOLLINS UNIVERSITY

Roanoke, Virginia

NCAA III ◆ Centennial Conference; Old Dominion Conference ◆ http://www.hollins.edu/

Independent comprehensive, founded 1842
Women only, 812 undergraduate students, 97% full-time, 100% women
Suburban 475-acre campus
Moderately difficult entrance level, 86% of applicants were admitted

Freshmen *Admission:* 813 applied, 701 were accepted, 202 enrolled. *Test scores:* SAT verbal scores over 500: 89%; SAT math scores over 500: 77%; SAT verbal scores over 600: 53%; SAT math scores over 600: 26%; SAT verbal scores over 700: 12%; SAT math scores over 700: 2%.
Tuition and fees (2003–04): $20,675 (full-time). *Room and board:* $7290 (room only: $4374).
Financial Aid (All incoming freshmen): *Average need-based gift aid:* $12,089. *Average non-need based aid:* $6305. *Average aid to full-time undergraduates:* $16,739.

Athletic Department: *Director of Athletics:* Lynda Calkins; Phone: 540-362-6435; Fax: 540-362-6553; E-mail: lcalkins@hollins.edu.

WOMEN'S COACHES

Basketball: Karen Harvey; Phone: 540-362-6424; E-mail: kharvey@hollins.edu.

Cross Country: J.P. Widner; Phone: 540-362-7436; E-mail: jwidner@hollins.edu.

Field Hockey: Sarah Copplestone; Phone: 540-362-6539; E-mail: scopplestone@hollins.edu.

Golf: Lanetta Ware; Phone: 540-362-6329; E-mail: lware@hollins.edu.

Lacrosse: Rachel Cress; Phone: 540-362-6597; E-mail: rscanlon@hollins.edu.

Soccer: Lynda Calkins; Phone: 540-362-6436; E-mail: lcalkins@hollins.edu.

Swimming: Lynda Calkins; Phone: 540-362-6435; E-mail: lcalkins@hollins.edu.

Tennis: Leslie Bernard; Phone: 540-362-6206; E-mail: lbernard@hollins.edu.

Volleyball: Kim Martinez; Phone: 540-362-6573; E-mail: kmartinez@hollins.edu.

HOLY FAMILY UNIVERSITY
Philadelphia, Pennsylvania

Tigers ◆ NCAA II ◆ Central Atlantic Collegiate Conference ◆ http://www.holyfamily.edu/

Independent Roman Catholic comprehensive, founded 1954
Coed, 1,782 undergraduate students, 61% full-time, 74% women, 26% men
Suburban 47-acre campus
Moderately difficult entrance level, 82% of applicants were admitted

Freshmen *Admission:* 573 applied, 441 were accepted, 230 enrolled. *Test scores:* SAT verbal scores over 500: 36%; SAT math scores over 500: 39%; SAT verbal scores over 600: 7%; SAT math scores over 600: 5%.
Tuition and fees (2003–04): $15,490 (full-time).
Financial Aid (All incoming freshmen): *Average need-based gift aid:* $5195. *Average non-need based aid:* $4488. *Average aid to full-time undergraduates:* $12,097.
Athletic Department: *Director of Athletics:* Sandra Michael; Phone: 215-637-7700; Fax: 215-637-6675; E-mail: smichael@holyfamily.edu.

MEN'S COACHES

Basketball: Alfred Johnson; Phone: 215-637-7700; E-mail: dwilliams@holyfamily.edu.

Cheerleading: Phone: 215-637-7700; E-mail: mmbobholz@holyfamily.edu.

Cross Country: Greg Hunger; Phone: 215-637-7700; E-mail: athletics@holyfamily.edu.

Golf: Mike Sulpizio; Phone: 215-637-7700; E-mail: athletics@holyfamily.edu.

Soccer: John Amorim; Phone: 215-637-7700; E-mail: athletics@holyfamily.edu.

WOMEN'S COACHES

Basketball: Mike McLaughlin; Phone: 215-637-7700; E-mail: athletics@holyfamily.edu.

Cheerleading: Phone: 215-637-7700; E-mail: mmbobholz@holyfamily.edu.

Cross Country: Kelly Hunger; Phone: 215-637-7700; E-mail: athletics@holyfamily.edu.

Soccer: Joe Mikolajewski; Phone: 215-637-7700; E-mail: athletics@holyfamily.edu.

Softball: Mickey McGroarty; Phone: 215-637-7700; E-mail: athletics@holyfamily.edu.

Volleyball: Joanna Pennell; Phone: 215-637-7700; E-mail: athletics@holyfamily.edu.

HOLY NAMES UNIVERSITY
Oakland, California

Hawks ◆ NAIA ◆ California Pacific Conference ◆ http://www.hnu.edu/

Independent Roman Catholic comprehensive, founded 1868
Coed, primarily women, 593 undergraduate students, 66% full-time, 78% women, 22% men
Urban 60-acre campus with easy access to San Francisco
Moderately difficult entrance level, 6% of applicants were admitted

Freshmen *Admission:* 211 applied, 131 were accepted, 58 enrolled. *Test scores:* SAT verbal scores over 500: 50%; SAT math scores over 500: 50%; SAT verbal scores over 600: 8%; SAT math scores over 600: 8%.
Tuition and fees (2004–05): $20,980 (full-time). *Room and board:* $7800 (room only: $4000).
Financial Aid (All incoming freshmen): *Average need-based gift aid:* $9918. *Average non-need based aid:* $3000. *Average aid to full-time undergraduates:* $22,883.
Athletic Department: *Director of Athletics:* Marc Gordon; Phone: 510-436-1491; Fax: 510-436-1259; E-mail: gordon@hnc.edu. *Sports Information Director:* Steve Spencer; Phone: 510-436-1584; E-mail: spencer@hnc.edu.

MEN'S COACHES

Basketball: Conn Dunning; Phone: 510-436-1582; E-mail: dunning@hnc.edu.

Cross Country: Jim McKinnon; Phone: 510-436-1613; E-mail: mckinnon@hnc.edu.

Golf: Siegfried Wroebel; Phone: 510-436-1584; E-mail: wroebel@hnc.edu.

Soccer: Marc Gordon; Phone: 510-436-1491; E-mail: gordon@hnc.edu.

WOMEN'S COACHES

Basketball: Dennis Jones; Phone: 510-436-1583; E-mail: jones@hnc.edu.

Cross Country: Jim McKinnon; Phone: 510-436-1613; E-mail: mckinnon@hnc.edu.

Soccer: d'Alary Dalton; Phone: 510-436-1613; E-mail: dalton@hnc.edu.

Volleyball: Jesse Knight; Phone: 510-436-1246; E-mail: knight@hnc.edu.

HOOD COLLEGE
Frederick, Maryland

Blazers ◆ NCAA III ◆ Atlantic Women's Colleges Conference ◆ http://www.hood.edu/

Independent comprehensive, founded 1893
Coed, 864 undergraduate students, 80% full-time, 85% women, 15% men
Suburban 50-acre campus with easy access to Baltimore and Washington, DC
Moderately difficult entrance level, 45% of applicants were admitted

Freshmen *Admission:* 1,001 applied, 546 were accepted, 181 enrolled. *Test scores:* SAT verbal scores over 500: 71%; SAT math scores over 500: 71%; SAT verbal scores over 600: 31%; SAT math scores over 600: 26%; SAT verbal scores over 700: 5%; SAT math scores over 700: 2%.
Tuition and fees (2003–04): $20,275 (full-time). *Room and board:* $7520 (room only: $3920).
Financial Aid (All incoming freshmen): *Average need-based gift aid:* $15,974. *Average non-need based aid:* $15,275. *Average aid to full-time undergraduates:* $19,565.
Athletic Department: *Director of Athletics:* Gib Romaine; Phone: 301-696-3493; Fax: 301-696-3488. *Sports Information Director:* Jason Brennan; Phone: 301-696-3978; E-mail: brennan@hood.edu.

MEN'S COACHES

Basketball: Tom Dickman; Phone: 301-696-3494; E-mail: dickman@hood.edu.

Cross Country: Brent Ayer; Phone: 301-696-3465; E-mail: ayer@hood.edu.

Golf: J.P. Lunn; Phone: 301-696-3491; E-mail: lunn@hood.edu.

Hood College (continued)

Swimming: Don Feinberg; Phone: 301-696-3484; E-mail: feinberg@hood.edu.
Tennis: Scott Eyler; Phone: 301-696-3491; E-mail: eyler@hood.edu.

WOMEN'S COACHES

Basketball: Rod Liller; Phone: 301-696-3468; E-mail: lillmill@starpower.net.
Cross Country: Brent Ayer; Phone: 301-696-3465; E-mail: ayer@hood.edu.
Field Hockey: Staci Thomson; Phone: 301-696-3785; E-mail: thomson@hood.edu.
Golf: J.P. Lunn; Phone: 301-696-3491; E-mail: lunn@hood.edu.
Lacrosse: Staci Thomson; Phone: 301-696-3785; E-mail: thomson@hood.edu.
Soccer: Zak Zakhnini; Phone: 301-696-9883; E-mail: zakhnini@earthlink.net.
Softball: Tricia Fiut; Phone: 301-696-3465; E-mail: fiut@hood.edu.
Swimming: Don Feinberg; Phone: 301-696-3484; E-mail: feinberg@hood.edu.
Tennis: Len Latkovski; Phone: 301-696-3722; E-mail: latkovski@hood.edu.
Volleyball: Judy Whims; Phone: 301-696-3491.

HOPE COLLEGE
Holland, Michigan

Flying Dutchman ◆ NCAA III ◆ Michigan Intercollegiate Conference ◆ http://www.hope.edu/

Independent religious 4-year, founded 1866, affiliated with Reformed Church in America
Coed, 3,068 undergraduate students, 96% full-time, 62% women, 38% men
Small-town 45-acre campus with easy access to Grand Rapids
Moderately difficult entrance level, 77% of applicants were admitted

Freshmen Admission: 2,481 applied, 2,056 were accepted, 811 enrolled. Test scores: SAT verbal scores over 500: 88%; SAT math scores over 500: 89%; SAT verbal scores over 600: 49%; SAT math scores over 600: 52%; SAT verbal scores over 700: 13%; SAT math scores over 700: 13%.
Tuition and fees (2003–04): $19,322 (full-time). Room and board: $6018 (room only: $2744).
Financial Aid (All incoming freshmen): Average need-based gift aid: $12,975. Average non-need based aid: $6070. Average aid to full-time undergraduates: $17,365.
Athletic Department: Director of Athletics: Ray Smith; Phone: 616-395-7698; Fax: 616-395-7175; E-mail: resmith@hope.edu. Sports Information Director: Tom Renner; Phone: 616-395-7860; E-mail: trenner@hope.edu.

MEN'S COACHES

Baseball: Stu Fritz; Phone: 616-395-7692; E-mail: fritz@hope.edu.
Basketball: Glenn Van Wieren; Phone: 616-395-7699; E-mail: gvanwieren@hope.edu.
Cheerleading: Wes Wooley; Phone: 616-393-9588; E-mail: wooley@hope.edu.
Cross Country: Mark Northuis; Phone: 616-395-7689; E-mail: northuis@hope.edu.
Diving: Jim Mitchell; Phone: 616-395-7690.
Football: Dean Kreps; Phone: 616-395-7704; E-mail: kreps@hope.edu.
Golf: Bob Ebels; Phone: 616-738-3800; E-mail: ebels@hope.edu.
Soccer: Steve Smith; Phone: 616-395-7569; E-mail: sdsmith@hope.edu.
Swimming: John Patnott; Phone: 616-395-7697; E-mail: patnott@hope.edu.
Tennis: Steve Gorno; Phone: 616-394-1192; E-mail: steven.m.gorno@jci.com.
Track and Field: Dereck Chavis; Phone: 616-395-7455; E-mail: chavis@hope.edu.

WOMEN'S COACHES

Basketball: Brian Morehouse; Phone: 616-395-7853; E-mail: morehouse@hope.edu.
Cheerleading: Wes Wooley; Phone: 616-393-9588; E-mail: wooley@hope.edu.
Cross Country: Mark Northuis; Phone: 616-395-7689; E-mail: northuis@hope.edu.

Diving: Jim Mitchell; Phone: 616-395-7690.
Golf: Tom Smith; Phone: 616-395-7979; E-mail: tsmith@hope.edu.
Soccer: Leigh Sears; Phone: 616-395-7690; E-mail: sears@hope.edu.
Softball: Karla Wolters; Phone: 616-395-7701; E-mail: wolters@hope.edu.
Swimming: John Patnott; Phone: 616-395-7697; E-mail: patnott@hope.edu.
Tennis: Karen Page; Phone: 616-395-4965; E-mail: page@hope.edu.
Track and Field: Dereck Chavis; Phone: 616-395-7455; E-mail: chavis@hope.edu.
Volleyball: Maureen Dunn; Phone: 616-395-7690; E-mail: dunnm@hope.edu.

HOPE INTERNATIONAL UNIVERSITY
Fullerton, California

Royals ◆ NAIA ◆ Golden State Conference ◆ http://www.hiu.edu/

Independent religious comprehensive, founded 1928, affiliated with Christian Churches and Churches of Christ
Coed, 926 undergraduate students, 50% full-time, 64% women, 36% men
Suburban 16-acre campus with easy access to Los Angeles
Moderately difficult entrance level, 4% of applicants were admitted

Freshmen Admission: 368 applied, 156 were accepted, 121 enrolled.
Tuition and fees (2003–04): $15,200 (full-time). Room and board: $5874 (room only: $3098).
Financial Aid (All incoming freshmen): Average need-based gift aid: $9086. Average non-need based aid: $9454. Average aid to full-time undergraduates: $11,849.
Athletic Department: Director of Athletics: Glenn Snyder; Phone: 714-879-3901; Fax: 714-879-0231; E-mail: gsnyder@hiu.edu. Sports Information Director: Mark Colachico; Phone: 714-879-3901; E-mail: mpcolachico@hiu.edu.

MEN'S COACHES

Basketball: Tim Sweeney; Phone: 714-879-3901; E-mail: tssweeney@hiu.edu.
Soccer: Bill Schnobrich; Phone: 714-879-3901; E-mail: brschnobrich@hiu.edu.
Tennis: Dave Radford; Phone: 714-879-3901; E-mail: saintdavid@aol.com.
Volleyball: Shawn Hunter; Phone: 714-879-3901; E-mail: swhunter@hiu.edu.

WOMEN'S COACHES

Basketball: Holley Limpach; Phone: 714-879-3901; E-mail: hjlimpach@hiu.edu.
Soccer: Jennifer Connell; Phone: 714-879-3901; E-mail: jeconnell@hiu.edu.
Softball: David Shawver; Phone: 714-879-3901; E-mail: djshawver@hiu.edu.
Tennis: Dave Radford; Phone: 714-879-3901; E-mail: saintdavid@aol.com.
Volleyball: Chris Keife; Phone: 714-879-3901; E-mail: cmkeife@hiu.edu.

HOUGHTON COLLEGE
Houghton, New York

Highlanders ◆ NAIA ◆ American Mideast Conference ◆ http://www.houghton.edu/

Independent Wesleyan 4-year, founded 1883
Coed, 1,458 undergraduate students, 94% full-time, 65% women, 35% men
Rural 1,300-acre campus with easy access to Buffalo and Rochester
Moderately difficult entrance level, 83% of applicants were admitted

Freshmen Admission: 1,071 applied, 911 were accepted, 304 enrolled. Test scores: SAT verbal scores over 500: 84%; SAT math scores over

500: 82%; SAT verbal scores over 600: 48%; SAT math scores over 600: 37%; SAT verbal scores over 700: 13%; SAT math scores over 700: 6%.
Tuition and fees (2003–04): $17,984 (full-time). *Room and board:* $6000 (room only: $3000).
Financial Aid (All incoming freshmen): *Average need-based gift aid:* $9941. *Average non-need based aid:* $7392. *Average aid to full-time undergraduates:* $14,342.
Athletic Department: *Director of Athletics:* Skip Lord; Phone: 585-567-9645; Fax: 585-567-9365; E-mail: harold.lord@houghton.edu. *Sports Information Director:* Jason Mucher; Phone: 585-567-9559; E-mail: jason.mucher@houghton.edu.

MEN'S COACHES
Basketball: Brad Zarges; Phone: 585-567-9368; E-mail: brad.zarges@houghton.edu.
Cross Country: Robert Smalley; Phone: 585-567-9389; E-mail: robert.smalley@houghton.edu.
Soccer: Dwight Hornibrook; Phone: 585-567-9489; E-mail: dwight.hornibrook@houghton.edu.
Track and Field: Robert Smalley; Phone: 585-567-9389; E-mail: robert.smalley@houghton.edu.

WOMEN'S COACHES
Basketball: Skip Lord; Phone: 585-567-9645; E-mail: harold.lord@houghton.edu.
Basketball: Skip Lord; Phone: 585-567-9645; E-mail: harold.lord@houghton.edu.
Cross Country: Robert Smalley; Phone: 585-567-9389; E-mail: robert.smalley@houghton.edu.
Field Hockey: Donna Hornibrook; Phone: 585-567-9268; E-mail: donna.hornibrook@houghton.edu.
Soccer: David Lewis; Phone: 585-567-9548; E-mail: david.lewis@houghton.edu.
Track and Field: Robert Smalley; Phone: 585-567-9389; E-mail: robert.smalley@houghton.edu.
Volleyball: Nancy Cole; Phone: 585-567-9292; E-mail: nancy.cole@houghton.edu.

HOUSTON BAPTIST UNIVERSITY
Houston, Texas
Huskies ◆ NAIA ◆ Red River Conference ◆ http://www.hbu.edu/

Independent Baptist comprehensive, founded 1960
Coed, 1,866 undergraduate students, 87% full-time, 69% women, 31% men
Urban 100-acre campus
Moderately difficult entrance level, 62% of applicants were admitted

Freshmen *Admission:* 896 applied, 559 were accepted, 280 enrolled. *Test scores:* SAT verbal scores over 500: 69%; SAT math scores over 500: 68%; SAT verbal scores over 600: 23%; SAT math scores over 600: 27%; SAT verbal scores over 700: 3%; SAT math scores over 700: 4%.
Tuition and fees (2003–04): $12,180 (full-time). *Room and board:* $4680.
Financial Aid (All incoming freshmen): *Average need-based gift aid:* $7010. *Average non-need based aid:* $14,647. *Average aid to full-time undergraduates:* $9405.
Athletic Department: *Director of Athletics:* Ron Cottrell; Phone: 281-649-3250; Fax: 281-649-3496; E-mail: rcottrell@hbu.edu. *Sports Information Director:* Steven Key; Phone: 281-649-3271; E-mail: skey@hbuhuskies.com.

MEN'S COACHES
Baseball: Brian Huddleston; Phone: 281-649-3332; E-mail: bhuddleston@hbu.edu.
Basketball: Ron Cottrell; Phone: 281-649-3250; E-mail: rcottrell@hbu.edu.

WOMEN'S COACHES
Basketball: Shane Brown; Phone: 281-649-3105; E-mail: sbrown@hbu.edu.
Softball: Mary Ellen Hall; Phone: 281-649-3248; E-mail: mehallhbu@aol.com.
Volleyball: Kaddie Platt; Phone: 281-649-3316; E-mail: kaddieplatt@yahoo.com.

HOWARD PAYNE UNIVERSITY
Brownwood, Texas
Yellow Jackets ◆ NCAA III ◆ American Southwest Conference ◆ http://www.hputx.edu/

Independent religious 4-year, founded 1889, affiliated with Baptist General Convention of Texas
Coed, 1,385 undergraduate students, 78% full-time, 49% women, 51% men
Small-town 30-acre campus
Minimally difficult entrance level, 76% of applicants were admitted

Freshmen *Admission:* 904 applied, 717 were accepted, 345 enrolled. *Test scores:* SAT verbal scores over 500: 52%; SAT math scores over 500: 52%; SAT verbal scores over 600: 20%; SAT math scores over 600: 14%; SAT verbal scores over 700: 2%; SAT math scores over 700: %.
Tuition and fees (2003–04): $11,150 (full-time). *Room and board:* $4026 (room only: $1660).
Financial Aid (All incoming freshmen): *Average need-based gift aid:* $7091. *Average non-need based aid:* $4010. *Average aid to full-time undergraduates:* $9756.
Athletic Department: *Director of Athletics:* Vance Gibson; Phone: 915-649-8109; Fax: 325-649-8920; E-mail: vgibson@hputx.edu. *Sports Information Director:* Nadir Dalleh; Phone: 325-649-8111; E-mail: ndalleh@hputx.edu.

MEN'S COACHES
Baseball: Mike Kennemer; Phone: 915-649-8117; E-mail: mkennemer@hputx.edu.
Basketball: Charles Pattillo; Phone: 915-649-8104; E-mail: cpattillo@hputx.edu.
Cheerleading: Torri Choate; Phone: 915-646-2502; E-mail: tchoate@hputx.edu.
Football: Vance Gibson; Phone: 915-649-8109; E-mail: vgibson@hputx.edu.
Tennis: Shane Wiliford; Phone: 915-649-8827; E-mail: swilliford@hputx.edu.
Track and Field: Darren Kight; Phone: 915-649-8115; E-mail: dkight@hputx.edu.

WOMEN'S COACHES
Basketball: Chris Kiclsmeier; Phone: 915-649-8110; E-mail: ckielsmeier@hputx.edu.
Cheerleading: Torri Choate; Phone: 915-646-2502; E-mail: tchoate@hputx.edu.
Softball: Angela Froboese; Phone: 915-649-8970; E-mail: afroboese@hputx.edu.
Tennis: Shane Wiliford; Phone: 915-649-8827; E-mail: swilliford@hputx.edu.
Track and Field: Darren Kight; Phone: 915-649-8115; E-mail: dkight@hputx.edu.
Volleyball: Leslie Walker; Phone: 915-649-8107; E-mail: lwalker@hputx.edu.

HOWARD UNIVERSITY
Washington, District of Columbia
Bison ◆ NCAA I ◆ Atlantic Soccer Conference; Mid-Eastern Athletic Conference; Northeast Conference ◆ http://www.howard.edu/

Independent university, founded 1867
Coed, 7,059 undergraduate students, 94% full-time, 67% women, 33% men
Urban 256-acre campus
Moderately difficult entrance level, 53% of applicants were admitted

Freshmen *Admission:* 7,057 applied, 3,982 were accepted, 1,455 enrolled.
Tuition and fees (2003–04): $10,935 (full-time). *Room and board:* $5570 (room only: $2182).
Financial Aid (All incoming freshmen): *Average need-based gift aid:* $3417. *Average aid to full-time undergraduates:* $16,879.
Athletic Department: *Director of Athletics:* Sondra Norrell-Thomas; Phone: 202-806-7141; Fax: 202-806-9090; E-mail: snorrell-thomas@

Howard University *(continued)*

howard.edu. *Sports Information Director:* Edward Hill; Phone: 202-806-7184; E-mail: ehill@howard.edu.

MEN'S COACHES

Basketball: Frankie Allen; Phone: 202-806-5202; E-mail: fwallen@howard.edu.

Cheerleading: Rasheem Ameid-Rooke; Phone: 202-806-7000; E-mail: r_rooke@howard.edu.

Cross Country: Michael Merritt; Phone: 202-806-5162; E-mail: mmerritt@howard.edu.

Football: Rayford Petty; Phone: 202-806-7151; E-mail: rpetty@howard.edu.

Soccer: Keith Tucker; Phone: 202-806-7174; E-mail: ktucker@howard.edu.

Swimming: Roy Fagin; Phone: 202-806-6793; E-mail: rfagin@howard.edu.

Tennis: Larry Strickland; Phone: 202-806-7162; E-mail: lstrickland@howard.edu.

Track and Field: Michael Merritt; Phone: 202-806-5162; E-mail: mmerritt@howard.edu.

WOMEN'S COACHES

Basketball: Cathy Parson; Phone: 202-806-7950; E-mail: cparson@howard.edu.

Cheerleading: Rasheem Ameid-Rooke; Phone: 202-806-7000; E-mail: r_rooke@howard.edu.

Cross Country: Michael Merritt; Phone: 202-806-5162; E-mail: mmerritt@howard.edu.

Lacrosse: Melinda Vaughn; Phone: 202-806-6804; E-mail: mlvaughn@howard.edu.

Soccer: Michell Street; Phone: 202-806-7147; E-mail: mstreet@howard.edu.

Softball: Tonja Braxton; Phone: 202-806-5165; E-mail: tbraxtonhusb@msn.com.

Swimming: Roy Fagin; Phone: 202-806-6793; E-mail: rfagin@howard.edu.

Tennis: Larry Strickland; Phone: 202-806-7162; E-mail: lstrickland@howard.edu.

Track and Field: Michael Merritt; Phone: 202-806-5162; E-mail: mmerritt@howard.edu.

Volleyball: Linda Spencer; Phone: 202-806-5204; E-mail: lspencer@howard.edu.

HUMBOLDT STATE UNIVERSITY
Arcata, California

Lumberjacks ◆ NCAA II ◆ Great Northwest Athletic Conference ◆ http://www.humboldt.edu/

State-supported comprehensive, founded 1913, part of California State University System
Coed, 6,682 undergraduate students, 89% full-time, 55% women, 45% men
Rural 161-acre campus
Moderately difficult entrance level, 65% of applicants were admitted

Freshmen *Admission:* 5,521 applied, 3,677 were accepted, 861 enrolled. *Test scores:* SAT verbal scores over 500: 66%; SAT math scores over 500: 65%; SAT verbal scores over 600: 26%; SAT math scores over 600: 20%; SAT verbal scores over 700: 3%; SAT math scores over 700: 2%.
Tuition and fees (2003–04): $2539 (resident), $9307 (nonresident). *Room and board:* $6861 (room only: $3595).
Financial Aid (All incoming freshmen): *Average need-based gift aid:* $5100. *Average aid to full-time undergraduates:* $8550.
Athletic Department: *Director of Athletics:* Dan Collen; Phone: 707-826-3666; Fax: 707-826-5446; E-mail: dgc7001@humboldt.edu. *Sports Information Director:* Dan Pambianco; Phone: 707-826-3631; E-mail: dmp1@humboldt.edu.

MEN'S COACHES

Basketball: Tom Wood; Phone: 707-826-3463; E-mail: tmw2@axe.humboldt.edu.

Cross Country: David Wells; Phone: 707-826-5955; E-mail: dcw3@axe.humboldt.edu.

Football: Doug Adkins; Phone: 707-826-5947; E-mail: da7002@humboldt.edu.

Soccer: Alan Exley; Phone: 707-826-5941; E-mail: aje2@axe.humboldt.edu.

Track and Field: David Wells; Phone: 707-826-5955; E-mail: dcw3@axe.humboldt.edu.

WOMEN'S COACHES

Basketball: Carol Harrison; Phone: 707-826-5942; E-mail: cah5mailto:pjm2@axe.humboldt.edu.

Cross Country: David Wells; Phone: 707-826-5955; E-mail: dcw3@axe.humboldt.edu.

Soccer: Andy Cumbo; Phone: 707-826-4129; E-mail: ac11@humboldt.edu.

Softball: Frank Cheek; Phone: 707-826-5952; E-mail: fjc2@axe.humboldt.edu.

Track and Field: David Wells; Phone: 707-826-5955; E-mail: dcw3@axe.humboldt.edu.

Volleyball: Sue Woodstra; Phone: 707-826-6017; E-mail: sjw7002@humboldt.edu.

HUNTER COLLEGE OF THE CITY UNIVERSITY OF NEW YORK
New York, New York

Hawks ◆ NCAA III ◆ CUNY Athletic Conference ◆ http://www.hunter.cuny.edu/

State and locally supported comprehensive, founded 1870, part of City University of New York System
Coed, 15,906 undergraduate students, 66% full-time, 70% women, 30% men
Urban campus
Moderately difficult entrance level, 27% of applicants were admitted

Freshmen *Admission:* 12,345 applied, 3,659 were accepted, 1,691 enrolled. *Test scores:* SAT verbal scores over 500: 62%; SAT math scores over 500: 72%; SAT verbal scores over 600: 19%; SAT math scores over 600: 23%; SAT verbal scores over 700: 4%; SAT math scores over 700: 4%.
Tuition and fees (2003–04): $4164 (resident).
Athletic Department: *Director of Athletics:* Terry Wansart; Phone: 212-772-4783; Fax: 212-772-4739; E-mail: terry.wansart@hunter.cuny.edu. *Sports Information Director:* Damion Jones; Phone: 212-772-4631; E-mail: damion.jones@hunter.cuny.edu.

MEN'S COACHES

Basketball: Bill Healy; Phone: 212-772-4643; E-mail: william.healy@hunter.cuny.edu.

Cross Country: Ed Zarowin; Phone: 212-772-4791.

Soccer: Ivan Matteoni; Phone: 212-772-3901.

Tennis: Mel Kerper; Phone: 212-772-4790.

Track and Field: Ed Zarowin; Phone: 212-772-4791.

Volleyball: Lauren Caiaccia; Phone: 212-772-4797; E-mail: lauren.caiaccia@hunter.cuny.edu.

Wrestling: Bob Gaudenzi; Phone: 212-772-4654; E-mail: rgaudenz@hchs.hunter.cuny.edu.

WOMEN'S COACHES

Basketball: Jackie Meadow; Phone: 212-772-4912; E-mail: jackee.meadow@hunter.cuny.edu.

Cross Country: Ed Zarowin; Phone: 212-772-4791.

Softball: Betsy Hipple; Phone: 212-650-3264; E-mail: betsy.hipple@hunter.cuny.edu.

Swimming: Delon Callender; Phone: 212-650-3502.

Tennis: Jocelyn Cruz; Phone: 212-772-4790.

Track and Field: Ed Zarowin; Phone: 212-772-4791.

Volleyball: Lauren Caiaccia; Phone: 212-772-4797; E-mail: lauren.caiaccia@hunter.cuny.edu.

HUNTINGDON COLLEGE
Montgomery, Alabama

Hawks ◆ NCAA III ◆ Great South Conference; Independent ◆ http://www.huntingdon.edu/

Independent United Methodist 4-year, founded 1854
Coed, 660 undergraduate students, 96% full-time, 55% women, 45% men
Suburban 71-acre campus with easy access to Birmingham
Moderately difficult entrance level, 49% of applicants were admitted

Freshmen *Admission:* 1,108 applied, 650 were accepted, 201 enrolled. *Test scores:* SAT verbal scores over 500: 91%; SAT math scores over 500: 76%; SAT verbal scores over 600: 39%; SAT math scores over 600: 48%; SAT verbal scores over 700: 4%; SAT math scores over 700: 7%.
Tuition and fees (2004–05): $15,250 (full-time). *Room and board:* $6000.
Financial Aid (All incoming freshmen): *Average need-based gift aid:* $6186. *Average non-need based aid:* $5987. *Average aid to full-time undergraduates:* $9989.
Athletic Department: *Director of Athletics:* Duane Trogdon; Phone: 334-833-4581; Fax: 334-833-4486; E-mail: dtrogdon@huntingdon.edu. *Sports Information Director:* Jay Holcey; Phone: 334-833-4579; E-mail: jholcey@huntingdon.edu.

MEN'S COACHES
Baseball: Scott Paterson; Phone: 334-833-4501; E-mail: spatterson@huntingdon.edu.
Basketball: Tony Duckworth; Phone: 334-833-4399; E-mail: tduckworth@huntingdon.edu.
Football: Duane Trogdon; Phone: 334-833-4581; E-mail: dtrogdon@huntingdon.edu.
Golf: Duane Trojdan; Phone: 334-833-4581; E-mail: dtrogdon@huntingdon.edu.
Soccer: Ryan Cabarrao; Phone: 334-833-4316; E-mail: rcabarrao@huntingdon.edu.

WOMEN'S COACHES
Basketball: Forrest Smith; Phone: 334-833-4319; E-mail: fsmith@huntingdon.edu.
Soccer: Amy Stockton; Phone: 334-833-4468; E-mail: astockton@huntingdon.edu.
Softball: Angela Cook; Phone: 334-833-4561; E-mail: acook@huntingdon.edu.
Tennis: Ximena Moore; Phone: 334-833-4505; E-mail: xmoore@huntingdon.edu.
Volleyball: Terina Ganntt; Phone: 334-833-4411; E-mail: tgantt@huntingdon.edu.

HUNTINGTON COLLEGE
Huntington, Indiana

Foresters ◆ NAIA ◆ Mid-Central Conference ◆ http://www.huntington.edu/

Independent religious comprehensive, founded 1897, affiliated with Church of the United Brethren in Christ
Coed, 923 undergraduate students, 92% full-time, 57% women, 43% men
Small-town 200-acre campus with easy access to Fort Wayne
Moderately difficult entrance level, 93% of applicants were admitted

Freshmen *Admission:* 620 applied, 570 were accepted, 192 enrolled. *Test scores:* SAT verbal scores over 500: 78%; SAT math scores over 500: 79%; SAT verbal scores over 600: 33%; SAT math scores over 600: 33%; SAT verbal scores over 700: 8%; SAT math scores over 700: 6%.
Tuition and fees (2003–04): $17,700 (full-time). *Room and board:* $5890.
Financial Aid (All incoming freshmen): *Average need-based gift aid:* $9734. *Average non-need based aid:* $5492. *Average aid to full-time undergraduates:* $12,192.
Athletic Department: *Director of Athletics:* Gary Turner; Phone: 260-359-4284; Fax: 260-359-4295; E-mail: gturner@huntington.edu. *Sports Information Director:* Lori Culler; Phone: 260-359-4213; E-mail: lculler@huntington.edu.

MEN'S COACHES
Baseball: Mike Frame; Phone: 260-359-4212; E-mail: mframe@huntington.edu.
Basketball: Steve Platt; Phone: 260-359-4217; E-mail: splatt@huntington.edu.
Cheerleading: Candace Cooper; Phone: 260-359-4212.
Cross Country: Tom King; Phone: 260-359-4256; E-mail: tking@huntington.edu.
Golf: Pete Schownir; Phone: 260-359-4212; E-mail: pschownir@huntington.edu.
Soccer: Steve DeCou; Phone: 260-359-4289; E-mail: sdecou@huntington.edu.
Tennis: Gary Turner; Phone: 260-359-4284.
Track and Field: Tom King; Phone: 260-359-4256; E-mail: tking@huntington.edu.

WOMEN'S COACHES
Basketball: Lori Culler; Phone: 260-359-4213.
Cheerleading: Candace Cooper; Phone: 260-359-4212.
Cross Country: Tom King; Phone: 260-359-4256; E-mail: tking@huntington.edu.
Soccer: Tom Datema; Phone: 260-359-4212; E-mail: tdatema@huntington.edu.
Softball: Mike Tribolet; Phone: 260-359-4212; E-mail: mtribolet@huntington.edu.
Tennis: Gary Turner; Phone: 260-359-4284.
Track and Field: Tom King; Phone: 260-359-4256; E-mail: tking@huntington.edu.
Volleyball: David Schroeder; Phone: 260-359-4212.

HUSSON COLLEGE
Bangor, Maine

Braves ◆ NCAA III ◆ Independent; Sunrise Conference ◆ http://www.husson.edu/

Independent comprehensive, founded 1898
Coed, 1,767 undergraduate students, 64% full-time, 60% women, 40% men
Suburban 170-acre campus
Moderately difficult entrance level, 97% of applicants were admitted

Freshmen *Admission:* 656 applied, 639 were accepted, 305 enrolled. *Test scores:* SAT verbal scores over 500: 32%; SAT math scores over 500: 34%; SAT verbal scores over 600: 4%; SAT math scores over 600: 7%; SAT math scores over 700: 1%.
Tuition and fees (2003–04): $10,700 (full-time). *Room and board:* $5680.
Financial Aid (All incoming freshmen): *Average need-based gift aid:* $6457. *Average non-need based aid:* $5028. *Average aid to full-time undergraduates:* $8476.
Athletic Department: *Director of Athletics:* Gabby Price; Phone: 207-941-7029; Fax: 207-973-1015. *Sports Information Director:* Keith Bosley; Phone: 207-941-7017.

MEN'S COACHES
Baseball: John Kolasinski; Phone: 207-941-7700; E-mail: kolasinskij@husson.edu.
Basketball: Warren Caruso; Phone: 207-941-7112.
Cross Country: Dereck Treadwell; Phone: 207-941-5191.
Golf: Bruce MacGregor; Phone: 207-941-7011.
Soccer: Scott Warman; Phone: 207-941-7942.

WOMEN'S COACHES
Basketball: Kissy Walker; Phone: 207-941-7019; E-mail: walkerk@husson.edu.
Cross Country: Dereck Treadwell; Phone: 207-941-5191.
Field Hockey: Sharon Connolly; Phone: 207-941-7197.
Soccer: Keith Bosley; Phone: 207-941-7017.
Softball: Randy Dodge; Phone: 207-941-7025.
Volleyball: Pat Debeck; Phone: 207-941-7942.

HUSTON-TILLOTSON COLLEGE
Austin, Texas

Rams ◆ NAIA ◆ Red River Conference
◆ http://www.htc.edu/

Independent interdenominational 4-year, founded 1875
Coed, 583 undergraduate students, 94% full-time, 54% women, 46% men
Urban 23-acre campus
Moderately difficult entrance level, 98% of applicants were admitted

Freshmen *Admission:* 332 applied, 325 were accepted, 175 enrolled. *Test scores:* SAT verbal scores over 500: 16%; SAT math scores over 500: 15%; SAT verbal scores over 600: 1%; SAT math scores over 600: 1%.
Tuition and fees (2003–04): $8110 (full-time). *Room and board:* $5376 (room only: $3000).
Financial Aid (All incoming freshmen): *Average need-based gift aid:* $8989. *Average aid to full-time undergraduates:* $9184.
Athletic Department: *Director of Athletics:* Rozena McCabe; Phone: 512-505-3050; Fax: 512-505-3190.

MEN'S COACHES
Baseball: Alvin Moore; Phone: 512-505-3051; E-mail: almoore@htc.edu.
Basketball: Terrence Littlefield; Phone: 512-505-3050.
Soccer: Phone: 512-505-3050.
Track and Field: Howard Ware; Phone: 512-505-3049; E-mail: hhware@htc.edu.

WOMEN'S COACHES
Basketball: Walter Golden; Phone: 512-505-3050.
Soccer: Phone: 512-505-3050.
Track and Field: Howard Ware; Phone: 512-505-3049; E-mail: hhware@htc.edu.
Volleyball: Christiana Carter; Phone: 512-505-3050.

IDAHO STATE UNIVERSITY
Pocatello, Idaho

Bengals ◆ NCAA I ◆ Big Sky Conference
◆ http://www.isu.edu/

State-supported university, founded 1901
Coed, 11,451 undergraduate students, 69% full-time, 55% women, 45% men
Small-town 972-acre campus
Minimally difficult entrance level, 71% of applicants were admitted

Freshmen *Admission:* 3,573 applied, 2,644 were accepted, 1,971 enrolled. *Test scores:* SAT verbal scores over 500: 63%; SAT math scores over 500: 57%; SAT verbal scores over 600: 21%; SAT math scores over 600: 27%; SAT verbal scores over 700: 4%; SAT math scores over 700: 2%.
Tuition and fees (2003–04): $3448 (resident), $10,048 (nonresident). *Room and board:* $4680 (room only: $1980).
Athletic Department: *Director of Athletics:* Jim Senter; Phone: 208-282-4064; Fax: 208-282-4063; E-mail: sentjame@isu.edu. *Sports Information Director:* Frank Mercogliano; Phone: 208-282-2621; E-mail: mercfran@isu.edu.

MEN'S COACHES
Basketball: Doug Oliver; Phone: 208-282-4492; E-mail: olivdoug@isu.edu.
Cheerleading: Hillary Hofmaier; Phone: 208-282-4547; E-mail: johnhill@isu.edu.
Cross Country: Brian Janssen; Phone: 208-282-3297; E-mail: jansbria@isu.edu.
Football: Larry Lewis; Phone: 208-282-2779; E-mail: shermary@isu.edu.
Golf: Scott Busch; Phone: 208-282-5921; E-mail: buscscot@isu.edu.
Tennis: Bobby Goeltz; Phone: 208-282-4742; E-mail: goelrobe@isu.edu.
Track and Field: Dave Nielsen; Phone: 208-282-3299; E-mail: nieldave@isu.edu.

WOMEN'S COACHES
Basketball: Jon Newlee; Phone: 208-282-4492; E-mail: newljon@isu.edu.

Cheerleading: Hillary Hofmaier; Phone: 208-282-4547; E-mail: johnhill@isu.edu.
Cross Country: Brian Janssen; Phone: 208-282-3297; E-mail: jansbria@isu.edu.
Golf: Scott Busch; Phone: 208-282-5921; E-mail: buscscot@isu.edu.
Soccer: Mark Salisbury; Phone: 208-282-2925.
Tennis: Bobby Goeltz; Phone: 208-282-4742; E-mail: goelrobe@isu.edu.
Track and Field: Dave Nielsen; Phone: 208-282-3299; E-mail: nieldave@isu.edu.
Volleyball: Mike Welch; Phone: 208-282-4065; E-mail: welcmike@isu.edu.

ILLINOIS COLLEGE
Jacksonville, Illinois

Blue Boys ◆ NCAA III ◆ Midwest Conference ◆ http://www.ic.edu/

Independent interdenominational 4-year, founded 1829
Coed, 1,016 undergraduate students, 98% full-time, 56% women, 44% men
Small-town 62-acre campus with easy access to St. Louis
Moderately difficult entrance level, 71% of applicants were admitted

Freshmen *Admission:* 1,005 applied, 723 were accepted, 318 enrolled. *Test scores:* SAT verbal scores over 500: 86%; SAT math scores over 500: 90%; SAT verbal scores over 600: 48%; SAT math scores over 600: 52%; SAT verbal scores over 700: 10%; SAT math scores over 700: 14%.
Tuition and fees (2003–04): $13,300 (full-time). *Room and board:* $5800.
Financial Aid (All incoming freshmen): *Average need-based gift aid:* $5954. *Average non-need based aid:* $5487. *Average aid to full-time undergraduates:* $13,221.
Athletic Department: *Director of Athletics:* Gale Vaughn; Phone: 217-245-3400; Fax: 217-245-3398; E-mail: gfvaughn@ic.edu. *Sports Information Director:* Jim Murphy; Phone: 217-245-3048; E-mail: jtmurphy@ic.edu.

MEN'S COACHES
Baseball: Jay Eckhouse; Phone: 217-245-3381; E-mail: jeckhous@ic.edu.
Basketball: Mike Worrell; Phone: 217-245-3402; E-mail: mlworrel@ic.edu.
Cross Country: Laura Rodholm; Phone: 217-245-3400; E-mail: lrodholm@ic.edu.
Football: Aaron Keen; Phone: 217-245-3403; E-mail: akeen@ic.edu.
Golf: Jim Cisne; Phone: 217-245-3400; E-mail: jcisne@ic.edu.
Soccer: Russ Bogdanovich; Phone: 217-245-7838; E-mail: rbogdano@ic.edu.
Tennis: Joe Hankins; Phone: 217-245-3400; E-mail: jhankins@ic.edu.
Track and Field: Mike Brooks; Phone: 217-245-3400; E-mail: mbrooks@ic.edu.
Wrestling: Tom Rowland; Phone: 217-245-3403; E-mail: tlrowlan@ic.edu.

WOMEN'S COACHES
Basketball: Brenna Kelly; Phone: 217-245-3404; E-mail: bkelly@ic.edu.
Cross Country: Laura Rodholm; Phone: 217-245-3400; E-mail: lrodholm@ic.edu.
Golf: Brenna Kelly; Phone: 217-245-3404; E-mail: bkelly@ic.edu.
Soccer: Brett Berry; Phone: 217-245-3395; E-mail: bberry@ic.edu.
Softball: Jennifer Hanely; Phone: 217-245-3400; E-mail: jhanely@ic.edu.
Tennis: Joe Hankins; Phone: 217-245-3400; E-mail: jhankins@ic.edu.
Track and Field: Mike Brooks; Phone: 217-245-3400; E-mail: mbrooks@ic.edu.
Volleyball: Jennifer Hanely; Phone: 217-245-3391; E-mail: jhanely@ic.edu.

ILLINOIS INSTITUTE OF TECHNOLOGY
Chicago, Illinois

Scarlet Hawks ◆ NAIA ◆ Chicagoland Collegiate Conference ◆ http://www.iit.edu/

Independent university, founded 1890
Coed, 1,941 undergraduate students, 86% full-time, 25% women, 75% men
Urban 120-acre campus
Very difficult entrance level, 61% of applicants were admitted

Freshmen *Admission:* 2,538 applied, 1,502 were accepted, 398 enrolled. *Test scores:* SAT verbal scores over 500: 92%; SAT math scores over 500: 99%; SAT verbal scores over 600: 63%; SAT math scores over 600: 84%; SAT verbal scores over 700: 18%; SAT math scores over 700: 41%.
Tuition and fees (2004–05): $21,342 (full-time). *Room and board:* $6946.
Financial Aid (All incoming freshmen): *Average need-based gift aid:* $14,141. *Average non-need based aid:* $11,900. *Average aid to full-time undergraduates:* $19,663.
Athletic Department: *Director of Athletics:* Lee Hitchen; Phone: 312-567-7126; Fax: 312-567-7133; E-mail: hitchen@iit.edu. *Sports Information Director:* Chris Meyer; Phone: 312-567-7127; E-mail: meyer@iit.edu.

MEN'S COACHES
Baseball: JohnFitzgerald; Phone: 312-567-7128; E-mail: fitzgeraldj@iit.edu.
Basketball: Kenny Battle; Phone: 312-567-3299; E-mail: battlek@iit.edu.
Cross Country: Phil Kopinski; Phone: 312-567-7126; E-mail: kopinski@iit.edu.
Soccer: Lee Hitchen; Phone: 312-567-7126; E-mail: hitchen@iit.edu.
Swimming: Rob Bond; Phone: 312-567-7126; E-mail: bondr@iit.edu.

WOMEN'S COACHES
Basketball: Annie Basic; Phone: 312-567-3298; E-mail: basic@iit.edu.
Cross Country: Phil Kopinski; Phone: 312-567-7126; E-mail: kopinski@iit.edu.
Soccer: Lee Hitchen; Phone: 312-567-7126; E-mail: hitchen@iit.edu.
Swimming: Rob Bond; Phone: 312-567-7126; E-mail: bondr@iit.edu.
Volleyball: Phone: 312-567-3296; E-mail: basic@iit.edu.

ILLINOIS STATE UNIVERSITY
Normal, Illinois

NCAA I ◆ Gateway Football Conference; Missouri Valley Conference ◆ http://www.ilstu.edu/

State-supported university, founded 1857
Coed, 18,097 undergraduate students, 93% full-time, 58% women, 42% men
Urban 850-acre campus
Moderately difficult entrance level, 72% of applicants were admitted

Freshmen *Admission:* 10,075 applied, 7,570 were accepted, 3,097 enrolled.
Tuition and fees (2003–04): $5530 (resident), $10,000 (nonresident). *Room and board:* $5414 (room only: $2682).
Financial Aid (All incoming freshmen): *Average need-based gift aid:* $5664. *Average non-need based aid:* $2963. *Average aid to full-time undergraduates:* $6777.
Athletic Department: *Director of Athletics:* John Weisenburger; Phone: 309-438-3636; Fax: 309-438-2323; E-mail: jweisen@ilstu.edu. *Sports Information Director:* Todd Kober; Phone: 309-438-3805; E-mail: gtkober@ilstu.edu.

MEN'S COACHES
Baseball: Jim Brownlee; Phone: 309-438-5151; E-mail: jhbrown@ilstu.edu.
Basketball: Porter Moser; Phone: 309-438-8681; E-mail: pamoser@ilstu.edu.
Cheerleading: Erik Rankin; Phone: 309-438-3639; E-mail: etranki@ilstu.edu.
Cross Country: Elvis Forde; Phone: 309-438-3639; E-mail: eaforde@ilstu.edu.

Football: Denver Johnson; Phone: 309-438-8671; E-mail: pjmerna@ilstu.edu.
Golf: Harland Kilborn; Phone: 309-438-3635; E-mail: hrkilbo@ilstu.edu.
Tennis: Greg Kennett; Phone: 309-438-5577; E-mail: gfkenne@ilstu.edu.
Track and Field: Elvis Forde; Phone: 309-438-3639; E-mail: eaforde@ilstu.edu.

WOMEN'S COACHES
Basketball: Robin Pingeton; Phone: 309-438-2567; E-mail: rrpinge@ilstu.edu.
Cheerleading: Erik Rankin; Phone: 309-438-3639; E-mail: etranki@ilstu.edu.
Cross Country: Elvis Forde; Phone: 309-438-3639; E-mail: eaforde@ilstu.edu.
Diving: Carly Weiden; Phone: 309-438-7946.
Golf: Ray Kralis; Phone: 309-438-7962; E-mail: rakrali@ilstu.edu.
Gymnastics: Kristen Montero; Phone: 309-438-3639; E-mail: kmmonte@ilstu.edu.
Soccer: Pete Kowall; Phone: 309-438-7074; E-mail: pmkowal@ilstu.edu.
Softball: Melinda Fischer; Phone: 309-438-5807; E-mail: msfisch@ilstu.edu.
Swimming: Steve Paska; Phone: 309-438-7946; E-mail: sepaska@ilstu.edu.
Tennis: Chris Hoover; Phone: 309-438-5338; E-mail: cjhoove@ilstu.edu.
Track and Field: Elvis Forde; Phone: 309-438-3639; E-mail: eaforde@ilstu.edu.
Volleyball: Sharon Dingman; Phone: 309-438-2567; E-mail: psrexro@ilstu.edu.

ILLINOIS WESLEYAN UNIVERSITY
Bloomington, Illinois

Titans ◆ NCAA III ◆ College Conference of Illinois and Wisconsin Conference ◆ http://www.iwu.edu/

Independent 4-year, founded 1850
Coed, 2,106 undergraduate students, 100% full-time, 57% women, 43% men
Suburban 79-acre campus
Very difficult entrance level, 5% of applicants were admitted

Freshmen *Admission:* 3,331 applied, 1,431 were accepted, 578 enrolled. *Test scores:* SAT verbal scores over 500: 98%; SAT math scores over 500: 99%; SAT verbal scores over 600: 68%; SAT math scores over 600: 77%; SAT verbal scores over 700: 23%; SAT math scores over 700: 23%.
Tuition and fees (2004–05): $26,130 (full-time). *Room and board:* $6140 (room only: $3680).
Financial Aid (All incoming freshmen): *Average need-based gift aid:* $11,895. *Average aid to full-time undergraduates:* $16,561.
Athletic Department: *Director of Athletics:* Dennie Bridges; Phone: 309-556-3345; Fax: 309-556-3484; E-mail: dbridges@titan.iwu.edu. *Sports Information Director:* Stew Salowitz; Phone: 309-556-3206; E-mail: salowitz@titan.iwu.edu.

MEN'S COACHES
Baseball: Dennis Martel; Phone: 309-556-3335; E-mail: dmartel@titan.iwu.edu.
Basketball: Scott Trost; Phone: 309-556-3340; E-mail: strost@titan.iwu.edu.
Cross Country: Chris Schumacher; Phone: 309-556-3624; E-mail: cschumac@titan.iwu.edu.
Diving: Teresa Fish; Phone: 309-556-3382; E-mail: tfish@titan.iwu.edu.
Football: Norm Eash; Phone: 309-556-3344; E-mail: neash@titan.iwu.edu.
Golf: Jim Ott; Phone: 309-556-3612; E-mail: ottjim@hotmail.com.
Soccer: Dave Barrett; Phone: 309-556-3343; E-mail: dbarrett@titan.iwu.edu.
Swimming: Teresa Fish; Phone: 309-556-3382; E-mail: tfish@titan.iwu.edu.
Tennis: John Fish; Phone: 309-556-3626; E-mail: jfish@titan.iwu.edu.
Track and Field: Jason Williams; Phone: 309-556-2033; E-mail: jmwillia@titan.iwu.edu.

Illinois Wesleyan University *(continued)*
WOMEN'S COACHES
Basketball: Mia Smith; Phone: 309-556-3611; E-mail: msmith@titan. iwu.edu.
Cross Country: Chris Schumacher; Phone: 309-556-3624; E-mail: cschumac@titan.iwu.edu.
Diving: Teresa Fish; Phone: 309-556-3382; E-mail: tfish@titan.iwu.edu.
Golf: Kathy Niepagen; Phone: 309-556-3612; E-mail: niepy@aol.com.
Soccer: Dave Barnett; Phone: 309-556-3343; E-mail: dbarrett@titan. iwu.edu.
Softball: Beth Williams; Phone: 309-556-3348; E-mail: bhasheid@iwu. edu.
Swimming: Teresa Fish; Phone: 309-556-3382; E-mail: tfish@titan.iwu. edu.
Tennis: Sally Mangina; Phone: 309-556-3626; E-mail: sally.mangina. a2ev@statefarm.com.
Track and Field: Chris Schumacher; Phone: 309-556-3624; E-mail: cschumac@titan.iwu.edu.
Volleyball: Kim Nelson-Brown; Phone: 309-556-3349; E-mail: knbrown@titan.iwu.edu.

IMMACULATA UNIVERSITY
Immaculata, Pennsylvania

Mighty Macs ◆ NCAA III ◆ Pennsylvania Athletic Conference ◆ http://www.immaculata.edu/

Independent Roman Catholic comprehensive, founded 1920
Coed, 2,575 undergraduate students, 18% full-time, 84% women, 16% men
Suburban 400-acre campus with easy access to Philadelphia
Moderately difficult entrance level, 85% of applicants were admitted

Freshmen *Admission:* 346 applied, 295 were accepted, 82 enrolled. *Test scores:* SAT verbal scores over 500: 48%; SAT math scores over 500: 33%; SAT verbal scores over 600: 17%; SAT math scores over 600: 9%; SAT verbal scores over 700: 4%; SAT math scores over 700: 1%.
Tuition and fees (2003–04): $17,200 (full-time). *Room and board:* $8000 (room only: $4300).
Financial Aid (All incoming freshmen): *Average need-based gift aid:* $2800. *Average non-need based aid:* $5000. *Average aid to full-time undergraduates:* $13,100.
Athletic Department: *Director of Athletics:* Patty Canterino; Phone: 610-647-4400; Fax: 610-647-8482; E-mail: pcanterino@immaculata.edu. *Sports Information Director:* Kelly Donohue; Phone: 610-647-4400; E-mail: kdonohue@immaculata.edu.
WOMEN'S COACHES
Basketball: Patty Canterino; Phone: 610-647-4440; E-mail: pcanterino@immaculata.edu.
Cross Country: Kendra Weible; Phone: 610-647-4440.
Field Hockey: Erin McDonnell; Phone: 610-647-4440.
Lacrosse: Susan smith; Phone: 610-647-4440.
Soccer: Robert Miller; Phone: 610-647-4440.
Softball: Erin McDonnell; Phone: 610-647-4440.
Tennis: Lynn Winters; Phone: 610-647-4440.
Volleyball: Pam Criswell; Phone: 610-647-4440.

INDIANA INSTITUTE OF TECHNOLOGY
Fort Wayne, Indiana

Warriors ◆ NAIA ◆ Wolverine-Hoosier Conference ◆ http:// www.indtech.edu/

Independent comprehensive, founded 1930
Coed, 2,971 undergraduate students, 52% full-time, 56% women, 44% men
Urban 25-acre campus
Moderately difficult entrance level, 93% of applicants were admitted

Freshmen *Admission:* 1,989 applied, 1,826 were accepted, 749 enrolled. *Test scores:* SAT verbal scores over 500: 55%; SAT math scores over

500: 46%; SAT verbal scores over 600: 22%; SAT math scores over 600: 12%; SAT verbal scores over 700: 2%.
Tuition and fees (2004–05): $16,680 (full-time). *Room and board:* $6272 (room only: $3136).
Athletic Department: *Director of Athletics:* Dan Kline; Phone: 260-422-5561; Fax: 260-422-4584; E-mail: kline.d@indtech.edu. *Sports Information Director:* Chris Dickson; Phone: 260-422-5561.
MEN'S COACHES
Baseball: Steve Devine; Phone: 260-422-5561.
Basketball: Jason Kline; Phone: 260-422-5561; E-mail: kline.j@indtech. edu.
Cheerleading: Erin Erb; Phone: 260-422-5561.
Soccer: Martin Neuhoff; Phone: 260-422-5561; E-mail: neuhoff@ indtech.edu.
WOMEN'S COACHES
Basketball: Gary Cobb; Phone: 260-422-5561; E-mail: cobb@indtech. edu.
Cheerleading: Erin Erb; Phone: 260-422-5561.
Soccer: David Allway; Phone: 260-422-5561.
Softball: Brenda James; Phone: 260-422-5561; E-mail: bjames@indtech. edu.

INDIANA STATE UNIVERSITY
Terre Haute, Indiana

Sycamores ◆ NCAA I ◆ Gateway Football Conference; Missouri Valley Conference ◆ http://www.indstate.edu/

State-supported university, founded 1865
Coed, 9,615 undergraduate students, 88% full-time, 52% women, 48% men
Small-town 91-acre campus with easy access to Indianapolis
Moderately difficult entrance level, 85% of applicants were admitted

Freshmen *Admission:* 5,568 applied, 4,800 were accepted, 2,016 enrolled. *Test scores:* SAT verbal scores over 500: 38%; SAT math scores over 500: 38%; SAT verbal scores over 600: 7%; SAT math scores over 600: 6%; SAT verbal scores over 700: %; SAT math scores over 700: %.
Tuition and fees (2003–04): $5422 (resident), $11,890 (nonresident). *Room and board:* $5297 (room only: $2790).
Financial Aid (All incoming freshmen): *Average need-based gift aid:* $4277. *Average non-need based aid:* $3326. *Average aid to full-time undergraduates:* $5793.
Athletic Department: *Director of Athletics:* Andrea Myers; Phone: 812-237-3356; Fax: 812-237-2913; E-mail: athandi@isugw.indstate.edu. *Sports Information Director:* Jason Yaman; Phone: 812-237-4161; E-mail: athjason@isugw.indstate.edu.
MEN'S COACHES
Baseball: Bob Warn; Phone: 812-237-4051; E-mail: rwarn@indstate. edu.
Basketball: Royce Waltman; Phone: 812-237-4022; E-mail: rwaltman@ indstate.edu.
Cheerleading: Kimberly Keyes; Phone: 812-237-4082; E-mail: athletics@ indstate.edu.
Cross Country: John McNichols; Phone: 812-237-4164; E-mail: jmcnichols@indstate.edu.
Football: Tim McGuire; Phone: 812-237-4076; E-mail: t-mcguire@ indstate.edu.
Tennis: Ryan Ray; Phone: 812-237-4162; E-mail: athrayr@isugw. indstate.edu.
Track and Field: John McNichols; Phone: 812-237-4164; E-mail: jmcnichols@indstate.edu.
WOMEN'S COACHES
Basketball: Jim Wiedie; Phone: 812-237-8233; E-mail: athwied@isugw. indstate.edu.
Cheerleading: Kimberly Keyes; Phone: 812-237-4082; E-mail: athletics@ indstate.edu.
Cross Country: John Gartland; Phone: 812-237-4019; E-mail: jgartland@ indstate.edu.
Soccer: Vernon Croft; Phone: 812-237-7738; E-mail: vcroft@indstate. edu.
Softball: Brenda Coldren; Phone: 812-237-4166; E-mail: bcoldren@ indstate.edu.
Tennis: Mary Stadler; Phone: 812-237-4173; E-mail: athmstad@isugw. indstate.edu.

Track and Field: John Gartland; Phone: 812-237-4019; E-mail: jgartland@indstate.edu.
Volleyball: Julie Krofcheck; Phone: 812-237-4171; E-mail: athjulie@ isugw.indstate.edu.

INDIANA UNIVERSITY BLOOMINGTON
Bloomington, Indiana

Hoosiers ◆ NCAA I ◆ Big Ten Conference
◆ http://www.iu.edu/

State-supported university, founded 1820, part of Indiana University System
Coed, 30,319 undergraduate students, 94% full-time, 52% women, 48% men
Small-town 1,931-acre campus with easy access to Indianapolis
Moderately difficult entrance level, 77% of applicants were admitted

Freshmen *Admission:* 22,178 applied, 17,992 were accepted, 6,784 enrolled. *Test scores:* SAT verbal scores over 500: 73%; SAT math scores over 500: 76%; SAT verbal scores over 600: 28%; SAT math scores over 600: 35%; SAT verbal scores over 700: 4%; SAT math scores over 700: 6%.
Tuition and fees (2003–04): $6517 (resident), $17,552 (nonresident). *Room and board:* $5872 (room only: $3482).
Financial Aid (All incoming freshmen): *Average need-based gift aid:* $4964. *Average non-need based aid:* $3721. *Average aid to full-time undergraduates:* $10,512.
Athletic Department: *Director of Athletics:* Terry Clapacs; Phone: 812-855-1966; Fax: 812-856-5155. *Sports Information Director:* Jeff Fanter; Phone: 812-855-9399; E-mail: jfanter@indiana.edu.

MEN'S COACHES
Baseball: Bob Morgan; Phone: 812-855-1680; E-mail: rgmorgan@ indiana.edu.
Basketball: Mike Davis; Phone: 812-855-2238.
Cheerleading: Julie Horine; Phone: 812-855-2794.
Cross Country: Robert Chapman; Phone: 812-855-8583; E-mail: rfchapma@indiana.edu.
Diving: Jeff Huber; Phone: 812-855-5710; E-mail: jhuber@indiana.edu.
Football: Gerry Dinardo; Phone: 812-855-9618; E-mail: football@ indiana.edu.
Golf: Mike Mayer; Phone: 812-855-7950; E-mail: mbmayer@indiana. edu.
Soccer: Jerry Yeagley; Phone: 812-855-0051; E-mail: yeagley@indiana. edu.
Swimming: Ray Looze; Phone: 812-855-0106; E-mail: rlooze@indiana. edu.
Tennis: Ken Hydinger; Phone: 812-855-1006; E-mail: khydinge@ indiana.edu.
Track and Field: Randy Heisler; Phone: 812-855-8583.
Wrestling: Duane Goldman; Phone: 812-855-6941; E-mail: dlgoldma@ indiana.edu.

WOMEN'S COACHES
Basketball: Kathi Bennett; Phone: 812-855-3955; E-mail: katkaben@ indiana.edu.
Cheerleading: Julie Horine; Phone: 812-855-2794.
Cross Country: Judy Wilson; Phone: 812-855-8583; E-mail: jbogensc@ indiana.edu.
Diving: Jeff Huber; Phone: 812-855-5710; E-mail: jhuber@indiana.edu.
Field Hockey: Amy Robertson; Phone: 812-856-2171; E-mail: adrobert@ indiana.edu.
Golf: Sam Carmichael; Phone: 765-352-0766; E-mail: shcarmic@ indiana.edu.
Soccer: Mike Lyon; Phone: 812-855-0051; E-mail: wsoccer@indiana. edu.
Softball: Sara Hayes; Phone: 812-855-3569; E-mail: sarhayes@indiana. edu.
Swimming: Dorsey Tierney; Phone: 812-855-3031; E-mail: atierney@ indiana.edu.
Tennis: Lin Loring; Phone: 812-855-4791; E-mail: lloring@indiana.edu.
Track and Field: Randy Heisler; Phone: 812-855-8583.
Volleyball: Katie Weismiller; Phone: 812-855-3989; E-mail: kweismil@ indiana.edu.

INDIANA UNIVERSITY NORTHWEST
Gary, Indiana

Redhawks ◆ NAIA ◆ Independent ◆ http://www.iu.edu/

State-supported comprehensive, founded 1959, part of Indiana University System
Coed, 4,476 undergraduate students, 54% full-time, 69% women, 31% men
Urban 38-acre campus with easy access to Chicago
Minimally difficult entrance level, 7% of applicants were admitted

Freshmen *Admission:* 1,803 applied, 1,212 were accepted, 860 enrolled. *Test scores:* SAT verbal scores over 500: 34%; SAT math scores over 500: 28%; SAT verbal scores over 600: 10%; SAT math scores over 600: 6%; SAT verbal scores over 700: %; SAT math scores over 700: %.
Tuition and fees (2003–04): $4538 (resident), $10,488 (nonresident).
Financial Aid (All incoming freshmen): *Average need-based gift aid:* $4569. *Average non-need based aid:* $1821. *Average aid to full-time undergraduates:* $6515.
Athletic Department: *Director of Athletics:* Linda Anderson; Phone: 219-980-6793; Fax: 219-981-4233; E-mail: landers@iun.edu.

MEN'S COACHES
Baseball: Tom Bainbridge; Phone: 219-980-6945; E-mail: tbain@iun. edu.
Basketball: Tom Bainbridge; Phone: 219-980-6945; E-mail: tbain@iun. edu.
Cheerleading: T.J. Stoops; Phone: 219-980-6832; E-mail: tkstoops@iun. edu.
Golf: Darryl Baker; Phone: 219-980-6945; E-mail: darbaker@iun.edu.

WOMEN'S COACHES
Basketball: Tony Zezovski; Phone: 219-980-6746; E-mail: tzezovsk@ iun.edu.
Cheerleading: T.J. Stoops; Phone: 219-980-6832; E-mail: tkstoops@iun. edu.
Volleyball: Matt Zima; Phone: 219-980-6945; E-mail: mzima@iun.edu.

INDIANA UNIVERSITY OF PENNSYLVANIA
Indiana, Pennsylvania

Indians ◆ NCAA II ◆ Pennsylvania State Athletic Conference
◆ http://www.iup.edu/

State-supported university, founded 1875, part of Pennsylvania State System of Higher Education
Coed, 12,119 undergraduate students, 92% full-time, 56% women, 44% men
Small-town 350-acre campus with easy access to Pittsburgh
Moderately difficult entrance level, 57% of applicants were admitted

Freshmen *Admission:* 8,618 applied, 5,136 were accepted, 2,761 enrolled. *Test scores:* SAT verbal scores over 500: 61%; SAT math scores over 500: 59%; SAT verbal scores over 600: 15%; SAT math scores over 600: 15%; SAT verbal scores over 700: 3%; SAT math scores over 700: 2%.
Tuition and fees (2003–04): $5785 (resident), $12,683 (nonresident). *Room and board:* $4704 (room only: $2826).
Financial Aid (All incoming freshmen): *Average need-based gift aid:* $3948. *Average non-need based aid:* $1964. *Average aid to full-time undergraduates:* $7461.
Athletic Department: *Director of Athletics:* Frank Condino; Phone: 724-357-2782; Fax: 724-357-7804; E-mail: fcondino@iup.edu. *Sports Information Director:* Mike Hoffman; Phone: 724-357-2747; E-mail: mhoffman@iup.edu.

MEN'S COACHES
Baseball: Tom Kennedy; Phone: 724-357-7830; E-mail: tkennedy@iup. edu.
Basketball: Gary Edwards; Phone: 724-357-6287; E-mail: gedwards@ iup.edu.
Cheerleading: Jeff Hill; Phone: 724-357-2100; E-mail: ylnf@iup.edu.
Cross Country: Ed Fry; Phone: 724-357-2393; E-mail: edfry@iup.edu.

Indiana University of Pennsylvania *(continued)*

Football: Frank Cignetti; Phone: 724-357-2780; E-mail: cignetti@iup.edu.
Golf: Fred Joseph; Phone: 724-357-3277; E-mail: fajoseph@iup.edu.
Swimming: Dave Caldwell; Phone: 724-357-2779; E-mail: dcadlwel@iup.edu.
Track and Field: Brian Spickler; Phone: 724-357-2464; E-mail: bspick@iup.edu.

WOMEN'S COACHES
Basketball: Justin English; Phone: 724-357-2722; E-mail: jenglish@iup.edu.
Cheerleading: Jeff Hill; Phone: 724-357-2100; E-mail: ylnf@iup.edu.
Cross Country: Ed Fry; Phone: 724-357-2393; E-mail: edfry@iup.edu.
Field Hockey: Rutger Wiese; Phone: 724-357-7756; E-mail: rwiese@iup.edu.
Lacrosse: Rutger Wiese; Phone: 724-357-7756; E-mail: rwiese@iup.edu.
Soccer: Adel Heder; Phone: 724-357-6245; E-mail: aheder@iup.edu.
Softball: Sue Snyder; Phone: 724-357-7761; E-mail: slsnyder@iup.edu.
Swimming: Dave Caldwell; Phone: 724-357-2779; E-mail: dcadlwel@iup.edu.
Tennis: Tony Medvetz; Phone: 724-357-2462; E-mail: amedvetz@iup.edu.
Track and Field: Brian Spickler; Phone: 724-357-2464; E-mail: bspick@iup.edu.
Volleyball: Carmine Cortazzo; Phone: 724-357-4421; E-mail: cjcortaz@iup.edu.

INDIANA UNIVERSITY–PURDUE UNIVERSITY FORT WAYNE
Fort Wayne, Indiana

Mastodons ◆ NCAA II ◆ Great Lakes Valley Conference; Mid-American Conference; Midwestern Intercollegiate Volleyball Conference ◆ http://www.iu.edu/

State-supported comprehensive, founded 1917, part of Indiana University System and Purdue University System
Coed, 11,068 undergraduate students, 57% full-time, 58% women, 42% men
Urban 565-acre campus
Minimally difficult entrance level, 96% of applicants were admitted

Freshmen *Admission:* 2,486 applied, 2,402 were accepted, 1,643 enrolled. *Test scores:* SAT verbal scores over 500: 40%; SAT math scores over 500: 42%; SAT verbal scores over 600: 9%; SAT math scores over 600: 10%; SAT verbal scores over 700: 1%; SAT math scores over 700: 1%.
Tuition and fees (2003–04): $5108 (resident), $11,556 (nonresident).
Financial Aid (All incoming freshmen): *Average need-based gift aid:* $3585. *Average non-need based aid:* $982. *Average aid to full-time undergraduates:* $4320.
Athletic Department: *Director of Athletics:* Mark Pope; Phone: 260-481-5443; Fax: 260-481-6002; E-mail: popem@ipfw.edu. *Sports Information Director:* Rudy Yovich; Phone: 260-481-6646; E-mail: yovichr@ipfw.edu.

MEN'S COACHES
Baseball: Billy Gernon; Phone: 260-481-5480; E-mail: gernonw@ipfw.edu.
Basketball: Doug Noll; Phone: 260-481-6889; E-mail: nolld@ipfw.edu.
Cheerleading: Le'Kresia Outlaw; Phone: 260-348-0287; E-mail: borshia@ipfw.edu.
Cross Country: Mike Fruchey; Phone: 260-481-5713; E-mail: mike.fruchey@ci.ft-wayne.in.us.
Golf: Jeff Marsh; Phone: 260-481-6643.
Soccer: Terry Stefankiewicz; Phone: 260-481-6594; E-mail: stefanke@ipfw.edu.
Tennis: Eric Burns; Phone: 260-481-6642; E-mail: burns@ipfw.edu.
Volleyball: Arnie Ball; Phone: 260-481-6648; E-mail: balla@ipfw.edu.

WOMEN'S COACHES
Basketball: Bruce Patterson; Phone: 260-481-6957; E-mail: pattersb@ipfw.edu.
Cheerleading: Le'Kresia Outlaw; Phone: 260-348-0287; E-mail: borshia@ipfw.edu.

Cross Country: Mike Fruchey; Phone: 260-481-5713; E-mail: mike.fruchy@ci.ft-wayne.in.us.
Golf: Jeff Marsh; Phone: 260-481-6643.
Soccer: Terry Stefankiewicz; Phone: 260-481-6643; E-mail: stefanke@ipfw.edu.
Softball: Keith Fisher; Phone: 260-481-6910; E-mail: fisherk@ipfw.edu.
Tennis: Eric Burns; Phone: 260-481-6642; E-mail: burns@ipfw.edu.
Track and Field: Mike Fruchey; Phone: 260-481-5713; E-mail: mike.fruchy@ci.ft-wayne.in.us.
Volleyball: Kelly Hartley; Phone: 260-481-6021; E-mail: hartleyk@ipfw.edu.

INDIANA UNIVERSITY–PURDUE UNIVERSITY INDIANAPOLIS
Indianapolis, Indiana

Jaguars ◆ NCAA I ◆ Mid-Continent Conference ◆ http://www.iu.edu/

State-supported university, founded 1969, part of Indiana University System
Coed, 21,388 undergraduate students, 63% full-time, 59% women, 41% men
Urban 511-acre campus
Moderately difficult entrance level, 73% of applicants were admitted

Freshmen *Admission:* 5,698 applied, 4,373 were accepted, 2,826 enrolled. *Test scores:* SAT verbal scores over 500: 48%; SAT math scores over 500: 47%; SAT verbal scores over 600: 10%; SAT math scores over 600: 12%; SAT verbal scores over 700: 1%; SAT math scores over 700: 1%.
Tuition and fees (2003–04): $5703 (resident), $14,886 (nonresident). *Room only:* $2554.
Financial Aid (All incoming freshmen): *Average need-based gift aid:* $4984. *Average non-need based aid:* $2088. *Average aid to full-time undergraduates:* $6074.
Athletic Department: *Director of Athletics:* Michael Moore; Phone: 317-278-5247; Fax: 317-274-0609; E-mail: mmoore1@iupui.edu. *Sports Information Director:* Kevin Buerge; Phone: 317-278-3619; E-mail: kbuerge@iupui.edu.

MEN'S COACHES
Basketball: Ron Hunter; Phone: 317-278-5247; E-mail: rehunter@iupui.edu.
Cheerleading: Kris Greene; Phone: 317-278-5247; E-mail: krisjoan@aol.com.
Cross Country: Scott Williams; Phone: 317-278-7863; E-mail: sctwilli@iupui.edu.
Diving: Johanna Doecke; Phone: 317-278-2656.
Golf: John Andrews; Phone: 317-278-2658; E-mail: iupuigolf@aol.com.
Soccer: Steve Franklin; Phone: 317-274-1823; E-mail: sfrankli@iupui.edu.
Swimming: Jim Schuck; Phone: 317-278-2656; E-mail: jshuck@iupui.edu.
Tennis: Rich Lord; Phone: 317-274-2108; E-mail: rilord@iupui.edu.

WOMEN'S COACHES
Basketball: Kris Simpson; Phone: 317-278-5247; E-mail: ksimpson@iupui.edu.
Cheerleading: Kris Greene; Phone: 317-278-5247; E-mail: krisjoan@aol.com.
Cross Country: Scott Williams; Phone: 317-278-7863; E-mail: sctwilli@iupui.edu.
Diving: Johanna Doecke; Phone: 317-278-2656.
Golf: John Andrews; Phone: 317-278-2658; E-mail: iupuigolf@aol.com.
Soccer: Chris Johnson; Phone: 317-274-1447; E-mail: johnsojc@iupui.edu.
Softball: Julie Pratt; Phone: 317-278-1584; E-mail: jbias@iupui.edu.
Swimming: Jim Schuck; Phone: 317-278-2656; E-mail: jshuck@iupui.edu.
Tennis: Andrea Lord; Phone: 317-274-1254; E-mail: amlord@iupui.edu.
Volleyball: Steve Payne; Phone: 317-274-0620; E-mail: scpayne@iupui.edu.

INDIANA UNIVERSITY SOUTH BEND
South Bend, Indiana

Titans ◆ NAIA ◆ Chicagoland Collegiate Conference ◆ http://www.iu.edu/

State-supported comprehensive, founded 1922, part of Indiana University System
Coed, 6,093 undergraduate students, 56% full-time, 63% women, 37% men
Suburban 73-acre campus with easy access to Chicago
Moderately difficult entrance level, 84% of applicants were admitted

Freshmen *Admission:* 1,553 applied, 1,292 were accepted, 895 enrolled. *Test scores:* SAT verbal scores over 500: 43%; SAT math scores over 500: 42%; SAT verbal scores over 600: 9%; SAT math scores over 600: 8%; SAT verbal scores over 700: 1%; SAT math scores over 700: 1%.
Tuition and fees (2003–04): $4571 (resident), $11,163 (nonresident).
Financial Aid (All incoming freshmen): *Average need-based gift aid:* $3448. *Average non-need based aid:* $1710. *Average aid to full-time undergraduates:* $4895.
Athletic Department: *Director of Athletics:* Mary Wisniewski; Phone: 574-237-4457; Fax: 574-239-5041; E-mail: mwisniew@iusb.edu. *Sports Information Director:* Mary Wisniewski; Phone: 574-237-4457; E-mail: mwisniew@iusb.edu.

MEN'S COACHES
Basketball: Jim Parent; Phone: 574-237-4587.

WOMEN'S COACHES
Basketball: Mary Wisniewski; Phone: 574-237-4457; E-mail: mwisniew@iusb.edu.

INDIANA UNIVERSITY SOUTHEAST
New Albany, Indiana

Grenadiers ◆ NAIA ◆ Kentucky Intercollegiate Conference ◆ http://www.iu.edu/

State-supported comprehensive, founded 1941, part of Indiana University System
Coed, 5,581 undergraduate students, 56% full-time, 62% women, 38% men
Suburban 177-acre campus with easy access to Louisville
Minimally difficult entrance level, 83% of applicants were admitted

Freshmen *Admission:* 1,268 applied, 1,083 were accepted, 824 enrolled. *Test scores:* SAT verbal scores over 500: 38%; SAT math scores over 500: 37%; SAT verbal scores over 600: 8%; SAT math scores over 600: 6%; SAT verbal scores over 700: 1%; SAT math scores over 700: %.
Tuition and fees (2003–04): $4504 (resident), $10,454 (nonresident).
Financial Aid (All incoming freshmen): *Average need-based gift aid:* $4202. *Average non-need based aid:* $1582. *Average aid to full-time undergraduates:* $5023.
Athletic Department: *Director of Athletics:* Pat Mrozowski; Phone: 812-941-2177; Fax: 812-941-2434; E-mail: pmrozows@ius.edu. *Sports Information Director:* Michea Embry; Phone: 812-941-2450; E-mail: membry@ius.edu.

MEN'S COACHES
Baseball: Joe Decker; Phone: 812-941-2435; E-mail: jdecker@ius.edu.
Basketball: Walt Corbean; Phone: 812-941-2515; E-mail: wcorbean@ius.edu.
Cross Country: Steve Fleenor; Phone: 812-941-2450; E-mail: sfleenor@aol.com.
Tennis: Kevin Fulton; Phone: 812-941-2432; E-mail: wryall@ius.edu.

WOMEN'S COACHES
Basketball: Robin Farris; Phone: 812-941-2438; E-mail: rafarris @ius.edu.
Cross Country: Steve Fleenor; Phone: 812-941-2450; E-mail: sfleenor@aol.com.

Tennis: Bill Ryall; Phone: 812-941-2178; E-mail: wryall@ius.edu.
Volleyball: Robin Farris; Phone: 812-941-2438; E-mail: rafarris @ius.edu.

INDIANA WESLEYAN UNIVERSITY
Marion, Indiana

Wildcats ◆ NAIA ◆ Mid-Central Conference ◆ http://www.indwes.edu/

Independent Wesleyan comprehensive, founded 1920
Coed, 6,204 undergraduate students, 90% full-time, 63% women, 37% men
Small-town 132-acre campus with easy access to Indianapolis
Moderately difficult entrance level, 94% of applicants were admitted

Freshmen *Admission:* 2,577 applied, 2,315 were accepted, 1,036 enrolled. *Test scores:* SAT verbal scores over 500: 68%; SAT math scores over 500: 70%; SAT verbal scores over 600: 28%; SAT math scores over 600: 27%; SAT verbal scores over 700: 5%; SAT math scores over 700: 4%.
Tuition and fees (2003–04): $14,420 (full-time). *Room and board:* $5480 (room only: $2550).
Athletic Department: *Director of Athletics:* Mike Fratzke; Phone: 765-677-2317; Fax: 765-677-2328. *Sports Information Director:* Thomas Young; Phone: 765-677-2989.

MEN'S COACHES
Baseball: Mark DeMichael; Phone: 765-677-2324; E-mail: mark.demichael@indwes.edu.
Basketball: Mark Fleming; Phone: 765-677-2320; E-mail: mark.fleming@indwes.edu.
Cheerleading: Marcy Moreillon; Phone: 765-677-2519.
Cross Country: John Foss; Phone: 765-677-2336; E-mail: john.foss@indwes.edu.
Golf: Steve Evans; Phone: 765-677-2585.
Soccer: John Bratcher; Phone: 765-677-2321; E-mail: john.bratcher@indwes.edu.
Tennis: Bill May; Phone: 765-677-2546.
Track and Field: John Foss; Phone: 765-677-2336; E-mail: john.foss@indwes.edu.

WOMEN'S COACHES
Basketball: Steve Brooks; Phone: 765-677-2234; E-mail: steve.brooks@indwes.edu.
Cheerleading: Marcy Moreillon; Phone: 765-677-2519.
Cross Country: John Foss; Phone: 765-677-2336; E-mail: john.foss@indwes.edu.
Soccer: John Bratcher; Phone: 765-677-2321; E-mail: john.bratcher@indwes.edu.
Softball: Sue Bowman; Phone: 765-677-2319; E-mail: sue.bowman@indwes.edu.
Tennis: Terry Porter; Phone: 765-677-2323; E-mail: terry.porter@indwes.edu.
Track and Field: John Foss; Phone: 765-677-2336; E-mail: john.foss@indwes.edu.
Volleyball: Candace Moats; Phone: 765-677-2322; E-mail: candace.moats@indwes.edu.

IONA COLLEGE
New Rochelle, New York

Gaels ◆ NCAA I ◆ Metro Atlantic Athletic Conference ◆ http://www.iona.edu/

Independent religious comprehensive, founded 1940, affiliated with Roman Catholic Church
Coed, 3,395 undergraduate students, 88% full-time, 53% women, 47% men
Suburban 35-acre campus with easy access to New York City
Moderately difficult entrance level, 65% of applicants were admitted

Freshmen *Admission:* 4,196 applied, 2,696 were accepted, 860 enrolled. *Test scores:* SAT verbal scores over 500: 74%; SAT math scores over

Iona College *(continued)*

500: 75%; SAT verbal scores over 600: 25%; SAT math scores over 600: 25%; SAT verbal scores over 700: 2%; SAT math scores over 700: 1%.

Tuition and fees (2003–04): $18,290 (full-time). *Room and board:* $9698 (room only: $6826).

Financial Aid (All incoming freshmen): *Average need-based gift aid:* $2967. *Average non-need based aid:* $9716. *Average aid to full-time undergraduates:* $14,520.

Athletic Department: *Director of Athletics:* Shawn Brennan; Phone: 914-633-2311; Fax: 914-633-2072; E-mail: sbrennan@iona.edu. *Sports Information Director:* Mike Laprey; Phone: 914-633-2334; E-mail: mlaprey@iona.edu.

MEN'S COACHES

Baseball: Al Zoccolillo; Phone: 914-633-2319; E-mail: azoccolillo@iona.edu.

Basketball: Jeff Ruland; Phone: 914-633-2304; E-mail: jruland@iona.edu.

Cross Country: Mick Byrne; Phone: 914-633-2314; E-mail: mbyrne@iona.edu.

Diving: Kieran Smyth; Phone: 914-633-2323; E-mail: ncavataro@iona.edu.

Football: Fred Mariana; Phone: 914-633-2316; E-mail: fmariani@iona.edu.

Golf: Vince McDermott; Phone: 914-633-2305.

Ice Hockey: Frank Bretti; Phone: 914-633-2306; E-mail: fbretti@iona.edu.

Soccer: Fernando Barboto; Phone: 914-633-2315; E-mail: fbarboto@iona.edu.

Swimming: Nick Cavataro; Phone: 914-633-2323; E-mail: ncavataro@iona.edu.

Track and Field: Mick Byrne; Phone: 914-633-2314; E-mail: mbyrne@iona.edu.

WOMEN'S COACHES

Basketball: Anthony Bozzella; Phone: 914-633-2321; E-mail: abozella@iona.edu.

Cross Country: Mick Byrne; Phone: 914-633-2314; E-mail: mbyrne@iona.edu.

Diving: Kieran Smyth; Phone: 914-633-2323; E-mail: ncavataro@iona.edu.

Soccer: Emma Hayes; Phone: 914-633-2131; E-mail: ehayes@iona.edu.

Softball: Andrea Farquhar; Phone: 914-633-7756; E-mail: afarquhar@iona.edu.

Swimming: Nick Cavataro; Phone: 914-633-2323; E-mail: ncavataro@iona.edu.

Track and Field: Mick Byrne; Phone: 914-633-2314; E-mail: mbyrne@iona.edu.

Volleyball: Bob Weiner; Phone: 914-633-2317; E-mail: rweiner@iona.edu.

IOWA STATE UNIVERSITY OF SCIENCE AND TECHNOLOGY
Ames, Iowa

Cyclones ◆ NCAA I ◆ Big 12 Conference ◆ http://www.iastate.edu/

State-supported university, founded 1858
Coed, 22,230 undergraduate students, 93% full-time, 44% women, 56% men
Suburban 1,788-acre campus
Moderately difficult entrance level, 89% of applicants were admitted

Freshmen *Admission:* 9,035 applied, 8,116 were accepted, 3,897 enrolled. *Test scores:* SAT verbal scores over 500: 82%; SAT math scores over 500: 89%; SAT verbal scores over 600: 48%; SAT math scores over 600: 61%; SAT verbal scores over 700: 14%; SAT math scores over 700: 20%.

Tuition and fees (2004–05): $5426 (resident), $15,128 (nonresident). *Room and board:* $6121 (room only: $3350).

Financial Aid (All incoming freshmen): *Average need-based gift aid:* $3413. *Average non-need based aid:* $3042. *Average aid to full-time undergraduates:* $6712.

Athletic Department: *Director of Athletics:* Bruce Van De Velde; Phone: 515-294-0123; Fax: 515-294-0104; E-mail: bvelde@iastate.edu. *Sports Information Director:* Tom Kroeschell; Phone: 515-294-3372; E-mail: tkroesch@iastate.edu.

MEN'S COACHES

Basketball: Wayne Morgan; Phone: 515-294-8232; E-mail: wmorgan@iastate.edu.

Cheerleading: Misty Hade; Phone: 515-294-3558; E-mail: cheersquad@iastate.edu.

Cross Country: Corey Iameis; Phone: 515-294-1069; E-mail: cihmels@iastate.edu.

Football: Dan McCarney; Phone: 515-294-6721; E-mail: dmccarn@iastate.edu.

Golf: Jay Horton; Phone: 515-294-3823; E-mail: jhorton@iastate.edu.

Track and Field: Steve Lynn; Phone: 515-294-7088; E-mail: srlynn@mail.adp.iastate.edu.

Wrestling: Bobby Douglas; Phone: 515-294-4643; E-mail: bobbyd@iastate.edu.

WOMEN'S COACHES

Basketball: Bill Fennelly; Phone: 515-294-3436; E-mail: coachf@iastate.edu.

Cheerleading: Misty Hade; Phone: 515-294-3558; E-mail: cheersquad@iastate.edu.

Cross Country: Dick Lee; Phone: 515-294-1013; E-mail: dklee@iastate.edu.

Diving: Jeff Warrick; Phone: 515-294-5342; E-mail: jwarrick@iastate.edu.

Golf: Julie Manning; Phone: 515-294-9959; E-mail: manning@iastate.edu.

Gymnastics: K.J. Kindler; Phone: 515-294-4182; E-mail: kkindler@iastate.edu.

Soccer: Rebecca Hornbacher; Phone: 515-294-5328; E-mail: rhornbac@iastate.edu.

Softball: Ruth Crowe; Phone: 515-294-3426; E-mail: recrowe@iastate.edu.

Swimming: Duane Sorenson; Phone: 515-294-3185; E-mail: dsoren@iastate.edu.

Tennis: Michele Conlon; Phone: 515-294-3418; E-mail: mconlon@iastate.edu.

Track and Field: Dick Lee; Phone: 515-294-1013; E-mail: dklee@iastate.edu.

Volleyball: Linda Crum; Phone: 515-294-3395; E-mail: grensing@iastate.edu.

IOWA WESLEYAN COLLEGE
Mount Pleasant, Iowa

Tigers ◆ NAIA ◆ Mid-States Football Conference; Midwest Classic Conference ◆ http://www.iwc.edu/

Independent United Methodist 4-year, founded 1842
Coed, 753 undergraduate students, 71% full-time, 60% women, 40% men
Small-town 60-acre campus
Moderately difficult entrance level, 48% of applicants were admitted

Freshmen *Admission:* 680 applied, 358 were accepted, 118 enrolled.
Tuition and fees (2004–05): $16,070 (full-time). *Room and board:* $4920 (room only: $2050).

Financial Aid (All incoming freshmen): *Average need-based gift aid:* $6180. *Average non-need based aid:* $3037. *Average aid to full-time undergraduates:* $12,478.

Athletic Department: *Director of Athletics:* Mike Hampton; Phone: 319-385-6303; Fax: 319-385-6384; E-mail: mhampton@iwc.edu. *Sports Information Director:* Keith Kohorst; Phone: 319-385-6306; E-mail: kkohorst@iwc.edu.

MEN'S COACHES

Baseball: Todd Huckabone; Phone: 319-385-6349; E-mail: huckabon@iwc.edu.

Basketball: Al Magnani; Phone: 319-385-6307; E-mail: amagnani@iwc.edu.

Football: Todd Mcghghy; Phone: 319-385-6377; E-mail: toddam@iwc.edu.

Golf: Ted Peetz; Phone: 319-385-6301; E-mail: tpeetz@iwc.edu.

Soccer: Michael Sheerin; Phone: 319-385-6314; E-mail: msheerin@iwc.edu.

Track and Field: Stacy Boudreau; Phone: 319-385-6305; E-mail: sboudreau@iwc.edu.

WOMEN'S COACHES
Basketball: Seychelle Bruton; Phone: 319-385-6332; E-mail: sbruton@iwc.edu.
Golf: Ted Peetz; Phone: 319-385-6301; E-mail: tpeetz@iwc.edu.
Soccer: Michael Sheerin; Phone: 319-385-6332; E-mail: msheerin@iwc.edu.
Softball: Mike Hampton; Phone: 319-385-6303; E-mail: mhampton@iwc.edu.
Track and Field: Stacy Boudreau; Phone: 319-385-6305; E-mail: sboudreau@iwc.edu.
Volleyball: Stacy Boudreau; Phone: 319-385-6305; E-mail: sboudreau@iwc.edu.

ITHACA COLLEGE
Ithaca, New York

Bombers ◆ NCAA III ◆ Empire 8 Conference ◆ http://www.ithaca.edu/

Independent comprehensive, founded 1892
Coed, 6,260 undergraduate students, 98% full-time, 57% women, 43% men
Small-town 757-acre campus with easy access to Syracuse
Moderately difficult entrance level, 58% of applicants were admitted

Freshmen *Admission:* 10,650 applied, 6,756 were accepted, 1,585 enrolled. *Test scores:* SAT verbal scores over 500: 90%; SAT math scores over 500: 93%; SAT verbal scores over 600: 46%; SAT math scores over 600: 49%; SAT verbal scores over 700: 8%; SAT math scores over 700: 7%.
Tuition and fees (2003–04): $22,264 (full-time). *Room and board:* $9466 (room only: $4802).
Financial Aid (All incoming freshmen): *Average need-based gift aid:* $13,476. *Average non-need based aid:* $8961. *Average aid to full-time undergraduates:* $20,340.
Athletic Department: *Director of Athletics:* Ken Kutler; Phone: 607-274-3209; Fax: 607-274-1667; E-mail: kcutler@ithaca.edu. *Sports Information Director:* Mike Warwick; Phone: 607-274-1401; E-mail: mwarwick@ithaca.edu.

MEN'S COACHES
Baseball: George Valesente; Phone: 607-274-3749; E-mail: gvalesente@ithaca.edu.
Basketball: Jim Mullins; Phone: 607-274-1265; E-mail: jmullins@ithaca.edu.
Cross Country: Jim Nichols; Phone: 607-274-3745; E-mail: jnichols@ithaca.edu.
Diving: Karen LaFace; Phone: 607-274-3119.
Football: Michael Welch; Phone: 607-274-1143; E-mail: mwelch@ithaca.edu.
Lacrosse: Jeff Long; Phone: 607-274-3747; E-mail: jlong@ithaca.edu.
Soccer: Andy Byrne; Phone: 607-274-3337; E-mail: icsoccer@ithaca.edu.
Swimming: Kevin Markwardt; Phone: 607-274-3181; E-mail: kmarkwardt@ithaca.edu.
Tennis: Bill Austin; Phone: 607-274-1661; E-mail: baustin@ithaca.edu.
Track and Field: Jim Nichols; Phone: 607-274-1141; E-mail: jnichols@ithaca.edu.
Wrestling: Marty Nichols; Phone: 607-274-3660; E-mail: mnichols@ithaca.edu.

WOMEN'S COACHES
Basketball: Dan Raymond; Phone: 607-274-3179; E-mail: draymond@ithaca.edu.
Cross Country: Bill Ware; Phone: 607-274-3746; E-mail: wware@ithaca.edu.
Diving: Karen LaFace; Phone: 607-274-3119.
Field Hockey: Tracey Houk; Phone: 607-274-3140; E-mail: thouk@ithaca.edu.
Gymnastics: Rick Suddaby; Phone: 607-274-3148; E-mail: rsuddaby@ithaca.edu.
Lacrosse: Karen Hollands; Phone: 607-274-3663; E-mail: khollands@ithaca.edu.
Soccer: Mindy Quigg; Phone: 607-274-3180; E-mail: mquigg@ithaca.edu.

Softball: Deb Pallozzi; Phone: 607-274-1270; E-mail: dpallozzi@ithaca.edu.
Swimming: Paula Miller; Phone: 607-274-3119; E-mail: pmiller@ithaca.edu.
Tennis: Bill Austin; Phone: 607-274-1661; E-mail: baustin@ithaca.edu.
Track and Field: Jennifer Potter; Phone: 607-274-1757; E-mail: jpotter@ithaca.edu.
Volleyball: Janet Donovan; Phone: 607-274-1269; E-mail: jdonovan@ithaca.edu.

JACKSON STATE UNIVERSITY
Jackson, Mississippi

Tigers ◆ NCAA I ◆ Southwestern Athletic Conference ◆ http://www.jsums.edu/

State-supported university, founded 1877, part of Mississippi Institutions of Higher Learning
Coed, 6,292 undergraduate students, 86% full-time, 61% women, 39% men
Urban 150-acre campus
Minimally difficult entrance level, 43% of applicants were admitted

Freshmen *Admission:* 5,937 applied, 2,542 were accepted, 949 enrolled.
Tuition and fees (2004–05): $3612 (resident), $8116 (nonresident). *Room and board:* $4770 (room only: $2724).
Athletic Department: *Director of Athletics:* Roy Culberson; Phone: 601-979-2316; Fax: 601-979-7008; E-mail: roy.e.culberson@jsums.edu. *Sports Information Director:* Deidre Bell; Phone: 601-979-2273; E-mail: deidre.m.bell@jsums.edu.

MEN'S COACHES
Baseball: Mark Salter; Phone: 601-979-3928; E-mail: mark.l.salter@jsums.edu.
Basketball: Tevester Anderson; Phone: 601-979-2417; E-mail: andrew.stoglin@jsums.edu.
Cross Country: Edmond Donald; Phone: 601-979-5889; E-mail: edmond.donald@jsums.edu.
Football: James Bell; Phone: 601-979-2295.
Golf: Eddie Payton; Phone: 601-979-2430; E-mail: eddie.payton@jsums.edu.
Tennis: Willie Shepard; Phone: 601-979-2425; E-mail: willie.shepard@jsums.edu.
Track and Field: Edmond Donald; Phone: 601-979-5889; E-mail: edmond.donald@jsums.edu.

WOMEN'S COACHES
Basketball: Denise Taylor; Phone: 601-979-2818; E-mail: denise.taylor@jsums.edu.
Cross Country: Edmond Donald; Phone: 601-979-5889; E-mail: edmond.donald@jsums.edu.
Golf: Eddie Payton; Phone: 601-979-2430; E-mail: eddie.payton@jsums.edu.
Soccer: Niji Olagbegi; Phone: 601-979-2863; E-mail: adeniji.n.olagbegi@jsums.edu.
Softball: Jack Lott; Phone: 601-979-3929; E-mail: jack.w.lott@jsums.edu.
Tennis: Willie Shepard; Phone: 601-979-2425; E-mail: willie.shepard@jsums.edu.
Track and Field: Edmond Donald; Phone: 601-979-5889; E-mail: edmond.donald@jsums.edu.
Volleyball: Rose Washington; Phone: 601-979-1097; E-mail: rose.washington@jsums.edu.

JACKSONVILLE STATE UNIVERSITY
Jacksonville, Alabama

Gamecocks ◆ NCAA I ◆ Ohio Valley Conference ◆ http://www.jsu.edu/

State-supported comprehensive, founded 1883
Coed, 7,289 undergraduate students, 79% full-time, 58% women, 42% men
Small-town 459-acre campus with easy access to Birmingham
Minimally difficult entrance level, 5% of applicants were admitted

Freshmen *Admission:* 2,452 applied, 1,078 were accepted, 1,078 enrolled. *Test scores:* SAT verbal scores over 500: 36%; SAT math scores over 500: 37%; SAT verbal scores over 600: 8%; SAT math scores over 600: 8%; SAT verbal scores over 700: 1%; SAT math scores over 700: %.
Tuition and fees (2003–04): $3540 (resident), $7080 (nonresident). *Room and board:* $3288 (room only: $1150).
Financial Aid (All incoming freshmen): *Average non-need based aid:* $2400.
Athletic Department: *Director of Athletics:* Jim Fuller; Phone: 256-782-5368; Fax: 256-782-5666; E-mail: jfuller@jsucc.jsu.edu. *Sports Information Director:* Greg Seitz; Phone: 256-782-5279; E-mail: gseitz@jsucc.jsu.edu.

MEN'S COACHES
Baseball: Jim Case; Phone: 256-782-5367; E-mail: jwcase@jsucc.jsu.edu.
Basketball: Mike LaPlante; Phone: 256-782-5535.
Cheerleading: Brittany Ishee; Phone: 256-782-5536; E-mail: bishee@jsucc.jsu.edu.
Cross Country: Heath Dudley; Phone: 256-782-8068; E-mail: hdudley@jsucc.jsu.edu.
Football: Jack Crowe; Phone: 256-782-5365; E-mail: jcrowe@jsucc.jsu.edu.
Golf: James Hobbs; Phone: 256-782-5840; E-mail: jhobbs@jsucc.jsu.edu.
Tennis: Steve Bailey; Phone: 256-782-5887; E-mail: sbailey@jsucc.jsu.edu.

WOMEN'S COACHES
Basketball: Dave Dagostino; Phone: 256-782-8066; E-mail: dagostinodm@yahoo.com.
Cheerleading: Brittany Ishee; Phone: 256-782-5536; E-mail: bishee@jsucc.jsu.edu.
Cross Country: Heath Dudley; Phone: 256-782-8068; E-mail: hdudley@jsucc.jsu.edu.
Golf: James Hobbs; Phone: 256-782-5840; E-mail: jhobbs@jsucc.jsu.edu.
Soccer: Lisa Howe; Phone: 256-782-5679; E-mail: lhowe@jsucc.jsu.edu.
Softball: Jana McGinnis; Phone: 256-782-5524; E-mail: mcginnis@jsucc.jsu.edu.
Tennis: Steve Bailey; Phone: 256-782-5887; E-mail: sbailey@jsucc.jsu.edu.
Track and Field: Heath Dudley; Phone: 256-782-8068; E-mail: hdudley@jsucc.jsu.edu.
Volleyball: Rick Nold; Phone: 256-782-5521; E-mail: rnold@jsucc.jsu.edu.

JACKSONVILLE UNIVERSITY
Jacksonville, Florida

Dolphins ◆ NCAA I ◆ Atlantic Sun Conference; Pioneer Football League Conference ◆ http://www.jacksonville.edu/

Independent comprehensive, founded 1934
Coed, 2,214 undergraduate students, 86% full-time, 50% women, 50% men
Suburban 260-acre campus
Moderately difficult entrance level, 70% of applicants were admitted

Freshmen *Admission:* 1,684 applied, 1,179 were accepted, 451 enrolled. *Test scores:* SAT verbal scores over 500: 62%; SAT math scores over 500: 65%; SAT verbal scores over 600: 18%; SAT math scores over 600: 24%; SAT verbal scores over 700: 2%; SAT math scores over 700: 3%.

Tuition and fees (2003–04): $17,940 (full-time). *Room and board:* $6100 (room only: $2800).
Financial Aid (All incoming freshmen): *Average need-based gift aid:* $13,338. *Average non-need based aid:* $5435. *Average aid to full-time undergraduates:* $15,326.
Athletic Department: *Director of Athletics:* Hugh Durham; Phone: 904-256-7406; Fax: 904-256-7424. *Sports Information Director:* Jamie Zeitz; Phone: 904-256-7409; E-mail: jzeitz@ju.edu.

MEN'S COACHES
Baseball: Terry Alexander; Phone: 904-256-7412; E-mail: baseball@ju.edu.
Basketball: Hugh Durham; Phone: 904-256-7415.
Cross Country: Ron Grigg; Phone: 904-256-7408; E-mail: rgrigg@ju.edu.
Football: Steve Gilbert; Phone: 904-256-7549; E-mail: sgilber@ju.edu.
Golf: Mike Flemming; Phone: 904-256-7479; E-mail: mflemmi@ju.edu.
Soccer: Bob Moullin; Phone: 904-256-7470; E-mail: rmoulli@ju.edu.
Tennis: Andre Herke; Phone: 904-256-7411; E-mail: jutennis@yahoo.com.

WOMEN'S COACHES
Basketball: Melissa Taketa; Phone: 904-256-7236; E-mail: mtaketa@ju.edu.
Cross Country: Ron Grigg; Phone: 904-256-7408; E-mail: rgrigg@ju.edu.
Golf: Mike Flemming; Phone: 904-256-7479; E-mail: mflemmi@ju.edu.
Soccer: Mike Johnson; Phone: 904-256-7704; E-mail: mjohnso@ju.edu.
Softball: Jeff Franquet; Phone: 904-256-7361; E-mail: softball@ju.edu.
Tennis: Andre Herke; Phone: 904-256-7411; E-mail: jutennis@yahoo.com.
Track and Field: Ron Grigg; Phone: 904-256-7408; E-mail: rgrigg@ju.edu.
Volleyball: Courtney Dipert; Phone: 904-256-7405; E-mail: cdipert@ju.edu.

JAMES MADISON UNIVERSITY
Harrisonburg, Virginia

Dukes ◆ NCAA I ◆ Atlantic 10 Conference; Colonial Athletic Conference ◆ http://www.jmu.edu/

State-supported comprehensive, founded 1908
Coed, 14,991 undergraduate students, 96% full-time, 60% women, 40% men
Small-town 605-acre campus
Very difficult entrance level, 55% of applicants were admitted

Freshmen *Admission:* 15,056 applied, 9,404 were accepted, 3,388 enrolled. *Test scores:* SAT verbal scores over 500: 89%; SAT math scores over 500: 89%; SAT verbal scores over 600: 35%; SAT math scores over 600: 39%; SAT verbal scores over 700: 3%; SAT math scores over 700: 3%.
Tuition and fees (2003–04): $5058 (resident), $13,280 (nonresident). *Room and board:* $5966 (room only: $3088).
Financial Aid (All incoming freshmen): *Average need-based gift aid:* $4375. *Average non-need based aid:* $1706. *Average aid to full-time undergraduates:* $6443.
Athletic Department: *Director of Athletics:* Jeff Bourne; Phone: 540-568-6164; Fax: 540-568-3489; E-mail: jeff bournebournejt@jmu.edu. *Sports Information Director:* Gary Michael; Phone: 540-568-6154; E-mail: michaelgl@jmu.edu.

MEN'S COACHES
Baseball: Spanky McFarland; Phone: 540-568-3932; E-mail: mcfarlje@jmu.edu.
Basketball: Sherman Dillard; Phone: 540-568-6462; E-mail: dillarsd@jmu.edu.
Cheerleading: Greg Whitesell; Phone: 540-568-3596; E-mail: whitesgs@jmu.edu.
Cross Country: Dave Rinker; Phone: 540-568-3354; E-mail: rinkerld@jmu.edu.
Diving: Warrick Mann; Phone: 540-568-6574; E-mail: mannwd@jmu.edu.
Football: Mickey Matthews; Phone: 540-568-6715; E-mail: comerjm@jmu.edu.
Golf: Paul Gooden; Phone: 540-568-6988; E-mail: goodenpw@jmu.edu.
Soccer: Tom Martin; Phone: 540-568-6518; E-mail: martintr@jmu.edu.
Swimming: Matt Barany; Phone: 540-568-6528; E-mail: baranymj@jmu.edu.

Tennis: Stephen Second; Phone: 540-568-3950; E-mail: secordss@jmu.edu.
Track and Field: Dave Rinker; Phone: 540-568-3354; E-mail: rinkerld@jmu.edu.
Wrestling: Chris Elliot; Phone: 540-568-3958; E-mail: elliotca@jmu.edu.

WOMEN'S COACHES
Basketball: Kenny Brooks; Phone: 540-568-6513; E-mail: childebd@jmu.edu.
Cheerleading: Greg Whitesell; Phone: 540-568-3596; E-mail: whitesgs@jmu.edu.
Cross Country: Kelly Cox; Phone: 540-568-6544; E-mail: coxka@jmu.cdu.
Diving: Warrick Mann; Phone: 540-568-6574; E-mail: mannwd@jmu.edu.
Field Hockey: Antoinette Lucas; Phone: 540-568-3331; E-mail: fieldhockey@jmu.edu.
Golf: Paul Gooden; Phone: 540-568-3934; E-mail: goodenpw@jmu.edu.
Gymnastics: Roger Burke; Phone: 540-568-3684; E-mail: burkerj@jmu.edu.
Lacrosse: Kellie Young; Phone: 540-568-3618; E-mail: youngka@jmu.edu.
Soccer: Dave Lombardo; Phone: 540-568-3452; E-mail: lombardm@jmu.edu.
Softball: Katie Flynn; Phone: 540-568-2967; E-mail: flynnko@jmu.edu.
Swimming: Nancy Bercaw; Phone: 540-568-3948; E-mail: bercawns@jmu.edu.
Tennis: Maria Malerba; Phone: 540-568-6527; E-mail: malerbma@jmu.edu.
Track and Field: Kelly Cox; Phone: 540-568-6544; E-mail: coxka@jmu.edu.
Volleyball: Disa Garner; Phone: 540-568-6463; E-mail: garnerda@jmu.edu.

JAMESTOWN COLLEGE
Jamestown, North Dakota

Jimmies ◆ NAIA ◆ Dakota Conference ◆ http://www.jc.edu/

Independent Presbyterian 4-year, founded 1883
Coed, 1,152 undergraduate students, 94% full-time, 55% women, 45% men
Small-town 107-acre campus
Minimally difficult entrance level, 96% of applicants were admitted

Freshmen *Admission:* 781 applied, 762 were accepted, 293 enrolled.
Tuition and fees (2004–05): $9400 (full-time). *Room and board:* $3970 (room only: $1700).
Financial Aid (All incoming freshmen): *Average need-based gift aid:* $4543. *Average non-need based aid:* $7231. *Average aid to full-time undergraduates:* $7373.
Athletic Department: *Director of Athletics:* Brad Huse; Phone: 701-252-3467; Fax: 701-253-4318; E-mail: huse@jc.edu.

MEN'S COACHES
Baseball: Tom Hager; Phone: 701-252-3467; E-mail: thager@jc.edu.
Basketball: Brad Huse; Phone: 701-252-3467; E-mail: huse@jc.edu.
Cross Country: Josh Roberts; Phone: 701-252-3467; E-mail: jroberts@jc.edu.
Football: Curt Skotnicki; Phone: 701-252-3467; E-mail: cskotnic@jc.edu.
Golf: Shawn Stimmel; Phone: 701-252-3467; E-mail: sstimmel@jc.edu.
Track and Field: Josh Roberts; Phone: 701-252-3467; E-mail: jroberts@jc.edu.
Wrestling: James McCloud; Phone: 701-252-3467; E-mail: jmccloud@jc.edu.

WOMEN'S COACHES
Basketball: Lawrie Paulson; Phone: 701-252-3467; E-mail: paulson@jc.edu.
Cross Country: Josh Roberts; Phone: 701-252-3467; E-mail: jroberts@jc.edu.
Golf: Shawn Stimmel; Phone: 701-252-3467; E-mail: sstimmel@jc.edu.
Soccer: Shelley Osmond; Phone: 701-252-3467; E-mail: sosmond@jc.edu.
Softball: Chad Buchman; Phone: 701-252-3467; E-mail: buchmann@jc.edu.

Track and Field: Josh Roberts; Phone: 701-252-3467; E-mail: jroberts@jc.edu.
Volleyball: Chris Mahoney; Phone: 701-252-3467; E-mail: mahoney@jc.edu.

JARVIS CHRISTIAN COLLEGE
Hawkins, Texas

Bulldogs ◆ NAIA ◆ Red River Conference
◆ http://www.jarvis.edu/

Independent religious 4-year, founded 1912, affiliated with Christian Church (Disciples of Christ)
Coed, 654 undergraduate students, 100% full-time, 60% women, 40% men
Rural 465-acre campus
Minimally difficult entrance level, 50% of applicants were admitted

Freshmen *Admission:* 594 applied, 298 were accepted, 132 enrolled.
Test scores: SAT math scores over 600: 1%.
Tuition and fees (2003–04): $6330 (full-time). *Room and board:* $3485 (room only: $1610).
Financial Aid (All incoming freshmen): *Average aid to full-time undergraduates:* $9217.
Athletic Department: *Director of Athletics:* Elissa Burwell; Phone: 903-769-5766; Fax: 903-769-4842; E-mail: elissa_burwell@jarvis.edu.

MEN'S COACHES
Baseball: Robert Thomas; Phone: 903-769-5762; E-mail: robert_thomas@jarvis.edu.
Basketball: Byron Rimm; Phone: 903-769-5766; E-mail: byron_rimm@jarvis.edu.
Track and Field: Phone: 903-769-5766.

WOMEN'S COACHES
Basketball: Elissa Burwell; Phone: 903-769-5766; E-mail: elissa_burwell@jarvis.edu.
Track and Field: Phone: 903-769-5766.
Volleyball: Clara Kay; Phone: 903-769-5761; E-mail: clara_kay@jarvis.edu.

JOHN BROWN UNIVERSITY
Siloam Springs, Arkansas

Golden Eagles ◆ NAIA ◆ Sooner Conference ◆ http://www.jbu.edu/

Independent interdenominational comprehensive, founded 1919
Coed, 1,652 undergraduate students
Small-town 200-acre campus
Moderately difficult entrance level, 83% of applicants were admitted

Freshmen *Admission:* 620 applied, 511 were accepted. *Test scores:* SAT verbal scores over 500: 78%; SAT math scores over 500: 85%; SAT verbal scores over 600: 37%; SAT math scores over 600: 35%; SAT verbal scores over 700: 11%; SAT math scores over 700: 9%.
Tuition and fees (2003–04): $14,356 (full-time). *Room and board:* $5040.
Financial Aid (All incoming freshmen): *Average need-based gift aid:* $7508. *Average non-need based aid:* $3535. *Average aid to full-time undergraduates:* $12,121.
Athletic Department: *Director of Athletics:* Bob Burns; Phone: 479-524-7305; Fax: 479-524-7412; E-mail: rburns@jbu.edu. *Sports Information Director:* Ed Renfrow; Phone: 479-524-7304; E-mail: erenfrow@jbu.edu.

MEN'S COACHES
Basketball: John Sheehy; Phone: 479-524-7307; E-mail: jsheehy@jbu.edu.
Cheerleading: Kristen Shaw; Phone: 479-524-7300.
Diving: Mark England; Phone: 479-524-7316; E-mail: mengland@jbu.edu.
Soccer: Bob Gustavson; Phone: 479-524-7321; E-mail: rgustavs@jbu.edu.
Swimming: Brandi Harris; Phone: 479-524-7316; E-mail: bharris@jbu.edu.

John Brown University *(continued)*

Tennis: Robert Walker; Phone: 479-524-7302; E-mail: rwalker@jbu.edu.

WOMEN'S COACHES

Basketball: Jeff Soderquist; Phone: 479-524-7307; E-mail: jsoderqu@jbu.edu.
Cheerleading: Kristen Shaw; Phone: 479-524-7300.
Diving: Mark England; Phone: 479-524-7316; E-mail: mengland@jbu.edu.
Soccer: Joe Thoma; Phone: 479-238-8629; E-mail: jthoma@jbu.edu.
Swimming: Brandi Harris; Phone: 479-524-7316; E-mail: bharris@jbu.edu.
Tennis: Robert Walker; Phone: 479-524-7302; E-mail: rwalker@jbu.edu.
Volleyball: Robyn Gordon; Phone: 479-524-7301; E-mail: rgordon@jbu.edu.

JOHN CARROLL UNIVERSITY
University Heights, Ohio

Blue Streaks ◆ NCAA III ◆ Ohio Athletic Conference
◆ http://www.jcu.edu/

Independent Roman Catholic (Jesuit) comprehensive, founded 1886
Coed, 3,279 undergraduate students
Suburban 60-acre campus with easy access to Cleveland
Moderately difficult entrance level, 81% of applicants were admitted

Freshmen *Admission:* 2,764 applied, 2,387 were accepted. *Test scores:* SAT verbal scores over 500: 84%; SAT math scores over 500: 88%; SAT verbal scores over 600: 32%; SAT math scores over 600: 43%; SAT verbal scores over 700: 6%; SAT math scores over 700: 4%.
Tuition and fees (2003–04): $20,766 (full-time). *Room and board:* $6892.
Athletic Department: *Director of Athletics:* Gretchen Weitbrecht; Phone: 216-397-4194; Fax: 216-397-3043; E-mail: gweitbrecht@jcu.edu. *Sports Information Director:* Christopher Wenzler; Phone: 216-397-4676; E-mail: cwenzler@jcu.edu.

MEN'S COACHES

Baseball: Marc Thibeault; Phone: 216-397-4660; E-mail: mthibeault@jcu.edu.
Basketball: Mike Moran; Phone: 216-397-4505; E-mail: mmoran@jcu.edu.
Cross Country: Mark McClure; Phone: 216-397-4515; E-mail: mamcclure@jcu.edu.
Diving: Lewis Fellinger; Phone: 216-397-1624; E-mail: lfellinger@jcu.edu.
Football: Regis Scafe; Phone: 216-397-1681; E-mail: rscafe@jcu.edu.
Golf: Mike Moran; Phone: 216-397-4505; E-mail: mmoran@jcu.edu.
Soccer: Ali Kazemaini; Phone: 216-397-3041; E-mail: akazemaini@jcu.edu.
Swimming: Matt Lenhart; Phone: 216-397-4368; E-mail: mlenhart@jcu.edu.
Tennis: Bruce Thomas; Phone: 216-397-4396; E-mail: bthomas@jcu.edu.
Track and Field: Mark McClure; Phone: 216-397-4515; E-mail: mamcclure@jcu.edu.
Wrestling: Kerry Volkmann; Phone: 216-397-4464; E-mail: kvolkmann@jcu.edu.

WOMEN'S COACHES

Basketball: Kristie Maravalli; Phone: 216-397-4414; E-mail: kmaravalli@jcu.edu.
Cross Country: Mark McClure; Phone: 216-397-4515; E-mail: mamcclure@jcu.edu.
Diving: Lewis Fellinger; Phone: 216-397-1624; E-mail: lfellinger@jcu.edu.
Soccer: Tracy Blasius; Phone: 216-397-4527; E-mail: tblasius@jcu.edu.
Softball: Gretchen Weitbrecht; Phone: 216-397-4194; E-mail: gweitbrecht@jcu.edu.
Swimming: Matt Lenhart; Phone: 216-397-4368; E-mail: mlenhart@jcu.edu.
Tennis: Bruce Thomas; Phone: 216-397-4396; E-mail: bthomas@jcu.edu.
Track and Field: Mark McClure; Phone: 216-397-4515; E-mail: mamcclure@jcu.edu.
Volleyball: Regan Pore; Phone: 216-397-3060; E-mail: rpore06@jcu.edu.

JOHN JAY COLLEGE OF CRIMINAL JUSTICE OF THE CITY UNIVERSITY OF NEW YORK
New York, New York

Bloodhounds ◆ NCAA III ◆ CUNY Athletic Conference
◆ http://www.jjay.cuny.edu/

State and locally supported comprehensive, founded 1964, part of City University of New York System
Coed, 11,515 undergraduate students
Urban campus
Moderately difficult entrance level, 73% of applicants were admitted

Freshmen *Admission:* 3,144 applied, 2,299 were accepted.
Tuition and fees (2003–04): $4259 (resident), $8899 (nonresident).
Financial Aid (All incoming freshmen): *Average non-need based aid:* $500. *Average aid to full-time undergraduates:* $5100.
Athletic Department: *Director of Athletics:* Susan Larkin; Phone: 212-237-8371; Fax: 212-237-8474; E-mail: slarkin@jjay.cuny.edu. *Sports Information Director:* Jerry Albig; Phone: 212-237-8395; E-mail: jalbig@jjay.cuny.edu.

MEN'S COACHES

Baseball: Dan Palumbo; Phone: 212-237-8369; E-mail: dpalumbo@jjay.cuny.edu.
Basketball: Mike Brown; Phone: 212-237-8372; E-mail: mikebrown35@hotmail.com.
Cross Country: Robert Fox; Phone: 212-237-8373; E-mail: rfox@jjay.cuny.edu.
Soccer: John Ramirez; Phone: 212-237-8879; E-mail: jramirez@jjay.cuny.edu.
Tennis: Sebastien Barrois; Phone: 212-237-8322; E-mail: sbisfm@aol.com.

WOMEN'S COACHES

Basketball: John McGraw; Phone: 212-237-8431.
Cross Country: Robert Fox; Phone: 212-237-8373; E-mail: rfox@jjay.cuny.edu.
Softball: Patrick Malia; Phone: 212-237-8080; E-mail: pmalia@jjay.cuny.edu.
Swimming: Jane Katz; Phone: 212-237-8394; E-mail: jkatz@jjay.cuny.edu.
Tennis: Sebastien Barrois; Phone: 212-237-8322; E-mail: sbisfm@aol.com.
Volleyball: Mamdouh Hassan; Phone: 212-237-8396; E-mail: mhassan@jjay.cuny.edu.

THE JOHNS HOPKINS UNIVERSITY
Baltimore, Maryland

Blue Jays ◆ NCAA III ◆ American Lacrosse Conference; Centennial Conference; Independent ◆ http://www.jhu.edu/

Independent university, founded 1876
Coed, 4,177 undergraduate students, 99% full-time, 43% women, 57% men
Urban 140-acre campus with easy access to Washington, DC
Most difficult entrance level, 31% of applicants were admitted

Freshmen *Admission:* 10,022 applied, 3,052 were accepted, 1,048 enrolled. *Test scores:* SAT verbal scores over 500: 99%; SAT math scores over 500: 100%; SAT verbal scores over 600: 88%; SAT math scores over 600: 94%; SAT verbal scores over 700: 38%; SAT math scores over 700: 59%.
Tuition and fees (2003–04): $29,230 (full-time). *Room and board:* $9142.
Financial Aid (All incoming freshmen): *Average need-based gift aid:* $21,375. *Average non-need based aid:* $3000. *Average aid to full-time undergraduates:* $25,875.
Athletic Department: *Director of Athletics:* Tom Calder; Phone: 410-516-7490; Fax: 410-516-5376; E-mail: tcalder@jhu.edu. *Sports Information Director:* Ernie Larossa; Phone: 410-516-0552; E-mail: elarossa@jhu.edu.

MEN'S COACHES

Baseball: Bob Babb; Phone: 410-516-7485; E-mail: rbabb@jhunix.hcf.jhu.edu.

Basketball: Bill Nelson; Phone: 410-516-7483; E-mail: wnelson@jhunix. hcf.jhu.edu.
Cross Country: Bobby Van Allen; Phone: 410-516-3802; E-mail: vanallen.hcf.jhu.edu.
Football: Jim Margraff; Phone: 410-516-8423; E-mail: margraff@ jhunix.hcf.jhu.edu.
Lacrosse: Dave Pietramala; Phone: 410-516-7479; E-mail: dp43@jhu. edu.
Soccer: Matt Smith; Phone: 410-516-5099; E-mail: msmith@jhunix. hcf.jhu.edu.
Swimming: George Kennedy; Phone: 410-516-7484; E-mail: gkennedy@ jhunix.hcf.jhu.edu.
Tennis: Ben Baron; Phone: 410-516-7490; E-mail: benbaron@comcast. net.
Track and Field: Bobby Van Allen; Phone: 410-516-3802; E-mail: vanallen@jhunix.hcf.jhu.edu.
Wrestling: Kirk Salvo; Phone: 410-516-7490; E-mail: ksalvo@bcpl.net.

WOMEN'S COACHES
Basketball: Nancy Funk; Phone: 410-516-7486; E-mail: nfunk@jhu.edu.
Cross Country: Bobby Van Allen; Phone: 410-516-3802; E-mail: vanallen@jhunix.hcf.jhu.edu.
Field Hockey: Megan Callahan; Phone: 410-516-7490; E-mail: meganc@ jhunix.hcf.jhu.edu.
Lacrosse: Janine Tucker; Phone: 410-516-7722; E-mail: jrt@jhunix.hcf. jhu.edu.
Soccer: Leo Weil; Phone: 410-516-7967; E-mail: coachweil@aol.com.
Swimming: George Kennedy; Phone: 410-516-7484; E-mail: gkennedy@ jhunix.hcf.jhu.edu.
Tennis: Ben Baron; Phone: 410-516-7490; E-mail: benbaron@comcast. net.
Track and Field: Bobby Van Allen; Phone: 410-516-3802; E-mail: vanallen@jhunix.hcf.jhu.edu.
Volleyball: Scott Pennewill; Phone: 410-516-7968; E-mail: pennewill623@earthlink.net.

JOHNSON & WALES UNIVERSITY
Denver, Colorado

Wildcats ◆ NAIA ◆ Independent ◆ http://www.jwu.edu/

Independent 4-year, founded 1993
Coed, 1,328 undergraduate students
Small-town campus
Minimally difficult entrance level, 86% of applicants were admitted

Freshmen *Admission:* 2,024 applied, 1,789 were accepted. *Test scores:* SAT verbal scores over 500: 45%; SAT math scores over 500: 48%; SAT verbal scores over 600: 14%; SAT math scores over 600: 14%; SAT verbal scores over 700: 1%; SAT math scores over 700: 2%.
Tuition and fees (2004–05): $19,992 (full-time). *Room and board:* $8115.
Financial Aid (All incoming freshmen): *Average need-based gift aid:* $4490. *Average non-need based aid:* $4695. *Average aid to full-time undergraduates:* $13,733.
Athletic Department: *Director of Athletics:* Tim Corrigan; Phone: 303-256-9330; Fax: 303-256-9386; E-mail: tim.corrigan@jwu.edu. *Sports Information Director:* Mark Gentry; Phone: 303-256-9307; E-mail: mark.gentry@jwu.edu.

MEN'S COACHES
Baseball: Mark Gentry; Phone: 303-256-9307; E-mail: mark.gentry@ jwu.edu.
Basketball: Bill Perkins; Phone: 303-256-9446; E-mail: bill.perkins@ jwu.edu.
Golf: Joel Michor; Phone: 303-256-9346; E-mail: joel.michor@jwu.edu.
Soccer: Mike Flaherty; Phone: 303-256-9346; E-mail: mike.flaherty@ jwu.edu.
Volleyball: Josh Crosier; Phone: 303-256-9346; E-mail: josh.crosier@ jwu.edu.

WOMEN'S COACHES
Basketball: Regina Pollard; Phone: 303-256-9447; E-mail: regina. pollard@jwu.edu.
Soccer: Mike Baldwin; Phone: 303-256-9346; E-mail: mike.baldwin@ jwu.edu.
Softball: Bryon Rutherford; Phone: 303-256-9346; E-mail: bryon. rutherford@jwu.edu.
Volleyball: Liz Reid; Phone: 303-256-9346; E-mail: liz.reid@jwu.edu.

JOHNSON & WALES UNIVERSITY
North Miami, Florida

Wildcats ◆ NAIA ◆ Independent ◆ http://www.jwu.edu/

Independent 4-year, founded 1992
Coed, 2,379 undergraduate students
Suburban 8-acre campus with easy access to Miami
Minimally difficult entrance level, 84% of applicants were admitted

Freshmen *Admission:* 4,954 applied, 4,296 were accepted. *Test scores:* SAT verbal scores over 500: 31%; SAT math scores over 500: 31%; SAT verbal scores over 600: 7%; SAT math scores over 600: 8%; SAT verbal scores over 700: 1%.
Tuition and fees (2004–05): $19,992 (full-time). *Room only:* $7185.
Financial Aid (All incoming freshmen): *Average need-based gift aid:* $5462. *Average non-need based aid:* $5254. *Average aid to full-time undergraduates:* $14,511.

MEN'S COACHES
Basketball: David Graham; Phone: 305-892-7000.
Golf: Dave Adamonis; Phone: 305-892-7000.

JOHNSON & WALES UNIVERSITY
Providence, Rhode Island

Wildcats ◆ NCAA III ◆ Great Northeast Athletic Conference; New England College Wrestling Conference ◆ http://www.jwu.edu/

Independent comprehensive, founded 1914
Coed, 9,220 undergraduate students, 90% full-time, 52% women, 48% men
Urban 47-acre campus with easy access to Boston
Minimally difficult entrance level, 82% of applicants were admitted

Freshmen *Admission:* 11,174 applied, 9,548 were accepted, 2,388 enrolled. *Test scores:* SAT verbal scores over 500: 37%; SAT math scores over 500: 37%; SAT verbal scores over 600: 6%; SAT math scores over 600: 7%.
Tuition and fees (2004–05): $17,460 (full-time). *Room and board:* $7185.
Financial Aid (All incoming freshmen): *Average need-based gift aid:* $4560. *Average non-need based aid:* $3633. *Average aid to full-time undergraduates:* $12,848.
Athletic Department: *Director of Athletics:* John Parente; Phone: 401-598-1604; Fax: 401-598-1601; E-mail: john.parente@jwu.edu. *Sports Information Director:* Daniel Booth; Phone: 401-598-1632; E-mail: daniel.booth@jwu.edu.

MEN'S COACHES
Baseball: John Larose; Phone: 401-598-1609; E-mail: jclarose@jwu. edu.
Basketball: Todd Finn; Phone: 401-598-1621; E-mail: jwuwildcathoop@aol.com.
Cross Country: Tom Spann; Phone: 401-598-1615.
Golf: Mike Lurgio; Phone: 401-598-1600; E-mail: lizlurgio@aol.com.
Ice Hockey: Erik Noack; Phone: 401-598-1636; E-mail: dinonoack@ hotmail.com.
Soccer: Gregg Miller; Phone: 401-598-1614; E-mail: gmiller@jwu.edu.
Tennis: Adam Spring; Phone: 401-598-1635; E-mail: ajspringer@aol. com.
Volleyball: Neil Nachbar; Phone: 401-598-1611; E-mail: nnachbar@ jwu.edu.
Wrestling: Lonnie Morris; Phone: 401-598-1610; E-mail: jwuwrestle@ aol.com.

WOMEN'S COACHES
Basketball: Stephanie Brown; Phone: 401-598-1606; E-mail: sbrown@ jwu.edu.
Cross Country: Hollie Walton; Phone: 401-598-1615.
Soccer: Luis Faria; Phone: 401-598-1608; E-mail: luis.faria@jwu.edu.
Softball: Lance Howlett; Phone: 401-598-1607; E-mail: howie7801@ comcast.net.
Tennis: Allan Freedman; Phone: 401-598-1021; E-mail: afreedman@ jwu.edu.
Volleyball: Jamie Marcoux; Phone: 401-598-1605; E-mail: jmarcoux@ jwu.edu.

JOHNSON C. SMITH UNIVERSITY
Charlotte, North Carolina

Golden Bulls ◆ NCAA II ◆ Central Intercollegiate Athletic Conference ◆ http://www.jcsu.edu/

Independent 4-year, founded 1867
Coed, 1,474 undergraduate students, 95% full-time, 58% women, 42% men
Urban 105-acre campus
Minimally difficult entrance level, 5% of applicants were admitted

Freshmen *Admission:* 3,171 applied, 1,532 were accepted, 461 enrolled. *Test scores:* SAT verbal scores over 500: 12%; SAT math scores over 500: 8%; SAT verbal scores over 600: %; SAT math scores over 600: %.
Tuition and fees (2003–04): $13,062 (full-time). *Room and board:* $5046 (room only: $2904).
Financial Aid (All incoming freshmen): *Average need-based gift aid:* $1500. *Average aid to full-time undergraduates:* $5600.
Athletic Department: *Director of Athletics:* Helen Caldwell; Phone: 704-378-1164; Fax: 704-378-1073. *Sports Information Director:* Kristene Brathwaite; Phone: 704-378-1118.
MEN'S COACHES
Basketball: Steve Joyner; Phone: 704-378-1206; E-mail: sjoyner@jcsu.edu.
Cheerleading: Peggy Lide; Phone: 704-378-1205.
Cross Country: Mark Sherrill; Phone: 704-378-1255; E-mail: msherrill@jcsu.edu.
Football: Tim Harkness; Phone: 704-378-1208; E-mail: tharkness@jcsu.edu.
Golf: James Saunders; Phone: 704-378-1116; E-mail: jsaunders@jcsu.edu.
Tennis: James Cuthbertson; Phone: 704-378-1282; E-mail: jcuthbertson@jcsu.edu.
Track and Field: Jonathan Kelly; Phone: 704-378-1255; E-mail: jkelly@jcsu.edu.
WOMEN'S COACHES
Basketball: Vanessa Taylor; Phone: 704-378-1203; E-mail: vtaylor@jcsu.edu.
Cheerleading: Peggy Lide; Phone: 704-378-1205.
Cross Country: Ed Joyner; Phone: 704-378-1211.
Softball: Mark Raley; Phone: 704-378-1081; E-mail: mraley@jcsu.edu.
Tennis: James Cuthbertson; Phone: 704-378-1282; E-mail: jcuthbertson@jcsu.edu.
Track and Field: Jonathan Kelly; Phone: 704-378-1255; E-mail: jkelly@jcsu.edu.
Volleyball: Mark Raley; Phone: 704-378-1081; E-mail: mraley@jcsu.edu.

JOHNSON STATE COLLEGE
Johnson, Vermont

Badgers ◆ NCAA III ◆ North Atlantic Conference; North Coast Athletic Conference ◆ http://www.johnsonstatecollege.edu/

State-supported comprehensive, founded 1828, part of Vermont State Colleges System
Coed, 1,532 undergraduate students, 73% full-time, 60% women, 40% men
Rural 350-acre campus with easy access to Montreal
Moderately difficult entrance level, 87% of applicants were admitted

Freshmen *Admission:* 1,076 applied, 934 were accepted, 277 enrolled. *Test scores:* SAT verbal scores over 500: 45%; SAT math scores over 500: 36%; SAT verbal scores over 600: 11%; SAT math scores over 600: 6%; SAT verbal scores over 700: 1%.
Tuition and fees (2003–04): $5876 (resident), $12,430 (nonresident). *Room and board:* $6013 (room only: $3517).
Financial Aid (All incoming freshmen): *Average aid to full-time undergraduates:* $7835.
Athletic Department: *Director of Athletics:* Barbara Lougee-Fountain; Phone: 802-635-1485; Fax: 802-635-1497; E-mail: lougeeb@badger.

jsc.vsc.edu. *Sports Information Director:* Greg Dixon; Phone: 802-635-1470; E-mail: dixong@badger.jsc.vsc.edu.
MEN'S COACHES
Basketball: Greg Dixon; Phone: 802-635-1470; E-mail: dixong@mail.jsc.vsc.edu.
Cross Country: James Roy; Phone: 802-635-1468; E-mail: mrhehheh@aol.com.
Lacrosse: Phone: 802-635-1468.
Soccer: Brian Buczek; Phone: 802-635-1468; E-mail: buczeks@cs.com.
Tennis: Dain LaRoche; Phone: 802-635-1468; E-mail: laroched@mail.jsc.vsc.edu.
WOMEN'S COACHES
Basketball: Barbara Lougee Fountain; Phone: 802-635-1485; E-mail: lougeeb@mail.jsc.vsc.edu.
Cross Country: James Roy; Phone: 802-635-1468; E-mail: mrhehheh@aol.com.
Soccer: Angeline Faraci; Phone: 802-635-1468; E-mail: faracia@mail.jsc.vsc.edu.
Softball: Renee Breault; Phone: 802-635-1468; E-mail: breaultr@mail.jsc.vsc.edu.
Tennis: Nelson Murray; Phone: 802-635-1468; E-mail: murr13jr@hotmail.com.

JUDSON COLLEGE
Elgin, Illinois

Eagles ◆ NAIA ◆ Chicagoland Collegiate Conference ◆ http://www.judsoncollege.edu/

Independent Baptist 4-year, founded 1963
Coed, 1,123 undergraduate students, 79% full-time, 57% women, 43% men
Suburban 80-acre campus with easy access to Chicago
Moderately difficult entrance level, 80% of applicants were admitted

Freshmen *Admission:* 532 applied, 420 were accepted, 132 enrolled. *Test scores:* SAT verbal scores over 500: 60%; SAT math scores over 500: 63%; SAT verbal scores over 600: 20%; SAT math scores over 600: 33%; SAT math scores over 700: 3%.
Tuition and fees (2003–04): $16,050 (full-time). *Room and board:* $6000.
Athletic Department: *Director of Athletics:* Steve Burke; Phone: 847-628-1575; Fax: 847-628-1591; E-mail: sburke@judsoncollege.edu. *Sports Information Director:* Nancy Severson; Phone: 847-628-1581; E-mail: nseverson@judsoncollege.edu.
MEN'S COACHES
Baseball: Loren Torres; Phone: 847-628-2523; E-mail: ltorres@judsoncollege.edu.
Basketball: Jim Condill; Phone: 847-628-1576; E-mail: jcondill@judsoncollege.edu.
Soccer: Steve Burke; Phone: 847-628-1575; E-mail: sburke@judsoncollege.edu.
WOMEN'S COACHES
Basketball: Tory Gum; Phone: 847-628-1580; E-mail: tgum@judsoncollege.edu.
Soccer: Freddie King; Phone: 847-628-1589; E-mail: fking@judsoncollege.edu.
Softball: Mike Hawkins; Phone: 847-628-2499; E-mail: mhawkins@judsoncollege.edu.
Volleyball: Jennfier Tynis; Phone: 847-628-1588; E-mail: jtynis@judsoncollege.edu.

JUNIATA COLLEGE
Huntingdon, Pennsylvania

Eagles ◆ NCAA III ◆ Commonwealth Conference ◆ http://www.juniata.edu/

Independent religious 4-year, founded 1876, affiliated with Church of the Brethren
Coed, 1,396 undergraduate students, 96% full-time, 56% women, 44% men
Small-town 110-acre campus
Moderately difficult entrance level, 73% of applicants were admitted

Freshmen *Admission:* 1,578 applied, 1,179 were accepted, 381 enrolled. *Test scores:* SAT verbal scores over 500: 89%; SAT math scores over

500: 92%; SAT verbal scores over 600: 42%; SAT math scores over 600: 45%; SAT verbal scores over 700: 7%; SAT math scores over 700: 7%.
Tuition and fees (2004–05): $24,270 (full-time). *Room and board:* $6770 (room only: $3550).
Financial Aid (All incoming freshmen): *Average need-based gift aid:* $15,078. *Average non-need based aid:* $11,044. *Average aid to full-time undergraduates:* $18,316.
Athletic Department: *Director of Athletics:* Larry Bock; Phone: 814-641-3512; Fax: 814-641-3508; E-mail: bockl@juniata.edu. *Sports Information Director:* Joel Cookson; Phone: 814-641-3134; E-mail: cooksoj@juniata.edu.

MEN'S COACHES
Baseball: George Zanic; Phone: 814-641-3515; E-mail: zanicg@juniata.edu.
Basketball: Greg Curley; Phone: 814-641-3521; E-mail: curleyg@juniata.edu.
Cheerleading: Kristina Launtz; Phone: 814-641-3515; E-mail: launtzk@juniata.edu.
Cross Country: Jon Cutright; Phone: 814-641-3520; E-mail: cutrigj@juniata.edu.
Football: Kevin Burke; Phone: 814-641-3522; E-mail: burkek@juniata.edu.
Soccer: Scott McKenzie; Phone: 814-641-3503; E-mail: mckenzs@juniata.edu.
Tennis: Klaus Jaeger; Phone: 814-641-3527; E-mail: jaeger@juniata.edu.
Track and Field: Jon Cutright; Phone: 814-641-3520; E-mail: cutrigj@juniata.edu.
Volleyball: Ken Shibuya; Phone: 814-641-3514; E-mail: shibuyk@juniata.edu.

WOMEN'S COACHES
Basketball: Danny Young; Phone: 814-641-3518; E-mail: youngd@juniata.edu.
Cheerleading: Kristina Launtz; Phone: 814-641-3515; E-mail: launtzk@juniata.edu.
Cross Country: Jon Cutright; Phone: 814-641-3520; E-mail: cutrigj@juniata.edu.
Field Hockey: Caroline Gillich; Phone: 814-641-3519; E-mail: gillicc@juniata.edu.
Soccer: Scott McKenzie; Phone: 814-641-3503; E-mail: mckenzs@juniata.edu.
Softball: John Houck; Phone: 814-641-5305; E-mail: houckj@juniata.edu.
Swimming: Brian McGrath; Phone: 814-641-3717; E-mail: mcgratb@juniata.edu.
Tennis: Gala Baker; Phone: 814-641-3527; E-mail: bakerg@juniata.edu.
Track and Field: Jon Cutright; Phone: 814-641-3520; E-mail: cutrigj@juniata.edu.
Volleyball: Larry Bock; Phone: 814-641-3512; E-mail: bockl@juniata.edu.

KALAMAZOO COLLEGE
Kalamazoo, Michigan
Hornets ◆ NCAA III ◆ Michigan Intercollegiate Conference
◆ http://www.kzoo.edu/

Independent religious 4-year, founded 1833, affiliated with American Baptist Churches in the U.S.A.
Coed, 1,280 undergraduate students, 100% full-time, 56% women, 44% men
Suburban 60-acre campus
Very difficult entrance level, 68% of applicants were admitted

Freshmen *Admission:* 1,603 applied, 1,127 were accepted, 383 enrolled. *Test scores:* SAT verbal scores over 500: 99%; SAT math scores over 500: 98%; SAT verbal scores over 600: 83%; SAT math scores over 600: 81%; SAT verbal scores over 700: 32%; SAT math scores over 700: 25%.
Tuition and fees (2003–04): $22,908 (full-time). *Room and board:* $6480 (room only: $3210).
Financial Aid (All incoming freshmen): *Average need-based gift aid:* $13,414. *Average non-need based aid:* $8800. *Average aid to full-time undergraduates:* $19,334.

Athletic Department: *Director of Athletics:* Timon Corwin; Phone: 269-337-7079; Fax: 269-337-7401; E-mail: tcorwin@kzoo.edu. *Sports Information Director:* Steve Wideen; Phone: 269-337-7287; E-mail: swideen@kzoo.edu.

MEN'S COACHES
Baseball: Steve Wideen; Phone: 269-337-7287; E-mail: swideen@kzoo.edu.
Basketball: Rob Passage; Phone: 269-337-5804; E-mail: rpassage@kzoo.edu.
Cheerleading: Barb Vogelsang; Phone: 269-337-7210; E-mail: vogelsan@kzoo.edu.
Cross Country: Andy Strickler; Phone: 269-337-7169; E-mail: stricklr@kzoo.edu.
Diving: Ron Bramble; Phone: 269-337-7091.
Football: Tim Rogers; Phone: 269-337-7085; E-mail: trogers@kzoo.edu.
Golf: Rob Passage; Phone: 269-337-5804; E-mail: rpassage@kzoo.edu.
Soccer: Tim Halloran; Phone: 269-337-7454; E-mail: halloran@portageps.org.
Swimming: Kathy Milliken; Phone: 269-337-7091; E-mail: milliken@kzoo.edu.
Tennis: Timon Corwin; Phone: 269-337-7079; E-mail: tcorwin@kzoo.edu.

WOMEN'S COACHES
Basketball: Michele Fortimer; Phone: 269-337-5752; E-mail: mfortier@kzoo.edu.
Cheerleading: Barb Vogelsang; Phone: 269-337-7210; E-mail: vogelsan@kzoo.edu.
Cross Country: Andy Strickler; Phone: 269-337-7169; E-mail: stricklr@kzoo.edu.
Diving: Ron Bramble; Phone: 269-337-7091.
Golf: Dean Marks; Phone: 269-337-7082; E-mail: jabbergolf@aol.com.
Soccer: Matt Kellog; Phone: 269-337-7454; E-mail: mkellogg616@yahoo.com.
Softball: Tracy Ciucci; Phone: 269-337-7082; E-mail: tcoochi@hotmail.com.
Swimming: Kathy Milliken; Phone: 269-337-7091; E-mail: milliken@kzoo.edu.
Tennis: Alison Frye; Phone: 269-337-7289; E-mail: afrye@kzoo.edu.
Volleyball: Jeanne Hess; Phone: 269-337-7086; E-mail: jhess@kzoo.edu.

KANSAS STATE UNIVERSITY
Manhattan, Kansas
Wildcats ◆ NCAA I ◆ Big 12 Conference
◆ http://www.ksu.edu/

State-supported university, founded 1863, part of Kansas Board of Regents
Coed, 19,083 undergraduate students, 85% full-time, 48% women, 52% men
Suburban 668-acre campus with easy access to Kansas City
Noncompetitive entrance level, 61% of applicants were admitted

Freshmen *Admission:* 7,952 applied, 4,736 were accepted, 3,439 enrolled.
Tuition and fees (2003–04): $4059 (resident), $11,949 (nonresident). *Room and board:* $5080.
Financial Aid (All incoming freshmen): *Average need-based gift aid:* $1251. *Average non-need based aid:* $1944. *Average aid to full-time undergraduates:* $4972.
Athletic Department: *Director of Athletics:* Tim Weiser; Phone: 785-532-6912; Fax: 785-532-2340; E-mail: ksuad@k-state.edu. *Sports Information Director:* Garry Bowman; Phone: 785-532-7977; E-mail: gbowman@k-state.edu.

MEN'S COACHES
Baseball: Brad Hill; Phone: 785-532-5723.
Basketball: Jim Wooldridge; Phone: 785-532-6531; E-mail: jaw@ksu.edu.
Cheerleading: Damian Hilton; Phone: 785-532-7983; E-mail: damianh@k-state.edu.
Cross Country: Randy Cole; Phone: 785-532-6567; E-mail: coler@ksu.edu.
Football: Bill Snyder; Phone: 785-532-5876; E-mail: bssnyder@ksu.edu.
Golf: Tim Norris; Phone: 785-532-7931; E-mail: mengolf@ksu.edu.
Track and Field: Cliff Rovelto; Phone: 785-532-6567; E-mail: cliff@ksu.edu.

Kansas State University *(continued)*

WOMEN'S COACHES

Basketball: Deb Patterson; Phone: 785-532-6970; E-mail: dlpip@ksu. edu.

Cheerleading: Damian Hilton; Phone: 785-532-7983; E-mail: damianh@ k-state.edu.

Cross Country: Randy Cole; Phone: 785-532-6567; E-mail: coler@ksu. edu.

Golf: Kristi Knight; Phone: 785-532-7799; E-mail: ksugolf@ksu.edu.

Tennis: Steve Bietau; Phone: 785-532-7198; E-mail: ksuten@ksu.edu.

Track and Field: Cliff Rovelto; Phone: 785-532-6567; E-mail: cliff@ksu. edu.

Volleyball: Suzie Fritz; Phone: 785-532-5935; E-mail: sfritz@ksu.edu.

KANSAS WESLEYAN UNIVERSITY
Salina, Kansas

Coyotes ◆ NAIA ◆ Kansas Collegiate Conference ◆ http:// www.kwu.edu/

Independent United Methodist comprehensive, founded 1886
Coed, 768 undergraduate students, 78% full-time, 59% women, 41% men
Urban 28-acre campus
Moderately difficult entrance level, 47% of applicants were admitted

Freshmen *Admission:* 1,097 applied, 577 were accepted, 147 enrolled.
Tuition and fees (2004–05): $15,000 (full-time). *Room and board:* $5400 (room only: $2400).
Financial Aid (All incoming freshmen): *Average need-based gift aid:* $3890. *Average non-need based aid:* $6553. *Average aid to full-time undergraduates:* $10,901.
Athletic Department: *Director of Athletics:* Jerry Jones; Phone: 785-827-5541; Fax: 785-827-0927; E-mail: jones@kwu.edu. *Sports Information Director:* David Toelle; Phone: 785-827-5541; E-mail: sportsinfo@ kwu.edu.

MEN'S COACHES

Baseball: Tim Bellew; Phone: 785-827-5541; E-mail: timbel@kwu.edu.

Basketball: Jerry Jones; Phone: 785-827-5541; E-mail: jones@kwu.edu.

Cheerleading: Georgia Rupp; Phone: 785-827-5541.

Cross Country: John Pickens; Phone: 785-827-5541; E-mail: pickens@ kwu.edu.

Football: Dave Dallas; Phone: 785-827-5541; E-mail: dallas@kwu.edu.

Golf: Brad Gibson; Phone: 785-827-5541; E-mail: bradg@kwu.edu.

Soccer: Brian Berner; Phone: 785-827-5541; E-mail: soccer@kwu.edu.

Tennis: Brandon Lesovsky; Phone: 785-827-5541; E-mail: brales@kwu. edu.

Track and Field: John Pickens; Phone: 785-827-5541; E-mail: pickens@ kwu.edu.

WOMEN'S COACHES

Basketball: Cary Wilson; Phone: 785-827-5541; E-mail: cwilson@kwu. edu.

Cheerleading: Georgia Rupp; Phone: 785-827-5541.

Cross Country: John Pickens; Phone: 785-827-5541; E-mail: pickens@ kwu.edu.

Soccer: Brian Berner; Phone: 785-827-5541; E-mail: soccer@kwu.edu.

Softball: Mike Smith; Phone: 785-827-5541; E-mail: softball@kwu.edu.

Tennis: Brandon Lesovsky; Phone: 785-827-5541; E-mail: brales@kwu. edu.

Track and Field: John Pickens; Phone: 785-827-5541; E-mail: pickens@ kwu.edu.

Volleyball: Cary Wilson; Phone: 785-827-5541; E-mail: cwilson@kwu. edu.

KEAN UNIVERSITY
Union, New Jersey

Cougars ◆ NCAA III ◆ Knickerbocker Lacrosse Conference; New Jersey Athletic Conference ◆ http://www.kean.edu/

State-supported comprehensive, founded 1855, part of New Jersey State College System
Coed, 10,179 undergraduate students, 73% full-time, 64% women, 36% men
Urban 151-acre campus with easy access to New York City
Moderately difficult entrance level, 67% of applicants were admitted

Freshmen *Admission:* 4,225 applied, 2,723 were accepted, 1,376 enrolled. *Test scores:* SAT verbal scores over 500: 36%; SAT math scores over 500: 44%; SAT verbal scores over 600: 5%; SAT math scores over 600: 5%; SAT math scores over 700: %.
Tuition and fees (2003–04): $6724 (resident), $9086 (nonresident). *Room and board:* $7755 (room only: $5355).
Financial Aid (All incoming freshmen): *Average need-based gift aid:* $4257. *Average aid to full-time undergraduates:* $6759.
Athletic Department: *Director of Athletics:* Glenn Hedden; Phone: 908-737-5820; Fax: 908-737-5805; E-mail: ghedden@kean.edu. *Sports Information Director:* Jack McKiernan; Phone: 908-737-5979; E-mail: jmckiern@kean.edu.

MEN'S COACHES

Baseball: Neil Ioviero; Phone: 908-737-5452; E-mail: nioviero@kean. edu.

Basketball: Bruce Hamburger; Phone: 908-737-5456; E-mail: bhamburg@kean.edu.

Cheerleading: Cheree Berry; Phone: 732-669-0722; E-mail: berryc@ kean.edu.

Cross Country: Shelly Hollingsworth; Phone: 908-737-5817; E-mail: shollings@kean.edu.

Football: Charlie Cocuzza; Phone: 908-737-5813; E-mail: ccocuzza@ kean.edu.

Lacrosse: Shelley Scheiner; Phone: 908-737-5820.

Soccer: Tony Ochrimenko; Phone: 908-737-5807; E-mail: tko@kean. edu.

Track and Field: Shelly Hollingsworth; Phone: 908-737-5817; E-mail: shollings@kean.edu.

WOMEN'S COACHES

Basketball: Michele Sharp; Phone: 908-737-5458; E-mail: msharp@ kean.edu.

Cheerleading: Cheree Berry; Phone: 732-669-0722; E-mail: berryc@ kean.edu.

Cross Country: Shelly Hollingsworth; Phone: 908-737-5817; E-mail: shollings@kean.edu.

Field Hockey: Dipi Bhaya; Phone: 908-737-5810; E-mail: dbhaya@kean. edu.

Lacrosse: Dipi Bhaya; Phone: 908-737-5810; E-mail: dbhaya@kean. edu.

Soccer: Brian Doherty; Phone: 908-737-5826; E-mail: bdoherty@kean. edu.

Softball: Margie Acker; Phone: 908-737-5816; E-mail: macker@kean. edu.

Swimming: Phone: 908-737-5820.

Tennis: Kristen Higgins; Phone: 908-737-5806.

Track and Field: Shelly Hollingsworth; Phone: 908-737-5817; E-mail: shollings@kean.edu.

Volleyball: Bridget White; Phone: 908-737-5823; E-mail: mwhite@kean. edu.

KEENE STATE COLLEGE
Keene, New Hampshire
Owls ◆ NCAA III ◆ Little East Conference
◆ http://www.keene.edu/

State-supported comprehensive, founded 1909, part of University System of New Hampshire
Coed, 444 undergraduate students, 10% full-time, 52% women, 48% men
Small-town 160-acre campus
Moderately difficult entrance level, 64% of applicants were admitted

Freshmen *Admission:* 4,207 applied, 2,997 were accepted. *Test scores:* SAT verbal scores over 500: 52%; SAT math scores over 500: 51%; SAT verbal scores over 600: 11%; SAT math scores over 600: 9%; SAT verbal scores over 700: 1%; SAT math scores over 700: %.
Tuition and fees (2004–05): $6530 (resident), $12,580 (nonresident). *Room and board:* $5682 (room only: $3870).
Financial Aid (All incoming freshmen): *Average need-based gift aid:* $4339. *Average non-need based aid:* $2059. *Average aid to full-time undergraduates:* $6961.
Athletic Department: *Director of Athletics:* John Ratliff; Phone: 603-358-2813; Fax: 603-358-2888; E-mail: jratliff@keene.edu. *Sports Information Director:* Stuart Kaufman; Phone: 603-358-2630; E-mail: skaufman@keene.edu.

MEN'S COACHES
Baseball: Ken Howe; Phone: 603-358-2809; E-mail: khowe@keene.edu.
Basketball: Rob Colbert; Phone: 603-358-2806; E-mail: rcolbert@keene.edu.
Cheerleading: Karen Wilson; Phone: 603-358-7777; E-mail: kdwilson@prodigy.net.
Cross Country: Peter Thomas; Phone: 603-358-2834; E-mail: pthomas@keene.edu.
Diving: Gene Leonard; Phone: 603-358-2833; E-mail: eleonard@keene.edu.
Lacrosse: Mark Theriault; Phone: 603-358-2822; E-mail: mtheriau@keene.edu.
Soccer: Ron Butcher; Phone: 603-358-2805; E-mail: rbutcher@keene.edu.
Swimming: Gene Leonard; Phone: 603-358-2833; E-mail: eleonard@keene.edu.
Track and Field: Peter Thomas; Phone: 603-358-2834; E-mail: pthomas@keene.edu.

WOMEN'S COACHES
Basketball: Keith Boucher; Phone: 603-358-2802; E-mail: kboucher@keene.edu.
Cheerleading: Karen Wilson; Phone: 603-358-7777; E-mail: kdwilson@prodigy.net.
Cross Country: Peter Thomas; Phone: 603-358-2834; E-mail: pthomas@keene.edu.
Diving: Gene Leonard; Phone: 603-358-2833; E-mail: eleonard@keene.edu.
Field Hockey: Amy Watson; Phone: 603-358-2835; E-mail: keep99@msn.com.
Lacrosse: Emily Johnson; Phone: 603-358-2889; E-mail: ejohnson1@keene.edu.
Soccer: Denise Lyons; Phone: 603-358-2852; E-mail: dlyons@keene.edu.
Softball: Charlie Beach; Phone: 603-358-2820; E-mail: cbeach@keene.edu.
Swimming: Gene Leonard; Phone: 603-358-2833; E-mail: eleonard@keene.edu.
Track and Field: Peter Thomas; Phone: 603-358-2834; E-mail: pthomas@keene.edu.
Volleyball: Matora Fiorey; Phone: 603-358-2883; E-mail: mfiorey@keene.edu.

KENDALL COLLEGE
Chicago, Illinois
Vikings ◆ NAIA ◆ Chicagoland Collegiate Conference
◆ http://www.kendall.edu/

Independent United Methodist 4-year, founded 1934
Coed, 628 undergraduate students, 72% full-time, 54% women, 46% men
Urban 1-acre campus
Minimally difficult entrance level, 79% of applicants were admitted

Freshmen *Admission:* 629 applied, 496 were accepted, 70 enrolled.
Tuition and fees (2003–04): $14,750 (full-time). *Room and board:* $6828.
Financial Aid (All incoming freshmen): *Average need-based gift aid:* $1000.
Athletic Department: *Director of Athletics:* John Bongiorno; Phone: 847-448-2470; Fax: 847-448-2551; E-mail: jbongiorno@kendall.edu.

MEN'S COACHES
Basketball: John Bongiorno; Phone: 847-448-2470; E-mail: jbongiorno@kendall.edu.
Soccer: Tim Donahue; Phone: 847-448-2065; E-mail: tdonahue@kendall.edu.
Volleyball: Phone: 847-448-2000.

WOMEN'S COACHES
Basketball: Michele Miller; Phone: 847-448-2000.
Volleyball: John Wyatt Greenlee; Phone: 847-448-2000.

KENNESAW STATE UNIVERSITY
Kennesaw, Georgia
Fighting Owls ◆ NCAA II ◆ Peach Belt Conference ◆ http://www.kennesaw.edu/

State-supported comprehensive, founded 1963, part of University System of Georgia
Coed, 15,581 undergraduate students, 64% full-time, 62% women, 38% men
Suburban 185-acre campus with easy access to Atlanta
Moderately difficult entrance level, 69% of applicants were admitted

Freshmen *Admission:* 5,738 applied, 4,035 were accepted, 2,345 enrolled. *Test scores:* SAT verbal scores over 500: 65%; SAT math scores over 500: 60%; SAT verbal scores over 600: 17%; SAT math scores over 600: 14%; SAT verbal scores over 700: 1%; SAT math scores over 700: 1%.
Tuition and fees (2003–04): $3344 (resident), $9980 (nonresident). *Room only:* $3897.
Financial Aid (All incoming freshmen): *Average need-based gift aid:* $1379. *Average non-need based aid:* $760. *Average aid to full-time undergraduates:* $4062.
Athletic Department: *Director of Athletics:* Dave Waples; Phone: 770-423-6210; Fax: 770-423-6665; E-mail: dwaples@kennesaw.edu. *Sports Information Director:* Mark Toma; Phone: 770-499-3217; E-mail: mtoma@kennesaw.edu.

MEN'S COACHES
Baseball: Mike Sansing; Phone: 770-423-6264; E-mail: msansing@kennesaw.edu.
Basketball: Tony Ingle; Phone: 770-423-6388; E-mail: tingle@kennesaw.edu.
Cheerleading: Felecia Ingle; Phone: 770-423-6264; E-mail: fmulkey@kennesaw.edu.
Cross Country: Stan Sims; Phone: 770-423-6376; E-mail: ssims@kennesaw.edu.
Golf: Jon Dunlap; Phone: 770-862-8570; E-mail: jdunlap@kennesaw.edu.
Track and Field: Stan Sims; Phone: 770-423-6103; E-mail: ssims@kennesaw.edu.

WOMEN'S COACHES
Basketball: Colby Tilley; Phone: 770-423-6413; E-mail: ctilley@kennesaw.edu.
Cheerleading: Felecia Ingle; Phone: 770-423-6264; E-mail: fmulkey@kennesaw.edu.
Cross Country: Stan Sims; Phone: 770-423-6103; E-mail: ssims@kennesaw.edu.

Kennesaw State University *(continued)*

Soccer: Rob King; Phone: 770-423-6615; E-mail: rking2@kennesaw.edu.
Softball: Scott Whitlock; Phone: 770-423-6387; E-mail: swhitloc@kennesaw.edu.
Tennis: David Haliburton; Phone: 770-862-8560; E-mail: davidhaliburton@msn.com.
Track and Field: Stan Sims; Phone: 770-423-6103; E-mail: ssims@kennesaw.edu.

KENT STATE UNIVERSITY
Kent, Ohio

Golden Flashes ◆ NCAA I ◆ Mid-American Conference ◆ http://www.kent.edu/

State-supported university, founded 1910, part of Kent State University System
Coed, 19,173 undergraduate students, 83% full-time, 59% women, 41% men
Suburban 1,347-acre campus with easy access to Cleveland
Moderately difficult entrance level, 86% of applicants were admitted

Freshmen *Admission:* 11,098 applied, 9,922 were accepted, 3,822 enrolled. *Test scores:* SAT verbal scores over 500: 58%; SAT math scores over 500: 56%; SAT verbal scores over 600: 18%; SAT math scores over 600: 17%; SAT verbal scores over 700: 2%; SAT math scores over 700: 1%.
Tuition and fees (2003–04): $6882 (resident), $13,314 (nonresident). *Room and board:* $7920 (room only: $3540).
Financial Aid (All incoming freshmen): *Average need-based gift aid:* $4771. *Average non-need based aid:* $3584. *Average aid to full-time undergraduates:* $6822.
Athletic Department: *Director of Athletics:* Laing Kennedy; Phone: 330-672-3120; Fax: 330-672-5978; E-mail: lkennedy@kent.edu. *Sports Information Director:* Jeff Schaefer; Phone: 330-672-2110; E-mail: jschaef1@kent.edu.

MEN'S COACHES
Baseball: Rick Rembielak; Phone: 330-672-3696; E-mail: rrembiel@kent.edu.
Basketball: Jim Christian; Phone: 330-672-2470; E-mail: jchrist1@kent.edu.
Cheerleading: Lenee Buchman; Phone: 330-672-3990; E-mail: buchman@ameritech.net.
Cross Country: Wendel McRavien; Phone: 330-672-3991; E-mail: wmcraven@kent.edu.
Football: Dean Pees; Phone: 330-672-3350; E-mail: rpees@kent.edu.
Golf: Herb Page; Phone: 330-672-4629; E-mail: hpage@kent.edu.
Track and Field: Wendel McRavien; Phone: 330-672-3991; E-mail: wmcraven@kent.edu.
Wrestling: Jim Andrassy; Phone: 330-672-2820; E-mail: jandrass@kent.edu.

WOMEN'S COACHES
Basketball: Bob Lindsay; Phone: 330-672-3717; E-mail: rlindsay@kent.edu.
Cheerleading: Lenee Buchman; Phone: 330-672-3990; E-mail: buchman@ameritech.net.
Cross Country: Wendel McRavien; Phone: 330-672-3991; E-mail: wmcraven@kent.edu.
Field Hockey: Kerry DeVries; Phone: 330-672-3990; E-mail: kerrydevries@yahoo.com.
Golf: Mike Morrow; Phone: 330-672-4629; E-mail: mkmorrow@kent.edu.
Gymnastics: Brice Biggin; Phone: 330-672-2822; E-mail: bbiggin@kent.edu.
Soccer: Rob Marinaro; Phone: 330-672-9517; E-mail: rmarinar@kent.edu.
Softball: Karen Linder; Phone: 330-672-2162; E-mail: klinder@kent.edu.
Track and Field: Wendel McRavien; Phone: 330-672-3991; E-mail: wmcraven@kent.edu.
Volleyball: Mora Kanim; Phone: 330-672-2821; E-mail: mkanim@kent.edu.

KENTUCKY STATE UNIVERSITY
Frankfort, Kentucky

Thorobreds ◆ NCAA II ◆ Southern Intercollegiate Athletic Conference ◆ http://www.kysu.edu/

State-related comprehensive, founded 1886
Coed, 2,166 undergraduate students, 77% full-time, 59% women, 41% men
Small-town 485-acre campus with easy access to Louisville
Minimally difficult entrance level, 5% of applicants were admitted

Freshmen *Admission:* 2,200 applied, 1,147 were accepted, 333 enrolled. *Test scores:* SAT verbal scores over 500: 14%; SAT math scores over 500: 15%; SAT verbal scores over 600: 2%; SAT math scores over 600: 5%.
Tuition and fees (2003–04): $3370 (resident), $9014 (nonresident). *Room and board:* $5394 (room only: $2366).
Financial Aid (All incoming freshmen): *Average non-need based aid:* $2000. *Average aid to full-time undergraduates:* $6000.
Athletic Department: *Director of Athletics:* Derrick Ramsey; Phone: 502-597-6014; Fax: 502-597-6466; E-mail: dramsey@gwmail.kysu.edu. *Sports Information Director:* Ron Braden; Phone: 502-597-6019; E-mail: rbraden@gwmail.kysu.edu.

MEN'S COACHES
Baseball: Elwood Johnson; Phone: 502-597-6018; E-mail: ejohnson@gwmail.kysu.edu.
Basketball: Tom Patterson; Phone: 502-597-6888; E-mail: tpatterson@gwmail.kysu.edu.
Cheerleading: Cheryl Craig; Phone: 502-597-6117; E-mail: ccraig@gwmail.kysu.edu.
Cross Country: Von Smith; Phone: 502-597-6020; E-mail: vsmith@gwmail.kysu.edu.
Football: Donald Smith; Phone: 502-597-6731.
Golf: Ron Braden; Phone: 502-597-6019; E-mail: rbraden@gwmail.kysu.edu.
Track and Field: Von Smith; Phone: 502-597-6020; E-mail: vsmith@gwmail.kysu.edu.

WOMEN'S COACHES
Basketball: Carol Clark; Phone: 502-597-5974; E-mail: cclark@gwmail.kysu.edu.
Cheerleading: Cheryl Craig; Phone: 502-597-6117; E-mail: ccraig@gwmail.kysu.edu.
Cross Country: Von Smith; Phone: 502-597-6020; E-mail: vsmith@gwmail.kysu.edu.
Softball: Oscar Downs; Phone: 502-597-6021; E-mail: odowns@gwmail.kysu.edu.
Track and Field: Von Smith; Phone: 502-597-6020; E-mail: vsmith@gwmail.kysu.edu.
Volleyball: Walter Pauly; Phone: 502-597-5551; E-mail: wpauly@gwmail.kysu.edu.

KENTUCKY WESLEYAN COLLEGE
Owensboro, Kentucky

Panthers ◆ NCAA II ◆ Great Lakes Valley Conference ◆ http://www.kwc.edu/

Independent Methodist 4-year, founded 1858
Coed, 614 undergraduate students, 93% full-time, 51% women, 49% men
Suburban 52-acre campus
Moderately difficult entrance level, 74% of applicants were admitted

Freshmen *Admission:* 813 applied, 611 were accepted, 165 enrolled. *Test scores:* SAT verbal scores over 500: 49%; SAT math scores over 500: 42%; SAT verbal scores over 600: 6%; SAT math scores over 600: 11%.
Tuition and fees (2004–05): $12,510 (full-time). *Room and board:* $5450 (room only: $2500).
Financial Aid (All incoming freshmen): *Average need-based gift aid:* $9686. *Average non-need based aid:* $9520. *Average aid to full-time undergraduates:* $11,345.
Athletic Department: *Director of Athletics:* Larry Moore; Phone: 270-852-3330; Fax: 270-852-3356; E-mail: lmoore@kwc.edu. *Sports Information Director:* Roy Pickerill; Phone: 270-852-3143; E-mail: pickeril@kwc.edu.

MEN'S COACHES

Baseball: Todd Lillpop; Phone: 270-852-3342; E-mail: tlillpop@kwc.edu.
Basketball: Ray Harper; Phone: 270-852-3339.
Cheerleading: Jean Saalwaechter; Phone: 270-852-3330; E-mail: jeans@kwc.edu.
Football: Brent Holscaw; Phone: 270-852-3350; E-mail: holsclaw@kwc.edu.
Golf: Chris Cary; Phone: 270-852-8717; E-mail: ccary@kwc.edu.
Soccer: Scott Wilson; Phone: 270-852-3347; E-mail: scwilson@kwc.edu.

WOMEN'S COACHES

Basketball: Ron Williams; Phone: 270-852-3344; E-mail: rwilliam@kwc.edu.
Cheerleading: Jean Saalwaechter; Phone: 270-852-3330; E-mail: jeans@kwc.edu.
Golf: Chris Cary; Phone: 270-852-8717; E-mail: ccary@kwc.edu.
Soccer: Larry Kirk; Phone: 270-852-3348; E-mail: lkirk@kwc.edu.
Softball: Rob Wimsatt; Phone: 270-852-3313; E-mail: rwimsatt@kwc.edu.
Tennis: Eric Sherrard; Phone: 270-852-3330; E-mail: esherrar@kwc.edu.
Volleyball: Karie Jarrett; Phone: 270-852-3335; E-mail: karieja@kwc.edu.

KENYON COLLEGE
Gambier, Ohio

(M) Lords, (W) Ladies ◆ NCAA III ◆ North Coast Athletic Conference ◆ http://www.kenyon.edu/

Independent 4-year, founded 1824
Coed, 1,612 undergraduate students, 99% full-time, 55% women, 45% men
Rural 1,200-acre campus with easy access to Columbus
Very difficult entrance level, 4% of applicants were admitted

Freshmen *Admission:* 3,360 applied, 1,534 were accepted, 454 enrolled. *Test scores:* SAT verbal scores over 500: 99%; SAT math scores over 500: 99%; SAT verbal scores over 600: 86%; SAT math scores over 600: 78%; SAT verbal scores over 700: 40%; SAT math scores over 700: 23%.
Tuition and fees (2003–04): $30,330 (full-time). *Room and board:* $5040 (room only: $2340).
Financial Aid (All incoming freshmen): *Average need-based gift aid:* $18,990. *Average non-need based aid:* $9870. *Average aid to full-time undergraduates:* $21,630.
Athletic Department: *Director of Athletics:* Peter Smith; Phone: 740-427-5811; Fax: 740-427-5402; E-mail: smithp@kenyon.edu. *Sports Information Director:* Marty Fuller; Phone: 740-427-5471; E-mail: fullerm@kenyon.edu.

MEN'S COACHES

Baseball: Matt Burdette; Phone: 740-427-5810; E-mail: burdettem@kenyon.edu.
Basketball: Matt Croci; Phone: 740-427-5556; E-mail: crocim@kenyon.edu.
Cross Country: Duane Gomez; Phone: 740-427-5273; E-mail: gomez@kenyon.edu.
Diving: Andrew Campbell; Phone: 740-427-5554; E-mail: campbella@kenyon.edu.
Football: Ted Stanley; Phone: 740-427-5260; E-mail: stanleyt@kenyon.edu.
Golf: Bob O'Hara; Phone: 740-427-5907; E-mail: oharar@kenyon.edu.
Lacrosse: Brendan McWilliams; Phone: 740-427-5261; E-mail: mcwilliamsb@kenyon.edu.
Soccer: Des Lawless; Phone: 740-427-5564; E-mail: lawlessd@kenyon.edu.
Swimming: Jim Steen; Phone: 740-427-5554; E-mail: steen@kenyon.edu.
Tennis: Scott Thielke; Phone: 740-427-5620; E-mail: thielkes@kenyon.edu.
Track and Field: Duane Gomez; Phone: 740-427-5273; E-mail: gomez@kenyon.edu.

WOMEN'S COACHES

Basketball: Suzanne Helfant; Phone: 740-427-5222; E-mail: helfants@kenyon.edu.

Cross Country: Duane Gomez; Phone: 740-427-5273; E-mail: gomez@kenyon.edu.
Diving: Andrew Campbell; Phone: 740-427-5554; E-mail: campbella@kenyon.edu.
Field Hockey: Robin Cash; Phone: 740-427-5232; E-mail: cashr@kenyon.edu.
Lacrosse: Robin Cash; Phone: 740-427-5232; E-mail: cashr@kenyon.edu.
Soccer: Kelly Walters; Phone: 740-427-5796; E-mail: waltersk@kenyon.edu.
Softball: Joanne Ferguson; Phone: 740-427-5263; E-mail: fergusonj@kenyon.edu.
Swimming: Jim Steen; Phone: 740-427-5554; E-mail: steen@kenyon.edu.
Tennis: Scott Thielke; Phone: 740-427-5620; E-mail: thielkes@kenyon.edu.
Track and Field: Duane Gomez; Phone: 740-427-5273; E-mail: gomez@kenyon.edu.
Volleyball: Pam MacPherson; Phone: 740-427-5164; E-mail: macphersonp@kenyon.edu.

KEUKA COLLEGE
Keuka Park, New York

Storm ◆ NCAA III ◆ Eastern College Athletic Conference ◆ http://www.keuka.edu/

Independent religious comprehensive, founded 1890, affiliated with American Baptist Churches in the U.S.A.
Coed, 1,148 undergraduate students, 93% full-time, 70% women, 30% men
Rural 173-acre campus with easy access to Rochester
Moderately difficult entrance level, 80% of applicants were admitted

Freshmen *Admission:* 777 applied, 639 were accepted, 266 enrolled. *Test scores:* SAT verbal scores over 500: 41%; SAT math scores over 500: 42%; SAT verbal scores over 600: 7%; SAT math scores over 600: 6%; SAT verbal scores over 700: 1%.
Tuition and fees (2004–05): $16,660 (full-time). *Room and board:* $7800 (room only: $3700).
Financial Aid (All incoming freshmen): *Average need-based gift aid:* $11,109. *Average non-need based aid:* $11,736. *Average aid to full-time undergraduates:* $15,430.
Athletic Department: *Director of Athletics:* David Sweet; Phone: 315-279-5682; Fax: 315-279-5325; E-mail: dsweet@mail.keuka.edu. *Sports Information Director:* Jason Baribeau; Phone: 315-279-5681; E-mail: jbaribea@mail.keuka.edu.

MEN'S COACHES

Baseball: Bob Bergohltz; Phone: 315-279-5687; E-mail: bbergohl@mail.keuka.edu.
Basketball: George Wunder; Phone: 315-279-5637; E-mail: gwunder@mail.keuka.edu.
Cross Country: George Wunder; Phone: 315-279-5637; E-mail: gwunder@mail.keuka.edu.
Lacrosse: Jason Paige; Phone: 315-531-5689; E-mail: jpaige@mail.keuka.edu.
Soccer: Bob Friske; Phone: 315-279-5648; E-mail: rfriske@mail.keuka.edu.

WOMEN'S COACHES

Basketball: David Sweet; Phone: 315-279-5682; E-mail: dsweet@mail.keuka.edu.
Cross Country: George Wunder; Phone: 315-279-5637; E-mail: gwunder@mail.keuka.edu.
Soccer: Tim Moody; Phone: 315-279-5409; E-mail: tmoody@mail.keuka.edu.
Softball: Paul Bonus; Phone: 315-279-5648; E-mail: ccondron@mail.keuka.edu.
Volleyball: David Sweet; Phone: 315-279-5682; E-mail: dsweet@mail.keuka.edu.

KING COLLEGE
Bristol, Tennessee

Tornadoes ◆ NAIA ◆ Appalachian Conference ◆ http://www.king.edu/

Independent religious comprehensive, founded 1867, affiliated with Presbyterian Church (U.S.A.)
Coed, 687 undergraduate students, 85% full-time, 62% women, 38% men
Suburban 135-acre campus
Moderately difficult entrance level, 87% of applicants were admitted

Freshmen *Admission:* 627 applied, 545 were accepted, 98 enrolled. *Test scores:* SAT verbal scores over 500: 76%; SAT math scores over 500: 67%; SAT verbal scores over 600: 45%; SAT math scores over 600: 34%; SAT verbal scores over 700: 7%; SAT math scores over 700: 10%.
Tuition and fees (2004–05): $17,040 (full-time). *Room and board:* $5460 (room only: $2700).
Financial Aid (All incoming freshmen): *Average need-based gift aid:* $11,422. *Average non-need based aid:* $8687. *Average aid to full-time undergraduates:* $13,540.
Athletic Department: *Director of Athletics:* Scott Polsgrove; Phone: 423-652-4781; Fax: 423-652-6041; E-mail: sapolsgr@king.edu. *Sports Information Director:* Craig Kleinmann; Phone: 423-652-6017; E-mail: cjkleinm@king.edu.

MEN'S COACHES
Baseball: Craig Kleinmann; Phone: 423-652-6017; E-mail: cjkleinm@king.edu.
Basketball: Scott Polsgrove; Phone: 423-652-4781; E-mail: sapolsgr@king.edu.
Cross Country: Tracy Parkinson; Phone: 423-652-6008; E-mail: tsparkin@king.edu.
Golf: Jason Allison; Phone: 423-652-6031; E-mail: jralliso@king.edu.
Soccer: Matt Lavinder; Phone: 423-652-4815; E-mail: tmlavind@king.edu.
Tennis: Chris Toomey; Phone: 423-652-4754; E-mail: crtoomey@king.edu.

WOMEN'S COACHES
Basketball: Brad Horstmann; Phone: 423-652-4779; E-mail: bdhorstm@king.edu.
Cross Country: Tracy Parkinson; Phone: 423-652-6008; E-mail: tsparkin@king.edu.
Soccer: Adam Neder; Phone: 423-652-4849.
Tennis: Chris Toomey; Phone: 423-652-4754; E-mail: crtoomey@king.edu.
Volleyball: Susie Toomey; Phone: 423-652-4782; E-mail: sktoomey@king.edu.

KING'S COLLEGE
Wilkes-Barre, Pennsylvania

Monarchs ◆ NCAA III ◆ Freedom Conference ◆ http://www.kings.edu/

Independent Roman Catholic comprehensive, founded 1946
Coed, 2,064 undergraduate students, 86% full-time, 49% women, 51% men
Suburban 48-acre campus
Moderately difficult entrance level, 78% of applicants were admitted

Freshmen *Admission:* 1,623 applied, 1,308 were accepted, 450 enrolled. *Test scores:* SAT verbal scores over 500: 63%; SAT math scores over 500: 65%; SAT verbal scores over 600: 17%; SAT math scores over 600: 22%; SAT verbal scores over 700: 2%; SAT math scores over 700: 2%.
Tuition and fees (2003–04): $19,060 (full-time). *Room and board:* $7930 (room only: $3750).
Financial Aid (All incoming freshmen): *Average need-based gift aid:* $6818. *Average non-need based aid:* $8058. *Average aid to full-time undergraduates:* $16,497.
Athletic Department: *Director of Athletics:* Tom Baker; Phone: 570-208-5900; Fax: 570-208-5937; E-mail: tcbaker@kings.edu. *Sports Information Director:* Bob Ziadie; Phone: 570-208-5900; E-mail: raziadie@kings.edu.

MEN'S COACHES
Baseball: Jerry Greeley; Phone: 570-208-5900; E-mail: gpgreele@kings.edu.
Basketball: J.P. Andrejko; Phone: 570-208-5900.
Cheerleading: Heidi Hinz; Phone: 570-208-5900; E-mail: heinz@pgenergy.com.
Cross Country: Mike Kolinovsky; Phone: 570-208-5900; E-mail: mkolinov@kings.edu.
Football: Rich Mannello; Phone: 570-208-5900; E-mail: ramannel@kings.edu.
Golf: Tom Davis; Phone: 570-208-5900; E-mail: t_davis@kings.edu.
Lacrosse: Keith Lowthert; Phone: 717-822-5900; E-mail: kalowthe@kings.edu.
Soccer: Michael Davitt; Phone: 570-208-5900; E-mail: mdavitt@kings.edu.
Swimming: Suzanne Youngblood; Phone: 570-208-5900; E-mail: heartbc@hotmail.com.
Tennis: Bill Eydler; Phone: 570-208-5900; E-mail: be10scoach@aol.com.
Wrestling: Ned McGinley; Phone: 570-208-5900; E-mail: epmcginl@kings.edu.

WOMEN'S COACHES
Basketball: Bryan Whitten; Phone: 570-208-5900; E-mail: btwhitte@kings.edu.
Cheerleading: Heidi Hinz; Phone: 570-208-5900; E-mail: heinz@pgenergy.com.
Cross Country: Mike Kolinovsky; Phone: 570-208-5900; E-mail: mkolinov@kings.edu.
Field Hockey: Cheryl Ish; Phone: 570-208-5900; E-mail: cjish@kings.edu.
Lacrosse: Kathy Kerr; Phone: 570-208-5900; E-mail: krkerr@kings.edu.
Soccer: Kathy Kerr; Phone: 570-208-5900; E-mail: krkerr@kings.edu.
Softball: Lisa Gigliello; Phone: 570-208-5900; E-mail: lgigliel@kings.edu.
Swimming: Suzanne Youngblood; Phone: 570-208-5900; E-mail: heartbc@hotmail.com.
Tennis: Bill Eydler; Phone: 570-208-5900; E-mail: be10scoach@aol.com.
Volleyball: Bernie Kachinko; Phone: 570-208-5900; E-mail: raziadie@kings.edu.

KNOX COLLEGE
Galesburg, Illinois

Prairie Fire ◆ NCAA III ◆ Midwest Conference ◆ http://www.knox.edu/

Independent 4-year, founded 1837
Coed, 1,127 undergraduate students, 98% full-time, 53% women, 47% men
Small-town 82-acre campus with easy access to Peoria
Very difficult entrance level, 68% of applicants were admitted

Freshmen *Admission:* 1,538 applied, 1,129 were accepted, 268 enrolled. *Test scores:* SAT verbal scores over 500: 88%; SAT math scores over 500: 87%; SAT verbal scores over 600: 59%; SAT math scores over 600: 56%; SAT verbal scores over 700: 23%; SAT math scores over 700: 9%.
Tuition and fees (2004–05): $25,236 (full-time). *Room and board:* $6102 (room only: $2703).
Financial Aid (All incoming freshmen): *Average need-based gift aid:* $16,166. *Average non-need based aid:* $10,807. *Average aid to full-time undergraduates:* $20,857.
Athletic Department: *Director of Athletics:* Dan Calandro; Phone: 309-341-7280; Fax: 309-341-7806; E-mail: dcalandr@knox.edu. *Sports Information Director:* Kevin Walden; Phone: 309-341-7714; E-mail: kwalden@knox.edu.

MEN'S COACHES
Baseball: Jami Isaacson; Phone: 309-341-7456; E-mail: jwisaacs@knox.edu.
Basketball: Tim Heimann; Phone: 309-341-7285; E-mail: theimann@knox.edu.
Cross Country: Chris Pio; Phone: 309-341-7801; E-mail: cpio@knox.edu.
Diving: Heidi Rajsky; Phone: 309-341-7544; E-mail: hrajsky@knox.edu.

Football: Andy Gibbons; Phone: 309-341-7379; E-mail: agibbons@ knox.edu.
Golf: John Wozniak; Phone: 309-341-7282; E-mail: jwozniak@knox. edu.
Soccer: Luke Robison; Phone: 309-341-7954; E-mail: lrobison@knox. edu.
Swimming: Heidi Rajsky; Phone: 309-341-7544; E-mail: hrajsky@knox. edu.
Tennis: Sean Jennings; Phone: 309-341-7508; E-mail: sjenning@knox. edu.
Track and Field: Chris Pio; Phone: 309-341-7801; E-mail: cpio@knox. edu.
Wrestling: Tony Islas; Phone: 309-341-7443; E-mail: tislas@knox.edu.

WOMEN'S COACHES

Basketball: Nichole Leibold; Phone: 309-341-7484; E-mail: nleibold@ knox.edu.
Cross Country: Chris Pio; Phone: 309-341-7801; E-mail: cpio@knox.edu.
Diving: Heidi Rajsky; Phone: 309-341-7544; E-mail: hrajsky@knox. edu.
Golf: Mary Burgland; Phone: 309-341-7782; E-mail: mburglan@knox. edu.
Soccer: Jim Carothers; Phone: 309-341-7484; E-mail: jcarothe@knox. edu.
Softball: Kathy Wagoner; Phone: 309-341-7284; E-mail: kwagoner@ knox.edu.
Swimming: Heidi Rajsky; Phone: 309-341-7544; E-mail: hrajsky@knox. edu.
Tennis: Tim Heimann; Phone: 309-341-7285; E-mail: theimann@knox. edu.
Track and Field: Chris Pio; Phone: 309-341-7801; E-mail: cpio@knox. edu.
Volleyball: Kathy Wagoner; Phone: 309-341-7284; E-mail: kwagoner@ knox.edu.

KUTZTOWN UNIVERSITY OF PENNSYLVANIA
Kutztown, Pennsylvania

Golden Bears ◆ NCAA II ◆ Pennsylvania State Athletic Conference ◆ http://www.kutztown.edu/

State-supported comprehensive, founded 1866, part of Pennsylvania State System of Higher Education
Coed, 8,058 undergraduate students, 90% full-time, 60% women, 40% men
Rural 326-acre campus with easy access to Philadelphia
Moderately difficult entrance level, 68% of applicants were admitted

Freshmen *Admission:* 7,240 applied, 5,055 were accepted, 1,908 enrolled. *Test scores:* SAT verbal scores over 500: 54%; SAT math scores over 500: 46%; SAT verbal scores over 600: 16%; SAT math scores over 600: 7%; SAT verbal scores over 700: 7%.
Tuition and fees (2003–04): $5776 (resident), $12,674 (nonresident). *Room and board:* $4812 (room only: $3410).
Financial Aid (All incoming freshmen): *Average need-based gift aid:* $3791. *Average non-need based aid:* $1342. *Average aid to full-time undergraduates:* $5482.
Athletic Department: *Director of Athletics:* Clark Yeager; Phone: 610-683-4094; Fax: 610-683-1379; E-mail: yeager@kutztown.edu. *Sports Information Director:* Josh Leiboff; Phone: 610-683-4182; E-mail: leiboff@kutztown.edu.

MEN'S COACHES

Baseball: Chris Blum; Phone: 610-683-4063; E-mail: blum@kutztown. edu.
Basketball: Bernie Driscoll; Phone: 610-683-4064; E-mail: driscoll@ kutztown.edu.
Cheerleading: Jackie Bellanca; Phone: 610-916-6440; E-mail: jnkbellanca@aol.com.
Cross Country: Ray Hoffman; Phone: 610-683-1334; E-mail: hoffman@ kutztown.edu.
Football: Dave Keeney; Phone: 610-683-4362; E-mail: dkeeny@ kutztown.edu.
Soccer: Otto Ormosi; Phone: 610-683-1517; E-mail: ormosi@ kutztown.edu.

Swimming: Tim Flannery; Phone: 610-683-4359; E-mail: flannery@ kutztown.edu.
Tennis: Suresh Ramamurthi; Phone: 610-683-4380; E-mail: ramamurt@ kutztown.edu.
Track and Field: Brian Mondschein; Phone: 610-683-4666; E-mail: bmondsch@kutztown.edu.
Wrestling: Robert Fisher; Phone: 610-683-1536; E-mail: rfisher@ kutztown.edu.

WOMEN'S COACHES

Basketball: Janet Malouf; Phone: 610-683-4667; E-mail: malouf@ kutztown.edu.
Cheerleading: Jackie Bellanca; Phone: 610-916-6440; E-mail: jnkbellanca@aol.com.
Cross Country: Ray Hoffman; Phone: 610-683-1334; E-mail: hoffman@ kutztown.edu.
Field Hockey: Betty Wesner; Phone: 610-683-4378; E-mail: wesner@ kutztown.edu.
Golf: Robert Fisher; Phone: 610-683-1536; E-mail: rfisher@kutztown. edu.
Soccer: Jeff Schellenberger; Phone: 610-683-1522; E-mail: jschelle@ kutztown.edu.
Softball: Judy Lawes; Phone: 610-683-4665; E-mail: lawes@kutztown. edu.
Swimming: Tim Flannery; Phone: 610-683-4359; E-mail: flannery@ kutztown.edu.
Tennis: Suresh Ramamurthi; Phone: 610-683-4380; E-mail: ramamurt@ kutztown.edu.
Track and Field: Brian Mondschein; Phone: 610-683-4666; E-mail: bmondsch@kutztown.edu.
Volleyball: John Gump; Phone: 610-683-1333; E-mail: gump@ kutztown.edu.

LAFAYETTE COLLEGE
Easton, Pennsylvania

Leopards ◆ NCAA I ◆ Patriot League Conference ◆ http://www.lafayette.edu/

Independent religious 4-year, founded 1826, affiliated with Presbyterian Church (U.S.A.)
Coed, 2,285 undergraduate students, 97% full-time, 47% women, 53% men
Suburban 340-acre campus with easy access to New York City and Philadelphia
Most difficult entrance level, 34% of applicants were admitted

Freshmen *Admission:* 5,835 applied, 2,122 were accepted, 584 enrolled. *Test scores:* SAT verbal scores over 500: 97%; SAT math scores over 500: 99%; SAT verbal scores over 600: 64%; SAT math scores over 600: 79%; SAT verbal scores over 700: 15%; SAT math scores over 700: 25%.
Tuition and fees (2004–05): $27,328 (full-time). *Room and board:* $8418 (room only: $4740).
Financial Aid (All incoming freshmen): *Average need-based gift aid:* $21,191. *Average non-need based aid:* $13,186. *Average aid to full-time undergraduates:* $22,794.
Athletic Department: *Director of Athletics:* Bruce McCutcheon; Phone: 610-330-5470; Fax: 610-330-5702; E-mail: mccutchb@lafayette.edu. *Sports Information Director:* Phillip Labella; Phone: 610-330-5122; E-mail: labellap@lafayette.edu.

MEN'S COACHES

Baseball: Joe Kinney; Phone: 610-330-5476; E-mail: kinneyj@lafayette. edu.
Basketball: Fran O'Hanlon; Phone: 610-330-5475; E-mail: ohanlonf@ lafayette.edu.
Cheerleading: Priscilla Mint; Phone: 610-330-5470; E-mail: mintp@ lafayette.edu.
Cross Country: Julio Piazza; Phone: 610-330-5481; E-mail: piazzaj@ lafayette.edu.
Diving: James Dailey; Phone: 610-330-5483; E-mail: daileyj@lafayette. edu.
Football: Frank Tavani; Phone: 610-330-5485; E-mail: football@ lafayette.edu.
Golf: Jim Hutnik; Phone: 610-330-5487; E-mail: jhutlaf10@aol.com.
Lacrosse: Terry Mangan; Phone: 610-330-5482; E-mail: mangant@ lafayette.edu.

Lafayette College *(continued)*

Soccer: Dennis Bohn; Phone: 610-330-5495; E-mail: bohnd@lafayette.edu.

Swimming: James Dailey; Phone: 610-330-5483; E-mail: daileyj@lafayette.edu.

Tennis: Eric Ratchford; Phone: 610-330-5480; E-mail: ratchfoe@lafayette.edu.

Track and Field: Julio Piazza; Phone: 610-330-5481; E-mail: piazzaj@lafayette.edu.

WOMEN'S COACHES

Basketball: Tammy Smith; Phone: 610-330-5475; E-mail: smithta@lafayette.edu.

Cheerleading: Priscilla Mint; Phone: 610-330-5470; E-mail: mintp@lafayette.edu.

Cross Country: Julio Piazza; Phone: 610-330-5481; E-mail: piazzaj@lafayette.edu.

Diving: James Dailey; Phone: 610-330-5483; E-mail: daileyj@lafayette.edu.

Field Hockey: Ann Gold; Phone: 610-330-5479; E-mail: goldann@lafayette.edu.

Lacrosse: Melissa Michels; Phone: 610-330-5716; E-mail: michelsm@lafayette.edu.

Soccer: Wayne Miller; Phone: 610-330-5458; E-mail: millerw@lafayette.edu.

Softball: John Wong; Phone: 610-330-5764; E-mail: wongj@lafayette.edu.

Swimming: James Dailey; Phone: 610-330-5483; E-mail: daileyj@lafayette.edu.

Tennis: Eric Ratchford; Phone: 610-330-5480; E-mail: ratchfoe@lafayette.edu.

Track and Field: Julio Piazza; Phone: 610-330-5481; E-mail: piazzaj@lafayette.edu.

Volleyball: Terri Dadio Campbell; Phone: 610-330-5473; E-mail: campbelt@lafayette.edu.

LAGRANGE COLLEGE
LaGrange, Georgia

Panthers ◆ NCAA III ◆ Independent
◆ http://www.lagrange.edu/

Independent United Methodist comprehensive, founded 1831
Coed, 971 undergraduate students, 88% full-time, 62% women, 38% men
Small-town 120-acre campus with easy access to Atlanta
Moderately difficult entrance level, 81% of applicants were admitted

Freshmen *Admission:* 563 applied, 506 were accepted, 195 enrolled. *Test scores:* SAT verbal scores over 500: 62%; SAT math scores over 500: 54%; SAT verbal scores over 600: 20%; SAT math scores over 600: 16%; SAT verbal scores over 700: 1%.
Tuition and fees (2003–04): $14,482 (full-time). *Room and board:* $6018.
Financial Aid (All incoming freshmen): *Average need-based gift aid:* $10,515. *Average non-need based aid:* $2651. *Average aid to full-time undergraduates:* $12,267.
Athletic Department: *Director of Athletics:* Phil Williamson; Phone: 706-880-8262; Fax: 706-880-8350; E-mail: bstorie@lagrange.edu. *Sports Information Director:* John Hughes; Phone: 706-880-8318; E-mail: jhughes@lagrange.edu.

MEN'S COACHES

Baseball: Kevin Howard; Phone: 706-880-8295; E-mail: khoward@lagrange.edu.

Basketball: Warren Haynes; Phone: 706-880-8328; E-mail: whaynes@lagrange.edu.

Cheerleading: Tiffany Mixon; Phone: 706-880-8049; E-mail: tmixon@lagrange.edu.

Cross Country: Bryan Burgess; Phone: 706-880-8307; E-mail: bburgess@lagrange.edu.

Golf: Lee Richter; Phone: 706-880-8343; E-mail: lrichter@lagrange.edu.

Soccer: Jeff Geeter; Phone: 706-880-8283; E-mail: jgeeter@lagrange.edu.

Swimming: Susan Brown; Phone: 706-880-8018; E-mail: sbrown@lagrange.edu.

Tennis: Ryan Horn; Phone: 706-880-8105; E-mail: rhorn@lagrange.edu.

WOMEN'S COACHES

Basketball: Kelly Britsky; Phone: 706-880-8342; E-mail: kbritsky@lagrange.edu.

Cheerleading: Tiffany Mixon; Phone: 706-880-8049; E-mail: tmixon@lagrange.edu.

Cross Country: Bryan Burgess; Phone: 706-880-8307; E-mail: bburgess@lagrange.edu.

Soccer: Jeff Geeter; Phone: 706-880-8283; E-mail: jgeeter@lagrange.edu.

Softball: Jennifer Claybrook; Phone: 706-880-8032; E-mail: jclaybrook@lagrange.edu.

Swimming: Susan Brown; Phone: 706-880-8018; E-mail: sbrown@lagrange.edu.

Tennis: Ryan Horn; Phone: 706-880-8105; E-mail: rhorn@lagrange.edu.

Volleyball: Kelly Britsky; Phone: 706-880-8342; E-mail: kbritsky@lagrange.edu.

LAKE ERIE COLLEGE
Painesville, Ohio

Storm ◆ NCAA III ◆ Allegheny Mountain Conference
◆ http://www.lec.edu/

Independent comprehensive, founded 1856
Coed, 720 undergraduate students, 78% full-time, 76% women, 24% men
Small-town 57-acre campus with easy access to Cleveland
Minimally difficult entrance level, 43% of applicants were admitted

Freshmen *Admission:* 509 applied, 281 were accepted, 121 enrolled. *Test scores:* SAT verbal scores over 500: 52%; SAT math scores over 500: 42%; SAT verbal scores over 600: 15%; SAT math scores over 600: 7%; SAT verbal scores over 700: 1%.
Tuition and fees (2003–04): $17,720 (full-time). *Room and board:* $5830 (room only: $3120).
Athletic Department: *Director of Athletics:* Ken Krolovic; Phone: 440-375-7470; Fax: 440-375-7474; E-mail: krsolovic@lec.edu. *Sports Information Director:* Jason Stronz; Phone: 440-375-7475; E-mail: stronz@lec.edu.

MEN'S COACHES

Baseball: Ken Krolovic; Phone: 440-639-7470; E-mail: krsolovic@lec.edu.

Basketball: Jim Dolan; Phone: 440-375-7477; E-mail: jdolan@lec.edu.

Cross Country: Bryan Wadsworth; Phone: 440-375-7479; E-mail: bwadsworth@lec.edu.

Golf: Milt Johnson; Phone: 440-375-7478; E-mail: miltonjohnson@lec.edu.

Soccer: Dale Sheptak; Phone: 440-375-7473; E-mail: dsheptak@lec.edu.

WOMEN'S COACHES

Basketball: Carla Richardson; Phone: 440-375-7476; E-mail: crichardson@lec.edu.

Cross Country: Bryan Wadsworth; Phone: 440-375-7479; E-mail: bwadsworth@lec.edu.

Soccer: Laureen Ferullo; Phone: 440-375-7472; E-mail: lferullo@lec.edu.

Softball: Gary Van Cauwenberge; Phone: 440-375-7471; E-mail: garyv@lec.edu.

Volleyball: Gary Van Cauwenberge; Phone: 440-375-7471; E-mail: garyv@lec.edu.

LAKE FOREST COLLEGE
Lake Forest, Illinois

Foresters ◆ NCAA III ◆ Midwest Conference; Northern Collegiate Hockey Conference ◆ http://www.lakeforest.edu/

Independent comprehensive, founded 1857
Coed, 1,336 undergraduate students, 98% full-time, 57% women, 43% men
Suburban 110-acre campus with easy access to Chicago
Very difficult entrance level, 6% of applicants were admitted

Freshmen *Admission:* 1,835 applied, 1,240 were accepted, 347 enrolled. *Test scores:* SAT verbal scores over 500: 82%; SAT math scores over

500: 85%; SAT verbal scores over 600: 44%; SAT math scores over 600: 44%; SAT verbal scores over 700: 8%; SAT math scores over 700: 8%.
Tuition and fees (2003–04): $24,406 (full-time). *Room and board:* $5764 (room only: $3164).
Financial Aid (All incoming freshmen): *Average need-based gift aid:* $16,486. *Average non-need based aid:* $8808. *Average aid to full-time undergraduates:* $19,209.
Athletic Department: *Director of Athletics:* Jackie Slaats; Phone: 847-735-5290; Fax: 847-735-6290; E-mail: slaats@lfc.edu. *Sports Information Director:* Mike Wajerski; Phone: 847-735-6136; E-mail: wajerski@lfc.edu.

MEN'S COACHES
Basketball: Chris Conger; Phone: 847-735-5292; E-mail: conger@lfc.edu.
Cross Country: Tina McDonie; Phone: 847-735-6142; E-mail: mcdonie@lfc.edu.
Diving: Susan Bromberg; Phone: 847-735-5289.
Football: Chad Eisele; Phone: 847-735-5286; E-mail: eisele@lfc.edu.
Ice Hockey: Tony Fritz; Phone: 847-735-5294; E-mail: fritz@lfc.edu.
Soccer: Ed Kositzki; Phone: 847-735-5249; E-mail: ekositzki@lfc.edu.
Swimming: Alec Webster; Phone: 847-735-5289; E-mail: webster@lfc.edu.
Tennis: Chad Eisele; Phone: 847-735-5286; E-mail: eisele@lfc.edu.

WOMEN'S COACHES
Basketball: Jackie Slaats; Phone: 847-735-5290; E-mail: slaats@lfc.edu.
Cross Country: Tina McDonie; Phone: 847-735-6142; E-mail: mcdonie@lfc.edu.
Diving: Susan Bromberg; Phone: 847-735-5289.
Soccer: T.R. Bell; Phone: 847-735-6132; E-mail: tbell@lfc.edu.
Softball: Chris Kane; Phone: 847-735-6154; E-mail: kane@lfc.edu.
Swimming: Alec Webster; Phone: 847-735-5289; E-mail: webster@lfc.edu.
Tennis: Chris Conger; Phone: 847-735-5292; E-mail: conger@lfc.edu.
Volleyball: Beth Pier; Phone: 847-735-5295; E-mail: pier@lfc.edu.

LAKELAND COLLEGE
Sheboygan, Wisconsin
Muskies ◆ NCAA III ◆ Illini-Badger Football Conference; Lake Michigan Conference ◆ http://www.lakeland.edu/

Independent religious comprehensive, founded 1862, affiliated with United Church of Christ
Coed, 3,399 undergraduate students, 40% full-time, 61% women, 39% men
Rural 240-acre campus with easy access to Milwaukee
Minimally difficult entrance level, 63% of applicants were admitted

Freshmen *Admission:* 584 applied, 399 were accepted, 155 enrolled.
Tuition and fees (2004–05): $14,900 (full-time). *Room and board:* $5655 (room only: $2655).
Financial Aid (All incoming freshmen): *Average need-based gift aid:* $8659. *Average non-need based aid:* $7079. *Average aid to full-time undergraduates:* $11,267.
Athletic Department: *Director of Athletics:* Jane Bouche; Phone: 920-565-1240; Fax: 920-565-1399; E-mail: boucheja@lakeland.edu. *Sports Information Director:* John Weber; Phone: 920-565-1411; E-mail: weberjj@lakeland.edu.

MEN'S COACHES
Baseball: John Weber; Phone: 920-565-1411; E-mail: weberjj@lakeland.edu.
Basketball: Gary Grzesk; Phone: 920-565-1309; E-mail: grzeskga@lakeland.edu.
Cross Country: Phone: 920-565-1366.
Football: Jim Zebrowski; Phone: 920-565-1246; E-mail: zebrowskijp@lakeland.edu.
Golf: Phone: 920-565-1244.
Soccer: Marc Colwell; Phone: 920-565-1244; E-mail: colwellmj@lakeland.edu.
Tennis: Dave Lauer; Phone: 920-565-1284; E-mail: lauerd@lakeland.edu.
Wrestling: Phone: 920-565-1411.

WOMEN'S COACHES
Basketball: April Arvan; Phone: 920-565-1222; E-mail: arvanaa@lakeland.edu.

Cross Country: Phone: 920-565-1366.
Golf: Phone: 920-565-1309.
Soccer: Marc Colwell; Phone: 920-565-1244; E-mail: colwellmj@lakeland.edu.
Softball: Jim Staff; Phone: 920-565-1435; E-mail: staafjc@lakeland.edu.
Tennis: Mike Devaney; Phone: 920-565-1262; E-mail: devaneym@lakeland.edu.
Volleyball: Chad Schreiber; Phone: 920-565-1232; E-mail: schreibercp@lakeland.edu.

LAKE SUPERIOR STATE UNIVERSITY
Sault Sainte Marie, Michigan
Lakers ◆ NCAA II ◆ Central Collegiate Hockey Conference; Great Lakes Intercollegiate Conference ◆ http://www.lssu.edu/

State-supported 4-year, founded 1946
Coed, 3,258 undergraduate students, 76% full-time, 49% women, 51% men
Small-town 121-acre campus
Moderately difficult entrance level, 90% of applicants were admitted

Freshmen *Admission:* 1,557 applied, 1,388 were accepted, 541 enrolled.
Tuition and fees (2003–04): $5454 (resident), $10,380 (nonresident). *Room and board:* $5993 (room only: $5334).
Financial Aid (All incoming freshmen): *Average need-based gift aid:* $2968. *Average non-need based aid:* $2366. *Average aid to full-time undergraduates:* $6718.
Athletic Department: *Director of Athletics:* Bill Crawford; Phone: 906-635-2878; Fax: 906-635-2753; E-mail: bcrawford@lssu.edu. *Sports Information Director:* Linda Bouvet; Phone: 906-635-2601; E-mail: lbouvet@lssu.edu.

MEN'S COACHES
Basketball: Mike Fitzner; Phone: 906-635-2607; E-mail: mfitzner@lssu.edu.
Cheerleading: Phone: 906-635-2627; E-mail: lssucheer@yahoo.com.
Cross Country: Drew Ludtke; Phone: 906-635-2765; E-mail: dludtke@lssu.edu.
Golf: Brady Larson; Phone: 906-635-2607; E-mail: blarson@lssu.edu.
Ice Hockey: Frank Anzalone; Phone: 906-635-2605; E-mail: fanzalone@lssu.edu.
Tennis: Jon Coles; Phone: 906-635-2606; E-mail: jcoles@lssu.edu.
Track and Field: Drew Ludtke; Phone: 906-635-2765; E-mail: dludtke@lssu.edu.

WOMEN'S COACHES
Basketball: Kris Dunbar; Phone: 906-635-2625; E-mail: kdunbar@lssu.edu.
Cheerleading: Phone: 906-635-2627; E-mail: lssucheer@yahoo.com.
Cross Country: Drew Ludtke; Phone: 906-635-2765; E-mail: dludtke@lssu.edu.
Softball: Don Myers; Phone: 906-635-2637; E-mail: dmyers@lssu.edu.
Tennis: Jon Coles; Phone: 906-635-2606; E-mail: jcoles@lssu.edu.
Track and Field: Drew Ludtke; Phone: 906-635-2765; E-mail: dludtke@lssu.edu.
Volleyball: Mark Engle; Phone: 906-635-2809; E-mail: mengle@lssu.edu.

LAMAR UNIVERSITY
Beaumont, Texas
Cardinals ◆ NCAA I ◆ Southland Conference ◆ http://www.lamar.edu/

State-supported university, founded 1923, part of Texas State University System
Coed, 9,184 undergraduate students, 68% full-time, 60% women, 40% men
Suburban 200-acre campus with easy access to Houston
Minimally difficult entrance level, 69% of applicants were admitted

Freshmen *Admission:* 4,147 applied, 2,834 were accepted, 1,411 enrolled. *Test scores:* SAT verbal scores over 500: 39%; SAT math scores

Lamar University *(continued)*

over 500: 37%; SAT verbal scores over 600: 9%; SAT math scores over 600: 9%; SAT verbal scores over 700: 1%; SAT math scores over 700: 2%.
Tuition and fees (2003–04): $3260 (resident), $11,270 (nonresident). *Room and board:* $5760 (room only: $3960).
Financial Aid (All incoming freshmen): *Average non-need based aid:* $1300. *Average aid to full-time undergraduates:* $1300.
Athletic Department: *Director of Athletics:* Billy Tubbs; Phone: 409-880-8323; Fax: 409-880-1814; E-mail: tubbsbd@hal.lamar.edu. *Sports Information Director:* Daucy Crizer; Phone: 409-880-8329; E-mail: crizerdc@hal.lamar.edu.

MEN'S COACHES
Baseball: Jim Gilligan; Phone: 409-880-8315; E-mail: gilliganjp@hal.lamar.edu.
Basketball: Billy Tubbs; Phone: 409-880-2337; E-mail: tubbsbd@hal.lamar.edu.
Cross Country: Trey Clark; Phone: 409-880-8318; E-mail: clarkwg@hal.lamar.edu.
Golf: Brad McMakin; Phone: 409-880-8334; E-mail: mcmakinbe@hal.lamar.edu.
Tennis: David Wong; Phone: 409-880-8056; E-mail: wongdc@hal.lamar.edu.
Track and Field: Trey Clark; Phone: 409-880-8318; E-mail: clarkwg@hal.lamar.edu.

WOMEN'S COACHES
Basketball: Leonard Drake; Phone: 409-880-2238; E-mail: drakelu@hal.lamar.edu.
Cross Country: Trey Clark; Phone: 409-880-8318; E-mail: clarkwg@hal.lamar.edu.
Golf: Brad McMakin; Phone: 409-880-8334; E-mail: mcmakinbe@hal.lamar.edu.
Tennis: David Wong; Phone: 409-880-8056; E-mail: wongdc@hal.lamar.edu.
Track and Field: Trey Clark; Phone: 409-880-8318; E-mail: clarkwg@hal.lamar.edu.
Volleyball: Fiona Bolten; Phone: 409-880-8717; E-mail: fiona.simmons@lamar.edu.

LAMBUTH UNIVERSITY
Jackson, Tennessee

Eagles ◆ NAIA ◆ Mid-South Conference ◆ http://www.lambuth.edu/

Independent United Methodist 4-year, founded 1843
Coed, 836 undergraduate students, 93% full-time, 52% women, 48% men
Urban 50-acre campus with easy access to Memphis
Moderately difficult entrance level, 60% of applicants were admitted

Freshmen *Admission:* 881 applied, 575 were accepted, 181 enrolled. *Test scores:* SAT verbal scores over 500: 70%; SAT math scores over 500: 70%; SAT verbal scores over 600: 31%; SAT math scores over 600: 28%; SAT verbal scores over 700: 6%; SAT math scores over 700: 6%.
Tuition and fees (2003–04): $11,590 (full-time). *Room and board:* $5178 (room only: $2364).
Financial Aid (All incoming freshmen): *Average need-based gift aid:* $7518. *Average non-need based aid:* $6102. *Average aid to full-time undergraduates:* $11,410.
Athletic Department: *Director of Athletics:* Vic Wallace; Phone: 731-425-3368; Fax: 731-425-3498; E-mail: wallace-v@lambuth.edu. *Sports Information Director:* Will Atkinson; Phone: 731-425-3256; E-mail: atkinson@lambuth.edu.

MEN'S COACHES
Baseball: Wayne Albury; Phone: 731-425-3385; E-mail: albury@lambuth.edu.
Basketball: Kent Thomas; Phone: 731-425-3368; E-mail: thomas@lambuth.edu.
Cheerleading: Lisa Warmath; Phone: 731-425-3368; E-mail: warmath@lambuth.edu.
Cross Country: Phone: 731-425-3368.
Football: Vic Wallace; Phone: 731-425-3368; E-mail: wallace-v@lambuth.edu.

Golf: Phone: 731-425-3368; E-mail: atkinson@lambuth.edu.
Soccer: Paul Conway; Phone: 731-425-3368; E-mail: conway@lambuth.edu.
Tennis: Jackie Johnson; Phone: 731-425-3368.

WOMEN'S COACHES
Basketball: James Walker; Phone: 731-425-3368; E-mail: walker@lambuth.edu.
Cheerleading: Lisa Warmath; Phone: 731-425-3368; E-mail: warmath@lambuth.edu.
Cross Country: Phone: 731-425-3368.
Soccer: Ted Flogaites; Phone: 731-425-3368; E-mail: flogaites@lambuth.edu.
Softball: Will Atkinson; Phone: 731-425-3368; E-mail: atkinson@lambuth.edu.
Tennis: Jackie Johnson; Phone: 731-425-3368.
Volleyball: Amy Verseman; Phone: 731-425-3368.

LANDER UNIVERSITY
Greenwood, South Carolina

Bearcats ◆ NCAA II ◆ Peach Belt Conference ◆ http://www.lander.edu/

State-supported comprehensive, founded 1872, part of South Carolina Commission on Higher Education
Coed, 2,634 undergraduate students, 87% full-time, 65% women, 35% men
Small-town 100-acre campus
Moderately difficult entrance level, 8% of applicants were admitted

Freshmen *Admission:* 1,668 applied, 1,351 were accepted, 547 enrolled. *Test scores:* SAT verbal scores over 500: 45%; SAT math scores over 500: 50%; SAT verbal scores over 600: 8%; SAT math scores over 600: 10%.
Tuition and fees (2003–04): $5550 (resident), $11,200 (nonresident). *Room and board:* $4946 (room only: $3016).
Financial Aid (All incoming freshmen): *Average need-based gift aid:* $1861. *Average non-need based aid:* $2665. *Average aid to full-time undergraduates:* $4616.
Athletic Department: *Director of Athletics:* Jeff May; Phone: 864-388-8316; Fax: 864-388-8898; E-mail: jmay@lander.edu. *Sports Information Director:* Bob Stoner; Phone: 864-388-8962; E-mail: bstoner@lander.edu.

MEN'S COACHES
Baseball: Mike McGuire; Phone: 864-388-8961; E-mail: mmcguire@lander.edu.
Basketball: Chipper Bagwell; Phone: 864-388-8758; E-mail: rbagwell@lander.edu.
Cheerleading: Jodi Yates; Phone: 864-229-0694.
Soccer: Van Taylor; Phone: 864-388-8291; E-mail: vtaylor@lander.edu.
Tennis: Joe Cabri; Phone: 864-388-8214; E-mail: jcabri@lander.edu.

WOMEN'S COACHES
Basketball: Jon Norton; Phone: 864-388-8257; E-mail: jnorton@lander.edu.
Cheerleading: Jodi Yates; Phone: 864-229-0694.
Cross Country: Bob Stoner; Phone: 864-388-8962; E-mail: bstoner@lander.edu.
Soccer: George Sugden; Phone: 864-388-8960; E-mail: gsugden@lander.edu.
Softball: Doug Spears; Phone: 864-388-8691; E-mail: dspears@lander.edu.
Volleyball: Angela Kearns; Phone: 864-388-8963; E-mail: akearns@lander.edu.

LANE COLLEGE
Jackson, Tennessee

Dragons ◆ NCAA II ◆ Southern Intercollegiate Athletic Conference ◆ http://www.lanecollege.edu/

Independent religious 4-year, founded 1882, affiliated with Christian Methodist Episcopal Church
Coed, 952 undergraduate students, 99% full-time, 52% women, 48% men
Suburban 25-acre campus with easy access to Memphis
Minimally difficult entrance level, 3% of applicants were admitted

Freshmen *Admission:* 2,636 applied, 733 were accepted, 296 enrolled.
Tuition and fees (2003–04): $6812 (full-time). *Room and board:* $4366.
Financial Aid (All incoming freshmen): *Average need-based gift aid:* $6125. *Average aid to full-time undergraduates:* $8256.
Athletic Department: *Director of Athletics:* J.L. Perry; Phone: 731-426-7568; Fax: 731-421-7107; E-mail: jlperry@lanecollege.edu.
MEN'S COACHES
Baseball: Wesley Green; Phone: 731-426-7568.
Basketball: J.L. Perry; Phone: 731-426-7568; E-mail: jlperry@lanecollege.edu.
Cheerleading: Nicole Hewitt; Phone: 731-426-7625; E-mail: nhewitt@lanecollege.edu.
Cross Country: Fredrick Summers; Phone: 731-426-7109.
Football: Brandon Miles; Phone: 731-426-7213; E-mail: mbrandon@lanecollege.edu.
Tennis: James Walker; Phone: 731-426-7569.
Track and Field: Brandon Miles; Phone: 731-426-7213; E-mail: mbrandon@lanecollege.edu.
WOMEN'S COACHES
Basketball: Anita Harris; Phone: 731-426-7570.
Cheerleading: Nicole Hewitt; Phone: 731-426-7625; E-mail: nhewitt@lanecollege.edu.
Cross Country: Fredrick Summers; Phone: 731-426-7109.
Softball: Olabanji Abanishe; Phone: 731-426-7568.
Tennis: James Walker; Phone: 731-426-7569.
Track and Field: Brandon Miles; Phone: 731-426-7213; E-mail: mbrandon@lanecollege.edu.
Volleyball: Terance Plumer; Phone: 731-426-7570.

LANGSTON UNIVERSITY
Langston, Oklahoma

Lions ◆ NAIA ◆ Central States Football Conference; Red River Conference ◆ http://www.lunet.edu/

State-supported comprehensive, founded 1897, part of Oklahoma State Regents for Higher Education
Coed, 2,896 undergraduate students, 77% full-time, 57% women, 43% men
Rural 40-acre campus with easy access to Oklahoma City
Minimally difficult entrance level, 6% of applicants were admitted

Freshmen *Admission:* 2,088 applied, 1,034 were accepted, 481 enrolled.
Tuition and fees (2003–04): $2787 (resident), $6399 (nonresident). *Room and board:* $4380 (room only: $2400).
Financial Aid (All incoming freshmen): *Average need-based gift aid:* $1065. *Average non-need based aid:* $2975. *Average aid to full-time undergraduates:* $7167.
Athletic Department: *Director of Athletics:* Rozalyn Washington; Phone: 405-466-3626; Fax: 405-466-3461; E-mail: rlwashington@lunet.edu. *Sports Information Director:* James Hiliard; Phone: 405-466-3243; E-mail: jwhilliard@lunet.edu.
MEN'S COACHES
Basketball: Gregory Webb; Phone: 405-466-3351; E-mail: gewebb@lunet.edu.
Cheerleading: Rozalyn Washington; Phone: 405-466-3349; E-mail: rlwashington@lunet.edu.
Cross Country: James Hiliard; Phone: 405-466-3243; E-mail: jwhilliard@lunet.edu.
Football: Phone: 405-466-3353.
Golf: Jerome Willis; Phone: 405-466-3380; E-mail: jwillisjr@lunet.edu.
Track and Field: James Hiliard; Phone: 405-466-3243; E-mail: jwhilliard@lunet.edu.
WOMEN'S COACHES
Basketball: Donnita Drain; Phone: 405-466-3352; E-mail: drdrain@lunet.edu.
Cheerleading: Rozalyn Washington; Phone: 405-466-3349; E-mail: rlwashington@lunet.edu.
Cross Country: James Hiliard; Phone: 405-466-3243; E-mail: jwhilliard@lunet.edu.
Track and Field: James Hiliard; Phone: 405-466-3243; E-mail: jwhilliard@lunet.edu.

LA ROCHE COLLEGE
Pittsburgh, Pennsylvania

Red Hawks ◆ NCAA III ◆ Allegheny Mountain Conference ◆ http://www.laroche.edu/

Independent religious comprehensive, founded 1963, affiliated with Roman Catholic Church
Coed, 1,551 undergraduate students, 76% full-time, 63% women, 37% men
Suburban 80-acre campus
Minimally difficult entrance level, 68% of applicants were admitted

Freshmen *Admission:* 528 applied, 365 were accepted, 175 enrolled.
Test scores: SAT verbal scores over 500: 38%; SAT math scores over 500: 49%; SAT verbal scores over 600: 11%; SAT math scores over 600: 11%; SAT math scores over 700: 1%.
Tuition and fees (2004–05): $16,582 (full-time). *Room and board:* $6862 (room only: $4250).
Financial Aid (All incoming freshmen): *Average need-based gift aid:* $4057. *Average non-need based aid:* $4000. *Average aid to full-time undergraduates:* $14,465.
Athletic Department: *Director of Athletics:* Jim Tinkey; Phone: 412-536-1011; Fax: 412-536-1012; E-mail: tinkeyd1@laroche.edu. *Sports Information Director:* Rich Pasquale; Phone: 412-536-1046; E-mail: pasquar1@laroche.edu.
MEN'S COACHES
Baseball: Rich Pasquale; Phone: 412-536-1046; E-mail: pasquar1@laroche.edu.
Basketball: Scott Lange; Phone: 412-536-1004; E-mail: langs1@laroche.edu.
Cheerleading: Beth Ann DeFazio; Phone: 412-536-1014.
Cross Country: George Guiley; Phone: 412-536-1005; E-mail: guileyg1@laroche.edu.
Golf: Jim Tinkey; Phone: 412-536-1011; E-mail: tinkeyd1@laroche.edu.
Soccer: Weston Hawley; Phone: 412-536-1002; E-mail: hawleyw1@laroche.edu.
WOMEN'S COACHES
Basketball: Tamica Hunter; Phone: 412-536-1003; E-mail: huntert1@laroche.edu.
Cheerleading: Beth Ann DeFazio; Phone: 412-536-1014.
Cross Country: George Guiley; Phone: 412-536-1005; E-mail: guileyg1@laroche.edu.
Soccer: Miguel Lozano; Phone: 412-536-1016; E-mail: lozanom1@laroche.edu.
Softball: Orie Gentile; Phone: 412-536-1028; E-mail: gentilo1@laroche.edu.
Volleyball: Kassie Ott; Phone: 412-536-1056; E-mail: ottk1@laroche.edu.

LA SALLE UNIVERSITY
Philadelphia, Pennsylvania

Explorers ◆ NCAA I ◆ Atlantic 10 Conference; Metro Atlantic Athletic Conference ◆ http://www.lasalle.edu/

Independent Roman Catholic comprehensive, founded 1863
Coed, 4,099 undergraduate students, 83% full-time, 58% women, 42% men
Urban 100-acre campus
Moderately difficult entrance level, 68% of applicants were admitted

Freshmen *Admission:* 4,701 applied, 3,177 were accepted, 866 enrolled.
Test scores: SAT verbal scores over 500: 75%; SAT math scores over

La Salle University *(continued)*

500: 73%; SAT verbal scores over 600: 28%; SAT math scores over 600: 25%; SAT verbal scores over 700: 4%; SAT math scores over 700: 3%.

Tuition and fees (2003–04): $22,960 (full-time). *Room and board:* $8770 (room only: $4420).

Financial Aid (All incoming freshmen): *Average need-based gift aid:* $12,436. *Average non-need based aid:* $9274. *Average aid to full-time undergraduates:* $16,082.

Athletic Department: *Director of Athletics:* Tom Brennan; Phone: 215-951-1425; Fax: 215-951-1694; E-mail: brennan@lasalle.edu. *Sports Information Director:* Kale Beers; Phone: 215-951-1513; E-mail: beers@lasalle.edu.

MEN'S COACHES

Baseball: Lee Saverio; Phone: 215-951-1995; E-mail: saverio@lasalle.edu.

Basketball: Billy Hahn; Phone: 215-951-1518; E-mail: hahn@lasalle.edu.

Cheerleading: Bob Arra; Phone: 215-951-5090; E-mail: baspirit5@aol.com.

Cross Country: Charles Torpey; Phone: 215-951-1992; E-mail: torpey@lasalle.edu.

Diving: Diane Maiese; Phone: 215-951-1520.

Football: Archie Stalcup; Phone: 215-951-1857; E-mail: stalcup@lasalle.edu.

Golf: Tim Kelly; Phone: 215-951-5090; E-mail: kellyt@lasalle.edu.

Soccer: Pat Farrell; Phone: 215-951-1993; E-mail: farrell@lasalle.edu.

Swimming: Matt Nunnally; Phone: 215-951-1520; E-mail: nunnally@lasalle.edu.

Tennis: Ed Colfer; Phone: 215-951-1528; E-mail: colfer@lasalle.edu.

Track and Field: Charles Torpey; Phone: 215-951-1992; E-mail: torpey@lasalle.edu.

WOMEN'S COACHES

Basketball: John Miller; Phone: 215-951-1518; E-mail: millerj@lasalle.edu.

Cheerleading: Bob Arra; Phone: 215-951-5090; E-mail: baspirit5@aol.com.

Cross Country: Charles Torpey; Phone: 215-951-1992; E-mail: torpey@lasalle.edu.

Diving: Diane Maiese; Phone: 215-951-1520.

Field Hockey: Sarah Catlin; Phone: 215-951-5190; E-mail: catlin@lasalle.edu.

Lacrosse: Julie Weiss; Phone: 215-951-1994; E-mail: weiss@lasalle.edu.

Soccer: Paul Royal; Phone: 215-951-1523; E-mail: royal@lasalle.edu.

Softball: Joe Dipietro; Phone: 215-951-1695; E-mail: dieptro@lasalle.edu.

Swimming: Matt Nunnally; Phone: 215-951-1520; E-mail: nunnally@lasalle.edu.

Tennis: Ed Colfer; Phone: 215-951-1528; E-mail: colfer@lasalle.edu.

Track and Field: Charles Torpey; Phone: 215-951-1992; E-mail: torpey@lasalle.edu.

Volleyball: Dave Stever; Phone: 215-951-1727; E-mail: stever@lasalle.edu.

LASELL COLLEGE
Newton, Massachusetts

Lasers ◆ NCAA III ◆ New England Women's Lacrosse Conference; North Atlantic Conference
◆ http://www.lasell.edu/

Independent comprehensive, founded 1851
Coed, 1,081 undergraduate students, 98% full-time, 73% women, 27% men
Suburban 50-acre campus with easy access to Boston
Moderately difficult entrance level, 68% of applicants were admitted

Freshmen *Admission:* 2,283 applied, 1,557 were accepted, 367 enrolled. *Test scores:* SAT verbal scores over 500: 41%; SAT math scores over 500: 36%; SAT verbal scores over 600: 4%; SAT math scores over 600: 5%.

Tuition and fees (2003–04): $17,500 (full-time). *Room and board:* $8500.

Financial Aid (All incoming freshmen): *Average need-based gift aid:* $11,500. *Average non-need based aid:* $5500. *Average aid to full-time undergraduates:* $14,800.

Athletic Department: *Director of Athletics:* Kristy Walter; Phone: 617-243-2147; Fax: 617-243-2389; E-mail: kwalter@lasell.edu. *Sports Information Director:* Jessica King; Phone: 617-243-2232; E-mail: jeking@lasell.edu.

MEN'S COACHES

Basketball: Chris Harvey; Phone: 617-243-2188; E-mail: charvey@lasell.edu.

Cross Country: Larry Sullivan; Phone: 617-243-2137; E-mail: lasullivan@lasell.edu.

Lacrosse: Tim Dunton; Phone: 617-243-2213; E-mail: tdunton@lasell.edu.

Soccer: Giovanni Pacini; Phone: 617-243-2118; E-mail: gpacini@attbi.com.

Volleyball: Mike Starr; Phone: 617-243-2137; E-mail: mstarr@lasell.edu.

WOMEN'S COACHES

Basketball: Stephanie Tobey; Phone: 617-243-2035; E-mail: stobey@lasell.edu.

Cross Country: Larry Sullivan; Phone: 617-243-2137; E-mail: lasullivan@lasell.edu.

Field Hockey: Jessica King; Phone: 617-243-2232; E-mail: jeking@lasell.edu.

Lacrosse: Jill Smock; Phone: 617-243-2247; E-mail: jsmock@lasell.edu.

Soccer: Lisa McNamara; Phone: 617-243-2106; E-mail: lmcnamara@lasell.edu.

Softball: Bob McKinley; Phone: 617-243-2137; E-mail: bmckinley@lasell.edu.

Volleyball: Mary Toms; Phone: 617-243-2147; E-mail: mtom@rcn.com.

LAWRENCE UNIVERSITY
Appleton, Wisconsin

Vikings ◆ NCAA III ◆ Midwest Conference
◆ http://www.lawrence.edu/

Independent 4-year, founded 1847
Coed, 1,407 undergraduate students, 95% full-time, 53% women, 47% men
Small-town 84-acre campus
Very difficult entrance level, 6% of applicants were admitted

Freshmen *Admission:* 2,044 applied, 1,192 were accepted, 356 enrolled. *Test scores:* SAT verbal scores over 500: 93%; SAT math scores over 500: 96%; SAT verbal scores over 600: 63%; SAT math scores over 600: 62%; SAT verbal scores over 700: 19%; SAT math scores over 700: 18%.

Tuition and fees (2003–04): $25,089 (full-time). *Room and board:* $5652.

Financial Aid (All incoming freshmen): *Average need-based gift aid:* $15,906. *Average non-need based aid:* $10,249. *Average aid to full-time undergraduates:* $21,094.

Athletic Department: *Director of Athletics:* Dave Brown; Phone: 920-832-7347; Fax: 920-832-7349; E-mail: david.d.brown@lawrence.edu. *Sports Information Director:* Joe Vander Acker; Phone: 920-832-6878; E-mail: joseph.m.vandenacker@lawrence.edu.

MEN'S COACHES

Baseball: Korey Krueger; Phone: 920-832-7346; E-mail: korey.j.krueger@lawrence.edu.

Basketball: John Tharp; Phone: 920-832-6761; E-mail: john.s.tharp@lawrence.edu.

Cross Country: Lee Watson; Phone: 920-832-7033; E-mail: lee.watson@lawrence.edu.

Diving: Kurt Kirner; Phone: 920-832-6638; E-mail: kurt.kirner@lawrence.edu.

Football: Dave Brown; Phone: 920-832-7347; E-mail: david.d.brown@lawrence.edu.

Golf: Dave Ruhly; Phone: 920-832-6761; E-mail: david.ruhly@lawrence.edu.

Ice Hockey: David Ruhly; Phone: 920-832-7348; E-mail: david.ruhly@lawrence.edu.

Soccer: Blake Johnson; Phone: 920-832-7034; E-mail: blake.f.johnson@lawrence.edu.

Swimming: Kurt Kirner; Phone: 920-832-6638; E-mail: kurt.kirner@lawrence.edu.

Tennis: Dennis Niemi; Phone: 920-832-7272.

Track and Field: Matt Kehrein; Phone: 920-832-6759; E-mail: matthew.j.kehrein@lawrence.edu.

Wrestling: Dave Novickis; Phone: 920-832-6763; E-mail: david.novickis@lawrence.edu.

WOMEN'S COACHES

Basketball: Amy Proctor; Phone: 920-832-6513; E-mail: amy.proctor@lawrence.edu.
Cross Country: Lee Watson; Phone: 920-832-7033; E-mail: lee.watson@lawrence.edu.
Diving: Kurt Kirner; Phone: 920-832-6638; E-mail: kurt.kirner@lawrence.edu.
Soccer: Moira Runly; Phone: 920-832-6974; E-mail: moira.ruhly@lawrence.edu.
Softball: Kim Tatro; Phone: 920-832-6975; E-mail: kimberly.n.tatro@lawrence.edu.
Swimming: Kurt Kirner; Phone: 920-832-6638; E-mail: kurt.kirner@lawrence.edu.
Tennis: Asma Ali; Phone: 920-832-7272; E-mail: asma.a.ali@lawrence.edu.
Track and Field: Matt Kehrein; Phone: 920-832-6759; E-mail: matthew.j.kehrein@lawrence.edu.
Volleyball: Kendra Marlowe; Phone: 920-993-6144; E-mail: kendra.a.marlowe@lawrence.edu.

LEBANON VALLEY COLLEGE
Annville, Pennsylvania

Flying Dutchmen ◆ NCAA III ◆ Commonwealth Conference ◆ http://www.lvc.edu/

Independent United Methodist comprehensive, founded 1866
Coed, 1,765 undergraduate students, 87% full-time, 58% women, 42% men
Small-town 275-acre campus
Moderately difficult entrance level, 6% of applicants were admitted

Freshmen Admission: 2,083 applied, 1,520 were accepted, 429 enrolled. Test scores: SAT verbal scores over 500: 75%; SAT math scores over 500: 80%; SAT verbal scores over 600: 27%; SAT math scores over 600: 36%; SAT verbal scores over 700: 2%; SAT math scores over 700: 4%.
Tuition and fees (2003–04): $22,510 (full-time). Room and board: $6360 (room only: $3110).
Financial Aid (All incoming freshmen): Average need-based gift aid: $14,098. Average non-need based aid: $8908. Average aid to full-time undergraduates: $17,318.
Athletic Department: Director of Athletics: Kathy Tierney; Phone: 717-867-6261; Fax: 717-867-6990; E-mail: tierney@lvc.edu. Sports Information Director: Braden Snyder; Phone: 717-867-6033; E-mail: bsnyder@lvc.edu.

MEN'S COACHES

Baseball: Keith evans; Phone: 717-867-6271; E-mail: kevans@lvc.edu.
Basketball: Brad McAlester; Phone: 717-867-6263; E-mail: mcaleste@lvc.edu.
Cross Country: Kent Reed; Phone: 717-867-6364; E-mail: reed@lvc.edu.
Football: Mike Silecchia; Phone: 717-867-6264; E-mail: silecchi@lvc.edu.
Golf: Lou Sorrentino; Phone: 717-867-6991; E-mail: sorrenti@lvc.edu.
Ice Hockey: Al MacCormack; Phone: 717-867-6258; E-mail: maccorma@lvc.edu.
Soccer: Mark Pulisic; Phone: 717-867-6267; E-mail: pulisic@lvc.edu.
Swimming: Mary Gardner; Phone: 717-867-6367; E-mail: gardner@lvc.edu.
Tennis: Cliff Myers; Phone: 717-867-6992.
Track and Field: Kent Reed; Phone: 717-867-6364; E-mail: reed@lvc.edu.

WOMEN'S COACHES

Basketball: Peg Kauffman; Phone: 717-867-6272; E-mail: kauffman@lvc.edu.
Cross Country: Kent Reed; Phone: 717-867-6364; E-mail: reed@lvc.edu.
Field Hockey: Laurel Martin; Phone: 717-867-6268; E-mail: martin@lvc.edu.
Soccer: Mark Pulisic; Phone: 717-867-6267; E-mail: pulisic@lvc.edu.
Softball: Stacey Hollinger; Phone: 717-867-6891; E-mail: st_holli@lvc.edu.
Swimming: Mary Gardner; Phone: 717-867-6367; E-mail: gardner@lvc.edu.
Tennis: Cliff Myers; Phone: 717-867-6992.

Track and Field: Kent Reed; Phone: 717-867-6364; E-mail: reed@lvc.edu.
Volleyball: Wayne Perry; Phone: 717-867-6273; E-mail: perry@lvc.edu.

LEES-MCRAE COLLEGE
Banner Elk, North Carolina

Bobcats ◆ NCAA II ◆ Carolinas-Virginia Athletics Conference; Deep South Lacrosse Conference ◆ http://www.lmc.edu/

Independent religious 4-year, founded 1900, affiliated with Presbyterian Church (U.S.A.)
Coed, 792 undergraduate students, 96% full-time, 57% women, 43% men
Rural 400-acre campus
Minimally difficult entrance level, 79% of applicants were admitted

Freshmen Admission: 799 applied, 629 were accepted, 199 enrolled. Test scores: SAT verbal scores over 500: 43%; SAT math scores over 500: 35%; SAT verbal scores over 600: 5%; SAT math scores over 600: 10%.
Tuition and fees (2003–04): $14,500 (full-time). Room and board: $5440 (room only: $2550).
Financial Aid (All incoming freshmen): Average need-based gift aid: $4739. Average non-need based aid: $4500. Average aid to full-time undergraduates: $11,178.
Athletic Department: Director of Athletics: Ried Estus; Phone: 828-898-8903; Fax: 828-898-8742; E-mail: estus@lmc.edu. Sports Information Director: Julie Kennedy; Phone: 828-898-8904; E-mail: kennedyj@lmc.edu.

MEN'S COACHES

Basketball: Randy Unger; Phone: 828-898-8897; E-mail: unger@lmc.edu.
Cheerleading: Showalter; Phone: 828-898-5241; E-mail: showalter@lmc.edu.
Cross Country: Craig McPhail; Phone: 828-898-2483; E-mail: mcphail@lmc.edu.
Golf: Randy Unger; Phone: 828-898-8897; E-mail: unger@lmc.edu.
Lacrosse: Chris Perkinson; Phone: 828-898-2480; E-mail: perkinson@lmc.edu.
Soccer: Adrian Blenitt; Phone: 828-898-8801; E-mail: blewitt@lmc.edu.
Tennis: Patric Hynes; Phone: 828-898-2547; E-mail: hynes@lmc.edu.
Track and Field: Craig McPhail; Phone: 828-898-2483; E-mail: mcphail@lmc.edu.
Volleyball: Robert Manosca; Phone: 828-898-8714; E-mail: manosca@lmc.edu.

WOMEN'S COACHES

Basketball: Gene Joiner; Phone: 828-898-2482; E-mail: joinerg@lmc.edu.
Cheerleading: Showalter; Phone: 828-898-5241; E-mail: showalter@lmc.edu.
Cross Country: Craig McPhail; Phone: 828-898-2483; E-mail: mcphail@lmc.edu.
Lacrosse: Shaun Williamson; Phone: 828-898-2583; E-mail: williamson@lmc.edu.
Soccer: Tracey Leipold; Phone: 828-898-8771; E-mail: leipoldt@lmc.edu.
Softball: Julie Kennedy; Phone: 828-898-8904; E-mail: kennedyj@lmc.edu.
Tennis: Patric Hynes; Phone: 828-898-2547; E-mail: hynes@lmc.edu.
Track and Field: Craig McPhail; Phone: 828-898-2483; E-mail: mcphail@lmc.edu.
Track and Field: Craig McPhail; Phone: 828-898-2483; E-mail: mcphail@lmc.edu.
Volleyball: Tony Fontanelle; Phone: 828-898-8891; E-mail: fontanelle@lmc.edu.

LEE UNIVERSITY
Cleveland, Tennessee

Flames ◆ NAIA ◆ TranSouth Conference
◆ http://www.leeuniversity.edu/

Independent religious comprehensive, founded 1918, affiliated with Church of God
Coed, 3,555 undergraduate students, 90% full-time, 57% women, 43% men
Small-town 115-acre campus
Minimally difficult entrance level, 57% of applicants were admitted

Freshmen *Admission:* 1,204 applied, 676 were accepted, 654 enrolled. *Test scores:* SAT verbal scores over 500: 66%; SAT math scores over 500: 58%; SAT verbal scores over 600: 28%; SAT math scores over 600: 21%; SAT verbal scores over 700: 5%; SAT math scores over 700: 3%.
Tuition and fees (2004–05): $9075 (full-time). *Room and board:* $4560 (room only: $2350).
Financial Aid (All incoming freshmen): *Average need-based gift aid:* $5750. *Average non-need based aid:* $5247. *Average aid to full-time undergraduates:* $7042.
Athletic Department: *Director of Athletics:* Larry Carpenter; Phone: 423-614-8440; Fax: 423-614-8443; E-mail: lcarpenter@leeuniversity.edu. *Sports Information Director:* George Starr; Phone: 423-614-8440; E-mail: gstarr@leeuniversity.edu.

MEN'S COACHES
Baseball: David Altopp; Phone: 423-614-8440; E-mail: daltopp@leeuniversity.edu.
Basketball: Rick Hughes; Phone: 423-614-8440; E-mail: rhughes@leeuniversity.edu.
Cheerleading: Farrah Still; Phone: 423-614-8440.
Cross Country: Matt Farmer; Phone: 423-614-8440.
Golf: Jack Souther; Phone: 423-614-8440; E-mail: osouther@leeuniversity.edu.
Soccer: Henry Moyo; Phone: 423-614-8440.
Tennis: Tony Cavett; Phone: 423-614-8440.

WOMEN'S COACHES
Basketball: Tiffany Hill; Phone: 423-614-8440; E-mail: thill@leeuniversity.edu.
Cheerleading: Farrah Still; Phone: 423-614-8440.
Cross Country: Matt Farmer; Phone: 423-614-8440.
Soccer: Matt Yelton; Phone: 423-614-8440.
Softball: Emily Moore; Phone: 423-614-8440.
Tennis: Tony Cavett; Phone: 423-614-8440.
Volleyball: Andrea Hudson; Phone: 423-614-8440; E-mail: aorr@leeuniversity.edu.

LEHIGH UNIVERSITY
Bethlehem, Pennsylvania

Mountain Hawks ◆ NCAA I ◆ Eastern Intercollegiate Wrestling Association Conference; Patriot League Conference ◆ http://www.lehigh.edu/

Independent university, founded 1865
Coed, 4,679 undergraduate students, 99% full-time, 40% women, 60% men
Suburban 1,600-acre campus with easy access to Philadelphia
Most difficult entrance level, 40% of applicants were admitted

Freshmen *Admission:* 9,087 applied, 3,678 were accepted, 1,125 enrolled. *Test scores:* SAT verbal scores over 500: 97%; SAT math scores over 500: 99%; SAT verbal scores over 600: 71%; SAT math scores over 600: 87%; SAT verbal scores over 700: 12%; SAT math scores over 700: 35%.
Tuition and fees (2004–05): $29,340 (full-time). *Room and board:* $8230 (room only: $4700).
Financial Aid (All incoming freshmen): *Average need-based gift aid:* $17,677. *Average non-need based aid:* $13,935. *Average aid to full-time undergraduates:* $22,226.
Athletic Department: *Director of Athletics:* Joe Sterrett; Phone: 610-758-4320; Fax: 610-758-6629; E-mail: jds7@lehigh.edu. *Sports Information Director:* Jeff Tourial; Phone: 610-758-3158; E-mail: jat8@lehigh.edu.

MEN'S COACHES
Baseball: Sean Leary; Phone: 610-758-4315; E-mail: spl3@lehigh.edu.
Basketball: Billy Taylor; Phone: 610-758-4188; E-mail: wpt2@lehigh.edu.
Cross Country: Debbie Utesch; Phone: 610-758-4303; E-mail: deu3@lehigh.edu.
Diving: Taryn Gall; Phone: 610-758-4607; E-mail: taf6@lehigh.edu.
Football: Pete Lembo; Phone: 610-758-4356; E-mail: jpl5@lehigh.edu.
Golf: Kelly Gutshall; Phone: 610-758-5176; E-mail: fbg0@lehigh.edu.
Lacrosse: Chris Wakely; Phone: 610-758-4917; E-mail: cjw5@lehigh.edu.
Soccer: Dean Koski; Phone: 610-758-5355; E-mail: dk0f@lehigh.edu.
Swimming: John Morrison; Phone: 610-758-4309; E-mail: jhm3@lehigh.edu.
Tennis: Dave Shook; Phone: 610-758-6576; E-mail: dasf@lehigh.edu.
Track and Field: Matt Utesch; Phone: 610-758-5188; E-mail: mau4@lehigh.edu.
Wrestling: Greg Strobel; Phone: 610-758-4302; E-mail: gos2@lehigh.edu.

WOMEN'S COACHES
Basketball: Sue Troyan; Phone: 610-758-4458; E-mail: srb1@lehigh.edu.
Cross Country: Debbie Utesch; Phone: 610-758-4303; E-mail: deu3@lehigh.edu.
Diving: Taryn Gall; Phone: 610-758-4607; E-mail: taf6@lehigh.edu.
Field Hockey: Julie Mazer; Phone: 610-758-4388; E-mail: jum2@lehigh.edu.
Golf: Kelly Gutshall; Phone: 610-758-5176; E-mail: fbg0@lehigh.edu.
Lacrosse: Jim Shreve; Phone: 610-758-4321; E-mail: jlsi@lehigh.edu.
Soccer: Manny Oudin; Phone: 610-758-4346; E-mail: mao2@lehigh.edu.
Softball: Fran Troyan; Phone: 610-758-4387; E-mail: fgt2@lehigh.edu.
Swimming: John Morrison; Phone: 610-758-4309; E-mail: jhm3@lehigh.edu.
Tennis: Dave Shook; Phone: 610-758-6576; E-mail: dasf@lehigh.edu.
Track and Field: Matt Utesch; Phone: 610-758-5188; E-mail: mau4@lehigh.edu.
Volleyball: Patrick Nicholas; Phone: 610-758-6111; E-mail: phn3@lehigh.edu.

LEHMAN COLLEGE OF THE CITY UNIVERSITY OF NEW YORK
Bronx, New York

Lightning ◆ NCAA III ◆ CUNY Athletic Conference ◆ http://www.lehman.cuny.edu/

State and locally supported comprehensive, founded 1931, part of City University of New York System
Coed, 7,594 undergraduate students, 60% full-time, 72% women, 28% men
Urban 37-acre campus
Moderately difficult entrance level, 3% of applicants were admitted

Freshmen *Admission:* 4,553 applied, 1,370 were accepted, 819 enrolled. *Test scores:* SAT verbal scores over 500: 19%; SAT math scores over 500: 20%; SAT verbal scores over 600: 3%; SAT math scores over 600: 4%; SAT verbal scores over 700: 1%; SAT math scores over 700: 1%.
Tuition and fees (2003–04): $4270 (resident), $8910 (nonresident).
Financial Aid (All incoming freshmen): *Average need-based gift aid:* $2132. *Average aid to full-time undergraduates:* $8025.
Athletic Department: *Director of Athletics:* Martin Zwiren; Phone: 718-960-1117; Fax: 718-960-1132; E-mail: martinz@lehman.cuny.edu. *Sports Information Director:* Eric Harrison; Phone: 718-960-7175; E-mail: eharriso@lehman.cuny.edu.

MEN'S COACHES
Baseball: Kiko Reyes; Phone: 718-960-7746; E-mail: khit2000@aol.com.
Basketball: Steve Schulman; Phone: 718-960-7745; E-mail: sschulma@lehman.cuny.edu.
Cheerleading: Stacy Ann Letford; Phone: 718-960-8101.
Cross Country: Lesleigh Hogg; Phone: 718-960-1144; E-mail: lhogg@lehman.cuny.edu.

Swimming: Peter Kiernan; Phone: 718-960-7123; E-mail: apexswim@usa.net.
Tennis: Steven Schulman; Phone: 718-960-7199; E-mail: sschulma@lehman.cuny.edu.
Track and Field: Lesleigh Hogg; Phone: 718-960-1144; E-mail: lhogg@lehman.cuny.edu.
Volleyball: Junior Garcia; Phone: 718-960-7176; E-mail: elsocio1@aol.com.

WOMEN'S COACHES
Basketball: Eric Harrison; Phone: 718-960-7175; E-mail: eharriso@lehman.cuny.edu.
Cheerleading: Stacy Ann Letford; Phone: 718-960-8101.
Cross Country: Lesleigh Hogg; Phone: 718-960-1144; E-mail: lhogg@lehman.cuny.edu.
Softball: Kim Santoiemma; Phone: 718-960-1130; E-mail: kimmi3126@aol.com.
Swimming: Peter Kiernan; Phone: 718-960-7123; E-mail: apexswim@usa.net.
Tennis: Steven Schulman; Phone: 718-960-7199; E-mail: sschulma@lehman.cuny.edu.
Track and Field: Lesleigh Hogg; Phone: 718-960-1144; E-mail: lhogg@lehman.cuny.edu.
Volleyball: Junior Garcia; Phone: 718-960-7176; E-mail: elsocio1@aol.com.

LE MOYNE COLLEGE
Syracuse, New York

Dolphins ◆ NCAA II ◆ Metro Atlantic Athletic Conference; Northeast-10 Conference; Upstate Collegiate Athletic Conference ◆ http://www.lemoyne.edu/

Independent Roman Catholic (Jesuit) comprehensive, founded 1946
Coed, 2,691 undergraduate students, 84% full-time, 63% women, 37% men
Suburban 151-acre campus
Moderately difficult entrance level, 71% of applicants were admitted

Freshmen *Admission:* 2,940 applied, 2,118 were accepted, 503 enrolled. *Test scores:* SAT verbal scores over 500: 79%; SAT math scores over 500: 84%; SAT verbal scores over 600: 26%; SAT math scores over 600: 29%; SAT verbal scores over 700: 3%; SAT math scores over 700: 3%.
Tuition and fees (2003–04): $18,950 (full-time). *Room and board:* $7450 (room only: $4710).
Financial Aid (All incoming freshmen): *Average need-based gift aid:* $15,856. *Average non-need based aid:* $8789. *Average aid to full-time undergraduates:* $18,904.
Athletic Department: *Director of Athletics:* Dick Rockwell; Phone: 315-445-4414; Fax: 315-445-4678; E-mail: rockwerw@lemoyne.edu. *Sports Information Director:* Mike Donlin; Phone: 315-445-4412; E-mail: donlinm@lemoyne.edu.

MEN'S COACHES
Baseball: Steve Owens; Phone: 315-445-4415; E-mail: owenssc@lemoyne.edu.
Basketball: Steven Evans; Phone: 315-445-4416; E-mail: evanssw@lemoyne.edu.
Cross Country: Gerry Mahon; Phone: 315-470-7950; E-mail: mahongp@lemoyne.edu.
Diving: Joe Hannah; Phone: 315-445-4452; E-mail: hannahjm@lemoyne.edu.
Golf: Nick Masterpole; Phone: 315-445-4411; E-mail: masternc@lemoyne.edu.
Lacrosse: Dan Sheehan; Phone: 315-445-4463; E-mail: sheehadj@lemoyne.edu.
Soccer: Tom Bonus; Phone: 315-445-4713; E-mail: bonustp@lemoyne.edu.
Swimming: Joe Hannah; Phone: 315-445-4452; E-mail: hannahjm@lemoyne.edu.
Tennis: Steve Underwood; Phone: 315-445-4411; E-mail: underwsb@lemoyne.edu.

WOMEN'S COACHES
Basketball: Jeanne Dupree; Phone: 315-445-4413; E-mail: dupreejc@lemoyne.edu.
Cross Country: Gerry Mahon; Phone: 315-470-7950; E-mail: mahongp@lemoyne.edu.
Diving: Joe Hannah; Phone: 315-445-4452; E-mail: hannahjm@lemoyne.edu.
Lacrosse: Laureen O'Connor; Phone: 315-445-4634; E-mail: oconnole@lemoyne.edu.
Soccer: Matt Townsend; Phone: 315-445-4421; E-mail: townsend@lemoyne.edu.
Softball: Ken King; Phone: 315-445-4420; E-mail: kingk@lemoyne.edu.
Swimming: Joe Hannah; Phone: 315-445-4452; E-mail: hannahjm@lemoyne.edu.
Tennis: Steve Underwood; Phone: 315-445-4411; E-mail: underwsb@lemoyne.edu.
Volleyball: Ken King; Phone: 315-445-4420; E-mail: kingk@lemoyne.edu.

LEMOYNE-OWEN COLLEGE
Memphis, Tennessee

Magicians ◆ NCAA II ◆ Southern Intercollegiate Athletic Conference ◆ http://www.lemoyne-owen.edu/

Independent religious 4-year, founded 1862, affiliated with United Church of Christ
Coed, 734 undergraduate students, 85% full-time, 70% women, 30% men
Urban 15-acre campus
Minimally difficult entrance level, 100% of applicants were admitted

Freshmen *Admission:* 203 applied, 203 were accepted, 162 enrolled.
Tuition and fees (2003–04): $8450 (full-time). *Room and board:* $4620 (room only: $2420).
Financial Aid (All incoming freshmen): *Average need-based gift aid:* $6522. *Average non-need based aid:* $10,799. *Average aid to full-time undergraduates:* $8121.
Athletic Department: *Director of Athletics:* E.D. Wilkens; Phone: 901-942-7327; Fax: 901-942-6272.

MEN'S COACHES
Baseball: Eric Lee; Phone: 901-942-6237.
Basketball: Willie Patterson; Phone: 901-774-9090.
Cross Country: Curtis Hollowell; Phone: 901-942-7329.
Tennis: William Anderson; Phone: 901-774-9090.

WOMEN'S COACHES
Basketball: William Anderson; Phone: 901-774-9090.
Cross Country: Curtis Hollowell; Phone: 901-942-7329.
Softball: Nedra Brown; Phone: 901-942-9090.
Tennis: William Anderson; Phone: 901-774-9090.
Volleyball: Nedra Brown; Phone: 901-942-9090.

LENOIR-RHYNE COLLEGE
Hickory, North Carolina

Bears ◆ NCAA II ◆ South Atlantic Conference ◆ http://www.lrc.edu/

Independent Lutheran comprehensive, founded 1891
Coed, 1,348 undergraduate students, 92% full-time, 64% women, 36% men
Small-town 100-acre campus with easy access to Charlotte
Moderately difficult entrance level, 75% of applicants were admitted

Freshmen *Admission:* 1,563 applied, 1,261 were accepted, 310 enrolled. *Test scores:* SAT verbal scores over 500: 52%; SAT math scores over 500: 58%; SAT verbal scores over 600: 14%; SAT math scores over 600: 18%; SAT verbal scores over 700: 1%; SAT math scores over 700: 2%.
Tuition and fees (2004–05): $17,850 (full-time). *Room and board:* $6300.
Financial Aid (All incoming freshmen): *Average need-based gift aid:* $9712. *Average non-need based aid:* $13,778. *Average aid to full-time undergraduates:* $11,985.
Athletic Department: *Director of Athletics:* Neil Geachy; Phone: 828-328-7128; Fax: 828-267-3445; E-mail: mcgeachy@lrc.edu. *Sports Information Director:* John Karrs; Phone: 828-328-7174; E-mail: karrsjd@lrc.edu.

Lenoir-Rhyne College (continued)

MEN'S COACHES
Baseball: Frank Pait; Phone: 828-328-7136; E-mail: paitf@lrc.edu.
Basketball: John Lentz; Phone: 828-328-7122; E-mail: lentz@lrc.edu.
Cross Country: Jason Stewart; Phone: 828-328-7140; E-mail: stewartjd@lrc.edu.
Football: Wayne Hicks; Phone: 828-328-7117; E-mail: hicksw@lrc.edu.
Golf: Brian Bailie; Phone: 828-328-7620; E-mail: bailieb@lrc.edu.
Soccer: Bobby Ladimir; Phone: 828-328-7137; E-mail: ladimarb@lrc.edu.

WOMEN'S COACHES
Basketball: Karen Barefoot; Phone: 828-328-7132; E-mail: barefootk@lrc.edu.
Cross Country: Jason Stewart; Phone: 828-328-7140; E-mail: stewartjd@lrc.edu.
Golf: Brian Bailie; Phone: 828-328-7620; E-mail: bailieb@lrc.edu.
Soccer: Will Beddingfield; Phone: 828-328-7169; E-mail: beddingfieldw@lrc.edu.
Softball: Shena Hollar; Phone: 828-328-7133; E-mail: hollars@lrc.edu.
Volleyball: Dave Markland; Phone: 828-328-7215; E-mail: marklandd@lrc.edu.

LESLEY UNIVERSITY
Cambridge, Massachusetts

Lynx ◆ NCAA III ◆ Independent ◆ http://www.lesley.edu/

Independent comprehensive, founded 1909
Coed, primarily women, 516 undergraduate students, 97% full-time, 100% women, 100% men
Urban 5-acre campus with easy access to Boston
Moderately difficult entrance level, 77% of applicants were admitted

Freshmen *Admission:* 365 applied, 281 were accepted, 102 enrolled. *Test scores:* SAT verbal scores over 500: 71%; SAT math scores over 500: 58%; SAT verbal scores over 600: 17%; SAT math scores over 600: 11%; SAT verbal scores over 700: 3%.
Tuition and fees (2004–05): $21,275 (full-time). *Room and board:* $9370 (room only: $5645).
Financial Aid (All incoming freshmen): *Average need-based gift aid:* $10,785. *Average non-need based aid:* $6650. *Average aid to full-time undergraduates:* $16,441.
Athletic Department: *Director of Athletics:* Stanley Viera; Phone: 617-349-8498; Fax: 617-349-8558; E-mail: sviera@mail.lesley.edu.

WOMEN'S COACHES
Basketball: Jim Burfoot; Phone: 617-349-8976; E-mail: bball@mail.lesley.edu.
Soccer: Christina Belisle; Phone: 617-349-8361; E-mail: cbelisle@mail.lesley.edu.
Softball: Jen Benway; Phone: 617-349-8183; E-mail: jbenway@mail.lesley.edu.
Volleyball: Jennifer Voegeli; Phone: 617-349-8976; E-mail: vball@mail.lesley.edu.

LETOURNEAU UNIVERSITY
Longview, Texas

Yellow Jackets ◆ NCAA III ◆ American Southwest Conference ◆ http://www.letu.edu/

Independent nondenominational comprehensive, founded 1946
Coed, 3,175 undergraduate students, 40% full-time, 53% women, 47% men
Suburban 162-acre campus
84% of applicants were admitted

Freshmen *Admission:* 849 applied, 680 were accepted, 340 enrolled. *Test scores:* SAT verbal scores over 500: 81%; SAT math scores over 500: 85%; SAT verbal scores over 600: 48%; SAT math scores over 600: 46%; SAT verbal scores over 700: 13%; SAT math scores over 700: 12%.
Tuition and fees (2004–05): $15,030 (full-time). *Room and board:* $6050.

Financial Aid (All incoming freshmen): *Average need-based gift aid:* $5724. *Average non-need based aid:* $3964. *Average aid to full-time undergraduates:* $12,728.
Athletic Department: *Director of Athletics:* Bernie Balikian; Phone: 903-233-3371; Fax: 903-233-3822; E-mail: berniebalikian@letu.edu. *Sports Information Director:* Shane Meling; Phone: 903-233-3378; E-mail: shanemeling@letu.edu.

MEN'S COACHES
Baseball: Bernie Martinez; Phone: 903-233-3372; E-mail: berniemartinez@letu.edu.
Basketball: Bernie Balikian; Phone: 903-233-3371; E-mail: berniebalikian@letu.edu.
Cross Country: Minnette Langley; Phone: 903-233-3497; E-mail: minnettelangley@letu.edu.
Golf: Andy Woodring; Phone: 903-233-3303; E-mail: andywoodring@letu.edu.
Soccer: Art Busha; Phone: 903-233-3374; E-mail: artbusha@letu.edu.
Tennis: Pedro Blanco; Phone: 903-233-3531; E-mail: pedroblanco@letu.edu.

WOMEN'S COACHES
Basketball: Jamy Bechler; Phone: 903-233-3390; E-mail: jamybechler@letu.edu.
Cross Country: Minnette Langley; Phone: 903-233-3497; E-mail: minnettelangley@letu.edu.
Golf: Andy Woodring; Phone: 903-233-3303; E-mail: andywoodring@letu.edu.
Soccer: Pedro Blanco; Phone: 903-233-3531; E-mail: pedroblanco@letu.edu.
Softball: Jay Terry; Phone: 903-233-3373; E-mail: jayterry@letu.edu.
Tennis: Pedro Blanco; Phone: 903-233-3531; E-mail: pedroblanco@letu.edu.
Volleyball: Jay Terry; Phone: 903-233-3373; E-mail: jayterry@letu.edu.

LEWIS & CLARK COLLEGE
Portland, Oregon

Pioneers ◆ NCAA III ◆ Northwest Conference ◆ http://www.lclark.edu/

Independent comprehensive, founded 1867
Coed, 1,792 undergraduate students, 98% full-time, 61% women, 39% men
Suburban 137-acre campus
Very difficult entrance level, 62% of applicants were admitted

Freshmen *Admission:* 3,405 applied, 2,310 were accepted, 493 enrolled. *Test scores:* SAT verbal scores over 500: 99%; SAT math scores over 500: 99%; SAT verbal scores over 600: 78%; SAT math scores over 600: 68%; SAT verbal scores over 700: 30%; SAT math scores over 700: 17%.
Tuition and fees (2003–04): $24,670 (full-time). *Room and board:* $7030 (room only: $3710).
Financial Aid (All incoming freshmen): *Average need-based gift aid:* $19,568. *Average non-need based aid:* $7387. *Average aid to full-time undergraduates:* $20,114.
Athletic Department: *Director of Athletics:* Steve Wallo; Phone: 503-768-7548; Fax: 503-768-7058; E-mail: wallo@lclark.edu. *Sports Information Director:* Melissa Dudek; Phone: 503-768-7067; E-mail: mdudek@lclark.edu.

MEN'S COACHES
Baseball: Reed Rainey; Phone: 503-768-7059; E-mail: rainey@lclark.edu.
Basketball: Bob Gaillard; Phone: 503-768-7072; E-mail: gaillard@lclark.edu.
Cross Country: David Fix; Phone: 503-768-7068; E-mail: fix@lclark.edu.
Football: Mike Fanger; Phone: 503-768-7069; E-mail: fanger@lclark.edu.
Golf: Pat Smith; Phone: 503-768-7808; E-mail: psmith@lclark.edu.
Swimming: Matt Sellman; Phone: 503-768-7189; E-mail: sellman@lclark.edu.
Tennis: Gundars Tilmanis; Phone: 503-768-7033; E-mail: tiltennis@lclark.edu.
Track and Field: David Fix; Phone: 503-768-7068; E-mail: fix@lclark.edu.

WOMEN'S COACHES
Basketball: Missy Smith; Phone: 503-768-7557; E-mail: masmith@lclark.edu.

Cross Country: David Fix; Phone: 503-768-7068; E-mail: fix@lclark.edu.

Golf: Mary Jo McCloskey; Phone: 503-768-7176; E-mail: maryjo@lclark.edu.

Soccer: Todd Anckaitis; Phone: 503-768-7550; E-mail: todd@lclark.edu.

Softball: Jennifer Piper; Phone: 503-768-7552; E-mail: jpiper@lclark.edu.

Swimming: Matt Sellman; Phone: 503-768-7189; E-mail: sellman@lclark.edu.

Tennis: Gundars Tilmanis; Phone: 503-768-7033; E-mail: tiltennis@lclark.edu.

Track and Field: David Fix; Phone: 503-768-7068; E-mail: fix@lclark.edu.

Volleyball: Lori Jepsen; Phone: 503-768-7547; E-mail: jepsen@lclark.edu.

LEWIS-CLARK STATE COLLEGE
Lewiston, Idaho

Warriors ◆ NAIA ◆ Frontier Conference
◆ http://www.lcsc.edu/

State-supported 4-year, founded 1893
Coed, 3,471 undergraduate students, 65% full-time, 61% women, 39% men
Small-town 44-acre campus
Minimally difficult entrance level, 58% of applicants were admitted

Freshmen *Admission:* 1,246 applied, 796 were accepted, 514 enrolled. *Test scores:* SAT verbal scores over 500: 45%; SAT math scores over 500: 50%; SAT verbal scores over 600: 12%; SAT math scores over 600: 14%; SAT verbal scores over 700: 2%; SAT math scores over 700: 2%.
Tuition and fees (2003–04): $3126 (resident), $9124 (nonresident). *Room and board:* $4336 (room only: $1880).
Financial Aid (All incoming freshmen): *Average need-based gift aid:* $2458. *Average non-need based aid:* $2289. *Average aid to full-time undergraduates:* $4064.
Athletic Department: *Director of Athletics:* Dene Thomas; Phone: 208-792-2275; Fax: 208-792-2801; E-mail: dkthomas@lcsc.edu. *Sports Information Director:* Lance Acord; Phone: 208-792-2289; E-mail: ldacord@lcsc.edu.

MEN'S COACHES
Baseball: Ed Cheff; Phone: 208-792-2272; E-mail: echeff@lcsc.edu.
Basketball: George Pfeifer; Phone: 208-792-2271; E-mail: gpfeifer@lcsc.edu.
Cross Country: Mike Collins; Phone: 208-792-2308; E-mail: mcollins@lewiston.com.
Golf: Paul Thompson; Phone: 208-792-2088; E-mail: pethompson@lcsc.edu.
Tennis: Kai Fong; Phone: 208-792-2309; E-mail: kfong@lcsc.edu.
Track and Field: Mike Collins; Phone: 208-792-2308; E-mail: mcollins@lewiston.com.

WOMEN'S COACHES
Basketball: Brian Orr; Phone: 208-792-2274; E-mail: rborr@lcsc.edu.
Cross Country: Mike Collins; Phone: 208-792-2308; E-mail: mcollins@lewiston.com.
Golf: Paul Thompson; Phone: 208-792-2088; E-mail: pethompson@lcsc.edu.
Tennis: Kai Fong; Phone: 208-792-2309; E-mail: kfong@lcsc.edu.
Track and Field: Mike Collins; Phone: 208-792-2308; E-mail: mcollins@lewiston.com.
Volleyball: Jerry Pruitt; Phone: 208-792-2258; E-mail: jnpruitt@lcsc.edu.

LEWIS UNIVERSITY
Romeoville, Illinois

Flyers ◆ NCAA II ◆ Great Lakes Valley Conference; Midwestern Intercollegiate Volleyball Conference ◆ http://www.lewisu.edu/

Independent religious comprehensive, founded 1932, affiliated with Roman Catholic Church
Coed, 3,214 undergraduate students, 70% full-time, 59% women, 41% men
Small-town 375-acre campus with easy access to Chicago
Moderately difficult entrance level, 69% of applicants were admitted

Freshmen *Admission:* 1,595 applied, 1,056 were accepted, 458 enrolled. *Test scores:* SAT verbal scores over 500: 75%; SAT math scores over 500: 75%; SAT verbal scores over 600: 25%; SAT math scores over 600: 25%.
Tuition and fees (2004–05): $16,906 (full-time). *Room and board:* $7200 (room only: $4850).
Financial Aid (All incoming freshmen): *Average need-based gift aid:* $6134. *Average non-need based aid:* $6309. *Average aid to full-time undergraduates:* $13,200.
Athletic Department: *Director of Athletics:* Paul Zakowski; Phone: 815-836-5937; Fax: 815-836-5835; E-mail: zakowspa@lewisu.edu. *Sports Information Director:* Mickey Smith; Phone: 815-836-5248; E-mail: smithmh@lewisu.edu.

MEN'S COACHES
Baseball: Irish O'Reilly; Phone: 815-836-5255; E-mail: oreillir@lewisu.edu.
Basketball: Jim Whitesell; Phone: 815-836-5451; E-mail: whitesja@lewisu.edu.
Cheerleading: Suzanne Stamm; Phone: 815-836-5933; E-mail: oreillir@lewisu.edu.
Cross Country: Bob Schultz; Phone: 815-836-5406; E-mail: schultbo@lewisu.edu.
Golf: Dennis Troy; Phone: 815-836-5932.
Soccer: Evan Fiffels; Phone: 815-836-5495; E-mail: fiffleev@lewisu.edu.
Swimming: Jennifer Arndt; Phone: 815-836-5526; E-mail: arndtje@lewisu.edu.
Tennis: Eric Perez; Phone: 815-836-5612.
Track and Field: Bob Schultz; Phone: 815-836-5406; E-mail: schultbo@lewisu.edu.
Volleyball: Dave Deuser; Phone: 815-836-5447.

WOMEN'S COACHES
Basketball: Lynn Plett; Phone: 815-836-5876; E-mail: plettly@lewisu.edu.
Cheerleading: Suzanne Stamm; Phone: 815-836-5933; E-mail: oreillir@lewisu.edu.
Cross Country: Bob Schultz; Phone: 815-836-5406; E-mail: schultbo@lewisu.edu.
Golf: Phone: 815-836-5510.
Soccer: Bill Bruno; Phone: 815-836-5496; E-mail: brunowi@lewisu.edu.
Softball: George Dimatteo; Phone: 815-836-5547; E-mail: dimattge@lewisu.edu.
Swimming: Jennifer Arndt; Phone: 815-836-5526; E-mail: arndtje@lewisu.edu.
Tennis: Jill Siegfried; Phone: 815-836-5277; E-mail: siegfrji@lewisu.edu.
Track and Field: Bob Schultz; Phone: 815-836-5406; E-mail: schultbo@lewisu.edu.
Volleyball: Karen Lockyer; Phone: 815-836-5454; E-mail: lockyeka@lewisu.edu.

LIBERTY UNIVERSITY
Lynchburg, Virginia

Flames ◆ NCAA I ◆ Big South Conference
◆ http://www.liberty.edu/

Independent nondenominational comprehensive, founded 1971
Coed, 7,613 undergraduate students, 85% full-time, 52% women, 48% men
Suburban 230-acre campus
Minimally difficult entrance level, 96% of applicants were admitted

Freshmen *Admission:* 4,055 applied, 3,883 were accepted, 1,897 enrolled. *Test scores:* SAT verbal scores over 500: 56%; SAT math scores over 500: 46%; SAT verbal scores over 600: 18%; SAT math scores over 600: 13%; SAT verbal scores over 700: 3%; SAT math scores over 700: 1%.
Tuition and fees (2004–05): $13,150 (full-time). *Room and board:* $5400.
Financial Aid (All incoming freshmen): *Average need-based gift aid:* $3917. *Average non-need based aid:* $5594. *Average aid to full-time undergraduates:* $9685.
Athletic Department: *Director of Athletics:* Kim Graham; Phone: 434-582-2100; Fax: 434-582-2205; E-mail: kgraham@liberty.edu. *Sports Information Director:* Todd Wetmore; Phone: 434-582-2292; E-mail: twetmore@liberty.edu.

MEN'S COACHES
Baseball: Matt Royer; Phone: 434-582-2103; E-mail: mroyer@liberty.edu.
Basketball: Randy Dunton; Phone: 434-582-2337; E-mail: rdunton@liberty.edu.
Cheerleading: Tim McTee; Phone: 434-582-2100; E-mail: tmmctee@liberty.edu.
Cross Country: Brant Tolsma; Phone: 434-582-2100; E-mail: bctolsma@liberty.edu.
Football: Ken Karcher; Phone: 434-582-2040; E-mail: kkarcher@liberty.edu.
Golf: Frank Landrey; Phone: 434-385-0061; E-mail: lugolf@aol.com.
Soccer: Jeff Alder; Phone: 434-582-2381; E-mail: jtalder@liberty.edu.
Tennis: Larry Hubbard; Phone: 434-582-2100; E-mail: lhubbard@liberty.edu.
Track and Field: Brant Tolsma; Phone: 434-582-2100; E-mail: bctolsma@liberty.edu.

WOMEN'S COACHES
Basketball: Carey Green; Phone: 434-582-2907; E-mail: cgreen@liberty.edu.
Cheerleading: Tim McTee; Phone: 434-582-2100; E-mail: tmmctee@liberty.edu.
Cross Country: Brant Tolsma; Phone: 434-582-2100; E-mail: bctolsma@liberty.edu.
Soccer: James Price; Phone: 434-582-2100; E-mail: wsoccer@liberty.edu.
Softball: Paul Wetmore; Phone: 434-582-7255; E-mail: pawetmor@liberty.edu.
Tennis: Larry Hubbard; Phone: 434-582-2100; E-mail: lhubbard@liberty.edu.
Track and Field: Brant Tolsma; Phone: 434-582-2100; E-mail: bctolsma@liberty.edu.
Volleyball: Chris Phillips; Phone: 434-582-2100; E-mail: cfphilli@liberty.edu.

LIMESTONE COLLEGE
Gaffney, South Carolina

Saints ◆ NCAA II ◆ California Collegiate Athletic Conference; Carolinas-Virginia Athletics Conference; Deep South Lacrosse Conference ◆ http://www.limestone.edu/

Independent 4-year, founded 1845
Coed, 552 undergraduate students, 97% full-time, 48% women, 52% men
Suburban 115-acre campus with easy access to Charlotte
Minimally difficult entrance level, 2% of applicants were admitted

Freshmen *Admission:* 758 applied, 145 were accepted, 136 enrolled. *Test scores:* SAT verbal scores over 500: 36%; SAT math scores over 500: 38%; SAT verbal scores over 600: 4%; SAT math scores over 600: 9%.

Tuition and fees (2004–05): $13,200 (full-time). *Room and board:* $5400.
Financial Aid (All incoming freshmen): *Average need-based gift aid:* $6597. *Average non-need based aid:* $6864. *Average aid to full-time undergraduates:* $8271.
Athletic Department: *Director of Athletics:* Dennis Bloomer; Phone: 864-488-4561; Fax: 864-902-0714; E-mail: dbloomer@limestone.edu.

MEN'S COACHES
Baseball: Chico Lombardo; Phone: 864-488-4565; E-mail: alombardo@limestone.edu.
Basketball: Larry Epperly; Phone: 864-488-4564; E-mail: lepperly@limestone.edu.
Cheerleading: Jennifer Dawson; Phone: 864-488-4561.
Cross Country: Corey Fox; Phone: 864-488-4572; E-mail: cfox@limestone.edu.
Golf: Doc Lemmons; Phone: 864-488-4560; E-mail: dlemmons@limestone.edu.
Lacrosse: T.W. Johnson; Phone: 864-488-4562; E-mail: tjohnson@limestone.edu.
Soccer: Eric Alsop; Phone: 864-488-4584; E-mail: ealsop@limestone.edu.
Tennis: Stephen Monge; Phone: 864-488-8350; E-mail: smonge@limestone.edu.
Wrestling: Ben Stehura; Phone: 800-795-7251; E-mail: bstehura@limestone.edu.

WOMEN'S COACHES
Basketball: Dennis Bloomer; Phone: 864-488-4561; E-mail: dbloomer@limestone.edu.
Cheerleading: Jennifer Dawson; Phone: 864-488-4561.
Cross Country: Corey Fox; Phone: 864-488-4572; E-mail: cfox@limestone.edu.
Golf: Doc Lemmons; Phone: 864-488-4560; E-mail: dlemmons@limestone.edu.
Lacrosse: Scott Tucker; Phone: 864-488-4561; E-mail: stucker@limestone.edu.
Soccer: Eric Alsop; Phone: 864-488-4584; E-mail: ealsop@limestone.edu.
Softball: Jimmy Martin; Phone: 864-488-4566; E-mail: jmartin@limestone.edu.
Swimming: Carl Brown; Phone: 864-488-4570; E-mail: cbrown@limestone.edu.
Tennis: Stephen Monge; Phone: 864-488-8350; E-mail: smonge@limestone.edu.
Volleyball: Alison Maybry; Phone: 864-488-4568; E-mail: amaybry@limestone.edu.

LINCOLN MEMORIAL UNIVERSITY
Harrogate, Tennessee

Railsplitters ◆ NCAA II ◆ Gulf South Conference ◆ http://www.lmunet.edu/

Independent comprehensive, founded 1897
Coed, 1,117 undergraduate students, 77% full-time, 73% women, 27% men
Small-town 1,000-acre campus
Moderately difficult entrance level, 85% of applicants were admitted

Freshmen *Admission:* 577 applied, 488 were accepted, 279 enrolled.
Tuition and fees (2004–05): $12,600 (full-time). *Room and board:* $4910 (room only: $2250).
Financial Aid (All incoming freshmen): *Average need-based gift aid:* $5410. *Average non-need based aid:* $6550. *Average aid to full-time undergraduates:* $10,750.
Athletic Department: *Director of Athletics:* Jack Bondurant; Phone: 423-869-6399; Fax: 423-869-6382; E-mail: jbondurant@lmunet.edu. *Sports Information Director:* Rusty Peace; Phone: 423-869-6236; E-mail: rpeace@lmunet.edu.

MEN'S COACHES
Baseball: Jeff Sziksai; Phone: 423-869-6345; E-mail: jsziksai@lmunet.edu.
Basketball: Jeff Tungate; Phone: 423-869-6240; E-mail: jtungate@lmunet.edu.
Cheerleading: Elizabeth Warren; Phone: 423-869-6239; E-mail: athletics@lmunet.edu.
Cross Country: Brandon Gibbs; Phone: 423-869-6201; E-mail: bgibbs@lmunet.edu.

Golf: Travis Mucey; Phone: 423-869-6285.
Soccer: Helio D'Anna; Phone: 423-869-6245; E-mail: hdanna@lmunet.edu.
Tennis: Charles Poteat; Phone: 423-869-6371; E-mail: cpoteat@lmunet.edu.

WOMEN'S COACHES

Basketball: Roger Vannoy; Phone: 423-869-6241; E-mail: rvannoy@lmunet.edu.
Cheerleading: Elizabeth Warren; Phone: 423-869-6239; E-mail: athletics@lmunet.edu.
Cross Country: Brandon Gibbs; Phone: 423-869-6201; E-mail: bgibbs@lmunet.edu.
Golf: Greg Lasley; Phone: 423-869-6209; E-mail: glasley@lmunet.edu.
Soccer: Helio D'Anna; Phone: 423-869-6245; E-mail: hdanna@lmunet.edu.
Softball: Dan Burns; Phone: 423-869-6242; E-mail: cen01554@centurytel.net.
Tennis: Jack Bondurant; Phone: 423-869-6399; E-mail: jbondurant@lmunet.edu.
Volleyball: Mike Smith; Phone: 423-869-6239; E-mail: msmith@lmunet.edu.

LINCOLN UNIVERSITY
Jefferson City, Missouri

Blue Tigers ◆ NCAA II ◆ Heartland Conference; Independent ◆ http://www.lincolnu.edu/

State-supported comprehensive, founded 1866, part of Missouri Coordinating Board for Higher Education
Coed, 2,910 undergraduate students, 65% full-time, 61% women, 39% men
Small-town 152-acre campus
Noncompetitive entrance level, 97% of applicants were admitted

Freshmen *Admission:* 1,155 applied, 1,109 were accepted, 533 enrolled.
Tuition and fees (2003–04): $4562 (resident), $8102 (nonresident). *Room and board:* $3790 (room only: $1850).
Financial Aid (All incoming freshmen): *Average need-based gift aid:* $1000. *Average non-need based aid:* $600. *Average aid to full-time undergraduates:* $5400.
Athletic Department: *Director of Athletics:* Tim Abney; Phone: 573-681-5325; Fax: 573-681-5998; E-mail: abneyt@lincolnu.edu. *Sports Information Director:* Larry Mendez; Phone: 573-681-5343.

MEN'S COACHES

Baseball: Earl Wheeler; Phone: 573-681-5334; E-mail: wheelere@lincolnu.edu.
Basketball: Charles Terry; Phone: 573-681-5332; E-mail: popew@lincolnu.edu.
Cheerleading: Billie Coachman; Phone: 573-499-2972.
Football: Fred Manuel; Phone: 573-681-5904; E-mail: manuelf@lincolnu.edu.
Golf: Jerry Coffman; Phone: 573-681-5330; E-mail: coffmanj@lincolnu.edu.
Track and Field: Victor Thomas; Phone: 573-681-5339; E-mail: thomasv@lincolnu.edu.

WOMEN'S COACHES

Basketball: Tim Abney; Phone: 573-681-5336; E-mail: abneyt@lincolnu.edu.
Cheerleading: Billie Coachman; Phone: 573-499-2972.
Cross Country: Victor Thomas; Phone: 573-681-5339; E-mail: thomasv@lincolnu.edu.
Softball: Betty Kemna; Phone: 573-681-5953; E-mail: kemnab@lincolnu.edu.
Tennis: Jenone Bell; Phone: 573-681-5338; E-mail: bellj@lincolnu.edu.
Track and Field: Victor Thomas; Phone: 573-681-5339; E-mail: thomasv@lincolnu.edu.

LINCOLN UNIVERSITY
Lincoln University, Pennsylvania

Lions ◆ NCAA III ◆ Eastern College Athletic Conference ◆ http://www.lincoln.edu/

State-related comprehensive, founded 1854
Coed, 1,530 undergraduate students, 96% full-time, 60% women, 40% men
Rural 422-acre campus with easy access to Philadelphia
Moderately difficult entrance level, 35% of applicants were admitted

Freshmen *Admission:* 3,973 applied, 1,586 were accepted, 462 enrolled. *Test scores:* SAT verbal scores over 500: 22%; SAT math scores over 500: 18%; SAT verbal scores over 600: 3%; SAT math scores over 600: 4%; SAT verbal scores over 700: 1%; SAT math scores over 700: 1%.
Tuition and fees (2003–04): $6952 (resident), $10,350 (nonresident). *Room and board:* $6368 (room only: $3462).
Financial Aid (All incoming freshmen): *Average need-based gift aid:* $5500. *Average non-need based aid:* $2625. *Average aid to full-time undergraduates:* $13,000.
Athletic Department: *Director of Athletics:* Cyrus Jones; Phone: 610-932-8300; Fax: 610-932-1220; E-mail: cjones@lu.lincoln.edu.

MEN'S COACHES

Baseball: Paul Johnson; Phone: 610-932-8300.
Basketball: Robert Byars; Phone: 610-932-3586; E-mail: mbyars@lu.lincoln.edu.
Cheerleading: Antoinette Wallace; Phone: 610-932-8300; E-mail: wallace@lu.lincoln.edu.
Cross Country: Cyrus Jones; Phone: 610-932-8300; E-mail: cjones@lu.lincoln.edu.
Soccer: Sylvester Corbie; Phone: 610-932-8300.
Tennis: Eugene Thompson; Phone: 610-932-8300.
Track and Field: Cyrus Jones; Phone: 610-932-8300; E-mail: cjones@lu.lincoln.edu.

WOMEN'S COACHES

Basketball: Alfred Mikes; Phone: 610-932-8300.
Cheerleading: Antoinette Wallace; Phone: 610-932-8300; E-mail: wallace@lu.lincoln.edu.
Cross Country: Cyrus Jones; Phone: 610-932-8300; E-mail: cjones@lu.lincoln.edu.
Soccer: Michael Spencer; Phone: 610-932-8300.
Tennis: Eugene Thompson; Phone: 610-932-8300.
Track and Field: Cyrus Jones; Phone: 610-932-8300; E-mail: cjones@lu.lincoln.edu.
Volleyball: Darnell Edwards; Phone: 610-932-8300; E-mail: dedwards@lu.lincoln.edu.

LINDENWOOD UNIVERSITY
St. Charles, Missouri

Lions ◆ NAIA ◆ Heart of America Conference ◆ http://www.lindenwood.edu/

Independent Presbyterian comprehensive, founded 1827
Coed, 4,923 undergraduate students, 89% full-time, 56% women, 44% men
Suburban 420-acre campus with easy access to St. Louis
Moderately difficult entrance level, 4% of applicants were admitted

Freshmen *Admission:* 2,428 applied, 1,112 were accepted, 784 enrolled.
Tuition and fees (2004–05): $11,650 (full-time). *Room and board:* $5400 (room only: $2700).
Athletic Department: *Director of Athletics:* Phone: 636-949-4777; Fax: 636-949-4636.

MEN'S COACHES

Baseball: Brian Behrens; Phone: 636-949-4185.
Basketball: Don Mulhern; Phone: 636-949-4633.
Cross Country: Lane Lohr; Phone: 636-949-4801.
Diving: Craig Penrose; Phone: 636-949-4999.
Football: Rick Gorzynski; Phone: 636-949-4800.
Golf: Roger Ellis; Phone: 636-949-4839.
Lacrosse: Troy Hood; Phone: 636-949-4945.
Soccer: Hutter; Phone: 636-949-4651.

Lindenwood University *(continued)*

Swimming: Craig Penrose; Phone: 636-949-4999.
Tennis: Phone: 636-949-4118.
Track and Field: Lane Lohr; Phone: 636-949-4801.
Volleyball: Phone: 636-949-4634.
Wrestling: Phone: 636-949-4827.

WOMEN'S COACHES
Basketball: Chandra Jackson; Phone: 636-949-4632.
Cross Country: Lane Lohr; Phone: 636-949-4801.
Diving: Craig Penrose; Phone: 636-949-4999.
Field Hockey: Lauren Worley Cornthwaite; Phone: 636-949-4782.
Lacrosse: Meghan McLaughlin; Phone: 636-949-4945.
Soccer: Thomas Champion; Phone: 636-949-4651.
Softball: Austene; Phone: 636-949-4995; E-mail: kaustene@lindenwood.edu.
Swimming: Craig Penrose; Phone: 636-949-4999.
Tennis: Phone: 636-949-4118.
Track and Field: Lane Lohr; Phone: 636-949-4801.
Volleyball: Phone: 636-949-4634.

LINDSEY WILSON COLLEGE
Columbia, Kentucky

Blue Raiders ◆ NAIA ◆ Mid-South Conference ◆ http://www.lindsey.edu/

Independent United Methodist comprehensive, founded 1903
Coed, 1,536 undergraduate students, 88% full-time, 65% women, 35% men
Rural 45-acre campus
Minimally difficult entrance level, 73% of applicants were admitted

Freshmen *Admission:* 1,270 applied, 932 were accepted, 434 enrolled.
Tuition and fees (2003–04): $12,602 (full-time). *Room and board:* $5484 (room only: $2024).
Athletic Department: *Director of Athletics:* Willis Pooler; Phone: 270-384-8186; Fax: 270-384-8078; E-mail: poolerw@lindsey.edu. *Sports Information Director:* Chris Wells; Phone: 270-384-8071; E-mail: wellsc@lindsey.edu.

MEN'S COACHES
Baseball: Mike Talley; Phone: 270-384-8074; E-mail: talleym@lindsey.edu.
Basketball: Paul Peck; Phone: 270-384-8072; E-mail: peckp@lindsey.edu.
Cheerleading: LaQuita Goodin; Phone: 270-384-8515; E-mail: goodinl@lindsey.edu.
Cross Country: Stu Melby; Phone: 270-384-8175; E-mail: melbys@lindsey.edu.
Golf: Jeff Lambert; Phone: 270-384-8188; E-mail: lambertj@lindsey.edu.
Soccer: Ray Wells; Phone: 270-384-8069; E-mail: wellsr@lindsey.edu.
Tennis: Audra Nothwehr; Phone: 270-384-8058; E-mail: nothwehra@lindsey.edu.
Track and Field: Stu Melby; Phone: 270-384-8175; E-mail: melbys@lindsey.edu.

WOMEN'S COACHES
Basketball: John Wethington; Phone: 270-384-8073; E-mail: wethingt@lindsey.edu.
Cheerleading: LaQuita Goodin; Phone: 270-384-8515; E-mail: goodinl@lindsey.edu.
Cross Country: Stu Melby; Phone: 270-384-8175; E-mail: melbys@lindsey.edu.
Golf: Jeff Lambert; Phone: 270-384-8188; E-mail: lambertj@lindsey.edu.
Soccer: Willis Pooler; Phone: 270-384-8186; E-mail: poolerw@lindsey.edu.
Softball: Tom Openbrouw; Phone: 270-384-8076; E-mail: opdenbt@lindsey.edu.
Tennis: Audra Nothwehr; Phone: 270-384-8058; E-mail: nothwehra@lindsey.edu.
Track and Field: Stu Melby; Phone: 270-384-8175; E-mail: melbys@lindsey.edu.
Volleyball: Audra Nothwehr; Phone: 270-384-8058; E-mail: nothwehra@lindsey.edu.

LINFIELD COLLEGE
McMinnville, Oregon

Wildcats ◆ NCAA III ◆ Northwest Conference ◆ http://www.linfield.edu/

Independent American Baptist Churches in the USA 4-year, founded 1849
Coed, 1,659 undergraduate students, 97% full-time, 55% women, 45% men
Small-town 193-acre campus with easy access to Portland
Moderately difficult entrance level, 8% of applicants were admitted

Freshmen *Admission:* 1,903 applied, 1,482 were accepted, 453 enrolled.
Test scores: SAT verbal scores over 500: 75%; SAT math scores over 500: 82%; SAT verbal scores over 600: 29%; SAT math scores over 600: 35%; SAT verbal scores over 700: 5%; SAT math scores over 700: 5%.
Tuition and fees (2003–04): $20,970 (full-time). *Room and board:* $6120 (room only: $3200).
Financial Aid (All incoming freshmen): *Average need-based gift aid:* $4976. *Average non-need based aid:* $9588. *Average aid to full-time undergraduates:* $17,001.
Athletic Department: *Director of Athletics:* Scott Carnahan; Phone: 503-883-2229; Fax: 503-883-2453; E-mail: scarnah@linfield.edu. *Sports Information Director:* Kelly Bitd; Phone: 503-883-2439; E-mail: kbird@linfield.edu.

MEN'S COACHES
Baseball: Scott Carnahan; Phone: 503-883-2229; E-mail: scarnah@linfield.edu.
Basketball: Larry Doty; Phone: 503-883-2416; E-mail: ldoty@linfield.edu.
Cross Country: Garry Kilgore; Phone: 503-883-2410; E-mail: gkillgor@linfield.edu.
Football: Jay Locey; Phone: 503-883-2415; E-mail: jlocey@linfield.edu.
Golf: Greg Copeland; Phone: 503-883-2501; E-mail: gcopelan@linfield.edu.
Soccer: Eric Watson; Phone: 503-883-2528; E-mail: ewatson@linfield.edu.
Swimming: Gary Gutierrez; Phone: 503-883-2526; E-mail: ggutierr@linfield.edu.
Tennis: Carl Swanson; Phone: 503-883-2414; E-mail: cswanson@linfield.edu.
Track and Field: Garry Kilgore; Phone: 503-883-2410; E-mail: gkillgor@linfield.edu.

WOMEN'S COACHES
Basketball: Robyn Stewart; Phone: 503-883-2412; E-mail: rstewart@linfield.edu.
Cross Country: Garry Kilgore; Phone: 503-883-2410; E-mail: gkillgor@linfield.edu.
Golf: Marty Bergan; Phone: 503-883-2530; E-mail: mbergan@linfield.edu.
Lacrosse: Bill Hander; Phone: 503-883-2619; E-mail: bhander@linfield.edu.
Soccer: Eric Watson; Phone: 503-883-2528; E-mail: ewatson@linfield.edu.
Softball: Jackson Vaughan; Phone: 503-883-2413; E-mail: jvaughan@linfield.edu.
Swimming: Gary Gutierrez; Phone: 503-883-2526; E-mail: ggutierr@linfield.edu.
Tennis: Amy Dames; Phone: 503-883-2710; E-mail: adames@linfield.edu.
Track and Field: Garry Kilgore; Phone: 503-883-2410; E-mail: gkillgor@linfield.edu.
Volleyball: Shane Kimura; Phone: 503-883-2532; E-mail: skimura@linfield.edu.

LIPSCOMB UNIVERSITY
Nashville, Tennessee

Bisons ◆ NCAA I ◆ Atlantic Sun Conference ◆ http://www.lipscomb.edu/

Independent religious comprehensive, founded 1891, affiliated with Church of Christ
Coed, 2,433 undergraduate students, 90% full-time, 56% women, 44% men
Urban 65-acre campus
Moderately difficult entrance level, 73% of applicants were admitted

Freshmen *Admission:* 2,344 applied, 1,700 were accepted, 596 enrolled. *Test scores:* SAT verbal scores over 500: 76%; SAT math scores over 500: 70%; SAT verbal scores over 600: 30%; SAT math scores over 600: 28%; SAT verbal scores over 700: 7%; SAT math scores over 700: 7%.
Tuition and fees (2004–05): $13,447 (full-time). *Room and board:* $5590.
Financial Aid (All incoming freshmen): *Average need-based gift aid:* $2447. *Average non-need based aid:* $5037. *Average aid to full-time undergraduates:* $8840.
Athletic Department: *Director of Athletics:* Steve Potts; Phone: 615-279-5850; Fax: 615-269-1806; E-mail: steve.potts@lipscomb.edu. *Sports Information Director:* Paul Nance; Phone: 615-279-5967; E-mail: paul.nance@lipscomb.edu.

MEN'S COACHES
Baseball: Wynn Fletcher; Phone: 615-279-5716; E-mail: wynn.fletcher@lipscomb.edu.
Basketball: Scott Sanderson; Phone: 615-269-5791; E-mail: scott.sanderson@lipscomb.edu.
Cheerleading: Renee French; Phone: 615-662-9469; E-mail: kreneefrench@hotmail.com.
Cross Country: Clay Nicks; Phone: 615-269-7152; E-mail: clay.nicks@lipscomb.edu.
Golf: Ralph Samples; Phone: 615-269-5815; E-mail: ralph.samples@lipscomb.edu.
Soccer: Jon Goad; Phone: 615-269-5866; E-mail: jon.goad@lipscomb.edu.
Tennis: Lynn Griffith; Phone: 615-269-5751; E-mail: lynn.griffith@lipscomb.edu.

WOMEN'S COACHES
Basketball: Frank Bennett; Phone: 615-269-5856; E-mail: frank.bennett@lipscomb.edu.
Cheerleading: Renee French; Phone: 615-662-9469; E-mail: kreneefrench@hotmail.com.
Cross Country: Clay Nicks; Phone: 615-269-7152; E-mail: clay.nicks@lipscomb.edu.
Golf: Ralph Samples; Phone: 615-269-5815; E-mail: ralph.samples@lipscomb.edu.
Soccer: Jenger Parrish; Phone: 615-269-7036; E-mail: jenger.parrish@lipscomb.edu.
Softball: Andy Lane; Phone: 615-269-5853; E-mail: andy.lane@lipscomb.edu.
Tennis: Lynn Griffith; Phone: 615-269-5751; E-mail: lynn.griffith@lipscomb.edu.
Track and Field: Clay Nicks; Phone: 615-269-7152; E-mail: clay.nicks@lipscomb.edu.
Volleyball: Brandon Rosenthal; Phone: 615-269-5857; E-mail: brandon.rosenthal@lipscomb.edu.

LIVINGSTONE COLLEGE
Salisbury, North Carolina

Blue Bears ◆ NCAA II ◆ Central Intercollegiate Athletic Conference ◆ http://www.livingstone.edu/

Independent religious 4-year, founded 1879, affiliated with African Methodist Episcopal Zion Church
Coed, 1,005 undergraduate students, 98% full-time, 52% women, 48% men
Small-town 272-acre campus
Minimally difficult entrance level, 5% of applicants were admitted

Freshmen *Admission:* 1,792 applied, 802 were accepted, 286 enrolled. *Test scores:* SAT verbal scores over 500: 10%; SAT math scores over 500: 7%; SAT verbal scores over 600: 2%; SAT math scores over 700: %.
Tuition and fees (2003–04): $12,298 (full-time). *Room and board:* $5803 (room only: $2725).
Athletic Department: *Director of Athletics:* Clifton Huff; Phone: 704-216-6013; Fax: 704-216-6278; E-mail: chuff@livingstone.edu. *Sports Information Director:* Adrian Ferguson; Phone: 704-216-6179; E-mail: aferguson@livingstone.edu.

MEN'S COACHES
Basketball: Westley Gillum; Phone: 704-216-6016; E-mail: jgillum@livingstone.edu.
Cheerleading: Holly Zacharias; Phone: 704-216-6911; E-mail: hzacharias@livingstone.edu.
Cross Country: Cliffton Huff; Phone: 704-797-1013; E-mail: chuff@livingstone.edu.
Football: George Johnson; Phone: 704-797-1089.
Track and Field: Cliffton Huff; Phone: 704-797-1013; E-mail: chuff@livingstone.edu.

WOMEN'S COACHES
Basketball: Andrew Mitchell; Phone: 704-216-6017; E-mail: amitchell@livingstone.edu.
Cheerleading: Holly Zacharias; Phone: 704-216-6911; E-mail: hzacharias@livingstone.edu.
Cross Country: Cliffton Huff; Phone: 704-797-1013; E-mail: chuff@livingstone.edu.
Softball: Linda Bell; Phone: 704-216-6317; E-mail: lbell@livingstone.edu.
Tennis: Bill Woods; Phone: 704-797-6243; E-mail: wwood@livingstone.edu.
Track and Field: Cliffton Huff; Phone: 704-797-1013; E-mail: chuff@livingstone.edu.
Volleyball: Linda Bell; Phone: 704-216-6317; E-mail: lbell@livingstone.edu.

LOCK HAVEN UNIVERSITY OF PENNSYLVANIA
Lock Haven, Pennsylvania

Bald Eagles ◆ NCAA II ◆ Pennsylvania State Athletic Conference ◆ http://www.lhup.edu/

State-supported comprehensive, founded 1870, part of Pennsylvania State System of Higher Education
Coed, 4,696 undergraduate students, 91% full-time, 59% women, 41% men
Rural 165-acre campus
Moderately difficult entrance level, 78% of applicants were admitted

Freshmen *Admission:* 3,932 applied, 3,199 were accepted, 1,184 enrolled. *Test scores:* SAT verbal scores over 500: 40%; SAT math scores over 500: 54%; SAT verbal scores over 600: 6%; SAT math scores over 600: 11%; SAT verbal scores over 700: %; SAT math scores over 700: %.
Tuition and fees (2003–04): $5874 (resident), $10,772 (nonresident). *Room and board:* $5224 (room only: $2944).
Financial Aid (All incoming freshmen): *Average need-based gift aid:* $3900. *Average non-need based aid:* $1000. *Average aid to full-time undergraduates:* $5540.

Lock Haven University of Pennsylvania *(continued)*

Athletic Department: *Director of Athletics:* Sharon Taylor; Phone: 570-893-2093; Fax: 570-893-2414; E-mail: staylor@lhup.edu. *Sports Information Director:* Danielle Barney; Phone: 570-893-2350; E-mail: dbarney@lhup.edu.

MEN'S COACHES

Baseball: Smokey Stover; Phone: 570-893-2245; E-mail: pstover@lhup.edu.
Basketball: John Wilson; Phone: 570-893-2097; E-mail: jwilson2@lhup.edu.
Cheerleading: Dennis Strouse; Phone: 570-893-2101.
Cross Country: Aaron Russell; Phone: 570-893-2261; E-mail: arussell@lhup.edu.
Football: Mark Luther; Phone: 570-893-2250; E-mail: mluther@lhup.edu.
Soccer: Doug Moore; Phone: 570-893-2192; E-mail: bmoore4@lhup.edu.
Track and Field: Mark Elliston; Phone: 570-893-2635; E-mail: mellisto@lhup.edu.
Wrestling: Rocky Bonomo; Phone: 570-893-2304; E-mail: abonomo@lhup.edu.

WOMEN'S COACHES

Basketball: Britt King; Phone: 570-893-2329; E-mail: bking@lhup.edu.
Cheerleading: Dennis Strouse; Phone: 570-893-2101.
Cross Country: Aaron Russell; Phone: 570-893-2261; E-mail: arussell@lhup.edu.
Field Hockey: Pat Rudy; Phone: 570-893-2722; E-mail: prudy@lhup.edu.
Lacrosse: Kristen Geissler; Phone: 570-893-2571; E-mail: kgeissle@lhup.edu.
Soccer: Shannon Champ; Phone: 570-893-2459; E-mail: schamp@lhup.edu.
Softball: Kelly Green; Phone: 570-893-2574; E-mail: kgreen@lhup.edu.
Swimming: Bart Garlick; Phone: 570-893-2820; E-mail: ggarlick@lhup.edu.
Track and Field: Mark Elliston; Phone: 570-893-2635; E-mail: mellisto@lhup.edu.
Volleyball: Tom Justice; Phone: 570-893-2388; E-mail: tjustice@lhup.edu.

LONG ISLAND UNIVERSITY, BROOKLYN CAMPUS
Brooklyn, New York

Blackbirds ◆ NCAA I ◆ Northeast Conference ◆ http://www.brooklyn.liu.edu/

Independent university, founded 1926, part of Long Island University
Coed, 5,380 undergraduate students, 82% full-time, 73% women, 27% men
Urban 10-acre campus
Minimally difficult entrance level, 68% of applicants were admitted

Freshmen *Admission:* 3,604 applied, 2,479 were accepted, 967 enrolled. *Test scores:* SAT verbal scores over 500: 67%; SAT math scores over 500: 73%; SAT verbal scores over 600: 26%; SAT math scores over 600: 35%; SAT verbal scores over 700: 4%; SAT math scores over 700: 13%.
Tuition and fees (2003–04): $17,122 (full-time). *Room and board:* $6480 (room only: $4200).
Financial Aid (All incoming freshmen): *Average need-based gift aid:* $9180. *Average non-need based aid:* $12,963. *Average aid to full-time undergraduates:* $13,428.
Athletic Department: *Director of Athletics:* John Suarez; Phone: 718-488-1030; E-mail: jsuarez@liu.edu. *Sports Information Director:* Stacey Brann; Phone: 718-488-1307; E-mail: dcrudele@liu.edu.

MEN'S COACHES

Baseball: Frank Giannone; Phone: 718-488-1538.
Basketball: Jim Ferry; Phone: 718-488-1528; E-mail: jim.ferry@liu.edu.
Cheerleading: Pia Stevens Haynes; Phone: 718-488-1216.
Cross Country: Julia Sandiford; Phone: 718-780-4094; E-mail: jn_sandi@hotmail.com.
Golf: Lonnie Barton; Phone: 718-488-1074; E-mail: lbarton@liu.edu.
Soccer: T.J. Kostecky; Phone: 718-488-1530; E-mail: kostecky@liu.edu.

Track and Field: Julia Sandiford; Phone: 718-780-4094; E-mail: jn_sandi@hotmail.com.

WOMEN'S COACHES

Basketball: Stephanie Gaitley; Phone: 718-488-1531; E-mail: stephanie.gaitley@liu.edu.
Cheerleading: Pia Stevens Haynes; Phone: 718-488-1216.
Cross Country: Julia Sandiford; Phone: 718-780-4094; E-mail: jn_sandi@hotmail.com.
Golf: Lonnie Barton; Phone: 718-488-1074; E-mail: lbarton@liu.edu.
Lacrosse: Dawn Strunk; Phone: 718-246-6156; E-mail: dstrunk@liu.edu.
Soccer: Tracey Bartholomew; Phone: 718-488-3496; E-mail: tbarthol@liu.edu.
Softball: Roy Kortmann; Phone: 718-488-1523; E-mail: rkortman@liu.edu.
Tennis: Wayne Martin; Phone: 718-488-3497; E-mail: wayne.martin@liu.edu.
Track and Field: Julia Sandiford; Phone: 718-780-4094; E-mail: jn_sandi@hotmail.com.
Volleyball: Toby Rens; Phone: 718-488-1532; E-mail: toby.rens@liu.edu.

LONG ISLAND UNIVERSITY, C.W. POST CAMPUS
Brookville, New York

Pioneers ◆ NCAA II ◆ New York Collegiate Athletic Conference ◆ http://www.cwpost.liunet.edu/cwis/cwp/post.html

Independent comprehensive, founded 1954, part of Long Island University
Coed, 4,716 undergraduate students, 85% full-time, 61% women, 39% men
Suburban 308-acre campus with easy access to New York City
Moderately difficult entrance level, 75% of applicants were admitted

Freshmen *Admission:* 4,418 applied, 3,382 were accepted, 806 enrolled. *Test scores:* SAT verbal scores over 500: 48%; SAT math scores over 500: 48%; SAT verbal scores over 600: 11%; SAT math scores over 600: 12%; SAT verbal scores over 700: 1%; SAT math scores over 700: 1%.
Tuition and fees (2003–04): $20,490 (full-time). *Room and board:* $7730 (room only: $5150).
Financial Aid (All incoming freshmen): *Average need-based gift aid:* $6400. *Average non-need based aid:* $4500. *Average aid to full-time undergraduates:* $9800.
Athletic Department: *Director of Athletics:* Vincent Salamone; Phone: 516-299-2288; Fax: 516-299-3155; E-mail: vsalam@liu.edu. *Sports Information Director:* Brad Sullivan; Phone: 516-299-4156; E-mail: bsulliva@liu.edu.

MEN'S COACHES

Baseball: Dick Vining; Phone: 516-299-2938.
Basketball: Tom Galeazzi; Phone: 516-299-2939.
Cheerleading: Jessica Rector; Phone: 516-299-2684.
Cross Country: Andy Young; Phone: 516-299-3855; E-mail: posttf@cs.com.
Lacrosse: Tom Postel; Phone: 516-299-3851; E-mail: tpostel370@aol.com.
Soccer: Danny Longo; Phone: 516-299-3856.
Track and Field: Andy Young; Phone: 516-299-3855; E-mail: posttf@cs.com.

WOMEN'S COACHES

Basketball: Patrick Walker; Phone: 516-299-3853; E-mail: patrice.walker@liu.edu.
Cheerleading: Jessica Rector; Phone: 516-299-2684.
Cross Country: Andy Young; Phone: 516-299-3855; E-mail: posttf@cs.com.
Field Hockey: Raenee Savin; Phone: 516-299-3857.
Lacrosse: Karen MacCrate; Phone: 516-299-2286; E-mail: karen.maccrate@liu.edu.
Soccer: Drayson Hounsome; Phone: 516-299-3856.
Softball: Jamie Apicella; Phone: 516-299-3857; E-mail: james.apicella@liu.edu.

Swimming: Maureen Travers; Phone: 516-299-3371; E-mail: maureen.travers@liu.edu.
Tennis: Renie Sokdowski; Phone: 516-299-4187.
Track and Field: Andy Young; Phone: 516-299-3855; E-mail: posttf@cs.com.
Volleyball: Sue Cassidy; Phone: 516-299-3854; E-mail: postvbcoach@aol.com.

LONG ISLAND UNIVERSITY, SOUTHAMPTON COLLEGE
Southampton, New York

Colonials ◆ NCAA II ◆ New York Collegiate Athletic Conference ◆ http://www.southampton.liu.edu/

Independent comprehensive, founded 1963, part of Long Island University
Coed, 1,196 undergraduate students, 89% full-time, 67% women, 33% men
Small-town 110-acre campus
Moderately difficult entrance level, 61% of applicants were admitted

Freshmen *Admission:* 1,354 applied, 856 were accepted, 224 enrolled. *Test scores:* SAT verbal scores over 500: 64%; SAT math scores over 500: 60%; SAT verbal scores over 600: 21%; SAT math scores over 600: 21%; SAT verbal scores over 700: 2%; SAT math scores over 700: 2%.
Tuition and fees (2003–04): $20,560 (full-time). *Room and board:* $8810 (room only: $5030).
Financial Aid (All incoming freshmen): *Average need-based gift aid:* $14,875. *Average non-need based aid:* $8000. *Average aid to full-time undergraduates:* $23,500.
Athletic Department: *Director of Athletics:* Mary Topping; Phone: 631-287-8385; Fax: 631-287-8188; E-mail: mtopping@southampton.liu.edu. *Sports Information Director:* Darren Johnson; Phone: 631-287-8360; E-mail: djohnson@southampton.liu.edu.
MEN'S COACHES
Basketball: Peter Quinn; Phone: 631-287-8386; E-mail: pquinn@southampton.liu.edu.
Lacrosse: Ralph Pepe; Phone: 631-287-8386.
Soccer: Andreas Lindberg; Phone: 631-287-8386; E-mail: alindberg@southampton.liu.edu.
Tennis: Marcus Donahue; Phone: 631-287-8386.
Volleyball: John Lenihan; Phone: 631-287-8386.
WOMEN'S COACHES
Basketball: Pat McGunnigle; Phone: 631-287-8386; E-mail: pmcgunnigle@southampton.liu.edu.
Soccer: Mark Dawson; Phone: 631-287-8386; E-mail: wsoccer@southampton.liu.edu.
Softball: Cassie Arroyo; Phone: 631-287-8387; E-mail: carroyo@southampton.liu.edu.
Tennis: Marcus Donahue; Phone: 631-287-8386.
Volleyball: Toby Pantophlet; Phone: 631-287-8386.

LONGWOOD UNIVERSITY
Farmville, Virginia

Lancers ◆ NCAA II ◆ Carolinas-Virginia Athletics Conference ◆ http://www.longwood.edu/

State-supported comprehensive, founded 1839, part of The State Council of Higher Education for Virginia (SCHEV)
Coed, 3,685 undergraduate students, 97% full-time, 66% women, 34% men
Small-town 160-acre campus with easy access to Richmond
Moderately difficult entrance level, 66% of applicants were admitted

Freshmen *Admission:* 3,472 applied, 2,441 were accepted, 880 enrolled. *Test scores:* SAT verbal scores over 500: 79%; SAT math scores over 500: 75%; SAT verbal scores over 600: 19%; SAT math scores over 600: 15%; SAT verbal scores over 700: 1%; SAT math scores over 700: 1%.

Tuition and fees (2003–04): $5877 (resident), $11,803 (nonresident). *Room and board:* $5298 (room only: $3114).
Financial Aid (All incoming freshmen): *Average need-based gift aid:* $3954. *Average non-need based aid:* $3357. *Average aid to full-time undergraduates:* $6528.
Athletic Department: *Director of Athletics:* Rick Mazzuto; Phone: 434-395-2057; Fax: 434-395-2568; E-mail: rmazzuto@longwood.edu. *Sports Information Director:* Greg Prouty; Phone: 434-395-2097; E-mail: gprouty@longwood.edu.
MEN'S COACHES
Baseball: Buddy Bolding; Phone: 434-395-2352; E-mail: bbolding@longwood.edu.
Basketball: Mike Gillian; Phone: 434-395-2838; E-mail: mgillian@longwood.edu.
Cheerleading: Jennifer Stanley; Phone: 434-395-2000.
Cross Country: Rich Firth; Phone: 434-395-2132; E-mail: rfirth@longwood.edu.
Golf: Kevin Fillman; Phone: 434-395-2563; E-mail: kfillman@longwood.edu.
Soccer: Dave Barrueta; Phone: 434-395-2681; E-mail: dbarruet@longwood.edu.
Tennis: Pat Breen; Phone: 434-395-2757; E-mail: pbreen@longwood.edu.
WOMEN'S COACHES
Basketball: Shirley Duncan; Phone: 434-395-2559; E-mail: sduncan@longwood.edu.
Cheerleading: Jennifer Stanley; Phone: 434-395-2000.
Cross Country: Rich Firth; Phone: 434-395-2132; E-mail: rfirth@longwood.edu.
Field Hockey: Nancy Joel; Phone: 434-395-2562; E-mail: njoel@longwood.edu.
Golf: Lane Pace; Phone: 434-395-2565; E-mail: lpace@longwood.edu.
Lacrosse: Janet Grubbs; Phone: 434-395-2566; E-mail: lpace@longwood.edu.
Soccer: Todd Dyer; Phone: 434-395-2794; E-mail: tdyer@longwood.edu.
Softball: Kathy Riley; Phone: 434-395-2353; E-mail: kriley@longwood.edu.
Tennis: Pat Breen; Phone: 434-395-2757; E-mail: pbreen@longwood.edu.

LORAS COLLEGE
Dubuque, Iowa

Duhawks ◆ NCAA III ◆ Iowa Athletic Conference ◆ http://www.loras.edu/

Independent Roman Catholic comprehensive, founded 1839
Coed, 1,613 undergraduate students, 96% full-time, 51% women, 49% men
Suburban 60-acre campus
Moderately difficult entrance level, 93% of applicants were admitted

Freshmen *Admission:* 1,453 applied, 1,388 were accepted, 414 enrolled. *Test scores:* SAT verbal scores over 500: 77%; SAT math scores over 500: 81%; SAT verbal scores over 600: 15%; SAT math scores over 600: 19%; SAT verbal scores over 700: 10%; SAT math scores over 700: 5%.
Tuition and fees (2003–04): $18,338 (full-time). *Room and board:* $5895 (room only: $2900).
Financial Aid (All incoming freshmen): *Average need-based gift aid:* $6585. *Average non-need based aid:* $6469. *Average aid to full-time undergraduates:* $17,834.
Athletic Department: *Director of Athletics:* Greg Capell; Phone: 563-588-7112; Fax: 563-557-4087; E-mail: greg.capell@loras.edu. *Sports Information Director:* Tom Galbraith; Phone: 563-588-7407; E-mail: thomas.galbrai@loras.edu.
MEN'S COACHES
Baseball: Carl Tebon; Phone: 563-588-7732; E-mail: ctebon@loras.edu.
Basketball: Chad Walthall; Phone: 563-588-7736; E-mail: chad.walthall@loras.edu.
Cross Country: Gary Wittman; Phone: 563-588-7216; E-mail: gary.wittman@loras.edu.
Diving: Doug Collin; Phone: 563-588-7525; E-mail: douglas.colin@loras.edu.

Loras College *(continued)*

Football: Bob Bierie; Phone: 563-588-7208; E-mail: bob.bierie@loras. edu.
Golf: Denise Udelhofen; Phone: 563-588-7742; E-mail: denise. udelhofen@loras.edu.
Soccer: Dan Rothert; Phone: 563-588-4936; E-mail: daniel.rothert@ loras.edu.
Swimming: Doug Collin; Phone: 563-588-7525; E-mail: douglas.colin@ loras.edu.
Tennis: Alejandro Pino; Phone: 563-588-7205; E-mail: alejandro.pino@ loras.edu.
Track and Field: Desiree Orwig-Gremmel; Phone: 563-588-7491; E-mail: desiree.gremmel@loras.edu.
Wrestling: Randy Steward; Phone: 563-588-7925; E-mail: randy.steward@loras.edu.

WOMEN'S COACHES

Basketball: Larry Lawlor; Phone: 563-588-7947; E-mail: llawler@loras. edu.
Cross Country: Gary Wittman; Phone: 563-588-7216; E-mail: gary. wittman@loras.edu.
Diving: Doug Collin; Phone: 563-588-7525; E-mail: douglas.colin@ loras.edu.
Golf: Denise Udelhofen; Phone: 563-588-7742; E-mail: denise. udelhofen@loras.edu.
Soccer: Dan Rothert; Phone: 563-588-4936; E-mail: daniel.rothert@ loras.edu.
Softball: Sarah Anderson; Phone: 563-588-7156; E-mail: sarah. anderson@loras.edu.
Swimming: Doug Collin; Phone: 563-588-7525; E-mail: douglas.colin@ loras.edu.
Tennis: Alejandro Pino; Phone: 563-588-7205; E-mail: alejandro.pino@ loras.edu.
Track and Field: Desiree Orwig-Gremmel; Phone: 563-588-7491; E-mail: desiree.gremmel@loras.edu.
Volleyball: Brian Meeter; Phone: 563-588-7459; E-mail: brian.meeter@ loras.edu.

LOUISIANA COLLEGE
Pineville, Louisiana

Wildcats ◆ NCAA III ◆ American Southwest Conference ◆ http://www.lacollege.edu/

Independent Southern Baptist 4-year, founded 1906
Coed, 1,135 undergraduate students, 86% full-time, 57% women, 43% men
Small-town 81-acre campus
Moderately difficult entrance level, 79% of applicants were admitted

Freshmen *Admission:* 727 applied, 618 were accepted, 266 enrolled. *Test scores:* SAT verbal scores over 500: 43%; SAT math scores over 500: 47%; SAT verbal scores over 600: 9%; SAT math scores over 600: 25%; SAT math scores over 700: 3%.
Tuition and fees (2003–04): $9650 (full-time). *Room and board:* $3610 (room only: $1550).
Financial Aid (All incoming freshmen): *Average need-based gift aid:* $3267. *Average non-need based aid:* $4216. *Average aid to full-time undergraduates:* $9366.
Athletic Department: *Director of Athletics:* Tim Whitman; Phone: 318-487-7559; Fax: 318-487-7174; E-mail: whitman@lacollege.edu. *Sports Information Director:* Alex Goodling; Phone: 318-487-7590; E-mail: goodling@lacollege.edu.

MEN'S COACHES

Baseball: Mike Byrnes; Phone: 318-487-7322; E-mail: byrnes@ lacollege.edu.
Basketball: Gene Rushing; Phone: 318-487-7503; E-mail: rushing@ lacollege.edu.
Football: Marty Secord; Phone: 318-487-7725; E-mail: secord@ lacollege.edu.
Golf: Billy Brooks; Phone: 318-487-7502; E-mail: brooks@lacollege. edu.
Soccer: James Decker; Phone: 318-487-7559; E-mail: decker@lacollege. edu.

WOMEN'S COACHES

Basketball: Tonya Sanders McIntosh; Phone: 318-487-7432; E-mail: sanders@lacollege.edu.

Cross Country: Philip Perrin; Phone: 318-487-7432; E-mail: perrin@ lacollege.edu.
Soccer: James Decker; Phone: 318-487-7559; E-mail: decker@lacollege. edu.
Softball: Tim Whitman; Phone: 318-487-7131; E-mail: whitman@ lacollege.edu.
Tennis: Mona Lonesberry; Phone: 318-487-7559; E-mail: ramona11@ cox-internet.com.

LOUISIANA STATE UNIVERSITY AND AGRICULTURAL AND MECHANICAL COLLEGE
Baton Rouge, Louisiana

Tigers ◆ NCAA I ◆ Southeastern Conference ◆ http://www.lsu.edu/

State-supported university, founded 1860, part of Louisiana State University System
Coed, 26,156 undergraduate students, 91% full-time, 53% women, 47% men
Urban 2,000-acre campus with easy access to New Orleans
Moderately difficult entrance level, 79% of applicants were admitted

Freshmen *Admission:* 10,147 applied, 8,171 were accepted, 5,428 enrolled.
Tuition and fees (2003–04): $3910 (resident), $9210 (nonresident). *Room and board:* $5216 (room only: $3150).
Financial Aid (All incoming freshmen): *Average need-based gift aid:* $4194. *Average non-need based aid:* $3575. *Average aid to full-time undergraduates:* $5184.
Athletic Department: *Director of Athletics:* Skip Bertman; Phone: 225-578-3600; Fax: 225-578-2430; E-mail: skipbertman@lsu.edu. *Sports Information Director:* Michael Bonnette; Phone: 225-578-8226; E-mail: mbonnet@lsu.edu.

MEN'S COACHES

Baseball: Smoke Laval; Phone: 225-578-4148; E-mail: rlaval1@lsu.edu.
Basketball: John Brady; Phone: 225-578-8217; E-mail: jbrady2@lsu. edu.
Cheerleading: Pauline Zernott; Phone: 225-578-8001.
Cross Country: Pat Henry; Phone: 225-578-8627; E-mail: phenry1@lsu. edu.
Diving: Doug Shaffer; Phone: 225-578-3947; E-mail: djshaffer@lsu.edu.
Football: Nick Saban; Phone: 225-578-1151; E-mail: football@lsu.edu.
Golf: Greg Jones; Phone: 225-578-0494; E-mail: gjones3@lsu.edu.
Swimming: Jeff Cavana; Phone: 225-578-3947; E-mail: jcavana@lsu. edu.
Tennis: Jeff Brown; Phone: 225-578-3947; E-mail: jbrow29@lsu.edu.
Track and Field: Pat Henry; Phone: 225-578-8627; E-mail: phenry1@lsu. edu.

WOMEN'S COACHES

Basketball: Sue Gunter; Phone: 225-578-6643; E-mail: sgunte1@lsu. edu.
Cheerleading: Pauline Zernott; Phone: 225-578-8001.
Cross Country: Pat Henry; Phone: 225-578-8627; E-mail: phenry1@lsu. edu.
Diving: Doug Shaffer; Phone: 225-578-3947; E-mail: djshaffer@lsu.edu.
Golf: Karen Bahnsen; Phone: 225-578-1281; E-mail: kbahnse@lsu.edu.
Gymnastics: D.D.Breaux; Phone: 225-578-5050; E-mail: dbreaux@lsu. edu.
Soccer: George Fotopolous; Phone: 225-578-8769; E-mail: gfotop1@ lsu.edu.
Softball: Yvette Girouard; Phone: 225-578-3947; E-mail: ygirouard@ yahoo.com.
Swimming: Jeff Cavana; Phone: 225-578-3947; E-mail: jcavana@lsu. edu.
Tennis: Tony Minnis; Phone: 225-578-8627; E-mail: tminni2@lsu.edu.
Track and Field: Pat Henry; Phone: 225-578-8627; E-mail: phenry1@lsu. edu.
Volleyball: Fran Flory; Phone: 225-578-5050; E-mail: frflory@lsu.edu.

LOUISIANA STATE UNIVERSITY IN SHREVEPORT
Shreveport, Louisiana

Pilots ◆ NAIA ◆ Gulf Coast Conference
◆ http://www.lsus.edu/

State-supported comprehensive, founded 1965, part of Louisiana State University System
Coed, 3,655 undergraduate students, 70% full-time, 62% women, 38% men
Urban 200-acre campus
Noncompetitive entrance level, 68% of applicants were admitted

Freshmen *Admission:* 848 applied, 579 were accepted, 579 enrolled.
Tuition and fees (2003–04): $2884 (resident), $7214 (nonresident). *Room only:* $2196.
Athletic Department: *Director of Athletics:* Doug Robinson; Phone: 318-798-4107; Fax: 318-798-4179; E-mail: drobinso@pilot.lsus.edu. *Sports Information Director:* Rocke Musgraves; Phone: 318-798-4106; E-mail: rmusgrav@pilot.lsus.edu.

MEN'S COACHES
Baseball: Rocke Musgraves; Phone: 318-798-4106; E-mail: rmusgrav@pilot.lsus.edu.
Basketball: Chad McDowell; Phone: 318-798-4110; E-mail: cmcdowel@pilot.lsus.edu.

WOMEN'S COACHES
Basketball: Ronnie Howell; Phone: 318-798-4111; E-mail: rhowell@pilot.lsus.edu.
Soccer: Phone: 318-798-4107.

LOUISIANA TECH UNIVERSITY
Ruston, Louisiana

Bulldogs ◆ NCAA I ◆ Western Athletic Conference ◆ http://www.latech.edu/

State-supported university, founded 1894, part of University of Louisiana System
Coed, 9,739 undergraduate students, 82% full-time, 48% women, 52% men
Small-town 247-acre campus
Moderately difficult entrance level, 92% of applicants were admitted

Freshmen *Admission:* 3,768 applied, 3,454 were accepted, 2,107 enrolled.
Tuition and fees (2003–04): $3270 (resident), $7065 (nonresident). *Room and board:* $3885 (room only: $2025).
Financial Aid (All incoming freshmen): *Average need-based gift aid:* $4396. *Average non-need based aid:* $5010. *Average aid to full-time undergraduates:* $5382.
Athletic Department: *Director of Athletics:* Jim Oakes; Phone: 318-257-4111; Fax: 318-257-4437; E-mail: jimoakes@latech.edu. *Sports Information Director:* Malcolm Butler; Phone: 318-257-4111; E-mail: mbutler@latech.edu.

MEN'S COACHES
Baseball: Wade Simoneaux; Phone: 318-257-4111; E-mail: wade@latech.edu.
Basketball: Keith Richard; Phone: 318-257-4111; E-mail: ltbbball@latech.edu.
Cross Country: Gary Stanley; Phone: 318-257-4111; E-mail: runfast@latech.edu.
Football: Jack Bicknell; Phone: 318-257-4546; E-mail: bicknell@latech.edu.
Golf: Tom Stinson; Phone: 318-257-4111; E-mail: tstinson@latech.edu.
Track and Field: Gary Stanley; Phone: 318-257-4111; E-mail: runfast@latech.edu.

WOMEN'S COACHES
Basketball: Kurt Budke; Phone: 318-257-4111; E-mail: kbudke@latech.edu.
Cross Country: Gary Stanley; Phone: 318-257-4111; E-mail: runfast@latech.edu.
Softball: Sarah Dawson; Phone: 318-257-4111; E-mail: sdgirlfive@aol.com.

Tennis: Greg Hearn; Phone: 318-257-4111; E-mail: g10s@yahoo.com.
Track and Field: Gary Stanley; Phone: 318-257-4111; E-mail: runfast@latech.edu.
Volleyball: Heather Mazeitis; Phone: 318-257-4111; E-mail: mazeitis@latech.edu.

LOYOLA COLLEGE IN MARYLAND
Baltimore, Maryland

Greyhounds ◆ NCAA I ◆ Metro Atlantic Athletic Conference
◆ http://www.loyola.edu/

Independent Roman Catholic (Jesuit) comprehensive, founded 1852
Coed, 3,413 undergraduate students, 98% full-time, 58% women, 42% men
Urban 89-acre campus with easy access to Washington, DC
Moderately difficult entrance level, 71% of applicants were admitted

Freshmen *Admission:* 6,611 applied, 4,675 were accepted, 916 enrolled. *Test scores:* SAT verbal scores over 500: 96%; SAT math scores over 500: 97%; SAT verbal scores over 600: 52%; SAT math scores over 600: 62%; SAT verbal scores over 700: 11%; SAT math scores over 700: 10%.
Tuition and fees (2003–04): $26,610 (full-time). *Room and board:* $8630 (room only: $6630).
Financial Aid (All incoming freshmen): *Average need-based gift aid:* $11,215. *Average non-need based aid:* $10,733. *Average aid to full-time undergraduates:* $18,700.
Athletic Department: *Director of Athletics:* Joe Boylan; Phone: 410-617-2553; Fax: 410-617-5029; E-mail: jboylan@loyola.edu. *Sports Information Director:* Tom Milajecki; Phone: 410-617-2777; E-mail: twmilajecki@loyola.edu.

MEN'S COACHES
Basketball: Scott Hicks; Phone: 410-617-2437; E-mail: shicks@loyola.edu.
Cheerleading: Denise Thomas; Phone: 410-617-7419; E-mail: dmthomas@loyola.edu.
Cross Country: Chris Bayless; Phone: 410-617-2076; E-mail: runcoach@aol.com.
Diving: Meghan Devine; Phone: 410-617-2388.
Golf: Tom Beidleman; Phone: 410-617-2683; E-mail: tsbpro1@comcast.net.
Lacrosse: Bill Dirrigl; Phone: 410-617-2041; E-mail: ctoomey1@loyola.edu.
Soccer: Mark Mettrick; Phone: 410-617-2379; E-mail: mmettrick@loyola.edu.
Swimming: Brian Loeffler; Phone: 410-617-2388; E-mail: bloeffler@loyola.edu.
Tennis: Rick McClure; Phone: 410-617-2081; E-mail: rmcclure@loyola.edu.

WOMEN'S COACHES
Basketball: Candy Cage; Phone: 410-617-2283; E-mail: ccage@loyola.edu.
Cheerleading: Denise Thomas; Phone: 410-617-7419; E-mail: dmthomas@loyola.edu.
Cross Country: Chris Bayless; Phone: 410-617-2076; E-mail: runcoach@aol.com.
Diving: Meghan Devine; Phone: 410-617-2388.
Lacrosse: Kerri Johnson; Phone: 410-617-2535; E-mail: daikens@loyola.edu.
Soccer: Joe Mallia; Phone: 410-617-5279; E-mail: jmallia@loyola.edu.
Swimming: Brian Loeffler; Phone: 410-617-2388; E-mail: bloeffler@loyola.edu.
Tennis: Rick McClure; Phone: 410-617-2081; E-mail: rmcclure@loyola.edu.
Volleyball: Jennifer Briggs; Phone: 410-617-2772; E-mail: jbriggs2@loyola.edu.

LOYOLA MARYMOUNT UNIVERSITY
Los Angeles, California

Lions ◆ NCAA I ◆ West Coast Conference; Western Athletic Conference ◆ http://www.lmu.edu/

Independent Roman Catholic comprehensive, founded 1911
Coed, 5,699 undergraduate students, 93% full-time, 60% women, 40% men
Suburban 128-acre campus
Very difficult entrance level, 54% of applicants were admitted

Freshmen *Admission:* 7,833 applied, 4,568 were accepted, 1,335 enrolled. *Test scores:* SAT verbal scores over 500: 87%; SAT math scores over 500: 88%; SAT verbal scores over 600: 36%; SAT math scores over 600: 42%; SAT verbal scores over 700: 4%; SAT math scores over 700: 6%.
Tuition and fees (2003–04): $23,934 (full-time). *Room and board:* $8260 (room only: $6010).
Financial Aid (All incoming freshmen): *Average need-based gift aid:* $13,159. *Average non-need based aid:* $6919. *Average aid to full-time undergraduates:* $18,342.
Athletic Department: *Director of Athletics:* William Husak; Phone: 310-338-5940; Fax: 310-338-5915; E-mail: whusak@lmu.edu. *Sports Information Director:* John Shaffer; Phone: 310-338-7643; E-mail: jshaffer@lmu.edu.

MEN'S COACHES
Baseball: Frank Cruz; Phone: 310-338-2949; E-mail: fcruz@lmu.edu.
Basketball: Steve Aggers; Phone: 310-338-4530; E-mail: lmuhoops@lmu.edu.
Cheerleading: Niki Neville; Phone: 310-258-8608; E-mail: khandela@lmu.edu.
Cross Country: Scott Guerrero; Phone: 310-338-7630; E-mail: sguerrer@lmu.edu.
Golf: Alex Galvan; Phone: 310-258-8619; E-mail: agalvan@lmu.edu.
Soccer: Paul Krumpe; Phone: 310-338-7640; E-mail: pkrumpe@lmu.edu.
Tennis: Nik Devore; Phone: 310-338-7589; E-mail: ndevore@lmu.edu.

WOMEN'S COACHES
Basketball: Julie Wilhoit; Phone: 310-338-4530; E-mail: jwilhoit@lmu.edu.
Cheerleading: Niki Neville; Phone: 310-258-8608; E-mail: khandela@lmu.edu.
Cross Country: Scott Guerrero; Phone: 310-338-7630; E-mail: sguerrer@lmu.edu.
Diving: John Loughran; Phone: 310-338-1844; E-mail: jloughra@lmu.edu.
Soccer: Gregg Murphy; Phone: 310-338-2795; E-mail: gmurphy@lmu.edu.
Softball: Gary Ferrin; Phone: 310-338-7651; E-mail: gferrin@lmu.edu.
Swimming: John Loughran; Phone: 310-338-1844; E-mail: jloughra@lmu.edu.
Tennis: Jamie Sanchez; Phone: 310-338-7506.
Volleyball: Steve Stratos; Phone: 310-338-4528; E-mail: sstratos@lmu.edu.

LOYOLA UNIVERSITY CHICAGO
Chicago, Illinois

Ramblers ◆ NCAA I ◆ Horizon League Conference; Midwestern Intercollegiate Volleyball Conference ◆ http://www.luc.edu/

Independent Roman Catholic (Jesuit) university, founded 1870
Coed, 7,916 undergraduate students, 83% full-time, 66% women, 34% men
Urban 105-acre campus
Moderately difficult entrance level, 81% of applicants were admitted

Freshmen *Admission:* 11,009 applied, 9,078 were accepted, 1,915 enrolled. *Test scores:* SAT verbal scores over 500: 86%; SAT math scores over 500: 80%; SAT verbal scores over 600: 44%; SAT math scores over 600: 40%; SAT verbal scores over 700: 8%; SAT math scores over 700: 5%.

Tuition and fees (2004–05): $22,340 (full-time). *Room and board:* $8824 (room only: $5974).
Financial Aid (All incoming freshmen): *Average need-based gift aid:* $16,813. *Average non-need based aid:* $7956. *Average aid to full-time undergraduates:* $20,241.
Athletic Department: *Director of Athletics:* John Planek; Phone: 773-508-2560; Fax: 773-508-3884; E-mail: jplanek@luc.edu. *Sports Information Director:* Bill Behrns; Phone: 773-508-2575; E-mail: bbehrns@luc.edu.

MEN'S COACHES
Basketball: Larry Farmer; Phone: 773-508-2564; E-mail: lfarme1@luc.edu.
Cheerleading: Beccy Sullivan; Phone: 773-869-9405.
Cross Country: Marc Burns; Phone: 773-508-2582; E-mail: mburns2@luc.edu.
Golf: Pat Dorgan; Phone: 773-508-2493; E-mail: pdorgan@luc.edu.
Soccer: Ray O'Connell; Phone: 773-508-2570; E-mail: roconne@luc.edu.
Track and Field: Marc Burns; Phone: 773-508-2582; E-mail: mburns2@luc.edu.
Volleyball: Shane Davis; Phone: 773-508-8897; E-mail: sdavis6@luc.edu.

WOMEN'S COACHES
Basketball: Mary Walker; Phone: 773-508-2558; E-mail: mwalke1@luc.edu.
Cheerleading: Beccy Sullivan; Phone: 773-869-9405.
Cross Country: Marc Burns; Phone: 773-508-2582; E-mail: mburns2@luc.edu.
Golf: Nate Miklos; Phone: 773-350-1511; E-mail: n8miklos@hotmail.com.
Soccer: Brendan Eitz; Phone: 773-508-2561; E-mail: beitz@luc.edu.
Softball: Jamie Gillies; Phone: 773-508-2580; E-mail: jgillie@luc.edu.
Track and Field: Marc Burns; Phone: 773-508-2582; E-mail: mburns2@luc.edu.
Volleyball: Liz Nelson; Phone: 773-508-8749; E-mail: enelso1@luc.edu.

LOYOLA UNIVERSITY NEW ORLEANS
New Orleans, Louisiana

Wolfpack ◆ NAIA ◆ Gulf Coast Conference ◆ http://www.loyno.edu/

Independent Roman Catholic (Jesuit) comprehensive, founded 1912
Coed, 3,747 undergraduate students, 88% full-time, 62% women, 38% men
Urban 26-acre campus
Moderately difficult entrance level, 66% of applicants were admitted

Freshmen *Admission:* 3,609 applied, 2,485 were accepted, 864 enrolled. *Test scores:* SAT verbal scores over 500: 96%; SAT math scores over 500: 96%; SAT verbal scores over 600: 66%; SAT math scores over 600: 59%; SAT verbal scores over 700: 11%; SAT math scores over 700: 6%.
Tuition and fees (2004–05): $23,618 (full-time). *Room and board:* $7994 (room only: $4924).
Financial Aid (All incoming freshmen): *Average need-based gift aid:* $13,693. *Average non-need based aid:* $10,197. *Average aid to full-time undergraduates:* $18,470.
Athletic Department: *Director of Athletics:* Jerry Hernandez; Phone: 504-864-7711; Fax: 504-864-7380; E-mail: gjhernan@loyno.edu. *Sports Information Director:* Brett Simpson; Phone: 504-864-7396; E-mail: bsimpson@loyno.edu.

MEN'S COACHES
Baseball: Gregg Mucerino; Phone: 504-864-7392; E-mail: gmucerin@loyno.edu.
Basketball: Jerry Hernandez; Phone: 504-864-7225; E-mail: gjhernan@loyno.edu.
Cross Country: Al Seither; Phone: 504-864-7395; E-mail: aseither@loyno.edu.
Track and Field: Al Seither; Phone: 504-864-7395; E-mail: aseither@loyno.edu.

WOMEN'S COACHES
Basketball: DoBee Plaisance; Phone: 504-864-7577; E-mail: mplaisan@loyno.edu.

Cross Country: Al Seither; Phone: 504-864-7395; E-mail: aseither@loyno.edu.
Soccer: Emmy Therrell; Phone: 504-864-7398; E-mail: therrell@loyno.edu.
Track and Field: Al Seither; Phone: 504-864-7395; E-mail: aseither@loyno.edu.
Volleyball: Tommy Harold; Phone: 504-864-7397; E-mail: tharold@loyno.edu.

LUBBOCK CHRISTIAN UNIVERSITY
Lubbock, Texas

Chaparrals ◆ NAIA ◆ Sooner Conference
◆ http://www.lcu.edu/

Independent religious comprehensive, founded 1957, affiliated with Church of Christ
Coed, 1,759 undergraduate students, 77% full-time, 58% women, 42% men
Suburban 120-acre campus
Moderately difficult entrance level, 73% of applicants were admitted

Freshmen *Admission:* 807 applied, 579 were accepted, 298 enrolled. *Test scores:* SAT verbal scores over 500: 57%; SAT math scores over 500: 50%; SAT verbal scores over 600: 16%; SAT math scores over 600: 11%; SAT verbal scores over 700: 1%.
Tuition and fees (2003–04): $11,452 (full-time). *Room and board:* $4380 (room only: $2460).
Financial Aid (All incoming freshmen): *Average need-based gift aid:* $7658. *Average non-need based aid:* $9096. *Average aid to full-time undergraduates:* $11,057.
Athletic Department: *Director of Athletics:* John Copeland; Phone: 806-796-8800; Fax: 806-796-8642; E-mail: john.copeland@lcu.edu. *Sports Information Director:* Kelly Robinson; Phone: 806-796-8800.

MEN'S COACHES
Baseball: Nathan Blackwood; Phone: 806-796-8800; E-mail: nathan.blackwood@lcu.edu.
Basketball: John Copeland; Phone: 806-796-8800; E-mail: john.copeland@lcu.edu.

WOMEN'S COACHES
Basketball: Steve Gomez; Phone: 806-796-8800; E-mail: steve.gomez@lcu.edu.
Volleyball: Steven McRoberts; Phone: 806-796-8800; E-mail: steven.mcroberts@lcu.edu.

LUTHER COLLEGE
Decorah, Iowa

Norse ◆ NCAA III ◆ Iowa Athletic Conference ◆ http://www.luther.edu/

Independent religious 4-year, founded 1861, affiliated with Evangelical Lutheran Church in America
Coed, 2,565 undergraduate students, 98% full-time, 60% women, 40% men
Small-town 800-acre campus
Moderately difficult entrance level, 7% of applicants were admitted

Freshmen *Admission:* 1,998 applied, 1,537 were accepted, 668 enrolled. *Test scores:* SAT verbal scores over 500: 86%; SAT math scores over 500: 88%; SAT verbal scores over 600: 44%; SAT math scores over 600: 54%; SAT verbal scores over 700: 12%; SAT math scores over 700: 10%.
Tuition and fees (2004–05): $23,070 (full-time). *Room and board:* $4170 (room only: $2040).
Financial Aid (All incoming freshmen): *Average need-based gift aid:* $11,410. *Average non-need based aid:* $6584. *Average aid to full-time undergraduates:* $16,803.
Athletic Department: *Director of Athletics:* Joe Thompson; Phone: 563-387-1583; Fax: 563-387-1458; E-mail: thompsjo@luther.edu. *Sports Information Director:* Dave Blanchard; Phone: 563-387-1583; E-mail: blanchda@luther.edu.

MEN'S COACHES
Baseball: Brian Gillobly; Phone: 563-387-1590; E-mail: gillbr01@luther.edu.
Basketball: Jeff Olinger; Phone: 563-387-1588; E-mail: olingeje@luther.edu.
Cross Country: Jeff Wettach; Phone: 563-387-1577; E-mail: wettacje@luther.edu.
Diving: Lance Huber; Phone: 563-387-1578; E-mail: hubela01@luther.edu.
Football: Paul Hefty; Phone: 563-387-2491; E-mail: heftpa01@luther.edu.
Golf: Scott Fjelstul; Phone: 563-387-5210; E-mail: fjelstul@rconnect.com.
Soccer: Doug Mello; Phone: 563-387-2161; E-mail: mellodou@luther.edu.
Swimming: Lance Huber; Phone: 563-387-1578; E-mail: hubela01@luther.edu.
Tennis: Brian Huinker; Phone: 563-387-2181; E-mail: huinbr01@luther.edu.
Track and Field: Jeff Wettach; Phone: 563-387-1577; E-mail: wettacje@luther.edu.
Wrestling: Dave Mitchell; Phone: 563-387-1713; E-mail: mitcheda@luther.edu.

WOMEN'S COACHES
Basketball: Jane Hildebrand; Phone: 563-387-1580; E-mail: hildebja@luther.edu.
Cross Country: Betsy Emerson; Phone: 563-387-1589; E-mail: emersoel@luther.edu.
Diving: Lance Huber; Phone: 563-387-1578; E-mail: hubela01@luther.edu.
Golf: Jason Berg; Phone: 563-387-2128; E-mail: bergjaso@luther.edu.
Softball: Renae Hartl; Phone: 563-387-1244; E-mail: hartre01@luther.edu.
Swimming: Lance Huber; Phone: 563-387-1578; E-mail: hubela01@luther.edu.
Tennis: Su Oertel; Phone: 563-387-1582; E-mail: oertelsu@luther.edu.
Track and Field: Betsy Emerson; Phone: 563-387-1589; E-mail: emersoel@luther.edu.
Volleyball: Ellen Drewes-Stoew; Phone: 563-387-1587; E-mail: drewesel@luther.edu.

LYCOMING COLLEGE
Williamsport, Pennsylvania

Warriors ◆ NCAA III ◆ Freedom Conference ◆ http://www.lycoming.edu/

Independent United Methodist 4-year, founded 1812
Coed, 1,417 undergraduate students, 97% full-time, 55% women, 45% men
Small-town 35-acre campus
Moderately difficult entrance level, 77% of applicants were admitted

Freshmen *Admission:* 1,449 applied, 1,156 were accepted, 366 enrolled. *Test scores:* SAT verbal scores over 500: 74%; SAT math scores over 500: 72%; SAT verbal scores over 600: 26%; SAT math scores over 600: 27%; SAT verbal scores over 700: 2%; SAT math scores over 700: 1%.
Tuition and fees (2003–04): $21,723 (full-time). *Room and board:* $5866.
Financial Aid (All incoming freshmen): *Average need-based gift aid:* $13,827. *Average non-need based aid:* $9279. *Average aid to full-time undergraduates:* $15,818.
Athletic Department: *Director of Athletics:* Frank Girardi; Phone: 570-321-4260; Fax: 570-321-4158; E-mail: girardi@lycoming.edu. *Sports Information Director:* Robb Dietrich; Phone: 570-321-4208; E-mail: dietrich@lycoming.edu.

MEN'S COACHES
Basketball: Don Friday; Phone: 570-321-4262; E-mail: friday@lycoming.edu.
Cross Country: George Camp; Phone: 570-321-4020.
Football: Frank Girardi; Phone: 570-321-4260; E-mail: girardi@lycoming.edu.
Golf: James Spencer; Phone: 570-321-4251; E-mail: spencer@lycoming.edu.
Lacrosse: Shawn Rosa; Phone: 570-321-4251; E-mail: rosa@lycoming.edu.

Lycoming College *(continued)*

Soccer: Scott Kennell; Phone: 570-321-4308; E-mail: kennell@lycoming.edu.
Swimming: Jerry Hammaker; Phone: 570-321-4304; E-mail: hammaker@lycoming.edu.
Track and Field: Adrienne Wydra; Phone: 570-321-4308; E-mail: wydadri@lycoming.edu.
Wrestling: Roger Crebs; Phone: 570-321-4264; E-mail: crebs@lycoming.edu.

WOMEN'S COACHES

Basketball: Christen Ditzler; Phone: 570-321-4261; E-mail: ditzler@lycoming.edu.
Cross Country: George Camp; Phone: 570-321-4020.
Lacrosse: Kara Bates; Phone: 570-321-4254; E-mail: bates@lycoming.edu.
Soccer: Scott Kennell; Phone: 570-321-4254; E-mail: kennell@lycoming.edu.
Softball: Christen Ditzler; Phone: 570-321-4261; E-mail: ditzler@lycoming.edu.
Swimming: Jerry Hammaker; Phone: 570-321-4304; E-mail: hammaker@lycoming.edu.
Tennis: Deb Holmes; Phone: 570-321-4263; E-mail: holmes@lycoming.edu.
Track and Field: Adrienne Wydra; Phone: 570-321-4308; E-mail: wydadri@lycoming.edu.
Volleyball: Tim McMahon; Phone: 570-321-4252; E-mail: mcmahon@lycoming.edu.

LYNCHBURG COLLEGE

Lynchburg, Virginia

Hornets ◆ NCAA III ◆ Old Dominion Conference ◆ http://www.lynchburg.edu/

Independent religious comprehensive, founded 1903, affiliated with Christian Church (Disciples of Christ)
Coed, 1,777 undergraduate students, 93% full-time, 60% women, 40% men
Suburban 214-acre campus
Moderately difficult entrance level, 78% of applicants were admitted

Freshmen *Admission:* 3,119 applied, 2,380 were accepted, 589 enrolled. *Test scores:* SAT verbal scores over 500: 56%; SAT math scores over 500: 58%; SAT verbal scores over 600: 14%; SAT math scores over 600: 15%; SAT verbal scores over 700: 1%; SAT math scores over 700: 1%.
Tuition and fees (2003–04): $21,515 (full-time). *Room and board:* $4800 (room only: $2800).
Financial Aid (All incoming freshmen): *Average need-based gift aid:* $14,205. *Average non-need based aid:* $8238. *Average aid to full-time undergraduates:* $17,325.
Athletic Department: *Director of Athletics:* Jack Toms; Phone: 434-544-8498; Fax: 434-544-8365; E-mail: toms@lynchburg.edu. *Sports Information Director:* Mike Carpenter; Phone: 434-544-8495; E-mail: carpenter@lynchburg.edu.

MEN'S COACHES

Baseball: Percy Abell; Phone: 434-544-8496; E-mail: abell@lynchburg.edu.
Basketball: John Swickrath; Phone: 434-544-8490; E-mail: swickrath@lynchburg.edu.
Cheerleading: Gail Olsen; Phone: 434-544-8498; E-mail: olsen.g@lynchburg.edu.
Cross Country: Jack Toms; Phone: 434-544-8498; E-mail: toms@lynchburg.edu.
Golf: Will Andrews; Phone: 434-544-8429; E-mail: andrews.w@lynchburg.edu.
Lacrosse: Steve Koudelka; Phone: 434-544-8494; E-mail: koudelka@lynchburg.edu.
Soccer: Chris Yeager; Phone: 434-544-8326; E-mail: yeager@lynchburg.edu.
Tennis: Neal Cassidy; Phone: 434-544-8287; E-mail: cassidy.j@lynchburg.edu.
Track and Field: Jack Toms; Phone: 434-544-8498; E-mail: toms@lynchburg.edu.

WOMEN'S COACHES

Basketball: Richie Waggoner; Phone: 434-544-8684; E-mail: waggoner@lynchburg.edu.
Cheerleading: Gail Olsen; Phone: 434-544-8498; E-mail: olsen.g@lynchburg.edu.
Cross Country: Jack Toms; Phone: 434-544-8498; E-mail: toms@lynchburg.edu.
Field Hockey: Enza Steele; Phone: 434-544-8492; E-mail: steele@lynchburg.edu.
Lacrosse: Bruce Reid; Phone: 434-544-8429; E-mail: reid.ba@lynchburg.edu.
Soccer: Todd Olsen; Phone: 434-544-8491; E-mail: olsen.t@lynchburg.edu.
Softball: Dawn Simmons; Phone: 434-544-8493; E-mail: simmons@lynchburg.edu.
Tennis: Neal Cassidy; Phone: 434-544-8287; E-mail: cassidy.j@lynchburg.edu.
Track and Field: Jack Toms; Phone: 434-544-8498; E-mail: toms@lynchburg.edu.
Volleyball: Marie Lewis; Phone: 434-544-8388; E-mail: lewis.d@lynchburg.edu.

LYNDON STATE COLLEGE

Lyndonville, Vermont

Hornets ◆ NAIA ◆ Sunrise Conference
◆ http://www.lyndonstate.edu/

State-supported comprehensive, founded 1911, part of Vermont State Colleges System
Coed, 1,384 undergraduate students, 81% full-time, 55% women, 45% men
Rural 175-acre campus
Moderately difficult entrance level, 93% of applicants were admitted

Freshmen *Admission:* 941 applied, 881 were accepted, 368 enrolled. *Test scores:* SAT verbal scores over 500: 42%; SAT math scores over 500: 39%; SAT verbal scores over 600: 8%; SAT math scores over 600: 7%.
Tuition and fees (2003–04): $5806 (resident), $12,360 (nonresident). *Room and board:* $6014 (room only: $3518).
Athletic Department: *Director of Athletics:* Darrell Pound; Phone: 802-626-6477; Fax: 802-626-4806; E-mail: pounds@lyndonstate.edu. *Sports Information Director:* Christopher Ummer; Phone: 802-626-6224; E-mail: ummerc@lyndonstate.edu.

MEN'S COACHES

Baseball: Darrell Pound; Phone: 802-626-6477; E-mail: pounds@lyndonstate.edu.
Basketball: Eric Berry; Phone: 802-626-3928; E-mail: eric.berry@lyndonstate.edu.
Cross Country: Christopher Ummer; Phone: 802-626-6224; E-mail: ummerc@lyndonstate.edu.
Soccer: Darrell Pound; Phone: 802-626-6477; E-mail: pounds@lyndonstate.edu.
Tennis: Michael Smookler; Phone: 802-626-6706; E-mail: msmookler@surgarbush.com.

WOMEN'S COACHES

Basketball: Dave Mellor; Phone: 802-626-6244; E-mail: mellord@lyndonstate.edu.
Cross Country: Christopher Ummer; Phone: 802-626-6224; E-mail: ummerc@lyndonstate.edu.
Soccer: Miles Etter; Phone: 802-695-8834; E-mail: mmkirby5@hotmail.com.
Softball: Leigh Chamberlain; Phone: 802-626-4000; E-mail: leighc@kingcon.com.
Tennis: Mary Lou Bell; Phone: 802-626-5013; E-mail: mlbell@hcr.net.

LYNN UNIVERSITY
Boca Raton, Florida

Fighting Knights ◆ NCAA II ◆ Sunshine State Conference
◆ http://www.lynn.edu/

Independent comprehensive, founded 1962
Coed, 1,620 undergraduate students, 94% full-time, 48% women,
52% men
Suburban 123-acre campus with easy access to Fort Lauderdale
Minimally difficult entrance level, 78% of applicants were admitted

Freshmen *Admission:* 2,607 applied, 2,017 were accepted, 501 enrolled.
Test scores: SAT verbal scores over 500: 25%; SAT math scores over
500: 26%; SAT verbal scores over 600: 3%; SAT math scores over
600: 5%.
Tuition and fees (2003–04): $22,750 (full-time). *Room and board:* $8000.
Financial Aid (All incoming freshmen): *Average need-based gift aid:*
$10,880. *Average non-need based aid:* $9432. *Average aid to full-time
undergraduates:* $19,691.
Athletic Department: *Director of Athletics:* John McCarthy; Phone: 561-
237-7279; Fax: 561-237-7273; E-mail: jmccarthy@lynn.edu. *Sports
Information Director:* Ross Blacker; Phone: 561-237-7341; E-mail:
rblacker@lynn.edu.

MEN'S COACHES
Baseball: Rudy Garbalosa; Phone: 561-237-7242; E-mail: rgarbalosa@
lynn.edu.
Basketball: Scott McMillin; Phone: 561-237-7053.
Cheerleading: Kathleen Cosgrove; Phone: 561-237-7281.
Golf: Eric Abreu; Phone: 561-237-7238; E-mail: eabreu@lynn.edu.
Soccer: Shaun Pendleton; Phone: 561-237-7243; E-mail: spendleton@
lynn.edu.
Tennis: Mike Perez; Phone: 561-237-7241; E-mail: mperez@lynn.edu.

WOMEN'S COACHES
Basketball: Pam DeCosta; Phone: 561-237-7282; E-mail: pdecosta@
lynn.edu.
Cheerleading: Kathleen Cosgrove; Phone: 561-237-7281.
Golf: Courtney Krell; Phone: 561-237-7281; E-mail: ckrell@lynn.edu.
Soccer: Rocky Orezzoli; Phone: 561-237-7244; E-mail: rorezzoli@lynn.
edu.
Softball: Amy Youngblood; Phone: 561-237-7261; E-mail: aalderman@
lynn.edu.
Tennis: Mike Perez; Phone: 561-237-7241; E-mail: mperez@lynn.edu.
Volleyball: Ginny Kelly; Phone: 561-237-7951.

LYON COLLEGE
Batesville, Arkansas

Scots ◆ NAIA ◆ TranSouth Conference
◆ http://www.lyon.edu/

Independent Presbyterian 4-year, founded 1872
Coed, 490 undergraduate students, 92% full-time, 52% women,
48% men
Small-town 136-acre campus
Very difficult entrance level, 69% of applicants were admitted

Freshmen *Admission:* 427 applied, 309 were accepted, 120 enrolled.
Test scores: SAT verbal scores over 500: 81%; SAT math scores over
500: 74%; SAT verbal scores over 600: 37%; SAT math scores over
600: 30%; SAT verbal scores over 700: 11%; SAT math scores over
700: 8%.
Tuition and fees (2004–05): $13,130 (full-time). *Room and board:* $5820
(room only: $2390).
Financial Aid (All incoming freshmen): *Average need-based gift aid:*
$11,070. *Average non-need based aid:* $9625. *Average aid to full-time
undergraduates:* $13,728.
Athletic Department: *Director of Athletics:* Terry Garner; Phone: 870-
698-4221; Fax: 870-793-1763; E-mail: tgarner@lyon.edu. *Sports Information Director:* Monty McCurley; Phone: 870-793-1781; E-mail:
mmccurley@lyon.edu.

MEN'S COACHES
Baseball: Kirk Kelley; Phone: 870-698-4337; E-mail: kkelley@lyon.edu.
Basketball: Kevin Jenkins; Phone: 870-698-4220; E-mail: kjenkins@
lyon.edu.

Cross Country: Be Pham; Phone: 870-698-1788; E-mail: bpham@lyon.
edu.
Golf: Kevin Jenkins; Phone: 870-698-4220; E-mail: kjenkins@lyon.edu.
Soccer: Jeremy Bishop; Phone: 870-698-4245; E-mail: jbishop@lyon.
edu.
Tennis: Be Pham; Phone: 870-698-1788; E-mail: bpham@lyon.edu.

WOMEN'S COACHES
Basketball: David McClure; Phone: 870-698-4248; E-mail: dmcclure@
lyon.edu.
Cross Country: Be Pham; Phone: 870-698-1788; E-mail: bpham@lyon.
edu.
Golf: Brian King; Phone: 870-698-4222; E-mail: gmcdowell@lyon.edu.
Soccer: Derek Nichols; Phone: 870-793-1757; E-mail: dnichols@lyon.
edu.
Tennis: Be Pham; Phone: 870-698-1788; E-mail: bpham@lyon.edu.
Volleyball: Michele Jacobs; Phone: 870-698-4223; E-mail: mjacobs@
lyon.edu.

MACALESTER COLLEGE
St. Paul, Minnesota

Scots ◆ NCAA III ◆ Minnesota Intercollegiate Athletic
Conference ◆ http://www.macalester.edu/

Independent Presbyterian 4-year, founded 1874
Coed, 1,884 undergraduate students, 97% full-time, 58% women,
42% men
Urban 53-acre campus
Very difficult entrance level, 42% of applicants were admitted

Freshmen *Admission:* 4,341 applied, 1,920 were accepted, 513 enrolled.
Test scores: SAT verbal scores over 500: 100%; SAT math scores over
500: 100%; SAT verbal scores over 600: 90%; SAT math scores over
600: 87%; SAT verbal scores over 700: 50%; SAT math scores over
700: 30%.
Tuition and fees (2004–05): $26,806 (full-time). *Room and board:* $7350
(room only: $3820).
Financial Aid (All incoming freshmen): *Average need-based gift aid:*
$16,568. *Average non-need based aid:* $5263. *Average aid to full-time
undergraduates:* $20,302.
Athletic Department: *Director of Athletics:* Irv Cross; Phone: 651-696-
6164; Fax: 651-696-6328; E-mail: cross@macalester.edu. *Sports Information Director:* Andy Johnson; Phone: 651-696-6533; E-mail:
johnsona@macalester.edu.

MEN'S COACHES
Baseball: Matt Parrington; Phone: 651-696-6770; E-mail: parrington@
macalester.edu.
Basketball: Curt Kietzer; Phone: 651-696-6245; E-mail: kietzer@
macalester.edu.
Cross Country: Matt Haugen; Phone: 651-696-6649; E-mail: haugen@
macalester.edu.
Diving: Bob Pearson; Phone: 651-696-6463; E-mail: pearson@
macalester.edu.
Football: Dennis Czech; Phone: 651-696-6286; E-mail: czech@
macalester.edu.
Golf: Martha Nause; Phone: 651-696-6774; E-mail: nause@macalester.
edu.
Soccer: John Leaney; Phone: 651-696-6737; E-mail: leaney@
macalester.edu.
Swimming: Bob Pearson; Phone: 651-696-6463; E-mail: pearson@
macalester.edu.
Tennis: Eric Eberhardt; Phone: 651-696-6718; E-mail: eberhardt@
macalester.edu.
Track and Field: Martin Peper; Phone: 651-696-6167; E-mail: peper@
macalester.edu.

WOMEN'S COACHES
Basketball: Mary Orsted; Phone: 651-696-6477; E-mail: orsted@
macalester.edu.
Cross Country: Jordan Cushing; Phone: 651-696-6717; E-mail: cushing@
macalester.edu.
Diving: Bob Pearson; Phone: 651-696-6463; E-mail: pearson@
macalester.edu.
Golf: Martha Nause; Phone: 651-696-6774; E-mail: nause@macalester.
edu.
Soccer: John Leaney; Phone: 651-696-6737; E-mail: leaney@
macalester.edu.

Macalester College (continued)

Softball: Tina Johnson; Phone: 651-696-6165; E-mail: johnsont@macalester.edu.
Swimming: Bob Pearson; Phone: 651-696-6463; E-mail: pearson@macalester.edu.
Tennis: Eric Eberhardt; Phone: 651-696-6718; E-mail: eberhardt@macalester.edu.
Track and Field: Martin Peper; Phone: 651-696-6167; E-mail: peper@macalester.edu.
Volleyball: Stephanie Schleuder; Phone: 651-696-6467; E-mail: schleuder@macalester.edu.

MACMURRAY COLLEGE
Jacksonville, Illinois

Highlanders ◆ NCAA III ◆ Illini-Badger Football Conference; St. Louis Athletic Conference ◆ http://www.mac.edu/

Independent United Methodist 4-year, founded 1846
Coed, 673 undergraduate students, 91% full-time, 59% women, 41% men
Small-town 60-acre campus
Moderately difficult entrance level, 59% of applicants were admitted

Freshmen Admission: 1,082 applied, 690 were accepted, 162 enrolled. Test scores: SAT verbal scores over 500: 31%; SAT math scores over 500: 31%; SAT verbal scores over 600: 15%; SAT math scores over 600: 8%.
Tuition and fees (2004–05): $14,650 (full-time). Room and board: $5620 (room only: $2850).
Financial Aid (All incoming freshmen): Average need-based gift aid: $12,042. Average non-need based aid: $4800. Average aid to full-time undergraduates: $13,361.
Athletic Department: Director of Athletics: Bob Gay; Phone: 217-479-7142; Fax: 217-479-7147; E-mail: bobgay@mac.edu. Sports Information Director: Larry Bostwick; Phone: 217-479-7143; E-mail: sid@mac.edu.

MEN'S COACHES
Baseball: Kevin Vest; Phone: 217-479-7153; E-mail: kvest@mac.edu.
Basketball: Bob Gay; Phone: 217-479-7142; E-mail: bobgay@mac.edu.
Cross Country: Teri Moore; Phone: 217-479-7143; E-mail: crosscountry@mac.edu.
Football: Brandon McCray; Phone: 217-479-7148; E-mail: bmccray@mac.edu.
Golf: Jim Cimarossa; Phone: 217-479-7148.
Soccer: Bill Killen; Phone: 217-479-7154; E-mail: bkillen@mac.edu.
Tennis: Neal Hart; Phone: 217-479-7143; E-mail: nealhart@mac.edu.
Wrestling: Jerry Kelly; Phone: 217-479-7156; E-mail: jkelly@mac.edu.

WOMEN'S COACHES
Basketball: Amy Wilson; Phone: 217-479-7143; E-mail: awilson@mac.edu.
Cross Country: Teri Moore; Phone: 217-479-7143; E-mail: crosscountry@mac.edu.
Golf: Ellen Crowe; Phone: 217-479-7143; E-mail: ecrowe@mac.edu.
Soccer: Greg Walter; Phone: 217-479-7143; E-mail: athletics@mac.edu.
Tennis: Neal Hart; Phone: 217-479-7143; E-mail: nealhart@mac.edu.
Volleyball: Darrin DeNeve; Phone: 217-479-7143; E-mail: ddeneve@mac.edu.

MADONNA UNIVERSITY
Livonia, Michigan

Crusaders ◆ NAIA ◆ Wolverine-Hoosier Conference ◆ http://www.munet.edu/

Independent Roman Catholic comprehensive, founded 1947
Coed, 3,243 undergraduate students, 47% full-time, 74% women, 26% men
Suburban 49-acre campus with easy access to Detroit
Moderately difficult entrance level, 81% of applicants were admitted

Freshmen Admission: 673 applied, 579 were accepted, 241 enrolled.

Tuition and fees (2004–05): $9800 (full-time). Room and board: $5612 (room only: $2550).
Financial Aid (All incoming freshmen): Average need-based gift aid: $3000. Average non-need based aid: $500. Average aid to full-time undergraduates: $1800.
Athletic Department: Director of Athletics: Bryan Rizzo; Phone: 734-432-5604; Fax: 734-432-5611; E-mail: brizzo@madonna.edu. Sports Information Director: Matt Fancett; Phone: 734-432-5610; E-mail: mfancett@madonna.edu.

MEN'S COACHES
Baseball: Greg Haeger; Phone: 734-432-5609; E-mail: ghaeger@madonna.edu.
Basketball: Bernie Holowicki; Phone: 734-432-5591; E-mail: bholowicki@madonna.edu.
Golf: Bill Durham; Phone: 734-432-5608; E-mail: billdurham@pga.com.
Soccer: Tino Scicluna; Phone: 734-432-5607; E-mail: tscicluna@madonna.edu.

WOMEN'S COACHES
Basketball: Marylou Jansen; Phone: 734-432-5606; E-mail: madonnabball@aol.com.
Golf: Bill Durham; Phone: 734-432-5608; E-mail: billdurham@pga.com.
Soccer: Mark Zathey; Phone: 734-432-5882; E-mail: mzathey@madonna.edu.
Softball: Al White; Phone: 734-432-5783; E-mail: awhite@madonna.edu.
Volleyball: Jerry Abraham; Phone: 734-432-5612; E-mail: jabraham@madonna.edu.

MAINE MARITIME ACADEMY
Castine, Maine

Mariners ◆ NCAA III ◆ New England Football Conference; North Atlantic Conference ◆ http://www.mainemaritime.edu/

State-supported comprehensive, founded 1941
Coed, primarily men, 846 undergraduate students, 88% full-time, 16% women, 84% men
Small-town 35-acre campus
Moderately difficult entrance level, 7% of applicants were admitted

Freshmen Admission: 659 applied, 449 were accepted, 241 enrolled.
Tuition and fees (2003–04): $6560 (resident), $11,610 (nonresident). Room and board: $5820 (room only: $2020).
Financial Aid (All incoming freshmen): Average need-based gift aid: $4837. Average non-need based aid: $6515. Average aid to full-time undergraduates: $8065.
Athletic Department: Director of Athletics: William Mottolla; Phone: 207-326-2451; Fax: 207-326-2513; E-mail: wmottala@mma.edu.

MEN'S COACHES
Basketball: Chris Murphy; Phone: 207-326-2452; E-mail: cmurphy@mma.edu.
Cross Country: Mark Cote; Phone: 207-326-2102; E-mail: mcote@mma.edu.
Football: Chris McKenny; Phone: 207-326-2453; E-mail: cmckenney@mma.edu.
Golf: Bill Mottola; Phone: 207-326-2451; E-mail: wmottola@mma.edu.
Lacrosse: Dave LaChapelle; Phone: 207-326-9560; E-mail: dlachapelle@mma.edu.
Soccer: Mike Keller; Phone: 207-326-2484; E-mail: mkeller@mma.edu.

WOMEN'S COACHES
Basketball: Craig Dagan; Phone: 207-326-2372; E-mail: cdagan@mma.edu.
Cross Country: Mark Cote; Phone: 207-326-2102; E-mail: mcote@mma.edu.
Soccer: Craig Dagan; Phone: 207-326-2372; E-mail: cdagan@mma.edu.
Softball: Mike Keller; Phone: 207-326-2484; E-mail: mkeller@mma.edu.

MALONE COLLEGE
Canton, Ohio

Pioneers ◆ NAIA ◆ American Mideast Conference; Mid-States Football Conference ◆ http://www.malone.edu/

Independent religious comprehensive, founded 1892, affiliated with Evangelical Friends Church–Eastern Region
Coed, 1,937 undergraduate students, 86% full-time, 61% women, 39% men
Suburban 78-acre campus with easy access to Cleveland
Moderately difficult entrance level, 82% of applicants were admitted

Freshmen *Admission:* 992 applied, 842 were accepted, 401 enrolled. *Test scores:* SAT verbal scores over 500: 69%; SAT math scores over 500: 61%; SAT verbal scores over 600: 30%; SAT math scores over 600: 22%; SAT verbal scores over 700: 3%; SAT math scores over 700: 5%.
Tuition and fees (2003–04): $14,995 (full-time). *Room and board:* $6000 (room only: $3200).
Financial Aid (All incoming freshmen): *Average need-based gift aid:* $8687. *Average non-need based aid:* $4464. *Average aid to full-time undergraduates:* $12,067.
Athletic Department: *Director of Athletics:* Hal Smith; Phone: 330-471-8296; Fax: 330-471-8298; E-mail: hsmith@malone.edu. *Sports Information Director:* Mark Bankert; Phone: 330-471-8293; E-mail: mbankert@malone.edu.

MEN'S COACHES
Baseball: Tom Crank; Phone: 330-471-8286; E-mail: tcrank@malone.edu.
Basketball: Hal Smith; Phone: 330-471-8296; E-mail: hsmith@malone.edu.
Cheerleading: Phone: 330-471-8300; E-mail: cheerleading@malone.edu.
Cross Country: Jack Hazen; Phone: 330-471-8291; E-mail: hazen@malone.edu.
Football: Dan Hanson; Phone: 330-471-8385; E-mail: dhanson@malone.edu.
Golf: Ken Hyland; Phone: 330-471-8300; E-mail: khyland@malone.edu.
Soccer: Todd Clark; Phone: 330-471-8295; E-mail: tclark@malone.edu.
Tennis: Kevin Knoch; Phone: 330-471-8300; E-mail: kknoch@malone.edu.
Track and Field: Charlie Grimes; Phone: 330-471-8438; E-mail: cgrimes@malone.edu.

WOMEN'S COACHES
Basketball: Lori Wynn; Phone: 330-471-8422; E-mail: lwynn@malone.edu.
Cheerleading: Phone: 330-471-8300; E-mail: cheerleading@malone.edu.
Cross Country: Jack Hazen; Phone: 330-471-8291; E-mail: hazen@malone.edu.
Golf: Max Baker; Phone: 330-471-8300; E-mail: mbaker@malone.edu.
Soccer: Todd Clark; Phone: 330-471-8295; E-mail: tclark@malone.edu.
Softball: Missi Wing; Phone: 330-471-8294; E-mail: mwing@malone.edu.
Tennis: Kevin Knoch; Phone: 330-471-8300; E-mail: kknoch@malone.edu.
Track and Field: Charlie Grimes; Phone: 330-471-8438; E-mail: cgrimes@malone.edu.
Volleyball: Tanya Hockman; Phone: 330-471-8287; E-mail: thockman@malone.edu.

MANCHESTER COLLEGE
North Manchester, Indiana

Spartans ◆ NCAA III ◆ Heartland Collegiate Conference ◆ http://www.manchester.edu/

Independent religious comprehensive, founded 1889, affiliated with Church of the Brethren
Coed, 1,153 undergraduate students, 96% full-time, 55% women, 45% men
Small-town 125-acre campus
Moderately difficult entrance level, 73% of applicants were admitted

Freshmen *Admission:* 1,085 applied, 854 were accepted, 335 enrolled. *Test scores:* SAT verbal scores over 500: 56%; SAT math scores over 500: 51%; SAT verbal scores over 600: 18%; SAT math scores over 600: 14%; SAT verbal scores over 700: 2%; SAT math scores over 700: 1%.
Tuition and fees (2004–05): $18,060 (full-time). *Room and board:* $6650 (room only: $4150).
Financial Aid (All incoming freshmen): *Average need-based gift aid:* $13,516. *Average non-need based aid:* $6777. *Average aid to full-time undergraduates:* $16,412.
Athletic Department: *Director of Athletics:* Tom Jarman; Phone: 260-982-5390; Fax: 260-982-5032; E-mail: tsjarman@manchester.edu. *Sports Information Director:* Doug Shoemaker; Phone: 260-982-5035; E-mail: dashoemaker@manchester.edu.

MEN'S COACHES
Baseball: Rick Espeset; Phone: 219-982-5034; E-mail: rbespeset@manchester.edu.
Basketball: Jamie Matthews; Phone: 219-982-5040; E-mail: jamatthews@manchester.edu.
Cheerleading: Laura Sloop; Phone: 219-982-5233; E-mail: llsloop@manchester.edu.
Cross Country: Brian Cashdollar; Phone: 219-982-5378; E-mail: brcashdollar@manchester.edu.
Football: Shannon Griffith; Phone: 219-982-5377; E-mail: wsgriffith@manchester.edu.
Golf: Roger Lundy; Phone: 219-982-5385; E-mail: ralundy@manchester.edu.
Soccer: Dave Good; Phone: 219-982-5332; E-mail: dlgood@manchester.edu.
Tennis: Todd Hartsough; Phone: 219-982-5946; E-mail: tmhartsough@manchester.edu.
Track and Field: Brian Cashdollar; Phone: 219-982-5378; E-mail: brcashdollar@manchester.edu.
Wrestling: Tom Jarman; Phone: 219-982-5390; E-mail: tsjarman@manchester.edu.

WOMEN'S COACHES
Basketball: Michelle Gill; Phone: 219-982-5379; E-mail: mmgill@manchester.edu.
Cheerleading: Laura Sloop; Phone: 219-982-5233; E-mail: llsloop@manchester.edu.
Cross Country: Brian Cashdollar; Phone: 219-982-5378; E-mail: brcashdollar@manchester.edu.
Golf: Roger Lundy; Phone: 219-982-5385; E-mail: ralundy@manchester.edu.
Soccer: Scott Stan; Phone: 219-982-5046; E-mail: jsstan@manchester.edu.
Softball: Martha Judge; Phone: 219-982-5356; E-mail: mejudge@manchester.edu.
Tennis: Todd Hartsough; Phone: 219-982-5946; E-mail: tmhartsough@manchester.edu.
Track and Field: Brian Cashdollar; Phone: 219-982-5378; E-mail: brcashdollar@manchester.edu.
Volleyball: Wayne Chadwick; Phone: 219-982-5358; E-mail: whchadwick@manchester.edu.

MANHATTAN COLLEGE
Riverdale, New York

Jaspers ◆ NCAA I ◆ Metro Atlantic Athletic Conference ◆ http://www.manhattan.edu/

Independent religious comprehensive, founded 1853, affiliated with Roman Catholic Church
Coed, 2,879 undergraduate students, 94% full-time, 50% women, 50% men
Urban 31-acre campus with easy access to New York City
Moderately difficult entrance level, 53% of applicants were admitted

Freshmen *Admission:* 4,414 applied, 2,332 were accepted, 651 enrolled. *Test scores:* SAT verbal scores over 500: 73%; SAT math scores over 500: 79%; SAT verbal scores over 600: 18%; SAT math scores over 600: 27%; SAT verbal scores over 700: 2%; SAT math scores over 700: 3%.
Tuition and fees (2003–04): $19,300 (full-time). *Room and board:* $8100.
Financial Aid (All incoming freshmen): *Average need-based gift aid:* $7179. *Average non-need based aid:* $6988. *Average aid to full-time undergraduates:* $12,688.

Manhattan College *(continued)*

Athletic Department: *Director of Athletics:* Bob Byrnes; Phone: 718-862-7227; Fax: 718-862-8020; E-mail: robert.byrnes@manhattan.edu. *Sports Information Director:* Michael Antonaccio; Phone: 718-862-7228; E-mail: michael.antonaccio@manhattan.edu.

MEN'S COACHES

Baseball: Steve Trimper; Phone: 718-862-7486; E-mail: steve.trimper@manhattan.edu.
Basketball: Bobby Gonzalez; Phone: 718-862-7180; E-mail: robert.gonzalez@manhattan.edu.
Cross Country: Dan Mecca; Phone: 718-862-7229; E-mail: danmecca@hotmail.com.
Golf: Walter Olsewski; Phone: 718-862-7859; E-mail: jasperalum@aol.com.
Lacrosse: Tim McIntee; Phone: 718-862-7841; E-mail: timothy.mcintee@manhattan.edu.
Soccer: Billy Walsh; Phone: 718-862-7844; E-mail: bwalsh2@aol.com.
Tennis: Arthur Bobko; Phone: 718-862-7858; E-mail: arthur.bobko@manhattan.edu.
Track and Field: Dan Mecca; Phone: 718-862-7229; E-mail: danmecca@hotmail.com.

WOMEN'S COACHES

Basketball: Myndi Hill; Phone: 718-862-7935; E-mail: myndi.hill@manhattan.edu.
Cross Country: Dan Mecca; Phone: 718-862-7229; E-mail: danmecca@hotmail.com.
Lacrosse: Jill Donovan; Phone: 718-862-7842; E-mail: jill.donovan@manhattan.edu.
Soccer: John Sanchez; Phone: 718-862-7936; E-mail: john.sanchez@manhattan.edu.
Softball: Jennifer Fisher; Phone: 718-862-7835; E-mail: jennifer.fisher@manhattan.edu.
Swimming: Walter Olsewski; Phone: 718-862-7859; E-mail: jasperalum@aol.com.
Tennis: Liz Shweky; Phone: 718-862-7856; E-mail: lshweky@aol.com.
Track and Field: Dan Mecca; Phone: 718-862-7229; E-mail: danmecca@hotmail.com.
Volleyball: Pete Volkert; Phone: 718-862-7839; E-mail: peterstaceyv@aol.com.

MANHATTANVILLE COLLEGE
Purchase, New York

Valiants ◆ NCAA III ◆ Freedom Conference; Knickerbocker Lacrosse Conference; Skyline Conference ◆ http://www.manhattanville.edu/

Independent comprehensive, founded 1841
Coed, 1,671 undergraduate students, 91% full-time, 68% women, 32% men
Suburban 100-acre campus with easy access to New York City
Moderately difficult entrance level, 5% of applicants were admitted

Freshmen *Admission:* 2,450 applied, 1,348 were accepted, 420 enrolled. *Test scores:* SAT verbal scores over 500: 65%; SAT math scores over 500: 63%; SAT verbal scores over 600: 20%; SAT math scores over 600: 15%; SAT verbal scores over 700: 2%; SAT math scores over 700: 1%.
Tuition and fees (2004–05): $24,570 (full-time). *Room and board:* $10,130 (room only: $6020).
Financial Aid (All incoming freshmen): *Average need-based gift aid:* $9927. *Average non-need based aid:* $8664. *Average aid to full-time undergraduates:* $15,500.
Athletic Department: *Director of Athletics:* Keith Levinthal; Phone: 914-323-7277; Fax: 914-323-5130; E-mail: levinthalk@mville.edu. *Sports Information Director:* Michael LaPlaca; Phone: 914-323-7280; E-mail: laplacam@mville.edu.

MEN'S COACHES

Baseball: Joe Ferraro; Phone: 914-323-7284; E-mail: ferrarojo@mville.edu.
Basketball: Dean Meminger; Phone: 914-323-7271.
Cheerleading: Chezdis Sanchez; Phone: 914-323-5280; E-mail: sanchezch@mville.edu.
Golf: Oly Hicks; Phone: 914-323-7281.

Ice Hockey: Keith Levinthal; Phone: 914-323-7277; E-mail: levinthalk@mville.edu.
Lacrosse: Dan Mulholland; Phone: 914-323-7286; E-mail: mulhollandd@mville.edu.
Soccer: Chris Smith; Phone: 914-323-7272; E-mail: smithc@mville.edu.
Tennis: Eric Ratchford; Phone: 914-323-7135; E-mail: ratchfordc@mville.edu.

WOMEN'S COACHES

Basketball: Shawn Lincoln; Phone: 914-323-7282; E-mail: lincolnc@mville.edu.
Cheerleading: Chezdis Sanchez; Phone: 914-323-5280; E-mail: sanchezch@mville.edu.
Field Hockey: Heather-lyn Memmis; Phone: 914-323-3175.
Lacrosse: Jenna Szyluk; Phone: 914-323-3185.
Soccer: Jenna Szyluk; Phone: 914-323-7275.
Softball: Dale Martin; Phone: 914-323-7283; E-mail: martind@mville.edu.
Tennis: Jorg Rauthe; Phone: 914-323-7135; E-mail: jorg.rauthe@verizon.net.

MANSFIELD UNIVERSITY OF PENNSYLVANIA
Mansfield, Pennsylvania

Mountaineers ◆ NCAA II ◆ Pennsylvania State Athletic Conference ◆ http://www.mansfield.edu/

State-supported comprehensive, founded 1857, part of Pennsylvania State System of Higher Education
Coed, 3,168 undergraduate students, 91% full-time, 61% women, 39% men
Small-town 205-acre campus
Moderately difficult entrance level, 77% of applicants were admitted

Freshmen *Admission:* 2,348 applied, 1,801 were accepted, 710 enrolled. *Test scores:* SAT verbal scores over 500: 44%; SAT math scores over 500: 41%; SAT verbal scores over 600: 10%; SAT math scores over 600: 9%; SAT verbal scores over 700: 1%; SAT math scores over 700: 1%.
Tuition and fees (2003–04): $5972 (resident), $12,870 (nonresident). *Room and board:* $5248.
Athletic Department: *Director of Athletics:* Roger Maisner; Phone: 570-662-4636; Fax: 570-662-4116; E-mail: rmaisner@mnsfld.edu. *Sports Information Director:* Steve McCloskey; Phone: 570-662-4845; E-mail: smcclosk@mansfield.edu.

MEN'S COACHES

Baseball: Harry Hillson; Phone: 570-662-4457; E-mail: hhillson@mansfield.edu.
Basketball: Vince Alexander; Phone: 570-662-4453; E-mail: valexand@mansfield.edu.
Cheerleading: Robert Maris; Phone: 570-662-4537; E-mail: rmaris@mnsfld.edu.
Cross Country: Michael Rohl; Phone: 570-662-4645; E-mail: mrohl@mansfield.edu.
Football: Chris Woods; Phone: 570-662-4460; E-mail: cwoods@mansfield.edu.
Track and Field: Michael Rohl; Phone: 570-662-4645; E-mail: mrohl@mansfield.edu.

WOMEN'S COACHES

Basketball: Ruth Henderson; Phone: 570-662-4456; E-mail: rhenders@mansfield.edu.
Cheerleading: Robert Maris; Phone: 570-662-4537; E-mail: rmaris@mnsfld.edu.
Cross Country: Michael Rohl; Phone: 570-662-4645; E-mail: mrohl@mansfield.edu.
Field Hockey: Diane Monkiewicz; Phone: 570-662-4637; E-mail: dmonkiew@mansfield.edu.
Soccer: Tim Dempsey; Phone: 570-662-4454; E-mail: tdempsey@mansfield.edu.
Softball: Edith Gallagher; Phone: 570-662-4633; E-mail: egallagh@mansfield.edu.
Swimming: Danita Fox; Phone: 570-662-4464; E-mail: dfox@mansfield.edu.
Track and Field: Michael Rohl; Phone: 570-662-4645; E-mail: mrohl@mansfield.edu.

MARANATHA BAPTIST BIBLE COLLEGE
Watertown, Wisconsin

Crusaders ◆ NCAA III ◆ Lake Michigan Conference ◆ http://www.mbbc.edu/

Independent Baptist comprehensive, founded 1968
Coed, 776 undergraduate students, 100% full-time, 53% women, 47% men
Small-town 60-acre campus with easy access to Milwaukee
Noncompetitive entrance level, 70% of applicants were admitted

Freshmen *Admission:* 308 applied, 215 were accepted, 186 enrolled.
Tuition and fees (2003–04): $7780 (full-time). *Room and board:* $4520.
Financial Aid (All incoming freshmen): *Average need-based gift aid:* $834. *Average non-need based aid:* $680. *Average aid to full-time undergraduates:* $4073.
Athletic Department: *Director of Athletics:* Terry Price; Phone: 920-206-2376; Fax: 920-261-9109; E-mail: tprice@mbbc.edu.

MEN'S COACHES
Baseball: Jerry Terrill; Phone: 920-206-2376; E-mail: jterrill@mbbc.edu.
Basketball: Jerry Terrill; Phone: 920-206-2376; E-mail: jterrill@mbbc.edu.
Cross Country: Robert Montgomery; Phone: 920-206-2381; E-mail: rmontgomery@mbbc.edu.
Football: Terry Price; Phone: 920-206-2377; E-mail: tprice@mbbc.edu.
Soccer: Max Schuyler; Phone: 920-206-2491.
Wrestling: Dave Wredberg; Phone: 920-206-8071; E-mail: dwredberg@mbbc.edu.

WOMEN'S COACHES
Basketball: Clayton Morrison; Phone: 920-206-2379; E-mail: cmorrison@mbbc.edu.
Cross Country: Robert Montgomery; Phone: 920-206-2381; E-mail: rmontgomery@mbbc.edu.
Soccer: Josh Caucutt; Phone: 920-206-2508.
Softball: Clayton Morrison; Phone: 920-206-2379; E-mail: cmorrison@mbbc.edu.
Volleyball: Marsha Jackson; Phone: 920-206-2351; E-mail: mjackson@mbbc.edu.

MARIAN COLLEGE
Indianapolis, Indiana

Knights ◆ NAIA ◆ Mid-Central Conference ◆ http://www.marian.edu/

Independent Roman Catholic comprehensive, founded 1851
Coed, 1,547 undergraduate students, 67% full-time, 74% women, 26% men
Urban 114-acre campus
Moderately difficult entrance level, 79% of applicants were admitted

Freshmen *Admission:* 859 applied, 640 were accepted, 471 enrolled.
Test scores: SAT verbal scores over 500: 49%; SAT math scores over 500: 46%; SAT verbal scores over 600: 12%; SAT math scores over 600: 7%.
Tuition and fees (2003–04): $17,460 (full-time). *Room and board:* $5800.
Financial Aid (All incoming freshmen): *Average need-based gift aid:* $8243. *Average non-need based aid:* $8485. *Average aid to full-time undergraduates:* $16,123.
Athletic Department: *Director of Athletics:* John Grimes; Phone: 317-955-6118; Fax: 920-923-8134; E-mail: jgrimes@marian.edu. *Sports Information Director:* Brett Cope; Phone: 317-955-6122; E-mail: bcope@marian.edu.

MEN'S COACHES
Baseball: Kurt Guldner; Phone: 317-955-6310; E-mail: guldner@marian.edu.
Basketball: John Grimes; Phone: 317-955-6118; E-mail: jgrimes@marian.edu.
Cheerleading: Miranda Fischer; Phone: 317-205-9302; E-mail: mcfischer77@msn.com.
Cross Country: Dave Roberts; Phone: 317-955-6341; E-mail: ddroberts@marian.edu.
Golf: John Shelton; Phone: 317-955-6040; E-mail: jshelton@marian.edu.
Soccer: Matt Nirrengarten; Phone: 317-955-6117; E-mail: mnirreng@indygov.org.
Tennis: Todd Bacon; Phone: 317-955-6119; E-mail: toddba@marian.edu.
Track and Field: Dave Roberts; Phone: 317-955-6341; E-mail: ddroberts@marian.edu.

WOMEN'S COACHES
Basketball: Todd Bacon; Phone: 317-955-6119; E-mail: toddba@marian.edu.
Cheerleading: Miranda Fischer; Phone: 317-205-9302; E-mail: mcfischer77@msn.com.
Cross Country: Dave Roberts; Phone: 317-955-6341; E-mail: ddroberts@marian.edu.
Soccer: Kurt Guldner; Phone: 317-205-6118; E-mail: guldner@marian.edu.
Softball: Scott Fleming; Phone: 317-955-6106; E-mail: sflemming@marian.edu.
Tennis: Todd Bacon; Phone: 317-955-6119; E-mail: toddba@marian.edu.
Track and Field: Dave Roberts; Phone: 317-955-6341; E-mail: ddroberts@marian.edu.
Volleyball: Dan Findley; Phone: 317-955-6165; E-mail: dfindley@marian.edu.

MARIAN COLLEGE OF FOND DU LAC
Fond du Lac, Wisconsin

Sabres ◆ NCAA III ◆ Lake Michigan Conference ◆ http://www.mariancollege.edu/

Independent Roman Catholic comprehensive, founded 1936
Coed, 1,856 undergraduate students, 66% full-time, 70% women, 30% men
Small-town 77-acre campus with easy access to Milwaukee
Moderately difficult entrance level, 70% of applicants were admitted

Freshmen *Admission:* 884 applied, 684 were accepted, 251 enrolled.
Tuition and fees (2003–04): $15,025 (full-time). *Room and board:* $4600 (room only: $2600).
Financial Aid (All incoming freshmen): *Average need-based gift aid:* $6727. *Average non-need based aid:* $3902. *Average aid to full-time undergraduates:* $14,683.
Athletic Department: *Director of Athletics:* Doug Hammonds; Phone: 920-923-7178; Fax: 920-923-8134; E-mail: dhammonds@mariancollege.edu. *Sports Information Director:* Chris Zills; Phone: 920-923-8155; E-mail: czills@mariancollege.edu.

MEN'S COACHES
Baseball: Jason Bartelt; Phone: 920-923-8090; E-mail: jbartelt@mariancollege.edu.
Basketball: Mark Boyle; Phone: 920-923-7627; E-mail: mboyle@mariancollege.edu.
Golf: Chris Brown; Phone: 920-923-7667; E-mail: cbrown@mariancollege.edu.
Ice Hockey: Chris Brown; Phone: 920-923-7667; E-mail: cbrown@mariancollege.edu.
Soccer: Craig Peltonen; Phone: 920-923-7626; E-mail: cpeltonen@mariancollege.edu.
Tennis: Craig Peltonen; Phone: 920-923-7626; E-mail: cpeltonen@mariancollege.edu.

WOMEN'S COACHES
Basketball: Doug Neumann; Phone: 920-923-8154; E-mail: dneumann@mariancollege.edu.
Golf: Ann Felker; Phone: 920-923-8140; E-mail: afelker@mariancollege.edu.
Soccer: Craig Peltonen; Phone: 920-923-7626; E-mail: cpeltonen@mariancollege.edu.
Softball: Ann Felker; Phone: 920-923-8140; E-mail: afelker@mariancollege.edu.
Tennis: Donna Whealon; Phone: 920-923-7147.
Volleyball: Doug Hammonds; Phone: 920-923-7178; E-mail: dhammonds@mariancollege.edu.

MARIETTA COLLEGE
Marietta, Ohio

Pioneers ◆ NCAA III ◆ Ohio Athletic Conference ◆ http://www.marietta.edu/

Independent comprehensive, founded 1835
Coed, 1,222 undergraduate students, 94% full-time, 49% women, 51% men
Small-town 120-acre campus
Moderately difficult entrance level, 76% of applicants were admitted

Freshmen *Admission:* 1,912 applied, 1,486 were accepted, 378 enrolled. *Test scores:* SAT verbal scores over 500: 70%; SAT math scores over 500: 62%; SAT verbal scores over 600: 24%; SAT math scores over 600: 21%; SAT verbal scores over 700: 3%; SAT math scores over 700: 3%.
Tuition and fees (2003–04): $20,892 (full-time). *Room and board:* $5946 (room only: $3176).
Financial Aid (All incoming freshmen): *Average need-based gift aid:* $7575. *Average non-need based aid:* $6406. *Average aid to full-time undergraduates:* $18,374.
Athletic Department: *Director of Athletics:* Debora Lazorik; Phone: 740-376-4665; Fax: 740-376-4666; E-mail: lazorikd@marietta.edu. *Sports Information Director:* Dan May; Phone: 740-376-4665; E-mail: mayd@marietta.edu.

MEN'S COACHES
Baseball: Brian Brewer; Phone: 740-376-4517; E-mail: brewerb@marietta.edu.
Basketball: Doug Foote; Phone: 740-376-4612; E-mail: footed@marietta.edu.
Cross Country: Derek Stanley; Phone: 740-376-4656; E-mail: stanleyd@marietta.edu.
Football: Todd Glaser; Phone: 740-376-4676; E-mail: glaserr@marietta.edu.
Soccer: Patrick Holguin; Phone: 740-376-4672; E-mail: holguinp@marietta.edu.
Tennis: Phil Inman; Phone: 740-376-4577; E-mail: phil_iman@hotmail.com.
Track and Field: Derek Stanley; Phone: 740-376-4656; E-mail: stanleyd@marietta.edu.

WOMEN'S COACHES
Basketball: Vicki Giffin; Phone: 740-376-4669; E-mail: giffinv@marietta.edu.
Cross Country: Derek Stanley; Phone: 740-376-4656; E-mail: stanleyd@marietta.edu.
Soccer: Patrick Holguin; Phone: 740-376-4672; E-mail: holguinp@marietta.edu.
Softball: Jeanne Arbuckle; Phone: 740-376-4668; E-mail: arbucklj@marietta.edu.
Tennis: Suzy Haddox; Phone: 740-376-4577; E-mail: suzyhaddox@charter.net.
Track and Field: Derek Stanley; Phone: 740-376-4656; E-mail: stanleyd@marietta.edu.
Volleyball: Eric Viney; Phone: 740-376-4902; E-mail: vineye@marietta.edu.

MARIST COLLEGE
Poughkeepsie, New York

Red Foxes ◆ NCAA I ◆ Metro Atlantic Athletic Conference ◆ http://www.marist.edu/

Independent comprehensive, founded 1929
Coed, 4,773 undergraduate students, 88% full-time, 57% women, 43% men
Small-town 150-acre campus with easy access to Albany and New York City
Moderately difficult entrance level, 54% of applicants were admitted

Freshmen *Admission:* 6,606 applied, 4,664 were accepted, 1,125 enrolled. *Test scores:* SAT verbal scores over 500: 91%; SAT math scores over 500: 95%; SAT verbal scores over 600: 37%; SAT math scores over 600: 44%; SAT verbal scores over 700: 2%; SAT math scores over 700: 3%.

Tuition and fees (2003–04): $18,962 (full-time). *Room and board:* $8634 (room only: $5460).
Financial Aid (All incoming freshmen): *Average need-based gift aid:* $6737. *Average non-need based aid:* $5605. *Average aid to full-time undergraduates:* $13,195.
Athletic Department: *Director of Athletics:* Tim Murray; Phone: 845-575-3699; Fax: 845-452-7028; E-mail: athletics@marist.edu. *Sports Information Director:* Chris O'Connor; Phone: 845-575-3699; E-mail: christopher.o'connor@marist.edu.

MEN'S COACHES
Baseball: Joe Raccuia; Phone: 845-575-3699; E-mail: jim.tyrrell@marist.edu.
Basketball: Dave Magarity; Phone: 845-575-3699; E-mail: david.magarity@marist.edu.
Cross Country: Pete Colaizzo; Phone: 845-575-3699; E-mail: peter.colaizzo@marist.edu.
Diving: Melanie Bolstad; Phone: 845-575-3699; E-mail: melanie.bolstad@marist.edu.
Football: Jim Parady; Phone: 845-575-3699; E-mail: jim.parady@marist.edu.
Lacrosse: Andrew Copelan; Phone: 845-575-3699; E-mail: edgar.glascott@marist.edu.
Soccer: Robert Herodes; Phone: 845-575-3699; E-mail: bobby.herodes@marist.edu.
Swimming: Larry Van Wagner; Phone: 845-575-3699; E-mail: larry.vanwagner@marist.edu.
Tennis: Tim Smith; Phone: 845-575-3699; E-mail: timothy.smith@marist.edu.
Track and Field: Pete Colaizzo; Phone: 845-575-3699; E-mail: peter.colaizzo@marist.edu.

WOMEN'S COACHES
Basketball: Brian Giorgis; Phone: 845-575-3699; E-mail: brian.giorgis@marist.edu.
Cross Country: Phil Kelly; Phone: 845-575-3699; E-mail: philip.kelly@marist.edu.
Diving: Melanie Bolstad; Phone: 845-575-3699; E-mail: melanie.bolstad@marist.edu.
Lacrosse: Noelle Cebron; Phone: 845-575-3699; E-mail: noelle.cebron@marist.edu.
Soccer: Sheri Huckleberry; Phone: 845-575-3699; E-mail: sheri.huckleberry@marist.edu.
Softball: Melissa Tucci; Phone: 845-575-3699; E-mail: melissa.tucci@marist.edu.
Swimming: Larry VanWagner; Phone: 845-575-3699; E-mail: larry.vanwagner@marist.edu.
Tennis: Peter Angarola; Phone: 845-575-3699; E-mail: peter.angarola@marist.edu.
Track and Field: Phil Kelly; Phone: 845-575-3699; E-mail: philip.kelly@marist.edu.
Volleyball: Sarah Watters; Phone: 845-575-3699; E-mail: sarah.watters@marist.edu.

MARQUETTE UNIVERSITY
Milwaukee, Wisconsin

Golden Eagles ◆ NCAA I ◆ Conference USA Conference ◆ http://www.marquette.edu/

Independent Roman Catholic (Jesuit) university, founded 1881
Coed, 7,775 undergraduate students, 93% full-time, 55% women, 45% men
Urban 80-acre campus
Moderately difficult entrance level, 80% of applicants were admitted

Freshmen *Admission:* 8,232 applied, 6,817 were accepted, 1,889 enrolled. *Test scores:* SAT verbal scores over 500: 86%; SAT math scores over 500: 84%; SAT verbal scores over 600: 42%; SAT math scores over 600: 49%; SAT verbal scores over 700: 7%; SAT math scores over 700: 9%.
Tuition and fees (2003–04): $20,710 (full-time). *Room and board:* $7000 (room only: $4550).
Financial Aid (All incoming freshmen): *Average need-based gift aid:* $11,087. *Average non-need based aid:* $6744. *Average aid to full-time undergraduates:* $15,966.
Athletic Department: *Director of Athletics:* Bill Cords; Phone: 414-288-5249; Fax: 414-288-7341; E-mail: bill.cords@marquette.edu. *Sports Information Director:* Blain Fowler; Phone: 414-288-6980; E-mail: blain.fowler@marquette.edu.

MEN'S COACHES

Basketball: Tom Crean; Phone: 414-288-7130; E-mail: tom.crean@marquette.edu.
Cross Country: Dave Uhrich; Phone: 414-288-5105; E-mail: david.uhrich@marquette.edu.
Golf: Tim Grogan; Phone: 414-288-5156; E-mail: tim.grogan@marquette.edu.
Soccer: Steve Adlard; Phone: 414-288-3069; E-mail: steve.adlard@marquette.edu.
Tennis: Steve Rodecap; Phone: 414-288-3775.
Track and Field: Dave Uhrich; Phone: 414-288-5105; E-mail: david.uhrich@marquette.edu.

WOMEN'S COACHES

Basketball: Terri Mitchell; Phone: 414-288-5784; E-mail: terri.mitchell@marquette.edu.
Cross Country: Dave Uhrich; Phone: 414-288-5105; E-mail: david.uhrich@marquette.edu.
Soccer: Markus Roeders; Phone: 414-288-7414; E-mail: markus.roeders@marquette.edu.
Tennis: Jody Bronson; Phone: 414-288-5146; E-mail: jody.bronson@marquette.edu.
Track and Field: Dave Uhrich; Phone: 414-288-5105; E-mail: david.uhrich@marquette.edu.
Volleyball: Pati Rolf; Phone: 414-288-5157; E-mail: pati.rolf@marquette.edu.

MARSHALL UNIVERSITY
Huntington, West Virginia

Thundering Herd ◆ NCAA I ◆ Mid-American Conference ◆ http://www.marshall.edu/

State-supported university, founded 1837, part of University System of West Virginia
Coed, 9,958 undergraduate students, 85% full-time, 56% women, 44% men
Urban 70-acre campus
Minimally difficult entrance level, 87% of applicants were admitted

Freshmen *Admission:* 2,578 applied, 2,274 were accepted, 1,938 enrolled. *Test scores:* SAT verbal scores over 500: 49%; SAT math scores over 500: 50%; SAT verbal scores over 600: 15%; SAT math scores over 600: 18%; SAT verbal scores over 700: 3%; SAT math scores over 700: 1%.
Tuition and fees (2003–04): $3260 (resident), $8944 (nonresident). *Room and board:* $5856.
Financial Aid (All incoming freshmen): *Average need-based gift aid:* $3948. *Average non-need based aid:* $4392. *Average aid to full-time undergraduates:* $6435.
Athletic Department: *Director of Athletics:* Bob Marcum; Phone: 304-696-4304; Fax: 304-696-6448; E-mail: marcum@marshall.edu. *Sports Information Director:* Randy Burnside; Phone: 304-696-4660; E-mail: burnsid2@marshall.edu.

MEN'S COACHES

Baseball: David Piepenbrink; Phone: 304-696-5277; E-mail: piepenb2@marshall.edu.
Basketball: Ron Jirsa; Phone: 304-696-6460; E-mail: jirsa@marshall.edu.
Cheerleading: Donna Dunn; Phone: 304-696-6707.
Cross Country: Jeff Small; Phone: 304-696-5412; E-mail: small@marshall.edu.
Football: Bob Pruett; Phone: 304-696-6464; E-mail: pruett@marshall.edu.
Golf: Joe Feaganes; Phone: 304-696-5401; E-mail: feaganes@marshall.edu.
Soccer: Bob Gray; Phone: 304-696-4659; E-mail: grayr@marshall.edu.
Track and Field: Jeff Small; Phone: 304-696-2431; E-mail: small@marshall.edu.

WOMEN'S COACHES

Basketball: Royce Chadwick; Phone: 304-696-5447; E-mail: chadwickr@marshall.edu.
Cheerleading: Donna Dunn; Phone: 304-696-6707.
Cross Country: Jeff Small; Phone: 304-696-2431; E-mail: small@marshall.edu.
Diving: Ryan Donley; Phone: 304-696-2573.
Golf: Joe Feaganes; Phone: 304-696-5401; E-mail: feaganes@marshall.edu.
Soccer: Chris Kane; Phone: 304-696-6388; E-mail: kane@marshall.edu.
Softball: Shonda Stanton; Phone: 304-696-4370; E-mail: stantons@marshall.edu.
Swimming: Leonard Kraus; Phone: 304-696-2573; E-mail: kraus@marshall.edu.
Tennis: John Mercer; Phone: 304-696-2431; E-mail: merceratmarshall@msn.com.
Track and Field: Jeff Small; Phone: 304-696-2431; E-mail: small@marshall.edu.
Volleyball: Mitch Jacobs; Phone: 304-696-3980; E-mail: jacobsm@marshall.edu.

MARS HILL COLLEGE
Mars Hill, North Carolina

Lions ◆ NCAA II ◆ Deep South Lacrosse Conference; South Atlantic Conference ◆ http://www.mhc.edu/

Independent Baptist 4-year, founded 1856
Coed, 1,351 undergraduate students
Small-town 194-acre campus
Moderately difficult entrance level, 83% of applicants were admitted

Freshmen *Admission:* 1,006 applied, 856 were accepted. *Test scores:* SAT verbal scores over 500: 47%; SAT math scores over 500: 46%; SAT verbal scores over 600: 13%; SAT math scores over 600: 11%; SAT verbal scores over 700: 1%; SAT math scores over 700: 2%.
Tuition and fees (2003–04): $15,458 (full-time). *Room and board:* $6760.
Financial Aid (All incoming freshmen): *Average need-based gift aid:* $9404. *Average non-need based aid:* $6799. *Average aid to full-time undergraduates:* $12,132.
Athletic Department: *Director of Athletics:* David Riggins; Phone: 828-689-1215; Fax: 828-689-1501; E-mail: driggins@mhc.edu. *Sports Information Director:* Rick Baker; Phone: 828-689-1373; E-mail: rbaker@mhc.edu.

MEN'S COACHES

Baseball: Dan Taylor; Phone: 828-689-1173; E-mail: dtaylor@mhc.edu.
Basketball: Terry Rogers; Phone: 828-689-1223; E-mail: trogers@mhc.edu.
Cheerleading: Robin Cole; Phone: 828-689-1408; E-mail: rcole@mhc.edu.
Cross Country: Mike Owens; Phone: 828-689-1178; E-mail: mowens@mhc.edu.
Football: Tim Clifton; Phone: 828-689-1375; E-mail: tclifton@mhc.edu.
Golf: Brian Gordner; Phone: 828-689-1219; E-mail: bgordner@mhc.edu.
Lacrosse: Brian Anken; Phone: 828-689-1441; E-mail: banken@mhc.edu.
Soccer: Trei Morrison; Phone: 828-689-1227; E-mail: tmorrison@mhc.edu.
Tennis: Tom Schrecengost; Phone: 828-689-1170; E-mail: tschrecengost@mhc.edu.
Track and Field: Mike Owens; Phone: 828-689-1178; E-mail: mowens@mhc.edu.

WOMEN'S COACHES

Basketball: Mandy Mattox; Phone: 828-689-1229; E-mail: mmattox@mhc.edu.
Cheerleading: Robin Cole; Phone: 828-689-1408; E-mail: rcole@mhc.edu.
Cross Country: Mike Owens; Phone: 828-689-1178; E-mail: mowens@mhc.edu.
Soccer: Scott Ginn; Phone: 828-689-1171.
Softball: Fred Gillum; Phone: 828-689-1219; E-mail: fgillum@mhc.edu.
Tennis: Tom Schrecengost; Phone: 828-689-1170; E-mail: tschrecengost@mhc.edu.
Track and Field: Mike Owens; Phone: 828-689-1178; E-mail: mowens@mhc.edu.
Volleyball: Bill Shook; Phone: 828-689-1497; E-mail: bshook@mhc.edu.

MARTIN LUTHER COLLEGE
New Ulm, Minnesota

Knights ◆ NCAA III ◆ Independent ◆ http://www.mlc-wels.edu/

Independent religious 4-year, founded 1995, affiliated with Wisconsin Evangelical Lutheran Synod
Coed, 1,020 undergraduate students, 99% full-time, 49% women, 51% men
Small-town 50-acre campus
Moderately difficult entrance level, 99% of applicants were admitted

Freshmen *Admission:* 322 applied, 315 were accepted, 222 enrolled.
Tuition and fees (2004–05): $8500 (full-time). *Room and board:* $3300.
Financial Aid (All incoming freshmen): *Average need-based gift aid:* $4107. *Average non-need based aid:* $801. *Average aid to full-time undergraduates:* $5435.
Athletic Department: *Director of Athletics:* James Unke; Phone: 507-354-8221; Fax: 507-233-9115; E-mail: unkejm@mlc-wels.edu. *Sports Information Director:* Jeremy Belter; Phone: 507-354-8221; E-mail: sid@mlc-wels.edu.

MEN'S COACHES
Baseball: Drew Buck; Phone: 507-354-8221; E-mail: buckdm@mlc-wels.edu.
Basketball: James Unke; Phone: 507-354-8221; E-mail: unkejm@mlc-wels.edu.
Cross Country: Chuck Hussman; Phone: 507-354-8221; E-mail: hussmace@mlc-wels.edu.
Football: Dennis Gorsline; Phone: 507-354-8221; E-mail: gorslidd@mlc-wels.edu.
Golf: Jeff Schone; Phone: 507-354-8221; E-mail: schonejl@mlc-wels.edu.
Soccer: Paul Koelpin; Phone: 507-354-8221; E-mail: koelpipe@mlc-wels.edu.
Tennis: Arien Koestler; Phone: 507-354-8221; E-mail: koestlal@mlc-wels.edu.
Track and Field: Chuck Hussman; Phone: 507-354-8221; E-mail: hussmace@mlc-wels.edu.

WOMEN'S COACHES
Basketball: Gene Pfeifer; Phone: 507-354-8221; E-mail: pfeifegr@mlc-wels.edu.
Cross Country: Chuck Hussman; Phone: 507-354-8221; E-mail: hussmace@mlc-wels.edu.
Soccer: John Gronholz; Phone: 507-354-8221; E-mail: gronhojh@mlc-wels.edu.
Softball: Barb Leopold; Phone: 507-354-8221; E-mail: leopolbl@mlc-wels.edu.
Tennis: Gary Dallmann; Phone: 507-354-8221; E-mail: dallmagl@mlc-wels.edu.
Track and Field: Chuck Hussman; Phone: 507-354-8221; E-mail: hussmace@mlc-wels.edu.
Volleyball: Drew Buck; Phone: 507-354-8221; E-mail: buckdm@mlc-wels.edu.

MARTIN METHODIST COLLEGE
Pulaski, Tennessee

Red Hawks ◆ NAIA ◆ TranSouth Conference ◆ http://www.martinmethodist.edu/

Independent United Methodist 4-year, founded 1870
Coed, 631 undergraduate students, 65% full-time, 61% women, 39% men
Small-town 6-acre campus with easy access to Nashville
Minimally difficult entrance level, 97% of applicants were admitted

Freshmen *Admission:* 377 applied, 364 were accepted, 157 enrolled.
Tuition and fees (2003–04): $13,000 (full-time). *Room and board:* $4000.
Financial Aid (All incoming freshmen): *Average need-based gift aid:* $4100. *Average non-need based aid:* $1872. *Average aid to full-time undergraduates:* $7228.
Athletic Department: *Director of Athletics:* Jeff Bain; Fax: 931-363-9873; E-mail: jbain@martinmethodist.edu. *Sports Information Director:* Pat Ford; Phone: 931-363-9883; E-mail: pford@martinmethodist.edu.

MEN'S COACHES
Baseball: George Ogilvie; Phone: 931-363-9827; E-mail: gogilvie@martinmethodist.edu.
Basketball: Chris Croft; Phone: 931-363-9826; E-mail: ccroft@martinmethodist.edu.
Cheerleading: Royce Hughes; Phone: 931-363-9828; E-mail: rhughes@martinmethodist.edu.
Golf: Jamie Morefield; Phone: 931-363-9881; E-mail: jmorefield@martinmethodist.edu.
Soccer: Paschal Dunne; Phone: 931-363-9880; E-mail: pdunne@martinmethodist.edu.
Tennis: Melinda Sevier; Phone: 931-363-9885; E-mail: msevier@martinmethodist.edu.

WOMEN'S COACHES
Basketball: Randy Roberts; Phone: 931-363-9829; E-mail: rroberts@martinmethodist.edu.
Cheerleading: Royce Hughes; Phone: 931-363-9828; E-mail: rhughes@martinmethodist.edu.
Soccer: Paschal Dunne; Phone: 931-363-9880; E-mail: pdunne@martinmethodist.edu.
Softball: Brandie Paul; Phone: 931-363-9879; E-mail: bpaul@martinmethodist.edu.
Tennis: Melinda Sevier; Phone: 931-363-9885; E-mail: msevier@martinmethodist.edu.
Volleyball: Rose Magers-Powell; Phone: 931-363-9878; E-mail: rpowell@martinmethodist.edu.

MARY BALDWIN COLLEGE
Staunton, Virginia

Fighting Squirrels ◆ NCAA III ◆ Atlantic Women's Colleges Conference ◆ http://www.mbc.edu/

Independent comprehensive, founded 1842
Coed, 1,565 undergraduate students, 70% full-time, 94% women, 6% men
Small-town 54-acre campus
Moderately difficult entrance level, 76% of applicants were admitted

Freshmen *Admission:* 1,443 applied, 1,094 were accepted, 278 enrolled. *Test scores:* SAT verbal scores over 500: 71%; SAT math scores over 500: 56%; SAT verbal scores over 600: 30%; SAT math scores over 600: 13%; SAT verbal scores over 700: 5%; SAT math scores over 700: 5%.
Tuition and fees (2003–04): $19,414 (full-time). *Room and board:* $5525 (room only: $3525).
Financial Aid (All incoming freshmen): *Average need-based gift aid:* $12,371. *Average non-need based aid:* $12,391. *Average aid to full-time undergraduates:* $21,693.
Athletic Department: *Director of Athletics:* Donna Miller; Phone: 540-887-7160; Fax: 540-887-7322; E-mail: dmiller@mbc.edu. *Sports Information Director:* Jackie Bryan; Phone: 540-887-7320; E-mail: jbryan@mbc.edu.

WOMEN'S COACHES
Basketball: Jackie Bryan; Phone: 540-887-7320; E-mail: jbryan@mbc.edu.
Cross Country: Gary Kessler; Phone: 540-887-7165; E-mail: gkessler@mbc.edu.
Field Hockey: Holly Russell; Phone: 540-887-7356; E-mail: hrussell@mbc.edu.
Soccer: Andrew Green; Phone: 540-887-7160; E-mail: greenaj5975@mbc.edu.
Softball: Christy Shelton; Phone: 540-887-7321; E-mail: cshelton@mbc.edu.
Swimming: Amy Darby; Phone: 540-887-7185; E-mail: adarby@mbc.edu.
Tennis: Bev Coffman; Phone: 540-887-7185; E-mail: bcoffman@mbc.edu.
Volleyball: Tiffany Barnes; Phone: 540-887-7153; E-mail: tbarnes@mbc.edu.

MARYMOUNT UNIVERSITY
Arlington, Virginia

Saints ◆ NCAA III ◆ Capital Athletic Conference ◆ http://www.marymount.edu/

Independent religious comprehensive, founded 1950, affiliated with Roman Catholic Church
Coed, 2,179 undergraduate students, 79% full-time, 75% women, 25% men
Suburban 21-acre campus with easy access to Washington, DC
Moderately difficult entrance level, 74% of applicants were admitted

Freshmen *Admission:* 1,665 applied, 1,349 were accepted, 386 enrolled. *Test scores:* SAT verbal scores over 500: 56%; SAT math scores over 500: 48%; SAT verbal scores over 600: 14%; SAT math scores over 600: 10%; SAT verbal scores over 700: 2%; SAT math scores over 700: 2%.
Tuition and fees (2003–04): $16,438 (full-time). *Room and board:* $7230.
Financial Aid (All incoming freshmen): *Average need-based gift aid:* $6510. *Average non-need based aid:* $8535. *Average aid to full-time undergraduates:* $13,689.
Athletic Department: *Director of Athletics:* Bill Finney; Phone: 703-284-1619; Fax: 703-284-3684; E-mail: bfinney@marymount.edu. *Sports Information Director:* Judy Finney; Phone: 703-284-3838; E-mail: jfinney@marymount.edu.

MEN'S COACHES
Basketball: Scott McClary; Phone: 703-284-1515; E-mail: scott.mcclary@marymount.edu.
Cheerleading: Jen Barthle; Phone: 703-966-8958; E-mail: jbotchie@yahoo.com.
Golf: Patrick Aylward; Phone: 703-284-6946; E-mail: patrick.aylward@marymount.edu.
Lacrosse: Chris Swanenburg; Phone: 703-284-1690; E-mail: chris.swanenburg@marymount.edu.
Soccer: Keith Moser; Phone: 703-284-1574; E-mail: william.moser@marymount.edu.
Swimming: Mike Clark; Phone: 703-284-3832; E-mail: mclark@marymount.edu.

WOMEN'S COACHES
Basketball: Bill Finney; Phone: 703-284-1619; E-mail: bfinney@marymount.edu.
Cheerleading: Jen Barthle; Phone: 703-966-8958; E-mail: jbotchie@yahoo.com.
Lacrosse: Darcy Littlefield; Phone: 703-284-3831; E-mail: darcy.littlefield@marymount.edu.
Soccer: Bob Meden; Phone: 703-284-1574; E-mail: rmeden@marymount.edu.
Swimming: Mike Clark; Phone: 703-284-3832; E-mail: mclark@marymount.edu.
Volleyball: Beth Ann Wilson; Phone: 703-284-3834; E-mail: bethannwilson@aol.com.

MARYVILLE COLLEGE
Maryville, Tennessee

Fighting Scots ◆ NCAA III ◆ Independent ◆ http://www.maryvillecollege.edu/

Independent Presbyterian 4-year, founded 1819
Coed, 1,052 undergraduate students, 98% full-time, 56% women, 44% men
Suburban 350-acre campus with easy access to Knoxville
Moderately difficult entrance level, 79% of applicants were admitted

Freshmen *Admission:* 1,378 applied, 1,112 were accepted, 292 enrolled. *Test scores:* SAT verbal scores over 500: 72%; SAT math scores over 500: 69%; SAT verbal scores over 600: 39%; SAT math scores over 600: 40%; SAT verbal scores over 700: 4%; SAT math scores over 700: 7%.
Tuition and fees (2004–05): $21,065 (full-time). *Room and board:* $6500 (room only: $3200).
Financial Aid (All incoming freshmen): *Average need-based gift aid:* $13,226. *Average non-need based aid:* $13,370. *Average aid to full-time undergraduates:* $19,076.

Athletic Department: *Director of Athletics:* Randy Lambert; Phone: 865-981-8287; Fax: 865-981-8285; E-mail: randy.lambert@maryvillecollege.edu. *Sports Information Director:* Eric Etchison; Phone: 865-981-8283; E-mail: eric.etchison@maryvillecollege.edu.

MEN'S COACHES
Baseball: Eric Etchison; Phone: 865-981-8283; E-mail: eric.etchison@maryvillecollege.edu.
Basketball: Randy Lambert; Phone: 865-981-8287; E-mail: randy.lambert@maryvillecollege.edu.
Cheerleading: Andy Lewter; Phone: 865-981-8215; E-mail: andy.lewter@maryvillecollege.edu.
Cross Country: Beth Coppenger; Phone: 865-981-8099; E-mail: beth.coppenger@maryvillecollege.edu.
Football: Tony Ierulli; Phone: 865-981-8282; E-mail: tony.ierulli@maryvillecollege.edu.
Soccer: Pepe Fernadez; Phone: 865-981-8284; E-mail: pepe.fernandez@maryvillecollege.edu.
Tennis: Chad Tracy; Phone: 865-981-8280; E-mail: chad.tracy@maryvillecollege.edu.

WOMEN'S COACHES
Basketball: Dee Bell; Phone: 865-981-8291; E-mail: dee.bell@maryvillecollege.edu.
Cheerleading: Andy Lewter; Phone: 865-981-8215; E-mail: andy.lewter@maryvillecollege.edu.
Cross Country: Beth Coppenger; Phone: 865-981-8099; E-mail: beth.coppenger@maryvillecollege.edu.
Soccer: Pepe Fernadez; Phone: 865-981-8284; E-mail: pepe.fernandez@maryvillecollege.edu.
Softball: Danny Fish; Phone: 865-981-8228; E-mail: danny.fish@maryvillecollege.edu.
Tennis: Chad Tracy; Phone: 865-981-8280; E-mail: chad.tracy@maryvillecollege.edu.
Volleyball: Kandis Schram; Phone: 865-981-8290; E-mail: kandis.schram@maryvillecollege.edu.

MARYVILLE UNIVERSITY OF SAINT LOUIS
St. Louis, Missouri

Saints ◆ NCAA III ◆ St. Louis Athletic Conference ◆ http://www.maryville.edu/

Independent comprehensive, founded 1872
Coed, 2,705 undergraduate students, 56% full-time, 76% women, 24% men
Suburban 130-acre campus
Moderately difficult entrance level, 71% of applicants were admitted

Freshmen *Admission:* 1,154 applied, 844 were accepted, 335 enrolled.
Tuition and fees (2004–05): $16,300 (full-time). *Room and board:* $7000.
Financial Aid (All incoming freshmen): *Average need-based gift aid:* $9806. *Average non-need based aid:* $3558. *Average aid to full-time undergraduates:* $12,787.
Athletic Department: *Director of Athletics:* Matt Rogers; Phone: 314-529-9878; Fax: 314-529-9947; E-mail: mrogers@maryville.edu. *Sports Information Director:* Nicole Peloquin; Phone: 314-529-9312; E-mail: npeloquin@maryville.edu.

MEN'S COACHES
Baseball: Tracy Schmidt; Phone: 314-529-9483; E-mail: tschmidt@maryville.edu.
Basketball: Matt Rogers; Phone: 314-529-9878; E-mail: mrogers@maryville.edu.
Cheerleading: Sharron Luellen; Phone: 314-529-9483; E-mail: sluellen@maryville.edu.
Cross Country: Glen House; Phone: 314-529-9483; E-mail: glenh@maryville.edu.
Golf: Glenn Paulus; Phone: 314-529-9484; E-mail: gpaulus@maryville.edu.
Soccer: Eric Delabar; Phone: 314-529-9483; E-mail: edelabar@maryville.edu.
Tennis: Karim Madatali; Phone: 314-529-9483; E-mail: kmadatali@maryville.edu.

WOMEN'S COACHES
Basketball: Chris Ellis; Phone: 314-529-9483; E-mail: cellis@maryville.edu.

Maryville University of Saint Louis *(continued)*

Cheerleading: Sharron Luellen; Phone: 314-529-9483; E-mail: sluellen@maryville.edu.

Cross Country: Glen House; Phone: 314-529-9483; E-mail: glenh@maryville.edu.

Soccer: Eric Delabar; Phone: 314-529-9483; E-mail: edelabar@maryville.edu.

Softball: Charlie Kennedy; Phone: 314-529-9483; E-mail: kennedy@maryville.edu.

Tennis: Erica Crowell-Hoffman; Phone: 314-529-9483; E-mail: ecrowellhoffman@maryville.edu.

Volleyball: Brian Dodillet; Phone: 314-529-9483; E-mail: bdodillet@maryville.edu.

MARYWOOD UNIVERSITY
Scranton, Pennsylvania

Pacers ◆ NCAA III ◆ Pennsylvania Athletic Conference ◆ http://www.marywood.edu/

Independent Roman Catholic comprehensive, founded 1915
Coed, 1,751 undergraduate students, 87% full-time, 72% women, 28% men
Suburban 115-acre campus
Moderately difficult entrance level, 72% of applicants were admitted

Freshmen *Admission:* 1,275 applied, 1,011 were accepted, 286 enrolled. *Test scores:* SAT verbal scores over 500: 60%; SAT math scores over 500: 48%; SAT verbal scores over 600: 13%; SAT math scores over 600: 11%; SAT verbal scores over 700: 1%; SAT math scores over 700: 1%.
Tuition and fees (2003–04): $19,475 (full-time). *Room and board:* $8134 (room only: $4200).
Financial Aid (All incoming freshmen): *Average need-based gift aid:* $11,073. *Average non-need based aid:* $8110. *Average aid to full-time undergraduates:* $14,467.
Athletic Department: *Director of Athletics:* Mary Jo Gunning; Phone: 570-961-4724; Fax: 570-961-4730; E-mail: gunning@ac.marywood.edu. *Sports Information Director:* Will Donohoe; Phone: 570-961-4724; E-mail: donohoe@ac.marywood.edu.

MEN'S COACHES
Baseball: Joe Ross; Phone: 570-961-4724; E-mail: jross@es.marywood.edu.

Basketball: Eric Grundman; Phone: 570-961-4724; E-mail: grundman@es.marywood.edu.

Cross Country: John Kirby; Phone: 570-961-4724; E-mail: kamplot343@hotmail.com.

Soccer: Hector Uribe; Phone: 570-961-4724; E-mail: coachuribe@hotmail.com.

Tennis: Keith Hetsko; Phone: 570-961-4724; E-mail: vunomeme@aol.com.

WOMEN'S COACHES
Basketball: Teri Snyder; Phone: 570-961-4724; E-mail: snydert@ns.neiu.k12.pa.us.

Cross Country: John Kirby; Phone: 570-961-4724; E-mail: kamplot343@hotmail.com.

Field Hockey: Samantha Merrill; Phone: 570-961-4724; E-mail: merrill@es.marywood.edu.

Soccer: Julie Heincelman; Phone: 570-961-4724; E-mail: jheincelman@hotmail.com.

Softball: Bob Fitzsimmons; Phone: 570-961-4724.

Tennis: Janice Winslow; Phone: 570-961-4724; E-mail: kanej1@scranton.edu.

Volleyball: Jennifer Newton; Phone: 570-961-4724; E-mail: rjnhome@epix.net.

MASSACHUSETTS COLLEGE OF LIBERAL ARTS
North Adams, Massachusetts

Trailblazers ◆ NCAA III ◆ Massachusetts State College Athletic Conference ◆ http://www.mcla.edu/

State-supported comprehensive, founded 1894, part of Massachusetts Public Higher Education System
Coed, 1,458 undergraduate students, 82% full-time, 61% women, 39% men
Small-town 80-acre campus
Moderately difficult entrance level, 64% of applicants were admitted

Freshmen *Admission:* 1,206 applied, 805 were accepted, 257 enrolled. *Test scores:* SAT verbal scores over 500: 68%; SAT math scores over 500: 58%; SAT verbal scores over 600: 26%; SAT math scores over 600: 14%; SAT verbal scores over 700: 4%; SAT math scores over 700: 1%.
Tuition and fees (2003–04): $5397 (resident), $14,342 (nonresident). *Room and board:* $5620 (room only: $2946).
Financial Aid (All incoming freshmen): *Average need-based gift aid:* $4241. *Average non-need based aid:* $2998. *Average aid to full-time undergraduates:* $6389.
Athletic Department: *Director of Athletics:* Scott Nichols; Phone: 413-662-5412; Fax: 413-662-5357; E-mail: snichols@mcla.mass.edu. *Sports Information Director:* Deb Raber; Phone: 413-662-5355; E-mail: draber@mcla.mass.edu.

MEN'S COACHES
Baseball: Jeff Puleri; Phone: 413-662-5403; E-mail: jpuleri@mcla.mass.edu.

Basketball: Devin Gotham; Phone: 413-662-5352; E-mail: dgotham@mcla.edu.

Cross Country: Devin Gotham; Phone: 413-662-5352; E-mail: dgotham@mcla.edu.

Golf: Jack Tosone; Phone: 413-662-5411; E-mail: snichols@mcla.mass.edu.

Soccer: Ron Shewcraft; Phone: 413-662-5354; E-mail: rshewcra@mcla.mass.edu.

WOMEN'S COACHES
Basketball: Tez Kraft; Phone: 413-662-5130; E-mail: tkraft@mcla.mass.edu.

Cross Country: Devin Gotham; Phone: 413-662-5352; E-mail: dgotham@mcla.edu.

Soccer: Deb Rader; Phone: 413-662-5355; E-mail: draber@mcla.mass.edu.

Softball: Brian Claypool; Phone: 413-662-5411.

Tennis: Whitney Suters; Phone: 413-662-5411; E-mail: snichols@mcla.mass.edu.

Volleyball: Ed Paquette; Phone: 413-662-5549; E-mail: snichols@mcla.mass.edu.

MASSACHUSETTS INSTITUTE OF TECHNOLOGY
Cambridge, Massachusetts

Engineers ◆ NCAA III ◆ New England Women's & Men's Athletics Conference ◆ http://web.mit.edu/

Independent university, founded 1861
Coed, 4,112 undergraduate students, 99% full-time, 42% women, 58% men
Urban 154-acre campus with easy access to Boston
Most difficult entrance level, 1% of applicants were admitted

Freshmen *Admission:* 10,549 applied, 1,735 were accepted, 1,019 enrolled. *Test scores:* SAT verbal scores over 500: 99%; SAT verbal scores over 600: 95%; SAT math scores over 600: 100%; SAT verbal scores over 700: 63%; SAT math scores over 700: 89%.
Tuition and fees (2003–04): $29,600 (full-time). *Room and board:* $8710 (room only: $4560).
Financial Aid (All incoming freshmen): *Average need-based gift aid:* $20,659. *Average non-need based aid:* $8158. *Average aid to full-time undergraduates:* $22,464.

Athletic Department: *Director of Athletics:* Candace Royer; Phone: 617-253-4497; Fax: 617-258-7343; E-mail: clroyer@mit.edu. *Sports Information Director:* James Kramer; Phone: 617-258-5265; E-mail: jdkramer@mit.edu.

MEN'S COACHES

Baseball: Andrew Barlow; Phone: 617-258-7310; E-mail: anbarlow@mit.edu.
Basketball: Larry Anderson; Phone: 617-253-5007; E-mail: landerso@mit.edu.
Cheerleading: Maritza Rodriguez; Phone: 617-258-4498.
Cross Country: Halston Taylor; Phone: 617-253-4918; E-mail: hwtaylor@mit.edu.
Football: Dwight Smith; Phone: 617-253-5018; E-mail: desmith@mit.edu.
Golf: Jim Burke; Phone: 617-253-4919; E-mail: jrbjr6@aol.com.
Lacrosse: Walter Alessi; Phone: 617-258-5782; E-mail: waalessi@mit.edu.
Soccer: Walter Alessi; Phone: 617-258-5782; E-mail: waalessi@mit.edu.
Swimming: Dawn Gerken; Phone: 617-253-4490; E-mail: dgerken@mit.edu.
Tennis: Jeff Hamilton; Phone: 617-258-0333; E-mail: coach@mit.edu.
Track and Field: Halston Taylor; Phone: 617-253-4918; E-mail: hwtaylor@mit.edu.
Volleyball: Paul Dill; Phone: 617-258-0331; E-mail: pdill@mit.edu.
Wrestling: Tom Layte; Phone: 617-253-0332; E-mail: tlayte@mit.edu.

WOMEN'S COACHES

Basketball: Kristi Straub; Phone: 617-253-5006; E-mail: sprtegal@mit.edu.
Cheerleading: Maritza Rodriguez; Phone: 617-258-4498.
Cross Country: Paul Slovenski; Phone: 617-253-3633; E-mail: sluggo@mit.edu.
Field Hockey: Cheryl Silva; Phone: 617-253-4910; E-mail: fhlxc@mit.edu.
Gymnastics: Eduardo Ovalle; Phone: 617-258-0330; E-mail: eduardo@mit.edu.
Lacrosse: Cheryl Silva; Phone: 617-253-4910; E-mail: fhlxc@mit.edu.
Soccer: Kristi Straub; Phone: 617-253-5006; E-mail: sprtegal@mit.edu.
Softball: Lisa Naas; Phone: 617-353-8703; E-mail: lnaas@mit.edu.
Swimming: Dawn Gerken; Phone: 617-253-4490; E-mail: dgerken@mit.edu.
Tennis: Carol Matsuzaki; Phone: 617-253-1451; E-mail: handy@mit.edu.
Track and Field: Paul Slovenski; Phone: 617-253-3633; E-mail: sluggo@mit.edu.
Volleyball: Paul Dill; Phone: 617-258-0331; E-mail: pdill@mit.edu.

MASSACHUSETTS MARITIME ACADEMY
Buzzards Bay, Massachusetts

Buccaneers ◆ NCAA III ◆ Massachusetts State College Athletic Conference ◆ http://www.maritime.edu/

State-supported 4-year, founded 1891, part of Massachusetts Public Higher Education System
Coed, primarily men, 927 undergraduate students, 97% full-time, 12% women, 88% men
Small-town 55-acre campus with easy access to Boston
Moderately difficult entrance level, 6% of applicants were admitted

Freshmen *Admission:* 808 applied, 485 were accepted, 275 enrolled. *Test scores:* SAT verbal scores over 500: 52%; SAT math scores over 500: 64%; SAT verbal scores over 600: 10%; SAT math scores over 600: 17%; SAT verbal scores over 700: 1%; SAT math scores over 700: 1%.
Tuition and fees (2004–05): $4663 (resident), $15,143 (nonresident). *Room and board:* $5809 (room only: $2884).
Financial Aid (All incoming freshmen): *Average need-based gift aid:* $1943. *Average non-need based aid:* $1943. *Average aid to full-time undergraduates:* $6087.
Athletic Department: *Director of Athletics:* Bob Corradi; Phone: 508-830-5055; Fax: 508-830-5056; E-mail: rcorradi@mma.mass.edu.

MEN'S COACHES

Baseball: Bob Corradi; Phone: 508-830-5055; E-mail: rcorradi@mma.mass.edu.
Cross Country: Chris Ryan; Phone: 508-830-5003; E-mail: cryan@mma.mass.edu.
Football: Joe Domingos; Phone: 508-830-5046; E-mail: jdomingos@mma.mass.edu.
Lacrosse: Ed Egan; Phone: 508-830-5054.
Soccer: Greg Perry; Phone: 508-830-5000.

WOMEN'S COACHES

Cross Country: Linda Letourneau; Phone: 508-830-5000; E-mail: lletourneau@mma.mass.edu.
Softball: Maureen Holden; Phone: 508-830-5000.
Volleyball: Chris Ratches; Phone: 508-830-5000.

THE MASTER'S COLLEGE AND SEMINARY
Santa Clarita, California

Mustangs ◆ NAIA ◆ Golden State Conference ◆ http://www.masters.edu/

Independent nondenominational comprehensive, founded 1927
Coed, 1,132 undergraduate students, 86% full-time, 51% women, 49% men
Suburban 110-acre campus with easy access to Los Angeles
Moderately difficult entrance level, 54% of applicants were admitted

Freshmen *Admission:* 412 applied, 221 were accepted, 209 enrolled. *Test scores:* SAT verbal scores over 500: 81%; SAT math scores over 500: 80%; SAT verbal scores over 600: 40%; SAT math scores over 600: 32%; SAT verbal scores over 700: 6%; SAT math scores over 700: 5%.
Tuition and fees (2003–04): $17,200 (full-time). *Room and board:* $6050 (room only: $3370).
Financial Aid (All incoming freshmen): *Average need-based gift aid:* $10,900. *Average non-need based aid:* $5399. *Average aid to full-time undergraduates:* $13,910.
Athletic Department: *Director of Athletics:* Paul Berry; Phone: 661-259-3540; Fax: 661-254-6129. *Sports Information Director:* Dan Waldeck; Phone: 661-259-3540; E-mail: athletics@masters.edu.

MEN'S COACHES

Baseball: Monte Brooks; Phone: 661-254-3540.
Basketball: Bill Oates; Phone: 661-254-3540.
Cross Country: Dan Waldeck; Phone: 661-254-3540.
Golf: Jim Lundstrom; Phone: 661-254-3540.
Soccer: Jim Rickard; Phone: 661-254-3540.

WOMEN'S COACHES

Basketball: Ken Sugarman; Phone: 661-254-3540.
Cross Country: Dan Waldeck; Phone: 661-254-3540.
Soccer: Allan Bowden; Phone: 661-254-3540.
Tennis: Alan Harvey; Phone: 661-254-3540.
Volleyball: Beth Avila; Phone: 661-254-3540.

MAYVILLE STATE UNIVERSITY
Mayville, North Dakota

Comets ◆ NAIA ◆ Dakota Conference ◆ http://www.mayvillestate.edu/

State-supported 4-year, founded 1889, part of North Dakota University System
Coed, 817 undergraduate students, 75% full-time, 57% women, 43% men
Rural 60-acre campus
Noncompetitive entrance level

Freshmen *Admission:* 222 enrolled.
Tuition and fees (2004–05): $4356 (resident), $8877 (nonresident). *Room and board:* $3508 (room only: $1452).
Financial Aid (All incoming freshmen): *Average need-based gift aid:* $2747. *Average non-need based aid:* $1442. *Average aid to full-time undergraduates:* $5554.
Athletic Department: *Director of Athletics:* Terry Layton; Phone: 701-786-4834; Fax: 701-788-4669; E-mail: terry_layton@mail.masu.nodak.edu.

Mayville State University *(continued)*

MEN'S COACHES

Baseball: Scott Berry; Phone: 701-788-4771; E-mail: scott_berry@mail.masu.nodak.edu.
Basketball: Terry Layton; Phone: 701-788-4834; E-mail: terry_layton@mail.masu.nodak.edu.
Cheerleading: Rebecca Gunderson; Phone: 701-788-4841; E-mail: bgunderson@mail.masu.nodak.edu.
Football: Kelly Jeffrey; Phone: 701-788-4659; E-mail: k_jeffrey@mail.masu.nodak.edu.

WOMEN'S COACHES

Basketball: Jay Tschetter; Phone: 701-788-4665; E-mail: tschetter@mail.masu.nodak.edu.
Cheerleading: Rebecca Gunderson; Phone: 701-788-4841; E-mail: bgunderson@mail.masu.nodak.edu.
Softball: Cari Boe; Phone: 701-788-4658; E-mail: c_boe@mail.masu.nodak.edu.
Volleyball: Chris Rodgers; Phone: 701-788-4837; E-mail: c_rodgers@mail.maus.nodak.edu.

MCDANIEL COLLEGE
Westminster, Maryland

Green Terror ◆ NCAA III ◆ Centennial Conference ◆ http://www.mcdaniel.edu/

Independent comprehensive, founded 1867
Coed, 1,744 undergraduate students, 97% full-time, 57% women, 43% men
Suburban 160-acre campus with easy access to Baltimore and Washington, DC
Moderately difficult entrance level, 80% of applicants were admitted

Freshmen *Admission:* 2,008 applied, 1,676 were accepted, 451 enrolled. *Test scores:* SAT verbal scores over 500: 74%; SAT math scores over 500: 78%; SAT verbal scores over 600: 28%; SAT math scores over 600: 28%; SAT verbal scores over 700: 5%; SAT math scores over 700: 3%.
Tuition and fees (2003–04): $23,160 (full-time). *Room and board:* $5280 (room only: $2690).
Financial Aid (All incoming freshmen): *Average need-based gift aid:* $8023. *Average non-need based aid:* $7640. *Average aid to full-time undergraduates:* $18,674.
Athletic Department: *Director of Athletics:* David Melendez; Phone: 410-848-7000; E-mail: dmelendez@mcdaniel.edu. *Sports Information Director:* Phone: 410-848-2291; E-mail: sid@mcdaniel.edu.

MEN'S COACHES

Baseball: Dave Seibert; Phone: 410-848-7000; E-mail: dseibert@mcdaniel.edu.
Basketball: Jay Dull; Phone: 410-848-7000; E-mail: jdull@mcdaniel.edu.
Cross Country: Doug Renner; Phone: 410-848-7000; E-mail: drenner@mcdaniel.edu.
Football: Tim Keating; Phone: 410-848-7000; E-mail: football@mcdaniel.edu.
Golf: Scott Moyer; Phone: 410-848-7000; E-mail: grnterror@qis.net.
Lacrosse: Jim Townsend; Phone: 410-848-7000; E-mail: jtownsen@mcdaniel.edu.
Soccer: John Plevyak; Phone: 410-848-7000; E-mail: dplevyak@mcdaniel.edu.
Swimming: Kim Easterday; Phone: 410-848-7000; E-mail: keasterd@mcdaniel.edu.
Tennis: Kevin Klunk; Phone: 410-848-7000; E-mail: kklunk@mcdaniel.edu.
Track and Field: Doug Renner; Phone: 410-848-7000; E-mail: drenner@mcdaniel.edu.
Wrestling: Sam Gardner; Phone: 410-848-7000.

WOMEN'S COACHES

Basketball: Becky Martin; Phone: 410-848-7000; E-mail: rmartin@mcdaniel.edu.
Cross Country: Doug Renner; Phone: 410-848-7000; E-mail: drenner@mcdaniel.edu.
Field Hockey: Mindy McCord; Phone: 410-848-7000; E-mail: mmccord@mcdaniel.edu.
Golf: Michael Diehl; Phone: 410-848-7000; E-mail: grnterror@qis.net.
Lacrosse: Marjorie Bliss; Phone: 410-386-4611; E-mail: mmccord@mcdaniel.edu.
Soccer: Scott Swanson; Phone: 410-848-7000; E-mail: scswanson1@aol.com.
Softball: George Dix; Phone: 410-848-7000; E-mail: gdix@mcdaniel.edu.
Swimming: Kim Easterday; Phone: 410-848-7000; E-mail: keasterd@mcdaniel.edu.
Tennis: Kevin Klunk; Phone: 410-848-7000; E-mail: kklunk@mcdaniel.edu.
Track and Field: Doug Renner; Phone: 410-848-7000; E-mail: drenner@mcdaniel.edu.
Volleyball: Carole Molloy; Phone: 410-848-7000; E-mail: cmolloy@mcdaniel.edu.

MCKENDREE COLLEGE
Lebanon, Illinois

Bearcats ◆ NAIA ◆ American Midwest Conference; Mid-States Football Conference ◆ http://www.mckendree.edu/

Independent religious 4-year, founded 1828, affiliated with United Methodist Church
Coed, 2,115 undergraduate students, 74% full-time, 61% women, 39% men
Small-town 80-acre campus with easy access to St. Louis
Moderately difficult entrance level, 73% of applicants were admitted

Freshmen *Admission:* 1,182 applied, 865 were accepted, 310 enrolled.
Tuition and fees (2003–04): $15,200 (full-time). *Room and board:* $5920.
Financial Aid (All incoming freshmen): *Average need-based gift aid:* $10,926. *Average non-need based aid:* $9734. *Average aid to full-time undergraduates:* $12,907.
Athletic Department: *Director of Athletics:* Harry Statham; Phone: 618-537-6871; Fax: 618-537-6876; E-mail: hstatham@mckendree.edu. *Sports Information Director:* Scott Cummings; Phone: 618-537-6879; E-mail: secummin@mckendree.edu.

MEN'S COACHES

Baseball: Jim Boehne; Phone: 618-537-6906; E-mail: jboehne@mckendree.edu.
Basketball: Harry Statham; Phone: 618-537-6871; E-mail: hstatham@mckendree.edu.
Cheerleading: Rosalie Wand; Phone: 800-232-7228.
Cross Country: Gary White; Phone: 618-537-6442; E-mail: bgwhite@mckendree.edu.
Football: Carl Poelker; Phone: 618-537-6446.
Golf: Fred Underwood; Phone: 618-537-6852; E-mail: funderwo@mckendree.edu.
Soccer: Tim Strange; Phone: 618-537-6910; E-mail: tstrange@mckendree.edu.
Tennis: Bill Rusick; Phone: 618-537-6873.
Track and Field: Gary White; Phone: 618-537-6442; E-mail: bgwhite@mckendree.edu.
Wrestling: James Kisgen; Phone: 618-537-6872; E-mail: jjkisgen@mckendree.edu.

WOMEN'S COACHES

Basketball: Melissa Ringhausen; Phone: 618-537-6874; E-mail: mringhau@mckendree.edu.
Cheerleading: Rosalie Wand; Phone: 800-232-7228.
Cross Country: Gary White; Phone: 618-537-6442; E-mail: bgwhite@mckendree.edu.
Golf: Fred Underwood; Phone: 618-537-6852; E-mail: funderwo@mckendree.edu.
Soccer: Tim Strange; Phone: 618-537-6910; E-mail: tstrange@mckendree.edu.
Softball: Evelyn Bean; Phone: 618-537-6908; E-mail: eybean@mckendree.edu.
Tennis: Maureen Moore; Phone: 618-537-6912.
Track and Field: Gary White; Phone: 618-537-6442; E-mail: bgwhite@mckendree.edu.
Volleyball: Evelyn Bean; Phone: 618-537-6908; E-mail: eybean@mckendree.edu.

MCMURRY UNIVERSITY
Abilene, Texas

Indians ◆ NCAA III ◆ American Southwest Conference ◆ http://www.mcm.edu/

Independent United Methodist 4-year, founded 1923
Coed, 1,376 undergraduate students, 84% full-time, 49% women, 51% men
Urban 41-acre campus
Moderately difficult entrance level, 60% of applicants were admitted

Freshmen *Admission:* 908 applied, 556 were accepted, 258 enrolled. *Test scores:* SAT verbal scores over 500: 36%; SAT math scores over 500: 45%; SAT verbal scores over 600: 9%; SAT math scores over 600: 11%; SAT verbal scores over 700: 1%; SAT math scores over 700: 2%.
Tuition and fees (2003–04): $12,980 (full-time). *Room and board:* $5046 (room only: $2350).
Financial Aid (All incoming freshmen): *Average need-based gift aid:* $6567. *Average non-need based aid:* $5039. *Average aid to full-time undergraduates:* $12,895.
Athletic Department: *Director of Athletics:* Jerry Larned; Phone: 325-793-4631; Fax: 325-793-4659; E-mail: jlarned@mcm.edu. *Sports Information Director:* Patrick Stewart; Phone: 325-793-4612; E-mail: stewartp@mcmurryadm.mcm.edu.

MEN'S COACHES
Baseball: Lee Driggers; Phone: 325-793-4650; E-mail: driggerl@mcmurryadm.mcm.edu.
Basketball: Ron Holmes; Phone: 325-793-4647; E-mail: holmesr@mcmurryadm.mcm.edu.
Cheerleading: Susan Hunter; Phone: 325-793-4870; E-mail: hunters@mcmurryadm.mcm.edu.
Cross Country: David Chandler; Phone: 325-793-4939; E-mail: chandled@mcmurryadm.mcm.edu.
Football: Steve Keenum; Phone: 325-793-4640; E-mail: keenums@mcmurryadm.mcm.edu.
Golf: Russ Evans; Phone: 325-793-4653; E-mail: evansr@mcmurryadm.mcm.edu.
Soccer: Steve Allan; Phone: 325-793-4656.
Swimming: Bev Ball; Phone: 325-793-4869; E-mail: ballb@mcmurryadm.mcm.edu.
Tennis: Mark Hathorn; Phone: 325-793-4657; E-mail: hathornm@mcmurryadm.mcm.edu.
Track and Field: Barbara Crousen; Phone: 325-793-4646; E-mail: crousenb@mcmurryadm.mcm.edu.

WOMEN'S COACHES
Basketball: Sam Nichols; Phone: 325-793-4638; E-mail: nicholss@mcmurryadm.mcm.edu.
Cheerleading: Susan Hunter; Phone: 325-793-4870; E-mail: hunters@mcmurryadm.mcm.edu.
Cross Country: David Chandler; Phone: 325-793-4939; E-mail: chandled@mcmurryadm.mcm.edu.
Golf: Russ Evans; Phone: 325-793-4653; E-mail: evansr@mcmurryadm.mcm.edu.
Soccer: Christy Cousins; Phone: 325-793-4630; E-mail: cousinsc@mcmurryadm.mcm.edu.
Swimming: Bev Ball; Phone: 325-793-4869; E-mail: ballb@mcmurryadm.mcm.edu.
Tennis: Mark Hathorn; Phone: 325-793-4657; E-mail: hathornm@mcmurryadm.mcm.edu.
Track and Field: Barbara Crousen; Phone: 325-793-4646; E-mail: crousenb@mcmurryadm.mcm.edu.
Volleyball: Cammrie Petree; Phone: 325-793-4635; E-mail: petreec@mcmurryadm.mcm.edu.

MCNEESE STATE UNIVERSITY
Lake Charles, Louisiana

Cowboys ◆ NCAA I ◆ Southland Conference ◆ http://www.mcneese.edu/

State-supported comprehensive, founded 1939, part of University of Louisiana System
Coed, 7,330 undergraduate students, 82% full-time, 58% women, 42% men
Suburban 580-acre campus
Moderately difficult entrance level, 87% of applicants were admitted

Freshmen *Admission:* 2,183 applied, 1,927 were accepted, 1,563 enrolled.
Tuition and fees (2003–04): $2772 (resident), $8838 (nonresident). *Room and board:* $3788.
Athletic Department: *Director of Athletics:* Harold Watkins; Phone: 337-475-5908; Fax: 337-475-5202. *Sports Information Director:* Louis Bonnette; Phone: 337-475-5207; E-mail: lbonnette@structurex.net.

MEN'S COACHES
Baseball: Todd Butler; Phone: 337-475-5484.
Basketball: George Price; Phone: 337-475-5480.
Cross Country: Russ Buller; Phone: 337-475-5482.
Football: Tommy Tate; Phone: 337-475-5214.
Golf: Don Meadows; Phone: 337-475-5382.
Track and Field: Russ Buller; Phone: 337-475-5482.

WOMEN'S COACHES
Basketball: Carol Sensley; Phone: 337-475-5935; E-mail: csensley@mail.mcneese.edu.
Cross Country: Russ Buller; Phone: 337-475-5482.
Golf: Don Meadows; Phone: 337-475-5382.
Soccer: Scooter Savoie; Phone: 337-475-5216; E-mail: rpsavoie01@yahoo.com.
Softball: Scott Eastman; Phone: 337-475-5475.
Tennis: Pat McCain; Phone: 337-475-5382; E-mail: pmccain@mail.mcneese.edu.
Track and Field: Russ Buller; Phone: 337-475-5482.
Volleyball: Lee McBride; Phone: 337-475-5474; E-mail: lmcbride@mail.mcneese.edu.

MCPHERSON COLLEGE
McPherson, Kansas

Bulldogs ◆ NAIA ◆ Kansas Collegiate Conference ◆ http://www.mcpherson.edu/

Independent religious 4-year, founded 1887, affiliated with Church of the Brethren
Coed, 436 undergraduate students, 89% full-time, 39% women, 61% men
Small-town 26-acre campus
Moderately difficult entrance level, 72% of applicants were admitted

Freshmen *Admission:* 532 applied, 390 were accepted, 133 enrolled. *Test scores:* SAT verbal scores over 500: 56%; SAT math scores over 500: 52%; SAT verbal scores over 600: 9%; SAT math scores over 600: 22%.
Tuition and fees (2004–05): $14,645 (full-time). *Room and board:* $5620 (room only: $2345).
Financial Aid (All incoming freshmen): *Average need-based gift aid:* $5315. *Average non-need based aid:* $6273. *Average aid to full-time undergraduates:* $15,951.
Athletic Department: *Director of Athletics:* Bart Gray; Phone: 620-241-0731; Fax: 620-241-8443; E-mail: grayb@mcpherson.edu. *Sports Information Director:* Carol Swenson; Phone: 620-241-0731; E-mail: swensonc@mcpherson.edu.

MEN'S COACHES
Basketball: Roger Trimmell; Phone: 620-241-0731; E-mail: trimmelr@mcpherson.edu.
Cheerleading: Janice Haldi; Phone: 620-241-0731.
Cross Country: Bart Gray; Phone: 620-241-0731; E-mail: grayb@mcpherson.edu.
Football: David Cunningham; Phone: 620-241-0731; E-mail: cunningd@mcpherson.edu.

McPherson College *(continued)*

Soccer: Doug Quint; Phone: 620-241-0731; E-mail: quintd@ mcpherson.edu.
Track and Field: Bart Gray; Phone: 620-241-0731; E-mail: grayb@ mcpherson.edu.

WOMEN'S COACHES

Basketball: Mel Wright; Phone: 620-241-0731; E-mail: wrightm@ mcpherson.edu.
Cheerleading: Janice Haldi; Phone: 620-241-0731.
Cross Country: Bart Gray; Phone: 620-241-0731; E-mail: grayb@ mcpherson.edu.
Soccer: Doug Quint; Phone: 620-241-0731; E-mail: quintd@ mcpherson.edu.
Softball: Mike Mccormick; Phone: 620-241-0731; E-mail: mccormim@ mcpherson.edu.
Track and Field: Bart Gray; Phone: 620-241-0731; E-mail: grayb@ mcpherson.edu.
Volleyball: Nathalea Stephenson; Phone: 620-241-0731; E-mail: stephenn@mcpherson.edu.

MEDAILLE COLLEGE
Buffalo, New York

Mavericks ◆ NCAA III ◆ Allegheny Mountain Conference; Independent ◆ http://www.medaille.edu/

Independent comprehensive, founded 1875
Coed, 1,655 undergraduate students, 91% full-time, 67% women, 33% men
Urban 13-acre campus
Moderately difficult entrance level, 66% of applicants were admitted

Freshmen *Admission:* 772 applied, 508 were accepted, 288 enrolled. *Test scores:* SAT verbal scores over 500: 32%; SAT math scores over 500: 32%; SAT verbal scores over 600: 5%; SAT math scores over 600: 5%.
Tuition and fees (2003–04): $13,660 (full-time). *Room and board:* $6400.
Financial Aid (All incoming freshmen): *Average need-based gift aid:* $2500. *Average non-need based aid:* $1500. *Average aid to full-time undergraduates:* $11,500.
Athletic Department: *Director of Athletics:* Dick Hack; Phone: 716-884-3411; Fax: 716-884-0291; E-mail: dhack@medaille.edu. *Sports Information Director:* Mike Carbery; Phone: 716-884-3411; E-mail: mcarbery@medaille.edu.

MEN'S COACHES

Baseball: Ron Nero; Phone: 716-884-3411.
Basketball: Richard Jacob; Phone: 716-884-3411; E-mail: rjacob@ medaille.edu.
Lacrosse: Mike Carbery; Phone: 716-884-3411; E-mail: mcarbery@ medaille.edu.
Soccer: Dan Krzyzanowicz; Phone: 716-884-3411; E-mail: dkrzyzanowicz@e1b.org.
Volleyball: Keith Koch; Phone: 716-884-3281; E-mail: cmkkoch@aol.com.

WOMEN'S COACHES

Basketball: Peter Lonergan; Phone: 716-884-3411; E-mail: plonergan@ medaille.edu.
Cross Country: Peter Jererko; Phone: 716-884-3411; E-mail: pjerebko@ medaille.edu.
Lacrosse: Dan Krzyzanowicz; Phone: 716-884-3411; E-mail: dkrzyzanowicz@e1b.org.
Soccer: Dan Krzyzanowicz; Phone: 716-884-3411; E-mail: dkrzyzanowicz@e1b.org.
Softball: Robyn Ventura; Phone: 716-884-3411; E-mail: rventura@ mbaum.com.
Volleyball: Laura Edholm; Phone: 716-884-3411; E-mail: ledholm@ medaille.edu.

MEDGAR EVERS COLLEGE OF THE CITY UNIVERSITY OF NEW YORK
Brooklyn, New York

Cougars ◆ NCAA III ◆ CUNY Athletic Conference ◆ http://www.mec.cuny.edu/

State and locally supported 4-year, founded 1969, part of City University of New York System
Coed, 4,722 undergraduate students, 55% full-time, 78% women, 22% men
Urban 1-acre campus
Noncompetitive entrance level, 7% of applicants were admitted

Freshmen *Admission:* 1,701 applied, 1,299 were accepted, 671 enrolled.
Tuition and fees (2003–04): $4230 (resident), $8870 (nonresident).
Athletic Department: *Director of Athletics:* Roy Anderson; Phone: 718-270-6071; Fax: 718-270-6198; E-mail: roy@mec.cuny.edu.

MEN'S COACHES

Basketball: Robert Holford; Phone: 718-270-6072.
Cross Country: Alphonso Dance; Phone: 718-270-6404.
Soccer: Stanle Harmon; Phone: 718-270-6403.
Track and Field: Alphonso Dance; Phone: 718-270-6071.
Volleyball: Phone: 718-270-6071.

WOMEN'S COACHES

Basketball: Roy Anderson; Phone: 718-270-6071; E-mail: roy@mec.cuny.edu.
Cross Country: Alphonso Dance; Phone: 718-270-6404.
Softball: Safiyyah Wilson; Phone: 718-270-6403.
Track and Field: Alphonso Dance; Phone: 718-270-6071.
Volleyball: Avril O'Neal; Phone: 718-270-6402.

MENLO COLLEGE
Atherton, California

Oaks ◆ NCAA III ◆ California Pacific Conference ◆ http://www.menlo.edu/

Independent 4-year, founded 1927
Coed, 660 undergraduate students, 91% full-time, 37% women, 63% men
Small-town 45-acre campus with easy access to San Francisco
Moderately difficult entrance level, 59% of applicants were admitted

Freshmen *Admission:* 1,061 applied, 598 were accepted, 172 enrolled. *Test scores:* SAT verbal scores over 500: 29%; SAT math scores over 500: 42%; SAT verbal scores over 600: 3%; SAT math scores over 600: 9%; SAT math scores over 700: 1%.
Tuition and fees (2003–04): $21,780 (full-time). *Room and board:* $9080.
Financial Aid (All incoming freshmen): *Average need-based gift aid:* $17,446. *Average non-need based aid:* $10,508. *Average aid to full-time undergraduates:* $20,315.
Athletic Department: *Director of Athletics:* Caitlin Collier; Phone: 650-543-3770; Fax: 650-543-3769; E-mail: ccollier@menlo.edu. *Sports Information Director:* Nicholas Enriquez; Phone: 650-543-4124; E-mail: nenriquez@menlo.edu.

MEN'S COACHES

Baseball: Ken Bowman; Phone: 650-543-3932; E-mail: kbowman@ menlo.edu.
Basketball: Kevin Nosek; Phone: 650-543-3760; E-mail: knosek@ menlo.edu.
Cross Country: Tim Dempsey; Phone: 650-463-1920; E-mail: tdempsey@ menlo.edu.
Football: Mark Kaanapu; Phone: 650-556-3772; E-mail: mkaanapu@ menlo.edu.
Golf: Bill Imwalle; Phone: 650-543-4122; E-mail: blowfishimwalle@aol.com.
Soccer: Len Renery; Phone: 650-543-4121; E-mail: lrenery@ sequoiainstitute.com.
Wrestling: Keith Spataro; Phone: 650-543-3853; E-mail: kspataro@ menlo.edu.

WOMEN'S COACHES

Basketball: Caitlin Coller; Phone: 650-543-3770; E-mail: ccollier@ menlo.edu.

Cross Country: Tim Dempsey; Phone: 650-463-1920; E-mail: tdempsey@menlo.edu.
Soccer: Owen Flannery; Phone: 650-543-3765; E-mail: oflannery@menlo.edu.
Softball: Kyle Brumbaugh; Phone: 650-543-4386; E-mail: oakssoftbl@aol.com.
Volleyball: Bill Imwalle; Phone: 650-543-4122; E-mail: blowfishimwalle@aol.com.

MERCER UNIVERSITY
Macon, Georgia

Bears ◆ NCAA I ◆ Atlantic Sun Conference
◆ http://www.mercer.edu/

Independent Baptist comprehensive, founded 1833
Coed, 4,580 undergraduate students, 84% full-time, 67% women, 33% men
Suburban 150-acre campus with easy access to Atlanta
Moderately difficult entrance level, 82% of applicants were admitted

Freshmen *Admission:* 3,034 applied, 2,403 were accepted, 696 enrolled. *Test scores:* SAT verbal scores over 500: 89%; SAT math scores over 500: 89%; SAT verbal scores over 600: 42%; SAT math scores over 600: 50%; SAT verbal scores over 700: 8%; SAT math scores over 700: 11%.
Tuition and fees (2004–05): $22,050 (full-time). *Room and board:* $7060 (room only: $3400).
Financial Aid (All incoming freshmen): *Average need-based gift aid:* $14,103. *Average non-need based aid:* $15,031. *Average aid to full-time undergraduates:* $22,119.
Athletic Department: *Director of Athletics:* Bobby Pope; Phone: 478-301-2994; Fax: 478-301-2061; E-mail: pope_ba@mercer.edu. *Sports Information Director:* Joel Lamp; Phone: 478-301-2994; E-mail: lamp_js@mercer.edu.

MEN'S COACHES
Baseball: Craig Gibson; Phone: 478-752-2738; E-mail: gibson_c@mercer.edu.
Basketball: Mark Slonaker; Phone: 478-752-2736; E-mail: slonaker_mw@mercer.edu.
Cross Country: Jeremy Luther; Phone: 478-752-2509; E-mail: luther_jr@mercer.edu.
Golf: Jason Payne; Phone: 478-752-2994; E-mail: payne_jc@mercer.edu.
Soccer: Tom Melville; Phone: 478-752-2994; E-mail: melville_t@mercer.edu.
Tennis: Nick Stutsman; Phone: 478-752-2269; E-mail: stutsman_n@mercer.edu.

WOMEN'S COACHES
Basketball: Brenda Welch-Nichols; Phone: 478-752-2994; E-mail: nichols_bw@mercer.edu.
Cross Country: Jeremy Luther; Phone: 478-752-2509; E-mail: luther_jr@mercer.edu.
Golf: Charlotte Grant; Phone: 478-752-2994; E-mail: cgrant@plantationcable.net.
Soccer: Brianna Heffington; Phone: 478-752-2060; E-mail: heffington_bk@med.mercer.edu.
Softball: Tony Foti; Phone: 478-752-2263; E-mail: foti_t@mercer.edu.
Tennis: Nick Stutsman; Phone: 478-752-2269; E-mail: stutsman_n@mercer.edu.
Volleyball: Alan Edwards; Phone: 478-752-2268; E-mail: edwards_ab@mercer.edu.

MERCY COLLEGE
Dobbs Ferry, New York

Flyers ◆ NCAA II ◆ New York Collegiate Athletic Conference
◆ http://www.mercynet.edu/

Independent comprehensive, founded 1951
Coed, 6,208 undergraduate students, 29% full-time, 35% women, 65% men
Suburban 60-acre campus with easy access to New York City

Freshmen *Admission:* 2,708 applied, 693 enrolled.
Tuition and fees (2003–04): $10,844 (full-time). *Room and board:* $8180.

Athletic Department: *Director of Athletics:* Neil Judge; Phone: 914-674-6595; Fax: 914-674-7281. *Sports Information Director:* Steve Balsan; Phone: 914-674-7566.

MEN'S COACHES
Baseball: Bill Sullivan; Phone: 914-674-7566; E-mail: athletics@mercy.edu.
Basketball: Steve Kelly; Phone: 914-674-7566; E-mail: athletics@mercy.edu.
Cross Country: Darryl Bullock; Phone: 914-674-7566; E-mail: athletics@mercy.edu.
Golf: Tony Macellaro; Phone: 914-674-7566; E-mail: athletics@mercy.edu.
Soccer: Christian Gonzalez; Phone: 914-674-7566; E-mail: athletics@mercy.edu.
Tennis: Barbaros Ozdogan; Phone: 914-674-7566; E-mail: athletics@mercy.edu.

WOMEN'S COACHES
Basketball: Kent Washington; Phone: 914-674-7566; E-mail: athletics@mercy.edu.
Cross Country: Darryl Bullock; Phone: 914-674-7566; E-mail: athletics@mercy.edu.
Soccer: Victor Acosta; Phone: 914-674-7590; E-mail: athletics@mercy.edu.
Softball: Phone: 914-674-7566; E-mail: athletics@mercy.edu.
Volleyball: Jennifer Addison; Phone: 914-674-7566; E-mail: athletics@mercy.edu.

MERCYHURST COLLEGE
Erie, Pennsylvania

Lakers ◆ NCAA II ◆ Great Lakes Intercollegiate Conference; Midwestern Intercollegiate Volleyball Conference ◆ http://www.mercyhurst.edu/

Independent Roman Catholic comprehensive, founded 1926
Coed, 3,610 undergraduate students, 87% full-time, 62% women, 38% men
Suburban 88-acre campus with easy access to Buffalo
Moderately difficult entrance level, 71% of applicants were admitted

Freshmen *Admission:* 2,523 applied, 1,934 were accepted, 1,020 enrolled. *Test scores:* SAT verbal scores over 500: 73%; SAT math scores over 500: 72%; SAT verbal scores over 600: 21%; SAT math scores over 600: 20%; SAT verbal scores over 700: 2%; SAT math scores over 700: 1%.
Tuition and fees (2003–04): $16,980 (full-time). *Room and board:* $6414 (room only: $3264).
Financial Aid (All incoming freshmen): *Average need-based gift aid:* $9912. *Average non-need based aid:* $5359. *Average aid to full-time undergraduates:* $12,832.
Athletic Department: *Director of Athletics:* Pete Russo; Phone: 814-824-2226; Fax: 814-824-2204; E-mail: prusso@mercyhurst.edu. *Sports Information Director:* John Leisering; Phone: 814-824-2525; E-mail: jleisering@mercyhurst.edu.

MEN'S COACHES
Baseball: Joe Spano; Phone: 814-824-2441; E-mail: jspano@mercyhurst.edu.
Basketball: Gary Manchel; Phone: 814-824-2223; E-mail: gmanchel@mercyhurst.edu.
Cheerleading: Heather Kirsch; Phone: 814-453-6471; E-mail: ccccheercamps@aol.com.
Cross Country: Mike Fraley; Phone: 814-824-2228; E-mail: mfraley@mercyhurst.edu.
Football: Marty Schaetzle; Phone: 814-824-2222; E-mail: mschaetzle@mercyhurst.edu.
Golf: Dave Hewett; Phone: 814-824-2283; E-mail: dhewett@mercyhurst.edu.
Ice Hockey: Rick Gotkin; Phone: 814-824-2542; E-mail: rgotkin@mercyhurst.edu.
Lacrosse: Chris Ryan; Phone: 814-824-2138; E-mail: cryan@mercyhurst.edu.
Soccer: Keith Cammidge; Phone: 814-824-2128; E-mail: kcammidge@mercyhurst.edu.
Tennis: Heather Kirsch; Phone: 814-824-9632; E-mail: rman50@aol.com.

Mercyhurst College *(continued)*

Volleyball: Craig Davic; Phone: 814-824-2227; E-mail: cdavic@ mercyhurst.edu.

Wrestling: Tony Cipollone; Phone: 814-824-3101; E-mail: athletics@ mercyhurst.edu.

WOMEN'S COACHES

Basketball: Bo Kuntz; Phone: 814-824-2207; E-mail: bokuntz@ mercyhurst.edu.

Cheerleading: Heather Kirsch; Phone: 814-453-6471; E-mail: ccccheercamps@aol.com.

Cross Country: Mike Fraley; Phone: 814-824-2228; E-mail: kfrakey@ mercyhurst.edu.

Field Hockey: Stacey Gaudette; Phone: 814-824-3066; E-mail: sgaudette@mercyhurst.edu.

Golf: Dave Hewett; Phone: 814-824-2283; E-mail: dhewett@ mercyhurst.edu.

Lacrosse: Stacey Gaudette; Phone: 814-824-2079; E-mail: sgaudette@ mercyhurst.edu.

Soccer: Heather Kirsch; Phone: 814-824-2128; E-mail: kcammidge@ mercyhurst.edu.

Softball: Sara Headley; Phone: 814-824-2342; E-mail: sheadley@ mercyhurst.edu.

Tennis: Keith Cammidge; Phone: 814-824-9632; E-mail: rman50@aol.com.

Volleyball: Missy Soboleski; Phone: 814-824-2221; E-mail: msoboles@ mercyhurst.edu.

MEREDITH COLLEGE
Raleigh, North Carolina

Angels ◆ NCAA III ◆ Independent
◆ http://www.meredith.edu/

Independent comprehensive, founded 1891
Women only, 2,000 undergraduate students, 78% full-time, 99% women, 1% men
Urban 225-acre campus
Moderately difficult entrance level, 87% of applicants were admitted

Freshmen *Admission:* 1,026 applied, 895 were accepted, 344 enrolled. *Test scores:* SAT verbal scores over 500: 61%; SAT math scores over 500: 60%; SAT verbal scores over 600: 19%; SAT math scores over 600: 17%; SAT verbal scores over 700: 2%; SAT math scores over 700: 1%.
Tuition and fees (2004–05): $19,000 (full-time). *Room and board:* $5350.
Financial Aid (All incoming freshmen): *Average need-based gift aid:* $11,396. *Average non-need based aid:* $6132. *Average aid to full-time undergraduates:* $13,989.
Athletic Department: *Director of Athletics:* Jackie Myers; Phone: 919-760-8198; Fax: 919-760-2828.

WOMEN'S COACHES

Basketball: Carl Hatchell; Phone: 919-760-8310; E-mail: hatchellc@ meredith.edu.

Soccer: Paul Smith; Phone: 919-760-2250; E-mail: coachpauls@aol.com.

Softball: Carl Hatchell; Phone: 919-760-8310.

Tennis: Mary Kovell; Phone: 919-760-2250.

Volleyball: Kathy Mayberry; Phone: 919-760-2374; E-mail: mayberryk@meredith.edu.

MERRIMACK COLLEGE
North Andover, Massachusetts

Warriors ◆ NCAA II ◆ Hockey East Conference; Northeast-10 Conference ◆ http://www.merrimack.edu/

Independent Roman Catholic comprehensive, founded 1947
Coed, 2,389 undergraduate students, 86% full-time, 55% women, 45% men
Suburban 220-acre campus with easy access to Boston
Moderately difficult entrance level, 55% of applicants were admitted

Freshmen *Admission:* 3,353 applied, 2,000 were accepted, 590 enrolled. *Test scores:* SAT verbal scores over 500: 80%; SAT math scores over 500: 90%; SAT verbal scores over 600: 16%; SAT math scores over 600: 21%; SAT math scores over 700: 2%.
Tuition and fees (2003–04): $20,875 (full-time). *Room and board:* $8750 (room only: $4900).
Financial Aid (All incoming freshmen): *Average need-based gift aid:* $10,000. *Average non-need based aid:* $5000. *Average aid to full-time undergraduates:* $15,125.
Athletic Department: *Director of Athletics:* Chris Serino; Phone: 978-837-5000; Fax: 978-837-5032; E-mail: christie.serino@merrimack.edu. *Sports Information Director:* Thomas O'Brien; Phone: 978-837-5000; E-mail: tobrien@merrimack.edu.

MEN'S COACHES

Baseball: Joseph Sarno; Phone: 978-837-5000; E-mail: joseph.sarno@ merrimack.edu.

Basketball: Bert Hammel; Phone: 978-837-5000; E-mail: bert.hammel@ merrimack.edu.

Cheerleading: Angela Caira; Phone: 978-837-5341; E-mail: angela.caira@merrimack.edu.

Cross Country: Chris Cameron; Phone: 978-837-5000; E-mail: christopher.cameron@merrimack.edu.

Football: James Murphy; Phone: 978-837-5000; E-mail: james.murphy@merrimack.edu.

Ice Hockey: Chris Serino; Phone: 978-837-5000; E-mail: christie.serino@merrimack.edu.

Lacrosse: Ryan Polley; Phone: 978-837-5000; E-mail: ryan.polley@ merrimack.edu.

Soccer: Tony Martone; Phone: 978-837-5000; E-mail: anthony.martone@merrimack.edu.

Tennis: Scott Wilkins; Phone: 978-837-5000; E-mail: scott.wilkins@ merrimack.edu.

WOMEN'S COACHES

Basketball: Ann McInerney; Phone: 978-837-5000; E-mail: ann.mcinerney@merrimack.edu.

Cheerleading: Angela Caira; Phone: 978-837-5341; E-mail: angela.caira@merrimack.edu.

Cross Country: Chris Cameron; Phone: 978-837-5000; E-mail: christopher.cameron@merrimack.edu.

Field Hockey: Carolyn Cahill; Phone: 978-837-5000; E-mail: carolyn.cahill@merrimack.edu.

Lacrosse: Karen Lahey; Phone: 978-837-5000; E-mail: karen.lahey@ merrimack.edu.

Soccer: Gabe Mejail; Phone: 978-837-5000; E-mail: gabriel.mejail@ merrimack.edu.

Softball: Michele Myslinski; Phone: 978-837-5000; E-mail: michele.myslinski@merrimack.edu.

Tennis: Scott Wilkins; Phone: 978-837-5000; E-mail: scott.wilkins@ merrimack.edu.

Volleyball: Joey Pacis; Phone: 978-837-5000; E-mail: joey.pacis@ merrimack.edu.

MESA STATE COLLEGE
Grand Junction, Colorado

Mavericks ◆ NCAA II ◆ Rocky Mountain Athletic Conference ◆ http://www.mesastate.edu/

State-supported comprehensive, founded 1925, part of State Colleges in Colorado
Coed, 5,463 undergraduate students, 76% full-time, 57% women, 43% men
Small-town 42-acre campus
Minimally difficult entrance level, 91% of applicants were admitted

Freshmen *Admission:* 2,361 applied, 2,182 were accepted, 1,112 enrolled. *Test scores:* SAT verbal scores over 500: 50%; SAT math scores over 500: 51%; SAT verbal scores over 600: 14%; SAT math scores over 600: 13%; SAT verbal scores over 700: 2%; SAT math scores over 700: 1%.
Tuition and fees (2003–04): $2516 (resident), $8168 (nonresident). *Room and board:* $6266 (room only: $3106).
Financial Aid (All incoming freshmen): *Average need-based gift aid:* $2678. *Average aid to full-time undergraduates:* $6206.
Athletic Department: *Director of Athletics:* Clarence Ross; Phone: 970-248-1659; Fax: 970-248-1980; E-mail: cross@mesastate.edu. *Sports Information Director:* Tish Elliott; Phone: 970-248-1143; E-mail: telliott@mesastate.edu.

MEN'S COACHES

Baseball: Chris Hanks; Phone: 970-248-1891; E-mail: chanks@mesastate.edu.
Basketball: Jim Heaps; Phone: 970-248-1714; E-mail: jheaps@mesastate.edu.
Football: Joe Ramunno; Phone: 970-248-1103; E-mail: jramunno@mesastate.edu.
Tennis: David Elliott; Phone: 970-248-1937; E-mail: delliott@mesastate.edu.

WOMEN'S COACHES

Basketball: Steve Kirkham; Phone: 970-248-1716; E-mail: skirkham@mesastate.edu.
Cross Country: Gig Leadbetter; Phone: 970-248-1194; E-mail: gleadbet@mesastate.edu.
Golf: Dan Sommers; Phone: 970-248-1503; E-mail: sbeaureg@mesastate.edu.
Soccer: Jim Buchan; Phone: 970-248-1042; E-mail: jbuchan@mesastate.edu.
Softball: Kris Mort; Phone: 970-248-1908; E-mail: kmort@mesastate.edu.
Tennis: David Elliott; Phone: 970-248-1937; E-mail: delliott@mesastate.edu.
Volleyball: Rusty Crick; Phone: 970-248-1362; E-mail: rcrick@mesastate.edu.

MESSIAH COLLEGE
Grantham, Pennsylvania

Falcons ◆ NCAA III ◆ Commonwealth Conference ◆ http://www.messiah.edu/

Independent interdenominational 4-year, founded 1909
Coed, 2,952 undergraduate students, 98% full-time, 63% women, 37% men
Small-town 400-acre campus
Moderately difficult entrance level, 83% of applicants were admitted

Freshmen *Admission:* 2,252 applied, 1,790 were accepted, 736 enrolled. *Test scores:* SAT verbal scores over 500: 93%; SAT math scores over 500: 93%; SAT verbal scores over 600: 52%; SAT math scores over 600: 48%; SAT verbal scores over 700: 11%; SAT math scores over 700: 11%.
Tuition and fees (2003–04): $19,550 (full-time). *Room and board:* $6340 (room only: $3280).
Financial Aid (All incoming freshmen): *Average need-based gift aid:* $4879. *Average non-need based aid:* $5906. *Average aid to full-time undergraduates:* $12,417.
Athletic Department: *Director of Athletics:* Jerry Chaplin; Phone: 717-766-2511; Fax: 717-691-6044; E-mail: jchaplin@messiah.edu. *Sports Information Director:* Scott Frey; Phone: 717-796-5359; E-mail: sfrey@messiah.edu.

MEN'S COACHES

Baseball: Frank Montgomery; Phone: 717-766-2511; E-mail: fmontgom@messiah.edu.
Basketball: Rick Van Pelt; Phone: 717-766-2511; E-mail: rvanpelt@messiah.edu.
Cross Country: Dale Fogelanger; Phone: 717-766-2511; E-mail: dfogelsa@messiah.edu.
Golf: Alex Lemmon; Phone: 717-766-2511; E-mail: alemmon@messiah.edu.
Lacrosse: Jerry Stanford; Phone: 717-766-2511; E-mail: jstandfo@messiah.edu.
Soccer: Dave Brandt; Phone: 717-766-2511; E-mail: dbrandt@messiah.edu.
Tennis: Sheila Bush; Phone: 717-766-2511.
Track and Field: Dale Fogelanger; Phone: 717-766-2511; E-mail: dfogelsa@messiah.edu.
Wrestling: Bryan Brunk; Phone: 717-766-2511; E-mail: bbrunk@messiah.edu.

WOMEN'S COACHES

Basketball: Mike Miller; Phone: 717-766-2511; E-mail: mmiller@messiah.edu.
Cross Country: Dale Fogelanger; Phone: 717-766-2511; E-mail: dfogelsa@messiah.edu.
Field Hockey: Jan Trapp; Phone: 717-766-2511; E-mail: jtrapp@messiah.edu.

Lacrosse: Rob Pepper; Phone: 717-766-2511; E-mail: rpepper@messiah.edu.
Soccer: Scott Frey; Phone: 717-796-5359; E-mail: sfrey@messiah.edu.
Softball: Amy Weaver; Phone: 717-766-2511; E-mail: aweaver@messiah.edu.
Tennis: Sheila Bush; Phone: 717-766-2511.
Track and Field: Dale Fogelanger; Phone: 717-766-2511; E-mail: dfogelsa@messiah.edu.
Volleyball: Judi Tobias; Phone: 717-766-2511; E-mail: jtobias@messiah.edu.

METHODIST COLLEGE
Fayetteville, North Carolina

Monarchs ◆ NCAA III ◆ USA South Athletic Conference ◆ http://www.methodist.edu/

Independent United Methodist comprehensive, founded 1956
Coed, 2,210 undergraduate students, 75% full-time, 42% women, 58% men
Suburban 600-acre campus with easy access to Raleigh-Durham
Moderately difficult entrance level, 73% of applicants were admitted

Freshmen *Admission:* 1,935 applied, 1,465 were accepted, 430 enrolled. *Test scores:* SAT verbal scores over 500: 44%; SAT math scores over 500: 54%; SAT verbal scores over 600: 7%; SAT math scores over 600: 15%; SAT math scores over 700: 1%.
Tuition and fees (2004–05): $16,760 (full-time). *Room and board:* $6370.
Financial Aid (All incoming freshmen): *Average need-based gift aid:* $6774. *Average non-need based aid:* $2081. *Average aid to full-time undergraduates:* $11,749.
Athletic Department: *Director of Athletics:* Bob McEvoy; Phone: 910-630-7175; Fax: 910-630-7676; E-mail: mcevoy@methodist.edu. *Sports Information Director:* Lee Wright; Phone: 910-630-7172; E-mail: sportsinfo@methodist.edu.

MEN'S COACHES

Baseball: Tom Austin; Phone: 910-630-7176; E-mail: taustin@methodist.edu.
Basketball: David Smith; Phone: 910-630-7185; E-mail: dgsmith@methodist.edu.
Cheerleading: Rickey Hill; Phone: 910-630-7154; E-mail: rhill@methodist.edu.
Cross Country: Halcyon Blake; Phone: 910-630-7181; E-mail: tudyb@methodist.edu.
Football: Jim Sypult; Phone: 910-630-7178; E-mail: jsypult@methodist.edu.
Golf: Steve Conley; Phone: 910-630-7146; E-mail: sconley@methodist.edu.
Soccer: Justin Terranova; Phone: 910-630-7097; E-mail: jterranova@methodist.edu.
Tennis: Mike Roberts; Phone: 910-630-7493; E-mail: mroberts@methodist.edu.
Track and Field: Halcyon Blake; Phone: 910-630-7181; E-mail: tudyb@methodist.edu.

WOMEN'S COACHES

Basketball: Deedee Jarman; Phone: 910-630-7283; E-mail: djarman@methodist.edu.
Cheerleading: Rickey Hill; Phone: 910-630-7154; E-mail: rhill@methodist.edu.
Cross Country: Halcyon Blake; Phone: 910-630-7181; E-mail: tudyb@methodist.edu.
Golf: Vici Pate; Phone: 910-630-7689; E-mail: vpate@methodist.edu.
Lacrosse: Jill Penrose; Phone: 910-630-7510; E-mail: jpenrose@methodist.edu.
Soccer: Robert Graham; Phone: 910-630-7096; E-mail: bgraham@methodist.edu.
Softball: Ron Simpson; Phone: 910-630-7290; E-mail: rsimpson@methodist.edu.
Tennis: Kelly Brown; Phone: 910-630-7315; E-mail: kebrown@methodist.edu.
Track and Field: Halcyon Blake; Phone: 910-630-7181; E-mail: tudyb@methodist.edu.
Volleyball: Ed Matthews; Phone: 910-630-7187; E-mail: ematthews@methodist.edu.

METROPOLITAN STATE COLLEGE OF DENVER
Denver, Colorado

Roadrunners ◆ NCAA II ◆ Rocky Mountain Athletic Conference ◆ http://www.mscd.edu/

State-supported 4-year, founded 1963
Coed, 20,261 undergraduate students, 58% full-time, 56% women, 44% men
Urban 175-acre campus
Minimally difficult entrance level, 79% of applicants were admitted

Freshmen *Admission:* 4,550 applied, 3,575 were accepted, 2,330 enrolled. *Test scores:* SAT verbal scores over 500: 54%; SAT math scores over 500: 53%; SAT verbal scores over 600: 13%; SAT math scores over 600: 11%; SAT verbal scores over 700: 2%; SAT math scores over 700: %.
Tuition and fees (2003–04): $2668 (resident), $9275 (nonresident).
Financial Aid (All incoming freshmen): *Average need-based gift aid:* $3919. *Average non-need based aid:* $1577. *Average aid to full-time undergraduates:* $4941.
Athletic Department: *Director of Athletics:* Joan McDermott; Phone: 303-556-8300; Fax: 303-556-2720. *Sports Information Director:* Trent Nielsen; Phone: 303-556-3431; E-mail: nielent@mscd.edu.

MEN'S COACHES
Baseball: Vince Porreco; Phone: 303-556-3301; E-mail: porrecov@mscd.edu.
Basketball: Mike Dunlap; Phone: 303-556-3309; E-mail: dunlapm@mscd.edu.
Cheerleading: Brianna Newland; Phone: 303-556-2730.
Soccer: Brian Crookham; Phone: 303-556-4875; E-mail: crookhab@mscd.edu.
Swimming: Rich LeDuc; Phone: 303-556-6447; E-mail: leducr@mscd.edu.
Tennis: Eduardo Provencio; Phone: 303-556-8141; E-mail: provenc@mscd.edu.

WOMEN'S COACHES
Basketball: Dave Murphy; Phone: 303-556-8426; E-mail: murpdavi@mscd.edu.
Cheerleading: Brianna Newland; Phone: 303-556-2730.
Soccer: Danny Sanchez; Phone: 303-556-4874; E-mail: sanchdan@mscd.edu.
Swimming: Rich LeDuc; Phone: 303-556-6447; E-mail: leducr@mscd.edu.
Tennis: Eduardo Provencio; Phone: 303-556-8141; E-mail: provenc@mscd.edu.
Volleyball: Debbie Hendricks; Phone: 303-556-2875; E-mail: hendricd@mscd.edu.

MIAMI UNIVERSITY
Oxford, Ohio

Redhawks ◆ NCAA I ◆ Central Collegiate Hockey Conference; Mid-American Conference
◆ http://www.muohio.edu/

State-related university, founded 1809, part of Miami University System
Coed, 15,174 undergraduate students, 97% full-time, 54% women, 46% men
Small-town 2,000-acre campus with easy access to Cincinnati
Moderately difficult entrance level, 68% of applicants were admitted

Freshmen *Admission:* 13,859 applied, 9,842 were accepted, 3,309 enrolled. *Test scores:* SAT verbal scores over 500: 97%; SAT math scores over 500: 98%; SAT verbal scores over 600: 55%; SAT math scores over 600: 70%; SAT verbal scores over 700: 8%; SAT math scores over 700: 11%.
Tuition and fees (2003–04): $8353 (resident), $18,123 (nonresident).
Room and board: $6680 (room only: $3340).
Financial Aid (All incoming freshmen): *Average need-based gift aid:* $4030. *Average non-need based aid:* $4527. *Average aid to full-time undergraduates:* $6648.

Athletic Department: *Director of Athletics:* Brad Bates; Phone: 513-529-7286; Fax: 513-529-6729; E-mail: batesbj@muohio.edu. *Sports Information Director:* Mike Harris; Phone: 513-529-4327; E-mail: harrismr@muohio.edu.

MEN'S COACHES
Baseball: Tracy Smith; Phone: 513-529-6631; E-mail: smithtj@muohio.edu.
Basketball: Charlie Coles; Phone: 513-529-1650; E-mail: osterbc@muohio.edu.
Cheerleading: Cindi McDaniel; Phone: 513-529-1662; E-mail: byrgecl@muohio.edu.
Cross Country: Warren Mandrell; Phone: 513-529-3105; E-mail: mandrewh@muohio.edu.
Diving: Todd Spohn; Phone: 513-529-8156; E-mail: spohntm@muohio.edu.
Football: Terry Hoeppner; Phone: 513-529-3319; E-mail: football@muohio.edu.
Golf: John Wiler; Phone: 513-529-2119; E-mail: wilerj@muohio.edu.
Ice Hockey: Enrico Blasi; Phone: 513-529-3343; E-mail: blasie@muohio.edu.
Swimming: Pete Lindsay; Phone: 513-529-8150; E-mail: lindsapr@muohio.edu.
Track and Field: Warren Mandrell; Phone: 513-529-3105; E-mail: mandrewh@muohio.edu.

WOMEN'S COACHES
Basketball: Maria Fantanarosa; Phone: 513-529-3300; E-mail: fantanml@muohio.edu.
Cheerleading: Cindi McDaniel; Phone: 513-529-1662; E-mail: byrgecl@muohio.edu.
Cross Country: Richard Cerone; Phone: 513-529-3106; E-mail: ceronirj@muohio.edu.
Diving: Todd Spohn; Phone: 513-529-8156; E-mail: spohntm@muohio.edu.
Field Hockey: Lil Fesperman; Phone: 513-529-7290; E-mail: fesperld@muohio.edu.
Soccer: Bobby Kramig; Phone: 513-529-1767; E-mail: kramigre@muohio.edu.
Softball: Angie Jacobs; Phone: 513-529-3999; E-mail: musoftball@muohio.edu.
Swimming: Dave Jennings; Phone: 513-529-8153; E-mail: jenninda@muohio.edu.
Tennis: Ray Reppert; Phone: 513-529-7088; E-mail: repperre@muohio.edu.
Track and Field: Richard Cerone; Phone: 513-529-3106; E-mail: ceronirj@muohio.edu.
Volleyball: Carolyn Condit; Phone: 513-529-6922; E-mail: muvb@muohio.edu.

MICHIGAN STATE UNIVERSITY
East Lansing, Michigan

Spartans ◆ NCAA I ◆ Big Ten Conference; Central Collegiate Hockey Conference ◆ http://www.msu.edu/

State-supported university, founded 1855
Coed, 34,853 undergraduate students, 89% full-time, 54% women, 46% men
Suburban 5,192-acre campus with easy access to Detroit
Moderately difficult entrance level, 67% of applicants were admitted

Freshmen *Admission:* 24,973 applied, 17,690 were accepted, 7,122 enrolled. *Test scores:* SAT verbal scores over 500: 76%; SAT math scores over 500: 84%; SAT verbal scores over 600: 36%; SAT math scores over 600: 47%; SAT verbal scores over 700: 7%; SAT math scores over 700: 11%.
Tuition and fees (2003–04): $6703 (resident), $16,663 (nonresident).
Room and board: $5230 (room only: $2250).
Financial Aid (All incoming freshmen): *Average need-based gift aid:* $4372. *Average non-need based aid:* $3173. *Average aid to full-time undergraduates:* $8348.
Athletic Department: *Director of Athletics:* Clarence Underwood; Phone: 517-355-1623; Fax: 517-432-1047; E-mail: underw12@msu.edu. *Sports Information Director:* John Lewandowski; Phone: 517-355-2271; E-mail: lewand19@msu.edu.

MEN'S COACHES
Baseball: Ted Mahan; Phone: 517-355-4486; E-mail: mahant@msu.edu.

Basketball: Tom Izzo; Phone: 517-355-1643; E-mail: izzo@msu.edu.
Cheerleading: Zoe Yockey; Phone: 517-355-7499; E-mail: cheer@msu.edu.
Cross Country: Jim Stintzi; Phone: 517-355-1640; E-mail: stintzi@msu.edu.
Diving: Eric Best; Phone: 517-353-0652; E-mail: bester@msu.edu.
Football: John Smith; Phone: 517-355-1647; E-mail: jlsmith@msu.edu.
Golf: Mark Hankins; Phone: 517-432-2950; E-mail: hankins@msu.edu.
Ice Hockey: Rick Comley; Phone: 517-355-1639; E-mail: comley@msu.edu.
Swimming: Matt Gianiodis; Phone: 517-432-2054; E-mail: gianiodi@msu.edu.
Tennis: Gene Orlando; Phone: 517-355-2209; E-mail: orlando@msu.edu.
Track and Field: Darroll Gatson; Phone: 517-355-1641; E-mail: gatson@msu.edu.
Wrestling: Tom Minkel; Phone: 517-355-5270; E-mail: minkel@msu.edu.

WOMEN'S COACHES

Basketball: Joanne McCallie; Phone: 517-353-8613; E-mail: mccallie@msu.edu.
Cheerleading: Zoe Yockey; Phone: 517-355-7499; E-mail: cheer@msu.edu.
Cross Country: Jim Stintzi; Phone: 517-355-1641; E-mail: gatson@msu.edu.
Diving: Eric Best; Phone: 517-353-0652; E-mail: bester@msu.edu.
Field Hockey: Michele Madison; Phone: 517-355-7157; E-mail: madisonm@msu.edu.
Golf: Stacy Slobodnik; Phone: 517-432-1438; E-mail: slobodni@pilot.msu.edu.
Gymnastics: Kathie Klages; Phone: 517-355-4708; E-mail: klages@msu.edu.
Soccer: Tom Saxton; Phone: 517-355-3152; E-mail: saxtont@msu.edu.
Softball: Jacquie Joseph; Phone: 517-355-4752; E-mail: josephj@msu.edu.
Swimming: Matt Gianiodis; Phone: 517-432-2054; E-mail: gianiodi@msu.edu.
Tennis: Tim Bauer; Phone: 517-432-0636; E-mail: bauerti@msu.edu.
Track and Field: Angela Goodman; Phone: 517-353-9229; E-mail: agoodman@msu.edu.
Volleyball: Chuck Erbe; Phone: 517-355-4750; E-mail: erbe@msu.edu.

MICHIGAN TECHNOLOGICAL UNIVERSITY
Houghton, Michigan

Huskies ◆ NCAA II ◆ Great Lakes Intercollegiate Conference; Western Collegiate Hockey Conference
◆ http://www.mtu.edu/

State-supported university, founded 1885
Coed, 5,765 undergraduate students, 86% full-time, 24% women, 76% men
Small-town 240-acre campus
Moderately difficult entrance level, 92% of applicants were admitted

Freshmen *Admission:* 3,080 applied, 2,861 were accepted, 1,187 enrolled. *Test scores:* SAT verbal scores over 500: 83%; SAT math scores over 500: 92%; SAT verbal scores over 600: 41%; SAT math scores over 600: 62%; SAT verbal scores over 700: 10%; SAT math scores over 700: 14%.
Tuition and fees (2003–04): $7440 (resident), $18,330 (nonresident). *Room and board:* $5795 (room only: $2759).
Financial Aid (All incoming freshmen): *Average need-based gift aid:* $5224. *Average non-need based aid:* $2542. *Average aid to full-time undergraduates:* $7560.
Athletic Department: *Director of Athletics:* Rick Yeo; Phone: 906-487-3070; Fax: 906-487-3062; E-mail: ryeo@mtu.edu. *Sports Information Director:* Dave Fischer; Phone: 906-487-2350; E-mail: dfischer@mtu.edu.

MEN'S COACHES

Basketball: Kevin Luke; Phone: 906-487-2988; E-mail: keluke@mtu.edu.
Cheerleading: Phone: 906-487-3070; E-mail: stuntteam-l@mtu.edu.
Cross Country: Joe Haggenmiller; Phone: 906-487-2986; E-mail: jjhaggen@mtu.edu.
Football: Bernie Anderson; Phone: 906-487-2718; E-mail: banderso@mtu.edu.
Ice Hockey: Jamie Russell; Phone: 906-487-2104; E-mail: jrussell@mtu.edu.
Tennis: Mike Axford; Phone: 906-487-2718; E-mail: mhaxford@mtu.edu.
Track and Field: Joe Haggenmiller; Phone: 906-487-2986; E-mail: jjhaggen@mtu.edu.

WOMEN'S COACHES

Basketball: John Barnes; Phone: 906-487-2222; E-mail: jmbarnes@mtu.edu.
Cheerleading: Phone: 906-487-3070; E-mail: stuntteam-l@mtu.edu.
Cross Country: Joe Haggenmiller; Phone: 906-487-2986; E-mail: jjhaggen@mtu.edu.
Tennis: Mike Axford; Phone: 906-487-2718; E-mail: mhaxford@mtu.edu.
Track and Field: Joe Haggenmiller; Phone: 906-487-2986; E-mail: jjhaggen@mtu.edu.
Volleyball: Krista Mikesch; Phone: 906-487-2427; E-mail: kmikesch@mtu.edu.

MIDAMERICA NAZARENE UNIVERSITY
Olathe, Kansas

Pioneers ◆ NAIA ◆ Heart of America Conference ◆ http://www.mnu.edu/

Independent religious comprehensive, founded 1966, affiliated with Church of the Nazarene
Coed, 1,438 undergraduate students, 89% full-time, 54% women, 46% men
Suburban 105-acre campus with easy access to Kansas City
Minimally difficult entrance level, 42% of applicants were admitted

Freshmen *Admission:* 629 applied, 260 were accepted, 260 enrolled. *Test scores:* SAT verbal scores over 500: 56%; SAT math scores over 500: 52%; SAT verbal scores over 600: 22%; SAT math scores over 600: 22%; SAT verbal scores over 700: 3%; SAT math scores over 700: 3%.
Tuition and fees (2003–04): $12,910 (full-time). *Room and board:* $5828.
Financial Aid (All incoming freshmen): *Average need-based gift aid:* $7333. *Average non-need based aid:* $3508. *Average aid to full-time undergraduates:* $10,917.
Athletic Department: *Director of Athletics:* Ron Hill; Phone: 913-782-3750; Fax: 913-791-3290; E-mail: rhill@mnu.edu. *Sports Information Director:* Lance Beeson; Phone: 913-782-3750; E-mail: ldbeeson@mnu.edu.

MEN'S COACHES

Baseball: Todd Garrett; Phone: 913-782-3750; E-mail: tgarrett@mnu.edu.
Basketball: Rocky Lamar; Phone: 913-782-3750; E-mail: rlamar@mnu.edu.
Cheerleading: Lois Perrigo; Phone: 913-782-3750.
Cross Country: Curt Ammons; Phone: 913-782-3750; E-mail: cammons@mnu.edu.
Football: Mike Cochran; Phone: 913-782-3750; E-mail: mcochran@mnu.edu.
Soccer: Kevin Wardlaw; Phone: 913-782-3750; E-mail: kpwardlaw@mnu.edu.
Track and Field: Curt Ammons; Phone: 913-782-3750; E-mail: cammons@mnu.edu.

WOMEN'S COACHES

Basketball: Bill Olin; Phone: 913-782-3750; E-mail: bolin@mnu.edu.
Cheerleading: Lois Perrigo; Phone: 913-782-3750.
Cross Country: Curt Ammons; Phone: 913-782-3750; E-mail: cammons@mnu.edu.
Soccer: Rocky Orton; Phone: 913-782-3750; E-mail: rlorton@mnu.edu.
Softball: Krystal Kennard; Phone: 913-782-3750; E-mail: kkennard@mnu.edu.
Track and Field: Curt Ammons; Phone: 913-782-3750; E-mail: cammons@mnu.edu.
Volleyball: Ken Carver; Phone: 913-782-3750; E-mail: kdcarver@mnu.edu.

MID-CONTINENT COLLEGE
Mayfield, Kentucky

Cougars ◆ NAIA ◆ Kentucky Intercollegiate Conference
◆ http://www.midcontinent.edu/

Independent Southern Baptist 4-year, founded 1949
Coed, 683 undergraduate students, 88% full-time, 48% women, 52% men
Small-town 60-acre campus
Minimally difficult entrance level, 87% of applicants were admitted

Freshmen *Admission:* 99 applied, 87 were accepted, 75 enrolled. *Test scores:* SAT verbal scores over 500: 50%; SAT math scores over 500: 50%.
Tuition and fees (2003–04): $9080 (full-time). *Room and board:* $5400.
Financial Aid (All incoming freshmen): *Average need-based gift aid:* $5488. *Average non-need based aid:* $6445. *Average aid to full-time undergraduates:* $7069.
Athletic Department: *Director of Athletics:* Joe Zakowicz; Phone: 270-247-8521; Fax: 270-247-3115; E-mail: jzakowicz@midcontinent.edu.
MEN'S COACHES
Baseball: Seth Zartman; Phone: 270-247-8521.
Cross Country: Seth Hawkins; Phone: 270-247-8521; E-mail: shawkins@midcontinent.edu.
Soccer: Joe Zakowicz; Phone: 270-247-8521; E-mail: jzakowicz@midcontinent.edu.
WOMEN'S COACHES
Cross Country: Seth Hawkins; Phone: 270-247-8521; E-mail: shawkins@midcontinent.edu.
Softball: Taralee Pringle; Phone: 270-247-8521; E-mail: tpringle@midcontinent.edu.
Volleyball: Taralee Pringle; Phone: 270-247-8521; E-mail: tpringle@midcontinent.edu.

MIDDLEBURY COLLEGE
Middlebury, Vermont

Panthers ◆ NCAA III ◆ New England Small College
Conference ◆ http://www.middlebury.edu/

Independent comprehensive, founded 1800
Coed, 2,424 undergraduate students, 99% full-time, 53% women, 47% men
Small-town 350-acre campus
Most difficult entrance level, 2% of applicants were admitted

Freshmen *Admission:* 5,468 applied, 1,273 were accepted, 580 enrolled. *Test scores:* SAT verbal scores over 500: 99%; SAT math scores over 500: 99%; SAT verbal scores over 600: 97%; SAT math scores over 600: 95%; SAT verbal scores over 700: 69%; SAT math scores over 700: 61%.
Tuition and fees (2003–04): Comprehensive fee (includes tuition, fees, and room and board): $38,100.
Financial Aid (All incoming freshmen): *Average need-based gift aid:* $20,653. *Average aid to full-time undergraduates:* $25,166.
Athletic Department: *Director of Athletics:* Russ Reilly; Phone: 802-443-5253; Fax: 802-443-2124; E-mail: reilly@middlebury.edu. *Sports Information Director:* Brad Nadeau; Phone: 802-443-5193; E-mail: bnadeau@middlebury.edu.
MEN'S COACHES
Baseball: Bob Smith; Phone: 802-443-5264; E-mail: rsmith@middlebury.edu.
Basketball: Jeff Brown; Phone: 802-443-5269; E-mail: jeffreyb@middlebury.edu.
Cross Country: Terry Aldrich; Phone: 802-443-5271; E-mail: aldrich@middlebury.edu.
Diving: Peter Solomon; Phone: 802-443-5010; E-mail: solomon@middlebury.edu.
Football: Bob Ritter; Phone: 802-443-5681; E-mail: ritter@middlebury.edu.
Golf: Bill Beaney; Phone: 802-443-5268; E-mail: beaney@middlebury.edu.
Ice Hockey: Bill Beaney; Phone: 802-443-5268; E-mail: beaney@middlebury.edu.

Lacrosse: Erin Quinn; Phone: 802-443-5263; E-mail: quinn@middlebury.edu.
Soccer: David Saward; Phone: 802-443-5255; E-mail: saward@middlebury.edu.
Swimming: Peter Solomon; Phone: 802-443-5010; E-mail: solomon@middlebury.edu.
Tennis: Dave Schwartz; Phone: 802-443-3207; E-mail: dschwar@middlebury.edu.
Track and Field: Martin Beatty; Phone: 802-443-5956; E-mail: beatty@middlebury.edu.
WOMEN'S COACHES
Basketball: Noreen Pecsok; Phone: 802-443-2287; E-mail: npecsok@middlebury.edu.
Cross Country: Terry Aldrich; Phone: 802-443-5271; E-mail: aldrich@middlebury.edu.
Diving: Peter Solomon; Phone: 802-443-5010; E-mail: solomon@middlebury.edu.
Field Hockey: Katharine Delorenzo; Phone: 802-443-5422; E-mail: kdeloren@middlebury.edu.
Golf: Bill Beaney; Phone: 802-443-5268; E-mail: beaney@middlebury.edu.
Lacrosse: Missy Foote; Phone: 802-443-5262; E-mail: foote@middlebury.edu.
Soccer: Dianne Boettcher; Phone: 802-443-5410; E-mail: dboettch@middlebury.edu.
Swimming: Peter Solomon; Phone: 802-443-5010; E-mail: solomon@middlebury.edu.
Tennis: Nate Simms; Phone: 802-443-5242; E-mail: nsimms@middlebury.edu.
Track and Field: Martin Beatty; Phone: 802-443-5956; E-mail: beatty@middlebury.edu.
Volleyball: Sarah Raunecker; Phone: 802-443-5613; E-mail: srauneck@middlebury.edu.

MIDDLE TENNESSEE STATE UNIVERSITY
Murfreesboro, Tennessee

Blue Raiders ◆ NCAA I ◆ Sun Belt Conference ◆ http://www.mtsu.edu/

State-supported university, founded 1911, part of Tennessee Board of Regents
Coed, 19,754 undergraduate students, 84% full-time, 53% women, 47% men
Urban 500-acre campus with easy access to Nashville
Moderately difficult entrance level, 73% of applicants were admitted

Freshmen *Admission:* 7,206 applied, 5,398 were accepted, 3,037 enrolled.
Tuition and fees (2003–04): $3910 (resident), $11,842 (nonresident). *Room only:* $2386).
Financial Aid (All incoming freshmen): *Average need-based gift aid:* $1618. *Average non-need based aid:* $3823. *Average aid to full-time undergraduates:* $5340.
Athletic Department: *Director of Athletics:* Boots Donnelly; Phone: 615-898-2452; Fax: 615-898-5626. *Sports Information Director:* Mark Owens; Phone: 615-898-2450; E-mail: mrowens@mtsu.edu.
MEN'S COACHES
Baseball: Steve Paterson; Phone: 615-898-2450; E-mail: pfones@mtsu.edu.
Basketball: Kermit Davis; Phone: 615-898-2916; E-mail: cvaughn@mtsu.edu.
Cheerleading: Jonathan Pursley; Phone: 615-898-5812; E-mail: jpursley@mtsu.edu.
Cross Country: Dean Hayes; Phone: 615-898-2571; E-mail: dhayes@mtsu.edu.
Football: Andy McCollum; Phone: 615-898-2926; E-mail: nworley@mtsu.edu.
Golf: Johnny Moore; Phone: 615-898-5685; E-mail: chughes@mtsu.edu.
Tennis: Dale Short; Phone: 615-898-2957; E-mail: coachshort@aol.com.
Track and Field: Dean Hayes; Phone: 615-898-2571; E-mail: dhayes@mtsu.edu.

WOMEN'S COACHES

Basketball: Stephany Smith; Phone: 615-898-2968; E-mail: rbforth@mtsu.edu.

Cheerleading: Jonathan Pursley; Phone: 615-898-5812; E-mail: jpursley@mtsu.edu.

Cross Country: Dean Hayes; Phone: 615-898-2571; E-mail: dhayes@mtsu.edu.

Golf: Rachael Moore; Phone: 615-898-5404; E-mail: rmoore@mtsu.edu.

Soccer: Aston Rhoden; Phone: 615-898-5316; E-mail: agrhoden@mtsu.edu.

Softball: Cindy Connelley; Phone: 615-898-5018; E-mail: cconnelley@mtsu.edu.

Tennis: Randy Holden; Phone: 615-898-5154; E-mail: coachrholden@yahoo.com.

Track and Field: Dean Hayes; Phone: 615-898-2571; E-mail: dhayes@mtsu.edu.

Volleyball: Lisa Kissee; Phone: 615-898-2230; E-mail: lkissee@mtsu.edu.

MIDLAND LUTHERAN COLLEGE
Fremont, Nebraska

Warriors ◆ NAIA ◆ Great Plains Conference ◆ http://www.mlc.edu/

Independent Lutheran 4-year, founded 1883
Coed, 946 undergraduate students, 97% full-time, 58% women, 42% men
Small-town 27-acre campus with easy access to Omaha
Moderately difficult entrance level, 86% of applicants were admitted

Freshmen *Admission:* 937 applied, 802 were accepted, 261 enrolled.
Tuition and fees (2003–04): $16,310 (full-time). *Room and board:* $4420 (room only: $1950).
Financial Aid (All incoming freshmen): *Average need-based gift aid:* $10,453. *Average non-need based aid:* $9073. *Average aid to full-time undergraduates:* $14,160.
Athletic Department: *Director of Athletics:* Steve Schneider; Phone: 402-941-6361; Fax: 402-721-9406; E-mail: schneiders@mlc.edu. *Sports Information Director:* Keith Kramme; Phone: 402-941-6059; E-mail: kkramme@mlc.edu.

MEN'S COACHES

Baseball: Jef Field; Phone: 402-941-6371; E-mail: jfield@mlc.edu.

Basketball: Rich McGill; Phone: 402-941-6378; E-mail: mcgill@mlc.edu.

Cross Country: Jim McMahon; Phone: 402-941-6365; E-mail: track@mlc.edu.

Football: Bob Dzuris; Phone: 402-941-6364; E-mail: dzuris@mlc.edu.

Golf: Al Pokorski; Phone: 402-941-6511; E-mail: pokorski@mlc.edu.

Soccer: Dan Sullivan; Phone: 402-941-6372; E-mail: sullivan@mlc.edu.

Tennis: Doug Hartman; Phone: 402-941-6059; E-mail: hartman@mlc.edu.

Track and Field: Jim McMahon; Phone: 402-941-6365; E-mail: track@mlc.edu.

WOMEN'S COACHES

Basketball: Joanne Bracker; Phone: 402-941-6362; E-mail: bracker@mlc.edu.

Cross Country: Jim McMahon; Phone: 402-941-6365; E-mail: track@mlc.edu.

Golf: Al Pokorski; Phone: 402-941-6511; E-mail: pokorski@mlc.edu.

Soccer: Dan Sullivan; Phone: 402-941-6372; E-mail: sullivan@mlc.edu.

Softball: Keith Kramme; Phone: 402-941-6059; E-mail: kkramme@mlc.edu.

Tennis: Doug Hartman; Phone: 402-941-6059; E-mail: hartman@mlc.edu.

Track and Field: Jim McMahon; Phone: 402-941-6365; E-mail: track@mlc.edu.

Volleyball: Joan Rickert; Phone: 402-941-6512; E-mail: rickert@mlc.edu.

MIDWAY COLLEGE
Midway, Kentucky

Eagles ◆ NAIA ◆ Kentucky Intercollegiate Conference ◆ http://www.midway.edu/

Independent religious 4-year, founded 1847, affiliated with Christian Church (Disciples of Christ)
Women only, 1,154 undergraduate students, 62% full-time, 88% women, 12% men
Small-town 105-acre campus with easy access to Louisville and Lexington
Minimally difficult entrance level, 77% of applicants were admitted

Freshmen *Admission:* 342 applied, 252 were accepted, 121 enrolled.
Test scores: SAT verbal scores over 500: 70%; SAT math scores over 500: 55%; SAT verbal scores over 600: 10%; SAT math scores over 600: 20%; SAT verbal scores over 700: 5%; SAT math scores over 700: 5%.
Tuition and fees (2003–04): $11,850 (full-time). *Room and board:* $5800 (room only: $2800).
Financial Aid (All incoming freshmen): *Average need-based gift aid:* $7268. *Average non-need based aid:* $2000. *Average aid to full-time undergraduates:* $10,764.
Athletic Department: *Director of Athletics:* Timothy Southers; Phone: 859-846-5758; Fax: 859-846-5754; E-mail: tsouthers@midway.edu. *Sports Information Director:* Timothy Southers; Phone: 859-846-5758; E-mail: tsouthers@midway.edu.

WOMEN'S COACHES

Basketball: Timothy Southers; Phone: 859-846-5758; E-mail: tsouthers@midway.edu.

Soccer: Sufian Rayan; Phone: 859-846-5386.

Softball: Greg Dempsey; Phone: 859-846-5824; E-mail: gdempsey@midway.edu.

Tennis: Wendy Hoffman; Phone: 859-846-5805; E-mail: whoffman@midway.edu.

MIDWESTERN STATE UNIVERSITY
Wichita Falls, Texas

Indians ◆ NCAA II ◆ Lone Star Conference ◆ http://www.mwsu.edu/

State-supported comprehensive, founded 1922
Coed, 5,645 undergraduate students, 70% full-time, 57% women, 43% men
Urban 172-acre campus
Minimally difficult entrance level, 6% of applicants were admitted

Freshmen *Admission:* 2,294 applied, 1,496 were accepted, 702 enrolled.
Test scores: SAT verbal scores over 500: 40%; SAT math scores over 500: 38%; SAT verbal scores over 600: 11%; SAT math scores over 600: 6%; SAT verbal scores over 700: 1%; SAT math scores over 700: %.
Tuition and fees (2004–05): $3650 (resident), $10,730 (nonresident). *Room and board:* $4630 (room only: $2260).
Financial Aid (All incoming freshmen): *Average need-based gift aid:* $3924. *Average non-need based aid:* $3924. *Average aid to full-time undergraduates:* $4409.
Athletic Department: *Director of Athletics:* Jeff Ray; Phone: 940-397-4779; Fax: 940-397-4892; E-mail: jeff.ray@mwsu.edu. *Sports Information Director:* Andy Austin; Phone: 940-397-4769; E-mail: andy.austin@mwsu.edu.

MEN'S COACHES

Basketball: Jeff Ray; Phone: 940-397-4774; E-mail: jeff.ray@mwsu.edu.

Cheerleading: Leslee Ponder; Phone: 940-397-4501; E-mail: leslee.ponder@mwsu.edu.

Football: Bill Maskill; Phone: 940-397-4421; E-mail: bill.maskill@mwsu.edu.

Soccer: Doug Elder; Phone: 940-397-4772; E-mail: doug.elder@mwsu.edu.

Tennis: Larry Wiggins; Phone: 940-397-4766; E-mail: larry.wiggins@mwsu.edu.

WOMEN'S COACHES

Basketball: Shannon Burks; Phone: 940-397-4776; E-mail: shannon.burks@mwsu.edu.

Midwestern State University *(continued)*

Cheerleading: Leslee Ponder; Phone: 940-397-4501; E-mail: leslee.ponder@mwsu.edu.
Soccer: Jeff Trimble; Phone: 940-397-4823; E-mail: jeff.trimble@mwsu.edu.
Softball: Brady Tigert; Phone: 940-397-6329; E-mail: brady.tigert@mwsu.edu.
Tennis: Larry Wiggins; Phone: 940-397-4766; E-mail: larry.wiggins@mwsu.edu.
Volleyball: Pam Peetz; Phone: 940-397-4471; E-mail: pam.peetz@mwsu.edu.

MILES COLLEGE
Fairfield, Alabama

Golden Bears ◆ NCAA II ◆ Southern Intercollegiate Athletic Conference ◆ http://www.miles.edu/

Independent Christian Methodist Episcopal 4-year, founded 1905
Coed, 1,660 undergraduate students, 93% full-time, 57% women, 43% men
Small-town 35-acre campus
Noncompetitive entrance level, 58% of applicants were admitted

Freshmen *Admission:* 829 applied, 477 were accepted, 352 enrolled.
Tuition and fees (2003–04): $5470 (full-time). *Room and board:* $4338 (room only: $2370).
Financial Aid (All incoming freshmen): *Average need-based gift aid:* $3131. *Average non-need based aid:* $976. *Average aid to full-time undergraduates:* $6702.
Athletic Department: *Director of Athletics:* Augustus James; Phone: 205-929-1615; Fax: 205-929-1616. *Sports Information Director:* Latanya Barnes; Phone: 205-929-1821.

MEN'S COACHES
Baseball: Ken Hatcher; Phone: 205-929-1617.
Basketball: Roosevelt Sanders; Phone: 205-929-1612.
Cross Country: Oliver Smith; Phone: 205-929-1621.
Football: Wade Streeter; Phone: 205-929-1622.
Track and Field: Oliver Smith; Phone: 205-929-1621.

WOMEN'S COACHES
Basketball: Phone: 205-929-1615.
Cross Country: Oliver Smith; Phone: 205-929-1621.
Softball: Phone: 205-929-1615.
Track and Field: Oliver Smith; Phone: 205-929-1621.
Volleyball: Dionne Williams; Phone: 205-929-1621.

MILLERSVILLE UNIVERSITY OF PENNSYLVANIA
Millersville, Pennsylvania

Marauders ◆ NCAA II ◆ Pennsylvania State Athletic Conference ◆ http://www.millersville.edu/

State-supported comprehensive, founded 1855, part of Pennsylvania State System of Higher Education
Coed, 6,820 undergraduate students, 90% full-time, 56% women, 44% men
Small-town 190-acre campus
Moderately difficult entrance level, 59% of applicants were admitted

Freshmen *Admission:* 6,217 applied, 3,786 were accepted, 1,353 enrolled. *Test scores:* SAT verbal scores over 500: 68%; SAT math scores over 500: 69%; SAT verbal scores over 600: 17%; SAT math scores over 600: 20%; SAT verbal scores over 700: 2%; SAT math scores over 700: 1%.
Tuition and fees (2003–04): $5819 (resident), $12,717 (nonresident). *Room and board:* $5450 (room only: $3150).
Financial Aid (All incoming freshmen): *Average need-based gift aid:* $4286. *Average non-need based aid:* $4349. *Average aid to full-time undergraduates:* $6293.
Athletic Department: *Director of Athletics:* Daniel Audette; Phone: 717-872-3361; Fax: 717-872-2125; E-mail: daniel.audette@millersville.edu.

Sports Information Director: Greg Wright; Phone: 717-872-3100; E-mail: greg.wright@millersville.edu.

MEN'S COACHES
Baseball: Glenn Gallagher; Phone: 717-871-2411.
Basketball: Fred Thompson; Phone: 717-872-2047; E-mail: fthompson@millersville.edu.
Cheerleading: Matt Null; Phone: 717-872-2402.
Cross Country: Keith White; Phone: 717-872-3769; E-mail: kwhite@millersville.edu.
Football: Kevin Kiesel; Phone: 717-872-3012; E-mail: kkiesel@millersville.edu.
Golf: Scott Vandegrift; Phone: 717-872-3361; E-mail: svandegrift@millersville.edu.
Soccer: Bob Charles; Phone: 717-872-3491; E-mail: bob.charles@millersville.edu.
Tennis: Dewitt Boyd; Phone: 717-872-3818; E-mail: dboyd@millersville.edu.
Track and Field: Keith White; Phone: 717-872-3769; E-mail: kwhite@millersville.edu.
Wrestling: Steve Capoferri; Phone: 717-872-3795; E-mail: steve.capoferri@millersville.edu.

WOMEN'S COACHES
Basketball: Mary Fleig; Phone: 717-872-3706; E-mail: mfleig@millersville.edu.
Cheerleading: Matt Null; Phone: 717-872-2402.
Cross Country: Keith White; Phone: 717-872-3769; E-mail: kwhite@millersville.edu.
Field Hockey: Mary Gigliotti; Phone: 717-872-3834.
Lacrosse: Barbara Waltman; Phone: 717-872-3833; E-mail: bwaltman@millersville.edu.
Soccer: Trevor Hershey; Phone: 717-872-2370; E-mail: trevor.hershey@millersville.edu.
Softball: Kathy Cummings; Phone: 717-871-5503; E-mail: kcummings@millersville.edu.
Swimming: Mark Daum; Phone: 717-872-3872; E-mail: mdaum@millersville.edu.
Tennis: Dewitt Boyd; Phone: 717-872-3818; E-mail: dboyd@millersville.edu.
Track and Field: Keith White; Phone: 717-872-3769; E-mail: kwhite@millersville.edu.
Volleyball: Gary Lee; Phone: 717-872-3946; E-mail: gary.lee@millersville.edu.

MILLIGAN COLLEGE
Milligan College, Tennessee

Buffaloes ◆ NAIA ◆ Appalachian Conference ◆ http://www.milligan.edu/

Independent Christian comprehensive, founded 1866
Coed, 733 undergraduate students, 97% full-time, 61% women, 39% men
Suburban 145-acre campus
Moderately difficult entrance level, 72% of applicants were admitted

Freshmen *Admission:* 613 applied, 466 were accepted, 179 enrolled. *Test scores:* SAT verbal scores over 500: 81%; SAT math scores over 500: 75%; SAT verbal scores over 600: 31%; SAT math scores over 600: 26%; SAT verbal scores over 700: 4%; SAT math scores over 700: 4%.
Tuition and fees (2003–04): $15,260 (full-time). *Room and board:* $4600 (room only: $2250).
Financial Aid (All incoming freshmen): *Average need-based gift aid:* $1737. *Average non-need based aid:* $3770. *Average aid to full-time undergraduates:* $14,188.
Athletic Department: *Director of Athletics:* Ray Smith; Phone: 423-461-8990; Fax: 423-461-8740; E-mail: resmith@milligan.edu. *Sports Information Director:* Chandrea Shell; Phone: 423-461-8756; E-mail: chshell@milligan.edu.

MEN'S COACHES
Baseball: Danny Clark; Phone: 423-461-8722; E-mail: djclark@milligan.edu.
Basketball: Tony Wallingford; Phone: 423-461-8783; E-mail: twallingford@milligan.edu.
Cross Country: Chris Layne; Phone: 423-461-8992; E-mail: cclayne@milligan.edu.

Golf: .
Golf: Tony Wallingford; Phone: 423-461-8783; E-mail: twallingford@ milligan.edu.
Soccer: Marty Shirley; Phone: 423-461-8469; E-mail: amshirley@ milligan.edu.
Tennis: Rich Aubrey; Phone: 423-975-8029; E-mail: raubrey@milligan. edu.
Track and Field: .

WOMEN'S COACHES
Basketball: Rich Aubrey; Phone: 423-975-8029; E-mail: raubrey@ milligan.edu.
Cross Country: Chris Layne; Phone: 423-461-8992; E-mail: cclayne@ milligan.edu.
Soccer: David Dixon; Phone: 423-461-8993; E-mail: ddixon@milligan. edu.
Softball: Wes Holly; Phone: 423-461-8951; E-mail: weholly@milligan. edu.
Tennis: Kim Hyatt; Phone: 423-975-8724; E-mail: khyatt@milligan. edu.

MILLIKIN UNIVERSITY
Decatur, Illinois

Big Blue ◆ NCAA III ◆ College Conference of Illinois and Wisconsin Conference ◆ http://www.millikin.edu/

Independent religious comprehensive, founded 1901, affiliated with Presbyterian Church (U.S.A.)
Coed, 2,602 undergraduate students, 97% full-time, 56% women, 44% men
Suburban 70-acre campus
Moderately difficult entrance level, 70% of applicants were admitted

Freshmen *Admission:* 2,823 applied, 2,097 were accepted, 598 enrolled. *Test scores:* SAT verbal scores over 500: 67%; SAT math scores over 500: 66%; SAT verbal scores over 600: 32%; SAT math scores over 600: 28%; SAT verbal scores over 700: 6%; SAT math scores over 700: 2%.
Tuition and fees (2003–04): $19,234 (full-time). *Room and board:* $6123 (room only: $3315).
Financial Aid (All incoming freshmen): *Average need-based gift aid:* $11,990. *Average non-need based aid:* $6546. *Average aid to full-time undergraduates:* $17,086.
Athletic Department: *Director of Athletics:* Lori Kerans; Phone: 217-424-6344; Fax: 217-424-6629; E-mail: lkerans@mail.millikin.edu. *Sports Information Director:* Julie Farr; Phone: 217-362-6429; E-mail: jfarr@ mail.millikin.edu.

MEN'S COACHES
Baseball: Josh Manning; Phone: 217-424-3608; E-mail: jmanning@ mail.millikin.edu.
Basketball: Tim Littrell; Phone: 217-362-6480; E-mail: tlittrell@mail. millikin.edu.
Cross Country: Chad Sloan; Phone: 217-420-6625.
Football: Doug Neibuhr; Phone: 217-420-6621; E-mail: dneibuhr@mail. millikin.edu.
Golf: Pat Allgeier; Phone: 217-420-3605; E-mail: pallgeier@mail. millikin.edu.
Soccer: Craig lee; Phone: 217-420-3607; E-mail: crlee@mail.millikin. edu.
Swimming: Frank Sampson; Phone: 217-420-6676; E-mail: fsampson@ mail.millikin.edu.
Track and Field: Don Luy; Phone: 217-420-6625; E-mail: dluy@mail. millikin.edu.
Wrestling: Mike Poe; Phone: 217-420-3603; E-mail: mpoe@mail. millikin.edu.

WOMEN'S COACHES
Basketball: Lori Kerans; Phone: 217-420-6621; E-mail: lkerans@mail. millikin.edu.
Cross Country: Chad Sloan; Phone: 217-420-6625.
Golf: Marilyn Dechart; Phone: 217-420-3502.
Soccer: Ryan Lakin; Phone: 217-420-3607; E-mail: crlee@mail. millikin.edu.
Softball: Jim Mills; Phone: 217-420-3602; E-mail: jmills@mail.millikin. edu.
Swimming: Frank Sampson; Phone: 217-420-6676; E-mail: fsampson@ mail.millikin.edu.

Tennis: Mike Brannon; Phone: 217-424-3611.
Track and Field: Don Luy; Phone: 217-420-6625; E-mail: dluy@mail. millikin.edu.
Volleyball: Debbie Kiick; Phone: 217-420-6344; E-mail: dkiick@mail. millikin.edu.

MILLSAPS COLLEGE
Jackson, Mississippi

Majors ◆ NCAA III ◆ Southern Collegiate Athletic Conference ◆ http://www.millsaps.edu/

Independent United Methodist comprehensive, founded 1890
Coed, 1,123 undergraduate students, 96% full-time, 54% women, 46% men
Urban 100-acre campus
Moderately difficult entrance level, 82% of applicants were admitted

Freshmen *Admission:* 1,045 applied, 880 were accepted, 259 enrolled. *Test scores:* SAT verbal scores over 500: 93%; SAT math scores over 500: 80%; SAT verbal scores over 600: 48%; SAT math scores over 600: 38%; SAT verbal scores over 700: 12%; SAT math scores over 700: 10%.
Tuition and fees (2003–04): $18,414 (full-time). *Room and board:* $6768.
Financial Aid (All incoming freshmen): *Average need-based gift aid:* $13,656. *Average non-need based aid:* $11,516. *Average aid to full-time undergraduates:* $17,152.
Athletic Department: *Director of Athletics:* Ron Jurney; Phone: 601-974-1243; Fax: 601-974-1209; E-mail: jurnerw@millsaps.edu. *Sports Information Director:* Denny Hayles; Phone: 601-974-1394; E-mail: hayled@millsaps.edu.

MEN'S COACHES
Baseball: Jim Page; Phone: 601-974-1196; E-mail: pagejj@millsaps.edu.
Basketball: Tim Wise; Phone: 601-974-1188; E-mail: wiseta@millsaps. edu.
Cross Country: Eric Navarre; Phone: 601-974-1190; E-mail: navarej@ millsaps.edu.
Football: David Saunders; Phone: 601-974-1194; E-mail: saundde@ millsaps.edu.
Golf: Dill Gunn; Phone: 601-974-1190; E-mail: gunnwd@millsaps.edu.
Soccer: Lee Johnson; Phone: 601-974-1894; E-mail: johnsls@millsaps. edu.
Tennis: Scott Pennington; Phone: 601-974-1347.

WOMEN'S COACHES
Basketball: Robin Jeffries; Phone: 601-974-1297; E-mail: jeffrrl@ millsaps.edu.
Cross Country: Eric Navarre; Phone: 601-974-1190; E-mail: navarej@ millsaps.edu.
Golf: Denny Hayles; Phone: 601-974-1394; E-mail: hayled@millsaps. edu.
Soccer: Paul Van Hooydonk; Phone: 601-974-1198; E-mail: vanhopa@ millsaps.edu.
Softball: Joe Kinsella; Phone: 601-974-1195; E-mail: kinsejs@millsaps. edu.
Tennis: Scott Pennington; Phone: 601-974-1347.
Volleyball: Peter Cosmiano; Phone: 601-974-1197; E-mail: cosmipc@ millsaps.edu.

MILLS COLLEGE
Oakland, California

Cyclones ◆ NAIA ◆ California Pacific Conference ◆ http:// www.mills.edu/

Independent comprehensive, founded 1852
Women only, 735 undergraduate students, 92% full-time, 100% women, 100% men
Urban 135-acre campus with easy access to San Francisco
Moderately difficult entrance level, 73% of applicants were admitted

Freshmen *Admission:* 537 applied, 393 were accepted, 115 enrolled. *Test scores:* SAT verbal scores over 500: 80%; SAT math scores over

Mills College *(continued)*

500: 74%; SAT verbal scores over 600: 48%; SAT math scores over 600: 27%; SAT verbal scores over 700: 12%; SAT math scores over 700: 5%.
Tuition and fees (2003–04): $24,441 (full-time). *Room and board:* $8930.
Financial Aid (All incoming freshmen): *Average need-based gift aid:* $15,125. *Average non-need based aid:* $10,000. *Average aid to full-time undergraduates:* $23,913.
Athletic Department: *Director of Athletics:* Themy Adachi; Phone: 510-430-3285; Fax: 510-430-2276; E-mail: themy@mills.edu. *Sports Information Director:* Kara Riley; Phone: 510-430-2232; E-mail: kara@mills.edu.

WOMEN'S COACHES

Cross Country: Sharon Chiong; Phone: 510-430-3282; E-mail: chiong@mills.edu.
Soccer: Colette Bowler; Phone: 510-430-2395; E-mail: colette@mills.edu.
Swimming: Neil Virtue; Phone: 510-430-3384; E-mail: nvirtue@mills.edu.
Tennis: Judy Newman; Phone: 510-430-3257; E-mail: jrakaela@mills.edu.
Volleyball: Marla Mundis; Phone: 510-430-3283; E-mail: mmundis@mills.edu.

MILWAUKEE SCHOOL OF ENGINEERING
Milwaukee, Wisconsin

Raiders ◆ NCAA III ◆ Lake Michigan Conference ◆ http://www.msoe.edu/

Independent comprehensive, founded 1903
Coed, primarily men, 2,101 undergraduate students, 84% full-time, 17% women, 83% men
Urban 15-acre campus
Moderately difficult entrance level, 67% of applicants were admitted

Freshmen *Admission:* 1,809 applied, 1,177 were accepted, 439 enrolled. *Test scores:* SAT verbal scores over 500: 89%; SAT math scores over 500: 93%; SAT verbal scores over 600: 43%; SAT math scores over 600: 61%; SAT verbal scores over 700: 9%; SAT math scores over 700: 16%.
Tuition and fees (2003–04): $23,034 (full-time). *Room and board:* $5445 (room only: $3500).
Financial Aid (All incoming freshmen): *Average need-based gift aid:* $11,548. *Average non-need based aid:* $7200. *Average aid to full-time undergraduates:* $13,366.
Athletic Department: *Director of Athletics:* Dan Harris; Phone: 414-277-7230; Fax: 414-221-0610; E-mail: harris@msoe.edu. *Sports Information Director:* Mark Ostapina; Phone: 414-277-7565; E-mail: ostapina@msoe.edu.

MEN'S COACHES

Baseball: Len Vandenboom; Phone: 414-277-7154; E-mail: vandenbo@msoe.edu.
Basketball: Brian Good; Phone: 414-277-6947; E-mail: good@msoe.edu.
Cross Country: Patrick Pretty; Phone: 414-277-4552.
Golf: Joe Meloy; Phone: 414-277-7227; E-mail: meloy@msoe.edu.
Ice Hockey: Mark Ostapina; Phone: 414-277-7565; E-mail: ostapina@msoe.edu.
Soccer: Jimmy Banks; Phone: 414-277-7493; E-mail: banks@msoe.edu.
Tennis: Larry Gagnon; Phone: 414-277-4552.
Track and Field: Patrick Pretty; Phone: 414-277-4552.
Volleyball: Dan Kirchhoff; Phone: 414-277-6762.
Wrestling: Kevin Morin; Phone: 414-277-7129; E-mail: morin@msoe.edu.

WOMEN'S COACHES

Basketball: Jessica Ott; Phone: 414-277-2411; E-mail: ott@msoe.edu.
Cross Country: Patrick Pretty; Phone: 414-277-4552.
Golf: Jill Friauf; Phone: 414-277-7365; E-mail: friauf@msoe.edu.
Soccer: Michelle Alioto; Phone: 414-277-2412; E-mail: alioto@msoe.edu.
Softball: Dan Bantin; Phone: 414-277-7413; E-mail: bdbant@execpc.com.
Tennis: Larry Gagnon; Phone: 414-277-4552.

Track and Field: Patrick Pretty; Phone: 414-277-4552.
Volleyball: Adam Stikel; Phone: 414-277-4552; E-mail: astikel@wi.rr.com.

MINNESOTA STATE UNIVERSITY MANKATO
Mankato, Minnesota

Mavericks ◆ NCAA II ◆ North Central Intercollegiate Conference; Western Collegiate Hockey Conference ◆ http://www.mnsu.edu/

State-supported comprehensive, founded 1868, part of Minnesota State Colleges and Universities System
Coed, 12,390 undergraduate students, 90% full-time, 53% women, 47% men
Small-town 303-acre campus with easy access to Minneapolis–St. Paul
Moderately difficult entrance level, 84% of applicants were admitted

Freshmen *Admission:* 5,660 applied, 4,956 were accepted, 2,287 enrolled.
Tuition and fees (2003–04): $4506 (resident), $8775 (nonresident). *Room and board:* $4297.
Financial Aid (All incoming freshmen): *Average need-based gift aid:* $3399. *Average non-need based aid:* $1193. *Average aid to full-time undergraduates:* $5822.
Athletic Department: *Director of Athletics:* Kevin Buisman; Phone: 507-389-6111; Fax: 507-389-2904; E-mail: kevin.buisman@mnsu.edu. *Sports Information Director:* Paul Allan; Phone: 507-389-2625; E-mail: paul.allan@mnsu.edu.

MEN'S COACHES

Baseball: Dean Bowyer; Phone: 507-389-2689; E-mail: dean.bowyer@mnsu.edu.
Basketball: Matt Margenthaler; Phone: 507-389-2311; E-mail: matthew.margenthaler@mnsu.edu.
Cheerleading: Stefanie Kelly; Phone: 507-389-6111; E-mail: stefanie.kelly@mnsu.edu.
Cross Country: Mark Schuck; Phone: 507-389-5486; E-mail: mark.schuck@mnsu.edu.
Diving: Gretchen Wiley; Phone: 507-389-2538.
Football: Clarence Holley; Phone: 507-389-1072; E-mail: clarence.holley@mnsu.edu.
Golf: Mike Zinni; Phone: 507-389-6111; E-mail: pgamzinni@aol.com.
Ice Hockey: Troy Jutting; Phone: 507-389-5196; E-mail: troy.jutting@mnsu.edu.
Swimming: Libor Janek; Phone: 507-389-6326; E-mail: libor.janek@mnsu.edu.
Tennis: Todd Scott; Phone: 507-389-6111; E-mail: todd.scott@mnsu.edu.
Track and Field: Mark Schuck; Phone: 507-389-5486; E-mail: mark.schuck@mnsu.edu.
Wrestling: Jim Makovsky; Phone: 507-389-6521; E-mail: james.makovsky@mnsu.edu.

WOMEN'S COACHES

Basketball: Ann Walker; Phone: 507-389-2678; E-mail: ann.walker@mnsu.edu.
Cheerleading: Stefanie Kelly; Phone: 507-389-6111; E-mail: stefanie.kelly@mnsu.edu.
Cross Country: Jenny Blue; Phone: 507-389-6415; E-mail: jennifer.blue@mnsu.edu.
Diving: Gretchen Wiley; Phone: 507-389-2538.
Golf: Nick Campa; Phone: 507-389-5235; E-mail: nicholas.campa@mnsu.edu.
Soccer: Christine Miskec; Phone: 507-389-2671; E-mail: christine.miskec@mnsu.edu.
Softball: Lori Meyer; Phone: 507-389-1521; E-mail: lori.meyer@mnsu.edu.
Swimming: Libor Janek; Phone: 507-389-6326; E-mail: libor.janek@mnsu.edu.
Tennis: Phil Brauer; Phone: 507-389-6111.
Track and Field: Mark Schuck; Phone: 507-389-5486; E-mail: mark.schuck@mnsu.edu.
Volleyball: Doug Tully; Phone: 507-389-2673; E-mail: douglas.tully@mnsu.edu.

MINNESOTA STATE UNIVERSITY MOORHEAD
Moorhead, Minnesota

Dragons ◆ NCAA II ◆ Northern Sun Intercollegiate
Conference ◆ http://www.mnstate.edu/

State-supported comprehensive, founded 1885, part of Minnesota State Colleges and Universities System
Coed, 7,282 undergraduate students, 86% full-time, 61% women, 39% men
Urban 118-acre campus
Moderately difficult entrance level, 80% of applicants were admitted

Freshmen *Admission:* 2,764 applied, 2,375 were accepted, 1,291 enrolled.
Tuition and fees (2003–04): $4254 (resident), $4254 (nonresident). *Room and board:* $4340 (room only: $2560).
Financial Aid (All incoming freshmen): *Average need-based gift aid:* $3746. *Average non-need based aid:* $761. *Average aid to full-time undergraduates:* $3370.
Athletic Department: *Director of Athletics:* David Crockett; Phone: 218-477-2070; Fax: 218-477-3291; E-mail: crockett@mnstate.edu. *Sports Information Director:* Larry Scott; Phone: 218-477-2113; E-mail: scotty@mnstate.edu.

MEN'S COACHES
Basketball: Stu Engen; Phone: 218-477-2293; E-mail: stuengen@mnstate.edu.
Cheerleading: Phone: 218-477-2622.
Cross Country: Keith Barnier; Phone: 218-477-2294; E-mail: barnierk@mnstate.edu.
Football: Ralph Micheli; Phone: 218-477-2051; E-mail: rosenfde@mnstate.edu.
Track and Field: Keith Barnier; Phone: 218-477-2294; E-mail: barnierk@mnstate.edu.
Wrestling: Keenan Spiess; Phone: 218-477-2309; E-mail: spiess@mnstate.edu.

WOMEN'S COACHES
Basketball: Karla Nelson; Phone: 218-477-2421; E-mail: nelsnkar@mnstate.edu.
Cheerleading: Phone: 218-477-2622.
Cross Country: Keith Barnier; Phone: 218-477-2294; E-mail: barnierk@mnstate.edu.
Golf: Tracie Bents; Phone: 218-477-2622; E-mail: bents@west-fargo.k12.nd.us.
Soccer: Eric Swanbeck; Phone: 218-477-2320; E-mail: swanbeck@mnstate.edu.
Softball: Jason Sobolik; Phone: 218-477-5052; E-mail: sobolik@mnstate.edu.
Swimming: Todd Peters; Phone: 218-477-2305; E-mail: petrstod@mnstate.edu.
Tennis: Gary Harris; Phone: 218-477-2622; E-mail: harrismktg@lakesnet.net.
Track and Field: Keith Barnier; Phone: 218-477-2294; E-mail: barnierk@mnstate.edu.
Volleyball: Tammy Blake; Phone: 218-477-2321; E-mail: blake@mnstate.edu.

MINOT STATE UNIVERSITY
Minot, North Dakota

Beavers ◆ NAIA ◆ Dakota Conference
◆ http://www.minotstateu.edu/

State-supported comprehensive, founded 1913, part of North Dakota University System
Coed, 3,594 undergraduate students, 70% full-time, 62% women, 38% men
Small-town 103-acre campus
Minimally difficult entrance level, 83% of applicants were admitted

Freshmen *Admission:* 720 applied, 619 were accepted, 568 enrolled.
Tuition and fees (2003–04): $3228 (resident), $7787 (nonresident). *Room and board:* $3274 (room only: $1200).

Financial Aid (All incoming freshmen): *Average need-based gift aid:* $2149. *Average aid to full-time undergraduates:* $6489.
Athletic Department: *Director of Athletics:* Rick Hedberg; Phone: 701-858-3042; Fax: 701-858-3136; E-mail: rhedberg@minotstateu.edu. *Sports Information Director:* Sheila Green Gerding; Phone: 701-858-3042; E-mail: greensh@minotstateu.edu.

MEN'S COACHES
Baseball: Dick Limke; Phone: 701-858-4328; E-mail: rlimke@ndak.net.
Basketball: Mike Hultz; Phone: 701-858-3278; E-mail: hultz@minotstateu.edu.
Cross Country: Scott Simmons; Phone: 701-858-3268; E-mail: simmons@minotstateu.edu.
Football: Mike Sivertson; Phone: 701-858-4450; E-mail: sivertm@minotstateu.edu.
Golf: Mike Hultz; Phone: 701-858-3278; E-mail: hultz@minotstateu.edu.
Track and Field: Scott Simmons; Phone: 701-858-3268; E-mail: simmons@minotstateu.edu.

WOMEN'S COACHES
Basketball: Sheila Green Gerding; Phone: 701-858-3042; E-mail: greensh@minotstateu.edu.
Cross Country: Scott Simmons; Phone: 701-858-3268; E-mail: simmons@minotstateu.edu.
Golf: Mike Hultz; Phone: 701-858-3278; E-mail: hultz@minotstateu.edu.
Softball: Dana Fieldler; Phone: 701-858-3169; E-mail: fiedlerd@minotstateu.edu.
Track and Field: Scott Simmons; Phone: 701-858-3268; E-mail: simmons@minotstateu.edu.
Volleyball: Dana Fieldler; Phone: 701-858-3169; E-mail: fiedlerd@minotstateu.edu.

MISSISSIPPI COLLEGE
Clinton, Mississippi

Choctaws ◆ NCAA III ◆ American Southwest Conference
◆ http://www.mc.edu/

Independent Southern Baptist comprehensive, founded 1826
Coed, 2,367 undergraduate students, 91% full-time, 58% women, 42% men
Suburban 320-acre campus
Moderately difficult entrance level, 66% of applicants were admitted

Freshmen *Admission:* 1,646 applied, 949 were accepted, 425 enrolled.
Tuition and fees (2003–04): $11,529 (full-time). *Room and board:* $5396 (room only: $2830).
Financial Aid (All incoming freshmen): *Average need-based gift aid:* $10,216. *Average non-need based aid:* $9636. *Average aid to full-time undergraduates:* $12,380.
Athletic Department: *Director of Athletics:* Mike Jones; Phone: 601-925-3819; Fax: 601-925-7081; E-mail: jones01@mc.edu. *Sports Information Director:* Chris Brooks; Phone: 601-925-3234; E-mail: cbrooks@mc.edu.

MEN'S COACHES
Baseball: Lee Kuyrkendall; Phone: 601-925-3346; E-mail: kuyrkend@mc.edu.
Basketball: Don Lofton; Phone: 601-925-3364; E-mail: dlofton@mc.edu.
Cheerleading: Cheryl Moss; Phone: 601-925-3365; E-mail: cmoss@mc.edu.
Cross Country: Butch Ard; Phone: 601-925-7653; E-mail: bard@mc.edu.
Football: Johnny Mills; Phone: 601-925-3347; E-mail: jmills@mc.edu.
Soccer: Kevin Johns; Phone: 601-925-3934; E-mail: kjohns@mc.edu.
Tennis: David Boteler; Phone: 601-925-3959; E-mail: dboteler@mc.edu.
Track and Field: Butch Ard; Phone: 601-925-7653; E-mail: bard@mc.edu.

WOMEN'S COACHES
Basketball: Paul Allen Duke; Phone: 601-925-3360; E-mail: duke@mc.edu.
Cheerleading: Cheryl Moss; Phone: 601-925-3365; E-mail: cmoss@mc.edu.
Cross Country: Butch Ard; Phone: 601-925-7653; E-mail: bard@mc.edu.
Soccer: Darryl Longabaugh; Phone: 601-925-3892; E-mail: longabau@mc.edu.

Mississippi College *(continued)*

Softball: Susan Musselwhite; Phone: 601-925-3362; E-mail: musselwh@mc.edu.
Tennis: David Boteler; Phone: 601-925-3959; E-mail: dboteler@mc.edu.edu.
Track and Field: Butch Ard; Phone: 601-925-7653; E-mail: bard@mc.edu.
Volleyball: Anna McReynolds; Phone: 601-925-3357; E-mail: amcreyno@mc.edu.

MISSISSIPPI STATE UNIVERSITY
Mississippi State, Mississippi

Bulldogs ◆ NCAA I ◆ Southeastern Conference ◆ http://www.msstate.edu/

State-supported university, founded 1878, part of Mississippi Board of Trustees of State Institutions of Higher Learning
Coed, 12,839 undergraduate students, 87% full-time, 47% women, 53% men
Small-town 4,200-acre campus
Moderately difficult entrance level, 75% of applicants were admitted

Freshmen *Admission:* 4,646 applied, 3,492 were accepted, 1,688 enrolled.
Tuition and fees (2003–04): $3874 (resident), $8780 (nonresident). *Room and board:* $5265 (room only: $2230).
Financial Aid (All incoming freshmen): *Average need-based gift aid:* $3223. *Average non-need based aid:* $2530. *Average aid to full-time undergraduates:* $6367.
Athletic Department: *Director of Athletics:* Larry Templeton; Phone: 662-325-8082; Fax: 662-325-7904. *Sports Information Director:* David Rosinski; Phone: 662-325-3595; E-mail: rosinski@athletics.msstate.edu.

MEN'S COACHES
Baseball: Ron Polk; Phone: 662-325-3597.
Basketball: Rick Stansbury; Phone: 662-325-3800.
Cheerleading: Darryl Lyons; Phone: 662-325-9843; E-mail: msu-spirit@athletics.msstate.edu.
Cross Country: Steve Dudley; Phone: 662-325-8333; E-mail: sdudley@athletics.msstate.edu.
Football: Sylvester Croom; Phone: 662-325-2532.
Golf: Clay Homan; Phone: 662-325-2722; E-mail: choman@athletics.msstate.edu.
Tennis: Sylvain Guichard; Phone: 662-325-2896; E-mail: sguichard@athletics.msstate.edu.
Track and Field: Al Schmidt; Phone: 662-325-2892; E-mail: aschmidt@athletics.msstate.edu.

WOMEN'S COACHES
Basketball: Sharon Fanning; Phone: 662-325-0198; E-mail: bonnie@athletics.msstate.edu.
Cheerleading: Darryl Lyons; Phone: 662-325-9843; E-mail: msu-spirit@athletics.msstate.edu.
Cross Country: Al Schmidt; Phone: 662-325-2892; E-mail: aschmidt@athletics.msstate.edu.
Golf: Christi Sanders; Phone: 662-325-2722; E-mail: csanders@athletics.msstate.edu.
Soccer: Neal McGuire; Phone: 662-325-0718; E-mail: nmcguire@athletics.msstate.edu.
Softball: Jay Miller; Phone: 662-325-0573; E-mail: millercj@athletics.msstate.edu.
Tennis: Tracy Lane; Phone: 662-325-2896; E-mail: tlane@athletics.msstate.edu.
Track and Field: Al Schmidt; Phone: 662-325-2892; E-mail: aschmidt@athletics.msstate.edu.
Volleyball: Tina Burcham Seals; Phone: 662-325-2722.

MISSISSIPPI UNIVERSITY FOR WOMEN
Columbus, Mississippi

Blues ◆ NCAA II ◆ Gulf South Conference ◆ http://www.muw.edu/

State-supported comprehensive, founded 1884, part of Mississippi Institutions of Higher Learning
Coed, primarily women, 2,166 undergraduate students
Small-town 110-acre campus
Moderately difficult entrance level, 65% of applicants were admitted

Freshmen *Admission:* 609 applied, 395 were accepted.
Tuition and fees (2003–04): $3298 (resident), $7965 (nonresident). *Room and board:* $3230.
Financial Aid (All incoming freshmen): *Average need-based gift aid:* $2440. *Average non-need based aid:* $3176. *Average aid to full-time undergraduates:* $4475.
Athletic Department: *Director of Athletics:* Jo Spearman; Phone: 662-329-7225; Fax: 662-329-8554; E-mail: jspearma@muw.edu. *Sports Information Director:* Bobby Galinsky; Phone: 662-329-7127; E-mail: bgalinsky@muw.edu.

MEN'S COACHES
Cheerleading: Eric Harlan; Phone: 662-329-7261; E-mail: eharlan@muw.edu.

WOMEN'S COACHES
Basketball: Glenn Schmidt; Phone: 662-329-7241; E-mail: gschmidt@muw.edu.
Cheerleading: Eric Harlan; Phone: 662-329-7261; E-mail: eharlan@muw.edu.
Softball: Rita Higginbotham; Phone: 662-329-7229; E-mail: ritah@muw.edu.
Tennis: Jay Pacelli; Phone: 662-329-7179; E-mail: jpacelli@muw.edu.
Volleyball: Chris Campbell; Phone: 662-329-7228.

MISSISSIPPI VALLEY STATE UNIVERSITY
Itta Bena, Mississippi

Delta Devils ◆ NCAA I ◆ Southwestern Athletic Conference ◆ http://www.mvsu.edu/

State-supported comprehensive, founded 1946, part of Mississippi Institutions of Higher Learning
Coed, 3,259 undergraduate students, 89% full-time, 72% women, 28% men
Small-town 450-acre campus
Minimally difficult entrance level, 99% of applicants were admitted

Freshmen *Admission:* 3,486 applied, 3,447 were accepted, 331 enrolled.
Tuition and fees (2003–04): $3411 (resident), $7965 (nonresident). *Room and board:* $3544.
Financial Aid (All incoming freshmen): *Average aid to full-time undergraduates:* $7000.
Athletic Department: *Director of Athletics:* Lonza Hardy Jr.; Phone: 662-254-3550; Fax: 662-254-3639. *Sports Information Director:* Marlon Reed; Phone: 662-254-3011.

MEN'S COACHES
Baseball: Dough Shanks; Phone: 662-254-3834.
Basketball: Lafayette Stribling; Phone: 662-254-3546.
Cross Country: Charles Ruth; Phone: 662-254-3559.
Football: Willie Totten; Phone: 662-254-3566.
Golf: Roger Totten; Phone: 662-254-3567.
Tennis: Arthur Moore; Phone: 662-254-3550.
Track and Field: Charles Ruth; Phone: 662-254-3559.

WOMEN'S COACHES
Basketball: Nathaniel Kilbert; Phone: 662-254-3549.
Cross Country: Charles Ruth; Phone: 662-254-3559.
Golf: Roger Totten; Phone: 662-254-3567.
Softball: Lee Smith; Phone: 662-254-3721.
Tennis: Arthur Moore; Phone: 662-254-3550.
Track and Field: Charles Ruth; Phone: 662-254-3559.
Volleyball: Alyse Wells-Kilbert; Phone: 662-254-3552.

MISSOURI BAPTIST UNIVERSITY
St. Louis, Missouri

Spartans ◆ NAIA ◆ American Midwest Conference ◆ http://www.mobap.edu/

Independent Southern Baptist comprehensive, founded 1964
Coed, 2,947 undergraduate students, 35% full-time, 61% women, 39% men
Suburban 65-acre campus
Moderately difficult entrance level, 71% of applicants were admitted

Freshmen *Admission:* 712 applied, 507 were accepted, 210 enrolled.
Tuition and fees (2003–04): $12,280 (full-time). *Room and board:* $5800.
Athletic Department: *Director of Athletics:* Tom Smith; Phone: 314-392-2264; Fax: 314-392-2371; E-mail: smitht@mobap.edu. *Sports Information Director:* Danny Wingate; Phone: 314-392-2268; E-mail: wingate@mobap.edu.

MEN'S COACHES
Baseball: Eddie Uschold; Phone: 314-392-2384; E-mail: uschoer@mobap.edu.
Basketball: Tony Tompkins; Phone: 314-392-2267; E-mail: thompkar@mobap.edu.
Cheerleading: Marnie Walters; Phone: 314-392-2397; E-mail: waltemj@mobap.edu.
Cross Country: Josh Buffington; Phone: 314-392-2270; E-mail: buffington@mobap.edu.
Golf: Randy Carstens; Phone: 314-434-0753; E-mail: rcarstens@kirkofthehills.org.
Soccer: Jim Embick; Phone: 314-392-2391; E-mail: embickj@mobap.edu.
Volleyball: John Yehling; Phone: 314-392-2395; E-mail: yehling@mobap.edu.
Wrestling: Tom Smith; Phone: 314-392-2264; E-mail: smitht@mobap.edu.

WOMEN'S COACHES
Basketball: Danny Wingate; Phone: 314-392-2268; E-mail: wingate@mobap.edu.
Cheerleading: Marnie Walters; Phone: 314-392-2397; E-mail: waltemj@mobap.edu.
Cross Country: Josh Buffington; Phone: 314-392-2270; E-mail: buffington@mobap.edu.
Golf: Randy Carstens; Phone: 314-434-0753; E-mail: rcarstens@kirkofthehills.org.
Soccer: Juan Mares; Phone: 314-392-2274; E-mail: maresj@mobap.edu.
Softball: Kelley Bryant; Phone: 314-392-2394; E-mail: brent@mobap.edu.
Volleyball: Jay Potter; Phone: 314-392-2266; E-mail: pottejs@mobap.edu.

MISSOURI SOUTHERN STATE UNIVERSITY
Joplin, Missouri

Lions ◆ NCAA II ◆ Mid-America Intercollegiate Conference ◆ http://www.mssu.edu/

State-supported 4-year, founded 1937
Coed, 5,410 undergraduate students, 65% full-time, 59% women, 41% men
Small-town 350-acre campus
Moderately difficult entrance level, 7% of applicants were admitted

Freshmen *Admission:* 1,771 applied, 1,317 were accepted, 692 enrolled.
Tuition and fees (2004–05): $3976 (resident), $7786 (nonresident). *Room and board:* $4770.
Financial Aid (All incoming freshmen): *Average need-based gift aid:* $3699. *Average non-need based aid:* $2209. *Average aid to full-time undergraduates:* $5591.
Athletic Department: *Director of Athletics:* Sallie Beard; Phone: 417-625-9574; Fax: 417-625-9397; E-mail: beard-s@mssu.edu. *Sports Information Director:* J.R. Belew; Phone: 417-625-9359; E-mail: belew-j@mssu.edu.

MEN'S COACHES
Baseball: Warren Turner; Phone: 417-625-9312; E-mail: turner-w@mail.mssc.edu.
Basketball: Warren Turner; Phone: 417-625-9312; E-mail: turner-w@mssu.edu.
Cross Country: Tom Rutledge; Phone: 417-625-9554; E-mail: rutledge-t@mail.mssc.edu.
Football: Phone: 417-625-9358; E-mail: cooke-b@mail.mssc.edu.
Golf: Scott Stettes; Phone: 417-850-8248; E-mail: stettes@pga.com.
Soccer: Kiley Cirillo; Phone: 417-659-4458; E-mail: cirillo-k@mssu.edu.
Track and Field: Tom Rutledge; Phone: 417-625-9554; E-mail: rutledge-t@mail.mssu.edu.

WOMEN'S COACHES
Basketball: Maryann Mitts; Phone: 417-625-9581; E-mail: mitts-m@mail.mssc.edu.
Cross Country: Patty Vavra; Phone: 417-625-3063; E-mail: vavra-p@mail.mssc.edu.
Soccer: Trevor Wachsman; Phone: 417-625-3014; E-mail: wachsman-t@mssu.edu.
Softball: Crystal Turner; Phone: 417-625-9317.
Tennis: Julie Wengert; Phone: 417-625-9316; E-mail: wengert-j@mail.mssc.edu.
Track and Field: Patty Vavra; Phone: 417-625-3063; E-mail: vavra-p@mail.mssc.edu.
Volleyball: Debbie Traywick; Phone: 417-625-9705; E-mail: traywick-d@mail.mssc.edu.

MISSOURI VALLEY COLLEGE
Marshall, Missouri

Vikings ◆ NAIA ◆ Heart of America Conference ◆ http://www.moval.edu/

Independent religious 4-year, founded 1889, affiliated with Presbyterian Church
Coed, 1,623 undergraduate students, 85% full-time, 47% women, 53% men
Small-town 140-acre campus with easy access to Kansas City
Minimally difficult entrance level, 60% of applicants were admitted

Freshmen *Admission:* 1,345 applied, 898 were accepted, 405 enrolled. *Test scores:* SAT verbal scores over 500: 20%; SAT math scores over 500: 35%; SAT verbal scores over 600: 3%; SAT math scores over 600: 13%.
Tuition and fees (2004–05): $13,500 (full-time). *Room and board:* $5200.
Financial Aid (All incoming freshmen): *Average need-based gift aid:* $9750. *Average aid to full-time undergraduates:* $11,402.
Athletic Department: *Director of Athletics:* Tom Fifer; Phone: 660-831-4219; Fax: 660-831-4038; E-mail: fifert@moval.edu. *Sports Information Director:* Scott Latham; Phone: 660-831-4230; E-mail: lathams@moval.edu.

MEN'S COACHES
Baseball: Dan Bowers; Phone: 660-831-4113; E-mail: bowersd@moval.edu.
Basketball: Chad Lance; Phone: 660-831-4189; E-mail: lancec@moval.edu.
Cheerleading: Tatiana Toliver; Phone: 660-831-4631; E-mail: tolivert@moval.edu.
Cross Country: Jim Anderson; Phone: 660-831-4114; E-mail: andersonj@moval.edu.
Football: Paul Troth; Phone: 660-831-4118; E-mail: trothp@moval.edu.
Golf: Jim Anderson; Phone: 660-831-4114; E-mail: andersonj@moval.edu.
Soccer: Vladimir Simic; Phone: 660-831-4217; E-mail: simicv@moval.edu.
Tennis: Ryan Carney; Phone: 660-831-4090; E-mail: carneyr@moval.edu.
Track and Field: Charlie McFail; Phone: 660-831-4161; E-mail: mcfailc@moval.edu.
Volleyball: Ed Johnson; Phone: 660-831-4194; E-mail: johnsonce@moval.edu.
Wrestling: Mike Machholz; Phone: 660-831-4158; E-mail: machholzm@moval.edu.

WOMEN'S COACHES
Basketball: Bill Wolf; Phone: 660-831-4104; E-mail: wolfb@moval.edu.

Missouri Valley College *(continued)*

Cheerleading: Tatiana Toliver; Phone: 660-831-4631; E-mail: tolivert@moval.edu.
Cross Country: Jim Anderson; Phone: 660-831-4114; E-mail: andersonj@moval.edu.
Golf: Jim Anderson; Phone: 660-831-4114; E-mail: andersonj@moval.edu.
Soccer: Derek Burton; Phone: 660-831-4217; E-mail: burtond@moval.edu.
Softball: Kyle Mason; Phone: 660-831-4111; E-mail: masonk@moval.edu.
Tennis: Ryan Carney; Phone: 660-831-4090; E-mail: carneyr@moval.edu.
Track and Field: Charlie McFail; Phone: 660-831-4161; E-mail: mcfailc@moval.edu.
Volleyball: Jonea Rima; Phone: 660-831-4201; E-mail: rimaj@moval.edu.

MISSOURI WESTERN STATE COLLEGE
St. Joseph, Missouri

Griffons ◆ NCAA II ◆ Mid-America Intercollegiate Conference ◆ http://www.mwsc.edu/

State-supported 4-year, founded 1915
Coed, 4,928 undergraduate students, 75% full-time, 60% women, 40% men
Suburban 744-acre campus with easy access to Kansas City
100% of applicants were admitted

Freshmen *Admission:* 2,421 applied, 2,421 were accepted, 1,045 enrolled.
Tuition and fees (2003–04): $4464 (resident), $8040 (nonresident). *Room and board:* $4058.
Athletic Department: *Director of Athletics:* Mark Linder; Phone: 816-271-5623; Fax: 816-271-5901; E-mail: linder@mwsc.edu. *Sports Information Director:* Brett King; Phone: 816-271-4257; E-mail: king@mwsc.edu.

MEN'S COACHES
Baseball: Buzz Verduzco; Phone: 816-271-4484; E-mail: verduzco@mwsc.edu.
Basketball: Tom Smith; Phone: 816-271-4486; E-mail: tomsmith@mwsc.edu.
Cheerleading: Pat Stillman; Phone: 816-271-5981; E-mail: stillman@mwsc.edu.
Football: Jerry Partridge; Phone: 816-271-4499; E-mail: partjer@mwsc.edu.
Golf: Jim Perry; Phone: 816-271-5350; E-mail: haber@mwsc.edu.

WOMEN'S COACHES
Basketball: Dave Slifer; Phone: 816-271-4509; E-mail: slifer@mwsc.edu.
Cheerleading: Pat Stillman; Phone: 816-271-5981; E-mail: stillman@mwsc.edu.
Golf: Randy McGohan; Phone: 816-271-4481; E-mail: mrandygolf@aol.com.
Softball: Jennifer Bagley; Phone: 816-271-4480; E-mail: bagley@mwsc.edu.
Tennis: Josh Keister; Phone: 816-271-5863; E-mail: keister@mwsc.edu.
Volleyball: Cindy Brauck; Phone: 816-271-4209; E-mail: cdb7971@mwsc.edu.

MOLLOY COLLEGE
Rockville Centre, New York

Lions ◆ NCAA II ◆ New York Collegiate Athletic Conference ◆ http://www.molloy.edu/

Independent comprehensive, founded 1955
Coed, 2,311 undergraduate students, 70% full-time, 77% women, 23% men
Suburban 30-acre campus with easy access to New York City
Moderately difficult entrance level, 74% of applicants were admitted

Freshmen *Admission:* 918 applied, 617 were accepted, 275 enrolled.
Test scores: SAT verbal scores over 500: 62%; SAT math scores over 500: 63%; SAT verbal scores over 600: 15%; SAT math scores over 600: 17%; SAT verbal scores over 700: 1%; SAT math scores over 700: 2%.
Tuition and fees (2003–04): $15,130 (full-time).
Athletic Department: *Director of Athletics:* Harry Herman; Phone: 516-678-5000; Fax: 516-256-2210; E-mail: hherman@molloy.edu. *Sports Information Director:* Dan Drutz; Phone: 516-678-5000; E-mail: ddrutz@molloy.edu.

MEN'S COACHES
Baseball: Bernie Havern; Phone: 516-678-5000; E-mail: bhavern@molloy.edu.
Basketball: Charles Marquardt; Phone: 516-678-5000; E-mail: cmarquardt@molloy.edu.
Cross Country: Ray Gilliam; Phone: 516-678-5000; E-mail: rgilliam@molloy.edu.
Lacrosse: Joe Catolanotti; Phone: 516-678-5000; E-mail: jcatalanotti@molloy.edu.
Soccer: Phone: 516-678-5000; E-mail: athletics@molloy.edu.
Track and Field: Ray Gilliam; Phone: 516-678-5000; E-mail: rgilliam@molloy.edu.

WOMEN'S COACHES
Basketball: Tyler Zanghi; Phone: 516-678-5000; E-mail: tzanghi@molloy.edu.
Cross Country: Ray Gilliam; Phone: 516-678-5000; E-mail: rgilliam@molloy.edu.
Soccer: Steve Cadet; Phone: 516-678-5000; E-mail: molloysoccer@aol.com.
Softball: Phone: 516-678-5000; E-mail: athletics@molloy.edu.
Tennis: Nino Moukhatsov; Phone: 516-678-5000; E-mail: athletics@molloy.edu.
Track and Field: Ray Gilliam; Phone: 516-678-5000; E-mail: rgilliam@molloy.edu.
Volleyball: Lynn Higgins; Phone: 516-678-5000; E-mail: lhiggins@molloy.edu.

MONMOUTH COLLEGE
Monmouth, Illinois

Fighting Scots ◆ NCAA III ◆ Midwest Conference ◆ http://www.monm.edu/

Independent religious 4-year, founded 1853, affiliated with Presbyterian Church
Coed, 1,162 undergraduate students, 99% full-time, 52% women, 48% men
Small-town 80-acre campus with easy access to Peoria
Moderately difficult entrance level, 74% of applicants were admitted

Freshmen *Admission:* 1,480 applied, 1,128 were accepted, 357 enrolled. *Test scores:* SAT verbal scores over 500: 72%; SAT math scores over 500: 14%; SAT verbal scores over 600: 43%; SAT verbal scores over 700: 14%.
Tuition and fees (2004–05): $19,350 (full-time). *Room and board:* $5450.
Financial Aid (All incoming freshmen): *Average need-based gift aid:* $12,808. *Average non-need based aid:* $9499. *Average aid to full-time undergraduates:* $15,772.
Athletic Department: *Director of Athletics:* Terry Glasgow; Phone: 309-457-2176; Fax: 309-457-2168; E-mail: kathy@monm.edu. *Sports Information Director:* Barry McNamara; Phone: 309-457-2322; E-mail: mcnamara@monm.edu.

MEN'S COACHES
Baseball: Roger Sander; Phone: 309-457-2176; E-mail: kathy@monm.edu.
Basketball: Terry Glasgow; Phone: 309-457-2176; E-mail: terryg@monm.edu.
Cross Country: Roger Haynes; Phone: 309-457-2176; E-mail: rogerh@monm.edu.
Football: Steve Bell; Phone: 309-457-2176; E-mail: sbell@monm.edu.
Golf: Dave Ragone; Phone: 309-457-2178; E-mail: dragone@monm.edu.
Soccer: Rue Casthew; Phone: 309-457-2176; E-mail: kathy@monm.edu.
Swimming: Keith Crawford; Phone: 309-457-2215; E-mail: kcrawfor@monm.edu.
Tennis: Chad Braun; Phone: 309-457-2163; E-mail: chbraun@monm.edu.

Track and Field: Roger Haynes; Phone: 309-457-2177; E-mail: rogerh@monm.edu.

WOMEN'S COACHES

Basketball: Dennis Mann; Phone: 309-457-2176; E-mail: kathy@monm.edu.

Cross Country: Roger Haynes; Phone: 309-457-2176; E-mail: rogerh@monm.edu.

Golf: Bill Pieper; Phone: 309-457-2176; E-mail: kathy@monm.edu.

Soccer: Barry McNamara; Phone: 309-457-2117; E-mail: mcnamara@monm.edu.

Softball: Leann Hagen; Phone: 309-457-2174; E-mail: lhakeman@monm.edu.

Swimming: Keith Crawford; Phone: 309-457-2215; E-mail: kcrawfor@monm.edu.

Tennis: LeAnn Hagen; Phone: 309-457-2174; E-mail: lhakeman@monm.edu.

Track and Field: Roger Haynes; Phone: 309-457-2176; E-mail: rogerh@monm.edu.

Volleyball: Kari Shimmin; Phone: 309-457-2176; E-mail: kshimmin@monm.edu.

MONMOUTH UNIVERSITY
West Long Branch, New Jersey

Hawks ◆ NCAA I ◆ Northeast Conference
◆ http://www.monmouth.edu/

Independent comprehensive, founded 1933
Coed, 4,381 undergraduate students, 89% full-time, 58% women, 42% men
Suburban 153-acre campus with easy access to New York City and Philadelphia
Moderately difficult entrance level, 65% of applicants were admitted

Freshmen *Admission:* 5,772 applied, 3,785 were accepted, 905 enrolled. *Test scores:* SAT verbal scores over 500: 67%; SAT math scores over 500: 73%; SAT verbal scores over 600: 11%; SAT math scores over 600: 17%; SAT verbal scores over 700: 1%; SAT math scores over 700: 1%.
Tuition and fees (2003–04): $18,766 (full-time). *Room and board:* $7568 (room only: $4028).
Financial Aid (All incoming freshmen): *Average need-based gift aid:* $7783. *Average non-need based aid:* $5019. *Average aid to full-time undergraduates:* $11,219.
Athletic Department: *Director of Athletics:* Marilyn McNeil; Phone: 732-571-3414; Fax: 732-571-3535; E-mail: mmcneil@monmouth.edu. *Sports Information Director:* Thomas Dick; Phone: 732-571-4447; E-mail: tdick@monmouth.edu.

MEN'S COACHES

Baseball: Dean Ehehalt; Phone: 732-263-5186; E-mail: dehehalt@monmouth.edu.

Baseball: Dean Ehehalt; Phone: 732-263-5186; E-mail: dehehalt@monmouth.edu.

Basketball: Dave Calloway; Phone: 732-571-7584; E-mail: callow@monmouth.edu.

Cheerleading: Amanda Morris; Phone: 732-263-5350; E-mail: amorris@monmouth.edu.

Cross Country: Joe Compagni; Phone: 732-571-3676; E-mail: jcompagn@monmouth.edu.

Football: Kevin Callahan; Phone: 732-571-7582; E-mail: kcallaha@monmouth.edu.

Golf: Dennis Shea; Phone: 732-263-5177; E-mail: dshea@monmouth.edu.

Soccer: Shannon Poser; Phone: 732-263-5150; E-mail: sposer@monmouth.edu.

Tennis: Joe Cascone; Phone: 732-571-5387; E-mail: jcascone@monmouth.edu.

Track and Field: Joe Compagni; Phone: 732-571-3676; E-mail: jcompagn@monmouth.edu.

WOMEN'S COACHES

Basketball: Jackie Devane; Phone: 732-571-3565; E-mail: jdevane@monmouth.edu.

Cheerleading: Amanda Morris; Phone: 732-263-5350; E-mail: amorris@monmouth.edu.

Cross Country: Joe Compagni; Phone: 732-571-3676; E-mail: jcompagn@monmouth.edu.

Field Hockey: Monica Levy; Phone: 732-263-5322; E-mail: mmorgan@monmouth.edu.

Golf: Sherri McDonald; Phone: 732-571-4426; E-mail: smcdonal@monmouth.edu.

Lacrosse: Sue Cowperthwait; Phone: 732-263-5556; E-mail: scowpert@monmouth.edu.

Soccer: Kristine Turner; Phone: 732-571-4410; E-mail: kturner@monmouth.edu.

Softball: Carol Sullivan; Phone: 732-571-3648; E-mail: csulliva@monmouth.edu.

Tennis: Patrice Murray; Phone: 732-263-5175; E-mail: pmurray@monmouth.edu.

Track and Field: Joe Compagni; Phone: 732-571-3676; E-mail: jcompagn@monmouth.edu.

MONTANA STATE UNIVERSITY–BILLINGS
Billings, Montana

Yellowjackets ◆ NCAA II ◆ Pacific West Conference ◆ http://www.msubillings.edu/

State-supported comprehensive, founded 1927, part of Montana University System
Coed, 4,139 undergraduate students, 77% full-time, 63% women, 37% men
Urban 92-acre campus
Moderately difficult entrance level, 96% of applicants were admitted

Freshmen *Admission:* 996 applied, 956 were accepted, 845 enrolled. *Test scores:* SAT verbal scores over 500: 57%; SAT math scores over 500: 56%; SAT verbal scores over 600: 15%; SAT math scores over 600: 21%; SAT verbal scores over 700: 4%; SAT math scores over 700: 6%.
Tuition and fees (2003–04): $4180 (resident), $11,540 (nonresident). *Room and board:* $4430.
Financial Aid (All incoming freshmen): *Average need-based gift aid:* $3632. *Average non-need based aid:* $3579. *Average aid to full-time undergraduates:* $5790.
Athletic Department: *Director of Athletics:* Gary Gray; Phone: 406-657-2282; Fax: 406-657-2919; E-mail: ggray@msubillings.edu. *Sports Information Director:* Travis Elam; Phone: 406-657-2100; E-mail: telam@msubillings.edu.

MEN'S COACHES

Basketball: Craig Carse; Phone: 406-657-2371; E-mail: ccarse@msubillings.edu.

Cheerleading: Dani Ruoff; Phone: 406-657-2011; E-mail: druoff@msubillings.edu.

Cross Country: Dave Coppock; Phone: 406-657-2374; E-mail: run_msub@hotmail.com.

Golf: Roger Burckley; Phone: 406-657-2369.

Soccer: Doug Seigle; Phone: 406-657-2394; E-mail: dseigle@msubillings.edu.

Tennis: Jerry Peach; Phone: 406-657-2111; E-mail: jpeach@msubillings.edu.

WOMEN'S COACHES

Basketball: Melissa Slone; Phone: 406-657-2368; E-mail: mslone@msubillings.edu.

Cheerleading: Dani Ruoff; Phone: 406-657-2011; E-mail: druoff@msubillings.edu.

Cross Country: Dave Coppock; Phone: 406-657-2374; E-mail: run_msub@hotmail.com.

Golf: Roger Burckley; Phone: 406-657-2369.

Soccer: Don Trentham; Phone: 406-657-2373; E-mail: dtrentham@msubillings.edu.

Softball: Jeff Aumend; Phone: 406-657-2398; E-mail: jaumend@msubillings.edu.

Tennis: Jerry Peach; Phone: 406-657-2111; E-mail: jpeach@msubillings.edu.

Volleyball: Pa' Ulasi Matavao; Phone: 406-657-2603; E-mail: pmatavao@msubillings.edu.

MONTANA STATE UNIVERSITY–BOZEMAN

Bozeman, Montana

Bobcats ◆ NCAA I ◆ Big Sky Conference
◆ http://www.montana.edu/

State-supported university, founded 1893, part of Montana University System
Coed, 10,750 undergraduate students, 86% full-time, 46% women, 54% men
Small-town 1,170-acre campus
Moderately difficult entrance level, 82% of applicants were admitted

Freshmen *Admission:* 4,380 applied, 3,547 were accepted, 2,149 enrolled. *Test scores:* SAT verbal scores over 500: 73%; SAT math scores over 500: 76%; SAT verbal scores over 600: 27%; SAT math scores over 600: 34%; SAT verbal scores over 700: 3%; SAT math scores over 700: 6%.
Tuition and fees (2003–04): $4145 (resident), $12,707 (nonresident). *Room and board:* $5370.
Financial Aid (All incoming freshmen): *Average need-based gift aid:* $3624. *Average non-need based aid:* $2455. *Average aid to full-time undergraduates:* $6400.
Athletic Department: *Director of Athletics:* Peter Fields; Phone: 406-994-4221; Fax: 406-994-2278; E-mail: pfields@msubobcats.com. *Sports Information Director:* Tom Schulz; Phone: 406-994-5130; E-mail: tschulz@msubobcats.com.

MEN'S COACHES
Basketball: Mick Durham; Phone: 406-994-4221; E-mail: mdurham@msubobcats.com.
Cheerleading: Mary Kay Minor; Phone: 406-994-4221.
Cross Country: Dale Kennedy; Phone: 406-994-6261; E-mail: dkennedy@msubobcats.com.
Football: Mike Kramer; Phone: 406-994-4221; E-mail: mkramer@msubobcats.com.
Tennis: Mike Phillips; Phone: 406-994-6263; E-mail: mphillips@msubobcats.com.
Track and Field: Dale Kennedy; Phone: 406-994-6261; E-mail: dkennedy@msubobcats.com.

WOMEN'S COACHES
Basketball: Robin Potero-Haskins; Phone: 406-994-4221; E-mail: rpotera@msubobcats.com.
Cheerleading: Mary Kay Minor; Phone: 406-994-4221.
Cross Country: Dale Kennedy; Phone: 406-994-6261; E-mail: dkennedy@msubobcats.com.
Golf: Brittany Basye; Phone: 406-994-7216; E-mail: bbasye@msubobcats.com.
Tennis: Denise Albrecht; Phone: 406-994-4221; E-mail: dalbrecht@msubobcats.com.
Track and Field: Dale Kennedy; Phone: 406-994-6261; E-mail: dkennedy@msubobcats.com.
Volleyball: Miya Malauulu; Phone: 406-994-6258; E-mail: mmalauulu@msubobcats.com.

MONTANA STATE UNIVERSITY–NORTHERN

Havre, Montana

Skylights ◆ NAIA ◆ Frontier Conference
◆ http://www.msun.edu/

State-supported comprehensive, founded 1929, part of Montana University System
Coed, 1,428 undergraduate students, 74% full-time, 53% women, 47% men
Small-town 105-acre campus
Moderately difficult entrance level, 82% of applicants were admitted

Freshmen *Admission:* 868 applied, 709 were accepted, 234 enrolled.
Tuition and fees (2003–04): $4100 (resident), $11,220 (nonresident). *Room and board:* $5600.
Financial Aid (All incoming freshmen): *Average need-based gift aid:* $3372. *Average non-need based aid:* $1680. *Average aid to full-time undergraduates:* $5829.

Athletic Department: *Director of Athletics:* Byron Ophus; Phone: 406-265-3761; Fax: 406-265-4129; E-mail: bophus@msun.edu. *Sports Information Director:* Nate Larson; Phone: 406-265-3700; E-mail: nlarson@msun.edu.

MEN'S COACHES
Basketball: Shawn Huse; Phone: 406-265-3700; E-mail: shuse@msun.edu.
Football: Walt Currie; Phone: 406-265-3746; E-mail: ericksonm@msun.edu.
Wrestling: David Ray; Phone: 406-265-3761; E-mail: rayd@msun.edu.

WOMEN'S COACHES
Basketball: Mike Erickson; Phone: 406-265-3700; E-mail: ericksonm@msun.edu.
Golf: Warren Quick; Phone: 406-265-3700; E-mail: wquick@msun.edu.
Volleyball: Lisa Handley; Phone: 406-265-3700; E-mail: lhandley@msun.edu.

MONTANA TECH OF THE UNIVERSITY OF MONTANA

Butte, Montana

Orediggers ◆ NAIA ◆ Frontier Conference
◆ http://www.mtech.edu/

State-supported comprehensive, founded 1895, part of Montana University System
Coed, 2,142 undergraduate students, 83% full-time, 46% women, 54% men
Small-town 56-acre campus
Moderately difficult entrance level

Freshmen *Admission:* 410 enrolled. *Test scores:* SAT verbal scores over 500: 66%; SAT math scores over 500: 74%; SAT verbal scores over 600: 20%; SAT math scores over 600: 28%; SAT verbal scores over 700: 1%; SAT math scores over 700: 7%.
Tuition and fees (2003–04): $4350 (resident), $9060 (nonresident). *Room and board:* $4980 (room only: $2120).
Financial Aid (All incoming freshmen): *Average need-based gift aid:* $1000. *Average non-need based aid:* $2500. *Average aid to full-time undergraduates:* $5000.
Athletic Department: *Director of Athletics:* Bob Green; Phone: 406-496-4292; Fax: 406-496-4711. *Sports Information Director:* Mike Bauer; Phone: 406-496-4205; E-mail: mtechbauer@yahoo.edu.

MEN'S COACHES
Basketball: Mike Bauer; Phone: 406-496-4205.
Football: Bob Green; Phone: 406-496-4292.

WOMEN'S COACHES
Basketball: Meg Murphy; Phone: 406-496-4288.
Volleyball: Marilyn Tobin; Phone: 406-496-4337.

MONTCLAIR STATE UNIVERSITY

Upper Montclair, New Jersey

Red Hawks ◆ NCAA III ◆ Knickerbocker Lacrosse Conference; New Jersey Athletic Conference
◆ http://www.montclair.edu/

State-supported comprehensive, founded 1908
Coed, 11,375 undergraduate students, 79% full-time, 62% women, 38% men
Suburban 275-acre campus with easy access to New York City
Moderately difficult entrance level, 50% of applicants were admitted

Freshmen *Admission:* 8,335 applied, 4,257 were accepted, 1,647 enrolled. *Test scores:* SAT verbal scores over 500: 59%; SAT math scores over 500: 65%; SAT verbal scores over 600: 16%; SAT math scores over 600: 18%; SAT verbal scores over 700: 1%; SAT math scores over 700: 2%.
Tuition and fees (2003–04): $6410 (resident), $9409 (nonresident). *Room and board:* $7902 (room only: $5442).

Financial Aid (All incoming freshmen): *Average need-based gift aid:* $2197. *Average non-need based aid:* $2623. *Average aid to full-time undergraduates:* $8325.
Athletic Department: *Director of Athletics:* Holly Gera; Phone: 973-655-5234; Fax: 973-655-5390; E-mail: gerah@mail.montclair.edu. *Sports Information Director:* Mike Scala; Phone: 973-655-6787; E-mail: scalam@mail.montclair.edu.

MEN'S COACHES
Baseball: Norm Schoenig; Phone: 973-655-5281; E-mail: honekerc@mail.montclair.edu.
Basketball: Ted Fiore; Phone: 973-655-7608; E-mail: fioret@mail.montclair.edu.
Cross Country: Bennie Benson; Phone: 973-655-4468; E-mail: cb5125@aol.com.
Football: Rick Giancola; Phone: 973-655-5238; E-mail: oconnor@mail.montclair.edu.
Lacrosse: John Greco; Phone: 973-655-4066; E-mail: jgreco24@att.net.
Soccer: Brian Sentowski; Phone: 973-655-6791; E-mail: sentowskib@mail.montclair.edu.
Swimming: Brian McLaughlin; Phone: 973-655-5242; E-mail: mclaughlinb@mail.montclair.edu.
Track and Field: Bennie Benson; Phone: 973-655-4468; E-mail: cb5125@aol.com.
Wrestling: Steve Strellner; Phone: 973-655-5259.

WOMEN'S COACHES
Basketball: Brian Sentowski; Phone: 973-655-6791; E-mail: sentowskib@mail.montclair.edu.
Cross Country: Bennie Benson; Phone: 973-655-4468; E-mail: cb5125@aol.com.
Field Hockey: Beth Gottung; Phone: 973-655-6937; E-mail: gottungb@mail.montclair.edu.
Lacrosse: Beth Gottung; Phone: 973-655-6258; E-mail: gottungb@mail.montclair.edu.
Soccer: Eileen Blair; Phone: 973-655-6805; E-mail: eileen.blair@us.pwcglobal.com.
Softball: Anita Kubicka; Phone: 973-655-6790; E-mail: kubickaa@mail.montclair.edu.
Swimming: Brian McLaughlin; Phone: 973-655-5242; E-mail: mclaughlinb@mail.montclair.edu.
Tennis: Brian McLaughlin; Phone: 973-655-5242; E-mail: mclaughlinb@mail.montclair.edu.
Track and Field: Bennie Benson; Phone: 973-655-4468; E-mail: cb5125@aol.com.
Volleyball: Sandra Sanchez-Lombeyda; Phone: 973-655-7830.

MONTREAT COLLEGE
Montreat, North Carolina
Cavaliers ◆ NAIA ◆ Appalachian Conference ◆ http://www.montreat.edu/

Independent religious comprehensive, founded 1916, affiliated with Presbyterian Church (U.S.A.)
Coed, 943 undergraduate students, 99% full-time, 62% women, 38% men
Small-town 112-acre campus
Moderately difficult entrance level, 78% of applicants were admitted

Freshmen *Admission:* 409 applied, 320 were accepted, 126 enrolled. *Test scores:* SAT verbal scores over 500: 59%; SAT math scores over 500: 56%; SAT verbal scores over 600: 25%; SAT math scores over 600: 13%; SAT verbal scores over 700: 4%; SAT math scores over 700: 3%.
Tuition and fees (2004–05): $15,108 (full-time). *Room and board:* $4862.
Financial Aid (All incoming freshmen): *Average need-based gift aid:* $6220. *Average non-need based aid:* $4877. *Average aid to full-time undergraduates:* $9956.
Athletic Department: *Director of Athletics:* Bill Robinson; Phone: 828-669-8011; Fax: 828-669-8014; E-mail: wrobinson@montreat.edu. *Sports Information Director:* Joe Hagan; Phone: 828-669-8011; E-mail: jhagan@montreat.edu.

MEN'S COACHES
Baseball: Darin Chaplin; Phone: 828-669-8011; E-mail: dchaplain@montreat.edu.
Basketball: Bill Robinson; Phone: 828-669-8011; E-mail: wrobinson@montreat.edu.

Cross Country: Don McMahill; Phone: 828-669-8011; E-mail: dmcmahill@montreat.edu.
Soccer: Desmond Armstrong; Phone: 828-669-8011; E-mail: darmstrong@montreat.edu.
Tennis: Phone: 828-669-8011.

WOMEN'S COACHES
Basketball: Joe Hagan; Phone: 828-669-8011; E-mail: jhagan@montreat.edu.
Cross Country: Don McMahill; Phone: 828-669-8011; E-mail: dmcmahill@montreat.edu.
Golf: Bill Robinson; Phone: 828-669-8011; E-mail: wrobinson@montreat.edu.
Soccer: Phone: 828-669-8011.
Softball: Ken Sigler; Phone: 828-669-8011; E-mail: ksigler@montreat.edu.
Tennis: Phone: 828-669-8011.
Volleyball: Stephanie Pace; Phone: 828-669-8011; E-mail: space@montreat.edu.

MORAVIAN COLLEGE
Bethlehem, Pennsylvania
Greyhounds ◆ NCAA III ◆ Commonwealth Conference ◆ http://www.moravian.edu/

Independent religious comprehensive, founded 1742, affiliated with Moravian Church
Coed, 1,850 undergraduate students, 83% full-time, 64% women, 36% men
Suburban 65-acre campus with easy access to Philadelphia
Moderately difficult entrance level, 62% of applicants were admitted

Freshmen *Admission:* 1,670 applied, 1,143 were accepted, 380 enrolled. *Test scores:* SAT verbal scores over 500: 79%; SAT math scores over 500: 86%; SAT verbal scores over 600: 29%; SAT math scores over 600: 34%; SAT verbal scores over 700: 4%; SAT math scores over 700: 3%.
Tuition and fees (2004–05): $23,574 (full-time). *Room and board:* $7310 (room only: $4105).
Financial Aid (All incoming freshmen): *Average need-based gift aid:* $12,098. *Average non-need based aid:* $10,917. *Average aid to full-time undergraduates:* $16,586.
Athletic Department: *Director of Athletics:* Paul Moyer; Phone: 610-861-1534; Fax: 610-625-7954; E-mail: meprm01@moravian.edu. *Sports Information Director:* Mark Fleming; Phone: 610-861-1472; E-mail: sportsinfo@moravian.edu.

MEN'S COACHES
Baseball: Ed Little; Phone: 610-861-1536; E-mail: baseball@moravian.edu.
Basketball: Jim Walker; Phone: 610-861-1531; E-mail: mensbasketball@moravian.edu.
Cheerleading: Erin Kratzer; Phone: 610-861-1534; E-mail: athletics@moravian.edu.
Cross Country: Mark Will-Weber; Phone: 610-625-7848; E-mail: crosscountry@moravian.edu.
Football: Scot Dapp; Phone: 610-861-1533; E-mail: football@moravian.edu.
Golf: John Makuvek; Phone: 610-861-1535; E-mail: golf@moravian.edu.
Lacrosse: Fran Meagher; Phone: 610-861-1534; E-mail: menslacrosse@moravian.edu.
Soccer: Eric Lambinus; Phone: 610-625-7953; E-mail: soccer@moravian.edu.
Tennis: Jim Walker; Phone: 610-625-1531; E-mail: menstennis@moravian.edu.
Track and Field: Doug Pollard; Phone: 610-861-1568; E-mail: trackandfield@moravian.edu.

WOMEN'S COACHES
Basketball: Mary Beth Spirk; Phone: 610-861-1424; E-mail: womensbasketball@moravian.edu.
Cheerleading: Erin Kratzer; Phone: 610-861-1534; E-mail: athletics@moravian.edu.
Cross Country: Mark Will-Weber; Phone: 610-625-7848; E-mail: crosscountry@moravian.edu.
Field Hockey: Amy Endler; Phone: 610-861-1404; E-mail: fieldhockey@moravian.edu.

Moravian College *(continued)*

Lacrosse: Kate Miller; Phone: 610-625-7850; E-mail: womenslacrosse@moravian.edu.

Soccer: Eric Lambinus; Phone: 610-625-7953; E-mail: soccer@moravian.edu.

Softball: John Byrne; Phone: 610-861-1321; E-mail: softball@moravian.edu.

Tennis: Dawn Benner; Phone: 610-861-1530; E-mail: mekns01@moravian.edu.

Track and Field: Doug Pollard; Phone: 610-861-1568; E-mail: trackandfield@moravian.edu.

Volleyball: Shelly Bauder; Phone: 610-625-7849; E-mail: mekns01@moravian.edu.

MOREHEAD STATE UNIVERSITY
Morehead, Kentucky

Eagles ◆ NCAA I ◆ Ohio Valley Conference; Pioneer Football League Conference ◆ http://www.moreheadstate.edu/

State-supported comprehensive, founded 1922
Coed, 7,921 undergraduate students, 84% full-time, 60% women, 40% men
Small-town 1,016-acre campus
Minimally difficult entrance level, 71% of applicants were admitted

Freshmen *Admission:* 5,183 applied, 3,686 were accepted, 1,520 enrolled.
Tuition and fees (2003–04): $3364 (resident), $8948 (nonresident). *Room and board:* $4100.
Financial Aid (All incoming freshmen): *Average need-based gift aid:* $3960. *Average non-need based aid:* $2427. *Average aid to full-time undergraduates:* $6216.
Athletic Department: *Director of Athletics:* Chip Smith; Phone: 606-783-2089; Fax: 606-783-5035; E-mail: c.smith@moreheadstate.edu. *Sports Information Director:* Randy Stacy; Phone: 606-783-2500; E-mail: r.stacy@moreheadstate.edu.

MEN'S COACHES
Baseball: John Jarnagin; Phone: 606-783-2882; E-mail: j.jarnagin@moreheadstate.edu.
Basketball: Kyle Macy; Phone: 606-783-2087; E-mail: k.macy@moreheadstate.edu.
Cheerleading: Myron Doan; Phone: 606-783-2014; E-mail: m.doan@moreheadstate.edu.
Cross Country: Dan Lindsey; Phone: 606-783-2653; E-mail: dklinsdey@yesconnect.net.
Football: Matt Ballard; Phone: 606-783-2020; E-mail: dm.ballard@moreheadstate.edu.
Golf: Rex Chaney; Phone: 606-783-2396; E-mail: r.chaney@moreheadstate.cdu.
Tennis: David Vest; Phone: 606-783-5408; E-mail: davidvest12345@hotmail.com.
Track and Field: Dan Lindsey; Phone: 606-783-2653; E-mail: dklinsdey@yesconnect.net.

WOMEN'S COACHES
Basketball: Laura Litter; Phone: 606-783-2126; E-mail: l.litter@moreheadstate.edu.
Cheerleading: Myron Doan; Phone: 606-783-2014; E-mail: m.doan@moreheadstate.edu.
Cross Country: Dan Lindsey; Phone: 606-783-2653; E-mail: dklinsdey@yesconnect.net.
Soccer: Phone: 606-783-2589.
Softball: Jill Karwoski; Phone: 606-783-5283; E-mail: jillkarwoski@msn.com.
Tennis: David Vest; Phone: 606-783-5408; E-mail: davidvest12345@hotmail.com.
Track and Field: Dan Lindsey; Phone: 606-783-2653; E-mail: dklinsdey@yesconnect.net.
Volleyball: Jaime Gordon; Phone: 606-783-2122; E-mail: j.gordon@moreheadstate.edu.

MOREHOUSE COLLEGE
Atlanta, Georgia

Tigers ◆ NCAA II ◆ Southern Intercollegiate Athletic Conference ◆ http://www.morehouse.edu/

Independent 4-year, founded 1867
Men only, 2,859 undergraduate students, 95% full-time, 95% women, 100% men
Urban 61-acre campus
Moderately difficult entrance level, 72% of applicants were admitted

Freshmen *Admission:* 2,225 applied, 1,606 were accepted, 766 enrolled. *Test scores:* SAT verbal scores over 500: 63%; SAT math scores over 500: 66%; SAT verbal scores over 600: 18%; SAT math scores over 600: 24%; SAT verbal scores over 700: 2%; SAT math scores over 700: 2%.
Tuition and fees (2003–04): $14,310 (full-time). *Room and board:* $8418 (room only: $4814).
Financial Aid (All incoming freshmen): *Average need-based gift aid:* $3960. *Average non-need based aid:* $11,120. *Average aid to full-time undergraduates:* $10,950.
Athletic Department: *Director of Athletics:* Andre Patillo; Phone: 404-215-2669; Fax: 404-521-9073; E-mail: apattill@morehouse.edu. *Sports Information Director:* James Nix; Phone: 404-215-3501; E-mail: jnix@morehouse.edu.

MEN'S COACHES
Basketball: Grady Brewer; Phone: 404-215-2752; E-mail: gbrewer@morehouse.edu.
Cross Country: Willie Hill; Phone: 404-215-2686; E-mail: whill@morehouse.edu.
Football: Anthony Jones; Phone: 404-215-2752.
Golf: William Lewis; Phone: 404-215-2752.
Soccer: Phone: 404-215-2752.
Tennis: Terry Alexander; Phone: 404-681-2800; E-mail: talexand@morehouse.edu.
Track and Field: Willie Hill; Phone: 404-215-2686; E-mail: whill@morehouse.edu.

MORGAN STATE UNIVERSITY
Baltimore, Maryland

Golden Bears ◆ NCAA I ◆ Mid-Eastern Atlantic Conference ◆ http://www.morgan.edu/

State-supported university, founded 1867
Coed, 6,005 undergraduate students, 89% full-time, 58% women, 42% men
Urban 143-acre campus with easy access to Washington, DC
Moderately difficult entrance level, 35% of applicants were admitted

Freshmen *Admission:* 11,387 applied, 3,900 were accepted, 1,285 enrolled. *Test scores:* SAT verbal scores over 500: 24%; SAT math scores over 500: 25%; SAT verbal scores over 600: 3%; SAT math scores over 600: 3%.
Tuition and fees (2004–05): $5718 (resident), $12,958 (nonresident). *Room and board:* $6780 (room only: $4303).
Athletic Department: *Director of Athletics:* David Thomas; Phone: 443-885-3575; Fax: 443-319-4011; E-mail: dthomas@moac.morgan.edu. *Sports Information Director:* Joseph McIver; Phone: 443-885-4675; E-mail: jmciver@moac.morgan .edu.

MEN'S COACHES
Basketball: Butch Beard; Phone: 443-885-3050; E-mail: abeard@moac.morgan.edu.
Cheerleading: Theresa Gibson; Phone: 443-885-3105; E-mail: tgibson@moac.morgan.edu.
Cross Country: Neville Hodge; Phone: 443-885-3105; E-mail: nhodge@moac.morgan.edu.
Football: Donald Hill; Phone: 443-885-3610; E-mail: dhill@moac.morgan.edu.
Tennis: Sean Hendricks; Phone: 443-885-2015.
Track and Field: Neville Hodge; Phone: 443-885-3105; E-mail: nhodge@moac.morgan.edu.

WOMEN'S COACHES
Basketball: Felicia Kemp; Phone: 443-885-3480; E-mail: fkemp51@excite.com.

Cheerleading: Theresa Gibson; Phone: 443-885-3105; E-mail: tgibson@ moac.morgan.edu.
Cross Country: Neville Hodge; Phone: 443-885-3105; E-mail: nhodge@ moac.morgan.edu.
Softball: Ramona Riley-Bozier; Phone: 443-885-3887; E-mail: rbozier@ moac.morgan.edu.
Tennis: Sean Hendricks; Phone: 443-885-2015.
Track and Field: Neville Hodge; Phone: 443-885-3105; E-mail: nhodge@ moac.morgan.edu.
Volleyball: Ramona Riley-Bozier; Phone: 443-885-3887; E-mail: rbozier@moac.morgan.edu.

MORNINGSIDE COLLEGE
Sioux City, Iowa

Mustangs ◆ NAIA ◆ Great Plains Conference ◆ http:// www.morningside.edu/

Independent religious comprehensive, founded 1894, affiliated with United Methodist Church
Coed, 942 undergraduate students, 92% full-time, 57% women, 43% men
Suburban 41-acre campus
Moderately difficult entrance level, 71% of applicants were admitted

Freshmen *Admission:* 1,130 applied, 839 were accepted, 273 enrolled.
Tuition and fees (2003–04): $16,350 (full-time). *Room and board:* $5260 (room only: $2750).
Financial Aid (All incoming freshmen): *Average need-based gift aid:* $5950. *Average non-need based aid:* $8193. *Average aid to full-time under- graduates:* $16,450.
Athletic Department: *Director of Athletics:* Jerry Schmutte; Phone: 712- 274-5313; Fax: 712-274-5333; E-mail: schmutte@morningside.edu. *Sports Information Director:* Dave Rebstock; Phone: 712-274-5127; E-mail: rebstock@morningside.edu.

MEN'S COACHES
Baseball: Jim Scholten; Phone: 712-274-5248; E-mail: scholten@ morningside.edu.
Basketball: Jerry Schmutte; Phone: 712-274-5313; E-mail: schmutte@ morningside.edu.
Cross Country: Dave Nash; Phone: 712-274-5334; E-mail: nash@ morningside.edu.
Football: Steve Ryan; Phone: 712-274-5283; E-mail: ryan@morningside. edu.
Golf: Michele Bailey; Phone: 712-274-5434; E-mail: bailey@ morningside.edu.
Soccer: Tom Maxon; Phone: 712-274-5343; E-mail: maxon@ morningside.edu.
Swimming: Rory Coleman; Phone: 712-274-5367; E-mail: coleman@ morningside.edu.
Track and Field: Dave Nash; Phone: 712-274-5334; E-mail: nash@ morningside.edu.
Wrestling: Tim Jager; Phone: 712-274-5282; E-mail: jager@ morningside.edu.

WOMEN'S COACHES
Basketball: Jamie Sale; Phone: 712-274-5474; E-mail: sale@ morningside.edu.
Cross Country: Dave Nash; Phone: 712-274-5334; E-mail: nash@ morningside.edu.
Golf: Michele Bailey; Phone: 712-274-5434; E-mail: bailey@ morningside.edu.
Soccer: Tom Maxon; Phone: 712-274-5343; E-mail: maxon@ morningside.edu.
Softball: Jessica Jones-Sitzmann; Phone: 712-274-5223; E-mail: jonessitzmann@morningside.edu.
Swimming: Rory Coleman; Phone: 712-274-5367; E-mail: coleman@ morningside.edu.
Tennis: Jay Menke; Phone: 712-274-5372; E-mail: menke@ morningside.edu.
Track and Field: Dave Nash; Phone: 712-274-5334; E-mail: nash@ morningside.edu.
Volleyball: Jessica Phillips; Phone: 712-274-5317; E-mail: phillipsj@ morningside.edu.

MORRIS COLLEGE
Sumter, South Carolina

Hornets ◆ NAIA ◆ Eastern Intercollegiate Conference ◆ http://www.morris.edu/

Independent religious 4-year, founded 1908, affiliated with Baptist Educational and Missionary Convention of South Carolina
Coed, 1,007 undergraduate students, 98% full-time, 62% women, 38% men
Small-town 34-acre campus
Minimally difficult entrance level, 89% of applicants were admitted

Freshmen *Admission:* 1,778 applied, 1,677 were accepted, 276 enrolled. *Test scores:* SAT verbal scores over 500: 4%; SAT math scores over 500: 5%.
Tuition and fees (2003–04): $7410 (full-time). *Room and board:* $3564.
Financial Aid (All incoming freshmen): *Average need-based gift aid:* $1500. *Average aid to full-time undergraduates:* $11,000.
Athletic Department: *Director of Athletics:* Clarence Houck; Phone: 803- 934-3235; Fax: 803-773-3687; E-mail: chouch@morris.edu.

MEN'S COACHES
Baseball: Clarence Houck; Phone: 803-934-3235; E-mail: chouck@ morris.edu.
Basketball: Phone: 803-934-3200.
Cross Country: Rodney Johnson; Phone: 803-934-3200; E-mail: johnsonrod@morris.edu.
Golf: Phone: 903-934-3200.
Tennis: Phone: 803-934-3200.
Track and Field: Rodney Johnson; Phone: 803-934-3200; E-mail: johnsonrod@morris.edu.

WOMEN'S COACHES
Basketball: Gilbert Wilson; Phone: 803-934-3235; E-mail: gwilson@ morris.edu.
Cross Country: Rodney Johnson; Phone: 803-934-3200; E-mail: johnsonrod@morris.edu.
Softball: Gilbert Wilson; Phone: 803-934-3235; E-mail: gwilson@ morris.edu.
Tennis: Phone: 803-934-3200.
Track and Field: Rodney Johnson; Phone: 803-934-3200; E-mail: johnsonrod@morris.edu.
Volleyball: Glenda Fulwood; Phone: 803-934-3200; E-mail: gfulwood@ morris.edu.

MOUNTAIN STATE UNIVERSITY
Beckley, West Virginia

Cougars ◆ NAIA ◆ Independent ◆ http://www.mountainstate.edu/

Independent comprehensive, founded 1933
Coed, 3,644 undergraduate students, 76% full-time, 66% women, 34% men
Small-town 7-acre campus
Noncompetitive entrance level, 96% of applicants were admitted

Freshmen *Admission:* 1,448 applied, 1,394 were accepted, 1,282 en- rolled. *Test scores:* SAT verbal scores over 500: 40%; SAT math scores over 500: 40%; SAT verbal scores over 600: 10%; SAT math scores over 600: 20%.
Tuition and fees (2003–04): $6300 (full-time). *Room and board:* $5172 (room only: $2672).
Financial Aid (All incoming freshmen): *Average need-based gift aid:* $3158. *Average non-need based aid:* $2710. *Average aid to full-time under- graduates:* $4333.
Athletic Department: *Director of Athletics:* Bob Bolen; Phone: 304-929- 1405; E-mail: bobbolen@mountainstate.edu. *Sports Information Di- rector:* Dave Barksdale; Phone: 304-929-1407; E-mail: barksdale@ mountainstate.edu.

MEN'S COACHES
Basketball: Bob Bolen; Phone: 304-929-1405; E-mail: bobbolen@ mountainstate.edu.
Cheerleading: Ashlee Skeens; Phone: 304-929-1589; E-mail: askeens@ mountainstate.edu.

Mountain State University (continued)

WOMEN'S COACHES

Cheerleading: Ashlee Skeens; Phone: 304-929-1589; E-mail: askeens@ mountainstate.edu.
Softball: Tim Berry; Phone: 304-929-1509; E-mail: softball@ mountainstate.edu.
Volleyball: Tim Berry; Phone: 304-929-1509; E-mail: softball@ mountainstate.edu.

MOUNT HOLYOKE COLLEGE
South Hadley, Massachusetts

Lyons ◆ NCAA III ◆ New England Women's & Men's Athletics Conference ◆ http://www.mtholyoke.edu/

Independent comprehensive, founded 1837
Women only, 2,148 undergraduate students, 97% full-time, 100% women
Small-town 800-acre campus with easy access to Springfield
Very difficult entrance level, 52% of applicants were admitted

Freshmen Admission: 2,845 applied, 1,477 were accepted, 508 enrolled. Test scores: SAT verbal scores over 500: 99%; SAT math scores over 500: 99%; SAT verbal scores over 600: 86%; SAT math scores over 600: 74%; SAT verbal scores over 700: 28%; SAT math scores over 700: 14%.
Tuition and fees (2003–04): $29,338 (full-time). Room and board: $8580 (room only: $4200).
Financial Aid (All incoming freshmen): Average need-based gift aid: $20,042. Average non-need based aid: $10,100. Average aid to full-time undergraduates: $23,887.
Athletic Department: Director of Athletics: Laurie Priest; Phone: 413-538-2310; Fax: 413-538-2183; E-mail: lpriest@mtholyoke.edu. Sports Information Director: Bridget Gunn; Phone: 413-538-2469; E-mail: bgunn@mtholyoke.edu.

WOMEN'S COACHES

Basketball: Megan Henry; Phone: 413-538-2850; E-mail: mhenry@ mtholyoke.edu.
Cross Country: Tina Lee; Phone: 413-538-2501; E-mail: clee@mtholyoke. edu.
Diving: David Allen; Phone: 413-538-2314; E-mail: dmallen@ mtholyoke.edu.
Field Hockey: Andy Whitcomb; Phone: 413-538-2847; E-mail: awhitcom@mtholyoke.edu.
Golf: Shawn Durocher; Phone: 413-538-3087; E-mail: sduroche@ mtholyoke.edu.
Lacrosse: Michael Hyer; Phone: 413-538-2154; E-mail: mhyer@ mtholyoke.edu.
Soccer: Kristen Martini; Phone: 413-538-2112; E-mail: kmartini@ mtholyoke.edu.
Softball: Andy Whitcomb; Phone: 413-538-2846; E-mail: awhitcom@ mtholyoke.edu.
Swimming: David Allen; Phone: 413-538-2314; E-mail: dmallen@ mtholyoke.edu.
Tennis: Aldo Santiago; Phone: 413-538-2852; E-mail: asantiag@ mtholyoke.edu.
Track and Field: Tina Lee; Phone: 413-538-2501; E-mail: clee@ mtholyoke.edu.
Volleyball: Kristen Eberhart-Parker; Phone: 413-538-2639; E-mail: keberhar@mtholyoke.edu.

MOUNT IDA COLLEGE
Newton Center, Massachusetts

Mustangs ◆ NCAA III ◆ North Atlantic Conference ◆ http:// www.mountida.edu/

Independent 4-year, founded 1899
Coed, 1,076 undergraduate students
Suburban 72-acre campus with easy access to Boston
Moderately difficult entrance level, 72% of applicants were admitted

Freshmen Admission: 2,203 applied, 1,736 were accepted. Test scores: SAT verbal scores over 500: 24%; SAT math scores over 500: 16%;

SAT verbal scores over 600: 5%; SAT math scores over 600: 2%; SAT verbal scores over 700: 2%; SAT math scores over 700: 1%.
Tuition and fees (2004–05): $17,075 (full-time). Room and board: $9400.
Financial Aid (All incoming freshmen): Average need-based gift aid: $7960. Average non-need based aid: $4926. Average aid to full-time undergraduates: $10,767.
Athletic Department: Director of Athletics: Jacqueline Palmer; Phone: 617-928-7201; Fax: 617-928-4036; E-mail: jpalmer@mountida.edu. Sports Information Director: Jennifer Starek; Phone: 617-928-7202; E-mail: jstarek@mountida.edu.

MEN'S COACHES

Basketball: Rico Cabral; Phone: 617-928-7203; E-mail: rcabral@ mountida.edu.
Football: Edward Sweeney; Phone: 617-928-4083; E-mail: esweeney@ mountida.edu.
Lacrosse: Andrew Fink; Phone: 617-928-7207; E-mail: afink@ mountida.edu.
Soccer: Steve D'Arcy; Phone: 617-928-4576; E-mail: scdarcy@ mountida.edu.
Volleyball: Mike Chin; Phone: 617-928-7204.

WOMEN'S COACHES

Basketball: Natalie Nakic; Phone: 617-928-7208; E-mail: nnakic@ mountida.edu.
Cross Country: Marianne Croft; Phone: 617-928-4504; E-mail: mcroft@ mountida.edu.
Soccer: Laura Halfpenny; Phone: 617-928-7211; E-mail: llhalfpenny@ mountida.edu.
Softball: Jennifer Starek; Phone: 617-928-7202; E-mail: jstarek@ mountida.edu.
Volleyball: Skip Tately; Phone: 617-928-7204; E-mail: stately@ mountida.edu.

MOUNT MARTY COLLEGE
Yankton, South Dakota

Lancers ◆ NAIA ◆ Great Plains Conference ◆ http://www.mtmc.edu/

Independent Roman Catholic comprehensive, founded 1936
Coed, 1,095 undergraduate students, 67% full-time, 69% women, 31% men
Small-town 80-acre campus
Moderately difficult entrance level, 79% of applicants were admitted

Freshmen Admission: 439 applied, 352 were accepted, 184 enrolled. Test scores: SAT math scores over 600: 17%; SAT verbal scores over 700: 17%.
Tuition and fees (2003–04): $14,186 (full-time). Room and board: $4670.
Financial Aid (All incoming freshmen): Average need-based gift aid: $8437. Average non-need based aid: $5908. Average aid to full-time undergraduates: $11,859.
Athletic Department: Director of Athletics: Chuck Iverson; Phone: 605-668-1529; Fax: 605-668-1357; E-mail: civerson@mtmc.edu. Sports Information Director: Cynthia Sohler; Phone: 605-668-1241; E-mail: csohler@mtmc.edu.

MEN'S COACHES

Baseball: Kelly Heller; Phone: 605-668-1548; E-mail: kheller@mtmc. edu.
Basketball: Jim Thorson; Phone: 605-668-1501; E-mail: jthorson@ mtmc.edu.
Cross Country: Jim Miner; Phone: 605-668-1588; E-mail: jminer@mtmc. edu.
Golf: Noel Nafziger; Phone: 605-668-1238; E-mail: nnafziger@mtmc. edu.
Soccer: Charlie Long; Phone: 605-668-1268; E-mail: clong@mtmc.edu.
Track and Field: Jim Miner; Phone: 605-668-1588; E-mail: jminer@ mtmc.edu.

WOMEN'S COACHES

Basketball: Chuck Iverson; Phone: 605-668-1529; E-mail: civerson@ mtmc.edu.
Cross Country: Jim Miner; Phone: 605-668-1588; E-mail: jminer@mtmc. edu.
Golf: Noel Nafziger; Phone: 605-668-1238; E-mail: nnafziger@mtmc. edu.
Soccer: Charlie Long; Phone: 605-668-1268; E-mail: clong@mtmc.edu.

Softball: Clint Frederiksen; Phone: 605-668-1395; E-mail: rkline@mtmc.edu.
Track and Field: Jim Miner; Phone: 605-668-1588; E-mail: jminer@mtmc.edu.
Volleyball: Tracey Grotenhuis; Phone: 605-668-1366; E-mail: tgrotenhuis@mtmc.edu.

MOUNT MERCY COLLEGE
Cedar Rapids, Iowa

Mustangs ◆ NAIA ◆ Midwest Classic Conference ◆ http://www.mtmercy.edu/

Independent Roman Catholic 4-year, founded 1928
Coed, 1,473 undergraduate students, 66% full-time, 70% women, 30% men
Suburban 40-acre campus
Moderately difficult entrance level, 72% of applicants were admitted

Freshmen *Admission:* 488 applied, 408 were accepted, 196 enrolled.
Tuition and fees (2003–04): $16,070 (full-time). *Room and board:* $5330 (room only: $2164).
Financial Aid (All incoming freshmen): *Average need-based gift aid:* $10,577. *Average non-need based aid:* $11,496. *Average aid to full-time undergraduates:* $14,418.
Athletic Department: *Director of Athletics:* Don McCormick; Phone: 319-363-1323; Fax: 319-363-6341; E-mail: mccormic@mtmercy.edu. *Sports Information Director:* Jason Furler; Phone: 319-363-1323; E-mail: furler@mtmercy.edu.

MEN'S COACHES
Baseball: Justin Schulte; Phone: 319-363-1323; E-mail: jschulte@mtmercy.edu.
Basketball: Paul Gavin; Phone: 319-363-1323; E-mail: pgavin@mtmercy.edu.
Cross Country: Ryan Scheckel; Phone: 319-363-1323; E-mail: ryanscheckel@hotmail.com.
Golf: Paul Gavin; Phone: 319-363-1323; E-mail: pgavin@mtmercy.edu.
Soccer: Amir Hadzic; Phone: 319-363-1323; E-mail: ahadzic@mtmercy.edu.
Track and Field: Ryan Scheckel; Phone: 319-363-1323; E-mail: ryanscheckel@hotmail.com.

WOMEN'S COACHES
Basketball: Shawn Gilbert; Phone: 319-363-1323; E-mail: sgilbert@mtmercy.edu.
Cross Country: Ryan Scheckel; Phone: 319-363-1323; E-mail: ryanscheckel@hotmail.com.
Golf: Paul Gavin; Phone: 319-363-1323; E-mail: pgavin@mtmercy.edu.
Soccer: Amir Hadzic; Phone: 319-363-1323; E-mail: ahadzic@mtmercy.edu.
Softball: Gary Stamp; Phone: 319-363-1323; E-mail: rmartin@mtmercy.edu.
Track and Field: Ryan Scheckel; Phone: 319-363-1323; E-mail: ryanscheckel@hotmail.com.
Volleyball: JoAnn Jennings; Phone: 319-363-1323; E-mail: sjennings@uswest.edu.

MOUNT OLIVE COLLEGE
Mount Olive, North Carolina

Trojans ◆ NCAA II ◆ Carolinas-Virginia Athletics Conference ◆ http://www.moc.edu/

Independent Free Will Baptist 4-year, founded 1951
Coed, 2,289 undergraduate students, 82% full-time, 57% women, 43% men
Small-town 123-acre campus with easy access to Raleigh
Minimally difficult entrance level, 74% of applicants were admitted

Freshmen *Admission:* 617 applied, 455 were accepted, 249 enrolled.
Test scores: SAT verbal scores over 500: 37%; SAT math scores over 500: 44%; SAT verbal scores over 600: 5%; SAT math scores over 600: 4%; SAT verbal scores over 700: 1%; SAT math scores over 700: 1%.

Tuition and fees (2004–05): $11,220 (full-time). *Room and board:* $4600 (room only: $2000).
Financial Aid (All incoming freshmen): *Average need-based gift aid:* $5079. *Average non-need based aid:* $2757. *Average aid to full-time undergraduates:* $6387.
Athletic Department: *Director of Athletics:* Mac Cassell; Phone: 919-658-5056; Fax: 919-658-1753; E-mail: mcassell@moc.edu. *Sports Information Director:* David Shulimson; Phone: 919-658-5056; E-mail: dshulimson@moc.edu.

MEN'S COACHES
Baseball: Carl Lancaster; Phone: 919-658-7669; E-mail: clancaster@moc.edu.
Basketball: Bill Clingan; Phone: 919-658-5056; E-mail: wclingan@moc.edu.
Cheerleading: Heather Astopenia; Phone: 919-658-5056; E-mail: hastopenia@moc.edu.
Cross Country: Jennifer Lancaster; Phone: 919-658-5056; E-mail: jlancaster@moc.edu.
Golf: Chip Spiron; Phone: 919-658-5056; E-mail: cspiron@moc.edu.
Soccer: Jerry Riggs; Phone: 919-658-5056; E-mail: jriggs@moc.edu.
Tennis: Burt Lewis; Phone: 919-658-5056; E-mail: blewis@moc.edu.
Volleyball: Sasha Gutor; Phone: 919-658-5056.

WOMEN'S COACHES
Basketball: Wendy Lawrence; Phone: 919-658-5056; E-mail: wlawrence@moc.edu.
Cheerleading: Heather Astopenia; Phone: 919-658-5056; E-mail: hastopenia@moc.edu.
Cross Country: Jennifer Lancaster; Phone: 919-658-5056; E-mail: jlancaster@moc.edu.
Soccer: Chris Shaw; Phone: 919-658-5056; E-mail: cshaw@moc.edu.
Softball: Jaime Kylie; Phone: 919-658-5056; E-mail: jkylis@moc.edu.
Tennis: Burt Lewis; Phone: 919-658-5056; E-mail: blewis@moc.edu.
Volleyball: Sasha Gutor; Phone: 919-658-5056.

MOUNT SAINT MARY COLLEGE
Newburgh, New York

Knights ◆ NCAA III ◆ Skyline Conference ◆ http://www.msmc.edu/

Independent comprehensive, founded 1960
Coed, 2,130 undergraduate students, 73% full-time, 73% women, 27% men
Suburban 72-acre campus with easy access to New York City
Moderately difficult entrance level, 8% of applicants were admitted

Freshmen *Admission:* 1,404 applied, 1,154 were accepted, 349 enrolled. *Test scores:* SAT verbal scores over 500: 53%; SAT math scores over 500: 54%; SAT verbal scores over 600: 11%; SAT math scores over 600: 12%; SAT verbal scores over 700: 1%; SAT math scores over 700: 1%.
Tuition and fees (2003–04): $14,290 (full-time). *Room and board:* $6980 (room only: $3940).
Financial Aid (All incoming freshmen): *Average need-based gift aid:* $5836. *Average aid to full-time undergraduates:* $11,682.
Athletic Department: *Director of Athletics:* John Wright; Phone: 845-569-3592; Fax: 845-569-3589; E-mail: wright@msmc.edu. *Sports Information Director:* Dan Twomey; Phone: 845-569-3591; E-mail: dtwomey@msmc.edu.

MEN'S COACHES
Baseball: Matt Dembinsky; Phone: 845-569-3253; E-mail: dembinsk@msmc.edu.
Basketball: Duane Davis; Phone: 845-569-3593; E-mail: davisbball@yahoo.com.
Soccer: Doug Stahl; Phone: 845-569-3167; E-mail: stahl@msmc.edu.
Swimming: Gene Damm; Phone: 845-569-3481; E-mail: edammswim@aol.com.
Tennis: Chris Trieste; Phone: 845-569-3594; E-mail: ctrieste94@yahoo.com.

WOMEN'S COACHES
Basketball: Randy Ognibene; Phone: 845-569-3255; E-mail: ognibene@msmc.edu.
Soccer: John Westbrook; Phone: 845-569-3594; E-mail: westbroo@acc.msmc.edu.
Softball: Janice Pettit-Brundage; Phone: 845-569-3594.

Mount Saint Mary College *(continued)*
Swimming: Mary Damm; Phone: 845-569-3481; E-mail: edammswim@aol.com.
Tennis: Lorraine Brady; Phone: 845-569-3594.
Volleyball: Mike Strano; Phone: 845-569-3594; E-mail: mstrano@acc.msmc.edu.

MOUNT SAINT MARY'S UNIVERSITY
Emmitsburg, Maryland

Mountaineers ◆ NCAA I ◆ Metro Atlantic Athletic Conference; Northeast Conference ◆ http://www.msmary.edu/

Independent Roman Catholic comprehensive, founded 1808
Coed, 1,593 undergraduate students, 86% full-time, 57% women, 43% men
Rural 1,400-acre campus with easy access to Baltimore and Washington, DC
Moderately difficult entrance level, 89% of applicants were admitted

Freshmen *Admission:* 1,803 applied, 1,624 were accepted, 396 enrolled. *Test scores:* SAT verbal scores over 500: 71%; SAT math scores over 500: 70%; SAT verbal scores over 600: 27%; SAT math scores over 600: 26%; SAT verbal scores over 700: 4%; SAT math scores over 700: 3%.
Tuition and fees (2003–04): $21,000 (full-time). *Room and board:* $7400 (room only: $3600).
Financial Aid (All incoming freshmen): *Average need-based gift aid:* $11,990. *Average non-need based aid:* $14,336. *Average aid to full-time undergraduates:* $14,887.
Athletic Department: *Director of Athletics:* Harold Menninger; Phone: 301-447-5292; Fax: 301-447-5300; E-mail: menninge@msmary.edu. *Sports Information Director:* Mark Vandergrift; Phone: 301-447-5384; E-mail: vandergrift@msmary.edu.

MEN'S COACHES
Baseball: Scott Thomson; Phone: 301-447-3806; E-mail: sthomson@msmary.edu.
Basketball: Milan Brown; Phone: 301-447-5388; E-mail: brown@msmary.edu.
Cheerleading: Chris Bucklaew; Phone: 301-447-5360; E-mail: bucklaew@msmary.edu.
Cross Country: Jim Stevenson; Phone: 301-447-5391; E-mail: stevenso@msmary.edu.
Golf: Josh Leibfreid; Phone: 301-447-3804; E-mail: leibfreid@msmary.edu.
Lacrosse: Tom Gravante; Phone: 301-447-5356; E-mail: gravante@msmary.edu.
Soccer: Rob Ryerson; Phone: 301-447-5383; E-mail: ryerson@msmary.edu.
Tennis: Mary Ann Narutowitz; Phone: 301-447-3805; E-mail: narutowi@msmary.edu.
Track and Field: Jim Stevenson; Phone: 301-447-5389; E-mail: deegan@msmary.edu.

WOMEN'S COACHES
Basketball: Vanessa Blair; Phone: 301-447-5390; E-mail: blair@msmary.edu.
Cheerleading: Chris Bucklaew; Phone: 301-447-5360; E-mail: bucklaew@msmary.edu.
Cross Country: Jim Stevenson; Phone: 301-447-5391; E-mail: stevenso@msmary.edu.
Golf: Bud Nason; Phone: 301-447-3804; E-mail: nason@msmary.edu.
Lacrosse: Courtney Connor; Phone: 301-447-3802; E-mail: connor@msmary.edu.
Soccer: Paul Wood; Phone: 301-447-3803; E-mail: pwood@msmary.edu.
Softball: Shana Gary; Phone: 301-447-3807; E-mail: sgary2@msmary.edu.
Tennis: Mary Ann Narutowitz; Phone: 301-447-3805; E-mail: narutowi@msmary.edu.
Track and Field: Jim Deegan; Phone: 301-447-5389; E-mail: deegan@msmary.edu.

MOUNT UNION COLLEGE
Alliance, Ohio

Purple Raiders ◆ NCAA III ◆ Ohio Athletic Conference ◆ http://www.muc.edu/

Independent United Methodist 4-year, founded 1846
Coed, 2,425 undergraduate students, 87% full-time, 55% women, 45% men
Suburban 105-acre campus with easy access to Cleveland
Moderately difficult entrance level, 75% of applicants were admitted

Freshmen *Admission:* 2,177 applied, 1,632 were accepted, 586 enrolled.
Tuition and fees (2004–05): $18,810 (full-time). *Room and board:* $5630 (room only: $2360).
Financial Aid (All incoming freshmen): *Average need-based gift aid:* $11,283. *Average non-need based aid:* $7489. *Average aid to full-time undergraduates:* $15,735.
Athletic Department: *Director of Athletics:* Larry Kehres; Phone: 330-823-4880; Fax: 330-823-2399; E-mail: kehreslt@muc.edu. *Sports Information Director:* Michael DeMatteis; Phone: 330-823-6093; E-mail: demattmm@muc.edu.

MEN'S COACHES
Baseball: Paul Hesse; Phone: 330-823-4878; E-mail: hessepr@muc.edu.
Basketball: Lee Hood; Phone: 330-823-4771; E-mail: hoodln@muc.edu.
Cheerleading: Stephanie Unckrich; Phone: 330-823-4880; E-mail: unckrist@muc.edu.
Cross Country: John Homon; Phone: 330-823-4780; E-mail: homonjh@muc.edu.
Diving: Russell Morrison; Phone: 330-823-4880.
Football: Larry Kehres; Phone: 330-823-4880; E-mail: kehreslt@muc.edu.
Golf: Terry Weigand; Phone: 330-823-4773; E-mail: weigantr@muc.edu.
Soccer: Josh Eaton; Phone: 330-823-4792; E-mail: eatonja@muc.edu.
Swimming: Kathie Lavery; Phone: 330-823-4666; E-mail: laverykj@muc.edu.
Tennis: Jeff Wojowicz; Phone: 330-823-4798; E-mail: wojtowjm@muc.edu.
Track and Field: John Homon; Phone: 330-823-4780; E-mail: homonjh@muc.edu.
Wrestling: Marc Lambdin; Phone: 330-829-6651; E-mail: lambdim@muc.edu.

WOMEN'S COACHES
Basketball: Jennifer Henley; Phone: 330-823-4678; E-mail: henleyj@muc.edu.
Cheerleading: Stephanie Unckrich; Phone: 330-823-4880; E-mail: unckrist@muc.edu.
Cross Country: Deana Fresenko; Phone: 330-823-4786; E-mail: fresendl@muc.edu.
Diving: Russell Morrison; Phone: 330-823-4880.
Golf: Shawn Grimes; Phone: 330-862-2034; E-mail: pvgc@cannet.com.
Soccer: Scott Langone; Phone: 330-829-2817; E-mail: langonsa@muc.edu.
Softball: Sandy Douglas; Phone: 330-823-4779; E-mail: douglass@muc.edu.
Swimming: Kathie Lavery; Phone: 330-823-4666; E-mail: laverykj@muc.edu.
Tennis: Jeff Wojtowicz; Phone: 330-823-4798; E-mail: langonsa@muc.edu.
Track and Field: Deana Fresenko; Phone: 330-823-4786; E-mail: fresendl@muc.edu.
Volleyball: Sandy Douglas; Phone: 330-823-4779; E-mail: douglass@muc.edu.

MOUNT VERNON NAZARENE UNIVERSITY
Mount Vernon, Ohio

Cougars ◆ NAIA ◆ American Mideast Conference ◆ http://www.mvnu.edu/

Independent Nazarene comprehensive, founded 1964
Coed, 2,206 undergraduate students, 88% full-time, 57% women, 43% men
Small-town 401-acre campus with easy access to Columbus
Moderately difficult entrance level, 89% of applicants were admitted

Freshmen *Admission:* 699 applied, 602 were accepted, 375 enrolled. *Test scores:* SAT verbal scores over 500: 70%; SAT math scores over 500: 71%; SAT verbal scores over 600: 34%; SAT math scores over 600: 28%; SAT verbal scores over 700: 4%; SAT math scores over 700: 3%.
Tuition and fees (2004–05): $14,976 (full-time). *Room and board:* $4734 (room only: $2619).
Financial Aid (All incoming freshmen): *Average need-based gift aid:* $5508. *Average non-need based aid:* $1405. *Average aid to full-time undergraduates:* $10,969.
Athletic Department: *Director of Athletics:* Scott Flemming; Phone: 740-392-6868; Fax: 740-392-5079; E-mail: sflemmin@mvnu.edu. *Sports Information Director:* Dave Parsons; Phone: 740-392-6868; E-mail: dparsons@mvnu.edu.

MEN'S COACHES
Baseball: Keith Veale; Phone: 740-392-6868; E-mail: kveale@mvnu.edu.
Basketball: Scott Flemming; Phone: 740-392-6868; E-mail: sflemmin@mvnu.edu.
Golf: Mike Meeks; Phone: 740-392-6868; E-mail: chuff@mvnu.edu.
Soccer: Paul Furey; Phone: 740-392-6868; E-mail: pfurey@mvnu.edu.

WOMEN'S COACHES
Basketball: Steve Gregory; Phone: 740-392-6868; E-mail: sgregory@mvnu.edu.
Soccer: Jonathan Meade; Phone: 740-392-6868; E-mail: jmeade@mvnu.edu.
Softball: Jeana Howald; Phone: 740-392-6868; E-mail: jhowald@mvnu.edu.
Volleyball: Paul Swanson; Phone: 740-392-6868; E-mail: pswanson@mvnu.edu.

MUHLENBERG COLLEGE
Allentown, Pennsylvania

Mules ◆ NCAA III ◆ Centennial Conference ◆ http://www.muhlenberg.edu/

Independent religious 4-year, founded 1848, affiliated with Lutheran Church
Coed, 2,452 undergraduate students, 93% full-time, 58% women, 42% men
Suburban 75-acre campus with easy access to Philadelphia
Very difficult entrance level, 38% of applicants were admitted

Freshmen *Admission:* 4,111 applied, 1,743 were accepted, 589 enrolled. *Test scores:* SAT verbal scores over 500: 94%; SAT math scores over 500: 96%; SAT verbal scores over 600: 56%; SAT math scores over 600: 60%; SAT verbal scores over 700: 8%; SAT math scores over 700: 9%.
Tuition and fees (2003–04): $25,160 (full-time). *Room and board:* $6540 (room only: $3490).
Financial Aid (All incoming freshmen): *Average need-based gift aid:* $14,454. *Average non-need based aid:* $10,105. *Average aid to full-time undergraduates:* $16,767.
Athletic Department: *Director of Athletics:* Sam Beidleman; Phone: 484-664-3380; Fax: 484-664-3537; E-mail: beidlemn@muhlenberg.edu. *Sports Information Director:* Corey Goff; Phone: 484-664-3395; E-mail: cgoff@muhlenberg.edu.

MEN'S COACHES
Baseball: Bob Macaluso; Phone: 484-664-3684; E-mail: macaluso@muhlenberg.edu.

Basketball: Dave Madeira; Phone: 484-664-3387; E-mail: madeira@muhlenberg.edu.
Cheerleading: Misty Armstrong; Phone: 484-664-3788; E-mail: armstron@muhlenberg.edu.
Cross Country: Linda Andrews; Phone: 484-664-3381; E-mail: landrews@muhlenberg.edu.
Football: Mike Donnelly; Phone: 484-664-3385; E-mail: mdonnell@muhlenberg.edu.
Golf: Kevin Edwards; Phone: 484-664-3785; E-mail: edzgolf@aol.com.
Lacrosse: Dave Cornell; Phone: 484-664-3763; E-mail: cornell@muhlenberg.edu.
Soccer: Sean Topping; Phone: 484-664-3383; E-mail: topping@muhlenberg.edu.
Tennis: George Henry; Phone: 484-664-3785; E-mail: gthenry1@aol.com.
Track and Field: Brad Hackett; Phone: 484-664-3590; E-mail: bhackett@muhlenberg.edu.
Wrestling: Tom Schleicher; Phone: 484-664-3386; E-mail: schleich@muhlenberg.edu.

WOMEN'S COACHES
Basketball: Ron Rohn; Phone: 484-664-3394; E-mail: rohn@muhlenberg.edu.
Cheerleading: Misty Armstrong; Phone: 484-664-3788; E-mail: armstron@muhlenberg.edu.
Cross Country: Linda Andrews; Phone: 484-664-3381; E-mail: landrews@muhlenberg.edu.
Field Hockey: Kristen Stuckel; Phone: 484-664-3384; E-mail: kstuckel@muhlenberg.edu.
Golf: Ron Rohn; Phone: 484-664-3394; E-mail: rohn@muhlenberg.edu.
Lacrosse: Kristen Stuckel; Phone: 484-664-3384; E-mail: kstuckel@muhlenberg.edu.
Soccer: Leslie Benintend; Phone: 484-664-3382; E-mail: beninten@muhlenberg.edu.
Softball: Ruth Gibbs; Phone: 484-664-3415; E-mail: rgibbs@muhlenberg.edu.
Tennis: Linda Andrews; Phone: 484-664-3381; E-mail: landrews@muhlenberg.edu.
Track and Field: Brad Hackett; Phone: 484-664-3590; E-mail: bhackett@muhlenberg.edu.
Volleyball: Jenny Warmack-Chipman; Phone: 484-664-3669; E-mail: jchipman@muhlenberg.edu.

MURRAY STATE UNIVERSITY
Murray, Kentucky

Racers ◆ NCAA I ◆ Ohio Valley Conference ◆ http://www.murraystate.edu/

State-supported comprehensive, founded 1922, part of Kentucky Council on Post Secondary Education
Coed, 8,378 undergraduate students, 82% full-time, 59% women, 41% men
Small-town 238-acre campus
Moderately difficult entrance level, 56% of applicants were admitted

Freshmen *Admission:* 2,972 applied, 1,873 were accepted, 1,511 enrolled.
Tuition and fees (2003–04): $3436 (resident), $5492 (nonresident). *Room and board:* $4380 (room only: $2174).
Financial Aid (All incoming freshmen): *Average need-based gift aid:* $2255. *Average non-need based aid:* $2515. *Average aid to full-time undergraduates:* $4589.
Athletic Department: *Director of Athletics:* E.W. Dennison; Phone: 270-762-6800; Fax: 270-762-6814; E-mail: athletics@murraystate.edu. *Sports Information Director:* Steve Parker; Phone: 270-762-6800; E-mail: steve.parker@murraystate.edu.

MEN'S COACHES
Baseball: Rob McDonald; Phone: 270-762-6800; E-mail: rob.mcdonald@murraystate.edu.
Basketball: Mick Cronin; Phone: 270-762-6804; E-mail: cheryl.whitaker@murraystate.edu.
Cheerleading: Rollie Erb; Phone: 270-762-3825; E-mail: rollieqp@yahoo.com.
Cross Country: Norbert Elliot; Phone: 270-762-6800; E-mail: norbert.elliott@murraystate.edu.

Murray State University *(continued)*

Football: Joe Pannunzio; Phone: 270-762-6181; E-mail: joe.pannunzio@murraystate.edu.
Golf: Eddie Hunt; Phone: 270-762-6800; E-mail: athletics@murraystate.edu.
Tennis: Mel Purcell; Phone: 270-762-6813; E-mail: mel.purcell@murraystate.edu.
Track and Field: Norbert Elliot; Phone: 270-762-6800; E-mail: norbert.elliott@murraystate.edu.

WOMEN'S COACHES

Basketball: Joi Williams; Phone: 270-762-6288; E-mail: sharon.russell@murraystate.edu.
Cheerleading: Rollie Erb; Phone: 270-762-3825; E-mail: rollieqp@yahoo.com.
Cross Country: Norbert Elliot; Phone: 270-762-6800; E-mail: norbert.elliott@murraystate.edu.
Golf: Velvet Milkman; Phone: 270-762-5408; E-mail: velvet.milkman@murraystate.edu.
Soccer: Mike Minielli; Phone: 270-762-3136; E-mail: mike.minielli@murraystate.edu.
Tennis: Connie Keasling; Phone: 270-762-5407; E-mail: connie.keasling@murraystate.edu.
Track and Field: Norbert Elliot; Phone: 270-762-6800; E-mail: norbert.elliott@murraystate.edu.
Volleyball: Dave Schwepker; Phone: 270-762-3825; E-mail: dave.schwepker@murraystate.edu.

MUSKINGUM COLLEGE
New Concord, Ohio

Fighting Muskies ◆ NCAA III ◆ Ohio Athletic Conference ◆ http://www.muskingum.edu/

Independent religious comprehensive, founded 1837, affiliated with Presbyterian Church (U.S.A.)
Coed, 1,622 undergraduate students, 95% full-time, 50% women, 50% men
Small-town 215-acre campus with easy access to Columbus
Moderately difficult entrance level, 74% of applicants were admitted

Freshmen *Admission:* 1,703 applied, 1,360 were accepted, 386 enrolled. *Test scores:* SAT verbal scores over 500: 55%; SAT math scores over 500: 56%; SAT verbal scores over 600: 25%; SAT math scores over 600: 26%; SAT verbal scores over 700: 5%; SAT math scores over 700: 2%.
Tuition and fees (2004–05): $15,630 (full-time). *Room and board:* $6200.
Financial Aid (All incoming freshmen): *Average need-based gift aid:* $10,102. *Average non-need based aid:* $4680. *Average aid to full-time undergraduates:* $14,067.
Athletic Department: *Director of Athletics:* Larry Shank; Phone: 740-826-6109; Fax: 740-826-8300; E-mail: lshank@muskingum.edu. *Sports Information Director:* Tom Caudill; Phone: 740-826-8022; E-mail: tcaudill@muskingum.edu.

MEN'S COACHES

Baseball: Gregg Thompson; Phone: 740-826-8318; E-mail: greggt@muskingum.edu.
Basketball: Jim Burson; Phone: 740-826-8321; E-mail: jburson@muskingum.edu.
Cheerleading: Cindy Basham; Phone: 740-826-8137; E-mail: cbasham@muskingum.edu.
Cross Country: William Cooper; Phone: 740-826-8018; E-mail: wcooper@muskingum.edu.
Football: Jeff Heacock; Phone: 740-826-8325; E-mail: jheacock@muskingum.edu.
Golf: Dave Kirby; Phone: 740-826-8322; E-mail: dkirby@muskingum.edu.
Soccer: Seamus Reilly; Phone: 740-826-8019; E-mail: sreilly@muskingum.edu.
Tennis: Seamus Reilly; Phone: 740-826-8019; E-mail: sreilly@muskingum.edu.
Track and Field: William Cooper; Phone: 740-826-8018; E-mail: wcooper@muskingum.edu.
Wrestling: Dan Inglis; Phone: 740-826-8329; E-mail: dinglis@muskingum.edu.

WOMEN'S COACHES

Basketball: Keri Hamsher; Phone: 740-826-8317; E-mail: khamsher@muskingum.edu.
Cheerleading: Cindy Basham; Phone: 740-826-8137; E-mail: cbasham@muskingum.edu.
Cross Country: William Cooper; Phone: 740-826-8018; E-mail: wcooper@muskingum.edu.
Golf: Beth Fox; Phone: 740-826-8323; E-mail: bfox@muskingum.edu.
Soccer: Mary Beth Caudill; Phone: 740-826-8319; E-mail: marybeth@muskingum.edu.
Softball: Donna Newberry; Phone: 740-826-8324; E-mail: newberry@muskingum.edu.
Tennis: Mary Beth Caudill; Phone: 740-826-8319; E-mail: marybeth@muskingum.edu.
Track and Field: William Cooper; Phone: 740-826-8018; E-mail: wcooper@muskingum.edu.
Volleyball: Elizabeth Zicha; Phone: 740-826-8328; E-mail: ezicha@muskingum.edu.

NATIONAL AMERICAN UNIVERSITY
Rapid City, South Dakota

Mavericks ◆ NAIA ◆ Independent ◆ http://www.national.edu/

Proprietary comprehensive, founded 1941, part of National College
Coed, 714 undergraduate students, 46% full-time, 48% women, 52% men
Urban 8-acre campus
Noncompetitive entrance level

Freshmen *Admission:* 166 enrolled.
Tuition and fees (2003–04): $9990 (full-time). *Room and board:* $3720 (room only: $1725).
Athletic Department: *Director of Athletics:* Luis Usera; Phone: 605-394-4834; Fax: 605-394-4871.

MEN'S COACHES

Baseball: Rich Downs; Phone: 605-394-4834.
Soccer: Wulf Deiter-Koch; Phone: 605-394-4825.

WOMEN'S COACHES

Soccer: Luis Usera; Phone: 605-394-4834.
Volleyball: Todd Lowery; Phone: 605-394-4834.

NAZARETH COLLEGE OF ROCHESTER
Rochester, New York

Golden Flyers ◆ NCAA III ◆ Empire 8 Conference ◆ http://www.naz.edu/

Independent comprehensive, founded 1924
Coed, 1,997 undergraduate students, 88% full-time, 76% women, 24% men
Suburban 150-acre campus
Moderately difficult entrance level, 81% of applicants were admitted

Freshmen *Admission:* 1,627 applied, 1,352 were accepted, 383 enrolled. *Test scores:* SAT verbal scores over 500: 82%; SAT math scores over 500: 85%; SAT verbal scores over 600: 38%; SAT math scores over 600: 33%; SAT verbal scores over 700: 5%; SAT math scores over 700: 4%.
Tuition and fees (2004–05): $18,574 (full-time). *Room and board:* $7700 (room only: $4400).
Financial Aid (All incoming freshmen): *Average need-based gift aid:* $9785. *Average non-need based aid:* $6539. *Average aid to full-time undergraduates:* $14,219.
Athletic Department: *Director of Athletics:* Peter Bothner; Phone: 716-389-2196; Fax: 716-389-2839; E-mail: pgbothne@naz.edu. *Sports Information Director:* Joe Seil; Phone: 585-389-2452; E-mail: jeseil@naz.edu.

MEN'S COACHES

Basketball: Mike Daley; Phone: 716-389-2814; E-mail: mjdaley@naz.edu.
Cheerleading: Phone: 716-389-2853.
Cross Country: Scott Love; Phone: 716-389-2852; E-mail: elove9@naz.edu.
Diving: Dave Marsh; Phone: 716-389-2198; E-mail: dmarsh3@naz.edu.
Golf: Marty Coddington; Phone: 716-317-2195; E-mail: macoddin@naz.edu.
Lacrosse: Rob Randall; Phone: 716-389-2194; E-mail: rarandal@naz.edu.
Soccer: Doug May; Phone: 716-389-2191; E-mail: djmay@naz.edu.
Swimming: Rick Aronberg; Phone: 716-389-2198; E-mail: rxaronbe@naz.edu.
Tennis: Annette Shapiro; Phone: 716-389-2853; E-mail: axshapir@naz.edu.
Track and Field: Scott Love; Phone: 716-389-2852; E-mail: elove9@naz.edu.

WOMEN'S COACHES

Basketball: Diane Williams; Phone: 716-389-2190; E-mail: dmwillia@naz.edu.
Cheerleading: Phone: 716-389-2853.
Cross Country: Scott Love; Phone: 716-389-2852; E-mail: elove9@naz.edu.
Diving: Dave Marsh; Phone: 716-389-2198; E-mail: dmarsh3@naz.edu.
Field Hockey: Kathy Satterley; Phone: 716-389-2199; E-mail: katsat14@aol.com.
Lacrosse: Sue Behme; Phone: 716-389-2835; E-mail: sebehme@naz.edu.
Soccer: Gail Mann; Phone: 716-389-2813; E-mail: gemann@naz.edu.
Swimming: Rick Aronberg; Phone: 716-389-2198; E-mail: rxaronbe@naz.edu.
Tennis: Annette Shapiro; Phone: 716-389-2853; E-mail: axshapir@naz.edu.
Track and Field: Scott Love; Phone: 716-389-2852; E-mail: elove9@naz.edu.
Volleyball: Cal Wickens; Phone: 716-389-2189; E-mail: cwicken0@naz.edu.

NEBRASKA WESLEYAN UNIVERSITY
Lincoln, Nebraska

Prairie Wolves ◆ NAIA ◆ Great Plains Conference ◆ http://www.nebrwesleyan.edu/

Independent United Methodist comprehensive, founded 1887
Coed, 1,687 undergraduate students, 91% full-time, 56% women, 44% men
Suburban 50-acre campus with easy access to Omaha
Moderately difficult entrance level, 90% of applicants were admitted

Freshmen *Admission:* 1,312 applied, 1,214 were accepted, 420 enrolled.
Tuition and fees (2003–04): $16,430 (full-time). *Room and board:* $4530.
Financial Aid (All incoming freshmen): *Average need-based gift aid:* $9863. *Average non-need based aid:* $6526. *Average aid to full-time undergraduates:* $12,365.
Athletic Department: *Director of Athletics:* Ira Zeff; Phone: 402-465-2360; Fax: 402-465-2170; E-mail: izeff@nebrwesleyan.edu. *Sports Information Director:* Karl Skinner; Phone: 402-465-2151; E-mail: kws@nebrwesleyan.edu.

MEN'S COACHES

Baseball: Mark Mancuso; Phone: 402-465-2171; E-mail: mmancuso@nebrwesleyan.edu.
Basketball: Todd Raridon; Phone: 402-465-2367; E-mail: tdr@nebrwesleyan.edu.
Cross Country: Ted Bulling; Phone: 402-465-2369; E-mail: tab@nebrwesleyan.edu.
Football: Brian Keller; Phone: 402-465-2354; E-mail: bjk@nebrwesleyan.edu.
Golf: Brett Balak; Phone: 402-465-2150; E-mail: bcb@nebrwesleyan.edu.
Soccer: James Beckmann; Phone: 402-465-7516; E-mail: jlb2446@mail.com.
Tennis: Rick Harley; Phone: 402-465-2372; E-mail: rharley@nebrwesleyan.edu.

Track and Field: Ted Bulling; Phone: 402-465-2369; E-mail: tab@nebrwesleyan.edu.

WOMEN'S COACHES

Basketball: Brad White; Phone: 402-465-2163; E-mail: bww@nebrwesleyan.edu.
Cross Country: Ted Bulling; Phone: 402-465-2369; E-mail: tab@nebrwesleyan.edu.
Golf: Stacy Smith; Phone: 402-465-2357; E-mail: ssmith2@nebrwesleyan.edu.
Soccer: Taylor Haynes; Phone: 402-465-7507; E-mail: thaynes@nebrwesleyan.edu.
Softball: Lance Kingery; Phone: 402-465-7515; E-mail: lak@nebrwesleyan.edu.
Tennis: Rick Harley; Phone: 402-465-2372; E-mail: rharley@nebrwesleyan.edu.
Track and Field: Ted Bulling; Phone: 402-465-2369; E-mail: tab@nebrwesleyan.edu.
Volleyball: Tom Symons; Phone: 402-465-2373; E-mail: tes@nebrwesleyan.edu.

NEUMANN COLLEGE
Aston, Pennsylvania

Knights ◆ NCAA III ◆ Pennsylvania Athletic Conference ◆ http://www.neumann.edu/

Independent Roman Catholic comprehensive, founded 1965
Coed, 2,112 undergraduate students, 79% full-time, 66% women, 34% men
Suburban 50-acre campus with easy access to Philadelphia
Moderately difficult entrance level, 96% of applicants were admitted

Freshmen *Admission:* 1,641 applied, 1,579 were accepted, 525 enrolled.
Test scores: SAT verbal scores over 500: 18%; SAT math scores over 500: 20%; SAT verbal scores over 600: 3%; SAT math scores over 600: 3%.
Tuition and fees (2004–05): $17,190 (full-time). *Room and board:* $7740 (room only: $4600).
Financial Aid (All incoming freshmen): *Average need-based gift aid:* $10,000. *Average aid to full-time undergraduates:* $15,000.
Athletic Department: *Director of Athletics:* Charles Sack; Phone: 610-558-5327; Fax: 610-459-1370; E-mail: sackc@neumann.edu. *Sports Information Director:* leigh Matejkovic; Phone: 610-558-5639; E-mail: matejkol@neumann.edu.

MEN'S COACHES

Baseball: Len Schuler; Phone: 610-558-4505; E-mail: lschuler@neumann.edu.
Basketball: Brian Nugent; Phone: 610-361-5227; E-mail: nugentb@neumann.edu.
Golf: Frank Sill; Phone: 610-361-5284; E-mail: knarfllis@aol.com.
Ice Hockey: Nick Russo; Phone: 610-361-5230; E-mail: nrusso@neumann.edu.
Lacrosse: Tom Wyatt; Phone: 610-361-5412; E-mail: wyattt@neumann.edu.
Soccer: Bill Smith; Phone: 610-361-2482; E-mail: smithw@neumann.edu.
Tennis: Bob Spickler; Phone: 610-361-5286; E-mail: rspickler@aol.com.

WOMEN'S COACHES

Basketball: Colette Dugan; Phone: 610-361-5289; E-mail: duganc@neumann.edu.
Field Hockey: Carol Digirolamo; Phone: 610-361-5322; E-mail: digirolc@neumann.edu.
Lacrosse: Carol DiGirolamo; Phone: 610-361-5322; E-mail: digirolc@neumann.edu.
Soccer: Kenneth Leeder; Phone: 610-358-4503; E-mail: leederk@neumann.edu.
Softball: William Saar; Phone: 610-358-4501; E-mail: saarw@neumann.edu.
Tennis: Bob Spickler; Phone: 610-361-5286; E-mail: rspickler@aol.com.
Volleyball: Maggie Smyth; Phone: 610-361-5288; E-mail: digirolc@neumann.edu.

NEWBERRY COLLEGE
Newberry, South Carolina

Indians ◆ NCAA II ◆ South Atlantic Conference ◆ http://www.newberry.edu/

Independent Evangelical Lutheran 4-year, founded 1856
Coed, 744 undergraduate students, 96% full-time, 43% women, 57% men
Small-town 60-acre campus
Moderately difficult entrance level, 80% of applicants were admitted

Freshmen *Admission:* 1,057 applied, 744 were accepted, 206 enrolled. *Test scores:* SAT verbal scores over 500: 40%; SAT math scores over 500: 45%; SAT verbal scores over 600: 6%; SAT math scores over 600: 10%; SAT verbal scores over 700: 1%; SAT math scores over 700: 1%.
Tuition and fees (2003–04): $17,251 (full-time). *Room and board:* $5620 (room only: $2620).
Financial Aid (All incoming freshmen): *Average need-based gift aid:* $11,553. *Average non-need based aid:* $11,852. *Average aid to full-time undergraduates:* $13,857.
Athletic Department: *Director of Athletics:* Andy Carter; Phone: 803-321-5166; Fax: 803-321-5169; E-mail: acarter@newberry.edu. *Sports Information Director:* Ryan Rose; Phone: 803-321-5667; E-mail: rrose@newberry.edu.

MEN'S COACHES
Baseball: Tim Medlin; Phone: 803-321-5162.
Basketball: David Conrady; Phone: 803-321-5153; E-mail: dconrady@newberry.edu.
Cheerleading: Erica James; Phone: 803-321-5010.
Cross Country: Tony Jasick; Phone: 803-321-5665; E-mail: tony.jasick@newberry.edu.
Football: Zach Willis; Phone: 803-321-5159; E-mail: zak.willis@newberry.edu.
Golf: John Casey; Phone: 803-321-2065; E-mail: john.casey@newberry.edu.
Soccer: Joel Harrison; Phone: 803-321-5640; E-mail: joel.harrison@newberry.edu.
Tennis: David Staniford; Phone: 803-321-5123; E-mail: david.staniford@newberry.edu.

WOMEN'S COACHES
Basketball: Jason Brink; Phone: 803-321-5160; E-mail: brink@newberry.edu.
Cheerleading: Erica James; Phone: 803-321-5010.
Cross Country: Audrey Ramsey; Phone: 803-321-5123; E-mail: audrey.ramsey@newberry.edu.
Golf: John Casey; Phone: 803-321-2065; E-mail: john.casey@newberry.edu.
Soccer: Juan Pablo Favero; Phone: 803-321-5656; E-mail: juan.favero@newberry.edu.
Softball: Erica Graham; Phone: 803-321-5164; E-mail: egraham@newberry.edu.
Tennis: David Staniford; Phone: 803-321-5123.
Volleyball: Nicole Swaback; Phone: 803-321-5165; E-mail: nswaback@newberry.edu.

NEWBURY COLLEGE
Brookline, Massachusetts

Nighthawks ◆ NCAA III ◆ Independent
◆ http://www.newbury.edu/

Independent 4-year, founded 1962
Coed, 1,167 undergraduate students, 62% full-time, 62% women, 38% men
Suburban 10-acre campus with easy access to Boston
Minimally difficult entrance level, 86% of applicants were admitted

Freshmen *Admission:* 964 applied, 850 were accepted, 356 enrolled. *Test scores:* SAT verbal scores over 500: 32%; SAT math scores over 500: 24%; SAT verbal scores over 600: 7%; SAT math scores over 600: 6%.
Tuition and fees (2004–05): $16,125 (full-time). *Room and board:* $7575.

Financial Aid (All incoming freshmen): *Average non-need based aid:* $4255. *Average aid to full-time undergraduates:* $2500.
Athletic Department: *Director of Athletics:* Peter Centola; Phone: 617-730-7091; Fax: 617-738-2414; E-mail: pcentola@newbury.edu. *Sports Information Director:* John Roberto; Phone: 617-730-7221; E-mail: jroberto@newbury.edu.

MEN'S COACHES
Basketball: Adam Nelson; Phone: 617-730-7165; E-mail: anelson@newbury.edu.
Cross Country: Andrea Bertini; Phone: 617-738-2412; E-mail: abertini@newbury.edu.
Golf: Lawrence Coletti; Phone: 617-730-2478; E-mail: lcoletti@newbury.edu.
Soccer: Gisle Sorli; Phone: 617-730-7223; E-mail: gsorli@newbury.edu.
Tennis: Colleen Nattrass; Phone: 617-730-7223; E-mail: cnattrass@newbury.edu.
Volleyball: David Hildenbrandt; Phone: 617-730-7207; E-mail: dhildebrandt@newbury.edu.

WOMEN'S COACHES
Basketball: Andrea Bertini; Phone: 617-730-2412; E-mail: abertini@newbury.edu.
Cross Country: Andrea Bertini; Phone: 617-738-2412; E-mail: abertini@newbury.edu.
Softball: Christin Santiago; Phone: 617-738-2478; E-mail: csantiago@newbury.edu.
Tennis: Colleen Nattrass; Phone: 617-730-7223; E-mail: cnattrass@newbury.edu.
Volleyball: David Hildenbrandt; Phone: 617-730-7207; E-mail: dhildebrandt@newbury.edu.

NEW ENGLAND COLLEGE
Henniker, New Hampshire

Pilgrims ◆ NCAA III ◆ Commonwealth Coast Conference ◆ http://www.nec.edu/

Independent comprehensive, founded 1946
Coed, 878 undergraduate students, 95% full-time, 53% women, 47% men
Small-town 225-acre campus with easy access to Boston
Moderately difficult entrance level, 96% of applicants were admitted

Freshmen *Admission:* 1,023 applied, 994 were accepted, 273 enrolled. *Test scores:* SAT verbal scores over 500: 37%; SAT math scores over 500: 29%; SAT verbal scores over 600: 7%; SAT math scores over 600: 7%; SAT verbal scores over 700: 1%.
Tuition and fees (2003–04): $21,120 (full-time). *Room and board:* $7740 (room only: $4026).
Financial Aid (All incoming freshmen): *Average need-based gift aid:* $13,437. *Average non-need based aid:* $8530. *Average aid to full-time undergraduates:* $25,247.
Athletic Department: *Director of Athletics:* Lori Runksmeier; Phone: 603-428-2292; Fax: 603-428-6023; E-mail: lrunksmei@nec.edu.

MEN'S COACHES
Baseball: Dave DeCew; Phone: 603-428-2447; E-mail: ddecew@nec.edu.
Basketball: Charlie Mason; Phone: 603-428-2396; E-mail: cmason@nec.edu.
Cross Country: Elliot Nott; Phone: 603-428-2292; E-mail: enott@nec.edu.
Ice Hockey: Tom Carroll; Phone: 603-428-2294; E-mail: tcarroll@nec.edu.
Lacrosse: Todd Sharp; Phone: 603-428-2313; E-mail: tsharp@nec.edu.
Soccer: Dave DeCew; Phone: 603-428-2447; E-mail: ddecew@nec.edu.

WOMEN'S COACHES
Basketball: Erica Ledy; Phone: 603-428-2435; E-mail: eledy@nec.edu.
Cross Country: Elliot Nott; Phone: 603-428-2292; E-mail: enott@nec.edu.
Field Hockey: Susan Murray; Phone: 603-428-2367; E-mail: smurray@nec.edu.
Lacrosse: Kristie Baldwin; Phone: 603-428-2401; E-mail: kbaldwin@nec.edu.
Soccer: Emily Houghton; Phone: 603-428-2263; E-mail: ehoughton@nec.edu.
Softball: Carrah Fisk Hennessey; Phone: 603-428-2213; E-mail: cfisk@nec.edu.

NEW JERSEY CITY UNIVERSITY
Jersey City, New Jersey

Gothic Knights ◆ NCAA III ◆ New Jersey Athletic Conference ◆ http://www.njcu.edu/

State-supported comprehensive, founded 1927
Coed, 6,174 undergraduate students, 68% full-time, 62% women, 38% men
Urban 46-acre campus with easy access to New York City
Moderately difficult entrance level, 5% of applicants were admitted

Freshmen *Admission:* 2,689 applied, 1,400 were accepted, 754 enrolled. *Test scores:* SAT verbal scores over 500: 21%; SAT math scores over 500: 24%; SAT verbal scores over 600: 2%; SAT math scores over 600: 1%.
Tuition and fees (2003–04): $6051 (resident), $10,359 (nonresident). *Room and board:* $6586 (room only: $4160).
Financial Aid (All incoming freshmen): *Average need-based gift aid:* $6296. *Average non-need based aid:* $3191. *Average aid to full-time undergraduates:* $8641.
Athletic Department: *Director of Athletics:* Larry Schiner; Phone: 201-200-3317; Fax: 201-200-2365; E-mail: lschiner@njcu.edu. *Sports Information Director:* Ira Thor; Phone: 201-200-3301; E-mail: ithor@njcu.edu.

MEN'S COACHES
Baseball: Ken Heaton; Phone: 201-200-3079; E-mail: kheaton@njcu.edu.
Basketball: Charlie Brown; Phone: 201-200-3303; E-mail: cbrown@njcu.edu.
Cross Country: Charlie Mays; Phone: 201-200-3365; E-mail: camays2@aol.com.
Soccer: Kevin East; Phone: 201-200-3209; E-mail: keast@njcu.edu.
Track and Field: Mark Griffin; Phone: 201-200-3365; E-mail: mgriffin@njcu.edu.
Volleyball: Christopher Feliciano; Phone: 201-200-2567; E-mail: njcucac@aol.com.

WOMEN'S COACHES
Basketball: Alice Defazio; Phone: 201-200-2243; E-mail: adefazio@njcu.edu.
Cross Country: Charlie Mays; Phone: 201-200-3365; E-mail: camays2@aol.com.
Soccer: Kevin East; Phone: 201-200-3209; E-mail: keast@njcu.edu.
Softball: Bridgette Quimpo; Phone: 201-200-2560; E-mail: bquimpo@njcu.edu.
Track and Field: Mark Griffin; Phone: 201-200-3365; E-mail: mgriffin@njcu.edu.
Volleyball: Christopher Feliciano; Phone: 201-200-2567; E-mail: njcucac@aol.com.

NEW JERSEY INSTITUTE OF TECHNOLOGY
Newark, New Jersey

Highlanders ◆ NCAA II ◆ Central Atlantic Collegiate Conference ◆ http://www.njit.edu/

State-supported university, founded 1881
Coed, 5,712 undergraduate students, 74% full-time, 21% women, 79% men
Urban 45-acre campus with easy access to New York City
Moderately difficult entrance level, 68% of applicants were admitted

Freshmen *Admission:* 2,566 applied, 1,747 were accepted, 709 enrolled. *Test scores:* SAT verbal scores over 500: 69%; SAT math scores over 500: 96%; SAT verbal scores over 600: 23%; SAT math scores over 600: 54%; SAT verbal scores over 700: 2%; SAT math scores over 700: 12%.
Tuition and fees (2003–04): $8500 (resident), $13,868 (nonresident). *Room and board:* $8076 (room only: $5494).
Financial Aid (All incoming freshmen): *Average need-based gift aid:* $4200. *Average non-need based aid:* $2420. *Average aid to full-time undergraduates:* $5980.

Athletic Department: *Director of Athletics:* Lenny Kaplan; Phone: 973-596-3638; Fax: 973-596-8295; E-mail: kaplan@adm.njit.edu. *Sports Information Director:* Mark Mentone; Phone: 973-596-8324; E-mail: mentone@adm.njit.edu.

MEN'S COACHES
Baseball: Brian Callahan; Phone: 973-596-5827; E-mail: callahan@njit.edu.
Basketball: Jim Casciano; Phone: 973-596-5727; E-mail: casciano@adm.njit.edu.
Cross Country: Al Alonzo; Phone: 973-596-3636; E-mail: alonso@njit.edu.
Soccer: Pedro Lopes; Phone: 973-596-5219; E-mail: pedro.j.lopes@njit.edu.
Swimming: Mary Kate Romano; Phone: 973-596-8238; E-mail: mkr5@njit.edu.
Tennis: Frank Koe; Phone: 973-642-7449; E-mail: koe@adm.njit.edu.
Volleyball: Mike Borga; Phone: 973-596-5380; E-mail: jsvba@aol.com.

WOMEN'S COACHES
Basketball: Kim Bowen; Phone: 973-596-3633; E-mail: bowen@adm.njit.edu.
Cross Country: Al Alonzo; Phone: 973-596-3636; E-mail: alonso@njit.edu.
Soccer: Phone: 973-596-2928; E-mail: coachnjit@aol.com.
Swimming: Mary Kate Romano; Phone: 973-596-8238; E-mail: mkr5@njit.edu.
Tennis: Phil Baboulis; Phone: 973-596-3636; E-mail: pbtennis@optonline.net.
Volleyball: Pavlina Klimova; Phone: 973-596-5380; E-mail: njitvolleyball@hotmail.com.

NEWMAN UNIVERSITY
Wichita, Kansas

Jets ◆ NAIA ◆ Midlands Collegiate Conference ◆ http://www.newmanu.edu/

Independent Roman Catholic comprehensive, founded 1933
Coed, 1,757 undergraduate students
Urban 61-acre campus
Minimally difficult entrance level

Freshmen *Admission:* 188 were accepted. *Test scores:* SAT verbal scores over 500: 67%; SAT math scores over 500: 73%; SAT verbal scores over 600: 11%; SAT math scores over 600: 12%; SAT math scores over 700: 6%.
Tuition and fees (2003–04): $13,348 (full-time). *Room and board:* $4820.
Financial Aid (All incoming freshmen): *Average need-based gift aid:* $3951. *Average non-need based aid:* $3593. *Average aid to full-time undergraduates:* $10,135.
Athletic Department: *Director of Athletics:* Curtis Hammeke; Phone: 316-942-4291; Fax: 316-942-4483; E-mail: hammekec@newmanu.edu.

MEN'S COACHES
Baseball: Kevin Ulwelling; Phone: 316-942-4291; E-mail: ulwelling@newmanu.edu.
Basketball: Mark Potter; Phone: 316-942-4291; E-mail: potter@newmanu.edu.
Cheerleading: Karen Peck; Phone: 316-942-4291; E-mail: peckk@newmanu.edu.
Cross Country: Josh Schepis; Phone: 316-942-4291; E-mail: schepisj@newmanu.edu.
Golf: Brad Sexson; Phone: 316-942-4291; E-mail: sexsonb@newmanu.edu.
Soccer: Cliff Brown; Phone: 316-942-4291; E-mail: browncw@newmanu.edu.
Volleyball: Dan Friend; Phone: 316-942-4291; E-mail: friendd@newmanu.edu.

WOMEN'S COACHES
Basketball: Rod Scheer; Phone: 316-942-4291; E-mail: scheerr@newmanu.edu.
Cheerleading: Karen Peck; Phone: 316-942-4291; E-mail: peckk@newmanu.edu.
Cross Country: Josh Schepis; Phone: 316-942-4291; E-mail: schepisj@newmanu.edu.
Golf: Brad Sexson; Phone: 316-942-4291; E-mail: sexsonb@newmanu.edu.
Soccer: Alan Sheperd; Phone: 316-942-4291.

Newman University *(continued)*

Softball: Steve Harshberger; Phone: 316-942-4291; E-mail: harshbergers@newmanu.edu.
Volleyball: Dan Friend; Phone: 316-942-4291; E-mail: friendd@newmanu.edu.

NEW MEXICO HIGHLANDS UNIVERSITY
Las Vegas, New Mexico

Cowboys ◆ NCAA II ◆ Rocky Mountain Athletic Conference ◆ http://www.nmhu.edu/

State-supported comprehensive, founded 1893
Coed, 2,103 undergraduate students, 66% full-time, 59% women, 41% men
Small-town 120-acre campus
Minimally difficult entrance level, 100% of applicants were admitted

Freshmen *Admission:* 880 applied, 880 were accepted, 255 enrolled.
Tuition and fees (2003–04): $2229 (resident), $9141 (nonresident). *Room and board:* $4085 (room only: $1973).
Financial Aid (All incoming freshmen): *Average need-based gift aid:* $2593. *Average non-need based aid:* $687. *Average aid to full-time under-graduates:* $3410.
Athletic Department: *Director of Athletics:* John Lumley; Phone: 505-454-3351; Fax: 505-426-2014; E-mail: jlumley@nmhu.edu. *Sports Information Director:* Tim Gotto; Phone: 505-426-2018; E-mail: tgotto@nmhu.edu.

MEN'S COACHES
Baseball: Steve Jones; Phone: 505-454-3587; E-mail: coachjones99@hotmail.com.
Basketball: Ed Manzanares; Phone: 505-454-3489; E-mail: manz21@yahoo.com.
Cheerleading: Jesse Lopez; Phone: 505-454-3368; E-mail: nmhuspirit2002@hotmail.com.
Cross Country: Bob Devries; Phone: 505-454-3368; E-mail: bob_devries@hotmail.com.
Football: John Fassel; Phone: 505-454-3551; E-mail: jwfassel@nmhu.edu.

WOMEN'S COACHES
Basketball: Lynn Kennedy; Phone: 505-454-3217; E-mail: kennedyl@nmhu.edu.
Cheerleading: Jesse Lopez; Phone: 505-454-3368; E-mail: nmhuspirit2002@hotmail.com.
Cross Country: Bob Devries; Phone: 505-454-3368; E-mail: bob_devries@hotmail.com.
Soccer: Ron Blue; Phone: 505-454-2019; E-mail: ronblue@nmhu.edu.
Softball: Dave Philop; Phone: 505-454-3487; E-mail: daphilop@nmhu.edu.
Volleyball: Tom Duke; Phone: 505-454-3206; E-mail: twduke@nmhu.edu.

NEW MEXICO STATE UNIVERSITY
Las Cruces, New Mexico

Aggies ◆ NCAA I ◆ Sun Belt Conference ◆ http://www.nmsu.edu/

State-supported university, founded 1888, part of New Mexico State University System
Coed, 12,797 undergraduate students, 82% full-time, 55% women, 45% men
Suburban 900-acre campus with easy access to El Paso
Moderately difficult entrance level, 83% of applicants were admitted

Freshmen *Admission:* 5,630 applied, 4,739 were accepted, 2,067 enrolled.
Tuition and fees (2003–04): $3372 (resident), $11,250 (nonresident). *Room and board:* $4560 (room only: $2440).

Financial Aid (All incoming freshmen): *Average need-based gift aid:* $5564. *Average non-need based aid:* $2413. *Average aid to full-time under-graduates:* $7096.
Athletic Department: *Director of Athletics:* Brian Faison; Phone: 505-646-1211; Fax: 505-646-5221; E-mail: bfaison@nmsu.edu. *Sports Information Director:* Sean Johnson; Phone: 505-646-1805; E-mail: seajohns@nmsu.edu.

MEN'S COACHES
Baseball: Rocky Ward; Phone: 505-646-5813; E-mail: rockyward32@yahoo.com.
Basketball: Lou Henson; Phone: 505-646-1324.
Cheerleading: Alysia Tucker; Phone: 505-646-1571.
Cross Country: Ed Crawford; Phone: 505-646-1538; E-mail: tcrawfor@nmsu.edu.
Football: Tony Samuel; Phone: 505-646-1234; E-mail: msamuel@nmsu.edu.
Golf: Larry Beem; Phone: 505-646-4131; E-mail: lbeem@nmsu.edu.
Tennis: Don Ball; Phone: 505-646-1942; E-mail: donball@nmsu.edu.

WOMEN'S COACHES
Basketball: Darin Spence; Phone: 505-646-1923; E-mail: spence@nmsu.edu.
Cheerleading: Alysia Tucker; Phone: 505-646-1571.
Cross Country: Ed Crawford; Phone: 505-646-1538; E-mail: tcrawfor@nmsu.edu.
Diving: Mark McFarland; Phone: 505-646-3120; E-mail: sw_coach@nmsu.edu.
Golf: Joann Cox; Phone: 505-646-3905.
Softball: Kathy Rodolph; Phone: 505-646-5793; E-mail: krodolph@nmsu.edu.
Swimming: Mark McFarland; Phone: 505-646-3120; E-mail: sw_coach@nmsu.edu.
Tennis: Don Ball; Phone: 505-646-1942; E-mail: donball@nmsu.edu.
Track and Field: Ed Crawford; Phone: 505-646-1538; E-mail: tcrawfor@nmsu.edu.
Volleyball: Michael Jordan; Phone: 505-646-4921; E-mail: micjorda@nmsu.edu.

NEW YORK CITY COLLEGE OF TECHNOLOGY OF THE CITY UNIVERSITY OF NEW YORK
Brooklyn, New York

Yellow Jackets ◆ NCAA III ◆ CUNY Athletic Conference ◆ http://www.citytech.cuny.edu/

State and locally supported primarily 2-year, founded 1946, part of City University of New York System
Coed, 11,380 undergraduate students, 62% full-time, 49% women, 51% men
Urban campus
Noncompetitive entrance level, 84% of applicants were admitted

Freshmen *Admission:* 5,833 applied, 4,916 were accepted, 2,184 enrolled. *Test scores:* SAT verbal scores over 500: 29%; SAT math scores over 500: 37%; SAT verbal scores over 600: 4%; SAT math scores over 600: 6%; SAT math scores over 700: 1%.
Tuition and fees (2003–04): $4269 (resident), $8909 (nonresident).
Athletic Department: *Director of Athletics:* Ray Amalbert; Phone: 718-260-5102; Fax: 718-260-5107; E-mail: ramalbert@citytech.cuny.edu. *Sports Information Director:* Steve Kahn; Phone: 718-260-5102; E-mail: stevenk577@aol.com.

MEN'S COACHES
Basketball: Ray Amalbert; Phone: 718-260-5102; E-mail: ramalbert@citytech.cuny.edu.
Cross Country: John Strickland; Phone: 718-260-5104; E-mail: jstrickland@citytech.cuny.edu.
Soccer: Andy Haynes; Phone: 718-260-5097; E-mail: ahaynes_03@netzero.com.
Tennis: Frank Rivera; Phone: 718-260-5110; E-mail: puerto105@yahoo.com.
Track and Field: John Strickland; Phone: 718-260-5104; E-mail: jstrickland@citytech.cuny.edu.
Volleyball: Greg Nosarzewski; Phone: 718-260-5110; E-mail: gnosarzewski@hotmail.com.

WOMEN'S COACHES

Basketball: Brenda Alexander; Phone: 718-260-5103; E-mail: balexander@citytech.cuny.edu.
Cross Country: John Strickland; Phone: 718-260-5104; E-mail: jstrickland@citytech.cuny.edu.
Softball: Greg Bowen; Phone: 718-260-5110.
Tennis: Frank Rivera; Phone: 718-260-5110; E-mail: puerto105@yahoo.com.
Track and Field: John Strickland; Phone: 718-260-5104; E-mail: jstrickland@citytech.cuny.edu.
Volleyball: Greg Nosarzewski; Phone: 718-260-5110; E-mail: gnosarzewski@hotmail.com.

NEW YORK INSTITUTE OF TECHNOLOGY
Old Westbury, New York

Bears ◆ NCAA II ◆ New York Collegiate Athletic Conference ◆ http://www.nyit.edu/

Independent university, founded 1955
Coed, 5,602 undergraduate students, 74% full-time, 39% women, 61% men
Suburban 1,050-acre campus with easy access to New York City
Moderately difficult entrance level, 79% of applicants were admitted

Freshmen *Admission:* 3,511 applied, 2,678 were accepted, 874 enrolled. *Test scores:* SAT verbal scores over 500: 69%; SAT math scores over 500: 86%; SAT verbal scores over 600: 24%; SAT math scores over 600: 42%; SAT verbal scores over 700: 2%; SAT math scores over 700: 8%.
Tuition and fees (2003–04): $17,226 (full-time). *Room and board:* $7780 (room only: $4080).
Financial Aid (All incoming freshmen): *Average need-based gift aid:* $7607. *Average non-need based aid:* $9978. *Average aid to full-time undergraduates:* $10,936.
Athletic Department: *Director of Athletics:* Clyde Doughty; Phone: 516-686-1133; Fax: 516-626-0750; E-mail: cdoughty@nyit.edu. *Sports Information Director:* Ben Arcuri; Phone: 516-686-7504; E-mail: barcuri@nyit.edu.

MEN'S COACHES

Baseball: Bob Hirschfield; Phone: 516-686-7513; E-mail: bhirsch19@hotmail.com.
Basketball: Sal Lagano; Phone: 516-686-7643; E-mail: slagano@hotmail.com.
Cross Country: Peter Zinno; Phone: 516-686-7627; E-mail: pzinno@hotmail.com.
Lacrosse: Jack Kaley; Phone: 516-686-7620; E-mail: jbkaley@cs.com.
Soccer: Carlos Delcid; Phone: 516-686-1214; E-mail: carlos_delcid@hotmail.com.
Track and Field: Peter Zinno; Phone: 516-686-7627; E-mail: pzinno@hotmail.com.

WOMEN'S COACHES

Basketball: Joe Hennie; Phone: 516-348-3043; E-mail: jhennie@nyit.edu.
Cross Country: Peter Zinno; Phone: 516-686-7627; E-mail: pzinno@hotmail.com.
Soccer: Joe Zyder; Phone: 516-686-1215; E-mail: adidasno13@hotmail.com.
Softball: Joe Hennie; Phone: 516-686-3043; E-mail: jhennie@nyit.edu.
Track and Field: Peter Zinno; Phone: 516-686-7627; E-mail: pzinno@hotmail.com.
Volleyball: Gail Wasmus; Phone: 516-686-7447; E-mail: glw08@aol.com.

NEW YORK UNIVERSITY
New York, New York

Violets ◆ NCAA III ◆ University Athletic Conference ◆ http://www.nyu.edu/

Independent university, founded 1831
Coed, 19,506 undergraduate students, 91% full-time, 60% women, 40% men
Urban campus
Most difficult entrance level, 3% of applicants were admitted

Freshmen *Admission:* 33,776 applied, 10,843 were accepted, 4,254 enrolled. *Test scores:* SAT verbal scores over 500: 99%; SAT math scores over 500: 99%; SAT verbal scores over 600: 81%; SAT math scores over 600: 83%; SAT verbal scores over 700: 29%; SAT math scores over 700: 32%.
Tuition and fees (2003–04): $28,496 (full-time). *Room and board:* $10,910.
Financial Aid (All incoming freshmen): *Average need-based gift aid:* $13,127. *Average non-need based aid:* $6270. *Average aid to full-time undergraduates:* $18,310.
Athletic Department: *Director of Athletics:* Christopher Bledsoe; Phone: 212-998-2021; Fax: 212-998-4591; E-mail: christopher.bledsoe@nyu.edu. *Sports Information Director:* Jeff Bernstein; Phone: 212-998-2031; E-mail: jmb14@nyu.edu.

MEN'S COACHES

Basketball: Joe Nesci; Phone: 212-998-2056; E-mail: jn3@nyu.edu.
Cheerleading: Gail Stentiford; Phone: 212-992-2018; E-mail: nyucheer@yahoo.com.
Cross Country: Nick McDonough; Phone: 212-998-2051; E-mail: npm1@nyu.edu.
Diving: Scott Donie; Phone: 212-992-2064; E-mail: scott.donie@nyu.edu.
Golf: Rich Mueller; Phone: 212-998-2049; E-mail: rkm3056@nyu.edu.
Soccer: Joe Behan; Phone: 212-998-2072; E-mail: jmb1184@nyu.edu.
Swimming: Bob Sorensen; Phone: 212-992-8531; E-mail: robert.sorensen@nyu.edu.
Tennis: John Curtis; Phone: 212-998-2054; E-mail: jc74@nyu.edu.
Track and Field: Nick McDonough; Phone: 212-998-2051; E-mail: npm1@nyu.edu.
Volleyball: Jose Pina; Phone: 212-998-2084; E-mail: jap3@nyu.edu.
Wrestling: Bruce Haberli; Phone: 212-998-2050; E-mail: bh7@nyu.edu.

WOMEN'S COACHES

Basketball: Janice Quinn; Phone: 212-998-2033; E-mail: jq1@nyu.edu.
Cheerleading: Gail Stentiford; Phone: 212-992-2018; E-mail: nyucheer@yahoo.com.
Cross Country: Jeff Smith; Phone: 212-998-2076; E-mail: jls14@nyu.edu.
Diving: Scott Donie; Phone: 212-992-2064; E-mail: scott.donie@nyu.edu.
Soccer: Amanda Vandervost; Phone: 212-998-2041.
Swimming: Mariejo Pasion; Phone: 212-992-8529; E-mail: mrp3325@nyu.edu.
Tennis: Horace Choy; Phone: 212-998-2054; E-mail: hc7@nyu.edu.
Track and Field: Jeff Smith; Phone: 212-998-2076; E-mail: jls14@nyu.edu.
Volleyball: Ed Caesar; Phone: 212-998-2068; E-mail: ejc1@nyu.edu.

NIAGARA UNIVERSITY
Niagara Falls, New York

Purple Eagles ◆ NCAA I ◆ College Hockey America Conference; Metro Atlantic Athletic Conference ◆ http://www.niagara.edu/

Independent religious comprehensive, founded 1856, affiliated with Roman Catholic Church
Coed, 2,734 undergraduate students, 95% full-time, 61% women, 39% men
Suburban 160-acre campus with easy access to Buffalo and Toronto
Moderately difficult entrance level, 79% of applicants were admitted

Freshmen *Admission:* 2,658 applied, 2,130 were accepted, 686 enrolled. *Test scores:* SAT verbal scores over 500: 58%; SAT math scores over

Niagara University *(continued)*

500: 63%; SAT verbal scores over 600: 14%; SAT math scores over 600: 18%; SAT verbal scores over 700: 1%; SAT math scores over 700: 2%.

Tuition and fees (2003–04): $17,380 (full-time). *Room and board:* $7670.

Financial Aid (All incoming freshmen): *Average need-based gift aid:* $11,598. *Average non-need based aid:* $7557. *Average aid to full-time undergraduates:* $15,136.

Athletic Department: *Director of Athletics:* Mike Hermann; Phone: 716-286-8601; Fax: 716-286-8609; E-mail: mjh@niagara.edu. *Sports Information Director:* Michele Dubert; Phone: 716-286-8588; E-mail: mdubert@niagara.edu.

MEN'S COACHES

Baseball: Mike McRae; Phone: 716-286-8624; E-mail: mmcrae@niagara.edu.

Basketball: Joe Mihalich; Phone: 716-286-8604; E-mail: jam@niagara.edu.

Cross Country: Dan Courtney; Phone: 716-286-8644; E-mail: dcourtney@niagara.edu.

Diving: Peter Thompson; Phone: 716-286-8053; E-mail: pthompson@niagara.edu.

Golf: Ryan Higgins; Phone: 716-286-8600; E-mail: rhiggins@niagara.edu.

Ice Hockey: Dave Burkholder; Phone: 716-286-8239; E-mail: db@niagara.edu.

Soccer: Dermot McGrane; Phone: 716-286-8661; E-mail: dmcgrane@niagara.edu.

Swimming: Peter Thompson; Phone: 716-286-8053; E-mail: pthompson@niagara.edu.

Tennis: Jason Joseph; Phone: 716-839-2881; E-mail: jjoseph@niagara.edu.

WOMEN'S COACHES

Basketball: Bill Argonin; Phone: 716-286-8618; E-mail: bagronin@niagara.edu.

Cross Country: Dan Courtney; Phone: 716-286-8644; E-mail: dcourtney@niagara.edu.

Diving: Peter Thompson; Phone: 716-286-8053; E-mail: pthompson@niagara.edu.

Lacrosse: Anne Windover; Phone: 716-286-8380; E-mail: acw@niagara.edu.

Soccer: Peter Veltri; Phone: 716-286-8617; E-mail: pveltri@niagara.edu.

Softball: Al Dirschberger; Phone: 716-286-8662; E-mail: afd@acsu.buffalo.edu.

Swimming: Peter Thompson; Phone: 716-286-8053; E-mail: pthompson@niagara.edu.

Tennis: Paul Calkins; Phone: 716-286-8641; E-mail: pcalkins@niagara.edu.

Volleyball: Rocco Lucci; Phone: 716-286-8540; E-mail: muvb@muohio.edu.

NICHOLLS STATE UNIVERSITY
Thibodaux, Louisiana

Colonels ◆ NCAA I ◆ Southland Conference ◆ http://www.nicholls.edu/

State-supported comprehensive, founded 1948, part of University of Louisiana System

Coed, 6,517 undergraduate students, 81% full-time, 62% women, 38% men

Small-town 210-acre campus with easy access to New Orleans

Noncompetitive entrance level, 99% of applicants were admitted

Freshmen *Admission:* 2,472 applied, 2,447 were accepted, 1,456 enrolled. *Test scores:* SAT verbal scores over 500: 36%; SAT math scores over 500: 44%; SAT verbal scores over 600: 12%; SAT math scores over 600: 3%.

Tuition and fees (2003–04): $2993 (resident), $8441 (nonresident). *Room and board:* $3402 (room only: $1750).

Financial Aid (All incoming freshmen): *Average need-based gift aid:* $2843. *Average non-need based aid:* $2596. *Average aid to full-time undergraduates:* $4443.

Athletic Department: *Director of Athletics:* Rob Bernardi; Phone: 985-448-4795; Fax: 985-448-4814; E-mail: ath-rob@nicholls.edu. *Sports Information Director:* Bobby Galinsky; Phone: 985-448-4281; E-mail: sid-reg@nicholls.edu.

MEN'S COACHES

Baseball: B.D. Parker; Phone: 985-446-4808; E-mail: ath-bdp@nicholls.edu.

Basketball: Ricky Blanton; Phone: 985-446-4287; E-mail: ath-rb@nicholls.edu.

Cheerleading: Eric Gueniot; Phone: 985-446-4422; E-mail: mus-ejg@nicholls.edu.

Cross Country: Agapius Amo; Phone: 985-446-7101.

Football: Daryl Daye; Phone: 985-446-4807; E-mail: ath-dld@nicholls.edu.

Golf: James Schilling; Phone: 985-493-2495; E-mail: ath-jcs@nicholls.edu.

Track and Field: Agapius Amo; Phone: 985-446-7101.

WOMEN'S COACHES

Basketball: Sue Syljebeck; Phone: 985-446-4265; E-mail: ath-sms@nicholls.edu.

Cheerleading: Eric Gueniot; Phone: 985-446-4422; E-mail: mus-ejg@nicholls.edu.

Cross Country: Agapius Amo; Phone: 985-446-7101.

Golf: James Schilling; Phone: 985-493-2495; E-mail: ath-jcs@nicholls.edu.

Soccer: Jim Zakel; Phone: 985-446-4956; E-mail: ath-jpz@nicholls.edu.

Softball: Phyllis Guedry; Phone: 985-448-4263; E-mail: ath-pmg@nicholls.edu.

Tennis: Scott Robinson; Phone: 985-446-4264.

Track and Field: Agapius Amo; Phone: 985-446-7101.

Volleyball: Mary Engstrom; Phone: 985-446-4283; E-mail: ath-mje@nicholls.edu.

NICHOLS COLLEGE
Dudley, Massachusetts

Bison ◆ NCAA III ◆ Commonwealth Coast Conference; New England Football Conference ◆ http://www.nichols.edu/

Independent comprehensive, founded 1815

Coed, 825 undergraduate students, 100% full-time, 33% women, 67% men

Rural 210-acre campus with easy access to Boston

Moderately difficult entrance level, 83% of applicants were admitted

Freshmen *Admission:* 1,017 applied, 845 were accepted, 256 enrolled. *Test scores:* SAT verbal scores over 500: 24%; SAT math scores over 500: 30%; SAT verbal scores over 600: 2%; SAT math scores over 600: 3%.

Tuition and fees (2003–04): $19,723 (full-time). *Room and board:* $7810.

Financial Aid (All incoming freshmen): *Average need-based gift aid:* $9354. *Average non-need based aid:* $10,384. *Average aid to full-time undergraduates:* $14,800.

Athletic Department: *Director of Athletics:* Charlyn Robert; Phone: 508-213-2368; Fax: 508-213-2384; E-mail: robertca@nichols.edu. *Sports Information Director:* Michael Serijan; Phone: 508-213-2352; E-mail: serijamt@nichols.edu.

MEN'S COACHES

Baseball: Steve Nadeau; Phone: 508-213-2363; E-mail: nadeausl@nichols.edu.

Basketball: Dave Sokolnicki; Phone: 508-213-2357; E-mail: sokolndj@nichols.edu.

Football: Bill Carven; Phone: 508-213-2362; E-mail: carvenwr@nichols.edu.

Golf: Mike Serijan; Phone: 508-213-2352; E-mail: serijamt@nichols.edu.

Ice Hockey: Mark Jargo; Phone: 508-213-2356; E-mail: mfjbison@aol.com.

Lacrosse: Tom Langan; Phone: 508-213-2351; E-mail: tom.langan@nichols.edu.

Soccer: Stephen Starr; Phone: 508-213-2360; E-mail: starrs@nichols.edu.

Tennis: Sean Cote; Phone: 508-213-2244; E-mail: scote@nichols.edu.

WOMEN'S COACHES

Basketball: Joanne Grzemski; Phone: 508-213-2239; E-mail: grzembjb@nichols.edu.

Field Hockey: Christy Deliberto; Phone: 508-213-2368; E-mail: cedeliberto@nichols.edu.

Lacrosse: Janna Cunningham; Phone: 508-213-2369; E-mail: jkcunningham@nichols.edu.

Soccer: Chris Traina; Phone: 508-213-2355; E-mail: cstraina@nichols.edu.

Softball: Linda Hendrickson; Phone: 508-213-2354; E-mail: lahendrickson@nichols.edu.

Tennis: Sean Cote; Phone: 508-213-2244; E-mail: scote@nichols.edu.

NORFOLK STATE UNIVERSITY
Norfolk, Virginia

Spartans ◆ NCAA I ◆ Mid-Eastern Athletic Conference
◆ http://www.nsu.edu/

State-supported comprehensive, founded 1935, part of State Council of Higher Education for Virginia
Coed, 6,039 undergraduate students, 79% full-time, 63% women, 37% men
Urban 134-acre campus
Moderately difficult entrance level, 72% of applicants were admitted

Freshmen *Admission:* 4,627 applied, 3,297 were accepted, 1,154 enrolled. *Test scores:* SAT verbal scores over 500: 21%; SAT math scores over 500: 19%; SAT verbal scores over 600: 3%; SAT math scores over 600: 3%.
Tuition and fees (2003–04): $3840 (resident), $13,260 (nonresident). *Room and board:* $5882 (room only: $3718).
Financial Aid (All incoming freshmen): *Average need-based gift aid:* $5615. *Average non-need based aid:* $3467. *Average aid to full-time undergraduates:* $8244.
Athletic Department: *Director of Athletics:* Orby Moss; Phone: 757-823-8152; Fax: 757-823-2566; E-mail: omoss@nsu.edu. *Sports Information Director:* Matt Michalec; Phone: 757-823-2628; E-mail: mmichalec@nsu.edu.

MEN'S COACHES

Baseball: Marty Miller; Phone: 757-823-9539; E-mail: mlmiller@nsu.edu.

Basketball: Dwight Freeman; Phone: 757-823-9192; E-mail: dfreeman@nsu.edu.

Cheerleading: Tiffany Watson; Phone: 757-823-8627; E-mail: twatson@nsu.edu.

Cross Country: Kenneth Giles; Phone: 757-823-2104; E-mail: kgiles@nsu.edu.

Football: Willie Gillus; Phone: 757-823-8824; E-mail: wgillus@nsu.edu.

Tennis: Nat Warren; Phone: 757-823-8821; E-mail: nwarren@nsu.edu.

Track and Field: Laverne Sweat; Phone: 757-823-2504; E-mail: fconley@nsu.edu.

WOMEN'S COACHES

Basketball: James Sweat; Phone: 757-823-8441; E-mail: jesweat@nsu.edu.

Cheerleading: Tiffany Watson; Phone: 757-823-8627; E-mail: twatson@nsu.edu.

Cross Country: Laverne Sweat; Phone: 757-823-2504; E-mail: plsweat@nsu.edu.

Softball: Chris Ake; Phone: 757-823-2118; E-mail: cjake@nsu.edu.

Tennis: Nat Warren; Phone: 757-823-8222; E-mail: nwarren@nsu.edu.

Track and Field: Laverne Sweat; Phone: 757-823-2504; E-mail: plsweat@nsu.edu.

Volleyball: Allison Millette; Phone: 757-823-2804; E-mail: almillette@nsu.edu.

NORTH CAROLINA AGRICULTURAL AND TECHNICAL STATE UNIVERSITY
Greensboro, North Carolina

Aggies ◆ NCAA I ◆ Mid-Eastern Athletic Conference
◆ http://www.ncat.edu/

State-supported university, founded 1891, part of University of North Carolina System
Coed, 7,331 undergraduate students, 90% full-time, 52% women, 48% men
Urban 191-acre campus
Moderately difficult entrance level, 80% of applicants were admitted

Freshmen *Admission:* 5,636 applied, 4,572 were accepted, 1,771 enrolled. *Test scores:* SAT verbal scores over 500: 20%; SAT math scores over 500: 23%; SAT verbal scores over 600: 2%; SAT math scores over 600: 3%.
Tuition and fees (2003–04): $2722 (resident), $12,089 (nonresident). *Room and board:* $4968 (room only: $2768).
Financial Aid (All incoming freshmen): *Average need-based gift aid:* $3573. *Average non-need based aid:* $3109. *Average aid to full-time undergraduates:* $5001.
Athletic Department: *Director of Athletics:* Charles Davis; Phone: 336-334-7686; Fax: 336-334-7272; E-mail: charles.davis@ncat.edu. *Sports Information Director:* Jim McNally; Phone: 336-334-7141; E-mail: jrmcnall@ncat.edu.

MEN'S COACHES

Baseball: Keith Shumate; Phone: 336-334-7371; E-mail: shumate@ncat.edu.

Basketball: Jerry Eaves; Phone: 336-334-7689.

Cross Country: Roy Thompson; Phone: 336-334-7374; E-mail: roy@ncat.edu.

Football: George Small; Phone: 336-334-7655.

Tennis: James Dunwoody; Phone: 336-334-7686.

Track and Field: Roy Thompson; Phone: 336-334-7374; E-mail: roy@ncat.edu.

WOMEN'S COACHES

Basketball: Saudia Rountree; Phone: 336-334-7891; E-mail: sroundtr@ncat.edu.

Cross Country: Tonya White; Phone: 336-334-7375.

Softball: Mamie Jones; Phone: 336-334-7370; E-mail: mjones@ncat.edu.

Swimming: Shawn Hendrix; Phone: 336-334-7918; E-mail: sh011231@ncat.edu.

Tennis: James Dunwoody; Phone: 336-334-7686.

Track and Field: Roy Thompson; Phone: 336-334-7374; E-mail: roy@ncat.edu.

Volleyball: Kathy Roulhac; Phone: 336-334-7373; E-mail: roulhack@ncat.edu.

NORTH CAROLINA CENTRAL UNIVERSITY
Durham, North Carolina

Eagles ◆ NCAA II ◆ Central Intercollegiate Athletic Conference ◆ http://www.nccu.edu/

State-supported comprehensive, founded 1910, part of University of North Carolina System
Coed, 5,362 undergraduate students, 79% full-time, 67% women, 33% men
Urban 103-acre campus
Minimally difficult entrance level, 84% of applicants were admitted

Freshmen *Admission:* 2,423 applied, 2,146 were accepted, 1,053 enrolled. *Test scores:* SAT verbal scores over 500: 16%; SAT math scores over 500: 15%; SAT verbal scores over 600: 3%; SAT math scores over 600: 2%; SAT verbal scores over 700: 1%.
Tuition and fees (2003–04): $3218 (resident), $12,587 (nonresident). *Room and board:* $4311 (room only: $2464).

North Carolina Central University *(continued)*

Financial Aid (All incoming freshmen): *Average need-based gift aid:* $3421. *Average non-need based aid:* $6600. *Average aid to full-time undergraduates:* $6456.

Athletic Department: *Director of Athletics:* William Hayes; Phone: 919-530-7057; Fax: 919-530-5426; E-mail: bhayes@wpo.nccu.edu. *Sports Information Director:* Kyle Serba; Phone: 919-530-7054; E-mail: kserba@nccu.edu.

MEN'S COACHES

Basketball: Phil Spence; Phone: 919-530-7059; E-mail: pspence@wpo.nccu.edu.

Cheerleading: LuAnn Edmonds-Harris; Phone: 919-530-7349; E-mail: lharris@wpo.nccu.edu.

Cross Country: Michael Lawson; Phone: 919-530-5121; E-mail: mlawson@wpo.nccu.edu.

Golf: Pete Hayes; Phone: 919-530-5124.

Tennis: David Nass; Phone: 919-530-5127; E-mail: dnass@wpo.nccu.edu.

Track and Field: Michael Lawson; Phone: 919-530-5121; E-mail: mlawson@wpo.nccu.edu.

WOMEN'S COACHES

Basketball: Joli Robinson; Phone: 919-530-7051; E-mail: jrobinson@wpo.nccu.edu.

Cheerleading: LuAnn Edmonds-Harris; Phone: 919-530-7349; E-mail: lharris@wpo.nccu.edu.

Cross Country: Michael Lawson; Phone: 919-530-5121; E-mail: mlawson@wpo.nccu.edu.

Golf: Pete Hayes; Phone: 919-530-5124.

Softball: Larry Keen; Phone: 919-530-5000; E-mail: lkeen@wpo.nccu.edu.

Tennis: David Nass; Phone: 919-530-5127; E-mail: dnass@wpo.nccu.edu.

Track and Field: Michael Lawson; Phone: 919-530-5121; E-mail: mlawson@wpo.nccu.edu.

Volleyball: Ingrid Wicker; Phone: 919-530-7053; E-mail: iwicker@wpo.nccu.edu.

NORTH CAROLINA STATE UNIVERSITY
Raleigh, North Carolina

Wolfpack ◆ NCAA I ◆ Atlantic Coast Conference ◆ http://www.ncsu.edu/

State-supported university, founded 1887, part of University of North Carolina System
Coed, 22,971 undergraduate students, 82% full-time, 42% women, 58% men
Suburban 1,623-acre campus
Very difficult entrance level, 59% of applicants were admitted

Freshmen *Admission:* 12,852 applied, 7,947 were accepted, 3,931 enrolled. *Test scores:* SAT verbal scores over 500: 88%; SAT math scores over 500: 95%; SAT verbal scores over 600: 42%; SAT math scores over 600: 60%; SAT verbal scores over 700: 6%; SAT math scores over 700: 14%.
Tuition and fees (2004–05): $4344 (resident), $16,192 (nonresident). *Room and board:* $6496 (room only: $3920).
Financial Aid (All incoming freshmen): *Average need-based gift aid:* $5700. *Average non-need based aid:* $6153. *Average aid to full-time undergraduates:* $7365.
Athletic Department: *Director of Athletics:* Lee Fowler; Phone: 919-515-2109; Fax: 919-515-3624; E-mail: lee_fowler@ncsu.edu. *Sports Information Director:* Annabelle Vaughan; Phone: 919-515-1181; E-mail: annabelle_vaughan@ncsu.edu.

MEN'S COACHES

Baseball: Eliott Avent; Phone: 919-515-3613; E-mail: elliott_avent@ncsu.edu.

Basketball: Herb Sendek; Phone: 919-515-3134; E-mail: herb_sendek@ncsu.edu.

Cheerleading: Lisa James; Phone: 919-515-2101.

Cross Country: Rollie Geiger; Phone: 919-515-3959; E-mail: rolland_geiger@ncsu.edu.

Diving: Brook Teal; Phone: 919-515-2849; E-mail: brooks_teal@ncsu.edu.

Football: Chuck Amato; Phone: 919-515-2432.

Golf: Richard Sykes; Phone: 919-515-3317; E-mail: richard_sykes@ncsu.edu.

Soccer: George Taratini; Phone: 919-515-3013.

Swimming: Brook Teal; Phone: 919-515-2849; E-mail: brooks_teal@ncsu.edu.

Tennis: Jon Choboy; Phone: 919-515-8786.

Track and Field: Rollie Geiger; Phone: 919-515-3959; E-mail: rolland_geiger@ncsu.edu.

Wrestling: Bob Guzzo; Phone: 919-515-3548.

WOMEN'S COACHES

Basketball: Kay Yow; Phone: 919-515-2880; E-mail: kay_yow@ncsu.edu.

Cheerleading: Lisa James; Phone: 919-515-2101.

Cross Country: Rollie Geiger; Phone: 919-515-3959; E-mail: rolland_geiger@ncsu.edu.

Diving: Brook Teal; Phone: 919-515-2849; E-mail: brooks_teal@ncsu.edu.

Golf: Page Marsh; Phone: 919-515-4169; E-mail: page_lee@ncsu.edu.

Gymnastics: Mark Stevenson; Phone: 919-515-2938; E-mail: ncsugym@ibm.net.

Soccer: Laura Kerrigan; Phone: 919-515-3476; E-mail: laura_kerrigan@ncsu.edu.

Swimming: Brook Teal; Phone: 919-515-2849; E-mail: brooks_teal@ncsu.edu.

Tennis: Hans Olsen; Phone: 919-515-2101.

Track and Field: Rollie Geiger; Phone: 919-515-3959; E-mail: rolland_geiger@ncsu.edu.

Volleyball: Mary Byrne; Phone: 919-515-3826; E-mail: mary_byrne@ncsu.edu.

NORTH CAROLINA WESLEYAN COLLEGE
Rocky Mount, North Carolina

Battling Bishops ◆ NCAA III ◆ USA South Athletic Conference ◆ http://www.ncwc.edu/

Independent religious 4-year, founded 1956, affiliated with United Methodist Church
Coed, 1,695 undergraduate students, 66% full-time, 59% women, 41% men
Suburban 200-acre campus
Moderately difficult entrance level, 87% of applicants were admitted

Freshmen *Admission:* 651 applied, 542 were accepted, 200 enrolled. *Test scores:* SAT verbal scores over 500: 26%; SAT math scores over 500: 26%; SAT verbal scores over 600: 6%; SAT math scores over 600: 6%; SAT verbal scores over 700: 1%.
Tuition and fees (2003–04): $12,279 (full-time). *Room and board:* $6555 (room only: $3000).
Athletic Department: *Director of Athletics:* John Thompson; Phone: 252-985-5218; Fax: 252-985-5252; E-mail: jthompson@ncwc.edu. *Sports Information Director:* Renny Taylor; Phone: 252-985-5214; E-mail: rtaylor@ncwc.edu.

MEN'S COACHES

Baseball: Charlie Long; Phone: 252-985-5219; E-mail: clong@ncwc.edu.

Basketball: John Thompson; Phone: 252-985-5218; E-mail: jthompson@ncwc.edu.

Football: Jack Ginn; Phone: 252-985-5226; E-mail: jginn@ncwc.edu.

Golf: Aaron Palen; Phone: 252-985-5271; E-mail: agpalen@ncwc.edu.

Soccer: Jason Kilby; Phone: 252-985-5209; E-mail: jakilby@ncwc.edu.

Tennis: Eric Allen; Phone: 252-985-5121; E-mail: ea162118@mail.ncwc.edu.

WOMEN'S COACHES

Basketball: John Brackett; Phone: 252-985-5217; E-mail: jbrackett@ncwc.edu.

Soccer: Tory Lukasina; Phone: 252-985-5215; E-mail: tlukasina@ncwc.edu.

Softball: John Brackett; Phone: 252-985-5217; E-mail: jbrackett@ncwc.edu.

Tennis: Eric Allen; Phone: 252-985-5121; E-mail: ea162118@mail.ncwc.edu.

Volleyball: Robin Pietryk; Phone: 252-985-5216; E-mail: rmpietryk@ncwc.edu.

NORTH CENTRAL COLLEGE
Naperville, Illinois

Cardinals ◆ NCAA III ◆ College Conference of Illinois and Wisconsin Conference ◆ http://www.northcentralcollege.edu/

Independent United Methodist comprehensive, founded 1861
Coed, 2,086 undergraduate students, 86% full-time, 59% women, 41% men
Suburban 56-acre campus with easy access to Chicago
Moderately difficult entrance level, 64% of applicants were admitted

Freshmen *Admission:* 1,654 applied, 1,171 were accepted, 408 enrolled. *Test scores:* SAT verbal scores over 500: 82%; SAT math scores over 500: 84%; SAT verbal scores over 600: 44%; SAT math scores over 600: 47%; SAT verbal scores over 700: 12%; SAT math scores over 700: 12%.
Tuition and fees (2003–04): $19,281 (full-time). *Room and board:* $6375.
Financial Aid (All incoming freshmen): *Average need-based gift aid:* $13,237. *Average non-need based aid:* $8725. *Average aid to full-time undergraduates:* $19,081.
Athletic Department: *Director of Athletics:* Walter Johnson; Phone: 630-637-5501; Fax: 630-637-5521; E-mail: wajohnso@noctrl.edu. *Sports Information Director:* Josh Hendricks; Phone: 630-637-5302; E-mail: johendricks@noctrl.edu.

MEN'S COACHES
Baseball: Brian Milchalak; Phone: 630-637-5512; E-mail: brmichalak@noctrl.edu.
Basketball: Benjy Taylor; Phone: 630-637-5517; E-mail: betaylor@noctrl.edu.
Cross Country: Al Carius; Phone: 630-637-5504; E-mail: alcarius@noctrl.edu.
Football: John Thorne; Phone: 630-637-5506; E-mail: jothorne@noctrl.edu.
Golf: Pat Bowler; Phone: 630-961-2429.
Soccer: Ed Vucinic; Phone: 630-637-5516.
Swimming: Dennis Ryan; Phone: 630-637-5514; E-mail: der@noctrl.edu.
Tennis: Craig Swanson; Phone: 630-961-2429; E-mail: crswanson@noctrl.edu.
Track and Field: Al Carius; Phone: 630-637-5504; E-mail: alcarius@noctrl.edu.
Wrestling: Jim Miller; Phone: 630-637-5513; E-mail: jamiller@noctrl.edu.

WOMEN'S COACHES
Basketball: Emily Bauer; Phone: 630-637-5531; E-mail: embauer@noctrl.edu.
Cross Country: Kari Kluckhohn; Phone: 630-637-5503; E-mail: kakluckhohn@noctrl.edu.
Golf: Maria Long; Phone: 630-983-5497.
Soccer: Dimitre Gueorguiev; Phone: 630-637-5516.
Softball: Jim Kulawiak; Phone: 630-637-5509; E-mail: jakulawi@noctrl.edu.
Swimming: Dennis Ryan; Phone: 630-637-5514; E-mail: der@noctrl.edu.
Tennis: Vanessa Vaughn; Phone: 630-637-5500.
Track and Field: Kari Kluckhohn; Phone: 630-637-5503; E-mail: kakluckhohn@noctrl.edu.
Volleyball: Rita Adolphson; Phone: 630-637-5162; E-mail: riadolphson@noctrl.edu.

NORTH DAKOTA STATE UNIVERSITY
Fargo, North Dakota

Bison ◆ NCAA II ◆ North Central Intercollegiate Conference ◆ http://www.ndsu.edu/

State-supported university, founded 1890, part of North Dakota University System
Coed, 10,148 undergraduate students, 89% full-time, 44% women, 56% men
Urban 2,100-acre campus
Moderately difficult entrance level, 6% of applicants were admitted

Freshmen *Admission:* 3,245 applied, 1,986 were accepted, 1,974 enrolled. *Test scores:* SAT verbal scores over 500: 76%; SAT math scores over 500: 86%; SAT verbal scores over 600: 43%; SAT math scores over 600: 54%; SAT verbal scores over 700: 11%; SAT math scores over 700: 13%.
Tuition and fees (2003–04): $4190 (resident), $9599 (nonresident). *Room and board:* $4471 (room only: $1711).
Financial Aid (All incoming freshmen): *Average need-based gift aid:* $3736. *Average non-need based aid:* $2039. *Average aid to full-time undergraduates:* $5462.
Athletic Department: *Director of Athletics:* Gene Taylor; Phone: 701-231-8985; Fax: 701-231-8022; E-mail: gene.taylor@ndsu.nodak.edu. *Sports Information Director:* George Ellis; Phone: 701-231-8331; E-mail: george.ellis@ndsu.nodak.edu.

MEN'S COACHES
Baseball: Mitch McCleod; Phone: 701-231-8853; E-mail: mitch.mcleod@ndsu.nodak.edu.
Basketball: Tim Miles; Phone: 701-231-7805; E-mail: tim.miles@ndsu.nodak.edu.
Cheerleading: Pat Fredrickson; Phone: 701-231-8086; E-mail: pat.fredrickson@ndsu.nodak.edu.
Cross Country: Don Larson; Phone: 701-231-7793; E-mail: donald.larson@ndsu.nodak.edu.
Football: Craig Bohl; Phone: 701-231-7796; E-mail: craig.bohl@ndsu.nodak.edu.
Golf: Matt Johnson; Phone: 701-280-0824; E-mail: mjohnson@thesportsbubble.com.
Track and Field: Don Larson; Phone: 701-231-7793; E-mail: donald.larson@ndsu.nodak.edu.
Wrestling: Bucky Maughan; Phone: 701-231-8983; E-mail: bucky.maughan@ndsu.nodak.edu.

WOMEN'S COACHES
Basketball: Amy Ruley; Phone: 701-231-8875; E-mail: amy.ruley@ndsu.nodak.edu.
Cheerleading: Pat Fredrickson; Phone: 701-231-8086; E-mail: pat.fredrickson@ndsu.nodak.edu.
Cross Country: Ryun Godfrey; Phone: 701-231-8867; E-mail: v.godfrey@ndsu.nodak.edu.
Golf: Diane Fedje-Weisgarber; Phone: 701-39-9062; E-mail: weisgad@fargo.k12.nd.us.
Soccer: Pete Cuadrado; Phone: 701-231-9471; E-mail: pete.cuadrado@ndsu.nodak.edu.
Softball: Darren Mueller; Phone: 701-231-6160; E-mail: darren.mueller@ndsu.nodak.edu.
Track and Field: Ryun Godfrey; Phone: 701-231-8867; E-mail: v.godfrey@ndsu.nodak.edu.
Volleyball: Zaundra Bina; Phone: 701-231-8859; E-mail: zaundra.bina@ndsu.nodak.edu.

NORTHEASTERN STATE UNIVERSITY
Tahlequah, Oklahoma

Redmen ◆ NCAA II ◆ Lone Star Conference ◆ http://www.nsuok.edu/

State-supported comprehensive, founded 1846, part of Oklahoma State Regents for Higher Education
Coed, 8,313 undergraduate students, 78% full-time, 59% women, 41% men
Small-town 160-acre campus with easy access to Tulsa
Moderately difficult entrance level, 89% of applicants were admitted

Freshmen *Admission:* 2,223 applied, 1,976 were accepted, 1,294 enrolled.
Tuition and fees (2003–04): $2700 (resident), $6600 (nonresident). *Room and board:* $3080.
Financial Aid (All incoming freshmen): *Average need-based gift aid:* $2695. *Average non-need based aid:* $750. *Average aid to full-time undergraduates:* $6400.
Athletic Department: *Director of Athletics:* Eddie Griffin; Phone: 908-456-5511; E-mail: griff001@nsuok.edu. *Sports Information Director:* Scott Pettus; Phone: 908-456-5511; E-mail: pettusr@nsuok.edu.

MEN'S COACHES
Baseball: Sergio Espinal; Phone: 918-456-5511; E-mail: espinal@nsuok.edu.
Basketball: Larry Gipson; Phone: 918-456-5511; E-mail: gipsonrm@nsuok.edu.
Football: John Horner; Phone: 918-456-5511.
Golf: Scott Varner; Phone: 918-456-5511; E-mail: varnersm@nsuok.edu.
Soccer: Charlie Mitchell; Phone: 918-456-5511; E-mail: mitchcha@nsuok.edu.

WOMEN'S COACHES
Basketball: Randy Gipson; Phone: 918-456-5511; E-mail: gipsonrm@nsuok.edu.
Golf: Scott Varner; Phone: 918-458-2071; E-mail: varnersm@nsuok.edu.
Soccer: Charlie Mitchell; Phone: 918-458-2071; E-mail: mitchcha@nsuok.edu.
Softball: Dee Gerlach; Phone: 918-456-5511; E-mail: gerlach@nsuok.edu.
Tennis: Ron Cox; Phone: 918-456-5511; E-mail: coxr@nsuok.edu.

NORTHEASTERN UNIVERSITY
Boston, Massachusetts

Huskies ◆ NCAA I ◆ America East Conference; Atlantic 10 Conference; Hockey East Conference ◆ http://www.northeastern.edu/

Independent university, founded 1898
Coed, 3,194 undergraduate students, 100% full-time, 53% women, 47% men
Urban 67-acre campus
Moderately difficult entrance level, 5% of applicants were admitted

Freshmen *Admission:* 21,484 applied, 10,200 were accepted, 3,194 enrolled. *Test scores:* SAT verbal scores over 500: 90%; SAT math scores over 500: 94%; SAT verbal scores over 600: 49%; SAT math scores over 600: 63%; SAT verbal scores over 700: 6%; SAT math scores over 700: 11%.
Tuition and fees (2003–04): $25,840 (full-time). *Room and board:* $9810 (room only: $5260).
Financial Aid (All incoming freshmen): *Average need-based gift aid:* $13,920. *Average non-need based aid:* $14,197. *Average aid to full-time undergraduates:* $17,334.
Athletic Department: *Director of Athletics:* Dave O'Brien; Phone: 617-373-7590; Fax: 617-373-8988; E-mail: da.o'brien@neu.edu. *Sports Information Director:* Dave Henry; Phone: 617-373-3643; E-mail: dave@gonu.com.

MEN'S COACHES
Baseball: Neil Mc Phee; Phone: 617-373-3657; E-mail: n.mcphee@neu.edu.

Basketball: Ron Everhart; Phone: 617-373-4464; E-mail: r.everhart@neu.edu.
Cheerleading: Lorrie Wright; Phone: 617-436-0458; E-mail: nucheer@lynx.neu.edu.
Cross Country: Sherman Hart; Phone: 617-373-3555; E-mail: s.hart@neu.edu.
Football: Don Brown; Phone: 617-373-5549; E-mail: do.brown@neu.edu.
Ice Hockey: Bruce Crowder; Phone: 617-373-2631; E-mail: b.crowder@neu.edu.
Soccer: Ed Matz; Phone: 617-373-4465; E-mail: e.matz@neu.edu.
Track and Field: Sherman Hart; Phone: 617-373-3555; E-mail: s.hart@neu.edu.

WOMEN'S COACHES
Basketball: Willette White; Phone: 617-373-2702; E-mail: w.white@neu.edu.
Cheerleading: Lorrie Wright; Phone: 617-436-0458; E-mail: nucheer@lynx.neu.edu.
Cross Country: Sherman Hart; Phone: 617-373-3555; E-mail: s.hart@neu.edu.
Diving: Roy Coates; Phone: 617-373-2676; E-mail: r.coates@neu.edu.
Field Hockey: Cheryl Murtagh; Phone: 617-373-2828; E-mail: c.murtagh@neu.edu.
Soccer: Ed Matz; Phone: 617-373-4465; E-mail: e.matz@neu.edu.
Swimming: Roy Coates; Phone: 617-373-2676; E-mail: r.coates@neu.edu.
Track and Field: Sherman Hart; Phone: 617-373-3555; E-mail: s.hart@neu.edu.
Volleyball: Ken Nichols; Phone: 617-373-3556; E-mail: k.nichols@neu.edu.

NORTHERN ARIZONA UNIVERSITY
Flagstaff, Arizona

Lumberjacks ◆ NCAA I ◆ Big Sky Conference ◆ http://www.nau.edu/

State-supported university, founded 1899, part of Arizona University System
Coed, 13,015 undergraduate students
Small-town 730-acre campus
Moderately difficult entrance level

Freshmen *Test scores:* SAT verbal scores over 500: 67%; SAT math scores over 500: 63%; SAT verbal scores over 600: 23%; SAT math scores over 600: 22%; SAT verbal scores over 700: 3%; SAT math scores over 700: 2%.
Tuition and fees (2003–04): $3628 (resident), $12,148 (nonresident). *Room and board:* $5374 (room only: $2708).
Financial Aid (All incoming freshmen): *Average need-based gift aid:* $5168. *Average non-need based aid:* $5484. *Average aid to full-time undergraduates:* $7896.
Athletic Department: *Director of Athletics:* Dave Brown; Phone: 928-523-3440; Fax: 928-523-6035; E-mail: dave.brown@nau.edu. *Sports Information Director:* Steve Shaff; Phone: 928-523-6792; E-mail: steven.shaff@nau.edu.

MEN'S COACHES
Basketball: Mike Adras; Phone: 928-523-5630; E-mail: michael.adras@nau.edu.
Cheerleading: Tom Shrake; Phone: 928-523-1299; E-mail: tom.shrake@nauathletics.com.
Cross Country: Ron Mann; Phone: 928-523-5646; E-mail: ron.mann@nau.edu.
Football: Jerome Souers; Phone: 928-523-6787; E-mail: jerome.souers@nau.edu.
Tennis: Albin Polonyi; Phone: 928-523-7465; E-mail: albin.polonyi@nau.edu.
Track and Field: Ron Mann; Phone: 928-523-5646; E-mail: ron.mann@nau.edu.

WOMEN'S COACHES
Basketball: Laurie Kelly; Phone: 928-523-6035; E-mail: laura.kelly@nau.edu.
Cheerleading: Tom Shrake; Phone: 928-523-1299; E-mail: tom.shrake@nauathletics.com.

Cross Country: Ron Mann; Phone: 928-523-5646; E-mail: ron.mann@nau.edu.
Diving: Nikki Kelsy-Huffman; Phone: 928-523-6035; E-mail: nicole.kelsey@nau.edu.
Golf: Tom McCurdy; Phone: 928-523-1668; E-mail: tom.mccurdy@nau.edu.
Soccer: Andre Luciano; Phone: 928-523-2021; E-mail: andre.luciano@nau.edu.
Swimming: Andy Johns; Phone: 928-523-6035; E-mail: robert.johns@nau.edu.
Tennis: Albin Polonyi; Phone: 928-523-7465; E-mail: albin.polonyi@nau.edu.
Track and Field: Ron Mann; Phone: 928-523-5646; E-mail: ron.mann@nau.edu.
Volleyball: Michelle Hansen; Phone: 928-218-6550; E-mail: mlh29@dana.ucc.nau.edu.

NORTHERN ILLINOIS UNIVERSITY
De Kalb, Illinois

Huskies ◆ NCAA I ◆ Mid-American Conference ◆ http://www.niu.edu/

State-supported university, founded 1895
Coed, 18,275 undergraduate students, 90% full-time, 53% women, 47% men
Small-town 589-acre campus with easy access to Chicago
Moderately difficult entrance level, 62% of applicants were admitted

Freshmen *Admission:* 16,128 applied, 10,028 were accepted, 3,253 enrolled.
Tuition and fees (2003–04): $5164 (resident), $9076 (nonresident). *Room and board:* $5360.
Financial Aid (All incoming freshmen): *Average need-based gift aid:* $6221. *Average non-need based aid:* $2834. *Average aid to full-time undergraduates:* $8239.
Athletic Department: *Director of Athletics:* Cary Groth; Phone: 815-753-7370; Fax: 815-753-7700; E-mail: cgroth@niu.edu. *Sports Information Director:* Mike Korcek; Phone: 815-753-1706; E-mail: mkorcek@niu.edu.

MEN'S COACHES
Baseball: Ed Mathey; Phone: 815-753-2225; E-mail: emathey@niu.edu.
Basketball: Rob Judson; Phone: 815-753-1633; E-mail: rjudson@niu.edu.
Cheerleading: Al Enlow; Phone: 815-753-0801; E-mail: aenlow@niu.edu.
Football: Joe Novak; Phone: 815-753-1825; E-mail: joenovak@niu.edu.
Golf: John Cleary; Phone: 815-753-1816; E-mail: johncleary@niu.edu.
Soccer: Steve Simmons; Phone: 815-753-1372; E-mail: smsimmons@niu.edu.
Tennis: Pontus Hiort; Phone: 815-753-6845.
Wrestling: David Grant; Phone: 815-753-9478; E-mail: dgrant@niu.edu.

WOMEN'S COACHES
Basketball: Carol Hammerle; Phone: 815-753-9936; E-mail: chammerle@niu.edu.
Cheerleading: Al Enlow; Phone: 815-753-0801; E-mail: aenlow@niu.edu.
Cross Country: Shantel Twiggs; Phone: 815-753-0836; E-mail: stwiggs@niu.edu.
Golf: Pam Tyska; Phone: 815-753-1548; E-mail: ptyska@niu.edu.
Gymnastics: Mark Sontag; Phone: 815-753-1498; E-mail: msontag@niu.edu.
Soccer: Frank Horvat; Phone: 815-753-9535; E-mail: fhorvat@niu.edu.
Softball: Donna Martin; Phone: 815-753-1497; E-mail: dmartin1@niu.edu.
Tennis: Laura Scott; Phone: 815-753-9536; E-mail: lascott@niu.edu.
Track and Field: Shantel Twiggs; Phone: 815-753-0571; E-mail: stwiggs@niu.edu.
Volleyball: Ray Gooden; Phone: 815-753-9533; E-mail: rgooden@niu.edu.

NORTHERN KENTUCKY UNIVERSITY
Highland Heights, Kentucky

Norse ◆ NCAA II ◆ Great Lakes Valley Conference ◆ http://www.nku.edu/

State-supported comprehensive, founded 1968
Coed, 12,188 undergraduate students, 75% full-time, 58% women, 42% men
Suburban 320-acre campus with easy access to Cincinnati
Noncompetitive entrance level, 86% of applicants were admitted

Freshmen *Admission:* 3,779 applied, 3,378 were accepted, 2,002 enrolled. *Test scores:* SAT verbal scores over 500: 42%; SAT math scores over 500: 40%; SAT verbal scores over 600: 14%; SAT math scores over 600: 9%; SAT verbal scores over 700: 1%; SAT math scores over 700: 2%.
Tuition and fees (2003–04): $3744 (resident), $7992 (nonresident). *Room and board:* $5066 (room only: $3026).
Financial Aid (All incoming freshmen): *Average need-based gift aid:* $3744. *Average non-need based aid:* $2872. *Average aid to full-time undergraduates:* $5554.
Athletic Department: *Director of Athletics:* Jane Meier; Phone: 859-572-5631; Fax: 859-572-6089; E-mail: meierj@nku.edu. *Sports Information Director:* Don Owen; Phone: 859-572-5470; E-mail: owend@nku.edu.

MEN'S COACHES
Baseball: Todd Asalon; Phone: 859-572-6474; E-mail: asalont@nku.edu.
Basketball: Ken Shields; Phone: 859-572-5192; E-mail: shieldsr@nku.edu.
Cheerleading: Jaime Schaeffer; Phone: 859-393-7252; E-mail: jm09@hotmail.com.
Cross Country: Steve Kruse; Phone: 859-572-5193; E-mail: kruses@nku.edu.
Golf: Daryl Landrum; Phone: 859-572-5193; E-mail: landrumd@nku.edu.
Soccer: John Basalyga; Phone: 859-572-5193; E-mail: basalygaj@nku.edu.
Tennis: Geoff Crawford; Phone: 859-572-5193; E-mail: crawfordg@nku.edu.

WOMEN'S COACHES
Basketball: Nancy Winstel; Phone: 859-572-5195; E-mail: winstel@nku.edu.
Cheerleading: Jaime Schaeffer; Phone: 859-393-7252; E-mail: jm09@hotmail.com.
Cross Country: Steve Kruse; Phone: 859-572-5193; E-mail: kruses@nku.edu.
Golf: Daryl Landrum; Phone: 859-572-5193; E-mail: landrumd@nku.edu.
Soccer: Bob Sheehan; Phone: 859-572-6314; E-mail: sheehanr@nku.edu.
Softball: Kathy Brown; Phone: 859-572-5939; E-mail: bownk@nku.edu.
Tennis: Geoff Crawford; Phone: 859-572-5193; E-mail: crawfordg@nku.edu.
Volleyball: Carlos Chia; Phone: 859-572-6372; E-mail: chia@nku.edu.

NORTHERN MICHIGAN UNIVERSITY
Marquette, Michigan

Wildcats ◆ NCAA II ◆ Central Collegiate Hockey Conference; Great Lakes Intercollegiate Conference ◆ http://www.nmu.edu/

State-supported comprehensive, founded 1899, part of Autonomous
Coed, 8,536 undergraduate students
Small-town 300-acre campus with easy access to Sawyer International
Minimally difficult entrance level, 84% of applicants were admitted

Freshmen *Admission:* 4,460 applied, 3,762 were accepted.

Northern Michigan University *(continued)*

Tuition and fees (2003–04): $5370 (resident), $8658 (nonresident). *Room and board:* $5724.
Financial Aid (All incoming freshmen): *Average need-based gift aid:* $3385. *Average aid to full-time undergraduates:* $6624.
Athletic Department: *Director of Athletics:* Brian Verigin; Phone: 906-227-2491; Fax: 906-227-2492; E-mail: bverigin@nmu.edu. *Sports Information Director:* David Faiella; Phone: 906-227-1013; E-mail: dfaiella@nmu.edu.

MEN'S COACHES
Basketball: Dean Ellis; Phone: 906-227-2106; E-mail: dellis@nmu.edu.
Cheerleading: LeAnn Foster; Phone: 906-227-2132; E-mail: lhebert@nmu.edu.
Football: Doug Sams; Phone: 906-227-2039; E-mail: dsams@nmu.edu.
Golf: Dean Ellis; Phone: 906-227-2106; E-mail: dellis@nmu.edu.
Ice Hockey: Walt Kyle; Phone: 906-227-1211; E-mail: wkyle@nmu.edu.

WOMEN'S COACHES
Basketball: Mike Geary; Phone: 906-227-2646; E-mail: mgeary@nmu.edu.
Cheerleading: LeAnn Foster; Phone: 906-227-2132; E-mail: lhebert@nmu.edu.
Cross Country: Sten Fjeldheim; Phone: 906-227-2049; E-mail: sfjeldhe@nmu.edu.
Diving: Jim Rainey; Phone: 906-227-2137; E-mail: jrainey@nmu.edu.
Soccer: Carl Gregon; Phone: 906-227-2139; E-mail: cgregor@nmu.edu.
Swimming: Jonathan Wilson; Phone: 906-227-2827; E-mail: jwilson@nmu.edu.
Track and Field: Sten Fjeldheim; Phone: 906-227-2049; E-mail: sfjeldhe@nmu.edu.
Volleyball: Jim Moore; Phone: 906-227-2378; E-mail: jamoore@nmu.edu.

NORTHERN STATE UNIVERSITY
Aberdeen, South Dakota

Wolves ◆ NCAA II ◆ Northern Sun Intercollegiate Conference ◆ http://www.northern.edu/

State-supported comprehensive, founded 1901, part of South Dakota Board of Regents
Coed, 2,842 undergraduate students, 57% full-time, 59% women, 41% men
Small-town 52-acre campus
Minimally difficult entrance level, 91% of applicants were admitted

Freshmen *Admission:* 902 applied, 833 were accepted, 434 enrolled.
Tuition and fees (2003–04): $4207 (resident), $8919 (nonresident). *Room and board:* $3306 (room only: $1478).
Financial Aid (All incoming freshmen): *Average need-based gift aid:* $2630. *Average non-need based aid:* $1788. *Average aid to full-time undergraduates:* $4510.
Athletic Department: *Director of Athletics:* Bob Olson; Phone: 605-626-7732; Fax: 605-626-2238; E-mail: olsonr@northern.edu. *Sports Information Director:* Mike Lefler; Phone: 605-626-7741; E-mail: leflerm@northern.edu.

MEN'S COACHES
Baseball: Curt Fredrickson; Phone: 605-626-7735; E-mail: fredricc@northern.edu.
Basketball: Dan Meyer; Phone: 605-626-7730; E-mail: meyerd@northern.edu.
Cheerleading: Shannon Westra-Imbery; Phone: 605-225-6390.
Cross Country: James Fuller; Phone: 605-626-7736; E-mail: fullerj@northern.edu.
Football: Ken Heufel; Phone: 605-626-2007; E-mail: heupelk@northern.edu.
Golf: Paul Sather; Phone: 605-626-2230; E-mail: satherp@northern.edu.
Track and Field: James Fuller; Phone: 605-626-7736; E-mail: fullerj@northern.edu.
Wrestling: Patrick Timm; Phone: 605-626-2489; E-mail: timmp@northern.edu.

WOMEN'S COACHES
Basketball: Curt Fredrickson; Phone: 605-626-7735; E-mail: fredricc@northern.edu.
Cheerleading: Shannon Westra-Imbery; Phone: 605-225-6390.

Cross Country: James Fuller; Phone: 605-626-7736; E-mail: fullerj@northern.edu.
Golf: Paul Sather; Phone: 605-626-7730; E-mail: satherpk@northern.edu.
Soccer: Steve Kehm; Phone: 605-626-3319; E-mail: kehms@northern.edu.
Softball: Paula Krueger; Phone: 605-626-2937; E-mail: kruegerp@northern.edu.
Track and Field: James Fuller; Phone: 605-626-7736; E-mail: fullerj@northern.edu.
Volleyball: Lisa Schriver; Phone: 605-626-7729; E-mail: schrivel@northern.edu.

NORTH GEORGIA COLLEGE & STATE UNIVERSITY
Dahlonega, Georgia

Saints ◆ NAIA ◆ Georgia Alabama Carolina Conference ◆ http://www.ngcsu.edu/

State-supported comprehensive, founded 1873, part of University System of Georgia
Coed, 3,946 undergraduate students, 80% full-time, 62% women, 38% men
Small-town 140-acre campus with easy access to Atlanta
Moderately difficult entrance level, 7% of applicants were admitted

Freshmen *Admission:* 1,797 applied, 1,133 were accepted, 728 enrolled.
Test scores: SAT verbal scores over 500: 70%; SAT math scores over 500: 68%; SAT verbal scores over 600: 17%; SAT math scores over 600: 18%; SAT verbal scores over 700: 1%; SAT math scores over 700: 1%.
Tuition and fees (2003–04): $2824 (resident), $9460 (nonresident). *Room and board:* $4160 (room only: $2080).
Financial Aid (All incoming freshmen): *Average need-based gift aid:* $2759. *Average non-need based aid:* $3191. *Average aid to full-time undergraduates:* $5623.
Athletic Department: *Director of Athletics:* Randy Dunn; Phone: 706-864-1758; Fax: 706-864-1868; E-mail: rdunn@ngcsu.edu. *Sports Information Director:* Denise Bryant; Phone: 706-864-2755; E-mail: dbryant@ngcsu.edu.

MEN'S COACHES
Baseball: Tom Cantrell; Phone: 706-867-2754; E-mail: thcantrell@ngcsu.edu.
Basketball: Chris Faulkner; Phone: 706-867-2808; E-mail: cfaulkner@ngcsu.edu.
Cheerleading: Kristen Thompson; Phone: 706-864-1758.
Cross Country: Jason Gibson; Phone: 706-867-1476.
Soccer: Chris Adams; Phone: 706-867-2849; E-mail: cadams@ngcsu.edu.
Tennis: Rick Case; Phone: 706-867-2921; E-mail: drcase@ngcsu.edu.

WOMEN'S COACHES
Basketball: Buffie Burson; Phone: 706-864-1628; E-mail: bbburson@ngcsu.edu.
Cheerleading: Kristen Thompson; Phone: 706-864-1758.
Cross Country: Jason Gibson; Phone: 706-867-1476.
Soccer: Chris Adams; Phone: 706-867-2849; E-mail: cadams@ngcsu.edu.
Softball: Mike Davenport; Phone: 706-864-1861; E-mail: mjdavenport@ngcsu.edu.
Tennis: Rick Case; Phone: 706-867-2921; E-mail: drcase@ngcsu.edu.

NORTH GREENVILLE COLLEGE
Tigerville, South Carolina

Crusaders ◆ NCAA II ◆ Independent ◆ http://www.ngc.edu/

Independent Southern Baptist 4-year, founded 1892
Coed, 1,615 undergraduate students, 93% full-time, 49% women, 51% men
Rural 500-acre campus with easy access to Greenville
Minimally difficult entrance level, 94% of applicants were admitted

Freshmen *Admission:* 769 applied, 731 were accepted, 408 enrolled.
Test scores: SAT verbal scores over 500: 61%; SAT math scores over

500: 62%; SAT verbal scores over 600: 21%; SAT math scores over 600: 18%; SAT verbal scores over 700: 2%; SAT math scores over 700: 1%.
Tuition and fees (2003–04): $9300 (full-time). *Room and board:* $5280.
Athletic Department: *Director of Athletics:* Jan McDonald; Phone: 864-977-7151; Fax: 864-977-7152; E-mail: jmcdonald@ngc.edu. *Sports Information Director:* Butch Dean; Phone: 864-977-7187; E-mail: bdean@ngc.edu.

MEN'S COACHES
Baseball: Tim Nihart; Phone: 864-977-7156; E-mail: tnihart@ngc.edu.
Basketball: Chad Lister; Phone: 864-977-7155; E-mail: clister@ngc.edu.
Cross Country: Micah Sepko; Phone: 864-977-7157; E-mail: msepko@ngc.edu.
Football: Brian Smith; Phone: 864-977-7112; E-mail: bsmith@ngc.edu.
Golf: Jeffrey Patillo; Phone: 864-977-7190; E-mail: jpatillio@ngc.edu.
Soccer: Chad Gfeller; Phone: 864-977-7189; E-mail: cgfeller@ngc.edu.
Tennis: Barry Quinn; Phone: 864-977-7254; E-mail: brquinn@mindspring.com.

WOMEN'S COACHES
Basketball: Jayne Arledge; Phone: 864-977-7154; E-mail: jarledge@ngc.edu.
Cross Country: Micah Sepko; Phone: 864-977-7156; E-mail: msepko@ngc.edu.
Soccer: Chad Gfeller; Phone: 864-977-7189; E-mail: cgfeller@ngc.edu.
Softball: Buster Sturkie; Phone: 864-977-7253; E-mail: bsturke@ngc.edu.
Tennis: Barry Quinn; Phone: 864-977-7254; E-mail: brquinn@mindspring.com.
Volleyball: Angie Cochran; Phone: 864-977-7110; E-mail: abennett@ngc.edu.

NORTHLAND COLLEGE
Ashland, Wisconsin
Lumberjacks ◆ NCAA III ◆ Independent ◆ http://www.northland.edu/

Independent religious 4-year, founded 1892, affiliated with United Church of Christ
Coed, 750 undergraduate students, 95% full-time, 54% women, 46% men
Small-town 130-acre campus
Moderately difficult entrance level, 72% of applicants were admitted

Freshmen *Admission:* 875 applied, 640 were accepted, 115 enrolled. *Test scores:* SAT verbal scores over 500: 79%; SAT math scores over 500: 78%; SAT verbal scores over 600: 25%; SAT math scores over 600: 20%; SAT verbal scores over 700: 5%; SAT math scores over 700: 5%.
Tuition and fees (2004–05): $18,715 (full-time). *Room and board:* $5390 (room only: $2170).
Financial Aid (All incoming freshmen): *Average need-based gift aid:* $10,899. *Average non-need based aid:* $7103. *Average aid to full-time undergraduates:* $14,594.
Athletic Department: *Director of Athletics:* Steve Wammer; Phone: 715-682-1244; Fax: 715-682-1248; E-mail: swammer@northland.edu. *Sports Information Director:* Rob Robinson; Phone: 715-682-1850; E-mail: rrobinson@northland.edu.

MEN'S COACHES
Baseball: Joel Barta; Phone: 715-682-1387; E-mail: jbarta@northland.edu.
Basketball: Kurt Soderberg; Phone: 715-682-1865.
Cross Country: Julie Gabert; Phone: 715-682-1395; E-mail: jgabert@northland.edu.
Ice Hockey: Dan Huntley; Phone: 715-682-1395; E-mail: dhuntley@northland.edu.
Soccer: Scott Mayforth; Phone: 715-682-1246; E-mail: smayforth@northland.edu.

WOMEN'S COACHES
Basketball: Rob Robinson; Phone: 715-682-1850; E-mail: rrobinson@northland.edu.
Cross Country: Julie Gabert; Phone: 715-682-1395; E-mail: jgabert@northland.edu.
Soccer: Scott Mayforth; Phone: 715-682-1246; E-mail: smayforth@northland.edu.

Softball: Steve Wammer; Phone: 715-682-1244; E-mail: swammer@northland.edu.
Volleyball: Angie Heifort; Phone: 715-682-1868; E-mail: aheifort@northland.edu.

NORTH PARK UNIVERSITY
Chicago, Illinois
Vikings ◆ NCAA III ◆ College Conference of Illinois and Wisconsin Conference ◆ http://www.northpark.edu/

Independent religious comprehensive, founded 1891, affiliated with Evangelical Covenant Church
Coed, 1,573 undergraduate students, 80% full-time, 62% women, 38% men
Urban 30-acre campus
Moderately difficult entrance level, 68% of applicants were admitted

Freshmen *Admission:* 1,068 applied, 791 were accepted, 320 enrolled. *Test scores:* SAT verbal scores over 500: 82%; SAT math scores over 500: 80%; SAT verbal scores over 600: 46%; SAT math scores over 600: 38%; SAT verbal scores over 700: 11%; SAT math scores over 700: 9%.
Tuition and fees (2004–05): $20,350 (full-time). *Room and board:* $6510.
Financial Aid (All incoming freshmen): *Average need-based gift aid:* $8200. *Average non-need based aid:* $6060. *Average aid to full-time undergraduates:* $11,575.
Athletic Department: *Director of Athletics:* Jack Surridge; Phone: 773-244-5685; Fax: 773-244-4952; E-mail: jsurridge@northpark.edu. *Sports Information Director:* Carrie Swenson; Phone: 773-244-5670; E-mail: cswenson1@northpark.edu.

MEN'S COACHES
Baseball: Steve Vandenbranden; Phone: 773-244-5675; E-mail: svandenbranden@northpark.edu.
Basketball: Rees Johnson; Phone: 773-244-5679; E-mail: pbrenegan@northpark.edu.
Cross Country: Emma Sandberg; Phone: 773-244-5689; E-mail: esandberg@northpark.edu.
Football: Robin Cooper; Phone: 773-244-5681; E-mail: rcooper@northpark.edu.
Golf: Paul Brenegan; Phone: 773-244-5651; E-mail: pbrenegan@northpark.edu.
Soccer: John Born; Phone: 773-244-5771; E-mail: jborn@northpark.edu.
Track and Field: Aleisha Morgan; Phone: 773-244-5678; E-mail: amorgan@northpark.edu.

WOMEN'S COACHES
Basketball: Jack Surridge; Phone: 773-244-5685; E-mail: jsurridge@northpark.edu.
Cross Country: Emma Sandberg; Phone: 773-244-5689; E-mail: esandberg@northpark.edu.
Golf: Paul Brenegan; Phone: 773-244-5651; E-mail: pbrenegan@northpark.edu.
Soccer: Erin Leinweber; Phone: 773-244-6251; E-mail: eleinweber-01@northpark.edu.
Softball: Dan Gooris; Phone: 773-244-5676; E-mail: dgooris@northpark.edu.
Track and Field: Aleisha Morgan; Phone: 773-244-5678; E-mail: amorgan@northpark.edu.
Volleyball: Sue Zimmer; Phone: 773-244-5673; E-mail: szimmer@northpark.edu.

NORTHWEST COLLEGE
Kirkland, Washington
Eagles ◆ NAIA ◆ Cascade Collegiate Conference ◆ http://www.nwcollege.edu/

Independent religious comprehensive, founded 1934, affiliated with Assemblies of God
Coed, 1,080 undergraduate students, 92% full-time, 62% women, 38% men
Suburban 56-acre campus with easy access to Seattle
Moderately difficult entrance level, 88% of applicants were admitted

Freshmen *Admission:* 357 applied, 320 were accepted, 174 enrolled. *Test scores:* SAT verbal scores over 500: 74%; SAT math scores over

Northwest College *(continued)*

500: 26%; SAT verbal scores over 600: 20%; SAT math scores over 600: 5%; SAT verbal scores over 700: 1%.
Tuition and fees (2004–05): $14,760 (full-time). *Room and board:* $6450.
Financial Aid (All incoming freshmen): *Average need-based gift aid:* $7631. *Average non-need based aid:* $7448. *Average aid to full-time undergraduates:* $11,128.
Athletic Department: *Director of Athletics:* Kristi Brodin; Phone: 425-889-5245; Fax: 425-889-5323; E-mail: kristi.brodin@ncag.edu. *Sports Information Director:* Shaun Kupferberg; Phone: 425-889-5341; E-mail: shaun.kupferberg@ncag.edu.

MEN'S COACHES
Basketball: John Van Dyke; Phone: 425-889-5275; E-mail: john.vandyke@ncag.edu.
Cross Country: Bill Taylor; Phone: 425-889-7785; E-mail: bill.taylor@ncag.edu.
Soccer: Gary McIntosh; Phone: 425-889-7790; E-mail: gary.mcintosh@ncag.edu.
Track and Field: Bill Taylor; Phone: 425-889-7785; E-mail: bill.taylor@ncag.edu.

WOMEN'S COACHES
Basketball: Lori Napier; Phone: 425-889-7795; E-mail: lori.napier@ncag.edu.
Cross Country: Bill Taylor; Phone: 425-889-7785; E-mail: bill.taylor@ncag.edu.
Track and Field: Bill Taylor; Phone: 425-889-7785; E-mail: bill.taylor@ncag.edu.
Volleyball: Shaun Kupferberg; Phone: 425-889-5341; E-mail: shaun.kupferberg@ncag.edu.

NORTHWESTERN COLLEGE
Orange City, Iowa

Red Raiders ◆ NAIA ◆ Great Plains Conference ◆ http://www.nwciowa.edu/

Independent religious 4-year, founded 1882, affiliated with Reformed Church in America
Coed, 1,285 undergraduate students, 95% full-time, 61% women, 39% men
Rural 45-acre campus
Moderately difficult entrance level, 80% of applicants were admitted

Freshmen *Admission:* 1,311 applied, 1,090 were accepted, 311 enrolled.
Tuition and fees (2003–04): $15,290 (full-time). *Room and board:* $4350 (room only: $1850).
Financial Aid (All incoming freshmen): *Average need-based gift aid:* $4997. *Average non-need based aid:* $1550. *Average aid to full-time undergraduates:* $13,534.
Athletic Department: *Director of Athletics:* Barry Brandt; Phone: 712-707-7280; Fax: 712-737-7290; E-mail: brandt@nwciowa.edu. *Sports Information Director:* Jen McAlpine; Phone: 712-707-7289; E-mail: jmcalpin@nwciowa.edu.

MEN'S COACHES
Baseball: Dave Nonnemacher; Phone: 712-707-7000; E-mail: baseball@nwciowa.edu.
Basketball: Kris Korver; Phone: 712-707-7000; E-mail: kkorver@nwciowa.edu.
Cross Country: Dale Thompson; Phone: 712-707-7000; E-mail: dalet@nwciowa.edu.
Football: Orv Otten; Phone: 712-707-7000; E-mail: otten@nwciowa.edu.
Golf: Mark Bloemendaal; Phone: 712-707-7000; E-mail: markb@nwciowa.edu.
Soccer: T.J. Buchholz; Phone: 712-707-7000; E-mail: tbuchhol@nwciowa.edu.
Track and Field: Mike Reed; Phone: 712-707-7000; E-mail: mreed@nwciowa.edu.
Wrestling: Paul Bartlett; Phone: 712-707-7000; E-mail: bartlett@nwciowa.edu.

WOMEN'S COACHES
Basketball: Earl Woudstra; Phone: 712-707-7000; E-mail: earl@nwciowa.edu.
Cross Country: Dale Thompson; Phone: 712-707-7000; E-mail: dalet@nwciowa.edu.

Golf: Harold Hoftyzer; Phone: 712-707-7000; E-mail: haroldh@nwciowa.edu.
Soccer: Tom Cliff; Phone: 712-707-7000; E-mail: tcliff@nwciowa.edu.
Softball: Melanie Mason; Phone: 712-707-7000; E-mail: mmason@nwciowa.edu.
Track and Field: Mike Reed; Phone: 712-707-7000; E-mail: mreed@nwciowa.edu.
Volleyball: Mike Meyer; Phone: 712-707-7000; E-mail: meyer@nwciowa.edu.

NORTHWESTERN COLLEGE
St. Paul, Minnesota

Eagles ◆ NAIA ◆ Upper Midwest Athletic Conference ◆ http://www.nwc.edu/

Independent nondenominational 4-year, founded 1902
Coed, 2,592 undergraduate students, 76% full-time, 63% women, 37% men
Suburban 100-acre campus
Moderately difficult entrance level, 93% of applicants were admitted

Freshmen *Admission:* 980 applied, 919 were accepted, 459 enrolled. *Test scores:* SAT verbal scores over 500: 74%; SAT math scores over 500: 77%; SAT verbal scores over 600: 48%; SAT math scores over 600: 39%; SAT verbal scores over 700: 22%; SAT math scores over 700: 8%.
Tuition and fees (2004–05): $18,370 (full-time). *Room and board:* $6020 (room only: $3300).
Financial Aid (All incoming freshmen): *Average need-based gift aid:* $9904. *Average non-need based aid:* $4422. *Average aid to full-time undergraduates:* $12,879.
Athletic Department: *Director of Athletics:* Matt Hill♂; Phone: 651-631-5362; Fax: 651-628-3350; E-mail: mbhill@nwc.edu. *Sports Information Director:* Corey Borchardt; Phone: 651-631-5363; E-mail: cpborchardt@nwc.edu.

MEN'S COACHES
Baseball: Dave Hieb; Phone: 651-631-5345; E-mail: dh1@nwc.edu.
Basketball: Tim Grosz; Phone: 651-631-5238; E-mail: tsg@nwc.edu.
Cross Country: Steve Thiessen; Phone: 651-631-5273; E-mail: st1@nwc.edu.
Football: Kirk Talley; Phone: 651-631-5283; E-mail: kat@nwc.edu.
Golf: Bill Aune; Phone: 651-631-5219; E-mail: bjaune@nwc.edu.
Soccer: Greg Wheaton; Phone: 651-631-5219; E-mail: athletics@nwc.edu.
Tennis: Sue Ek; Phone: 651-631-5327; E-mail: sde@nwc.edu.
Track and Field: Steve Thiessen; Phone: 651-631-5273; E-mail: st1@nwc.edu.

WOMEN'S COACHES
Basketball: Linda Schuck; Phone: 651-631-5219; E-mail: lss@nwc.edu.
Cross Country: Steve Thiessen; Phone: 651-631-5273; E-mail: st1@nwc.edu.
Soccer: Karin Meloch; Phone: 651-631-5219; E-mail: kjm@nwc.edu.
Softball: Tracy Cromer; Phone: 651-631-5219; E-mail: athletics@nwc.edu.
Tennis: Sue Ek; Phone: 651-631-5327; E-mail: sde@nwc.edu.
Track and Field: Steve Thiessen; Phone: 651-631-5273; E-mail: st1@nwc.edu.
Volleyball: Jill Peterson; Phone: 651-631-5219; E-mail: athletics@nwc.edu.

NORTHWESTERN OKLAHOMA STATE UNIVERSITY
Alva, Oklahoma

Rangers ◆ NAIA ◆ Central States Football Conference; Sooner Conference ◆ http://www.nwosu.edu/

State-supported comprehensive, founded 1897, part of Oklahoma State Regents for Higher Education
Coed, 1,874 undergraduate students, 73% full-time, 54% women, 46% men
Small-town 70-acre campus
Moderately difficult entrance level, 99% of applicants were admitted

Freshmen *Admission:* 525 applied, 522 were accepted, 313 enrolled.

Tuition and fees (2003–04): $2728 (resident), $6628 (nonresident). *Room and board:* $2720 (room only: $860).
Financial Aid (All incoming freshmen): *Average need-based gift aid:* $3112. *Average non-need based aid:* $1701. *Average aid to full-time undergraduates:* $3906.
Athletic Department: *Director of Athletics:* Milburn Barton; Phone: 580-327-8626; Fax: 580-327-8669; E-mail: mfbarton@nwosu.edu. *Sports Information Director:* Ryan Hintergardt; Phone: 580-327-8639; E-mail: rshintergardt@nwosu.edu.

MEN'S COACHES
Baseball: Joe Phillips; Phone: 580-327-8635; E-mail: jkphillips@nwosu.edu.
Basketball: Bob Battisti; Phone: 580-327-8632; E-mail: rfbattisti@nwosu.edu.
Cheerleading: Rhea Watson; Phone: 580-327-8627; E-mail: heyrhea@hotmail.com.
Cross Country: Phone: 580-327-8626.
Football: Garin Higgins; Phone: 580-327-8636; E-mail: ghhiggins@nwosu.edu.
Soccer: Steve Barrows; Phone: 580-327-8103; E-mail: sdbarrows@nwosu.edu.

WOMEN'S COACHES
Basketball: Todd Clark; Phone: 580-327-8634; E-mail: tqclark@nwosu.edu.
Cheerleading: Rhea Watson; Phone: 580-327-8627; E-mail: heyrhea@hotmail.com.
Cross Country: Phone: 580-327-8626.
Softball: Cody Hooper; Phone: 580-327-8102; E-mail: cwhooper@nwosu.edu.

NORTHWESTERN STATE UNIVERSITY OF LOUISIANA
Natchitoches, Louisiana
Demons ◆ NCAA I ◆ Southland Conference ◆ http://www.nsula.edu/

State-supported comprehensive, founded 1884, part of University of Louisiana System
Coed, 9,351 undergraduate students, 75% full-time, 66% women, 34% men
Small-town 916-acre campus
Noncompetitive entrance level, 98% of applicants were admitted

Freshmen *Admission:* 4,389 applied, 4,313 were accepted, 2,173 enrolled. *Test scores:* SAT verbal scores over 500: 57%; SAT math scores over 500: 48%; SAT verbal scores over 600: 19%; SAT math scores over 600: 21%; SAT verbal scores over 700: 2%; SAT math scores over 700: 1%.
Tuition and fees (2004–05): $3006 (resident), $9084 (nonresident). *Room and board:* $3326 (room only: $1850).
Financial Aid (All incoming freshmen): *Average need-based gift aid:* $2159. *Average non-need based aid:* $1789. *Average aid to full-time undergraduates:* $3002.
Athletic Department: *Director of Athletics:* Greg Burke; Phone: 318-357-5251; Fax: 318-357-4221; E-mail: burkeg@nsula.edu. *Sports Information Director:* Doug Ireland; Phone: 318-357-6467; E-mail: ireland@nsula.edu.

MEN'S COACHES
Baseball: Mitch Gaspard; Phone: 318-357-4139; E-mail: gaspardm@nsula.edu.
Basketball: Mike McConathy; Phone: 318-357-4274; E-mail: mikem@nsula.edu.
Football: Scott Stoker; Phone: 318-357-5252; E-mail: stokers@nsula.edu.
Track and Field: Leon Johnson; Phone: 318-357-4290; E-mail: nsutrack@nsula.edu.

WOMEN'S COACHES
Basketball: James Smith; Phone: 318-357-5891; E-mail: mandy@nsula.edu.
Soccer: Jimmy Mitchell; Phone: 318-357-4337; E-mail: jmitchell@soccermail.com.
Softball: Eileen Schmidt; Phone: 318-357-4234; E-mail: schmidte@nsula.edu.
Tennis: Willie Paz; Phone: 318-357-5251; E-mail: pazw@nsula.edu.

Track and Field: Dean Johnson; Phone: 318-357-4472; E-mail: nsutrack@nsula.edu.
Volleyball: Leigh Mullins; Phone: 318-357-4227; E-mail: northwestern_volleyball@hotmail.com.

NORTHWESTERN UNIVERSITY
Evanston, Illinois
Wildcats ◆ NCAA I ◆ Big Ten Conference
◆ http://www.northwestern.edu/

Independent university, founded 1851
Coed, 8,001 undergraduate students, 97% full-time, 53% women, 47% men
Suburban 250-acre campus with easy access to Chicago
Most difficult entrance level, 34% of applicants were admitted

Freshmen *Admission:* 14,137 applied, 4,702 were accepted, 1,941 enrolled. *Test scores:* SAT verbal scores over 500: 98%; SAT math scores over 500: 99%; SAT verbal scores over 600: 90%; SAT math scores over 600: 93%; SAT verbal scores over 700: 50%; SAT math scores over 700: 56%.
Tuition and fees (2004–05): $30,085 (full-time). *Room and board:* $9393 (room only: $5398).
Financial Aid (All incoming freshmen): *Average need-based gift aid:* $19,926. *Average non-need based aid:* $5750. *Average aid to full-time undergraduates:* $23,587.
Athletic Department: *Director of Athletics:* Mark Murphy; Phone: 847-491-8880; Fax: 847-491-4659; E-mail: mark-murphy@northwestern.edu. *Sports Information Director:* Mike Wolf; Phone: 847-491-7503; E-mail: mwolf@northwestern.edu.

MEN'S COACHES
Baseball: Paul Stevens; Phone: 847-491-4652; E-mail: p-stevens2@northwestern.edu.
Basketball: Bill Carmody; Phone: 847-491-7906; E-mail: bcarmo@northwestern.edu.
Cheerleading: Sarah Agne; Phone: 847-491-8880; E-mail: s-agne@northwestern.edu.
Diving: Tom Michael; Phone: 847-491-4276; E-mail: tom-michael@northwestern.edu.
Football: Randy Walker; Phone: 847-491-7274; E-mail: r-walker2@northwestern.edu.
Golf: Pat Goss; Phone: 847-491-4642; E-mail: p-goss@northwestern.edu.
Soccer: Tim Lenahan; Phone: 847-467-1312; E-mail: t-lenahan@northwestern.edu.
Swimming: Bob Groseth; Phone: 847-491-4276; E-mail: r-groseth@northwestern.edu.
Tennis: Paul Torricelli; Phone: 847-491-4644; E-mail: torch@northwestern.edu.
Wrestling: Tim Cysewski; Phone: 847-491-4799; E-mail: wrestling@northwestern.edu.

WOMEN'S COACHES
Basketball: June Olkowski; Phone: 847-491-5709; E-mail: j-olkowski@northwestern.edu.
Cheerleading: Sarah Agne; Phone: 847-491-8880; E-mail: s-agne@northwestern.edu.
Cross Country: Amy Tush; Phone: 847-491-4797; E-mail: a-tush@northwestern.edu.
Diving: Tom Michael; Phone: 847-491-4276; E-mail: tom-michael@northwestern.edu.
Field Hockey: Marisa Didio; Phone: 847-491-4641; E-mail: m-didio@northwestern.edu.
Golf: Chris Regenberg; Phone: 847-491-4795; E-mail: c-regenberg@northwestern.edu.
Lacrosse: Kelly Amonte-Hiller; Phone: 847-491-2796; E-mail: h-amonte@northwestern.edu.
Soccer: Jenny Haigh; Phone: 847-467-3151; E-mail: j-haigh@northwestern.edu.
Softball: Kate Drohan; Phone: 847-491-4650; E-mail: k-drohan@northwestern.edu.
Swimming: Jimmy Tierney; Phone: 847-491-4433; E-mail: j-tierney@northwestern.edu.
Tennis: Claire Pollard; Phone: 847-491-4643; E-mail: c-pollard@northwestern.edu.
Volleyball: Keylor Chan; Phone: 847-491-4638; E-mail: keychan@northwestern.edu.

NORTHWEST MISSOURI STATE UNIVERSITY
Maryville, Missouri

Bearcats ◆ NCAA II ◆ Mid-America Intercollegiate Conference ◆ http://www.nwmissouri.edu/

State-supported comprehensive, founded 1905, part of Missouri Coordinating Board for Higher Education
Coed, 5,601 undergraduate students, 88% full-time, 57% women, 43% men
Small-town 240-acre campus with easy access to Kansas City
Moderately difficult entrance level, 87% of applicants were admitted

Freshmen *Admission:* 2,764 applied, 2,394 were accepted, 1,198 enrolled.
Tuition and fees (2003–04): $5025 (resident), $8535 (nonresident). *Room and board:* $5042.
Financial Aid (All incoming freshmen): *Average need-based gift aid:* $2506. *Average non-need based aid:* $1699. *Average aid to full-time undergraduates:* $5709.
Athletic Department: *Director of Athletics:* Bob Boerigter; Phone: 660-562-1306; Fax: 660-562-1493; E-mail: bboer@mail.nwmissouri.edu. *Sports Information Director:* Andy Seeley; Phone: 660-562-1118; E-mail: nwsid@mail.nwmissouri.edu.

MEN'S COACHES
Baseball: Darin Loe; Phone: 660-562-1352; E-mail: dloe@mail.nwmissouri.edu.
Basketball: Steve Tappmeyer; Phone: 660-562-1309; E-mail: stappme@mail.nwmissouri.edu.
Cheerleading: Chris Andrews; Phone: 660-562-1581; E-mail: andrews@mail.nwmissouri.edu.
Cross Country: Richard Alsup; Phone: 660-562-1327; E-mail: ralsup@mail.nwmissouri.edu.
Football: Mel Tjeerdsma; Phone: 660-562-1311; E-mail: coacht@mail.nwmissouri.edu.
Tennis: Mark Rosewell; Phone: 660-562-1312; E-mail: mrosewe@mail.nwmissouri.edu.
Track and Field: Richard Alsup; Phone: 660-562-1327; E-mail: ralsup@mail.nwmissouri.edu.

WOMEN'S COACHES
Basketball: Gene Steinmeyer; Phone: 660-562-1299; E-mail: gstein@mail.nwmissouri.edu.
Cheerleading: Chris Andrews; Phone: 660-562-1581; E-mail: andrews@mail.nwmissouri.edu.
Cross Country: Vicki Wooten; Phone: 660-562-1303; E-mail: vwooton@mail.nwmissouri.edu.
Soccer: Tracy Cross; Phone: 660-562-1302; E-mail: tjcross@mail.nwmissouri.edu.
Softball: Susan Anderson; Phone: 660-562-1783; E-mail: punzos@mail.nwmissouri.edu.
Tennis: Mark Rosewell; Phone: 660-562-1312; E-mail: mrosewe@mail.nwmissouri.edu.
Track and Field: Vicki Wooten; Phone: 660-562-1303; E-mail: vwooton@mail.nwmissouri.edu.
Volleyball: Lori DeJongh-Slight; Phone: 660-562-1782; E-mail: lslight@mail.nwmissouri.edu.

NORTHWEST NAZARENE UNIVERSITY
Nampa, Idaho

Crusaders ◆ NCAA II ◆ Great Northwest Athletic Conference ◆ http://www.nnu.edu/

Independent religious comprehensive, founded 1913, affiliated with Church of the Nazarene
Coed, 1,156 undergraduate students, 94% full-time, 56% women, 44% men
Small-town 85-acre campus
Moderately difficult entrance level, 70% of applicants were admitted

Freshmen *Admission:* 814 applied, 571 were accepted, 283 enrolled.
Tuition and fees (2004–05): $16,570 (full-time). *Room and board:* $4630.

Financial Aid (All incoming freshmen): *Average need-based gift aid:* $2564. *Average non-need based aid:* $7813. *Average aid to full-time undergraduates:* $12,231.
Athletic Department: *Director of Athletics:* Rich Sanders; Phone: 208-467-8825; Fax: 208-467-8396; E-mail: rfsanders@nnu.edu. *Sports Information Director:* Craig Stensgaard; Phone: 208-467-8856; E-mail: cmstensgaard@nnu.edu.

MEN'S COACHES
Baseball: Tim Onofrei; Phone: 208-467-8351; E-mail: teonofrei@nnu.edu.
Basketball: Ed Weidenbach; Phone: 208-467-8400; E-mail: ejweidenbach@nnu.edu.
Cross Country: John Spatz; Phone: 208-467-8247; E-mail: jtspatz@nnu.edu.
Golf: Craig Stensgaard; Phone: 208-467-8856; E-mail: cmstensgaard@nnu.edu.
Track and Field: John Spatz; Phone: 208-467-8247; E-mail: jtspatz@nnu.edu.

WOMEN'S COACHES
Basketball: Kelli Kronberg; Phone: 208-467-8544; E-mail: kakronberger@nnu.edu.
Cross Country: John Spatz; Phone: 208-467-8247; E-mail: jtspatz@nnu.edu.
Soccer: Jamie Lindvall; Phone: 208-467-8862; E-mail: jllindvall@nnu.edu.
Softball: Julie Coert; Phone: 208-467-8868; E-mail: jrcoert@nnu.edu.
Track and Field: John Spatz; Phone: 208-467-8247; E-mail: jtspatz@nnu.edu.
Volleyball: Deb Bradburn; Phone: 208-467-8857; E-mail: dsbradburn@nnu.edu.

NORTHWOOD UNIVERSITY
Midland, Michigan

Timberwolves ◆ NCAA II ◆ Great Lakes Intercollegiate Conference ◆ http://www.northwood.edu/

Independent comprehensive, founded 1959
Coed, 3,472 undergraduate students, 65% full-time, 46% women, 54% men
Small-town 434-acre campus
Moderately difficult entrance level, 87% of applicants were admitted

Freshmen *Admission:* 1,387 applied, 1,200 were accepted, 394 enrolled. *Test scores:* SAT verbal scores over 500: 19%; SAT math scores over 500: 43%; SAT verbal scores over 600: 4%; SAT math scores over 600: 11%.
Tuition and fees (2003–04): $13,995 (full-time). *Room and board:* $6270.
Financial Aid (All incoming freshmen): *Average need-based gift aid:* $4912. *Average non-need based aid:* $4415. *Average aid to full-time undergraduates:* $11,722.
Athletic Department: *Director of Athletics:* Pat Riepma; Phone: 989-837-4385; Fax: 989-837-4484; E-mail: riepma@northwood.edu. *Sports Information Director:* Travis McCurdy; Phone: 989-837-4239; E-mail: mccurdyt@northwood.edu.

MEN'S COACHES
Baseball: Joe Dibenedetto; Phone: 989-837-4427; E-mail: joedi@northwood.edu.
Basketball: Bob Taylor; Phone: 989-837-4383; E-mail: btaylor@northwood.edu.
Cheerleading: Jukie Felske; Phone: 989-837-4178; E-mail: felske@northwood.edu.
Cross Country: Scott Cook; Phone: 989-837-4473; E-mail: cooksm@northwood.edu.
Football: Pat Riepma; Phone: 989-837-4385; E-mail: riepma@northwood.edu.
Golf: Dave Turner; Phone: 989-832-4837; E-mail: turnerda@northwood.edu.
Soccer: Doug Carter; Phone: 989-832-4759; E-mail: dccarter@northwood.edu.
Tennis: Zane Colestock; Phone: 989-832-4386; E-mail: zane@northwood.edu.
Track and Field: Scott Cook; Phone: 989-837-4473; E-mail: cooksm@northwood.edu.

WOMEN'S COACHES
Basketball: Kelli Parker; Phone: 989-832-4384; E-mail: kparker@northwood.edu.

Cheerleading: Jukie Felske; Phone: 989-837-4178; E-mail: felske@northwood.edu.

Cross Country: Scott Cook; Phone: 989-837-4473; E-mail: cooksm@northwood.edu.

Golf: Dave Turner; Phone: 989-832-6187; E-mail: turnerda@northwood.edu.

Soccer: Doug Carter; Phone: 989-832-4759; E-mail: dccarter@northwood.edu.

Softball: Heather Bruder; Phone: 989-832-4380; E-mail: bruder@northwood.edu.

Tennis: Zane Colestock; Phone: 989-832-4386; E-mail: zane@northwood.edu.

Track and Field: Scott Cook; Phone: 989-837-4473; E-mail: cooksm@northwood.edu.

Volleyball: Jeff Williams; Phone: 989-832-4390; E-mail: jeffw@northwood.edu.

NORTHWOOD UNIVERSITY, FLORIDA CAMPUS

West Palm Beach, Florida

Seahawks ◆ NAIA ◆ Florida Sun Conference ◆ http://www.northwood.edu/

Independent 4-year, founded 1982
Coed, 959 undergraduate students, 81% full-time, 46% women, 54% men
Suburban 90-acre campus with easy access to Miami
Moderately difficult entrance level, 61% of applicants were admitted

Freshmen *Admission:* 878 applied, 532 were accepted, 156 enrolled. *Test scores:* SAT verbal scores over 500: 33%; SAT math scores over 500: 45%; SAT verbal scores over 600: 3%; SAT math scores over 600: 13%.
Tuition and fees (2003–04): $13,995 (full-time). *Room and board:* $6840 (room only: $3420).
Financial Aid (All incoming freshmen): *Average need-based gift aid:* $9183. *Average non-need based aid:* $4699. *Average aid to full-time undergraduates:* $12,884.
Athletic Department: *Director of Athletics:* Rick Smoliak; Phone: 561-478-5552; Fax: 561-478-5593; E-mail: smoliak@northwood.edu. *Sports Information Director:* Bill Caudill; Phone: 561-478-5552; E-mail: bcaudill@northwood.edu.

MEN'S COACHES

Baseball: Rick Smoliak; Phone: 561-478-5593; E-mail: smoliak@northwood.edu.

Golf: Bill Caudill; Phone: 561-478-5593; E-mail: bcaudill@northwood.edu.

Soccer: Ty Brewer; Phone: 561-478-5593; E-mail: brewer@northwood.edu.

Tennis: Perry Sinett; Phone: 561-478-5593.

WOMEN'S COACHES

Golf: Bill Caudill; Phone: 561-478-5593; E-mail: bcaudill@northwood.edu.

Soccer: John Webb; Phone: 561-478-5593; E-mail: northwoodcoach@aol.com.

Softball: Katie Mahoney; Phone: 561-478-5593; E-mail: kmahoney@northwood.edu.

Tennis: Perry Sinett; Phone: 561-478-5593.

Volleyball: Kathy Esarey; Phone: 561-478-5593; E-mail: esareyk@northwood.edu.

NORTHWOOD UNIVERSITY, TEXAS CAMPUS

Cedar Hill, Texas

Knights ◆ NAIA ◆ Red River Conference ◆ http://www.northwood.edu/

Independent 4-year, founded 1966
Coed, 1,117 undergraduate students, 78% full-time, 59% women, 41% men
Small-town 360-acre campus with easy access to Dallas
Moderately difficult entrance level, 67% of applicants were admitted

Freshmen *Admission:* 864 applied, 508 were accepted, 188 enrolled. *Test scores:* SAT verbal scores over 500: 27%; SAT math scores over 500: 31%; SAT verbal scores over 600: 2%; SAT math scores over 600: 5%; SAT math scores over 700: 1%.
Tuition and fees (2003–04): $13,995 (full-time). *Room and board:* $5910 (room only: $3120).
Financial Aid (All incoming freshmen): *Average need-based gift aid:* $9211. *Average non-need based aid:* $4607. *Average aid to full-time undergraduates:* $11,609.
Athletic Department: *Director of Athletics:* Shawn Winget; Phone: 972-291-5423; Fax: 972-291-0662; E-mail: winget@northwood.edu.

MEN'S COACHES

Baseball: Pat Malcheski; Phone: 972-293-5493; E-mail: malchesk@northwood.edu.

Cross Country: Shawn Winget; Phone: 972-293-5423; E-mail: winget@northwood.edu.

Golf: Gary Belt; Phone: 972-293-5428; E-mail: belt@northwood.edu.

Soccer: Scott Turner; Phone: 972-293-5481; E-mail: sturner@northwood.edu.

Track and Field: Shawn Winget; Phone: 972-293-5423; E-mail: winget@northwood.edu.

WOMEN'S COACHES

Cross Country: Shawn Winget; Phone: 972-293-5423; E-mail: winget@northwood.edu.

Golf: Gary Belt; Phone: 972-293-5428; E-mail: belt@northwood.edu.

Soccer: Scott Turner; Phone: 972-293-5481; E-mail: sturner@northwood.edu.

Softball: Denise Panice; Phone: 972-293-5483; E-mail: paniced@northwood.edu.

Track and Field: Shawn Winget; Phone: 972-293-5423; E-mail: winget@northwood.edu.

NORWICH UNIVERSITY

Northfield, Vermont

Cadets ◆ NCAA III ◆ Freedom Football Conference; Great Northeast Athletic Conference; New England College Wrestling Conference ◆ http://www.norwich.edu/

Independent comprehensive, founded 1819
Coed, 2,129 undergraduate students
Small-town 1,125-acre campus with easy access to Burlington
Moderately difficult entrance level, 91% of applicants were admitted

Freshmen *Admission:* 1,472 applied, 1,340 were accepted. *Test scores:* SAT verbal scores over 500: 50%; SAT math scores over 500: 52%; SAT verbal scores over 600: 15%; SAT math scores over 600: 15%; SAT verbal scores over 700: 3%; SAT math scores over 700: 1%.
Tuition and fees (2003–04): $18,210 (full-time). *Room and board:* $6722.
Athletic Department: *Director of Athletics:* Tony Mariano; Phone: 802-485-2230; Fax: 802-485-2234; E-mail: tmariano@norwich.edu. *Sports Information Director:* David Caspole; Phone: 802-485-2160; E-mail: dcaspole@norwich.edu.

MEN'S COACHES

Baseball: Bill Barrale; Phone: 802-485-2233; E-mail: wbarrale@norwich.edu.

Basketball: Paul Booth; Phone: 802-485-2239; E-mail: pbooth@norwich.edu.

Cross Country: Chris Walczak; Phone: 802-485-2230; E-mail: marathoner68@norwich.edu.

Norwich University *(continued)*

Diving: Steve Looke; Phone: 802-485-2241; E-mail: slooke@norwich.edu.

Football: Mike Yesalonia; Phone: 802-485-2238; E-mail: myesalon@norwich.edu.

Ice Hockey: Mike McShane; Phone: 802-485-2242; E-mail: mmcshane@norwich.edu.

Lacrosse: Marc Klaiman; Phone: 802-485-2243; E-mail: mklaiman@norwich.edu.

Soccer: James Franklin; Phone: 802-485-2240; E-mail: jfrankli@norwich.edu.

Swimming: Steve Looke; Phone: 802-485-2241; E-mail: slooke@norwich.edu.

Tennis: James Franklin; Phone: 802-485-2240; E-mail: jfrankli@norwich.edu.

Wrestling: Rich Hasenfus; Phone: 802-485-2248; E-mail: hasenfus@norwich.edu.

WOMEN'S COACHES

Basketball: Steve Lanpher; Phone: 802-485-2229; E-mail: slanpher@norwich.edu.

Cross Country: Chris Walczak; Phone: 802-485-2230; E-mail: marathoner68@norwich.edu.

Diving: Steve Looke; Phone: 802-485-2241; E-mail: slooke@norwich.edu.

Soccer: Steve Looke; Phone: 802-485-2241; E-mail: slooke@norwich.edu.

Softball: Dennis Tyner; Phone: 802-485-2267; E-mail: dtyner@norwich.edu.

Swimming: Steve Looke; Phone: 802-485-2241; E-mail: slooke@norwich.edu.

NOTRE DAME COLLEGE
South Euclid, Ohio

Falcons ◆ NAIA ◆ American Mideast Conference ◆ http://www.notredamecollege.edu/

Independent Roman Catholic comprehensive, founded 1922
Coed, 766 undergraduate students, 43% full-time, 76% women, 24% men
Suburban 53-acre campus with easy access to Cleveland
Moderately difficult entrance level, 42% of applicants were admitted

Freshmen *Admission:* 138 applied, 65 were accepted, 64 enrolled. *Test scores:* SAT verbal scores over 500: 80%; SAT math scores over 500: 75%; SAT verbal scores over 600: 30%; SAT math scores over 600: 25%.
Tuition and fees (2003–04): $17,490 (full-time). *Room and board:* $6200 (room only: $3114).
Financial Aid (All incoming freshmen): *Average need-based gift aid:* $6011. *Average aid to full-time undergraduates:* $17,843.
Athletic Department: *Director of Athletics:* Susan Hlavacek; Phone: 216-373-5306; Fax: 216-373-5400; E-mail: shlavacek@ndc.edu. *Sports Information Director:* Kristy Booher; Phone: 216-373-5306; E-mail: kbooher@ndc.edu.

MEN'S COACHES

Basketball: Kevin Bille; Phone: 216-373-5306; E-mail: kbille@ndc.edu.
Cross Country: Patrick Bindis; Phone: 216-373-5306; E-mail: pbindis@ndc.edu.
Soccer: Michael McBride; Phone: 216-373-5306; E-mail: mmcbride@ndc.edu.
Tennis: Michael McBride; Phone: 216-373-5306; E-mail: mmcbride@ndc.edu.
Track and Field: Patrick Bindis; Phone: 216-373-5306; E-mail: pbindis@ndc.edu.

WOMEN'S COACHES

Basketball: Dick Deasy; Phone: 216-373-5306; E-mail: ddeasy@ndc.edu.
Cross Country: Patrick Bindis; Phone: 216-373-5306; E-mail: pbindis@ndc.edu.
Soccer: Mike Shiels; Phone: 216-373-5306; E-mail: mshiels@ndc.edu.
Softball: Ali Brian; Phone: 216-373-5306; E-mail: abrian@ndc.edu.
Track and Field: Patrick Bindis; Phone: 216-373-5306; E-mail: pbindis@ndc.edu.
Volleyball: Mark Ridley; Phone: 216-373-5306; E-mail: mridley@ndc.edu.

NOTRE DAME DE NAMUR UNIVERSITY
Belmont, California

Argonauts ◆ NAIA ◆ California Pacific Conference ◆ http://www.ndnu.edu/

Independent Roman Catholic comprehensive, founded 1851
Coed, 988 undergraduate students, 65% full-time, 68% women, 32% men
Suburban 80-acre campus with easy access to San Francisco
Moderately difficult entrance level, 86% of applicants were admitted

Freshmen *Admission:* 537 applied, 477 were accepted, 191 enrolled. *Test scores:* SAT verbal scores over 500: 44%; SAT math scores over 500: 53%; SAT verbal scores over 600: 9%; SAT math scores over 600: 15%; SAT verbal scores over 700: 2%; SAT math scores over 700: 1%.
Tuition and fees (2004–05): $21,500 (full-time). *Room and board:* $9650.
Athletic Department: *Director of Athletics:* Doug Locker; Phone: 650-508-3685; Fax: 650-508-3641; E-mail: dlocker@ndnu.edu. *Sports Information Director:* Stephanie Duke; Phone: 650-508-3690; E-mail: sduke@ndnu.edu.

MEN'S COACHES

Basketball: George Puou; Phone: 650-508-3655; E-mail: gpuou@ndnu.edu.
Cross Country: Jesse Torres; Phone: 650-508-3772; E-mail: jtorres@ndnu.edu.
Golf: George Puou; Phone: 650-508-3655; E-mail: gpuou@ndnu.edu.
Lacrosse: Joe Romano; Phone: 650-508-3589; E-mail: jromano@ndnu.edu.
Soccer: Joe Silveira; Phone: 650-508-3687; E-mail: jsilveira@ndnu.edu.

WOMEN'S COACHES

Basketball: Stephanie Duke; Phone: 650-508-3690; E-mail: sduke@ndnu.edu.
Cross Country: Jesse Torres; Phone: 650-508-3772; E-mail: jtorres@ndnu.edu.
Golf: George Puou; Phone: 650-508-3655; E-mail: gpuou@ndnu.edu.
Soccer: Joe Silveira; Phone: 650-508-3687; E-mail: jsilveira@ndnu.edu.
Softball: Steve Rianda; Phone: 650-508-3654; E-mail: srianda@ndnu.edu.
Volleyball: Devin Grant; Phone: 650-508-3688; E-mail: dgrant@ndnu.edu.

NOVA SOUTHEASTERN UNIVERSITY
Fort Lauderdale, Florida

Knights ◆ NCAA II ◆ Sunshine State Conference ◆ http://www.nova.edu/

Independent university, founded 1964
Coed, 5,223 undergraduate students, 60% full-time, 75% women, 25% men
Suburban 300-acre campus
Moderately difficult entrance level, 6% of applicants were admitted

Freshmen *Admission:* 1,550 applied, 993 were accepted, 393 enrolled. *Test scores:* SAT verbal scores over 500: 43%; SAT math scores over 500: 54%; SAT verbal scores over 600: 9%; SAT math scores over 600: 17%; SAT verbal scores over 700: 1%; SAT math scores over 700: 3%.
Tuition and fees (2003–04): $15,220 (full-time). *Room and board:* $8126 (room only: $5662).
Financial Aid (All incoming freshmen): *Average need-based gift aid:* $9211. *Average non-need based aid:* $11,655. *Average aid to full-time undergraduates:* $15,197.
Athletic Department: *Director of Athletics:* Michael Mominey; Phone: 954-262-8252; Fax: 954-262-3926; E-mail: mominey@nsu.nova.edu. *Sports Information Director:* Jennifer Meriam; Phone: 954-262-5355.

MEN'S COACHES

Baseball: Michael Mominey; Phone: 954-262-8252; E-mail: mominey@nsu.nova.edu.
Basketball: Tony McAndrews; Phone: 954-262-8263.

Golf: Duke Donahue; Phone: 954-262-8268; E-mail: ddonahue@nsu. nova.edu.
Soccer: Joe DePalo; Phone: 954-262-8250; E-mail: depalog@nsu.nova. edu.

WOMEN'S COACHES
Basketball: Marilyn Rule; Phone: 954-262-8078; E-mail: rulem@nsu. nova.edu.
Cross Country: Shannon Cain; Phone: 954-262-8266; E-mail: cain@nsu. nova.edu.
Golf: Duke Donahue; Phone: 954-262-8268; E-mail: ddonahue@nsu. nova.edu.
Soccer: Mike Goodrich; Phone: 954-262-3926; E-mail: goodm@nsu. nova.edu.
Softball: Lesa Bonee; Phone: 954-262-3926; E-mail: bonee@nsu.nova. edu.
Volleyball: Lisa Rembe; Phone: 954-262-8250; E-mail: rembe@nsu. nova.edu.

NYACK COLLEGE
Nyack, New York

The Purple Pride ◆ NCAA II ◆ Central Atlantic Collegiate Conference ◆ http://www.nyackcollege.edu/

Independent religious comprehensive, founded 1882, affiliated with The Christian and Missionary Alliance
Coed, 2,069 undergraduate students, 86% full-time, 60% women, 40% men
Suburban 102-acre campus with easy access to New York City
Moderately difficult entrance level

Freshmen *Admission:* 295 enrolled. *Test scores:* SAT verbal scores over 500: 40%; SAT math scores over 500: 35%; SAT verbal scores over 600: 14%; SAT math scores over 600: 8%; SAT verbal scores over 700: 1%; SAT math scores over 700: %.
Tuition and fees (2004–05): $14,790 (full-time). *Room and board:* $7250.
Financial Aid (All incoming freshmen): *Average need-based gift aid:* $8609. *Average non-need based aid:* $5388. *Average aid to full-time under-graduates:* $12,039.
Athletic Department: *Director of Athletics:* Keith Davie; Phone: 845-358-1710; Fax: 845-353-2147. *Sports Information Director:* Randy Bowman; Phone: 845-358-1710.

MEN'S COACHES
Baseball: Jason Beck; Phone: 845-358-1710.
Basketball: John Jones; Phone: 845-358-1710.
Cheerleading: Jen Delmanto; Phone: 845-358-1710.
Cross Country: Anita Reimer; Phone: 845-358-1710.
Golf: Randy Bowman; Phone: 845-358-1710.
Soccer: Keith Davie; Phone: 845-358-1710.

WOMEN'S COACHES
Basketball: Josh Thompson; Phone: 845-358-1710.
Cheerleading: Jen Delmanto; Phone: 845-358-1710.
Cross Country: Anita Reimer; Phone: 845-358-1710.
Soccer: Randy Bowman; Phone: 845-358-1710.
Softball: Ernie Armoogan; Phone: 845-358-1710.
Volleyball: Madaline Toliver; Phone: 845-358-1710.

OAKLAND CITY UNIVERSITY
Oakland City, Indiana

(M) Mighty Oaks (W) Lady Oaks ◆ NCAA II ◆ Independent ◆ http://www.oak.edu/

Independent General Baptist comprehensive, founded 1885
Coed, 1,486 undergraduate students, 82% full-time, 53% women, 47% men
Rural 20-acre campus
Minimally difficult entrance level, 99% of applicants were admitted

Freshmen *Admission:* 339 applied, 334 were accepted, 319 enrolled. *Test scores:* SAT verbal scores over 500: 29%; SAT math scores over 500: 36%; SAT math scores over 600: 10%.

Tuition and fees (2004–05): $12,920 (full-time). *Room and board:* $4800 (room only: $1550).
Athletic Department: *Director of Athletics:* Mike Sandifar; Phone: 812-749-1290; Fax: 812-749-1291; E-mail: msandifar@oak.edu.

MEN'S COACHES
Baseball: T. Ray Fletcher; Phone: 812-749-1576.
Basketball: Mike Sandifar; Phone: 812-749-1290; E-mail: msandifar@ oak.edu.
Cheerleading: Stephanie Powell; Phone: 812-749-1264; E-mail: spowell@oak.edu.
Cross Country: Jason Mayes; Phone: 812-749-1264; E-mail: jmayes@ oak.edu.
Golf: T-Ray Fletcher; Phone: 812-749-1264; E-mail: tfletche@oak.edu.
Soccer: Matt Baehr; Phone: 812-749-1584; E-mail: mbaehr@oak.edu.

WOMEN'S COACHES
Basketball: Charlie Brauser; Phone: 812-749-1586.
Cheerleading: Stephanie Powell; Phone: 812-749-1264; E-mail: spowell@oak.edu.
Cross Country: Jason Mayes; Phone: 812-749-1264; E-mail: jmayes@ oak.edu.
Golf: Patti Buchta; Phone: 812-749-1265; E-mail: pbuchta@oak.edu.
Soccer: Kevin Botterill; Phone: 812-749-1266; E-mail: kbotterill@oak. edu.
Softball: Patti Buchta; Phone: 812-749-1265; E-mail: pbuchta@oak.edu.
Volleyball: Mary Baehr; Phone: 812-749-1542; E-mail: mkbaehr@oak. edu.

OAKLAND UNIVERSITY
Rochester, Michigan

Golden Grizzlies ◆ NCAA I ◆ Mid-Continent Conference ◆ http://www.oakland.edu/

State-supported university, founded 1957
Coed, 12,958 undergraduate students, 72% full-time, 62% women, 38% men
Suburban 1,444-acre campus with easy access to Detroit
Moderately difficult entrance level, 76% of applicants were admitted

Freshmen *Admission:* 6,321 applied, 5,079 were accepted, 2,101 enrolled.
Tuition and fees (2003–04): $5260 (resident), $11,954 (nonresident). *Room and board:* $5540.
Financial Aid (All incoming freshmen): *Average need-based gift aid:* $3389. *Average non-need based aid:* $3081. *Average aid to full-time under-graduates:* $5470.
Athletic Department: *Director of Athletics:* Jack Mehl; Phone: 248-370-3190; Fax: 248-370-4056; E-mail: mehl@oakland.edu. *Sports Information Director:* Phil Hess; Phone: 248-370-4008; E-mail: hess@ oakland.edu.

MEN'S COACHES
Baseball: Mark Avery; Phone: 248-370-4059; E-mail: markavery@ comcast.net.
Basketball: Greg Kampe; Phone: 248-370-4005; E-mail: kampe@ oakland.edu.
Cheerleading: Teri Bossi; Phone: 248-370-3190; E-mail: teri5177@ comcast.net.
Cross Country: Paul Rice; Phone: 248-370-3107; E-mail: oucc1@aol. com.
Diving: Pete Hovland; Phone: 248-370-4001; E-mail: hovland@ oakland.edu.
Golf: Dave Dewulf; Phone: 248-370-3190; E-mail: dkdwulf@aol.com.
Soccer: Gary Parsons; Phone: 248-370-4007; E-mail: parsons@ oakland.edu.
Swimming: Pete Hovland; Phone: 248-370-4001; E-mail: hovland@ oakland.edu.

WOMEN'S COACHES
Basketball: Eileen Shea-Hiliard; Phone: 248-370-4006; E-mail: ehilliar@ oakland.edu.
Cheerleading: Teri Bossi; Phone: 248-370-3190; E-mail: teri5177@ comcast.net.
Cross Country: Paul Rice; Phone: 248-370-3107; E-mail: oucc1@aol. com.
Diving: Pete Hovland; Phone: 248-370-4001; E-mail: hovland@ oakland.edu.
Golf: Dave Dewulf; Phone: 248-370-3190; E-mail: dkdwulf@aol.com.

Oakland University *(continued)*

Soccer: Nick O'Shea; Phone: 248-370-4009; E-mail: nkoshea@oakland.edu.
Softball: Mike Tomlinson; Phone: 248-370-3103; E-mail: miketomlinson22@msn.com.
Swimming: Pete Hovland; Phone: 248-370-4001; E-mail: hovland@oakland.edu.
Tennis: Heather Redshaw; Phone: 248-370-3105; E-mail: shredsh@juno.com.
Volleyball: David Schmidlin; Phone: 248-370-4057; E-mail: schmidli@oakland.edu.

OBERLIN COLLEGE
Oberlin, Ohio

Yeomen ◆ NCAA III ◆ North Coast Athletic Conference ◆ http://www.oberlin.edu/

Independent comprehensive, founded 1833
Coed, 2,883 undergraduate students, 97% full-time, 55% women, 45% men
Small-town 440-acre campus with easy access to Cleveland
Very difficult entrance level, 36% of applicants were admitted

Freshmen *Admission:* 5,983 applied, 2,159 were accepted, 764 enrolled. *Test scores:* SAT verbal scores over 500: 98%; SAT math scores over 500: 97%; SAT verbal scores over 600: 86%; SAT math scores over 600: 79%; SAT verbal scores over 700: 43%; SAT math scores over 700: 30%.
Tuition and fees (2003–04): $29,688 (full-time). *Room and board:* $7250 (room only: $3800).
Financial Aid (All incoming freshmen): *Average need-based gift aid:* $17,622. *Average non-need based aid:* $12,506. *Average aid to full-time undergraduates:* $22,093.
Athletic Department: *Director of Athletics:* vin Lananna; Phone: 440-775-6401; Fax: 440-775-8597; E-mail: vin.lananna@oberlin.edu. *Sports Information Director:* Eric Lahetta; Phone: 440-775-8502; E-mail: eric.lahetta@oberlin.edu.

MEN'S COACHES
Baseball: Eric Lahetta; Phone: 440-775-8502; E-mail: eric.lahetta@oberlin.edu.
Basketball: Frank Dobbs; Phone: 440-775-8507; E-mail: frank.dobbs@oberlin.edu.
Cross Country: Jason Hudson; Phone: 440-775-8510; E-mail: jason.hudson@oberlin.edu.
Diving: Aaron Hillyer; Phone: 440-775-8501; E-mail: aaron.hillyer@hotmail.com.
Football: Jeff Ramsey; Phone: 440-775-8968; E-mail: jeff.ramsey@oberlin.edu.
Golf: Blake New; Phone: 440-775-8506; E-mail: blake.new@oberlin.edu.
Lacrosse: Rob Oldham; Phone: 440-775-8516; E-mail: rob.oldham@oberlin.edu.
Soccer: Blake New; Phone: 440-775-8506; E-mail: blake.new@oberlin.edu.
Swimming: Dick Michaels; Phone: 440-775-8501; E-mail: dick.michaels@oberlin.edu.
Tennis: Don Husinger; Phone: 440-775-8508; E-mail: don.hunsinger@oberlin.edu.
Track and Field: Jason Hudson; Phone: 440-775-8510; E-mail: jason.hudson@oberlin.edu.

WOMEN'S COACHES
Basketball: Christa Champion; Phone: 440-775-8546; E-mail: christa.champion@oberlin.edu.
Cross Country: Jason Hudson; Phone: 440-775-8510; E-mail: jason.hudson@oberlin.edu.
Diving: Aaron Hillyer; Phone: 440-775-8501; E-mail: aaron.hillyer@hotmail.com.
Field Hockey: Deb Ranieri; Phone: 440-775-8511; E-mail: deb.ranieri@oberlin.edu.
Golf: Blake New; Phone: 440-775-8506; E-mail: blake.new@oberlin.edu.
Lacrosse: Deb Ranieri; Phone: 440-775-8511; E-mail: deb.ranieri@oberlin.edu.

Soccer: Jane Wildman; Phone: 440-775-8509; E-mail: jane.wildman@oberlin.edu.
Softball: Tina Wood; Phone: 440-775-8536; E-mail: tina.wood@oberlin.edu.
Swimming: Dick Michaels; Phone: 440-775-8501; E-mail: dick.michaels@oberlin.edu.
Tennis: Don Hunsinger; Phone: 440-775-8508; E-mail: don.hunsinger@oberlin.edu.
Track and Field: Jason Hudson; Phone: 440-775-8510; E-mail: jason.hudson@oberlin.edu.
Volleyball: Kristen Surovjak; Phone: 440-775-8505; E-mail: kristen.surovjak@oberlin.edu.

OCCIDENTAL COLLEGE
Los Angeles, California

Tigers ◆ NCAA III ◆ Southern California Athletic Conference ◆ http://www.oxy.edu/

Independent comprehensive, founded 1887
Coed, 1,840 undergraduate students, 99% full-time, 58% women, 42% men
Urban 120-acre campus
Very difficult entrance level, 44% of applicants were admitted

Freshmen *Admission:* 4,513 applied, 1,964 were accepted, 441 enrolled. *Test scores:* SAT verbal scores over 500: 85%; SAT math scores over 500: 86%; SAT verbal scores over 600: 61%; SAT math scores over 600: 60%; SAT verbal scores over 700: 18%; SAT math scores over 700: 16%.
Tuition and fees (2003–04): $28,306 (full-time). *Room and board:* $7820 (room only: $4300).
Financial Aid (All incoming freshmen): *Average need-based gift aid:* $20,598. *Average non-need based aid:* $16,137. *Average aid to full-time undergraduates:* $25,537.
Athletic Department: *Director of Athletics:* Dixon Farmer; Phone: 323-259-2608; Fax: 323-341-4993; E-mail: dfarmer@oxy.edu.

MEN'S COACHES
Baseball: Denny Barrett; Phone: 323-259-2683; E-mail: dbarrett@oxy.edu.
Basketball: Brian Newhall; Phone: 323-259-2690; E-mail: bnewhall@oxy.edu.
Cross Country: Troy Engle; Phone: 323-259-2715; E-mail: tengle@oxy.edu.
Football: Dale Widolff; Phone: 323-259-2708; E-mail: dwidolff@oxy.edu.
Soccer: Colm McFeely; Phone: 323-259-2931; E-mail: cmcfeely@oxy.edu.
Swimming: Peggy Carl; Phone: 323-259-2703; E-mail: swimming@oxy.edu.
Tennis: David Bojalad; Phone: 323-259-2802; E-mail: bojalad@oxy.edu.
Track and Field: Troy Engle; Phone: 323-259-2715; E-mail: tengle@oxy.edu.

WOMEN'S COACHES
Basketball: Kevin Hall; Phone: 323-259-2682; E-mail: athletics@oxy.edu.
Cross Country: Troy Engle; Phone: 323-259-2715; E-mail: tengle@oxy.edu.
Soccer: Colm McFeely; Phone: 323-259-2931; E-mail: cmcfeely@oxy.edu.
Softball: Gene Shepherd; Phone: 323-259-2632; E-mail: softball@oxy.edu.
Swimming: Peggy Carl; Phone: 323-259-2703; E-mail: swimming@oxy.edu.
Tennis: CiCi Louie; Phone: 323-259-2802; E-mail: bbbccjj@aol.com.
Track and Field: Troy Engle; Phone: 323-259-2715; E-mail: tengle@oxy.edu.
Volleyball: Chris Hahn; Phone: 323-259-2702; E-mail: chahn@oxy.edu.

OGLETHORPE UNIVERSITY
Atlanta, Georgia

Stormy Petrels ◆ NCAA III ◆ Southern Collegiate Athletic Conference ◆ http://www.oglethorpe.edu/

Independent comprehensive, founded 1835
Coed, 945 undergraduate students, 83% full-time, 65% women, 35% men
Suburban 118-acre campus
Very difficult entrance level, 60% of applicants were admitted

Freshmen *Admission:* 746 applied, 492 were accepted, 167 enrolled. *Test scores:* SAT verbal scores over 500: 88%; SAT math scores over 500: 79%; SAT verbal scores over 600: 54%; SAT math scores over 600: 40%; SAT verbal scores over 700: 14%; SAT math scores over 700: 6%.
Tuition and fees (2003–04): $20,370 (full-time). *Room and board:* $6550.
Financial Aid (All incoming freshmen): *Average need-based gift aid:* $14,140. *Average non-need based aid:* $11,336. *Average aid to full-time undergraduates:* $23,190.
Athletic Department: *Director of Athletics:* Jack Berkshire; Phone: 404-364-8415; Fax: 404-364-8445.

MEN'S COACHES
Baseball: Bill Popp; Phone: 404-364-8417; E-mail: bpopp@oglethorpe.edu.
Basketball: Phil Ponder; Phone: 404-364-8422; E-mail: pponder@oglethorpe.edu.
Cross Country: Bob Unger; Phone: 404-364-8414; E-mail: bunger@oglethorpe.edu.
Golf: Jim Owen; Phone: 404-364-8420; E-mail: jowen@oglthorpe.edu.
Soccer: Jon Akin; Phone: 404-364-8416; E-mail: jakin@oglethorpe.edu.
Tennis: Phillip Ponder; Phone: 404-364-8422; E-mail: pponder@oglethorpe.edu.
Track and Field: Bob Unger; Phone: 404-364-8414; E-mail: bunger@oglethorpe.edu.

WOMEN'S COACHES
Basketball: Kathy Corbett; Phone: 404-364-8421; E-mail: kcorbett@oglethorpe.edu.
Cross Country: Bob Unger; Phone: 404-364-8414; E-mail: bunger@oglethorpe.edu.
Golf: Jim Owen; Phone: 404-364-8420; E-mail: jowen@oglthorpe.edu.
Soccer: Jon Akin; Phone: 404-364-8416; E-mail: jakin@oglethorpe.edu.
Tennis: Mike Scoggins; Phone: 404-364-8487.
Track and Field: Bob Unger; Phone: 404-364-8414; E-mail: bunger@oglethorpe.edu.
Volleyball: Dan Giordano; Phone: 404-364-8487; E-mail: dgiordano@oglethorpe.edu.

OHIO DOMINICAN UNIVERSITY
Columbus, Ohio

Panthers ◆ NAIA ◆ American Mideast Conference; Mid-States Football Conference ◆ http://www.ohiodominican.edu/

Independent Roman Catholic comprehensive, founded 1911
Coed, 2,308 undergraduate students, 73% full-time, 70% women, 30% men
Urban 62-acre campus
Moderately difficult entrance level, 77% of applicants were admitted

Freshmen *Admission:* 1,193 applied, 902 were accepted, 312 enrolled.
Tuition and fees (2004–05): $18,000 (full-time). *Room and board:* $5900.
Financial Aid (All incoming freshmen): *Average need-based gift aid:* $6108. *Average aid to full-time undergraduates:* $12,467.
Athletic Department: *Director of Athletics:* Paul Page; Phone: 614-251-4535; Fax: 614-252-2556; E-mail: pagep@ohiodominican.edu. *Sports Information Director:* Jeff Blair; Phone: 614-251-4577; E-mail: blairj2@ohiodominican.edu.

MEN'S COACHES
Baseball: Paul Page; Phone: 614-251-4535; E-mail: pagep@ohiodominican.edu.
Basketball: Dan Priest; Phone: 614-251-4533; E-mail: priestd@ohiodominican.edu.

Football: Dale Carlson; Phone: 614-251-4556; E-mail: carlsond@ohiodominican.edu.
Golf: Chris Deibel; Phone: 614-251-4537; E-mail: deibelc@ohiodominican.edu.
Soccer: David Mor; Phone: 614-251-4521; E-mail: mord@ohiodominican.edu.
Tennis: Mike Bonnell; Phone: 614-251-3482; E-mail: bonnellm@ohiodominican.edu.

WOMEN'S COACHES
Basketball: Kate Cummings; Phone: 614-251-5434; E-mail: cummingk@ohiodominican.edu.
Golf: Chris Deibel; Phone: 614-251-4537; E-mail: deibelc@ohiodominican.edu.
Soccer: Alan Green; Phone: 614-251-4635; E-mail: greena@ohiodominican.edu.
Softball: Marcella Vanlanadingham; Phone: 614-251-4532; E-mail: vanlandm@ohiodominican.edu.
Tennis: Mike Bonnell; Phone: 614-251-3482; E-mail: bonnellm@ohiodominican.edu.
Volleyball: Sandy Rowley; Phone: 614-251-4538; E-mail: rowleys@ohiodominican.edu.

OHIO NORTHERN UNIVERSITY
Ada, Ohio

Polar Bears ◆ NCAA III ◆ Ohio Athletic Conference ◆ http://www.onu.edu/

Independent religious comprehensive, founded 1871, affiliated with United Methodist Church
Coed, 2,214 undergraduate students, 93% full-time, 47% women, 53% men
Small-town 285-acre campus
Moderately difficult entrance level, 80% of applicants were admitted

Freshmen *Admission:* 2,841 applied, 2,277 were accepted, 554 enrolled. *Test scores:* SAT verbal scores over 500: 81%; SAT math scores over 500: 89%; SAT verbal scores over 600: 37%; SAT math scores over 600: 51%; SAT verbal scores over 700: 6%; SAT math scores over 700: 9%.
Tuition and fees (2003–04): $24,645 (full-time). *Room and board:* $6030 (room only: $3015).
Financial Aid (All incoming freshmen): *Average need-based gift aid:* $15,922. *Average non-need based aid:* $12,529. *Average aid to full-time undergraduates:* $21,577.
Athletic Department: *Director of Athletics:* Tom Simmons; Phone: 419-772-2450; Fax: 419-772-2470; E-mail: t-simmons@onu.edu. *Sports Information Director:* Tim Glon; Phone: 419-772-2046; E-mail: t-glon@onu.edu.

MEN'S COACHES
Baseball: Milan Rasic; Phone: 419-772-2442; E-mail: m-rasic@onu.edu.
Basketball: Joe Campoli; Phone: 419-772-2454; E-mail: j-campoli1@onu.edu.
Cross Country: Brian Cole; Phone: 419-772-2445; E-mail: b-cole@onu.edu.
Diving: Bud Harbison; Phone: 419-772-2243; E-mail: n-harbison@onu.edu.
Football: Dean Paul; Phone: 419-772-2448; E-mail: d-paul@onu.edu.
Golf: Jeff Coleman; Phone: 419-772-1497; E-mail: j-coleman@onu.edu.
Soccer: Brent Ridenour; Phone: 419-772-2458; E-mail: b-ridenour@onu.edu.
Swimming: Rock Snow; Phone: 419-772-2243; E-mail: r-snow@onu.edu.
Tennis: Brent Ridenour; Phone: 419-772-2458; E-mail: b-ridenour@onu.edu.
Track and Field: Brian Cole; Phone: 419-772-2445; E-mail: b-cole@onu.edu.
Wrestling: Ron Beaschler; Phone: 419-772-2453; E-mail: r-beaschler@onu.edu.

WOMEN'S COACHES
Basketball: Michele Durand; Phone: 419-772-2725; E-mail: m-durand@onu.edu.
Cross Country: Brian Cole; Phone: 419-772-2445; E-mail: b-cole@onu.edu.

Ohio Northern University (*continued*)

Diving: Bud Harbison; Phone: 419-772-2243; E-mail: n-harbison@onu.edu.
Golf: Stacy Hairston; Phone: 419-772-2455; E-mail: s-hairston@onu.edu.
Soccer: Annette Hunt; Phone: 419-772-2459; E-mail: a-hunt@onu.edu.
Softball: Jeff Nickerson; Phone: 419-772-2459; E-mail: j-nickerson@onu.edu.
Swimming: Rock Snow; Phone: 419-772-2243; E-mail: r-snow@onu.edu.
Tennis: Scott Wills; Phone: 419-772-2041; E-mail: s-wills@onu.edu.
Track and Field: Brian Cole; Phone: 419-772-2445; E-mail: b-cole@onu.edu.
Volleyball: Katie Witte; Phone: 419-772-2446; E-mail: k-witte@onu.edu.

THE OHIO STATE UNIVERSITY
Columbus, Ohio

Buckeyes ◆ NCAA I ◆ American Lacrosse Conference; Big Ten Conference; Midwestern Intercollegiate Volleyball Conference; Western Collegiate Hockey Conference ◆ http://www.osu.edu/

State-supported university, founded 1870
Coed, 37,605 undergraduate students, 89% full-time, 48% women, 52% men
Urban 3,117-acre campus
Moderately difficult entrance level, 70% of applicants were admitted

Freshmen *Admission:* 20,122 applied, 14,488 were accepted, 6,390 enrolled. *Test scores:* SAT verbal scores over 500: 86%; SAT math scores over 500: 90%; SAT verbal scores over 600: 43%; SAT math scores over 600: 53%; SAT verbal scores over 700: 8%; SAT math scores over 700: 12%.
Tuition and fees (2003–04): $6651 (resident), $16,638 (nonresident). *Room and board:* $6429.
Financial Aid (All incoming freshmen): *Average need-based gift aid:* $3283. *Average non-need based aid:* $3709. *Average aid to full-time undergraduates:* $8482.
Athletic Department: *Director of Athletics:* Andy Geiger; Phone: 614-292-2477; Fax: 614-292-0506. *Sports Information Director:* Steve Snapp; Phone: 614-292-3102; E-mail: snapp.1:@osu.edu.

MEN'S COACHES
Baseball: Bob Todd; Phone: 614-292-1075; E-mail: todd.10@osu.edu.
Basketball: Jim O'Brien; Phone: 614-292-0505.
Cheerleading: Judy Bunting; Phone: 614-688-3038; E-mail: bunting.1@osu.edu.
Cross Country: Russ Rogers; Phone: 614-292-2931; E-mail: rogers.3@osu.edu.
Diving: Vince Panzano; Phone: 614-292-1542; E-mail: panzano.1@osu.edu.
Football: Jim Tressell; Phone: 614-292-7620; E-mail: tressel.3@osu.edu.
Golf: Jim Brown; Phone: 614-292-4653; E-mail: brown.30@osu.edu.
Ice Hockey: John Markell; Phone: 614-688-5846; E-mail: markell.1@osu.edu.
Lacrosse: Joe Breschi; Phone: 614-292-6853; E-mail: breschi.1@osu.edu.
Soccer: John Bluem; Phone: 614-292-3139; E-mail: bluem.1@osu.edu.
Swimming: Bill Wadley; Phone: 614-292-1542; E-mail: wadley.1@osu.edu.
Tennis: Ty Tucker; Phone: 614-292-8994; E-mail: tucker.62@osu.edu.
Track and Field: Russ Rogers; Phone: 614-292-2931; E-mail: rogers.3@osu.edu.
Volleyball: Pete Hanson; Phone: 614-292-6452; E-mail: hanson.5@osu.edu.
Wrestling: Russ Hellickson; Phone: 614-292-6302; E-mail: hellickson.1@osu.edu.

WOMEN'S COACHES
Basketball: Jim Foster; Phone: 614-292-9270; E-mail: foster.384@osu.edu.
Cheerleading: Judy Bunting; Phone: 614-688-3038; E-mail: bunting.1@osu.edu.
Cross Country: Russ Rogers; Phone: 614-292-2931; E-mail: rogers.3@osu.edu.
Diving: Vince Panzano; Phone: 614-292-1542; E-mail: panzano.1@osu.edu.
Field Hockey: Anne Wilkinson; Phone: 614-292-6214; E-mail: wilkinson.48@osu.edu.
Golf: Therese Hession; Phone: 614-292-4653; E-mail: hession.1@osu.edu.
Gymnastics: Larry Cox; Phone: 614-292-4143; E-mail: cox.14@osu.edu.
Lacrosse: Sue Stimmel; Phone: 614-292-4178; E-mail: stimmel.1@osu.edu.
Soccer: Lori Walker; Phone: 614-292-8482; E-mail: walker.457@osu.edu.
Softball: Linda Kalafatis; Phone: 614-292-0856; E-mail: kalafatis.1@osu.edu.
Swimming: Jeanne Fleck; Phone: 614-292-4415; E-mail: fleck.22@osu.edu.
Tennis: Chuck Merzbacher; Phone: 614-292-6189; E-mail: merzbacher.1@osu.edu.
Track and Field: Russ Rogers; Phone: 614-292-2931; E-mail: rogers.3@osu.edu.
Volleyball: Jim Stone; Phone: 614-292-5382.

OHIO UNIVERSITY
Athens, Ohio

Bobcats ◆ NCAA I ◆ Mid-American Conference ◆ http://www.ohio.edu/

State-supported university, founded 1804, part of Ohio Board of Regents
Coed, 17,192 undergraduate students, 93% full-time, 54% women, 46% men
Small-town 1,700-acre campus
Moderately difficult entrance level, 76% of applicants were admitted

Freshmen *Admission:* 12,937 applied, 10,235 were accepted, 3,673 enrolled. *Test scores:* SAT verbal scores over 500: 77%; SAT math scores over 500: 77%; SAT verbal scores over 600: 28%; SAT math scores over 600: 28%; SAT verbal scores over 700: 3%; SAT math scores over 700: 3%.
Tuition and fees (2003–04): $7128 (resident), $15,351 (nonresident). *Room and board:* $7320 (room only: $3600).
Financial Aid (All incoming freshmen): *Average need-based gift aid:* $3376. *Average non-need based aid:* $4688. *Average aid to full-time undergraduates:* $5729.
Athletic Department: *Director of Athletics:* Thomas Boeh; Phone: 740-593-0982; Fax: 740-593-2420; E-mail: athletics@ohio.edu. *Sports Information Director:* Derek Scott; Phone: 740-593-0834; E-mail: scottd2@ohio.edu.

MEN'S COACHES
Baseball: Joe Carbone; Phone: 740-593-1180; E-mail: jcarbone1@ohio.edu.
Basketball: Tim O'Shea; Phone: 740-597-1668; E-mail: oshea@ohio.edu.
Cheerleading: Tricia Perry; Phone: 740-593-1174; E-mail: taggartt@ohio.edu.
Cross Country: Clay Calkins; Phone: 740-593-1191; E-mail: calkins@ohio.edu.
Diving: Rob Bitner; Phone: 740-593-9416; E-mail: bitner@ohio.edu.
Football: Brian Knorr; Phone: 740-593-1204; E-mail: knorr@ohio.edu.
Golf: Bob Cooley; Phone: 740-593-1177; E-mail: cooleyr@ohio.edu.
Swimming: Greg Werner; Phone: 740-593-1612; E-mail: werner@ohio.edu.
Track and Field: Clay Calkins; Phone: 740-593-1191; E-mail: calkins@ohio.edu.
Wrestling: Joel Greenlee; Phone: 740-593-1179; E-mail: greenlej@ohio.edu.

WOMEN'S COACHES
Basketball: Lynn Bria; Phone: 740-593-1193; E-mail: bria@ohio.edu.
Cheerleading: Tricia Perry; Phone: 740-593-1174; E-mail: taggartt@ohio.edu.
Cross Country: Clay Calkins; Phone: 740-593-1191; E-mail: calkins@ohio.edu.
Diving: Rob Bitner; Phone: 740-593-9416; E-mail: bitner@ohio.edu.
Field Hockey: Shelly Morris; Phone: 740-593-1196; E-mail: morriss@ohio.edu.
Golf: Bob Cooley; Phone: 740-593-9708; E-mail: cooleyr@ohio.edu.

Lacrosse: Kate Brew; Phone: 740-597-2970; E-mail: brew@ohio.edu.
Soccer: Stacy Strauss; Phone: 740-593-2990; E-mail: strauss@ohio.edu.
Softball: Roanna Brazier; Phone: 740-593-1175; E-mail: brazier@ohio.edu.
Swimming: Greg Werner; Phone: 740-593-1612; E-mail: werner@ohio.edu.
Track and Field: Clay Calkins; Phone: 740-593-1191; E-mail: calkins@ohio.edu.
Volleyball: Geoff Carlston; Phone: 740-593-1189; E-mail: carlston@ohio.edu.

OHIO VALLEY COLLEGE
Vienna, West Virginia

Fighting Scots ◆ NCAA II ◆ West Virginia Intercollegiate Athletic Conference ◆ http://www.ovc.edu/

Independent religious 4-year, founded 1960, affiliated with Church of Christ
Coed, 515 undergraduate students, 96% full-time, 50% women, 50% men
Small-town 299-acre campus
Minimally difficult entrance level, 50% of applicants were admitted

Freshmen *Admission:* 445 applied, 210 were accepted, 103 enrolled. *Test scores:* SAT verbal scores over 500: 55%; SAT math scores over 500: 42%; SAT verbal scores over 600: 7%; SAT math scores over 600: 12%; SAT math scores over 700: 5%.
Tuition and fees (2004–05): $12,012 (full-time). *Room and board:* $5380 (room only: $2930).
Financial Aid (All incoming freshmen): *Average need-based gift aid:* $3714. *Average non-need based aid:* $3303. *Average aid to full-time undergraduates:* $8722.
Athletic Department: *Director of Athletics:* Ron Pavan; Phone: 304-865-6041; Fax: 304—865-6001; E-mail: rpavan@wirefire.com. *Sports Information Director:* Mike Oblisk; Phone: 304-865-6050; E-mail: moblisk@hotmail.com.
MEN'S COACHES
Baseball: Chad Porter; Phone: 304-865-6209; E-mail: cporter@ovc.edu.
Basketball: Bill McGee; Phone: 304-865-6136; E-mail: billmcgee@ovc.edu.
Cheerleading: Natalie Fitch; Phone: 304-865-6000; E-mail: ndfitch@ovc.edu.
Cross Country: Tim Wiblin; Phone: 304-865-6136; E-mail: billmcgee@ovc.edu.
Golf: Larry Lyons; Phone: 304-865-6035; E-mail: lrlyons@ovc.edu.
Soccer: Dan Lyons; Phone: 304-685-6043; E-mail: dlyons@ovc.edu.
WOMEN'S COACHES
Basketball: Ron Pavan; Phone: 304-865-6041; E-mail: rpavan@wirefire.com.
Cheerleading: Natalie Fitch; Phone: 304-865-6000; E-mail: ndfitch@ovc.edu.
Cross Country: Tim Wiblin; Phone: 304-865-6136; E-mail: billmcgee@ovc.edu.
Soccer: Eric Taylor; Phone: 304-865-6047; E-mail: erockedfree@yahoo.com.
Softball: Heather Oblisk; Phone: 304-865-6054; E-mail: hoblisk@ovc.edu.
Volleyball: Paul Jacoby; Phone: 304-865-6052; E-mail: pjacoby@ovc.edu.

OHIO WESLEYAN UNIVERSITY
Delaware, Ohio

Battling Bishops ◆ NCAA III ◆ North Coast Athletic Conference ◆ http://web.owu.edu/

Independent United Methodist 4-year, founded 1842
Coed, 1,929 undergraduate students, 99% full-time, 54% women, 46% men
Small-town 200-acre campus with easy access to Columbus
Very difficult entrance level, 7% of applicants were admitted

Freshmen *Admission:* 2,580 applied, 1,910 were accepted, 567 enrolled. *Test scores:* SAT verbal scores over 500: 89%; SAT math scores over

500: 90%; SAT verbal scores over 600: 55%; SAT math scores over 600: 53%; SAT verbal scores over 700: 14%; SAT math scores over 700: 11%.
Tuition and fees (2003–04): $25,440 (full-time). *Room and board:* $7110 (room only: $3530).
Financial Aid (All incoming freshmen): *Average need-based gift aid:* $21,561. *Average non-need based aid:* $11,513. *Average aid to full-time undergraduates:* $23,268.
Athletic Department: *Director of Athletics:* Jay Martin; Phone: 740-368-3727; Fax: 740-368-3751; E-mail: jamartin@owu.edu. *Sports Information Director:* Mark Beckenbach; Phone: 740-368-3340; E-mail: mlbecken@owu.edu.
MEN'S COACHES
Baseball: Roger Ingles; Phone: 740-368-3738; E-mail: rdingles@owu.edu.
Basketball: Mike Dewitt; Phone: 740-368-3744; E-mail: mddewitt@owu.edu.
Cheerleading: Kay Durfey; Phone: 740-368-3726; E-mail: skdurfey@owu.edu.
Cross Country: Kris Boey; Phone: 740-368-3731; E-mail: kwboey@owu.edu.
Football: Mike Hollway; Phone: 740-368-3732; E-mail: mchollwa@owu.edu.
Golf: Jon Whithaus; Phone: 740-368-3742; E-mail: jewhitha@owu.edu.
Lacrosse: Sean Ryan; Phone: 740-368-3730; E-mail: smryan@owu.edu.
Soccer: Jay Martin; Phone: 740-368-3727; E-mail: jamartin@owu.edu.
Swimming: Dick Hawes; Phone: 740-368-3740; E-mail: rlhawes@owu.edu.
Tennis: Phone: 740-368-3741.
Track and Field: Kris Boey; Phone: 740-368-3731; E-mail: kwboey@owu.edu.
WOMEN'S COACHES
Basketball: Nan Carney-Debord; Phone: 740-368-3729; E-mail: nhcarney@owu.edu.
Cheerleading: Kay Durfey; Phone: 740-368-3726; E-mail: skdurfey@owu.edu.
Cross Country: Kris Boey; Phone: 740-368-3731; E-mail: kwboey@owu.edu.
Field Hockey: Marge Redmond; Phone: 740-368-3736; E-mail: meredmon@owu.edu.
Lacrosse: Kimberly Rocheleau; Phone: 740-368-3735; E-mail: karochel@owu.edu.
Soccer: Bob Barnes; Phone: 740-368-3757; E-mail: rcbarnes@owu.edu.
Softball: Heather Rakosik; Phone: 740-368-3737; E-mail: hmrakosi@owu.edu.
Swimming: Dick Hawes; Phone: 740-368-3740; E-mail: rlhawes@owu.edu.
Tennis: Sheri Courter; Phone: 740-368-3758; E-mail: smcourte@owu.edu.
Track and Field: Kris Boey; Phone: 740-368-3731; E-mail: kwboey@owu.edu.
Volleyball: Cynthia Holliday; Phone: 740-368-3746; E-mail: ccholliad@owu.edu.

OKLAHOMA BAPTIST UNIVERSITY
Shawnee, Oklahoma

Bison ◆ NAIA ◆ Sooner Conference ◆ http://www.okbu.edu/

Independent Southern Baptist comprehensive, founded 1910
Coed, 1,866 undergraduate students, 81% full-time, 56% women, 44% men
Small-town 125-acre campus with easy access to Oklahoma City
Moderately difficult entrance level, 88% of applicants were admitted

Freshmen *Admission:* 1,098 applied, 938 were accepted, 411 enrolled. *Test scores:* SAT verbal scores over 500: 84%; SAT math scores over 500: 79%; SAT verbal scores over 600: 48%; SAT math scores over 600: 38%; SAT verbal scores over 700: 12%; SAT math scores over 700: 9%.
Tuition and fees (2003–04): $11,580 (full-time). *Room and board:* $3640 (room only: $1690).
Financial Aid (All incoming freshmen): *Average need-based gift aid:* $3330. *Average non-need based aid:* $4716. *Average aid to full-time undergraduates:* $10,630.

Oklahoma Baptist University *(continued)*

Athletic Department: *Director of Athletics:* Norris Russell; Phone: 405-878-2136; Fax: 405-878-2152; E-mail: norris.russell@okbu.edu. *Sports Information Director:* Ray Fink; Phone: 405-878-2109; E-mail: ray_fink@mail.okbu.edu.

MEN'S COACHES

Baseball: Bobby Cox; Phone: 405-878-2136; E-mail: bobby.cox@okbu.edu.

Basketball: Doug Tolin; Phone: 405-878-2136; E-mail: doug_tolin@mail.okbu.edu.

Cheerleading: Linda McElroy; Phone: 405-878-2138; E-mail: linda.mcelroy@okbu.edu.

Cross Country: Ford Mastin; Phone: 405-878-2136; E-mail: ford.mastin@mokbu.edu.

Golf: Rick Cody; Phone: 405-878-2136.

Tennis: Sue Dick; Phone: 405-878-2136; E-mail: garyandsuedick@yahoo.com.

Track and Field: Ford Mastin; Phone: 405-878-2136; E-mail: ford.mastin@mokbu.edu.

WOMEN'S COACHES

Basketball: John McCullough; Phone: 405-878-2136; E-mail: john.mccullough@okbu.edu.

Cheerleading: Linda McElroy; Phone: 405-878-2138; E-mail: linda.mcelroy@okbu.edu.

Cross Country: Ford Mastin; Phone: 405-878-2136; E-mail: ford.mastin@mokbu.edu.

Golf: Rick Cody; Phone: 405-878-2136.

Softball: Pam Fink; Phone: 405-878-2136; E-mail: pam.fink@okbu.edu.

Tennis: Sue Dick; Phone: 405-878-2136; E-mail: garyandsuedick@yahoo.com.

Track and Field: Ford Mastin; Phone: 405-878-2136; E-mail: ford.mastin@mokbu.edu.

OKLAHOMA CHRISTIAN UNIVERSITY
Oklahoma City, Oklahoma

Eagles ◆ NAIA ◆ Sooner Conference ◆ http://www.oc.edu/

Independent religious comprehensive, founded 1950, affiliated with Church of Christ
Coed, 386 undergraduate students, 100% full-time, 55% women, 45% men
Suburban 200-acre campus
Noncompetitive entrance level, 30% of applicants were admitted

Freshmen *Admission:* 1,271 applied, 386 were accepted, 386 enrolled.
Tuition and fees (2004–05): $13,160 (full-time). *Room and board:* $4820.
Financial Aid (All incoming freshmen): *Average need-based gift aid:* $1881. *Average non-need based aid:* $1817. *Average aid to full-time undergraduates:* $12,220.
Athletic Department: *Director of Athletics:* Dan Hays; Phone: 405-425-5360; Fax: 405-425-5351; E-mail: dan.hays@oc.edu. *Sports Information Director:* Stan Green; Phone: 405-425-5363; E-mail: stan.green@oc.edu.

MEN'S COACHES

Basketball: Dan Hays; Phone: 405-425-5360; E-mail: dan.hays@oc.edu.
Cross Country: Randy Heath; Phone: 405-425-5353; E-mail: randy.heath@oc.edu.
Golf: David Lynn; Phone: 405-425-5645; E-mail: david.lynn@oc.edu.
Soccer: Adam Basic; Phone: 405-425-5386; E-mail: adam.basic@oc.edu.
Tennis: Chris Young; Phone: 405-425-5356; E-mail: chrisyoung@oc.edu.
Track and Field: Randy Heath; Phone: 405-425-5353; E-mail: randy.heath@oc.edu.

WOMEN'S COACHES

Basketball: Stephanie Findley; Phone: 405-425-5355; E-mail: stephanie.findley@oc.edu.
Cross Country: Randy Heath; Phone: 405-425-5353; E-mail: randy.heath@oc.edu.
Soccer: Adam Basic; Phone: 405-425-5386; E-mail: adam.basic@oc.edu.
Softball: Tom Heath; Phone: 405-425-5357; E-mail: tom.heath@oc.edu.

Tennis: Chris Young; Phone: 405-425-5356; E-mail: chrisyoung@oc.edu.
Track and Field: Randy Heath; Phone: 405-425-5353; E-mail: randy.heath@oc.edu.

OKLAHOMA CITY UNIVERSITY
Oklahoma City, Oklahoma

Stars ◆ NAIA ◆ Sooner Conference ◆ http://www.okcu.edu/

Independent United Methodist comprehensive, founded 1904
Coed, 1,793 undergraduate students, 75% full-time, 62% women, 38% men
Urban 68-acre campus
Moderately difficult entrance level, 79% of applicants were admitted

Freshmen *Admission:* 822 applied, 639 were accepted, 319 enrolled. *Test scores:* SAT verbal scores over 500: 82%; SAT math scores over 500: 72%; SAT verbal scores over 600: 33%; SAT math scores over 600: 37%; SAT verbal scores over 700: 1%; SAT math scores over 700: 4%.
Tuition and fees (2003–04): $14,030 (full-time). *Room and board:* $5550.
Financial Aid (All incoming freshmen): *Average need-based gift aid:* $7823. *Average non-need based aid:* $6463. *Average aid to full-time undergraduates:* $10,390.
Athletic Department: *Director of Athletics:* Jim Abbott; Phone: 405-521-5301; Fax: 405-521-5370; E-mail: jabbott@okcu.edu. *Sports Information Director:* Chris Doyle; Phone: 405-521-5304; E-mail: cdoyle@okcu.edu.

MEN'S COACHES

Baseball: Denney Crabaugh; Phone: 405-521-5156; E-mail: dcrabaugh@okcu.edu.
Basketball: Win Case; Phone: 405-521-5310; E-mail: wcase@okcu.edu.
Cheerleading: Anna Alexander; Phone: 405-521-5051; E-mail: annaalexander@okcu.edu.
Golf: Kyle Blaser; Phone: 405-521-5303; E-mail: kblaser@okcu.edu.
Soccer: Brian Harvey; Phone: 405-521-5800; E-mail: bharvey@okcu.edu.

WOMEN'S COACHES

Basketball: Janell Jones; Phone: 405-521-5868; E-mail: jljones@okcu.edu.
Cheerleading: Anna Alexander; Phone: 405-521-5051; E-mail: annaalexander@okcu.edu.
Golf: Derek Freeman; Phone: 405-521-5302; E-mail: dfreeman@okcu.edu.
Soccer: Brian Harvey; Phone: 405-521-5800; E-mail: bharvey@okcu.edu.
Softball: Phil McSpadden; Phone: 405-521-5311; E-mail: pmcspadden@okcu.edu.

OKLAHOMA PANHANDLE STATE UNIVERSITY
Goodwell, Oklahoma

(M) Aggies (W) Lady Aggies ◆ NCAA II ◆ Heartland Conference ◆ http://www.opsu.edu/

State-supported 4-year, founded 1909, part of Oklahoma State Regents for Higher Education
Coed, 1,226 undergraduate students, 67% full-time, 53% women, 47% men
Rural 40-acre campus
Noncompetitive entrance level

Freshmen *Admission:* 222 enrolled.
Tuition and fees (2004–05): $2970 (resident), $4470 (nonresident). *Room and board:* $2810 (room only: $930).
Financial Aid (All incoming freshmen): *Average need-based gift aid:* $2590. *Average aid to full-time undergraduates:* $8830.
Athletic Department: *Director of Athletics:* Wayne Stewart; Phone: 580-349-2611; Fax: 580-349-3375. *Sports Information Director:* Scott Puryear; Phone: 580-349-2611.

MEN'S COACHES

Baseball: Robert Rubel; Phone: 580-349-2611; E-mail: rrubel@opsu.edu.

Basketball: Charles Terry; Phone: 580-349-1324; E-mail: cterry@opsu.edu.

Football: Ryan Held; Phone: 580-349-1322; E-mail: rheld@opsu.edu.

Golf: Roger McKinnon; Phone: 580-349-1340.

WOMEN'S COACHES

Basketball: Deb McWilliams; Phone: 580-349-1344; E-mail: debm@opsu.edu.

Cross Country: Steve Kissel; Phone: 580-349-1342; E-mail: stevek@opsu.edu.

Golf: Roger McKinnon; Phone: 580-349-1340.

Softball: Steve Kissel; Phone: 580-349-1342; E-mail: stevek@opsu.edu.

OKLAHOMA STATE UNIVERSITY
Stillwater, Oklahoma

Cowboys ◆ NCAA I ◆ Big 12 Conference ◆ http://www.okstate.edu/

State-supported university, founded 1890, part of Oklahoma State University

Coed, 18,689 undergraduate students, 88% full-time, 49% women, 51% men

Small-town 840-acre campus with easy access to Oklahoma City and Tulsa

Moderately difficult entrance level, 89% of applicants were admitted

Freshmen *Admission:* 6,629 applied, 5,930 were accepted, 3,490 enrolled. *Test scores:* SAT verbal scores over 500: 75%; SAT math scores over 500: 76%; SAT verbal scores over 600: 26%; SAT math scores over 600: 31%; SAT verbal scores over 700: 4%; SAT math scores over 700: 4%.

Tuition and fees (2003–04): $3665 (resident), $9611 (nonresident). *Room and board:* $5468 (room only: $2468).

Financial Aid (All incoming freshmen): *Average need-based gift aid:* $3661. *Average non-need based aid:* $2492. *Average aid to full-time undergraduates:* $7250.

Athletic Department: *Director of Athletics:* Harry Birdwell; Phone: 405-744-7050; Fax: 405-744-4535; E-mail: miesner@okstate.edu. *Sports Information Director:* Steve Buzzard; Phone: 405-744-7714; E-mail: buzzars@okstate.edu.

MEN'S COACHES

Baseball: Frank Anderson; Phone: 405-744-5849; E-mail: thollid@okstate.edu.

Basketball: Eddie Sutton; Phone: 405-744-5845; E-mail: seddie@okstate.edu.

Cross Country: Dick Weis; Phone: 405-744-6782; E-mail: weis@okstate.edu.

Football: Les Miles; Phone: 405-744-3378.

Golf: Mike Holder; Phone: 405-744-7325; E-mail: holder@okstate.edu.

Tennis: James Wadley; Phone: 405-744-7529; E-mail: wadleyj@okstate.edu.

Track and Field: Dick Weis; Phone: 405-744-6782; E-mail: weis@okstate.edu.

Wrestling: Jon Smith; Phone: 405-744-4541.

WOMEN'S COACHES

Basketball: Julie Goodenough; Phone: 405-744-2490; E-mail: goodeno@okstate.edu.

Cross Country: Rene Sepulveda; Phone: 405-744-5573; E-mail: srene@okstate.edu.

Golf: Amy Weeks; Phone: 405-744-7681; E-mail: wamy@okstate.edu.

Soccer: Karen Hancock; Phone: 405-744-5603; E-mail: horstma@okstate.edu.

Softball: Margaret Rebenar; Phone: 405-744-5883; E-mail: rebenar@okstate.edu.

Tennis: Julius Majewski; Phone: 405-744-7343; E-mail: jlubicz@okstate.edu.

Track and Field: Rene Sepulveda; Phone: 405-744-5573; E-mail: srene@okstate.edu.

OKLAHOMA WESLEYAN UNIVERSITY
Bartlesville, Oklahoma

Eagles ◆ NAIA ◆ Midlands Collegiate Conference ◆ http://www.okwu.edu/

Independent religious comprehensive, founded 1909, affiliated with Wesleyan Church

Coed, 675 undergraduate students

Small-town 127-acre campus with easy access to Tulsa

Minimally difficult entrance level, 64% of applicants were admitted

Freshmen *Admission:* 427 applied, 257 were accepted. *Test scores:* SAT verbal scores over 500: 67%; SAT math scores over 500: 54%; SAT verbal scores over 600: 32%; SAT math scores over 600: 19%; SAT verbal scores over 700: 2%; SAT math scores over 700: 4%.

Tuition and fees (2003–04): $12,250 (full-time). *Room and board:* $4600 (room only: $2300).

Financial Aid (All incoming freshmen): *Average need-based gift aid:* $2414. *Average non-need based aid:* $2100. *Average aid to full-time undergraduates:* $7113.

Athletic Department: *Director of Athletics:* Chris Reese; Phone: 918-335-6843; E-mail: creese@okwu.edu.

MEN'S COACHES

Baseball: Bengie Rodriguez; Phone: 918-335-6848; E-mail: brodriguez@okwu.edu.

Basketball: Chris Reese; Phone: 918-335-9843; E-mail: creese@okwu.edu.

Golf: Phone: 918-335-6849; E-mail: kbashford@okwu.edu.

Soccer: Marcelo Galvao; Phone: 918-335-6297; E-mail: soccer@okwu.edu.

WOMEN'S COACHES

Basketball: Barney Hay; Phone: 918-335-6817; E-mail: ladyhoops@okwu.edu.

Soccer: Marcelo Galvao; Phone: 918-335-6297; E-mail: soccer@okwu.edu.

Softball: Kurt Bashford; Phone: 918-335-6849; E-mail: kbashford@okwu.edu.

Volleyball: Herb Whitehouse; Phone: 918-335-6283; E-mail: sswhitehouse@okwu.edu.

OLD DOMINION UNIVERSITY
Norfolk, Virginia

Monarchs ◆ NCAA I ◆ Colonial Athletic Conference ◆ http://www.odu.edu/

State-supported university, founded 1930

Coed, 14,209 undergraduate students, 69% full-time, 58% women, 42% men

Urban 188-acre campus with easy access to Virginia Beach

83% of applicants were admitted

Freshmen *Admission:* 5,425 applied, 4,444 were accepted, 2,047 enrolled. *Test scores:* SAT verbal scores over 500: 62%; SAT math scores over 500: 60%; SAT verbal scores over 600: 17%; SAT math scores over 600: 18%; SAT verbal scores over 700: 2%; SAT math scores over 700: 2%.

Tuition and fees (2003–04): $4928 (resident), $14,078 (nonresident). *Room and board:* $5513 (room only: $3704).

Financial Aid (All incoming freshmen): *Average need-based gift aid:* $4254. *Average non-need based aid:* $2694. *Average aid to full-time undergraduates:* $6916.

Athletic Department: *Director of Athletics:* Jim Jarrett; Phone: 757-683-3369; Fax: 757-683-3119; E-mail: jjarrett@odu.edu. *Sports Information Director:* Carol Hudson; Phone: 757-683-3372; E-mail: chudson@odu.edu.

MEN'S COACHES

Baseball: Tony Guzzo; Phone: 757-683-4360; E-mail: aguzzo@odu.edu.

Basketball: Blaine Taylor; Phone: 757-683-3362.

Cheerleading: Phone: 757-683-3359.

Diving: Chad Triolet; Phone: 757-683-3375.

Golf: Murray Rudisill; Phone: 757-683-3300; E-mail: mrudisil@odu.edu.

Old Dominion University *(continued)*

Soccer: Alan Dawson; Phone: 757-683-4360; E-mail: adawson@odu.edu.

Swimming: Carol Withus; Phone: 757-683-3375; E-mail: cwithus@odu.edu.

Tennis: Darryl Cummings; Phone: 757-683-5312; E-mail: dcumming@odu.edu.

Wrestling: Gary Simons; Phone: 757-683-3375; E-mail: gsimons@odu.edu.

WOMEN'S COACHES

Basketball: Wendy Larry; Phone: 757-683-3401; E-mail: wlarry@odu.edu.

Cheerleading: Phone: 757-683-3359.

Diving: Chad Triolet; Phone: 757-683-3375.

Field Hockey: Beth Anders; Phone: 757-683-3375; E-mail: odufieldhockey@sprintmail.com.

Lacrosse: Sue Stahl; Phone: 757-683-3375; E-mail: sstahl@odu.edu.

Soccer: Joe Pereira; Phone: 757-683-3375; E-mail: jpereira@odu.edu.

Swimming: Carol Withus; Phone: 757-683-3375; E-mail: cwithus@odu.edu.

Tennis: Darryl Cummings; Phone: 757-683-5312; E-mail: dcumming@odu.edu.

OLIVET COLLEGE
Olivet, Michigan

Comets ◆ NCAA III ◆ Michigan Intercollegiate Conference ◆ http://www.olivetcollege.edu/

Independent religious comprehensive, founded 1844, affiliated with Congregational Christian Church
Coed, 1,042 undergraduate students, 90% full-time, 43% women, 57% men
Small-town 92-acre campus
Minimally difficult entrance level, 59% of applicants were admitted

Freshmen *Admission:* 972 applied, 574 were accepted, 297 enrolled.
Tuition and fees (2004–05): $15,941 (full-time). *Room and board:* $5330 (room only: $2901).
Financial Aid (All incoming freshmen): *Average need-based gift aid:* $9675. *Average non-need based aid:* $8081. *Average aid to full-time undergraduates:* $12,701.
Athletic Department: *Director of Athletics:* Dave Price; Phone: 616-749-7593; Fax: 269-749-7229; E-mail: dprice@olivetcollege.edu. *Sports Information Director:* Geoff Henson; Phone: 269-749-7602; E-mail: ghenson@olivetcollege.edu.

MEN'S COACHES

Baseball: Carlton Hardy; Phone: 616-749-4184; E-mail: chardy@olivetcollege.edu.

Basketball: Steve Hettinga; Phone: 616-749-7674; E-mail: shettinga@olivetcollege.edu.

Cheerleading: Antoinette Gray; Phone: 616-749-6625; E-mail: agray@olivetcollege.edu.

Cross Country: Steve Laidacker; Phone: 616-749-7671; E-mail: slaidacker@olivetcollege.edu.

Diving: David Stubbs; Phone: 616-749-7195; E-mail: dstubbs@olivetcollege.edu.

Football: Irv Sigler; Phone: 616-749-7672; E-mail: isigler@olivetcollege.edu.

Golf: Gary Morrison; Phone: 616-749-7669; E-mail: gmorrison@olivetcollege.edu.

Soccer: Matt Wait; Phone: 616-749-6652; E-mail: mwait@olivetcollege.edu.

Swimming: David Stubbs; Phone: 616-749-7195; E-mail: dstubbs@olivetcollege.edu.

Track and Field: Brian Hug; Phone: 616-749-6654; E-mail: bhug@olivetcollege.edu.

Wrestling: Steve Laidacker; Phone: 616-749-7671; E-mail: slaidacker@olivetcollege.edu.

WOMEN'S COACHES

Basketball: Deanna Richard; Phone: 616-749-7156; E-mail: drichard@olivetcollege.edu.

Cheerleading: Antoinette Gray; Phone: 616-749-6625; E-mail: agray@olivetcollege.edu.

Cross Country: Steve Laidacker; Phone: 616-749-7671; E-mail: slaidacker@olivetcollege.edu.

Diving: David Stubbs; Phone: 616-749-7195; E-mail: dstubbs@olivetcollege.edu.

Golf: Bill Maas; Phone: 616-749-7567; E-mail: bmaas@olivetcollege.edu.

Soccer: Hans Morgan; Phone: 616-749-7155; E-mail: hmorgan@olivetcollege.edu.

Softball: James Farnum; Phone: 616-749-6604; E-mail: jfarnum@olivetcollege.edu.

Swimming: David Stubbs; Phone: 616-749-7195; E-mail: dstubbs@olivetcollege.edu.

Tennis: Mary Anne McMullen; Phone: 616-749-7131; E-mail: mmcmullen@olivetcollege.edu.

Track and Field: Brian Hug; Phone: 616-749-6654; E-mail: bhug@olivetcollege.edu.

Volleyball: Tamara Tranter; Phone: 616-749-6677; E-mail: ttranter@olivetcollege.edu.

OLIVET NAZARENE UNIVERSITY
Bourbonnais, Illinois

Tigers ◆ NAIA ◆ Chicagoland Collegiate Conference; Mid-States Football Conference ◆ http://www.olivet.edu/

Independent religious comprehensive, founded 1907, affiliated with Church of the Nazarene
Coed, 2,427 undergraduate students, 87% full-time, 59% women, 41% men
Small-town 200-acre campus with easy access to Chicago
Minimally difficult entrance level, 8% of applicants were admitted

Freshmen *Admission:* 1,902 applied, 1,493 were accepted, 594 enrolled.
Tuition and fees (2004–05): $15,740 (full-time). *Room and board:* $5800 (room only: $2900).
Financial Aid (All incoming freshmen): *Average need-based gift aid:* $4655. *Average non-need based aid:* $7101. *Average aid to full-time undergraduates:* $11,258.
Athletic Department: *Director of Athletics:* Jeff Schimmelpfennig; Phone: 815-939-5372; Fax: 815-939-7933; E-mail: jschimm@olivet.edu. *Sports Information Director:* Marc Shaner; Phone: 815-928-5561; E-mail: mshaner@olivet.edu.

MEN'S COACHES

Baseball: Elliot Johnson; Phone: 815-939-5119; E-mail: ejohnso1@olivet.edu.

Basketball: Ralph Hodge; Phone: 815-939-5124; E-mail: rhodge@olivet.edu.

Cheerleading: Karen Eylander; Phone: 815-932-7507; E-mail: keylande@olivet.edu.

Cross Country: Michael McDowell; Phone: 815-939-5165; E-mail: mmcdowel@olivet.edu.

Football: Gary Newsome; Phone: 815-939-5120; E-mail: gnewsome@olivet.edu.

Golf: Jeff Schimmelpfennig; Phone: 815-939-5372; E-mail: jschimm@olivet.edu.

Soccer: Mark Howard; Phone: 815-939-5123; E-mail: mhoward@olivet.edu.

Tennis: Obie Coomer; Phone: 815-939-5117; E-mail: ocoomer@olivet.edu.

Track and Field: Michael McDowell; Phone: 815-939-5165; E-mail: mmcdowel@olivet.edu.

WOMEN'S COACHES

Basketball: Doug Porter; Phone: 815-939-5164; E-mail: dporter@olivet.edu.

Cheerleading: Karen Eylander; Phone: 815-932-7507; E-mail: keylande@olivet.edu.

Cross Country: Michael McDowell; Phone: 815-939-5165; E-mail: mmcdowel@olivet.edu.

Golf: Jeff Schimmelpfennig; Phone: 815-939-5372; E-mail: jschimm@olivet.edu.

Soccer: Bill Bahr; Phone: 815-928-5464; E-mail: bbahr@olivet.edu.

Softball: Ritchie Richardson; Phone: 815-939-5166; E-mail: rrichard@olivet.edu.

Tennis: Obie Coomer; Phone: 815-939-5117; E-mail: ocoomer@olivet.edu.

Track and Field: Michael McDowell; Phone: 815-939-5165; E-mail: mmcdowel@olivet.edu.
Volleyball: Brenda Williams; Phone: 815-928-5411; E-mail: bwillia1@olivet.edu.

ORAL ROBERTS UNIVERSITY
Tulsa, Oklahoma

Golden Eagles ◆ NCAA I ◆ Mid-Continent Conference
◆ http://www.oru.edu/

Independent interdenominational comprehensive, founded 1963
Coed, 3,363 undergraduate students, 91% full-time, 61% women, 39% men
Urban 263-acre campus
Moderately difficult entrance level, 59% of applicants were admitted

Freshmen *Admission:* 1,363 applied, 867 were accepted, 644 enrolled. *Test scores:* SAT verbal scores over 500: 64%; SAT math scores over 500: 62%; SAT verbal scores over 600: 25%; SAT math scores over 600: 22%; SAT verbal scores over 700: 5%; SAT math scores over 700: 3%.
Tuition and fees (2003–04): $13,970 (full-time). *Room and board:* $5900 (room only: $2880).
Financial Aid (All incoming freshmen): *Average need-based gift aid:* $8499. *Average non-need based aid:* $6913. *Average aid to full-time undergraduates:* $13,752.
Athletic Department: *Director of Athletics:* Mike Carter; Phone: 918-495-7150; Fax: 918-495-7123; E-mail: mcarter@oru.edu. *Sports Information Director:* Cris Belvin; Phone: 918-495-7094; E-mail: cbelvin@oru.edu.

MEN'S COACHES
Baseball: Rob Walton; Phone: 918-495-7130; E-mail: rwalton@oru.edu.
Basketball: Scott Sutton; Phone: 918-495-7153; E-mail: ssutton@oru.edu.
Cheerleading: Paige White; Phone: 918-495-7151; E-mail: pwhite@oru.edu.
Cross Country: Alick Musukuma; Phone: 918-495-7251; E-mail: amusukuma@oru.edu.
Golf: Bob Canada; Phone: 918-495-6822; E-mail: bcanada@oru.edu.
Soccer: Steve Hayes; Phone: 918-495-6817; E-mail: shayes@oru.edu.
Tennis: Brad Richison; Phone: 918-495-6823; E-mail: brichison@oru.edu.
Track and Field: Joe Dial; Phone: 918-495-6839; E-mail: jdial@oru.edu.

WOMEN'S COACHES
Basketball: Jerry Finkbeiner; Phone: 918-495-7153; E-mail: jfinkbeiner@oru.edu.
Cheerleading: Paige White; Phone: 918-495-7151; E-mail: pwhite@oru.edu.
Cross Country: Alick Musukuma; Phone: 918-495-7251; E-mail: amusukuma@oru.edu.
Golf: Lance Watson; Phone: 918-495-7618; E-mail: lwatson@oru.edu.
Soccer: Kyle Cussen; Phone: 918-495-6830; E-mail: kcussen@oru.edu.
Tennis: Linda Breckenridge; Phone: 918-495-6671; E-mail: libreckenridge@oru.edu.
Track and Field: Joe Dial; Phone: 918-495-6839; E-mail: jdial@oru.edu.
Volleyball: Sheera Sirola; Phone: 918-495-6891; E-mail: ssirola@oru.edu.

OREGON INSTITUTE OF TECHNOLOGY
Klamath Falls, Oregon

Owls ◆ NAIA ◆ Cascade Collegiate Conference ◆ http://www.oit.edu/

State-supported 4-year, founded 1947, part of Oregon University System
Coed, 3,235 undergraduate students, 63% full-time, 46% women, 54% men
Small-town 173-acre campus
Moderately difficult entrance level, 53% of applicants were admitted

Freshmen *Admission:* 877 applied, 473 were accepted, 354 enrolled. *Test scores:* SAT verbal scores over 500: 58%; SAT math scores over 500: 67%; SAT verbal scores over 600: 20%; SAT math scores over 600: 23%; SAT verbal scores over 700: 4%; SAT math scores over 700: 3%.
Tuition and fees (2003–04): $4443 (resident), $13,623 (nonresident). *Room and board:* $6135.
Financial Aid (All incoming freshmen): *Average need-based gift aid:* $3682. *Average aid to full-time undergraduates:* $3561.
Athletic Department: *Director of Athletics:* Michael Schell; Phone: 541-885-1311; Fax: 541-885-1633; E-mail: schellm@oit.edu. *Sports Information Director:* Bobby Thompson; Phone: 541-885-1851; E-mail: thompsb@oit.edu.

MEN'S COACHES
Baseball: Pete Whisler; Phone: 541-885-1722; E-mail: whislerp@oit.edu.
Basketball: Dan Miles; Phone: 541-885-1625; E-mail: milesd@oit.edu.
Cross Country: Ken Coffman; Phone: 541-885-1399; E-mail: coffmank@oit.edu.
Track and Field: Ken Coffman; Phone: 541-885-1399; E-mail: coffmank@oit.edu.

WOMEN'S COACHES
Basketball: Tom Looney; Phone: 541-885-1632; E-mail: loneyt@oit.edu.
Cross Country: Ken Coffman; Phone: 541-885-1399; E-mail: coffmank@oit.edu.
Soccer: Kevin Sims; Phone: 541-885-1626; E-mail: simske@oit.edu.
Softball: Dan Miles; Phone: 541-885-1625; E-mail: milesd@oit.edu.
Track and Field: Ken Coffman; Phone: 541-885-1399; E-mail: coffmank@oit.edu.
Volleyball: Amanda Mitzner; Phone: 541-885-1632; E-mail: loneyt@oit.edu.

OREGON STATE UNIVERSITY
Corvallis, Oregon

Beavers ◆ NCAA I ◆ Pacific-10 Conference
◆ http://oregonstate.edu/

State-supported university, founded 1868, part of Oregon University System
Coed, 15,599 undergraduate students, 90% full-time, 47% women, 53% men
Small-town 422-acre campus with easy access to Portland
Moderately difficult entrance level, 86% of applicants were admitted

Freshmen *Admission:* 7,410 applied, 6,529 were accepted, 2,949 enrolled. *Test scores:* SAT verbal scores over 500: 65%; SAT math scores over 500: 72%; SAT verbal scores over 600: 24%; SAT math scores over 600: 30%; SAT verbal scores over 700: 3%; SAT math scores over 700: 5%.
Tuition and fees (2003–04): $4869 (resident), $17,625 (nonresident). *Room and board:* $6336.
Athletic Department: *Director of Athletics:* Bob De Carolis; Phone: 541-737-2547; Fax: 541-737-4002; E-mail: bob.decarolis@orst.edu. *Sports Information Director:* Hal Cowan; Phone: 541-737-3720; E-mail: hal.cowan@orst.edu.

MEN'S COACHES
Baseball: Pat Casey; Phone: 541-737-2825; E-mail: pat.casey@orst.edu.
Basketball: Jay John; Phone: 541-737-2076; E-mail: jay.john@orst.edu.
Cheerleading: Amber Bezates; Phone: 541-737-5593; E-mail: amber.bezates@orst.edu.
Football: Mike Riley; Phone: 541-737-2614.
Golf: Brian Watts; Phone: 541-737-7494; E-mail: brian.watts@orst.edu.
Soccer: Dana Taylor; Phone: 541-737-7489; E-mail: dana.taylor@orst.edu.
Wrestling: Joe Wells; Phone: 541-737-7493; E-mail: joe.wells@orst.edu.

WOMEN'S COACHES
Basketball: Judy Spoelstra; Phone: 541-737-7481; E-mail: judy.spoelstra@orst.edu.
Cheerleading: Amber Bezates; Phone: 541-737-5593; E-mail: amber.bezates@orst.edu.
Cross Country: Kelly Sullivan; Phone: 541-737-2547; E-mail: kelly.sullivan@oregonstate.edu.
Golf: Rise Lakawske; Phone: 541-737-6161; E-mail: rise.lakawske@orst.edu.
Gymnastics: Tanya Chaplin; Phone: 541-737-3889; E-mail: tanya.chaplin@orst.edu.

Oregon State University *(continued)*

Soccer: Steve Fennah; Phone: 541-737-3081; E-mail: steve.fennah@orst.edu.
Softball: Kirk Walker; Phone: 541-737-2789; E-mail: kirk.walker@orst.edu.
Swimming: Larry Liebowitz; Phone: 541-737-1075; E-mail: larry.liebowitz@oregonstate.edu.
Track and Field: Kelly Sullivan; Phone: 541-737-2547; E-mail: kelly.sullivan@oregonstate.edu.
Volleyball: Nancy Somera; Phone: 541-737-7491; E-mail: nancy.somera@orst.edu.

OTTAWA UNIVERSITY
Ottawa, Kansas

Braves ◆ NAIA ◆ Kansas Collegiate Conference ◆ http://www.ottawa.edu/

Independent American Baptist Churches in the USA comprehensive, founded 1865
Coed, 530 undergraduate students, 89% full-time, 45% women, 55% men
Small-town 60-acre campus with easy access to Kansas City
Moderately difficult entrance level, 32% of applicants were admitted

Freshmen *Admission:* 561 applied, 245 were accepted, 116 enrolled.
Tuition and fees (2004–05): $14,150 (full-time). *Room and board:* $5450 (room only: $2400).
Athletic Department: *Director of Athletics:* Andy Carrier; Phone: 785-242-5200; Fax: 785-229-1015; E-mail: acarrier@ottawa.edu. *Sports Information Director:* Jeffrey Wacker; Phone: 785-242-5200; E-mail: jwacker@ottawa.edu.

MEN'S COACHES
Baseball: Jarrod Titus; Phone: 785-242-5200; E-mail: titus@ottawa.edu.
Basketball: Andy Carrier; Phone: 785-242-5200; E-mail: acarrier@ottawa.edu.
Cheerleading: Kathy Hinderliter; Phone: 785-242-5200; E-mail: hinderl@ottawa.edu.
Cross Country: Kirk Wren; Phone: 785-242-5200; E-mail: wren@ottawa.edu.
Football: Patrick Ross; Phone: 785-242-5200; E-mail: rossp@ottawa.edu.
Golf: Pete Van Mullen; Phone: 785-242-5200; E-mail: vanmullemp@ottawa.edu.
Soccer: Chip Wiggins; Phone: 785-242-5200; E-mail: wigginsc@ottawa.edu.
Track and Field: Kirk Wren; Phone: 785-242-5200; E-mail: wren@ottawa.edu.

WOMEN'S COACHES
Basketball: Arabie Conner; Phone: 785-242-5200; E-mail: connera@ottawa.edu.
Cheerleading: Kathy Hinderliter; Phone: 785-242-5200; E-mail: hinderl@ottawa.edu.
Cross Country: Kirk Wren; Phone: 785-242-5200; E-mail: wren@ottawa.edu.
Soccer: Chip Wiggins; Phone: 785-242-5200; E-mail: wigginsc@ottawa.edu.
Softball: Jay Kahnt; Phone: 785-242-5200; E-mail: kahntj@ottawa.edu.
Track and Field: Kirk Wren; Phone: 785-242-5200; E-mail: wren@ottawa.edu.
Volleyball: Kendra Oberzank; Phone: 785-242-5200; E-mail: oberzank@ottawa.edu.

OTTERBEIN COLLEGE
Westerville, Ohio

Cardinals ◆ NCAA III ◆ Ohio Athletic Conference ◆ http://www.otterbein.edu/

Independent United Methodist comprehensive, founded 1847
Coed, 2,088 undergraduate students, 100% full-time, 63% women, 37% men
Suburban 142-acre campus with easy access to Columbus
Moderately difficult entrance level, 78% of applicants were admitted

Freshmen *Admission:* 2,305 applied, 1,929 were accepted, 632 enrolled. *Test scores:* SAT verbal scores over 500: 71%; SAT math scores over 500: 64%; SAT verbal scores over 600: 24%; SAT math scores over 600: 20%; SAT verbal scores over 700: 3%; SAT math scores over 700: 2%.
Tuition and fees (2003–04): $20,133 (full-time). *Room and board:* $5952 (room only: $2712).
Athletic Department: *Director of Athletics:* Dick Reynolds; Phone: 614-823-3529; Fax: 614-823-1966; E-mail: rreynolds@otterbein.edu. *Sports Information Director:* Ed Syguda; Phone: 614-823-3530; E-mail: esyguda@otterbein.edu.

MEN'S COACHES
Baseball: George Powell; Phone: 614-823-3529; E-mail: gpowell@otterbein.edu.
Basketball: Dick Reynolds; Phone: 614-823-3529; E-mail: rreynolds@otterbein.edu.
Cross Country: Ryan Borland; Phone: 614-823-3529; E-mail: dborland@otterbein.edu.
Football: Joe Loth; Phone: 614-823-3529; E-mail: jloth@otterbein.edu.
Golf: Matt Smith; Phone: 614-823-3529; E-mail: msmith@otterbein.edu.
Soccer: Gerald D'Arcy; Phone: 614-823-3529; E-mail: gdarcy@otterbein.edu.
Tennis: Gerald D'Arcy; Phone: 614-823-3529; E-mail: dmorris@otterbein.edu.
Track and Field: Doug Welsh; Phone: 614-823-3529; E-mail: dwelsh@otterbein.edu.

WOMEN'S COACHES
Basketball: Connie Richardson; Phone: 614-823-3529; E-mail: crichardson@otterbein.edu.
Cross Country: Ryan Borland; Phone: 614-823-3529; E-mail: dborland@otterbein.edu.
Golf: Sharon Sexton; Phone: 614-823-3529; E-mail: ssexton@otterbein.edu.
Soccer: Brandon Koons; Phone: 614-823-3529; E-mail: bkoons@otterbein.edu.
Softball: Deb Torman; Phone: 614-823-3529; E-mail: dtorman@otterbein.edu.
Tennis: Pat Anderson; Phone: 614-823-3529; E-mail: paanderson@otterbein.edu.
Track and Field: Doug Welsh; Phone: 614-823-3529; E-mail: dwelsh@otterbein.edu.
Volleyball: Sharon Sexton; Phone: 614-823-3529; E-mail: ssexton@otterbein.edu.

OUACHITA BAPTIST UNIVERSITY
Arkadelphia, Arkansas

Tigers ◆ NCAA II ◆ Gulf South Conference ◆ http://www.obu.edu/

Independent Baptist 4-year, founded 1886
Coed, 1,530 undergraduate students, 97% full-time, 54% women, 46% men
Small-town 84-acre campus with easy access to Little Rock
Moderately difficult entrance level, 78% of applicants were admitted

Freshmen *Admission:* 879 applied, 704 were accepted, 343 enrolled. *Test scores:* SAT verbal scores over 500: 70%; SAT math scores over 500: 74%; SAT verbal scores over 600: 32%; SAT math scores over 600: 29%; SAT verbal scores over 700: 8%; SAT math scores over 700: 7%.
Tuition and fees (2004–05): $15,170 (full-time). *Room and board:* $4800.

Financial Aid (All incoming freshmen): *Average need-based gift aid:* $5166. *Average non-need based aid:* $5058. *Average aid to full-time undergraduates:* $12,323.
Athletic Department: *Director of Athletics:* David Sharp; Phone: 870-245-5182; Fax: 870-245-5598; E-mail: sharpd@obu.edu. *Sports Information Director:* Chris Babb; Phone: 870-245-5186; E-mail: babbc@obu.edu.

MEN'S COACHES

Baseball: B.J. Brown; Phone: 870-245-4255; E-mail: brownb@obu.edu.
Basketball: Charlie Schaef; Phone: 870-245-5184; E-mail: schaefc@obu.edu.
Cheerleading: Sheila Baker; Phone: 870-245-5367.
Diving: Jim Dann; Phone: 870-245-5116; E-mail: dannj@obu.edu.
Football: Todd Knight; Phone: 870-245-5314; E-mail: knighttf@obu.edu.
Golf: David Sharp; Phone: 870-245-5182; E-mail: sharpd@obu.edu.
Soccer: Erik Forrest; Phone: 870-245-5187; E-mail: forreste@obu.edu.
Swimming: Jim Dann; Phone: 870-245-5116; E-mail: dannj@obu.edu.
Tennis: Craig Ward; Phone: 870-245-2441; E-mail: wardc@obu.edu.

WOMEN'S COACHES

Basketball: Garry Crowder; Phone: 870-245-5294; E-mail: crowderg@obu.edu.
Cheerleading: Sheila Baker; Phone: 870-245-5367.
Cross Country: Jason Jones; Phone: 870-245-5296; E-mail: jonesjw@obu.edu.
Diving: Jim Dann; Phone: 870-245-5116; E-mail: dannj@obu.edu.
Soccer: Erik Forrest; Phone: 870-245-5187; E-mail: forreste@obu.edu.
Softball: Marissa Lafitte; Phone: 870-245-5083; E-mail: lafittem@obu.edu.
Swimming: Jim Dann; Phone: 870-245-5116; E-mail: dannj@obu.edu.
Tennis: Betsy Danner; Phone: 870-245-5183; E-mail: dannerb@obu.edu.
Volleyball: Marissa Lafitte; Phone: 870-245-5083; E-mail: lafittem@obu.edu.

PACE UNIVERSITY
New York, New York

Setters ◆ NCAA II ◆ Northeast-10 Conference ◆ http://www.pace.edu/

Independent university, founded 1906
Coed, 8,871 undergraduate students, 78% full-time, 61% women, 39% men
Moderately difficult entrance level, 73% of applicants were admitted

Freshmen *Admission:* 7,973 applied, 5,906 were accepted, 1,657 enrolled. *Test scores:* SAT verbal scores over 500: 71%; SAT math scores over 500: 75%; SAT verbal scores over 600: 21%; SAT math scores over 600: 25%; SAT verbal scores over 700: 2%; SAT math scores over 700: 3%.
Tuition and fees (2003–04): $21,104 (full-time). *Room and board:* $7650.
Financial Aid (All incoming freshmen): *Average need-based gift aid:* $10,796. *Average non-need based aid:* $6765. *Average aid to full-time undergraduates:* $15,642.
Athletic Department: *Director of Athletics:* Joseph O'Donnell; Phone: 914-773-3481; Fax: 914-773-3441; E-mail: jodonnell@pace.edu. *Sports Information Director:* Ken Sweeten; Phone: 914-773-3888; E-mail: ksweeten@pace.edu.

MEN'S COACHES

Baseball: Henry Manning; Phone: 914-773-3413; E-mail: hmanning@pace.edu.
Basketball: Jim Harter; Phone: 212-773-3274; E-mail: jharter@pace.edu.
Cheerleading: Moire Givney; Phone: 914-773-3826.
Cross Country: Tim Fulton; Phone: 914-923-3727.
Diving: Greg Smith; Phone: 914-773-3279; E-mail: gsmith2@pace.edu.
Football: Gregory Lusardi; Phone: 914-773-2885; E-mail: glusardi@pace.edu.
Golf: Judy Carlson; Phone: 914-773-2790; E-mail: jcarlson@pace.edu.
Lacrosse: John Jez; Phone: 914-245-2903; E-mail: jjez@pace.edu.
Swimming: Greg Smith; Phone: 914-773-3279; E-mail: gsmith2@pace.edu.
Tennis: Rich Corsetti; Phone: 914-923-2788; E-mail: rcorsetti@pace.edu.
Track and Field: Tim Fulton; Phone: 914-923-3727.

WOMEN'S COACHES

Basketball: Carrie Seymour; Phone: 914-923-3970; E-mail: cseymour@pace.edu.
Cheerleading: Moire Givney; Phone: 914-773-3826.
Cross Country: Tim Fulton; Phone: 914-923-3727.
Diving: Greg Smith; Phone: 914-773-3279; E-mail: gsmith2@pace.edu.
Golf: Judy Carlson; Phone: 914-773-2790; E-mail: jcarlson@pace.edu.
Soccer: Mike Winn; Phone: 914-923-2904; E-mail: mwinn@pace.edu.
Softball: Claudia Stabile; Phone: 914-923-2902; E-mail: cstabile@pace.edu.
Swimming: Greg Smith; Phone: 914-773-3279; E-mail: gsmith2@pace.edu.
Tennis: Rich Corsetti; Phone: 914-923-2788; E-mail: rcorsetti@pace.edu.
Track and Field: Tim Fulton; Phone: 914-923-3727.
Volleyball: Phone: 914-773-3987.

PACIFIC LUTHERAN UNIVERSITY
Tacoma, Washington

Lutes ◆ NCAA III ◆ Northwest Conference ◆ http://www.plu.edu/

Independent religious comprehensive, founded 1890, affiliated with Evangelical Lutheran Church in America
Coed, 3,185 undergraduate students, 92% full-time, 63% women, 37% men
Suburban 126-acre campus with easy access to Seattle
Moderately difficult entrance level, 80% of applicants were admitted

Freshmen *Admission:* 1,973 applied, 1,575 were accepted, 694 enrolled. *Test scores:* SAT verbal scores over 500: 77%; SAT math scores over 500: 76%; SAT verbal scores over 600: 38%; SAT math scores over 600: 35%; SAT verbal scores over 700: 8%; SAT math scores over 700: 3%.
Tuition and fees (2003–04): $19,610 (full-time). *Room and board:* $6105 (room only: $3000).
Financial Aid (All incoming freshmen): *Average need-based gift aid:* $6966. *Average non-need based aid:* $5503. *Average aid to full-time undergraduates:* $17,194.
Athletic Department: *Director of Athletics:* Paul Hoseth; Phone: 253-535-7361; Fax: 253-535-7584; E-mail: hosethpe@plu.edu. *Sports Information Director:* Dave Girrard; Phone: 253-535-7356; E-mail: girrardl@plu.edu.

MEN'S COACHES

Baseball: Geoff Loomis; Phone: 253-535-8789; E-mail: loomisgs@plu.edu.
Basketball: Dave Harshman; Phone: 253-535-8706; E-mail: harshmdb@plu.edu.
Cheerleading: Kristen Kay; Phone: 253-548-2244.
Cross Country: Brad Moore; Phone: 253-535-7362; E-mail: mooreba@plu.edu.
Football: Frosty Westering; Phone: 253-535-8311; E-mail: westerse@plu.edu.
Golf: Gary Cinotto; Phone: 253-535-7393; E-mail: glcpro@aol.com.
Soccer: John Yorke; Phone: 253-535-6900; E-mail: jyorke3@aol.com.
Swimming: Jim Johnson; Phone: 253-535-7370; E-mail: johnsonjf@plu.edu.
Tennis: Craig Hamilton; Phone: 253-535-6900; E-mail: coachhams@hotmail.com.
Track and Field: Brad Moore; Phone: 253-535-7362; E-mail: mooreba@plu.edu.

WOMEN'S COACHES

Basketball: Gil Rigell; Phone: 253-535-7353; E-mail: rigellga@plu.edu.
Cheerleading: Kristen Kay; Phone: 253-548-2244.
Cross Country: Brad Moore; Phone: 253-535-7362; E-mail: mooreba@plu.edu.
Golf: Mike Quatsoe; Phone: 253-535-7393; E-mail: quatsomj@plu.edu.
Soccer: Jerrod Fleury; Phone: 253-531-6900; E-mail: fleuryjp@plu.edu.
Softball: Rick Noren; Phone: 253-535-7419; E-mail: norenre@plu.edu.
Swimming: Jim Johnson; Phone: 253-535-7370; E-mail: johnsonjf@plu.edu.
Tennis: Janel McFeat; Phone: 253-531-6900; E-mail: owendog@msn.com.
Track and Field: Brad Moore; Phone: 253-535-7362; E-mail: mooreba@plu.edu.
Volleyball: Kevin Aoki; Phone: 253-535-8799; E-mail: aokika@plu.edu.

PACIFIC UNION COLLEGE
Angwin, California

Pioneers ◆ NAIA ◆ California Pacific Conference ◆ http://www.puc.edu/

Independent Seventh-day Adventist comprehensive, founded 1882
Coed, 1,494 undergraduate students, 99% full-time, 54% women, 46% men
Rural 200-acre campus with easy access to San Francisco
Moderately difficult entrance level, 4% of applicants were admitted

Freshmen *Admission:* 1,688 applied, 589 were accepted, 282 enrolled. *Test scores:* SAT verbal scores over 500: 62%; SAT math scores over 500: 58%; SAT verbal scores over 600: 24%; SAT math scores over 600: 24%; SAT verbal scores over 700: 5%; SAT math scores over 700: 4%.
Tuition and fees (2003–04): $17,355 (full-time). *Room and board:* $4902 (room only: $2952).
Financial Aid (All incoming freshmen): *Average need-based gift aid:* $7940. *Average non-need based aid:* $6523. *Average aid to full-time undergraduates:* $11,652.
Athletic Department: *Director of Athletics:* Chuck Evans; Phone: 707-965-6796; Fax: 707-965-6390; E-mail: cgevans@puc.edu.

MEN'S COACHES
Basketball: Scott Blunt; Phone: 707-965-6347; E-mail: sblunt@puc.edu.
Cross Country: Bob Paulson; Phone: 707-965-6348; E-mail: bpaulson@puc.edu.
Volleyball: Robert Castillo; Phone: 707-965-6652; E-mail: rcastillo@puc.edu.

WOMEN'S COACHES
Basketball: Robert Castillo; Phone: 707-965-6652; E-mail: rcastillo@puc.edu.
Cross Country: Bob Paulson; Phone: 707-965-6348; E-mail: bpaulson@puc.edu.
Volleyball: Herschel Sandler; Phone: 707-965-6653; E-mail: hsandler@puc.edu.

PACIFIC UNIVERSITY
Forest Grove, Oregon

Boxers ◆ NCAA III ◆ Northwest Conference ◆ http://www.pacificu.edu/

Independent comprehensive, founded 1849
Coed, 1,203 undergraduate students, 93% full-time, 61% women, 39% men
Small-town 55-acre campus with easy access to Portland
Moderately difficult entrance level, 79% of applicants were admitted

Freshmen *Admission:* 1,214 applied, 1,020 were accepted, 303 enrolled. *Test scores:* SAT verbal scores over 500: 78%; SAT math scores over 500: 79%; SAT verbal scores over 600: 32%; SAT math scores over 600: 31%; SAT verbal scores over 700: 1%; SAT math scores over 700: 3%.
Tuition and fees (2003–04): $19,890 (full-time). *Room and board:* $5540 (room only: $2680).
Financial Aid (All incoming freshmen): *Average need-based gift aid:* $12,587. *Average non-need based aid:* $8923. *Average aid to full-time undergraduates:* $17,484.

MEN'S COACHES
Baseball: Greg Bradley; Phone: 503-352-2142; E-mail: brad0757@pacificu.edu.
Basketball: Ken Schumann; Phone: 503-352-2180; E-mail: schumank@pacificu.edu.
Cross Country: Ron Tabb; Phone: 503-352-2164; E-mail: tabb1112@pacificu.edu.
Golf: Richard Warren; Phone: 503-352-2271; E-mail: warr0773@pacificu.edu.
Soccer: Jim Brazeau; Phone: 503-352-2272; E-mail: jimbrazeau@pacificu.edu.
Tennis: Monika Kowalew; Phone: 503-352-2968; E-mail: kowa4033@pacificu.edu.
Track and Field: Ron Tabb; Phone: 503-352-2164; E-mail: tabb1112@pacificu.edu.

Wrestling: Scott Miller; Phone: 503-352-2827; E-mail: sdmiller@pacificu.edu.

WOMEN'S COACHES
Basketball: Jeff Thompson; Phone: 503-352-2166; E-mail: thom4046@pacificu.edu.
Cross Country: Ron Tabb; Phone: 503-352-2164; E-mail: tabb1112@pacificu.edu.
Soccer: Jim Brazeau; Phone: 503-352-2272; E-mail: jimbrazeau@pacificu.edu.
Softball: Tim Hill; Phone: 503-352-2167; E-mail: hill3383@pacificu.edu.
Tennis: Monika Kowalew; Phone: 503-352-2968; E-mail: kowa4033@pacificu.edu.
Track and Field: Ron Tabb; Phone: 503-352-2164; E-mail: tabb1112@pacificu.edu.
Volleyball: Chris Stanley; Phone: 503-352-3152; E-mail: stan9303@pacificu.edu.

PAINE COLLEGE
Augusta, Georgia

Lions ◆ NCAA II ◆ Southern Intercollegiate Athletic Conference ◆ http://www.paine.edu/

Independent Methodist 4-year, founded 1882
Coed, 972 undergraduate students, 88% full-time, 70% women, 30% men
Urban 55-acre campus with easy access to Atlanta
Minimally difficult entrance level, 1% of applicants were admitted

Freshmen *Admission:* 3,837 applied, 287 were accepted, 264 enrolled. *Test scores:* SAT verbal scores over 500: 9%; SAT math scores over 500: 13%; SAT verbal scores over 600: 1%; SAT math scores over 600: 1%.
Tuition and fees (2003–04): $9082 (full-time). *Room and board:* $3940.
Athletic Department: *Director of Athletics:* Ronnie Spry; Phone: 706-821-8353; Fax: 706-821-8376; E-mail: spryr@mail.paine.edu. *Sports Information Director:* Kimberly May; Phone: 706-821-8353; E-mail: mayk@mail.paine.edu.

MEN'S COACHES
Baseball: Pete Cardenas; Phone: 706-821-8200; E-mail: cardenasp@mail.paine.edu.
Basketball: Ron Spry; Phone: 706-821-8200; E-mail: spryr@mail.paine.edu.
Cross Country: Carlos McNair; Phone: 706-821-8200; E-mail: mcnairc@mail.paine.edu.
Track and Field: Carlos McNair; Phone: 706-821-8200; E-mail: mcnairc@mail.paine.edu.

WOMEN'S COACHES
Basketball: Selina Bynum Kohn; Phone: 706-821-8200; E-mail: bynums@mail.paine.edu.
Cross Country: Willie Adams; Phone: 706-821-8200; E-mail: adamsw@mail.paine.edu.
Softball: Zack Howard; Phone: 706-821-8200; E-mail: howardz@mail.paine.edu.
Track and Field: Willie Adams; Phone: 706-821-8200; E-mail: adamsw@mail.paine.edu.
Volleyball: Selina Bynum Kohn; Phone: 706-821-8200; E-mail: bynums@mail.paine.edu.

PARK UNIVERSITY
Parkville, Missouri

Pirates ◆ NAIA ◆ Midlands Collegiate Conference ◆ http://www.park.edu/

Independent comprehensive, founded 1875
Coed, 11,520 undergraduate students, 10% full-time, 48% women, 52% men
Suburban 800-acre campus with easy access to Kansas City
Moderately difficult entrance level

Freshmen *Admission:* 100 enrolled.
Tuition and fees (2003–04): $5600 (full-time). *Room and board:* $5180.

Financial Aid (All incoming freshmen): *Average need-based gift aid:* $2380. *Average non-need based aid:* $3748. *Average aid to full-time undergraduates:* $6593.
Athletic Department: *Director of Athletics:* Claude English; Phone: 816-584-6492; Fax: 816-741-4911; E-mail: cenglish@mail.park.edu. *Sports Information Director:* Derek Mueller; Phone: 816-584-6490; E-mail: dmueller@mail.park.edu.

MEN'S COACHES
Baseball: Cary Lundy; Phone: 816-584-6746; E-mail: clundy@mail.park.edu.
Basketball: Claude English; Phone: 816-584-6492; E-mail: cenglish@mail.park.edu.
Cross Country: Brian Renshaw; Phone: 816-584-6488; E-mail: brianrenshaw@hotmail.com.
Soccer: Efrem Shimlis; Phone: 816-584-6487; E-mail: eshimlis@mail.park.edu.
Track and Field: Brian Renshaw; Phone: 816-584-6488; E-mail: brianrenshaw@hotmail.com.
Volleyball: Lorenzo Barrientez; Phone: 816-584-6763; E-mail: lbarrientez@park.edu.

WOMEN'S COACHES
Basketball: Joe Meriweather; Phone: 816-584-6491; E-mail: coachmeriweather@mail.park.edu.
Cross Country: Brian Renshaw; Phone: 816-584-6488; E-mail: brianrenshaw@hotmail.com.
Cross Country: Pat Fayard; Phone: 816-584-6425; E-mail: pfayard@mail.park.edu.
Golf: Kelly Defeo; Phone: 816-584-6238; E-mail: kelly.defeo@park.edu.
Soccer: Scott Bowen; Phone: 816-584-6408; E-mail: sbowen@mail.park.edu.
Softball: Phone: 816-584-6443.
Track and Field: Brian Renshaw; Phone: 816-584-6488; E-mail: brianrenshaw@hotmail.com.
Volleyball: Peggy Tuter; Phone: 816-584-6493; E-mail: ptuter@mail.park.edu.

PATTEN UNIVERSITY
Oakland, California

NAIA ◆ Independent ◆ http://www.patten.edu/

Independent interdenominational comprehensive, founded 1944
Coed, 446 undergraduate students, 46% full-time, 40% women, 60% men
Urban 5-acre campus with easy access to San Francisco
Noncompetitive entrance level, 50% of applicants were admitted

Freshmen *Admission:* 67 applied, 39 were accepted, 10 enrolled.
Tuition and fees (2003–04): $9840 (full-time). *Room and board:* $5800.

MEN'S COACHES
Basketball: .

PAUL QUINN COLLEGE
Dallas, Texas

Tigers ◆ NAIA ◆ Red River Conference ◆ http://www.pqc.edu/

Independent African Methodist Episcopal 4-year, founded 1872
Coed, 871 undergraduate students, 84% full-time, 52% women, 48% men
Suburban 132-acre campus
Moderately difficult entrance level, 2% of applicants were admitted

Freshmen *Admission:* 3,221 applied, 867 were accepted, 154 enrolled.
Test scores: SAT verbal scores over 500: 10%; SAT math scores over 500: 5%.
Tuition and fees (2003–04): $4980 (full-time). *Room and board:* $3800 (room only: $1400).
Financial Aid (All incoming freshmen): *Average need-based gift aid:* $1265. *Average aid to full-time undergraduates:* $9900.
Athletic Department: *Director of Athletics:* Fax: 214-302-3559.

MEN'S COACHES
Baseball: Don Coffer; Phone: 214-302-3598; E-mail: dcofer@pqc.edu.
Basketball: Keith McKinnon; Phone: 214-302-3598; E-mail: kemckinn@pqc.edu.
Football: Archie Cooley; Phone: 214-302-3598; E-mail: acooley@pqc.edu.
Track and Field: Maurice West; Phone: 214-302-3598.

WOMEN'S COACHES
Basketball: Tina Wagoner; Phone: 214-302-3598.
Track and Field: Maurice West; Phone: 214-302-3598.
Volleyball: Tamara Brown; Phone: 214-302-3598; E-mail: tbrown@pqc.edu.

PEACE COLLEGE
Raleigh, North Carolina

Pride ◆ NCAA III ◆ USA South Athletic Conference ◆ http://www.peace.edu/

Independent religious 4-year, founded 1857, affiliated with Presbyterian Church (U.S.A.)
Women only, 701 undergraduate students, 95% full-time, 100% women, 100% men
Urban 19-acre campus
Moderately difficult entrance level, 35% of applicants were admitted

Freshmen *Admission:* 717 applied, 251 were accepted, 251 enrolled.
Test scores: SAT verbal scores over 500: 44%; SAT math scores over 500: 40%; SAT verbal scores over 600: 9%; SAT math scores over 600: 6%; SAT verbal scores over 700: 2%.
Tuition and fees (2004–05): $16,881 (full-time). *Room and board:* $6526.
Financial Aid (All incoming freshmen): *Average need-based gift aid:* $10,584. *Average non-need based aid:* $8510. *Average aid to full-time undergraduates:* $13,099.
Athletic Department: *Director of Athletics:* Christian Dystat; Phone: 919-508-2329; Fax: 919-508-2326; E-mail: cdysart@peace.edu. *Sports Information Director:* Heather Daniels; Phone: 919-508-2331; E-mail: hdaniels@peace.edu.

WOMEN'S COACHES
Basketball: Christian Dysart; Phone: 919-508-2329; E-mail: cdysart@peace.edu.
Cross Country: Rob King; Phone: 919-508-2334; E-mail: rking@peace.edu.
Soccer: Jennie Altherr; Phone: 919-508-2334; E-mail: jaltherr@peace.edu.
Softball: Charlie Dobbins; Phone: 919-508-2334; E-mail: cdobbins@peace.edu.
Tennis: Cy King; Phone: 919-508-2394; E-mail: cking@peace.edu.
Volleyball: Heather Daniels; Phone: 919-508-2223; E-mail: hdaniels@peace.edu.

THE PENNSYLVANIA STATE UNIVERSITY ALTOONA COLLEGE
Altoona, Pennsylvania

Cougars ◆ NCAA III ◆ Allegheny Mountain Conference ◆ http://www.aa.psu.edu/

State-related 4-year, founded 1939, part of Pennsylvania State University
Coed, 3,771 undergraduate students, 92% full-time, 50% women, 50% men
Suburban 106-acre campus
Moderately difficult entrance level, 71% of applicants were admitted

Freshmen *Admission:* 4,664 applied, 3,448 were accepted, 1,325 enrolled. *Test scores:* SAT verbal scores over 500: 55%; SAT math scores over 500: 60%; SAT verbal scores over 600: 9%; SAT math scores over 600: 16%; SAT verbal scores over 700: %; SAT math scores over 700: 1%.
Tuition and fees (2003–04): $9304 (resident), $14,124 (nonresident). *Room and board:* $5940 (room only: $3080).

The Pennsylvania State University Altoona College *(continued)*

Financial Aid (All incoming freshmen): *Average need-based gift aid:* $4137. *Average non-need based aid:* $1459. *Average aid to full-time undergraduates:* $9680.
Athletic Department: *Director of Athletics:* Fredina Ingold; Phone: 814-949-5410; Fax: 814-949-5416; E-mail: fmi1@psu.edu. *Sports Information Director:* Brent Baird; Phone: 814-949-5556; E-mail: rzb3@psu.edu.

MEN'S COACHES
Baseball: Joe Piotti; Phone: 814-949-5226; E-mail: xp50@psu.edu.
Basketball: Armon Gilliam; Phone: 814-949-5469; E-mail: alg954@psu.edu.
Cheerleading: John Anderson; Phone: 814-949-5300; E-mail: jandersonwillbe@hotmail.com.
Cross Country: Doug Hoover; Phone: 814-832-2857; E-mail: deh122@psu.edu.
Diving: Nanette Cummings; Phone: 814-949-5233; E-mail: ncummings1@yahoo.com.
Golf: Greg Johnson; Phone: 814-949-5234.
Soccer: John Parente; Phone: 814-949-5735; E-mail: jmp296@psu.edu.
Swimming: Nanette Cummings; Phone: 814-949-5233; E-mail: ncummings1@yahoo.com.
Tennis: Steve Genter; Phone: 814-944-9412; E-mail: jessgenter@yahoo.com.

WOMEN'S COACHES
Basketball: John Nardozza; Phone: 814-949-5234.
Cheerleading: John Anderson; Phone: 814-949-5300; E-mail: jandersonwillbe@hotmail.com.
Cross Country: Doug Hoover; Phone: 814-832-2857; E-mail: deh122@psu.edu.
Diving: Nanette Cummings; Phone: 814-949-5233; E-mail: ncummings1@yahoo.com.
Soccer: Jim Fee; Phone: 814-949-5234; E-mail: fjesoccer1@aol.com.
Softball: Brenda Palmer; Phone: 814-949-5234; E-mail: psusoftballbp@aol.com.
Swimming: Nanette Cummings; Phone: 814-949-5233; E-mail: ncummings1@yahoo.com.
Tennis: Steve Genter; Phone: 814-944-9412; E-mail: jessgenter@yahoo.com.
Volleyball: Aaron Bowers; Phone: 814-949-5234.

THE PENNSYLVANIA STATE UNIVERSITY AT ERIE, THE BEHREND COLLEGE
Erie, Pennsylvania

Lions ◆ NCAA III ◆ Allegheny Mountain Conference ◆ http://www.pserie.psu.edu/

State-related comprehensive, founded 1948, part of Pennsylvania State University
Coed, 3,554 undergraduate students, 93% full-time, 34% women, 66% men
Suburban 727-acre campus
Very difficult entrance level, 8% of applicants were admitted

Freshmen *Admission:* 3,045 applied, 2,411 were accepted, 844 enrolled. *Test scores:* SAT verbal scores over 500: 66%; SAT math scores over 500: 76%; SAT verbal scores over 600: 17%; SAT math scores over 600: 30%; SAT verbal scores over 700: 2%; SAT math scores over 700: 4%.
Tuition and fees (2003–04): $9304 (resident), $15,874 (nonresident). *Room and board:* $5940 (room only: $3080).
Financial Aid (All incoming freshmen): *Average need-based gift aid:* $4279. *Average non-need based aid:* $2217. *Average aid to full-time undergraduates:* $10,019.
Athletic Department: *Director of Athletics:* Brian Streeter; Phone: 814-898-6379; Fax: 814-898-6013; E-mail: bfs6@psu.edu. *Sports Information Director:* Paul Benim; Phone: 814-898-6322; E-mail: prb3@psu.edu.

MEN'S COACHES
Baseball: Paul Benim; Phone: 814-898-6322; E-mail: prb3@psu.edu.
Basketball: David Niland; Phone: 814-898-6398; E-mail: dfn1@psu.edu.

Cross Country: David Cooper; Phone: 814-898-6239; E-mail: dac26@psu.edu.
Diving: Gordy Schmidt; Phone: 814-898-7147.
Golf: Mark Murphy; Phone: 814-898-7566; E-mail: mpm249@psu.edu.
Soccer: Dan Perritano; Phone: 814-898-6296; E-mail: dpp2@psu.edu.
Swimming: Jennifer Slack; Phone: 814-898-7147; E-mail: jns11@psu.edu.
Tennis: Jeff Barger; Phone: 814-898-6017; E-mail: jrb35@psu.edu.
Track and Field: Dave Cooper; Phone: 814-898-6239; E-mail: dac26@psu.edu.

WOMEN'S COACHES
Basketball: Rosalyn Fornari; Phone: 814-898-6425; E-mail: rxf16@psu.edu.
Cross Country: David Cooper; Phone: 814-898-6239; E-mail: dac26@psu.edu.
Diving: Gordy Schmidt; Phone: 814-898-7147.
Golf: Mark Murphy; Phone: 814-898-7566; E-mail: mpm249@psu.edu.
Soccer: Dan Perritano; Phone: 814-898-6296; E-mail: dpp2@psu.edu.
Softball: Stacy Pondo; Phone: 814-898-6163; E-mail: slp15@psu.edu.
Swimming: Jennifer Slack; Phone: 814-898-7147; E-mail: jns11@psu.edu.
Tennis: Jeff Barger; Phone: 814-898-6017; E-mail: jrb35@psu.edu.
Track and Field: Dave Cooper; Phone: 814-898-7568; E-mail: dac26@psu.edu.
Volleyball: Phil Pisano; Phone: 814-898-6235; E-mail: pjo120@psu.edu.

THE PENNSYLVANIA STATE UNIVERSITY UNIVERSITY PARK CAMPUS
State College, Pennsylvania

Nittany Lions ◆ NCAA I ◆ American Lacrosse Conference; Big Ten Conference ◆ http://www.psu.edu/

State-related university, founded 1855, part of Pennsylvania State University
Coed, 35,002 undergraduate students, 96% full-time, 47% women, 53% men
Small-town 6,388-acre campus
Very difficult entrance level, 5% of applicants were admitted

Freshmen *Admission:* 31,264 applied, 17,174 were accepted, 6,048 enrolled. *Test scores:* SAT verbal scores over 500: 88%; SAT math scores over 500: 93%; SAT verbal scores over 600: 44%; SAT math scores over 600: 62%; SAT verbal scores over 700: 8%; SAT math scores over 700: 15%.
Tuition and fees (2003–04): $9706 (resident), $19,328 (nonresident). *Room and board:* $5940 (room only: $3080).
Financial Aid (All incoming freshmen): *Average need-based gift aid:* $4459. *Average non-need based aid:* $3849. *Average aid to full-time undergraduates:* $10,915.
Athletic Department: *Director of Athletics:* Tim Curley; Phone: 814-865-1086; Fax: 814-863-7955; E-mail: tmc3@psu.edu. *Sports Information Director:* Jeff Nelson; Phone: 814-865-1757; E-mail: jtn4@psu.edu.

MEN'S COACHES
Baseball: Joe Hindelang; Phone: 814-863-0239; E-mail: jjh15@psu.edu.
Basketball: Ed DeChellis; Phone: 814-863-5494; E-mail: jmd3@psu.edu.
Cheerleading: Curtis White; Phone: 814-865-1086; E-mail: cheerleading@psu.edu.
Cross Country: Harry Groves; Phone: 814-863-3147; E-mail: maa1@psu.edu.
Diving: Craig Brown; Phone: 814-863-4812; E-mail: crb1@psu.edu.
Football: Joe Paterno; Phone: 814-863-0411.
Golf: Greg Nye; Phone: 814-863-7469; E-mail: gan2@psu.edu.
Lacrosse: Glenn Thiel; Phone: 814-863-7476; E-mail: gft1@psu.edu.
Soccer: Barry Gorman; Phone: 814-863-7477; E-mail: tbg1@psu.edu.
Swimming: Bill Dorenkott; Phone: 814-863-5554; E-mail: wfd3@psu.edu.
Tennis: Jan Bortner; Phone: 814-863-3487; E-mail: jeb12@psu.edu.
Track and Field: Harry Groves; Phone: 814-863-3147; E-mail: maa1@psu.edu.
Volleyball: Mark Pavlik; Phone: 814-863-7464; E-mail: mtp7@psu.edu.
Wrestling: Troy Sunderland; Phone: 814-863-7460; E-mail: tls138@psu.edu.

WOMEN'S COACHES

Basketball: Rene Portland; Phone: 814-863-2672; E-mail: sfb3@psu. edu.
Cheerleading: Curtis White; Phone: 814-865-1086; E-mail: cheerleading@psu.edu.
Cross Country: Beth Alford-Sullivan; Phone: 814-863-3146; E-mail: bxa10@psu.edu.
Diving: Craig Brown; Phone: 814-863-4812; E-mail: crb1@psu.edu.
Field Hockey: Charlene Morett; Phone: 814-863-7467; E-mail: cxm12@psu.edu.
Golf: Denise St. Pierre; Phone: 814-863-2396; E-mail: dxs10@psu.edu.
Gymnastics: Steve Shephard; Phone: 814-863-7461; E-mail: ses13@psu.cdu.
Lacrosse: Suzanne Weinberg; Phone: 814-863-7470; E-mail: sdw114@psu.edu.
Soccer: Paula Wilkins; Phone: 814-863-5372; E-mail: plw6@psu.edu.
Softball: Robin Petrini; Phone: 814-863-7472; E-mail: rjp13@psu.edu.
Swimming: Bill Dorenkott; Phone: 814-863-5554; E-mail: wfd3@psu.edu.
Tennis: Buffy Baker; Phone: 814-863-7479; E-mail: blb27@psu.edu.
Track and Field: Beth Alford-Sullivan; Phone: 814-863-3146; E-mail: bxa10@psu.edu.
Volleyball: Russ Rose; Phone: 814-863-7474; E-mail: rdr5@psu.edu.

PEPPERDINE UNIVERSITY
Malibu, California

Waves ◆ NCAA I ◆ West Coast Conference
◆ http://www.pepperdine.edu/

Independent religious university, founded 1937, affiliated with Church of Christ
Coed, 3,098 undergraduate students, 83% full-time, 56% women, 44% men
Small-town 830-acre campus with easy access to Los Angeles
Very difficult entrance level, 2% of applicants were admitted

Freshmen *Admission:* 6,719 applied, 1,555 were accepted, 615 enrolled. *Test scores:* SAT verbal scores over 500: 90%; SAT math scores over 500: 90%; SAT verbal scores over 600: 48%; SAT math scores over 600: 58%; SAT verbal scores over 700: 11%; SAT math scores over 700: 13%.
Tuition and fees (2004–05): $28,720 (full-time). *Room and board:* $8640.
Financial Aid (All incoming freshmen): *Average need-based gift aid:* $17,511. *Average non-need based aid:* $16,389. *Average aid to full-time undergraduates:* $23,614.
Athletic Department: *Director of Athletics:* John Watson; Phone: 310-506-4242; Fax: 310-506-7459; E-mail: jgwatson@pepperdine.edu. *Sports Information Director:* Al Barba; Phone: 310-506-4455; E-mail: abarba@pepperdine.edu.

MEN'S COACHES

Baseball: Steve Rodriguez; Phone: 310-506-4371; E-mail: srodrigu@pepperdine.edu.
Basketball: Paul Westphal; Phone: 310-506-4161; E-mail: paul.westphal@pepperdine.edu.
Cheerleading: Sean Larsen; Phone: 310-506-4150; E-mail: cdeldoss@pepperdine.edu.
Cross Country: Dick Kampmann; Phone: 310-506-4165; E-mail: rkampman@pepperdine.edu.
Golf: John Geiberger; Phone: 310-506-4028; E-mail: jgeiberg@pepperdine.edu.
Tennis: Adam Steinberg; Phone: 310-506-4267; E-mail: asteinbe@pepperdine.edu.
Volleyball: Marv Dunphy; Phone: 310-506-4517; E-mail: mdunphy@pepperdine.edu.

WOMEN'S COACHES

Basketball: Mark Trakh; Phone: 310-506-4768; E-mail: mtrakh@pepperdine.edu.
Cheerleading: Scan Larsen; Phone: 310-506-4150; E-mail: cdeldoss@pepperdine.edu.
Cross Country: Dick Kampmann; Phone: 310-506-4165; E-mail: rkampman@pepperdine.edu.
Diving: Nick Rodionoff; Phone: 310-506-4124; E-mail: nrodiono@pepperdine.edu.
Golf: Laurie Gibbs; Phone: 310-506-4482; E-mail: lgibbs@pepperdine.edu.

Soccer: Tim Ward; Phone: 310-506-4338; E-mail: tward@pepperdine.edu.
Swimming: Nick Rodionoff; Phone: 310-506-4124; E-mail: nrodiono@pepperdine.edu.
Tennis: Gualberto Esudero; Phone: 310-506-4506; E-mail: gescuder@pepperdine.edu.
Volleyball: Nina Matthies; Phone: 310-506-4712; E-mail: nmatthie@pepperdine.edu.

PERU STATE COLLEGE
Peru, Nebraska

Bobcats ◆ NAIA ◆ Central States Football Conference; Midlands Collegiate Conference ◆ http://www.peru.edu/

State-supported comprehensive, founded 1867, part of Nebraska State College System
Coed, 1,467 undergraduate students, 61% full-time, 55% women, 45% men
Rural 104-acre campus
Noncompetitive entrance level, 57% of applicants were admitted

Freshmen *Admission:* 504 applied, 314 were accepted, 188 enrolled.
Tuition and fees (2003–04): $3284 (resident), $5894 (nonresident). *Room and board:* $4911 (room only: $2361).
Athletic Department: *Director of Athletics:* Ted Harshbarger; Phone: 402-872-2441; Fax: 402-872-2302; E-mail: tharshbarger@oakmail.peru.edu. *Sports Information Director:* Jerre Cole; Phone: 402-872-2441; E-mail: jcole@oakmail.peru.edu.

MEN'S COACHES

Baseball: Mark Bayliss; Phone: 402-872-2302; E-mail: mbayliss@oakmail.peru.edu.
Basketball: Jerre Cole; Phone: 402-872-2441; E-mail: jcole@oakmail.peru.edu.
Cheerleading: Nancy Merz; Phone: 402-872-2441.
Football: Terry Clark; Phone: 402-872-2443; E-mail: tclark@oakmail.peru.edu.
Volleyball: Geno Frugoli; Phone: 402-872-2441; E-mail: gfrugoli@oakmail.peru.edu.

WOMEN'S COACHES

Basketball: Dennis Prichard; Phone: 402-872-2217; E-mail: dprichard@oakmail.peru.edu.
Cheerleading: Nancy Merz; Phone: 402-872-2441.
Cross Country: Bryan Lee; Phone: 402-872-2393; E-mail: blee@oakmail.peru.edu.
Golf: Dennis Prichard; Phone: 402-872-2217; E-mail: dprichard@oakmail.peru.edu.
Softball: Mark Mathews; Phone: 402-872-2441; E-mail: mmathews@oakmail.peru.edu.
Volleyball: Geno Frugoli; Phone: 402-872-2441; E-mail: gfrugoli@oakmail.peru.edu.

PFEIFFER UNIVERSITY
Misenheimer, North Carolina

Falcons ◆ NCAA II ◆ Carolinas-Virginia Athletics Conference; Deep South Lacrosse Conference ◆ http://www.pfeiffer.edu/

Independent United Methodist comprehensive, founded 1885
Coed, 1,188 undergraduate students, 84% full-time, 58% women, 42% men
Rural 300-acre campus with easy access to Charlotte
Moderately difficult entrance level, 72% of applicants were admitted

Freshmen *Admission:* 586 applied, 419 were accepted, 170 enrolled. *Test scores:* SAT verbal scores over 500: 49%; SAT math scores over 500: 57%; SAT verbal scores over 600: 9%; SAT math scores over 600: 13%; SAT verbal scores over 700: 1%; SAT math scores over 700: 1%.
Tuition and fees (2004–05): $14,570 (full-time). *Room and board:* $5830 (room only: $3030).

Pfeiffer University (*continued*)

Financial Aid (All incoming freshmen): *Average need-based gift aid:* $9400. *Average non-need based aid:* $10,204. *Average aid to full-time undergraduates:* $11,647.
Athletic Department: *Director of Athletics:* Chris Pollard; Phone: 704-463-1360; Fax: 704-463-5051; E-mail: cpollard@pfeifer.edu. *Sports Information Director:* Jeff Childress; Phone: 704-463-1360; E-mail: jchildre@pfeifer.edu.

MEN'S COACHES
Baseball: Chris Pollard; Phone: 704-463-1360; E-mail: cpollard@pfeiffer.edu.
Basketball: Dave Davis; Phone: 704-463-1360; E-mail: ddavis@pfeiffer.edu.
Cheerleading: Micki Thompson; Phone: 704-463-1360; E-mail: mthompson@pfeiffer.edu.
Cross Country: Robert Marchinko; Phone: 704-463-1360; E-mail: bmarchinko@pfeiffer.edu.
Golf: Jim Haughey; Phone: 704-463-1360; E-mail: jhaughey@pfeifer.edu.
Lacrosse: Jason Dombrowski; Phone: 704-463-1360; E-mail: jdombrowski@pfeiffer.edu.
Soccer: Steve Brdarski; Phone: 704-463-1360; E-mail: srb@pfeiffer.edu.
Tennis: Jeff Childress; Phone: 704-463-1360; E-mail: jchildre@pfeiffer.edu.

WOMEN'S COACHES
Basketball: Rob Brafford; Phone: 704-463-1360; E-mail: rbrafford@pfeiffer.edu.
Cheerleading: Micki Thompson; Phone: 704-463-1360; E-mail: mthompson@pfeiffer.edu.
Cross Country: Robert Marchinko; Phone: 704-463-1360; E-mail: bmarchinko@pfeiffer.edu.
Golf: Jim Haughey; Phone: 704-463-1360; E-mail: jhaughey@pfeifer.edu.
Lacrosse: Julian Domenech; Phone: 704-463-1360; E-mail: jdomenech@pfeiffer.edu.
Soccer: Chad Miller; Phone: 704-463-1360; E-mail: cmiller@pfeiffer.edu.
Softball: Shane Prescott; Phone: 704-463-1360; E-mail: sprescott@pfeiffer.edu.
Swimming: Randy Duncan; Phone: 704-463-1360; E-mail: rduncan@pfeiffer.edu.
Tennis: Mary Ann Sunbury; Phone: 704-463-1360; E-mail: msunbury@pfeiffer.edu.
Volleyball: Dean Miller; Phone: 704-463-1360; E-mail: dmiller@pfeiffer.edu.

PHILADELPHIA BIBLICAL UNIVERSITY
Langhorne, Pennsylvania

Crimson Eagles ◆ NCAA III ◆ Independent ◆ http://www.pbu.edu/

Independent nondenominational comprehensive, founded 1913
Coed, 1,045 undergraduate students, 88% full-time, 54% women, 46% men
Suburban 105-acre campus with easy access to Philadelphia
Moderately difficult entrance level, 70% of applicants were admitted

Freshmen *Admission:* 412 applied, 313 were accepted, 187 enrolled. *Test scores:* SAT verbal scores over 500: 72%; SAT math scores over 500: 61%; SAT verbal scores over 600: 27%; SAT math scores over 600: 20%; SAT verbal scores over 700: 4%; SAT math scores over 700: 1%.
Tuition and fees (2004–05): $13,495 (full-time). *Room and board:* $5855 (room only: $2930).
Financial Aid (All incoming freshmen): *Average need-based gift aid:* $8269. *Average non-need based aid:* $4761. *Average aid to full-time undergraduates:* $9968.
Athletic Department: *Director of Athletics:* Dick Beach; Phone: 215-702-4403; Fax: 215-702-4401; E-mail: rbeach@pbu.edu. *Sports Information Director:* Drew Watson; Phone: 215-702-4404; E-mail: dwatson@pbu.edu.

MEN'S COACHES
Baseball: Bill Marshall; Phone: 215-702-4405.
Basketball: Dick Beach; Phone: 215-702-4403; E-mail: rbeach@pbu.edu.
Soccer: Tom Fink; Phone: 215-702-4263; E-mail: tfink@pbu.edu.
Tennis: Helen Hui; Phone: 215-702-4267; E-mail: hhui@pbu.edu.
Volleyball: Dave Emmons; Phone: 215-702-4405; E-mail: demmons@pbu.edu.

WOMEN'S COACHES
Basketball: Drew Watson; Phone: 215-702-4404; E-mail: dwatson@pbu.edu.
Field Hockey: Paula Beach; Phone: 215-702-4283; E-mail: pbeach@pbu.edu.
Soccer: Carolyn Burgman; Phone: 215-702-4405; E-mail: cburgman@pbu.edu.
Softball: Drew Watson; Phone: 215-702-4405; E-mail: dwatson@pbu.edu.
Tennis: Helen Hui; Phone: 215-702-4267; E-mail: hhui@pbu.edu.
Volleyball: Brad Jackson; Phone: 215-702-4405.

PHILADELPHIA UNIVERSITY
Philadelphia, Pennsylvania

NCAA II ◆ Atlantic Soccer Conference; Independent; New York Collegiate Athletic Conference ◆ http://www.philau.edu/

Independent comprehensive, founded 1884
Coed, 2,603 undergraduate students, 87% full-time, 68% women, 32% men
Suburban 100-acre campus
Moderately difficult entrance level, 66% of applicants were admitted

Freshmen *Admission:* 3,461 applied, 2,420 were accepted, 624 enrolled. *Test scores:* SAT verbal scores over 500: 70%; SAT math scores over 500: 72%; SAT verbal scores over 600: 19%; SAT math scores over 600: 21%; SAT verbal scores over 700: 1%; SAT math scores over 700: 1%.
Tuition and fees (2003–04): $20,022 (full-time). *Room and board:* $7370 (room only: $3630).
Financial Aid (All incoming freshmen): *Average need-based gift aid:* $10,866. *Average non-need based aid:* $4482. *Average aid to full-time undergraduates:* $15,352.
Athletic Department: *Director of Athletics:* Tom Shirley; Phone: 215-951-2720; Fax: 215-951-2775; E-mail: shirleyt@philau.edu. *Sports Information Director:* Tony Berich; Phone: 215-951-2852; E-mail: bericht@philau.edu.

MEN'S COACHES
Baseball: Don Flynn; Phone: 215-951-2630; E-mail: gilesw@philau.edu.
Basketball: Herb Magee; Phone: 215-951-2724; E-mail: mageeh@philau.edu.
Cheerleading: Wendy Gall; Phone: 215-951-2720; E-mail: gilesw@philau.edu.
Golf: Jerry Morse; Phone: 215-951-2724; E-mail: gilesw@philau.edu.
Soccer: Greg Wilson; Phone: 215-951-2725; E-mail: wilsong@philau.edu.
Tennis: Marty Gilbert; Phone: 215-951-2739; E-mail: gilesw@philau.edu.

WOMEN'S COACHES
Basketball: Tom Shirley; Phone: 215-951-2720; E-mail: shirleyt@philau.edu.
Cheerleading: Wendy Gall; Phone: 215-951-2720; E-mail: gilesw@philau.edu.
Field Hockey: Denise Junkerman; Phone: 215-951-2630; E-mail: junkermand@philau.edu.
Lacrosse: Christy Malone; Phone: 215-951-2630; E-mail: malonec@philau.edu.
Soccer: George Dunbar; Phone: 215-951-2739; E-mail: dunbarg@philau.edu.
Softball: Frank Fiorino; Phone: 215-951-5394; E-mail: gilesw@philau.edu.
Tennis: Marty Gilbert; Phone: 215-951-2739; E-mail: gilesw@philau.edu.
Volleyball: Phone: 215-951-2739.

PIEDMONT COLLEGE
Demorest, Georgia

Lions ◆ NCAA III ◆ Independent
◆ http://www.piedmont.edu/

Independent religious comprehensive, founded 1897, affiliated with United Church of Christ
Coed, 1,010 undergraduate students, 85% full-time, 63% women, 37% men
Rural 115-acre campus with easy access to Atlanta
Moderately difficult entrance level, 53% of applicants were admitted

Freshmen *Admission:* 542 applied, 291 were accepted, 142 enrolled. *Test scores:* SAT verbal scores over 500: 54%; SAT math scores over 500: 54%; SAT verbal scores over 600: 20%; SAT math scores over 600: 17%; SAT verbal scores over 700: 1%; SAT math scores over 700: 1%.
Tuition and fees (2004–05): $13,500 (full-time). *Room and board:* $4700 (room only: $2450).
Financial Aid (All incoming freshmen): *Average need-based gift aid:* $2891. *Average non-need based aid:* $2431. *Average aid to full-time undergraduates:* $8009.
Athletic Department: *Director of Athletics:* Delene Lee; Phone: 706-778-3000; Fax: 706-776-0145; E-mail: dlee@piedmont.edu. *Sports Information Director:* Richard Dombrowsky; Phone: 706-778-3000; E-mail: sportsinfo@piedmont.edu.

MEN'S COACHES
Baseball: Jim Peeples; Phone: 706-778-3000; E-mail: jpeeples@piedmont.edu.
Basketball: Lee Glenn; Phone: 706-778-3000; E-mail: lglenn@piedmont.edu.
Cheerleading: Lynn Miller; Phone: 706-778-3000; E-mail: lmiller@piedmont.edu.
Cross Country: Payton Capper; Phone: 706-778-3000; E-mail: pcapper@piedmont.edu.
Golf: Lee Glenn; Phone: 706-778-3000; E-mail: lglenn@piedmont.edu.
Soccer: Jason Smith; Phone: 706-778-3000; E-mail: jpsmith@piedmont.edu.
Tennis: Shane Wood; Phone: 706-778-3000; E-mail: swood1@piedmont.edu.

WOMEN'S COACHES
Basketball: Charles Cooper; Phone: 706-778-3000; E-mail: ccooper@piedmont.edu.
Cheerleading: Lynn Miller; Phone: 706-778-3000; E-mail: lmiller@piedmont.edu.
Cross Country: Payton Capper; Phone: 706-778-3000; E-mail: pcapper@piedmont.edu.
Golf: Lee Glenn; Phone: 706-778-3000; E-mail: lglenn@piedmont.edu.
Softball: Terry Martin; Phone: 706-778-3000; E-mail: wtmartin@piedmont.edu.
Tennis: Shane Wood; Phone: 706-778-3000; E-mail: swood1@piedmont.edu.
Volleyball: Katie O'Brien; Phone: 706-778-3000; E-mail: kobrien@piedmont.edu.

PIKEVILLE COLLEGE
Pikeville, Kentucky

Bears ◆ NAIA ◆ Mid-South Conference ◆ http://www.pc.edu/

Independent religious comprehensive, founded 1889, affiliated with Presbyterian Church (U.S.A.)
Coed, 762 undergraduate students, 94% full-time, 57% women, 43% men
Small-town 25-acre campus
Noncompetitive entrance level, 100% of applicants were admitted

Freshmen *Admission:* 615 applied, 615 were accepted, 149 enrolled.
Tuition and fees (2003–04): $9900 (full-time). *Room and board:* $5000 (room only: $2500).
Financial Aid (All incoming freshmen): *Average need-based gift aid:* $5904. *Average non-need based aid:* $2369. *Average aid to full-time undergraduates:* $11,278.

Athletic Department: *Director of Athletics:* Ron Damron; Phone: 606-218-5230; Fax: 606-218-5351; E-mail: rdamron@pc.edu. *Sports Information Director:* Rick Bently; Phone: 606-218-5350; E-mail: rbentley@pc.edu.

MEN'S COACHES
Baseball: Johnnie LeMaster; Phone: 606-218-5370; E-mail: athletics@pc.edu.
Basketball: Randy McCoy; Phone: 606-218-5352; E-mail: rmccoy@pc.edu.
Cheerleading: Jamie Fields; Phone: 606-218-5651; E-mail: kfields@pc.edu.
Cross Country: John Biery; Phone: 606-218-5223; E-mail: jbiery@pc.edu.
Football: Jerry Mynatt; Phone: 606-218-5350; E-mail: athletics@pc.edu.
Golf: James Riley; Phone: 606-218-5010; E-mail: jriley@pc.edu.
Tennis: John Kitchen; Phone: 606-218-5354; E-mail: jbkitchen@hotmail.com.
Tennis: John Kitchen; Phone: 606-218-5354; E-mail: jbkitchen@hotmail.com.

WOMEN'S COACHES
Basketball: Bill Watson; Phone: 606-218-5356; E-mail: bwatson@pc.edu.
Cheerleading: Jamie Fields; Phone: 606-218-5651; E-mail: kfields@pc.edu.
Cross Country: John Biery; Phone: 606-218-5223; E-mail: jbiery@pc.edu.
Golf: Roland Wierwille; Phone: 606-218-5769; E-mail: rwierwil@pc.edu.
Softball: Robert Staggs; Phone: 606-218-5357; E-mail: robstaggs@hotmail.com.
Tennis: John Kitchen; Phone: 606-218-5354; E-mail: jbkitchen@hotmail.com.
Volleyball: Robert Staggs; Phone: 606-218-5357; E-mail: robstaggs@hotmail.com.

PINE MANOR COLLEGE
Chestnut Hill, Massachusetts

Gators ◆ NCAA III ◆ Great Northeast Athletic Conference
◆ http://www.pmc.edu/

Independent 4-year, founded 1911
Women only, 487 undergraduate students, 98% full-time, 100% women, 100% men
Suburban 65-acre campus with easy access to Boston
Moderately difficult entrance level, 71% of applicants were admitted

Freshmen *Admission:* 601 applied, 427 were accepted, 159 enrolled. *Test scores:* SAT verbal scores over 500: 20%; SAT math scores over 500: 5%; SAT verbal scores over 600: 4%; SAT math scores over 600: 2%.
Tuition and fees (2003–04): $13,612 (full-time). *Room and board:* $8526.
Financial Aid (All incoming freshmen): *Average need-based gift aid:* $11,107. *Average non-need based aid:* $6872. *Average aid to full-time undergraduates:* $14,673.
Athletic Department: *Director of Athletics:* Bill Boffi; Phone: 617-731-7056; Fax: 617-731-7035; E-mail: boffiwil@pmc.edu. *Sports Information Director:* Amy Wilichoski; Phone: 617-731-7036; E-mail: wilichoa@pmc.edu.

WOMEN'S COACHES
Basketball: Kelly Barker; Phone: 617-731-7676; E-mail: barkerke@pmc.edu.
Cross Country: William Stargard; Phone: 617-731-7070; E-mail: stargarw@pmc.edu.
Lacrosse: Sarah Keating; Phone: 617-731-7058; E-mail: keatings@pmc.edu.
Soccer: Sarah Keating; Phone: 617-731-7058; E-mail: keatings@pmc.edu.
Softball: Amy Wilichoski; Phone: 617-731-7036; E-mail: wilichoa@pmc.edu.
Tennis: Lisa Breger; Phone: 617-731-7671; E-mail: bregerli@pmc.edu.
Volleyball: Kelly Barker; Phone: 617-731-7676; E-mail: barkerke@pmc.edu.

PITTSBURG STATE UNIVERSITY
Pittsburg, Kansas

Gorillas ◆ NCAA II ◆ Mid-America Intercollegiate
Conference ◆ http://www.pittstate.edu/

State-supported comprehensive, founded 1903, part of Kansas
Board of Regents
Coed, 5,531 undergraduate students
Small-town 233-acre campus
Noncompetitive entrance level, 54% of applicants were admitted

Freshmen *Admission:* 1,690 applied, 908 were accepted.
Tuition and fees (2003–04): $2962 (resident), $8784 (nonresident). *Room and board:* $4166.
Financial Aid (All incoming freshmen): *Average need-based gift aid:* $3209. *Average non-need based aid:* $1709. *Average aid to full-time undergraduates:* $5968.
Athletic Department: *Director of Athletics:* Chuck Broyles; Phone: 620-235-4651; Fax: 620-235-4661; E-mail: cbroyles@pittstate.edu. *Sports Information Director:* Dan Wilkes; Phone: 620-235-4147; E-mail: dwilkes@pittstate.edu.

MEN'S COACHES
Baseball: Steve Bever; Phone: 620-232-7951; E-mail: sbever@pittstate.edu.
Basketball: Gene Iba; Phone: 620-235-4649; E-mail: giba@pittstate.edu.
Cheerleading: Linda Graham; Phone: 620-235-4646; E-mail: pittcheer@hotmail.com.
Cross Country: Russ Jewett; Phone: 620-235-4659; E-mail: rjewett@pittstate.edu.
Football: Chuck Broyles; Phone: 620-235-4651; E-mail: cbroyles@pittstate.edu.
Golf: Jeff Hafer; Phone: 620-235-4649; E-mail: jhafer@pittstate.edu.
Track and Field: Russ Jewett; Phone: 620-235-4659; E-mail: rjewett@pittstate.edu.

WOMEN'S COACHES
Basketball: Steve High; Phone: 620-235-4647; E-mail: shigh@pittstate.edu.
Cheerleading: Linda Graham; Phone: 620-235-4646; E-mail: pittcheer@hotmail.com.
Cross Country: Russ Jewett; Phone: 620-235-4659; E-mail: rjewett@pittstate.edu.
Softball: Jenifer Wells; Phone: 620-232-7947; E-mail: jwells@pittstate.edu.
Track and Field: Russ Jewett; Phone: 620-235-4659; E-mail: rjewett@pittstate.edu.
Volleyball: Ibraheem Suberu; Phone: 620-235-4674; E-mail: isuberu@pittstate.edu.

PITZER COLLEGE
Claremont, California

Sagehens ◆ NCAA III ◆ Southern California Athletic
Conference ◆ http://www.pitzer.edu/

Independent 4-year, founded 1963, part of The Claremont Colleges
Consortium
Coed, 942 undergraduate students, 95% full-time, 60% women,
40% men
Suburban 35-acre campus with easy access to Los Angeles
Moderately difficult entrance level, 5% of applicants were admitted

Freshmen *Admission:* 2,425 applied, 1,215 were accepted, 230 enrolled.
Test scores: SAT verbal scores over 500: 93%; SAT math scores over 500: 90%; SAT verbal scores over 600: 61%; SAT math scores over 600: 60%; SAT verbal scores over 700: 15%; SAT math scores over 700: 12%.
Tuition and fees (2003–04): $29,794 (full-time). *Room and board:* $7796 (room only: $4880).
Financial Aid (All incoming freshmen): *Average need-based gift aid:* $23,490. *Average non-need based aid:* $10,000. *Average aid to full-time undergraduates:* $28,282.
Athletic Department: *Director of Athletics:* Charles Katsiaficas; Phone: 909-621-8423; Fax: 909-621-8547; E-mail: ckatsiaficas@pomona.edu.

Sports Information Director: Ben Belletto; Phone: 909-621-8427; E-mail: benjamin.belletto@pomona.edu.

MEN'S COACHES
Baseball: Frank Pericolosi; Phone: 909-621-8422; E-mail: frank.pericolosi@pomona.edu.
Basketball: Charles Katsiaficas; Phone: 909-621-8238; E-mail: charles.katsiaficas@pomona.edu.
Cross Country: Pat Mulcahy; Phone: 909-607-3819; E-mail: patrick.mulcahy@pomona.edu.
Diving: Gary Troyer; Phone: 909-607-4484; E-mail: gary.troyer@pomona.edu.
Football: Roger Caron; Phone: 909-607-1826; E-mail: roger.caron@pomona.edu.
Golf: Lorn Foster; Phone: 909-607-2263; E-mail: lorn.foster@pomona.edu.
Soccer: Bill Swartz; Phone: 909-607-2771; E-mail: william.swartz@pomona.edu.
Swimming: Gary Troyer; Phone: 909-607-4484; E-mail: gary.troyer@pomona.edu.
Tennis: Ben Belletto; Phone: 909-621-8427; E-mail: benjamin.belletto@pomona.edu.
Track and Field: Pat Mulcahy; Phone: 909-607-3819; E-mail: patrick.mulcahy@pomona.edu.

WOMEN'S COACHES
Basketball: Kathy Connell; Phone: 909-607-2247; E-mail: kathleen.connell@pomona.edu.
Cross Country: Kirk Reynolds; Phone: 909-621-8429; E-mail: kirk_reynolds@pomona.edu.
Diving: Penny Lee Dean; Phone: 909-607-4486; E-mail: penny.dean@pomona.edu.
Golf: Lorn Foster; Phone: 909-607-2263; E-mail: lorn.foster@pomona.edu.
Soccer: Eli Koenn-Bollinger; Phone: 909-607-5439.
Softball: Eli Koenn-Bollinger; Phone: 909-607-5439.
Swimming: Penny Lee Dean; Phone: 909-607-4486; E-mail: penny.dean@pomona.edu.
Tennis: Ann Lebedeff; Phone: 909-607-2492; E-mail: ann.lebedeff@pomona.edu.
Track and Field: Kirk Reynolds; Phone: 909-621-8016; E-mail: kirk_reynolds@pomona.edu.
Volleyball: Valerie Cowan; Phone: 909-607-6329; E-mail: valerie.cowan@pomona.edu.

PLYMOUTH STATE UNIVERSITY
Plymouth, New Hampshire

Panthers ◆ NCAA III ◆ Freedom Football Conference; Little
East Conference; New England College Wrestling Conference
◆ http://www.plymouth.edu/

State-supported comprehensive, founded 1871, part of University
System of New Hampshire
Coed, 3,967 undergraduate students, 93% full-time, 51% women,
49% men
Small-town 170-acre campus
Moderately difficult entrance level, 64% of applicants were admitted

Freshmen *Admission:* 3,685 applied, 2,601 were accepted, 903 enrolled.
Test scores: SAT verbal scores over 500: 43%; SAT math scores over 500: 43%; SAT verbal scores over 600: 7%; SAT math scores over 600: 8%; SAT verbal scores over 700: 1%; SAT math scores over 700: 1%.
Tuition and fees (2003–04): $6240 (resident), $12,290 (nonresident). *Room and board:* $6058 (room only: $4100).
Financial Aid (All incoming freshmen): *Average need-based gift aid:* $4248. *Average non-need based aid:* $1930. *Average aid to full-time undergraduates:* $6562.
Athletic Department: *Director of Athletics:* John Clark; Phone: 603-535-2751; Fax: 603-535-2758; E-mail: jpclark@mail.plymouth.edu. *Sports Information Director:* Kent Cherrington; Phone: 603-535-2477; E-mail: kcherrin@mail.plymouth.edu.

MEN'S COACHES
Baseball: Dennis McManus; Phone: 603-535-2756; E-mail: dmcmanus@mail.plymouth.edu.
Basketball: John Scheinman; Phone: 603-535-2753; E-mail: jscheinman@mail.plymouth.edu.

Football: Paul Castonia; Phone: 603-535-2761; E-mail: pfcastonia@ mail.plymouth.edu.
Ice Hockey: Brett Tryder; Phone: 603-535-2744; E-mail: brtryder@mail. plymouth.edu.
Lacrosse: Andrew Brauch; Phone: 603-535-2764; E-mail: anbrauch@ plymouth.edu.
Soccer: Rob Wright; Phone: 603-535-2516; E-mail: rjwright@mail. plymouth.edu.
Wrestling: Donald Perrin; Phone: 603-535-2774; E-mail: dperrin@mail. plymouth.edu.

WOMEN'S COACHES

Basketball: Lauren Lavigne; Phone: 603-535-2763; E-mail: l_lavign@ mail.plymouth.edu.
Diving: Al Switzer; Phone: 603-535-2765; E-mail: aswitzer@mail. plymouth.edu.
Field Hockey: Bonnie Lord; Phone: 603-535-2759; E-mail: blord@mail. plymouth.edu.
Lacrosse: Wynne Lobel; Phone: 603-535-3015; E-mail: wlobel@mail. plymouth.edu.
Soccer: Keith Scarlett; Phone: 603-535-2732; E-mail: kscarlett@mail. plymouth.edu.
Softball: Bruce Addison; Phone: 603-535-3016; E-mail: beaddison@ plymouth.edu.
Swimming: Al Switzer; Phone: 603-535-2765; E-mail: aswitzer@mail. plymouth.edu.
Tennis: Barbara Rawsky-Willett; Phone: 603-535-2768; E-mail: brwillett@plymouth.edu.
Volleyball: Moira Long; Phone: 603-535-2778; E-mail: mlong@mail. plymouth.edu.

POINT LOMA NAZARENE UNIVERSITY
San Diego, California

Sea Lions ◆ NAIA ◆ Golden State Conference ◆ http://www.ptloma.edu/

Independent Nazarene comprehensive, founded 1902
Coed, 2,375 undergraduate students, 95% full-time, 59% women, 41% men
Suburban 88-acre campus
Moderately difficult entrance level, 61% of applicants were admitted

Freshmen *Admission:* 1,672 applied, 1,076 were accepted, 555 enrolled. *Test scores:* SAT verbal scores over 500: 83%; SAT math scores over 500: 84%; SAT verbal scores over 600: 35%; SAT math scores over 600: 39%; SAT verbal scores over 700: 5%; SAT math scores over 700: 4%.
Tuition and fees (2003–04): $18,500 (full-time). *Room and board:* $6380.
Financial Aid (All incoming freshmen): *Average need-based gift aid:* $9242. *Average non-need based aid:* $7012. *Average aid to full-time undergraduates:* $11,249.
Athletic Department: *Director of Athletics:* Carroll Land; Phone: 619-849-2265; Fax: 619-849-2553. *Sports Information Director:* Jorge de la Torre; Phone: 619-849-2441.

MEN'S COACHES

Baseball: Scott Sarver; Phone: 619-849-2265; E-mail: ssarver@ptloma. edu.
Basketball: Art Wilmore; Phone: 619-849-2265; E-mail: artwilmore@ ptloma.edu.
Cross Country: Jerry Arvin; Phone: 619-849-2265; E-mail: jerryarvin@ ptloma.edu.
Golf: Ben Foster; Phone: 619-849-2283; E-mail: benfoster@ptloma.edu.
Soccer: Tim Hall; Phone: 619-849-2761; E-mail: timhall@ptloma.edu.
Tennis: Rich Hills; Phone: 619-849-2265; E-mail: richhills@ptloma.edu.
Track and Field: Jerry Arvin; Phone: 619-849-2265; E-mail: jerryarvin@ ptloma.edu.

WOMEN'S COACHES

Basketball: Bill Westphal; Phone: 619-849-2694; E-mail: billwestphal@ ptloma.edu.
Cross Country: Jerry Arvin; Phone: 619-849-2265; E-mail: jerryarvin@ ptloma.edu.
Soccer: Amy Colunga; Phone: 619-849-2557; E-mail: markhalpert@ ptloma.edu.

Softball: Dave Williams; Phone: 619-849-2439; E-mail: davewilliams@ ptloma.edu.
Tennis: Rich Hills; Phone: 619-849-2265; E-mail: richhills@ptloma.edu.
Track and Field: Jerry Arvin; Phone: 619-849-2265; E-mail: jerryarvin@ ptloma.edu.
Volleyball: Barb Wnek; Phone: 619-849-2589; E-mail: barbarawnek@ ptloma.edu.

POINT PARK UNIVERSITY
Pittsburgh, Pennsylvania

Pioneers ◆ NAIA ◆ American Mideast Conference ◆ http://www.ppc.edu/

Independent comprehensive, founded 1960
Coed, 2,827 undergraduate students, 73% full-time, 58% women, 42% men
Urban campus
Moderately difficult entrance level, 78% of applicants were admitted

Freshmen *Admission:* 1,715 applied, 1,391 were accepted, 439 enrolled. *Test scores:* SAT verbal scores over 500: 66%; SAT math scores over 500: 53%; SAT verbal scores over 600: 18%; SAT math scores over 600: 12%; SAT verbal scores over 700: 1%; SAT math scores over 700: 1%.
Tuition and fees (2003–04): $15,180 (full-time). *Room and board:* $6660 (room only: $3140).
Financial Aid (All incoming freshmen): *Average need-based gift aid:* $7194. *Average non-need based aid:* $5240. *Average aid to full-time undergraduates:* $12,369.
Athletic Department: *Director of Athletics:* Bob Rager; Phone: 412-392-3843; Fax: 412-392-4780; E-mail: brager@ppc.edu. *Sports Information Director:* Jim Cromie; Phone: 412-392-3997; E-mail: jcromie@ ppc.edu.

MEN'S COACHES

Baseball: Al Liberi; Phone: 412-392-3854; E-mail: alibei@ppc.edu.
Basketball: Bob Rager; Phone: 412-392-3843; E-mail: brager@ppc.edu.
Cross Country: Sam Kosanovich; Phone: 412-392-3854.
Soccer: Dama Fidelis; Phone: 412-392-2230.

WOMEN'S COACHES

Basketball: Jay Banaszak; Phone: 412-392-2224; E-mail: jbanaszak@ ppc.edu.
Cross Country: Sam Kosanovich; Phone: 412-392-3854.
Soccer: Jeroen Walstra; Phone: 412-392-2231; E-mail: etozzi@ppc.edu.
Softball: Ed Tozzi; Phone: 412-392-2229; E-mail: etozzi@ppc.edu.
Volleyball: Stephanie Szabo; Phone: 412-392-2225; E-mail: sszabo@ ppc.edu.

POLYTECHNIC UNIVERSITY, BROOKLYN CAMPUS
Brooklyn, New York

Bluejays ◆ NCAA III ◆ Eastern College Athletic Conference ◆ http://www.poly.edu/

Independent university, founded 1854
Coed, 1,559 undergraduate students, 95% full-time, 18% women, 82% men
Urban 3-acre campus
Very difficult entrance level, 74% of applicants were admitted

Freshmen *Admission:* 1,307 applied, 959 were accepted, 396 enrolled. *Test scores:* SAT verbal scores over 500: 74%; SAT math scores over 500: 96%; SAT verbal scores over 600: 24%; SAT math scores over 600: 68%; SAT verbal scores over 700: 2%; SAT math scores over 700: 20%.
Tuition and fees (2003–04): $25,772 (full-time). *Room and board:* $8000 (room only: $6500).
Financial Aid (All incoming freshmen): *Average need-based gift aid:* $9230. *Average non-need based aid:* $18,038. *Average aid to full-time undergraduates:* $22,311.

Polytechnic University, Brooklyn Campus *(continued)*

Athletic Department: *Director of Athletics:* Maureen Braziel; Phone: 718-260-3458; Fax: 718-260-3474; E-mail: mbraziel@poly.edu. *Sports Information Director:* Fred DeJesus; Phone: 718-260-3459; E-mail: fdejesus@poly.edu.

MEN'S COACHES
Baseball: Roger Perez; Phone: 718-260-3453.
Basketball: Laddy Baldwin; Phone: 718-260-3453.
Cross Country: Rick Tomlinson; Phone: 718-260-3453.
Soccer: Courtney Boothe; Phone: 718-260-3453.
Tennis: Steve Wen; Phone: 718-260-3453.
Track and Field: Rick Tomlinson; Phone: 718-260-3453.
Volleyball: James Zeng; Phone: 718-260-3453.

WOMEN'S COACHES
Basketball: Jimmy Barrett; Phone: 718-260-3453; E-mail: jbarrett@duke.poly.edu.
Cross Country: Rick Tomlinson; Phone: 718-260-3453.
Soccer: Ernest Barrington; Phone: 718-260-3453.
Softball: Jimmy Barrett; Phone: 718-260-3453; E-mail: jbarrett@duke.poly.edu.
Tennis: Francis Thomas; Phone: 718-260-3453.
Track and Field: Rick Tomlinson; Phone: 718-260-3453.
Volleyball: Richard Lam; Phone: 718-260-3453.

POMONA COLLEGE
Claremont, California

Sagehens ◆ NCAA III ◆ Southern California Athletic Conference ◆ http://www.pomona.edu/

Independent 4-year, founded 1887, part of The Claremont Colleges Consortium
Coed, 1,555 undergraduate students, 100% full-time, 51% women, 49% men
Suburban 140-acre campus with easy access to Los Angeles
Most difficult entrance level, 3% of applicants were admitted

Freshmen *Admission:* 4,539 applied, 968 were accepted, 399 enrolled. *Test scores:* SAT verbal scores over 500: 100%; SAT math scores over 500: 100%; SAT verbal scores over 600: 97%; SAT math scores over 600: 97%; SAT verbal scores over 700: 74%; SAT math scores over 700: 70%.
Tuition and fees (2003–04): $27,150 (full-time). *Room and board:* $9980.
Financial Aid (All incoming freshmen): *Average need-based gift aid:* $21,350. *Average non-need based aid:* $2500. *Average aid to full-time undergraduates:* $25,500.
Athletic Department: *Director of Athletics:* Charles Katsiaficas; Phone: 909-621-8423; Fax: 909-621-8547; E-mail: ckatsiaficas@pomona.edu. *Sports Information Director:* Ben Belletto; Phone: 909-621-8427; E-mail: benjamin.belletto@pomona.edu.

MEN'S COACHES
Baseball: Frank Pericolosi; Phone: 909-621-8422; E-mail: frank.pericolosi@pomona.edu.
Basketball: Charles Katsiaficas; Phone: 909-621-8238; E-mail: charles.katsiaficas@pomona.edu.
Cross Country: Pat Mulcahy; Phone: 909-607-3819; E-mail: patrick.mulcahy@pomona.edu.
Diving: Gary Troyer; Phone: 909-607-4484; E-mail: gary.troyer@pomona.edu.
Football: Roger Caron; Phone: 909-607-1826; E-mail: roger.caron@pomona.edu.
Golf: Lorn Foster; Phone: 909-607-2263; E-mail: lorn.foster@pomona.edu.
Soccer: Bill Swartz; Phone: 909-607-2771; E-mail: william.swartz@pomona.edu.
Swimming: Gary Troyer; Phone: 909-607-4484; E-mail: gary.troyer@pomona.edu.
Tennis: Ben Belletto; Phone: 909-621-8427; E-mail: benjamin.belletto@pomona.edu.
Track and Field: Pat Mulcahy; Phone: 909-607-3819; E-mail: patrick.mulcahy@pomona.edu.

WOMEN'S COACHES
Basketball: Kathy Connell; Phone: 909-607-2247; E-mail: kathleen.connell@pomona.edu.

Cross Country: Kirk Reynolds; Phone: 909-621-8429; E-mail: kirk_reynolds@pomona.edu.
Diving: Penny Lee Dean; Phone: 909-607-4486; E-mail: penny.dean@pomona.edu.
Golf: Lorn Foster; Phone: 909-607-2263; E-mail: lorn.foster@pomona.edu.
Soccer: Eli Koenn-Bollinger; Phone: 909-607-5439.
Softball: Eli Koenn-Bollinger; Phone: 909-607-5439.
Swimming: Penny Lee Dean; Phone: 909-607-4486; E-mail: penny.dean@pomona.edu.
Tennis: Ann Lebedeff; Phone: 909-607-2492; E-mail: ann.lebedeff@pomona.edu.
Track and Field: Kirk Reynolds; Phone: 909-621-8016; E-mail: kirk_reynolds@pomona.edu.
Volleyball: Valerie Cowan; Phone: 909-607-6329; E-mail: valerie.cowan@pomona.edu.

PORTLAND STATE UNIVERSITY
Portland, Oregon

Vikings ◆ NCAA I ◆ Big sky Conference; Pacific Coast Softball Conference; Pacific-10 Conference
◆ http://www.pdx.edu/

State-supported university, founded 1946, part of Oregon University System
Coed, 16,906 undergraduate students, 62% full-time, 54% women, 46% men
Urban 49-acre campus
Minimally difficult entrance level, 83% of applicants were admitted

Freshmen *Admission:* 3,344 applied, 2,832 were accepted, 1,538 enrolled. *Test scores:* SAT verbal scores over 500: 59%; SAT math scores over 500: 61%; SAT verbal scores over 600: 20%; SAT math scores over 600: 20%; SAT verbal scores over 700: 3%; SAT math scores over 700: 2%.
Tuition and fees (2003–04): $4278 (resident), $13,674 (nonresident). *Room and board:* $8175 (room only: $6075).
Financial Aid (All incoming freshmen): *Average need-based gift aid:* $3629. *Average non-need based aid:* $1979. *Average aid to full-time undergraduates:* $5986.
Athletic Department: *Director of Athletics:* Tom Burman; Phone: 503-725-2500; Fax: 503-725-5550; E-mail: burmant@pdx.edu. *Sports Information Director:* Mike Lund; Phone: 503-725-5602; E-mail: lundm@pdx.edu.

MEN'S COACHES
Basketball: Heath Schroyer; Phone: 503-725-5630; E-mail: schroyerh@pdx.edu.
Cheerleading: Darlene Brady; Phone: 503-871-4444; E-mail: bradyd@pdx.edu.
Cross Country: Kebba Tolbert; Phone: 503-725-4508; E-mail: tolbert@pdx.edu.
Football: Tim Walsh; Phone: 503-725-5625; E-mail: walsht@pdx.edu.
Track and Field: Kebba Tolbert; Phone: 503-725-4508; E-mail: tolbert@pdx.edu.
Wrestling: Marlin Grahn; Phone: 503-725-4688; E-mail: grahn@pdx.edu.

WOMEN'S COACHES
Basketball: George Wolfe; Phone: 503-725-4502; E-mail: wolfeg@pdx.edu.
Cheerleading: Darlene Brady; Phone: 503-871-4444; E-mail: bradyd@pdx.edu.
Cross Country: Kebba Tolbert; Phone: 503-725-4508; E-mail: tolbert@pdx.edu.
Golf: Felicia Johnston; Phone: 503-725-5619; E-mail: fmj@mail.pdx.edu.
Soccer: Tara Bilanski; Phone: 503-725-5632; E-mail: bilanski@pdx.edu.
Softball: Teri Mariani; Phone: 503-725-4400; E-mail: mariant@pdx.edu.
Track and Field: Kebba Tolbert; Phone: 503-725-4508; E-mail: tolbert@pdx.edu.
Volleyball: Jeff Mozzochi; Phone: 503-725-3853; E-mail: mozzochi@pdx.edu.

PRAIRIE VIEW A&M UNIVERSITY
Prairie View, Texas

Panthers ◆ NCAA I ◆ Southwestern Athletic Conference
◆ http://www.pvamu.edu/

State-supported comprehensive, founded 1878, part of Texas A&M University System
Coed, 6,042 undergraduate students, 89% full-time, 56% women, 44% men
Small-town 1,440-acre campus with easy access to Houston
Moderately difficult entrance level, 98% of applicants were admitted

Freshmen *Admission:* 2,767 applied, 2,710 were accepted, 1,459 enrolled.
Tuition and fees (2003–04): $3592 (resident), $10,672 (nonresident). *Room and board:* $5826 (room only: $3536).
Financial Aid (All incoming freshmen): *Average need-based gift aid:* $3300. *Average non-need based aid:* $1720. *Average aid to full-time undergraduates:* $6500.
Athletic Department: *Director of Athletics:* Charles McClelland; Phone: 936-857-2127; Fax: 936-857-2408; E-mail: charles_mcclelland@pvamu.edu. *Sports Information Director:* Stefann Robinson; Phone: 936-857-2114; E-mail: harlan_robinson@pvamu.edu.

MEN'S COACHES
Baseball: Michael Robertson; Phone: 936-857-2155; E-mail: michael_robertson@pvamu.edu.
Basketball: Jerome Francis; Phone: 936-857-4918; E-mail: jerome_francis@pvamu.edu.
Cheerleading: Pam Thomas; Phone: 936-857-2018; E-mail: pam_thomas@pvamu.edu.
Cross Country: Clifford Gilliard; Phone: 936-857-3019; E-mail: clifton_gilliard@pvamu.edu.
Football: Henry Frazier; Phone: 936-857-2413.
Golf: Vernon Perry; Phone: 936-857-2196; E-mail: vernon_perry@pvamu.edu.
Track and Field: Clifford Gilliard; Phone: 936-857-3019; E-mail: clifton_gilliard@pvamu.edu.

WOMEN'S COACHES
Basketball: Robert Atkins; Phone: 936-857-2115; E-mail: robert_atkins@pvamu.edu.
Cheerleading: Pam Thomas; Phone: 936-857-2018; E-mail: pam_thomas@pvamu.edu.
Cross Country: Essie Washington; Phone: 936-857-4319; E-mail: essie_washington@pvamu.edu.
Golf: Vernon Perry; Phone: 936-857-2196; E-mail: vernon_perry@pvamu.edu.
Soccer: Felicia Tarver; Phone: 936-857-4421.
Softball: A.D. James; Phone: 936-857-2422.
Track and Field: Essie Washington; Phone: 936-857-4319; E-mail: essie_washington@pvamu.edu.
Volleyball: Alicia Pete; Phone: 936-857-4416; E-mail: alicia_pete@pvamu.edu.

PRESBYTERIAN COLLEGE
Clinton, South Carolina

Blue Hose ◆ NCAA II ◆ South Atlantic Conference ◆ http://www.presby.edu/

Independent religious 4-year, founded 1880, affiliated with Presbyterian Church (U.S.A.)
Coed, 1,175 undergraduate students
Small-town 215-acre campus with easy access to Greenville - Spartanburg
Very difficult entrance level, 75% of applicants were admitted

Freshmen *Admission:* 1,103 applied, 865 were accepted. *Test scores:* SAT verbal scores over 500: 86%; SAT math scores over 500: 84%; SAT verbal scores over 600: 36%; SAT math scores over 600: 38%; SAT verbal scores over 700: 5%; SAT math scores over 700: 4%.
Tuition and fees (2003–04): $20,110 (full-time). *Room and board:* $5811 (room only: $2816).
Financial Aid (All incoming freshmen): *Average need-based gift aid:* $16,753. *Average non-need based aid:* $9850. *Average aid to full-time undergraduates:* $19,487.

Athletic Department: *Director of Athletics:* Bee Carlton; Phone: 864-833-8242; Fax: 864-833-8323; E-mail: wbcarlton@presby.edu. *Sports Information Director:* Al Ansley; Phone: 864-833-8252; E-mail: aansley@presby.edu.

MEN'S COACHES
Baseball: Doug Kovash; Phone: 864-833-8236; E-mail: dkovash@presby.edu.
Basketball: Greg Nibert; Phone: 864-833-8245; E-mail: gnibert@presby.edu.
Cross Country: Michele Karlon; Phone: 864-833-7094; E-mail: cmkarlon@presby.edu.
Football: Tommy Spangler; Phone: 864-833-8247; E-mail: tespangl@presby.edu.
Golf: Tommy Addison; Phone: 864-833-8537; E-mail: taddison@presby.edu.
Soccer: Bret Bouleware; Phone: 864-833-8255; E-mail: bboulwar@presby.edu.
Tennis: Paul Maxwell; Phone: 864-833-8251; E-mail: pmaxwell@presby.edu.

WOMEN'S COACHES
Basketball: Leigh Irwin; Phone: 864-833-8248; E-mail: lairwin@presby.edu.
Cross Country: Michele Karlon; Phone: 864-833-7094; E-mail: cmkarlon@presby.edu.
Soccer: Brian Purcell; Phone: 864-833-8327; E-mail: bpurcell@presby.edu.
Softball: Jeff Nickerson; Phone: 864-833-8192; E-mail: jnick@presby.edu.
Tennis: Bobby McKee; Phone: 864-833-8250; E-mail: rdmckee@presby.edu.
Volleyball: Ed Allen; Phone: 864-833-8538; E-mail: ewallen@presby.edu.

PRESENTATION COLLEGE
Aberdeen, South Dakota

Saints ◆ NAIA ◆ Upper Midwest Athletic Conference ◆ http://www.presentation.edu/

Independent Roman Catholic 4-year, founded 1951
Coed, 618 undergraduate students, 70% full-time, 88% women, 12% men
Small-town 100-acre campus
Noncompetitive entrance level

Freshmen *Admission:* 163 applied, 162 enrolled.
Tuition and fees (2003–04): $10,050 (full-time). *Room and board:* $4150 (room only: $3400).
Financial Aid (All incoming freshmen): *Average need-based gift aid:* $3664. *Average non-need based aid:* $2905. *Average aid to full-time undergraduates:* $7276.
Athletic Department: *Director of Athletics:* Jim Zimmerman; Phone: 605-229-8587; Fax: 605-229-8548; E-mail: zimmermanj@presentation.edu. *Sports Information Director:* Bob Schuchardt; Phone: 605-229-8575; E-mail: schuchardt_bob@presentation.edu.

MEN'S COACHES
Baseball: Rick Kline; Phone: 605-229-8406; E-mail: kline_rick@presentation.edu.
Basketball: Randy Jordan; Phone: 605-229-8515; E-mail: jordanrandy@presentation.edu.
Cross Country: Randy Mages; Phone: 605-229-8415; E-mail: magesr@presentation.edu.
Golf: Ed Miller; Phone: 605-229-8361; E-mail: emiller@presentation.edu.
Soccer: Bob Schuchardt; Phone: 605-229-8575; E-mail: schuchardt_bob@presentation.edu.

WOMEN'S COACHES
Basketball: Mark Wiest; Phone: 605-229-8487; E-mail: wiestm@presentation.edu.
Cross Country: Randy Mages; Phone: 605-229-8415; E-mail: magesr@presentation.edu.
Golf: Ed Miller; Phone: 605-229-8361; E-mail: emiller@presentation.edu.
Soccer: Bob Schuchardt; Phone: 605-229-8575; E-mail: schuchardt_bob@presentation.edu.

Presentation College *(continued)*

Softball: Ed Miller; Phone: 605-229-8361; E-mail: emiller@presentation.edu.
Volleyball: Kristin Salvevold; Phone: 605-229-8404; E-mail: krissalv@presentation.edu.

PRINCETON UNIVERSITY
Princeton, New Jersey

Tigers ◆ NCAA I ◆ Eastern College Athletic Conference; Ivy League Conference ◆ http://www.princeton.edu/

Independent university, founded 1746
Coed, 4,837 undergraduate students, 97% full-time, 48% women, 52% men
Suburban 600-acre campus with easy access to New York City and Philadelphia
Most difficult entrance level, 1% of applicants were admitted

Freshmen *Admission:* 15,726 applied, 1,601 were accepted, 1,168 enrolled. *Test scores:* SAT verbal scores over 500: 100%; SAT math scores over 500: 100%; SAT verbal scores over 600: 96%; SAT math scores over 600: 98%; SAT verbal scores over 700: 71%; SAT math scores over 700: 73%.
Tuition and fees (2004–05): $29,910 (full-time). *Room and board:* $8387 (room only: $4315).
Financial Aid (All incoming freshmen): *Average need-based gift aid:* $21,900. *Average aid to full-time undergraduates:* $22,020.
Athletic Department: *Director of Athletics:* Gary Walters; Phone: 609-258-3535; Fax: 609-258-4477; E-mail: walters@princeton.edu. *Sports Information Director:* Jerry Price; Phone: 609-258-3569; E-mail: jprice@princeton.edu.

MEN'S COACHES
Baseball: Scott Bradley; Phone: 609-258-5059; E-mail: sbradley@princeton.edu.
Basketball: John Thompson; Phone: 609-258-2459; E-mail: jrtiii@princeton.edu.
Cheerleading: Phone: 609-258-3531; E-mail: pucheer@princeton.edu.
Cross Country: Mike Brady; Phone: 609-258-3526; E-mail: bradymp@princeton.edu.
Diving: Rob Orr; Phone: 609-258-3544; E-mail: orr@princeton.edu.
Football: Roger Hughes; Phone: 609-258-3515; E-mail: rhughes@princeton.edu.
Golf: William Green; Phone: 609-258-1972; E-mail: golf@princeton.edu.
Ice Hockey: Len Quesnelle; Phone: 609-258-6616; E-mail: lenq@princeton.edu.
Lacrosse: Bill Tierney; Phone: 609-258-4978; E-mail: tierney@princeton.edu.
Soccer: Jim Barlow; Phone: 609-258-4977; E-mail: jimbarlo@princeton.edu.
Swimming: Rob Orr; Phone: 609-258-3544; E-mail: orr@princeton.edu.
Tennis: Glenn Michibata; Phone: 609-258-6990; E-mail: gmichiba@princeton.edu.
Track and Field: Fred Samara; Phone: 609-258-5007; E-mail: samara@princeton.edu.
Volleyball: Glenn Nelson; Phone: 609-258-3532; E-mail: gnelson@princeton.edu.
Wrestling: Michael New; Phone: 609-258-2197; E-mail: mlncu@princeton.edu.

WOMEN'S COACHES
Basketball: Richard Barron; Phone: 609-258-2721; E-mail: rbarron@princeton.edu.
Cheerleading: Phone: 609-258-3531; E-mail: pucheer@princeton.edu.
Cross Country: Peter Farrell; Phone: 609-258-3522; E-mail: pfarrell@princeton.edu.
Diving: Susan Teeter; Phone: 609-258-3562; E-mail: teeter@princeton.edu.
Field Hockey: Kristen Holmes-Winn; Phone: 609-258-4976; E-mail: kh@princeton.edu.
Golf: Eric Stein; Phone: 609-258-3531; E-mail: estein@princeton.edu.
Lacrosse: Chris Sailer; Phone: 609-258-6489; E-mail: wlax@princeton.edu.
Soccer: Julie Shackford; Phone: 609-258-5092; E-mail: jcs@princeton.edu.

Softball: Maureen Barron; Phone: 609-258-4669; E-mail: medavies@princeton.edu.
Swimming: Susan Teeter; Phone: 609-258-3562; E-mail: teeter@princeton.edu.
Tennis: Louise Gengler; Phone: 609-258-5087; E-mail: gengler@princeton.edu.
Track and Field: Peter Farrell; Phone: 609-258-3522; E-mail: pfarrell@princeton.edu.
Volleyball: Glenn Nelson; Phone: 609-258-3552; E-mail: gnelson@princeton.edu.

PRINCIPIA COLLEGE
Elsah, Illinois

Panthers ◆ NCAA III ◆ St. Louis Athletic Conference ◆ http://www.prin.edu/college/

Independent Christian Science 4-year, founded 1910
Coed, 552 undergraduate students, 99% full-time, 55% women, 45% men
Rural 2,600-acre campus with easy access to St. Louis
Moderately difficult entrance level, 80% of applicants were admitted

Freshmen *Admission:* 247 applied, 211 were accepted, 147 enrolled. *Test scores:* SAT verbal scores over 500: 81%; SAT math scores over 500: 87%; SAT verbal scores over 600: 49%; SAT math scores over 600: 45%; SAT verbal scores over 700: 13%; SAT math scores over 700: 14%.
Tuition and fees (2004–05): $19,455 (full-time). *Room and board:* $6831 (room only: $3315).
Financial Aid (All incoming freshmen): *Average need-based gift aid:* $11,014. *Average non-need based aid:* $12,986. *Average aid to full-time undergraduates:* $15,915.
Athletic Department: *Director of Athletics:* Lee Suarez; Phone: 618-374-5026; Fax: 618-374-5221; E-mail: las@prin.edu. *Sports Information Director:* Brian Peticolas; Phone: 618-374-5031; E-mail: bcpeticolas@principia.edu.

MEN'S COACHES
Baseball: Michael Barthelmess; Phone: 618-374-5036; E-mail: mjb@prin.edu.
Basketball: Garry Sprague; Phone: 618-374-5035; E-mail: gts@prin.edu.
Cross Country: Chuck Wilcoxen; Phone: 618-374-5032; E-mail: cew@prin.edu.
Football: Michael Barthelmess; Phone: 618-374-5036; E-mail: mjb@prin.edu.
Golf: Chuck Wilcoxen; Phone: 618-374-5032; E-mail: cew@prin.edu.
Soccer: Vitalis Otieno; Phone: 618-374-5025; E-mail: scj@prin.edu.
Swimming: Brian Peticolas; Phone: 618-374-5031; E-mail: bcpeticolas@principia.edu.
Tennis: Keith Pierson; Phone: 618-374-5033; E-mail: hkp@prin.edu.
Track and Field: Ann Pierson; Phone: 618-374-5028; E-mail: abp@prin.edu.

WOMEN'S COACHES
Basketball: Norm Purdy; Phone: 618-374-5021; E-mail: ncp@prin.edu.
Cross Country: Chuck Wilcoxen; Phone: 618-374-5032; E-mail: cew@prin.edu.
Soccer: Lee Ellis; Phone: 618-374-5030; E-mail: lee@prin.edu.
Swimming: Brian Peticolas; Phone: 618-374-5031; E-mail: bcpeticolas@principia.edu.
Tennis: Keith Pierson; Phone: 618-374-5033; E-mail: hkp@prin.edu.
Track and Field: Ann Pierson; Phone: 618-374-5028; E-mail: abp@prin.edu.
Volleyball: Mary Ann Sprague; Phone: 618-374-5038; E-mail: mas@prin.edu.

PROVIDENCE COLLEGE
Providence, Rhode Island

Friars ◆ NCAA I ◆ Big East Conference; Hockey East Conference; Metro Atlantic Athletic Conference ◆ http://www.providence.edu/

Independent Roman Catholic comprehensive, founded 1917
Coed, 4,342 undergraduate students, 86% full-time, 58% women, 42% men
Suburban 105-acre campus with easy access to Boston
Very difficult entrance level, 60% of applicants were admitted

Freshmen *Admission:* 7,397 applied, 3,906 were accepted, 975 enrolled. *Test scores:* SAT verbal scores over 500: 93%; SAT math scores over 500: 95%; SAT verbal scores over 600: 53%; SAT math scores over 600: 58%; SAT verbal scores over 700: 8%; SAT math scores over 700: 8%.
Tuition and fees (2003–04): $22,104 (full-time). *Room and board:* $8500 (room only: $4350).
Financial Aid (All incoming freshmen): *Average need-based gift aid:* $10,500. *Average non-need based aid:* $12,677. *Average aid to full-time undergraduates:* $15,500.
Athletic Department: *Director of Athletics:* Robert Driscoll; Phone: 401-865-2265; Fax: 401-865-2583; E-mail: rdriscol@providence.edu. *Sports Information Director:* Arthur Parks; Phone: 401-865-2759; E-mail: aparks@providence.edu.

MEN'S COACHES

Basketball: Tim Welsh; Phone: 401-865-2266; E-mail: twelsh@providence.edu.
Cross Country: Ray Treacy; Phone: 401-865-2427; E-mail: rtreacy@providence.edu.
Diving: Jon Caswell; Phone: 401-865-2268; E-mail: jcaswell@providence.edu.
Ice Hockey: Paul Pooley; Phone: 401-865-2551; E-mail: ppooley@providence.edu.
Lacrosse: Chris Burdick; Phone: 401-865-2007; E-mail: cburdick@providence.edu.
Soccer: Chaka Daley; Phone: 401-865-2005; E-mail: ckdaley@providence.edu.
Swimming: Jon Caswell; Phone: 401-865-2268; E-mail: jcaswell@providence.edu.
Track and Field: Ray Treacy; Phone: 401-865-2427; E-mail: rtreacy@providence.edu.

WOMEN'S COACHES

Basketball: Susan Yow; Phone: 401-865-2527; E-mail: syow@providence.edu.
Cross Country: Ray Treacy; Phone: 401-865-2969; E-mail: rtreacy@providence.edu.
Diving: Jon Caswell; Phone: 401-865-2268; E-mail: jcaswell@providence.edu.
Field Hockey: Diane Madl; Phone: 401-865-1518; E-mail: dmadl@providence.edu.
Soccer: Tracy Dimillio Kerr; Phone: 401-865-2032; E-mail: tkerr@providence.edu.
Softball: Dana Fulmer; Phone: 401-865-2967; E-mail: dfulmer@providence.edu.
Swimming: Jon Caswell; Phone: 401-865-2268; E-mail: jcaswell@providence.edu.
Track and Field: Ray Treacy; Phone: 401-865-2427; E-mail: rtreacy@providence.edu.
Volleyball: Margot Royer; Phone: 401-865-2028; E-mail: mroyer@providence.edu.

PURDUE UNIVERSITY
West Lafayette, Indiana

Boilermakers ◆ NCAA I ◆ Big Ten Conference ◆ http://www.purdue.edu/

State-supported university, founded 1869, part of Purdue University System
Coed, 30,851 undergraduate students, 94% full-time, 41% women, 59% men
Suburban 1,579-acre campus with easy access to Indianapolis
Moderately difficult entrance level, 76% of applicants were admitted

Freshmen *Admission:* 22,977 applied, 18,076 were accepted, 6,371 enrolled. *Test scores:* SAT verbal scores over 500: 78%; SAT math scores over 500: 83%; SAT verbal scores over 600: 31%; SAT math scores over 600: 42%; SAT verbal scores over 700: 5%; SAT math scores over 700: 10%.
Tuition and fees (2003–04): $5860 (resident), $17,480 (nonresident). *Room and board:* $6700.
Financial Aid (All incoming freshmen): *Average need-based gift aid:* $8370. *Average non-need based aid:* $12,878. *Average aid to full-time undergraduates:* $9391.
Athletic Department: *Director of Athletics:* Morgan Burke; Phone: 765-494-3189; Fax: 765-494-1280; E-mail: mjb@purdue.edu. *Sports Information Director:* Tom Schott; Phone: 765-494-3145; E-mail: tschott@purdue.edu.

MEN'S COACHES

Baseball: Doug Schreiber; Phone: 765-494-3998; E-mail: dschreiber@purdue.edu.
Basketball: Gene Keady; Phone: 765-494-3214.
Cheerleading: Sue Bayley; Phone: 765-494-3194; E-mail: cbailey@purdue.edu.
Cross Country: Mike Poehlein; Phone: 765-494-3218; E-mail: mpoehlein@purdue.edu.
Diving: Wenbo Chen; Phone: 765-494-2993; E-mail: wbch6177@purdue.edu.
Football: Joe Tiller; Phone: 765-494-3220.
Golf: Devon Brouse; Phone: 765-494-2290; E-mail: dbrouse@purdue.edu.
Swimming: Dan Ross; Phone: 765-494-3278; E-mail: dross@purdue.edu.
Tennis: Tim Madden; Phone: 765-494-1647; E-mail: madden@purdue.edu.
Track and Field: Lissa Olson; Phone: 765-494-1584; E-mail: mmolson@purdue.edu.
Wrestling: Jessie Reyes; Phone: 765-494-9137; E-mail: jvreyes@purdue.edu.

WOMEN'S COACHES

Basketball: Kristy Curry; Phone: 765-494-5853; E-mail: kscurry@purdue.edu.
Cheerleading: Sue Bayley; Phone: 765-494-3194; E-mail: cbailey@purdue.edu.
Cross Country: Mike Poehlein; Phone: 765-494-9126; E-mail: mpoehlein@purdue.edu.
Diving: Wenbo Chen; Phone: 765-494-2993; E-mail: wbch6177@purdue.edu.
Golf: Devon Brouse; Phone: 765-494-2290; E-mail: dbrouse@purdue.edu.
Soccer: Robert Klatte; Phone: 765-494-3396; E-mail: rklatte@purdue.edu.
Softball: Carol Bruggeman; Phone: 765-494-6914; E-mail: bruggeman@purdue.edu.
Swimming: Cathy Wright-Eger; Phone: 765-494-1294; E-mail: cwright-eger@purdue.edu.
Tennis: Mat Iandolo; Phone: 765-494-7783; E-mail: miandolo@purdue.edu.
Track and Field: Lissa Olson; Phone: 765-494-1584; E-mail: mmolson@purdue.edu.
Volleyball: Dave Shondell; Phone: 765-494-3206; E-mail: dshondell@purdue.edu.

PURDUE UNIVERSITY CALUMET
Hammond, Indiana

Lakers ◆ NAIA ◆ Chicagoland Collegiate Conference ◆ http://www.calumet.purdue.edu/

State-supported comprehensive, founded 1951, part of Purdue University System
Coed, 8,196 undergraduate students, 57% full-time, 56% women, 44% men
Urban 167-acre campus with easy access to Chicago
Minimally difficult entrance level, 9% of applicants were admitted

Freshmen *Admission:* 1,969 applied, 1,721 were accepted, 1,198 enrolled. *Test scores:* SAT verbal scores over 500: 52%; SAT math scores over 500: 48%; SAT verbal scores over 600: 7%; SAT math scores over 600: 7%; SAT verbal scores over 700: 1%; SAT math scores over 700: %.
Tuition and fees (2004–05): $4826 (resident), $10,256 (nonresident).
Financial Aid (All incoming freshmen): *Average need-based gift aid:* $4226. *Average non-need based aid:* $585. *Average aid to full-time undergraduates:* $4422.
Athletic Department: *Director of Athletics:* Rob Jensen; Phone: 219-989-2540; Fax: 219-989-2766; E-mail: rjensen@calumet.purdue.edu. *Sports Information Director:* J.B. Lyles; Phone: 219-989-2506; E-mail: lyles@calumet.purdue.edu.

MEN'S COACHES
Basketball: Gary Hayes; Phone: 219-989-2309.

WOMEN'S COACHES
Basketball: Dennis Smith; Phone: 219-989-2309.

PURDUE UNIVERSITY NORTH CENTRAL
Westville, Indiana

Panthers ◆ NAIA ◆ Chicagoland Collegiate Conference ◆ http://www.pnc.edu/

State-supported comprehensive, founded 1967, part of Purdue University System
Coed, 3,443 undergraduate students, 59% full-time, 60% women, 40% men
Rural 305-acre campus with easy access to Chicago
Minimally difficult entrance level, 88% of applicants were admitted

Freshmen *Admission:* 973 applied, 812 were accepted, 617 enrolled. *Test scores:* SAT verbal scores over 500: 38%; SAT math scores over 500: 37%; SAT verbal scores over 600: 7%; SAT math scores over 600: 7%; SAT math scores over 700: 1%.
Tuition and fees (2003–04): $4712 (resident), $10,871 (nonresident).
Financial Aid (All incoming freshmen): *Average need-based gift aid:* $4285. *Average non-need based aid:* $1343. *Average aid to full-time undergraduates:* $4099.
Athletic Department: *Director of Athletics:* Paul Gillikin; Phone: 219-785-5273; Fax: 219-785-5355; E-mail: paulg@purduenc.edu. *Sports Information Director:* Paul Gillikin; Phone: 219-785-5273; E-mail: paulg@purduenc.edu.

MEN'S COACHES
Baseball: Ryan Brown; Phone: 219-785-5273; E-mail: rwbrown@pnc.edu.
Basketball: Grayling Gordon; Phone: 219-785-5273; E-mail: ggordon@pnc.edu.
Cheerleading: Jean-Ann Morton; Phone: 219-785-5273; E-mail: jmorton@pnc.edu.

WOMEN'S COACHES
Cheerleading: Jean-Ann Morton; Phone: 219-785-5273; E-mail: jmorton@pnc.edu.
Softball: Gil Arzola; Phone: 219-785-5273; E-mail: garzola3@pnc.edu.

QUEENS COLLEGE OF THE CITY UNIVERSITY OF NEW YORK
Flushing, New York

Knights ◆ NCAA II ◆ New York Collegiate Athletic Conference ◆ http://www.qc.edu/

State and locally supported comprehensive, founded 1937, part of City University of New York System
Coed, 12,346 undergraduate students, 66% full-time, 63% women, 37% men
Urban 76-acre campus
Very difficult entrance level, 99% of applicants were admitted

Freshmen *Admission:* 2,503 applied, 2,468 were accepted, 1,330 enrolled. *Test scores:* SAT verbal scores over 500: 52%; SAT math scores over 500: 70%; SAT verbal scores over 600: 14%; SAT math scores over 600: 22%; SAT verbal scores over 700: 3%; SAT math scores over 700: 2%.
Tuition and fees (2004–05): $4361 (resident), $9001 (nonresident).
Financial Aid (All incoming freshmen): *Average need-based gift aid:* $3200. *Average aid to full-time undergraduates:* $4000.
Athletic Department: *Director of Athletics:* Richard Wettan; Phone: 718-997-2795; Fax: 718-997-2799; E-mail: richard_wettan@qc.edu. *Sports Information Director:* Neal Kaufer; Phone: 718-997-2758; E-mail: neal_kaufer@qc.edu.

MEN'S COACHES
Baseball: Frank Battaglia; Phone: 718-997-2781.
Basketball: Kyrk Peponakis; Phone: 718-997-2776.
Golf: Richard Wettan; Phone: 718-997-2795; E-mail: richard_wettan@qc.edu.
Swimming: Steve Sthab; Phone: 718-997-2752.
Tennis: Alan Landes; Phone: 718-997-2727.
Volleyball: Karl Pierre; Phone: 718-997-2761.

WOMEN'S COACHES
Basketball: Denis Conroy; Phone: 718-997-2774.
Diving: Alicia Lampasso-Dillon; Phone: 718-997-2767; E-mail: alicia_lampasso-dillon@qc.edu.
Soccer: Roby Young; Phone: 718-997-2755.
Softball: Brian Demasters; Phone: 718-997-2777; E-mail: brian_demasters@qc.edu.
Swimming: Alicia Lampasso-Dillon; Phone: 718-997-2767; E-mail: alicia_lampasso-dillon@qc.edu.
Tennis: Alan Nagel; Phone: 718-997-2756.
Volleyball: Pascale Lubin; Phone: 718-997-2761.

QUEENS UNIVERSITY OF CHARLOTTE
Charlotte, North Carolina

Royals ◆ NCAA II ◆ Carolinas-Virginia Athletics Conference; Deep South Lacrosse Conference ◆ http://www.queens.edu/

Independent Presbyterian comprehensive, founded 1857
Coed, 1,411 undergraduate students, 61% full-time, 77% women, 23% men
Suburban 25-acre campus
Moderately difficult entrance level, 71% of applicants were admitted

Freshmen *Admission:* 839 applied, 619 were accepted, 252 enrolled. *Test scores:* SAT verbal scores over 500: 69%; SAT math scores over 500: 66%; SAT verbal scores over 600: 24%; SAT math scores over 600: 20%; SAT verbal scores over 700: 3%; SAT math scores over 700: %.
Tuition and fees (2004–05): $17,008 (full-time). *Room and board:* $6190.
Financial Aid (All incoming freshmen): *Average need-based gift aid:* $8536. *Average non-need based aid:* $7999. *Average aid to full-time undergraduates:* $10,326.
Athletic Department: *Director of Athletics:* Jeannie King; Phone: 704-337-2509; Fax: 704-337-2237; E-mail: kingj@queens.edu. *Sports Information Director:* NA; Phone: 704-337-2585.

MEN'S COACHES
Basketball: Barclay Radebaugh; Phone: 704-337-2510; E-mail: radebaub@queens.edu.

Cheerleading: Jen Johnson; Phone: 704-337-2509; E-mail: cheer@
webmail.queens.edu.
Cross Country: Beth Gattuso; Phone: 704-337-2598; E-mail: gattusob@
queens.edu.
Golf: Todd Lawton; Phone: 803-634-9173; E-mail: lawtonl@queens.
edu.
Lacrosse: James Fritz; Phone: 704-688-2811; E-mail: fritzj@queens.edu.
Soccer: Fred Norchi; Phone: 704-337-2530; E-mail: norchif@queens.
edu.
Tennis: Charles Gordon; Phone: 704-337-2597; E-mail: gordonc@
queens.edu.
Track and Field: Beth Gattuso; Phone: 704-337-2598; E-mail: gattusob@
queens.edu.

WOMEN'S COACHES
Basketball: Beth Gattuso; Phone: 704-337-2598; E-mail: gattusob@
queens.edu.
Cheerleading: Jen Johnson; Phone: 704-337-2509; E-mail: cheer@
webmail.queens.edu.
Cross Country: Beth Gattuso; Phone: 704-337-2598; E-mail: gattusob@
queens.edu.
Golf: Laura Covington; Phone: 803-802-2053; E-mail: covingtl@
queens.edu.
Lacrosse: Kevin Cooke; Phone: 704-688-2810; E-mail: cookek@queens.
edu.
Soccer: Jonathan Brabson; Phone: 704-337-2540; E-mail: brabsonj@
queens.edu.
Softball: Adrian Ochoa; Phone: 704-337-2254; E-mail: ochoaa@queens.
edu.
Tennis: Scott Handback; Phone: 704-337-2346; E-mail: handbacs@
queens.edu.
Track and Field: Beth Gattuso; Phone: 704-337-2598; E-mail: gattusob@
queens.edu.
Volleyball: Chrys Baker; Phone: 704-337-2360; E-mail: bakerc@queens.
edu.

QUINCY UNIVERSITY
Quincy, Illinois

Hawks ◆ NCAA II ◆ Great Lakes Valley Conference;
Midwestern Intercollegiate Volleyball Conference ◆ http://
www.quincy.edu/

Independent Roman Catholic comprehensive, founded 1860
Coed, 1,130 undergraduate students, 86% full-time, 55% women,
45% men
Small-town 75-acre campus
Moderately difficult entrance level, 94% of applicants were admitted

Freshmen *Admission:* 1,056 applied, 988 were accepted, 222 enrolled.
Test scores: SAT verbal scores over 500: 53%; SAT math scores over
500: 53%; SAT verbal scores over 600: 13%; SAT math scores over
600: 20%.
Tuition and fees (2003–04): $16,850 (full-time). *Room and board:* $6735
(room only: $3265).
Financial Aid (All incoming freshmen): *Average need-based gift aid:*
$11,030. *Average non-need based aid:* $3715. *Average aid to full-time
undergraduates:* $16,220.
Athletic Department: *Director of Athletics:* Pat Atwell; Phone: 217-228-
5290; Fax: 217-228-5034; E-mail: atwelpt@quincy.edu. *Sports Information Director:* Ryan Dowd; Phone: 217-228-5290; E-mail:
dowdry@quincy.edu.

MEN'S COACHES
Baseball: Greg McVey; Phone: 217-228-5290; E-mail: mcveygr@quincy.
edu.
Basketball: Marty Bell; Phone: 217-228-5292; E-mail: bellma@quincy.
edu.
Cheerleading: Amy Anderson; Phone: 217-228-5290; E-mail: anderam@
quincy.edu.
Football: Bill Terlisner; Phone: 217-228-5578.
Golf: Alex Eichman; Phone: 217-228-7499; E-mail: alexeichman@
hotmail.com.
Soccer: Jack MacKenzie; Phone: 217-228-5591; E-mail: mackeja@
quincy.edu.
Tennis: Bill Latour; Phone: 217-228-5298; E-mail: blatour@quincy.edu.
Volleyball: Tim Koth; Phone: 217-228-5293; E-mail: kothti@quincy.
edu.

WOMEN'S COACHES
Basketball: Larry Just; Phone: 217-228-5206; E-mail: justla@quincy.
edu.
Cheerleading: Amy Anderson; Phone: 217-228-5290; E-mail: anderam@
quincy.edu.
Golf: Troy Conover; Phone: 217-228-5290.
Soccer: Bill Postiglione; Phone: 217-228-5483; E-mail: postiwi@quincy.
edu.
Softball: Sharlene Peter; Phone: 217-228-5308; E-mail: petersh@quincy.
edu.
Tennis: Bill Latour; Phone: 217-228-5298; E-mail: blatour@quincy.edu.
Volleyball: Tim Koth; Phone: 217-228-5293; E-mail: kothti@quincy.
edu.

QUINNIPIAC UNIVERSITY
Hamden, Connecticut

Braves ◆ NCAA I ◆ America East Conference; Atlantic
Hockey Conference; Northeast Conference
◆ http://www.quinnipiac.edu/

Independent comprehensive, founded 1929
Coed, 5,470 undergraduate students, 93% full-time, 62% women,
38% men
Suburban 400-acre campus with easy access to Hartford
Moderately difficult entrance level, 62% of applicants were admitted

Freshmen *Admission:* 8,881 applied, 5,503 were accepted, 1,318 enrolled. *Test scores:* SAT verbal scores over 500: 76%; SAT math scores
over 500: 84%; SAT verbal scores over 600: 18%; SAT math scores
over 600: 27%; SAT verbal scores over 700: 1%; SAT math scores
over 700: 2%.
Tuition and fees (2004–05): $22,500 (full-time). *Room and board:* $9900.
Financial Aid (All incoming freshmen): *Average need-based gift aid:* $8708.
Average non-need based aid: $5504. *Average aid to full-time under-
graduates:* $12,404.
Athletic Department: *Director of Athletics:* Jack McDonald; Phone: 203-
582-8621; Fax: 203-582-8716; E-mail: mcdonald@quinnipiac.edu.
Sports Information Director: Mike Kobylanski; Phone: 203-582-8625;
E-mail: michael.kobylanski@quinnipiac.edu.

MEN'S COACHES
Baseball: Dan Gooley; Phone: 203-582-8966; E-mail: gooley@
quinnipiac.edu.
Basketball: Joe Desantis; Phone: 203-582-5311.
Cheerleading: May Ann Powers; Phone: 203-582-5325; E-mail:
mapowercoach@aol.com.
Cross Country: Edward O'Connor; Phone: 203-582-5320; E-mail:
edward.oconnor@quinnipiac.edu.
Golf: Todd Howes; Phone: 203-582-5317; E-mail: todd.howes@
quinnipiac.edu.
Ice Hockey: Rand Pecknold; Phone: 203-582-5321; E-mail: pecknold@
quinnipiac.edu.
Lacrosse: Eric Fekete; Phone: 203-582-5318; E-mail: eric.fekete@
quinnipiac.edu.
Soccer: Sam Carrington; Phone: 203-582-5324; E-mail: samuel.
carrington@quinnipiac.edu.
Tennis: Mike Quitko; Phone: 203-582-5322; E-mail: quitko@
quinnipiac.edu.
Track and Field: Shawn Green; Phone: 203-582-8620; E-mail: shawn.
green@quinnipiac.edu.

WOMEN'S COACHES
Basketball: Tricia Sacca-Fabbri; Phone: 203-582-5362; E-mail: sacca@
quinnipiac.edu.
Cheerleading: May Ann Powers; Phone: 203-582-5325; E-mail:
mapowercoach@aol.com.
Cross Country: Shawn Green; Phone: 203-582-5314; E-mail: shawn.
green@quinnipiac.edu.
Field Hockey: Becca Kohli; Phone: 203-582-5319; E-mail: main@
quinnipiac.edu.
Lacrosse: Stephanie Samaras; Phone: 203-582-5323; E-mail: stephania.
samaras@quinnipiac.edu.
Soccer: David Clarke; Phone: 203-582-5315; E-mail: quwsoccer@aol.
com.
Softball: Germain Fairchild; Phone: 203-582-5316; E-mail: germaine.
fairchild@quinnipiac.edu.

Quinnipiac University *(continued)*

Tennis: Mike Quitko; Phone: 203-582-5322; E-mail: quitko@ quinnipiac.edu.
Track and Field: Shawn Green; Phone: 203-582-8620; E-mail: shawn. green@quinnipiac.edu.
Volleyball: Makeba Davis; Phone: 203-582-5313; E-mail: mdavis@ quinnipiac.edu.

RADFORD UNIVERSITY
Radford, Virginia

Highlanders ◆ NCAA I ◆ Big South Conference; Northern Pacific Field Hockey Conference ◆ http://www.radford.edu/

State-supported comprehensive, founded 1910
Coed, 8,167 undergraduate students, 95% full-time, 59% women, 41% men
Small-town 177-acre campus
Moderately difficult entrance level, 66% of applicants were admitted

Freshmen *Admission:* 6,379 applied, 4,709 were accepted, 1,806 enrolled. *Test scores:* SAT verbal scores over 500: 51%; SAT math scores over 500: 49%; SAT verbal scores over 600: 12%; SAT math scores over 600: 10%; SAT verbal scores over 700: 1%; SAT math scores over 700: 1%.
Tuition and fees (2003–04): $4140 (resident), $11,202 (nonresident). *Room and board:* $5660 (room only: $3034).
Financial Aid (All incoming freshmen): *Average need-based gift aid:* $3853. *Average non-need based aid:* $5402. *Average aid to full-time undergraduates:* $6545.
Athletic Department: *Director of Athletics:* Greig Denny; Phone: 540-831-5228; Fax: 540-831-6095; E-mail: gdenny@radford.edu. *Sports Information Director:* Drew Dickerson; Phone: 540-831-5726; E-mail: adickerso@radford.edu.

MEN'S COACHES
Baseball: Lew Kent; Phone: 540-831-5881; E-mail: lgkent@radford. edu.
Basketball: Byron Samuels; Phone: 540-831-5125; E-mail: brsamuels@ radford.edu.
Cross Country: Glenn Terry; Phone: 540-831-7823; E-mail: gterry@ radford.edu.
Golf: Michael Grant; Phone: 540-831-5228; E-mail: mgrant2@radford. edu.
Soccer: Spencer Smith; Phone: 540-831-7821; E-mail: s-smith@radford. edu.
Tennis: Mike Anderson; Phone: 540-831-5394; E-mail: mcanders@ radford.edu.
Track and Field: Glenn Terry; Phone: 540-831-7823; E-mail: gterry@ radford.edu.

WOMEN'S COACHES
Basketball: Jeri Porter; Phone: 540-831-5123; E-mail: jporter6@ radford.edu.
Cross Country: Glenn Terry; Phone: 540-831-7823; E-mail: gterry@ radford.edu.
Diving: Bill Beecher; Phone: 540-831-5240; E-mail: wbeecher@radford. edu.
Field Hockey: Jeff Woods; Phone: 540-831-5876; E-mail: jwoods@ radford.edu.
Golf: Michael Grant; Phone: 540-831-5228; E-mail: mgrant2@radford. edu.
Soccer: Ben Sohrabi; Phone: 540-831-7826; E-mail: bsohrabi@radford. edu.
Softball: Amy Kuilhaug; Phone: 540-831-5882; E-mail: akvilhaug@ radford.edu.
Swimming: Bill Beecher; Phone: 540-831-5240; E-mail: wbeecher@ radford.edu.
Tennis: Bruce Harrison; Phone: 540-831-5394; E-mail: bharrison@ radford.edu.
Track and Field: Glenn Terry; Phone: 540-831-7823; E-mail: gterry@ radford.edu.
Volleyball: Michael Burch; Phone: 540-831-5879; E-mail: meburch@ radford.edu.

RAMAPO COLLEGE OF NEW JERSEY
Mahwah, New Jersey

Roadrunners ◆ NCAA III ◆ New Jersey Athletic Conference ◆ http://www.ramapo.edu/

State-supported comprehensive, founded 1969, part of New Jersey State College System
Coed, 5,242 undergraduate students, 76% full-time, 60% women, 40% men
Suburban 300-acre campus with easy access to New York City
Moderately difficult entrance level, 44% of applicants were admitted

Freshmen *Admission:* 4,028 applied, 1,746 were accepted, 725 enrolled. *Test scores:* SAT verbal scores over 500: 93%; SAT math scores over 500: 93%; SAT verbal scores over 600: 33%; SAT math scores over 600: 40%; SAT verbal scores over 700: 4%; SAT math scores over 700: 4%.
Tuition and fees (2003–04): $7411 (resident), $11,666 (nonresident). *Room and board:* $7792 (room only: $5332).
Financial Aid (All incoming freshmen): *Average need-based gift aid:* $9909. *Average non-need based aid:* $8744. *Average aid to full-time undergraduates:* $10,680.
Athletic Department: *Director of Athletics:* Eugene Marshall; Phone: 201-684-7674; Fax: 201-684-7958. *Sports Information Director:* Rachel McCann; Phone: 201-684-7679; E-mail: rmccann@ramapo.edu.

MEN'S COACHES
Baseball: Rich Martin; Phone: 201-684-7066; E-mail: rmartin@ ramapo.edu.
Basketball: Chuck McBreen; Phone: 201-684-7073; E-mail: roadrunners121@hotmail.com.
Cheerleading: Cristina Lofaro; Phone: 201-684-7674; E-mail: lofaroc@ hotmail.com.
Cross Country: John Nepolitan; Phone: 201-684-7090.
Soccer: Peppe Pinton; Phone: 201-390-7065; E-mail: ppinton@ramapo. edu.
Tennis: Roy Innis; Phone: 201-684-7674; E-mail: yohim@msn.com.
Track and Field: John Nepolitan; Phone: 201-684-7090.
Volleyball: Don Vanderbeck; Phone: 201-684-7068; E-mail: ramapovb@ aol.com.

WOMEN'S COACHES
Basketball: Eugene Marshall; Phone: 201-684-7674.
Cheerleading: Cristina Lofaro; Phone: 201-684-7674; E-mail: lofaroc@ hotmail.com.
Cross Country: John Nepolitan; Phone: 201-684-7090.
Field Hockey: Leslie LaFronz; Phone: 201-684-7938; E-mail: llafronz@ ramapo.edu.
Soccer: Arnie Ramirez; Phone: 201-684-7678; E-mail: gringojuli@aol. com.
Softball: Ben Allen; Phone: 201-684-7680; E-mail: ballen@ramapo.edu.
Tennis: Roy Innis; Phone: 201-684-7674; E-mail: yohim@msn.com.
Track and Field: John Nepolitan; Phone: 201-684-7090.
Volleyball: Brett Killman; Phone: 201-684-7068; E-mail: killman15@ optonline.net.

RANDOLPH-MACON COLLEGE
Ashland, Virginia

Yellow Jackets ◆ NCAA III ◆ Old Dominion Conference ◆ http://www.rmc.edu/

Independent United Methodist 4-year, founded 1830
Coed, 1,118 undergraduate students, 97% full-time, 52% women, 48% men
Suburban 110-acre campus with easy access to Richmond
Moderately difficult entrance level, 75% of applicants were admitted

Freshmen *Admission:* 1,661 applied, 1,285 were accepted, 326 enrolled. *Test scores:* SAT verbal scores over 500: 82%; SAT math scores over 500: 74%; SAT verbal scores over 600: 30%; SAT math scores over 600: 27%; SAT verbal scores over 700: 3%; SAT math scores over 700: 1%.
Tuition and fees (2003–04): $21,160 (full-time). *Room and board:* $6030 (room only: $3160).

Financial Aid (All incoming freshmen): *Average need-based gift aid:* $11,136. *Average non-need based aid:* $12,495. *Average aid to full-time undergraduates:* $15,135.
Athletic Department: *Director of Athletics:* Jeff Burns; Phone: 804-752-7367; Fax: 804-752-3748; E-mail: jburns@rmc.edu. *Sports Information Director:* Ann Schlottman; Phone: 804-752-7387; E-mail: aschlott@rmc.edu.

MEN'S COACHES

Baseball: Gregg Waters; Phone: 804-752-7303; E-mail: gwaters@rmc.edu.
Basketball: Michael Rhoades; Phone: 804-752-4733; E-mail: mrhoades@rmc.edu.
Cheerleading: Tarnee Kendell; Phone: 804-752-7223.
Football: Allan Gerber; Phone: 804-752-3784; E-mail: agerber@rmc.edu.
Golf: Jeff Burns; Phone: 804-752-7367; E-mail: jburns@rmc.edu.
Lacrosse: Jim Woodcock; Phone: 804-752-7358; E-mail: jwoodcoc@rmc.edu.
Soccer: Helmut Werner; Phone: 804-752-7299; E-mail: hwerner@rmc.edu.
Swimming: David Holland; Phone: 804-752-3104; E-mail: dholland@rmc.edu.
Tennis: Jamal Brunt; Phone: 804-752-7397; E-mail: jbrunt@rmc.edu.

WOMEN'S COACHES

Basketball: Caroll LaHaye; Phone: 804-752-7365; E-mail: clahaye@rmc.edu.
Cheerleading: Tarnee Kendell; Phone: 804-752-7223.
Field Hockey: Sarah Sobon; Phone: 804-752-3778; E-mail: ssobon@rmc.edu.
Lacrosse: Jessica Spadafora; Phone: 804-752-7366; E-mail: jspadafo@rmc.edu.
Soccer: Jim Woodcock; Phone: 804-752-7358; E-mail: jwoodcoc@rmc.edu.
Softball: Kevin Proffitt; Phone: 804-752-3611; E-mail: kproffit@rmc.edu.
Swimming: David Holland; Phone: 804-752-3104; E-mail: dholland@rmc.edu.
Tennis: Ana Litton; Phone: 804-752-4714; E-mail: alitton@rmc.edu.
Volleyball: Bill Rogers; Phone: 804-752-7327; E-mail: brogers@rmc.edu.

RANDOLPH-MACON WOMAN'S COLLEGE
Lynchburg, Virginia

Wildcats ◆ NCAA III ◆ Old Dominion Conference ◆ http://www.rmwc.edu/

Independent Methodist 4-year, founded 1891
Women only, 737 undergraduate students, 96% full-time, 100% women
Suburban 100-acre campus
Moderately difficult entrance level, 86% of applicants were admitted

Freshmen *Admission:* 716 applied, 615 were accepted, 177 enrolled. *Test scores:* SAT verbal scores over 500: 92%; SAT math scores over 500: 79%; SAT verbal scores over 600: 54%; SAT math scores over 600: 32%; SAT verbal scores over 700: 14%; SAT math scores over 700: 4%.
Tuition and fees (2003–04): $20,530 (full-time). *Room and board:* $7900.
Financial Aid (All incoming freshmen): *Average need-based gift aid:* $15,490. *Average non-need based aid:* $14,470. *Average aid to full-time undergraduates:* $19,845.
Athletic Department: *Director of Athletics:* Valerie Cushman; Phone: 434-947-8536; Fax: 434-947-8706; E-mail: vcushman@rmwc.edu.

WOMEN'S COACHES

Basketball: Melissa Wiggins; Phone: 434-947-8536; E-mail: mwiggins@rmwc.edu.
Field Hockey: Jerri Lucas; Phone: 434-947-8536; E-mail: jlucido@rmwc.edu.
Soccer: Kevin Porterfield; Phone: 434-947-8536; E-mail: kporterfield@rmwc.edu.
Softball: Michelle Cunningham; Phone: 434-947-8536; E-mail: mcunningham@rmwc.edu.

Swimming: Donna Hodgert; Phone: 434-947-8536; E-mail: dhodgert@rmwc.edu.
Tennis: Amy Rowland; Phone: 434-947-8536; E-mail: arowland@rmwc.edu.
Volleyball: Heather Somers; Phone: 434-947-8536; E-mail: hsomers@rmwc.edu.

REGIS COLLEGE
Weston, Massachusetts

Pride ◆ NCAA III ◆ Commonwealth Coast Conference ◆ http://www.regiscollege.edu/

Independent Roman Catholic comprehensive, founded 1927
Women only, 800 undergraduate students, 74% full-time, 98% women, 2% men
Small-town 168-acre campus with easy access to Boston
Moderately difficult entrance level, 87% of applicants were admitted

Freshmen *Admission:* 569 applied, 497 were accepted, 156 enrolled. *Test scores:* SAT verbal scores over 500: 41%; SAT math scores over 500: 35%; SAT verbal scores over 600: 8%; SAT math scores over 600: 8%; SAT verbal scores over 700: 1%; SAT math scores over 700: 1%.
Tuition and fees (2003–04): $19,910 (full-time). *Room and board:* $9090.
Financial Aid (All incoming freshmen): *Average need-based gift aid:* $10,925. *Average non-need based aid:* $9000. *Average aid to full-time undergraduates:* $20,193.
Athletic Department: *Director of Athletics:* Marybeth Lamb; Phone: 781-768-7147; Fax: 781-768-7152; E-mail: marybeth.lamb@regiscollege.edu.

WOMEN'S COACHES

Basketball: Tony Staffiere; Phone: 781-768-7383; E-mail: anthony.staffiere@regiscollege.edu.
Cross Country: Christine Kloiber; Phone: 781-768-7141; E-mail: christine.kloiber@regiscollege.edu.
Diving: Christa Gillis; Phone: 781-768-7148; E-mail: christa.gillis@regiscollege.edu.
Field Hockey: Heather Gilmour; Phone: 781-768-7149; E-mail: heather.gilmour@regiscollege.edu.
Softball: Heather Gilmour; Phone: 781-768-7149; E-mail: heather.gilmour@regiscollege.edu.
Swimming: Christa Gillis; Phone: 781-768-7148; E-mail: christa.gillis@regiscollege.edu.
Tennis: Roberta Danielle; Phone: 781-837-2588; E-mail: athletics@regiscollege.edu.
Track and Field: Christine Kloiber; Phone: 781-768-7150; E-mail: christine.kloiber@regiscollege.edu.
Volleyball: Kelly Murphy; Phone: 781-768-7141; E-mail: kelly.murphy@regiscollege.edu.

REGIS UNIVERSITY
Denver, Colorado

Rangers ◆ NCAA II ◆ Rocky Mountain Athletic Conference ◆ http://www.regis.edu/

Independent Roman Catholic (Jesuit) comprehensive, founded 1877
Coed, 381 undergraduate students, 100% full-time, 56% women, 44% men
Suburban 90-acre campus
Moderately difficult entrance level, 81% of applicants were admitted

Freshmen *Admission:* 1,528 applied, 1,268 were accepted, 381 enrolled. *Test scores:* SAT verbal scores over 500: 71%; SAT math scores over 500: 66%; SAT verbal scores over 600: 23%; SAT math scores over 600: 21%; SAT verbal scores over 700: 1%; SAT math scores over 700: 2%.
Tuition and fees (2003–04): $20,900 (full-time). *Room and board:* $7600 (room only: $4300).
Financial Aid (All incoming freshmen): *Average need-based gift aid:* $11,736. *Average non-need based aid:* $6080. *Average aid to full-time undergraduates:* $21,548.

Regis University *(continued)*

Athletic Department: *Director of Athletics:* Barbara Schroeder; Phone: 303-458-4071; Fax: 303-964-5499; E-mail: bschroed@regis.edu. *Sports Information Director:* Jeff Duggan; Phone: 303-458-4052; E-mail: jduggan@regis.edu.

MEN'S COACHES

Baseball: Dan McDermott; Phone: 303-458-3519; E-mail: dmcdermo@regis.edu.
Basketball: Lonnie Porter; Phone: 303-458-4074; E-mail: aporter@regis.edu.
Cross Country: Mike Mittelstaedt; Phone: 303-458-4392; E-mail: mmittels@regis.edu.
Golf: Mike Kramer; Phone: 303-458-3586; E-mail: rcasper@regis.edu.
Soccer: Matt McDowell; Phone: 303-458-4359; E-mail: mmcdowel@regis.edu.

WOMEN'S COACHES

Basketball: Linda Raunig; Phone: 303-458-4203; E-mail: lraunig@regis.edu.
Cross Country: Mike Mittelstaedt; Phone: 303-458-4392; E-mail: mmittels@regis.edu.
Lacrosse: Karie Keane; Phone: 303-458-3681; E-mail: kwatts@regis.edu.
Soccer: J.B. Belzer; Phone: 303-458-4981; E-mail: jbelzer@regis.edu.
Softball: Dana Lillard; Phone: 303-458-4353; E-mail: dlillard@regis.edu.
Volleyball: Frank Lavrisha; Phone: 303-458-4053; E-mail: flavrisha@regis.edu.

REINHARDT COLLEGE
Waleska, Georgia

Eagles ◆ NAIA ◆ Georgia Alabama Carolina Conference ◆ http://www.reinhardt.edu/

Independent religious 4-year, founded 1883, affiliated with United Methodist Church
Coed, 1,308 undergraduate students, 89% full-time, 59% women, 41% men
Rural 600-acre campus with easy access to Atlanta
Moderately difficult entrance level, 95% of applicants were admitted

Freshmen *Admission:* 773 applied, 542 were accepted, 258 enrolled.
Tuition and fees (2004–05): $12,200 (full-time). *Room and board:* $5762.
Athletic Department: *Director of Athletics:* Steve Condon; Phone: 770-720-5538; Fax: 770-720-5622; E-mail: smc@reinhardt.edu. *Sports Information Director:* Amy Saxon; Phone: 770-720-9217; E-mail: ars@reinhardt.edu.

MEN'S COACHES

Basketball: Joe Kennamer; Phone: 770-720-9228; E-mail: tjk@reinhardt.edu.
Cross Country: Kevin Kelly; Phone: 770-720-5912; E-mail: kjk@reinhardt.edu.
Soccer: Dan Farnham; Phone: 770-720-5619; E-mail: drf@reinhardt.edu.
Tennis: Sam Allen.

WOMEN'S COACHES

Basketball: T.J. Rosene; Phone: 770-720-5614; E-mail: tjr@reinhardt.edu.
Cross Country: Kevin Kelly; Phone: 770-720-5912; E-mail: kjk@reinhardt.edu.
Soccer: Andy Kaplan; Phone: 770-720-5979; E-mail: aek@reinhardt.edu.
Tennis: Julie Fleming; E-mail: jcf@reinhardt.edu.
Volleyball: Amy Saxon; Phone: 770-720-9217; E-mail: ars@reinhardt.edu.

RENSSELAER POLYTECHNIC INSTITUTE
Troy, New York

Engineers ◆ NCAA III ◆ Eastern College Athletic Conference; Upstate Collegiate Athletic Conference ◆ http://www.rpi.edu/

Independent university, founded 1824
Coed, 5,210 undergraduate students, 99% full-time, 25% women, 75% men
Suburban 260-acre campus with easy access to Albany
Very difficult entrance level, 80% of applicants were admitted

Freshmen *Admission:* 5,252 applied, 4,216 were accepted, 1,341 enrolled. *Test scores:* SAT verbal scores over 500: 95%; SAT math scores over 500: 99%; SAT verbal scores over 600: 70%; SAT math scores over 600: 90%; SAT verbal scores over 700: 19%; SAT math scores over 700: 44%.
Tuition and fees (2003–04): $28,496 (full-time). *Room and board:* $9083 (room only: $5101).
Financial Aid (All incoming freshmen): *Average need-based gift aid:* $19,532. *Average non-need based aid:* $10,457. *Average aid to full-time undergraduates:* $24,967.
Athletic Department: *Director of Athletics:* Ken Ralph; Phone: 518-276-6702; Fax: 518-276-8997; E-mail: ralphk@rpi.edu. *Sports Information Director:* Kevin Beattie; Phone: 518-276-2187; E-mail: beattk@rpi.edu.

MEN'S COACHES

Baseball: Karl Steffen; Phone: 518-276-6185; E-mail: steffk@rpi.edu.
Basketball: Mike Griffin; Phone: 518-276-8624; E-mail: griffm@rpi.edu.
Cross Country: Colin Tory; Phone: 518-276-6184; E-mail: toryc@rpi.edu.
Diving: Maria Coomaraswamy; Phone: 518-276-2642; E-mail: crandm@rpi.edu.
Football: Joe King; Phone: 518-276-2556; E-mail: kingj@rpi.edu.
Golf: Miles Nolan; Phone: 518-276-8535.
Ice Hockey: Dan Fridgen; Phone: 518-276-8534; E-mail: fridgd@rpi.edu.
Lacrosse: Tom Korrie; Phone: 518-276-6181; E-mail: korrit@rpi.edu.
Soccer: Adam Clinton; Phone: 518-276-6563; E-mail: clinta@rpi.edu.
Swimming: Shannon O'Brien; Phone: 518-276-2642; E-mail: obries@rpi.edu.
Tennis: Carol Pillsworth; Phone: 518-276-6183; E-mail: pillsc@rpi.edu.
Track and Field: Colin Tory; Phone: 518-276-6184; E-mail: toryc@rpi.edu.

WOMEN'S COACHES

Basketball: John Greene; Phone: 518-276-8037; E-mail: greenj5@rpi.edu.
Cross Country: Colin Tory; Phone: 518-276-6184; E-mail: toryc@rpi.edu.
Diving: Maria Coomaraswamy; Phone: 518-276-2642; E-mail: crandm@rpi.edu.
Field Hockey: Bridget Lanoir; Phone: 518-276-8623; E-mail: lanoib2@rpi.edu.
Lacrosse: Leslie Khachadourian; Phone: 518-276-6182; E-mail: khachl@rpi.edu.
Soccer: Leslie Khachadourian; Phone: 518-276-6182; E-mail: khachl@rpi.edu.
Softball: Erika Lewis; Phone: 518-276-8373; E-mail: lewise@rpi.edu.
Swimming: Shannon O'Brien; Phone: 518-276-2642; E-mail: obries@rpi.edu.
Tennis: Carol Pillsworth; Phone: 518-276-6183; E-mail: pillsc@rpi.edu.
Track and Field: Colin Tory; Phone: 518-276-6184; E-mail: toryc@rpi.edu.

RHODE ISLAND COLLEGE
Providence, Rhode Island

Anchormen ◆ NCAA III ◆ Little East Conference ◆ http://www.ric.edu/

State-supported comprehensive, founded 1854
Coed, 7,305 undergraduate students, 68% full-time, 67% women, 33% men
Suburban 180-acre campus with easy access to Boston
Moderately difficult entrance level, 73% of applicants were admitted

Freshmen *Admission:* 3,088 applied, 2,257 were accepted, 1,043 enrolled. *Test scores:* SAT verbal scores over 500: 44%; SAT math scores over 500: 43%; SAT verbal scores over 600: 10%; SAT math scores over 600: 10%; SAT verbal scores over 700: 1%; SAT math scores over 700: %.
Tuition and fees (2004–05): $4270 (resident), $10,910 (nonresident). *Room and board:* $6650 (room only: $3500).
Athletic Department: *Director of Athletics:* Donald Tencher; Phone: 401-456-8007; Fax: 401-546-8514; E-mail: dtencher@ric.edu. *Sports Information Director:* Scott Gibbons; Phone: 401-456-8516; E-mail: sgibbons@ric.edu.

MEN'S COACHES
Baseball: Jay Grenier; Phone: 401-456-8258; E-mail: jgrenier@ric.edu.
Basketball: Michael Kelly; Phone: 401-456-8075; E-mail: mkelly@ric.edu.
Cross Country: Kevin Jackson; Phone: 401-456-4617; E-mail: kjackson@ric.edu.
Golf: John Fitta; Phone: 401-456-8829; E-mail: jfitta@ric.edu.
Soccer: Len Mercurio; Phone: 401-456-8251; E-mail: lmercurio@ric.edu.
Tennis: Kelly Chartier; Phone: 401-456-1954; E-mail: klange01@ric.edu.
Track and Field: Kevin Jackson; Phone: 401-456-4617; E-mail: kjackson@ric.edu.
Wrestling: Jay Jones; Phone: 401-456-4615; E-mail: jjones@ric.edu.

WOMEN'S COACHES
Basketball: Spencer Manning; Phone: 401-456-8156; E-mail: smanning@ric.edu.
Cross Country: Kevin Jackson; Phone: 401-456-4617; E-mail: kjackson@ric.edu.
Gymnastics: Bob Nannig; Phone: 401-456-8215; E-mail: rnannig@ric.edu.
Lacrosse: Ryan Angel; Phone: 401-456-8252; E-mail: rangel@ric.edu.
Soccer: Ryan Angel; Phone: 401-456-8252; E-mail: rangel@ric.edu.
Softball: Maria Morin; Phone: 401-456-8259; E-mail: mmorin@ric.edu.
Tennis: Kelly Chartier; Phone: 401-456-1954; E-mail: klange01@ric.edu.
Track and Field: Kevin Jackson; Phone: 401-456-4617; E-mail: kjackson@ric.edu.
Volleyball: Craig Letourneau; Phone: 401-456-8641; E-mail: cletourneau@ric.edu.

RHODES COLLEGE
Memphis, Tennessee

Lynx ◆ NCAA III ◆ Southern Collegiate Athletic Conference ◆ http://www.rhodes.edu/

Independent Presbyterian comprehensive, founded 1848
Coed, 1,551 undergraduate students, 98% full-time, 58% women, 42% men
Suburban 100-acre campus
Very difficult entrance level, 66% of applicants were admitted

Freshmen *Admission:* 2,326 applied, 1,686 were accepted, 457 enrolled. *Test scores:* SAT verbal scores over 500: 99%; SAT math scores over 500: 99%; SAT verbal scores over 600: 75%; SAT math scores over 600: 68%; SAT verbal scores over 700: 22%; SAT math scores over 700: 16%.
Tuition and fees (2004–05): $24,278 (full-time). *Room and board:* $6638.
Financial Aid (All incoming freshmen): *Average need-based gift aid:* $11,678. *Average non-need based aid:* $8384. *Average aid to full-time undergraduates:* $15,815.

Athletic Department: *Director of Athletics:* Mike Clary; Phone: 901-843-3939; Fax: 901-843-3749; E-mail: clary@rhodes.edu. *Sports Information Director:* Matt Dean; Phone: 901-843-3946; E-mail: mdean@rhodes.edu.

MEN'S COACHES
Baseball: Jeff Cleanthes; Phone: 901-843-3456; E-mail: areynolds@rhodes.edu.
Basketball: Herb Hilgeman; Phone: 901-843-3942; E-mail: hilgeman@rhodes.edu.
Cross Country: Robert Shankman; Phone: 901-843-3950; E-mail: shankman@rhodes.edu.
Football: Joe White; Phone: 901-843-3019; E-mail: white@rhodes.edu.
Golf: Bill Cochran; Phone: 901-843-3460; E-mail: cochranb@rhodes.edu.
Soccer: Andy Marcinko; Phone: 901-843-3948; E-mail: marcinko@rhodes.edu.
Swimming: Mike Clary; Phone: 901-843-3939; E-mail: clary@rhodes.edu.
Tennis: Sarah Hatgas; Phone: 901-843-3949; E-mail: hatgas@rhodes.edu.
Track and Field: Robert Shankman; Phone: 901-843-3950; E-mail: shankman@rhodes.edu.

WOMEN'S COACHES
Basketball: Matt Dean; Phone: 901-843-3946; E-mail: mdean@rhodes.edu.
Cross Country: Robert Shankman; Phone: 901-843-3950; E-mail: shankman@rhodes.edu.
Field Hockey: David Norton; Phone: 901-843-3954; E-mail: nortond@rhodes.edu.
Golf: Bill Cochran; Phone: 901-843-3460; E-mail: cochranb@rhodes.edu.
Soccer: Laura Whiteley; Phone: 901-843-3452; E-mail: whiteley@rhodes.edu.
Softball: Neil Cordell; Phone: 901-843-3454; E-mail: cordelln@rhodes.edu.
Swimming: Mike Clary; Phone: 901-843-3939; E-mail: clary@rhodes.edu.
Tennis: Sarah Hatgas; Phone: 901-843-3949; E-mail: hatgas@rhodes.edu.
Track and Field: Robert Shankman; Phone: 901-843-3950; E-mail: shankman@rhodes.edu.
Volleyball: Samantha Lambert; Phone: 901-843-3168; E-mail: wolinski@rhodes.edu.

RICE UNIVERSITY
Houston, Texas

Owls ◆ NCAA I ◆ Western Athletic Conference ◆ http://www.rice.edu/

Independent university, founded 1912
Coed, 2,921 undergraduate students, 98% full-time, 48% women, 52% men
Urban 300-acre campus
Most difficult entrance level, 2% of applicants were admitted

Freshmen *Admission:* 7,501 applied, 1,821 were accepted, 715 enrolled. *Test scores:* SAT verbal scores over 500: 98%; SAT math scores over 500: 100%; SAT verbal scores over 600: 91%; SAT math scores over 600: 94%; SAT verbal scores over 700: 57%; SAT math scores over 700: 64%.
Tuition and fees (2003–04): $19,670 (full-time). *Room and board:* $7880 (room only: $4800).
Financial Aid (All incoming freshmen): *Average need-based gift aid:* $12,226. *Average non-need based aid:* $4999. *Average aid to full-time undergraduates:* $13,970.
Athletic Department: *Director of Athletics:* Bobby May; Phone: 281-348-6900; Fax: 281-527-6019; E-mail: bmay@rice.edu. *Sports Information Director:* Bill Cousins; Phone: 281-348-5775; E-mail: bcuz@rice.edu.

MEN'S COACHES
Baseball: Wayne Graham; Phone: 713-348-6022; E-mail: baseball@rice.edu.
Basketball: Willis Wilson; Phone: 713-348-4075; E-mail: wtwilson@rice.edu.
Cross Country: Jon Warren; Phone: 713-348-6021; E-mail: jhwarren@rice.edu.

Rice University *(continued)*

Football: Ken Hatfield; Phone: 713-348-6900; E-mail: khatfiel@rice.edu.
Golf: Dick Ellis; Phone: 713-348-6913; E-mail: choman@rice.edu.
Tennis: Ron Smarr; Phone: 713-348-5716.
Track and Field: Jon Warren; Phone: 713-348-6021; E-mail: jhwarren@rice.edu.

WOMEN'S COACHES
Basketball: Cristy McKinney; Phone: 713-348-5677; E-mail: mckinney@rice.edu.
Cross Country: Victor Lopez; Phone: 713-348-6023; E-mail: lopezwtr@rice.edu.
Soccer: Chris Huston; Phone: 713-348-6955; E-mail: chuston@rice.edu.
Swimming: Seth Huston; Phone: 713-348-4710; E-mail: shuston@rice.edu.
Tennis: Roger White; Phone: 713-348-6035; E-mail: rlwhite@rice.edu.
Track and Field: Victor Lopez; Phone: 713-348-6023; E-mail: lopezwtr@rice.edu.
Volleyball: Phone: 713-348-8884.

THE RICHARD STOCKTON COLLEGE OF NEW JERSEY
Pomona, New Jersey

Ospreys ◆ NCAA III ◆ Knickerbocker Lacrosse Conference; New Jersey Athletic Conference ◆ http://www.stockton.edu/

State-supported comprehensive, founded 1969, part of New Jersey State College System
Coed, 6,540 undergraduate students, 83% full-time, 59% women, 41% men
Suburban 1,600-acre campus with easy access to Philadelphia
Very difficult entrance level, 43% of applicants were admitted

Freshmen *Admission:* 3,795 applied, 1,624 were accepted, 825 enrolled. *Test scores:* SAT verbal scores over 500: 75%; SAT math scores over 500: 79%; SAT verbal scores over 600: 19%; SAT math scores over 600: 22%; SAT verbal scores over 700: 2%; SAT math scores over 700: 2%.
Tuition and fees (2003–04): $6224 (resident), $9168 (nonresident). *Room and board:* $6748 (room only: $4300).
Financial Aid (All incoming freshmen): *Average need-based gift aid:* $5892. *Average non-need based aid:* $1494. *Average aid to full-time undergraduates:* $9552.
Athletic Department: *Director of Athletics:* Lonnie Folks; Phone: 609-652-4877; Fax: 609-748-5510; E-mail: lonnie.folks@stockton.edu. *Sports Information Director:* Chris Rollman; Phone: 609-748-6011; E-mail: chris.rollman@stockton.edu.

MEN'S COACHES
Baseball: Marty Kavanagh; Phone: 609-652-6010; E-mail: kavanagm@stockton.edu.
Basketball: Gerry Matthews; Phone: 609-748-6008; E-mail: matthewg@stockton.edu.
Cheerleading: Phone: 609-652-4217.
Cross Country: Bill Preston; Phone: 609-748-6007; E-mail: prestonw@stockton.edu.
Lacrosse: Dick Rizk; Phone: 609-748-6004; E-mail: rizkr@stockton.edu.
Soccer: Jeff Haines; Phone: 609-748-6005; E-mail: hainesj@stockton.edu.
Track and Field: Bill Preston; Phone: 609-748-6007; E-mail: prestonw@stockton.edu.

WOMEN'S COACHES
Basketball: Joe Fussner; Phone: 609-748-6009; E-mail: fussnerj@stockton.edu.
Cheerleading: Phone: 609-652-4217.
Cross Country: Bill Preston; Phone: 609-748-6007; E-mail: prestonw@stockton.edu.
Soccer: Nick Juengert; Phone: 609-748-6006; E-mail: juengern@stockton.edu.
Softball: Val Julien; Phone: 609-748-6012; E-mail: julienv@stockton.edu.
Tennis: Phil Birnbaum; Phone: 609-748-6082; E-mail: phil.birnbaum@stockton.edu.

Track and Field: Bill Preston; Phone: 609-748-6007; E-mail: prestonw@stockton.edu.
Volleyball: Eric Illjes; Phone: 609-748-6038; E-mail: illjese@stockton.edu.

RIDER UNIVERSITY
Lawrenceville, New Jersey

Broncs ◆ NCAA I ◆ Colonial Athletic Conference; Metro Atlantic Athletic Conference; Northeast Conference ◆ http://www.rider.edu/

Independent comprehensive, founded 1865
Coed, 4,329 undergraduate students, 82% full-time, 59% women, 41% men
Suburban 340-acre campus with easy access to New York City and Philadelphia
Moderately difficult entrance level, 76% of applicants were admitted

Freshmen *Admission:* 4,329 applied, 3,394 were accepted, 950 enrolled. *Test scores:* SAT verbal scores over 500: 60%; SAT math scores over 500: 64%; SAT verbal scores over 600: 15%; SAT math scores over 600: 18%; SAT verbal scores over 700: 1%; SAT math scores over 700: 1%.
Tuition and fees (2003–04): $21,050 (full-time). *Room and board:* $8060.
Financial Aid (All incoming freshmen): *Average need-based gift aid:* $8693. *Average non-need based aid:* $7879. *Average aid to full-time undergraduates:* $17,875.
Athletic Department: *Director of Athletics:* Curt Blake; Phone: 609-896-5338; Fax: 609-896-0341; E-mail: blake@rider.edu. *Sports Information Director:* Bud Focht; Phone: 609-896-5138; E-mail: focht@rider.edu.

MEN'S COACHES
Baseball: Sonny Pittaro; Phone: 609-896-5055; E-mail: spittaro@rider.edu.
Basketball: Don Hamum; Phone: 609-896-5076; E-mail: harnum@rider.edu.
Cheerleading: CL Kravitsky; Phone: 609-896-5000; E-mail: kravitsky@rider.edu.
Cross Country: Bill Hodge; Phone: 609-896-5317; E-mail: whodge@rider.edu.
Diving: Dennis Ceppa; Phone: 609-896-5024.
Golf: Chet Dalgewicz; Phone: 609-896-5642; E-mail: dalgewic@rider.edu.
Soccer: Russ Fager; Phone: 609-896-5319; E-mail: fager@rider.edu.
Swimming: Steve Fletcher; Phone: 609-896-5024; E-mail: fletcher@rider.edu.
Tennis: Ed Torres; Phone: 609-895-5654.
Track and Field: Bill Hodge; Phone: 609-896-5317; E-mail: whodge@rider.edu.
Wrestling: Gary Taylor; Phone: 609-896-5201; E-mail: gtaylor@rider.edu.

WOMEN'S COACHES
Basketball: Eldon Price; Phone: 609-896-5383; E-mail: pricee@rider.edu.
Cheerleading: CL Kravitsky; Phone: 609-896-5000; E-mail: kravitsky@rider.edu.
Cross Country: Bill Hodge; Phone: 609-896-5317; E-mail: whodge@rider.edu.
Diving: Dennis Ceppa; Phone: 609-896-5024.
Field Hockey: Lori Hussong; Phone: 609-895-5629; E-mail: lhussong@rider.edu.
Soccer: Kevin Long; Phone: 609-896-5359; E-mail: klong@rider.edu.
Softball: Tricia Carroll; Phone: 609-896-5396; E-mail: carrollp@rider.edu.
Swimming: Steve Fletcher; Phone: 609-896-5024; E-mail: fletcher@rider.edu.
Tennis: Ed Torres; Phone: 609-896-5654.
Track and Field: Bill Hodge; Phone: 609-896-5317; E-mail: whodge@rider.edu.
Volleyball: Emily Ahlquist; Phone: 609-896-5239; E-mail: eahlquist@rider.edu.

RIPON COLLEGE
Ripon, Wisconsin
Red Hawks ◆ NCAA III ◆ Midwest Conference ◆ http://www.ripon.edu/

Independent 4-year, founded 1851
Coed, 998 undergraduate students, 98% full-time, 52% women, 48% men
Small-town 250-acre campus with easy access to Milwaukee
Moderately difficult entrance level, 83% of applicants were admitted

Freshmen *Admission:* 959 applied, 809 were accepted, 259 enrolled. *Test scores:* SAT verbal scores over 500: 81%; SAT math scores over 500: 76%; SAT verbal scores over 600: 51%; SAT math scores over 600: 46%; SAT verbal scores over 700: 14%; SAT math scores over 700: 25%.
Tuition and fees (2004–05): $20,730 (full-time). *Room and board:* $5360 (room only: $2530).
Financial Aid (All incoming freshmen): *Average need-based gift aid:* $13,825. *Average non-need based aid:* $15,811. *Average aid to full-time undergraduates:* $17,300.
Athletic Department: *Director of Athletics:* Bob Gillespie; Phone: 920-748-8774; Fax: 920-748-7386; E-mail: gillespier@ripon.edu. *Sports Information Director:* Chris Graham; Phone: 920-748-8157; E-mail: grahamc@ripon.edu.

MEN'S COACHES
Baseball: Gordon Gillespie; Phone: 920-748-8776; E-mail: jessl@ripon.edu.
Basketball: Bob Gillespie; Phone: 920-748-8774; E-mail: gillespier@ripon.edu.
Cross Country: Bob Duley; Phone: 920-748-8778; E-mail: duleyr@westfield.k12.wi.us.
Football: Ron Ernst; Phone: 920-748-8708; E-mail: ernstr@ripon.edu.
Golf: Ron Ernst; Phone: 920-748-8708; E-mail: ernstr@ripon.edu.
Soccer: Andy Haskell; Phone: 920-748-8133; E-mail: haskella@ripon.edu.
Swimming: Elizabeth Tierney; Phone: 920-748-8780; E-mail: tierneye@ripon.edu.
Tennis: Chuck Larson; Phone: 920-748-8133; E-mail: larsonc@ripon.edu.
Track and Field: Bob Duley; Phone: 920-748-8778; E-mail: duleyr@westfield.k12.wi.us.

WOMEN'S COACHES
Basketball: Julie Johnson; Phone: 920-748-8772; E-mail: johnsonj@ripon.edu.
Cross Country: Bob Duley; Phone: 920-748-8778; E-mail: duleyr@westfield.k12.wi.us.
Golf: Julie Johnson; Phone: 920-748-8772; E-mail: johnsonj@ripon.edu.
Soccer: Andy Haskell; Phone: 920-748-8133; E-mail: haskella@ripon.edu.
Softball: Kelly Witte; Phone: 920-748-8133; E-mail: wittek@ripon.edu.
Swimming: Elizabeth Tierney; Phone: 920-748-8780; E-mail: tierneye@ripon.edu.
Tennis: Kevin Francis; Phone: 920-748-8764; E-mail: jessl@ripon.edu.
Track and Field: Bob Duley; Phone: 920-748-8778; E-mail: duleyr@westfield.k12.wi.us.
Volleyball: Kelly Witte; Phone: 920-748-8133; E-mail: wittek@ripon.edu.

RIVIER COLLEGE
Nashua, New Hampshire
Raiders ◆ NCAA III ◆ Great Northeast Athletic Conference ◆ http://www.rivier.edu/

Independent Roman Catholic comprehensive, founded 1933
Coed, 1,452 undergraduate students, 56% full-time, 82% women, 18% men
Suburban 64-acre campus with easy access to Boston
Moderately difficult entrance level, 78% of applicants were admitted

Freshmen *Admission:* 899 applied, 715 were accepted, 221 enrolled. *Test scores:* SAT verbal scores over 500: 49%; SAT math scores over 500: 38%; SAT verbal scores over 600: 11%; SAT math scores over 600: 9%.

Tuition and fees (2003–04): $18,450 (full-time). *Room and board:* $7092.
Financial Aid (All incoming freshmen): *Average need-based gift aid:* $8592. *Average non-need based aid:* $6000. *Average aid to full-time undergraduates:* $14,625.
Athletic Department: *Director of Athletics:* Joanne Merrill; Phone: 603-897-8257; Fax: 603-897-8886; E-mail: jmerrill@rivier.edu. *Sports Information Director:* Joanne Merrill; Phone: 603-897-8257; E-mail: jmerrill@rivier.edu.

MEN'S COACHES
Baseball: Bill Maniotis; Phone: 603-897-8257; E-mail: bmaniotis@rivier.edu.
Basketball: Dave Morissette; Phone: 603-897-8579; E-mail: dmorissette@rivier.edu.
Cheerleading: Jessica Gillis; Phone: 603-897-8257.
Cross Country: Dave Morissette; Phone: 603-897-8579; E-mail: dmorissette@rivier.edu.
Soccer: Jeff Simoneau; Phone: 603-897-8657; E-mail: jsimoneau@rivier.edu.
Volleyball: Craig Kolek; Phone: 603-897-8467; E-mail: ckolek@rivier.edu.

WOMEN'S COACHES
Basketball: Bob Ward; Phone: 603-897-8257; E-mail: bward@rivier.edu.
Cheerleading: Jessica Gillis; Phone: 603-897-8257.
Cross Country: Dave Morissette; Phone: 603-897-8579; E-mail: dmorissette@rivier.edu.
Soccer: Jennifer Craft; Phone: 603-897-8657; E-mail: jcraft@rivier.edu.
Softball: Jennifer Craft; Phone: 603-897-8657; E-mail: jcraft@rivier.edu.
Volleyball: Craig Kolek; Phone: 603-897-8467; E-mail: ckolek@rivier.edu.

ROANOKE COLLEGE
Salem, Virginia
Maroons ◆ NCAA III ◆ Old Dominion Conference ◆ http://www.roanoke.edu/

Independent religious 4-year, founded 1842, affiliated with Evangelical Lutheran Church in America
Coed, 1,899 undergraduate students, 93% full-time, 58% women, 42% men
Suburban 68-acre campus
Moderately difficult entrance level, 74% of applicants were admitted

Freshmen *Admission:* 2,827 applied, 2,164 were accepted, 519 enrolled. *Test scores:* SAT verbal scores over 500: 78%; SAT math scores over 500: 78%; SAT verbal scores over 600: 30%; SAT math scores over 600: 26%; SAT verbal scores over 700: 4%; SAT math scores over 700: 3%.
Tuition and fees (2003–04): $20,865 (full-time). *Room and board:* $6528 (room only: $3168).
Financial Aid (All incoming freshmen): *Average need-based gift aid:* $14,101. *Average non-need based aid:* $9041. *Average aid to full-time undergraduates:* $17,670.
Athletic Department: *Director of Athletics:* Scott Allison; Phone: 540-375-2337; Fax: 540-375-2382; E-mail: allison@roanoke.edu. *Sports Information Director:* Chris Cummings; Phone: 540-375-2344; E-mail: cummings@roanoke.edu.

MEN'S COACHES
Baseball: Richard Morris; Phone: 540-378-5147; E-mail: rmorris@roanoke.edu.
Basketball: Page Moir; Phone: 540-375-2336; E-mail: moir@roanoke.edu.
Cross Country: Finn Pincus; Phone: 540-375-2384; E-mail: pincus@roanoke.edu.
Golf: Mike Flanary; Phone: 540-375-2338; E-mail: flanary@roanoke.edu.
Lacrosse: Bill Pilat; Phone: 540-375-2340; E-mail: pilat@roanoke.edu.
Soccer: Scott Allison; Phone: 540-375-2337; E-mail: allison@roanoke.edu.
Tennis: Phil Benne; Phone: 540-375-2480; E-mail: pbenne@roanoke.edu.
Track and Field: Finn Pincus; Phone: 540-375-2384; E-mail: pincus@roanoke.edu.

WOMEN'S COACHES
Basketball: Susan Dunagan; Phone: 540-375-2339; E-mail: dunagan@roanoke.edu.

Roanoke College (*continued*)

Cross Country: Finn Pincus; Phone: 540-375-2384; E-mail: pincus@roanoke.edu.
Field Hockey: Emily Stone; Phone: 540-375-2334; E-mail: estone@roanoke.edu.
Lacrosse: Tammy Dixon; Phone: 540-375-2572; E-mail: dixon@roanoke.edu.
Soccer: Phil Benne; Phone: 540-375-2480; E-mail: pbenne@roanoke.edu.
Softball: Alan Bayse; Phone: 540-378-5130; E-mail: albayse@earthlink.net.
Tennis: Scott Gibson; Phone: 540-375-2051; E-mail: gibson@roanoke.edu.
Track and Field: Finn Pincus; Phone: 540-375-2384; E-mail: pincus@roanoke.edu.
Volleyball: Blair Trail; Phone: 540-378-5131; E-mail: bcalvert@roanoke.edu.

ROBERT MORRIS COLLEGE
Chicago, Illinois

Eagles ◆ NAIA ◆ Chicagoland Collegiate Conference ◆ http://www.robertmorris.edu/

Independent 4-year, founded 1913
Coed, 5,139 undergraduate students, 91% full-time, 68% women, 32% men
Urban campus
Minimally difficult entrance level, 75% of applicants were admitted

Freshmen *Admission:* 3,043 applied, 2,310 were accepted, 1,011 enrolled.
Tuition and fees (2004–05): $14,250 (full-time).
Financial Aid (All incoming freshmen): *Average need-based gift aid:* $8582. *Average non-need based aid:* $7234. *Average aid to full-time undergraduates:* $10,515.
Athletic Department: *Director of Athletics:* Steve Mendelson; Phone: 312-935-6801; Fax: 312-935-6804; E-mail: smendelson@robertmorris.edu. *Sports Information Director:* Tom Czop; Phone: 312-935-6217; E-mail: tczop@robertmorris.edu.

MEN'S COACHES
Baseball: Woody Urchak; Phone: 312-838-9965.
Basketball: Al Bruehl; Phone: 312-935-6808.
Cross Country: Mary Ellen Schoenjohn; Phone: 312-838-9965.
Golf: Jim Dennor; Phone: 312-935-6801.

WOMEN'S COACHES
Basketball: E.C. Hill; Phone: 312-935-6801.
Cross Country: Mary Ellen Schoenjohn; Phone: 312-838-9965.
Golf: Bob Franz; Phone: 312-935-6801; E-mail: rfranz@robertmorris.edu.
Soccer: Kurt Melcher; Phone: 312-935-6801.
Softball: Scott Wesley; Phone: 312-935-6801.
Tennis: Phone: 312-935-6801.
Volleyball: Chris Pruitt; Phone: 312-935-6801.

ROBERT MORRIS UNIVERSITY
Moon Township, Pennsylvania

Colonials ◆ NCAA I ◆ Northeast Conference ◆ http://www.rmu.edu/

Independent comprehensive, founded 1921
Coed, 3,735 undergraduate students, 74% full-time, 48% women, 52% men
Suburban 230-acre campus with easy access to Pittsburgh
Moderately difficult entrance level, 91% of applicants were admitted

Freshmen *Admission:* 1,816 applied, 1,645 were accepted, 557 enrolled.
Test scores: SAT verbal scores over 500: 48%; SAT math scores over 500: 54%; SAT verbal scores over 600: 8%; SAT math scores over 600: 16%; SAT math scores over 700: 1%.
Tuition and fees (2003–04): $13,484 (full-time). *Room and board:* $6954 (room only: $4138).

Financial Aid (All incoming freshmen): *Average need-based gift aid:* $7880. *Average non-need based aid:* $7408. *Average aid to full-time undergraduates:* $12,247.
Athletic Department: *Director of Athletics:* Susan Hofacre; Phone: 412-262-8302; Fax: 412-262-8557; E-mail: hofacre@rmu.edu. *Sports Information Director:* James Duzyk; Phone: 412-262-8314; E-mail: duzyk@rmu.edu.

MEN'S COACHES
Basketball: Mark Schmidt; Phone: 412-262-8297; E-mail: schmidtm@rmu.edu.
Cheerleading: Melissa Hay; Phone: 412-262-8295; E-mail: hay@rmu.edu.
Cross Country: Michael Smith; Phone: 412-262-2562; E-mail: smithm@rmu.edu.
Football: Joe Walton; Phone: 412-262-8296.
Golf: Jerry Stone; Phone: 412-262-8295; E-mail: stone@rmu.edu.
Ice Hockey: Derek Schooley; Phone: 412-269-4477; E-mail: schoolcy@rmu.edu.
Lacrosse: Ken Davis; Phone: 412-262-8295; E-mail: davisk@rmu.edu.
Soccer: Bill Denniston; Phone: 412-262-8446; E-mail: denniston@rmu.edu.
Tennis: Evan Schermer; Phone: 412-262-8587.
Track and Field: Michael Smith; Phone: 412-262-8513; E-mail: smithm@rmu.edu.

WOMEN'S COACHES
Basketball: Sal Buscaglia; Phone: 412-262-8419; E-mail: buscaglia@rmu.edu.
Cheerleading: Melissa Hay; Phone: 412-262-8295; E-mail: hay@rmu.edu.
Cross Country: Michael Smith; Phone: 412-262-2562; E-mail: smithm@rmu.edu.
Golf: Margot Turner; Phone: 412-262-8295; E-mail: turner@rmu.edu.
Lacrosse: Katy Phillips; Phone: 412-262-3889; E-mail: phillips@rmu.edu.
Soccer: John Kowalski; Phone: 412-262-8631; E-mail: kowalski@rmu.edu.
Softball: Craig Coleman; Phone: 412-262-8295; E-mail: colemanc@rmu.edu.
Tennis: Evan Schermer; Phone: 412-262-8587.
Track and Field: Michael Smith; Phone: 412-262-8513; E-mail: smithm@rmu.edu.
Volleyball: Rob Thomas; Phone: 412-262-8603; E-mail: thomasr@rmu.edu.

ROBERTS WESLEYAN COLLEGE
Rochester, New York

Raiders ◆ NAIA ◆ American Mideast Conference ◆ http://www.roberts.edu/

Independent religious comprehensive, founded 1866, affiliated with Free Methodist Church of North America
Coed, 1,292 undergraduate students, 91% full-time, 66% women, 34% men
Suburban 75-acre campus
Moderately difficult entrance level, 81% of applicants were admitted

Freshmen *Admission:* 689 applied, 554 were accepted, 253 enrolled.
Test scores: SAT verbal scores over 500: 71%; SAT verbal scores over 600: 29%; SAT math scores over 600: 27%; SAT verbal scores over 700: 2%; SAT math scores over 700: 3%.
Tuition and fees (2003–04): $16,752 (full-time). *Room and board:* $6200 (room only: $4420).
Financial Aid (All incoming freshmen): *Average need-based gift aid:* $10,536. *Average non-need based aid:* $8930. *Average aid to full-time undergraduates:* $15,613.
Athletic Department: *Director of Athletics:* Mike Faro; Phone: 585-594-6512; Fax: 585-594-6580; E-mail: farom@roberts.edu. *Sports Information Director:* Jason Blom; Phone: 585-594-6855; E-mail: blom_jason@roberts.com.

MEN'S COACHES
Basketball: Rob McCoy; Phone: 585-594-6515; E-mail: mccoy_robert@roberts.edu.
Cross Country: Paul Kurtz; Phone: 585-594-6513; E-mail: kurtzp@roberts.edu.

Golf: Ken Starkweather; Phone: 585-594-6891; E-mail: starkweather_ken@roberts.edu.
Soccer: Greg Gidman; Phone: 585-594-6514; E-mail: gidmang@roberts.edu.
Tennis: Mike Faro; Phone: 585-594-6512; E-mail: farom@roberts.edu.
Track and Field: Adam Steinwachs; Phone: 585-594-6891; E-mail: steinwachs_adam@roberts.edu.

WOMEN'S COACHES

Basketball: Chris Williams; Phone: 585-594-6357; E-mail: williamsc@roberts.edu.
Cross Country: Paul Kurtz; Phone: 585-594-6513; E-mail: kurtzp@roberts.edu.
Soccer: Andrea Boon; Phone: 585-594-6962; E-mail: boon_andrea@roberts.edu.
Tennis: Mike Faro; Phone: 585-594-6512; E-mail: farom@roberts.edu.
Track and Field: Adam Steinwachs; Phone: 585-594-6891; E-mail: steinwachs_adam@roberts.edu.
Volleyball: Jim Vanderhoof; Phone: 585-594-6565; E-mail: vanderhoofj@roberts.edu.

ROCHESTER INSTITUTE OF TECHNOLOGY
Rochester, New York

Tigers ◆ NCAA III ◆ Empire 8 Conference
◆ http://www.rit.edu/

Independent comprehensive, founded 1829
Coed, 12,381 undergraduate students, 86% full-time, 31% women, 69% men
Suburban 1,300-acre campus with easy access to Buffalo
Moderately difficult entrance level, 70% of applicants were admitted

Freshmen *Admission:* 8,317 applied, 5,784 were accepted, 2,203 enrolled. *Test scores:* SAT verbal scores over 500: 89%; SAT math scores over 500: 96%; SAT verbal scores over 600: 46%; SAT math scores over 600: 65%; SAT verbal scores over 700: 8%; SAT math scores over 700: 16%.
Tuition and fees (2003–04): $21,384 (full-time). *Room and board:* $7833 (room only: $4452).
Financial Aid (All incoming freshmen): *Average need-based gift aid:* $10,000. *Average non-need based aid:* $5900. *Average aid to full-time undergraduates:* $16,500.
Athletic Department: *Director of Athletics:* Janet Jones; Phone: 585-475-2329; Fax: 716-475-5675; E-mail: jejatl@rit.edu. *Sports Information Director:* Stephen Jaynes; Phone: 585-475-6154; E-mail: skjsid@rit.edu.

MEN'S COACHES

Baseball: Rob Grow; Phone: 716-475-7374; E-mail: rcg1221@rit.edu.
Basketball: Bob McVean; Phone: 716-475-2580; E-mail: rhmatl@rit.edu.
Cheerleading: Hysha Robinson; Phone: 716-475-7699; E-mail: hlrsfa@rit.edu.
Cross Country: Dave Warth; Phone: 716-475-6666; E-mail: djwatl@rit.edu.
Ice Hockey: Wayne Wilson; Phone: 716-475-5615; E-mail: jwwatl1@rit.edu.
Lacrosse: Gene Peluso; Phone: 716-475-2131; E-mail: coachpeluso@hotmail.com.
Soccer: Bill Garno; Phone: 716-475-2618; E-mail: wtgter@rit.edu.
Swimming: Mike Cahill; Phone: 716-475-5082; E-mail: sksatl@rit.edu.
Tennis: Ann Nealon; Phone: 716-475-6562; E-mail: amnped@rit.edu.
Track and Field: Dave Warth; Phone: 716-475-6666; E-mail: djwatl@rit.edu.
Wrestling: Scott Stever; Phone: 716-475-7476; E-mail: sastever@yahoo.com.

WOMEN'S COACHES

Basketball: Deborah Buff; Phone: 716-475-5666; E-mail: dxbchp@rit.edu.
Cheerleading: Hysha Robinson; Phone: 716-475-7699; E-mail: hlrsfa@rit.edu.
Cross Country: Dave Warth; Phone: 716-475-6666; E-mail: djwatl@rit.edu.
Lacrosse: Tricia Manley; Phone: 716-475-6961; E-mail: triciamanley9@hotmail.com.

Soccer: Tom Natalie; Phone: 716-475-7373; E-mail: tfnatl@rit.edu.
Softball: Jack Carpenter; Phone: 716-475-7770; E-mail: ritfastpitch@hotmail.com.
Swimming: Mike Cahill; Phone: 716-475-5004; E-mail: sksatl@rit.edu.
Tennis: Ann Nealon; Phone: 716-475-6562; E-mail: amnped@rit.edu.
Track and Field: Dave Warth; Phone: 716-475-6666; E-mail: djwatl@rit.edu.
Volleyball: Roger Worsley; Phone: 716-475-5295; E-mail: rwwatl@rit.edu.

ROCKFORD COLLEGE
Rockford, Illinois

Regents ◆ NCAA III ◆ Northern Illinois-Iowa Conference
◆ http://www.rockford.edu/

Independent comprehensive, founded 1847
Coed, 976 undergraduate students, 79% full-time, 62% women, 38% men
Suburban 130-acre campus with easy access to Chicago
Moderately difficult entrance level, 52% of applicants were admitted

Freshmen *Admission:* 654 applied, 384 were accepted, 131 enrolled. *Test scores:* SAT verbal scores over 500: 60%; SAT math scores over 500: 63%; SAT verbal scores over 600: 28%; SAT math scores over 600: 23%; SAT verbal scores over 700: 14%; SAT math scores over 700: 5%.
Tuition and fees (2004–05): $21,200 (full-time).
Athletic Department: *Director of Athletics:* Kristyn King; Phone: 815-394-5061; Fax: 815-226-4166; E-mail: kristyn_king@rockford.edu. *Sports Information Director:* Dave Beyer; Phone: 815-394-5060; E-mail: dave_beyer@rockford.edu.

MEN'S COACHES

Baseball: Brian Nelson; Phone: 815-394-5062; E-mail: brian_nelson@rockford.edu.
Basketball: Bill Lavery; Phone: 815-226-5063; E-mail: bill_lavery@rockford.edu.
Cross Country: Frank Mateus; Phone: 815-226-4085; E-mail: dactyls3@aol.com.
Football: Mike Hoskins; Phone: 815-394-3728; E-mail: mike_hoskins@rockford.edu.
Golf: Bill Lavery; Phone: 815-226-5063; E-mail: bill_lavery@rockford.edu.
Soccer: Frank Mateus; Phone: 815-226-4085; E-mail: dactyls3@aol.com.
Tennis: Steve Price; Phone: 815-226-4085; E-mail: ustaguru@aol.com.

WOMEN'S COACHES

Basketball: Bob Amsberry; Phone: 815-226-5065; E-mail: bob_amsberry@rockford.edu.
Cross Country: Frank Mateus; Phone: 815-226-4085; E-mail: dactyls3@aol.com.
Soccer: Frank Mateus; Phone: 815-226-4085; E-mail: dactyls3@aol.com.
Softball: Kristyn King; Phone: 815-226-5061; E-mail: kristyn_king@rockford.edu.
Tennis: Steve Price; Phone: 815-226-4085; E-mail: ustaguru@aol.com.
Volleyball: Julian Jacques; Phone: 815-226-4085; E-mail: idigur31@aol.com.

ROCKHURST UNIVERSITY
Kansas City, Missouri

Hawks ◆ NCAA II ◆ Heartland Conference
◆ http://www.rockhurst.edu/

Independent Roman Catholic (Jesuit) comprehensive, founded 1910
Coed, 1,957 undergraduate students, 55% full-time, 57% women, 43% men
Urban 35-acre campus
Moderately difficult entrance level, 81% of applicants were admitted

Freshmen *Admission:* 960 applied, 766 were accepted, 245 enrolled. *Test scores:* SAT verbal scores over 500: 81%; SAT math scores over

Rockhurst University *(continued)*

500: 81%; SAT verbal scores over 600: 48%; SAT math scores over 600: 38%; SAT verbal scores over 700: 19%; SAT math scores over 700: 14%.
Tuition and fees (2003–04): $17,410 (full-time). *Room and board:* $5750.
Financial Aid (All incoming freshmen): *Average need-based gift aid:* $5760. *Average non-need based aid:* $5258. *Average aid to full-time undergraduates:* $16,502.
Athletic Department: *Director of Athletics:* Frank Diskin; Phone: 816-501-4141; Fax: 816-501-4119; E-mail: frank.diskin@rockhurst.edu. *Sports Information Director:* Sid Bordman; Phone: 816-501-4141; E-mail: athletics@rockhurst.edu.

MEN'S COACHES

Baseball: Gary Burns; Phone: 816-501-4851; E-mail: gary.burns@rockhurst.edu.
Basketball: Bill O'Connor; Phone: 816-501-4586; E-mail: william.oconnor@rockhurst.edu.
Cheerleading: Tricia McCracken; Phone: 816-501-4141.
Golf: Carl Capra; Phone: 816-501-4851; E-mail: carl.capra@rockhurst.edu.
Soccer: Tony Tocco; Phone: 816-501-4852; E-mail: anthony.tocco@rockhurst.edu.
Tennis: Kendell Hale; Phone: 816-501-4141; E-mail: kendell.hale@rockhurst.edu.

WOMEN'S COACHES

Basketball: Rebecca Morrisey; Phone: 816-501-4141; E-mail: rebecca.morrisey@rockhurst.edu.
Cheerleading: Tricia McCracken; Phone: 816-501-4141.
Golf: Carl Cadra; Phone: 816-501-4851; E-mail: carl.capra@rockhurst.edu.
Soccer: Greg Herdlick; Phone: 816-501-4141; E-mail: greg.herdlick@rockhurst.edu.
Tennis: Kendell Hale; Phone: 816-501-4141; E-mail: kendell.hale@rockhurst.edu.
Volleyball: Tracy Rietzke; Phone: 816-501-4853; E-mail: tracy.rietzke@rockhurst.edu.

ROCKY MOUNTAIN COLLEGE
Billings, Montana

Bears ◆ NAIA ◆ Frontier Conference
◆ http://www.rocky.edu/

Independent interdenominational 4-year, founded 1878
Coed, 919 undergraduate students, 94% full-time, 56% women, 44% men
Urban 60-acre campus
Moderately difficult entrance level, 84% of applicants were admitted

Freshmen *Admission:* 720 applied, 611 were accepted, 233 enrolled. *Test scores:* SAT verbal scores over 500: 73%; SAT math scores over 500: 70%; SAT verbal scores over 600: 22%; SAT math scores over 600: 15%; SAT verbal scores over 700: 4%; SAT math scores over 700: 1%.
Tuition and fees (2003–04): $14,115 (full-time). *Room and board:* $4900 (room only: $2112).
Financial Aid (All incoming freshmen): *Average need-based gift aid:* $8739. *Average non-need based aid:* $5871. *Average aid to full-time undergraduates:* $12,949.
Athletic Department: *Director of Athletics:* Terry Corey; Phone: 406-657-1124; Fax: 406-657-1185; E-mail: coreyt@rocky.edu. *Sports Information Director:* Chris Mouat; Phone: 406-657-1001; E-mail: mouatc@rocky.edu.

MEN'S COACHES

Basketball: Bill Dreikosen; Phone: 406-657-1034; E-mail: dreikosw@rocky.edu.
Football: Clay Moose; Phone: 406-657-1065; E-mail: moosec@rocky.edu.
Golf: Randy Northrop; Phone: 406-656-8099.

WOMEN'S COACHES

Basketball: Brian Henderson; Phone: 406-657-1038; E-mail: hendersb@rocky.edu.
Golf: Randy Northrop; Phone: 406-656-8099.
Soccer: Richard Duffy; Phone: 406-657-1122; E-mail: duffyr@rocky.edu.
Volleyball: Wade Wells; Phone: 406-657-1119; E-mail: wellsw@rocky.edu.

ROGER WILLIAMS UNIVERSITY
Bristol, Rhode Island

Hawks ◆ NCAA III ◆ Commonwealth Coast Conference; New England College Wrestling Conference
◆ http://www.rwu.edu/

Independent comprehensive, founded 1956
Coed, 4,110 undergraduate students, 82% full-time, 50% women, 50% men
Small-town 140-acre campus with easy access to Boston
Moderately difficult entrance level, 76% of applicants were admitted

Freshmen *Admission:* 5,438 applied, 4,326 were accepted, 959 enrolled. *Test scores:* SAT verbal scores over 500: 66%; SAT math scores over 500: 70%; SAT verbal scores over 600: 18%; SAT math scores over 600: 22%; SAT verbal scores over 700: 2%; SAT math scores over 700: 2%.
Tuition and fees (2003–04): $20,840 (full-time). *Room and board:* $9456 (room only: $4860).
Financial Aid (All incoming freshmen): *Average need-based gift aid:* $7659. *Average non-need based aid:* $5429. *Average aid to full-time undergraduates:* $12,432.
Athletic Department: *Director of Athletics:* George Kolb; Phone: 401-254-3129; Fax: 401-254-3535; E-mail: gkolb@rwu.edu. *Sports Information Director:* David Kemmy; Phone: 401-254-3428; E-mail: dkemmy@rwu.edu.

MEN'S COACHES

Baseball: Derek Carlson; Phone: 401-254-3163; E-mail: dcarlson@rwu.edu.
Basketball: Michael Tully; Phone: 401-254-3298; E-mail: mtully@rwu.edu.
Cheerleading: Patricia Lavier; Phone: 401-254-3050; E-mail: plavier@rwu.edu.
Cross Country: Todd Deely; Phone: 401-254-3408; E-mail: deelyworm@aol.com.
Lacrosse: Marty Kelly; Phone: 401-254-3073; E-mail: mkelly@rwu.edu.
Soccer: James Cook; Phone: 401-254-3091; E-mail: jcook@rwu.edu.
Tennis: Chris O'Brien; Phone: 401-254-3579.
Volleyball: Michael Holden; Phone: 401-254-3050; E-mail: mdhvball@aol.com.
Wrestling: David Kemmy; Phone: 401-254-3428; E-mail: dkemmy@rwu.edu.

WOMEN'S COACHES

Basketball: Rachel Madsen; Phone: 401-254-3748; E-mail: rmadsen@rwu.edu.
Cheerleading: Patricia Lavier; Phone: 401-254-3050; E-mail: plavier@rwu.edu.
Cross Country: Todd Deely; Phone: 401-254-3408; E-mail: deelyworm@aol.com.
Lacrosse: Emily Kiablick; Phone: 401-254-3450; E-mail: ekiablick@rwu.edu.
Soccer: Emily Kiablick; Phone: 401-254-3450; E-mail: ekiablick@rwu.edu.
Softball: Stephen Pappas; Phone: 401-254-3763; E-mail: spappas@rwu.edu.
Tennis: Chris O'Brien; Phone: 401-254-3579; E-mail: cobrien@rwu.edu.
Volleyball: Ben Heroux; Phone: 401-254-3050; E-mail: bheroux@rwu.edu.

ROLLINS COLLEGE
Winter Park, Florida

Tars ◆ NCAA II ◆ Sunshine State Conference ◆ http://www.rollins.edu/

Independent comprehensive, founded 1885
Coed, 1,733 undergraduate students, 100% full-time, 61% women, 39% men
Suburban 70-acre campus with easy access to Orlando
Very difficult entrance level, 6% of applicants were admitted

Freshmen *Admission:* 2,271 applied, 1,510 were accepted, 497 enrolled. *Test scores:* SAT verbal scores over 500: 89%; SAT math scores over

500: 90%; SAT verbal scores over 600: 39%; SAT math scores over 600: 42%; SAT verbal scores over 700: 6%; SAT math scores over 700: 6%.

Tuition and fees (2003–04): $26,250 (full-time). *Room and board:* $8050 (room only: $4650).

Financial Aid (All incoming freshmen): *Average need-based gift aid:* $21,352. *Average non-need based aid:* $10,010. *Average aid to full-time undergraduates:* $25,127.

Athletic Department: *Director of Athletics:* Phillip Roach; Phone: 407-646-2198; Fax: 407-646-1562; E-mail: proach@rollins.edu. *Sports Information Director:* Dean Hybl; Phone: 407-646-2661; E-mail: dhybl@rollins.edu.

MEN'S COACHES

Baseball: Bob Rikeman; Phone: 407-646-2328; E-mail: rike27@atlantic.net.
Basketball: Tom Klusman; Phone: 407-646-2291; E-mail: tklusman@rollins.edu.
Cheerleading: Bess Auer; Phone: 407-646-2366; E-mail: tarcheerleading@yahoo.com.
Cross Country: Brad Ash; Phone: 407-691-1732; E-mail: bash@rollins.edu.
Golf: Kyle Frakes; Phone: 407-646-2566; E-mail: ofrakes@rollins.edu.
Soccer: Keith Buckley; Phone: 407-646-2513; E-mail: kbuckley@rollins.edu.
Swimming: Rich Morris; Phone: 407-628-6387; E-mail: rmorris@rollins.edu.
Tennis: Ron Bohrnstedt; Phone: 407-646-2665; E-mail: rbohrnstedt@rollins.edu.

WOMEN'S COACHES

Basketball: Glenn Wilkes; Phone: 407-646-2476; E-mail: gwilkes@rollins.edu.
Cheerleading: Bess Auer; Phone: 407-646-2366; E-mail: tarcheerleading@yahoo.com.
Cross Country: Brad Ash; Phone: 407-691-1732; E-mail: bash@rollins.edu.
Golf: Julie Garner; Phone: 407-646-2601; E-mail: jgarner@rollins.edu.
Soccer: Tony Amato; Phone: 407-646-2142; E-mail: aamato@rollins.edu.
Softball: Michelle Frew; Phone: 407-646-2412; E-mail: mfrew@rollins.edu.
Swimming: Rich Morris; Phone: 407-628-6387; E-mail: rmorris@rollins.edu.
Tennis: Beverly Buckley; Phone: 407-646-2482; E-mail: bbuckley@rollins.edu.
Volleyball: Sindge Snow; Phone: 407-646-2631; E-mail: ssnow@rollins.edu.

ROSE-HULMAN INSTITUTE OF TECHNOLOGY
Terre Haute, Indiana

Fighting Engineers ◆ NCAA III ◆ Southern Collegiate Athletic Conference ◆ http://www.rose-hulman.edu/

Independent comprehensive, founded 1874
Coed, primarily men, 1,721 undergraduate students, 99% full-time, 18% women, 82% men
Suburban 200-acre campus with easy access to Indianapolis
Very difficult entrance level, 70% of applicants were admitted

Freshmen *Admission:* 3,188 applied, 2,261 were accepted, 490 enrolled. *Test scores:* SAT verbal scores over 500: 99%; SAT math scores over 500: 100%; SAT verbal scores over 600: 64%; SAT math scores over 600: 90%; SAT verbal scores over 700: 22%; SAT math scores over 700: 47%.

Tuition and fees (2003–04): $24,705 (full-time). *Room and board:* $6720 (room only: $3840).

Financial Aid (All incoming freshmen): *Average need-based gift aid:* $6570. *Average non-need based aid:* $6969. *Average aid to full-time undergraduates:* $17,373.

Athletic Department: *Director of Athletics:* Jeff Jenkins; Phone: 812-877-8209; Fax: 812-877-8407; E-mail: jeffrey.jenkins@rose-hulman.edu. *Sports Information Director:* Kevin Lanke; Phone: 812-877-8180; E-mail: kevin.lanke@rose-hulman.edu.

MEN'S COACHES

Baseball: Jeff Jenkins; Phone: 812-877-8209; E-mail: jeffrey.jenkins@rose-hulman.edu.
Basketball: Jim Shaw; Phone: 812-877-8497; E-mail: james.shaw@rose-hulman.edu.
Cross Country: Larry Cole; Phone: 812-877-8509; E-mail: larry.cole@rose-hulman.edu.
Diving: Michael Caruso; Phone: 812-877-8052; E-mail: caruso@rose-hulman.edu.
Football: Ted Karras; Phone: 812-877-8496; E-mail: ted.karras@rose-hulman.edu.
Golf: Jon Prevo; Phone: 812-877-8932; E-mail: jon.prevo@rose-hulman.edu.
Soccer: Brad Hauter; Phone: 812-877-8461; E-mail: brad.hauter@rose-hulman.edu.
Swimming: Michael Caruso; Phone: 812-877-8052; E-mail: caruso@rose-hulman.edu.
Tennis: Dan Hopkins; Phone: 812-877-8252; E-mail: j.d.hopkins@rose-hulman.edu.
Track and Field: Larry Cole; Phone: 812-877-8509; E-mail: larry.cole@rose-hulman.edu.
Wrestling: Mark Buti; Phone: 812-877-8252; E-mail: mark.buti@rose-hulman.edu.

WOMEN'S COACHES

Basketball: Tony Hill; Phone: 812-877-8197; E-mail: tony.hill@rose-hulman.edu.
Cross Country: Joe Houghtelin; Phone: 812-877-8252; E-mail: joseph.houghtelin@rose-hulman.edu.
Diving: Michael Caruso; Phone: 812-877-8052; E-mail: caruso@rose-hulman.edu.
Golf: Jon Prevo; Phone: 812-877-8932; E-mail: jon.prevo@rose-hulman.edu.
Golf: Jon Prevo; Phone: 812-877-8932; E-mail: jon.prevo@rose-hulman.edu.
Soccer: Brad Hauter; Phone: 812-877-8461; E-mail: brad.hauter@rose-hulman.edu.
Softball: Brian Shearer; Phone: 812-877-8058; E-mail: brian.shearer@rose-hulman.edu.
Swimming: Michael Caruso; Phone: 812-877-8052; E-mail: caruso@rose-hulman.edu.
Tennis: Brenda Davis; Phone: 812-877-8017; E-mail: brenda.davis@rose-hulman.edu.
Track and Field: Larry Cole; Phone: 812-877-8509; E-mail: larry.cole@rose-hulman.edu.
Volleyball: Brenda Davis; Phone: 812-877-8017; E-mail: brenda.davis@rose-hulman.edu.

ROSEMONT COLLEGE
Rosemont, Pennsylvania

Ramblers ◆ NCAA III ◆ Pennsylvania Athletic Conference ◆ http://www.rosemont.edu/

Independent Roman Catholic comprehensive, founded 1921
Women only, 697 undergraduate students, 60% full-time, 90% women, 10% men
Suburban 56-acre campus with easy access to Philadelphia
Moderately difficult entrance level, 70% of applicants were admitted

Freshmen *Admission:* 337 applied, 235 were accepted, 97 enrolled. *Test scores:* SAT verbal scores over 500: 76%; SAT math scores over 500: 61%; SAT verbal scores over 600: 37%; SAT math scores over 600: 24%; SAT verbal scores over 700: 10%; SAT math scores over 700: 8%.

Tuition and fees (2004–05): $19,470 (full-time). *Room and board:* $8400.

Financial Aid (All incoming freshmen): *Average need-based gift aid:* $11,970. *Average non-need based aid:* $9340. *Average aid to full-time undergraduates:* $17,325.

Athletic Department: *Director of Athletics:* Pamela Wojnar; Phone: 610-527-0200; Fax: 610-526-2956.

WOMEN'S COACHES

Basketball: Andy McGovern; Phone: 610-527-0200; E-mail: amcgovern@rosemont.edu.
Field Hockey: Lynn Rothenhoefer; Phone: 610-527-0200; E-mail: lrothenhoefer@rosemont.edu.

Rosemont College (continued)

Lacrosse: Lynn Rothenhoefer; Phone: 610-853-3846; E-mail: lrothenhoefer@rosemont.edu.
Softball: Marie Bray; Phone: 610-527-0200; E-mail: mbray@rosemont.edu.
Tennis: Joe Kissel; Phone: 610-527-0200; E-mail: jkissel@rosemont.edu.
Volleyball: Amy Miller; Phone: 610-527-0200.

ROWAN UNIVERSITY
Glassboro, New Jersey

Profs ◆ NCAA III ◆ New Jersey Athletic Conference ◆ http://www.rowan.edu/

State-supported comprehensive, founded 1923, part of New Jersey State College System
Coed, 8,311 undergraduate students, 82% full-time, 57% women, 43% men
Small-town 200-acre campus with easy access to Philadelphia
Moderately difficult entrance level, 52% of applicants were admitted

Freshmen *Admission:* 6,208 applied, 3,190 were accepted, 1,239 enrolled. *Test scores:* SAT verbal scores over 500: 77%; SAT math scores over 500: 82%; SAT verbal scores over 600: 22%; SAT math scores over 600: 34%; SAT verbal scores over 700: 2%; SAT math scores over 700: 4%.
Tuition and fees (2003–04): $7222 (resident), $12,618 (nonresident). *Room and board:* $7394 (room only: $4478).
Financial Aid (All incoming freshmen): *Average need-based gift aid:* $5064. *Average non-need based aid:* $974. *Average aid to full-time undergraduates:* $8855.
Athletic Department: *Director of Athletics:* Joy Solomen; Phone: 856-256-4686; Fax: 856-256-4916; E-mail: solomen@rowan.edu. *Sports Information Director:* Sheila Stevenson; Phone: 856-256-4252; E-mail: stevenson@rowan.edu.

MEN'S COACHES
Baseball: John Cole; Phone: 856-256-4687; E-mail: cole@rowan.edu.
Basketball: Joe Cassidy; Phone: 856-256-4685; E-mail: jcassidy@rowan.edu.
Cross Country: Bill Fritz; Phone: 856-256-4683; E-mail: fritz@kwiknet.net.
Diving: Tony Lisa; Phone: 856-256-4682; E-mail: lisa@rowan.edu.
Football: Jay Accorsi; Phone: 856-256-4697; E-mail: accorsi@rowan.edu.
Soccer: Dan Gilmore; Phone: 856-256-4684; E-mail: gilmore@rowan.edu.
Swimming: Tony Lisa; Phone: 856-256-4682; E-mail: lisa@rowan.edu.
Track and Field: Bill Fritz; Phone: 856-256-4683; E-mail: fritz@kwiknet.net.

WOMEN'S COACHES
Basketball: Gabby Liselle; Phone: 856-256-4681; E-mail: lisella@rowan.edu.
Cross Country: Bill Fritz; Phone: 856-256-4683; E-mail: fritz@kwiknet.net.
Diving: Tony Lisa; Phone: 856-256-4682; E-mail: lisa@rowan.edu.
Field Hockey: Penny Kempf; Phone: 856-256-4679; E-mail: kempf@rowan.edu.
Lacrosse: Mary Marino; Phone: 856-256-4680; E-mail: marinom@rowan.edu.
Soccer: Scott Leacott; Phone: 856-256-4694; E-mail: leacott@rowan.edu.
Softball: Kim Wilson; Phone: 856-256-4688; E-mail: wilson@rowan.edu.
Swimming: Tony Lisa; Phone: 856-256-4682; E-mail: lisa@rowan.edu.
Track and Field: Bill Fritz; Phone: 856-256-4683; E-mail: fritz@kwiknet.net.
Volleyball: Noelle Hughes; Phone: 856-256-4693; E-mail: hughesn@rowan.edu.

RUSSELL SAGE COLLEGE
Troy, New York

Gators ◆ NCAA III ◆ New York Women's Athletic Conference ◆ http://www.sage.edu/RSC/

Independent 4-year, founded 1916, part of The Sage Colleges
Women only, 824 undergraduate students, 92% full-time, 100% women, 100% men
Urban 8-acre campus
Moderately difficult entrance level, 82% of applicants were admitted

Freshmen *Admission:* 365 applied, 301 were accepted, 130 enrolled. *Test scores:* SAT verbal scores over 500: 69%; SAT math scores over 500: 63%; SAT verbal scores over 600: 20%; SAT math scores over 600: 14%; SAT verbal scores over 700: 2%.
Tuition and fees (2003–04): $19,945 (full-time). *Room and board:* $6866 (room only: $3316).
Financial Aid (All incoming freshmen): *Average non-need based aid:* $8100.
Athletic Department: *Director of Athletics:* Candice Poiss; Phone: 518-244-2274; Fax: 518-244-3107; E-mail: poissc@sage.edu. *Sports Information Director:* Kelly Thompson; Phone: 518-244-2418; E-mail: thompk2@sage.edu.

WOMEN'S COACHES
Basketball: Kelly Thompson; Phone: 518-244-2418; E-mail: thompk2@sage.edu.
Soccer: Barry Balkwell; Phone: 518-244-2415; E-mail: balkwb@sage.edu.
Softball: James Buffoline; Phone: 518-244-2417; E-mail: athletics@sage.edu.
Tennis: Candice Poiss; Phone: 518-244-2274; E-mail: poissc@sage.edu.
Volleyball: Lisa Greiner; Phone: 518-244-2417; E-mail: greinl@sage.edu.

RUST COLLEGE
Holly Springs, Mississippi

Bearcats ◆ NCAA III ◆ Independent ◆ http://www.rustcollege.edu/

Independent United Methodist 4-year, founded 1866
Coed, 988 undergraduate students, 80% full-time, 64% women, 36% men
Rural 126-acre campus with easy access to Memphis
Moderately difficult entrance level, 47% of applicants were admitted

Freshmen *Admission:* 3,295 applied, 1,603 were accepted, 325 enrolled.
Tuition and fees (2003–04): $5935 (full-time). *Room and board:* $2600 (room only: $1162).
Financial Aid (All incoming freshmen): *Average need-based gift aid:* $3574. *Average non-need based aid:* $2010. *Average aid to full-time undergraduates:* $6424.
Athletic Department: *Director of Athletics:* Ishmell Edwards; Phone: 662-252-4661; Fax: 662-252-6107.

MEN'S COACHES
Baseball: Avery Mason; Phone: 662-252-8000.
Basketball: Rodney Stennis; Phone: 662-252-4661.
Cross Country: Daniel Henry; Phone: 662-252-8200.
Soccer: Roderick Mabry; Phone: 662-252-4661.
Tennis: Rodney Stennis; Phone: 662-252-4661.
Track and Field: Daniel Henry; Phone: 662-252-8200.
Volleyball: Phone: 662-252-4661.

WOMEN'S COACHES
Basketball: Priscilla Fisher; Phone: 662-252-4661.
Cross Country: Daniel Henry; Phone: 662-252-8200.
Tennis: Rodney Stennis; Phone: 662-252-4661.
Track and Field: Daniel Henry; Phone: 662-252-8200.
Volleyball: Avery Mason; Phone: 662-252-8101.

RUTGERS, THE STATE UNIVERSITY OF NEW JERSEY, CAMDEN

Camden, New Jersey

Scarlet Raptors ◆ NCAA III ◆ New Jersey Athletic Conference ◆ http://www.rutgers.edu/

State-supported university, founded 1927, part of Rutgers, The State University of New Jersey
Coed, 3,969 undergraduate students, 77% full-time, 58% women, 42% men
Moderately difficult entrance level, 59% of applicants were admitted

Freshmen *Admission:* 4,697 applied, 2,717 were accepted, 499 enrolled. *Test scores:* SAT verbal scores over 500: 74%; SAT math scores over 500: 78%; SAT verbal scores over 600: 22%; SAT math scores over 600: 33%; SAT verbal scores over 700: 4%; SAT math scores over 700: 6%.
Tuition and fees (2003–04): $7756 (resident), $14,270 (nonresident).
Room and board: $7552 (room only: $5152).
Financial Aid (All incoming freshmen): *Average need-based gift aid:* $6732. *Average non-need based aid:* $4234. *Average aid to full-time undergraduates:* $9253.
Athletic Department: *Director of Athletics:* Jeffrey Dean; Phone: 856-225-6698; Fax: 856-225-6024; E-mail: jldean@camden.rutgers.edu. *Sports Information Director:* Michael Ballard; Phone: 856-225-6198; E-mail: mballard@camden.rutgers.edu.

MEN'S COACHES
Baseball: Keith Williams; Phone: 856-225-6197; E-mail: kwilly@camden.rutgers.edu.
Basketball: Bill Culbertson; Phone: 856-225-6195.
Cheerleading: Linda Chapman; Phone: 856-225-6197.
Cross Country: Joe Puleo; Phone: 856-225-6197.
Golf: Robert Cardea; Phone: 856-225-6197.
Track and Field: Joe Puleo; Phone: 856-225-6197.

WOMEN'S COACHES
Basketball: Jackie Trakimas; Phone: 856-225-6197.
Cheerleading: Linda Chapman; Phone: 856-225-6197.
Cross Country: Joe Puleo; Phone: 856-225-6197.
Soccer: Brian Sheehan; Phone: 856-225-6197.
Softball: Carl Taylor; Phone: 856-225-6197.
Track and Field: Joe Puleo; Phone: 856-225-6197.
Volleyball: Joe Gillespie; Phone: 856-225-6197.

RUTGERS, THE STATE UNIVERSITY OF NEW JERSEY, NEWARK

Newark, New Jersey

Scarlet Raiders ◆ NCAA III ◆ New Jersey Athletic Conference ◆ http://www.rutgers.edu/

State-supported university, founded 1892, part of Rutgers, The State University of New Jersey
Coed, 6,784 undergraduate students, 75% full-time, 58% women, 42% men
Moderately difficult entrance level, 50% of applicants were admitted

Freshmen *Admission:* 7,835 applied, 3,681 were accepted, 987 enrolled. *Test scores:* SAT verbal scores over 500: 68%; SAT math scores over 500: 78%; SAT verbal scores over 600: 19%; SAT math scores over 600: 36%; SAT verbal scores over 700: 1%; SAT math scores over 700: 5%.
Tuition and fees (2003–04): $7580 (resident), $14,094 (nonresident).
Room and board: $8140 (room only: $5090).
Financial Aid (All incoming freshmen): *Average need-based gift aid:* $7009. *Average non-need based aid:* $2701. *Average aid to full-time undergraduates:* $9222.
Athletic Department: *Director of Athletics:* Mary Wessely; Phone: 973-353-5474; Fax: 973-353-1431; E-mail: mews@andromeda.rutgers.edu.

MEN'S COACHES
Baseball: Mark Rizzi; Phone: 973-353-5474; E-mail: mrizzi@andromeda.rutgers.edu.

Basketball: Joe Loughran; Phone: 973-353-5474; E-mail: loughran@andromeda.rutgers.edu.
Soccer: Chris Condron; Phone: 973-353-5474; E-mail: ccondron@andromeda.rutgers.edu.
Tennis: Bil Liepold; Phone: 973-353-5474; E-mail: bleipold@andromeda.rutgers.edu.
Volleyball: Sean Byron; Phone: 973-353-5474; E-mail: sbyron@andromeda.rutgers.edu.

WOMEN'S COACHES
Basketball: Kevin Morris; Phone: 973-353-5474; E-mail: sraiders@andromeda.rutgers.edu.
Soccer: Erik Burstein; Phone: 973-353-5474; E-mail: burstein@andromeda.rutgers.edu.
Softball: Al Fecso; Phone: 973-353-5474; E-mail: afecso@netscape.net.
Tennis: Kevin Morris; Phone: 973-353-5474; E-mail: sraiders@andromeda.rutgers.edu.
Volleyball: Sean Byron; Phone: 973-353-5474; E-mail: sbyron@andromeda.rutgers.edu.

RUTGERS, THE STATE UNIVERSITY OF NEW JERSEY, NEW BRUNSWICK/PISCATAWAY

New Brunswick, New Jersey

Scarlet Knights ◆ NCAA I ◆ Big East Conference ◆ http://www.rutgers.edu/

State-supported university, founded 1766, part of Rutgers, The State University of New Jersey
Coed, 27,365 undergraduate students, 91% full-time, 52% women, 48% men
Moderately difficult entrance level, 5% of applicants were admitted

Freshmen *Admission:* 26,175 applied, 14,180 were accepted, 4,717 enrolled. *Test scores:* SAT verbal scores over 500: 92%; SAT math scores over 500: 95%; SAT verbal scores over 600: 47%; SAT math scores over 600: 63%; SAT verbal scores over 700: 9%; SAT math scores over 700: 17%.
Tuition and fees (2003–04): $7927 (resident), $14,441 (nonresident).
Room and board: $7711.
Financial Aid (All incoming freshmen): *Average need-based gift aid:* $7082. *Average non-need based aid:* $4613. *Average aid to full-time undergraduates:* $10,216.
Athletic Department: *Director of Athletics:* Robert Mulcahy; Phone: 732-445-8610; Fax: 732-445-8616; E-mail: ad@scarletknights.com. *Sports Information Director:* John Wooding; Phone: 732-445-4200; E-mail: jwooding@scarletknights.com.

MEN'S COACHES
Baseball: Fred Hill; Phone: 732-445-7834; E-mail: baseball@scarletknights.com.
Basketball: Gary Waters; Phone: 732-445-4291; E-mail: mbball@scarletknights.com.
Cheerleading: Christine Zoffinger; Phone: 732-445-1766; E-mail: cmzoff@aol.com.
Cross Country: Mike Mulqueen; Phone: 732-445-4323; E-mail: rutgers_mtrack@hotmail.com.
Diving: Fred Woodruff; Phone: 732-445-0467; E-mail: jhodgson@@rci.rutgers.edu.
Football: Greg Schiano; Phone: 732-445-5100; E-mail: football@scarletknights.com.
Golf: Maura Waters; Phone: 732-445-7844; E-mail: mawaters@rci.rutgers.edu.
Lacrosse: Jim Stagnitta; Phone: 732-445-4211; E-mail: rulax@scarletknights.com.
Soccer: Bob Reasso; Phone: 732-445-4206; E-mail: br1@rci.rutgers.edu.
Swimming: Chuck Warner; Phone: 732-445-0467; E-mail: abashor@scarletknights.com.
Tennis: Mickey Cook; Phone: 732-445-7834; E-mail: mcook@scarletknights.com.
Track and Field: Mike Mulqueen; Phone: 732-445-4323; E-mail: rutgers_mtrack@hotmail.com.
Wrestling: John Sacchi; Phone: 732-932-6500; E-mail: wrestlin@rci.rutgers.edu.

Rutgers, The State University of New Jersey, New Brunswick/Piscataway *(continued)*

WOMEN'S COACHES

Basketball: Vivian Stringer; Phone: 732-445-4251; E-mail: cvstring@rci.rutgers.edu.
Cheerleading: Christine Zoffinger; Phone: 732-445-1766; E-mail: cmzoff@aol.com.
Cross Country: Mike Mulqueen; Phone: 732-445-4324; E-mail: ranthes@scarletknights.com.
Diving: Fred Woodruff; Phone: 732-445-0467; E-mail: jhodgson@@rci.rutgers.edu.
Field Hockey: Elizabeth Tchou; Phone: 732-445-4235; E-mail: etchou@scarletknights.com.
Golf: Maura Waters; Phone: 732-445-7844; E-mail: mawaters@rci.rutgers.edu.
Gymnastics: Chrystal Chollet-Norton; Phone: 732-445-6502; E-mail: ccnorton@rci.rutgers.edu.
Lacrosse: Laura Brand; Phone: 732-445-3843; E-mail: lbrand@scarletknights.com.
Soccer: Glenn Crooks; Phone: 732-445-4073; E-mail: gcrooks@scarletknights.com.
Softball: Pat Willis; Phone: 732-445-4234; E-mail: willisp@rci.rutgers.edu.
Swimming: Chuck Warner; Phone: 732-445-0467; E-mail: abashor@scarletknights.com.
Tennis: Marian Rosenwasser; Phone: 732-445-7834; E-mail: ruace@scarletknights.com.
Track and Field: Mike Mulqueen; Phone: 732-445-4324; E-mail: ranthes@scarletknights.com.
Volleyball: Ann Leonard-House; Phone: 732-932-6501; E-mail: adlhouse@rci.rutgers.edu.

SACRED HEART UNIVERSITY
Fairfield, Connecticut

Pioneers ◆ NCAA I ◆ Atlantic Hockey Conference; Colonial Athletic Conference; Northeast Conference ◆ http://www.sacredheart.edu/

Independent Roman Catholic comprehensive, founded 1963
Coed, 4,100 undergraduate students, 74% full-time, 61% women, 39% men
Suburban 56-acre campus with easy access to New York City
Moderately difficult entrance level, 63% of applicants were admitted

Freshmen *Admission:* 4,701 applied, 3,219 were accepted, 816 enrolled. *Test scores:* SAT verbal scores over 500: 66%; SAT math scores over 500: 86%; SAT verbal scores over 600: 12%; SAT math scores over 600: 35%; SAT verbal scores over 700: 1%; SAT math scores over 700: 1%.
Tuition and fees (2003–04): $20,268 (full-time). *Room and board:* $8910 (room only: $6490).
Financial Aid (All incoming freshmen): *Average need-based gift aid:* $9213. *Average non-need based aid:* $10,682. *Average aid to full-time undergraduates:* $13,441.
Athletic Department: *Director of Athletics:* Don Cook; Phone: 203-365-7696; Fax: 203-365-7696; E-mail: cookd@sacredheart.edu. *Sports Information Director:* Gene Gumbs; Phone: 203-396-8127; E-mail: gumbsg@sacredheart.edu.

MEN'S COACHES

Baseball: Nick Giaquinto; Phone: 203-365-7632; E-mail: giaquinton@sacredheart.edu.
Basketball: Dave Bike; Phone: 203-371-7848; E-mail: biked@sacredheart.edu.
Cheerleading: Kelly Tedesco; Phone: 203-922-1353; E-mail: coachkel01@aol.com.
Cross Country: Christian Morrison; Phone: 203-365-7618; E-mail: morrisonc@sacredheart.edu.
Football: Bill Lacey; Phone: 203-396-8105; E-mail: laceyb@sacredheart.edu.
Golf: Mike Giaquinto; Phone: 203-365-7574; E-mail: giaquintom@sacredheart.edu.
Ice Hockey: Shaun Hannah; Phone: 203-876-2480; E-mail: hannahs@sacredheart.edu.
Lacrosse: Tom Mariano; Phone: 203-365-7563; E-mail: marianot@sacredheart.edu.

Soccer: Joe McGuigan; Phone: 203-365-7604; E-mail: mcguiganj@sacredheart.edu.
Tennis: Mike Guastelle; Phone: 203-371-7885; E-mail: guastellem@sacredheart.edu.
Track and Field: Christian Morrison; Phone: 203-365-7618; E-mail: morrisonc@sacredheart.edu.
Volleyball: Craig Boston; Phone: 203-365-7526; E-mail: bostonc@sacredheart.edu.
Wrestling: Andy Seras; Phone: 203-426-8230; E-mail: thedr68kg@earthlink.net.

WOMEN'S COACHES

Basketball: Ed Swanson; Phone: 203-365-7698; E-mail: swansone@sacredheart.edu.
Cheerleading: Kelly Tedesco; Phone: 203-922-1353; E-mail: coachkel01@aol.com.
Cross Country: Christian Morrison; Phone: 203-365-7618; E-mail: morrisonc@sacredheart.edu.
Diving: Greg Zacholl; Phone: 203-359-3551.
Field Hockey: Christine Blais; Phone: 203-365-7534; E-mail: blaisc@sacredheart.edu.
Golf: Jamie Romeo; Phone: 203-365-4735; E-mail: romeoj@sacredheart.edu.
Lacrosse: Laura Korutz; Phone: 203-396-8128; E-mail: korutzl@sacredheart.edu.
Soccer: Joe Barroso; Phone: 203-396-8123; E-mail: barrosoj@sacredheart.edu.
Softball: Elizabeth Luckie; Phone: 203-371-7826; E-mail: luckiee@sacredheart.edu.
Swimming: Dan Maloney; Phone: 203-359-3551; E-mail: maloneydb@yahoo.com.
Tennis: Mike Guastelle; Phone: 203-371-7885; E-mail: guastellem@sacredheart.edu.
Track and Field: Christian Morrison; Phone: 203-365-7618; E-mail: morrisonc@sacredheart.edu.
Volleyball: Elizabeth McGreevy; Phone: 203-371-7647; E-mail: mcgreevye@sacredheart.edu.

SAGINAW VALLEY STATE UNIVERSITY
University Center, Michigan

Cardinals ◆ NCAA II ◆ Great Lakes Intercollegiate Conference ◆ http://www.svsu.edu/

State-supported comprehensive, founded 1963
Coed, 7,580 undergraduate students, 73% full-time, 60% women, 40% men
Rural 782-acre campus
Moderately difficult entrance level, 88% of applicants were admitted

Freshmen *Admission:* 3,324 applied, 2,985 were accepted, 1,181 enrolled.
Tuition and fees (2003–04): $5410 (resident), $11,009 (nonresident). *Room and board:* $5645 (room only: $3530).
Financial Aid (All incoming freshmen): *Average need-based gift aid:* $2676. *Average non-need based aid:* $4059. *Average aid to full-time undergraduates:* $5760.
Athletic Department: *Director of Athletics:* Joe Vogl; Phone: 989-790-4053; Fax: 989-790-0545; E-mail: javogl@svsu.edu. *Sports Information Director:* Ryan Thompson; Phone: 989-790-4053; E-mail: rgthomps@svsu.edu.

MEN'S COACHES

Baseball: Walt Head; Phone: 989-791-7334; E-mail: whead@svsu.edu.
Basketball: Dean Lockwood; Phone: 989-791-7314; E-mail: dloc@svsu.edu.
Cheerleading: Jill Tetloff; Phone: 989-791-4053.
Cross Country: Jim Nesbitt; Phone: 989-791-4322; E-mail: jnesbitt@svsu.edu.
Football: Randy Awrey; Phone: 989-791-7315; E-mail: rawrey@svsu.edu.
Golf: Andy Bethune; Phone: 989-791-7310; E-mail: andy@thesawmill.com.
Soccer: Dean Pappas; Phone: 989-791-7308; E-mail: dnpappas@svsu.edu.

Track and Field: Jim Nesbitt; Phone: 989-791-4322; E-mail: jnesbitt@svsu.edu.

WOMEN'S COACHES

Basketball: Kim Chandler; Phone: 989-964-7312; E-mail: kchandle@svsu.edu.
Cheerleading: Jill Tetloff; Phone: 989-791-4053.
Cross Country: Jim Nesbitt; Phone: 989-791-4322; E-mail: jnesbitt@svsu.edu.
Soccer: Drago Dumbovic; Phone: 989-791-7313; E-mail: ddumbovic@svsu.edu.
Softball: Sabrina Lane; Phone: 989-791-7300; E-mail: slane@svsu.edu.
Tennis: Mike Major; Phone: 989-791-7309; E-mail: mmajor@svsu.edu.
Track and Field: Jim Nesbitt; Phone: 989-791-4322; E-mail: jnesbitt@svsu.edu.
Volleyball: Will Stanton; Phone: 989-790-7023; E-mail: wstanto@svsu.edu.

ST. AMBROSE UNIVERSITY
Davenport, Iowa

Fighting Bees ◆ NAIA ◆ Midwest Classic Conference ◆ http://www.sau.edu/

Independent Roman Catholic comprehensive, founded 1882
Coed, 2,483 undergraduate students, 80% full-time, 59% women, 41% men
Urban 11-acre campus
Moderately difficult entrance level, 87% of applicants were admitted

Freshmen *Admission:* 1,112 applied, 971 were accepted, 436 enrolled.
Tuition and fees (2004–05): $17,565 (full-time). *Room and board:* $6635 (room only: $3380).
Financial Aid (All incoming freshmen): *Average need-based gift aid:* $4340. *Average non-need based aid:* $6251. *Average aid to full-time undergraduates:* $13,066.
Athletic Department: *Director of Athletics:* Ray Shovlain; Phone: 563-333-6229; Fax: 563-333-6239; E-mail: shovlainraymondj@ambrose.sau.edu. *Sports Information Director:* Jeff Griebel; Phone: 563-333-6305; E-mail: griebeljefferyk@ambrose.sau.edu.

MEN'S COACHES

Baseball: Jim Callahan; Phone: 563-333-6237; E-mail: callahanjamesr@ambrose.sau.edu.
Basketball: Ray Shovlain; Phone: 563-333-6229; E-mail: shovlainraymondj@ambrose.sau.edu.
Cheerleading: Deanna Richardson; Phone: 563-333-6229; E-mail: richardsondeannam@ambrose.sau.edu.
Cross Country: Carrie Lane; Phone: 563-333-6229; E-mail: billingsleybrucea@ambrose.sau.edu.
Football: Todd Sturdy; Phone: 563-333-6240; E-mail: sturdytodda@ambrose.sau.edu.
Golf: Jeff Griebel; Phone: 563-333-6305; E-mail: griebeljefferyk@ambrose.sau.edu.
Soccer: Bud Grant; Phone: 563-333-6419; E-mail: grantrobert@ambrose.sau.edu.
Tennis: Rich Blomgren; Phone: 563-333-6229; E-mail: billingsleybrucea@ambrose.sau.edu.
Track and Field: Ryan Saddler; Phone: 563-333-3275; E-mail: saddlerryanc@ambrose.sau.edu.
Volleyball: Bruce Billingsley; Phone: 563-333-6452; E-mail: billingsleybrucea@ambrose.sau.edu.

WOMEN'S COACHES

Basketball: Ted Eskildsen; Phone: 563-333-6230; E-mail: billingsleybrucea@ambrose.sau.edu.
Cheerleading: Deanna Richardson; Phone: 563-333-6229; E-mail: richardsondeannam@ambrose.sau.edu.
Cross Country: Carrie Lane; Phone: 563-333-6229; E-mail: billingsleybrucea@ambrose.sau.edu.
Golf: Laura Ekizian; Phone: 563-333-6229; E-mail: ekizianlaural@ambrose.sau.edu.
Soccer: Laura Klutsaritis; Phone: 563-333-6476; E-mail: klutsaritslauraj@ambrose.sau.edu.
Softball: Sarah Anderson; Phone: 563-333-6476; E-mail: sausoftball@hotmail.com.
Tennis: Nada Diab; Phone: 563-333-6229.
Track and Field: Ryan Saddler; Phone: 563-333-3275; E-mail: saddlerryanc@ambrose.sau.edu.

Volleyball: Bruce Billingsley; Phone: 563-333-6452; E-mail: billingsleybrucea@ambrose.sau.edu.

ST. ANDREWS PRESBYTERIAN COLLEGE
Laurinburg, North Carolina

Knights ◆ NCAA II ◆ Carolinas-Virginia Athletics Conference; Deep South Lacrosse Conference ◆ http://www.sapc.edu/

Independent Presbyterian 4-year, founded 1958
Coed, 693 undergraduate students, 91% full-time, 60% women, 40% men
Small-town 600-acre campus
Moderately difficult entrance level, 83% of applicants were admitted

Freshmen *Admission:* 668 applied, 562 were accepted, 196 enrolled.
Test scores: SAT verbal scores over 500: 45%; SAT math scores over 500: 46%; SAT verbal scores over 600: 15%; SAT math scores over 600: 8%; SAT verbal scores over 700: 2%.
Tuition and fees (2003–04): $15,115 (full-time). *Room and board:* $5410 (room only: $2200).
Financial Aid (All incoming freshmen): *Average need-based gift aid:* $10,403. *Average non-need based aid:* $9010. *Average aid to full-time undergraduates:* $12,936.
Athletic Department: *Director of Athletics:* Carl Ullrich; Phone: 910-277-5275; Fax: 910-277-5272; E-mail: ullrichcf@sapc.edu. *Sports Information Director:* Kevin Buczek; Phone: 910-277-5751; E-mail: buczekkc@sapc.edu.

MEN'S COACHES

Baseball: Bobby Simmons; Phone: 910-277-5426; E-mail: simmonsbo@sapc.edu.
Basketball: Rob Perron; Phone: 910-277-5727; E-mail: perronrj@sapc.edu.
Cross Country: Gary Aycock; Phone: 910-277-5434; E-mail: aycockgp@sapc.edu.
Golf: Jason Hughes; Phone: 910-277-5055; E-mail: hughesjc@sapc.edu.
Lacrosse: John Brubaker; Phone: 910-277-5279; E-mail: brubakerj@sapc.edu.
Soccer: Tom Frambach; Phone: 910-277-5428; E-mail: frambacht@sapc.edu.

WOMEN'S COACHES

Basketball: William Carter; Phone: 910-277-3940; E-mail: carterwe@sapc.edu.
Cross Country: Gary Aycock; Phone: 910-277-5434; E-mail: aycockgp@sapc.edu.
Soccer: Stevan Hernandez; Phone: 910-277-5277; E-mail: hernandz@sapc.edu.
Softball: Stevan Hernandez; Phone: 910-277-5277; E-mail: hernandz@sapc.edu.
Tennis: William Carter; Phone: 910-277-3940; E-mail: carterwe@sapc.edu.
Volleyball: Bill Rude; Phone: 910-277-5429; E-mail: rudebl@sapc.edu.

SAINT ANSELM COLLEGE
Manchester, New Hampshire

Hawks ◆ NCAA II ◆ Northeast-10 Conference ◆ http://www.anselm.edu/

Independent Roman Catholic 4-year, founded 1889
Coed, 2,008 undergraduate students, 97% full-time, 57% women, 43% men
Suburban 450-acre campus with easy access to Boston
Moderately difficult entrance level, 66% of applicants were admitted

Freshmen *Admission:* 3,033 applied, 2,140 were accepted, 588 enrolled.
Test scores: SAT verbal scores over 500: 81%; SAT math scores over 500: 82%; SAT verbal scores over 600: 29%; SAT math scores over 600: 28%; SAT verbal scores over 700: 2%; SAT math scores over 700: 2%.
Tuition and fees (2004–05): $23,710 (full-time). *Room and board:* $8580.

Saint Anselm College *(continued)*

Financial Aid (All incoming freshmen): *Average need-based gift aid:* $13,411. *Average non-need based aid:* $5261. *Average aid to full-time undergraduates:* $18,246.
Athletic Department: *Director of Athletics:* Ed Cannon; Phone: 603-641-7800; Fax: 603-641-7550; E-mail: ecannon@anselm.edu. *Sports Information Director:* Kurt Svoboda; Phone: 603-641-7810; E-mail: ksvoboda@anselm.edu.

MEN'S COACHES

Baseball: Ken Harring Jr.; Phone: 603-656-6016; E-mail: kharring@anselm.edu.
Basketball: Keith Dickson; Phone: 603-641-7805; E-mail: kdickson@anselm.edu.
Cross Country: Paul Finn; Phone: 603-656-6017; E-mail: menscrosscountry@anselm.edu.
Football: Geoff Harlan; Phone: 603-656-6010; E-mail: gharlan@anselm.edu.
Golf: Frank Driscoll; Phone: 603-656-6016; E-mail: golf@anselm.edu.
Ice Hockey: Ed Seney; Phone: 603-641-7803; E-mail: eseney@anselm.edu.
Lacrosse: Gerry Byrne; Phone: 603-656-6017; E-mail: menslacrosse@anselm.edu.
Soccer: Ed Cannon; Phone: 603-641-7800; E-mail: menssoccer@anselm.edu.
Tennis: Roberta Cullity; Phone: 603-641-7247; E-mail: tennis@anselm.edu.

WOMEN'S COACHES

Basketball: Monica McCarthy-Galamaga; Phone: 603-641-7804; E-mail: mgalamaga@anselm.edu.
Cross Country: Kevin O'Neil; Phone: 603-656-6017; E-mail: koneil@anselm.edu.
Field Hockey: Kristie Baldwin; Phone: 603-656-6014; E-mail: fieldhockey@anselm.edu.
Lacrosse: Emily Frawley; Phone: 603-656-6014; E-mail: efrawley@anselm.edu.
Soccer: Dean Schneider; Phone: 603-656-7247; E-mail: womenssoccer@anselm.edu.
Softball: Don Huot; Phone: 603-656-7247; E-mail: softball@anselm.edu.
Tennis: Roberta Cullity; Phone: 603-641-7247; E-mail: tennis@anselm.edu.
Volleyball: Donald Ferguson; Phone: 603-656-6016; E-mail: volleyball@anselm.edu.

SAINT AUGUSTINE'S COLLEGE
Raleigh, North Carolina

Mighty Falcons ◆ NCAA II ◆ Central Intercollegiate Athletic Conference ◆ http://www.st-aug.edu/

Independent Episcopal 4-year, founded 1867
Coed, 1,635 undergraduate students, 95% full-time, 49% women, 51% men
Urban 105-acre campus
Minimally difficult entrance level, 62% of applicants were admitted

Freshmen *Admission:* 1,957 applied, 1,181 were accepted, 548 enrolled. *Test scores:* SAT verbal scores over 500: 10%; SAT math scores over 500: 11%.
Tuition and fees (2003–04): $9530 (full-time). *Room and board:* $4960 (room only: $2084).
Financial Aid (All incoming freshmen): *Average non-need based aid:* $9319. *Average aid to full-time undergraduates:* $12,541.
Athletic Department: *Director of Athletics:* George Williams; Phone: 919-516-4236; Fax: 919-828-9731; E-mail: gdwilliams@st-aug.edu. *Sports Information Director:* Oralia Washington; Phone: 919-516-4172; E-mail: onwashington@st-aug.edu.

MEN'S COACHES

Baseball: Rashem Wynn; Phone: 919-516-4470; E-mail: rwynn@st-aug.edu.
Basketball: Thomas Hargrove; Phone: 919-516-4077; E-mail: thargrove@st-aug.edu.
Cheerleading: Sheryl Ximines; Phone: 919-516-4343; E-mail: sximines@st-aug.edu.

Cross Country: George Williams; Phone: 919-516-4236; E-mail: gdwilliams@st-aug.edu.
Football: Michael Costa; Phone: 919-516-5180; E-mail: mecosta@st-aug.edu.
Golf: Larry Coleman; Phone: 919-516-4202; E-mail: lcoleman@st-aug.edu.
Tennis: Leon Carrington; Phone: 919-516-4174; E-mail: lcarrington@st-aug.edu.
Track and Field: George Williams; Phone: 919-516-4236; E-mail: gdwilliams@st-aug.edu.

WOMEN'S COACHES

Basketball: Antonio Davis; Phone: 919-516-4119; E-mail: aodavis@st-aug.edu.
Cheerleading: Sheryl Ximines; Phone: 919-516-4343; E-mail: sximines@st-aug.edu.
Cross Country: George Williams; Phone: 919-516-4236; E-mail: gdwilliams@st-aug.edu.
Softball: Dot Neal; Phone: 919-516-4174; E-mail: dmneal@cs.com.
Tennis: Leon Carrington; Phone: 919-516-4174; E-mail: lcarrington@st-aug.edu.
Track and Field: George Williams; Phone: 919-516-4236; E-mail: gdwilliams@st-aug.edu.
Volleyball: Edric Poitier; Phone: 919-516-4468.

ST. BONAVENTURE UNIVERSITY
St. Bonaventure, New York

Bonnies ◆ NCAA I ◆ Atlantic 10 Conference ◆ http://www.sbu.edu/

Independent religious comprehensive, founded 1858, affiliated with Roman Catholic Church
Coed, 2,291 undergraduate students, 95% full-time, 51% women, 49% men
Small-town 600-acre campus
Moderately difficult entrance level, 9% of applicants were admitted

Freshmen *Admission:* 1,990 applied, 1,728 were accepted, 596 enrolled. *Test scores:* SAT verbal scores over 500: 67%; SAT math scores over 500: 65%; SAT verbal scores over 600: 18%; SAT math scores over 600: 19%; SAT verbal scores over 700: 2%; SAT math scores over 700: 2%.
Tuition and fees (2003–04): $17,925 (full-time). *Room and board:* $6530 (room only: $3300).
Financial Aid (All incoming freshmen): *Average need-based gift aid:* $10,928. *Average non-need based aid:* $7042. *Average aid to full-time undergraduates:* $15,270.
Athletic Department: *Director of Athletics:* Ron Zwierlein; Phone: 716-375-2280; Fax: 716-375-2383; E-mail: %ronz@sbu.edu. *Sports Information Director:* Steve Mest; Phone: 716-375-2319; E-mail: smest@sbu.edu.

MEN'S COACHES

Baseball: Larry Sudbrook; Phone: 716-375-2641; E-mail: lsudbrk@sbu.edu.
Basketball: Anthony Solomon; Phone: 716-375-2257; E-mail: asolomon@sbu.edu.
Cross Country: Tom Hagen; Phone: 716-375-2287; E-mail: thagen@sbu.edu.
Diving: Allison Manion; Phone: 716-375-2254; E-mail: amanion@sbu.edu.
Golf: Steve Campbell; Phone: 716-375-2599; E-mail: scamp@sbu.edu.
Soccer: Bill Brady; Phone: 716-375-2642; E-mail: wbrady@sbu.edu.
Swimming: Sean McNamee; Phone: 716-375-2254; E-mail: smcnamee@sbu.edu.
Tennis: Mike Bates; Phone: 716-375-2293; E-mail: mbates@sbu.edu.

WOMEN'S COACHES

Basketball: Jim Crowley; Phone: 716-375-2285; E-mail: jcrowley@sbu.edu.
Cross Country: Tom Hagen; Phone: 716-375-2287; E-mail: thagen@sbu.edu.
Diving: Allison Manion; Phone: 716-375-2254; E-mail: amanion@sbu.edu.
Lacrosse: Tony Zostant; Phone: 716-375-2640; E-mail: tzostant@sbu.edu.
Soccer: Dan Magner; Phone: 716-375-2286; E-mail: dmagner@sbu.edu.

Softball: Mike Threehouse; Phone: 716-375-2289; E-mail: mthreeho@sbu.edu.
Swimming: Lance Brennan; Phone: 716-375-2211; E-mail: lbrennan@sbu.edu.
Tennis: Mike Bates; Phone: 716-375-2293; E-mail: mbates@sbu.edu.

ST. CLOUD STATE UNIVERSITY
St. Cloud, Minnesota

Huskies ◆ NCAA II ◆ North Central Intercollegiate Conference; Western Collegiate Hockey Conference ◆ http://www.stcloudstate.edu/

State-supported comprehensive, founded 1869, part of Minnesota State Colleges and Universities System
Coed, 14,483 undergraduate students, 81% full-time, 55% women, 45% men
Suburban 922-acre campus with easy access to Minneapolis–St. Paul
Moderately difficult entrance level, 71% of applicants were admitted

Freshmen *Admission:* 6,011 applied, 4,581 were accepted, 2,298 enrolled.
Tuition and fees (2003–04): $4550 (resident), $9209 (nonresident). *Room and board:* $3812 (room only: $2548).
Financial Aid (All incoming freshmen): *Average need-based gift aid:* $1929. *Average non-need based aid:* $309. *Average aid to full-time undergraduates:* $6204.
Athletic Department: *Director of Athletics:* Morris Kurtz; Phone: 320-308-3102; Fax: 320-203-6146; E-mail: mkurtz@stcloudstate.edu. *Sports Information Director:* Anne Abicht; Phone: 320-308-2141; E-mail: aabicht@stcloudstate.edu.

MEN'S COACHES
Baseball: Dennis Lorsung; Phone: 320-308-3208; E-mail: dklorsung@stcloudstate.edu.
Basketball: Kevin Schlagel; Phone: 320-308-3297; E-mail: klschlagel@stcloudstate.edu.
Cheerleading: Tracy Dill; Phone: 320-308-4924; E-mail: tldill@stcloudstate.edu.
Cross Country: Seth Mischke; Phone: 320-308-2242; E-mail: scmischke@stcloudstate.edu.
Diving: Jeff Hegle; Phone: 320-308-3102; E-mail: jmhegle@stcloudstate.edu.
Football: Randy Hedberg; Phone: 320-308-3070; E-mail: rhedberg@stcloudstate.edu.
Golf: Judy Larkin; Phone: 320-259-7745.
Ice Hockey: Craig Dahl; Phone: 320-308-4806; E-mail: cadahl@stcloudstate.edu.
Swimming: Jeff Hegle; Phone: 320-308-3102; E-mail: jmhegle@stcloudstate.edu.
Tennis: Jerry Anderson; Phone: 320-654-5269; E-mail: jlanderson@stcloudstate.edu.
Track and Field: Seth Mischke; Phone: 320-308-2242; E-mail: scmischke@stcloudstate.edu.
Wrestling: Steve Grimit; Phone: 320-308-2996; E-mail: srgrimit@stcloudstate.edu.

WOMEN'S COACHES
Basketball: Lori Ufferts; Phone: 320-308-2230; E-mail: lkulferts@stcloudstate.edu.
Cheerleading: Tracy Dill; Phone: 320-308-4924; E-mail: tldill@stcloudstate.edu.
Cross Country: Seth Mischke; Phone: 320-308-2242; E-mail: scmischke@stcloudstate.edu.
Diving: Jeff Hegle; Phone: 320-308-3102; E-mail: jmhegle@stcloudstate.edu.
Golf: Judy Larkin; Phone: 320-259-3102.
Soccer: Stephanie McGuinness; Phone: 320-308-2143; E-mail: smcguinness@stcloudstate.edu.
Softball: Paul U'Ren; Phone: 320-308-2900; E-mail: pjuren@stcloudstate.edu.
Tennis: Larry Sundby; Phone: 320-252-0847; E-mail: sundby@astound.net.
Track and Field: Seth Mischke; Phone: 320-308-2242; E-mail: scmischke@stcloudstate.edu.
Volleyball: Patricia Mickow; Phone: 320-308-2242; E-mail: pamickow@stcloudstate.edu.

ST. EDWARD'S UNIVERSITY
Austin, Texas

Hilltoppers ◆ NCAA II ◆ Heartland Conference ◆ http://www.stedwards.edu/

Independent Roman Catholic comprehensive, founded 1885
Coed, 3,531 undergraduate students, 70% full-time, 57% women, 43% men
Urban 160-acre campus
Moderately difficult entrance level, 7% of applicants were admitted

Freshmen *Admission:* 2,005 applied, 1,396 were accepted, 563 enrolled. *Test scores:* SAT verbal scores over 500: 77%; SAT math scores over 500: 73%; SAT verbal scores over 600: 28%; SAT math scores over 600: 27%; SAT verbal scores over 700: 3%; SAT math scores over 700: 1%.
Tuition and fees (2003–04): $14,710 (full-time). *Room and board:* $6018.
Financial Aid (All incoming freshmen): *Average need-based gift aid:* $8873. *Average non-need based aid:* $5876. *Average aid to full-time undergraduates:* $11,777.
Athletic Department: *Director of Athletics:* Debbie Taylor; Phone: 512-448-8744; Fax: 512-416-5834; E-mail: deboraw@admin.stedwards.edu. *Sports Information Director:* Naveen Boppana; Phone: 512-464-8810; E-mail: naveenb@admin.stedwards.edu.

MEN'S COACHES
Baseball: Jeremy Farber; Phone: 512-448-8497; E-mail: jeremyf@admin.stedwards.edu.
Basketball: Mike Jones; Phone: 512-448-8591; E-mail: mikej@admin.stedwards.edu.
Cheerleading: Mia Allen; Phone: 512-448-8740; E-mail: mias@admin.stedwards.edu.
Cross Country: Kevin Felts; Phone: 512-428-1053; E-mail: kevinf@admin.stedwards.edu.
Golf: Mark McEntire; Phone: 512-448-8604; E-mail: markm@admin.stedwards.edu.
Soccer: Mike Smith; Phone: 512-448-8507; E-mail: michaels@admin.stedwards.edu.
Tennis: Russell Sterns; Phone: 512-448-8743; E-mail: russells@admin.stedwards.edu.

WOMEN'S COACHES
Basketball: Jennifer White; Phone: 512-448-8590; E-mail: jennw@admin.stedwards.edu.
Cheerleading: Mia Allen; Phone: 512-448-8740; E-mail: mias@admin.stedwards.edu.
Cross Country: Kevin Felts; Phone: 512-428-1053; E-mail: kevinf@admin.stedwards.edu.
Golf: Mark McEntire; Phone: 512-448-8604; E-mail: markm@admin.stedwards.edu.
Soccer: Erin Lynch; Phone: 512-428-1052; E-mail: erinl@admin.stedwards.edu.
Softball: Amy Coulter; Phone: 512-448-8494; E-mail: amyc@admin.stedwards.edu.
Tennis: Russell Sterns; Phone: 512-448-8743; E-mail: russells@admin.stedwards.edu.
Volleyball: Sean Donahue; Phone: 512-428-1386; E-mail: seand@admin.stedwards.edu.

ST. FRANCIS COLLEGE
Brooklyn Heights, New York

Terriers ◆ NCAA I ◆ Northeast Conference ◆ http://www.stfranciscollege.edu/

Independent Roman Catholic 4-year, founded 1884
Coed, 2,468 undergraduate students, 80% full-time, 58% women, 42% men
Urban 1-acre campus with easy access to New York City
Moderately difficult entrance level, 87% of applicants were admitted

Freshmen *Admission:* 1,304 applied, 1,149 were accepted, 434 enrolled. *Test scores:* SAT verbal scores over 500: 41%; SAT math scores over 500: 35%; SAT verbal scores over 600: 10%; SAT math scores over 600: 5%; SAT verbal scores over 700: 1%.
Tuition and fees (2003–04): $10,880 (full-time).

St. Francis College *(continued)*

Athletic Department: *Director of Athletics:* Edward Aquilone; Phone: 718-489-5486; Fax: 718-797-2140; E-mail: eaquilone@stfranciscollege.edu. *Sports Information Director:* Angela Merlino; Phone: 718-489-5369; E-mail: amerlino@stfranciscollege.edu.

MEN'S COACHES

Baseball: Frank Del George; Phone: 718-489-5365; E-mail: fdg5@aol.com.
Basketball: Ron Ganulim; Phone: 718-489-5265.
Cross Country: Anthony Kurtin; Phone: 718-489-5469; E-mail: akurtin@stfranciscollege.edu.
Soccer: Carlos Acquista; Phone: 718-489-5469; E-mail: cacquista@aol.com.
Swimming: Juan Trinidad; Phone: 718-489-5252; E-mail: nelson262@aol.com.
Tennis: Zach Davis; Phone: 718-489-5365.
Track and Field: Anthony Kurtin; Phone: 718-489-5469; E-mail: akurtin@stfranciscollege.edu.

WOMEN'S COACHES

Basketball: Brenda Milano; Phone: 718-489-5421.
Cross Country: Anthony Kurtin; Phone: 718-489-5469; E-mail: akurtin@stfranciscollege.edu.
Softball: Nicki Trani; Phone: 718-489-5365.
Swimming: Juan Trinidad; Phone: 718-489-5252; E-mail: nelson262@aol.com.
Tennis: Zach Davis; Phone: 718-489-5365.
Track and Field: Anthony Kurtin; Phone: 718-489-5469; E-mail: akurtin@stfranciscollege.edu.
Volleyball: Rony Gilot; Phone: 718-489-5365; E-mail: rony_gilot@hotmail.com.

SAINT FRANCIS UNIVERSITY
Loretto, Pennsylvania

Red Flash ◆ NCAA I ◆ Northeast Conference ◆ http://www.sfcpa.edu/

Independent Roman Catholic comprehensive, founded 1847
Coed, 1,401 undergraduate students, 83% full-time, 60% women, 40% men
Rural 600-acre campus
Moderately difficult entrance level, 83% of applicants were admitted

Freshmen *Admission:* 1,280 applied, 1,116 were accepted, 335 enrolled. *Test scores:* SAT verbal scores over 500: 59%; SAT math scores over 500: 60%; SAT verbal scores over 600: 12%; SAT math scores over 600: 18%; SAT verbal scores over 700: 1%; SAT math scores over 700: 3%.
Tuition and fees (2003–04): $19,342 (full-time). *Room and board:* $7346 (room only: $3564).
Financial Aid (All incoming freshmen): *Average need-based gift aid:* $12,996. *Average non-need based aid:* $9439. *Average aid to full-time undergraduates:* $16,943.
Athletic Department: *Director of Athletics:* Jeffrey Eisen; Phone: 814-472-3276; Fax: 814-472-3209; E-mail: jeisen@francis.edu. *Sports Information Director:* Pat Farabaugh; Phone: 814-472-3128.

MEN'S COACHES

Basketball: Bobby Jones; Phone: 814-472-3018; E-mail: bjones@francis.edu.
Cross Country: Scott Cantone; Phone: 814-472-3018; E-mail: scatone@francis.edu.
Football: Dave Opfar; Phone: 814-472-3018; E-mail: dopfar@francis.edu.
Soccer: B.J. Craig; Phone: 814-472-3018; E-mail: bjcraig@francis.edu.
Tennis: Bob Phillips; Phone: 814-472-3018; E-mail: iwrite@penn.com.
Track and Field: Scott Cantone; Phone: 814-472-3018; E-mail: scatonc@francis.edu.
Volleyball: Mike Rumbaugh; Phone: 814-472-3018; E-mail: mrumbaugh@francis.edu.

WOMEN'S COACHES

Basketball: Myndi Hill; Phone: 814-472-3018; E-mail: mhill@francis.edu.
Cross Country: Scott Cantone; Phone: 814-472-3018; E-mail: scatone@francis.edu.
Field Hockey: Phone: 814-472-3018; E-mail: wlax@francis.edu.

Golf: Darrell Jones; Phone: 814-472-3018; E-mail: djones@francis.edu.
Lacrosse: Martin Romeril; Phone: 814-472-3018; E-mail: wlax@francis.edu.
Soccer: Michael Coll; Phone: 814-472-3018; E-mail: mcoll@francis.edu.
Softball: Laura Cymmerman; Phone: 814-472-3018; E-mail: lcymmerman@francis.edu.
Swimming: Patrick Gallagher; Phone: 814-472-3018; E-mail: pgallagher@francis.edu.
Tennis: Frank Spaid; Phone: 814-472-3018; E-mail: jtaylor@francis.edu.
Track and Field: Scott Cantone; Phone: 814-472-3018; E-mail: scatone@francis.edu.
Volleyball: Scott Gleason; Phone: 814-472-3018.

ST. GREGORY'S UNIVERSITY
Shawnee, Oklahoma

Cavaliers ◆ NAIA ◆ Sooner Conference
◆ http://www.stgregorys.edu/

Independent Roman Catholic 4-year, founded 1875
Coed, 705 undergraduate students, 75% full-time, 54% women, 46% men
Small-town 640-acre campus with easy access to Oklahoma City
Minimally difficult entrance level, 62% of applicants were admitted

Freshmen *Admission:* 473 applied, 292 were accepted, 120 enrolled.
Tuition and fees (2004–05): $11,076 (full-time). *Room and board:* $4888.
Financial Aid (All incoming freshmen): *Average need-based gift aid:* $4635. *Average non-need based aid:* $3823. *Average aid to full-time undergraduates:* $8734.
Athletic Department: *Director of Athletics:* Jim Gasso; Phone: 405-878-5124; Fax: 405-878-5198; E-mail: jagasso@stgregorys.edu. *Sports Information Director:* Bill Foutch; Phone: 405-878-5184; E-mail: bjfoutch@stgregorys.edu.

MEN'S COACHES

Baseball: Chris Pingry; Phone: 405-878-5151; E-mail: cdpingry@stgregorys.edu.
Basketball: Kevin Johnson; Phone: 405-878-5293; E-mail: kjjohnson@stgregorys.edu.
Cross Country: Michael Houston; Phone: 405-878-5245; E-mail: mlhouston@stgregorys.edu.
Golf: Jimmy Roye; Phone: 405-878-5246; E-mail: jroy@stgregorys.edu.
Soccer: Mauro Cichero; Phone: 405-878-5341; E-mail: lmcichero@stgregorys.edu.
Track and Field: Michael Houston; Phone: 405-878-5245; E-mail: mlhouston@stgregorys.edu.

WOMEN'S COACHES

Basketball: George Torres; Phone: 405-878-5661; E-mail: gtorres@stgregorys.edu.
Cross Country: Michael Houston; Phone: 405-878-5245; E-mail: mlhouston@stgregorys.edu.
Golf: Jimmy Roye; Phone: 405-878-5246; E-mail: jroy@stgregorys.edu.
Soccer: Kara Lowery; Phone: 405-878-5242; E-mail: kdlowery@stgregorys.edu.
Softball: Heather Shanahan; Phone: 405-878-5429; E-mail: hashanahan@stgregorys.edu.
Track and Field: Michael Houston; Phone: 405-878-5245; E-mail: mlhouston@stgregorys.edu.

ST. JOHN FISHER COLLEGE
Rochester, New York

Cardinals ◆ NCAA III ◆ Empire 8 Conference ◆ http://www.sjfc.edu/

Independent religious comprehensive, founded 1948, affiliated with Roman Catholic Church
Coed, 2,496 undergraduate students, 88% full-time, 58% women, 42% men
Suburban 136-acre campus
Moderately difficult entrance level, 7% of applicants were admitted

Freshmen *Admission:* 2,263 applied, 1,617 were accepted, 540 enrolled. *Test scores:* SAT verbal scores over 500: 68%; SAT math scores over

500: 75%; SAT verbal scores over 600: 15%; SAT math scores over 600: 19%; SAT verbal scores over 700: 2%; SAT math scores over 700: 1%.
Tuition and fees (2003–04): $17,450 (full-time). *Room and board:* $7420 (room only: $4780).
Financial Aid (All incoming freshmen): *Average need-based gift aid:* $11,602. *Average non-need based aid:* $5648. *Average aid to full-time undergraduates:* $15,600.
Athletic Department: *Director of Athletics:* Bob Ward; Phone: 585-385-8310; Fax: 585-385-7308; E-mail: ward@sjfc.edu. *Sports Information Director:* Norm Kieffer; Phone: 585-385-8421; E-mail: kieffer@sjfc.edu.

MEN'S COACHES
Baseball: Dan Pepicelli; Phone: 585-385-8419; E-mail: pepicell@sjfc.edu.
Basketball: Rob Kornaker; Phone: 585-385-8391; E-mail: kornaker@sjfc.edu.
Football: Paul Vosburgh; Phone: 585-385-8433; E-mail: vosburgh@sjfc.edu.
Golf: Bob Simms; Phone: 585-385-8420; E-mail: simms@sjfc.edu.
Lacrosse: Craig Camp; Phone: 585-385-8485; E-mail: camp@sjfc.edu.
Soccer: Rob Searl; Phone: 585-385-8459; E-mail: rsearl@sjfc.edu.
Tennis: Linda Gohagan; Phone: 585-385-8484; E-mail: lgohagan@sjfc.edu.

WOMEN'S COACHES
Basketball: Phil Kahler; Phone: 585-385-8311; E-mail: ermi@sjfc.edu.
Lacrosse: Shannon McHale; Phone: 585-385-5219; E-mail: mchale@sjfc.edu.
Soccer: Jill McCabe; Phone: 585-385-8312; E-mail: mccabe@sjfc.edu.
Softball: Len Maiorani; Phone: 585-385-8487; E-mail: kelly@sjfc.edu.
Tennis: Linda Gohagan; Phone: 585-385-8484; E-mail: lgohagan@sjfc.edu.
Volleyball: Jim Chan; Phone: 585-385-8486; E-mail: jchan@sjfc.edu.

SAINT JOHN'S UNIVERSITY
Collegeville, Minnesota

Johnnies ◆ NCAA III ◆ Minnesota Intercollegiate Athletic Conference ◆ http://www.csbsju.edu/

Independent Roman Catholic comprehensive, founded 1857
Coed, primarily men, 1,940 undergraduate students, 98% full-time, 98% women, 100% men
Rural 2,400-acre campus with easy access to Minneapolis–St. Paul
Moderately difficult entrance level, 89% of applicants were admitted

Freshmen *Admission:* 1,049 applied, 932 were accepted, 490 enrolled. *Test scores:* SAT verbal scores over 500: 90%; SAT math scores over 500: 90%; SAT verbal scores over 600: 45%; SAT math scores over 600: 53%; SAT verbal scores over 700: 5%; SAT math scores over 700: 10%.
Tuition and fees (2003–04): $20,685 (full-time). *Room and board:* $5788 (room only: $2900).
Financial Aid (All incoming freshmen): *Average need-based gift aid:* $12,781. *Average non-need based aid:* $5761. *Average aid to full-time undergraduates:* $18,050.
Athletic Department: *Director of Athletics:* Jim Smith; Phone: 320-363-2500; Fax: 320-363-3130; E-mail: jsmith@csbsju.edu. *Sports Information Director:* Michael Hemmesch; Phone: 320-363-2595; E-mail: mhemmesch@csbsju.edu.

MEN'S COACHES
Baseball: Jerry Haugen; Phone: 320-363-2756; E-mail: jthaugen@csbsju.edu.
Basketball: Jim Smith; Phone: 320-363-2500; E-mail: jsmith@csbsju.edu.
Cross Country: Tim Miles; Phone: 320-363-2787; E-mail: tmiles@csbsju.edu.
Diving: Bill Saxton; Phone: 320-363-3352; E-mail: wsaxton@csbsju.edu.
Football: John Gagliardi; Phone: 320-363-3387; E-mail: jgagliardi@csbsju.edu.
Golf: Bob Alpers; Phone: 320-363-3088; E-mail: ralpers@csbsju.edu.
Ice Hockey: John Harrington; Phone: 320-363-2242; E-mail: jharrington@csbsju.edu.
Soccer: Pat Haws; Phone: 320-363-2758; E-mail: phaws@csbsju.edu.

Swimming: Bill Saxton; Phone: 320-363-3352; E-mail: wsaxton@csbsju.edu.
Tennis: Jack Bowe; Phone: 320-363-2442; E-mail: jbowe@csbsju.edu.
Track and Field: Tim Miles; Phone: 320-363-2787; E-mail: tmiles@csbsju.edu.
Wrestling: John Elton; Phone: 320-363-2243; E-mail: jelton@csbsju.edu.

ST. JOHN'S UNIVERSITY
Jamaica, New York

Red Storm ◆ NCAA I ◆ Big East Conference; Eastern College Athletic Conference ◆ http://www.stjohns.edu/

Independent religious university, founded 1870, affiliated with Roman Catholic Church
Coed, 14,908 undergraduate students, 79% full-time, 59% women, 41% men
Urban 98-acre campus with easy access to New York City
Moderately difficult entrance level, 69% of applicants were admitted

Freshmen *Admission:* 15,383 applied, 10,515 were accepted, 2,976 enrolled. *Test scores:* SAT verbal scores over 500: 55%; SAT math scores over 500: 64%; SAT verbal scores over 600: 15%; SAT math scores over 600: 23%; SAT verbal scores over 700: 1%; SAT math scores over 700: 5%.
Tuition and fees (2003–04): $20,080 (full-time). *Room and board:* $10,100 (room only: $6300).
Financial Aid (All incoming freshmen): *Average need-based gift aid:* $8655. *Average non-need based aid:* $8613. *Average aid to full-time undergraduates:* $18,025.
Athletic Department: *Director of Athletics:* David Wegrzyn; Phone: 718-990-1806; Fax: 718-990-2197; E-mail: athleticdirector@stjohns.edu. *Sports Information Director:* Dominic Scianna; Phone: 718-990-6367; E-mail: sciannad@stjohns.edu.

MEN'S COACHES
Baseball: Ed Blankmeyer; Phone: 718-990-6148; E-mail: blankmee@stjohns.edu.
Basketball: Kevin Clark; Phone: 718-990-6160; E-mail: clarkk@stjohns.edu.
Cheerleading: Matt Sonberg; Phone: 718-990-2315; E-mail: sonbergm@stjohns.edu.
Diving: John Skudin; Phone: 718-990-1689; E-mail: skudinj@stjohns.edu.
Golf: Frank Darby; Phone: 718-990-2058; E-mail: darbyf@stjohns.edu.
Lacrosse: Rick Sowell; Phone: 718-990-5599; E-mail: sowellr@stjohns.edu.
Soccer: Marc Reeves; Phone: 718-990-2098; E-mail: reevesm@stjohns.edu.
Swimming: John Skudin; Phone: 718-990-1689; E-mail: skudinj@stjohns.edu.
Tennis: Eric Rebhuhn; Phone: 718-990-5549; E-mail: rebhuhne@stjohns.edu.

WOMEN'S COACHES
Basketball: Kim Barnes Arcio; Phone: 718-990-6139; E-mail: barnesak@stjohns.edu.
Cheerleading: Matt Sonberg; Phone: 718-990-2315; E-mail: sonbergm@stjohns.edu.
Cross Country: Jim Hunt; Phone: 718-990-6159; E-mail: hurtj@stjohns.edu.
Diving: John Skudin; Phone: 718-990-1689; E-mail: skudinj@stjohns.edu.
Soccer: Ian Stone; Phone: 718-990-6163; E-mail: stonei@stjohns.edu.
Softball: Melody Cope; Phone: 718-990-6149; E-mail: copem@stjohns.edu.
Swimming: John Skudin; Phone: 718-990-1689; E-mail: skudinj@stjohns.edu.
Tennis: Gemma Alexander-Mozeak; Phone: 718-990-2026; E-mail: copelank@stjohns.edu.
Track and Field: Jim Hunt; Phone: 718-990-6159; E-mail: hurtj@stjohns.edu.
Volleyball: Joanne Persico-Smith; Phone: 718-990-1872; E-mail: persicoj@stjohns.edu.

SAINT JOSEPH COLLEGE
West Hartford, Connecticut

Bluejays ◆ NCAA III ◆ Great Northeast Athletic Conference ◆ http://www.sjc.edu/

Independent Roman Catholic comprehensive, founded 1932
Women only, 1,193 undergraduate students, 71% full-time, 98% women, 2% men
Suburban 84-acre campus with easy access to Hartford
Moderately difficult entrance level, 68% of applicants were admitted

Freshmen *Admission:* 709 applied, 485 were accepted, 215 enrolled. *Test scores:* SAT verbal scores over 500: 46%; SAT math scores over 500: 34%; SAT verbal scores over 600: 12%; SAT math scores over 600: 6%; SAT verbal scores over 700: 1%.
Tuition and fees (2003–04): $20,900 (full-time). *Room and board:* $8785 (room only: $4140).
Financial Aid (All incoming freshmen): *Average need-based gift aid:* $13,586. *Average non-need based aid:* $12,642. *Average aid to full-time undergraduates:* $17,174.
Athletic Department: *Director of Athletics:* William Cardarelli; Phone: 860—231-5246; Fax: 860—570-2423; E-mail: bcardarelli@sjc.edu. *Sports Information Director:* Chris Legates; Phone: 860—232-5422; E-mail: clegates@sjc.edu.

WOMEN'S COACHES
Basketball: Gary Sirois; Phone: 860-231-5423.
Cross Country: Antonella Maccarone; Phone: 860-232-3777.
Diving: Kieran Myers-Osgood; Phone: 860-232-5768; E-mail: wmyers@sjc.edu.
Soccer: Chris Legates; Phone: 860-232-5422; E-mail: clegates@sjc.edu.
Softball: Kerilyn Rostowsky; Phone: 860-232-3777; E-mail: krostowsky@sjc.edu.
Swimming: Kieran Myers-Osgood; Phone: 860-232-5768; E-mail: wmyers@sjc.edu.
Tennis: Tom Walsh; Phone: 860-232-5423.
Volleyball: Jeanne Digiacomo; Phone: 860-231-5421; E-mail: jdigiacomo@sjc.edu.

SAINT JOSEPH'S COLLEGE
Rensselaer, Indiana

Pumas ◆ NCAA II ◆ Great Lakes Valley Conference ◆ http://www.saintjoe.edu/

Independent Roman Catholic comprehensive, founded 1889
Coed, 998 undergraduate students, 84% full-time, 58% women, 42% men
Small-town 180-acre campus with easy access to Chicago
Moderately difficult entrance level, 73% of applicants were admitted

Freshmen *Admission:* 1,169 applied, 885 were accepted, 259 enrolled. *Test scores:* SAT verbal scores over 500: 52%; SAT math scores over 500: 46%; SAT verbal scores over 600: 9%; SAT math scores over 600: 15%; SAT verbal scores over 700: 2%; SAT math scores over 700: 2%.
Tuition and fees (2004–05): $19,160 (full-time). *Room and board:* $6300.
Financial Aid (All incoming freshmen): *Average need-based gift aid:* $11,500. *Average non-need based aid:* $5500. *Average aid to full-time undergraduates:* $14,500.
Athletic Department: *Director of Athletics:* Bill Massoels; Phone: 219-866-6184; Fax: 219-866-6276; E-mail: billm@saintjoe.edu. *Sports Information Director:* Clark Teuscher; Phone: 219-866-6141; E-mail: clark@saintjoe.edu.

MEN'S COACHES
Baseball: Rick O'Dette; Phone: 219-866-6399; E-mail: ricko@saintjoe.edu.
Basketball: Linc Darner; Phone: 219-866-0000; E-mail: ldarner@saintjoe.edu.
Cheerleading: Michelle Resendez; Phone: 219-866-6127; E-mail: micheller@saintjoe.edu.
Cross Country: Bill Massoels; Phone: 219-866-6184; E-mail: billm@saintjoe.edu.
Football: Tim Lester; Phone: 219-866-6222; E-mail: tlester@saintjoe.edu.
Golf: Doug Knutson; Phone: 219-866-6306; E-mail: dknutson13@hotmail.com.
Soccer: Rob Cummings; Phone: 219-866-6314; E-mail: cummings@saintjoe.edu.
Tennis: Donn Gobbie; Phone: 219-866-6335; E-mail: dgobbie@saintjoe.edu.
Track and Field: Bill Massoels; Phone: 219-866-6184; E-mail: billm@saintjoe.edu.

WOMEN'S COACHES
Basketball: John Raff; Phone: 219-866-6286; E-mail: jraff@saintjoe.edu.
Cheerleading: Michelle Resendez; Phone: 219-866-6127; E-mail: micheller@saintjoe.edu.
Cross Country: Bill Massoels; Phone: 219-866-6184; E-mail: billm@saintjoe.edu.
Golf: Doug Knutson; Phone: 219-866-6306; E-mail: dknutson13@hotmail.com.
Soccer: Rob Cummings; Phone: 219-866-6335; E-mail: cummings@saintjoe.edu.
Softball: Frank Wilkins; Phone: 219-866-6339; E-mail: fpwilk@saintjoe.edu.
Tennis: Donn Gobbie; Phone: 219-866-6335; E-mail: dgobbie@saintjoe.edu.
Track and Field: Bill Massoels; Phone: 219-866-6184; E-mail: billm@saintjoe.edu.
Volleyball: Ken Murczek; Phone: 219-866-0000; E-mail: kmurczek@saintjoe.edu.

SAINT JOSEPH'S COLLEGE OF MAINE
Standish, Maine

Monks ◆ NCAA III ◆ Independent ◆ http://www.sjcme.edu/

Independent religious comprehensive, founded 1912, affiliated with Roman Catholic Church
Coed, 953 undergraduate students, 97% full-time, 66% women, 34% men
Small-town 330-acre campus
Moderately difficult entrance level, 81% of applicants were admitted

Freshmen *Admission:* 962 applied, 763 were accepted, 247 enrolled. *Test scores:* SAT verbal scores over 500: 51%; SAT math scores over 500: 47%; SAT verbal scores over 600: 13%; SAT math scores over 600: 11%; SAT verbal scores over 700: 1%.
Tuition and fees (2003–04): $18,070 (full-time). *Room and board:* $7530.
Financial Aid (All incoming freshmen): *Average need-based gift aid:* $10,271. *Average non-need based aid:* $11,154. *Average aid to full-time undergraduates:* $15,096.
Athletic Department: *Director of Athletics:* David Roussel; Phone: 207-893-6670; Fax: 207-893-7860; E-mail: droussel@sjcme.edu.

MEN'S COACHES
Baseball: Will Sanborn; Phone: 207-893-6675; E-mail: wsanborn@sjcme.edu.
Basketball: Robert Sanicola; Phone: 207-893-6673; E-mail: rsimonds@sjcme.edu.
Cross Country: Tom Dann; Phone: 207-893-6678; E-mail: tdann@sjcme.edu.
Golf: Mike McDevitt; Phone: 207-893-6671; E-mail: mmcdevit@sjcme.edu.

WOMEN'S COACHES
Basketball: Mark McCaleb; Phone: 207-893-7667; E-mail: mmccaleb@sjcme.edu.
Cross Country: Tom Dann; Phone: 207-893-6678; E-mail: tdann@sjcme.edu.
Field Hockey: Carolyn Vail; Phone: 207-893-7661; E-mail: cvail@sjcme.edu.
Soccer: Todd Sniper; Phone: 207-893-7665; E-mail: tsniper@sjcme.edu.
Softball: Jamie Smyth; Phone: 207-893-7663; E-mail: jsmyth@sjcme.edu.
Volleyball: Kara Johnson; Phone: 207-893-7662; E-mail: kljohnson@sjcme.edu.

ST. JOSEPH'S COLLEGE, SUFFOLK CAMPUS
Patchogue, New York

Golden Eagles ◆ NCAA III ◆ Skyline Conference ◆ http://www.sjcny.edu/

Independent comprehensive, founded 1916
Coed, 3,692 undergraduate students, 71% full-time, 75% women, 25% men
Small-town 28-acre campus with easy access to New York City
Moderately difficult entrance level, 78% of applicants were admitted

Freshmen *Admission:* 1,050 applied, 810 were accepted, 421 enrolled. *Test scores:* SAT verbal scores over 500: 70%; SAT math scores over 500: 78%; SAT verbal scores over 600: 17%; SAT math scores over 600: 25%; SAT verbal scores over 700: 1%; SAT math scores over 700: 1%.
Tuition and fees (2003–04): $11,297 (full-time).
Financial Aid (All incoming freshmen): *Average need-based gift aid:* $8136. *Average non-need based aid:* $5085. *Average aid to full-time undergraduates:* $9798.
Athletic Department: *Director of Athletics:* Don Lizak; Phone: 631-447-3290; Fax: 631-447-3347. *Sports Information Director:* Frank Flandina; Phone: 631-447-3352; E-mail: fflandina@sjcny.edu.

MEN'S COACHES
Baseball: Randy Caden; Phone: 631-447-3349.
Basketball: John Mateyko; Phone: 631-447-3314.
Cross Country: Jim Crowley; Phone: 631-447-3349.
Golf: Donald Lizak; Phone: 631-447-3290.
Soccer: Gary Smith; Phone: 631-447-3351.
Tennis: Ken Kramer; Phone: 631-447-3370.

WOMEN'S COACHES
Basketball: Dennis Case; Phone: 631-447-3314.
Cross Country: Jim Crowley; Phone: 631-447-3349.
Soccer: Joseph Lee; Phone: 631-447-3292.
Softball: Gary Smith; Phone: 631-447-3351.
Swimming: Jayne Foster; Phone: 631-447-3346.
Tennis: Glenn Nathan; Phone: 631-447-3291.
Volleyball: Sean Holden; Phone: 631-447-3292.

SAINT JOSEPH'S UNIVERSITY
Philadelphia, Pennsylvania

Hawks ◆ NCAA I ◆ Atlantic 10 Conference; Metro Atlantic Athletic Conference ◆ http://www.sju.edu/

Independent Roman Catholic (Jesuit) comprehensive, founded 1851
Coed, 4,656 undergraduate students, 82% full-time, 53% women, 47% men
Suburban 65-acre campus
Very difficult entrance level, 50% of applicants were admitted

Freshmen *Admission:* 7,765 applied, 3,753 were accepted, 998 enrolled. *Test scores:* SAT verbal scores over 500: 86%; SAT math scores over 500: 88%; SAT verbal scores over 600: 33%; SAT math scores over 600: 40%; SAT verbal scores over 700: 5%; SAT math scores over 700: 6%.
Tuition and fees (2003–04): $24,230 (full-time). *Room and board:* $9400 (room only: $5950).
Financial Aid (All incoming freshmen): *Average need-based gift aid:* $7902. *Average non-need based aid:* $7410. *Average aid to full-time undergraduates:* $11,727.
Athletic Department: *Director of Athletics:* Don DiJulia; Phone: 610-660-1707; Fax: 610-660-1716; E-mail: ddijulia@sju.edu. *Sports Information Director:* Marie Wozniak; Phone: 610-660-1727; E-mail: mwozniak@sju.edu.

MEN'S COACHES
Baseball: Jim Ertel; Phone: 610-660-1718; E-mail: jertel@sju.edu.
Basketball: Phil Martelli; Phone: 610-660-1706; E-mail: cariano@sju.edu.
Cross Country: Mike Glavin; Phone: 610-660-1731; E-mail: mglavin@netreach.net.
Golf: Bob Lynch; Phone: 610-660-1759; E-mail: blynch@gospike.com.
Lacrosse: Paul Perdue; Phone: 610-660-1733; E-mail: pperdue@sju.edu.
Soccer: Tom Turner; Phone: 610-660-1764; E-mail: mic30tur@comcast.net.
Tennis: Al Laveson; Phone: 610-660-3368; E-mail: alaveson@sju.edu.
Track and Field: Mike Glavin; Phone: 610-660-1731; E-mail: mglavin@netreach.net.

WOMEN'S COACHES
Basketball: Cindy Griffin; Phone: 610-660-1736; E-mail: cgriffin@sju.edu.
Cross Country: Kevin Quinn; Phone: 610-660-1731; E-mail: quinn@sju.edu.
Field Hockey: Michelle Finegan; Phone: 610-660-1763; E-mail: mfinegan@sju.edu.
Lacrosse: Denise Szatkowski; Phone: 610-660-2585; E-mail: deniseski4_@hotmail.com.
Soccer: Jess Reynolds; Phone: 610-660-3367; E-mail: jreynold@sju.edu.
Softball: Moo Moyer; Phone: 610-660-1734; E-mail: hmoyer3002@aol.com.
Tennis: Al Laveson; Phone: 610-660-3368; E-mail: alaveson@sju.edu.
Track and Field: Kevin Quinn; Phone: 610-660-1731; E-mail: quinn@sju.edu.

ST. LAWRENCE UNIVERSITY
Canton, New York

Saints ◆ NCAA III ◆ Eastern College Athletic Conference; Upstate Collegiate Athletic Conference ◆ http://www.stlawu.edu/

Independent comprehensive, founded 1856
Coed, 2,148 undergraduate students, 98% full-time, 53% women, 47% men
Small-town 1,000-acre campus with easy access to Ottawa
Very difficult entrance level, 5% of applicants were admitted

Freshmen *Admission:* 3,082 applied, 1,767 were accepted, 566 enrolled. *Test scores:* SAT verbal scores over 500: 83%; SAT math scores over 500: 86%; SAT verbal scores over 600: 38%; SAT math scores over 600: 40%; SAT verbal scores over 700: 5%; SAT math scores over 700: 4%.
Tuition and fees (2003–04): $28,190 (full-time). *Room and board:* $7755 (room only: $4170).
Financial Aid (All incoming freshmen): *Average need-based gift aid:* $20,310. *Average non-need based aid:* $9318. *Average aid to full-time undergraduates:* $26,725.
Athletic Department: *Director of Athletics:* Margie Strait; Phone: 315-229-5784; Fax: 315-229-5589; E-mail: mstrait@stlawu.edu. *Sports Information Director:* Wally Johnson; Phone: 315-229-5588; E-mail: wjohnson@stlawu.edu.

MEN'S COACHES
Baseball: Tom Fay; Phone: 315-229-5882; E-mail: tfay@stlawu.edu.
Basketball: Chris Downs; Phone: 315-229-5836; E-mail: cdowns@stlawu.edu.
Cross Country: John Newman; Phone: 315-229-5779; E-mail: jnewman@stlawu.edu.
Diving: Beth Nee; Phone: 315-229-5884; E-mail: efesko@stlawu.edu.
Football: Chris Phelps; Phone: 315-229-5785; E-mail: cphelps@stlawu.edu.
Golf: Mary Lawrence; Phone: 315-229-5789; E-mail: malawrence@stlawu.edu.
Ice Hockey: Joe Marsh; Phone: 315-229-5881; E-mail: jmarsh@stlawu.edu.
Lacrosse: Mike Mahoney; Phone: 315-229-5786; E-mail: mmahoney@stlawu.edu.
Soccer: Bob Durocher; Phone: 315-229-5870; E-mail: bdur@mail.stlawu.edu.
Swimming: Bob Clemmer; Phone: 315-229-5884; E-mail: rclemmer@stlawu.edu.
Tennis: Jeremy Freeman; Phone: 315-229-5787; E-mail: jfreeman@stlawu.edu.
Track and Field: John Newman; Phone: 315-229-5779; E-mail: jnewman@stlawu.edu.

WOMEN'S COACHES
Basketball: G.P. Gromacki; Phone: 315-229-5839; E-mail: ggromacki@stlawu.edu.
Cross Country: Deb Lyndaker; Phone: 315-229-5813; E-mail: dlyndaker@stlawu.edu.

St. Lawrence University (continued)

Diving: Beth Nee; Phone: 315-229-5884; E-mail: efesko@stlawu.edu.
Field Hockey: Fran Grembowicz; Phone: 315-229-5780; E-mail: fgrembowicz@stlawu.edu.
Golf: Mary Lawrence; Phone: 315-229-5789; E-mail: malawrence@stlawu.edu.
Lacrosse: Jodi Axtell; Phone: 315-229-5874; E-mail: jaxtell@stlawu.edu.
Soccer: Deb Biche; Phone: 315-229-5790; E-mail: dbiche@stlawu.edu.
Softball: Fran Grembowicz; Phone: 315-229-5780; E-mail: fgrembowicz@stlawu.edu.
Swimming: Bob Clemmer; Phone: 315-229-5884; E-mail: rclemmer@stlawu.edu.
Tennis: Jeremy Freeman; Phone: 315-229-5787; E-mail: jfreeman@stlawu.edu.
Track and Field: Mike Howard; Phone: 315-229-5883; E-mail: mhoward@stlawu.edu.
Volleyball: Anne Schneider; Phone: 315-229-5883; E-mail: aschneider@stlawu.edu.

SAINT LEO UNIVERSITY
Saint Leo, Florida

Lions ◆ NCAA II ◆ Sunshine State Conference ◆ http://www.saintleo.edu/

Independent Roman Catholic comprehensive, founded 1889
Coed, 1,083 undergraduate students, 95% full-time, 55% women, 45% men
Rural 186-acre campus with easy access to Tampa and Orlando
Moderately difficult entrance level, 6% of applicants were admitted

Freshmen *Admission:* 1,933 applied, 1,145 were accepted, 376 enrolled. *Test scores:* SAT verbal scores over 500: 46%; SAT math scores over 500: 46%; SAT verbal scores over 600: 8%; SAT math scores over 600: 7%; SAT verbal scores over 700: 1%; SAT math scores over 700: 1%.
Tuition and fees (2003–04): $13,570 (full-time). *Room and board:* $7030 (room only: $3700).
Financial Aid (All incoming freshmen): *Average need-based gift aid:* $10,381. *Average non-need based aid:* $6238. *Average aid to full-time undergraduates:* $16,345.
Athletic Department: *Director of Athletics:* Fran Reidy; Phone: 352-588-8246; Fax: 352-588-8290; E-mail: fran.reidy@saintleo.edu. *Sports Information Director:* Walter Riddle; Phone: 352-588-8506; E-mail: walt.riddle@saintleo.edu.

MEN'S COACHES
Baseball: Ricky Ware; Phone: 352-588-8227; E-mail: ricky.ware@saintleo.edu.
Basketball: Mike Madagan; Phone: 352-588-8224; E-mail: mike.madagan@saintleo.edu.
Cheerleading: Suzanne Hollis; Phone: 352-588-8358; E-mail: suzanne.hollis@saintleo.edu.
Cross Country: Cyle Sage; Phone: 352-588-8221; E-mail: cyle.sage@saintleo.edu.
Golf: Tim Holt; Phone: 352-588-8366; E-mail: tim.holt@saintleo.edu.
Soccer: Greg Vallee; Phone: 352-588-8843; E-mail: gregory.vallee@saintleo.edu.
Tennis: Tim Crosby; Phone: 352-588-8226; E-mail: thomas.crosby@saintleo.edu.

WOMEN'S COACHES
Basketball: Kerri Reaves; Phone: 352-588-8447; E-mail: kerri.reaves@saintleo.edu.
Cheerleading: Suzanne Hollis; Phone: 352-588-8358; E-mail: suzanne.hollis@saintleo.edu.
Cross Country: Cyle Sage; Phone: 352-588-8221; E-mail: cyle.sage@saintleo.edu.
Golf: Melissa Lynn; Phone: 352-588-8684; E-mail: melissa.lynn@saintleo.edu.
Soccer: Tony Paris; Phone: 352-588-8843; E-mail: tony.paris@saintleo.edu.
Softball: Christi Wade; Phone: 352-588-8451; E-mail: christi.wade@saintleo.edu.
Tennis: Tim Crosby; Phone: 352-588-8226; E-mail: thomas.crosby@saintleo.edu.
Volleyball: Stephanie Radecki; Phone: 352-588-8448; E-mail: stephanie.radecki@saintleo.edu.

ST. LOUIS COLLEGE OF PHARMACY
St. Louis, Missouri

Eutectics ◆ NAIA ◆ Independent ◆ http://www.stlcop.edu/

Independent comprehensive, founded 1864
Coed, 170 undergraduate students, 98% full-time, 65% women, 35% men
Urban 5-acre campus
Moderately difficult entrance level, 43% of applicants were admitted

Freshmen *Admission:* 514 applied, 228 were accepted.
Tuition and fees (2004–05): $17,260 (full-time). *Room and board:* $7350.
Financial Aid (All incoming freshmen): *Average need-based gift aid:* $4159. *Average non-need based aid:* $7541. *Average aid to full-time undergraduates:* $9667.
Athletic Department: *Director of Athletics:* Briana Hepfinger; Phone: 314-446-8346; E-mail: bhepfinger@stlcop.edu.

MEN'S COACHES
Basketball: Evan Pedersen; Phone: 314-446-8347; E-mail: epedersen@stlcop.edu.
Cross Country: Ember Knobeloch; Phone: 314-446-8347; E-mail: eknobeloch@stlcop.edu.

WOMEN'S COACHES
Basketball: Chad Gregory; Phone: 314-446-8347; E-mail: cgregory@stlcop.edu.
Cross Country: Ember Knobeloch; Phone: 314-446-8347; E-mail: eknobeloch@stlcop.edu.
Volleyball: Ryan VonFeldt; Phone: 314-446-8347; E-mail: rvonfeldt@stlcop.edu.

SAINT LOUIS UNIVERSITY
St. Louis, Missouri

Billikens ◆ NCAA I ◆ Conference USA Conference; Northern Pacific Field Hockey Conference ◆ http://www.slu.edu/

Independent Roman Catholic (Jesuit) university, founded 1818
Coed, 7,091 undergraduate students, 91% full-time, 55% women, 45% men
Urban 373-acre campus
Moderately difficult entrance level, 70% of applicants were admitted

Freshmen *Admission:* 6,405 applied, 4,500 were accepted, 1,526 enrolled. *Test scores:* SAT verbal scores over 500: 90%; SAT math scores over 500: 89%; SAT verbal scores over 600: 48%; SAT math scores over 600: 54%; SAT verbal scores over 700: 9%; SAT math scores over 700: 11%.
Tuition and fees (2003–04): $22,218 (full-time). *Room and board:* $7740 (room only: $4240).
Financial Aid (All incoming freshmen): *Average need-based gift aid:* $13,266. *Average non-need based aid:* $7628. *Average aid to full-time undergraduates:* $18,249.
Athletic Department: *Director of Athletics:* Doug Woolard; Phone: 314-977-3167; Fax: 314-977-3178; E-mail: woolardd@slu.edu. *Sports Information Director:* Doug McIlhagga; Phone: 314-977-2524; E-mail: mcilhad2@slu.edu.

MEN'S COACHES
Baseball: Bob Hughes; Phone: 314-977-3172; E-mail: hughesj3@slu.edu.
Basketball: Brad Soderberg; Phone: 314-977-3173; E-mail: soderbbw@slu.edu.
Cross Country: Mike Uhrich; Phone: 314-977-3253; E-mail: uhrichm3@slu.edu.
Diving: Elizzabeth Frost; Phone: 314-977-3256.
Diving: Meredith Kieersznowski; Phone: 314-977-3252.
Golf: Ed Schwent; Phone: 314-977-3981; E-mail: schwente@slu.edu.
Soccer: Dan Donigan; Phone: 314-977-3266; E-mail: donigand@slu.edu.
Swimming: Jim Halliburton; Phone: 314-977-3252; E-mail: hallibje@slu.edu.
Tennis: Jonathan Zych; Phone: 314-977-8421; E-mail: zychjd@slu.edu.

WOMEN'S COACHES
Basketball: Jill Pizzotti; Phone: 314-977-3177; E-mail: pizzotti@slu.edu.

Cross Country: Mike Uhrich; Phone: 314-977-3253; E-mail: uhrichm3@slu.edu.

Diving: Meredith Kiersznowski; Phone: 314-977-3252.

Field Hockey: Maria Whitehead; Phone: 314-977-3186; E-mail: whitehme@slu.edu.

Soccer: Tim Champion; Phone: 314-977-3271; E-mail: champion@slu.edu.

Softball: Jim Molloy; Phone: 314-977-3284; E-mail: molloyjj@slu.edu.

Swimming: Jim Halliburton; Phone: 314-977-3252; E-mail: hallibje@slu.edu.

Tennis: Jonathan Zych; Phone: 314-977-8421; E-mail: zychjd@slu.edu.

Volleyball: Anne Kordes; Phone: 314-977-3254; E-mail: nolenmm@slu.edu.

SAINT MARTIN'S COLLEGE
Lacey, Washington

Saints ◆ NCAA II ◆ Great Northwest Athletic Conference ◆ http://www.stmartin.edu/

Independent Roman Catholic comprehensive, founded 1895
Coed, 1,246 undergraduate students, 66% full-time, 56% women, 44% men
Suburban 300-acre campus with easy access to Tacoma
Moderately difficult entrance level, 74% of applicants were admitted

Freshmen *Admission:* 462 applied, 352 were accepted, 145 enrolled. *Test scores:* SAT verbal scores over 500: 53%; SAT math scores over 500: 48%; SAT verbal scores over 600: 15%; SAT math scores over 600: 18%; SAT verbal scores over 700: 2%; SAT math scores over 700: 2%.
Tuition and fees (2004–05): $18,950 (full-time). *Room and board:* $5720 (room only: $2420).
Financial Aid (All incoming freshmen): *Average need-based gift aid:* $14,215. *Average non-need based aid:* $10,982. *Average aid to full-time undergraduates:* $18,108.
Athletic Department: *Director of Athletics:* Bob Grisham; Phone: 360-438-4368; Fax: 360-412-6191; E-mail: bgrisham@stmartin.edu. *Sports Information Director:* Mark McGreevy; Phone: 360-438-4328; E-mail: mmcgreevy@stmartin.edu.

MEN'S COACHES
Baseball: Joe Dominiak; Phone: 360-438-4531; E-mail: jdominiak@stmartin.edu.

Basketball: Keith Cooper; Phone: 360-438-4551; E-mail: kcooper@stmartin.edu.

Cross Country: Brad Hooper; Phone: 360-438-4523; E-mail: bhooper@stmartin.edu.

Golf: Kurt Kageler; Phone: 360-438-4366; E-mail: kkageler@stmartin.edu.

Track and Field: Brad Hooper; Phone: 360-438-4523; E-mail: bhooper@stmartin.edu.

WOMEN'S COACHES
Basketball: Tim Healy; Phone: 360-438-4369; E-mail: thealy@stmartin.edu.

Cross Country: Brad Hooper; Phone: 360-438-4523; E-mail: bhooper@stmartin.edu.

Golf: Kurt Kageler; Phone: 360-438-4366; E-mail: kkageler@stmartin.edu.

Softball: Scott Gottberg; Phone: 360-438-4296.

Track and Field: Brad Hooper; Phone: 360-438-4523; E-mail: bhooper@stmartin.edu.

Volleyball: Clyde Reis; Phone: 360-438-4535; E-mail: creis@stmartin.edu.

SAINT MARY'S COLLEGE
Notre Dame, Indiana

Belles ◆ NCAA III ◆ Michigan Intercollegiate Conference ◆ http://www.saintmarys.edu/

Independent Roman Catholic 4-year, founded 1844
Women only, 1,475 undergraduate students, 98% full-time, 100% women
Suburban 275-acre campus
Moderately difficult entrance level, 82% of applicants were admitted

Freshmen *Admission:* 1,014 applied, 828 were accepted, 402 enrolled. *Test scores:* SAT verbal scores over 500: 78%; SAT math scores over 500: 81%; SAT verbal scores over 600: 32%; SAT math scores over 600: 31%; SAT verbal scores over 700: 4%; SAT math scores over 700: 3%.
Tuition and fees (2003–04): $21,974 (full-time). *Room and board:* $7289.
Financial Aid (All incoming freshmen): *Average need-based gift aid:* $8931. *Average non-need based aid:* $6969. *Average aid to full-time undergraduates:* $19,176.
Athletic Department: *Director of Athletics:* Lynn Kacharik; Phone: 574-284-5547; Fax: 574-284-4797; E-mail: kachmarik@saintmarys.edu. *Sports Information Director:* Gregg Petcoff; Phone: 574-284-5290; E-mail: gpetcoff@saintmarys.edu.

WOMEN'S COACHES
Basketball: Suzanne Bellina; Phone: 574-284-4907; E-mail: ssmith@saintmarys.edu.

Cheerleading: Angela Layman; Phone: 574-284-4907; E-mail: mag5l@aol.com.

Cross Country: David Barstis; Phone: 574-284-4027; E-mail: dbarstis@saintmarys.edu.

Diving: Nick Farmer; Phone: 574-284-5290.

Golf: Mark Hamilton; Phone: 574-284-4817; E-mail: markh@saintmarys.edu.

Soccer: Caryn Mackenzie; Phone: 574-284-4909; E-mail: cmack@stanleyclark.org.

Softball: Anna Welsh; Phone: 574-284-4910; E-mail: awelsh@saintmarys.edu.

Swimming: Gregg Petcoff; Phone: 574-284-5290; E-mail: gpetcoff@saintmarys.edu.

Tennis: Dee Stevenson; Phone: 574-284-5546; E-mail: stevensn@saintmarys.edu.

Volleyball: Julie Schroeder-Biek; Phone: 574-284-4908; E-mail: jsbiek@saintmarys.edu.

SAINT MARY'S COLLEGE OF CALIFORNIA
Moraga, California

Gaels ◆ NCAA I ◆ Pacific Coast Softball Conference; West Coast Conference ◆ http://www.stmarys-ca.edu/

Independent Roman Catholic comprehensive, founded 1863
Coed, 3,337 undergraduate students, 72% full-time, 60% women, 40% men
Suburban 420-acre campus with easy access to San Francisco
Moderately difficult entrance level, 79% of applicants were admitted

Freshmen *Admission:* 3,172 applied, 2,590 were accepted, 562 enrolled. *Test scores:* SAT verbal scores over 500: 75%; SAT math scores over 500: 76%; SAT verbal scores over 600: 22%; SAT math scores over 600: 27%; SAT verbal scores over 700: 3%; SAT math scores over 700: 2%.
Tuition and fees (2003–04): $23,775 (full-time). *Room and board:* $9075 (room only: $5065).
Financial Aid (All incoming freshmen): *Average need-based gift aid:* $17,027. *Average non-need based aid:* $11,000. *Average aid to full-time undergraduates:* $21,443.
Athletic Department: *Director of Athletics:* Carl Clapp; Phone: 925-631-4399; Fax: 925-376-0829; E-mail: kdwillia@stmarys-ca.edu. *Sports Information Director:* Rich Davi; Phone: 925-631-4402; E-mail: rdavi@stmarys-ca.edu.

MEN'S COACHES
Baseball: Jedd Soto; Phone: 925-631-4637; E-mail: jsoto@stmarys-ca.edu.

Saint Mary's College of California (continued)

Basketball: Randy Bennett; Phone: 925-631-8848; E-mail: rbennett@stmarys-ca.edu.
Cheerleading: Dianna Rowley; Phone: 925-631-8805; E-mail: dancingdianna@hotmail.com.
Cross Country: Randy Rau; Phone: 925-631-4294; E-mail: runforsmc@earthlink.net.
Football: Vincent White; Phone: 925-631-4395; E-mail: vwhite@stmarys-ca.edu.
Golf: Scott Hardy; Phone: 925-631-4954; E-mail: stmarysgolf@hotmail.com.
Soccer: Steve Rammel; Phone: 925-631-4657; E-mail: srammel@stmarys-ca.edu.
Tennis: Michael Wayman; Phone: 925-631-4401; E-mail: mwayman@stmarys-ca.edu.

WOMEN'S COACHES

Basketball: Michelle Jacoby; Phone: 925-631-4712; E-mail: msasaki@stmarys-ca.edu.
Cheerleading: Dianna Rowley; Phone: 925-631-8805; E-mail: dancingdianna@hotmail.com.
Cross Country: Randy Rau; Phone: 925-631-4294; E-mail: runforsmc@earthlink.net.
Lacrosse: Brandon Badgley; Phone: 925-631-4959; E-mail: bbadgley@stmarys-ca.edu.
Soccer: Paul Sapsford; Phone: 925-631-4415; E-mail: smcwsoccer@yahoo.com.
Softball: Megumi Takasaki; Phone: 925-631-4550; E-mail: mtakasak@stmarys-ca.edu.
Tennis: Lisa Alioaz; Phone: 925-631-4711; E-mail: lalipaz@stmarys-ca.edu.
Volleyball: Jon Stevenson; Phone: 925-631-4444; E-mail: jstevens@stmarys-ca.edu.

ST. MARY'S COLLEGE OF MARYLAND
St. Mary's City, Maryland

Seahawks ◆ NCAA III ◆ Capital Athletic Conference ◆ http://www.smcm.edu/

State-supported 4-year, founded 1840, part of Maryland State Colleges and Universities System
Coed, 1,922 undergraduate students, 92% full-time, 60% women, 40% men
Rural 319-acre campus
Very difficult entrance level, 6% of applicants were admitted

Freshmen Admission: 2,262 applied, 1,243 were accepted, 421 enrolled. Test scores: SAT verbal scores over 500: 95%; SAT math scores over 500: 95%; SAT verbal scores over 600: 72%; SAT math scores over 600: 66%; SAT verbal scores over 700: 20%; SAT math scores over 700: 15%.
Tuition and fees (2004–05): $9680 (resident), $17,160 (nonresident). Room and board: $7400 (room only: $4165).
Financial Aid (All incoming freshmen): Average need-based gift aid: $3500. Average non-need based aid: $4000. Average aid to full-time undergraduates: $7072.
Athletic Department: Director of Athletics: Scott Devine; Phone: 240-895-4295; Fax: 240-895-4480; E-mail: swdevine@smcm.edu. Sports Information Director: Shawne McCoy; Phone: 240-895-4482; E-mail: smmccoy@smcm.edu.

MEN'S COACHES

Baseball: Lew Jenkins; Phone: 240-895-4312; E-mail: lwjenkins@smcm.edu.
Basketball: Brock Kantrow; Phone: 240-895-4318; E-mail: pbkantrow@smcm.edu.
Cheerleading: Donna Fitzgerald; Phone: 240-895-4295; E-mail: dhfitzgerald@smcm.edu.
Lacrosse: Jayme Block; Phone: 240-895-4324; E-mail: jeblock@smcm.edu.
Soccer: Herb Gainey; Phone: 240-895-4321; E-mail: whgainey@smcm.edu.
Swimming: Andre Barbins; Phone: 240-895-4798; E-mail: arbarbins@smcm.edu.

Tennis: Lisa McCoy; Phone: 240-895-3304; E-mail: lrmccoy@smcm.edu.

WOMEN'S COACHES

Basketball: Nan Hambrose; Phone: 240-895-4323; E-mail: nmhambrose@smcm.edu.
Cheerleading: Donna Fitzgerald; Phone: 240-895-4295; E-mail: dhfitzgerald@smcm.edu.
Field Hockey: Megan Block; Phone: 240-895-4319; E-mail: mblock@smcm.edu.
Lacrosse: Megan Block; Phone: 240-895-4319; E-mail: mblock@smcm.edu.
Soccer: Mark Mermelstein; Phone: 240-895-4350; E-mail: mamermelstein@smcm.edu.
Swimming: Andre Barbins; Phone: 240-895-4798; E-mail: arbarbins@smcm.edu.
Tennis: Lisa McCoy; Phone: 240-895-3304; E-mail: lrmccoy@smcm.edu.
Volleyball: Morris Davis; Phone: 240-895-2054; E-mail: midavis@smcm.edu.

SAINT MARY'S UNIVERSITY OF MINNESOTA
Winona, Minnesota

Cardinals ◆ NCAA III ◆ Minnesota Intercollegiate Athletic Conference ◆ http://www.smumn.edu/

Independent Roman Catholic comprehensive, founded 1912
Coed, 1,704 undergraduate students, 78% full-time, 55% women, 45% men
Small-town 350-acre campus
Moderately difficult entrance level, 62% of applicants were admitted

Freshmen Admission: 1,312 applied, 981 were accepted, 369 enrolled. Test scores: SAT verbal scores over 500: 75%; SAT math scores over 500: 70%; SAT verbal scores over 600: 27%; SAT math scores over 600: 29%; SAT verbal scores over 700: 5%; SAT math scores over 700: 2%.
Tuition and fees (2004–05): $17,925 (full-time). Room and board: $5450 (room only: $3050).
Financial Aid (All incoming freshmen): Average need-based gift aid: $6425. Average non-need based aid: $5495. Average aid to full-time undergraduates: $14,305.
Athletic Department: Director of Athletics: Chris Kendall; Phone: 507-457-1781; Fax: 507-457-6640; E-mail: ckendall@smumn.edu. Sports Information Director: Nikki Fennern; Phone: 507-457-1638; E-mail: nfennern@smumn.edu.

MEN'S COACHES

Baseball: Nick Whaley; Phone: 507-457-1577; E-mail: nwhaley@smumn.edu.
Basketball: Mark Lovelace; Phone: 507-457-8729; E-mail: mlovelacl@smumn.edu.
Cross Country: John Skemp; Phone: 507-457-1574.
Diving: Debi Piscitiello; Phone: 507-457-7413; E-mail: dpisciti@smumn.edu.
Golf: Tom Farren; Phone: 507-457-1608; E-mail: dblank@smumn.edu.
Ice Hockey: Don Olsen; Phone: 507-457-1578; E-mail: dolson@smumn.edu.
Soccer: Eric Luzzi; Phone: 507-457-6967; E-mail: eluzzi@smumn.edu.
Swimming: Eric Lindquist; Phone: 507-457-1622; E-mail: elindqui@smumn.edu.
Tennis: Jeff Halberg; Phone: 507-453-5555; E-mail: jhalberg@smumn.edu.
Track and Field: Kirk Nauman; Phone: 507-457-1623; E-mail: knauman@smumn.edu.

WOMEN'S COACHES

Basketball: Dan Messemann; Phone: 507-457-6955; E-mail: dmessman@smumn.edu.
Cross Country: John Skemp; Phone: 507-457-1574.
Diving: Debi Piscitiello; Phone: 507-457-7413; E-mail: dpisciti@smumn.edu.
Golf: Dan Messman; Phone: 507-457-1623; E-mail: dmessman@smumn.edu.
Soccer: Dan Blank; Phone: 507-457-1583; E-mail: dblank@smumn.edu.

Swimming: Eric Lindquist; Phone: 507-457-1622; E-mail: elindqui@smumn.edu.
Tennis: Jeff Halberg; Phone: 507-453-5555; E-mail: jhalberg@smumn.edu.
Track and Field: Kirk Nauman; Phone: 507-457-1623; E-mail: knauman@smumn.edu.
Volleyball: Mike Lester; Phone: 507-457-6973; E-mail: mlester@smumn.edu.

ST. MARY'S UNIVERSITY OF SAN ANTONIO
San Antonio, Texas

Rattlers ◆ NCAA II ◆ Heartland Conference ◆ http://www.stmarytx.edu/

Independent Roman Catholic comprehensive, founded 1852
Coed, 2,582 undergraduate students, 92% full-time, 59% women, 41% men
Urban 135-acre campus
Moderately difficult entrance level, 82% of applicants were admitted

Freshmen *Admission:* 1,464 applied, 1,189 were accepted, 472 enrolled. *Test scores:* SAT verbal scores over 500: 69%; SAT math scores over 500: 72%; SAT verbal scores over 600: 22%; SAT math scores over 600: 20%; SAT verbal scores over 700: 1%; SAT math scores over 700: 3%.
Tuition and fees (2004–05): $17,756 (full-time). *Room and board:* $6498 (room only: $3802).
Financial Aid (All incoming freshmen): *Average need-based gift aid:* $6965. *Average non-need based aid:* $8479. *Average aid to full-time undergraduates:* $14,481.
Athletic Department: *Director of Athletics:* Charlie Migl; Phone: 210-436-3528; Fax: 210-436-3040; E-mail: cmigl@alvin.stmarytx.edu. *Sports Information Director:* Pat Abernathey; Phone: 210-431-4379; E-mail: jabernathey@stmarytx.edu.

MEN'S COACHES
Baseball: Charlie Migl; Phone: 210-436-3528; E-mail: cmigl@stmarytx.edu.
Basketball: Buddy Meyer; Phone: 210-436-3528; E-mail: bmeyer@stmarytx.edu.
Cheerleading: Bridget O'Connor; Phone: 210-436-3126; E-mail: boconnor@stmarytx.edu.
Golf: Wes Skidmore; Phone: 210-431-6720; E-mail: wskidmore@stmarytx.edu.
Soccer: Que Willis; Phone: 210-436-3248; E-mail: qwillis@stmarytx.edu.
Tennis: Brad Bulyck; Phone: 210-431-4246; E-mail: bbulycz@stmarytx.edu.

WOMEN'S COACHES
Basketball: Paige Clawson; Phone: 210-436-3528; E-mail: pclawson@stmarytx.edu.
Cheerleading: Bridget O'Connor; Phone: 210-436-3126; E-mail: boconnor@stmarytx.edu.
Cross Country: Ricardo Guerra; Phone: 210-431-6765; E-mail: rguerra@stmarytx.edu.
Golf: Cindy Krause; Phone: 210-436-3004; E-mail: ckrause@stmarytx.edu.
Soccer: Que Willis; Phone: 210-436-3248; E-mail: qwillis@stmarytx.edu.
Softball: Donna Fields; Phone: 210-431-5034; E-mail: dfields@stmarytx.edu.
Tennis: Brad Bulyck; Phone: 210-431-4246; E-mail: bbulycz@stmarytx.edu.
Volleyball: Todd Caughlin; Phone: 210-436-3661; E-mail: tcaughlin@stmarytx.edu.

SAINT MICHAEL'S COLLEGE
Colchester, Vermont

Purple Knights ◆ NCAA II ◆ Northeast-10 Conference ◆ http://www.smcvt.edu/

Independent Roman Catholic comprehensive, founded 1904
Coed, 1,991 undergraduate students, 96% full-time, 54% women, 46% men
Small-town 440-acre campus with easy access to Montreal
Moderately difficult entrance level, 60% of applicants were admitted

Freshmen *Admission:* 2,777 applied, 1,872 were accepted, 512 enrolled. *Test scores:* SAT verbal scores over 500: 82%; SAT math scores over 500: 83%; SAT verbal scores over 600: 30%; SAT math scores over 600: 30%; SAT verbal scores over 700: 3%; SAT math scores over 700: 2%.
Tuition and fees (2003–04): $22,420 (full-time). *Room and board:* $7680 (room only: $4775).
Financial Aid (All incoming freshmen): *Average need-based gift aid:* $12,792. *Average non-need based aid:* $7483. *Average aid to full-time undergraduates:* $17,699.
Athletic Department: *Director of Athletics:* Geri Knortz; Phone: 802-654-2200; Fax: 802-654-2497; E-mail: gknortz@smcvt.edu. *Sports Information Director:* Seth Cole; Phone: 802-654-2537; E-mail: scole2@smcvt.edu.

MEN'S COACHES
Baseball: Perry Bove; Phone: 802-654-2725; E-mail: pbove@smcvt.edu.
Basketball: Tom O'Shea; Phone: 802-654-2675; E-mail: toshea@smcvt.edu.
Cheerleading: Robyn Myers; Phone: 802-654-9774; E-mail: rmyers@smcvt.edu.
Cross Country: Joe Connelly; Phone: 802-654-2616; E-mail: jconnelly@smcvt.edu.
Diving: Jame Donoghue; Phone: 802-654-2500; E-mail: jdonoghue@smcvt.edu.
Golf: Erie Rich; Phone: 802-654-2676; E-mail: erich@smcvt.edu.
Ice Hockey: Lou Dimasi; Phone: 802-654-2566; E-mail: ldimasi@smcvt.edu.
Lacrosse: Paul Schimoler; Phone: 802-654-2745; E-mail: pschimoler@smcvt.edu.
Soccer: Tim Kaleita; Phone: 802-654-2693; E-mail: tkaleita@smcvt.edu.
Swimming: Jim Donoghue; Phone: 802-654-2500; E-mail: jdonoghue@smcvt.edu.
Tennis: Robert Fleming; Phone: 802-654-2725; E-mail: rfleming@smcvt.edu.

WOMEN'S COACHES
Basketball: Jen Niebling; Phone: 802-654-2505; E-mail: jniebling@smcvt.edu.
Cheerleading: Robyn Myers; Phone: 802-654-9774; E-mail: rmyers@smcvt.edu.
Cross Country: Larry Kimball; Phone: 802-654-2616; E-mail: lkimball@smcvt.edu.
Diving: Jame Donoghue; Phone: 802-654-2500; E-mail: jdonoghue@smcvt.edu.
Field Hockey: Carla Hesler; Phone: 802-654-2634; E-mail: chesler@smcvt.edu.
Lacrosse: Carla Hesler; Phone: 802-654-2725; E-mail: chesler@smcvt.edu.
Soccer: Marcel Choquette; Phone: 802-654-2903; E-mail: mchoquette@smcvt.edu.
Softball: Robyn Newton; Phone: 802-654-2676; E-mail: rnewton@smcvt.edu.
Swimming: Jame Donoghue; Phone: 802-654-2500; E-mail: jdonoghue@smcvt.edu.
Tennis: Greg Cluff; Phone: 802-654-2725; E-mail: gcluff@smcvt.edu.
Volleyball: J.P. Farineau; Phone: 802-654-2498; E-mail: jfarineau@smcvt.edu.

ST. NORBERT COLLEGE
De Pere, Wisconsin

Green Knights ◆ NCAA III ◆ Midwest Conference; Northern Collegiate Hockey Conference ◆ http://www.snc.edu/

Independent Roman Catholic comprehensive, founded 1898
Coed, 2,086 undergraduate students, 96% full-time, 57% women, 43% men
Suburban 92-acre campus
Moderately difficult entrance level, 82% of applicants were admitted

Freshmen *Admission:* 1,658 applied, 1,432 were accepted, 529 enrolled.
Tuition and fees (2004–05): $21,510 (full-time). *Room and board:* $5980 (room only: $3160).
Financial Aid (All incoming freshmen): *Average need-based gift aid:* $12,245. *Average non-need based aid:* $11,262. *Average aid to full-time undergraduates:* $15,813.
Athletic Department: *Director of Athletics:* Don Maslinski; Phone: 920-403-3128; Fax: 920-403-3128; E-mail: don.maslinski@snc.edu. *Sports Information Director:* Dan Lukes; Phone: 920-403-3031; E-mail: lukedr@mail.snc.edu.

MEN'S COACHES
Baseball: Tom Winske; Phone: 920-403-3345.
Basketball: Paul DeNoble; Phone: 920-403-3137; E-mail: paul.denoble@snc.edu.
Cheerleading: Cheryl Reed; Phone: 920-403-3030; E-mail: cheryl.reed@snc.edu.
Cross Country: Joe Dunham; Phone: 920-403-3547; E-mail: jerome.feldhausen@snc.edu.
Football: Jim Purtill; Phone: 920-403-3172; E-mail: james.purtill@snc.edu.
Golf: Paul DeNoble; Phone: 920-403-3137; E-mail: paul.denoble@snc.edu.
Ice Hockey: Tim Coghlin; Phone: 920-403-2025; E-mail: tim.coghlin@snc.edu.
Soccer: Dale Rhodes; Phone: 920-403-3546; E-mail: dale.rhodes@snc.edu.
Tennis: Dave Shalkhauser; Phone: 920-403-3928; E-mail: dave.shalkhauser@snc.edu.
Track and Field: Joe Dunham; Phone: 920-403-3456; E-mail: joseph.dunham@snc.edu.

WOMEN'S COACHES
Basketball: Connie Tilley; Phone: 920-403-3033; E-mail: connie.tilley@snc.edu.
Cheerleading: Cheryl Reed; Phone: 920-403-3030; E-mail: cheryl.reed@snc.edu.
Cross Country: Nancy Gritt; Phone: 920-403-3521; E-mail: nancy.gritt@snc.edu.
Golf: Connie Tilley; Phone: 920-403-3033; E-mail: connie.tilley@snc.edu.
Soccer: Dennis Detrie; Phone: 920-403-3031; E-mail: dennis.detrie@snc.edu.
Softball: JoAnn Krueger; Phone: 920-403-4080; E-mail: joann.krueger@snc.edu.
Swimming: Jeremy Moeller; Phone: 920-403-3031.
Tennis: Kathryn Ullman; Phone: 920-403-3031; E-mail: kathryn.petersen@snc.edu.
Track and Field: Joe Dunham; Phone: 920-403-3547.
Volleyball: Lori Sadewater; Phone: 920-403-3138; E-mail: lori.sadewater@snc.edu.

ST. OLAF COLLEGE
Northfield, Minnesota

Oles ◆ NCAA III ◆ Minnesota Intercollegiate Athletic Conference ◆ http://www.stolaf.edu/

Independent Lutheran 4-year, founded 1874
Coed, 2,994 undergraduate students, 98% full-time, 59% women, 41% men
Small-town 300-acre campus with easy access to Minneapolis-St. Paul
Very difficult entrance level, 77% of applicants were admitted

Freshmen *Admission:* 2,517 applied, 1,894 were accepted, 720 enrolled.
Test scores: SAT verbal scores over 500: 95%; SAT math scores over 500: 95%; SAT verbal scores over 600: 70%; SAT math scores over 600: 72%; SAT verbal scores over 700: 26%; SAT math scores over 700: 21%.
Tuition and fees (2004–05): $25,150 (full-time). *Room and board:* $5800 (room only: $2750).
Financial Aid (All incoming freshmen): *Average need-based gift aid:* $12,834. *Average non-need based aid:* $6137. *Average aid to full-time undergraduates:* $18,186.
Athletic Department: *Director of Athletics:* Matt McDonald; Phone: 507-646-3638; Fax: 507-646-3572; E-mail: mcdonamc@stolaf.edu. *Sports Information Director:* LeAnn Finger; Phone: 507-646-3834; E-mail: finger@stolaf.edu.

MEN'S COACHES
Baseball: Matt McDonald; Phone: 507-646-3638; E-mail: mcdonamc@stolaf.edu.
Basketball: Dan Kosmoski; Phone: 507-646-3252; E-mail: kosmoski@stolaf.edu.
Cross Country: Bill Thornton; Phone: 507-646-3256; E-mail: thorntow@stolaf.edu.
Diving: Dave Hauck; Phone: 507-646-3259; E-mail: hauckd@stolaf.edu.
Football: Chris Meidt; Phone: 507-646-3768; E-mail: meidt@stolaf.edu.
Golf: LeAnn Finger; Phone: 507-646-3834; E-mail: finger@stolaf.edu.
Ice Hockey: Sean Goldsworthy; Phone: 507-646-3456; E-mail: goldswor@stolaf.edu.
Soccer: Kurt Anderson; Phone: 507-646-3253; E-mail: anderk@stolaf.edu.
Swimming: Dave Hauck; Phone: 507-646-3259; E-mail: hauckd@stolaf.edu.
Tennis: Scott Nesbit; Phone: 507-646-3812; E-mail: nesbit@stolaf.edu.
Track and Field: Bill Thornton; Phone: 507-646-3256; E-mail: thorntow@stolaf.edu.
Wrestling: Ken Pratt; Phone: 507-646-3409; E-mail: prattk@stolaf.edu.

WOMEN'S COACHES
Basketball: Pat Buresh; Phone: 507-646-3258; E-mail: buresh@stolaf.edu.
Cross Country: Chris Daymont; Phone: 507-646-3810; E-mail: daymont@stolaf.edu.
Diving: Dave Hauck; Phone: 507-646-3259; E-mail: hauckd@stolaf.edu.
Golf: Leann Finger; Phone: 507-646-3834; E-mail: finger@stolaf.edu.
Soccer: Kurt Anderson; Phone: 507-646-3253; E-mail: anderk@stolaf.edu.
Softball: Lori Cooling; Phone: 507-646-3975; E-mail: littleto@stolaf.edu.
Swimming: Dave Hauck; Phone: 507-646-3259; E-mail: hauckd@stolaf.edu.
Tennis: Scott Nesbit; Phone: 507-646-3812; E-mail: nesbit@stolaf.edu.
Track and Field: Chris Daymont; Phone: 507-646-3810; E-mail: daymont@stolaf.edu.
Volleyball: Traci Cook; Phone: 507-646-3250; E-mail: tracilynncook@hotmail.com.

SAINT PAUL'S COLLEGE
Lawrenceville, Virginia

Tigers ◆ NCAA II ◆ Central Intercollegiate Athletic Conference ◆ http://www.saintpauls.edu/

Independent Episcopal 4-year, founded 1888
Coed, 531 undergraduate students
Small-town 75-acre campus with easy access to Richmond
Minimally difficult entrance level, 87% of applicants were admitted

Freshmen *Admission:* 408 applied, 359 were accepted.
Tuition and fees (2003–04): $9156 (full-time). *Room and board:* $5187.
Financial Aid (All incoming freshmen): *Average need-based gift aid:* $4969. *Average aid to full-time undergraduates:* $8273.
Athletic Department: *Director of Athletics:* Fax: 434-848-2001. *Sports Information Director:* Tiffani-Dawn Sykes; Phone: 434-848-1828; E-mail: tsykes@saintpauls.edu.

MEN'S COACHES
Baseball: Oliver Harrison; Phone: 434-848-1828; E-mail: athletics@saintpauls.edu.
Basketball: Jerry Seale; Phone: 434-848-1831; E-mail: athletics@saintpauls.edu.
Cross Country: Ralph Hawkins; Phone: 434-848-6440; E-mail: rhawkins@saintpauls.edu.

Football: Bob Smith; Phone: 434-848-6494; E-mail: bsmith@saintpauls.edu.
Golf: Phone: 434-848-1828; E-mail: athletics@saintpauls.edu.
Tennis: Joe Carey; Phone: 434-848-1828; E-mail: athletics@saintpauls.edu.
Track and Field: Ralph Hawkins; Phone: 434-848-6440; E-mail: rhawkins@saintpauls.edu.

WOMEN'S COACHES

Basketball: Anthony Portley; Phone: 434-848-1832; E-mail: athletics@saintpauls.edu.
Cross Country: Ralph Hawkins; Phone: 434-848-6440; E-mail: rhawkins@saintpauls.edu.
Golf: Phone: 434-848-1828; E-mail: athletics@saintpauls.edu.
Softball: John Hill; Phone: 434-848-1828; E-mail: athletics@saintpauls.edu.
Tennis: Joe Carey; Phone: 434-848-1828; E-mail: athletics@saintpauls.edu.
Track and Field: Ralph Hawkins; Phone: 434-848-6440; E-mail: rhawkins@saintpauls.edu.
Volleyball: Arila Washington; Phone: 434-848-1828; E-mail: athletics@saintpauls.edu.

SAINT PETER'S COLLEGE
Jersey City, New Jersey

Peacocks ◆ NCAA I ◆ Metro Atlantic Athletic Conference ◆ http://www.spc.edu/

Independent Roman Catholic (Jesuit) comprehensive, founded 1872
Coed, 2,000 undergraduate students
Urban 15-acre campus with easy access to New York City
Moderately difficult entrance level, 67% of applicants were admitted

Freshmen *Admission:* 2,041 applied, 1,359 were accepted. *Test scores:* SAT verbal scores over 500: 29%; SAT math scores over 500: 36%; SAT verbal scores over 600: 6%; SAT math scores over 600: 8%; SAT verbal scores over 700: 1%; SAT math scores over 700: 1%.
Tuition and fees (2003–04): $18,592 (full-time). *Room and board:* $7800 (room only: $4933).
Financial Aid (All incoming freshmen): *Average need-based gift aid:* $8171. *Average non-need based aid:* $7776. *Average aid to full-time undergraduates:* $15,190.
Athletic Department: *Director of Athletics:* William Stein; Phone: 201-915-9100; Fax: 201-915-9102. *Sports Information Director:* Tim Camp; Phone: 201-915-9100.

MEN'S COACHES

Baseball: Jimmy Walsh; Phone: 201-915-9100.
Basketball: Bob Leckie; Phone: 201-915-9103.
Cheerleading: Juli Peterson; Phone: 201-915-9300.
Cross Country: Bob Oppici; Phone: 201-915-9090.
Diving: Tom Romano; Phone: 201-915-9110; E-mail: tromano@spc.edu.
Football: Scott Kochman; Phone: 201-915-9300.
Golf: John Koblan; Phone: 201-915-9100.
Soccer: Phone: 201-915-9068.
Swimming: Tom Romano; Phone: 201-915-9110; E-mail: tromano@spc.edu.
Tennis: Michael Scolamieri; Phone: 201-915-9109.
Track and Field: Bob Oppici; Phone: 201-915-9090.

WOMEN'S COACHES

Basketball: Mike Granelli; Phone: 201-915-9118; E-mail: sdewolfe@spc.edu.
Cheerleading: Juli Peterson; Phone: 201-915-9300.
Cross Country: Jana Burton; Phone: 201-915-9090.
Diving: Tom Romano; Phone: 201-915-9110; E-mail: tromano@spc.edu.
Soccer: Elizabeth Roper; Phone: 201-915-9108.
Softball: Jeff Horohonich; Phone: 201-915-9125.
Swimming: Tom Romano; Phone: 201-915-9110; E-mail: tromano@spc.edu.
Tennis: Dave Cortez; Phone: 201-915-9100.
Track and Field: Jana Burton; Phone: 201-915-9090.
Volleyball: Mikhail Sigalov; Phone: 201-915-7208; E-mail: msigalov@spc.edu.

ST. THOMAS AQUINAS COLLEGE
Sparkill, New York

Spartans ◆ NCAA II ◆ New York Collegiate Athletic Conference ◆ http://www.stac.edu/

Independent comprehensive, founded 1952
Coed, 2,148 undergraduate students, 63% full-time, 58% women, 42% men
Suburban 46-acre campus with easy access to New York City
Moderately difficult entrance level, 74% of applicants were admitted

Freshmen *Admission:* 1,269 applied, 947 were accepted, 343 enrolled. *Test scores:* SAT verbal scores over 500: 35%; SAT math scores over 500: 33%; SAT verbal scores over 600: 8%; SAT math scores over 600: 8%; SAT verbal scores over 700: 1%; SAT math scores over 700: 1%.
Tuition and fees (2004–05): $15,700 (full-time). *Room and board:* $8590 (room only: $4640).
Athletic Department: *Director of Athletics:* Gerald Oswald; Phone: 845-398-4186; Fax: 845-398-4071; E-mail: goswald@stac.edu. *Sports Information Director:* Michael McManus; Phone: 845-398-4091; E-mail: mmcmanus@stac.edu.

MEN'S COACHES

Baseball: Scott Muscat; Phone: 845-398-4027; E-mail: smuscat@stac.edu.
Basketball: Dennis O'Donnell; Phone: 845-398-4056; E-mail: dodonnel@stac.edu.
Cross Country: John O'Donnell; Phone: 845-398-4053; E-mail: jodonnel@stac.edu.
Golf: Ken Bortner; Phone: 845-398-4186.
Soccer: Graham Brown; Phone: 845-398-4163.

WOMEN'S COACHES

Basketball: Mike McManus; Phone: 845-398-4091; E-mail: mmcmanus@stac.edu.
Cross Country: John O'Donnell; Phone: 845-398-4053; E-mail: jodonnel@stac.edu.
Lacrosse: Chris Grange; Phone: 845-398-4085.
Soccer: Al Moroni; Phone: 845-398-4163; E-mail: amoroni@stac.edu.
Softball: Tom Slocum; Phone: 845-398-4053.
Tennis: Vincent Ceci; Phone: 845-398-4085; E-mail: vceci@stac.edu.
Volleyball: Dan Altro; Phone: 845-398-4058.

ST. THOMAS UNIVERSITY
Miami Gardens, Florida

Bobcats ◆ NAIA ◆ Florida Sun Conference ◆ http://www.stu.edu/

Independent Roman Catholic comprehensive, founded 1961
Coed, 1,171 undergraduate students, 93% full-time, 61% women, 39% men
Suburban 140-acre campus
Moderately difficult entrance level, 57% of applicants were admitted

Freshmen *Admission:* 818 applied, 349 were accepted, 209 enrolled. *Test scores:* SAT verbal scores over 500: 22%; SAT math scores over 500: 25%; SAT verbal scores over 600: 2%; SAT math scores over 600: 6%; SAT verbal scores over 700: 1%.
Tuition and fees (2003–04): $16,200 (full-time). *Room and board:* $10,200.
Financial Aid (All incoming freshmen): *Average non-need based aid:* $5000.
Athletic Department: *Director of Athletics:* Laura Courtley-Todd; Phone: 305-625-6677; Fax: 305-628-6591; E-mail: lcourtle@stu.edu. *Sports Information Director:* Ross Devonport; Phone: 305-628-6681; E-mail: rdevonport@stu.edu.

MEN'S COACHES

Baseball: Manny Mantrana; Phone: 305-628-6730; E-mail: jhoerner@stu.edu.
Cross Country: Adrian Melero; Phone: 305-474-6678; E-mail: coachamelero@aol.com.
Golf: Michael Moore; Phone: 305-474-6678; E-mail: moorem815@aol.com.
Soccer: Fernando Valenzuela; Phone: 305-628-6679; E-mail: fvalenzuela@stu.edu.

St. Thomas University (*continued*)

Tennis: Bruce Carrington; Phone: 305-474-6816; E-mail: tenitron@aol.com.

WOMEN'S COACHES

Cross Country: Adrian Melero; Phone: 305-474-6678; E-mail: coachamelero@aol.com.
Soccer: Jeff Hoerner; Phone: 305-474-6889; E-mail: jhoerner@stu.edu.
Tennis: Bruce Carrington; Phone: 305-474-6816; E-mail: tenitron@aol.com.
Volleyball: Hector Martinez; Phone: 305-628-6680; E-mail: stuvolleyball@hotmail.com.

SAINT VINCENT COLLEGE
Latrobe, Pennsylvania

Bearcats ◆ NAIA ◆ American Mideast Conference ◆ http://www.stvincent.edu/

Independent Roman Catholic comprehensive, founded 1846
Coed, 1,440 undergraduate students, 88% full-time, 50% women, 50% men
Suburban 200-acre campus with easy access to Pittsburgh
Moderately difficult entrance level, 90% of applicants were admitted

Freshmen *Admission:* 1,327 applied, 989 were accepted, 361 enrolled. *Test scores:* SAT verbal scores over 500: 72%; SAT math scores over 500: 68%; SAT verbal scores over 600: 22%; SAT math scores over 600: 25%; SAT verbal scores over 700: 3%; SAT math scores over 700: 3%.
Tuition and fees (2003–04): $19,470 (full-time). *Room and board:* $6060 (room only: $3080).
Financial Aid (All incoming freshmen): *Average need-based gift aid:* $11,031. *Average non-need based aid:* $6616. *Average aid to full-time undergraduates:* $15,176.
Athletic Department: *Director of Athletics:* Myron Kirsch; Phone: 724-805-2111; Fax: 724-532-5050; E-mail: myron.kirsch@email.stvincent.edu. *Sports Information Director:* Jeff Zidek; Phone: 724-805-2476; E-mail: jeff.zidek@email.stvincent.edu.

MEN'S COACHES

Baseball: Mick Janosko; Phone: 724-532-6600.
Basketball: D.P. Harris; Phone: 724-532-6600; E-mail: dharris@email.stvincent.edu.
Cross Country: Andy Herr; Phone: 724-532-6600; E-mail: andy.herr@email.stvincent.edu.
Golf: Thomas Cline; Phone: 724-532-6600; E-mail: thomas.cline@email.stvincent.edu.
Lacrosse: Peter Tulk; Phone: 724-532-6600.
Soccer: Keith Harmon; Phone: 724-532-6600; E-mail: keith.harmon@email.stvincent.edu.
Tennis: Keith Harmon; Phone: 724-532-6600; E-mail: enrico.campi@email.stvincent.edu.

WOMEN'S COACHES

Basketball: Kristen Zawacki; Phone: 724-532-6600; E-mail: kristen.zawacki@email.stvincent.edu.
Cross Country: Tom Harbert; Phone: 724-532-6600; E-mail: tom.harbert@email.stvincent.edu.
Golf: Thomas Cline; Phone: 724-532-6600; E-mail: thomas.cline@email.stvincent.edu.
Lacrosse: Tom Harbert; Phone: 724-532-6600; E-mail: tom.harbert@email.stvincent.edu.
Soccer: Keith Harmon; Phone: 724-532-6600; E-mail: keith.harmon@email.stvincent.edu.
Softball: Kristen Zawacki; Phone: 724-532-6600; E-mail: kristen.zawacki@email.stvincent.edu.
Tennis: James Bendel; Phone: 724-532-6600.

SAINT XAVIER UNIVERSITY
Chicago, Illinois

Cougars ◆ NAIA ◆ Chicagoland Collegiate Conference ◆ http://www.sxu.edu/

Independent Roman Catholic comprehensive, founded 1847
Coed, 3,062 undergraduate students, 76% full-time, 71% women, 29% men
Urban 70-acre campus
Moderately difficult entrance level, 7% of applicants were admitted

Freshmen *Admission:* 1,701 applied, 1,159 were accepted, 384 enrolled.
Tuition and fees (2003–04): $16,680 (full-time). *Room and board:* $6464 (room only: $3688).
Financial Aid (All incoming freshmen): *Average need-based gift aid:* $10,123. *Average non-need based aid:* $4297. *Average aid to full-time undergraduates:* $15,197.
Athletic Department: *Director of Athletics:* Bob Hallberg; Phone: 773-298-3109; Fax: 773-298-3111; E-mail: hallberg@sxu.edu. *Sports Information Director:* Rob Huizenga; Phone: 773-298-3110; E-mail: huizenga@sxu.edu.

MEN'S COACHES

Baseball: Mike Dooley; Phone: 773-298-3103; E-mail: dooley@sxu.edu.
Basketball: Tom O'Malley; Phone: 773-298-3104; E-mail: omalley@sxu.edu.
Cheerleading: Amy Ballard; Phone: 773-298-3101; E-mail: a.ballard@mail.sxu.edu.
Football: Mike Feminis; Phone: 773-298-3107; E-mail: feminis@sxu.edu.
Soccer: Henry Barsch; Phone: 773-298-3775; E-mail: barsch@sxu.edu.

WOMEN'S COACHES

Basketball: Bob Hallberg; Phone: 773-298-3109; E-mail: hallberg@sxu.edu.
Cheerleading: Amy Ballard; Phone: 773-298-3101; E-mail: a.ballard@mail.sxu.edu.
Cross Country: Karen Clifton; Phone: 773-298-3101; E-mail: hallberg@sxu.edu.
Soccer: Derek Begich; Phone: 773-298-3112; E-mail: begich@sxu.edu.
Softball: Myra Minuskin; Phone: 773-298-3100; E-mail: minuskin@sxu.edu.
Volleyball: Bob Heersema; Phone: 773-298-3105; E-mail: heersema@sxu.edu.

SALEM INTERNATIONAL UNIVERSITY
Salem, West Virginia

Tigers ◆ NCAA II ◆ West Virginia Intercollegiate Athletic Conference ◆ http://www.salemiu.edu/

Independent comprehensive, founded 1888
Coed, 443 undergraduate students, 81% full-time, 47% women, 53% men
Rural 300-acre campus
Minimally difficult entrance level, 99% of applicants were admitted

Freshmen *Admission:* 251 applied, 249 were accepted, 51 enrolled. *Test scores:* SAT verbal scores over 500: 50%; SAT math scores over 500: 67%; SAT verbal scores over 600: 7%; SAT math scores over 600: 17%.
Tuition and fees (2003–04): $15,005 (full-time). *Room and board:* $4785 (room only: $1845).
Financial Aid (All incoming freshmen): *Average need-based gift aid:* $5268. *Average non-need based aid:* $9803. *Average aid to full-time undergraduates:* $18,575.
Athletic Department: *Director of Athletics:* Lou Talerico; Phone: 304-782-5573; Fax: 304-782-5516; E-mail: talerico@salemiu.edu. *Sports Information Director:* David Zinn; Phone: 304-782-5602; E-mail: dzinn@salemiu.edu.

MEN'S COACHES

Baseball: Rich Leitch; Phone: 304-782-5632; E-mail: leitch@salemiu.edu.

Basketball: Clark Malone; Phone: 304-782-5379; E-mail: maloney@salemiu.edu.
Cross Country: Ron Weist; Phone: 304-782-5299; E-mail: weist@salemiu.edu.
Golf: Lou Talerico; Phone: 304-782-5573; E-mail: talerico@salemiu.edu.
Soccer: Florin Marton; Phone: 304-782-5252; E-mail: marton@salemiu.edu.
Swimming: Keith Bullion; Phone: 304-782-5262; E-mail: bullion@salemiu.edu.
Tennis: Florin Martin; Phone: 304-782-5252; E-mail: marton@salemiu.edu.

WOMEN'S COACHES

Basketball: David Zinn; Phone: 304-782-5602; E-mail: dzinn@salemiu.edu.
Cross Country: Ron Weist; Phone: 304-782-5299; E-mail: weist@salemiu.edu
Soccer: Glenn Beggin; Phone: 304-782-5646; E-mail: beggin@salemiu.edu.
Softball: Amy Schmaltz; Phone: 304-782-5394; E-mail: schmaltz@salemiu.edu.
Swimming: Keith Bullion; Phone: 304-782-5262; E-mail: bullion@salemiu.edu.
Volleyball: Amy Schmaltz; Phone: 304-782-5394; E-mail: schmaltz@salemiu.edu.

SALEM STATE COLLEGE
Salem, Massachusetts

Vikings ◆ NCAA III ◆ Little East Conference; Massachusetts State College Athletic Conference
◆ http://www.salemstate.edu/

State-supported comprehensive, founded 1854, part of Massachusetts Public Higher Education System
Coed, 6,508 undergraduate students, 72% full-time, 64% women, 36% men
Small-town 62-acre campus with easy access to Boston
Minimally difficult entrance level, 78% of applicants were admitted

Freshmen *Admission:* 4,018 applied, 3,313 were accepted, 1,016 enrolled. *Test scores:* SAT verbal scores over 500: 40%; SAT math scores over 500: 37%; SAT verbal scores over 600: 8%; SAT math scores over 600: 6%; SAT verbal scores over 700: 1%; SAT math scores over 700: %.
Tuition and fees (2003–04): $5038 (resident), $11,178 (nonresident). *Room and board:* $5940.
Financial Aid (All incoming freshmen): *Average need-based gift aid:* $4882. *Average non-need based aid:* $838. *Average aid to full-time undergraduates:* $3680.
Athletic Department: *Director of Athletics:* Tim Shea; Phone: 978-542-6517; Fax: 978-542-2926. *Sports Information Director:* Thomas Roundy; Phone: 978-542-6549.

MEN'S COACHES

Baseball: Ken Perrone; Phone: 978-542-6622; E-mail: kenneth.perrone@salemstate.edu.
Basketball: Sean Doherty; Phone: 978-542-6564; E-mail: sdoherty@salemstate.edu.
Cross Country: Dennis Floyd; Phone: 978-542-6233; E-mail: dennis.floyd@salemstate.edu.
Golf: Steve Campbell; Phone: 978-542-6570; E-mail: steve.campbell@salemstate.edu.
Ice Hockey: Bill O'Neill; Phone: 978-542-6575; E-mail: william.oneil@salemstate.edu.
Soccer: Mike Kersker; Phone: 978-542-6570; E-mail: michael.kersker@salemstate.edu.
Tennis: Greg Labelle; Phone: 978-542-6570; E-mail: greg.labelle@salemstate.edu.
Track and Field: Dennis Floyd; Phone: 978-542-6233; E-mail: dennis.floyd@salemstate.edu.

WOMEN'S COACHES

Basketball: Tim Shea; Phone: 978-542-6517; E-mail: timothy.shea@salemstate.edu.
Cross Country: Dennis Floyd; Phone: 978-542-6233; E-mail: dennis.floyd@salemstate.edu.

Field Hockey: Holly Brennan Sheehan; Phone: 978-542-6570; E-mail: holly.sheehan@salemstate.edu.
Soccer: Alvaro Ibanez; Phone: 978-542-6570; E-mail: alvaro.ibanez@salemstate.edu.
Softball: Wendy Rogers; Phone: 978-542-6569; E-mail: wendy.rogers@salemstate.edu.
Tennis: Joe Dunn; Phone: 978-542-6537; E-mail: joseph.dunn@salemstate.edu.
Track and Field: Dennis Floyd; Phone: 978-542-6233; E-mail: dennis.floyd@salemstate.edu.
Volleyball: Bette Bailey; Phone: 978-542-6586; E-mail: bette.bailey@salemstate.edu.

SALISBURY UNIVERSITY
Salisbury, Maryland

Seagulls ◆ NCAA III ◆ Capital Athletic Conference ◆ http://www.ssu.edu/

State-supported comprehensive, founded 1925, part of University System of Maryland
Coed, 6,199 undergraduate students, 88% full-time, 57% women, 43% men
Small-town 144-acre campus
Moderately difficult entrance level, 2% of applicants were admitted

Freshmen *Admission:* 5,550 applied, 950 were accepted, 950 enrolled. *Test scores:* SAT verbal scores over 500: 84%; SAT math scores over 500: 90%; SAT verbal scores over 600: 25%; SAT math scores over 600: 38%; SAT verbal scores over 700: 2%; SAT math scores over 700: 4%.
Tuition and fees (2003–04): $6994 (resident), $13,882 (nonresident). *Room and board:* $6900 (room only: $3350).
Financial Aid (All incoming freshmen): *Average need-based gift aid:* $3925. *Average non-need based aid:* $3126. *Average aid to full-time undergraduates:* $5379.
Athletic Department: *Director of Athletics:* Michael Vienna; Phone: 410-548-3503; Fax: 410-546-2639; E-mail: mpvienna@salisbury.edu. *Sports Information Director:* Paul Ohanian; Phone: 410-543-6016; E-mail: gpohanian@salisbury.edu.

MEN'S COACHES

Baseball: Doug Fleetwood; Phone: 410-543-6034; E-mail: edfleetwood@salisbury.edu.
Basketball: Steve Holmes; Phone: 410-548-4163; E-mail: smholmes@salisbury.edu.
Cheerleading: Pam Phillips; Phone: 410-548-3503; E-mail: pnprocks@aol.com.
Cross Country: Jim Jones; Phone: 410-543-6337; E-mail: jajones@salisbury.edu.
Football: Sherman Wood; Phone: 410-543-6356; E-mail: slwood@salisbury.edu.
Lacrosse: Jim Berkman; Phone: 410-543-6389; E-mail: jjberkman@salisbury.edu.
Soccer: Gerry Dibartolo; Phone: 410-548-5338; E-mail: grdibartolo@salisbury.edu.
Swimming: Jill Stephenson; Phone: 410-543-6357; E-mail: jastephenson@salisbury.edu.
Tennis: Randy Halfpap; Phone: 410-543-6248; E-mail: rbhalfpap@salisbury.edu.
Track and Field: Jim Jones; Phone: 410-543-6337; E-mail: jajones@salisbury.edu.

WOMEN'S COACHES

Basketball: Bridget Benshetler; Phone: 410-543-6003; E-mail: babenshetler@salisbury.edu.
Cheerleading: Pam Phillips; Phone: 410-548-3503; E-mail: pnprocks@aol.com.
Cross Country: Jim Jones; Phone: 410-543-6337; E-mail: jajones@salisbury.edu.
Field Hockey: Dawn Chamberlin; Phone: 410-548-2588; E-mail: drchamberlin@salisbury.edu.
Lacrosse: Jim Nestor; Phone: 410-677-5338; E-mail: jpnestor@salisbury.edu.
Soccer: Jim Nestor; Phone: 410-677-5338; E-mail: jpnestor@salisbury.edu.
Softball: Margie Knight; Phone: 410-543-6352; E-mail: mjknight@salisbury.edu.

Salisbury University *(continued)*

Swimming: Jill Stephenson; Phone: 410-543-6357; E-mail: jastephenson@salisbury.edu.
Tennis: Randy Halfpap; Phone: 410-543-6248; E-mail: rbhalfpap@salisbury.edu.
Track and Field: Jim Jones; Phone: 410-543-6337; E-mail: jajones@salisbury.edu.
Volleyball: Margie Knight; Phone: 410-543-6352; E-mail: mjknight@salisbury.edu.

SALVE REGINA UNIVERSITY
Newport, Rhode Island

Seahawks ◆ NCAA III ◆ Commonwealth Coast Conference; New England Football Conference; New England Women's Lacrosse Conference ◆ http://www.salve.edu/

Independent Roman Catholic comprehensive, founded 1934
Coed, 2,026 undergraduate students, 95% full-time, 69% women, 31% men
Suburban 70-acre campus with easy access to Boston and Providence
Moderately difficult entrance level, 52% of applicants were admitted

Freshmen *Admission:* 4,131 applied, 2,294 were accepted, 571 enrolled. *Test scores:* SAT verbal scores over 500: 76%; SAT math scores over 500: 71%; SAT verbal scores over 600: 16%; SAT math scores over 600: 15%; SAT verbal scores over 700: 1%.
Tuition and fees (2003–04): $20,510 (full-time). *Room and board:* $8700.
Financial Aid (All incoming freshmen): *Average need-based gift aid:* $12,283. *Average non-need based aid:* $9919. *Average aid to full-time undergraduates:* $16,383.
Athletic Department: *Director of Athletics:* Del Malloy; Phone: 401-341-2268; Fax: 401-341-2907; E-mail: malloyd@salve.edu. *Sports Information Director:* Ed Habershaw; Phone: 401-341-2271; E-mail: habershe@salve.edu.

MEN'S COACHES
Baseball: Steve Cirella; Phone: 401-341-2267.
Basketball: Sean Foster; Phone: 401-341-2257; E-mail: fosters@salve.edu.
Football: Art Bell; Phone: 401-341-3264.
Ice Hockey: Chris MacPherson; Phone: 401-341-2242.
Lacrosse: Pascale Musto; Phone: 401-847-6650.
Soccer: Keith Cory; Phone: 401-341-2273; E-mail: coryk@salve.edu.
Tennis: Brian Shanley; Phone: 401-341-3166; E-mail: shanleyb@salve.edu.

WOMEN'S COACHES
Basketball: Amanda Van Voorhis; Phone: 401-341-2272; E-mail: vanvoora@salve.edu.
Cross Country: Pam St. Martin; Phone: 401-341-2458.
Field Hockey: Kristen Gangemi; Phone: 401-341-2427.
Lacrosse: Kristen Gangemi; Phone: 401-341-2269.
Soccer: Lisa Yenush; Phone: 401-341-2247; E-mail: yenushl@salve.edu.
Softball: Lisa Yenush; Phone: 401-341-2247; E-mail: yenushl@salve.edu.
Tennis: Meghan Daniels; Phone: 401-341-2333; E-mail: danielsm@salve.edu.
Track and Field: Mike Rogers; Phone: 401-341-2238.
Volleyball: Erin McGlove; Phone: 401-341-2239.

SAMFORD UNIVERSITY
Birmingham, Alabama

Bulldogs ◆ NCAA I ◆ Ohio Valley Conference ◆ http://www.samford.edu/

Independent Baptist university, founded 1841
Coed, 2,882 undergraduate students, 93% full-time, 64% women, 36% men
Suburban 180-acre campus
Moderately difficult entrance level, 86% of applicants were admitted

Freshmen *Admission:* 2,074 applied, 1,859 were accepted, 684 enrolled. *Test scores:* SAT verbal scores over 500: 85%; SAT math scores over 500: 83%; SAT verbal scores over 600: 35%; SAT math scores over 600: 38%; SAT verbal scores over 700: 10%; SAT math scores over 700: 6%.
Tuition and fees (2003–04): $13,154 (full-time). *Room and board:* $5244 (room only: $2554).
Financial Aid (All incoming freshmen): *Average need-based gift aid:* $7527. *Average non-need based aid:* $5584. *Average aid to full-time undergraduates:* $9977.
Athletic Department: *Director of Athletics:* Bob Roller; Phone: 205-726-2131; Fax: 205-726-2132; E-mail: rlroller@samford.edu. *Sports Information Director:* Everett Hutto; Phone: 205-726-2802; E-mail: eehutto@samford.edu.

MEN'S COACHES
Baseball: Tim Parenton; Phone: 205-726-2134; E-mail: tmparent@samford.edu.
Basketball: Jim Tillette; Phone: 205-726-2920; E-mail: jatillett@samford.edu.
Cross Country: Glenn McWaters; Phone: 205-726-2081; E-mail: jgmcwate@samford.edu.
Football: Bill Gray; Phone: 205-726-2575; E-mail: wagray@samford.edu.
Golf: Woody Eubanks; Phone: 205-726-2355; E-mail: wdeubank@samford.edu.
Tennis: Kemper Baker; Phone: 205-726-2592; E-mail: kwbaker@samford.edu.
Track and Field: Glenn McWaters; Phone: 205-726-2081; E-mail: jgmcwate@samford.edu.

WOMEN'S COACHES
Basketball: Mike Morris; Phone: 205-726-4072; E-mail: mwmorris@samford.edu.
Cross Country: Glenn McWaters; Phone: 205-726-2081; E-mail: jgmcwate@samford.edu.
Golf: Ian Thompson; Phone: 205-726-2942; E-mail: iithomps@samford.edu.
Soccer: Todd Yelton; Phone: 205-726-4039; E-mail: atyelton@samford.edu.
Softball: Beanie Ketcham; Phone: 205-726-2218; E-mail: laketcha@samford.edu.
Tennis: Terri Sisk; Phone: 205-726-4254; E-mail: tsisk@samford.edu.
Track and Field: Glenn McWaters; Phone: 205-726-2081; E-mail: jgmcwate@samford.edu.
Volleyball: Michelle Durban; Phone: 205-726-2969; E-mail: mldurban@samford.edu.

SAM HOUSTON STATE UNIVERSITY
Huntsville, Texas

Bearkats ◆ NCAA I ◆ Southland Conference ◆ http://www.shsu.edu/

State-supported university, founded 1879, part of The Texas State University System
Coed, 11,504 undergraduate students, 85% full-time, 58% women, 42% men
Small-town 1,256-acre campus with easy access to Houston
Moderately difficult entrance level, 73% of applicants were admitted

Freshmen *Admission:* 5,182 applied, 3,915 were accepted, 1,810 enrolled. *Test scores:* SAT verbal scores over 500: 54%; SAT math scores over 500: 56%; SAT verbal scores over 600: 13%; SAT math scores over 600: 12%; SAT verbal scores over 700: 1%; SAT math scores over 700: 1%.
Tuition and fees (2003–04): $3652 (resident), $10,732 (nonresident). *Room and board:* $4160 (room only: $2112).
Financial Aid (All Incoming freshmen): *Average need-based gift aid:* $3431. *Average non-need based aid:* $1884. *Average aid to full-time undergraduates:* $5158.
Athletic Department: *Director of Athletics:* Bobby Williams; Phone: 936-294-4205; Fax: 936-294-4266; E-mail: ath_brw@shsu.edu. *Sports Information Director:* Paul Ridings; Phone: 936-294-1764; E-mail: ridings@shsu.edu.

MEN'S COACHES
Baseball: Chris Rupp; Phone: 936-294-1731; E-mail: ath_cwr@shsu.edu.

Basketball: Bob Marlin; Phone: 936-294-1747; E-mail: ath_rlm@shsu.edu.
Cheerleading: Phone: 936-294-4239; E-mail: spirit@shsu.edu.
Cross Country: Curtis Collier; Phone: 936-294-3539; E-mail: ath_ccc@shsu.edu.
Football: Ron Randleman; Phone: 936-294-1735; E-mail: ath_rjr@shsu.edu.
Golf: Craig Rex; Phone: 936-294-1051; E-mail: ath_car@shsu.edu.
Track and Field: Curtis Collier; Phone: 936-294-3539; E-mail: ath_ccc@shsu.edu.

WOMEN'S COACHES

Basketball: Wooly Hatchell; Phone: 936-294-1994; E-mail: wooly@shsu.edu.
Cheerleading: Phone: 936-294-4239; E-mail: spirit@shsu.edu.
Cross Country: Curtis Collier; Phone: 936-294-3539; E-mail: ath_ccc@shsu.edu.
Golf: Craig Rex; Phone: 936-294-1051; E-mail: ath_car@shsu.edu.
Soccer: Marcia Oliveira; Phone: 936-294-1244; E-mail: ath_mxo@shsu.edu.
Softball: Bob Brock; Phone: 936-294-3920; E-mail: ath_rlb@shsu.edu.
Tennis: Scott Shankles; Phone: 936-294-1744; E-mail: ath_jss@shsu.edu.
Track and Field: Curtis Collier; Phone: 936-294-3539; E-mail: ath_ccc@shsu.edu.
Volleyball: Brenda Gray; Phone: 936-294-1736; E-mail: ath_bxg@shsu.edu.

SAN DIEGO STATE UNIVERSITY
San Diego, California

Aztecs ◆ NCAA I ◆ Mountain West Conference ◆ http://www.sdsu.edu/

State-supported university, founded 1897, part of California State University System
Coed, 27,345 undergraduate students, 79% full-time, 58% women, 42% men
Urban 300-acre campus
Moderately difficult entrance level, 5% of applicants were admitted

Freshmen *Admission:* 29,129 applied, 14,454 were accepted, 3,730 enrolled. *Test scores:* SAT verbal scores over 500: 66%; SAT math scores over 500: 75%; SAT verbal scores over 600: 17%; SAT math scores over 600: 26%; SAT verbal scores over 700: 1%; SAT math scores over 700: 2%.
Tuition and fees (2003–04): $2488 (resident), $10,948 (nonresident).
Room and board: $8787 (room only: $5096).
Financial Aid (All incoming freshmen): *Average need-based gift aid:* $3300. *Average non-need based aid:* $2200. *Average aid to full-time undergraduates:* $6300.
Athletic Department: *Director of Athletics:* Mike Bohn; Phone: 619-594-6357; Fax: 619-582-6541; E-mail: martel@mail.sdsu.edu. *Sports Information Director:* Kevin Klintworth; Phone: 619-594-5547; E-mail: kklintwo@mail.sdsu.edu.

MEN'S COACHES

Baseball: Tony Gwynn; Phone: 619-594-6889.
Basketball: Steve Fischer; Phone: 619-594-6249; E-mail: sfisher1@mail.sdsu.edu.
Cheerleading: Jennifer Robison; Phone: 760-788-2906; E-mail: jrobison@sdsucheer.com.
Football: Tom Craft; Phone: 619-594-6769; E-mail: aztecfootball@mail.sdsu.edu.
Golf: Dale Walker; Phone: 619-594-4334; E-mail: sdsumensgolf@cox.net.
Soccer: Lev Kirshner; Phone: 619-594-0136; E-mail: aztecsoccer@mail.sdsu.edu.
Tennis: Gene Carswell; Phone: 619-594-5084; E-mail: carswell@mail.sdsu.edu.

WOMEN'S COACHES

Basketball: Jim Tomey; Phone: 619-594-4095; E-mail: jtomey@mail.sdsu.edu.
Cheerleading: Jennifer Robison; Phone: 760-788-2906; E-mail: jrobison@sdsucheer.com.
Cross Country: Rahn Sheffield; Phone: 619-594-5514; E-mail: sheffiel@mail.sdsu.edu.

Diving: Deena Schmidt; Phone: 619-594-5883; E-mail: ddschmid@mail.sdsu.edu.
Golf: Felicia Brown; Phone: 619-594-7665; E-mail: fbrown@mail.sdsu.edu.
Soccer: Angela M orrison; Phone: 619-594-3749; E-mail: amorriso@mail.sdsu.edu.
Softball: Kathy Van Wyk; Phone: 619-594-1952; E-mail: vanwyk@mail.sdsu.edu.
Swimming: Deena Schmidt; Phone: 619-594-5883; E-mail: ddschmid@mail.sdsu.edu.
Tennis: Peter Mattera; Phone: 619-594-6505; E-mail: mattera@mail.sdsu.edu.
Track and Field: Rahn Sheffield; Phone: 619-594-5514; E-mail: sheffiel@mail.sdsu.edu.
Volleyball: Mark Warner; Phone: 619-594-5064; E-mail: warner@mail.sdsu.edu.

SAN FRANCISCO STATE UNIVERSITY
San Francisco, California

Gators ◆ NCAA II ◆ California Collegiate Athletic Conference; Rocky Mountain Athletic Conference ◆ http://www.sfsu.edu/

State-supported comprehensive, founded 1899, part of California State University System
Coed, 21,892 undergraduate students, 75% full-time, 59% women, 41% men
Urban 90-acre campus
Moderately difficult entrance level, 12% of applicants were admitted

Freshmen *Admission:* 16,221 applied, 10,417 were accepted, 2,499 enrolled. *Test scores:* SAT verbal scores over 500: 50%; SAT math scores over 500: 55%; SAT verbal scores over 600: 15%; SAT math scores over 600: 15%; SAT verbal scores over 700: 1%; SAT math scores over 700: 1%.
Tuition and fees (2003–04): $2498 (resident), $10,958 (nonresident).
Room and board: $8090 (room only: $5030).
Financial Aid (All incoming freshmen): *Average need-based gift aid:* $6136. *Average non-need based aid:* $1062. *Average aid to full-time undergraduates:* $8377.
Athletic Department: *Director of Athletics:* Michael Simpson; Phone: 415-338-2218; Fax: 415-338-1967; E-mail: msimpson@sfsu.edu. *Sports Information Director:* Joe Danahey; Phone: 415-338-1579; E-mail: joed@sfsu.edu.

MEN'S COACHES

Baseball: Matt Markovich; Phone: 415-338-1226; E-mail: mmarko@sfsu.edu.
Basketball: Charlie Thomas; Phone: 415-338-1729; E-mail: cltsfsumbb24@sfsu.edu.
Cheerleading: Dr. Saffold; Phone: 415-338-4920; E-mail: cheer@sfsu.edu.
Cross Country: John Johnson; Phone: 415-338-1561; E-mail: trackjj@sfsu.edu.
Soccer: Joe Hunter; Phone: 415-338-7571; E-mail: hunterj@sfsu.edu.
Swimming: Chris Culp; Phone: 415-338-2148; E-mail: cculp@sfsu.edu.
Track and Field: John Johnson; Phone: 415-338-1561; E-mail: trackjj@sfsu.edu.
Wrestling: Lars Jensen; Phone: 415-338-2301; E-mail: ljensen@sfsu.edu.

WOMEN'S COACHES

Basketball: Arden Kragalott; Phone: 415-338-1084; E-mail: kragalot@sfsu.edu.
Cheerleading: Dr. Saffold; Phone: 415-338-4920; E-mail: cheer@sfsu.edu.
Cross Country: John Johnson; Phone: 415-338-1561; E-mail: trackjj@sfsu.edu.
Soccer: Jack Hyde; Phone: 415-338-1804; E-mail: jhyde@sfsu.edu.
Softball: Kristi Lansford; Phone: 415-338-1063; E-mail: lansford@sfsu.edu.
Swimming: Chris Culp; Phone: 415-338-2148; E-mail: cculp@sfsu.edu.
Tennis: Marla Reid; Phone: 415-338-2219; E-mail: mreid@sfsu.edu.
Track and Field: John Johnson; Phone: 415-338-1561; E-mail: trackjj@sfsu.edu.
Volleyball: Heather Sisneros; Phone: 415-338-2707; E-mail: sfsuvb@sfsu.edu.

SAN JOSE STATE UNIVERSITY
San Jose, California

Spartans ◆ NCAA I ◆ Western Athletic Conference ◆ http://www.sjsu.edu/

State-supported comprehensive, founded 1857, part of California State University System
Coed, 21,396 undergraduate students, 72% full-time, 51% women, 49% men
Urban 104-acre campus
Moderately difficult entrance level, 50% of applicants were admitted

Freshmen *Admission:* 13,065 applied, 6,785 were accepted, 1,978 enrolled. *Test scores:* SAT verbal scores over 500: 42%; SAT math scores over 500: 56%; SAT verbal scores over 600: 9%; SAT math scores over 600: 16%; SAT verbal scores over 700: %; SAT math scores over 700: 2%.
Tuition and fees (2003–04): $2562 (resident), $9330 (nonresident). *Room and board:* $8465.
Financial Aid (All incoming freshmen): *Average need-based gift aid:* $5523. *Average non-need based aid:* $3432. *Average aid to full-time undergraduates:* $6815.
Athletic Department: *Director of Athletics:* Chuck Bell; Phone: 408-924-1200; Fax: 408-924-1291; E-mail: cebell@email.sjsu.edu. *Sports Information Director:* Lawrence Fan; Phone: 408-924-1217; E-mail: ltfan@email.sjsu.edu.

MEN'S COACHES
Baseball: Sam Piraro; Phone: 408-924-1255.
Basketball: Phil Johnson; Phone: 408-924-1245.
Cheerleading: Jenise Mills; Phone: 408-924-1693; E-mail: cheercoach@sjsu.edu.
Cross Country: Augie Argabright; Phone: 408-924-1465; E-mail: sjsuspartancc@yahoo.com.
Football: Fitz Hill; Phone: 408-924-1266; E-mail: fitzhill@hotmail.com.
Golf: Nancy Lewis; Phone: 408-924-1206; E-mail: nlewis2@email.sjsu.edu.
Soccer: Gary St. Clair; Phone: 408-924-1261; E-mail: gstclair@email.sjsu.edu.

WOMEN'S COACHES
Basketball: Janice Richard; Phone: 408-924-1226; E-mail: jjrich@email.sjsu.edu.
Cheerleading: Jenise Mills; Phone: 408-924-1693; E-mail: cheercoach@sjsu.edu.
Cross Country: Augie Argabright; Phone: 408-924-1465; E-mail: sjsuspartancc@yahoo.com.
Diving: Phone: 408-924-1225.
Golf: Nancy Lewis; Phone: 408-924-1206; E-mail: nlewis2@email.sjsu.edu.
Gymnastics: Wayne Wright; Phone: 408-924-1390; E-mail: wwright@sjsu.edu.
Soccer: Dave Siracusa; Phone: 408-924-1718.
Softball: Dee Dee Enabenter; Phone: 408-924-1253; E-mail: aenabent@email.sjsu.edu.
Swimming: Victor Wales; Phone: 408-924-1225; E-mail: mnwales@aol.com.
Tennis: Anh-Dao Nguyen; Phone: 408-924-1327; E-mail: adn10s@yahoo.com.
Volleyball: Craig Choate; Phone: 408-924-1242; E-mail: cchoate@email.sjsu.edu.

SANTA CLARA UNIVERSITY
Santa Clara, California

Broncos ◆ NCAA I ◆ West Coast Conference ◆ http://www.scu.edu/

Independent Roman Catholic (Jesuit) university, founded 1851
Coed, 4,298 undergraduate students, 97% full-time, 55% women, 45% men
Suburban 104-acre campus with easy access to San Francisco and San Jose
Moderately difficult entrance level, 63% of applicants were admitted

Freshmen *Admission:* 6,388 applied, 4,223 were accepted, 897 enrolled. *Test scores:* SAT verbal scores over 500: 87%; SAT math scores over 500: 94%; SAT verbal scores over 600: 43%; SAT math scores over 600: 58%; SAT verbal scores over 700: 6%; SAT math scores over 700: 10%.
Tuition and fees (2003–04): $25,365 (full-time). *Room and board:* $9336.
Financial Aid (All incoming freshmen): *Average need-based gift aid:* $14,297. *Average non-need based aid:* $4971. *Average aid to full-time undergraduates:* $16,309.
Athletic Department: *Director of Athletics:* Jonathan Clough; Phone: 408-554-6920; Fax: 408-554-6969; E-mail: jclough@scu.edu. *Sports Information Director:* Lisa Eskey; Phone: 408-554-4659; E-mail: leskey@scu.edu.

MEN'S COACHES
Baseball: Mark O'Brien; Phone: 408-554-4680; E-mail: msobrien@scu.edu.
Basketball: Dick Davey; Phone: 408-554-4563; E-mail: rdavey@scu.edu.
Cheerleading: Cheryl Levick; Phone: 408-554-4063; E-mail: scucheer@yahoo.com.
Cross Country: John Maloney; Phone: 408-554-4886; E-mail: jmaloney@scu.edu.
Golf: John Kennady; Phone: 408-554-5741; E-mail: jkennaday@scu.edu.
Soccer: Cameron Rast; Phone: 408-554-4784; E-mail: crast@scu.edu.
Tennis: George Husack; Phone: 408-554-4069; E-mail: ghusack@scu.edu.

WOMEN'S COACHES
Basketball: Michelle Bento; Phone: 408-554-6988; E-mail: mbento@scu.edu.
Cheerleading: Cheryl Levick; Phone: 408-554-4063; E-mail: scucheer@yahoo.com.
Cross Country: Tom Service; Phone: 408-554-4688; E-mail: tservice@scu.edu.
Golf: Polly Schulze; Phone: 408-554-5742; E-mail: pschulze@scu.edu.
Soccer: Jerry Smith; Phone: 408-554-6989; E-mail: jsmith@scu.edu.
Softball: Marcy Crouch; Phone: 408-554-5063; E-mail: mcrouch@scu.edu.
Tennis: Tricia Guidace; Phone: 408-554-5761; E-mail: tguidace@scu.edu.
Volleyball: Jon Wallace; Phone: 408-554-6981; E-mail: jwallace@scu.edu.

SAVANNAH COLLEGE OF ART AND DESIGN
Savannah, Georgia

Bees ◆ NAIA ◆ Independent ◆ http://www.scad.edu/

Independent comprehensive, founded 1978
Coed, 5,318 undergraduate students, 91% full-time, 49% women, 51% men
Urban campus
Moderately difficult entrance level, 75% of applicants were admitted

Freshmen *Admission:* 3,515 applied, 2,648 were accepted, 1,041 enrolled. *Test scores:* SAT verbal scores over 500: 72%; SAT math scores over 500: 65%; SAT verbal scores over 600: 29%; SAT math scores over 600: 25%; SAT verbal scores over 700: 4%; SAT math scores over 700: 3%.
Tuition and fees (2004–05): $20,250 (full-time). *Room and board:* $8330 (room only: $5300).
Financial Aid (All incoming freshmen): *Average need-based gift aid:* $3019. *Average non-need based aid:* $3546. *Average aid to full-time undergraduates:* $7268.
Athletic Department: *Director of Athletics:* Jud Damon; Phone: 912-525-4781; Fax: 912-525-4814; E-mail: jdamon@scad.edu. *Sports Information Director:* Michael MacEachern; Phone: 912-525-4815; E-mail: mmaceach@scad.edu.

MEN'S COACHES
Baseball: Doug Wollenburg; Phone: 912-525-4782; E-mail: dwollenbu@scad.edu.
Basketball: Cazzie Russell; Phone: 912-525-4809; E-mail: crussell@scad.edu.
Cheerleading: Wayne Evans; Phone: 912-525-4780; E-mail: wevans@scad.edu.

Cross Country: Gabi Hauck; Phone: 912-525-6001; E-mail: ghauck@scad.edu.
Golf: Fred Fruisen; Phone: 912-525-4812; E-mail: golf@scad.edu.
Lacrosse: Mike Avery; Phone: 912-525-4810; E-mail: mavery@scad.edu.
Soccer: Bryan Thorp; Phone: 912-525-4816; E-mail: brthorp@scad.edu.
Swimming: Scott Rabalais; Phone: 912-525-4824; E-mail: srabalai@scad.edu.
Tennis: Chuck Keenan; Phone: 912-525-4817; E-mail: ckeenan@scad.edu.

WOMEN'S COACHES

Basketball: Eddie Concepcion; Phone: 912-525-4803; E-mail: econcepc@scad.edu.
Cheerleading: Wayne Evans; Phone: 912-525-4780; E-mail: wevans@scad.edu.
Cross Country: Gabi Hauck; Phone: 912-525-6001; E-mail: ghauck@scad.edu.
Golf: Amanda Workman; Phone: 912-525-4779; E-mail: aworkman@scad.edu.
Lacrosse: Phone: 912-525-4812.
Soccer: Andy Williamson; Phone: 912-525-4777; E-mail: anwillia@scad.edu.
Softball: Terri Knecht; Phone: 912-525-4825; E-mail: tknecht@scad.edu.
Swimming: Scott Rabalais; Phone: 912-525-4824; E-mail: srabalai@scad.edu.
Tennis: Chuck Keenan; Phone: 912-525-4817; E-mail: ckeenan@scad.edu.
Volleyball: Glenn Cox; Phone: 912-525-4806; E-mail: gcox@scad.edu.

SAVANNAH STATE UNIVERSITY
Savannah, Georgia

Tigers ◆ NCAA II ◆ Independent ◆ http://www.savstate.edu/

State-supported comprehensive, founded 1890, part of University System of Georgia
Coed, 2,595 undergraduate students, 85% full-time, 58% women, 42% men
Suburban 165-acre campus
Minimally difficult entrance level, 4% of applicants were admitted

Freshmen *Admission:* 3,220 applied, 1,192 were accepted, 631 enrolled. *Test scores:* SAT verbal scores over 500: 18%; SAT math scores over 500: 17%; SAT verbal scores over 600: 2%; SAT math scores over 600: 1%; SAT verbal scores over 700: %; SAT math scores over 700: %.
Tuition and fees (2003–04): $2830 (resident), $9466 (nonresident). *Room and board:* $4498.
Financial Aid (All incoming freshmen): *Average aid to full-time undergraduates:* $3200.
Athletic Department: *Director of Athletics:* Hank Ford; Phone: 912-356-5181; Fax: 912-353-5287. *Sports Information Director:* Lee Grant Pearson; Phone: 912-356-2446.

MEN'S COACHES

Baseball: Jamie Rigdon; Phone: 912-356-2801.
Basketball: Ed Daniels; Phone: 912-353-2210.
Cheerleading: Cynthia Stephens; Phone: 912-353-5181; E-mail: stephenc@savstate.edu.
Cross Country: Ted Whitaker; Phone: 912-351-3506.
Football: Richard Basil; Phone: 912-353-3031.
Golf: Ivy Williams; Phone: 912-303-1899.
Tennis: Craig Payne; Phone: 912-353-3033.
Track and Field: Ted Whitaker; Phone: 912-351-3506.

WOMEN'S COACHES

Cheerleading: Cynthia Stephens; Phone: 912-353-5181; E-mail: stephenc@savstate.edu.
Cross Country: Ted Whitaker; Phone: 912-351-3506.
Golf: Ivy Williams; Phone: 912-303-1899.
Softball: Stephanie Anderson; Phone: 912-353-5181.
Tennis: Craig Payne; Phone: 912-353-3033.
Track and Field: Ted Whitaker; Phone: 912-351-3506.
Volleyball: Alvin Jones; Phone: 912-353-5181.

SCHREINER UNIVERSITY
Kerrville, Texas

Mountaineers ◆ NCAA III ◆ American Southwest Conference ◆ http://www.schreiner.edu/

Independent Presbyterian comprehensive, founded 1923
Coed, 732 undergraduate students, 90% full-time, 58% women, 42% men
Small-town 175-acre campus with easy access to San Antonio and Austin
Moderately difficult entrance level, 68% of applicants were admitted

Freshmen *Admission:* 570 applied, 359 were accepted, 173 enrolled. *Test scores:* SAT verbal scores over 500: 45%; SAT math scores over 500: 48%; SAT verbal scores over 600: 16%; SAT math scores over 600: 9%; SAT verbal scores over 700: 2%.
Tuition and fees (2003–04): $13,640 (full-time). *Room and board:* $6800 (room only: $3500).
Financial Aid (All incoming freshmen): *Average need-based gift aid:* $9168. *Average non-need based aid:* $9483. *Average aid to full-time undergraduates:* $11,373.
Athletic Department: *Director of Athletics:* Barry Shaw; Phone: 830-792-7421; Fax: 830-792-7483; E-mail: bshaw@schreiner.edu. *Sports Information Director:* David Nichols; Phone: 830-792-7285; E-mail: dfnichols@schreiner.edu.

MEN'S COACHES

Baseball: Joe Castillo; Phone: 830-792-7292; E-mail: jcastillo@schreiner.edu.
Basketball: Thirman Dimery; Phone: 830-792-7306; E-mail: tmdimery@schreiner.edu.
Golf: Frank Boynton; Phone: 830-792-7289; E-mail: fboyton@ktc.com.
Soccer: Paul Hayes; Phone: 830-792-7293; E-mail: pmhayes@schreiner.edu.
Tennis: Lee Jennings; Phone: 830-792-7291; E-mail: hljennings@schreiner.edu.

WOMEN'S COACHES

Basketball: Leigh Anne Owens; Phone: 830-792-7308; E-mail: laownes@schreiner.edu.
Soccer: Gavin Rogers; Phone: 830-792-7449; E-mail: gjrogers@schreiner.edu.
Softball: Rhonda Ruesch; Phone: 830-792-7309; E-mail: rkruesch@schreiner.edu.
Tennis: Lee Jennings; Phone: 830-792-7291; E-mail: hljennings@schreiner.edu.
Volleyball: Rhonda Ruesch; Phone: 830-792-7309; E-mail: rkruesch@schreiner.edu.

SEATTLE PACIFIC UNIVERSITY
Seattle, Washington

Falcons ◆ NCAA II ◆ Great Northwest Athletic Conference ◆ http://www.spu.edu/

Independent Free Methodist comprehensive, founded 1891
Coed, 2,859 undergraduate students, 92% full-time, 67% women, 33% men
Urban 35-acre campus
Moderately difficult entrance level, 90% of applicants were admitted

Freshmen *Admission:* 1,778 applied, 1,635 were accepted, 683 enrolled. *Test scores:* SAT verbal scores over 500: 84%; SAT math scores over 500: 80%; SAT verbal scores over 600: 42%; SAT math scores over 600: 40%; SAT verbal scores over 700: 9%; SAT math scores over 700: 5%.
Tuition and fees (2003–04): $19,158 (full-time). *Room and board:* $7017 (room only: $3762).
Financial Aid (All incoming freshmen): *Average need-based gift aid:* $13,945. *Average non-need based aid:* $9759. *Average aid to full-time undergraduates:* $15,978.
Athletic Department: *Director of Athletics:* Tom Box; Phone: 206-281-2175; Fax: 206-281-2266; E-mail: twb@spu.edu. *Sports Information Director:* Frank MacDonald; Phone: 206-281-2772; E-mail: frmacdon@spu.edu.

Seattle Pacific University *(continued)*

MEN'S COACHES

Basketball: Jeff Hironaka; Phone: 206-281-2963; E-mail: jhironak@spu.edu.

Cross Country: Doris Heritage; Phone: 206-281-2880; E-mail: doris@spu.edu.

Soccer: Cliff McCrath; Phone: 206-281-2968; E-mail: cmccrath@spu.edu.

Track and Field: Jack Hoyt; Phone: 206-281-2897; E-mail: jchoyt@spu.edu.

WOMEN'S COACHES

Basketball: Gordy Presnell; Phone: 206-281-2851; E-mail: presnell@spu.edu.

Cross Country: Doris Heritage; Phone: 206-281-2880; E-mail: doris@spu.edu.

Gymnastics: Laurel Tindall; Phone: 206-281-2883; E-mail: ltindall@spu.edu.

Soccer: Chuck Sekyra; Phone: 206-281-2859; E-mail: csekyra@spu.edu.

Track and Field: Jack Hoyt; Phone: 206-281-2897; E-mail: jchoyt@spu.edu.

Volleyball: Kellie Ryan; Phone: 206-281-2854; E-mail: kryan@spu.edu.

SEATTLE UNIVERSITY
Seattle, Washington

Redhawks ◆ NCAA II ◆ Great Northwest Athletic Conference ◆ http://www.seattleu.edu/

Independent Roman Catholic comprehensive, founded 1891
Coed, 3,765 undergraduate students, 92% full-time, 62% women, 38% men
Urban 46-acre campus
Moderately difficult entrance level, 76% of applicants were admitted

Freshmen *Admission:* 2,985 applied, 2,321 were accepted, 665 enrolled. *Test scores:* SAT verbal scores over 500: 83%; SAT math scores over 500: 79%; SAT verbal scores over 600: 38%; SAT math scores over 600: 35%; SAT verbal scores over 700: 6%; SAT math scores over 700: 4%.
Tuition and fees (2003–04): $20,070 (full-time). *Room and board:* $6858 (room only: $4473).
Financial Aid (All incoming freshmen): *Average need-based gift aid:* $10,932. *Average non-need based aid:* $2361. *Average aid to full-time undergraduates:* $19,409.
Athletic Department: *Director of Athletics:* Nancy Gerou; Phone: 206-296-6400; Fax: 206-296-2154; E-mail: ngerou@seattleu.edu. *Sports Information Director:* Jason Lichtenberger; Phone: 206-296-5915; E-mail: jasonl@seattleu.edu.

MEN'S COACHES

Basketball: Joe Callero; Phone: 206-296-5872; E-mail: calleroj@seattleu.edu.

Cheerleading: Mary Galvez; Phone: 206-296-5811.

Cross Country: Brian Montgomery; Phone: 206-296-5772; E-mail: suxc@seattleu.edu.

Soccer: Peter Fewing; Phone: 206-296-5498; E-mail: fewingp@seattleu.edu.

Swimming: Craig Mallery; Phone: 206-296-6423; E-mail: mallery@seattleu.edu.

WOMEN'S COACHES

Basketball: Dave Cox; Phone: 206-296-5483; E-mail: dwc1089@seattleu.edu.

Cheerleading: Mary Galvez; Phone: 206-296-5811.

Cross Country: Brian Montgomery; Phone: 206-296-5772; E-mail: suxc@seattleu.edu.

Soccer: Julie Woodward; Phone: 206-296-5482; E-mail: woodward@seattleu.edu.

Softball: Dan Powers; Phone: 206-296-5905; E-mail: powersd@seattleu.edu.

Swimming: Craig Mallery; Phone: 206-296-6423; E-mail: mallery@seattleu.edu.

Volleyball: Steve Nimocks; Phone: 206-296-6426; E-mail: suvb@seattleu.edu.

SETON HALL UNIVERSITY
South Orange, New Jersey

Pirates ◆ NCAA I ◆ Big East Conference ◆ http://www.shu.edu/

Independent Roman Catholic university, founded 1856
Coed, 5,238 undergraduate students, 89% full-time, 52% women, 48% men
Suburban 58-acre campus with easy access to New York City
Moderately difficult entrance level, 81% of applicants were admitted

Freshmen *Admission:* 5,750 applied, 4,707 were accepted, 1,248 enrolled. *Test scores:* SAT verbal scores over 500: 73%; SAT math scores over 500: 76%; SAT verbal scores over 600: 29%; SAT math scores over 600: 32%; SAT verbal scores over 700: 6%; SAT math scores over 700: 5%.
Tuition and fees (2003–04): $21,580 (full-time). *Room and board:* $9546 (room only: $6068).
Financial Aid (All incoming freshmen): *Average need-based gift aid:* $4589. *Average non-need based aid:* $12,165. *Average aid to full-time undergraduates:* $14,743.
Athletic Department: *Director of Athletics:* Jeff Fogelson; Phone: 973-761-9498; Fax: 973-761-9675; E-mail: fogelsje@shu.edu. *Sports Information Director:* Jeff Andriesse; Phone: 973-761-9556.

MEN'S COACHES

Baseball: Rob Sheppard; Phone: 973-761-9557; E-mail: shepparo@shu.edu.

Basketball: Louis Orr; Phone: 973-761-9070.

Cross Country: John Moon; Phone: 973-761-9639; E-mail: moonjohn@shu.edu.

Diving: Leslie Woodruff; Phone: 973-761-9594.

Golf: Scott Allen; Phone: 973-761-9406; E-mail: allensco@shu.edu.

Soccer: Manfred Schellscheidt; Phone: 973-761-9693.

Swimming: Ron Farina; Phone: 973-761-9594; E-mail: farinaro@shu.edu.

Track and Field: John Moon; Phone: 973-761-9639; E-mail: moonjohn@shu.edu.

WOMEN'S COACHES

Basketball: Phyllis Mangina; Phone: 973-761-9298; E-mail: manginph@shu.edu.

Cross Country: John Moon; Phone: 973-761-9639; E-mail: moonjohn@shu.edu.

Diving: Leslie Woodruff; Phone: 973-761-9594.

Soccer: Betty Ann Kempf; Phone: 973-761-9777; E-mail: kempfeli@shu.edu.

Softball: Ray Vander May; Phone: 973-761-2408; E-mail: vanderra@shu.edu.

Swimming: Ron Farina; Phone: 973-761-9594; E-mail: farinaro@shu.edu.

Tennis: Betsy Purpura; Phone: 973-761-7946; E-mail: purpurbe@shu.edu.

Track and Field: John Moon; Phone: 973-761-9639; E-mail: moonjohn@shu.edu.

Volleyball: Richard Pickrell; Phone: 973-761-2083; E-mail: pickreri@shu.edu.

SETON HILL UNIVERSITY
Greensburg, Pennsylvania

Griffins ◆ NAIA ◆ American Mideast Conference ◆ http://www.setonhill.edu/

Independent Roman Catholic comprehensive, founded 1883
Coed, 1,292 undergraduate students, 74% full-time, 74% women, 26% men
Small-town 200-acre campus with easy access to Pittsburgh
Moderately difficult entrance level, 83% of applicants were admitted

Freshmen *Admission:* 945 applied, 798 were accepted, 231 enrolled.
Tuition and fees (2003–04): $18,930 (full-time). *Room and board:* $6000.
Financial Aid (All incoming freshmen): *Average need-based gift aid:* $11,421. *Average non-need based aid:* $8406. *Average aid to full-time undergraduates:* $15,782.

Athletic Department: *Director of Athletics:* John Fogle; Phone: 724-838-4259; Fax: 724-830-1296; E-mail: fogle@setonhill.edu. *Sports Information Director:* Marc Marizzaldi; Phone: 724-830-1169; E-mail: marizzaldi@setonhill.edu.

MEN'S COACHES

Baseball: Marc Marizzaldi; Phone: 724-830-1169; E-mail: marizzaldi@setonhill.edu.
Basketball: Tony Morocco; Phone: 724-830-1413; E-mail: morocco@setonhill.edu.
Golf: Dan McCarty; Phone: 724-830-1143; E-mail: mccarty@setonhill.edu.
Lacrosse: Rick Matthews; Phone: 724-830-1298; E-mail: cmatthews@setonhill.edu.
Tennis: Tim Creamer; Phone: 724-830-1872; E-mail: tcreamer@setonhill.edu.

WOMEN'S COACHES

Basketball: Scott Breegle; Phone: 724-836-0013.
Cross Country: Tim Creamer; Phone: 724-830-1872; E-mail: tcreamer@setonhill.edu.
Field Hockey: Jessie Black; Phone: 724-830-1170; E-mail: jblack@setonhill.edu.
Golf: Paul Dominic; Phone: 724-838-9727; E-mail: domsports@msn.com.
Lacrosse: Rick Matthews; Phone: 724-830-1298; E-mail: cmatthews@setonhill.edu.
Soccer: John Fogle; Phone: 724-838-4259; E-mail: fogle@setonhill.edu.
Softball: Jessie Black; Phone: 724-830-1170; E-mail: jblack@setonhill.edu.
Tennis: Tim Creamer; Phone: 724-830-1872; E-mail: tcreamer@setonhill.edu.
Volleyball: Rick Hall; Phone: 724-537-5651; E-mail: hall@setonhill.edu.

SHAWNEE STATE UNIVERSITY
Portsmouth, Ohio

Bears ◆ NAIA ◆ American Mideast Conference ◆ http://www.shawnee.edu/

State-supported 4-year, founded 1986, part of Ohio Board of Regents
Coed, 3,693 undergraduate students, 83% full-time, 60% women, 40% men
Small-town 52-acre campus
Noncompetitive entrance level, 100% of applicants were admitted

Freshmen *Admission:* 2,610 applied, 2,610 were accepted, 709 enrolled.
Tuition and fees (2003–04): $4734 (resident), $8019 (nonresident). *Room and board:* $6297 (room only: $4155).
Financial Aid (All incoming freshmen): *Average need-based gift aid:* $2788. *Average aid to full-time undergraduates:* $3881.
Athletic Department: *Director of Athletics:* Jim Arnzen; Phone: 740-351-3263; Fax: 740-351-3381; E-mail: jarnzen@shawnee.edu. *Sports Information Director:* Jared Shoemaker; Phone: 740-351-3313; E-mail: jshoemaker@shawnee.edu.

MEN'S COACHES

Baseball: Tom Bergan; Phone: 740-351-3537; E-mail: tbergan@shawnee.edu.
Basketball: Jeff Hamilton; Phone: 740-351-3393; E-mail: jhamilton@shawnee.edu.
Cheerleading: Pam Hutchinson; Phone: 740-351-3285; E-mail: pkhutch@falcon1.net.
Cross Country: Larry Mangus; Phone: 740-351-3280; E-mail: lmangus@shawnee.edu.
Golf: Roger Merb; Phone: 740-351-3602; E-mail: rmerb@shawnee.edu.
Soccer: Ron Goodson; Phone: 740-351-3528; E-mail: rgoodson@shawnee.edu.

WOMEN'S COACHES

Basketball: Robin Hagen Smith; Phone: 740-351-3271; E-mail: rhagen_smith@shawnee.edu.
Cheerleading: Pam Hutchinson; Phone: 740-351-3285; E-mail: pkhutch@falcon1.net.
Cross Country: Larry Mangus; Phone: 740-351-3280; E-mail: lmangus@shawnee.edu.
Soccer: Bryan Smith; Phone: 740-351-3528; E-mail: bsmith3@shawnee.edu.
Softball: Ralph Cole; Phone: 740-351-3144.

Tennis: Jeff Hamilton; Phone: 740-351-3602; E-mail: jhamilton@shawnee.edu.
Volleyball: Steven Rader; Phone: 740-351-3633; E-mail: srader@shawnee.edu.

SHAW UNIVERSITY
Raleigh, North Carolina

Bears ◆ NCAA II ◆ Central Intercollegiate Athletic Conference ◆ http://www.shawuniversity.edu/

Independent Baptist comprehensive, founded 1865
Coed, 2,446 undergraduate students, 87% full-time, 63% women, 37% men
Urban 30-acre campus
Minimally difficult entrance level, 47% of applicants were admitted

Freshmen *Admission:* 3,854 applied, 1,707 were accepted, 509 enrolled. *Test scores:* SAT verbal scores over 500: 13%; SAT math scores over 500: 14%; SAT verbal scores over 600: 1%; SAT math scores over 600: 3%.
Tuition and fees (2003–04): $9178 (full-time). *Room and board:* $5654 (room only: $2448).
Financial Aid (All incoming freshmen): *Average need-based gift aid:* $6045. *Average non-need based aid:* $6481. *Average aid to full-time undergraduates:* $8613.
Athletic Department: *Director of Athletics:* Alfonza Carter; Phone: 919-546-8281; Fax: 919-546-8444; E-mail: alcarter@shawu.edu. *Sports Information Director:* Donal Ware; Phone: 919-546-8279; E-mail: dware@shawu.edu.

MEN'S COACHES

Baseball: Bobby Sanders; Phone: 919-546-8278; E-mail: bsanders@shawu.edu.
Basketball: Michael Bernard; Phone: 919-546-8289; E-mail: mbernard@shawu.edu.
Cheerleading: Sherby Rodgers-Speight; Phone: 919-546-8281; E-mail: sspeight@shawu.edu.
Cross Country: William Montague; Phone: 919-546-8596; E-mail: wmontague@shawu.edu.
Football: Deondri Clark; Phone: 919-546-5710; E-mail: dclark@shawu.edu.
Tennis: Sunday Enitan; Phone: 919-546-8482; E-mail: senitan@shawu.edu.
Track and Field: William Montague; Phone: 919-546-8596; E-mail: wmontague@shawu.edu.

WOMEN'S COACHES

Basketball: Jacques Curtis; Phone: 919-546-8597; E-mail: jcurtis@shawu.edu.
Cheerleading: Sherby Rodgers-Speight; Phone: 919-546-8281; E-mail: sspeight@shawu.edu.
Cross Country: William Montague; Phone: 919-546-8596; E-mail: wmontague@shawu.edu.
Softball: Dianthia Ford-Kee; Phone: 919-546-8290; E-mail: dfordkee@shawu.edu.
Tennis: Sunday Enitan; Phone: 919-546-8482; E-mail: senitan@shawu.edu.
Track and Field: William Montague; Phone: 919-546-8596; E-mail: wmontague@shawu.edu.
Volleyball: Dianthia Ford-Kee; Phone: 919-546-8290; E-mail: dfkee@shawu.edu.

SHENANDOAH UNIVERSITY
Winchester, Virginia

Hornets ◆ NCAA III ◆ Pennsylvania Athletic Conference; USA South Athletic Conference ◆ http://www.su.edu/

Independent United Methodist comprehensive, founded 1875
Coed, 1,415 undergraduate students, 94% full-time, 58% women, 42% men
Small-town 100-acre campus with easy access to Baltimore and Washington, DC
Moderately difficult entrance level, 72% of applicants were admitted

Freshmen *Admission:* 1,319 applied, 961 were accepted, 329 enrolled. *Test scores:* SAT verbal scores over 500: 55%; SAT math scores over

Shenandoah University *(continued)*

500: 51%; SAT verbal scores over 600: 17%; SAT math scores over 600: 15%; SAT verbal scores over 700: 2%; SAT math scores over 700: 1%.
Tuition and fees (2003–04): $18,390 (full-time). *Room and board:* $6800.
Financial Aid (All incoming freshmen): *Average need-based gift aid:* $4154. *Average non-need based aid:* $4069. *Average aid to full-time undergraduates:* $13,419.
Athletic Department: *Director of Athletics:* John Hill; Phone: 540-665-4566; Fax: 540-665-4934; E-mail: jhil2@su.edu. *Sports Information Director:* Scott Musa; Phone: 540-665-5417; E-mail: smusa@su.edu.

MEN'S COACHES
Baseball: Kevin Anderson; Phone: 540-665-4531; E-mail: kanders2@su.edu.
Basketball: Robert Harris; Phone: 540-665-4567; E-mail: rharris@su.edu.
Cheerleading: Sandra Barry; Phone: 540-545-7364; E-mail: sbarry@su.edu.
Cross Country: Sam Karns; Phone: 540-665-5579; E-mail: skarns@su.edu.
Football: Paul Barnes; Phone: 540-678-4306; E-mail: pbarnes@su.edu.
Golf: Rob Kulton; Phone: 540-665-4519; E-mail: rkulton@su.edu.
Lacrosse: Brian Jenkins; Phone: 540-665-5415; E-mail: bjenkins@su.edu.
Soccer: Rob Kulton; Phone: 540-665-4519; E-mail: rkulton@su.edu.

WOMEN'S COACHES
Basketball: Kathy Orsini; Phone: 540-665-5400; E-mail: korsini@su.edu.
Cheerleading: Sandra Barry; Phone: 540-545-7364; E-mail: sbarry@su.edu.
Cross Country: Sam Karns; Phone: 540-665-5579; E-mail: skarns@su.edu.
Lacrosse: Lois Bowers; Phone: 540-545-7368; E-mail: lbower2@su.edu.
Soccer: Miranda Armstrong; Phone: 540-665-5538; E-mail: marmstro@su.edu.
Softball: Michelle Manning; Phone: 540-665-5580; E-mail: mmanning@su.edu.
Tennis: Colin Clark; Phone: 540-545-7360; E-mail: kanders2@su.edu.
Volleyball: Sarah Pelster; Phone: 540-545-7366; E-mail: spelster@su.edu.

SHEPHERD UNIVERSITY
Shepherdstown, West Virginia
Rams ◆ NCAA II ◆ West Virginia Intercollegiate Athletic Conference ◆ http://www.shepherd.edu/

State-supported comprehensive, founded 1871, part of West Virginia Higher Education Policy Commission
Coed, 4,804 undergraduate students, 65% full-time, 60% women, 40% men
Small-town 320-acre campus with easy access to Washington, DC
Moderately difficult entrance level, 90% of applicants were admitted

Freshmen *Admission:* 1,061 applied, 948 were accepted, 845 enrolled. *Test scores:* SAT verbal scores over 500: 57%; SAT math scores over 500: 54%; SAT verbal scores over 600: 13%; SAT math scores over 600: 9%.
Tuition and fees (2003–04): $3270 (resident), $8030 (nonresident). *Room and board:* $5338.
Financial Aid (All incoming freshmen): *Average need-based gift aid:* $3546. *Average non-need based aid:* $5654. *Average aid to full-time undergraduates:* $5994.
Athletic Department: *Director of Athletics:* Monte Cater; Phone: 304-876-5263; Fax: 304-876-3267; E-mail: mcater@shepherd.edu. *Sports Information Director:* Charles Ransom; Phone: 304-876-5228; E mail: cransom@shepherd.edu.

MEN'S COACHES
Baseball: Wayne Riser; Phone: 304-876-5231; E-mail: kriser@shepherd.edu.
Basketball: Ken Tyler; Phone: 304-876-5264; E-mail: ktyler@shepherd.edu.
Cheerleading: Buffy Ashcroft; Phone: 304-876-5231.
Cross Country: Moe Morris; Phone: 304-876-5481; E-mail: rmorris@shepherd.edu.

Football: Monte Cater; Phone: 304-876-5263; E-mail: mcater@shepherd.edu.
Golf: Mike Jacobs; Phone: 304-876-5233; E-mail: mjacobs@shepherd.edu.
Soccer: Joseph Okoh; Phone: 304-876-5639; E-mail: jokoh@shepherd.edu.
Tennis: Chris Stambaugh; Phone: 304-876-5466; E-mail: cstambau@shepherd.edu.

WOMEN'S COACHES
Basketball: Jodie Runner; Phone: 304-876-5170; E-mail: jrunner@shepherd.edu.
Cheerleading: Buffy Ashcroft; Phone: 304-876-5231.
Cross Country: Moe Morris; Phone: 304-876-5481; E-mail: rmorris@shepherd.edu.
Soccer: Jim Sweeney; Phone: 304-876-5231; E-mail: jsweeney@shepherd.edu.
Softball: David Trail; Phone: 304-876-5481; E-mail: dtrail@shepherd.edu.
Tennis: Chris Stambaugh; Phone: 304-876-5466; E-mail: cstambau@shepherd.edu.
Volleyball: Lu Kormeluk; Phone: 304-876-5481.

SHIPPENSBURG UNIVERSITY OF PENNSYLVANIA
Shippensburg, Pennsylvania
Raiders ◆ NCAA II ◆ Pennsylvania State Athletic Conference ◆ http://www.ship.edu/

State-supported comprehensive, founded 1871, part of Pennsylvania State System of Higher Education
Coed, 6,567 undergraduate students, 96% full-time, 53% women, 47% men
Rural 200-acre campus
Moderately difficult entrance level, 65% of applicants were admitted

Freshmen *Admission:* 5,863 applied, 3,916 were accepted, 1,493 enrolled. *Test scores:* SAT verbal scores over 500: 64%; SAT math scores over 500: 68%; SAT verbal scores over 600: 15%; SAT math scores over 600: 18%; SAT verbal scores over 700: 1%; SAT math scores over 700: 2%.
Tuition and fees (2003–04): $5746 (resident), $12,694 (nonresident). *Room and board:* $5080 (room only: $3086).
Financial Aid (All incoming freshmen): *Average need-based gift aid:* $3614. *Average non-need based aid:* $2166. *Average aid to full-time undergraduates:* $5329.
Athletic Department: *Director of Athletics:* Roberta Page; Phone: 717-477-1541; Fax: 717-477-4045; E-mail: rlpage@ship.edu. *Sports Information Director:* John Alosi; Phone: 717-477-1541; E-mail: sid@ship.edu.

MEN'S COACHES
Baseball: Bruce Peddie; Phone: 717-477-1508; E-mail: bdpedd@ship.edu.
Basketball: David Springer; Phone: 717-477-1449; E-mail: cdspri@ship.edu.
Cheerleading: Heidi Whittaker; Phone: 717-477-1322; E-mail: heidiwhittaker@yahoo.com.
Cross Country: Steve Spence; Phone: 717-477-1284; E-mail: saspen@ship.edu.
Football: Rocky Rees; Phone: 717-477-1758; E-mail: wmrees@ship.edu.
Soccer: Guy Furfaro; Phone: 717-477-1740; E-mail: gtfurf@ship.edu.
Swimming: Tim Verge; Phone: 717-477-1457; E-mail: tpverg@wharf.ship.edu.
Track and Field: Steve Spence; Phone: 717-477-1284; E-mail: saspen@ship.cdu.
Wrestling: Donald Tabar; Phone: 717-477-1238; E-mail: djtaba@ship.edu.

WOMEN'S COACHES
Basketball: Kristy Trn; Phone: 717-477-1543; E-mail: kktrn@wharf.ship.edu.
Cheerleading: Heidi Whittaker; Phone: 717-477-1322; E-mail: heidiwhittaker@yahoo.com.
Cross Country: Steve Spence; Phone: 717-477-1284; E-mail: saspen@ship.edu.

Field Hockey: Bertie Landes; Phone: 717-477-1711; E-mail: blland@ship.edu.
Lacrosse: Bertie Landes; Phone: 717-477-1542; E-mail: blland@ship.edu.
Soccer: Guy Furfaro; Phone: 717-477-1740; E-mail: gtfurf@ship.edu.
Softball: Bob Brookers; Phone: 717-477-1328; E-mail: rgbroo@ship.edu.
Swimming: Tim Verge; Phone: 717-477-1457; E-mail: tpverg@wharf.ship.edu.
Tennis: Walter Manderson; Phone: 717-477-1283; E-mail: wemand@wharf.ship.edu.
Track and Field: Steve Spence; Phone: 717-477-1284; E-mail: saspen@ship.edu.
Volleyball: Randy Hood; Phone: 717-477-1322; E-mail: rmhood@wharf.ship.edu.

SHORTER COLLEGE
Rome, Georgia

Hawks ◆ NAIA ◆ Georgia Alabama Carolina Conference ◆ http://www.shorter.edu/

Independent Baptist comprehensive, founded 1873
Coed, 884 undergraduate students, 95% full-time, 61% women, 39% men
Small-town 155-acre campus with easy access to Atlanta
Moderately difficult entrance level, 83% of applicants were admitted

Freshmen *Admission:* 555 applied, 460 were accepted, 185 enrolled. *Test scores:* SAT verbal scores over 500: 64%; SAT math scores over 500: 64%; SAT verbal scores over 600: 22%; SAT math scores over 600: 20%; SAT verbal scores over 700: 4%; SAT math scores over 700: 1%.
Tuition and fees (2003–04): $11,705 (full-time). *Room and board:* $5665 (room only: $3165).
Financial Aid (All incoming freshmen): *Average need-based gift aid:* $7818. *Average non-need based aid:* $8873. *Average aid to full-time undergraduates:* $9606.
Athletic Department: *Director of Athletics:* Ricci Lattanzi; Phone: 706-233-7347; Fax: 706-291-7080; E-mail: rlattanzi@shorter.edu.

MEN'S COACHES
Baseball: Matt Larry; Phone: 706-233-7510; E-mail: mlarry@shorter.edu.
Basketball: Ricky Williams; Phone: 706-233-7343; E-mail: rwilliams@shorter.edu.
Golf: Ahmad Hayat; Phone: 706-233-7371; E-mail: ahayat@shorter.edu.
Soccer: Gordon Leslie; Phone: 706-233-7346; E-mail: gleslie@shorter.edu.
Tennis: Walt Attaway; Phone: 706-233-7345; E-mail: wattaway@shorter.edu.

WOMEN'S COACHES
Basketball: Vic Mitchell; Phone: 706-233-7344; E-mail: vmitchell@shorter.edu.
Golf: Vic Mitchell; Phone: 706-233-7344; E-mail: vmitchell@shorter.edu.
Soccer: Orville Adams; Phone: 706-233-7384; E-mail: oadams@shorter.edu.
Softball: Jaleel Riaz; Phone: 706-233-7376; E-mail: jriaz@shorter.edu.
Tennis: Walt Attaway; Phone: 706-233-7345; E-mail: wattaway@shorter.edu.
Volleyball: Jaleel Riaz; Phone: 706-233-7376; E-mail: jriaz@shorter.edu.

SIENA COLLEGE
Loudonville, New York

Saints ◆ NCAA I ◆ Metro Atlantic Athletic Conference; Northeast Conference ◆ http://www.siena.edu/

Independent Roman Catholic 4-year, founded 1937
Coed, 3,379 undergraduate students, 90% full-time, 56% women, 44% men
Suburban 163-acre campus
Moderately difficult entrance level, 59% of applicants were admitted

Freshmen *Admission:* 4,112 applied, 2,599 were accepted, 759 enrolled. *Test scores:* SAT verbal scores over 500: 81%; SAT math scores over

500: 88%; SAT verbal scores over 600: 25%; SAT math scores over 600: 36%; SAT verbal scores over 700: 2%; SAT math scores over 700: 3%.
Tuition and fees (2004–05): $19,130 (full-time). *Room and board:* $7575 (room only: $4750).
Financial Aid (All incoming freshmen): *Average need-based gift aid:* $9402. *Average non-need based aid:* $4537. *Average aid to full-time undergraduates:* $11,892.
Athletic Department: *Director of Athletics:* John D'Argenio; Phone: 518-783-2450; Fax: 518-783-2992; E-mail: dargenio@siena.edu. *Sports Information Director:* Jason Rich; Phone: 518-783-2411; E-mail: jrich@siena.edu.

MEN'S COACHES
Baseball: Tony Rossi; Phone: 518-786-5044; E-mail: rossi@siena.edu.
Basketball: Rob Lanier; Phone: 518-783-2551; E-mail: rlanier@siena.edu.
Cheerleading: Lynn Grasso; Phone: 518-786-2451; E-mail: kerry.spilman@students.siena.edu.
Cross Country: Jim Bowles; Phone: 518-786-5064; E-mail: jbowles@siena.edu.
Football: Phone: 518-786-6106.
Golf: Tom Wronowski; Phone: 518-782-6106; E-mail: twronowski@siena.edu.
Lacrosse: Roger Manion; Phone: 518-786-5043; E-mail: rmanion@siena.edu.
Soccer: Charlie Curto; Phone: 518-786-5042; E-mail: ccurto@siena.edu.
Tennis: Jim Serbalik; Phone: 518-783-2368; E-mail: serbalik@siena.edu.

WOMEN'S COACHES
Basketball: Gina Castelli; Phone: 518-783-2484; E-mail: castelli@siena.edu.
Cheerleading: Lynn Grasso; Phone: 518-786-2451; E-mail: kerry.spilman@students.siena.edu.
Cross Country: Jim Bowles; Phone: 518-786-5064; E-mail: jbowles@siena.edu.
Diving: Jim Serbalik; Phone: 518-783-2368; E-mail: serbalik@siena.edu.
Field Hockey: Lynda Lareau; Phone: 518-783-2939; E-mail: llareau@siena.edu.
Golf: Theresa Wenzel; Phone: 518-783-2940; E-mail: twenzel@siena.edu.
Lacrosse: Jake McHerron; Phone: 518-786-5043; E-mail: jmcherron@siena.edu.
Soccer: Steve Karbowski; Phone: 518-786-5042; E-mail: skarbowski@siena.edu.
Softball: Patti Brun; Phone: 518-783-2916; E-mail: pbrun@siena.edu.
Swimming: Jeff Maxwell; Phone: 518-786-5037; E-mail: jmaxwell@siena.edu.
Tennis: Tim O'Brien; Phone: 518-783-6454; E-mail: tobrien@siena.edu.

SIENA HEIGHTS UNIVERSITY
Adrian, Michigan

Saints ◆ NAIA ◆ Wolverine-Hoosier Conference ◆ http://www.sienahts.edu/

Independent Roman Catholic comprehensive, founded 1919
Coed, 1,886 undergraduate students
Small-town 140-acre campus with easy access to Detroit
Moderately difficult entrance level, 64% of applicants were admitted

Freshmen *Admission:* 979 applied, 631 were accepted.
Tuition and fees (2004–05): $15,520 (full-time). *Room and board:* $5455.
Financial Aid (All incoming freshmen): *Average aid to full-time undergraduates:* $12,200.
Athletic Department: *Director of Athletics:* Fred Smith; Phone: 517-264-7876; Fax: 517-264-7737; E-mail: fsmith@sienahts.edu. *Sports Information Director:* Scott Oliver; Phone: 517-264-7879; E-mail: soliver@sienahts.edu.

MEN'S COACHES
Baseball: John Kolansinski; Phone: 517-264-7872; E-mail: jkolasin@sineahts.edu.
Basketball: Fred Smith; Phone: 517-264-7876; E-mail: fsmith@sienahts.edu.
Cross Country: Tim Bauer; Phone: 517-264-7878; E-mail: tbauer@sienahts.edu.
Golf: Al Sandifer; Phone: 517-264-7879; E-mail: asandife@sienahts.edu.

Siena Heights University *(continued)*

Soccer: Aldo Zid; Phone: 517-264-7873; E-mail: azid@sienahts.edu.
Track and Field: Tim Bauer; Phone: 517-264-7878; E-mail: tbauer@sienahts.edu.

WOMEN'S COACHES

Basketball: Renee Kudzia; Phone: 517-264-7871; E-mail: rkudzia@sienahts.edu.
Cross Country: Don Kleinow; Phone: 517-264-7878.
Soccer: Scott Oliver; Phone: 517-264-7879; E-mail: soliver@sienahts.edu.
Softball: Lynnette Overstreet; Phone: 517-264-7874; E-mail: loverstr@sienahts.edu.
Track and Field: Tim Bauer; Phone: 517-264-7878; E-mail: tbauer@sienahts.edu.
Volleyball: Craig Vlietstra; Phone: 517-264-7875; E-mail: cvlietst@sienahts.edu.

SIMMONS COLLEGE
Boston, Massachusetts

Sharks ◆ NCAA III ◆ Great Northeast Athletic Conference; North Atlantic Conference ◆ http://www.simmons.edu/

Independent university, founded 1899
Women only, 1,555 undergraduate students, 88% full-time, 100% women, 100% men
Urban 12-acre campus
Moderately difficult entrance level, 68% of applicants were admitted

Freshmen *Admission:* 1,895 applied, 1,291 were accepted, 419 enrolled. *Test scores:* SAT verbal scores over 500: 79%; SAT math scores over 500: 74%; SAT verbal scores over 600: 32%; SAT math scores over 600: 19%; SAT verbal scores over 700: 5%; SAT math scores over 700: 1%.
Tuition and fees (2004–05): $24,490 (full-time). *Room and board:* $9820.
Financial Aid (All incoming freshmen): *Average need-based gift aid:* $15,518. *Average non-need based aid:* $11,430. *Average aid to full-time undergraduates:* $17,255.
Athletic Department: *Director of Athletics:* Alice Kantor; Phone: 617-521-1041; Fax: 617-521-1026; E-mail: alice.kantor@simmons.edu. *Sports Information Director:* Mary Taylor; Phone: 617-521-1040; E-mail: mary.taylor2@simmons.edu.

WOMEN'S COACHES

Basketball: Tony Price; Phone: 617-521-1036; E-mail: pricea@simmons.edu.
Diving: Douglas Backlund; Phone: 617-521-1023; E-mail: dbacklund@simmons.edu.
Field Hockey: Jane Mollo; Phone: 617-521-1039; E-mail: jane.mollo@simmons.edu.
Soccer: Dick Dawson; Phone: 617-521-1037; E-mail: dick.dawson@simmons.edu.
Softball: Doug Backlund; Phone: 617-521-1032; E-mail: richard.backlund@simmons.edu.
Swimming: Douglas Backlund; Phone: 617-521-1023; E-mail: dbacklund@simmons.edu.
Tennis: Elinor Ross; Phone: 617-521-1043; E-mail: elinor.ross@simmons.edu.
Volleyball: David Wong; Phone: 617-521-1042; E-mail: david.wong@simmons.edu.

SIMPSON COLLEGE
Indianola, Iowa

Storm; Vanguards ◆ NCAA III ◆ California Pacific Conference; Iowa Athletic Conference ◆ http://www.simpson.edu/

Independent United Methodist 4-year, founded 1860
Coed, 1,937 undergraduate students, 74% full-time, 59% women, 41% men
Small-town 74-acre campus
Moderately difficult entrance level, 84% of applicants were admitted

Freshmen *Admission:* 1,271 applied, 1,097 were accepted, 413 enrolled.

Tuition and fees (2003–04): $18,097 (full-time). *Room and board:* $6062 (room only: $3170).
Financial Aid (All incoming freshmen): *Average need-based gift aid:* $12,112. *Average non-need based aid:* $7499. *Average aid to full-time undergraduates:* $17,184.
Athletic Department: *Director of Athletics:* John Sirianni; Phone: 515-961-1620; Fax: 515-961-1279; E-mail: siriannj@simpson.edu. *Sports Information Director:* Matt Turk; Phone: 515-961-1577; E-mail: turk@simpson.edu.

MEN'S COACHES

Baseball: Gary Ledbetter; Phone: 530-226-4703; E-mail: quickhandle@email.msn.com.
Baseball: John Sirianni; Phone: 515-961-1620; E-mail: smithl@simpson.edu.
Basketball: Bruce Wilson; Phone: 515-961-1651; E-mail: smithl@simpson.edu.
Basketball: Wayne Mendezona; Phone: 530-226-4703; E-mail: quickhandle@email.msn.com.
Cheerleading: Debra Lord; Phone: 515-961-1624; E-mail: lord@simpson.edu.
Cross Country: Erin Bresnan; Phone: 515-961-1640; E-mail: smithl@simpson.edu.
Football: Jay Niemann; Phone: 515-961-1691; E-mail: smithl@simpson.edu.
Golf: Larry Shoop; Phone: 515-961-5445; E-mail: smithl@simpson.edu.
Soccer: Aziz Haffar; Phone: 515-961-1643; E-mail: smithl@simpson.edu.
Soccer: Lee McKenzie; Phone: 530-226-4703; E-mail: lslcmckenzie@cs.com.
Tennis: Bob Nutgrass; Phone: 515-961-1678; E-mail: smithl@simpson.edu.
Track and Field: Wayne Stacy; Phone: 515-961-1402; E-mail: smithl@simpson.edu.
Wrestling: Ron Peterson; Phone: 515-961-1718; E-mail: smithl@simpson.edu.

WOMEN'S COACHES

Basketball: Brian Neimuth; Phone: 515-961-1670; E-mail: smithl@simpson.edu.
Basketball: Steve Sain; Phone: 530-226-4731; E-mail: ssain@simpsonca.edu.
Cheerleading: Debra Lord; Phone: 515-961-1624; E-mail: lord@simpson.edu.
Cross Country: Erin Bresnan; Phone: 515-961-1640; E-mail: smithl@simpson.edu.
Golf: Bob Darrah; Phone: 515-961-1864; E-mail: smithl@simpson.edu.
Soccer: Aziz Haffar; Phone: 515-961-1643; E-mail: smithl@simpson.edu.
Soccer: Dan Woerner; Phone: 530-226-4976; E-mail: dwoerner@simpsonca.edu.
Softball: Henry Christowski; Phone: 515-961-1337; E-mail: smithl@simpson.edu.
Swimming: Mark Corley; Phone: 515-961-1342; E-mail: smithl@simpson.edu.
Tennis: Bob Nutgrass; Phone: 515-961-1678; E-mail: smithl@simpson.edu.
Track and Field: Wayne Stacy; Phone: 515-961-1402; E-mail: smithl@simpson.edu.
Volleyball: Lana Smith; Phone: 515-961-1641; E-mail: smithl@simpson.edu.
Volleyball: Sean Porter; Phone: 530-226-4938; E-mail: sporter@simpsonca.edu.

SI TANKA HURON UNIVERSITY
Huron, South Dakota

Eagles ◆ NAIA ◆ Dakota Conference ◆ http://www.sitanka.net/1.5/

Proprietary 4-year, founded 1883
Coed, 528 undergraduate students, 84% full-time, 45% women, 55% men
Small-town 15-acre campus
Minimally difficult entrance level, 39% of applicants were admitted

Freshmen *Admission:* 622 applied, 242 were accepted, 175 enrolled.

Financial Aid (All incoming freshmen): *Average need-based gift aid:* $4138. *Average aid to full-time undergraduates:* $5000.
Athletic Department: *Director of Athletics:* Garney Henley; Phone: 605-352-8721; Fax: 605-352-7421.

MEN'S COACHES
Baseball: Dean Berry; Phone: 605-352-8721.
Basketball: Shane Warick; Phone: 605-352-8721.
Football: Paul Troth; Phone: 605-352-8721.
Soccer: Brad Smith; Phone: 605-352-8721.
Track and Field: Phone: 605-352-8721.
Wrestling: Mark Blaschko; Phone: 605-352-8721.

WOMEN'S COACHES
Basketball: Laura Merritt; Phone: 605-352-8721.
Soccer: Sean Fleming; Phone: 605-352-8721.
Softball: Terri Holmes; Phone: 605-352-8721.
Track and Field: Phone: 605-352-8721.
Volleyball: Terri Holmes; Phone: 605-352-8721.

SKIDMORE COLLEGE
Saratoga Springs, New York

Thoroughbreds ◆ NCAA III ◆ Upstate Collegiate Athletic Conference ◆ http://www.skidmore.edu/

Independent comprehensive, founded 1903
Coed, 2,532 undergraduate students, 90% full-time, 59% women, 41% men
Small-town 800-acre campus with easy access to Albany
Very difficult entrance level, 51% of applicants were admitted

Freshmen *Admission:* 5,903 applied, 2,724 were accepted, 642 enrolled. *Test scores:* SAT verbal scores over 500: 95%; SAT math scores over 500: 97%; SAT verbal scores over 600: 67%; SAT math scores over 600: 69%; SAT verbal scores over 700: 16%; SAT math scores over 700: 12%.
Tuition and fees (2003–04): $29,630 (full-time). *Room and board:* $8300 (room only: $4630).
Financial Aid (All incoming freshmen): *Average need-based gift aid:* $19,072. *Average non-need based aid:* $10,000. *Average aid to full-time undergraduates:* $22,920.
Athletic Department: *Director of Athletics:* Jeffrey Segrave; Phone: 518-580-5370; Fax: 518-580-5395; E-mail: jsegrave@skidmore.edu. *Sports Information Director:* Bill Jones; Phone: 518-580-5364; E-mail: bjones@skidmore.edu.

MEN'S COACHES
Baseball: Ron Plourde; Phone: 518-580-5380; E-mail: rplourde@skidmore.edu.
Basketball: John Quattrochi; Phone: 518-580-5384; E-mail: jquattro@skidmore.edu.
Diving: Jill Belding; Phone: 518-580-5368; E-mail: jbelding@skidmore.edu.
Golf: Tim Brown; Phone: 518-580-5372; E-mail: tbrown@skidmore.edu.
Ice Hockey: Paul Dion; Phone: 518-580-5374; E-mail: pdion@skidmore.edu.
Lacrosse: Terry Cochran; Phone: 518-580-5362; E-mail: tcorcora@skidmore.edu.
Soccer: Ron McEachen; Phone: 518-580-5381; E-mail: rmceache@skidmore.edu.
Swimming: Jill Belding; Phone: 518-580-5368; E-mail: jbelding@skidmore.edu.
Tennis: Paul Arciero; Phone: 518-580-5366; E-mail: parciero@skidmore.edu.

WOMEN'S COACHES
Basketball: Lisa Pleban; Phone: 518-580-5363; E-mail: lpleban@skidmore.edu.
Diving: Jill Belding; Phone: 518-580-5368; E-mail: jbelding@skidmore.edu.
Field Hockey: Beth Hallenbeck; Phone: 518-580-5373; E-mail: bhallen@skidmore.edu.
Lacrosse: Mark McCormick; Phone: 518-580-5397; E-mail: mmccormick@skidmore.edu.
Soccer: Sarah Cooper; Phone: 518-580-5385; E-mail: scooper@skidmore.edu.
Softball: Larry Ramos; Phone: 518-580-5380.

Swimming: Jill Belding; Phone: 518-580-5368; E-mail: jbelding@skidmore.edu.
Tennis: Heather Wood; Phone: 518-580-8361; E-mail: hwood@skidmore.edu.
Volleyball: Hilda Arrechea; Phone: 518-580-5367; E-mail: harreche@skidmore.edu.

SLIPPERY ROCK UNIVERSITY OF PENNSYLVANIA
Slippery Rock, Pennsylvania

The Rockets ◆ NCAA II ◆ Pennsylvania State Athletic Conference ◆ http://www.sru.edu/

State-supported comprehensive, founded 1889, part of Pennsylvania State System of Higher Education
Coed, 7,054 undergraduate students, 91% full-time, 56% women, 44% men
Rural 600-acre campus with easy access to Pittsburgh
Moderately difficult entrance level, 78% of applicants were admitted

Freshmen *Admission:* 4,310 applied, 3,481 were accepted, 1,491 enrolled. *Test scores:* SAT verbal scores over 500: 48%; SAT math scores over 500: 47%; SAT verbal scores over 600: 8%; SAT math scores over 600: 9%; SAT verbal scores over 700: 1%; SAT math scores over 700: 1%.
Tuition and fees (2003–04): $5801 (resident), $12,699 (nonresident). *Room and board:* $4542 (room only: $2438).
Financial Aid (All incoming freshmen): *Average need-based gift aid:* $2907. *Average non-need based aid:* $3590. *Average aid to full-time undergraduates:* $6074.
Athletic Department: *Director of Athletics:* Paul Lueken; Phone: 724-738-2767; Fax: 724-738-2626; E-mail: paul.lueken@sru.edu. *Sports Information Director:* Bob McComas; Phone: 724-738-2777; E-mail: robert.mccomas@sru.edu.

MEN'S COACHES
Baseball: Jeff Messer; Phone: 724-738-2813; E-mail: jeffrey.messer@sru.edu.
Basketball: John Marhefka; Phone: 724-738-2826; E-mail: john.marhefka@sru.edu.
Cheerleading: Gemma Fotia; Phone: 724-738-4790; E-mail: gemma.fotia@sru.edu.
Cross Country: John Papa; Phone: 724-738-2798; E-mail: john.papa@sru.edu.
Football: George Mihalik; Phone: 724-738-2780; E-mail: george.mihalik@sru.edu.
Golf: Dave Crunkelton; Phone: 724-738-4404; E-mail: dcrunk@nauticom.net.
Soccer: Matt Thompson; Phone: 724-738-2822; E-mail: matthew.thompson@sru.edu.
Swimming: Andrew Waeger; Phone: 724-738-2896; E-mail: andrew.waeger@sru.edu.
Tennis: Matt Meridith; Phone: 724-738-4504; E-mail: mattmeredith@hotmail.com.
Track and Field: John Papa; Phone: 724-738-2798; E-mail: john.papa@sru.edu.
Wrestling: Jim Harshaw; Phone: 724-738-2722; E-mail: james.harshaw@sru.edu.

WOMEN'S COACHES
Basketball: Laurel Heilman; Phone: 724-738-2399; E-mail: laurel.heilman@sru.edu.
Cheerleading: Gemma Fotia; Phone: 724-738-4790; E-mail: gemma.fotia@sru.edu.
Cross Country: John Papa; Phone: 724-738-2798; E-mail: john.papa@sru.edu.
Field Hockey: Sarah Dunn; Phone: 724-738-2786; E-mail: sarah.dunn@sru.edu.
Soccer: Noreen Herlihy; Phone: 724-738-2946; E-mail: noreen.herlihy@sru.edu.
Softball: Vashion Johnson; Phone: 724-738-4959; E-mail: vashion.johnson@sru.edu.
Swimming: Andrew Waeger; Phone: 724-738-2896; E-mail: andrew.waeger@sru.edu.
Tennis: Matt Meridith; Phone: 724-738-4504; E-mail: mattmeredith@hotmail.com.

Slippery Rock University of Pennsylvania (continued)

Track and Field: John Papa; Phone: 724-738-2798; E-mail: john.papa@sru.edu.

Volleyball: Laurie Lokash; Phone: 724-738-2817; E-mail: laureen.lokash@sru.edu.

SMITH COLLEGE
Northampton, Massachusetts

Pioneers ◆ NCAA III ◆ New England Women's & Men's Athletics Conference ◆ http://www.smith.edu/

Independent comprehensive, founded 1871
Women only, 2,682 undergraduate students, 98% full-time, 100% women, 100% men
Small-town 125-acre campus with easy access to Hartford
Very difficult entrance level, 52% of applicants were admitted

Freshmen *Admission:* 3,304 applied, 1,705 were accepted, 635 enrolled. *Test scores:* SAT verbal scores over 500: 93%; SAT math scores over 500: 96%; SAT verbal scores over 600: 70%; SAT math scores over 600: 62%; SAT verbal scores over 700: 27%; SAT math scores over 700: 15%.
Tuition and fees (2003–04): $27,544 (full-time). *Room and board:* $9490.
Financial Aid (All incoming freshmen): *Average need-based gift aid:* $22,716. *Average non-need based aid:* $6754. *Average aid to full-time undergraduates:* $26,692.
Athletic Department: *Director of Athletics:* Lynn Oberbillig; Phone: 413-584-2701; Fax: 413-585-2712; E-mail: loberbil@email.smith.edu. *Sports Information Director:* Carole Grills; Phone: 413-585-2703; E-mail: cgrills@email.smith.edu.

WOMEN'S COACHES
Basketball: Liz Feeley; Phone: 413-585-2719; E-mail: lfeeley@smith.edu.
Cross Country: Ellen O'Neil; Phone: 413-585-2718.
Diving: Kim Bierwert; Phone: 413-585-2722; E-mail: kbierwer@smith.edu.
Field Hockey: Judy Strong; Phone: 413-585-2714; E-mail: jstrong@smith.edu.
Lacrosse: Wendy Walker; Phone: 413-585-2714; E-mail: jstrong@smith.edu.
Soccer: Phil Nielson; Phone: 413-585-3983; E-mail: pnielsen@smith.edu.
Softball: Bonnie May; Phone: 413-585-2713; E-mail: bmay@email.smith.edu.
Swimming: Kim Bierwert; Phone: 413-585-2722; E-mail: kbierwer@smith.edu.
Tennis: Christine Davis; Phone: 413-585-2716; E-mail: cdavis@smith.edu.
Track and Field: Carla Coffey; Phone: 413-585-2718; E-mail: ccoffey@email.smith.edu.
Volleyball: Bonnie May; Phone: 413-585-2713; E-mail: bmay@smith.edu.

SONOMA STATE UNIVERSITY
Rohnert Park, California

Seawolves ◆ NCAA II ◆ California Collegiate Athletic Conference ◆ http://www.sonoma.edu/

State-supported comprehensive, founded 1960, part of California State University System
Coed, 6,996 undergraduate students, 86% full-time, 63% women, 37% men
Small-town 280-acre campus with easy access to San Francisco
Moderately difficult entrance level, 80% of applicants were admitted

Freshmen *Admission:* 6,366 applied, 5,361 were accepted, 1,303 enrolled. *Test scores:* SAT verbal scores over 500: 61%; SAT math scores over 500: 63%; SAT verbal scores over 600: 17%; SAT math scores over 600: 16%; SAT verbal scores over 700: 2%; SAT math scores over 700: 1%.

Tuition and fees (2003–04): $3010 (resident), $11,470 (nonresident). *Room and board:* $7411 (room only: $4645).
Financial Aid (All incoming freshmen): *Average need-based gift aid:* $4778. *Average non-need based aid:* $2643. *Average aid to full-time undergraduates:* $4997.
Athletic Department: *Director of Athletics:* Bill Fusco; Phone: 707-664-2639; Fax: 707-664-4104; E-mail: bill.fusco@sonoma.edu. *Sports Information Director:* Brandon Bronzan; Phone: 707-664-2358; E-mail: brandon.bronzan@sonoma.edu.

MEN'S COACHES
Baseball: John Goelz; Phone: 707-664-2524; E-mail: john.goelz@sonoma.edu.
Basketball: Pat Fuscaldo; Phone: 707-664-2110; E-mail: fuscaldo@sonoma.edu.
Golf: Val Verhunce; Phone: 707-664-3320; E-mail: zholen1@pacbell.net.
Soccer: Marcus Ziemer; Phone: 707-664-2614; E-mail: marcus.ziemer@sonoma.edu.
Tennis: Steve Cunninghame; Phone: 707-664-2657; E-mail: steve.cunninghame@sonoma.edu.

WOMEN'S COACHES
Basketball: Mark Rigby; Phone: 707-664-2498; E-mail: mark.rigby@sonoma.edu.
Cross Country: Jim Hiserman; Phone: 707-664-2290; E-mail: jim.hiserman@sonoma.edu.
Soccer: Luke Oberkirch; Phone: 707-664-2481; E-mail: luke.oberkirch@sonoma.edu.
Softball: Chris Elze; Phone: 707-664-4054; E-mail: chris.elze@sonoma.edu.
Tennis: Tracy Prince; Phone: 707-664-2291; E-mail: tracey.prince@sonoma.edu.
Track and Field: Jim Hiserman; Phone: 707-664-2290; E-mail: jim.hiserman@sonoma.edu.
Volleyball: Ed Grassl; Phone: 707-664-2656; E-mail: bear.grassl@sonoma.edu.

SOUTH CAROLINA STATE UNIVERSITY
Orangeburg, South Carolina

Bulldogs ◆ NCAA I ◆ Mid-Eastern Athletic Conference ◆ http://www.scsu.edu/

State-supported comprehensive, founded 1896, part of South Carolina Commission on Higher Education
Coed, 3,585 undergraduate students, 90% full-time, 58% women, 42% men
Small-town 160-acre campus
Minimally difficult entrance level, 80% of applicants were admitted

Freshmen *Admission:* 2,558 applied, 2,045 were accepted, 810 enrolled. *Test scores:* SAT verbal scores over 500: 17%; SAT math scores over 500: 23%; SAT verbal scores over 600: 4%; SAT math scores over 600: 6%; SAT verbal scores over 700: 1%; SAT math scores over 700: 1%.
Tuition and fees (2003–04): $5755 (resident), $11,035 (nonresident). *Room and board:* $4672 (room only: $2826).
Athletic Department: *Director of Athletics:* Tim Autry; Phone: 803-536-8578; Fax: 803-536-3634; E-mail: tjautry@scsu.edu. *Sports Information Director:* Bill Hamilton; Phone: 803-536-7060; E-mail: whamilton@scsu.edu.

MEN'S COACHES
Basketball: Ben Betts; Phone: 803-536-8586.
Cross Country: Ernest Tche; Phone: 803-536-8715.
Football: Buddy Pough; Phone: 803-536-7242.
Golf: Richard Arrington; Phone: 803-536-3620.
Tennis: Hardeep Judge; Phone: 803-536-7242.
Track and Field: Ernest Tche; Phone: 803-536-8715.

WOMEN'S COACHES
Basketball: Keshia Campbell; Phone: 803-536-7242.
Cross Country: Ernest Tche; Phone: 803-536-8715.
Soccer: Sonia King; Phone: 803-536-7242.
Softball: Mary Hill; Phone: 803-533-3783.
Tennis: Hardeep Judge; Phone: 803-536-7242.

Track and Field: Ernest Tche; Phone: 803-536-8715.
Volleyball: Mary Hill; Phone: 803-536-3783.

SOUTH DAKOTA SCHOOL OF MINES AND TECHNOLOGY
Rapid City, South Dakota

Hardrockers ◆ NAIA ◆ Dakota Conference
◆ http://www.sdsmt.edu/

State-supported university, founded 1885, part of South Dakota State University System
Coed, 2,112 undergraduate students, 82% full-time, 31% women, 69% men
Suburban 120-acre campus
Moderately difficult entrance level, 94% of applicants were admitted

Freshmen *Admission:* 811 applied, 762 were accepted, 420 enrolled. *Test scores:* SAT verbal scores over 500: 71%; SAT math scores over 500: 85%; SAT verbal scores over 600: 30%; SAT math scores over 600: 46%; SAT verbal scores over 700: 7%; SAT math scores over 700: 8%.
Tuition and fees (2003–04): $4293 (resident), $9005 (nonresident). *Room and board:* $3561 (room only: $1625).
Financial Aid (All incoming freshmen): *Average need-based gift aid:* $3093. *Average non-need based aid:* $2537. *Average aid to full-time undergraduates:* $5107.
Athletic Department: *Director of Athletics:* Hugh Welsh; Phone: 605-394-2352; Fax: 605-394-3375; E-mail: hugh.welsh@sdsmt.edu. *Sports Information Director:* Tom Rudebusch; Phone: 605-394-2601; E-mail: thomas.rudebusch@sdsmt.edu.

MEN'S COACHES
Basketball: Hugh Welsh; Phone: 605-394-2352; E-mail: hugh.welsh@sdsmt.edu.
Cross Country: Jerry Schafer; Phone: 605-394-2603; E-mail: jerald.schafer@sdsmt.edu.
Football: Darren Soucy; Phone: 605-394-2604; E-mail: darren.soucy@sdsmt.edu.
Golf: Aaron Roeber; Phone: 605-394-2352.
Track and Field: Jerry Schafer; Phone: 605-394-2603; E-mail: jerald.schafer@sdsmt.edu.

WOMEN'S COACHES
Basketball: Barb Felderman; Phone: 605-394-2602; E-mail: barbara.felderman@sdsmt.edu.
Cross Country: Jerry Schafer; Phone: 605-394-2603; E-mail: jerald.schafer@sdsmt.edu.
Golf: Aaron Roeber; Phone: 605-394-2352.
Track and Field: Jerry Schafer; Phone: 605-394-2603; E-mail: jerald.schafer@sdsmt.edu.
Volleyball: Doug Tabbert; Phone: 605-394-2605; E-mail: douglas.tabbert@sdsmt.edu.

SOUTH DAKOTA STATE UNIVERSITY
Brookings, South Dakota

Jackrabbits ◆ NCAA II ◆ North Central Intercollegiate Conference ◆ http://www.sdstate.edu/

State-supported university, founded 1881
Coed, 9,284 undergraduate students, 80% full-time, 53% women, 47% men
Small-town 272-acre campus
Moderately difficult entrance level, 96% of applicants were admitted

Freshmen *Admission:* 3,748 applied, 3,586 were accepted, 2,073 enrolled.
Tuition and fees (2003–04): $4536 (resident), $9560 (nonresident). *Room and board:* $3586 (room only: $1862).
Financial Aid (All incoming freshmen): *Average need-based gift aid:* $3070. *Average non-need based aid:* $982. *Average aid to full-time undergraduates:* $6094.

Athletic Department: *Director of Athletics:* Fred Oien; Phone: 605-688-5625; Fax: 605-688-5999; E-mail: fred_oien@sdstate.edu. *Sports Information Director:* Ron Lenz; Phone: 605-688-4623; E-mail: ronald_lenz@sdstate.edu.

MEN'S COACHES
Baseball: Mark Ekeland; Phone: 605-688-5027; E-mail: mark_ekeland@sdstate.edu.
Basketball: Scott Nagy; Phone: 605-688-5626; E-mail: scott_nagy@sdstate.edu.
Cross Country: Paul Danger; Phone: 605-688-5994; E-mail: paul_danger@sdstate.edu.
Football: John Stiegelmeier; Phone: 605-688-5525; E-mail: john_stiegelmeier@sdstate.edu.
Golf: Jim Booher; Phone: 605-691-1592; E-mail: james_booher@sdstate.edu.
Swimming: Brad Erickson; Phone: 605-688-6527; E-mail: bradley_erickson@sdstate.edu.
Tennis: Don Hanson; Phone: 605-688-5625; E-mail: donald_hanson@sdstate.edu.
Track and Field: Paul Danger; Phone: 605-688-5994; E-mail: paul_danger@sdstate.edu.
Wrestling: Jason Liles; Phone: 605-688-5026; E-mail: jason_liles@sdstate.edu.

WOMEN'S COACHES
Basketball: Aaron Johnston; Phone: 605-688-6336; E-mail: aaron_johnston@sdstate.edu.
Cross Country: Paul Danger; Phone: 605-688-5994; E-mail: paul_danger@sdstate.edu.
Golf: Jim Booher; Phone: 605-691-1592; E-mail: james_booher@sdstate.edu.
Soccer: Lang Wedemeyer; Phone: 605-688-4070; E-mail: lang_wedemeyer@sdstate.edu.
Softball: Shane Bouman; Phone: 605-688-6510; E-mail: shane_bouman@sdstate.edu.
Swimming: Brad Erickson; Phone: 605-688-6527; E-mail: bradley_erickson@sdstate.edu.
Tennis: Don Hanson; Phone: 605-688-5625; E-mail: donald_hanson@sdstate.edu.
Track and Field: Paul Danger; Phone: 605-688-5994; E-mail: paul_danger@sdstate.edu.
Volleyball: Andrew Palileo; Phone: 605-688-5819; E-mail: andrew_palileo@sdstate.edu.

SOUTHEASTERN LOUISIANA UNIVERSITY
Hammond, Louisiana

Lions ◆ NCAA I ◆ Southland Conference
◆ http://www.selu.edu/

State-supported comprehensive, founded 1925, part of University of Louisiana System
Coed, 13,629 undergraduate students, 84% full-time, 62% women, 38% men
Small-town 375-acre campus with easy access to New Orleans
95% of applicants were admitted

Freshmen *Admission:* 3,488 applied, 3,341 were accepted, 2,681 enrolled.
Tuition and fees (2003–04): $2951 (resident), $8279 (nonresident). *Room and board:* $3840 (room only: $1900).
Financial Aid (All incoming freshmen): *Average need-based gift aid:* $3076. *Average non-need based aid:* $2379. *Average aid to full-time undergraduates:* $4005.
Athletic Department: *Director of Athletics:* Frank Pergolizzi; Phone: 985-549-2420; Fax: 985-549-3495; E-mail: fpergolizzi@selu.edu. *Sports Information Director:* Dart Volz; Phone: 985-549-2142; E-mail: dvolz@selu.edu.

MEN'S COACHES
Baseball: Dan Canevari; Phone: 985-549-2896; E-mail: dcanevari@selu.edu.
Basketball: Billy Kennedy; Phone: 985-549-3744; E-mail: bkennedy@selu.edu.
Cheerleading: Lorry Perry; Phone: 985-549-2900; E-mail: lperry@selu.edu.

Southeastern Louisiana University *(continued)*

Cross Country: Sean Brady; Phone: 985-549-5188; E-mail: sbrady@selu.edu.

Football: Hal Mumme; Phone: 985-549-2395; E-mail: sportsinfo@selu.edu.

Golf: Tim Baldwin; Phone: 985-549-5186; E-mail: tbaldwin@selu.edu.

Tennis: Jason Hayes; Phone: 985-549-5193; E-mail: hayes_jason@hotmail.com.

Track and Field: Sean Brady; Phone: 985-549-5188; E-mail: sbrady@selu.edu.

WOMEN'S COACHES

Basketball: Lori Davis Jones; Phone: 985-549-3744; E-mail: ljones@selu.edu.

Cheerleading: Lorry Perry; Phone: 985-549-2900; E-mail: lperry@selu.edu.

Cross Country: Sean Brady; Phone: 985-549-5188; E-mail: sbrady@selu.edu.

Soccer: Blake Hornbuckle; Phone: 985-549-5185; E-mail: bhornbuckle@selu.edu.

Softball: Pete Langlois; Phone: 985-549-5192; E-mail: planglois@selu.edu.

Tennis: Jason Hayes; Phone: 985-549-5193; E-mail: hayes_jason@hotmail.com.

Track and Field: Sean Brady; Phone: 985-549-5188; E-mail: sbrady@selu.edu.

Volleyball: Roni Armeda Hipp; Phone: 985-549-5189; E-mail: rarmeda@selu.edu.

SOUTHEASTERN OKLAHOMA STATE UNIVERSITY
Durant, Oklahoma

Savages ◆ NCAA II ◆ Lone Star Conference ◆ http://www.sosu.edu/

State-supported comprehensive, founded 1909, part of Oklahoma State Regents for Higher Education
Coed, 3,738 undergraduate students, 79% full-time, 54% women, 46% men
Small-town 177-acre campus
Moderately difficult entrance level, 80% of applicants were admitted

Freshmen *Admission:* 1,067 applied, 856 were accepted, 646 enrolled.
Tuition and fees (2003–04): $2947 (resident), $6847 (nonresident). *Room and board:* $3200 (room only: $1400).
Financial Aid (All incoming freshmen): *Average need-based gift aid:* $1171. *Average non-need based aid:* $809. *Average aid to full-time undergraduates:* $2585.
Athletic Department: *Director of Athletics:* Don Parham; Phone: 580-745-2250; Fax: 580-745-7493; E-mail: dparham@sosu.edu. *Sports Information Director:* Dave Wester; Phone: 580-745-2646; E-mail: dwester@sosu.edu.

MEN'S COACHES

Baseball: Mike Metheny; Phone: 580-745-2478; E-mail: mmetheny@sosu.edu.

Basketball: Tony Robinson; Phone: 580-745-2458; E-mail: trobinson@sosu.edu.

Cheerleading: Liz McCraw; Phone: 580-745-2360; E-mail: lmccraw@sosu.edu.

Football: Keith Baxter; Phone: 580-745-2468; E-mail: kbaxter@sosu.edu.

Tennis: Bill Troeger; Phone: 580-745-2486; E-mail: btroeger@sosu.edu.

WOMEN'S COACHES

Basketball: Nick Keith; Phone: 580-745-2472; E-mail: nkeith@sosu.edu.

Cheerleading: Liz McCraw; Phone: 580-745-2360; E-mail: lmccraw@sosu.edu.

Cross Country: Brad Ludrick; Phone: 580-745-2668; E-mail: bludrick@sosu.edu.

Softball: Ron Faubion; Phone: 580-745-2474; E-mail: rfaubion@sosu.edu.

Tennis: Pat Mauldin; Phone: 580-745-2480; E-mail: pmauldin@sosu.edu.

Volleyball: Cherrie Wilmoth; Phone: 580-745-2690; E-mail: cwilmoth@sosu.edu.

SOUTHEAST MISSOURI STATE UNIVERSITY
Cape Girardeau, Missouri

(M) Indians (W) Otahkians ◆ NCAA I ◆ Ohio Valley Conference ◆ http://www.semo.edu/

State-supported comprehensive, founded 1873, part of Missouri Coordinating Board for Higher Education
Coed, 8,483 undergraduate students, 78% full-time, 58% women, 42% men
Small-town 693-acre campus with easy access to St. Louis
Moderately difficult entrance level, 84% of applicants were admitted

Freshmen *Admission:* 3,910 applied, 3,238 were accepted, 1,495 enrolled.
Tuition and fees (2003–04): $4575 (resident), $8160 (nonresident). *Room and board:* $5450 (room only: $3505).
Financial Aid (All incoming freshmen): *Average need-based gift aid:* $3947. *Average non-need based aid:* $2764. *Average aid to full-time undergraduates:* $5665.
Athletic Department: *Director of Athletics:* Don Kaverman; Phone: 573-651-2229; Fax: 573-651-2959; E-mail: dkaverman@semo.edu. *Sports Information Director:* Ron Hines; Phone: 573-651-2294; E-mail: rhines@semo.edu.

MEN'S COACHES

Baseball: Mark Hogan; Phone: 573-651-2645; E-mail: baseball@semo.edu.

Basketball: Gary Garner; Phone: 573-651-2160; E-mail: ggarner@semo.edu.

Cheerleading: Nancy Greaser; Phone: 573-986-6194; E-mail: ngreaser@semo.edu.

Cross Country: Joey Haines; Phone: 573-651-5994; E-mail: f262ath@semo.edu.

Football: Tim Billings; Phone: 573-651-2561; E-mail: tbillings@semo.edu.

Golf: Carroll WIlliams; Phone: 573-651-2467; E-mail: c248edh@semo.edu.

Track and Field: Joey Haines; Phone: 573-651-5994; E-mail: f262ath@semo.edu.

WOMEN'S COACHES

Basketball: B.J. Smith; Phone: 573-651-2643; E-mail: bjsmith@semo.edu.

Cheerleading: Nancy Greaser; Phone: 573-986-6194; E-mail: ngreaser@semo.edu.

Cross Country: Joey Haines; Phone: 573-651-5994; E-mail: f262ath@semo.edu.

Gymnastics: Tom Farden; Phone: 573-651-2604; E-mail: tfarden@semo.edu.

Soccer: Heather Nelson; Phone: 573-651-6013; E-mail: hnelson@semo.edu.

Softball: Lana Richmond; Phone: 573-651-2993; E-mail: lrichmond@semo.edu.

Tennis: Jay Pacelli; Phone: 573-651-2548; E-mail: jpacelli@semo.edu.

Track and Field: Joey Haines; Phone: 573-651-5994; E-mail: f262ath@semo.edu.

Volleyball: Cindy Gannon; Phone: 573-651-2997; E-mail: cmgannon@semo.edu.

SOUTHERN ARKANSAS UNIVERSITY–MAGNOLIA
Magnolia, Arkansas

(M)Muleriders (W) Riderettes ◆ NCAA II ◆ Gulf South Conference ◆ http://www.saumag.edu/

State-supported comprehensive, founded 1909, part of Southern Arkansas University System
Coed, 2,804 undergraduate students, 87% full-time, 56% women, 44% men
Small-town 781-acre campus
Moderately difficult entrance level, 82% of applicants were admitted

Freshmen *Admission:* 1,155 applied, 939 were accepted, 565 enrolled.

Tuition and fees (2003–04): $3496 (resident), $5186 (nonresident). *Room and board:* $3460.
Financial Aid (All incoming freshmen): *Average need-based gift aid:* $3662. *Average non-need based aid:* $3110. *Average aid to full-time undergraduates:* $6074.
Athletic Department: *Director of Athletics:* Jay Adcox; Phone: 870-235-4132; Fax: 870-235-4988; E-mail: jdadcox@saumag.edu. *Sports Information Director:* Houston Taylor; Phone: 870-235-4104; E-mail: hdtaylor@saumag.edu.

MEN'S COACHES
Baseball: Steve Goodheart; Phone: 870-235-4127; E-mail: sdgoodheart@saumag.edu.
Basketball: Brian Daugherty; Phone: 870-235-4131; E-mail: bcdaugherty@saumag.edu.
Cheerleading: Ceil Bridges; Phone: 870-235-4092; E-mail: cbridges@saumag.edu.
Cross Country: Dan Veach; Phone: 870-235-4154; E-mail: dtveach@saumag.edu.
Football: Steve Quinn; Phone: 870-235-4105; E-mail: smquinn@saumag.edu.
Golf: Dave Graham; Phone: 870-235-4041.
Track and Field: Dan Veach; Phone: 870-235-4154; E-mail: dtveach@saumag.edu.

WOMEN'S COACHES
Basketball: Sam Biley; Phone: 870-235-4134; E-mail: sbiley@saumag.edu.
Cheerleading: Ceil Bridges; Phone: 870-235-4092; E-mail: cbridges@saumag.edu.
Cross Country: Dan Veach; Phone: 870-235-4154; E-mail: dtveach@saumag.edu.
Softball: Kevin Blaskowski; Phone: 870-235-4384; E-mail: klblaskowski@saumag.edu.
Tennis: Wayne Garner; Phone: 870-235-4146; E-mail: wdgarner@saumag.edu.
Track and Field: Dan Veach; Phone: 870-235-4154; E-mail: dtveach@saumag.edu.
Volleyball: Shawna Laurendine; Phone: 870-235-4128; E-mail: sllaurendine@saumag.edu.

SOUTHERN CONNECTICUT STATE UNIVERSITY
New Haven, Connecticut
Owls ◆ NCAA II ◆ Northeast-10 Conference ◆ http://www.southernct.edu/

State-supported comprehensive, founded 1893, part of Connecticut State University System
Coed, 8,123 undergraduate students, 78% full-time, 60% women, 40% men
Urban 168-acre campus with easy access to New York City
Moderately difficult entrance level, 57% of applicants were admitted

Freshmen *Admission:* 4,829 applied, 2,936 were accepted, 1,337 enrolled. *Test scores:* SAT verbal scores over 500: 43%; SAT math scores over 500: 41%; SAT verbal scores over 600: 7%; SAT math scores over 600: 6%; SAT math scores over 700: 1%.
Tuition and fees (2004–05): $5622 (resident), $12,356 (nonresident). *Room and board:* $7019 (room only: $3865).
Financial Aid (All incoming freshmen): *Average need-based gift aid:* $3732. *Average non-need based aid:* $3428. *Average aid to full-time undergraduates:* $7444.
Athletic Department: *Director of Athletics:* Tony Aceto; Phone: 203-392-6003; Fax: 203-392-6006; E-mail: acetoa1@southernct.edu. *Sports Information Director:* Ricky Leddy; Phone: 203-392-6004; E-mail: leddyr1@southernct.edu.

MEN'S COACHES
Baseball: Tim Shea; Phone: 203-392-6021; E-mail: sheat1@southernct.edu.
Basketball: Art Leary; Phone: 203-392-6015; E-mail: scsuhoops@yahoo.com.
Cross Country: Jack Maloney; Phone: 203-392-6023; E-mail: maloneyj1@southernct.edu.
Football: Rich Cavanaugh; Phone: 203-392-6010; E-mail: cavanaughr1@southernct.edu.
Soccer: Tom Lang; Phone: 203-392-6018; E-mail: scsusoccer@yahoo.com.
Swimming: Tim Quill; Phone: 203-392-6026; E-mail: quillt1@southernct.edu.
Track and Field: Jack Maloney; Phone: 203-392-6023; E-mail: maloneyj1@southernct.edu.

WOMEN'S COACHES
Basketball: Joe Frager; Phone: 203-392-6002; E-mail: fragerj1@southernct.edu.
Cross Country: Nancy Gouthro; Phone: 203-392-6000; E-mail: nvgouthro@aol.com.
Field Hockey: Kelly Kimball Frassinelli; Phone: 203-392-5981; E-mail: coachkimball@yahoo.com.
Gymnastics: Pat Danichas; Phone: 203-392-6082; E-mail: panichasp1@southernct.edu.
Lacrosse: Kelly Kimball Frassinelli; Phone: 203-392-5981; E-mail: coachkimball@yahoo.com.
Soccer: Jim O'Brien; Phone: 203-392-5759; E-mail: coachob@hotmail.com.
Softball: Pat Fernandes; Phone: 203-392-6022; E-mail: fernandesp1@southernct.edu.
Swimming: Tim Quill; Phone: 203-392-6026; E-mail: quillt1@southernct.edu.
Track and Field: Jim Barber; Phone: 203-392-6814; E-mail: barberj1@southernct.edu.
Volleyball: Pat Fernandes; Phone: 203-392-6022; E-mail: fernandesp1@southernct.edu.

SOUTHERN ILLINOIS UNIVERSITY CARBONDALE
Carbondale, Illinois
Salukis ◆ NCAA I ◆ Gateway Football Conference; Missouri Valley Conference ◆ http://www.siuc.edu/

State-supported university, founded 1869, part of Southern Illinois University
Coed, 16,366 undergraduate students, 90% full-time, 44% women, 56% men
Rural 1,133-acre campus with easy access to St. Louis
Moderately difficult entrance level, 73% of applicants were admitted

Freshmen *Admission:* 8,627 applied, 6,665 were accepted, 2,624 enrolled. *Test scores:* SAT verbal scores over 500: 59%; SAT math scores over 500: 60%; SAT verbal scores over 600: 25%; SAT math scores over 600: 28%; SAT verbal scores over 700: 4%; SAT math scores over 700: 7%.
Tuition and fees (2004–05): $5981 (resident), $10,541 (nonresident). *Room and board:* $5200 (room only: $2640).
Financial Aid (All incoming freshmen): *Average need-based gift aid:* $4933. *Average non-need based aid:* $2668. *Average aid to full-time undergraduates:* $7329.
Athletic Department: *Director of Athletics:* Paul Kowalczyk; Phone: 618-453-7250; Fax: 618-453-5152; E-mail: pkowal@siu.edu. *Sports Information Director:* Tom Weber; Phone: 618-453-7236; E-mail: tomweber@siu.edu.

MEN'S COACHES
Baseball: Dan Callahan; Phone: 618-453-2802; E-mail: dcal@siu.edu.
Basketball: Matt Painter; Phone: 618-453-4667; E-mail: mpainter@siu.edu.
Cheerleading: Nancy Esling; Phone: 618-453-2221; E-mail: spirit@siu.edu.
Cross Country: Cameron Wright; Phone: 618-453-7242; E-mail: saluki2000@aol.com.
Diving: Joy Zhao; Phone: 618-453-5461; E-mail: zhaoc@siu.edu.
Football: Jerry Kill; Phone: 618-453-3331; E-mail: jkill@siu.edu.
Golf: Leroy Newton; Phone: 618-453-7248; E-mail: lnewton@siu.edu.
Swimming: Rick Walker; Phone: 618-453-7230; E-mail: rwalker@siu.edu.
Tennis: Missy Jeffrey; Phone: 618-453-7247; E-mail: jeffrey@siu.edu.
Track and Field: Cameron Wright; Phone: 618-453-7242; E-mail: saluki2000@aol.com.

WOMEN'S COACHES
Basketball: Lori Opp; Phone: 618-453-5484; E-mail: loriopp@siu.edu.

Southern Illinois University Carbondale *(continued)*

Cheerleading: Nancy Esling; Phone: 618-453-2221; E-mail: spirit@siu.edu.
Cross Country: Matt Sparks; Phone: 618-453-8375; E-mail: msparks@siu.edu.
Diving: Joy Zhao; Phone: 618-453-5461; E-mail: zhaoc@siu.edu.
Golf: Diane Daugherty; Phone: 618-453-5469; E-mail: ddgolf@siu.edu.
Softball: Kerri Blaylock; Phone: 618-453-5466; E-mail: mook@siu.edu.
Swimming: Jeff Goelz; Phone: 618-453-5461; E-mail: jgoelz@siu.edu.
Tennis: Judy Auld; Phone: 618-453-5462; E-mail: jauld@siu.edu.
Track and Field: Connie Price-Smith; Phone: 618-453-5460; E-mail: psmith@siu.edu.
Volleyball: Sonya Locke; Phone: 618-453-5473; E-mail: salooki@siu.edu.

SOUTHERN ILLINOIS UNIVERSITY EDWARDSVILLE
Edwardsville, Illinois

Cougars ◆ NCAA II ◆ Great Lakes Valley Conference ◆ http://www.siue.edu/

State-supported comprehensive, founded 1957, part of Southern Illinois University
Coed, 10,563 undergraduate students, 84% full-time, 55% women, 45% men
Suburban 2,660-acre campus with easy access to St. Louis
Moderately difficult entrance level, 80% of applicants were admitted

Freshmen *Admission:* 4,383 applied, 3,542 were accepted, 1,743 enrolled.
Tuition and fees (2003–04): $4183 (resident), $7543 (nonresident). *Room and board:* $5364 (room only: $3077).
Financial Aid (All incoming freshmen): *Average need-based gift aid:* $5119. *Average non-need based aid:* $3284. *Average aid to full-time undergraduates:* $7211.
Athletic Department: *Director of Athletics:* Brad Hewitt; Phone: 618-650-2869; Fax: 618-650-3369; E-mail: bhewitt@siue.edu. *Sports Information Director:* Eric Hess; Phone: 618-650-3608; E-mail: ehess@siue.edu.

MEN'S COACHES
Baseball: Gary Collins; Phone: 618-650-2872; E-mail: gcollin@siue.edu.
Basketball: Marty Simmons; Phone: 618-650-2866; E-mail: masimmo@siue.edu.
Cheerleading: Ariene Cheney; Phone: 618-650-3695; E-mail: acheney@siue.edu.
Cross Country: Darryl Frerker; Phone: 618-650-2877; E-mail: dfrerke@siue.edu.
Soccer: Ed Huneke; Phone: 618-650-2868; E-mail: ehuneke@siue.edu.
Tennis: William Logan; Phone: 618-650-2867; E-mail: wlogan@siue.edu.
Track and Field: Darryl Frerker; Phone: 618-650-2877; E-mail: dfrerke@siue.edu.
Wrestling: Booker Benford; Phone: 618-650-3715; E-mail: bbenfor@siue.edu.

WOMEN'S COACHES
Basketball: Wendy Hedberg; Phone: 618-650-2880; E-mail: whedber@siue.edu.
Cheerleading: Ariene Cheney; Phone: 618-650-3695; E-mail: acheney@siue.edu.
Cross Country: Darryl Frerker; Phone: 618-650-2877; E-mail: dfrerke@siue.edu.
Golf: Larry Bennett; Phone: 618-650-3236; E-mail: lbennett@siue.edu.
Soccer: Lynda Bowers; Phone: 618-650-3738; E-mail: lbowers@siue.edu.
Softball: Sandy Montgomery; Phone: 618-650-2870; E-mail: smontgo@siue.edu.
Tennis: William Logan; Phone: 618-650-2867; E-mail: wlogan@siue.edu.
Track and Field: Darryl Frerker; Phone: 618-650-2877; E-mail: dfrerke@siue.edu.
Volleyball: Todd Gober; Phone: 618-650-5923; E-mail: tgober@siue.edu.

SOUTHERN METHODIST UNIVERSITY
Dallas, Texas

Mustangs ◆ NCAA I ◆ Missouri Valley Conference; Western Athletic Conference ◆ http://www.smu.edu/

Independent religious university, founded 1911, affiliated with United Methodist Church
Coed, 6,299 undergraduate students, 94% full-time, 55% women, 45% men
Suburban 165-acre campus
Moderately difficult entrance level, 58% of applicants were admitted

Freshmen *Admission:* 6,293 applied, 4,076 were accepted, 1,383 enrolled. *Test scores:* SAT verbal scores over 500: 92%; SAT math scores over 500: 94%; SAT verbal scores over 600: 48%; SAT math scores over 600: 57%; SAT verbal scores over 700: 8%; SAT math scores over 700: 11%.
Tuition and fees (2004–05): $25,358 (full-time). *Room and board:* $8852.
Financial Aid (All incoming freshmen): *Average need-based gift aid:* $14,909. *Average non-need based aid:* $6137. *Average aid to full-time undergraduates:* $22,817.
Athletic Department: *Director of Athletics:* Jim Copeland; Phone: 214-768-4301; E-mail: jcopelan@mail.smu.edu. *Sports Information Director:* Brad Sutton; Phone: 214-768-1651; E-mail: bsutton@mail.smu.edu.

MEN'S COACHES
Basketball: Mike Dement; Phone: 214-768-3504; E-mail: mdement@mail.smu.edu.
Cheerleading: Sara O'Connell; Phone: 214-768-1500; E-mail: soconnel@mail.smu.edu.
Cross Country: Dave Wollman; Phone: 214-768-3517; E-mail: dwollman@mail.smu.edu.
Diving: Jim Stillson; Phone: 214-768-1640; E-mail: stillson@mail.smu.edu.
Football: Phil Bennett; Phone: 214-768-3667; E-mail: pbennett@mail.smu.edu.
Golf: Jay Loar; Phone: 214-768-3283; E-mail: jloar@mail.smu.edu.
Soccer: Schellas Hyndman; Phone: 214-768-2875; E-mail: shyndman@mail.smu.edu.
Swimming: Eddie Sinnot; Phone: 214-768-2311; E-mail: esinnott@mail.smu.edu.
Tennis: Carl Neufeld; Phone: 214-768-2664; E-mail: cneufeld@mail.smu.edu.
Track and Field: Dave Wollman; Phone: 214-768-3517; E-mail: dwollman@mail.smu.edu.

WOMEN'S COACHES
Basketball: Rhonda Rompola; Phone: 214-768-3536; E-mail: rrompola@mail.smu.edu.
Cheerleading: Sara O'Connell; Phone: 214-768-1500; E-mail: soconnel@mail.smu.edu.
Cross Country: Dave Wollman; Phone: 214-768-3517; E-mail: dwollman@mail.smu.edu.
Diving: Jim Stillson; Phone: 214-768-1640; E-mail: stillson@mail.smu.edu.
Golf: Todd Selders; Phone: 214-768-2884; E-mail: tselders@mail.smu.edu.
Soccer: John Cossaboon; Phone: 214-768-4030; E-mail: jcossabo@mail.smu.edu.
Swimming: Steve Collins; Phone: 214-768-2944; E-mail: collins@mail.smu.edu.
Tennis: Stephen Moore; Phone: 214-768-3830; E-mail: smoore@mail.smu.edu.
Track and Field: Dave Wollman; Phone: 214-768-3517; E-mail: dwollman@mail.smu.edu.
Volleyball: Lisa Seifert; Phone: 214-768-4227; E-mail: lseifert@mail.smu.edu.

SOUTHERN NAZARENE UNIVERSITY
Bethany, Oklahoma

Crimson Storm ◆ NAIA ◆ Central States Football Conference; Sooner Conference ◆ http://www.snu.edu/

Independent Nazarene comprehensive, founded 1899
Coed, 1,803 undergraduate students, 96% full-time, 53% women, 47% men
Suburban 40-acre campus with easy access to Oklahoma City
Noncompetitive entrance level, 41% of applicants were admitted

Freshmen *Admission:* 735 applied, 304 were accepted, 304 enrolled.
Tuition and fees (2004–05): $12,834 (full-time). *Room and board:* $5110 (room only: $2410).
Athletic Department: *Director of Athletics:* Bobby Martin; Phone: 405-491-6339; Fax: 405-491-6387; E-mail: bgmartin@snu.edu. *Sports Information Director:* Scott Secor; Phone: 405-491-6619; E-mail: ssecor@snu.edu.

MEN'S COACHES
Baseball: Scott Selby; Phone: 405-491-6630; E-mail: sselby@snu.edu.
Basketball: Michael Broughton; Phone: 405-491-6623; E-mail: mibrough@snu.edu.
Cheerleading: Misty Jaggers; Phone: 405-491-6559; E-mail: mjaggers@snu.edu.
Cross Country: Billy Miller; Phone: 405-717-6227.
Football: Paul McGrady; Phone: 405-491-6338; E-mail: pmcgrady@snu.edu.
Golf: Steve Hulsey; Phone: 405-491-6699; E-mail: shulsey@snu.edu.
Soccer: Mark Persson; Phone: 405-491-6629; E-mail: mpersson@snu.edu.
Tennis: Phil White; Phone: 405-491-6326; E-mail: pwhite@snu.edu.
Track and Field: Tim McMichael; Phone: 405-717-6227; E-mail: tmcmicha@snu.edu.

WOMEN'S COACHES
Basketball: Lori Carter; Phone: 405-491-6303; E-mail: lcarter@snu.edu.
Cheerleading: Misty Jaggers; Phone: 405-491-6559; E-mail: mjaggers@snu.edu.
Cross Country: Billy Miller; Phone: 405-717-6227.
Golf: Steve Hulsey; Phone: 405-491-6699; E-mail: shulsey@snu.edu.
Soccer: Patty Naumoska; Phone: 405-491-6238; E-mail: @snu.edu.
Softball: Jimmy Knight; Phone: 405-491-6621; E-mail: jknight@snu.edu.
Tennis: Phil White; Phone: 405-491-6326; E-mail: pwhite@snu.edu.
Track and Field: Tim McMichael; Phone: 405-717-6227; E-mail: tmcmicha@snu.edu.
Volleyball: Kevin Ingram; Phone: 405-717-6221; E-mail: kingram@snu.edu.

SOUTHERN NEW HAMPSHIRE UNIVERSITY
Manchester, New Hampshire

Penmen ◆ NCAA II ◆ Northeast-10 Conference ◆ http://www.snhu.edu/

Independent comprehensive, founded 1932
Coed, 3,907 undergraduate students, 62% full-time, 55% women, 45% men
Suburban 280-acre campus with easy access to Boston
Moderately difficult entrance level, 82% of applicants were admitted

Freshmen *Admission:* 1,953 applied, 1,602 were accepted, 806 enrolled. *Test scores:* SAT verbal scores over 500: 35%; SAT math scores over 500: 41%; SAT verbal scores over 600: 7%; SAT math scores over 600: 9%.
Tuition and fees (2004–05): $19,314 (full-time). *Room and board:* $7866.
Athletic Department: *Director of Athletics:* Chip Polak; Phone: 603-645-9604; Fax: 603-645-9686; E-mail: j.polak@snhu.edu. *Sports Information Director:* Tom McDermott; Phone: 603-645-9638; E-mail: t.mcdermott@snhu.edu.

MEN'S COACHES
Baseball: Bruce Joyce; Phone: 603-645-9637; E-mail: b.joyce@snhu.edu.
Basketball: Stan Spirou; Phone: 603-645-9649; E-mail: s.spirou@snhu.edu.
Cheerleading: Amy Slattum; Phone: 603-645-9768; E-mail: a.slattum@snhu.edu.
Cross Country: Adrien Cooper; Phone: 603-645-9746; E-mail: a.cooper@snhu.edu.
Golf: Jozef Maston; Phone: 603-645-9747; E-mail: j.maston@snhu.edu.
Ice Hockey: Rene LeClerc; Phone: 603-645-9769; E-mail: r.leclerc@snhu.edu.
Lacrosse: Paul Calkins; Phone: 603-645-9759; E-mail: p.calkins@snhu.edu.
Soccer: Dave Anderson; Phone: 603-645-9703; E-mail: d.anderson@snhu.edu.
Tennis: Brian Horan; Phone: 603-645-9748; E-mail: b.horan@snhu.edu.

WOMEN'S COACHES
Basketball: Dennis Masi; Phone: 603-645-9662; E-mail: d.masi@snhu.edu.
Cheerleading: Amy Slattum; Phone: 603-645-9768; E-mail: a.slattum@snhu.edu.
Cross Country: Sid Slark; Phone: 603-645-9773; E-mail: s.slark@snhu.edu.
Lacrosse: Mary Squire; Phone: 603-645-9749; E-mail: m.squire@snhu.edu.
Soccer: Terry Prouty; Phone: 603-645-9641; E-mail: t.prouty@snhu.edu.
Softball: Terry Prouty; Phone: 603-645-9641; E-mail: t.prouty@snhu.edu.
Tennis: Hugh Mallet; Phone: 603-645-9604; E-mail: h.mallett@snhu.edu.
Volleyball: John Vaughn; Phone: 603-645-9764; E-mail: j.vaughn@snhu.edu.

SOUTHERN OREGON UNIVERSITY
Ashland, Oregon

Raiders ◆ NAIA ◆ Cascade Collegiate Conference ◆ http://www.sou.edu/

State-supported comprehensive, founded 1926, part of Oregon University System
Coed, 4,964 undergraduate students, 78% full-time, 55% women, 45% men
Small-town 175-acre campus
Moderately difficult entrance level, 89% of applicants were admitted

Freshmen *Admission:* 2,176 applied, 1,960 were accepted, 968 enrolled. *Test scores:* SAT verbal scores over 500: 61%; SAT math scores over 500: 59%; SAT verbal scores over 600: 22%; SAT math scores over 600: 17%; SAT verbal scores over 700: 3%; SAT math scores over 700: 2%.
Tuition and fees (2003–04): $4153 (resident), $12,823 (nonresident). *Room and board:* $6039.
Financial Aid (All incoming freshmen): *Average need-based gift aid:* $4374. *Average non-need based aid:* $6496. *Average aid to full-time undergraduates:* $5978.
Athletic Department: *Director of Athletics:* Phil Pifer; Phone: 541-552-6727; Fax: 541-552-6543; E-mail: pifer@sou.edu. *Sports Information Director:* Rich Rosenthal; Phone: 541-552-6824; E-mail: rosenthal@sou.edu.

MEN'S COACHES
Basketball: Brian McDermott; Phone: 541-552-8554; E-mail: mcdermott@sou.edu.
Cross Country: Grier Gatlin; Phone: 541-552-6735; E-mail: gatling@sou.edu.
Football: Jeff Olson; Phone: 541-552-6659; E-mail: jolson@sou.edu.
Tennis: Gail Patton; Phone: 541-552-6563; E-mail: pattong@sou.edu.
Track and Field: Grier Gatlin; Phone: 541-552-6735; E-mail: gatling@sou.edu.
Wrestling: Mike Ritchey; Phone: 541-552-6363; E-mail: ritchey@sou.edu.

WOMEN'S COACHES
Basketball: Kevin Wilson; Phone: 541-552-6044; E-mail: wilsonk@sou.edu.
Cross Country: Grier Gatlin; Phone: 541-552-6735; E-mail: gatling@sou.edu.

Southern Oregon University *(continued)*

Soccer: Jose Chavez; Phone: 541-552-6735; E-mail: chavezj@sou.edu.
Softball: Larry Binney; Phone: 541-552-8285; E-mail: binneyl@sou.edu.
Tennis: Gail Patton; Phone: 541-552-6563; E-mail: pattong@sou.edu.
Track and Field: Grier Gatlin; Phone: 541-552-6735; E-mail: gatling@sou.edu.
Volleyball: Paul Elliot; Phone: 541-552-6728; E-mail: pelliott@sou.edu.

SOUTHERN POLYTECHNIC STATE UNIVERSITY
Marietta, Georgia

Hornets ◆ NAIA ◆ Georgia Alabama Carolina Conference ◆ http://www.spsu.edu/

State-supported comprehensive, founded 1948, part of University System of Georgia
Coed, 3,185 undergraduate students, 63% full-time, 18% women, 82% men
Suburban 200-acre campus with easy access to Atlanta
Moderately difficult entrance level, 87% of applicants were admitted

Freshmen *Admission:* 779 applied, 666 were accepted, 472 enrolled. *Test scores:* SAT verbal scores over 500: 75%; SAT math scores over 500: 88%; SAT verbal scores over 600: 22%; SAT math scores over 600: 35%; SAT verbal scores over 700: 2%; SAT math scores over 700: 2%.
Tuition and fees (2003–04): $2754 (resident), $9690 (nonresident). *Room and board:* $4866 (room only: $2660).
Financial Aid (All incoming freshmen): *Average need-based gift aid:* $2700. *Average non-need based aid:* $2230. *Average aid to full-time undergraduates:* $6954.
Athletic Department: *Director of Athletics:* Karl Stabler; Phone: 770-528-7349; Fax: 770-528-5515; E-mail: kstaber@spsu.edu.

MEN'S COACHES
Baseball: Matt Griffin; Phone: 770-528-5445; E-mail: mgriffin@spsu.edu.
Basketball: Michael Helfer; Phone: 770-528-7360; E-mail: mhelfer@spsu.edu.
Tennis: Pascual Herrera; Phone: 770-528-5477; E-mail: patherrera8783@msn.com.

WOMEN'S COACHES
Basketball: Alisa Niederstadt Staude; Phone: 770-528-5514; E-mail: astaude@spsu.edu.
Tennis: Pascual Herrera; Phone: 770-528-5477; E-mail: patherrera8783@msn.com.

SOUTHERN UNIVERSITY AND AGRICULTURAL AND MECHANICAL COLLEGE
Baton Rouge, Louisiana

Jaguars ◆ NCAA I ◆ Southwestern Athletic Conference ◆ http://www.subr.edu/

State-supported comprehensive, founded 1880, part of Southern University System
Coed, 7,571 undergraduate students, 92% full-time, 60% women, 40% men
Suburban 964-acre campus
Moderately difficult entrance level, 55% of applicants were admitted

Freshmen *Admission:* 4,217 applied, 2,389 were accepted, 1,298 enrolled. *Test scores:* SAT verbal scores over 500: 20%; SAT math scores over 500: 20%; SAT verbal scores over 600: 5%; SAT math scores over 600: 5%.
Tuition and fees (2003–04): $3066 (resident), $8858 (nonresident). *Room and board:* $4306.
Financial Aid (All incoming freshmen): *Average need-based gift aid:* $3200. *Average non-need based aid:* $2625. *Average aid to full-time undergraduates:* $7000.

Athletic Department: *Director of Athletics:* Floyd Kerr; Phone: 225-771-2712; Fax: 225-771-4400. *Sports Information Director:* Kevin Manns; Phone: 225-771-2601; E-mail: kmanns@aol.com.

MEN'S COACHES
Baseball: Roger Cador; Phone: 225-771-2513; E-mail: roger_cador@cxs.subr.edu.
Basketball: Ben Jobe; Phone: 225-771-2403.
Cross Country: Johnny Thomas; Phone: 225-771-2476.
Football: Pete Richardson; Phone: 225-771-5900.
Golf: Willie Williams; Phone: 225-771-2956.
Tennis: Jeffrey Conyers; Phone: 225-771-2956.
Track and Field: Johnny Thomas; Phone: 225-771-2476.

WOMEN'S COACHES
Basketball: Sandy Pugh; Phone: 225-771-2412.
Cross Country: Johnny Thomas; Phone: 225-771-2476.
Softball: Nancy Marshall; Phone: 225-771-3170.
Tennis: Jeffrey Conyers; Phone: 225-771-2956.
Track and Field: Johnny Thomas; Phone: 225-771-2476.
Volleyball: Nathanial Denu; Phone: 225-771-4326.

SOUTHERN UNIVERSITY AT NEW ORLEANS
New Orleans, Louisiana

Knights ◆ NAIA ◆ Gulf Coast Conference ◆ http://www.suno.edu/

State-supported comprehensive, founded 1959, part of Southern University System
Coed
17-acre campus
Noncompetitive entrance level, 100% of applicants were admitted

Freshmen *Admission:* 1,000 applied, 1,000 were accepted.
Tuition and fees (2003–04): $2828 (resident), $6566 (nonresident).
Athletic Department: *Director of Athletics:* Earl Hill; Phone: 504-286-5195; Fax: 504-286-5328.

MEN'S COACHES
Basketball: Earl Hill; Phone: 504-286-5195.
Track and Field: Stephanie Minto; Phone: 504-286-5195.

WOMEN'S COACHES
Basketball: Elston King; Phone: 504-286-5195.
Track and Field: Stephanie Minto; Phone: 504-286-5195.

SOUTHERN UTAH UNIVERSITY
Cedar City, Utah

Thunderbirds ◆ NCAA I ◆ Mid-Continent Conference ◆ http://www.suu.edu/

State-supported comprehensive, founded 1897, part of Utah System of Higher Education
Coed, 5,840 undergraduate students, 74% full-time, 55% women, 45% men
Small-town 113-acre campus
Moderately difficult entrance level, 79% of applicants were admitted

Freshmen *Admission:* 1,355 applied, 1,054 were accepted, 725 enrolled. *Test scores:* SAT verbal scores over 500: 58%; SAT math scores over 500: 62%; SAT verbal scores over 600: 13%; SAT math scores over 600: 19%.
Tuition and fees (2003–04): $2794 (resident), $8158 (nonresident). *Room and board:* $5400 (room only: $2400).
Financial Aid (All incoming freshmen): *Average need-based gift aid:* $2620. *Average non-need based aid:* $2539. *Average aid to full-time undergraduates:* $2830.
Athletic Department: *Director of Athletics:* Thomas Douple; Phone: 435-865-8354; Fax: 435-586-5444; E-mail: douple@suu.edu. *Sports Information Director:* Neil Gardner; Phone: 435-586-7753; E-mail: gardner@suu.edu.

MEN'S COACHES

Baseball: Kurt Palmer; Phone: 435-586-7932; E-mail: palmer@suu.edu.
Basketball: Bill Evans; Phone: 435-586-7824; E-mail: evans_b@suu.edu.
Cheerleading: Tami Melton; Phone: 435-586-8332; E-mail: melton@suu.edu.
Cross Country: Eric Houle; Phone: 435-586-1982; E-mail: houle@suu.edu.
Football: Gary Andersen; Phone: 435-586-5471; E-mail: anderseng@suu.edu.
Golf: Richard Church; Phone: 435-586-7805; E-mail: churchr@suu.edu.
Track and Field: Eric Houle; Phone: 435-586-1982; E-mail: houle@suu.edu.

WOMEN'S COACHES

Basketball: Joe Hillock; Phone: 435-586-8061; E-mail: hillock@suu.edu.
Cheerleading: Tami Melton; Phone: 435-586-8332; E-mail: melton@suu.edu.
Cross Country: Eric Houle; Phone: 435-586-1982; E-mail: houle@suu.edu.
Gymnastics: Scott Bauman; Phone: 435-586-7825; E-mail: bauman@suu.edu.
Soccer: Brian Stock; Phone: 435-586-8513; E-mail: stock@suu.edu.
Softball: Laurel Simmons; Phone: 435-586-8536; E-mail: simmons@suu.edu.
Tennis: Lenny Lee; Phone: 435-586-8164; E-mail: lee_l@suu.edu.
Track and Field: Eric Houle; Phone: 435-586-1982; E-mail: houle@suu.edu.

SOUTHERN VERMONT COLLEGE
Bennington, Vermont

Mountaineers ◆ NCAA III ◆ Great Northeast Athletic Conference ◆ http://www.svc.edu/

Independent 4-year, founded 1926
Coed, 464 undergraduate students
Small-town 371-acre campus with easy access to Albany
Minimally difficult entrance level, 67% of applicants were admitted

Freshmen *Admission:* 373 applied, 264 were accepted. *Test scores:* SAT verbal scores over 500: 36%; SAT math scores over 500: 19%; SAT verbal scores over 600: 8%; SAT math scores over 600: 4%.
Tuition and fees (2003–04): $11,996 (full-time). *Room and board:* $6230 (room only: $2900).
Financial Aid (All incoming freshmen): *Average need-based gift aid:* $10,669. *Average non-need based aid:* $2500. *Average aid to full-time undergraduates:* $12,320.
Athletic Department: *Director of Athletics:* Scott Kilgallon; Phone: 802-447-4660; E-mail: skilgall@svc.edu.

MEN'S COACHES

Baseball: Ryan Marks; Phone: 802-447-5648; E-mail: rmarks@svc.edu.
Basketball: Ryan Marks; Phone: 802-447-4658; E-mail: rmarks@svc.edu.
Cross Country: Scott Kilgallon; Phone: 802-447-4660; E-mail: skilgall@svc.edu.
Soccer: Dan Dubois; Phone: 802-447-4662; E-mail: ddubois@svc.edu.
Track and Field: Scott Kilgallon; Phone: 802-447-4660; E-mail: skilgall@svc.edu.

WOMEN'S COACHES

Basketball: Robin Finnegan; Phone: 802-447-4659; E-mail: finnegan@svc.edu.
Cross Country: Scott Kilgallon; Phone: 802-447-4660; E-mail: skilgall@svc.edu.
Soccer: Robin Finnegan; Phone: 802-447-4659; E-mail: finnegan@svc.edu.
Softball: John Tetrault; Phone: 802-447-4671; E-mail: tetrault@svc.edu.
Track and Field: Scott Kilgallon; Phone: 802-447-4660; E-mail: skilgall@svc.edu.
Volleyball: John Tetrault; Phone: 802-447-4671; E-mail: tetrault@svc.edu.

SOUTHERN VIRGINIA UNIVERSITY
Buena Vista, Virginia

Knights ◆ NAIA ◆ Independent
◆ http://www.southernvirginia.edu/

Independent Latter-day Saints 4-year, founded 1867
Coed, 579 undergraduate students, 84% full-time, 53% women, 47% men
Small-town 155-acre campus
52% of applicants were admitted

Freshmen *Admission:* 1,394 applied, 730 were accepted, 271 enrolled.
Tuition and fees (2004–05): $14,640 (full-time). *Room and board:* $5300.
Financial Aid (All incoming freshmen): *Average need-based gift aid:* $6735. *Average non-need based aid:* $5500. *Average aid to full-time undergraduates:* $9268.
Athletic Department: *Director of Athletics:* Don Chamberlain; Phone: 540-261-8418; Fax: 540-261-8434; E-mail: dchamberlain@southernvirginia.edu.

MEN'S COACHES

Baseball: Jerry Schlegelmilch; Phone: 540-261-4276; E-mail: jschlegelmilch@southernvirginia.edu.
Basketball: Don Chamberlain; Phone: 540-261-8418; E-mail: dchamberlain@southernvirginia.edu.
Cheerleading: Valerie Smith; Phone: 540-261-8410.
Cross Country: Paul Wright; Phone: 540-261-4094; E-mail: pwright@southernvirginia.edu.
Football: Gary Buer; Phone: 540-261-4283; E-mail: gbuer@southernvirginia.edu.
Lacrosse: Dave Mercer; Phone: 540-261-4503.
Soccer: Paul Wright; Phone: 540-261-4094; E-mail: pwright@southernvirginia.edu.
Track and Field: Paul Wright; Phone: 540-261-4094; E-mail: pwright@southernvirginia.edu.
Wrestling: Michael Flood; Phone: 540-261-4520.

WOMEN'S COACHES

Basketball: Michael Harmon; Phone: 540-261-4268; E-mail: mharmon@southernvirginia.edu.
Cheerleading: Valerie Smith; Phone: 540-261-8410.
Cross Country: Paul Wright; Phone: 540-261-4094; E-mail: pwright@southernvirginia.edu.
Soccer: John Butler; Phone: 540-261-8406; E-mail: jbutler@southernvirginia.edu.
Softball: Deidra Dryden; Phone: 540-261-4244; E-mail: ddryden@southernvirginia.edu.
Track and Field: Paul Wright; Phone: 540-261-4094; E-mail: pwright@southernvirginia.edu.
Volleyball: Michael Harmon; Phone: 540-261-4268; E-mail: mharmon@southernvirginia.edu.

SOUTHERN WESLEYAN UNIVERSITY
Central, South Carolina

Warriors ◆ NAIA ◆ Georgia Alabama Carolina Conference
◆ http://www.swu.edu/

Independent religious comprehensive, founded 1906, affiliated with Wesleyan Church
Coed, 1,965 undergraduate students, 93% full-time, 64% women, 36% men
Small-town 230-acre campus
Minimally difficult entrance level, 66% of applicants were admitted

Freshmen *Admission:* 516 applied, 350 were accepted, 129 enrolled. *Test scores:* SAT verbal scores over 500: 57%; SAT math scores over 500: 57%; SAT verbal scores over 600: 19%; SAT math scores over 600: 18%; SAT verbal scores over 700: 3%; SAT math scores over 700: 2%.
Tuition and fees (2004–05): $14,100 (full-time). *Room and board:* $4935.
Financial Aid (All incoming freshmen): *Average need-based gift aid:* $9209. *Average non-need based aid:* $7928. *Average aid to full-time undergraduates:* $10,769.

Southern Wesleyan University *(continued)*

Athletic Department: *Director of Athletics:* Keith Connor; Phone: 864-644-5303; Fax: 864-644-5903. *Sports Information Director:* Mike Gillespie; Phone: 864-644-5305; E-mail: mgillespie@swu.edu.

MEN'S COACHES

Baseball: Mike Gillespie; Phone: 864-644-5305; E-mail: mgillespie@swu.edu.

Basketball: Charles Wimphrie; Phone: 864-644-5306; E-mail: cwimphrie@swu.edu.

Cheerleading: Julia Brackett-Cook; Phone: 864-644-5556; E-mail: jbcook@swu.edu.

Cross Country: Chad Peters; Phone: 864-644-5558; E-mail: cpeters@swu.edu.

Golf: Don Wood; Phone: 864-644-5303.

Soccer: Claudia Arias; Phone: 864-644-5302; E-mail: carias@swu.edu.

WOMEN'S COACHES

Basketball: Drew Brauer; Phone: 864-644-5301; E-mail: abrauer@swu.edu.

Cheerleading: Julia Brackett-Cook; Phone: 864-644-5556; E-mail: jbcook@swu.edu.

Cross Country: Chad Peters; Phone: 864-644-5558; E-mail: cpeters@swu.edu.

Soccer: Todd Eason; Phone: 864-644-5308; E-mail: teason@swu.edu.

Softball: Dave Seamans; Phone: 864-644-5304; E-mail: dseamans@swu.edu.

Volleyball: Larry Hinshaw; Phone: 864-644-5310; E-mail: lhinshaw@swu.edu.

SOUTHWEST BAPTIST UNIVERSITY
Bolivar, Missouri

Bearcats ◆ NCAA II ◆ Mid-America Intercollegiate Conference ◆ http://www.sbuniv.edu/

Independent Southern Baptist comprehensive, founded 1878
Coed, 2,746 undergraduate students, 66% full-time, 66% women, 34% men
Small-town 152-acre campus
Moderately difficult entrance level, 86% of applicants were admitted

Freshmen *Admission:* 768 applied, 661 were accepted, 470 enrolled.
Tuition and fees (2004–05): $12,332 (full-time). *Room and board:* $3888 (room only: $2088).
Financial Aid (All incoming freshmen): *Average need-based gift aid:* $3720. *Average non-need based aid:* $4378. *Average aid to full-time undergraduates:* $9901.
Athletic Department: *Director of Athletics:* Jim Middleton; Phone: 417-328-1795; Fax: 417-328-2009; E-mail: jmiddlet@sbuniv.edu. *Sports Information Director:* Adam Ledyard; Phone: 417-328-1797; E-mail: sbusid@hotmail.com.

MEN'S COACHES

Baseball: Sam Berg; Phone: 417-328-1794; E-mail: sberg@sbuniv.edu.
Basketball: Darin Archer; Phone: 417-328-1785; E-mail: darcher@sbuniv.edu.
Cheerleading: Shayla Hale; Phone: 417-328-1564; E-mail: shale@sbuniv.edu.
Cross Country: Mark Misch; Phone: 417-328-1874; E-mail: mmisch@sbuniv.edu.
Football: Ray Richards; Phone: 417-328-1798; E-mail: rrichard@sbuniv.edu.
Golf: Kevin Cribbs; Phone: 417-777-6500; E-mail: kcribbs@sbuniv.edu.
Tennis: John Bryant; Phone: 417-328-1747; E-mail: jbryant@sbuniv.edu.
Track and Field: Mark Misch; Phone: 417-328-1874; E-mail: mmisch@sbuniv.edu.

WOMEN'S COACHES

Basketball: Jim Middleton; Phone: 417-328-1795; E-mail: jmiddlet@sbuniv.edu.
Cheerleading: Shayla Hale; Phone: 417-328-1564; E-mail: shale@sbuniv.edu.
Cross Country: Mark Misch; Phone: 417-328-1874; E-mail: mmisch@sbuniv.edu.
Soccer: Peter McGovern; Phone: 417-326-1739; E-mail: pmcgover@sbuniv.edu.

Softball: Dana Bradshaw; Phone: 417-328-1791; E-mail: dbradsha@sbuniv.edu.
Tennis: Ray Still; Phone: 417-326-1790; E-mail: rstill@sbuniv.edu.
Track and Field: Mark Misch; Phone: 417-328-1874; E-mail: mmisch@sbuniv.edu.
Volleyball: Leslie Howe; Phone: 417-328-1709; E-mail: lhowe@sbuniv.edu.

SOUTHWESTERN ASSEMBLIES OF GOD UNIVERSITY
Waxahachie, Texas

Lions ◆ NAIA ◆ Central States Football Conference; Red River Conference ◆ http://www.sagu.edu/

Independent religious comprehensive, founded 1927, affiliated with Assemblies of God
Coed, 1,527 undergraduate students
Small-town 70-acre campus with easy access to Dallas
Noncompetitive entrance level, 34% of applicants were admitted

Freshmen *Admission:* 1,676 applied, 569 were accepted. *Test scores:* SAT verbal scores over 500: 56%; SAT math scores over 500: 48%; SAT verbal scores over 600: 20%; SAT math scores over 600: 20%; SAT verbal scores over 700: 8%; SAT math scores over 700: 4%.
Tuition and fees (2003–04): $8430 (full-time). *Room and board:* $4470 (room only: $3000).
Financial Aid (All incoming freshmen): *Average need-based gift aid:* $3630. *Average aid to full-time undergraduates:* $6135.
Athletic Department: *Director of Athletics:* Scott Vaughan; Phone: 972-937-4010; Fax: 972-937-0488; E-mail: svaughan@sagu.edu. *Sports Information Director:* Jeff Mills; Phone: 972-937-4010; E-mail: jmills@sagu.edu.

MEN'S COACHES

Baseball: Paul Burgard; Phone: 972-937-4010; E-mail: pburgard@sagu.edu.
Basketball: Scott Vaughan; Phone: 972-937-4010; E-mail: svaughan@sagu.edu.
Cheerleading: Beverly Robinson; Phone: 214-682-5292; E-mail: brobinson@sagu.edu.
Football: Jesse Godding; Phone: 972-937-4010; E-mail: pburgard@sagu.edu.
Soccer: Austin Guest; Phone: 214-682-5292; E-mail: pburgard@sagu.edu.
Track and Field: Phone: 972-937-4010.

WOMEN'S COACHES

Basketball: Scott Vaughan; Phone: 972-937-4010; E-mail: svaughan@sagu.edu.
Cheerleading: Beverly Robinson; Phone: 214-682-5292; E-mail: brobinson@sagu.edu.
Track and Field: Phone: 972-937-4010.
Volleyball: Hank Moore; Phone: 214-682-5292; E-mail: hmoore@sagu.edu.

SOUTHWESTERN COLLEGE
Winfield, Kansas

Moundbuilders ◆ NAIA ◆ Kansas Collegiate Conference ◆ http://www.sckans.edu/

Independent United Methodist comprehensive, founded 1885
Coed, 1,218 undergraduate students, 63% full-time, 47% women, 53% men
Small-town 70-acre campus with easy access to Wichita
Moderately difficult entrance level, 63% of applicants were admitted

Freshmen *Admission:* 540 applied, 385 were accepted, 177 enrolled. *Test scores:* SAT verbal scores over 500: 36%; SAT math scores over 500: 46%; SAT verbal scores over 600: 9%; SAT math scores over 600: 12%; SAT verbal scores over 700: 2%; SAT math scores over 700: 2%.
Tuition and fees (2004–05): $15,349 (full-time). *Room and board:* $5098 (room only: $2288).

Financial Aid (All incoming freshmen): *Average need-based gift aid:* $9333. *Average non-need based aid:* $7400. *Average aid to full-time undergraduates:* $13,664.
Athletic Department: *Director of Athletics:* Bill Stephens; Phone: 620-229-6128; Fax: 620-229-6124; E-mail: stephens@sckans.edu. *Sports Information Director:* Mike Kirkland; Phone: 620-229-6359; E-mail: kake@sckans.edu.

MEN'S COACHES
Basketball: Doug Hall; Phone: 620-229-6128; E-mail: dhall@sckans.edu.
Cheerleading: Jennifer Dougherty; Phone: 620-229-6128; E-mail: jed@sckans.edu.
Cross Country: Jim Helmer; Phone: 620-229-6217; E-mail: jhelm@sckans.edu.
Football: Chris Douglas; Phone: 620-229-6359; E-mail: cdouglas@sckans.edu.
Golf: Mike Fluty; Phone: 620-221-3478; E-mail: jinxpro@kcist.net.
Soccer: Phone: 620-221-6128.
Tennis: John Paulin; Phone: 620-221-6128; E-mail: jpaulin@sckans.edu.
Track and Field: Jim Helmer; Phone: 620-229-6217; E-mail: jhelm@sckans.edu.

WOMEN'S COACHES
Basketball: Dave Denly; Phone: 620-229-6128.
Cheerleading: Jennifer Dougherty; Phone: 620-229-6128; E-mail: jed@sckans.edu.
Cross Country: Jim Helmer; Phone: 620-229-6217; E-mail: jhelm@sckans.edu.
Golf: Mike Fluty; Phone: 620-221-3478; E-mail: jinxpro@kcist.net.
Soccer: Phone: 620-221-6128.
Softball: Phone: 620-221-6128.
Tennis: John Paulin; Phone: 620-221-6128; E-mail: jpaulin@sckans.edu.
Track and Field: Mike Kirkland; Phone: 620-229-6359; E-mail: kake@sckans.edu.
Volleyball: Julie Konrade; Phone: 620-221-6128; E-mail: jkonrade@sckans.edu.

SOUTHWESTERN OKLAHOMA STATE UNIVERSITY
Weatherford, Oklahoma
Bulldogs ◆ NCAA II ◆ Lone Star Conference ◆ http://www.swosu.edu/

State-supported comprehensive, founded 1901, part of Southwestern Oklahoma State University
Coed, 4,181 undergraduate students, 89% full-time, 54% women, 46% men
Small-town 73-acre campus with easy access to Oklahoma City
Moderately difficult entrance level, 92% of applicants were admitted

Freshmen *Admission:* 1,470 applied, 1,362 were accepted, 964 enrolled.
Tuition and fees (2003–04): $2758 (resident), $6658 (nonresident). *Room and board:* $2910 (room only: $1230).
Financial Aid (All incoming freshmen): *Average need-based gift aid:* $1054. *Average non-need based aid:* $755. *Average aid to full-time undergraduates:* $3063.
Athletic Department: *Director of Athletics:* Cecil Perkins; Phone: 580-774-3182; Fax: 580-774-7106; E-mail: perkinc@swosu.edu. *Sports Information Director:* Mike Bond; Phone: 580-774-7122; E-mail: bondm@swosu.edu.

MEN'S COACHES
Baseball: Charles Teasley; Phone: 580-774-3263; E-mail: teaslec@swosu.edu.
Basketball: Scott Reed; Phone: 580-774-3701; E-mail: reeds@swosu.edu.
Cheerleading: Pam Nichols; Phone: 580-774-3068; E-mail: nicholp@swosu.edu.
Football: Paul Sharp; Phone: 580-774-3703; E-mail: sharpp@swosu.edu.
Golf: Rocky Powell; Phone: 580-774-3702; E-mail: powellr@swosu.edu.
Soccer: Joe Bradley; Phone: 580-774-7047; E-mail: bradlej@swosu.edu.

WOMEN'S COACHES
Basketball: Shelly Pond; Phone: 580-774-3290; E-mail: ponds@swosu.edu.

Cheerleading: Pam Nichols; Phone: 580-774-3068; E-mail: nicholp@swosu.edu.
Cross Country: Adina Peters; Phone: 580-774-7047; E-mail: gorjus@hotmail.com.
Golf: Jerry Keeling; Phone: 580-774-7036; E-mail: keelingj@swosu.edu.
Soccer: Joe Bradley; Phone: 580-774-7047; E-mail: bradlej@swosu.edu.
Softball: Tammy Loy; Phone: 580-774-3226; E-mail: loyt@swosu.edu.

SOUTHWESTERN UNIVERSITY
Georgetown, Texas
Pirates ◆ NCAA III ◆ Southern Collegiate Athletic Conference ◆ http://www.southwestern.edu/

Independent Methodist 4-year, founded 1840
Coed, 1,265 undergraduate students, 98% full-time, 58% women, 42% men
Suburban 700-acre campus with easy access to Austin
Very difficult entrance level, 7% of applicants were admitted

Freshmen *Admission:* 1,765 applied, 1,115 were accepted, 343 enrolled. *Test scores:* SAT verbal scores over 500: 96%; SAT math scores over 500: 96%; SAT verbal scores over 600: 64%; SAT math scores over 600: 64%; SAT verbal scores over 700: 17%; SAT math scores over 700: 12%.
Tuition and fees (2003–04): $18,870 (full-time). *Room and board:* $6540 (room only: $3240).
Financial Aid (All incoming freshmen): *Average need-based gift aid:* $12,116. *Average non-need based aid:* $6791. *Average aid to full-time undergraduates:* $15,469.
Athletic Department: *Director of Athletics:* Glada Munt; Phone: 512-863-1381; Fax: 512-863-1393; E-mail: muntg@southwestern.edu. *Sports Information Director:* James Shelton; Phone: 512-863-1381; E-mail: sheltonj@southwestern.edu.

MEN'S COACHES
Baseball: Jim Mallon; Phone: 512-863-1383; E-mail: mallonj@southwestern.edu.
Basketball: Bill Raleigh; Phone: 512-863-1611; E-mail: raleighb@southwestern.edu.
Cross Country: Francie Smith; Phone: 512-863-1615; E-mail: flsmith@southwestern.edu.
Diving: Tim Pukys; Phone: 512-863-1399; E-mail: pukyst@southwestern.edu.
Golf: Dan Ruyle; Phone: 512-863-1641; E-mail: ruyled@southwestern.edu.
Soccer: Don Gregory; Phone: 512-863-1532; E-mail: gregoryd@southwestern.edu.
Swimming: Tim Pukys; Phone: 512-863-1399; E-mail: pukyst@southwestern.edu.
Tennis: Chad Cage; Phone: 512-863-1789; E-mail: cagec@southwestern.edu.
Track and Field: Francie Smith; Phone: 512-863-1615; E-mail: flsmith@southwestern.edu.

WOMEN'S COACHES
Basketball: Kerri Brinkoeter; Phone: 512-863-1381; E-mail: brinkoek@southwestern.edu.
Cross Country: Francie Smith; Phone: 512-863-1615; E-mail: flsmith@southwestern.edu.
Diving: Tim Pukys; Phone: 512-863-1399; E-mail: pukyst@southwestern.edu.
Golf: Dan Ruyle; Phone: 512-863-1641; E-mail: ruyled@southwestern.edu.
Soccer: Jack Flatau; Phone: 512-863-1531; E-mail: flatauj@southwestern.edu.
Swimming: Tim Pukys; Phone: 512-863-1399; E-mail: pukyst@southwestern.edu.
Tennis: Chad Cage; Phone: 512-863-1789; E-mail: cagec@southwestern.edu.
Track and Field: Francie Smith; Phone: 512-863-1615; E-mail: flsmith@southwestern.edu.
Volleyball: Shannon Carlson; Phone: 512-863-1533; E-mail: carlsons@southwestern.edu.

SOUTHWEST MINNESOTA STATE UNIVERSITY
Marshall, Minnesota

Mustangs ◆ NCAA II ◆ Northern Sun Intercollegiate Conference ◆ http://www.southwest.msus.edu/

State-supported comprehensive, founded 1963, part of Minnesota State Colleges and Universities System
Coed, 5,167 undergraduate students, 45% full-time, 60% women, 40% men
Small-town 216-acre campus
Minimally difficult entrance level

Freshmen *Admission:* 1,232 enrolled.
Tuition and fees (2003–04): $4615 (resident), $4615 (nonresident). *Room and board:* $4491.
Financial Aid (All incoming freshmen): *Average need-based gift aid:* $3255. *Average non-need based aid:* $1533. *Average aid to full-time undergraduates:* $5687.

MEN'S COACHES
Baseball: Paul Blanchard; Phone: 507-537-7021.
Basketball: Greg Stemen; Phone: 507-537-7021.
Football: Curt Straheim; Phone: 507-537-7021.
Wrestling: John Sterner; Phone: 507-537-7021.

WOMEN'S COACHES
Basketball: Kelly Kruger; Phone: 507-537-7021.
Golf: Greg Stemen; Phone: 507-537-7021.
Soccer: Jill McCartney; Phone: 507-537-7021.
Softball: Pat Toews; Phone: 507-537-7021.
Tennis: George Seldat; Phone: 507-537-7021.
Volleyball: Deb Denbeck; Phone: 507-537-7021.

SOUTHWEST MISSOURI STATE UNIVERSITY
Springfield, Missouri

Bears ◆ NCAA I ◆ Gateway Football Conference; Missouri Valley Conference; Northern Pacific Field Hockey Conference ◆ http://www.smsu.edu/

State-supported comprehensive, founded 1905
Coed, 15,771 undergraduate students, 79% full-time, 56% women, 44% men
Suburban 225-acre campus
Moderately difficult entrance level, 84% of applicants were admitted

Freshmen *Admission:* 6,316 applied, 5,446 were accepted, 2,695 enrolled.
Tuition and fees (2003–04): $4636 (resident), $8776 (nonresident). *Room and board:* $4282 (room only: $2982).
Financial Aid (All incoming freshmen): *Average need-based gift aid:* $3149. *Average non-need based aid:* $3531. *Average aid to full-time undergraduates:* $6495.
Athletic Department: *Director of Athletics:* Bill Rowe; Phone: 417-836-5244; Fax: 417-836-6344; E-mail: ble232t@smsu.edu. *Sports Information Director:* Mark Stillwell; Phone: 417-836-5402; E-mail: mrs509t@smsu.edu.

MEN'S COACHES
Baseball: Keith Guttin; Phone: 417-836-5242; E-mail: keg849t@smsu.edu.
Basketball: Barry Hinson; Phone: 417-836-5250; E-mail: bdh862t@smsu.edu.
Cheerleading: Randy Blackwood; Phone: 417-836-5240; E-mail: rrb988t@smsu.edu.
Cross Country: Ronald Boyce; Phone: 417-836-5242; E-mail: rib040t@smsu.edu.
Diving: Chris Waters; Phone: 417-836-5466; E-mail: caw212t@smsu.edu.
Football: Randy Ball; Phone: 417-836-5343; E-mail: rrb549t@smsu.edu.
Golf: Kory Bowman; Phone: 417-836-5242; E-mail: kob646t@smsu.edu.
Soccer: Jon Leamy; Phone: 417-836-5242; E-mail: jhl928t@smsu.edu.

Swimming: Jack Steck; Phone: 417-836-5466; E-mail: jns842t@smsu.edu.
Tennis: Jim Klousia; Phone: 417-836-5242; E-mail: jhk787t@smsu.edu.
Track and Field: Ronald Boyce; Phone: 417-836-5242; E-mail: rib040t@smsu.edu.

WOMEN'S COACHES
Basketball: Katie Abrahamson-Henderson; Phone: 417-836-4136; E-mail: kna989t@smsu.edu.
Cheerleading: Randy Blackwood; Phone: 417-836-5240; E-mail: rrb988t@smsu.edu.
Cross Country: Ronald Boyce; Phone: 417-836-5242; E-mail: rib040t@smsu.edu.
Diving: Chris Waters; Phone: 417-836-5466; E-mail: caw212t@smsu.edu.
Field Hockey: Dawn Porter; Phone: 417-836-5242; E-mail: dap352t@smsu.edu.
Golf: Kevin Kane; Phone: 417-836-5242; E-mail: kck535t@smsu.edu.
Soccer: Rob Brewer; Phone: 417-836-5242; E-mail: rab660t@smsu.edu.
Softball: Holly Hesse; Phone: 417-836-8384; E-mail: hrh224t@smsu.edu.
Swimming: Jack Steck; Phone: 417-836-5466; E-mail: jns842t@smsu.edu.
Tennis: Jim Giachino; Phone: 417-836-5242; E-mail: jjg009t@smsu.edu.
Track and Field: Ronald Boyce; Phone: 417-836-5242; E-mail: rib040t@smsu.edu.
Volleyball: Melissa Stokes; Phone: 417-836-8384; E-mail: mks833t@smsu.edu.

SPALDING UNIVERSITY
Louisville, Kentucky

NAIA ◆ Kentucky Intercollegiate Conference ◆ http://www.spalding.edu/

Independent religious comprehensive, founded 1814, affiliated with Roman Catholic Church
Coed, 964 undergraduate students, 65% full-time, 76% women, 24% men
Urban 5-acre campus
Moderately difficult entrance level, 73% of applicants were admitted

Freshmen *Admission:* 373 applied, 275 were accepted, 118 enrolled. *Test scores:* SAT verbal scores over 500: 80%; SAT math scores over 500: 85%; SAT verbal scores over 600: 28%; SAT math scores over 600: 31%.
Tuition and fees (2003–04): $13,990 (full-time). *Room and board:* $5334 (room only: $2569).
Financial Aid (All incoming freshmen): *Average aid to full-time undergraduates:* $11,700.
Athletic Department: *Director of Athletics:* Chris Perkins; Phone: 502-585-9911; Fax: 502-585-7158.

MEN'S COACHES
Baseball: Kevin Kocks; Phone: 502-452-2508.
Basketball: Kevin Gray; Phone: 502-585-9911; E-mail: kgray@spalding.edu.
Soccer: Roy Webster; Phone: 502-585-9911.

WOMEN'S COACHES
Basketball: Chris Perkins; Phone: 502-585-9911.
Soccer: Paul Patton; Phone: 502-585-9911.
Softball: Allen Benz; Phone: 502-585-9911.
Volleyball: Bridget Yates; Phone: 502-585-9911.

SPELMAN COLLEGE
Atlanta, Georgia

Jaguars ◆ NCAA III ◆ Great South Conference ◆ http://www.spelman.edu/

Independent 4-year, founded 1881
Women only, 2,063 undergraduate students, 96% full-time, 100% women, 100% men
Urban 32-acre campus
Very difficult entrance level, 39% of applicants were admitted

Freshmen *Admission:* 4,345 applied, 1,689 were accepted, 493 enrolled. *Test scores:* SAT verbal scores over 500: 77%; SAT math scores over 500: 72%; SAT verbal scores over 600: 20%; SAT math scores over 600: 17%; SAT verbal scores over 700: 3%; SAT math scores over 700: 1%.
Tuition and fees (2003–04): $14,125 (full-time). *Room and board:* $7625.
Financial Aid (All incoming freshmen): *Average need-based gift aid:* $2000. *Average non-need based aid:* $2000. *Average aid to full-time undergraduates:* $8625.
Athletic Department: *Director of Athletics:* Germaine McAuley; Phone: 404-681-3643; Fax: 404-270-5714. *Sports Information Director:* Vicki Mangram; Phone: 404-270-5715; E-mail: vmangram@spelman.edu.

WOMEN'S COACHES
Basketball: Lavon Mercer; Phone: 404-270-5736; E-mail: lmercer@spelman.edu.
Cheerleading: Doris Terrel; Phone: 404-270-5716; E-mail: dllacyt@aol.com.
Cross Country: Kevin Foster; Phone: 404-270-5716; E-mail: kevfost@bellsouth.net.
Golf: Willie Burkes; Phone: 404-270-5716.
Soccer: Phan Bach Holland; Phone: 404-270-5716; E-mail: mystiquefilms@hotmail.com.
Tennis: Doris Terrel; Phone: 404-270-5716; E-mail: dllacyt@aol.com.
Volleyball: Michael Carter; Phone: 404-270-5716.

SPRING ARBOR UNIVERSITY
Spring Arbor, Michigan

Cougars ◆ NAIA ◆ Wolverine-Hoosier Conference ◆ http://www.arbor.edu/

Independent Free Methodist comprehensive, founded 1873
Coed, 2,623 undergraduate students, 79% full-time, 69% women, 31% men
Small-town 123-acre campus
Moderately difficult entrance level, 84% of applicants were admitted

Freshmen *Admission:* 850 applied, 730 were accepted, 312 enrolled.
Tuition and fees (2003–04): $14,916 (full-time). *Room and board:* $5290 (room only: $2420).
Financial Aid (All incoming freshmen): *Average need-based gift aid:* $8237. *Average non-need based aid:* $1704. *Average aid to full-time undergraduates:* $15,134.
Athletic Department: *Director of Athletics:* Hank Burbridge; Phone: 517-750-6503; Fax: 517-750-2745; E-mail: hankb@arbor.edu. *Sports Information Director:* Joel Maust; Phone: 517-750-6359; E-mail: jmaust@arbor.edu.

MEN'S COACHES
Baseball: Hank Burbridge; Phone: 517-750-6502; E-mail: hankb@arbor.edu.
Basketball: Ryan Cottingham; Phone: 517-750-6502; E-mail: ryanc@arbor.edu.
Cross Country: Bill Bippes; Phone: 517-750-6502; E-mail: bbippes@arbor.edu.
Golf: Bill Bockwitz; Phone: 517-750-6502; E-mail: bockwitz@arbor.edu.
Soccer: Anil Joseph; Phone: 517-750-6502; E-mail: anilj@arbor.edu.
Tennis: Terry Darling; Phone: 517-750-6502; E-mail: tdarling@arbor.edu.
Track and Field: Bill Bippes; Phone: 517-750-6502; E-mail: bbippes@arbor.edu.

WOMEN'S COACHES
Basketball: Tom Britsch; Phone: 517-750-6502.

Cross Country: Bill Bippes; Phone: 517-750-6502; E-mail: bbippes@arbor.edu.
Soccer: Jason Crist; Phone: 517-750-6502; E-mail: jcrist@arbor.edu.
Softball: Deb Thompson; Phone: 517-750-6502; E-mail: debt@arbor.edu.
Tennis: Terry Darling; Phone: 517-750-6502; E-mail: tdarling@arbor.edu.
Track and Field: Bill Bippes; Phone: 517-750-6502; E-mail: bbippes@arbor.edu.
Volleyball: Vince Beresford; Phone: 517-750-6502; E-mail: vberesfo@arbor.edu.

SPRINGFIELD COLLEGE
Springfield, Massachusetts

Pride ◆ NCAA III ◆ New England Women's & Men's Athletics Conference ◆ http://www.spfldcol.edu/

Independent comprehensive, founded 1885
Coed, 2,238 undergraduate students, 96% full-time, 48% women, 52% men
Suburban 167-acre campus
Moderately difficult entrance level, 70% of applicants were admitted

Freshmen *Admission:* 2,110 applied, 1,558 were accepted, 553 enrolled. *Test scores:* SAT verbal scores over 500: 52%; SAT math scores over 500: 62%; SAT verbal scores over 600: 9%; SAT math scores over 600: 16%; SAT verbal scores over 700: %; SAT math scores over 700: 2%.
Tuition and fees (2003–04): $19,610 (full-time). *Room and board:* $7520 (room only: $3780).
Financial Aid (All incoming freshmen): *Average need-based gift aid:* $11,064. *Average non-need based aid:* $11,635. *Average aid to full-time undergraduates:* $15,354.
Athletic Department: *Director of Athletics:* Cathie Schweitzer; Phone: 413-748-3333; Fax: 413-748-3855. *Sports Information Director:* John White; Phone: 413-748-3342; E-mail: jawhite@spfldcol.edu.

MEN'S COACHES
Baseball: Mark Simeone; Phone: 413-748-3274; E-mail: mark_a_simeone@spfldcol.edu.
Basketball: Charlie Brock; Phone: 413-748-3229; E-mail: charles_r_brock@spfldcol.edu.
Cross Country: Mike Gauvin; Phone: 413-748-3760; E-mail: mikegauvin@aol.com.
Diving: Pete Avdoulos; Phone: 413-748-2445; E-mail: john_taffe@spfldcol.edu.
Football: Mike Delong; Phone: 413-748-3156; E-mail: michael_delong@spfldcol.edu.
Golf: Joe Eadie; Phone: 413-748-3332.
Lacrosse: Keith Bugbee; Phone: 413-748-3154; E-mail: keith_bugbee@spfldcol.edu.
Soccer: Peter Haley; Phone: 413-748-3368; E-mail: peter_haley@spfldcol.edu.
Swimming: John Taffe; Phone: 413-748-3169; E-mail: john_taffe@spfldcol.edu.
Tennis: Michael Myers; Phone: 413-748-3760; E-mail: michaelmyers@hotmail.com.
Track and Field: Ken Klata; Phone: 413-748-3230; E-mail: kenneth_klatka@spfldcol.edu.
Volleyball: Charlie Sullivan; Phone: 413-748-3850; E-mail: csulliva@spfldcol.edu.
Wrestling: Daryl Arroyo; Phone: 413-748-3276; E-mail: daryl_arroyo@spfldcol.edu.

WOMEN'S COACHES
Basketball: Naomi Graves; Phone: 413-748-3415; E-mail: naomi_graves@spfldcol.edu.
Cross Country: Jim Pennington; Phone: 413-748-3351; E-mail: james_pennington@spfldcol.edu.
Diving: Pete Avdoulos; Phone: 413-748-2445; E-mail: john_taffe@spfldcol.edu.
Field Hockey: Dottie Zenaty; Phone: 413-748-3167; E-mail: dorothy_zenaty@spfldcol.edu.
Gymnastics: Cheryl Raymond; Phone: 413-748-3363; E-mail: cheryl_raymond@spfldcol.edu.
Lacrosse: Rachel Bugbee; Phone: 413-748-3760; E-mail: keith_bugbee@spfldcol.edu.

Springfield College *(continued)*

Soccer: John Gibson; Phone: 413-748-3170; E-mail: jgibson@spfldcol. edu.

Softball: Kathy Mangano; Phone: 413-748-3147; E-mail: kathleen_mangano@spfldcol.edu.

Swimming: John Taffe; Phone: 413-748-3169; E-mail: john_taffe@ spfldcol.edu.

Tennis: Michael Myers; Phone: 413-748-3760; E-mail: michaelemyers@ hotmail.com.

Track and Field: Jim Pennington; Phone: 413-748-3351; E-mail: james_pennington@spfldcol.edu.

Volleyball: Joel Dearing; Phone: 413-748-3438; E-mail: joel_dearing@ spfldcol.edu.

SPRING HILL COLLEGE
Mobile, Alabama

Badgers ◆ NAIA ◆ Gulf Coast Conference ◆ http://www.shc.edu/

Independent Roman Catholic (Jesuit) comprehensive, founded 1830
Coed, 1,211 undergraduate students, 86% full-time, 62% women, 38% men
Suburban 450-acre campus
Moderately difficult entrance level, 78% of applicants were admitted

Freshmen *Admission:* 1,122 applied, 892 were accepted, 309 enrolled. *Test scores:* SAT verbal scores over 500: 73%; SAT math scores over 500: 73%; SAT verbal scores over 600: 40%; SAT math scores over 600: 29%; SAT verbal scores over 700: 4%; SAT math scores over 700: 3%.
Tuition and fees (2003–04): $19,000 (full-time). *Room and board:* $6868 (room only: $3466).
Financial Aid (All incoming freshmen): *Average need-based gift aid:* $13,842. *Average non-need based aid:* $7350. *Average aid to full-time undergraduates:* $18,085.
Athletic Department: *Director of Athletics:* Doug Mosley; Phone: 251-380-4461; Fax: 251-460-2196; E-mail: dmosley@shc.edu. *Sports Information Director:* Matthew DeWitt; Phone: 251-380-4468; E-mail: mdewitt@shc.edu.

MEN'S COACHES
Baseball: Frank Sims; Phone: 251-380-3486; E-mail: fsims@shc.edu.
Basketball: Robert Thompson; Phone: 251-380-4460; E-mail: rthompson@shc.edu.
Cross Country: Michelle Cook; Phone: 251-380-3485; E-mail: mhoobler@shc.edu.
Golf: Steve Hodges; Phone: 251-380-4659; E-mail: shcgolf1@aol.com.
Soccer: Wulf-Dieter Koch; Phone: 251-380-3491; E-mail: wkoch@shc. edu.
Swimming: John Hartman; Phone: 251-380-4462; E-mail: jhartman@ shc.edu.
Tennis: Kelly Williamson; Phone: 251-380-3490; E-mail: kwilliamson@ shc.edu.

WOMEN'S COACHES
Basketball: Terry Fowler; Phone: 251-380-3488; E-mail: tfowler@shc. edu.
Cross Country: Michelle Cook; Phone: 251-380-3485; E-mail: mhoobler@shc.edu.
Golf: Duke Ankiewcz; Phone: 251-380-4659; E-mail: dankie572@aol. com.
Soccer: Wulf-Dieter Koch; Phone: 251-380-3491; E-mail: wkoch@shc. edu.
Softball: Coby Mackin; Phone: 251-380-3489; E-mail: cmackin@shc. edu.
Swimming: John Hartman; Phone: 251-380-4462; E-mail: jhartman@ shc.edu.
Tennis: Kelly Williamson; Phone: 251-380-3490; E-mail: kwilliamson@ shc.edu.
Volleyball: Gretchen Speed; Phone: 251-380-4475; E-mail: gspeed@shc. edu.

STANFORD UNIVERSITY
Stanford, California

Cardinal ◆ NCAA I ◆ Northern Pacific Field Hockey Conference; Pacific-10 Conference ◆ http://www.stanford.edu/

Independent university, founded 1891
Coed, 7,054 undergraduate students, 91% full-time, 50% women, 50% men
Suburban 8,180-acre campus with easy access to San Francisco
Most difficult entrance level, 13% of applicants were admitted

Freshmen *Admission:* 18,628 applied, 2,343 were accepted, 1,640 enrolled. *Test scores:* SAT verbal scores over 500: 99%; SAT math scores over 500: 99%; SAT verbal scores over 600: 91%; SAT math scores over 600: 94%; SAT verbal scores over 700: 63%; SAT math scores over 700: 69%.
Tuition and fees (2004–05): $29,847 (full-time). *Room and board:* $9500 (room only: $5012).
Financial Aid (All incoming freshmen): *Average need-based gift aid:* $23,216. *Average non-need based aid:* $1974. *Average aid to full-time undergraduates:* $25,564.
Athletic Department: *Director of Athletics:* Ted Leland; Phone: 650-723-4596; Fax: 650-725-8642; E-mail: tleland@stanford.edu. *Sports Information Director:* Gary Migdol; Phone: 650-725-2958; E-mail: gmigdol@stanford.edu.

MEN'S COACHES
Baseball: Mark Marquess; Phone: 650-723-4528; E-mail: kwolff@ stanford.edu.
Basketball: Phone: 650-723-0562; E-mail: sandrap@stanford.edu.
Cross Country: Andrew Gerard; Phone: 650-736-1125; E-mail: agerard@ stanford.edu.
Diving: Rick Schavone; Phone: 650-723-9159; E-mail: schavone@ stanford.edu.
Football: Buddy Teevens; Phone: 650-723-5665; E-mail: teevens@ stanford.edu.
Golf: Jeff Mitchell; Phone: 650-323-0939; E-mail: jkmitch@stanford. edu.
Soccer: Bret Simon; Phone: 650-723-9375; E-mail: basimon@stanford. edu.
Swimming: Skip Kenney; Phone: 650-723-4416; E-mail: skenney@ stanford.edu.
Tennis: Dick Gould; Phone: 650-723-1160; E-mail: dgould@stanford. edu.
Track and Field: Robert Weir; Phone: 650-725-0760; E-mail: weir@ stanford.edu.
Volleyball: Don Shaw; Phone: 650-725-0763; E-mail: donshaw@ stanford.edu.
Wrestling: Steve Buddie; Phone: 650-723-9486; E-mail: buddie@ stanford.edu.

WOMEN'S COACHES
Basketball: Tara Vanderveer; Phone: 650-723-0284; E-mail: tarahoop@ stanford.edu.
Cross Country: Dena Evans; Phone: 650-725-0761; E-mail: islander@ stanford.edu.
Diving: Rick Schavone; Phone: 650-723-9159; E-mail: schavone@ stanford.edu.
Field Hockey: Leslie Irvine; Phone: 650-725-2578.
Golf: Caroline O'Connor; Phone: 650-723-0938; E-mail: coconnor@ stanford.edu.
Gymnastics: Kristen Smyth; Phone: 650-725-6143; E-mail: kristen. smyth@stanford.edu.
Lacrosse: Michele Uhfelder; Phone: 650-725-1994; E-mail: muhlfeld@ stanford.edu.
Soccer: Paul Ratcliffe; Phone: 650-725-2425; E-mail: pratclif@ stanford.edu.
Softball: John Rittman; Phone: 650-725-0736; E-mail: jrittman@ stanford.edu.
Swimming: Richard Quick; Phone: 650-735-0923; E-mail: rwquick@ stanford.edu.
Tennis: Lele Forood; Phone: 650-723-9540; E-mail: lelef@stanford.edu.
Track and Field: Edrick Floreal; Phone: 650-725-0759; E-mail: floreal@ stanford.edu.
Volleyball: John Dunning; Phone: 650-723-1997; E-mail: jdunning@ stanford.edu.

STATE UNIVERSITY OF NEW YORK AT BINGHAMTON
Binghamton, New York

Bearcats ◆ NCAA I ◆ America East Conference; Colonial Athletic Conference ◆ http://www.binghamton.edu/

State-supported university, founded 1946, part of State University of New York System
Coed, 10,563 undergraduate students, 97% full-time, 52% women, 48% men
Suburban 887-acre campus
Very difficult entrance level, 4% of applicants were admitted

Freshmen *Admission:* 19,076 applied, 8,521 were accepted, 2,291 enrolled. *Test scores:* SAT verbal scores over 500: 95%; SAT math scores over 500: 98%; SAT verbal scores over 600: 53%; SAT math scores over 600: 73%; SAT verbal scores over 700: 7%; SAT math scores over 700: 17%.
Tuition and fees (2003–04): $5687 (resident), $11,637 (nonresident). *Room and board:* $7100 (room only: $4384).
Financial Aid (All incoming freshmen): *Average need-based gift aid:* $4639. *Average non-need based aid:* $1754. *Average aid to full-time undergraduates:* $9641.
Athletic Department: *Director of Athletics:* Joel Thirer; Phone: 607-777-2043; Fax: 607-777-2495; E-mail: jthirer@binghamton.edu. *Sports Information Director:* John Hartrick; Phone: 607-777-6800; E-mail: hartrick@binghamton.edu.

MEN'S COACHES
Baseball: Tim Sinicki; Phone: 607-777-2525; E-mail: tsinicki@binghamton.edu.
Basketball: Al Walker; Phone: 607-777-2118; E-mail: awalker@binghamton.edu.
Cheerleading: Kristi Putrino; Phone: 607-777-4255; E-mail: kmp4vca@aol.com.
Cross Country: Annette Acuff; Phone: 607-777-2109; E-mail: aacuff@binghamton.edu.
Diving: Chris Zoltoski; Phone: 607-777-7946; E-mail: czoltoski@binghamton.edu.
Golf: Nick Lasky; Phone: 607-777-3928; E-mail: nlasky@binghamton.edu.
Lacrosse: Ed Stephenson; Phone: 607-777-3154; E-mail: estephen@binghamton.edu.
Soccer: Paul Marco; Phone: 607-777-4571; E-mail: pmarco@binghamton.edu.
Swimming: Patrice Back; Phone: 607-777-7946; E-mail: pback@binghamton.edu.
Tennis: Michael Starke; Phone: 607-777-4255; E-mail: mstarke@tennisctr.com.
Track and Field: Mike Thompson; Phone: 607-777-4458; E-mail: mthomps@binghamton.edu.
Wrestling: Mike Fusilli; Phone: 607-777-6367; E-mail: mfusilli@binghamton.edu.

WOMEN'S COACHES
Basketball: Rich Conover; Phone: 607-777-6339; E-mail: rconover@binghamton.edu.
Cheerleading: Kristi Putrino; Phone: 607-777-4255; E-mail: kmp4vca@aol.com.
Cross Country: Annette Acuff; Phone: 607-777-2109; E-mail: aacuff@binghamton.edu.
Diving: Chris Zoltoski; Phone: 607-777-7946; E-mail: czoltoski@binghamton.edu.
Lacrosse: Sue Frost; Phone: 607-777-3159; E-mail: sfrost@binghamton.edu.
Soccer: Jeff Leightman; Phone: 607-777-6439; E-mail: jleight@binghamton.edu.
Softball: Holly Brown; Phone: 607-777-6838; E-mail: hbrown@binghamton.edu.
Swimming: Patrice Back; Phone: 607-777-7946; E-mail: pback@binghamton.edu.

Tennis: Mike Stevens; Phone: 607-777-6682; E-mail: mstevens@binghamton.edu.
Track and Field: Mike Thompson; Phone: 607-777-4458; E-mail: mthomps@binghamton.edu.
Volleyball: Glenn Kiriyama; Phone: 607-777-2842; E-mail: kiriyama@binghamton.edu.

STATE UNIVERSITY OF NEW YORK AT NEW PALTZ
New Paltz, New York

Hawks ◆ NCAA III ◆ SUNY Athletic Conference ◆ http://www.newpaltz.edu/

State-supported comprehensive, founded 1828, part of State University of New York System
Coed, 6,292 undergraduate students, 87% full-time, 64% women, 36% men
Small-town 216-acre campus
Moderately difficult entrance level, 30% of applicants were admitted

Freshmen *Admission:* 10,942 applied, 3,768 were accepted, 916 enrolled. *Test scores:* SAT verbal scores over 500: 78%; SAT math scores over 500: 80%; SAT verbal scores over 600: 29%; SAT math scores over 600: 25%; SAT verbal scores over 700: 3%; SAT math scores over 700: 3%.
Tuition and fees (2003–04): $5145 (resident), $11,095 (nonresident). *Room and board:* $6420 (room only: $3880).
Financial Aid (All incoming freshmen): *Average need-based gift aid:* $2045. *Average non-need based aid:* $1029. *Average aid to full-time undergraduates:* $1946.
Athletic Department: *Director of Athletics:* Stuart Robinson; Phone: 845-257-3908; Fax: 845-257-3920; E-mail: robinsos@newpaltz.edu. *Sports Information Director:* Mike Salerno; Phone: 845-257-3927; E-mail: salernom@newpaltz.edu.

MEN'S COACHES
Baseball: Mike Juhl; Phone: 845-257-3915; E-mail: juhlm@newpaltz.edu.
Basketball: Doug Pasquerella; Phone: 845-257-3917; E-mail: pasquerd@newpaltz.edu.
Cross Country: Cassandra Quackenbush; Phone: 845-257-3922; E-mail: quackenc@lan.newpaltz.edu.
Soccer: Stuart Robinson; Phone: 845-257-3908; E-mail: robinsos@newpaltz.edu.
Swimming: Brian Williams; Phone: 845-257-3912; E-mail: williamb@newpaltz.edu.
Tennis: Robert Bruley; Phone: 845-257-3931; E-mail: bruleyr@lan.newpaltz.edu.
Track and Field: Cassandra Quackenbush; Phone: 845-257-3922; E-mail: quackenc@lan.newpaltz.edu.
Volleyball: Ian Walker; Phone: 845-257-3919; E-mail: walkeri@newpaltz.edu.

WOMEN'S COACHES
Cross Country: Cassandra Quackenbush; Phone: 845-257-3922; E-mail: quackenc@lan.newpaltz.edu.
Field Hockey: Bil Davidson; Phone: 845-257-3929; E-mail: davidsob@newpaltz.edu.
Soccer: Colleen Bruley; Phone: 845-257-3918; E-mail: bruleyc@lan.newpaltz.edu.
Softball: Brad Duckworth; Phone: 845-257-3923; E-mail: duckworb@lan.newpaltz.edu.
Swimming: Brian Williams; Phone: 845-257-3912; E-mail: williamb@newpaltz.edu.
Tennis: Robert Bruley; Phone: 845-257-3931; E-mail: bruleyr@lan.newpaltz.edu.
Track and Field: Cassandra Quackenbush; Phone: 845-257-3922; E-mail: quackenc@lan.newpaltz.edu.
Volleyball: Matt Giufre; Phone: 845-257-3919; E-mail: giufrem@newpaltz.edu.

STATE UNIVERSITY OF NEW YORK AT OSWEGO
Oswego, New York

Lakers ◆ NCAA III ◆ SUNY Athletic Conference ◆ http://www.oswego.edu/

State-supported comprehensive, founded 1861, part of State University of New York System
Coed, 7,181 undergraduate students, 91% full-time, 54% women, 46% men
Small-town 696-acre campus with easy access to Syracuse
Moderately difficult entrance level, 54% of applicants were admitted

Freshmen *Admission:* 7,438 applied, 4,223 were accepted, 1,336 enrolled. *Test scores:* SAT verbal scores over 500: 75%; SAT math scores over 500: 80%; SAT verbal scores over 600: 17%; SAT math scores over 600: 20%; SAT verbal scores over 700: 2%; SAT math scores over 700: 1%.
Tuition and fees (2003–04): $5176 (resident), $11,126 (nonresident). *Room and board:* $7540 (room only: $4490).
Financial Aid (All incoming freshmen): *Average need-based gift aid:* $4097. *Average non-need based aid:* $4012. *Average aid to full-time undergraduates:* $7392.
Athletic Department: *Director of Athletics:* Tim Hale; Phone: 315-312-2378; Fax: 315-312-6397; E-mail: thale@oswego.edu. *Sports Information Director:* Lyle Fulton; Phone: 315-312-2488; E-mail: lfulton@oswego.edu.

MEN'S COACHES
Baseball: Frank Paino; Phone: 315-312-2405; E-mail: paino@oswego.edu.
Basketball: Kevin Broderick; Phone: 315-312-2379; E-mail: kbroderi@oswego.edu.
Cross Country: Tim Boyce; Phone: 315-312-4149; E-mail: tboyce@oswego.edu.
Diving: Kami Matthews; Phone: 315-312-3366; E-mail: kmathews@oswego.edu.
Golf: Mike Howard; Phone: 315-312-2402; E-mail: howard@oswego.edu.
Ice Hockey: Ed Gosek; Phone: 315-312-4145; E-mail: egosek@oswego.edu.
Lacrosse: Dan Witmer; Phone: 315-312-2407; E-mail: witmer@oswego.edu.
Soccer: Ken Peterson; Phone: 315-312-4142; E-mail: kpeterso@oswego.edu.
Swimming: Kami Matthews; Phone: 315-312-3366; E-mail: kmathews@oswego.edu.
Tennis: Stan Gosek; Phone: 315-312-2922.
Track and Field: Tim Boyce; Phone: 315-312-4149; E-mail: tboyce@oswego.edu.
Wrestling: Mike Howard; Phone: 315-312-2402; E-mail: howard@oswego.edu.

WOMEN'S COACHES
Basketball: Michele Collins; Phone: 315-312-2404; E-mail: mcollin1@oswego.edu.
Cross Country: Tim Boyce; Phone: 315-312-4149; E-mail: tboyce@oswego.edu.
Diving: Kami Matthews; Phone: 315-312-3366; E-mail: kmathews@oswego.edu.
Field Hockey: Adair Milmoe; Phone: 315-312-2881; E-mail: amilmoe@hotmail.com.
Lacrosse: Adair Milmoe; Phone: 315-637-2881; E-mail: milmoe@oswego.edu.
Soccer: Ken Peterson; Phone: 315-312-4142; E-mail: kpeterso@oswego.edu.
Softball: Chyrisse Conte; Phone: 315-312-2828; E-mail: cconte@oswego.edu.
Swimming: Kami Matthews; Phone: 315-312-3366; E-mail: kmathews@oswego.edu.
Tennis: Stan Gosek; Phone: 315-312-2922.
Track and Field: Tim Boyce; Phone: 315-312-4149; E-mail: tboyce@oswego.edu.
Volleyball: Dani Drews; Phone: 315-312-3330; E-mail: drews@oswego.edu.

STATE UNIVERSITY OF NEW YORK AT PLATTSBURGH
Plattsburgh, New York

Cardinals ◆ NCAA III ◆ SUNY Athletic Conference ◆ http://www.plattsburgh.edu/

State-supported comprehensive, founded 1889, part of State University of New York System
Coed, 5,403 undergraduate students, 92% full-time, 58% women, 42% men
Small-town 265-acre campus with easy access to Montreal
Moderately difficult entrance level, 61% of applicants were admitted

Freshmen *Admission:* 6,798 applied, 4,232 were accepted, 967 enrolled. *Test scores:* SAT verbal scores over 500: 61%; SAT math scores over 500: 66%; SAT verbal scores over 600: 13%; SAT math scores over 600: 15%; SAT verbal scores over 700: 1%; SAT math scores over 700: 1%.
Tuition and fees (2003–04): $5200 (resident), $11,150 (nonresident). *Room and board:* $6448 (room only: $4040).
Financial Aid (All incoming freshmen): *Average need-based gift aid:* $4486. *Average non-need based aid:* $3535. *Average aid to full-time undergraduates:* $7753.
Athletic Department: *Director of Athletics:* Peter Luguri; Phone: 518-564-4153; Fax: 518-564-4155; E-mail: luguripp@plattsburgh.edu. *Sports Information Director:* Kelly Vergin; Phone: 518-564-4148; E-mail: verginkl@plattsburgh.edu.

MEN'S COACHES
Baseball: Kris Doorey; Phone: 518-564-4136; E-mail: dooreykm@plattsburgh.edu.
Basketball: Tom Curle; Phone: 518-564-4143; E-mail: curleto@plattsburgh.edu.
Cross Country: Brett Willmott; Phone: 518-564-4145; E-mail: willmobd@plattsburgh.edu.
Golf: Matt Salvatore; Phone: 518-564-3142; E-mail: salvatm@plattsburgh.edu.
Ice Hockey: Bob Emery; Phone: 518-564-3607; E-mail: emeryrd@plattsburgh.edu.
Lacrosse: Scott DeMonte; Phone: 518-564-3139; E-mail: scott.demonte@plattsburgh.edu.
Soccer: Chris Waterbury; Phone: 518-564-4142; E-mail: waterbcp@plattsburgh.edu.
Track and Field: Brett Willmott; Phone: 518-564-4145; E-mail: willmobd@plattsburgh.edu.

WOMEN'S COACHES
Basketball: Cheryl Cole; Phone: 518-564-4147; E-mail: coleca@plattsburgh.edu.
Cross Country: Brett Willmott; Phone: 518-564-4145; E-mail: willmobd@plattsburgh.edu.
Golf: Matt Salvatore; Phone: 518-564-3142; E-mail: salvatm@plattsburgh.edu.
Soccer: Karen Waterbury; Phone: 518-564-4141; E-mail: karen.waterbury@plattsburgh.edu.
Softball: Sean Cotter; Phone: 518-564-4144; E-mail: cottersm@plattsburgh.edu.
Tennis: Matt Mero; Phone: 518-564-2066; E-mail: meromv@plattsburgh.edu.
Track and Field: Brett Willmott; Phone: 518-564-4145; E-mail: willmobd@plattsburgh.edu.
Volleyball: Dena O'Connell; Phone: 518-564-4244; E-mail: oconnedq@plattsburgh.edu.

STATE UNIVERSITY OF NEW YORK COLLEGE AT BROCKPORT
Brockport, New York

Golden Eagles ◆ NCAA III ◆ SUNY Athletic Conference
◆ http://www.brockport.edu/

State-supported comprehensive, founded 1867, part of State University of New York System
Coed, 6,962 undergraduate students, 88% full-time, 57% women, 43% men
Small-town 435-acre campus with easy access to Rochester
Moderately difficult entrance level, 48% of applicants were admitted

Freshmen *Admission:* 7,214 applied, 3,701 were accepted, 1,046 enrolled. *Test scores:* SAT verbal scores over 500: 74%; SAT math scores over 500: 68%; SAT verbal scores over 600: 20%; SAT math scores over 600: 16%; SAT verbal scores over 700: 2%; SAT math scores over 700: 2%.
Tuition and fees (2004–05): $5221 (resident), $11,171 (nonresident). *Room and board:* $6890 (room only: $4240).
Financial Aid (All incoming freshmen): *Average need-based gift aid:* $2667. *Average non-need based aid:* $2717. *Average aid to full-time undergraduates:* $7343.
Athletic Department: *Director of Athletics:* Lin Case; Phone: 585-395-5328; Fax: 585-395-2160; E-mail: lcase@brockport.edu. *Sports Information Director:* Eric McDowell; Phone: 585-395-2218; E-mail: emcdowel@brockport.edu.

MEN'S COACHES
Baseball: Mark Rowland; Phone: 716-395-5329; E-mail: mrowland@brockport.edu.
Basketball: Nelson Whitmore; Phone: 716-395-2235; E-mail: nwhitmor@brockport.edu.
Cross Country: Mark Krueger; Phone: 716-395-5353; E-mail: mkrueger@brockport.edu.
Diving: Greg Kenney; Phone: 716-395-5344; E-mail: gkenney@brockport.edu.
Football: Rocco Salomone; Phone: 716-395-5348; E-mail: rsalomon@brockport.edu.
Ice Hockey: Brian Dickison; Phone: 716-395-5351; E-mail: bdickins@brockport.edu.
Lacrosse: Ben Wineburg; Phone: 716-395-5067; E-mail: bwinebur@brockport.edu.
Soccer: Gary Lapietra; Phone: 716-395-5448; E-mail: glapietr@brockport.edu.
Swimming: Greg Kenney; Phone: 716-395-5344; E-mail: gkenney@brockport.edu.
Track and Field: Mark Krueger; Phone: 716-395-5353; E-mail: mkrueger@brockport.edu.
Wrestling: Don Murray; Phone: 716-395-5360; E-mail: dmurray@brockport.edu.

WOMEN'S COACHES
Basketball: Michele Carron; Phone: 716-395-5359; E-mail: mcarron@brockport.edu.
Cross Country: Mark Krueger; Phone: 716-395-5353; E-mail: mkrueger@brockport.edu.
Diving: Greg Kenney; Phone: 716-395-5344; E-mail: gkenney@brockport.edu.
Field Hockey: Andrea Zurlo; Phone: 716-395-5977; E-mail: azurlo@brockport.edu.
Lacrosse: Traci Hay Lian; Phone: 716-395-5347; E-mail: thay@brockport.edu.
Soccer: Joan Schockow; Phone: 716-395-5350; E-mail: jschocko@brockport.edu.
Softball: John Dumaw; Phone: 716-395-5955; E-mail: jdumaw@brockport.edu.
Swimming: Greg Kenney; Phone: 716-395-5344; E-mail: gkenney@brockport.edu.
Tennis: Ed Gonzalez; Phone: 716-395-5614; E-mail: egonzale@brockport.edu.
Track and Field: Mark Krueger; Phone: 716-395-5353; E-mail: mkrueger@brockport.edu.
Volleyball: John Tuttle; Phone: 716-395-5841; E-mail: jtuttle@brockport.edu.

STATE UNIVERSITY OF NEW YORK COLLEGE AT CORTLAND
Cortland, New York

Red Dragons ◆ NCAA III ◆ New Jersey Athletic Conference; SUNY Athletic Conference ◆ http://www.cortland.edu/

State-supported comprehensive, founded 1868, part of State University of New York System
Coed, 5,796 undergraduate students, 95% full-time, 58% women, 42% men
Small-town 191-acre campus with easy access to Syracuse
Moderately difficult entrance level, 43% of applicants were admitted

Freshmen *Admission:* 9,327 applied, 4,532 were accepted, 1,134 enrolled. *Test scores:* SAT verbal scores over 500: 80%; SAT math scores over 500: 67%; SAT verbal scores over 600: 17%; SAT math scores over 600: 11%; SAT verbal scores over 700: 1%; SAT math scores over 700: 1%.
Tuition and fees (2003–04): $5235 (resident), $11,185 (nonresident). *Room and board:* $6860 (room only: $3960).
Financial Aid (All incoming freshmen): *Average need-based gift aid:* $2489. *Average non-need based aid:* $5248. *Average aid to full-time undergraduates:* $7420.
Athletic Department: *Director of Athletics:* Joan Sitterly; Phone: 607-753-4953; Fax: 607-753-4929; E-mail: sitterly@cortland.edu. *Sports Information Director:* Fran Elia; Phone: 607-753-5673; E-mail: eliaf@cortland.edu.

MEN'S COACHES
Baseball: Joe Brown; Phone: 607-753-4950; E-mail: jbrown@cortland.edu.
Basketball: Tom Spanbauer; Phone: 607-753-4906; E-mail: spanbauer@cortland.edu.
Cheerleading: Justin Hobbie; Phone: 607-753-4953; E-mail: cheerleading@cortland.edu.
Cross Country: Jack Daniels; Phone: 607-753-4948; E-mail: danielsj@cortland.edu.
Diving: Brian Tobin; Phone: 607-753-5709; E-mail: tobinb@cortland.edu.
Football: Daniel MacNeil; Phone: 607-753-5711; E-mail: football@cortland.edu.
Ice Hockey: Tom Cranfield; Phone: 607-753-4990; E-mail: cranfieldt@cortland.edu.
Lacrosse: Lelan Rogers; Phone: 607-753-4993; E-mail: rogersl@cortland.edu.
Soccer: Mike Middleton; Phone: 607-753-4958; E-mail: middletonm@cortland.edu.
Swimming: Brian Tobin; Phone: 607-753-5709; E-mail: tobinb@cortland.edu.
Track and Field: John Crawford; Phone: 607-753-5012; E-mail: crawfordj@cortland.edu.
Wrestling: Brad Bruhn; Phone: 607-753-5718; E-mail: bruhnb@cortland.edu.

WOMEN'S COACHES
Basketball: Jeanette Yeoman; Phone: 607-753-5788; E-mail: yeomanj@cortland.edu.
Cheerleading: Justin Hobbie; Phone: 607-753-4953; E-mail: cheerleading@cortland.edu.
Cross Country: Jack Daniels; Phone: 607-753-4948; E-mail: danielsj@cortland.edu.
Diving: Brian Tobin; Phone: 607-753-5709; E-mail: tobinb@cortland.edu.
Field Hockey: Cynthia Wetmore; Phone: 607-753-5706; E-mail: wetmorec@cortland.edu.
Golf: Karen Lang; Phone: 607-753-4923; E-mail: langk@cortland.edu.
Gymnastics: Gary Babjack; Phone: 607-753-4999; E-mail: babjackg@cortland.edu.
Lacrosse: Cynthia Wetmore; Phone: 607-753-5706; E-mail: wetmorec@cortland.edu.
Soccer: Laura Ray; Phone: 607-753-5715; E-mail: rayla@cortland.edu.
Softball: Julie Lenhart; Phone: 607-753-5712; E-mail: lenhartj@cortland.edu.
Swimming: Brian Tobin; Phone: 607-753-5709; E-mail: tobinb@cortland.edu.
Tennis: Pete Cahill; Phone: 607-753-4903; E-mail: cahill@cortland.edu.

State University of New York College at Cortland *(continued)*

Track and Field: John Crawford; Phone: 607-753-5012; E-mail: crawfordj@cortland.edu.
Volleyball: Joan Sitterly; Phone: 607-753-4992; E-mail: sitterly@cortland.edu.

STATE UNIVERSITY OF NEW YORK COLLEGE AT FREDONIA
Fredonia, New York

Blue Devils ◆ NCAA III ◆ SUNY Athletic Conference ◆ http://www.fredonia.edu/

State-supported comprehensive, founded 1826, part of State University of New York System
Coed, 4,852 undergraduate students, 96% full-time, 59% women, 41% men
Small-town 266-acre campus with easy access to Buffalo
Moderately difficult entrance level, 55% of applicants were admitted

Freshmen *Admission:* 5,961 applied, 3,377 were accepted, 1,074 enrolled. *Test scores:* SAT verbal scores over 500: 81%; SAT math scores over 500: 83%; SAT verbal scores over 600: 22%; SAT math scores over 600: 24%; SAT verbal scores over 700: 4%; SAT math scores over 700: 3%.
Tuition and fees (2004–05): $5362 (resident), $11,312 (nonresident). *Room and board:* $6120 (room only: $4050).
Financial Aid (All incoming freshmen): *Average need-based gift aid:* $3643. *Average non-need based aid:* $1547. *Average aid to full-time undergraduates:* $6769.
Athletic Department: *Director of Athletics:* Greg Prechtl; Phone: 716-673-3101; Fax: 716-673-3624; E-mail: gregory.prechtl@fredonia.edu. *Sports Information Director:* Jerry Reilly; Phone: 716-673-3100; E-mail: jerome.reilly@fredonia.edu.

MEN'S COACHES
Baseball: Matt Palisan; Phone: 716-673-3743; E-mail: matthew.palisin@fredonia.edu.
Basketball: Kevin Moore; Phone: 716-673-3108; E-mail: kevin.moore@fredonia.edu.
Cheerleading: Monica Brown; Phone: 716-673-3767; E-mail: monica.brown@fredonia.edu.
Cross Country: Adrian Barr; Phone: 716-673-3700; E-mail: adarian.barr@fredonia.edu.
Diving: Arthur Wang; Phone: 716-673-3643; E-mail: arthur.wang@fredonia.edu.
Ice Hockey: Jeffrey Meredith; Phone: 716-673-3334; E-mail: jeffrey.meredith@fredonia.edu.
Soccer: P.J. Gondek; Phone: 716-673-3366; E-mail: patrick.gondek@fredonia.edu.
Swimming: Arthur Wang; Phone: 716-673-3643; E-mail: arthur.wang@fredonia.edu.
Tennis: Joseph Calarco; Phone: 716-673-3101; E-mail: joseph.calarco@fredonia.edu.
Track and Field: Adarian Barr; Phone: 716-673-3700; E-mail: adarian.barr@fredonia.edu.

WOMEN'S COACHES
Basketball: Donna Wise; Phone: 716-673-3120; E-mail: donna.wise@fredonia.edu.
Cheerleading: Monica Brown; Phone: 716-673-3767; E-mail: monica.brown@fredonia.edu.
Cross Country: Adarian Barr; Phone: 716-673-3700; E-mail: adarian.barr@fredonia.edu.
Diving: Arthur Wang; Phone: 716-673-3643; E-mail: arthur.wang@fredonia.edu.
Lacrosse: Chris Case; Phone: 716-673-3279; E-mail: christopher.case@fredonia.edu.
Softball: Lorrie Corsi; Phone: 716-673-3101; E-mail: lorrie.corsi@fredonia.edu.
Swimming: Arthur Wang; Phone: 716-673-3643; E-mail: arthur.wang@fredonia.edu.
Tennis: Joseph Calarco; Phone: 716-673-3101; E-mail: joseph.calarco@fredonia.edu.
Track and Field: Penny Hite; Phone: 716-673-3159; E-mail: penny.hite@fredonia.edu.
Volleyball: Geoff Braun; Phone: 716-673-3687; E-mail: geoffrey.braun@fredonia.edu.

STATE UNIVERSITY OF NEW YORK COLLEGE AT GENESEO
Geneseo, New York

Knights ◆ NCAA III ◆ SUNY Athletic Conference ◆ http://www.geneseo.edu/

State-supported comprehensive, founded 1871, part of State University of New York System
Coed, 5,307 undergraduate students, 98% full-time, 63% women, 37% men
Small-town 220-acre campus with easy access to Rochester
Very difficult entrance level, 40% of applicants were admitted

Freshmen *Admission:* 8,783 applied, 3,684 were accepted, 996 enrolled. *Test scores:* SAT verbal scores over 500: 97%; SAT math scores over 500: 99%; SAT verbal scores over 600: 70%; SAT math scores over 600: 77%; SAT verbal scores over 700: 12%; SAT math scores over 700: 9%.
Tuition and fees (2003–04): $5390 (resident), $11,340 (nonresident). *Room and board:* $6750 (room only: $3700).
Financial Aid (All incoming freshmen): *Average need-based gift aid:* $2790. *Average non-need based aid:* $1560. *Average aid to full-time undergraduates:* $8040.

MEN'S COACHES
Basketball: Steve Minton; Phone: 716-245-5359; E-mail: minton@geneseo.edu.
Cheerleading: Caroline Haddad; Phone: 716-245-5211; E-mail: haddad@geneseo.edu.
Cross Country: Mike Woods; Phone: 716-245-5340; E-mail: woodsm@geneseo.edu.
Diving: Paul Dotterweich; Phone: 716-245-5352; E-mail: dotter@geneseo.edu.
Ice Hockey: Brian Hills; Phone: 716-245-5356; E-mail: hills@geneseo.edu.
Lacrosse: Jim Lyons; Phone: 716-245-5450; E-mail: lyons@geneseo.edu.
Soccer: Mike Mooney; Phone: 716-245-5343; E-mail: mooney@geneseo.edu.
Swimming: Paul Dotterweich; Phone: 716-245-5352; E-mail: dotter@geneseo.edu.
Track and Field: Mike Woods; Phone: 716-245-5340; E-mail: woodsm@geneseo.edu.

WOMEN'S COACHES
Basketball: Kris Ruffo; Phone: 716-245-5354; E-mail: ruffo@geneseo.edu.
Cheerleading: Caroline Haddad; Phone: 716-245-5211; E-mail: haddad@geneseo.edu.
Cross Country: Mike Woods; Phone: 716-245-5340; E-mail: woodsm@geneseo.edu.
Diving: Paul Dotterweich; Phone: 716-245-5352; E-mail: dotter@geneseo.edu.
Field Hockey: Liz Monte; Phone: 716-245-5342; E-mail: monte@geneseo.edu.
Lacrosse: Carly Peters; Phone: 716-245-5342; E-mail: petersc@geneseo.edu.
Soccer: Aimee Canale; Phone: 716-245-5146; E-mail: canale@geneseo.edu.
Softball: Tony Ciccarello; Phone: 716-245-5183; E-mail: ciccarel@geneseo.edu.
Swimming: Paul Dotterweich; Phone: 716-245-5352; E-mail: dotter@geneseo.edu.
Tennis: Jim Chen; Phone: 716-245-5146; E-mail: jchen001@rochester.rr.com.
Track and Field: Mike Woods; Phone: 716-245-5340; E-mail: woodsm@geneseo.edu.
Volleyball: Maggie Loncz; Phone: 716-245-5353; E-mail: loncz@geneseo.edu.

STATE UNIVERSITY OF NEW YORK COLLEGE AT OLD WESTBURY

Old Westbury, New York

Panthers ◆ NCAA III ◆ Skyline Conference
◆ http://www.oldwestbury.edu/

State-supported comprehensive, founded 1965, part of State University of New York System
Coed, 3,227 undergraduate students, 76% full-time, 59% women, 41% men
Suburban 605-acre campus with easy access to New York City
Moderately difficult entrance level, 6% of applicants were admitted

Freshmen *Admission:* 2,844 applied, 1,635 were accepted, 334 enrolled. *Test scores:* SAT verbal scores over 500: 28%; SAT math scores over 500: 39%; SAT verbal scores over 600: 4%; SAT math scores over 600: 4%.
Tuition and fees (2003–04): $5041 (resident), $10,991 (nonresident). *Room and board:* $7749 (room only: $5459).
Financial Aid (All incoming freshmen): *Average need-based gift aid:* $6357. *Average aid to full-time undergraduates:* $7539.
Athletic Department: *Director of Athletics:* John Lonardo; Phone: 516-876-3241; Fax: 516-876-3230; E-mail: lonardoj@oldwestbury.edu. *Sports Information Director:* Matt Farrand; Phone: 516-876-3032; E-mail: farrandm@oldwestbury.edu.

MEN'S COACHES
Baseball: Hector Aristy; Phone: 516-876-3461.
Basketball: Bernard Tomlin; Phone: 516-876-3466; E-mail: tomlinb@oldwestbury.edu.
Cheerleading: Kate Honan; Phone: 516-876-3244.
Cross Country: Leonard Pitt; Phone: 516-876-3463.
Soccer: Mark Prizant; Phone: 516-876-3462; E-mail: prizantm@oldwestbury.edu.
Swimming: Sigitas Rudokas; Phone: 516-876-3351.

WOMEN'S COACHES
Basketball: Mik Krasnoff; Phone: 516-876-3241.
Cheerleading: Kate Honan; Phone: 516-876-3244.
Cross Country: Leonard Pitt; Phone: 516-876-3463.
Softball: Keri Boller; Phone: 516-876-3467; E-mail: bollerk@oldwestbury.edu.
Swimming: Sigitas Rudokas; Phone: 516-876-3351.
Volleyball: Brian Donaghy; Phone: 516-876-3465; E-mail: bollerk@oldwestbury.edu.

STATE UNIVERSITY OF NEW YORK COLLEGE AT ONEONTA

Oneonta, New York

Red Dragons ◆ NCAA III ◆ Atlantic Soccer Conference; SUNY Athletic Conference ◆ http://www.oneonta.edu/

State-supported comprehensive, founded 1889, part of State University of New York System
Coed, 5,506 undergraduate students, 97% full-time, 59% women, 41% men
Small-town 250-acre campus
Moderately difficult entrance level, 46% of applicants were admitted

Freshmen *Admission:* 10,200 applied, 4,880 were accepted, 1,201 enrolled. *Test scores:* SAT verbal scores over 500: 76%; SAT math scores over 500: 84%; SAT verbal scores over 600: 16%; SAT math scores over 600: 19%; SAT verbal scores over 700: 1%; SAT math scores over 700: 1%.
Tuition and fees (2003–04): $5256 (resident), $11,206 (nonresident). *Room and board:* $6458 (room only: $3688).
Financial Aid (All incoming freshmen): *Average need-based gift aid:* $2985. *Average non-need based aid:* $750. *Average aid to full-time undergraduates:* $6546.
Athletic Department: *Director of Athletics:* Steve Garner; Phone: 607-436-3494; Fax: 607-436-3088; E-mail: garnerse@oneonta.edu. *Sports Information Director:* Geoff Hassard; Phone: 607-436-2106; E-mail: hassargj@oneonta.edu.

MEN'S COACHES
Baseball: Rick Ferchen; Phone: 607-436-2661; E-mail: fercherk@oneonta.edu.
Basketball: Paul Clune; Phone: 607-436-3280; E-mail: clunepg@oneonta.edu.
Cross Country: Matt Lopiccolo; Phone: 607-436-2436; E-mail: lopiccmj@oneonta.edu.
Lacrosse: Stewart Moan; Phone: 607-436-2103; E-mail: moansj@oneonta.edu.
Soccer: Iain Byrne; Phone: 607-436-2102; E-mail: byrneij@oneonta.edu.
Swimming: Chris Schuler-Ghiorse; Phone: 607-436-2505; E-mail: schulee@oneonta.edu.
Tennis: Phone: 607-436-3594.
Track and Field: Matt Lopiccolo; Phone: 607-436-2436; E-mail: lopiccmj@oneonta.edu.
Wrestling: Al Sosa; Phone: 607-436-2100; E-mail: sosaah@oneonta.edu.

WOMEN'S COACHES
Basketball: Dan McGraw; Phone: 607-436-2360; E-mail: mcgrawdt@oneonta.edu.
Cross Country: Matt Lopiccolo; Phone: 607-436-2436; E-mail: lopiccmj@oneonta.edu.
Field Hockey: Michele Dombrowski; Phone: 607-436-2104; E-mail: dombroml@oneonta.edu.
Lacrosse: Laura Moan; Phone: 607-436-2902; E-mail: moanlb@oneonta.edu.
Soccer: Tracy Ranieri; Phone: 607-436-2446; E-mail: raniertm@oneonta.edu.
Softball: Denise Marchese; Phone: 607-436-3590; E-mail: marchedl@oneonta.edu.
Swimming: Chris Schuler-Ghiorse; Phone: 607-436-2505; E-mail: schulee@oneonta.edu.
Tennis: Phone: 607-436-3348.
Track and Field: Matt Lopiccolo; Phone: 607-436-2436; E-mail: lopiccmj@oneonta.edu.
Volleyball: Colleen Cashman; Phone: 607-436-2145; E-mail: cashmacm@oneonta.edu.

STATE UNIVERSITY OF NEW YORK COLLEGE AT POTSDAM

Potsdam, New York

Bears ◆ NCAA III ◆ SUNY Athletic Conference ◆ http://www.potsdam.edu/

State-supported comprehensive, founded 1816, part of State University of New York System
Coed, 3,484 undergraduate students, 96% full-time, 59% women, 41% men
Small-town 240-acre campus
Moderately difficult entrance level, 68% of applicants were admitted

Freshmen *Admission:* 3,418 applied, 2,366 were accepted, 677 enrolled. *Test scores:* SAT verbal scores over 500: 68%; SAT math scores over 500: 70%; SAT verbal scores over 600: 22%; SAT math scores over 600: 24%; SAT verbal scores over 700: 3%; SAT math scores over 700: 3%.
Tuition and fees (2003–04): $5190 (resident), $11,140 (nonresident). *Room and board:* $6970 (room only: $4070).
Financial Aid (All incoming freshmen): *Average need-based gift aid:* $4491. *Average non-need based aid:* $7057. *Average aid to full-time undergraduates:* $11,706.
Athletic Department: *Director of Athletics:* Jim Zalacca; Phone: 315-267-3135; Fax: 315-267-2316; E-mail: zalaccja@potsdam.edu. *Sports Information Director:* Boyd Jones; Phone: 315-267-2315; E-mail: joneswb@potsdam.edu.

MEN'S COACHES
Basketball: Bill Mitchell; Phone: 315-267-2307; E-mail: mitchewj@potsdam.edu.
Cheerleading: Lisa_aucoin@yahoo.ca; Phone: 315-267-2311; E-mail: lisa_aucoin@yahoo.ca.
Cross Country: Matt Tessier; Phone: 315-267-2310; E-mail: tessiemj@potsdam.edu.
Diving: Ken McLaughlin; Phone: 315-267-2311; E-mail: mclaugdk@potsdam.edu.

State University of New York College at Potsdam (*continued*)

Golf: Rick Berkman; Phone: 315-267-2317; E-mail: berkmarw@potsdam.edu.
Ice Hockey: Glenn Thomaris; Phone: 315-267-2301; E-mail: thomargf@potsdam.edu.
Lacrosse: Rick Berkman; Phone: 315-267-2317; E-mail: berkmarw@potsdam.edu.
Soccer: Joe Vaadi; Phone: 315-267-2313; E-mail: vaadijs@potsdam.edu.
Swimming: Ken McLaughlin; Phone: 315-267-2311; E-mail: mclaugdk@potsdam.edu.

WOMEN'S COACHES
Basketball: Devonna Williams; Phone: 315-267-3708.
Cheerleading: Lisa_aucoin@yahoo.ca; Phone: 315-267-2311; E-mail: lisa_aucoin@yahoo.ca.
Cross Country: Matt Tessier; Phone: 315-267-2310; E-mail: tessiemj@potsdam.edu.
Diving: Ken McLaughlin; Phone: 315-267-2311; E-mail: mclaugdk@potsdam.edu.
Lacrosse: Lauren Bruce; Phone: 315-267-2322.
Soccer: Lauren Bruce; Phone: 315-267-2322.
Softball: Steve Pike; Phone: 315-267-2309; E-mail: pikesm@potsdam.edu.
Swimming: Ken McLaughlin; Phone: 315-267-2311; E-mail: mclaugdk@potsdam.edu.
Tennis: Cynthia Morin; Phone: 315-267-2310; E-mail: morincm@potsdam.edu.
Volleyball: Steve Pike; Phone: 315-267-2309; E-mail: morincm@potsdam.edu.

STATE UNIVERSITY OF NEW YORK COLLEGE OF TECHNOLOGY AT DELHI
Delhi, New York

Broncos ◆ NAIA ◆ Independent ◆ http://www.delhi.edu/

State-supported primarily 2-year, founded 1913, part of State University of New York System
Coed, 2,281 undergraduate students, 90% full-time, 42% women, 58% men
Rural 405-acre campus
Moderately difficult entrance level, 60% of applicants were admitted

Freshmen *Admission:* 3,462 applied, 2,091 were accepted, 945 enrolled.
Tuition and fees (2004–05): $5325 (resident), $11,275 (nonresident).
Room and board: $6390.
Athletic Department: *Director of Athletics:* Gary Cole; Phone: 607-746-4677; E-mail: colegs@delhi.edu. *Sports Information Director:* Tom Fisher; Phone: 607-746-4604; E-mail: fishertw@delhi.edu.

MEN'S COACHES
Basketball: Anthony Flores; Phone: 607-746-4676; E-mail: foresap@delhi.edu.
Cross Country: Bob Backus; Phone: 607-746-4680; E-mail: backusrh@delhi.edu.
Golf: Dave Arehart; Phone: 607-746-4550; E-mail: arehardb@delhi.edu.
Lacrosse: Robert Leary; Phone: 607-746-4610; E-mail: learyrt@delhi.edu.
Soccer: Doug McKee; Phone: 607-746-4550; E-mail: mckeedm@delhi.edu.
Swimming: John Kolodziej; Phone: 607-746-4263; E-mail: kolodzje@delhi.edu.
Tennis: Charles Mole; Phone: 607-746-4316; E-mail: molecc@delhi.edu.
Track and Field: Bob Backus; Phone: 607-746-4680; E-mail: backusrh@delhi.edu.

WOMEN'S COACHES
Basketball: Glen LePinnet; Phone: 607-746-4229; E-mail: lepinngg@delhi.edu.
Cross Country: Bob Backus; Phone: 607-746-4680; E-mail: backusrh@delhi.edu.
Golf: Gary Cole; Phone: 607-746-4677; E-mail: colegs@delhi.edu.
Soccer: Robert Leary; Phone: 607-746-4610; E-mail: learyrt@delhi.edu.

Softball: Tom Fisher; Phone: 607-746-4604; E-mail: fishertw@delhi.edu.
Swimming: John Kolodziej; Phone: 607-746-4263; E-mail: kolodzje@delhi.edu.
Tennis: Charles Mole; Phone: 607-746-4316; E-mail: molecc@delhi.edu.
Track and Field: Bob Backus; Phone: 607-746-4680; E-mail: backusrh@delhi.edu.
Volleyball: Michelle Barber; Phone: 607-746-4214; E-mail: michelle.barber@co.delaware.ny.us.

STATE UNIVERSITY OF NEW YORK INSTITUTE OF TECHNOLOGY
Utica, New York

Wildcats ◆ NCAA III ◆ SUNY Athletic Conference ◆ http://www.sunyit.edu/

State-supported comprehensive, founded 1966, part of State University of New York System
Coed, 2,059 undergraduate students, 62% full-time, 50% women, 50% men
Suburban 850-acre campus
Minimally difficult entrance level, 23% of applicants were admitted

Freshmen *Admission:* 868 applied, 200 were accepted, 105 enrolled.
Test scores: SAT verbal scores over 500: 92%; SAT math scores over 500: 97%; SAT verbal scores over 600: 35%; SAT math scores over 600: 60%; SAT verbal scores over 700: 5%; SAT math scores over 700: 6%.
Tuition and fees (2003–04): $5154 (resident), $11,104 (nonresident).
Room and board: $6800.
Athletic Department: *Director of Athletics:* Kevin Grimmer; Phone: 315-792-7520; Fax: 315-792-7536; E-mail: grimmek@sunyit.edu. *Sports Information Director:* Shawn Lincoln; Phone: 315-792-7521; E-mail: edickk@sunyit.edu.

MEN'S COACHES
Baseball: Kevin Edick; Phone: 315-792-7520; E-mail: edickk@sunyit.edu.
Basketball: Thomas Curle; Phone: 315-792-7512; E-mail: curlet@sunyit.edu.
Golf: John Randall; Phone: 315-792-7520.
Lacrosse: Mark Murphy; Phone: 315-792-7520; E-mail: murphym9@sunyit.edu.
Soccer: Bob Leary; Phone: 315-792-7520.

WOMEN'S COACHES
Basketball: David Katz; Phone: 315-792-7520; E-mail: katzd@sunyit.edu.
Soccer: James Lipocky; Phone: 315-792-7834; E-mail: lipockj@sunyit.edu.
Softball: Michele Decoursey; Phone: 315-792-7539; E-mail: decourm@sunyit.edu.
Volleyball: Michele Decoursey; Phone: 315-792-7539; E-mail: decourm@sunyit.edu.

STATE UNIVERSITY OF NEW YORK MARITIME COLLEGE
Throggs Neck, New York

Privateers ◆ NCAA III ◆ Knickerbocker Lacrosse Conference; Skyline Conference ◆ http://www.sunymaritime.edu/

State-supported comprehensive, founded 1874, part of State University of New York System
Coed, primarily men, 951 undergraduate students, 97% full-time, 11% women, 89% men
Suburban 56-acre campus
Moderately difficult entrance level, 88% of applicants were admitted

Freshmen *Admission:* 888 applied, 772 were accepted, 319 enrolled.
Test scores: SAT verbal scores over 500: 64%; SAT math scores over

500: 74%; SAT verbal scores over 600: 19%; SAT math scores over 600: 26%; SAT verbal scores over 700: 2%; SAT math scores over 700: 1%.
Tuition and fees (2003–04): $5850 (resident), $11,800 (nonresident). *Room and board:* $7046.
Athletic Department: *Director of Athletics:* William Martinov; Phone: 718-409-7331; Fax: 718-409-7404; E-mail: wmartinov@sunymaritime.edu. *Sports Information Director:* Chris Morello; Phone: 718-409-6981; E-mail: cmorello@sunymaritime.edu.

MEN'S COACHES
Baseball: Frank Menna; Phone: 718-409-7755.
Basketball: David Summa; Phone: 718-409-7787; E-mail: dsumma@sunymaritime.edu.
Cross Country: Paul Acquaro; Phone: 718-409-7452; E-mail: pacquaro@sunymaritime.edu.
Lacrosse: Kelly Curtin; Phone: 718-409-6800; E-mail: kcurtin@sunymaritime.edu.
Soccer: Andrew McCarthy; Phone: 718-409-6659; E-mail: amccarthy@sunymaritime.edu.
Swimming: Peter Vecchio; Phone: 718-409-7774; E-mail: pvecchio@sunymaritime.edu.
Wrestling: Israel Medina; Phone: 718-409-7785; E-mail: izzyhere@optonline.net.

WOMEN'S COACHES
Basketball: John Wilson; Phone: 718-409-7775; E-mail: net-jaminc@aol.com.
Cross Country: Paul Acquaro; Phone: 718-409-7452; E-mail: pacquaro@sunymaritime.edu.
Softball: Paul Acquaro; Phone: 718-409-7452; E-mail: pacquaro@sunymaritime.edu.
Swimming: Peter Vecchio; Phone: 718-409-7774; E-mail: pvecchio@sunymaritime.edu.
Volleyball: Ennio Escoto; Phone: 718-409-7703; E-mail: eescoto@sunymaritime.edu.

STATE UNIVERSITY OF WEST GEORGIA
Carrollton, Georgia

Braves ◆ NCAA II ◆ Gulf South Conference ◆ http://www.westga.edu/

State-supported comprehensive, founded 1933, part of University System of Georgia
Coed, 8,045 undergraduate students, 84% full-time, 60% women, 40% men
Small-town 394-acre campus with easy access to Atlanta
Minimally difficult entrance level, 92% of applicants were admitted

Freshmen *Admission:* 4,848 applied, 3,026 were accepted, 1,788 enrolled. *Test scores:* SAT verbal scores over 500: 54%; SAT math scores over 500: 51%; SAT verbal scores over 600: 12%; SAT math scores over 600: 11%; SAT verbal scores over 700: 2%; SAT math scores over 700: 1%.
Tuition and fees (2003–04): $2774 (resident), $9410 (nonresident). *Room and board:* $4406 (room only: $2420).
Financial Aid (All incoming freshmen): *Average need-based gift aid:* $4604. *Average non-need based aid:* $2660. *Average aid to full-time undergraduates:* $6727.
Athletic Department: *Director of Athletics:* Ed Murphy; Phone: 770-836-6533; Fax: 770-836-6792; E-mail: emurphy@westga.edu. *Sports Information Director:* Mitch Gray; Phone: 770-836-6542; E-mail: mgray@westga.edu.

MEN'S COACHES
Baseball: Doc Fowlkes; Phone: 770-836-6537; E-mail: dfowlkes@westga.edu.
Basketball: Ed Murphy; Phone: 770-836-6533; E-mail: emurphy@westga.edu.
Cheerleading: Sherry Cooney; Phone: 770-836-6533.
Cross Country: Don Medeiros; Phone: 770-836-4623; E-mail: dmedeiro@westga.edu.
Football: Mike Ledford; Phone: 770-836-6539; E-mail: mledford@westga.edu.
Track and Field: Don Medeiros; Phone: 770-836-6533; E-mail: dmedeiro@westga.edu.

WOMEN'S COACHES
Basketball: Craig Roden; Phone: 770-836-4625; E-mail: croden@westga.edu.
Cheerleading: Sherry Cooney; Phone: 770-836-6533.
Cross Country: Don Medeiros; Phone: 770-836-4623; E-mail: dmedeiro@westga.edu.
Softball: Erika Swanson; Phone: 770-828-3140; E-mail: eswanson@westga.edu.
Track and Field: Don Medeiros; Phone: 770-836-6533; E-mail: dmedeiro@westga.edu.
Volleyball: Amy Draper; Phone: 770-836-4621; E-mail: adraper@westga.edu.

STEPHEN F. AUSTIN STATE UNIVERSITY
Nacogdoches, Texas

Lumberjacks ◆ NCAA I ◆ Southland Conference ◆ http://www.sfasu.edu/

State-supported comprehensive, founded 1923
Coed, 9,747 undergraduate students, 86% full-time, 59% women, 41% men
Small-town 400-acre campus
Moderately difficult entrance level, 70% of applicants were admitted

Freshmen *Admission:* 5,750 applied, 4,198 were accepted, 1,754 enrolled. *Test scores:* SAT verbal scores over 500: 53%; SAT math scores over 500: 53%; SAT verbal scores over 600: 14%; SAT math scores over 600: 11%; SAT verbal scores over 700: 1%; SAT math scores over 700: %.
Tuition and fees (2003–04): $2639 (resident), $8307 (nonresident). *Room and board:* $4766.
Financial Aid (All incoming freshmen): *Average need-based gift aid:* $2050. *Average non-need based aid:* $2327. *Average aid to full-time undergraduates:* $4013.
Athletic Department: *Director of Athletics:* Steve McCarty; Phone: 409-468-4540; Fax: 409-468-4593; E-mail: smccarty@sfasu.edu. *Sports Information Director:* Rob Meyers; Phone: 409-468-2606; E-mail: rmeyers@sfasu.edu.

MEN'S COACHES
Basketball: Danny Kaspar; Phone: 936-468-3108; E-mail: dkaspar@sfasu.edu.
Cheerleading: Beverly Farmer; Phone: 936-468-3703; E-mail: bfarmer@sfasu.edu.
Cross Country: Phil Olson; Phone: 936-468-4140; E-mail: polson@sfasu.edu.
Football: Mike Santiago; Phone: 936-468-3502; E-mail: msantiago@sfasu.edu.
Golf: Mike Hopson; Phone: 936-468-4462; E-mail: mhhopson@sfasu.edu.
Track and Field: Phil Olson; Phone: 936-468-4140; E-mail: polson@sfasu.edu.

WOMEN'S COACHES
Basketball: Lee Ann Riley; Phone: 936-468-3208; E-mail: lriley@sfasu.edu.
Cheerleading: Beverly Farmer; Phone: 936-468-3703; E-mail: bfarmer@sfasu.edu.
Cross Country: Phil Olson; Phone: 936-468-4140; E-mail: polson@sfasu.edu.
Soccer: Nicole Nelson; Phone: 936-468-4207; E-mail: nnelson@sfasu.edu.
Softball: Jennifer Poulsen; Phone: 936-468-4011; E-mail: jpoulsen@sfasu.edu.
Tennis: Bret Arrant; Phone: 936-468-1643; E-mail: barrant@sfasu.edu.
Track and Field: Phil Olson; Phone: 936-468-4140; E-mail: polson@sfasu.edu.
Volleyball: Debbie Humphreys; Phone: 936-468-4014; E-mail: dhumphreys@sfasu.edu.

STEPHENS COLLEGE
Columbia, Missouri

Stars ◆ NCAA III ◆ Independent ◆ http://www.stephens.edu/

Independent comprehensive, founded 1833
Women only, 577 undergraduate students, 77% full-time, 97% women, 3% men
Urban 86-acre campus
Moderately difficult entrance level, 98% of applicants were admitted

Freshmen *Admission:* 393 applied, 311 were accepted, 139 enrolled. *Test scores:* SAT verbal scores over 500: 88%; SAT math scores over 500: 73%; SAT verbal scores over 600: 34%; SAT math scores over 600: 24%; SAT verbal scores over 700: 2%; SAT math scores over 700: 2%.
Tuition and fees (2003–04): $17,360 (full-time). *Room and board:* $6900 (room only: $3050).
Financial Aid (All incoming freshmen): *Average need-based gift aid:* $5622. *Average non-need based aid:* $8411. *Average aid to full-time undergraduates:* $15,631.
Athletic Department: *Director of Athletics:* Deb Duren; Phone: 573-876-7212; Fax: 573-876-7248; E-mail: debd@stephens.edu.

WOMEN'S COACHES
Basketball: Dane Pavlovich; Phone: 573-876-7212; E-mail: dpavlovich@stephens.edu.
Soccer: Carrie Crossett; Phone: 573-876-7212.
Swimming: Laura Wacker; Phone: 573-876-7212.
Tennis: Lori Towle; Phone: 573-876-7212.
Volleyball: Deb Duren; Phone: 573-876-7212; E-mail: debd@stephens.edu.

STERLING COLLEGE
Sterling, Kansas

Warriors ◆ NAIA ◆ Kansas Collegiate Conference ◆ http://www.sterling.edu/

Independent Presbyterian 4-year, founded 1887
Coed, 495 undergraduate students, 87% full-time, 51% women, 49% men
Rural 46-acre campus
Moderately difficult entrance level, 51% of applicants were admitted

Freshmen *Admission:* 465 applied, 263 were accepted, 126 enrolled. *Test scores:* SAT verbal scores over 500: 24%; SAT math scores over 500: 19%; SAT math scores over 600: 5%.
Tuition and fees (2003–04): $13,520 (full-time). *Room and board:* $5513 (room only: $2170).
Financial Aid (All incoming freshmen): *Average need-based gift aid:* $7912. *Average non-need based aid:* $5216. *Average aid to full-time undergraduates:* $12,619.
Athletic Department: *Director of Athletics:* Lonnie Kruse; Phone: 620-278-4285; Fax: 620-278-4319; E-mail: lkruse@sterling.edu. *Sports Information Director:* Shawn Reed; Phone: 620-278-4282; E-mail: sreed@sterling.edu.

MEN'S COACHES
Baseball: Scott Norwood; Phone: 620-278-4227; E-mail: snorwood@sterling.edu.
Basketball: Tommy DeSalme; Phone: 620-278-4277; E-mail: tdesalme@sterling.edu.
Cross Country: Matt Canterbury; Phone: 620-278-4224; E-mail: mcanterbury@sterling.edu.
Football: Phone: 620-278-4239.
Soccer: Justin Morris; Phone: 620-278-4324; E-mail: jmorris@sterling.edu.
Track and Field: Matt Canterbury; Phone: 620-278-4224; E-mail: mcanterbury@sterling.edu.

WOMEN'S COACHES
Basketball: Lonnie Kruse; Phone: 620-278-4285; E-mail: lkruse@sterling.edu.
Cross Country: Matt Canterbury; Phone: 620-278-4224; E-mail: mcanterbury@sterling.edu.
Soccer: Justin Morris; Phone: 620-278-4324; E-mail: jmorris@sterling.edu.

Softball: Pam Bell; Phone: 620-278-4338; E-mail: pbell@sterling.edu.
Track and Field: Matt Canterbury; Phone: 620-278-4224; E-mail: mcanterbury@sterling.edu.
Volleyball: Mary Ver Steeg; Phone: 620-278-4257; E-mail: mversteeg@sterling.edu.

STETSON UNIVERSITY
DeLand, Florida

Hatters ◆ NCAA I ◆ Atlantic Sun Conference ◆ http://www.stetson.edu/

Independent comprehensive, founded 1883
Coed, 2,161 undergraduate students, 96% full-time, 57% women, 43% men
Small-town 170-acre campus with easy access to Orlando
Moderately difficult entrance level, 8% of applicants were admitted

Freshmen *Admission:* 1,992 applied, 1,510 were accepted, 529 enrolled. *Test scores:* SAT verbal scores over 500: 86%; SAT math scores over 500: 82%; SAT verbal scores over 600: 36%; SAT math scores over 600: 33%; SAT verbal scores over 700: 7%; SAT math scores over 700: 4%.
Tuition and fees (2003–04): $22,380 (full-time). *Room and board:* $6855 (room only: $3845).
Financial Aid (All incoming freshmen): *Average need-based gift aid:* $16,751. *Average non-need based aid:* $12,311. *Average aid to full-time undergraduates:* $20,535.
Athletic Department: *Director of Athletics:* Jeff Altier; Phone: 386-822-8120; Fax: 386-822-8148; E-mail: jaltier@stetson.edu. *Sports Information Director:* Jamie Bataille; Phone: 386-822-8120; E-mail: jbataill@stetson.edu.

MEN'S COACHES
Baseball: Pete Dunn; Phone: 386-822-8106; E-mail: pdunn@stetson.edu.
Basketball: Derek Waugh; Phone: 386-822-8118; E-mail: dwaugh@stetson.edu.
Cheerleading: Salina Hood; Phone: 386-822-8131; E-mail: shood@stetson.edu.
Cross Country: John Boyle; Phone: 386-822-8120; E-mail: jboyle@stetson.edu.
Golf: Robert Weickel; Phone: 386-822-8154; E-mail: rweickel@stetson.edu.
Soccer: Sean Murphy; Phone: 386-822-8123; E-mail: smurphy@stetson.edu.
Tennis: Pierre Pilote; Phone: 386-822-8146; E-mail: ppilote@stetson.edu.

WOMEN'S COACHES
Basketball: Dee Romine; Phone: 386-822-8116; E-mail: dromine@stetson.edu.
Cheerleading: Salina Hood; Phone: 386-822-8131; E-mail: shood@stetson.edu.
Cross Country: John Boyle; Phone: 386-822-8120; E-mail: jboyle@stetson.edu.
Golf: Nancy Rubin-Sharff; Phone: 386-822-8137; E-mail: nrubinsh@stetson.edu.
Soccer: Julie Orlowski; Phone: 386-822-8139; E-mail: jorlowsk@stetson.edu.
Softball: Frank Griffin; Phone: 386-822-8129; E-mail: fgriffin@stetson.edu.
Tennis: Sasha Schmid; Phone: 386-822-8100; E-mail: sschmid@stetson.edu.
Volleyball: Becky Thyhsen; Phone: 386-822-8117; E-mail: bthyhsen@stetson.edu.

STEVENS INSTITUTE OF TECHNOLOGY
Hoboken, New Jersey

Ducks ◆ NCAA III ◆ Knickerbocker Lacrosse Conference; Skyline Conference ◆ http://www.stevens.edu/

Independent university, founded 1870
Coed, 1,707 undergraduate students, 100% full-time, 25% women, 75% men
Urban 55-acre campus with easy access to New York City
Very difficult entrance level, 50% of applicants were admitted

Freshmen *Admission:* 1,999 applied, 1,026 were accepted, 395 enrolled. *Test scores:* SAT verbal scores over 500: 95%; SAT math scores over 500: 99%; SAT verbal scores over 600: 56%; SAT math scores over 600: 87%; SAT verbal scores over 700: 12%; SAT math scores over 700: 34%.
Tuition and fees (2003–04): $26,960 (full-time). *Room and board:* $8500 (room only: $4400).
Financial Aid (All incoming freshmen): *Average need-based gift aid:* $15,021. *Average non-need based aid:* $7878. *Average aid to full-time undergraduates:* $21,842.
Athletic Department: *Director of Athletics:* Russell Rogers; Phone: 201-216-5688; Fax: 201-216-8244; E-mail: rrogers@stevens.edu. *Sports Information Director:* Tracy King; Phone: 201-216-5078; E-mail: tking@stevens.edu.

MEN'S COACHES
Baseball: John Crane; Phone: 201-216-8033; E-mail: jcrane@stevens-tech.edu.
Basketball: Steve Hayn; Phone: 201-216-5690; E-mail: shayn@stevens-tech.edu.
Cross Country: Kevin McGinn; Phone: 201-216-8086; E-mail: kmcginn@stevens-tech.edu.
Lacrosse: Bryon Collins; Phone: 201-216-5692; E-mail: bcollins@stevens-tech.edu.
Soccer: Tim O'Donohue; Phone: 201-216-5244; E-mail: todonohu@stevens-tech.edu.
Swimming: J. Earl Walton; Phone: 201-216-5696; E-mail: ewalton@stevens-tech.edu.
Tennis: Jeff Bloomberg; Phone: 201-216-5694; E-mail: jbloombe@stevens.edu.
Track and Field: Kevin McGinn; Phone: 201-216-8086; E-mail: kmcginn@stevens-tech.edu.
Volleyball: Patrick Dorywalski; Phone: 201-216-5691; E-mail: pdorywal@stevens-tech.edu.
Wrestling: Andy Lausier; Phone: 201-216-8244; E-mail: alausier@stevens.edu.

WOMEN'S COACHES
Basketball: Susan Roarke; Phone: 201-216-8087; E-mail: sroarke@stevens-tech.edu.
Cross Country: Kevin McGinn; Phone: 201-216-8086; E-mail: kmcginn@stevens-tech.edu.
Field Hockey: Jessica Reed; Phone: 201-216-8040.
Lacrosse: Celine Cunningham; Phone: 201-216-8056; E-mail: ccunning@stevens-tech.edu.
Soccer: Jeff Parker; Phone: 201-216-8112; E-mail: jparker1@stevens-tech.edu.
Swimming: J. Earl Walton; Phone: 201-216-5696; E-mail: ewalton@stevens-tech.edu.
Tennis: Jeff Bloomberg; Phone: 201-216-5694; E-mail: jbloombe@stevens.edu.
Track and Field: Kevin McGinn; Phone: 201-216-8086; E-mail: kmcginn@stevens-tech.edu.
Volleyball: J.J. O'Connell; Phone: 201-216-5685; E-mail: joconnel@stevens-tech.edu.

STILLMAN COLLEGE
Tuscaloosa, Alabama

Tigers ◆ NCAA III ◆ Independent ◆ http://www.stillman.edu/

Independent religious 4-year, founded 1876, affiliated with Presbyterian Church (U.S.A.)
Coed, 1,458 undergraduate students
Urban 100-acre campus with easy access to Birmingham
Minimally difficult entrance level, 50% of applicants were admitted

Freshmen *Admission:* 2,591 applied, 1,291 were accepted.
Tuition and fees (2003–04): $8718 (full-time). *Room and board:* $4200 (room only: $2000).
Athletic Department: *Director of Athletics:* Richard Cosby; Phone: 205-366-8987; Fax: 205-366-8988; E-mail: rcosby@stillman.edu. *Sports Information Director:* Wesley Peterson; Phone: 205-366-8101; E-mail: wpeterson@stillman.edu.

MEN'S COACHES
Baseball: Randy Jennings; Phone: 205-366-8980.
Basketball: Shawn Parks; Phone: 205-366-8842.
Cross Country: Shawn Parks; Phone: 205-366-8842.
Football: Theophilus Danzy; Phone: 205-247-8172.
Tennis: Will Riley; Phone: 205-366-8964.
Track and Field: Jake Irby; Phone: 205-366-8965.

WOMEN'S COACHES
Basketball: Linda Burgess; Phone: 205-366-8180.
Cross Country: Jake Irby; Phone: 205-366-8965.
Softball: Albert Stinson; Phone: 205-366-8180.
Tennis: Will Riley; Phone: 205-366-8964.
Track and Field: Jake Irby; Phone: 205-366-8965.
Volleyball: Will Riley; Phone: 205-366-8964.

STONEHILL COLLEGE
Easton, Massachusetts

Chieftans ◆ NCAA II ◆ Northeast-10 Conference ◆ http://www.stonehill.edu/

Independent Roman Catholic comprehensive, founded 1948
Coed, 2,567 undergraduate students, 87% full-time, 59% women, 41% men
Suburban 375-acre campus with easy access to Boston
Very difficult entrance level, 57% of applicants were admitted

Freshmen *Admission:* 4,808 applied, 2,366 were accepted, 568 enrolled. *Test scores:* SAT verbal scores over 500: 93%; SAT math scores over 500: 96%; SAT verbal scores over 600: 48%; SAT math scores over 600: 54%; SAT verbal scores over 700: 5%; SAT math scores over 700: 5%.
Tuition and fees (2003–04): $21,302 (full-time). *Room and board:* $9450.
Financial Aid (All incoming freshmen): *Average need-based gift aid:* $12,113. *Average non-need based aid:* $11,038. *Average aid to full-time undergraduates:* $16,968.
Athletic Department: *Director of Athletics:* Paula Sullivan; Phone: 508-565-1391; Fax: 508-565-1460; E-mail: psullivan@stonehill.edu. *Sports Information Director:* Jim Seavey; Phone: 508-565-1352; E-mail: jseavey@stonehill.edu.

MEN'S COACHES
Baseball: Patrick Boen; Phone: 508-565-1351; E-mail: pboen@stonehill.edu.
Basketball: David McLaughlin; Phone: 508-565-1385; E-mail: damclaughlin@stonehill.edu.
Cross Country: Karen Boen; Phone: 508-565-1142; E-mail: kboen@stonehill.edu.
Football: Chris Woods; Phone: 508-565-1318; E-mail: cjwoods@stonehill.edu.
Ice Hockey: Scott Harlow; Phone: 508-565-1598; E-mail: sharlow@stonehill.edu.
Soccer: Jose Gomes; Phone: 508-565-1523; E-mail: jgomes@stonehill.edu.
Tennis: Peter Miller; Phone: 508-565-1529; E-mail: pmiller@stonehill.edu.
Track and Field: Karen Boen; Phone: 508-565-1142; E-mail: kboen@stonehill.edu.

Stonehill College *(continued)*

WOMEN'S COACHES

Basketball: Trisha Brown; Phone: 508-565-1124; E-mail: trishab@stonehill.edu.

Cross Country: Karen Boen; Phone: 508-565-1142; E-mail: kboen@stonehill.edu.

Field Hockey: Pam Arpe; Phone: 508-565-1704; E-mail: parpe@stonehill.edu.

Lacrosse: Michael Daly; Phone: 508-565-1518; E-mail: mdaly@stonehill.edu.

Soccer: Kathy Brophy; Phone: 508-565-1677; E-mail: kmbrophy@stonehill.edu.

Softball: Julie Szala; Phone: 508-565-1523; E-mail: jszala@stonehill.edu.

Tennis: Sandy Xenos; Phone: 508-565-1523; E-mail: sxenos@stonehill.edu.

Track and Field: Karen Boen; Phone: 508-565-1142; E-mail: kboen@stonehill.edu.

Volleyball: Brad Alexander; Phone: 508-565-1529; E-mail: balexander@stonehill.edu.

STONY BROOK UNIVERSITY, STATE UNIVERSITY OF NEW YORK
Stony Brook, New York

Sea Wolves ◆ NCAA I ◆ America East Conference; Northeast Conference ◆ http://www.sunysb.edu/

State-supported university, founded 1957, part of State University of New York System
Coed, 14,072 undergraduate students, 90% full-time, 49% women, 51% men
Small-town 1,100-acre campus with easy access to New York City
Very difficult entrance level, 52% of applicants were admitted

Freshmen *Admission:* 16,909 applied, 8,564 were accepted, 2,181 enrolled. *Test scores:* SAT verbal scores over 500: 93%; SAT math scores over 500: 99%; SAT verbal scores over 600: 40%; SAT math scores over 600: 62%; SAT verbal scores over 700: 5%; SAT math scores over 700: 13%.
Tuition and fees (2003–04): $5316 (resident), $11,266 (nonresident). *Room and board:* $7458.
Financial Aid (All incoming freshmen): *Average need-based gift aid:* $2936. *Average non-need based aid:* $2883. *Average aid to full-time undergraduates:* $8841.
Athletic Department: *Director of Athletics:* Jim Fiore; Phone: 631-632-7131; Fax: 631-632-7122; E-mail: james.fiore@stonybrook.edu. *Sports Information Director:* Rob Emmerich; Phone: 631-632-6312; E-mail: robert.emmerich@notes.cc.sunysb.edu.

MEN'S COACHES

Baseball: Matt Senk; Phone: 631-632-9226; E-mail: matthew.senk@notes.cc.sunysb.edu.

Basketball: Nick Macarchuk; Phone: 631-632-7201; E-mail: nicholas.macarchuk@notes.cc.sunysb.edu.

Cross Country: Andy Ronan; Phone: 631-632-7214; E-mail: andrew.ronan@notes.cc.sunysb.edu.

Diving: Brian Yodice; Phone: 631-632-4318; E-mail: david.alexander@notes.cc.sunysb.edu.

Football: Sam Kornhauser; Phone: 631-632-7198; E-mail: samuel.kornhauser@notes.cc.sunysb.edu.

Lacrosse: John Espey; Phone: 631-632-7219; E-mail: john.espey@notes.cc.sunysb.edu.

Soccer: Cesar Markovic; Phone: 631-632-7203; E-mail: scott.a.dean@notes.cc.sunysb.edu.

Swimming: Dave Alexander; Phone: 631-632-7204; E-mail: david.alexander@notes.cc.sunysb.edu.

Tennis: Gary Glassman; Phone: 631-632-7208; E-mail: gary.glassman@notes.cc.sunysb.edu.

Track and Field: Andy Ronan; Phone: 631-632-7214; E-mail: andrew.ronan@notes.cc.sunysb.edu.

WOMEN'S COACHES

Basketball: Trish Roberts; Phone: 631-632-7199; E-mail: patricia.roberts@notes.cc.sunysb.edu.

Cross Country: Andy Ronan; Phone: 631-632-7214; E-mail: andrew.ronan@notes.cc.sunysb.edu.

Diving: Brian Yodice; Phone: 631-632-4318; E-mail: david.alexander@notes.cc.sunysb.edu.

Lacrosse: Danie Caro; Phone: 631-632-4089; E-mail: danielle.caro@notes.cc.sunysb.edu.

Soccer: Sue Ryan; Phone: 631-632-7216; E-mail: sryan@notes.cc.sunysb.edu.

Softball: Megan Bryant; Phone: 631-632-7282; E-mail: megan.bryant@notes.cc.sunysb.edu.

Swimming: Dave Alexander; Phone: 631-632-7204; E-mail: david.alexander@notes.cc.sunysb.edu.

Tennis: Gary Glassman; Phone: 631-632-7208; E-mail: gary.glassman@notes.cc.sunysb.edu.

Track and Field: Andy Ronan; Phone: 631-632-7214; E-mail: andrew.ronan@notes.cc.sunysb.edu.

Volleyball: Deborah Matejka; Phone: 631-632-7212; E-mail: deborah.matejka@notes.cc.sunysb.edu.

SUFFOLK UNIVERSITY
Boston, Massachusetts

Rams ◆ NCAA III ◆ Great Northeast Athletic Conference ◆ http://www.suffolk.edu/

Independent comprehensive, founded 1906
Coed, 4,181 undergraduate students, 81% full-time, 59% women, 41% men
Urban 2-acre campus
Moderately difficult entrance level, 77% of applicants were admitted

Freshmen *Admission:* 4,464 applied, 3,658 were accepted, 925 enrolled. *Test scores:* SAT verbal scores over 500: 56%; SAT math scores over 500: 53%; SAT verbal scores over 600: 14%; SAT math scores over 600: 12%; SAT verbal scores over 700: 1%; SAT math scores over 700: 1%.
Tuition and fees (2003–04): $17,690 (full-time). *Room and board:* $10,290.
Financial Aid (All incoming freshmen): *Average need-based gift aid:* $6340. *Average non-need based aid:* $5555. *Average aid to full-time undergraduates:* $12,078.
Athletic Department: *Director of Athletics:* Jim Nelson; Phone: 617-573-8379; Fax: 617-227-4935; E-mail: jnelson@suffolk.edu. *Sports Information Director:* Brenda Laymance; Phone: 617-573-8379; E-mail: blaymanc@suffolk.edu.

MEN'S COACHES

Baseball: Cary McConnell; Phone: 617-573-8379; E-mail: cmcconne@suffolk.edu.

Basketball: Dennis McHugh; Phone: 617-573-8379; E-mail: djmchugh@rcn.com.

Cheerleading: Elaine Schwager; Phone: 617-573-8379; E-mail: eschwage@suffolk.edu.

Cross Country: Don Murray; Phone: 617-573-8379.

Golf: Ed McMellen; Phone: 617-573-8379.

Ice Hockey: Brian Horan; Phone: 617-573-8379; E-mail: surams@hockeymail.com.

Soccer: Nick Papadopoulos; Phone: 617-573-8379.

Tennis: Seth Joyal; Phone: 617-573-8379.

WOMEN'S COACHES

Basketball: Ed Leyden; Phone: 617-573-8379; E-mail: eleyden@hotmail.com.

Cheerleading: Elaine Schwager; Phone: 617-573-8379; E-mail: eschwage@suffolk.edu.

Cross Country: Don Murray; Phone: 617-573-8379.

Softball: Elaine Schwager; Phone: 617-573-8379; E-mail: eschwage@suffolk.edu.

Tennis: Seth Joyal; Phone: 617-573-8379.

Volleyball: Elaine Schwager; Phone: 617-573-8379; E-mail: eschwage@suffolk.edu.

SUL ROSS STATE UNIVERSITY
Alpine, Texas

Lobos ◆ NCAA III ◆ American Southwest Conference
◆ http://www.sulross.edu/

State-supported comprehensive, founded 1920, part of Texas State
University System
Coed, 1,402 undergraduate students, 88% full-time, 48% women,
52% men
Small-town 640-acre campus
Noncompetitive entrance level, 80% of applicants were admitted

Freshmen *Admission:* 1,021 applied, 750 were accepted, 323 enrolled.
Test scores: SAT verbal scores over 500: 19%; SAT math scores over
500: 19%; SAT verbal scores over 600: 3%; SAT math scores over
600: 3%; SAT verbal scores over 700: 1%.
Tuition and fees (2003–04): $3402 (resident), $9702 (nonresident). *Room
and board:* $3850 (room only: $1700).
Athletic Department: *Director of Athletics:* Kay Whitley; Phone: 432-837-
8229; Fax: 432-837-8234; E-mail: kwhitley@sulross.edu. *Sports Information Director:* Steve Lang; Phone: 432-837-8226.
MEN'S COACHES
Baseball: Mike Pallanez; Phone: 432-837-8231; E-mail: mpallane@
sulross.edu.
Basketball: Doug Davalos; Phone: 432-837-8093; E-mail: ddavalos@
sulross.edu.
Cheerleading: Nory Callaway; Phone: 432-837-8299; E-mail: btelesca@
sulross.edu.
Football: Steve Wright; Phone: 432-837-8228; E-mail: swright@sulross.
edu.
Tennis: Kay Whitley; Phone: 432-837-8229; E-mail: kwhitley@sulross.
edu.
Track and Field: Ke Koa Kealoha; Phone: 432-837-8663; E-mail:
kkealoha@sulross.edu.
WOMEN'S COACHES
Basketball: David Tandy; Phone: 432-837-8230; E-mail: dtandy@
sulross.edu.
Cheerleading: Nory Callaway; Phone: 432-837-8299; E-mail: btelesca@
sulross.edu.
Cross Country: Ke Koa Kealoha; Phone: 432-837-8663; E-mail:
kkealoha@sulross.edu.
Softball: Rick Garcia; Phone: 432-837-8256; E-mail: rgarcia@sulross.
edu.
Tennis: Kay Whitley; Phone: 432-837-8229; E-mail: kwhitley@sulross.
edu.
Track and Field: Ke Koa Kealoha; Phone: 432-837-8663; E-mail:
kkealoha@sulross.edu.
Volleyball: Rick Garcia; Phone: 432-837-8256; E-mail: rgarcia@sulross.
edu.

SUSQUEHANNA UNIVERSITY
Selinsgrove, Pennsylvania

Crusaders ◆ NCAA III ◆ Commonwealth Conference
◆ http://www.susqu.edu/

Independent religious 4-year, founded 1858, affiliated with
Evangelical Lutheran Church in America
Coed, 2,009 undergraduate students, 96% full-time, 57% women,
43% men
Suburban 220-acre campus with easy access to Harrisburg
Moderately difficult entrance level, 7% of applicants were admitted

Freshmen *Admission:* 2,373 applied, 1,660 were accepted, 499 enrolled.
Test scores: SAT verbal scores over 500: 89%; SAT math scores over
500: 90%; SAT verbal scores over 600: 33%; SAT math scores over
600: 42%; SAT verbal scores over 700: 3%; SAT math scores over
700: 3%.
Tuition and fees (2003–04): $23,480 (full-time). *Room and board:* $6510
(room only: $3440).
Financial Aid (All incoming freshmen): *Average need-based gift aid:*
$13,534. *Average non-need based aid:* $9452. *Average aid to full-time
undergraduates:* $16,780.

Athletic Department: *Director of Athletics:* Pam Samuelson; Phone: 570-
372-4272; Fax: 570-372-2758; E-mail: samuelson@susqu.edu. *Sports
Information Director:* Jim Miller; Phone: 570-372-4119; E-mail:
jmiller@susqu.edu.
MEN'S COACHES
Baseball: Matt Karchner; Phone: 570-372-4417; E-mail: karchner@
susqu.edu.
Basketball: Frank Marcinek; Phone: 570-372-4230; E-mail: marcinek@
susqu.edu.
Cheerleading: Kathleen Lybarger; Phone: 570-372-4080.
Cross Country: Marty Owens; Phone: 570-372-4416; E-mail: owensm@
susqu.edu.
Football: Steve Briggs; Phone: 570-372-4123; E-mail: briggs@susqu.edu.
Golf: Don Harnum; Phone: 570-372-4457; E-mail: harnumd@susqu.
edu.
Lacrosse: Ron Miller; Phone: 570-372-4069; E-mail: rjmiller@susqu.
edu.
Soccer: Jim Findlay; Phone: 570-372-4277; E-mail: findlay@susqu.edu.
Swimming: Ged Schwieikert; Phone: 570-372-4299; E-mail: schweike@
susqu.edu.
Tennis: Rob Logan; Phone: 570-372-4537; E-mail: loganrob@susqu.
edu.
Track and Field: Jim Taylor; Phone: 570-372-4416; E-mail: taylor@
susqu.edu.
WOMEN'S COACHES
Basketball: Liz Cranmer-Briggs; Phone: 570-372-4276; E-mail:
briggse@susqu.edu.
Cheerleading: Kathleen Lybarger; Phone: 570-372-4080.
Cross Country: Marty Owens; Phone: 570-372-4416; E-mail: owensm@
susqu.edu.
Field Hockey: Amy Zimmerman; Phone: 570-372-4271; E-mail:
zimmermana@susqu.edu.
Golf: Liz Cranmer Briggs; Phone: 570-372-4276; E-mail: briggse@
susqu.edu.
Lacrosse: Kate Scattergood; Phone: 570-372-4275; E-mail:
scattergood@susqu.edu.
Soccer: Jim Findlay; Phone: 570-372-4277; E-mail: findlay@susqu.edu.
Softball: Kathy Kroupa; Phone: 570-372-4532; E-mail: kkroupa@aol.
com.
Swimming: Ged Schwieikert; Phone: 570-372-4299; E-mail: schweike@
susqu.edu.
Tennis: Bob Jordan; Phone: 570-374-2011; E-mail: jordrip@mail.
sunlink.net.
Track and Field: Marty Owens; Phone: 570-372-4416; E-mail: owensm@
susqu.edu.
Volleyball: John Tom; Phone: 570-372-4080; E-mail: tom@susqu.edu.

SWARTHMORE COLLEGE
Swarthmore, Pennsylvania

Garnet ◆ NCAA III ◆ Centennial Conference ◆ http://
www.swarthmore.edu/

Independent 4-year, founded 1864
Coed, 1,500 undergraduate students, 99% full-time, 53% women,
47% men
Suburban 357-acre campus with easy access to Philadelphia
Most difficult entrance level, 3% of applicants were admitted

Freshmen *Admission:* 3,908 applied, 920 were accepted, 368 enrolled.
Test scores: SAT verbal scores over 500: 99%; SAT math scores over
500: 100%; SAT verbal scores over 600: 93%; SAT math scores over
600: 93%; SAT verbal scores over 700: 67%; SAT math scores over
700: 65%.
Tuition and fees (2003–04): $28,802 (full-time). *Room and board:* $8914
(room only: $4572).
Financial Aid (All incoming freshmen): *Average need-based gift aid:*
$23,789. *Average non-need based aid:* $28,500. *Average aid to full-
time undergraduates:* $26,395.
Athletic Department: *Director of Athletics:* Adam Hertz; Phone: 610-328-
8325; Fax: 610-328-7798; E-mail: ahertz1@swarthmore.edu. *Sports
Information Director:* Mark Duzenski; Phone: 610-328-8206; E-mail:
mduzens1@swarthmore.edu.
MEN'S COACHES
Baseball: Frank Agovino; Phone: 610-328-8216; E-mail: fagovin1@
swarthmore.edu.

Swarthmore College *(continued)*

Basketball: Lee Wimberly; Phone: 610-328-8219; E-mail: lwimber1@swarthmore.edu.
Cross Country: Peter Carroll; Phone: 610-328-8683; E-mail: pcarrol2@swarthmore.edu.
Golf: Mark Duzenski; Phone: 610-328-8206; E-mail: mduzens1@swarthmore.edu.
Lacrosse: Pat Gress; Phone: 610-328-8208; E-mail: pgress1@swarthmore.edu.
Soccer: Eric Wagner; Phone: 610-690-6822; E-mail: ewagner1@swarthmore.edu.
Swimming: Sue Davis; Phone: 610-328-8211; E-mail: sdavis1@swarthmore.edu.
Tennis: Mike Mullan; Phone: 610-328-8212; E-mail: mmullan3@swarthmore.edu.
Track and Field: Peter Carroll; Phone: 610-328-8683; E-mail: pcarrol2@swarthmore.edu.

WOMEN'S COACHES
Basketball: Adrienne Shibles; Phone: 610-328-8089; E-mail: ashible1@swarthmore.edu.
Cross Country: Peter Carroll; Phone: 610-328-8683; E-mail: pcarrol2@swarthmore.edu.
Field Hockey: Kelly Wilcox; Phone: 610-690-6884; E-mail: kwilcox1@swarthmore.edu.
Lacrosse: Karen Borbee; Phone: 610-328-8209; E-mail: kborbee1@swarthmore.edu.
Soccer: Amy Brunner; Phone: 610-328-8210; E-mail: abrunne1@swarthmore.edu.
Softball: Renee Clarke; Phone: 610-690-6883; E-mail: rclarke1@swarthmore.edu.
Swimming: Sue Davis; Phone: 610-328-8211; E-mail: sdavis1@swarthmore.edu.
Tennis: Jeremy Loomis; Phone: 610-328-8204; E-mail: jloomis1@swarthmore.edu.
Track and Field: Peter Carroll; Phone: 610-328-8683; E-mail: pcarrol2@swarthmore.edu.
Volleyball: Harleigh Leach; Phone: 610-328-8217; E-mail: hleach1@swarthmore.edu.

SWEET BRIAR COLLEGE
Sweet Briar, Virginia

Vixens ◆ NCAA III ◆ Old Dominion Conference ◆ http://www.sbc.edu/

Independent 4-year, founded 1901
Women only, 709 undergraduate students, 93% full-time, 96% women, 4% men
Rural 3,250-acre campus
Moderately difficult entrance level, 88% of applicants were admitted

Freshmen *Admission:* 404 applied, 355 were accepted, 133 enrolled. *Test scores:* SAT verbal scores over 500: 80%; SAT math scores over 500: 69%; SAT verbal scores over 600: 36%; SAT math scores over 600: 20%; SAT verbal scores over 700: 10%; SAT math scores over 700: 2%.
Tuition and fees (2004–05): $21,080 (full-time). *Room and board:* $8520 (room only: $3420).
Financial Aid (All incoming freshmen): *Average need-based gift aid:* $11,809. *Average non-need based aid:* $10,469. *Average aid to full-time undergraduates:* $13,193.
Athletic Department: *Director of Athletics:* Milly MacDonell; Phone: 434-381-6337; Fax: 434-381-6487; E-mail: morrison@sbc.edu. *Sports Information Director:* Jennifer Crispen; Phone: 434-381-6338; E-mail: crispen@sbc.edu.

WOMEN'S COACHES
Field Hockey: Jennifer Crispen; Phone: 434-381-6338; E-mail: crispen@sbc.edu.
Lacrosse: Missy Ackerman; Phone: 434-381-6291; E-mail: mackerman@sbc.edu.
Soccer: Paul Shaw; Phone: 434-381-6149; E-mail: pshaw@sbc.edu.
Swimming: Jason Gallher; Phone: 434-381-6336; E-mail: jgallaher@sbc.edu.
Tennis: Kelly Morrison; Phone: 434-381-6337; E-mail: morrison@sbc.edu.
Volleyball: Beth Huus; Phone: 434-381-6149; E-mail: bhuus@sbc.edu.

SYRACUSE UNIVERSITY
Syracuse, New York

Orangemen ◆ NCAA I ◆ Big East Conference ◆ http://www.syracuse.edu/

Independent university, founded 1870
Coed, 10,840 undergraduate students, 99% full-time, 56% women, 44% men
Urban 200-acre campus
Very difficult entrance level, 61% of applicants were admitted

Freshmen *Admission:* 14,144 applied, 8,718 were accepted, 2,650 enrolled. *Test scores:* SAT verbal scores over 500: 96%; SAT math scores over 500: 95%; SAT verbal scores over 600: 55%; SAT math scores over 600: 63%; SAT verbal scores over 700: 9%; SAT math scores over 700: 14%.
Tuition and fees (2003–04): $24,830 (full-time). *Room and board:* $9590.
Financial Aid (All incoming freshmen): *Average need-based gift aid:* $14,221. *Average non-need based aid:* $9080. *Average aid to full-time undergraduates:* $18,780.
Athletic Department: *Director of Athletics:* Jake Crouthamel; Phone: 315-443-2385; Fax: 315-443-2076; E-mail: jjcrouth@syr.edu. *Sports Information Director:* Sue Edson; Phone: 315-443-2608; E-mail: sedson@syr.edu.

MEN'S COACHES
Basketball: Jim Boeheim; Phone: 315-443-2082.
Cross Country: Andy Roberts; Phone: 315-443-5054; E-mail: robertsa@syr.edu.
Diving: Jeff Keck; Phone: 315-443-1924; E-mail: wjkeck@syr.edu.
Football: Paul Pasqualoni; Phone: 315-443-4791; E-mail: kmpasqa@syr.edu.
Lacrosse: John Desko; Phone: 315-443-1503; E-mail: jtdesko@syr.edu.
Soccer: Dean Foti; Phone: 315-443-3025; E-mail: dtfoti@syr.edu.
Swimming: Lou Walker; Phone: 315-443-4151; E-mail: lrwalker@syr.edu.
Track and Field: Andy Roberts; Phone: 315-443-5054; E-mail: robertsa@syr.edu.

WOMEN'S COACHES
Basketball: Keith Cieplicki; Phone: 315-443-3761; E-mail: kcieplic@syr.edu.
Cross Country: Andy Roberts; Phone: 315-443-5054; E-mail: robertsa@syr.edu.
Diving: Jeff Keck; Phone: 315-443-1924; E-mail: wjkeck@syr.edu.
Field Hockey: Kathleen Parker; Phone: 315-443-1421; E-mail: kparker@syr.edu.
Lacrosse: Lisa Miller; Phone: 315-443-4258; E-mail: lmmille0@syr.edu.
Soccer: April Kater; Phone: 315-443-5859; E-mail: askater@syr.edu.
Softball: Mary Jo Fimbach; Phone: 315-443-4591; E-mail: mafirnba@syr.edu.
Swimming: Lou Walker; Phone: 315-443-4151; E-mail: lrwalker@syr.edu.
Tennis: Mac Gifford; Phone: 315-443-3552; E-mail: rmgiffor@syr.edu.
Track and Field: Andy Roberts; Phone: 315-443-5054; E-mail: robertsa@syr.edu.
Volleyball: Jing Pu; Phone: 315-443-4149; E-mail: jpu@syr.edu.

TABOR COLLEGE
Hillsboro, Kansas

Bluejays ◆ NAIA ◆ Kansas Collegiate Conference ◆ http://www.tabor.edu/

Independent Mennonite Brethren comprehensive, founded 1908
Coed, 522 undergraduate students, 79% full-time, 48% women, 52% men
Small-town 26-acre campus with easy access to Wichita
Moderately difficult entrance level, 3% of applicants were admitted

Freshmen *Admission:* 382 applied, 153 were accepted, 86 enrolled.
Tuition and fees (2003–04): $14,350 (full-time). *Room and board:* $5150 (room only: $2000).
Financial Aid (All incoming freshmen): *Average need-based gift aid:* $3756. *Average non-need based aid:* $5022. *Average aid to full-time undergraduates:* $13,196.

Athletic Department: *Director of Athletics:* Don Brubacher; Phone: 620-947-3121; Fax: 620-947-3789; E-mail: donb@tabor.edu.

MEN'S COACHES

Baseball: John Sparks; Phone: 620-947-3121; E-mail: johns@tabor.edu.
Basketball: Don Brubacher; Phone: 620-947-3121; E-mail: donb@tabor.edu.
Cross Country: Karol Hunt; Phone: 620-947-3121; E-mail: karolh@tabor.edu.
Football: Tim McCarty; Phone: 620-947-3121; E-mail: timm@tabor.edu.
Golf: Randy Keck; Phone: 620-947-3120; E-mail: randyk@tabor.edu.
Soccer: Lincoln Wulf; Phone: 620-947-3121.
Tennis: Lonnie Isaac; Phone: 620-947-3121.
Track and Field: Dave Kroeker; Phone: 620-947-3120; E-mail: davidk@tabor.edu.

WOMEN'S COACHES

Basketball: Rusty Allen; Phone: 620-947-3121.
Cross Country: Karol Hunt; Phone: 620-947-3121; E-mail: karolh@tabor.edu.
Golf: Randy Keck; Phone: 620-947-3120; E-mail: randyk@tabor.edu.
Soccer: Dylan Pohlman; Phone: 620-947-3121.
Softball: Tina King; Phone: 620-947-3121.
Tennis: Lonnie Isaac; Phone: 620-947-3121.
Track and Field: Dave Kroeker; Phone: 620-947-3120; E-mail: davidk@tabor.edu.
Volleyball: Amy Ratzlaff; Phone: 620-947-3121.

TARLETON STATE UNIVERSITY
Stephenville, Texas

Texans ◆ NCAA II ◆ Lone Star Conference
◆ http://www.tarleton.edu/

State-supported comprehensive, founded 1899, part of Texas A&M University System
Coed, 7,429 undergraduate students, 77% full-time, 56% women, 44% men
Small-town 125-acre campus with easy access to Fort Worth
Moderately difficult entrance level, 89% of applicants were admitted

Freshmen *Admission:* 3,181 applied, 2,867 were accepted, 1,313 enrolled. *Test scores:* SAT verbal scores over 500: 39%; SAT math scores over 500: 40%; SAT verbal scores over 600: 7%; SAT math scores over 600: 6%; SAT verbal scores over 700: 1%; SAT math scores over 700: 1%.
Tuition and fees (2003–04): $3505 (resident), $10,585 (nonresident). *Room and board:* $4804.
Financial Aid (All incoming freshmen): *Average need-based gift aid:* $2571. *Average aid to full-time undergraduates:* $5827.
Athletic Department: *Director of Athletics:* Lonn Reisman; Phone: 254-968-9178; Fax: 254-968-9674; E-mail: reisman@tarleton.edu. *Sports Information Director:* Stan Wagnon; E-mail: wagnon@tarleton.edu.

MEN'S COACHES

Baseball: Trey Felan; Phone: 254-968-9182; E-mail: felan@tarleton.edu.
Basketball: Lonn Reisman; Phone: 254-968-9178; E-mail: reisman@tarleton.edu.
Cheerleading: Misti Reisman; Phone: 254-968-9755; E-mail: riebock@tarleton.edu.
Cross Country: Clint Strickland; Phone: 254-968-9174; E-mail: cstrick@tarleton.edu.
Football: Todd Whitten; Phone: 254-968-9518; E-mail: twhitten@tarleton.edu.
Track and Field: Clint Strickland; Phone: 254-968-9174; E-mail: cstrick@tarleton.edu.

WOMEN'S COACHES

Basketball: Ronnie Hearne; Phone: 254-968-9184.
Cheerleading: Misti Reisman; Phone: 254-968-9755; E-mail: riebock@tarleton.edu.
Cross Country: Clint Strickland; Phone: 254-968-9174; E-mail: cstrick@tarleton.edu.
Golf: Jerry Doyle; Phone: 254-968-9986; E-mail: doyle@tarleton.edu.
Softball: Julia Mata; Phone: 254-968-9522; E-mail: coachmata1@yahoo.com.
Tennis: Lance Drake; Phone: 254-968-9370; E-mail: drake@tarleton.edu.

Track and Field: Clint Strickland; Phone: 254-968-9174; E-mail: cstrick@tarleton.edu.
Volleyball: Hadley Foster; Phone: 254-968-9542; E-mail: gfoster@tarleton.edu.

TAYLOR UNIVERSITY
Upland, Indiana

Trojans ◆ NAIA ◆ Mid-Central Conference; Mid-States Football Conference ◆ http://www.tayloru.edu/

Independent interdenominational comprehensive, founded 1846
Coed, 1,834 undergraduate students, 98% full-time, 53% women, 47% men
Rural 250-acre campus with easy access to Indianapolis
Very difficult entrance level, 86% of applicants were admitted

Freshmen *Admission:* 1,312 applied, 1,100 were accepted, 470 enrolled. *Test scores:* SAT verbal scores over 500: 88%; SAT math scores over 500: 84%; SAT verbal scores over 600: 52%; SAT math scores over 600: 44%; SAT verbal scores over 700: 10%; SAT math scores over 700: 10%.
Tuition and fees (2003–04): $18,528 (full-time). *Room and board:* $5292 (room only: $2572).
Financial Aid (All incoming freshmen): *Average need-based gift aid:* $9773. *Average non-need based aid:* $3183. *Average aid to full-time undergraduates:* $12,890.
Athletic Department: *Director of Athletics:* David Bireline; Phone: 765-998-5181; Fax: 765-998-4920; E-mail: dvbirelin@tayloru.edu. *Sports Information Director:* Ted Bowers; Phone: 765-998-5181; E-mail: tdbowers@tayloru.edu.

MEN'S COACHES

Baseball: Mark Raikes; Phone: 765-998-5181; E-mail: mrraikes@tayloru.edu.
Basketball: Paul Patterson; Phone: 765-998-5181; E-mail: plpatters@tayloru.edu.
Cross Country: Troy Friedersdorf; Phone: 765-998-5181; E-mail: tfriedersdorf@eastbrook.k12.in.us.
Football: Steve Wilt; Phone: 765-998-5181; E-mail: stwilt@tayloru.edu.
Golf: Joe Romine; Phone: 765-998-5181; E-mail: joromine@tayloru.edu.
Soccer: Joe Lund; Phone: 765-998-5181; E-mail: jslund@tayloru.edu.
Tennis: Don Taylor; Phone: 765-998-5181; E-mail: dntaylor@tayloru.edu.
Track and Field: Ted Bowers; Phone: 765-998-5181; E-mail: tdbowers@tayloru.edu.

WOMEN'S COACHES

Basketball: Tena Krause; Phone: 765-998-5181; E-mail: tnkrause@tayloru.edu.
Cross Country: Cindy Callison; Phone: 765-998-5181; E-mail: tdbowers@tayloru.edu.
Soccer: Ed Meadors; Phone: 765-998-5181; E-mail: edmeadors@tayloru.edu.
Softball: Stephanie Smith; Phone: 765-998-5181; E-mail: smsmith@tayloru.edu.
Tennis: Dara Syswerda; Phone: 765-998-5181; E-mail: tdsyswerda@bpsinet.com.
Track and Field: Ted Bowers; Phone: 765-998-5181; E-mail: tdbowers@tayloru.edu.
Volleyball: Angie Fincannon; Phone: 765-998-5181; E-mail: anfincann@tayloru.edu.

TEIKYO POST UNIVERSITY
Waterbury, Connecticut

Eagles ◆ NCAA II ◆ Central Atlantic Collegiate Conference
◆ http://teikyopost.edu/

Independent 4-year, founded 1890
Coed, 1,325 undergraduate students, 54% full-time, 64% women, 36% men
Suburban 70-acre campus with easy access to Hartford
Minimally difficult entrance level, 63% of applicants were admitted

Freshmen *Admission:* 1,111 applied, 733 were accepted, 197 enrolled. *Test scores:* SAT verbal scores over 500: 18%; SAT math scores over

Teikyo Post University (continued)

500: 16%; SAT verbal scores over 600: 2%; SAT math scores over 600: 5%; SAT verbal scores over 700: 1%; SAT math scores over 700: 1%.
Tuition and fees (2003–04): $17,500 (full-time). *Room and board:* $7375.
Financial Aid (All incoming freshmen): *Average need-based gift aid:* $5500. *Average non-need based aid:* $5333. *Average aid to full-time undergraduates:* $8951.
Athletic Department: *Director of Athletics:* Daniel Mara; Phone: 203-596-4531; Fax: 203-596-4695; E-mail: dmara@teikyopost.edu.

MEN'S COACHES
Baseball: Wayne Mazzoni; Phone: 203-596-4690; E-mail: wmazzoni@teikyopost.edu.
Basketball: Mike Donnelly; Phone: 203-596-4688; E-mail: mdonnelly@teikyopost.edu.
Cross Country: Paul Ebbs; Phone: 203-596-4534; E-mail: pebbs@teikyopost.edu.
Golf: Pete Stevens; Phone: 203-596-4535; E-mail: pstevens@teikyopost.edu.
Soccer: Rick Bryant; Phone: 203-596-4568; E-mail: rbryant@teikyopost.edu.

WOMEN'S COACHES
Basketball: Paul Ebbs; Phone: 203-596-4534; E-mail: pebbs@teikyopost.edu.
Cross Country: Paul Ebbs; Phone: 203-596-4534; E-mail: pebbs@teikyopost.edu.
Soccer: Rick Bryant; Phone: 203-596-4568; E-mail: rbryant@teikyopost.edu.
Softball: Dawn Spellman; Phone: 203-596-4556; E-mail: dspellman@teikyopost.edu.
Volleyball: Dawn Spellman; Phone: 203-596-4556; E-mail: dspellman@teikyopost.edu.

TEMPLE UNIVERSITY
Philadelphia, Pennsylvania

Owls ◆ NCAA I ◆ Atlantic 10 Conference; Big East Conference ◆ http://www.temple.edu/

State-related university, founded 1884
Coed, 22,215 undergraduate students, 85% full-time, 57% women, 43% men
Urban 110-acre campus
Moderately difficult entrance level, 60% of applicants were admitted

Freshmen *Admission:* 16,758 applied, 10,058 were accepted, 3,606 enrolled. *Test scores:* SAT verbal scores over 500: 75%; SAT math scores over 500: 76%; SAT verbal scores over 600: 28%; SAT math scores over 600: 25%; SAT verbal scores over 700: 2%; SAT math scores over 700: 2%.
Tuition and fees (2003–04): $8594 (resident), $15,354 (nonresident). *Room and board:* $7276 (room only: $4668).
Financial Aid (All incoming freshmen): *Average need-based gift aid:* $4712. *Average non-need based aid:* $2808. *Average aid to full-time undergraduates:* $11,601.
Athletic Department: *Director of Athletics:* Bill Bradshaw; Phone: 215-204-7447; Fax: 215-204-7770; E-mail: bill.bradshaw@temple.edu. *Sports Information Director:* Larry Dougherty; Phone: 215-204-2588; E-mail: larry.dougherty@temple.edu.

MEN'S COACHES
Baseball: Skip Wilson; Phone: 215-204-3146.
Basketball: John Chaney; Phone: 215-204-7443; E-mail: dleibovi@temple.edu.
Cheerleading: Alan Avayou; Phone: 215-204-2789; E-mail: amavayou@juno.com.
Football: Bobby Wallace; Phone: 215-204-0858; E-mail: edda.alicea@temple.edu.
Golf: Bill Mannino; Phone: 215-204-8224; E-mail: bmannino@brownandpartners.com.
Soccer: Dave Mac Williams; Phone: 215-204-8477; E-mail: macpsa6@cs.com.
Tennis: Bill Hoehne; Phone: 215-204-0157.
Track and Field: George Phillips; Phone: 215-204-8258; E-mail: gphill01@temple.edu.

WOMEN'S COACHES
Basketball: Dawn Staley; Phone: 215-204-1955; E-mail: owlhoops@temple.edu.
Cheerleading: Alan Avayou; Phone: 215-204-2789; E-mail: amavayou@juno.com.
Field Hockey: Lauren Fuchs; Phone: 215-204-6288; E-mail: ltaz6@aol.com.
Gymnastics: Ken Anderson; Phone: 215-204-6667; E-mail: kander03@temple.edu.
Lacrosse: Kim Ciarrocca; Phone: 215-204-6668; E-mail: kimlax@unix.temple.edu.
Soccer: David Jones; Phone: 215-204-3162.
Softball: Rocci Pignoli; Phone: 215-204-8742; E-mail: rocci@juno.com.
Tennis: Tracey Tooke; Phone: 215-204-8619; E-mail: ttooke@temple.edu.
Track and Field: George Phillips; Phone: 215-204-8258; E-mail: gphill01@temple.edu.
Volleyball: Robert Bertucci; Phone: 215-204-6289; E-mail: bertucci@temple.edu.

TENNESSEE STATE UNIVERSITY
Nashville, Tennessee

Tigers ◆ NCAA I ◆ Ohio Valley Conference ◆ http://www.tnstate.edu/

State-supported comprehensive, founded 1912, part of Tennessee Board of Regents
Coed, 7,118 undergraduate students, 84% full-time, 63% women, 37% men
Urban 450-acre campus
Minimally difficult entrance level, 35% of applicants were admitted

Freshmen *Admission:* 7,850 applied, 2,711 were accepted, 1,188 enrolled.
Tuition and fees (2003–04): $3818 (resident), $11,750 (nonresident). *Room and board:* $4270 (room only: $2460).
Financial Aid (All incoming freshmen): *Average need-based gift aid:* $719. *Average non-need based aid:* $8640. *Average aid to full-time undergraduates:* $6075.
Athletic Department: *Director of Athletics:* Teresa Phillips; Phone: 615-963-1545; Fax: 615-963-5911; E-mail: tphillips@tnstate.edu. *Sports Information Director:* Lee Wilmot; Phone: 615-963-5674; E-mail: lwilmot@tnstate.edu.

MEN'S COACHES
Basketball: Cy Alexander; Phone: 615-963-5900; E-mail: calexander1@tnstate.edu.
Cheerleading: Dwight Pope; Phone: 615-963-5861; E-mail: tsucheer@aol.com.
Cross Country: Kelly Carter; Phone: 615-963-5890; E-mail: kcarter@tnstate.edu.
Football: James Reese; Phone: 615-963-5920; E-mail: jreese@tnstate.edu.
Golf: Catana Starks; Phone: 615-963-5604; E-mail: cstarks@tnstate.edu.
Tennis: Gerald Robinson; Phone: 615-963-5897; E-mail: grobinson@tnstate.edu.
Track and Field: Kelly Carter; Phone: 615-963-5890; E-mail: kcarter@tnstate.edu.

WOMEN'S COACHES
Basketball: Sharon Allen; Phone: 615-963-5903; E-mail: vjordan@tnstate.edu.
Cheerleading: Dwight Pope; Phone: 615-963-5861; E-mail: tsucheer@aol.com.
Cross Country: Chandra Cheeseborough; Phone: 615-963-5906; E-mail: ccheeseborough@tnstate.edu.
Golf: Glenn Steimling; Phone: 615-963-2172; E-mail: gsteimling@tnstate.edu.
Softball: Joyce Maudie; Phone: 615-963-1543; E-mail: jmaudie@tnstate.edu.
Tennis: Gerald Robinson; Phone: 615-963-5897; E-mail: grobinson@tnstate.edu.
Track and Field: Chandra Cheeseborough; Phone: 615-963-5906; E-mail: ccheeseborough@tnstate.edu.
Volleyball: Dawn Reese; Phone: 615-963-5010; E-mail: ddonaldson@tnstate.edu.

TENNESSEE TECHNOLOGICAL UNIVERSITY

Cookeville, Tennessee

Golden Eagles ◆ NCAA I ◆ Ohio Valley Conference ◆ http://www.tntech.edu/

State-supported university, founded 1915, part of Tennessee Board of Regents
Coed, 7,273 undergraduate students, 88% full-time, 45% women, 55% men
Small-town 235-acre campus
Moderately difficult entrance level, 82% of applicants were admitted

Freshmen *Admission:* 3,182 applied, 2,570 were accepted, 1,388 enrolled. *Test scores:* SAT verbal scores over 500: 76%; SAT math scores over 500: 78%; SAT verbal scores over 600: 36%; SAT math scores over 600: 40%; SAT verbal scores over 700: 6%; SAT math scores over 700: 6%.
Tuition and fees (2003–04): $3778 (resident), $11,710 (nonresident). *Room and board:* $5092 (room only: $2300).
Financial Aid (All incoming freshmen): *Average need-based gift aid:* $2712. *Average non-need based aid:* $3978. *Average aid to full-time undergraduates:* $5627.
Athletic Department: *Director of Athletics:* Frank Harrell; Phone: 931-372-3939; Fax: 931-372-3114; E-mail: fharrell@tntech.edu. *Sports Information Director:* Rob Schabert; Phone: 931-372-3088; E-mail: rschabert@tntech.edu.

MEN'S COACHES

Baseball: Matt Bragga; Phone: 931-372-3925; E-mail: mbragga@tntech.edu.
Basketball: Mike Sutton; Phone: 931-372-3956; E-mail: msutton@tntech.edu.
Cheerleading: Laura Rojas; Phone: 931-372-3928; E-mail: pparrott@tntech.edu.
Cross Country: Jim Greeson; Phone: 931-372-3749; E-mail: jgreeson@tntech.edu.
Football: Mike Hennigan; Phone: 931-372-3930; E-mail: pparrott@tntech.edu.
Golf: Bobby Nichols; Phone: 931-372-2331; E-mail: nicholstntechgolf@citlink.net.
Tennis: Al Campos; Phone: 931-372-3322; E-mail: acampos@tntech.edu.

WOMEN'S COACHES

Basketball: Bill Worrell; Phone: 931-372-3921; E-mail: bworrell@tntech.edu.
Cheerleading: Laura Rojas; Phone: 931-372-3928; E-mail: pparrott@tntech.edu.
Cross Country: Jim Greeson; Phone: 931-372-3749; E-mail: jgreeson@tntech.edu.
Golf: Bobby Nichols; Phone: 931-372-2331; E-mail: nicholstntechgolf@citlink.net.
Soccer: Patrick Farmer; Phone: 931-372-6200; E-mail: pfarmer@tntech.edu.
Softball: Tory Acheson; Phone: 931-372-6552; E-mail: tacheson@tntech.edu.
Tennis: Al Campos; Phone: 931-372-3322; E-mail: acampos@tntech.edu.
Track and Field: Jim Greeson; Phone: 931-372-3749; E-mail: jgreeson@tntech.edu.
Volleyball: John Blair; Phone: 931-372-3924; E-mail: jblair@tntech.edu.

TENNESSEE WESLEYAN COLLEGE

Athens, Tennessee

Bulldogs ◆ NAIA ◆ Appalachian Conference ◆ http://www.twcnet.edu/

Independent United Methodist 4-year, founded 1857
Coed, 793 undergraduate students, 81% full-time, 68% women, 32% men
Small-town 40-acre campus with easy access to Knoxville and Chattanooga
Moderately difficult entrance level, 85% of applicants were admitted

Freshmen *Admission:* 452 applied, 376 were accepted, 106 enrolled. *Test scores:* SAT verbal scores over 500: 50%; SAT math scores over 500: 50%; SAT verbal scores over 600: 25%; SAT math scores over 600: 25%.
Tuition and fees (2004–05): $12,340 (full-time). *Room and board:* $4850.
Financial Aid (All incoming freshmen): *Average need-based gift aid:* $6976. *Average non-need based aid:* $6210. *Average aid to full-time undergraduates:* $8444.
Athletic Department: *Director of Athletics:* Stan Harrison; Phone: 423-746-5253; Fax: 423-744-9968; E-mail: sharrison@twcnet.edu. *Sports Information Director:* Richard Northcutt; Phone: 423-746-5225; E-mail: rnorthcutt@twcnet.edu.

MEN'S COACHES

Baseball: Ashley Lawson; Phone: 423-746-5277; E-mail: alawson@twcnet.edu.
Basketball: Steve Adams; Phone: 423-746-5264; E-mail: stevea@twcnet.edu.
Cross Country: Crystal Lingerfelt; Phone: 423-746-5256; E-mail: lingerfeltc@twcnet.edu.
Soccer: Richard Northcutt; Phone: 423-746-5225; E-mail: rnorthcutt@twcnet.edu.
Tennis: Louie Royal; Phone: 423-746-5253; E-mail: lroyal@twcnet.edu.

WOMEN'S COACHES

Basketball: Stan Harrison; Phone: 423-746-5253; E-mail: sharrison@twcnet.edu.
Cross Country: Crystal Lingerfelt; Phone: 423-746-5256; E-mail: lingerfeltc@twcnet.edu.
Soccer: Tom Condone; Phone: 423-746-5273; E-mail: tcondone@twcnet.edu.
Softball: Jeff Rice; Phone: 423-746-5256; E-mail: coach_rice@twcnet.edu.
Tennis: Louie Royal; Phone: 423-746-5253; E-mail: lroyal@twcnet.edu.
Volleyball: Toby Brooks; Phone: 423-746-5254; E-mail: tbrooks@twcnet.edu.

TEXAS A&M INTERNATIONAL UNIVERSITY

Laredo, Texas

Dustdevils ◆ NAIA ◆ Red River Conference ◆ http://www.tamiu.edu/

State-supported comprehensive, founded 1969, part of Texas A&M University System
Coed, 3,116 undergraduate students, 67% full-time, 64% women, 36% men
Urban 300-acre campus
Moderately difficult entrance level, 48% of applicants were admitted

Freshmen *Admission:* 1,494 applied, 780 were accepted, 497 enrolled. *Test scores:* SAT verbal scores over 500: 24%; SAT math scores over 500: 27%; SAT verbal scores over 600: 4%; SAT math scores over 600: 4%; SAT verbal scores over 700: 1%; SAT math scores over 700: 1%.
Tuition and fees (2004–05): $3833 (resident), $11,573 (nonresident). *Room and board:* $5240 (room only: $3400).
Financial Aid (All incoming freshmen): *Average need-based gift aid:* $6275. *Average non-need based aid:* $3297. *Average aid to full-time undergraduates:* $7690.
Athletic Department: *Director of Athletics:* Steven Garippa; Phone: 956-326-2891; Fax: 519-661-2889; E-mail: sgarippa@tamiu.edu.

Texas A&M International University *(continued)*

MEN'S COACHES

Basketball: Tarvish Felton; Phone: 956-326-2891; E-mail: tfelton@tamiu.edu.

Cross Country: Javier Coronado; Phone: 956-326-2891; E-mail: jacoronado@tamiu.edu.

Golf: Lance Noble; Phone: 956-326-2891; E-mail: lnoble@tamiu.edu.

Soccer: Lance Noble; Phone: 956-326-2891; E-mail: lnoble@tamiu.edu.

WOMEN'S COACHES

Basketball: Marc Garcia; Phone: 956-326-2891; E-mail: marc@tamiu.edu.

Cross Country: Javier Coronado; Phone: 956-326-2891; E-mail: jacoronado@tamiu.edu.

Golf: Sandra Forestier; Phone: 956-326-2891; E-mail: sforestier@tamiu.edu.

Soccer: Sandra Forestier; Phone: 956-326-2891; E-mail: sforestier@tamiu.edu.

Volleyball: Binny Canales; Phone: 956-326-2891; E-mail: acanales@tamiu.edu.

TEXAS A&M UNIVERSITY
College Station, Texas

Aggies ◆ NCAA I ◆ Big 12 Conference
◆ http://www.tamu.edu/

State-supported university, founded 1876, part of Texas A&M University System

Coed, 36,066 undergraduate students, 91% full-time, 49% women, 51% men

Suburban 5,200-acre campus with easy access to Houston

Moderately difficult entrance level, 64% of applicants were admitted

Freshmen *Admission:* 17,250 applied, 11,639 were accepted, 6,726 enrolled. *Test scores:* SAT verbal scores over 500: 83%; SAT math scores over 500: 92%; SAT verbal scores over 600: 43%; SAT math scores over 600: 58%; SAT verbal scores over 700: 8%; SAT math scores over 700: 17%.

Tuition and fees (2003–04): $5051 (resident), $12,131 (nonresident). *Room and board:* $6030 (room only: $3192).

Financial Aid (All incoming freshmen): *Average need-based gift aid:* $6990. *Average non-need based aid:* $7466. *Average aid to full-time undergraduates:* $8375.

Athletic Department: *Director of Athletics:* Bill Byrne; Phone: 979-845-3129; Fax: 979-845-6825; E-mail: b-byrne@tamu.edu. *Sports Information Director:* Alan Cannon; Phone: 979-845-0563; E-mail: a-cannon@tamu.edu.

MEN'S COACHES

Baseball: Mark Johnson; Phone: 979-845-1991; E-mail: m-johnson80173@tamu.edu.

Basketball: Melvin Watkins; Phone: 979-845-4531; E-mail: melvin-l-watkins@tamu.edu.

Cheerleading: Tim Sweeney; Phone: 979-845-1133; E-mail: jtsweeney@tamu.edu.

Cross Country: Dave Hartman; Phone: 979-845-0530; E-mail: david-e-hartman@tamu.edu.

Diving: Kevin Wright; Phone: 979-862-4250; E-mail: k-wright13488@tamu.edu.

Football: Dennis Franchione; Phone: 979-845-3500.

Golf: JT Higgins; Phone: 979-845-4533.

Swimming: Mel Nash; Phone: 979-845-3710; E-mail: m-nash5035@tamu.edu.

Tennis: Tim Cass; Phone: 979-845-2816; E-mail: timothy-d-cass@tamu.edu.

Track and Field: Ted Nelson; Phone: 979-845-8842; E-mail: f-nelson6612@tamu.edu.

WOMEN'S COACHES

Basketball: Gary Blair; Phone: 979-862-3218.

Cheerleading: Tim Sweeney; Phone: 979-845-1133; E-mail: jtsweeney@tamu.edu.

Cross Country: Dave Hartman; Phone: 979-845-0530; E-mail: david-e-hartman@tamu.edu.

Diving: Kevin Wright; Phone: 979-862-4250; E-mail: k-wright13488@tamu.edu.

Golf: Jeanne Sutherland; Phone: 979-845-1070; E-mail: j-sutherland1278@tamu.edu.

Soccer: G. Guerrieri; Phone: 979-862-4248; E-mail: g-guerrieri@tamu.edu.

Softball: Jo Evans; Phone: 979-845-1770; E-mail: joleen-evans@tamu.edu.

Swimming: Steve Bultman; Phone: 979-845-4058; E-mail: ernest-s-bultman@tamu.edu.

Tennis: Bobby Kleinecke; Phone: 979-845-4591; E-mail: r-kleinecke@tamu.edu.

Track and Field: Ted Nelson; Phone: 979-845-9534; E-mail: f-nelson6612@tamu.edu.

Volleyball: Laurie Corbelli; Phone: 979-845-3266; E-mail: l-corbelli@tamu.edu.

TEXAS A&M UNIVERSITY–COMMERCE
Commerce, Texas

Lions ◆ NCAA II ◆ Lone Star Conference
◆ http://www.tamu-commerce.edu/

State-supported university, founded 1889, part of Texas A&M University System

Coed, 5,066 undergraduate students

Small-town 140-acre campus with easy access to Dallas–Fort Worth

Moderately difficult entrance level, 6% of applicants were admitted

Freshmen *Admission:* 1,910 applied, 1,075 were accepted.

Tuition and fees (2003–04): $4578 (resident), $11,658 (nonresident). *Room and board:* $5004 (room only: $2610).

Financial Aid (All incoming freshmen): *Average need-based gift aid:* $5875. *Average non-need based aid:* $1473. *Average aid to full-time undergraduates:* $6736.

Athletic Department: *Director of Athletics:* Paul Peak; Phone: 903-886-5554; Fax: 903-468-3033; E-mail: paul_peak@tamu-commerce.edu. *Sports Information Director:* Bill Powers; Phone: 903-886-5131; E-mail: bill_powers@tamu-commerce.edu.

MEN'S COACHES

Basketball: Sam Walker; Phone: 903-886-5558; E-mail: sam_walker@tamu-commerce.edu.

Cheerleading: Kristi Frost; Phone: 903-468-3091; E-mail: kristi_frost@tamu-commerce.edu.

Cross Country: Pat Ponder; Phone: 903-886-5574; E-mail: patrick_ponder@tamu-commerce.edu.

Football: Scotty Conely; Phone: 903-886-5566; E-mail: eddie_brister@tamu-commerce.edu.

Golf: Jason Price; Phone: 903-886-5558; E-mail: jason_price@tamu-commerce.edu.

Track and Field: Pat Ponder; Phone: 903-886-5574; E-mail: patrick_ponder@tamu-commerce.edu.

WOMEN'S COACHES

Basketball: Denny Downing; Phone: 903-886-5575; E-mail: denny_downing@tamu-commerce.edu.

Cheerleading: Kristi Frost; Phone: 903-468-3091; E-mail: kristi_frost@tamu-commerce.edu.

Cross Country: Pat Ponder; Phone: 903-886-5574; E-mail: patrick_ponder@tamu-commerce.edu.

Golf: Jason Price; Phone: 903-886-5558; E-mail: jason_price@tamu-commerce.edu.

Soccer: Neil Piper; Phone: 903-886-5571; E-mail: neil_piper@tamu-commerce.edu.

Track and Field: Pat Ponder; Phone: 903-886-5572; E-mail: patrick_ponder@tamu-commerce.edu.

Volleyball: Gwendolyn Adams; Phone: 903-886-5576; E-mail: gwendolyn_adams@tamu-commerce.edu.

TEXAS A&M UNIVERSITY–CORPUS CHRISTI
Corpus Christi, Texas

Islanders ◆ NCAA I ◆ Big South Conference; Independent
◆ http://www.tamucc.edu/

State-supported comprehensive, founded 1947, part of Texas A&M University System
Coed, 6,330 undergraduate students, 76% full-time, 60% women, 40% men
Suburban 240-acre campus
Moderately difficult entrance level, 77% of applicants were admitted

Freshmen *Admission:* 2,841 applied, 2,379 were accepted, 1,170 enrolled. *Test scores:* SAT verbal scores over 500: 51%; SAT math scores over 500: 52%; SAT verbal scores over 600: 12%; SAT math scores over 600: 11%; SAT verbal scores over 700: 1%; SAT math scores over 700: 1%.
Tuition and fees (2003–04): $3833 (resident), $10,913 (nonresident). *Room and board:* $7688 (room only: $5088).
Financial Aid (All incoming freshmen): *Average need-based gift aid:* $3616. *Average non-need based aid:* $3314. *Average aid to full-time undergraduates:* $5422.
Athletic Department: *Director of Athletics:* Dan Viola; Phone: 361-825-5541; Fax: 361-825-3218; E-mail: dan.viola@tamucc.edu. *Sports Information Director:* Craig Merriman; Phone: 361-825-3410; E-mail: craig.merriman@tamucc.edu.

MEN'S COACHES
Baseball: Hector Salinas; Phone: 361-825-3252; E-mail: hector.salinas@mail.tamucc.edu.
Basketball: Ronnie Arrow; Phone: 361-825-3417; E-mail: ronnie.arrow@mail.tamucc.edu.
Cross Country: Shawn Flanagan; Phone: 361-825-3212; E-mail: shawn.flanagan@mail.tamucc.edu.
Tennis: Steve Denton; Phone: 361-825-6013; E-mail: steve.denton@mail.tamucc.edu.
Track and Field: Shawn Flanagan; Phone: 361-825-3212; E-mail: shawn.flanagan@mail.tamucc.edu.

WOMEN'S COACHES
Basketball: Jodi Kest; Phone: 361-825-2319; E-mail: jodi.kest@mail.tamucc.edu.
Cross Country: Shawn Flanagan; Phone: 361-825-3212; E-mail: shawn.flanagan@mail.tamucc.edu.
Golf: Carol Blackmar; Phone: 361-825-1395.
Softball: Missy Phillips-Dickerson; Phone: 361-825-3253; E-mail: missy.phillips@mail.tamucc.edu.
Tennis: Ken De Koning; Phone: 361-825-5541; E-mail: ken.dekoning@mail.tamucc.edu.
Track and Field: Shawn Flanagan; Phone: 361-825-3212; E-mail: shawn.flanagan@mail.tamucc.edu.
Volleyball: Frances Kinnison; Phone: 361-825-3232; E-mail: frances.kinnison@mail.tamucc.edu.

TEXAS A&M UNIVERSITY–KINGSVILLE
Kingsville, Texas

Javelinas ◆ NCAA II ◆ Lone Star Conference ◆ http://www.tamuk.edu/

State-supported university, founded 1925, part of Texas A&M University System
Coed, 5,546 undergraduate students, 73% full-time, 51% women, 49% men
Small-town 255-acre campus
Moderately difficult entrance level, 99% of applicants were admitted

Freshmen *Admission:* 2,105 applied, 2,092 were accepted, 844 enrolled. *Test scores:* SAT verbal scores over 500: 30%; SAT math scores over 500: 38%; SAT verbal scores over 600: 8%; SAT math scores over 600: 12%; SAT verbal scores over 700: 1%; SAT math scores over 700: 1%.

Tuition and fees (2003–04): $3846 (resident), $10,926 (nonresident). *Room and board:* $3966 (room only: $2166).
Financial Aid (All incoming freshmen): *Average need-based gift aid:* $6625. *Average aid to full-time undergraduates:* $6625.
Athletic Department: *Director of Athletics:* Jill Willson; Phone: 361-593-2414; Fax: 361-593-3587; E-mail: kfjow00@tamuk.edu. *Sports Information Director:* Fred Nuesch; Phone: 361-593-3908.

MEN'S COACHES
Baseball: Russell Stockton; Phone: 361-593-3487; E-mail: kfrbs00@tamuk.edu.
Basketball: Pete Peterson; Phone: 361-593-2412; E-mail: rick.peterson@tamuk.edu.
Cheerleading: Romy Timmons; Phone: 361-593-3065.
Cross Country: Brent Ericksen; Phone: 361-593-2424; E-mail: brent_ericksen@hotmail.com.
Football: Richard Cundiff; Phone: 361-593-2496; E-mail: richard.cundiff@tamuk.edu.
Track and Field: Brent Ericksen; Phone: 361-593-2424; E-mail: brent_ericksen@hotmail.com.

WOMEN'S COACHES
Basketball: Dina Kangas; Phone: 361-593-4029; E-mail: kadlk00@tamuk.edu.
Cheerleading: Romy Timmons; Phone: 361-593-3065.
Cross Country: Brent Ericksen; Phone: 361-593-2424; E-mail: brent_ericksen@hotmail.com.
Softball: Jake Schumann; Phone: 361-593-3388; E-mail: kajes01@tamuk.edu.
Track and Field: Brent Erickson; Phone: 361-593-2424; E-mail: brent_ericksen@hotmail.com.
Volleyball: Jane Atzenhoffer; Phone: 361-593-2413; E-mail: kfjak01@tamuk.edu.

TEXAS CHRISTIAN UNIVERSITY
Fort Worth, Texas

Horned Frogs ◆ NCAA I ◆ Conference USA Conference
◆ http://www.tcu.edu/

Independent religious university, founded 1873, affiliated with Christian Church (Disciples of Christ)
Coed, 6,933 undergraduate students, 92% full-time, 59% women, 41% men
Suburban 260-acre campus
Moderately difficult entrance level, 61% of applicants were admitted

Freshmen *Admission:* 7,654 applied, 4,971 were accepted, 1,596 enrolled.
Tuition and fees (2003–04): $17,630 (full-time). *Room and board:* $5780 (room only: $3780).
Financial Aid (All incoming freshmen): *Average need-based gift aid:* $9233. *Average non-need based aid:* $6722. *Average aid to full-time undergraduates:* $12,587.
Athletic Department: *Director of Athletics:* Eric Hyman; Phone: 817-257-7965; Fax: 817-257-7656; E-mail: e.hyman@tcu.edu. *Sports Information Director:* Steve Fink; Phone: 817-257-5394; E-mail: s.fink@tcu.edu.

MEN'S COACHES
Baseball: Jim Schlossnagle; Phone: 817-257-5354; E-mail: j.schlossnagle@tcu.edu.
Basketball: Neil Dougherty; Phone: 817-257-7968; E-mail: n.dougherty@tcu.edu.
Cheerleading: Jeff Tucker; Phone: 817-257-6561; E-mail: tcucheer@tcu.edu.
Cross Country: Monte Stratton; Phone: 817-257-7983; E-mail: m.stratton@tcu.edu.
Diving: Wayne Chester; Phone: 817-257-7963; E-mail: w.chester@tcu.edu.
Football: Gary Patterson; Phone: 817-257-7970; E-mail: g.patterson@tcu.edu.
Golf: Bill Montigel; Phone: 817-257-7646; E-mail: b.montigel@tcu.edu.
Swimming: Richard Sybesma; Phone: 817-257-7963; E-mail: r.sybesma@tcu.edu.
Tennis: Joey Rive; Phone: 817-257-5782; E-mail: j.rive@tcu.edu.
Track and Field: Monte Stratton; Phone: 817-257-7983; E-mail: m.stratton@tcu.edu.

Texas Christian University *(continued)*

WOMEN'S COACHES

Basketball: Jeff Mittie; Phone: 817-257-7962; E-mail: j.mittie@tcu.edu.
Cheerleading: Jeff Tucker; Phone: 817-257-6561; E-mail: tcucheer@tcu.edu.
Cross Country: Monte Stratton; Phone: 817-257-7983; E-mail: m.stratton@tcu.edu.
Diving: Wayne Chester; Phone: 817-257-7963; E-mail: w.chester@tcu.edu.
Golf: Angie Ravaiola Larkin; Phone: 817-257-7941.
Soccer: Dave Rubinson; Phone: 817-257-7096; E-mail: d.rubinson@tcu.edu.
Swimming: Richard Sybesma; Phone: 817-257-7962; E-mail: r.sybesma@tcu.edu.
Tennis: Dave Borelli; Phone: 817-257-7639; E-mail: d.borelli@tcu.edu.
Track and Field: Monte Stratton; Phone: 817-257-7983; E-mail: m.stratton@tcu.edu.
Volleyball: Prentice Lewis; Phone: 817-257-7360; E-mail: p.lewis@tcu.edu.

TEXAS COLLEGE
Tyler, Texas

Steers ◆ NAIA ◆ Central States Football Conference; Red River Conference ◆ http://www.texascollege.edu/

Independent religious 4-year, founded 1894, affiliated with Christian Methodist Episcopal Church
Coed, 617 undergraduate students, 96% full-time, 64% women, 36% men
Noncompetitive entrance level

Freshmen *Admission:* 182 enrolled.
Tuition and fees (2003–04): $7680 (full-time). *Room and board:* $4730.
Financial Aid (All incoming freshmen): *Average need-based gift aid:* $1000. *Average aid to full-time undergraduates:* $3500.
Athletic Department: *Director of Athletics:* Emanuel Brown; Phone: 903-593-8311; Fax: 903-593-2342; E-mail: ejbrown@texascollege.edu.

MEN'S COACHES

Baseball: Malcolm Walker; Phone: 903-593-8311; E-mail: mwalker@texascollege.edu.
Basketball: Andre Payne; Phone: 903-593-8311; E-mail: apayne@texascollege.edu.
Football: Emanuel Brown; Phone: 903-593-8311; E-mail: ejbrown@texascollege.edu.

WOMEN'S COACHES

Basketball: Stephen Burns; Phone: 903-593-8311.
Soccer: Phone: 903-593-8311.
Softball: Phone: 903-593-8311.
Volleyball: Phone: 903-593-8311.

TEXAS LUTHERAN UNIVERSITY
Seguin, Texas

Bulldogs ◆ NCAA III ◆ American Southwest Conference ◆ http://www.tlu.edu/

Independent religious 4-year, founded 1891, affiliated with Evangelical Lutheran Church
Coed, 1,410 undergraduate students, 92% full-time, 55% women, 45% men
Suburban 196-acre campus with easy access to San Antonio
Moderately difficult entrance level, 75% of applicants were admitted

Freshmen *Admission:* 1,065 applied, 831 were accepted, 377 enrolled. *Test scores:* SAT verbal scores over 500: 62%; SAT math scores over 500: 67%; SAT verbal scores over 600: 17%; SAT math scores over 600: 25%; SAT verbal scores over 700: 3%; SAT math scores over 700: 2%.
Tuition and fees (2003–04): $15,590 (full-time). *Room and board:* $4780 (room only: $2230).
Financial Aid (All incoming freshmen): *Average non-need based aid:* $8039. *Average aid to full-time undergraduates:* $13,859.

Athletic Department: *Director of Athletics:* Bill Miller; Phone: 830-372-8124; Fax: 830-372-8135; E-mail: bmiller@tlu.edu. *Sports Information Director:* Tim Clark; Phone: 830-372-6877; E-mail: tclark@tlu.edu.

MEN'S COACHES

Baseball: Bill Miller; Phone: 830-372-8124; E-mail: bmiller@tlu.edu.
Basketball: Tom Oswald; Phone: 830-372-8122; E-mail: toswald@tlu.edu.
Cheerleading: Emily King; Phone: 830-372-6578; E-mail: eking@tlu.edu.
Football: Tom Mueller; Phone: 830-372-8126; E-mail: tmueller@tlu.edu.
Golf: HC Tran; Phone: 830-372-8144; E-mail: htran@tlu.edu.
Soccer: Mike Alderson; Phone: 830-372-6577; E-mail: malderson@tlu.edu.
Tennis: Bill Lehman; Phone: 830-372-8128; E-mail: wlehman@tlu.edu.

WOMEN'S COACHES

Basketball: Ashley Smith; Phone: 830-372-8125; E-mail: asmith@tlu.edu.
Cheerleading: Emily King; Phone: 830-372-6578; E-mail: eking@tlu.edu.
Cross Country: Kandice Holaman; Phone: 830-372-6578; E-mail: kholamon@tlu.edu.
Golf: HC Tran; Phone: 830-372-8144; E-mail: htran@tlu.edu.
Soccer: Tony Tommasi; Phone: 830-372-6807; E-mail: ttommasi@tlu.edu.
Softball: Missy McCaughey; Phone: 830-372-8129; E-mail: mmccaughey@tlu.edu.
Tennis: Bill Lehman; Phone: 830-372-8128; E-mail: wlehman@tlu.edu.
Track and Field: Kandice Holaman; Phone: 830-372-6578; E-mail: mmccaughey@tlu.edu.
Volleyball: Brandi Bradley; Phone: 830-372-8130; E-mail: bbradley@tlu.edu.

TEXAS SOUTHERN UNIVERSITY
Houston, Texas

Tigers ◆ NCAA I ◆ Southwestern Athletic Conference ◆ http://www.tsu.edu/

State-supported university, founded 1947, part of Texas Higher Education Coordinating Board
Coed, 8,920 undergraduate students, 88% full-time, 57% women, 43% men
Urban 147-acre campus
Noncompetitive entrance level, 48% of applicants were admitted

Freshmen *Admission:* 5,574 applied, 2,448 were accepted, 2,448 enrolled. *Test scores:* SAT verbal scores over 500: 86%; SAT math scores over 500: 100%; SAT math scores over 600: 14%.
Tuition and fees (2003–04): $3096 (resident), $8760 (nonresident). *Room and board:* $5824.
Financial Aid (All incoming freshmen): *Average need-based gift aid:* $9050. *Average aid to full-time undergraduates:* $14,065.
Athletic Department: *Director of Athletics:* Alois Blackwell; Phone: 713-313-7216; Fax: 713-313-7273.

MEN'S COACHES

Baseball: Candy Robinson; Phone: 713-313-7993.
Basketball: Ronnie Courtney; Phone: 713-313-4372.
Cheerleading: Alice Rogers; Phone: 713-313-7271.
Cross Country: Clyde Duncan; Phone: 713-313-7632.
Football: Steve Wilson; Phone: 713-313-7047.
Golf: Hank Stewart; Phone: 713-313-7920.
Tennis: Albert Rojo; Phone: 713-313-6830.
Track and Field: Clyde Duncan; Phone: 713-313-7620.

WOMEN'S COACHES

Basketball: Claude Cummings; Phone: 713-313-1910.
Cheerleading: Alice Rogers; Phone: 713-313-7271.
Cross Country: Clyde Duncan; Phone: 713-313-7620.
Golf: Hank Stewart; Phone: 713-313-7920.
Softball: Yolanda Sinegal; Phone: 713-313-1938.
Tennis: Albert Rojo; Phone: 713-313-6830.
Track and Field: Clyde Duncan; Phone: 713-313-7620.
Volleyball: Dwalah Fisher; Phone: 713-313-7272.

TEXAS STATE UNIVERSITY-SAN MARCOS

San Marcos, Texas

Bobcats ◆ NCAA I ◆ Southland Conference
◆ http://www.txstate.edu/

State-supported university, founded 1899, part of Texas State University System
Coed, 21,974 undergraduate students, 80% full-time, 55% women, 45% men
Suburban 423-acre campus with easy access to San Antonio and Austin
Moderately difficult entrance level, 53% of applicants were admitted

Freshmen *Admission:* 11,483 applied, 6,435 were accepted, 2,874 enrolled. *Test scores:* SAT verbal scores over 500: 74%; SAT math scores over 500: 77%; SAT verbal scores over 600: 20%; SAT math scores over 600: 22%; SAT verbal scores over 700: 1%; SAT math scores over 700: 1%.
Tuition and fees (2003–04): $4010 (resident), $11,090 (nonresident). *Room and board:* $5310 (room only: $3224).
Financial Aid (All incoming freshmen): *Average need-based gift aid:* $4214. *Average non-need based aid:* $6942. *Average aid to full-time undergraduates:* $7780.
Athletic Department: *Director of Athletics:* Fax: 512-245-2967. *Sports Information Director:* Tony Brubaker; Phone: 512-245-2996; E-mail: ab17@swt.edu.

MEN'S COACHES
Baseball: Ty Harrington; Phone: 512-245-3586; E-mail: th18@swt.edu.
Basketball: Dennis Nutt; Phone: 512-245-2987; E-mail: dn10@swt.edu.
Cheerleading: Jeff Nixon; Phone: 512-353-4380; E-mail: cheernix@hotmail.com.
Cross Country: Galina Bukharina; Phone: 512-245-9281; E-mail: gb15@swt.edu.
Football: David Bailiff; Phone: 512-245-2977.
Golf: Bill Woodley; Phone: 512-245-9190; E-mail: ww12@swt.edu.
Track and Field: Galina Bukharina; Phone: 512-245-9281; E-mail: gb15@swt.edu.

WOMEN'S COACHES
Basketball: Suzanne Fox; Phone: 512-245-2981; E-mail: sf11@swt.edu.
Cheerleading: Jeff Nixon; Phone: 512-353-4380; E-mail: cheernix@hotmail.com.
Cross Country: Galina Bukharina; Phone: 512-245-9281; E-mail: gb15@swt.edu.
Golf: Bill Woodley; Phone: 512-245-9190; E-mail: ww12@swt.edu.
Soccer: Kat Conner; Phone: 512-245-9264; E-mail: kc13@swt.edu.
Softball: Ricci Woodard; Phone: 512-245-7753; E-mail: rw15@swt.edu.
Tennis: Tory Plunkett; Phone: 512-245-2965; E-mail: tp16@swt.edu.
Track and Field: Galina Bukharina; Phone: 512-245-9281; E-mail: gb15@swt.edu.
Volleyball: Karen Chisum; Phone: 512-245-2983; E-mail: kc06@swt.edu.

TEXAS TECH UNIVERSITY

Lubbock, Texas

Red Raiders ◆ NCAA I ◆ Big 12 Conference ◆ http://www.ttu.edu/

State-supported university, founded 1923, part of Texas Tech University System
Coed, 23,595 undergraduate students, 89% full-time, 45% women, 55% men
Urban 1,839-acre campus
Moderately difficult entrance level, 67% of applicants were admitted

Freshmen *Admission:* 13,755 applied, 9,257 were accepted, 4,445 enrolled. *Test scores:* SAT verbal scores over 500: 78%; SAT math scores over 500: 86%; SAT verbal scores over 600: 26%; SAT math scores over 600: 37%; SAT verbal scores over 700: 3%; SAT math scores over 700: 5%.
Tuition and fees (2003–04): $4745 (resident), $11,825 (nonresident). *Room and board:* $6023 (room only: $3308).

Financial Aid (All incoming freshmen): *Average need-based gift aid:* $4534. *Average non-need based aid:* $2337. *Average aid to full-time undergraduates:* $6236.
Athletic Department: *Director of Athletics:* Gerald Myers; Phone: 806-742-3355; Fax: 806-742-1970. *Sports Information Director:* Chris Cook; Phone: 806-742-2770; E-mail: chris.cook@ttu.edu.

MEN'S COACHES
Baseball: Larry Hays; Phone: 806-742-3355; E-mail: haysjk@ttu.edu.
Basketball: Bobby Knight; Phone: 806-742-7600.
Cross Country: Mike Jarvinen; Phone: 806-742-2771; E-mail: mika.jarvinen@ttu.edu.
Football: Mike Leach; Phone: 806-742-3355; E-mail: mike.leach@ttu.edu.
Golf: Greg Sands; Phone: 806-742-3355; E-mail: greg.sands@ttu.edu.
Tennis: Tim Siegel; Phone: 806-742-3355; E-mail: tim.siegel@ttu.edu.
Track and Field: Wes Kittley; Phone: 806-742-3355; E-mail: wes.kittley@ttu.edu.

WOMEN'S COACHES
Basketball: Marsha Sharp; Phone: 806-742-7000; E-mail: marsha.sharp@ttu.edu.
Cross Country: Mike Jarvinen; Phone: 806-742-2771; E-mail: mika.jarvinen@ttu.edu.
Golf: Stacey Totman; Phone: 806-742-3355; E-mail: stacey.totman@ttu.edu.
Soccer: Felix Oskam; Phone: 806-742-3355; E-mail: felix.oskam@ttu.edu.
Softball: Bobby Reeves; Phone: 806-742-3355; E-mail: bobby.reeves@ttu.edu.
Tennis: Cari Groce; Phone: 806-742-3355; E-mail: cari.groce@ttu.edu.
Track and Field: Wes Kittley; Phone: 806-742-3355; E-mail: wes.kittley@ttu.edu.
Volleyball: Nancy Todd; Phone: 806-742-7545; E-mail: nancy.todd@ttu.edu.

TEXAS WESLEYAN UNIVERSITY

Fort Worth, Texas

Rams ◆ NAIA ◆ Red River Conference
◆ http://www.txwesleyan.edu/

Independent United Methodist comprehensive, founded 1890
Coed, 1,506 undergraduate students, 69% full-time, 62% women, 38% men
Urban 74-acre campus
Moderately difficult entrance level, 40% of applicants were admitted

Freshmen *Admission:* 411 applied, 175 were accepted, 175 enrolled. *Test scores:* SAT verbal scores over 500: 40%; SAT math scores over 500: 38%; SAT verbal scores over 600: 8%; SAT math scores over 600: 10%; SAT verbal scores over 700: 1%; SAT math scores over 700: 1%.
Tuition and fees (2003–04): $11,960 (full-time). *Room and board:* $5242 (room only: $1680).
Athletic Department: *Director of Athletics:* Terry Waldrop; Phone: 817-531-4851; Fax: 817-531-4208; E-mail: waldropt@txwes.edu. *Sports Information Director:* Logan Lawrence; Phone: 817-531-4855; E-mail: llawrence@txwes.edu.

MEN'S COACHES
Baseball: Mike Jeffcoat; Phone: 817-531-7547; E-mail: mjeffcoat@txwes.edu.
Basketball: .
Basketball: Terry Waldrop; Phone: 817-531-4851; E-mail: waldropt@txwes.edu.
Cheerleading: Danelle Rodruiguez; Phone: 817-531-4401; E-mail: drodriguez@txwes.edu.
Golf: Kevin Millikan; Phone: 817-531-4874; E-mail: millikak@txwes.edu.
Soccer: Steve Jones; Phone: 817-531-7556; E-mail: sjones@txwes.edu.

WOMEN'S COACHES
Basketball: Stacy Francis; Phone: 817-531-6599; E-mail: franciss@txwes.edu.
Cheerleading: Danelle Rodruiguez; Phone: 817-531-4401; E-mail: drodriguez@txwes.edu.
Soccer: Steve Jones; Phone: 817-531-7556; E-mail: sjones@txwes.edu.

Texas Wesleyan University (continued)

Softball: David Barrientes; Phone: 817-531-4852; E-mail: dbarrientes@txwes.edu.
Volleyball: Rick Johansen; Phone: 817-531-4850; E-mail: ne14vb@aol.com.

TEXAS WOMAN'S UNIVERSITY
Denton, Texas

Pioneers ◆ NCAA II ◆ Lone Star Conference ◆ http://www.twu.edu/

State-supported university, founded 1901
Coed, primarily women, 5,344 undergraduate students, 72% full-time, 95% women, 5% men
Suburban 270-acre campus with easy access to Dallas–Fort Worth
Minimally difficult entrance level, 70% of applicants were admitted

Freshmen *Admission:* 1,964 applied, 1,413 were accepted, 616 enrolled. *Test scores:* SAT verbal scores over 500: 75%; SAT math scores over 500: 75%.
Tuition and fees (2003–04): $2964 (resident), $8628 (nonresident). *Room and board:* $4780 (room only: $2420).
Financial Aid (All incoming freshmen): *Average need-based gift aid:* $4094. *Average non-need based aid:* $2187. *Average aid to full-time undergraduates:* $9647.
Athletic Department: *Director of Athletics:* Chalese Connors; Phone: 940-898-2378; Fax: 940-898-2372; E-mail: cconnors@twu.edu. *Sports Information Director:* Courtney Archer; Phone: 940-898-2373; E-mail: carcher@twu.edu.

WOMEN'S COACHES
Basketball: Devin Gabbard; Phone: 940-898-2388; E-mail: dgabbard@twu.edu.
Gymnastics: Frank Kudlac; Phone: 940-898-2384; E-mail: fkudlac@twu.edu.
Soccer: Fleur Benatar; Phone: 940-898-2379; E-mail: fbenatar@twu.edu.
Softball: Dianne Baker; Phone: 940-898-2383; E-mail: dbaker@twu.edu.
Volleyball: Shelly Barberee; Phone: 940-898-2416; E-mail: mbarberee@twu.edu.

THIEL COLLEGE
Greenville, Pennsylvania

Tomcats ◆ NCAA III ◆ Presidents' Athletic Conference ◆ http://www.thiel.edu/

Independent religious 4-year, founded 1866, affiliated with Evangelical Lutheran Church in America
Coed, 1,261 undergraduate students, 94% full-time, 47% women, 53% men
Rural 135-acre campus with easy access to Cleveland and Pittsburgh
Moderately difficult entrance level, 73% of applicants were admitted

Freshmen *Admission:* 1,557 applied, 1,182 were accepted, 349 enrolled. *Test scores:* SAT verbal scores over 500: 45%; SAT math scores over 500: 42%; SAT verbal scores over 600: 10%; SAT math scores over 600: 7%; SAT verbal scores over 700: 1%; SAT math scores over 700: 1%.
Tuition and fees (2003–04): $14,386 (full-time). *Room and board:* $6584 (room only: $3396).
Financial Aid (All incoming freshmen): *Average need-based gift aid:* $9889. *Average non-need based aid:* $4600. *Average aid to full-time undergraduates:* $13,500.
Athletic Department: *Director of Athletics:* Joe Schaly; Phone: 724-589-2138; Fax: 724-589-2880; E-mail: jschaly@thiel.edu. *Sports Information Director:* Kevin Fenstermacher; Phone: 724-589-2187; E-mail: kfenstermacher@thiel.edu.

MEN'S COACHES
Baseball: Joe Schaly; Phone: 724-589-2138; E-mail: jschaly@thiel.edu.
Basketball: Mike Snell; Phone: 724-589-2134; E-mail: msnell@thiel.edu.
Cheerleading: Lynsey Wilkins; Phone: 724-589-2165.
Cross Country: Gloria Pacsi; Phone: 724-589-2141; E-mail: gpacsi@thiel.edu.
Football: Jack Leipheimer; Phone: 724-589-2212; E-mail: jleip@thiel.edu.
Golf: John Dickason; Phone: 724-589-2147; E-mail: jdickaso@thiel.edu.
Soccer: Bryan Williams; Phone: 724-589-2869; E-mail: bwilliam@thiel.edu.
Tennis: Mike Snell; Phone: 724-589-2134; E-mail: msnell@thiel.edu.
Track and Field: Bryan Williams; Phone: 724-589-2869; E-mail: bwilliam@thiel.edu.
Wrestling: Craig Thurber; Phone: 724-589-2814.

WOMEN'S COACHES
Basketball: Gloria Pacsi; Phone: 724-589-2141; E-mail: gpacsi@thiel.edu.
Cheerleading: Lynsey Wilkins; Phone: 724-589-2165.
Cross Country: Gloria Pacsi; Phone: 724-589-2141; E-mail: gpacsi@thiel.edu.
Golf: Kurt Reiser; Phone: 724-589-2137; E-mail: kreiser@thiel.edu.
Softball: Sarah Roseto; Phone: 724-589-2164; E-mail: sroseto@thiel.edu.
Tennis: Mike Snell; Phone: 724-589-2814; E-mail: msnell@thiel.edu.
Track and Field: Bryan Williams; Phone: 724-589-2869; E-mail: bwilliam@thiel.edu.
Volleyball: Sarah Roseto; Phone: 724-589-2164; E-mail: sroseto@thiel.edu.

THOMAS COLLEGE
Waterville, Maine

Terriers ◆ NCAA III ◆ North Atlantic Conference ◆ http://www.thomas.edu/

Independent comprehensive, founded 1894
Coed, 695 undergraduate students, 78% full-time, 53% women, 47% men
Small-town 70-acre campus
Minimally difficult entrance level, 70% of applicants were admitted

Freshmen *Admission:* 588 applied, 428 were accepted, 179 enrolled. *Test scores:* SAT verbal scores over 500: 23%; SAT math scores over 500: 31%; SAT verbal scores over 600: 2%; SAT math scores over 600: 6%.
Tuition and fees (2004–05): $15,870 (full-time). *Room and board:* $6760.
Financial Aid (All incoming freshmen): *Average need-based gift aid:* $9379. *Average non-need based aid:* $9304. *Average aid to full-time undergraduates:* $12,332.
Athletic Department: *Director of Athletics:* Chris Young; Phone: 207-859-1404; Fax: 207-859-1107; E-mail: youngc@thomas.edu. *Sports Information Director:* Mark Tardif; Phone: 207-859-1221; E-mail: pr@thomas.edu.

MEN'S COACHES
Baseball: Greg King; Phone: 207-859-1208; E-mail: kingg@thomas.edu.
Basketball: James Libby; Phone: 207-859-1404; E-mail: libbyj@thomas.edu.
Golf: Mitch Orser; Phone: 207-859-1228; E-mail: orserm@thomas.edu.
Lacrosse: Stephen Graustein; Phone: 207-859-1208; E-mail: grausteins@thomas.edu.
Soccer: Christopher Aube; Phone: 207-859-1404; E-mail: aube@thomas.edu.
Tennis: Phone: 207-859-1404.

WOMEN'S COACHES
Basketball: Christopher Aube; Phone: 207-859-1404; E-mail: aube@thomas.edu.
Field Hockey: Lisa Gibbs; Phone: 207-859-1404; E-mail: gibbsl@thomas.edu.
Lacrosse: Phone: 207-859-1312.
Soccer: Kelly Smith; Phone: 207-859-1314.
Softball: Paul Rodrigue; Phone: 207-859-1207; E-mail: rodriguep@thomas.edu.
Volleyball: Michele Collins; Phone: 207-859-1319; E-mail: collinsm@thomas.edu.

THOMAS MORE COLLEGE
Crestview Hills, Kentucky

Saints ◆ NCAA III ◆ Independent
◆ http://www.thomasmore.edu/

Independent Roman Catholic comprehensive, founded 1921
Coed, 1,390 undergraduate students
Suburban 100-acre campus with easy access to Cincinnati
Moderately difficult entrance level, 62% of applicants were admitted

Freshmen *Admission:* 1,363 applied, 835 were accepted. *Test scores:* SAT verbal scores over 500: 63%; SAT math scores over 500: 58%; SAT verbal scores over 600: 21%; SAT math scores over 600: 27%; SAT math scores over 700: 3%.
Tuition and fees (2003–04): $16,000 (full-time). *Room and board:* $5400 (room only: $2600).
Financial Aid (All incoming freshmen): *Average need-based gift aid:* $4421. *Average non-need based aid:* $2882. *Average aid to full-time undergraduates:* $12,764.
Athletic Department: *Director of Athletics:* Terry Connor; Phone: 859-344-3308; Fax: 859-344-3632; E-mail: terry.connor@thomasmore.edu. *Sports Information Director:* Jason Eichelberger; Phone: 859-344-3672; E-mail: jason.eichelberger@thomasmore.edu.

MEN'S COACHES
Baseball: Jeff Hetzer; Phone: 859-344-3532; E-mail: jeff.hetzer@thomasmore.edu.
Basketball: Terry Connor; Phone: 859-344-3308; E-mail: terry.connor@thomasmore.edu.
Cross Country: Del Walters; Phone: 859-344-3630; E-mail: del.walters@thomasmore.edu.
Football: Mike Hallet; Phone: 859-344-3516; E-mail: mike.hallett@thomasmore.edu.
Golf: Steve Sigler; Phone: 859-344-3674; E-mail: steve.sigler@thomasmore.edu.
Soccer: Jason Burr; Phone: 859-344-4053; E-mail: jason.burr@thomasmore.edu.
Tennis: Del Walters; Phone: 859-344-3630; E-mail: del.walters@thomasmore.edu.

WOMEN'S COACHES
Basketball: Jeff Hetzer; Phone: 859-344-3532; E-mail: jeff.hetzer@thomasmore.edu.
Cross Country: Del Walters; Phone: 859-344-3630; E-mail: del.walters@thomasmore.edu.
Golf: Steve Sigler; Phone: 859-344-3390; E-mail: steve.sigler@thomasmore.edu.
Soccer: Jason Burr; Phone: 859-344-4053; E-mail: jason.burr@thomasmore.edu.
Softball: Everett Roper; Phone: 859-344-3628; E-mail: everett.roper@thomasmore.edu.
Tennis: John Spinney; Phone: 859-344-3634; E-mail: john.spinney@thomasmore.edu.
Volleyball: John Spinney; Phone: 859-344-3634; E-mail: john.spinney@thomasmore.edu.

THOMAS UNIVERSITY
Thomasville, Georgia

Night Hawks ◆ NAIA ◆ http://www.thomasu.edu/

Independent comprehensive, founded 1950
Coed, 674 undergraduate students, 74% full-time, 69% women, 31% men
Small-town 24-acre campus
Noncompetitive entrance level

Freshmen *Admission:* 62 applied, 68 enrolled.
Tuition and fees (2003–04): $9020 (full-time). *Room only:* $2400.
Financial Aid (All incoming freshmen): *Average need-based gift aid:* $2963. *Average aid to full-time undergraduates:* $4823.
Athletic Department: *Director of Athletics:* Mike Lee; Phone: 229-226-1621; Fax: 229-227-6885; E-mail: mlee@thomasu.edu. *Sports Information Director:* Eric Faulconer; Phone: 229-226-1621; E-mail: efaulconer@thomasu.edu.

MEN'S COACHES
Baseball: Mike Lee; Phone: 229-226-1621; E-mail: mlee@thomasu.edu.
Golf: Jack Megahee; Phone: 229-226-1621.

Soccer: Vinny Gill; Phone: 229-226-1621; E-mail: vgill@thomasu.edu.

WOMEN'S COACHES
Soccer: Eric Faulconer; Phone: 229-226-1621; E-mail: efaulconer@thomasu.edu.
Softball: Thomas Macera; Phone: 229-226-1621; E-mail: thmacera@thomasu.edu.
Tennis: Ann Castorri; Phone: 229-226-1621; E-mail: castorri@rose.net.

TIFFIN UNIVERSITY
Tiffin, Ohio

Dragons ◆ NAIA ◆ Independent ◆ http://www.tiffin.edu/

Independent comprehensive, founded 1888
Coed, 1,026 undergraduate students, 85% full-time, 54% women, 46% men
Small-town 110-acre campus with easy access to Toledo
Minimally difficult entrance level, 88% of applicants were admitted

Freshmen *Admission:* 1,000 applied, 911 were accepted, 262 enrolled. *Test scores:* SAT verbal scores over 500: 32%; SAT math scores over 500: 32%; SAT math scores over 600: 4%; SAT math scores over 700: 1%.
Tuition and fees (2004–05): $14,290 (full-time). *Room and board:* $6075 (room only: $3075).
Financial Aid (All incoming freshmen): *Average need-based gift aid:* $2853. *Average non-need based aid:* $1241. *Average aid to full-time undergraduates:* $15,682.
Athletic Department: *Director of Athletics:* Ian Day; Phone: 419-448-3452; Fax: 419-443-5007; E-mail: iday@tiffin.edu. *Sports Information Director:* Shane O'Donnell; Phone: 419-448-3288; E-mail: sodonnel@tiffin.edu.

MEN'S COACHES
Baseball: Lonny Allen; Phone: 419-448-3359.
Basketball: Andre'as James; Phone: 419-448-3266; E-mail: jamesa@tiffin.edu.
Cheerleading: Darby Roggow; Phone: 419-448-3425; E-mail: droggow@tiffin.edu.
Cross Country: Jeremy Croy; Phone: 419-448-3338; E-mail: croyjn@tiffin.edu.
Football: Nathan Cole; Phone: 419-448-3331; E-mail: ncole@tiffin.edu.
Golf: Darby Roggow; Phone: 419-448-3425; E-mail: droggow@tiffin.edu.
Soccer: Ian Day; Phone: 419-448-3452; E-mail: iday@tiffin.edu.
Tennis: Terry Sullivan; Phone: 419-448-3290; E-mail: tsullivan@tiffin.edu.
Track and Field: Jeremy Croy; Phone: 419-448-3338; E-mail: croyjn@tiffin.edu.

WOMEN'S COACHES
Basketball: Leslie Mugg; Phone: 419-448-3260; E-mail: lmugg@tiffin.edu.
Cheerleading: Darby Roggow; Phone: 419-448-3425; E-mail: droggow@tiffin.edu.
Cross Country: Jeremy Croy; Phone: 419-448-3338; E-mail: croyjn@tiffin.edu.
Soccer: Rudy Brownell; Phone: 419-448-3290; E-mail: rbrownel@tiffin.edu.
Softball: Brian Campbell; Phone: 419-448-3337; E-mail: bcampbel@tiffin.edu.
Tennis: Bonnie Tiell; Phone: 419-448-3261; E-mail: btiell@tiffin.edu.
Track and Field: Jeremy Croy; Phone: 419-448-3338; E-mail: croyjn@tiffin.edu.
Volleyball: Michelle Vlietstra; Phone: 419-448-3280; E-mail: vlietstraml@tiffin.edu.

TOUGALOO COLLEGE
Tougaloo, Mississippi

Bulldogs ◆ NAIA ◆ Gulf Coast Conference
◆ http://www.tougaloo.edu/

Independent religious 4-year, founded 1869, affiliated with United Church of Christ
Coed, 940 undergraduate students, 94% full-time, 70% women, 30% men
Suburban 500-acre campus
Minimally difficult entrance level, 94% of applicants were admitted

Freshmen *Admission:* 627 applied, 621 were accepted, 222 enrolled.
Tuition and fees (2004–05): $8700 (full-time). *Room and board:* $5080 (room only: $3310).
Financial Aid (All incoming freshmen): *Average aid to full-time undergraduates:* $10,500.
Athletic Department: *Director of Athletics:* James Turner; Phone: 601-977-7809; Fax: 601-978-1309; E-mail: james.turner@tougaloo.edu. *Sports Information Director:* Vanetta Kelso; Phone: 601-977-7809.

MEN'S COACHES
Basketball: James Turner; Phone: 601-977-7809; E-mail: james.turner@tougaloo.edu.
Cheerleading: Tamia Herndon; Phone: 601-977-7899; E-mail: tamia.herndon@tougaloo.edu.
Cross Country: Amir Hamlin; Phone: 601-977-7809.
Golf: Jim Coleman; Phone: 601-977-7887; E-mail: james.coleman@tougaloo.edu.
Tennis: Curtis Shaw; Phone: 601-977-7719; E-mail: curtis.shaw@tougaloo.edu.

WOMEN'S COACHES
Basketball: Vanetta Kelso; Phone: 601-977-7809.
Cheerleading: Tamia Herndon; Phone: 601-977-7899; E-mail: tamia.herndon@tougaloo.edu.
Cross Country: Amir Hamlin; Phone: 601-977-7809.

TOWSON UNIVERSITY
Towson, Maryland

Tigers ◆ NCAA I ◆ Colonial Athletic Conference; Patriot League Conference ◆ http://www.towson.edu/

State-supported university, founded 1866, part of University System of Maryland
Coed, 13,981 undergraduate students, 86% full-time, 61% women, 39% men
Suburban 321-acre campus with easy access to Baltimore and Washington, DC
Moderately difficult entrance level, 44% of applicants were admitted

Freshmen *Admission:* 11,289 applied, 5,818 were accepted, 1,754 enrolled. *Test scores:* SAT verbal scores over 500: 75%; SAT math scores over 500: 79%; SAT verbal scores over 600: 21%; SAT math scores over 600: 26%; SAT verbal scores over 700: 2%; SAT math scores over 700: 2%.
Tuition and fees (2004–05): $6672 (resident), $15,352 (nonresident). *Room and board:* $6468 (room only: $3816).
Financial Aid (All incoming freshmen): *Average need-based gift aid:* $4874. *Average non-need based aid:* $4087. *Average aid to full-time undergraduates:* $7398.
Athletic Department: *Director of Athletics:* Wayne Edwards; Phone: 410-704-2758; Fax: 410-704-4322; E-mail: wedwards@towson.edu. *Sports Information Director:* Peter Schlehr; Phone: 410-704-2232; E-mail: pschlehr@towson.edu.

MEN'S COACHES
Baseball: Mike Gottlieb; Phone: 410-704-3775; E-mail: mgottlieb@towson.edu.
Basketball: Michael Hunt; Phone: 410-704-3173; E-mail: mhunt@towson.edu.
Cross Country: Roger Erricker; Phone: 410-704-3972; E-mail: rerricker@towson.edu.
Diving: Pat Mead; Phone: 410-704-3577; E-mail: pmead@towson.edu.
Football: Gordy Combs; Phone: 410-704-3155; E-mail: gcombs@towson.edu.
Golf: Brian Yaniker; Phone: 410-704-2758; E-mail: coachby1@aol.com.
Lacrosse: Tony Seaman; Phone: 410-704-4698; E-mail: tseaman@towson.edu.
Soccer: Frank Olszewski; Phone: 410-704-3260; E-mail: folszewski@towson.edu.
Swimming: Pat Mead; Phone: 410-704-3577; E-mail: pmead@towson.edu.
Tennis: Peter Walten; Phone: 410-704-6399; E-mail: pwalten@towson.edu.
Track and Field: Roger Erricker; Phone: 410-704-3972; E-mail: rerricker@towson.edu.

WOMEN'S COACHES
Basketball: Joe Matthews; Phone: 410-704-5787; E-mail: jmathews@towson.edu.
Cross Country: Roger Erricker; Phone: 410-704-3972; E-mail: rerricker@towson.edu.
Diving: Pat Mead; Phone: 410-704-3577; E-mail: pmead@towson.edu.
Field Hockey: Lynette Mitzel; Phone: 410-704-3159; E-mail: lmitzel@towson.edu.
Gymnastics: Dick Filbert; Phone: 410-704-3895; E-mail: rfilbert@towson.edu.
Lacrosse: Missy Holmes; Phone: 410-704-3572.
Soccer: Leslie Wray; Phone: 410-704-3165; E-mail: lwray@towson.edu.
Softball: Lisa Costello; Phone: 410-704-3164; E-mail: lcostello@towson.edu.
Swimming: Pat Mead; Phone: 410-704-3577; E-mail: pmead@towson.edu.
Tennis: Peter Walten; Phone: 410-704-6399; E-mail: pwalten@towson.edu.
Track and Field: Roger Erricker; Phone: 410-704-3972; E-mail: rerricker@towson.edu.
Volleyball: Chris Riley; Phone: 410-704-4028; E-mail: criley@towson.edu.

TRANSYLVANIA UNIVERSITY
Lexington, Kentucky

Pioneers ◆ NCAA III ◆ Heartland Collegiate Conference ◆ http://www.transy.edu/

Independent religious 4-year, founded 1780, affiliated with Christian Church (Disciples of Christ)
Coed, 1,134 undergraduate students, 99% full-time, 57% women, 43% men
Urban 35-acre campus with easy access to Cincinnati and Louisville
Very difficult entrance level, 89% of applicants were admitted

Freshmen *Admission:* 1,098 applied, 965 were accepted, 300 enrolled. *Test scores:* SAT verbal scores over 500: 86%; SAT math scores over 500: 84%; SAT verbal scores over 600: 49%; SAT math scores over 600: 51%; SAT verbal scores over 700: 15%; SAT math scores over 700: 10%.
Tuition and fees (2003–04): $17,660 (full-time). *Room and board:* $6120 (room only: $3420).
Financial Aid (All incoming freshmen): *Average need-based gift aid:* $11,343. *Average non-need based aid:* $9996. *Average aid to full-time undergraduates:* $14,549.
Athletic Department: *Director of Athletics:* Cindy Jacobelli; Phone: 859-233-8270; Fax: 859-233-8638; E-mail: cjacobelli@transy.edu. *Sports Information Director:* Glenn Osborne; Phone: 859-233-8284; E-mail: gosborne@transy.edu.

MEN'S COACHES
Baseball: Shayne Stock; Phone: 859-233-8699; E-mail: sstock@transy.edu.
Basketball: Brian Lane; Phone: 859-233-8136; E-mail: blane@mail.transy.edu.
Cheerleading: Sherri Gibson Patterson; Phone: 859-233-8893.
Cross Country: Toby Carrigan; Phone: 859-233-8663; E-mail: tcarrigan@transy.edu.
Diving: Billy Bradford; Phone: 859-233-8165.
Golf: Brian Lane; Phone: 859-233-8136; E-mail: blane@mail.transy.edu.
Soccer: Brandon Bowman; Phone: 859-281-8612; E-mail: bbowman@transy.edu.
Swimming: Jack Ebel; Phone: 859-233-8165; E-mail: jebel@transy.edu.
Tennis: Chuck Brown; Phone: 859-233-8772; E-mail: chuckb0489@msn.com.

WOMEN'S COACHES

Basketball: Mark Turner; Phone: 859-233-8267; E-mail: mturner@transy.edu.
Cheerleading: Sherri Gibson Patterson; Phone: 859-233-8893.
Cross Country: Toby Carrigan; Phone: 859-233-8663; E-mail: tcarrigan@transy.edu.
Diving: Billy Bradford; Phone: 859-233-8165.
Field Hockey: Beth Lucas; Phone: 859-233-8194; E-mail: elucas@transy.edu.
Golf: Mark Turner; Phone: 859-281-8267; E-mail: mturner@transy.edu.
Soccer: Michael Fulton; Phone: 859-233-8612.
Softball: Kelly Anderson; Phone: 859-233-3613; E-mail: rsscan@aol.com.
Swimming: Jack Ebel; Phone: 859-233-8165; E-mail: jebel@transy.edu.
Tennis: Chuck Brown; Phone: 859-233-8772; E-mail: chuckb0489@msn.com.
Volleyball: Cindy Jacobelli; Phone: 859-233-8663; E-mail: cjacobelli@transy.edu.

TREVECCA NAZARENE UNIVERSITY
Nashville, Tennessee

Trojans ◆ NAIA ◆ TranSouth Conference ◆ http://www.trevecca.edu/

Independent Nazarene comprehensive, founded 1901
Coed, 1,232 undergraduate students, 77% full-time, 59% women, 41% men
Urban 65-acre campus
Moderately difficult entrance level, 66% of applicants were admitted

Freshmen *Admission:* 680 applied, 454 were accepted, 224 enrolled.
Tuition and fees (2004–05): $12,792 (full-time). *Room and board:* $5868 (room only: $2648).
Financial Aid (All incoming freshmen): *Average need-based gift aid:* $4040. *Average non-need based aid:* $3710. *Average aid to full-time undergraduates:* $10,880.
Athletic Department: *Director of Athletics:* Alan Smith; Phone: 615-248-1275; Fax: 615-248-7798; E-mail: asmith@trevecca.edu. *Sports Information Director:* Greg Ruff; Phone: 615-248-1606; E-mail: gruff@trevecca.edu.

MEN'S COACHES

Baseball: Jeff Forehand; Phone: 615-248-1276; E-mail: jforehand@trevecca.edu.
Basketball: Sam Harris; Phone: 615-248-1603; E-mail: sharris2@trevecca.edu.
Cheerleading: Julie Conley; Phone: 615-480-8113; E-mail: julieconley24@hotmail.com.
Golf: Jacob Ward; Phone: 615-337-2396; E-mail: jacobward2003@msn.com.
Soccer: Stan Herod; Phone: 615-248-1440; E-mail: sherod@trevecca.edu.

WOMEN'S COACHES

Basketball: Julie Van Beek; Phone: 615-248-1273; E-mail: jvanbeek@trevecca.edu.
Cheerleading: Julie Conley; Phone: 615-480-8113; E-mail: julieconley24@hotmail.com.
Golf: Michael Johnson; Phone: 615-248-7735; E-mail: mjohnson@trevecca.edu.
Soccer: Stan Herod; Phone: 615-248-1440; E-mail: sherod@trevecca.edu.
Softball: Angela Sullivan; Phone: 615-248-1277; E-mail: asullivan@trevecca.edu.
Volleyball: Scott Jones; Phone: 615-248-1317; E-mail: sjaspike@yahoo.com.

TRINITY CHRISTIAN COLLEGE
Palos Heights, Illinois

Trolls ◆ NAIA ◆ Chicagoland Collegiate Conference ◆ http://www.trnty.edu/

Independent Christian Reformed 4-year, founded 1959
Coed, 1,263 undergraduate students, 82% full-time, 63% women, 37% men
Suburban 53-acre campus with easy access to Chicago
Moderately difficult entrance level, 90% of applicants were admitted

Freshmen *Admission:* 589 applied, 548 were accepted, 255 enrolled. *Test scores:* SAT verbal scores over 500: 71%; SAT math scores over 500: 66%; SAT verbal scores over 600: 21%; SAT math scores over 600: 24%; SAT math scores over 700: 3%.
Tuition and fees (2003–04): $15,490 (full-time). *Room and board:* $6000 (room only: $3100).
Financial Aid (All incoming freshmen): *Average need-based gift aid:* $2680. *Average non-need based aid:* $2972. *Average aid to full-time undergraduates:* $10,420.
Athletic Department: *Director of Athletics:* Tim Walker; Phone: 708-239-4782; Fax: 708-396-7460; E-mail: tim.walker@trnty.edu. *Sports Information Director:* Amy Strong; Phone: 708-239-4778; E-mail: amy.strong@trnty.edu.

MEN'S COACHES

Baseball: Matt Schans; Phone: 708-239-4780; E-mail: matt.schans@trnty.edu.
Basketball: Tim Walker; Phone: 708-239-4782; E-mail: tim.walker@trnty.edu.
Cross Country: Laura Schnyders; Phone: 708-239-4783; E-mail: laura.schnyders@trnty.edu.
Soccer: Jonathan Lenarz; Phone: 708-239-4781; E-mail: jonathan.lenarz@trnty.edu.
Track and Field: Laura Schnyders; Phone: 708-239-4783; E-mail: laura.schnyders@trnty.edu.
Volleyball: Chadd Grevengoed; Phone: 708-239-4783; E-mail: weatherbee15@go.com.

WOMEN'S COACHES

Basketball: Amy Strong; Phone: 708-239-4778; E-mail: amy.strong@trnty.edu.
Cross Country: Laura Schnyders; Phone: 708-239-4783; E-mail: laura.schnyders@trnty.edu.
Soccer: Josh Lenarz; Phone: 708-239-4824; E-mail: josh.lenarz@trnty.edu.
Softball: Sue Gasperec; Phone: 708-239-4805; E-mail: sue.gasperec@trnty.edu.
Track and Field: Laura Schnyders; Phone: 708-239-4783; E-mail: laura.schnyders@trnty.edu.
Volleyball: Sue Gasperec; Phone: 708-239-4805; E-mail: sue.gasperec@trnty.edu.

TRINITY COLLEGE
Hartford, Connecticut

Bantams ◆ NCAA III ◆ New England Small College Conference ◆ http://www.trincoll.edu/

Independent comprehensive, founded 1823
Coed, 2,188 undergraduate students, 91% full-time, 51% women, 49% men
Urban 100-acre campus
Very difficult entrance level, 35% of applicants were admitted

Freshmen *Admission:* 5,510 applied, 1,993 were accepted, 550 enrolled. *Test scores:* SAT verbal scores over 500: 97%; SAT math scores over 500: 99%; SAT verbal scores over 600: 73%; SAT math scores over 600: 83%; SAT verbal scores over 700: 26%; SAT math scores over 700: 30%.
Tuition and fees (2003–04): $30,230 (full-time). *Room and board:* $7810 (room only: $5020).
Financial Aid (All incoming freshmen): *Average need-based gift aid:* $21,503. *Average non-need based aid:* $23,113. *Average aid to full-time undergraduates:* $24,821.

Trinity College *(continued)*

Athletic Department: *Director of Athletics:* Richard Hazelton; Phone: 860-297-2055; Fax: 860-297-2492; E-mail: richard.hazelton@trincoll.edu. *Sports Information Director:* David Kingsley; Phone: 860-297-2137; E-mail: david.kingsley@trincoll.edu.

MEN'S COACHES

Baseball: Bill Decker; Phone: 860-297-2066; E-mail: william.decker@trincoll.edu.
Basketball: Stan Ogrodnik; Phone: 860-297-2061; E-mail: stanley.ogrodnik@trincoll.edu.
Cross Country: George Suitor; Phone: 860-297-5128; E-mail: george.suitor@trincoll.edu.
Diving: Peter Suydam; Phone: 860-297-2057; E-mail: peter.suydam@trincoll.edu.
Football: Chuck Priore; Phone: 860-297-4130; E-mail: charles.priore@trincoll.edu.
Golf: Bill Detrick; Phone: 860-297-2057; E-mail: william.detrick@trincoll.edu.
Ice Hockey: John Dunham; Phone: 860-297-5176.
Lacrosse: Brian Silcott; Phone: 860-297-4247; E-mail: brian.silcott@trincoll.edu.
Soccer: Ed Mighten; Phone: 860-297-2063; E-mail: edmond.mighten@trincoll.edu.
Swimming: Kristen Noone; Phone: 860-297-2064; E-mail: kristen.noone@trincoll.edu.
Tennis: Paul Assaiante; Phone: 860-297-2590; E-mail: paul.assaiante@trincoll.edu.
Track and Field: George Suitor; Phone: 860-297-5128; E-mail: george.suitor@trincoll.edu.
Wrestling: Sebastian Amato; Phone: 860-297-2057; E-mail: sebbyamato@peoplepc.com.

WOMEN'S COACHES

Basketball: Maureen Pine; Phone: 860-297-2069; E-mail: maureen.pine@trincoll.edu.
Cross Country: George Suitor; Phone: 860-297-5128; E-mail: george.suitor@trincoll.edu.
Diving: Peter Suydam; Phone: 860-297-2057; E-mail: peter.suydam@trincoll.edu.
Field Hockey: Anne Parmenter; Phone: 860-297-4189; E-mail: anne.parmenter@trincoll.edu.
Lacrosse: Kara Tierney; Phone: 860-297-4140; E-mail: kara.tierney@trincoll.edu.
Soccer: Michael Smith; Phone: 860-297-4263; E-mail: michael.smith.3@trincoll.edu.
Softball: Caitlin Luz; Phone: 860-297-4032; E-mail: caitlin.luz@trincoll.edu.
Swimming: Kristen Noone; Phone: 860-297-2064; E-mail: kristen.noone@trincoll.edu.
Tennis: Wendy Bartlett; Phone: 860-297-2068; E-mail: wendy.bartlett@trincoll.edu.
Track and Field: George Suitor; Phone: 860-297-5128; E-mail: george.suitor@trincoll.edu.
Volleyball: Angela Mills; Phone: 860-297-2079; E-mail: angela.mills@trincoll.edu.

TRINITY COLLEGE
Washington, District of Columbia

Tigers ◆ NCAA III ◆ Atlantic Women's Colleges Conference ◆ http://www.trinitydc.edu/

Independent Roman Catholic comprehensive, founded 1897
Women only, 1,011 undergraduate students, 55% full-time, 98% women, 2% men
Urban 26-acre campus
Moderately difficult entrance level, 78% of applicants were admitted

Freshmen *Admission:* 423 applied, 331 were accepted, 162 enrolled. *Test scores:* SAT verbal scores over 500: 22%; SAT math scores over 500: 19%; SAT verbal scores over 600: 5%; SAT math scores over 600: 1%.
Tuition and fees (2004–05): $16,860 (full-time). *Room and board:* $7290 (room only: $3190).
Financial Aid (All incoming freshmen): *Average need-based gift aid:* $11,236. *Average non-need based aid:* $10,279. *Average aid to full-time undergraduates:* $14,537.

Athletic Department: *Director of Athletics:* Christy Neff; Phone: 202-884-9606; Fax: 202-884-9229; E-mail: neffc@trinitydc.edu. *Sports Information Director:* Christy Germani; Phone: 202-884-9656; E-mail: germanic@trinitydc.edu.

WOMEN'S COACHES

Basketball: Christy Neff; Phone: 202-884-9606; E-mail: neffc@trinitydc.edu.
Field Hockey: Christy Germani; Phone: 202-884-9656; E-mail: germanic@trinitydc.edu.
Lacrosse: Roger Palmisano; Phone: 202-884-9658; E-mail: palmisanor@trinitydc.edu.
Soccer: Jody Bergstrom; Phone: 202-884-9658; E-mail: bergstromj@trinitydc.edu.
Softball: Stephen Christianson; Phone: 202-884-9656; E-mail: christiansons@trinitydc.edu.
Swimming: Eric Waananen; Phone: 202-884-9656; E-mail: waananene@trinitydc.edu.
Tennis: Derek Jones; Phone: 202-884-9658; E-mail: jonesd@trinitydc.edu.
Track and Field: Michelle Latimer; Phone: 202-884-9606; E-mail: latimerm@trinitydc.edu.
Volleyball: Christy Neff; Phone: 202-884-9606; E-mail: neffc@trinitydc.edu.

TRINITY INTERNATIONAL UNIVERSITY
Deerfield, Illinois

Trojans ◆ NAIA ◆ Chicagoland Collegiate Conference; Mid-States Football Conference ◆ http://www.tiu.edu/

Independent religious university, founded 1897, affiliated with Evangelical Free Church of America
Coed, 1,428 undergraduate students, 91% full-time, 59% women, 41% men
Suburban 108-acre campus with easy access to Chicago
Moderately difficult entrance level, 83% of applicants were admitted

Freshmen *Admission:* 498 applied, 431 were accepted, 431 enrolled. *Test scores:* SAT verbal scores over 500: 85%; SAT math scores over 500: 76%; SAT verbal scores over 600: 39%; SAT math scores over 600: 44%; SAT verbal scores over 700: 10%; SAT math scores over 700: 10%.
Tuition and fees (2003–04): $17,150 (full-time). *Room and board:* $5830 (room only: $3060).
Financial Aid (All incoming freshmen): *Average need-based gift aid:* $7692. *Average non-need based aid:* $2500. *Average aid to full-time undergraduates:* $14,247.
Athletic Department: *Director of Athletics:* Patrick Gilliam; Phone: 847-317-7094; Fax: 847-317-8056; E-mail: pgilliam@tiu.edu. *Sports Information Director:* Matt Callahan; Phone: 847-317-7024; E-mail: mcallaha@tiu.edu.

MEN'S COACHES

Baseball: Mike Manes; Phone: 847-317-7093; E-mail: mmanes@tiu.edu.
Basketball: Dean Jaderston; Phone: 847-317-7098; E-mail: djaderst@tiu.edu.
Football: Andy Lambert; Phone: 847-317-7092; E-mail: alambert@tiu.edu.
Soccer: Stosh Walsh; Phone: 847-317-7095; E-mail: swalsh@tiu.edu.

WOMEN'S COACHES

Basketball: Matt Callahan; Phone: 847-317-7024; E-mail: mcallaha@tiu.edu.
Soccer: Patrick Gilliam; Phone: 847-317-7094; E-mail: pgilliam@tiu.edu.
Softball: John Bernard; Phone: 847-317-6434; E-mail: jbernard@tiu.edu.
Volleyball: Linsey Ebert; Phone: 847-317-6486; E-mail: lebert@tiu.edu.

TRINITY UNIVERSITY
San Antonio, Texas

Tigers ◆ NCAA III ◆ Southern Collegiate Athletic Conference ◆ http://www.trinity.edu/

Independent religious comprehensive, founded 1869, affiliated with Presbyterian Church
Coed, 2,407 undergraduate students, 99% full-time, 52% women, 48% men
Urban 113-acre campus
Very difficult entrance level, 62% of applicants were admitted

Freshmen *Admission:* 3,675 applied, 2,360 were accepted, 633 enrolled. *Test scores:* SAT verbal scores over 500: 98%; SAT math scores over 500: 100%; SAT verbal scores over 600: 78%; SAT math scores over 600: 84%; SAT verbal scores over 700: 21%; SAT math scores over 700: 22%.
Tuition and fees (2003–04): $19,176 (full-time). *Room and board:* $7290 (room only: $4590).
Financial Aid (All incoming freshmen): *Average need-based gift aid:* $11,811. *Average non-need based aid:* $6264. *Average aid to full-time undergraduates:* $16,046.
Athletic Department: *Director of Athletics:* Bob King; Phone: 210-999-8237; Fax: 210-999-8292; E-mail: bob.king@trinity.edu. *Sports Information Director:* Justin Parker; Phone: 210-999-8447; E-mail: jparker@trinity.edu.

MEN'S COACHES
Baseball: Tim Scannell; Phone: 210-999-8287; E-mail: tscannel@trinity.edu.
Basketball: Pat Cunningham; Phone: 210-999-8275; E-mail: pcunning@trinity.edu.
Cheerleading: Wendi Landrum; Phone: 210-999-8222; E-mail: wendi.landrum@trinity.edu.
Cross Country: Jenny Breuer; Phone: 210-999-8289; E-mail: jennifer.breuer@trinity.edu.
Diving: John Ryan; Phone: 210-999-8273; E-mail: jryan@trinity.edu.
Football: Steve Mohr; Phone: 210-999-8285; E-mail: smohr@trinity.edu.
Golf: Carla Spenkoch; Phone: 210-999-8046; E-mail: cspenko@trinity.edu.
Soccer: Paul McGinlay; Phone: 210-999-8270; E-mail: pmcginla@trinity.edu.
Swimming: John Ryan; Phone: 210-999-8273; E-mail: jryan@trinity.edu.
Tennis: Butch Newman; Phone: 210-999-8271; E-mail: bnewman@trinity.edu.
Track and Field: Jenny Breuer; Phone: 210-999-8289; E-mail: jennifer.breuer@trinity.edu.

WOMEN'S COACHES
Basketball: Becky Geyer; Phone: 210-999-8276; E-mail: bgeyer@trinity.edu.
Cheerleading: Wendi Landrum; Phone: 210-999-8222; E-mail: wendi.landrum@trinity.edu.
Cross Country: Jenny Breuer; Phone: 210-999-8289; E-mail: jennifer.breuer@trinity.edu.
Diving: John Ryan; Phone: 210-999-8273; E-mail: jryan@trinity.edu.
Golf: Carla Spenkoch; Phone: 210-999-8046; E-mail: cspenko@trinity.edu.
Soccer: Greg Ashton; Phone: 210-999-8286; E-mail: gashton@trinity.edu.
Softball: Roland Rodriguez; Phone: 210-999-8023; E-mail: rrodrigu@trinity.edu.
Swimming: John Ryan; Phone: 210-999-8273; E-mail: jryan@trinity.edu.
Tennis: Butch Newman; Phone: 210-999-8271; E-mail: bnewman@trinity.edu.
Track and Field: Jenny Breuer; Phone: 210-999-8289; E-mail: jennifer.breuer@trinity.edu.
Volleyball: Julie Jenkins; Phone: 210-999-8274; E-mail: jjenkins@trinity.edu.

TRI-STATE UNIVERSITY
Angola, Indiana

Thunder ◆ NAIA ◆ Mid-States Football Conference; Wolverine-Hoosier Conference ◆ http://www.tristate.edu/

Independent comprehensive, founded 1884
Coed, 1,186 undergraduate students, 87% full-time, 36% women, 64% men
Small-town 400-acre campus
Moderately difficult entrance level, 73% of applicants were admitted

Freshmen *Admission:* 1,852 applied, 1,330 were accepted, 335 enrolled. *Test scores:* SAT verbal scores over 500: 62%; SAT math scores over 500: 76%; SAT verbal scores over 600: 19%; SAT math scores over 600: 38%; SAT verbal scores over 700: 1%; SAT math scores over 700: 6%.
Tuition and fees (2003–04): $18,000 (full-time). *Room and board:* $5600.
Financial Aid (All incoming freshmen): *Average need-based gift aid:* $4225. *Average non-need based aid:* $775. *Average aid to full-time undergraduates:* $11,725.
Athletic Department: *Director of Athletics:* Rob Harmon; Phone: 260-665-4149; Fax: 260-665-4839; E-mail: harmonr@tristate.edu. *Sports Information Director:* Melissa Cope; Phone: 260-665-4446; E-mail: copem@tristate.edu.

MEN'S COACHES
Baseball: Greg Perschke; Phone: 260-665-4135; E-mail: perschkeg@tristate.edu.
Basketball: Rob Harmon; Phone: 260-665-4149; E-mail: harmonr@tristate.edu.
Cheerleading: Dee Davis; Phone: 260-665-4285; E-mail: davisd@tristate.edu.
Cross Country: Mike Cole; Phone: 260-665-4146; E-mail: colem@tristate.edu.
Football: Bob Frey; Phone: 260-665-4142; E-mail: freyr@tristate.edu.
Golf: Bill SanGiacomo; Phone: 260-665-4203; E-mail: sangiacomow@tristate.edu.
Soccer: Mike Ferrell; Phone: 260-665-4294; E-mail: ferrellm@tristate.edu.
Tennis: Bill Maddock; Phone: 260-665-4845; E-mail: maddockb@tristate.edu.

WOMEN'S COACHES
Basketball: Jennifer Rushton; Phone: 260-665-4144; E-mail: rushtonj@tristate.edu.
Cheerleading: Dee Davis; Phone: 260-665-4285; E-mail: davisd@tristate.edu.
Cross Country: Mike Cole; Phone: 260-665-4146; E-mail: colem@tristate.edu.
Golf: Bill Maddock; Phone: 260-665-4845; E-mail: maddockb@tristate.edu.
Soccer: Tom Pawlik; Phone: 260-665-4841; E-mail: pawlikt@tristate.edu.
Softball: Henry Smith; Phone: 260-665-4444; E-mail: smithh@tristate.edu.
Tennis: Bill Maddock; Phone: 260-665-4845; E-mail: maddockb@tristate.edu.
Volleyball: Alena Krug; Phone: 260-665-4145; E-mail: kruga@tristate.edu.

TROY STATE UNIVERSITY
Troy, Alabama

Trojans ◆ NCAA I ◆ Atlantic Sun Conference; Sun Belt Conference ◆ http://www.troyst.edu/

State-supported comprehensive, founded 1887, part of Troy State University System
Coed, 5,205 undergraduate students, 80% full-time, 59% women, 41% men
Small-town 577-acre campus
Moderately difficult entrance level, 64% of applicants were admitted

Freshmen *Admission:* 3,507 applied, 2,335 were accepted, 1,007 enrolled.

Troy State University *(continued)*

Tuition and fees (2003–04): $3842 (resident), $7372 (nonresident). *Room and board:* $4580 (room only: $2240).

Financial Aid (All incoming freshmen): *Average need-based gift aid:* $5000. *Average aid to full-time undergraduates:* $6000.

Athletic Department: *Director of Athletics:* Johnny Williams; Phone: 334-670-3482; Fax: 334-670-3724; E-mail: hricks@troyst.edu. *Sports Information Director:* Tom Strother; Phone: 334-670-3229; E-mail: stroth@troyst.edu.

MEN'S COACHES

Baseball: Bobby Pierce; Phone: 334-670-3489; E-mail: pierceb@troyst.edu.

Basketball: Don Maestri; Phone: 334-670-3685.

Cheerleading: Traci McCall; Phone: 334-670-3480; E-mail: hricks@troyst.edu.

Cross Country: Bob Lambert; Phone: 334-670-3275; E-mail: rlambert@troyst.edu.

Football: Larry Blakeney; Phone: 334-670-3682; E-mail: blakeney@troyst.edu.

Golf: Matt Terry; Phone: 334-670-3249; E-mail: mterry@troyst.edu.

Tennis: Eric Hayes; Phone: 334-670-3649; E-mail: hayes@642002@yahoo.com.

Track and Field: Bob Lambert; Phone: 334-670-3275; E-mail: rlambert@troyst.edu.

WOMEN'S COACHES

Basketball: Mike Murphy; Phone: 334-670-3688; E-mail: mmurphy@troyst.edu.

Cheerleading: Traci McCall; Phone: 334-670-3480; E-mail: hricks@troyst.edu.

Cross Country: Bob Lambert; Phone: 334-670-3275; E-mail: rlambert@troyst.edu.

Golf: Matt Terry; Phone: 334-670-3249; E-mail: mterry@troyst.edu.

Soccer: John Garvilla; Phone: 334-670-5652; E-mail: garvilla@troyst.edu.

Softball: Melanie Davis; Phone: 334-670-3446; E-mail: mcdavis@troyst.edu.

Tennis: Eric Hayes; Phone: 334-670-3649; E-mail: hayes@642002@yahoo.com.

Track and Field: Bob Lambert; Phone: 334-670-3275; E-mail: rlambert@troyst.edu.

Volleyball: Phone: 334-670-3926.

TRUMAN STATE UNIVERSITY
Kirksville, Missouri

Bulldogs ◆ NCAA II ◆ Mid-America Intercollegiate Conference ◆ http://www.truman.edu/

State-supported comprehensive, founded 1867

Coed, 5,479 undergraduate students, 97% full-time, 59% women, 41% men

Small-town 140-acre campus

Moderately difficult entrance level, 83% of applicants were admitted

Freshmen *Admission:* 4,334 applied, 3,622 were accepted, 1,317 enrolled. *Test scores:* SAT verbal scores over 500: 94%; SAT math scores over 500: 92%; SAT verbal scores over 600: 59%; SAT math scores over 600: 58%; SAT verbal scores over 700: 18%; SAT math scores over 700: 12%.

Tuition and fees (2003–04): $4656 (resident), $8456 (nonresident). *Room and board:* $5072.

Financial Aid (All incoming freshmen): *Average need-based gift aid:* $2858. *Average non-need based aid:* $4470. *Average aid to full-time undergraduates:* $6232.

Athletic Department: *Director of Athletics:* Jerry Wollmering; Phone: 660-785-4235; Fax: 660-785-4189; E-mail: jerryw@truman.edu. *Sports Information Director:* Melissa Ware; Phone: 660-785-4276; E-mail: mware@truman.edu.

MEN'S COACHES

Baseball: Lawrence Scully; Phone: 660-785-6003; E-mail: lscully@truman.edu.

Basketball: Jack Schrader; Phone: 660-785-4171; E-mail: schrader@truman.edu.

Cheerleading: Leah Hettinger; Phone: 660-785-4222; E-mail: leah@truman.edu.

Cross Country: Ed Schneider; Phone: 660-785-4342; E-mail: pe09@truman.edu.

Football: John Ware; Phone: 660-785-4252; E-mail: jware@truman.edu.

Golf: Tom Drennan; Phone: 660-665-5335; E-mail: athletics@truman.edu.

Soccer: Alf Bilbao; Phone: 660-785-4168; E-mail: abilbao@truman.edu.

Swimming: Colleen Murphy; Phone: 660-785-7219; E-mail: cmurphy@truman.edu.

Tennis: Peter Kendall; Phone: 660-785-7258; E-mail: pkendall@truman.edu.

Track and Field: Ed Schneider; Phone: 660-785-4342; E-mail: pe09@truman.edu.

Wrestling: David Schutter; Phone: 660-785-7257; E-mail: schutter@truman.edu.

WOMEN'S COACHES

Basketball: John Sloop; Phone: 660-785-4459; E-mail: jsloop@truman.edu.

Cheerleading: Leah Hettinger; Phone: 660-785-4222; E-mail: leah@truman.edu.

Cross Country: John Cochrane; Phone: 660-785-4341; E-mail: cochrane@truman.edu.

Golf: Sam Lesseig; Phone: 660-785-4090; E-mail: slesseig@truman.edu.

Soccer: Mike Cannon; Phone: 660-785-4463; E-mail: mcannon@truman.edu.

Softball: Lacey Schanz; Phone: 660-785-4343; E-mail: lschanz@truman.edu.

Swimming: Colleen Murphy; Phone: 660-785-7219; E-mail: cmurphy@truman.edu.

Tennis: Peter Kendall; Phone: 660-785-7258; E-mail: pkendall@truman.edu.

Track and Field: John Cochrane; Phone: 660-785-4341; E-mail: cochrane@truman.edu.

Volleyball: Qi Wang; Phone: 660-785-4468; E-mail: vball@truman.edu.

TUFTS UNIVERSITY
Medford, Massachusetts

Jumbos ◆ NCAA III ◆ New England Small College Conference ◆ http://www.tufts.edu/

Independent university, founded 1852

Coed, 4,892 undergraduate students, 98% full-time, 54% women, 46% men

Suburban 150-acre campus with easy access to Boston

Most difficult entrance level, 29% of applicants were admitted

Freshmen *Admission:* 14,528 applied, 3,830 were accepted, 1,282 enrolled. *Test scores:* SAT verbal scores over 500: 98%; SAT math scores over 500: 99%; SAT verbal scores over 600: 82%; SAT math scores over 600: 88%; SAT verbal scores over 700: 31%; SAT math scores over 700: 44%.

Tuition and fees (2003–04): $29,593 (full-time). *Room and board:* $8640 (room only: $4420).

Financial Aid (All incoming freshmen): *Average need-based gift aid:* $22,577. *Average non-need based aid:* $500. *Average aid to full-time undergraduates:* $24,482.

Athletic Department: *Director of Athletics:* Bill Gehling; Phone: 617-627-3232; Fax: 617-627-3614; E-mail: bill.gehling@tufts.edu. *Sports Information Director:* Paul Sweeney; Phone: 617-627-3586; E-mail: paul.sweeney@tufts.edu.

MEN'S COACHES

Baseball: John Casey; Phone: 617-627-5218; E-mail: john.casey@tufts.edu.

Basketball: Bob Sheldon; Phone: 617-627-5012; E-mail: bob.sheldon_jr@tufts.edu.

Cross Country: Connie Putnam; Phone: 617-627-5062; E-mail: connie.putnam@tufts.edu.

Diving: Brad Snodgrass; Phone: 617-627-5112.

Football: Bill Samko; Phone: 617-627-5111; E-mail: w.samko@tufts.edu.

Golf: Bob Sheldon; Phone: 617-627-5012; E-mail: bob.sheldon_jr@tufts.edu.

Ice Hockey: Brian Murphy; Phone: 617-627-5286; E-mail: brian.murphy@tufts.edu.

Lacrosse: Mike Daley; Phone: 617-627-3757; E-mail: michael.daly@tufts.edu.
Soccer: Ralph Ferrigno; Phone: 617-627-5152; E-mail: ralph.ferrigno@tufts.edu.
Swimming: Don Megerle; Phone: 617-627-5143; E-mail: donald.megerle@tufts.edu.
Tennis: Jim Watson; Phone: 617-627-5076; E-mail: tuftstennis2000@yahoo.com.
Track and Field: Connie Putnam; Phone: 617-627-5062; E-mail: connie.putnam@tufts.edu.

WOMEN'S COACHES
Basketball: Carla Berube; Phone: 617-627-5491; E-mail: carla.berube@tufts.edu.
Cross Country: Kristen Morwick; Phone: 617-627-5625; E-mail: kristen.morwick@tufts.edu.
Diving: Brad Snodgrass; Phone: 617-627-5112.
Field Hockey: Carol Rappoli; Phone: 617-627-5235; E-mail: carol.rappoli@tufts.edu.
Lacrosse: Carol Rappoli; Phone: 617-627-5235; E-mail: carol.rappoli@tufts.edu.
Soccer: Martha Whiting; Phone: 617-627-5743; E-mail: martha.whiting@tufts.edu.
Softball: Kris Talon; Phone: 617-627-5241; E-mail: kris.talon@tufts.edu.
Swimming: Nancy Bigelow; Phone: 617-627-5112; E-mail: nancy.bigelow@tufts.edu.
Tennis: Jim Watson; Phone: 617-627-5076; E-mail: tuftstennis2000@yahoo.com.
Track and Field: Kristen Morwick; Phone: 617-627-5625; E-mail: kristen.morwick@tufts.edu.
Volleyball: Cora Thompson; Phone: 617-627-5471; E-mail: cora.thompson@tufts.edu.

TULANE UNIVERSITY
New Orleans, Louisiana
Green Wave ◆ NCAA I ◆ Conference USA Conference ◆ http://www.tulane.edu/

Independent university, founded 1834
Coed, 7,862 undergraduate students, 76% full-time, 53% women, 47% men
Urban 110-acre campus
Very difficult entrance level, 62% of applicants were admitted

Freshmen *Admission:* 13,931 applied, 7,801 were accepted, 1,678 enrolled. *Test scores:* SAT verbal scores over 500: 97%; SAT math scores over 500: 98%; SAT verbal scores over 600: 84%; SAT math scores over 600: 79%; SAT verbal scores over 700: 32%; SAT math scores over 700: 25%.
Tuition and fees (2003–04): $32,120 (full-time). *Room and board:* $7641 (room only: $4541).
Financial Aid (All incoming freshmen): *Average need-based gift aid:* $15,918. *Average non-need based aid:* $14,128. *Average aid to full-time undergraduates:* $21,980.
Athletic Department: *Director of Athletics:* Rick Dickson; Phone: 504-865-5500; Fax: 504-865-5512. *Sports Information Director:* Donna Turner; Phone: 504-865-5506; E-mail: dturner1@tulane.edu.

MEN'S COACHES
Baseball: Rick Jones; Phone: 504-862-8239.
Basketball: Shawn Finney; Phone: 504-865-5505; E-mail: sfinney@tulane.edu.
Cheerleading: Raymond Williams; Phone: 504-486-6141; E-mail: raytucheer@aol.com.
Cross Country: Heather Van Norman; Phone: 504-865-5514; E-mail: hvannorm@tulane.edu.
Football: Chris Scelfo; Phone: 504-865-5355; E-mail: cscelfo@tulane.edu.
Golf: Tom Shaw; Phone: 504-865-5507; E-mail: tshaw@tulane.edu.
Tennis: Robert Klein; Phone: 504-865-8237; E-mail: rklein@tulane.edu.
Track and Field: Heather Van Norman; Phone: 504-865-5514; E-mail: hvannorm@tulane.edu.

WOMEN'S COACHES
Basketball: Lisa Stockton; Phone: 504-865-5672; E-mail: lstockt@tulane.edu.

Cheerleading: Raymond Williams; Phone: 504-486-6141; E-mail: raytucheer@aol.com.
Cross Country: Heather Van Norman; Phone: 504-865-5514; E-mail: hvannorm@tulane.edu.
Golf: Sue Bower; Phone: 504-865-5513; E-mail: sbower@tulane.edu.
Soccer: Betsy Anderson; Phone: 504-865-5574; E-mail: eanders@tulane.edu.
Tennis: David Schumacher; Phone: 504-865-5503; E-mail: dschuma@tulane.edu.
Track and Field: Heather Van Norman; Phone: 504-865-5514; E-mail: hvannorm@tulane.edu.
Volleyball: Betsy Becker; Phone: 504-865-5570; E-mail: ebecker@tulane.edu.

TUSCULUM COLLEGE
Greeneville, Tennessee
Pioneers ◆ NCAA II ◆ South Atlantic Conference ◆ http://www.tusculum.edu/

Independent Presbyterian comprehensive, founded 1794
Coed, 1,914 undergraduate students, 99% full-time, 53% women, 47% men
Small-town 140-acre campus
Moderately difficult entrance level, 76% of applicants were admitted

Freshmen *Admission:* 1,381 applied, 1,050 were accepted, 303 enrolled. *Test scores:* SAT verbal scores over 500: 39%; SAT math scores over 500: 43%; SAT verbal scores over 600: 8%; SAT math scores over 600: 12%; SAT verbal scores over 700: 1%; SAT math scores over 700: 1%.
Tuition and fees (2003–04): $14,410 (full-time). *Room and board:* $5880.
Financial Aid (All incoming freshmen): *Average need-based gift aid:* $1467. *Average non-need based aid:* $6438. *Average aid to full-time undergraduates:* $11,945.
Athletic Department: *Director of Athletics:* Ed Hoffmeyer; Phone: 423-636-7300; Fax: 423-636-7370; E-mail: ehoffmey@tusculum.edu. *Sports Information Director:* Dom Donnelly; Phone: 423-636-7326; E-mail: ddonnell@tusculum.edu.

MEN'S COACHES
Baseball: Doug Jones; Phone: 423-636-7322; E-mail: djones@tusculum.edu.
Basketball: Duggar Baucom; Phone: 423-636-0575; E-mail: dbaucom@tusculum.edu.
Cheerleading: Robin Brown; Phone: 423-636-7830; E-mail: rbrown@tusculum.edu.
Cross Country: Jim Fields; Phone: 423-636-7300; E-mail: jfields@tusculum.edu.
Football: Frankie DeBusk; Phone: 423-636-7302; E-mail: fdebusk@tusculum.edu.
Golf: Bob Dibble; Phone: 423-636-7300; E-mail: bdibble@tusculum.edu.
Soccer: Tony Castainca; Phone: 423-636-7496; E-mail: tcastain@tusculum.edu.
Tennis: Tommy Amett; Phone: 423-636-7300; E-mail: tarnett@tusculum.edu.

WOMEN'S COACHES
Basketball: Suzanne McBride; Phone: 423-636-7329; E-mail: smcbride@tusculum.edu.
Cheerleading: Robin Brown; Phone: 423-636-7830; E-mail: rbrown@tusculum.edu.
Cross Country: Jim Fields; Phone: 423-636-7300; E-mail: jfields@tusculum.edu.
Golf: Bob Dibble; Phone: 423-636-7323; E-mail: bdibble@tusculum.edu.
Soccer: Mike Joy; Phone: 423-636-7321; E-mail: mjoy@tusculum.edu.
Softball: Lisa Minton-Dean; Phone: 423-636-7300; E-mail: lminton@tusculum.edu.
Tennis: Tommy Arnett; Phone: 423-636-7300; E-mail: tarnett@tusculum.edu.
Volleyball: Missy Gragg; Phone: 423-636-7328; E-mail: mgragg@tusculum.edu.

TUSKEGEE UNIVERSITY
Tuskegee, Alabama

Golden Tigers ◆ NCAA II ◆ Southern Intercollegiate Athletic Conference ◆ http://www.tuskegee.edu/

Independent comprehensive, founded 1881
Coed, 2,804 undergraduate students, 96% full-time, 63% women, 37% men
Small-town 4,390-acre campus
Moderately difficult entrance level, 80% of applicants were admitted

Freshmen *Admission:* 1,326 applied, 1,068 were accepted, 518 enrolled. *Test scores:* SAT verbal scores over 500: 22%; SAT math scores over 500: 29%; SAT verbal scores over 600: 5%; SAT math scores over 600: 6%; SAT verbal scores over 700: 1%; SAT math scores over 700: 3%.
Tuition and fees (2003–04): $11,310 (full-time). *Room and board:* $5940.
Financial Aid (All incoming freshmen): *Average need-based gift aid:* $8000. *Average non-need based aid:* $6000. *Average aid to full-time undergraduates:* $13,824.
Athletic Department: *Director of Athletics:* Rick Comegy; Phone: 334-724-4800; Fax: 334-724-4233; E-mail: rcomegy@tuskegee.edu. *Sports Information Director:* Arnold Houston; Phone: 334-727-8150; E-mail: alhouston@tuskegee.edu.

MEN'S COACHES
Baseball: Antonio Knight; Phone: 334-727-8485; E-mail: adknight@tuskegee.edu.
Basketball: Oliver Jones; Phone: 334-727-8681; E-mail: joneso@tuskegee.edu.
Cheerleading: Velma Moore; Phone: 334-727-8096; E-mail: moorev@tuskegee.edu.
Cross Country: Ondray Wagner; Phone: 334-727-8276; E-mail: wagneroj@tuskegee.edu.
Football: Rick Comegy; Phone: 334-724-4800; E-mail: rcomegy@tuskegee.edu.
Tennis: Gregory Green; Phone: 334-727-8902; E-mail: ggreen@tuskegee.edu.
Track and Field: Keith Higdon; Phone: 334-724-4300; E-mail: klhigdon@tuskegee.edu.

WOMEN'S COACHES
Basketball: Belinda Roby; Phone: 334-724-8848; E-mail: broby@tuskegee.edu.
Cheerleading: Velma Moore; Phone: 334-727-8096; E-mail: moorev@tuskegee.edu.
Cross Country: Ondray Wagner; Phone: 334-727-8276; E-mail: wagneroj@tuskegee.edu.
Softball: Tarsha Askew; Phone: 334-724-8680; E-mail: tyaskew@tuskegee.edu.
Tennis: Gregory Green; Phone: 334-727-8902; E-mail: ggreen@tuskegee.edu.
Track and Field: Keith Higdon; Phone: 334-724-4300; E-mail: klhigdon@tuskegee.edu.
Volleyball: Tarsha Askew; Phone: 334-724-8680; E-mail: tyaskew@tuskegee.edu.

UNION COLLEGE
Barbourville, Kentucky

Bulldogs ◆ NAIA ◆ Appalachian Conference ◆ http://www.unionky.edu/

Independent United Methodist comprehensive, founded 1879
Coed, 589 undergraduate students, 94% full-time, 51% women, 49% men
Small-town 110-acre campus
Moderately difficult entrance level, 73% of applicants were admitted

Freshmen *Admission:* 579 applied, 422 were accepted, 130 enrolled.
Tuition and fees (2003–04): $13,200 (full-time). *Room and board:* $4400 (room only: $1600).
Financial Aid (All incoming freshmen): *Average need-based gift aid:* $7458. *Average non-need based aid:* $9178. *Average aid to full-time undergraduates:* $10,715.
Athletic Department: *Director of Athletics:* Darin Wilson; Phone: 606-546-1308; Fax: 606-546-1286; E-mail: dswilson@unionky.edu. *Sports Information Director:* Jay Stancil; Phone: 606-546-1292; E-mail: jstancil@unionky.edu.

MEN'S COACHES
Baseball: Bart Osborne; Phone: 606-546-1355; E-mail: bosborne@unionky.edu.
Basketball: Kelly Combs; Phone: 606-546-1705; E-mail: kellycombs@unionky.edu.
Cheerleading: Judy Eaton; Phone: 606-546-1724; E-mail: jeaton@unionky.edu.
Football: Tommy Reid; Phone: 606-546-1707; E-mail: treid@unionky.edu.
Golf: Kelly Combs; Phone: 606-546-1705; E-mail: kellycombs@unionky.edu.
Soccer: Tyler Brock; Phone: 606-546-1307; E-mail: tbrock@unionky.edu.

WOMEN'S COACHES
Basketball: Tim Curry; Phone: 606-546-1682; E-mail: tcurry@unionky.edu.
Cheerleading: Judy Eaton; Phone: 606-546-1724; E-mail: jeaton@unionky.edu.
Golf: Larry Inkster; Phone: 606-546-1234; E-mail: linkster@unionky.edu.
Soccer: Tyler Brock; Phone: 606-546-1307; E-mail: tbrock@unionky.edu.
Softball: Tim Curry; Phone: 606-546-1682; E-mail: tcurry@unionky.edu.
Volleyball: Phone: 606-546-1365; E-mail: tbrock@unionky.edu.

UNION COLLEGE
Schenectady, New York

Bulldogs ◆ NCAA III ◆ Eastern College Athletic Conference; Upstate Collegiate Athletic Conference ◆ http://www.union.edu/

Independent 4-year, founded 1795
Coed, 2,174 undergraduate students, 99% full-time, 47% women, 53% men
Suburban 100-acre campus
Very difficult entrance level, 4% of applicants were admitted

Freshmen *Admission:* 4,159 applied, 1,822 were accepted, 559 enrolled. *Test scores:* SAT verbal scores over 500: 97%; SAT math scores over 500: 99%; SAT verbal scores over 600: 60%; SAT math scores over 600: 72%; SAT verbal scores over 700: 12%; SAT math scores over 700: 22%.
Tuition and fees (2003–04): $28,928 (full-time). *Room and board:* $7077 (room only: $3882).
Financial Aid (All incoming freshmen): *Average need-based gift aid:* $18,291. *Average non-need based aid:* $20,000. *Average aid to full-time undergraduates:* $23,156.
Athletic Department: *Director of Athletics:* Val Belmonte; Phone: 518-388-6284; Fax: 518-388-6695; E-mail: belmontv@union.edu. *Sports Information Director:* George Cuttita; Phone: 518-388-6170; E-mail: cuttitag@alice.union.edu.

MEN'S COACHES
Baseball: Jeremy Rivenburg; Phone: 518-388-8025; E-mail: rivenbuj@union.edu.
Basketball: Bob Montana; Phone: 518-388-6595; E-mail: montanar@idol.union.edu.
Cross Country: Dave Riggi; Phone: 518-388-8350; E-mail: riggid@union.edu.
Diving: Aaron D'Addario; Phone: 518-388-6331; E-mail: daddaria@union.edu.
Football: John Audino; Phone: 518-388-6152; E-mail: audinoj@union.edu.
Ice Hockey: Nate Leaman; Phone: 518-388-6134; E-mail: leaman@union.edu.
Lacrosse: Erv Chambliss; Phone: 518-388-6199; E-mail: chamblie@union.edu.
Soccer: Jeff Guinn; Phone: 518-388-6287; E-mail: guinnj@union.edu.
Swimming: Scott Felix; Phone: 518-388-8039; E-mail: felixs@union.edu.
Tennis: Wayne Emerick; Phone: 518-463-0037; E-mail: wemerick11@aol.com.

WOMEN'S COACHES

Basketball: Marry Ellen Burt; Phone: 518-388-6546; E-mail: burtm@idol.union.edu.
Cross Country: Dave Riggi; Phone: 518-388-8350; E-mail: riggid@union.edu.
Diving: Aaron D'Addario; Phone: 518-388-6331; E-mail: daddaria@union.edu.
Field Hockey: Lacey French; Phone: 518-388-6508; E-mail: frenchl@union.edu.
Lacrosse: Linda Bevelander; Phone: 518-388-6040; E-mail: bevelanl@union.edu.
Soccer: Brian Speck; Phone: 518-388-6191; E-mail: speckb@idol.union.edu.
Softball: Peter Brown; Phone: 518-388-6363; E-mail: brownp@union.edu.
Swimming: Scott Felix; Phone: 518-388-8039; E-mail: felixs@union.edu.
Tennis: Wayne Emerick; Phone: 518-463-0037; E-mail: wemerick11@aol.com.
Track and Field: Larry Cottrell; Phone: 518-388-6547; E-mail: cottrell@union.edu.
Volleyball: Sandy Collins; Phone: 518-388-6491; E-mail: collinss@union.edu.

UNION UNIVERSITY
Jackson, Tennessee

Bulldogs ◆ NAIA ◆ TranSouth Conference ◆ http://www.uu.edu/

Independent Southern Baptist comprehensive, founded 1823
Coed, 2,022 undergraduate students, 80% full-time, 61% women, 39% men
Small-town 290-acre campus with easy access to Memphis
Moderately difficult entrance level, 6% of applicants were admitted

Freshmen *Admission:* 1,461 applied, 893 were accepted, 450 enrolled. *Test scores:* SAT verbal scores over 500: 75%; SAT math scores over 500: 84%; SAT verbal scores over 600: 33%; SAT math scores over 600: 36%; SAT verbal scores over 700: 9%; SAT math scores over 700: 16%.
Tuition and fees (2004–05): $15,350 (full-time). *Room and board:* $4970 (room only: $2990).
Financial Aid (All incoming freshmen): *Average need-based gift aid:* $2585. *Average non-need based aid:* $5475. *Average aid to full-time undergraduates:* $10,402.
Athletic Department: *Director of Athletics:* David Blackstone; Phone: 731-661-5277; Fax: 731-661-5182; E-mail: dblackst@uu.edu. *Sports Information Director:* Steven Aldridge; Phone: 731-661-5027; E-mail: saldridg@uu.edu.

MEN'S COACHES

Baseball: Andy Rushing; Phone: 731-661-5333; E-mail: arushing@uu.edu.
Basketball: Ralph Turner; Phone: 731-661-5286; E-mail: rturner@uu.edu.
Cheerleading: Tina Giddens; Phone: 731-661-5299; E-mail: tgiddens@uu.edu.
Cross Country: Gary Johnson; Phone: 731-661-5246; E-mail: gjohnson@uu.edu.
Golf: Don Morris; Phone: 731-661-5130.
Soccer: Darin White; Phone: 731-661-5108; E-mail: dwhite@uu.edu.

WOMEN'S COACHES

Basketball: Mark Campbell; Phone: 731-661-5344; E-mail: mcampbel@uu.edu.
Cheerleading: Tina Giddens; Phone: 731-661-5299; E-mail: tgiddens@uu.edu.
Cross Country: Gary Johnson; Phone: 731-661-5246; E-mail: gjohnson@uu.edu.
Softball: Brian Dunn; Phone: 731-661-5451; E-mail: bdunn@uu.edu.
Volleyball: Brian Dunn; Phone: 731-661-5451; E-mail: bdunn@uu.edu.

UNITED STATES AIR FORCE ACADEMY
Colorado Springs, Colorado

Falcons ◆ NCAA I ◆ College Hockey America Conference; Great Western Lacrosse Conference; Mountain West Conference ◆ http://www.usafa.edu/

Federally supported 4-year, founded 1954
Coed, primarily men, 4,157 undergraduate students, 100% full-time, 17% women, 83% men
Suburban 18,000-acre campus with easy access to Denver
Most difficult entrance level, 1% of applicants were admitted

Freshmen *Admission:* 10,780 applied, 1,291 were accepted, 1,214 enrolled. *Test scores:* SAT verbal scores over 500: 96%; SAT math scores over 500: 99%; SAT verbal scores over 600: 70%; SAT math scores over 600: 84%; SAT verbal scores over 700: 16%; SAT math scores over 700: 28%.
Athletic Department: *Director of Athletics:* Randy Spetman; Phone: 719-333-4008; Fax: 719-333-4009; E-mail: randall.spetman@usafa.af.mil. *Sports Information Director:* Troy Garnhart; Phone: 719-333-9263; E-mail: troy.garnhart@usafa.af.mil.

MEN'S COACHES

Baseball: Mike Hutcheon; Phone: 719-333-4008; E-mail: michael.hutcheon@usafa.af.mil.
Basketball: Joe Scott; Phone: 719-333-9076; E-mail: joe.scott@usafa.af.mil.
Cross Country: Mark Stanforth; Phone: 719-333-3602; E-mail: mark.stanforth@usafa.af.mil.
Diving: Stan Curnow; Phone: 719-333-4765; E-mail: stan.curnow@usafa.af.mil.
Football: Fischer Deberry; Phone: 719-333-3836; E-mail: fisher.deberry@usafa.af.mil.
Golf: George Koury; Phone: 719-333-2280; E-mail: george.koury@usafa.af.mil.
Ice Hockey: Frank Serratore; Phone: 719-333-2188; E-mail: frank.serratore@usafa.af.mil.
Lacrosse: Fred Acee; Phone: 719-333-7544; E-mail: frederick.acee@usafa.af.mil.
Soccer: Lou Sagastume; Phone: 719-333-2174; E-mail: luis.sagastume@usafa.af.mil.
Swimming: Rob Clayton; Phone: 719-333-4726; E-mail: rob.clayton@usafa.af.mil.
Tennis: Rich Gugat; Phone: 719-333-2564; E-mail: richard.gugat@usafa.af.mil.
Track and Field: Ralph Lindeman; Phone: 719-333-2173; E-mail: ralph.lindeman@usafa.af.mil.
Wrestling: Wayne Baughman; Phone: 719-333-2811; E-mail: richard.baughman@usafa.af.mil.

WOMEN'S COACHES

Basketball: Ardie McInelly; Phone: 719-333-4008; E-mail: ardie.mcinelly@usafa.af.mil.
Cross Country: Mark Stanforth; Phone: 719-333-3602; E-mail: mark.stanforth@usafa.af.mil.
Diving: Stan Curnow; Phone: 719-333-4765; E-mail: stan.curnow@usafa.af.mil.
Gymnastics: Lisa Woody; Phone: 719-333-2422; E-mail: lisa.woody@usafa.af.mil.
Soccer: Marty Buckley; Phone: 719-333-2201; E-mail: marty.buckley@usafa.af.mil.
Swimming: Casey Converse; Phone: 719-333-4765; E-mail: keith.converse@usafa.af.mil.
Tennis: Kim Gidley; Phone: 719-333-2489; E-mail: kim.gidley@usafa.af.mil.
Track and Field: Ralph Lindeman; Phone: 719-333-2173; E-mail: ralph.lindeman@usafa.af.mil.
Volleyball: Penny Lucas-White; Phone: 719-333-2897; E-mail: penny.lucas-white@usafa.af.mil.

UNITED STATES COAST GUARD ACADEMY

New London, Connecticut

Bears ◆ NCAA III ◆ New England Women's & Men's Athletics Conference ◆ http://www.cga.edu/

Federally supported 4-year, founded 1876
Coed, 1,016 undergraduate students, 100% full-time, 30% women, 70% men
Suburban 110-acre campus with easy access to Providence and Hartford
Very difficult entrance level, 1% of applicants were admitted

Freshmen *Admission:* 6,028 applied, 429 were accepted, 309 enrolled. *Test scores:* SAT verbal scores over 500: 97%; SAT math scores over 500: 100%; SAT math scores over 600: 64%; SAT verbal scores over 600: 83%; SAT verbal scores over 700: 15%; SAT math scores over 700: 18%.
Athletic Department: *Director of Athletics:* Ray Cieplik; Phone: 860-444-8600; Fax: 860-444-8607; E-mail: rcieplik@exmail.uscga.edu. *Sports Information Director:* Jason Southard; Phone: 860-701-6800; E-mail: jsouthard@cga.uscg.mil.

MEN'S COACHES
Baseball: Pete Barry; Phone: 860-701-6132; E-mail: pbarry@exmail.uscga.edu.
Basketball: Pete Barry; Phone: 860-701-6132; E-mail: pbarry@exmail.uscga.edu.
Cross Country: Steve Eldridge; Phone: 860-444-8587; E-mail: seldridge@exmail.uscga.edu.
Diving: Bob Brooks; Phone: 860-701-8586.
Football: Bill George; Phone: 860-701-8584; E-mail: bgeorge@exmail.uscga.edu.
Soccer: Chris Parsons; Phone: 860-701-6197; E-mail: cparsons@exmail.uscga.edu.
Swimming: John Westkott; Phone: 860-701-8586; E-mail: jwestkott@exmail.uscga.edu.
Tennis: Mike Turdo; Phone: 860-701-8236; E-mail: mturdo@exmail.uscga.edu.
Track and Field: Dan Rose; Phone: 860-701-8590; E-mail: drose@exmail.uscga.edu.
Wrestling: Steve Eldridge; Phone: 860-444-8587; E-mail: seldridge@exmail.uscga.edu.

WOMEN'S COACHES
Basketball: Alex Simonka; Phone: 860-444-8602; E-mail: asimonka@exmail.uscga.edu.
Cross Country: Larry Falconi; Phone: 860-444-8267; E-mail: lfalconi@exmail.uscga.edu.
Diving: Bob Brooks; Phone: 860-701-8586.
Soccer: Carla DeSantis; Phone: 860-701-8582; E-mail: cdesantis@exmail.uscga.edu.
Softball: Donna Koczajowski; Phone: 860-701-8604; E-mail: dkoczajowski@exmail.uscga.edu.
Swimming: John Westkott; Phone: 860-701-8586; E-mail: jwestkott@exmail.uscga.edu.
Track and Field: Dan Rose; Phone: 860-701-8590; E-mail: drose@exmail.uscga.edu.
Volleyball: Patty Giannattasio; Phone: 860-701-8589; E-mail: pgiannattasio@exmail.uscga.edu.

UNITED STATES MERCHANT MARINE ACADEMY

Kings Point, New York

Mariners ◆ NCAA III ◆ Freedom Football Conference; Knickerbocker Lacrosse Conference; Skyline Conference ◆ http://www.usmma.edu/

Federally supported 4-year, founded 1943
Coed, 971 undergraduate students, 100% full-time, 13% women, 87% men
Suburban 82-acre campus with easy access to New York City
Very difficult entrance level, 2% of applicants were admitted

Freshmen *Admission:* 1,919 applied, 303 were accepted, 303 enrolled. *Test scores:* SAT verbal scores over 500: 100%; SAT math scores over 500: 100%; SAT verbal scores over 600: 64%; SAT math scores over 600: 61%; SAT verbal scores over 700: 22%; SAT math scores over 700: 8%.
Athletic Department: *Director of Athletics:* Susan Peterson Lublow; Phone: 516-773-5859; Fax: 516-773-5469; E-mail: lublows@usmma.edu. *Sports Information Director:* Tom Emberley; Phone: 516-773-5455; E-mail: emberleyt@usmma.edu.

MEN'S COACHES
Baseball: Dennis Gagnon; Phone: 516-773-5273; E-mail: gagnond@usmma.edu.
Basketball: Chris Carideo; Phone: 516-773-5266; E-mail: carideoc@usmma.edu.
Cross Country: Yolanda Flamino; Phone: 516-773-5322; E-mail: flaminoy@usmma.edu.
Diving: Kevin Ryan; Phone: 516-773-5859; E-mail: ryank@usmma.edu.
Football: Tim McNulty; Phone: 516-773-5519; E-mail: mcnultyt@usmma.edu.
Golf: Bill McCumisky; Phone: 516-773-5859; E-mail: mccumiskyb@usmma.edu.
Lacrosse: Tom Gill; Phone: 516-773-5330; E-mail: gillt@usmma.edu.
Soccer: Michael Smolens; Phone: 516-773-5321; E-mail: smolensm@usmma.edu.
Swimming: Sean Tedesco; Phone: 516-773-5265; E-mail: tedescos@usmma.edu.
Tennis: Sean Perera; Phone: 516-773-5859; E-mail: pereras@usmma.edu.
Track and Field: Yolanda Flamino; Phone: 516-773-5322; E-mail: flaminoy@usmma.edu.
Wrestling: Tim Alger; Phone: 516-773-5262; E-mail: algert@usmma.edu.

WOMEN'S COACHES
Basketball: Michael Murray; Phone: 516-773-5326; E-mail: murraym@usmma.edu.
Cross Country: Yolanda Flamino; Phone: 516-773-5322; E-mail: flaminoy@usmma.edu.
Diving: Kevin Ryan; Phone: 516-773-5859; E-mail: ryank@usmma.edu.
Softball: Heather Stone; Phone: 516-773-5276; E-mail: stoneh@usmma.edu.
Swimming: Sean Tedesco; Phone: 516-773-5265; E-mail: tedescos@usmma.edu.
Track and Field: Yolanda Flamino; Phone: 516-773-5322; E-mail: flaminoy@usmma.edu.
Volleyball: James Wilroy; Phone: 516-773-5394; E-mail: wilroyj@usmma.edu.

UNITED STATES MILITARY ACADEMY

West Point, New York

Black Knights ◆ NCAA I ◆ Atlantic Hockey Conference; Conference USA Conference; Patriot League Conference ◆ http://www.usma.edu/

Federally supported 4-year, founded 1802
Coed, primarily men, 4,242 undergraduate students, 100% full-time, 15% women, 85% men
Small-town 16,080-acre campus with easy access to New York City
Most difficult entrance level, 1% of applicants were admitted

Freshmen *Admission:* 12,688 applied, 1,314 were accepted, 1,314 enrolled. *Test scores:* SAT verbal scores over 500: 98%; SAT math scores over 500: 100%; SAT verbal scores over 600: 69%; SAT math scores over 600: 82%; SAT verbal scores over 700: 18%; SAT math scores over 700: 25%.
Athletic Department: *Director of Athletics:* Rick Greenspan; Phone: 845-938-3701; Fax: 845-938-8707; E-mail: wr7639@usma.edu. *Sports Information Director:* Bob Beretta; Phone: 845-938-3303; E-mail: yr7587@usma.edu.

MEN'S COACHES
Baseball: Joe Soholano; Phone: 845-938-3712; E-mail: wj9188@usma.edu.
Basketball: Jim Crews; Phone: 845-938-2419.
Cross Country: Jerry Quiller; Phone: 845-938-3008; E-mail: wj1372@usma.edu.

Diving: Jonathan Johnson; Phone: 845-938-4207; E-mail: jonathan.johnson@usma.edu.
Football: Bobby Ross; Phone: 845-938-6266; E-mail: armyfootball@usma.edu.
Golf: Jimmy Ray Clevenger; Phone: 845-938-3819; E-mail: wj5639@usma.edu.
Ice Hockey: Bob Riley; Phone: 845-938-4614; E-mail: wr6684@usma.edu.
Lacrosse: Jack Emmer; Phone: 845-938-2429; E-mail: wj3427@usma.edu.
Soccer: Kurt Swanbeck; Phone: 845-938-2463; E-mail: kurt.swanbeck@usma.edu.
Swimming: John O'Neill; Phone: 845-938-3604; E-mail: wj8437@usma.edu.
Tennis: Jim Poling; Phone: 845-938-6011; E-mail: james.poling@usma.edu.
Track and Field: Jerry Quiller; Phone: 845-938-8008; E-mail: wj1372@usma.edu.
Wrestling: Chuck Barbee; Phone: 845-938-3123; E-mail: wc8171@usma.edu.

WOMEN'S COACHES
Basketball: Sherri Abbey-Nowatzki; Phone: 845-938-2796; E-mail: ws0141@usma.edu.
Cross Country: Jerry Quiller; Phone: 845-938-8008; E-mail: wj1372@usma.edu.
Diving: Jonathan Johnson; Phone: 845-938-4207; E-mail: jonathan.johnson@usma.edu.
Soccer: Gene Ventriglia; Phone: 845-938-4826; E-mail: wg8129@usma.edu.
Softball: Jim Flowers; Phone: 845-938-4443; E-mail: wj4453@usma.edu.
Swimming: John O'Neill; Phone: 845-938-2809; E-mail: wj8437@usma.edu.
Tennis: Paul Peck; Phone: 845-938-4452; E-mail: pp3828@usma.edu.
Track and Field: Jerry Quiller; Phone: 845-938-8008; E-mail: wj1372@usma.edu.
Volleyball: Glen Conley; Phone: 845-938-4382; E-mail: wg6544@usma.edu.

UNITED STATES NAVAL ACADEMY
Annapolis, Maryland

Midshipmen ◆ NCAA I ◆ Patriot League Conference ◆ http://www.usna.edu/

Federally supported 4-year, founded 1845
Coed, primarily men, 4,335 undergraduate students, 100% full-time, 16% women, 84% men
Small-town 329-acre campus with easy access to Baltimore and Washington, DC
Very difficult entrance level, 1% of applicants were admitted

Freshmen *Admission:* 14,101 applied, 1,479 were accepted, 1,178 enrolled. *Test scores:* SAT verbal scores over 500: 100%; SAT math scores over 500: 100%; SAT verbal scores over 600: 75%; SAT math scores over 600: 86%; SAT verbal scores over 700: 24%; SAT math scores over 700: 35%.
Athletic Department: *Director of Athletics:* Chet Gladchuk; Phone: 410-293-2700; Fax: 410-293-8954; E-mail: gladchuk@usna.edu. *Sports Information Director:* Scott Strasemeier; Phone: 410-293-2700; E-mail: sstrasem@nadn.navy.mil.

MEN'S COACHES
Baseball: Steve Whitmeyer; Phone: 410-293-5571; E-mail: whitmyer@usna.edu.
Basketball: Don Devoe; Phone: 410-293-2627; E-mail: devoe@usna.edu.
Cheerleading: Dana Kessler; Phone: 410-293-1000.
Cross Country: Al Cantello; Phone: 410-293-5574; E-mail: cantello@usna.edu.
Diving: Joe Suriano; Phone: 410-293-2970; E-mail: suriano@usna.edu.
Football: Paul Johnson; Phone: 410-293-2241; E-mail: gareis@usna.edu.
Golf: Pat Owen; Phone: 410-293-3544; E-mail: powen@usna.edu.
Lacrosse: Ritchie Meade; Phone: 410-293-5547; E-mail: meade@usna.edu.
Soccer: Greg Myers; Phone: 410-293-5542; E-mail: myers@usna.edu.

Swimming: Bill Roberts; Phone: 410-293-3012; E-mail: robertsw@usna.edu.
Tennis: John Officer; Phone: 410-293-5589; E-mail: jco@usna.edu.
Track and Field: Steve Cooksey; Phone: 410-293-5568; E-mail: cooksey@usna.edu.
Wrestling: Bruce Burnett; Phone: 410-293-3011; E-mail: bburnett@usna.edu.

WOMEN'S COACHES
Basketball: Tom Marryott; Phone: 410-293-5577; E-mail: tmarryot@usna.edu.
Cheerleading: Dana Kessler; Phone: 410-293-1000.
Cross Country: Karen Boyle; Phone: 410-293-5579; E-mail: boyle@usna.edu.
Soccer: Carin Caberra; Phone: 410-293-5562; E-mail: gabarra@usna.edu.
Swimming: Dick Purdy; Phone: 410-293-3081; E-mail: dwpurdy@usna.edu.
Track and Field: Carla Criste; Phone: 410-293-5580; E-mail: criste@usna.edu.
Volleyball: Mike Schwob; Phone: 410-293-5546; E-mail: schwob@usna.edu.

UNIVERSITY AT ALBANY, STATE UNIVERSITY OF NEW YORK
Albany, New York

Great Danes ◆ NCAA I ◆ America East Conference; Northeast Conference ◆ http://www.albany.edu/

State-supported university, founded 1844, part of State University of New York System
Coed, 11,796 undergraduate students, 91% full-time, 50% women, 50% men
Suburban 560-acre campus
Moderately difficult entrance level, 55% of applicants were admitted

Freshmen *Admission:* 17,328 applied, 9,672 were accepted, 2,161 enrolled. *Test scores:* SAT verbal scores over 500: 82%; SAT math scores over 500: 87%; SAT verbal scores over 600: 31%; SAT math scores over 600: 39%; SAT verbal scores over 700: 3%; SAT math scores over 700: 5%.
Tuition and fees (2003–04): $5770 (resident), $11,720 (nonresident). *Room and board:* $7181 (room only: $4417).
Financial Aid (All incoming freshmen): *Average need-based gift aid:* $4593. *Average non-need based aid:* $3883. *Average aid to full-time undergraduates:* $8065.
Athletic Department: *Director of Athletics:* Lee McElroy; Phone: 518-442-2562; Fax: 518-442-3031; E-mail: lmcelroy@uamail.albany.edu. *Sports Information Director:* Brian DePasquale; Phone: 518-442-3072; E-mail: bdepasquale@uamail.albany.edu.

MEN'S COACHES
Baseball: Jon Mueller; Phone: 518-442-3014; E-mail: jmueller@uamail.albany.edu.
Basketball: Will Brown; Phone: 518-442-3036; E-mail: wbrown@uamail.albany.edu.
Cheerleading: Patty Palmer; Phone: 518-442-3339; E-mail: ppalmer@uamail.albany.edu.
Cross Country: Craig McVey; Phone: 518-442-3057; E-mail: cmcvey@uamail.albany.edu.
Football: Bob Ford; Phone: 518-442-3052; E-mail: rford@uamail.albany.edu.
Lacrosse: Scott Marr; Phone: 518-442-3015; E-mail: smarr@uamail.albany.edu.
Soccer: Johan Aamio; Phone: 518-442-3065; E-mail: jaarnio@uamail.albany.edu.
Track and Field: Roberto Vives; Phone: 518-442-3064; E-mail: rvives@uamail.albany.edu.

WOMEN'S COACHES
Basketball: Trina Patterson; Phone: 518-442-3062; E-mail: tpatterson@uamail.albany.edu.
Cheerleading: Patty Palmer; Phone: 518-442-3339; E-mail: ppalmer@uamail.albany.edu.
Cross Country: Craig McVey; Phone: 518-442-3057; E-mail: cmcvey@uamail.albany.edu.

University at Albany, State University of New York (continued)

Field Hockey: Deborah Fiore; Phone: 518-442-3017; E-mail: albanyfieldhockey@uamail.albany.edu.
Golf: Richard Sauers; Phone: 518-442-3811; E-mail: rsauers@uamail.albany.edu.
Lacrosse: Dennis Short; Phone: 518-442-3204; E-mail: dshort@uamail.albany.edu.
Soccer: Kalekeni Banda; Phone: 518-442-3043; E-mail: kbanda@uamail.albany.edu.
Softball: Chris Cannata; Phone: 518-442-4391; E-mail: ccannata@uamail.albany.edu.
Tennis: Chrissy Short; Phone: 518-442-3048; E-mail: cshort@uamail.albany.edu.
Track and Field: Roberto Vives; Phone: 518-442-3064; E-mail: rvives@uamail.albany.edu.
Volleyball: Kelly Sheffield; Phone: 518-442-3039; E-mail: ksheffield@uamail.albany.edu.

UNIVERSITY AT BUFFALO, THE STATE UNIVERSITY OF NEW YORK
Buffalo, New York

Bulls ◆ NCAA I ◆ Mid-American Conference ◆ http://www.buffalo.edu/

State-supported university, founded 1846, part of State University of New York System
Coed, 17,818 undergraduate students, 91% full-time, 45% women, 55% men
Suburban 1,350-acre campus
Moderately difficult entrance level, 63% of applicants were admitted

Freshmen *Admission:* 17,448 applied, 10,890 were accepted, 3,593 enrolled. *Test scores:* SAT verbal scores over 500: 77%; SAT math scores over 500: 88%; SAT verbal scores over 600: 28%; SAT math scores over 600: 42%; SAT verbal scores over 700: 4%; SAT math scores over 700: 6%.
Tuition and fees (2003–04): $5850 (resident), $11,800 (nonresident). *Room and board:* $6816 (room only: $4036).
Financial Aid (All incoming freshmen): *Average need-based gift aid:* $2364. *Average non-need based aid:* $2700. *Average aid to full-time undergraduates:* $5727.
Athletic Department: *Director of Athletics:* William Maher; Phone: 716-645-3454; Fax: 716-645-3754; E-mail: wm4@buffalo.edu. *Sports Information Director:* Paul Vecchio; Phone: 716-645-6311; E-mail: pvecchio@buffalo.edu.

MEN'S COACHES
Baseball: Bill Breene; Phone: 716-645-6808; E-mail: breene@buffalo.edu.
Basketball: Reggie Witherspoon; Phone: 716-645-3025; E-mail: prw@buffalo.edu.
Cheerleading: Justin Bridenbaker; Phone: 716-645-6436; E-mail: jb5@buffalo.edu.
Cross Country: Vicki Mitchell; Phone: 716-645-6815; E-mail: vam3@buffalo.edu.
Diving: Kara Sixbury; Phone: 716-645-3628; E-mail: sixbury@buffalo.edu.
Football: Jim Hofher; Phone: 716-645-3177; E-mail: jhofher@buffalo.edu.
Soccer: John Astudillo; Phone: 716-645-3144; E-mail: jaa@buffalo.edu.
Swimming: Budd Termin; Phone: 716-645-3130; E-mail: btermin@buffalo.edu.
Tennis: Russ Crispell; Phone: 716-645-6669; E-mail: crispell@buffalo.edu.
Track and Field: Perry Jenkins; Phone: 716-645-6801; E-mail: pjenkins@buffalo.edu.
Wrestling: Jim Beichner; Phone: 716-645-6876; E-mail: beichner@buffalo.edu.

WOMEN'S COACHES
Basketball: Cheryl Dozier; Phone: 716-645-5985; E-mail: cldozier@buffalo.edu.
Cheerleading: Justin Bridenbaker; Phone: 716-645-6436; E-mail: jb5@buffalo.edu.
Cross Country: Vicki Mitchell; Phone: 716-645-6815; E-mail: vam3@buffalo.edu.
Diving: Kara Sixbury; Phone: 716-645-3628; E-mail: sixbury@buffalo.edu.
Soccer: Jean-A. Tassy; Phone: 716-645-6664; E-mail: tassy@buffalo.edu.
Softball: Marie Curran; Phone: 716-645-6517; E-mail: mcurran@buffalo.edu.
Swimming: Dorsi Raynolds; Phone: 716-645-3145; E-mail: raynolds@buffalo.edu.
Tennis: Kathy Twist; Phone: 716-645-6866; E-mail: twist@buffalo.edu.
Track and Field: Vicki Mitchell; Phone: 716-645-6815; E-mail: vam3@buffalo.edu.
Volleyball: Sally Kus; Phone: 716-645-3149; E-mail: skus@buffalo.edu.

THE UNIVERSITY OF AKRON
Akron, Ohio

Zips ◆ NCAA I ◆ Mid-American Conference ◆ http://www.uakron.edu/

State-supported university, founded 1870
Coed, 20,111 undergraduate students, 69% full-time, 54% women, 46% men
Urban 170-acre campus with easy access to Cleveland
Minimally difficult entrance level, 87% of applicants were admitted

Freshmen *Admission:* 7,113 applied, 6,216 were accepted, 3,715 enrolled. *Test scores:* SAT verbal scores over 500: 50%; SAT math scores over 500: 52%; SAT verbal scores over 600: 16%; SAT math scores over 600: 21%; SAT verbal scores over 700: 2%; SAT math scores over 700: 4%.
Tuition and fees (2004–05): $7510 (resident), $15,179 (nonresident). *Room and board:* $6660 (room only: $4240).
Financial Aid (All incoming freshmen): *Average need-based gift aid:* $1710. *Average non-need based aid:* $2202. *Average aid to full-time undergraduates:* $1879.
Athletic Department: *Director of Athletics:* Michael Thomas; Phone: 330-972-7080; Fax: 330-972-5473; E-mail: mthomas@uakron.edu. *Sports Information Director:* Shawn Nestor; Phone: 330-972-6292; E-mail: nestor@uakron.edu.

MEN'S COACHES
Baseball: Tim Berenyi; Phone: 330-972-7290; E-mail: tab3@uakron.edu.
Basketball: Dan Hipsher; Phone: 330-972-7678; E-mail: deh@uakron.edu.
Cheerleading: Sean Wade; Phone: 330-972-7468; E-mail: swade9156@yahoo.com.
Cross Country: Dennis Mitchell; Phone: 330-972-7964; E-mail: dwmitch@uakron.edu.
Football: J.D. Brookhart; Phone: 330-972-7493; E-mail: nstott@uakron.edu.
Golf: Steve Parker; Phone: 330-972-6290; E-mail: msp1@uakron.edu.
Soccer: Ken Lolla; Phone: 330-972-7990; E-mail: lolla@uakron.edu.
Track and Field: Dennis Mitchell; Phone: 330-972-7964; E-mail: dwmitch@uakron.edu.

WOMEN'S COACHES
Basketball: Kelly Kennedy; Phone: 330-972-7433; E-mail: kkebe@uakron.edu.
Cheerleading: Sean Wade; Phone: 330-972-7468; E-mail: swade9156@yahoo.com.
Cross Country: Dennis Mitchell; Phone: 330-972-7964; E-mail: dwmitch@uakron.edu.
Diving: Chris Medvedeff; Phone: 330-972-2339.
Soccer: Catherine Byrne; Phone: 330-972-2167; E-mail: cbyrne@uakron.edu.
Softball: Deanna Parks; Phone: 330-972-7578; E-mail: dmparks@uakron.edu.
Swimming: Brian Vereb; Phone: 330-972-5984; E-mail: bvereb@uakron.edu.
Tennis: Tony Fox; Phone: 330-972-7312; E-mail: afox@uakron.edu.
Track and Field: Dennis Mitchell; Phone: 330-972-7964; E-mail: dwmitch@uakron.edu.
Volleyball: Mike Sweitzer; Phone: 330-972-7338; E-mail: msweitz@uakron.edu.

THE UNIVERSITY OF ALABAMA
Tuscaloosa, Alabama

Crimson Tide ◆ NCAA I ◆ Southeastern Conference ◆ http://www.ua.edu/

State-supported university, founded 1831, part of The University of Alabama System
Coed, 15,889 undergraduate students, 90% full-time, 54% women, 46% men
Suburban 1,000-acre campus with easy access to Birmingham
Moderately difficult entrance level, 86% of applicants were admitted

Freshmen *Admission:* 8,298 applied, 7,194 were accepted, 3,077 enrolled. *Test scores:* SAT verbal scores over 500: 78%; SAT math scores over 500: 75%; SAT verbal scores over 600: 30%; SAT math scores over 600: 29%; SAT verbal scores over 700: 8%; SAT math scores over 700: 6%.
Tuition and fees (2003–04): $4134 (resident), $11,294 (nonresident). *Room and board:* $4906 (room only: $2788).
Financial Aid (All incoming freshmen): *Average need-based gift aid:* $3381. *Average non-need based aid:* $4377. *Average aid to full-time undergraduates:* $7167.
Athletic Department: *Director of Athletics:* Mal Moore; Phone: 205-348-3697; Fax: 205-348-2196; E-mail: mmoore@ia.ua.edu. *Sports Information Director:* Larry White; Phone: 205-348-6084.
MEN'S COACHES
Baseball: Jim Wells; Phone: 205-348-4029; E-mail: tbutler@ia.ua.edu.
Basketball: Mark Gottfried; Phone: 205-348-4551.
Cheerleading: Debbie Greenwell; Phone: 205-348-3636; E-mail: dgreenwell@ia.ua.edu.
Diving: Patrick Greenwell; Phone: 205-348-3915; E-mail: pgreenwell@ia.ua.edu.
Football: Mike Shula; Phone: 205-348-3600.
Golf: Jay Seawell; Phone: 205-348-0383; E-mail: jseawell@ia.ua.edu.
Swimming: Eric McIlquham; Phone: 205-348-3912; E-mail: emcilquham@ia.ua.edu.
Tennis: Billy Pate; Phone: 205-348-2467; E-mail: bpate@ia.ua.edu.
Track and Field: Harvey Glance; Phone: 205-348-2467; E-mail: hglance@ia.ua.edu.
WOMEN'S COACHES
Basketball: Rick Moody; Phone: 205-348-7077.
Cheerleading: Debbie Greenwell; Phone: 205-348-3636; E-mail: dgreenwell@ia.ua.edu.
Diving: Patrick Greenwell; Phone: 205-348-3915; E-mail: pgreenwell@ia.ua.edu.
Golf: Betty Palmer; Phone: 205-348-0526.
Gymnastics: Sarah Patterson; Phone: 205-348-7600; E-mail: spatterson@ia.ua.edu.
Soccer: Don Staley; Phone: 205-348-0526; E-mail: dstaley@ia.ua.edu.
Softball: Patrick Murphy; Phone: 205-348-0526; E-mail: pmurphy@ia.ua.edu.
Swimming: Eric McIlquham; Phone: 205-348-3912; E-mail: emcilquham@ia.ua.edu.
Tennis: Jenny Mainz; Phone: 205-348-2467; E-mail: jmainz@ia.ua.edu.
Track and Field: Sandy Fowler; Phone: 205-348-2467; E-mail: sfowler@ia.ua.edu.
Volleyball: Judy Green; Phone: 205-348-2467; E-mail: jgreen@ia.ua.edu.

THE UNIVERSITY OF ALABAMA AT BIRMINGHAM
Birmingham, Alabama

Blazers ◆ NCAA I ◆ Conference USA Conference ◆ http://www.uab.edu/

State-supported university, founded 1969, part of University of Alabama System
Coed, 11,046 undergraduate students, 70% full-time, 60% women, 40% men
Urban 265-acre campus
Moderately difficult entrance level, 79% of applicants were admitted

Freshmen *Admission:* 4,710 applied, 3,807 were accepted, 1,708 enrolled.

Tuition and fees (2003–04): $4274 (resident), $9494 (nonresident). *Room only:* $2588.
Financial Aid (All incoming freshmen): *Average need-based gift aid:* $3227. *Average non-need based aid:* $5159. *Average aid to full-time undergraduates:* $7966.
Athletic Department: *Director of Athletics:* Watson Brown; Phone: 205-934-7586; Fax: 205-934-7286. *Sports Information Director:* Norm Reilly; Phone: 205-934-0722; E-mail: nreilly@uab.edu.
MEN'S COACHES
Baseball: Larry Giangrosso; Phone: 205-934-5181; E-mail: gino@uab.edu.
Basketball: Mike Anderson; Phone: 205-934-3402; E-mail: manders@its.uab.edu.
Cheerleading: Ashelie Halla; Phone: 205-934-8224; E-mail: ahalla@uab.edu.
Football: Watson Brown; Phone: 205-934-7586.
Golf: Alan Kaufman; Phone: 205-975-4653.
Soccer: Mike Getman; Phone: 205-934-8066; E-mail: uabsoccer@its.uab.edu.
Tennis: Derek Tarr; Phone: 205-934-3989; E-mail: tarrdj@aol.com.
WOMEN'S COACHES
Basketball: Jeannie Milling; Phone: 205-934-2048; E-mail: milling@uab.edu.
Cheerleading: Ashelie Halla; Phone: 205-934-8224; E-mail: ahalla@uab.edu.
Cross Country: Ray Stanfield; Phone: 205-934-7236; E-mail: rstan@uab.edu.
Golf: Kim Wilcox; Phone: 205-934-4009.
Soccer: Paul Harbin; Phone: 205-934-4756; E-mail: pharbin@uab.edu.
Softball: Marla Townsend; Phone: 205-975-7800; E-mail: softball@uab.edu.
Tennis: Mert Ertunga; Phone: 205-934-3976; E-mail: mertov@bjk.com.
Track and Field: Ray Stanfield; Phone: 205-934-7236; E-mail: rstan@uab.edu.
Volleyball: Melinda Claiborne; Phone: 205-934-8010; E-mail: melindac@uab.edu.

THE UNIVERSITY OF ALABAMA IN HUNTSVILLE
Huntsville, Alabama

Chargers ◆ NCAA II ◆ College Hockey America Conference; Gulf South Conference ◆ http://www.uah.edu/

State-supported university, founded 1950, part of University of Alabama System
Coed, 5,481 undergraduate students, 71% full-time, 49% women, 51% men
Suburban 376-acre campus
Moderately difficult entrance level, 89% of applicants were admitted

Freshmen *Admission:* 1,785 applied, 1,563 were accepted, 798 enrolled. *Test scores:* SAT verbal scores over 500: 83%; SAT math scores over 500: 82%; SAT verbal scores over 600: 38%; SAT math scores over 600: 37%; SAT verbal scores over 700: 8%; SAT math scores over 700: 7%.
Tuition and fees (2003–04): $4126 (resident), $8702 (nonresident). *Room and board:* $5000 (room only: $3400).
Financial Aid (All incoming freshmen): *Average need-based gift aid:* $2957. *Average non-need based aid:* $2370. *Average aid to full-time undergraduates:* $4942.
Athletic Department: *Director of Athletics:* Jim Harris; Phone: 256-824-6144; Fax: 256-824-7306; E-mail: harrisj@email.uah.edu. *Sports Information Director:* Jamie Gilliam; Phone: 256-824-2201; E-mail: gilliaj@email.uah.edu.
MEN'S COACHES
Baseball: David Keel; Phone: 256-824-2206; E-mail: keelc@email.uah.edu.
Basketball: Lennie Acuff; Phone: 256-824-2212; E-mail: acuffl@email.uah.edu.
Cheerleading: Ann Finney; Phone: 256-582-7060; E-mail: finneya@email.uah.edu.
Cross Country: David Cain; Phone: 256-824-2222; E-mail: caind@email.uah.edu.
Ice Hockey: Doug Ross; Phone: 256-824-2205.

The University of Alabama in Huntsville *(continued)*

Soccer: Carlos Peterson; Phone: 256-824-2207; E-mail: petersc@email.
uah.edu.
Tennis: Julie Woltjen; Phone: 256-824-7853; E-mail: woltjenj@email.
uah.edu.

WOMEN'S COACHES

Basketball: Jeff Keller; Phone: 256-824-2208; E-mail: kellerj@email.
uah.edu.
Cheerleading: Ann Finney; Phone: 256-582-7060; E-mail: finneya@
email.uah.edu.
Cross Country: David Cain; Phone: 256-824-2222; E-mail: caind@email.
uah.edu.
Soccer: Lincoln Ziyenge; Phone: 256-824-5425; E-mail: ziyengel@
email.uah.edu.
Softball: Les Stuedeman; Phone: 256-824-2204; E-mail: stuedel@email.
uah.edu.
Tennis: Julie Woltjen; Phone: 256-824-7853; E-mail: woltjenj@email.
uah.edu.
Track and Field: David Cain; Phone: 256-824-2222; E-mail: caind@
email.uah.edu.
Volleyball: Laura Taube; Phone: 256-824-2203; E-mail: taubel@email.
uah.edu.

UNIVERSITY OF ALASKA ANCHORAGE
Anchorage, Alaska

Seawolves ◆ NCAA II ◆ Great Northwest Athletic
Conference; Western Collegiate Hockey Conference ◆ http://
www.uaa.alaska.edu/

State-supported comprehensive, founded 1954, part of University of
Alaska System
Coed, 15,810 undergraduate students, 42% full-time, 62% women,
38% men
Urban 428-acre campus
Noncompetitive entrance level, 74% of applicants were admitted

Freshmen *Admission:* 2,516 applied, 1,922 were accepted, 1,379 enrolled. *Test scores:* SAT verbal scores over 500: 48%; SAT math scores
over 500: 52%; SAT verbal scores over 600: 13%; SAT math scores
over 600: 13%; SAT verbal scores over 700: 1%; SAT math scores
over 700: 1%.
Tuition and fees (2003–04): $2656 (resident), $7152 (nonresident). *Room
and board:* $6830 (room only: $3730).
Athletic Department: *Director of Athletics:* Steve Cobb; Phone: 907-786-
1225; Fax: 907-786-1142; E-mail: ansrc@uaa.alaska.edu. *Sports Information Director:* Nathan Sagan; Phone: 907-786-1295; E-mail:
annss@uaa.alaska.edu.

MEN'S COACHES

Basketball: Charlie Bruns; Phone: 907-786-1286; E-mail: chazmister@
msn.com.
Cheerleading: Phone: 907-786-1800; E-mail: uaacheer@uaa.alaska.edu.
Cross Country: Michael Friess; Phone: 907-786-1325; E-mail: anmaf@
uaa.alaska.edu.
Ice Hockey: John Hill; Phone: 907-786-1227; E-mail: anjh@uaa.alaska.
edu.
Track and Field: Michael Friess; Phone: 907-786-1325; E-mail: anmaf@
uaa.alaska.edu.

WOMEN'S COACHES

Basketball: Jody Henson; Phone: 907-786-1040; E-mail: coachhensen@
uaa.alaska.edu.
Cheerleading: Phone: 907-786-1800; E-mail: uaacheer@uaa.alaska.edu.
Cross Country: Michael Friess; Phone: 907-786-1325; E-mail: anmaf@
uaa.alaska.edu.
Gymnastics: Paul Stoklos; Phone: 907-786-1229; E-mail: anps1@uaa.
alaska.edu.
Track and Field: Michael Friess; Phone: 907-786-1325; E-mail: anmaf@
uaa.alaska.edu.
Volleyball: Kim Lauwers; Phone: 907-786-1226; E-mail: ankal@uaa.
alaska.edu.

UNIVERSITY OF ALASKA FAIRBANKS
Fairbanks, Alaska

Nanooks ◆ NCAA II ◆ Central Collegiate Hockey
Conference; Great Northwest Athletic Conference ◆ http://
www.uaf.edu/

State-supported university, founded 1917, part of University of
Alaska System
Coed, 7,708 undergraduate students, 46% full-time, 59% women,
41% men
Small-town 2,250-acre campus
Minimally difficult entrance level, 8% of applicants were admitted

Freshmen *Admission:* 1,895 applied, 1,587 were accepted, 1,021 enrolled. *Test scores:* SAT verbal scores over 500: 58%; SAT math scores
over 500: 58%; SAT verbal scores over 600: 23%; SAT math scores
over 600: 22%; SAT verbal scores over 700: 5%; SAT math scores
over 700: 3%.
Tuition and fees (2004–05): $4165 (resident), $11,195 (nonresident).
Room and board: $5130 (room only: $2690).
Financial Aid (All incoming freshmen): *Average need-based gift aid:* $4516.
Average non-need based aid: $2753. *Average aid to full-time under-
graduates:* $8600.
Athletic Department: *Director of Athletics:* Cory Schwartz; Phone: 907-
474-7780; Fax: 907-474-5162; E-mail: cory.schwartz@uaf.edu. *Sports
Information Director:* Kevin Raap; Phone: 907-474-5162; E-mail:
sports.info@uaf.edu.

MEN'S COACHES

Basketball: Al Sokaitis; Phone: 907-474-6636; E-mail: fnajs@uaf.edu.
Cheerleading: Lydia Anderson; Phone: 907-474-7037; E-mail: fnlma@
uaf.edu.
Cross Country: Bill McDonnell; Phone: 907-474-6802; E-mail: fnwbm@
uaf.edu.
Ice Hockey: Guy Gadowsky; Phone: 907-474-6869; E-mail: guy.
gadowsky@uaf.edu.

WOMEN'S COACHES

Basketball: Jenny Benson; Phone: 907-474-6813; E-mail: fnjlb@uaf.edu.
Cheerleading: Lydia Anderson; Phone: 907-474-7037; E-mail: fnlma@
uaf.edu.
Cross Country: Bill McDonnell; Phone: 907-474-6802; E-mail: fnwbm@
uaf.edu.
Volleyball: Phil Shoemaker; Phone: 907-474-6809; E-mail: fnprs@uaf.
edu.

THE UNIVERSITY OF ARIZONA
Tucson, Arizona

Wildcats ◆ NCAA I ◆ Pacific-10 Conference ◆ http://
www.arizona.edu/

State-supported university, founded 1885, part of Arizona Board of
Regents
Coed, 28,482 undergraduate students, 85% full-time, 53% women,
47% men
Urban 362-acre campus
Moderately difficult entrance level, 8% of applicants were admitted

Freshmen *Admission:* 20,924 applied, 17,796 were accepted, 5,958 enrolled. *Test scores:* SAT verbal scores over 500: 74%; SAT math scores
over 500: 77%; SAT verbal scores over 600: 30%; SAT math scores
over 600: 36%; SAT verbal scores over 700: 5%; SAT math scores
over 700: 6%.
Tuition and fees (2003–04): $3603 (resident), $12,373 (nonresident).
Room and board: $6810 (room only: $3570).
Financial Aid (All incoming freshmen): *Average aid to full-time undergraduates:* $8878.
Athletic Department: *Director of Athletics:* Jim Livengood; Phone: 520-
621-4622; Fax: 520-621-2681; E-mail: livengood@arizona.edu. *Sports
Information Director:* Tom Duddleston; Phone: 520-621-4163; E-mail:
tduddles@arizona.edu.

MEN'S COACHES

Baseball: Andy Lopez; Phone: 502-621-4102; E-mail: lopeza@u.
arizona.edu.

Basketball: Lute Olson; Phone: 502-621-4142; E-mail: lute@email.arizona.edu.
Cheerleading: Phoebe Chalk; Phone: 502-621-2331; E-mail: pchalk@u.arizona.edu.
Cross Country: Fred Harvey; Phone: 502-621-2124; E-mail: flh@u.arizona.edu.
Diving: Michele Mitchell-Rocha; Phone: 502-621-2750; E-mail: mmrocha@u.arizona.edu.
Football: Mike Stoops; Phone: 502-621-4917.
Golf: Rick Larose; Phone: 502-621-4658; E-mail: larose@u.arizona.edu.
Swimming: Frank Busch; Phone: 502-621-2131; E-mail: mgarcia@u.arizona.edu.
Tennis: Bill Wright; Phone: 502-621-4626; E-mail: bwright@arizona.edu.
Track and Field: Fred Harvey; Phone: 502-621-2124; E-mail: flh@u.arizona.edu.

WOMEN'S COACHES
Basketball: Joan Bonvicini; Phone: 502-621-4014; E-mail: jbonvici@u.arizona.edu.
Cheerleading: Phoebe Chalk; Phone: 502-621-2331; E-mail: pchalk@u.arizona.edu.
Cross Country: Fred Harvey; Phone: 502-621-2124; E-mail: flh@u.arizona.edu.
Diving: Michele Mitchell-Rocha; Phone: 502-621-2750; E-mail: mmrocha@u.arizona.edu.
Golf: Greg Allen; Phone: 502-621-5777; E-mail: gallen@u.arizona.edu.
Gymnastics: Bill Ryden; Phone: 502-621-4777; E-mail: ryden@u.arizona.edu.
Soccer: Dan Tobias; Phone: 502-621-7771; E-mail: tobiasd@u.arizona.edu.
Softball: Mike Candrea; Phone: 502-621-4920; E-mail: candrea@u.arizona.edu.
Swimming: Frank Busch; Phone: 502-621-2131; E-mail: mgarcia@u.arizona.edu.
Tennis: Vicky Maes; Phone: 502-621-4915; E-mail: maes@u.arizona.edu.
Track and Field: Fred Harvey; Phone: 502-621-2124; E-mail: flh@u.arizona.edu.
Volleyball: David Rubio; Phone: 502-621-2856; E-mail: drubio@u.arizona.edu.

UNIVERSITY OF ARKANSAS
Fayetteville, Arkansas
Razorbacks ◆ NCAA I ◆ Southeastern Conference ◆ http://www.uark.edu/

State-supported university, founded 1871, part of University of Arkansas System
Coed, 13,083 undergraduate students, 84% full-time, 49% women, 51% men
Suburban 357-acre campus
Moderately difficult entrance level, 84% of applicants were admitted

Freshmen *Admission:* 5,491 applied, 4,661 were accepted, 2,357 enrolled. *Test scores:* SAT verbal scores over 500: 84%; SAT math scores over 500: 83%; SAT verbal scores over 600: 45%; SAT math scores over 600: 49%; SAT verbal scores over 700: 10%; SAT math scores over 700: 13%.
Tuition and fees (2003–04): $4768 (resident), $11,518 (nonresident). *Room and board:* $5087 (room only: $2812).
Financial Aid (All incoming freshmen): *Average need-based gift aid:* $3604. *Average non-need based aid:* $5786. *Average aid to full-time undergraduates:* $8433.
Athletic Department: *Director of Athletics:* Frank Broyles; Phone: 501-575-2755; Fax: 501-575-7501; E-mail: jbroyle@uark.edu. *Sports Information Director:* Kevin Trainor; Phone: 501-575-2751; E-mail: ktrainor@uark.edu.

MEN'S COACHES
Baseball: Dave Van Horn; Phone: 479-575-3655; E-mail: dvanhor@uark.edu.
Basketball: Stan Heath; Phone: 479-575-4555; E-mail: heath@uark.edu.
Cheerleading: Jana Bolding; Phone: 479-575-4959; E-mail: jbolding@uark.edu.
Cross Country: John McDonnell; Phone: 479-575-5403; E-mail: mcdonnel@uark.edu.

Football: Houston Nutt; Phone: 479-575-4849; E-mail: hnutt@uark.edu.
Golf: Mike Ketcham; Phone: 479-575-2000; E-mail: mketchu@uark.edu.
Tennis: Robert Cox; Phone: 479-575-2758; E-mail: rocox@uark.edu.
Track and Field: John McDonnell; Phone: 479-575-5403; E-mail: mcdonnel@uark.edu.

WOMEN'S COACHES
Basketball: Susie Gardner; Phone: 479-575-3000; E-mail: gardner@uark.edu.
Cheerleading: Jana Bolding; Phone: 479-575-4959; E-mail: jbolding@uark.edu.
Cross Country: Lance Harter; Phone: 479-575-3014; E-mail: kharter@uark.edu.
Diving: Scott Reich; Phone: 479-575-3014; E-mail: sreich@uark.edu.
Golf: Kelley Hester; Phone: 479-575-3014; E-mail: khester@uark.edu.
Gymnastics: Rene Cook; Phone: 479-575-3014; E-mail: rcook@uark.edu.
Soccer: Gordon Henderson; Phone: 479-575-4959; E-mail: gjhende@uark.edu.
Softball: Carie Dever Boaz; Phone: 479-575-6620; E-mail: cdboaz@uark.edu.
Swimming: Anne Goodman James; Phone: 479-575-3014; E-mail: agjames@uark.edu.
Tennis: Kevin Platt; Phone: 479-575-3014; E-mail: platt@uark.edu.
Track and Field: Lance Harter; Phone: 479-575-3014; E-mail: kharter@uark.edu.
Volleyball: Chris Poole; Phone: 479-575-4959; E-mail: cpoole@uark.edu.

UNIVERSITY OF ARKANSAS AT LITTLE ROCK
Little Rock, Arkansas
Trojans ◆ NCAA I ◆ Sun Belt Conference
◆ http://www.ualr.edu/

State-supported university, founded 1927, part of University of Arkansas System
Coed, 9,330 undergraduate students, 61% full-time, 62% women, 38% men
Urban 150-acre campus
Minimally difficult entrance level, 99% of applicants were admitted

Freshmen *Admission:* 2,531 applied, 2,514 were accepted, 777 enrolled.
Tuition and fees (2003–04): $4598 (resident), $10,538 (nonresident). *Room only:* $2700.
Financial Aid (All incoming freshmen): *Average aid to full-time undergraduates:* $7190.
Athletic Department: *Director of Athletics:* Chris Peterson; Phone: 501-569-3167; Fax: 501-569-3030; E-mail: tlcampbell@ualr.edu. *Sports Information Director:* Kevin Tankersley; Phone: 501-569-3449; E-mail: kxtankersley@ualr.edu.

MEN'S COACHES
Baseball: Brian Rhees; Phone: 501-663-8095; E-mail: brhees25@hotmail.com.
Basketball: Steve Shields; Phone: 501-569-3304; E-mail: slshields@ualr.edu.
Cheerleading: Sunshine Barnett; Phone: 501-569-8050; E-mail: sbarnett@nationalspirit.com.
Cross Country: Kirk Elias; Phone: 501-569-8921; E-mail: kdelias@aol.com.
Golf: Wyn Norwood; Phone: 501-868-1756; E-mail: wcnorwood@ualr.edu.
Tennis: Tommy McDonald; Phone: 501-569-3447; E-mail: trmcdonald@ualr.edu.
Track and Field: Kirk Elias; Phone: 501-569-8921; E-mail: kdelias@aol.com.

WOMEN'S COACHES
Basketball: Joe Foley; Phone: 501-569-3464; E-mail: jmfoley@ualr.edu.
Cheerleading: Sunshine Barnett; Phone: 501-569-8050; E-mail: sbarnett@nationalspirit.com.
Cross Country: Kirk Elias; Phone: 501-569-8921; E-mail: kdelias@aol.com.

University of Arkansas at Little Rock *(continued)*

Diving: Richard Turner; Phone: 501-569-3322; E-mail: crturner@ualr.edu.
Golf: Bridgett Norwood; Phone: 501-569-1756; E-mail: golfbridg@aol.com.
Soccer: Gregg Hess; Phone: 501-569-3452; E-mail: gk00ghess@hotmail.com.
Swimming: Richard Turner; Phone: 501-569-3322; E-mail: crturner@ualr.edu.
Tennis: Tommy McDonald; Phone: 501-569-3447; E-mail: trmcdonald@ualr.edu.
Track and Field: Kirk Elias; Phone: 501-569-8921; E-mail: kdelias@aol.com.
Volleyball: Van Compton; Phone: 501-569-3371; E-mail: vxcompton@ualr.edu.

UNIVERSITY OF ARKANSAS AT MONTICELLO
Monticello, Arkansas

Cotton Blossoms; Bollweevils ◆ NCAA II ◆ Gulf South Conference ◆ http://www.uamont.edu/

State-supported comprehensive, founded 1909, part of University of Arkansas System
Coed, 2,694 undergraduate students, 84% full-time, 60% women, 40% men
Small-town 400-acre campus
Noncompetitive entrance level, 72% of applicants were admitted

Freshmen *Admission:* 1,208 applied, 880 were accepted, 751 enrolled.
Tuition and fees (2003–04): $3385 (resident), $6805 (nonresident). *Room and board:* $3150.
Athletic Department: *Director of Athletics:* Alvy Early; Phone: 870-460-1068; Fax: 870-460-1458; E-mail: early@uamont.edu. *Sports Information Director:* Stephen Fuller; Phone: 870-460-1574; E-mail: fullers@uamont.edu.

MEN'S COACHES
Baseball: Kevin Downing; Phone: 870-460-1257; E-mail: downing@uamont.edu.
Basketball: Mike Newell; Phone: 870-460-1258; E-mail: newell@uamont.edu.
Football: Gregg Ricono; Phone: 870-460-1817; E-mail: ricono@uamont.edu.
Golf: Jeff Handly; Phone: 870-367-8585; E-mail: jeffery_handly@afbic.com.

WOMEN'S COACHES
Basketball: Jill Lewis; Phone: 870-460-1357; E-mail: lewisj@uamont.edu.
Cross Country: Fred Cooper; Phone: 870-460-1736; E-mail: cooperf@uamont.edu.
Softball: Alvy Early; Phone: 870-460-1058; E-mail: early@uamont.edu.
Tennis: Fred Cooper; Phone: 870-460-1736; E-mail: cooperf@uamont.edu.

UNIVERSITY OF ARKANSAS AT PINE BLUFF
Pine Bluff, Arkansas

Golden Lions ◆ NCAA I ◆ Southwestern Athletic Conference ◆ http://www.uapb.edu/

State-supported comprehensive, founded 1873, part of University of Arkansas System
Coed, 3,136 undergraduate students, 90% full-time, 55% women, 45% men
Urban 327-acre campus
Minimally difficult entrance level, 74% of applicants were admitted

Freshmen *Admission:* 1,636 applied, 1,114 were accepted, 746 enrolled.
Test scores: SAT verbal scores over 500: 19%; SAT math scores over 500: 28%; SAT verbal scores over 600: 5%; SAT math scores over 600: 7%; SAT math scores over 700: 2%.
Tuition and fees (2003–04): $3687 (resident), $7437 (nonresident). *Room and board:* $5180.
Athletic Department: *Director of Athletics:* Craig Curry; Phone: 870-543-8675; Fax: 870-543-8114; E-mail: curry_c@uapb.edu. *Sports Information Director:* Tamara Williams; Phone: 870-575-7174; E-mail: bynum_t@vx4500.uapb.edu.

MEN'S COACHES
Baseball: Elbert Bennet; Phone: 870-575-8938; E-mail: bennett_e@vx4500.uapb.edu.
Basketball: Harold Blevins; Phone: 870-575-8694.
Cheerleading: Karen Blunt; Phone: 870-575-7702; E-mail: blunt_k@vx4500.uapb.edu.
Football: Lee Hardman; Phone: 870-575-8689; E-mail: hardman_l@vx4500.uapb.edu.
Golf: Joe Lambert; Phone: 870-575-8675; E-mail: lambert_j@uapb.edu.
Tennis: Mark Conley; Phone: 870-575-8675; E-mail: conley_m@vx4500.uapb.edu.
Track and Field: Curtis Pittman; Phone: 870-575-8677.

WOMEN'S COACHES
Basketball: Angela Daniels; Phone: 870-575-8681; E-mail: daniels_a@uapb.edu.
Cheerleading: Karen Blunt; Phone: 870-575-7702; E-mail: blunt_k@vx4500.uapb.edu.
Golf: Mike Ketcham; Phone: 870-575-8675.
Softball: Betty Hayes; Phone: 870-575-8675; E-mail: hayes_b@vx4500.uapb.edu.
Tennis: Mark Conley; Phone: 870-575-8675; E-mail: conley_m@vx4500.uapb.edu.
Track and Field: Curtis Pittman; Phone: 870-575-8677.
Volleyball: Kawanza Bibles; Phone: 870-575-8668; E-mail: bibles_k@uapb.edu.

UNIVERSITY OF BRIDGEPORT
Bridgeport, Connecticut

Purple Knights ◆ NCAA II ◆ New York Collegiate Athletic Conference ◆ http://www.bridgeport.edu/

Independent comprehensive, founded 1927
Coed, 1,261 undergraduate students, 80% full-time, 59% women, 41% men
Urban 86-acre campus with easy access to New York City
Moderately difficult entrance level, 9% of applicants were admitted

Freshmen *Admission:* 1,796 applied, 1,514 were accepted, 293 enrolled.
Test scores: SAT verbal scores over 500: 21%; SAT math scores over 500: 26%; SAT verbal scores over 600: 6%; SAT math scores over 600: 6%; SAT verbal scores over 700: 1%; SAT math scores over 700: 1%.
Tuition and fees (2003–04): $17,924 (full-time). *Room and board:* $8000.
Athletic Department: *Director of Athletics:* Joe DiPuma; Phone: 203-576-4735; Fax: 203-576-4057; E-mail: jdipuma@bridgeport.edu. *Sports Information Director:* Ken Johnson; Phone: 203-576-4726; E-mail: kjohnson@bridgeport.edu.

MEN'S COACHES
Baseball: John Anquillare; Phone: 203-576-4059; E-mail: johnanq@yahoo.com.
Basketball: Mike Ruane; Phone: 203-576-4721; E-mail: mruane@bridgeport.edu.
Cheerleading: Katsai Augustin; Phone: 203-576-4936; E-mail: kat01_06902@yahoo.com.
Cross Country: Mike Ruane; Phone: 203-576-4721; E-mail: mruane@bridgeport.edu.
Soccer: Brian Quinn; Phone: 203-576-4723; E-mail: bquinn@bridgeport.edu.

WOMEN'S COACHES
Basketball: Henry Rondon; Phone: 203-576-4728; E-mail: coachrondon16@aol.com.
Cheerleading: Katsai Augustin; Phone: 203-576-4936; E-mail: kat01_06902@yahoo.com.
Gymnastics: Shawn Simpson; Phone: 203-576-4242; E-mail: ubgymcoach@aol.com.
Soccer: Magnus Nilerud; Phone: 203-576-4723; E-mail: nilerud@bridgeport.edu.

Softball: Valerie Steen; Phone: 203-576-4736; E-mail: vsteen@bridgeport.edu.
Volleyball: Analia Carcer; Phone: 203-576-4936; E-mail: acarcer@bridgeport.edu.

UNIVERSITY OF CALIFORNIA, BERKELEY
Berkeley, California

Golden Bears ◆ NCAA I ◆ Northern Pacific Field Hockey Conference; Pacific-10 Conference ◆ http://www.berkeley.edu/

State-supported university, founded 1868, part of University of California System
Coed, 23,206 undergraduate students, 95% full-time, 54% women, 46% men
Urban 1,232-acre campus with easy access to San Francisco
Very difficult entrance level, 24% of applicants were admitted

Freshmen *Admission:* 36,976 applied, 8,832 were accepted, 3,653 enrolled. *Test scores:* SAT verbal scores over 500: 90%; SAT math scores over 500: 95%; SAT verbal scores over 600: 67%; SAT math scores over 600: 80%; SAT verbal scores over 700: 28%; SAT math scores over 700: 45%.
Tuition and fees (2003–04): $5250 (resident), $19,460 (nonresident). *Room and board:* $11,212.
Financial Aid (All incoming freshmen): *Average need-based gift aid:* $10,647. *Average non-need based aid:* $2677. *Average aid to full-time undergraduates:* $14,683.
Athletic Department: *Director of Athletics:* Steve Gladstone; Phone: 510-642-5316; Fax: 510-642-3399. *Sports Information Director:* Bob Rose; E-mail: bobrose@uclink.berkeley.edu.

MEN'S COACHES
Baseball: David Esquer; Phone: 510-642-6006; E-mail: dcesquer@uclink4.berkeley.edu.
Basketball: Ben Braun; Phone: 510-642-0361.
Cross Country: Tony Sandoval; Phone: 510-642-3158; E-mail: tsandovl@uclink4.berkeley.edu.
Diving: Phil Tonne; Phone: 510-642-7470; E-mail: ptonne@uclink4.berkeley.edu.
Football: Jeff Tedford; Phone: 510-642-3857.
Golf: Steve Desimone; Phone: 510-642-5914; E-mail: desimone@uclink4.berkeley.edu.
Soccer: Kevin Grimes; Phone: 510-642-5916.
Swimming: Nort Thornton; Phone: 510-642-5917; E-mail: thornton@uclink4.berkeley.edu.
Tennis: Peter Wright; Phone: 510-642-1153; E-mail: pwright@uclink4.berkeley.edu.
Track and Field: Chris Huffins; Phone: 510-642-3158; E-mail: chuffins@uclink.berkeley.edu.

WOMEN'S COACHES
Basketball: Caren Horstmeyer; Phone: 510-642-3839; E-mail: chorstme@uclink.berkeley.edu.
Cross Country: Tony Sandoval; Phone: 510-642-3158; E-mail: tsandovl@uclink4.berkeley.edu.
Diving: Phil Tonne; Phone: 510-642-7470; E-mail: ptonne@uclink4.berkeley.edu.
Field Hockey: Shellie Onstead; Phone: 510-642-9415.
Golf: Nancy McDaniel; Phone: 510-642-7940; E-mail: nmcdan@uclink4.berkeley.edu.
Gymnastics: Cari DuBois; Phone: 510-642-9411; E-mail: cadubois@uclink.berkeley.edu.
Lacrosse: Jill Malko; Phone: 510-642-2580; E-mail: malkoj@uclink4.berkeley.edu.
Soccer: Kevin Boyd; Phone: 510-642-8100; E-mail: boydk@uclink4.berkeley.edu.
Softball: Diane Ninemire; Phone: 510-642-1449; E-mail: ninemire@uclink4.berkeley.edu.
Swimming: Teri McKeever; Phone: 510-642-9450; E-mail: mckeever@uclink4.berkeley.edu.
Tennis: Jan Brogan; Phone: 510-642-9449; E-mail: jbrogan@uclink4.berkeley.edu.
Track and Field: Chris Huffins; Phone: 510-642-3158; E-mail: chuffins@uclink.berkeley.edu.
Volleyball: Rich Feller; Phone: 510-642-0978; E-mail: rifeller@uclink4.berkeley.edu.

UNIVERSITY OF CALIFORNIA, DAVIS
Davis, California

Aggies ◆ NCAA II ◆ California Collegiate Athletic Conference; Pacific-10 Conference ◆ http://www.ucdavis.edu/

State-supported university, founded 1905, part of University of California System
Coed, 23,472 undergraduate students, 89% full-time, 56% women, 44% men
Suburban 5,993-acre campus with easy access to San Francisco
Very difficult entrance level, 58% of applicants were admitted

Freshmen *Admission:* 32,506 applied, 19,367 were accepted, 4,786 enrolled. *Test scores:* SAT verbal scores over 500: 80%; SAT math scores over 500: 92%; SAT verbal scores over 600: 41%; SAT math scores over 600: 63%; SAT verbal scores over 700: 8%; SAT math scores over 700: 16%.
Tuition and fees (2003–04): $5853 (resident), $20,063 (nonresident). *Room and board:* $9143.
Financial Aid (All incoming freshmen): *Average need-based gift aid:* $7818. *Average non-need based aid:* $2024. *Average aid to full-time undergraduates:* $10,410.
Athletic Department: *Director of Athletics:* Greg Warzecka; Phone: 530-752-1111; Fax: 530-752-6681; E-mail: gdwarzecka@ucdavis.edu. *Sports Information Director:* Mike Robles; Phone: 530-752-3680; E-mail: merobles@ucdavis.edu.

MEN'S COACHES
Baseball: Rex Peters; Phone: 530-752-7513; E-mail: rwpeters@ucdavis.edu.
Basketball: Gary Stewart; Phone: 530-752-3501; E-mail: glstewart@ucdavis.edu.
Cheerleading: Maria Zalesky; Phone: 530-752-0111; E-mail: mazalesky@ucdavis.edu.
Cross Country: Sue Williams; Phone: 530-752-1942; E-mail: suewilliams@ucdavis.edu.
Diving: Peter Motekaitis; Phone: 530-752-9467; E-mail: pjmotekaitis@ucdavis.edu.
Football: Bob Biggs; Phone: 530-752-1356; E-mail: grbiggs@ucdavis.edu.
Golf: Cy Williams; Phone: 530-752-0639; E-mail: cywilliams@ucdavis.edu.
Soccer: Dwayne Schaffer; Phone: 530-752-8892; E-mail: dlshaffer@ucdavis.edu.
Swimming: Peter Motekaitis; Phone: 530-752-9467; E-mail: pjmotekaitis@ucdavis.edu.
Tennis: Daryl Lee; Phone: 530-752-9365; E-mail: darlee@ucdavis.edu.
Track and Field: Jon Vochatzer; Phone: 530-752-8608; E-mail: jevochatzer@ucdavis.edu.
Wrestling: Lennie Zalesky; Phone: 530-752-3686; E-mail: ljzalesky@ucdavis.edu.

WOMEN'S COACHES
Basketball: Sandy Simpson; Phone: 530-752-0315; E-mail: slsimpson@ucdavis.edu.
Cheerleading: Maria Zalesky; Phone: 530-752-0111; E-mail: mazalesky@ucdavis.edu.
Cross Country: Sue Williams; Phone: 530-752-1942; E-mail: suewilliams@ucdavis.edu.
Diving: Barbara Jahn; Phone: 530-752-9271; E-mail: bajahn@ucdavis.edu.
Gymnastics: Ray Goldbar; Phone: 530-752-1188; E-mail: rsgoldbar@ucdavis.edu.
Lacrosse: Elaine Jones; Phone: 530-752-2039; E-mail: ejjones@ucdavis.edu.
Soccer: Mary Claire Robinson; Phone: 530-752-0735; E-mail: mkrobinson@ucdavis.edu.
Softball: Kathy DeYoung; Phone: 530-752-1053; E-mail: kmdeyoung@ucdavis.edu.
Swimming: Barbara Jahn; Phone: 530-752-9271; E-mail: bajahn@ucdavis.edu.
Tennis: Bill Maze; Phone: 530-752-7511; E-mail: bsmaze@ucdavis.edu.
Track and Field: Deanne Vochatzer; Phone: 530-752-5057; E-mail: dmvochatzer@ucdavis.edu.
Volleyball: Stephanie Hawbecker; Phone: 530-752-0644; E-mail: shawbecker@ucdavis.edu.

UNIVERSITY OF CALIFORNIA, IRVINE

Irvine, California

Anteaters ◆ NCAA I ◆ Big West Conference ◆ http://www.uci.edu/

State-supported university, founded 1965, part of University of California System
Coed, 19,967 undergraduate students, 96% full-time, 50% women, 50% men
Suburban 1,477-acre campus with easy access to Los Angeles
Moderately difficult entrance level, 5% of applicants were admitted

Freshmen *Admission:* 34,417 applied, 18,517 were accepted, 4,043 enrolled. *Test scores:* SAT verbal scores over 500: 86%; SAT math scores over 500: 94%; SAT verbal scores over 600: 39%; SAT math scores over 600: 65%; SAT verbal scores over 700: 7%; SAT math scores over 700: 19%.
Tuition and fees (2003–04): $6165 (resident), $20,375 (nonresident). *Room and board:* $8055.
Financial Aid (All incoming freshmen): *Average need-based gift aid:* $7131. *Average non-need based aid:* $3013. *Average aid to full-time undergraduates:* $9753.
Athletic Department: *Director of Athletics:* Bob Chichester; Phone: 949-824-6932; Fax: 949-824-8492; E-mail: rchiches@uci.edu. *Sports Information Director:* Bob Olson; Phone: 949-824-5814; E-mail: rkolson@uci.edu.

MEN'S COACHES

Baseball: John Savage; Phone: 949-824-4292; E-mail: savage@uci.edu.
Basketball: Pat Douglass; Phone: 949-824-6840; E-mail: jdouglas@uci.edu.
Cheerleading: Jennifer Villasenor; Phone: 949-824-6931; E-mail: jennyvil@uci.edu.
Cross Country: Vince O'Boyle; Phone: 949-824-6080; E-mail: vboboyle@uci.edu.
Diving: Curt Wilson; Phone: 949-824-5071; E-mail: wilsoncg@uci.edu.
Golf: Paul Smolinski; Phone: 949-824-1097; E-mail: psmolins@uci.edu.
Soccer: George Kuntz; Phone: 949-824-8158; E-mail: gekuntz@uci.edu.
Swimming: Brian Pajer; Phone: 949-824-9034; E-mail: bpajer@uci.edu.
Tennis: Steve Clark; Phone: 949-824-8366; E-mail: srclark@uci.edu.
Track and Field: Vince O'Boyle; Phone: 949-824-6080; E-mail: vboboyle@uci.edu.
Volleyball: John Speraw; Phone: 949-824-5908; E-mail: jsperaw@uci.edu.

WOMEN'S COACHES

Basketball: Mark Adams; Phone: 949-824-7595; E-mail: mradams@uci.edu.
Cheerleading: Jennifer Villasenor; Phone: 949-824-6931; E-mail: jennyvil@uci.edu.
Cross Country: Vince O'Boyle; Phone: 949-824-6080; E-mail: vboboyle@uci.edu.
Diving: Curt Wilson; Phone: 949-824-5071; E-mail: wilsoncg@uci.edu.
Golf: Kelly Crawford; Phone: 949-824-7868; E-mail: kcrawfor@uci.edu.
Soccer: Marine Cano; Phone: 949-824-7432; E-mail: mcano@uci.edu.
Swimming: Brian Pajer; Phone: 949-824-9034; E-mail: bpajer@uci.edu.
Tennis: Mike Edles; Phone: 949-824-6960; E-mail: medles@uci.edu.
Track and Field: Vince O'Boyle; Phone: 949-824-6080; E-mail: vboboyle@uci.edu.
Volleyball: Charlie Brande; Phone: 949-824-6682; E-mail: wcbrande@uci.edu.

UNIVERSITY OF CALIFORNIA, LOS ANGELES

Los Angeles, California

Bruins ◆ NCAA I ◆ Pacific-10 Conference ◆ http://www.ucla.edu/

State-supported university, founded 1919, part of University of California System
Coed, 25,715 undergraduate students, 96% full-time, 56% women, 44% men
Urban 419-acre campus
Very difficult entrance level, 2% of applicants were admitted

Freshmen *Admission:* 44,994 applied, 10,581 were accepted, 4,268 enrolled. *Test scores:* SAT verbal scores over 500: 89%; SAT math scores over 500: 95%; SAT verbal scores over 600: 63%; SAT math scores over 600: 76%; SAT verbal scores over 700: 20%; SAT math scores over 700: 39%.
Tuition and fees (2003–04): $5820 (resident), $20,030 (nonresident). *Room and board:* $10,452.
Financial Aid (All incoming freshmen): *Average need-based gift aid:* $10,014. *Average non-need based aid:* $3711. *Average aid to full-time undergraduates:* $12,842.
Athletic Department: *Director of Athletics:* Dan Guerrero; Phone: 310-206-6382; Fax: 310-794-2143; E-mail: dguerrero@athletics.ucla.edu. *Sports Information Director:* Marc Dellins; Phone: 310-206-8194; E-mail: mdellins@athletics.ucla.edu.

MEN'S COACHES

Baseball: Gary Adams; Phone: 310-206-8210; E-mail: gadams@athletics.ucla.edu.
Basketball: Ben Howland; Phone: 310-206-6276; E-mail: bhowland@athletics.ucla.edu.
Cheerleading: Mollie Vehling; Phone: 310-206-8210; E-mail: mvehling@saonet.ucla.edu.
Cross Country: Eric Peterson; Phone: 310-206-8497; E-mail: ericp@athletics.ucla.edu.
Football: Karl Dorrell; Phone: 310-206-6290; E-mail: kdorrell@athletics.ucla.edu.
Golf: O.D. Vincent; Phone: 310-206-6588; E-mail: ovincent@athletics.ucla.edu.
Soccer: Tom Fitzgerald; Phone: 310-206-1777; E-mail: tfitzgerald@athletics.ucla.edu.
Tennis: Billy Martin; Phone: 310-206-6375; E-mail: bmartin@athletics.ucla.edu.
Track and Field: Art Venegas; Phone: 310-206-6690; E-mail: avenegas@athletics.ucla.edu.
Volleyball: Al Scates; Phone: 310-206-5683; E-mail: ascates@athletics.ucla.edu.

WOMEN'S COACHES

Basketball: Kathy Olivier; Phone: 310-206-6350; E-mail: kolivier@athletics.ucla.edu.
Cheerleading: Mollie Vehling; Phone: 310-206-8210; E-mail: mvehling@saonet.ucla.edu.
Cross Country: Eric Peterson; Phone: 310-206-8497; E-mail: ericp@athletics.ucla.edu.
Diving: Tom Stebbins; Phone: 310-825-9536; E-mail: bruindiver@uclaswimanddive.com.
Golf: Carrie Leary; Phone: 310-206-6799; E-mail: cleary@athletics.ucla.edu.
Gymnastics: Valorie Kondos; Phone: 310-206-6420; E-mail: vkondos@athletics.ucla.edu.
Soccer: Jillian Ellis; Phone: 310-206-2377; E-mail: jellis@athletics.ucla.edu.
Softball: Sue Enquist; Phone: 310-206-6779; E-mail: senquist@athletics.ucla.edu.
Swimming: Cyndi Gallagher; Phone: 310-206-6784; E-mail: cgallagher@athletics.ucla.edu.
Tennis: Stella Sampras; Phone: 310-206-6787; E-mail: ssampras@athletics.ucla.edu.
Track and Field: Jeanette Bolden; Phone: 310-206-6769; E-mail: jbolden@athletics.ucla.edu.
Volleyball: Andy Banachowski; Phone: 310-206-6839; E-mail: andyb@athletics.ucla.edu.

UNIVERSITY OF CALIFORNIA, RIVERSIDE

Riverside, California

Highlanders ◆ NCAA I ◆ Big West Conference ◆ http://www.ucr.edu/

State-supported university, founded 1954, part of University of California System
Coed, 15,282 undergraduate students, 97% full-time, 54% women, 46% men
Urban 1,200-acre campus with easy access to Los Angeles
Very difficult entrance level, 8% of applicants were admitted

Freshmen *Admission:* 20,060 applied, 15,862 were accepted, 3,889 enrolled. *Test scores:* SAT verbal scores over 500: 55%; SAT math scores over 500: 72%; SAT verbal scores over 600: 16%; SAT math scores over 600: 33%; SAT verbal scores over 700: 2%; SAT math scores over 700: 6%.
Tuition and fees (2003–04): $5950 (resident), $19,681 (nonresident). *Room and board:* $9350.
Financial Aid (All incoming freshmen): *Average need-based gift aid:* $8536. *Average non-need based aid:* $3593. *Average aid to full-time undergraduates:* $11,429.
Athletic Department: *Director of Athletics:* Stan Morrison; Phone: 909—787-5432; Fax: 909—787-5889; E-mail: stan.morrison@ucr.edu. *Sports Information Director:* Ross French; Phone: 909—787-5438; E-mail: ross.french@ucr.edu.

MEN'S COACHES

Baseball: Jack Smitheran; Phone: 909-787-5441; E-mail: jack.smitheran@ucr.edu.
Basketball: John Masi; Phone: 909-787-5496; E-mail: john.masi@ucr.edu.
Cheerleading: Tim Black; Phone: 909-784-9496; E-mail: flip4tim@yahoo.com.
Cross Country: Irv Ray; Phone: 909-787-5207; E-mail: irv.ray@ucr.edu.
Golf: Paul Hjulberg; Phone: 909-787-2120; E-mail: paul.hjulberg@ucr.edu.
Soccer: Nate Gonzalez; Phone: 909-787-5022; E-mail: nat.gonzalez@ucr.edu.
Tennis: York Strother; Phone: 909-787-2669; E-mail: york.strother@ucr.edu.
Track and Field: Irv Ray; Phone: 909-787-5207; E-mail: irv.ray@ucr.edu.

WOMEN'S COACHES

Basketball: Jennifer Young; Phone: 909-787-3811; E-mail: jennifer.young@ucr.edu.
Cheerleading: Tim Black; Phone: 909-784-9496; E-mail: flip4tim@yahoo.com.
Cross Country: Irv Ray; Phone: 909-787-5207; E-mail: irv.ray@ucr.edu.
Golf: Paul Hjulberg; Phone: 909-787-2120; E-mail: paul.hjulberg@ucr.edu.
Soccer: Veronica O'Brien; Phone: 909-787-2575; E-mail: veronica.obrien@ucr.edu.
Softball: Connie Miner; Phone: 909-787-2218; E-mail: connie.miner@ucr.edu.
Tennis: Mark Henry; Phone: 909-787-4758; E-mail: mark.henry@ucr.edu.
Track and Field: Irv Ray; Phone: 909-787-5207; E-mail: irv.ray@ucr.edu.
Volleyball: Sue Gozawsky; Phone: 909-787-5439; E-mail: sue.gozansky@ucr.edu.

UNIVERSITY OF CALIFORNIA, SAN DIEGO

La Jolla, California

Tritons ◆ NCAA II ◆ California Collegiate Athletic Conference ◆ http://www.ucsd.edu/

State-supported university, founded 1959, part of University of California System
Coed, 19,872 undergraduate students, 100% full-time, 52% women, 48% men
Suburban 1,976-acre campus with easy access to San Diego
Very difficult entrance level, 36% of applicants were admitted

Freshmen *Admission:* 43,438 applied, 18,118 were accepted, 3,799 enrolled. *Test scores:* SAT verbal scores over 500: 89%; SAT math scores over 500: 96%; SAT verbal scores over 600: 56%; SAT math scores over 600: 77%; SAT verbal scores over 700: 13%; SAT math scores over 700: 30%.
Tuition and fees (2003–04): $5507 (resident), $19,237 (nonresident). *Room and board:* $8620.
Financial Aid (All incoming freshmen): *Average need-based gift aid:* $8495. *Average non-need based aid:* $7588. *Average aid to full-time undergraduates:* $12,468.
Athletic Department: *Director of Athletics:* Earl Edwards; Phone: 858-534-4211; Fax: 858-534-8475; E-mail: ewedwards@ucsd.edu. *Sports Information Director:* Doga Gur; Phone: 858-534-8451; E-mail: dgur@ucsd.edu.

MEN'S COACHES

Baseball: Dan O'Brien; Phone: 858-534-8162; E-mail: dobrien@ucsd.edu.
Basketball: Greg Lanthier; Phone: 858-534-8453; E-mail: hoops@ucsd.edu.
Cheerleading: Irazmi Perez; Phone: 858-822-3324; E-mail: cheer@ucsd.edu.
Cross Country: Ted Van Ardsdale; Phone: 858-534-0328; E-mail: tvanarsdale@ucsd.edu.
Diving: Jessica Pilger; Phone: 858-534-8462.
Golf: Mike Wydra; Phone: 858-534-4211; E-mail: mtwydra2@aol.com.
Soccer: Derek Armstrong; Phone: 858-534-8165; E-mail: darmstrong@ucsd.edu.
Swimming: Scott McGihon; Phone: 858-534-8462; E-mail: smcgihon@ucsd.edu.
Tennis: Eric Steidlmayer; Phone: 858-534-8457; E-mail: esteidlm@ucsd.edu.
Track and Field: Tony Salerno; Phone: 858-534-2833; E-mail: asalerno@ucsd.edu.
Volleyball: Ron Larsen; Phone: 858-534-8458; E-mail: mvball@ucsd.edu.

WOMEN'S COACHES

Basketball: Judy Malone; Phone: 858-534-8441; E-mail: jmalone@ucsd.edu.
Cheerleading: Irazmi Perez; Phone: 858-822-3324; E-mail: cheer@ucsd.edu.
Cross Country: Ted Van Ardsdale; Phone: 858-534-0328; E-mail: tvanarsdale@ucsd.edu.
Diving: Jessica Pilger; Phone: 858-534-8462.
Soccer: Brian McManus; Phone: 858-534-8456; E-mail: bmmcmanus@ucsd.edu.
Softball: Patti Gerckens; Phone: 858-534-8442; E-mail: pgerckens@ucsd.edu.
Swimming: Scott McGihon; Phone: 858-534-8462; E-mail: smcgihon@ucsd.edu.
Tennis: Liz LaPlante; Phone: 858-534-8455; E-mail: liztens@aol.com.
Track and Field: Tony Salerno; Phone: 858-534-2833; E-mail: asalerno@ucsd.edu.
Volleyball: Duncan McFarland; Phone: 858-534-8443; E-mail: dmcfarland@ucsd.edu.

UNIVERSITY OF CALIFORNIA, SANTA BARBARA

Santa Barbara, California

Gauchos ◆ NCAA I ◆ Big West Conference
◆ http://www.ucsb.edu/

State-supported university, founded 1909, part of University of California System
Coed, 17,844 undergraduate students, 96% full-time, 55% women, 45% men
Suburban 989-acre campus
Very difficult entrance level, 47% of applicants were admitted

Freshmen *Admission:* 37,599 applied, 18,780 were accepted, 3,993 enrolled. *Test scores:* SAT verbal scores over 500: 85%; SAT math scores over 500: 90%; SAT verbal scores over 600: 45%; SAT math scores over 600: 57%; SAT verbal scores over 700: 8%; SAT math scores over 700: 12%.
Tuition and fees (2003–04): $5639 (resident), $19,370 (nonresident). *Room and board:* $9236 (room only: $6849).
Financial Aid (All incoming freshmen): *Average need-based gift aid:* $7009. *Average non-need based aid:* $3890. *Average aid to full-time undergraduates:* $10,235.
Athletic Department: *Director of Athletics:* Gary Cunningham; Phone: 805-893-3400; Fax: 805-893-8640; E-mail: gary.cunningham@athletics.ucsb.edu. *Sports Information Director:* Bill Mahoney; Phone: 805-893-3428; E-mail: bill.mahoney@athletics.ucsb.edu.

MEN'S COACHES

Baseball: Bob Brontsema; Phone: 858-534-3690; E-mail: bob.brontsema@athletics.ucsb.edu.
Basketball: Bob Williams; Phone: 858-534-2141; E-mail: robert.williams@athletics.ucsb.edu.
Cheerleading: Brandon Parish; Phone: 858-534-3291; E-mail: sbgr8one@aol.com.
Cross Country: Pete Dolan; Phone: 858-893-8276; E-mail: pete.dolan@athletics.ucsb.edu.
Diving: Gregg Wilson; Phone: 858-534-2989; E-mail: gregg.wilson@athletics.ucsb.edu.
Golf: Steve Lass; Phone: 858-534-4587; E-mail: steve.lass@athletics.ucsb.edu.
Soccer: Tim Vom Steeg; Phone: 858-534-3473; E-mail: menssoccer@athletics.ucsb.edu.
Swimming: Gregg Wilson; Phone: 858-534-2989; E-mail: gregg.wilson@athletics.ucsb.edu.
Tennis: Marty Davis; Phone: 858-534-3956; E-mail: marty.davis@athletics.ucsb.edu.
Track and Field: Pete Dolan; Phone: 858-893-8276; E-mail: pete.dolan@athletics.ucsb.edu.
Volleyball: Ken Preston; Phone: 858-893-2200; E-mail: ken.preston@athletics.ucsb.edu.

WOMEN'S COACHES

Basketball: Mark French; Phone: 858-534-7875; E-mail: mark.french@athletics.ucsb.edu.
Cheerleading: Brandon Parish; Phone: 858-534-3291; E-mail: sbgr8one@aol.com.
Cross Country: Pete Dolan; Phone: 858-893-8276; E-mail: pete.dolan@athletics.ucsb.edu.
Diving: Gregg Wilson; Phone: 858-534-2989; E-mail: gregg.wilson@athletics.ucsb.edu.
Soccer: Paul Stumpf; Phone: 858-534-2715; E-mail: paul.stumpf@athletics.ucsb.edu.
Softball: Kristy Schroeder; Phone: 858-534-3335; E-mail: kristy.schroeder@athletics.ucsb.edu.
Swimming: Gregg Wilson; Phone: 858-534-2989; E-mail: gregg.wilson@athletics.ucsb.edu.
Tennis: Pete Kirkwood; Phone: 858-534-3747; E-mail: peter.kirkwood@athletics.ucsb.edu.
Track and Field: Pete Dolan; Phone: 858-893-8276; E-mail: pete.dolan@athletics.ucsb.edu.
Volleyball: Kathy Gregory; Phone: 858-534-4881; E-mail: kathy.gregory@athletics.ucsb.edu.

UNIVERSITY OF CALIFORNIA, SANTA CRUZ

Santa Cruz, California

Banana Slugs ◆ NCAA III ◆ Independent
◆ http://www.ucsc.edu/

State-supported university, founded 1965, part of University of California System
Coed, 13,660 undergraduate students, 95% full-time, 55% women, 45% men
Small-town 2,000-acre campus with easy access to San Francisco and San Jose
Very difficult entrance level, 8% of applicants were admitted

Freshmen *Admission:* 21,525 applied, 17,284 were accepted, 3,434 enrolled. *Test scores:* SAT verbal scores over 500: 80%; SAT math scores over 500: 84%; SAT verbal scores over 600: 40%; SAT math scores over 600: 42%; SAT verbal scores over 700: 8%; SAT math scores over 700: 6%.
Tuition and fees (2003–04): $4629 (resident), $22,738 (nonresident). *Room and board:* $10,314.
Financial Aid (All incoming freshmen): *Average need-based gift aid:* $8483. *Average non-need based aid:* $6233. *Average aid to full-time undergraduates:* $12,642.
Athletic Department: *Director of Athletics:* Greg Harshaw; Phone: 831-459-2531; Fax: 831-459-4070; E-mail: harshaw@ucsc.edu. *Sports Information Director:* Adam Boothe; Phone: 831-459-5574; E-mail: aboothe@ucsc.edu.

MEN'S COACHES

Basketball: Gordon Johnson; Phone: 831-459-4532; E-mail: gdjohnso@ucsc.edu.
Diving: Joan Pegoda; Phone: 831-459-3372; E-mail: joaninjesus@aol.com.
Soccer: Paul Holocher; Phone: 831-459-3211; E-mail: holocher@ucsc.edu.
Swimming: Kim Musch; Phone: 831-459-3372; E-mail: kmusch@cats.ucsc.edu.
Tennis: Bob Hansen; Phone: 831-459-4694; E-mail: bwhansen@ucsc.edu.
Volleyball: Jay Hosack; Phone: 831-459-5982; E-mail: jhosack@ucsc.edu.

WOMEN'S COACHES

Basketball: Steve Spencer; Phone: 831-459-4962; E-mail: spencah@hotmail.com.
Cross Country: Adam Boothe; Phone: 831-459-5574; E-mail: aboothe@ucsc.edu.
Diving: Joan Pegoda; Phone: 831-459-3372; E-mail: joaninjesus@aol.com.
Golf: Paulette Pera; Phone: 831-459-2531; E-mail: cruzgolf@earthlink.net.
Soccer: Mike Runeare; Phone: 831-459-3362; E-mail: wmsoccer@ucsc.edu.
Swimming: Kim Musch; Phone: 831-459-3372; E-mail: kmusch@cats.ucsc.edu.
Tennis: Dave Muldawer; Phone: 831-459-4537; E-mail: muldawer@ucsc.edu.
Volleyball: Jay Hosack; Phone: 831-459-5982; E-mail: jhosack@ucsc.edu.

UNIVERSITY OF CENTRAL ARKANSAS

Conway, Arkansas

(W)Bears, (W) Sugar Bears ◆ NCAA II ◆ Gulf South Conference ◆ http://www.uca.edu/

State-supported comprehensive, founded 1907
Coed, 8,580 undergraduate students, 94% full-time, 60% women, 40% men
Small-town 365-acre campus
Moderately difficult entrance level, 72% of applicants were admitted

Freshmen *Admission:* 5,655 applied, 3,979 were accepted, 2,428 enrolled.

Tuition and fees (2003–04): $4505 (resident), $7817 (nonresident). *Room and board:* $3786 (room only: $2112).
Athletic Department: *Director of Athletics:* Vance Strange; Phone: 501-450-3150; Fax: 501-450-3151; E-mail: vances@mail.uca.edu. *Sports Information Director:* Steve East; Phone: 501-450-5743; E-mail: seast@mail.uca.edu.

MEN'S COACHES

Baseball: Doug Clark; Phone: 501-450-3407; E-mail: dclark@mail.uca.edu.
Basketball: Rand Chappell; Phone: 501-450-5867; E-mail: chappell@mail.uca.edu.
Cheerleading: Ashley Childers; Phone: 501-329-4646.
Football: Clint Conque; Phone: 501-450-3153; E-mail: cconque@mail.uca.edu.
Golf: Ryke Dismuke; Phone: 501-450-3638; E-mail: ryked@mail.uca.edu.
Soccer: Chad Flanders; Phone: 870-328-0279; E-mail: flanders@ucasoccer.com.

WOMEN'S COACHES

Basketball: Ron Marvel; Phone: 501-450-3157; E-mail: ronm@mail.uca.edu.
Cheerleading: Ashley Childers; Phone: 501-329-4646.
Cross Country: Richard Martin; Phone: 501-450-5786; E-mail: richardm@mail.uca.edu.
Golf: Ryke Dismuke; Phone: 501-450-3638; E-mail: ryked@mail.uca.edu.
Soccer: Tina Conley; Phone: 501-450-0801; E-mail: tinasoccer@ucasoccer.com.
Softball: Natalie Shock; Phone: 501-450-5797; E-mail: natalies@mail.uca.edu.
Tennis: Cendey Roberts; Phone: 501-450-3141; E-mail: cendey@conwaycorp.net.
Volleyball: Kris Peterson; Phone: 501-450-3154; E-mail: krisp@mail.uca.edu.

UNIVERSITY OF CENTRAL FLORIDA
Orlando, Florida

Golden Knights ◆ NCAA I ◆ Atlantic Sun Conference; Mid-American Conference ◆ http://www.ucf.edu/

State-supported university, founded 1963, part of State University System of Florida
Coed, 34,170 undergraduate students, 75% full-time, 55% women, 45% men
Suburban 1,415-acre campus
Moderately difficult entrance level, 6% of applicants were admitted

Freshmen *Admission:* 20,533 applied, 12,289 were accepted, 5,965 enrolled. *Test scores:* SAT verbal scores over 500: 84%; SAT math scores over 500: 87%; SAT verbal scores over 600: 32%; SAT math scores over 600: 38%; SAT verbal scores over 700: 4%; SAT math scores over 700: 5%.
Tuition and fees (2003–04): $3013 (resident), $14,041 (nonresident). *Room and board:* $7026 (room only: $4200).
Financial Aid (All incoming freshmen): *Average need-based gift aid:* $3543. *Average non-need based aid:* $1885. *Average aid to full-time undergraduates:* $4642.
Athletic Department: *Director of Athletics:* Steve Orsini; Phone: 407-823-2261; Fax: 407-823-5293; E-mail: sorsini@mail.ucf.edu. *Sports Information Director:* John Marini; Phone: 407-823-2729; E-mail: jmarini@mail.ucf.edu.

MEN'S COACHES

Baseball: Jay Bergman; Phone: 407-823-0140; E-mail: jbergman@mail.ucf.edu.
Basketball: Kirk Speraw; Phone: 407-823-5805; E-mail: ksperaw@mail.ucf.edu.
Cheerleading: Linda Gooch; Phone: 407-823-2143; E-mail: lgooch@mail.ucf.edu.
Cross Country: Marcia Wentworth; Phone: 407-823-0096; E-mail: mmansur@mail.ucf.edu.
Football: George O'Leary; Phone: 407-823-2342; E-mail: football@mail.ucf.edu.
Golf: Nick Clinard; Phone: 407-823-1465; E-mail: nclinard@mail.ucf.edu.
Soccer: Bob Winch; Phone: 407-823-2262; E-mail: rwinch@mail.ucf.edu.
Tennis: Bobby Cashman; Phone: 407-823-2257; E-mail: bcashman@mail.ucf.edu.

WOMEN'S COACHES

Basketball: Gail Striegler; Phone: 407-823-5802; E-mail: gstriegl@mail.ucf.edu.
Cheerleading: Linda Gooch; Phone: 407-823-2143; E-mail: lgooch@mail.ucf.edu.
Cross Country: Marcia Wentworth; Phone: 407-823-0096; E-mail: mmansur@mail.ucf.edu.
Golf: Jill Fjelstul; Phone: 407-823-6448; E-mail: jfjelstu@mail.ucf.edu.
Soccer: Amanda Cromwell; Phone: 407-823-6345; E-mail: acromwel@mail.ucf.edu.
Softball: Renee Gillispie; Phone: 407-823-6891; E-mail: rgillisp@mail.ucf.edu.
Tennis: Patricia Allison; Phone: 407-823-6563; E-mail: pallison@mail.ucf.edu.
Track and Field: Marcia Wentworth; Phone: 407-823-0096; E-mail: mmansur@mail.ucf.edu.
Volleyball: Meg Colado; Phone: 407-823-6229; E-mail: mfitzger@mail.ucf.edu.

UNIVERSITY OF CENTRAL OKLAHOMA
Edmond, Oklahoma

Bronchos ◆ NCAA II ◆ Lone Star Conference ◆ http://www.ucok.edu/

State-supported comprehensive, founded 1890, part of Oklahoma State Regents for Higher Education
Coed, 13,566 undergraduate students, 71% full-time, 58% women, 42% men
Suburban 200-acre campus with easy access to Oklahoma City
Minimally difficult entrance level, 84% of applicants were admitted

Freshmen *Admission:* 3,791 applied, 3,346 were accepted, 2,049 enrolled.
Tuition and fees (2003–04): $2649 (resident), $6549 (nonresident). *Room and board:* $3670.
Financial Aid (All incoming freshmen): *Average need-based gift aid:* $1300. *Average aid to full-time undergraduates:* $3350.
Athletic Department: *Director of Athletics:* Bill Farley; Phone: 405-974-2502; Fax: 405-974-3820; E-mail: bfarley@ucok.edu. *Sports Information Director:* Mike Kirk; Phone: 405-974-2142; E-mail: mkirk@ucok.edu.

MEN'S COACHES

Baseball: Wendell Simmons; Phone: 405-974-2506; E-mail: wsimmons@ucok.edu.
Basketball: Terry Evans; Phone: 405-974-2145; E-mail: tevans@ucok.edu.
Football: Chuck Langston; Phone: 405-974-2147; E-mail: clangston@ucok.edu.
Golf: Dax Johnston; Phone: 405-974-2139; E-mail: djohnston@ucok.edu.
Tennis: Francis Baxter; Phone: 405-974-2138; E-mail: fbaxter@ucok.edu.
Wrestling: David James; Phone: 405-974-2509; E-mail: djames@ucok.edu.

WOMEN'S COACHES

Basketball: John Keely; Phone: 405-974-2141; E-mail: jkeely@ucok.edu.
Cross Country: Tavia Briscoe; Phone: 405-974-2501.
Golf: Dax Johnston; Phone: 405-974-2139; E-mail: djohnston@ucok.edu.
Soccer: Mike Cook; Phone: 405-974-2136; E-mail: mcook@ucok.edu.
Softball: Genny Honea; Phone: 405-974-2144; E-mail: ghonea@ucok.edu.
Tennis: Francis Baxter; Phone: 405-974-2138; E-mail: fbaxter@ucok.edu.
Volleyball: Jeff Boyland; Phone: 405-974-2148; E-mail: jboyland1@ucok.edu.

UNIVERSITY OF CHARLESTON
Charleston, West Virginia

Golden Eagles ◆ NCAA II ◆ West Virginia Intercollegiate Athletic Conference ◆ http://www.ucwv.edu/

Independent comprehensive, founded 1888
Coed, 981 undergraduate students, 85% full-time, 63% women, 37% men
Urban 40-acre campus
Moderately difficult entrance level, 60% of applicants were admitted

Freshmen *Admission:* 1,160 applied, 725 were accepted, 205 enrolled. *Test scores:* SAT verbal scores over 500: 43%; SAT math scores over 500: 54%; SAT verbal scores over 600: 10%; SAT math scores over 600: 7%.
Tuition and fees (2004–05): $19,400 (full-time). *Room and board:* $7200.
Financial Aid (All incoming freshmen): *Average need-based gift aid:* $6850. *Average non-need based aid:* $5875. *Average aid to full-time undergraduates:* $16,800.

MEN'S COACHES
Baseball: Tom Nozica; Phone: 304-357-4820.
Basketball: Jayson Gee; Phone: 304-357-4831.
Cross Country: Jason Henley; Phone: 304-357-4819.
Golf: Mike Good; Phone: 304-357-4827.
Soccer: Marty Martinez; Phone: 304-357-4899.
Swimming: Kim Duff; Phone: 304-357-4826.
Tennis: Sean Murphy; Phone: 304-357-4816.
Track and Field: Jason Henley; Phone: 304-357-4819.

WOMEN'S COACHES
Basketball: Sherry Winn; Phone: 304-357-4821.
Cross Country: Bruce Cox; Phone: 304-357-4819.
Soccer: Todd Diuguid; Phone: 304-357-4827.
Softball: Karen Pauley; Phone: 304-357-4976.
Swimming: Kim Duff; Phone: 304-357-4826.
Tennis: Shari Reed; Phone: 304-357-4816.
Track and Field: Bruce Cox; Phone: 304-357-4819.
Volleyball: Bren Stevens; Phone: 304-357-4911.

UNIVERSITY OF CHICAGO
Chicago, Illinois

Maroons ◆ NCAA III ◆ University Athletic Conference ◆ http://www.uchicago.edu/

Independent university, founded 1891
Coed, 4,355 undergraduate students, 98% full-time, 51% women, 49% men
Urban 211-acre campus
Most difficult entrance level, 39% of applicants were admitted

Freshmen *Admission:* 9,100 applied, 3,605 were accepted, 1,155 enrolled. *Test scores:* SAT verbal scores over 500: 99%; SAT math scores over 500: 99%; SAT verbal scores over 600: 90%; SAT math scores over 600: 91%; SAT verbal scores over 700: 57%; SAT math scores over 700: 53%.
Tuition and fees (2003–04): $29,238 (full-time). *Room and board:* $9315.
Athletic Department: *Director of Athletics:* Tom Weingartner; Phone: 773-702-7684; Fax: 773-702-6517; E-mail: tweingar@uchicago.edu. *Sports Information Director:* Dave Hilbert; Phone: 773-702-4638; E-mail: dhilbert@uchicago.edu.

MEN'S COACHES
Baseball: Brian Baldea; Phone: 773-702-4643; E-mail: bbaldea@uchicago.edu.
Basketball: Mike McGrath; Phone: 773-702-4647; E-mail: mmcgrath@uchicago.edu.
Cheerleading: Phone: 773-702-4643; E-mail: stephani@uchicago.edu.
Cross Country: Chris Hall; Phone: 773-702-4640; E-mail: hallc@uchicago.edu.
Football: Dick Maloney; Phone: 773-702-9035; E-mail: rmaloney@uchicago.edu.
Soccer: John O'Connor; Phone: 773-702-4660; E-mail: joconnor@uchicago.edu.
Swimming: George Villarreal; Phone: 773-702-4657; E-mail: scain1@uchicago.edu.
Tennis: Marty Perry; Phone: 773-702-4656; E-mail: scain1@uchicago.edu.
Track and Field: Chris Hall; Phone: 773-702-4640; E-mail: hallc@uchicago.edu.
Wrestling: Leo Kocher; Phone: 773-702-4641; E-mail: lkocher@uchicago.edu.

WOMEN'S COACHES
Basketball: Jennifer Kroll; Phone: 773-702-4639; E-mail: jkroll@uchicago.edu.
Cheerleading: Phone: 773-702-4643; E-mail: stephani@uchicago.edu.
Cross Country: Chris Hall; Phone: 773-702-4640; E-mail: hallc@uchicago.edu.
Soccer: Amy Reifert; Phone: 773-702-4655; E-mail: areifert@uchicago.edu.
Softball: Ruth Kmak; Phone: 773-702-4642; E-mail: ruthkmak@uchicago.edu.
Swimming: Sheila O'Connor; Phone: 773-702-4657; E-mail: scain1@uchicago.edu.
Tennis: Marty Perry; Phone: 773-702-4656; E-mail: scain1@uchicago.edu.
Track and Field: Chris Hall; Phone: 773-702-4640; E-mail: hallc@uchicago.edu.
Volleyball: Dorinda Von Tersh; Phone: 773-702-5145; E-mail: dvtersch@uchicago.edu.

UNIVERSITY OF CINCINNATI
Cincinnati, Ohio

Bearcats ◆ NCAA I ◆ Conference USA Conference ◆ http://www.uc.edu/

State-supported university, founded 1819, part of University of Cincinnati System
Coed, 19,159 undergraduate students, 82% full-time, 48% women, 52% men
Urban 137-acre campus
Moderately difficult entrance level, 91% of applicants were admitted

Freshmen *Admission:* 10,958 applied, 9,673 were accepted, 3,820 enrolled. *Test scores:* SAT verbal scores over 500: 63%; SAT math scores over 500: 65%; SAT verbal scores over 600: 24%; SAT math scores over 600: 30%; SAT verbal scores over 700: 3%; SAT math scores over 700: 5%.
Tuition and fees (2003–04): $7623 (resident), $19,230 (nonresident). *Room and board:* $7113.
Financial Aid (All incoming freshmen): *Average need-based gift aid:* $3175. *Average non-need based aid:* $4387. *Average aid to full-time undergraduates:* $7003.
Athletic Department: *Director of Athletics:* Bob Goin; Phone: 513-556-4603; Fax: 513-556-2209. *Sports Information Director:* Tom Hathaway; Phone: 513-556-0616; E-mail: tom.hathaway@uc.edu.

MEN'S COACHES
Baseball: Brian Cleary; Phone: 513-556-1577; E-mail: brian.cleary@uc.edu.
Basketball: Bob Huggins; Phone: 513-556-5847.
Cheerleading: Tabby Fagin; Phone: 513-556-3463; E-mail: uccheerleading@yahoo.com.
Cross Country: Bill Schnier; Phone: 513-556-0562; E-mail: bill.schnier@uc.edu.
Diving: Monty Hopkins; Phone: 513-556-0564; E-mail: monty.hopkins@uc.edu.
Football: Mark Dantonio; Phone: 513-556-5986; E-mail: john.widecan@uc.edu.
Golf: Kerry Sahms; Phone: 513-556-0829; E-mail: ksahms@cinci.rr.com.
Soccer: Hylton Dayes; Phone: 513-556-0568; E-mail: hylton.dayes@uc.edu.
Swimming: Monty Hopkins; Phone: 513-556-0564; E-mail: monty.hopkins@uc.edu.
Track and Field: Bill Schnier; Phone: 513-556-0562; E-mail: bill.schnier@uc.edu.

WOMEN'S COACHES
Basketball: Laurie Pirtle; Phone: 513-556-2255; E-mail: laurie.pirtle@uc.edu.
Cheerleading: Tabby Fagin; Phone: 513-556-3463; E-mail: uccheerleading@yahoo.com.

Cross Country: Bill Schnier; Phone: 513-556-0562; E-mail: bill.schnier@uc.edu.

Diving: Monty Hopkins; Phone: 513-556-0564; E-mail: monty.hopkins@uc.edu.

Golf: Kerry Sahms; Phone: 513-556-0829; E-mail: ksahms@cinci.rr.com.

Soccer: Meridy Glenn; Phone: 513-556-0567; E-mail: meridy.glenn@uc.edu.

Swimming: Monty Hopkins; Phone: 513-556-0564; E-mail: monty.hopkins@uc.edu.

Tennis: Kimberly Jones; Phone: 513-556-0845; E-mail: kimberly.jones@uc.edu.

Track and Field: Jim Schnur; Phone: 513-556-0563; E-mail: jim.schnur@uc.edu.

Volleyball: Reed Sunahara; Phone: 513-556-2877; E-mail: reed.sunahara@uc.edu.

UNIVERSITY OF COLORADO AT BOULDER
Boulder, Colorado

Buffaloes ◆ NCAA I ◆ Big 12 Conference
◆ http://www.colorado.edu/

State-supported university, founded 1876, part of University of Colorado System
Coed, 26,186 undergraduate students, 91% full-time, 47% women, 53% men
Suburban 600-acre campus with easy access to Denver
Moderately difficult entrance level, 8% of applicants were admitted

Freshmen *Admission:* 20,920 applied, 16,790 were accepted, 5,630 enrolled. *Test scores:* SAT verbal scores over 500: 89%; SAT math scores over 500: 91%; SAT verbal scores over 600: 41%; SAT math scores over 600: 51%; SAT verbal scores over 700: 6%; SAT math scores over 700: 9%.
Tuition and fees (2003–04): $4020 (resident), $20,336 (nonresident). *Room and board:* $6754.
Financial Aid (All incoming freshmen): *Average need-based gift aid:* $4336. *Average non-need based aid:* $3876. *Average aid to full-time undergraduates:* $8563.

MEN'S COACHES
Basketball: Ricardo Patton; Phone: 303-492-6877; E-mail: cumbball@colorado.edu.
Cross Country: Mark Wetmore; Phone: 303-492-5227; E-mail: mark.wetmore@colorado.edu.
Football: Gary Barnett; Phone: 303-492-5330; E-mail: cufb@colorado.edu.
Golf: Mark Simpson; Phone: 303-492-4653; E-mail: m.simpson@colorado.edu.
Tennis: Sam Winterbotham; Phone: 303-492-5885; E-mail: sam.winterbotham@colorado.edu.
Track and Field: Mark Wetmore; Phone: 303-492-5227; E-mail: mark.wetmore@colorado.edu.

WOMEN'S COACHES
Basketball: Ceal Barry; Phone: 303-492-6086; E-mail: ceal.barry@colorado.edu.
Cross Country: Mark Wetmore; Phone: 303-492-5227; E-mail: mark.wetmore@colorado.edu.
Golf: Anne Kelley; Phone: 303-492-5885; E-mail: anne.kelly@colorado.edu.
Soccer: Bill Hempen; Phone: 303-492-0632; E-mail: bill.hempen@colorado.edu.
Tennis: Nicole Kenneally; Phone: 303-492-5885; E-mail: nicole.kenneally@colorado.edu.
Track and Field: Mark Wetmore; Phone: 303-492-5227; E-mail: mark.wetmore@colorado.edu.
Volleyball: Pi'i Aiu; Phone: 303-492-5227; E-mail: piimauna.aiu@colorado.edu.

UNIVERSITY OF COLORADO AT COLORADO SPRINGS
Colorado Springs, Colorado

Mountain Lions ◆ NCAA II ◆ Rocky Mountain Athletic Conference ◆ http://www.uccs.edu/

State-supported comprehensive, founded 1965
Coed, 5,875 undergraduate students, 78% full-time, 62% women, 38% men
Suburban 400-acre campus with easy access to Denver
Moderately difficult entrance level, 74% of applicants were admitted

Freshmen *Admission:* 2,551 applied, 1,886 were accepted, 690 enrolled. *Test scores:* SAT verbal scores over 500: 71%; SAT math scores over 500: 72%; SAT verbal scores over 600: 24%; SAT math scores over 600: 31%; SAT verbal scores over 700: 5%; SAT math scores over 700: 3%.
Tuition and fees (2003–04): $5156 (resident), $19,988 (nonresident). *Room and board:* $6729.
Financial Aid (All incoming freshmen): *Average need-based gift aid:* $3538. *Average non-need based aid:* $1776. *Average aid to full-time undergraduates:* $5157.
Athletic Department: *Director of Athletics:* Randy Cubero; Phone: 719-262-3075; Fax: 719-262-3131; E-mail: rcubero@uccs.edu. *Sports Information Director:* Doug Fitzgerald; Phone: 719-262-3003; E-mail: dfitzger@uccs.edu.

MEN'S COACHES
Basketball: Marty Fletcher; Phone: 719-262-3680; E-mail: mfletch2@uccs.edu.
Cheerleading: Stephanie Morran; Phone: 719-262-3000; E-mail: cheer@uccs.edu.
Cross Country: Graeme Badger; Phone: 719-262-3005; E-mail: coachbadger@msn.com.
Golf: Phil Trujillo; Phone: 719-633-1355; E-mail: ptrujill@uccs.edu.
Soccer: Flavio Mazzetti; Phone: 719-262-3448; E-mail: fmazzett@uccs.edu.
Tennis: Sarah Cartwright; Phone: 719-262-3057; E-mail: scart20@yahoo.com.
Track and Field: Graeme Badger; Phone: 719-262-3005; E-mail: coachbadger@msn.com.

WOMEN'S COACHES
Basketball: Marty Fletcher; Phone: 719-262-3602; E-mail: mfletch2@uccs.edu.
Cheerleading: Stephanie Morran; Phone: 719-262-3000; E-mail: cheer@uccs.edu.
Cross Country: Graeme Badger; Phone: 719-262-3005; E-mail: coachbadger@msn.com.
Softball: Scott Peterson; Phone: 719-262-3006; E-mail: speters4@uccs.edu.
Tennis: Sarah Cartwright; Phone: 719-262-3601; E-mail: scart20@yahoo.com.
Track and Field: Graeme Badger; Phone: 719-262-3005; E-mail: coachbadger@msn.com.
Volleyball: Tara Miller; Phone: 719-262-3679; E-mail: tmiller4@uccs.edu.

UNIVERSITY OF CONNECTICUT
Storrs, Connecticut

Huskies ◆ NCAA I ◆ Atlantic Hockey Conference; Big East Conference ◆ http://www.uconn.edu/

State-supported university, founded 1881
Coed, 15,184 undergraduate students, 94% full-time, 52% women, 48% men
Rural 4,104-acre campus
Moderately difficult entrance level, 50% of applicants were admitted

Freshmen *Admission:* 17,666 applied, 9,287 were accepted, 3,208 enrolled. *Test scores:* SAT verbal scores over 500: 89%; SAT math scores over 500: 91%; SAT verbal scores over 600: 37%; SAT math scores over 600: 48%; SAT verbal scores over 700: 5%; SAT math scores over 700: 8%.

University of Connecticut *(continued)*

Tuition and fees (2004–05): $7308 (resident), $19,036 (nonresident). *Room and board:* $7300 (room only: $3872).
Financial Aid (All incoming freshmen): *Average need-based gift aid:* $5086. *Average non-need based aid:* $4572. *Average aid to full-time undergraduates:* $8142.
Athletic Department: *Director of Athletics:* Jeff Hathaway; Phone: 860-486-2725; Fax: 860-486-3300; E-mail: jeffrey.hathaway@uconn.edu. *Sports Information Director:* Mike Enright; Phone: 860-486-3531; E-mail: menright@athletics.ath.uconn.edu.

MEN'S COACHES

Baseball: Jim Penders; Phone: 860-486-4089; E-mail: baseball@athletics.ath.uconn.edu.
Basketball: Jim Calhoun; Phone: 860-486-2720.
Cheerleading: Neal Kearney; Phone: 860-951-3279; E-mail: n.kearney@snet.net.
Cross Country: Greg Roy; Phone: 860-486-2365; E-mail: mtrack@athletics.ath.uconn.edu.
Diving: John Bransfield; Phone: 860-486-3155; E-mail: jbransfield@athletics.ath.uconn.edu.
Football: Randy Edsall; Phone: 860-486-2718; E-mail: randy.edsall@uconn.edu.
Golf: Ron Dubois; Phone: 860-486-6058; E-mail: colonel@athletics.ath.uconn.edu.
Ice Hockey: Bruce Marshall; Phone: 860-486-3072; E-mail: bruce.marshall@uconn.edu.
Soccer: Ray Reid; Phone: 860-486-4231; E-mail: ray.reid@uconn.edu.
Swimming: Bob Goldberg; Phone: 860-486-3155; E-mail: ucswim@athletics.ath.uconn.edu.
Tennis: Glenn Marshall; Phone: 860-486-0766; E-mail: marshall@athletics.ath.uconn.edu.
Track and Field: Greg Roy; Phone: 860-486-2365; E-mail: mtrack@athletics.ath.uconn.edu.

WOMEN'S COACHES

Basketball: Geno Auriemma; Phone: 860-486-4756; E-mail: geno.auriemma@uconn.edu.
Cheerleading: Neal Kearney; Phone: 860-951-3279; E-mail: n.kearney@snet.net.
Cross Country: Bill Morgan; Phone: 860-486-4840; E-mail: morgan@athletics.ath.uconn.edu.
Diving: John Bransfield; Phone: 860-486-3155; E-mail: jbransfield@athletics.ath.uconn.edu.
Field Hockey: Nancy Stevens; Phone: 860-486-4162; E-mail: nancy@athletics.ath.uconn.edu.
Lacrosse: Bonnie Rosen; Phone: 860-486-0888; E-mail: brosen@athletics.ath.uconn.edu.
Soccer: Len Tsantiris; Phone: 860-486-4204; E-mail: wsoccer@athletics.ath.uconn.edu.
Softball: Karen Mullins; Phone: 860-486-5020; E-mail: karen.mullins@uconn.edu.
Swimming: Bob Goldberg; Phone: 860-486-3155; E-mail: ucswim@athletics.ath.uconn.edu.
Tennis: Glenn Marshall; Phone: 860-486-0766; E-mail: marshall@athletics.ath.uconn.edu.
Track and Field: Bill Morgan; Phone: 860-486-4840; E-mail: morgan@athletics.ath.uconn.edu.
Volleyball: Kelli Myers; Phone: 860-486-4486; E-mail: kmyers@athletics.ath.uconn.edu.

UNIVERSITY OF DALLAS
Irving, Texas

Crusaders ◆ NCAA III ◆ Independent ◆ http://www.udallas.edu/

Independent Roman Catholic university, founded 1955
Coed, 1,250 undergraduate students, 90% full-time, 56% women, 44% men
Suburban 750-acre campus with easy access to Dallas–Fort Worth
Moderately difficult entrance level, 89% of applicants were admitted

Freshmen *Admission:* 1,080 applied, 956 were accepted, 299 enrolled. *Test scores:* SAT verbal scores over 500: 89%; SAT math scores over 500: 85%; SAT verbal scores over 600: 53%; SAT math scores over 600: 47%; SAT verbal scores over 700: 18%; SAT math scores over 700: 7%.

Tuition and fees (2004–05): $19,162 (full-time). *Room and board:* $6736 (room only: $3200).
Financial Aid (All incoming freshmen): *Average need-based gift aid:* $11,426. *Average non-need based aid:* $8802. *Average aid to full-time undergraduates:* $14,004.
Athletic Department: *Director of Athletics:* Richard Strockbine; Phone: 972-721-5207; Fax: 972-721-5208; E-mail: dick@acad.udallas.edu. *Sports Information Director:* Anjie Coplin; Phone: 972-721-5009; E-mail: acoplin@udallas.edu.

MEN'S COACHES

Baseball: Sam Blackmon; Phone: 972-721-5117; E-mail: blackmon@udallas.edu.
Basketball: Brian Stanfield; Phone: 972-721-5028; E-mail: bstan@udallas.edu.
Cross Country: Brian Borski; Phone: 972-721-4101; E-mail: btborski@udallas.edu.
Golf: Brian Stanfield; Phone: 972-721-5028; E-mail: bstan@udallas.edu.
Soccer: David Hoffman; Phone: 972-721-4026; E-mail: hoffmann@udallas.edu.
Tennis: Chris Hill; Phone: 972-721-4036; E-mail: chill@udallas.edu.
Track and Field: Brian Borski; Phone: 972-721-4101; E-mail: btborski@udallas.edu.

WOMEN'S COACHES

Basketball: Chris Hill; Phone: 972-721-4036; E-mail: chill@udallas.edu.
Cross Country: Brian Borski; Phone: 972-721-4101; E-mail: btborski@udallas.edu.
Golf: Brian Stanfield; Phone: 972-721-5028; E-mail: bstan@udallas.edu.
Lacrosse: Stefani Papageorge Webb; Phone: 972-721-5188; E-mail: spwebb@udallas.edu.
Soccer: Stefani Papageorge Webb; Phone: 972-721-5188; E-mail: spwebb@udallas.edu.
Softball: Venera Flores; Phone: 972-721-4035; E-mail: vflores@udallas.edu.
Tennis: Chris Hill; Phone: 972-721-4036; E-mail: chill@udallas.edu.
Track and Field: Brian Borski; Phone: 972-721-4101; E-mail: btborski@udallas.edu.
Volleyball: Venera Flores; Phone: 972-721-4035; E-mail: vflores@udallas.edu.

UNIVERSITY OF DAYTON
Dayton, Ohio

Flyers ◆ NCAA I ◆ Atlantic 10 Conference; Colonial Athletic Conference; Pioneer Football League Conference ◆ http://www.udayton.edu/

Independent Roman Catholic university, founded 1850
Coed, 7,103 undergraduate students, 93% full-time, 50% women, 50% men
Suburban 110-acre campus with easy access to Cincinnati
Moderately difficult entrance level, 102% of applicants were admitted

Freshmen *Admission:* 7,052 applied, 6,821 were accepted, 1,858 enrolled. *Test scores:* SAT verbal scores over 500: 79%; SAT math scores over 500: 83%; SAT verbal scores over 600: 34%; SAT math scores over 600: 45%; SAT verbal scores over 700: 6%; SAT math scores over 700: 10%.
Tuition and fees (2004–05): $20,630 (full-time). *Room and board:* $6300 (room only: $2700).
Financial Aid (All incoming freshmen): *Average need-based gift aid:* $8691. *Average non-need based aid:* $3812. *Average aid to full-time undergraduates:* $13,418.
Athletic Department: *Director of Athletics:* Ted Kissell; Phone: 937-229-2165; Fax: 937-229-4461; E-mail: ted.kissell@notes.udayton.edu. *Sports Information Director:* Doug Hauschild; Phone: 937-229-4390; E-mail: sid@udayton.edu.

MEN'S COACHES

Baseball: Tony Vittorio; Phone: 937-229-4456; E-mail: tony.vittorio@notes.udayton.edu.
Basketball: Brian Gregory; Phone: 937-229-4421; E-mail: mens-basketball@udayton.edu.
Cheerleading: Hope Hemminger; Phone: 937-229-4877; E-mail: daytoncheer@yahoo.com.
Cross Country: Rich Davis; Phone: 937-229-4293; E-mail: richard.davis@notes.udayton.edu.

Football: Mike Kelly; Phone: 937-229-4423; E-mail: michael.kelly@notes.udayton.edu.
Golf: Brad Smith; Phone: 937-229-4271; E-mail: brad.smith@notes.udayton.edu.
Soccer: Dave Schureck; Phone: 937-229-2492; E-mail: david.schureck@notes.udayton.edu.
Tennis: Steve Brumbaugh; Phone: 937-229-4279; E-mail: steve.brumbaugh@notes.udayton.edu.

WOMEN'S COACHES

Basketball: Jim Jabir; Phone: 937-229-4447; E-mail: jim.jabir@notes.udayton.edu.
Cheerleading: Hope Hemminger; Phone: 937-229-4877; E-mail: daytoncheer@yahoo.com.
Cross Country: George Brose; Phone: 937-229-4124; E-mail: george.brose@notes.udayton.edu.
Golf: Brad Smith; Phone: 937-229-4271; E-mail: brad.smith@notes.udayton.edu.
Soccer: Mike Tucker; Phone: 937-229-4459; E-mail: michael.tucker@notes.udayton.edu.
Softball: Jody Eickemeyer; Phone: 937-229-4399; E-mail: jodi.eickemeyer@notes.udayton.edu.
Tennis: Mike Unger; Phone: 937-229-4279; E-mail: michael.unger@notes.udayton.edu.
Track and Field: D'Andre Hill; Phone: 937-229-4249; E-mail: d'andre.hill@notes.udayton.edu.
Volleyball: Tim Horsmon; Phone: 937-229-4428; E-mail: timothy.horsmon@notes.udayton.edu.

UNIVERSITY OF DELAWARE
Newark, Delaware

Blue Hens ◆ NCAA I ◆ Atlantic 10 Conference; Colonial Athletic Conference ◆ http://www.udel.edu/

State-related university, founded 1743
Coed, 17,200 undergraduate students, 86% full-time, 58% women, 42% men
Small-town 1,000-acre campus with easy access to Philadelphia and Baltimore
Moderately difficult entrance level, 4% of applicants were admitted

Freshmen *Admission:* 22,020 applied, 9,267 were accepted, 3,384 enrolled. *Test scores:* SAT verbal scores over 500: 88%; SAT math scores over 500: 91%; SAT verbal scores over 600: 42%; SAT math scores over 600: 54%; SAT verbal scores over 700: 6%; SAT math scores over 700: 9%.
Tuition and fees (2003–04): $6498 (resident), $16,028 (nonresident). *Room and board:* $6118 (room only: $3428).
Financial Aid (All incoming freshmen): *Average need-based gift aid:* $6000. *Average non-need based aid:* $3800. *Average aid to full-time undergraduates:* $9250.
Athletic Department: *Director of Athletics:* Edgar Johnson; Phone: 302-831-4006; Fax: 302-831-8653; E-mail: edgarj@udel.edu. *Sports Information Director:* Scott Selheimer; Phone: 302-831-2186; E-mail: selheime@udel.edu.

MEN'S COACHES

Baseball: Jim Sherman; Phone: 302-831-8596; E-mail: sherman@udel.edu.
Basketball: David Henderson; Phone: 302-831-2724; E-mail: davidh@udel.edu.
Cheerleading: Joe Mackley; Phone: 302-831-1581; E-mail: jmackley@udel.edu.
Cross Country: Jim Fischer; Phone: 302-831-8846; E-mail: jfischer@udel.edu.
Diving: Peter Metrinko; Phone: 302-831-3208; E-mail: pjmetrinko@hotmail.com.
Football: K.C. Keeler; Phone: 302-831-2253; E-mail: keeler@udel.edu.
Golf: Mike Keogh; Phone: 302-454-2151; E-mail: mkeogh@udel.edu.
Lacrosse: Bob Shillinglaw; Phone: 302-831-8661; E-mail: bobshil@udel.edu.
Soccer: Marc Samonisky; Phone: 302-831-8603; E-mail: marcsamo@udel.edu.
Swimming: John Hayman; Phone: 302-831-8604; E-mail: hayman@udel.edu.
Tennis: Laura Travis; Phone: 302-831-8651; E-mail: leroy@udel.edu.

Track and Field: Jim Fischer; Phone: 302-831-8846; E-mail: jfischer@udel.edu.

WOMEN'S COACHES

Basketball: Tina Martin; Phone: 302-831-8663; E-mail: tmartin@udel.edu.
Cheerleading: Joe Mackley; Phone: 302-831-1581; E-mail: jmackley@udel.edu.
Cross Country: Sue McGrath-Powell; Phone: 302-831-8738; E-mail: suemcpow@udel.edu.
Diving: Peter Metrinko; Phone: 302-831-3208; E-mail: pjmetrinko@hotmail.com.
Field Hockey: Carol Miller; Phone: 302-831-6721; E-mail: camiller@udel.edu.
Lacrosse: Denise Wescott; Phone: 302-831-4057; E-mail: dwescott@udel.edu.
Soccer: Scott Grzenda; Phone: 302-831-8915; E-mail: sag@udel.edu.
Softball: Bonnie Jill Ferguson; Phone: 302-831-8608; E-mail: bferguso@udel.edu.
Swimming: John Hayman; Phone: 302-831-8604; E-mail: hayman@udel.edu.
Tennis: Laura Travis; Phone: 302-831-8651; E-mail: leroy@udel.edu.
Track and Field: Sue McGrath-Powell; Phone: 302-831-8738; E-mail: suemcpow@udel.edu.
Volleyball: Bonnie Kelly; Phone: 302-831-8606; E-mail: bjkenny@udel.edu.

UNIVERSITY OF DENVER
Denver, Colorado

Pioneers ◆ NCAA I ◆ Great Western Lacrosse Conference; Independent; Mountain Pacific Sports Conference; Sun Belt Conference; Western Collegiate Hockey Conference ◆ http://www.du.edu/

Independent university, founded 1864
Coed, 4,456 undergraduate students, 89% full-time, 56% women, 44% men
Suburban 125-acre campus
Moderately difficult entrance level, 73% of applicants were admitted

Freshmen *Admission:* 4,334 applied, 3,405 were accepted, 1,031 enrolled. *Test scores:* SAT verbal scores over 500: 79%; SAT math scores over 500: 82%; SAT verbal scores over 600: 37%; SAT math scores over 600: 40%; SAT verbal scores over 700: 6%; SAT math scores over 700: 6%.
Tuition and fees (2004–05): $26,610 (full-time). *Room and board:* $8363 (room only: $5093).
Financial Aid (All incoming freshmen): *Average need-based gift aid:* $14,195. *Average non-need based aid:* $6297. *Average aid to full-time undergraduates:* $17,955.
Athletic Department: *Director of Athletics:* Dianne Murphy; Phone: 303-871-3399; Fax: 303-871-3040; E-mail: mdmurphy@du.edu. *Sports Information Director:* Marla Rodriguez; Phone: 303-871-4990; E-mail: marrodri@du.edu.

MEN'S COACHES

Basketball: Terry Carroll; Phone: 303-871-4918; E-mail: dalbo@du.edu.
Diving: Jeff Carter; Phone: 303-871-3906; E-mail: jcarter4@du.edu.
Golf: Eric Hoos; Phone: 303-871-4915; E-mail: ehoos@du.edu.
Ice Hockey: George Gwozdecky; Phone: 303-871-3844; E-mail: ggwozdec@du.edu.
Lacrosse: Jamie Munro; Phone: 303-871-3531; E-mail: jmunro@du.edu.
Soccer: Chad Ashton; Phone: 303-871-4945; E-mail: cashton@du.edu.
Swimming: Jim Henry; Phone: 303-871-3906; E-mail: jhenry@du.edu.
Tennis: Geoff Young; Phone: 303-871-2512; E-mail: gyoung@du.edu.

WOMEN'S COACHES

Basketball: Pam Tanner; Phone: 303-871-3926; E-mail: ptanner@du.edu.
Diving: Jeff Carter; Phone: 303-871-3906; E-mail: jcarter4@du.edu.
Golf: Sammie Chergo; Phone: 303-871-7461; E-mail: schergo@du.edu.
Gymnastics: Melissa Kutcher-Rinehart; Phone: 303-871-3395; E-mail: mkutcher@du.edu.
Lacrosse: Abby Burbank; Phone: 303-871-4703; E-mail: aburbank@du.edu.
Soccer: Jeff Hooker; Phone: 303-871-3154; E-mail: jhooker@du.edu.
Swimming: Jim Henry; Phone: 303-871-3906; E-mail: jhenry@du.edu.

University of Denver *(continued)*

Tennis: Dana Young; Phone: 303-871-7425; E-mail: danayoun@du.edu.
Volleyball: Beth Kuwata; Phone: 303-871-3944; E-mail: bkuwata@du.edu.

UNIVERSITY OF DETROIT MERCY
Detroit, Michigan

Titans ◆ NCAA I ◆ Horizon League Conference ◆ http://www.udmercy.edu/

Independent Roman Catholic (Jesuit) university, founded 1877
Coed, 3,383 undergraduate students, 56% full-time, 66% women, 34% men
Urban 70-acre campus
Moderately difficult entrance level, 81% of applicants were admitted

Freshmen *Admission:* 2,181 applied, 1,768 were accepted, 486 enrolled.
Tuition and fees (2004–05): $20,970 (full-time). *Room and board:* $7040 (room only: $4128).
Financial Aid (All incoming freshmen): *Average need-based gift aid:* $23,989. *Average non-need based aid:* $13,109. *Average aid to full-time undergraduates:* $22,851.
Athletic Department: *Director of Athletics:* Brad Kinsman; Phone: 313-993-1700; Fax: 313-993-2449; E-mail: kinsmanb@udmercy.edu. *Sports Information Director:* Mark Engel; Phone: 313-993-1745; E-mail: engelml@udmercy.edu.

MEN'S COACHES
Baseball: Chris Czarnik; Phone: 313-993-1725; E-mail: czarnicj@udmercy.edu.
Basketball: Perry Watson; Phone: 313-993-1731; E-mail: watsonpa@udmercy.edu.
Cheerleading: Tonya Carper; Phone: 313-993-1712.
Cross Country: Guy Murray; Phone: 313-993-1724; E-mail: murraygr@udmercy.edu.
Golf: Mark Engel; Phone: 313-993-1745; E-mail: engelml@udmercy.edu.
Soccer: Morris Lupenec; Phone: 313-993-1912; E-mail: lupenecm@udmercy.edu.
Track and Field: Guy Murray; Phone: 313-993-1724; E-mail: murraygr@udmercy.edu.

WOMEN'S COACHES
Basketball: Mickey Barrett; Phone: 313-993-1723; E-mail: barretmt@udmercy.edu.
Cheerleading: Tonya Carper; Phone: 313-993-1712.
Cross Country: Guy Murray; Phone: 313-993-1724; E-mail: murraygr@udmercy.edu.
Soccer: Mike Lupenec; Phone: 313-993-1739; E-mail: lupenecm@udmercy.edu.
Softball: Bob Wilkerson; Phone: 313-993-1728; E-mail: wilkerrj@udmercy.edu.
Tennis: Daron Montgomery; Phone: 313-993-1700; E-mail: montgodl@udmercy.edu.
Track and Field: Guy Murray; Phone: 313-993-1724; E-mail: murraygr@udmercy.edu.

UNIVERSITY OF DUBUQUE
Dubuque, Iowa

Spartans ◆ NCAA III ◆ Iowa Athletic Conference ◆ http://www.dbq.edu/

Independent Presbyterian comprehensive, founded 1852
Coed, 990 undergraduate students, 95% full-time, 35% women, 65% men
Suburban 56-acre campus
Moderately difficult entrance level, 80% of applicants were admitted

Freshmen *Admission:* 746 applied, 609 were accepted, 313 enrolled.
Test scores: SAT verbal scores over 500: 38%; SAT math scores over 500: 44%; SAT verbal scores over 600: 10%; SAT math scores over 600: 15%; SAT verbal scores over 700: 1%.

Tuition and fees (2004–05): $16,260 (full-time). *Room and board:* $5420 (room only: $2610).
Financial Aid (All incoming freshmen): *Average need-based gift aid:* $8219. *Average non-need based aid:* $16,285. *Average aid to full-time undergraduates:* $15,801.
Athletic Department: *Director of Athletics:* Dan Runkle; Phone: 563-589-3599; Fax: 563-589-3425; E-mail: drunkle@dbq.edu.

MEN'S COACHES
Baseball: Shane Schellsmidt; Phone: 563-589-3124; E-mail: sschells@dbq.edu.
Basketball: Marty McDermott; Phone: 563-589-3230; E-mail: mmcdermo@dbq.edu.
Cheerleading: Kelly Munter; Phone: 563-589-3227; E-mail: kmunter@dbq.edu.
Cross Country: Greta Pemsl; Phone: 563-589-3590; E-mail: gpemsl@dbq.edu.
Football: Vince Brautigam; Phone: 563-589-3173; E-mail: vbrautig@dbq.edu.
Golf: Marty McDermott; Phone: 563-589-3230; E-mail: mmcdermo@dbq.edu.
Soccer: Jason Berna; Phone: 563-589-3786; E-mail: jberna@dbq.edu.
Tennis: Greg Ray; Phone: 563-589-3227.
Track and Field: Jeremy Fellows; Phone: 563-589-3727; E-mail: jfellows@dbq.edu.
Wrestling: Jon McGovern; Phone: 563-589-3685; E-mail: jmcgover@dbq.edu.

WOMEN'S COACHES
Basketball: Todd Huffman; Phone: 563-589-3279; E-mail: thuffman@dbq.edu.
Cheerleading: Kelly Munter; Phone: 563-589-3227; E-mail: kmunter@dbq.edu.
Cross Country: Greta Pemsl; Phone: 563-589-3590; E-mail: gpemsl@dbq.edu.
Golf: Bobbi Endress; Phone: 563-589-3415; E-mail: bendress@dbq.edu.
Soccer: Jason Berna; Phone: 563-589-3786; E-mail: jberna@dbq.edu.
Softball: Todd Huffman; Phone: 563-589-3279; E-mail: thuffman@dbq.edu.
Tennis: Greg Ray; Phone: 563-589-3227.
Track and Field: Greta Pemsl; Phone: 563-589-3590; E-mail: gpemsl@dbq.edu.
Volleyball: Stacy Ruff; Phone: 563-589-3231; E-mail: sruff@dbq.edu.

UNIVERSITY OF EVANSVILLE
Evansville, Indiana

Aces ◆ NCAA I ◆ Missouri Valley Conference ◆ http://www.evansville.edu/

Independent religious comprehensive, founded 1854, affiliated with United Methodist Church
Coed, 2,566 undergraduate students, 89% full-time, 62% women, 38% men
Suburban 75-acre campus
Moderately difficult entrance level, 85% of applicants were admitted

Freshmen *Admission:* 2,292 applied, 1,972 were accepted, 663 enrolled.
Test scores: SAT verbal scores over 500: 79%; SAT math scores over 500: 81%; SAT verbal scores over 600: 41%; SAT math scores over 600: 39%; SAT verbal scores over 700: 9%; SAT math scores over 700: 7%.
Tuition and fees (2003–04): $19,230 (full-time). *Room and board:* $5510 (room only: $2600).
Financial Aid (All incoming freshmen): *Average need-based gift aid:* $15,016. *Average non-need based aid:* $8819. *Average aid to full-time undergraduates:* $18,362.
Athletic Department: *Director of Athletics:* Bill McGillis; Phone: 812-479-2238; Fax: 812-479-2199; E-mail: bm79@evansville.edu. *Sports Information Director:* Bob Boxell; Phone: 812-479-2285; E-mail: bb33@evansville.edu.

MEN'S COACHES
Baseball: Dave Schrage; Phone: 812-479-2059; E-mail: ds89@evansville.edu.
Basketball: Steve Merfeld; Phone: 812-479-2762.
Cheerleading: Jamie Elkins; Phone: 812-479-2266; E-mail: je5@evansville.edu.

Cross Country: Don Walters; Phone: 812-488-1370; E-mail: coachdw2000@aol.com.
Diving: Denise Atkins; Phone: 812-488-1028; E-mail: cooldeepygirl@hotmail.com.
Golf: Mary Pat Boarman; Phone: 812-426-2166; E-mail: mpboarman@aol.com.
Soccer: Dave Golan; Phone: 812-479-2294; E-mail: dg45@evansville.edu.
Swimming: Rickey Perkins; Phone: 812-479-2290; E-mail: rp38@evansville.edu.
Tennis: Tomas Johansson; Phone: 812-479-2293; E-mail: kadetom@sigecom.net.

WOMEN'S COACHES

Basketball: Tricia Cullop; Phone: 812-479-2289; E-mail: tc38@evansville.edu.
Cheerleading: Jamie Elkins; Phone: 812-479-2266; E-mail: je5@evansville.edu.
Cross Country: Don Walters; Phone: 812-488-1370; E-mail: coachdw2000@aol.com.
Diving: Denise Atkins; Phone: 812-488-1028; E-mail: cooldeepygirl@hotmail.com.
Golf: Jim Hamilton; Phone: 812-426-2166; E-mail: mpboarman@aol.com.
Soccer: Rob Raab; Phone: 812-479-2084; E-mail: rr46@evansville.edu.
Softball: Gwen Lewis; Phone: 812-479-2620; E-mail: gl2@evansville.edu.
Swimming: Rickey Perkins; Phone: 812-479-2290; E-mail: rp38@evansville.edu.
Tennis: Chris Payne; Phone: 812-479-2074; E-mail: cp24@evansville.edu.
Volleyball: Mike Swan; Phone: 812-479-2755; E-mail: ms281@evansville.edu.

THE UNIVERSITY OF FINDLAY
Findlay, Ohio

Oilers ◆ NCAA II ◆ Great Lakes Intercollegiate Conference; Midwestern Intercollegiate Volleyball Conference ◆ http://www.findlay.edu/

Independent religious comprehensive, founded 1882, affiliated with Church of God
Coed, 3,432 undergraduate students, 78% full-time, 58% women, 42% men
Small-town 200-acre campus with easy access to Toledo
Moderately difficult entrance level, 77% of applicants were admitted

Freshmen *Admission:* 2,682 applied, 1,980 were accepted, 998 enrolled. *Test scores:* SAT verbal scores over 500: 60%; SAT math scores over 500: 61%; SAT verbal scores over 600: 19%; SAT math scores over 600: 16%; SAT verbal scores over 700: 2%.
Tuition and fees (2003–04): $19,952 (full-time). *Room and board:* $7062 (room only): $3540).
Financial Aid (All incoming freshmen): *Average need-based gift aid:* $10,765. *Average non-need based aid:* $8400. *Average aid to full-time undergraduates:* $15,500.
Athletic Department: *Director of Athletics:* Steven Rackley; Phone: 419-434-4651; Fax: 419-434-4125; E-mail: rackley@findlay.edu. *Sports Information Director:* David Buck; Phone: 419-434-4727; E-mail: buckd@findlay.edu.

MEN'S COACHES
Baseball: Troy Berry; Phone: 800-472-9502; E-mail: berry@findlay.edu.
Basketball: Ron Niekamp; Phone: 800-472-9502; E-mail: niekamp@findlay.edu.
Cheerleading: Stacey Endicott; Phone: 800-548-0932; E-mail: endicotts@findlay.edu.
Cross Country: Marc Arce; Phone: 800-472-9502; E-mail: arce@findlay.edu.
Diving: Wayne Norris; Phone: 800-472-9502; E-mail: norris@findlay.edu.
Football: Dan Simrell; Phone: 800-472-9502.
Golf: Al Baker; Phone: 800-472-9502; E-mail: abaker@findlay.edu.
Ice Hockey: Pat Ford; Phone: 800-548-0932; E-mail: pford@findlay.edu.
Soccer: Andy Smyth; Phone: 800-472-9502; E-mail: smyth@findlay.edu.

Swimming: Wayne Norris; Phone: 800-472-9502; E-mail: norris@findlay.edu.
Tennis: Cindy Brown; Phone: 800-472-9502; E-mail: brown@findlay.edu.
Track and Field: Marc Arce; Phone: 800-472-9502; E-mail: arce@findlay.edu.
Volleyball: Wick Colchagoff; Phone: 800-472-9502; E-mail: colchagoff@findlay.edu.
Wrestling: Shawn Nelson; Phone: 800-472-9502; E-mail: shawnelson@hotmail.com.

WOMEN'S COACHES
Basketball: Carolyn Mair; Phone: 800-472-9502; E-mail: mair@findlay.edu.
Cheerleading: Stacey Endicott; Phone: 800-548-0932; E-mail: endicotts@findlay.edu.
Cross Country: Marc Arce; Phone: 800-472-9502; E-mail: arce@findlay.edu.
Diving: Wayne Norris; Phone: 800-472-9502; E-mail: norris@findlay.edu.
Golf: Al Baker; Phone: 800-472-9502; E-mail: abaker@findlay.edu.
Soccer: Andy Smyth; Phone: 800-472-9502; E-mail: smyth@findlay.edu.
Softball: Ron Ammons; Phone: 800-472-9502; E-mail: ammons@findlay.edu.
Swimming: Wayne Norris; Phone: 800-472-9502; E-mail: norris@findlay.edu.
Tennis: Cindy Brown; Phone: 800-472-9502; E-mail: brown@findlay.edu.
Track and Field: Marc Arce; Phone: 800-472-9502; E-mail: arce@findlay.edu.
Volleyball: Wick Colchagoff; Phone: 800-472-9502; E-mail: colchagoff@findlay.edu.

UNIVERSITY OF FLORIDA
Gainesville, Florida

Gators ◆ NCAA I ◆ Southeastern Conference ◆ http://www.ufl.edu/

State-supported university, founded 1853, part of State University System of Florida
Coed, 33,982 undergraduate students, 92% full-time, 53% women, 47% men
Suburban 2,000-acre campus with easy access to Jacksonville
Very difficult entrance level, 5% of applicants were admitted

Freshmen *Admission:* 22,973 applied, 12,029 were accepted, 6,596 enrolled. *Test scores:* SAT verbal scores over 500: 92%; SAT math scores over 500: 95%; SAT verbal scores over 600: 59%; SAT math scores over 600: 69%; SAT verbal scores over 700: 14%; SAT math scores over 700: 19%.
Tuition and fees (2003–04): $2780 (resident), $13,808 (nonresident). *Room and board:* $5800 (room only): $3580).
Financial Aid (All incoming freshmen): *Average need-based gift aid:* $4400. *Average non-need based aid:* $4122. *Average aid to full-time undergraduates:* $8559.
Athletic Department: *Director of Athletics:* Jeremy Foley; Phone: 352-375-4683; Fax: 352-377-8971; E-mail: administration@gators.uaa.ufl.edu. *Sports Information Director:* Mary Howard; Phone: 352-375-4683; E-mail: sportsinfo@gators.uaa.ufl.edu.

MEN'S COACHES
Baseball: Pat McMahon; Phone: 352-375-4683.
Basketball: Billy Donovan; Phone: 352-375-4683; E-mail: billyd@gators.uaa.ufl.edu.
Cheerleading: Donni Frazier; Phone: 352-375-4683; E-mail: donnif@gators.uaa.ufl.edu.
Cross Country: Jeff Pigg; Phone: 352-375-4683.
Diving: Donnie Craine; Phone: 352-375-4683; E-mail: donc@gators.uaa.ufl.edu.
Football: Ron Zook; Phone: 352-375-4683.
Golf: Buddy Alexander; Phone: 352-375-4683.
Swimming: Gregg Troy; Phone: 352-375-4683.
Tennis: Andy Jackson; Phone: 352-375-4683.
Track and Field: Mike Holloway; Phone: 352-375-4683; E-mail: mouse@gators.uaa.ufl.edu.

University of Florida (continued)

WOMEN'S COACHES

Basketball: Carolyn Peck; Phone: 352-375-4683; E-mail: carolynp@gators.uaa.ufl.edu.
Cheerleading: Donni Frazier; Phone: 352-375-4683; E-mail: donnif@gators.uaa.ufl.edu.
Cross Country: Jeff Pigg; Phone: 352-375-4683.
Diving: Donnie Craine; Phone: 352-375-4683; E-mail: donc@gators.uaa.ufl.edu.
Golf: Jill Briles-Hinton; Phone: 352-375-4683.
Gymnastics: Rhonda Faehn; Phone: 352-375-4683.
Soccer: Becky Burleigh; Phone: 352-375-4683; E-mail: becky@gators.uaa.ufl.edu.
Softball: Karen Johns; Phone: 352-375-4683; E-mail: karenj@gators.uaa.ufl.edu.
Swimming: Gregg Troy; Phone: 352-375-4683.
Tennis: Roland Thornqvist; Phone: 352-375-4683.
Track and Field: Tom Jones; Phone: 352-375-4683.
Volleyball: Mary Wise; Phone: 352-375-4683; E-mail: mary@gators.uaa.ufl.edu.

UNIVERSITY OF GEORGIA
Athens, Georgia

Bulldogs ◆ NCAA I ◆ Southeastern Conference ◆ http://www.uga.edu/

State-supported university, founded 1785, part of University System of Georgia
Coed, 25,415 undergraduate students, 90% full-time, 57% women, 43% men
Suburban 1,289-acre campus with easy access to Atlanta
Moderately difficult entrance level, 71% of applicants were admitted

Freshmen *Admission:* 11,813 applied, 8,885 were accepted, 5,177 enrolled. *Test scores:* SAT verbal scores over 500: 93%; SAT math scores over 500: 94%; SAT verbal scores over 600: 52%; SAT math scores over 600: 56%; SAT verbal scores over 700: 10%; SAT math scores over 700: 10%.
Tuition and fees (2003–04): $4078 (resident), $14,854 (nonresident). *Room and board:* $5756 (room only: $3182).
Financial Aid (All incoming freshmen): *Average need-based gift aid:* $6203. *Average non-need based aid:* $1909. *Average aid to full-time undergraduates:* $7183.
Athletic Department: *Director of Athletics:* Vince Dooley; Fax: 706-542-1621. *Sports Information Director:* Claude Felton; Phone: 706-542-1621; E-mail: cfelton@sports.uga.edu.

MEN'S COACHES

Baseball: David Permo; Phone: 706-542-9036; E-mail: dperno@sports.uga.edu.
Basketball: Dennis Felton; Phone: 706-542-1432.
Cheerleading: Marilou Braswell; Phone: 706-542-1172.
Cross Country: Wayne Norton; Phone: 706-542-7915; E-mail: wnorton@sports.uga.edu.
Diving: Dan Laak; Phone: 706-542-7946.
Football: Mark Richt; Phone: 706-542-1515; E-mail: boca@sports.uga.edu.
Golf: Chris Haack; Phone: 706-369-5932; E-mail: haack@sports.uga.edu.
Swimming: Jack Bauerle; Phone: 706-542-7958.
Tennis: Manuel Diaz; Phone: 706-542-8066.
Track and Field: Wayne Norton; Phone: 706-542-7915; E-mail: wnorton@sports.uga.edu.

WOMEN'S COACHES

Basketball: Andy Landers; Phone: 706-542-1176; E-mail: landers@sports.uga.edu.
Cheerleading: Marilou Braswell; Phone: 706-542-1172.
Cross Country: Wayne Norton; Phone: 706-542-7915; E-mail: wnorton@sports.uga.edu.
Diving: Dan Laak; Phone: 706-542-7946.
Golf: Todd McCorkle; Phone: 706-542-1170; E-mail: mccorkle@sports.uga.edu.
Gymnastics: Suzanne Yoculan; Phone: 706-542-7934; E-mail: syoculan@sports.uga.edu.

Soccer: Sue Patberg; Phone: 706-542-9036; E-mail: smp@sports.uga.edu.
Softball: Lu Harris-Champer; Phone: 706-542-1170; E-mail: lharris@sports.uga.edu.
Swimming: Jach Bauerle; Phone: 706-542-7958; E-mail: jbauerle@sports.uga.edu.
Tennis: Jeff Wallace; Phone: 706-542-5817; E-mail: jwallace@sports.uga.edu.
Track and Field: Wayne Norton; Phone: 706-542-7915; E-mail: wnorton@sports.uga.edu.
Volleyball: Mary Buczeki; Phone: 706-542-7915; E-mail: mjbuczek@sports.uga.edu.

UNIVERSITY OF GREAT FALLS
Great Falls, Montana

Argonauts ◆ NAIA ◆ Frontier Conference
◆ http://www.ugf.edu/

Independent Roman Catholic comprehensive, founded 1932
Coed, 682 undergraduate students, 68% full-time, 71% women, 29% men
Urban 40-acre campus
Noncompetitive entrance level, 8% of applicants were admitted

Freshmen *Admission:* 192 applied, 154 were accepted, 84 enrolled. *Test scores:* SAT verbal scores over 500: 55%; SAT math scores over 500: 37%; SAT verbal scores over 600: 5%; SAT math scores over 600: 5%.
Tuition and fees (2003–04): $11,940 (full-time). *Room and board:* $5100 (room only: $2100).
Financial Aid (All incoming freshmen): *Average need-based gift aid:* $3185. *Average non-need based aid:* $2903. *Average aid to full-time undergraduates:* $8356.
Athletic Department: *Director of Athletics:* Antonio Veloso; Phone: 406-791-5920; Fax: 406-791-5994; E-mail: aveloso01@ugf.edu. *Sports Information Director:* NA; Phone: 406-791-5925.

MEN'S COACHES

Basketball: Antonio Veloso; Phone: 406-791-5920; E-mail: aveloso01@ugf.edu.

WOMEN'S COACHES

Basketball: Roger Hatler; Phone: 406-791-5921; E-mail: rhatler01@ugf.edu.
Volleyball: Dick Scott; Phone: 406-791-5922; E-mail: dscott01@ugf.edu.

UNIVERSITY OF HARTFORD
West Hartford, Connecticut

Hawks ◆ NCAA I ◆ America East Conference ◆ http://www.hartford.edu/

Independent comprehensive, founded 1877
Coed, 5,612 undergraduate students, 81% full-time, 52% women, 48% men
Suburban 320-acre campus with easy access to Hartford
Moderately difficult entrance level, 66% of applicants were admitted

Freshmen *Admission:* 12,009 applied, 7,658 were accepted, 1,448 enrolled. *Test scores:* SAT verbal scores over 500: 67%; SAT math scores over 500: 71%; SAT verbal scores over 600: 18%; SAT math scores over 600: 19%; SAT verbal scores over 700: 1%; SAT math scores over 700: 2%.
Tuition and fees (2003–04): $22,470 (full-time). *Room and board:* $8610 (room only: $5310).
Financial Aid (All incoming freshmen): *Average need-based gift aid:* $9192. *Average non-need based aid:* $8106. *Average aid to full-time undergraduates:* $16,046.
Athletic Department: *Director of Athletics:* Pat Meiser-McKnett; Phone: 860-768-4145; Fax: 860-768-5047; E-mail: mcknett@hartford.edu. *Sports Information Director:* Jim Keener; Phone: 860-768-5063; E-mail: jkeener@hartford.edu.

MEN'S COACHES

Baseball: Harvey Shapiro; Phone: 860-768-4656; E-mail: hshapiro@hartford.edu.
Basketball: Larry Harrison; Phone: 860-768-4660; E-mail: lharrison@hartford.edu.
Cheerleading: Stacy Roos; Phone: 860-768-4658; E-mail: roos@hartford.edu.
Cross Country: Kathy Manizza; Phone: 860-768-5710; E-mail: manizza@hartford.edu.
Golf: Jim Pinto; Phone: 860-768-4848; E-mail: jpinto@hartford.edu.
Lacrosse: Andrew Towers; Phone: 860-768-5203; E-mail: atowers@hartford.edu.
Soccer: Jim Evans; Phone: 860-768-4470; E-mail: jevans@hartford.edu.
Tennis: Tyler Gibson; Phone: 860-768-4949; E-mail: gibson@hartford.edu.
Track and Field: Kathy Manizza; Phone: 860-768-5710; E-mail: manizza@hartford.edu.

WOMEN'S COACHES

Basketball: Jennifer Rizzotti; Phone: 860-768-4653.
Cheerleading: Stacy Roos; Phone: 860-768-4658; E-mail: roos@hartford.edu.
Cross Country: Kathy Manizza; Phone: 860-768-5710; E-mail: manizza@hartford.edu.
Golf: Donna Harris; Phone: 860-768-5060; E-mail: harris@hartford.edu.
Soccer: Eva Bergsten; Phone: 860-768-4676; E-mail: bergsten@hartford.edu.
Softball: Todd Randall; Phone: 860-768-5157; E-mail: randall@hartford.edu.
Tennis: Donna Hornish Lisevick; Phone: 860-768-4949; E-mail: lisevick@hartford.edu.
Track and Field: Kathy Manizza; Phone: 860-768-5710; E-mail: manizza@hartford.edu.
Volleyball: Maria Stutsman y Marquez; Phone: 860-768-4659; E-mail: marquez@hartford.edu.

UNIVERSITY OF HAWAII AT HILO
Hilo, Hawaii

Vulcans ◆ NCAA II ◆ Pacific West Conference ◆ http://www.uhh.hawaii.edu/

State-supported comprehensive, founded 1970, part of University of Hawaii System
Coed, 3,214 undergraduate students
Small-town 115-acre campus
Moderately difficult entrance level, 66% of applicants were admitted

Freshmen *Admission:* 1,470 applied, 967 were accepted. *Test scores:* SAT verbal scores over 500: 47%; SAT math scores over 500: 56%; SAT verbal scores over 600: 12%; SAT math scores over 600: 15%; SAT verbal scores over 700: 2%; SAT math scores over 700: 2%.
Tuition and fees (2004–05): $2538 (resident), $8106 (nonresident). *Room and board:* $5081 (room only: $2360).
Financial Aid (All incoming freshmen): *Average need-based gift aid:* $2390. *Average non-need based aid:* $600. *Average aid to full-time undergraduates:* $3216.
Athletic Department: *Director of Athletics:* Kathleen McNally; Phone: 808-974-7621; Fax: 808-974-7711; E-mail: kmcnally@hawaii.edu. *Sports Information Director:* Kelly Leong; Phone: 808-974-7606; E-mail: kellyl@hawaii.edu.

MEN'S COACHES

Baseball: Joey Estrella; Phone: 808-974-7700; E-mail: josephe@hawaii.edu.
Basketball: Jeff Law; Phone: 808-974-7701; E-mail: jlaw@hawaii.edu.
Cross Country: Jaime Guerro; Phone: 808-974-7704; E-mail: guerpo@hawaii.edu.
Golf: Earl Tamiya; Phone: 808-974-7493; E-mail: tamiya@hawaii.edu.
Tennis: Kula Oda; Phone: 808-974-7704; E-mail: koda@hawaii.edu.

WOMEN'S COACHES

Cross Country: Jaime Guerro; Phone: 808-974-7704; E-mail: guerpo@hawaii.edu.
Softball: Callen Perreira; Phone: 808-974-7703; E-mail: callenp@hawaii.edu.
Tennis: Kula Oda; Phone: 808-974-7704; E-mail: koda@hawaii.edu.
Volleyball: Julie Morgan; Phone: 808-974-7698; E-mail: morganju@hawaii.edu.

UNIVERSITY OF HAWAII AT MANOA
Honolulu, Hawaii

Rainbows ◆ NCAA I ◆ Western Athletic Conference ◆ http://www.uhm.hawaii.edu/

State-supported university, founded 1907
Coed, 13,755 undergraduate students, 81% full-time, 56% women, 44% men
Urban 300-acre campus
Moderately difficult entrance level, 59% of applicants were admitted

Freshmen *Admission:* 6,028 applied, 3,566 were accepted, 1,996 enrolled. *Test scores:* SAT verbal scores over 500: 65%; SAT math scores over 500: 82%; SAT verbal scores over 600: 19%; SAT math scores over 600: 34%; SAT verbal scores over 700: 2%; SAT math scores over 700: 5%.
Tuition and fees (2003–04): $3561 (resident), $10,041 (nonresident). *Room and board:* $5675 (room only: $3314).
Financial Aid (All incoming freshmen): *Average need-based gift aid:* $3289. *Average non-need based aid:* $5537. *Average aid to full-time undergraduates:* $4943.
Athletic Department: *Director of Athletics:* Herman Frazier; Phone: 808-956-7301; Fax: 808-956-4470; E-mail: hfrazier@hawaii.edu. *Sports Information Director:* Phone: 808-956-4480; E-mail: manin@hawaii.edu.

MEN'S COACHES

Baseball: Mike Trapasso; Phone: 808-956-6247; E-mail: trapasso@hawaii.edu.
Basketball: Riley Wallace; Phone: 808-956-6501; E-mail: wallacer@hawaii.edu.
Cheerleading: Heidi Deininger; Phone: 808-956-4503; E-mail: uhcheer@hawaii.edu.
Diving: Mike Brown; Phone: 808-956-7510.
Football: June Jones; Phone: 808-956-6508; E-mail: junej@hawaii.edu.
Golf: Ronn Miyashiro; Phone: 808-956-4527; E-mail: ronnm@hawaii.edu.
Swimming: Mike Anderson; Phone: 808-956-7510; E-mail: swimmike@usa.net.
Tennis: John Nelson; Phone: 808-956-4528; E-mail: johnnels@hawaii.edu.
Volleyball: Mike Wilton; Phone: 808-956-4505; E-mail: uhmvball@hawaii.edu.

WOMEN'S COACHES

Basketball: Vince Goo; Phone: 808-956-6518; E-mail: vgoo@hawaii.edu.
Cheerleading: Heidi Deininger; Phone: 808-956-4503; E-mail: uhcheer@hawaii.edu.
Cross Country: Carmyn James; Phone: 808-956-2143; E-mail: carmyn@hawaii.edu.
Diving: Mike Brown; Phone: 808-956-7510.
Golf: Marga Stubblefield; Phone: 808-956-4333; E-mail: wmnsgolf@hawaii.edu.
Soccer: Pinsoom Tenzing; Phone: 808-956-4525; E-mail: pinsoom@hawaii.edu.
Softball: Bob Coolen; Phone: 808-956-4506; E-mail: coolen@hawaii.edu.
Swimming: Mike Anderson; Phone: 808-956-7510; E-mail: swimmike@usa.net.
Tennis: Carolyn Katayama; Phone: 808-956-3655; E-mail: carolynk@hawaii.edu.
Track and Field: Carmyn James; Phone: 808-956-2143; E-mail: carmyn@hawaii.edu.
Volleyball: Dave Shoji; Phone: 808-956-6229; E-mail: wvball@hawaii.edu.

UNIVERSITY OF HOUSTON
Houston, Texas

Cougars ◆ NCAA I ◆ Conference USA Conference ◆ http://www.uh.edu/

State-supported university, founded 1927, part of University of Houston System
Coed, 27,048 undergraduate students, 71% full-time, 52% women, 48% men
Urban 550-acre campus
Moderately difficult entrance level, 79% of applicants were admitted

Freshmen *Admission:* 8,177 applied, 6,380 were accepted, 3,325 enrolled. *Test scores:* SAT verbal scores over 500: 57%; SAT math scores over 500: 67%; SAT verbal scores over 600: 18%; SAT math scores over 600: 26%; SAT verbal scores over 700: 3%; SAT math scores over 700: 4%.
Tuition and fees (2003–04): $3948 (resident), $11,028 (nonresident). *Room and board:* $5870 (room only: $3290).
Financial Aid (All incoming freshmen): *Average need-based gift aid:* $5250. *Average non-need based aid:* $1900. *Average aid to full-time undergraduates:* $10,080.
Athletic Department: *Director of Athletics:* Dave Maggard; Phone: 713-743-9370; Fax: 713-743-9375; E-mail: dmaggard@uh.edu. *Sports Information Director:* Chris Burkhalter; Phone: 713-743-9404; E-mail: cburkha@mail.uh.edu.

MEN'S COACHES
Baseball: Rayner Noble; Phone: 713-743-9396; E-mail: jnoble@bayou.uh.edu.
Basketball: Ray McCallum; Phone: 713-743-9430; E-mail: rmccallum@uh.edu.
Cross Country: Theresa Fuqua; Phone: 713-743-9465; E-mail: tdunn2@uh.edu.
Football: Art Briles; Phone: 713-743-9388; E-mail: abriles@uh.edu.
Golf: Vince Jarrett; Phone: 713-743-9397; E-mail: rvjarrett@uh.edu.
Track and Field: Leroy Burrell; Phone: 713-743-9465; E-mail: leroyburrell@uh.edu.

WOMEN'S COACHES
Basketball: Joe Curl; Phone: 713-743-9460; E-mail: jcurl@uh.edu.
Cross Country: Theresa Fuqua; Phone: 713-743-9465; E-mail: tdunn2@uh.edu.
Diving: Jane Figueiredo; Phone: 713-743-9373; E-mail: janefig@msn.com.
Soccer: Bill Solberg; Phone: 713-743-9377; E-mail: bsol@mail.uh.edu.
Softball: Kyla Holas; Phone: 713-743-9339; E-mail: kholas@uh.edu.
Swimming: Mark Taylor; Phone: 713-743-9373; E-mail: mtaylor14@uh.edu.
Tennis: Jennifer Hyde; Phone: 713-743-0836; E-mail: jhyde@mail.uh.edu.
Track and Field: Leroy Burrell; Phone: 713-743-9465; E-mail: leroyburrell@uh.edu.
Volleyball: Bill Walton; Phone: 713-743-9474; E-mail: wwalton@bayou.uh.edu.

UNIVERSITY OF IDAHO
Moscow, Idaho

Vandels ◆ NCAA I ◆ Big West Conference; Sun Belt Conference ◆ http://www.uidaho.edu/

State-supported university, founded 1889
Coed, 9,607 undergraduate students, 87% full-time, 45% women, 55% men
Small-town 1,450-acre campus
Moderately difficult entrance level, 79% of applicants were admitted

Freshmen *Admission:* 3,973 applied, 3,202 were accepted, 1,650 enrolled. *Test scores:* SAT verbal scores over 500: 72%; SAT math scores over 500: 75%; SAT verbal scores over 600: 30%; SAT math scores over 600: 34%; SAT verbal scores over 700: 5%; SAT math scores over 700: 5%.
Tuition and fees (2003–04): $3348 (resident), $10,740 (nonresident). *Room and board:* $4868.

Financial Aid (All incoming freshmen): *Average need-based gift aid:* $3036. *Average non-need based aid:* $3194. *Average aid to full-time undergraduates:* $8079.
Athletic Department: *Director of Athletics:* Mike Bohn; Phone: 208-885-0200; Fax: 208-885-2862. *Sports Information Director:* Becky Paull; Phone: 208-885-0245; E-mail: bpaull@uidaho.edu.

MEN'S COACHES
Basketball: Leonard Perry; Phone: 208-885-0243; E-mail: lperry@uidaho.edu.
Cheerleading: Shelly Femreite; Phone: 208-885-0200.
Cross Country: Wayne Phipps; Phone: 208-885-0210; E-mail: wphipps@uidaho.edu.
Football: Nick Holt; Phone: 208-885-0208; E-mail: nickh@uidaho.edu.
Golf: Brad Rickel; Phone: 208-885-5244; E-mail: brickel@uidaho.edu.
Tennis: Greg South; Phone: 208-885-0247; E-mail: gsouth@uidaho.edu.
Track and Field: Wayne Phipps; Phone: 208-885-0210; E-mail: wphipps@uidaho.edu.

WOMEN'S COACHES
Basketball: Mike Divilbliss; Phone: 208-885-0277; E-mail: mdivilbi@uidaho.edu.
Cheerleading: Shelly Femreite; Phone: 208-885-0200.
Cross Country: Wayne Phipps; Phone: 208-885-0210; E-mail: wphipps@uidaho.edu.
Golf: Brad Rickel; Phone: 208-885-5244; E-mail: brickel@uidaho.edu.
Soccer: Arby Busey; Phone: 208-885-4804; E-mail: rbusey@uidaho.edu.
Tennis: Greg South; Phone: 208-885-0247; E-mail: gsouth@uidaho.edu.
Track and Field: Yogi Teevens; Phone: 208-885-0251; E-mail: yogi@uidaho.edu.
Volleyball: Debbie Bucanan; Phone: 208-885-4804; E-mail: debbieb@uidaho.edu.

UNIVERSITY OF ILLINOIS AT CHICAGO
Chicago, Illinois

Flames ◆ NCAA I ◆ Horizon League Conference ◆ http://www.uic.edu/

State-supported university, founded 1946, part of University of Illinois System
Coed, 16,012 undergraduate students, 89% full-time, 55% women, 45% men
Urban 240-acre campus
Moderately difficult entrance level, 58% of applicants were admitted

Freshmen *Admission:* 12,250 applied, 7,425 were accepted, 2,942 enrolled.
Tuition and fees (2004–05): $7860 (resident), $19,108 (nonresident). *Room and board:* $6884.
Financial Aid (All incoming freshmen): *Average need-based gift aid:* $7422. *Average non-need based aid:* $2301. *Average aid to full-time undergraduates:* $11,400.
Athletic Department: *Director of Athletics:* James Schmidt; Phone: 312-996-2695; Fax: 312-996-8349; E-mail: jschmidt@uic.edu. *Sports Information Director:* Mike Cassidy; Phone: 312-413-8199; E-mail: cassidy@uic.edu.

MEN'S COACHES
Baseball: Mike Dee; Phone: 312-996-8645; E-mail: mdee@uic.edu.
Basketball: Jimmy Collins; Phone: 312-996-8690.
Cheerleading: Randy Santiago; Phone: 312-355-0716; E-mail: cheercoach4uic@aol.com.
Cross Country: James Knoedel; Phone: 312-996-8644; E-mail: jknoedel@uic.edu.
Soccer: Sasha Begovic; Phone: 312-996-6999; E-mail: sasha@uic.edu.
Swimming: Paul Moniak; Phone: 312-996-2255; E-mail: pmoniak@uic.edu.
Tennis: Hans Neufeld; Phone: 312-996-2140; E-mail: hneufeld@uic.edu.
Track and Field: James Knoedel; Phone: 312-996-8644; E-mail: jknoedel@uic.edu.

WOMEN'S COACHES
Basketball: Lisa Rykbosch; Phone: 312-996-6962; E-mail: lisar@uic.edu.

Cheerleading: Randy Santiago; Phone: 312-355-0716; E-mail: cheercoach4uic@aol.com.
Cross Country: James Knoedel; Phone: 312-996-8644; E-mail: jknoedel@uic.edu.
Diving: Larry Barcheski; Phone: 312-996-2255; E-mail: caryle2@aol.com.
Gymnastics: Peter Jansson; Phone: 312-996-3557; E-mail: pjansson@uic.edu.
Softball: Sara O'Malley; Phone: 312-996-5305; E-mail: somall1@uic.edu.
Swimming: Paul Moniak; Phone: 312-996-2255; E-mail: pmoniak@uic.edu.
Tennis: Shannon Tully; Phone: 312-996-0866; E-mail: stully@uic.edu.
Track and Field: James Knoedel; Phone: 312-996-8644; E-mail: jknoedel@uic.edu.
Volleyball: Don August; Phone: 312-996-2056; E-mail: daugust@uic.edu.

UNIVERSITY OF ILLINOIS AT SPRINGFIELD

Springfield, Illinois

Prairie Stars ◆ NAIA ◆ American Midwest Conference
◆ http://www.uis.edu/

State-supported upper-level, founded 1969, part of University of Illinois
Coed, 2,569 undergraduate students, 58% full-time, 61% women, 39% men
Suburban 746-acre campus
Minimally difficult entrance level, 49% of applicants were admitted

Freshmen *Admission:* 481 applied, 248 were accepted, 116 enrolled.
Tuition and fees (2003–04): $4310 (resident), $11,210 (nonresident). *Room and board:* $7000.
Financial Aid (All incoming freshmen): *Average need-based gift aid:* $4927. *Average non-need based aid:* $2882. *Average aid to full-time undergraduates:* $6864.
Athletic Department: *Director of Athletics:* Nick Adams; Phone: 217-206-7592; Fax: 217-206-7706; E-mail: adams.nick@uis.edu. *Sports Information Director:* Paul MacDonna; Phone: 217-206-6752; E-mail: macdonna.paul@uis.edu.

MEN'S COACHES
Basketball: Kevin Gamble; Phone: 217-206-7591; E-mail: gamble.kevin@uis.edu.
Cheerleading: Amy Franks; Phone: 217-206-6674; E-mail: amyabarnes@aol.com.
Soccer: Joe Eck; Phone: 217-206-7392; E-mail: eck.joe@uis.edu.
Tennis: Manny Velasco; Phone: 217-206-6674; E-mail: velasco.manny@uis.edu.

WOMEN'S COACHES
Basketball: Wanda Nettles; Phone: 217-206-7901; E-mail: nettles.wanda@uis.edu.
Cheerleading: Amy Franks; Phone: 217-206-6674; E-mail: amyabarnes@aol.com.
Softball: Joe Fisher; Phone: 217-206-7900; E-mail: fisher.joe@uis.edu.
Tennis: Dom Giacomini; Phone: 217-206-6674; E-mail: giacomini.dominic@uis.edu.
Volleyball: Joe Fisher; Phone: 217-206-7900; E-mail: fisher.joe@uis.edu.

UNIVERSITY OF ILLINOIS AT URBANA–CHAMPAIGN

Champaign, Illinois

Illini ◆ NCAA I ◆ Big Ten Conference
◆ http://www.uiuc.edu/

State-supported university, founded 1867, part of University of Illinois System
Coed, 29,226 undergraduate students, 96% full-time, 47% women, 53% men
Small-town 1,470-acre campus
Very difficult entrance level, 6% of applicants were admitted

Freshmen *Admission:* 22,269 applied, 13,939 were accepted, 6,811 enrolled. *Test scores:* SAT verbal scores over 500: 90%; SAT math scores over 500: 97%; SAT verbal scores over 600: 58%; SAT math scores over 600: 79%; SAT verbal scores over 700: 14%; SAT math scores over 700: 37%.
Tuition and fees (2004–05): $9384 (resident), $20,866 (nonresident). *Room and board:* $6848 (room only: $2831).
Financial Aid (All incoming freshmen): *Average need-based gift aid:* $6589. *Average non-need based aid:* $2916. *Average aid to full-time undergraduates:* $8238.
Athletic Department: *Director of Athletics:* Ron Guenther; Phone: 217-333-3631; Fax: 217-244-9753; E-mail: rguenthe@uiuc.edu. *Sports Information Director:* Kent Brown; Phone: 217-244-6533; E-mail: kwbrown3@uiuc.edu.

MEN'S COACHES
Baseball: Richard Jones; Phone: 217-244-8138; E-mail: r-jones@uiuc.edu.
Basketball: Bruce Weber; Phone: 217-333-3400; E-mail: gnott@uiuc.edu.
Cheerleading: Stephanie Record; Phone: 217-333-3630; E-mail: record1@uiuc.edu.
Cross Country: Wayne Angel; Phone: 217-333-7968; E-mail: wangel@uiuc.edu.
Football: Ron Turner; Phone: 217-333-1400; E-mail: rdturner@uiuc.edu.
Golf: Mike Small; Phone: 217-333-8604; E-mail: small@uiuc.edu.
Tennis: Craig Tiley; Phone: 217-333-7971; E-mail: ctiley1@uiuc.edu.
Track and Field: Wayne Angel; Phone: 217-333-7968; E-mail: wangel@uiuc.edu.
Wrestling: Mark Johnson; Phone: 217-333-5853; E-mail: majohns@uiuc.edu.

WOMEN'S COACHES
Basketball: Theresa Grentz; Phone: 217-333-8612; E-mail: grentz@uiuc.edu.
Cheerleading: Stephanie Record; Phone: 217-333-3630; E-mail: record1@uiuc.edu.
Cross Country: Gary Winckler; Phone: 217-333-7970; E-mail: gwinckle@uiuc.edu.
Diving: Billy McGowan; Phone: 217-333-5213; E-mail: wmcgowan@uiuc.edu.
Golf: Paula Smith; Phone: 217-333-8610; E-mail: p-smith4@uiuc.edu.
Gymnastics: Bob Starkell; Phone: 217-333-7974; E-mail: starkell@uiuc.edu.
Soccer: Janet Rayfield; Phone: 217-333-4783; E-mail: rayfield@uiuc.edu.
Softball: Terri Sullivan; Phone: 217-333-8229; E-mail: tsullivn@uiuc.edu.
Swimming: Susan Novitsky; Phone: 217-333-5213; E-mail: novitsky@uiuc.edu.
Tennis: Sujay Lama; Phone: 217-333-8622; E-mail: lama@uiuc.edu.
Track and Field: Gary Winckler; Phone: 217-333-7970; E-mail: gwinckle@uiuc.edu.
Volleyball: Don Hardin; Phone: 217-333-8606; E-mail: dhardin@uiuc.edu.

UNIVERSITY OF INDIANAPOLIS
Indianapolis, Indiana

Greyhounds ◆ NCAA II ◆ Great Lakes Intercollegiate
Conference ◆ http://www.uindy.edu/

Independent religious comprehensive, founded 1902, affiliated with United Methodist Church
Coed, 3,007 undergraduate students, 70% full-time, 66% women, 34% men
Suburban 60-acre campus
Moderately difficult entrance level, 66% of applicants were admitted

Freshmen *Admission:* 2,828 applied, 2,103 were accepted, 661 enrolled. *Test scores:* SAT verbal scores over 500: 52%; SAT math scores over 500: 60%; SAT verbal scores over 600: 12%; SAT math scores over 600: 16%; SAT verbal scores over 700: 2%; SAT math scores over 700: 1%.
Tuition and fees (2004–05): $17,200 (full-time). *Room and board:* $6150.
Financial Aid (All incoming freshmen): *Average need-based gift aid:* $7686. *Average non-need based aid:* $7462. *Average aid to full-time undergraduates:* $14,380.
Athletic Department: *Director of Athletics:* Sue Wiley; Phone: 317-788-3412; Fax: 317-788-3472; E-mail: swiley@uindy.edu. *Sports Information Director:* Joe Gentry; Phone: 317-788-3494; E-mail: jgentry@uindy.edu.

MEN'S COACHES
Baseball: Gary Vaught; Phone: 317-788-3414; E-mail: gvaught@uindy.edu.
Basketball: Todd Sturgeon; Phone: 317-788-3418; E-mail: tsturgeon@uindy.edu.
Cheerleading: Kendra Holmes; Phone: 317-788-3368; E-mail: kholmes@uindy.edu.
Cross Country: Kathy Casey; Phone: 317-788-6146; E-mail: kcasey@uindy.edu.
Diving: Gary Kinkead; Phone: 317-788-3427; E-mail: gkinkead@uindy.edu.
Football: Joe Polizzi; Phone: 317-788-3413; E-mail: jpolizzi@uindy.edu.
Golf: Ken Partridge; Phone: 317-788-3273; E-mail: kpartridge@uindy.edu.
Soccer: Bob Kouril; Phone: 317-788-6111; E-mail: drkouril@aol.com.
Swimming: Gary Kinkead; Phone: 317-788-3427; E-mail: gkinkead@uindy.edu.
Tennis: Pat Nickell; Phone: 317-788-3270; E-mail: pnickell@uindy.edu.
Track and Field: Scott Fanghan; Phone: 317-788-3416.
Wrestling: Wiley Craft; Phone: 317-788-3417; E-mail: wcraft@uindy.edu.

WOMEN'S COACHES
Basketball: Teri Moren; Phone: 317-788-3443; E-mail: tmoren@uindy.edu.
Cheerleading: Kendra Holmes; Phone: 317-788-3368; E-mail: kholmes@uindy.edu.
Cross Country: Kathy Casey; Phone: 317-788-6146; E-mail: kcasey@uindy.edu.
Diving: Gary Kinkead; Phone: 317-788-3427; E-mail: gkinkead@uindy.edu.
Golf: Kelli Tungate; Phone: 317-788-6138; E-mail: ktungate@uindy.edu.
Soccer: Aaron Blessing; Phone: 317-788-3578; E-mail: ablessing@indy.edu.
Softball: Jackie Nebelsiek; Phone: 317-788-2198; E-mail: nebelsiekja@uindy.edu.
Swimming: Gary Kinkead; Phone: 317-788-3427; E-mail: gkinkead@uindy.edu.
Tennis: John Venter; Phone: 317-788-3411; E-mail: jventer@uindy.edu.
Track and Field: Scott Fanghan; Phone: 317-788-3416.
Volleyball: Jody Rogers-Butera; Phone: 317-788-6147; E-mail: jrogers@uindy.edu.

THE UNIVERSITY OF IOWA
Iowa City, Iowa

Hawkeyes ◆ NCAA I ◆ Big Ten Conference
◆ http://www.uiowa.edu/

State-supported university, founded 1847
Coed, 20,233 undergraduate students, 88% full-time, 54% women, 46% men
Small-town 1,900-acre campus
Moderately difficult entrance level, 79% of applicants were admitted

Freshmen *Admission:* 13,337 applied, 10,979 were accepted, 4,083 enrolled. *Test scores:* SAT verbal scores over 500: 84%; SAT math scores over 500: 88%; SAT verbal scores over 600: 47%; SAT math scores over 600: 53%; SAT verbal scores over 700: 11%; SAT math scores over 700: 14%.
Tuition and fees (2004–05): $5396 (resident), $16,048 (nonresident). *Room and board:* $6350.
Financial Aid (All incoming freshmen): *Average need-based gift aid:* $4526. *Average non-need based aid:* $4180. *Average aid to full-time undergraduates:* $7111.
Athletic Department: *Director of Athletics:* Robert Bowlsby; Phone: 319-335-9435; Fax: 319-335-9333; E-mail: robert-bowlsby@uiowa.edu. *Sports Information Director:* Phil Haddy; Phone: 319-335-9411; E-mail: phillip-haddy@uiowa.edu.

MEN'S COACHES
Baseball: Jack Dahm; Phone: 319-335-9329.
Basketball: Steve Alford; Phone: 319-335-9444; E-mail: steve-alford@uiowa.edu.
Cheerleading: Leslie Steenlage; Phone: 319-335-9438; E-mail: les-steenlage@uiowa.edu.
Cross Country: Larry Wieczorek; Phone: 319-335-9429; E-mail: larry-wieczorek@uiowa.edu.
Diving: Bob Rydze; Phone: 319-335-9432; E-mail: robert-rydze@uiowa.edu.
Football: Kirk Ferentz; Phone: 319-335-8945; E-mail: kirk-ferentz@uiowa.edu.
Golf: Terry Anderson; Phone: 319-335-9245; E-mail: terrance-anderson@uiowa.edu.
Swimming: John Davey; Phone: 319-335-9432; E-mail: john-davey@hawkeyeswimming.com.
Tennis: Steve Houghton; Phone: 319-335-9428; E-mail: steve-houghton@hawkeyetennis.com.
Track and Field: Larry Wieczorek; Phone: 319-335-9429; E-mail: larry-wieczorek@uiowa.edu.
Wrestling: Jim Zalesky; Phone: 319-335-9405; E-mail: jim-zalesky@uiowa.edu.

WOMEN'S COACHES
Basketball: Lisa Bluder; Phone: 319-335-9258; E-mail: lisa-bluder@uiowa.edu.
Cheerleading: Leslie Steenlage; Phone: 319-335-9438; E-mail: les-steenlage@uiowa.edu.
Cross Country: Jim Grant; Phone: 319-335-9257; E-mail: james-grant@iowatrack.com.
Diving: Bob Rydze; Phone: 319-335-9432; E-mail: robert-rydze@uiowa.edu.
Field Hockey: Tracy Griesbaum; Phone: 319-335-9259; E-mail: tracey-griesbaum@iowafieldhockey.com.
Golf: Bobbe Carney; Phone: 319-335-9259; E-mail: bobbe-carney@uiowa.edu.
Gymnastics: Mike Lorenzen; Phone: 319-335-9432; E-mail: michael-lorenzen@iowagymnastics.com.
Soccer: Carla Baker; Phone: 319-335-9251; E-mail: carla-baker@iowasoccer.com.
Softball: Gayle Blevins; Phone: 319-335-9257; E-mail: gayle-blevins@iowasoftball.com.
Swimming: Garland O'Keefe; Phone: 319-335-9257; E-mail: garland-okeeffe@iowaswimming.com.
Tennis: Paul Wardlaw; Phone: 319-335-9265; E-mail: paul-wardlaw@iowatennis.com.
Track and Field: Jim Grant; Phone: 319-335-9257; E-mail: james-grant@iowatrack.com.
Volleyball: Rita Buck-Crockett; Phone: 319-335-9259; E-mail: rita-crockett@iowavolleyball.com.

UNIVERSITY OF KANSAS
Lawrence, Kansas

Jayhawks ◆ NCAA I ◆ Big 12 Conference
◆ http://www.ku.edu/

State-supported university, founded 1866
Coed, 20,866 undergraduate students, 88% full-time, 52% women, 48% men
Suburban 1,100-acre campus with easy access to Kansas City
Moderately difficult entrance level, 67% of applicants were admitted

Freshmen *Admission:* 9,573 applied, 6,458 were accepted, 4,066 enrolled.
Tuition and fees (2003–04): $4101 (resident), $11,577 (nonresident). *Room and board:* $4822 (room only: $2498).
Financial Aid (All incoming freshmen): *Average need-based gift aid:* $3228. *Average non-need based aid:* $3007. *Average aid to full-time undergraduates:* $5540.
Athletic Department: *Director of Athletics:* Lew Perkins; Phone: 785-864-3143; Fax: 785-864-5525; E-mail: lperkins@ku.edu. *Sports Information Director:* Mitch Germann; Phone: 785-864-3474; E-mail: germann@ku.edu.

MEN'S COACHES
Baseball: Ritch Price; Phone: 785-864-4196; E-mail: rprice@ku.edu.
Basketball: Bill Self; Phone: 785-864-3056; E-mail: mensbasketball@jayhawks.org.
Cross Country: Stanley Redwine; Phone: 785-864-3486; E-mail: sredwine@ku.edu.
Football: Mark Mangino; Phone: 785-864-3142; E-mail: football@jayhawks.org.
Golf: Ross Randall; Phone: 785-864-1907; E-mail: rossran@ku.edu.
Track and Field: Stanley Redwine; Phone: 785-864-3486; E-mail: sredwine@ku.edu.

WOMEN'S COACHES
Basketball: Marian Washington; Phone: 785-864-4938; E-mail: mewash@ku.edu.
Cross Country: Stanley Redwine; Phone: 785-864-3486; E-mail: sredwine@ku.edu.
Diving: Brad Szurgot; Phone: 785-864-7924; E-mail: ccswim@ku.edu.
Golf: Megan Menzel; Phone: 785-864-4122; E-mail: mmenzel@ku.edu.
Soccer: Mark Francis; Phone: 785-864-3556; E-mail: mfrancis@ku.edu.
Softball: Tracy Bunge; Phone: 785-864-4737; E-mail: bunge@ku.edu.
Swimming: Clark Campbell; Phone: 785-864-4177; E-mail: ccswim@ku.edu.
Tennis: Amy Hall; Phone: 785-864-7992.
Track and Field: Stanley Redwine; Phone: 785-864-3486; E-mail: sredwine@ku.edu.
Volleyball: Ray Bechard; Phone: 785-864-5077; E-mail: rayb@ku.edu.

UNIVERSITY OF KENTUCKY
Lexington, Kentucky

Wildcats ◆ NCAA I ◆ Mid-American Conference; Southeastern Conference ◆ http://www.uky.edu/

State-supported university, founded 1865
Coed, 18,108 undergraduate students, 90% full-time, 52% women, 48% men
Urban 685-acre campus with easy access to Cincinnati and Louisville
Moderately difficult entrance level, 80% of applicants were admitted

Freshmen *Admission:* 9,418 applied, 7,603 were accepted, 3,688 enrolled. *Test scores:* SAT verbal scores over 500: 79%; SAT math scores over 500: 80%; SAT verbal scores over 600: 33%; SAT math scores over 600: 39%; SAT verbal scores over 700: 6%; SAT math scores over 700: 7%.
Tuition and fees (2003–04): $4546 (resident), $11,226 (nonresident). *Room and board:* $4285 (room only: $2785).
Financial Aid (All incoming freshmen): *Average need-based gift aid:* $5446. *Average non-need based aid:* $4048. *Average aid to full-time undergraduates:* $7262.
Athletic Department: *Director of Athletics:* Mitch Barnhart; Phone: 859-257-8000; Fax: 859-257-6303. *Sports Information Director:* Scott Stricklin; Phone: 859-257-8000; E-mail: stricklin@uky.edu.

MEN'S COACHES
Baseball: John Cohen; Phone: 859-257-6500.
Basketball: Tubby Smith; Phone: 859-257-1916.
Cheerleading: Jomo Thompson; Phone: 859-257-9080; E-mail: jkthom1@email.uky.edu.
Cross Country: Don Weber; Phone: 859-257-3002; E-mail: dweber@uky.edu.
Diving: Mike Lyden; Phone: 859-257-7944; E-mail: mlyden@uky.edu.
Football: Rich Brooks; Phone: 859-257-3611; E-mail: rbrooks@uky.edu.
Golf: Brian Craig; Phone: 859-257-6506; E-mail: bcrai2@uky.edu.
Soccer: Ian Collins; Phone: 859-257-4059; E-mail: icoll@uky.edu.
Swimming: Gary Conelly; Phone: 859-257-7944; E-mail: conelly@uky.edu.
Tennis: Dennis Emery; Phone: 859-257-7707; E-mail: dennisgemcry@aol.com.
Track and Field: Don Weber; Phone: 859-257-3002; E-mail: dweber@uky.edu.

WOMEN'S COACHES
Basketball: Mickie DeMoss; Phone: 859-257-6046; E-mail: demoss@uky.edu.
Cheerleading: Jomo Thompson; Phone: 859-257-9080; E-mail: jkthom1@email.uky.edu.
Cross Country: Don Weber; Phone: 859-257-3002; E-mail: dweber@uky.edu.
Diving: Mike Lyden; Phone: 859-257-7944; E-mail: mlyden@uky.edu.
Golf: Stephanie Martin; Phone: 859-257-4861; E-mail: smart2@uky.edu.
Gymnastics: Mo Muhammad; Phone: 859-257-6483.
Soccer: Warren Lipka; Phone: 859-257-4971; E-mail: lipka@pop.uky.edu.
Softball: Beth Pruitt; Phone: 859-257-9037; E-mail: kirchne@pop.uky.edu.
Swimming: Gary Conelly; Phone: 859-257-7944; E-mail: conelly@uky.edu.
Tennis: Mark Guilbeau; Phone: 859-257-7707; E-mail: markg@uky.edu.
Track and Field: Don Weber; Phone: 859-257-3002; E-mail: dweber@uky.edu.
Volleyball: Jona Braden; Phone: 859-257-6500; E-mail: jbrad1@email.uky.edu.

UNIVERSITY OF LA VERNE
La Verne, California

Leopards ◆ NCAA III ◆ Southern California Athletic Conference ◆ http://www.ulv.edu/

Independent university, founded 1891
Coed, 1,396 undergraduate students, 96% full-time, 63% women, 37% men
Suburban 26-acre campus with easy access to Los Angeles
Moderately difficult entrance level, 49% of applicants were admitted

Freshmen *Admission:* 1,432 applied, 805 were accepted, 290 enrolled. *Test scores:* SAT verbal scores over 500: 48%; SAT math scores over 500: 54%; SAT verbal scores over 600: 6%; SAT math scores over 600: 9%; SAT verbal scores over 700: 1%; SAT math scores over 700: 1%.
Tuition and fees (2004–05): $21,500 (full-time). *Room and board:* $8510 (room only: $4150).
Financial Aid (All incoming freshmen): *Average need-based gift aid:* $10,182. *Average non-need based aid:* $8414. *Average aid to full-time undergraduates:* $23,895.
Athletic Department: *Director of Athletics:* Chris Ragsdale; Phone: 909-593-3511; Fax: 909-596-9280; E-mail: cragsdale@ulv.edu. *Sports Information Director:* Gabe Duran; Phone: 909-593-3511; E-mail: durang@ulv.edu.

MEN'S COACHES
Baseball: Scott Winterburn; Phone: 909-593-3511; E-mail: winterbu@ulv.edu.
Basketball: Phone: 909-593-3511.
Cross Country: Pat Widolff; Phone: 909-593-5311; E-mail: widolffp@ulv.edu.
Diving: Toby Reclusado; Phone: 909-593-3511.
Football: Don Morel; Phone: 909-593-3511; E-mail: dmorel@ulv.edu.
Golf: Rex Huigens; Phone: 909-593-3511; E-mail: huigensr@ulv.edu.

University of La Verne *(continued)*

Soccer: Cres Gonzalez; Phone: 909-593-3511; E-mail: gonzalez@ulv.edu.
Swimming: John Hallman; Phone: 909-593-3511; E-mail: hallmanj@ulv.edu.
Tennis: Steven Bergovoy; Phone: 909-593-3511; E-mail: bergovo@ulv.edu.
Track and Field: Pat Widolff; Phone: 909-593-5311; E-mail: widolffp@ulv.edu.
Volleyball: Jack Coberly; Phone: 909-593-3511; E-mail: coberlym@ulv.edu.

WOMEN'S COACHES

Basketball: Julie Kline; Phone: 909-593-3511; E-mail: klinej@ulv.edu.
Cross Country: Pat Widolff; Phone: 909-593-5311; E-mail: widolffp@ulv.edu.
Diving: Toby Reclusado; Phone: 909-593-3511.
Soccer: Wendy Zwissler; Phone: 909-593-3511; E-mail: zwissler@ulv.edu.
Softball: Julie Kline; Phone: 909-593-3511; E-mail: klinej@ulv.edu.
Swimming: John Hallman; Phone: 909-593-3511; E-mail: hallmanj@ulv.edu.
Tennis: Steven Bergovoy; Phone: 909-593-3511; E-mail: bergovo@ulv.edu.
Track and Field: Pat Widolff; Phone: 909-593-5311; E-mail: widolffp@ulv.edu.
Volleyball: Don Flora; Phone: 909-593-3511; E-mail: florad@ulv.edu.

UNIVERSITY OF LOUISIANA AT LAFAYETTE
Lafayette, Louisiana

Ragincajuns ◆ NCAA I ◆ Sun Belt Conference ◆ http://www.louisiana.edu/

State-supported university, founded 1898, part of University of Louisiana System
Coed, 14,585 undergraduate students, 82% full-time, 57% women, 43% men
Urban 1,375-acre campus
Moderately difficult entrance level, 88% of applicants were admitted

Freshmen *Admission:* 4,431 applied, 3,888 were accepted, 2,683 enrolled.
Tuition and fees (2003–04): $2700 (resident), $8960 (nonresident). *Room and board:* $3126.
Financial Aid (All incoming freshmen): *Average need-based gift aid:* $2200. *Average non-need based aid:* $2746. *Average aid to full-time undergraduates:* $3690.
Athletic Department: *Director of Athletics:* Nelson Schexnayder; Phone: 337-482-5393; Fax: 337-482-1041; E-mail: athdir@louisiana.edu. *Sports Information Director:* Daryl Cetnar; Phone: 337-482-6331; E-mail: sportsinfo@louisiana.edu.

MEN'S COACHES

Baseball: Tony Robichaux; Phone: 337-482-6189; E-mail: cajunbaseball@cox-internet.com.
Basketball: Jessie Evans; Phone: 337-482-1421.
Cross Country: Charles Lancon; Phone: 337-482-6313.
Football: Rickey Bustle; Phone: 337-482-6318; E-mail: rnb9999@louisiana.edu.
Golf: Bob Bass; Phone: 337-482-6130; E-mail: rmb3845@louisiana.edu.
Tennis: Justin McGrath; Phone: 337-482-6328; E-mail: jrm2982@louisiana.edu.
Track and Field: Lance Veazey; Phone: 337-482-6313.

WOMEN'S COACHES

Basketball: Kelly Hall; Phone: 337-482-6978; E-mail: kxh8888@louisiana.edu.
Cross Country: Charles Lancon; Phone: 337-482-6313.
Soccer: Dave Poggi; Phone: 337-482-5165; E-mail: dep5418@louisiana.edu.
Softball: Stefni Lotief; Phone: 337-482-6334; E-mail: slotief@louisiana.edu.
Tennis: Justin McGrath; Phone: 337-482-6328; E-mail: jrm2982@louisiana.edu.

Track and Field: Lance Veazey; Phone: 337-482-6313.
Volleyball: Becky Madden; Phone: 337-482-6327; E-mail: bsm7985@louisiana.edu.

UNIVERSITY OF LOUISIANA AT MONROE
Monroe, Louisiana

Indians ◆ NCAA I ◆ Southland Conference; Sun Belt Conference ◆ http://www.ulm.edu/

State-supported university, founded 1931
Coed, 7,231 undergraduate students, 81% full-time, 65% women, 35% men
Urban 238-acre campus
Noncompetitive entrance level, 98% of applicants were admitted

Freshmen *Admission:* 1,405 applied, 1,387 were accepted, 1,364 enrolled.
Tuition and fees (2003–04): $2910 (resident), $8862 (nonresident). *Room and board:* $1645 (room only: $2200).
Athletic Department: *Director of Athletics:* Bruce Hanks; Phone: 318-342-5361; Fax: 318-342-5367; E-mail: hanks@ulm.edu. *Sports Information Director:* Hank Largin; Phone: 318-342-5442; E-mail: largin@ulm.edu.

MEN'S COACHES

Baseball: Brad Holland; Phone: 318-342-3591; E-mail: bholland@ulm.edu.
Basketball: Mike Vining; Phone: 318-342-5401.
Cheerleading: Jennifer Hyde; Phone: 318-342-5293; E-mail: hyde@ulm.edu.
Cross Country: J.D. Malone; Phone: 318-342-5390; E-mail: malone@ulm.edu.
Diving: Sean Braud; Phone: 318-342-5316.
Football: Charlie Weatherbie; Phone: 318-342-3575; E-mail: weatherbie@ulm.edu.
Golf: Rick Merritt; Phone: 318-342-3569; E-mail: merritt@ulm.edu.
Swimming: John Pittington; Phone: 318-342-5316; E-mail: pittington@ulm.edu.
Track and Field: J.D. Malone; Phone: 318-342-5390; E-mail: malone@ulm.edu.

WOMEN'S COACHES

Basketball: Mona Martin; Phone: 318-342-5407; E-mail: martin@ulm.edu.
Cheerleading: Jennifer Hyde; Phone: 318-342-5293; E-mail: hyde@ulm.edu.
Cross Country: J.D. Malone; Phone: 318-342-5390; E-mail: malone@ulm.edu.
Diving: Sean Braud; Phone: 318-342-5316.
Soccer: Stacy Lamb; Phone: 318-342-5090; E-mail: lamb@ulm.edu.
Softball: Rosemary Holloway; Phone: 318-342-5408; E-mail: roholloway@ulm.edu.
Swimming: John Pittington; Phone: 318-342-5316; E-mail: pittington@ulm.edu.
Tennis: Maria Zavala; Phone: 318-342-5394; E-mail: zavala@ulm.edu.
Track and Field: J.D. Malone; Phone: 318-342-5390; E-mail: malone@ulm.edu.
Volleyball: Alycia Varytimidis; Phone: 318-342-5406; E-mail: varytimidis@ulm.edu.

UNIVERSITY OF LOUISVILLE
Louisville, Kentucky

Cardinals ◆ NCAA I ◆ Conference USA Conference; Mid-American Conference ◆ http://www.louisville.edu/

State-supported university, founded 1798
Coed, 14,724 undergraduate students, 73% full-time, 53% women, 47% men
Urban 169-acre campus
Moderately difficult entrance level, 78% of applicants were admitted

Freshmen *Admission:* 5,284 applied, 4,189 were accepted, 2,251 enrolled.

Tuition and fees (2003–04): $4344 (resident), $11,856 (nonresident).
Room and board: $4312 (room only: $2772).
Financial Aid (All incoming freshmen): *Average need-based gift aid:* $5512.
Average non-need based aid: $4659. *Average aid to full-time under-graduates:* $7452.
Athletic Department: *Director of Athletics:* Tom Jurich; *Phone:* 502-852-5732; *Fax:* 502-852-6557; *E-mail:* jurich@louisville.edu. *Sports Information Director:* Kenny Klein; *Phone:* 502-852-6581; *E-mail:* kenny.klein@louisville.edu.

MEN'S COACHES

Baseball: Lelo Prado; *Phone:* 502-852-0103; *E-mail:* a0prad01@gwise.louisville.edu.
Basketball: Rick Pitino; *Phone:* 502-852-6651; *E-mail:* rapiti01@louisville.edu.
Cheerleading: Misty Hodges; *Phone:* 502-969-4111; *E-mail:* mistykatul@msn.com.
Cross Country: Gene Weis; *Phone:* 502-852-0106; *E-mail:* gmweis01@gwise.louisville.edu.
Diving: Mike Zehnder; *Phone:* 502-852-8848.
Football: Booby Petrino; *Phone:* 502-852-7775; *E-mail:* bobby.petrino@louisville.edu.
Golf: Mark Crabtree; *Phone:* 502-852-8452; *E-mail:* mlcrab01@gwise.louisville.edu.
Soccer: Tony Colvecchia; *Phone:* 502-852-0105; *E-mail:* a0cola01@gwise.louisville.edu.
Swimming: Arthur Albiero; *Phone:* 502-852-8848; *E-mail:* arthur.albiero@louisville.edu.
Tennis: Rex Ecarma; *Phone:* 502-852-0217; *E-mail:* rrecar01@gwise.louisville.edu.
Track and Field: Gene Weis; *Phone:* 502-852-0106; *E-mail:* gmweis01@gwise.louisville.edu.

WOMEN'S COACHES

Basketball: Tom Collen; *Phone:* 502-852-0221; *E-mail:* t0coll01@gwise.louisville.edu.
Cheerleading: Misty Hodges; *Phone:* 502-969-4111; *E-mail:* mistykatul@msn.com.
Cross Country: Warren Bye; *Phone:* 502-852-0194; *E-mail:* jwbye001@gwise.louisville.edu.
Diving: Mike Zehnder; *Phone:* 502-852-8848.
Field Hockey: Pam Bustin; *Phone:* 502-852-0215; *E-mail:* plbust01@gwise.louisville.edu.
Golf: Kelly Meyers; *Phone:* 502-852-1768; *E-mail:* kellym@louisville.edu.
Soccer: Karen Ferguson; *Phone:* 502-852-0104; *E-mail:* kferguson@louisville.edu.
Softball: Sandy Pearsall; *Phone:* 502-852-1782; *E-mail:* sjpear01@gwise.louisville.edu.
Swimming: Arthur Albiero; *Phone:* 502-852-8848; *E-mail:* arthur.albiero@louisville.edu.
Tennis: Greg Davis; *Phone:* 502-852-3357; *E-mail:* gedavi01@gwise.louisville.edu.
Track and Field: Warren Bye; *Phone:* 502-852-0194; *E-mail:* jwbye001@gwise.louisville.edu.
Volleyball: Leonid Yelin; *Phone:* 502-852-0218; *E-mail:* yelin@louisville.edu.

UNIVERSITY OF MAINE
Orono, Maine

Black Bears ◆ NCAA I ◆ America East Conference; Atlantic 10 Conference; Hockey East Conference ◆ http://www.umaine.edu/

State-supported university, founded 1865, part of University of Maine System
Coed, 8,972 undergraduate students, 82% full-time, 52% women, 48% men
Small-town 3,300-acre campus
Moderately difficult entrance level, 73% of applicants were admitted

Freshmen *Admission:* 5,540 applied, 4,204 were accepted, 1,662 enrolled. *Test scores:* SAT verbal scores over 500: 69%; SAT math scores over 500: 72%; SAT verbal scores over 600: 24%; SAT math scores over 600: 28%; SAT verbal scores over 700: 3%; SAT math scores over 700: 4%.

Tuition and fees (2003–04): $5914 (resident), $14,614 (nonresident).
Room and board: $6166 (room only: $3182).
Financial Aid (All incoming freshmen): *Average need-based gift aid:* $5667. *Average non-need based aid:* $3882. *Average aid to full-time under-graduates:* $9047.
Athletic Department: *Director of Athletics:* Patrick Nero; *Phone:* 207-581-1052; *Fax:* 207-581-3070. *Sports Information Director:* Brent Williamson; *Phone:* 207-581-4158; *E-mail:* brent.williamson@umit.maine.edu.

MEN'S COACHES

Baseball: Phil Kostacopoulos; *Phone:* 207-581-1090; *E-mail:* paul_kostacopoulos@umit.maine.edu.
Basketball: John Giannini; *Phone:* 207-581-1059.
Cheerleading: Melinda Kenny; *Phone:* 207-581-1485; *E-mail:* mparent@bucksportschools.com.
Cross Country: Jim Ballinger; *Phone:* 207-581-1078; *E-mail:* jim_ballinger@umit.maine.edu.
Diving: Jaret Lizzotte; *Phone:* 207-581-1076.
Football: Jack Cosgrove; *Phone:* 207-581-1061; *E-mail:* jack_cosgrove@umit.maine.edu.
Ice Hockey: Tim Whitehead; *Phone:* 207-581-1108; *E-mail:* tim_whitehead@umit.maine.edu.
Soccer: Travers Evans; *Phone:* 207-581-4777; *E-mail:* travers_evans@umit.maine.edu.
Swimming: Jeff Wren; *Phone:* 207-581-1076; *E-mail:* jeff_wren@umit.maine.edu.
Track and Field: Jim Ballinger; *Phone:* 207-581-1078; *E-mail:* jim_ballinger@umit.maine.edu.

WOMEN'S COACHES

Basketball: Sharon Versyp; *Phone:* 207-581-4067; *E-mail:* sharon_versyp@umit.maine.edu.
Cheerleading: Melinda Kenny; *Phone:* 207-581-1485; *E-mail:* mparent@bucksportschools.com.
Cross Country: Marck Lech; *Phone:* 207-581-1079; *E-mail:* mark_lech@umit.maine.edu.
Diving: Jaret Lizzotte; *Phone:* 207-581-1076.
Field Hockey: Terry Kix; *Phone:* 207-581-2004; *E-mail:* terry_kix@umit.maine.edu.
Soccer: Scott Atherley; *Phone:* 207-581-3050; *E-mail:* scott_atherley@umit.maine.edu.
Softball: Deb Smith; *Phone:* 207-581-4065; *E-mail:* deb_smith@umit.maine.edu.
Swimming: Jeff Wren; *Phone:* 207-581-1076; *E-mail:* jeff_wren@umit.maine.edu.
Track and Field: Jim Ballinger; *Phone:* 207-581-1078; *E-mail:* jim_ballinger@umit.maine.edu.
Volleyball: Sue Medley; *Phone:* 207-581-1048; *E-mail:* sue_medley@umit.maine.edu.

UNIVERSITY OF MAINE AT FARMINGTON
Farmington, Maine

Beavers ◆ NCAA III ◆ North Atlantic Conference ◆ http://www.umf.maine.edu/

State-supported 4-year, founded 1863, part of University of Maine System
Coed, 2,420 undergraduate students, 87% full-time, 67% women, 33% men
Small-town 50-acre campus
Moderately difficult entrance level, 7% of applicants were admitted

Freshmen *Admission:* 1,521 applied, 1,095 were accepted, 523 enrolled. *Test scores:* SAT verbal scores over 500: 64%; SAT math scores over 500: 62%; SAT verbal scores over 600: 22%; SAT math scores over 600: 16%; SAT verbal scores over 700: 2%; SAT math scores over 700: 2%.
Tuition and fees (2003–04): $4872 (resident), $11,052 (nonresident).
Room and board: $5318 (room only: $2848).
Financial Aid (All incoming freshmen): *Average need-based gift aid:* $4640. *Average non-need based aid:* $1947. *Average aid to full-time under-graduates:* $7869.
Athletic Department: *Director of Athletics:* Julie Davis; *Phone:* 207-778-7264; *Fax:* 207-778-8177; *E-mail:* jadavis@maine.edu. *Sports Information Director:* Jamie Beaudoin; *Phone:* 207-778-8168; *E-mail:* jbeaudoin@maine.edu.

University of Maine at Farmington (continued)

MEN'S COACHES

Baseball: Dick Meader; Phone: 207-778-7148; E-mail: meader@maine.edu.

Basketball: Dick Meader; Phone: 207-778-7148; E-mail: meader@maine.edu.

Cross Country: Arvid Cullenburg; Phone: 207-778-7567; E-mail: arvid.cullenberg@maine.edu.

Golf: Jon Moody; Phone: 207-778-7566; E-mail: jmoody@sad47.k12.me.us.

Soccer: Bob Leib; Phone: 207-778-7144; E-mail: rbleib@maine.edu.

WOMEN'S COACHES

Basketball: Jamie Beaudoin; Phone: 207-778-8168; E-mail: jbeaudoin@maine.edu.

Cross Country: Julie Davis; Phone: 207-778-7264; E-mail: jadavis@maine.edu.

Field Hockey: Beth Evans; Phone: 207-778-7375; E-mail: eevans@maine.edu.

Soccer: Bob Leib; Phone: 207-778-7144; E-mail: rbleib@maine.edu.

Softball: Bob Leib; Phone: 207-778-7144; E-mail: rbleib@maine.edu.

Volleyball: Jim Gallagher; Phone: 207-778-7143; E-mail: jim.gallagher@maine.edu.

UNIVERSITY OF MAINE AT FORT KENT

Fort Kent, Maine

Tigers ◆ NAIA ◆ Sunrise Conference
◆ http://www.umfk.maine.edu/

State-supported 4-year, founded 1878, part of University of Maine System

Coed, 924 undergraduate students

Rural 52-acre campus

Moderately difficult entrance level, 91% of applicants were admitted

Freshmen *Admission:* 292 applied, 267 were accepted. *Test scores:* SAT verbal scores over 500: 24%; SAT math scores over 500: 34%; SAT verbal scores over 600: 8%; SAT math scores over 600: 14%; SAT math scores over 700: 2%.

Tuition and fees (2004–05): $4514 (resident), $10,154 (nonresident). *Room and board:* $5564 (room only: $3026).

Financial Aid (All incoming freshmen): *Average need-based gift aid:* $3561. *Average non-need based aid:* $2819. *Average aid to full-time undergraduates:* $3648.

Athletic Department: *Director of Athletics:* John Murphy; Phone: 207-834-7571; Fax: 207-834-3144; E-mail: jdmurphy@maine.edu. *Sports Information Director:* James Graffam; Phone: 207-834-7571; E-mail: jgraffam@maine.edu.

MEN'S COACHES

Basketball: Eric Werntgen; Phone: 207-834-7571; E-mail: werntgen@maine.edu.

Soccer: Melik Khoury; Phone: 207-834-7571; E-mail: mkhoury@maine.edu.

WOMEN'S COACHES

Basketball: Lucas Levesque; Phone: 207-834-7571.

Soccer: Eric Werntgen; Phone: 207-834-7571; E-mail: werntgen@maine.edu.

UNIVERSITY OF MAINE AT MACHIAS

Machias, Maine

Clippers ◆ NAIA ◆ Sunrise Conference
◆ http://www.umm.maine.edu/

State-supported 4-year, founded 1909, part of University of Maine System

Coed, 1,313 undergraduate students, 44% full-time, 72% women, 28% men

Rural 42-acre campus

Moderately difficult entrance level, 82% of applicants were admitted

Freshmen *Admission:* 510 applied, 416 were accepted, 160 enrolled. *Test scores:* SAT verbal scores over 500: 35%; SAT math scores over

500: 34%; SAT verbal scores over 600: 10%; SAT math scores over 600: 5%; SAT verbal scores over 700: 1%.

Tuition and fees (2003–04): $4121 (resident), $10,115 (nonresident). *Room and board:* $5150 (room only: $2592).

Financial Aid (All incoming freshmen): *Average need-based gift aid:* $5099. *Average non-need based aid:* $3654. *Average aid to full-time undergraduates:* $7088.

Athletic Department: *Director of Athletics:* Bob Helper; Phone: 207-255-1403; Fax: 207-255-4864; E-mail: rhepler@maine.edu.

MEN'S COACHES

Basketball: Randy Lee; Phone: 207-255-1290; E-mail: rlee@maine.edu.

Cross Country: Randy Lee; Phone: 207-255-1290; E-mail: rlee@maine.edu.

Soccer: M.J. Ball; Phone: 207-255-1387; E-mail: mjball@maine.edu.

WOMEN'S COACHES

Basketball: Dean Preston; Phone: 207-255-1379; E-mail: prestond@maine.edu.

Cross Country: Randy Lee; Phone: 207-255-1290; E-mail: rlee@maine.edu.

Soccer: M.J. Ball; Phone: 207-255-1387; E-mail: mjball@maine.edu.

Volleyball: Coral Snowdeal; Phone: 207-255-1394; E-mail: csnowdeal@maine.edu.

UNIVERSITY OF MAINE AT PRESQUE ISLE

Presque Isle, Maine

Owls ◆ NAIA ◆ Sunrise Conference
◆ http://www.umpi.maine.edu/

State-supported 4-year, founded 1903, part of University of Maine System

Coed, 1,546 undergraduate students, 70% full-time, 67% women, 33% men

Small-town 150-acre campus

Minimally difficult entrance level, 85% of applicants were admitted

Freshmen *Admission:* 520 applied, 454 were accepted, 222 enrolled. *Test scores:* SAT verbal scores over 500: 32%; SAT math scores over 500: 30%; SAT verbal scores over 600: 7%; SAT math scores over 600: 6%; SAT math scores over 700: 1%.

Tuition and fees (2003–04): $4190 (resident), $9740 (nonresident). *Room and board:* $4965 (room only: $2835).

Financial Aid (All incoming freshmen): *Average need-based gift aid:* $5014. *Average non-need based aid:* $3372. *Average aid to full-time undergraduates:* $6625.

Athletic Department: *Director of Athletics:* Rich Ward; Phone: 207-768-9475; Fax: 207-768-9476; E-mail: wardr@polaris.umpi.maine.edu.

MEN'S COACHES

Baseball: Leo Saucier; Phone: 207-768-9421; E-mail: saucierl@polaris.umpi.maine.edu.

Basketball: Rich Ward; Phone: 207-768-9475; E-mail: wardr@polaris.umpi.maine.edu.

Cross Country: Chris Smith; Phone: 207-768-9472; E-mail: carlosm@polaris.umpi.maine.edu.

Golf: Joe Zubrick; Phone: 207-768-9689; E-mail: zubrickj@polaris.umpi.maine.edu.

Soccer: Alan Gordon; Phone: 207-768-9473; E-mail: gordona@polaris.umpi.maine.edu.

WOMEN'S COACHES

Basketball: Alan Gordon; Phone: 207-768-9473; E-mail: gordona@polaris.umpi.maine.edu.

Cross Country: Chris Smith; Phone: 207-768-9472; E-mail: carlosm@polaris.umpi.maine.edu.

Soccer: Michael Carlos; Phone: 207-768-9477; E-mail: carlosm@polaris.umpi.maine.edu.

Softball: Michael Carlos; Phone: 207-768-9477; E-mail: carlosm@polaris.umpi.maine.edu.

Volleyball: Serge Bodreau; Phone: 207-768-9475.

UNIVERSITY OF MARY
Bismarck, North Dakota

Marauders ◆ NAIA ◆ Dakota Conference
◆ http://www.umary.edu/

Independent Roman Catholic comprehensive, founded 1959
Coed, 2,152 undergraduate students, 90% full-time, 61% women, 39% men
Suburban 107-acre campus
Moderately difficult entrance level, 88% of applicants were admitted

Freshmen *Admission:* 890 applied, 804 were accepted, 391 enrolled.
Tuition and fees (2004–05): $10,290 (full-time). *Room and board:* $4080 (room only: $1940).
Athletic Department: *Director of Athletics:* Al Bortke; Phone: 701-255-7500; Fax: 701-255-7687; E-mail: abortke@umary.edu. *Sports Information Director:* Heidi Bale; Phone: 701-355-7500; E-mail: hbale@umary.edu.

MEN'S COACHES
Baseball: Van Vanatta; Phone: 701-355-8270; E-mail: vvanatta@umary.edu.
Basketball: Jim Feeney; Phone: 701-355-8220; E-mail: jfeeney@umary.edu.
Cheerleading: Tammi Perry; Phone: 701-255-7500.
Cross Country: Mike Thorson; Phone: 701-355-8280; E-mail: mthorson@umary.edu.
Football: Myron Schultz; Phone: 701-355-8230; E-mail: mschulz@umary.edu.
Soccer: Tim Mueller; Phone: 701-355-8144; E-mail: tmueller@umary.edu.
Tennis: Mike Skytland; Phone: 701-355-8200.
Track and Field: Mike Thorson; Phone: 701-355-8280; E-mail: mthorson@umary.edu.
Wrestling: Josh Kerbaugh; Phone: 701-355-8034; E-mail: kerbaugh@umary.edu.

WOMEN'S COACHES
Basketball: Fred Fridley; Phone: 701-355-8230; E-mail: ffridley@umary.edu.
Cheerleading: Tammi Perry; Phone: 701-255-7500.
Cross Country: Mike Thorson; Phone: 701-355-8280; E-mail: mthorson@umary.edu.
Soccer: Brock Thompson; Phone: 701-355-8260; E-mail: thompsonb@umary.edu.
Softball: Brad Walsh; Phone: 701-355-8232; E-mail: bwalsh@umary.edu.
Tennis: Mike Skytland; Phone: 701-355-8200.
Track and Field: Mike Thorson; Phone: 701-355-8280; E-mail: mthorson@umary.edu.
Volleyball: Heidi Sunderland; Phone: 701-355-8250; E-mail: hsunde@umary.edu.

UNIVERSITY OF MARY HARDIN-BAYLOR
Belton, Texas

Crusaders ◆ NCAA III ◆ American Southwest Conference
◆ http://www.umhb.edu/

Independent Southern Baptist comprehensive, founded 1845
Coed, 2,479 undergraduate students, 88% full-time, 65% women, 35% men
Small-town 100-acre campus with easy access to Austin
Moderately difficult entrance level, 71% of applicants were admitted

Freshmen *Admission:* 1,173 applied, 890 were accepted, 508 enrolled.
Test scores: SAT verbal scores over 500: 59%; SAT math scores over 500: 61%; SAT verbal scores over 600: 16%; SAT math scores over 600: 18%; SAT verbal scores over 700: 2%; SAT math scores over 700: 2%.
Tuition and fees (2003–04): $11,540 (full-time). *Room and board:* $4000.
Financial Aid (All incoming freshmen): *Average need-based gift aid:* $4922. *Average non-need based aid:* $3141. *Average aid to full-time undergraduates:* $9028.

Athletic Department: *Director of Athletics:* Ben Shipp; Phone: 254-295-4618; Fax: 254-295-4614; E-mail: bshipp@umhb.edu. *Sports Information Director:* Jon Wallin; Phone: 254-295-4611; E-mail: jwallin@umhb.edu.

MEN'S COACHES
Baseball: Micah Wells; Phone: 254-295-4619; E-mail: mwells@umhb.edu.
Basketball: Ken Deweese; Phone: 254-295-4594; E-mail: kdeweese@umhb.edu.
Football: Pete Fredenburg; Phone: 254-295-4226; E-mail: kgoff@umhb.edu.
Golf: Randy Mann; Phone: 254-295-4216; E-mail: rmann@umhb.edu.
Soccer: David Plunk; Phone: 254-295-4488; E-mail: dplunk@umhb.edu.
Tennis: James Cohagan; Phone: 254-295-4617; E-mail: jcohagan@umhb.edu.

WOMEN'S COACHES
Basketball: Margie Williamson; Phone: 254-295-4240; E-mail: mwilliamson@umhb.edu.
Golf: Darla Kirby; Phone: 254-295-5046; E-mail: dkirby@umhb.edu.
Soccer: Meghann Brown; Phone: 254-295-4215; E-mail: mbrown@umhb.edu.
Softball: Kasey Blomquist; Phone: 254-295-4170; E-mail: kblomquist@umhb.edu.
Tennis: James Cohagan; Phone: 254-295-4617; E-mail: jcohagan@umhb.edu.
Volleyball: Alice Taylor; Phone: 254-295-4616; E-mail: ataylor@umhb.edu.

UNIVERSITY OF MARYLAND, BALTIMORE COUNTY
Baltimore, Maryland

Retrievers ◆ NCAA I ◆ America East Conference ◆ http://www.umbc.edu/

State-supported university, founded 1963, part of University System of Maryland
Coed, 9,646 undergraduate students, 83% full-time, 47% women, 53% men
Suburban 530-acre campus with easy access to Washington, D.C.
Moderately difficult entrance level, 64% of applicants were admitted

Freshmen *Admission:* 5,501 applied, 3,167 were accepted, 1,505 enrolled. *Test scores:* SAT verbal scores over 500: 91%; SAT math scores over 500: 97%; SAT verbal scores over 600: 47%; SAT math scores over 600: 65%; SAT verbal scores over 700: 9%; SAT math scores over 700: 17%.
Tuition and fees (2003–04): $7388 (resident), $14,240 (nonresident). *Room and board:* $7007 (room only: $4714).
Financial Aid (All incoming freshmen): *Average need-based gift aid:* $3677. *Average non-need based aid:* $6341. *Average aid to full-time undergraduates:* $6023.
Athletic Department: *Director of Athletics:* Charles Brown; Phone: 410-455-2207; Fax: 410-455-1536; E-mail: chbrown@umbc.edu. *Sports Information Director:* Steve Levy; Phone: 410-455-2197; E-mail: slevy@umbc.edu.

MEN'S COACHES
Baseball: John Jancuska; Phone: 410-455-2239; E-mail: jancuska@umbc.edu.
Basketball: Tom Sullivan; Phone: 410-455-2864; E-mail: tsulliva@umbc.edu.
Cross Country: Murray Davis; Phone: 410-455-1579; E-mail: jdavis@umbc.edu.
Diving: Vic Corbin; Phone: 410-455-2679; E-mail: corbin@umbc.edu.
Lacrosse: Don Zimmerman; Phone: 410-455-1323; E-mail: dzimmerm@umbc.edu.
Soccer: Pete Caringi; Phone: 410-455-3003; E-mail: caringij@umbc.edu.
Swimming: Chad Cradrock; Phone: 410-455-2670; E-mail: ccradock@umbc.edu.
Tennis: Keith Puryear; Phone: 410-455-1327; E-mail: puryear@umbc.edu.
Track and Field: David Bobb; Phone: 410-455-6588; E-mail: dbobb1@umbc.edu.

University of Maryland, Baltimore County (continued)

WOMEN'S COACHES

Basketball: Phil Stern; Phone: 410-455-3279; E-mail: pstern@umbc.edu.

Cross Country: Murray Davis; Phone: 410-455-1579; E-mail: jdavis@umbc.edu.

Diving: Vic Corbin; Phone: 410-455-2679; E-mail: corbin@umbc.edu.

Field Hockey: Kristy Hartman; Phone: 410-455-1282; E-mail: fieldhockey@umbc.edu.

Lacrosse: Monica Yeakel; Phone: 410-455-6355; E-mail: dicandil@umbc.edu.

Soccer: Michelle Salmon; Phone: 410-455-2013; E-mail: salmon@umbc.edu.

Softball: Joe French; Phone: 410-455-1325; E-mail: jfrench@umbc.edu.

Swimming: Chad Cradrock; Phone: 410-455-2670; E-mail: ccradock@umbc.edu.

Tennis: Keith Puryear; Phone: 410-455-1327; E-mail: puryear@umbc.edu.

Track and Field: David Bobb; Phone: 410-455-6588; E-mail: dbobb1@umbc.edu.

Volleyball: Greg Giovanazzi; Phone: 410-455-3241.

UNIVERSITY OF MARYLAND, COLLEGE PARK

College Park, Maryland

Terrapins ◆ NCAA I ◆ Atlantic Coast Conference ◆ http://www.maryland.edu/

State-supported university, founded 1856, part of University System of Maryland

Coed, 25,379 undergraduate students, 91% full-time, 49% women, 51% men

Suburban 3,688-acre campus with easy access to Baltimore and Washington, DC

Moderately difficult entrance level, 4% of applicants were admitted

Freshmen Admission: 25,028 applied, 10,679 were accepted, 4,063 enrolled. Test scores: SAT verbal scores over 500: 92%; SAT math scores over 500: 95%; SAT verbal scores over 600: 63%; SAT math scores over 600: 77%; SAT verbal scores over 700: 14%; SAT math scores over 700: 26%.

Tuition and fees (2003–04): $6758 (resident), $17,432 (nonresident). Room and board: $7608 (room only: $4556).

Financial Aid (All incoming freshmen): Average need-based gift aid: $5194. Average non-need based aid: $4251. Average aid to full-time undergraduates: $8656.

Athletic Department: Director of Athletics: Deborah Yow; Phone: 301-314-7075; Fax: 301-314-7149; E-mail: dyow@umd.edu. Sports Information Director: Dave Haglund; Phone: 301-314-9433; E-mail: haglund@umd.edu.

MEN'S COACHES

Baseball: Terry Rupp; Phone: 301-314-7122; E-mail: rr202@umail.umd.edu.

Basketball: Gary Williams; Phone: 301-314-7029.

Cheerleading: Lura Fleece; Phone: 301-314-7075.

Cross Country: Trent Sanderson; Phone: 301-314-3330; E-mail: ts205@umail.umd.edu.

Diving: Michael Tober; Phone: 301-314-7031; E-mail: mtober@umd.edu.

Football: Ralph Friedgen; Phone: 301-314-7096.

Golf: Tom Hanna; Phone: 301-314-8157.

Lacrosse: Dave Cottle; Phone: 301-314-7117; E-mail: dc264@umail.umd.edu.

Soccer: Sasho Cirovski; Phone: 301-314-4161; E-mail: sc140@umail.umd.edu.

Swimming: Jim Wenhold; Phone: 301-314-7031; E-mail: jw40@umail.umd.edu.

Tennis: Jim Laitta; Phone: 301-314-7131; E-mail: laitta@wam.umd.edu.

Track and Field: Andrew Valmon; Phone: 301-314-6675; E-mail: avalmon@umd.edu.

Wrestling: Pat Santoro; Phone: 301-314-7134; E-mail: psantoro@umd.edu.

WOMEN'S COACHES

Basketball: Brenda Frese; Phone: 301-314-1747.

Cheerleading: Lura Fleece; Phone: 301-314-7075.

Cross Country: Trent Sanderson; Phone: 301-314-3330; E-mail: ts205@umail.umd.edu.

Diving: Michael Tober; Phone: 301-314-7031; E-mail: mtober@umd.edu.

Field Hockey: Missy Meharg; Phone: 301-314-3895; E-mail: mlmterp@wam.umd.edu.

Golf: Jason Rodenhaver; Phone: 301-314-4181; E-mail: rody@wam.umd.edu.

Gymnastics: Bob Nelligan; Phone: 301-314-7007; E-mail: rn@wam.umd.edu.

Lacrosse: Cindy Timchal; Phone: 301-314-4273; E-mail: cdtimcha@wam.umd.edu.

Soccer: Shannon Cirovski; Phone: 301-314-7034; E-mail: cirovski@aol.com.

Softball: Gina Lamandre; Phone: 301-314-6699; E-mail: lamandre@wam.umd.edu.

Swimming: Jim Wenhold; Phone: 301-314-7031; E-mail: jw40@umail.umd.edu.

Tennis: Martin Novak; Phone: 301-314-6601; E-mail: mn81@umail.umd.edu.

Track and Field: Andrew Valmon; Phone: 301-314-6675; E-mail: avalmon@umd.edu.

Volleyball: Janice Kruger; Phone: 301-314-9839; E-mail: jtkruger@wam.umd.edu.

UNIVERSITY OF MARYLAND EASTERN SHORE

Princess Anne, Maryland

Hawks ◆ NCAA I ◆ Mid-Eastern Athletic Conference ◆ http://www.umes.edu/

State-supported university, founded 1886, part of University System of Maryland

Coed, 3,326 undergraduate students, 87% full-time, 59% women, 41% men

Rural 700-acre campus

Moderately difficult entrance level, 58% of applicants were admitted

Freshmen Admission: 3,714 applied, 2,165 were accepted, 846 enrolled. Test scores: SAT verbal scores over 500: 18%; SAT math scores over 500: 16%; SAT verbal scores over 600: 2%; SAT math scores over 600: 2%; SAT verbal scores over 700: %; SAT math scores over 700: %.

Tuition and fees (2003–04): $5105 (resident), $10,440 (nonresident). Room and board: $5630 (room only: $3130).

Financial Aid (All incoming freshmen): Average need-based gift aid: $6350. Average non-need based aid: $2276. Average aid to full-time undergraduates: $10,150.

Athletic Department: Director of Athletics: Nelson Townsend; Phone: 410-651-6496; Fax: 410-651-7600; E-mail: netownsend@mail.umes.edu. Sports Information Director: Stan Bradley; Phone: 410-651-6499; E-mail: gsbradley@mail.umes.edu.

MEN'S COACHES

Baseball: Robert Rodriguez; Phone: 410-651-8158; E-mail: rerodriquez@mail.umes.edu.

Basketball: Thomas Trotter; Phone: 410-651-6541; E-mail: tctrotter@umes.edu.

Cross Country: Ernest Barrett; Phone: 410-651-6710; E-mail: egbarrett@umes.edu.

Tennis: Doug Wright; Phone: 410-651-7837; E-mail: drwright@umes.edu.

Track and Field: Ernest Barrett; Phone: 410-651-6710; E-mail: egbarrett@umes.edu.

WOMEN'S COACHES

Basketball: Surina Dixon; Phone: 410-651-6537; E-mail: sdixon@umes.edu.

Cross Country: Ernest Barrett; Phone: 410-651-6710; E-mail: egbarrett@umes.edu.

Softball: Barbara Hicks; Phone: 410-651-6535; E-mail: bshicks@mail.umes.edu.

Tennis: Doug Wright; Phone: 410-651-7837; E-mail: drwright@umes.edu.

Track and Field: Ernest Barrett; Phone: 410-651-6710; E-mail: egbarrett@umes.edu.

Volleyball: Toby Rens; Phone: 410-651-6538; E-mail: trens@umes.edu.

UNIVERSITY OF MARY WASHINGTON

Fredericksburg, Virginia

Eagles ◆ NCAA III ◆ Capital Athletic Conference ◆ http://www.umw.edu/

State-supported comprehensive, founded 1908
Coed, 4,220 undergraduate students, 85% full-time, 67% women, 33% men
Small-town 176-acre campus with easy access to Richmond and Washington, DC
Very difficult entrance level, 60% of applicants were admitted

Freshmen *Admission:* 4,472 applied, 2,676 were accepted, 869 enrolled. *Test scores:* SAT verbal scores over 500: 96%; SAT math scores over 500: 96%; SAT verbal scores over 600: 63%; SAT math scores over 600: 57%; SAT verbal scores over 700: 11%; SAT math scores over 700: 8%.
Tuition and fees (2003–04): $4424 (resident), $12,172 (nonresident). *Room and board:* $5478 (room only: $3160).
Financial Aid (All incoming freshmen): *Average need-based gift aid:* $2825. *Average non-need based aid:* $1080. *Average aid to full-time undergraduates:* $4450.
Athletic Department: *Director of Athletics:* Edward Hegmann; Phone: 540-654-1876; Fax: 540-654-1892; E-mail: ehegmann@mwc.edu. *Sports Information Director:* Clint Often; Phone: 540-654-1743; E-mail: coften@mwc.edu.

MEN'S COACHES

Baseball: Tom Sheridan; Phone: 540-654-1882; E-mail: tsherida@mwc.edu.
Basketball: Rod Wood; Phone: 540-654-1887; E-mail: rwood@mwc.edu.
Cross Country: Stan Soper; Phone: 540-654-1886; E-mail: dsoper@mwc.edu.
Lacrosse: Kurt Glaeser; Phone: 540-654-1883; E-mail: kglaeser@mwc.edu.
Soccer: Roy Gordon; Phone: 540-654-1875; E-mail: rgordon@mwc.edu.
Swimming: Matt Kinney; Phone: 540-654-1889; E-mail: mkinney@mwc.edu.
Tennis: Todd Helbing; Phone: 540-654-1908; E-mail: thelblin@mwc.edu.
Track and Field: Stan Soper; Phone: 540-654-1886; E-mail: dsoper@mwc.edu.

WOMEN'S COACHES

Basketball: Deena Applebury; Phone: 540-654-1888; E-mail: dapplebu@mwc.edu.
Cross Country: Stan Soper; Phone: 540-654-1886; E-mail: dsoper@mwc.edu.
Field Hockey: Dana Hall; Phone: 540-654-1890; E-mail: dhall@mwc.edu.
Lacrosse: Dana Hall; Phone: 540-654-1890; E-mail: dhall@mwc.edu.
Soccer: Kurt Glaeser; Phone: 540-654-1883; E-mail: kglaeser@mwc.edu.
Softball: Dee Conway; Phone: 540-654-1885; E-mail: dconway@mwc.edu.
Swimming: Matt Kinney; Phone: 540-654-1889; E-mail: mkinney@mwc.edu.
Tennis: Cindy Vanderberg; Phone: 540-654-1871; E-mail: cvanderb@mwc.edu.
Track and Field: Stan Soper; Phone: 540-654-1886; E-mail: dsoper@mwc.edu.
Volleyball: Dee Conway; Phone: 540-654-1885; E-mail: dconway@mwc.edu.

UNIVERSITY OF MASSACHUSETTS AMHERST

Amherst, Massachusetts

Minutemen ◆ NCAA I ◆ Atlantic 10 Conference; Hockey East Conference ◆ http://www.umass.edu/

State-supported university, founded 1863, part of University of Massachusetts
Coed, 18,718 undergraduate students, 93% full-time, 50% women, 50% men
Small-town 1,463-acre campus with easy access to Hartford
Moderately difficult entrance level, 81% of applicants were admitted

Freshmen *Admission:* 16,427 applied, 13,461 were accepted, 4,194 enrolled. *Test scores:* SAT verbal scores over 500: 80%; SAT math scores over 500: 85%; SAT verbal scores over 600: 33%; SAT math scores over 600: 39%; SAT verbal scores over 700: 5%; SAT math scores over 700: 7%.
Tuition and fees (2003–04): $8410 (resident), $16,633 (nonresident). *Room and board:* $5748 (room only: $3235).
Financial Aid (All incoming freshmen): *Average need-based gift aid:* $5557. *Average non-need based aid:* $4708. *Average aid to full-time undergraduates:* $8084.
Athletic Department: *Director of Athletics:* John McCutcheon; Phone: 413-545-9652; Fax: 413-545-1556; E-mail: jmccutch@admin.umass.edu. *Sports Information Director:* Charles Bare; Phone: 413-545-2439; E-mail: cbare@admin.umass.edu.

MEN'S COACHES

Baseball: Mike Stone; Phone: 413-545-3120; E-mail: mstone@admin.umass.edu.
Basketball: Steve Lappas; Phone: 413-545-2610; E-mail: slappas@admin.umass.edu.
Cheerleading: Kelly Proctor; Phone: 413-545-1928; E-mail: docproc117@aol.com.
Cross Country: Ken O'Brien; Phone: 413-545-0097; E-mail: obumass@aol.com.
Diving: Mandy Hixon; Phone: 413-545-1813; E-mail: aghixon@admin.umass.edu.
Football: Mark Whipple; Phone: 413-545-2026.
Ice Hockey: Don Cahoon; Phone: 413-545-5175; E-mail: dcahoon@admin.umass.edu.
Lacrosse: Greg Cannella; Phone: 413-545-3782; E-mail: cannella@admin.umass.edu.
Soccer: Sam Koch; Phone: 413-545-4341; E-mail: skoch@admin.umass.edu.
Swimming: Russ Yarworth; Phone: 413-545-0093; E-mail: yarworth@admin.umass.edu.
Track and Field: Ken O'Brien; Phone: 413-545-0097; E-mail: obumass@aol.com.

WOMEN'S COACHES

Basketball: Marnie Dacko; Phone: 413-545-2726; E-mail: marnie@admin.umass.edu.
Cheerleading: Kelly Proctor; Phone: 413-545-1928; E-mail: docproc117@aol.com.
Cross Country: Julie Lafreniere; Phone: 413-545-2759; E-mail: julie@admin.umass.edu.
Diving: Mandy Hixon; Phone: 413-545-1813; E-mail: aghixon@admin.umass.edu.
Field Hockey: Pat Shea; Phone: 413-545-1942; E-mail: fldhcky@admin.umass.edu.
Lacrosse: Carrie Bolduc; Phone: 413-545-3157; E-mail: csbolduc@admin.umass.edu.
Soccer: Jim Rudy; Phone: 413-545-4343; E-mail: wsoccer@admin.umass.edu.
Softball: Elaine Sortino; Phone: 413-545-0038; E-mail: elaine@admin.umass.edu.
Swimming: Robert Newcomb; Phone: 413-545-4342; E-mail: rnewc@admin.umass.edu.
Tennis: Judy Dixon; Phone: 413-545-1593; E-mail: dixon@admin.umass.edu.
Track and Field: Julie Lafreniere; Phone: 413-545-2759; E-mail: julie@admin.umass.edu.

UNIVERSITY OF MASSACHUSETTS BOSTON

Boston, Massachusetts

Beacons ◆ NCAA III ◆ Little East Conference ◆ http://www.umb.edu/

State-supported university, founded 1964, part of University of Massachusetts
Coed, 9,650 undergraduate students, 60% full-time, 58% women, 42% men
Urban 177-acre campus
Moderately difficult entrance level, 5% of applicants were admitted

Freshmen *Admission:* 2,834 applied, 1,561 were accepted, 610 enrolled. *Test scores:* SAT verbal scores over 500: 55%; SAT math scores over 500: 63%; SAT verbal scores over 600: 15%; SAT math scores over 600: 16%; SAT verbal scores over 700: 1%; SAT math scores over 700: 3%.
Tuition and fees (2003–04): $6977 (resident), $17,637 (nonresident).
Financial Aid (All incoming freshmen): *Average need-based gift aid:* $4878. *Average non-need based aid:* $2424. *Average aid to full-time undergraduates:* $8617.
Athletic Department: *Director of Athletics:* Charlie Titus; Phone: 617-287-7810; Fax: 617-287-7840; E-mail: charlie.titus@umb.edu. *Sports Information Director:* Alan Wickstrom; Phone: 617-287-7815; E-mail: alan.wickstrom@umb.edu.

MEN'S COACHES

Baseball: Mark Bettencourt; Phone: 617-287-7817; E-mail: mark.bettencourt@umb.edu.
Basketball: Charlie Titus; Phone: 617-287-7810; E-mail: charlie.titus@umb.edu.
Cross Country: Chris Fitzgerald; Phone: 617-287-6788; E-mail: chris.fitzgerald@umb.edu.
Ice Hockey: Jack Foley; Phone: 617-287-7812; E-mail: jack.foley@umb.edu.
Lacrosse: Myles Berry; Phone: 617-287-7822; E-mail: myles.berry@umb.edu.
Soccer: Myles Berry; Phone: 617-287-7822; E-mail: myles.berry@umb.edu.
Tennis: Phone: 617-287-7846.

WOMEN'S COACHES

Basketball: Shawn Polk; Phone: 617-287-7848; E-mail: shawn.polk@umb.edu.
Cross Country: Chris Fitzgerald; Phone: 617-287-6788; E-mail: chris.fitzgerald@umb.edu.
Soccer: Gretchen Randall; Phone: 617-287-7851; E-mail: gretchen.randall@umb.edu.
Softball: Gretchen Randall; Phone: 617-287-7851; E-mail: gretchen.randall@umb.edu.
Tennis: Phone: 617-287-7846.
Volleyball: Ken Goon; Phone: 617-287-7859; E-mail: ken.goon@umb.edu.

UNIVERSITY OF MASSACHUSETTS DARTMOUTH

North Dartmouth, Massachusetts

Corsairs ◆ NCAA III ◆ Little East Conference; New England Football Conference ◆ http://www.umassd.edu/

State-supported comprehensive, founded 1895, part of University of Massachusetts
Coed, 7,359 undergraduate students, 80% full-time, 52% women, 48% men
Suburban 710-acre campus with easy access to Boston and Providence
Moderately difficult entrance level, 70% of applicants were admitted

Freshmen *Admission:* 6,049 applied, 4,268 were accepted, 1,523 enrolled. *Test scores:* SAT verbal scores over 500: 67%; SAT math scores over 500: 71%; SAT verbal scores over 600: 17%; SAT math scores over 600: 19%; SAT verbal scores over 700: 1%; SAT math scores over 700: 2%.

Tuition and fees (2003–04): $6129 (resident), $12,811 (nonresident). *Room and board:* $7099 (room only: $4076).
Financial Aid (All incoming freshmen): *Average need-based gift aid:* $4828. *Average non-need based aid:* $2963. *Average aid to full-time undergraduates:* $6709.
Athletic Department: *Director of Athletics:* Robert Mullen; Phone: 508-999-8720; Fax: 508-999-8867; E-mail: rmullen@umassd.edu. *Sports Information Director:* Bill Gathright; Phone: 508-999-8727.

MEN'S COACHES

Baseball: Bruce Wheeler; Phone: 508-999-8721; E-mail: bwheeler@umassd.edu.
Basketball: Brian Baptiste; Phone: 508-999-8724; E-mail: bbaptiste@umassd.edu.
Cheerleading: Lisa Cabral; Phone: 508-999-9173; E-mail: l1cabral@umassd.edu.
Cross Country: Jon Hird; Phone: 508-999-8725; E-mail: jhird@umassd.edu.
Diving: Catherine Motta; Phone: 508-999-8720; E-mail: cmotta@umassd.edu.
Football: William Kavanaugh; Phone: 508-999-8738; E-mail: wkavanaugh@umassd.edu.
Golf: Paul Fistori; Phone: 508-999-3015; E-mail: pfistori@umassd.edu.
Ice Hockey: John Rolli; Phone: 508-999-8723; E-mail: jrolli@umassd.edu.
Lacrosse: Kevin Mahoney; Phone: 508-999-9179; E-mail: mahoneyk@seekonk.k12.ma.us.
Soccer: Ray Cabral; Phone: 508-999-8170; E-mail: rcabral@umassd.edu.
Swimming: Catherine Motta; Phone: 508-999-8720; E-mail: cmotta@umassd.edu.
Tennis: Tom Mendell; Phone: 508-999-8720; E-mail: tmendell@umassd.edu.
Track and Field: Jon Hird; Phone: 508-999-8725; E-mail: jhird@umassd.edu.

WOMEN'S COACHES

Basketball: Mick Klitzner; Phone: 508-999-9114; E-mail: jklitzner@umassd.edu.
Cheerleading: Lisa Cabral; Phone: 508-999-9173; E-mail: l1cabral@umassd.edu.
Cross Country: Jon Hird; Phone: 508-999-8725; E-mail: jhird@umassd.edu.
Diving: Catherine Motta; Phone: 508-999-8720; E-mail: cmotta@umassd.edu.
Field Hockey: Marilyn Ritz; Phone: 508-999-8733; E-mail: mritz@umassd.edu.
Golf: Paul Fistori; Phone: 508-999-3015; E-mail: pfistori@umassd.edu.
Lacrosse: Jerry Jennings; Phone: 508-999-9255; E-mail: gjennings@umassd.edu.
Soccer: Alex Silva; Phone: 508-999-8842; E-mail: asilva@umassd.edu.
Softball: Marilyn Ritz; Phone: 508-999-8733; E-mail: mritz@umassd.edu.
Swimming: Catherine Motta; Phone: 508-999-8720; E-mail: cmotta@umassd.edu.
Tennis: Ralph Perry; Phone: 508-999-8124; E-mail: rperry@umassd.edu.
Track and Field: Jon Hird; Phone: 508-999-8725; E-mail: jhird@umassd.edu.
Volleyball: Richard Quintin; Phone: 508-999-8717; E-mail: rquintin@umassd.edu.

UNIVERSITY OF MASSACHUSETTS LOWELL

Lowell, Massachusetts

River Hawks ◆ NCAA II ◆ Hockey East Conference; Northeast-10 Conference ◆ http://www.uml.edu/

State-supported university, founded 1894, part of University of Massachusetts
Coed, 9,006 undergraduate students, 65% full-time, 41% women, 59% men
Urban 100-acre campus with easy access to Boston
Moderately difficult entrance level, 63% of applicants were admitted

Freshmen *Admission:* 4,233 applied, 2,630 were accepted, 1,020 enrolled. *Test scores:* SAT verbal scores over 500: 71%; SAT math scores

over 500: 82%; SAT verbal scores over 600: 21%; SAT math scores over 600: 29%; SAT verbal scores over 700: 3%; SAT math scores over 700: 3%.
Tuition and fees (2003–04): $6213 (resident), $13,326 (nonresident). *Room and board:* $5724 (room only: $3486).
Financial Aid (All incoming freshmen): *Average need-based gift aid:* $3580. *Average non-need based aid:* $3221. *Average aid to full-time undergraduates:* $7015.
Athletic Department: *Director of Athletics:* Dana Skinner; Phone: 978-934-2310; Fax: 978-934-2313; E-mail: dana_skinner@uml.edu. *Sports Information Director:* Chris O'Donnell; Phone: 978-934-2306; E-mail: chris_odonnell@uml.edu.

MEN'S COACHES
Baseball: Ken Connerty; Phone: 978-934-2344; E-mail: athletics@uml.edu.
Basketball: Ken Barer; Phone: 978-934-2340; E-mail: ken_barer@uml.edu.
Cross Country: Gary Gardner; Phone: 978-934-2342; E-mail: umltrack@uml.edu.
Ice Hockey: Blaise MacDonald; Phone: 978-934-2339; E-mail: blaise_macdonald@uml.edu.
Soccer: Ted Priestly; Phone: 978-934-2317; E-mail: edward_priestly@uml.edu.
Track and Field: Gary Gardner; Phone: 978-934-2342; E-mail: umltrack@uml.edu.

WOMEN'S COACHES
Basketball: Kathy O'Neil; Phone: 978-934-2325; E-mail: kathleen_oneil@uml.edu.
Cross Country: Gary Gardner; Phone: 978-934-2342; E-mail: umltrack@uml.edu.
Field Hockey: Shannon Hlebichuk; Phone: 978-934-3976; E-mail: shannon_hlebichuk@uml.edu.
Soccer: Elie Monteiro; Phone: 978-934-2346; E-mail: elie_montiero@uml.edu.
Softball: Harry Sauter; Phone: 978-934-3977; E-mail: hcsauter@aol.com.
Track and Field: Gary Gardner; Phone: 978-934-2342; E-mail: umltrack@uml.edu.
Volleyball: Karen McNulty; Phone: 978-934-2319; E-mail: karen_mcnulty@uml.edu.

THE UNIVERSITY OF MEMPHIS
Memphis, Tennessee
Tigers ◆ NCAA I ◆ Conference USA Conference ◆ http://www.memphis.edu/

State-supported university, founded 1912, part of Tennessee Board of Regents
Coed, 15,209 undergraduate students
Urban 1,100-acre campus
Moderately difficult entrance level, 70% of applicants were admitted

Freshmen *Admission:* 4,764 applied, 3,471 were accepted. *Test scores:* SAT verbal scores over 500: 67%; SAT math scores over 500: 65%; SAT verbal scores over 600: 27%; SAT math scores over 600: 26%; SAT verbal scores over 700: 4%; SAT math scores over 700: 4%.
Tuition and fees (2003–04): $4234 (resident), $12,388 (nonresident). *Room and board:* $4690 (room only: $2700).
Financial Aid (All incoming freshmen): *Average need-based gift aid:* $3676. *Average non-need based aid:* $3614. *Average aid to full-time undergraduates:* $5017.
Athletic Department: *Director of Athletics:* R.C. Johnson; Phone: 901-678-5395; Fax: 901-678-5078; E-mail: rjohnson@memphis.edu. *Sports Information Director:* Bob Winn; Phone: 901-678-2337; E-mail: bwinn@memphis.edu.

MEN'S COACHES
Baseball: Dave Anderson; Phone: 901-678-4137; E-mail: dcandrsn@memphis.edu.
Basketball: John Calipari; Phone: 901-678-2346; E-mail: jcalipar@memphis.edu.
Cross Country: Glenn Hays; Phone: 901-678-4138; E-mail: ghays@memphis.edu.
Football: Tommy West; Phone: 901-678-2341; E-mail: tcwest@memphis.edu.
Golf: Grant Robbins; Phone: 901-678-4136; E-mail: crobbins@memphis.edu.
Soccer: Richie Grant; Phone: 901-678-4141; E-mail: rjgrant@memphis.edu.
Tennis: Phil Chamberlain; Phone: 901-678-5309; E-mail: pchmbrln@memphis.edu.
Track and Field: Glenn Hays; Phone: 901-678-2452; E-mail: ghays@memphis.edu.

WOMEN'S COACHES
Basketball: Joye Lee-McNelis; Phone: 901-678-4120; E-mail: jmcnelis@memphis.edu.
Cross Country: Brenda Cash; Phone: 901-678-4119; E-mail: bcash@memphis.edu.
Golf: Sheryl Maize; Phone: 901-678-4121; E-mail: smaize@memphis.edu.
Soccer: Brooks Monaghan; Phone: 901-678-3427; E-mail: bmonaghn@memphis.edu.
Tennis: Charlotte Peterson; Phone: 901-678-2328; E-mail: cepetrsn@memphis.edu.
Track and Field: Brenda Cash; Phone: 901-678-2315; E-mail: ghays@memphis.edu.
Volleyball: Carrie Couturier-Yerty; Phone: 901-678-3570; E-mail: memphisvb@memphis.edu.

UNIVERSITY OF MIAMI
Coral Gables, Florida
Hurricanes ◆ NCAA I ◆ Big East Conference ◆ http://www.miami.edu/

Independent university, founded 1925
Coed, 9,996 undergraduate students, 92% full-time, 58% women, 42% men
Suburban 260-acre campus with easy access to Miami
Very difficult entrance level, 42% of applicants were admitted

Freshmen *Admission:* 16,851 applied, 7,490 were accepted, 2,078 enrolled. *Test scores:* SAT verbal scores over 500: 93%; SAT math scores over 500: 95%; SAT verbal scores over 600: 54%; SAT math scores over 600: 64%; SAT verbal scores over 700: 13%; SAT math scores over 700: 18%.
Tuition and fees (2003–04): $26,722 (full-time). *Room and board:* $8323 (room only: $4858).
Financial Aid (All incoming freshmen): *Average need-based gift aid:* $16,448. *Average non-need based aid:* $13,976. *Average aid to full-time undergraduates:* $22,077.
Athletic Department: *Director of Athletics:* Paul Dee; Phone: 305-284-2673; Fax: 304-284-2703; E-mail: pdee@miami.edu. *Sports Information Director:* Mark Pray; Phone: 305-284-3244; E-mail: mpray@miami.edu.

MEN'S COACHES
Baseball: Jim Morris; Phone: 305-284-4171; E-mail: jmorris@miami.edu.
Basketball: Perry Clark; Phone: 305-284-2673.
Cheerleading: Heather Almaguer; Phone: 305-284-8309; E-mail: heatheralmaguer@hotmail.com.
Cross Country: Mike Ward; Phone: 305-284-3821; E-mail: mjward@miami.edu.
Diving: Dario Di Fazio; Phone: 305-284-3593.
Football: Larry Coker; Phone: 305-284-2563; E-mail: lcoker@miami.edu.
Swimming: Mariusz Podkoscielny; Phone: 305-284-3593.
Tennis: Bryan Getz; Phone: 305-284-4166; E-mail: bgetz@miami.edu.
Track and Field: Mike Ward; Phone: 305-284-3821; E-mail: mjward@miami.edu.

WOMEN'S COACHES
Basketball: Ferne Labati; Phone: 305-284-5801; E-mail: flabati@miami.edu.
Cheerleading: Heather Almaguer; Phone: 305-284-8309; E-mail: heatheralmaguer@hotmail.com.
Cross Country: Amy Deem; Phone: 305-284-5029; E-mail: adeem@miami.edu.
Diving: Dario Di Fazio; Phone: 305-284-3593.
Golf: Lela Cannon; Phone: 305-284-4385; E-mail: lcannon@miami.edu.
Soccer: Tricia Taliaferro; Phone: 305-284-3640; E-mail: ttaliaferro@miami.edu.

University of Miami *(continued)*
Swimming: Mariusz Podkoscielny; Phone: 305-284-3593.
Tennis: Paige Yaroshuk; Phone: 305-284-3822; E-mail: pyaroshuk@miami.edu.
Track and Field: Amy Deem; Phone: 305-284-5029; E-mail: adeem@miami.edu.
Volleyball: Nicole Lantagne Welch; Phone: 305-284-3822; E-mail: nlantagne@miami.edu.

UNIVERSITY OF MICHIGAN
Ann Arbor, Michigan

Wolverines ◆ NCAA I ◆ Big Ten Conference; Central Collegiate Hockey Conference ◆ http://www.umich.edu/

State-supported university, founded 1817
Coed, 24,517 undergraduate students, 95% full-time, 51% women, 49% men
Suburban 8,070-acre campus with easy access to Detroit
Very difficult entrance level, 5% of applicants were admitted

Freshmen *Admission:* 25,943 applied, 13,814 were accepted, 5,551 enrolled. *Test scores:* SAT verbal scores over 500: 95%; SAT math scores over 500: 97%; SAT verbal scores over 600: 70%; SAT math scores over 600: 84%; SAT verbal scores over 700: 20%; SAT math scores over 700: 39%.
Tuition and fees (2003–04): $7975 (resident), $24,777 (nonresident). *Room and board:* $6704.
Financial Aid (All incoming freshmen): *Average need-based gift aid:* $7324. *Average non-need based aid:* $4728. *Average aid to full-time undergraduates:* $10,461.
Athletic Department: *Director of Athletics:* William Martin; Phone: 734-647-2583; Fax: 734-764-3221. *Sports Information Director:* Phone: 734-647-4423.

MEN'S COACHES
Baseball: Rich Maloney; Phone: 734-647-4550; E-mail: rmaloney@umich.edu.
Basketball: Tommy Amaker; Phone: 734-647-5504; E-mail: amakerht@umich.edu.
Cheerleading: Pam St. John; Phone: 734-764-1562; E-mail: cheerleading@umich.edu.
Cross Country: Ron Warhurst; Phone: 734-647-1221; E-mail: verynice@umich.edu.
Diving: Christopher Bergere; Phone: 734-647-1289; E-mail: cbergere@umich.edu.
Football: Lloyd Carr; Phone: 734-647-4422; E-mail: lhcarr@umich.edu.
Golf: Andrew Sapp; Phone: 734-647-9761; E-mail: asapp@umich.edu.
Ice Hockey: Red Berenson; Phone: 734-647-1201; E-mail: redbaron@umich.edu.
Soccer: Stephen Burns; Phone: 734-647-4546; E-mail: burnss@umich.edu.
Swimming: Jon Urbanchek; Phone: 734-647-1287; E-mail: jurban@umich.edu.
Tennis: Mark Mees; Phone: 734-998-8846; E-mail: mmees@umich.edu.
Track and Field: Ron Warhurst; Phone: 734-647-1221; E-mail: verynice@umich.edu.
Wrestling: Joe McFarland; Phone: 734-647-1223; E-mail: joemcfar@umich.edu.

WOMEN'S COACHES
Basketball: Cheryl Burnett; Phone: 734-647-2918; E-mail: coachcb@umich.edu.
Cheerleading: Pam St. John; Phone: 734-764-1562; E-mail: cheerleading@umich.edu.
Cross Country: Mike McGuire; Phone: 734-647-0121; E-mail: mikemac@umich.edu.
Diving: Christopher Bergere; Phone: 734-647-1289; E-mail: cbergere@umich.edu.
Field Hockey: Marcia Pankratz; Phone: 734-647-1271; E-mail: mpank@umich.edu.
Golf: Kathy Teichert; Phone: 734-998-6313; E-mail: kteich@umich.edu.
Gymnastics: Beverly Plocki; Phone: 734-647-1259; E-mail: bplocki@umich.edu.
Soccer: Debbie Rademacher; Phone: 734-647-4530; E-mail: dbelk@umich.edu.

Softball: Carol Hutchins; Phone: 734-647-1269; E-mail: hutch@umich.edu.
Swimming: Jim Richardson; Phone: 734-647-0500; E-mail: jimrich@umich.edu.
Tennis: Betsy Ritt; Phone: 734-647-2583; E-mail: bitritt@umich.edu.
Track and Field: James Henry; Phone: 734-647-1266; E-mail: jehenry@umich.edu.
Volleyball: Mark Rosen; Phone: 734-647-3035; E-mail: rosenma@umich.edu.

UNIVERSITY OF MICHIGAN–DEARBORN
Dearborn, Michigan

Wolves ◆ NAIA ◆ Central States Collegiate Hockey League Conference; Independent ◆ http://www.umd.umich.edu/

State-supported comprehensive, founded 1959, part of University of Michigan System
Coed, 6,646 undergraduate students, 56% full-time, 53% women, 47% men
Suburban 210-acre campus with easy access to Detroit
Moderately difficult entrance level, 7% of applicants were admitted

Freshmen *Admission:* 2,679 applied, 1,785 were accepted, 767 enrolled.
Tuition and fees (2003–04): $5946 (resident), $13,018 (nonresident).
Financial Aid (All incoming freshmen): *Average need-based gift aid:* $3604. *Average non-need based aid:* $2014. *Average aid to full-time undergraduates:* $6173.
Athletic Department: *Director of Athletics:* Peggy Foss; Phone: 313-593-5540; Fax: 313-593-5436; E-mail: pjfoss@umd.umich.edu. *Sports Information Director:* Josh Brandwene; Phone: 313-593-5671; E-mail: jabrand@umd.umich.edu.

MEN'S COACHES
Basketball: Phone: 313-593-5540.
Ice Hockey: Josh Brandwene; Phone: 313-593-5671; E-mail: jabrand@umd.umich.edu.
Lacrosse: Owen Blank; Phone: 734-593-3751.
Soccer: Bilel Hussein; Phone: 313-231-0539.

WOMEN'S COACHES
Basketball: Vince Proctor; Phone: 313-593-5540.
Volleyball: Mike Gibson; Phone: 313-593-5673; E-mail: mikegib@umich.edu.

UNIVERSITY OF MINNESOTA, CROOKSTON
Crookston, Minnesota

Golden Eagles ◆ NCAA II ◆ Northern Sun Intercollegiate Conference ◆ http://www.crk.umn.edu/

State-supported 4-year, founded 1966, part of University of Minnesota System
Coed, 2,320 undergraduate students, 47% full-time, 52% women, 48% men
Rural 95-acre campus
Moderately difficult entrance level, 89% of applicants were admitted

Freshmen *Admission:* 487 applied, 431 were accepted, 247 enrolled.
Tuition and fees (2003–04): $6780 (resident), $6780 (nonresident). *Room and board:* $4684.
Financial Aid (All incoming freshmen): *Average need-based gift aid:* $4896. *Average non-need based aid:* $2542. *Average aid to full-time undergraduates:* $9424.
Athletic Department: *Director of Athletics:* Stephanie Helgeson; Phone: 218-281-8422; Fax: 218-281-8430; E-mail: helgeson@mail.crk.umn.edu. *Sports Information Director:* Nick Kornder; Phone: 218-281-8414; E-mail: sid@mail.crk.umn.edu.

MEN'S COACHES
Baseball: Steve Olson; Phone: 218-281-8419; E-mail: stolson@mail.crk.umn.edu.

Basketball: Jeff Oseth; Phone: 218-281-8426; E-mail: joseth@mail.crk.umn.edu.
Cheerleading: Rose Ulseth; Phone: 218-281-8439; E-mail: rulseth@mail.crk.umn.edu.
Football: Shannon Stassen; Phone: 218-281-8425; E-mail: sstassen@mail.crk.umn.edu.
Golf: Jason Tangquist; Phone: 218-281-8424; E-mail: jtangqui@mail.crk.umn.edu.
Ice Hockey: Gary Warren; Phone: 218-281-8428; E-mail: gwarren@mail.crk.umn.edu.

WOMEN'S COACHES
Basketball: Michael Curfman; Phone: 218-281-8423; E-mail: mcurfman@mail.crk.umn.edu.
Cheerleading: Rose Ulseth; Phone: 218-281-8439; E-mail: rulseth@mail.crk.umn.edu.
Golf: Rosalie Hayenga; Phone: 218-281-8429; E-mail: rhayenga@mail.crk.umn.edu.
Soccer: Chris Przemieniecki; Phone: 218-281-8420; E-mail: cprzem@mail.crk.umn.edu.
Softball: Ryan Anderson; Phone: 218-281-8412; E-mail: ande3814@mail.crk.umn.edu.
Volleyball: Dave Simon; Phone: 218-281-8418; E-mail: dsimon@mail.crk.umn.edu.

UNIVERSITY OF MINNESOTA, DULUTH
Duluth, Minnesota

Bulldogs ◆ NCAA II ◆ Northern Sun Intercollegiate Conference; Western Collegiate Hockey Conference ◆ http://www.d.umn.edu/

State-supported comprehensive, founded 1947, part of University of Minnesota System
Coed, 9,288 undergraduate students, 95% full-time, 49% women, 51% men
Suburban 250-acre campus
Moderately difficult entrance level, 74% of applicants were admitted

Freshmen *Admission:* 6,900 applied, 5,133 were accepted, 2,194 enrolled.
Tuition and fees (2003–04): $7370 (resident), $17,735 (nonresident). *Room and board:* $5100.
Financial Aid (All incoming freshmen): *Average need-based gift aid:* $4715. *Average non-need based aid:* $1549. *Average aid to full-time undergraduates:* $6803.
Athletic Department: *Director of Athletics:* Bob Nielson; Phone: 218-726-7121; Fax: 218-726-6529; E-mail: rnielson@d.umn.edu. *Sports Information Director:* Bob Nygaard; Phone: 218-726-8191; E-mail: bnygaard@d.umn.edu.

MEN'S COACHES
Baseball: Scott Hanna; Phone: 218-726-7967; E-mail: hbhanna@d.umn.edu.
Basketball: Gary Holquist; Phone: 218-726-6185; E-mail: gholquis@d.umn.edu.
Cheerleading: Paula LeBlanc; Phone: 218-726-6341; E-mail: pleblanc@d.umn.edu.
Cross Country: Steve Fulkrod; Phone: 218-726-7061; E-mail: jfulkrod@d.umn.edu.
Football: Bob Nielson; Phone: 218-726-7121; E-mail: rnielson@d.umn.edu.
Ice Hockey: Scott Sandelin; Phone: 218-726-8579; E-mail: sandelin@d.umn.edu.
Track and Field: Bill Hudspith; Phone: 218-726-8168; E-mail: whudspit@pop3.cloquet.k12.mn.us.

WOMEN'S COACHES
Basketball: Karen Stromme; Phone: 218-726-7143; E-mail: kstromme@d.umn.edu.
Cheerleading: Paula LeBlanc; Phone: 218-726-6341; E-mail: pleblanc@d.umn.edu.
Cross Country: Steve Fulkrod; Phone: 218-726-7061; E-mail: jfulkrod@d.umn.edu.
Soccer: Greg Cane; Phone: 218-726-6229; E-mail: gcane1@d.umn.edu.
Softball: Bill Haller; Phone: 218-726-8168; E-mail: bhaller@d.umn.edu.

Tennis: Dan Doyle; Phone: 218-726-8168; E-mail: doyledan@hotmail.com.
Track and Field: John Fulkrod; Phone: 218-726-7061; E-mail: jfulkrod@d.umn.edu.
Volleyball: Jim Boos; Phone: 218-726-7968; E-mail: jboos@d.umn.edu.

UNIVERSITY OF MINNESOTA, MORRIS
Morris, Minnesota

Cougars ◆ NCAA II ◆ Northern Sun Intercollegiate Conference; Upper Midwest Athletic Conference ◆ http://www.mrs.umn.edu/

State-supported 4-year, founded 1959, part of University of Minnesota System
Coed, 1,861 undergraduate students, 93% full-time, 60% women, 40% men
Small-town 130-acre campus
Moderately difficult entrance level, 81% of applicants were admitted

Freshmen *Admission:* 1,117 applied, 922 were accepted, 412 enrolled. *Test scores:* SAT verbal scores over 500: 87%; SAT math scores over 500: 80%; SAT verbal scores over 600: 59%; SAT math scores over 600: 46%; SAT verbal scores over 700: 14%; SAT math scores over 700: 6%.
Tuition and fees (2003–04): $8096 (resident), $8096 (nonresident). *Room and board:* $4800 (room only: $2260).
Financial Aid (All incoming freshmen): *Average need-based gift aid:* $5669. *Average non-need based aid:* $2719. *Average aid to full-time undergraduates:* $9477.
Athletic Department: *Director of Athletics:* Mark Fohl; Phone: 320-589-6421; Fax: 320-589-6428; E-mail: fohlmv@mrs.umn.edu. *Sports Information Director:* Brian Curtis; Phone: 320-589-6423; E-mail: brummond@mrs.umn.edu.

MEN'S COACHES
Baseball: Mark Fohl; Phone: 320-589-6421; E-mail: fohlmv@mrs.umn.edu.
Basketball: Paul Grove; Phone: 320-589-6433; E-mail: grovep@mrs.umn.edu.
Cheerleading: Aaron Wise; Phone: 320-589-6425.
Football: Ken Crandall; Phone: 320-589-6432; E-mail: crandaka@mrs.umn.edu.
Golf: Mark Fohl; Phone: 320-589-6421; E-mail: fohlmv@mrs.umn.edu.
Tennis: Tim Droske; Phone: 320-589-6045; E-mail: drosket@mrs.umn.edu.
Track and Field: Jerry Monner; Phone: 320-589-6427; E-mail: monnerj@mrs.umn.edu.
Wrestling: Doug Reese; Phone: 320-589-6437; E-mail: reesedc@mrs.umn.edu.

WOMEN'S COACHES
Basketball: Jim Hall; Phone: 320-589-6434; E-mail: jimhall@mrs.umn.edu.
Cheerleading: Aaron Wise; Phone: 320-589-6425.
Cross Country: Jerry Monner; Phone: 320-589-6427; E-mail: monnerj@mrs.umn.edu.
Golf: Jana Koehler; Phone: 320-589-6406; E-mail: koehlerj@mrs.umn.edu.
Soccer: Christian De Vries; Phone: 320-589-6422; E-mail: devriesc@mrs.umn.edu.
Softball: Heather Pennie; Phone: 320-589-6429; E-mail: penniehl@mrs.umn.edu.
Tennis: Daniel Mowry; Phone: 320-589-6443; E-mail: mowryd@mrs.umn.edu.
Track and Field: Jerry Monner; Phone: 320-589-6427; E-mail: monnerj@mrs.umn.edu.
Volleyball: Heather Pennie; Phone: 320-589-6429; E-mail: penniehl@mrs.umn.edu.

UNIVERSITY OF MINNESOTA, TWIN CITIES CAMPUS
Minneapolis, Minnesota

Golden Gophers ◆ NCAA I ◆ Big Ten Conference; Western Collegiate Hockey Conference ◆ http://www1.umn.edu/twincities/index.php

State-supported university, founded 1851, part of University of Minnesota System
Coed, 32,474 undergraduate students, 81% full-time, 53% women, 47% men
Urban 2,000-acre campus
Moderately difficult entrance level, 73% of applicants were admitted

Freshmen *Admission:* 17,164 applied, 13,038 were accepted, 5,186 enrolled. *Test scores:* SAT verbal scores over 500: 86%; SAT math scores over 500: 89%; SAT verbal scores over 600: 56%; SAT math scores over 600: 61%; SAT verbal scores over 700: 12%; SAT math scores over 700: 18%.
Tuition and fees (2003–04): $7116 (resident), $18,746 (nonresident). *Room and board:* $6044.
Financial Aid (All incoming freshmen): *Average need-based gift aid:* $6463. *Average non-need based aid:* $3892. *Average aid to full-time undergraduates:* $9377.
Athletic Department: *Director of Athletics:* Joel Maturi; Phone: 612-624-4497; Fax: 612-626-7859; E-mail: icaadmin@tc.umn.edu. *Sports Information Director:* Mike Lockrem; Phone: 612-624-7345; E-mail: gophers@tc.umn.edu.

MEN'S COACHES
Baseball: John Anderson; Phone: 612-625-4057; E-mail: ander014@umn.edu.
Basketball: Dan Monson; Phone: 612-625-3085; E-mail: monso028@umn.edu.
Cheerleading: Dane Campbell; Phone: 612-624-7367.
Cross Country: Steve Plasencia; Phone: 612-625-0592; E-mail: plase001@umn.edu.
Diving: Mike Martens; Phone: 612-625-1585; E-mail: mart0068@umn.edu.
Football: Glen Mason; Phone: 612-624-6004; E-mail: mase@umn.edu.
Golf: Brad James; Phone: 612-625-6063; E-mail: james034@umn.edu.
Ice Hockey: Don Lucia; Phone: 612-625-2886; E-mail: lucia004@umn.edu.
Swimming: Dennis Dale; Phone: 612-625-1585; E-mail: dalex001@umn.edu.
Tennis: David Geatz; Phone: 612-625-1013; E-mail: geatz001@umn.edu.
Track and Field: Phil Lundin; Phone: 612-625-6063; E-mail: lundi001@umn.edu.
Wrestling: J Robinson; Phone: 612-625-1013; E-mail: robin002@umn.edu.

WOMEN'S COACHES
Basketball: Pam Borton; Phone: 612-624-3563; E-mail: borton@umn.edu.
Cheerleading: Dane Campbell; Phone: 612-624-7367.
Cross Country: Gary Wilson; Phone: 612-625-0188; E-mail: wilso003@umn.edu.
Diving: Mike Martens; Phone: 612-625-1585; E-mail: mart0068@umn.edu.
Golf: Katie Weiss; Phone: 612-624-7599; E-mail: weiss065@umn.edu.
Gymnastics: Jim Stephenson; Phone: 612-624-4331; E-mail: steph007@umn.edu.
Soccer: Mickki Denney Wright; Phone: 612-626-1381.
Softball: Julie Standering; Phone: 612-624-7856; E-mail: stand004@umn.edu.
Swimming: Jean Freeman; Phone: 612-626-1320; E-mail: freem002@umn.edu.
Tennis: Tyler Thomson; Phone: 612-625-1013; E-mail: thoms016@umn.edu.
Track and Field: Gary Wilson; Phone: 612-625-0188; E-mail: wilso003@umn.edu.
Volleyball: Mike Hebert; Phone: 612-624-6533; E-mail: heber012@umn.edu.

UNIVERSITY OF MISSISSIPPI
Oxford, Mississippi

Rebels ◆ NCAA I ◆ Southeastern Conference ◆ http://www.olemiss.edu/

State-supported university, founded 1844, part of Mississippi Institutions of Higher Learning
Coed, 11,250 undergraduate students, 86% full-time, 53% women, 47% men
Small-town 2,500-acre campus with easy access to Memphis
Moderately difficult entrance level, 80% of applicants were admitted

Freshmen *Admission:* 6,601 applied, 5,287 were accepted, 2,380 enrolled.
Tuition and fees (2003–04): $3916 (resident), $8826 (nonresident). *Room and board:* $5300.
Financial Aid (All incoming freshmen): *Average need-based gift aid:* $3838. *Average non-need based aid:* $3822. *Average aid to full-time undergraduates:* $6892.
Athletic Department: *Director of Athletics:* Pete Boone; Phone: 662-915-7546; Fax: 662-915-7683. *Sports Information Director:* Langston Rogers; Phone: 662-915-7522; E-mail: lrogers@olemiss.edu.

MEN'S COACHES
Baseball: Mike Bianco; Phone: 662-915-7519; E-mail: mbianco@olemiss.edu.
Basketball: Rod Barnes; Phone: 662-915-7534.
Cross Country: Joe Walker; Phone: 662-915-7506; E-mail: jwalkerj@olemiss.edu.
Football: David Cutcliffe; Phone: 662-915-7535; E-mail: chyna@olemiss.edu.
Golf: Woody Cowart; Phone: 662-234-8368; E-mail: rebgolf62@hotmail.com.
Tennis: Billy Chadwick; Phone: 662-915-7532; E-mail: coachchadwick@hotmail.com.
Track and Field: Joe Walker; Phone: 662-915-7506; E-mail: jwalkerj@olemiss.edu.

WOMEN'S COACHES
Basketball: Carol Ross; Phone: 662-915-3944; E-mail: jcross1@olemiss.edu.
Cross Country: Joe Walker; Phone: 662-915-7506; E-mail: jwalkerj@olemiss.edu.
Golf: Meghan Bolger; Phone: 662-234-1831; E-mail: meghanbolger@hotmail.com.
Soccer: Steve Holeman; Phone: 662-915-7859; E-mail: sholeman@olemiss.edu.
Softball: Candi Letts; Phone: 662-915-7971; E-mail: sbletts@olemiss.edu.
Tennis: Mark Beyers; Phone: 662-915-7501; E-mail: beyersmark@olemiss.edu.
Track and Field: Joe Walker; Phone: 662-915-7506; E-mail: jwalkerj@olemiss.edu.
Volleyball: Joe Getzin; Phone: 662-915-7540; E-mail: jgetzin@olemiss.edu.

UNIVERSITY OF MISSOURI–COLUMBIA
Columbia, Missouri

Tigers ◆ NCAA I ◆ Big 12 Conference ◆ http://www.missouri.edu/

State-supported university, founded 1839, part of University of Missouri System
Coed, 20,441 undergraduate students, 93% full-time, 52% women, 48% men
Small-town 1,358-acre campus
Moderately difficult entrance level, 90% of applicants were admitted

Freshmen *Admission:* 10,449 applied, 9,327 were accepted, 4,669 enrolled.
Tuition and fees (2003–04): $6558 (resident), $16,005 (nonresident). *Room and board:* $5770.
Financial Aid (All incoming freshmen): *Average need-based gift aid:* $5721. *Average non-need based aid:* $4200. *Average aid to full-time undergraduates:* $9758.

Athletic Department: *Director of Athletics:* Michael Alden; Phone: 573-882-2055; E-mail: aldenm@missouri.edu. *Sports Information Director:* Chad Moller; Phone: 573-882-0712; E-mail: mollerc@missouri.edu.

MEN'S COACHES

Baseball: Tim Jamieson; Phone: 573-882-0731; E-mail: jamiesont@missouri.edu.

Basketball: Quin Snyder; Phone: 573-882-0715.

Cheerleading: Suzy Thompson; Phone: 573-228-0907.

Cross Country: Jared Wilmes; Phone: 573-882-0728; E-mail: wilmesj@missouri.edu.

Diving: Greg Triefenbach; Phone: 573-882-4669.

Football: Gary Pinkel; Phone: 573-882-2404.

Golf: Tim Robyn; Phone: 573-882-0740; E-mail: robynt@missouri.edu.

Swimming: Brian Hoffer; Phone: 573-882-4669; E-mail: hofferb@missouri.edu.

Track and Field: Rick McGuire; Phone: 573-882-0727; E-mail: mcguirer@missouri.edu.

Wrestling: Brian Smith; Phone: 573-882-0735.

WOMEN'S COACHES

Basketball: Cindy Stein; Phone: 573-882-1002; E-mail: steinc@missouri.edu.

Cheerleading: Suzy Thompson; Phone: 573-228-0907.

Cross Country: Jared Wilmes; Phone: 573-882-0728; E-mail: wilmesj@missouri.edu.

Diving: Greg Triefenbach; Phone: 573-882-4669.

Golf: Stephanie Cooper; Phone: 573-882-1672; E-mail: coopers@missouri.edu.

Gymnastics: Rob Drass; Phone: 573-882-0736; E-mail: drassr@missouri.edu.

Soccer: Bryan Blitz; Phone: 573-884-7914; E-mail: blitzb@missouri.edu.

Softball: Ty Singleton; Phone: 573-882-0730; E-mail: singletonts@missouri.edu.

Swimming: Brian Hoffer; Phone: 573-882-4669; E-mail: hofferb@missouri.edu.

Tennis: Blake Starkey; Phone: 573-882-4588; E-mail: starkeyb@missouri.edu.

Track and Field: Rick McGuire; Phone: 573-882-0722; E-mail: mcguirer@missouri.edu.

Volleyball: Susan Kreklow; Phone: 573-882-9600; E-mail: kreklows@missouri.edu.

UNIVERSITY OF MISSOURI–KANSAS CITY
Kansas City, Missouri

Kangaroos ◆ NCAA I ◆ Mid-Continent Conference ◆ http://www.umkc.edu/

State-supported university, founded 1929, part of University of Missouri System

Coed, 9,167 undergraduate students, 55% full-time, 60% women, 40% men

Urban 191-acre campus

Moderately difficult entrance level, 93% of applicants were admitted

Freshmen *Admission:* 1,884 applied, 1,746 were accepted, 785 enrolled.

Tuition and fees (2003–04): $6146 (resident), $14,964 (nonresident).

Room and board: $7270 (room only: $3170).

Financial Aid (All incoming freshmen): *Average need-based gift aid:* $4597. *Average non-need based aid:* $4989. *Average aid to full-time undergraduates:* $16,206.

Athletic Department: *Director of Athletics:* Robert Thomas; Phone: 816-235-1048; Fax: 816-235-1035; E-mail: thomasrw@umkc.edu. *Sports Information Director:* Pat Madden; Phone: 816-235-1034; E-mail: maddenp@umkc.edu.

MEN'S COACHES

Basketball: Rick Zvosec; Phone: 816-235-1140; E-mail: zvosecr@umkc.edu.

Cheerleading: Terri Freeman; Phone: 816-678-3438; E-mail: umkcspirit@earthlink.net.

Cross Country: Theo Hamilton; Phone: 816-235-5309; E-mail: hamiltonthe@umkc.edu.

Golf: J.W. VanDenBorn; Phone: 816-235-5989; E-mail: dub1763@aol.com.

Soccer: Rick Benben; Phone: 816-235-5469; E-mail: benbenr@umkc.edu.

Tennis: Cameron Macdonald; Phone: 816-235-1036; E-mail: macdonaldc@umkc.edu.

Track and Field: Theo Hamilton; Phone: 816-235-5309; E-mail: hamiltonthe@umkc.edu.

WOMEN'S COACHES

Basketball: Dana Eikenerg; Phone: 816-235-1264; E-mail: eikenbergd@umkc.edu.

Cheerleading: Terri Freeman; Phone: 816-678-3438; E-mail: umkcspirit@earthlink.net.

Cross Country: Theo Hamilton; Phone: 816-235-5309; E-mail: hamiltonthe@umkc.edu.

Golf: Mike Rhoades; Phone: 816-235-5989; E-mail: rhoadesm@umkc.edu.

Softball: Carla Marchetti; Phone: 816-235-5837; E-mail: marchettic@umkc.edu.

Tennis: Angela Blair-Garbe; Phone: 816-235-1036; E-mail: cgarbe@planetkc.com.

Track and Field: Theo Hamilton; Phone: 816-235-5309; E-mail: hamiltonthe@umkc.edu.

Volleyball: Steve Dallman; Phone: 816-235-1037; E-mail: dallmans@umkc.edu.

UNIVERSITY OF MISSOURI–ROLLA
Rolla, Missouri

Miners ◆ NCAA II ◆ Mid-America Intercollegiate Conference ◆ http://www.umr.edu/

State-supported university, founded 1870, part of University of Missouri System

Coed, 4,089 undergraduate students, 90% full-time, 23% women, 77% men

Small-town 284-acre campus

Very difficult entrance level, 91% of applicants were admitted

Freshmen *Admission:* 1,942 applied, 1,753 were accepted, 878 enrolled.

Tuition and fees (2003–04): $6839 (resident), $16,286 (nonresident).

Room and board: $5453.

Financial Aid (All incoming freshmen): *Average need-based gift aid:* $6700. *Average non-need based aid:* $6820. *Average aid to full-time undergraduates:* $9350.

Athletic Department: *Director of Athletics:* Mark Mullin; Phone: 573-341-4175; Fax: 573-341-4880; E-mail: memullin@umr.edu. *Sports Information Director:* John Kean; Phone: 573-341-4140; E-mail: jkean@umr.edu.

MEN'S COACHES

Baseball: Todd DeGraffenreid; Phone: 570-341-7506; E-mail: degraff@umr.edu.

Basketball: Dale Martin; Phone: 570-341-4101; E-mail: dwmartin@umr.edu.

Cross Country: Sterling Martin; Phone: 570-341-4971; E-mail: martinsb@umr.edu.

Football: Kirby Cannon; Phone: 570-341-4957; E-mail: kcannon@umr.edu.

Soccer: Vince Darnell; Phone: 570-341-4102; E-mail: darnellv@umr.edu.

Swimming: Doug Grooms; Phone: 570-341-6149; E-mail: dougg@umr.edu.

Track and Field: Sterling Martin; Phone: 570-341-4971; E-mail: martinsb@umr.edu.

WOMEN'S COACHES

Basketball: Alan Eads; Phone: 570-341-4105; E-mail: eadsa@umr.edu.

Cross Country: Sterling Martin; Phone: 570-341-4971; E-mail: martinsb@umr.edu.

Soccer: Diana Niland; Phone: 570-341-7032; E-mail: dniland@umr.edu.

Softball: Ryan Anderson; Phone: 570-341-4968; E-mail: andersr@umr.edu.

Track and Field: Sterling Martin; Phone: 570-341-4971; E-mail: martinsb@umr.edu.

UNIVERSITY OF MISSOURI–ST. LOUIS

St. Louis, Missouri

Rivermen ◆ NCAA II ◆ Great Lakes Valley Conference
◆ http://www.umsl.edu/

State-supported university, founded 1963, part of University of Missouri System
Coed, 12,630 undergraduate students, 45% full-time, 61% women, 39% men
Suburban 350-acre campus
Moderately difficult entrance level, 48% of applicants were admitted

Freshmen *Admission:* 2,433 applied, 1,178 were accepted, 534 enrolled. *Test scores:* SAT verbal scores over 500: 84%; SAT math scores over 500: 86%; SAT verbal scores over 600: 46%; SAT math scores over 600: 32%; SAT verbal scores over 700: 3%; SAT math scores over 700: 8%.
Tuition and fees (2003–04): $6866 (resident), $16,313 (nonresident). *Room and board:* $5600 (room only: $4300).
Financial Aid (All incoming freshmen): *Average need-based gift aid:* $4019. *Average non-need based aid:* $3679. *Average aid to full-time undergraduates:* $7623.
Athletic Department: *Director of Athletics:* Patricia Dolan; Phone: 314-516-5657; Fax: 314-516-5503; E-mail: dolan@umsl.edu. *Sports Information Director:* Todd Addington; Phone: 314-516-5660; E-mail: todd.addington@umsl.edu.

MEN'S COACHES
Baseball: Jim Brady; Phone: 314-516-5647; E-mail: bradyja@msx.umsl.edu.
Basketball: Chris Pilz; Phone: 314-516-5638; E-mail: pilzc@umsl.edu.
Cheerleading: Phone: 314-516-5661; E-mail: cheerleadingumsl@hotmail.com.
Golf: James Trittle; Phone: 314-516-5661; E-mail: trittlerj@umsl.edu.
Soccer: Dan King; Phone: 314-516-7027; E-mail: kingdm@msx.umsl.edu.
Tennis: Rick Gyllenborg; Phone: 314-516-7016; E-mail: athrgyll@msx.umsl.edu.

WOMEN'S COACHES
Basketball: Lee Buchanan; Phone: 314-516-5640; E-mail: buchananl@umsl.edu.
Cheerleading: Phone: 314-516-5661; E-mail: cheerleadingumsl@hotmail.com.
Golf: James Earle; Phone: 314-516-5661; E-mail: earleja@umsl.edu.
Soccer: Beth Goetz; Phone: 314-516-5646; E-mail: goetzm@msx.umsl.edu.
Softball: Nicole Durnin; Phone: 314-516-5685; E-mail: durninn@msx.umsl.edu.
Tennis: Rick Gyllenborg; Phone: 314-516-7016; E-mail: athrgyll@msx.umsl.edu.
Volleyball: Denise Silvester; Phone: 314-516-5643; E-mail: denise_silvester@umsl.edu.

UNIVERSITY OF MOBILE

Mobile, Alabama

Rams ◆ NAIA ◆ Gulf Coast Conference
◆ http://www.umobile.edu/

Independent Southern Baptist comprehensive, founded 1961
Coed, 1,663 undergraduate students, 74% full-time, 71% women, 29% men
Suburban 830-acre campus
Moderately difficult entrance level, 71% of applicants were admitted

Freshmen *Admission:* 413 applied, 276 were accepted, 212 enrolled.
Tuition and fees (2003–04): $9520 (full-time). *Room and board:* $5440.
Financial Aid (All incoming freshmen): *Average need-based gift aid:* $3201. *Average aid to full-time undergraduates:* $6800.
Athletic Department: *Director of Athletics:* Craig Bogar; Phone: 251-442-2279; Fax: 251-442-2499; E-mail: cbogar@mail.umobile.edu. *Sports Information Director:* Josh Ginsburg; Phone: 251-442-2257; E-mail: walkmobile@aol.com.

MEN'S COACHES
Baseball: Mike Jacobs; Phone: 251-442-2228; E-mail: majacobs19@hotmail.com.
Basketball: Joe Niland; Phone: 251-442-2288; E-mail: jnmobile@hotmail.com.
Cheerleading: Michael Lenz; Phone: 251-442-2365; E-mail: rmlenz@netzero.net.
Cross Country: Craig Bogar; Phone: 251-442-2279; E-mail: cbogar@mail.umobile.edu.
Golf: Terry Hopper; Phone: 251-442-2264.
Soccer: Peter Fuller; Phone: 251-442-2363.
Track and Field: Craig Bogar; Phone: 251-442-2279; E-mail: cbogar@mail.umobile.edu.

WOMEN'S COACHES
Basketball: Martha Gore-Algernon; Phone: 251-442-2260; E-mail: goremartha@hotmail.com.
Cheerleading: Michael Lenz; Phone: 251-442-2365; E-mail: rmlenz@netzero.net.
Cross Country: Craig Bogar; Phone: 251-442-2279; E-mail: cbogar@mail.umobile.edu.
Golf: Terry Hopper; Phone: 251-442-2264.
Soccer: Uwe Tittl; Phone: 251-442-2364.
Softball: Becky Clark; Phone: 251-442-2264.
Tennis: Uwe Tittl; Phone: 251-442-2364.
Track and Field: Craig Bogar; Phone: 251-442-2279; E-mail: cbogar@mail.umobile.edu.

THE UNIVERSITY OF MONTANA–MISSOULA

Missoula, Montana

Grizzlies ◆ NCAA I ◆ Big Sky Conference
◆ http://www.umt.edu/

State-supported university, founded 1893, part of Montana University System
Coed, 11,343 undergraduate students, 84% full-time, 53% women, 47% men
Urban 220-acre campus
Moderately difficult entrance level, 92% of applicants were admitted

Freshmen *Admission:* 4,112 applied, 3,813 were accepted, 2,286 enrolled. *Test scores:* SAT verbal scores over 500: 70%; SAT math scores over 500: 68%; SAT verbal scores over 600: 28%; SAT math scores over 600: 25%; SAT verbal scores over 700: 4%; SAT math scores over 700: 2%.
Tuition and fees (2004–05): $4377 (resident), $12,368 (nonresident). *Room and board:* $5432 (room only: $2448).
Financial Aid (All incoming freshmen): *Average need-based gift aid:* $4070. *Average non-need based aid:* $3024. *Average aid to full-time undergraduates:* $6599.
Athletic Department: *Director of Athletics:* Wayne Hogan; Phone: 406-243-5348; Fax: 406-243-2264; E-mail: hoganwc@mso.umt.edu. *Sports Information Director:* Dave Guffey; Phone: 406-243-5402; E-mail: guffeydb@mso.umt.edu.

MEN'S COACHES
Basketball: Pat Kennedy; Phone: 406-243-2157; E-mail: basketball@montanagrizzlies.com.
Cheerleading: Christie Anderson; Phone: 406-370-2212; E-mail: rahgriz@hotmail.com.
Cross Country: Tom Raunig; Phone: 406-243-5413; E-mail: raunigta@mso.umt.edu.
Football: Bobby Hauck; Phone: 406-243-2969; E-mail: football@montanagrizzlies.com.
Tennis: Kris Nord; Phone: 406-243-5410; E-mail: nordkm@mso.umt.edu.
Track and Field: Tom Raunig; Phone: 406-243-5413; E-mail: raunigta@mso.umt.edu.

WOMEN'S COACHES
Basketball: Robin Selvig; Phone: 406-243-5412; E-mail: selvigr@mso.umt.edu.
Cheerleading: Christie Anderson; Phone: 406-370-2212; E-mail: rahgriz@hotmail.com.
Cross Country: Tom Raunig; Phone: 406-243-5413; E-mail: raunigta@mso.umt.edu.

Golf: Joanne Steele; Phone: 406-243-4377; E-mail: steelejm@mso.umt.edu.
Soccer: Betsy Duerksen; Phone: 406-243-2760; E-mail: soccer@montanagrizzlies.com.
Tennis: Kris Nord; Phone: 406-243-5410; E-mail: nordkm@mso.umt.edu.
Track and Field: Tom Raunig; Phone: 406-243-5413; E-mail: raunigta@mso.umt.edu.
Volleyball: Nikki Best; Phone: 406-243-5411; E-mail: bestn@mso.umt.edu.

THE UNIVERSITY OF MONTANA–WESTERN
Dillon, Montana

Bulldogs ◆ NAIA ◆ Frontier Conference
◆ http://www.umwestern.edu/

State-supported 4-year, founded 1893, part of Montana University System
Coed, 1,160 undergraduate students, 75% full-time, 60% women, 40% men
Small-town 36-acre campus
Minimally difficult entrance level, 100% of applicants were admitted

Freshmen *Admission:* 291 applied, 291 were accepted, 171 enrolled. *Test scores:* SAT verbal scores over 500: 39%; SAT math scores over 500: 38%; SAT verbal scores over 600: 2%; SAT math scores over 600: 9%; SAT math scores over 700: 3%.
Tuition and fees (2004–05): $3780 (resident), $11,610 (nonresident). *Room and board:* $4600 (room only: $1800).
Financial Aid (All incoming freshmen): *Average need-based gift aid:* $3139. *Average non-need based aid:* $843. *Average aid to full-time undergraduates:* $3805.
Athletic Department: *Director of Athletics:* Pat Yeager; Phone: 406-683-7220; E-mail: p_yeager@umwestern.edu. *Sports Information Director:* Wally Feldt; Phone: 406-683-7201; E-mail: w_feldt@umwestern.edu.

MEN'S COACHES
Basketball: Mark Durham; Phone: 406-683-7509; E-mail: c_royer@umwestern.edu.
Cheerleading: Cris Royer; Phone: 406-683-7311; E-mail: c_royer@umwestern.edu.
Football: Tommy Lee; Phone: 406-683-7346; E-mail: c_royer@umwestern.edu.
Golf: Mark Durham; Phone: 406-683-7509; E-mail: c_royer@umwestern.edu.

WOMEN'S COACHES
Basketball: Kevin Engellant; Phone: 406-683-7317; E-mail: c_royer@umwestern.edu.
Cheerleading: Cris Royer; Phone: 406-683-7311; E-mail: c_royer@umwestern.edu.
Golf: Mark Durham; Phone: 406-683-7509; E-mail: c_royer@umwestern.edu.
Volleyball: Jenny Peterson; Phone: 406-683-7441; E-mail: c_royer@umwestern.edu.

UNIVERSITY OF MONTEVALLO
Montevallo, Alabama

Falcons ◆ NCAA II ◆ Gulf South Conference ◆ http://www.montevallo.edu/

State-supported comprehensive, founded 1896
Coed, 2,644 undergraduate students, 89% full-time, 67% women, 33% men
Small-town 106-acre campus with easy access to Birmingham
Moderately difficult entrance level, 79% of applicants were admitted

Freshmen *Admission:* 1,334 applied, 1,050 were accepted, 539 enrolled.
Tuition and fees (2003–04): $4784 (resident), $9284 (nonresident). *Room and board:* $3638 (room only: $2318).

Financial Aid (All incoming freshmen): *Average need-based gift aid:* $4425. *Average non-need based aid:* $3910. *Average aid to full-time undergraduates:* $5867.
Athletic Department: *Director of Athletics:* Michael Cancilla; Phone: 205-665-6594; Fax: 205-665-6587; E-mail: cancillama@montevallo.edu. *Sports Information Director:* Alfred Kojima; Phone: 205-665-6606; E-mail: kojimaa@montevallo.edu.

MEN'S COACHES
Baseball: Gregg Goff; Phone: 205-665-6760; E-mail: goffga@montevallo.edu.
Basketball: Danny Young; Phone: 205-665-6593; E-mail: youngd@montevallo.edu.
Cheerleading: Robyn Boyd; Phone: 205-665-6565; E-mail: boydrw@montevallo.edu.
Golf: Paula Floyd; Phone: 205-665-6583.
Soccer: Ryan Pratt; Phone: 205-665-6601; E-mail: prattrm@montevallo.edu.

WOMEN'S COACHES
Basketball: Lou DiFeo; Phone: 205-665-6592; E-mail: difeol@montevallo.edu.
Cheerleading: Robyn Boyd; Phone: 205-665-6565; E-mail: boydrw@montevallo.edu.
Golf: Paula Floyd; Phone: 205-665-6583.
Soccer: Patricia Hughes; Phone: 205-665-6604; E-mail: hughespm@montevallo.edu.
Tennis: Sandi Horsley; Phone: 205-665-6600.
Volleyball: C.J. Sherman; Phone: 205-665-6598; E-mail: shermanm@montevallo.edu.

UNIVERSITY OF NEBRASKA AT KEARNEY
Kearney, Nebraska

Antelopes ◆ NCAA II ◆ Rocky Mountain Athletic Conference
◆ http://www.unk.edu/

State-supported comprehensive, founded 1903, part of University of Nebraska System
Coed, 5,366 undergraduate students, 89% full-time, 55% women, 45% men
Small-town 235-acre campus
Moderately difficult entrance level, 88% of applicants were admitted

Freshmen *Admission:* 2,599 applied, 2,284 were accepted, 1,138 enrolled.
Tuition and fees (2003–04): $3885 (resident), $7147 (nonresident). *Room and board:* $4436.
Financial Aid (All incoming freshmen): *Average need-based gift aid:* $3527. *Average non-need based aid:* $1187. *Average aid to full-time undergraduates:* $6266.
Athletic Department: *Director of Athletics:* Jon McBride; Phone: 308-865-8332; Fax: 308-865-8187; E-mail: mcbridejl@unk.edu. *Sports Information Director:* Peter Yazvac; Phone: 308-865-8334; E-mail: yazvacpa@unk.edu.

MEN'S COACHES
Baseball: Damon Day; Phone: 308-865-8022; E-mail: daydd@unk.edu.
Basketball: Tom Kropp; Phone: 308-865-8021; E-mail: kroppt@unk.edu.
Cheerleading: Karla Falk; Phone: 308-865-8523; E-mail: falkka@unk.edu.
Cross Country: Shawn Wheelock; Phone: 308-865-8024; E-mail: wheelocks1@unk.edu.
Football: Darrell Morris; Phone: 308-865-8033; E-mail: morrisdw@unk.edu.
Golf: Dick Beechner; Phone: 308-865-8330; E-mail: golopers@aol.com.
Tennis: Patrick Fischer; Phone: 308-865-8514; E-mail: fischerpy@unk.edu.
Track and Field: Andy Meyer; Phone: 308-865-8010; E-mail: meyeraj@unk.edu.
Wrestling: Marc Bauer; Phone: 308-865-8019; E-mail: bauermd@unk.edu.

WOMEN'S COACHES
Basketball: Carol Russell; Phone: 308-865-8030; E-mail: russellcj1@unk.edu.

University of Nebraska at Kearney *(continued)*

Cheerleading: Karla Falk; Phone: 308-865-8523; E-mail: falkka@unk.edu.

Cross Country: Shawn Wheelock; Phone: 308-865-8024; E-mail: wheelocks1@unk.edu.

Golf: Mark Brosamie; Phone: 308-865-8727; E-mail: brosamlem@unk.edu.

Softball: Holly Carnes; Phone: 308-865-8010; E-mail: carnesha@unk.edu.

Swimming: Teresa Osmanski; Phone: 308-865-8024; E-mail: stratmanosmt@unk.edu.

Tennis: Patrick Fischer; Phone: 308-865-8514; E-mail: fischerpy@unk.edu.

Track and Field: Andy Meyer; Phone: 308-865-8010; E-mail: meyeraj@unk.edu.

Volleyball: Rick Squiers; Phone: 308-865-8031; E-mail: squiersr@unk.edu.

UNIVERSITY OF NEBRASKA AT OMAHA
Omaha, Nebraska

Mavericks ◆ NCAA II ◆ Central Collegiate Hockey Conference; North Central Intercollegiate Conference ◆ http://www.unomaha.edu/

State-supported university, founded 1908, part of University of Nebraska System
Coed, 11,102 undergraduate students, 73% full-time, 53% women, 47% men
Urban 158-acre campus
Minimally difficult entrance level, 84% of applicants were admitted

Freshmen *Admission:* 3,994 applied, 3,383 were accepted, 1,537 enrolled. *Test scores:* SAT verbal scores over 500: 62%; SAT math scores over 500: 58%; SAT verbal scores over 600: 24%; SAT math scores over 600: 25%; SAT verbal scores over 700: 5%; SAT math scores over 700: 4%.
Tuition and fees (2003–04): $4082 (resident), $10,922 (nonresident). *Room and board:* $3998 (room only: $3078).
Athletic Department: *Director of Athletics:* Bob Danenhauer; Phone: 402-554-3389; Fax: 402-554-3694; E-mail: rdanenhauer@mail.unomaha.edu. *Sports Information Director:* Gary Anderson; Phone: 402-554-3387; E-mail: ganderson@mail.unomaha.edu.

MEN'S COACHES
Baseball: Bob Herold; Phone: 402-554-3388; E-mail: bherold@mail.unomaha.edu.

Basketball: Kevin McKenna; Phone: 402-554-2631; E-mail: kmckenna@mail.unomaha.edu.

Cheerleading: Liz Higgins; Phone: 402-291-6848; E-mail: lizziebiz@cs.com.

Football: Pat Behrns; Phone: 402-554-3394; E-mail: pbehrns@mail.unomaha.edu.

Ice Hockey: Mike Kemp; Phone: 402-554-3629; E-mail: mkemp@mail.unomaha.edu.

Wrestling: Mike Denney; Phone: 402-554-3384; E-mail: mdenney@mail.unomaha.edu.

WOMEN'S COACHES
Basketball: Lisa Carlsen; Phone: 402-554-3269; E-mail: lcarlsen@mail.unomaha.edu.

Cheerleading: Liz Higgins; Phone: 402-291-6848; E-mail: lizziebiz@cs.com.

Cross Country: Tim Hendricks; Phone: 402-554-3265; E-mail: thendricks@mail.unomaha.edu.

Golf: Tim Nelson; Phone: 402-554-2013; E-mail: tlnelson@mail.unomaha.edu.

Soccer: Don Klosterman; Phone: 402-554-4962; E-mail: dklosterman@mail.unomaha.edu.

Softball: Jeanne Tostenson; Phone: 402-554-3266; E-mail: jtostenson@mail.unomaha.edu.

Swimming: Todd Samland; Phone: 402-554-2346; E-mail: tsamland@mail.unomaha.edu.

Tennis: Bill Nichols; Phone: 402-554-3931; E-mail: bnichols@mail.unomaha.edu.

Track and Field: Tim Hendricks; Phone: 402-554-3265; E-mail: thendricks@mail.unomaha.edu.

Volleyball: Rose Shires; Phone: 402-554-3407; E-mail: rshires@mail.unomaha.edu.

UNIVERSITY OF NEBRASKA–LINCOLN
Lincoln, Nebraska

Cornhuskers ◆ NCAA I ◆ Big 12 Conference ◆ http://www.unl.edu/

State-supported university, founded 1869, part of University of Nebraska System
Coed, 17,851 undergraduate students, 91% full-time, 48% women, 52% men
Urban 623-acre campus with easy access to Omaha
Moderately difficult entrance level, 75% of applicants were admitted

Freshmen *Admission:* 7,375 applied, 5,586 were accepted, 3,679 enrolled. *Test scores:* SAT verbal scores over 500: 82%; SAT math scores over 500: 84%; SAT verbal scores over 600: 45%; SAT math scores over 600: 51%; SAT verbal scores over 700: 14%; SAT math scores over 700: 16%.
Tuition and fees (2003–04): $4711 (resident), $12,293 (nonresident). *Room and board:* $5204 (room only: $2404).
Financial Aid (All incoming freshmen): *Average need-based gift aid:* $4653. *Average non-need based aid:* $3391. *Average aid to full-time undergraduates:* $7043.
Athletic Department: *Director of Athletics:* Steve Pederson; Phone: 402-472-3011; Fax: 402-472-9675; E-mail: steve@huskers.com. *Sports Information Director:* Chris Anderson; Phone: 402-472-2263; E-mail: canderson@huskers.com.

MEN'S COACHES
Baseball: Mike Anderson; Phone: 402-472-2269; E-mail: manderson@huskers.unl.edu.

Basketball: Barry Collier; Phone: 402-472-2265; E-mail: eshutts@huskers.unl.edu.

Cross Country: Jay Dirksen; Phone: 402-472-1136; E-mail: jd64726@alltel.net.

Football: Bill Callahan; Phone: 402-472-3116; E-mail: mwininger@huskers.com.

Golf: Bill Spangler; Phone: 402-472-6466; E-mail: wspangler@huskers.unl.edu.

Tennis: Kerry McDermott; Phone: 402-472-6464; E-mail: kmcdermott@huskers.unl.edu.

Track and Field: Gary Pepin; Phone: 402-472-1135; E-mail: gpepin@huskers.unl.edu.

Wrestling: Mark Manning; Phone: 402-472-9430; E-mail: mmanning@huskers.unl.edu.

WOMEN'S COACHES
Basketball: Connie Yori; Phone: 402-472-6462; E-mail: cyori@huskers.unl.edu.

Cross Country: Jay Dirksen; Phone: 402-472-6461; E-mail: jd64726@alltel.net.

Diving: Jeff DiNicola; Phone: 402-472-3186; E-mail: jdinicola@huskers.com.

Golf: Robin Krapfl; Phone: 402-472-1415; E-mail: rkrapfl@huskers.unl.edu.

Gymnastics: Dan Kendig; Phone: 402-472-3808; E-mail: dkendig@huskers.unl.edu.

Soccer: John Walker; Phone: 402-472-0456; E-mail: jwalker@huskers.unl.edu.

Softball: Rhonda Revelle; Phone: 402-472-6465; E-mail: rrevelle@huskers.unl.edu.

Swimming: Pablo Morales; Phone: 402-472-3186; E-mail: pmorales@huskers.unl.edu.

Tennis: Scott Jacobson; Phone: 402-472-6473; E-mail: sjacobson@huskers.unl.edu.

Track and Field: Gary Pepin; Phone: 402-472-1135; E-mail: gpepin@huskers.unl.edu.

Volleyball: John Cook; Phone: 402-472-2399; E-mail: jcook@huskers.unl.edu.

UNIVERSITY OF NEVADA, LAS VEGAS
Las Vegas, Nevada

Runnin' Rebels ◆ NCAA I ◆ Mountain West Conference ◆ http://www.unlv.edu/

State-supported university, founded 1957, part of University and Community College System of Nevada
Coed, 20,680 undergraduate students, 70% full-time, 56% women, 44% men
Urban 335-acre campus
Moderately difficult entrance level, 77% of applicants were admitted

Freshmen *Admission:* 6,162 applied, 4,938 were accepted, 2,976 enrolled. *Test scores:* SAT verbal scores over 500: 56%; SAT math scores over 500: 59%; SAT verbal scores over 600: 14%; SAT math scores over 600: 19%; SAT verbal scores over 700: 1%; SAT math scores over 700: 2%.
Tuition and fees (2004–05): $3006 (resident), $11,680 (nonresident). *Room and board:* $8258 (room only: $5200).
Financial Aid (All incoming freshmen): *Average need-based gift aid:* $2913. *Average non-need based aid:* $1200. *Average aid to full-time undergraduates:* $5681.
Athletic Department: *Director of Athletics:* Mike Hamrick; Phone: 702-895-4729; Fax: 702-895-4468; E-mail: mike.hamrick@ccmail.nevada.edu. *Sports Information Director:* Terry Cottle; Phone: 702-895-3454; E-mail: tcottle@ccmail.nevada.edu.

MEN'S COACHES
Baseball: Buddy Gouldsmith; Phone: 702-895-3499; E-mail: buddy.gouldsmith@ccmail.nevada.edu.
Basketball: Charlie Spoonhour; Phone: 702-895-3295; E-mail: deangelis@ccmail.nevada.edu.
Cheerleading: Nakia Jackson; Phone: 702-895-3715.
Diving: Julie Whitehead; Phone: 702-895-6211; E-mail: julie.whitehead@ccmail.nevada.edu.
Football: John Robinson; Phone: 702-895-3400.
Golf: Dwaine Knight; Phone: 702-895-3715; E-mail: golf@ccmail.nevada.edu.
Soccer: Barry Barto; Phone: 702-895-4175; E-mail: barry.barto@ccmail.nevada.edu.
Swimming: Jim Reitz; Phone: 702-895-3636; E-mail: jreitz@ccmail.nevada.edu.
Tennis: Owen Hambrook; Phone: 702-895-4322; E-mail: owen.hambrook@ccmail.nevada.edu.

WOMEN'S COACHES
Basketball: Regina Miller; Phone: 702-895-3151; E-mail: rmiller@ccmail.nevada.edu.
Cheerleading: Nakia Jackson; Phone: 702-895-3715.
Cross Country: Barbara Ferrell-Edmonson; Phone: 702-895-3256; E-mail: barbara.edmonson@ccmail.nevada.edu.
Diving: Julie Whitehead; Phone: 702-895-6211; E-mail: julie.whitehead@ccmail.nevada.edu.
Golf: Melissa Ringler; Phone: 702-895-2091; E-mail: melissa.ringler@ccmail.nevada.edu.
Soccer: Dan Abdalla; Phone: 702-895-4176; E-mail: abdalld1@nevada.edu.
Softball: Lonni Alameda; Phone: 702-895-3916; E-mail: lonni.alameda@ccmail.nevada.edu.
Swimming: Jim Reitz; Phone: 702-895-3636; E-mail: jreitz@ccmail.nevada.edu.
Tennis: Kevin Cory; Phone: 702-895-3009; E-mail: kcory@nevada.edu.
Track and Field: Barbara Ferrell-Edmonson; Phone: 702-895-3256; E-mail: barbara.edmonson@ccmail.nevada.edu.
Volleyball: Deitre Collins; Phone: 702-895-1898; E-mail: dcollins@ccmail.nevada.edu.

UNIVERSITY OF NEVADA, RENO
Reno, Nevada

Wolf Pack ◆ NCAA I ◆ Western Athletic Conference ◆ http://www.unr.edu/

State-supported university, founded 1874, part of University and Community College System of Nevada
Coed, 12,118 undergraduate students, 78% full-time, 55% women, 45% men
Urban 200-acre campus
Moderately difficult entrance level, 86% of applicants were admitted

Freshmen *Admission:* 4,024 applied, 3,551 were accepted, 2,097 enrolled. *Test scores:* SAT verbal scores over 500: 66%; SAT math scores over 500: 69%; SAT verbal scores over 600: 23%; SAT math scores over 600: 26%; SAT verbal scores over 700: 3%; SAT math scores over 700: 3%.
Financial Aid (All incoming freshmen): *Average need-based gift aid:* $2908. *Average non-need based aid:* $2735. *Average aid to full-time undergraduates:* $5940.
Athletic Department: *Director of Athletics:* Chris Ault; Phone: 775-784-6900; Fax: 775-784-4497; E-mail: cault@unr.edu. *Sports Information Director:* Jamie Klund; Phone: 775-784-6900; E-mail: jklund@unr.edu.

MEN'S COACHES
Baseball: Gary Powers; Phone: 775-784-6900; E-mail: gpowers@unr.edu.
Basketball: Trent Johnson; Phone: 775-784-6900; E-mail: tjohnson@unr.edu.
Cheerleading: Michael Gill; Phone: 775-784-6900; E-mail: mgill@unr.edu.
Football: Chris Tormey; Phone: 775-784-4438; E-mail: cjt@unr.edu.
Golf: Tom Duncan; Phone: 775-784-6900.
Tennis: Ryan Johnston; Phone: 775-784-6900; E-mail: ryanj@unr.edu.

WOMEN'S COACHES
Basketball: Kim Gervasoni; Phone: 775-784-6900; E-mail: gervason@unr.edu.
Cheerleading: Michael Gill; Phone: 775-784-6900; E-mail: mgill@unr.edu.
Cross Country: Kay Gooch; Phone: 775-784-6154; E-mail: kgooch@unr.edu.
Diving: Jian Li You; Phone: 775-784-6900; E-mail: jlyou@yahoo.com.
Golf: Carl Laib; Phone: 775-784-6900; E-mail: laibc@unr.edu.
Soccer: Dang Pibulvech; Phone: 775-784-6900; E-mail: dpibulvec@unr.edu.
Softball: Michele Gardner; Phone: 775-784-6900; E-mail: gmichell@unr.nevada.edu.
Swimming: Mike Shrader; Phone: 775-784-6900; E-mail: mshrader@unr.edu.
Tennis: Kurt Richter; Phone: 775-784-6900; E-mail: unrtennis@yahoo.com.
Track and Field: Curtis Kraft; Phone: 775-784-6900; E-mail: ckraft@unr.edu.
Volleyball: Devin Scruggs; Phone: 775-784-6900; E-mail: dscruggs@unr.edu.

UNIVERSITY OF NEW ENGLAND
Biddeford, Maine

Nor'easters ◆ NCAA III ◆ Commonwealth Coast Conference ◆ http://www.une.edu/

Independent comprehensive, founded 1831
Coed, 1,541 undergraduate students, 82% full-time, 76% women, 24% men
Small-town 410-acre campus
Moderately difficult entrance level, 96% of applicants were admitted

Freshmen *Admission:* 1,487 applied, 1,435 were accepted, 392 enrolled. *Test scores:* SAT verbal scores over 500: 57%; SAT math scores over 500: 59%; SAT verbal scores over 600: 15%; SAT math scores over 600: 17%; SAT verbal scores over 700: 1%; SAT math scores over 700: %.
Tuition and fees (2003–04): $19,640 (full-time). *Room and board:* $7560.

University of New England (continued)

Financial Aid (All incoming freshmen): *Average need-based gift aid: $8759. Average non-need based aid: $5509. Average aid to full-time undergraduates:* $16,048.
Athletic Department: *Director of Athletics:* Karol L'Heureux; Phone: 207-283-2376; Fax: 207-294-5903; E-mail: klheureux@une.edu. *Sports Information Director:* Curt Smyth; Phone: 207-283-2429; E-mail: csmyth@une.edu.

MEN'S COACHES
Basketball: David Labbe; Phone: 207-283-2551; E-mail: djlabbe@une.edu.
Cross Country: Ron Ouellette; Phone: 207-283-2161; E-mail: rouellette@une.edu.
Golf: Curt Smyth; Phone: 207-283-2429; E-mail: csmyth@une.edu.
Lacrosse: Bob Watson; Phone: 207-283-2418; E-mail: rwatson@une.edu.
Soccer: Doug Biggs; Phone: 207-283-2326; E-mail: dbiggs@une.edu.

WOMEN'S COACHES
Basketball: Curt Smyth; Phone: 207-283-2429; E-mail: csmyth@une.edu.
Cross Country: Ron Ouellette; Phone: 207-283-2161; E-mail: rouellette@une.edu.
Field Hockey: Julie Redman; Phone: 207-283-2907; E-mail: jredman@une.edu.
Lacrosse: Julie Redman; Phone: 207-283-2907; E-mail: jredman@une.edu.
Soccer: Doug Biggs; Phone: 207-283-2326; E-mail: dbiggs@une.edu.
Softball: David Labbe; Phone: 207-283-2551; E-mail: djlabbe@une.edu.
Volleyball: Karol L'Heureaux; Phone: 207-283-2376; E-mail: klheureux@une.edu.

UNIVERSITY OF NEW HAMPSHIRE
Durham, New Hampshire

Wildcats ◆ NCAA I ◆ America East Conference; Atlantic 10 Conference; Hockey East Conference ◆ http://www.unh.edu/

State-supported university, founded 1866, part of University System of New Hampshire
Coed, 11,516 undergraduate students, 93% full-time, 57% women, 43% men
Small-town 2,600-acre campus with easy access to Boston
Moderately difficult entrance level, 63% of applicants were admitted

Freshmen *Admission:* 10,798 applied, 7,502 were accepted, 2,636 enrolled. *Test scores:* SAT verbal scores over 500: 78%; SAT math scores over 500: 81%; SAT verbal scores over 600: 26%; SAT math scores over 600: 33%; SAT verbal scores over 700: 3%; SAT math scores over 700: 4%.
Tuition and fees (2003–04): $8664 (resident), $19,024 (nonresident). *Room and board:* $6234 (room only: $3636).
Financial Aid (All incoming freshmen): *Average need-based gift aid:* $2581. *Average non-need based aid:* $4445. *Average aid to full-time undergraduates:* $14,578.
Athletic Department: *Director of Athletics:* Marty Scarano; Phone: 603-862-2013; Fax: 603-862-3839; E-mail: marty.scarano@unh.edu. *Sports Information Director:* Scott Stapin; Phone: 603-862-3906; E-mail: smstapin@hopper.unh.edu.

MEN'S COACHES
Basketball: Phil Rowe; Phone: 603-862-3881; E-mail: prowe@cisunix.unh.edu.
Cheerleading: Lisa Wells; Phone: 603-862-5828; E-mail: unhcheer@aol.com.
Cross Country: Jim Boulanger; Phone: 603-862-3888; E-mail: jhb@christa.unh.edu.
Diving: Carol Stevenson; Phone: 603-862-3400; E-mail: cts3@cisunix.unh.edu.
Football: Sean McDonnell; Phone: 603-862-1852; E-mail: spmd@cisunix.unh.edu.
Ice Hockey: Richie Umile; Phone: 603-862-1161; E-mail: yaa@hopper.unh.edu.
Soccer: Robert Thompson; Phone: 603-862-3211; E-mail: robt@hopper.unh.edu.
Swimming: Josh Willman; Phone: 603-862-3832; E-mail: jwillman@christa.unh.edu.

Tennis: Anthony Sillitta; Phone: 603-862-3454; E-mail: asillitta@aol.com.
Track and Field: Jim Boulanger; Phone: 603-862-3888; E-mail: jhb@christa.unh.edu.

WOMEN'S COACHES
Basketball: Susan Johnson; Phone: 603-862-0282; E-mail: sej@hopper.unh.edu.
Cheerleading: Lisa Wells; Phone: 603-862-5828; E-mail: unhcheer@aol.com.
Cross Country: Rob Hoppler; Phone: 603-862-4740; E-mail: rhoppler@cisunix.unh.edu.
Diving: Carol Stevenson; Phone: 603-862-3400; E-mail: cts3@cisunix.unh.edu.
Field Hockey: Robin Balducci; Phone: 603-862-4345; E-mail: robinb@hopper.unh.edu.
Gymnastics: Gail Goodspeed; Phone: 603-862-3834; E-mail: gailg@hopper.unh.edu.
Lacrosse: Sandra Bridgeman; Phone: 603-862-4481; E-mail: sandrab@christa.unh.edu.
Soccer: Michael Jackson; Phone: 603-862-3822; E-mail: mdj@cisunix.unh.edu.
Swimming: Josh Willman; Phone: 603-862-3832; E-mail: jwillman@christa.unh.edu.
Tennis: Anthony Sillitta; Phone: 603-862-3454; E-mail: asillitta@aol.com.
Track and Field: Jim Boulanger; Phone: 603-862-3888; E-mail: jhb@christa.unh.edu.
Volleyball: Jill Hirschinger; Phone: 603-862-0296; E-mail: jillh@hopper.unh.edu.

UNIVERSITY OF NEW HAVEN
West Haven, Connecticut

Chargers ◆ NCAA II ◆ New York Collegiate Athletic Conference ◆ http://www.newhaven.edu/

Independent comprehensive, founded 1920
Coed, 2,621 undergraduate students, 76% full-time, 46% women, 54% men
Suburban 78-acre campus with easy access to Hartford, New Haven
Moderately difficult entrance level, 66% of applicants were admitted

Freshmen *Admission:* 3,025 applied, 2,039 were accepted, 631 enrolled. *Test scores:* SAT verbal scores over 500: 56%; SAT math scores over 500: 57%; SAT verbal scores over 600: 16%; SAT math scores over 600: 18%; SAT verbal scores over 700: 1%; SAT math scores over 700: 2%.
Tuition and fees (2003–04): $20,735 (full-time). *Room and board:* $8500 (room only: $5160).
Financial Aid (All incoming freshmen): *Average need-based gift aid:* $10,956. *Average non-need based aid:* $10,583. *Average aid to full-time undergraduates:* $15,256.
Athletic Department: *Director of Athletics:* Debbie Chin; Phone: 203-932-7016; Fax: 203-932-7470. *Sports Information Director:* Jason Sullivan; Phone: 203-932-7025; E-mail: jsullivan@newhaven.edu.

MEN'S COACHES
Baseball: Frank Vieira; Phone: 203-932-7018.
Basketball: Jay Young; Phone: 203-932-7024; E-mail: jyoung@newhaven.edu.
Cheerleading: Kirsten Smith; Phone: 203-932-7017.
Cross Country: John Sagnelli; Phone: 203-932-7021; E-mail: jsagnelli@newhaven.edu.
Football: Dave Patenaude; Phone: 203-932-7017.
Golf: Tom McQueeney; Phone: 203-932-7471.
Lacrosse: Dmitri Anufijevas; Phone: 203-479-4512.
Soccer: Chris Payne; Phone: 203-932-7027; E-mail: cpayne@newhaven.edu.
Track and Field: John Sagnelli; Phone: 203-932-7021; E-mail: jsagnelli@newhaven.edu.
Volleyball: Hugo Montesinos; Phone: 203-932-7278; E-mail: hmontesinos@newhaven.edu.

WOMEN'S COACHES
Basketball: Mimi Walters; Phone: 203-932-7098; E-mail: mwalters@newhaven.edu.
Cheerleading: Kirsten Smith; Phone: 203-932-7017.

Cross Country: John Sagnelli; Phone: 203-932-7021; E-mail: jhanneken@newhaven.edu.

Golf: Tony Amaral; Phone: 203-397-9651; E-mail: hobesound00@aol.com.

Lacrosse: Alan MacDougall; Phone: 203-932-7054; E-mail: alanm@newhaven.edu.

Soccer: Brendan Faherty; Phone: 203-932-7044; E-mail: bfaherty@newhaven.edu.

Softball: Becky Snow; Phone: 203-932-7045; E-mail: rsnow@newhaven.edu.

Tennis: Al South; Phone: 203-932-7347.

Track and Field: John Sagnelli; Phone: 203-932-7021; E-mail: jsagnelli@newhaven.edu.

Volleyball: Robin Salters; Phone: 203-932-7022; E-mail: rsalters@newhaven.edu.

UNIVERSITY OF NEW MEXICO
Albuquerque, New Mexico

Lobos ◆ NCAA I ◆ Mountain West Conference ◆ http://www.unm.edu/

State-supported university, founded 1889
Coed, 17,932 undergraduate students, 79% full-time, 57% women, 43% men
Urban 875-acre campus with easy access to Albuquerque
Moderately difficult entrance level, 74% of applicants were admitted

Freshmen *Admission:* 6,752 applied, 5,095 were accepted, 3,004 enrolled. *Test scores:* SAT verbal scores over 500: 80%; SAT math scores over 500: 71%; SAT verbal scores over 600: 43%; SAT math scores over 600: 26%; SAT verbal scores over 700: 9%; SAT math scores over 700: 4%.
Tuition and fees (2003–04): $3313 (resident), $11,954 (nonresident). *Room and board:* $5910 (room only: $3410).
Financial Aid (All incoming freshmen): *Average need-based gift aid:* $4792. *Average non-need based aid:* $2770. *Average aid to full-time undergraduates:* $6893.
Athletic Department: *Director of Athletics:* Rudy Davalos; Phone: 505-925-5510; Fax: 505-925-5509; E-mail: rudydav@unm.edu. *Sports Information Director:* Greg Remington; Phone: 505-925-5520; E-mail: gregrem@unm.edu.

MEN'S COACHES
Baseball: Rick Alday; Phone: 505-925-5720; E-mail: ambrose@unm.edu.

Basketball: Ritchie McKay; Phone: 505-925-5750; E-mail: lobobb@unm.edu.

Cheerleading: Tracy Denton; Phone: 505-925-8195; E-mail: unmcheer@comcast.net.

Cross Country: Matt Henry; Phone: 505-925-5735; E-mail: mathenry@unm.edu.

Football: Rocky Long; Phone: 505-925-5700; E-mail: lobofb@unm.edu.

Golf: Glen Millican; Phone: 505-925-4530; E-mail: unmgolf@unm.edu.

Soccer: Jeremy Fishbein; Phone: 505-925-9798; E-mail: lobosocr@unm.edu.

Tennis: Alan Dils; Phone: 505-925-5730; E-mail: aldils@aol.com.

Track and Field: Matt Henry; Phone: 505-925-5735; E-mail: mathenry@unm.edu.

WOMEN'S COACHES
Basketball: Don Flanagan; Phone: 505-925-5770; E-mail: donflan@unm.edu.

Cheerleading: Tracy Denton; Phone: 505-925-8195; E-mail: unmcheer@comcast.net.

Cross Country: Matt Henry; Phone: 505-925-5735; E-mail: mathenry@unm.edu.

Diving: Carlos Castillo; Phone: 505-277-2208; E-mail: coachc@unm.edu.

Golf: Jackie Booth; Phone: 505-277-4527; E-mail: jackicb@unm.edu.

Soccer: Kit Vela; Phone: 505-277-4358; E-mail: velascr@aol.com.

Softball: Kim Newbern; Phone: 505-277-2362; E-mail: newbern@unm.edu.

Swimming: Bill Spahn; Phone: 505-277-2208; E-mail: spahnb@unm.edu.

Tennis: Kathy Kolankiewicz; Phone: 505-925-5780; E-mail: kathykolan@aol.com.

Track and Field: Matt Henry; Phone: 505-925-5735; E-mail: mathenry@unm.edu.

Volleyball: Kelly Sliva; Phone: 505-277-3804; E-mail: sliva@unm.edu.

UNIVERSITY OF NEW ORLEANS
New Orleans, Louisiana

Privateers ◆ NCAA I ◆ Sun Belt Conference ◆ http://www.uno.edu/

State-supported university, founded 1958, part of Louisiana State University System
Coed, 13,338 undergraduate students, 72% full-time, 56% women, 44% men
Urban 345-acre campus
Moderately difficult entrance level, 72% of applicants were admitted

Freshmen *Admission:* 5,467 applied, 3,810 were accepted, 2,284 enrolled. *Test scores:* SAT verbal scores over 500: 65%; SAT math scores over 500: 58%; SAT verbal scores over 600: 30%; SAT math scores over 600: 24%; SAT verbal scores over 700: 6%; SAT math scores over 700: 5%.
Tuition and fees (2004–05): $3234 (resident), $10,278 (nonresident). *Room only:* $4122.
Financial Aid (All incoming freshmen): *Average need-based gift aid:* $3245. *Average non-need based aid:* $1288. *Average aid to full-time undergraduates:* $3373.
Athletic Department: *Director of Athletics:* Jim Miller; Phone: 504-280-6102; Fax: 504-280-7240; E-mail: jwmiller@uno.edu. *Sports Information Director:* Jack Duggan; Phone: 504-280-7027; E-mail: sid@uno.edu.

MEN'S COACHES
Baseball: Randy Bush; Phone: 504-280-7021; E-mail: rbush@uno.edu.

Basketball: Monte Towe; Phone: 504-280-6100; E-mail: mtowe@uno.edu.

Cross Country: Willie Randolph; Phone: 504-280-3979; E-mail: wrandolph@uno.edu.

Golf: Chris McCarter; Phone: 504-245-7347; E-mail: cpmcc@bellsouth.net.

Tennis: Burzis Kanga; Phone: 504-280-1065.

Track and Field: Willie Randolph; Phone: 504-280-3979; E-mail: wrandolph@uno.edu.

WOMEN'S COACHES
Basketball: Joey Favaloro; Phone: 504-280-7022; E-mail: coach.fav@uno.edu.

Cross Country: Willie Randolph; Phone: 504-280-3979; E-mail: wrandolph@uno.edu.

Golf: John Muller; Phone: 504-245-7347; E-mail: golfinfo@eastovercc.com.

Tennis: Burzis Kanga; Phone: 504-280-1065.

Track and Field: Willie Randolph; Phone: 504-280-3979; E-mail: wrandolph@uno.edu.

Volleyball: Julie Stempel-Ibieta; Phone: 504-280-7055; E-mail: jibieta@uno.edu.

UNIVERSITY OF NORTH ALABAMA
Florence, Alabama

Lions ◆ NCAA II ◆ Gulf South Conference ◆ http://www.una.edu/

State-supported comprehensive, founded 1830, part of Alabama Commission on Higher Education
Coed, 4,995 undergraduate students, 82% full-time, 58% women, 42% men
Urban 125-acre campus
Minimally difficult entrance level, 79% of applicants were admitted

Freshmen *Admission:* 1,635 applied, 1,298 were accepted, 803 enrolled.
Tuition and fees (2003–04): $3458 (resident), $6506 (nonresident). *Room and board:* $4272 (room only: $1960).

University of North Alabama (*continued*)

Financial Aid (All incoming freshmen): *Average need-based gift aid:* $2098. *Average aid to full-time undergraduates:* $4188.
Athletic Department: *Director of Athletics:* Joel Erdmann; Phone: 256-765-4397; Fax: 256-765-4685; E-mail: jwerdmann@una.edu. *Sports Information Director:* Jeff Hodges; Phone: 256-765-4595; E-mail: sportsinformation@una.edu.

MEN'S COACHES

Baseball: Mike Lane; Phone: 256-765-4615; E-mail: mlane@unanov.una.edu.
Basketball: Robert Champagne; Phone: 256-765-4398; E-mail: rjchampagne@una.edu.
Cross Country: Rodney Deline; Phone: 256-765-4161; E-mail: rcdeline@una.edu.
Football: Mark Hudspeth; Phone: 256-765-4565; E-mail: mdhudspeth@unanov.una.edu.
Golf: Billy Gamble; Phone: 256-765-4113; E-mail: bgamble@unanov.una.edu.
Tennis: Brice Bishop; Phone: 256-765-4617; E-mail: bbishop@unanov.una.edu.

WOMEN'S COACHES

Basketball: Flora Willie; Phone: 256-765-4616; E-mail: flwillie@una.edu.
Cross Country: Rodney Deline; Phone: 256-765-4161; E-mail: rcdeline@una.edu.
Soccer: Graham Winkworth; Phone: 256-765-4845; E-mail: gjwinkworth@una.edu.
Softball: Jeremy Reece; Phone: 256-765-5993; E-mail: jwreece@una.edu.
Tennis: Brice Bishop; Phone: 256-765-4617; E-mail: bbishop@unanov.una.edu.
Volleyball: Matt Peck; Phone: 256-765-4556; E-mail: mpeck@unanov.una.edu.

THE UNIVERSITY OF NORTH CAROLINA AT ASHEVILLE
Asheville, North Carolina

Bulldogs ◆ NCAA I ◆ Big South Conference ◆ http://www.unca.edu/

State-supported comprehensive, founded 1927, part of University of North Carolina System
Coed, 3,410 undergraduate students, 80% full-time, 57% women, 43% men
Suburban 265-acre campus
Moderately difficult entrance level, 7% of applicants were admitted

Freshmen *Admission:* 2,293 applied, 1,663 were accepted, 599 enrolled. *Test scores:* SAT verbal scores over 500: 84%; SAT math scores over 500: 86%; SAT verbal scores over 600: 38%; SAT math scores over 600: 38%; SAT verbal scores over 700: 5%; SAT math scores over 700: 3%.
Tuition and fees (2003–04): $3101 (resident), $11,926 (nonresident). *Room and board:* $4978 (room only: $2548).
Financial Aid (All incoming freshmen): *Average need-based gift aid:* $3162. *Average non-need based aid:* $3184. *Average aid to full-time undergraduates:* $6327.
Athletic Department: *Director of Athletics:* Mike Gore; Phone: 828-251-6923; Fax: 828-251-6386; E-mail: mgore@unca.edu. *Sports Information Director:* Mike Gore; Phone: 828-251-6923; E-mail: mgore@unca.edu.

MEN'S COACHES

Baseball: Matt Myers; Phone: 828-251-6920; E-mail: mmyers@unca.edu.
Basketball: Eddie Biedenbach; Phone: 828-251-6826; E-mail: ebiedenbach@unca.edu.
Cheerleading: Jamie Osteen; Phone: 828-232-5000; E-mail: josteen@unca.edu.
Cross Country: Dean Duncan; Phone: 828-251-6921; E-mail: dduncan@unca.edu.
Soccer: Steve Cornish; Phone: 828-251-6938; E-mail: scornish@unca.edu.
Tennis: Chase Hodges; Phone: 828-251-6888; E-mail: chodges@unca.edu.

Track and Field: Dean Duncan; Phone: 828-251-6921; E-mail: dduncan@unca.edu.

WOMEN'S COACHES

Basketball: Betsy Blose; Phone: 828-251-6907; E-mail: bblose@unca.edu.
Cheerleading: Jamie Osteen; Phone: 828-232-5000; E-mail: josteen@unca.edu.
Cross Country: Dean Duncan; Phone: 828-251-6921; E-mail: dduncan@unca.edu.
Soccer: Michele Cornish; Phone: 828-251-6933; E-mail: mcornish@unca.edu.
Tennis: Chase Hodges; Phone: 828-251-6888; E-mail: chodges@unca.edu.
Track and Field: Dean Duncan; Phone: 828-251-6921; E-mail: dduncan@unca.edu.
Volleyball: Julie Torbett; Phone: 828-251-5659; E-mail: jtorbett@unca.edu.

THE UNIVERSITY OF NORTH CAROLINA AT CHAPEL HILL
Chapel Hill, North Carolina

Tarheels ◆ NCAA I ◆ Atlantic Coast Conference ◆ http://www.unc.edu/

State-supported university, founded 1789, part of University of North Carolina System
Coed, 16,144 undergraduate students, 95% full-time, 59% women, 41% men
Suburban 729-acre campus with easy access to Raleigh-Durham
Very difficult entrance level, 4% of applicants were admitted

Freshmen *Admission:* 17,591 applied, 6,441 were accepted, 3,516 enrolled. *Test scores:* SAT verbal scores over 500: 96%; SAT math scores over 500: 98%; SAT verbal scores over 600: 72%; SAT math scores over 600: 78%; SAT verbal scores over 700: 21%; SAT math scores over 700: 26%.
Tuition and fees (2003–04): $4072 (resident), $15,920 (nonresident). *Room and board:* $6045 (room only: $3220).
Financial Aid (All incoming freshmen): *Average need-based gift aid:* $5524. *Average non-need based aid:* $4740. *Average aid to full-time undergraduates:* $8693.
Athletic Department: *Director of Athletics:* Dick Baddour; Phone: 919-962-8200; Fax: 919-962-6002; E-mail: dbaddour@uncaa.unc.edu. *Sports Information Director:* Steve Kirschner; Phone: 919-962-7258; E-mail: skirschner@uncaa.unc.edu.

MEN'S COACHES

Baseball: Mike Fox; Phone: 919-962-2351.
Basketball: Roy Williams; Phone: 919-962-6000.
Cheerleading: Don Collins; Phone: 919-843-7884; E-mail: dlcollin@email.unc.edu.
Cross Country: Dennis Craddock; Phone: 919-962-5411; E-mail: craddock@uncaa.unc.edu.
Diving: Kevin Lawrence; Phone: 919-962-7261.
Football: John Bunting; Phone: 919-962-2575.
Golf: John Inman; Phone: 919-962-5411; E-mail: jinman@uncaa.unc.edu.
Lacrosse: John Haus; Phone: 919-962-5216; E-mail: heel37@uncaa.unc.edu.
Soccer: Elmar Bolowich; Phone: 919-962-5411; E-mail: ebolowich@uncaa.unc.edu.
Swimming: Frank Comfort; Phone: 919-962-5411; E-mail: fcswim@uncaa.unc.edu.
Tennis: Sam Paul; Phone: 919-962-5411; E-mail: sampaul@email.unc.edu.
Track and Field: Dennis Craddock; Phone: 919-962-5411; E-mail: craddock@uncaa.unc.edu.
Wrestling: C.D. Mock; Phone: 919-962-6000.

WOMEN'S COACHES

Basketball: Sylvia Hatchell; Phone: 919-962-5187.
Cheerleading: Don Collins; Phone: 919-843-7884; E-mail: dlcollin@email.unc.edu.
Cross Country: Dennis Craddock; Phone: 919-962-5411; E-mail: craddock@uncaa.unc.edu.
Diving: Kevin Lawrence; Phone: 919-962-7261.

Field Hockey: Karen Shelton; Phone: 919-962-5411; E-mail: kcs@uncaa. unc.edu.
Golf: Sally Austin; Phone: 919-962-5411; E-mail: saustin@uncaa.unc. edu.
Gymnastics: Derek Galvin; Phone: 919-962-5213; E-mail: derekg@ uncaa.unc.edu.
Lacrosse: Jenny Slingluff Levy; Phone: 919-962-0740; E-mail: uncwlax@uncaa.unc.edu.
Soccer: Anson Dorrance; Phone: 919-962-4100; E-mail: anson@email. unc.edu.
Softball: Donna Papa; Phone: 919-962-5223; E-mail: djp@uncaa.unc. edu.
Swimming: Frank Comfort; Phone: 919-962-5411; E-mail: fcswim@ uncaa.unc.edu.
Tennis: Brian Kalbas; Phone: 919-962-6000.
Track and Field: Dennis Craddock; Phone: 919-962-5411; E-mail: craddock@uncaa.unc.edu.
Volleyball: Joe Sagula; Phone: 919-962-5228; E-mail: jsagula@uncaa. unc.edu.

THE UNIVERSITY OF NORTH CAROLINA AT CHARLOTTE
Charlotte, North Carolina

49ers ◆ NCAA I ◆ Conference USA Conference ◆ http:// www.uncc.edu/

State-supported university, founded 1946, part of University of North Carolina System
Coed, 15,694 undergraduate students, 78% full-time, 54% women, 46% men
Suburban 1,000-acre campus
Moderately difficult entrance level, 73% of applicants were admitted

Freshmen *Admission:* 8,478 applied, 6,085 were accepted, 2,519 enrolled. *Test scores:* SAT verbal scores over 500: 64%; SAT math scores over 500: 73%; SAT math scores over 600: 15%; SAT math scores over 600: 23%; SAT verbal scores over 700: 2%; SAT math scores over 700: 2%.
Tuition and fees (2003–04): $3105 (resident), $13,142 (nonresident). *Room and board:* $5076 (room only: $2596).
Financial Aid (All incoming freshmen): *Average need-based gift aid:* $3896. *Average non-need based aid:* $1732. *Average aid to full-time undergraduates:* $6678.
Athletic Department: *Director of Athletics:* Judy Rose; Phone: 704-687-6245; Fax: 704-687-4918; E-mail: jwrose@email.uncc.edu. *Sports Information Director:* Brent Stastny; Phone: 704-687-6313; E-mail: bmstastn@email.uncc.edu.

MEN'S COACHES
Baseball: Loren Hibbs; Phone: 704-687-3935; E-mail: lshibbs@email. uncc.edu.
Basketball: Bobby Lutz; Phone: 704-687-4939; E-mail: bmlutz@email. uncc.edu.
Cheerleading: Adam Thomas; Phone: 704-821-5591; E-mail: adamthomas@carolina.rr.com.
Cross Country: Brad Herbster; Phone: 704-687-6332; E-mail: bjherbst@ email.uncc.edu.
Golf: Jamie Green; Phone: 704-687-6303.
Soccer: John Tart; Phone: 704-687-3988; E-mail: jmtartsr@email.uncc. edu.
Tennis: Jim Boykin; Phone: 704-687-6316; E-mail: jcboykin@email. uncc.edu.
Track and Field: Robert Olesen; Phone: 704-687-6315; E-mail: rjolesen@ email.uncc.edu.

WOMEN'S COACHES
Basketball: Katie Meier; Phone: 704-687-3927; E-mail: kameier@email. uncc.edu.
Cheerleading: Adam Thomas; Phone: 704-821-5591; E-mail: adamthomas@carolina.rr.com.
Cross Country: Brad Herbster; Phone: 704-687-6332; E-mail: bjherbst@ email.uncc.edu.
Soccer: Neil Roberts; Phone: 704-687-3984; E-mail: nroberts@email. uncc.edu.
Softball: Aimee Devos; Phone: 704-687-3992; E-mail: amdevos@email. uncc.edu.

Tennis: Michaela Quinn; Phone: 704-687-6317.
Track and Field: Robert Olesen; Phone: 704-687-6315; E-mail: rjolesen@ email.uncc.edu.
Volleyball: Lisa Marston; Phone: 704-687-6321; E-mail: ermarsto@ email.uncc.edu.

THE UNIVERSITY OF NORTH CAROLINA AT GREENSBORO
Greensboro, North Carolina

Spartans ◆ NCAA I ◆ Southern Conference
◆ http://www.uncg.edu/

State-supported university, founded 1891, part of University of North Carolina System
Coed, 11,106 undergraduate students, 84% full-time, 68% women, 32% men
Urban 200-acre campus
Moderately difficult entrance level, 44% of applicants were admitted

Freshmen *Admission:* 6,968 applied, 3,297 were accepted, 2,056 enrolled. *Test scores:* SAT verbal scores over 500: 60%; SAT math scores over 500: 62%; SAT verbal scores over 600: 18%; SAT math scores over 600: 18%; SAT verbal scores over 700: 2%; SAT math scores over 700: 2%.
Tuition and fees (2003–04): $3038 (resident), $13,412 (nonresident). *Room and board:* $4760.
Financial Aid (All incoming freshmen): *Average need-based gift aid:* $2480. *Average non-need based aid:* $3025. *Average aid to full-time undergraduates:* $7706.
Athletic Department: *Director of Athletics:* Nelson Bobb; Phone: 336-334-5649; Fax: 336-334-4063; E-mail: nelson_bobb@uncg.edu. *Sports Information Director:* Jake Keys; Phone: 336-334-5615; E-mail: jmkeys@uncg.edu.

MEN'S COACHES
Baseball: Mike Gaski; Phone: 336-334-3247; E-mail: mggaski@uncg. edu.
Basketball: Fran McCaffrey; Phone: 336-334-3003; E-mail: basketball@ uncg.edu.
Cheerleading: Jennifer Desrosiers; Phone: 336-334-5952.
Cross Country: Dan Dachelet; Phone: 336-334-4157; E-mail: drdachel@ uncg.edu.
Golf: Terrance Stewart; Phone: 336-334-3122; E-mail: tcstewar@uncg. edu.
Soccer: Michael Parker; Phone: 336-334-5222; E-mail: mhparker@ uncg.edu.
Tennis: Jeff Trivette; Phone: 336-334-5581; E-mail: uncgtennis@uncg. edu.
Track and Field: Dan Dachelet; Phone: 336-334-4157; E-mail: drdachel@ uncg.edu.
Wrestling: Tom Shifflet; Phone: 336-334-5050; E-mail: thshiffl@uncg. edu.

WOMEN'S COACHES
Basketball: Lynne Agee; Phone: 336-334-3002; E-mail: lcagee@uncg. edu.
Cheerleading: Jennifer Desrosiers; Phone: 336-334-5952.
Cross Country: Dan Dachelet; Phone: 336-334-4157; E-mail: drdachel@ uncg.edu.
Golf: Emily Marron; Phone: 336-334-5316; E-mail: elmarron@uncg. edu.
Soccer: Eddie Radwanski; Phone: 336-334-4474; E-mail: eddie_rad@ uncg.edu.
Softball: Stephanie DeFeo; Phone: 336-334-5057; E-mail: stdefeo@ uncg.edu.
Tennis: Jeff Trivette; Phone: 336-334-5581; E-mail: uncgtennis@uncg. edu.
Track and Field: Dan Dachelet; Phone: 336-334-4157; E-mail: drdachel@ uncg.edu.
Volleyball: Stacy Meadows; Phone: 336-334-5303; E-mail: sbmeadow@ uncg.edu.

THE UNIVERSITY OF NORTH CAROLINA AT PEMBROKE
Pembroke, North Carolina

Braves ◆ NCAA II ◆ Peach Belt Conference
◆ http://www.uncp.edu/

State-supported comprehensive, founded 1887, part of University of North Carolina System
Coed, 4,253 undergraduate students, 77% full-time, 64% women, 36% men
Rural 152-acre campus
Moderately difficult entrance level, 4% of applicants were admitted

---

Freshmen *Admission:* 1,902 applied, 809 were accepted, 809 enrolled. *Test scores:* SAT verbal scores over 500: 33%; SAT math scores over 500: 38%; SAT verbal scores over 600: 6%; SAT math scores over 600: 7%; SAT verbal scores over 700: 1%; SAT math scores over 700: 1%.
Tuition and fees (2003–04): $2565 (resident), $11,929 (nonresident). *Room and board:* $4364 (room only: $2510).
Financial Aid (All incoming freshmen): *Average need-based gift aid:* $4281. *Average non-need based aid:* $1195. *Average aid to full-time undergraduates:* $5683.
Athletic Department: *Director of Athletics:* Dan Kenney; Phone: 910-521-6560; Fax: 910-521-6540; E-mail: daniel.kenney@uncp.edu. *Sports Information Director:* Rikki Cockrell; Phone: 910-521-6371; E-mail: rikki.cockrell@uncp.edu.

MEN'S COACHES
Baseball: Paul O'Neil; Phone: 910-521-6810; E-mail: paul.oneil@uncp.edu.
Basketball: Bryan Garmroth; Phone: 910-521-6344; E-mail: bryan.garmroth@uncp.edu.
Cheerleading: Chris McIntyre; Phone: 910-521-6220; E-mail: passenger06@hotmail.com.
Cross Country: Larry Rodgers; Phone: 910-521-6307; E-mail: larry.rodgers@uncp.edu.
Golf: John Haskins; Phone: 910-521-6345; E-mail: john.haskins@uncp.edu.
Soccer: Mike Schaeffer; Phone: 910-521-6342; E-mail: michael.schaeffer@uncp.edu.
Track and Field: Larry Rodgers; Phone: 910-521-6307; E-mail: larry.rodgers@uncp.edu.
Wrestling: P.J. Smith; Phone: 910-521-6261; E-mail: pj.smith@uncp.edu.

WOMEN'S COACHES
Basketball: Sandi Littleton; Phone: 910-521-6810; E-mail: sandi.mitchell@uncp.edu.
Cheerleading: Chris McIntyre; Phone: 910-521-6220; E-mail: passenger06@hotmail.com.
Cross Country: Larry Rodgers; Phone: 910-521-6307; E-mail: larry.rodgers@uncp.edu.
Soccer: Lars Andersson; Phone: 910-521-6442; E-mail: lars.andersson@uncp.edu.
Softball: Steve Johnson; Phone: 910-521-6308; E-mail: steven.johnson@uncp.edu.
Tennis: Robin Langley; Phone: 910-521-6809; E-mail: rbnlangley@aol.com.
Track and Field: Larry Rodgers; Phone: 910-521-6307; E-mail: larry.rodgers@uncp.edu.
Volleyball: Beverly Justice; Phone: 910-521-6273; E-mail: beverly.justice@uncp.edu.

THE UNIVERSITY OF NORTH CAROLINA AT WILMINGTON
Wilmington, North Carolina

Seahawks ◆ NCAA I ◆ Big South Conference; Colonial Athletic Conference ◆ http://www.uncw.edu/

State-supported comprehensive, founded 1947, part of University of North Carolina System
Coed, 9,974 undergraduate students, 90% full-time, 60% women, 40% men
Urban 650-acre campus
Moderately difficult entrance level, 50% of applicants were admitted

---

Freshmen *Admission:* 8,325 applied, 4,522 were accepted, 1,772 enrolled. *Test scores:* SAT verbal scores over 500: 71%; SAT math scores over 500: 80%; SAT verbal scores over 600: 17%; SAT math scores over 600: 26%; SAT verbal scores over 700: 1%; SAT math scores over 700: 2%.
Tuition and fees (2003–04): $3362 (resident), $12,937 (nonresident). *Room and board:* $5578.
Financial Aid (All incoming freshmen): *Average need-based gift aid:* $3425. *Average aid to full-time undergraduates:* $5721.
Athletic Department: *Director of Athletics:* Peg Bradley-Doppes; Phone: 910-962-3232; Fax: 910-962-3002; E-mail: pbd@uncw.edu. *Sports Information Director:* Joe Browning; Phone: 910-962-3236; E-mail: browningj@uncw.edu.

MEN'S COACHES
Baseball: Mark Scalf; Phone: 910-962-3570; E-mail: scalfm@uncw.edu.
Basketball: Brad Brownell; Phone: 910-962-3568; E-mail: brownellb@uncw.edu.
Cross Country: Jim Sprecher; Phone: 910-962-7233; E-mail: sprecherj@uncw.edu.
Diving: Dan Forrester; Phone: 910-962-7945; E-mail: forresterd@uncw.edu.
Golf: Jason Widener; Phone: 910-962-7204; E-mail: widenerj@uncw.edu.
Soccer: Aidan Heaney; Phone: 910-962-7057; E-mail: heaneya@uncw.edu.
Swimming: Dave Allen; Phone: 910-962-3237; E-mail: allend@uncw.edu.
Tennis: Allen Farfour; Phone: 910-962-3989; E-mail: farfoura@uncw.edu.
Track and Field: Jim Sprecher; Phone: 910-962-7233; E-mail: sprecherj@uncw.edu.

WOMEN'S COACHES
Basketball: Anne Hancock; Phone: 910-962-4085; E-mail: leee@uncw.edu.
Cross Country: Jim Sprecher; Phone: 910-962-7233; E-mail: sprecherj@uncw.edu.
Diving: Dan Forrester; Phone: 910-962-7945; E-mail: forresterd@uncw.edu.
Golf: Cindy Ho; Phone: 910-962-4163; E-mail: hoc@uncw.edu.
Soccer: Paul Cairney; Phone: 910-962-3932; E-mail: cairneyp@uncw.edu.
Softball: Melissa Jarrell; Phone: 910-962-3984; E-mail: jarrellm@uncw.edu.
Swimming: Dave Allen; Phone: 910-962-3237; E-mail: allend@uncw.edu.
Tennis: Jenny Garrity; Phone: 910-962-7714; E-mail: garrityjj@uncw.edu.
Track and Field: Jim Sprecher; Phone: 910-962-7233; E-mail: sprecherj@uncw.edu.
Volleyball: Jennifer McCall; Phone: 910-962-3232; E-mail: jennmccall13@hotmail.com.

UNIVERSITY OF NORTH DAKOTA
Grand Forks, North Dakota

Fighting Sioux ◆ NCAA II ◆ North Central Intercollegiate Conference; Western Collegiate Hockey Conference ◆ http://www.und.edu/

State-supported university, founded 1883, part of North Dakota University System
Coed, 10,711 undergraduate students, 90% full-time, 47% women, 53% men
Small-town 543-acre campus
Minimally difficult entrance level, 73% of applicants were admitted

Freshmen *Admission:* 4,066 applied, 3,096 were accepted, 2,233 enrolled.
Tuition and fees (2003–04): $4156 (resident), $9902 (nonresident). *Room and board:* $4234 (room only: $1706).
Financial Aid (All incoming freshmen): *Average need-based gift aid:* $2999. *Average non-need based aid:* $2770. *Average aid to full-time undergraduates:* $8566.
Athletic Department: *Director of Athletics:* Roger Thomas; Phone: 701-777-2234; Fax: 701-777-2285; E-mail: roger.thomas@mail.und.nodak.edu. *Sports Information Director:* Dan Benson; Phone: 701-777-2985; E-mail: dan.benson@mail.und.nodak.edu.

MEN'S COACHES

Baseball: Kevin Ziegler; Phone: 701-777-4038; E-mail: kelvin_ziegler@und.nodak.edu.
Basketball: Rich Glas; Phone: 701-777-2974; E-mail: rich.glas@mail.und.nodak.edu.
Cheerleading: Shannon O'Connor; Phone: 701-777-3594; E-mail: shan@undalumni.org.
Cross Country: Mike Grandall; Phone: 701-777-2973; E-mail: michael_grandall@und.nodak.edu.
Diving: Brian Strom; Phone: 701-777-2766; E-mail: brian.strom@mail.und.nodak.edu.
Football: Dale Lennon; Phone: 701-777-4192; E-mail: dale_lennon@und.nodak.edu.
Golf: Rob Stiles; Phone: 701-777-2155; E-mail: robert_stiles@und.nodak.edu.
Ice Hockey: Dean Blais; Phone: 701-777-3103; E-mail: dean.blais@mail.und.nodak.edu.
Swimming: Maviael Sampaio; Phone: 701-777-2766; E-mail: maviael_sampaio@und.nodak.edu.
Track and Field: Mike Grandall; Phone: 701-777-2973; E-mail: michael_grandall@und.nodak.edu.

WOMEN'S COACHES

Basketball: Gene Roebuck; Phone: 701-777-2980; E-mail: roebuck@bball.und.edu.
Cheerleading: Shannon O'Connor; Phone: 701-777-3594; E-mail: shan@undalumni.org.
Cross Country: Dick Clay; Phone: 701-777-2979; E-mail: richard_clay@und.nodak.edu.
Diving: Brian Strom; Phone: 701-777-2766; E-mail: brian.strom@mail.und.nodak.edu.
Golf: Steve Christian; Phone: 701-885-1249; E-mail: steven.christian@und.nodak.edu.
Soccer: Matt Granstrand; Phone: 701-777-3684; E-mail: matthew.granstrand@und.nodak.edu.
Softball: Tracy Marback; Phone: 701-777-4952; E-mail: tracy.marback@und.nodak.edu.
Swimming: Maviael Sampaio; Phone: 701-777-2766; E-mail: maviael_sampaio@und.nodak.edu.
Tennis: Tom Wynne; Phone: 701-746-2790; E-mail: wynnert@hotmail.com.
Track and Field: Dick Clay; Phone: 701-777-2979; E-mail: richard_clay@und.nodak.edu.
Volleyball: Maria Bruggeman; Phone: 701-777-2508; E-mail: maria.bruggeman@und.nodak.edu.

UNIVERSITY OF NORTHERN COLORADO
Greeley, Colorado

Bears ◆ NCAA II ◆ North Central Intercollegiate Conference ◆ http://www.unco.edu/

State-supported university, founded 1890
Coed, 10,664 undergraduate students, 89% full-time, 62% women, 38% men
Suburban 240-acre campus with easy access to Denver
Moderately difficult entrance level, 65% of applicants were admitted

Freshmen *Admission:* 7,172 applied, 5,063 were accepted, 2,140 enrolled. *Test scores:* SAT verbal scores over 500: 62%; SAT math scores over 500: 63%; SAT verbal scores over 600: 20%; SAT math scores over 600: 19%; SAT verbal scores over 700: 2%; SAT math scores over 700: 1%.
Tuition and fees (2003–04): $3205 (resident), $12,331 (nonresident). *Room and board:* $5782 (room only: $2704).
Financial Aid (All incoming freshmen): *Average need-based gift aid:* $3061. *Average non-need based aid:* $2280. *Average aid to full-time undergraduates:* $6228.
Athletic Department: *Director of Athletics:* Jim Fallis; Phone: 970-351-2534; Fax: 970-351-2018; E-mail: jim.fallis@unco.edu. *Sports Information Director:* Colin McDonough; Phone: 970-351-1065; E-mail: colin.mcdonough@unco.edu.

MEN'S COACHES

Baseball: Kevin Smallcomb; Phone: 970-351-1714; E-mail: baseball@unco.edu.
Basketball: Craig Rasmuson; Phone: 970-351-1716; E-mail: craig.rasmuson@unco.edu.
Cheerleading: Courtney Pederson; Phone: 970-351-2534.
Football: Kay Dalton; Phone: 970-351-1733; E-mail: kay.dalton@unco.edu.
Golf: Wally Goodwin; Phone: 970-351-2075; E-mail: rafterybanner@yahoo.com.
Tennis: Johnathan Casper; Phone: 970-351-1362; E-mail: jonathan.casper@unco.edu.
Track and Field: Phone: 970-351-1721.
Wrestling: Jack Maughan; Phone: 970-351-1815; E-mail: jack.maughan@unco.edu.

WOMEN'S COACHES

Basketball: Ron Vlasin; Phone: 970-351-1713; E-mail: ron.vlasin@unco.edu.
Cheerleading: Courtney Pederson; Phone: 970-351-2534.
Cross Country: Annie Ford; Phone: 970-351-1721; E-mail: ford6834@blue.unco.edu.
Diving: Jeff Noble; Phone: 970-351-2565.
Golf: Jack Maughan; Phone: 970-351-1815; E-mail: jack.maughan@unco.edu.
Soccer: Tim Barrera; Phone: 970-351-1758; E-mail: tim.barrera@unco.edu.
Softball: Linda Witt; Phone: 970-351-2055; E-mail: linda.witt@unco.edu.edu.
Swimming: Nancy Hinrichs; Phone: 970-351-1741; E-mail: nancy.hinrichs@unco.edu.
Tennis: Rosemary Fri; Phone: 970-351-1498; E-mail: rosemary.fri@unco.edu.
Track and Field: Phone: 970-351-1721.
Volleyball: Ron Alexander; Phone: 970-351-1719; E-mail: ron.alexander@unco.edu.

UNIVERSITY OF NORTHERN IOWA
Cedar Falls, Iowa

Panthers ◆ NCAA I ◆ Gateway Football Conference; Missouri Valley Conference ◆ http://www.uni.edu/

State-supported comprehensive, founded 1876, part of Board of Regents, State of Iowa
Coed, 11,910 undergraduate students, 88% full-time, 58% women, 42% men
Small-town 916-acre campus
Moderately difficult entrance level, 75% of applicants were admitted

Freshmen *Admission:* 4,375 applied, 3,509 were accepted, 1,785 enrolled. *Test scores:* SAT verbal scores over 500: 60%; SAT math scores over 500: 60%; SAT verbal scores over 600: 31%; SAT math scores over 600: 39%; SAT verbal scores over 700: 7%; SAT math scores over 700: 6%.
Tuition and fees (2003–04): $4916 (resident), $11,874 (nonresident). *Room and board:* $4918 (room only: $2272).
Financial Aid (All incoming freshmen): *Average need-based gift aid:* $2764. *Average non-need based aid:* $1894. *Average aid to full-time undergraduates:* $5880.
Athletic Department: *Director of Athletics:* Rick Hartzell; Phone: 319-273-2470; Fax: 319-273-3602; E-mail: rick.hartzell@uni.edu. *Sports Information Director:* Nancy Justis; Phone: 319-273-6354; E-mail: nancy.justis@uni.edu.

MEN'S COACHES
Baseball: Rick Heller; Phone: 319-273-6323; E-mail: rick.heller@uni.edu.
Basketball: Greg McDermott; Phone: 319-273-7609; E-mail: greg.mcdermott@uni.edu.
Cheerleading: Phone: 319-273-3100; E-mail: uni-cheer@uni.edu.
Cross Country: Chris Bucknam; Phone: 319-273-6481; E-mail: christopher.bucknam@uni.edu.
Football: Mark Farley; Phone: 319-273-6175; E-mail: mark.farley@uni.edu.
Golf: John Bermel; Phone: 319-273-3100; E-mail: john.bermel@uni.edu.
Track and Field: Chris Bucknam; Phone: 319-273-6481; E-mail: christopher.bucknam@uni.edu.
Wrestling: Brad Penrith; Phone: 319-273-5860; E-mail: brad.penrith@uni.edu.

WOMEN'S COACHES
Basketball: Tony Dicecco; Phone: 319-273-6443; E-mail: tony.dicecco@uni.edu.
Cheerleading: Phone: 319-273-3100; E-mail: uni-cheer@uni.edu.
Cross Country: Chris Bucknam; Phone: 319-273-6481; E-mail: christopher.bucknam@uni.edu.
Diving: Victor Laughlin; Phone: 319-273-3483.
Golf: John Bermel; Phone: 319-273-3100; E-mail: john.bermel@uni.edu.
Soccer: Linda Whitehead; Phone: 319-273-4625.
Softball: Christy Hebert; Phone: 319-273-2520.
Swimming: Stacey Simmer; Phone: 319-273-7946.
Tennis: Sachin Kirtane; Phone: 319-273-3901; E-mail: sachin.kirtane@uni.edu.
Track and Field: Chris Bucknam; Phone: 319-273-6481; E-mail: christopher.bucknam@uni.edu.
Volleyball: Bobbi Petersen; Phone: 319-273-7170.

UNIVERSITY OF NORTH FLORIDA
Jacksonville, Florida

Osprey ◆ NCAA II ◆ Peach Belt Conference ◆ http://www.unf.edu/

State-supported comprehensive, founded 1965, part of State University System of Florida
Coed, 11,970 undergraduate students, 69% full-time, 58% women, 42% men
Urban 1,300-acre campus
Very difficult entrance level, 66% of applicants were admitted

Freshmen *Admission:* 7,887 applied, 5,224 were accepted, 1,998 enrolled. *Test scores:* SAT verbal scores over 500: 79%; SAT math scores over 500: 78%; SAT verbal scores over 600: 28%; SAT math scores over 600: 29%; SAT verbal scores over 700: 4%; SAT math scores over 700: 3%.
Tuition and fees (2003–04): $2913 (resident), $13,268 (nonresident). *Room and board:* $5856 (room only: $3574).
Financial Aid (All incoming freshmen): *Average need-based gift aid:* $1696. *Average non-need based aid:* $2495. *Average aid to full-time undergraduates:* $1889.
Athletic Department: *Director of Athletics:* Richard Gropper; Phone: 904-620-2833; Fax: 904-620-2836; E-mail: rgropper@unf.edu. *Sports Information Director:* Shawn LaFata; Phone: 904-620-4025; E-mail: slafata@unf.edu.

MEN'S COACHES
Baseball: Dusty Rhodes; Phone: 904-620-2556; E-mail: jrhodes@unf.edu.
Basketball: Matt Kilcullen; Phone: 904-620-2494; E-mail: mkilcull@unf.edu.
Cheerleading: Christian Minnicks; Phone: 904-620-2833.
Cross Country: Mark Van Alstyne; Phone: 904-620-2559; E-mail: mvanal@unf.edu.
Golf: John Sadie; Phone: 904-620-4653; E-mail: jsadie@unf.edu.
Soccer: Ray Bunch; Phone: 904-620-2948; E-mail: rbunch@unf.edu.
Tennis: Tom Schrader; Phone: 904-620-2558; E-mail: tschrade@unf.edu.
Track and Field: Mark Van Alstyne; Phone: 904-620-2559; E-mail: mvanal@unf.edu.

WOMEN'S COACHES
Basketball: Mary Tappmeyer; Phone: 904-620-4667; E-mail: mtappmey@unf.edu.
Cheerleading: Christian Minnicks; Phone: 904-620-2833.
Cross Country: Mark Van Alstyne; Phone: 904-620-2559; E-mail: mvanal@unf.edu.
Diving: Emily Rokosch; Phone: 904-620-1420.
Soccer: Mike Munch; Phone: 904-620-1072; E-mail: mmunch@unf.edu.
Softball: Sonya Wilmoth; Phone: 904-620-2947; E-mail: swilmoth@unf.edu.
Swimming: Beth Harrell; Phone: 904-620-1420.
Tennis: Tom Schrader; Phone: 904-620-2558; E-mail: tschrade@unf.edu.
Track and Field: Mark Van Alstyne; Phone: 904-620-2559; E-mail: mvanal@unf.edu.
Volleyball: Bryan Bunn; Phone: 904-620-2897; E-mail: bbunn@unf.edu.

UNIVERSITY OF NORTH TEXAS
Denton, Texas

Mean Green ◆ NCAA I ◆ Sun Belt Conference ◆ http://www.unt.edu/

State-supported university, founded 1890
Coed, 23,862 undergraduate students, 78% full-time, 55% women, 45% men
Suburban 744-acre campus with easy access to Dallas–Fort Worth
Moderately difficult entrance level, 63% of applicants were admitted

Freshmen *Admission:* 10,335 applied, 7,046 were accepted, 3,618 enrolled. *Test scores:* SAT verbal scores over 500: 72%; SAT math scores over 500: 69%; SAT verbal scores over 600: 29%; SAT math scores over 600: 27%; SAT verbal scores over 700: 4%; SAT math scores over 700: 5%.
Tuition and fees (2003–04): $3782 (resident), $9448 (nonresident). *Room and board:* $4885 (room only: $2726).
Financial Aid (All incoming freshmen): *Average need-based gift aid:* $3538. *Average non-need based aid:* $2489. *Average aid to full-time undergraduates:* $5365.
Athletic Department: *Director of Athletics:* Rick Villarreal; Phone: 940-565-3646; Fax: 940-565-3470; E-mail: rickv@unt.edu. *Sports Information Director:* Eric Capper; Phone: 940-565-2476; E-mail: ecapper@unt.edu.

MEN'S COACHES
Basketball: Johnny Jones; Phone: 940-565-3649; E-mail: jones@unt.edu.
Cheerleading: Scotty Brown; Phone: 940-565-2662; E-mail: jcloutier@unt.edu.

Cross Country: Rick Watkins; Phone: 940-565-4753; E-mail: rwatkins@unt.edu.
Football: Darrell Dickey; Phone: 940-565-2451; E-mail: hardin@unt.edu.
Golf: Jim Bob Jackson; Phone: 940-565-2668; E-mail: jjackson@unt.edu.
Track and Field: Rick Watkins; Phone: 940-565-4753; E-mail: rwatkins@unt.edu.

WOMEN'S COACHES
Basketball: Tina Slinker; Phone: 940-565-3667; E-mail: slinker@unt.edu.
Cheerleading: Scotty Brown; Phone: 940-565-2662; E-mail: jcloutier@unt.edu.
Cross Country: Rick Watkins; Phone: 940-565-4753; E-mail: rwatkins@unt.edu.
Golf: Jim Bob Jackson; Phone: 940-565-2668; E-mail: jjackson@unt.edu.
Soccer: John Hedlund; Phone: 940-565-3669; E-mail: jhedlund@unt.edu.
Softball: Stacey Segal; Phone: 940-565-2662; E-mail: ssegal@unt.edu.
Swimming: Mona Nyheim-Canales; Phone: 940-565-7528; E-mail: mcanales@unt.edu.
Tennis: Dawna Denny; Phone: 940-565-2139; E-mail: ddenny@unt.edu.
Track and Field: Rick Watkins; Phone: 940-565-4753; E-mail: rwatkins@unt.edu.
Volleyball: Cassie Headrick; Phone: 940-565-3666; E-mail: headrick@unt.edu.

UNIVERSITY OF NOTRE DAME
Notre Dame, Indiana

Irish ◆ NCAA I ◆ Big East Conference; Central Collegiate Hockey Conference; Great Western Lacrosse Conference ◆ http://www.nd.edu/

Independent Roman Catholic university, founded 1842
Coed, 8,311 undergraduate students, 100% full-time, 47% women, 53% men
Suburban 1,250-acre campus
Most difficult entrance level, 29% of applicants were admitted

Freshmen *Admission:* 12,095 applied, 3,524 were accepted, 1,996 enrolled. *Test scores:* SAT verbal scores over 500: 97%; SAT math scores over 500: 99%; SAT verbal scores over 600: 84%; SAT math scores over 600: 90%; SAT verbal scores over 700: 39%; SAT math scores over 700: 51%.
Tuition and fees (2003–04): $27,612 (full-time). *Room and board:* $6930.
Financial Aid (All incoming freshmen): *Average need-based gift aid:* $17,663. *Average non-need based aid:* $5848. *Average aid to full-time undergraduates:* $22,902.
Athletic Department: *Director of Athletics:* Kevin White; Phone: 574-631-7546; Fax: 574-631-8231; E-mail: kevin.m.white.107@nd.edu. *Sports Information Director:* John Heisler; Phone: 574-631-7516♂; E-mail: john.e.heisler.1@nd.edu.

MEN'S COACHES
Baseball: Paul Mainieri; Phone: 574-631-6366; E-mail: paul.mainieri.1@nd.edu.
Basketball: Mike Brey; Phone: 574-631-5222; E-mail: michael.p.brey.2@nd.edu.
Cheerleading: Jo Minton; Phone: 574-631-9126; E-mail: jonette.minton.1@nd.edu.
Cross Country: Joe Piane; Phone: 574-631-6135; E-mail: joseph.p.piane.1@nd.edu.
Diving: Caiming Xie; Phone: 574-631-7020; E-mail: caiming.xie.2@nd.edu.
Football: Tyrone Willingham; Phone: 574-631-6107; E-mail: tyrone.l.willingham.2@nd.edu.
Golf: John Jasinski; Phone: 574-631-5907; E-mail: john.jasinski.2@nd.edu.
Ice Hockey: Dave Poulin; Phone: 574-631-5050; E-mail: david.j.poulin.1@nd.edu.
Lacrosse: Kevin Corrigan; Phone: 574-631-5108; E-mail: kevin.m.corrigan.1@nd.edu.
Soccer: Bobby Clark; Phone: 574-631-3381; E-mail: robert.b.clark.136@nd.edu.

Swimming: Tim Welsh; Phone: 574-631-7042; E-mail: timothy.f.welsh.1@nd.edu.
Tennis: Bob Bayliss; Phone: 574-631-6113; E-mail: robert.e.bayliss.1@nd.edu.
Track and Field: Joe Piane; Phone: 574-631-6135; E-mail: joseph.p.piane.1@nd.edu.

WOMEN'S COACHES
Basketball: Muffet McGraw; Phone: 574-631-5420.
Cheerleading: Jo Minton; Phone: 574-631-9126; E-mail: jonette.minton.1@nd.edu.
Cross Country: Tim Connelly; Phone: 574-631-6989; E-mail: timothy.g.connelly.1@nd.edu.
Diving: Caiming Xie; Phone: 574-631-7020; E-mail: caiming.xie.2@nd.edu.
Golf: Debby King; Phone: 574-631-8406; E-mail: debby.king.108@nd.edu.
Lacrosse: Tracy Coyne; Phone: 574-631-4719; E-mail: teresa.a.coyne.7@nd.edu.
Soccer: Randy Waldrum; Phone: 574-631-3376; E-mail: randy.waldrum.1@nd.edu.
Softball: Deanna Gumf; Phone: 574-631-6107.
Swimming: Bailey Weathers; Phone: 574-631-8359; E-mail: bailey.weathers.3@nd.edu.
Tennis: Jay Louderback; Phone: 574-631-5149; E-mail: jay.a.louderback.1@nd.edu.
Track and Field: Tim Connelly; Phone: 574-631-6989; E-mail: timothy.g.connelly.1@nd.edu.
Volleyball: Debbie Brown; Phone: 574-631-6307; E-mail: debra.l.brown.19@nd.edu.

UNIVERSITY OF OKLAHOMA
Norman, Oklahoma

Sooners ◆ NCAA I ◆ Big 12 Conference ◆ http://www.ou.edu/

State-supported university, founded 1890
Coed, 20,254 undergraduate students, 87% full-time, 49% women, 51% men
Suburban 3,500-acre campus with easy access to Oklahoma City
Moderately difficult entrance level, 83% of applicants were admitted

Freshmen *Admission:* 8,140 applied, 6,638 were accepted, 3,808 enrolled.
Tuition and fees (2003–04): $3741 (resident), $10,254 (nonresident). *Room and board:* $5485 (room only: $2797).
Financial Aid (All incoming freshmen): *Average need-based gift aid:* $3627. *Average non-need based aid:* $1085. *Average aid to full-time undergraduates:* $6519.
Athletic Department: *Director of Athletics:* Joe Castiglione; Phone: 405-325-8200. *Sports Information Director:* Kenny Mossman; Phone: 405-325-8231; E-mail: kmossman@ou.edu.

MEN'S COACHES
Baseball: Larry Cochell; Phone: 405-325-8354; E-mail: larry.l.cochell-1@ou.edu.
Basketball: Kelvin Sampson; Phone: 405-325-4732; E-mail: ksampson@ou.edu.
Cheerleading: Lori Kemmet; Phone: 405-325-8366; E-mail: lkemmet@ou.edu.
Cross Country: Rodney Rothoff; Phone: 405-325-8272; E-mail: runfast@ou.edu.
Football: Bob Stoops; Phone: 405-325-2345.
Golf: Jim Ragan; Phone: 405-325-8342; E-mail: jimragan@ou.edu.
Tennis: Paul Lockwood; Phone: 405-325-8362; E-mail: plockwood@ou.edu.
Track and Field: Rodney Price; Phone: 405-325-8361; E-mail: needle52@ou.edu.
Wrestling: Jack Spates; Phone: 405-325-8209; E-mail: jspates@ou.edu.

WOMEN'S COACHES
Basketball: Sherri Coale; Phone: 405-325-8322; E-mail: scoale@ou.edu.
Cheerleading: Lori Kemmet; Phone: 405-325-8366; E-mail: lkemmet@ou.edu.
Cross Country: Rodney Rothoff; Phone: 405-325-8272; E-mail: runfast@ou.edu.
Golf: Carol Ludvigson; Phone: 405-325-8343; E-mail: ouwomensgolf@ou.edu.

University of Oklahoma *(continued)*

Gymnastics: Steve Nunno; Phone: 405-325-8333; E-mail: snunno@ou.edu.

Soccer: Randy Evans; Phone: 405-325-8296; E-mail: evansr@ou.edu.

Softball: Patty Gasso; Phone: 405-325-8361; E-mail: pgasso@ou.edu.

Tennis: Mark Johnson; Phone: 405-325-8325; E-mail: mrjohnson@ou.edu.

Track and Field: Jill Lancaster; Phone: 405-325-8361; E-mail: jllancaster@ou.edu.

Volleyball: Phone: 405-325-8365.

UNIVERSITY OF OREGON
Eugene, Oregon

Ducks ◆ NCAA I ◆ Pacific-10 Conference ◆ http://www.uoregon.edu/

State-supported university, founded 1872, part of Oregon University System

Coed, 15,983 undergraduate students, 90% full-time, 53% women, 47% men

Urban 295-acre campus

Moderately difficult entrance level, 79% of applicants were admitted

Freshmen *Admission:* 10,193 applied, 8,602 were accepted, 2,865 enrolled. *Test scores:* SAT verbal scores over 500: 74%; SAT math scores over 500: 77%; SAT verbal scores over 600: 30%; SAT math scores over 600: 33%; SAT verbal scores over 700: 5%; SAT math scores over 700: 5%.

Tuition and fees (2003–04): $4914 (resident), $16,350 (nonresident). *Room and board:* $6981.

Financial Aid (All incoming freshmen): *Average need-based gift aid:* $3725. *Average non-need based aid:* $1583. *Average aid to full-time undergraduates:* $7118.

Athletic Department: *Director of Athletics:* Bill Moos; Phone: 541-346-4481; Fax: 541-346-5031. *Sports Information Director:* Andrew Longeteig; Phone: 541-346-2253.

MEN'S COACHES

Basketball: Ernie Kent; Phone: 541-346-0490; E-mail: ekent@oregon.uoregon.edu.

Cheerleading: Laraine Raish; Phone: 541-346-5485; E-mail: lraish@oregon.uoregon.edu.

Cross Country: Martin Smith; Phone: 541-346-5493; E-mail: martins@oregon.uoregon.edu.

Football: Mike Bellotti; Phone: 541-346-5469; E-mail: mbellott@oregon.uoregon.edu.

Golf: Steve Nosler; Phone: 541-346-3372; E-mail: snosler@oregon.uoregon.edu.

Tennis: Chris Russell; Phone: 541-346-5570; E-mail: crussell@oregon.uoregon.edu.

Track and Field: Martin Smith; Phone: 541-346-2260; E-mail: martins@oregon.uoregon.edu.

Wrestling: Chuck Kearney; Phone: 541-346-6113; E-mail: ckearney@oregon.uoregon.edu.

WOMEN'S COACHES

Basketball: Bev Smith; Phone: 541-346-3392; E-mail: bevsmith@oregon.uoregon.edu.

Cheerleading: Laraine Raish; Phone: 541-346-5485; E-mail: lraish@oregon.uoregon.edu.

Cross Country: Marnie Mason; Phone: 541-346-2260.

Golf: Shannon Rouillard; Phone: 541-346-5917; E-mail: shannonr@uoregon.oregon.edu.

Lacrosse: Jen Larsen; Phone: 541-346-5399; E-mail: jlarsen@uoregon.edu.

Soccer: Bill Steffen; Phone: 541-346-5506; E-mail: steffen@oregon.uoregon.edu.

Softball: Kathy Arendsen; Phone: 541-346-5305; E-mail: kja@darkwing.uoregon.edu.

Tennis: Nils Schyllander; Phone: 541-346-5379; E-mail: nils@oregon.uoregon.edu.

Track and Field: Martin Smith; Phone: 541-346-2260; E-mail: martins@oregon.uoregon.edu.

Volleyball: Carl Ferreira; Phone: 541-346-5410; E-mail: ferreira@oregon.uoregon.edu.

UNIVERSITY OF PENNSYLVANIA
Philadelphia, Pennsylvania

Quakers ◆ NCAA I ◆ Ivy League Conference ◆ http://www.upenn.edu/

Independent university, founded 1740

Coed, 9,836 undergraduate students, 96% full-time, 50% women, 50% men

Urban 269-acre campus

Most difficult entrance level, 19% of applicants were admitted

Freshmen *Admission:* 18,831 applied, 3,837 were accepted, 2,419 enrolled. *Test scores:* SAT verbal scores over 500: 100%; SAT math scores over 500: 100%; SAT verbal scores over 600: 93%; SAT math scores over 600: 96%; SAT verbal scores over 700: 51%; SAT math scores over 700: 65%.

Tuition and fees (2003–04): $29,318 (full-time). *Room and board:* $8642 (room only: $5130).

Financial Aid (All incoming freshmen): *Average need-based gift aid:* $21,152. *Average aid to full-time undergraduates:* $25,279.

Athletic Department: *Director of Athletics:* Steve Bilsky; Phone: 215-898-6121; Fax: 215-573-2095; E-mail: colbert@pobox.upenn.edu. *Sports Information Director:* Carla Zighelboim; Phone: 215-898-9232; E-mail: carlars@pobox.upenn.edu.

MEN'S COACHES

Baseball: Bob Seddon; Phone: 215-898-6282; E-mail: bseddon@pobox.upenn.edu.

Basketball: Fran Dunphy; Phone: 215-898-7966; E-mail: dunphy@pobox.upenn.edu.

Cheerleading: John Ceralde; Phone: 215-898-5316; E-mail: jceralde@pobox.upenn.edu.

Cross Country: Charlie Powell; Phone: 215-898-6149; E-mail: mwp@pobox.upenn.edu.

Diving: Anitra Kass; Phone: 215-898-4495.

Football: Al Bagnoli; Phone: 215-573-9229; E-mail: abagnoli@pobox.upenn.edu.

Golf: Heath Davidson; Phone: 215-898-3483; E-mail: heathd@pobox.upenn.edu.

Lacrosse: Brian Voelker; Phone: 215-898-6140; E-mail: bvoelker@pobox.upenn.edu.

Soccer: Rudy Fuller; Phone: 215-898-4815; E-mail: bfuller@pobox.upenn.edu.

Swimming: Mike Schnur; Phone: 215-898-4495; E-mail: mschnur@pobox.upenn.edu.

Tennis: Mark Riley; Phone: 215-898-2406; E-mail: mjriley@pobox.upenn.edu.

Track and Field: Charlie Powell; Phone: 215-898-6149; E-mail: mwp@pobox.upenn.edu.

Wrestling: Roger Reina; Phone: 215-898-9504; E-mail: rreina@pobox.upenn.edu.

WOMEN'S COACHES

Basketball: Kelly Greenberg; Phone: 215-898-6089; E-mail: greenbe2@pobox.upenn.edu.

Cheerleading: John Ceralde; Phone: 215-898-5316; E-mail: jceralde@pobox.upenn.edu.

Cross Country: Gwen Harris; Phone: 215-898-7666; E-mail: harrisgc@pobox.upenn.edu.

Diving: Anitra Kass; Phone: 215-898-4495.

Field Hockey: Val Cloud; Phone: 215-898-6308; E-mail: vcloud@pobox.upenn.edu.

Golf: Francis Vaughn; Phone: 215-898-3483; E-mail: fsv@pobox.upenn.edu.

Gymnastics: Tom Kovic; Phone: 215-898-5316; E-mail: kovic@pobox.upenn.edu.

Lacrosse: Karin Brower; Phone: 215-898-8278; E-mail: kbrower@pobox.upenn.edu.

Soccer: Darren Ambrose; Phone: 215-898-2923; E-mail: dvambros@pobox.upenn.edu.

Softball: Leslie King Moore; Phone: 215-898-3442; E-mail: lcmoore@pobox.upenn.edu.

Swimming: Mike Schnur; Phone: 215-898-4495; E-mail: mschnur@pobox.upenn.edu.

Tennis: Michael Dowd; Phone: 215-898-6958; E-mail: mdowd@pobox.upenn.edu.

Track and Field: Gwen Harris; Phone: 215-898-7666; E-mail: harrisgc@pobox.upenn.edu.
Volleyball: Kerry Major Carr; Phone: 215-898-6495; E-mail: kmajor@pobox.upenn.edu.

UNIVERSITY OF PITTSBURGH
Pittsburgh, Pennsylvania

Panthers ◆ NCAA I ◆ Big East Conference
◆ http://www.pitt.edu/

State-related university, founded 1787, part of Commonwealth System of Higher Education
Coed, 17,413 undergraduate students, 87% full-time, 52% women, 48% men
Urban 132-acre campus
Moderately difficult entrance level, 48% of applicants were admitted

Freshmen *Admission:* 17,494 applied, 8,413 were accepted, 2,964 enrolled. *Test scores:* SAT verbal scores over 500: 93%; SAT math scores over 500: 94%; SAT verbal scores over 600: 51%; SAT math scores over 600: 61%; SAT verbal scores over 700: 11%; SAT math scores over 700: 13%.
Tuition and fees (2003–04): $9274 (resident), $18,586 (nonresident). *Room and board:* $6800 (room only: $4050).
Financial Aid (All incoming freshmen): *Average need-based gift aid:* $7518. *Average non-need based aid:* $8530. *Average aid to full-time undergraduates:* $10,118.
Athletic Department: *Director of Athletics:* Jeff Long; Phone: 412-648-8230; Fax: 412-648-8248; E-mail: jlong@athletics.pitt.edu. *Sports Information Director:* E.J. Borghetti; Phone: 412-648-8240; E-mail: eborghetti@athletics.pitt.edu.

MEN'S COACHES
Baseball: Joe Jordano; Phone: 412-648-8208; E-mail: josephj@pitt.edu.
Basketball: Jamie Dixon; Phone: 412-648-8350.
Cheerleading: Theresa Nuzzo; Phone: 412-381-5024; E-mail: tan8@pitt.edu.
Cross Country: Alonzo Webb; Phone: 412-648-8212; E-mail: aww3@pitt.edu.
Diving: Julian Krug; Phone: 412-648-8299; E-mail: jkrug@pitt.edu.
Football: Walt Harris; Phone: 412-648-8711; E-mail: vkline@pitt.edu.
Soccer: Joe Luxbacher; Phone: 412-648-8217; E-mail: jlux@pitt.edu.
Swimming: Chuck Knoles; Phone: 412-648-8342; E-mail: cknoles@pitt.edu.
Track and Field: Alonzo Webb; Phone: 412-648-8212; E-mail: aww3@pitt.edu.
Wrestling: Rande Stottlemyer; Phone: 412-648-9176; E-mail: rjs@pitt.edu.

WOMEN'S COACHES
Basketball: Agnus Berenato; Phone: 412-648-8360; E-mail: amb63@pitt.edu.
Cheerleading: Theresa Nuzzo; Phone: 412-381-5024; E-mail: tan8@pitt.edu.
Cross Country: Alonzo Webb; Phone: 412-648-8212; E-mail: aww3@pitt.edu.
Diving: Julian Krug; Phone: 412-648-8299; E-mail: jkrug@pitt.edu.
Gymnastics: Debra Yohman; Phone: 412-648-8328; E-mail: dyohman@pitt.edu.
Soccer: Sue-Moy Chin; Phone: 412-648-8701; E-mail: suc22@pitt.edu.
Softball: Michele Phalen; Phone: 412-383-7351; E-mail: mdp5@pitt.edu.
Swimming: Chuck Knoles; Phone: 412-648-8200; E-mail: cknoles@pitt.edu.
Tennis: George Dieffenbach; Phone: 412-648-9715; E-mail: gdief@pitt.edu.
Track and Field: Alonzo Webb; Phone: 412-648-8212; E-mail: aww3@pitt.edu.
Volleyball: Chris Beerman; Phone: 412-648-8337; E-mail: cbeerman@pitt.edu.

UNIVERSITY OF PITTSBURGH AT BRADFORD
Bradford, Pennsylvania

Panthers ◆ NCAA III ◆ Allegheny Mountain Conference
◆ http://www.upb.pitt.edu/

State-related 4-year, founded 1963, part of University of Pittsburgh System
Coed, 1,417 undergraduate students, 73% full-time, 60% women, 40% men
Small-town 170-acre campus with easy access to Buffalo
Minimally difficult entrance level, 80% of applicants were admitted

Freshmen *Admission:* 677 applied, 555 were accepted, 315 enrolled. *Test scores:* SAT verbal scores over 500: 52%; SAT math scores over 500: 54%; SAT verbal scores over 600: 15%; SAT math scores over 600: 14%; SAT verbal scores over 700: 2%; SAT math scores over 700: 2%.
Tuition and fees (2003–04): $9264 (resident), $18,576 (nonresident). *Room and board:* $6030 (room only: $3340).
Athletic Department: *Director of Athletics:* Lori Mazza; Phone: 814-362-7523; Fax: 814-362-7503; E-mail: mazza@pitt.edu. *Sports Information Director:* Greg Clark; Phone: 814-362-7564; E-mail: grc21@pitt.edu.

MEN'S COACHES
Baseball: Bret Butler; Phone: 814-362-5093; E-mail: bab15@pitt.edu.
Basketball: Andy Moore; Phone: 814-362-5276; E-mail: ajm8@pitt.edu.
Cross Country: Travis Faulkner; Phone: 814-362-5093; E-mail: twf1@pitt.edu.
Golf: Keith Stauffner; Phone: 814-362-7520; E-mail: stauffner@pitt.edu.
Soccer: Peter Butler; Phone: 814-362-7537; E-mail: prb8@pitt.edu.

WOMEN'S COACHES
Basketball: Dalyann Fuller; Phone: 814-362-7521; E-mail: daf16@pitt.edu.
Cross Country: Travis Faulkner; Phone: 814-362-5055; E-mail: twf1@pitt.edu.
Golf: Keith Stauffner; Phone: 814-362-7520; E-mail: stauffner@pitt.edu.
Soccer: Peter Butler; Phone: 814-362-7537; E-mail: prb8@pitt.edu.
Softball: Tina Phillips; Phone: 814-362-5086; E-mail: tmp14@pitt.edu.
Volleyball: Tina Phillips; Phone: 814-362-5086; E-mail: tmp14@pitt.edu.

UNIVERSITY OF PITTSBURGH AT GREENSBURG
Greensburg, Pennsylvania

Bobcats ◆ NCAA III ◆ Allegheny Mountain Conference
◆ http://www.upg.pitt.edu/

State-related 4-year, founded 1963, part of University of Pittsburgh System
Coed, 1,918 undergraduate students, 89% full-time, 52% women, 48% men
Small-town 219-acre campus with easy access to Pittsburgh
Moderately difficult entrance level, 89% of applicants were admitted

Freshmen *Admission:* 4,381 applied, 3,895 were accepted, 525 enrolled. *Test scores:* SAT verbal scores over 500: 68%; SAT math scores over 500: 71%; SAT verbal scores over 600: 15%; SAT math scores over 600: 16%; SAT verbal scores over 700: 1%; SAT math scores over 700: 1%.
Tuition and fees (2003–04): $9214 (resident), $18,526 (nonresident). *Room and board:* $6770 (room only: $3870).
Financial Aid (All incoming freshmen): *Average need-based gift aid:* $5563. *Average non-need based aid:* $2500. *Average aid to full-time undergraduates:* $8225.
Athletic Department: *Director of Athletics:* Dan Swalga; Phone: 724-836-9949; Fax: 724-836-7134; E-mail: das6@pitt.edu. *Sports Information Director:* Mark Katarski; Phone: 724-836-7183; E-mail: mjk1@pitt.edu.

University of Pittsburgh at Greensburg *(continued)*

MEN'S COACHES
Baseball: Joe Hill; Phone: 724-836-7185; E-mail: joehill@pitt.edu.
Basketball: Marcus Kahn; Phone: 724-836-7076; E-mail: mnkahn@pitt.edu.
Cheerleading: Kellie Wilson; Phone: 724-853-6075; E-mail: kaw8@pitt.edu.
Cross Country: Joyce Brobeck; Phone: 724-836-7489; E-mail: jmb81@pitt.edu.
Golf: Scott Statler; Phone: 724-836-7038; E-mail: srs19@pitt.edu.
Soccer: Ted Wanrzyniak; Phone: 724-836-7487; E-mail: tew9@pitt.edu.
Tennis: Marcus Kahn; Phone: 724-836-7076; E-mail: mnkahn@pitt.edu.

WOMEN'S COACHES
Basketball: Mark Katarski; Phone: 724-836-7183; E-mail: mjk1@pitt.edu.
Cheerleading: Kellie Wilson; Phone: 724-853-6075; E-mail: kaw8@pitt.edu.
Cross Country: Joyce Brobeck; Phone: 724-836-7489; E-mail: jmb81@pitt.edu.
Golf: Scott Statler; Phone: 724-836-7038; E-mail: srs19@pitt.edu.
Soccer: John Beatty; Phone: 724-836-7038; E-mail: jmb11@pitt.edu.
Softball: Mark Katarski; Phone: 724-836-7183; E-mail: mjk1@pitt.edu.
Volleyball: Leroy Simms; Phone: 724-836-7038; E-mail: als71@pitt.edu.

UNIVERSITY OF PITTSBURGH AT JOHNSTOWN
Johnstown, Pennsylvania

(M)Mountain Cats (W) Lady Cats ◆ NCAA II ◆ Independent ◆ http://www.upj.pitt.edu/

State-related 4-year, founded 1927, part of University of Pittsburgh System
Coed, 3,146 undergraduate students, 90% full-time, 52% women, 48% men
Suburban 650-acre campus with easy access to Pittsburgh
Moderately difficult entrance level, 85% of applicants were admitted

Freshmen *Admission:* 2,955 applied, 2,479 were accepted, 881 enrolled. *Test scores:* SAT verbal scores over 500: 57%; SAT math scores over 500: 63%; SAT verbal scores over 600: 8%; SAT math scores over 600: 14%; SAT verbal scores over 700: 1%; SAT math scores over 700: 1%.
Tuition and fees (2003–04): $9256 (resident), $18,568 (nonresident). *Room and board:* $5760 (room only: $3480).
Financial Aid (All incoming freshmen): *Average need-based gift aid:* $4295. *Average non-need based aid:* $2263. *Average aid to full-time undergraduates:* $6958.
Athletic Department: *Director of Athletics:* Michael Castner; Phone: 814-269-2000; Fax: 814-269-2026; E-mail: castner@pitt.edu. *Sports Information Director:* Chris Caputo; Phone: 814-269-2031; E-mail: ccaputo@pitt.edu.

MEN'S COACHES
Baseball: Todd Williams; Phone: 814-269-7170; E-mail: twillms@pitt.edu.
Basketball: Bob Rukavina; Phone: 814-269-2005; E-mail: rukavina@pitt.edu.
Soccer: Eric Kinsey; Phone: 814-535-2034; E-mail: upjsoccer@aol.com.
Wrestling: Pat Pecora; Phone: 814-535-2004; E-mail: ppecora@pitt.edu.

WOMEN'S COACHES
Basketball: Jodi Gault; Phone: 814-535-7173; E-mail: jgault@pitt.edu.
Cross Country: Mary Krestar; Phone: 814-535-2003; E-mail: upjxc@aol.com.
Track and Field: Clyde Horner; Phone: 814-535-7174; E-mail: chorner@pitt.edu.
Volleyball: Clyde Horner; Phone: 814-535-7174; E-mail: chorner@pitt.edu.

UNIVERSITY OF PORTLAND
Portland, Oregon

Pilots ◆ NCAA I ◆ West Coast Conference
◆ http://www.up.edu/

Independent Roman Catholic comprehensive, founded 1901
Coed, 2,739 undergraduate students, 96% full-time, 60% women, 40% men
Urban 125-acre campus
Moderately difficult entrance level, 72% of applicants were admitted

Freshmen *Admission:* 2,964 applied, 2,136 were accepted, 674 enrolled. *Test scores:* SAT verbal scores over 500: 86%; SAT math scores over 500: 90%; SAT verbal scores over 600: 47%; SAT math scores over 600: 47%; SAT verbal scores over 700: 8%; SAT math scores over 700: 8%.
Tuition and fees (2003–04): $22,140 (full-time). *Room and board:* $6670.
Financial Aid (All incoming freshmen): *Average need-based gift aid:* $12,697. *Average non-need based aid:* $10,563. *Average aid to full-time undergraduates:* $18,354.
Athletic Department: *Director of Athletics:* Joe Etzel; Phone: 503-943-7117; Fax: 503-943-8082; E-mail: etzel@up.edu. *Sports Information Director:* Julia Lapomarda; Phone: 503-943-7731; E-mail: lapomard@up.edu.

MEN'S COACHES
Baseball: Chris Sperry; Phone: 503-943-7707; E-mail: sperry@up.edu.
Basketball: Michael Holton; Phone: 503-943-7711; E-mail: holton@up.edu.
Cross Country: Rob Conner; Phone: 503-943-7716; E-mail: conner@up.edu.
Golf: Bill Winter; Phone: 503-943-7837; E-mail: winter@up.edu.
Soccer: Bill Irwin; Phone: 503-943-7715; E-mail: irwin@up.edu.
Tennis: Aaron Gross; Phone: 503-943-7733; E-mail: sagross@aol.com.
Track and Field: Rob Conner; Phone: 503-943-7716; E-mail: conner@up.edu.

WOMEN'S COACHES
Basketball: Jim Sollars; Phone: 503-943-7718; E-mail: sollars@up.edu.
Cross Country: Rob Conner; Phone: 503-943-7716; E-mail: conner@up.edu.
Golf: Paul Hanson; Phone: 503-943-7717; E-mail: hanson@up.edu.
Soccer: Garrett Smith; Phone: 503-943-7715; E-mail: smithg@up.edu.
Tennis: Susan Campbell-Gross; Phone: 503-943-7734.
Track and Field: Rob Conner; Phone: 503-943-7716; E-mail: conner@up.edu.
Volleyball: Doug Sparks; Phone: 503-943-7737; E-mail: sparksd@up.edu.

UNIVERSITY OF PUERTO RICO AT BAYAMÓN
Bayamón, Puerto Rico

Cowboys ◆ NCAA II ◆ Independent ◆ http://www.uprb.edu/

Commonwealth-supported 4-year, founded 1971, part of University of Puerto Rico System
Coed, 5,826 undergraduate students, 78% full-time, 58% women, 42% men
Urban 78-acre campus with easy access to San Juan
Very difficult entrance level, 78% of applicants were admitted

Freshmen *Admission:* 1,986 applied, 1,557 were accepted, 1,475 enrolled.

MEN'S COACHES
Baseball: Samuel Martinez; Phone: 787-786-2885.
Basketball: Carlos Calcano; Phone: 787-786-2885.
Cross Country: Antonio Vallejo; Phone: 787-786-2885.
Swimming: Phone: 787-786-2885.
Tennis: Phone: 787-786-2885.
Track and Field: Ray Quinonez; Phone: 787-786-2885.
Volleyball: Milton Crespo; Phone: 787-786-2885.
Wrestling: Pedro Rojas; Phone: 787-786-2885.

WOMEN'S COACHES
Basketball: Gerardo Batista; Phone: 787-786-2885.
Cross Country: Antonio Vallejo; Phone: 787-786-2885.

Tennis: Phone: 787-786-2885.
Track and Field: Ray Quinonez; Phone: 787-786-2885.
Volleyball: Tony Sanchez; Phone: 787-786-2885.

UNIVERSITY OF PUERTO RICO AT HUMACAO
Humacao, Puerto Rico

NCAA II ◆ Independent ◆ http://cuhwww.upr.clu.edu/

Commonwealth-supported 4-year, founded 1962, part of University of Puerto Rico System
Coed, 4,507 undergraduate students, 79% full-time, 71% women, 29% men
Suburban 62-acre campus with easy access to San Juan
Moderately difficult entrance level, 4% of applicants were admitted

Freshmen *Admission:* 2,137 applied, 1,027 were accepted, 883 enrolled.
Tuition and fees (2003–04): $1090 (resident).
Financial Aid (All incoming freshmen): *Average need-based gift aid:* $3999. *Average aid to full-time undergraduates:* $4013.

MEN'S COACHES
Baseball: Phone: 787-850-9345.
Basketball: Phone: 787-850-9345.
Cross Country: Phone: 787-850-9345.
Swimming: Phone: 787-850-9345.
Track and Field: Phone: 787-850-9345.
Volleyball: Phone: 787-850-9345.
Wrestling: Phone: 787-850-9345.

WOMEN'S COACHES
Basketball: Phone: 787-850-9345.
Cross Country: Phone: 787-850-9345.
Softball: Phone: 787-850-9345.
Swimming: Phone: 787-850-9345.
Track and Field: Phone: 787-850-9345.
Volleyball: Phone: 787-850-9345.

UNIVERSITY OF PUERTO RICO, CAYEY UNIVERSITY COLLEGE
Cayey, Puerto Rico

NCAA II ◆ Independent ◆ http://www.upr.clu.edu/

Commonwealth-supported 4-year, founded 1967, part of University of Puerto Rico System
Coed, 3,987 undergraduate students, 90% full-time, 72% women, 28% men
Urban 177-acre campus with easy access to San Juan
Very difficult entrance level, 22% of applicants were admitted

Freshmen *Admission:* 4,084 applied, 891 were accepted, 814 enrolled.
Financial Aid (All incoming freshmen): *Average need-based gift aid:* $3300. *Average aid to full-time undergraduates:* $4200.

MEN'S COACHES
Baseball: Phone: 787-738-2161.
Basketball: Phone: 787-738-2161.
Cross Country: Phone: 787-738-2161.
Tennis: Phone: 787-738-2161.
Track and Field: Phone: 787-738-2161.
Volleyball: Phone: 787-738-2161.
Wrestling: Phone: 787-738-2161.

WOMEN'S COACHES
Basketball: Phone: 787-738-2161.
Cross Country: Phone: 787-738-2161.
Softball: Phone: 787-738-2161.
Track and Field: Phone: 787-738-2161.
Volleyball: Phone: 787-738-2161.

UNIVERSITY OF PUERTO RICO, MAYAGÜEZ CAMPUS
Mayagüez, Puerto Rico

(M) Tarzans, (W) Janes ◆ NCAA II ◆ Independent ◆ http://www.uprm.edu/

Commonwealth-supported university, founded 1911, part of University of Puerto Rico System
Coed, 11,564 undergraduate students, 91% full-time, 50% women, 50% men
Urban 315-acre campus
Very difficult entrance level, 64% of applicants were admitted

Freshmen *Admission:* 3,780 applied, 2,636 were accepted, 2,179 enrolled. *Test scores:* SAT verbal scores over 500: 89%; SAT math scores over 500: 93%; SAT verbal scores over 600: 44%; SAT math scores over 600: 64%; SAT verbal scores over 700: 2%; SAT math scores over 700: 22%.
Financial Aid (All incoming freshmen): *Average need-based gift aid:* $3902. *Average aid to full-time undergraduates:* $3902.

MEN'S COACHES
Baseball: Felix Vega Del Valle; Phone: 787-265-3866.
Basketball: Juan Flores; Phone: 787-265-3866.
Cross Country: Cesar Santiago; Phone: 787-265-3866.
Soccer: Abner Rodriguez; Phone: 787-265-3866.
Swimming: Phone: 787-265-3866.
Tennis: Eduardo Solero; Phone: 787-265-3866.
Track and Field: Jorge Garcia; Phone: 787-265-3866.
Volleyball: Israel Garcia; Phone: 787-265-3866.
Wrestling: Leonell Pereira; Phone: 787-265-3866.

WOMEN'S COACHES
Basketball: Pedro Vargasi; Phone: 787-265-3866.
Cross Country: Cesar Santiago; Phone: 787-265-3866.
Softball: Franciscom Cintron; Phone: 787-265-3866.
Swimming: Phone: 787-265-3866.
Tennis: Marta Mora; Phone: 787-265-3866.
Track and Field: Jorge Garcia; Phone: 787-265-3866.
Volleyball: Marta Mora; Phone: 787-265-3866.

UNIVERSITY OF PUERTO RICO, RÍO PIEDRAS
San Juan, Puerto Rico

(M) Gallitos, (W) Gamecocks ◆ NCAA II ◆ Independent ◆ http://www.rrp.upr.edu/

Commonwealth-supported university, founded 1903, part of University of Puerto Rico System
Coed, 17,746 undergraduate students, 82% full-time, 67% women, 33% men
Urban 281-acre campus
Very difficult entrance level, 64% of applicants were admitted

Freshmen *Admission:* 6,043 applied, 3,983 were accepted, 3,109 enrolled. *Test scores:* SAT verbal scores over 500: 84%; SAT math scores over 500: 83%; SAT verbal scores over 600: 41%; SAT math scores over 600: 50%; SAT verbal scores over 700: 4%; SAT math scores over 700: 15%.
Tuition and fees (2003–04): $1383 (resident), $3063 (nonresident). *Room and board:* $4940.

MEN'S COACHES
Baseball: Tony Rosa; Phone: 787-764-0000.
Basketball: Danny Ortiz; Phone: 787-764-0000.
Cross Country: Luis Alers; Phone: 787-764-0000.
Soccer: Artennio Lopez; Phone: 787-764-0000.
Tennis: Angel Diaz; Phone: 787-764-0000.
Track and Field: Luis Alers; Phone: 787-764-0000.
Volleyball: Javier Gaspar; Phone: 787-764-0000.
Wrestling: Luis Martinez; Phone: 787-764-0000.

WOMEN'S COACHES
Basketball: Grimaldo Maldonado; Phone: 787-764-0000.
Cross Country: Luis Alers; Phone: 787-764-0000.
Soccer: Felix Joglar; Phone: 787-764-0000.

University of Puerto Rico, Río Piedras *(continued)*
Softball: Edwin Ramos; Phone: 787-764-0000.
Tennis: Angel Diaz; Phone: 787-764-0000.
Track and Field: Luis Alers; Phone: 787-764-0000.
Volleyball: Xiomara Molero; Phone: 787-764-0000.

UNIVERSITY OF PUGET SOUND
Tacoma, Washington

Loggers ◆ NCAA III ◆ Northwest Conference ◆ http://www.ups.edu/

Independent comprehensive, founded 1888
Coed, 2,516 undergraduate students, 98% full-time, 59% women, 41% men
Suburban 97-acre campus with easy access to Seattle
Very difficult entrance level, 70% of applicants were admitted

Freshmen *Admission:* 4,237 applied, 3,022 were accepted, 641 enrolled. *Test scores:* SAT verbal scores over 500: 96%; SAT math scores over 500: 95%; SAT verbal scores over 600: 66%; SAT math scores over 600: 60%; SAT verbal scores over 700: 19%; SAT math scores over 700: 14%.
Tuition and fees (2003–04): $25,360 (full-time). *Room and board:* $6400 (room only: $3500).
Financial Aid (All incoming freshmen): *Average need-based gift aid:* $13,825. *Average non-need based aid:* $6697. *Average aid to full-time undergraduates:* $19,365.
Athletic Department: *Director of Athletics:* Amy Hackett; Phone: 253-879-3426; Fax: 253-879-3634; E-mail: ahackett@ups.edu. *Sports Information Director:* Brian Sponsler; Phone: 253-879-3974; E-mail: bsponsler@ups.edu.

MEN'S COACHES
Baseball: Brian Billings; Phone: 253-879-3265; E-mail: bbillings@ups.edu.
Basketball: Eric Bridgeland; Phone: 253-879-3414; E-mail: ebridgeland@ups.edu.
Cross Country: Mike Orechia; Phone: 253-879-3453; E-mail: morechia@ups.edu.
Football: Phil Willenbrock; Phone: 253-879-3457; E-mail: pwillenbrock@ups.edu.
Golf: Richard Ulrich; Phone: 253-879-3426; E-mail: rulrich@ups.edu.
Soccer: Reece Olney; Phone: 253-879-3586; E-mail: rolney@ups.edu.
Swimming: Chris Myhre; Phone: 253-879-3146; E-mail: cmyhre@ups.edu.
Tennis: Steve Bowen; Phone: 253-879-2670.
Track and Field: Mike Orechia; Phone: 253-879-3453; E-mail: morechia@ups.edu.

WOMEN'S COACHES
Basketball: Suzy Barcomb; Phone: 253-879-3421; E-mail: sbarcomb@ups.edu.
Cross Country: Mike Orechia; Phone: 253-879-3453; E-mail: morechia@ups.edu.
Golf: Richard Ulrich; Phone: 253-879-3426; E-mail: rulrich@ups.edu.
Lacrosse: Beth Bricker; Phone: 253-879-3430; E-mail: bbricker@ups.edu.
Soccer: Randy Hanson; Phone: 253-879-3587; E-mail: rhanson@ups.edu.
Softball: Robin Hamilton; Phone: 253-879-3141; E-mail: rhamilton@ups.edu.
Swimming: Chris Myhre; Phone: 253-879-3146; E-mail: cmyhre@ups.edu.
Tennis: Steve Bowen; Phone: 253-879-2670.
Track and Field: Mike Orechia; Phone: 253-879-3453; E-mail: morechia@ups.edu.
Volleyball: Mark Massey; Phone: 253-879-3412; E-mail: mmassey@ups.edu.

UNIVERSITY OF REDLANDS
Redlands, California

Bulldogs ◆ NCAA III ◆ Southern California Athletic Conference ◆ http://www.redlands.edu/

Independent comprehensive, founded 1907
Coed, 2,223 undergraduate students, 99% full-time, 59% women, 41% men
Small-town 140-acre campus with easy access to Los Angeles
Moderately difficult entrance level, 68% of applicants were admitted

Freshmen *Admission:* 2,669 applied, 1,890 were accepted, 574 enrolled. *Test scores:* SAT verbal scores over 500: 89%; SAT math scores over 500: 89%; SAT verbal scores over 600: 39%; SAT math scores over 600: 38%; SAT verbal scores over 700: 5%; SAT math scores over 700: 6%.
Tuition and fees (2003–04): $24,096 (full-time). *Room and board:* $8478.
Financial Aid (All incoming freshmen): *Average need-based gift aid:* $13,462. *Average non-need based aid:* $9877. *Average aid to full-time undergraduates:* $23,946.
Athletic Department: *Director of Athletics:* Jeff Martinez; Phone: 909-335-4004; Fax: 909-335-4088; E-mail: jeff_martinez@redlands.edu. *Sports Information Director:* Rachel Johnson; Phone: 909-335-4031; E-mail: rachel_johnson@redlands.edu.

MEN'S COACHES
Baseball: Scott Lauerty; Phone: 909-335-4004; E-mail: scott_laverty@redlands.edu.
Basketball: Gary Smith; Phone: 909-335-4004; E-mail: gary_smith@redlands.edu.
Cheerleading: Danelle Afflerbaugh; Phone: 909-335-4004; E-mail: danelle_afflerbaugh@redlands.edu.
Cross Country: Mike Erb; Phone: 909-335-4004; E-mail: mike_erb@redlands.edu.
Diving: Jaime Herrera; Phone: 909-335-5222; E-mail: leslie_evans@redlands.edu.
Football: Mike Maynard; Phone: 909-335-4004; E-mail: mike_maynard@redlands.edu.
Golf: Art Salvesen; Phone: 909-335-4004; E-mail: rgolfcoach@aol.com.
Soccer: Rob Becerra; Phone: 909-335-4004; E-mail: rob_becerra@redlands.edu.
Swimming: Leslie Evans; Phone: 909-335-5222; E-mail: leslie_evans@redlands.edu.
Tennis: Geoff Roche; Phone: 909-335-4004; E-mail: geoff_roche@redlands.edu.
Track and Field: Mike Erb; Phone: 909-335-4004; E-mail: mike_erb@redlands.edu.

WOMEN'S COACHES
Basketball: Jim Ducey; Phone: 909-335-4004; E-mail: jim_ducey@redlands.edu.
Cheerleading: Danelle Afflerbaugh; Phone: 909-335-4004; E-mail: danelle_afflerbaugh@redlands.edu.
Cross Country: Mike Erb; Phone: 909-335-4004; E-mail: mike_erb@redlands.edu.
Diving: Jaime Herrera; Phone: 909-335-5222; E-mail: leslie_evans@redlands.edu.
Lacrosse: Suzette Soboti; Phone: 909-335-4004; E-mail: suzette_soboti@redlands.edu.
Soccer: Suzette Soboti; Phone: 909-335-4004; E-mail: suzette_soboti@redlands.edu.
Softball: Amanda Peterson; Phone: 909-335-4004; E-mail: amanda_peterson@redlands.edu.
Swimming: Leslie Evans; Phone: 909-335-5222; E-mail: leslie_evans@redlands.edu.
Tennis: Geoff Roche; Phone: 909-335-4004; E-mail: geoff_roche@redlands.edu.
Track and Field: Mike Erb; Phone: 909-335-4004; E-mail: mike_erb@redlands.edu.
Volleyball: Becky Schmidt; Phone: 909-335-4004; E-mail: becky_schmidt@redlands.edu.

UNIVERSITY OF RHODE ISLAND
Kingston, Rhode Island

Rams ◆ NCAA I ◆ Atlantic 10 Conference
◆ http://www.uri.edu/

State-supported university, founded 1892, part of Rhode Island State System of Higher Education
Coed, 11,298 undergraduate students, 83% full-time, 57% women, 43% men
Small-town 1,200-acre campus
Moderately difficult entrance level, 67% of applicants were admitted

Freshmen *Admission:* 12,963 applied, 9,074 were accepted, 2,590 enrolled. *Test scores:* SAT verbal scores over 500: 79%; SAT math scores over 500: 84%; SAT verbal scores over 600: 25%; SAT math scores over 600: 32%; SAT verbal scores over 700: 3%; SAT math scores over 700: 4%.
Tuition and fees (2003–04): $6202 (resident), $16,334 (nonresident). *Room and board:* $7518 (room only: $4256).
Financial Aid (All incoming freshmen): *Average need-based gift aid:* $5821. *Average non-need based aid:* $4025. *Average aid to full-time undergraduates:* $9480.
Athletic Department: *Director of Athletics:* Ron Petro; Phone: 401-874-5245; Fax: 401-874-5354; E-mail: ronp@uri.edu. *Sports Information Director:* Mike Ballweg; Phone: 401-874-2401; E-mail: mballweg@uri.edu.

MEN'S COACHES
Baseball: Frank Leoni; Phone: 401-874-4550; E-mail: fleoni@etal.uri.edu.
Basketball: Jim Baron; Phone: 401-874-2544; E-mail: mbkb@etal.uri.edu.
Cheerleading: Bil Bowers; Phone: 401-874-4513; E-mail: uricheer@cox.net.
Cross Country: John Copeland; Phone: 401-874-2163; E-mail: jco2653u@postoffice.uri.edu.
Diving: Lindsay Moore; Phone: 401-874-2005; E-mail: linzdiver@aol.com.
Football: Tim Stowers; Phone: 401-874-2406; E-mail: jillcoon@uri.edu.
Golf: Tom Drennan; Phone: 401-874-7443; E-mail: dtom@uri.edu.
Soccer: Ed Bradley; Phone: 401-874-2560; E-mail: ebradley@uri.edu.
Swimming: Mike Westrott; Phone: 401-792-9430; E-mail: westkott@postoffice.uri.edu.
Tennis: John Spears; Phone: 401-874-2867; E-mail: coachspears@aol.com.
Track and Field: John Copeland; Phone: 401-874-2163; E-mail: jco2653u@postoffice.uri.edu.

WOMEN'S COACHES
Basketball: Boe Pearman; Phone: 401-874-2235; E-mail: wbb@etal.uri.edu.
Cheerleading: Bil Bowers; Phone: 401-874-4513; E-mail: uricheer@cox.net.
Cross Country: Laurie Feit-Melnick; Phone: 401-874-5234; E-mail: lauriefm@uri.edu.
Diving: Lindsay Moore; Phone: 401-874-2005; E-mail: linzdiver@aol.com.
Field Hockey: Stacey Bean; Phone: 401-874-5276; E-mail: bean@uri.edu.
Gymnastics: Chelle Kassabian; Phone: 401-874-4687; E-mail: chelle@uri.edu.
Soccer: Lisa Cole; Phone: 401-874-5233; E-mail: lcole@mail.uri.edu.
Softball: Christina Sutcliffe; Phone: 401-874-5232; E-mail: csutcliffe@uri.edu.
Swimming: Mike Westrott; Phone: 401-874-2005; E-mail: westkott@postoffice.uri.edu.
Tennis: Valerie Villucci; Phone: 401-874-4204; E-mail: villucci@etal.uri.edu.
Track and Field: John Melnick; Phone: 401-874-5234; E-mail: lauriefm@uri.edu.
Volleyball: Bob Schneck; Phone: 401-874-5231; E-mail: bschneck@uri.edu.

UNIVERSITY OF RICHMOND
Richmond, Virginia

Spiders ◆ NCAA I ◆ Atlantic 10 Conference; Colonial Athletic Conference ◆ http://www.richmond.edu/

Independent comprehensive, founded 1830
Coed, 2,926 undergraduate students, 98% full-time, 51% women, 49% men
Suburban 350-acre campus
Very difficult entrance level, 48% of applicants were admitted

Freshmen *Admission:* 6,079 applied, 2,560 were accepted, 835 enrolled. *Test scores:* SAT verbal scores over 500: 97%; SAT math scores over 500: 98%; SAT verbal scores over 600: 81%; SAT math scores over 600: 87%; SAT verbal scores over 700: 21%; SAT math scores over 700: 28%.
Tuition and fees (2003–04): $24,940 (full-time). *Room and board:* $5160 (room only: $2810).
Financial Aid (All incoming freshmen): *Average need-based gift aid:* $16,573. *Average non-need based aid:* $19,860. *Average aid to full-time undergraduates:* $19,790.
Athletic Department: *Director of Athletics:* Jim Miller; Phone: 804-289-8694; Fax: 804-289-8820; E-mail: athletics@richmond.edu. *Sports Information Director:* Simon Gray; Phone: 804-289-8320; E-mail: sgray2@richmond.edu.

MEN'S COACHES
Baseball: Ron Atkins; Phone: 804-289-8391; E-mail: ratkins@richmond.edu.
Basketball: Jerry Wainwright; Phone: 804-289-8384; E-mail: mwinieck@richmond.edu.
Cheerleading: Alison Crowder; Phone: 804-747-4895; E-mail: acrowder@richmond.edu.
Cross Country: Steve Taylor; Phone: 804-287-1935; E-mail: staylor7@richmond.edu.
Football: Jim Reid; Phone: 804-289-8372; E-mail: jreid2@richmond.edu.
Golf: Kevin Lynch; Phone: 804-289-8095; E-mail: klynch@richmond.edu.
Soccer: Jeff Gettler; Phone: 804-289-8357; E-mail: jgettler@richmond.edu.
Tennis: Steve Gerstenfeld; Phone: 804-289-8915; E-mail: sgersten@richmond.edu.
Track and Field: Steve Taylor; Phone: 804-287-1935; E-mail: staylor7@richmond.edu.

WOMEN'S COACHES
Basketball: Joanne Boyle; Phone: 804-289-8366; E-mail: jboyle@richmond.edu.
Cheerleading: Alison Crowder; Phone: 804-747-4895; E-mail: acrowder@richmond.edu.
Cross Country: Lori Taylor; Phone: 804-289-8362; E-mail: ltaylor2@richmond.edu.
Diving: Eliot Clark; Phone: 804-747-8750.
Field Hockey: Ange Bradley; Phone: 804-289-8646; E-mail: spiderhockey@richmond.edu.
Golf: Laree Pearl Sugg; Phone: 804-287-6371; E-mail: lsugg@richmond.edu.
Lacrosse: Sue Murphy; Phone: 804-289-6680; E-mail: smurphy4@richmond.edu.
Soccer: Peter Albright; Phone: 804-289-6013; E-mail: palbrigh@richmond.edu.
Swimming: Matt Kredich; Phone: 804-289-8750; E-mail: mkredich@richmond.edu.
Tennis: Mark Wesselink; Phone: 804-289-8648; E-mail: mwesseli@richmond.edu.
Track and Field: Lori Taylor; Phone: 804-289-8362; E-mail: ltaylor2@richmond.edu.

UNIVERSITY OF RIO GRANDE
Rio Grande, Ohio

Redmen ◆ NAIA ◆ American Mideast Conference ◆ http://www.rio.edu/

Independent comprehensive, founded 1876
Coed, 1,932 undergraduate students, 80% full-time, 59% women, 41% men
Rural 170-acre campus
Noncompetitive entrance level, 100% of applicants were admitted

Freshmen *Admission:* 597 applied, 597 were accepted, 343 enrolled.
Tuition and fees (2003–04): $10,238 (resident), $11,052 (nonresident). *Room and board:* $5768.
Financial Aid (All incoming freshmen): *Average need-based gift aid:* $2640. *Average aid to full-time undergraduates:* $5265.
Athletic Department: *Director of Athletics:* Paul Harrison; Phone: 740-245-7203; Fax: 740-245-7555; E-mail: harrison@rio.edu. *Sports Information Director:* Mark Williams; Phone: 740-245-7213; E-mail: markw@rio.edu.

MEN'S COACHES
Baseball: Brad Warnimont; Phone: 740-245-7486; E-mail: bradw@rio.edu.
Basketball: Earl Thomas; Phone: 740-245-7489; E-mail: ethomas@rio.edu.
Cross Country: Bob Willey; Phone: 740-245-7487; E-mail: rwilley@rio.edu.
Soccer: Scott Morrissey; Phone: 740-245-7126; E-mail: scottm@rio.edu.
Track and Field: Bob Willey; Phone: 740-245-7487; E-mail: rwilley@rio.edu.

WOMEN'S COACHES
Basketball: David Smalley; Phone: 740-245-7491; E-mail: dsmalley@rio.edu.
Cross Country: Bob Willey; Phone: 740-245-7487; E-mail: rwilley@rio.edu.
Softball: David Pyles; Phone: 740-245-7490; E-mail: dpyles@rio.edu.
Track and Field: Bob Willey; Phone: 740-245-7487; E-mail: rwilley@rio.edu.
Volleyball: Patty Fields; Phone: 740-245-7492; E-mail: pfields@rio.edu.

UNIVERSITY OF ROCHESTER
Rochester, New York

Yellow Jackets ◆ NCAA III ◆ University Athletic Conference ◆ http://www.rochester.edu/

Independent university, founded 1850
Coed, 4,581 undergraduate students, 95% full-time, 47% women, 53% men
Suburban 534-acre campus
Very difficult entrance level, 49% of applicants were admitted

Freshmen *Admission:* 10,486 applied, 5,096 were accepted, 1,091 enrolled. *Test scores:* SAT verbal scores over 500: 95%; SAT math scores over 500: 99%; SAT verbal scores over 600: 73%; SAT math scores over 600: 84%; SAT verbal scores over 700: 22%; SAT math scores over 700: 35%.
Tuition and fees (2003–04): $27,573 (full-time). *Room and board:* $8770 (room only: $5250).
Financial Aid (All incoming freshmen): *Average need-based gift aid:* $18,490. *Average non-need based aid:* $9522. *Average aid to full-time undergraduates:* $22,901.
Athletic Department: *Director of Athletics:* George VanderZwaag; Phone: 585-275-4301; Fax: 585-461-5081; E-mail: zwaag@sports.rochester.edu. *Sports Information Director:* Dennis O'Donnell; Phone: 585-275-5955; E-mail: dennis.odonnell@rochester.edu.

MEN'S COACHES
Baseball: Joe Reina; Phone: 716-275-6027; E-mail: jreina@sports.rochester.edu.
Basketball: Mike Neer; Phone: 716-275-4306; E-mail: miken@sports.rochester.edu.
Cross Country: John Izzo; Phone: 716-275-5510; E-mail: jizzo@sports.rochester.edu.
Football: Mark Kreydt; Phone: 716-275-9458; E-mail: mkreydt@sports.rochester.edu.
Golf: Rich Johnson; Phone: 716-275-7102; E-mail: rich@sports.rochester.edu.
Soccer: Chris Apple; Phone: 716-275-5630; E-mail: capple@sports.rochester.edu.
Swimming: Eric Stefanski; Phone: 716-275-4883; E-mail: estefanski@sports.rochester.edu.
Tennis: Anna Khvalina; Phone: 716-275-1661; E-mail: akhvalina@sports.rochester.edu.
Track and Field: John Izzo; Phone: 716-275-5510; E-mail: jizzo@sports.rochester.edu.

WOMEN'S COACHES
Basketball: Jim Scheible; Phone: 716-275-4281; E-mail: jscheible@sports.rochester.edu.
Cross Country: Barbara Hartwig; Phone: 716-275-5271; E-mail: barb@sports.rochester.edu.
Field Hockey: Michele Andre; Phone: 716-275-4274; E-mail: mandre@sports.rochester.edu.
Lacrosse: Elizabeth Monte; Phone: 716-275-1030; E-mail: lmonte@sports.rochester.edu.
Soccer: Terry Gurnett; Phone: 716-275-6698; E-mail: tgurnett@sports.rochester.edu.
Softball: Michelle Andre; Phone: 716-275-4274; E-mail: mandre@sports.rochester.edu.
Swimming: Eric Stefanski; Phone: 716-275-4883; E-mail: estefanski@sports.rochester.edu.
Tennis: Anna Khvalina; Phone: 716-275-1661; E-mail: akhvalina@sports.rochester.edu.
Track and Field: Barbara Hartwig; Phone: 716-275-5271; E-mail: barb@sports.rochester.edu.
Volleyball: Linda Downey; Phone: 716-275-9461; E-mail: ladowney@sports.rochester.edu.

UNIVERSITY OF ST. FRANCIS
Joliet, Illinois

Fighting Saints ◆ NAIA ◆ Chicagoland Collegiate Conference; Mid-States Football Conference ◆ http://www.stfrancis.edu/

Independent Roman Catholic comprehensive, founded 1920
Coed, 1,143 undergraduate students, 92% full-time, 67% women, 33% men
Suburban 17-acre campus with easy access to Chicago
Moderately difficult entrance level, 53% of applicants were admitted

Freshmen *Admission:* 768 applied, 443 were accepted, 189 enrolled.
Tuition and fees (2003–04): $16,840 (full-time). *Room and board:* $6030 (room only: $2930).
Financial Aid (All incoming freshmen): *Average need-based gift aid:* $8986. *Average non-need based aid:* $6010. *Average aid to full-time undergraduates:* $14,509.
Athletic Department: *Director of Athletics:* Dave Laketa; Phone: 815-740-3842; Fax: 815-740-3841; E-mail: dlaketa@stfrancis.edu. *Sports Information Director:* Ed Schaffer; Phone: 815-740-3614; E-mail: eschaffer@stfrancis.edu.

MEN'S COACHES
Baseball: Tony Delgado; Phone: 815-740-3406; E-mail: tdelgado@stfrancis.edu.
Basketball: Pat Sullivan; Phone: 815-740-3409; E-mail: psullivan@stfrancis.edu.
Football: Mike Slovick; Phone: 815-740-3410; E-mail: mslovick@stfrancis.edu.
Golf: Paul Downey; Phone: 815-740-3464.
Soccer: Art Garza; Phone: 815-740-3464.
Tennis: Kevin Togliatti; Phone: 815-740-3464.

WOMEN'S COACHES
Basketball: Frank Kaminsky; Phone: 815-740-5031; E-mail: fkaminsky@stfrancis.edu.
Cross Country: Matt Haffner; Phone: 815-740-3464.
Golf: Tom O'Connor; Phone: 815-740-3464.
Soccer: Tony Mravle; Phone: 815-740-2274; E-mail: amravle@stfrancis.edu.
Softball: Dick Smith; Phone: 815-740-3464.
Tennis: Ralph Kwilosz; Phone: 815-740-3464.

Track and Field: Matt Haffner; Phone: 815-740-3464.
Volleyball: Cara Currier; Phone: 815-740-3407; E-mail: ccirrier@stfrancis.edu.

UNIVERSITY OF SAINT FRANCIS
Fort Wayne, Indiana

Cougars ◆ NAIA ◆ Mid-Central Conference; Mid-States
Football Conference ◆ http://www.sf.edu/

Independent Roman Catholic comprehensive, founded 1890
Coed, 1,608 undergraduate students, 76% full-time, 71% women, 29% men
Suburban 73-acre campus
Moderately difficult entrance level, 73% of applicants were admitted

Freshmen *Admission:* 931 applied, 684 were accepted, 348 enrolled.
Test scores: SAT verbal scores over 500: 38%; SAT math scores over 500: 44%; SAT verbal scores over 600: 9%; SAT math scores over 600: 7%.
Tuition and fees (2003–04): $15,514 (full-time). *Room and board:* $5450.
Financial Aid (All incoming freshmen): *Average need-based gift aid:* $10,191. *Average non-need based aid:* $9495. *Average aid to full-time undergraduates:* $13,059.
Athletic Department: *Director of Athletics:* Kevin Donley; Phone: 260-434-7400; Fax: 260-434-7446; E-mail: kdonley@sf.edu. *Sports Information Director:* Bill Scott; Phone: 260-434-7433; E-mail: toliver@sf.edu.

MEN'S COACHES
Baseball: Doug Coate; Phone: 260-434-7414; E-mail: dcoate@sf.edu.
Basketball: Jeff Rekeweg; Phone: 260-434-3243; E-mail: jrekeweg@sf.edu.
Cheerleading: Nicole Henline; Phone: 260-434-7500; E-mail: nhenline@sf.edu.
Cross Country: Gary Andrews; Phone: 260-434-3238; E-mail: gandrews@sf.edu.
Football: Kevin Donley; Phone: 260-434-7400; E-mail: kdonley@sf.edu.
Golf: Jeff Rekeweg; Phone: 260-434-3243; E-mail: jrekeweg@sf.edu.
Soccer: Mitch Ellisen; Phone: 260-434-7559; E-mail: mellisen@sf.edu.
Track and Field: James Bettcher; Phone: 260-434-7525; E-mail: ashreffler@sf.edu.

WOMEN'S COACHES
Basketball: Gary Andrews; Phone: 260-434-3238; E-mail: gandrews@sf.edu.
Cheerleading: Nicole Henline; Phone: 260-434-7500; E-mail: nhenline@sf.edu.
Cross Country: Gary Andrews; Phone: 260-434-3238; E-mail: gandrews@sf.edu.
Soccer: Ken Nuber; Phone: 260-434-3269; E-mail: knuber@sf.edu.
Softball: Lindsay Schott; Phone: 260-434-7556; E-mail: knuber@sf.edu.
Tennis: Babs Sullivan; Phone: 260-434-7556; E-mail: rkrahn@sf.edu.
Track and Field: James Bettcher; Phone: 260-434-7525; E-mail: ashreffler@sf.edu.
Volleyball: Hector Kiely; Phone: 260-434-7476; E-mail: dschmidlin@sf.edu.

UNIVERSITY OF SAINT MARY
Leavenworth, Kansas

Spires ◆ NAIA ◆ Kansas Collegiate Conference ◆ http://www.stmary.edu/

Independent Roman Catholic comprehensive, founded 1923
Coed, 580 undergraduate students, 67% full-time, 54% women, 46% men
Small-town 240-acre campus with easy access to Kansas City
Moderately difficult entrance level, 42% of applicants were admitted

Freshmen *Admission:* 541 applied, 252 were accepted, 91 enrolled.
Tuition and fees (2003–04): $13,734 (full-time). *Room and board:* $5294 (room only: $2300).

Athletic Department: *Director of Athletics:* Darrell Phipps; Phone: 913-758-4337; Fax: 913-758-6140; E-mail: phippsd@stmary.edu. *Sports Information Director:* Phil Connor; Phone: 913-758-6311; E-mail: connorp@stmary.edu.

MEN'S COACHES
Baseball: Rob Miller; Phone: 913-758-6160; E-mail: millerro@stmary.edu.
Basketball: Phil Connor; Phone: 913-758-6311; E-mail: connorp@stmary.edu.
Football: Scott Frear; Phone: 913-758-4340; E-mail: frears@stmary.edu.
Soccer: Jon Parry; Phone: 913-758-6164; E-mail: parryj@stmary.edu.

WOMEN'S COACHES
Basketball: Bob Kickner; Phone: 913-758-4339; E-mail: kicknerr@stmary.edu.
Soccer: Jon Parry; Phone: 913-758-6164; E-mail: parryj@stmary.edu.
Softball: Darrell Phipps; Phone: 913-758-4337; E-mail: phippsd@stmary.edu.
Volleyball: Paul Lawson; Phone: 913-758-6120; E-mail: lawsonp@stmary.edu.

UNIVERSITY OF ST. THOMAS
St. Paul, Minnesota

Tommies ◆ NCAA III ◆ Minnesota Intercollegiate Athletic Conference ◆ http://www.stthomas.edu/

Independent Roman Catholic university, founded 1885
Coed, 5,236 undergraduate students, 88% full-time, 51% women, 49% men
Urban 78-acre campus with easy access to Minneapolis
Moderately difficult entrance level, 84% of applicants were admitted

Freshmen *Admission:* 2,979 applied, 2,583 were accepted, 1,039 enrolled. *Test scores:* SAT verbal scores over 500: 85%; SAT math scores over 500: 89%; SAT verbal scores over 600: 38%; SAT math scores over 600: 43%; SAT verbal scores over 700: 10%; SAT math scores over 700: 9%.
Tuition and fees (2003–04): $19,343 (full-time). *Room and board:* $6484 (room only: $3774).
Financial Aid (All incoming freshmen): *Average need-based gift aid:* $9786. *Average non-need based aid:* $6845. *Average aid to full-time undergraduates:* $16,152.
Athletic Department: *Director of Athletics:* Steve Fritz; Phone: 651-962-5901; Fax: 651-962-5910; E-mail: sjfritz@stthomas.edu. *Sports Information Director:* Gene McGivern; Phone: 651-962-5901; E-mail: ejmcgivern@stthomas.edu.

MEN'S COACHES
Baseball: Dennis Denning; Phone: 651-962-5924; E-mail: dldenning@stthomas.edu.
Basketball: Steve Fritz; Phone: 651-962-5901; E-mail: sjfritz@stthomas.edu.
Cheerleading: Anita Vogel; Phone: 651-962-5924; E-mail: amvogel@stthomas.edu.
Cross Country: Pete Wareham; Phone: 651-962-5913; E-mail: pjwareham@stthomas.edu.
Diving: Tom Hodgson; Phone: 651-962-5976; E-mail: tahodgson@stthomas.edu.
Football: Don Roney; Phone: 651-962-5908; E-mail: djroney@stthomas.edu.
Golf: Dave Landry; Phone: 651-962-5379; E-mail: dtlandry@stthomas.edu.
Ice Hockey: Terry Skrypek; Phone: 651-962-5911; E-mail: tpskrypek@stthomas.edu.
Soccer: Aaron Macke; Phone: 651-962-5900; E-mail: ammacke@stthomas.edu.
Swimming: Tom Hodgson; Phone: 651-962-5976; E-mail: tahodgson@stthomas.edu.
Tennis: Terry Peck; Phone: 651-962-5918; E-mail: stbennie@aol.com.
Track and Field: Steve Mathre; Phone: 651-962-5915; E-mail: samathre@stthomas.edu.

WOMEN'S COACHES
Basketball: Tricia Dornisch; Phone: 651-962-5931; E-mail: pmdornisch@stthomas.edu.
Cheerleading: Anita Vogel; Phone: 651-962-5924; E-mail: amvogel@stthomas.edu.

University of St. Thomas *(continued)*

Cross Country: Joe Sweeney; Phone: 651-962-5914; E-mail: jvsweeney@stthomas.edu.
Diving: Tom Hodgson; Phone: 651-962-5976; E-mail: tahodgson@stthomas.edu.
Golf: Cathy Lombritto; Phone: 651-962-5921; E-mail: golf@underpar.com.
Soccer: Colleen Carey; Phone: 651-962-6450; E-mail: cdcarey@stthomas.edu.
Softball: John Tschida; Phone: 651-962-5922; E-mail: jbtschida@stthomas.edu.
Swimming: Tom Hodgson; Phone: 651-962-5976; E-mail: tahodgson@stthomas.edu.
Tennis: Terry Peck; Phone: 651-962-5918; E-mail: stbennie@aol.com.
Track and Field: Joe Sweeney; Phone: 651-962-5914; E-mail: jvsweeney@stthomas.edu.
Volleyball: Thanh Pham; Phone: 651-962-5912; E-mail: tpham@stthomas.edu.

UNIVERSITY OF SAN DIEGO
San Diego, California

Toreros ◆ NCAA I ◆ Pacific Coast Softball Conference; Pioneer Football League Conference; West Coast Conference
◆ http://www.sandiego.edu/

Independent Roman Catholic university, founded 1949
Coed, 4,803 undergraduate students, 97% full-time, 62% women, 38% men
Urban 180-acre campus
Very difficult entrance level, 44% of applicants were admitted

Freshmen *Admission:* 7,273 applied, 3,709 were accepted, 1,064 enrolled. *Test scores:* SAT verbal scores over 500: 85%; SAT math scores over 500: 90%; SAT verbal scores over 600: 42%; SAT math scores over 600: 52%; SAT verbal scores over 700: 3%; SAT math scores over 700: 9%.
Tuition and fees (2003–04): $23,518 (full-time). *Room and board:* $9630 (room only: $6970).
Financial Aid (All incoming freshmen): *Average need-based gift aid:* $17,508. *Average non-need based aid:* $6268. *Average aid to full-time undergraduates:* $20,708.
Athletic Department: *Director of Athletics:* Jo-Ann Nester; Phone: 619-260-4803; Fax: 619-260-2213; E-mail: jnester@sandiego.edu. *Sports Information Director:* Ted Gosen; Phone: 619-260-4745; E-mail: tgosen@sandiego.edu.

MEN'S COACHES
Baseball: Rick Hill; Phone: 619-260-5953; E-mail: rhill@sandiego.edu.
Basketball: Brad Holland; Phone: 619-260-2843; E-mail: holland@sandiego.edu.
Cross Country: Will Guarino; Phone: 619-260-2847; E-mail: wguarino@sandiego.edu.
Football: Jason DesJarlias; Phone: 619-260-4740; E-mail: jasond@sandiego.edu.
Golf: Tim Mickelson; Phone: 619-260-2371; E-mail: mickelson@sandiego.edu.
Soccer: Seamus McFadden; Phone: 619-260-2305; E-mail: seamusm@sandiego.edu.
Tennis: Tom Hagedom; Phone: 619-260-8889; E-mail: hagedorn@sandiego.edu.

WOMEN'S COACHES
Basketball: Kathy Marpe; Phone: 619-260-4278; E-mail: kmarpe@sandiego.edu.
Cross Country: Rick Cota; Phone: 619-260-2847; E-mail: wguarino@sandiego.edu.
Diving: Michelle Sekeres; Phone: 619-260-4803.
Soccer: Ada Greenwood; Phone: 619-260-2306; E-mail: hadriang@sandiego.edu.
Softball: Melissa McElvain; Phone: 619-260-4281; E-mail: mcelvain@sandiego.edu.
Swimming: Mike Keeler; Phone: 619-260-2372; E-mail: keelerm@sandiego.edu.
Tennis: Sherri Stephens; Phone: 619-260-8893; E-mail: sherris@sandiego.edu.
Volleyball: Jennifer Petrie; Phone: 619-260-5909; E-mail: jenniferpetrie@sandiego.edu.

UNIVERSITY OF SAN FRANCISCO
San Francisco, California

Dons ◆ NCAA I ◆ West Coast Conference
◆ http://www.usfca.edu/

Independent Roman Catholic (Jesuit) university, founded 1855
Coed, 4,718 undergraduate students, 95% full-time, 65% women, 35% men
Urban 55-acre campus with easy access to in San Francisco
Moderately difficult entrance level, 76% of applicants were admitted

Freshmen *Admission:* 4,634 applied, 3,798 were accepted, 918 enrolled. *Test scores:* SAT verbal scores over 500: 79%; SAT math scores over 500: 80%; SAT verbal scores over 600: 31%; SAT math scores over 600: 31%; SAT verbal scores over 700: 7%; SAT math scores over 700: 4%.
Tuition and fees (2004–05): $24,920 (full-time). *Room and board:* $9780 (room only: $6180).
Financial Aid (All incoming freshmen): *Average need-based gift aid:* $14,867. *Average non-need based aid:* $15,959. *Average aid to full-time undergraduates:* $19,107.
Athletic Department: *Director of Athletics:* Bill Hogan; Phone: 415-422-2923; Fax: 415-422-2510; E-mail: hogan@usfca.edu. *Sports Information Director:* Ryan McCrary; Phone: 415-422-6162; E-mail: mccrary@usfca.edu.

MEN'S COACHES
Baseball: Nino Giarratano; Phone: 415-422-2934; E-mail: giarratano@usfca.edu.
Basketball: Phil Matthews; Phone: 415-422-5993; E-mail: mathewsp@usfca.edu.
Cross Country: Helen Lehman-Winters; Phone: 415-422-6026; E-mail: hlehmanwinters@usfca.edu.
Golf: Dick Nicolopulos; Phone: 415-422-2415; E-mail: nicolopulos@usfca.edu.
Soccer: Erik Visser; Phone: 415-422-2909; E-mail: visser@usfca.edu.
Tennis: Peter Bartlett; Phone: 415-422-6073; E-mail: bartlett@usfca.edu.

WOMEN'S COACHES
Basketball: Mary Hile-Nepfel; Phone: 415-422-2931; E-mail: hile@usfca.edu.
Cross Country: Helen Lehman-Winters; Phone: 415-422-6026; E-mail: hlehmanwinters@usfca.edu.
Golf: Sara Range; Phone: 415-422-2921; E-mail: range@usfca.edu.
Soccer: Pamela Kalinoski; Phone: 415-422-6001; E-mail: kalinoskip@usfca.edu.
Tennis: Hilary Somers; Phone: 415-422-2952; E-mail: somers@norcal.usta.com.
Track and Field: Helen Lehman-Winters; Phone: 415-422-6026; E-mail: hlehmanwinters@usfca.edu.
Volleyball: Jeff Nelson; Phone: 415-422-2908; E-mail: jjnelson@usfca.edu.

UNIVERSITY OF SCIENCE AND ARTS OF OKLAHOMA
Chickasha, Oklahoma

Drovers ◆ NAIA ◆ Sooner Conference
◆ http://www.usao.edu/

State-supported 4-year, founded 1908, part of Oklahoma State Regents for Higher Education
Coed, 1,449 undergraduate students, 73% full-time, 64% women, 36% men
Small-town 75-acre campus with easy access to Oklahoma City
Moderately difficult entrance level, 88% of applicants were admitted

Freshmen *Admission:* 523 applied, 448 were accepted, 296 enrolled.
Tuition and fees (2003–04): $2890 (resident), $6790 (nonresident). *Room and board:* $3530.
Financial Aid (All incoming freshmen): *Average need-based gift aid:* $4319. *Average non-need based aid:* $1809. *Average aid to full-time undergraduates:* $5303.

Athletic Department: *Director of Athletics:* Brisco McPherson; Phone: 405-574-1249; E-mail: facmcphersonb@usao.edu. *Sports Information Director:* Jason Jewell; Phone: 405-574-1210; E-mail: jjewell@usao.edu.

MEN'S COACHES

Baseball: L.J. Powell; Phone: 405-574-1228; E-mail: facpowelllj@usao.edu.
Basketball: Brisco McPherson; Phone: 405-574-1249; E-mail: facmcphersonb@usao.edu.
Soccer: Jimmy Johnson; Phone: 405-574-1358; E-mail: fachamptonj@usao.edu.

WOMEN'S COACHES

Basketball: Jay Niehues; E-mail: facniehuesj@usao.edu.
Soccer: Jimmy Johnson; Phone: 405-574-1358; E-mail: fachamptonj@usao.edu.
Softball: Julie Vergenz; Phone: 405-574-1260; E-mail: facvergenzj@usao.edu.

THE UNIVERSITY OF SCRANTON
Scranton, Pennsylvania

Royals ◆ NCAA III ◆ Freedom Conference ◆ http://www.scranton.edu/

Independent Roman Catholic (Jesuit) comprehensive, founded 1888
Coed, 4,073 undergraduate students, 93% full-time, 57% women, 43% men
Urban 50-acre campus
Moderately difficult entrance level, 73% of applicants were admitted

Freshmen *Admission:* 5,669 applied, 4,270 were accepted, 980 enrolled. *Test scores:* SAT verbal scores over 500: 80%; SAT math scores over 500: 85%; SAT verbal scores over 600: 27%; SAT math scores over 600: 32%; SAT verbal scores over 700: 3%; SAT math scores over 700: 4%.
Tuition and fees (2003–04): $21,408 (full-time). *Room and board:* $9335 (room only: $5532).
Financial Aid (All incoming freshmen): *Average need-based gift aid:* $10,771. *Average non-need based aid:* $7635. *Average aid to full-time undergraduates:* $14,317.
Athletic Department: *Director of Athletics:* Toby Lovecchio; Phone: 570-941-7440; Fax: 570-941-4223; E-mail: lovecchiof2@scranton.edu. *Sports Information Director:* Kevin Southard; Phone: 570-941-7571; E-mail: southardk2@scranton.edu.

MEN'S COACHES

Baseball: Mike Bartoletti; Phone: 570-941-7440; E-mail: bartolettim2@scranton.edu.
Basketball: Carl Danzig; Phone: 570-941-7478; E-mail: danzigc2@scranton.edu.
Cheerleading: Danielle West; Phone: 570-563-7440; E-mail: westd2@uofs.edu.
Cross Country: Bill King; Phone: 570-941-4349; E-mail: bking@scrsd.org.
Golf: Ed Karpovich; Phone: 570-941-7440; E-mail: southardk2@scranton.edu.
Ice Hockey: Bill Fitzgerald; Phone: 570-941-7440; E-mail: southardk2@scranton.edu.
Lacrosse: Warren Breig; Phone: 570-563-2221; E-mail: breigfw3ko@aol.com.
Soccer: Matt Pivirotto; Phone: 570-941-6191; E-mail: pivirottom2@scranton.edu.
Swimming: Tomm Evans; Phone: 570-941-6204; E-mail: evanst2@scranton.edu.
Tennis: Jack Lennox; Phone: 570-348-5351; E-mail: lennoxj3@scranton.edu.
Wrestling: Brett Owen; Phone: 570-941-7440; E-mail: owen_ship@yahoo.com.

WOMEN'S COACHES

Basketball: Michael Strong; Phone: 570-941-7605; E-mail: strongj1@scranton.edu.
Cheerleading: Danielle West; Phone: 570-563-7440; E-mail: westd2@uofs.edu.
Cross Country: Bill King; Phone: 570-941-4349; E-mail: bking@scrsd.org.
Field Hockey: Brenda Brewer; Phone: 570-941-4243; E-mail: minerb1@scranton.edu.

Lacrosse: Brenda Brewer; Phone: 570-941-4243; E-mail: minerb1@scranton.edu.
Soccer: Joe Bochicchio; Phone: 570-941-6191; E-mail: bochicchioj2@scranton.edu.
Softball: Gerald Alunni; Phone: 570-941-7571; E-mail: alunnig2@scranton.edu.
Swimming: Tomm Evans; Phone: 570-941-6204; E-mail: evanst2@scranton.edu.
Tennis: Jane Johnson; Phone: 570-941-5982; E-mail: johnsonj1@scranton.edu.
Volleyball: Jud Holdredge; Phone: 570-941-7440; E-mail: jeat@epix.net.

UNIVERSITY OF SIOUX FALLS
Sioux Falls, South Dakota

Cougars ◆ NAIA ◆ Great Plains Conference ◆ http://www.usiouxfalls.edu/

Independent American Baptist Churches in the USA comprehensive, founded 1883
Coed, 1,260 undergraduate students, 82% full-time, 56% women, 44% men
Suburban 22-acre campus
Moderately difficult entrance level, 99% of applicants were admitted

Freshmen *Admission:* 774 applied, 732 were accepted, 236 enrolled.
Tuition and fees (2004–05): $14,900 (full-time). *Room and board:* $4200 (room only: $1830).
Athletic Department: *Director of Athletics:* William Sanchez; Phone: 605-575-2038; Fax: 605-331-6792; E-mail: william.sanchez@usiouxfalls.edu. *Sports Information Director:* Ryan Streit; Phone: 605-331-6695; E-mail: ryan.streit@usiouxfalls.edu.

MEN'S COACHES

Baseball: Luke Langenfeld; Phone: 605-331-6638; E-mail: luke.langenfeld@usiouxfalls.edu.
Basketball: Shane Murphy; Phone: 605-331-6702; E-mail: shane.murphy@usiouxfalls.edu.
Cross Country: Rich Greeno; Phone: 605-331-6727; E-mail: rich.greeno@usiouxfalls.edu.
Football: Bob Young; Phone: 605-331-6742; E-mail: bob.young@usiouxfalls.edu.
Golf: Sid Kortemeyer; Phone: 605-331-6656; E-mail: sid.kortemeyer@usiouxfalls.edu.
Soccer: Brock Hickam; Phone: 605-331-6797; E-mail: brock.hickam@usiouxfalls.edu.
Tennis: Jeff Nelson; Phone: 605-331-6791; E-mail: jeff.nelson@usiouxfalls.edu.
Track and Field: Rich Greeno; Phone: 605-331-6727; E-mail: rich.greeno@usiouxfalls.edu.

WOMEN'S COACHES

Basketball: Katie Dailey; Phone: 605-331-6658; E-mail: katie.dailey@usiouxfalls.edu.
Cross Country: Rich Greeno; Phone: 605-331-6727; E-mail: rich.greeno@usiouxfalls.edu.
Golf: Sid Kortemeyer; Phone: 605-331-6656; E-mail: sid.kortemeyer@usiouxfalls.edu.
Soccer: Brock Hickam; Phone: 605-331-6797; E-mail: brock.hickam@usiouxfalls.edu.
Softball: Steph Kelly; Phone: 605-575-2035; E-mail: steph.kelley@usiouxfalls.edu.
Tennis: Jeff Nelson; Phone: 605-331-6791; E-mail: jeff.nelson@usiouxfalls.edu.
Track and Field: Rich Greeno; Phone: 605-331-6727; E-mail: rich.greeno@usiouxfalls.edu.
Volleyball: Lori Huisken; Phone: 605-331-6749; E-mail: lori.huisken@usiouxfalls.edu.

UNIVERSITY OF SOUTH ALABAMA
Mobile, Alabama

Jaguars ◆ NCAA I ◆ Sun Belt Conference
◆ http://www.usouthal.edu/

State-supported university, founded 1963
Coed, 10,171 undergraduate students, 74% full-time, 59% women, 41% men
Suburban 1,225-acre campus
Moderately difficult entrance level, 75% of applicants were admitted

Freshmen *Admission:* 2,930 applied, 2,217 were accepted, 1,376 enrolled.
Tuition and fees (2003–04): $3770 (resident), $7160 (nonresident). *Room and board:* $3990 (room only: $2220).
Financial Aid (All incoming freshmen): *Average non-need based aid:* $2350. *Average aid to full-time undergraduates:* $4046.
Athletic Department: *Director of Athletics:* Joe Gottfried; Phone: 251-460-7121; Fax: 251-460-6505; E-mail: jgottfried@usouthal.edu. *Sports Information Director:* Matt Smith; Phone: 251-460-7035; E-mail: msmith@usouthal.edu.

MEN'S COACHES
Baseball: Steve Kittrell; Phone: 251-461-1397; E-mail: skittrell@usouthal.edu.
Basketball: John Pelphrey; Phone: 251-460-6104; E-mail: jpelphrey@usouthal.edu.
Cheerleading: David Pearson; Phone: 251-610-7483.
Cross Country: Lee Evans; Phone: 251-460-6875; E-mail: levans@usouthal.edu.
Golf: Ben Hannan; Phone: 251-460-6213.
Tennis: Scott Novak; Phone: 251-460-6873; E-mail: snovak@usouthal.edu.
Track and Field: Lee Evans; Phone: 251-460-6875; E-mail: levans@usouthal.edu.

WOMEN'S COACHES
Basketball: Rick Pietri; Phone: 251-414-8298; E-mail: rpietri@usouthal.edu.
Cheerleading: David Pearson; Phone: 251-610-7483.
Cross Country: Lee Evans; Phone: 251-460-6875; E-mail: levans@usouthal.edu.
Golf: T.J. Jackson; Phone: 251-460-6446; E-mail: tjjackson@usouthal.edu.
Soccer: Mike Varga; Phone: 251-460-8253; E-mail: mvarga@usouthal.edu.
Tennis: Jaco Keyser; Phone: 251-460-6266; E-mail: jkeyser@usouthal.edu.
Track and Field: Lee Evans; Phone: 251-460-6875; E-mail: levans@usouthal.edu.
Volleyball: Nicole Keshock; Phone: 251-460-7124; E-mail: nkeshock@usouthal.edu.

UNIVERSITY OF SOUTH CAROLINA
Columbia, South Carolina

Gamecocks ◆ NCAA I ◆ Southeastern Conference ◆ http://www.sc.edu/

State-supported university, founded 1801, part of University of South Carolina System
Coed, 17,133 undergraduate students, 87% full-time, 55% women, 45% men
Urban 315-acre campus
Moderately difficult entrance level, 64% of applicants were admitted

Freshmen *Admission:* 12,817 applied, 8,260 were accepted, 3,491 enrolled. *Test scores:* SAT verbal scores over 500: 82%; SAT math scores over 500: 86%; SAT verbal scores over 600: 35%; SAT math scores over 600: 40%; SAT verbal scores over 700: 7%; SAT math scores over 700: 7%.
Tuition and fees (2003–04): $5748 (resident), $15,086 (nonresident). *Room and board:* $5327 (room only: $3040).
Financial Aid (All incoming freshmen): *Average need-based gift aid:* $3019. *Average non-need based aid:* $5287. *Average aid to full-time undergraduates:* $8745.

Athletic Department: *Director of Athletics:* Mike McGee; Phone: 803-777-8881; E-mail: mcgee-mike@sc.edu. *Sports Information Director:* Kerry Tharp; Phone: 803-777-7987.

MEN'S COACHES
Baseball: Ray Tanner; Phone: 803-777-4273.
Basketball: Dave Odom; Phone: 803-777-4197; E-mail: cherylh@gwm.sc.edu.
Cheerleading: Toni Karl; Phone: 803-777-4202; E-mail: usccheerleading@hotmail.com.
Diving: Todd Sherritt; Phone: 803-777-6065.
Football: Lou Holtz; Phone: 803-777-4273.
Golf: Puggy Blackmon; Phone: 803-777-0362; E-mail: puggyb@gwm.sc.edu.
Soccer: Mark Berson; Phone: 803-777-7901; E-mail: markb@uscround.ad.sc.edu.
Swimming: Don Gibb; Phone: 803-777-6065.
Tennis: Kent Demars; Phone: 803-777-7899.
Track and Field: Curtis Frye; Phone: 803-777-7915; E-mail: cafrye@gwm.sc.edu.

WOMEN'S COACHES
Basketball: Susan Walvius; Phone: 803-777-7836; E-mail: susanwalvius@sc.edu.
Cheerleading: Toni Karl; Phone: 803-777-4202; E-mail: usccheerleading@hotmail.com.
Cross Country: Stan Rosenthal; Phone: 803-777-7925; E-mail: stanrosenthal@hotmail.com.
Diving: Todd Sherritt; Phone: 803-777-6065.
Golf: Kristi Coggins; Phone: 803-777-7923; E-mail: kcog@sc.edu.
Soccer: Shelley Smith; Phone: 803-777-1353; E-mail: smithsa7@gwm.sc.edu.
Softball: Joyce Compton; Phone: 803-777-7858; E-mail: jcompton@gwm.sc.edu.
Swimming: Don Gibb; Phone: 803-777-6065.
Tennis: Arlo Elkins; Phone: 803-777-7857.
Track and Field: Curtis Frye; Phone: 803-777-7915; E-mail: cafrye@gwm.sc.edu.
Volleyball: Kim Hudson; Phone: 803-777-7883.

UNIVERSITY OF SOUTH CAROLINA AIKEN
Aiken, South Carolina

Pacers ◆ NCAA II ◆ Peach Belt Conference
◆ http://www.usca.edu/

State-supported comprehensive, founded 1961, part of University of South Carolina System
Coed, 3,247 undergraduate students, 72% full-time, 68% women, 32% men
Suburban 453-acre campus with easy access to Columbia
Minimally difficult entrance level, 68% of applicants were admitted

Freshmen *Admission:* 1,336 applied, 907 were accepted, 564 enrolled. *Test scores:* SAT verbal scores over 500: 46%; SAT math scores over 500: 52%; SAT verbal scores over 600: 10%; SAT math scores over 600: 12%; SAT verbal scores over 700: 1%; SAT math scores over 700: 1%.
Tuition and fees (2003–04): $5084 (resident), $10,224 (nonresident). *Room and board:* $4400 (room only: $2750).
Athletic Department: *Director of Athletics:* Randy Warrick; Phone: 803-641-3406; Fax: 803-641-3441; E-mail: randyw@usca.edu. *Sports Information Director:* Brad Fields; Phone: 803-641-3252; E-mail: bradf@usca.edu.

MEN'S COACHES
Baseball: Ken Thomas; Phone: 803-641-3410; E-mail: kennyt@usca.edu.
Basketball: Mike Roberts; Phone: 803-641-3260; E-mail: miker@usca.edu.
Cheerleading: Angie Osbon; Phone: 803-641-3588; E-mail: angieo@usca.edu.
Golf: Michael Carlisle; Phone: 803-641-3528; E-mail: mikec@usca.edu.
Soccer: Ike Ofoje; Phone: 803-641-3717; E-mail: ikeo@usca.edu.
Tennis: Steve Dahm; Phone: 803-641-3529; E-mail: stevend@usca.edu.

WOMEN'S COACHES
Basketball: Mike Brandt; Phone: 803-641-3491; E-mail: mikeb@usca.edu.

Cheerleading: Angie Osbon; Phone: 803-641-3588; E-mail: angieo@usca.edu.

Cross Country: Dana Richter; Phone: 803-641-3638; E-mail: danar@usca.edu.

Soccer: Ike Ofoje; Phone: 803-641-3717; E-mail: ikeo@usca.edu.

Softball: Jerry Snyder; Phone: 803-641-3462; E-mail: jerrys@usca.edu.

Tennis: Steve Dahm; Phone: 803-641-3529; E-mail: stevend@usca.edu.

Volleyball: Will Condon; Phone: 803-641-3373; E-mail: willc@usca.edu.

UNIVERSITY OF SOUTH CAROLINA SPARTANBURG

Spartanburg, South Carolina

Rifles ◆ NCAA II ◆ Peach Belt Conference
◆ http://www.uscs.edu/

State-supported comprehensive, founded 1967, part of University of South Carolina System
Coed, 4,397 undergraduate students, 78% full-time, 65% women, 35% men
Urban 300-acre campus with easy access to Charlotte
Moderately difficult entrance level, 5% of applicants were admitted

Freshmen *Admission:* 1,904 applied, 938 were accepted, 701 enrolled. *Test scores:* SAT verbal scores over 500: 45%; SAT math scores over 500: 47%; SAT verbal scores over 600: 10%; SAT math scores over 600: 9%; SAT verbal scores over 700: 1%; SAT math scores over 700: 1%.
Tuition and fees (2003–04): $5586 (resident), $11,212 (nonresident). *Room and board:* $4310 (room only: $2900).
Financial Aid (All incoming freshmen): *Average need-based gift aid:* $3331. *Average non-need based aid:* $3655. *Average aid to full-time undergraduates:* $6761.
Athletic Department: *Director of Athletics:* Mike Hall; Phone: 864-503-5140; Fax: 864-503-5130; E-mail: mhall@uscs.edu. *Sports Information Director:* Bill English; Phone: 864-503-5129; E-mail: benglish@uscs.edu.

MEN'S COACHES
Baseball: Matt Fincher; Phone: 864-503-5135; E-mail: mfincher@uscs.edu.

Basketball: Eddie Payne; Phone: 864-503-5177; E-mail: epayne@uscs.edu.

Cheerleading: Jennie Fowler; Phone: 864-503-5135.

Cross Country: Tim Gibboms; Phone: 864-503-5152; E-mail: tgibbons@uscs.edu.

Soccer: Greg Hooks; Phone: 864-503-5117; E-mail: ghooks@uscs.edu.

Tennis: Josh Hausman; Phone: 864-503-5131; E-mail: jhausman@uscs.edu.

WOMEN'S COACHES
Basketball: Laura Timmons; Phone: 864-503-5173; E-mail: ltimmons@uscs.edu.

Cheerleading: Jennie Fowler; Phone: 864-503-5135.

Cross Country: Tim Gibboms; Phone: 864-503-5152; E-mail: tgibbons@uscs.edu.

Soccer: Kendall Reyes; Phone: 864-503-5128; E-mail: kreyes@uscs.edu.

Softball: Chris Hawkins; Phone: 864-503-5171; E-mail: chawkins@uscs.edu.

Tennis: Josh Hausman; Phone: 864-503-5131; E-mail: jhausman@uscs.edu.

Volleyball: Jennifer Calloway; Phone: 864-503-5161; E-mail: jcalloway@uscs.edu.

THE UNIVERSITY OF SOUTH DAKOTA

Vermillion, South Dakota

Coyotes ◆ NCAA II ◆ North Central Intercollegiate Conference ◆ http://www.usd.edu/

State-supported university, founded 1862
Coed, 5,851 undergraduate students, 70% full-time, 61% women, 39% men
Small-town 216-acre campus
Moderately difficult entrance level, 85% of applicants were admitted

Freshmen *Admission:* 2,570 applied, 2,134 were accepted, 1,078 enrolled. *Test scores:* SAT verbal scores over 500: 86%; SAT math scores over 500: 80%; SAT verbal scores over 600: 43%; SAT math scores over 600: 33%; SAT verbal scores over 700: 6%; SAT math scores over 700: 6%.
Tuition and fees (2003–04): $4205 (resident), $8917 (nonresident). *Room and board:* $3504 (room only: $1777).
Financial Aid (All incoming freshmen): *Average need-based gift aid:* $2940. *Average non-need based aid:* $4821. *Average aid to full-time undergraduates:* $4176.
Athletic Department: *Director of Athletics:* Joel Nielsen; Phone: 605-677-5309; Fax: 605-677-5618; E-mail: jnielsen@usd.edu. *Sports Information Director:* Dan Genzler; Phone: 605-677-5927; E-mail: dgenzler@usd.edu.

MEN'S COACHES
Baseball: Brian Atchinson; Phone: 605-677-6259; E-mail: batchiso@usd.edu.

Basketball: Dave Boots; Phone: 605-677-5309; E-mail: dboots@usd.edu.

Cross Country: Rob Kinnunen; Phone: 605-677-5044; E-mail: rkinnune@usd.edu.

Diving: Ron Allen; Phone: 605-677-5931; E-mail: rlallen@usd.edu.

Football: Ed Meierkort; Phone: 605-677-5309.

Golf: Dennis Chandler; Phone: 605-677-5743; E-mail: chandler@usd.edu.

Swimming: Ron Allen; Phone: 605-677-5931; E-mail: rlallen@usd.edu.

Track and Field: Dave Gottsleben; Phone: 605-677-5942; E-mail: dgottsle@usd.edu.

WOMEN'S COACHES
Basketball: Chad Lavin; Phone: 605-677-5309; E-mail: clavin@usd.edu.

Cross Country: Rob Kinnunen; Phone: 605-677-5309; E-mail: rkinnune@usd.edu.

Diving: Ron Allen; Phone: 605-677-5931; E-mail: rlallen@usd.edu.

Golf: Dennis Chandler; Phone: 605-677-5743; E-mail: chandler@usd.edu.

Soccer: Jessica Maddox; Phone: 605-677-5516; E-mail: jmaddox@usd.edu.

Softball: Kim Zarling; Phone: 605-677-6587; E-mail: kzarling@usd.edu.

Swimming: Ron Allen; Phone: 605-677-5931; E-mail: rlallen@usd.edu.

Tennis: Greg Mahosky; Phone: 605-677-5309; E-mail: garth1223@aol.com.

Track and Field: Lucky Huber; Phone: 605-677-5939; E-mail: track@usd.edu.

Volleyball: Brian Lamppa; Phone: 605-677-5936; E-mail: blamppa@usd.edu.

UNIVERSITY OF SOUTHERN CALIFORNIA

Los Angeles, California

Trojans/Women of Troy ◆ NCAA I ◆ Pacific-10 Conference
◆ http://www.usc.edu/

Independent university, founded 1880
Coed, 16,381 undergraduate students, 96% full-time, 50% women, 50% men
Urban 155-acre campus
Most difficult entrance level, 3% of applicants were admitted

Freshmen *Admission:* 29,278 applied, 8,718 were accepted, 2,976 enrolled. *Test scores:* SAT verbal scores over 500: 99%; SAT math scores

University of Southern California (continued)

over 500: 100%; SAT verbal scores over 600: 81%; SAT math scores over 600: 91%; SAT verbal scores over 700: 28%; SAT math scores over 700: 42%.

Tuition and fees (2003–04): $28,692 (full-time). *Room and board:* $8632 (room only: $4750).

Financial Aid (All incoming freshmen): *Average need-based gift aid:* $21,859. *Average non-need based aid:* $11,732. *Average aid to full-time undergraduates:* $26,364.

Athletic Department: *Director of Athletics:* Mike Garrett; Phone: 213-740-3843; Fax: 213-740-1306; E-mail: lemoore@usc.edu. *Sports Information Director:* Tim Tessalone; Phone: 213-740-8480; E-mail: tessalon@usc.edu.

MEN'S COACHES

Baseball: Mike Gillespie; Phone: 213-740-5762; E-mail: gillespi@usc.edu.

Basketball: Henry Bibby; Phone: 213-740-3815; E-mail: bibby@usc.edu.

Cheerleading: Justine Gilman; Phone: 213-740-5127; E-mail: jgilman@usc.edu.

Diving: Hongping Li; Phone: 213-740-8450; E-mail: hli7788@aol.com.

Football: Pete Carroll; Phone: 213-740-4204; E-mail: pcarroll@usc.edu.

Golf: Tim Gleason; Phone: 213-821-3010; E-mail: tgleason@usc.edu.

Swimming: Mark Schubert; Phone: 213-740-8450; E-mail: mschu47573@aol.com.

Tennis: Peter Smith; Phone: 213-740-3829; E-mail: peterlsm@usc.edu.

Track and Field: Ron Allice; Phone: 213-740-4204; E-mail: rallice@usc.edu.

Volleyball: Turnhan Douglas; Phone: 213-740-3843; E-mail: douglas@usc.edu.

WOMEN'S COACHES

Basketball: Chris Gobrecht; Phone: 213-740-7204; E-mail: gobrecht@usc.edu.

Cheerleading: Justine Gilman; Phone: 213-740-5127; E-mail: jgilman@usc.edu.

Cross Country: Tom Walsh; Phone: 213-740-2171; E-mail: thomaswa@usc.edu.

Diving: Hongping Li; Phone: 213-740-8450; E-mail: hli7788@aol.com.

Golf: Andrea Gaston; Phone: 213-740-5421; E-mail: agaston@usc.edu.

Soccer: Jim Millinder; Phone: 213-740-3849; E-mail: scrjames@aol.com.

Swimming: Mark Schubert; Phone: 213-740-8450; E-mail: mschu47573@aol.com.

Tennis: Richard Gallien; Phone: 213-740-6560; E-mail: gallien@usc.edu.

Track and Field: Ron Allice; Phone: 213-740-4204; E-mail: rallice@usc.edu.

Volleyball: Mick Haley; Phone: 213-740-4151; E-mail: haleym@usc.edu.

UNIVERSITY OF SOUTHERN INDIANA
Evansville, Indiana

Screaming Eagles ◆ NCAA II ◆ Great Lakes Valley Conference ◆ http://www.usi.edu/

State-supported comprehensive, founded 1965, part of Indiana Commission for Higher Education
Coed, 9,154 undergraduate students, 80% full-time, 60% women, 40% men
Suburban 330-acre campus
Noncompetitive entrance level, 91% of applicants were admitted

Freshmen *Admission:* 4,368 applied, 4,048 were accepted, 2,079 enrolled. *Test scores:* SAT verbal scores over 500: 40%; SAT math scores over 500: 37%; SAT verbal scores over 600: 10%; SAT math scores over 600: 8%; SAT verbal scores over 700: 1%.
Tuition and fees (2003–04): $3885 (resident), $9188 (nonresident). *Room and board:* $5140 (room only: $2740).
Financial Aid (All incoming freshmen): *Average need-based gift aid:* $4233. *Average non-need based aid:* $2174. *Average aid to full-time undergraduates:* $4927.

Athletic Department: *Director of Athletics:* Jon Mark Hall; Phone: 812-465-7164; Fax: 812-465-7094; E-mail: jmhall@usi.edu. *Sports Information Director:* Ray Simmons; Phone: 812-465-7094; E-mail: rsimmons@usi.edu.

MEN'S COACHES

Baseball: Mike Goedde; Phone: 812-464-1943; E-mail: mjgoedde@usi.edu.

Basketball: Rick Herdes; Phone: 812-465-1639; E-mail: rherdes@usi.edu.

Cheerleading: Jeff Francis; Phone: 812-464-1846.

Cross Country: Mike Hillyard; Phone: 812-465-1232; E-mail: mhillyar@usi.edu.

Golf: Matt Scheessele; Phone: 812-464-1898; E-mail: mjscheessee@usi.edu.

Soccer: Dan Hogan; Phone: 812-464-1946; E-mail: dhogan@usi.edu.

Tennis: Ross Brown; Phone: 812-464-1814; E-mail: rhjlbrown@aol.com.

Track and Field: Mike Hillyard; Phone: 812-465-1232; E-mail: mhillyar@usi.edu.

WOMEN'S COACHES

Basketball: Rick Stein; Phone: 812-465-7108; E-mail: rstein@usi.edu.

Cheerleading: Jeff Francis; Phone: 812-464-1846.

Cross Country: Mike Hillyard; Phone: 812-465-1232; E-mail: mhillyar@usi.edu.

Golf: Don Bisesi; Phone: 812-464-5861; E-mail: bisesigolf@aol.com.

Soccer: Krissy Meek-Engelbrecht; Phone: 812-465-1041; E-mail: kenglbre@usi.edu.

Softball: Sue Kunkle; Phone: 812-465-1664; E-mail: kunkle@usi.edu.

Tennis: Keely Porter; Phone: 812-461-5235; E-mail: kporter@usi.edu.

Track and Field: Mike Hillyard; Phone: 812-465-1232; E-mail: mhillyar@usi.edu.

Volleyball: Craig Bere; Phone: 812-464-1789; E-mail: cbere@usi.edu.

UNIVERSITY OF SOUTHERN MAINE
Portland, Maine

Huskies ◆ NCAA III ◆ Little East Conference; New England College Wrestling Conference; New England Women's Lacrosse Conference ◆ http://www.usm.maine.edu/

State-supported comprehensive, founded 1878, part of University of Maine System
Coed, 8,613 undergraduate students, 54% full-time, 61% women, 39% men
Suburban 144-acre campus
Moderately difficult entrance level, 72% of applicants were admitted

Freshmen *Admission:* 3,585 applied, 2,588 were accepted, 934 enrolled. *Test scores:* SAT verbal scores over 500: 62%; SAT math scores over 500: 58%; SAT verbal scores over 600: 18%; SAT math scores over 600: 12%; SAT verbal scores over 700: 1%; SAT math scores over 700: 1%.
Tuition and fees (2003–04): $5198 (resident), $12,878 (nonresident). *Room and board:* $6014 (room only: $3224).
Financial Aid (All incoming freshmen): *Average need-based gift aid:* $4078. *Average non-need based aid:* $3000. *Average aid to full-time undergraduates:* $7460.
Athletic Department: *Director of Athletics:* Albert Bean; Phone: 207-780-5588; Fax: 207-780-5182; E-mail: albean@usm.maine.edu. *Sports Information Director:* B.L. Elfring; Phone: 207-780-5434; E-mail: elfring@usm.maine.edu.

MEN'S COACHES

Baseball: Ed Flaherty; Phone: 207-780-5474; E-mail: edwardf@usm.maine.edu.

Basketball: Karl Henrikson; Phone: 207-780-5432; E-mail: karlh@usm.maine.edu.

Cheerleading: Kae Loveless; Phone: 207-780-5993.

Cross Country: Bruce Bickford; Phone: 207-780-5776; E-mail: bruceb@usm.maine.edu.

Ice Hockey: Jeff Beaney; Phone: 207-780-5987; E-mail: jbeaney@usm.maine.edu.

Lacrosse: Ben Raymond; Phone: 207-780-8589; E-mail: braymond@usm.maine.edu.

Soccer: Eric Miller; Phone: 207-780-5594; E-mail: emiller@usm.maine.edu.
Tennis: Phil Cole; Phone: 207-780-4554; E-mail: pcole@usm.maine.edu.
Track and Field: Bruce Bickford; Phone: 207-780-5776; E-mail: bruceb@usm.maine.edu.
Wrestling: Joe Pistone; Phone: 207-780-5992; E-mail: jpistone@usm.maine.edu.

WOMEN'S COACHES

Basketball: Gary Fifield; Phone: 207-780-5475; E-mail: gfifield@usm.maine.edu.
Cheerleading: Kae Loveless; Phone: 207-780-5993.
Cross Country: George Towle; Phone: 207-780-5595; E-mail: gtowle@usm.maine.edu.
Field Hockey: Bonny Brown-Denico; Phone: 207-780-5519; E-mail: bbdenico@usm.maine.edu.
Lacrosse: David Venditti; Phone: 207-780-5996; E-mail: venditti@usm.maine.edu.
Soccer: Steve Quinones; Phone: 207-780-5328; E-mail: quinones@usm.maine.edu.
Softball: Bonny Brown-Denico; Phone: 207-780-5519; E-mail: bbdenico@usm.maine.edu.
Tennis: Wayne St. Peter; Phone: 207-780-5574; E-mail: wstpeter@usm.maine.edu.
Track and Field: George Towle; Phone: 207-780-5595; E-mail: gtowle@usm.maine.edu.
Volleyball: John Razsa; Phone: 207-780-5764; E-mail: jrazsa@usm.maine.edu.

UNIVERSITY OF SOUTHERN MISSISSIPPI
Hattiesburg, Mississippi

Golden Eagles ◆ NCAA I ◆ Conference USA Conference ◆ http://www.usm.edu/

State-supported university, founded 1910
Coed, 12,215 undergraduate students, 82% full-time, 60% women, 40% men
Suburban 1,090-acre campus with easy access to New Orleans
Moderately difficult entrance level, 46% of applicants were admitted

Freshmen *Admission:* 6,432 applied, 3,169 were accepted, 1,453 enrolled. *Test scores:* SAT verbal scores over 500: 65%; SAT math scores over 500: 63%; SAT verbal scores over 600: 29%; SAT math scores over 600: 27%; SAT verbal scores over 700: 4%; SAT math scores over 700: 4%.
Tuition and fees (2003–04): $3874 (resident), $8752 (nonresident). *Room and board:* $4785 (room only: $3045).
Financial Aid (All incoming freshmen): *Average need-based gift aid:* $3258. *Average non-need based aid:* $2062. *Average aid to full-time undergraduates:* $6266.
Athletic Department: *Director of Athletics:* Richard Giannini; Phone: 601-266-5017; Fax: 601-266-6595. *Sports Information Director:* Mike Montoro; Phone: 601-266-5017; E-mail: michael.montoro@usm.edu.

MEN'S COACHES

Baseball: Corky Palmer; Phone: 601-266-5017; E-mail: baseball@usm.edu.
Basketball: James Green; Phone: 601-266-6355.
Cheerleading: Brian Hunt; Phone: 601-266-5017; E-mail: brian.hunt@usm.edu.
Football: Jeff Bower; Phone: 601-266-4567; E-mail: football@usm.edu.
Golf: Steve Johnson; Phone: 601-266-4836; E-mail: stephen.johnson@usm.edu.
Tennis: Teddy Viator; Phone: 601-266-5318.
Track and Field: Wayne Williams; Phone: 601-266-5017.

WOMEN'S COACHES

Basketball: Rick Reeves; Phone: 601-266-6355; E-mail: rick.reeves@usm.edu.
Cheerleading: Brian Hunt; Phone: 601-266-5017; E-mail: brian.hunt@usm.edu.
Cross Country: Deb Osteen; Phone: 601-266-5017.
Golf: Julie Gallup; Phone: 601-266-5017.

Soccer: Matt Clark; Phone: 601-266-5017; E-mail: matthew.clark@usm.edu.
Softball: Gay McNutt; Phone: 601-266-6749.
Tennis: Randy Rowley; Phone: 601-266-6870; E-mail: randy.rowley@usm.edu.
Track and Field: Wayne Williams; Phone: 601-266-5017.
Volleyball: Santiago Restrepo; Phone: 601-266-6355; E-mail: santi.r@usm.edu.

UNIVERSITY OF SOUTH FLORIDA
Tampa, Florida

Bulls ◆ NCAA I ◆ Conference USA Conference ◆ http://usfweb.usf.edu/

State-supported university, founded 1956, part of State University System of Florida
Coed, 32,127 undergraduate students, 67% full-time, 59% women, 41% men
Urban 1,913-acre campus
Moderately difficult entrance level, 61% of applicants were admitted

Freshmen *Admission:* 15,491 applied, 9,567 were accepted, 5,051 enrolled. *Test scores:* SAT verbal scores over 500: 71%; SAT math scores over 500: 75%; SAT verbal scores over 600: 22%; SAT math scores over 600: 26%; SAT verbal scores over 700: 2%; SAT math scores over 700: 3%.
Tuition and fees (2003–04): $2983 (resident), $14,011 (nonresident). *Room and board:* $6508 (room only: $3408).
Financial Aid (All incoming freshmen): *Average need-based gift aid:* $3566. *Average non-need based aid:* $4037. *Average aid to full-time undergraduates:* $7408.
Athletic Department: *Director of Athletics:* Lee Roy Selmon; Phone: 813-974-2125; Fax: 813-974-4028; E-mail: selmon@admin.usf.edu. *Sports Information Director:* John Gerdes; Phone: 813-974-4086; E-mail: gerdes@admin.usf.edu.

MEN'S COACHES

Baseball: Ed Cardieri; Phone: 813-974-2504; E-mail: cardieri@admin.usf.edu.
Basketball: Robert Mccullum; Phone: 813-974-3252; E-mail: mccullum@admin.usf.edu.
Cheerleading: Erika Meyer; Phone: 813-974-2125; E-mail: usfcheer@hotmail.com.
Cross Country: Greg Thiel; Phone: 813-974-4667; E-mail: gthiel@admin.usf.edu.
Football: Jim Leavitt; Phone: 813-974-7177; E-mail: football@admin.usf.edu.
Golf: Jim Fee; Phone: 813-974-6893; E-mail: fee@admin.usf.edu.
Soccer: George Kiefer; Phone: 813-974-4149; E-mail: gkiefer@admin.usf.edu.
Tennis: Don Barr; Phone: 813-974-4112; E-mail: barr@admin.usf.edu.
Track and Field: Greg Thiel; Phone: 813-974-4094; E-mail: gthiel@admin.usf.edu.

WOMEN'S COACHES

Basketball: Jose Fernandez; Phone: 813-974-7472; E-mail: josef@admin.usf.edu.
Cheerleading: Erika Meyer; Phone: 813-974-2125; E-mail: usfcheer@hotmail.com.
Cross Country: Greg Thiel; Phone: 813-974-4094; E-mail: gthiel@admin.usf.edu.
Golf: Susan Holt; Phone: 813-974-6893; E-mail: smholt@aol.com.
Soccer: Logan Fleck; Phone: 813-974-4026; E-mail: fleck@admin.usf.edu.
Softball: Ken Erikson; Phone: 813-974-4111; E-mail: eriksen@admin.usf.edu.
Tennis: Gigi Fernandez; Phone: 813-974-4121; E-mail: gigif@admin.usf.edu.
Track and Field: Greg Thiel; Phone: 813-974-4094; E-mail: gthiel@admin.usf.edu.
Volleyball: Nancy Mueller; Phone: 813-974-4023; E-mail: mueller@admin.usf.edu.

THE UNIVERSITY OF TAMPA
Tampa, Florida

Spartans ◆ NCAA II ◆ Sunshine State Conference ◆ http://www.ut.edu/

Independent comprehensive, founded 1931
Coed, 4,125 undergraduate students, 88% full-time, 63% women, 37% men
Urban 90-acre campus
Moderately difficult entrance level, 65% of applicants were admitted

---

Freshmen *Admission:* 5,269 applied, 3,202 were accepted, 1,079 enrolled. *Test scores:* SAT verbal scores over 500: 70%; SAT math scores over 500: 70%; SAT verbal scores over 600: 20%; SAT math scores over 600: 20%; SAT verbal scores over 700: 1%; SAT math scores over 700: 2%.
Tuition and fees (2003–04): $17,572 (full-time). *Room and board:* $6410 (room only: $3430).
Financial Aid (All incoming freshmen): *Average need-based gift aid:* $5690. *Average non-need based aid:* $7102. *Average aid to full-time undergraduates:* $14,980.
Athletic Department: *Director of Athletics:* Larry Marfise; Phone: 813-253-3333; Fax: 813-253-6288; E-mail: lmarfise@ut.edu. *Sports Information Director:* Gil Swalls; Phone: 813-253-3333; E-mail: gswalls@ut.edu.

MEN'S COACHES
Baseball: Joe Urso; Phone: 813-253-3333; E-mail: jurso@ut.edu.
Basketball: Richard Schmidt; Phone: 813-253-3333; E-mail: rschmidt@ut.edu.
Cross Country: Jarrett Slaven; Phone: 813-253-3333; E-mail: jslaven@ut.edu.
Golf: Rick Christie; Phone: 813-253-3333; E-mail: rchristie@ut.edu.
Soccer: Tom Fitzgerald; Phone: 813-253-3333.
Swimming: Ed Brennan; Phone: 813-259-3333; E-mail: ebrennan@ut.edu.

WOMEN'S COACHES
Basketball: Thomas Jessee; Phone: 813-253-3333; E-mail: tjessee@ut.edu.
Cross Country: Jarrett Slaven; Phone: 813-253-3333; E-mail: jslaven@ut.edu.
Soccer: Bobby Johnston; Phone: 813-253-3333; E-mail: johnstonr@ut.edu.
Softball: Leslie Kanter; Phone: 813-253-3333; E-mail: lkanter@ut.edu.
Swimming: Ed Brennan; Phone: 813-259-3333; E-mail: ebrennan@ut.edu.
Tennis: Al Du Faux; Phone: 813-253-3333; E-mail: adufaux@ut.edu.
Volleyball: Chris Catanach; Phone: 813-253-3333; E-mail: ccatanach@ut.edu.

THE UNIVERSITY OF TENNESSEE
Knoxville, Tennessee

Volunteers ◆ NCAA I ◆ Southeastern Conference ◆ http://www.tennessee.edu/

State-supported university, founded 1794, part of University of Tennessee System
Coed, 19,224 undergraduate students, 91% full-time, 51% women, 49% men
Urban 533-acre campus
Moderately difficult entrance level, 72% of applicants were admitted

---

Freshmen *Admission:* 9,514 applied, 6,790 were accepted, 3,579 enrolled. *Test scores:* SAT verbal scores over 500: 76%; SAT math scores over 500: 78%; SAT verbal scores over 600: 32%; SAT math scores over 600: 33%; SAT verbal scores over 700: 6%; SAT math scores over 700: 5%.
Tuition and fees (2003–04): $4950 (resident), $13,532 (nonresident). *Room and board:* $5110 (room only: $2490).
Financial Aid (All incoming freshmen): *Average need-based gift aid:* $6225. *Average non-need based aid:* $10,905. *Average aid to full-time undergraduates:* $6925.
Athletic Department: *Director of Athletics:* Mike Hamilton; Phone: 865-974-1218; Fax: 865-974-1269; E-mail: mhamilton@tennessee.edu. *Sports Information Director:* Debby Jennings; Phone: 865-974-4275; E-mail: jennin00@utk.edu.

MEN'S COACHES
Baseball: Rod Delmonico; Phone: 865-974-2056; E-mail: delmon00@utk.edu.
Basketball: Buzz Patterson; Phone: 865-974-1206.
Cheerleading: Joy Postell; Phone: 865-974-1000.
Cross Country: George Watts; Phone: 865-974-2240; E-mail: gwatts@utk.edu.
Diving: Dave Parrington; Phone: 865-974-8102; E-mail: parrin00@utk.edu.
Football: Phillip Fulmer; Phone: 865-974-1235.
Golf: Jim Kelson; Phone: 865-974-3834; E-mail: jkelson@utk.edu.
Swimming: John Trembley; Phone: 865-974-2292; E-mail: trembl00@utk.edu.
Swimming: John Trembley; Phone: 865-974-2292; E-mail: trembl00@utk.edu.
Tennis: Michael Fancutt; Phone: 865-974-1253; E-mail: mfancutt@utk.edu.
Track and Field: Bill Webb; Phone: 865-974-1256; E-mail: billwebb@utk.edu.

WOMEN'S COACHES
Basketball: Pat Summitt; Phone: 865-974-0600.
Cheerleading: Joy Postell; Phone: 865-974-1000.
Cross Country: JJ Clark; Phone: 865-974-4275.
Diving: Dave Parrington; Phone: 865-974-8102; E-mail: parrin00@utk.edu.
Golf: Judi Pavon; Phone: 865-974-4275; E-mail: jpavon@utk.edu.
Soccer: Angela Kelly; Phone: 865-974-4275; E-mail: akelly@utk.edu.
Softball: Karen Weekly; Phone: 865-974-4275; E-mail: kweekly@utk.edu.
Swimming: Dan Colella; Phone: 865-974-0832; E-mail: dcolella@utk.edu.
Tennis: Mike Patrick; Phone: 865-974-6883; E-mail: mpatrick@utk.edu.
Track and Field: JJ Clark; Phone: 865-974-4275.
Volleyball: Rob Patrick; Phone: 865-974-4275; E-mail: rpatric1@utk.edu.

THE UNIVERSITY OF TENNESSEE AT CHATTANOOGA
Chattanooga, Tennessee

Moccasins ◆ NCAA I ◆ Southern Conference ◆ http://www.utc.edu/

State-supported comprehensive, founded 1886, part of University of Tennessee System
Coed, 7,197 undergraduate students, 83% full-time, 58% women, 42% men
Urban 117-acre campus with easy access to Atlanta
Moderately difficult entrance level, 5% of applicants were admitted

---

Freshmen *Admission:* 3,156 applied, 1,638 were accepted, 1,410 enrolled.
Tuition and fees (2003–04): $3852 (resident), $11,504 (nonresident). *Room only:* $3000.
Financial Aid (All incoming freshmen): *Average need-based gift aid:* $3600. *Average non-need based aid:* $3000. *Average aid to full-time undergraduates:* $8050.
Athletic Department: *Director of Athletics:* Steve Sloan; Phone: 423-425-4495; Fax: 423-425-2160; E-mail: steve-sloan@utc.edu. *Sports Information Director:* Jeff Romero; Phone: 423-425-5292; E-mail: jeff-romero@utc.edu.

MEN'S COACHES
Basketball: Jeff Lebo; Phone: 423-425-4681; E-mail: jeff-lebo@utc.edu.
Cheerleading: Ellen Neufeldt; Phone: 423-425-4260; E-mail: ellen-neufeldt@utc.edu.
Cross Country: Bill Gautier; Phone: 423-425-4782; E-mail: bill-gautier@utc.edu.
Football: Rodney Allison; Phone: 423-425-4558; E-mail: teresa-adcox@utc.edu.
Golf: Reed Sanderlin; Phone: 423-425-4625; E-mail: reed-sanderlin@utc.edu.
Tennis: Carlos Garcia; Phone: 423-425-4359; E-mail: carlos-garcia@utc.edu.

Track and Field: Bill Gautier; Phone: 423-425-4782; E-mail: bill-gautier@utc.edu.
Wrestling: Terry Brands; Phone: 423-425-4287; E-mail: terry-brands@utc.edu.

WOMEN'S COACHES

Basketball: Wes Moore; Phone: 423-425-4376; E-mail: wes-moore@utc.edu.
Cheerleading: Ellen Neufeldt; Phone: 423-425-4260; E-mail: ellen-neufeldt@utc.edu.
Cross Country: Bill Gautier; Phone: 423-425-4782; E-mail: bill-gautier@utc.edu.
Soccer: J.D. Kyzer; Phone: 423-425-5302; E-mail: jd-kyzer@utc.edu.
Softball: Frank Reed; Phone: 423-425-2163; E-mail: frank-reed@utc.edu.
Tennis: Carlos Garcia; Phone: 423-425-4359; E-mail: carlos-garcia@utc.edu.
Track and Field: Bill Gautier; Phone: 423-425-4782; E-mail: bill-gautier@utc.edu.
Volleyball: Lisa Rhodes; Phone: 423-425-4069; E-mail: lisa-rhodes@utc.edu.

THE UNIVERSITY OF TENNESSEE AT MARTIN
Martin, Tennessee

Skyhawks ◆ NCAA I ◆ Ohio Valley Conference ◆ http://www.utm.edu/

State-supported comprehensive, founded 1900, part of University of Tennessee System
Coed, 5,404 undergraduate students, 84% full-time, 58% women, 42% men
Small-town 250-acre campus
Moderately difficult entrance level, 5% of applicants were admitted

Freshmen *Admission:* 2,627 applied, 1,341 were accepted, 1,000 enrolled.
Tuition and fees (2003–04): $3846 (resident), $11,496 (nonresident). *Room and board:* $3800 (room only: $1910).
Financial Aid (All incoming freshmen): *Average need-based gift aid:* $3740. *Average non-need based aid:* $2524. *Average aid to full-time undergraduates:* $6555.
Athletic Department: *Director of Athletics:* Phil Dane; Phone: 731-587-7661; Fax: 731-587-7962; E-mail: pdane@utm.edu. *Sports Information Director:* Joe Lofaro; Phone: 731-587-7632; E-mail: jlofaro@utm.edu.

MEN'S COACHES

Baseball: Bubba Cates; Phone: 731-587-7337; E-mail: vcates@utm.edu.
Basketball: Bret Campbell; Phone: 731-587-7659; E-mail: bretcamp@utm.edu.
Cheerleading: Fran Spear; Phone: 731-587-7951; E-mail: spears@utmcheer.com.
Cross Country: Jason McKinney; Phone: 731-587-7930; E-mail: mckinney@utm.edu.
Football: Matt Griffin; Phone: 731-587-7671; E-mail: mgriffin@utm.edu.
Golf: Jerry Carpenter; Phone: 731-587-7665; E-mail: jecgolf@utm.edu.
Tennis: Dennis Taylor; Phone: 731-587-7683; E-mail: dtaylor@utm.edu.

WOMEN'S COACHES

Basketball: Gary Vanatta; Phone: 731-587-7317; E-mail: gvanatta@utm.edu.
Cheerleading: Fran Spear; Phone: 731-587-7951; E-mail: spears@utmcheer.com.
Cross Country: Jason McKinney; Phone: 731-587-7930; E-mail: mckinney@utm.edu.
Soccer: Nathan Pifer; Phone: 731-587-7931; E-mail: npifer@utm.edu.
Softball: Donley Canary; Phone: 731-587-7162; E-mail: dcanary@utm.edu.
Tennis: Dennis Taylor; Phone: 731-587-7683; E-mail: dtaylor@utm.edu.
Volleyball: Chris Rushing; Phone: 731-587-7332; E-mail: crushing@utm.edu.

THE UNIVERSITY OF TEXAS AT ARLINGTON
Arlington, Texas

Mavericks ◆ NCAA I ◆ Southland Conference ◆ http://www.uta.edu/

State-supported university, founded 1895, part of University of Texas System
Coed, 18,870 undergraduate students, 71% full-time, 53% women, 47% men
Urban 395-acre campus with easy access to Dallas–Fort Worth
Moderately difficult entrance level, 80% of applicants were admitted

Freshmen *Admission:* 5,092 applied, 3,928 were accepted, 1,986 enrolled. *Test scores:* SAT verbal scores over 500: 65%; SAT math scores over 500: 71%; SAT verbal scores over 600: 19%; SAT math scores over 600: 25%; SAT verbal scores over 700: 2%; SAT math scores over 700: 3%.
Tuition and fees (2003–04): $4423 (resident), $11,503 (nonresident). *Room and board:* $4829 (room only: $2643).
Financial Aid (All incoming freshmen): *Average need-based gift aid:* $4892. *Average non-need based aid:* $2097. *Average aid to full-time undergraduates:* $6875.
Athletic Department: *Director of Athletics:* Pete Carlon; Phone: 817-272-5039; Fax: 817-272-5037; E-mail: carlon@uta.edu. *Sports Information Director:* Bill Petitt; Phone: 817-272-2239; E-mail: wpetitt@uta.edu.

MEN'S COACHES

Baseball: Jeff Curtis; Phone: 817-272-2060; E-mail: jcurtis@uta.edu.
Basketball: Eddie McCarter; Phone: 817-272-5754; E-mail: mccarter@uta.edu.
Cheerleading: Chris Lawrence; Phone: 817-272-2963; E-mail: cheerleading@uta.edu.
Cross Country: John Sauerhage; Phone: 817-272-5753; E-mail: hog34536@uta.edu.
Golf: Jay Rees; Phone: 817-272-5038; E-mail: jrees@uta.edu.
Tennis: Christian Wassmer; Phone: 817-272-2546; E-mail: moose@uta.edu.
Track and Field: John Sauerhage; Phone: 817-272-5753; E-mail: hog34536@uta.edu.

WOMEN'S COACHES

Basketball: Donna Capps; Phone: 817-272-7165; E-mail: capps@uta.edu.
Cheerleading: Chris Lawrence; Phone: 817-272-2963; E-mail: cheerleading@uta.edu.
Cross Country: John Sauerhage; Phone: 817-272-5753; E-mail: hog34536@uta.edu.
Softball: Debbie Hedrick; Phone: 817-272-5756; E-mail: hedrick@uta.edu.
Tennis: Christian Wassmer; Phone: 817-272-2546; E-mail: moose@uta.edu.
Track and Field: John Sauerhage; Phone: 817-272-5753; E-mail: hog34536@uta.edu.
Volleyball: Janine Smith; Phone: 817-272-5755; E-mail: jsmith@uta.edu.

THE UNIVERSITY OF TEXAS AT AUSTIN
Austin, Texas

Longhorns ◆ NCAA I ◆ Big 12 Conference ◆ http://www.utexas.edu/

State-supported university, founded 1883, part of University of Texas System
Coed, 38,383 undergraduate students, 90% full-time, 51% women, 49% men
Urban 350-acre campus with easy access to San Antonio
Very difficult entrance level, 4% of applicants were admitted

Freshmen *Admission:* 24,519 applied, 11,504 were accepted, 6,544 enrolled. *Test scores:* SAT verbal scores over 500: 88%; SAT math scores over 500: 93%; SAT verbal scores over 600: 55%; SAT math scores over 600: 68%; SAT verbal scores over 700: 15%; SAT math scores over 700: 24%.

The University of Texas at Austin *(continued)*

Tuition and fees (2003–04): $4548 (resident), $11,668 (nonresident).
Room and board: $6082 (room only: $3499).
Financial Aid (All incoming freshmen): *Average need-based gift aid:* $6120.
Average non-need based aid: $4470. *Average aid to full-time under-graduates:* $8670.
Athletic Department: *Director of Athletics:* DeLoss Dodds; Phone: 512-471-5757; Fax: 512-471-6040; E-mail: ddodds@mail.utexas.edu.
Sports Information Director: John Bianco; Phone: 512-471-1346;
E-mail: jbianco@mail.utexas.edu.

MEN'S COACHES

Baseball: Augie Garrido; Phone: 512471-471-5732; E-mail: agarrido@mail.utexas.edu.
Basketball: Rick Barnes; Phone: 512471-471-5816; E-mail: barnesbkball@mail.utexas.edu.
Cheerleading: Jeff Dieta; Phone: 512471-232-2911; E-mail: jeffdieta@mail.utexas.edu.
Cross Country: Bubba Thornton; Phone: 512471-471-1372; E-mail: bthornton@mail.utexas.edu.
Diving: Matt Scoggin; Phone: 512471-471-7794; E-mail: scoggin@mail.utexas.edu.
Football: Mack Brown; Phone: 512471-471-3050; E-mail: kaseylj@mail.utexas.edu.
Golf: John Fields; Phone: 512471-471-1385; E-mail: jfields@mail.utexas.edu.
Swimming: Eddie Reese; Phone: 512471-471-1384; E-mail: ereese@mail.utexas.edu.
Tennis: Michael Center; Phone: 512471-471-1376; E-mail: mcenter@mail.utexas.edu.
Track and Field: Bubba Thornton; Phone: 512471-471-1372; E-mail: bthornton@mail.utexas.edu.

WOMEN'S COACHES

Basketball: Jody Conradt; Phone: 512471-471-9802; E-mail: jconradt@mail.utexas.edu.
Cheerleading: Jeff Dieta; Phone: 512471-232-2911; E-mail: jeffdieta@mail.utexas.edu.
Cross Country: Beverly Kearney; Phone: 512471-471-9146; E-mail: bkearney@mail.utexas.edu.
Diving: Matt Scoggin; Phone: 512471-471-7794; E-mail: scoggin@mail.utexas.edu.
Golf: Susan Watkins; Phone: 512471-471-9278; E-mail: swatkins@mail.utexas.edu.
Soccer: Chris Petrucelli; Phone: 512471-471-9968; E-mail: cpetrucelli@mail.utexas.edu.
Softball: Connie Clark; Phone: 512471-471-7884; E-mail: cclark@mail.utexas.edu.
Swimming: Jill Sterkel; Phone: 512471-471-7790; E-mail: jsterkel@mail.utexas.edu.
Tennis: Jeff Moore; Phone: 512471-471-1049; E-mail: jeffmoore@mail.utexas.edu.
Track and Field: Beverly Kearney; Phone: 512471-471-9146; E-mail: bkearney@mail.utexas.edu.
Volleyball: Jerritt Elliott; Phone: 512471-471-9148; E-mail: jelliott@mail.utexas.edu.

THE UNIVERSITY OF TEXAS AT DALLAS

Richardson, Texas

Comets ◆ NCAA III ◆ American Southwest Conference
◆ http://www.utdallas.edu/

State-supported university, founded 1969, part of University of Texas System
Coed, 8,688 undergraduate students, 69% full-time, 49% women, 51% men
Suburban 455-acre campus with easy access to Dallas
Very difficult entrance level, 54% of applicants were admitted

Freshmen *Admission:* 5,048 applied, 2,501 were accepted, 1,060 enrolled. *Test scores:* SAT verbal scores over 500: 90%; SAT math scores over 500: 97%; SAT verbal scores over 600: 55%; SAT math scores over 600: 66%; SAT verbal scores over 700: 14%; SAT math scores over 700: 21%.

Tuition and fees (2003–04): $5493 (resident), $12,573 (nonresident).
Room and board: $6122.
Financial Aid (All incoming freshmen): *Average need-based gift aid:* $3134.
Average non-need based aid: $4799. *Average aid to full-time under-graduates:* $7993.
Athletic Department: *Director of Athletics:* Chris Gage; Phone: 972-883-2055; Fax: 972-883-2026; E-mail: ccg034000@utdallas.edu. *Sports Information Director:* Bruce Unrue; Phone: 972-883-6308; E-mail: bruceunrue@utdallas.edu.

MEN'S COACHES

Baseball: Shane Shewmake; Phone: 972-883-2392; E-mail: shewmk@utdallas.edu.
Basketball: Terry Butterfield; Phone: 972-883-4063; E-mail: tbutter@utdallas.edu.
Cheerleading: Phone: 972-883-6158.
Cross Country: Brandon Rains; Phone: 972-883-2392; E-mail: gbr032000@utdallas.edu.
Golf: Chet Cook; Phone: 972-883-4063; E-mail: chet.cook@utdallas.edu.
Soccer: Jack Peel; Phone: 972-883-4062; E-mail: jpeel@utdallas.edu.
Tennis: Jeremy Morse; Phone: 972-883-4068; E-mail: jsm019000@utdallas.edu.

WOMEN'S COACHES

Basketball: Rachelle Leonard; Phone: 972-883-4064; E-mail: rachell@utdallas.edu.
Cheerleading: Phone: 972-883-6158.
Cross Country: Brandon Rains; Phone: 972-883-2392; E-mail: gbr032000@utdallas.edu.
Golf: Katherine Salerno; Phone: 972-883-4064; E-mail: kcs0121000@utdallas.edu.
Soccer: John Antonisse; Phone: 972-883-4061; E-mail: johna@utdallas.edu.
Softball: Tricia Hoffman; Phone: 972-883-2394; E-mail: coachp@utdallas.edu.
Tennis: Jenny Dunn; Phone: 972-883-4068; E-mail: jrd013300@utdallas.edu.
Volleyball: Marci Sanders; Phone: 972-883-2012; E-mail: marci.sanders@utdallas.edu.

THE UNIVERSITY OF TEXAS AT EL PASO

El Paso, Texas

Miners ◆ NCAA I ◆ Western Athletic Conference ◆ http://www.utep.edu/

State-supported university, founded 1913
Coed, 15,085 undergraduate students, 73% full-time, 54% women, 46% men
Urban 360-acre campus
Minimally difficult entrance level, 98% of applicants were admitted

Freshmen *Admission:* 4,020 applied, 3,958 were accepted, 2,538 enrolled. *Test scores:* SAT verbal scores over 500: 31%; SAT math scores over 500: 29%; SAT verbal scores over 600: 5%; SAT math scores over 600: 5%; SAT verbal scores over 700: %; SAT math scores over 700: %.
Tuition and fees (2003–04): $3948 (resident), $11,028 (nonresident).
Room only: $38,352.
Financial Aid (All incoming freshmen): *Average need-based gift aid:* $5034.
Average non-need based aid: $875. *Average aid to full-time under-graduates:* $7755.
Athletic Department: *Director of Athletics:* Bob Stull; Phone: 915-747-6822; Fax: 915-747-5162; E-mail: rilerma@utep.edu. *Sports Information Director:* Jeff Darby; Phone: 915-747-6652; E-mail: jdarby@utep.edu.

MEN'S COACHES

Basketball: Billy Gillispie; Phone: 915-747-5323; E-mail: acrowther@utep.edu.
Cheerleading: David Vasquez; Phone: 915-747-5330; E-mail: vasdavid@utep.edu.
Cross Country: David Welsh; Phone: 915-747-6840; E-mail: dwelsh@utep.edu.
Football: Mike Price; Phone: 915-747-5224; E-mail: mgarrido@utep.edu.

Golf: Rick Todd; Phone: 915-747-5396; E-mail: rtodd@utep.edu.
Track and Field: Bob Kitchens; Phone: 915-747-5819; E-mail: rkitchen@utep.edu.

WOMEN'S COACHES

Basketball: Keitha Green; Phone: 915-747-8609; E-mail: kgreen@utep.edu.
Cheerleading: David Vasquez; Phone: 915-747-5330; E-mail: vasdavid@utep.edu.
Cross Country: David Welsh; Phone: 915-747-6840; E-mail: dwelsh@utep.edu.
Golf: Jere Pelletier; Phone: 915-747-5395; E-mail: jere@utep.edu.
Soccer: Kevin Cross; Phone: 915-747-5872; E-mail: kcross@utep.edu.
Softball: Kathleen Rodriguez; Phone: 915-747-8833; E-mail: kaguilar2@utep.edu.
Tennis: Jaime Campbell; Phone: 915-747-6660; E-mail: jcampbell3@utep.edu.
Track and Field: Bob Kitchens; Phone: 915-747-5819; E-mail: rkitchen@utep.edu.
Volleyball: Scott Swanson; Phone: 915-747-6656; E-mail: sswanson@utep.edu.

THE UNIVERSITY OF TEXAS AT SAN ANTONIO

San Antonio, Texas

Roadrunners ◆ NCAA I ◆ Southland Conference ◆ http://www.utsa.edu/

State-supported university, founded 1969, part of University of Texas System
Coed, 21,217 undergraduate students, 73% full-time, 54% women, 46% men
Suburban 600-acre campus with easy access to San Antonio, Texas
Moderately difficult entrance level, 99% of applicants were admitted

Freshmen *Admission:* 9,685 applied, 9,618 were accepted, 3,077 enrolled. *Test scores:* SAT verbal scores over 500: 44%; SAT math scores over 500: 46%; SAT verbal scores over 600: 9%; SAT math scores over 600: 9%; SAT verbal scores over 700: 1%; SAT math scores over 700: 1%.
Tuition and fees (2003–04): $4319 (resident), $11,399 (nonresident).
Room and board: $7898 (room only: $3339).
Athletic Department: *Director of Athletics:* Lynn Hickey; Phone: 210-458-4444; Fax: 210-458-4569; E-mail: lhickey@utsa.edu. *Sports Information Director:* Rick Nixon; Phone: 210-458-4551; E-mail: rnixon@utsa.edu.

MEN'S COACHES

Baseball: Sherman Corbett; Phone: 210-458-4805; E-mail: scorbett@utsa.edu.
Basketball: Tim Carter; Phone: 210-458-4162; E-mail: tcarter@utsa.edu.
Cheerleading: Melissa Rodriguez; Phone: 210-458-4164.
Cross Country: Aaron Fox; Phone: 210-458-4205; E-mail: acfox@utsa.edu.
Golf: Chris Donielson; Phone: 210-458-4198; E-mail: golfcoach69@aol.com.
Tennis: Oliver Trittenwein; Phone: 210-458-4193; E-mail: otrittenwein@utsa.edu.
Track and Field: Aaron Fox; Phone: 210-458-4176; E-mail: acfox@utsa.edu.

WOMEN'S COACHES

Basketball: Rae Blair; Phone: 210-458-4179; E-mail: rblair@utsa.edu.
Cheerleading: Melissa Rodriguez; Phone: 210-458-4164.
Cross Country: Rose Monday; Phone: 210-458-4667; E-mail: rosarita@swbell.net.
Softball: Corrie Hill; Phone: 210-458-4804; E-mail: chill@utsa.edu.
Tennis: Brenda Niemeyer; Phone: 210-458-4177; E-mail: bniemeyer@utsa.edu.
Track and Field: James Blackwood; Phone: 210-458-4191; E-mail: jblackwood@utsa.edu.
Volleyball: Laura Groff; Phone: 210-458-4192; E-mail: lgroff@utsa.edu.

THE UNIVERSITY OF TEXAS OF THE PERMIAN BASIN

Odessa, Texas

Falcons ◆ NAIA ◆ Red River Conference
◆ http://www.utpb.edu/

State-supported comprehensive, founded 1969, part of University of Texas System
Coed, 2,012 undergraduate students, 69% full-time, 65% women, 35% men
Urban 600-acre campus
Moderately difficult entrance level, 84% of applicants were admitted

Freshmen *Admission:* 453 applied, 398 were accepted, 226 enrolled. *Test scores:* SAT verbal scores over 500: 45%; SAT math scores over 500: 37%; SAT verbal scores over 600: 8%; SAT math scores over 600: 6%; SAT math scores over 700: 1%.
Tuition and fees (2003–04): $3900 (resident), $10,980 (nonresident).
Room and board: $4176 (room only: $2526).
Financial Aid (All incoming freshmen): *Average need-based gift aid:* $6536. *Average non-need based aid:* $2070. *Average aid to full-time undergraduates:* $6573.
Athletic Department: *Director of Athletics:* Steve Aicinena; Phone: 432-552-2675; Fax: 432-552-3676; E-mail: aicinena_s@utpb.edu.

MEN'S COACHES

Basketball: Keith Thompson; Phone: 432-552-3677; E-mail: kthomp8754@aol.com.
Soccer: Dennis Peterson; Phone: 432-552-0575; E-mail: peterson_d@utpb.edu.
Swimming: Rob Rankin; Phone: 432-552-2335; E-mail: rankin_r@utpb.edu.

WOMEN'S COACHES

Basketball: John Hufford; Phone: 432-552-3679; E-mail: hufford_j@utpb.edu.
Soccer: Dennis Peterson; Phone: 432-552-0575; E-mail: peterson_d@utpb.edu.
Softball: Danny Dunaway; Phone: 432-552-2676; E-mail: dunaway_d@utpb.edu.
Swimming: Rob Rankin; Phone: 432-552-2335; E-mail: rankin_r@utpb.edu.
Volleyball: Steve Aicinena; Phone: 432-552-2675; E-mail: aicinena_s@utpb.edu.

THE UNIVERSITY OF TEXAS–PAN AMERICAN

Edinburg, Texas

Broncs ◆ NCAA I ◆ Independent; Southland Conference
◆ http://www.panam.edu/

State-supported comprehensive, founded 1927, part of University of Texas System
Coed, 13,868 undergraduate students, 70% full-time, 58% women, 42% men
Small-town 238-acre campus with easy access to McAllen-Edinburg-Mission MSA
Noncompetitive entrance level, 63% of applicants were admitted

Freshmen *Admission:* 6,622 applied, 4,257 were accepted, 2,420 enrolled. *Test scores:* SAT verbal scores over 500: 32%; SAT math scores over 500: 36%; SAT verbal scores over 600: 7%; SAT math scores over 600: 9%; SAT verbal scores over 700: 1%; SAT math scores over 700: 1%.
Tuition and fees (2003–04): $4075 (resident), $11,851 (nonresident).
Room and board: $3488 (room only: $2406).
Financial Aid (All incoming freshmen): *Average need-based gift aid:* $6810. *Average non-need based aid:* $3376. *Average aid to full-time undergraduates:* $6858.
Athletic Department: *Director of Athletics:* William Weidner; Phone: 956-381-2221; Fax: 956-381-2261; E-mail: weidnerw@panam.edu. *Sports Information Director:* Mike Bond; Phone: 956-381-2240; E-mail: mibond@panam.edu.

The University of Texas–Pan American *(continued)*

MEN'S COACHES

Baseball: Willie Gawlik; Phone: 956-381-2235; E-mail: gawlikw@panam.edu.

Basketball: Bob Hoffman; Phone: 956-381-2870; E-mail: bhoffman@panam.edu.

Cheerleading: Charlie Caceres; Phone: 956-292-0839; E-mail: caceresc@panam.edu.

Cross Country: Ricky Vaughn; Phone: 956-381-7113; E-mail: rvaughn@panam.edu.

Golf: Drew Scott; Phone: 956-381-7103; E-mail: drewscott@panam.edu.

Tennis: Eduardo Provencio; Phone: 956-381-2223; E-mail: provenc@mscd.edu.

Track and Field: Ricky Vaughn; Phone: 956-381-7113; E-mail: rvaughn@panam.edu.

WOMEN'S COACHES

Basketball: DeAnn Craft; Phone: 956-381-2974; E-mail: craftd@panam.edu.

Cheerleading: Charlie Caceres; Phone: 956-292-0839; E-mail: caceresc@panam.edu.

Cross Country: Ricky Vaughn; Phone: 956-381-7113; E-mail: rvaughn@panam.edu.

Golf: Barb Odale; Phone: 956-381-7109; E-mail: odaleb@panam.edu.

Tennis: Eduardo Provencio; Phone: 956-381-2223; E-mail: provenc@mscd.edu.

Track and Field: Ricky Vaughn; Phone: 956-381-7113; E-mail: rvaughn@panam.edu.

Volleyball: Dave Thorn; Phone: 956-316-7007; E-mail: thorndm@panam.edu.

UNIVERSITY OF THE DISTRICT OF COLUMBIA

Washington, District of Columbia

Firebirds ◆ NCAA II ◆ Independent ◆ http://www.udc.edu/

District-supported comprehensive, founded 1976
Coed, 5,006 undergraduate students, 37% full-time, 62% women, 38% men
Urban 28-acre campus
Noncompetitive entrance level, 91% of applicants were admitted

Freshmen *Admission:* 2,002 applied, 1,825 were accepted, 720 enrolled.
Tuition and fees (2004–05): $2070 (resident), $4710 (nonresident).
Financial Aid (All incoming freshmen): *Average need-based gift aid:* $2746. *Average non-need based aid:* $3625. *Average aid to full-time undergraduates:* $4821.
Athletic Department: *Director of Athletics:* Michael McLeese; Phone: 202-274-5024; Fax: 202-274-5065; E-mail: mmcleese@udc.edu. *Sports Information Director:* Bernard Payton; Phone: 202-274-5064; E-mail: bpayton@udc.edu.

MEN'S COACHES

Basketball: Michael McLeesie; Phone: 202-274-5024; E-mail: mmcleese@udc.edu.

Cross Country: Lorenzo Roach; Phone: 202-274-5094.

Soccer: Osman Orlando; Phone: 202-274-5074.

Tennis: Saundra Woods; Phone: 202-274-5077.

WOMEN'S COACHES

Basketball: Stephanie Evans-Suber; Phone: 202-274-5085.

Cross Country: Lorenzo Roach; Phone: 202-274-5094.

Soccer: Osman Orlando; Phone: 202-274-5074.

Tennis: Saundra Woods; Phone: 202-274-5077.

Volleyball: Bessie Stockard; Phone: 202-274-5076; E-mail: bstockard@udc.edu.

UNIVERSITY OF THE INCARNATE WORD

San Antonio, Texas

Crusaders ◆ NCAA II ◆ Heartland Conference ◆ http://www.uiw.edu/

Independent Roman Catholic comprehensive, founded 1881
Coed, 3,665 undergraduate students, 58% full-time, 67% women, 33% men
Urban 200-acre campus
Moderately difficult entrance level, 9% of applicants were admitted

Freshmen *Admission:* 1,422 applied, 1,234 were accepted, 406 enrolled. *Test scores:* SAT verbal scores over 500: 48%; SAT math scores over 500: 41%; SAT verbal scores over 600: 14%; SAT math scores over 600: 12%; SAT verbal scores over 700: 2%; SAT math scores over 700: 1%.
Tuition and fees (2004–05): $16,082 (full-time). *Room and board:* $5690 (room only: $3590).
Financial Aid (All incoming freshmen): *Average need-based gift aid:* $7605. *Average non-need based aid:* $6646. *Average aid to full-time undergraduates:* $12,349.
Athletic Department: *Director of Athletics:* Mark Papich; Phone: 210-829-6053; Fax: 210-805-3574; E-mail: papich@universe.uiwtx.edu. *Sports Information Director:* Wayne Witt; Phone: 210-829-3828; E-mail: witt@universe.uiwtx.edu.

MEN'S COACHES

Baseball: Danny Heep; Phone: 210-829-3830; E-mail: heep@universe.uiwtx.edu.

Basketball: Al Gushkin; Phone: 210-829-6052; E-mail: algrushkin@aol.com.

Cross Country: Tomas Ramos; Phone: 210-805-3566; E-mail: ramos@universe.uiwtx.edu.

Golf: Brent Powell; Phone: 210-829-2795; E-mail: bw_powell@hotmail.com.

Soccer: Dennis Currier; Phone: 210-841-7396; E-mail: currier@universe.uiwtx.edu.

Swimming: Adrian Montoya; Phone: 210-912-2256; E-mail: montoya@universe.uiwtx.edu.

Tennis: John Newman; Phone: 210-829-5006; E-mail: newman@universe.uiwtx.edu.

Track and Field: Tomas Ramos; Phone: 210-805-3566; E-mail: ramos@universe.uiwtx.edu.

WOMEN'S COACHES

Basketball: Angela Lawson; Phone: 210-829-3827; E-mail: lawson@universe.uiwtx.edu.

Cross Country: Tomas Ramos; Phone: 210-805-3566; E-mail: ramos@universe.uiwtx.edu.

Golf: Brent Powell; Phone: 210-829-2795; E-mail: bw_powell@hotmail.com.

Soccer: Tina Patterson; Phone: 210-829-3941; E-mail: tpatters@universe.uiwtx.edu.

Softball: Kevin Jannusch; Phone: 210-829-3969; E-mail: jannusch@universe.uiwtx.edu.

Swimming: Adrian Montoya; Phone: 210-912-2256; E-mail: montoya@universe.uiwtx.edu.

Tennis: John Newman; Phone: 210-829-5006; E-mail: newman@universe.uiwtx.edu.

Track and Field: Tomas Ramos; Phone: 210-805-3566; E-mail: ramos@universe.uiwtx.edu.

Volleyball: Mark Papich; Phone: 210-805-6053; E-mail: papich@universe.uiwtx.edu.

UNIVERSITY OF THE OZARKS
Clarksville, Arkansas

Eagles ◆ NCAA III ◆ American Southwest Conference
◆ http://www.ozarks.edu/

Independent Presbyterian 4-year, founded 1834
Coed, 734 undergraduate students, 94% full-time, 57% women, 43% men
Small-town 56-acre campus with easy access to Little Rock
Moderately difficult entrance level, 84% of applicants were admitted

Freshmen *Admission:* 654 applied, 548 were accepted, 214 enrolled. *Test scores:* SAT verbal scores over 500: 94%; SAT math scores over 500: 43%; SAT verbal scores over 600: 17%; SAT math scores over 600: 10%; SAT verbal scores over 700: 6%; SAT math scores over 700: 3%.
Tuition and fees (2003–04): $11,880 (full-time). *Room and board:* $4580.
Financial Aid (All incoming freshmen): *Average need-based gift aid:* $11,806. *Average non-need based aid:* $11,632. *Average aid to full-time undergraduates:* $12,816.
Athletic Department: *Director of Athletics:* Dave De Hart; Phone: 479-979-1210; Fax: 479-979-1330; E-mail: ddehart@ozarks.edu. *Sports Information Director:* Josh Peppas; Phone: 479-979-1465; E-mail: jpeppas@ozarks.edu.

MEN'S COACHES
Baseball: Jimmy Clark; Phone: 479-979-1409; E-mail: jclark@ozarks.edu.
Basketball: Matt O'Connor; Phone: 479-979-1326; E-mail: moconnor@ozarks.edu.
Cheerleading: Lisa Hollis; Phone: 479-979-1311; E-mail: lhollis@ozarks.edu.
Cross Country: Jon Janssen; Phone: 479-979-1463; E-mail: jjanssen@ozarks.edu.
Golf: Jack Jones; Phone: 479-979-1325; E-mail: jcjones@ozarks.edu.
Soccer: Dave DeHart; Phone: 479-979-1210; E-mail: ddehart@ozarks.edu.
Tennis: Sally Wood; Phone: 479-979-1332; E-mail: swood@ozarks.edu.

WOMEN'S COACHES
Basketball: Jack Jones; Phone: 479-979-1325; E-mail: jcjones@ozarks.edu.
Cheerleading: Lisa Hollis; Phone: 479-979-1311; E-mail: lhollis@ozarks.edu.
Cross Country: Jon Janssen; Phone: 479-979-1463; E-mail: jjanssen@ozarks.edu.
Soccer: Jeremy Bernard; Phone: 479-979-1334; E-mail: jbernard@ozarks.edu.
Softball: Jon Janssen; Phone: 479-979-1463; E-mail: jjanssen@ozarks.edu.
Tennis: Sally Wood; Phone: 479-979-1332; E-mail: swood@ozarks.edu.

UNIVERSITY OF THE PACIFIC
Stockton, California

Tigers ◆ NCAA I ◆ Big West Conference; Northern Pacific Field Hockey Conference ◆ http://www.pacific.edu/

Independent university, founded 1851
Coed, 3,357 undergraduate students, 96% full-time, 58% women, 42% men
Suburban 175-acre campus with easy access to Sacramento
Moderately difficult entrance level, 71% of applicants were admitted

Freshmen *Admission:* 4,501 applied, 3,173 were accepted, 818 enrolled. *Test scores:* SAT verbal scores over 500: 82%; SAT math scores over 500: 90%; SAT verbal scores over 600: 35%; SAT math scores over 600: 50%; SAT verbal scores over 700: 3%; SAT math scores over 700: 12%.
Tuition and fees (2003–04): $23,600 (full-time). *Room and board:* $7490 (room only: $3736).
Financial Aid (All incoming freshmen): *Average need-based gift aid:* $17,227. *Average non-need based aid:* $7973. *Average aid to full-time undergraduates:* $20,205.
Athletic Department: *Director of Athletics:* Lynn King; Phone: 209-946-2472; Fax: 209-946-2731; E-mail: lynnking@pacific.edu. *Sports Information Director:* Mike Millerick; Phone: 209-946-2479; E-mail: mmontgomery@pacific.edu.

MEN'S COACHES
Baseball: Ed Sprague; Phone: 209-946-2709; E-mail: esprague@pacific.edu.
Basketball: Bob Thomason; Phone: 209-946-2341; E-mail: bthomaso@uop.edu.
Golf: Jason Preeo; Phone: 209-946-2713; E-mail: jpreeo@uop.edu.
Swimming: Danny May; Phone: 209-946-2710; E-mail: dmay@uop.edu.
Tennis: Guido Baumann; Phone: 209-946-2219; E-mail: gbaumann@uop.edu.
Volleyball: Joe Wortmann; Phone: 209-946-2724; E-mail: jwortman@uop.edu.

WOMEN'S COACHES
Basketball: Craig Jackson; Phone: 209-946-2745; E-mail: cjackson@uop.edu.
Cross Country: Tim Teeter; Phone: 209-946-2710; E-mail: tteeter@uop.edu.
Field Hockey: Linda MacDonald; Phone: 209-946-2249; E-mail: lmacdona@uop.edu.
Soccer: Keith Coleman; Phone: 209-946-2129; E-mail: kcoleman@uop.edu.
Softball: Brian Kolze; Phone: 209-946-2699; E-mail: bkolze@uop.edu.
Swimming: Danny May; Phone: 209-946-2710; E-mail: dmay@uop.edu.
Tennis: Bob Chiene; Phone: 209-946-2128; E-mail: bchiene@pacific.edu.
Volleyball: Jayne McHugh; Phone: 209-946-2389; E-mail: jmchugh@uop.edu.

UNIVERSITY OF THE SCIENCES IN PHILADELPHIA
Philadelphia, Pennsylvania

Devils ◆ NAIA ◆ Central Atlantic Collegiate Conference
◆ http://www.usip.edu/

Independent university, founded 1821
Coed, 2,323 undergraduate students, 95% full-time, 67% women, 33% men
Urban 35-acre campus
Moderately difficult entrance level, 71% of applicants were admitted

Freshmen *Admission:* 2,966 applied, 2,029 were accepted, 532 enrolled. *Test scores:* SAT verbal scores over 500: 73%; SAT math scores over 500: 91%; SAT verbal scores over 600: 20%; SAT math scores over 600: 39%; SAT verbal scores over 700: 1%; SAT math scores over 700: 5%.
Tuition and fees (2003–04): $20,958 (full-time). *Room and board:* $8352 (room only: $5134).
Athletic Department: *Director of Athletics:* Robert Morgan; Phone: 215-596-8916; E-mail: r.morgan@usip.edu. *Sports Information Director:* Bob Heller; Phone: 215-895-3133; E-mail: r.heller@usip.edu.

MEN'S COACHES
Baseball: Jack Bilbee; Phone: 215-596-8782; E-mail: j.bilbee@usip.edu.
Basketball: David Pauley; Phone: 215-596-8817; E-mail: d.pauley@usip.edu.
Cross Country: Bob Heller; Phone: 215-596-3133; E-mail: r.heller@usip.edu.
Tennis: Julian Snow; Phone: 215-596-8837; E-mail: j.snow@usip.edu.

WOMEN'S COACHES
Basketball: Nate Ware; Phone: 215-596-8782; E-mail: n.ware@usip.edu.
Cross Country: Bob Heller; Phone: 215-596-3133; E-mail: r.heller@usip.edu.
Softball: Joseph Long; Phone: 215-596-8782; E-mail: eastfallsauto@msn.com.
Tennis: Bob Flitter; Phone: 215-596-8782; E-mail: r.flitter@usip.edu.
Volleyball: Mike Sinesi; Phone: 215-596-8782.

UNIVERSITY OF THE SOUTH
Sewanee, Tennessee

Tigers ◆ NCAA III ◆ Southern Collegiate Athletic Conference ◆ http://www.sewanee.edu/

Independent Episcopal comprehensive, founded 1857
Coed, 1,374 undergraduate students, 99% full-time, 54% women, 46% men
Small-town 10,000-acre campus
Very difficult entrance level, 66% of applicants were admitted

Freshmen *Admission:* 1,825 applied, 1,316 were accepted, 427 enrolled. *Test scores:* SAT verbal scores over 500: 97%; SAT math scores over 500: 96%; SAT verbal scores over 600: 63%; SAT math scores over 600: 63%; SAT verbal scores over 700: 16%; SAT math scores over 700: 10%.
Tuition and fees (2003–04): $24,135 (full-time). *Room and board:* $6720 (room only: $3440).
Financial Aid (All incoming freshmen): *Average need-based gift aid:* $16,918. *Average non-need based aid:* $11,880. *Average aid to full-time undergraduates:* $20,358.
Athletic Department: *Director of Athletics:* Mark Webb; Phone: 931-598-1388; Fax: 931-598-1673; E-mail: mwebb@sewanee.edu.

MEN'S COACHES
Baseball: Scott Baker; Phone: 931-598-1455; E-mail: sbaker@sewanee.edu.
Basketball: Joe Thoni; Phone: 931-598-1298; E-mail: jthoni@sewanee.edu.
Cross Country: Jeff Heitzenrater; Phone: 931-598-1285; E-mail: jheitzen@sewanee.edu.
Diving: Max Obermiller; Phone: 931-598-1546; E-mail: mobermil@sewanee.edu.
Football: John Windham; Phone: 931-598-1593; E-mail: jwindham@sewanee.edu.
Golf: Tim Whittle; Phone: 931-598-3381; E-mail: twhittle@sewanee.edu.
Soccer: Qasim Sheikh; Phone: 931-598-1582; E-mail: qsheikh@sewanee.edu.
Swimming: Max Obermiller; Phone: 931-598-1546; E-mail: mobermil@sewanee.edu.
Tennis: John Shackleford; Phone: 931-598-1485; E-mail: jshackel@sewanee.edu.
Track and Field: Jeff Heitzenrater; Phone: 931-598-1285; E-mail: jheitzen@sewanee.edu.

WOMEN'S COACHES
Basketball: Dickie McCarthy; Phone: 931-598-1284; E-mail: dmccarth@sewanee.edu.
Cross Country: Jeff Heitzenrater; Phone: 931-598-1285; E-mail: jheitzen@sewanee.edu.
Diving: Max Obermiller; Phone: 931-598-1546; E-mail: mobermil@sewanee.edu.
Field Hockey: Barb Taylor; Phone: 931-598-1380; E-mail: btaylor@sewanee.edu.
Golf: Nancy Ladd; Phone: 931-598-1320; E-mail: nladd@sewanee.edu.
Soccer: Nick Cowell; Phone: 931-598-1545; E-mail: nconwell@sewanee.edu.
Softball: Heather Windham; Phone: 931-598-1465; E-mail: hwindham@sewanee.edu.
Swimming: Max Obermiller; Phone: 931-598-1546; E-mail: mobermil@sewanee.edu.
Tennis: Conchie Shackleford; Phone: 931-598-1485; E-mail: cshackel@sewanee.edu.
Track and Field: Jeff Heitzenrater; Phone: 931-598-1285; E-mail: jheitzen@sewanee.edu.
Volleyball: Nancy Ladd; Phone: 931-598-1320; E-mail: nladd@sewanee.edu.

UNIVERSITY OF TOLEDO
Toledo, Ohio

Rockets ◆ NCAA I ◆ Mid-American Conference ◆ http://www.utoledo.edu/

State-supported university, founded 1872
Coed, 17,388 undergraduate students, 79% full-time, 51% women, 49% men
Suburban 407-acre campus with easy access to Detroit
Noncompetitive entrance level, 97% of applicants were admitted

Freshmen *Admission:* 8,877 applied, 8,650 were accepted, 3,884 enrolled. *Test scores:* SAT verbal scores over 500: 69%; SAT math scores over 500: 60%; SAT verbal scores over 600: 29%; SAT math scores over 600: 25%; SAT verbal scores over 700: 4%; SAT math scores over 700: 4%.
Tuition and fees (2003–04): $6414 (resident), $15,052 (nonresident). *Room and board:* $6834.
Financial Aid (All incoming freshmen): *Average need-based gift aid:* $3873. *Average non-need based aid:* $2814. *Average aid to full-time undergraduates:* $5594.
Athletic Department: *Director of Athletics:* Mike O'Brien; Phone: 419-530-4987; Fax: 419-530-4428; E-mail: mobrien6@utnet.utoledo.edu. *Sports Information Director:* Paul Helgren; Phone: 419-530-4918; E-mail: phelgre@utnet.utoledo.edu.

MEN'S COACHES
Baseball: Cory Mee; Phone: 419-530-6263; E-mail: cmee@utnet.utoledo.edu.
Basketball: Stan Joplin; Phone: 419-530-4187; E-mail: stan.joplin@utoledo.edu.
Cheerleading: Ron Ott; Phone: 419-530-5521; E-mail: ronan.ott@utoledo.edu.
Cross Country: Kevin Hadsell; Phone: 419-530-7813; E-mail: kevin.hadsell@utoledo.edu.
Football: Tom Amstutz; Phone: 419-530-3500; E-mail: thomas.amstutz@utoledo.edu.
Golf: Jamie Mauntler; Phone: 419-530-4218; E-mail: jmauntl2@utnet.utoledo.edu.
Tennis: Al Wermer; Phone: 419-530-4374; E-mail: alwermer@hotmail.com.

WOMEN'S COACHES
Basketball: Marie Ehlen; Phone: 419-530-2530; E-mail: dehlen@pop3.utoledo.edu.
Cheerleading: Ron Ott; Phone: 419-530-5521; E-mail: ronan.ott@utoledo.edu.
Cross Country: Kevin Hadsell; Phone: 419-530-7813; E-mail: kevin.hadsell@utoledo.edu.
Diving: Kelly Lajiness; Phone: 419-530-2532; E-mail: klajine@utnet.utoledo.edu.
Golf: Nicole Hollingsworth; Phone: 419-530-7761; E-mail: nhollin@utnet.utoledo.edu.
Soccer: Brad Evans; Phone: 419-530-6250; E-mail: soccer@utoledo.edu.
Softball: Jo Ann Gordon; Phone: 419-530-6258; E-mail: jgordon8@utnet.utoledo.edu.
Swimming: Brian Sharer; Phone: 419-530-2782; E-mail: brian.sharar@utoledo.edu.
Tennis: Tracy Honko; Phone: 419-530-2499; E-mail: thonko@utnet.utoledo.edu.
Track and Field: Kevin Hadsell; Phone: 419-530-7813; E-mail: kevin.hadsell@utoledo.edu.
Volleyball: Kent Miller; Phone: 419-530-7740; E-mail: rocketvb@utnet.utoledo.edu.

UNIVERSITY OF TULSA
Tulsa, Oklahoma

Golden Hurricane ◆ NCAA I ◆ Missouri Valley Conference; Western Athletic Conference ◆ http://www.utulsa.edu/

Independent religious university, founded 1894, affiliated with Presbyterian Church (U.S.A.)
Coed, 2,672 undergraduate students, 92% full-time, 50% women, 50% men
Urban 200-acre campus with easy access to Tulsa
Very difficult entrance level, 8% of applicants were admitted

Freshmen *Admission:* 2,292 applied, 1,747 were accepted, 590 enrolled. *Test scores:* SAT verbal scores over 500: 83%; SAT math scores over 500: 83%; SAT verbal scores over 600: 54%; SAT math scores over 600: 51%; SAT verbal scores over 700: 22%; SAT math scores over 700: 18%.
Tuition and fees (2003–04): $15,736 (full-time). *Room and board:* $5610 (room only: $3060).
Financial Aid (All incoming freshmen): *Average need-based gift aid:* $4681. *Average non-need based aid:* $8553. *Average aid to full-time undergraduates:* $14,035.
Athletic Department: *Director of Athletics:* Judy MacLeod; Phone: 918-631-2181; Fax: 918-631-3670; E-mail: judy-macleod@utulsa.edu. *Sports Information Director:* Don Tomkalski; Phone: 918-631-3200; E-mail: donald-tomkalski@utulsa.edu.

MEN'S COACHES
Basketball: John Phillips; Phone: 918-631-2747; E-mail: john-phillips@utulsa.edu.
Cheerleading: Scott Gund; Phone: 918-631-5496; E-mail: spiritgroup@utulsa.edu.
Cross Country: Steve Gulley; Phone: 918-631-2545; E-mail: steven-gulley@utulsa.edu.
Football: Steve Kragthorpe; Phone: 918-631-3112.
Golf: Bill Brogden; Phone: 918-631-2394; E-mail: william-brogden@utulsa.edu.
Soccer: Tom McIntosh; Phone: 918-631-3789; E-mail: thomas-mcintosh@utulsa.edu.
Tennis: Vince Westbrook; Phone: 918-631-5090; E-mail: vincent-westbrook@utulsa.edu.
Track and Field: Steve Gulley; Phone: 918-631-2545; E-mail: steven-gulley@utulsa.edu.

WOMEN'S COACHES
Basketball: Kathy McConnell-Miller; Phone: 918-631-2391.
Cheerleading: Scott Gund; Phone: 918-631-5496; E-mail: spiritgroup@utulsa.edu.
Cross Country: Steve Gulley; Phone: 918-631-2545; E-mail: steven-gulley@utulsa.edu.
Golf: Holly Hair; Phone: 918-631-2325; E-mail: holley-hair@utulsa.edu.
Soccer: Rena Richardson; Phone: 918-631-2123.
Tennis: Paige McMurray; Phone: 918-631-3186; E-mail: jennifer-mcmurray@utulsa.edu.
Track and Field: Steve Gulley; Phone: 918-631-2545; E-mail: steven-gulley@utulsa.edu.
Volleyball: Matt Sonnichsen; Phone: 918-631-2128; E-mail: matthew-sonnichsen@utulsa.edu.

UNIVERSITY OF UTAH
Salt Lake City, Utah

Utes ◆ NCAA I ◆ Mountain West Conference ◆ http://www.utah.edu/

State-supported university, founded 1850, part of Utah System of Higher Education
Coed, 22,421 undergraduate students, 68% full-time, 45% women, 55% men
Urban 1,500-acre campus
Moderately difficult entrance level, 86% of applicants were admitted

Freshmen *Admission:* 5,842 applied, 5,036 were accepted, 2,653 enrolled.

Tuition and fees (2003–04): $3647 (resident), $11,293 (nonresident). *Room and board:* $5036 (room only: $2472).
Financial Aid (All incoming freshmen): *Average need-based gift aid:* $4401. *Average non-need based aid:* $3211. *Average aid to full-time undergraduates:* $6776.
Athletic Department: *Director of Athletics:* Chris Hill; Phone: 801-581-3508; Fax: 801-581-4358. *Sports Information Director:* Liz Abel; Phone: 801-581-3511; E-mail: label@huntsman.utah.edu.

MEN'S COACHES
Baseball: Tim Esmay; Phone: 801-581-3526.
Basketball: Rick Majerus; Phone: 801-581-5451; E-mail: rmajerus@huntsman.utah.edu.
Cross Country: Brian Appell; Phone: 801-581-3525; E-mail: bappell@huntsman.utah.edu.
Diving: Rachel Degener; Phone: 801-585-3955; E-mail: rae023@yahoo.com.
Football: Urban Meyer; Phone: 801-581-7684.
Golf: Wayne Fisher; Phone: 801-581-1041.
Swimming: Mike Litzinger; Phone: 801-581-5480; E-mail: mlitzinger@huntsman.utah.edu.
Tennis: F.D. Robbins; Phone: 801-581-4755.
Track and Field: Lisa Collet; Phone: 801-585-6858.

WOMEN'S COACHES
Basketball: Elaine Elliot; Phone: 801-581-7037; E-mail: eelliott@huntsman.utah.edu.
Cross Country: Brian Appell; Phone: 801-581-3525; E-mail: bappell@huntsman.utah.edu.
Diving: Rachel Degener; Phone: 801-585-3955; E-mail: rae023@yahoo.com.
Gymnastics: Greg Marsden; Phone: 801-581-3513; E-mail: gmarsden@huntsman.utah.edu.
Soccer: Rich Manning; Phone: 801-581-7250.
Softball: Mona Stevens; Phone: 801-581-3514; E-mail: mstevens@huntsman.utah.edu.
Swimming: Mike Litzinger; Phone: 801-581-5480; E-mail: mlitzinger@huntsman.utah.edu.
Tennis: Megan Dorny; Phone: 801-581-7229; E-mail: m.payne@m.cc.utah.edu.
Track and Field: Lisa Collet; Phone: 801-585-6858.
Track and Field: Lisa Collet; Phone: 801-585-6858.
Volleyball: Beth Launiere; Phone: 801-581-6843; E-mail: elauniere@huntsman.utah.edu.

UNIVERSITY OF VERMONT
Burlington, Vermont

Catamounts ◆ NCAA I ◆ America East Conference; Eastern College Athletic Conference ◆ http://www.uvm.edu/

State-supported university, founded 1791
Coed, 9,234 undergraduate students, 84% full-time, 57% women, 43% men
Suburban 425-acre campus
Moderately difficult entrance level, 69% of applicants were admitted

Freshmen *Admission:* 10,456 applied, 7,792 were accepted, 1,923 enrolled. *Test scores:* SAT verbal scores over 500: 87%; SAT math scores over 500: 87%; SAT verbal scores over 600: 38%; SAT math scores over 600: 42%; SAT verbal scores over 700: 4%; SAT math scores over 700: 4%.
Tuition and fees (2003–04): $9636 (resident), $22,688 (nonresident). *Room and board:* $6680 (room only: $4464).
Financial Aid (All incoming freshmen): *Average need-based gift aid:* $11,360. *Average non-need based aid:* $2006. *Average aid to full-time undergraduates:* $11,929.
Athletic Department: *Director of Athletics:* Robert Corran; Phone: 802-656-3075; Fax: 802-656-0949; E-mail: robert.corran@uvm.edu. *Sports Information Director:* Gordon Woodworth; Phone: 802-656-1110; E-mail: gordon.woodworth@uvm.edu.

MEN'S COACHES
Baseball: Bill Currier; Phone: 802-656-7701; E-mail: willard.currier@uvm.edu.
Basketball: Tom Brennan; Phone: 802-656-3165; E-mail: thomas.j.brennan@uvm.edu.
Cross Country: Joe Gingras; Phone: 802-656-7687; E-mail: joseph.gingras@uvm.edu.

University of Vermont (*continued*)

Diving: Gerry Cournoyer; Phone: 802-656-7702; E-mail: gerry.cournoyer@uvm.edu.
Golf: Mike Gilligan; Phone: 802-656-7698; E-mail: michael.gilligan@uvm.edu.
Ice Hockey: Kevin Sneddon; Phone: 802-656-7698; E-mail: kevin.sneddon@uvm.edu.
Lacrosse: Steve Beville; Phone: 802-656-7683; E-mail: stephen.beville@uvm.edu.
Soccer: Jesse Cormier; Phone: 802-656-7694.
Swimming: Gerry Cournoyer; Phone: 802-656-7702; E-mail: gerry.cournoyer@uvm.edu.
Tennis: Dave Moore; Phone: 802-656-7690; E-mail: david.moore@uvm.edu.

WOMEN'S COACHES
Basketball: Sharon Dawley; Phone: 802-656-7695; E-mail: sharon.dawley@uvm.edu.
Cross Country: Joe Gingras; Phone: 802-656-7687; E-mail: joseph.gingras@uvm.edu.
Diving: Gerry Cournoyer; Phone: 802-656-7702; E-mail: gerry.cournoyer@uvm.edu.
Field Hockey: Nicole Houghton; Phone: 802-656-7700; E-mail: nicole.houghton@uvm.edu.
Lacrosse: Tracy Scott; Phone: 802-656-7709; E-mail: court7680@aol.com.
Soccer: Kerry Dziczkaniec; Phone: 802-656-7740; E-mail: wsoccer@uvm.edu.
Softball: Pam Childs; Phone: 802-656-7676; E-mail: pamela.childs@uvm.edu.
Swimming: Gerry Cournoyer; Phone: 802-656-7702; E-mail: gerry.cournoyer@uvm.edu.
Tennis: Muff Parsons-Reinhart; Phone: 802-656-7710; E-mail: muff.parsons@uvm.edu.
Track and Field: Joe Gingras; Phone: 802-656-7687; E-mail: joseph.gingras@uvm.edu.

UNIVERSITY OF VIRGINIA
Charlottesville, Virginia

(M) Cavaiers (W) Wahoos ◆ NCAA I ◆ Atlantic Coast Conference ◆ http://www.virginia.edu/

State-supported university, founded 1819
Coed, 13,829 undergraduate students, 94% full-time, 53% women, 47% men
Suburban 1,160-acre campus with easy access to Richmond
Most difficult entrance level, 40% of applicants were admitted

Freshmen *Admission:* 14,627 applied, 5,775 were accepted, 3,101 enrolled. *Test scores:* SAT verbal scores over 500: 98%; SAT math scores over 500: 97%; SAT verbal scores over 600: 80%; SAT math scores over 600: 84%; SAT verbal scores over 700: 32%; SAT math scores over 700: 39%.
Tuition and fees (2003–04): $6149 (resident), $22,119 (nonresident). *Room and board:* $5591 (room only: $2711).
Financial Aid (All incoming freshmen): *Average need-based gift aid:* $9190. *Average non-need based aid:* $5122. *Average aid to full-time undergraduates:* $12,069.
Athletic Department: *Director of Athletics:* Craig Littlepage; Phone: 434-982-5100; Fax: 434-982-5212; E-mail: ckl9e@virginia.edu. *Sports Information Director:* Rich Murray; Phone: 434-982-5500; E-mail: rjm4e@virginia.edu.

MEN'S COACHES
Baseball: Brian O'Connor; Phone: 434-982-4932; E-mail: bpo8n@virginia.edu.
Basketball: Pete Gillen; Phone: 434-982-5400; E-mail: pjg4n@virginia.edu.
Cheerleading: Kelley Carter; Phone: 434-975-6499; E-mail: klc4z@virginia.edu.
Cross Country: Randy Bungard; Phone: 434-982-5760; E-mail: trackcoach@virginia.edu.
Diving: Dave Fafara; Phone: 434-975-5756; E-mail: djf2h@virginia.edu.
Football: Al Groh; Phone: 434-982-5900; E-mail: algroh@virginia.edu.
Golf: Michael Moraghan; Phone: 434-982-5730; E-mail: moraghan@virginia.edu.

Lacrosse: Don Starsia; Phone: 434-982-5715; E-mail: ds3s@virginia.edu.
Soccer: George Gelnovatch; Phone: 434-982-5125; E-mail: gelnovatch@virginia.edu.
Swimming: Mark Bernardino; Phone: 434-982-5755; E-mail: p.m.bernardino@virginia.edu.
Tennis: Brian Boland; Phone: 434-982-5732; E-mail: uvatennis@virginia.edu.
Track and Field: Randy Bungard; Phone: 434-982-5760; E-mail: trackcoach@virginia.edu.
Wrestling: Lenny Bernstein; Phone: 434-982-5738; E-mail: lenny.h.bernstein@virginia.edu.

WOMEN'S COACHES
Basketball: Debbie Ryan; Phone: 434-982-5800; E-mail: dar2h@virginia.edu.
Cheerleading: Kelley Carter; Phone: 434-975-6499; E-mail: klc4z@virginia.edu.
Cross Country: Randy Bungard; Phone: 434-982-5760; E-mail: trackcoach@virginia.edu.
Diving: Dave Fafara; Phone: 434-975-5756; E-mail: djf2h@virginia.edu.
Field Hockey: Jessica Wilk; Phone: 434-982-5751; E-mail: jwilk@virginia.edu.
Golf: Jan Mann; Phone: 434-243-5361; E-mail: janmann@virginia.edu.
Lacrosse: Julie Myers; Phone: 434-982-5061; E-mail: jap2v@virginia.edu.
Soccer: Steve Swanson; Phone: 434-982-5710; E-mail: sswanson@virginia.edu.
Softball: Cheryl Sprangel; Phone: 434-982-5736; E-mail: cts6n@virginia.edu.
Swimming: Mark Bernardino; Phone: 434-982-5755; E-mail: p.m.bernardino@virginia.edu.
Tennis: Phil Rogers; Phone: 434-982-5734; E-mail: pcr8f@virginia.edu.
Track and Field: Randy Bungard; Phone: 434-982-5760; E-mail: trackcoach@virginia.edu.
Volleyball: Melissa Shelton; Phone: 434-982-5712; E-mail: vball@virginia.edu.

THE UNIVERSITY OF VIRGINIA'S COLLEGE AT WISE
Wise, Virginia

Cavaliers ◆ NAIA ◆ Appalachian Conference ◆ http://www.uvawise.edu/

State-supported 4-year, founded 1954, part of University of Virginia
Coed, 1,703 undergraduate students, 80% full-time, 56% women, 44% men
Small-town 396-acre campus
Moderately difficult entrance level, 84% of applicants were admitted

Freshmen *Admission:* 987 applied, 766 were accepted, 349 enrolled. *Test scores:* SAT verbal scores over 500: 48%; SAT math scores over 500: 49%; SAT verbal scores over 600: 13%; SAT math scores over 600: 10%; SAT verbal scores over 700: 2%; SAT math scores over 700: 1%.
Tuition and fees (2003–04): $4530 (resident), $13,418 (nonresident). *Room and board:* $5586 (room only: $3104).
Financial Aid (All incoming freshmen): *Average need-based gift aid:* $3413. *Average non-need based aid:* $1507. *Average aid to full-time undergraduates:* $5197.
Athletic Department: *Director of Athletics:* Ray Spenilla; Phone: 276-328-0204; Fax: 276-376-1023; E-mail: r_spenilla@uvawise.edu. *Sports Information Director:* Chad Osborne; Phone: 276-328-0188; E-mail: c_osborne@uvawise.edu.

MEN'S COACHES
Baseball: Hank Banner; Phone: 276-376-4504; E-mail: alc5d@uvawise.edu.
Basketball: Lee Clark; Phone: 276-328-0207; E-mail: alc5d@uvawise.edu.
Cross Country: Jamie Trent; Phone: 276-328-0206.
Football: Bruce Wasem; Phone: 276-328-0208; E-mail: bww2e@uvawise.edu.
Golf: Jim Stewart; Phone: 276-328-0206.
Tennis: Danny Rowland; Phone: 276-328-0206; E-mail: impressions@mounet.com.

Basketball: Rachel Clay-Keohane; Phone: 276-328-0205; E-mail: rlc4m@uvawise.edu.
Cross Country: Jamie Trent; Phone: 276-328-0206.
Tennis: Danny Rowland; Phone: 276-328-0206; E-mail: impressions@mounet.com.
Volleyball: Kim Mathes; Phone: 276-328-4584; E-mail: kimmathes@hotmail.com.

UNIVERSITY OF WASHINGTON
Seattle, Washington

Huskies ◆ NCAA I ◆ Pacific-10 Conference
◆ http://www.washington.edu/

State-supported university, founded 1861
Coed, 28,362 undergraduate students, 83% full-time, 52% women, 48% men
Urban 703-acre campus
Moderately difficult entrance level, 64% of applicants were admitted

Freshmen *Admission:* 15,950 applied, 10,884 were accepted, 4,771 enrolled. *Test scores:* SAT verbal scores over 500: 83%; SAT math scores over 500: 91%; SAT verbal scores over 600: 44%; SAT math scores over 600: 58%; SAT verbal scores over 700: 10%; SAT math scores over 700: 15%.
Tuition and fees (2003–04): $4968 (resident), $16,124 (nonresident). *Room and board:* $6726.
Financial Aid (All incoming freshmen): *Average need-based gift aid:* $5572. *Average non-need based aid:* $1362. *Average aid to full-time undergraduates:* $8970.
Athletic Department: *Director of Athletics:* Barbara Hedges; Phone: 206-543-2212; Fax: 206-685-4668; E-mail: bhedges@u.washington.edu. *Sports Information Director:* Jim Daves; Phone: 206-543-2230; E-mail: jdaves@u.washington.edu.

MEN'S COACHES

Baseball: Ken Knutson; Phone: 206-616-4335; E-mail: coachk@u.washington.edu.
Basketball: Lorenzo Romar; Phone: 206-543-5260; E-mail: romar@u.washington.edu.
Cross Country: Gregg Metcalf; Phone: 206-543-0811; E-mail: gmetcalf@u.washington.edu.
Diving: Mickey Wender; Phone: 206-685-1536; E-mail: mwender@u.washington.edu.
Football: Keith Gilbertson; Phone: 206-543-2223; E-mail: gilbs@u.washington.edu.
Golf: Matt Thurmond; Phone: 206-685-7632; E-mail: mthurm@u.washington.edu.
Soccer: Dean Wurzberger; Phone: 206-543-4209; E-mail: wdeanw@u.washington.edu.
Swimming: Mickey Wender; Phone: 206-685-1536; E-mail: mwender@u.washington.edu.
Tennis: Matt Anger; Phone: 206-543-1131; E-mail: manger@u.washington.edu.
Track and Field: Greg Metcalf; Phone: 206-543-7429; E-mail: gmetcalf@u.washington.edu.

WOMEN'S COACHES

Basketball: June Daugherty; Phone: 206-543-0732; E-mail: juned@u.washington.edu.
Cross Country: Greg Metcalf; Phone: 206-543-0811; E-mail: gmetcalf@u.washington.edu.
Diving: Mickey Wender; Phone: 206-685-1536; E-mail: mwender@u.washington.edu.
Golf: Mary Lou Mulflur; Phone: 206-543-0348; E-mail: mlmulf@u.washington.edu.
Gymnastics: Bob Levesque; Phone: 206-543-1826; E-mail: lbob@u.washington.edu.
Soccer: Leslie Gallimore; Phone: 206-685-3966; E-mail: lesleg@u.washington.edu.
Softball: Teresa Wilson; Phone: 206-543-5872; E-mail: twilson@u.washington.edu.
Swimming: Mickey Wender; Phone: 206-685-1536; E-mail: mwender@u.washington.edu.
Tennis: Patty McCain; Phone: 206-543-1116; E-mail: coachn10s@u.washington.edu.
Track and Field: Greg Metcalf; Phone: 206-543-7429; E-mail: gmetcalf@u.washington.edu.
Volleyball: Jim McLaughlin; Phone: 206-616-9060; E-mail: jimmc@u.washington.edu.

THE UNIVERSITY OF WEST ALABAMA
Livingston, Alabama

Tigers ◆ NCAA II ◆ Gulf South Conference
◆ http://www.uwa.edu/

State-supported comprehensive, founded 1835
Coed, 1,692 undergraduate students, 90% full-time, 56% women, 44% men
Small-town 595-acre campus
Minimally difficult entrance level, 77% of applicants were admitted

Freshmen *Admission:* 730 applied, 572 were accepted, 322 enrolled.
Tuition and fees (2003–04): $3710 (resident), $6950 (nonresident). *Room and board:* $2986 (room only: $1460).
Athletic Department: *Director of Athletics:* Dee Outlaw; Phone: 205-652-3784; Fax: 205-652-3600; E-mail: cdo@uwa.edu. *Sports Information Director:* Jason Hughes; Phone: 205-652-3596; E-mail: jhughes@uwa.edu.

MEN'S COACHES

Baseball: Gary Rundles; Phone: 205-652-3870; E-mail: rrundles@uwa.edu.
Basketball: Rick Ready; Phone: 205-652-3525; E-mail: rdr@uwa.edu.
Cross Country: Jenny Schoenfeld; Phone: 205-652-3671; E-mail: jschoenfeld@uwa.edu.
Football: Sam McCorkle; Phone: 205-652-3483.

WOMEN'S COACHES

Basketball: Amanda Marks; Phone: 205-652-3506; E-mail: amarks@uwa.edu.
Cross Country: Jenny Schoenfeld; Phone: 205-652-3671; E-mail: jschoenfeld@uwa.edu.
Softball: Janet Montgomery; Phone: 205-652-3630; E-mail: jlm@uwa.edu.
Volleyball: Karisa Wesley; Phone: 205-652-3712; E-mail: kwesley@uwa.edu.

UNIVERSITY OF WEST FLORIDA
Pensacola, Florida

Argonauts ◆ NCAA II ◆ Gulf South Conference ◆ http://uwf.edu/

State-supported comprehensive, founded 1963, part of State University System of Florida
Coed, 7,911 undergraduate students, 71% full-time, 59% women, 41% men
Suburban 1,600-acre campus
Moderately difficult entrance level, 65% of applicants were admitted

Freshmen *Admission:* 3,011 applied, 1,996 were accepted, 940 enrolled. *Test scores:* SAT verbal scores over 500: 77%; SAT math scores over 500: 79%; SAT verbal scores over 600: 28%; SAT math scores over 600: 26%; SAT verbal scores over 700: 3%; SAT math scores over 700: 2%.
Tuition and fees (2003–04): $2855 (resident), $13,883 (nonresident). *Room and board:* $6000.
Athletic Department: *Director of Athletics:* Richard Berg; Phone: 850-474-3003; Fax: 850-474-3342; E-mail: rberg@uwf.edu. *Sports Information Director:* Cara Lynn Teague; Phone: 850-474-2428; E-mail: cteague@uwf.edu.

MEN'S COACHES

Baseball: Jim Spooner; Phone: 850-474-2488; E-mail: jspooner@uwf.edu.
Basketball: Don Hogan; Phone: 850-474-3319; E-mail: dhogan@uwf.edu.
Cheerleading: Karen Seals; Phone: 850-474-2985; E-mail: kseals@uwf.edu.

University of West Florida (continued)

Cross Country: Matthew Dobson; Phone: 850-474-2141; E-mail: rdobson@uwf.edu.
Golf: Steve Fell; Phone: 850-474-3005; E-mail: sfell@uwf.edu.
Soccer: Bill Elliott; Phone: 850-474-2584; E-mail: belliot@uwf.edu.
Tennis: Derrick Racine; Phone: 850-474-3006; E-mail: dracine@uwf.edu.

WOMEN'S COACHES

Basketball: Shannan Bergen; Phone: 850-474-3235; E-mail: sbergen@uwf.edu.
Cheerleading: Karen Seals; Phone: 850-474-2985; E-mail: kseals@uwf.edu.
Cross Country: Dan Keely; Phone: 850-474-2141; E-mail: dkeely@uwf.edu.
Soccer: Joe Bartlinski; Phone: 850-501-8501; E-mail: jbartlinski@uwf.edu.
Softball: Tami Cyr; Phone: 850-474-3316; E-mail: tcyr@uwf.edu.
Tennis: Derrick Racine; Phone: 850-474-3006; E-mail: dracine@uwf.edu.
Track and Field: Dan Keely; Phone: 850-474-2141; E-mail: dkeely@uwf.edu.
Volleyball: Melissa Wolter; Phone: 850-474-7073; E-mail: mwolter@uwf.edu.

UNIVERSITY OF WISCONSIN–EAU CLAIRE
Eau Claire, Wisconsin

Blugolds ◆ NCAA III ◆ Northern Collegiate Hockey Conference; Wisconsin Athletic Conference ◆ http://www.uwec.edu/

State-supported comprehensive, founded 1916, part of University of Wisconsin System
Coed, 10,059 undergraduate students, 92% full-time, 60% women, 40% men
Urban 333-acre campus
Moderately difficult entrance level, 58% of applicants were admitted

Freshmen *Admission:* 7,055 applied, 4,258 were accepted, 1,879 enrolled. *Test scores:* SAT verbal scores over 500: 81%; SAT math scores over 500: 84%; SAT verbal scores over 600: 51%; SAT math scores over 600: 46%; SAT verbal scores over 700: 13%; SAT math scores over 700: 8%.
Tuition and fees (2003–04): $4313 (resident), $14,360 (nonresident). *Room and board:* $4150 (room only: $2410).
Financial Aid (All incoming freshmen): *Average need-based gift aid:* $3604. *Average non-need based aid:* $1133. *Average aid to full-time undergraduates:* $5514.
Athletic Department: *Director of Athletics:* Tim Petermann; Phone: 715-836-4184; Fax: 715-836-4074; E-mail: petermta@uwec.edu. *Sports Information Director:* Tim Petermann; Phone: 715-836-4184; E-mail: petermta@uwec.edu.

MEN'S COACHES

Basketball: Terry Gibbons; Phone: 715-836-5480; E-mail: gibbontm@uwec.edu.
Cross Country: Chip Schneider; Phone: 715-836-5016; E-mail: schnechi@uwec.edu.
Diving: Rob Welcher; Phone: 715-836-4422; E-mail: welcherl@uwec.edu.
Football: Todd Hoffner; Phone: 715-836-3093; E-mail: hoffnert@uwec.edu.
Golf: John Rawdon; Phone: 715-836-5913; E-mail: rawdonjg@uwec.edu.
Ice Hockey: Jean Laforest; Phone: 715-836-4516; E-mail: laforejd@uwec.edu.
Swimming: Rob Welcher; Phone: 715-836-4422; E-mail: welcherl@uwec.edu.
Tennis: Tom Gillman; Phone: 715-836-5017; E-mail: gillmatm@uwec.edu.
Track and Field: Chip Schneider; Phone: 715-836-5016; E-mail: schnechi@uwec.edu.
Wrestling: Don Parker; Phone: 715-836-3404; E-mail: parkerdc@uwec.edu.

WOMEN'S COACHES

Basketball: Tonja Englund; Phone: 715-836-3489; E-mail: engluntj@uwec.edu.
Cross Country: Tracy Yengo; Phone: 715-836-2649; E-mail: santante@uwec.edu.
Diving: Rob Welcher; Phone: 715-836-4422; E-mail: welcherl@uwec.edu.
Golf: John Rawdon; Phone: 715-836-5913; E-mail: rawdonjg@uwec.edu.
Gymnastics: Jean DeLisle; Phone: 715-836-3991; E-mail: delisljm@uwec.edu.
Soccer: Sean Yengo; Phone: 715-836-4097; E-mail: yengosp@uwec.edu.
Softball: Leslie Huntington; Phone: 715-836-2663; E-mail: huntinla@uwec.edu.
Swimming: Rob Welcher; Phone: 715-836-4422; E-mail: welcherl@uwec.edu.
Tennis: Tom Gillman; Phone: 715-836-5017; E-mail: gillmatm@uwec.edu.
Track and Field: Tracy Yengo; Phone: 715-836-2649; E-mail: santante@uwec.edu.
Volleyball: Lisa Herb; Phone: 715-836-5475; E-mail: herblk@uwec.edu.

UNIVERSITY OF WISCONSIN–GREEN BAY
Green Bay, Wisconsin

Phoenix ◆ NCAA I ◆ Horizon League Conference ◆ http://www.uwgb.edu/

State-supported comprehensive, founded 1968, part of University of Wisconsin System
Coed, 5,256 undergraduate students, 83% full-time, 66% women, 34% men
Suburban 700-acre campus
Moderately difficult entrance level, 72% of applicants were admitted

Freshmen *Admission:* 2,979 applied, 2,322 were accepted, 964 enrolled.
Tuition and fees (2003–04): $4654 (resident), $14,701 (nonresident). *Room and board:* $4500 (room only: $2500).
Financial Aid (All incoming freshmen): *Average need-based gift aid:* $3420. *Average non-need based aid:* $2068. *Average aid to full-time undergraduates:* $6273.
Athletic Department: *Director of Athletics:* Ken Bothof; Phone: 920-465-2145; Fax: 920-465-2652; E-mail: bothofk@uwgb.edu. *Sports Information Director:* Brian Nicol; Phone: 920-465-2498; E-mail: nicolb@uwgb.edu.

MEN'S COACHES

Basketball: Tod Kowalczyk; Phone: 920-465-2145; E-mail: kowalczt@uwgb.edu.
Cross Country: Mike Kline; Phone: 920-465-2145.
Diving: Laurie Miller; Phone: 920-465-2367.
Golf: Shaun Rezachek; Phone: 920-465-2145; E-mail: rezaches@uwgb.edu.
Soccer: Tom Poitras; Phone: 920-465-2092; E-mail: poitrast@uwgb.edu.
Swimming: Jim Merner; Phone: 920-465-2367; E-mail: mernerj@uwgb.edu.
Tennis: Dan Oliver; Phone: 920-465-2145; E-mail: oliverd@uwgb.edu.

WOMEN'S COACHES

Basketball: Kevin Borseth; Phone: 920-465-2145; E-mail: borsethk@uwgb.edu.
Cross Country: Mike Kline; Phone: 920-465-2145.
Diving: Laurie Miller; Phone: 920-465-2367.
Soccer: Quinn Ross; Phone: 920-465-2836; E-mail: rossq@uwgb.edu.
Softball: Susan Beeck; Phone: 920-465-2145; E-mail: beecks@uwgb.edu.
Swimming: Jim Merner; Phone: 920-465-2367; E-mail: mernerj@uwgb.edu.
Tennis: Karen Neuman; Phone: 920-465-2145; E-mail: neumank@uwgb.edu.
Volleyball: Debbie Kirch; Phone: 920-465-2573; E-mail: kirchd@uwgb.edu.

UNIVERSITY OF WISCONSIN–LA CROSSE
La Crosse, Wisconsin

Eagles ◆ NCAA III ◆ Wisconsin Athletic Conference ◆ http://www.uwlax.edu/

State-supported comprehensive, founded 1909, part of University of Wisconsin System
Coed, 8,100 undergraduate students, 93% full-time, 60% women, 40% men
Suburban 121-acre campus
Moderately difficult entrance level, 47% of applicants were admitted

Freshmen *Admission:* 6,376 applied, 3,357 were accepted, 1,509 enrolled. *Test scores:* SAT verbal scores over 500: 88%; SAT math scores over 500: 94%; SAT verbal scores over 600: 45%; SAT math scores over 600: 61%; SAT verbal scores over 700: 6%; SAT math scores over 700: 9%.
Tuition and fees (2003–04): $4741 (resident), $14,404 (nonresident). *Room and board:* $4050 (room only: $2200).
Financial Aid (All incoming freshmen): *Average need-based gift aid:* $1419. *Average non-need based aid:* $394. *Average aid to full-time undergraduates:* $4316.
Athletic Department: *Director of Athletics:* Joe Baker; Phone: 608-785-8616; Fax: 608-785-8674; E-mail: baker.jose@uwlax.edu. *Sports Information Director:* David Johnson; Phone: 608-785-8493; E-mail: johnson.dav2@uwlax.edu.

MEN'S COACHES
Baseball: George Williams; Phone: 608-785-6540; E-mail: williams.geor@uwlax.edu.
Basketball: Ken Koelbe; Phone: 608-785-8819; E-mail: koelbl.kenn@uwlax.edu.
Cheerleading: Gil Standridge; Phone: 608-785-5221; E-mail: standrid.gil@uwlax.edu.
Cross Country: Don Fritsch; Phone: 608-785-6548; E-mail: fritsch.dona@uwlax.edu.
Diving: Richard Pein; Phone: 608-785-8185; E-mail: pein.rich@uwlax.edu.
Football: Larry Terry; Phone: 608-785-8680; E-mail: terry.lawr@uwlax.edu.
Swimming: Richard Pein; Phone: 608-785-8185; E-mail: pein.rich@uwlax.edu.
Tennis: Bill Hehli; Phone: 608-785-8676; E-mail: hehli.will@uwlax.edu.
Track and Field: Mark Guthrie; Phone: 608-785-8679; E-mail: guthrie.mark@uwlax.edu.
Wrestling: Tim Fader; Phone: 608-785-6515; E-mail: fader.timo@uwlax.edu.

WOMEN'S COACHES
Basketball: Lois Heeren; Phone: 608-785-8618; E-mail: heeren.lois@uwlax.edu.
Cheerleading: Gil Standridge; Phone: 608-785-5221; E-mail: standrid.gil@uwlax.edu.
Cross Country: Pat Healy; Phone: 608-785-6531; E-mail: healy.patr@uwlax.edu.
Diving: Richard Pein; Phone: 608-785-8185; E-mail: pein.rich@uwlax.edu.
Gymnastics: Barbara Gibson; Phone: 608-785-8677; E-mail: gibson.barb@uwlax.edu.
Soccer: Sara Burton; Phone: 608-785-6534; E-mail: burton.sara@uwlax.edu.
Softball: Vicki Schull; Phone: 608-785-6536; E-mail: schull.vick@uwlax.edu.
Swimming: Richard Pein; Phone: 608-785-8185; E-mail: pein.rich@uwlax.edu.
Tennis: Bill Hehli; Phone: 608-785-8676; E-mail: hehli.will@uwlax.edu.
Track and Field: Pat Healy; Phone: 608-785-6531; E-mail: healy.patr@uwlax.edu.
Volleyball: Sheila Perkins; Phone: 608-785-8170; E-mail: perkins.shei@uwlax.edu.

UNIVERSITY OF WISCONSIN–MADISON
Madison, Wisconsin

Badgers ◆ NCAA I ◆ Big Ten Conference; Western Collegiate Hockey Conference ◆ http://www.wisc.edu/

State-supported university, founded 1848, part of University of Wisconsin System
Coed, 28,583 undergraduate students
Urban 1,050-acre campus with easy access to Milwaukee
Very difficult entrance level, 61% of applicants were admitted

Freshmen *Admission:* 21,335 applied, 12,931 were accepted. *Test scores:* SAT verbal scores over 500: 97%; SAT math scores over 500: 98%; SAT verbal scores over 600: 71%; SAT math scores over 600: 79%; SAT verbal scores over 700: 26%; SAT math scores over 700: 25%.
Tuition and fees (2003–04): $5140 (resident), $19,150 (nonresident). *Room and board:* $6130.
Financial Aid (All incoming freshmen): *Average need-based gift aid:* $5920. *Average non-need based aid:* $2632. *Average aid to full-time undergraduates:* $10,172.
Athletic Department: *Director of Athletics:* Pat Richter; Phone: 608-262-5068; Fax: 608-265-3036; E-mail: pat@athletics.wisc.edu. *Sports Information Director:* Justin Doherty; Phone: 608-262-1811; E-mail: jmd@athletics.wisc.edu.

MEN'S COACHES
Basketball: Bo Ryan; Phone: 608-262-4597.
Cheerleading: Josette Scheer; Phone: 608-262-6703; E-mail: jrs@athletics.wisc.edu.
Cross Country: Jerry Schumacher; Phone: 608-262-5729; E-mail: jhs@athletics.wisc.edu.
Diving: Josh Seykora; Phone: 608-262-4958; E-mail: js4@athletics.wisc.edu.
Football: Barry Alvarez; Phone: 608-262-1861.
Golf: Jim Schuman; Phone: 608-265-3114; E-mail: js6@athletics.wisc.edu.
Ice Hockey: Mike Eaves; Phone: 608-262-3932; E-mail: mge@athletics.wisc.edu.
Soccer: Jeff Rohrman; Phone: 608-262-7749; E-mail: jr2@athletics.wisc.edu.
Swimming: Eric Hansen; Phone: 608-262-3336; E-mail: ehansen@chem.wisc.edu.
Tennis: Pat Klingelhoets; Phone: 608-262-0997; E-mail: pxk@athletics.wisc.edu.
Track and Field: Ed Nuttycombe; Phone: 608-262-4397; E-mail: ehn@athletics.wisc.edu.
Wrestling: Barry Davis; Phone: 608-262-4399; E-mail: bad@athletics.wisc.edu.

WOMEN'S COACHES
Basketball: Lisa Stone; Phone: 608-262-5506; E-mail: lls@athletics.wisc.edu.
Cheerleading: Josette Scheer; Phone: 608-262-6703; E-mail: jrs@athletics.wisc.edu.
Cross Country: Peter Tegen; Phone: 608-262-5109; E-mail: pit@athletics.wisc.edu.
Diving: Josh Seykora; Phone: 608-262-4958; E-mail: js4@athletics.wisc.edu.
Golf: Todd Oehrlein; Phone: 608-265-3117; E-mail: tso@athletics.wisc.edu.
Soccer: Dean Duerst; Phone: 608-262-2974; E-mail: dmd@athletics.wisc.edu.
Softball: Karen Gallagher; Phone: 608-265-6152; E-mail: kpg@athletics.wisc.edu.
Swimming: Eric Hansen; Phone: 608-262-3336; E-mail: ehansen@chem.wisc.edu.
Tennis: Patti Henderson; Phone: 608-263-6304; E-mail: plh@athletics.wisc.edu.
Track and Field: Peter Tegen; Phone: 608-262-5109; E-mail: pit@athletics.wisc.edu.
Volleyball: Peter Waite; Phone: 608-263-5670; E-mail: wpw@athletics.wisc.edu.

UNIVERSITY OF WISCONSIN–MILWAUKEE

Milwaukee, Wisconsin

Panthers ◆ NCAA I ◆ Horizon League Conference ◆ http://www.uwm.edu/

State-supported university, founded 1956, part of University of Wisconsin System
Coed, 21,052 undergraduate students, 80% full-time, 55% women, 45% men
Urban 90-acre campus
Moderately difficult entrance level, 79% of applicants were admitted

Freshmen *Admission:* 9,918 applied, 7,881 were accepted, 3,855 enrolled. *Test scores:* SAT verbal scores over 500: 59%; SAT math scores over 500: 71%; SAT verbal scores over 600: 19%; SAT math scores over 600: 23%; SAT math scores over 700: 1%.
Tuition and fees (2003–04): $5107 (resident), $17,858 (nonresident). *Room and board:* $4320 (room only: $2540).
Financial Aid (All incoming freshmen): *Average need-based gift aid:* $1642. *Average non-need based aid:* $1481. *Average aid to full-time undergraduates:* $5170.
Athletic Department: *Director of Athletics:* Bud Haidet; Phone: 414-229-5669; Fax: 414-229-6759; E-mail: haidet@uwm.edu. *Sports Information Director:* Kevin O'Connor; Phone: 414-229-5674; E-mail: kjoc@uwm.edu.

MEN'S COACHES

Baseball: Jerry Augustine; Phone: 414-229-5670.
Basketball: Bruce Pearl; Phone: 414-229-3738; E-mail: bpearl@uwm.edu.
Cheerleading: Mary Ann Kelling; Phone: 414-229-6433; E-mail: kelling@uwm.edu.
Cross Country: Pete Corfield; Phone: 414-229-5149; E-mail: knutcor@aol.com.
Diving: Dave Clark; Phone: 414-229-5153; E-mail: h2o@uwm.edu.
Soccer: Louis Bennett; Phone: 414-229-5377; E-mail: loobe@uwm.edu.
Swimming: Dave Clark; Phone: 414-229-5153; E-mail: h2o@uwm.edu.
Track and Field: Pete Corfield; Phone: 414-229-5149; E-mail: knutcor@aol.com.

WOMEN'S COACHES

Basketball: Sandy Botham; Phone: 414-229-4405; E-mail: sbotham@uwm.edu.
Cheerleading: Mary Ann Kelling; Phone: 414-229-6433; E-mail: kelling@uwm.edu.
Cross Country: Pete Corfield; Phone: 414-229-5149; E-mail: knutcor@aol.com.
Diving: Dave Clark; Phone: 414-229-5153; E-mail: h2o@uwm.edu.
Soccer: Mike Moynihan; Phone: 414-229-4554; E-mail: moynihan@uwm.edu.
Swimming: Dave Clark; Phone: 414-229-5153; E-mail: h2o@uwm.edu.
Tennis: Erika Wentz; Phone: 414-229-5523; E-mail: emwentz@uwm.edu.
Track and Field: Pete Corfield; Phone: 414-229-5149; E-mail: knutcor@aol.com.
Volleyball: Kathy Lizau; Phone: 414-229-3739; E-mail: kclitzau@uwm.edu.

UNIVERSITY OF WISCONSIN–OSHKOSH

Oshkosh, Wisconsin

Titans ◆ NCAA III ◆ Wisconsin Athletic Conference ◆ http://www.uwosh.edu/

State-supported comprehensive, founded 1871, part of University of Wisconsin System
Coed, 9,804 undergraduate students, 86% full-time, 60% women, 40% men
Suburban 192-acre campus with easy access to Milwaukee
Moderately difficult entrance level, 44% of applicants were admitted

Freshmen *Admission:* 5,395 applied, 2,553 were accepted, 1,780 enrolled.

Tuition and fees (2004–05): $4044 (resident), $14,320 (nonresident). *Room and board:* $4100 (room only: $2278).
Financial Aid (All incoming freshmen): *Average need-based gift aid:* $2200. *Average non-need based aid:* $2511. *Average aid to full-time undergraduates:* $4876.
Athletic Department: *Director of Athletics:* Allen Ackerman; Phone: 920-424-1034; Fax: 920-424-7445; E-mail: ackerman@uwosh.edu. *Sports Information Director:* Kennan Timm; Phone: 920-424-0365; E-mail: timmk@uwosh.edu.

MEN'S COACHES

Baseball: Tom Lechnir; Phone: 920-424-0374; E-mail: lechnir@uwosh.edu.
Basketball: Ted Van Dellen; Phone: 920-424-2211; E-mail: vandelle@uwosh.edu.
Cheerleading: Darcell Salm; Phone: 920-424-1034; E-mail: darcsalm@csd.k12.wi.us.
Cross Country: John Zupanc; Phone: 920-424-7140; E-mail: zupanc@uwosh.edu.
Diving: Paula Struwing; Phone: 920-424-0385; E-mail: struwing@uwosh.edu.
Football: Phil Meyer; Phone: 920-424-3121; E-mail: meyer@uwosh.edu.
Soccer: Toby Bares; Phone: 920-424-1282; E-mail: bares@uwosh.edu.
Swimming: Paula Struwing; Phone: 920-424-0385; E-mail: struwing@uwosh.edu.
Tennis: Steve Francour; Phone: 920-424-1203; E-mail: francour@uwosh.edu.
Track and Field: Bruce Coleman; Phone: 920-424-1226; E-mail: coleman@uwosh.edu.
Wrestling: Larry Marchionda; Phone: 920-424-1201; E-mail: marchion@uwosh.edu.

WOMEN'S COACHES

Basketball: Pam Ruder; Phone: 920-424-7132; E-mail: ruder@uwosh.edu.
Cheerleading: Darcell Salm; Phone: 920-424-1034; E-mail: darcsalm@csd.k12.wi.us.
Cross Country: Deb Vercauteren; Phone: 920-424-1384; E-mail: vercaute@uwosh.edu.
Diving: Paula Struwing; Phone: 920-424-0385; E-mail: struwing@uwosh.edu.
Golf: Tim Gaubatz; Phone: 920-424-1225; E-mail: gaubatz@uwosh.edu.
Gymnastics: Nadalie Walsh; Phone: 920-424-7299; E-mail: walsh@uwosh.edu.
Soccer: Erin O'Driscoll; Phone: 920-424-1312; E-mail: ebod11@hotmail.com.
Softball: Amy Smith; Phone: 920-424-3236; E-mail: sipp30@hotmail.com.
Swimming: Paula Struwing; Phone: 920-424-0385; E-mail: struwing@uwosh.edu.
Tennis: Steve Francour; Phone: 920-424-1203; E-mail: francour@uwosh.edu.
Track and Field: Deb Vercauteren; Phone: 920-424-1384; E-mail: vercaute@uwosh.edu.
Volleyball: Marty Peterson; Phone: 920-424-1392; E-mail: petersen@uwosh.edu.

UNIVERSITY OF WISCONSIN–PARKSIDE

Kenosha, Wisconsin

Rangers ◆ NCAA II ◆ Great Lakes Valley Conference ◆ http://www.uwp.edu/

State-supported comprehensive, founded 1968, part of University of Wisconsin System
Coed, 4,939 undergraduate students, 71% full-time, 57% women, 43% men
Suburban 700-acre campus with easy access to Chicago and Milwaukee
Moderately difficult entrance level, 6% of applicants were admitted

Freshmen *Admission:* 2,096 applied, 1,262 were accepted, 975 enrolled.
Tuition and fees (2004–05): $3532 (resident), $13,578 (nonresident). *Room and board:* $5056 (room only: $3156).

Financial Aid (All incoming freshmen): *Average need-based gift aid: $4055. Average non-need based aid: $1770. Average aid to full-time undergraduates: $5175.*
Athletic Department: *Director of Athletics:* David Williams; Phone: 262-595-2485; Fax: 262-595-2225; E-mail: williamsd@uwp.edu. *Sports Information Director:* Steve Kratochvil; Phone: 262-595-2045; E-mail: kratochv@uwp.edu.

MEN'S COACHES
Baseball: Tracey Archuletta; Phone: 262-595-2317; E-mail: archulet@uwp.edu.
Basketball: Luke Reigel; Phone: 262-595-2468; E-mail: reigel@uwp.edu.
Cross Country: Lucian Rosa; Phone: 262-595-3225; E-mail: rosa@uwp.edu.
Golf: Mark Olsen; Phone: 262-595-3357; E-mail: mark.olsen@uwp.edu.
Soccer: Rick Kilps; Phone: 262-595-2257; E-mail: kilps@uwp.edu.
Track and Field: Lucian Rosa; Phone: 262-595-3225; E-mail: rosa@uwp.edu.
Wrestling: Jim Koch; Phone: 262-595-2267; E-mail: koch@uwp.edu.

WOMEN'S COACHES
Basketball: Jenny Knight; Phone: 262-595-3345; E-mail: knightj@uwp.edu.
Cross Country: Mike Dewitt; Phone: 262-595-2405; E-mail: dewitt@uwp.edu.
Soccer: Troy Fabiano; Phone: 262-595-3347; E-mail: fabiano@uwp.edu.
Softball: Laura Fillipp; Phone: 262-595-2412; E-mail: fillipp@uwp.edu.
Track and Field: Mike Dewitt; Phone: 262-595-2405; E-mail: dewitt@uwp.edu.
Volleyball: Nichole Roethig; Phone: 262-595-2127; E-mail: roethig@uwp.edu.

UNIVERSITY OF WISCONSIN–PLATTEVILLE
Platteville, Wisconsin

Pioneers ◆ NCAA III ◆ Wisconsin Athletic Conference
◆ http://www.uwplatt.edu/

State-supported comprehensive, founded 1866, part of University of Wisconsin System
Coed, 5,541 undergraduate students, 91% full-time, 39% women, 61% men
Small-town 380-acre campus
Moderately difficult entrance level, 79% of applicants were admitted

Freshmen *Admission:* 2,789 applied, 2,229 were accepted, 1,103 enrolled.
Tuition and fees (2003–04): $4254 (resident), $14,300 (nonresident).
Room and board: $4196 (room only: $2120).
Financial Aid (All incoming freshmen): *Average need-based gift aid: $3660. Average non-need based aid: $1459. Average aid to full-time undergraduates: $5809.*
Athletic Department: *Director of Athletics:* Mark Molesworth; Phone: 608-342-1567; Fax: 608-342-1576; E-mail: moleswom@uwplatt.edu. *Sports Information Director:* Paul Erickson; Phone: 608-342-1574; E-mail: ericksop@uwplatt.edu.

MEN'S COACHES
Baseball: Jamie Sailors; Phone: 608-342-1843; E-mail: sailorsj@uwplatt.edu.
Basketball: Paul Combs; Phone: 608-342-1278; E-mail: combsp@uwplatt.edu.
Cheerleading: Renee Ringgenberg; Phone: 608-342-1573; E-mail: athletics@uwplatt.edu.
Cross Country: Tom Antczak; Phone: 608-342-1504; E-mail: antczak@uwplatt.edu.
Football: Mike Emendorfer; Phone: 608-342-1801; E-mail: emendorm@uwplatt.edu.
Soccer: Chris Bianchi; Phone: 608-342-1343; E-mail: bianchic@uwplatt.edu.
Track and Field: Jim Nickasch; Phone: 608-342-1263; E-mail: nickascj@uwplatt.edu.
Wrestling: Chris Walter; Phone: 608-342-1572; E-mail: walterc@uwplatt.edu.

WOMEN'S COACHES
Basketball: Denise Dunbar; Phone: 608-342-1477; E-mail: dunbarde@uwplatt.edu.
Cheerleading: Renee Ringgenberg; Phone: 608-342-1573; E-mail: athletics@uwplatt.edu.
Cross Country: Tom Antczak; Phone: 608-342-1504; E-mail: antczak@uwplatt.edu.
Golf: Pete Reif; Phone: 608-348-4653; E-mail: reifp@uwplatt.edu.
Soccer: Chris Bianchi; Phone: 608-342-1343; E-mail: bianchic@uwplatt.edu.
Softball: Janet James; Phone: 608-342-1677; E-mail: jamesj@uwplatt.edu.
Track and Field: Jim Nickasch; Phone: 608-342-1263; E-mail: nickascj@uwplatt.edu.
Volleyball: Deb Schulman; Phone: 608-342-1255; E-mail: schulman@uwplatt.edu.

UNIVERSITY OF WISCONSIN–RIVER FALLS
River Falls, Wisconsin

Falcons ◆ NCAA III ◆ Northern Collegiate Hockey Conference; Wisconsin Athletic Conference
◆ http://www.uwrf.edu/

State-supported comprehensive, founded 1874, part of University of Wisconsin System
Coed, 5,413 undergraduate students, 93% full-time, 61% women, 39% men
Suburban 225-acre campus with easy access to Minneapolis–St. Paul
Moderately difficult entrance level, 76% of applicants were admitted

Freshmen *Admission:* 2,786 applied, 2,108 were accepted, 1,227 enrolled.
Tuition and fees (2003–04): $4450 (resident), $14,496 (nonresident).
Room and board: $3968 (room only: $2248).
Financial Aid (All incoming freshmen): *Average need-based gift aid: $1777. Average non-need based aid: $3035. Average aid to full-time undergraduates: $3764.*
Athletic Department: *Director of Athletics:* Rick Bowen; Phone: 715-425-3246; Fax: 715-425-3696; E-mail: rick.h.bowen@uwrf.edu. *Sports Information Director:* Jim Thies; Phone: 715-425-3846; E-mail: james.g.thies@uwrf.edu.

MEN'S COACHES
Basketball: Rick Bowen; Phone: 715-425-3726; E-mail: rick.h.bowen@uwrf.edu.
Cross Country: Don Glover; Phone: 715-425-0705; E-mail: drglover@ties.k12.mn.us.
Diving: Bill Henderson; Phone: 715-425-0636; E-mail: william.henderson@uwrf.edu.
Football: John O'Grady; Phone: 715-425-3135; E-mail: john.f.ogrady@uwrf.edu.
Ice Hockey: Steve Freeman; Phone: 715-425-3252; E-mail: steven.c.freeman@uwrf.edu.
Swimming: Bill Henderson; Phone: 715-425-0636; E-mail: william.henderson@uwrf.edu.
Track and Field: Don Glover; Phone: 715-425-3241; E-mail: drglover@ties.k12.mn.us.

WOMEN'S COACHES
Basketball: Cindy Hovet; Phone: 715-425-3250; E-mail: cindy.hovet@uwrf.edu.
Cross Country: Don Glover; Phone: 715-425-0705; E-mail: drglover@ties.k12.mn.us.
Diving: Bill Henderson; Phone: 715-425-0636; E-mail: william.henderson@uwrf.edu.
Golf: Jeff Berkhof; Phone: 715-425-3726; E-mail: jeffrey.d.berkhof@uwrf.edu.
Soccer: Sean McKuras; Phone: 715-425-3829; E-mail: sean.m.mckuras@uwrf.edu.
Softball: Faye Perkins; Phone: 715-425-3966; E-mail: faye.j.perkins@uwrf.edu.
Swimming: Bill Henderson; Phone: 715-425-0636; E-mail: william.henderson@uwrf.edu.

University of Wisconsin–River Falls *(continued)*

Tennis: Lee Lueck; Phone: 715-425-3521; E-mail: leland.lueck@uwrf. edu.

Track and Field: Don Glover; Phone: 715-425-3241; E-mail: drglover@ ties.k12.mn.us.

Volleyball: Patti Ford; Phone: 715-425-3244; E-mail: patricia.kay.ford@ uwrf.edu.

UNIVERSITY OF WISCONSIN–STEVENS POINT

Stevens Point, Wisconsin

Pointers ◆ NCAA III ◆ Northern Collegiate Hockey Conference; Wisconsin Athletic Conference ◆ http://www.uwsp.edu/

State-supported comprehensive, founded 1894, part of University of Wisconsin System

Coed, 8,503 undergraduate students, 91% full-time, 56% women, 44% men

Small-town 335-acre campus

Moderately difficult entrance level, 70% of applicants were admitted

Freshmen *Admission:* 4,621 applied, 3,484 were accepted, 1,506 enrolled. *Test scores:* SAT verbal scores over 500: 92%; SAT math scores over 500: 84%; SAT verbal scores over 600: 36%; SAT math scores over 600: 60%; SAT verbal scores over 700: 12%; SAT math scores over 700: 4%.

Tuition and fees (2003–04): $4148 (resident), $14,195 (nonresident). *Room and board:* $3964 (room only: $2324).

Financial Aid (All incoming freshmen): *Average need-based gift aid:* $3834. *Average non-need based aid:* $1964. *Average aid to full-time undergraduates:* $4894.

Athletic Department: *Director of Athletics:* Frank O'Brien; Phone: 715-346-3888; Fax: 715-346-4655; E-mail: fobrien@uwsp.edu. *Sports Information Director:* Jim Strick; Phone: 715-346-2840; E-mail: jstrick@ uwsp.edu.

MEN'S COACHES

Baseball: Pat Bloom; Phone: 715-346-4412; E-mail: pbloom@uwsp. edu.

Basketball: Jack Bennett; Phone: 715-346-4025; E-mail: jbennett@ uwsp.edu.

Cross Country: Rick Witt; Phone: 715-346-3677; E-mail: rwitt@uwsp. edu.

Diving: Alan Boelk; Phone: 715-346-2200; E-mail: aboelk@uwsp.edu.

Football: John Miech; Phone: 715-346-3758; E-mail: jmiech@uwsp.edu.

Ice Hockey: Joe Baldarotta; Phone: 715-346-3332; E-mail: jbaldaro@ uwsp.edu.

Swimming: Alan Boelk; Phone: 715-346-2200; E-mail: aboelk@uwsp. edu.

Track and Field: Rick Witt; Phone: 715-346-3677; E-mail: rwitt@uwsp. edu.

Wrestling: Johnny Johnson; Phone: 715-346-4184; E-mail: jjohnson@ uwsp.edu.

WOMEN'S COACHES

Basketball: Shirley Egner; Phone: 715-346-3397; E-mail: segner@uwsp. edu.

Cross Country: Len Hill; Phone: 715-346-4415; E-mail: lhill@uwsp.edu.

Diving: Alan Boelk; Phone: 715-346-2200; E-mail: aboelk@uwsp.edu.

Golf: Mike Okray; Phone: 715-346-3620; E-mail: mokray@uwsp.edu.

Soccer: Sheila Miech; Phone: 715-346-2462; E-mail: smiech@uwsp. edu.

Softball: Kelly Erickson; Phone: 715-346-4277; E-mail: kerickso@uwsp. edu.

Swimming: Alan Boelk; Phone: 715-346-2200; E-mail: aboelk@uwsp. edu.

Tennis: Karlyn Jakusz; Phone: 715-346-4716; E-mail: kjakusz@uwsp. edu.

Track and Field: Len Hill; Phone: 715-346-4415; E-mail: lhill@uwsp.edu.

Volleyball: Stacy White; Phone: 715-346-2151; E-mail: swhite@uwsp. edu.

UNIVERSITY OF WISCONSIN–STOUT

Menomonie, Wisconsin

Blue Devils ◆ NCAA III ◆ Wisconsin Athletic Conference ◆ http://www.uwstout.edu/

State-supported comprehensive, founded 1891, part of University of Wisconsin System

Coed, 7,101 undergraduate students, 90% full-time, 49% women, 51% men

Small-town 120-acre campus with easy access to Minneapolis–St. Paul

Moderately difficult entrance level, 67% of applicants were admitted

Freshmen *Admission:* 3,876 applied, 2,576 were accepted, 1,275 enrolled. *Test scores:* SAT verbal scores over 500: 66%; SAT math scores over 500: 72%; SAT verbal scores over 600: 14%; SAT math scores over 600: 19%.

Tuition and fees (2003–04): $5680 (resident), $16,016 (nonresident). *Room and board:* $4038 (room only: $2292).

Financial Aid (All incoming freshmen): *Average need-based gift aid:* $4087. *Average non-need based aid:* $1251. *Average aid to full-time undergraduates:* $6336.

Athletic Department: *Director of Athletics:* Steve Terry; Phone: 715-232-2161; Fax: 715-232-1684; E-mail: terrys@uwstout.edu. *Sports Information Director:* Layne Pitt; Phone: 715-232-2275; E-mail: pittl@ uwstout.edu.

MEN'S COACHES

Baseball: Craig Walter; Phone: 715-232-1459; E-mail: walterc@ uwstout.edu.

Basketball: Ed Andrist; Phone: 715-232-1162; E-mail: andriste@ uwstout.edu.

Cheerleading: Jeff Richards; Phone: 715-232-2118; E-mail: richardsj@ uwstout.edu.

Cross Country: Josh Buchholtz; Phone: 715-232-3491; E-mail: buchholtzjos@uwstout.edu.

Football: Todd Strop; Phone: 715-232-1424; E-mail: stropt@uwstout. edu.

Ice Hockey: Terry Watkins; Phone: 715-232-1258; E-mail: watkinsd@ uwstout.edu.

Track and Field: Josh Buchholtz; Phone: 715-232-3491; E-mail: buchholtzjos@uwstout.edu.

WOMEN'S COACHES

Basketball: Mark Thomas; Phone: 715-232-2465; E-mail: thomasm@ uwstout.edu.

Cheerleading: Jeff Richards; Phone: 715-232-2118; E-mail: richardsj@ uwstout.edu.

Cross Country: Joe Harlan; Phone: 715-232-5243; E-mail: harlanj@ uwstout.edu.

Gymnastics: Jeff Richards; Phone: 715-232-2118; E-mail: richardsj@ uwstout.edu.

Soccer: David Morris; Phone: 715-232-1312; E-mail: morrisd@ uwstout.edu.

Softball: Chris Stainer; Phone: 715-232-1336; E-mail: stainerc@ uwstout.edu.

Tennis: Mark Noll; Phone: 715-232-2106; E-mail: nollma@uwstout. edu.

Track and Field: Joe Harlan; Phone: 715-232-5243; E-mail: harlanj@ uwstout.edu.

Volleyball: Jim Joliff; Phone: 715-232-1689; E-mail: jolliffj@uwstout. edu.

UNIVERSITY OF WISCONSIN–SUPERIOR

Superior, Wisconsin

Yellow Jackets ◆ NCAA III ◆ Northern Collegiate Hockey Conference; Wisconsin Athletic Conference

◆ http://www.uwsuper.edu/

State-supported comprehensive, founded 1893, part of University of Wisconsin System

Coed, 2,530 undergraduate students, 77% full-time, 59% women, 41% men

Small-town 230-acre campus

Moderately difficult entrance level, 72% of applicants were admitted

Freshmen *Admission:* 869 applied, 673 were accepted, 352 enrolled. *Test scores:* SAT verbal scores over 500: 50%; SAT math scores over 500: 66%; SAT math scores over 600: 33%.

Tuition and fees (2003–04): $4276 (resident), $14,322 (nonresident). *Room and board:* $4246 (room only: $2406).

Financial Aid (All incoming freshmen): *Average need-based gift aid:* $4376. *Average non-need based aid:* $1657. *Average aid to full-time undergraduates:* $7069.

Athletic Department: *Director of Athletics:* Steve Nelson; Phone: 715-395-4693; Fax: 715-394-8110; E-mail: snelson@uwsuper.edu. *Sports Information Director:* Steve Kirk; Phone: 715-395-4671; E-mail: skirk@uwsuper.edu.

MEN'S COACHES

Baseball: Chris Vito; Phone: 715-395-4671; E-mail: cvito@uwsuper.edu.

Basketball: Jeff Kaminsky; Phone: 715-395-4619; E-mail: jkaminsk@uwsuper.edu.

Cheerleading: Susie Bednar; Phone: 715-395-4601; E-mail: sbednar@uwsuper.edu.

Cross Country: Paul Nisius; Phone: 715-395-4601; E-mail: pnisius@uwsuper.edu.

Ice Hockey: Dan Stauber; Phone: 715-394-8362; E-mail: dstauber@uwsuper.edu.

Soccer: Chris Perez; Phone: 715-395-4663; E-mail: cperez@uwsuper.edu.

Track and Field: Paul Nisius; Phone: 715-395-4601; E-mail: pnisius@uwsuper.edu.

WOMEN'S COACHES

Basketball: Sandy Eilertsen; Phone: 715-395-4672; E-mail: seilerts@uwsuper.edu.

Cheerleading: Susie Bednar; Phone: 715-395-4601; E-mail: sbednar@uwsuper.edu.

Cross Country: Paul Nisius; Phone: 715-395-4601; E-mail: pnisius@uwsuper.edu.

Golf: Roger Plachta; Phone: 715-395-4622; E-mail: rplachta@uwsuper.edu.

Soccer: Chris Perez; Phone: 715-395-4663; E-mail: cperez@uwsuper.edu.

Softball: Roger Plachta; Phone: 715-395-4622; E-mail: rplachta@uwsuper.edu.

Track and Field: Paul Nisius; Phone: 715-395-4601; E-mail: pnisius@uwsuper.edu.

Volleyball: Lynne Deadrick; Phone: 715-395-4612; E-mail: ldeadric@uwsuper.edu.

UNIVERSITY OF WISCONSIN–WHITEWATER

Whitewater, Wisconsin

Warhawks ◆ NCAA III ◆ Wisconsin Athletic Conference ◆ http://www.uww.edu/

State-supported comprehensive, founded 1868, part of University of Wisconsin System

Coed, 9,429 undergraduate students, 92% full-time, 53% women, 47% men

Small-town 385-acre campus with easy access to Milwaukee

Moderately difficult entrance level, 68% of applicants were admitted

Freshmen *Admission:* 5,639 applied, 3,821 were accepted, 1,832 enrolled.

Tuition and fees (2003–04): $4934 (resident), $14,980 (nonresident). *Room and board:* $3742 (room only: $2232).

Financial Aid (All incoming freshmen): *Average non-need based aid:* $1472. *Average aid to full-time undergraduates:* $5692.

MEN'S COACHES

Baseball: John Vodenlich; Phone: 262-472-1420; E-mail: vodenlij@mail.uww.edu.

Basketball: Pat Miller; Phone: 262-472-1146; E-mail: millerp@mail.uww.edu.

Cross Country: Jeff Miller; Phone: 262-472-5648; E-mail: millerjr@mail.uww.edu.

Football: Bob Berezowitz; Phone: 262-472-1453; E-mail: berezowr@mail.uww.edu.

Soccer: Greghen Schel; Phone: 262-472-1153; E-mail: henscheg@mail.uww.edu.

Swimming: Debbie Thompson; Phone: 262-472-6235; E-mail: thompsod@mail.uww.edu.

Tennis: Frank Barnes; Phone: 262-472-6201; E-mail: barnesf@mail.uww.edu.

Track and Field: Darren Scheider; Phone: 262-472-1367; E-mail: schneidd@mail.uww.edu.

Wrestling: Willie Myers; Phone: 262-472-1867; E-mail: myersw@mail.uww.edu.

WOMEN'S COACHES

Basketball: Keri Carollo; Phone: 262-472-5782; E-mail: carollok@mail.uww.edu.

Cross Country: Jeff Miller; Phone: 262-472-5648; E-mail: millerjr@mail.uww.edu.

Golf: Brett Weber; Phone: 262-472-5678; E-mail: weberb@mail.uww.edu.

Gymnastics: Jennifer White; Phone: 262-472-5647; E-mail: whitej@mail.uww.edu.

Soccer: Greghen Schel; Phone: 262-472-1153; E-mail: henscheg@mail.uww.edu.

Softball: Brenda Volk; Phone: 262-472-1155; E-mail: volkb@mail.uww.edu.

Swimming: Debbie Thompson; Phone: 262-472-6235; E-mail: thompsod@mail.uww.edu.

Tennis: Debbie Burgess; Phone: 262-472-1461; E-mail: burgessd@mail.uww.edu.

Track and Field: Darren Scheider; Phone: 262-472-1367; E-mail: schneidd@mail.uww.edu.

Volleyball: Kris Russell; Phone: 262-472-5645; E-mail: russellk@mail.uww.edu.

UNIVERSITY OF WYOMING

Laramie, Wyoming

Cowboys ◆ NCAA I ◆ Mountain West Conference ◆ http://www.uwyo.edu/

State-supported university, founded 1886

Coed, 9,385 undergraduate students, 81% full-time, 53% women, 47% men

Small-town 785-acre campus

Moderately difficult entrance level, 93% of applicants were admitted

Freshmen *Admission:* 2,948 applied, 2,796 were accepted, 1,416 enrolled. *Test scores:* SAT verbal scores over 500: 66%; SAT math scores

University of Wyoming *(continued)*

over 500: 72%; SAT verbal scores over 600: 24%; SAT math scores over 600: 30%; SAT verbal scores over 700: 3%; SAT math scores over 700: 5%.

Tuition and fees (2003–04): $3090 (resident), $8940 (nonresident). *Room and board:* $5546 (room only: $2372).

Financial Aid (All incoming freshmen): *Average need-based gift aid:* $3823. *Average non-need based aid:* $1955. *Average aid to full-time undergraduates:* $7698.

Athletic Department: *Director of Athletics:* Gary Barta; Phone: 307-766-2292; Fax: 307-766-5414; E-mail: gbarta@uwyo.edu. *Sports Information Director:* Kevin McKinney; Phone: 307-766-2256; E-mail: kevinm@uwyo.edu.

MEN'S COACHES

Basketball: Steve McClain; Phone: 307-766-5144; E-mail: ksmhoops@uwyo.edu.

Cheerleading: Traci Parks; Phone: 307-766-6247; E-mail: truce@uwyo.edu.

Cross Country: Randy Cole; Phone: 307-766-5364; E-mail: coler@uwyo.edu.

Diving: Russ Dekker; Phone: 307-766-2441; E-mail: rdekker@uwyo.edu.

Football: Joe Glenn; Phone: 307-766-3155; E-mail: jglenn@uwyo.edu.

Golf: Joe Jensen; Phone: 307-766-3111; E-mail: joej@uwyo.edu.

Swimming: Tom Johnson; Phone: 307-766-6265; E-mail: tomj@uwyo.edu.

Track and Field: Don Yentes; Phone: 307-766-5365; E-mail: dyentes@uwyo.edu.

Wrestling: Steve Suder; Phone: 307-766-5382; E-mail: hiplains@uwyo.edu.

WOMEN'S COACHES

Basketball: Joe Legerski; Phone: 307-766-6291; E-mail: legerski@uwyo.edu.

Cheerleading: Traci Parks; Phone: 307-766-6247; E-mail: truce@uwyo.edu.

Cross Country: Randy Cole; Phone: 307-766-5364; E-mail: coler@uwyo.edu.

Diving: Russ Dekker; Phone: 307-766-2441; E-mail: rdekker@uwyo.edu.

Golf: Jill Rettinger; Phone: 307-766-5369; E-mail: undapar@uwyo.edu.

Soccer: Anne Moore; Phone: 307-766-5508; E-mail: abmoore@uwyo.edu.

Swimming: Tom Johnson; Phone: 307-766-6265; E-mail: tomj@uwyo.edu.

Tennis: Pam Wildt; Phone: 307-766-5065; E-mail: pwildt@uwyo.edu.

Track and Field: Don Yentes; Phone: 307-766-5365; E-mail: dyentes@uwyo.edu.

Volleyball: Jim Barnes; Phone: 307-766-4941; E-mail: jbarnes@uwyo.edu.

UPPER IOWA UNIVERSITY
Fayette, Iowa

Peacocks ◆ NCAA III ◆ Iowa Athletic Conference ◆ http://www.uiu.edu/

Independent comprehensive, founded 1857
Coed, 683 undergraduate students, 92% full-time, 40% women, 60% men
Rural 80-acre campus
Moderately difficult entrance level, 56% of applicants were admitted

Freshmen *Admission:* 853 applied, 479 were accepted, 146 enrolled.
Tuition and fees (2004–05): $16,556 (full-time). *Room and board:* $5272 (room only: $2188).
Athletic Department: *Director of Athletics:* Gil Cloud; Phone: 563-425-5293; Fax: 563-425-5334; E-mail: cloudg@uiu.edu. *Sports Information Director:* Brian Thiessen; Phone: 563-425-5307; E-mail: thiessenb@uiu.edu.

MEN'S COACHES

Baseball: Mark Danker; Phone: 563-425-5290; E-mail: dankerm@uiu.edu.

Basketball: Dave Martin; Phone: 563-425-5294; E-mail: martind@uiu.edu.

Cheerleading: Marie Summers; Phone: 563-425-5668; E-mail: summersm@uiu.edu.

Cross Country: Dawn Abernathy-Fassbinder; Phone: 563-425-5705; E-mail: abernathyd@uiu.edu.

Football: Courtney Messingham; Phone: 563-425-5313; E-mail: messinghamc@uiu.edu.

Golf: Chad Markuson; Phone: 563-425-5820; E-mail: markusonc@uiu.edu.

Soccer: Troy Otradovec; Phone: 563-425-5382; E-mail: otradovect@uiu.edu.

Tennis: Chad Leonard; Phone: 563-425-5369; E-mail: leonardc@uiu.edu.

Track and Field: Dawn Abernathy-Fassbinder; Phone: 563-425-5705; E-mail: abernathyd@uiu.edu.

Wrestling: Heath Grimm; Phone: 563-425-5291; E-mail: grimmh@uiu.edu.

WOMEN'S COACHES

Basketball: Bill Wilson; Phone: 563-425-5292; E-mail: wilsonb@uiu.edu.

Cheerleading: Marie Summers; Phone: 563-425-5668; E-mail: summersm@uiu.edu.

Cross Country: Dawn Abernathy-Fassbinder; Phone: 563-425-5705; E-mail: abernathyd@uiu.edu.

Golf: Chad Markuson; Phone: 563-425-5820; E-mail: markusonc@uiu.edu.

Soccer: Chad Leonard; Phone: 563-425-5369; E-mail: leonardc@uiu.edu.

Softball: Brent Kuker; Phone: 563-425-5370; E-mail: kukerb@uiu.edu.

Tennis: Teri Hepler; Phone: 563-425-5295; E-mail: heplert@uiu.edu.

Track and Field: Dawn Abernathy-Fassbinder; Phone: 563-425-5705; E-mail: abernathyd@uiu.edu.

Volleyball: Julia Fielder; Phone: 563-425-5763; E-mail: fielderj@uiu.edu.

URBANA UNIVERSITY
Urbana, Ohio

Blue Knights ◆ NAIA ◆ American Mideast Conference; Mid-States Football Conference ◆ http://www.urbana.edu/

Independent comprehensive, founded 1850, affiliated with Church of the New Jerusalem
Coed, 1,441 undergraduate students, 61% full-time, 55% women, 45% men
Small-town 128-acre campus with easy access to Columbus and Dayton
Moderately difficult entrance level, 55% of applicants were admitted

Freshmen *Admission:* 538 applied, 312 were accepted, 261 enrolled.
Tuition and fees (2004–05): $14,220 (full-time). *Room and board:* $5680 (room only: $1920).
Financial Aid (All incoming freshmen): *Average need-based gift aid:* $1804. *Average aid to full-time undergraduates:* $11,342.
Athletic Department: *Director of Athletics:* Bill Blazer; Phone: 937-448-1391; Fax: 937-484-1389; E-mail: bblazer@urbana.edu. *Sports Information Director:* Krystal Kessler; Phone: 937-484-1320; E-mail: sid@urbana.edu.

MEN'S COACHES

Baseball: Scott Spriggs; Phone: 937-484-1351; E-mail: spriggs@urbana.edu.

Basketball: Paul Bryant; Phone: 937-484-1393; E-mail: pbryant@urbana.edu.

Football: Todd Murgatroyd; Phone: 937-484-1325; E-mail: toddm@urbana.edu.

Golf: Bill Blazer; Phone: 937-484-1391; E-mail: bblazer@urbana.edu.

Soccer: Jim Wendling; Phone: 937-484-1385; E-mail: athletics@urbana.edu.

WOMEN'S COACHES

Basketball: Rod Phillips; Phone: 937-484-1392; E-mail: rphillilps@urbana.edu.

Soccer: Jim Wendling; Phone: 937-484-1385; E-mail: athletics@urbana.edu.

Softball: Rod Phillips; Phone: 937-484-1392; E-mail: rphillilps@urbana.edu.

Volleyball: Jeremy Wise; Phone: 937-484-1384; E-mail: jerm50@hotmail.com.

URSINUS COLLEGE
Collegeville, Pennsylvania

Bears ◆ NCAA III ◆ Centennial Conference
◆ http://www.ursinus.edu/

Independent 4-year, founded 1869
Coed, 1,485 undergraduate students, 99% full-time, 54% women, 46% men
Suburban 168-acre campus with easy access to Philadelphia
Very difficult entrance level, 71% of applicants were admitted

Freshmen *Admission:* 1,775 applied, 1,322 were accepted, 454 enrolled. *Test scores:* SAT verbal scores over 500: 93%; SAT math scores over 500: 91%; SAT verbal scores over 600: 52%; SAT math scores over 600: 57%; SAT verbal scores over 700: 12%; SAT math scores over 700: 12%.
Tuition and fees (2003–04): $27,500 (full-time). *Room and board:* $6900.
Financial Aid (All incoming freshmen): *Average need-based gift aid:* $17,048. *Average non-need based aid:* $11,500. *Average aid to full-time undergraduates:* $22,606.
Athletic Department: *Director of Athletics:* Brian Thomas; Phone: 610-409-3611; Fax: 610-409-3620; E-mail: bthomas@ursinus.edu. *Sports Information Director:* Bill Stiles; Phone: 610-409-3612; E-mail: bstiles@ursinus.edu.

MEN'S COACHES
Baseball: Brian Thomas; Phone: 610-409-3606; E-mail: bthomas@ursinus.edu.
Basketball: Kevin Small; Phone: 610-409-3606; E-mail: ksmall@ursinus.edu.
Cross Country: Neil Schafer; Phone: 610-409-3606; E-mail: nschafer@ursinus.edu.
Football: Peter Gallagher; Phone: 610-409-3606; E-mail: pgallagher@ursinus.edu.
Golf: Ted McKenzie; Phone: 610-409-3606; E-mail: tmckenzie@ursinus.edu.
Lacrosse: Glenn Carter; Phone: 610-409-3606; E-mail: gcarter@ursinus.edu.
Soccer: Wayne McKinney; Phone: 610-409-3606; E-mail: wmckinney@ursinus.edu.
Swimming: Sue Hadfield; Phone: 610-409-3606; E-mail: shadfield@ursinus.edu.
Tennis: Steve Mauro; Phone: 610-409-3606; E-mail: smauro@ursinus.edu.
Track and Field: Dean Lent; Phone: 610-409-3606; E-mail: dlent@ursinus.edu.
Wrestling: Bill Racich; Phone: 610-409-3606; E-mail: wracich@ursinus.edu.

WOMEN'S COACHES
Basketball: Jim Buckley; Phone: 610-409-3606; E-mail: jbuckley@ursinus.edu.
Cross Country: Neil Schafer; Phone: 610-409-3606; E-mail: nschafer@ursinus.edu.
Field Hockey: Laura Moliken; Phone: 610-409-3606; E-mail: lmoliken@ursinus.edu.
Golf: Chris Pincince; Phone: 610-409-3606; E-mail: cpincince@ursinus.edu.
Gymnastics: Jeff Schepers; Phone: 610-409-3606; E-mail: jschepers@ursinus.edu.
Lacrosse: Carrie Kirk; Phone: 610-409-3761; E-mail: ckirk@ursinus.edu.
Soccer: Jeff Ykoruk; Phone: 610-409-3606; E-mail: jykoruk@ursinus.edu.
Softball: Terry McGowan; Phone: 610-409-3606; E-mail: tmcgowan@ursinus.edu.
Swimming: Sue Hadfield; Phone: 610-409-3606; E-mail: shadfield@ursinus.edu.
Tennis: Sue McDonough; Phone: 610-409-3606; E-mail: smcdonough@ursinus.edu.
Track and Field: Dean Lent; Phone: 610-409-3606; E-mail: dlent@ursinus.edu.
Volleyball: Diane Hagan; Phone: 610-409-3606; E-mail: dhagan@ursinus.edu.

URSULINE COLLEGE
Pepper Pike, Ohio

Arrows ◆ NAIA ◆ American Mideast Conference ◆ http://www.ursuline.edu/

Independent Roman Catholic comprehensive, founded 1871
Women only, 1,095 undergraduate students, 60% full-time, 91% women, 9% men
Suburban 112-acre campus with easy access to Cleveland
Minimally difficult entrance level, 40% of applicants were admitted

Freshmen *Admission:* 351 applied, 244 were accepted, 118 enrolled. *Test scores:* SAT verbal scores over 500: 41%; SAT math scores over 500: 39%; SAT verbal scores over 600: 10%; SAT math scores over 600: 6%.
Tuition and fees (2003–04): $17,270 (full-time). *Room and board:* $5458.
Financial Aid (All incoming freshmen): *Average need-based gift aid:* $8055. *Average non-need based aid:* $6875. *Average aid to full-time undergraduates:* $15,901.
Athletic Department: *Director of Athletics:* Cindy McKnight; Phone: 440-684-6102; Fax: 440-684-6097; E-mail: cmcknigh@ursuline.edu. *Sports Information Director:* Deborah Wordell; Phone: 440-684-6094; E-mail: dwordell@ursuline.edu.

WOMEN'S COACHES
Basketball: Nelson Schorr; Phone: 440-646-8306; E-mail: nschorr@ursuline.edu.
Cross Country: Nelson Schorr; Phone: 440-646-8306; E-mail: nschorr@ursuline.edu.
Golf: June Poole; Phone: 440-646-8308; E-mail: jpoole@ursuline.edu.
Soccer: Irenna Lawrence; Phone: 440-684-6095; E-mail: ilawrence@ursuline.edu.
Softball: Claudette Farrell; Phone: 440-449-4204; E-mail: cfarrell@ursuline.edu.
Tennis: Irenna Lawrence; Phone: 440-684-6095; E-mail: ilawrence@ursuline.edu.
Volleyball: Deborah Wordell; Phone: 440-684-6094; E-mail: dwordell@ursuline.edu.

UTAH STATE UNIVERSITY
Logan, Utah

Aggies ◆ NCAA I ◆ Big West Conference; Sun Belt Conference ◆ http://www.usu.edu/

State-supported university, founded 1888, part of Utah System of Higher Education
Coed, 13,958 undergraduate students, 84% full-time, 49% women, 51% men
Urban 456-acre campus
Moderately difficult entrance level, 92% of applicants were admitted

Freshmen *Admission:* 5,165 applied, 4,851 were accepted, 2,548 enrolled. *Test scores:* SAT verbal scores over 500: 72%; SAT math scores over 500: 75%; SAT verbal scores over 600: 31%; SAT math scores over 600: 39%; SAT verbal scores over 700: 7%; SAT math scores over 700: 8%.
Tuition and fees (2003–04): $3141 (resident), $8946 (nonresident). *Room and board:* $3930 (room only: $1550).
Financial Aid (All incoming freshmen): *Average need-based gift aid:* $2800. *Average non-need based aid:* $2300. *Average aid to full-time undergraduates:* $3600.
Athletic Department: *Director of Athletics:* Rance Pugmire; Phone: 435-797-2060; Fax: 435-797-2615; E-mail: rance.pugmire@usu.edu. *Sports Information Director:* Mike Strauss; Phone: 435-797-1361; E-mail: mike.strauss@usu.edu.

MEN'S COACHES
Basketball: Stew Morrill; Phone: 435-797-2060; E-mail: ronda.christoffersen@usu.edu.
Cheerleading: Linda Zimmerman; Phone: 435-797-3384; E-mail: lindaz@cc.usu.edu.
Cross Country: Gregg Gensel; Phone: 435-797-2061; E-mail: gregg.gensel@usu.edu.
Football: Mike Dennehy; Phone: 435-797-1850; E-mail: vfonz@cc.usu.edu.

Utah State University (continued)

Golf: Dean Johansen; Phone: 435-797-6050.
Tennis: Chris Wright; Phone: 435-797-2593; E-mail: cwrightennis@ hotmail.com.
Track and Field: Gregg Gensel; Phone: 435-797-2061; E-mail: gregg. gensel@usu.edu.

WOMEN'S COACHES
Basketball: Raegan Pebley; Phone: 435-797-2583.
Cheerleading: Linda Zimmerman; Phone: 435-797-3384; E-mail: lindaz@cc.usu.edu.
Cross Country: Gregg Gensel; Phone: 435-797-2061; E-mail: gregg. gensel@usu.edu.
Gymnastics: Ray Corn; Phone: 435-797-1494; E-mail: raycorn@cc.usu. edu.
Soccer: Heather Cairns; Phone: 435-797-0900; E-mail: hcairns@cc.usu. edu.
Softball: Debbie Bilbao; Phone: 435-797-2069; E-mail: debbie.bilbao@ usu.edu.
Tennis: Chris Wright; Phone: 435-797-2593; E-mail: cwrightennis@ hotmail.com.
Track and Field: Gregg Gensel; Phone: 435-797-2061; E-mail: gregg. gensel@usu.edu.
Volleyball: Burt Fuller; Phone: 435-797-2068; E-mail: bfuller@cc.usu. edu.

UTICA COLLEGE
Utica, New York

Pioneers ◆ NCAA III ◆ Empire 8 Conference ◆ http:// www.utica.edu/

Independent comprehensive, founded 1946
Coed, 2,170 undergraduate students, 86% full-time, 59% women, 41% men
Suburban 128-acre campus
Moderately difficult entrance level, 75% of applicants were admitted

Freshmen *Admission:* 2,946 applied, 2,273 were accepted, 449 enrolled. *Test scores:* SAT verbal scores over 500: 45%; SAT math scores over 500: 49%; SAT verbal scores over 600: 8%; SAT math scores over 600: 13%; SAT verbal scores over 700: 1%; SAT math scores over 700: 1%.
Tuition and fees (2003–04): $20,270 (full-time). *Room and board:* $8070 (room only: $4200).
Financial Aid (All incoming freshmen): *Average need-based gift aid:* $15,293. *Average non-need based aid:* $9000.
Athletic Department: *Director of Athletics:* Jim Spartano; Phone: 315-792-3051; Fax: 315-792-3211; E-mail: jspartano@utica.edu. *Sports Information Director:* Ryan Hyland; Phone: 315-792-3772; E-mail: rhyland@utica.edu.

MEN'S COACHES
Baseball: Don Guido; Phone: 315-792-3378; E-mail: dguido@utica.edu.
Basketball: Andy Goodemote; Phone: 315-792-3121; E-mail: agoodemote@utica.edu.
Diving: Eric Stilz; Phone: 315-792-3103; E-mail: estilz@utica.edu.
Football: Mike Kemp; Phone: 315-792-3713; E-mail: mkemp@utica. edu.
Golf: Charles Lewis; Phone: 315-792-3272; E-mail: athletics@utica.edu.
Ice Hockey: Gary Heenan; Phone: 315-792-3726; E-mail: gheenan@ utica.edu.
Lacrosse: Tim Nelson; Phone: 315-792-3706; E-mail: tnelson@utica. edu.
Soccer: Dariusz Panol; Phone: 315-792-3255; E-mail: dpanol@utica. edu.
Swimming: Eric Stilz; Phone: 315-792-3103; E-mail: estilz@utica.edu.
Tennis: John Nigro; Phone: 315-792-3097; E-mail: athletics@utica.edu.

WOMEN'S COACHES
Basketball: Michele Davis; Phone: 315-792-3052; E-mail: mdavis@ utica.edu.
Diving: Eric Stilz; Phone: 315-792-3103; E-mail: estilz@utica.edu.
Field Hockey: Patricia Mihalko; Phone: 315-792-3776; E-mail: athletics@utica.edu.
Lacrosse: Jessica Critchlow; Phone: 315-792-3182; E-mail: jcritchlow@ utica.edu.
Soccer: Jessica Critchlow; Phone: 315-792-3182; E-mail: jcritchlow@ utica.edu.
Softball: Jim Murnane; Phone: 315-792-3281; E-mail: jmurnane@utica. edu.
Swimming: Eric Stilz; Phone: 315-792-3103; E-mail: estilz@utica.edu.
Tennis: John Nigro; Phone: 315-792-3097; E-mail: athletics@utica.edu.
Volleyball: Darin Lynch; Phone: 315-792-3791; E-mail: athletics@utica. edu.

VALDOSTA STATE UNIVERSITY
Valdosta, Georgia

Blazers ◆ NCAA II ◆ Gulf South Conference ◆ http:// www.valdosta.edu/

State-supported university, founded 1906, part of University System of Georgia
Coed, 8,801 undergraduate students, 80% full-time, 60% women, 40% men
Small-town 200-acre campus with easy access to Jacksonville
Moderately difficult entrance level, 69% of applicants were admitted

Freshmen *Admission:* 5,400 applied, 3,694 were accepted, 2,001 enrolled. *Test scores:* SAT verbal scores over 500: 54%; SAT math scores over 500: 52%; SAT verbal scores over 600: 10%; SAT math scores over 600: 11%; SAT verbal scores over 700: 1%; SAT math scores over 700: 1%.
Tuition and fees (2003–04): $2860 (resident), $9496 (nonresident). *Room and board:* $5002 (room only: $2556).
Financial Aid (All incoming freshmen): *Average need-based gift aid:* $3145. *Average non-need based aid:* $5416. *Average aid to full-time undergraduates:* $6424.
Athletic Department: *Director of Athletics:* Herb Reinhard; Phone: 229-245-3761; Fax: 229-333-5972; E-mail: hreinhar@valdosta.edu. *Sports Information Director:* Steve Roberts; Phone: 229-333-5903; E-mail: sroberts@valdosta.edu.

MEN'S COACHES
Baseball: Tommy Thomas; Phone: 229-333-5562; E-mail: tjthomas@ valdosta.edu.
Basketball: Jim Yarbrough; Phone: 229-333-5893; E-mail: jdyarbro@ valdosta.edu.
Cheerleading: Dante Tennant; Phone: 229-333-5890; E-mail: dantetennant@aol.com.
Cross Country: Johnny Lancaster; Phone: 229-333-5890; E-mail: jelancas@valdosta.edu.
Football: Chris Hatcher; Phone: 229-333-5970; E-mail: cmhatch@ valdosta.edu.
Golf: Jared Purvis; Phone: 229-333-5890; E-mail: jaredpurvis@hotmail. com.
Tennis: John Hansen; Phone: 229-333-5902; E-mail: jhansen@valdosta. edu.

WOMEN'S COACHES
Basketball: Kiley Hill; Phone: 229-333-5892; E-mail: khill@valdosta. edu.
Cheerleading: Dante Tennant; Phone: 229-333-5890; E-mail: dantetennant@aol.com.
Cross Country: Johnny Lancaster; Phone: 229-333-5890; E-mail: jelancas@valdosta.edu.
Softball: Kendra McDaniel; Phone: 229-333-7405; E-mail: kdmcdani@ valdosta.edu.
Tennis: John Hansen; Phone: 229-333-5902; E-mail: jhansen@valdosta. edu.
Volleyball: Jon Teetzel; Phone: 229-333-5894; E-mail: jteetzel@valdosta. edu.

VALLEY CITY STATE UNIVERSITY
Valley City, North Dakota

Vikings ◆ NAIA ◆ Dakota Conference
◆ http://www.vcsu.edu/

State-supported 4-year, founded 1890, part of North Dakota University System
Coed, 998 undergraduate students, 74% full-time, 55% women, 45% men
Small-town 55-acre campus
Noncompetitive entrance level, 90% of applicants were admitted

Freshmen *Admission:* 264 applied, 240 were accepted, 166 enrolled.
Tuition and fees (2003–04): $3249 (resident), $7677 (nonresident). *Room and board:* $3254 (room only: $1230).
Financial Aid (All incoming freshmen): *Average need-based gift aid:* $3670. *Average non-need based aid:* $1725. *Average aid to full-time undergraduates:* $5958.
Athletic Department: *Director of Athletics:* Don Bauer; Phone: 701-845-7160; Fax: 701-845-7211; E-mail: don.bauer@vcsu.edu. *Sports Information Director:* Cory Anderson; Phone: 701-845-7413; E-mail: cory.anderson@vcsu.edu.

MEN'S COACHES
Baseball: Cory Anderson; Phone: 701-845-7413; E-mail: cory.anderson@vcsu.edu.
Basketball: Adam DeHaan; Phone: 701-845-7240; E-mail: adam.dehaan@vcsu.edu.
Cheerleading: Tiffany Hieb; Phone: 800-532-8641; E-mail: tiffany_hieb@mail.vcsu.nodak.edu.
Football: Dennis McCulloch; Phone: 701-845-7425; E-mail: dennis.mcculloch@vcsu.edu.

WOMEN'S COACHES
Basketball: Jill DeVries; Phone: 701-845-7164; E-mail: jill.devries@vcsu.edu.
Cheerleading: Tiffany Hieb; Phone: 800-532-8641; E-mail: tiffany_hieb@mail.vcsu.nodak.edu.
Softball: Chad Slyter; Phone: 701-845-7161; E-mail: chad.slyter@vcsu.edu.
Volleyball: Diane Burr; Phone: 701-845-7242; E-mail: diane.burr@vcsu.edu.

VALPARAISO UNIVERSITY
Valparaiso, Indiana

Crusaders ◆ NCAA I ◆ Mid-Continent Conference; Pioneer Football League Conference ◆ http://www.valpo.edu/

Independent religious comprehensive, founded 1859, affiliated with Lutheran Church
Coed, 3,026 undergraduate students, 94% full-time, 53% women, 47% men
Small-town 310-acre campus with easy access to Chicago
Moderately difficult entrance level, 89% of applicants were admitted

Freshmen *Admission:* 3,576 applied, 2,929 were accepted, 795 enrolled. *Test scores:* SAT verbal scores over 500: 84%; SAT math scores over 500: 83%; SAT verbal scores over 600: 41%; SAT math scores over 600: 45%; SAT verbal scores over 700: 10%; SAT math scores over 700: 12%.
Tuition and fees (2003–04): $20,632 (full-time). *Room and board:* $5480 (room only: $3480).
Financial Aid (All incoming freshmen): *Average non-need based aid:* $7085. *Average aid to full-time undergraduates:* $18,168.
Athletic Department: *Director of Athletics:* William Steinbrecher; Phone: 219-464-6894; Fax: 219-464-5762; E-mail: bill.steinbrecher@valpo.edu. *Sports Information Director:* Bill Rogers; Phone: 219-464-5232; E-mail: bill.rogers@valpo.edu.

MEN'S COACHES
Baseball: Paul Twenge; Phone: 219-464-5239; E-mail: deacon.twenge@valpo.edu.
Basketball: Homer Drew; Phone: 219-464-5231; E-mail: homer.drew@valpo.edu.
Cheerleading: Jenifer Crosby; Phone: 219-738-2195; E-mail: cbcrosby@msn.com.

Cross Country: Mike Straubel; Phone: 219-465-7812; E-mail: mike.straubel@valpo.edu.
Diving: Nathan Mundt; Phone: 219-464-5014; E-mail: nathan.mundt@valpo.edu.
Football: Tom Horne; Phone: 219-464-5229; E-mail: thomas.horne@valpo.edu.
Soccer: Mis Mrak; Phone: 219-464-5783; E-mail: mis.mrak@valpo.edu.
Swimming: Nathan Mundt; Phone: 219-464-5014; E-mail: nathan.mundt@valpo.edu.
Tennis: Jim Daugherty; Phone: 219-464-5257; E-mail: james.daugherty@valpo.edu.
Track and Field: Tyler Wingard; Phone: 219-464-6118; E-mail: tyler.wingard@valpo.edu.

WOMEN'S COACHES
Basketball: Keith Freeman; Phone: 219-464-5238; E-mail: keith.freeman@valpo.edu.
Cheerleading: Jenifer Crosby; Phone: 219-738-2195; E-mail: cbcrosby@msn.com.
Cross Country: Mike Straubel; Phone: 219-465-7812; E-mail: mike.straubel@valpo.edu.
Diving: Nathan Mundt; Phone: 219-464-5014; E-mail: nathan.mundt@valpo.edu.
Soccer: Stephen Anthony; Phone: 219-464-5242; E-mail: stephen.anthony@valpo.edu.
Softball: Randy Schneider; Phone: 219-464-5047; E-mail: randy.schneider@valpo.edu.
Swimming: Nathan Mundt; Phone: 219-464-5014; E-mail: nathan.mundt@valpo.edu.
Tennis: Tim Maluga; Phone: 219-464-5760; E-mail: tim.maluga@valpo.edu.
Track and Field: Tyler Wingard; Phone: 219-464-6118; E-mail: tyler.wingard@valpo.edu.
Volleyball: Carin Avery; Phone: 219-464-5323; E-mail: carin.avery@valpo.edu.

VANDERBILT UNIVERSITY
Nashville, Tennessee

Commodores ◆ NCAA I ◆ Missouri Valley Conference; Southeastern Conference ◆ http://www.vanderbilt.edu/

Independent university, founded 1873
Coed, 6,283 undergraduate students, 99% full-time, 52% women, 48% men
Urban 330-acre campus
Very difficult entrance level, 41% of applicants were admitted

Freshmen *Admission:* 10,960 applied, 4,405 were accepted, 1,546 enrolled. *Test scores:* SAT verbal scores over 500: 98%; SAT math scores over 500: 99%; SAT verbal scores over 600: 84%; SAT math scores over 600: 89%; SAT verbal scores over 700: 31%; SAT math scores over 700: 39%.
Tuition and fees (2003–04): $28,440 (full-time). *Room and board:* $9457 (room only: $6182).
Financial Aid (All incoming freshmen): *Average need-based gift aid:* $22,592. *Average non-need based aid:* $16,196. *Average aid to full-time undergraduates:* $29,352.
Athletic Department: *Director of Athletics:* NA; Fax: 615-343-7064. *Sports Information Director:* Rod Williamson; Phone: 615-322-4121; E-mail: rodney.h.williamson@vanderbilt.edu.

MEN'S COACHES
Baseball: Tim Corbin; Phone: 615-322-7725; E-mail: t.corbin@vanderbilt.edu.
Basketball: Kevin Stallings; Phone: 615-322-6530; E-mail: kevin.stallings@vanderbilt.edu.
Cheerleading: Pam Pearson; Phone: 270-622-7910; E-mail: ppearson@nationalspirit.com.
Cross Country: Don Bailey; Phone: 615-298-3533; E-mail: donald.bailey@vanderbilt.edu.
Football: Bobby Johnson; Phone: 615-322-3565; E-mail: football.johnson@vanderbilt.edu.
Golf: Press McPhaul; Phone: 615-343-5342; E-mail: press.mcphaul@vanderbilt.edu.
Soccer: Tim McClements; Phone: 615-343-8098; E-mail: tim.mcclements@vanderbilt.edu.

Vanderbilt University (continued)

Tennis: Ken Flach; Phone: 615-322-4102; E-mail: ken.flach@vanderbilt.edu.

WOMEN'S COACHES

Basketball: Melanie Balcomb; Phone: 615-343-8482; E-mail: melanie.balcomb@vanderbilt.edu.

Cheerleading: Pam Pearson; Phone: 270-622-7910; E-mail: ppearson@nationalspirit.com.

Cross Country: Jim Spivey; Phone: 615-343-8558; E-mail: jim.spivey@vanderbilt.edu.

Golf: Martha Freitag; Phone: 615-343-8097; E-mail: martha.freitag@vanderbilt.edu.

Lacrosse: Cathy Swezey; Phone: 615-343-8526.

Soccer: Ronnie Hill; Phone: 615-343-8099; E-mail: ronnie.hill@vanderbilt.edu.

Tennis: Geoff MacDonald; Phone: 615-343-8940; E-mail: geoff.macdonald@vanderbilt.edu.

Track and Field: Lori Shepard; Phone: 615-343-2897; E-mail: lori.shepard@vanderbilt.edu.

VANGUARD UNIVERSITY OF SOUTHERN CALIFORNIA
Costa Mesa, California

Lions ◆ NAIA ◆ Golden State Conference ◆ http://www.vanguard.edu/

Independent religious comprehensive, founded 1920, affiliated with Assemblies of God
Coed, 1,340 undergraduate students, 98% full-time, 64% women, 36% men
Suburban 38-acre campus with easy access to Los Angeles
Moderately difficult entrance level, 76% of applicants were admitted

Freshmen *Admission:* 746 applied, 599 were accepted, 347 enrolled. *Test scores:* SAT verbal scores over 500: 57%; SAT math scores over 500: 53%; SAT verbal scores over 600: 22%; SAT math scores over 600: 15%; SAT verbal scores over 700: 2%; SAT math scores over 700: 1%.
Tuition and fees (2003–04): $16,358 (full-time). *Room and board:* $5510 (room only: $3060).
Financial Aid (All incoming freshmen): *Average need-based gift aid:* $7400. *Average non-need based aid:* $4051. *Average aid to full-time undergraduates:* $9700.
Athletic Department: *Director of Athletics:* Bob Wilson; Phone: 714-556-3610; Fax: 714-668-6144; E-mail: bwilson@vanguard.edu. *Sports Information Director:* Beth Renkoski; Phone: 714-556-3610; E-mail: brenkoski@vanguard.edu.

MEN'S COACHES

Baseball: Kevin Kasper; Phone: 714-556-3610; E-mail: kkasper@vanguard.edu.

Basketball: Bob Wilson; Phone: 714-556-3610; E-mail: bwilson@vanguard.edu.

Cross Country: Bryan Wilkins; Phone: 714-556-3610; E-mail: bwilkins@vanguard.edu.

Soccer: Randy Dodge; Phone: 714-556-3610; E-mail: rdodge@vanguard.edu.

Tennis: Mattias Johansson; Phone: 714-556-3610; E-mail: kamadrutt@aol.com.

Track and Field: Bryan Wilkins; Phone: 714-556-3610; E-mail: bwilkins@vanguard.edu.

WOMEN'S COACHES

Basketball: Russ Davis; Phone: 714-556-3610; E-mail: rdavis@vanguard.edu.

Cross Country: Bryan Wilkins; Phone: 714-556-3610; E-mail: bwilkins@vanguard.edu.

Soccer: Kerry McGrath; Phone: 714-556-3610; E-mail: kmcgrathcrooks@vanguard.edu.

Softball: Beth Renkoski; Phone: 714-556-3610; E-mail: brenkoski@vanguard.edu.

Tennis: Mattias Johansson; Phone: 714-556-3610; E-mail: kamadrutt@aol.com.

Track and Field: Bryan Wilkins; Phone: 714-556-3610; E-mail: bwilkins@vanguard.edu.

Volleyball: Erikks Gulbranson; Phone: 714-556-3610; E-mail: egulbranson@vanguard.edu.

VASSAR COLLEGE
Poughkeepsie, New York

Brewers ◆ NCAA III ◆ Upstate Collegiate Athletic Conference ◆ http://www.vassar.edu/

Independent 4-year, founded 1861
Coed, 2,444 undergraduate students, 98% full-time, 60% women, 40% men
Suburban 1,000-acre campus with easy access to New York City
Very difficult entrance level, 36% of applicants were admitted

Freshmen *Admission:* 6,207 applied, 1,806 were accepted, 632 enrolled. *Test scores:* SAT verbal scores over 500: 100%; SAT math scores over 500: 100%; SAT verbal scores over 600: 96%; SAT math scores over 600: 92%; SAT verbal scores over 700: 50%; SAT math scores over 700: 37%.
Tuition and fees (2003–04): $29,540 (full-time). *Room and board:* $7490 (room only: $3980).
Financial Aid (All incoming freshmen): *Average need-based gift aid:* $20,302. *Average aid to full-time undergraduates:* $24,075.
Athletic Department: *Director of Athletics:* Andy Jennings; Phone: 845-437-7452; Fax: 845-437-7033; E-mail: anjennings@vassar.edu. *Sports Information Director:* Casey Hager; Phone: 845-437-7469; E-mail: cahager@vassar.edu.

MEN'S COACHES

Baseball: Chris Campassi; Phone: 845-437-7469; E-mail: chcampassi@vassar.edu.

Basketball: Mike Dutton; Phone: 845-437-7535; E-mail: midutton@vassar.edu.

Cross Country: Ron Stonitsch; Phone: 845-473-9089; E-mail: rostonitsch@vassar.edu.

Diving: Tom Albright; Phone: 845-437-7461.

Lacrosse: Brian Rhoads; Phone: 845-437-7456; E-mail: brrhoads@vassar.edu.

Soccer: Andy Jennings; Phone: 845-437-7452; E-mail: anjennings@vassar.edu.

Swimming: Lisl Prater-Lee; Phone: 845-437-7461; E-mail: lipraterlee@vassar.edu.

Tennis: Roman Czula; Phone: 845-437-7471; E-mail: roczula@vassar.edu.

Volleyball: Jonathan Penn; Phone: 845-437-7458; E-mail: jopenn@vassar.edu.

WOMEN'S COACHES

Basketball: Steve Buonfiglio; Phone: 845-437-5347; E-mail: stbuonfiglio@vassar.edu.

Cross Country: Ron Stonitsch; Phone: 845-437-9089; E-mail: rostonitsch@vassar.edu.

Diving: Tom Albright; Phone: 845-437-7461.

Field Hockey: Judy Finerghty; Phone: 845-437-7459; E-mail: jufinerghty@vassar.edu.

Lacrosse: Judy Finerghty; Phone: 845-437-7459; E-mail: jufinerghty@vassar.edu.

Soccer: Erin DeMarco; Phone: 845-437-7817; E-mail: erdemarco@vassar.edu.

Swimming: Lisl Prater-Lee; Phone: 845-437-7461; E-mail: lipraterlee@vassar.edu.

Tennis: Kathy Campbell; Phone: 845-437-7460; E-mail: kacampbell@vassar.edu.

Volleyball: Jonathan Penn; Phone: 845-437-7458; E-mail: jopenn@vassar.edu.

VILLA JULIE COLLEGE
Stevenson, Maryland

Mustangs ◆ NCAA III ◆ Independent; Pennsylvania Athletic Conference ◆ http://www.vjc.edu/

Independent comprehensive, founded 1952
Coed, 2,656 undergraduate students, 78% full-time, 73% women, 27% men
Suburban 60-acre campus with easy access to Baltimore
Moderately difficult entrance level, 63% of applicants were admitted

Freshmen *Admission:* 2,195 applied, 1,382 were accepted, 545 enrolled. *Test scores:* SAT verbal scores over 500: 59%; SAT math scores over

500: 62%; SAT verbal scores over 600: 16%; SAT math scores over 600: 21%; SAT verbal scores over 700: 1%; SAT math scores over 700: 1%.

Tuition and fees (2003–04): $13,693 (full-time). *Room only:* $4700.

Financial Aid (All incoming freshmen): *Average need-based gift aid:* $8031. *Average non-need based aid:* $5593. *Average aid to full-time undergraduates:* $9016.

Athletic Department: *Director of Athletics:* Brett Adams; Phone: 443-334-2250; Fax: 410-602-6564; E-mail: ath-bret@mail.vjc.edu. *Sports Information Director:* Jeb Barber; Phone: 443-334-2469; E-mail: ath-jeb@mail.vjc.edu.

MEN'S COACHES

Baseball: Jason Tawney; Phone: 410-602-7334; E-mail: ath-jaso@mail.vjc.edu.

Basketball: Brett Adams; Phone: 410-602-7250; E-mail: ath-bret@mail.vjc.edu.

Cheerleading: Jill Matheny; Phone: 410-248-2272; E-mail: jillscott1@aol.com.

Cross Country: Bryan Gunning; Phone: 410-602-7250.

Golf: Jay German; Phone: 410-602-7133; E-mail: j_german_2000@yahoo.com.

Lacrosse: Whit Morrill; Phone: 410-602-6730.

Soccer: Kevin Cromwell; Phone: 410-602-7273; E-mail: ath-kevi@mail.vjc.edu.

Tennis: Brad Friedel; Phone: 410-602-6763; E-mail: ath-brad@mail.vjc.edu.

Volleyball: Herb Simon; Phone: 410-602-7115; E-mail: simoncoach@juno.com.

WOMEN'S COACHES

Basketball: Chris Ramer; Phone: 410-602-7482; E-mail: ath-chri@mail.vjc.edu.

Cheerleading: Jill Matheny; Phone: 410-248-2272; E-mail: jillscott1@aol.com.

Cross Country: Bryan Gunning; Phone: 410-602-7250.

Field Hockey: Christine Jackson; Phone: 410-602-7183; E-mail: christinejackson@netzero.net.

Lacrosse: Brenda Yoo; Phone: 410-602-7162; E-mail: ath-bren@mail.vjc.edu.

Soccer: Lynnette Buffington; Phone: 410-602-7453; E-mail: ath-lynn@mail.vjc.edu.

Softball: Stephanie Meyerson; Phone: 410-602-7444; E-mail: ath-stef@mail.vjc.edu.

Tennis: Brad Friedel; Phone: 410-602-6763; E-mail: ath-brad@mail.vjc.edu.

Volleyball: Peter LeTourneau; Phone: 410-602-7115; E-mail: ath-pete@mail.vjc.edu.

VILLANOVA UNIVERSITY
Villanova, Pennsylvania

Wildcats ◆ NCAA I ◆ Atlantic 10 Conference; Big East Conference; Colonial Athletic Conference; Patriot League Conference ◆ http://www.villanova.edu/

Independent Roman Catholic comprehensive, founded 1842
Coed, 7,267 undergraduate students, 90% full-time, 51% women, 49% men
Suburban 254-acre campus with easy access to Philadelphia
Very difficult entrance level, 55% of applicants were admitted

Freshmen *Admission:* 10,896 applied, 5,781 were accepted, 1,566 enrolled. *Test scores:* SAT verbal scores over 500: 96%; SAT math scores over 500: 97%; SAT verbal scores over 600: 61%; SAT math scores over 600: 77%; SAT verbal scores over 700: 10%; SAT math scores over 700: 17%.

Tuition and fees (2003–04): $26,223 (full-time). *Room and board:* $8827 (room only: $4667).

Financial Aid (All incoming freshmen): *Average need-based gift aid:* $13,490. *Average non-need based aid:* $9569. *Average aid to full-time undergraduates:* $18,900.

Athletic Department: *Director of Athletics:* Vince Nicastro; Phone: 610-519-4110; Fax: 610-519-7987; E-mail: vincent.nicastro@villanova.edu. *Sports Information Director:* Dean Kenefick; Phone: 610-519-4120; E-mail: dean.kenefick@villanova.edu.

MEN'S COACHES

Baseball: Joe Godri; Phone: 610-519-4529; E-mail: jgodri@earthlink.net.

Basketball: Jay Wright; Phone: 610-519-4287.

Cheerleading: Phil O'Neill; Phone: 610-519-4110; E-mail: villanovacheer@aol.com.

Cross Country: Marcus O'Sullivan; Phone: 610-519-4147; E-mail: marcus.osullivan@villanova.edu.

Diving: Gary Elder; Phone: 610-519-4417; E-mail: gary.elder@villanova.edu.

Football: Andy Talley; Phone: 610-519-4105; E-mail: andy.talley@villanova.edu.

Golf: Joe Moran; Phone: 610-519-4093.

Lacrosse: Randy Marks; Phone: 610-519-4146; E-mail: randy.marks@villanova.edu.

Soccer: Larry Sullivan; Phone: 610-519-7266; E-mail: larry.sullivan@villanova.edu.

Swimming: Rick Simpson; Phone: 610-519-4136; E-mail: richard.simpson@villanova.edu.

Tennis: Bob Batman; Phone: 610-519-7619; E-mail: bob.batman@villanova.edu.

Track and Field: Marcus O'Sullivan; Phone: 610-519-4110; E-mail: marcus.osullivan@villanova.edu.

WOMEN'S COACHES

Basketball: Harry Perretta; Phone: 610-519-4113; E-mail: harry.perretta@villanova.edu.

Cheerleading: Phil O'Neill; Phone: 610-519-4110; E-mail: villanovacheer@aol.com.

Cross Country: Marcus O'Sullivan; Phone: 610-519-4147; E-mail: marcus.osullivan@villanova.edu.

Diving: Gary Elder; Phone: 610-519-4417; E-mail: gary.elder@villanova.edu.

Field Hockey: Joan Milhous; Phone: 610-519-4132; E-mail: joan.milhous@villanova.edu.

Lacrosse: Shannon O'Neil; Phone: 610-519-6453; E-mail: shannon.oneil@villanova.edu.

Soccer: Ann Clifton; Phone: 610-519-4135; E-mail: ann.clifton@villanova.edu.

Softball: Maria Dibernardi; Phone: 610-519-4138; E-mail: maria.dibernardi@villanova.edu.

Swimming: Rick Simpson; Phone: 610-519-4136; E-mail: richard.simpson@villanova.edu.

Tennis: Steve Reiniger; Phone: 610-519-4184; E-mail: steven.reiniger@villanova.edu.

Track and Field: Gina Procaccio; Phone: 610-519-6196; E-mail: gina.procaccio@villanova.edu.

Volleyball: Allison Keeley; Phone: 610-519-4137; E-mail: allison.keeley@villanova.edu.

VIRGINIA COMMONWEALTH UNIVERSITY
Richmond, Virginia

Rams ◆ NCAA I ◆ Colonial Athletic Conference ◆ http://www.vcu.edu/

State-supported university, founded 1838
Coed, 18,312 undergraduate students, 76% full-time, 58% women, 42% men
Urban 126-acre campus
Moderately difficult entrance level, 74% of applicants were admitted

Freshmen *Admission:* 9,435 applied, 6,993 were accepted, 3,326 enrolled. *Test scores:* SAT verbal scores over 500: 68%; SAT math scores over 500: 62%; SAT verbal scores over 600: 24%; SAT math scores over 600: 21%; SAT verbal scores over 700: 3%; SAT math scores over 700: 3%.

Tuition and fees (2004–05): $5138 (resident), $17,262 (nonresident). *Room and board:* $6920 (room only: $3980).

Financial Aid (All incoming freshmen): *Average need-based gift aid:* $3482. *Average non-need based aid:* $2648. *Average aid to full-time undergraduates:* $6562.

Athletic Department: *Director of Athletics:* Richard Sander; Phone: 804-828-8110; Fax: 804-828-7526; E-mail: bhopcrof@vcu.edu. *Sports Information Director:* Phil Stanton; Phone: 804-828-7000; E-mail: pdstanton@vcu.edu.

MEN'S COACHES

Baseball: Paul Keyes; Phone: 804-828-4820; E-mail: pakeyes@vcu.edu.

Basketball: Jeff Capel; Phone: 804-828-1278; E-mail: dalong@vcu.edu.

Virginia Commonwealth University *(continued)*

Cheerleading: Tim Morgan; Phone: 804-389-4074; E-mail: vcucheer@aol.com.
Cross Country: Julian Spooner; Phone: 804-828-0945; E-mail: jmspoone@vcu.edu.
Golf: Matt Ball; Phone: 804-828-3027; E-mail: mcball@vcu.edu.
Soccer: Tim O'Sullivan; Phone: 804-828-4839; E-mail: tvosulli@vcu.edu.
Tennis: Paul Kostin; Phone: 804-828-4817; E-mail: pkostin@vcu.edu.
Track and Field: Julian Spooner; Phone: 804-828-0945; E-mail: jmspoone@vcu.edu.

WOMEN'S COACHES

Basketball: Beth Cunningham; Phone: 804-828-4366; E-mail: bacunningham@vcu.edu.
Cheerleading: Tim Morgan; Phone: 804-389-4074; E-mail: vcucheer@aol.com.
Cross Country: Dena Reif; Phone: 804-828-0946; E-mail: dmreif@vcu.edu.
Field Hockey: Shelly Behrens; Phone: 804-828-3025; E-mail: mmbehrens@vcu.edu.
Soccer: Denise Schilte-Brown; Phone: 804-828-7617; E-mail: dcschilt@saturn.vcu.edu.
Tennis: Paul Kostin; Phone: 804-828-4817; E-mail: pkostin@vcu.edu.
Track and Field: Dena Reif; Phone: 804-828-0946; E-mail: dmreif@vcu.edu.
Volleyball: Perri Hankins; Phone: 804-828-3024; E-mail: phankins@vcu.edu.

VIRGINIA INTERMONT COLLEGE
Bristol, Virginia

Cobras ♦ NAIA ♦ Appalachian Conference
♦ http://www.vic.edu/

Independent religious 4-year, founded 1884, affiliated with Baptist Church
Coed, 1,147 undergraduate students, 86% full-time, 73% women, 27% men
Small-town 13-acre campus
Minimally difficult entrance level, 61% of applicants were admitted

Freshmen *Admission:* 831 applied, 542 were accepted, 191 enrolled. *Test scores:* SAT verbal scores over 500: 40%; SAT math scores over 500: 39%; SAT verbal scores over 600: 12%; SAT math scores over 600: 11%; SAT verbal scores over 700: 1%; SAT math scores over 700: 1%.
Tuition and fees (2003–04): $14,400 (full-time). *Room and board:* $5400 (room only: $2600).
Financial Aid (All incoming freshmen): *Average need-based gift aid:* $3255. *Average non-need based aid:* $5422. *Average aid to full-time undergraduates:* $12,138.
Athletic Department: *Director of Athletics:* Phillip Worrell; Phone: 276-466-7940; Fax: 276-466-7164; E-mail: pworrell@vic.edu. *Sports Information Director:* Terrie Oliver; Phone: 276-466-7944; E-mail: toliver@vic.edu.

MEN'S COACHES

Baseball: Christopher Holt; Phone: 276-466-7945; E-mail: chrisholt@vic.edu.
Basketball: Thad Johnson; Phone: 276-466-7166; E-mail: thadjohnson@vic.edu.
Cross Country: Matt High; Phone: 276-645-6386; E-mail: matthigh@vic.edu.
Golf: Thad Johnson; Phone: 276-466-7166; E-mail: thadjohnson@vic.edu.
Soccer: Dan Balaguero; Phone: 276-645-6495; E-mail: danbalaguero@vic.edu.
Tennis: Ron Worrell; Phone: 276-466-7943; E-mail: rworrell@vic.edu.
Track and Field: Matt High; Phone: 276-645-6386; E-mail: matthigh@vic.edu.

WOMEN'S COACHES

Basketball: Heather Conley; Phone: 276-466-7942; E-mail: hconley@vic.edu.
Cross Country: Matt High; Phone: 276-645-6386; E-mail: matthigh@vic.edu.

Soccer: Michael Swan; Phone: 276-645-6389; E-mail: michaelswan@vic.edu.
Softball: Jimmy Nelson; Phone: 276-466-7946; E-mail: jamesnelson@vic.edu.
Tennis: Mary Lou Smith; Phone: 276-466-7941; E-mail: mlsmith@vic.edu.
Track and Field: Matt High; Phone: 276-645-6386; E-mail: matthigh@vic.edu.
Volleyball: Dale Martin; Phone: 276-466-7171; E-mail: dalemartin@vic.edu.

VIRGINIA MILITARY INSTITUTE
Lexington, Virginia

Keydets ♦ NCAA I ♦ Big South Conference; Metro Atlantic Athletic Conference; Southern Conference
♦ http://www.vmi.edu/

State-supported 4-year, founded 1839
Coed, primarily men, 1,333 undergraduate students, 100% full-time, 6% women, 94% men
Small-town 134-acre campus
Moderately difficult entrance level, 48% of applicants were admitted

Freshmen *Admission:* 1,609 applied, 813 were accepted, 338 enrolled. *Test scores:* SAT verbal scores over 500: 87%; SAT math scores over 500: 88%; SAT verbal scores over 600: 33%; SAT math scores over 600: 37%; SAT verbal scores over 700: 6%; SAT math scores over 700: 3%.
Tuition and fees (2003–04): $6181 (resident), $18,893 (nonresident). *Room and board:* $5266.
Financial Aid (All incoming freshmen): *Average need-based gift aid:* $10,172. *Average non-need based aid:* $4441. *Average aid to full-time undergraduates:* $12,071.
Athletic Department: *Director of Athletics:* Donny White; Phone: 540-464-7251; Fax: 540-464-7622; E-mail: white dt@vmi.edu. *Sports Information Director:* Wade Branner; Phone: 540-464-7515; E-mail: brannerwh@vmi.edu.

MEN'S COACHES

Baseball: Tom Slater; Phone: 540-464-7609; E-mail: slatertg@mail.vmi.edu.
Basketball: Bart Bellairs; Phone: 540-464-7384; E-mail: bellairswb@mail.vmi.edu.
Cross Country: Michael Bozeman; Phone: 540-464-7324; E-mail: bozemanml@mail.vmi.edu.
Diving: Bill Nicholson; Phone: 540-464-7737; E-mail: nicholsonwj@mail.vmi.edu.
Football: Cal McCombs; Phone: 540-464-7264; E-mail: mccombswc@mail.vmi.edu.
Lacrosse: Doug Bartlett; Phone: 540-464-7512; E-mail: bartlettdp@mail.vmi.edu.
Soccer: Steve Ross; Phone: 540-464-7611; E-mail: rossst@mail.vmi.edu.
Swimming: Bill Nicholson; Phone: 540-464-7737; E-mail: nicholsonwj@mail.vmi.edu.
Track and Field: Michael Bozeman; Phone: 540-464-7324; E-mail: bozemanml@mail.vmi.edu.
Wrestling: John Trudgeon; Phone: 540-464-7513; E-mail: trudgeonjs@mail.vmi.edu.

WOMEN'S COACHES

Cross Country: Michael Bozeman; Phone: 540-464-7324; E-mail: bozemanml@mail.vmi.edu.
Soccer: Julie Davis; Phone: 540-464-7608; E-mail: davisj@mail.vmi.edu.
Track and Field: Michael Bozeman; Phone: 540-464-7324; E-mail: bozemanml@mail.vmi.edu.

VIRGINIA POLYTECHNIC INSTITUTE AND STATE UNIVERSITY
Blacksburg, Virginia

Gobblers & Hokies ◆ NCAA I ◆ Big East Conference
◆ http://www.vt.edu/

State-supported university, founded 1872
Coed, 21,343 undergraduate students, 97% full time, 41% women, 59% men
Small-town 2,600-acre campus
Moderately difficult entrance level, 67% of applicants were admitted

Freshmen *Admission:* 18,028 applied, 12,387 were accepted, 5,874 enrolled. *Test scores:* SAT verbal scores over 500: 88%; SAT math scores over 500: 91%; SAT verbal scores over 600: 39%; SAT math scores over 600: 52%; SAT verbal scores over 700: 5%; SAT math scores over 700: 11%.
Tuition and fees (2004–05): $5095 (resident), $14,979 (nonresident). *Room and board:* $4146 (room only: $2064).
Financial Aid (All incoming freshmen): *Average need-based gift aid:* $4313. *Average non-need based aid:* $1413. *Average aid to full-time undergraduates:* $7088.
Athletic Department: *Director of Athletics:* Jim Weaver; Phone: 540-231-3977; Fax: 540-231-3020; E-mail: weaverj@vt.edu. *Sports Information Director:* Dave Smith; Phone: 540-231-9965; E-mail: vtsid@vt.edu.

MEN'S COACHES
Baseball: Chuck Hartman; Phone: 540-231-9974; E-mail: chartman@vt.edu.
Basketball: Seth Greenberg; Phone: 540-231-6725; E-mail: sgreenbe@vt.edu.
Cheerleading: Brad Grigg; Phone: 540-231-6796; E-mail: bgrigg@vt.edu.
Cross Country: Dave Cianelli; Phone: 540-231-3094; E-mail: dcianell@vt.edu.
Diving: Bert Locklin; Phone: 540-231-3301; E-mail: blocklin@vt.edu.
Football: Frank Beamer; Phone: 540-231-4132; E-mail: fbeamer@vt.edu.
Golf: Jay Hardwick; Phone: 540-231-3222.
Soccer: Oliver Weiss; Phone: 540-231-7143; E-mail: oweiss@vt.edu.
Swimming: Ned Skinner; Phone: 540-231-5086; E-mail: nskinner@vt.edu.
Tennis: Jim Thompson; Phone: 540-231-4589; E-mail: jthomp@vt.edu.
Track and Field: Dave Cianelli; Phone: 540-231-3094; E-mail: dcianell@vt.edu.
Wrestling: Keith Mourlam; Phone: 540-231-9357; E-mail: kmourlam@vt.edu.

WOMEN'S COACHES
Basketball: Bonnie Henrickson; Phone: 540-231-4998; E-mail: bonnieh@vt.edu.
Cheerleading: Brad Grigg; Phone: 540-231-6796; E-mail: bgrigg@vt.edu.
Cross Country: Dave Cianelli; Phone: 540-231-3094; E-mail: dcianell@vt.edu.
Diving: Bert Locklin; Phone: 540-231-3301; E-mail: blocklin@vt.edu.
Lacrosse: Tami Riley; Phone: 540-231-2776; E-mail: triley@vt.edu.
Soccer: Kelly Cagle; Phone: 540-231-5128; E-mail: kcagle@vt.edu.
Softball: Scott Thomas; Phone: 540-231-3671; E-mail: swthomas@vt.edu.
Swimming: Ned Skinner; Phone: 540-231-5086; E-mail: nskinner@vt.edu.
Tennis: Terry Ann Zawacki-Woods; Phone: 540-231-9971; E-mail: tzawacki@vt.edu.
Track and Field: Dave Cianelli; Phone: 540-231-3094; E-mail: dcianell@vt.edu.
Volleyball: Greg Smith; Phone: 540-231-9972; E-mail: grsmith1@vt.edu.

VIRGINIA STATE UNIVERSITY
Petersburg, Virginia

Trojans ◆ NCAA II ◆ Central Intercollegiate Athletic Conference ◆ http://www.vsu.edu/

State-supported comprehensive, founded 1882, part of State Council of Higher Education for Virginia
Coed, 4,033 undergraduate students, 92% full-time, 57% women, 43% men
Suburban 236-acre campus with easy access to Richmond
Minimally difficult entrance level, 66% of applicants were admitted

Freshmen *Admission:* 3,675 applied, 2,442 were accepted, 964 enrolled. *Test scores:* SAT verbal scores over 500: 11%; SAT math scores over 500: 8%; SAT verbal scores over 600: 1%.
Tuition and fees (2003–04): $4530 (resident), $11,390 (nonresident). *Room and board:* $6008 (room only: $3464).
Financial Aid (All incoming freshmen): *Average need-based gift aid:* $4150. *Average non-need based aid:* $6125. *Average aid to full-time undergraduates:* $7300.
Athletic Department: *Director of Athletics:* Peggy Davis; Phone: 804-524-5650; Fax: 804-524-5763; E-mail: pdavis@vsu.edu. *Sports Information Director:* Paul Williams; Phone: 804-524-5028; E-mail: pwilliams@vsu.edu.

MEN'S COACHES
Baseball: Merrill Morgan; Phone: 804-524-5816; E-mail: mmorgan@vsu.edu.
Basketball: John Hill; Phone: 804-524-5029; E-mail: jhill@vsu.edu.
Cheerleading: Paulette Johnson; Phone: 804-524-5783; E-mail: pjohnson@vsu.edu.
Cross Country: Andre Moore; Phone: 804-524-5392; E-mail: amoore@vsu.edu.
Football: Andrew Faison; Phone: 804-524-5600; E-mail: afaison@vsu.edu.
Golf: Serena Reese; Phone: 804-524-5777; E-mail: sreese@vsu.edu.
Tennis: Phone: 804-524-5393.
Track and Field: Andre Moore; Phone: 804-524-5392; E-mail: amoore@vsu.edu.

WOMEN'S COACHES
Basketball: Stephanie Evans; Phone: 804-524-6817; E-mail: evanss@vsu.edu.
Cheerleading: Paulette Johnson; Phone: 804-524-5783; E-mail: pjohnson@vsu.edu.
Cross Country: Andre Moore; Phone: 804-524-5392; E-mail: amoore@vsu.edu.
Golf: Serena Reese; Phone: 804-524-5777; E-mail: sreese@vsu.edu.
Softball: Shonda Pegram; Phone: 804-524-5391; E-mail: spegram@vsu.edu.
Tennis: Linda Person; Phone: 804-524-5780; E-mail: lperson@vsu.edu.
Track and Field: Andre Moore; Phone: 804-524-5392; E-mail: amoore@vsu.edu.
Volleyball: Steve Wallace; Phone: 804-524-5390; E-mail: swallace@vsu.edu.

VIRGINIA UNION UNIVERSITY
Richmond, Virginia

Panthers ◆ NCAA II ◆ Central Intercollegiate Athletic Conference ◆ http://www.vuu.edu/

Independent Baptist comprehensive, founded 1865
Coed, 1,286 undergraduate students, 97% full-time, 57% women, 43% men
Urban 72-acre campus
Moderately difficult entrance level, 56% of applicants were admitted

Freshmen *Admission:* 3,251 applied, 1,981 were accepted, 491 enrolled.
Tuition and fees (2004–05): $12,205 (full-time). *Room and board:* $5420 (room only: $2755).
Financial Aid (All incoming freshmen): *Average need-based gift aid:* $4202. *Average non-need based aid:* $5617. *Average aid to full-time undergraduates:* $6983.
Athletic Department: *Director of Athletics:* Michael Bailey; Phone: 804-342-1495; Fax: 804-342-1485; E-mail: mbailey@vuu.edu. *Sports Information Director:* Jim Junot; Phone: 804-342-1495.

Virginia Union University *(continued)*

MEN'S COACHES

Basketball: Charles Robbins; Phone: 804-257-5790; E-mail: crobbins@vuu.edu.
Cheerleading: Valerie Briggs; Phone: 804-342-1484.
Cross Country: Marcus Clarke; Phone: 804-342-1495.
Football: Willard Bailey; Phone: 804-257-5766.
Golf: Donald Coleman; Phone: 804-342-1495.
Tennis: Guy Walton; Phone: 804-342-1495.
Track and Field: Marcus Clarke; Phone: 804-342-1495.

WOMEN'S COACHES

Basketball: Barbara Burgess; Phone: 804-257-5872.
Cheerleading: Valerie Briggs; Phone: 804-342-1484.
Cross Country: Marcus Clarke; Phone: 804-342-1495.
Golf: Donald Coleman; Phone: 804-342-1495.
Softball: Reva Green; Phone: 804-257-5872.
Tennis: Guy Walton; Phone: 804-342-1495.
Track and Field: Sabrina Clarke; Phone: 804-342-1495.
Volleyball: Queen Frazier; Phone: 804-355-5689; E-mail: qzfrazier@vuu.edu.

VIRGINIA WESLEYAN COLLEGE
Norfolk, Virginia

Marlins ◆ NCAA III ◆ Old Dominion Conference ◆ http://www.vwc.edu/

Independent United Methodist 4-year, founded 1961
Coed, 1,429 undergraduate students
Urban 300-acre campus with easy access to Norfolk/Virginia Beach
Moderately difficult entrance level, 75% of applicants were admitted

Freshmen *Admission:* 1,147 applied, 920 were accepted. *Test scores:* SAT verbal scores over 500: 47%; SAT math scores over 500: 44%; SAT verbal scores over 600: 10%; SAT math scores over 600: 9%; SAT verbal scores over 700: 1%; SAT math scores over 700: 1%.
Tuition and fees (2003–04): $19,200 (full-time). *Room and board:* $6150.
Financial Aid (All incoming freshmen): *Average need-based gift aid:* $4061. *Average non-need based aid:* $5458. *Average aid to full-time undergraduates:* $13,341.
Athletic Department: *Director of Athletics:* Sonny Travis; Phone: 757-455-3303; Fax: 757-461-2262. *Sports Information Director:* Joe Wasiluk; Phone: 757-455-3393; E-mail: jwasiluk@vwc.edu.

MEN'S COACHES

Baseball: Nick Boothe; Phone: 757-455-3348; E-mail: nboothe@vwc.edu.
Basketball: David Macedo; Phone: 757-455-3307; E-mail: dmacedo@vwc.edu.
Cross Country: Mat Littleton; Phone: 757-455-3303.
Golf: Jeremy Marks; Phone: 757-455-3347; E-mail: jmarks@vwc.edu.
Lacrosse: J.P. Stewart; Phone: 757-455-3135; E-mail: jpstewart@vwc.edu.
Soccer: Sonny Travis; Phone: 757-455-3387; E-mail: stravis@vwc.edu.
Tennis: John Brinkman; Phone: 757-455-8703; E-mail: jbrinkman@vwc.edu.

WOMEN'S COACHES

Basketball: Joanne Renn; Phone: 757-455-5723; E-mail: jrenn@vwc.edu.
Cross Country: Mat Littleton; Phone: 757-455-3303.
Field Hockey: Kim-Michael Mertes; Phone: 757-455-3396; E-mail: kmertes@vwc.edu.
Lacrosse: Kim-Michael Mertes; Phone: 757-455-3396; E-mail: kmertes@vwc.edu.
Lacrosse: Kim-Michael Mertes; Phone: 757-455-3396; E-mail: kmertes@vwc.edu.
Soccer: Jeff Bowers; Phone: 757-455-3285; E-mail: jbowers@vwc.edu.
Softball: Conrad Parker; Phone: 757-455-3307; E-mail: cparker@vwc.edu.
Tennis: John Brinkman; Phone: 757-233-8703; E-mail: jbrinkman@vwc.edu.
Volleyball: Jenn Strauss; Phone: 757-455-3136; E-mail: jstrauss@vwc.edu.

VITERBO UNIVERSITY
La Crosse, Wisconsin

Hawks ◆ NAIA ◆ Midwest Classic Conference ◆ http://www.viterbo.edu/

Independent Roman Catholic comprehensive, founded 1890
Coed, 1,862 undergraduate students, 81% full-time, 75% women, 25% men
Suburban 72-acre campus
Moderately difficult entrance level, 87% of applicants were admitted

Freshmen *Admission:* 1,293 applied, 1,136 were accepted, 356 enrolled.
Tuition and fees (2004–05): $15,990 (full-time). *Room and board:* $5220 (room only: $2250).
Financial Aid (All incoming freshmen): *Average need-based gift aid:* $9989. *Average non-need based aid:* $6200. *Average aid to full-time undergraduates:* $13,559.
Athletic Department: *Director of Athletics:* Barry Fried; Phone: 608-796-3812; Fax: 608-796-3818; E-mail: bjfried@viterbo.edu. *Sports Information Director:* Nels Popp; Phone: 608-796-3820; E-mail: nkpopp@viterbo.edu.

MEN'S COACHES

Baseball: Larry Lipker; Phone: 608-796-3824; E-mail: lflipker@viterbo.edu.
Basketball: Wayne Wagner; Phone: 608-796-3814; E-mail: wrwagner@viterbo.edu.
Soccer: Mark Brandenburgh; Phone: 608-796-3822; E-mail: mtbrandenburgh@viterbo.edu.

WOMEN'S COACHES

Basketball: Bobbi Vandenberg; Phone: 608-796-3813; E-mail: blvandenberg@viterbo.edu.
Soccer: Will Lemke; Phone: 608-796-3821; E-mail: whlemke@viterbo.edu.
Softball: Jaimi Dutton; Phone: 608-796-3819; E-mail: jmstejskal@viterbo.edu.
Volleyball: Kelly Aspen; Phone: 608-796-3823; E-mail: kmaspen@viterbo.edu.

VOORHEES COLLEGE
Denmark, South Carolina

Tigers ◆ NAIA ◆ Eastern Intercollegiate Conference ◆ http://www.voorhees.edu/

Independent Episcopal 4-year, founded 1897
Coed, 847 undergraduate students, 95% full-time, 65% women, 35% men
Rural 350-acre campus
Moderately difficult entrance level, 4% of applicants were admitted

Freshmen *Admission:* 2,624 applied, 1,066 were accepted, 156 enrolled. *Test scores:* SAT verbal scores over 500: 16%; SAT math scores over 500: 13%.
Tuition and fees (2004–05): $7276 (full-time). *Room and board:* $4572 (room only: $1904).
Financial Aid (All incoming freshmen): *Average need-based gift aid:* $6391. *Average non-need based aid:* $8387. *Average aid to full-time undergraduates:* $8945.
Athletic Department: *Director of Athletics:* Willie Jefferson; Phone: 864-703-7173; Fax: 803-793-4584.

MEN'S COACHES

Baseball: Adrian West; Phone: 803-703-7173.
Basketball: Andre Williams; Phone: 803-703-7173.
Cross Country: Frank Hyland; Phone: 803-703-7173.
Track and Field: Frank Hyland; Phone: 803-703-7173.

WOMEN'S COACHES

Basketball: Edward Glover; Phone: 803-703-7173.
Cross Country: Frank Hyland; Phone: 803-703-7173.
Softball: Hercules Davis; Phone: 803-703-7173.
Track and Field: Frank Hyland; Phone: 803-703-7173.
Volleyball: Hercules Davis; Phone: 803-703-7173.

WABASH COLLEGE
Crawfordsville, Indiana

Little Giants ◆ NCAA III ◆ North Coast Athletic Conference ◆ http://www.wabash.edu/

Independent 4-year, founded 1832
Men only, 863 undergraduate students, 100% full-time, 100% women, 100% men
Small-town 50-acre campus with easy access to Indianapolis
Moderately difficult entrance level, 50% of applicants were admitted

Freshmen *Admission:* 1,299 applied, 647 were accepted, 239 enrolled. *Test scores:* SAT verbal scores over 500: 83%; SAT math scores over 500: 88%; SAT verbal scores over 600: 39%; SAT math scores over 600: 56%; SAT verbal scores over 700: 9%; SAT math scores over 700: 14%.
Tuition and fees (2004–05): $22,275 (full-time). *Room and board:* $7053 (room only: $2609).
Financial Aid (All incoming freshmen): *Average need-based gift aid:* $16,610. *Average non-need based aid:* $12,475. *Average aid to full-time undergraduates:* $20,645.
Athletic Department: *Director of Athletics:* Vernon Mummert; Phone: 765-361-6233; Fax: 765-361-6447; E-mail: mummertv@wabash.edu. *Sports Information Director:* Brent Harris; Phone: 765-361-6165; E-mail: harrisb@wabash.edu.

MEN'S COACHES
Baseball: Tom Flynn; Phone: 765-361-6209; E-mail: flynnt@wabash.edu.
Basketball: Malcolm Petty; Phone: 765-361-6238; E-mail: pettym@wabash.edu.
Cross Country: Rob Johnson; Phone: 765-361-6279; E-mail: johnsonr@wabash.edu.
Football: Chris Creighton; Phone: 765-361-6300; E-mail: creightc@wabash.edu.
Golf: Brian Ward; Phone: 765-361-6287; E-mail: wardb@wabash.edu.
Soccer: George Perry; Phone: 765-361-6208; E-mail: perryg@wabash.edu.
Swimming: Peter Casares; Phone: 765-361-6272; E-mail: casaresp@wabash.edu.
Tennis: Elana Engleman; Phone: 765-361-6353; E-mail: englemae@wabash.edu.
Track and Field: Rob Johnson; Phone: 765-361-6279; E-mail: johnsonr@wabash.edu.
Wrestling: Eric Reed; Phone: 765-361-6190; E-mail: reede@wabash.edu.

WAGNER COLLEGE
Staten Island, New York

Sea Hawks ◆ NCAA I ◆ Colonial Athletic Conference; Metro Atlantic Athletic Conference; Northeast Conference ◆ http://www.wagner.edu/

Independent comprehensive, founded 1883
Coed, 1,826 undergraduate students, 97% full-time, 60% women, 40% men
Urban 105-acre campus with easy access to New York City
Moderately difficult entrance level, 6% of applicants were admitted

Freshmen *Admission:* 2,425 applied, 1,209 were accepted, 540 enrolled. *Test scores:* SAT verbal scores over 500: 79%; SAT math scores over 500: 78%; SAT verbal scores over 600: 24%; SAT math scores over 600: 25%; SAT verbal scores over 700: 3%; SAT math scores over 700: 4%.
Tuition and fees (2004–05): $23,900 (full-time). *Room and board:* $7500.
Financial Aid (All incoming freshmen): *Average need-based gift aid:* $10,576. *Average non-need based aid:* $7624. *Average aid to full-time undergraduates:* $12,605.
Athletic Department: *Director of Athletics:* Walt Hameline; Phone: 718-390-3488; Fax: 718-390-3347; E-mail: whamelin@wagner.edu. *Sports Information Director:* Ben Shove; Phone: 718-390-3227; E-mail: bshove@wagner.edu.

MEN'S COACHES
Baseball: Joe Litterio; Phone: 718-390-3154; E-mail: jlitteri@wagner.edu.

Basketball: Mike Deane; Phone: 718-390-3468; E-mail: mdeane@wagner.edu.
Cheerleading: Pam Coppola; Phone: 718-390-3209.
Cross Country: Joe Stasi; Phone: 718-390-3155; E-mail: jstasi@wagner.edu.
Football: Walt Hameline; Phone: 718-390-3488; E-mail: whamelin@wagner.edu.
Golf: John Garland; Phone: 718-390-3229; E-mail: jgarland@wagner.edu.
Lacrosse: Chris Lukowski; Phone: 718-390-3231; E-mail: clukowsk@wagner.edu.
Tennis: Ed Perpetua; Phone: 718-390-3188; E-mail: eperpetu@wagner.edu.
Track and Field: Joe Stasi; Phone: 718-390-3155; E-mail: jstasi@wagner.edu.
Wrestling: Joe Ryan; Phone: 718-390-3160; E-mail: jryan@wagner.edu.

WOMEN'S COACHES
Basketball: Tara Gallagher; Phone: 718-390-3198; E-mail: tgallagh@wagner.edu.
Cheerleading: Pam Coppola; Phone: 718-390-3209.
Cross Country: Joe Stasi; Phone: 718-390-3155; E-mail: jstasi@wagner.edu.
Golf: John Garland; Phone: 718-390-3229; E-mail: jgarland@wagner.edu.
Lacrosse: Lee Daignault; Phone: 718-390-3200; E-mail: ldaignau@wagner.edu.
Soccer: Hope Troman; Phone: 718-390-3156; E-mail: htroman@wagner.edu.
Softball: Glen Payne; Phone: 718-390-3201; E-mail: gpayne@wagner.edu.
Swimming: Katie Dolan; Phone: 718-390-3191; E-mail: kdolan@wagner.edu.
Tennis: Ed Perpetua; Phone: 718-390-3188; E-mail: eperpetu@wagner.edu.
Track and Field: Joe Stasi; Phone: 718-390-3155; E-mail: jstasi@wagner.edu.
Volleyball: Kevin Papa; Phone: 718-390-3199; E-mail: kpapa@wagner.edu.

WAKE FOREST UNIVERSITY
Winston-Salem, North Carolina

Demon Deacons ◆ NCAA I ◆ Atlantic Coast Conference ◆ http://www.wfu.edu/

Independent university, founded 1834
Coed, 4,031 undergraduate students, 99% full-time, 51% women, 49% men
Suburban 340-acre campus
Very difficult entrance level, 50% of applicants were admitted

Freshmen *Admission:* 5,752 applied, 2,599 were accepted, 1,004 enrolled. *Test scores:* SAT verbal scores over 500: 96%; SAT math scores over 500: 98%; SAT verbal scores over 600: 82%; SAT math scores over 600: 87%; SAT verbal scores over 700: 24%; SAT math scores over 700: 31%.
Tuition and fees (2004–05): $28,310 (full-time). *Room and board:* $8000 (room only: $4900).
Financial Aid (All incoming freshmen): *Average need-based gift aid:* $15,933. *Average non-need based aid:* $9435. *Average aid to full-time undergraduates:* $20,767.
Athletic Department: *Director of Athletics:* Ron Wellman; Phone: 336-758-5616; Fax: 336-758-6090; E-mail: wellmanr@wfu.edu. *Sports Information Director:* Mike Vest; Phone: 336-758-1880; E-mail: vestma@wfu.edu.

MEN'S COACHES
Baseball: George Greer; Phone: 336-758-5570; E-mail: greerge@wfu.edu.
Basketball: Skip Prosser; Phone: 336-758-5622; E-mail: heflinlg@wfu.edu.
Cheerleading: Brent Campbell; Phone: 336-758-4902; E-mail: bc91573@wfu.edu.
Cross Country: Scott Hall; Phone: 336-758-5860; E-mail: hallsa@wfu.edu.
Football: Jim Grobe; Phone: 330-490-5633; E-mail: grobejb@wfu.edu.
Golf: Jerry Haas; Phone: 336-758-6000; E-mail: haasjl@wfu.edu.

Wake Forest University (continued)

Soccer: Jay Vidovich; Phone: 336-758-5783; E-mail: vidovijm@wfu.edu.
Tennis: Jeff Zinn; Phone: 336-758-5886; E-mail: zinnjt@wfu.edu.
Track and Field: Annie Bennett; Phone: 336-758-4871; E-mail: bennetas@wfu.edu.

WOMEN'S COACHES

Basketball: Charlene Curtis; Phone: 336-758-5862; E-mail: curtisca@wfu.edu.
Cheerleading: Brent Campbell; Phone: 336-758-4902; E-mail: bc91573@wfu.edu.
Cross Country: Annie Bennett; Phone: 336-758-4871; E-mail: bennetas@wfu.edu.
Field Hockey: Jennifer Averill; Phone: 336-758-5859; E-mail: averiljd@wfu.edu.
Golf: Diane Dailey; Phone: 336-758-5858; E-mail: dianned@wfu.edu.
Soccer: Tony Da luz; Phone: 336-758-4375; E-mail: daluz@wfu.edu.
Tennis: Brian Fleishman; Phone: 336-758-5752; E-mail: fleishbe@wfu.edu.
Track and Field: Annie Bennett; Phone: 336-758-4871; E-mail: bennetas@wfu.edu.
Volleyball: Valorie Baker; Phone: 336-758-6993; E-mail: bakervg@wfu.edu.

WALDORF COLLEGE
Forest City, Iowa

Warriors ◆ NAIA ◆ Midwest Classic Conference ◆ http://www.waldorf.edu/

Independent Lutheran 4-year, founded 1903
Coed, 592 undergraduate students, 83% full-time, 50% women, 50% men
Small-town 29-acre campus
Moderately difficult entrance level, 68% of applicants were admitted

Freshmen *Admission:* 585 applied, 424 were accepted, 295 enrolled.
Tuition and fees (2003–04): $13,662 (full-time). *Room and board:* $4200 (room only: $2100).
Financial Aid (All incoming freshmen): *Average need-based gift aid:* $11,140. *Average non-need based aid:* $8089. *Average aid to full-time undergraduates:* $15,307.
Athletic Department: *Director of Athletics:* Denny Jerome; Phone: 641-585-8183; Fax: 641-585-8184; E-mail: jeromed@waldorf.edu. *Sports Information Director:* Denny Gilbertson; Phone: 641-585-8271; E-mail: gilbertsd@waldorf.edu.

MEN'S COACHES

Baseball: Brian Grunzke; Phone: 641-585-8263; E-mail: grunzkeb@waldorf.edu.
Basketball: Chad Brown; Phone: 641-585-8262; E-mail: brownc@waldorf.edu.
Cheerleading: Teresa Hanna; Phone: 641-585-8185; E-mail: hannat@waldorf.edu.
Football: David Bolstorf; Phone: 641-585-8166; E-mail: bolstorff@waldorf.edu.
Golf: Neil Boyd; Phone: 641-585-8232.
Soccer: Alan Seldon; Phone: 641-585-8266; E-mail: seldona@waldorf.edu.
Wrestling: Steve Kelly; Phone: 641-585-8261; E-mail: kellys@waldorf.edu.

WOMEN'S COACHES

Basketball: Denny Jerome; Phone: 641-585-8183; E-mail: jeromed@waldorf.edu.
Cheerleading: Teresa Hanna; Phone: 641-585-8185; E-mail: hannat@waldorf.edu.
Golf: Neil Boyd; Phone: 641-585-8232.
Soccer: Julie Seldon; Phone: 641-585-8262; E-mail: seldonj@waldorf.edu.
Softball: Denny Gilbertson; Phone: 641-585-8271; E-mail: gilbertsd@waldorf.edu.
Volleyball: Jody Dosser; Phone: 641-585-8230; E-mail: dosserj@waldorf.edu.

WALSH UNIVERSITY
North Canton, Ohio

Cavaliers ◆ NAIA ◆ American Mideast Conference; Mid-States Football Conference ◆ http://www.walsh.edu/

Independent Roman Catholic comprehensive, founded 1958
Coed, 1,573 undergraduate students, 73% full-time, 60% women, 40% men
Small-town 107-acre campus with easy access to Cleveland
Moderately difficult entrance level, 80% of applicants were admitted

Freshmen *Admission:* 970 applied, 792 were accepted, 294 enrolled.
Tuition and fees (2004–05): $15,610 (full-time). *Room and board:* $7700 (room only: $4500).
Financial Aid (All incoming freshmen): *Average need-based gift aid:* $6144. *Average non-need based aid:* $4545. *Average aid to full-time undergraduates:* $10,632.
Athletic Department: *Director of Athletics:* Jim Dennison; Phone: 330-490-7035; Fax: 330-490-7038; E-mail: jdennison@walsh.edu. *Sports Information Director:* Jim Clark; Phone: 330-490-7017; E-mail: jclark@walsh.edu.

MEN'S COACHES

Basketball: Steve Loy; Phone: 330-490-7015; E-mail: sloy@walsh.edu.
Cheerleading: Nikki Caldwell; Phone: 330-490-7035; E-mail: ncaldwell@walsh.edu.
Cross Country: Al Campbell; Phone: 330-490-7023; E-mail: acampbell@walsh.edu.
Football: Jim Dennison; Phone: 330-490-7035; E-mail: jdennison@walsh.edu.
Golf: Jeff Young; Phone: 330-490-7020; E-mail: jyoung@walsh.edu.
Tennis: Sherry Bossart; Phone: 330-490-7019; E-mail: sbossart@walsh.edu.

WOMEN'S COACHES

Basketball: Theresa Berg; Phone: 330-490-7012; E-mail: tberg@walsh.edu.
Cheerleading: Nikki Caldwell; Phone: 330-490-7035; E-mail: ncaldwell@walsh.edu.
Cross Country: Al Campbell; Phone: 330-490-7023; E-mail: acampbell@walsh.edu.
Golf: Jeff Young; Phone: 330-490-7020; E-mail: jyoung@walsh.edu.
Soccer: Ed Vargo; Phone: 330-490-7034; E-mail: evargo@walsh.edu.
Softball: Ed Vargo; Phone: 330-490-7034; E-mail: evargo@walsh.edu.
Tennis: Sherry Bossart; Phone: 330-490-7019; E-mail: sbossart@walsh.edu.
Track and Field: Al Campbell; Phone: 330-490-7023; E-mail: acampbell@walsh.edu.
Track and Field: Al Campbell; Phone: 330-490-7023; E-mail: acampbell@walsh.edu.
Volleyball: Cassandra Dixon; Phone: 330-490-7028; E-mail: cdixon@walsh.edu.

WARNER PACIFIC COLLEGE
Portland, Oregon

Knights ◆ NAIA ◆ Cascade Collegiate Conference ◆ http://www.warnerpacific.edu/

Independent religious comprehensive, founded 1937, affiliated with Church of God
Coed, 504 undergraduate students, 83% full-time, 61% women, 39% men
Urban 15-acre campus
Moderately difficult entrance level, 44% of applicants were admitted

Freshmen *Admission:* 802 applied, 355 were accepted, 68 enrolled.
Tuition and fees (2003–04): $16,910 (full-time). *Room and board:* $4990.
Financial Aid (All incoming freshmen): *Average need-based gift aid:* $3561. *Average non-need based aid:* $10,175. *Average aid to full-time undergraduates:* $17,409.
Athletic Department: *Director of Athletics:* Bart Valentine; Phone: 503-517-1125; Fax: 503-517-1250; E-mail: bvalentine@warnerpacific.edu. *Sports Information Director:* Troy Hutchinson; Phone: 503-517-1370; E-mail: sid@warnerpacific.edu.

MEN'S COACHES

Basketball: Bart Valentine; Phone: 503-517-1125; E-mail: bvalentine@ warnerpacific.edu.
Cross Country: Dave Lee; Phone: 503-517-1370; E-mail: dlee@ warnerpacific.edu.
Soccer: Bernie Fagan; Phone: 503-517-1069; E-mail: bfagan@ warnerpacific.edu.
Track and Field: Dave Lee; Phone: 503-517-1370; E-mail: dlee@ warnerpacific.edu.

WOMEN'S COACHES

Basketball: Katy Steding; Phone: 503-517-1369; E-mail: ksteding@ warnerpacific.edu.
Cross Country: Dave Lee; Phone: 503-517-1370; E-mail: dlee@ warnerpacific.edu.
Soccer: Phone: 503-517-1370.
Track and Field: Dave Lee; Phone: 503-517-1370; E-mail: dlee@ warnerpacific.edu.
Volleyball: Tom Russell; Phone: 503-517-1368; E-mail: trussell@ warnerpacific.edu.

WARNER SOUTHERN COLLEGE
Lake Wales, Florida

Royals ◆ NAIA ◆ Florida Sun Conference ◆ http://www.warner.edu/

Independent religious comprehensive, founded 1968, affiliated with Church of God
Coed, 1,144 undergraduate students, 86% full-time, 57% women, 43% men
Rural 320-acre campus with easy access to Tampa and Orlando
Minimally difficult entrance level, 63% of applicants were admitted

Freshmen *Admission:* 279 applied, 194 were accepted, 120 enrolled. *Test scores:* SAT verbal scores over 500: 32%; SAT math scores over 500: 31%; SAT verbal scores over 600: 4%; SAT math scores over 600: 4%; SAT verbal scores over 700: 2%; SAT math scores over 700: 2%.
Tuition and fees (2003–04): $11,380 (full-time). *Room and board:* $5271 (room only: $2640).
Financial Aid (All incoming freshmen): *Average need-based gift aid:* $1813. *Average non-need based aid:* $7033. *Average aid to full-time undergraduates:* $11,601.
Athletic Department: *Director of Athletics:* Gary Bays; Phone: 863-638-1464; Fax: 863-638-3776; E-mail: baysg@warner.edu.

MEN'S COACHES

Baseball: Jeff Sikes; Phone: 863-638-1464; E-mail: sikesj@warner.edu.
Basketball: Kory Bays; Phone: 863-638-1464; E-mail: baysk@warner.edu.
Cheerleading: Heather Snively; Phone: 863-638-1464; E-mail: j.snively@warner.edu.
Cross Country: Jose Larios; Phone: 863-638-1464; E-mail: lariosj@warner.edu.
Golf: Phone: 863-638-1464.
Soccer: Bob Lennon; Phone: 863-638-1464; E-mail: lennonb@warner.edu.
Track and Field: Jose Larios; Phone: 863-638-1464; E-mail: lariosj@warner.edu.

WOMEN'S COACHES

Basketball: Gary Bays; Phone: 863-638-1464; E-mail: baysg@warner.edu.
Cheerleading: Heather Snively; Phone: 863-638-1464; E-mail: j.snively@warner.edu.
Cross Country: Jose Larios; Phone: 863-638-1464; E-mail: lariosj@warner.edu.
Golf: Phone: 863-638-1464.
Soccer: Shawn Gary; Phone: 863-638-1464; E-mail: garys@warner.edu.
Softball: Shawn Gary; Phone: 863-638-1464; E-mail: garys@warner.edu.
Track and Field: Jose Larios; Phone: 863-638-1464; E-mail: lariosj@warner.edu.
Volleyball: Phone: 863-638-1464; E-mail: garys@warner.edu.

WARTBURG COLLEGE
Waverly, Iowa

Knights ◆ NCAA III ◆ Iowa Athletic Conference ◆ http://www.wartburg.edu/

Independent Lutheran 4-year, founded 1852
Coed, 1,775 undergraduate students, 96% full-time, 55% women, 45% men
Small-town 118-acre campus
Moderately difficult entrance level, 78% of applicants were admitted

Freshmen *Admission:* 1,841 applied, 1,531 were accepted, 504 enrolled. *Test scores:* SAT verbal scores over 500: 71%; SAT math scores over 500: 70%; SAT verbal scores over 600: 38%; SAT math scores over 600: 53%; SAT verbal scores over 700: 5%; SAT math scores over 700: 5%.
Tuition and fees (2003–04): $18,550 (full-time). *Room and board:* $5180 (room only: $2530).
Financial Aid (All incoming freshmen): *Average need-based gift aid:* $12,420. *Average non-need based aid:* $18,453. *Average aid to full-time undergraduates:* $17,415.
Athletic Department: *Director of Athletics:* Gary Grace; Phone: 319-352-8470; Fax: 319-352-8528; E-mail: gary.grace@wartburg.edu. *Sports Information Director:* Mark Adkins; Phone: 319-352-8208; E-mail: mark.adkins@wartburg.edu.

MEN'S COACHES

Baseball: Joel Holst; Phone: 319-352-8532; E-mail: joel.holst@ wartburg.edu.
Basketball: Dick Peth; Phone: 319-352-8483; E-mail: dick.peth@ wartburg.edu.
Cheerleading: Kathy Franken; Phone: 319-352-8612; E-mail: kathy. franken@wartburg.edu.
Cross Country: Steve Johnson; Phone: 319-352-8292; E-mail: steven. johnson@wartburg.edu.
Football: Rick Willis; Phone: 319-352-8467; E-mail: rick.willis@ wartburg.edu.
Golf: Mark Franzen; Phone: 319-352-8362; E-mail: mark.franzen@ wartburg.edu.
Soccer: Jim Conlon; Phone: 319-352-8355; E-mail: james.conlon@ wartburg.edu.
Tennis: Jim Willis; Phone: 319-352-2901; E-mail: james.willis@ wartburg.edu.
Track and Field: Marcus Newsom; Phone: 319-352-8356; E-mail: marcus.newsom@wartburg.edu.
Wrestling: Jim Miller; Phone: 319-352-8310; E-mail: james.miller@ wartburg.edu.

WOMEN'S COACHES

Basketball: Monica Severson; Phone: 319-352-8469; E-mail: monica. severson@wartburg.edu.
Cheerleading: Kathy Franken; Phone: 319-352-8612; E-mail: kathy. franken@wartburg.edu.
Cross Country: Steve Johnson; Phone: 319-352-8292; E-mail: steven. johnson@wartburg.edu.
Golf: Mark Franzen; Phone: 319-352-8362; E-mail: mark.franzen@ wartburg.edu.
Soccer: Jim Conlon; Phone: 319-352-8355; E-mail: james.conlon@ wartburg.edu.
Softball: Kara Kehe; Phone: 319-352-8663; E-mail: kara.kehe@ wartburg.edu.
Tennis: Jim Willis; Phone: 319-352-2901; E-mail: james.willis@ wartburg.edu.
Track and Field: Marcus Newsom; Phone: 319-352-8356; E-mail: marcus.newsom@wartburg.edu.
Volleyball: Jennifer Walker; Phone: 319-352-8468; E-mail: jennifer. walker@wartburg.edu.

WASHBURN UNIVERSITY
Topeka, Kansas

(M) Ichabods (W) Lady Blues ◆ NCAA II ◆ Mid-America Intercollegiate Conference ◆ http://www.washburn.edu/

City-supported comprehensive, founded 1865
Coed, 6,045 undergraduate students
Urban 160-acre campus with easy access to Kansas City
Noncompetitive entrance level, 100% of applicants were admitted

Freshmen *Admission:* 1,705 applied, 1,705 were accepted.
Tuition and fees (2004–05): *Room and board:* $4860.
Financial Aid (All incoming freshmen): *Average need-based gift aid:* $1350. *Average non-need based aid:* $1551. *Average aid to full-time undergraduates:* $2125.
Athletic Department: *Director of Athletics:* Loren Ferre; Phone: 785-231-1010; Fax: 785-231-1091; E-mail: loren.ferre@washburn.edu. *Sports Information Director:* Gene Cassell; E-mail: cassell@washburn.edu.

MEN'S COACHES
Baseball: Steve Anson; Phone: 785-231-1010; E-mail: steve.anson@washburn.edu.
Basketball: Bob Chipman; Phone: 785-231-1010; E-mail: bob.chipman@washburn.edu.
Football: Craig Schurig; Phone: 785-231-1010; E-mail: craig.schurig@washburn.edu.
Golf: Doug Hamilton; Phone: 785-231-1010; E-mail: doug.hamilton@washburn.edu.
Tennis: Jennifer Hastert; Phone: 785-231-1010; E-mail: jennifer.hastert@washburn.edu.

WOMEN'S COACHES
Basketball: Ron McHenry; Phone: 785-231-1010; E-mail: ron.mchenry@washburn.edu.
Soccer: Tim Collins; Phone: 785-231-1010; E-mail: tim.collins@washburn.edu.
Softball: Lisa Carey; Phone: 785-231-1010; E-mail: lisa.carey@washburn.edu.
Tennis: Jennifer Hastert; Phone: 785-231-1010; E-mail: jennifer.hastert@washburn.edu.
Volleyball: Chris Herron; Phone: 785-231-1010; E-mail: chris.herron@washburn.edu.

WASHINGTON & JEFFERSON COLLEGE
Washington, Pennsylvania

Presidents ◆ NCAA III ◆ Presidents' Athletic Conference ◆ http://www.washjeff.edu/

Independent 4-year, founded 1781
Coed, 1,233 undergraduate students, 99% full-time, 48% women, 52% men
Small-town 51-acre campus with easy access to Pittsburgh
Very difficult entrance level, 4% of applicants were admitted

Freshmen *Admission:* 3,135 applied, 1,260 were accepted, 347 enrolled. *Test scores:* SAT verbal scores over 500: 84%; SAT math scores over 500: 87%; SAT verbal scores over 600: 32%; SAT math scores over 600: 40%; SAT verbal scores over 700: 4%; SAT math scores over 700: 6%.
Tuition and fees (2003–04): $23,260 (full-time). *Room and board:* $6310 (room only: $3440).
Financial Aid (All incoming freshmen): *Average need-based gift aid:* $10,871. *Average non-need based aid:* $7270. *Average aid to full-time undergraduates:* $17,146.
Athletic Department: *Director of Athletics:* Rick Creehan; Phone: 724-503-1001; Fax: 724-250-3329; E-mail: rcreehan@washjeff.edu. *Sports Information Director:* Scott McGuinness; Phone: 724-503-1001; E-mail: smcguinness@washjeff.edu.

MEN'S COACHES
Baseball: Jeff Mountain; Phone: 724-503-1001; E-mail: jmountain@washjeff.edu.
Basketball: Karel Jelinek; Phone: 724-223-6064; E-mail: kjelinek@washjeff.edu.

Cross Country: Mark Fitzpatrick; Phone: 724-223-6054; E-mail: mfitzpatrick@washjeff.edu.
Diving: Mike Orstein; Phone: 724-503-1001; E-mail: morstein@washjeff.edu.
Football: Mike Sirianni; Phone: 724-223-6061; E-mail: msirianni@washjeff.edu.
Golf: Pete Coughlin; Phone: 724-503-1001; E-mail: terpgolf99@yahoo.com.
Lacrosse: Chad Moore; Phone: 724-223-6062; E-mail: cmoore@washjeff.edu.
Soccer: Ian Mcdonald; Phone: 724-503-1001; E-mail: imcdonald@washjeff.edu.
Swimming: Mike Orstein; Phone: 724-503-1001; E-mail: morstein@washjeff.edu.
Tennis: John Delaura; Phone: 724-223-5001; E-mail: jdelaura@washjeff.edu.
Track and Field: Mike Sirinni; Phone: 724-250-3305; E-mail: msirianni@washjeff.edu.
Wrestling: Angelo Morascyzk; Phone: 724-223-6054; E-mail: amorascyzk@falconplastics.com.

WOMEN'S COACHES
Basketball: Carrie Zickefoose; Phone: 724-250-3461; E-mail: czickefoose@washjeff.edu.
Cross Country: Mark Fitzpatrick; Phone: 724-223-6054; E-mail: mfitzpatrick@washjeff.edu.
Diving: Mike Orstein; Phone: 724-503-1001; E-mail: morstein@washjeff.edu.
Field Hockey: Jenny Dumas; Phone: 724-223-6055; E-mail: jdumas@washjeff.edu.
Golf: Pete Coughlin; Phone: 724-503-1001; E-mail: terpgolf99@yahoo.com.
Soccer: Melissa Joseph; Phone: 724-503-1001; E-mail: mjoseph@washjeff.edu.
Softball: Stephani Ehrenfeld; Phone: 724-503-1001; E-mail: sehrenfeld@washjeff.edu.
Swimming: Mike Orstein; Phone: 724-503-1001; E-mail: morstein@washjeff.edu.
Tennis: John Delaura; Phone: 724-503-1001; E-mail: jdelaura@washjeff.edu.
Track and Field: Mike Sirinni; Phone: 724-250-3305; E-mail: msirianni@washjeff.edu.
Volleyball: Fred Wallace; Phone: 724-503-1001; E-mail: fwallace@washjeff.edu.

WASHINGTON AND LEE UNIVERSITY
Lexington, Virginia

Generals ◆ NCAA III ◆ Centennial Conference; Old Dominion Conference ◆ http://www.wlu.edu/

Independent comprehensive, founded 1749
Coed, 1,740 undergraduate students, 100% full-time, 48% women, 52% men
Small-town 322-acre campus
Most difficult entrance level, 3% of applicants were admitted

Freshmen *Admission:* 3,185 applied, 996 were accepted, 453 enrolled. *Test scores:* SAT verbal scores over 500: 100%; SAT math scores over 500: 100%; SAT verbal scores over 600: 92%; SAT math scores over 600: 96%; SAT verbal scores over 700: 44%; SAT math scores over 700: 46%.
Tuition and fees (2003–04): $23,295 (full-time). *Room and board:* $6368 (room only: $2698).
Financial Aid (All incoming freshmen): *Average need-based gift aid:* $16,969. *Average non-need based aid:* $6557. *Average aid to full-time undergraduates:* $22,272.
Athletic Department: *Director of Athletics:* Mike Walsh; Phone: 540-458-8671; Fax: 540-464-7622; E-mail: walshm@wlu.edu. *Sports Information Director:* Brian Laubscher; Phone: 540-458-8676; E-mail: blaubsch@wlu.edu.

MEN'S COACHES
Baseball: Marlin Ikenberry; Phone: 540-458-7609; E-mail: ikenberrymm@vmi.edu.

Basketball: Adam Hutchinson; Phone: 540-458-8691; E-mail: hutchinsona@wlu.edu.

Cross Country: John Tucker; Phone: 540-458-8667; E-mail: tuckerj@wlu.edu.

Football: Frank Miriello; Phone: 540-458-8686; E-mail: miriellof@wlu.edu.

Golf: Gavin Colliton; Phone: 540-458-8682; E-mail: collitong@wlu.edu.

Lacrosse: Mike Cerino; Phone: 540-458-8678; E-mail: cerinom@wlu.edu.

Soccer: Rolf Piranian; Phone: 540-458-8685; E-mail: piranianr@wlu.edu.

Swimming: Joel Shinofield; Phone: 540-458-8693; E-mail: shinofieldj@wlu.edu.

Tennis: David Detwiller; Phone: 540-458-8118; E-mail: detwilerd@wlu.edu.

Track and Field: Nate Hoey; Phone: 540-458-8965; E-mail: hoeyn@wlu.edu.

Wrestling: Gary Franke; Phone: 540-458-8666; E-mail: frankeg@wlu.edu.

WOMEN'S COACHES

Basketball: Mandy King; Phone: 540-458-8202; E-mail: kingma@wlu.edu.

Cross Country: Kris Hoey; Phone: 540-458-8679; E-mail: hoeyk@wlu.edu.

Field Hockey: Wendy Orrison; Phone: 540-458-8675; E-mail: orrisonw@wlu.edu.

Lacrosse: Jamie Hathorn; Phone: 540-458-8668; E-mail: hathornj@wlu.edu.

Soccer: Neil Cunningham; Phone: 540-458-8056; E-mail: cunninghamn@wlu.edu.

Swimming: Kiki Jacobs; Phone: 540-458-8481; E-mail: jacobsk@wlu.edu.

Track and Field: John Tucker; Phone: 540-458-8667; E-mail: tuckerj@wlu.edu.

Volleyball: Bryan Snyder; Phone: 540-458-8946; E-mail: snyderb@wlu.edu.

WASHINGTON COLLEGE
Chestertown, Maryland

Sho'men ◆ NCAA III ◆ Centennial Conference ◆ http://www.washcoll.edu/

Independent comprehensive, founded 1782
Coed, 1,398 undergraduate students, 96% full-time, 63% women, 37% men
Small-town 120-acre campus with easy access to Baltimore and Washington, DC
Moderately difficult entrance level, 6% of applicants were admitted

Freshmen *Admission:* 2,114 applied, 1,290 were accepted, 359 enrolled. *Test scores:* SAT verbal scores over 500: 90%; SAT math scores over 500: 86%; SAT verbal scores over 600: 44%; SAT math scores over 600: 33%; SAT verbal scores over 700: 7%; SAT math scores over 700: 4%.
Tuition and fees (2003–04): $24,300 (full-time). *Room and board:* $5740 (room only: $2600).
Financial Aid (All incoming freshmen): *Average need-based gift aid:* $14,631. *Average non-need based aid:* $11,026. *Average aid to full-time undergraduates:* $18,283.
Athletic Department: *Director of Athletics:* Bryan Matthews; Phone: 410-778-7231; Fax: 410-778-7741; E-mail: athletic_director@washcoll.edu. *Sports Information Director:* Phil Ticknor; Phone: 410-778-7238; E-mail: sports_information@washcoll.edu.

MEN'S COACHES

Baseball: Al Streelman; Phone: 410-778-7239; E-mail: baseball_coach@washcoll.edu.

Basketball: Rob Nugent; Phone: 410-778-7258; E-mail: m_basketball@washcoll.edu.

Lacrosse: J.B. Clarke; Phone: 410-778-7248; E-mail: m_lacrosse@washcoll.edu.

Soccer: Lin Outten; Phone: 410-778-7240; E-mail: m_soccer@washcoll.edu.

Swimming: Kim Lessard; Phone: 410-778-7241; E-mail: swimming_coach@washcoll.edu.

Tennis: Constantine Ananiadis; Phone: 410-778-7259; E-mail: tennis_coach@washcoll.edu.

WOMEN'S COACHES

Basketball: Gail Gilchrest; Phone: 410-778-7462; E-mail: w_basketball@washcoll.edu.

Field Hockey: Rachel Boyce; Phone: 410-778-7236; E-mail: field_hockey@washcoll.edu.

Lacrosse: Suzie Friedrich; Phone: 410-778-7257; E-mail: w_lacrosse@washcoll.edu.

Soccer: Suzie Friedrich; Phone: 410-778-7257; E-mail: w_soccer@washcoll.edu.

Softball: Lin Outten; Phone: 410-778-7240; E-mail: m_soccer@washcoll.edu.

Swimming: Kim Lessard; Phone: 410-778-7241; E-mail: swimming_coach@washcoll.edu.

Tennis: Constantine Ananiadis; Phone: 410-778-7259; E-mail: tennis_coach@washcoll.edu.

Volleyball: KJ Welcenbach; Phone: 410-778-7463; E-mail: volleyball_coach@washcoll.edu.

WASHINGTON STATE UNIVERSITY
Pullman, Washington

Cougars ◆ NCAA I ◆ Pacific-10 Conference ◆ http://www.wsu.edu/

State-supported university, founded 1890
Coed, 18,746 undergraduate students, 84% full-time, 53% women, 47% men
Rural 620-acre campus
Moderately difficult entrance level, 75% of applicants were admitted

Freshmen *Admission:* 9,182 applied, 7,206 were accepted, 3,043 enrolled. *Test scores:* SAT verbal scores over 500: 66%; SAT math scores over 500: 70%; SAT verbal scores over 600: 21%; SAT math scores over 600: 25%; SAT verbal scores over 700: 2%; SAT math scores over 700: 3%.
Tuition and fees (2003–04): $5210 (resident), $13,312 (nonresident). *Room and board:* $6054 (room only: $3010).
Financial Aid (All incoming freshmen): *Average need-based gift aid:* $4522. *Average non-need based aid:* $3751. *Average aid to full-time undergraduates:* $8166.
Athletic Department: *Director of Athletics:* Jim Sterk; Phone: 509-335-0200; Fax: 509-335-0328; E-mail: sterkj@wsu.edu. *Sports Information Director:* Rod Commons; Phone: 509-335-0269; E-mail: rodco@wsu.edu.

MEN'S COACHES

Baseball: Tim Mooney; Phone: 509-335-0211; E-mail: tmooney@wsu.edu.

Basketball: Dick Bennett; Phone: 509-335-0240; E-mail: bennettr@wsu.edu.

Cross Country: Rick Sloan; Phone: 509-335-0248; E-mail: ricks@wsu.edu.

Football: Bill Doba; Phone: 509-335-0250; E-mail: billdoba@wsu.edu.

Golf: Walt Williams; Phone: 509-335-0224; E-mail: wwilliams@wsu.edu.

Track and Field: Rick Sloan; Phone: 509-335-0248; E-mail: ricks@wsu.edu.

WOMEN'S COACHES

Basketball: Sherri Murell; Phone: 509-335-0276.

Cross Country: Rick Sloan; Phone: 509-335-0248; E-mail: ricks@wsu.edu.

Diving: Erica Quam; Phone: 509-335-0273; E-mail: ericaq@wsu.edu.

Golf: Walt Williams; Phone: 509-335-0224; E-mail: wwilliams@wsu.edu.

Soccer: Matt Potter; Phone: 509-335-0306; E-mail: mjpotter@wsu.edu.

Swimming: Erica Quam; Phone: 509-335-0273; E-mail: ericaq@wsu.edu.

Tennis: Lisa Hart; Phone: 509-335-0308.

Track and Field: Rick Sloan; Phone: 509-335-0248; E-mail: ricks@wsu.edu.

Volleyball: Cindy Fredrick; Phone: 509-335-0277; E-mail: cindyf@wsu.edu.

WASHINGTON UNIVERSITY IN ST. LOUIS
St. Louis, Missouri

Bears ◆ NCAA III ◆ University Athletic Conference ◆ http://www.wustl.edu/

Independent university, founded 1853
Coed, 7,188 undergraduate students, 82% full-time, 53% women, 47% men
Suburban 169-acre campus
Most difficult entrance level, 2% of applicants were admitted

Freshmen *Admission:* 20,378 applied, 4,080 were accepted, 1,367 enrolled. *Test scores:* SAT verbal scores over 500: 100%; SAT math scores over 500: 100%; SAT verbal scores over 600: 94%; SAT math scores over 600: 98%; SAT verbal scores over 700: 47%; SAT math scores over 700: 60%.
Tuition and fees (2004–05): $30,546 (full-time). *Room and board:* $9640 (room only: $5750).
Financial Aid (All incoming freshmen): *Average need-based gift aid:* $21,404. *Average non-need based aid:* $10,813. *Average aid to full-time undergraduates:* $25,010.
Athletic Department: *Director of Athletics:* John Schael; Phone: 314-935-5288; Fax: 314-935-5545; E-mail: schael@athletics.wustl.edu. *Sports Information Director:* Chris Mitchell; Phone: 314-935-5077; E-mail: mitchell@wustl.edu.

MEN'S COACHES
Baseball: Ric Lessmann; Phone: 314-935-5945; E-mail: lessmann@athletics.wustl.edu.
Basketball: Mark Edwards; Phone: 314-935-5168; E-mail: marke@athletics.wustl.edu.
Cheerleading: Tracy Zuckett; Phone: 314-244-2212; E-mail: tzuckett@moser.com.
Cross Country: Jeff Stiles; Phone: 314-935-7307; E-mail: stiles@athletics.wustl.edu.
Diving: Meg Dierkes; Phone: 314-935-7490.
Football: Larry Kindbom; Phone: 314-935-7308; E-mail: larryki@athletics.wustl.edu.
Soccer: Joe Clarke; Phone: 314-935-5174; E-mail: joec@athletics.wustl.edu.
Swimming: Brad Shively; Phone: 314-935-7490; E-mail: bkswim@athletics.wustl.edu.
Tennis: Roger Follmer; Phone: 314-935-6801; E-mail: follmer@athletics.wustl.edu.
Track and Field: Paul Thornton; Phone: 314-935-9089; E-mail: thornton@athletics.wustl.edu.

WOMEN'S COACHES
Basketball: Nancy Fahey; Phone: 314-935-4702; E-mail: nancyf@athletics.wustl.edu.
Cheerleading: Tracy Zuckett; Phone: 314-244-2212; E-mail: tzuckett@moser.com.
Diving: Meg Dierkes; Phone: 314-935-7490.
Soccer: Wendy Dillinger; Phone: 314-935-4706; E-mail: wendyd@athletics.wustl.edu.
Softball: Cindy Zelinsky; Phone: 314-935-8549; E-mail: cindyz@athletics.wustl.edu.
Swimming: Brad Shively; Phone: 314-935-7490; E-mail: bkswim@athletics.wustl.edu.
Tennis: Lynn Imergoot; Phone: 314-935-5204; E-mail: imergoot@athletics.wustl.edu.
Track and Field: Paul Thornton; Phone: 314-935-9089; E-mail: thornton@athletics.wustl.edu.
Volleyball: Rich Luenemann; Phone: 314-935-4713; E-mail: luenemann@athletics.wustl.edu.

WAYLAND BAPTIST UNIVERSITY
Plainview, Texas

Pioneers ◆ NAIA ◆ Sooner Conference ◆ http://www.wbu.edu/

Independent Baptist comprehensive, founded 1908
Coed, 998 undergraduate students, 81% full-time, 59% women, 41% men
Small-town 80-acre campus
Minimally difficult entrance level, 99% of applicants were admitted

Freshmen *Admission:* 303 applied, 296 were accepted, 215 enrolled. *Test scores:* SAT verbal scores over 500: 55%; SAT math scores over 500: 59%; SAT verbal scores over 600: 18%; SAT math scores over 600: 17%; SAT verbal scores over 700: 4%; SAT math scores over 700: 1%.
Tuition and fees (2003–04): $8500 (full-time). *Room and board:* $3354 (room only: $1276).
Financial Aid (All incoming freshmen): *Average need-based gift aid:* $6055. *Average non-need based aid:* $6807. *Average aid to full-time undergraduates:* $7552.
Athletic Department: *Director of Athletics:* Greg Feris; Phone: 806-291-1137; Fax: 806-291-1962; E-mail: gferis@wbu.edu. *Sports Information Director:* Rhane Jeffress; Phone: 806-291-1136; E-mail: jeffress@wbu.edu.

MEN'S COACHES
Baseball: Brad Bass; Phone: 806-291-1132; E-mail: bradbass@wbu.edu.
Basketball: Todd Thurman; Phone: 806-291-1155; E-mail: @wbu.edu.
Cross Country: Chris Beene; Phone: 806-291-1143; E-mail: beene@wbu.edu.
Golf: Tom Harp; Phone: 806-291-1156; E-mail: tomharp@wbu.edu.
Track and Field: Chris Beene; Phone: 806-291-1143; E-mail: beene@wbu.edu.

WOMEN'S COACHES
Basketball: Will Flemons; Phone: 806-291-1145; E-mail: flemonsw@wbu.edu.
Cross Country: Chris Beene; Phone: 806-291-1143; E-mail: beene@wbu.edu.
Soccer: Brent Camp; Phone: 806-291-1149; E-mail: campb@wbu.edu.
Track and Field: Chris Beene; Phone: 806-291-1143; E-mail: beene@wbu.edu.
Volleyball: Kristee Turpin; Phone: 806-291-1144; E-mail: turpin@wbu.edu.

WAYNESBURG COLLEGE
Waynesburg, Pennsylvania

Yellow Jackets ◆ NCAA III ◆ Presidents' Athletic Conference ◆ http://www.waynesburg.edu/

Independent religious comprehensive, founded 1849, affiliated with Presbyterian Church (U.S.A.)
Coed, 1,530 undergraduate students, 83% full-time, 58% women, 42% men
Small-town 30-acre campus with easy access to Pittsburgh
Moderately difficult entrance level, 75% of applicants were admitted

Freshmen *Admission:* 1,467 applied, 1,147 were accepted, 330 enrolled.
Tuition and fees (2003–04): $13,850 (full-time). *Room and board:* $5520 (room only: $2820).
Financial Aid (All incoming freshmen): *Average need-based gift aid:* $7359. *Average non-need based aid:* $2900. *Average aid to full-time undergraduates:* $9510.
Athletic Department: *Director of Athletics:* Rudy Marisa; Phone: 724-852-3246; Fax: 724-852-4122; E-mail: rmarisa@waynesburg.edu. *Sports Information Director:* Justin Zackal; Phone: 724-852-3334; E-mail: jzackal@waynesburg.edu.

MEN'S COACHES
Baseball: Duane Lanzy; Phone: 724-852-3229; E-mail: dlanzy@waynesburg.edu.
Basketball: Frank Ferraro; Phone: 724-852-3466; E-mail: rmarisa@waynesburg.edu.
Football: Jeff Hand; Phone: 724-852-3245; E-mail: jhand@waynesburg.edu.

Golf: John Garber; Phone: 724-852-3230.
Soccer: Jim Balach; Phone: 724-852-3230.
Tennis: Ron Christman; Phone: 724-852-3365; E-mail: rchristm@waynesburg.edu.
Wrestling: Dave Thomas; Phone: 724-852-3338; E-mail: dthomas@waynesburg.edu.

WOMEN'S COACHES
Basketball: Terry Acker; Phone: 724-852-3292; E-mail: tacker@waynesburg.edu.
Cross Country: Blair Zimmerman; Phone: 724-852-3438; E-mail: bzimmerm@waynesburg.edu.
Golf: John Garber; Phone: 724-852-3230.
Soccer: Jim Rue; Phone: 724-852-3292.
Tennis: Ron Christman; Phone: 724-852-3365; E-mail: rchristm@waynesburg.edu.
Volleyball: Mike Bruno; Phone: 724-852-3230; E-mail: mbruno@waynesburg.edu.

WAYNE STATE COLLEGE
Wayne, Nebraska

Wildcats ◆ NCAA II ◆ Northern Sun Intercollegiate Conference ◆ http://www.wsc.edu/

State-supported comprehensive, founded 1910, part of Nebraska State College System
Coed, 2,769 undergraduate students, 93% full-time, 56% women, 44% men
Small-town 128-acre campus
Noncompetitive entrance level, 100% of applicants were admitted

Freshmen *Admission:* 1,321 applied, 1,321 were accepted, 610 enrolled. **Tuition and fees (2003–04):** $3432 (resident), $6042 (nonresident). *Room and board:* $3920 (room only: $1860).
Financial Aid (All incoming freshmen): *Average need-based gift aid:* $1385. *Average aid to full-time undergraduates:* $3470.
Athletic Department: *Director of Athletics:* Todd Barry; Phone: 402-375-7520; Fax: 402-375-7271; E-mail: tobarry1@wsc.edu. *Sports Information Director:* Steve Schafer; Phone: 402-375-7326; E-mail: stschaf1@wsc.edu.

MEN'S COACHES
Baseball: John Manganaro; Phone: 402-375-7499; E-mail: jomanga1@wsc.edu.
Basketball: Rico Burkett; Phone: 402-375-7303; E-mail: riburke1@wsc.edu.
Cross Country: Marion Brink; Phone: 402-375-7507; E-mail: mabrink1@wsc.edu.
Football: Scott Hoffman; Phone: 402-375-7315; E-mail: schoffm1@wsc.edu.
Golf: Eric Henderson; Phone: 402-375-7515; E-mail: erhende1@wsc.edu.
Track and Field: Marion Brink; Phone: 402-375-7507; E-mail: mabrink1@wsc.edu.

WOMEN'S COACHES
Basketball: Ryun Williams; Phone: 402-375-7311; E-mail: rywilli1@wsc.edu.
Cross Country: Marion Brink; Phone: 402-375-7507; E-mail: mabrink1@wsc.edu.
Golf: Jon Misfeldt; Phone: 402-375-7522; E-mail: jomisfe1@wsc.edu.
Soccer: Rollie Bullock; Phone: 402-375-7506; E-mail: robuloc1@wsc.edu.
Softball: Jon Misfeldt; Phone: 402-375-7522; E-mail: jomisfe1@wsc.edu.
Track and Field: Marion Brink; Phone: 402-375-7507; E-mail: mabrink1@wsc.edu.
Volleyball: Sharon Vanis; Phone: 402-375-7303; E-mail: shvanis1@wsc.edu.

WAYNE STATE UNIVERSITY
Detroit, Michigan

Warriors ◆ NCAA II ◆ College Hockey America Conference; Great Lakes Intercollegiate Conference
◆ http://www.wayne.edu/

State-supported university, founded 1868
Coed, 20,150 undergraduate students
Urban 203-acre campus
Moderately difficult entrance level, 68% of applicants were admitted

Freshmen *Admission:* 8,477 applied, 5,764 were accepted.
Tuition and fees (2003–04): $5190 (resident), $11,211 (nonresident). *Room and board:* $6500.
Financial Aid (All incoming freshmen): *Average need-based gift aid:* $3833. *Average non-need based aid:* $4720. *Average aid to full-time undergraduates:* $6473.
Athletic Department: *Director of Athletics:* Rob Fournier; Phone: 313-577-4280; Fax: 313-577-5997; E-mail: ai5611@wayne.edu. *Sports Information Director:* Jeff Weiss; Phone: 313-577-7542; E-mail: jeff.weiss@wayne.edu.

MEN'S COACHES
Baseball: Jay Alexander; Phone: 313-577-2749; E-mail: jayalexander@wayne.edu.
Basketball: David Greer; Phone: 313-577-7515; E-mail: ak1733@wayne.edu.
Cheerleading: Viola Sprague; Phone: 586-263-6101; E-mail: ac2185@wayne.edu.
Cross Country: Rick Cummins; Phone: 313-577-4293; E-mail: rickcummins@wayne.edu.
Diving: Kelly LaCroix; Phone: 313-577-4263; E-mail: wsudiving@aol.com.
Football: Paul Winter; Phone: 313-577-4288.
Golf: Mike Horn; Phone: 313-577-4280; E-mail: mikidiway@wideopenwest.com.
Ice Hockey: Bill Wilkinson; Phone: 313-577-9173; E-mail: william.wilkinson@wayne.edu.
Swimming: Sean Peters; Phone: 313-577-4263; E-mail: wsuaqua@hotmail.com.
Swimming: Sean Peters; Phone: 313-577-4263; E-mail: wsuaqua@hotmail.com.
Tennis: Rick Cummins; Phone: 313-577-4293; E-mail: rickcummins@wayne.edu.

WOMEN'S COACHES
Basketball: Gloria Bradley; Phone: 313-577-7543; E-mail: ai6039@wayne.edu.
Cheerleading: Viola Sprague; Phone: 586-263-6101; E-mail: ac2185@wayne.edu.
Cross Country: Rick Cummins; Phone: 313-577-4293; E-mail: rickcummins@wayne.edu.
Diving: Kelly LaCroix; Phone: 313-577-4263; E-mail: wsudiving@aol.com.
Softball: Gary Bryce; Phone: 313-577-7513; E-mail: ab6905@wayne.edu.
Swimming: Sean Peters; Phone: 313-577-4463; E-mail: wsuaqua@hotmail.com.
Tennis: Rick Cummins; Phone: 313-577-4291; E-mail: rickcummins@wayne.edu.
Volleyball: Limin Jin; Phone: 313-577-7541; E-mail: ak5390@wayne.edu.

WEBBER INTERNATIONAL UNIVERSITY
Babson Park, Florida

Warriors ◆ NAIA ◆ Florida Sun Conference ◆ http://www.webber.edu/

Independent comprehensive, founded 1927
Coed, 588 undergraduate students, 90% full-time, 40% women, 60% men
Small-town 110-acre campus with easy access to Orlando
Moderately difficult entrance level, 5% of applicants were admitted

Freshmen *Admission:* 418 applied, 209 were accepted, 121 enrolled. *Test scores:* SAT verbal scores over 500: 18%; SAT math scores over 500: 22%; SAT math scores over 600: 3%.
Tuition and fees (2004–05): $12,930 (full-time). *Room and board:* $4510.
Financial Aid (All incoming freshmen): *Average need-based gift aid:* $8377. *Average non-need based aid:* $2041. *Average aid to full-time undergraduates:* $10,742.
Athletic Department: *Director of Athletics:* Nancy Nichols; Phone: 863-638-2953; Fax: 863-638-2915; E-mail: nancynic@aol.com. *Sports Information Director:* Jim Cappello; Phone: 863-638-2980; E-mail: blazefc@aol.com.

MEN'S COACHES
Baseball: Brad Niethammer; Phone: 863-638-2951; E-mail: bdhammer17@aol.com.
Basketball: Therman Bronaugh; Phone: 863-638-2961; E-mail: thermanb@hotmail.com.
Cheerleading: Vicky Harris; Phone: 863-638-1431; E-mail: vharriswiu@aol.com.
Cross Country: Harry Wooddell; Phone: 863-638-2952; E-mail: hwawooddell@juno.com.
Football: Rod Shafer; Phone: 863-638-2958; E-mail: wiuwarriorfootball@yahoo.com.
Golf: Nancy Nichols; Phone: 863-638-2953; E-mail: nancynic@aol.com.
Soccer: Ian Barritt; Phone: 863-638-2980; E-mail: ibarritt@hotmail.com.
Tennis: Bill Heath; Phone: 863-638-2970; E-mail: bhtennnis@hotmail.com.
Track and Field: Harry Wooddell; Phone: 863-638-2952; E-mail: hwawooddell@juno.com.

WOMEN'S COACHES
Basketball: Therman Bronaugh; Phone: 863-638-2961; E-mail: thermanb@hotmail.com.
Cheerleading: Vicky Harris; Phone: 863-638-1431; E-mail: vharriswiu@aol.com.
Cross Country: Harry Wooddell; Phone: 863-638-2952; E-mail: hwawooddell@juno.com.
Golf: Nancy Nichols; Phone: 863-638-2953; E-mail: nancynic@aol.com.
Soccer: Jim Cappello; Phone: 863-638-2980; E-mail: blazefc@aol.com.
Softball: Gina Dube; Phone: 863-638-1431; E-mail: gina_dube@yahoo.com.
Tennis: Bill Heath; Phone: 863-638-2970; E-mail: bhtennnis@hotmail.com.
Track and Field: Harry Wooddell; Phone: 863-638-2952; E-mail: hwawooddell@juno.com.
Volleyball: Laura Kinder; Phone: 863-638-2963; E-mail: lkinder34@hotmail.com.

WEBER STATE UNIVERSITY
Ogden, Utah

Wildcats ◆ NCAA I ◆ Big Sky Conference ◆ http://weber.edu/

State-supported comprehensive, founded 1889, part of Utah System of Higher Education
Coed, 18,452 undergraduate students, 60% full-time, 51% women, 49% men
Urban 526-acre campus with easy access to Salt Lake City
Noncompetitive entrance level, 100% of applicants were admitted

Freshmen *Admission:* 5,893 applied, 5,893 were accepted, 2,878 enrolled. *Test scores:* SAT verbal scores over 500: 55%; SAT math scores

over 500: 52%; SAT verbal scores over 600: 16%; SAT math scores over 600: 18%; SAT verbal scores over 700: 3%; SAT math scores over 700: 2%.
Tuition and fees (2003–04): $3134 (resident), $8460 (nonresident). *Room and board:* $5313 (room only: $2223).
Financial Aid (All incoming freshmen): *Average need-based gift aid:* $3125. *Average aid to full-time undergraduates:* $5800.
Athletic Department: *Director of Athletics:* John Johnson; Phone: 801-626-7738; Fax: 801-626-6490; E-mail: jjohnson22@weber.edu. *Sports Information Director:* Brad Larsen; Phone: 801-626-6010; E-mail: blarsen3@weber.edu.

MEN'S COACHES
Basketball: Joe Cravens; Phone: 801-626-7292; E-mail: jcravens@weber.edu.
Cheerleading: Summer Willis; Phone: 801-626-7163.
Cross Country: Chick Hislop; Phone: 801-626-6940; E-mail: chislop@weber.edu.
Football: Jerry Graybeal; Phone: 801-626-6928; E-mail: jgraybeal@weber.edu.
Golf: Dave Kearl; Phone: 801-626-6013.
Tennis: Keith Cox; Phone: 801-626-6537; E-mail: wsuten@aol.com.
Track and Field: Chick Hislop; Phone: 801-626-6940; E-mail: chislop@weber.edu.

WOMEN'S COACHES
Basketball: Carla Taylor; Phone: 801-626-6502; E-mail: ctaylor3@weber.edu.
Cheerleading: Summer Willis; Phone: 801-626-7163.
Cross Country: Jim Blaisdell; Phone: 801-626-6497; E-mail: jblaisdell@weber.edu.
Golf: Jeff Smith; Phone: 801-626-7219; E-mail: jsmith13@weber.edu.
Soccer: Lynn Kofoed; Phone: 801-626-7291; E-mail: lkofoed@weber.edu.
Tennis: Wendy Compton; Phone: 801-626-7513; E-mail: wsuten@aol.com.
Track and Field: Jim Blaisdell; Phone: 801-626-6497; E-mail: jblaisdell@weber.edu.
Volleyball: Al Givens; Phone: 801-626-7091; E-mail: agivens@weber.edu.

WEBSTER UNIVERSITY
St. Louis, Missouri

Gorloks ◆ NCAA III ◆ St. Louis Athletic Conference ◆ http://www.webster.edu/

Independent comprehensive, founded 1915
Coed, 3,559 undergraduate students, 70% full-time, 63% women, 37% men
Suburban 47-acre campus
Moderately difficult entrance level, 55% of applicants were admitted

Freshmen *Admission:* 1,282 applied, 738 were accepted, 453 enrolled. *Test scores:* SAT verbal scores over 500: 89%; SAT math scores over 500: 75%; SAT verbal scores over 600: 54%; SAT math scores over 600: 35%; SAT verbal scores over 700: 9%; SAT math scores over 700: 7%.
Tuition and fees (2003–04): $15,480 (full-time). *Room and board:* $6368 (room only: $3140).
Financial Aid (All incoming freshmen): *Average need-based gift aid:* $5084. *Average non-need based aid:* $9033. *Average aid to full-time undergraduates:* $16,024.
Athletic Department: *Director of Athletics:* Tom Hart; Phone: 314-961-2660; Fax: 314-968-6092; E-mail: harttr@webster.edu. *Sports Information Director:* Merry Graf; Phone: 314-961-2660; E-mail: mgraf@webster.edu.

MEN'S COACHES
Baseball: Marty Hunsucker; Phone: 314-961-2660; E-mail: hunsucma@webster.edu.
Basketball: Chris Bunch; Phone: 314-961-2660; E-mail: bunch@webster.edu.
Cheerleading: Pam Miller; Phone: 314-961-2660; E-mail: millerpb@webster.edu.
Golf: Tom Hart; Phone: 314-961-2660; E-mail: harttr@webster.edu.
Soccer: Marty Todt; Phone: 314-968-6984; E-mail: scirela@webster.edu.

Swimming: Matt Gardner; Phone: 314-494-2616; E-mail: gardnerm@webster.edu.
Tennis: Kate Malesevich; Phone: 314-961-2660; E-mail: malesevi@webster.edu.

WOMEN'S COACHES

Basketball: Ryan Barke; Phone: 314-961-2660; E-mail: rbarke@webster.edu.
Cheerleading: Pam Miller; Phone: 314-961-2660; E-mail: millerpb@webster.edu.
Cross Country: Chris Bunch; Phone: 314-961-2660; E-mail: bunch@webster.edu.
Soccer: Luigi Scire; Phone: 314-961-2660; E-mail: scirela@webster.edu.
Softball: Craig Walston; Phone: 314-961-2660; E-mail: cwally_2000@yahoo.com.
Swimming: Matt Gardner; Phone: 314-494-2616; E-mail: gardnerm@webster.edu.
Tennis: Kate Malesevich; Phone: 314-961-2660; E-mail: malesevi@webster.edu.
Volleyball: Merry Graf; Phone: 314-961-2660; E-mail: mgraf@webster.edu.

WELLESLEY COLLEGE
Wellesley, Massachusetts

Blue ◆ NCAA III ◆ New England Women's & Men's Athletics Conference ◆ http://www.wellesley.edu/

Independent 4-year, founded 1870
Women only, 2,312 undergraduate students, 96% full-time, 99% women, 1% men
Suburban 500-acre campus with easy access to Boston
Most difficult entrance level, 41% of applicants were admitted

Freshmen *Admission:* 3,434 applied, 1,394 were accepted, 591 enrolled. *Test scores:* SAT verbal scores over 500: 99%; SAT math scores over 500: 99%; SAT verbal scores over 600: 88%; SAT math scores over 600: 87%; SAT verbal scores over 700: 45%; SAT math scores over 700: 41%.
Tuition and fees (2003–04): $27,724 (full-time). *Room and board:* $8612 (room only: $4362).
Financial Aid (All incoming freshmen): *Average need-based gift aid:* $23,969. *Average aid to full-time undergraduates:* $25,407.
Athletic Department: *Director of Athletics:* Louise O'Neal; Phone: 781-283-2001; Fax: 781-283-3641; E-mail: loneal@wellesley.edu. *Sports Information Director:* Christina Cracolici; Phone: 781-283-2003.

WOMEN'S COACHES

Basketball: Kathy Hagerstrom; Phone: 781-283-2013; E-mail: khagerstrom@wellesley.edu.
Cross Country: John Babington; Phone: 781-283-2435; E-mail: jbabington@wellesley.edu.
Diving: Kelly Magennis; Phone: 781-283-2019; E-mail: kmagennis@wellesley.edu.
Field Hockey: Nicole Smith; Phone: 781-283-2011.
Golf: Bill McInerney; Phone: 781-283-2005; E-mail: wmcinernery@wellesley.edu.
Lacrosse: Nicole Smith; Phone: 781-283-2011.
Soccer: Liz Driscoll; Phone: 781-283-2012; E-mail: edriscol@wellesley.edu.
Swimming: Bonnie Dix; Phone: 781-283-2021; E-mail: bdix@wellesley.edu.
Tennis: Christine Franek; Phone: 781-283-2014; E-mail: cfranek@wellesley.edu.
Track and Field: John Babington; Phone: 781-283-2435; E-mail: jbabington@wellesley.edu.
Volleyball: Dorothy Webb; Phone: 781-283-2010; E-mail: dwebb1@wellesley.edu.

WELLS COLLEGE
Aurora, New York

Express ◆ NCAA III ◆ Atlantic Women's Colleges Conference ◆ http://www.wells.edu/

Independent 4-year, founded 1868
Women only, 420 undergraduate students, 95% full-time, 100% women, 100% men
Rural 365-acre campus with easy access to Syracuse
Moderately difficult entrance level, 84% of applicants were admitted

Freshmen *Admission:* 410 applied, 345 were accepted, 100 enrolled. *Test scores:* SAT verbal scores over 500: 83%; SAT math scores over 500: 67%; SAT verbal scores over 600: 43%; SAT math scores over 600: 27%; SAT verbal scores over 700: 4%; SAT math scores over 700: 1%.
Tuition and fees (2003–04): $14,292 (full-time). *Room and board:* $6830 (room only: $3415).
Financial Aid (All incoming freshmen): *Average need-based gift aid:* $11,925. *Average non-need based aid:* $5121. *Average aid to full-time undergraduates:* $15,560.
Athletic Department: *Director of Athletics:* Lyn Labar; Phone: 315-364-3410; Fax: 315-364-3433; E-mail: llabar@wells.edu.

WOMEN'S COACHES

Field Hockey: Lyn Labar; Phone: 315-364-3410; E-mail: llabar@wells.edu.
Lacrosse: Chris Perkins; Phone: 315-364-3409; E-mail: cperkins@wells.edu.
Soccer: Chris Perkins; Phone: 315-364-3409; E-mail: cperkins@wells.edu.
Softball: Ace Dolan; Phone: 315-364-3461; E-mail: adolan@wells.edu.
Swimming: Danielle Herring; Phone: 315-364-3413; E-mail: dherring@wells.edu.
Tennis: Katie Somerville; Phone: 315-364-3249; E-mail: csomerville@wells.edu.

WENTWORTH INSTITUTE OF TECHNOLOGY
Boston, Massachusetts

Leopards ◆ NCAA III ◆ Commonwealth Coast Conference ◆ http://www.wit.edu/

Independent 4-year, founded 1904
Coed, 3,273 undergraduate students, 77% full-time, 18% women, 82% men
Urban 35-acre campus
Moderately difficult entrance level, 71% of applicants were admitted

Freshmen *Admission:* 3,623 applied, 2,548 were accepted, 1,064 enrolled. *Test scores:* SAT verbal scores over 500: 42%; SAT math scores over 500: 61%; SAT verbal scores over 600: 10%; SAT math scores over 600: 17%; SAT verbal scores over 700: 1%; SAT math scores over 700: 2%.
Tuition and fees (2003–04): $15,000 (full-time). *Room and board:* $8200.
Financial Aid (All incoming freshmen): *Average need-based gift aid:* $1125. *Average non-need based aid:* $2645. *Average aid to full-time undergraduates:* $7625.
Athletic Department: *Director of Athletics:* Lee Conrad; Phone: 617-989-4146; Fax: 617-989-4150; E-mail: conradl@wit.edu. *Sports Information Director:* Bill Gorman; Phone: 617-989-4147; E-mail: gormanb@wit.edu.

MEN'S COACHES

Baseball: Tom Randolph; Phone: 617-989-4824; E-mail: thomas_randolph@hotmail.com.
Basketball: Tom Devitt; Phone: 617-989-4154; E-mail: devittt@wit.edu.
Golf: David Pierce; Phone: 617-989-4655; E-mail: pierce61@attbi.com.
Ice Hockey: Jonathan Deptula; Phone: 617-989-4149; E-mail: deptulaj@wit.edu.
Lacrosse: Paul Murphy; Phone: 617-989-4823; E-mail: murphyp4@wit.edu.
Soccer: Bob Long; Phone: 617-989-4145; E-mail: bmscr5@aol.com.
Tennis: Eddie Davis; Phone: 617-989-4820; E-mail: edit9@comcast.net.

Wentworth Institute of Technology *(continued)*

Volleyball: Jason Jeffers; Phone: 617-989-4821; E-mail: jeffersj@wit.edu.

WOMEN'S COACHES

Basketball: Carrie Crawford; Phone: 617-989-4148; E-mail: crawfordc@wit.edu.
Soccer: Angel Schofield; Phone: 617-989-4159; E-mail: schofielda@wit.edu.
Softball: Bob Long; Phone: 617-989-4145; E-mail: bmscr5@aol.com.
Tennis: Eddie Davis; Phone: 617-989-4655; E-mail: edit9@comcast.net.
Volleyball: Jason Jeffers; Phone: 617-989-4821; E-mail: jeffersj@wit.edu.

WESLEYAN COLLEGE
Macon, Georgia

Pioneers ◆ NCAA III ◆ Independent
◆ http://www.wesleyancollege.edu/

Independent United Methodist comprehensive, founded 1836
Women only, 661 undergraduate students, 79% full-time, 100% women, 100% men
Suburban 200-acre campus with easy access to Atlanta
Moderately difficult entrance level, 77% of applicants were admitted

Freshmen *Admission:* 323 applied, 250 were accepted, 92 enrolled. *Test scores:* SAT verbal scores over 500: 73%; SAT math scores over 500: 62%; SAT verbal scores over 600: 33%; SAT math scores over 600: 24%; SAT verbal scores over 700: 5%; SAT math scores over 700: 6%.
Tuition and fees (2003–04): $10,420 (full-time). *Room and board:* $7450.
Financial Aid (All incoming freshmen): *Average need-based gift aid:* $8998. *Average non-need based aid:* $12,441. *Average aid to full-time undergraduates:* $11,101.
Athletic Department: *Director of Athletics:* Ellen Lord; Phone: 478-757-5253; Fax: 478-757-2486; E-mail: elord@wesleyancollege.edu.

WOMEN'S COACHES

Basketball: James Taylor; Phone: 478-477-1110.
Soccer: Ellen Lord; Phone: 478-757-5253; E-mail: elord@wesleyancollege.edu.
Softball: Joanna Lane; Phone: 478-757-5255; E-mail: jlane@wesleyancollege.edu.
Tennis: James Pettis; Phone: 478-757-2488; E-mail: jpettis@wesleyancollege.edu.
Volleyball: James Pettis; Phone: 478-757-2488; E-mail: jpettis@wesleyancollege.edu.

WESLEYAN UNIVERSITY
Middletown, Connecticut

Cardinals ◆ NCAA III ◆ New England Small College Conference ◆ http://www.wesleyan.edu/

Independent university, founded 1831
Coed, 2,730 undergraduate students, 99% full-time, 53% women, 47% men
Small-town 120-acre campus
Most difficult entrance level, 29% of applicants were admitted

Freshmen *Admission:* 6,955 applied, 1,854 were accepted, 715 enrolled. *Test scores:* SAT verbal scores over 500: 99%; SAT math scores over 500: 100%; SAT verbal scores over 600: 87%; SAT math scores over 600: 92%; SAT verbal scores over 700: 51%; SAT math scores over 700: 44%.
Tuition and fees (2003–04): $29,998 (full-time). *Room and board:* $8226 (room only: $5138).
Financial Aid (All incoming freshmen): *Average need-based gift aid:* $20,183. *Average aid to full-time undergraduates:* $23,650.
Athletic Department: *Director of Athletics:* John Biddiscombe; Phone: 860-685-2895; Fax: 860-685-2691; E-mail: jbiddiscombe@wesleyan.edu. *Sports Information Director:* Brian Katten; Phone: 860-685-2887; E-mail: bkatten@wesleyan.edu.

MEN'S COACHES

Baseball: Mark Woodworth; Phone: 860-685-2924; E-mail: mwoodworthl@wesleyan.edu.
Basketball: Gerry McDowell; Phone: 860-685-2918; E-mail: gmcdowell@wesleyan.edu.
Cross Country: John Crooke; Phone: 860-685-5320; E-mail: jcrooke@wesleyan.edu.
Diving: Pat Pyrch; Phone: 860-685-2874; E-mail: ppyrch@wesleyan.edu.
Football: Frank Hauser; Phone: 860-685-2908; E-mail: fhauser@wesleyan.edu.
Golf: Chris Potter; Phone: 860-685-2927; E-mail: cjpotter@wesleyan.edu.
Ice Hockey: Chris Potter; Phone: 860-685-2927; E-mail: cjpotter@wesleyan.edu.
Lacrosse: John Raba; Phone: 860-685-3917; E-mail: jraba@wesleyan.edu.
Soccer: Geoff Wheeler; Phone: 860-685-2898; E-mail: gwheeler@wesleyan.edu.
Swimming: Mary Bolich; Phone: 860-685-2929; E-mail: mbolich@wesleyan.edu.
Tennis: Tom Cutone; Phone: 860-685-2926; E-mail: tcutone@wesleyan.edu.
Track and Field: Walter Curry; Phone: 860-685-2905; E-mail: wcurry@wesleyan.edu.
Wrestling: Drew Black; Phone: 860-685-2907; E-mail: dblack@wesleyan.edu.

WOMEN'S COACHES

Basketball: Kate Mullen; Phone: 860-685-2888; E-mail: kmullen@wesleyan.edu.
Cross Country: John Crooke; Phone: 860-685-5320; E-mail: jcrooke@wesleyan.edu.
Diving: Pat Pyrch; Phone: 860-685-2874; E-mail: ppyrch@wesleyan.edu.
Field Hockey: Patti Klecha-Porter; Phone: 860-685-2899; E-mail: pklechaporte@wesleyan.edu.
Lacrosse: Holly Wheeler; Phone: 860-685-2906; E-mail: hwheeler@wesleyan.edu.
Soccer: Holly Wheeler; Phone: 860-685-2906; E-mail: hwheeler@wesleyan.edu.
Softball: Jen Shea; Phone: 860-685-2436; E-mail: jashea@wesleyan.edu.
Swimming: Mary Bolich; Phone: 860-685-2929; E-mail: mbolich@wesleyan.edu.
Tennis: Tom Cutone; Phone: 860-685-2926; E-mail: tcutone@wesleyan.edu.
Track and Field: Walter Curry; Phone: 860-685-2905; E-mail: wcurry@wesleyan.edu.
Volleyball: Gale Lackey; Phone: 860-685-2925; E-mail: glackey@wesleyan.edu.

WESLEY COLLEGE
Dover, Delaware

Wolverines ◆ NCAA III ◆ Pennsylvania Athletic Conference
◆ http://www.wesley.edu/

Independent United Methodist comprehensive, founded 1873
Coed, 2,000 undergraduate students, 83% full-time, 55% women, 45% men
Small-town 40-acre campus
Moderately difficult entrance level, 68% of applicants were admitted

Freshmen *Admission:* 1,842 applied, 1,253 were accepted, 429 enrolled. *Test scores:* SAT verbal scores over 500: 42%; SAT math scores over 500: 49%; SAT verbal scores over 600: 8%; SAT math scores over 600: 8%; SAT verbal scores over 700: 1%; SAT math scores over 700: 1%.
Tuition and fees (2004–05): $14,364 (full-time). *Room and board:* $6480.
Financial Aid (All incoming freshmen): *Average need-based gift aid:* $5810. *Average non-need based aid:* $8920. *Average aid to full-time undergraduates:* $7900.
Athletic Department: *Director of Athletics:* Michele Stabley; Phone: 302-736-2545; Fax: 302-736-2308; E-mail: stablemi@wesley.edu. *Sports Information Director:* John Davis; Phone: 302-736-2450; E-mail: davisjoh@wesley.edu.

MEN'S COACHES

Baseball: Matt Addonizio; Phone: 302-735-5939; E-mail: addonima@wesley.edu.

Basketball: Chris Wentworth; Phone: 302-736-2555; E-mail: wentwoch@wesley.edu.
Cheerleading: Serena Swann; Phone: 302-739-2545; E-mail: swannser@wesley.edu.
Cross Country: Steve Pickering; Phone: 302-736-7050; E-mail: pickerst@wesley.edu.
Football: Mike Drass; Phone: 302-736-2363; E-mail: drassmi@wesley.edu.
Golf: Rick McCall; Phone: 302-674-2877.
Lacrosse: Christian Zwickert; Phone: 302-736-2460; E-mail: zwickech@wesley.edu.
Soccer: Steve Clark; Phone: 302-736-2557; E-mail: clarkst@wesley.edu.
Tennis: Ed Muntz; Phone: 302-736-2516; E-mail: muntzed@wesley.edu.

WOMEN'S COACHES

Basketball: Michele Stabley; Phone: 302-736-2545; E-mail: stablemi@wesley.edu.
Cheerleading: Serena Swann; Phone: 302-739-2545; E-mail: swannser@wesley.edu.
Cross Country: Steve Pickering; Phone: 302-736-7050; E-mail: pickerst@wesley.edu.
Field Hockey: Tracey Short; Phone: 302-736-2458; E-mail: shorttr@wesley.edu.
Lacrosse: Kristen Calore; Phone: 302-736-2450; E-mail: calorekr@wesley.edu.
Soccer: Ed Muntz; Phone: 302-736-2516; E-mail: muntzed@wesley.edu.
Softball: Stacy Trice; Phone: 302-736-2541; E-mail: tricesta@wesley.edu.
Tennis: Dave Sweeney; Phone: 302-736-2404; E-mail: sweeneda@wesley.edu.

WEST CHESTER UNIVERSITY OF PENNSYLVANIA
West Chester, Pennsylvania

Golden Rams ◆ NCAA II ◆ Atlantic 10 Conference; Pennsylvania State Athletic Conference ◆ http://www.wcupa.edu/

State-supported comprehensive, founded 1871, part of Pennsylvania State System of Higher Education
Coed, 10,562 undergraduate students, 87% full-time, 61% women, 39% men
Suburban 547-acre campus with easy access to Philadelphia
Moderately difficult entrance level, 43% of applicants were admitted

Freshmen *Admission:* 10,207 applied, 4,720 were accepted, 1,729 enrolled. *Test scores:* SAT verbal scores over 500: 71%; SAT math scores over 500: 70%; SAT verbal scores over 600: 15%; SAT math scores over 600: 16%; SAT verbal scores over 700: 1%; SAT math scores over 700: 1%.
Tuition and fees (2003–04): $4598 (resident), $11,496 (nonresident). *Room and board:* $5642 (room only: $4960).
Athletic Department: *Director of Athletics:* Edward Matejkovic; Phone: 610-436-3555; E-mail: ematejkovi@wcupa.edu. *Sports Information Director:* Tom DiCamillo; Phone: 610-436-3316; E-mail: tdicamillo@wcupa.edu.

MEN'S COACHES

Baseball: Chris Calciano; Phone: 610-436-2152; E-mail: ccalciano@wcupa.edu.
Basketball: Dick Delaney; Phone: 610-436-2136; E-mail: rdelaney@wcupa.edu.
Cheerleading: Julie Smink; Phone: 610-436-3420; E-mail: wcucheer@yahoo.com.
Cross Country: James Williams; Phone: 610-436-2468; E-mail: jwilliams3@wcupa.edu.
Diving: Ronn Jenkins; Phone: 610-436-2127; E-mail: rjenkins@wcupa.edu.
Football: Bill Zwaan; Phone: 610-436-2159; E-mail: wzwaan@wcupa.edu.
Golf: Mark Maurer; Phone: 610-436-3420; E-mail: coachmaurer@aol.com.
Soccer: Kendall Wilkes; Phone: 610-436-2221; E-mail: kwalkes@wcupa.edu.

Swimming: Jamie Rudisill; Phone: 610-436-2127; E-mail: jrudisill@wcupa.edu.
Tennis: Dennis Olenik; Phone: 610-436-6946; E-mail: shearwater02@hotmail.com.
Track and Field: James Williams; Phone: 610-436-2468; E-mail: jwilliams3@wcupa.edu.

WOMEN'S COACHES

Basketball: Deirdre Kane; Phone: 610-436-3399; E-mail: dkane@wcupa.edu.
Cheerleading: Julie Smink; Phone: 610-436-3420; E-mail: wcucheer@yahoo.com.
Cross Country: James Williams; Phone: 610-436-2468; E-mail: jwilliams3@wcupa.edu.
Diving: Ronn Jenkins; Phone: 610-436-2127; E-mail: rjenkins@wcupa.edu.
Field Hockey: Kathy Krannebitter; Phone: 610-436-2144; E-mail: kkrannebit@wcupa.edu.
Golf: Mark Maurer; Phone: 610-436-3420; E-mail: coachmaurer@aol.com.
Gymnastics: Jen Teneza; Phone: 610-436-3215.
Lacrosse: Ginny Martino; Phone: 610-436-2394; E-mail: vmartino@wcupa.edu.
Soccer: Deb Flaherty; Phone: 610-436-6903; E-mail: dflaherty@wcupa.edu.
Softball: Diane Lokey; Phone: 610-436-2170; E-mail: dlokey@wcupa.edu.
Swimming: Jamie Rudisill; Phone: 610-436-2127; E-mail: jrudisill@wcupa.edu.
Tennis: Lisa Haldes; Phone: 610-436-6946; E-mail: lisehal@aol.com.
Track and Field: James Williams; Phone: 610-436-2468; E-mail: jwilliams3@wcupa.edu.
Volleyball: Sharon Bonaventure; Phone: 610-436-3237; E-mail: sbonaventu@wcupa.edu.

WESTERN BAPTIST COLLEGE
Salem, Oregon

Warriors ◆ NAIA ◆ Cascade Collegiate Conference ◆ http://www.wbc.edu/

Independent religious 4-year, founded 1935
Coed, 737 undergraduate students, 84% full-time, 59% women, 41% men
Suburban 107-acre campus with easy access to Portland
Moderately difficult entrance level, 79% of applicants were admitted

Freshmen *Admission:* 550 applied, 460 were accepted, 167 enrolled. *Test scores:* SAT verbal scores over 500: 76%; SAT math scores over 500: 69%; SAT verbal scores over 600: 31%; SAT math scores over 600: 26%; SAT verbal scores over 700: 3%; SAT math scores over 700: 3%.
Tuition and fees (2004–05): $17,035 (full-time). *Room and board:* $6065.
Financial Aid (All incoming freshmen): *Average need-based gift aid:* $9235. *Average non-need based aid:* $8619. *Average aid to full-time undergraduates:* $13,467.
Athletic Department: *Director of Athletics:* John Nelson; Phone: 503-589-8119; Fax: 503-589-2947; E-mail: jnelson@wbc.edu. *Sports Information Director:* Tim Smith; Phone: 503-589-8121; E-mail: tismith@wbc.edu.

MEN'S COACHES

Baseball: Paul Gale; Phone: 503-589-8183; E-mail: pgale@wbc.edu.
Basketball: Justin Sherwood; Phone: 503-589-8196; E-mail: jsherwood@wbc.edu.
Cross Country: Norm Berney; Phone: 503-589-8157; E-mail: nberney@wbc.edu.
Golf: Phone: 503-375-7021.
Soccer: Justin Rivard; Phone: 503-589-8157; E-mail: jrivard@wbc.edu.

WOMEN'S COACHES

Basketball: Dave Bale; Phone: 503-589-8104; E-mail: dbale@wbc.edu.
Cross Country: Norm Berney; Phone: 503-589-8157; E-mail: nberney@wbc.edu.
Soccer: Marty Ziesemer; Phone: 503-375-7115; E-mail: mziesemer@wbc.edu.
Softball: Todd Bradley; Phone: 503-589-8107; E-mail: tbradley@wbc.edu.
Volleyball: Tracy Smith; Phone: 503-375-7021; E-mail: tsmith@wbc.edu.

WESTERN CAROLINA UNIVERSITY
Cullowhee, North Carolina

Catamounts ◆ NCAA I ◆ Southern Conference ◆ http://www.wcu.edu/

State-supported comprehensive, founded 1889, part of University of North Carolina System
Coed, 6,087 undergraduate students, 87% full-time, 52% women, 48% men
Rural 260-acre campus
Moderately difficult entrance level, 73% of applicants were admitted

Freshmen *Admission:* 4,606 applied, 3,392 were accepted, 1,495 enrolled. *Test scores:* SAT verbal scores over 500: 54%; SAT math scores over 500: 56%; SAT verbal scores over 600: 14%; SAT math scores over 600: 15%; SAT verbal scores over 700: 2%; SAT math scores over 700: 1%.
Tuition and fees (2003–04): $2806 (resident), $12,167 (nonresident). *Room and board:* $3826 (room only: $2026).
Financial Aid (All incoming freshmen): *Average need-based gift aid:* $3693. *Average non-need based aid:* $2085. *Average aid to full-time undergraduates:* $5939.
Athletic Department: *Director of Athletics:* Jeff Compher; Phone: 828-227-7338; Fax: 828-227-7688; E-mail: jcompher@email.wcu.edu. *Sports Information Director:* Rebecca Vick; Phone: 828-227-2339; E-mail: rvick@email.wcu.edu.

MEN'S COACHES
Baseball: Todd Raleigh; Phone: 828-227-2021; E-mail: traleigh@email.wcu.edu.
Basketball: Steve Shurina; Phone: 828-227-2017; E-mail: shurina@email.wcu.edu.
Cheerleading: Charity Moon; Phone: 828-227-7338; E-mail: charityleigh@hotmail.com.
Cross Country: Danny Williamson; Phone: 828-227-2026; E-mail: dwilliams@email.wcu.edu.
Football: Kent Briggs; Phone: 828-227-7395; E-mail: kbriggs@email.wcu.edu.
Golf: Johnny Wike; Phone: 828-227-3794; E-mail: wikej@wcu.edu.
Track and Field: Danny Williamson; Phone: 828-227-2026; E-mail: dwilliams@email.wcu.edu.

WOMEN'S COACHES
Basketball: Beth Dunkenberger; Phone: 828-227-2028; E-mail: dunk@email.wcu.edu.
Cheerleading: Charity Moon; Phone: 828-227-7338; E-mail: charityleigh@hotmail.com.
Cross Country: Danny Williamson; Phone: 828-227-2026; E-mail: dwilliams@email.wcu.edu.
Golf: Steve Lott; Phone: 828-227-3797; E-mail: wcugolf1@aol.com.
Soccer: Debbie Hensley; Phone: 828-227-2337; E-mail: dhensley@email.wcu.edu.
Tennis: Jan Stubbs; Phone: 828-227-2338; E-mail: stubbs@email.wcu.edu.
Track and Field: Danny Williamson; Phone: 828-227-2026; E-mail: dwilliams@email.wcu.edu.
Volleyball: Angell Benson; Phone: 828-227-2032; E-mail: abenson@wcu.edu.

WESTERN CONNECTICUT STATE UNIVERSITY
Danbury, Connecticut

Colonials ◆ NCAA III ◆ Freedom Football Conference; Little East Conference; New England Women's Lacrosse Conference ◆ http://www.wcsu.edu/

State-supported comprehensive, founded 1903, part of Connecticut State University System
Coed, 5,236 undergraduate students, 73% full-time, 55% women, 45% men
Urban 340-acre campus with easy access to New York City
Moderately difficult entrance level, 53% of applicants were admitted

Freshmen *Admission:* 3,626 applied, 2,008 were accepted, 820 enrolled. *Test scores:* SAT verbal scores over 500: 47%; SAT math scores over 500: 43%; SAT verbal scores over 600: 8%; SAT math scores over 600: 10%; SAT verbal scores over 700: 1%; SAT math scores over 700: 1%.
Tuition and fees (2003–04): $5044 (resident), $12,032 (nonresident). *Room and board:* $6580 (room only: $4240).
Financial Aid (All incoming freshmen): *Average need-based gift aid:* $3959. *Average non-need based aid:* $1749. *Average aid to full-time undergraduates:* $5746.
Athletic Department: *Director of Athletics:* Ed Farrington; Phone: 203-837-9013; Fax: 203-837-9050; E-mail: farringtone@wcsu.edu. *Sports Information Director:* Scott Ames; Phone: 203-837-9014; E-mail: amess@wcsu.edu.

MEN'S COACHES
Baseball: John Susi; Phone: 203-837-8608; E-mail: susij@wcsu.edu.
Basketball: Bob Campbell; Phone: 203-837-9017; E-mail: campbellr@wcsu.edu.
Football: John Burrell; Phone: 203-837-9028; E-mail: burrellj@wcsu.edu.
Lacrosse: Rick McCarthy; Phone: 203-837-9053; E-mail: mccarthyf@wcsu.edu.
Soccer: Wayne Mones; Phone: 203-837-9057; E-mail: yankeeunitedheat@aol.com.
Tennis: Alex Aitchison; Phone: 203-837-9021.

WOMEN'S COACHES
Basketball: Kimberly Rybczyk; Phone: 203-837-9018; E-mail: rybczykk@wcsu.edu.
Lacrosse: Denna Stachelek Grasso; Phone: 203-837-9042; E-mail: stachelekd@wcsu.edu.
Soccer: Joe Mingchos; Phone: 203-837-9020; E-mail: mingachosj@wcsu.edu.
Softball: Alicia O'Brien; Phone: 203-837-9019; E-mail: obriena@wcsu.edu.
Swimming: Jill Cook; Phone: 203-837-8624; E-mail: cookj@wcsu.edu.
Tennis: Alex Aitchison; Phone: 203-837-9021.
Volleyball: Richard Myers; Phone: 203-837-9022; E-mail: myersr@wcsu.edu.

WESTERN ILLINOIS UNIVERSITY
Macomb, Illinois

Leathernecks(M), Westerwinds(W) ◆ NCAA I ◆ Gateway Football Conference; Mid-Continent Conference ◆ http://www.wiu.edu/

State-supported comprehensive, founded 1899
Coed, 11,027 undergraduate students, 89% full-time, 49% women, 51% men
Small-town 1,050-acre campus
Moderately difficult entrance level, 66% of applicants were admitted

Freshmen *Admission:* 7,612 applied, 5,032 were accepted, 1,961 enrolled.
Tuition and fees (2003–04): $5402 (resident), $9317 (nonresident). *Room and board:* $5366 (room only: $3122).
Financial Aid (All incoming freshmen): *Average need-based gift aid:* $4941. *Average non-need based aid:* $2233. *Average aid to full-time undergraduates:* $6222.
Athletic Department: *Director of Athletics:* Tim Van Alstine; Phone: 309-298-1106; Fax: 309-298-2009; E-mail: t-vanalstine@wiu.edu. *Sports Information Director:* Jason Kaufman; Phone: 309-298-1133; E-mail: jp-kaufman@wiu.edu.

MEN'S COACHES
Baseball: Stan Hyman; Phone: 309-298-1521; E-mail: sd-hyman@wiu.edu.
Basketball: Derek Thomas; Phone: 309-298-1224; E-mail: d-thomas2@wiu.edu.
Cheerleading: Cindy Green; Phone: 309-298-1190; E-mail: cm-green@wiu.edu.
Cross Country: Matt Roe; Phone: 309-298-1716; E-mail: mc-roe@wiu.edu.
Diving: Aaron Hintz; Phone: 309-298-1432; E-mail: ra-hintz@wiu.edu.
Football: Don Patterson; Phone: 309-298-1221; E-mail: d-patterson@wiu.edu.
Golf: Mel Blasi; Phone: 309-298-3676; E-mail: mb-blasi@wiu.edu.
Soccer: Eric Johnson; Phone: 309-298-1954; E-mail: ep-johnson@wiu.edu.

Swimming: Kelly Byrne; Phone: 309-298-1432; E-mail: kk-byrne@wiu. edu.

Tennis: Dann Nelson; Phone: 309-298-1731; E-mail: dd-nelson@wiu. edu.

Track and Field: Mike Stevensen; Phone: 309-298-1716; E-mail: m-stevenson@wiu.edu.

WOMEN'S COACHES

Basketball: Leslie Crane; Phone: 309-298-1703; E-mail: ls-crane@wiu. edu.

Cheerleading: Cindy Green; Phone: 309-298-1190; E-mail: cm-green@ wiu.edu.

Cross Country: Matt Roe; Phone: 309-298-1716; E-mail: mc-roe@wiu. edu.

Diving: Aaron Hintz; Phone: 309-298-1432; E-mail: ra-hintz@wiu.edu.

Golf: Andrea Keene; Phone: 309-298-3676; E-mail: al-keene@wiu.edu.

Soccer: Richard Moller; Phone: 309-298-1906; E-mail: r-moller@wiu. edu.

Softball: Kathy Veroni; Phone: 309-298-1753; E-mail: kj-veroni@wiu. edu.

Swimming: Kelly Byrne; Phone: 309-298-1432; E-mail: kk-byrne@wiu. edu.

Tennis: Dann Nelson; Phone: 309-298-1731; E-mail: dd-nelson@wiu. edu.

Track and Field: Mike Stevensen; Phone: 309-298-1716; E-mail: m-stevenson@wiu.edu.

Volleyball: Kym McKay; Phone: 309-298-1855; E-mail: k-mckay@wiu. edu.

WESTERN KENTUCKY UNIVERSITY
Bowling Green, Kentucky

Hilltoppers ◆ NCAA I ◆ Gateway Football Conference; Missouri Valley Conference; Sun Belt Conference ◆ http:// www.wku.edu/

State-supported comprehensive, founded 1906
Coed, 15,787 undergraduate students, 82% full-time, 59% women, 41% men
Suburban 223-acre campus with easy access to Nashville
Moderately difficult entrance level, 92% of applicants were admitted

Freshmen *Admission:* 6,373 applied, 5,927 were accepted, 3,076 enrolled. *Test scores:* SAT verbal scores over 500: 52%; SAT math scores over 500: 56%; SAT verbal scores over 600: 15%; SAT math scores over 600: 12%; SAT verbal scores over 700: 2%; SAT math scores over 700: 2%.
Financial Aid (All incoming freshmen): *Average need-based gift aid:* $3516. *Average non-need based aid:* $2024. *Average aid to full-time undergraduates:* $5701.
Athletic Department: *Director of Athletics:* Camden Wood Selig; Phone: 270-745-3542; Fax: 270-745-6187; E-mail: wood.selig@wku.edu. *Sports Information Director:* Brian Fremund; Phone: 270-745-5045; E-mail: brian.fremund@wku.edu.

MEN'S COACHES

Baseball: Joel Murrie; Phone: 270-745-6023; E-mail: joel.murrie@wku. edu.

Basketball: Darrin Horn; Phone: 270-745-2131.

Cross Country: Curtiss Long; Phone: 270-745-6025; E-mail: curtiss. long@wku.edu.

Football: David Elson; Phone: 270-745-2984; E-mail: david.elson@wku. edu.

Golf: Brian Tirpak; Phone: 270-745-5036.

Soccer: David Holmes; Phone: 270-745-6068; E-mail: david.holmes@ wku.edu.

Swimming: Bill Powell; Phone: 270-745-6075; E-mail: bill.powell@wku. edu.

Tennis: Jeff True; Phone: 270-745-6485; E-mail: jeff.true@wku.edu.

Track and Field: Curtiss Long; Phone: 270-745-6025; E-mail: curtiss. long@wku.edu.

WOMEN'S COACHES

Basketball: Mary Taylor Cowles; Phone: 270-745-2133; E-mail: mary. cowles@wku.edu.

Cross Country: Curtiss Long; Phone: 270-745-6025; E-mail: curtiss. long@wku.edu.

Golf: Chuck Eison; Phone: 270-745-6269; E-mail: chuck.eison@wku. edu.

Soccer: Jason Neidell; Phone: 270-745-6563; E-mail: jason.neidell@ wku.edu.

Softball: Leslie Phelan; Phone: 270-745-6269; E-mail: leslie.phelan@ wku.edu.

Swimming: Bill Powell; Phone: 270-745-6075; E-mail: bill.powell@wku. edu.

Tennis: Jeff True; Phone: 270-745-6485; E-mail: jeff.true@wku.edu.

Track and Field: Curtiss Long; Phone: 270-745-6025; E-mail: curtiss. long@wku.edu.

Volleyball: Travis Hudson; Phone: 270-745-6496; E-mail: travis. hudson@wku.edu.

WESTERN MICHIGAN UNIVERSITY
Kalamazoo, Michigan

Broncos ◆ NCAA I ◆ Central Collegiate Hockey Conference; Mid-American Conference ◆ http://www.wmich.edu/

State-supported university, founded 1903
Coed, 23,309 undergraduate students, 87% full-time, 51% women, 49% men
Urban 1,200-acre campus
Moderately difficult entrance level, 86% of applicants were admitted

Freshmen *Admission:* 15,100 applied, 12,923 were accepted, 4,258 enrolled.
Tuition and fees (2003–04): $5536 (resident), $13,048 (nonresident). *Room and board:* $6496 (room only: $3350).
Financial Aid (All incoming freshmen): *Average need-based gift aid:* $4300. *Average non-need based aid:* $2500. *Average aid to full-time undergraduates:* $7200.
Athletic Department: *Director of Athletics:* Kathy Beauregard; Phone: 269-387-3061; Fax: 616-387-3668; E-mail: kathy.beauregard@wmich. edu. *Sports Information Director:* Daniel Jankowski; Phone: 269-387-4122; E-mail: daniel.jankowski@wmich.edu.

MEN'S COACHES

Baseball: Fred Decker; Phone: 616-387-8149; E-mail: fred.decker@ wmich.edu.

Basketball: Steve Hawkins; Phone: 616-387-3127; E-mail: steve. hawkins@wmich.edu.

Cheerleading: Tracy Lentz; Phone: 616-387-2352; E-mail: wmu-cheer@ wmich.edu.

Cross Country: Mike Turk; Phone: 616-387-3111; E-mail: michael.turk@ wmich.edu.

Football: Gary Darnell; Phone: 616-387-8620; E-mail: gary.darnell@ wmich.edu.

Ice Hockey: Jim Culhane; Phone: 616-387-3053; E-mail: james. culhane@wmich.edu.

Soccer: Chris Karwoski; Phone: 616-387-3059; E-mail: christopher. karwoski@wmich.edu.

Tennis: Dave Morin; Phone: 616-387-3125; E-mail: david.morin@ wmich.edu.

Track and Field: Mike Turk; Phone: 616-387-3111; E-mail: michael. turk@wmich.edu.

WOMEN'S COACHES

Basketball: Ron Stewart; Phone: 616-387-3119; E-mail: ronald. stewart@wmich.edu.

Cheerleading: Tracy Lentz; Phone: 616-387-2352; E-mail: wmu-cheer@ wmich.edu.

Cross Country: Kelly Lycan; Phone: 616-387-3884; E-mail: kelly.lycan@ wmich.edu.

Golf: Cindy Trout; Phone: 616-387-3878; E-mail: cindy.trout@wmich. edu.

Gymnastics: Terry Karwoski; Phone: 616-387-3129; E-mail: terry. karwoski@wmich.edu.

Soccer: Mike Haines; Phone: 616-387-0350; E-mail: michael.haines@ wmich.edu.

Softball: Kathy Leitke; Phone: 616-387-8602; E-mail: kathy.leitke@ wmich.edu.

Tennis: Betsy Kuhle; Phone: 616-387-3102; E-mail: elizabeth.kuhle@ wmich.edu.

Track and Field: Kelly Lycan; Phone: 616-387-3884; E-mail: kelly.lycan@ wmich.edu.

Volleyball: Cathy George; Phone: 616-387-3940; E-mail: cathy.george@ wmich.edu.

WESTERN NEW ENGLAND COLLEGE
Springfield, Massachusetts

Golden Bear ◆ NCAA III ◆ Great Northeast Athletic Conference; New England College Wrestling Conference; New England Football Conference; New England Women's Lacrosse Conference; North Atlantic Conference ◆ http://www.wnec.edu/

Independent comprehensive, founded 1919
Coed, 3,168 undergraduate students, 71% full-time, 37% women, 63% men
Suburban 215-acre campus
Moderately difficult entrance level, 73% of applicants were admitted

Freshmen *Admission:* 4,517 applied, 3,415 were accepted, 704 enrolled. *Test scores:* SAT verbal scores over 500: 64%; SAT math scores over 500: 70%; SAT verbal scores over 600: 15%; SAT math scores over 600: 24%; SAT verbal scores over 700: 1%; SAT math scores over 700: 2%.
Tuition and fees (2003–04): $20,824 (full-time). *Room and board:* $8100.
Financial Aid (All incoming freshmen): *Average need-based gift aid:* $7490. *Average non-need based aid:* $6288. *Average aid to full-time undergraduates:* $11,255.
Athletic Department: *Director of Athletics:* Mike Theulen; Phone: 413-782-1202; Fax: 413-796-2121; E-mail: mtheulen@wnec.edu. *Sports Information Director:* Ken Cerino; Phone: 413-782-1227; E-mail: kcerino@wnec.edu.

MEN'S COACHES
Baseball: Matt Labranche; Phone: 413-782-1792; E-mail: mlabranc@wnec.edu.
Basketball: Doug Pearson; Phone: 413-782-1209; E-mail: dpearson@wnec.edu.
Cross Country: Brian Walsh; Phone: 413-796-1202; E-mail: bwalsh@wnec.edu.
Football: Gerry Martin; Phone: 413-796-2208; E-mail: gmartin@wnec.edu.
Golf: Bill Downes; Phone: 413-782-1551; E-mail: mluciano@wnec.edu.
Ice Hockey: Karl Enroth; Phone: 413-782-2283; E-mail: kenroth@wnec.edu.
Lacrosse: John Klepacki; Phone: 413-782-1367; E-mail: jklepack@wnec.edu.
Soccer: Erin Sullivan; Phone: 413-782-1764; E-mail: esulliva@wnec.edu.
Tennis: Jennifer Kolins; Phone: 413-796-2229; E-mail: jkolins@wnec.edu.
Wrestling: Bob Skelton; Phone: 413-782-1609; E-mail: bskelton@wnec.edu.

WOMEN'S COACHES
Basketball: Wendy Davis; Phone: 413-796-2206; E-mail: wdavis@wnec.edu.
Cross Country: Brian Walsh; Phone: 413-796-1202; E-mail: bwalsh@wnec.edu.
Field Hockey: Sarah Kelly; Phone: 413-796-2289; E-mail: skelly0@wnec.edu.
Lacrosse: Aimee Klepacki; Phone: 413-796-2227; E-mail: aklepack@wnec.edu.
Soccer: Ron Dias; Phone: 413-782-1632; E-mail: rdias@wnec.edu.
Softball: Lori Mayhen; Phone: 413-796-2230; E-mail: lmayhew@wnec.edu.
Swimming: Andrea Daley; Phone: 413-796-2228; E-mail: adaley@wnec.edu.
Tennis: Jennifer Kolins; Phone: 413-796-2229; E-mail: jkolins@wnec.edu.
Volleyball: Greg Poole; Phone: 413-782-1550; E-mail: gpoole@wnec.edu.

WESTERN NEW MEXICO UNIVERSITY
Silver City, New Mexico

Mustangs ◆ NCAA II ◆ Pacific West Conference ◆ http://www.wnmu.edu/

State-supported comprehensive, founded 1893
Coed, 2,555 undergraduate students
Rural 83-acre campus
Noncompetitive entrance level

Tuition and fees (2003–04): $2451 (resident), $9003 (nonresident). *Room and board:* $4280 (room only: $1550).
Financial Aid (All incoming freshmen): *Average need-based gift aid:* $3374. *Average non-need based aid:* $504. *Average aid to full-time undergraduates:* $4579.
Athletic Department: *Director of Athletics:* Scott Woodard; Phone: 505-538-3966; Fax: 505-538-6163; E-mail: woodards@iron.wnmu.edu. *Sports Information Director:* Kent Beatty; Phone: 505-538-5729; E-mail: wnmugolf@aol.com.

MEN'S COACHES
Basketball: Mark Coleman; Phone: 505-534-1329; E-mail: colemanm1@wnmu.edu.
Cross Country: Brent Hansen; Phone: 505-538-6237; E-mail: hansenb@email.wnmu.edu.
Football: Charley Wade; Phone: 505-534-0344; E-mail: wadec@iron.wnmu.edu.
Golf: Kent Beatty; Phone: 505-538-6235; E-mail: wnmugolf@aol.com.
Tennis: Robert Benavidez; Phone: 505-388-9177; E-mail: benavidezrm@silver.wnmu.edu.

WOMEN'S COACHES
Basketball: Samantha Ezell; Phone: 505-538-6218; E-mail: ezells@pyrite.wnmu.edu.
Cross Country: Brent Hansen; Phone: 505-538-6237; E-mail: hansenb@email.wnmu.edu.
Golf: Kent Beatty; Phone: 505-538-6235; E-mail: wnmugolf@aol.com.
Softball: Freddy Flores; Phone: 505-388-8630; E-mail: floresb@iron.wnmu.edu.
Tennis: Robert Benavidez; Phone: 505-388-9177; E-mail: benavidezrm@silver.wnmu.edu.
Volleyball: James Callendar; Phone: 505-538-9866; E-mail: callenderj@iron.wnmu.edu.

WESTERN OREGON UNIVERSITY
Monmouth, Oregon

Wolves ◆ NCAA II ◆ Great Northwest Athletic Conference ◆ http://www.wou.edu/

State-supported comprehensive, founded 1856, part of Oregon University System
Coed, 4,470 undergraduate students, 90% full-time, 59% women, 41% men
Rural 157-acre campus with easy access to Portland
Moderately difficult entrance level, 93% of applicants were admitted

Freshmen *Admission:* 1,809 applied, 1,694 were accepted, 926 enrolled. *Test scores:* SAT verbal scores over 500: 48%; SAT math scores over 500: 45%; SAT verbal scores over 600: 11%; SAT math scores over 600: 10%; SAT math scores over 700: 1%.
Tuition and fees (2003–04): $4305 (resident), $12,570 (nonresident). *Room and board:* $5976.
Financial Aid (All incoming freshmen): *Average need-based gift aid:* $3844. *Average non-need based aid:* $6959. *Average aid to full-time undergraduates:* $5707.
Athletic Department: *Director of Athletics:* Jon Carey; Phone: 503-838-8252; Fax: 503-838-8370; E-mail: careyj@wou.edu. *Sports Information Director:* Russ Blunck; Phone: 503-838-8160; E-mail: blunckr@wou.edu.

MEN'S COACHES
Baseball: Terry Baumgartner; Phone: 503-838-8448; E-mail: baumgat@wou.edu.
Basketball: Tim Hills; Phone: 503-838-8919; E-mail: hillst@wou.edu.

Cross Country: Rob Wood; Phone: 503-838-8068; E-mail: woodr@wou.edu.

Football: Duke Iverson; Phone: 503-838-8255; E-mail: iversond@wou.edu.

Track and Field: Mike Johnson; Phone: 503-838-8420; E-mail: johnsonm@wou.edu.

WOMEN'S COACHES

Basketball: Paula Pietrok; Phone: 503-838-8177; E-mail: pietrokp@wou.edu.

Cross Country: Rob Wood; Phone: 503-838-8068; E-mail: woodr@wou.edu.

Soccer: Rod Fretz; Phone: 503-838-8448; E-mail: fretzr@wou.edu.

Softball: Pam Knox; Phone: 503-838-8438; E-mail: knoxp@wou.edu.

Track and Field: Mike Johnson; Phone: 503-838-8420; E-mail: johnsonm@wou.edu.

Volleyball: Judy Lovre; Phone: 503-838-8384; E-mail: lovrej@wou.edu.

WESTERN STATE COLLEGE OF COLORADO
Gunnison, Colorado

Mountaineers ◆ NCAA II ◆ Rocky Mountain Athletic Conference ◆ http://www.western.edu/

State-supported 4-year, founded 1901
Coed, 2,385 undergraduate students, 91% full-time, 41% women, 59% men
Small-town 381-acre campus
Moderately difficult entrance level, 80% of applicants were admitted

Freshmen *Admission:* 2,077 applied, 1,643 were accepted, 634 enrolled. *Test scores:* SAT verbal scores over 500: 51%; SAT math scores over 500: 49%; SAT verbal scores over 600: 15%; SAT math scores over 600: 13%; SAT verbal scores over 700: 2%; SAT math scores over 700: 1%.
Tuition and fees (2003–04): $2564 (resident), $9746 (nonresident). *Room and board:* $5680 (room only: $3524).
Financial Aid (All incoming freshmen): *Average need-based gift aid:* $2500. *Average non-need based aid:* $1000. *Average aid to full-time undergraduates:* $6625.
Athletic Department: *Director of Athletics:* Greg Waggoner; Phone: 970-943-2079; Fax: 970-943-2754; E-mail: gwaggoner@western.edu. *Sports Information Director:* Bobby Heiken; Phone: 970-943-2831; E-mail: bheiken@western.edu.

MEN'S COACHES

Basketball: Steve Phillips; Phone: 970-943-2134; E-mail: sphillips@western.edu.

Cross Country: Duane Vandenbusche; Phone: 970-943-2068; E-mail: wsctrack@hotmail.com.

Football: Jeff Zenisek; Phone: 970-943-2056; E-mail: jzenisek@western.edu.

Track and Field: Scott Lorek; Phone: 970-943-3257; E-mail: slorek@western.edu.

Wrestling: Miles Van Hee; Phone: 970-943-2089; E-mail: mvanhee@western.edu.

WOMEN'S COACHES

Basketball: Sandee Mott; Phone: 970-943-2652; E-mail: smott@western.edu.

Cross Country: Duane Vandenbusche; Phone: 970-943-2068; E-mail: wsctrack@hotmail.com.

Track and Field: Scott Lorek; Phone: 970-943-3257; E-mail: slorek@western.edu.

Volleyball: Shawn Back; Phone: 970-943-2834; E-mail: sback@western.edu.

WESTERN WASHINGTON UNIVERSITY
Bellingham, Washington

Vikings ◆ NCAA II ◆ Great Northwest Athletic Conference ◆ http://www.wwu.edu/

State-supported comprehensive, founded 1893
Coed, 12,477 undergraduate students, 92% full-time, 57% women, 43% men
Small-town 223-acre campus with easy access to Seattle and Vancouver
Moderately difficult entrance level, 72% of applicants were admitted

Freshmen *Admission:* 7,652 applied, 5,843 were accepted, 2,214 enrolled. *Test scores:* SAT verbal scores over 500: 79%; SAT math scores over 500: 81%; SAT verbal scores over 600: 35%; SAT math scores over 600: 31%; SAT verbal scores over 700: 5%; SAT math scores over 700: 3%.
Tuition and fees (2003–04): $4182 (resident), $12,954 (nonresident). *Room and board:* $5945 (room only: $3902).
Financial Aid (All incoming freshmen): *Average need-based gift aid:* $4579. *Average non-need based aid:* $3303. *Average aid to full-time undergraduates:* $7535.
Athletic Department: *Director of Athletics:* Lynda Goodrich; Phone: 360-650-3109; Fax: 360-650-3495; E-mail: lynda.goodrich@wwu.edu. *Sports Information Director:* Paul Madison; Phone: 360-650-3108; E-mail: paul.madison@wwu.edu.

MEN'S COACHES

Basketball: Brad Jackson; Phone: 360-650-3024; E-mail: brad.jackson@wwu.edu.

Cheerleading: Tonja Gilbert; Phone: 360-650-3211; E-mail: wwucheer@hotmail.com.

Cross Country: Pee Wee Halsell; Phone: 360-650-3103; E-mail: peewee.halsell@wwu.edu.

Football: Rob Smith; Phone: 360-650-3211; E-mail: rsmith@cc.wwu.edu.

Golf: Steve Card; Phone: 360-650-3489; E-mail: steve.card@wwu.edu.

Soccer: Travis Connell; Phone: 360-650-3493; E-mail: travis.connell@wwu.edu.

Track and Field: Pee Wee Halsell; Phone: 360-650-3103; E-mail: peewee.halsell@wwu.edu.

WOMEN'S COACHES

Basketball: Sara Nichols; Phone: 360-650-4933; E-mail: sara.nichols@wwu.edu.

Cheerleading: Tonja Gilbert; Phone: 360-650-3211; E-mail: wwucheer@hotmail.com.

Cross Country: Pee Wee Halsell; Phone: 360-650-3103; E-mail: peewee.halsell@wwu.edu.

Golf: Dean Russell; Phone: 360-650-3109.

Soccer: Travis Connell; Phone: 360-650-3493; E-mail: travis.connell@wwu.edu.

Softball: Lonnie Hicks; Phone: 360-650-7783; E-mail: lonnie.hicks@wwu.edu.

Track and Field: Pee Wee Halsell; Phone: 360-650-3103; E-mail: peewee.halsell@wwu.edu.

Volleyball: Diane Flick; Phone: 360-650-2849; E-mail: diane.flick@wwu.edu.

WESTFIELD STATE COLLEGE
Westfield, Massachusetts

Owls ◆ NCAA III ◆ Little East Conference; Massachusetts State College Athletic Conference; New England Football Conference ◆ http://www.wsc.ma.edu/

State-supported comprehensive, founded 1838, part of Massachusetts Public Higher Education System
Coed, 4,292 undergraduate students, 87% full-time, 56% women, 44% men
Small-town 227-acre campus
Moderately difficult entrance level, 60% of applicants were admitted

Freshmen *Admission:* 3,838 applied, 2,521 were accepted, 854 enrolled. *Test scores:* SAT verbal scores over 500: 60%; SAT math scores over

Westfield State College *(continued)*

500: 58%; SAT verbal scores over 600: 10%; SAT math scores over 600: 9%; SAT verbal scores over 700: 1%; SAT math scores over 700: %.

Tuition and fees (2003–04): $4557 (resident), $10,637 (nonresident). *Room and board:* $5290 (room only: $3250).

Financial Aid (All incoming freshmen): *Average need-based gift aid: $3764. Average non-need based aid: $3442. Average aid to full-time undergraduates: $4878.*

Athletic Department: *Director of Athletics:* Ken Magarian; Phone: 413-572-5405; Fax: 413-572-5477; E-mail: kmagarian@wsc.ma.edu. *Sports Information Director:* Mickey Curtis; Phone: 413-572-5433; E-mail: mcurtis@wsc.ma.edu.

MEN'S COACHES

Baseball: Tom Lo Ricco; Phone: 413-572-5633; E-mail: tloricco@earthlink.net.

Basketball: Rich Sutter; Phone: 413-572-5509; E-mail: rsutter@wisdom.wsc.ma.edu.

Cheerleading: Lisa Moskow; Phone: 413-532-1701; E-mail: lmoskow@uca.com.

Cross Country: Bob Rausch; Phone: 413-572-5392; E-mail: rrausch@wisdom.wsc.ma.edu.

Football: Steve Marino; Phone: 413-572-5420; E-mail: stcm@samnet.net.

Ice Hockey: Sean Provost; Phone: 413-349-8269; E-mail: sprovost@attbi.com.

Soccer: Fred Broxton; Phone: 413-627-7872; E-mail: fbroxton@aol.com.

Track and Field: Sean O'Brien; Phone: 413-572-5510; E-mail: sobrien@wsc.ma.edu.

WOMEN'S COACHES

Basketball: Steve Marcil; Phone: 413-572-5405; E-mail: marcilsteven26@hotmail.com.

Cheerleading: Lisa Moskow; Phone: 413-532-1701; E-mail: lmoskow@uca.com.

Cross Country: Bob Rausch; Phone: 413-572-5392; E-mail: rrausch@wisdom.wsc.ma.edu.

Diving: Dave Laing; Phone: 413-572-5395; E-mail: dlaing@wsc.ma.edu.

Field Hockey: Heather Cabral; Phone: 413-572-5405; E-mail: heatherc12@yahoo.com.

Soccer: Heather Boisvere-Langone; Phone: 413-572-5405; E-mail: hboisvere@juno.com.

Softball: Lou Ann Simchak; Phone: 413-572-5417; E-mail: lsimchak@wsc.ma.edu.

Swimming: Dave Laing; Phone: 413-572-5395; E-mail: dlaing@wsc.ma.edu.

Track and Field: Sean O'Brien; Phone: 413-572-5510; E-mail: sobrien@wsc.ma.edu.

Volleyball: Fred Glanville; Phone: 413-572-5405; E-mail: glanville215@charter.net.

WEST LIBERTY STATE COLLEGE
West Liberty, West Virginia

Hilltoppers ◆ NCAA II ◆ West Virginia Intercollegiate Athletic Conference ◆ http://www.wlsc.edu/

State-supported 4-year, founded 1837, part of West Virginia Higher Education Policy Commission
Coed, 2,491 undergraduate students, 87% full-time, 55% women, 45% men
Rural 290-acre campus with easy access to Pittsburgh
Minimally difficult entrance level, 84% of applicants were admitted

Freshmen *Admission:* 1,309 applied, 1,120 were accepted, 463 enrolled. *Test scores:* SAT verbal scores over 500: 22%; SAT math scores over 500: 18%; SAT verbal scores over 600: 10%; SAT math scores over 600: 4%.

Tuition and fees (2003–04): $3138 (resident), $7790 (nonresident). *Room and board:* $4730 (room only: $2750).

Financial Aid (All incoming freshmen): *Average need-based gift aid: $3829. Average non-need based aid: $2509. Average aid to full-time undergraduates: $4709.*

Athletic Department: *Director of Athletics:* James Watson; Phone: 304-336-8046; Fax: 304-336-8304; E-mail: watsonjw@wlsc.wvnet.edu. *Sports Information Director:* Lynn Ullom; Phone: 304-336-8320; E-mail: ullomlyn@wlsc.wvnet.edu.

MEN'S COACHES

Baseball: Bo McConnaughy; Phone: 304-336-8235; E-mail: mcconnbo@wlsc.wvnet.edu.

Basketball: Dan Petri; Phone: 304-336-8234.

Cheerleading: Patty Hendershot; Phone: 304-336-8235.

Cross Country: Stu Rynkievich; Phone: 304-336-8416; E-mail: srynkiev@wlsc.wvnet.edu.

Football: Bob Eaton; Phone: 304-336-8042; E-mail: eatonbob@wlsc.edu.

Golf: Roger Waialae; Phone: 304-336-8294; E-mail: rwaialae@wlsc.wvnet.edu.

Tennis: Jim Crutchfield; Phone: 304-336-8232.

Track and Field: Carl Bowman; Phone: 304-336-8368; E-mail: cbowman@wlsc.evnet.edu.

Wrestling: Vince Monseau; Phone: 304-336-8230; E-mail: monseauv@wlsc.evnet.edu.

WOMEN'S COACHES

Basketball: Lynn Ullom; Phone: 304-336-8320; E-mail: ullomlyn@wlsc.edu.

Cheerleading: Patty Hendershot; Phone: 304-336-8235.

Cross Country: Stu Rynkievich; Phone: 304-336-8416; E-mail: srynkiev@wlsc.wvnet.edu.

Golf: Karen Murphy Waialae; Phone: 304-336-8294; E-mail: rwaialae@wlsc.wvnet.edu.

Softball: Herb Minch; Phone: 304-336-8093; E-mail: minchhp@wlsc.evnet.edu.

Tennis: Jim Crutchfield; Phone: 304-336-8232.

Track and Field: Carl Bowman; Phone: 304-336-8046; E-mail: cbowman@wlsc.evnet.edu.

Volleyball: Jackie Goldstein; Phone: 304-336-8844.

WESTMINSTER COLLEGE
Salt Lake City, Utah

Griffins ◆ NAIA ◆ Frontier Conference ◆ http://www.westminstercollege.edu/

Independent comprehensive, founded 1875
Coed, 2,017 undergraduate students, 89% full-time, 58% women, 42% men
Suburban 27-acre campus
Moderately difficult entrance level, 73% of applicants were admitted

Freshmen *Admission:* 865 applied, 713 were accepted, 374 enrolled.

Tuition and fees (2003–04): $16,994 (full-time). *Room and board:* $5300.

Financial Aid (All incoming freshmen): *Average need-based gift aid: $10,350. Average non-need based aid: $7203. Average aid to full-time undergraduates: $14,651.*

Athletic Department: *Director of Athletics:* Tommy Connor; Phone: 801-484-7651; Fax: 801-474-2511; E-mail: tconnor@westminstercollege.edu.

MEN'S COACHES

Basketball: Tommy Connor; E-mail: tconnor@westminstercollege.edu.

Cross Country: Phone: 801-484-7651.

Golf: Daron Park; Phone: 801-832-2335; E-mail: dpark@westminstercollege.edu.

Soccer: Chris Dorich; Phone: 801-832-2337; E-mail: cdorich@westminstercollege.edu.

WOMEN'S COACHES

Basketball: Daron Park; Phone: 801-832-2335; E-mail: dpark@westminstercollege.edu.

Cross Country: Phone: 801-484-7651.

Golf: Daron Park; Phone: 801-832-2335; E-mail: dpark@westminstercollege.edu.

Volleyball: Tasha Poduska; Phone: 801-832-2343; E-mail: tpoduska@westminstercollege.edu.

WESTMINSTER COLLEGE
Fulton, Missouri

Blue Jays ◆ NCAA III ◆ St. Louis Athletic Conference
◆ http://www.westminster-mo.edu/

Independent religious 4-year, founded 1851, affiliated with Presbyterian Church
Coed, 821 undergraduate students, 98% full-time, 42% women, 58% men
Small-town 65-acre campus
Moderately difficult entrance level, 74% of applicants were admitted

Freshmen *Admission:* 846 applied, 634 were accepted, 240 enrolled. *Test scores:* SAT verbal scores over 500: 78%; SAT math scores over 500: 75%; SAT verbal scores over 600: 42%; SAT math scores over 600: 36%; SAT verbal scores over 700: 6%; SAT math scores over 700: 9%.
Tuition and fees (2004–05): $13,410 (full-time). *Room and board:* $5650 (room only: $2880).
Financial Aid (All incoming freshmen): *Average need-based gift aid:* $11,300. *Average non-need based aid:* $5026. *Average aid to full-time undergraduates:* $13,684.
Athletic Department: *Director of Athletics:* Terry Logue; Phone: 573-592-5200; Fax: 573-592-5366; E-mail: loguet@jaynet.wcmo.edu. *Sports Information Director:* Beth Usewicz; Phone: 573-592-5200; E-mail: sid@jaynet.wcmo.edu.

MEN'S COACHES
Baseball: Scott Pritchard; Phone: 573-592-5200; E-mail: pritchs@jaynet.wcmo.edu.
Basketball: Matt Mitchell; Phone: 573-592-5200; E-mail: mitchem@jaynet.wcmo.edu.
Football: John Welty; Phone: 573-592-5200; E-mail: weltyj@jaynet.wcmo.edu.
Golf: Matt Mitchell; Phone: 573-592-5200; E-mail: mitchem@jaynet.wcmo.edu.
Soccer: Joel Wallace; Phone: 573-592-5200; E-mail: wallacj@jaynet.wcmo.edu.
Tennis: Jeff Borengasser; Phone: 573-592-5200; E-mail: borengasserj@jaynet.wcmo.edu.

WOMEN'S COACHES
Basketball: Tracey Dailey; Phone: 573-592-5200; E-mail: daileyt@jaynet.wcmo.edu.
Golf: Matt Mitchell; Phone: 573-592-5200; E-mail: mitchem@jaynet.wcmo.edu.
Soccer: Heidi Kocher; Phone: 573-592-5200; E-mail: kocherh@jaynet.wcmo.edu.
Softball: Chris Viers; Phone: 573-592-5200; E-mail: viersc@jaynet.wcmo.edu.
Tennis: Jeff Borengasser; Phone: 573-592-5200; E-mail: borengasserj@jaynet.wcmo.edu.
Volleyball: Chris Viers; Phone: 573-592-5200; E-mail: viersc@jaynet.wcmo.edu.

WESTMINSTER COLLEGE
New Wilmington, Pennsylvania

Titans ◆ NCAA II ◆ Presidents' Athletic Conference ◆ http://www.westminster.edu/

Independent religious comprehensive, founded 1852, affiliated with Presbyterian Church (U.S.A.)
Coed, 1,425 undergraduate students, 96% full-time, 61% women, 39% men
Small-town 350-acre campus with easy access to Pittsburgh
Moderately difficult entrance level, 73% of applicants were admitted

Freshmen *Admission:* 1,244 applied, 953 were accepted, 339 enrolled. *Test scores:* SAT verbal scores over 500: 73%; SAT math scores over 500: 72%; SAT verbal scores over 600: 28%; SAT math scores over 600: 29%; SAT verbal scores over 700: 2%; SAT math scores over 700: 3%.
Tuition and fees (2004–05): $21,470 (full-time). *Room and board:* $6360 (room only: $3360).

Financial Aid (All incoming freshmen): *Average need-based gift aid:* $7309. *Average non-need based aid:* $8517. *Average aid to full-time undergraduates:* $17,737.
Athletic Department: *Director of Athletics:* Jim Dafler; Phone: 724-946-7313; Fax: 724-946-7021; E-mail: daflerje@westminster.edu. *Sports Information Director:* Joe Onderko; Phone: 724-946-6357; E-mail: onderkjm@westminster.edu.

MEN'S COACHES
Baseball: Carmen Nocera; Phone: 724-946-7312; E-mail: noceract@westminster.edu.
Basketball: Larry Ondako; Phone: 724-946-6342; E-mail: ondakolr@westminster.edu.
Cheerleading: Bess Ondako; Phone: 724-946-6160; E-mail: ondakoba@westminster.edu.
Cross Country: Gary Lilly; Phone: 724-946-7250; E-mail: glilly@westminster.edu.
Football: Jerry Schmitt; Phone: 724-946-7310; E-mail: schmitjm@westminster.edu.
Golf: Gene Nicholson; Phone: 724-946-7308; E-mail: nicholbe@westminster.edu.
Soccer: Girish Thacker; Phone: 724-946-7316; E-mail: thakargs@westminster.edu.
Swimming: Rob Klamut; Phone: 724-946-7315; E-mail: klamutrg@westminster.edu.
Tennis: Scott Renninger; Phone: 724-946-7311; E-mail: renninds@westminster.edu.
Track and Field: Don Augustine; Phone: 724-946-6213; E-mail: augustd@westminster.edu.

WOMEN'S COACHES
Basketball: Rosanne Scott; Phone: 724-946-7157; E-mail: scottrm@westminster.edu.
Cheerleading: Bess Ondako; Phone: 724-946-6160; E-mail: ondakoba@westminster.edu.
Cross Country: Gary Lilly; Phone: 724-946-7250; E-mail: glilly@westminster.edu.
Golf: Debi Behr; Phone: 724-946-6164; E-mail: behrd@westminster.edu.
Soccer: Girish Thaker; Phone: 724-946-7316; E-mail: thakargs@westminster.edu.
Softball: Jan Reddinger; Phone: 724-946-7319; E-mail: reddinjm@westminster.edu.
Swimming: Rob Klamut; Phone: 724-946-7315; E-mail: klamutrg@westminster.edu.
Tennis: S. Kipley Hass; Phone: 724-946-7318; E-mail: haassk@westminster.edu.
Track and Field: Don Augustine; Phone: 724-946-6213; E-mail: augustd@westminster.edu.
Volleyball: Tammy Swearingen; Phone: 724-946-7320; E-mail: swearitl@westminster.edu.

WESTMONT COLLEGE
Santa Barbara, California

Warriors ◆ NAIA ◆ Golden State Conference ◆ http://www.westmont.edu/

Independent nondenominational 4-year, founded 1937
Coed, 1,343 undergraduate students, 100% full-time, 65% women, 35% men
Suburban 133-acre campus with easy access to Los Angeles
Moderately difficult entrance level, 82% of applicants were admitted

Freshmen *Admission:* 1,404 applied, 1,188 were accepted, 355 enrolled. *Test scores:* SAT verbal scores over 500: 92%; SAT math scores over 500: 94%; SAT verbal scores over 600: 57%; SAT math scores over 600: 62%; SAT verbal scores over 700: 12%; SAT math scores over 700: 21%.
Tuition and fees (2003–04): $24,890 (full-time). *Room and board:* $8390 (room only: $4888).
Financial Aid (All incoming freshmen): *Average need-based gift aid:* $10,944. *Average non-need based aid:* $10,355. *Average aid to full-time undergraduates:* $14,900.
Athletic Department: *Director of Athletics:* Dave Wolf; Phone: 805-565-6106; Fax: 805-565-6221; E-mail: wolf@westmont.edu. *Sports Information Director:* Jeff Raymond; Phone: 805-565-7012; E-mail: jraymond@westmont.edu.

Westmont College *(continued)*

MEN'S COACHES

Baseball: Rob Crawford; Phone: 805-565-6012; E-mail: crawford@westmont.edu.

Basketball: John Moore; Phone: 805-565-6013; E-mail: moore@westmont.edu.

Cross Country: Russell Smelley; Phone: 805-565-6108; E-mail: smelley@westmont.edu.

Soccer: Dave Wolf; Phone: 805-565-6106; E-mail: wolf@westmont.edu.

Tennis: Chris Elwood; Phone: 805-565-6241; E-mail: celwood@westmont.edu.

Track and Field: Russell Smelley; Phone: 805-565-6108; E-mail: smelley@westmont.edu.

WOMEN'S COACHES

Basketball: Gregg Afman; Phone: 805-565-7005; E-mail: afman@westmont.edu.

Cross Country: Russell Smelley; Phone: 805-565-6108; E-mail: smelley@westmont.edu.

Soccer: Mike Giuliano; Phone: 805-565-6134; E-mail: giuliano@westmont.edu.

Tennis: Kathy LeSage; Phone: 805-565-6120; E-mail: lesage@westmont.edu.

Track and Field: Russell Smelley; Phone: 805-565-6108; E-mail: smelley@westmont.edu.

Volleyball: Jim Smoot; Phone: 805-565-7303; E-mail: smoot@westmont.edu.

WEST TEXAS A&M UNIVERSITY
Canyon, Texas

Buffaloes ◆ NCAA II ◆ Lone Star Conference ◆ http://www.wtamu.edu/

State-supported comprehensive, founded 1909, part of Texas A&M University System
Coed, 5,583 undergraduate students, 78% full-time, 56% women, 44% men
Small-town 128-acre campus
Moderately difficult entrance level, 69% of applicants were admitted

Freshmen *Admission:* 1,899 applied, 1,341 were accepted, 799 enrolled. *Test scores:* SAT verbal scores over 500: 48%; SAT math scores over 500: 50%; SAT verbal scores over 600: 13%; SAT math scores over 600: 12%; SAT verbal scores over 700: 1%; SAT math scores over 700: 2%.
Tuition and fees (2003–04): $3227 (resident), $10,307 (nonresident). *Room and board:* $4342 (room only: $1930).
Financial Aid (All incoming freshmen): *Average need-based gift aid:* $3830. *Average non-need based aid:* $3064. *Average aid to full-time undergraduates:* $5422.
Athletic Department: *Director of Athletics:* Ed Harris; Phone: 806-651-4400; Fax: 806-651-4409; E-mail: eharris@mail.wtamu.edu. *Sports Information Director:* Zach Fisher; Phone: 806-651-4406; E-mail: zfisher@mail.wtamu.edu.

MEN'S COACHES

Baseball: Mark Jones; Phone: 806-651-2676; E-mail: mjones@mail.wtamu.edu.

Basketball: Rick Cooper; Phone: 806-651-2697; E-mail: rcooper@mail.wtamu.edu.

Cheerleading: Nathan Gonzales; Phone: 806-651-4400; E-mail: nathang@sprintpcs.com.

Cross Country: Eric Lathrop; Phone: 806-651-2339; E-mail: elathrop@mail.wtamu.edu.

Football: Ronnie Jones; Phone: 806-651-4410; E-mail: rjones@mail.wtamu.edu.

Golf: Brad Borden; Phone: 806-651-2701; E-mail: beborden@mail.wtamu.edu.

Soccer: Butch Lauffer; Phone: 806-651-2678; E-mail: rlauffer@mail.wtamu.edu.

WOMEN'S COACHES

Basketball: Bob Schneider; Phone: 806-651-2692; E-mail: bschneider@mail.wtamu.edu.

Cheerleading: Nathan Gonzales; Phone: 806-651-4400; E-mail: nathang@sprintpcs.com.

Cross Country: Kimberly Dudley; Phone: 806-651-8483; E-mail: kdudley@mail.wtamu.edu.

Golf: Brad Borden; Phone: 806-651-2701; E-mail: beborden@mail.wtamu.edu.

Soccer: Butch Lauffer; Phone: 806-651-2678; E-mail: rlauffer@mail.wtamu.edu.

Volleyball: Tony Graystone; Phone: 806-651-2695; E-mail: tgraystone@mail.wtamu.edu.

WEST VIRGINIA STATE COLLEGE
Institute, West Virginia

Yellow Jackets ◆ NCAA II ◆ West Virginia Intercollegiate Athletic Conference ◆ http://www.wvsc.edu/

State-supported comprehensive, founded 1891, part of State College System of West Virginia
Coed, 4,992 undergraduate students, 64% full-time, 60% women, 40% men
Suburban 90-acre campus
Minimally difficult entrance level

Freshmen *Admission:* 732 enrolled.
Tuition and fees (2003–04): $2814 (resident), $6394 (nonresident). *Room and board:* $4400 (room only: $2100).
Athletic Department: *Director of Athletics:* Bob Parker; Phone: 304-766-3165; Fax: 304-766-3364. *Sports Information Director:* Sean McAndrews; Phone: 304-766-4122; E-mail: mcandrse@wvsc.edu.

MEN'S COACHES

Baseball: Calvin Bailey; Phone: 304-766-3208; E-mail: loyds@mail.wvsc.edu.

Basketball: Brian Poore; Phone: 304-766-3226; E-mail: poorebr@wvsc.edu.

Cheerleading: Lisa Bradley; Phone: 304-766-3165; E-mail: bradleyk@wvsc.edu.

Football: Carl Lee; Phone: 304-766-3228; E-mail: leecr@wvsc.edu.

Tennis: John Simms; Phone: 304-766-2260; E-mail: simsy1@aol.com.

Track and Field: Chip Ferrel; Phone: 304-766-5748; E-mail: ferrellw@wvsc.edu.

WOMEN'S COACHES

Basketball: Gill Heasley; Phone: 304-766-3227; E-mail: heasleyg@wvsc.edu.

Cheerleading: Lisa Bradley; Phone: 304-766-3165; E-mail: bradleyk@wvsc.edu.

Softball: Denise Dietrich; Phone: 304-766-3229; E-mail: dietride@wvsc.edu.

Tennis: John Simms; Phone: 304-766-2260; E-mail: simsy1@aol.com.

Track and Field: Chip Ferrel; Phone: 304-766-5748; E-mail: ferrellw@wvsc.edu.

Volleyball: Shannon Gerenicir; Phone: 304-766-5750; E-mail: payteesmom@aol.com.

WEST VIRGINIA UNIVERSITY
Morgantown, West Virginia

Mountaineers ◆ NCAA I ◆ Big East Conference ◆ http://www.wvu.edu/

State-supported university, founded 1867, part of West Virginia Higher Education System
Coed, 17,517 undergraduate students, 94% full-time, 47% women, 53% men
Small-town 913-acre campus with easy access to Pittsburgh
Moderately difficult entrance level, 92% of applicants were admitted

Freshmen *Admission:* 10,049 applied, 9,281 were accepted, 4,415 enrolled. *Test scores:* SAT verbal scores over 500: 63%; SAT math scores over 500: 67%; SAT verbal scores over 600: 15%; SAT math scores over 600: 20%; SAT verbal scores over 700: 1%; SAT math scores over 700: 2%.
Tuition and fees (2003–04): $3548 (resident), $10,768 (nonresident). *Room and board:* $5822 (room only: $3074).

Financial Aid (All incoming freshmen): *Average need-based gift aid: $3348. Average non-need based aid: $5337. Average aid to full-time undergraduates: $6580.*
Athletic Department: *Director of Athletics:* Ed Pastilong; Phone: 304-293-5621; Fax: 304-293-4105; E-mail: edpastilong@mail.wvu.edu. *Sports Information Director:* Shelly Poe; Phone: 304-293-2821; E-mail: shelly.poe@mail.wvu.edu.

MEN'S COACHES
Baseball: Greg Van Zant; Phone: 304-293-2300; E-mail: gregvanzant@mail.wvu.edu.
Basketball: John Beilein; Phone: 304-293-2193; E-mail: wvuhoop@mail.wvu.edu.
Cheerleading: Christy Bryan-Davis; Phone: 304-293-5621; E-mail: wvucheer@mail.wvu.edu.
Diving: Steve Phillips; Phone: 304-293-2289; E-mail: steven.phillips@mail.wvu.edu.
Football: Rich Rodriquez; Phone: 304-293-4194.
Soccer: Mike Seabolt; Phone: 304-293-2300.
Swimming: Steve Phillips; Phone: 304-293-2289; E-mail: steven.phillips@mail.wvu.edu.
Wrestling: Craig Tumbull; Phone: 304-293-5383; E-mail: craig.turnbull@mail.wvu.edu.

WOMEN'S COACHES
Basketball: Mike Carey; Phone: 304-293-3508; E-mail: mike.carey@mail.wvu.edu.
Cheerleading: Christy Bryan-Davis; Phone: 304-293-5621; E-mail: wvucheer@mail.wvu.edu.
Cross Country: Jeff Huntoun; Phone: 304-293-2300; E-mail: jeff.huntoon@mail.wvu.edu.
Diving: Steve Phillips; Phone: 304-293-2289; E-mail: steven.phillips@mail.wvu.edu.
Gymnastics: Linda Burdette; Phone: 304-293-3294; E-mail: linda.burdette@mail.wvu.edu.
Soccer: Nikki Izzo-Brown; Phone: 304-293-5621; E-mail: nikki.izzo-brown@mail.wvu.edu.
Swimming: Steve Phillips; Phone: 304-293-2289; E-mail: steven.phillips@mail.wvu.edu.
Tennis: Dan Silverstein; Phone: 304-293-5621; E-mail: dan.silverstein@mail.wvu.edu.
Track and Field: Jeff Huntoun; Phone: 304-293-2300; E-mail: jeff.huntoon@mail.wvu.edu.
Volleyball: Veronica Hammersmith; Phone: 304-293-4811; E-mail: veronica.hammersmith@mail.wvu.edu.

WEST VIRGINIA UNIVERSITY INSTITUTE OF TECHNOLOGY
Montgomery, West Virginia
Golden Bears ◆ NCAA II ◆ West Virginia Intercollegiate Athletic Conference ◆ http://www.wvutech.edu/

State-supported comprehensive, founded 1895, part of University System of West Virginia
Coed, 2,435 undergraduate students, 70% full-time, 40% women, 60% men
Small-town 200-acre campus with easy access to Charleston
Noncompetitive entrance level, 75% of applicants were admitted

Freshmen *Admission:* 1,191 applied, 883 were accepted, 417 enrolled. *Test scores:* SAT verbal scores over 500: 47%; SAT math scores over 500: 51%; SAT verbal scores over 600: 14%; SAT math scores over 600: 18%; SAT math scores over 700: 2%.
Tuition and fees (2003–04): $3488 (resident), $8371 (nonresident). *Room and board:* $4832 (room only: $2259).
Financial Aid (All incoming freshmen): *Average need-based gift aid: $3086. Average non-need based aid: $2994. Average aid to full-time undergraduates: $6270.*
Athletic Department: *Director of Athletics:* Reggie Smith; Phone: 304-442-3181; Fax: 304-442-3499; E-mail: rsmith4@wvutech.edu. *Sports Information Director:* Dan Conley; Phone: 304-442-3286; E-mail: dconley@wvutech.edu.

MEN'S COACHES
Baseball: Tom Eppling; Phone: 304-442-3831.
Basketball: Robert Williams; Phone: 304-442-3250; E-mail: rwilliams@wvutech.edu.

Cheerleading: Debbie Oliver; Phone: 304-442-3104; E-mail: doliver@wvutech.edu.
Football: Mauro Monz; Phone: 304-442-3255.
Golf: Jim Kerrigan; Phone: 304-442-3100; E-mail: jkerrigan@wvutech.edu.
Tennis: Tom Watkins; Phone: 304-442-3121.

WOMEN'S COACHES
Basketball: LeAnn Bird; Phone: 304-442-3855.
Cheerleading: Debbie Oliver; Phone: 304-442-3104; E-mail: doliver@wvutech.edu.
Soccer: Reggie Smith; Phone: 304-442-3181; E-mail: rsmith4@wvutech.edu.
Softball: Leann Bird; Phone: 304-442-3855.
Tennis: Tom Watkins; Phone: 304-442-3121.
Volleyball: Steve Davis; Phone: 304-442-3121.

WEST VIRGINIA WESLEYAN COLLEGE
Buckhannon, West Virginia
Bobcats ◆ NCAA II ◆ West Virginia Intercollegiate Athletic Conference ◆ http://www.wvwc.edu/

Independent religious comprehensive, founded 1890, affiliated with United Methodist Church
Coed, 1,589 undergraduate students, 98% full-time, 55% women, 45% men
Small-town 80-acre campus
Moderately difficult entrance level, 79% of applicants were admitted

Freshmen *Admission:* 1,461 applied, 1,155 were accepted, 464 enrolled. *Test scores:* SAT verbal scores over 500: 62%; SAT math scores over 500: 60%; SAT verbal scores over 600: 20%; SAT math scores over 600: 17%; SAT verbal scores over 700: 2%; SAT math scores over 700: 2%.
Tuition and fees (2004–05): $20,450 (full-time). *Room and board:* $5200.
Financial Aid (All incoming freshmen): *Average need-based gift aid: $15,853. Average non-need based aid: $9309. Average aid to full-time undergraduates: $18,658.*
Athletic Department: *Director of Athletics:* George Klebez; Phone: 304-473-8099; Fax: 304-473-8056; E-mail: klebez@wvwc.edu. *Sports Information Director:* Andrea Wesp; Phone: 304-473-8102; E-mail: wesp_ae@wvwc.edu.

MEN'S COACHES
Baseball: Randy Tenney; Phone: 304-473-8054; E-mail: tenney_r@wvwc.edu.
Basketball: Charles Miller; Phone: 304-473-8053; E-mail: miller_c@wvwc.edu.
Cross Country: Jesse Skiles; Phone: 304-473-8056; E-mail: skiles_j@wvwc.edu.
Diving: Denton Quick; Phone: 304-473-8507; E-mail: quick_d@wvwc.edu.
Football: Bill Struble; Phone: 304-473-8257; E-mail: struble_w@wvwc.edu.
Golf: John Barbour; Phone: 304-473-8244; E-mail: barbor_j@wvwc.edu.
Soccer: Gavin Donaldson; Phone: 304-473-8195; E-mail: donaldson@wvwc.edu.
Swimming: Denton Quick; Phone: 304-473-8507; E-mail: quick_d@wvwc.edu.
Tennis: Matt Bohman; Phone: 304-473-8702; E-mail: bohman_m@wvwc.edu.
Track and Field: Jesse Skiles; Phone: 304-473-8056; E-mail: skiles_j@wvwc.edu.

WOMEN'S COACHES
Basketball: Steve Tierney; Phone: 304-473-8057; E-mail: tierney_s@wvwc.edu.
Cross Country: Jesse Skiles; Phone: 304-473-8056; E-mail: skiles_j@wvwc.edu.
Diving: Denton Quick; Phone: 304-473-8507; E-mail: quick_d@wvwc.edu.
Soccer: Anthony James; Phone: 304-473-8101; E-mail: james_a@wvwc.edu.
Softball: Steve Warner; Phone: 304-473-8005; E-mail: warner_s@wvwc.edu.

West Virginia Wesleyan College *(continued)*

Swimming: Denton Quick; Phone: 304-473-8507; E-mail: quick_d@
wvwc.edu.
Tennis: Matt Bohman; Phone: 304-473-8702; E-mail: bohman_m@
wvwc.edu.
Track and Field: Jesse Skiles; Phone: 304-473-8056; E-mail: skiles_j@
wvwc.edu.
Volleyball: Melissa Klein; Phone: 304-473-8219; E-mail: klein_mf@
wvwc.edu.

WHEATON COLLEGE
Wheaton, Illinois

Thunder ◆ NCAA III ◆ College Conference of Illinois and
Wisconsin Conference ◆ http://www.wheaton.edu/

Independent nondenominational comprehensive, founded 1860
Coed, 2,430 undergraduate students, 97% full-time, 51% women,
49% men
Suburban 80-acre campus with easy access to Chicago
Very difficult entrance level, 6% of applicants were admitted

Freshmen *Admission:* 2,170 applied, 1,146 were accepted, 576 enrolled.
Test scores: SAT verbal scores over 500: 100%; SAT math scores over
500: 98%; SAT verbal scores over 600: 85%; SAT math scores over
600: 82%; SAT verbal scores over 700: 37%; SAT math scores over
700: 29%.
Tuition and fees (2004–05): $20,000 (full-time). *Room and board:* $6466
(room only: $3784).
Financial Aid (All incoming freshmen): *Average need-based gift aid:*
$11,446. *Average non-need based aid:* $2123. *Average aid to full-time
undergraduates:* $17,092.
Athletic Department: *Director of Athletics:* Tony Ladd; Phone: 630-752-
5748; Fax: 630-752-7007; E-mail: tony.ladd@wheaton.edu. *Sports
Information Director:* Brett Marhanka; Phone: 630-752-5747; E-mail:
brett.w.marhanka@wheaton.edu.

MEN'S COACHES
Baseball: Bobby Elder; Phone: 630-752-7164; E-mail: bobby.v.elder@
wheaton.edu.
Basketball: Bill Harris; Phone: 630-752-5735; E-mail: william.r.harris@
wheaton.edu.
Cross Country: Scott Bradley; Phone: 630-752-7059; E-mail: scott.s.
bradley@wheaton.edu.
Football: Mike Swider; Phone: 630-752-5741; E-mail: michael.o.
swider@wheaton.edu.
Golf: Joe Bean; Phone: 630-752-5123; E-mail: joseph.w.bean@wheaton.
edu.
Soccer: Joe Bean; Phone: 630-752-5123; E-mail: joseph.w.bean@
wheaton.edu.
Swimming: Jon Lederhouse; Phone: 630-752-5411; E-mail: jonathan.e.
lederhouse@wheaton.edu.
Tennis: David Webster; Phone: 630-752-5167; E-mail: david.m.
webster@wheaton.edu.
Track and Field: Scott Bradley; Phone: 630-752-7059; E-mail: scott.s.
bradley@wheaton.edu.
Wrestling: Seth Norton; Phone: 630-752-5310; E-mail: seth.norton@
wheaton.edu.

WOMEN'S COACHES
Basketball: Beth Baker; Phone: 630-752-5736; E-mail: beth.baker@
wheaton.edu.
Cross Country: Scott Bradley; Phone: 630-752-7059; E-mail: scott.s.
bradley@wheaton.edu.
Golf: Kent Madsen; Phone: 630-752-7057; E-mail: kent.r.madsen@
wheaton.edu.
Soccer: Pete Felske; Phone: 630-752-7003; E-mail: pete.b.felske@
wheaton.edu.
Softball: Pete Felske; Phone: 630-752-7003; E-mail: pete.b.felske@
wheaton.edu.
Swimming: Jon Lederhouse; Phone: 630-752-5411; E-mail: jonathan.e.
lederhouse@wheaton.edu.
Tennis: Jane Nelson; Phone: 630-752-5907; E-mail: jane.nelson@
wheaton.edu.
Track and Field: Scott Bradley; Phone: 630-752-7059; E-mail: scott.s.
bradley@wheaton.edu.

Volleyball: Jennifer Soderquist; Phone: 630-752-5733; E-mail: jennifer.
k.soderquist@wheaton.edu.

WHEATON COLLEGE
Norton, Massachusetts

Lyons ◆ NCAA III ◆ New England Women's & Men's
Athletics Conference ◆ http://www.wheatoncollege.edu/

Independent 4-year, founded 1834
Coed, 1,565 undergraduate students, 99% full-time, 64% women,
36% men
Small-town 385-acre campus with easy access to Boston
Moderately difficult entrance level, 4% of applicants were admitted

Freshmen *Admission:* 3,465 applied, 1,492 were accepted, 445 enrolled.
Test scores: SAT verbal scores over 500: 97%; SAT math scores over
500: 97%; SAT verbal scores over 600: 63%; SAT math scores over
600: 56%; SAT verbal scores over 700: 11%; SAT math scores over
700: 6%.
Tuition and fees (2003–04): $28,900 (full-time). *Room and board:* $7430
(room only: $3920).
Financial Aid (All incoming freshmen): *Average need-based gift aid:*
$16,421. *Average non-need based aid:* $8688. *Average aid to full-time
undergraduates:* $19,777.
Athletic Department: *Director of Athletics:* Chad Yowell; Phone: 508-
286-3998; Fax: 508-286-8273; E-mail: cyowell@wheatonma.edu.
Sports Information Director: Scott Dietz; Phone: 508-286-3768;
E-mail: sdietz@wheatonma.edu.

MEN'S COACHES
Baseball: Eric Podbelski; Phone: 508-286-3394; E-mail: epodbels@
wheatonma.edu.
Basketball: Brian Walmsley; Phone: 508-286-3991; E-mail: bwalmsle@
wheatonma.edu.
Cross Country: Paul Carr; Phone: 508-286-3762; E-mail: pcarr@
wheatonma.edu.
Diving: Danielle Petrone; Phone: 508-286-3989.
Lacrosse: Brad Jorgensen; Phone: 508-286-3906; E-mail: bjorgens@
wheatonma.edu.
Soccer: Matt Cushing; Phone: 508-286-3996; E-mail: mcushing@
wheatonma.edu.
Swimming: Jean-Paul Gowdy; Phone: 508-286-3989; E-mail:
gowdy_jp@wheatonma.edu.
Tennis: Lynn Miller; Phone: 508-286-3992; E-mail: lmiller@
wheatonma.edu.
Track and Field: Paul Souza; Phone: 508-286-3982; E-mail: psouza@
wheatonma.edu.

WOMEN'S COACHES
Basketball: Melissa Hodgdon; Phone: 508-286-3990; E-mail:
mhodgdon@wheatonma.edu.
Cross Country: Paul Carr; Phone: 508-286-3762; E-mail: pcarr@
wheatonma.edu.
Diving: Danielle Petrone; Phone: 508-286-3989.
Field Hockey: Rebecca Begley; Phone: 508-286-3755; E-mail: rbegley@
wheatonma.edu.
Lacrosse: Rebecca Begley; Phone: 508-286-3755; E-mail: rbegley@
wheatonma.edu.
Soccer: Luis Reis; Phone: 508-286-3997; E-mail: lreis@wheatonma.
edu.
Softball: Gina Loudenburg; Phone: 508-286-3360; E-mail: gloudenb@
wheatonma.edu.
Swimming: Jean-Paul Gowdy; Phone: 508-286-3989; E-mail:
gowdy_jp@wheatonma.edu.
Tennis: Lynn Miller; Phone: 508-286-3992; E-mail: lmiller@
wheatonma.edu.
Track and Field: Paul Souza; Phone: 508-286-3982; E-mail: psouza@
wheatonma.edu.
Volleyball: Elizabeth Rey; Phone: 508-286-5684; E-mail: erey@
wheatonma.edu.

WHEELING JESUIT UNIVERSITY
Wheeling, West Virginia

Cardinals ◆ NCAA II ◆ West Virginia Intercollegiate Athletic Conference ◆ http://www.wju.edu/

Independent Roman Catholic (Jesuit) comprehensive, founded 1954
Coed, 1,251 undergraduate students, 84% full-time, 61% women, 39% men
Suburban 65-acre campus with easy access to Pittsburgh, PA
Moderately difficult entrance level, 78% of applicants were admitted

Freshmen *Admission:* 1,188 applied, 919 were accepted, 247 enrolled. *Test scores:* SAT verbal scores over 500: 71%; SAT math scores over 500: 66%; SAT verbal scores over 600: 37%; SAT math scores over 600: 26%; SAT verbal scores over 700: 10%; SAT math scores over 700: 9%.
Tuition and fees (2004–05): $20,340 (full-time). *Room and board:* $6305 (room only: $2925).
Financial Aid (All incoming freshmen): *Average need-based gift aid:* $5273. *Average non-need based aid:* $8455. *Average aid to full-time undergraduates:* $18,509.
Athletic Department: *Director of Athletics:* Jay DeFruscio; Phone: 304-243-2365; Fax: 304-243-2265; E-mail: jayd@wju.edu.

MEN'S COACHES
Basketball: Jay DeFruscio; Phone: 304-243-2365; E-mail: jayd@wju.edu.
Cheerleading: Holly Cefaldo; Phone: 304-243-2365.
Cross Country: Trent Huntsinger; Phone: 304-243-2365; E-mail: thuntsinger@wju.edu.
Golf: Dan Sancomb; Phone: 304-243-2083; E-mail: dsancomb@wju.edu.
Lacrosse: Tim Florence; Phone: 304-243-2102.
Soccer: James Regan; Phone: 304-243-2314; E-mail: jregan@wju.edu.
Swimming: Jeff Stewart; Phone: 304-243-2399; E-mail: jstewart@wju.edu.
Track and Field: Trent Huntsinger; Phone: 304-243-2365; E-mail: thuntsinger@wju.edu.

WOMEN'S COACHES
Basketball: Joe Key; Phone: 304-243-2365; E-mail: jkey@wju.edu.
Cheerleading: Holly Cefaldo; Phone: 304-243-2365.
Cross Country: Trent Huntsinger; Phone: 304-243-2365; E-mail: thuntsinger@wju.edu.
Golf: Susan Vail; Phone: 304-243-4451.
Soccer: Carrie Hanna; Phone: 304-243-2365; E-mail: channa@wju.edu.
Softball: Melissa Frost; Phone: 304-243-2212; E-mail: mfrost@wju.edu.
Swimming: Jeff Stewart; Phone: 304-243-2399; E-mail: jstewart@wju.edu.
Track and Field: Trent Huntsinger; Phone: 304-243-2365; E-mail: thuntsinger@wju.edu.
Volleyball: Christy Benner; Phone: 304-243-8700; E-mail: volleyball@wju.edu.

WHEELOCK COLLEGE
Boston, Massachusetts

Wildcats ◆ NCAA III ◆ North Atlantic Conference ◆ http://www.wheelock.edu/

Independent comprehensive, founded 1888
Coed, primarily women, 587 undergraduate students, 98% full-time, 94% women, 6% men
Urban 7-acre campus
Moderately difficult entrance level, 47% of applicants were admitted

Freshmen *Admission:* 609 applied, 407 were accepted, 139 enrolled. *Test scores:* SAT verbal scores over 500: 68%; SAT math scores over 500: 57%; SAT verbal scores over 600: 23%; SAT math scores over 600: 15%; SAT verbal scores over 700: 4%.
Tuition and fees (2003–04): $20,400 (full-time). *Room and board:* $8600.
Financial Aid (All incoming freshmen): *Average need-based gift aid:* $9605. *Average non-need based aid:* $11,548. *Average aid to full-time undergraduates:* $13,435.
Athletic Department: *Director of Athletics:* Nicole Viele; Phone: 617-879-2238; Fax: 617-879-2277; E-mail: nvielve@wheelock.edu.

WOMEN'S COACHES
Basketball: Jason Cacciapuoti; Phone: 617-879-2238; E-mail: jcacciapuoti@wheelock.edu.
Diving: Kristy Krugh; Phone: 617-879-2238; E-mail: kkrugh@wheelock.edu.
Field Hockey: Nicole Viele; Phone: 617-879-2238; E-mail: nvielve@wheelock.edu.
Soccer: Lee Pippen; Phone: 617-879-2238; E-mail: lpippen@wheelock.edu.
Softball: Nicole Viele; Phone: 617-879-2238; E-mail: nvielve@wheelock.edu.
Swimming: Kristy Krugh; Phone: 617-879-2238; E-mail: kkrugh@wheelock.edu.

WHITMAN COLLEGE
Walla Walla, Washington

Missionaires ◆ NCAA III ◆ Northwest Conference ◆ http://www.whitman.edu/

Independent 4-year, founded 1859
Coed, 1,454 undergraduate students, 97% full-time, 56% women, 44% men
Small-town 117-acre campus
Very difficult entrance level, 6% of applicants were admitted

Freshmen *Admission:* 2,143 applied, 1,196 were accepted, 362 enrolled. *Test scores:* SAT verbal scores over 500: 98%; SAT math scores over 500: 100%; SAT verbal scores over 600: 85%; SAT math scores over 600: 83%; SAT verbal scores over 700: 40%; SAT math scores over 700: 28%.
Tuition and fees (2003–04): $25,626 (full-time). *Room and board:* $6900 (room only: $3170).
Financial Aid (All incoming freshmen): *Average need-based gift aid:* $11,900. *Average non-need based aid:* $6850. *Average aid to full-time undergraduates:* $19,550.
Athletic Department: *Director of Athletics:* Travis Feezell; Phone: 509-527-5288; Fax: 509-527-5960; E-mail: feezelt@whitman.edu. *Sports Information Director:* Dave Holden; Phone: 509-527-5902; E-mail: holden@whitman.edu.

MEN'S COACHES
Baseball: Casey Powell; Phone: 509-527-4931; E-mail: powellct@whitman.edu.
Basketball: Skip Molitor; Phone: 509-527-4970; E-mail: molitore@whitman.edu.
Cross Country: Carol Feezell; Phone: 509-522-5263; E-mail: feezelca@whitman.edu.
Golf: Peter McClure; Phone: 509-527-5059; E-mail: mcclurp@whitman.edu.
Soccer: Mike Washington; Phone: 509-527-5286; E-mail: washinmj@whitman.edu.
Swimming: Jennifer Blomme; Phone: 509-527-5287; E-mail: blommejb@whitman.edu.
Tennis: Jeff Northam; Phone: 509-527-5886; E-mail: northajw@whitman.edu.

WOMEN'S COACHES
Basketball: Michele Ferenz; Phone: 509-527-5261; E-mail: ferenzmk@whitman.edu.
Cross Country: Carol Feezell; Phone: 509-522-5263; E-mail: feezelca@whitman.edu.
Golf: Peter McClure; Phone: 509-527-5059; E-mail: mcclurp@whitman.edu.
Soccer: Scott Shields; Phone: 509-527-5414; E-mail: shieldsp@whitman.edu.
Swimming: Jennifer Blomme; Phone: 509-527-5287; E-mail: blommejb@whitman.edu.
Tennis: Heidi Tate; Phone: 509-527-5262; E-mail: tateha@whitman.edu.
Volleyball: Dean Snider; Phone: 509-527-5264; E-mail: sniderdc@whitman.edu.

WHITTIER COLLEGE
Whittier, California

Poets ◆ NCAA III ◆ Southern California Athletic Conference ◆ http://www.whittier.edu/

Independent comprehensive, founded 1887
Coed, 1,263 undergraduate students, 98% full-time, 58% women, 42% men
Suburban 95-acre campus with easy access to Los Angeles
Moderately difficult entrance level, 75% of applicants were admitted

Freshmen *Admission:* 1,511 applied, 1,209 were accepted, 348 enrolled. *Test scores:* SAT verbal scores over 500: 69%; SAT math scores over 500: 67%; SAT verbal scores over 600: 28%; SAT math scores over 600: 23%; SAT verbal scores over 700: 6%; SAT math scores over 700: 4%.
Tuition and fees (2003–04): $23,492 (full-time). *Room and board:* $7588 (room only: $4162).
Financial Aid (All incoming freshmen): *Average need-based gift aid:* $10,946. *Average non-need based aid:* $11,365. *Average aid to full-time undergraduates:* $26,518.
Athletic Department: *Director of Athletics:* Jack Wendell; Phone: 562-907-4268; Fax: 562-945-8024; E-mail: wjack@whittier.edu. *Sports Information Director:* Rock Carter; Phone: 562-907-4972; E-mail: rcarter@whittier.edu.

MEN'S COACHES
Baseball: Mike Rizzo; Phone: 562-907-4967; E-mail: mrizzo@whittier.edu.
Basketball: Rock Carter; Phone: 562-907-4972; E-mail: rcarter@whittier.edu.
Cross Country: Greg Phillips; Phone: 562-907-4975; E-mail: gphillips@whittier.edu.
Football: Greg Carlson; Phone: 562-907-4269; E-mail: gcarlson@whittier.edu.
Golf: B.J. Hammer; Phone: 562-907-4869; E-mail: whammer@whittier.edu.
Lacrosse: Dave Schaller; Phone: 562-907-4895; E-mail: dschaller@whittier.edu.
Soccer: Dave Shaller; Phone: 562-907-4895; E-mail: dschaller@whittier.edu.
Swimming: Mitch Carty; Phone: 562-907-4916; E-mail: mcarty@whittier.edu.
Tennis: Jeff Kizer; Phone: 562-907-4952.
Track and Field: Greg Phillips; Phone: 562-907-4975; E-mail: gphillips@whittier.edu.

WOMEN'S COACHES
Basketball: Will Morris; Phone: 562-907-4932; E-mail: wmorris@whittier.edu.
Cross Country: Greg Phillips; Phone: 562-907-4975; E-mail: gphillips@whittier.edu.
Lacrosse: Will Morris; Phone: 562-907-4932; E-mail: wmorris@whittier.edu.
Soccer: Skelly Miller; Phone: 562-907-4872; E-mail: smiller@whittier.edu.
Softball: Erin Bridges; Phone: 562-907-4935; E-mail: mmcbride@whittier.edu.
Swimming: Mitch Carty; Phone: 562-907-4916; E-mail: mcarty@whittier.edu.
Tennis: Jeff Kizer; Phone: 562-907-4952.
Track and Field: Greg Phillips; Phone: 562-907-4975; E-mail: gphillips@whittier.edu.
Volleyball: Kristi Vanderberg; Phone: 562-907-4976; E-mail: kvandenberg@whittier.edu.

WHITWORTH COLLEGE
Spokane, Washington

Pirates ◆ NCAA III ◆ Northwest Conference ◆ http://www.whitworth.edu/

Independent Presbyterian comprehensive, founded 1890
Coed, 2,071 undergraduate students
Suburban 200-acre campus
Very difficult entrance level, 75% of applicants were admitted

Freshmen *Admission:* 1,890 applied, 1,413 were accepted. *Test scores:* SAT verbal scores over 500: 86%; SAT math scores over 500: 88%; SAT verbal scores over 600: 40%; SAT math scores over 600: 40%; SAT verbal scores over 700: 7%; SAT math scores over 700: 5%.
Tuition and fees (2003–04): $20,078 (full-time). *Room and board:* $6350.
Financial Aid (All incoming freshmen): *Average need-based gift aid:* $13,429. *Average non-need based aid:* $6295. *Average aid to full-time undergraduates:* $18,618.
Athletic Department: *Director of Athletics:* Scott McQuilkin; Phone: 509-777-4392; Fax: 509-777-3720; E-mail: smcquilkin@whitworth.edu. *Sports Information Director:* Steve Flegel; E-mail: sflegel@whitworth.edu.

MEN'S COACHES
Baseball: Keith Ward; Phone: 509-777-4394; E-mail: kward@whitworth.edu.
Basketball: Jim Hayford; Phone: 509-777-4422; E-mail: jhayford@whitworth.edu.
Cross Country: Toby Schwarz; Phone: 509-777-4361; E-mail: tschwarz@whitworth.edu.
Football: John Tully; Phone: 509-777-4416; E-mail: jtully@whitworth.edu.
Golf: Warren Friedrichs; Phone: 509-777-3224; E-mail: wfriedrichs@whitworth.edu.
Soccer: Sean Bushey; Phone: 509-777-3224; E-mail: sbushey@whitworth.edu.
Tennis: Mike Shanks; Phone: 509-777-3726; E-mail: mshanks@whitworth.edu.
Track and Field: Toby Schwarz; Phone: 509-777-4361; E-mail: tschwarz@whitworth.edu.

WOMEN'S COACHES
Basketball: Helen Higgs; Phone: 509-777-4376; E-mail: hhiggs@whitworth.edu.
Cross Country: Toby Schwarz; Phone: 509-777-4361; E-mail: tschwarz@whitworth.edu.
Golf: Warren Friedrichs; Phone: 509-777-3224; E-mail: wfriedrichs@whitworth.edu.
Soccer: Sean Bushey; Phone: 509-777-3224; E-mail: sbushey@whitworth.edu.
Softball: Teresa Hansen; Phone: 509-777-4397; E-mail: thansen@whitworth.edu.
Tennis: Jo Ann Wagstaff; Phone: 509-777-4311; E-mail: jwagstaff@whitworth.edu.
Track and Field: Toby Schwarz; Phone: 509-777-4361; E-mail: tschwarz@whitworth.edu.
Volleyball: Steve Rupe; Phone: 509-777-4391; E-mail: srupe@whitworth.edu.

WICHITA STATE UNIVERSITY
Wichita, Kansas

Shockers ◆ NCAA I ◆ Missouri Valley Conference ◆ http://www.wichita.edu/

State-supported university, founded 1895, part of Kansas Board of Regents
Coed, 11,692 undergraduate students, 63% full-time, 56% women, 44% men
Urban 335-acre campus
Noncompetitive entrance level, 6% of applicants were admitted

Freshmen *Admission:* 3,037 applied, 1,917 were accepted, 1,211 enrolled.
Tuition and fees (2003–04): $3506 (resident), $10,960 (nonresident). *Room and board:* $4620.

Financial Aid (All incoming freshmen): *Average need-based gift aid: $3213. Average non-need based aid: $2259. Average aid to full-time undergraduates: $4648.*
Athletic Department: *Director of Athletics:* Jim Schaus; Phone: 316-978-3250; Fax: 316-978-3336; E-mail: jschaus@goshockers.com. *Sports Information Director:* Larry Rankin; Phone: 316-978-3265; E-mail: lrankin@goshockers.com.

MEN'S COACHES
Baseball: Gene Stephenson; Phone: 316-978-3636; E-mail: gene.stephenson@wichita.edu.
Basketball: Mack Turgeon; Phone: 316-978-3252; E-mail: mturgeon@goshockers.com.
Cheerleading: Jay Grayson; Phone: 316-978-3251.
Golf: Grier Jones; Phone: 316-978-5548.
Tennis: Kevin Kowauk; Phone: 316-978-3183; E-mail: kkowalik@goshockers.com.
Track and Field: Steve Rainbolt; Phone: 316-978-3362; E-mail: srainbolt@goshockers.com.

WOMEN'S COACHES
Basketball: Jane Albright; Phone: 316-978-3257; E-mail: jalbright@goshockers.com.
Cheerleading: Jay Grayson; Phone: 316-978-3251.
Cross Country: Randy Hasenbank; Phone: 316-978-3362; E-mail: rhasenbank@goshockers.com.
Golf: Shelly Hogan; Phone: 316-978-3362; E-mail: shogan@goshockers.com.
Softball: Tim Walton; Phone: 316-978-3257; E-mail: twalton@goshockers.com.
Tennis: Les Stafford; Phone: 316-978-3183; E-mail: lstafford@goshockers.com.
Track and Field: Steve Rainbolt; Phone: 316-978-3362; E-mail: srainbolt@goshockers.com.
Volleyball: Chris Lamb; Phone: 316-978-3257; E-mail: clamb@goshockers.com.

WIDENER UNIVERSITY
Chester, Pennsylvania

Pioneers ◆ NCAA III ◆ Commonwealth Conference ◆ http://www.widener.edu/

Independent comprehensive, founded 1821
Coed, 2,400 undergraduate students, 94% full-time, 46% women, 54% men
Suburban 110-acre campus with easy access to Philadelphia
Moderately difficult entrance level, 73% of applicants were admitted

Freshmen *Admission:* 3,008 applied, 2,229 were accepted, 715 enrolled. *Test scores:* SAT verbal scores over 500: 46%; SAT math scores over 500: 53%; SAT verbal scores over 600: 10%; SAT math scores over 600: 15%; SAT verbal scores over 700: 1%; SAT math scores over 700: 2%.
Tuition and fees (2003–04): $21,500 (full-time). *Room and board:* $8795 (room only: $4095).
Financial Aid (All incoming freshmen): *Average need-based gift aid: $14,068. Average non-need based aid: $8069. Average aid to full-time undergraduates: $20,319.*
Athletic Department: *Director of Athletics:* Dave Duda; Phone: 610-499-4454; E-mail: david.duda@widener.edu. *Sports Information Director:* Susan Fumagalli; Phone: 610-499-4436; E-mail: susan.e.fumagalli@widener.edu.

MEN'S COACHES
Baseball: Steve Carcarey; Phone: 610-499-4446; E-mail: widenerbaseball@aol.com.
Basketball: Dave Dupa; Phone: 610-499-4454; E-mail: david.duda@widener.edu.
Cheerleading: Nicole Daliessio; Phone: 610-499-4441; E-mail: missdelval2000@yahoo.com.
Cross Country: Vince Touey; Phone: 610-499-4453; E-mail: vince.touey@widener.edu.
Football: David Wood; Phone: 610-499-4665; E-mail: david.wood@widener.edu.
Golf: David Wood; Phone: 610-499-4665; E-mail: david.wood@widener.edu.
Lacrosse: Jamie Steele; Phone: 610-499-4455; E-mail: jamie@bostonpost.com.

Soccer: Fred Dohrmann; Phone: 610-499-4450; E-mail: fred.dohrmann@widener.edu.
Swimming: Bob Piotti; Phone: 610-499-4448; E-mail: bob.piotti@widener.edu.
Tennis: Dan Sears; Phone: 610-499-4447; E-mail: dhs0302@mail.widener.edu.
Track and Field: Vince Touey; Phone: 610-499-4453; E-mail: vince.touey@widener.edu.

WOMEN'S COACHES
Basketball: Alisa DiBonaventura; Phone: 610-499-4428; E-mail: adibonaventura@mail.widener.edu.
Cheerleading: Nicole Daliessio; Phone: 610-499-4441; E-mail: missdelval2000@yahoo.com.
Cross Country: Vince Touey; Phone: 610-499-4453; E-mail: vince.touey@widener.edu.
Field Hockey: Larissa Gillespie; Phone: 610-499-4434; E-mail: wucoachg@hotmail.com.
Lacrosse: Larissa Gillespie; Phone: 610-499-4434; E-mail: wucoachg@hotmail.com.
Soccer: Jack Shafer; Phone: 610-499-4437; E-mail: jack_shafer@hotmail.com.
Softball: Fred Dohrmann; Phone: 610-499-4450; E-mail: fred.dohrmann@widener.edu.
Swimming: Bob Piotti; Phone: 610-499-4448; E-mail: bob.piotti@widener.edu.
Tennis: Dan Sears; Phone: 610-499-4447; E-mail: dhs0302@mail.widener.edu.
Track and Field: Vince Touey; Phone: 610-499-4453; E-mail: vince.touey@widener.edu.
Volleyball: Diane Felker; Phone: 610-499-4571; E-mail: diana.m.felker@widener.edu.

WILBERFORCE UNIVERSITY
Wilberforce, Ohio

Bulldogs ◆ NAIA ◆ American Mideast Conference ◆ http://www.wilberforce.edu/

Independent religious 4-year, founded 1856, affiliated with African Methodist Episcopal Church
Coed, 1,180 undergraduate students, 99% full-time, 60% women, 40% men
Rural 125-acre campus with easy access to Dayton
Minimally difficult entrance level, 2% of applicants were admitted

Freshmen *Admission:* 2,405 applied, 521 were accepted, 190 enrolled.
Tuition and fees (2003–04): $10,770 (full-time). *Room and board:* $5320 (room only: $2820).
Athletic Department: *Director of Athletics:* John Freeman; Phone: 937-708-5611; Fax: 937-708-5535; E-mail: jfreeman@wilberforce.edu. *Sports Information Director:* Ronnie Bennett; Phone: 937-708-5746; E-mail: rbennett@wilberforce.edu.

MEN'S COACHES
Basketball: Geoff Warren; Phone: 937-708-5611.

WOMEN'S COACHES
Basketball: Torrance Hill; Phone: 937-708-5611.

WILEY COLLEGE
Marshall, Texas

NAIA ◆ Red River Conference ◆ http://www.wileyc.edu/

Independent religious 4-year, founded 1873, affiliated with United Methodist Church
Coed, 666 undergraduate students, 97% full-time, 56% women, 44% men
Small-town 58-acre campus
Minimally difficult entrance level, 46% of applicants were admitted

Freshmen *Admission:* 725 applied, 320 were accepted, 165 enrolled. *Test scores:* SAT verbal scores over 500: 8%; SAT math scores over 500: 6%; SAT math scores over 600: 3%.

Wiley College (*continued*)

Tuition and fees (2003–04): $6376 (full-time). *Room and board:* $4092 (room only: $1966).
Financial Aid (All incoming freshmen): *Average need-based gift aid:* $4436. *Average non-need based aid:* $6144. *Average aid to full-time undergraduates:* $5322.
Athletic Department: *Director of Athletics:* James Hodges; Phone: 903-927-3350; Fax: 903-938-4310. *Sports Information Director:* Jim McCutchens; Phone: 903-938-4319; E-mail: ffjimmc@shreve.net.

MEN'S COACHES
Baseball: Austin Reece; Phone: 903-927-3350.
Basketball: Eddie Ray Watson; Phone: 903-927-3350.
Soccer: Phone: 903-927-3350.
Track and Field: Jesse Johnson; Phone: 903-927-3350.

WOMEN'S COACHES
Basketball: Jesse Johnson; Phone: 903-927-3350.
Track and Field: Jesse Johnson; Phone: 903-927-3350.
Volleyball: Charlette Mask; Phone: 903-927-3350.

WILKES UNIVERSITY
Wilkes-Barre, Pennsylvania

Colonels ◆ NCAA III ◆ Freedom Conference ◆ http://www.wilkes.edu/

Independent comprehensive, founded 1933
Coed, 2,055 undergraduate students, 87% full-time, 50% women, 50% men
Urban 25-acre campus
Moderately difficult entrance level, 8% of applicants were admitted

Freshmen *Admission:* 2,332 applied, 1,878 were accepted, 523 enrolled. *Test scores:* SAT verbal scores over 500: 68%; SAT math scores over 500: 71%; SAT verbal scores over 600: 24%; SAT math scores over 600: 31%; SAT verbal scores over 700: 3%; SAT math scores over 700: 6%.
Tuition and fees (2003–04): $19,630 (full-time). *Room and board:* $8430 (room only: $5080).
Financial Aid (All incoming freshmen): *Average need-based gift aid:* $12,683. *Average non-need based aid:* $8708. *Average aid to full-time undergraduates:* $16,855.
Athletic Department: *Director of Athletics:* Addy Malatesta; Phone: 570-408-4024; Fax: 570-408-7818; E-mail: malatest@wilkes.edu. *Sports Information Director:* John Seitzinger; Phone: 570-408-4777; E-mail: seitzing@wilkes.edu.

MEN'S COACHES
Baseball: Joe Folek; Phone: 570-408-4020; E-mail: folek@wilkes.edu.
Basketball: Jerry Rickrode; Phone: 570-408-4033; E-mail: rickrodj@wilkes.edu.
Football: Frank Sheptock; Phone: 570-714-4750; E-mail: sheptock@wilkes.edu.
Golf: Art Brunn; Phone: 570-408-4020; E-mail: brunn@wilkes.edu.
Soccer: Phil Wingert; Phone: 570-408-4024; E-mail: wingert@wilkes.edu.
Tennis: Chris Leicht; Phone: 570-408-4353; E-mail: leicht@wilkes.edu.
Wrestling: Jon Laudenslager; Phone: 570-408-4035; E-mail: laudensl@wilkes.edu.

WOMEN'S COACHES
Basketball: Jim Reed; Phone: 570-408-4022; E-mail: reed@wilkes.edu.
Field Hockey: Todd Broxmeyer; Phone: 570-408-4018; E-mail: broxmeye@wilkes.edu.
Lacrosse: Nancy Billger; Phone: 570-408-4019; E-mail: billger@wilkes.edu.
Soccer: John Sumoski; Phone: 570-408-4017; E-mail: sumoski@wilkes.edu.
Softball: Frank Matthews; Phone: 570-408-4031; E-mail: matthews@wilkes.edu.
Tennis: Chris Leicht; Phone: 570-408-4353; E-mail: leicht@wilkes.edu.
Volleyball: Scott Vanvalkenburgh; Phone: 570-408-4016; E-mail: vanvalke@wilkes.edu.

WILLAMETTE UNIVERSITY
Salem, Oregon

Bearcats ◆ NCAA III ◆ Northwest Conference ◆ http://www.willamette.edu/

Independent United Methodist comprehensive, founded 1842
Coed, 1,945 undergraduate students, 93% full-time, 55% women, 45% men
Urban 72-acre campus with easy access to Portland
Very difficult entrance level, 7% of applicants were admitted

Freshmen *Admission:* 2,164 applied, 1,603 were accepted, 541 enrolled. *Test scores:* SAT verbal scores over 500: 94%; SAT math scores over 500: 96%; SAT verbal scores over 600: 64%; SAT math scores over 600: 65%; SAT verbal scores over 700: 17%; SAT math scores over 700: 14%.
Tuition and fees (2003–04): $25,462 (full-time). *Room and board:* $6600.
Financial Aid (All incoming freshmen): *Average need-based gift aid:* $17,920. *Average non-need based aid:* $11,645. *Average aid to full-time undergraduates:* $21,119.
Athletic Department: *Director of Athletics:* Mark Majeski; Phone: 530-30-6420; Fax: 503-370-6379; E-mail: mmajeski@willamette.edu. *Sports Information Director:* Aina Williams; Phone: 503-370-6110; E-mail: william@willamette.edu.

MEN'S COACHES
Baseball: Matt Allison; Phone: 503-370-6011; E-mail: mallison@willamette.edu.
Basketball: Gordie James; Phone: 503-370-6063; E-mail: gjames@willamette.edu.
Cross Country: Matt McGuirk; Phone: 503-370-6803; E-mail: mmcguirk@willamette.edu.
Football: Mark Speckman; Phone: 503-375-5350; E-mail: mspeckma@willamette.edu.
Golf: Steve Prothero; Phone: 503-370-6484; E-mail: prothero@willamette.edu.
Soccer: Jeff Enquist; Phone: 503-370-6132; E-mail: jenquist@willamette.edu.
Swimming: Al Stephenson; Phone: 503-370-6601; E-mail: astephen@willamette.edu.
Tennis: Becky Roberts; Phone: 503-370-6804; E-mail: rbrobert@willamette.edu.
Track and Field: Matt McGuirk; Phone: 503-370-6803; E-mail: mmcguirk@willamette.edu.

WOMEN'S COACHES
Basketball: Tom Steers; Phone: 503-370-6132; E-mail: tsteers@willamette.edu.
Cross Country: Matt McGuirk; Phone: 503-370-6803; E-mail: mmcguirk@willamette.edu.
Golf: Tom Hibbard; Phone: 503-370-6317; E-mail: thibbard@willamette.edu.
Soccer: Jim Tursi; Phone: 503-370-6657; E-mail: jtursi@willamette.edu.
Softball: Damian Williams; Phone: 503-370-6656; E-mail: williamr@willamette.edu.
Swimming: Al Stephenson; Phone: 503-370-6601; E-mail: astephen@willamette.edu.
Tennis: Becky Roberts; Phone: 503-370-6804; E-mail: rbrobert@willamette.edu.
Track and Field: Matt McGuirk; Phone: 503-370-6803; E-mail: mmcguirk@willamette.edu.
Volleyball: Tricia Wright; Phone: 503-370-6230; E-mail: twright@willamette.edu.

WILLIAM CAREY COLLEGE
Hattiesburg, Mississippi

Crusaders ◆ NAIA ◆ Gulf Coast Conference ◆ http://www.wmcarey.edu/

Independent Southern Baptist comprehensive, founded 1906
Coed, 1,762 undergraduate students, 84% full-time, 70% women, 30% men
Small-town 64-acre campus with easy access to New Orleans
Moderately difficult entrance level, 8% of applicants were admitted

Freshmen *Admission:* 233 applied, 169 were accepted, 168 enrolled. *Test scores:* SAT verbal scores over 500: 27%; SAT math scores over 500: 40%; SAT verbal scores over 600: 7%; SAT math scores over 600: 7%.
Tuition and fees (2003–04): $7815 (full-time). *Room and board:* $3390 (room only: $1305).
Athletic Department: *Director of Athletics:* Steve Knight; Phone: 601-318-6415; Fax: 601-318-6200; E-mail: sknight@wmcarey.edu. *Sports Information Director:* Joe Garvin; Phone: 601-318-6431; E-mail: joe.garvin@wmcarey.edu.

MEN'S COACHES
Baseball: Bobby Halford; Phone: 601-318-6110; E-mail: bhalford@wmcarey.edu.
Basketball: Steve Knight; Phone: 601-318-6415; E-mail: sknight@wmcarey.edu.
Golf: Tracy English; Phone: 601-318-6111; E-mail: tenglish@wmcarey.edu.
Soccer: Nigel Boulton; Phone: 601-318-6401; E-mail: nigel.boulton@wmcarey.edu.

WOMEN'S COACHES
Basketball: Tracy English; Phone: 601-318-6111; E-mail: tenglish@wmcarey.edu.
Soccer: Nigel Boulton; Phone: 601-318-6401; E-mail: nigel.boulton@wmcarey.edu.
Softball: Jack Lott; Phone: 601-318-6551; E-mail: jgarvin@wmcarey.edu.

WILLIAM JEWELL COLLEGE
Liberty, Missouri

Cardinals ◆ NAIA ◆ Heart of America Conference ◆ http://www.jewell.edu/

Independent Baptist 4-year, founded 1849
Coed, 1,274 undergraduate students, 97% full-time, 59% women, 41% men
Small-town 200-acre campus with easy access to Kansas City
Moderately difficult entrance level, 94% of applicants were admitted

Freshmen *Admission:* 907 applied, 864 were accepted, 358 enrolled. *Test scores:* SAT verbal scores over 500: 80%; SAT math scores over 500: 87%; SAT verbal scores over 600: 45%; SAT math scores over 600: 46%; SAT verbal scores over 700: 7%; SAT math scores over 700: 10%.
Tuition and fees (2003–04): $16,500 (full-time). *Room and board:* $4820.
Financial Aid (All incoming freshmen): *Average need-based gift aid:* $9337. *Average aid to full-time undergraduates:* $13,896.
Athletic Department: *Director of Athletics:* Larry Hamilton; Phone: 816-781-7700; Fax: 816-415-5029; E-mail: hamiltonl@william.jewell.edu. *Sports Information Director:* Gail Stewart; Phone: 816-781-7700; E-mail: stewartg@william.jewell.edu.

MEN'S COACHES
Baseball: Mike Stockton; Phone: 816-415-5962.
Basketball: Larry Holley; Phone: 816-415-5947; E-mail: holleyl@william.jewell.edu.
Basketball: Larry Holly; Phone: 816-781-7700; E-mail: holleyl@william.jewell.edu.
Cheerleading: Beed Harris; Phone: 816-781-7700.
Cross Country: Steve Lucito; Phone: 816-415-5952; E-mail: lucitos@william.jewell.edu.
Football: David Bassore; Phone: 816-781-7700; E-mail: bassored@william.jewell.edu.
Golf: Bill Skolaut; Phone: 816-781-6522.

Soccer: Chris Cissell; Phone: 816-415-5935; E-mail: cissellc@william.jewell.edu.
Tennis: Rob Thomson; Phone: 816-781-7700.
Track and Field: Steve Lucito; Phone: 816-415-5952; E-mail: lucitos@william.jewell.edu.

WOMEN'S COACHES
Basketball: Jill Cress; Phone: 816-415-5937; E-mail: cressj@william.jewell.edu.
Cheerleading: Beed Harris; Phone: 816-781-7700.
Cross Country: Steve Lucito; Phone: 816-415-5952; E-mail: lucitos@william.jewell.edu.
Golf: Walt Tabory; Phone: 816-781-7700.
Soccer: Chris Cissell; Phone: 816-415-5935; E-mail: cissellc@william.jewell.edu.
Softball: Ed Hornback; Phone: 816-415-5948; E-mail: hornbacke@william.jewell.edu.
Tennis: Rob Thomson; Phone: 816-781-7700.
Track and Field: Steve Lucito; Phone: 816-415-5952; E-mail: lucitos@william.jewell.edu.
Volleyball: Ed Hornback; Phone: 816-415-5948; E-mail: albitzf@william.jewell.edu.

WILLIAM PATERSON UNIVERSITY OF NEW JERSEY
Wayne, New Jersey

Pioneers ◆ NCAA III ◆ New Jersey Athletic Conference ◆ http://ww2.wpunj.edu/

State-supported comprehensive, founded 1855, part of New Jersey State College System
Coed, 9,302 undergraduate students, 79% full-time, 59% women, 41% men
Suburban 300-acre campus with easy access to New York City
Moderately difficult entrance level, 64% of applicants were admitted

Freshmen *Admission:* 5,704 applied, 3,469 were accepted, 1,365 enrolled. *Test scores:* SAT verbal scores over 500: 54%; SAT math scores over 500: 57%; SAT verbal scores over 600: 11%; SAT math scores over 600: 11%; SAT verbal scores over 700: 1%; SAT math scores over 700: 1%.
Tuition and fees (2003–04): $7120 (resident), $11,510 (nonresident). *Room and board:* $7630 (room only: $4990).
Financial Aid (All incoming freshmen): *Average need-based gift aid:* $5789. *Average non-need based aid:* $5561. *Average aid to full-time undergraduates:* $9113.
Athletic Department: *Director of Athletics:* Sabrina Grant; Phone: 973-720-2754; Fax: 973-595-3017; E-mail: grantsa@wpunj.edu. *Sports Information Director:* Brian Falzarano; Phone: 973-720-2705; E-mail: falzaranob@wpunj.edu.

MEN'S COACHES
Baseball: Jeff Albies; Phone: 973-720-2210; E-mail: albiesj@wpunj.edu.
Basketball: Jose Rebimbas; Phone: 973-720-2170; E-mail: rebimbasj@wpunj.edu.
Cheerleading: Kathy Gasalberti; Phone: 973-720-2000; E-mail: kathyg1118@aol.com.
Cross Country: Horace Perkins; Phone: 973-720-2750; E-mail: perkinsh@wpunj.edu.
Diving: Steve McDonough; Phone: 973-720-3267.
Football: Larry Arico; Phone: 973-720-2326; E-mail: aricol@wpunj.edu.
Soccer: Brian Woods; Phone: 973-720-3120; E-mail: woodsb@wpunj.edu.
Swimming: Ed Gurka; Phone: 973-720-3267; E-mail: gurkae@wpunj.edu.
Track and Field: Horace Perkins; Phone: 973-720-2750; E-mail: perkinsh@wpunj.edu.

WOMEN'S COACHES
Basketball: Erin Monahan; Phone: 973-720-2647; E-mail: monahane@wpunj.edu.
Cheerleading: Kathy Gasalberti; Phone: 973-720-2000; E-mail: kathyg1118@aol.com.
Cross Country: Horace Perkins; Phone: 973-720-2750; E-mail: perkinsh@wpunj.edu.
Diving: Steve McDonough; Phone: 973-720-3267.

William Paterson University of New Jersey *(continued)*

Field Hockey: Hallie Cohen; Phone: 973-720-3016; E-mail: cohenh@wpunj.edu.

Soccer: Keith Woods; Phone: 973-720-3010; E-mail: woodsk@wpunj.edu.

Softball: Hallie Cohen; Phone: 973-720-3016; E-mail: cohenh@wpunj.edu.

Swimming: Ed Gurka; Phone: 973-720-3267; E-mail: gurkae@wpunj.edu.

Track and Field: Horace Perkins; Phone: 973-720-2750; E-mail: perkinsh@wpunj.edu.

Volleyball: Sandy Ferrella; Phone: 973-720-3012; E-mail: ferrarellas@wpunj.edu.

WILLIAM PENN UNIVERSITY
Oskaloosa, Iowa

Statesmen ♦ NAIA ♦ Mid-States Football Conference; Midwest Classic Conference ♦ http://www.wmpenn.edu/

Independent religious 4-year, founded 1873, affiliated with Society of Friends
Coed, 1,499 undergraduate students, 94% full-time, 48% women, 52% men
Rural 60-acre campus with easy access to Des Moines
Moderately difficult entrance level, 69% of applicants were admitted

Freshmen *Admission:* 717 applied, 465 were accepted, 230 enrolled.
Tuition and fees (2004–05): $14,604 (full-time). *Room and board:* $4746 (room only: $1852).
Athletic Department: *Director of Athletics:* John Ottoson; Phone: 641-673-1048; Fax: 641-673-1373; E-mail: ottossonj@wmpenn.edu. *Sports Information Director:* Sunny Eigmy; Phone: 319-326-9561; E-mail: eighmys@wmpenn.edu.

MEN'S COACHES
Baseball: Mike Laird; Phone: 641-673-1018; E-mail: lairdm@wmpenn.edu.
Basketball: John Henry; Phone: 641-673-1108; E-mail: henryj@wmpenn.edu.
Cross Country: Brandon Lenhart; Phone: 641-673-1108; E-mail: lenhartb@wmpenn.edu.
Football: Jim Cox; Phone: 641-673-9653; E-mail: coxj@wmpenn.edu.
Golf: Dean Mattix; Phone: 641-673-1018; E-mail: mattixd@wmpenn.edu.
Soccer: Ammon Bennett; Phone: 641-673-1706; E-mail: bennetta@wmpenn.edu.
Track and Field: Brian Spielbauer; Phone: 641-673-1018; E-mail: spielbauerb@wmpenn.edu.
Wrestling: Gary Garvis; Phone: 641-673-1084; E-mail: garvisg@wmpenn.edu.

WOMEN'S COACHES
Basketball: Tom Burger; Phone: 641-673-1019; E-mail: burgert@wmpenn.edu.
Cross Country: Brandon Lenhart; Phone: 641-673-1108; E-mail: lenhartb@wmpenn.edu.
Soccer: Ammon Bennett; Phone: 641-673-1706; E-mail: bennetta@wmpenn.edu.
Softball: Mike Christner; Phone: 641-673-1707; E-mail: christnerm@wmpenn.edu.
Track and Field: Brian Spielbauer; Phone: 641-673-1018; E-mail: spielbauerb@wmpenn.edu.
Volleyball: Christopher Brees; Phone: 641-673-1024; E-mail: breesc@wmpenn.edu.

WILLIAMS BAPTIST COLLEGE
Walnut Ridge, Arkansas

Eagles ♦ NAIA ♦ American Midwest Conference ♦ http://www.wbcoll.edu/

Independent Southern Baptist 4-year, founded 1941
Coed, 653 undergraduate students, 78% full-time, 56% women, 44% men
Rural 180-acre campus
Minimally difficult entrance level, 69% of applicants were admitted

Freshmen *Admission:* 407 applied, 281 were accepted, 121 enrolled.
Tuition and fees (2004–05): $8600 (full-time). *Room and board:* $4000.
Financial Aid (All incoming freshmen): *Average need-based gift aid:* $2704. *Average non-need based aid:* $3097. *Average aid to full-time undergraduates:* $8403.
Athletic Department: *Director of Athletics:* Carol Halford; Phone: 870-886-6741; Fax: 870-886-3924; E-mail: chalford@wbcoll.edu. *Sports Information Director:* Brett Cooper; Phone: 870-759-4107; E-mail: bcooper@wbcoll.edu.

MEN'S COACHES
Baseball: Josh Katrosh; Phone: 870-886-6741.
Basketball: Jeff Rider; Phone: 870-886-6741; E-mail: jrider@wbcoll.edu.
Golf: Jeff Rider; Phone: 870-886-6741; E-mail: jrider@wbcoll.edu.
Soccer: Bob Culbreath; Phone: 870-886-6741; E-mail: bculbreath@wbcoll.edu.

WOMEN'S COACHES
Basketball: Carol Halford; Phone: 870-886-6741; E-mail: chalford@wbcoll.edu.
Softball: Angie Pastiva; Phone: 870-886-6741; E-mail: apastiva@wbcoll.edu.
Volleyball: Angie Pastiva; Phone: 870-886-6741; E-mail: apastiva@wbcoll.edu.

WILLIAMS COLLEGE
Williamstown, Massachusetts

Ephs ♦ NCAA III ♦ New England Small College Conference ♦ http://www.williams.edu/

Independent comprehensive, founded 1793
Coed, 2,045 undergraduate students, 98% full-time, 50% women, 50% men
Small-town 450-acre campus with easy access to Albany
Most difficult entrance level, 2% of applicants were admitted

Freshmen *Admission:* 5,341 applied, 1,133 were accepted, 533 enrolled. *Test scores:* SAT verbal scores over 500: 100%; SAT math scores over 500: 99%; SAT verbal scores over 600: 92%; SAT math scores over 600: 93%; SAT verbal scores over 700: 60%; SAT math scores over 700: 60%.
Tuition and fees (2003–04): $28,090 (full-time). *Room and board:* $7660 (room only: $3840).
Financial Aid (All incoming freshmen): *Average need-based gift aid:* $23,435. *Average aid to full-time undergraduates:* $25,153.
Athletic Department: *Director of Athletics:* Harry Sheehy; Phone: 413-597-2366; Fax: 413-597-4272; E-mail: harry.c.sheehy@williams.edu. *Sports Information Director:* Dick Quinn; Phone: 413-597-4982; E-mail: dick.quinn@williams.edu.

MEN'S COACHES
Baseball: Dave Barnard; Phone: 413-597-3326; E-mail: david.e.barnard@williams.edu.
Basketball: Dave Paulsen; Phone: 413-597-2201; E-mail: david.r.paulsen@williams.edu.
Cross Country: Peter Farwell; Phone: 413-597-3249; E-mail: peter.k.farwell@williams.edu.
Diving: Kathleen Callahan Koch; Phone: 413-597-3255; E-mail: kit.c.koch@williams.edu.
Football: Mike Whalen; Phone: 413-597-3023; E-mail: michael.f.whalen@williams.edu.
Golf: Rick Pohle; Phone: 413-458-3997; E-mail: rickpga@msn.com.
Ice Hockey: Bill Kangas; Phone: 413-458-3201; E-mail: william.r.kangas@williams.edu.

Lacrosse: George McCormick; Phone: 413-597-4230; E-mail: george.m. mccormack@williams.edu.
Soccer: Mike Russo; Phone: 413-597-3329; E-mail: t. michael.russo@ williams.edu.
Swimming: Steven Kuster; Phone: 413-597-4372; E-mail: steven.j. kuster@williams.edu.
Tennis: Dave Johnson; Phone: 413-597-3295; E-mail: david.c.johnson@ williams.edu.
Track and Field: Ralph White; Phone: 413-597-2447; E-mail: ralph.e. white@williams.edu.
Wrestling: Mike Whalen; Phone: 413-597-3023; E-mail: michael.f. whalen@williams.edu.

WOMEN'S COACHES
Basketball: Pat Manning; Phone: 413-597-3256; E-mail· patricia.m. manning@williams.edu.
Cross Country: Peter Farwell; Phone: 413-597-3249; E-mail: peter.k. farwell@williams.edu.
Diving: Kathleen Callahan Koch; Phone: 413-597-3255; E-mail: kit.c. koch@williams.edu.
Field Hockey: Alix Rorke; Phone: 413-597-4543; E-mail: alix.h.rorke@ williams.edu.
Lacrosse: Chris Mason; Phone: 413-597-2249; E-mail: christine.l.mason@williams.edu.
Soccer: Michelyne Pinard; Phone: 413-597-4599; E-mail: michelyne.j. pinard@williams.edu.
Softball: Kris Herman; Phone: 413-597-3323; E-mail: kristin.herman@ williams.edu.
Swimming: Steven Kuster; Phone: 413-597-4372; E-mail: steven.j. kuster@williams.edu.
Tennis: Julie Greenwood; Phone: 413-597-2427; E-mail: julie.a.greenwood@williams.edu.
Track and Field: Ralph White; Phone: 413-597-2447; E-mail: ralph.e. white@williams.edu.
Volleyball: Fran Vandermeer; Phone: 413-597-4381; E-mail: frances.d. vandermeer@williams.edu.

WILLIAM WOODS UNIVERSITY
Fulton, Missouri

Owls ◆ NAIA ◆ American Midwest Conference ◆ http:// www.williamwoods.edu/

Independent religious comprehensive, founded 1870, affiliated with Christian Church (Disciples of Christ)
Coed, 1,132 undergraduate students, 91% full-time, 72% women, 28% men
Small-town 170-acre campus with easy access to St. Louis
Moderately difficult entrance level

Freshmen *Admission:* 612 applied, 254 enrolled. *Test scores:* SAT verbal scores over 500: 58%; SAT math scores over 500: 46%; SAT verbal scores over 600: 20%; SAT math scores over 600: 8%; SAT verbal scores over 700: 5%.
Tuition and fees (2004–05): $14,420 (full-time). *Room and board:* $5700.
Financial Aid (All incoming freshmen): *Average need-based gift aid:* $1794. *Average non-need based aid:* $3608. *Average aid to full-time undergraduates:* $13,775.
Athletic Department: *Director of Athletics:* Larry York; Phone: 573-592-4387; Fax: 573-592-4386; E-mail: lyork@williamwoods.edu. *Sports Information Director:* Shawn Snider; Phone: 573-592-1627; E-mail: shawn.snider@williamwoods.edu.

MEN'S COACHES
Basketball: Ryan Bay; Phone: 573-592-1187; E-mail: rbay@ williamwoods.edu.
Cross Country: Jamie Moreno; Phone: 573-592-1642; E-mail: jamie. moreno@williamwoods.edu.
Golf: Barry Doty; Phone: 573-592-4387; E-mail: bdoty@williamwoods. edu.
Soccer: Rob Podeyn; Phone: 573-592-1156; E-mail: rpodeyn@ williamwoods.edu.
Volleyball: Bob Hadaway; Phone: 573-592-4340; E-mail: bob. hadaway@williamwoods.edu.

WOMEN'S COACHES
Basketball: Melissa Brooks; Phone: 573-592-4206; E-mail: mbrooks@ williamwoods.edu.

Cross Country: Jamie Moreno; Phone: 573-592-1642; E-mail: jamie. moreno@williamwoods.edu.
Golf: Barry Doty; Phone: 573-592-4387; E-mail: bdoty@williamwoods. edu.
Soccer: Rob Podeyn; Phone: 573-592-1156; E-mail: rpodeyn@ williamwoods.edu.
Softball: Tracy Gastineau; Phone: 573-592-4326; E-mail: tgastine@ williamwoods.edu.
Volleyball: Bob Hadaway; Phone: 573-592-4340; E-mail: bob. hadaway@williamwoods.edu.

WILMINGTON COLLEGE
New Castle, Delaware

Wildcats ◆ NCAA II ◆ Central Atlantic Collegiate Conference ◆ http://www.wilmcoll.edu/

Independent comprehensive, founded 1967
Coed, 4,110 undergraduate students, 46% full-time, 67% women, 33% men
Suburban 17-acre campus with easy access to Philadelphia
Noncompetitive entrance level

Freshmen *Admission:* 494 enrolled.
Tuition and fees (2003–04): $6980 (full-time).
Financial Aid (All incoming freshmen): *Average need-based gift aid:* $1450. *Average non-need based aid:* $2300. *Average aid to full-time undergraduates:* $5467.
Athletic Department: *Director of Athletics:* Frank Aiello; Phone: 302-328-9441; Fax: 302-328-8045; E-mail: faiel@wilmcoll.edu. *Sports Information Director:* Linda Doran; Phone: 302-328-9441; E-mail: ldora@wilmcoll.edu.

MEN'S COACHES
Baseball: Matt Brainard; Phone: 302-328-9435; E-mail: mbrai@ wilmcoll.edu.
Basketball: Scott Barker; Phone: 302-328-9435; E-mail: mbasketball@ wilmcoll.edu.
Cheerleading: Tina Scott; Phone: 302-328-9401; E-mail: tscot@ wilmcoll.edu.
Cross Country: Keith Jones; Phone: 302-328-9435; E-mail: crosscountry@wilmcoll.edu.
Soccer: Matt Digney; Phone: 302-328-9435.

WOMEN'S COACHES
Basketball: Bill Cleary; Phone: 302-328-9435.
Cheerleading: Tina Scott; Phone: 302-328-9401; E-mail: tscot@ wilmcoll.edu.
Cross Country: Keith Jones; Phone: 302-328-9435; E-mail: crosscountry@wilmcoll.edu.
Soccer: Bob Varell; Phone: 302-328-9435; E-mail: wsoccer@wilmcoll. edu.
Softball: Gretchen Loose; Phone: 302-328-9435; E-mail: softball@ wilmcoll.edu.
Volleyball: Amanda Moran; Phone: 302-328-9435; E-mail: volleyball@ wilmcoll.edu.

WILMINGTON COLLEGE
Wilmington, Ohio

Quakers ◆ NCAA III ◆ Ohio Athletic Conference ◆ http:// www.wilmington.edu/

Independent Friends comprehensive, founded 1870
Coed, 1,231 undergraduate students, 96% full-time, 56% women, 44% men
Small-town 1,465-acre campus with easy access to Cincinnati and Columbus
Moderately difficult entrance level, 76% of applicants were admitted

Freshmen *Admission:* 988 applied, 819 were accepted, 339 enrolled.
Tuition and fees (2003–04): $17,682 (full-time). *Room and board:* $6490 (room only: $3080).

Wilmington College *(continued)*

Financial Aid (All incoming freshmen): *Average need-based gift aid:* $12,262. *Average non-need based aid:* $7253. *Average aid to full-time undergraduates:* $16,828.
Athletic Department: *Director of Athletics:* Terry Rupert; Phone: 937-382-6661; Fax: 937-382-8566. *Sports Information Director:* Bill Salyer; Phone: 937-382-6661; E-mail: bill_salyer@wilmington.edu.

MEN'S COACHES
Baseball: Tony Haley; Phone: 937-382-6661.
Basketball: Will Rey; Phone: 937-382-6661; E-mail: will_rey@wilmington.edu.
Cross Country: Ron Combs; Phone: 937-382-6661; E-mail: ron_combs@wilmington.edu.
Football: Mike Wallace; Phone: 937-382-6661; E-mail: mike_wallace@wilmington.edu.
Golf: Bill Glaspey; Phone: 937-382-6661.
Soccer: Bud Lewis; Phone: 937-382-6661; E-mail: bud_lewis@wilmington.edu.
Swimming: Trip Breen; Phone: 937-382-6661; E-mail: trip_breen@wilmington.edu.
Tennis: Ken Lundy; Phone: 937-382-6661.
Track and Field: Ron Combs; Phone: 937-382-6661; E-mail: ron_combs@wilmington.edu.
Wrestling: Jim Marsh; Phone: 937-382-6661; E-mail: jim_marsh@wilmington.edu.

WOMEN'S COACHES
Basketball: Jerry Scheve; Phone: 937-382-6661; E-mail: jerry_scheve@wilmington.edu.
Cross Country: Ron Combs; Phone: 937-382-6661; E-mail: ron_combs@wilmington.edu.
Golf: Sharon Sims; Phone: 937-382-6661; E-mail: sharon_sims@wilmington.edu.
Soccer: Steve Spirk; Phone: 937-382-6661; E-mail: steve_spirk@wilmington.edu.
Softball: Quyen Tran; Phone: 937-382-6661; E-mail: quyen_tran@wilmington.edu.
Swimming: Trip Breen; Phone: 937-382-6661; E-mail: trip_breen@wilmington.edu.
Tennis: Ken Lundy; Phone: 937-382-6661.
Track and Field: Ron Combs; Phone: 937-382-6661; E-mail: ron_combs@wilmington.edu.
Volleyball: James Neyhouse; Phone: 937-382-6661; E-mail: james_neyhouse@wilmington.edu.

WILSON COLLEGE
Chambersburg, Pennsylvania

Phoenix ◆ NCAA III ◆ Atlantic Women's Colleges Conference ◆ http://www.wilson.edu/

Independent religious 4-year, founded 1869, affiliated with Presbyterian Church (U.S.A.)
Women only, 791 undergraduate students, 50% full-time, 85% women, 15% men
Small-town 300-acre campus
Moderately difficult entrance level, 68% of applicants were admitted

Freshmen *Admission:* 349 applied, 239 were accepted, 88 enrolled. *Test scores:* SAT verbal scores over 500: 42%; SAT math scores over 500: 53%; SAT verbal scores over 600: 10%; SAT math scores over 600: 20%; SAT verbal scores over 700: 1%; SAT math scores over 700: 3%.
Tuition and fees (2003–04): $16,916 (full-time). *Room and board:* $6996 (room only: $3604).
Financial Aid (All incoming freshmen): *Average need-based gift aid:* $12,196. *Average non-need based aid:* $10,719. *Average aid to full-time undergraduates:* $14,715.
Athletic Department: *Director of Athletics:* Lori Frey; Phone: 717-262-2012; Fax: 717-264-1578; E-mail: lfrey@wilson.edu. *Sports Information Director:* Shelly Novak; Phone: 717-264-4141; E-mail: snovak@wilson.edu.

WOMEN'S COACHES
Basketball: Allison Steiger; Phone: 717-262-2012.
Field Hockey: Shelly Novak; Phone: 717-264-4141; E-mail: snovak@wilson.edu.
Gymnastics: Toby Townson; Phone: 717-262-2012.
Soccer: Anne Marie Hollinshead; Phone: 717-262-2012.
Softball: Brett Cline; Phone: 717-262-2012.
Tennis: Allison Steiger; Phone: 717-262-2012.
Volleyball: Amy Pastorak; Phone: 717-262-2012.

WINGATE UNIVERSITY
Wingate, North Carolina

Bulldogs ◆ NCAA II ◆ Deep South Lacrosse Conference; South Atlantic Conference ◆ http://www.wingate.edu/

Independent Baptist comprehensive, founded 1896
Coed, 1,324 undergraduate students, 96% full-time, 54% women, 46% men
Small-town 330-acre campus with easy access to Charlotte
Moderately difficult entrance level, 80% of applicants were admitted

Freshmen *Admission:* 1,235 applied, 1,011 were accepted, 372 enrolled. *Test scores:* SAT verbal scores over 500: 59%; SAT math scores over 500: 63%; SAT verbal scores over 600: 16%; SAT math scores over 600: 20%; SAT verbal scores over 700: 1%; SAT math scores over 700: 1%.
Tuition and fees (2004–05): $16,000 (full-time). *Room and board:* $6200.
Financial Aid (All incoming freshmen): *Average need-based gift aid:* $3920. *Average non-need based aid:* $5202. *Average aid to full-time undergraduates:* $12,008.
Athletic Department: *Director of Athletics:* Steve Poston; Phone: 704-233-8194; Fax: 704-233-8170; E-mail: poston@wingate.edu. *Sports Information Director:* David Sherwood; Phone: 704-233-8186; E-mail: dsherwod@wingate.edu.

MEN'S COACHES
Baseball: Bill Nash; Phone: 704-233-8242; E-mail: bilnash@wingate.edu.
Basketball: Parker Laketa; Phone: 704-233-8171; E-mail: plaketa@wingate.edu.
Cheerleading: Beverly Wingate; Phone: 704-233-8193; E-mail: bburnette@wingate.edu.
Cross Country: Dennis Johnson; Phone: 704-233-8182; E-mail: djohnson@wingate.edu.
Football: Joe Reich; Phone: 704-233-8197; E-mail: reich@wingate.edu.
Golf: Holly Burns; Phone: 704-233-8385; E-mail: hsburns@wingate.edu.
Lacrosse: Sonny Ziegler; Phone: 704-233-8196; E-mail: sziegler@wingate.edu.
Soccer: Gary Hamill; Phone: 704-233-8175; E-mail: hamill@wingate.edu.
Tennis: Bill Cooper; Phone: 704-233-8384; E-mail: bcooper@wingate.edu.

WOMEN'S COACHES
Basketball: Johnny Jacumin; Phone: 704-233-8172; E-mail: johnjac@wingate.edu.
Cheerleading: Beverly Wingate; Phone: 704-233-8193; E-mail: bburnette@wingate.edu.
Cross Country: Dennis Johnson; Phone: 704-233-8182; E-mail: djohnson@wingate.edu.
Golf: Holly Burns; Phone: 704-233-8385; E-mail: hsburns@wingate.edu.
Soccer: Andy Thompson; Phone: 704-233-8166; E-mail: athompso@wingate.edu.
Softball: Michelle Caddigan; Phone: 704-233-8174; E-mail: caddigan@wingate.edu.
Swimming: Kirk Sanocki; Phone: 704-233-8167; E-mail: ksanocki@wingate.edu.
Tennis: Nicole Smith; Phone: 704-233-8195; E-mail: rohr@wingate.edu.
Volleyball: Shelton Collier; Phone: 704-233-8251; E-mail: scollier@wingate.edu.

WINONA STATE UNIVERSITY
Winona, Minnesota

Warriors ◆ NCAA II ◆ Northern Sun Intercollegiate
Conference ◆ http://www.winona.edu/

State-supported comprehensive, founded 1858, part of Minnesota State Colleges and Universities System
Coed, 7,569 undergraduate students, 90% full-time, 63% women, 37% men
Small-town 40-acre campus
Moderately difficult entrance level, 79% of applicants were admitted

Freshmen *Admission:* 4,802 applied, 3,798 were accepted, 1,552 enrolled.
Tuition and fees (2003–04): $4800 (resident), $9260 (nonresident). *Room and board:* $4640.
Financial Aid (All incoming freshmen): *Average need-based gift aid:* $3006. *Average non-need based aid:* $1275. *Average aid to full-time undergraduates:* $4538.
Athletic Department: *Director of Athletics:* Larry Holstad; Phone: 507-457-5212; Fax: 507-457-5479; E-mail: lholstad@winona.edu. *Sports Information Director:* Michael Herzberg; Phone: 507-457-5576; E-mail: mherzberg@winona.edu.

MEN'S COACHES
Baseball: Kyle Poock; Phone: 507-457-2332; E-mail: kpoock@winona.edu.
Basketball: Mike Leaf; Phone: 507-457-5530; E-mail: mleaf@winona.edu.
Cheerleading: Rob Murray; Phone: 507-457-5556; E-mail: rmurray@winona.edu.
Cross Country: Neal Mundahl; Phone: 507-457-5695; E-mail: nmundahl@winona.edu.
Football: Tom Sawyer; Phone: 507-457-5213; E-mail: tsawyer@winona.edu.
Golf: Mark Bambenek; Phone: 507-457-5528; E-mail: mbambeneck@winona.edu.
Tennis: Sean Kangrga; Phone: 507-269-9302; E-mail: seaner_k@winona.edu.

WOMEN'S COACHES
Basketball: Terri Sheridan; Phone: 507-457-5577; E-mail: tsheridan@winona.edu.
Cheerleading: Rob Murray; Phone: 507-457-5556; E-mail: rmurray@winona.edu.
Cross Country: Neal Mundahl; Phone: 507-457-5695; E-mail: nmundahl@winona.edu.
Golf: Robert Newberry; Phone: 507-457-5621; E-mail: rnewberry@winona.edu.
Gymnastics: Rob Murray; Phone: 507-457-5556; E-mail: rmurray@winona.edu.
Soccer: Ali Omar; Phone: 507-457-5646; E-mail: aomar@winona.edu.
Softball: Greg Jones; Phone: 507-457-5284; E-mail: gjones@winona.edu.
Tennis: Sean Kangrga; Phone: 507-269-9302; E-mail: seaner_k@winona.edu.
Track and Field: Kim Blum; Phone: 507-457-5211; E-mail: kblum@winona.edu.
Volleyball: Connie Mettille; Phone: 507-457-5456; E-mail: cmettille@winona.edu.

WINSTON-SALEM STATE UNIVERSITY
Winston-Salem, North Carolina

Rams ◆ NCAA II ◆ Central Intercollegiate Athletic
Conference ◆ http://www.wssu.edu/

State-supported comprehensive, founded 1892, part of University of North Carolina System
Coed, 3,929 undergraduate students, 84% full-time, 68% women, 32% men
Urban 94-acre campus
Minimally difficult entrance level, 71% of applicants were admitted

Freshmen *Admission:* 2,597 applied, 1,994 were accepted, 897 enrolled.

Tuition and fees (2003–04): $2394 (resident), $10,659 (nonresident). *Room and board:* $5306 (room only: $3300).
Financial Aid (All incoming freshmen): *Average need-based gift aid:* $2381. *Average non-need based aid:* $2125. *Average aid to full-time undergraduates:* $3462.
Athletic Department: *Director of Athletics:* Chico Caldwell; Phone: 336-750-2141; Fax: 336-750-2144; E-mail: caldwellp@wssu.edu. *Sports Information Director:* Chris Zona; Phone: 336-750-2143; E-mail: zonac@wssu.edu.

MEN'S COACHES
Basketball: Philip Stitt; Phone: 336-750-2140; E-mail: stittp@wssu.edu.
Cheerleading: Kim Reese; Phone: 336-750-3145; E-mail: reesekf@wssu.edu.
Cross Country: Philip Stitt; Phone: 336-750-2137; E-mail: stittp@wssu.edu.
Football: Kermit Blount; Phone: 336-750-2148; E-mail: blountk@wssu.edu.
Tennis: Leon Kay; Phone: 336-750-2141; E-mail: kayl@wssu.edu.

WOMEN'S COACHES
Basketball: John Williams; Phone: 336-750-2596; E-mail: williamsj@wssu.edu.
Cheerleading: Kim Reese; Phone: 336-750-3145; E-mail: reesekf@wssu.edu.
Cross Country: Philip Stitt; Phone: 336-750-2137; E-mail: stittp@wssu.edu.
Softball: Lataya Hillard-Gray; Phone: 336-750-2598; E-mail: latayash@hotmail.com.
Volleyball: Lataya Hillard-Gray; Phone: 336-750-2598; E-mail: latayash@hotmail.com.

WINTHROP UNIVERSITY
Rock Hill, South Carolina

Eagles ◆ NCAA I ◆ Big South Conference
◆ http://www.winthrop.edu/

State-supported comprehensive, founded 1886, part of South Carolina Commission on Higher Education
Coed, 5,161 undergraduate students, 89% full-time, 70% women, 30% men
Suburban 418-acre campus with easy access to Charlotte
Moderately difficult entrance level, 60% of applicants were admitted

Freshmen *Admission:* 3,965 applied, 2,632 were accepted, 1,074 enrolled. *Test scores:* SAT verbal scores over 500: 67%; SAT math scores over 500: 66%; SAT verbal scores over 600: 22%; SAT math scores over 600: 18%; SAT verbal scores over 700: 3%; SAT math scores over 700: 2%.
Tuition and fees (2003–04): $6672 (resident), $12,278 (nonresident). *Room and board:* $4630 (room only: $2770).
Financial Aid (All incoming freshmen): *Average need-based gift aid:* $6599. *Average non-need based aid:* $4200. *Average aid to full-time undergraduates:* $7310.
Athletic Department: *Director of Athletics:* Tom Hickman; Phone: 803-323-2129; Fax: 803-323-2433; E-mail: hickmant@winthrop.edu. *Sports Information Director:* Jack Frost; Phone: 803-323-2129; E-mail: frostj@winthrop.edu.

MEN'S COACHES
Baseball: Joe Hudak; Phone: 803-323-2129; E-mail: hudakj@winthrop.edu.
Basketball: Greg Marshall; Phone: 803-323-2129; E-mail: marshallg@winthrop.edu.
Cheerleading: Phone: 803-323-2129; E-mail: winthropcheer@yahoo.com.
Cross Country: Ben Paxton; Phone: 803-323-2129; E-mail: paxtonb@winthrop.edu.
Golf: Eddie Weldon; Phone: 803-323-2129; E-mail: weldone@winthrop.edu.
Soccer: Rich Posipanko; Phone: 803-323-2129; E-mail: posipankor@winthrop.edu.
Tennis: Cid Carvalho; Phone: 803-323-2129; E-mail: carvalhoa@winthrop.edu.
Track and Field: Ben Paxton; Phone: 803-323-2129; E-mail: paxtonb@winthrop.edu.

WOMEN'S COACHES
Basketball: Darrah Metz; Phone: 803-323-2129; E-mail: metzd@winthrop.edu.

Winthrop University (*continued*)

Cheerleading: Phone: 803-323-2129; E-mail: winthropcheer@yahoo. com.

Cross Country: Ben Paxton; Phone: 803-323-2129; E-mail: paxtonb@ winthrop.edu.

Golf: Eddie Weldon; Phone: 803-323-2129; E-mail: weldone@winthrop. edu.

Soccer: Melissa Heinz; Phone: 803-323-2129; E-mail: heinzm@ winthrop.edu.

Softball: Mark Cooke; Phone: 803-323-2129; E-mail: cookem@ winthrop.edu.

Tennis: Cid Carvalho; Phone: 803-323-2129; E-mail: carvalhoa@ winthrop.edu.

Track and Field: Ben Paxton; Phone: 803-323-2129; E-mail: paxtonb@ winthrop.edu.

Volleyball: Joel McCartney; Phone: 803-323-2129; E-mail: mccartneyj@ winthrop.edu.

WISCONSIN LUTHERAN COLLEGE
Milwaukee, Wisconsin

Warriors ◆ NCAA III ◆ Lake Michigan Conference; Michigan Intercollegiate Conference ◆ http://www.wlc.edu/

Independent religious 4-year, founded 1973, affiliated with Wisconsin Evangelical Lutheran Synod
Coed, 706 undergraduate students, 95% full-time, 60% women, 40% men
Suburban 21-acre campus
Moderately difficult entrance level, 77% of applicants were admitted

Freshmen *Admission:* 531 applied, 444 were accepted, 207 enrolled.
Tuition and fees (2003–04): $15,850 (full-time). *Room and board:* $5325 (room only: $2775).
Financial Aid (All incoming freshmen): *Average need-based gift aid:* $9800. *Average non-need based aid:* $9456. *Average aid to full-time undergraduates:* $12,810.
Athletic Department: *Director of Athletics:* Skip Noon; Phone: 414-443-8871; Fax: 414-443-8508; E-mail: edward_noon@wlc.edu. *Sports Information Director:* Cheryl Pasbrig; Phone: 414-443-8876; E-mail: cheryl_pasbrig@wlc.edu.

MEN'S COACHES
Baseball: Brook Smith; Phone: 414-443-8990; E-mail: brook_smith@ wlc.edu.

Basketball: Skip Noon; Phone: 414-443-8871; E-mail: edward_noon@ wlc.edu.

Cheerleading: Jody Brill; Phone: 414-443-8808; E-mail: jody_brill@wlc. edu.

Cross Country: Steve Travis; Phone: 414-443-8872; E-mail: steve_travis@ wlc.edu.

Football: Dennis Miller; Phone: 414-443-8708; E-mail: dennis_miller@ wlc.edu.

Golf: Roger Fleming; Phone: 414-443-8817; E-mail: roger_fleming@ wlc.edu.

Soccer: Joe Luedke; Phone: 414-443-8716; E-mail: joseph_luedke@wlc. edu.

Track and Field: Steve Travis; Phone: 414-443-8872; E-mail: steve_travis@wlc.edu.

WOMEN'S COACHES
Basketball: Wayne Smith; Phone: 414-443-8869; E-mail: wayne_smith@ wlc.edu.

Cheerleading: Jody Brill; Phone: 414-443-8808; E-mail: jody_brill@wlc. edu.

Cross Country: Steve Travis; Phone: 414-443-8872; E-mail: steve_travis@ wlc.edu.

Golf: Chuck Garbedian; Phone: 414-443-8808; E-mail: chuck_garbedian@wlc.edu.

Softball: Rachel Kuehl; Phone: 414-443-8885; E-mail: rachel_kuehl@ wlc.edu.

Tennis: Dave Larson; Phone: 414-443-8889; E-mail: dave_larson@wlc. edu.

Track and Field: Steve Travis; Phone: 414-443-8872; E-mail: steve_travis@wlc.edu.

Volleyball: Rachel Kuehl; Phone: 414-443-8885; E-mail: rachel_kuehl@ wlc.edu.

WITTENBERG UNIVERSITY
Springfield, Ohio

Tigers ◆ NCAA III ◆ North Coast Athletic Conference ◆ http://www.wittenberg.edu/

Independent religious comprehensive, founded 1845, affiliated with Evangelical Lutheran Church
Coed, 2,152 undergraduate students, 95% full-time, 58% women, 42% men
Suburban 71-acre campus with easy access to Columbus and Dayton
Moderately difficult entrance level, 68% of applicants were admitted

Freshmen *Admission:* 3,048 applied, 2,263 were accepted, 549 enrolled. *Test scores:* SAT verbal scores over 500: 85%; SAT math scores over 500: 85%; SAT verbal scores over 600: 39%; SAT math scores over 600: 39%; SAT verbal scores over 700: 7%; SAT math scores over 700: 5%.
Tuition and fees (2004–05): $26,196 (full-time). *Room and board:* $6686 (room only: $3454).
Financial Aid (All incoming freshmen): *Average need-based gift aid:* $17,056. *Average non-need based aid:* $9655. *Average aid to full-time undergraduates:* $22,234.

MEN'S COACHES
Baseball: Jay Lewis; Phone: 937-327-6494; E-mail: jlewis@wittenberg. edu.

Basketball: Bill Brown; Phone: 937-327-6454; E-mail: wbrown@ wittenberg.edu.

Cross Country: Steve Shutt; Phone: 937-327-6493; E-mail: sshutt@ wittenberg.edu.

Football: Joe Fincham; Phone: 937-327-6498; E-mail: wfincham@ wittenberg.edu.

Golf: Scott Isphording; Phone: 937-327-6462; E-mail: sisphording@ wittenberg.edu.

Lacrosse: Vinnie Lang; Phone: 937-327-6451; E-mail: vlang@ wittenberg.edu.

Soccer: Steve Dawson; Phone: 937-327-6456; E-mail: sdawson@ wittenberg.edu.

Swimming: Leslie Ramsey; Phone: 937-327-6446; E-mail: lramsey@ wittenberg.edu.

Tennis: Dave Engle; Phone: 937-327-6453; E-mail: ovta@voyager.net.

Track and Field: Steve Shutt; Phone: 937-327-6493; E-mail: sshutt@ wittenberg.edu.

WOMEN'S COACHES
Basketball: Pam Smith; Phone: 937-327-6463; E-mail: psmith@ wittenberg.edu.

Cross Country: Steve Shutt; Phone: 937-327-6493; E-mail: sshutt@ wittenberg.edu.

Field Hockey: Marianne Beshara; Phone: 937-327-6499; E-mail: mbeshara@wittenberg.edu.

Lacrosse: Nancy Beck; Phone: 937-327-6457; E-mail: pclouse@ wittenberg.edu.

Soccer: Norm Riker; Phone: 937-327-6496; E-mail: nriker@wittenberg. edu.

Softball: Becky Hall; Phone: 937-327-6460; E-mail: rhall@wittenberg. edu.

Swimming: Leslie Ramsey; Phone: 937-327-6446; E-mail: lramsey@ wittenberg.edu.

Tennis: Dave Engle; Phone: 937-327-6453; E-mail: ovta@voyager.net.

Track and Field: Steve Shutt; Phone: 937-327-6493; E-mail: sshutt@ wittenberg.edu.

Volleyball: Paco Labrador; Phone: 937-327-6492; E-mail: flabrador@ wittenberg.edu.

WOFFORD COLLEGE
Spartanburg, South Carolina

Terriers ◆ NCAA I ◆ Southern Conference
◆ http://www.wofford.edu/

Independent religious 4-year, founded 1854, affiliated with United Methodist Church
Coed, 1,132 undergraduate students, 99% full-time, 51% women, 49% men
Urban 140-acre campus with easy access to Charlotte
Very difficult entrance level, 78% of applicants were admitted

Freshmen *Admission:* 1,317 applied, 1,053 were accepted, 330 enrolled. *Test scores:* SAT verbal scores over 500: 93%; SAT math scores over 500: 98%; SAT verbal scores over 600: 62%; SAT math scores over 600: 68%; SAT verbal scores over 700: 13%; SAT math scores over 700: 17%.
Tuition and fees (2003–04): $20,610 (full-time). *Room and board:* $6100 (room only: $3280).
Financial Aid (All incoming freshmen): *Average need-based gift aid:* $15,481. *Average non-need based aid:* $8004. *Average aid to full-time undergraduates:* $20,302.
Athletic Department: *Director of Athletics:* David Wood; Phone: 864-597-4232; Fax: 864-597-4129; E-mail: woodds@wofford.edu. *Sports Information Director:* Mark Cohen; Phone: 864-597-4093; E-mail: cohenm@wofford.edu.

MEN'S COACHES
Baseball: Steve Traylor; Phone: 864-597-4126; E-mail: traylorse@wofford.edu.
Basketball: Mike Young; Phone: 864-597-4117; E-mail: youngmk@wofford.edu.
Cheerleading: Heather Morrow; Phone: 864-597-4048; E-mail: morrowhj@wofford.edu.
Cross Country: Roger Saltsman; Phone: 864-597-4109; E-mail: saltsmanrs@wofford.edu.
Football: Mike Ayers; Phone: 864-597-4100; E-mail: ayersmw@wofford.edu.
Golf: Dan O'Connell; Phone: 864-597-0260; E-mail: dan2.o@prodigy.net.
Soccer: Matt Kern; Phone: 864-597-4125; E-mail: kernme@wofford.edu.
Tennis: Rod Ray; Phone: 864-597-4154; E-mail: rayra@wofford.edu.
Track and Field: Freddie Brown; Phone: 864-597-4111.

WOMEN'S COACHES
Basketball: Samantha Young; Phone: 864-597-4119.
Cheerleading: Heather Morrow; Phone: 864-597-4048; E-mail: morrowhj@wofford.edu.
Cross Country: Roger Saltsman; Phone: 864-597-4109; E-mail: saltsmanrs@wofford.edu.
Golf: Randy Mahaffey; Phone: 864-597-4496; E-mail: mahaffeycr@wofford.edu.
Soccer: Amy Kiah; Phone: 864-597-4153; E-mail: burnsam@wofford.edu.
Tennis: Rod Ray; Phone: 864-597-4154; E-mail: rayra@wofford.edu.
Track and Field: Freddie Brown; Phone: 864-597-4111.
Volleyball: Corey Helle; Phone: 864-597-4152; E-mail: hellecj@wofford.edu.

WORCESTER POLYTECHNIC INSTITUTE
Worcester, Massachusetts

Engineers ◆ NCAA III ◆ New England Women's & Men's Athletics Conference ◆ http://www.wpi.edu/

Independent university, founded 1865
Coed, 2,785 undergraduate students, 97% full-time, 24% women, 76% men
Suburban 80-acre campus with easy access to Boston
Very difficult entrance level, 69% of applicants were admitted

Freshmen *Admission:* 3,576 applied, 2,547 were accepted, 633 enrolled. *Test scores:* SAT verbal scores over 500: 96%; SAT math scores over 500: 100%; SAT verbal scores over 600: 61%; SAT math scores over 600: 87%; SAT verbal scores over 700: 15%; SAT math scores over 700: 32%.
Tuition and fees (2003–04): $28,620 (full-time). *Room and board:* $8984 (room only: $5184).
Financial Aid (All incoming freshmen): *Average need-based gift aid:* $17,134. *Average non-need based aid:* $16,201. *Average aid to full-time undergraduates:* $20,878.

MEN'S COACHES
Baseball: Chris Robertson; Phone: 508-831-5243; E-mail: crob@wpi.edu.
Basketball: Chris Bartley; Phone: 508-831-5760; E-mail: cbartley@wpi.edu.
Cross Country: Brian Savilonis; Phone: 508-831-5686; E-mail: bjs@wpi.edu.
Football: Ed Zaloom; Phone: 508-831-5624; E-mail: ezaloom@wpi.edu.
Golf: bob McNeil; Phone: 508-831-5243; E-mail: colonelbob@wpi.edu.
Soccer: Malcolm Macpherson; Phone: 508-831-5841; E-mail: mjm@wpi.edu.
Swimming: Natalie Koukis; Phone: 508-831-5625; E-mail: nkoukis@wpi.edu.
Tennis: Robert Palmer; Phone: 508-831-5243; E-mail: rpalmer@wpi.edu.
Track and Field: Dan Green; Phone: 508-831-6022; E-mail: dgreen@wpi.edu.
Wrestling: Phil Grebinar; Phone: 508-831-5623; E-mail: grebinar@wpi.edu.

WOMEN'S COACHES
Basketball: Cherise Galasso; Phone: 508-831-5063; E-mail: cgalasso@wpi.edu.
Cross Country: Brian Savilonis; Phone: 508-831-5686; E-mail: bjs@wpi.edu.
Field Hockey: Johanna Dicarlo; Phone: 508-831-5588; E-mail: jdicarlo@wpi.edu.
Soccer: Stepahnie Carlson; Phone: 508-831-5975; E-mail: scarlson@wpi.edu.
Softball: Johanna Dicarlo; Phone: 508-831-5588; E-mail: jdicarlo@wpi.edu.
Swimming: Natalie Koukis; Phone: 508-831-5625; E-mail: nkoukis@wpi.edu.
Tennis: Robert Palmer; Phone: 508-831-5243; E-mail: rpalmer@wpi.edu.
Track and Field: Dan Green; Phone: 508-831-6022; E-mail: dgreen@wpi.edu.
Volleyball: Nancy Vaskas; Phone: 508-831-5588; E-mail: nvaskas@aol.com.

WORCESTER STATE COLLEGE
Worcester, Massachusetts

Lancers ◆ NCAA III ◆ Little East Conference; Massachusetts State College Athletic Conference; New England Football Conference; New England Women's Lacrosse Conference ◆ http://www.worcester.edu/

State-supported comprehensive, founded 1874, part of Massachusetts Public Higher Education System
Coed, 4,665 undergraduate students, 66% full-time, 60% women, 40% men
Urban 53-acre campus with easy access to Boston
Moderately difficult entrance level, 5% of applicants were admitted

Freshmen *Admission:* 2,939 applied, 1,634 were accepted, 628 enrolled. *Test scores:* SAT verbal scores over 500: 53%; SAT math scores over 500: 52%; SAT verbal scores over 600: 8%; SAT math scores over 600: 11%; SAT verbal scores over 700: %; SAT math scores over 700: %.
Tuition and fees (2003–04): $4123 (resident), $10,203 (nonresident). *Room and board:* $5500.
Financial Aid (All incoming freshmen): *Average need-based gift aid:* $1717. *Average non-need based aid:* $2199. *Average aid to full-time undergraduates:* $5494.

MEN'S COACHES
Baseball: Dirk Baker; Phone: 508-929-8852; E-mail: dbaker1@worcester.edu.

Worcester State College *(continued)*

Basketball: Dave Lindberg; Phone: 508-929-8593; E-mail: dlindberg@worcester.edu.
Cross Country: Chris D'Aniello; Phone: 508-929-8034.
Football: Brien Cullen; Phone: 508-929-8598; E-mail: bcullen@worcester.edu.
Golf: Rick Korzec; Phone: 508-929-8152; E-mail: rkorzec@worcester.edu.
Ice Hockey: John Guiney; Phone: 508-929-8510; E-mail: jguiney@worcester.edu.
Soccer: Dave Morris; Phone: 508-929-8906; E-mail: dmorris@worcester.edu.
Tennis: Ed Titus; Phone: 508-929-8034.
Track and Field: Chris D'Aniello; Phone: 508-929-8034.

WOMEN'S COACHES

Basketball: Karen Tessmer; Phone: 508-929-8769; E-mail: ktessmer@worcester.edu.
Cross Country: Alan Halper; Phone: 508-929-8581; E-mail: ahalper@worcester.edu.
Field Hockey: Meighan Guiney; Phone: 508-929-8919; E-mail: mguiney@worcester.edu.
Lacrosse: Jim Grandose; Phone: 508-929-8643; E-mail: jgrandone@worcester.edu.
Soccer: Mike Webber; Phone: 508-929-8924; E-mail: mwebber@worcester.edu.
Softball: Lynne Olson; Phone: 508-929-8034.
Tennis: Ed Titus; Phone: 508-929-8034.
Track and Field: Alan Halper; Phone: 508-929-8581; E-mail: ahalper@worcester.edu.
Volleyball: Patryce Hudspeth; Phone: 508-929-8919; E-mail: phudspeth@worcester.edu.

WRIGHT STATE UNIVERSITY
Dayton, Ohio

Raiders ◆ NCAA I ◆ Horizon League Conference ◆ http://www.wright.edu/

State-supported university, founded 1964
Coed, 11,787 undergraduate students, 85% full-time, 57% women, 43% men
Suburban 557-acre campus with easy access to Cincinnati
Minimally difficult entrance level, 90% of applicants were admitted

Freshmen *Admission:* 5,104 applied, 4,650 were accepted, 2,282 enrolled. *Test scores:* SAT verbal scores over 500: 52%; SAT math scores over 500: 51%; SAT verbal scores over 600: 14%; SAT math scores over 600: 16%; SAT verbal scores over 700: 1%; SAT math scores over 700: 2%.
Tuition and fees (2003–04): $5892 (resident), $10,524 (nonresident). *Room and board:* $6019.
Financial Aid (All incoming freshmen): *Average aid to full-time undergraduates:* $7857.
Athletic Department: *Director of Athletics:* Michael Cusack; Phone: 937-775-2771; Fax: 937-775-2368; E-mail: mcusack@wright.edu. *Sports Information Director:* Robert Noss; Phone: 937-775-2771; E-mail: rnoss@wright.edu.

MEN'S COACHES

Baseball: Ron Nischwitz; Phone: 937-775-2771; E-mail: ron.nischwitz@wright.edu.
Basketball: Paul Biancardi; Phone: 937-775-2271; E-mail: christina.brame@wright.edu.
Cheerleading: Joyce Whitaker; Phone: 937-775-2771; E-mail: wsucheerdanz@aol.com.
Cross Country: Bob Schul; Phone: 937-775-2771; E-mail: bobschul@sprintmail.com.
Diving: Liyi Wang; Phone: 937-775-2771.
Golf: Fred Jefferson; Phone: 937-775-2771; E-mail: fjeffers@discover.wright.edu.
Soccer: Mike Tracy; Phone: 937-775-2771; E-mail: michael.tracy@wright.edu.
Swimming: Matt Liddy; Phone: 937-775-2771; E-mail: mliddy@wright.edu.
Tennis: Herb Foster; Phone: 937-775-2771; E-mail: herbert.foster@wright.edu.

WOMEN'S COACHES

Basketball: Bridgett Williams; Phone: 937-775-2771; E-mail: christina.brame@wright.edu.
Cheerleading: Joyce Whitaker; Phone: 937-775-2771; E-mail: wsucheerdanz@aol.com.
Cross Country: Bob Schul; Phone: 937-775-2771; E-mail: bobschul@sprintmail.com.
Diving: Liyi Wang; Phone: 937-775-2771.
Soccer: Scott Rodgers; Phone: 937-775-2771; E-mail: b.rodgers@wright.edu.
Softball: Sheila Nahrgang; Phone: 937-775-2771; E-mail: sheila.nahrgang@wright.edu.
Swimming: Matt Liddy; Phone: 937-775-2771; E-mail: mliddy@wright.edu.
Tennis: Herb Foster; Phone: 937-775-2771; E-mail: herbert.foster@wright.edu.
Track and Field: Bob Schul; Phone: 937-775-2771; E-mail: bobschul@sprintmail.com.
Volleyball: Joylynn Tracy; Phone: 937-775-2771; E-mail: joylynn.tracy@wright.edu.

XAVIER UNIVERSITY
Cincinnati, Ohio

Muskateers ◆ NCAA I ◆ Atlantic 10 Conference; Colonial Athletic Conference ◆ http://www.xavier.edu/

Independent Roman Catholic comprehensive, founded 1831
Coed, 3,915 undergraduate students, 84% full-time, 56% women, 44% men
Suburban 130-acre campus
Moderately difficult entrance level, 77% of applicants were admitted

Freshmen *Admission:* 4,364 applied, 3,420 were accepted, 786 enrolled. *Test scores:* SAT verbal scores over 500: 88%; SAT math scores over 500: 90%; SAT verbal scores over 600: 45%; SAT math scores over 600: 44%; SAT verbal scores over 700: 8%; SAT math scores over 700: 8%.
Tuition and fees (2003–04): $19,150 (full-time). *Room and board:* $8000 (room only: $4400).
Financial Aid (All incoming freshmen): *Average need-based gift aid:* $10,512. *Average non-need based aid:* $8859. *Average aid to full-time undergraduates:* $13,960.
Athletic Department: *Director of Athletics:* Mike Bobinski; Phone: 513-745-3417; Fax: 513-745-4390; E-mail: bobinski@xavier.edu. *Sports Information Director:* Dawn Rogers; Phone: 513-745-2854; E-mail: rogers@xavier.edu.

MEN'S COACHES

Baseball: John Morrey; Phone: 513-745-2890; E-mail: regruth@xu.edu.
Basketball: Thad Matta; Phone: 513-745-3417; E-mail: matta@xavier.edu.
Cheerleading: Jim Ray; Phone: 513-745-3044; E-mail: rayjim@xu.edu.
Cross Country: Steve Nester; Phone: 513-745-2849; E-mail: nester@xavier.edu.
Golf: Doug Steiner; Phone: 513-745-3465; E-mail: steiner@xavier.edu.
Soccer: Jack Hermans; Phone: 513-745-3879; E-mail: hermans@xavier.edu.
Swimming: George Rathmann; Phone: 513-745-2855; E-mail: rathman@xu.edu.
Tennis: Jim Brockhoff; Phone: 513-745-2840; E-mail: brockhoffj@xavier.edu.

WOMEN'S COACHES

Basketball: Kevin McGuff; Phone: 513-745-3414; E-mail: mcguff@xu.edu.
Cheerleading: Jim Ray; Phone: 513-745-3044; E-mail: rayjim@xu.edu.
Cross Country: Steve Nester; Phone: 513-745-2849; E-mail: nester@xavier.edu.
Golf: Gina Yoder-Davies; Phone: 513-745-2895; E-mail: yoder@xu.edu.
Soccer: Ron Quinn; Phone: 513-745-1084; E-mail: quinnr@xu.edu.
Swimming: George Rathmann; Phone: 513-745-2855; E-mail: rathman@xu.edu.
Tennis: Jim Brockhoff; Phone: 513-745-3413; E-mail: brockhoffj@xavier.edu.
Volleyball: Floydd Deaton; Phone: 513-745-3198; E-mail: deaton@xavier.edu.

XAVIER UNIVERSITY OF LOUISIANA
New Orleans, Louisiana

Gold Rush ◆ NAIA ◆ Gulf Coast Conference ◆ http://www.xula.edu/

Independent Roman Catholic comprehensive, founded 1925
Coed, 3,145 undergraduate students, 95% full-time, 75% women, 25% men
Urban 23-acre campus with easy access to New Orleans
Moderately difficult entrance level, 84% of applicants were admitted

Freshmen *Admission:* 4,172 applied, 3,508 were accepted, 913 enrolled. *Test scores:* SAT verbal scores over 500: 54%; SAT math scores over 500: 52%; SAT verbal scores over 600: 12%; SAT math scores over 600: 12%; SAT math scores over 700: 1%.
Tuition and fees (2003–04): $11,400 (full-time). *Room and board:* $6200.
Financial Aid (All incoming freshmen): *Average need-based gift aid:* $3866. *Average non-need based aid:* $2988. *Average aid to full-time undergraduates:* $4438.
Athletic Department: *Director of Athletics:* Steve Kalbaugh; Phone: 504-520-7330; Fax: 504-520-7934; E-mail: skalbaug@xula.edu. *Sports Information Director:* Bambi Hall; Phone: 504-520-5707; E-mail: brhall@xula.edu.

MEN'S COACHES
Basketball: Dannton Jackson; Phone: 504-520-5448; E-mail: djackson@xula.edu.
Cross Country: Steve Kalbaugh; Phone: 504-520-5008; E-mail: skalbaug@xula.edu.
Tennis: Alan Green; Phone: 504-520-5008; E-mail: amgreen@xula.edu.
Track and Field: Steve Kalbaugh; Phone: 504-520-5008; E-mail: skalbaug@xula.edu.

WOMEN'S COACHES
Basketball: Robert Browder; Phone: 504-520-7333; E-mail: rbrowder@xula.edu.
Cross Country: Steve Kalbaugh; Phone: 504-520-5008; E-mail: skalbaug@xula.edu.
Tennis: Alan Green; Phone: 504-520-5008; E-mail: amgreen@xula.edu.
Track and Field: Steve Kalbaugh; Phone: 504-520-5008; E-mail: skalbaug@xula.edu.
Volleyball: Greg Castillo; Phone: 504-520-5008.

YALE UNIVERSITY
New Haven, Connecticut

Bulldogs ◆ NCAA I ◆ Ivy League Conference ◆ http://www.yale.edu/

Independent university, founded 1701
Coed, 5,354 undergraduate students, 99% full-time, 50% women, 50% men
Urban 200-acre campus with easy access to New York City
Most difficult entrance level, 1% of applicants were admitted

Freshmen *Admission:* 17,735 applied, 2,014 were accepted, 1,352 enrolled.
Tuition and fees (2003–04): $28,400 (full-time). *Room and board:* $8600 (room only: $4700).
Financial Aid (All incoming freshmen): *Average need-based gift aid:* $24,685. *Average aid to full-time undergraduates:* $26,995.
Athletic Department: *Director of Athletics:* Thomas Beckett; Phone: 203-432-1414; Fax: 203-432-7772; E-mail: thomas.beckett@yale.edu. *Sports Information Director:* Steve Conn; Phone: 203-432-1455; E-mail: steve.conn@yale.edu.

MEN'S COACHES
Baseball: John Stuper; Phone: 203-432-1466; E-mail: john.stuper@yale.edu.
Basketball: James Jones; Phone: 203-432-1485; E-mail: j.jones@yale.edu.
Cross Country: Daniel Ireland; Phone: 203-432-1406; E-mail: daniel.ireland@yale.edu.
Diving: Ryan Moehnke; Phone: 203-432-2447; E-mail: mrfmdive@aol.com.
Football: Jack Siedlecki; Phone: 203-432-8587; E-mail: jack.siedlecki@yale.edu.
Golf: Dave Paterson; Phone: 203-432-8697; E-mail: david.paterson@yale.edu.
Ice Hockey: Tim Taylor; Phone: 203-432-1478; E-mail: tim.taylor@yale.edu.
Lacrosse: Andy Shay; Phone: 203-432-1494; E-mail: andrew.shay@yale.edu.
Soccer: Brian Tompkins; Phone: 203-432-1495; E-mail: brian.tompkins@yale.edu.
Swimming: Frank Keefe; Phone: 203-432-2447; E-mail: frank.keefe@yale.edu.
Tennis: Alex Dorato; Phone: 203-432-2498; E-mail: alex.dorato@yale.edu.
Track and Field: Mark Young; Phone: 203-432-1405; E-mail: mark.young@yale.edu.

WOMEN'S COACHES
Basketball: Amy Backus; Phone: 203-432-1488; E-mail: amy.backus@yale.edu.
Cross Country: Mark Young; Phone: 203-432-1405; E-mail: mark.young@yale.edu.
Diving: Ryan Moehnke; Phone: 203-432-2447; E-mail: mrfmdive@aol.com.
Field Hockey: Ainslee Lamb; Phone: 203-432-1479; E-mail: ainslee.lamb@yale.edu.
Golf: Mary Moan; Phone: 203-432-7370; E-mail: mary.moan@yale.edu.
Gymnastics: Barbara Tonry; Phone: 203-432-2138; E-mail: barbara.tonry@yale.edu.
Lacrosse: Amanda O'Leary; Phone: 203-432-1486; E-mail: amanda.oleary@pantheon.yale.edu.
Soccer: Rudy Meredith; Phone: 203-432-1492; E-mail: rudolph.meredith@yale.edu.
Softball: Andy Van Etten; Phone: 203-432-1407; E-mail: andrew.vanetten@yale.edu.
Swimming: Frank Keefe; Phone: 203-432-2447; E-mail: frank.keefe@yale.edu.
Tennis: Chad Skorupka; Phone: 203-432-1493; E-mail: chad.skorupka@yale.edu.
Track and Field: Mark Young; Phone: 203-432-1405; E-mail: mark.young@yale.edu.
Volleyball: Erin Appleman; Phone: 203-432-1408; E-mail: erin.appleman@yale.edu.

YESHIVA UNIVERSITY
New York, New York

Maccabees ◆ NCAA III ◆ Skyline Conference ◆ http://www.yu.edu/

Independent university, founded 1886
Coed, 2,819 undergraduate students, 99% full-time, 44% women, 56% men
Urban campus
Moderately difficult entrance level, 80% of applicants were admitted

Freshmen *Admission:* 1,768 applied, 1,372 were accepted, 755 enrolled.
Tuition and fees (2003–04): $22,240 (full-time). *Room and board:* $6980 (room only: $5050).
Financial Aid (All incoming freshmen): *Average need-based gift aid:* $12,020. *Average non-need based aid:* $4828. *Average aid to full-time undergraduates:* $11,488.

MEN'S COACHES
Basketball: Jonathan Halpert; Phone: 212-960-5211; E-mail: mamboa30@hotmail.com.
Cross Country: Stanley Watson; Phone: 212-960-5211.
Golf: David Neiss; Phone: 212-960-5211; E-mail: dneiss@sempratrading.com.
Soccer: Jack Thelusma; Phone: 212-960-5211; E-mail: theludon@aol.com.
Tennis: Jonathan Bandler; Phone: 212-960-5211; E-mail: scoopjonb@aol.com.
Volleyball: Juan Corona; Phone: 212-960-5211; E-mail: cjuan726@aol.com.
Wrestling: Neil Ellman; Phone: 212-960-5211.

YORK COLLEGE
York, Nebraska

Panthers ◆ NAIA ◆ Midlands Collegiate Conference ◆ http://www.york.edu/

Independent religious 4-year, founded 1890, affiliated with Church of Christ
Coed, 461 undergraduate students, 94% full-time, 52% women, 48% men
Small-town 44-acre campus
Moderately difficult entrance level, 61% of applicants were admitted

Freshmen *Admission:* 344 applied, 216 were accepted, 116 enrolled. *Test scores:* SAT verbal scores over 500: 57%; SAT math scores over 500: 73%; SAT verbal scores over 600: 10%; SAT math scores over 600: 26%; SAT verbal scores over 700: 5%.
Tuition and fees (2003–04): $11,400 (full-time). *Room and board:* $3575 (room only: $1375).
Athletic Department: *Director of Athletics:* Chris Luther; Phone: 402-363-5635; Fax: 402-363-5738; E-mail: cluther@york.edu.

MEN'S COACHES
Baseball: Jerry Laird; Phone: 402-363-5736.
Basketball: Derek Harrell; Phone: 402-363-5622; E-mail: dharrell@york.edu.
Cross Country: Roger Collins; Phone: 402-363-5877; E-mail: rlcollins@york.edu.
Golf: Frank Chapman; Phone: 402-363-5735; E-mail: fchapman@york.edu.
Soccer: Chris Luther; Phone: 402-363-5635; E-mail: cluther@york.edu.
Track and Field: Roger Collins; Phone: 402-363-5877; E-mail: rlcollins@york.edu.

WOMEN'S COACHES
Basketball: Gerry Nixon; Phone: 402-363-5720; E-mail: genixon@york.edu.
Cross Country: Roger Collins; Phone: 402-363-5877; E-mail: rlcollins@york.edu.
Golf: Frank Chapman; Phone: 402-363-5735; E-mail: fchapman@york.edu.
Soccer: Chris Luther; Phone: 402-363-5635; E-mail: cluther@york.edu.
Softball: Rex Reynolds; Phone: 402-363-5735; E-mail: rreynolds@york.edu.
Track and Field: Roger Collins; Phone: 402-363-5877; E-mail: rlcollins@york.edu.

YORK COLLEGE OF PENNSYLVANIA
York, Pennsylvania

Spartans ◆ NCAA III ◆ Capital Athletic Conference ◆ http://www.ycp.edu/

Independent comprehensive, founded 1787
Coed, 5,281 undergraduate students, 80% full-time, 60% women, 40% men
Suburban 118-acre campus with easy access to Baltimore
Moderately difficult entrance level, 75% of applicants were admitted

Freshmen *Admission:* 4,141 applied, 3,070 were accepted, 1,024 enrolled. *Test scores:* SAT verbal scores over 500: 83%; SAT math scores over 500: 83%; SAT verbal scores over 600: 28%; SAT math scores over 600: 23%; SAT verbal scores over 700: 4%; SAT math scores over 700: 2%.
Tuition and fees (2003–04): $8550 (full-time). *Room and board:* $5950 (room only: $3250).
Financial Aid (All incoming freshmen): *Average need-based gift aid:* $4111. *Average non-need based aid:* $2726. *Average aid to full-time undergraduates:* $6481.

MEN'S COACHES
Baseball: Paul Saikia; Phone: 717-815-1245; E-mail: psaikia@ycp.edu.
Basketball: Jeff Gamber; Phone: 717-894-1614; E-mail: jgamber@ycp.edu.
Cross Country: Rich Achtzehn; Phone: 717-815-1747; E-mail: rachtzeh@ycp.edu.
Golf: Jeff Gamber; Phone: 717-894-1614; E-mail: jgamber@ycp.edu.
Lacrosse: Rob Horrigan; Phone: 717-815-1949; E-mail: rhorriga@ycp.edu.
Soccer: Mark Ludwig; Phone: 717-894-1919; E-mail: mludwig@ycp.edu.
Swimming: Gina McHenry; Phone: 717-894-1517; E-mail: gmchenry@ycp.edu.
Tennis: Mark Ludwig; Phone: 717-894-1919; E-mail: mludwig@ycp.edu.
Track and Field: Eric Hue; Phone: 717-815-1948; E-mail: ehue@ycp.edu.
Wrestling: Tom Kessler; Phone: 717-894-1449; E-mail: tkessler@ycp.edu.

WOMEN'S COACHES
Basketball: Betsy Witman; Phone: 717-894-1537; E-mail: bwitman@ycp.edu.
Cross Country: Rich Achtzehn; Phone: 717-815-1747; E-mail: rachtzeh@ycp.edu.
Field Hockey: Vicki Sutton; Phone: 717-815-1516; E-mail: vsutton@ycp.edu.
Soccer: Vicki Sterner; Phone: 717-894-1517; E-mail: vsterner@ycp.edu.
Softball: Becky Bliss; Phone: 717-894-1940; E-mail: rbliss@ycp.edu.
Swimming: Gina McHenry; Phone: 717-894-1517; E-mail: gmchenry@ycp.edu.
Tennis: Tammy Myers; Phone: 717-894-1789; E-mail: tmyers@ycp.edu.
Track and Field: Rebecca Lankford; Phone: 717-815-1774; E-mail: rlankfor@ycp.edu.
Volleyball: Sue Dumars; Phone: 717-894-1770; E-mail: sdumars@ycp.edu.

YORK COLLEGE OF THE CITY UNIVERSITY OF NEW YORK
Jamaica, New York

Cardinals ◆ NCAA III ◆ CUNY Athletic Conference ◆ http://www.york.cuny.edu/

State and locally supported 4-year, founded 1967, part of City University of New York System
Coed, 5,672 undergraduate students, 60% full-time, 70% women, 30% men
Urban 50-acre campus with easy access to New York City
Moderately difficult entrance level, 3% of applicants were admitted

Freshmen *Admission:* 2,389 applied, 738 were accepted, 599 enrolled. *Test scores:* SAT verbal scores over 500: 14%; SAT math scores over 500: 16%; SAT verbal scores over 600: 1%; SAT math scores over 600: 2%.
Tuition and fees (2004–05): $4242 (resident), $8882 (nonresident).

MEN'S COACHES
Basketball: Ronald St. John; Phone: 718-262-5100; E-mail: rstjohn43@hotmail.com.
Cross Country: Thomas Pope; Phone: 718-262-5100.
Soccer: Richard Packard; Phone: 718-262-5100.
Swimming: George Taylor; Phone: 718-262-5100.
Tennis: Richard Packard; Phone: 718-262-5100.
Track and Field: Thomas Pope; Phone: 718-262-5100.
Volleyball: Andre Titus; Phone: 718-262-5100.

WOMEN'S COACHES
Basketball: Jacqueline Smith; Phone: 718-262-5100.
Cross Country: Thomas Pope; Phone: 718-262-5100.
Softball: Phone: 718-262-5100.
Swimming: George Taylor; Phone: 718-262-5100.
Track and Field: Thomas Pope; Phone: 718-262-5100.
Volleyball: Andre Titus; Phone: 718-262-5100.

YOUNGSTOWN STATE UNIVERSITY
Youngstown, Ohio

Penguins ◆ NCAA I ◆ Gateway Football Conference; Horizon League Conference ◆ http://www.ysu.edu/

State-supported comprehensive, founded 1908
Coed, 11,592 undergraduate students, 79% full-time, 55% women, 45% men
Urban 200-acre campus with easy access to Cleveland and Pittsburgh
Noncompetitive entrance level, 99% of applicants were admitted

Freshmen *Admission:* 3,760 applied, 3,738 were accepted, 2,029 enrolled.
Tuition and fees (2003–04): $5478 (resident), $10,686 (nonresident). *Room and board:* $5700.
Athletic Department: *Director of Athletics:* Ron Strollo; Phone: 330-941-2385; Fax: 330-941-2733; E-mail: rastrollo@ysu.edu. *Sports Information Director:* Trevor Parks; Phone: 330-941-3192; E-mail: tparks@ysu.edu.

MEN'S COACHES
Baseball: Mike Florak; Phone: 330-941-3485; E-mail: meflorak@ysu.edu.
Basketball: John Robic; Phone: 330-941-3386.
Cheerleading: Michelle Markota; Phone: 330-941-7227; E-mail: efbartley@ysu.edu.
Cross Country: Brian Gorby; Phone: 330-941-3395; E-mail: brian_gorby@hotmail.com.
Football: Joe Heacock; Phone: 330-941-3478; E-mail: jrheacoc@ysu.edu.
Golf: Tony Joy; Phone: 330-941-2166.
Tennis: Eric Ronan; Phone: 330-941-2762; E-mail: evronan@ysu.edu.
Track and Field: Brian Gorby; Phone: 330-941-3395; E-mail: brian_gorby@hotmail.com.

WOMEN'S COACHES
Basketball: Tisha Hill; Phone: 330-941-3743; E-mail: thill@ysu.edu.
Cheerleading: Michelle Markota; Phone: 330-941-7227; E-mail: efbartley@ysu.edu.
Cross Country: Brian Gorby; Phone: 330-941-3395; E-mail: brian_gorby@hotmail.com.
Diving: Nick Gavolas; Phone: 330-941-3189.
Golf: Roseann Schwartz; Phone: 330-941-2166; E-mail: pinesgolf@msn.com.
Soccer: Anthony James; Phone: 330-941-3629.
Swimming: Matt Anderson; Phone: 330-941-3673; E-mail: mlanderson.04@ysu.edu.
Tennis: Michele Grim; Phone: 330-941-2762; E-mail: penguin10s@aol.com.
Track and Field: Brian Gorby; Phone: 330-941-3395; E-mail: brian_gorby@hotmail.com.
Volleyball: Joe Conroy; Phone: 330-941-1920; E-mail: jcconroy@ysu.edu.

Indexes

Geographic Listing of College Athletic Programs

Colorado

Adams State College	37
Colorado Christian University	122
The Colorado College	122
Colorado School of Mines	123
Colorado State University	123
Colorado State University-Pueblo	124
Fort Lewis College	170
Johnson & Wales University	215
Mesa State College	260
Metropolitan State College of Denver	262
Regis University	327
United States Air Force Academy	405
University of Colorado at Boulder	419
University of Colorado at Colorado Springs	419
University of Denver	421
University of Northern Colorado	451
Western State College of Colorado	507

Connecticut

Albertus Magnus College	40
Central Connecticut State University	102
Connecticut College	130
Eastern Connecticut State University	148
Fairfield University	161
Quinnipiac University	325
Sacred Heart University	338
Saint Joseph College	344
Southern Connecticut State University	367
Teikyo Post University	389
Trinity College	399
United States Coast Guard Academy	406
University of Bridgeport	412
University of Connecticut	419
University of Hartford	424
University of New Haven	446
Wesleyan University	502
Western Connecticut State University	504
Yale University	525

Delaware

Delaware State University	138
Goldey-Beacom College	182
University of Delaware	421
Wesley College	502
Wilmington College	519

District of Columbia

American University	45
The Catholic University of America	99
Gallaudet University	175
Georgetown University	178
The George Washington University	179
Howard University	201
Trinity College	400
University of the District of Columbia	472

Florida

Barry University	59
Bethune-Cookman College	69
Eckerd College	153
Edward Waters College	154
Embry-Riddle Aeronautical University	157
Flagler College	166
Florida Agricultural and Mechanical University	166
Florida Atlantic University	166
Florida Gulf Coast University	167
Florida Institute of Technology	167
Florida International University	168
Florida Memorial College	168
Florida Southern College	168
Florida State University	169
Jacksonville University	212
Johnson & Wales University	215
Lynn University	245
Northwood University, Florida Campus	299
Nova Southeastern University	300
Rollins College	334
Saint Leo University	346
St. Thomas University	351
Stetson University	384
University of Central Florida	417
University of Florida	423
University of Miami	437
University of North Florida	452
University of South Florida	467
The University of Tampa	468
University of West Florida	477
Warner Southern College	495
Webber International University	500

Georgia

Agnes Scott College	38
Albany State University	39
Armstrong Atlantic State University	50
Atlanta Christian College	51
Augusta State University	54
Berry College	66
Brenau University	76
Brewton-Parker College	77
Clark Atlanta University	110
Clayton College & State University	112
Columbus State University	125
Covenant College	132
Emmanuel College	158
Emory University	159
Fort Valley State University	171
Georgia College & State University	179
Georgia Institute of Technology	179
Georgia Southern University	180
Georgia Southwestern State University	181
Georgia State University	181
Kennesaw State University	219
LaGrange College	224
Mercer University	259
Morehouse College	276
North Georgia College & State University	294
Oglethorpe University	303
Paine College	312
Piedmont College	317
Reinhardt College	328
Savannah College of Art and Design	356
Savannah State University	357
Shorter College	361
Southern Polytechnic State University	370
Spelman College	375
State University of West Georgia	383
Thomas University	397
University of Georgia	424
Valdosta State University	486
Wesleyan College	502

Hawaii

Brigham Young University–Hawaii	79
Chaminade University of Honolulu	105
Hawai'i Pacific University	195
University of Hawaii at Hilo	425
University of Hawaii at Manoa	425

Idaho

Albertson College of Idaho	39
Boise State University	73
Idaho State University	204
Lewis-Clark State College	233
Northwest Nazarene University	298
University of Idaho	426

Illinois

Augustana College	53
Aurora University	54
Benedictine University	65
Blackburn College	70
Bradley University	76
Chicago State University	106
Concordia University	127
DePaul University	140
Dominican University	143
Eastern Illinois University	149
Elmhurst College	155
Eureka College	160
Greenville College	187
Illinois College	204
Illinois Institute of Technology	205
Illinois State University	205
Illinois Wesleyan University	205
Judson College	216
Kendall College	219
Knox College	222
Lake Forest College	224
Lewis University	233
Loyola University Chicago	242
MacMurray College	246
McKendree College	256
Millikin University	267
Monmouth College	272
North Central College	291
Northern Illinois University	293
North Park University	295
Northwestern University	297
Olivet Nazarene University	308
Principia College	322
Quincy University	325
Robert Morris College	332
Rockford College	333
Saint Xavier University	352
Southern Illinois University Carbondale	367
Southern Illinois University Edwardsville	368
Trinity Christian College	399
Trinity International University	400
University of Chicago	418

Massachusetts

Michigan

Minnesota

Mississippi

Missouri

Montana

Nebraska

College Athletic Programs by Sport

Baseball

Abilene Christian University (TX) (m)
Adelphi University (NY) (m)
Adrian College (MI) (m)
Alabama Agricultural and Mechanical University (AL) (m)
Alabama State University (AL) (m)
Albany State University (GA) (m)
Albertson College of Idaho (ID) (m)
Albertus Magnus College (CT) (m)
Albion College (MI) (m)
Albright College (PA) (m)
Alcorn State University (MS) (m)
Alderson-Broaddus College (WV) (m)
Alice Lloyd College (KY) (m)
Allegheny College (PA) (m)
Allen University (SC) (m)
Alma College (MI) (m)
Alvernia College (PA) (m)
American International College (MA) (m)
Amherst College (MA) (m)
Anderson College (SC) (m)
Anderson University (IN) (m)
Angelo State University (TX) (m)
Anna Maria College (MA) (m)
Appalachian State University (NC) (m)
Aquinas College (MI) (m)
Arcadia University (PA) (m)
Arizona State University (AZ) (m)
Arkansas State University (AR) (m)
Arkansas Tech University (AR) (m)
Armstrong Atlantic State University (GA) (m)
Ashland University (OH) (m)
Assumption College (MA) (m)
Atlanta Christian College (GA) (m)
Auburn University (AL) (m)
Auburn University Montgomery (AL) (m)
Augsburg College (MN) (m)
Augustana College (IL) (m)
Augustana College (SD) (m)
Augusta State University (GA) (m)
Aurora University (IL) (m)
Austin College (TX) (m)
Austin Peay State University (TN) (m)
Averett University (VA) (m)
Avila University (MO) (m)
Azusa Pacific University (CA) (m)
Babson College (MA) (m)
Bacone College (OK) (m)
Baker University (KS) (m)
Baldwin-Wallace College (OH) (m)
Ball State University (IN) (m)
Barber-Scotia College (NC) (m)
Barry University (FL) (m)
Barton College (NC) (m)
Bates College (ME) (m)
Baylor University (TX) (m)
Belhaven College (MS) (m)
Bellarmine University (KY) (m)

Bellevue University (NE) (m)
Belmont Abbey College (NC) (m)
Belmont University (TN) (m)
Beloit College (WI) (m)
Bemidji State University (MN) (m)
Benedict College (SC) (m)
Benedictine College (KS) (m)
Benedictine University (IL) (m)
Bentley College (MA) (m)
Berea College (KY) (m)
Bernard M. Baruch College of the City University of New York (NY) (m)
Berry College (GA) (m)
Bethany College (KS) (m)
Bethany College (WV) (m)
Bethany College of the Assemblies of God (CA) (m)
Bethel College (IN) (m)
Bethel College (TN) (m)
Bethel University (MN) (m)
Bethune-Cookman College (FL) (m)
Birmingham-Southern College (AL) (m)
Blackburn College (IL) (m)
Bloomfield College (NJ) (m)
Bloomsburg University of Pennsylvania (PA) (m)
Bluefield College (VA) (m)
Bluefield State College (WV) (m)
Bluffton College (OH) (m)
Boston College (MA) (m)
Bowdoin College (ME) (m)
Bowling Green State University (OH) (m)
Bradley University (IL) (m)
Brandeis University (MA) (m)
Brescia University (KY) (m)
Brevard College (NC) (m)
Brewton-Parker College (GA) (m)
Briar Cliff University (IA) (m)
Bridgewater College (VA) (m)
Bridgewater State College (MA) (m)
Brigham Young University (UT) (m)
Brown University (RI) (m)
Bryan College (TN) (m)
Bryant College (RI) (m)
Bucknell University (PA) (m)
Buena Vista University (IA) (m)
Butler University (IN) (m)
Caldwell College (NJ) (m)
California Baptist University (CA) (m)
California Institute of Technology (CA) (m)
California Lutheran University (CA) (m)
California Polytechnic State University, San Luis Obispo (CA) (m)
California State Polytechnic University, Pomona (CA) (m)
California State University, Chico (CA) (m)
California State University, Dominguez Hills (CA) (m)
California State University, Fresno (CA) (m)

California State University, Fullerton (CA) (m)
California State University, Hayward (CA) (m)
California State University, Long Beach (CA) (m)
California State University, Los Angeles (CA) (m)
California State University, Northridge (CA) (m)
California State University, Sacramento (CA) (m)
California State University, San Bernardino (CA) (m)
California State University, Stanislaus (CA) (m)
California University of Pennsylvania (PA) (m)
Calumet College of Saint Joseph (IN) (m)
Calvin College (MI) (m)
Cameron University (OK) (m)
Campbellsville University (KY) (m)
Campbell University (NC) (m)
Canisius College (NY) (m)
Capital University (OH) (m)
Cardinal Stritch University (WI) (m)
Carleton College (MN) (m)
Carroll College (WI) (m)
Carson-Newman College (TN) (m)
Carthage College (WI) (m)
Case Western Reserve University (OH) (m)
Castleton State College (VT) (m)
Catawba College (NC) (m)
The Catholic University of America (DC) (m)
Cazenovia College (NY) (m)
Cedarville University (OH) (m)
Centenary College (NJ) (m)
Centenary College of Louisiana (LA) (m)
Central Christian College of Kansas (KS) (m)
Central College (IA) (m)
Central Connecticut State University (CT) (m)
Central Methodist College (MO) (m)
Central Michigan University (MI) (m)
Central Missouri State University (MO) (m)
Central Washington University (WA) (m)
Centre College (KY) (m)
Chapman University (CA) (m)
Charleston Southern University (SC) (m)
Chicago State University (IL) (m)
Chowan College (NC) (m)
Christian Brothers University (TN) (m)
Christopher Newport University (VA) (m)
The Citadel, The Military College of South Carolina (SC) (m)
Claflin University (SC) (m)
Claremont McKenna College (CA) (m)
Clarion University of Pennsylvania (PA) (m)
Clark Atlanta University (GA) (m)
Clarke College (IA) (m)

Clarkson University (NY) (m)
Clark University (MA) (m)
Clemson University (SC) (m)
Cleveland State University (OH) (m)
Coastal Carolina University (SC) (m)
Coe College (IA) (m)
Coker College (SC) (m)
Colby College (ME) (m)
Colby-Sawyer College (NH) (m)
College Misericordia (PA) (m)
College of Charleston (SC) (m)
College of Mount St. Joseph (OH) (m)
The College of New Jersey (NJ) (m)
The College of Saint Rose (NY) (m)
The College of St. Scholastica (MN) (m)
College of Staten Island of the City University
   of New York (NY) (m)
College of the Holy Cross (MA) (m)
College of the Ozarks (MO) (m)
College of the Southwest (NM) (m)
The College of William and Mary (VA) (m)
The College of Wooster (OH) (m)
Colorado School of Mines (CO) (m)
Colorado State University-Pueblo (CO) (m)
Columbia College (NY) (m)
Columbia Union College (MD) (m)
Columbus State University (GA) (m)
Concord College (WV) (m)
Concordia College (MN) (m)
Concordia College (NY) (m)
Concordia University (CA) (m)
Concordia University (IL) (m)
Concordia University (MI) (m)
Concordia University (NE) (m)
Concordia University (OR) (m)
Concordia University at Austin (TX) (m)
Concordia University, St. Paul (MN) (m)
Concordia University Wisconsin (WI) (m)
Coppin State University (MD) (m)
Cornell College (IA) (m)
Cornell University (NY) (m)
Creighton University (NE) (m)
Crown College (MN) (m)
Culver-Stockton College (MO) (m)
Cumberland College (KY) (m)
Cumberland University (TN) (m)
Curry College (MA) (m)
Dakota State University (SD) (m)
Dakota Wesleyan University (SD) (m)
Dallas Baptist University (TX) (m)
Dana College (NE) (m)
Daniel Webster College (NH) (m)
Dartmouth College (NH) (m)
Davidson College (NC) (m)
Davis & Elkins College (WV) (m)
Defiance College (OH) (m)
Delaware State University (DE) (m)
Delaware Valley College (PA) (m)
Delta State University (MS) (m)
Denison University (OH) (m)
DePauw University (IN) (m)
DeSales University (PA) (m)
Dickinson College (PA) (m)
Dickinson State University (ND) (m)
Doane College (NE) (m)
Dominican College (NY) (m)
Dominican University (IL) (m)
Dordt College (IA) (m)
Dowling College (NY) (m)
Drew University (NJ) (m)
Duke University (NC) (m)
Duquesne University (PA) (m)
D'Youville College (NY) (m)
Earlham College (IN) (m)
East Carolina University (NC) (m)

East Central University (OK) (m)
Eastern Connecticut State University (CT)
   (m)
Eastern Illinois University (IL) (m)
Eastern Kentucky University (KY) (m)
Eastern Mennonite University (VA) (m)
Eastern Michigan University (MI) (m)
Eastern Nazarene College (MA) (m)
Eastern New Mexico University (NM) (m)
Eastern Oregon University (OR) (m)
Eastern University (PA) (m)
East Stroudsburg University of Pennsylvania
   (PA) (m)
East Tennessee State University (TN) (m)
East Texas Baptist University (TX) (m)
Eckerd College (FL) (m)
Edgewood College (WI) (m)
Edward Waters College (FL) (m)
Elizabeth City State University (NC) (m)
Elizabethtown College (PA) (m)
Elmhurst College (IL) (m)
Elon University (NC) (m)
Embry-Riddle Aeronautical University (FL)
   (m)
Emerson College (MA) (m)
Emmanuel College (GA) (m)
Emory & Henry College (VA) (m)
Emory University (GA) (m)
Emporia State University (KS) (m)
Endicott College (MA) (m)
Erskine College (SC) (m)
Eureka College (IL) (m)
Evangel University (MO) (m)
Fairfield University (CT) (m)
Fairleigh Dickinson University, College at
   Florham (NJ) (m)
Fairmont State University (WV) (m)
Farmingdale State University of New York
   (NY) (m)
Faulkner University (AL) (m)
Felician College (NJ) (m)
Ferrum College (VA) (m)
Fisher College (MA) (m)
Fisk University (TN) (m)
Fitchburg State College (MA) (m)
Flagler College (FL) (m)
Florida Agricultural and Mechanical
   University (FL) (m)
Florida Atlantic University (FL) (m)
Florida Gulf Coast University (FL) (m)
Florida Institute of Technology (FL) (m)
Florida International University (FL) (m)
Florida Memorial College (FL) (m)
Florida Southern College (FL) (m)
Florida State University (FL) (m)
Fontbonne University (MO) (m)
Fordham University (NY) (m)
Fort Hays State University (KS) (m)
Framingham State College (MA) (m)
The Franciscan University (IA) (m)
Francis Marion University (SC) (m)
Franklin and Marshall College (PA) (m)
Franklin College (IN) (m)
Franklin Pierce College (NH) (m)
Freed-Hardeman University (TN) (m)
Friends University (KS) (m)
Frostburg State University (MD) (m)
Furman University (SC) (m)
Gallaudet University (DC) (m)
Gannon University (PA) (m)
Gardner-Webb University (NC) (m)
Geneva College (PA) (m)
George Fox University (OR) (m)
George Mason University (VA) (m)
Georgetown College (KY) (m)

Georgetown University (DC) (m)
The George Washington University (DC) (m)
Georgia College & State University (GA) (m)
Georgia Institute of Technology (GA) (m)
Georgia Southern University (GA) (m)
Georgia Southwestern State University (GA)
   (m)
Georgia State University (GA) (m)
Gettysburg College (PA) (m)
Gonzaga University (WA) (m)
Gordon College (MA) (m)
Goshen College (IN) (m)
Grace College (IN) (m)
Graceland University (IA) (m)
Grambling State University (LA) (m)
Grand Canyon University (AZ) (m)
Grand Valley State University (MI) (m)
Grand View College (IA) (m)
Greensboro College (NC) (m)
Greenville College (IL) (m)
Grinnell College (IA) (m)
Grove City College (PA) (m)
Guilford College (NC) (m)
Gustavus Adolphus College (MN) (m)
Gwynedd-Mercy College (PA) (m)
Hamilton College (NY) (m)
Hamline University (MN) (m)
Hampden-Sydney College (VA) (m)
Hannibal-LaGrange College (MO) (m)
Hanover College (IN) (m)
Harding University (AR) (m)
Hardin-Simmons University (TX) (m)
Harris-Stowe State College (MO) (m)
Hartwick College (NY) (m)
Harvard University (MA) (m)
Hastings College (NE) (m)
Haverford College (PA) (m)
Hawai'i Pacific University (HI) (m)
Heidelberg College (OH) (m)
Henderson State University (AR) (m)
Hendrix College (AR) (m)
High Point University (NC) (m)
Hilbert College (NY) (m)
Hillsdale College (MI) (m)
Hiram College (OH) (m)
Hofstra University (NY) (m)
Hope College (MI) (m)
Houston Baptist University (TX) (m)
Howard Payne University (TX) (m)
Huntingdon College (AL) (m)
Huntington College (IN) (m)
Husson College (ME) (m)
Huston-Tillotson College (TX) (m)
Illinois College (IL) (m)
Illinois Institute of Technology (IL) (m)
Illinois State University (IL) (m)
Illinois Wesleyan University (IL) (m)
Indiana Institute of Technology (IN) (m)
Indiana State University (IN) (m)
Indiana University Bloomington (IN) (m)
Indiana University Northwest (IN) (m)
Indiana University of Pennsylvania (PA) (m)
Indiana University–Purdue University Fort
   Wayne (IN) (m)
Indiana University Southeast (IN) (m)
Indiana Wesleyan University (IN) (m)
Iona College (NY) (m)
Iowa Wesleyan College (IA) (m)
Ithaca College (NY) (m)
Jackson State University (MS) (m)
Jacksonville State University (AL) (m)
Jacksonville University (FL) (m)
James Madison University (VA) (m)
Jamestown College (ND) (m)
Jarvis Christian College (TX) (m)

John Carroll University (OH) (m)
John Jay College of Criminal Justice of the City University of New York (NY) (m)
The Johns Hopkins University (MD) (m)
Johnson & Wales University (CO) (m)
Johnson & Wales University (RI) (m)
Judson College (IL) (m)
Juniata College (PA) (m)
Kalamazoo College (MI) (m)
Kansas State University (KS) (m)
Kansas Wesleyan University (KS) (m)
Kean University (NJ) (m)
Keene State College (NH) (m)
Kennesaw State University (GA) (m)
Kent State University (OH) (m)
Kentucky State University (KY) (m)
Kentucky Wesleyan College (KY) (m)
Kenyon College (OH) (m)
Keuka College (NY) (m)
King College (TN) (m)
King's College (PA) (m)
Knox College (IL) (m)
Kutztown University of Pennsylvania (PA) (m)
Lafayette College (PA) (m)
LaGrange College (GA) (m)
Lake Erie College (OH) (m)
Lakeland College (WI) (m)
Lamar University (TX) (m)
Lambuth University (TN) (m)
Lander University (SC) (m)
Lane College (TN) (m)
La Roche College (PA) (m)
La Salle University (PA) (m)
Lawrence University (WI) (m)
Lebanon Valley College (PA) (m)
Lee University (TN) (m)
Lehigh University (PA) (m)
Lehman College of the City University of New York (NY) (m)
Le Moyne College (NY) (m)
LeMoyne-Owen College (TN) (m)
Lenoir-Rhyne College (NC) (m)
LeTourneau University (TX) (m)
Lewis & Clark College (OR) (m)
Lewis-Clark State College (ID) (m)
Lewis University (IL) (m)
Liberty University (VA) (m)
Limestone College (SC) (m)
Lincoln Memorial University (TN) (m)
Lincoln University (MO) (m)
Lincoln University (PA) (m)
Lindenwood University (MO) (m)
Lindsey Wilson College (KY) (m)
Linfield College (OR) (m)
Lipscomb University (TN) (m)
Lock Haven University of Pennsylvania (PA) (m)
Long Island University, Brooklyn Campus (NY) (m)
Long Island University, C.W. Post Campus (NY) (m)
Longwood University (VA) (m)
Loras College (IA) (m)
Louisiana College (LA) (m)
Louisiana State University and Agricultural and Mechanical College (LA) (m)
Louisiana State University in Shreveport (LA) (m)
Louisiana Tech University (LA) (m)
Loyola Marymount University (CA) (m)
Loyola University New Orleans (LA) (m)
Lubbock Christian University (TX) (m)
Luther College (IA) (m)
Lynchburg College (VA) (m)

Lyndon State College (VT) (m)
Lynn University (FL) (m)
Lyon College (AR) (m)
Macalester College (MN) (m)
MacMurray College (IL) (m)
Madonna University (MI) (m)
Malone College (OH) (m)
Manchester College (IN) (m)
Manhattan College (NY) (m)
Manhattanville College (NY) (m)
Mansfield University of Pennsylvania (PA) (m)
Maranatha Baptist Bible College (WI) (m)
Marian College (IN) (m)
Marian College of Fond du Lac (WI) (m)
Marietta College (OH) (m)
Marist College (NY) (m)
Marshall University (WV) (m)
Mars Hill College (NC) (m)
Martin Luther College (MN) (m)
Martin Methodist College (TN) (m)
Maryville College (TN) (m)
Maryville University of Saint Louis (MO) (m)
University of Mary Washington (VA) (m)
Marywood University (PA) (m)
Massachusetts College of Liberal Arts (MA) (m)
Massachusetts Institute of Technology (MA) (m)
Massachusetts Maritime Academy (MA) (m)
The Master's College and Seminary (CA) (m)
Mayville State University (ND) (m)
McDaniel College (MD) (m)
McKendree College (IL) (m)
McMurry University (TX) (m)
McNeese State University (LA) (m)
Medaille College (NY) (m)
Menlo College (CA) (m)
Mercer University (GA) (m)
Mercy College (NY) (m)
Mercyhurst College (PA) (m)
Merrimack College (MA) (m)
Mesa State College (CO) (m)
Messiah College (PA) (m)
Methodist College (NC) (m)
Metropolitan State College of Denver (CO) (m)
Miami University (OH) (m)
Michigan State University (MI) (m)
MidAmerica Nazarene University (KS) (m)
Mid-Continent College (KY) (m)
Middlebury College (VT) (m)
Middle Tennessee State University (TN) (m)
Midland Lutheran College (NE) (m)
Miles College (AL) (m)
Millersville University of Pennsylvania (PA) (m)
Milligan College (TN) (m)
Millikin University (IL) (m)
Millsaps College (MS) (m)
Milwaukee School of Engineering (WI) (m)
Minnesota State University Mankato (MN) (m)
Minot State University (ND) (m)
Mississippi College (MS) (m)
Mississippi State University (MS) (m)
Mississippi Valley State University (MS) (m)
Missouri Baptist University (MO) (m)
Missouri Southern State University (MO) (m)
Missouri Valley College (MO) (m)
Missouri Western State College (MO) (m)
Molloy College (NY) (m)
Monmouth College (IL) (m)
Monmouth University (NJ) (m)
Montclair State University (NJ) (m)

Montreat College (NC) (m)
Moravian College (PA) (m)
Morehead State University (KY) (m)
Morningside College (IA) (m)
Morris College (SC) (m)
Mount Marty College (SD) (m)
Mount Mercy College (IA) (m)
Mount Olive College (NC) (m)
Mount Saint Mary College (NY) (m)
Mount Saint Mary's University (MD) (m)
Mount Union College (OH) (m)
Mount Vernon Nazarene University (OH) (m)
Muhlenberg College (PA) (m)
Murray State University (KY) (m)
Muskingum College (OH) (m)
National American University (SD) (m)
Nebraska Wesleyan University (NE) (m)
Neumann College (PA) (m)
Newberry College (SC) (m)
New England College (NH) (m)
New Jersey City University (NJ) (m)
New Jersey Institute of Technology (NJ) (m)
Newman University (KS) (m)
New Mexico Highlands University (NM) (m)
New Mexico State University (NM) (m)
New York Institute of Technology (NY) (m)
Niagara University (NY) (m)
Nicholls State University (LA) (m)
Nichols College (MA) (m)
Norfolk State University (VA) (m)
North Carolina Agricultural and Technical State University (NC) (m)
North Carolina State University (NC) (m)
North Carolina Wesleyan College (NC) (m)
North Central College (IL) (m)
North Dakota State University (ND) (m)
Northeastern State University (OK) (m)
Northeastern University (MA) (m)
Northern Illinois University (IL) (m)
Northern Kentucky University (KY) (m)
Northern State University (SD) (m)
North Georgia College & State University (GA) (m)
North Greenville College (SC) (m)
Northland College (WI) (m)
North Park University (IL) (m)
Northwestern College (IA) (m)
Northwestern College (MN) (m)
Northwestern Oklahoma State University (OK) (m)
Northwestern State University of Louisiana (LA) (m)
Northwestern University (IL) (m)
Northwest Missouri State University (MO) (m)
Northwest Nazarene University (ID) (m)
Northwood University (MI) (m)
Northwood University, Florida Campus (FL) (m)
Northwood University, Texas Campus (TX) (m)
Norwich University (VT) (m)
Nova Southeastern University (FL) (m)
Nyack College (NY) (m)
Oakland City University (IN) (m)
Oakland University (MI) (m)
Oberlin College (OH) (m)
Occidental College (CA) (m)
Oglethorpe University (GA) (m)
Ohio Dominican University (OH) (m)
Ohio Northern University (OH) (m)
The Ohio State University (OH) (m)
Ohio University (OH) (m)
Ohio Valley College (WV) (m)

Ohio Wesleyan University (OH) (m)
Oklahoma Baptist University (OK) (m)
Oklahoma City University (OK) (m)
Oklahoma Panhandle State University (OK) (m)
Oklahoma State University (OK) (m)
Oklahoma Wesleyan University (OK) (m)
Old Dominion University (VA) (m)
Olivet College (MI) (m)
Olivet Nazarene University (IL) (m)
Oral Roberts University (OK) (m)
Oregon Institute of Technology (OR) (m)
Oregon State University (OR) (m)
Ottawa University (KS) (m)
Otterbein College (OH) (m)
Ouachita Baptist University (AR) (m)
Pace University (NY) (m)
Pacific Lutheran University (WA) (m)
Pacific University (OR) (m)
Paine College (GA) (m)
Park University (MO) (m)
Paul Quinn College (TX) (m)
The Pennsylvania State University Altoona College (PA) (m)
The Pennsylvania State University at Erie, The Behrend College (PA) (m)
The Pennsylvania State University University Park Campus (PA) (m)
Pepperdine University (CA) (m)
Peru State College (NE) (m)
Pfeiffer University (NC) (m)
Philadelphia Biblical University (PA) (m)
Philadelphia University (PA) (m)
Piedmont College (GA) (m)
Pikeville College (KY) (m)
Pittsburg State University (KS) (m)
Pitzer College (CA) (m)
Plymouth State University (NH) (m)
Point Loma Nazarene University (CA) (m)
Point Park University (PA) (m)
Polytechnic University, Brooklyn Campus (NY) (m)
Pomona College (CA) (m)
Prairie View A&M University (TX) (m)
Presbyterian College (SC) (m)
Presentation College (SD) (m)
Princeton University (NJ) (m)
Principia College (IL) (m)
Purdue University (IN) (m)
Purdue University North Central (IN) (m)
Queens College of the City University of New York (NY) (m)
Quincy University (IL) (m)
Quinnipiac University (CT) (m)
Radford University (VA) (m)
Ramapo College of New Jersey (NJ) (m)
Randolph-Macon College (VA) (m)
Regis University (CO) (m)
Rensselaer Polytechnic Institute (NY) (m)
Rhode Island College (RI) (m)
Rhodes College (TN) (m)
Rice University (TX) (m)
The Richard Stockton College of New Jersey (NJ) (m)
Rider University (NJ) (m)
Ripon College (WI) (m)
Rivier College (NH) (m)
Roanoke College (VA) (m)
Robert Morris College (IL) (m)
Rochester Institute of Technology (NY) (m)
Rockford College (IL) (m)
Rockhurst University (MO) (m)
Roger Williams University (RI) (m)
Rollins College (FL) (m)

Rose-Hulman Institute of Technology (IN) (m)
Rowan University (NJ) (m)
Rust College (MS) (m)
Rutgers, The State University of New Jersey, Camden (NJ) (m)
Rutgers, The State University of New Jersey, Newark (NJ) (m)
Rutgers, The State University of New Jersey, New Brunswick/Piscataway (NJ) (m)
Sacred Heart University (CT) (m)
Saginaw Valley State University (MI) (m)
St. Ambrose University (IA) (m)
St. Andrews Presbyterian College (NC) (m)
Saint Anselm College (NH) (m)
Saint Augustine's College (NC) (m)
St. Bonaventure University (NY) (m)
St. Cloud State University (MN) (m)
St. Edward's University (TX) (m)
St. Francis College (NY) (m)
St. Gregory's University (OK) (m)
St. John Fisher College (NY) (m)
Saint John's University (MN) (m)
St. John's University (NY) (m)
Saint Joseph's College (IN) (m)
Saint Joseph's College of Maine (ME) (m)
St. Joseph's College, Suffolk Campus (NY) (m)
Saint Joseph's University (PA) (m)
St. Lawrence University (NY) (m)
Saint Leo University (FL) (m)
Saint Louis University (MO) (m)
Saint Martin's College (WA) (m)
Saint Mary's College of California (CA) (m)
St. Mary's College of Maryland (MD) (m)
Saint Mary's University of Minnesota (MN) (m)
St. Mary's University of San Antonio (TX) (m)
Saint Michael's College (VT) (m)
St. Norbert College (WI) (m)
St. Olaf College (MN) (m)
Saint Paul's College (VA) (m)
Saint Peter's College (NJ) (m)
St. Thomas Aquinas College (NY) (m)
St. Thomas University (FL) (m)
Saint Vincent College (PA) (m)
Saint Xavier University (IL) (m)
Salem International University (WV) (m)
Salem State College (MA) (m)
Salisbury University (MD) (m)
Salve Regina University (RI) (m)
Samford University (AL) (m)
Sam Houston State University (TX) (m)
San Diego State University (CA) (m)
San Francisco State University (CA) (m)
San Jose State University (CA) (m)
Santa Clara University (CA) (m)
Savannah College of Art and Design (GA) (m)
Savannah State University (GA) (m)
Schreiner University (TX) (m)
Seton Hall University (NJ) (m)
Seton Hill University (PA) (m)
Shawnee State University (OH) (m)
Shaw University (NC) (m)
Shenandoah University (VA) (m)
Shepherd University (WV) (m)
Shippensburg University of Pennsylvania (PA) (m)
Shorter College (GA) (m)
Siena College (NY) (m)
Siena Heights University (MI) (m)
Simpson College (IA) (m)
Si Tanka Huron University (SD) (m)

Skidmore College (NY) (m)
Slippery Rock University of Pennsylvania (PA) (m)
Sonoma State University (CA) (m)
South Dakota State University (SD) (m)
Southeastern Louisiana University (LA) (m)
Southeastern Oklahoma State University (OK) (m)
Southeast Missouri State University (MO) (m)
Southern Arkansas University–Magnolia (AR) (m)
Southern Connecticut State University (CT) (m)
Southern Illinois University Carbondale (IL) (m)
Southern Illinois University Edwardsville (IL) (m)
Southern Nazarene University (OK) (m)
Southern New Hampshire University (NH) (m)
Southern Polytechnic State University (GA) (m)
Southern University and Agricultural and Mechanical College (LA) (m)
Southern Utah University (UT) (m)
Southern Vermont College (VT) (m)
Southern Virginia University (VA) (m)
Southern Wesleyan University (SC) (m)
Southwest Baptist University (MO) (m)
Southwestern Assemblies of God University (TX) (m)
Southwestern Oklahoma State University (OK) (m)
Southwestern University (TX) (m)
Southwest Minnesota State University (MN) (m)
Southwest Missouri State University (MO) (m)
Spalding University (KY) (m)
Spring Arbor University (MI) (m)
Springfield College (MA) (m)
Spring Hill College (AL) (m)
Stanford University (CA) (m)
State University of New York at Binghamton (NY) (m)
State University of New York at New Paltz (NY) (m)
State University of New York at Oswego (NY) (m)
State University of New York at Plattsburgh (NY) (m)
State University of New York College at Brockport (NY) (m)
State University of New York College at Cortland (NY) (m)
State University of New York College at Fredonia (NY) (m)
State University of New York College at Old Westbury (NY) (m)
State University of New York College at Oneonta (NY) (m)
State University of New York Institute of Technology (NY) (m)
State University of New York Maritime College (NY) (m)
State University of West Georgia (GA) (m)
Sterling College (KS) (m)
Stetson University (FL) (m)
Stevens Institute of Technology (NJ) (m)
Stillman College (AL) (m)
Stonehill College (MA) (m)
Stony Brook University, State University of New York (NY) (m)
Suffolk University (MA) (m)

Sul Ross State University (TX) (m)
Susquehanna University (PA) (m)
Swarthmore College (PA) (m)
Tabor College (KS) (m)
Tarleton State University (TX) (m)
Taylor University (IN) (m)
Teikyo Post University (CT) (m)
Temple University (PA) (m)
Tennessee Technological University (TN) (m)
Tennessee Wesleyan College (TN) (m)
Texas A&M University (TX) (m)
Texas A&M University–Corpus Christi (TX) (m)
Texas A&M University–Kingsville (TX) (m)
Texas Christian University (TX) (m)
Texas College (TX) (m)
Texas Lutheran University (TX) (m)
Texas Southern University (TX) (m)
Texas State University-San Marcos (TX) (m)
Texas Tech University (TX) (m)
Texas Wesleyan University (TX) (m)
Thiel College (PA) (m)
Thomas College (ME) (m)
Thomas More College (KY) (m)
Thomas University (GA) (m)
Tiffin University (OH) (m)
Towson University (MD) (m)
Transylvania University (KY) (m)
Trevecca Nazarene University (TN) (m)
Trinity Christian College (IL) (m)
Trinity College (CT) (m)
Trinity International University (IL) (m)
Trinity University (TX) (m)
Tri-State University (IN) (m)
Troy State University (AL) (m)
Truman State University (MO) (m)
Tufts University (MA) (m)
Tulane University (LA) (m)
Tusculum College (TN) (m)
Tuskegee University (AL) (m)
Union College (KY) (m)
Union College (NY) (m)
Union University (TN) (m)
United States Air Force Academy (CO) (m)
United States Coast Guard Academy (CT) (m)
United States Merchant Marine Academy (NY) (m)
United States Military Academy (NY) (m)
United States Naval Academy (MD) (m)
University at Albany, State University of New York (NY) (m)
University at Buffalo, The State University of New York (NY) (m)
The University of Akron (OH) (m)
The University of Alabama (AL) (m)
The University of Alabama at Birmingham (AL) (m)
The University of Alabama in Huntsville (AL) (m)
The University of Arizona (AZ) (m)
University of Arkansas (AR) (m)
University of Arkansas at Little Rock (AR) (m)
University of Arkansas at Monticello (AR) (m)
University of Arkansas at Pine Bluff (AR) (m)
University of Bridgeport (CT) (m)
University of California, Berkeley (CA) (m)
University of California, Davis (CA) (m)
University of California, Irvine (CA) (m)
University of California, Los Angeles (CA) (m)
University of California, Riverside (CA) (m)
University of California, San Diego (CA) (m)

University of California, Santa Barbara (CA) (m)
University of Central Arkansas (AR) (m)
University of Central Florida (FL) (m)
University of Central Oklahoma (OK) (m)
University of Charleston (WV) (m)
University of Chicago (IL) (m)
University of Cincinnati (OH) (m)
University of Connecticut (CT) (m)
University of Dallas (TX) (m)
University of Dayton (OH) (m)
University of Delaware (DE) (m)
University of Detroit Mercy (MI) (m)
University of Dubuque (IA) (m)
University of Evansville (IN) (m)
The University of Findlay (OH) (m)
University of Florida (FL) (m)
University of Georgia (GA) (m)
University of Hartford (CT) (m)
University of Hawaii at Hilo (HI) (m)
University of Hawaii at Manoa (HI) (m)
University of Houston (TX) (m)
University of Illinois at Chicago (IL) (m)
University of Illinois at Urbana–Champaign (IL) (m)
University of Indianapolis (IN) (m)
The University of Iowa (IA) (m)
University of Kansas (KS) (m)
University of Kentucky (KY) (m)
University of La Verne (CA) (m)
University of Louisiana at Lafayette (LA) (m)
University of Louisiana at Monroe (LA) (m)
University of Louisville (KY) (m)
University of Maine (ME) (m)
University of Maine at Farmington (ME) (m)
University of Maine at Presque Isle (ME) (m)
University of Mary (ND) (m)
University of Mary Hardin-Baylor (TX) (m)
University of Maryland, Baltimore County (MD) (m)
University of Maryland, College Park (MD) (m)
University of Maryland Eastern Shore (MD) (m)
University of Massachusetts Amherst (MA) (m)
University of Massachusetts Boston (MA) (m)
University of Massachusetts Dartmouth (MA) (m)
University of Massachusetts Lowell (MA) (m)
The University of Memphis (TN) (m)
University of Miami (FL) (m)
University of Michigan (MI) (m)
University of Minnesota, Crookston (MN) (m)
University of Minnesota, Duluth (MN) (m)
University of Minnesota, Morris (MN) (m)
University of Minnesota, Twin Cities Campus (MN) (m)
University of Mississippi (MS) (m)
University of Missouri–Columbia (MO) (m)
University of Missouri–Rolla (MO) (m)
University of Missouri–St. Louis (MO) (m)
University of Mobile (AL) (m)
University of Montevallo (AL) (m)
University of Nebraska at Kearney (NE) (m)
University of Nebraska at Omaha (NE) (m)
University of Nebraska–Lincoln (NE) (m)
University of Nevada, Las Vegas (NV) (m)
University of Nevada, Reno (NV) (m)
University of New Haven (CT) (m)
University of New Mexico (NM) (m)
University of New Orleans (LA) (m)

University of North Alabama (AL) (m)
The University of North Carolina at Asheville (NC) (m)
The University of North Carolina at Chapel Hill (NC) (m)
The University of North Carolina at Charlotte (NC) (m)
The University of North Carolina at Greensboro (NC) (m)
The University of North Carolina at Pembroke (NC) (m)
The University of North Carolina at Wilmington (NC) (m)
University of North Dakota (ND) (m)
University of Northern Colorado (CO) (m)
University of Northern Iowa (IA) (m)
University of North Florida (FL) (m)
University of Notre Dame (IN) (m)
University of Oklahoma (OK) (m)
University of Pennsylvania (PA) (m)
University of Pittsburgh (PA) (m)
University of Pittsburgh at Bradford (PA) (m)
University of Pittsburgh at Greensburg (PA) (m)
University of Pittsburgh at Johnstown (PA) (m)
University of Portland (OR) (m)
University of Puerto Rico at Bayamón (PR) (m)
University of Puerto Rico at Humacao (PR) (m)
University of Puerto Rico, Cayey University College (PR) (m)
University of Puerto Rico, Mayagüez Campus (PR) (m)
University of Puerto Rico, Río Piedras (PR) (m)
University of Puget Sound (WA) (m)
University of Redlands (CA) (m)
University of Rhode Island (RI) (m)
University of Richmond (VA) (m)
University of Rio Grande (OH) (m)
University of Rochester (NY) (m)
University of St. Francis (IL) (m)
University of Saint Francis (IN) (m)
University of Saint Mary (KS) (m)
University of St. Thomas (MN) (m)
University of San Diego (CA) (m)
University of San Francisco (CA) (m)
University of Science and Arts of Oklahoma (OK) (m)
The University of Scranton (PA) (m)
University of Sioux Falls (SD) (m)
University of South Alabama (AL) (m)
University of South Carolina (SC) (m)
University of South Carolina Aiken (SC) (m)
University of South Carolina Spartanburg (SC) (m)
The University of South Dakota (SD) (m)
University of Southern California (CA) (m)
University of Southern Indiana (IN) (m)
University of Southern Maine (ME) (m)
University of Southern Mississippi (MS) (m)
University of South Florida (FL) (m)
The University of Tampa (FL) (m)
The University of Tennessee (TN) (m)
The University of Tennessee at Martin (TN) (m)
The University of Texas at Arlington (TX) (m)
The University of Texas at Austin (TX) (m)
The University of Texas at Dallas (TX) (m)
The University of Texas at San Antonio (TX) (m)

The University of Texas–Pan American (TX) (m)
University of the Incarnate Word (TX) (m)
University of the Ozarks (AR) (m)
University of the Pacific (CA) (m)
University of the Sciences in Philadelphia (PA) (m)
University of the South (TN) (m)
University of Toledo (OH) (m)
University of Utah (UT) (m)
University of Vermont (VT) (m)
University of Virginia (VA) (m)
The University of Virginia's College at Wise (VA) (m)
University of Washington (WA) (m)
The University of West Alabama (AL) (m)
University of West Florida (FL) (m)
University of Wisconsin–La Crosse (WI) (m)
University of Wisconsin–Milwaukee (WI) (m)
University of Wisconsin–Oshkosh (WI) (m)
University of Wisconsin–Parkside (WI) (m)
University of Wisconsin–Platteville (WI) (m)
University of Wisconsin–Stevens Point (WI) (m)
University of Wisconsin–Stout (WI) (m)
University of Wisconsin–Superior (WI) (m)
University of Wisconsin–Whitewater (WI) (m)
Upper Iowa University (IA) (m)
Urbana University (OH) (m)
Ursinus College (PA) (m)
Utica College (NY) (m)
Valdosta State University (GA) (m)
Valley City State University (ND) (m)
Valparaiso University (IN) (m)
Vanderbilt University (TN) (m)
Vanguard University of Southern California (CA) (m)
Vassar College (NY) (m)
Villa Julie College (MD) (m)
Villanova University (PA) (m)
Virginia Commonwealth University (VA) (m)
Virginia Intermont College (VA) (m)
Virginia Military Institute (VA) (m)
Virginia Polytechnic Institute and State University (VA) (m)
Virginia State University (VA) (m)
Virginia Wesleyan College (VA) (m)
Viterbo University (WI) (m)
Voorhees College (SC) (m)
Wabash College (IN) (m)
Wagner College (NY) (m)
Wake Forest University (NC) (m)
Waldorf College (IA) (m)
Warner Southern College (FL) (m)
Wartburg College (IA) (m)
Washburn University (KS) (m)
Washington & Jefferson College (PA) (m)
Washington and Lee University (VA) (m)
Washington College (MD) (m)
Washington State University (WA) (m)
Washington University in St. Louis (MO) (m)
Wayland Baptist University (TX) (m)
Waynesburg College (PA) (m)
Wayne State College (NE) (m)
Wayne State University (MI) (m)
Webber International University (FL) (m)
Webster University (MO) (m)
Wentworth Institute of Technology (MA) (m)
Wesleyan University (CT) (m)
Wesley College (DE) (m)
West Chester University of Pennsylvania (PA) (m)
Western Baptist College (OR) (m)
Western Carolina University (NC) (m)

Western Connecticut State University (CT) (m)
Western Illinois University (IL) (m)
Western Kentucky University (KY) (m)
Western Michigan University (MI) (m)
Western New England College (MA) (m)
Western Oregon University (OR) (m)
Westfield State College (MA) (m)
West Liberty State College (WV) (m)
Westminster College (MO) (m)
Westminster College (PA) (m)
Westmont College (CA) (m)
West Texas A&M University (TX) (m)
West Virginia State College (WV) (m)
West Virginia University (WV) (m)
West Virginia University Institute of Technology (WV) (m)
West Virginia Wesleyan College (WV) (m)
Wheaton College (IL) (m)
Wheaton College (MA) (m)
Whitman College (WA) (m)
Whittier College (CA) (m)
Whitworth College (WA) (m)
Wichita State University (KS) (m)
Widener University (PA) (m)
Wiley College (TX) (m)
Wilkes University (PA) (m)
Willamette University (OR) (m)
William Carey College (MS) (m)
William Jewell College (MO) (m)
William Paterson University of New Jersey (NJ) (m)
William Penn University (IA) (m)
Williams Baptist College (AR) (m)
Williams College (MA) (m)
Wilmington College (DE) (m)
Wilmington College (OH) (m)
Wingate University (NC) (m)
Winona State University (MN) (m)
Winthrop University (SC) (m)
Wisconsin Lutheran College (WI) (m)
Wittenberg University (OH) (m)
Wofford College (SC) (m)
Worcester Polytechnic Institute (MA) (m)
Worcester State College (MA) (m)
Wright State University (OH) (m)
Xavier University (OH) (m)
Yale University (CT) (m)
York College (NE) (m)
York College of Pennsylvania (PA) (m)
Youngstown State University (OH)(m)

Basketball

Abilene Christian University (TX) (m/w)
Adams State College (CO) (m/w)
Adelphi University (NY) (m/w)
Adrian College (MI) (m/w)
Agnes Scott College (GA) (w)
Alabama Agricultural and Mechanical University (AL) (m/w)
Alabama State University (AL) (m/w)
Albany State University (GA) (m/w)
Albertson College of Idaho (ID) (m/w)
Albertus Magnus College (CT) (m/w)
Albion College (MI) (m/w)
Albright College (PA) (m/w)
Alcorn State University (MS) (m/w)
Alderson-Broaddus College (WV) (m/w)
Alfred University (NY) (m/w)
Alice Lloyd College (KY) (m/w)
Allegheny College (PA) (m/w)
Allen University (SC) (m/w)
Alma College (MI) (m/w)
Alvernia College (PA) (m/w)

Alverno College (WI) (w)
American International College (MA) (m/w)
American University (DC) (m/w)
Amherst College (MA) (m/w)
Anderson College (SC) (m/w)
Anderson University (IN) (m/w)
Angelo State University (TX) (m/w)
Anna Maria College (MA) (m/w)
Appalachian State University (NC) (m/w)
Aquinas College (MI) (m/w)
Arcadia University (PA) (m/w)
Arizona State University (AZ) (m/w)
Arkansas State University (AR) (m/w)
Arkansas Tech University (AR) (m/w)
Armstrong Atlantic State University (GA) (m/w)
Asbury College (KY) (m/w)
Ashland University (OH) (m/w)
Assumption College (MA) (m/w)
Athens State University (AL) (m)
Atlanta Christian College (GA) (m/w)
Auburn University (AL) (m/w)
Auburn University Montgomery (AL) (m/w)
Augsburg College (MN) (m/w)
Augustana College (IL) (m/w)
Augustana College (SD) (m/w)
Augusta State University (GA) (m/w)
Aurora University (IL) (m/w)
Austin College (TX) (m/w)
Austin Peay State University (TN) (m/w)
Averett University (VA) (m/w)
Avila University (MO) (m/w)
Azusa Pacific University (CA) (m/w)
Babson College (MA) (m/w)
Bacone College (OK) (m)
Baker University (KS) (m/w)
Baldwin-Wallace College (OH) (m/w)
Ball State University (IN) (m/w)
Baptist Bible College of Pennsylvania (PA) (m/w)
Barber-Scotia College (NC) (m/w)
Bard College (NY) (m/w)
Barry University (FL) (m/w)
Barton College (NC) (m/w)
Bates College (ME) (m/w)
Baylor University (TX) (m/w)
Bay Path College (MA) (w)
Belhaven College (MS) (m/w)
Bellarmine University (KY) (m/w)
Bellevue University (NE) (m)
Belmont Abbey College (NC) (m/w)
Belmont University (TN) (m/w)
Beloit College (WI) (m/w)
Bemidji State University (MN) (m/w)
Benedict College (SC) (m/w)
Benedictine College (KS) (m/w)
Benedictine University (IL) (m/w)
Bennett College (NC) (w)
Bentley College (MA) (m/w)
Berea College (KY) (m/w)
Bernard M. Baruch College of the City University of New York (NY) (m/w)
Berry College (GA) (m/w)
Bethany College (KS) (m/w)
Bethany College (WV) (m/w)
Bethany College of the Assemblies of God (CA) (m/w)
Bethel College (IN) (m/w)
Bethel College (KS) (m/w)
Bethel College (TN) (m/w)
Bethel University (MN) (m/w)
Bethune-Cookman College (FL) (m/w)
Biola University (CA) (m/w)
Birmingham-Southern College (AL) (m/w)
Blackburn College (IL) (m/w)

Black Hills State University (SD) (m/w)
Bloomfield College (NJ) (m/w)
Bloomsburg University of Pennsylvania (PA) (m/w)
Bluefield College (VA) (m/w)
Bluefield State College (WV) (m/w)
Blue Mountain College (MS) (w)
Bluffton College (OH) (m/w)
Boise State University (ID) (m/w)
Boston College (MA) (m/w)
Boston University (MA) (m/w)
Bowdoin College (ME) (m/w)
Bowie State University (MD) (m/w)
Bowling Green State University (OH) (m/w)
Bradley University (IL) (m/w)
Brandeis University (MA) (m/w)
Brescia University (KY) (m/w)
Brevard College (NC) (m/w)
Brewton-Parker College (GA) (m/w)
Briar Cliff University (IA) (m/w)
Bridgewater College (VA) (m/w)
Bridgewater State College (MA) (m/w)
Brigham Young University (UT) (m/w)
Brigham Young University–Hawaii (HI) (m)
Brooklyn College of the City University of New York (NY) (m/w)
Brown University (RI) (m/w)
Bryan College (TN) (m/w)
Bryant College (RI) (m/w)
Bryn Mawr College (PA) (w)
Bucknell University (PA) (m/w)
Buena Vista University (IA) (m/w)
Buffalo State College, State University of New York (NY) (m/w)
Butler University (IN) (m/w)
Cabrini College (PA) (m/w)
Caldwell College (NJ) (m/w)
California Baptist University (CA) (m/w)
California Institute of Technology (CA) (m/w)
California Lutheran University (CA) (m/w)
California Maritime Academy (CA) (m)
California Polytechnic State University, San Luis Obispo (CA) (m/w)
California State Polytechnic University, Pomona (CA) (m/w)
California State University, Bakersfield (CA) (m/w)
California State University, Chico (CA) (m/w)
California State University, Dominguez Hills (CA) (m/w)
California State University, Fresno (CA) (m/w)
California State University, Fullerton (CA) (m/w)
California State University, Hayward (CA) (m/w)
California State University, Long Beach (CA) (m/w)
California State University, Los Angeles (CA) (m/w)
California State University, Monterey Bay (CA) (m/w)
California State University, Northridge (CA) (m/w)
California State University, Sacramento (CA) (m/w)
California State University, San Bernardino (CA) (m/w)
California State University, Stanislaus (CA) (m/w)
California University of Pennsylvania (PA) (m/w)
Calumet College of Saint Joseph (IN) (m/w)
Calvin College (MI) (m/w)

Cameron University (OK) (m/w)
Campbellsville University (KY) (m/w)
Campbell University (NC) (m/w)
Canisius College (NY) (m/w)
Capital University (OH) (m/w)
Cardinal Stritch University (WI) (m/w)
Carleton College (MN) (m/w)
Carlow College (PA) (w)
Carnegie Mellon University (PA) (m/w)
Carroll College (MT) (m/w)
Carroll College (WI) (m/w)
Carson-Newman College (TN) (m/w)
Carthage College (WI) (m/w)
Cascade College (OR) (m/w)
Case Western Reserve University (OH) (m/w)
Castleton State College (VT) (m/w)
Catawba College (NC) (m/w)
The Catholic University of America (DC) (m/w)
Cazenovia College (NY) (m/w)
Cedar Crest College (PA) (w)
Cedarville University (OH) (m/w)
Centenary College (NJ) (m/w)
Centenary College of Louisiana (LA) (m/w)
Central Christian College of Kansas (KS) (m/w)
Central College (IA) (m/w)
Central Connecticut State University (CT) (m/w)
Central Methodist College (MO) (m/w)
Central Michigan University (MI) (m/w)
Central Missouri State University (MO) (m/w)
Central Washington University (WA) (m/w)
Centre College (KY) (m/w)
Chadron State College (NE) (m/w)
Chaminade University of Honolulu (HI) (m)
Chapman University (CA) (m/w)
Charleston Southern University (SC) (m/w)
Chatham College (PA) (w)
Chestnut Hill College (PA) (m/w)
Cheyney University of Pennsylvania (PA) (m/w)
Chicago State University (IL) (m/w)
Chowan College (NC) (m/w)
Christian Brothers University (TN) (m/w)
Christian Heritage College (CA) (m/w)
Christopher Newport University (VA) (m/w)
The Citadel, The Military College of South Carolina (SC) (m)
City College of the City University of New York (NY) (m/w)
Claflin University (SC) (m/w)
Claremont McKenna College (CA) (m/w)
Clarion University of Pennsylvania (PA) (m/w)
Clark Atlanta University (GA) (m/w)
Clarke College (IA) (m/w)
Clarkson University (NY) (m/w)
Clark University (MA) (m/w)
Clayton College & State University (GA) (m/w)
Clemson University (SC) (m/w)
Cleveland State University (OH) (m/w)
Coastal Carolina University (SC) (m/w)
Coe College (IA) (m/w)
Coker College (SC) (m/w)
Colby College (ME) (m/w)
Colby-Sawyer College (NH) (m/w)
Colgate University (NY) (m/w)
College Misericordia (PA) (m/w)
College of Charleston (SC) (m/w)
College of Mount St. Joseph (OH) (m/w)
College of Mount Saint Vincent (NY) (m/w)
The College of New Jersey (NJ) (m/w)

The College of New Rochelle (NY) (w)
College of Notre Dame of Maryland (MD) (w)
College of Saint Benedict (MN) (w)
College of St. Catherine (MN) (w)
College of Saint Elizabeth (NJ) (w)
College of St. Joseph (VT) (m/w)
College of Saint Mary (NE) (w)
The College of Saint Rose (NY) (m/w)
The College of St. Scholastica (MN) (m/w)
College of Staten Island of the City University of New York (NY) (m/w)
College of the Holy Cross (MA) (m/w)
College of the Ozarks (MO) (m/w)
The College of William and Mary (VA) (m/w)
The College of Wooster (OH) (m/w)
Colorado Christian University (CO) (m/w)
The Colorado College (CO) (m/w)
Colorado School of Mines (CO) (m/w)
Colorado State University (CO) (m/w)
Colorado State University-Pueblo (CO) (m/w)
Columbia College (MO) (m/w)
Columbia College (NY) (m/w)
Columbia Union College (MD) (m/w)
Columbus State University (GA) (m/w)
Concord College (WV) (m/w)
Concordia College (MN) (m/w)
Concordia College (NY) (m/w)
Concordia University (CA) (m/w)
Concordia University (IL) (m/w)
Concordia University (MI) (m/w)
Concordia University (NE) (m/w)
Concordia University (OR) (m/w)
Concordia University at Austin (TX) (m/w)
Concordia University, St. Paul (MN) (m/w)
Concordia University Wisconsin (WI) (m/w)
Connecticut College (CT) (m/w)
Converse College (SC) (w)
Coppin State University (MD) (m/w)
Cornell College (IA) (m/w)
Cornell University (NY) (m/w)
Cornerstone University (MI) (m/w)
Covenant College (GA) (m/w)
Creighton University (NE) (m/w)
Crown College (MN) (m/w)
Culver-Stockton College (MO) (m/w)
Cumberland College (KY) (m/w)
Cumberland University (TN) (m/w)
Curry College (MA) (m/w)
Daemen College (NY) (m/w)
Dakota State University (SD) (m/w)
Dakota Wesleyan University (SD) (m/w)
Dana College (NE) (m/w)
Daniel Webster College (NH) (m/w)
Dartmouth College (NH) (m/w)
Davenport University (MI) (m/w)
Davidson College (NC) (m/w)
Davis & Elkins College (WV) (m/w)
Defiance College (OH) (m/w)
Delaware State University (DE) (m/w)
Delaware Valley College (PA) (m/w)
Delta State University (MS) (m/w)
Denison University (OH) (m/w)
DePaul University (IL) (m/w)
DePauw University (IN) (m/w)
DeSales University (PA) (m/w)
Dickinson College (PA) (m/w)
Dickinson State University (ND) (m/w)
Dillard University (LA) (m)
Doane College (NE) (m/w)
Dominican College (NY) (m/w)
Dominican University (IL) (m/w)

Dominican University of California (CA) (m/w)
Dordt College (IA) (m/w)
Dowling College (NY) (m/w)
Drake University (IA) (m/w)
Drew University (NJ) (m/w)
Drexel University (PA) (m/w)
Drury University (MO) (m/w)
Duke University (NC) (m/w)
Duquesne University (PA) (m/w)
D'Youville College (NY) (m/w)
Earlham College (IN) (m/w)
East Carolina University (NC) (m/w)
East Central University (OK) (m/w)
Eastern Connecticut State University (CT) (m/w)
Eastern Illinois University (IL) (m/w)
Eastern Kentucky University (KY) (m/w)
Eastern Mennonite University (VA) (m/w)
Eastern Michigan University (MI) (m/w)
Eastern Nazarene College (MA) (m/w)
Eastern New Mexico University (NM) (m/w)
Eastern Oregon University (OR) (m/w)
Eastern University (PA) (m/w)
Eastern Washington University (WA) (m/w)
East Stroudsburg University of Pennsylvania (PA) (m/w)
East Tennessee State University (TN) (m/w)
East Texas Baptist University (TX) (m/w)
Eckerd College (FL) (m/w)
Edgewood College (WI) (m/w)
Edinboro University of Pennsylvania (PA) (m/w)
Edward Waters College (FL) (m/w)
Elizabeth City State University (NC) (m/w)
Elizabethtown College (PA) (m/w)
Elmhurst College (IL) (m)
Elmira College (NY) (m/w)
Elms College (MA) (m/w)
Elon University (NC) (m/w)
Embry-Riddle Aeronautical University (FL) (m)
Emerson College (MA) (m/w)
Emmanuel College (GA) (m/w)
Emmanuel College (MA) (m/w)
Emory & Henry College (VA) (m/w)
Emory University (GA) (m/w)
Emporia State University (KS) (m/w)
Endicott College (MA) (m/w)
Erskine College (SC) (m/w)
Eureka College (IL) (m/w)
Evangel University (MO) (m/w)
The Evergreen State College (WA) (m/w)
Fairfield University (CT) (m/w)
Fairleigh Dickinson University, College at Florham (NJ) (m/w)
Fairmont State University (WV) (m/w)
Farmingdale State University of New York (NY) (m/w)
Faulkner University (AL) (m)
Fayetteville State University (NC) (m/w)
Felician College (NJ) (m/w)
Ferris State University (MI) (m/w)
Ferrum College (VA) (m/w)
Fisher College (MA) (m/w)
Fisk University (TN) (m/w)
Fitchburg State College (MA) (m/w)
Flagler College (FL) (m/w)
Florida Agricultural and Mechanical University (FL) (m/w)
Florida Atlantic University (FL) (m/w)
Florida Gulf Coast University (FL) (m/w)
Florida Institute of Technology (FL) (m/w)
Florida International University (FL) (m/w)
Florida Memorial College (FL) (m/w)

Florida Southern College (FL) (m/w)
Florida State University (FL) (m/w)
Fontbonne University (MO) (m/w)
Fordham University (NY) (m/w)
Fort Hays State University (KS) (m/w)
Fort Lewis College (CO) (m/w)
Fort Valley State University (GA) (m/w)
Framingham State College (MA) (m/w)
The Franciscan University (IA) (m/w)
Francis Marion University (SC) (m/w)
Franklin and Marshall College (PA) (m/w)
Franklin College (IN) (m/w)
Franklin Pierce College (NH) (m/w)
Freed-Hardeman University (TN) (m/w)
Fresno Pacific University (CA) (m/w)
Friends University (KS) (m/w)
Frostburg State University (MD) (m/w)
Furman University (SC) (m/w)
Gallaudet University (DC) (m/w)
Gannon University (PA) (m/w)
Gardner-Webb University (NC) (m/w)
Geneva College (PA) (m/w)
George Fox University (OR) (m/w)
George Mason University (VA) (m/w)
Georgetown College (KY) (m/w)
Georgetown University (DC) (m/w)
The George Washington University (DC) (m/w)
Georgia College & State University (GA) (m/w)
Georgia Institute of Technology (GA) (m/w)
Georgian Court University (NJ) (w)
Georgia Southern University (GA) (m/w)
Georgia Southwestern State University (GA) (m/w)
Georgia State University (GA) (m/w)
Gettysburg College (PA) (m/w)
Glenville State College (WV) (m/w)
Goldey-Beacom College (DE) (m/w)
Gonzaga University (WA) (m/w)
Gordon College (MA) (m/w)
Goshen College (IN) (m/w)
Goucher College (MD) (m/w)
Grace College (IN) (m/w)
Graceland University (IA) (m/w)
Grambling State University (LA) (m/w)
Grand Canyon University (AZ) (m/w)
Grand Valley State University (MI) (m/w)
Grand View College (IA) (m/w)
Green Mountain College (VT) (m/w)
Greensboro College (NC) (m/w)
Greenville College (IL) (m/w)
Grinnell College (IA) (m/w)
Grove City College (PA) (m)
Guilford College (NC) (m/w)
Gustavus Adolphus College (MN) (m/w)
Gwynedd-Mercy College (PA) (m/w)
Hamilton College (NY) (m/w)
Hamline University (MN) (m/w)
Hampden-Sydney College (VA) (m)
Hampton University (VA) (m/w)
Hannibal-LaGrange College (MO) (m/w)
Hanover College (IN) (m/w)
Harding University (AR) (m/w)
Hardin-Simmons University (TX) (m/w)
Harris-Stowe State College (MO) (m/w)
Hartwick College (NY) (m/w)
Harvard University (MA) (m/w)
Haskell Indian Nations University (KS) (m/w)
Hastings College (NE) (m/w)
Haverford College (PA) (m/w)
Hawai'i Pacific University (HI) (m)
Heidelberg College (OH) (m/w)
Henderson State University (AR) (m/w)

Hendrix College (AR) (m/w)
High Point University (NC) (m/w)
Hilbert College (NY) (m/w)
Hillsdale College (MI) (m/w)
Hiram College (OH) (m/w)
Hobart and William Smith Colleges (NY) (m/w)
Hofstra University (NY) (m/w)
Hollins University (VA) (w)
Holy Family University (PA) (m/w)
Holy Names University (CA) (m/w)
Hood College (MD) (m/w)
Hope College (MI) (m/w)
Hope International University (CA) (m/w)
Houghton College (NY) (m/w/w)
Houston Baptist University (TX) (m/w)
Howard Payne University (TX) (m/w)
Howard University (DC) (m/w)
Humboldt State University (CA) (m/w)
Hunter College of the City University of New York (NY) (m/w)
Huntingdon College (AL) (m/w)
Huntington College (IN) (m/w)
Husson College (ME) (m/w)
Huston-Tillotson College (TX) (m/w)
Idaho State University (ID) (m/w)
Illinois College (IL) (m/w)
Illinois Institute of Technology (IL) (m/w)
Illinois State University (IL) (m/w)
Illinois Wesleyan University (IL) (m/w)
Immaculata University (PA) (w)
Indiana Institute of Technology (IN) (m/w)
Indiana State University (IN) (m/w)
Indiana University Bloomington (IN) (m/w)
Indiana University Northwest (IN) (m/w)
Indiana University of Pennsylvania (PA) (m/w)
Indiana University–Purdue University Fort Wayne (IN) (m/w)
Indiana University–Purdue University Indianapolis (IN) (m/w)
Indiana University South Bend (IN) (m/w)
Indiana University Southeast (IN) (m/w)
Indiana Wesleyan University (IN) (m/w)
Iona College (NY) (m/w)
Iowa State University of Science and Technology (IA) (m/w)
Iowa Wesleyan College (IA) (m/w)
Ithaca College (NY) (m/w)
Jackson State University (MS) (m/w)
Jacksonville State University (AL) (m/w)
Jacksonville University (FL) (m/w)
James Madison University (VA) (m/w)
Jamestown College (ND) (m/w)
Jarvis Christian College (TX) (m/w)
John Brown University (AR) (m/w)
John Carroll University (OH) (m/w)
John Jay College of Criminal Justice of the City University of New York (NY) (m/w)
The Johns Hopkins University (MD) (m/w)
Johnson & Wales University (CO) (m/w)
Johnson & Wales University (FL) (m)
Johnson & Wales University (RI) (m)
Johnson C. Smith University (NC) (m/w)
Johnson State College (VT) (m/w)
Judson College (IL) (m/w)
Juniata College (PA) (m/w)
Kalamazoo College (MI) (m/w)
Kansas State University (KS) (m/w)
Kansas Wesleyan University (KS) (m/w)
Kean University (NJ) (m/w)
Keene State College (NH) (m/w)
Kendall College (IL) (m/w)
Kennesaw State University (GA) (m/w)
Kent State University (OH) (m/w)

Kentucky State University (KY) (m/w)
Kentucky Wesleyan College (KY) (m/w)
Kenyon College (OH) (m/w)
Keuka College (NY) (m/w)
King College (TN) (m/w)
King's College (PA) (m/w)
Knox College (IL) (m/w)
Kutztown University of Pennsylvania (PA)
  (m/w)
Lafayette College (PA) (m/w)
LaGrange College (GA) (m/w)
Lake Erie College (OH) (m/w)
Lake Forest College (IL) (m/w)
Lakeland College (WI) (m/w)
Lake Superior State University (MI) (m/w)
Lamar University (TX) (m/w)
Lambuth University (TN) (m/w)
Lander University (SC) (m/w)
Lane College (TN) (m/w)
Langston University (OK) (m/w)
La Roche College (PA) (m/w)
La Salle University (PA) (m/w)
Lasell College (MA) (m/w)
Lawrence University (WI) (m/w)
Lebanon Valley College (PA) (m/w)
Lees-McRae College (NC) (m/w)
Lee University (TN) (m/w)
Lehigh University (PA) (m/w)
Lehman College of the City University of
  New York (NY) (m/w)
Le Moyne College (NY) (m/w)
LeMoyne-Owen College (TN) (m/w)
Lenoir-Rhyne College (NC) (m/w)
Lesley University (MA) (w)
LeTourneau University (TX) (m/w)
Lewis & Clark College (OR) (m/w)
Lewis-Clark State College (ID) (m/w)
Lewis University (IL) (m/w)
Liberty University (VA) (m/w)
Limestone College (SC) (m/w)
Lincoln Memorial University (TN) (m/w)
Lincoln University (MO) (m/w)
Lincoln University (PA) (m/w)
Lindenwood University (MO) (m/w)
Lindsey Wilson College (KY) (m/w)
Linfield College (OR) (m/w)
Lipscomb University (TN) (m/w)
Livingstone College (NC) (m/w)
Lock Haven University of Pennsylvania (PA)
  (m/w)
Long Island University, Brooklyn Campus
  (NY) (m/w)
Long Island University, C.W. Post Campus
  (NY) (m/w)
Long Island University, Southampton College
  (NY) (m/w)
Longwood University (VA) (m/w)
Loras College (IA) (m/w)
Louisiana College (LA) (m/w)
Louisiana State University and Agricultural
  and Mechanical College (LA) (m/w)
Louisiana State University in Shreveport (LA)
  (m/w)
Louisiana Tech University (LA) (m/w)
Loyola College in Maryland (MD) (m/w)
Loyola Marymount University (CA) (m/w)
Loyola University Chicago (IL) (m/w)
Loyola University New Orleans (LA) (m/w)
Lubbock Christian University (TX) (m/w)
Luther College (IA) (m/w)
Lycoming College (PA) (m/w)
Lynchburg College (VA) (m/w)
Lyndon State College (VT) (m/w)
Lynn University (FL) (m/w)
Lyon College (AR) (m/w)

Macalester College (MN) (m/w)
MacMurray College (IL) (m/w)
Madonna University (MI) (m/w)
Maine Maritime Academy (ME) (m/w)
Malone College (OH) (m/w)
Manchester College (IN) (m/w)
Manhattan College (NY) (m/w)
Manhattanville College (NY) (m/w)
Mansfield University of Pennsylvania (PA)
  (m/w)
Maranatha Baptist Bible College (WI) (m/w)
Marian College (IN) (m/w)
Marian College of Fond du Lac (WI) (m/w)
Marietta College (OH) (m/w)
Marist College (NY) (m/w)
Marquette University (WI) (m/w)
Marshall University (WV) (m/w)
Mars Hill College (NC) (m/w)
Martin Luther College (MN) (m/w)
Martin Methodist College (TN) (m/w)
Mary Baldwin College (VA) (w)
Marymount University (VA) (m/w)
Maryville College (TN) (m/w)
Maryville University of Saint Louis (MO)
  (m/w)
University of Mary Washington (VA) (m/w)
Marywood University (PA) (m/w)
Massachusetts College of Liberal Arts (MA)
  (m/w)
Massachusetts Institute of Technology (MA)
  (m/w)
The Master's College and Seminary (CA)
  (m/w)
Mayville State University (ND) (m/w)
McDaniel College (MD) (m/w)
McKendree College (IL) (m/w)
McMurry University (TX) (m/w)
McNeese State University (LA) (m/w)
McPherson College (KS) (m/w)
Medaille College (NY) (m/w)
Medgar Evers College of the City University
  of New York (NY) (m/w)
Menlo College (CA) (m/w)
Mercer University (GA) (m/w)
Mercy College (NY) (m/w)
Mercyhurst College (PA) (m/w)
Meredith College (NC) (w)
Merrimack College (MA) (m/w)
Mesa State College (CO) (m/w)
Messiah College (PA) (m/w)
Methodist College (NC) (m/w)
Metropolitan State College of Denver (CO)
  (m/w)
Miami University (OH) (m/w)
Michigan State University (MI) (m/w)
Michigan Technological University (MI)
  (m/w)
MidAmerica Nazarene University (KS) (m/w)
Middlebury College (VT) (m/w)
Middle Tennessee State University (TN)
  (m/w)
Midland Lutheran College (NE) (m/w)
Midway College (KY) (w)
Midwestern State University (TX) (m/w)
Miles College (AL) (m/w)
Millersville University of Pennsylvania (PA)
  (m/w)
Milligan College (TN) (m/w)
Millikin University (IL) (m/w)
Millsaps College (MS) (m/w)
Milwaukee School of Engineering (WI) (m/w)
Minnesota State University Mankato (MN)
  (m/w)
Minnesota State University Moorhead (MN)
  (m/w)

Minot State University (ND) (m/w)
Mississippi College (MS) (m/w)
Mississippi State University (MS) (m/w)
Mississippi University for Women (MS) (w)
Mississippi Valley State University (MS)
  (m/w)
Missouri Baptist University (MO) (m/w)
Missouri Southern State University (MO)
  (m/w)
Missouri Valley College (MO) (m/w)
Missouri Western State College (MO) (m/w)
Molloy College (NY) (m/w)
Monmouth College (IL) (m/w)
Monmouth University (NJ) (m/w)
Montana State University–Billings (MT)
  (m/w)
Montana State University–Bozeman (MT)
  (m/w)
Montana State University–Northern (MT)
  (m/w)
Montana Tech of The University of Montana
  (MT) (m/w)
Montclair State University (NJ) (m/w)
Montreat College (NC) (m/w)
Moravian College (PA) (m/w)
Morehead State University (KY) (m/w)
Morehouse College (GA) (m)
Morgan State University (MD) (m/w)
Morningside College (IA) (m/w)
Morris College (SC) (m/w)
Mountain State University (WV) (m)
Mount Holyoke College (MA) (w)
Mount Ida College (MA) (m/w)
Mount Marty College (SD) (m/w)
Mount Mercy College (IA) (m/w)
Mount Olive College (NC) (m/w)
Mount Saint Mary College (NY) (m/w)
Mount Saint Mary's University (MD) (m/w)
Mount Union College (OH) (m/w)
Mount Vernon Nazarene University (OH)
  (m/w)
Muhlenberg College (PA) (m/w)
Murray State University (KY) (m/w)
Muskingum College (OH) (m/w)
Nazareth College of Rochester (NY) (m/w)
Nebraska Wesleyan University (NE) (m/w)
Neumann College (PA) (m/w)
Newberry College (SC) (m/w)
Newbury College (MA) (m/w)
New England College (NH) (m/w)
New Jersey City University (NJ) (m/w)
New Jersey Institute of Technology (NJ)
  (m/w)
Newman University (KS) (m/w)
New Mexico Highlands University (NM)
  (m/w)
New Mexico State University (NM) (m/w)
New York City College of Technology of the
  City University of New York (NY) (m/w)
New York Institute of Technology (NY)
  (m/w)
New York University (NY) (m/w)
Niagara University (NY) (m/w)
Nicholls State University (LA) (m/w)
Nichols College (MA) (m/w)
Norfolk State University (VA) (m/w)
North Carolina Agricultural and Technical
  State University (NC) (m/w)
North Carolina Central University (NC)
  (m/w)
North Carolina State University (NC) (m/w)
North Carolina Wesleyan College (NC)
  (m/w)
North Central College (IL) (m/w)
North Dakota State University (ND) (m/w)

Northeastern State University (OK) (m/w)
Northeastern University (MA) (m/w)
Northern Arizona University (AZ) (m/w)
Northern Illinois University (IL) (m/w)
Northern Kentucky University (KY) (m/w)
Northern Michigan University (MI) (m/w)
Northern State University (SD) (m/w)
North Georgia College & State University (GA) (m/w)
North Greenville College (SC) (m/w)
Northland College (WI) (m/w)
North Park University (IL) (m/w)
Northwest College (WA) (m/w)
Northwestern College (IA) (m/w)
Northwestern College (MN) (m/w)
Northwestern Oklahoma State University (OK) (m/w)
Northwestern State University of Louisiana (LA) (m/w)
Northwestern University (IL) (m/w)
Northwest Missouri State University (MO) (m/w)
Northwest Nazarene University (ID) (m/w)
Northwood University (MI) (m/w)
Norwich University (VT) (m/w)
Notre Dame College (OH) (m/w)
Notre Dame de Namur University (CA) (m/w)
Nova Southeastern University (FL) (m/w)
Nyack College (NY) (m/w)
Oakland City University (IN) (m/w)
Oakland University (MI) (m/w)
Oberlin College (OH) (m/w)
Occidental College (CA) (m/w)
Oglethorpe University (GA) (m/w)
Ohio Dominican University (OH) (m/w)
Ohio Northern University (OH) (m/w)
The Ohio State University (OH) (m/w)
Ohio University (OH) (m/w)
Ohio Valley College (WV) (m/w)
Ohio Wesleyan University (OH) (m/w)
Oklahoma Baptist University (OK) (m/w)
Oklahoma Christian University (OK) (m/w)
Oklahoma City University (OK) (m/w)
Oklahoma Panhandle State University (OK) (m/w)
Oklahoma State University (OK) (m/w)
Oklahoma Wesleyan University (OK) (m/w)
Old Dominion University (VA) (m/w)
Olivet College (MI) (m/w)
Olivet Nazarene University (IL) (m/w)
Oral Roberts University (OK) (m/w)
Oregon Institute of Technology (OR) (m/w)
Oregon State University (OR) (m/w)
Ottawa University (KS) (m/w)
Otterbein College (OH) (m/w)
Ouachita Baptist University (AR) (m/w)
Pace University (NY) (m/w)
Pacific Lutheran University (WA) (m/w)
Pacific Union College (CA) (m/w)
Pacific University (OR) (m/w)
Paine College (GA) (m/w)
Park University (MO) (m/w)
Patten University (CA) (m)
Paul Quinn College (TX) (m/w)
Peace College (NC) (w)
The Pennsylvania State University Altoona College (PA) (m/w)
The Pennsylvania State University at Erie, The Behrend College (PA) (m/w)
The Pennsylvania State University University Park Campus (PA) (m/w)
Pepperdine University (CA) (m/w)
Peru State College (NE) (m/w)
Pfeiffer University (NC) (m/w)

Philadelphia Biblical University (PA) (m/w)
Philadelphia University (PA) (m/w)
Piedmont College (GA) (m/w)
Pikeville College (KY) (m/w)
Pine Manor College (MA) (w)
Pittsburg State University (KS) (m/w)
Pitzer College (CA) (m/w)
Plymouth State University (NH) (m/w)
Point Loma Nazarene University (CA) (m/w)
Point Park University (PA) (m/w)
Polytechnic University, Brooklyn Campus (NY) (m/w)
Pomona College (CA) (m/w)
Portland State University (OR) (m/w)
Prairie View A&M University (TX) (m/w)
Presbyterian College (SC) (m/w)
Presentation College (SD) (m/w)
Princeton University (NJ) (m/w)
Principia College (IL) (m/w)
Providence College (RI) (m/w)
Purdue University (IN) (m/w)
Purdue University Calumet (IN) (m/w)
Purdue University North Central (IN) (m)
Queens College of the City University of New York (NY) (m/w)
Queens University of Charlotte (NC) (m/w)
Quincy University (IL) (m/w)
Quinnipiac University (CT) (m/w)
Radford University (VA) (m/w)
Ramapo College of New Jersey (NJ) (m/w)
Randolph-Macon College (VA) (m/w)
Randolph-Macon Woman's College (VA) (w)
Regis College (MA) (w)
Regis University (CO) (m/w)
Reinhardt College (GA) (m/w)
Rensselaer Polytechnic Institute (NY) (m/w)
Rhode Island College (RI) (m/w)
Rhodes College (TN) (m/w)
Rice University (TX) (m/w)
The Richard Stockton College of New Jersey (NJ) (m/w)
Rider University (NJ) (m/w)
Ripon College (WI) (m/w)
Rivier College (NH) (m/w)
Roanoke College (VA) (m/w)
Robert Morris College (IL) (m/w)
Robert Morris University (PA) (m/w)
Roberts Wesleyan College (NY) (m/w)
Rochester Institute of Technology (NY) (m/w)
Rockford College (IL) (m/w)
Rockhurst University (MO) (m/w)
Rocky Mountain College (MT) (m/w)
Roger Williams University (RI) (m/w)
Rollins College (FL) (m/w)
Rose-Hulman Institute of Technology (IN) (m/w)
Rosemont College (PA) (w)
Rowan University (NJ) (m/w)
Russell Sage College (NY) (w)
Rust College (MS) (m/w)
Rutgers, The State University of New Jersey, Camden (NJ) (m/w)
Rutgers, The State University of New Jersey, Newark (NJ) (m/w)
Rutgers, The State University of New Jersey, New Brunswick/Piscataway (NJ) (m/w)
Sacred Heart University (CT) (m/w)
Saginaw Valley State University (MI) (m/w)
St. Ambrose University (IA) (m/w)
St. Andrews Presbyterian College (NC) (m/w)
Saint Anselm College (NH) (m/w)
Saint Augustine's College (NC) (m/w)
St. Bonaventure University (NY) (m/w)
St. Cloud State University (MN) (m/w)

St. Edward's University (TX) (m/w)
St. Francis College (NY) (m/w)
Saint Francis University (PA) (m/w)
St. Gregory's University (OK) (m/w)
St. John Fisher College (NY) (m/w)
Saint John's University (MN) (m)
St. John's University (NY) (m/w)
Saint Joseph College (CT) (w)
Saint Joseph's College (IN) (m/w)
Saint Joseph's College of Maine (ME) (m/w)
St. Joseph's College, Suffolk Campus (NY) (m/w)
Saint Joseph's University (PA) (m/w)
St. Lawrence University (NY) (m/w)
Saint Leo University (FL) (m/w)
St. Louis College of Pharmacy (MO) (m/w)
Saint Louis University (MO) (m/w)
Saint Martin's College (WA) (m/w)
Saint Mary's College (IN) (w)
Saint Mary's College of California (CA) (m/w)
St. Mary's College of Maryland (MD) (m/w)
Saint Mary's University of Minnesota (MN) (m/w)
St. Mary's University of San Antonio (TX) (m/w)
Saint Michael's College (VT) (m/w)
St. Norbert College (WI) (m/w)
St. Olaf College (MN) (m/w)
Saint Paul's College (VA) (m/w)
Saint Peter's College (NJ) (m/w)
St. Thomas Aquinas College (NY) (m/w)
Saint Vincent College (PA) (m/w)
Saint Xavier University (IL) (m/w)
Salem International University (WV) (m/w)
Salem State College (MA) (m/w)
Salisbury University (MD) (m/w)
Salve Regina University (RI) (m/w)
Samford University (AL) (m/w)
Sam Houston State University (TX) (m/w)
San Diego State University (CA) (m/w)
San Francisco State University (CA) (m/w)
San Jose State University (CA) (m/w)
Santa Clara University (CA) (m/w)
Savannah College of Art and Design (GA) (m/w)
Savannah State University (GA) (m)
Schreiner University (TX) (m/w)
Seattle Pacific University (WA) (m/w)
Seattle University (WA) (m/w)
Seton Hall University (NJ) (m/w)
Seton Hill University (PA) (m/w)
Shawnee State University (OH) (m/w)
Shaw University (NC) (m/w)
Shenandoah University (VA) (m/w)
Shepherd University (WV) (m/w)
Shippensburg University of Pennsylvania (PA) (m/w)
Shorter College (GA) (m/w)
Siena College (NY) (m/w)
Siena Heights University (MI) (m/w)
Simmons College (MA) (w)
Simpson College (IA) (m/w/w)
Si Tanka Huron University (SD) (m/w)
Skidmore College (NY) (m/w)
Slippery Rock University of Pennsylvania (PA) (m/w)
Smith College (MA) (w)
Sonoma State University (CA) (m/w)
South Carolina State University (SC) (m/w)
South Dakota School of Mines and Technology (SD) (m/w)
South Dakota State University (SD) (m/w)
Southeastern Louisiana University (LA) (m/w)

Southeastern Oklahoma State University (OK) (m/w)

Southeast Missouri State University (MO) (m/w)

Southern Arkansas University–Magnolia (AR) (m/w)

Southern Connecticut State University (CT) (m/w)

Southern Illinois University Carbondale (IL) (m/w)

Southern Illinois University Edwardsville (IL) (m/w)

Southern Methodist University (TX) (m/w)

Southern Nazarene University (OK) (m/w)

Southern New Hampshire University (NH) (m/w)

Southern Oregon University (OR) (m/w)

Southern Polytechnic State University (GA) (m/w)

Southern University and Agricultural and Mechanical College (LA) (m/w)

Southern University at New Orleans (LA) (m/w)

Southern Utah University (UT) (m/w)

Southern Vermont College (VT) (m/w)

Southern Virginia University (VA) (m/w)

Southern Wesleyan University (SC) (m/w)

Southwest Baptist University (MO) (m/w)

Southwestern Assemblies of God University (TX) (m/w)

Southwestern College (KS) (m/w)

Southwestern Oklahoma State University (OK) (m/w)

Southwestern University (TX) (m/w)

Southwest Minnesota State University (MN) (m/w)

Southwest Missouri State University (MO) (m/w)

Spalding University (KY) (m/w)

Spelman College (GA) (w)

Spring Arbor University (MI) (m/w)

Springfield College (MA) (m/w)

Spring Hill College (AL) (m/w)

Stanford University (CA) (m/w)

State University of New York at Binghamton (NY) (m/w)

State University of New York at New Paltz (NY) (m)

State University of New York at Oswego (NY) (m/w)

State University of New York at Plattsburgh (NY) (m/w)

State University of New York College at Brockport (NY) (m/w)

State University of New York College at Cortland (NY) (m/w)

State University of New York College at Fredonia (NY) (m/w)

State University of New York College at Geneseo (NY) (m/w)

State University of New York College at Old Westbury (NY) (m/w)

State University of New York College at Oneonta (NY) (m/w)

State University of New York College at Potsdam (NY) (m/w)

State University of New York College of Technology at Delhi (NY) (m/w)

State University of New York Institute of Technology (NY) (m/w)

State University of New York Maritime College (NY) (m/w)

State University of West Georgia (GA) (m/w)

Stephen F. Austin State University (TX) (m/w)

Stephens College (MO) (w)

Sterling College (KS) (m/w)

Stetson University (FL) (m/w)

Stevens Institute of Technology (NJ) (m/w)

Stillman College (AL) (m/w)

Stonehill College (MA) (m/w)

Stony Brook University, State University of New York (NY) (m/w)

Suffolk University (MA) (m/w)

Sul Ross State University (TX) (m/w)

Susquehanna University (PA) (m/w)

Swarthmore College (PA) (m/w)

Syracuse University (NY) (m/w)

Tabor College (KS) (m/w)

Tarleton State University (TX) (m/w)

Taylor University (IN) (m/w)

Teikyo Post University (CT) (m/w)

Temple University (PA) (m/w)

Tennessee State University (TN) (m/w)

Tennessee Technological University (TN) (m/w)

Tennessee Wesleyan College (TN) (m/w)

Texas A&M International University (TX) (m/w)

Texas A&M University (TX) (m/w)

Texas A&M University–Commerce (TX) (m/w)

Texas A&M University–Corpus Christi (TX) (m/w)

Texas A&M University–Kingsville (TX) (m/w)

Texas Christian University (TX) (m/w)

Texas College (TX) (m/w)

Texas Lutheran University (TX) (m/w)

Texas Southern University (TX) (m/w)

Texas State University-San Marcos (TX) (m/w)

Texas Tech University (TX) (m/w)

Texas Wesleyan University (TX) (m/w)

Texas Woman's University (TX) (w)

Thiel College (PA) (m/w)

Thomas College (ME) (m/w)

Thomas More College (KY) (m/w)

Tiffin University (OH) (m/w)

Tougaloo College (MS) (m/w)

Towson University (MD) (m/w)

Transylvania University (KY) (m/w)

Trevecca Nazarene University (TN) (m/w)

Trinity Christian College (IL) (m/w)

Trinity College (CT) (m/w)

Trinity College (DC) (w)

Trinity International University (IL) (m/w)

Trinity University (TX) (m/w)

Tri-State University (IN) (m/w)

Troy State University (AL) (m/w)

Truman State University (MO) (m/w)

Tufts University (MA) (m/w)

Tulane University (LA) (m/w)

Tusculum College (TN) (m/w)

Tuskegee University (AL) (m/w)

Union College (KY) (m/w)

Union College (NY) (m/w)

Union University (TN) (m/w)

United States Air Force Academy (CO) (m/w)

United States Coast Guard Academy (CT) (m/w)

United States Merchant Marine Academy (NY) (m/w)

United States Military Academy (NY) (m/w)

United States Naval Academy (MD) (m/w)

University at Albany, State University of New York (NY) (m/w)

University at Buffalo, The State University of New York (NY) (m/w)

The University of Akron (OH) (m/w)

The University of Alabama (AL) (m/w)

The University of Alabama at Birmingham (AL) (m/w)

The University of Alabama in Huntsville (AL) (m/w)

University of Alaska Anchorage (AK) (m/w)

University of Alaska Fairbanks (AK) (m/w)

The University of Arizona (AZ) (m/w)

University of Arkansas (AR) (m/w)

University of Arkansas at Little Rock (AR) (m/w)

University of Arkansas at Monticello (AR) (m/w)

University of Arkansas at Pine Bluff (AR) (m/w)

University of Bridgeport (CT) (m/w)

University of California, Berkeley (CA) (m/w)

University of California, Davis (CA) (m/w)

University of California, Irvine (CA) (m/w)

University of California, Los Angeles (CA) (m/w)

University of California, Riverside (CA) (m/w)

University of California, San Diego (CA) (m/w)

University of California, Santa Barbara (CA) (m/w)

University of California, Santa Cruz (CA) (m/w)

University of Central Arkansas (AR) (m/w)

University of Central Florida (FL) (m/w)

University of Central Oklahoma (OK) (m/w)

University of Charleston (WV) (m/w)

University of Chicago (IL) (m/w)

University of Cincinnati (OH) (m/w)

University of Colorado at Boulder (CO) (m/w)

University of Colorado at Colorado Springs (CO) (m/w)

University of Connecticut (CT) (m/w)

University of Dallas (TX) (m/w)

University of Dayton (OH) (m/w)

University of Delaware (DE) (m/w)

University of Denver (CO) (m/w)

University of Detroit Mercy (MI) (m/w)

University of Dubuque (IA) (m/w)

University of Evansville (IN) (m/w)

The University of Findlay (OH) (m/w)

University of Florida (FL) (m/w)

University of Georgia (GA) (m/w)

University of Great Falls (MT) (m/w)

University of Hartford (CT) (m/w)

University of Hawaii at Hilo (HI) (m)

University of Hawaii at Manoa (HI) (m/w)

University of Houston (TX) (m/w)

University of Idaho (ID) (m/w)

University of Illinois at Chicago (IL) (m/w)

University of Illinois at Springfield (IL) (m/w)

University of Illinois at Urbana–Champaign (IL) (m/w)

University of Indianapolis (IN) (m/w)

The University of Iowa (IA) (m/w)

University of Kansas (KS) (m/w)

University of Kentucky (KY) (m/w)

University of La Verne (CA) (m/w)

University of Louisiana at Lafayette (LA) (m/w)

University of Louisiana at Monroe (LA) (m/w)

University of Louisville (KY) (m/w)

University of Maine (ME) (m/w)

University of Maine at Farmington (ME) (m/w)

University of Maine at Fort Kent (ME) (m/w)

University of Maine at Machias (ME) (m/w)

University of Maine at Presque Isle (ME) (m/w)

University of Mary (ND) (m/w)

University of Mary Hardin-Baylor (TX) (m/w)

University of Maryland, Baltimore County (MD) (m/w)

University of Maryland, College Park (MD) (m/w)

University of Maryland Eastern Shore (MD) (m/w)

University of Massachusetts Amherst (MA) (m/w)

University of Massachusetts Boston (MA) (m/w)

University of Massachusetts Dartmouth (MA) (m/w)

University of Massachusetts Lowell (MA) (m/w)

The University of Memphis (TN) (m/w)

University of Miami (FL) (m/w)

University of Michigan (MI) (m/w)

University of Michigan–Dearborn (MI) (m/w)

University of Minnesota, Crookston (MN) (m/w)

University of Minnesota, Duluth (MN) (m/w)

University of Minnesota, Morris (MN) (m/w)

University of Minnesota, Twin Cities Campus (MN) (m/w)

University of Mississippi (MS) (m/w)

University of Missouri–Columbia (MO) (m/w)

University of Missouri–Kansas City (MO) (m/w)

University of Missouri–Rolla (MO) (m/w)

University of Missouri–St. Louis (MO) (m/w)

University of Mobile (AL) (m/w)

The University of Montana–Missoula (MT) (m/w)

The University of Montana–Western (MT) (m/w)

University of Montevallo (AL) (m/w)

University of Nebraska at Kearney (NE) (m/w)

University of Nebraska at Omaha (NE) (m/w)

University of Nebraska–Lincoln (NE) (m/w)

University of Nevada, Las Vegas (NV) (m/w)

University of Nevada, Reno (NV) (m/w)

University of New England (ME) (m/w)

University of New Hampshire (NH) (m/w)

University of New Haven (CT) (m/w)

University of New Mexico (NM) (m/w)

University of New Orleans (LA) (m/w)

University of North Alabama (AL) (m/w)

The University of North Carolina at Asheville (NC) (m/w)

The University of North Carolina at Chapel Hill (NC) (m/w)

The University of North Carolina at Charlotte (NC) (m/w)

The University of North Carolina at Greensboro (NC) (m/w)

The University of North Carolina at Pembroke (NC) (m/w)

The University of North Carolina at Wilmington (NC) (m/w)

University of North Dakota (ND) (m/w)

University of Northern Colorado (CO) (m/w)

University of Northern Iowa (IA) (m/w)

University of North Florida (FL) (m/w)

University of North Texas (TX) (m/w)

University of Notre Dame (IN) (m/w)

University of Oklahoma (OK) (m/w)

University of Oregon (OR) (m/w)

University of Pennsylvania (PA) (m/w)

University of Pittsburgh (PA) (m/w)

University of Pittsburgh at Bradford (PA) (m/w)

University of Pittsburgh at Greensburg (PA) (m/w)

University of Pittsburgh at Johnstown (PA) (m/w)

University of Portland (OR) (m/w)

University of Puerto Rico at Bayamón (PR) (m/w)

University of Puerto Rico at Humacao (PR) (m/w)

University of Puerto Rico, Cayey University College (PR) (m/w)

University of Puerto Rico, Mayagüez Campus (PR) (m/w)

University of Puerto Rico, Río Piedras (PR) (m/w)

University of Puget Sound (WA) (m/w)

University of Redlands (CA) (m/w)

University of Rhode Island (RI) (m/w)

University of Richmond (VA) (m/w)

University of Rio Grande (OH) (m/w)

University of Rochester (NY) (m/w)

University of St. Francis (IL) (m/w)

University of Saint Francis (IN) (m/w)

University of Saint Mary (KS) (m/w)

University of St. Thomas (MN) (m/w)

University of San Diego (CA) (m/w)

University of San Francisco (CA) (m/w)

University of Science and Arts of Oklahoma (OK) (m/w)

The University of Scranton (PA) (m/w)

University of Sioux Falls (SD) (m/w)

University of South Alabama (AL) (m/w)

University of South Carolina (SC) (m/w)

University of South Carolina Aiken (SC) (m/w)

University of South Carolina Spartanburg (SC) (m/w)

The University of South Dakota (SD) (m/w)

University of Southern California (CA) (m/w)

University of Southern Indiana (IN) (m/w)

University of Southern Maine (ME) (m/w)

University of Southern Mississippi (MS) (m/w)

University of South Florida (FL) (m/w)

The University of Tampa (FL) (m/w)

The University of Tennessee (TN) (m/w)

The University of Tennessee at Chattanooga (TN) (m/w)

The University of Tennessee at Martin (TN) (m/w)

The University of Texas at Arlington (TX) (m/w)

The University of Texas at Austin (TX) (m/w)

The University of Texas at Dallas (TX) (m/w)

The University of Texas at El Paso (TX) (m/w)

The University of Texas at San Antonio (TX) (m/w)

The University of Texas of the Permian Basin (TX) (m/w)

The University of Texas–Pan American (TX) (m/w)

University of the District of Columbia (DC) (m/w)

University of the Incarnate Word (TX) (m/w)

University of the Ozarks (AR) (m/w)

University of the Pacific (CA) (m/w)

University of the Sciences in Philadelphia (PA) (m/w)

University of the South (TN) (m/w)

University of Toledo (OH) (m/w)

University of Tulsa (OK) (m/w)

University of Utah (UT) (m/w)

University of Vermont (VT) (m/w)

University of Virginia (VA) (m/w)

The University of Virginia's College at Wise (VA) (m/w)

University of Washington (WA) (m/w)

The University of West Alabama (AL) (m/w)

University of West Florida (FL) (m/w)

University of Wisconsin–Eau Claire (WI) (m/w)

University of Wisconsin–Green Bay (WI) (m/w)

University of Wisconsin–La Crosse (WI) (m/w)

University of Wisconsin–Madison (WI) (m/w)

University of Wisconsin–Milwaukee (WI) (m/w)

University of Wisconsin–Oshkosh (WI) (m/w)

University of Wisconsin–Parkside (WI) (m/w)

University of Wisconsin–Platteville (WI) (m/w)

University of Wisconsin–River Falls (WI) (m/w)

University of Wisconsin–Stevens Point (WI) (m/w)

University of Wisconsin–Stout (WI) (m/w)

University of Wisconsin–Superior (WI) (m/w)

University of Wisconsin–Whitewater (WI) (m/w)

University of Wyoming (WY) (m/w)

Upper Iowa University (IA) (m/w)

Urbana University (OH) (m/w)

Ursinus College (PA) (m/w)

Ursuline College (OH) (w)

Utah State University (UT) (m/w)

Utica College (NY) (m/w)

Valdosta State University (GA) (m/w)

Valley City State University (ND) (m/w)

Valparaiso University (IN) (m/w)

Vanderbilt University (TN) (m/w)

Vanguard University of Southern California (CA) (m/w)

Vassar College (NY) (m/w)

Villa Julie College (MD) (m/w)

Villanova University (PA) (m/w)

Virginia Commonwealth University (VA) (m/w)

Virginia Intermont College (VA) (m/w)

Virginia Military Institute (VA) (m)

Virginia Polytechnic Institute and State University (VA) (m/w)

Virginia State University (VA) (m/w)

Virginia Union University (VA) (m/w)

Virginia Wesleyan College (VA) (m/w)

Viterbo University (WI) (m/w)

Voorhees College (SC) (m/w)

Wabash College (IN) (m)

Wagner College (NY) (m/w)

Wake Forest University (NC) (m/w)

Waldorf College (IA) (m/w)

Walsh University (OH) (m/w)

Warner Pacific College (OR) (m/w)

Warner Southern College (FL) (m/w)

Wartburg College (IA) (m/w)

Washburn University (KS) (m/w)

Washington & Jefferson College (PA) (m/w)

Washington and Lee University (VA) (m/w)

Washington College (MD) (m/w)

Washington State University (WA) (m/w)

Washington University in St. Louis (MO) (m/w)

Wayland Baptist University (TX) (m/w)
Waynesburg College (PA) (m/w)
Wayne State College (NE) (m/w)
Wayne State University (MI) (m/w)
Webber International University (FL) (m/w)
Weber State University (UT) (m/w)
Webster University (MO) (m/w)
Wellesley College (MA) (w)
Wentworth Institute of Technology (MA)
  (m/w)
Wesleyan College (GA) (w)
Wesleyan University (CT) (m/w)
Wesley College (DE) (m/w)
West Chester University of Pennsylvania (PA)
  (m/w)
Western Baptist College (OR) (m/w)
Western Carolina University (NC) (m/w)
Western Connecticut State University (CT)
  (m/w)
Western Illinois University (IL) (m/w)
Western Kentucky University (KY) (m/w)
Western Michigan University (MI) (m/w)
Western New England College (MA) (m/w)
Western New Mexico University (NM)
  (m/w)
Western Oregon University (OR) (m/w)
Western State College of Colorado (CO)
  (m/w)
Western Washington University (WA) (m/w)
Westfield State College (MA) (m/w)
West Liberty State College (WV) (m/w)
Westminster College (UT) (m/w)
Westminster College (MO) (m/w)
Westminster College (PA) (m/w)
Westmont College (CA) (m/w)
West Texas A&M University (TX) (m/w)
West Virginia State College (WV) (m/w)
West Virginia University (WV) (m/w)
West Virginia University Institute of
  Technology (WV) (m/w)
West Virginia Wesleyan College (WV) (m/w)
Wheaton College (IL) (m/w)
Wheaton College (MA) (m/w)
Wheeling Jesuit University (WV) (m/w)
Wheelock College (MA) (w)
Whitman College (WA) (m/w)
Whittier College (CA) (m/w)
Whitworth College (WA) (m/w)
Wichita State University (KS) (m/w)
Widener University (PA) (m/w)
Wilberforce University (OH) (m/w)
Wiley College (TX) (m/w)
Wilkes University (PA) (m/w)
Willamette University (OR) (m/w)
William Carey College (MS) (m/w)
William Jewell College (MO) (m/w)
William Paterson University of New Jersey
  (NJ) (m/w)
William Penn University (IA) (m/w)
Williams Baptist College (AR) (m/w)
Williams College (MA) (m/w)
William Woods University (MO) (m/w)
Wilmington College (DE) (m/w)
Wilmington College (OH) (m/w)
Wilson College (PA) (w)
Wingate University (NC) (m/w)
Winona State University (MN) (m/w)
Winston-Salem State University (NC) (m/w)
Winthrop University (SC) (m/w)
Wisconsin Lutheran College (WI) (m/w)
Wittenberg University (OH) (m/w)
Wofford College (SC) (m/w)
Worcester Polytechnic Institute (MA) (m/w)
Worcester State College (MA) (m/w)
Wright State University (OH) (m/w)

Xavier University (OH) (m/w)
Xavier University of Louisiana (LA) (m/w)
Yale University (CT) (m/w)
Yeshiva University (NY) (m)
York College (NE) (m/w)
York College of Pennsylvania (PA) (m/w)
York College of the City University of New
  York (NY) (m/w)
Youngstown State University (OH)(m/w)

Cheerleading

Adelphi University (NY) (m/w)
Albany State University (GA) (m/w)
Albion College (MI) (m/w)
Albright College (PA) (m/w)
Alfred University (NY) (m/w)
Allegheny College (PA) (m/w)
Alma College (MI) (m/w)
Alverno College (WI) (w)
American University (DC) (m/w)
Anderson University (IN) (m/w)
Angelo State University (TX) (m/w)
Anna Maria College (MA) (m/w)
Appalachian State University (NC) (m/w)
Aquinas College (MI) (m/w)
Arkansas State University (AR) (m/w)
Arkansas Tech University (AR) (m/w)
Armstrong Atlantic State University (GA)
  (m/w)
Ashland University (OH) (m/w)
Auburn University (AL) (m/w)
Augsburg College (MN) (m/w)
Augustana College (IL) (m/w)
Augusta State University (GA) (m/w)
Aurora University (IL) (m/w)
Austin College (TX) (m/w)
Austin Peay State University (TN) (m/w)
Averett University (VA) (m/w)
Azusa Pacific University (CA) (m/w)
Bacone College (OK) (m/w)
Baker University (KS) (m/w)
Baldwin-Wallace College (OH) (m/w)
Ball State University (IN) (m/w)
Baptist Bible College of Pennsylvania (PA)
  (m/w)
Barry University (FL) (m/w)
Barton College (NC) (m/w)
Belhaven College (MS) (m/w)
Bellarmine University (KY) (m/w)
Belmont University (TN) (m/w)
Benedict College (SC) (m/w)
Benedictine College (KS) (m/w)
Bentley College (MA) (m/w)
Bethany College (KS) (m/w)
Bethel College (IN) (m/w)
Bethel College (TN) (m/w)
Bethune-Cookman College (FL) (m/w)
Bluefield State College (WV) (m/w)
Boise State University (ID) (m/w)
Boston College (MA) (m/w)
Bowie State University (MD) (m/w)
Bradley University (IL) (m/w)
Brandeis University (MA) (m/w)
Brevard College (NC) (m/w)
Bridgewater College (VA) (m/w)
Brigham Young University (UT) (m/w)
Brigham Young University–Hawaii (HI)
  (m/w)
Brown University (RI) (m/w)
Bryant College (RI) (m/w)
Bucknell University (PA) (m/w)
Buffalo State College, State University of
  New York (NY) (m/w)

California Polytechnic State University, San
  Luis Obispo (CA) (m/w)
California State University, Bakersfield (CA)
  (m/w)
California State University, Chico (CA) (m/w)
California State University, Hayward (CA)
  (m/w)
California State University, Los Angeles (CA)
  (m/w)
California State University, Sacramento (CA)
  (m/w)
California State University, San Bernardino
  (CA) (m/w)
California University of Pennsylvania (PA)
  (m/w)
Campbellsville University (KY) (m/w)
Campbell University (NC) (m/w)
Capital University (OH) (m/w)
Carnegie Mellon University (PA) (m/w)
Carroll College (WI) (m/w)
Carthage College (WI) (m/w)
Cascade College (OR) (m/w)
Case Western Reserve University (OH) (m/w)
Catawba College (NC) (m/w)
The Catholic University of America (DC)
  (m/w)
Cazenovia College (NY) (m/w)
Cedarville University (OH) (m/w)
Centenary College of Louisiana (LA) (m/w)
Central Christian College of Kansas (KS)
  (m/w)
Central College (IA) (m/w)
Central Connecticut State University (CT)
  (m/w)
Central Methodist College (MO) (m/w)
Central Michigan University (MI) (m/w)
Central Missouri State University (MO)
  (m/w)
Central Washington University (WA) (m/w)
Centre College (KY) (m/w)
Chadron State College (NE) (m/w)
Charleston Southern University (SC) (m/w)
Chowan College (NC) (m/w)
Christopher Newport University (VA) (m/w)
The Citadel, The Military College of South
  Carolina (SC) (m/w)
Claflin University (SC) (m/w)
Clarion University of Pennsylvania (PA)
  (m/w)
Clark Atlanta University (GA) (m/w)
Clayton College & State University (GA)
  (m/w)
Clemson University (SC) (m/w)
Cleveland State University (OH) (m/w)
Coastal Carolina University (SC) (m/w)
Colby-Sawyer College (NH) (m/w)
Colgate University (NY) (m/w)
College Misericordia (PA) (m/w)
College of Charleston (SC) (m/w)
College of Mount St. Joseph (OH) (m/w)
College of Staten Island of the City University
  of New York (NY) (m/w)
College of the Holy Cross (MA) (m/w)
College of the Ozarks (MO) (m/w)
The College of William and Mary (VA)
  (m/w)
Colorado School of Mines (CO) (m/w)
Colorado State University (CO) (m/w)
Columbia College (NY) (m/w)
Columbus State University (GA) (m/w)
Concord College (WV) (m/w)
Concordia University (IL) (m/w)
Concordia University Wisconsin (WI) (m/w)
Converse College (SC) (w)
Coppin State University (MD) (m/w)

Cornell College (IA) (m/w)
Creighton University (NE) (m/w)
Culver-Stockton College (MO) (m/w)
Curry College (MA) (m/w)
Dakota State University (SD) (m/w)
Dartmouth College (NH) (m/w)
Davidson College (NC) (m/w)
Delaware State University (DE) (m/w)
Delaware Valley College (PA) (m/w)
Delta State University (MS) (m/w)
Denison University (OH) (m/w)
DePaul University (IL) (m/w)
DePauw University (IN) (m/w)
DeSales University (PA) (m/w)
Dominican University of California (CA)
    (m/w)
Dowling College (NY) (m/w)
Drake University (IA) (m/w)
Drexel University (PA) (m/w)
Drury University (MO) (m/w)
Duke University (NC) (m/w)
Duquesne University (PA) (m/w)
East Carolina University (NC) (m/w)
East Central University (OK) (m/w)
Eastern Illinois University (IL) (m/w)
Eastern Kentucky University (KY) (m/w)
Eastern Michigan University (MI) (m/w)
Eastern New Mexico University (NM) (m/w)
Eastern Oregon University (OR) (m/w)
Eastern University (PA) (m/w)
Eastern Washington University (WA) (m/w)
East Tennessee State University (TN) (m/w)
Edinboro University of Pennsylvania (PA)
    (m/w)
Elmhurst College (IL) (m/w)
Elmira College (NY) (m/w)
Elon University (NC) (m/w)
Embry-Riddle Aeronautical University (FL)
    (m/w)
Emory & Henry College (VA) (m/w)
Emporia State University (KS) (m/w)
Endicott College (MA) (m/w)
Fairleigh Dickinson University, College at
    Florham (NJ) (m/w)
Fairmont State University (WV) (m/w)
Fayetteville State University (NC) (m/w)
Felician College (NJ) (m/w)
Ferris State University (MI) (m/w)
Ferrum College (VA) (m/w)
Fisk University (TN) (m/w)
Florida Atlantic University (FL) (m/w)
Florida Gulf Coast University (FL) (m/w)
Florida Institute of Technology (FL) (m/w)
Florida International University (FL) (m/w)
Florida Memorial College (FL) (m/w)
Florida Southern College (FL) (m/w)
Florida State University (FL) (m/w)
Fontbonne University (MO) (m/w)
Fort Hays State University (KS) (m/w)
Framingham State College (MA) (m/w)
Franklin College (IN) (m/w)
Freed-Hardeman University (TN) (m/w)
Frostburg State University (MD) (m/w)
Furman University (SC) (m/w)
Gallaudet University (DC) (m/w)
Gannon University (PA) (m/w)
Gardner-Webb University (NC) (m/w)
George Mason University (VA) (m/w)
Georgetown College (KY) (m/w)
Georgetown University (DC) (m/w)
Georgia College & State University (GA)
    (m/w)
Georgia Institute of Technology (GA) (m/w)
Georgia Southern University (GA) (m/w)
Georgia State University (GA) (m/w)

Gettysburg College (PA) (m/w)
Gonzaga University (WA) (m/w)
Grace College (IN) (m/w)
Grand Valley State University (MI) (m/w)
Grand View College (IA) (m/w)
Greensboro College (NC) (m/w)
Hampton University (VA) (m/w)
Hannibal-LaGrange College (MO) (m/w)
Harding University (AR) (m/w)
Haskell Indian Nations University (KS)
    (m/w)
Hastings College (NE) (m/w)
Hawai'i Pacific University (HI) (m/w)
Heidelberg College (OH) (m/w)
Hendrix College (AR) (m/w)
High Point University (NC) (m/w)
Hofstra University (NY) (m/w)
Holy Family University (PA) (m/w)
Hope College (MI) (m/w)
Howard Payne University (TX) (m/w)
Howard University (DC) (m/w)
Huntington College (IN) (m/w)
Idaho State University (ID) (m/w)
Illinois State University (IL) (m/w)
Indiana Institute of Technology (IN) (m/w)
Indiana State University (IN) (m/w)
Indiana University Bloomington (IN) (m/w)
Indiana University Northwest (IN) (m/w)
Indiana University of Pennsylvania (PA)
    (m/w)
Indiana University–Purdue University Fort
    Wayne (IN) (m/w)
Indiana University–Purdue University
    Indianapolis (IN) (m/w)
Indiana Wesleyan University (IN) (m/w)
Iowa State University of Science and
    Technology (IA) (m/w)
Jacksonville State University (AL) (m/w)
James Madison University (VA) (m/w)
John Brown University (AR) (m/w)
Johnson C. Smith University (NC) (m/w)
Juniata College (PA) (m/w)
Kalamazoo College (MI) (m/w)
Kansas State University (KS) (m/w)
Kansas Wesleyan University (KS) (m/w)
Kean University (NJ) (m/w)
Keene State College (NH) (m/w)
Kennesaw State University (GA) (m/w)
Kent State University (OH) (m/w)
Kentucky State University (KY) (m/w)
Kentucky Wesleyan College (KY) (m/w)
King's College (PA) (m/w)
Kutztown University of Pennsylvania (PA)
    (m/w)
Lafayette College (PA) (m/w)
LaGrange College (GA) (m/w)
Lake Superior State University (MI) (m/w)
Lambuth University (TN) (m/w)
Lander University (SC) (m/w)
Lane College (TN) (m/w)
Langston University (OK) (m/w)
La Roche College (PA) (m/w)
La Salle University (PA) (m/w)
Lees-McRae College (NC) (m/w)
Lee University (TN) (m/w)
Lehman College of the City University of
    New York (NY) (m/w)
Lewis University (IL) (m/w)
Liberty University (VA) (m/w)
Limestone College (SC) (m/w)
Lincoln Memorial University (TN) (m/w)
Lincoln University (MO) (m/w)
Lincoln University (PA) (m/w)
Lindsey Wilson College (KY) (m/w)
Lipscomb University (TN) (m/w)

Livingstone College (NC) (m/w)
Lock Haven University of Pennsylvania (PA)
    (m/w)
Long Island University, Brooklyn Campus
    (NY) (m/w)
Long Island University, C.W. Post Campus
    (NY) (m/w)
Longwood University (VA) (m/w)
Louisiana State University and Agricultural
    and Mechanical College (LA) (m/w)
Loyola College in Maryland (MD) (m/w)
Loyola Marymount University (CA) (m/w)
Loyola University Chicago (IL) (m/w)
Lynchburg College (VA) (m/w)
Lynn University (FL) (m/w)
Malone College (OH) (m/w)
Manchester College (IN) (m/w)
Manhattanville College (NY) (m/w)
Mansfield University of Pennsylvania (PA)
    (m/w)
Marian College (IN) (m/w)
Marshall University (WV) (m/w)
Mars Hill College (NC) (m/w)
Martin Methodist College (TN) (m/w)
Marymount University (VA) (m/w)
Maryville College (TN) (m/w)
Maryville University of Saint Louis (MO)
    (m/w)
Massachusetts Institute of Technology (MA)
    (m/w)
Mayville State University (ND) (m/w)
McKendree College (IL) (m/w)
McMurry University (TX) (m/w)
McPherson College (KS) (m/w)
Mercyhurst College (PA) (m/w)
Merrimack College (MA) (m/w)
Methodist College (NC) (m/w)
Metropolitan State College of Denver (CO)
    (m/w)
Miami University (OH) (m/w)
Michigan State University (MI) (m/w)
Michigan Technological University (MI)
    (m/w)
MidAmerica Nazarene University (KS) (m/w)
Middle Tennessee State University (TN)
    (m/w)
Midwestern State University (TX) (m/w)
Millersville University of Pennsylvania (PA)
    (m/w)
Minnesota State University Mankato (MN)
    (m/w)
Minnesota State University Moorhead (MN)
    (m/w)
Mississippi College (MS) (m/w)
Mississippi State University (MS) (m/w)
Mississippi University for Women (MS)
    (m/w)
Missouri Baptist University (MO) (m/w)
Missouri Valley College (MO) (m/w)
Missouri Western State College (MO) (m/w)
Monmouth University (NJ) (m/w)
Montana State University–Billings (MT)
    (m/w)
Montana State University–Bozeman (MT)
    (m/w)
Moravian College (PA) (m/w)
Morehead State University (KY) (m/w)
Morgan State University (MD) (m/w)
Mountain State University (WV) (m/w)
Mount Olive College (NC) (m/w)
Mount Saint Mary's University (MD) (m/w)
Mount Union College (OH) (m/w)
Muhlenberg College (PA) (m/w)
Murray State University (KY) (m/w)
Muskingum College (OH) (m/w)

Nazareth College of Rochester (NY) (m/w)
Newberry College (SC) (m/w)
Newman University (KS) (m/w)
New Mexico Highlands University (NM) (m/w)
New Mexico State University (NM) (m/w)
New York University (NY) (m/w)
Nicholls State University (LA) (m/w)
Norfolk State University (VA) (m/w)
North Carolina Central University (NC) (m/w)
North Carolina State University (NC) (m/w)
North Dakota State University (ND) (m/w)
Northeastern University (MA) (m/w)
Northern Arizona University (AZ) (m/w)
Northern Illinois University (IL) (m/w)
Northern Kentucky University (KY) (m/w)
Northern Michigan University (MI) (m/w)
Northern State University (SD) (m/w)
North Georgia College & State University (GA) (m/w)
Northwestern Oklahoma State University (OK) (m/w)
Northwestern University (IL) (m/w)
Northwest Missouri State University (MO) (m/w)
Northwood University (MI) (m/w)
Nyack College (NY) (m/w)
Oakland City University (IN) (m/w)
Oakland University (MI) (m/w)
The Ohio State University (OH) (m/w)
Ohio University (OH) (m/w)
Ohio Valley College (WV) (m/w)
Ohio Wesleyan University (OH) (m/w)
Oklahoma Baptist University (OK) (m/w)
Oklahoma City University (OK) (m/w)
Old Dominion University (VA) (m/w)
Olivet College (MI) (m/w)
Olivet Nazarene University (IL) (m/w)
Oral Roberts University (OK) (m/w)
Oregon State University (OR) (m/w)
Ottawa University (KS) (m/w)
Ouachita Baptist University (AR) (m/w)
Pace University (NY) (m/w)
Pacific Lutheran University (WA) (m/w)
The Pennsylvania State University Altoona College (PA) (m/w)
The Pennsylvania State University University Park Campus (PA) (m/w)
Pepperdine University (CA) (m/w)
Peru State College (NE) (m/w)
Pfeiffer University (NC) (m/w)
Philadelphia University (PA) (m/w)
Piedmont College (GA) (m/w)
Pikeville College (KY) (m/w)
Pittsburg State University (KS) (m/w)
Portland State University (OR) (m/w)
Prairie View A&M University (TX) (m/w)
Princeton University (NJ) (m/w)
Purdue University (IN) (m/w)
Purdue University North Central (IN) (m/w)
Queens University of Charlotte (NC) (m/w)
Quincy University (IL) (m/w)
Quinnipiac University (CT) (m/w)
Ramapo College of New Jersey (NJ) (m/w)
Randolph-Macon College (VA) (m/w)
The Richard Stockton College of New Jersey (NJ) (m/w)
Rider University (NJ) (m/w)
Rivier College (NH) (m/w)
Robert Morris University (PA) (m/w)
Rochester Institute of Technology (NY) (m/w)
Rockhurst University (MO) (m/w)
Roger Williams University (RI) (m/w)

Rollins College (FL) (m/w)
Rutgers, The State University of New Jersey, Camden (NJ) (m/w)
Rutgers, The State University of New Jersey, New Brunswick/Piscataway (NJ) (m/w)
Sacred Heart University (CT) (m/w)
Saginaw Valley State University (MI) (m/w)
St. Ambrose University (IA) (m/w)
Saint Augustine's College (NC) (m/w)
St. Cloud State University (MN) (m/w)
St. Edward's University (TX) (m/w)
St. John's University (NY) (m/w)
Saint Joseph's College (IN) (m/w)
Saint Leo University (FL) (m/w)
Saint Mary's College (IN) (w)
Saint Mary's College of California (CA) (m/w)
St. Mary's College of Maryland (MD) (m/w)
St. Mary's University of San Antonio (TX) (m/w)
Saint Michael's College (VT) (m/w)
St. Norbert College (WI) (m/w)
Saint Peter's College (NJ) (m/w)
Saint Xavier University (IL) (m/w)
Salisbury University (MD) (m/w)
Sam Houston State University (TX) (m/w)
San Diego State University (CA) (m/w)
San Francisco State University (CA) (m/w)
San Jose State University (CA) (m/w)
Santa Clara University (CA) (m/w)
Savannah College of Art and Design (GA) (m/w)
Savannah State University (GA) (m/w)
Seattle University (WA) (m/w)
Shawnee State University (OH) (m/w)
Shaw University (NC) (m/w)
Shenandoah University (VA) (m/w)
Shepherd University (WV) (m/w)
Shippensburg University of Pennsylvania (PA) (m/w)
Siena College (NY) (m/w)
Simpson College (IA) (m/w)
Slippery Rock University of Pennsylvania (PA) (m/w)
Southeastern Louisiana University (LA) (m/w)
Southeastern Oklahoma State University (OK) (m/w)
Southeast Missouri State University (MO) (m/w)
Southern Arkansas University–Magnolia (AR) (m/w)
Southern Illinois University Carbondale (IL) (m/w)
Southern Illinois University Edwardsville (IL) (m/w)
Southern Methodist University (TX) (m/w)
Southern Nazarene University (OK) (m/w)
Southern New Hampshire University (NH) (m/w)
Southern Utah University (UT) (m/w)
Southern Virginia University (VA) (m/w)
Southern Wesleyan University (SC) (m/w)
Southwest Baptist University (MO) (m/w)
Southwestern Assemblies of God University (TX) (m/w)
Southwestern College (KS) (m/w)
Southwestern Oklahoma State University (OK) (m/w)
Southwest Missouri State University (MO) (m/w)
Spelman College (GA) (w)
State University of New York at Binghamton (NY) (m/w)

State University of New York College at Cortland (NY) (m/w)
State University of New York College at Fredonia (NY) (m/w)
State University of New York College at Geneseo (NY) (m/w)
State University of New York College at Old Westbury (NY) (m/w)
State University of New York College at Potsdam (NY) (m/w)
State University of West Georgia (GA) (m/w)
Stephen F. Austin State University (TX) (m/w)
Stetson University (FL) (m/w)
Suffolk University (MA) (m/w)
Sul Ross State University (TX) (m/w)
Susquehanna University (PA) (m/w)
Tarleton State University (TX) (m/w)
Temple University (PA) (m/w)
Tennessee State University (TN) (m/w)
Tennessee Technological University (TN) (m/w)
Texas A&M University (TX) (m/w)
Texas A&M University–Commerce (TX) (m/w)
Texas A&M University–Kingsville (TX) (m/w)
Texas Christian University (TX) (m/w)
Texas Lutheran University (TX) (m/w)
Texas Southern University (TX) (m/w)
Texas State University-San Marcos (TX) (m/w)
Texas Wesleyan University (TX) (m/w)
Thiel College (PA) (m/w)
Tiffin University (OH) (m/w)
Tougaloo College (MS) (m/w)
Transylvania University (KY) (m/w)
Trevecca Nazarene University (TN) (m/w)
Trinity University (TX) (m/w)
Tri-State University (IN) (m/w)
Troy State University (AL) (m/w)
Truman State University (MO) (m/w)
Tulane University (LA) (m/w)
Tusculum College (TN) (m/w)
Tuskegee University (AL) (m/w)
Union College (KY) (m/w)
Union University (TN) (m/w)
United States Naval Academy (MD) (m/w)
University at Albany, State University of New York (NY) (m/w)
University at Buffalo, The State University of New York (NY) (m/w)
The University of Akron (OH) (m/w)
The University of Alabama (AL) (m/w)
The University of Alabama at Birmingham (AL) (m/w)
The University of Alabama in Huntsville (AL) (m/w)
University of Alaska Anchorage (AK) (m/w)
University of Alaska Fairbanks (AK) (m/w)
The University of Arizona (AZ) (m/w)
University of Arkansas (AR) (m/w)
University of Arkansas at Little Rock (AR) (m/w)
University of Arkansas at Pine Bluff (AR) (m/w)
University of Bridgeport (CT) (m/w)
University of California, Davis (CA) (m/w)
University of California, Irvine (CA) (m/w)
University of California, Los Angeles (CA) (m/w)
University of California, Riverside (CA) (m/w)
University of California, San Diego (CA) (m/w)

University of California, Santa Barbara (CA) (m/w)
University of Central Arkansas (AR) (m/w)
University of Central Florida (FL) (m/w)
University of Chicago (IL) (m/w)
University of Cincinnati (OH) (m/w)
University of Colorado at Colorado Springs (CO) (m/w)
University of Connecticut (CT) (m/w)
University of Dayton (OH) (m/w)
University of Delaware (DE) (m/w)
University of Detroit Mercy (MI) (m/w)
University of Dubuque (IA) (m/w)
University of Evansville (IN) (m/w)
The University of Findlay (OH) (m/w)
University of Florida (FL) (m/w)
University of Georgia (GA) (m/w)
University of Hartford (CT) (m/w)
University of Hawaii at Manoa (HI) (m/w)
University of Idaho (ID) (m/w)
University of Illinois at Chicago (IL) (m/w)
University of Illinois at Springfield (IL) (m/w)
University of Illinois at Urbana–Champaign (IL) (m/w)
University of Indianapolis (IN) (m/w)
The University of Iowa (IA) (m/w)
University of Kentucky (KY) (m/w)
University of Louisiana at Monroe (LA) (m/w)
University of Louisville (KY) (m/w)
University of Maine (ME) (m/w)
University of Mary (ND) (m/w)
University of Maryland, College Park (MD) (m/w)
University of Massachusetts Amherst (MA) (m/w)
University of Massachusetts Dartmouth (MA) (m/w)
University of Miami (FL) (m/w)
University of Michigan (MI) (m/w)
University of Minnesota, Crookston (MN) (m/w)
University of Minnesota, Duluth (MN) (m/w)
University of Minnesota, Morris (MN) (m/w)
University of Minnesota, Twin Cities Campus (MN) (m/w)
University of Missouri–Columbia (MO) (m/w)
University of Missouri–Kansas City (MO) (m/w)
University of Missouri–St. Louis (MO) (m/w)
University of Mobile (AL) (m/w)
The University of Montana–Missoula (MT) (m/w)
The University of Montana–Western (MT) (m/w)
University of Montevallo (AL) (m/w)
University of Nebraska at Kearney (NE) (m/w)
University of Nebraska at Omaha (NE) (m/w)
University of Nevada, Las Vegas (NV) (m/w)
University of Nevada, Reno (NV) (m/w)
University of New Hampshire (NH) (m/w)
University of New Haven (CT) (m/w)
University of New Mexico (NM) (m/w)
The University of North Carolina at Asheville (NC) (m/w)
The University of North Carolina at Chapel Hill (NC) (m/w)
The University of North Carolina at Charlotte (NC) (m/w)
The University of North Carolina at Greensboro (NC) (m/w)

The University of North Carolina at Pembroke (NC) (m/w)
University of North Dakota (ND) (m/w)
University of Northern Colorado (CO) (m/w)
University of Northern Iowa (IA) (m/w)
University of North Florida (FL) (m/w)
University of North Texas (TX) (m/w)
University of Notre Dame (IN) (m/w)
University of Oklahoma (OK) (m/w)
University of Oregon (OR) (m/w)
University of Pennsylvania (PA) (m/w)
University of Pittsburgh (PA) (m/w)
University of Pittsburgh at Greensburg (PA) (m/w)
University of Redlands (CA) (m/w)
University of Rhode Island (RI) (m/w)
University of Richmond (VA) (m/w)
University of Saint Francis (IN) (m/w)
University of St. Thomas (MN) (m/w)
The University of Scranton (PA) (m/w)
University of South Alabama (AL) (m/w)
University of South Carolina (SC) (m/w)
University of South Carolina Aiken (SC) (m/w)
University of South Carolina Spartanburg (SC) (m/w)
University of Southern California (CA) (m/w)
University of Southern Indiana (IN) (m/w)
University of Southern Maine (ME) (m/w)
University of Southern Mississippi (MS) (m/w)
University of South Florida (FL) (m/w)
The University of Tennessee (TN) (m/w)
The University of Tennessee at Chattanooga (TN) (m/w)
The University of Tennessee at Martin (TN) (m/w)
The University of Texas at Arlington (TX) (m/w)
The University of Texas at Austin (TX) (m/w)
The University of Texas at Dallas (TX) (m/w)
The University of Texas at El Paso (TX) (m/w)
The University of Texas at San Antonio (TX) (m/w)
The University of Texas–Pan American (TX) (m/w)
University of the Ozarks (AR) (m/w)
University of Toledo (OH) (m/w)
University of Tulsa (OK) (m/w)
University of Virginia (VA) (m/w)
University of West Florida (FL) (m/w)
University of Wisconsin–La Crosse (WI) (m/w)
University of Wisconsin–Madison (WI) (m/w)
University of Wisconsin–Milwaukee (WI) (m/w)
University of Wisconsin–Oshkosh (WI) (m/w)
University of Wisconsin–Platteville (WI) (m/w)
University of Wisconsin–Stout (WI) (m/w)
University of Wisconsin–Superior (WI) (m/w)
University of Wyoming (WY) (m/w)
Upper Iowa University (IA) (m/w)
Utah State University (UT) (m/w)
Valdosta State University (GA) (m/w)
Valley City State University (ND) (m/w)
Valparaiso University (IN) (m/w)
Vanderbilt University (TN) (m/w)
Villa Julie College (MD) (m/w)
Villanova University (PA) (m/w)
Virginia Commonwealth University (VA) (m/w)

Virginia Polytechnic Institute and State University (VA) (m/w)
Virginia State University (VA) (m/w)
Virginia Union University (VA) (m/w)
Wagner College (NY) (m/w)
Wake Forest University (NC) (m/w)
Waldorf College (IA) (m/w)
Walsh University (OH) (m/w)
Warner Southern College (FL) (m/w)
Wartburg College (IA) (m/w)
Washington University in St. Louis (MO) (m/w)
Wayne State University (MI) (m/w)
Webber International University (FL) (m/w)
Weber State University (UT) (m/w)
Webster University (MO) (m/w)
Wesley College (DE) (m/w)
West Chester University of Pennsylvania (PA) (m/w)
Western Carolina University (NC) (m/w)
Western Illinois University (IL) (m/w)
Western Michigan University (MI) (m/w)
Western Washington University (WA) (m/w)
Westfield State College (MA) (m/w)
West Liberty State College (WV) (m/w)
Westminster College (PA) (m/w)
West Texas A&M University (TX) (m/w)
West Virginia State College (WV) (m/w)
West Virginia University (WV) (m/w)
West Virginia University Institute of Technology (WV) (m/w)
Wheeling Jesuit University (WV) (m/w)
Wichita State University (KS) (m/w)
Widener University (PA) (m/w)
William Jewell College (MO) (m/w)
William Paterson University of New Jersey (NJ) (m/w)
Wilmington College (DE) (m/w)
Wingate University (NC) (m/w)
Winona State University (MN) (m/w)
Winston-Salem State University (NC) (m/w)
Winthrop University (SC) (m/w)
Wisconsin Lutheran College (WI) (m/w)
Wofford College (SC) (m/w)
Wright State University (OH) (m/w)
Xavier University (OH) (m/w)
Youngstown State University (OH)(m/w)

Cross Country

Abilene Christian University (TX) (m/w)
Adams State College (CO) (m/w)
Adelphi University (NY) (m/w)
Adrian College (MI) (m/w)
Agnes Scott College (GA) (w)
Alabama Agricultural and Mechanical University (AL) (m/w)
Alabama State University (AL) (m/w)
Albany State University (GA) (m/w)
Albertson College of Idaho (ID) (m/w)
Albertus Magnus College (CT) (m/w)
Albion College (MI) (m/w)
Albright College (PA) (m/w)
Alcorn State University (MS) (m/w)
Alderson-Broaddus College (WV) (m/w)
Alfred University (NY) (m/w)
Alice Lloyd College (KY) (m/w)
Allegheny College (PA) (m/w)
Allen University (SC) (m/w)
Alliant International University (CA) (m/w)
Alma College (MI) (m/w)
Alvernia College (PA) (m/w)
Alverno College (WI) (w)
American University (DC) (m/w)
Amherst College (MA) (m/w)

Anderson College (SC) (m/w)
Anderson University (IN) (m/w)
Angelo State University (TX) (m/w)
Anna Maria College (MA) (m)
Appalachian State University (NC) (m/w)
Aquinas College (MI) (m/w)
Arcadia University (PA) (m/w)
Arizona State University (AZ) (m/w)
Arkansas State University (AR) (m/w)
Arkansas Tech University (AR) (w)
Asbury College (KY) (m/w)
Ashland University (OH) (m/w)
Assumption College (MA) (m/w)
Auburn University (AL) (m/w)
Augsburg College (MN) (m/w)
Augustana College (IL) (m/w)
Augustana College (SD) (m/w)
Augusta State University (GA) (w)
Aurora University (IL) (m/w)
Austin Peay State University (TN) (m/w)
Averett University (VA) (m/w)
Azusa Pacific University (CA) (m/w)
Babson College (MA) (m/w)
Bacone College (OK) (m/w)
Baker University (KS) (m/w)
Baldwin-Wallace College (OH) (m/w)
Ball State University (IN) (m/w)
Baptist Bible College of Pennsylvania (PA)
    (m/w)
Barber-Scotia College (NC) (m/w)
Bard College (NY) (m/w)
Barton College (NC) (m/w)
Bates College (ME) (m/w)
Baylor University (TX) (m/w)
Bay Path College (MA) (w)
Belhaven College (MS) (m/w)
Bellarmine University (KY) (m/w)
Belmont Abbey College (NC) (m/w)
Belmont University (TN) (m/w)
Beloit College (WI) (m/w)
Bemidji State University (MN) (w)
Benedict College (SC) (m/w)
Benedictine College (KS) (m/w)
Benedictine University (IL) (m/w)
Bentley College (MA) (m/w)
Berea College (KY) (m/w)
Bernard M. Baruch College of the City
    University of New York (NY) (w)
Berry College (GA) (m/w)
Bethany College (KS) (m/w)
Bethany College (WV) (m/w)
Bethel College (IN) (m/w)
Bethel College (KS) (m/w)
Bethel College (TN) (m/w)
Bethel University (MN) (m/w)
Biola University (CA) (m/w)
Birmingham-Southern College (AL) (m/w)
Blackburn College (IL) (m/w)
Black Hills State University (SD) (m/w)
Bloomfield College (NJ) (m)
Bloomsburg University of Pennsylvania (PA)
    (m/w)
Bluefield State College (WV) (m/w)
Bluffton College (OH) (m/w)
Boise State University (ID) (m/w)
Boston College (MA) (m/w)
Boston University (MA) (m/w)
Bowdoin College (ME) (m/w)
Bowie State University (MD) (m/w)
Bowling Green State University (OH) (m/w)
Bradley University (IL) (m/w)
Brandeis University (MA) (m/w)
Brevard College (NC) (m/w)
Briar Cliff University (IA) (m/w)
Bridgewater College (VA) (m/w)

Bridgewater State College (MA) (m/w)
Brigham Young University (UT) (m/w)
Brigham Young University–Hawaii (HI)
    (m/w)
Brooklyn College of the City University of
    New York (NY) (m/w)
Brown University (RI) (m/w)
Bryant College (RI) (m/w)
Bryn Mawr College (PA) (w)
Bucknell University (PA) (m/w)
Buena Vista University (IA) (m/w)
Buffalo State College, State University of
    New York (NY) (m/w)
Butler University (IN) (m/w)
Cabrini College (PA) (m/w)
Caldwell College (NJ) (w)
California Baptist University (CA) (m/w)
California Institute of Technology (CA)
    (m/w)
California Lutheran University (CA) (m/w)
California Polytechnic State University, San
    Luis Obispo (CA) (m/w)
California State Polytechnic University,
    Pomona (CA) (m/w)
California State University, Bakersfield (CA)
    (w)
California State University, Chico (CA) (m/w)
California State University, Dominguez Hills
    (CA) (w)
California State University, Fresno (CA) (w)
California State University, Fullerton (CA)
    (m/w)
California State University, Hayward (CA)
    (m/w)
California State University, Long Beach (CA)
    (m/w)
California State University, Los Angeles (CA)
    (w)
California State University, Monterey Bay
    (CA) (m/w)
California State University, Northridge (CA)
    (m/w)
California State University, Sacramento (CA)
    (m/w)
California State University, San Bernardino
    (CA) (w)
California State University, San Marcos (CA)
    (m/w)
California State University, Stanislaus (CA)
    (m/w)
California University of Pennsylvania (PA)
    (m/w)
Calvin College (MI) (m/w)
Campbellsville University (KY) (m/w)
Campbell University (NC) (m/w)
Canisius College (NY) (m/w)
Capital University (OH) (m/w)
Cardinal Stritch University (WI) (m/w)
Carleton College (MN) (m/w)
Carnegie Mellon University (PA) (m/w)
Carroll College (WI) (m/w)
Carson-Newman College (TN) (m/w)
Carthage College (WI) (m/w)
Cascade College (OR) (m/w)
Case Western Reserve University (OH) (m/w)
Castleton State College (VT) (m/w)
Catawba College (NC) (m/w)
The Catholic University of America (DC)
    (m/w)
Cazenovia College (NY) (m/w)
Cedar Crest College (PA) (w)
Cedarville University (OH) (m/w)
Centenary College (NJ) (m/w)
Centenary College of Louisiana (LA) (m/w)

Central Christian College of Kansas (KS)
    (m/w)
Central College (IA) (m/w)
Central Connecticut State University (CT)
    (m/w)
Central Methodist College (MO) (m/w)
Central Michigan University (MI) (m/w)
Central Missouri State University (MO)
    (m/w)
Central Washington University (WA) (m/w)
Centre College (KY) (m/w)
Chaminade University of Honolulu (HI)
    (m/w)
Chapman University (CA) (m/w)
Charleston Southern University (SC) (m/w)
Cheyney University of Pennsylvania (PA)
    (m/w)
Chicago State University (IL) (m/w)
Chowan College (NC) (w)
Christian Brothers University (TN) (m/w)
Christian Heritage College (CA) (m/w)
Christopher Newport University (VA) (m/w)
The Citadel, The Military College of South
    Carolina (SC) (m/w)
Claflin University (SC) (m/w)
Claremont McKenna College (CA) (m/w)
Clarion University of Pennsylvania (PA)
    (m/w)
Clark Atlanta University (GA) (m/w)
Clarke College (IA) (m/w)
Clarkson University (NY) (m/w)
Clark University (MA) (m/w)
Clayton College & State University (GA)
    (m/w)
Cleveland State University (OH) (w)
Coastal Carolina University (SC) (m/w)
Coe College (IA) (m/w)
Coker College (SC) (m/w)
Colby College (ME) (m/w)
Colgate University (NY) (m/w)
College Misericordia (PA) (m/w)
College of Charleston (SC) (m/w)
College of Mount St. Joseph (OH) (m/w)
College of Mount Saint Vincent (NY) (m/w)
The College of New Jersey (NJ) (m/w)
The College of New Rochelle (NY) (w)
College of Saint Benedict (MN) (w)
College of St. Catherine (MN) (w)
College of Saint Mary (NE) (w)
The College of Saint Rose (NY) (m/w)
The College of St. Scholastica (MN) (m/w)
College of the Holy Cross (MA) (m/w)
The College of William and Mary (VA)
    (m/w)
The College of Wooster (OH) (m/w)
Colorado Christian University (CO) (m/w)
The Colorado College (CO) (m/w)
Colorado School of Mines (CO) (m/w)
Colorado State University (CO) (m/w)
Columbia College (NY) (m/w)
Columbia College (SC) (w)
Columbia Union College (MD) (m/w)
Columbus State University (GA) (m/w)
Concord College (WV) (m/w)
Concordia College (MN) (m/w)
Concordia College (NY) (m/w)
Concordia University (CA) (m/w)
Concordia University (IL) (m/w)
Concordia University (NE) (m/w)
Concordia University at Austin (TX) (m/w)
Concordia University, St. Paul (MN) (m/w)
Concordia University Wisconsin (WI) (m/w)
Connecticut College (CT) (m/w)
Converse College (SC) (w)
Coppin State University (MD) (m/w)

Cornell College (IA) (m/w)
Cornell University (NY) (m/w)
Cornerstone University (MI) (m/w)
Covenant College (GA) (m/w)
Creighton University (NE) (m/w)
Crown College (MN) (m/w)
Cumberland College (KY) (m/w)
Cumberland University (TN) (m/w)
Curry College (MA) (w)
Daemen College (NY) (m/w)
Dakota State University (SD) (m/w)
Dakota Wesleyan University (SD) (m/w)
Dallas Baptist University (TX) (m/w)
Dana College (NE) (m/w)
Daniel Webster College (NH) (m/w)
Dartmouth College (NH) (m/w)
Davidson College (NC) (m/w)
Davis & Elkins College (WV) (m/w)
Defiance College (OH) (m/w)
Delaware State University (DE) (m/w)
Delaware Valley College (PA) (m/w)
Delta State University (MS) (w)
Denison University (OH) (m/w)
DePaul University (IL) (m/w)
DePauw University (IN) (m/w)
DeSales University (PA) (m/w)
Dickinson College (PA) (m/w)
Dickinson State University (ND) (m/w)
Dillard University (LA) (m/w)
Doane College (NE) (m/w)
Dominican College (NY) (m/w)
Dominican University (IL) (m/w)
Dordt College (IA) (m/w)
Dowling College (NY) (w)
Drake University (IA) (m/w)
Drew University (NJ) (m/w)
Drury University (MO) (m/w)
Duke University (NC) (m/w)
Duquesne University (PA) (m/w)
D'Youville College (NY) (w)
Earlham College (IN) (m/w)
East Carolina University (NC) (m/w)
East Central University (OK) (m/w)
Eastern Connecticut State University (CT) (m/w)
Eastern Illinois University (IL) (m/w)
Eastern Kentucky University (KY) (m/w)
Eastern Mennonite University (VA) (m/w)
Eastern Michigan University (MI) (m/w)
Eastern Nazarene College (MA) (m/w)
Eastern New Mexico University (NM) (m/w)
Eastern Oregon University (OR) (m/w)
Eastern Washington University (WA) (m/w)
East Stroudsburg University of Pennsylvania (PA) (m/w)
East Tennessee State University (TN) (m/w)
East Texas Baptist University (TX) (m/w)
Eckerd College (FL) (w)
Edgewood College (WI) (m/w)
Edinboro University of Pennsylvania (PA) (m/w)
Elizabeth City State University (NC) (m/w)
Elizabethtown College (PA) (m/w)
Elmhurst College (IL) (m/w)
Elms College (MA) (m/w)
Elon University (NC) (m/w)
Embry-Riddle Aeronautical University (FL) (m/w)
Emerson College (MA) (m/w)
Emmanuel College (MA) (m/w)
Emory & Henry College (VA) (m/w)
Emory University (GA) (m/w)
Emporia State University (KS) (m/w)
Endicott College (MA) (m/w)
Erskine College (SC) (m/w)

Evangel University (MO) (m/w)
The Evergreen State College (WA) (m/w)
Fairfield University (CT) (m/w)
Fairleigh Dickinson University, College at Florham (NJ) (m/w)
Fairmont State University (WV) (m/w)
Farmingdale State University of New York (NY) (m/w)
Faulkner University (AL) (m/w)
Fayetteville State University (NC) (m/w)
Felician College (NJ) (m/w)
Ferris State University (MI) (m/w)
Ferrum College (VA) (m/w)
Fisk University (TN) (m/w)
Fitchburg State College (MA) (m/w)
Flagler College (FL) (m/w)
Florida Atlantic University (FL) (m/w)
Florida Gulf Coast University (FL) (m/w)
Florida Institute of Technology (FL) (m/w)
Florida International University (FL) (m/w)
Florida Memorial College (FL) (m/w)
Florida Southern College (FL) (m/w)
Florida State University (FL) (m/w)
Fontbonne University (MO) (m/w)
Fordham University (NY) (m/w)
Fort Hays State University (KS) (m/w)
Fort Lewis College (CO) (m/w)
Fort Valley State University (GA) (m/w)
Framingham State College (MA) (m/w)
The Franciscan University (IA) (m/w)
Francis Marion University (SC) (m/w)
Franklin and Marshall College (PA) (m/w)
Franklin College (IN) (m/w)
Franklin Pierce College (NH) (m/w)
Freed-Hardeman University (TN) (m/w)
Fresno Pacific University (CA) (m/w)
Friends University (KS) (m/w)
Frostburg State University (MD) (m/w)
Furman University (SC) (m/w)
Gallaudet University (DC) (m/w)
Gannon University (PA) (m/w)
Gardner-Webb University (NC) (m/w)
Geneva College (PA) (m/w)
George Fox University (OR) (m/w)
George Mason University (VA) (m/w)
Georgetown College (KY) (m/w)
Georgetown University (DC) (m/w)
The George Washington University (DC) (m/w)
Georgia College & State University (GA) (m/w)
Georgia Institute of Technology (GA) (m/w)
Georgian Court University (NJ) (w)
Georgia Southern University (GA) (w)
Georgia State University (GA) (m/w)
Gettysburg College (PA) (m/w)
Glenville State College (WV) (m/w)
Goldey-Beacom College (DE) (m/w)
Gonzaga University (WA) (m/w)
Gordon College (MA) (m/w)
Goshen College (IN) (m/w)
Goucher College (MD) (m/w)
Grace College (IN) (m/w)
Graceland University (IA) (m/w)
Grambling State University (LA) (m/w)
Grand Valley State University (MI) (m/w)
Grand View College (IA) (m/w)
Greensboro College (NC) (m/w)
Greenville College (IL) (m/w)
Grinnell College (IA) (m/w)
Grove City College (PA) (m/w)
Gustavus Adolphus College (MN) (m/w)
Gwynedd-Mercy College (PA) (m/w)
Hamilton College (NY) (m/w)
Hamline University (MN) (m/w)

Hampden-Sydney College (VA) (m)
Hampton University (VA) (m/w)
Hannibal-LaGrange College (MO) (m/w)
Hanover College (IN) (m/w)
Harding University (AR) (m/w)
Hartwick College (NY) (m/w)
Harvard University (MA) (m/w)
Haskell Indian Nations University (KS) (m/w)
Hastings College (NE) (m/w)
Haverford College (PA) (m/w)
Hawai'i Pacific University (HI) (m/w)
Heidelberg College (OH) (m/w)
Henderson State University (AR) (w)
Hendrix College (AR) (m/w)
High Point University (NC) (m/w)
Hilbert College (NY) (m/w)
Hillsdale College (MI) (m/w)
Hiram College (OH) (m/w)
Hobart and William Smith Colleges (NY) (m/w)
Hofstra University (NY) (m/w)
Hollins University (VA) (w)
Holy Family University (PA) (m/w)
Holy Names University (CA) (m/w)
Hood College (MD) (w)
Hope College (MI) (m/w)
Houghton College (NY) (m/w)
Howard University (DC) (m/w)
Humboldt State University (CA) (m/w)
Hunter College of the City University of New York (NY) (m/w)
Huntington College (IN) (m/w)
Husson College (ME) (m/w)
Idaho State University (ID) (m/w)
Illinois College (IL) (m/w)
Illinois Institute of Technology (IL) (m/w)
Illinois State University (IL) (m/w)
Illinois Wesleyan University (IL) (m/w)
Immaculata University (PA) (w)
Indiana State University (IN) (m/w)
Indiana University Bloomington (IN) (m/w)
Indiana University of Pennsylvania (PA) (m/w)
Indiana University–Purdue University Fort Wayne (IN) (m/w)
Indiana University–Purdue University Indianapolis (IN) (m/w)
Indiana University Southeast (IN) (m/w)
Indiana Wesleyan University (IN) (m/w)
Iona College (NY) (m/w)
Iowa State University of Science and Technology (IA) (m/w)
Ithaca College (NY) (m/w)
Jackson State University (MS) (m/w)
Jacksonville State University (AL) (m/w)
Jacksonville University (FL) (m/w)
James Madison University (VA) (m/w)
Jamestown College (ND) (m/w)
John Carroll University (OH) (m/w)
John Jay College of Criminal Justice of the City University of New York (NY) (m/w)
The Johns Hopkins University (MD) (m/w)
Johnson & Wales University (RI) (m/w)
Johnson C. Smith University (NC) (m/w)
Johnson State College (VT) (m/w)
Juniata College (PA) (m/w)
Kalamazoo College (MI) (m/w)
Kansas State University (KS) (m/w)
Kansas Wesleyan University (KS) (m/w)
Kean University (NJ) (m/w)
Keene State College (NH) (m/w)
Kennesaw State University (GA) (m/w)
Kent State University (OH) (m/w)
Kentucky State University (KY) (m/w)

Kenyon College (OH) (m/w)
Keuka College (NY) (m/w)
King College (TN) (m/w)
King's College (PA) (m/w)
Knox College (IL) (m/w)
Kutztown University of Pennsylvania (PA)
Lafayette College (PA) (m/w)
LaGrange College (GA) (m/w)
Lake Erie College (OH) (m/w)
Lake Forest College (IL) (m/w)
Lakeland College (WI) (m/w)
Lake Superior State University (MI) (m/w)
Lamar University (TX) (m/w)
Lambuth University (TN) (m/w)
Lander University (SC) (w)
Lane College (TN) (m/w)
Langston University (OK) (m/w)
La Roche College (PA) (m/w)
La Salle University (PA) (m/w)
Lasell College (MA) (m/w)
Lawrence University (WI) (m/w)
Lebanon Valley College (PA) (m/w)
Lees-McRae College (NC) (m/w)
Lee University (TN) (m/w)
Lehigh University (PA) (m/w)
Lehman College of the City University of
    New York (NY) (m/w)
Le Moyne College (NY) (m/w)
LeMoyne-Owen College (TN) (m/w)
Lenoir-Rhyne College (NC) (m/w)
LeTourneau University (TX) (m/w)
Lewis & Clark College (OR) (m/w)
Lewis-Clark State College (ID) (m/w)
Lewis University (IL) (m/w)
Liberty University (VA) (m/w)
Limestone College (SC) (m/w)
Lincoln Memorial University (TN) (m/w)
Lincoln University (MO) (w)
Lincoln University (PA) (m/w)
Lindenwood University (MO) (m/w)
Lindsey Wilson College (KY) (m/w)
Linfield College (OR) (m/w)
Lipscomb University (TN) (m/w)
Livingstone College (NC) (m/w)
Lock Haven University of Pennsylvania (PA)
    (m/w)
Long Island University, Brooklyn Campus
    (NY) (m/w)
Long Island University, C.W. Post Campus
    (NY) (m/w)
Longwood University (VA) (m/w)
Loras College (IA) (m/w)
Louisiana College (LA) (w)
Louisiana State University and Agricultural
    and Mechanical College (LA) (m/w)
Louisiana Tech University (LA) (m/w)
Loyola College in Maryland (MD) (m/w)
Loyola Marymount University (CA) (m/w)
Loyola University Chicago (IL) (m/w)
Loyola University New Orleans (LA) (m/w)
Luther College (IA) (m/w)
Lycoming College (PA) (m/w)
Lynchburg College (VA) (m/w)
Lyndon State College (VT) (m/w)
Lyon College (AR) (m/w)
Macalester College (MN) (m/w)
MacMurray College (IL) (m/w)
Maine Maritime Academy (ME) (m/w)
Malone College (OH) (m/w)
Manchester College (IN) (m/w)
Manhattan College (NY) (m/w)
Mansfield University of Pennsylvania (PA)
    (m/w)
Maranatha Baptist Bible College (WI) (m/w)

Marian College (IN) (m/w)
Marietta College (OH) (m/w)
Marist College (NY) (m/w)
Marquette University (WI) (m/w)
Marshall University (WV) (m/w)
Mars Hill College (NC) (m/w)
Martin Luther College (MN) (m/w)
Mary Baldwin College (VA) (w)
Maryville College (TN) (m/w)
Maryville University of Saint Louis (MO)
    (m/w)
University of Mary Washington (VA) (m/w)
Marywood University (PA) (m/w)
Massachusetts College of Liberal Arts (MA)
    (m/w)
Massachusetts Institute of Technology (MA)
    (m/w)
Massachusetts Maritime Academy (MA)
    (m/w)
The Master's College and Seminary (CA)
    (m/w)
McDaniel College (MD) (m/w)
McKendree College (IL) (m/w)
McMurry University (TX) (m/w)
McNeese State University (LA) (m/w)
McPherson College (KS) (m/w)
Medaille College (NY) (w)
Medgar Evers College of the City University
    of New York (NY) (m/w)
Menlo College (CA) (m/w)
Mercer University (GA) (m/w)
Mercy College (NY) (m/w)
Mercyhurst College (PA) (m/w)
Merrimack College (MA) (m/w)
Mesa State College (CO) (w)
Messiah College (PA) (m/w)
Methodist College (NC) (m/w)
Miami University (OH) (m/w)
Michigan State University (MI) (m/w)
Michigan Technological University (MI)
    (m/w)
MidAmerica Nazarene University (KS) (m/w)
Mid-Continent College (KY) (m/w)
Middlebury College (VT) (m/w)
Middle Tennessee State University (TN)
    (m/w)
Midland Lutheran College (NE) (m/w)
Miles College (AL) (m/w)
Millersville University of Pennsylvania (PA)
    (m/w)
Milligan College (TN) (m/w)
Millikin University (IL) (m/w)
Millsaps College (MS) (m/w)
Mills College (CA) (w)
Milwaukee School of Engineering (WI) (m/w)
Minnesota State University Mankato (MN)
    (m/w)
Minnesota State University Moorhead (MN)
    (m/w)
Minot State University (ND) (m/w)
Mississippi College (MS) (m/w)
Mississippi State University (MS) (m/w)
Mississippi Valley State University (MS)
    (m/w)
Missouri Baptist University (MO) (m/w)
Missouri Southern State University (MO)
    (m/w)
Missouri Valley College (MO) (m/w)
Molloy College (NY) (m/w)
Monmouth College (IL) (m/w)
Monmouth University (NJ) (m/w)
Montana State University–Billings (MT)
    (m/w)
Montana State University–Bozeman (MT)
    (m/w)

Montclair State University (NJ) (m/w)
Montreat College (NC) (m/w)
Moravian College (PA) (m/w)
Morehead State University (KY) (m/w)
Morehouse College (GA) (m)
Morgan State University (MD) (m/w)
Morningside College (IA) (m/w)
Morris College (SC) (m/w)
Mount Holyoke College (MA) (w)
Mount Ida College (MA) (w)
Mount Marty College (SD) (m/w)
Mount Mercy College (IA) (m/w)
Mount Olive College (NC) (m/w)
Mount Saint Mary's University (MD) (m/w)
Mount Union College (OH) (m/w)
Muhlenberg College (PA) (m/w)
Murray State University (KY) (m/w)
Muskingum College (OH) (m/w)
Nazareth College of Rochester (NY) (m/w)
Nebraska Wesleyan University (NE) (m/w)
Newberry College (SC) (m/w)
Newbury College (MA) (m/w)
New England College (NH) (m/w)
New Jersey City University (NJ) (m/w)
New Jersey Institute of Technology (NJ)
    (m/w)
Newman University (KS) (m/w)
New Mexico Highlands University (NM)
    (m/w)
New Mexico State University (NM) (m/w)
New York City College of Technology of the
    City University of New York (NY) (m/w)
New York Institute of Technology (NY)
    (m/w)
New York University (NY) (m/w)
Niagara University (NY) (m/w)
Nicholls State University (LA) (m/w)
Norfolk State University (VA) (m/w)
North Carolina Agricultural and Technical
    State University (NC) (m/w)
North Carolina Central University (NC)
    (m/w)
North Carolina State University (NC) (m/w)
North Central College (IL) (m/w)
North Dakota State University (ND) (m/w)
Northeastern University (MA) (m/w)
Northern Arizona University (AZ) (m/w)
Northern Illinois University (IL) (w)
Northern Kentucky University (KY) (m/w)
Northern Michigan University (MI) (m/w)
Northern State University (SD) (m/w)
North Georgia College & State University
    (GA) (m/w)
North Greenville College (SC) (m/w)
Northland College (WI) (m/w)
North Park University (IL) (m/w)
Northwest College (WA) (m/w)
Northwestern College (IA) (m/w)
Northwestern College (MN) (m/w)
Northwestern Oklahoma State University
    (OK) (m/w)
Northwestern University (IL) (w)
Northwest Missouri State University (MO)
    (m/w)
Northwest Nazarene University (ID) (m/w)
Northwood University (MI) (m/w)
Northwood University, Texas Campus (TX)
    (m/w)
Norwich University (VT) (m/w)
Notre Dame College (OH) (m/w)
Notre Dame de Namur University (CA)
    (m/w)
Nova Southeastern University (FL) (w)
Nyack College (NY) (m/w)
Oakland City University (IN) (m/w)

Oakland University (MI) (m/w)
Oberlin College (OH) (m/w)
Occidental College (CA) (m/w)
Oglethorpe University (GA) (m/w)
Ohio Northern University (OH) (m/w)
The Ohio State University (OH) (m/w)
Ohio University (OH) (m/w)
Ohio Valley College (WV) (m/w)
Ohio Wesleyan University (OH) (m/w)
Oklahoma Baptist University (OK) (m/w)
Oklahoma Christian University (OK) (m/w)
Oklahoma Panhandle State University (OK) (w)
Oklahoma State University (OK) (m/w)
Olivet College (MI) (m/w)
Olivet Nazarene University (IL) (m/w)
Oral Roberts University (OK) (m/w)
Oregon Institute of Technology (OR) (m/w)
Oregon State University (OR) (w)
Ottawa University (KS) (m/w)
Otterbein College (OH) (m/w)
Ouachita Baptist University (AR) (w)
Pace University (NY) (m/w)
Pacific Lutheran University (WA) (m/w)
Pacific Union College (CA) (m/w)
Pacific University (OR) (m/w)
Paine College (GA) (m/w)
Park University (MO) (m/w/w)
Peace College (NC) (w)
The Pennsylvania State University Altoona College (PA) (m/w)
The Pennsylvania State University at Erie, The Behrend College (PA) (m/w)
The Pennsylvania State University University Park Campus (PA) (m/w)
Pepperdine University (CA) (m/w)
Peru State College (NE) (w)
Pfeiffer University (NC) (m/w)
Piedmont College (GA) (m/w)
Pikeville College (KY) (m/w)
Pine Manor College (MA) (w)
Pittsburg State University (KS) (m/w)
Pitzer College (CA) (m/w)
Point Loma Nazarene University (CA) (m/w)
Point Park University (PA) (m/w)
Polytechnic University, Brooklyn Campus (NY) (m/w)
Pomona College (CA) (m/w)
Portland State University (OR) (m/w)
Prairie View A&M University (TX) (m/w)
Presbyterian College (SC) (m/w)
Presentation College (SD) (m/w)
Princeton University (NJ) (m/w)
Principia College (IL) (m/w)
Providence College (RI) (m/w)
Purdue University (IN) (m/w)
Queens University of Charlotte (NC) (m/w)
Quinnipiac University (CT) (m/w)
Radford University (VA) (m/w)
Ramapo College of New Jersey (NJ) (m/w)
Regis College (MA) (w)
Regis University (CO) (m/w)
Reinhardt College (GA) (m/w)
Rensselaer Polytechnic Institute (NY) (m/w)
Rhode Island College (RI) (m/w)
Rhodes College (TN) (m/w)
Rice University (TX) (m/w)
The Richard Stockton College of New Jersey (NJ) (m/w)
Rider University (NJ) (m/w)
Ripon College (WI) (m/w)
Rivier College (NH) (m/w)
Roanoke College (VA) (m/w)
Robert Morris College (IL) (m/w)
Robert Morris University (PA) (m/w)

Roberts Wesleyan College (NY) (m/w)
Rochester Institute of Technology (NY) (m/w)
Rockford College (IL) (m/w)
Roger Williams University (RI) (m/w)
Rollins College (FL) (m/w)
Rose-Hulman Institute of Technology (IN) (m/w)
Rowan University (NJ) (m/w)
Rust College (MS) (m/w)
Rutgers, The State University of New Jersey, Camden (NJ) (m/w)
Rutgers, The State University of New Jersey, New Brunswick/Piscataway (NJ) (m/w)
Sacred Heart University (CT) (m/w)
Saginaw Valley State University (MI) (m/w)
St. Ambrose University (IA) (m/w)
St. Andrews Presbyterian College (NC) (m/w)
Saint Anselm College (NH) (m/w)
Saint Augustine's College (NC) (m/w)
St. Bonaventure University (NY) (m/w)
St. Cloud State University (MN) (m/w)
St. Edward's University (TX) (m/w)
St. Francis College (NY) (m/w)
Saint Francis University (PA) (m/w)
St. Gregory's University (OK) (m/w)
Saint John's University (MN) (m)
St. John's University (NY) (w)
Saint Joseph College (CT) (w)
Saint Joseph's College (IN) (m/w)
Saint Joseph's College of Maine (ME) (m/w)
St. Joseph's College, Suffolk Campus (NY) (m/w)
Saint Joseph's University (PA) (m/w)
St. Lawrence University (NY) (m/w)
Saint Leo University (FL) (m/w)
St. Louis College of Pharmacy (MO) (m/w)
Saint Louis University (MO) (m/w)
Saint Martin's College (WA) (m/w)
Saint Mary's College (IN) (w)
Saint Mary's College of California (CA) (m/w)
Saint Mary's University of Minnesota (MN) (m/w)
St. Mary's University of San Antonio (TX) (w)
Saint Michael's College (VT) (m/w)
St. Norbert College (WI) (m/w)
St. Olaf College (MN) (m/w)
Saint Paul's College (VA) (m/w)
Saint Peter's College (NJ) (m/w)
St. Thomas Aquinas College (NY) (m/w)
St. Thomas University (FL) (m/w)
Saint Vincent College (PA) (m/w)
Saint Xavier University (IL) (w)
Salem International University (WV) (m/w)
Salem State College (MA) (m/w)
Salisbury University (MD) (m/w)
Salve Regina University (RI) (w)
Samford University (AL) (m/w)
Sam Houston State University (TX) (m/w)
San Diego State University (CA) (w)
San Francisco State University (CA) (m/w)
San Jose State University (CA) (m/w)
Santa Clara University (CA) (m/w)
Savannah College of Art and Design (GA) (m/w)
Savannah State University (GA) (m/w)
Seattle Pacific University (WA) (m/w)
Seattle University (WA) (m/w)
Seton Hall University (NJ) (m/w)
Seton Hill University (PA) (w)
Shawnee State University (OH) (m/w)
Shaw University (NC) (m/w)
Shenandoah University (VA) (m/w)

Shepherd University (WV) (m/w)
Shippensburg University of Pennsylvania (PA) (m/w)
Siena College (NY) (m/w)
Siena Heights University (MI) (m/w)
Simpson College (IA) (m/w)
Slippery Rock University of Pennsylvania (PA) (m/w)
Smith College (MA) (w)
Sonoma State University (CA) (w)
South Carolina State University (SC) (m/w)
South Dakota School of Mines and Technology (SD) (m/w)
South Dakota State University (SD) (m/w)
Southeastern Louisiana University (LA) (m/w)
Southeastern Oklahoma State University (OK) (m/w)
Southeast Missouri State University (MO) (m/w)
Southern Arkansas University–Magnolia (AR) (m/w)
Southern Connecticut State University (CT) (m/w)
Southern Illinois University Carbondale (IL) (m/w)
Southern Illinois University Edwardsville (IL) (m/w)
Southern Methodist University (TX) (m/w)
Southern Nazarene University (OK) (m/w)
Southern New Hampshire University (NH) (m/w)
Southern Oregon University (OR) (m/w)
Southern University and Agricultural and Mechanical College (LA) (m/w)
Southern Utah University (UT) (m/w)
Southern Vermont College (VT) (m/w)
Southern Virginia University (VA) (m/w)
Southern Wesleyan University (SC) (m/w)
Southwest Baptist University (MO) (m/w)
Southwestern College (KS) (m/w)
Southwestern Oklahoma State University (OK) (w)
Southwestern University (TX) (m/w)
Southwest Missouri State University (MO) (m/w)
Spelman College (GA) (w)
Spring Arbor University (MI) (m/w)
Springfield College (MA) (m/w)
Spring Hill College (AL) (m/w)
Stanford University (CA) (m/w)
State University of New York at Binghamton (NY) (m/w)
State University of New York at New Paltz (NY) (m/w)
State University of New York at Oswego (NY) (m/w)
State University of New York at Plattsburgh (NY) (m/w)
State University of New York College at Brockport (NY) (m/w)
State University of New York College at Cortland (NY) (m/w)
State University of New York College at Fredonia (NY) (m/w)
State University of New York College at Geneseo (NY) (m/w)
State University of New York College at Old Westbury (NY) (m/w)
State University of New York College at Oneonta (NY) (m/w)
State University of New York College at Potsdam (NY) (m/w)
State University of New York College of Technology at Delhi (NY) (m/w)

State University of New York Maritime
College (NY) (m/w)
State University of West Georgia (GA) (m/w)
Stephen F. Austin State University (TX)
(m/w)
Sterling College (KS) (m/w)
Stetson University (FL) (m/w)
Stevens Institute of Technology (NJ) (m/w)
Stillman College (AL) (m/w)
Stonehill College (MA) (m/w)
Stony Brook University, State University of
New York (NY) (m/w)
Suffolk University (MA) (m/w)
Sul Ross State University (TX) (w)
Susquehanna University (PA) (m/w)
Swarthmore College (PA) (m/w)
Syracuse University (NY) (m/w)
Tabor College (KS) (m/w)
Tarleton State University (TX) (m/w)
Taylor University (IN) (m/w)
Teikyo Post University (CT) (m/w)
Tennessee State University (TN) (m/w)
Tennessee Technological University (TN)
(m/w)
Tennessee Wesleyan College (TN) (m/w)
Texas A&M International University (TX)
(m/w)
Texas A&M University (TX) (m/w)
Texas A&M University–Commerce (TX)
(m/w)
Texas A&M University–Corpus Christi (TX)
(m/w)
Texas A&M University–Kingsville (TX)
(m/w)
Texas Christian University (TX) (m/w)
Texas Lutheran University (TX) (w)
Texas Southern University (TX) (m/w)
Texas State University-San Marcos (TX)
(m/w)
Texas Tech University (TX) (m/w)
Thiel College (PA) (m/w)
Thomas More College (KY) (m/w)
Tiffin University (OH) (m/w)
Tougaloo College (MS) (m/w)
Towson University (MD) (m/w)
Transylvania University (KY) (m/w)
Trinity Christian College (IL) (m/w)
Trinity College (CT) (m/w)
Trinity University (TX) (m/w)
Tri-State University (IN) (m/w)
Troy State University (AL) (m/w)
Truman State University (MO) (m/w)
Tufts University (MA) (m/w)
Tulane University (LA) (m/w)
Tusculum College (TN) (m/w)
Tuskegee University (AL) (m/w)
Union College (NY) (m/w)
Union University (TN) (m/w)
United States Air Force Academy (CO) (m/w)
United States Coast Guard Academy (CT)
(m/w)
United States Merchant Marine Academy
(NY) (m/w)
United States Military Academy (NY) (m/w)
United States Naval Academy (MD) (m/w)
University at Albany, State University of New
York (NY) (m/w)
University at Buffalo, The State University of
New York (NY) (m/w)
The University of Akron (OH) (m/w)
The University of Alabama at Birmingham
(AL) (w)
The University of Alabama in Huntsville
(AL) (m/w)
University of Alaska Anchorage (AK) (m/w)

University of Alaska Fairbanks (AK) (m/w)
The University of Arizona (AZ) (m/w)
University of Arkansas (AR) (m/w)
University of Arkansas at Little Rock (AR)
(m/w)
University of Arkansas at Monticello (AR)
(w)
University of Bridgeport (CT) (m)
University of California, Berkeley (CA) (m/w)
University of California, Davis (CA) (m/w)
University of California, Irvine (CA) (m/w)
University of California, Los Angeles (CA)
(m/w)
University of California, Riverside (CA)
(m/w)
University of California, San Diego (CA)
(m/w)
University of California, Santa Barbara (CA)
(m/w)
University of California, Santa Cruz (CA) (w)
University of Central Arkansas (AR) (w)
University of Central Florida (FL) (m/w)
University of Central Oklahoma (OK) (w)
University of Charleston (WV) (m/w)
University of Chicago (IL) (m/w)
University of Cincinnati (OH) (m/w)
University of Colorado at Boulder (CO)
(m/w)
University of Colorado at Colorado Springs
(CO) (m/w)
University of Connecticut (CT) (m/w)
University of Dallas (TX) (m/w)
University of Dayton (OH) (m/w)
University of Delaware (DE) (m/w)
University of Detroit Mercy (MI) (m/w)
University of Dubuque (IA) (m/w)
University of Evansville (IN) (m/w)
The University of Findlay (OH) (m/w)
University of Florida (FL) (m/w)
University of Georgia (GA) (m/w)
University of Hartford (CT) (m/w)
University of Hawaii at Hilo (HI) (m/w)
University of Hawaii at Manoa (HI) (w)
University of Houston (TX) (m/w)
University of Idaho (ID) (m/w)
University of Illinois at Chicago (IL) (m/w)
University of Illinois at Urbana–Champaign
(IL) (m/w)
University of Indianapolis (IN) (m/w)
The University of Iowa (IA) (m/w)
University of Kansas (KS) (m/w)
University of Kentucky (KY) (m/w)
University of La Verne (CA) (m/w)
University of Louisiana at Lafayette (LA)
(m/w)
University of Louisiana at Monroe (LA)
(m/w)
University of Louisville (KY) (m/w)
University of Maine (ME) (m/w)
University of Maine at Farmington (ME)
(m/w)
University of Maine at Machias (ME) (m/w)
University of Maine at Presque Isle (ME)
(m/w)
University of Mary (ND) (m/w)
University of Maryland, Baltimore County
(MD) (m/w)
University of Maryland, College Park (MD)
(m/w)
University of Maryland Eastern Shore (MD)
(m/w)
University of Massachusetts Amherst (MA)
(m/w)
University of Massachusetts Boston (MA)
(m/w)

University of Massachusetts Dartmouth
(MA) (m/w)
University of Massachusetts Lowell (MA)
(m/w)
The University of Memphis (TN) (m/w)
University of Miami (FL) (m/w)
University of Michigan (MI) (m/w)
University of Minnesota, Duluth (MN) (m/w)
University of Minnesota, Morris (MN) (w)
University of Minnesota, Twin Cities
Campus (MN) (m/w)
University of Mississippi (MS) (m/w)
University of Missouri–Columbia (MO)
(m/w)
University of Missouri–Kansas City (MO)
(m/w)
University of Missouri–Rolla (MO) (m/w)
University of Mobile (AL) (m/w)
The University of Montana–Missoula (MT)
(m/w)
University of Nebraska at Kearney (NE)
(m/w)
University of Nebraska at Omaha (NE) (w)
University of Nebraska–Lincoln (NE) (m/w)
University of Nevada, Las Vegas (NV) (w)
University of Nevada, Reno (NV) (w)
University of New England (ME) (m/w)
University of New Hampshire (NH) (m/w)
University of New Haven (CT) (m/w)
University of New Mexico (NM) (m/w)
University of New Orleans (LA) (m/w)
University of North Alabama (AL) (m/w)
The University of North Carolina at
Asheville (NC) (m/w)
The University of North Carolina at Chapel
Hill (NC) (m/w)
The University of North Carolina at
Charlotte (NC) (m/w)
The University of North Carolina at
Greensboro (NC) (m/w)
The University of North Carolina at
Pembroke (NC) (m/w)
The University of North Carolina at
Wilmington (NC) (m/w)
University of North Dakota (ND) (m/w)
University of Northern Colorado (CO) (w)
University of Northern Iowa (IA) (m/w)
University of North Florida (FL) (m/w)
University of North Texas (TX) (m/w)
University of Notre Dame (IN) (m/w)
University of Oklahoma (OK) (m/w)
University of Oregon (OR) (m/w)
University of Pennsylvania (PA) (m/w)
University of Pittsburgh (PA) (m/w)
University of Pittsburgh at Bradford (PA)
(m/w)
University of Pittsburgh at Greensburg (PA)
(m/w)
University of Pittsburgh at Johnstown (PA)
(w)
University of Portland (OR) (m/w)
University of Puerto Rico at Bayamón (PR)
(m/w)
University of Puerto Rico at Humacao (PR)
(m/w)
University of Puerto Rico, Cayey University
College (PR) (m/w)
University of Puerto Rico, Mayagüez
Campus (PR) (m/w)
University of Puerto Rico, Río Piedras (PR)
(m/w)
University of Puget Sound (WA) (m/w)
University of Redlands (CA) (m/w)
University of Rhode Island (RI) (m/w)
University of Richmond (VA) (m/w)

University of Rio Grande (OH) (m/w)
University of Rochester (NY) (m/w)
University of St. Francis (IL) (w)
University of Saint Francis (IN) (m/w)
University of St. Thomas (MN) (m/w)
University of San Diego (CA) (m/w)
University of San Francisco (CA) (m/w)
The University of Scranton (PA) (m/w)
University of Sioux Falls (SD) (m/w)
University of South Alabama (AL) (m/w)
University of South Carolina (SC) (w)
University of South Carolina Aiken (SC) (w)
University of South Carolina Spartanburg (SC) (m/w)
The University of South Dakota (SD) (m/w)
University of Southern California (CA) (w)
University of Southern Indiana (IN) (m/w)
University of Southern Maine (ME) (m/w)
University of Southern Mississippi (MS) (w)
University of South Florida (FL) (m/w)
The University of Tampa (FL) (m/w)
The University of Tennessee (TN) (m/w)
The University of Tennessee at Chattanooga (TN) (m/w)
The University of Tennessee at Martin (TN) (m/w)
The University of Texas at Arlington (TX) (m/w)
The University of Texas at Austin (TX) (m/w)
The University of Texas at Dallas (TX) (m/w)
The University of Texas at El Paso (TX) (m/w)
The University of Texas at San Antonio (TX) (m/w)
The University of Texas–Pan American (TX) (m/w)
University of the District of Columbia (DC) (m/w)
University of the Incarnate Word (TX) (m/w)
University of the Ozarks (AR) (m/w)
University of the Pacific (CA) (w)
University of the Sciences in Philadelphia (PA) (m/w)
University of the South (TN) (m/w)
University of Toledo (OH) (m/w)
University of Tulsa (OK) (m/w)
University of Utah (UT) (m/w)
University of Vermont (VT) (m/w)
University of Virginia (VA) (m/w)
The University of Virginia's College at Wise (VA) (m/w)
University of Washington (WA) (m/w)
The University of West Alabama (AL) (m/w)
University of West Florida (FL) (m/w)
University of Wisconsin–Eau Claire (WI) (m/w)
University of Wisconsin–Green Bay (WI) (m/w)
University of Wisconsin–La Crosse (WI) (m/w)
University of Wisconsin–Madison (WI) (m/w)
University of Wisconsin–Milwaukee (WI) (m/w)
University of Wisconsin–Oshkosh (WI) (m/w)
University of Wisconsin–Parkside (WI) (m/w)
University of Wisconsin–Platteville (WI) (m/w)
University of Wisconsin–River Falls (WI) (m/w)
University of Wisconsin–Stevens Point (WI) (m/w)
University of Wisconsin–Stout (WI) (m/w)
University of Wisconsin–Superior (WI) (m/w)

University of Wisconsin–Whitewater (WI) (m/w)
University of Wyoming (WY) (m/w)
Upper Iowa University (IA) (m/w)
Ursinus College (PA) (m/w)
Ursuline College (OH) (w)
Utah State University (UT) (m/w)
Valdosta State University (GA) (m/w)
Valparaiso University (IN) (m/w)
Vanderbilt University (TN) (m/w)
Vanguard University of Southern California (CA) (m/w)
Vassar College (NY) (m/w)
Villa Julie College (MD) (m/w)
Villanova University (PA) (m/w)
Virginia Commonwealth University (VA) (m/w)
Virginia Intermont College (VA) (m/w)
Virginia Military Institute (VA) (m/w)
Virginia Polytechnic Institute and State University (VA) (m/w)
Virginia State University (VA) (m/w)
Virginia Union University (VA) (m/w)
Virginia Wesleyan College (VA) (m/w)
Voorhees College (SC) (m/w)
Wabash College (IN) (m)
Wagner College (NY) (m/w)
Wake Forest University (NC) (m/w)
Walsh University (OH) (m/w)
Warner Pacific College (OR) (m/w)
Warner Southern College (FL) (m/w)
Wartburg College (IA) (m/w)
Washington & Jefferson College (PA) (m/w)
Washington and Lee University (VA) (m/w)
Washington State University (WA) (m/w)
Washington University in St. Louis (MO) (m)
Wayland Baptist University (TX) (m/w)
Waynesburg College (PA) (w)
Wayne State College (NE) (m/w)
Wayne State University (MI) (m/w)
Webber International University (FL) (m/w)
Weber State University (UT) (m/w)
Webster University (MO) (w)
Wellesley College (MA) (w)
Wesleyan University (CT) (m/w)
Wesley College (DE) (m/w)
West Chester University of Pennsylvania (PA) (m/w)
Western Baptist College (OR) (m/w)
Western Carolina University (NC) (m/w)
Western Illinois University (IL) (m/w)
Western Kentucky University (KY) (m/w)
Western Michigan University (MI) (m/w)
Western New England College (MA) (m/w)
Western New Mexico University (NM) (m/w)
Western Oregon University (OR) (m/w)
Western State College of Colorado (CO) (m/w)
Western Washington University (WA) (m/w)
Westfield State College (MA) (m/w)
West Liberty State College (WV) (m/w)
Westminster College (UT) (m/w)
Westminster College (PA) (m/w)
Westmont College (CA) (m/w)
West Texas A&M University (TX) (m/w)
West Virginia University (WV) (w)
West Virginia Wesleyan College (WV) (m/w)
Wheaton College (IL) (m/w)
Wheaton College (MA) (m/w)
Wheeling Jesuit University (WV) (m/w)
Whitman College (WA) (m/w)
Whittier College (CA) (m/w)
Whitworth College (WA) (m/w)
Wichita State University (KS) (w)

Widener University (PA) (m/w)
Willamette University (OR) (m/w)
William Jewell College (MO) (m/w)
William Paterson University of New Jersey (NJ) (m/w)
William Penn University (IA) (m/w)
Williams College (MA) (m/w)
William Woods University (MO) (m/w)
Wilmington College (DE) (m/w)
Wilmington College (OH) (m/w)
Wingate University (NC) (m/w)
Winona State University (MN) (m/w)
Winston-Salem State University (NC) (m/w)
Winthrop University (SC) (m/w)
Wisconsin Lutheran College (WI) (m/w)
Wittenberg University (OH) (m/w)
Wofford College (SC) (m/w)
Worcester Polytechnic Institute (MA) (m/w)
Worcester State College (MA) (m/w)
Wright State University (OH) (m/w)
Xavier University (OH) (m/w)
Xavier University of Louisiana (LA) (m/w)
Yale University (CT) (m/w)
Yeshiva University (NY) (m)
York College (NE) (m/w)
York College of Pennsylvania (PA) (m/w)
York College of the City University of New York (NY) (m/w)
Youngstown State University (OH)(m/w)

Diving

Albion College (MI) (m/w)
Alfred University (NY) (m/w)
Allegheny College (PA) (m/w)
Alma College (MI) (m/w)
American University (DC) (m/w)
Amherst College (MA) (m/w)
Arizona State University (AZ) (m/w)
Auburn University (AL) (m/w)
Augsburg College (MN) (m/w)
Augustana College (IL) (m/w)
Austin College (TX) (m/w)
Babson College (MA) (m/w)
Ball State University (IN) (m/w)
Bates College (ME) (m/w)
Bentley College (MA) (m/w)
Bernard M. Baruch College of the City University of New York (NY) (m/w)
Bethany College (WV) (m/w)
Boston College (MA) (m/w)
Boston University (MA) (m/w)
Bowdoin College (ME) (m/w)
Bowling Green State University (OH) (w)
Brandeis University (MA) (m/w)
Bridgewater State College (MA) (m/w)
Brigham Young University (UT) (m/w)
Brown University (RI) (m/w)
Bucknell University (PA) (m/w)
Buena Vista University (IA) (m/w)
Buffalo State College, State University of New York (NY) (m/w)
Butler University (IN) (m/w)
California Baptist University (CA) (m/w)
California Institute of Technology (CA) (m/w)
California Polytechnic State University, San Luis Obispo (CA) (m/w)
California State University, Fresno (CA) (w)
California State University, Northridge (CA) (m/w)
Calvin College (MI) (m/w)
Canisius College (NY) (m/w)
Carleton College (MN) (m/w)
Carnegie Mellon University (PA) (m/w)

Case Western Reserve University (OH) (m/w)
Central Connecticut State University (CT) (w)
Centre College (KY) (m/w)
Claremont McKenna College (CA) (m/w)
Clarion University of Pennsylvania (PA) (m/w)
Clark University (MA) (m/w)
Clemson University (SC) (m/w)
Cleveland State University (OH) (m/w)
Coe College (IA) (m/w)
Colby College (ME) (m/w)
Colby-Sawyer College (NH) (m/w)
Colgate University (NY) (m/w)
College of Charleston (SC) (m/w)
The College of New Jersey (NJ) (m)
College of Saint Benedict (MN) (w)
The College of Saint Rose (NY) (m/w)
College of the Holy Cross (MA) (m/w)
The College of William and Mary (VA) (m/w)
The Colorado College (CO) (m/w)
Colorado State University (CO) (w)
Columbia College (NY) (m/w)
Concordia College (MN) (w)
Connecticut College (CT) (m/w)
Cornell University (NY) (m/w)
Dartmouth College (NH) (m/w)
Davidson College (NC) (m/w)
Delta State University (MS) (m/w)
Denison University (OH) (m/w)
DePauw University (IN) (m/w)
Drexel University (PA) (m/w)
Drury University (MO) (m/w)
Duke University (NC) (m/w)
East Carolina University (NC) (m/w)
Eastern Michigan University (MI) (m/w)
Emory University (GA) (m/w)
Eureka College (IL) (m/w)
Fairfield University (CT) (m/w)
Florida Atlantic University (FL) (m/w)
Florida International University (FL) (w)
Florida State University (FL) (m/w)
Fordham University (NY) (m/w)
Frostburg State University (MD) (m/w)
George Mason University (VA) (m/w)
Georgetown University (DC) (m/w)
The George Washington University (DC) (m/w)
Georgia Institute of Technology (GA) (m/w)
Georgia Southern University (GA) (w)
Grinnell College (IA) (m/w)
Grove City College (PA) (m/w)
Gustavus Adolphus College (MN) (m/w)
Hamilton College (NY) (m/w)
Hamline University (MN) (m/w)
Hartwick College (NY) (m/w)
Harvard University (MA) (m/w)
Hendrix College (AR) (m/w)
Hiram College (OH) (m/w)
Hobart and William Smith Colleges (NY) (w)
Hope College (MI) (m/w)
Illinois State University (IL) (w)
Illinois Wesleyan University (IL) (m/w)
Indiana University Bloomington (IN) (m/w)
Indiana University–Purdue University Indianapolis (IN) (m/w)
Iona College (NY) (m/w)
Iowa State University of Science and Technology (IA) (w)
Ithaca College (NY) (m/w)
James Madison University (VA) (m/w)
John Brown University (AR) (m/w)
John Carroll University (OH) (m/w)
Kalamazoo College (MI) (m/w)

Keene State College (NH) (m/w)
Kenyon College (OH) (m/w)
Knox College (IL) (m/w)
Lafayette College (PA) (m/w)
Lake Forest College (IL) (m/w)
La Salle University (PA) (m/w)
Lawrence University (WI) (m/w)
Lehigh University (PA) (m/w)
Le Moyne College (NY) (m/w)
Lindenwood University (MO) (m/w)
Loras College (IA) (m/w)
Louisiana State University and Agricultural and Mechanical College (LA) (m/w)
Loyola College in Maryland (MD) (m/w)
Loyola Marymount University (CA) (w)
Luther College (IA) (m/w)
Macalester College (MN) (m/w)
Marist College (NY) (m/w)
Marshall University (WV) (w)
Miami University (OH) (m/w)
Michigan State University (MI) (m/w)
Middlebury College (VT) (m/w)
Minnesota State University Mankato (MN) (m/w)
Mount Holyoke College (MA) (w)
Mount Union College (OH) (m/w)
Nazareth College of Rochester (NY) (m/w)
New Mexico State University (NM) (w)
New York University (NY) (m/w)
Niagara University (NY) (m/w)
North Carolina State University (NC) (m/w)
Northeastern University (MA) (m/w)
Northern Arizona University (AZ) (w)
Northern Michigan University (MI) (w)
Northwestern University (IL) (m/w)
Norwich University (VT) (m/w)
Oakland University (MI) (m/w)
Oberlin College (OH) (m/w)
Ohio Northern University (OH) (m/w)
The Ohio State University (OH) (m/w)
Ohio University (OH) (m/w)
Old Dominion University (VA) (m/w)
Olivet College (MI) (m/w)
Ouachita Baptist University (AR) (m/w)
Pace University (NY) (m/w)
The Pennsylvania State University Altoona College (PA) (m/w)
The Pennsylvania State University at Erie, The Behrend College (PA) (m/w)
The Pennsylvania State University University Park Campus (PA) (m/w)
Pepperdine University (CA) (w)
Pitzer College (CA) (m/w)
Plymouth State University (NH) (w)
Pomona College (CA) (m/w)
Princeton University (NJ) (m/w)
Providence College (RI) (m/w)
Purdue University (IN) (m/w)
Queens College of the City University of New York (NY) (w)
Radford University (VA) (w)
Regis College (MA) (w)
Rensselaer Polytechnic Institute (NY) (m/w)
Rider University (NJ) (m/w)
Rose-Hulman Institute of Technology (IN) (m/w)
Rowan University (NJ) (m/w)
Rutgers, The State University of New Jersey, New Brunswick/Piscataway (NJ) (m/w)
Sacred Heart University (CT) (w)
St. Bonaventure University (NY) (m/w)
St. Cloud State University (MN) (m/w)
Saint John's University (MN) (m)
St. John's University (NY) (m/w)
Saint Joseph College (CT) (w)

St. Lawrence University (NY) (m/w)
Saint Louis University (MO) (m/w)
Saint Mary's College (IN) (w)
Saint Mary's University of Minnesota (MN) (m/w)
Saint Michael's College (VT) (m/w)
St. Olaf College (MN) (m/w)
Saint Peter's College (NJ) (m/w)
San Diego State University (CA) (w)
San Jose State University (CA) (w)
Seton Hall University (NJ) (m/w)
Siena College (NY) (w)
Simmons College (MA) (w)
Skidmore College (NY) (m/w)
Smith College (MA) (w)
Southern Illinois University Carbondale (IL) (m/w)
Southern Methodist University (TX) (m/w)
Southwestern University (TX) (m/w)
Southwest Missouri State University (MO) (m/w)
Springfield College (MA) (m/w)
Stanford University (CA) (m/w)
State University of New York at Binghamton (NY) (m/w)
State University of New York at Oswego (NY) (m/w)
State University of New York College at Brockport (NY) (m/w)
State University of New York College at Cortland (NY) (m/w)
State University of New York College at Fredonia (NY) (m/w)
State University of New York College at Geneseo (NY) (m/w)
State University of New York College at Potsdam (NY) (m/w)
Stony Brook University, State University of New York (NY) (m/w)
Syracuse University (NY) (m/w)
Texas A&M University (TX) (m/w)
Texas Christian University (TX) (m/w)
Towson University (MD) (m/w)
Transylvania University (KY) (m/w)
Trinity College (CT) (m/w)
Trinity University (TX) (m/w)
Tufts University (MA) (m/w)
Union College (NY) (m/w)
United States Air Force Academy (CO) (m/w)
United States Coast Guard Academy (CT) (m/w)
United States Merchant Marine Academy (NY) (m/w)
United States Military Academy (NY) (m/w)
United States Naval Academy (MD) (m)
University at Buffalo, The State University of New York (NY) (m/w)
The University of Akron (OH) (w)
The University of Alabama (AL) (m/w)
The University of Arizona (AZ) (m/w)
University of Arkansas (AR) (w)
University of Arkansas at Little Rock (AR) (w)
University of California, Berkeley (CA) (m/w)
University of California, Davis (CA) (m/w)
University of California, Irvine (CA) (m/w)
University of California, Los Angeles (CA) (w)
University of California, San Diego (CA) (m/w)
University of California, Santa Barbara (CA) (m/w)
University of California, Santa Cruz (CA) (m/w)
University of Cincinnati (OH) (m/w)

University of Connecticut (CT) (m/w)
University of Delaware (DE) (m/w)
University of Denver (CO) (m/w)
University of Evansville (IN) (m/w)
The University of Findlay (OH) (m/w)
University of Florida (FL) (m/w)
University of Georgia (GA) (m/w)
University of Hawaii at Manoa (HI) (m/w)
University of Houston (TX) (w)
University of Illinois at Chicago (IL) (w)
University of Illinois at Urbana–Champaign (IL) (w)
University of Indianapolis (IN) (m/w)
The University of Iowa (IA) (m/w)
University of Kansas (KS) (w)
University of Kentucky (KY) (m/w)
University of La Verne (CA) (m/w)
University of Louisiana at Monroe (LA) (m/w)
University of Louisville (KY) (m/w)
University of Maine (ME) (m/w)
University of Maryland, Baltimore County (MD) (m/w)
University of Maryland, College Park (MD) (m/w)
University of Massachusetts Amherst (MA) (m/w)
University of Massachusetts Dartmouth (MA) (m/w)
University of Miami (FL) (m/w)
University of Michigan (MI) (m/w)
University of Minnesota, Twin Cities Campus (MN) (m/w)
University of Missouri–Columbia (MO) (m/w)
University of Nebraska–Lincoln (NE) (w)
University of Nevada, Las Vegas (NV) (m/w)
University of Nevada, Reno (NV) (w)
University of New Hampshire (NH) (m/w)
University of New Mexico (NM) (w)
The University of North Carolina at Chapel Hill (NC) (m/w)
The University of North Carolina at Wilmington (NC) (m/w)
University of North Dakota (ND) (m/w)
University of Northern Colorado (CO) (w)
University of Northern Iowa (IA) (m/w)
University of North Florida (FL) (w)
University of Notre Dame (IN) (m/w)
University of Pennsylvania (PA) (m/w)
University of Pittsburgh (PA) (m/w)
University of Redlands (CA) (m/w)
University of Rhode Island (RI) (m/w)
University of Richmond (VA) (w)
University of St. Thomas (MN) (m/w)
University of San Diego (CA) (w)
University of South Carolina (SC) (m/w)
The University of South Dakota (SD) (m/w)
University of Southern California (CA) (m/w)
The University of Tennessee (TN) (m/w)
The University of Texas at Austin (TX) (m/w)
University of the South (TN) (m/w)
University of Toledo (OH) (w)
University of Utah (UT) (m/w)
University of Vermont (VT) (m/w)
University of Virginia (VA) (m/w)
University of Washington (WA) (m/w)
University of Wisconsin–Eau Claire (WI) (m/w)
University of Wisconsin–Green Bay (WI) (m/w)
University of Wisconsin–La Crosse (WI) (m/w)
University of Wisconsin–Madison (WI) (m/w)

University of Wisconsin–Milwaukee (WI) (m/w)
University of Wisconsin–Oshkosh (WI) (m/w)
University of Wisconsin–River Falls (WI) (m/w)
University of Wisconsin–Stevens Point (WI) (m/w)
University of Wyoming (WY) (m/w)
Utica College (NY) (m/w)
Valparaiso University (IN) (m/w)
Vassar College (NY) (m/w)
Villanova University (PA) (m/w)
Virginia Military Institute (VA) (m)
Virginia Polytechnic Institute and State University (VA) (m/w)
Washington & Jefferson College (PA) (m/w)
Washington State University (WA) (w)
Washington University in St. Louis (MO) (m/w)
Wayne State University (MI) (m/w)
Wellesley College (MA) (w)
Wesleyan University (CT) (m/w)
West Chester University of Pennsylvania (PA) (m/w)
Western Illinois University (IL) (m/w)
Westfield State College (MA) (w)
West Virginia University (WV) (m/w)
West Virginia Wesleyan College (WV) (m/w)
Wheaton College (MA) (m/w)
Wheelock College (MA) (w)
William Paterson University of New Jersey (NJ) (m/w)
Williams College (MA) (m/w)
Wright State University (OH) (m/w)
Yale University (CT) (m/w)
Youngstown State University (OH)(w)

Field Hockey

Albright College (PA) (w)
Alvernia College (PA) (w)
American International College (MA) (w)
American University (DC) (w)
Amherst College (MA) (w)
Anna Maria College (MA) (w)
Appalachian State University (NC) (w)
Arcadia University (PA) (w)
Assumption College (MA) (w)
Babson College (MA) (w)
Ball State University (IN) (w)
Bates College (ME) (w)
Bellarmine University (KY) (w)
Bentley College (MA) (w)
Bloomsburg University of Pennsylvania (PA) (w)
Boston College (MA) (w)
Boston University (MA) (w)
Bowdoin College (ME) (w)
Bridgewater College (VA) (w)
Bridgewater State College (MA) (w)
Brown University (RI) (w)
Bryant College (RI) (w)
Bryn Mawr College (PA) (w)
Bucknell University (PA) (w)
Cabrini College (PA) (w)
Castleton State College (VT) (w)
Catawba College (NC) (w)
The Catholic University of America (DC) (w)
Cedar Crest College (PA) (w)
Central Michigan University (MI) (w)
Centre College (KY) (w)
Chestnut Hill College (PA) (w)
Christopher Newport University (VA) (w)
Clark University (MA) (w)

Colby College (ME) (w)
Colgate University (NY) (w)
College Misericordia (PA) (w)
The College of New Jersey (NJ) (w)
College of Notre Dame of Maryland (MD) (w)
College of the Holy Cross (MA) (w)
The College of William and Mary (VA) (w)
The College of Wooster (OH) (w)
Columbia College (NY) (w)
Connecticut College (CT) (w)
Cornell University (NY) (w)
Dartmouth College (NH) (w)
Davidson College (NC) (w)
Delaware Valley College (PA) (w)
Denison University (OH) (w)
DePauw University (IN) (w)
Dickinson College (PA) (w)
Drew University (NJ) (w)
Drexel University (PA) (w)
Duke University (NC) (w)
Earlham College (IN) (w)
Eastern Connecticut State University (CT) (w)
Eastern Mennonite University (VA) (w)
Eastern University (PA) (w)
East Stroudsburg University of Pennsylvania (PA) (w)
Elizabethtown College (PA) (w)
Elmira College (NY) (w)
Elms College (MA) (w)
Endicott College (MA) (w)
Fairfield University (CT) (w)
Fairleigh Dickinson University, College at Florham (NJ) (w)
Fitchburg State College (MA) (w)
Framingham State College (MA) (w)
Franklin and Marshall College (PA) (w)
Franklin Pierce College (NH) (w)
Frostburg State University (MD) (w)
Georgetown University (DC) (w)
Gettysburg College (PA) (w)
Gordon College (MA) (w)
Goucher College (MD) (w)
Gwynedd-Mercy College (PA) (w)
Hamilton College (NY) (w)
Hartwick College (NY) (w)
Harvard University (MA) (w)
Haverford College (PA) (w)
Hobart and William Smith Colleges (NY) (w)
Hofstra University (NY) (w)
Hollins University (VA) (w)
Hood College (MD) (w)
Houghton College (NY) (w)
Husson College (ME) (w)
Immaculata University (PA) (w)
Indiana University Bloomington (IN) (w)
Indiana University of Pennsylvania (PA) (w)
Ithaca College (NY) (w)
James Madison University (VA) (w)
The Johns Hopkins University (MD) (w)
Juniata College (PA) (w)
Kean University (NJ) (w)
Keene State College (NH) (w)
Kent State University (OH) (w)
Kenyon College (OH) (w)
King's College (PA) (w)
Kutztown University of Pennsylvania (PA) (w)
Lafayette College (PA) (w)
La Salle University (PA) (w)
Lasell College (MA) (w)
Lebanon Valley College (PA) (w)
Lehigh University (PA) (w)
Lindenwood University (MO) (w)

Lock Haven University of Pennsylvania (PA) (w)
Long Island University, C.W. Post Campus (NY) (w)
Longwood University (VA) (w)
Lynchburg College (VA) (w)
Manhattanville College (NY) (w)
Mansfield University of Pennsylvania (PA) (w)
Mary Baldwin College (VA) (w)
University of Mary Washington (VA) (w)
Marywood University (PA) (w)
Massachusetts Institute of Technology (MA) (w)
McDaniel College (MD) (w)
Mercyhurst College (PA) (w)
Merrimack College (MA) (w)
Messiah College (PA) (w)
Miami University (OH) (w)
Michigan State University (MI) (w)
Middlebury College (VT) (w)
Millersville University of Pennsylvania (PA) (w)
Monmouth University (NJ) (w)
Montclair State University (NJ) (w)
Moravian College (PA) (w)
Mount Holyoke College (MA) (w)
Muhlenberg College (PA) (w)
Nazareth College of Rochester (NY) (w)
Neumann College (PA) (w)
New England College (NH) (w)
Nichols College (MA) (w)
Northeastern University (MA) (w)
Northwestern University (IL) (w)
Oberlin College (OH) (w)
The Ohio State University (OH) (w)
Ohio University (OH) (w)
Ohio Wesleyan University (OH) (w)
Old Dominion University (VA) (w)
The Pennsylvania State University University Park Campus (PA) (w)
Philadelphia Biblical University (PA) (w)
Philadelphia University (PA) (w)
Plymouth State University (NH) (w)
Princeton University (NJ) (w)
Providence College (RI) (w)
Quinnipiac University (CT) (w)
Radford University (VA) (w)
Ramapo College of New Jersey (NJ) (w)
Randolph-Macon College (VA) (w)
Randolph-Macon Woman's College (VA) (w)
Regis College (MA) (w)
Rensselaer Polytechnic Institute (NY) (w)
Rhodes College (TN) (w)
Rider University (NJ) (w)
Roanoke College (VA) (w)
Rosemont College (PA) (w)
Rowan University (NJ) (w)
Rutgers, The State University of New Jersey, New Brunswick/Piscataway (NJ) (w)
Sacred Heart University (CT) (w)
Saint Anselm College (NH) (w)
Saint Francis University (PA) (w)
Saint Joseph's College of Maine (ME) (w)
Saint Joseph's University (PA) (w)
St. Lawrence University (NY) (w)
Saint Louis University (MO) (w)
St. Mary's College of Maryland (MD) (w)
Saint Michael's College (VT) (w)
Salem State College (MA) (w)
Salisbury University (MD) (w)
Salve Regina University (RI) (w)
Seton Hill University (PA) (w)
Shippensburg University of Pennsylvania (PA) (w)

Siena College (NY) (w)
Simmons College (MA) (w)
Skidmore College (NY) (w)
Slippery Rock University of Pennsylvania (PA) (w)
Smith College (MA) (w)
Southern Connecticut State University (CT) (w)
Southwest Missouri State University (MO) (w)
Springfield College (MA) (w)
Stanford University (CA) (w)
State University of New York at New Paltz (NY) (w)
State University of New York at Oswego (NY) (w)
State University of New York College at Brockport (NY) (w)
State University of New York College at Cortland (NY) (w)
State University of New York College at Geneseo (NY) (w)
State University of New York College at Oneonta (NY) (w)
Stevens Institute of Technology (NJ) (w)
Stonehill College (MA) (w)
Susquehanna University (PA) (w)
Swarthmore College (PA) (w)
Sweet Briar College (VA) (w)
Syracuse University (NY) (w)
Temple University (PA) (w)
Thomas College (ME) (w)
Towson University (MD) (w)
Transylvania University (KY) (w)
Trinity College (CT) (w)
Trinity College (DC) (w)
Tufts University (MA) (w)
Union College (NY) (w)
University at Albany, State University of New York (NY) (w)
University of California, Berkeley (CA) (w)
University of Connecticut (CT) (w)
University of Delaware (DE) (w)
The University of Iowa (IA) (w)
University of Louisville (KY) (w)
University of Maine (ME) (w)
University of Maine at Farmington (ME) (w)
University of Maryland, Baltimore County (MD) (w)
University of Maryland, College Park (MD) (w)
University of Massachusetts Amherst (MA) (w)
University of Massachusetts Dartmouth (MA) (w)
University of Massachusetts Lowell (MA) (w)
University of Michigan (MI) (w)
University of New England (ME) (w)
University of New Hampshire (NH) (w)
The University of North Carolina at Chapel Hill (NC) (w)
University of Pennsylvania (PA) (w)
University of Rhode Island (RI) (w)
University of Richmond (VA) (w)
University of Rochester (NY) (w)
The University of Scranton (PA) (w)
University of Southern Maine (ME) (w)
University of the Pacific (CA) (w)
University of the South (TN) (w)
University of Vermont (VT) (w)
University of Virginia (VA) (w)
Ursinus College (PA) (w)
Utica College (NY) (w)
Vassar College (NY) (w)
Villa Julie College (MD) (w)

Villanova University (PA) (w)
Virginia Commonwealth University (VA) (w)
Virginia Wesleyan College (VA) (w)
Wake Forest University (NC) (w)
Washington & Jefferson College (PA) (w)
Washington and Lee University (VA) (w)
Washington College (MD) (w)
Wellesley College (MA) (w)
Wells College (NY) (w)
Wesleyan University (CT) (w)
Wesley College (DE) (w)
West Chester University of Pennsylvania (PA) (w)
Western New England College (MA) (w)
Westfield State College (MA) (w)
Wheaton College (MA) (w)
Wheelock College (MA) (w)
Widener University (PA) (w)
Wilkes University (PA) (w)
William Paterson University of New Jersey (NJ) (w)
Williams College (MA) (w)
Wilson College (PA) (w)
Wittenberg University (OH) (w)
Worcester Polytechnic Institute (MA) (w)
Worcester State College (MA) (w)
Yale University (CT) (w)
York College of Pennsylvania (PA)(w)

Football

Abilene Christian University (TX) (m)
Adams State College (CO) (m)
Adrian College (MI) (m)
Alabama Agricultural and Mechanical University (AL) (m)
Alabama State University (AL) (m)
Albany State University (GA) (m)
Albion College (MI) (m)
Albright College (PA) (m)
Alcorn State University (MS) (m)
Alfred University (NY) (m)
Allegheny College (PA) (m)
Allen University (SC) (m)
Alma College (MI) (m)
American International College (MA) (m)
Amherst College (MA) (m)
Anderson University (IN) (m)
Angelo State University (TX) (m)
Appalachian State University (NC) (m)
Arizona State University (AZ) (m)
Arkansas State University (AR) (m)
Arkansas Tech University (AR) (m)
Ashland University (OH) (m)
Assumption College (MA) (m)
Auburn University (AL) (m)
Augsburg College (MN) (m)
Augustana College (IL) (m)
Augustana College (SD) (m)
Aurora University (IL) (m)
Austin College (TX) (m)
Austin Peay State University (TN) (m)
Averett University (VA) (m)
Avila University (MO) (m)
Azusa Pacific University (CA) (m)
Bacone College (OK) (m)
Baker University (KS) (m)
Baldwin-Wallace College (OH) (m)
Ball State University (IN) (m)
Bates College (ME) (m)
Baylor University (TX) (m)
Belhaven College (MS) (m)
Beloit College (WI) (m)
Bemidji State University (MN) (m)
Benedict College (SC) (m)

Benedictine College (KS) (m)
Benedictine University (IL) (m)
Bentley College (MA) (m)
Bethany College (KS) (m)
Bethany College (WV) (m)
Bethel College (KS) (m)
Bethel College (TN) (m)
Bethel University (MN) (m)
Bethune-Cookman College (FL) (m)
Blackburn College (IL) (m)
Black Hills State University (SD) (m)
Bloomsburg University of Pennsylvania (PA) (m)
Bluffton College (OH) (m)
Boise State University (ID) (m)
Boston College (MA) (m)
Bowdoin College (ME) (m)
Bowie State University (MD) (m)
Bowling Green State University (OH) (m)
Briar Cliff University (IA) (m)
Bridgewater College (VA) (m)
Bridgewater State College (MA) (m)
Brigham Young University (UT) (m)
Brown University (RI) (m)
Bryant College (RI) (m)
Bucknell University (PA) (m)
Buena Vista University (IA) (m)
Buffalo State College, State University of New York (NY) (m)
Butler University (IN) (m)
Caldwell College (NJ) (m)
California Lutheran University (CA) (m)
California Polytechnic State University, San Luis Obispo (CA) (m)
California State University, Fresno (CA) (m)
California State University, Sacramento (CA) (m)
California University of Pennsylvania (PA) (m)
Campbellsville University (KY) (m)
Capital University (OH) (m)
Carleton College (MN) (m)
Carnegie Mellon University (PA) (m)
Carroll College (MT) (m)
Carroll College (WI) (m)
Carson-Newman College (TN) (m)
Carthage College (WI) (m)
Case Western Reserve University (OH) (m)
Catawba College (NC) (m)
The Catholic University of America (DC) (m)
Central College (IA) (m)
Central Connecticut State University (CT) (m)
Central Methodist College (MO) (m)
Central Michigan University (MI) (m)
Central Missouri State University (MO) (m)
Central Washington University (WA) (m)
Centre College (KY) (m)
Chadron State College (NE) (m)
Chapman University (CA) (m)
Charleston Southern University (SC) (m)
Cheyney University of Pennsylvania (PA) (m)
Chowan College (NC) (m)
Christopher Newport University (VA) (m)
The Citadel, The Military College of South Carolina (SC) (m)
Claremont McKenna College (CA) (m)
Clarion University of Pennsylvania (PA) (m)
Clark Atlanta University (GA) (m)
Clemson University (SC) (m)
Coastal Carolina University (SC) (m)
Coe College (IA) (m)
Colby College (ME) (m)
Colgate University (NY) (m)
College of Mount St. Joseph (OH) (m)

The College of New Jersey (NJ) (m)
College of the Holy Cross (MA) (m)
The College of William and Mary (VA) (m)
The College of Wooster (OH) (m)
The Colorado College (CO) (m)
Colorado School of Mines (CO) (m)
Colorado State University (CO) (m)
Columbia College (NY) (m)
Concord College (WV) (m)
Concordia College (MN) (m)
Concordia University (IL) (m)
Concordia University (NE) (m)
Concordia University, St. Paul (MN) (m)
Concordia University Wisconsin (WI) (m)
Cornell College (IA) (m)
Cornell University (NY) (m)
Crown College (MN) (m)
Culver-Stockton College (MO) (m)
Cumberland College (KY) (m)
Cumberland University (TN) (m)
Curry College (MA) (m)
Dakota State University (SD) (m)
Dakota Wesleyan University (SD) (m)
Dana College (NE) (m)
Dartmouth College (NH) (m)
Davidson College (NC) (m)
Defiance College (OH) (m)
Delaware State University (DE) (m)
Delaware Valley College (PA) (m)
Delta State University (MS) (m)
Denison University (OH) (m)
DePauw University (IN) (m)
Dickinson College (PA) (m)
Dickinson State University (ND) (m)
Doane College (NE) (m)
Drake University (IA) (m)
Duke University (NC) (m)
Duquesne University (PA) (m)
Earlham College (IN) (m)
East Carolina University (NC) (m)
East Central University (OK) (m)
Eastern Illinois University (IL) (m)
Eastern Kentucky University (KY) (m)
Eastern Michigan University (MI) (m)
Eastern New Mexico University (NM) (m)
Eastern Oregon University (OR) (m)
Eastern Washington University (WA) (m)
East Stroudsburg University of Pennsylvania (PA) (m)
East Tennessee State University (TN) (m)
East Texas Baptist University (TX) (m)
Edinboro University of Pennsylvania (PA) (m)
Edward Waters College (FL) (m)
Elizabeth City State University (NC) (m)
Elmhurst College (IL) (m)
Elon University (NC) (m)
Emory & Henry College (VA) (m)
Emporia State University (KS) (m)
Endicott College (MA) (m)
Eureka College (IL) (m)
Evangel University (MO) (m)
Fairleigh Dickinson University, College at Florham (NJ) (m)
Fairmont State University (WV) (m)
Fayetteville State University (NC) (m)
Ferris State University (MI) (m)
Ferrum College (VA) (m)
Fitchburg State College (MA) (m)
Florida Agricultural and Mechanical University (FL) (m)
Florida Atlantic University (FL) (m)
Florida International University (FL) (m)
Florida State University (FL) (m)
Fordham University (NY) (m)

Fort Hays State University (KS) (m)
Fort Lewis College (CO) (m)
Fort Valley State University (GA) (m)
Framingham State College (MA) (m)
Franklin and Marshall College (PA) (m)
Franklin College (IN) (m)
Friends University (KS) (m)
Frostburg State University (MD) (m)
Furman University (SC) (m)
Gallaudet University (DC) (m)
Gannon University (PA) (m)
Gardner-Webb University (NC) (m)
Geneva College (PA) (m)
Georgetown College (KY) (m)
Georgetown University (DC) (m)
Georgia Institute of Technology (GA) (m)
Georgia Southern University (GA) (m)
Gettysburg College (PA) (m)
Glenville State College (WV) (m)
Graceland University (IA) (m)
Grambling State University (LA) (m)
Grand Valley State University (MI) (m)
Greensboro College (NC) (m)
Greenville College (IL) (m)
Grinnell College (IA) (m)
Grove City College (PA) (m)
Guilford College (NC) (m)
Gustavus Adolphus College (MN) (m)
Hamilton College (NY) (m)
Hamline University (MN) (m)
Hampden-Sydney College (VA) (m)
Hampton University (VA) (m)
Hanover College (IN) (m)
Harding University (AR) (m)
Hardin-Simmons University (TX) (m)
Hartwick College (NY) (m)
Harvard University (MA) (m)
Haskell Indian Nations University (KS) (m)
Hastings College (NE) (m)
Heidelberg College (OH) (m)
Henderson State University (AR) (m)
Hillsdale College (MI) (m)
Hiram College (OH) (m)
Hobart and William Smith Colleges (NY) (m)
Hofstra University (NY) (m)
Hope College (MI) (m)
Howard Payne University (TX) (m)
Howard University (DC) (m)
Humboldt State University (CA) (m)
Huntingdon College (AL) (m)
Idaho State University (ID) (m)
Illinois College (IL) (m)
Illinois State University (IL) (m)
Illinois Wesleyan University (IL) (m)
Indiana State University (IN) (m)
Indiana University Bloomington (IN) (m)
Indiana University of Pennsylvania (PA) (m)
Iona College (NY) (m)
Iowa State University of Science and Technology (IA) (m)
Iowa Wesleyan College (IA) (m)
Ithaca College (NY) (m)
Jackson State University (MS) (m)
Jacksonville State University (AL) (m)
Jacksonville University (FL) (m)
James Madison University (VA) (m)
Jamestown College (ND) (m)
John Carroll University (OH) (m)
The Johns Hopkins University (MD) (m)
Johnson C. Smith University (NC) (m)
Juniata College (PA) (m)
Kalamazoo College (MI) (m)
Kansas State University (KS) (m)
Kansas Wesleyan University (KS) (m)

Kean University (NJ) (m)
Kent State University (OH) (m)
Kentucky State University (KY) (m)
Kentucky Wesleyan College (KY) (m)
Kenyon College (OH) (m)
King's College (PA) (m)
Knox College (IL) (m)
Kutztown University of Pennsylvania (PA) (m)
Lafayette College (PA) (m)
Lake Forest College (IL) (m)
Lakeland College (WI) (m)
Lambuth University (TN) (m)
Lane College (TN) (m)
Langston University (OK) (m)
La Salle University (PA) (m)
Lawrence University (WI) (m)
Lebanon Valley College (PA) (m)
Lehigh University (PA) (m)
Lenoir-Rhyne College (NC) (m)
Lewis & Clark College (OR) (m)
Liberty University (VA) (m)
Lincoln University (MO) (m)
Lindenwood University (MO) (m)
Linfield College (OR) (m)
Livingstone College (NC) (m)
Lock Haven University of Pennsylvania (PA) (m)
Loras College (IA) (m)
Louisiana College (LA) (m)
Louisiana State University and Agricultural and Mechanical College (LA) (m)
Louisiana Tech University (LA) (m)
Luther College (IA) (m)
Lycoming College (PA) (m)
Macalester College (MN) (m)
MacMurray College (IL) (m)
Maine Maritime Academy (ME) (m)
Malone College (OH) (m)
Manchester College (IN) (m)
Mansfield University of Pennsylvania (PA) (m)
Maranatha Baptist Bible College (WI) (m)
Marietta College (OH) (m)
Marist College (NY) (m)
Marshall University (WV) (m)
Mars Hill College (NC) (m)
Martin Luther College (MN) (m)
Maryville College (TN) (m)
Massachusetts Institute of Technology (MA) (m)
Massachusetts Maritime Academy (MA) (m)
Mayville State University (ND) (m)
McDaniel College (MD) (m)
McKendree College (IL) (m)
McMurry University (TX) (m)
McNeese State University (LA) (m)
McPherson College (KS) (m)
Menlo College (CA) (m)
Mercyhurst College (PA) (m)
Merrimack College (MA) (m)
Mesa State College (CO) (m)
Methodist College (NC) (m)
Miami University (OH) (m)
Michigan State University (MI) (m)
Michigan Technological University (MI) (m)
MidAmerica Nazarene University (KS) (m)
Middlebury College (VT) (m)
Middle Tennessee State University (TN) (m)
Midland Lutheran College (NE) (m)
Midwestern State University (TX) (m)
Miles College (AL) (m)
Millersville University of Pennsylvania (PA) (m)
Millikin University (IL) (m)

Millsaps College (MS) (m)
Minnesota State University Mankato (MN) (m)
Minnesota State University Moorhead (MN) (m)
Minot State University (ND) (m)
Mississippi College (MS) (m)
Mississippi State University (MS) (m)
Mississippi Valley State University (MS) (m)
Missouri Southern State University (MO) (m)
Missouri Valley College (MO) (m)
Missouri Western State College (MO) (m)
Monmouth College (IL) (m)
Monmouth University (NJ) (m)
Montana State University–Bozeman (MT) (m)
Montana State University–Northern (MT) (m)
Montana Tech of The University of Montana (MT) (m)
Montclair State University (NJ) (m)
Moravian College (PA) (m)
Morehead State University (KY) (m)
Morehouse College (GA) (m)
Morgan State University (MD) (m)
Morningside College (IA) (m)
Mount Ida College (MA) (m)
Mount Union College (OH) (m)
Muhlenberg College (PA) (m)
Murray State University (KY) (m)
Muskingum College (OH) (m)
Nebraska Wesleyan University (NE) (m)
Newberry College (SC) (m)
New Mexico Highlands University (NM) (m)
New Mexico State University (NM) (m)
Nicholls State University (LA) (m)
Nichols College (MA) (m)
Norfolk State University (VA) (m)
North Carolina Agricultural and Technical State University (NC) (m)
North Carolina State University (NC) (m)
North Carolina Wesleyan College (NC) (m)
North Central College (IL) (m)
North Dakota State University (ND) (m)
Northeastern State University (OK) (m)
Northeastern University (MA) (m)
Northern Arizona University (AZ) (m)
Northern Illinois University (IL) (m)
Northern Michigan University (MI) (m)
Northern State University (SD) (m)
North Greenville College (SC) (m)
North Park University (IL) (m)
Northwestern College (IA) (m)
Northwestern College (MN) (m)
Northwestern Oklahoma State University (OK) (m)
Northwestern State University of Louisiana (LA) (m)
Northwestern University (IL) (m)
Northwest Missouri State University (MO) (m)
Northwood University (MI) (m)
Norwich University (VT) (m)
Oberlin College (OH) (m)
Occidental College (CA) (m)
Ohio Dominican University (OH) (m)
Ohio Northern University (OH) (m)
The Ohio State University (OH) (m)
Ohio University (OH) (m)
Ohio Wesleyan University (OH) (m)
Oklahoma Panhandle State University (OK) (m)
Oklahoma State University (OK) (m)
Olivet College (MI) (m)
Olivet Nazarene University (IL) (m)

Oregon State University (OR) (m)
Ottawa University (KS) (m)
Otterbein College (OH) (m)
Ouachita Baptist University (AR) (m)
Pace University (NY) (m)
Pacific Lutheran University (WA) (m)
Paul Quinn College (TX) (m)
The Pennsylvania State University University Park Campus (PA) (m)
Peru State College (NE) (m)
Pikeville College (KY) (m)
Pittsburg State University (KS) (m)
Pitzer College (CA) (m)
Plymouth State University (NH) (m)
Pomona College (CA) (m)
Portland State University (OR) (m)
Prairie View A&M University (TX) (m)
Presbyterian College (SC) (m)
Princeton University (NJ) (m)
Principia College (IL) (m)
Purdue University (IN) (m)
Quincy University (IL) (m)
Randolph-Macon College (VA) (m)
Rensselaer Polytechnic Institute (NY) (m)
Rhodes College (TN) (m)
Rice University (TX) (m)
Ripon College (WI) (m)
Robert Morris University (PA) (m)
Rockford College (IL) (m)
Rocky Mountain College (MT) (m)
Rose-Hulman Institute of Technology (IN) (m)
Rowan University (NJ) (m)
Rutgers, The State University of New Jersey, New Brunswick/Piscataway (NJ) (m)
Sacred Heart University (CT) (m)
Saginaw Valley State University (MI) (m)
St. Ambrose University (IA) (m)
Saint Anselm College (NH) (m)
Saint Augustine's College (NC) (m)
St. Cloud State University (MN) (m)
Saint Francis University (PA) (m)
St. John Fisher College (NY) (m)
Saint John's University (MN) (m)
Saint Joseph's College (IN) (m)
St. Lawrence University (NY) (m)
Saint Mary's College of California (CA) (m)
St. Norbert College (WI) (m)
St. Olaf College (MN) (m)
Saint Paul's College (VA) (m)
Saint Peter's College (NJ) (m)
Saint Xavier University (IL) (m)
Salisbury University (MD) (m)
Salve Regina University (RI) (m)
Samford University (AL) (m)
Sam Houston State University (TX) (m)
San Diego State University (CA) (m)
San Jose State University (CA) (m)
Savannah State University (GA) (m)
Shaw University (NC) (m)
Shenandoah University (VA) (m)
Shepherd University (WV) (m)
Shippensburg University of Pennsylvania (PA) (m)
Siena College (NY) (m)
Simpson College (IA) (m)
Si Tanka Huron University (SD) (m)
Slippery Rock University of Pennsylvania (PA) (m)
South Carolina State University (SC) (m)
South Dakota School of Mines and Technology (SD) (m)
South Dakota State University (SD) (m)
Southeastern Louisiana University (LA) (m)

Southeastern Oklahoma State University (OK) (m)

Southeast Missouri State University (MO) (m)

Southern Arkansas University–Magnolia (AR) (m)

Southern Connecticut State University (CT) (m)

Southern Illinois University Carbondale (IL) (m)

Southern Methodist University (TX) (m)

Southern Nazarene University (OK) (m)

Southern Oregon University (OR) (m)

Southern University and Agricultural and Mechanical College (LA) (m)

Southern Utah University (UT) (m)

Southern Virginia University (VA) (m)

Southwest Baptist University (MO) (m)

Southwestern Assemblies of God University (TX) (m)

Southwestern College (KS) (m)

Southwestern Oklahoma State University (OK) (m)

Southwest Minnesota State University (MN) (m)

Southwest Missouri State University (MO) (m)

Springfield College (MA) (m)

Stanford University (CA) (m)

State University of New York College at Brockport (NY) (m)

State University of New York College at Cortland (NY) (m)

State University of West Georgia (GA) (m)

Stephen F. Austin State University (TX) (m)

Sterling College (KS) (m)

Stillman College (AL) (m)

Stonehill College (MA) (m)

Stony Brook University, State University of New York (NY) (m)

Sul Ross State University (TX) (m)

Susquehanna University (PA) (m)

Syracuse University (NY) (m)

Tabor College (KS) (m)

Tarleton State University (TX) (m)

Taylor University (IN) (m)

Temple University (PA) (m)

Tennessee State University (TN) (m)

Tennessee Technological University (TN) (m)

Texas A&M University (TX) (m)

Texas A&M University–Commerce (TX) (m)

Texas A&M University–Kingsville (TX) (m)

Texas Christian University (TX) (m)

Texas College (TX) (m)

Texas Lutheran University (TX) (m)

Texas Southern University (TX) (m)

Texas State University-San Marcos (TX) (m)

Texas Tech University (TX) (m)

Thiel College (PA) (m)

Thomas More College (KY) (m)

Tiffin University (OH) (m)

Towson University (MD) (m)

Trinity College (CT) (m)

Trinity International University (IL) (m)

Trinity University (TX) (m)

Tri-State University (IN) (m)

Troy State University (AL) (m)

Truman State University (MO) (m)

Tufts University (MA) (m)

Tulane University (LA) (m)

Tusculum College (TN) (m)

Tuskegee University (AL) (m)

Union College (KY) (m)

Union College (NY) (m)

United States Air Force Academy (CO) (m)

United States Coast Guard Academy (CT) (m)

United States Merchant Marine Academy (NY) (m)

United States Military Academy (NY) (m)

United States Naval Academy (MD) (m)

University at Albany, State University of New York (NY) (m)

University at Buffalo, The State University of New York (NY) (m)

The University of Akron (OH) (m)

The University of Alabama (AL) (m)

The University of Alabama at Birmingham (AL) (m)

The University of Arizona (AZ) (m)

University of Arkansas (AR) (m)

University of Arkansas at Monticello (AR) (m)

University of Arkansas at Pine Bluff (AR) (m)

University of California, Berkeley (CA) (m)

University of California, Davis (CA) (m)

University of California, Los Angeles (CA) (m)

University of Central Arkansas (AR) (m)

University of Central Florida (FL) (m)

University of Central Oklahoma (OK) (m)

University of Chicago (IL) (m)

University of Cincinnati (OH) (m)

University of Colorado at Boulder (CO) (m)

University of Connecticut (CT) (m)

University of Dayton (OH) (m)

University of Delaware (DE) (m)

University of Dubuque (IA) (m)

The University of Findlay (OH) (m)

University of Florida (FL) (m)

University of Georgia (GA) (m)

University of Hawaii at Manoa (HI) (m)

University of Houston (TX) (m)

University of Idaho (ID) (m)

University of Illinois at Urbana–Champaign (IL) (m)

University of Indianapolis (IN) (m)

The University of Iowa (IA) (m)

University of Kansas (KS) (m)

University of Kentucky (KY) (m)

University of La Verne (CA) (m)

University of Louisiana at Lafayette (LA) (m)

University of Louisiana at Monroe (LA) (m)

University of Louisville (KY) (m)

University of Maine (ME) (m)

University of Mary (ND) (m)

University of Mary Hardin-Baylor (TX) (m)

University of Maryland, College Park (MD) (m)

University of Massachusetts Amherst (MA) (m)

University of Massachusetts Dartmouth (MA) (m)

The University of Memphis (TN) (m)

University of Miami (FL) (m)

University of Michigan (MI) (m)

University of Minnesota, Crookston (MN) (m)

University of Minnesota, Duluth (MN) (m)

University of Minnesota, Morris (MN) (m)

University of Minnesota, Twin Cities Campus (MN) (m)

University of Mississippi (MS) (m)

University of Missouri–Columbia (MO) (m)

University of Missouri–Rolla (MO) (m)

The University of Montana–Missoula (MT) (m)

The University of Montana–Western (MT) (m)

University of Nebraska at Kearney (NE) (m)

University of Nebraska at Omaha (NE) (m)

University of Nebraska–Lincoln (NE) (m)

University of Nevada, Las Vegas (NV) (m)

University of Nevada, Reno (NV) (m)

University of New Hampshire (NH) (m)

University of New Haven (CT) (m)

University of New Mexico (NM) (m)

University of North Alabama (AL) (m)

The University of North Carolina at Chapel Hill (NC) (m)

University of North Dakota (ND) (m)

University of Northern Colorado (CO) (m)

University of Northern Iowa (IA) (m)

University of North Texas (TX) (m)

University of Notre Dame (IN) (m)

University of Oklahoma (OK) (m)

University of Oregon (OR) (m)

University of Pennsylvania (PA) (m)

University of Pittsburgh (PA) (m)

University of Puget Sound (WA) (m)

University of Redlands (CA) (m)

University of Rhode Island (RI) (m)

University of Richmond (VA) (m)

University of Rochester (NY) (m)

University of St. Francis (IL) (m)

University of Saint Francis (IN) (m)

University of Saint Mary (KS) (m)

University of St. Thomas (MN) (m)

University of San Diego (CA) (m)

University of Sioux Falls (SD) (m)

University of South Carolina (SC) (m)

The University of South Dakota (SD) (m)

University of Southern California (CA) (m)

University of Southern Mississippi (MS) (m)

University of South Florida (FL) (m)

The University of Tennessee (TN) (m)

The University of Tennessee at Chattanooga (TN) (m)

The University of Tennessee at Martin (TN) (m)

The University of Texas at Austin (TX) (m)

The University of Texas at El Paso (TX) (m)

University of the South (TN) (m)

University of Toledo (OH) (m)

University of Tulsa (OK) (m)

University of Utah (UT) (m)

University of Virginia (VA) (m)

The University of Virginia's College at Wise (VA) (m)

University of Washington (WA) (m)

The University of West Alabama (AL) (m)

University of Wisconsin–Eau Claire (WI) (m)

University of Wisconsin–La Crosse (WI) (m)

University of Wisconsin–Madison (WI) (m)

University of Wisconsin–Oshkosh (WI) (m)

University of Wisconsin–Platteville (WI) (m)

University of Wisconsin–River Falls (WI) (m)

University of Wisconsin–Stevens Point (WI) (m)

University of Wisconsin–Stout (WI) (m)

University of Wisconsin–Whitewater (WI) (m)

University of Wyoming (WY) (m)

Upper Iowa University (IA) (m)

Urbana University (OH) (m)

Ursinus College (PA) (m)

Utah State University (UT) (m)

Utica College (NY) (m)

Valdosta State University (GA) (m)

Valley City State University (ND) (m)

Valparaiso University (IN) (m)

Vanderbilt University (TN) (m)

Villanova University (PA) (m)

Virginia Military Institute (VA) (m)

Virginia Polytechnic Institute and State University (VA) (m)
Virginia State University (VA) (m)
Virginia Union University (VA) (m)
Wabash College (IN) (m)
Wagner College (NY) (m)
Wake Forest University (NC) (m)
Waldorf College (IA) (m)
Walsh University (OH) (m)
Wartburg College (IA) (m)
Washburn University (KS) (m)
Washington & Jefferson College (PA) (m)
Washington and Lee University (VA) (m)
Washington State University (WA) (m)
Washington University in St. Louis (MO) (m)
Waynesburg College (PA) (m)
Wayne State College (NE) (m)
Wayne State University (MI) (m)
Webber International University (FL) (m)
Weber State University (UT) (m)
Wesleyan University (CT) (m)
Wesley College (DE) (m)
West Chester University of Pennsylvania (PA) (m)
Western Carolina University (NC) (m)
Western Connecticut State University (CT) (m)
Western Illinois University (IL) (m)
Western Kentucky University (KY) (m)
Western Michigan University (MI) (m)
Western New England College (MA) (m)
Western New Mexico University (NM) (m)
Western Oregon University (OR) (m)
Western State College of Colorado (CO) (m)
Western Washington University (WA) (m)
Westfield State College (MA) (m)
West Liberty State College (WV) (m)
Westminster College (MO) (m)
Westminster College (PA) (m)
West Texas A&M University (TX) (m)
West Virginia State College (WV) (m)
West Virginia University (WV) (m)
West Virginia University Institute of Technology (WV) (m)
West Virginia Wesleyan College (WV) (m)
Wheaton College (IL) (m)
Whittier College (CA) (m)
Whitworth College (WA) (m)
Widener University (PA) (m)
Wilkes University (PA) (m)
Willamette University (OR) (m)
William Jewell College (MO) (m)
William Paterson University of New Jersey (NJ) (m)
William Penn University (IA) (m)
Williams College (MA) (m)
Wilmington College (OH) (m)
Wingate University (NC) (m)
Winona State University (MN) (m)
Winston-Salem State University (NC) (m)
Wisconsin Lutheran College (WI) (m)
Wittenberg University (OH) (m)
Wofford College (SC) (m)
Worcester Polytechnic Institute (MA) (m)
Worcester State College (MA) (m)
Yale University (CT) (m)
Youngstown State University (OH)(m)

Golf

Abilene Christian University (TX) (m)
Adams State College (CO) (m)
Adelphi University (NY) (m)
Adrian College (MI) (m/w)

Alabama Agricultural and Mechanical University (AL) (m/w)
Alabama State University (AL) (m/w)
Albertson College of Idaho (ID) (m/w)
Albion College (MI) (m/w)
Albright College (PA) (m)
Alcorn State University (MS) (m/w)
Allegheny College (PA) (m)
Alma College (MI) (m/w)
Alvernia College (PA) (m)
American International College (MA) (m)
American University (DC) (m)
Amherst College (MA) (m/w)
Anderson College (SC) (m/w)
Anderson University (IN) (m/w)
Anna Maria College (MA) (m)
Appalachian State University (NC) (m/w)
Aquinas College (MI) (m/w)
Arcadia University (PA) (m/w)
Arizona State University (AZ) (m/w)
Arkansas State University (AR) (m/w)
Arkansas Tech University (AR) (m/w)
Armstrong Atlantic State University (GA) (m)
Ashland University (OH) (m/w)
Assumption College (MA) (m)
Atlanta Christian College (GA) (m)
Auburn University (AL) (m/w)
Augsburg College (MN) (m/w)
Augustana College (IL) (m/w)
Augustana College (SD) (m/w)
Augusta State University (GA) (m/w)
Aurora University (IL) (m)
Austin College (TX) (m)
Austin Peay State University (TN) (m/w)
Averett University (VA) (m)
Avila University (MO) (w)
Babson College (MA) (m)
Bacone College (OK) (m)
Baker University (KS) (m/w)
Baldwin-Wallace College (OH) (m/w)
Ball State University (IN) (m/w)
Barry University (FL) (m/w)
Barton College (NC) (m)
Baylor University (TX) (m/w)
Belhaven College (MS) (m/w)
Bellarmine University (KY) (m/w)
Belmont Abbey College (NC) (m)
Belmont University (TN) (m/w)
Beloit College (WI) (m/w)
Bemidji State University (MN) (m/w)
Benedict College (SC) (m/w)
Benedictine College (KS) (m/w)
Benedictine University (IL) (m/w)
Bentley College (MA) (m)
Berea College (KY) (m)
Berry College (GA) (m/w)
Bethany College (KS) (m)
Bethany College of the Assemblies of God (CA) (m/w)
Bethel College (IN) (m)
Bethel College (KS) (m/w)
Bethel College (TN) (m/w)
Bethel University (MN) (m)
Bethune-Cookman College (FL) (m/w)
Birmingham-Southern College (AL) (m/w)
Blackburn College (IL) (m)
Bluefield College (VA) (m)
Bluefield State College (WV) (m)
Bluffton College (OH) (m/w)
Boise State University (ID) (m/w)
Boston College (MA) (m/w)
Boston University (MA) (m/w)
Bowdoin College (ME) (m)
Bowling Green State University (OH) (m/w)
Bradley University (IL) (m/w/w)

Brandeis University (MA) (m)
Brescia University (KY) (m/w)
Brevard College (NC) (m)
Briar Cliff University (IA) (m/w)
Bridgewater College (VA) (m)
Brigham Young University (UT) (m/w)
Brown University (RI) (m/w)
Bryant College (RI) (m/w)
Bucknell University (PA) (m/w)
Buena Vista University (IA) (m/w)
Butler University (IN) (m/w)
Cabrini College (PA) (m)
California Institute of Technology (CA) (m)
California Lutheran University (CA) (m)
California Maritime Academy (CA) (m)
California Polytechnic State University, San Luis Obispo (CA) (m/w)
California State University, Bakersfield (CA) (m)
California State University, Chico (CA) (m/w)
California State University, Dominguez Hills (CA) (m)
California State University, Fresno (CA) (m)
California State University, Hayward (CA) (m/w)
California State University, Long Beach (CA) (m/w)
California State University, Monterey Bay (CA) (m/w)
California State University, Northridge (CA) (m/w)
California State University, Sacramento (CA) (m/w)
California State University, San Bernardino (CA) (m)
California State University, San Marcos (CA) (m/w)
California State University, Stanislaus (CA) (m)
Calvin College (MI) (m/w)
Cameron University (OK) (m)
Campbellsville University (KY) (m/w)
Campbell University (NC) (m/w)
Canisius College (NY) (m)
Capital University (OH) (m/w)
Carleton College (MN) (m/w)
Carnegie Mellon University (PA) (m/w)
Carroll College (MT) (m/w)
Carroll College (WI) (m/w)
Carson-Newman College (TN) (m)
Carthage College (WI) (m/w)
Catawba College (NC) (m/w)
Cazenovia College (NY) (m)
Cedarville University (OH) (m)
Centenary College (NJ) (m/w)
Centenary College of Louisiana (LA) (m/w)
Central Christian College of Kansas (KS) (m/w)
Central College (IA) (m/w)
Central Connecticut State University (CT) (m/w)
Central Methodist College (MO) (m/w)
Central Missouri State University (MO) (m)
Centre College (KY) (m/w)
Chadron State College (NE) (w)
Chapman University (CA) (m)
Charleston Southern University (SC) (m/w)
Chicago State University (IL) (m/w)
Chowan College (NC) (m)
Christian Brothers University (TN) (m)
Christopher Newport University (VA) (m)
The Citadel, The Military College of South Carolina (SC) (m/w)
Claremont McKenna College (CA) (m)
Clarion University of Pennsylvania (PA) (m)

Clarke College (IA) (m/w)
Clarkson University (NY) (m)
Clayton College & State University (GA) (m)
Clemson University (SC) (m)
Cleveland State University (OH) (m/w)
Coastal Carolina University (SC) (m/w)
Coe College (IA) (m/w)
Coker College (SC) (m)
Colby College (ME) (m)
Colgate University (NY) (m)
College Misericordia (PA) (m)
College of Charleston (SC) (m/w)
College of Mount St. Joseph (OH) (m/w)
The College of New Jersey (NJ) (m)
College of Saint Benedict (MN) (w)
College of Saint Mary (NE) (w)
The College of Saint Rose (NY) (m)
College of the Holy Cross (MA) (m/w)
College of the Southwest (NM) (m/w)
The College of William and Mary (VA)
    (m/w)
The College of Wooster (OH) (m)
Colorado Christian University (CO) (m)
Colorado School of Mines (CO) (m)
Colorado State University (CO) (m/w)
Colorado State University-Pueblo (CO) (m)
Columbia College (NY) (m)
Columbus State University (GA) (m)
Concord College (WV) (m)
Concordia College (MN) (m/w)
Concordia University (NE) (m/w)
Concordia University (OR) (m/w)
Concordia University at Austin (TX) (m/w)
Concordia University Wisconsin (WI) (m/w)
Cornell College (IA) (m/w)
Cornell University (NY) (m)
Cornerstone University (MI) (m)
Creighton University (NE) (m/w)
Crown College (MN) (m)
Culver-Stockton College (MO) (m/w)
Cumberland College (KY) (m/w)
Cumberland University (TN) (m)
Daemen College (NY) (m)
Dakota State University (SD) (m/w)
Dakota Wesleyan University (SD) (m/w)
Dartmouth College (NH) (m/w)
Davenport University (MI) (m/w)
Davidson College (NC) (m)
Davis & Elkins College (WV) (m)
Defiance College (OH) (m/w)
Delaware Valley College (PA) (m)
Delta State University (MS) (m)
Denison University (OH) (m)
DePaul University (IL) (m)
DePauw University (IN) (m/w)
DeSales University (PA) (m)
Dickinson College (PA) (m/w)
Dickinson State University (ND) (m/w)
Doane College (NE) (m/w)
Dominican College (NY) (m)
Dordt College (IA) (m)
Dowling College (NY) (m)
Drake University (IA) (m)
Drexel University (PA) (m)
Drury University (MO) (m/w)
Duke University (NC) (m/w)
Duquesne University (PA) (m)
East Carolina University (NC) (m/w)
East Central University (OK) (m)
Eastern Illinois University (IL) (m/w)
Eastern Kentucky University (KY) (m/w)
Eastern Michigan University (MI) (m/w)
Eastern University (PA) (m)
Eastern Washington University (WA) (m/w)
East Tennessee State University (TN) (m/w)

Eckerd College (FL) (m)
Edgewood College (WI) (m/w)
Edward Waters College (FL) (m/w)
Elizabeth City State University (NC) (m)
Elizabethtown College (PA) (m)
Elmhurst College (IL) (m/w)
Elmira College (NY) (m/w)
Elms College (MA) (m)
Elon University (NC) (m/w)
Embry-Riddle Aeronautical University (FL)
    (m/w)
Emory & Henry College (VA) (m)
Emory University (GA) (m)
Endicott College (MA) (m/w)
Eureka College (IL) (m)
Evangel University (MO) (m/w)
Fairfield University (CT) (m/w)
Fairleigh Dickinson University, College at
    Florham (NJ) (m/w)
Fairmont State University (WV) (m/w)
Farmingdale State University of New York
    (NY) (m)
Fayetteville State University (NC) (m)
Ferris State University (MI) (m/w)
Ferrum College (VA) (m)
Fisk University (TN) (m/w)
Flagler College (FL) (m/w)
Florida Agricultural and Mechanical
    University (FL) (m)
Florida Atlantic University (FL) (m/w)
Florida Gulf Coast University (FL) (m/w)
Florida International University (FL) (w)
Florida Southern College (FL) (m/w)
Florida State University (FL) (m/w)
Fontbonne University (MO) (m)
Fordham University (NY) (m)
Fort Hays State University (KS) (m)
Fort Lewis College (CO) (m)
The Franciscan University (IA) (m)
Francis Marion University (SC) (m)
Franklin and Marshall College (PA) (m/w)
Franklin College (IN) (m/w)
Franklin Pierce College (NH) (m/w)
Freed-Hardeman University (TN) (m/w)
Friends University (KS) (m)
Furman University (SC) (m/w)
Gannon University (PA) (m/w)
Gardner-Webb University (NC) (m/w)
George Mason University (VA) (m)
Georgetown College (KY) (m/w)
Georgetown University (DC) (m/w)
The George Washington University (DC) (m)
Georgia College & State University (GA) (m)
Georgia Institute of Technology (GA) (m)
Georgia Southern University (GA) (m)
Georgia State University (GA) (m/w)
Gettysburg College (PA) (m/w)
Glenville State College (WV) (m/w)
Goldey-Beacom College (DE) (m/w)
Gonzaga University (WA) (m/w)
Goshen College (IN) (m)
Grace College (IN) (m)
Graceland University (IA) (m/w)
Grambling State University (LA) (m/w)
Grand Canyon University (AZ) (m/w)
Grand Valley State University (MI) (m/w)
Green Mountain College (VT) (m/w)
Greensboro College (NC) (m)
Grinnell College (IA) (m/w)
Grove City College (PA) (m/w)
Guilford College (NC) (m)
Gustavus Adolphus College (MN) (m/w)
Gwynedd-Mercy College (PA) (m/w)
Hamilton College (NY) (m)
Hampden-Sydney College (VA) (m)

Hampton University (VA) (m/w)
Hannibal-LaGrange College (MO) (m)
Hanover College (IN) (m/w)
Harding University (AR) (m)
Hardin-Simmons University (TX) (m/w)
Hartwick College (NY) (m)
Harvard University (MA) (m/w)
Haskell Indian Nations University (KS) (m)
Hastings College (NE) (m/w)
Heidelberg College (OH) (m/w)
Henderson State University (AR) (m)
Hendrix College (AR) (m)
High Point University (NC) (m/w)
Hilbert College (NY) (m)
Hillsdale College (MI) (m)
Hiram College (OH) (m/w)
Hobart and William Smith Colleges (NY)
    (m)
Hofstra University (NY) (m/w)
Hollins University (VA) (w)
Holy Family University (PA) (m)
Holy Names University (CA) (m)
Hood College (MD) (m/w)
Hope College (MI) (m/w)
Huntingdon College (AL) (m)
Huntington College (IN) (m)
Husson College (ME) (m)
Idaho State University (ID) (m/w)
Illinois College (IL) (m/w)
Illinois State University (IL) (m/w)
Illinois Wesleyan University (IL) (m/w)
Indiana University Bloomington (IN) (m/w)
Indiana University Northwest (IN) (m)
Indiana University of Pennsylvania (PA) (m)
Indiana University–Purdue University Fort
    Wayne (IN) (m/w)
Indiana University–Purdue University
    Indianapolis (IN) (m/w)
Indiana Wesleyan University (IN) (m)
Iona College (NY) (m)
Iowa State University of Science and
    Technology (IA) (m/w)
Iowa Wesleyan College (IA) (m/w)
Jackson State University (MS) (m/w)
Jacksonville State University (AL) (m/w)
Jacksonville University (FL) (m/w)
James Madison University (VA) (m/w)
Jamestown College (ND) (m/w)
John Carroll University (OH) (m)
Johnson & Wales University (CO) (m)
Johnson & Wales University (FL) (m)
Johnson & Wales University (RI) (m)
Johnson C. Smith University (NC) (m)
Kalamazoo College (MI) (m/w)
Kansas State University (KS) (m/w)
Kansas Wesleyan University (KS) (m)
Kennesaw State University (GA) (m)
Kent State University (OH) (m/w)
Kentucky State University (KY) (m)
Kentucky Wesleyan College (KY) (m/w)
Kenyon College (OH) (m)
King College (TN) (m)
King's College (PA) (m)
Knox College (IL) (m/w)
Kutztown University of Pennsylvania (PA)
    (w)
Lafayette College (PA) (m)
LaGrange College (GA) (m)
Lake Erie College (OH) (m)
Lakeland College (WI) (m/w)
Lake Superior State University (MI) (m)
Lamar University (TX) (m/w)
Lambuth University (TN) (m)
Langston University (OK) (m)
La Roche College (PA) (m)

La Salle University (PA) (m)
Lawrence University (WI) (m)
Lebanon Valley College (PA) (m)
Lees-McRae College (NC) (m)
Lee University (TN) (m)
Lehigh University (PA) (m/w)
Le Moyne College (NY) (m)
Lenoir-Rhyne College (NC) (m/w)
LeTourneau University (TX) (m/w)
Lewis & Clark College (OR) (m/w)
Lewis-Clark State College (ID) (m/w)
Lewis University (IL) (m/w)
Liberty University (VA) (m)
Limestone College (SC) (m/w)
Lincoln Memorial University (TN) (m/w)
Lincoln University (MO) (m)
Lindenwood University (MO) (m)
Lindsey Wilson College (KY) (m/w)
Linfield College (OR) (m/w)
Lipscomb University (TN) (m/w)
Long Island University, Brooklyn Campus
    (NY) (m/w)
Longwood University (VA) (m/w)
Loras College (IA) (m/w)
Louisiana College (LA) (m)
Louisiana State University and Agricultural
    and Mechanical College (LA) (m/w)
Louisiana Tech University (LA) (m)
Loyola College in Maryland (MD) (m)
Loyola Marymount University (CA) (m)
Loyola University Chicago (IL) (m/w)
Luther College (IA) (m/w)
Lycoming College (PA) (m)
Lynchburg College (VA) (m/w)
Lynn University (FL) (m/w)
Lyon College (AR) (m/w)
Macalester College (MN) (m/w)
MacMurray College (IL) (m/w)
Madonna University (MI) (m/w)
Maine Maritime Academy (ME) (m)
Malone College (OH) (m/w)
Manchester College (IN) (m/w)
Manhattan College (NY) (m)
Manhattanville College (NY) (m)
Marian College (IN) (m)
Marian College of Fond du Lac (WI) (m/w)
Marquette University (WI) (m)
Marshall University (WV) (m/w)
Mars Hill College (NC) (m)
Martin Luther College (MN) (m)
Martin Methodist College (TN) (m)
Marymount University (VA) (m)
Maryville University of Saint Louis (MO) (m)
Massachusetts College of Liberal Arts (MA)
    (m)
Massachusetts Institute of Technology (MA)
    (m)
The Master's College and Seminary (CA) (m)
McDaniel College (MD) (m/w)
McKendree College (IL) (m/w)
McMurry University (TX) (m/w)
McNeese State University (LA) (m/w)
Menlo College (CA) (m)
Mercer University (GA) (m/w)
Mercy College (NY) (m)
Mercyhurst College (PA) (m/w)
Mesa State College (CO) (w)
Messiah College (PA) (m)
Methodist College (NC) (m/w)
Miami University (OH) (m)
Michigan State University (MI) (m/w)
Middlebury College (VT) (m/w)
Middle Tennessee State University (TN)
    (m/w)
Midland Lutheran College (NE) (m/w)

Millersville University of Pennsylvania (PA)
    (m)
Milligan College (TN) (m)
Millikin University (IL) (m/w)
Millsaps College (MS) (m/w)
Milwaukee School of Engineering (WI) (m/w)
Minnesota State University Mankato (MN)
    (m/w)
Minnesota State University Moorhead (MN)
    (w)
Minot State University (ND) (m/w)
Mississippi State University (MS) (m/w)
Mississippi Valley State University (MS)
    (m/w)
Missouri Baptist University (MO) (m/w)
Missouri Southern State University (MO) (m)
Missouri Valley College (MO) (m/w)
Missouri Western State College (MO) (m/w)
Monmouth College (IL) (m/w)
Monmouth University (NJ) (m/w)
Montana State University–Billings (MT)
    (m/w)
Montana State University–Bozeman (MT)
    (w)
Montana State University–Northern (MT)
    (w)
Montreat College (NC) (w)
Moravian College (PA) (m)
Morehead State University (KY) (m)
Morehouse College (GA) (m)
Morningside College (IA) (m/w)
Morris College (SC) (m)
Mount Holyoke College (MA) (w)
Mount Marty College (SD) (m/w)
Mount Mercy College (IA) (m/w)
Mount Olive College (NC) (m)
Mount Saint Mary's University (MD) (m/w)
Mount Union College (OH) (m/w)
Mount Vernon Nazarene University (OH)
    (m)
Muhlenberg College (PA) (m/w)
Murray State University (KY) (m/w)
Muskingum College (OH) (m/w)
Nazareth College of Rochester (NY) (m)
Nebraska Wesleyan University (NE) (m/w)
Neumann College (PA) (m)
Newberry College (SC) (m/w)
Newbury College (MA) (m)
Newman University (KS) (m/w)
New Mexico State University (NM) (m/w)
New York University (NY) (m)
Niagara University (NY) (m)
Nicholls State University (LA) (m/w)
Nichols College (MA) (m)
North Carolina Central University (NC)
    (m/w)
North Carolina State University (NC) (m/w)
North Carolina Wesleyan College (NC) (m)
North Central College (IL) (m/w)
North Dakota State University (ND) (m/w)
Northeastern State University (OK) (m/w)
Northern Arizona University (AZ) (w)
Northern Illinois University (IL) (m/w)
Northern Kentucky University (KY) (m/w)
Northern Michigan University (MI) (m)
Northern State University (SD) (m/w)
North Greenville College (SC) (m)
North Park University (IL) (m/w)
Northwestern College (IA) (m/w)
Northwestern College (MN) (m)
Northwestern University (IL) (m/w)
Northwest Nazarene University (ID) (m)
Northwood University (MI) (m/w)
Northwood University, Florida Campus (FL)
    (m/w)

Northwood University, Texas Campus (TX)
    (m/w)
Notre Dame de Namur University (CA)
    (m/w)
Nova Southeastern University (FL) (m/w)
Nyack College (NY) (m)
Oakland City University (IN) (m/w)
Oakland University (MI) (m/w)
Oberlin College (OH) (m/w)
Oglethorpe University (GA) (m/w)
Ohio Dominican University (OH) (m/w)
Ohio Northern University (OH) (m/w)
The Ohio State University (OH) (m/w)
Ohio University (OH) (m/w)
Ohio Valley College (WV) (m)
Ohio Wesleyan University (OH) (m/w)
Oklahoma Baptist University (OK) (m/w)
Oklahoma Christian University (OK) (m)
Oklahoma City University (OK) (m/w)
Oklahoma Panhandle State University (OK)
    (m/w)
Oklahoma State University (OK) (m/w)
Oklahoma Wesleyan University (OK) (m)
Old Dominion University (VA) (m)
Olivet College (MI) (m/w)
Olivet Nazarene University (IL) (m/w)
Oral Roberts University (OK) (m/w)
Oregon State University (OR) (m/w)
Ottawa University (KS) (m)
Otterbein College (OH) (m/w)
Ouachita Baptist University (AR) (m)
Pace University (NY) (m/w)
Pacific Lutheran University (WA) (m/w)
Pacific University (OR) (m)
Park University (MO) (w)
The Pennsylvania State University Altoona
    College (PA) (m)
The Pennsylvania State University at Erie,
    The Behrend College (PA) (m/w)
The Pennsylvania State University University
    Park Campus (PA) (m/w)
Pepperdine University (CA) (m/w)
Peru State College (NE) (w)
Pfeiffer University (NC) (m/w)
Philadelphia University (PA) (m)
Piedmont College (GA) (m/w)
Pikeville College (KY) (m/w)
Pittsburg State University (KS) (m)
Pitzer College (CA) (m/w)
Point Loma Nazarene University (CA) (m)
Pomona College (CA) (m/w)
Portland State University (OR) (w)
Prairie View A&M University (TX) (m/w)
Presbyterian College (SC) (m)
Presentation College (SD) (m/w)
Princeton University (NJ) (m/w)
Principia College (IL) (m)
Purdue University (IN) (m/w)
Queens College of the City University of
    New York (NY) (m)
Queens University of Charlotte (NC) (m/w)
Quincy University (IL) (m/w)
Quinnipiac University (CT) (m)
Radford University (VA) (m/w)
Randolph-Macon College (VA) (m)
Regis University (CO) (m)
Rensselaer Polytechnic Institute (NY) (m)
Rhode Island College (RI) (m)
Rhodes College (TN) (m/w)
Rice University (TX) (m)
Rider University (NJ) (m)
Ripon College (WI) (m/w)
Roanoke College (VA) (m)
Robert Morris College (IL) (m/w)
Robert Morris University (PA) (m/w)

Roberts Wesleyan College (NY) (m)
Rockford College (IL) (m)
Rockhurst University (MO) (m/w)
Rocky Mountain College (MT) (m/w)
Rollins College (FL) (m/w)
Rose-Hulman Institute of Technology (IN) (m/w/w)
Rutgers, The State University of New Jersey, Camden (NJ) (m)
Rutgers, The State University of New Jersey, New Brunswick/Piscataway (NJ) (m/w)
Sacred Heart University (CT) (m/w)
Saginaw Valley State University (MI) (m)
St. Ambrose University (IA) (m/w)
St. Andrews Presbyterian College (NC) (m)
Saint Anselm College (NH) (m)
Saint Augustine's College (NC) (m)
St. Bonaventure University (NY) (m)
St. Cloud State University (MN) (m/w)
St. Edward's University (TX) (m/w)
Saint Francis University (PA) (w)
St. Gregory's University (OK) (m/w)
St. John Fisher College (NY) (m)
Saint John's University (MN) (m)
St. John's University (NY) (m)
Saint Joseph's College (IN) (m/w)
Saint Joseph's College of Maine (ME) (m)
St. Joseph's College, Suffolk Campus (NY) (m)
Saint Joseph's University (PA) (m)
St. Lawrence University (NY) (m/w)
Saint Leo University (FL) (m/w)
Saint Louis University (MO) (m)
Saint Martin's College (WA) (m/w)
Saint Mary's College (IN) (w)
Saint Mary's College of California (CA) (m)
Saint Mary's University of Minnesota (MN) (m/w)
St. Mary's University of San Antonio (TX) (m/w)
Saint Michael's College (VT) (m)
St. Norbert College (WI) (m/w)
St. Olaf College (MN) (m/w)
Saint Paul's College (VA) (m/w)
Saint Peter's College (NJ) (m)
St. Thomas Aquinas College (NY) (m)
St. Thomas University (FL) (m)
Saint Vincent College (PA) (m/w)
Salem International University (WV) (m)
Salem State College (MA) (m)
Samford University (AL) (m/w)
Sam Houston State University (TX) (m/w)
San Diego State University (CA) (m/w)
San Jose State University (CA) (m/w)
Santa Clara University (CA) (m/w)
Savannah College of Art and Design (GA) (m/w)
Savannah State University (GA) (m/w)
Schreiner University (TX) (m)
Seton Hall University (NJ) (m)
Seton Hill University (PA) (m/w)
Shawnee State University (OH) (m)
Shenandoah University (VA) (m)
Shepherd University (WV) (m)
Shorter College (GA) (m/w)
Siena College (NY) (m/w)
Siena Heights University (MI) (m)
Simpson College (IA) (m/w)
Skidmore College (NY) (m)
Slippery Rock University of Pennsylvania (PA) (m)
Sonoma State University (CA) (m)
South Carolina State University (SC) (m)
South Dakota School of Mines and Technology (SD) (m)

South Dakota State University (SD) (m/w)
Southeastern Louisiana University (LA) (m)
Southeast Missouri State University (MO) (m)
Southern Arkansas University–Magnolia (AR) (m)
Southern Illinois University Carbondale (IL) (m/w)
Southern Illinois University Edwardsville (IL) (w)
Southern Methodist University (TX) (m/w)
Southern Nazarene University (OK) (m/w)
Southern New Hampshire University (NH) (m)
Southern University and Agricultural and Mechanical College (LA) (m)
Southern Utah University (UT) (m)
Southern Wesleyan University (SC) (m)
Southwest Baptist University (MO) (m)
Southwestern College (KS) (m/w)
Southwestern Oklahoma State University (OK) (m/w)
Southwestern University (TX) (m/w)
Southwest Minnesota State University (MN) (w)
Southwest Missouri State University (MO) (m/w)
Spelman College (GA) (w)
Spring Arbor University (MI) (m)
Springfield College (MA) (m)
Spring Hill College (AL) (m/w)
Stanford University (CA) (m/w)
State University of New York at Binghamton (NY) (m)
State University of New York at Oswego (NY) (m)
State University of New York at Plattsburgh (NY) (m/w)
State University of New York College at Cortland (NY) (w)
State University of New York College at Potsdam (NY) (m)
State University of New York College of Technology at Delhi (NY) (m/w)
State University of New York Institute of Technology (NY) (m)
Stephen F. Austin State University (TX) (m)
Stetson University (FL) (m/w)
Suffolk University (MA) (m)
Susquehanna University (PA) (m/w)
Swarthmore College (PA) (m)
Tabor College (KS) (m/w)
Tarleton State University (TX) (w)
Taylor University (IN) (m)
Teikyo Post University (CT) (m)
Temple University (PA) (m)
Tennessee State University (TN) (m/w)
Tennessee Technological University (TN) (m/w)
Texas A&M International University (TX) (m/w)
Texas A&M University (TX) (m/w)
Texas A&M University–Commerce (TX) (m/w)
Texas A&M University–Corpus Christi (TX) (w)
Texas Christian University (TX) (m/w)
Texas Lutheran University (TX) (m/w)
Texas Southern University (TX) (m/w)
Texas State University-San Marcos (TX) (m/w)
Texas Tech University (TX) (m/w)
Texas Wesleyan University (TX) (m)
Thiel College (PA) (m/w)
Thomas College (ME) (m)

Thomas More College (KY) (m/w)
Thomas University (GA) (m)
Tiffin University (OH) (m)
Tougaloo College (MS) (m)
Towson University (MD) (m)
Transylvania University (KY) (m/w)
Trevecca Nazarene University (TN) (m/w)
Trinity College (CT) (m)
Trinity University (TX) (m/w)
Tri-State University (IN) (m/w)
Troy State University (AL) (m/w)
Truman State University (MO) (m/w)
Tufts University (MA) (m)
Tulane University (LA) (m/w)
Tusculum College (TN) (m/w)
Union College (KY) (m/w)
Union University (TN) (m)
United States Air Force Academy (CO) (m)
United States Merchant Marine Academy (NY) (m)
United States Military Academy (NY) (m)
United States Naval Academy (MD) (m)
University at Albany, State University of New York (NY) (w)
The University of Akron (OH) (m)
The University of Alabama (AL) (m/w)
The University of Alabama at Birmingham (AL) (m/w)
The University of Arizona (AZ) (m/w)
University of Arkansas (AR) (m/w)
University of Arkansas at Little Rock (AR) (m/w)
University of Arkansas at Monticello (AR) (m)
University of Arkansas at Pine Bluff (AR) (m/w)
University of California, Berkeley (CA) (m/w)
University of California, Davis (CA) (m)
University of California, Irvine (CA) (m/w)
University of California, Los Angeles (CA) (m/w)
University of California, Riverside (CA) (m/w)
University of California, San Diego (CA) (m)
University of California, Santa Barbara (CA) (m)
University of California, Santa Cruz (CA) (w)
University of Central Arkansas (AR) (m/w)
University of Central Florida (FL) (m/w)
University of Central Oklahoma (OK) (m/w)
University of Charleston (WV) (m)
University of Cincinnati (OH) (m/w)
University of Colorado at Boulder (CO) (m/w)
University of Colorado at Colorado Springs (CO) (m)
University of Connecticut (CT) (m)
University of Dallas (TX) (m/w)
University of Dayton (OH) (m/w)
University of Delaware (DE) (m)
University of Denver (CO) (m/w)
University of Detroit Mercy (MI) (m)
University of Dubuque (IA) (m/w)
University of Evansville (IN) (m/w)
The University of Findlay (OH) (m/w)
University of Florida (FL) (m/w)
University of Georgia (GA) (m/w)
University of Hartford (CT) (m/w)
University of Hawaii at Hilo (HI) (m)
University of Hawaii at Manoa (HI) (m/w)
University of Houston (TX) (m)
University of Idaho (ID) (m/w)
University of Illinois at Urbana–Champaign (IL) (m/w)
University of Indianapolis (IN) (m/w)

The University of Iowa (IA) (m/w)
University of Kansas (KS) (m/w)
University of Kentucky (KY) (m/w)
University of La Verne (CA) (m/w)
University of Louisiana at Lafayette (LA) (m)
University of Louisiana at Monroe (LA) (m)
University of Louisville (KY) (m/w)
University of Maine at Farmington (ME) (m)
University of Maine at Presque Isle (ME) (m)
University of Mary Hardin-Baylor (TX)
   (m/w)
University of Maryland, College Park (MD)
   (m/w)
University of Massachusetts Dartmouth
   (MA) (m/w)
The University of Memphis (TN) (m/w)
University of Miami (FL) (w)
University of Michigan (MI) (m/w)
University of Minnesota, Crookston (MN)
   (m/w)
University of Minnesota, Morris (MN) (m/w)
University of Minnesota, Twin Cities
   Campus (MN) (m/w)
University of Mississippi (MS) (m/w)
University of Missouri–Columbia (MO)
   (m/w)
University of Missouri–Kansas City (MO)
   (m/w)
University of Missouri–St. Louis (MO) (m/w)
University of Mobile (AL) (m/w)
The University of Montana–Missoula (MT)
   (w)
The University of Montana–Western (MT)
   (m/w)
University of Montevallo (AL) (m/w)
University of Nebraska at Kearney (NE)
   (m/w)
University of Nebraska at Omaha (NE) (w)
University of Nebraska–Lincoln (NE) (m/w)
University of Nevada, Las Vegas (NV) (m/w)
University of Nevada, Reno (NV) (m/w)
University of New England (ME) (m)
University of New Haven (CT) (m/w)
University of New Mexico (NM) (m/w)
University of New Orleans (LA) (m/w)
University of North Alabama (AL) (m)
The University of North Carolina at Chapel
   Hill (NC) (m/w)
The University of North Carolina at
   Charlotte (NC) (m)
The University of North Carolina at
   Greensboro (NC) (m/w)
The University of North Carolina at
   Pembroke (NC) (m)
The University of North Carolina at
   Wilmington (NC) (m/w)
University of North Dakota (ND) (m/w)
University of Northern Colorado (CO) (m/w)
University of Northern Iowa (IA) (m/w)
University of North Florida (FL) (m)
University of North Texas (TX) (m/w)
University of Notre Dame (IN) (m/w)
University of Oklahoma (OK) (m/w)
University of Oregon (OR) (m/w)
University of Pennsylvania (PA) (m/w)
University of Pittsburgh at Bradford (PA)
   (m/w)
University of Pittsburgh at Greensburg (PA)
   (m/w)
University of Portland (OR) (m/w)
University of Puget Sound (WA) (m/w)
University of Redlands (CA) (m)
University of Rhode Island (RI) (m)
University of Richmond (VA) (m/w)
University of Rochester (NY) (m)

University of St. Francis (IL) (m/w)
University of Saint Francis (IN) (m)
University of St. Thomas (MN) (m/w)
University of San Diego (CA) (m)
University of San Francisco (CA) (m/w)
The University of Scranton (PA) (m)
University of Sioux Falls (SD) (m/w)
University of South Alabama (AL) (m/w)
University of South Carolina (SC) (m/w)
University of South Carolina Aiken (SC) (m)
The University of South Dakota (SD) (m/w)
University of Southern California (CA) (m/w)
University of Southern Indiana (IN) (m/w)
University of Southern Mississippi (MS)
   (m/w)
University of South Florida (FL) (m/w)
The University of Tampa (FL) (m)
The University of Tennessee (TN) (m/w)
The University of Tennessee at Chattanooga
   (TN) (m)
The University of Tennessee at Martin (TN)
   (m)
The University of Texas at Arlington (TX)
   (m)
The University of Texas at Austin (TX) (m/w)
The University of Texas at Dallas (TX) (m/w)
The University of Texas at El Paso (TX)
   (m/w)
The University of Texas at San Antonio (TX)
   (m)
The University of Texas–Pan American (TX)
   (m/w)
University of the Incarnate Word (TX) (m/w)
University of the Ozarks (AR) (m)
University of the Pacific (CA) (m)
University of the South (TN) (m/w)
University of Toledo (OH) (m/w)
University of Tulsa (OK) (m/w)
University of Utah (UT) (m)
University of Vermont (VT) (m)
University of Virginia (VA) (m/w)
The University of Virginia's College at Wise
   (VA) (m)
University of Washington (WA) (m/w)
University of West Florida (FL) (m)
University of Wisconsin–Eau Claire (WI)
   (m/w)
University of Wisconsin–Green Bay (WI) (m)
University of Wisconsin–Madison (WI)
   (m/w)
University of Wisconsin–Oshkosh (WI) (w)
University of Wisconsin–Parkside (WI) (m)
University of Wisconsin–Platteville (WI) (w)
University of Wisconsin–River Falls (WI) (w)
University of Wisconsin–Stevens Point (WI)
   (w)
University of Wisconsin–Superior (WI) (w)
University of Wisconsin–Whitewater (WI)
   (w)
University of Wyoming (WY) (m/w)
Upper Iowa University (IA) (m/w)
Urbana University (OH) (m)
Ursinus College (PA) (m/w)
Ursuline College (OH) (w)
Utah State University (UT) (m)
Utica College (NY) (m)
Valdosta State University (GA) (m)
Vanderbilt University (TN) (m/w)
Villa Julie College (MD) (m)
Villanova University (PA) (m)
Virginia Commonwealth University (VA) (m)
Virginia Intermont College (VA) (m)
Virginia Polytechnic Institute and State
   University (VA) (m)
Virginia State University (VA) (m/w)

Virginia Union University (VA) (m/w)
Virginia Wesleyan College (VA) (m)
Wabash College (IN) (m)
Wagner College (NY) (m/w)
Wake Forest University (NC) (m/w)
Waldorf College (IA) (m/w)
Walsh University (OH) (m/w)
Warner Southern College (FL) (m/w)
Wartburg College (IA) (m/w)
Washburn University (KS) (m)
Washington & Jefferson College (PA) (m/w)
Washington and Lee University (VA) (m)
Washington State University (WA) (m/w)
Wayland Baptist University (TX) (m)
Waynesburg College (PA) (m/w)
Wayne State College (NE) (m/w)
Wayne State University (MI) (m)
Webber International University (FL) (m/w)
Weber State University (UT) (m/w)
Webster University (MO) (m)
Wellesley College (MA) (w)
Wentworth Institute of Technology (MA) (m)
Wesleyan University (CT) (m)
Wesley College (DE) (m)
West Chester University of Pennsylvania (PA)
   (m/w)
Western Baptist College (OR) (m)
Western Carolina University (NC) (m/w)
Western Illinois University (IL) (m/w)
Western Kentucky University (KY) (m/w)
Western Michigan University (MI) (w)
Western New England College (MA) (m)
Western New Mexico University (NM)
   (m/w)
Western Washington University (WA) (m/w)
West Liberty State College (WV) (m/w)
Westminster College (UT) (m/w)
Westminster College (MO) (m/w)
Westminster College (PA) (m/w)
West Texas A&M University (TX) (m/w)
West Virginia University Institute of
   Technology (WV) (m)
West Virginia Wesleyan College (WV) (m)
Wheaton College (IL) (m/w)
Wheeling Jesuit University (WV) (m/w)
Whitman College (WA) (m/w)
Whittier College (CA) (m)
Whitworth College (WA) (m/w)
Wichita State University (KS) (m/w)
Widener University (PA) (m)
Wilkes University (PA) (m)
Willamette University (OR) (m/w)
William Carey College (MS) (m)
William Jewell College (MO) (m/w)
William Penn University (IA) (m)
Williams Baptist College (AR) (m)
Williams College (MA) (m)
William Woods University (MO) (m/w)
Wilmington College (OH) (m/w)
Wingate University (NC) (m/w)
Winona State University (MN) (m/w)
Winthrop University (SC) (m/w)
Wisconsin Lutheran College (WI) (m/w)
Wittenberg University (OH) (m)
Wofford College (SC) (m)
Worcester Polytechnic Institute (MA) (m)
Worcester State College (MA) (m)
Wright State University (OH) (m)
Xavier University (OH) (m/w)
Yale University (CT) (m/w)
Yeshiva University (NY) (m)
York College (NE) (m)
York College of Pennsylvania (PA) (m)
Youngstown State University (OH)(m/w)

Gymnastics

Arizona State University (AZ) (w)
Auburn University (AL) (w)
Ball State University (IN) (w)
Boise State University (ID) (w)
Bowling Green State University (OH) (w)
Brigham Young University (UT) (w)
Brown University (RI) (w)
California State University, Fullerton (CA) (w)
California State University, Sacramento (CA) (w)
Centenary College of Louisiana (LA) (w)
Central Michigan University (MI) (w)
The College of William and Mary (VA) (w)
Cornell University (NY) (w)
Eastern Michigan University (MI) (w)
The George Washington University (DC) (w)
Gustavus Adolphus College (MN) (w)
Illinois State University (IL) (w)
Iowa State University of Science and Technology (IA) (w)
Ithaca College (NY) (w)
James Madison University (VA) (w)
Kent State University (OH) (w)
Louisiana State University and Agricultural and Mechanical College (LA) (w)
Massachusetts Institute of Technology (MA) (w)
Michigan State University (MI) (w)
North Carolina State University (NC) (w)
Northern Illinois University (IL) (w)
The Ohio State University (OH) (w)
Oregon State University (OR) (w)
The Pennsylvania State University University Park Campus (PA) (w)
Rhode Island College (RI) (w)
Rutgers, The State University of New Jersey, New Brunswick/Piscataway (NJ) (w)
San Jose State University (CA) (w)
Seattle Pacific University (WA) (w)
Southeast Missouri State University (MO) (w)
Southern Connecticut State University (CT) (w)
Southern Utah University (UT) (w)
Springfield College (MA) (w)
Stanford University (CA) (w)
State University of New York College at Cortland (NY) (w)
Temple University (PA) (w)
Texas Woman's University (TX) (w)
Towson University (MD) (w)
United States Air Force Academy (CO) (w)
The University of Alabama (AL) (w)
University of Alaska Anchorage (AK) (w)
The University of Arizona (AZ) (w)
University of Arkansas (AR) (w)
University of Bridgeport (CT) (w)
University of California, Berkeley (CA) (w)
University of California, Davis (CA) (w)
University of California, Los Angeles (CA) (w)
University of Denver (CO) (w)
University of Florida (FL) (w)
University of Georgia (GA) (w)
University of Illinois at Chicago (IL) (w)
University of Illinois at Urbana–Champaign (IL) (w)
The University of Iowa (IA) (w)
University of Kentucky (KY) (w)
University of Maryland, College Park (MD) (w)
University of Michigan (MI) (w)

University of Minnesota, Twin Cities Campus (MN) (w)
University of Missouri–Columbia (MO) (w)
University of Nebraska–Lincoln (NE) (w)
University of New Hampshire (NH) (w)
The University of North Carolina at Chapel Hill (NC) (w)
University of Oklahoma (OK) (w)
University of Pennsylvania (PA) (w)
University of Pittsburgh (PA) (w)
University of Rhode Island (RI) (w)
University of Utah (UT) (w)
University of Washington (WA) (w)
University of Wisconsin–Eau Claire (WI) (w)
University of Wisconsin–La Crosse (WI) (w)
University of Wisconsin–Oshkosh (WI) (w)
University of Wisconsin–Stout (WI) (w)
University of Wisconsin–Whitewater (WI) (w)
Ursinus College (PA) (w)
Utah State University (UT) (w)
West Chester University of Pennsylvania (PA) (w)
Western Michigan University (MI) (w)
West Virginia University (WV) (w)
Wilson College (PA) (w)
Winona State University (MN) (w)
Yale University (CT)(w)

Ice Hockey

American International College (MA) (m)
Amherst College (MA) (m)
Assumption College (MA) (m)
Augsburg College (MN) (m)
Babson College (MA) (m)
Bemidji State University (MN) (m)
Bentley College (MA) (m)
Bethel University (MN) (m)
Boston College (MA) (m)
Boston University (MA) (m)
Bowdoin College (ME) (m)
Bowling Green State University (OH) (m)
Brown University (RI) (m)
Buffalo State College, State University of New York (NY) (m)
Canisius College (NY) (m)
Castleton State College (VT) (m)
Clarkson University (NY) (m)
Colby College (ME) (m)
Colgate University (NY) (m)
The College of St. Scholastica (MN) (m)
College of the Holy Cross (MA) (m)
The Colorado College (CO) (m)
Concordia College (MN) (m)
Connecticut College (CT) (m)
Cornell University (NY) (m)
Curry College (MA) (m)
Dartmouth College (NH) (m)
Elmira College (NY) (m)
Ferris State University (MI) (m)
Fitchburg State College (MA) (m)
Framingham State College (MA) (m)
Franklin Pierce College (NH) (m)
Gustavus Adolphus College (MN) (m)
Hamilton College (NY) (m)
Hamline University (MN) (m)
Harvard University (MA) (m)
Hobart and William Smith Colleges (NY) (m)
Iona College (NY) (m)
Johnson & Wales University (RI) (m)
Lake Forest College (IL) (m)
Lake Superior State University (MI) (m)
Lawrence University (WI) (m)

Lebanon Valley College (PA) (m)
Manhattanville College (NY) (m)
Marian College of Fond du Lac (WI) (m)
Mercyhurst College (PA) (m)
Merrimack College (MA) (m)
Miami University (OH) (m)
Michigan State University (MI) (m)
Michigan Technological University (MI) (m)
Middlebury College (VT) (m)
Milwaukee School of Engineering (WI) (m)
Minnesota State University Mankato (MN) (m)
Neumann College (PA) (m)
New England College (NH) (m)
Niagara University (NY) (m)
Nichols College (MA) (m)
Northeastern University (MA) (m)
Northern Michigan University (MI) (m)
Northland College (WI) (m)
Norwich University (VT) (m)
The Ohio State University (OH) (m)
Plymouth State University (NH) (m)
Princeton University (NJ) (m)
Providence College (RI) (m)
Quinnipiac University (CT) (m)
Rensselaer Polytechnic Institute (NY) (m)
Robert Morris University (PA) (m)
Rochester Institute of Technology (NY) (m)
Sacred Heart University (CT) (m)
Saint Anselm College (NH) (m)
St. Cloud State University (MN) (m)
Saint John's University (MN) (m)
St. Lawrence University (NY) (m)
Saint Mary's University of Minnesota (MN) (m)
Saint Michael's College (VT) (m)
St. Norbert College (WI) (m)
St. Olaf College (MN) (m)
Salem State College (MA) (m)
Salve Regina University (RI) (m)
Skidmore College (NY) (m)
Southern New Hampshire University (NH) (m)
State University of New York at Oswego (NY) (m)
State University of New York at Plattsburgh (NY) (m)
State University of New York College at Brockport (NY) (m)
State University of New York College at Cortland (NY) (m)
State University of New York College at Fredonia (NY) (m)
State University of New York College at Geneseo (NY) (m)
State University of New York College at Potsdam (NY) (m)
Stonehill College (MA) (m)
Suffolk University (MA) (m)
Trinity College (CT) (m)
Tufts University (MA) (m)
Union College (NY) (m)
United States Air Force Academy (CO) (m)
United States Military Academy (NY) (m)
The University of Alabama in Huntsville (AL) (m)
University of Alaska Anchorage (AK) (m)
University of Alaska Fairbanks (AK) (m)
University of Connecticut (CT) (m)
University of Denver (CO) (m)
The University of Findlay (OH) (m)
University of Maine (ME) (m)
University of Massachusetts Amherst (MA) (m)

University of Massachusetts Boston (MA) (m)

University of Massachusetts Dartmouth (MA) (m)

University of Massachusetts Lowell (MA) (m)

University of Michigan (MI) (m)

University of Michigan–Dearborn (MI) (m)

University of Minnesota, Crookston (MN) (m)

University of Minnesota, Duluth (MN) (m)

University of Minnesota, Twin Cities Campus (MN) (m)

University of Nebraska at Omaha (NE) (m)

University of New Hampshire (NH) (m)

University of North Dakota (ND) (m)

University of Notre Dame (IN) (m)

University of St. Thomas (MN) (m)

The University of Scranton (PA) (m)

University of Southern Maine (ME) (m)

University of Vermont (VT) (m)

University of Wisconsin–Eau Claire (WI) (m)

University of Wisconsin–Madison (WI) (m)

University of Wisconsin–River Falls (WI) (m)

University of Wisconsin–Stevens Point (WI) (m)

University of Wisconsin–Stout (WI) (m)

University of Wisconsin–Superior (WI) (m)

Utica College (NY) (m)

Wayne State University (MI) (m)

Wentworth Institute of Technology (MA) (m)

Wesleyan University (CT) (m)

Western Michigan University (MI) (m)

Western New England College (MA) (m)

Westfield State College (MA) (m)

Williams College (MA) (m)

Worcester State College (MA) (m)

Yale University (CT)(m)

Lacrosse

Adelphi University (NY) (m/w)

Alfred University (NY) (m/w)

Allegheny College (PA) (w)

Alvernia College (PA) (w)

American International College (MA) (m/w)

American University (DC) (w)

Amherst College (MA) (m/w)

Arcadia University (PA) (w)

Assumption College (MA) (m/w)

Babson College (MA) (m/w)

Bates College (ME) (m/w)

Bentley College (MA) (m/w)

Bloomsburg University of Pennsylvania (PA) (w)

Boston College (MA) (w)

Boston University (MA) (w)

Bowdoin College (ME) (m/w)

Bridgewater College (VA) (w)

Bridgewater State College (MA) (w)

Brown University (RI) (m/w)

Bryant College (RI) (m/w)

Bryn Mawr College (PA) (w)

Bucknell University (PA) (m/w)

Buffalo State College, State University of New York (NY) (w)

Butler University (IN) (m)

Cabrini College (PA) (m/w)

Canisius College (NY) (m/w)

Castleton State College (VT) (m/w)

Catawba College (NC) (m)

The Catholic University of America (DC) (m/w)

Cazenovia College (NY) (m/w)

Cedar Crest College (PA) (w)

Centenary College (NJ) (m/w)

Central Connecticut State University (CT) (w)

Chapman University (CA) (m)

Chestnut Hill College (PA) (w)

Christopher Newport University (VA) (w)

City College of the City University of New York (NY) (m)

Claremont McKenna College (CA) (w)

Clarkson University (NY) (m/w)

Clark University (MA) (m)

Colby College (ME) (m/w)

Colby-Sawyer College (NH) (w)

Colgate University (NY) (m/w)

College Misericordia (PA) (m/w)

College of Mount Saint Vincent (NY) (m/w)

The College of New Jersey (NJ) (w)

College of Notre Dame of Maryland (MD) (w)

College of the Holy Cross (MA) (m/w)

The College of William and Mary (VA) (w)

The College of Wooster (OH) (m/w)

The Colorado College (CO) (m/w)

Columbia College (NY) (w)

Connecticut College (CT) (m/w)

Cornell University (NY) (m/w)

Curry College (MA) (m/w)

Daniel Webster College (NH) (m)

Dartmouth College (NH) (m/w)

Davidson College (NC) (w)

Denison University (OH) (m/w)

DeSales University (PA) (m)

Dickinson College (PA) (m/w)

Dominican College (NY) (m/w)

Dowling College (NY) (m)

Drew University (NJ) (m/w)

Drexel University (PA) (m/w)

Duke University (NC) (m/w)

Duquesne University (PA) (w)

Earlham College (IN) (w)

Eastern Connecticut State University (CT) (m/w)

Eastern University (PA) (w)

East Stroudsburg University of Pennsylvania (PA) (w)

Elizabethtown College (PA) (m/w)

Elmira College (NY) (m/w)

Elms College (MA) (w)

Emerson College (MA) (m/w)

Endicott College (MA) (m/w)

Fairfield University (CT) (m/w)

Fairleigh Dickinson University, College at Florham (NJ) (m/w)

Farmingdale State University of New York (NY) (m)

Ferrum College (VA) (w)

Franklin and Marshall College (PA) (m/w)

Franklin Pierce College (NH) (m/w)

Frostburg State University (MD) (w)

Gannon University (PA) (w)

George Mason University (VA) (w)

Georgetown University (DC) (m/w)

The George Washington University (DC) (w)

Gettysburg College (PA) (m/w)

Gordon College (MA) (m/w)

Goucher College (MD) (m/w)

Green Mountain College (VT) (m)

Greensboro College (NC) (m/w)

Guilford College (NC) (m/w)

Gwynedd-Mercy College (PA) (w)

Hamilton College (NY) (m/w)

Hampden-Sydney College (VA) (m)

Hartwick College (NY) (m/w)

Harvard University (MA) (m/w)

Haverford College (PA) (m/w)

Hobart and William Smith Colleges (NY) (m/w)

Hofstra University (NY) (m/w)

Hollins University (VA) (w)

Hood College (MD) (w)

Howard University (DC) (w)

Immaculata University (PA) (w)

Indiana University of Pennsylvania (PA) (w)

Ithaca College (NY) (m/w)

James Madison University (VA) (w)

The Johns Hopkins University (MD) (m/w)

Johnson State College (VT) (m)

Kean University (NJ) (m/w)

Keene State College (NH) (m/w)

Kenyon College (OH) (m/w)

Keuka College (NY) (m)

King's College (PA) (m/w)

Lafayette College (PA) (m/w)

La Salle University (PA) (w)

Lasell College (MA) (m/w)

Lees-McRae College (NC) (m/w)

Lehigh University (PA) (m/w)

Le Moyne College (NY) (m/w)

Limestone College (SC) (m/w)

Lindenwood University (MO) (m/w)

Linfield College (OR) (w)

Lock Haven University of Pennsylvania (PA) (w)

Long Island University, Brooklyn Campus (NY) (w)

Long Island University, C.W. Post Campus (NY) (m/w)

Long Island University, Southampton College (NY) (m)

Longwood University (VA) (w)

Loyola College in Maryland (MD) (m/w)

Lycoming College (PA) (m/w)

Lynchburg College (VA) (m/w)

Maine Maritime Academy (ME) (m)

Manhattan College (NY) (m/w)

Manhattanville College (NY) (m/w)

Marist College (NY) (m/w)

Mars Hill College (NC) (m)

Marymount University (VA) (m/w)

University of Mary Washington (VA) (m/w)

Massachusetts Institute of Technology (MA) (m/w)

Massachusetts Maritime Academy (MA) (m)

McDaniel College (MD) (m/w)

Medaille College (NY) (m/w)

Mercyhurst College (PA) (m/w)

Merrimack College (MA) (m/w)

Messiah College (PA) (m/w)

Methodist College (NC) (w)

Middlebury College (VT) (m/w)

Millersville University of Pennsylvania (PA) (w)

Molloy College (NY) (m)

Monmouth University (NJ) (w)

Montclair State University (NJ) (m/w)

Moravian College (PA) (m/w)

Mount Holyoke College (MA) (w)

Mount Ida College (MA) (m)

Mount Saint Mary's University (MD) (m/w)

Muhlenberg College (PA) (m/w)

Nazareth College of Rochester (NY) (m/w)

Neumann College (PA) (m/w)

New England College (NH) (m/w)

New York Institute of Technology (NY) (m)

Niagara University (NY) (w)

Nichols College (MA) (m/w)

Northwestern University (IL) (w)

Norwich University (VT) (m)

Notre Dame de Namur University (CA) (m)

Oberlin College (OH) (m/w)

The Ohio State University (OH) (m/w)
Ohio University (OH) (w)
Ohio Wesleyan University (OH) (m/w)
Old Dominion University (VA) (w)
Pace University (NY) (m)
The Pennsylvania State University University Park Campus (PA) (m/w)
Pfeiffer University (NC) (m/w)
Philadelphia University (PA) (w)
Pine Manor College (MA) (w)
Plymouth State University (NH) (m/w)
Princeton University (NJ) (m/w)
Providence College (RI) (m)
Queens University of Charlotte (NC) (m/w)
Quinnipiac University (CT) (m/w)
Randolph-Macon College (VA) (m/w)
Regis University (CO) (w)
Rensselaer Polytechnic Institute (NY) (m/w)
Rhode Island College (RI) (w)
The Richard Stockton College of New Jersey (NJ) (m)
Roanoke College (VA) (m/w)
Robert Morris University (PA) (m/w)
Rochester Institute of Technology (NY) (m/w)
Roger Williams University (RI) (m/w)
Rosemont College (PA) (w)
Rowan University (NJ) (w)
Rutgers, The State University of New Jersey, New Brunswick/Piscataway (NJ) (m/w)
Sacred Heart University (CT) (m/w)
St. Andrews Presbyterian College (NC) (m)
Saint Anselm College (NH) (m/w)
St. Bonaventure University (NY) (w)
Saint Francis University (PA) (w)
St. John Fisher College (NY) (m/w)
St. John's University (NY) (m)
Saint Joseph's University (PA) (m/w)
St. Lawrence University (NY) (m/w)
Saint Mary's College of California (CA) (w)
St. Mary's College of Maryland (MD) (m/w)
Saint Michael's College (VT) (m/w)
St. Thomas Aquinas College (NY) (w)
Saint Vincent College (PA) (m/w)
Salisbury University (MD) (m/w)
Salve Regina University (RI) (m/w)
Savannah College of Art and Design (GA) (m/w)
Seton Hill University (PA) (m/w)
Shenandoah University (VA) (m/w)
Shippensburg University of Pennsylvania (PA) (w)
Siena College (NY) (m/w)
Skidmore College (NY) (m/w)
Smith College (MA) (w)
Southern Connecticut State University (CT) (w)
Southern New Hampshire University (NH) (m/w)
Southern Virginia University (VA) (m)
Springfield College (MA) (m/w)
Stanford University (CA) (w)
State University of New York at Binghamton (NY) (m/w)
State University of New York at Oswego (NY) (m/w)
State University of New York at Plattsburgh (NY) (m)
State University of New York College at Brockport (NY) (m/w)
State University of New York College at Cortland (NY) (m/w)
State University of New York College at Fredonia (NY) (w)

State University of New York College at Geneseo (NY) (m/w)
State University of New York College at Oneonta (NY) (m/w)
State University of New York College at Potsdam (NY) (m/w)
State University of New York College of Technology at Delhi (NY) (m)
State University of New York Institute of Technology (NY) (m)
State University of New York Maritime College (NY) (m)
Stevens Institute of Technology (NJ) (m/w)
Stonehill College (MA) (w)
Stony Brook University, State University of New York (NY) (m/w)
Susquehanna University (PA) (m/w)
Swarthmore College (PA) (m/w)
Sweet Briar College (VA) (w)
Syracuse University (NY) (m/w)
Temple University (PA) (w)
Thomas College (ME) (m/w)
Towson University (MD) (m/w)
Trinity College (CT) (m/w)
Trinity College (DC) (w)
Tufts University (MA) (m/w)
Union College (NY) (m/w)
United States Air Force Academy (CO) (m)
United States Merchant Marine Academy (NY) (m)
United States Military Academy (NY) (m)
United States Naval Academy (MD) (m)
University at Albany, State University of New York (NY) (m/w)
University of California, Berkeley (CA) (w)
University of California, Davis (CA) (w)
University of Connecticut (CT) (w)
University of Dallas (TX) (w)
University of Delaware (DE) (m/w)
University of Denver (CO) (w)
University of Hartford (CT) (m)
University of Maryland, Baltimore County (MD) (m/w)
University of Maryland, College Park (MD) (m/w)
University of Massachusetts Amherst (MA) (m/w)
University of Massachusetts Boston (MA) (m)
University of Massachusetts Dartmouth (MA) (m/w)
University of Michigan–Dearborn (MI) (m)
University of New England (ME) (m/w)
University of New Hampshire (NH) (w)
University of New Haven (CT) (m/w)
The University of North Carolina at Chapel Hill (NC) (m/w)
University of Notre Dame (IN) (m/w)
University of Oregon (OR) (w)
University of Pennsylvania (PA) (m/w)
University of Puget Sound (WA) (w)
University of Redlands (CA) (w)
University of Richmond (VA) (w)
University of Rochester (NY) (w)
The University of Scranton (PA) (m/w)
University of Southern Maine (ME) (m/w)
University of Vermont (VT) (m/w)
University of Virginia (VA) (m/w)
Ursinus College (PA) (m/w)
Utica College (NY) (m/w)
Vassar College (NY) (m/w)
Villa Julie College (MD) (m/w)
Villanova University (PA) (m/w)
Virginia Military Institute (VA) (m)

Virginia Polytechnic Institute and State University (VA) (w)
Virginia Wesleyan College (VA) (m/w/w)
Wagner College (NY) (m/w)
Washington & Jefferson College (PA) (m)
Washington and Lee University (VA) (m/w)
Washington College (MD) (m/w)
Wellesley College (MA) (w)
Wells College (NY) (w)
Wentworth Institute of Technology (MA) (m)
Wesleyan University (CT) (m/w)
Wesley College (DE) (m/w)
West Chester University of Pennsylvania (PA) (w)
Western Connecticut State University (CT) (m/w)
Western New England College (MA) (m/w)
Wheaton College (MA) (m/w)
Wheeling Jesuit University (WV) (m)
Whittier College (CA) (m/w)
Widener University (PA) (m/w)
Wilkes University (PA) (w)
Williams College (MA) (m/w)
Wingate University (NC) (m)
Wittenberg University (OH) (m/w)
Worcester State College (MA) (w)
Yale University (CT) (m/w)
York College of Pennsylvania (PA)(m)

Soccer

Adams State College (CO) (w)
Adelphi University (NY) (m/w)
Adrian College (MI) (m/w)
Agnes Scott College (GA) (w)
Alabama Agricultural and Mechanical University (AL) (m/w)
Albertson College of Idaho (ID) (m/w)
Albertus Magnus College (CT) (m)
Albion College (MI) (m/w)
Albright College (PA) (m/w)
Alderson-Broaddus College (WV) (m)
Alfred University (NY) (m/w)
Allegheny College (PA) (m/w)
Alliant International University (CA) (m/w)
Alma College (MI) (m/w)
Alvernia College (PA) (m/w)
Alverno College (WI) (w)
American International College (MA) (m/w)
American University (DC) (m/w)
Amherst College (MA) (m/w)
Anderson College (SC) (m/w)
Anderson University (IN) (m/w)
Angelo State University (TX) (w)
Anna Maria College (MA) (m/w)
Appalachian State University (NC) (m/w)
Aquinas College (MI) (m/w)
Arcadia University (PA) (m/w)
Arizona State University (AZ) (w)
Arkansas State University (AR) (w)
Asbury College (KY) (m/w)
Ashland University (OH) (m/w)
Assumption College (MA) (m/w)
Atlanta Christian College (GA) (m/w)
Auburn University (AL) (w)
Auburn University Montgomery (AL) (m/w)
Augsburg College (MN) (m/w)
Augustana College (IL) (m/w)
Augustana College (SD) (m/w)
Aurora University (IL) (m/w)
Austin College (TX) (m/w)
Austin Peay State University (TN) (w)
Averett University (VA) (m/w)
Avila University (MO) (m/w)
Azusa Pacific University (CA) (m/w)

Babson College (MA) (m)
Bacone College (OK) (m/w)
Baker University (KS) (m/w)
Baldwin-Wallace College (OH) (m/w)
Ball State University (IN) (w)
Baptist Bible College of Pennsylvania (PA) (m/w)
Bard College (NY) (m/w)
Barry University (FL) (m/w)
Barton College (NC) (m/w)
Bates College (ME) (m/w)
Baylor University (TX) (w)
Bay Path College (MA) (w)
Belhaven College (MS) (m/w)
Bellarmine University (KY) (m/w)
Bellevue University (NE) (m/w)
Belmont Abbey College (NC) (m/w)
Belmont University (TN) (m/w)
Beloit College (WI) (m/w)
Bemidji State University (MN) (w)
Benedictine College (KS) (m/w)
Benedictine University (IL) (m/w)
Bentley College (MA) (m/w)
Berea College (KY) (m/w)
Bernard M. Baruch College of the City University of New York (NY) (m)
Berry College (GA) (m/w)
Bethany College (KS) (m/w)
Bethany College (WV) (m/w)
Bethany College of the Assemblies of God (CA) (m/w)
Bethel College (IN) (m/w)
Bethel College (KS) (m/w)
Bethel College (TN) (m/w)
Bethel University (MN) (m/w)
Biola University (CA) (m/w)
Birmingham-Southern College (AL) (m/w)
Blackburn College (IL) (m/w)
Bloomfield College (NJ) (m/w)
Bloomsburg University of Pennsylvania (PA) (m/w)
Bluefield College (VA) (m/w)
Bluffton College (OH) (m/w)
Boise State University (ID) (w)
Boston College (MA) (m/w)
Boston University (MA) (m/w)
Bowdoin College (ME) (m/w)
Bowling Green State University (OH) (m/w)
Bradley University (IL) (m)
Brandeis University (MA) (m/w)
Brenau University (GA) (w)
Brescia University (KY) (m/w)
Brevard College (NC) (m/w)
Brewton-Parker College (GA) (m/w)
Briar Cliff University (IA) (m/w)
Bridgewater College (VA) (m/w)
Bridgewater State College (MA) (m/w)
Brigham Young University (UT) (w)
Brooklyn College of the City University of New York (NY) (m)
Brown University (RI) (m/w)
Bryan College (TN) (m/w)
Bryant College (RI) (m/w)
Bryn Mawr College (PA) (w)
Bucknell University (PA) (m/w)
Buena Vista University (IA) (m/w)
Buffalo State College, State University of New York (NY) (m/w)
Butler University (IN) (m/w)
Cabrini College (PA) (m/w)
Caldwell College (NJ) (m/w)
California Baptist University (CA) (m/w)
California Institute of Technology (CA) (m)
California Lutheran University (CA) (m/w)
California Maritime Academy (CA) (m)

California Polytechnic State University, San Luis Obispo (CA) (m/w)
California State Polytechnic University, Pomona (CA) (m/w)
California State University, Bakersfield (CA) (m/w)
California State University, Chico (CA) (m/w)
California State University, Dominguez Hills (CA) (m/w)
California State University, Fresno (CA) (m/w)
California State University, Fullerton (CA) (m/w)
California State University, Hayward (CA) (m/w)
California State University, Long Beach (CA) (w)
California State University, Los Angeles (CA) (m/w)
California State University, Monterey Bay (CA) (m/w)
California State University, Northridge (CA) (m/w)
California State University, Sacramento (CA) (m/w)
California State University, San Bernardino (CA) (m/w)
California State University, Stanislaus (CA) (m/w)
California University of Pennsylvania (PA) (m/w)
Calumet College of Saint Joseph (IN) (w)
Calvin College (MI) (m/w)
Campbellsville University (KY) (m/w)
Campbell University (NC) (m/w)
Canisius College (NY) (m/w)
Capital University (OH) (m/w)
Cardinal Stritch University (WI) (m/w)
Carleton College (MN) (m/w)
Carlow College (PA) (w)
Carnegie Mellon University (PA) (m/w)
Carroll College (MT) (w)
Carroll College (WI) (m/w)
Carson-Newman College (TN) (m/w)
Carthage College (WI) (m/w)
Cascade College (OR) (m/w)
Case Western Reserve University (OH) (m/w)
Castleton State College (VT) (m/w)
Catawba College (NC) (m/w)
The Catholic University of America (DC) (m/w)
Cazenovia College (NY) (m/w)
Cedar Crest College (PA) (w)
Cedarville University (OH) (m/w)
Centenary College (NJ) (m/w)
Centenary College of Louisiana (LA) (m/w)
Central Christian College of Kansas (KS) (m/w)
Central College (IA) (m/w)
Central Connecticut State University (CT) (m/w)
Central Methodist College (MO) (m/w)
Central Michigan University (MI) (w)
Central Missouri State University (MO) (w)
Central Washington University (WA) (w)
Centre College (KY) (m/w)
Chapman University (CA) (m/w)
Charleston Southern University (SC) (w)
Chatham College (PA) (w)
Chestnut Hill College (PA) (w)
Chowan College (NC) (m/w)
Christian Brothers University (TN) (m/w)
Christian Heritage College (CA) (m/w)
Christopher Newport University (VA) (m/w)

The Citadel, The Military College of South Carolina (SC) (w)
City College of the City University of New York (NY) (m/w)
Claremont McKenna College (CA) (m/w)
Clarion University of Pennsylvania (PA) (w)
Clarke College (IA) (m/w)
Clarkson University (NY) (m/w)
Clark University (MA) (m/w)
Clayton College & State University (GA) (m/w)
Clemson University (SC) (m/w)
Cleveland State University (OH) (m)
Coastal Carolina University (SC) (m/w)
Coe College (IA) (m/w)
Coker College (SC) (m/w)
Colby College (ME) (m/w)
Colby-Sawyer College (NH) (m/w)
Colgate University (NY) (m/w)
College Misericordia (PA) (m/w)
College of Charleston (SC) (m/w)
College of Mount St. Joseph (OH) (w)
College of Mount Saint Vincent (NY) (m/w)
The College of New Jersey (NJ) (m/w)
College of Notre Dame of Maryland (MD) (w)
College of Saint Benedict (MN) (w)
College of St. Catherine (MN) (w)
College of Saint Elizabeth (NJ) (w)
College of St. Joseph (VT) (m/w)
College of Saint Mary (NE) (w)
The College of Saint Rose (NY) (m/w)
The College of St. Scholastica (MN) (m/w)
College of Staten Island of the City University of New York (NY) (m)
College of the Holy Cross (MA) (m/w)
College of the Southwest (NM) (m/w)
The College of William and Mary (VA) (m/w)
The College of Wooster (OH) (m/w)
Colorado Christian University (CO) (m/w)
The Colorado College (CO) (m/w)
Colorado School of Mines (CO) (m)
Colorado State University-Pueblo (CO) (m/w)
Columbia College (MO) (m)
Columbia College (NY) (m/w)
Columbia College (SC) (w)
Columbia Union College (MD) (m/w)
Columbus State University (GA) (w)
Concord College (WV) (m/w)
Concordia College (MN) (m/w)
Concordia College (NY) (m/w)
Concordia University (CA) (m/w)
Concordia University (IL) (m/w)
Concordia University (MI) (m/w)
Concordia University (NE) (m/w)
Concordia University (OR) (m/w)
Concordia University at Austin (TX) (m)
Concordia University, St. Paul (MN) (w)
Concordia University Wisconsin (WI) (m/w)
Connecticut College (CT) (m/w)
Converse College (SC) (w)
Cornell College (IA) (m/w)
Cornell University (NY) (m/w)
Cornerstone University (MI) (m/w)
Covenant College (GA) (m/w)
Creighton University (NE) (m/w)
Crown College (MN) (m/w)
Culver-Stockton College (MO) (m/w)
Cumberland College (KY) (m/w)
Cumberland University (TN) (m/w)
Curry College (MA) (m/w)
Daemen College (NY) (m/w)
Dallas Baptist University (TX) (m/w)

Dana College (NE) (m/w)
Daniel Webster College (NH) (m/w)
Dartmouth College (NH) (m/w)
Davenport University (MI) (m/w)
Davidson College (NC) (m/w)
Davis & Elkins College (WV) (m/w)
Defiance College (OH) (m/w)
Delaware State University (DE) (w)
Delaware Valley College (PA) (m/w)
Delta State University (MS) (m/w)
Denison University (OH) (m/w)
DePaul University (IL) (m/w)
DePauw University (IN) (m/w)
DeSales University (PA) (m/w)
Dickinson College (PA) (m/w)
Doane College (NE) (m/w)
Dominican College (NY) (m/w)
Dominican University (IL) (m/w)
Dominican University of California (CA)
   (m/w)
Dordt College (IA) (m/w)
Dowling College (NY) (m)
Drake University (IA) (m/w)
Drew University (NJ) (m/w)
Drexel University (PA) (m/w)
Drury University (MO) (m/w)
Duke University (NC) (m/w)
Duquesne University (PA) (m/w)
D'Youville College (NY) (m/w)
Earlham College (IN) (m/w)
East Carolina University (NC) (m/w)
East Central University (OK) (w)
Eastern Connecticut State University (CT)
   (m/w)
Eastern Illinois University (IL) (m/w)
Eastern Mennonite University (VA) (m/w)
Eastern Michigan University (MI) (w)
Eastern Nazarene College (MA) (m/w)
Eastern Oregon University (OR) (w)
Eastern University (PA) (m/w)
Eastern Washington University (WA) (w)
East Stroudsburg University of Pennsylvania
   (PA) (m/w)
East Tennessee State University (TN) (w)
East Texas Baptist University (TX) (m/w)
Eckerd College (FL) (m/w)
Edgewood College (WI) (m/w)
Edinboro University of Pennsylvania (PA) (w)
Elizabethtown College (PA) (m/w)
Elmhurst College (IL) (w)
Elmira College (NY) (m/w)
Elms College (MA) (m/w)
Elon University (NC) (m/w)
Embry-Riddle Aeronautical University (AZ)
   (m/w)
Embry-Riddle Aeronautical University (FL)
   (m)
Emerson College (MA) (m/w)
Emmanuel College (GA) (m/w)
Emmanuel College (MA) (m/w)
Emory & Henry College (VA) (m/w)
Emory University (GA) (m/w)
Emporia State University (KS) (w)
Endicott College (MA) (m/w)
Erskine College (SC) (m/w)
The Evergreen State College (WA) (m/w)
Fairfield University (CT) (m/w)
Fairleigh Dickinson University, College at
   Florham (NJ) (m/w)
Farmingdale State University of New York
   (NY) (m/w)
Felician College (NJ) (m/w)
Ferris State University (MI) (w)
Ferrum College (VA) (m/w)
Fisk University (TN) (m/w)

Fitchburg State College (MA) (m/w)
Flagler College (FL) (m/w)
Florida Atlantic University (FL) (m/w)
Florida Institute of Technology (FL) (m)
Florida International University (FL) (m/w)
Florida Southern College (FL) (m/w)
Florida State University (FL) (w)
Fontbonne University (MO) (m/w)
Fordham University (NY) (m/w)
Fort Lewis College (CO) (m/w)
Framingham State College (MA) (m/w)
The Franciscan University (IA) (m/w)
Francis Marion University (SC) (m/w)
Franklin and Marshall College (PA) (m/w)
Franklin College (IN) (m/w)
Franklin Pierce College (NH) (m/w)
Freed-Hardeman University (TN) (m/w)
Fresno Pacific University (CA) (m/w)
Friends University (KS) (m/w)
Frostburg State University (MD) (m/w)
Furman University (SC) (m/w)
Gallaudet University (DC) (m/w)
Gannon University (PA) (m/w)
Gardner-Webb University (NC) (m/w)
Geneva College (PA) (m/w)
George Fox University (OR) (m/w)
George Mason University (VA) (m/w)
Georgetown College (KY) (m/w)
Georgetown University (DC) (m/w)
The George Washington University (DC)
   (m/w)
Georgia College & State University (GA) (w)
Georgian Court University (NJ) (w)
Georgia Southern University (GA) (m/w)
Georgia State University (GA) (m/w)
Gettysburg College (PA) (m/w)
Goldey-Beacom College (DE) (m/w)
Gonzaga University (WA) (m/w)
Gordon College (MA) (m/w)
Goshen College (IN) (m/w)
Goucher College (MD) (m/w)
Grace College (IN) (m/w)
Graceland University (IA) (m/w)
Grand Canyon University (AZ) (m/w)
Grand Valley State University (MI) (w)
Grand View College (IA) (m/w)
Green Mountain College (VT) (m/w)
Greensboro College (NC) (m/w)
Greenville College (IL) (m/w)
Grinnell College (IA) (m/w)
Grove City College (PA) (m/w)
Guilford College (NC) (m/w)
Gustavus Adolphus College (MN) (m/w)
Gwynedd-Mercy College (PA) (m/w)
Hamilton College (NY) (m/w)
Hamline University (MN) (m/w)
Hampden-Sydney College (VA) (m)
Hannibal-LaGrange College (MO) (m/w)
Hanover College (IN) (m/w)
Harding University (AR) (m/w)
Hardin-Simmons University (TX) (m/w)
Harris-Stowe State College (MO) (m/w)
Hartwick College (NY) (m/w)
Harvard University (MA) (m/w)
Hastings College (NE) (m/w)
Haverford College (PA) (m/w)
Heidelberg College (OH) (m/w)
Hendrix College (AR) (m/w)
High Point University (NC) (m/w)
Hilbert College (NY) (m/w)
Hiram College (OH) (m/w)
Hobart and William Smith Colleges (NY)
   (m/w)
Hofstra University (NY) (m/w)
Hollins University (VA) (w)

Holy Family University (PA) (m/w)
Holy Names University (CA) (m/w)
Hood College (MD) (w)
Hope College (MI) (m/w)
Hope International University (CA) (m/w)
Houghton College (NY) (m/w)
Howard University (DC) (m/w)
Humboldt State University (CA) (m/w)
Hunter College of the City University of New
   York (NY) (m)
Huntingdon College (AL) (m/w)
Huntington College (IN) (m/w)
Husson College (ME) (m/w)
Huston-Tillotson College (TX) (m/w)
Idaho State University (ID) (w)
Illinois College (IL) (m/w)
Illinois Institute of Technology (IL) (m/w)
Illinois State University (IL) (w)
Illinois Wesleyan University (IL) (m/w)
Immaculata University (PA) (m/w)
Indiana Institute of Technology (IN) (m/w)
Indiana State University (IN) (w)
Indiana University Bloomington (IN) (m/w)
Indiana University of Pennsylvania (PA) (w)
Indiana University–Purdue University Fort
   Wayne (IN) (m/w)
Indiana University–Purdue University
   Indianapolis (IN) (m/w)
Indiana Wesleyan University (IN) (m/w)
Iona College (NY) (m/w)
Iowa State University of Science and
   Technology (IA) (w)
Iowa Wesleyan College (IA) (m/w)
Ithaca College (NY) (m/w)
Jackson State University (MS) (w)
Jacksonville State University (AL) (w)
Jacksonville University (FL) (m/w)
James Madison University (VA) (m/w)
Jamestown College (ND) (w)
John Brown University (AR) (m/w)
John Carroll University (OH) (m/w)
John Jay College of Criminal Justice of the
   City University of New York (NY) (m)
The Johns Hopkins University (MD) (m/w)
Johnson & Wales University (CO) (m/w)
Johnson & Wales University (RI) (m/w)
Johnson State College (VT) (m/w)
Judson College (IL) (m/w)
Juniata College (PA) (m/w)
Kalamazoo College (MI) (m/w)
Kansas Wesleyan University (KS) (m/w)
Kean University (NJ) (m/w)
Keene State College (NH) (m/w)
Kendall College (IL) (m)
Kennesaw State University (GA) (w)
Kent State University (OH) (w)
Kentucky Wesleyan College (KY) (m/w)
Kenyon College (OH) (m/w)
Keuka College (NY) (m/w)
King College (TN) (m/w)
King's College (PA) (m/w)
Knox College (IL) (m/w)
Kutztown University of Pennsylvania (PA)
   (m/w)
Lafayette College (PA) (m/w)
LaGrange College (GA) (m/w)
Lake Erie College (OH) (m/w)
Lake Forest College (IL) (m/w)
Lakeland College (WI) (m/w)
Lambuth University (TN) (m/w)
Lander University (SC) (m/w)
La Roche College (PA) (m/w)
La Salle University (PA) (m/w)
Lasell College (MA) (m/w)
Lawrence University (WI) (m/w)

Lebanon Valley College (PA) (m/w)
Lees-McRae College (NC) (m/w)
Lee University (TN) (m/w)
Lehigh University (PA) (m/w)
Le Moyne College (NY) (m/w)
Lenoir-Rhyne College (NC) (m/w)
Lesley University (MA) (w)
LeTourneau University (TX) (m/w)
Lewis & Clark College (OR) (w)
Lewis University (IL) (m/w)
Liberty University (VA) (m/w)
Limestone College (SC) (m/w)
Lincoln Memorial University (TN) (m/w)
Lincoln University (PA) (m/w)
Lindenwood University (MO) (m/w)
Lindsey Wilson College (KY) (m/w)
Linfield College (OR) (m/w)
Lipscomb University (TN) (m/w)
Lock Haven University of Pennsylvania (PA) (m/w)
Long Island University, Brooklyn Campus (NY) (m/w)
Long Island University, C.W. Post Campus (NY) (m/w)
Long Island University, Southampton College (NY) (m/w)
Longwood University (VA) (m/w)
Loras College (IA) (m/w)
Louisiana College (LA) (m/w)
Louisiana State University and Agricultural and Mechanical College (LA) (w)
Louisiana State University in Shreveport (LA) (w)
Loyola College in Maryland (MD) (m/w)
Loyola Marymount University (CA) (m/w)
Loyola University Chicago (IL) (m/w)
Loyola University New Orleans (LA) (w)
Luther College (IA) (m)
Lycoming College (PA) (m/w)
Lynchburg College (VA) (m/w)
Lyndon State College (VT) (m/w)
Lynn University (FL) (m/w)
Lyon College (AR) (m/w)
Macalester College (MN) (m/w)
MacMurray College (IL) (m/w)
Madonna University (MI) (m/w)
Maine Maritime Academy (ME) (m/w)
Malone College (OH) (m/w)
Manchester College (IN) (m/w)
Manhattan College (NY) (m/w)
Manhattanville College (NY) (m/w)
Mansfield University of Pennsylvania (PA) (w)
Maranatha Baptist Bible College (WI) (m/w)
Marian College (IN) (m/w)
Marian College of Fond du Lac (WI) (m/w)
Marietta College (OH) (m/w)
Marist College (NY) (m/w)
Marquette University (WI) (m/w)
Marshall University (WV) (m/w)
Mars Hill College (NC) (m/w)
Martin Luther College (MN) (m/w)
Martin Methodist College (TN) (m/w)
Mary Baldwin College (VA) (w)
Marymount University (VA) (m/w)
Maryville College (TN) (m/w)
Maryville University of Saint Louis (MO) (m/w)
University of Mary Washington (VA) (m/w)
Marywood University (PA) (m/w)
Massachusetts College of Liberal Arts (MA) (m/w)
Massachusetts Institute of Technology (MA) (m/w)
Massachusetts Maritime Academy (MA) (m)

The Master's College and Seminary (CA) (m/w)
McDaniel College (MD) (m/w)
McKendree College (IL) (m/w)
McMurry University (TX) (m/w)
McNeese State University (LA) (w)
McPherson College (KS) (m/w)
Medaille College (NY) (m/w)
Medgar Evers College of the City University of New York (NY) (m)
Menlo College (CA) (m/w)
Mercer University (GA) (m/w)
Mercy College (NY) (m/w)
Mercyhurst College (PA) (m/w)
Meredith College (NC) (w)
Merrimack College (MA) (m/w)
Mesa State College (CO) (w)
Messiah College (PA) (m/w)
Methodist College (NC) (m/w)
Metropolitan State College of Denver (CO) (m/w)
Miami University (OH) (w)
Michigan State University (MI) (w)
MidAmerica Nazarene University (KS) (m/w)
Mid-Continent College (KY) (m)
Middlebury College (VT) (m/w)
Middle Tennessee State University (TN) (w)
Midland Lutheran College (NE) (m/w)
Midway College (KY) (w)
Midwestern State University (TX) (m/w)
Millersville University of Pennsylvania (PA) (m/w)
Milligan College (TN) (m/w)
Millikin University (IL) (m/w)
Millsaps College (MS) (m/w)
Mills College (CA) (w)
Milwaukee School of Engineering (WI) (m/w)
Minnesota State University Mankato (MN) (w)
Minnesota State University Moorhead (MN) (w)
Mississippi College (MS) (m/w)
Mississippi State University (MS) (w)
Missouri Baptist University (MO) (m/w)
Missouri Southern State University (MO) (m/w)
Missouri Valley College (MO) (m/w)
Molloy College (NY) (m/w)
Monmouth College (IL) (m/w)
Monmouth University (NJ) (m/w)
Montana State University–Billings (MT) (m/w)
Montclair State University (NJ) (m/w)
Montreat College (NC) (m/w)
Moravian College (PA) (m/w)
Morehead State University (KY) (w)
Morehouse College (GA) (m)
Morningside College (IA) (m/w)
Mount Holyoke College (MA) (w)
Mount Ida College (MA) (m/w)
Mount Marty College (SD) (m/w)
Mount Mercy College (IA) (m/w)
Mount Olive College (NC) (m/w)
Mount Saint Mary College (NY) (m/w)
Mount Saint Mary's University (MD) (m/w)
Mount Union College (OH) (m/w)
Mount Vernon Nazarene University (OH) (m/w)
Muhlenberg College (PA) (m/w)
Murray State University (KY) (w)
Muskingum College (OH) (m/w)
National American University (SD) (m/w)
Nazareth College of Rochester (NY) (m/w)
Nebraska Wesleyan University (NE) (m/w)
Neumann College (PA) (m/w)

Newberry College (SC) (m/w)
Newbury College (MA) (m)
New England College (NH) (m/w)
New Jersey City University (NJ) (m/w)
New Jersey Institute of Technology (NJ) (m/w)
Newman University (KS) (m/w)
New Mexico Highlands University (NM) (w)
New York City College of Technology of the City University of New York (NY) (m)
New York Institute of Technology (NY) (m/w)
New York University (NY) (m/w)
Niagara University (NY) (m/w)
Nicholls State University (LA) (w)
Nichols College (MA) (m/w)
North Carolina State University (NC) (m/w)
North Carolina Wesleyan College (NC) (m/w)
North Central College (IL) (m/w)
North Dakota State University (ND) (w)
Northeastern State University (OK) (m/w)
Northeastern University (MA) (m/w)
Northern Arizona University (AZ) (w)
Northern Illinois University (IL) (m/w)
Northern Kentucky University (KY) (m/w)
Northern Michigan University (MI) (w)
Northern State University (SD) (w)
North Georgia College & State University (GA) (m/w)
North Greenville College (SC) (m/w)
Northland College (WI) (m/w)
North Park University (IL) (m/w)
Northwest College (WA) (m)
Northwestern College (IA) (m/w)
Northwestern College (MN) (m/w)
Northwestern Oklahoma State University (OK) (m)
Northwestern State University of Louisiana (LA) (w)
Northwestern University (IL) (m/w)
Northwest Missouri State University (MO) (w)
Northwest Nazarene University (ID) (w)
Northwood University (MI) (m/w)
Northwood University, Florida Campus (FL) (m/w)
Northwood University, Texas Campus (TX) (m/w)
Norwich University (VT) (m/w)
Notre Dame College (OH) (m/w)
Notre Dame de Namur University (CA) (m/w)
Nova Southeastern University (FL) (m/w)
Nyack College (NY) (m/w)
Oakland City University (IN) (m/w)
Oakland University (MI) (m/w)
Oberlin College (OH) (m/w)
Occidental College (CA) (m/w)
Oglethorpe University (GA) (m/w)
Ohio Dominican University (OH) (m/w)
Ohio Northern University (OH) (m/w)
The Ohio State University (OH) (m/w)
Ohio University (OH) (w)
Ohio Valley College (WV) (m/w)
Ohio Wesleyan University (OH) (m/w)
Oklahoma Christian University (OK) (m/w)
Oklahoma City University (OK) (m/w)
Oklahoma State University (OK) (w)
Oklahoma Wesleyan University (OK) (m/w)
Old Dominion University (VA) (m/w)
Olivet College (MI) (m/w)
Olivet Nazarene University (IL) (m/w)
Oral Roberts University (OK) (m/w)
Oregon Institute of Technology (OR) (w)

Oregon State University (OR) (m/w)
Ottawa University (KS) (m/w)
Otterbein College (OH) (m/w)
Ouachita Baptist University (AR) (m/w)
Pace University (NY) (w)
Pacific Lutheran University (WA) (m/w)
Pacific University (OR) (m/w)
Park University (MO) (m/w)
Peace College (NC) (w)
The Pennsylvania State University Altoona
  College (PA) (m/w)
The Pennsylvania State University at Erie,
  The Behrend College (PA) (m/w)
The Pennsylvania State University University
  Park Campus (PA) (m/w)
Pepperdine University (CA) (w)
Pfeiffer University (NC) (m/w)
Philadelphia Biblical University (PA) (m/w)
Philadelphia University (PA) (m/w)
Piedmont College (GA) (m)
Pine Manor College (MA) (w)
Pitzer College (CA) (m/w)
Plymouth State University (NH) (m/w)
Point Loma Nazarene University (CA) (m/w)
Point Park University (PA) (m/w)
Polytechnic University, Brooklyn Campus
  (NY) (m/w)
Pomona College (CA) (m/w)
Portland State University (OR) (w)
Prairie View A&M University (TX) (w)
Presbyterian College (SC) (m/w)
Presentation College (SD) (m/w)
Princeton University (NJ) (m/w)
Principia College (IL) (m/w)
Providence College (RI) (m/w)
Purdue University (IN) (w)
Queens College of the City University of
  New York (NY) (w)
Queens University of Charlotte (NC) (m/w)
Quincy University (IL) (m/w)
Quinnipiac University (CT) (m/w)
Radford University (VA) (m/w)
Ramapo College of New Jersey (NJ) (m/w)
Randolph-Macon College (VA) (m/w)
Randolph-Macon Woman's College (VA) (w)
Regis University (CO) (m/w)
Reinhardt College (GA) (m/w)
Rensselaer Polytechnic Institute (NY) (m/w)
Rhode Island College (RI) (m/w)
Rhodes College (TN) (m/w)
Rice University (TX) (w)
The Richard Stockton College of New Jersey
  (NJ) (m/w)
Rider University (NJ) (m/w)
Ripon College (WI) (m/w)
Rivier College (NH) (m/w)
Roanoke College (VA) (m/w)
Robert Morris College (IL) (w)
Robert Morris University (PA) (m/w)
Roberts Wesleyan College (NY) (m/w)
Rochester Institute of Technology (NY)
  (m/w)
Rockford College (IL) (m/w)
Rockhurst University (MO) (m/w)
Rocky Mountain College (MT) (w)
Roger Williams University (RI) (m/w)
Rollins College (FL) (m/w)
Rose-Hulman Institute of Technology (IN)
  (m/w)
Rowan University (NJ) (m/w)
Russell Sage College (NY) (w)
Rust College (MS) (m)
Rutgers, The State University of New Jersey,
  Camden (NJ) (w)

Rutgers, The State University of New Jersey,
  Newark (NJ) (m/w)
Rutgers, The State University of New Jersey,
  New Brunswick/Piscataway (NJ) (m/w)
Sacred Heart University (CT) (m/w)
Saginaw Valley State University (MI) (m/w)
St. Ambrose University (IA) (m/w)
St. Andrews Presbyterian College (NC) (m/w)
Saint Anselm College (NH) (m/w)
St. Bonaventure University (NY) (m/w)
St. Cloud State University (MN) (w)
St. Edward's University (TX) (m/w)
St. Francis College (NY) (m)
Saint Francis University (PA) (m/w)
St. Gregory's University (OK) (m/w)
St. John Fisher College (NY) (m/w)
Saint John's University (MN) (m)
St. John's University (NY) (m/w)
Saint Joseph College (CT) (w)
Saint Joseph's College (IN) (m/w)
Saint Joseph's College of Maine (ME) (w)
St. Joseph's College, Suffolk Campus (NY)
  (m/w)
Saint Joseph's University (PA) (m/w)
St. Lawrence University (NY) (m/w)
Saint Leo University (FL) (m/w)
Saint Louis University (MO) (m/w)
Saint Mary's College (IN) (w)
Saint Mary's College of California (CA)
  (m/w)
St. Mary's College of Maryland (MD) (m/w)
Saint Mary's University of Minnesota (MN)
  (m/w)
St. Mary's University of San Antonio (TX)
  (m/w)
Saint Michael's College (VT) (m/w)
St. Norbert College (WI) (m/w)
St. Olaf College (MN) (m/w)
Saint Peter's College (NJ) (m/w)
St. Thomas Aquinas College (NY) (m/w)
St. Thomas University (FL) (m/w)
Saint Vincent College (PA) (m/w)
Saint Xavier University (IL) (m/w)
Salem International University (WV) (m/w)
Salem State College (MA) (m/w)
Salisbury University (MD) (m/w)
Salve Regina University (RI) (m/w)
Samford University (AL) (w)
Sam Houston State University (TX) (w)
San Diego State University (CA) (m/w)
San Francisco State University (CA) (m/w)
San Jose State University (CA) (m/w)
Santa Clara University (CA) (m/w)
Savannah College of Art and Design (GA)
  (m/w)
Schreiner University (TX) (m/w)
Seattle Pacific University (WA) (m/w)
Seattle University (WA) (m/w)
Seton Hall University (NJ) (m/w)
Seton Hill University (PA) (w)
Shawnee State University (OH) (m/w)
Shenandoah University (VA) (m/w)
Shepherd University (WV) (m/w)
Shippensburg University of Pennsylvania
  (PA) (m/w)
Shorter College (GA) (m/w)
Siena College (NY) (m/w)
Siena Heights University (MI) (m/w)
Simmons College (MA) (w)
Simpson College (IA) (m/w/w)
Si Tanka Huron University (SD) (m/w)
Skidmore College (NY) (m/w)
Slippery Rock University of Pennsylvania
  (PA) (m/w)
Smith College (MA) (w)

Sonoma State University (CA) (m/w)
South Carolina State University (SC) (w)
South Dakota State University (SD) (w)
Southeastern Louisiana University (LA) (w)
Southeast Missouri State University (MO)
  (w)
Southern Connecticut State University (CT)
  (m/w)
Southern Illinois University Edwardsville (IL)
  (m/w)
Southern Methodist University (TX) (m/w)
Southern Nazarene University (OK) (m/w)
Southern New Hampshire University (NH)
  (m/w)
Southern Oregon University (OR) (w)
Southern Utah University (UT) (w)
Southern Vermont College (VT) (m/w)
Southern Virginia University (VA) (m/w)
Southern Wesleyan University (SC) (m/w)
Southwest Baptist University (MO) (w)
Southwestern Assemblies of God University
  (TX) (m)
Southwestern College (KS) (m/w)
Southwestern Oklahoma State University
  (OK) (m/w)
Southwestern University (TX) (m/w)
Southwest Minnesota State University (MN)
  (w)
Southwest Missouri State University (MO)
  (m/w)
Spalding University (KY) (m/w)
Spelman College (GA) (w)
Spring Arbor University (MI) (m/w)
Springfield College (MA) (m/w)
Spring Hill College (AL) (m/w)
Stanford University (CA) (m/w)
State University of New York at Binghamton
  (NY) (m/w)
State University of New York at New Paltz
  (NY) (m/w)
State University of New York at Oswego
  (NY) (m/w)
State University of New York at Plattsburgh
  (NY) (m/w)
State University of New York College at
  Brockport (NY) (m/w)
State University of New York College at
  Cortland (NY) (m/w)
State University of New York College at
  Fredonia (NY) (m)
State University of New York College at
  Geneseo (NY) (m/w)
State University of New York College at Old
  Westbury (NY) (m/w)
State University of New York College at
  Oneonta (NY) (m/w)
State University of New York College at
  Potsdam (NY) (m/w)
State University of New York College of
  Technology at Delhi (NY) (m/w)
State University of New York Institute of
  Technology (NY) (m/w)
State University of New York Maritime
  College (NY) (m)
Stephen F. Austin State University (TX) (w)
Stephens College (MO) (w)
Sterling College (KS) (m/w)
Stetson University (FL) (m/w)
Stevens Institute of Technology (NJ) (m/w)
Stonehill College (MA) (m/w)
Stony Brook University, State University of
  New York (NY) (m/w)
Suffolk University (MA) (m)
Susquehanna University (PA) (m/w)
Swarthmore College (PA) (m/w)

Sweet Briar College (VA) (w)
Syracuse University (NY) (m/w)
Tabor College (KS) (m/w)
Taylor University (IN) (m/w)
Teikyo Post University (CT) (m/w)
Temple University (PA) (m/w)
Tennessee Technological University (TN) (w)
Tennessee Wesleyan College (TN) (m/w)
Texas A&M International University (TX) (m/w)
Texas A&M University (TX) (w)
Texas A&M University–Commerce (TX) (w)
Texas Christian University (TX) (w)
Texas College (TX) (w)
Texas Lutheran University (TX) (m/w)
Texas State University-San Marcos (TX) (w)
Texas Tech University (TX) (w)
Texas Wesleyan University (TX) (m/w)
Texas Woman's University (TX) (w)
Thiel College (PA) (m)
Thomas College (ME) (m/w)
Thomas More College (KY) (m/w)
Thomas University (GA) (m/w)
Tiffin University (OH) (m/w)
Towson University (MD) (m/w)
Transylvania University (KY) (m/w)
Trevecca Nazarene University (TN) (m/w)
Trinity Christian College (IL) (m/w)
Trinity College (CT) (m/w)
Trinity College (DC) (w)
Trinity International University (IL) (m/w)
Trinity University (TX) (m/w)
Tri-State University (IN) (m/w)
Troy State University (AL) (w)
Truman State University (MO) (m/w)
Tufts University (MA) (m/w)
Tulane University (LA) (w)
Tusculum College (TN) (m/w)
Union College (KY) (m/w)
Union College (NY) (m/w)
Union University (TN) (m)
United States Air Force Academy (CO) (m/w)
United States Coast Guard Academy (CT) (m/w)
United States Merchant Marine Academy (NY) (m)
United States Military Academy (NY) (m/w)
United States Naval Academy (MD) (m/w)
University at Albany, State University of New York (NY) (m/w)
University at Buffalo, The State University of New York (NY) (m/w)
The University of Akron (OH) (m/w)
The University of Alabama (AL) (w)
The University of Alabama at Birmingham (AL) (m/w)
The University of Alabama in Huntsville (AL) (m/w)
The University of Arizona (AZ) (w)
University of Arkansas (AR) (w)
University of Arkansas at Little Rock (AR) (w)
University of Bridgeport (CT) (m/w)
University of California, Berkeley (CA) (m/w)
University of California, Davis (CA) (m/w)
University of California, Irvine (CA) (m/w)
University of California, Los Angeles (CA) (m/w)
University of California, Riverside (CA) (m/w)
University of California, San Diego (CA) (m/w)
University of California, Santa Barbara (CA) (m/w)

University of California, Santa Cruz (CA) (m/w)
University of Central Arkansas (AR) (m/w)
University of Central Florida (FL) (m/w)
University of Central Oklahoma (OK) (w)
University of Charleston (WV) (m/w)
University of Chicago (IL) (m/w)
University of Cincinnati (OH) (m/w)
University of Colorado at Boulder (CO) (w)
University of Colorado at Colorado Springs (CO) (m)
University of Connecticut (CT) (m/w)
University of Dallas (TX) (m/w)
University of Dayton (OH) (m/w)
University of Delaware (DE) (m/w)
University of Denver (CO) (m/w)
University of Detroit Mercy (MI) (m/w)
University of Dubuque (IA) (m/w)
University of Evansville (IN) (m/w)
The University of Findlay (OH) (m/w)
University of Florida (FL) (w)
University of Georgia (GA) (w)
University of Hartford (CT) (m/w)
University of Hawaii at Manoa (HI) (w)
University of Houston (TX) (w)
University of Idaho (ID) (w)
University of Illinois at Chicago (IL) (m)
University of Illinois at Springfield (IL) (m)
University of Illinois at Urbana–Champaign (IL) (w)
University of Indianapolis (IN) (m/w)
The University of Iowa (IA) (w)
University of Kansas (KS) (w)
University of Kentucky (KY) (m/w)
University of La Verne (CA) (m/w)
University of Louisiana at Lafayette (LA) (w)
University of Louisiana at Monroe (LA) (w)
University of Louisville (KY) (m/w)
University of Maine (ME) (m/w)
University of Maine at Farmington (ME) (m/w)
University of Maine at Fort Kent (ME) (m/w)
University of Maine at Machias (ME) (m/w)
University of Maine at Presque Isle (ME) (m/w)
University of Mary (ND) (m/w)
University of Mary Hardin-Baylor (TX) (m/w)
University of Maryland, Baltimore County (MD) (m/w)
University of Maryland, College Park (MD) (m/w)
University of Massachusetts Amherst (MA) (m/w)
University of Massachusetts Boston (MA) (m/w)
University of Massachusetts Dartmouth (MA) (m/w)
University of Massachusetts Lowell (MA) (m/w)
The University of Memphis (TN) (m/w)
University of Miami (FL) (w)
University of Michigan (MI) (m/w)
University of Michigan–Dearborn (MI) (m)
University of Minnesota, Crookston (MN) (w)
University of Minnesota, Duluth (MN) (w)
University of Minnesota, Morris (MN) (w)
University of Minnesota, Twin Cities Campus (MN) (w)
University of Mississippi (MS) (w)
University of Missouri–Columbia (MO) (w)
University of Missouri–Kansas City (MO) (m)
University of Missouri–Rolla (MO) (m/w)

University of Missouri–St. Louis (MO) (m/w)
University of Mobile (AL) (m/w)
The University of Montana–Missoula (MT) (w)
University of Montevallo (AL) (m/w)
University of Nebraska at Omaha (NE) (w)
University of Nebraska–Lincoln (NE) (w)
University of Nevada, Las Vegas (NV) (m/w)
University of Nevada, Reno (NV) (w)
University of New England (ME) (m/w)
University of New Hampshire (NH) (m/w)
University of New Haven (CT) (m/w)
University of New Mexico (NM) (m/w)
University of North Alabama (AL) (w)
The University of North Carolina at Asheville (NC) (m/w)
The University of North Carolina at Chapel Hill (NC) (m/w)
The University of North Carolina at Charlotte (NC) (m/w)
The University of North Carolina at Greensboro (NC) (m/w)
The University of North Carolina at Pembroke (NC) (m/w)
The University of North Carolina at Wilmington (NC) (m/w)
University of North Dakota (ND) (w)
University of Northern Colorado (CO) (w)
University of Northern Iowa (IA) (w)
University of North Florida (FL) (m/w)
University of North Texas (TX) (w)
University of Notre Dame (IN) (m/w)
University of Oklahoma (OK) (w)
University of Oregon (OR) (w)
University of Pennsylvania (PA) (m/w)
University of Pittsburgh (PA) (m/w)
University of Pittsburgh at Bradford (PA) (m/w)
University of Pittsburgh at Greensburg (PA) (m/w)
University of Pittsburgh at Johnstown (PA) (m)
University of Portland (OR) (m/w)
University of Puerto Rico, Mayagüez Campus (PR) (m)
University of Puerto Rico, Río Piedras (PR) (m/w)
University of Puget Sound (WA) (m/w)
University of Redlands (CA) (m/w)
University of Rhode Island (RI) (m/w)
University of Richmond (VA) (m/w)
University of Rio Grande (OH) (m)
University of Rochester (NY) (m/w)
University of St. Francis (IL) (m/w)
University of Saint Francis (IN) (m/w)
University of Saint Mary (KS) (m/w)
University of St. Thomas (MN) (m/w)
University of San Diego (CA) (m/w)
University of San Francisco (CA) (m/w)
University of Science and Arts of Oklahoma (OK) (m/w)
The University of Scranton (PA) (m/w)
University of Sioux Falls (SD) (m/w)
University of South Alabama (AL) (w)
University of South Carolina (SC) (m/w)
University of South Carolina Aiken (SC) (m/w)
University of South Carolina Spartanburg (SC) (m/w)
The University of South Dakota (SD) (w)
University of Southern California (CA) (w)
University of Southern Indiana (IN) (m/w)
University of Southern Maine (ME) (m/w)
University of Southern Mississippi (MS) (w)
University of South Florida (FL) (m/w)

The University of Tampa (FL) (m/w)
The University of Tennessee (TN) (w)
The University of Tennessee at Chattanooga (TN) (w)
The University of Tennessee at Martin (TN) (w)
The University of Texas at Austin (TX) (w)
The University of Texas at Dallas (TX) (m/w)
The University of Texas at El Paso (TX) (w)
The University of Texas of the Permian Basin (TX) (m/w)
University of the District of Columbia (DC) (m/w)
University of the Incarnate Word (TX) (m/w)
University of the Ozarks (AR) (m/w)
University of the Pacific (CA) (w)
University of the South (TN) (m/w)
University of Toledo (OH) (w)
University of Tulsa (OK) (m/w)
University of Utah (UT) (w)
University of Vermont (VT) (m/w)
University of Virginia (VA) (m/w)
University of Washington (WA) (m/w)
University of West Florida (FL) (m/w)
University of Wisconsin–Eau Claire (WI) (w)
University of Wisconsin–Green Bay (WI) (m/w)
University of Wisconsin–La Crosse (WI) (w)
University of Wisconsin–Madison (WI) (m/w)
University of Wisconsin–Milwaukee (WI) (m/w)
University of Wisconsin–Oshkosh (WI) (m/w)
University of Wisconsin–Parkside (WI) (m/w)
University of Wisconsin–Platteville (WI) (m/w)
University of Wisconsin–River Falls (WI) (w)
University of Wisconsin–Stevens Point (WI) (w)
University of Wisconsin–Stout (WI) (w)
University of Wisconsin–Superior (WI) (m/w)
University of Wisconsin–Whitewater (WI) (m/w)
University of Wyoming (WY) (w)
Upper Iowa University (IA) (m/w)
Urbana University (OH) (m/w)
Ursinus College (PA) (m/w)
Ursuline College (OH) (w)
Utah State University (UT) (w)
Utica College (NY) (m/w)
Valparaiso University (IN) (m/w)
Vanderbilt University (TN) (m/w)
Vanguard University of Southern California (CA) (m/w)
Vassar College (NY) (m/w)
Villa Julie College (MD) (m/w)
Villanova University (PA) (m/w)
Virginia Commonwealth University (VA) (m/w)
Virginia Intermont College (VA) (m/w)
Virginia Military Institute (VA) (m/w)
Virginia Polytechnic Institute and State University (VA) (m/w)
Virginia Wesleyan College (VA) (m/w)
Viterbo University (WI) (m/w)
Wabash College (IN) (m)
Wagner College (NY) (w)
Wake Forest University (NC) (m/w)
Waldorf College (IA) (m/w)
Walsh University (OH) (w)
Warner Pacific College (OR) (m/w)
Warner Southern College (FL) (m/w)
Wartburg College (IA) (m/w)
Washburn University (KS) (w)

Washington & Jefferson College (PA) (m/w)
Washington and Lee University (VA) (m/w)
Washington College (MD) (m/w)
Washington State University (WA) (w)
Washington University in St. Louis (MO) (m/w)
Wayland Baptist University (TX) (w)
Waynesburg College (PA) (m/w)
Wayne State College (NE) (w)
Webber International University (FL) (m/w)
Weber State University (UT) (w)
Webster University (MO) (m/w)
Wellesley College (MA) (w)
Wells College (NY) (w)
Wentworth Institute of Technology (MA) (m/w)
Wesleyan College (GA) (w)
Wesleyan University (CT) (m/w)
Wesley College (DE) (m/w)
West Chester University of Pennsylvania (PA) (m/w)
Western Baptist College (OR) (m/w)
Western Carolina University (NC) (w)
Western Connecticut State University (CT) (m/w)
Western Illinois University (IL) (m/w)
Western Kentucky University (KY) (m/w)
Western Michigan University (MI) (m/w)
Western New England College (MA) (m/w)
Western Oregon University (OR) (w)
Western Washington University (WA) (m/w)
Westfield State College (MA) (m/w)
Westminster College (UT) (m)
Westminster College (MO) (m/w)
Westminster College (PA) (m/w)
Westmont College (CA) (m/w)
West Texas A&M University (TX) (m/w)
West Virginia University (WV) (m/w)
West Virginia University Institute of Technology (WV) (w)
West Virginia Wesleyan College (WV) (m/w)
Wheaton College (IL) (m/w)
Wheaton College (MA) (m/w)
Wheeling Jesuit University (WV) (m/w)
Wheelock College (MA) (w)
Whitman College (WA) (m/w)
Whittier College (CA) (m/w)
Whitworth College (WA) (m/w)
Widener University (PA) (m/w)
Wiley College (TX) (m)
Wilkes University (PA) (m/w)
Willamette University (OR) (m/w)
William Carey College (MS) (m/w)
William Jewell College (MO) (m/w)
William Paterson University of New Jersey (NJ) (m/w)
William Penn University (IA) (m/w)
Williams Baptist College (AR) (m)
Williams College (MA) (m/w)
William Woods University (MO) (m/w)
Wilmington College (DE) (m/w)
Wilmington College (OH) (m/w)
Wilson College (PA) (w)
Wingate University (NC) (m/w)
Winona State University (MN) (w)
Winthrop University (SC) (m/w)
Wisconsin Lutheran College (WI) (m)
Wittenberg University (OH) (m/w)
Wofford College (SC) (m/w)
Worcester Polytechnic Institute (MA) (m/w)
Worcester State College (MA) (m/w)
Wright State University (OH) (m/w)
Xavier University (OH) (m/w)
Yale University (CT) (m/w)
Yeshiva University (NY) (m)

York College (NE) (m/w)
York College of Pennsylvania (PA) (m/w)
York College of the City University of New York (NY) (m)
Youngstown State University (OH)(w)

Softball

Abilene Christian University (TX) (w)
Adams State College (CO) (w)
Adrian College (MI) (w)
Agnes Scott College (GA) (w)
Alabama Agricultural and Mechanical University (AL) (w)
Alabama State University (AL) (w)
Albany State University (GA) (w)
Albertson College of Idaho (ID) (w)
Albertus Magnus College (CT) (w)
Albion College (MI) (w)
Albright College (PA) (w)
Alcorn State University (MS) (w)
Alderson-Broaddus College (WV) (w)
Alfred University (NY) (w)
Alice Lloyd College (KY) (w)
Allegheny College (PA) (w)
Allen University (SC) (w)
Alma College (MI) (w)
Alvernia College (PA) (w)
Alverno College (WI) (w)
American International College (MA) (w)
Amherst College (MA) (w)
Anderson College (SC) (w)
Anderson University (IN) (w)
Angelo State University (TX) (w)
Anna Maria College (MA) (w)
Appalachian State University (NC) (w)
Aquinas College (MI) (w)
Arcadia University (PA) (w)
Arizona State University (AZ) (w)
Arkansas Tech University (AR) (w)
Armstrong Atlantic State University (GA) (w)
Ashland University (OH) (w)
Assumption College (MA) (w)
Athens State University (AL) (w)
Auburn University (AL) (w)
Augsburg College (MN) (w)
Augustana College (IL) (w)
Augustana College (SD) (w)
Augusta State University (GA) (w)
Aurora University (IL) (w)
Austin Peay State University (TN) (w)
Averett University (VA) (w)
Avila University (MO) (w)
Azusa Pacific University (CA) (w)
Babson College (MA) (w)
Bacone College (OK) (w)
Baker University (KS) (w)
Baldwin-Wallace College (OH) (w)
Ball State University (IN) (w)
Baptist Bible College of Pennsylvania (PA) (w)
Barber-Scotia College (NC) (w)
Barry University (FL) (w)
Barton College (NC) (w)
Bates College (ME) (w)
Baylor University (TX) (w)
Bay Path College (MA) (w)
Belhaven College (MS) (w)
Bellarmine University (KY) (w)
Bellevue University (NE) (w)
Belmont Abbey College (NC) (w)
Belmont University (TN) (w)
Beloit College (WI) (w)
Bemidji State University (MN) (w)
Benedict College (SC) (w)

Benedictine College (KS) (w)
Benedictine University (IL) (w)
Bennett College (NC) (w)
Bentley College (MA) (w)
Berea College (KY) (w)
Bernard M. Baruch College of the City
  University of New York (NY) (w)
Bethany College (KS) (w)
Bethany College (WV) (w)
Bethany College of the Assemblies of God
  (CA) (w)
Bethel College (IN) (w)
Bethel College (TN) (w)
Bethel University (MN) (w)
Bethune-Cookman College (FL) (w)
Biola University (CA) (w)
Birmingham-Southern College (AL) (w)
Blackburn College (IL) (w)
Bloomfield College (NJ) (w)
Bloomsburg University of Pennsylvania (PA)
  (w)
Bluefield College (VA) (w)
Bluefield State College (WV) (w)
Bluffton College (OH) (w)
Boston College (MA) (w)
Boston University (MA) (w)
Bowdoin College (ME) (w)
Bowie State University (MD) (w)
Bowling Green State University (OH) (w)
Bradley University (IL) (w)
Brandeis University (MA) (w)
Brescia University (KY) (w)
Brevard College (NC) (w)
Brewton-Parker College (GA) (w)
Briar Cliff University (IA) (w)
Bridgewater College (VA) (w)
Bridgewater State College (MA) (w)
Brigham Young University (UT) (w)
Brigham Young University–Hawaii (HI) (w)
Brooklyn College of the City University of
  New York (NY) (w)
Brown University (RI) (w)
Bryant College (RI) (w)
Bucknell University (PA) (w)
Buena Vista University (IA) (w)
Buffalo State College, State University of
  New York (NY) (w)
Butler University (IN) (w)
Cabrini College (PA) (w)
Caldwell College (NJ) (w)
California Baptist University (CA) (w)
California Lutheran University (CA) (w)
California Polytechnic State University, San
  Luis Obispo (CA) (w)
California State University, Bakersfield (CA)
  (w)
California State University, Chico (CA) (w)
California State University, Dominguez Hills
  (CA) (w)
California State University, Fresno (CA) (w)
California State University, Fullerton (CA)
  (w)
California State University, Hayward (CA)
  (w)
California State University, Long Beach (CA)
  (w)
California State University, Northridge (CA)
  (w)
California State University, Sacramento (CA)
  (w)
California State University, San Bernardino
  (CA) (w)
California State University, Stanislaus (CA)
  (w)

California University of Pennsylvania (PA)
  (w)
Calumet College of Saint Joseph (IN) (w)
Calvin College (MI) (w)
Cameron University (OK) (w)
Campbellsville University (KY) (w)
Campbell University (NC) (w)
Canisius College (NY) (w)
Capital University (OH) (w)
Cardinal Stritch University (WI) (w)
Carleton College (MN) (w)
Carlow College (PA) (w)
Carroll College (WI) (w)
Carson-Newman College (TN) (w)
Carthage College (WI) (w)
Case Western Reserve University (OH) (w)
Castleton State College (VT) (w)
Catawba College (NC) (w)
The Catholic University of America (DC) (w)
Cazenovia College (NY) (w)
Cedar Crest College (PA) (w)
Cedarville University (OH) (w)
Centenary College (NJ) (w)
Centenary College of Louisiana (LA) (w)
Central Christian College of Kansas (KS) (w)
Central College (IA) (w)
Central Connecticut State University (CT)
  (w)
Central Methodist College (MO) (w)
Central Michigan University (MI) (w)
Central Missouri State University (MO) (w)
Central Washington University (WA) (w)
Centre College (KY) (w)
Chaminade University of Honolulu (HI) (w)
Chapman University (CA) (w)
Charleston Southern University (SC) (w)
Chatham College (PA) (w)
Chestnut Hill College (PA) (w)
Chowan College (NC) (w)
Christian Brothers University (TN) (w)
Christopher Newport University (VA) (w)
Claflin University (SC) (w)
Claremont McKenna College (CA) (w)
Clarion University of Pennsylvania (PA) (w)
Clark Atlanta University (GA) (w)
Clarke College (IA) (w)
Clark University (MA) (w)
Cleveland State University (OH) (w)
Coastal Carolina University (SC) (w)
Coe College (IA) (w)
Coker College (SC) (w)
Colby College (ME) (w)
Colgate University (NY) (w)
College Misericordia (PA) (w)
College of Charleston (SC) (w)
College of Mount St. Joseph (OH) (w)
College of Mount Saint Vincent (NY) (w)
The College of New Jersey (NJ) (w)
The College of New Rochelle (NY) (w)
College of Saint Benedict (MN) (w)
College of St. Catherine (MN) (w)
College of Saint Elizabeth (NJ) (w)
College of St. Joseph (VT) (w)
College of Saint Mary (NE) (w)
The College of Saint Rose (NY) (w)
The College of St. Scholastica (MN) (w)
College of Staten Island of the City University
  of New York (NY) (w)
College of the Holy Cross (MA) (w)
The College of Wooster (OH) (w)
The Colorado College (CO) (w)
Colorado School of Mines (CO) (w)
Colorado State University (CO) (w)
Colorado State University-Pueblo (CO) (w)
Columbia College (MO) (w)

Columbia College (NY) (w)
Columbia Union College (MD) (w)
Columbus State University (GA) (w)
Concord College (WV) (w)
Concordia College (MN) (w)
Concordia College (NY) (w)
Concordia University (CA) (w)
Concordia University (IL) (w)
Concordia University (MI) (w)
Concordia University (NE) (w)
Concordia University (OR) (w)
Concordia University at Austin (TX) (w)
Concordia University, St. Paul (MN) (w)
Concordia University Wisconsin (WI) (w)
Coppin State University (MD) (w)
Cornell College (IA) (w)
Cornell University (NY) (w)
Cornerstone University (MI) (w)
Creighton University (NE) (w)
Crown College (MN) (w)
Culver-Stockton College (MO) (w)
Cumberland College (KY) (w)
Cumberland University (TN) (w)
Curry College (MA) (w)
Dakota State University (SD) (w)
Dakota Wesleyan University (SD) (w)
Dana College (NE) (w)
Daniel Webster College (NH) (w)
Dartmouth College (NH) (w)
Davis & Elkins College (WV) (w)
Defiance College (OH) (w)
Delaware State University (DE) (w)
Delaware Valley College (PA) (w)
Delta State University (MS) (w)
Denison University (OH) (w)
DePaul University (IL) (w)
DePauw University (IN) (w)
DeSales University (PA) (w)
Dickinson College (PA) (w)
Dickinson State University (ND) (w)
Doane College (NE) (w)
Dominican College (NY) (w)
Dominican University (IL) (w)
Dominican University of California (CA) (w)
Dordt College (IA) (w)
Dowling College (NY) (w)
Drake University (IA) (w)
Drew University (NJ) (w)
Drexel University (PA) (w)
D'Youville College (NY) (w)
East Carolina University (NC) (w)
East Central University (OK) (w)
Eastern Connecticut State University (CT)
  (w)
Eastern Illinois University (IL) (w)
Eastern Kentucky University (KY) (w)
Eastern Mennonite University (VA) (w)
Eastern Michigan University (MI) (w)
Eastern Nazarene College (MA) (w)
Eastern New Mexico University (NM) (w)
Eastern Oregon University (OR) (w)
Eastern University (PA) (w)
East Stroudsburg University of Pennsylvania
  (PA) (w)
East Tennessee State University (TN) (w)
East Texas Baptist University (TX) (w)
Eckerd College (FL) (w)
Edgewood College (WI) (w)
Edinboro University of Pennsylvania (PA) (w)
Edward Waters College (FL) (w)
Elizabeth City State University (NC) (w)
Elizabethtown College (PA) (w)
Elmhurst College (IL) (w)
Elmira College (NY) (w)
Elms College (MA) (w)

Elon University (NC) (w)
Emerson College (MA) (w)
Emmanuel College (GA) (w)
Emmanuel College (MA) (w)
Emory & Henry College (VA) (w)
Emory University (GA) (w)
Emporia State University (KS) (w)
Endicott College (MA) (w)
Erskine College (SC) (w)
Eureka College (IL) (w)
Evangel University (MO) (w)
Fairfield University (CT) (w)
Fairleigh Dickinson University, College at
    Florham (NJ) (w)
Fairmont State University (WV) (w)
Farmingdale State University of New York
    (NY) (w)
Faulkner University (AL) (w)
Fayetteville State University (NC) (w)
Felician College (NJ) (w)
Ferris State University (MI) (w)
Ferrum College (VA) (w)
Fisher College (MA) (w)
Fisk University (TN) (w)
Fitchburg State College (MA) (w)
Florida Agricultural and Mechanical
    University (FL) (w)
Florida Atlantic University (FL) (w)
Florida Gulf Coast University (FL) (w)
Florida Institute of Technology (FL) (w)
Florida International University (FL) (w)
Florida Southern College (FL) (w)
Florida State University (FL) (w)
Fontbonne University (MO) (w)
Fordham University (NY) (w)
Fort Hays State University (KS) (w)
Fort Lewis College (CO) (w)
Fort Valley State University (GA) (w)
Framingham State College (MA) (w)
The Franciscan University (IA) (w)
Francis Marion University (SC) (w)
Franklin and Marshall College (PA) (w)
Franklin College (IN) (w)
Franklin Pierce College (NH) (w)
Freed-Hardeman University (TN) (w)
Friends University (KS) (w)
Frostburg State University (MD) (w)
Furman University (SC) (w)
Gallaudet University (DC) (w)
Gannon University (PA) (w)
Gardner-Webb University (NC) (w)
Geneva College (PA) (w)
George Fox University (OR) (w)
George Mason University (VA) (w)
Georgetown College (KY) (w)
The George Washington University (DC) (w)
Georgia College & State University (GA) (w)
Georgia Institute of Technology (GA) (w)
Georgian Court University (NJ) (w)
Georgia Southern University (GA) (w)
Georgia Southwestern State University (GA)
    (w)
Georgia State University (GA) (w)
Gettysburg College (PA) (w)
Glenville State College (WV) (w)
Goldey-Beacom College (DE) (w)
Gordon College (MA) (w)
Goshen College (IN) (w)
Grace College (IN) (w)
Graceland University (IA) (w)
Grambling State University (LA) (w)
Grand Canyon University (AZ) (w)
Grand Valley State University (MI) (w)
Grand View College (IA) (w)
Green Mountain College (VT) (w)

Greensboro College (NC) (w)
Greenville College (IL) (w)
Grinnell College (IA) (w)
Grove City College (PA) (w)
Guilford College (NC) (w)
Gustavus Adolphus College (MN) (w)
Gwynedd-Mercy College (PA) (w)
Hamilton College (NY) (w)
Hamline University (MN) (w)
Hampton University (VA) (w)
Hannibal-LaGrange College (MO) (w)
Hanover College (IN) (w)
Hardin-Simmons University (TX) (w)
Hartwick College (NY) (w)
Harvard University (MA) (w)
Haskell Indian Nations University (KS) (w)
Hastings College (NE) (w)
Haverford College (PA) (w)
Hawai'i Pacific University (HI) (w)
Heidelberg College (OH) (w)
Henderson State University (AR) (w)
Hendrix College (AR) (w)
Hilbert College (NY) (w)
Hillsdale College (MI) (w)
Hiram College (OH) (w)
Hofstra University (NY) (w)
Holy Family University (PA) (w)
Hood College (MD) (w)
Hope College (MI) (w)
Hope International University (CA) (w)
Houston Baptist University (TX) (w)
Howard Payne University (TX) (w)
Howard University (DC) (w)
Humboldt State University (CA) (w)
Hunter College of the City University of New
    York (NY) (w)
Huntingdon College (AL) (w)
Huntington College (IN) (w)
Husson College (ME) (w)
Illinois College (IL) (w)
Illinois State University (IL) (w)
Illinois Wesleyan University (IL) (w)
Immaculata University (PA) (w)
Indiana Institute of Technology (IN) (w)
Indiana State University (IN) (w)
Indiana University Bloomington (IN) (w)
Indiana University of Pennsylvania (PA) (w)
Indiana University–Purdue University Fort
    Wayne (IN) (w)
Indiana University–Purdue University
    Indianapolis (IN) (w)
Indiana Wesleyan University (IN) (w)
Iona College (NY) (w)
Iowa State University of Science and
    Technology (IA) (w)
Iowa Wesleyan College (IA) (w)
Ithaca College (NY) (w)
Jackson State University (MS) (w)
Jacksonville State University (AL) (w)
Jacksonville University (FL) (w)
James Madison University (VA) (w)
Jamestown College (ND) (w)
John Carroll University (OH) (w)
John Jay College of Criminal Justice of the
    City University of New York (NY) (w)
Johnson & Wales University (CO) (w)
Johnson & Wales University (RI) (w)
Johnson C. Smith University (NC) (w)
Johnson State College (VT) (w)
Judson College (IL) (w)
Juniata College (PA) (w)
Kalamazoo College (MI) (w)
Kansas Wesleyan University (KS) (w)
Kean University (NJ) (w)
Keene State College (NH) (w)

Kennesaw State University (GA) (w)
Kent State University (OH) (w)
Kentucky State University (KY) (w)
Kentucky Wesleyan College (KY) (w)
Kenyon College (OH) (w)
Keuka College (NY) (w)
King's College (PA) (w)
Knox College (IL) (w)
Kutztown University of Pennsylvania (PA)
    (w)
Lafayette College (PA) (w)
LaGrange College (GA) (w)
Lake Erie College (OH) (w)
Lake Forest College (IL) (w)
Lakeland College (WI) (w)
Lake Superior State University (MI) (w)
Lambuth University (TN) (w)
Lander University (SC) (w)
Lane College (TN) (w)
La Roche College (PA) (w)
La Salle University (PA) (w)
Lasell College (MA) (w)
Lawrence University (WI) (w)
Lebanon Valley College (PA) (w)
Lees-McRae College (NC) (w)
Lee University (TN) (w)
Lehigh University (PA) (w)
Lehman College of the City University of
    New York (NY) (w)
Le Moyne College (NY) (w)
LeMoyne-Owen College (TN) (w)
Lenoir-Rhyne College (NC) (w)
Lesley University (MA) (w)
LeTourneau University (TX) (w)
Lewis & Clark College (OR) (w)
Lewis University (IL) (w)
Liberty University (VA) (w)
Limestone College (SC) (w)
Lincoln Memorial University (TN) (w)
Lincoln University (MO) (w)
Lindenwood University (MO) (w)
Lindsey Wilson College (KY) (w)
Linfield College (OR) (w)
Lipscomb University (TN) (w)
Livingstone College (NC) (w)
Lock Haven University of Pennsylvania (PA)
    (w)
Long Island University, Brooklyn Campus
    (NY) (w)
Long Island University, C.W. Post Campus
    (NY) (w)
Long Island University, Southampton College
    (NY) (w)
Longwood University (VA) (w)
Loras College (IA) (w)
Louisiana College (LA) (w)
Louisiana State University and Agricultural
    and Mechanical College (LA) (w)
Louisiana Tech University (LA) (w)
Loyola Marymount University (CA) (w)
Loyola University Chicago (IL) (w)
Luther College (IA) (w)
Lycoming College (PA) (w)
Lynchburg College (VA) (w)
Lyndon State College (VT) (w)
Lynn University (FL) (w)
Macalester College (MN) (w)
Madonna University (MI) (w)
Maine Maritime Academy (ME) (w)
Malone College (OH) (w)
Manchester College (IN) (w)
Manhattan College (NY) (w)
Manhattanville College (NY) (w)
Mansfield University of Pennsylvania (PA)
    (w)

Maranatha Baptist Bible College (WI) (w)
Marian College (IN) (w)
Marian College of Fond du Lac (WI) (w)
Marietta College (OH) (w)
Marist College (NY) (w)
Marshall University (WV) (w)
Mars Hill College (NC) (w)
Martin Luther College (MN) (w)
Martin Methodist College (TN) (w)
Mary Baldwin College (VA) (w)
Maryville College (TN) (w)
Maryville University of Saint Louis (MO) (w)
University of Mary Washington (VA) (w)
Marywood University (PA) (w)
Massachusetts College of Liberal Arts (MA) (w)
Massachusetts Institute of Technology (MA) (w)
Massachusetts Maritime Academy (MA) (w)
Mayville State University (ND) (w)
McDaniel College (MD) (w)
McKendree College (IL) (w)
McNeese State University (LA) (w)
McPherson College (KS) (w)
Medaille College (NY) (w)
Medgar Evers College of the City University of New York (NY) (w)
Menlo College (CA) (w)
Mercer University (GA) (w)
Mercy College (NY) (w)
Mercyhurst College (PA) (w)
Meredith College (NC) (w)
Merrimack College (MA) (w)
Mesa State College (CO) (w)
Messiah College (PA) (w)
Methodist College (NC) (w)
Miami University (OH) (w)
Michigan State University (MI) (w)
MidAmerica Nazarene University (KS) (w)
Mid-Continent College (KY) (w)
Middle Tennessee State University (TN) (w)
Midland Lutheran College (NE) (w)
Midway College (KY) (w)
Midwestern State University (TX) (w)
Miles College (AL) (w)
Millersville University of Pennsylvania (PA) (w)
Milligan College (TN) (w)
Millikin University (IL) (w)
Millsaps College (MS) (w)
Milwaukee School of Engineering (WI) (w)
Minnesota State University Mankato (MN) (w)
Minnesota State University Moorhead (MN) (w)
Minot State University (ND) (w)
Mississippi College (MS) (w)
Mississippi State University (MS) (w)
Mississippi University for Women (MS) (w)
Mississippi Valley State University (MS) (w)
Missouri Baptist University (MO) (w)
Missouri Southern State University (MO) (w)
Missouri Valley College (MO) (w)
Missouri Western State College (MO) (w)
Molloy College (NY) (w)
Monmouth College (IL) (w)
Monmouth University (NJ) (w)
Montana State University–Billings (MT) (w)
Montclair State University (NJ) (w)
Montreat College (NC) (w)
Moravian College (PA) (w)
Morehead State University (KY) (w)
Morgan State University (MD) (w)
Morningside College (IA) (w)
Morris College (SC) (w)

Mountain State University (WV) (w)
Mount Holyoke College (MA) (w)
Mount Ida College (MA) (w)
Mount Marty College (SD) (w)
Mount Mercy College (IA) (w)
Mount Olive College (NC) (w)
Mount Saint Mary College (NY) (w)
Mount Saint Mary's University (MD) (w)
Mount Union College (OH) (w)
Mount Vernon Nazarene University (OH) (w)
Muhlenberg College (PA) (w)
Muskingum College (OH) (w)
Nebraska Wesleyan University (NE) (w)
Neumann College (PA) (w)
Newberry College (SC) (w)
Newbury College (MA) (w)
New England College (NH) (w)
New Jersey City University (NJ) (w)
Newman University (KS) (w)
New Mexico Highlands University (NM) (w)
New Mexico State University (NM) (w)
New York City College of Technology of the City University of New York (NY) (w)
New York Institute of Technology (NY) (w)
Niagara University (NY) (w)
Nicholls State University (LA) (w)
Nichols College (MA) (w)
Norfolk State University (VA) (w)
North Carolina Agricultural and Technical State University (NC) (w)
North Carolina Central University (NC) (w)
North Carolina Wesleyan College (NC) (w)
North Central College (IL) (w)
North Dakota State University (ND) (w)
Northeastern State University (OK) (w)
Northern Illinois University (IL) (w)
Northern Kentucky University (KY) (w)
Northern State University (SD) (w)
North Georgia College & State University (GA) (w)
North Greenville College (SC) (w)
Northland College (WI) (w)
North Park University (IL) (w)
Northwestern College (IA) (w)
Northwestern College (MN) (w)
Northwestern Oklahoma State University (OK) (w)
Northwestern State University of Louisiana (LA) (w)
Northwestern University (IL) (w)
Northwest Missouri State University (MO) (w)
Northwest Nazarene University (ID) (w)
Northwood University (MI) (w)
Northwood University, Florida Campus (FL) (w)
Northwood University, Texas Campus (TX) (w)
Norwich University (VT) (w)
Notre Dame College (OH) (w)
Notre Dame de Namur University (CA) (w)
Nova Southeastern University (FL) (w)
Nyack College (NY) (w)
Oakland City University (IN) (w)
Oakland University (MI) (w)
Oberlin College (OH) (w)
Occidental College (CA) (w)
Ohio Dominican University (OH) (w)
Ohio Northern University (OH) (w)
The Ohio State University (OH) (w)
Ohio University (OH) (w)
Ohio Valley College (WV) (w)
Ohio Wesleyan University (OH) (w)
Oklahoma Baptist University (OK) (w)

Oklahoma Christian University (OK) (w)
Oklahoma City University (OK) (w)
Oklahoma Panhandle State University (OK) (w)
Oklahoma State University (OK) (w)
Oklahoma Wesleyan University (OK) (w)
Olivet College (MI) (w)
Olivet Nazarene University (IL) (w)
Oregon Institute of Technology (OR) (w)
Oregon State University (OR) (w)
Ottawa University (KS) (w)
Otterbein College (OH) (w)
Ouachita Baptist University (AR) (w)
Pace University (NY) (w)
Pacific Lutheran University (WA) (w)
Pacific University (OR) (w)
Paine College (GA) (w)
Park University (MO) (w)
Peace College (NC) (w)
The Pennsylvania State University Altoona College (PA) (w)
The Pennsylvania State University at Erie, The Behrend College (PA) (w)
The Pennsylvania State University University Park Campus (PA) (w)
Peru State College (NE) (w)
Pfeiffer University (NC) (w)
Philadelphia Biblical University (PA) (w)
Philadelphia University (PA) (w)
Piedmont College (GA) (w)
Pikeville College (KY) (w)
Pine Manor College (MA) (w)
Pittsburg State University (KS) (w)
Pitzer College (CA) (w)
Plymouth State University (NH) (w)
Point Loma Nazarene University (CA) (w)
Point Park University (PA) (w)
Polytechnic University, Brooklyn Campus (NY) (w)
Pomona College (CA) (w)
Portland State University (OR) (w)
Prairie View A&M University (TX) (w)
Presbyterian College (SC) (w)
Presentation College (SD) (w)
Princeton University (NJ) (w)
Providence College (RI) (w)
Purdue University (IN) (w)
Purdue University North Central (IN) (w)
Queens College of the City University of New York (NY) (w)
Queens University of Charlotte (NC) (w)
Quincy University (IL) (w)
Quinnipiac University (CT) (w)
Radford University (VA) (w)
Ramapo College of New Jersey (NJ) (w)
Randolph-Macon College (VA) (w)
Randolph-Macon Woman's College (VA) (w)
Regis College (MA) (w)
Regis University (CO) (w)
Rensselaer Polytechnic Institute (NY) (w)
Rhode Island College (RI) (w)
Rhodes College (TN) (w)
The Richard Stockton College of New Jersey (NJ) (w)
Rider University (NJ) (w)
Ripon College (WI) (w)
Rivier College (NH) (w)
Roanoke College (VA) (w)
Robert Morris College (IL) (w)
Robert Morris University (PA) (w)
Rochester Institute of Technology (NY) (w)
Rockford College (IL) (w)
Roger Williams University (RI) (w)
Rollins College (FL) (w)

Rose-Hulman Institute of Technology (IN) (w)
Rosemont College (PA) (w)
Rowan University (NJ) (w)
Russell Sage College (NY) (w)
Rutgers, The State University of New Jersey, Camden (NJ) (w)
Rutgers, The State University of New Jersey, Newark (NJ) (w)
Rutgers, The State University of New Jersey, New Brunswick/Piscataway (NJ) (w)
Sacred Heart University (CT) (w)
Saginaw Valley State University (MI) (w)
St. Ambrose University (IA) (w)
St. Andrews Presbyterian College (NC) (w)
Saint Anselm College (NH) (w)
Saint Augustine's College (NC) (w)
St. Bonaventure University (NY) (w)
St. Cloud State University (MN) (w)
St. Edward's University (TX) (w)
St. Francis College (NY) (w)
Saint Francis University (PA) (w)
St. Gregory's University (OK) (w)
St. John Fisher College (NY) (w)
St. John's University (NY) (w)
Saint Joseph College (CT) (w)
Saint Joseph's College (IN) (w)
Saint Joseph's College of Maine (ME) (w)
St. Joseph's College, Suffolk Campus (NY) (w)
Saint Joseph's University (PA) (w)
St. Lawrence University (NY) (w)
Saint Leo University (FL) (w)
Saint Louis University (MO) (w)
Saint Martin's College (WA) (w)
Saint Mary's College (IN) (w)
Saint Mary's College of California (CA) (w)
St. Mary's University of San Antonio (TX) (w)
Saint Michael's College (VT) (w)
St. Norbert College (WI) (w)
St. Olaf College (MN) (w)
Saint Paul's College (VA) (w)
Saint Peter's College (NJ) (w)
St. Thomas Aquinas College (NY) (w)
Saint Vincent College (PA) (w)
Saint Xavier University (IL) (w)
Salem International University (WV) (w)
Salem State College (MA) (w)
Salisbury University (MD) (w)
Salve Regina University (RI) (w)
Samford University (AL) (w)
Sam Houston State University (TX) (w)
San Diego State University (CA) (w)
San Francisco State University (CA) (w)
San Jose State University (CA) (w)
Santa Clara University (CA) (w)
Savannah College of Art and Design (GA) (w)
Savannah State University (GA) (w)
Schreiner University (TX) (w)
Seattle University (WA) (w)
Seton Hall University (NJ) (w)
Seton Hill University (PA) (w)
Shawnee State University (OH) (w)
Shaw University (NC) (w)
Shenandoah University (VA) (w)
Shepherd University (WV) (w)
Shippensburg University of Pennsylvania (PA) (w)
Shorter College (GA) (w)
Siena College (NY) (w)
Siena Heights University (MI) (w)
Simmons College (MA) (w)
Simpson College (IA) (w)

Si Tanka Huron University (SD) (w)
Skidmore College (NY) (w)
Slippery Rock University of Pennsylvania (PA) (w)
Smith College (MA) (w)
Sonoma State University (CA) (w)
South Carolina State University (SC) (w)
South Dakota State University (SD) (w)
Southeastern Louisiana University (LA) (w)
Southeastern Oklahoma State University (OK) (w)
Southeast Missouri State University (MO) (w)
Southern Arkansas University–Magnolia (AR) (w)
Southern Connecticut State University (CT) (w)
Southern Illinois University Carbondale (IL) (w)
Southern Illinois University Edwardsville (IL) (w)
Southern Nazarene University (OK) (w)
Southern New Hampshire University (NH) (w)
Southern Oregon University (OR) (w)
Southern University and Agricultural and Mechanical College (LA) (w)
Southern Utah University (UT) (w)
Southern Vermont College (VT) (w)
Southern Virginia University (VA) (w)
Southern Wesleyan University (SC) (w)
Southwest Baptist University (MO) (w)
Southwestern College (KS) (w)
Southwestern Oklahoma State University (OK) (w)
Southwest Minnesota State University (MN) (w)
Southwest Missouri State University (MO) (w)
Spalding University (KY) (w)
Spring Arbor University (MI) (w)
Springfield College (MA) (w)
Spring Hill College (AL) (w)
Stanford University (CA) (w)
State University of New York at Binghamton (NY) (w)
State University of New York at New Paltz (NY) (w)
State University of New York at Oswego (NY) (w)
State University of New York at Plattsburgh (NY) (w)
State University of New York College at Brockport (NY) (w)
State University of New York College at Cortland (NY) (w)
State University of New York College at Fredonia (NY) (w)
State University of New York College at Geneseo (NY) (w)
State University of New York College at Old Westbury (NY) (w)
State University of New York College at Oneonta (NY) (w)
State University of New York College at Potsdam (NY) (w)
State University of New York College of Technology at Delhi (NY) (w)
State University of New York Institute of Technology (NY) (w)
State University of New York Maritime College (NY) (w)
State University of West Georgia (GA) (w)
Stephen F. Austin State University (TX) (w)
Sterling College (KS) (w)

Stetson University (FL) (w)
Stillman College (AL) (w)
Stonehill College (MA) (w)
Stony Brook University, State University of New York (NY) (w)
Suffolk University (MA) (w)
Sul Ross State University (TX) (w)
Susquehanna University (PA) (w)
Swarthmore College (PA) (w)
Syracuse University (NY) (w)
Tabor College (KS) (w)
Tarleton State University (TX) (w)
Taylor University (IN) (w)
Teikyo Post University (CT) (w)
Temple University (PA) (w)
Tennessee State University (TN) (w)
Tennessee Technological University (TN) (w)
Tennessee Wesleyan College (TN) (w)
Texas A&M University (TX) (w)
Texas A&M University–Corpus Christi (TX) (w)
Texas A&M University–Kingsville (TX) (w)
Texas College (TX) (w)
Texas Lutheran University (TX) (w)
Texas Southern University (TX) (w)
Texas State University-San Marcos (TX) (w)
Texas Tech University (TX) (w)
Texas Wesleyan University (TX) (w)
Texas Woman's University (TX) (w)
Thiel College (PA) (w)
Thomas College (ME) (w)
Thomas More College (KY) (w)
Thomas University (GA) (w)
Tiffin University (OH) (w)
Towson University (MD) (w)
Transylvania University (KY) (w)
Trevecca Nazarene University (TN) (w)
Trinity Christian College (IL) (w)
Trinity College (CT) (w)
Trinity College (DC) (w)
Trinity International University (IL) (w)
Trinity University (TX) (w)
Tri-State University (IN) (w)
Troy State University (AL) (w)
Truman State University (MO) (w)
Tufts University (MA) (w)
Tusculum College (TN) (w)
Tuskegee University (AL) (w)
Union College (KY) (w)
Union College (NY) (w)
Union University (TN) (w)
United States Coast Guard Academy (CT) (w)
United States Merchant Marine Academy (NY) (w)
United States Military Academy (NY) (w)
University at Albany, State University of New York (NY) (w)
University at Buffalo, The State University of New York (NY) (w)
The University of Akron (OH) (w)
The University of Alabama (AL) (w)
The University of Alabama at Birmingham (AL) (w)
The University of Alabama in Huntsville (AL) (w)
The University of Arizona (AZ) (w)
University of Arkansas (AR) (w)
University of Arkansas at Monticello (AR) (w)
University of Arkansas at Pine Bluff (AR) (w)
University of Bridgeport (CT) (w)
University of California, Berkeley (CA) (w)
University of California, Davis (CA) (w)

University of California, Los Angeles (CA) (w)
University of California, Riverside (CA) (w)
University of California, San Diego (CA) (w)
University of California, Santa Barbara (CA) (w)
University of Central Arkansas (AR) (w)
University of Central Florida (FL) (w)
University of Central Oklahoma (OK) (w)
University of Charleston (WV) (w)
University of Chicago (IL) (w)
University of Colorado at Colorado Springs (CO) (w)
University of Connecticut (CT) (w)
University of Dallas (TX) (w)
University of Dayton (OH) (w)
University of Delaware (DE) (w)
University of Detroit Mercy (MI) (w)
University of Dubuque (IA) (w)
University of Evansville (IN) (w)
The University of Findlay (OH) (w)
University of Florida (FL) (w)
University of Georgia (GA) (w)
University of Hartford (CT) (w)
University of Hawaii at Hilo (HI) (w)
University of Hawaii at Manoa (HI) (w)
University of Houston (TX) (w)
University of Illinois at Chicago (IL) (w)
University of Illinois at Springfield (IL) (w)
University of Illinois at Urbana–Champaign (IL) (w)
University of Indianapolis (IN) (w)
The University of Iowa (IA) (w)
University of Kansas (KS) (w)
University of Kentucky (KY) (w)
University of La Verne (CA) (w)
University of Louisiana at Lafayette (LA) (w)
University of Louisiana at Monroe (LA) (w)
University of Louisville (KY) (w)
University of Maine (ME) (w)
University of Maine at Farmington (ME) (w)
University of Maine at Presque Isle (ME) (w)
University of Mary (ND) (w)
University of Mary Hardin-Baylor (TX) (w)
University of Maryland, Baltimore County (MD) (w)
University of Maryland, College Park (MD) (w)
University of Maryland Eastern Shore (MD) (w)
University of Massachusetts Amherst (MA) (w)
University of Massachusetts Boston (MA) (w)
University of Massachusetts Dartmouth (MA) (w)
University of Massachusetts Lowell (MA) (w)
University of Michigan (MI) (w)
University of Minnesota, Crookston (MN) (w)
University of Minnesota, Duluth (MN) (w)
University of Minnesota, Morris (MN) (w)
University of Minnesota, Twin Cities Campus (MN) (w)
University of Mississippi (MS) (w)
University of Missouri–Columbia (MO) (w)
University of Missouri–Kansas City (MO) (w)
University of Missouri–Rolla (MO) (w)
University of Missouri–St. Louis (MO) (w)
University of Mobile (AL) (w)
University of Nebraska at Kearney (NE) (w)
University of Nebraska at Omaha (NE) (w)
University of Nebraska–Lincoln (NE) (w)
University of Nevada, Las Vegas (NV) (w)

University of Nevada, Reno (NV) (w)
University of New England (ME) (w)
University of New Haven (CT) (w)
University of New Mexico (NM) (w)
University of North Alabama (AL) (w)
The University of North Carolina at Chapel Hill (NC) (w)
The University of North Carolina at Charlotte (NC) (w)
The University of North Carolina at Greensboro (NC) (w)
The University of North Carolina at Pembroke (NC) (w)
The University of North Carolina at Wilmington (NC) (w)
University of North Dakota (ND) (w)
University of Northern Colorado (CO) (w)
University of Northern Iowa (IA) (w)
University of North Florida (FL) (w)
University of North Texas (TX) (w)
University of Notre Dame (IN) (w)
University of Oklahoma (OK) (w)
University of Oregon (OR) (w)
University of Pennsylvania (PA) (w)
University of Pittsburgh (PA) (w)
University of Pittsburgh at Bradford (PA) (w)
University of Pittsburgh at Greensburg (PA) (w)
University of Puerto Rico at Humacao (PR) (w)
University of Puerto Rico, Cayey University College (PR) (w)
University of Puerto Rico, Mayagüez Campus (PR) (w)
University of Puerto Rico, Río Piedras (PR) (w)
University of Puget Sound (WA) (w)
University of Redlands (CA) (w)
University of Rhode Island (RI) (w)
University of Rio Grande (OH) (w)
University of Rochester (NY) (w)
University of St. Francis (IL) (w)
University of Saint Francis (IN) (w)
University of Saint Mary (KS) (w)
University of St. Thomas (MN) (w)
University of San Diego (CA) (w)
University of Science and Arts of Oklahoma (OK) (w)
The University of Scranton (PA) (w)
University of Sioux Falls (SD) (w)
University of South Carolina (SC) (w)
University of South Carolina Aiken (SC) (w)
University of South Carolina Spartanburg (SC) (w)
The University of South Dakota (SD) (w)
University of Southern Indiana (IN) (w)
University of Southern Maine (ME) (w)
University of Southern Mississippi (MS) (w)
University of South Florida (FL) (w)
The University of Tampa (FL) (w)
The University of Tennessee (TN) (w)
The University of Tennessee at Chattanooga (TN) (w)
The University of Tennessee at Martin (TN) (w)
The University of Texas at Arlington (TX) (w)
The University of Texas at Austin (TX) (w)
The University of Texas at Dallas (TX) (w)
The University of Texas at El Paso (TX) (w)
The University of Texas at San Antonio (TX) (w)
The University of Texas of the Permian Basin (TX) (w)
University of the Incarnate Word (TX) (w)

University of the Ozarks (AR) (w)
University of the Pacific (CA) (w)
University of the Sciences in Philadelphia (PA) (w)
University of the South (TN) (w)
University of Toledo (OH) (w)
University of Utah (UT) (w)
University of Vermont (VT) (w)
University of Virginia (VA) (w)
University of Washington (WA) (w)
The University of West Alabama (AL) (w)
University of West Florida (FL) (w)
University of Wisconsin–Eau Claire (WI) (w)
University of Wisconsin–Green Bay (WI) (w)
University of Wisconsin–La Crosse (WI) (w)
University of Wisconsin–Madison (WI) (w)
University of Wisconsin–Oshkosh (WI) (w)
University of Wisconsin–Parkside (WI) (w)
University of Wisconsin–Platteville (WI) (w)
University of Wisconsin–River Falls (WI) (w)
University of Wisconsin–Stevens Point (WI) (w)
University of Wisconsin–Stout (WI) (w)
University of Wisconsin–Superior (WI) (w)
University of Wisconsin–Whitewater (WI) (w)
Upper Iowa University (IA) (w)
Urbana University (OH) (w)
Ursinus College (PA) (w)
Ursuline College (OH) (w)
Utah State University (UT) (w)
Utica College (NY) (w)
Valdosta State University (GA) (w)
Valley City State University (ND) (w)
Valparaiso University (IN) (w)
Vanguard University of Southern California (CA) (w)
Villa Julie College (MD) (w)
Villanova University (PA) (w)
Virginia Intermont College (VA) (w)
Virginia Polytechnic Institute and State University (VA) (w)
Virginia State University (VA) (w)
Virginia Union University (VA) (w)
Virginia Wesleyan College (VA) (w)
Viterbo University (WI) (w)
Voorhees College (SC) (w)
Wagner College (NY) (w)
Waldorf College (IA) (w)
Walsh University (OH) (w)
Warner Southern College (FL) (w)
Wartburg College (IA) (w)
Washburn University (KS) (w)
Washington & Jefferson College (PA) (w)
Washington College (MD) (w)
Washington University in St. Louis (MO) (w)
Wayne State College (NE) (w)
Wayne State University (MI) (w)
Webber International University (FL) (w)
Webster University (MO) (w)
Wells College (NY) (w)
Wentworth Institute of Technology (MA) (w)
Wesleyan College (GA) (w)
Wesleyan University (CT) (w)
Wesley College (DE) (w)
West Chester University of Pennsylvania (PA) (w)
Western Baptist College (OR) (w)
Western Connecticut State University (CT) (w)
Western Illinois University (IL) (w)
Western Kentucky University (KY) (w)
Western Michigan University (MI) (w)
Western New England College (MA) (w)
Western New Mexico University (NM) (w)

Western Oregon University (OR) (w)
Western Washington University (WA) (w)
Westfield State College (MA) (w)
West Liberty State College (WV) (w)
Westminster College (MO) (w)
Westminster College (PA) (w)
West Virginia State College (WV) (w)
West Virginia University Institute of
    Technology (WV) (w)
West Virginia Wesleyan College (WV) (w)
Wheaton College (IL) (w)
Wheaton College (MA) (w)
Wheeling Jesuit University (WV) (w)
Wheelock College (MA) (w)
Whittier College (CA) (w)
Whitworth College (WA) (w)
Wichita State University (KS) (w)
Widener University (PA) (w)
Wilkes University (PA) (w)
Willamette University (OR) (w)
William Carey College (MS) (w)
William Jewell College (MO) (w)
William Paterson University of New Jersey
    (NJ) (w)
William Penn University (IA) (w)
Williams Baptist College (AR) (w)
Williams College (MA) (w)
William Woods University (MO) (w)
Wilmington College (DE) (w)
Wilmington College (OH) (w)
Wilson College (PA) (w)
Wingate University (NC) (w)
Winona State University (MN) (w)
Winston-Salem State University (NC) (w)
Winthrop University (SC) (w)
Wisconsin Lutheran College (WI) (w)
Wittenberg University (OH) (w)
Worcester Polytechnic Institute (MA) (w)
Worcester State College (MA) (w)
Wright State University (OH) (w)
Yale University (CT) (w)
York College (NE) (w)
York College of Pennsylvania (PA) (w)
York College of the City University of New
    York (NY)(w)

Swimming

Adelphi University (NY) (m/w)
Agnes Scott College (GA) (w)
Albertson College of Idaho (ID) (m/w)
Albion College (MI) (m/w)
Albright College (PA) (m/w)
Alfred University (NY) (m/w)
Allegheny College (PA) (m/w)
Alma College (MI) (m/w)
American University (DC) (m/w)
Amherst College (MA) (m/w)
Arcadia University (PA) (m/w)
Arizona State University (AZ) (m/w)
Asbury College (KY) (m/w)
Ashland University (OH) (m/w)
Auburn University (AL) (m/w)
Augsburg College (MN) (m/w)
Augustana College (IL) (m/w)
Austin College (TX) (m/w)
Babson College (MA) (m/w)
Baldwin-Wallace College (OH) (m/w)
Ball State University (IN) (m/w)
Bates College (ME) (m/w)
Beloit College (WI) (m/w)
Benedictine University (IL) (m/w)
Bentley College (MA) (m/w)
Berea College (KY) (m/w)

Bernard M. Baruch College of the City
    University of New York (NY) (m/w)
Bethany College (WV) (m/w)
Biola University (CA) (m/w)
Bloomsburg University of Pennsylvania (PA)
    (m/w)
Boston College (MA) (m/w)
Boston University (MA) (m/w)
Bowdoin College (ME) (m/w)
Bowling Green State University (OH) (w)
Brandeis University (MA) (m/w)
Bridgewater State College (MA) (m/w)
Brigham Young University (UT) (m/w)
Brown University (RI) (m/w)
Bryn Mawr College (PA) (w)
Bucknell University (PA) (m/w)
Buena Vista University (IA) (m/w)
Buffalo State College, State University of
    New York (NY) (m/w)
Butler University (IN) (m/w)
California Baptist University (CA) (m/w)
California Institute of Technology (CA)
    (m/w)
California Polytechnic State University, San
    Luis Obispo (CA) (m/w)
California State University, Bakersfield (CA)
    (m/w)
California State University, Fresno (CA) (w)
California State University, Hayward (CA)
    (w)
California State University, Northridge (CA)
    (m/w)
California University of Pennsylvania (PA)
    (w)
Calvin College (MI) (m/w)
Campbell University (NC) (w)
Canisius College (NY) (m/w)
Carleton College (MN) (m/w)
Carnegie Mellon University (PA) (m/w)
Carthage College (WI) (m/w)
Case Western Reserve University (OH) (m/w)
Catawba College (NC) (w)
The Catholic University of America (DC)
    (m/w)
Centenary College of Louisiana (LA) (m/w)
Central Connecticut State University (CT)
    (w)
Central Washington University (WA) (m/w)
Centre College (KY) (m/w)
Chapman University (CA) (m/w)
Chatham College (PA) (w)
Claremont McKenna College (CA) (m/w)
Clarion University of Pennsylvania (PA)
    (m/w)
Clarkson University (NY) (m/w)
Clark University (MA) (m/w)
Clemson University (SC) (m/w)
Cleveland State University (OH) (m/w)
Coe College (IA) (m/w)
Colby College (ME) (m/w)
Colby-Sawyer College (NH) (m/w)
Colgate University (NY) (m/w)
College Misericordia (PA) (m/w)
College of Charleston (SC) (m/w)
College of Mount Saint Vincent (NY) (w)
The College of New Jersey (NJ) (m/w)
The College of New Rochelle (NY) (w)
College of Notre Dame of Maryland (MD)
    (w)
College of Saint Benedict (MN) (w)
College of St. Catherine (MN) (w)
College of Saint Elizabeth (NJ) (w)
The College of Saint Rose (NY) (m/w)
College of Staten Island of the City University
    of New York (NY) (m/w)

College of the Holy Cross (MA) (m/w)
The College of William and Mary (VA)
    (m/w)
The College of Wooster (OH) (m/w)
The Colorado College (CO) (m/w)
Colorado School of Mines (CO) (m/w)
Colorado State University (CO) (w)
Columbia College (NY) (m/w)
Concordia College (MN) (w)
Connecticut College (CT) (m/w)
Cornell University (NY) (m/w)
Cumberland College (KY) (m/w)
Dartmouth College (NH) (m/w)
Davidson College (NC) (m/w)
Delta State University (MS) (m/w)
Denison University (OH) (m/w)
DePauw University (IN) (m/w)
Dickinson College (PA) (m/w)
Drew University (NJ) (m/w)
Drexel University (PA) (m/w)
Drury University (MO) (m/w)
Duke University (NC) (m/w)
Duquesne University (PA) (m/w)
East Carolina University (NC) (m/w)
Eastern Connecticut State University (CT)
    (w)
Eastern Illinois University (IL) (m/w)
Eastern Michigan University (MI) (m/w)
East Stroudsburg University of Pennsylvania
    (PA) (w)
Edinboro University of Pennsylvania (PA)
    (m/w)
Elizabethtown College (PA) (m/w)
Elms College (MA) (m/w)
Emory University (GA) (m/w)
Eureka College (IL) (m/w)
Fairfield University (CT) (m/w)
Fairleigh Dickinson University, College at
    Florham (NJ) (m/w)
Fairmont State University (WV) (m/w)
Florida Agricultural and Mechanical
    University (FL) (m/w)
Florida Atlantic University (FL) (m/w)
Florida International University (FL) (w)
Florida Southern College (FL) (m/w)
Florida State University (FL) (m/w)
Fordham University (NY) (m/w)
Franklin and Marshall College (PA) (m/w)
Frostburg State University (MD) (m/w)
Gallaudet University (DC) (m/w)
Gannon University (PA) (m/w)
Gardner-Webb University (NC) (w)
George Mason University (VA) (m/w)
Georgetown University (DC) (m/w)
The George Washington University (DC)
    (m/w)
Georgia Institute of Technology (GA) (m/w)
Georgia Southern University (GA) (w)
Gettysburg College (PA) (m/w)
Gordon College (MA) (m/w)
Goucher College (MD) (m/w)
Grand Valley State University (MI) (m/w)
Greensboro College (NC) (w)
Grinnell College (IA) (m/w)
Grove City College (PA) (m/w)
Gustavus Adolphus College (MN) (m/w)
Hamilton College (NY) (m/w)
Hamline University (MN) (m/w)
Hartwick College (NY) (m/w)
Harvard University (MA) (m/w)
Henderson State University (AR) (m/w)
Hendrix College (AR) (m/w)
Hillsdale College (MI) (m/w)
Hiram College (OH) (m/w)
Hobart and William Smith Colleges (NY) (w)

Hollins University (VA) (w)
Hood College (MD) (m/w)
Hope College (MI) (m/w)
Howard University (DC) (m/w)
Hunter College of the City University of New
    York (NY) (w)
Illinois Institute of Technology (IL) (m/w)
Illinois State University (IL) (w)
Illinois Wesleyan University (IL) (m/w)
Indiana University Bloomington (IN) (m/w)
Indiana University of Pennsylvania (PA)
    (m/w)
Indiana University–Purdue University
    Indianapolis (IN) (m/w)
Iona College (NY) (m/w)
Iowa State University of Science and
    Technology (IA) (w)
Ithaca College (NY) (m/w)
James Madison University (VA) (m/w)
John Brown University (AR) (m/w)
John Carroll University (OH) (m/w)
John Jay College of Criminal Justice of the
    City University of New York (NY) (w)
The Johns Hopkins University (MD) (m/w)
Juniata College (PA) (w)
Kalamazoo College (MI) (m/w)
Kean University (NJ) (w)
Keene State College (NH) (m/w)
Kenyon College (OH) (m/w)
King's College (PA) (m/w)
Knox College (IL) (m/w)
Kutztown University of Pennsylvania (PA)
    (m/w)
Lafayette College (PA) (m/w)
LaGrange College (GA) (m/w)
Lake Forest College (IL) (m/w)
La Salle University (PA) (m/w)
Lawrence University (WI) (m/w)
Lebanon Valley College (PA) (m/w)
Lehigh University (PA) (m/w)
Lehman College of the City University of
    New York (NY) (m/w)
Le Moyne College (NY) (m/w)
Lewis & Clark College (OR) (m/w)
Lewis University (IL) (m/w)
Limestone College (SC) (w)
Lindenwood University (MO) (m/w)
Linfield College (OR) (m/w)
Lock Haven University of Pennsylvania (PA)
    (w)
Long Island University, C.W. Post Campus
    (NY) (w)
Loras College (IA) (m/w)
Louisiana State University and Agricultural
    and Mechanical College (LA) (m/w)
Loyola College in Maryland (MD) (m/w)
Loyola Marymount University (CA) (w)
Luther College (IA) (m/w)
Lycoming College (PA) (m/w)
Macalester College (MN) (m/w)
Manhattan College (NY) (w)
Mansfield University of Pennsylvania (PA)
    (w)
Marist College (NY) (m/w)
Marshall University (WV) (w)
Mary Baldwin College (VA) (w)
Marymount University (VA) (w)
University of Mary Washington (VA) (m/w)
Massachusetts Institute of Technology (MA)
    (m/w)
McDaniel College (MD) (m/w)
McMurry University (TX) (m/w)
Metropolitan State College of Denver (CO)
    (m/w)
Miami University (OH) (m/w)

Michigan State University (MI) (m/w)
Middlebury College (VT) (m/w)
Millersville University of Pennsylvania (PA)
    (w)
Millikin University (IL) (m/w)
Mills College (CA) (w)
Minnesota State University Mankato (MN)
    (m/w)
Minnesota State University Moorhead (MN)
    (w)
Monmouth College (IL) (m/w)
Montclair State University (NJ) (m/w)
Morningside College (IA) (m/w)
Mount Holyoke College (MA) (w)
Mount Saint Mary College (NY) (m/w)
Mount Union College (OH) (m/w)
Nazareth College of Rochester (NY) (m/w)
New Jersey Institute of Technology (NJ)
    (m/w)
New Mexico State University (NM) (w)
New York University (NY) (m/w)
Niagara University (NY) (m/w)
North Carolina Agricultural and Technical
    State University (NC) (w)
North Carolina State University (NC) (m/w)
North Central College (IL) (m/w)
Northeastern University (MA) (w)
Northern Arizona University (AZ) (w)
Northern Michigan University (MI) (w)
Northwestern University (IL) (m/w)
Norwich University (VT) (m/w)
Oakland University (MI) (m/w)
Oberlin College (OH) (m/w)
Occidental College (CA) (m/w)
Ohio Northern University (OH) (m/w)
The Ohio State University (OH) (m/w)
Ohio University (OH) (m/w)
Ohio Wesleyan University (OH) (m/w)
Old Dominion University (VA) (m/w)
Olivet College (MI) (m/w)
Oregon State University (OR) (w)
Ouachita Baptist University (AR) (m/w)
Pace University (NY) (m/w)
Pacific Lutheran University (WA) (m/w)
The Pennsylvania State University Altoona
    College (PA) (m/w)
The Pennsylvania State University at Erie,
    The Behrend College (PA) (m/w)
The Pennsylvania State University University
    Park Campus (PA) (m/w)
Pepperdine University (CA) (w)
Pfeiffer University (NC) (w)
Pitzer College (CA) (m/w)
Plymouth State University (NH) (w)
Pomona College (CA) (m/w)
Princeton University (NJ) (m/w)
Principia College (IL) (m/w)
Providence College (RI) (m/w)
Purdue University (IN) (m/w)
Queens College of the City University of
    New York (NY) (m/w)
Radford University (VA) (w)
Randolph-Macon College (VA) (m/w)
Randolph-Macon Woman's College (VA) (w)
Regis College (MA) (w)
Rensselaer Polytechnic Institute (NY) (m/w)
Rhodes College (TN) (m/w)
Rice University (TX) (w)
Rider University (NJ) (m/w)
Ripon College (WI) (m/w)
Rochester Institute of Technology (NY)
    (m/w)
Rollins College (FL) (m/w)
Rose-Hulman Institute of Technology (IN)
    (m/w)

Rowan University (NJ) (m/w)
Rutgers, The State University of New Jersey,
    New Brunswick/Piscataway (NJ) (m/w)
Sacred Heart University (CT) (w)
St. Bonaventure University (NY) (w)
St. Cloud State University (MN) (m)
St. Francis College (NY) (w)
Saint Francis University (PA) (w)
Saint John's University (MN) (m)
St. John's University (NY) (m/w)
Saint Joseph College (CT) (w)
St. Joseph's College, Suffolk Campus (NY)
    (w)
St. Lawrence University (NY) (m/w)
Saint Louis University (MO) (m/w)
Saint Mary's College (IN) (w)
St. Mary's College of Maryland (MD) (m/w)
Saint Mary's University of Minnesota (MN)
    (m/w)
Saint Michael's College (VT) (m/w)
St. Norbert College (WI) (w)
St. Olaf College (MN) (m/w)
Saint Peter's College (NJ) (m/w)
Salem International University (WV) (m/w)
Salisbury University (MD) (m/w)
San Diego State University (CA) (w)
San Francisco State University (CA) (m/w)
San Jose State University (CA) (w)
Savannah College of Art and Design (GA)
    (m/w)
Seattle University (WA) (m/w)
Seton Hall University (NJ) (m/w)
Shippensburg University of Pennsylvania
    (PA) (m/w)
Siena College (NY) (w)
Simmons College (MA) (w)
Simpson College (IA) (w)
Skidmore College (NY) (m/w)
Slippery Rock University of Pennsylvania
    (PA) (m/w)
Smith College (MA) (w)
South Dakota State University (SD) (m/w)
Southern Connecticut State University (CT)
    (m/w)
Southern Illinois University Carbondale (IL)
    (m/w)
Southern Methodist University (TX) (m/w)
Southwestern University (TX) (m/w)
Southwest Missouri State University (MO)
    (m/w)
Springfield College (MA) (m/w)
Spring Hill College (AL) (m/w)
Stanford University (CA) (m/w)
State University of New York at Binghamton
    (NY) (m/w)
State University of New York at New Paltz
    (NY) (m/w)
State University of New York at Oswego
    (NY) (m/w)
State University of New York College at
    Brockport (NY) (m/w)
State University of New York College at
    Cortland (NY) (m/w)
State University of New York College at
    Fredonia (NY) (m/w)
State University of New York College at
    Geneseo (NY) (m/w)
State University of New York College at Old
    Westbury (NY) (m/w)
State University of New York College at
    Oneonta (NY) (m/w)
State University of New York College at
    Potsdam (NY) (m/w)
State University of New York College of
    Technology at Delhi (NY) (m/w)

State University of New York Maritime College (NY) (m/w)
Stephens College (MO) (w)
Stevens Institute of Technology (NJ) (m/w)
Stony Brook University, State University of New York (NY) (m/w)
Susquehanna University (PA) (m/w)
Swarthmore College (PA) (m/w)
Sweet Briar College (VA) (w)
Syracuse University (NY) (m/w)
Texas A&M University (TX) (m/w)
Texas Christian University (TX) (m/w)
Towson University (MD) (m/w)
Transylvania University (KY) (m/w)
Trinity College (CT) (m/w)
Trinity College (DC) (w)
Trinity University (TX) (m/w)
Truman State University (MO) (m/w)
Tufts University (MA) (m/w)
Union College (NY) (m/w)
United States Air Force Academy (CO) (m/w)
United States Coast Guard Academy (CT) (m/w)
United States Merchant Marine Academy (NY) (m/w)
United States Military Academy (NY) (m/w)
United States Naval Academy (MD) (m/w)
University at Buffalo, The State University of New York (NY) (m/w)
The University of Akron (OH) (w)
The University of Alabama (AL) (m/w)
The University of Arizona (AZ) (m/w)
University of Arkansas (AR) (w)
University of Arkansas at Little Rock (AR) (w)
University of California, Berkeley (CA) (m/w)
University of California, Davis (CA) (m/w)
University of California, Irvine (CA) (m/w)
University of California, Los Angeles (CA) (w)
University of California, San Diego (CA) (m/w)
University of California, Santa Barbara (CA) (m/w)
University of California, Santa Cruz (CA) (m/w)
University of Charleston (WV) (m/w)
University of Chicago (IL) (m/w)
University of Cincinnati (OH) (m/w)
University of Connecticut (CT) (m/w)
University of Delaware (DE) (m/w)
University of Denver (CO) (m/w)
University of Evansville (IN) (m/w)
The University of Findlay (OH) (m/w)
University of Florida (FL) (m/w)
University of Georgia (GA) (m/w)
University of Hawaii at Manoa (HI) (m/w)
University of Houston (TX) (w)
University of Illinois at Chicago (IL) (m/w)
University of Illinois at Urbana–Champaign (IL) (w)
University of Indianapolis (IN) (m/w)
The University of Iowa (IA) (m/w)
University of Kansas (KS) (w)
University of Kentucky (KY) (m/w)
University of La Verne (CA) (m/w)
University of Louisiana at Monroe (LA) (m/w)
University of Louisville (KY) (m/w)
University of Maine (ME) (m/w)
University of Maryland, Baltimore County (MD) (m/w)
University of Maryland, College Park (MD) (m/w)

University of Massachusetts Amherst (MA) (m/w)
University of Massachusetts Dartmouth (MA) (m/w)
University of Miami (FL) (m/w)
University of Michigan (MI) (m/w)
University of Minnesota, Twin Cities Campus (MN) (m/w)
University of Missouri–Columbia (MO) (m/w)
University of Missouri–Rolla (MO) (m)
University of Nebraska at Kearney (NE) (w)
University of Nebraska at Omaha (NE) (w)
University of Nebraska–Lincoln (NE) (w)
University of Nevada, Las Vegas (NV) (m/w)
University of Nevada, Reno (NV) (w)
University of New Hampshire (NH) (m/w)
University of New Mexico (NM) (w)
The University of North Carolina at Chapel Hill (NC) (m/w)
The University of North Carolina at Wilmington (NC) (m/w)
University of North Dakota (ND) (m/w)
University of Northern Colorado (CO) (w)
University of Northern Iowa (IA) (m/w)
University of North Florida (FL) (w)
University of North Texas (TX) (w)
University of Notre Dame (IN) (m/w)
University of Pennsylvania (PA) (m/w)
University of Pittsburgh (PA) (m/w)
University of Puerto Rico at Bayamón (PR) (m)
University of Puerto Rico at Humacao (PR) (m/w)
University of Puerto Rico, Mayagüez Campus (PR) (m/w)
University of Puget Sound (WA) (m/w)
University of Redlands (CA) (m/w)
University of Rhode Island (RI) (m/w)
University of Richmond (VA) (w)
University of Rochester (NY) (m/w)
University of St. Thomas (MN) (m/w)
University of San Diego (CA) (w)
The University of Scranton (PA) (m/w)
University of South Carolina (SC) (m/w)
The University of South Dakota (SD) (m/w)
University of Southern California (CA) (m/w)
The University of Tampa (FL) (m/w)
The University of Tennessee (TN) (m/w)
The University of Texas at Austin (TX) (m/w)
The University of Texas of the Permian Basin (TX) (m/w)
University of the Incarnate Word (TX) (m/w)
University of the Pacific (CA) (m/w)
University of the South (TN) (m/w)
University of Toledo (OH) (w)
University of Utah (UT) (m/w)
University of Vermont (VT) (m/w)
University of Virginia (VA) (m/w)
University of Washington (WA) (m/w)
University of Wisconsin–Eau Claire (WI) (m/w)
University of Wisconsin–Green Bay (WI) (m/w)
University of Wisconsin–La Crosse (WI) (m/w)
University of Wisconsin–Madison (WI) (m/w)
University of Wisconsin–Milwaukee (WI) (m/w)
University of Wisconsin–Oshkosh (WI) (m/w)
University of Wisconsin–River Falls (WI) (m/w)

University of Wisconsin–Stevens Point (WI) (m/w)
University of Wisconsin–Whitewater (WI) (m/w)
University of Wyoming (WY) (m/w)
Ursinus College (PA) (m/w)
Utica College (NY) (m/w)
Valparaiso University (IN) (m/w)
Vassar College (NY) (m/w)
Villanova University (PA) (m/w)
Virginia Military Institute (VA) (m)
Virginia Polytechnic Institute and State University (VA) (m/w)
Wabash College (IN) (m)
Wagner College (NY) (w)
Washington & Jefferson College (PA) (m/w)
Washington and Lee University (VA) (m/w)
Washington College (MD) (m/w)
Washington State University (WA) (w)
Washington University in St. Louis (MO) (m/w)
Wayne State University (MI) (m/w)
Webster University (MO) (m/w)
Wellesley College (MA) (w)
Wells College (NY) (w)
Wesleyan University (CT) (m/w)
West Chester University of Pennsylvania (PA) (m/w)
Western Connecticut State University (CT) (w)
Western Illinois University (IL) (m/w)
Western Kentucky University (KY) (m/w)
Western New England College (MA) (w)
Westfield State College (MA) (w)
Westminster College (PA) (m/w)
West Virginia University (WV) (m/w)
West Virginia Wesleyan College (WV) (m/w)
Wheaton College (IL) (m/w)
Wheaton College (MA) (m/w)
Wheeling Jesuit University (WV) (m/w)
Wheelock College (MA) (w)
Whitman College (WA) (m/w)
Whittier College (CA) (m/w)
Widener University (PA) (m/w)
Willamette University (OR) (m/w)
William Paterson University of New Jersey (NJ) (m/w)
Williams College (MA) (m/w)
Wilmington College (OH) (m/w)
Wingate University (NC) (w)
Wittenberg University (OH) (m/w)
Worcester Polytechnic Institute (MA) (m/w)
Wright State University (OH) (m/w)
Xavier University (OH) (m/w)
Yale University (CT) (m/w)
York College of Pennsylvania (PA) (m/w)
York College of the City University of New York (NY) (m/w)
Youngstown State University (OH)(w)

Tennis

Abilene Christian University (TX) (m/w)
Adelphi University (NY) (m/w)
Adrian College (MI) (m/w)
Agnes Scott College (GA) (w)
Alabama Agricultural and Mechanical University (AL) (m/w)
Alabama State University (AL) (m/w)
Albany State University (GA) (w)
Albertson College of Idaho (ID) (w)
Albertus Magnus College (CT) (m/w)
Albion College (MI) (m/w)
Albright College (PA) (m/w)
Alcorn State University (MS) (m/w)

Alfred University (NY) (m/w)
Allegheny College (PA) (m/w)
Allen University (SC) (m/w)
Alliant International University (CA) (m/w)
Alma College (MI) (m/w)
Alvernia College (PA) (m/w)
American International College (MA) (m/w)
American University (DC) (m/w)
Amherst College (MA) (m/w)
Anderson College (SC) (m/w)
Anderson University (IN) (m/w)
Appalachian State University (NC) (m/w)
Aquinas College (MI) (m/w)
Arcadia University (PA) (m/w)
Arizona State University (AZ) (m/w)
Arkansas State University (AR) (w)
Arkansas Tech University (AR) (w)
Armstrong Atlantic State University (GA)
    (m/w)
Asbury College (KY) (m/w)
Ashland University (OH) (w)
Assumption College (MA) (m/w)
Auburn University (AL) (m/w)
Auburn University Montgomery (AL) (m/w)
Augustana College (IL) (m/w)
Augustana College (SD) (m/w)
Augusta State University (GA) (m/w)
Aurora University (IL) (m/w)
Austin College (TX) (m/w)
Austin Peay State University (TN) (m/w)
Averett University (VA) (m/w)
Azusa Pacific University (CA) (m/w)
Babson College (MA) (m/w)
Baker University (KS) (m/w)
Baldwin-Wallace College (OH) (m/w)
Ball State University (IN) (m/w)
Bard College (NY) (m/w)
Barry University (FL) (m/w)
Barton College (NC) (m/w)
Bates College (ME) (m/w)
Baylor University (TX) (m/w)
Belhaven College (MS) (m/w)
Bellarmine University (KY) (m/w)
Belmont Abbey College (NC) (m/w)
Belmont University (TN) (m/w)
Beloit College (WI) (m/w)
Bemidji State University (MN) (w)
Benedict College (SC) (m/w)
Benedictine College (KS) (m/w)
Benedictine University (IL) (w)
Bennett College (NC) (w)
Bentley College (MA) (m/w)
Berea College (KY) (m/w)
Bernard M. Baruch College of the City
    University of New York (NY) (m/w)
Berry College (GA) (m/w)
Bethany College (KS) (m/w)
Bethany College (WV) (m/w)
Bethel College (IN) (m/w)
Bethel College (KS) (m/w)
Bethel College (TN) (m/w)
Bethel University (MN) (m/w)
Bethune-Cookman College (FL) (m/w)
Biola University (CA) (w)
Birmingham-Southern College (AL) (m/w)
Blackburn College (IL) (w)
Bloomsburg University of Pennsylvania (PA)
    (m/w)
Bluefield State College (WV) (m/w)
Blue Mountain College (MS) (w)
Bluffton College (OH) (m/w)
Boise State University (ID) (m/w)
Boston College (MA) (m/w)
Boston University (MA) (m/w)
Bowdoin College (ME) (m/w)

Bowie State University (MD) (w)
Bowling Green State University (OH) (w)
Bradley University (IL) (m/w)
Brandeis University (MA) (m/w)
Brenau University (GA) (w)
Brescia University (KY) (w)
Bridgewater College (VA) (m/w)
Bridgewater State College (MA) (m/w)
Brigham Young University (UT) (m/w)
Brigham Young University–Hawaii (HI) (m)
Brooklyn College of the City University of
    New York (NY) (m/w)
Brown University (RI) (m/w)
Bryant College (RI) (m/w)
Bryn Mawr College (PA) (w)
Bucknell University (PA) (m/w)
Buena Vista University (IA) (m/w)
Butler University (IN) (m/w)
Cabrini College (PA) (m/w)
Caldwell College (NJ) (m/w)
California Institute of Technology (CA)
    (m/w)
California Lutheran University (CA) (m/w)
California Polytechnic State University, San
    Luis Obispo (CA) (m/w)
California State Polytechnic University,
    Pomona (CA) (m/w)
California State University, Bakersfield (CA)
    (w)
California State University, Fresno (CA)
    (m/w)
California State University, Fullerton (CA)
    (w)
California State University, Long Beach (CA)
    (w)
California State University, Los Angeles (CA)
    (m/w)
California State University, Northridge (CA)
    (w)
California State University, Sacramento (CA)
    (m/w)
California State University, San Bernardino
    (CA) (w)
California University of Pennsylvania (PA)
    (w)
Calvin College (MI) (m/w)
Cameron University (OK) (m/w)
Campbellsville University (KY) (m/w)
Campbell University (NC) (m/w)
Capital University (OH) (m/w)
Carleton College (MN) (m/w)
Carlow College (PA) (w)
Carnegie Mellon University (PA) (m/w)
Carroll College (WI) (m/w)
Carson-Newman College (TN) (m/w)
Carthage College (WI) (m/w)
Case Western Reserve University (OH) (m/w)
Castleton State College (VT) (m/w)
Catawba College (NC) (m/w)
The Catholic University of America (DC) (w)
Cedar Crest College (PA) (w)
Cedarville University (OH) (m/w)
Centenary College of Louisiana (LA) (m/w)
Central Christian College of Kansas (KS)
    (m/w)
Central College (IA) (m/w)
Centre College (KY) (m/w)
Chaminade University of Honolulu (HI)
    (m/w)
Chapman University (CA) (m/w)
Charleston Southern University (SC) (m/w)
Chatham College (PA) (w)
Chestnut Hill College (PA) (m/w)
Chicago State University (IL) (m/w)
Christian Brothers University (TN) (m/w)

Christopher Newport University (VA) (m/w)
The Citadel, The Military College of South
    Carolina (SC) (m)
City College of the City University of New
    York (NY) (m/w)
Claremont McKenna College (CA) (m/w)
Clarion University of Pennsylvania (PA) (w)
Clark Atlanta University (GA) (m/w)
Clarke College (IA) (m/w)
Clarkson University (NY) (m/w)
Clark University (MA) (m/w)
Clayton College & State University (GA) (w)
Clemson University (SC) (m/w)
Cleveland State University (OH) (m/w)
Coastal Carolina University (SC) (m/w)
Coe College (IA) (m/w)
Coker College (SC) (m/w)
Colby College (ME) (m/w)
Colby-Sawyer College (NH) (m/w)
Colgate University (NY) (m/w)
College Misericordia (PA) (w)
College of Charleston (SC) (m/w)
College of Mount St. Joseph (OH) (m/w)
College of Mount Saint Vincent (NY) (m/w)
The College of New Jersey (NJ) (m/w)
The College of New Rochelle (NY) (w)
College of Notre Dame of Maryland (MD)
    (w)
College of Saint Benedict (MN) (w)
College of St. Catherine (MN) (w)
College of Saint Elizabeth (NJ) (w)
The College of St. Scholastica (MN) (m/w)
College of Santa Fe (NM) (m/w)
College of Staten Island of the City University
    of New York (NY) (m/w)
College of the Holy Cross (MA) (m/w)
The College of William and Mary (VA)
    (m/w)
The College of Wooster (OH) (m/w)
Colorado Christian University (CO) (m/w)
The Colorado College (CO) (m/w)
Colorado School of Mines (CO) (m)
Colorado State University (CO) (w)
Colorado State University-Pueblo (CO)
    (m/w)
Columbia College (NY) (m/w)
Columbia College (SC) (w)
Columbus State University (GA) (m/w)
Concord College (WV) (m/w)
Concordia College (MN) (m/w)
Concordia College (NY) (m/w)
Concordia University (IL) (m/w)
Concordia University (NE) (m/w)
Concordia University at Austin (TX) (m/w)
Concordia University Wisconsin (WI) (m/w)
Connecticut College (CT) (m/w)
Converse College (SC) (w)
Coppin State University (MD) (m/w)
Cornell College (IA) (m)
Cornell University (NY) (m/w)
Creighton University (NE) (m/w)
Cumberland College (KY) (m/w)
Cumberland University (TN) (m/w)
Curry College (MA) (m/w)
Dallas Baptist University (TX) (m/w)
Dartmouth College (NH) (m/w)
Davidson College (NC) (m/w)
Davis & Elkins College (WV) (m/w)
Defiance College (OH) (m/w)
Delaware State University (DE) (m/w)
Delta State University (MS) (m)
Denison University (OH) (m/w)
DePaul University (IL) (m/w)
DePauw University (IN) (m/w)
DeSales University (PA) (m/w)

Dickinson College (PA) (m/w)
Dillard University (LA) (m/w)
Doane College (NE) (m/w)
Dominican University (IL) (m/w)
Dominican University of California (CA)
(m/w)
Dordt College (IA) (m/w)
Dowling College (NY) (m/w)
Drake University (IA) (m/w)
Drew University (NJ) (m/w)
Drexel University (PA) (m/w)
Drury University (MO) (m/w)
Duke University (NC) (m/w)
Duquesne University (PA) (m/w)
Earlham College (IN) (m/w)
East Carolina University (NC) (m/w)
East Central University (OK) (m/w)
Eastern Illinois University (IL) (m/w)
Eastern Kentucky University (KY) (m/w)
Eastern Mennonite University (VA) (m/w)
Eastern Michigan University (MI) (w)
Eastern Nazarene College (MA) (m)
Eastern New Mexico University (NM) (w)
Eastern University (PA) (m/w)
Eastern Washington University (WA) (m/w)
East Stroudsburg University of Pennsylvania
(PA) (m/w)
East Tennessee State University (TN) (m/w)
Eckerd College (FL) (m/w)
Edgewood College (WI) (w)
Elizabeth City State University (NC) (w)
Elizabethtown College (PA) (m/w)
Elmhurst College (IL) (m/w)
Elmira College (NY) (m/w)
Elon University (NC) (m/w)
Embry-Riddle Aeronautical University (FL)
(m/w)
Emerson College (MA) (m/w)
Emmanuel College (GA) (m/w)
Emmanuel College (MA) (w)
Emory & Henry College (VA) (m/w)
Emory University (GA) (m/w)
Emporia State University (KS) (m/w)
Endicott College (MA) (m/w)
Erskine College (SC) (m/w)
Eureka College (IL) (m/w)
Evangel University (MO) (w)
Fairfield University (CT) (m/w)
Fairleigh Dickinson University, College at
Florham (NJ) (m/w)
Fairmont State University (WV) (m/w)
Fayetteville State University (NC) (w)
Ferris State University (MI) (m/w)
Ferrum College (VA) (m/w)
Fisk University (TN) (m/w)
Flagler College (FL) (m/w)
Florida Agricultural and Mechanical
University (FL) (m/w)
Florida Atlantic University (FL) (m/w)
Florida Gulf Coast University (FL) (m/w)
Florida International University (FL) (w)
Florida Southern College (FL) (m/w)
Florida State University (FL) (m/w)
Fontbonne University (MO) (m/w)
Fordham University (NY) (m/w)
Fort Hays State University (KS) (w)
Fort Valley State University (GA) (m/w)
Francis Marion University (SC) (m/w)
Franklin and Marshall College (PA) (m/w)
Franklin College (IN) (m/w)
Franklin Pierce College (NH) (m/w)
Freed-Hardeman University (TN) (m/w)
Friends University (KS) (m/w)
Frostburg State University (MD) (m/w)
Furman University (SC) (m/w)

Gallaudet University (DC) (w)
Gardner-Webb University (NC) (m/w)
Geneva College (PA) (w)
George Fox University (OR) (m/w)
George Mason University (VA) (m/w)
Georgetown College (KY) (m/w)
Georgetown University (DC) (m/w)
The George Washington University (DC)
(m/w)
Georgia College & State University (GA)
(m/w)
Georgia Institute of Technology (GA) (m/w)
Georgian Court University (NJ) (w)
Georgia Southern University (GA) (m/w)
Georgia Southwestern State University (GA)
(m/w)
Georgia State University (GA) (m/w)
Gettysburg College (PA) (m/w)
Gonzaga University (WA) (m/w)
Gordon College (MA) (m/w)
Goshen College (IN) (m/w)
Goucher College (MD) (m/w)
Grace College (IN) (m/w)
Graceland University (IA) (m/w)
Grambling State University (LA) (m/w)
Grand Canyon University (AZ) (w)
Grand Valley State University (MI) (m/w)
Green Mountain College (VT) (m/w)
Greensboro College (NC) (m/w)
Greenville College (IL) (m/w)
Grinnell College (IA) (m/w)
Grove City College (PA) (m/w)
Guilford College (NC) (w)
Gustavus Adolphus College (MN) (m/w)
Gwynedd-Mercy College (PA) (m)
Hamilton College (NY) (m/w)
Hamline University (MN) (m/w)
Hampden-Sydney College (VA) (m)
Hampton University (VA) (m/w)
Hanover College (IN) (m/w)
Harding University (AR) (m/w)
Hardin-Simmons University (TX) (m/w)
Hartwick College (NY) (m/w)
Harvard University (MA) (m/w)
Hastings College (NE) (m/w)
Haverford College (PA) (m/w)
Hawai'i Pacific University (HI) (m/w)
Heidelberg College (OH) (m/w)
Henderson State University (AR) (w)
Hendrix College (AR) (m/w)
High Point University (NC) (m/w)
Hillsdale College (MI) (m/w)
Hiram College (OH) (m/w)
Hobart and William Smith Colleges (NY)
(m/w)
Hofstra University (NY) (m/w)
Hollins University (VA) (w)
Hood College (MD) (w)
Hope College (MI) (m/w)
Hope International University (CA) (m/w)
Howard Payne University (TX) (m/w)
Howard University (DC) (m/w)
Hunter College of the City University of New
York (NY) (m/w)
Huntingdon College (AL) (w)
Huntington College (IN) (m/w)
Idaho State University (ID) (m/w)
Illinois College (IL) (m/w)
Illinois State University (IL) (m/w)
Illinois Wesleyan University (IL) (m/w)
Immaculata University (PA) (w)
Indiana State University (IN) (m/w)
Indiana University Bloomington (IN) (m/w)
Indiana University of Pennsylvania (PA) (w)

Indiana University–Purdue University Fort
Wayne (IN) (m/w)
Indiana University–Purdue University
Indianapolis (IN) (m/w)
Indiana University Southeast (IN) (m/w)
Indiana Wesleyan University (IN) (m/w)
Iowa State University of Science and
Technology (IA) (w)
Ithaca College (NY) (m/w)
Jackson State University (MS) (m/w)
Jacksonville State University (AL) (m/w)
Jacksonville University (FL) (m/w)
James Madison University (VA) (m/w)
John Brown University (AR) (m/w)
John Carroll University (OH) (m/w)
John Jay College of Criminal Justice of the
City University of New York (NY) (m/w)
The Johns Hopkins University (MD) (m/w)
Johnson & Wales University (RI) (m/w)
Johnson C. Smith University (NC) (m/w)
Johnson State College (VT) (m/w)
Juniata College (PA) (m/w)
Kalamazoo College (MI) (m/w)
Kansas State University (KS) (w)
Kansas Wesleyan University (KS) (m/w)
Kean University (NJ) (w)
Kennesaw State University (GA) (w)
Kentucky Wesleyan College (KY) (w)
Kenyon College (OH) (m/w)
King College (TN) (m/w)
King's College (PA) (m/w)
Knox College (IL) (m/w)
Kutztown University of Pennsylvania (PA)
(m/w)
Lafayette College (PA) (m/w)
LaGrange College (GA) (m/w)
Lake Forest College (IL) (m/w)
Lakeland College (WI) (m/w)
Lake Superior State University (MI) (m/w)
Lamar University (TX) (m/w)
Lambuth University (TN) (m/w)
Lander University (SC) (m)
Lane College (TN) (m/w)
La Salle University (PA) (m/w)
Lawrence University (WI) (m/w)
Lebanon Valley College (PA) (m/w)
Lees-McRae College (NC) (m/w)
Lee University (TN) (m/w)
Lehigh University (PA) (m/w)
Lehman College of the City University of
New York (NY) (m/w)
Le Moyne College (NY) (m/w)
LeMoyne-Owen College (TN) (m/w)
LeTourneau University (TX) (m/w)
Lewis & Clark College (OR) (m/w)
Lewis-Clark State College (ID) (m/w)
Lewis University (IL) (m/w)
Liberty University (VA) (m/w)
Limestone College (SC) (m/w)
Lincoln Memorial University (TN) (m/w)
Lincoln University (MO) (w)
Lincoln University (PA) (m/w)
Lindenwood University (MO) (m/w)
Lindsey Wilson College (KY) (m/w)
Linfield College (OR) (m/w)
Lipscomb University (TN) (m/w)
Livingstone College (NC) (w)
Long Island University, Brooklyn Campus
(NY) (m/w)
Long Island University, C.W. Post Campus
(NY) (w)
Long Island University, Southampton College
(NY) (m/w)
Longwood University (VA) (m/w)
Loras College (IA) (m/w)

Louisiana College (LA) (w)
Louisiana State University and Agricultural and Mechanical College (LA) (m/w)
Louisiana Tech University (LA) (w)
Loyola College in Maryland (MD) (m/w)
Loyola Marymount University (CA) (m/w)
Luther College (IA) (m/w)
Lycoming College (PA) (w)
Lynchburg College (VA) (m/w)
Lyndon State College (VT) (m/w)
Lynn University (FL) (m/w)
Lyon College (AR) (m/w)
Macalester College (MN) (m/w)
MacMurray College (IL) (m/w)
Malone College (OH) (m/w)
Manchester College (IN) (m/w)
Manhattan College (NY) (m/w)
Manhattanville College (NY) (m/w)
Marian College (IN) (m/w)
Marian College of Fond du Lac (WI) (m/w)
Marietta College (OH) (m/w)
Marist College (NY) (m/w)
Marquette University (WI) (m/w)
Marshall University (WV) (w)
Mars Hill College (NC) (m/w)
Martin Luther College (MN) (m/w)
Martin Methodist College (TN) (m/w)
Mary Baldwin College (VA) (w)
Maryville College (TN) (m/w)
Maryville University of Saint Louis (MO) (m/w)
University of Mary Washington (VA) (m/w)
Marywood University (PA) (m/w)
Massachusetts College of Liberal Arts (MA) (w)
Massachusetts Institute of Technology (MA) (m/w)
The Master's College and Seminary (CA) (w)
McDaniel College (MD) (m/w)
McKendree College (IL) (m/w)
McMurry University (TX) (m/w)
McNeese State University (LA) (w)
Mercer University (GA) (m/w)
Mercy College (NY) (m)
Mercyhurst College (PA) (m/w)
Meredith College (NC) (w)
Merrimack College (MA) (m/w)
Mesa State College (CO) (m/w)
Messiah College (PA) (m/w)
Methodist College (NC) (m/w)
Metropolitan State College of Denver (CO) (m/w)
Miami University (OH) (w)
Michigan State University (MI) (m/w)
Michigan Technological University (MI) (m/w)
Middlebury College (VT) (m/w)
Middle Tennessee State University (TN) (m/w)
Midland Lutheran College (NE) (m/w)
Midway College (KY) (w)
Midwestern State University (TX) (m/w)
Millersville University of Pennsylvania (PA) (m/w)
Milligan College (TN) (m/w)
Millikin University (IL) (w)
Millsaps College (MS) (m/w)
Mills College (CA) (w)
Milwaukee School of Engineering (WI) (m/w)
Minnesota State University Mankato (MN) (m/w)
Minnesota State University Moorhead (MN) (w)
Mississippi College (MS) (m/w)
Mississippi State University (MS) (m/w)

Mississippi University for Women (MS) (w)
Mississippi Valley State University (MS) (m/w)
Missouri Southern State University (MO) (w)
Missouri Valley College (MO) (m/w)
Missouri Western State College (MO) (w)
Molloy College (NY) (w)
Monmouth College (IL) (m/w)
Monmouth University (NJ) (m/w)
Montana State University–Billings (MT) (m/w)
Montana State University–Bozeman (MT) (m/w)
Montclair State University (NJ) (w)
Montreat College (NC) (m/w)
Moravian College (PA) (m/w)
Morehead State University (KY) (m/w)
Morehouse College (GA) (m)
Morgan State University (MD) (m/w)
Morningside College (IA) (w)
Morris College (SC) (m/w)
Mount Holyoke College (MA) (w)
Mount Olive College (NC) (m/w)
Mount Saint Mary College (NY) (m/w)
Mount Saint Mary's University (MD) (m/w)
Mount Union College (OH) (m/w)
Muhlenberg College (PA) (m/w)
Murray State University (KY) (m/w)
Muskingum College (OH) (m/w)
Nazareth College of Rochester (NY) (m/w)
Nebraska Wesleyan University (NE) (m/w)
Neumann College (PA) (m/w)
Newberry College (SC) (m/w)
Newbury College (MA) (m/w)
New Jersey Institute of Technology (NJ) (m/w)
New Mexico State University (NM) (m/w)
New York City College of Technology of the City University of New York (NY) (m/w)
New York University (NY) (m/w)
Niagara University (NY) (m/w)
Nicholls State University (LA) (w)
Nichols College (MA) (m/w)
Norfolk State University (VA) (m/w)
North Carolina Agricultural and Technical State University (NC) (m/w)
North Carolina Central University (NC) (m/w)
North Carolina State University (NC) (m/w)
North Carolina Wesleyan College (NC) (m/w)
North Central College (IL) (m/w)
Northeastern State University (OK) (w)
Northern Arizona University (AZ) (m/w)
Northern Illinois University (IL) (m/w)
Northern Kentucky University (KY) (m/w)
North Georgia College & State University (GA) (m/w)
North Greenville College (SC) (m/w)
Northwestern College (MN) (m/w)
Northwestern State University of Louisiana (LA) (w)
Northwestern University (IL) (m/w)
Northwest Missouri State University (MO) (m/w)
Northwood University (MI) (m/w)
Northwood University, Florida Campus (FL) (m/w)
Norwich University (VT) (m)
Notre Dame College (OH) (m)
Oakland University (MI) (w)
Oberlin College (OH) (m/w)
Occidental College (CA) (m/w)
Oglethorpe University (GA) (m/w)
Ohio Dominican University (OH) (m/w)

Ohio Northern University (OH) (m/w)
The Ohio State University (OH) (m/w)
Ohio Wesleyan University (OH) (m/w)
Oklahoma Baptist University (OK) (m/w)
Oklahoma Christian University (OK) (m/w)
Oklahoma State University (OK) (m/w)
Old Dominion University (VA) (m/w)
Olivet College (MI) (w)
Olivet Nazarene University (IL) (m/w)
Oral Roberts University (OK) (m/w)
Otterbein College (OH) (m/w)
Ouachita Baptist University (AR) (m/w)
Pace University (NY) (m/w)
Pacific Lutheran University (WA) (m/w)
Pacific University (OR) (m/w)
Peace College (NC) (w)
The Pennsylvania State University Altoona College (PA) (m/w)
The Pennsylvania State University at Erie, The Behrend College (PA) (m/w)
The Pennsylvania State University University Park Campus (PA) (m/w)
Pepperdine University (CA) (m/w)
Pfeiffer University (NC) (m/w)
Philadelphia Biblical University (PA) (m/w)
Philadelphia University (PA) (m/w)
Piedmont College (GA) (m/w)
Pikeville College (KY) (m/w)
Pine Manor College (MA) (w)
Pitzer College (CA) (m/w)
Plymouth State University (NH) (w)
Point Loma Nazarene University (CA) (m/w)
Polytechnic University, Brooklyn Campus (NY) (m/w)
Pomona College (CA) (m/w)
Presbyterian College (SC) (m/w)
Princeton University (NJ) (m/w)
Principia College (IL) (m/w)
Purdue University (IN) (m/w)
Queens College of the City University of New York (NY) (m/w)
Queens University of Charlotte (NC) (m/w)
Quincy University (IL) (m/w)
Quinnipiac University (CT) (m/w)
Radford University (VA) (m/w)
Ramapo College of New Jersey (NJ) (m/w)
Randolph-Macon College (VA) (m/w)
Randolph-Macon Woman's College (VA) (w)
Regis College (MA) (w)
Reinhardt College (GA) (m/w)
Rensselaer Polytechnic Institute (NY) (m/w)
Rhode Island College (RI) (m/w)
Rhodes College (TN) (m/w)
Rice University (TX) (m/w)
The Richard Stockton College of New Jersey (NJ) (w)
Rider University (NJ) (m/w)
Ripon College (WI) (m/w)
Roanoke College (VA) (m/w)
Robert Morris College (IL) (w)
Robert Morris University (PA) (m/w)
Roberts Wesleyan College (NY) (m/w)
Rochester Institute of Technology (NY) (m/w)
Rockford College (IL) (m/w)
Rockhurst University (MO) (m/w)
Roger Williams University (RI) (m/w)
Rollins College (FL) (m/w)
Rose-Hulman Institute of Technology (IN) (m/w)
Rosemont College (PA) (w)
Russell Sage College (NY) (w)
Rust College (MS) (m/w)
Rutgers, The State University of New Jersey, Newark (NJ) (m/w)

Rutgers, The State University of New Jersey, New Brunswick/Piscataway (NJ) (m/w)
Sacred Heart University (CT) (m/w)
Saginaw Valley State University (MI) (w)
St. Ambrose University (IA) (m/w)
St. Andrews Presbyterian College (NC) (w)
Saint Anselm College (NH) (m/w)
Saint Augustine's College (NC) (m/w)
St. Bonaventure University (NY) (m/w)
St. Cloud State University (MN) (m/w)
St. Edward's University (TX) (m/w)
St. Francis College (NY) (m/w)
Saint Francis University (PA) (m/w)
St. John Fisher College (NY) (m/w)
Saint John's University (MN) (m)
St. John's University (NY) (m/w)
Saint Joseph College (CT) (w)
Saint Joseph's College (IN) (m/w)
St. Joseph's College, Suffolk Campus (NY) (m/w)
Saint Joseph's University (PA) (m/w)
St. Lawrence University (NY) (m/w)
Saint Leo University (FL) (m/w)
Saint Louis University (MO) (m/w)
Saint Mary's College (IN) (w)
Saint Mary's College of California (CA) (m/w)
St. Mary's College of Maryland (MD) (m/w)
Saint Mary's University of Minnesota (MN) (m/w)
St. Mary's University of San Antonio (TX) (m/w)
Saint Michael's College (VT) (m/w)
St. Norbert College (WI) (m/w)
St. Olaf College (MN) (m/w)
Saint Paul's College (VA) (m/w)
Saint Peter's College (NJ) (m/w)
St. Thomas Aquinas College (NY) (w)
St. Thomas University (FL) (m/w)
Saint Vincent College (PA) (m/w)
Salem International University (WV) (m)
Salem State College (MA) (m/w)
Salisbury University (MD) (m/w)
Salve Regina University (RI) (m/w)
Samford University (AL) (m/w)
Sam Houston State University (TX) (w)
San Diego State University (CA) (m/w)
San Francisco State University (CA) (w)
San Jose State University (CA) (w)
Santa Clara University (CA) (m/w)
Savannah College of Art and Design (GA) (m/w)
Savannah State University (GA) (m/w)
Schreiner University (TX) (m/w)
Seton Hall University (NJ) (w)
Seton Hill University (PA) (m/w)
Shawnee State University (OH) (w)
Shaw University (NC) (m/w)
Shenandoah University (VA) (w)
Shepherd University (WV) (m/w)
Shippensburg University of Pennsylvania (PA) (w)
Shorter College (GA) (m/w)
Siena College (NY) (m/w)
Simmons College (MA) (w)
Simpson College (IA) (m/w)
Skidmore College (NY) (m/w)
Slippery Rock University of Pennsylvania (PA) (m/w)
Smith College (MA) (w)
Sonoma State University (CA) (m/w)
South Carolina State University (SC) (m/w)
South Dakota State University (SD) (m/w)
Southeastern Louisiana University (LA) (m/w)

Southeastern Oklahoma State University (OK) (m/w)
Southeast Missouri State University (MO) (w)
Southern Arkansas University–Magnolia (AR) (w)
Southern Illinois University Carbondale (IL) (m/w)
Southern Illinois University Edwardsville (IL) (m/w)
Southern Methodist University (TX) (m/w)
Southern Nazarene University (OK) (m/w)
Southern New Hampshire University (NH) (m/w)
Southern Oregon University (OR) (m/w)
Southern Polytechnic State University (GA) (m/w)
Southern University and Agricultural and Mechanical College (LA) (m/w)
Southern Utah University (UT) (w)
Southwest Baptist University (MO) (m/w)
Southwestern College (KS) (m/w)
Southwestern University (TX) (m/w)
Southwest Minnesota State University (MN) (w)
Southwest Missouri State University (MO) (m/w)
Spelman College (GA) (w)
Spring Arbor University (MI) (m/w)
Springfield College (MA) (m/w)
Spring Hill College (AL) (m/w)
Stanford University (CA) (m/w)
State University of New York at Binghamton (NY) (m/w)
State University of New York at New Paltz (NY) (m/w)
State University of New York at Oswego (NY) (m/w)
State University of New York at Plattsburgh (NY) (w)
State University of New York College at Brockport (NY) (w)
State University of New York College at Cortland (NY) (w)
State University of New York College at Fredonia (NY) (m/w)
State University of New York College at Geneseo (NY) (w)
State University of New York College at Oneonta (NY) (m/w)
State University of New York College at Potsdam (NY) (w)
State University of New York College of Technology at Delhi (NY) (m/w)
Stephen F. Austin State University (TX) (w)
Stephens College (MO) (w)
Stetson University (FL) (m/w)
Stevens Institute of Technology (NJ) (m/w)
Stillman College (AL) (m/w)
Stonehill College (MA) (m/w)
Stony Brook University, State University of New York (NY) (m/w)
Suffolk University (MA) (m/w)
Sul Ross State University (TX) (m/w)
Susquehanna University (PA) (m/w)
Swarthmore College (PA) (m/w)
Sweet Briar College (VA) (w)
Syracuse University (NY) (w)
Tabor College (KS) (m/w)
Tarleton State University (TX) (w)
Taylor University (IN) (m/w)
Temple University (PA) (m/w)
Tennessee State University (TN) (m/w)
Tennessee Technological University (TN) (m/w)

Tennessee Wesleyan College (TN) (m/w)
Texas A&M University (TX) (m/w)
Texas A&M University–Corpus Christi (TX) (m/w)
Texas Christian University (TX) (m/w)
Texas Lutheran University (TX) (m/w)
Texas Southern University (TX) (m/w)
Texas State University-San Marcos (TX) (w)
Texas Tech University (TX) (m/w)
Thiel College (PA) (m/w)
Thomas College (ME) (m)
Thomas More College (KY) (m/w)
Thomas University (GA) (w)
Tiffin University (OH) (m/w)
Tougaloo College (MS) (m)
Towson University (MD) (m/w)
Transylvania University (KY) (m/w)
Trinity College (CT) (m/w)
Trinity College (DC) (w)
Trinity University (TX) (m/w)
Tri-State University (IN) (m/w)
Troy State University (AL) (m/w)
Truman State University (MO) (m/w)
Tufts University (MA) (m/w)
Tulane University (LA) (m/w)
Tusculum College (TN) (m/w)
Tuskegee University (AL) (m/w)
Union College (NY) (m/w)
United States Air Force Academy (CO) (m/w)
United States Coast Guard Academy (CT) (m)
United States Merchant Marine Academy (NY) (m)
United States Military Academy (NY) (m/w)
United States Naval Academy (MD) (m)
University at Albany, State University of New York (NY) (w)
University at Buffalo, The State University of New York (NY) (m/w)
The University of Akron (OH) (w)
The University of Alabama (AL) (m/w)
The University of Alabama at Birmingham (AL) (m/w)
The University of Alabama in Huntsville (AL) (m/w)
The University of Arizona (AZ) (m/w)
University of Arkansas (AR) (m/w)
University of Arkansas at Little Rock (AR) (m/w)
University of Arkansas at Monticello (AR) (w)
University of Arkansas at Pine Bluff (AR) (m/w)
University of California, Berkeley (CA) (m/w)
University of California, Davis (CA) (m/w)
University of California, Irvine (CA) (m/w)
University of California, Los Angeles (CA) (m/w)
University of California, Riverside (CA) (m/w)
University of California, San Diego (CA) (m/w)
University of California, Santa Barbara (CA) (m/w)
University of California, Santa Cruz (CA) (m/w)
University of Central Arkansas (AR) (w)
University of Central Florida (FL) (m/w)
University of Central Oklahoma (OK) (m/w)
University of Charleston (WV) (m/w)
University of Chicago (IL) (m/w)
University of Cincinnati (OH) (w)
University of Colorado at Boulder (CO) (m/w)

University of Colorado at Colorado Springs (CO) (m/w)

University of Connecticut (CT) (m/w)

University of Dallas (TX) (m/w)

University of Dayton (OH) (m/w)

University of Delaware (DE) (m/w)

University of Denver (CO) (m/w)

University of Detroit Mercy (MI) (w)

University of Dubuque (IA) (m/w)

University of Evansville (IN) (m/w)

The University of Findlay (OH) (m/w)

University of Florida (FL) (m/w)

University of Georgia (GA) (m/w)

University of Hartford (CT) (m/w)

University of Hawaii at Hilo (HI) (m/w)

University of Hawaii at Manoa (HI) (m/w)

University of Houston (TX) (w)

University of Idaho (ID) (m/w)

University of Illinois at Chicago (IL) (m/w)

University of Illinois at Springfield (IL) (m/w)

University of Illinois at Urbana–Champaign (IL) (m/w)

University of Indianapolis (IN) (m/w)

The University of Iowa (IA) (m/w)

University of Kansas (KS) (w)

University of Kentucky (KY) (m/w)

University of La Verne (CA) (m/w)

University of Louisiana at Lafayette (LA) (m/w)

University of Louisiana at Monroe (LA) (w)

University of Louisville (KY) (m/w)

University of Mary (ND) (m/w)

University of Mary Hardin-Baylor (TX) (m/w)

University of Maryland, Baltimore County (MD) (m/w)

University of Maryland, College Park (MD) (m/w)

University of Maryland Eastern Shore (MD) (m/w)

University of Massachusetts Amherst (MA) (w)

University of Massachusetts Boston (MA) (m/w)

University of Massachusetts Dartmouth (MA) (m/w)

The University of Memphis (TN) (m/w)

University of Miami (FL) (m/w)

University of Michigan (MI) (m/w)

University of Minnesota, Duluth (MN) (w)

University of Minnesota, Morris (MN) (m/w)

University of Minnesota, Twin Cities Campus (MN) (m/w)

University of Mississippi (MS) (m/w)

University of Missouri–Columbia (MO) (w)

University of Missouri–Kansas City (MO) (m/w)

University of Missouri–St. Louis (MO) (m/w)

University of Mobile (AL) (w)

The University of Montana–Missoula (MT) (m/w)

University of Montevallo (AL) (w)

University of Nebraska at Kearney (NE) (m/w)

University of Nebraska at Omaha (NE) (w)

University of Nebraska–Lincoln (NE) (m/w)

University of Nevada, Las Vegas (NV) (m/w)

University of Nevada, Reno (NV) (m/w)

University of New Hampshire (NH) (m/w)

University of New Haven (CT) (m/w)

University of New Mexico (NM) (m/w)

University of New Orleans (LA) (m/w)

University of North Alabama (AL) (m/w)

The University of North Carolina at Asheville (NC) (m/w)

The University of North Carolina at Chapel Hill (NC) (m/w)

The University of North Carolina at Charlotte (NC) (m/w)

The University of North Carolina at Greensboro (NC) (m/w)

The University of North Carolina at Pembroke (NC) (w)

The University of North Carolina at Wilmington (NC) (m/w)

University of North Dakota (ND) (w)

University of Northern Colorado (CO) (m/w)

University of Northern Iowa (IA) (w)

University of North Florida (FL) (m/w)

University of North Texas (TX) (w)

University of Notre Dame (IN) (m/w)

University of Oklahoma (OK) (m/w)

University of Oregon (OR) (m/w)

University of Pennsylvania (PA) (m/w)

University of Pittsburgh (PA) (w)

University of Pittsburgh at Greensburg (PA) (m)

University of Portland (OR) (m/w)

University of Puerto Rico at Bayamón (PR) (m/w)

University of Puerto Rico, Cayey University College (PR) (m)

University of Puerto Rico, Mayagüez Campus (PR) (m/w)

University of Puerto Rico, Río Piedras (PR) (m/w)

University of Puget Sound (WA) (m/w)

University of Redlands (CA) (m/w)

University of Rhode Island (RI) (m/w)

University of Richmond (VA) (m/w)

University of Rochester (NY) (m/w)

University of St. Francis (IL) (m/w)

University of Saint Francis (IN) (w)

University of St. Thomas (MN) (m/w)

University of San Diego (CA) (m/w)

University of San Francisco (CA) (m/w)

The University of Scranton (PA) (m/w)

University of Sioux Falls (SD) (m/w)

University of South Alabama (AL) (m/w)

University of South Carolina (SC) (m/w)

University of South Carolina Aiken (SC) (m/w)

University of South Carolina Spartanburg (SC) (m/w)

The University of South Dakota (SD) (w)

University of Southern California (CA) (m/w)

University of Southern Indiana (IN) (m/w)

University of Southern Maine (ME) (m/w)

University of Southern Mississippi (MS) (m/w)

University of South Florida (FL) (m/w)

The University of Tampa (FL) (w)

The University of Tennessee (TN) (m/w)

The University of Tennessee at Chattanooga (TN) (m/w)

The University of Tennessee at Martin (TN) (m/w)

The University of Texas at Arlington (TX) (m/w)

The University of Texas at Austin (TX) (m/w)

The University of Texas at Dallas (TX) (m/w)

The University of Texas at El Paso (TX) (w)

The University of Texas at San Antonio (TX) (m/w)

The University of Texas–Pan American (TX) (m/w)

University of the District of Columbia (DC) (m/w)

University of the Incarnate Word (TX) (m/w)

University of the Ozarks (AR) (m/w)

University of the Pacific (CA) (m/w)

University of the Sciences in Philadelphia (PA) (m/w)

University of the South (TN) (m/w)

University of Toledo (OH) (m/w)

University of Tulsa (OK) (m/w)

University of Utah (UT) (m/w)

University of Vermont (VT) (m/w)

University of Virginia (VA) (m/w)

The University of Virginia's College at Wise (VA) (m/w)

University of Washington (WA) (m/w)

University of West Florida (FL) (m/w)

University of Wisconsin–Eau Claire (WI) (m/w)

University of Wisconsin–Green Bay (WI) (m/w)

University of Wisconsin–La Crosse (WI) (m/w)

University of Wisconsin–Madison (WI) (m/w)

University of Wisconsin–Milwaukee (WI) (w)

University of Wisconsin–Oshkosh (WI) (m/w)

University of Wisconsin–River Falls (WI) (w)

University of Wisconsin–Stevens Point (WI) (w)

University of Wisconsin–Stout (WI) (w)

University of Wisconsin–Whitewater (WI) (m/w)

University of Wyoming (WY) (w)

Upper Iowa University (IA) (m/w)

Ursinus College (PA) (m/w)

Ursuline College (OH) (w)

Utah State University (UT) (m/w)

Utica College (NY) (m/w)

Valdosta State University (GA) (m/w)

Valparaiso University (IN) (m/w)

Vanderbilt University (TN) (m/w)

Vanguard University of Southern California (CA) (m/w)

Vassar College (NY) (m/w)

Villa Julie College (MD) (m/w)

Villanova University (PA) (m/w)

Virginia Commonwealth University (VA) (m/w)

Virginia Intermont College (VA) (m/w)

Virginia Polytechnic Institute and State University (VA) (m/w)

Virginia State University (VA) (m/w)

Virginia Union University (VA) (m/w)

Virginia Wesleyan College (VA) (m/w)

Wabash College (IN) (m)

Wagner College (NY) (m/w)

Wake Forest University (NC) (m/w)

Walsh University (OH) (m/w)

Wartburg College (IA) (m/w)

Washburn University (KS) (m/w)

Washington & Jefferson College (PA) (m/w)

Washington and Lee University (VA) (m)

Washington College (MD) (m/w)

Washington State University (WA) (w)

Washington University in St. Louis (MO) (m/w)

Waynesburg College (PA) (m/w)

Wayne State University (MI) (m/w)

Webber International University (FL) (m/w)

Weber State University (UT) (m/w)

Webster University (MO) (m/w)

Wellesley College (MA) (w)

Wells College (NY) (w)

Wentworth Institute of Technology (MA) (m/w)

Wesleyan College (GA) (w)

Wesleyan University (CT) (m/w)

Wesley College (DE) (m/w)
West Chester University of Pennsylvania (PA) (m/w)
Western Carolina University (NC) (w)
Western Connecticut State University (CT) (m/w)
Western Illinois University (IL) (m/w)
Western Kentucky University (KY) (m/w)
Western Michigan University (MI) (m/w)
Western New England College (MA) (m/w)
Western New Mexico University (NM) (m/w)
West Liberty State College (WV) (m/w)
Westminster College (MO) (m/w)
Westminster College (PA) (m/w)
Westmont College (CA) (m/w)
West Virginia State College (WV) (m/w)
West Virginia University (WV) (w)
West Virginia University Institute of Technology (WV) (m/w)
West Virginia Wesleyan College (WV) (m/w)
Wheaton College (IL) (m/w)
Wheaton College (MA) (m/w)
Whitman College (WA) (m/w)
Whittier College (CA) (m/w)
Whitworth College (WA) (m/w)
Wichita State University (KS) (m/w)
Widener University (PA) (m/w)
Wilkes University (PA) (m/w)
Willamette University (OR) (m/w)
William Jewell College (MO) (m/w)
Williams College (MA) (m/w)
Wilmington College (OH) (m/w)
Wilson College (PA) (w)
Wingate University (NC) (m/w)
Winona State University (MN) (m/w)
Winston-Salem State University (NC) (m)
Winthrop University (SC) (m/w)
Wisconsin Lutheran College (WI) (w)
Wittenberg University (OH) (m/w)
Wofford College (SC) (m/w)
Worcester Polytechnic Institute (MA) (m/w)
Worcester State College (MA) (m/w)
Wright State University (OH) (m/w)
Xavier University (OH) (m/w)
Xavier University of Louisiana (LA) (m/w)
Yale University (CT) (m/w)
Yeshiva University (NY) (m)
York College of Pennsylvania (PA) (m/w)
York College of the City University of New York (NY) (m)
Youngstown State University (OH)(m/w)

Track and Field

Abilene Christian University (TX) (m/w)
Adams State College (CO) (m/w)
Adelphi University (NY) (m)
Adrian College (MI) (m/w)
Alabama Agricultural and Mechanical University (AL) (m/w)
Alabama State University (AL) (m/w)
Albany State University (GA) (m/w)
Albertson College of Idaho (ID) (m/w)
Albion College (MI) (m/w)
Albright College (PA) (m/w)
Alcorn State University (MS) (m/w)
Alderson-Broaddus College (WV) (m/w)
Alfred University (NY) (m/w)
Allegheny College (PA) (m/w)
Allen University (SC) (m/w)
Alliant International University (CA) (m/w)
Alma College (MI) (m/w)
American University (DC) (m/w)
Amherst College (MA) (m/w)

Anderson College (SC) (m/w)
Anderson University (IN) (m/w)
Angelo State University (TX) (m/w)
Appalachian State University (NC) (m/w)
Aquinas College (MI) (m/w)
Arizona State University (AZ) (m/w)
Arkansas State University (AR) (m/w)
Ashland University (OH) (m/w)
Assumption College (MA) (m/w)
Auburn University (AL) (m/w)
Augsburg College (MN) (m/w)
Augustana College (IL) (m/w)
Augustana College (SD) (m/w)
Aurora University (IL) (m/w)
Austin Peay State University (TN) (w)
Azusa Pacific University (CA) (m/w)
Babson College (MA) (m/w)
Bacone College (OK) (m/w)
Baker University (KS) (m/w)
Baldwin-Wallace College (OH) (m/w)
Ball State University (IN) (m/w)
Baptist Bible College of Pennsylvania (PA) (m/w)
Barber-Scotia College (NC) (m/w)
Bates College (ME) (m/w)
Baylor University (TX) (m/w)
Bellarmine University (KY) (m/w)
Belmont University (TN) (m/w)
Beloit College (WI) (m/w)
Bemidji State University (MN) (m/w)
Benedict College (SC) (m/w)
Benedictine College (KS) (m/w)
Benedictine University (IL) (w)
Bennett College (NC) (w)
Bentley College (MA) (m/w)
Berea College (KY) (m/w)
Bethany College (KS) (m/w)
Bethany College (WV) (m/w)
Bethel College (IN) (m/w)
Bethel College (KS) (m/w)
Bethel College (TN) (m/w)
Bethel University (MN) (m/w)
Bethune-Cookman College (FL) (w)
Biola University (CA) (m/w)
Black Hills State University (SD) (m/w)
Bloomsburg University of Pennsylvania (PA) (m/w)
Bluffton College (OH) (m/w)
Boise State University (ID) (m/w)
Boston College (MA) (m/w)
Boston University (MA) (m/w)
Bowdoin College (ME) (m/w)
Bowie State University (MD) (m/w)
Bowling Green State University (OH) (w)
Bradley University (IL) (w)
Brandeis University (MA) (m/w)
Brevard College (NC) (m/w)
Briar Cliff University (IA) (m/w)
Bridgewater College (VA) (m/w)
Bridgewater State College (MA) (m/w)
Brigham Young University (UT) (m/w)
Brooklyn College of the City University of New York (NY) (m/w)
Brown University (RI) (m/w)
Bryant College (RI) (m/w)
Bryn Mawr College (PA) (w)
Bucknell University (PA) (m)
Buena Vista University (IA) (m/w)
Buffalo State College, State University of New York (NY) (m/w)
Butler University (IN) (m/w)
Cabrini College (PA) (m/w)
California Institute of Technology (CA) (m/w)
California Lutheran University (CA) (m/w)

California Polytechnic State University, San Luis Obispo (CA) (m/w)
California State Polytechnic University, Pomona (CA) (m/w)
California State University, Bakersfield (CA) (m/w)
California State University, Chico (CA) (m/w)
California State University, Dominguez Hills (CA) (w)
California State University, Fresno (CA) (m/w)
California State University, Fullerton (CA) (m/w)
California State University, Long Beach (CA) (m/w)
California State University, Los Angeles (CA) (m/w)
California State University, Northridge (CA) (m/w)
California State University, Sacramento (CA) (m/w)
California State University, San Marcos (CA) (m/w)
California State University, Stanislaus (CA) (m/w)
California University of Pennsylvania (PA) (m/w)
Calvin College (MI) (m/w)
Campbellsville University (KY) (m/w)
Campbell University (NC) (m/w)
Capital University (OH) (m/w)
Carleton College (MN) (m/w)
Carnegie Mellon University (PA) (m/w)
Carroll College (WI) (m/w)
Carson-Newman College (TN) (m/w)
Carthage College (WI) (m/w)
Cascade College (OR) (m/w)
Case Western Reserve University (OH) (m/w)
The Catholic University of America (DC) (m/w)
Cedarville University (OH) (m/w)
Central College (IA) (m/w)
Central Connecticut State University (CT) (m/w)
Central Methodist College (MO) (m/w)
Central Michigan University (MI) (m/w)
Central Missouri State University (MO) (m/w)
Central Washington University (WA) (m/w)
Centre College (KY) (m/w)
Chadron State College (NE) (m/w)
Chapman University (CA) (w)
Charleston Southern University (SC) (m/w)
Cheyney University of Pennsylvania (PA) (m/w)
Chicago State University (IL) (m/w)
Christopher Newport University (VA) (m/w)
The Citadel, The Military College of South Carolina (SC) (m/w)
City College of the City University of New York (NY) (m/w)
Claflin University (SC) (m/w)
Claremont McKenna College (CA) (m/w)
Clarion University of Pennsylvania (PA) (m/w)
Clark Atlanta University (GA) (m/w)
Clayton College & State University (GA) (m/w)
Clemson University (SC) (m/w)
Coastal Carolina University (SC) (m/w)
Coe College (IA) (m/w)
Colby College (ME) (m/w)
Colby-Sawyer College (NH) (m/w)
Colgate University (NY) (m/w)
College Misericordia (PA) (m/w)

College of Charleston (SC) (w)
College of Mount St. Joseph (OH) (m/w)
College of Mount Saint Vincent (NY) (w)
The College of New Jersey (NJ) (m/w)
College of Saint Benedict (MN) (w)
College of St. Catherine (MN) (w)
The College of St. Scholastica (MN) (w)
College of the Holy Cross (MA) (m/w)
The College of William and Mary (VA) (m/w)
The College of Wooster (OH) (m/w)
The Colorado College (CO) (m/w)
Colorado School of Mines (CO) (m/w)
Colorado State University (CO) (m/w)
Columbia College (NY) (m/w)
Columbia Union College (MD) (m/w)
Concord College (WV) (m/w)
Concordia College (MN) (m/w)
Concordia University (CA) (m/w)
Concordia University (IL) (m/w)
Concordia University (NE) (m/w)
Concordia University, St. Paul (MN) (m/w)
Concordia University Wisconsin (WI) (m/w)
Connecticut College (CT) (m/w)
Coppin State University (MD) (m/w)
Cornell College (IA) (m/w)
Cornell University (NY) (m/w)
Cornerstone University (MI) (m/w)
Cumberland College (KY) (m/w)
Dakota State University (SD) (m/w)
Dakota Wesleyan University (SD) (m/w)
Dallas Baptist University (TX) (m/w)
Dana College (NE) (m/w)
Dartmouth College (NH) (m/w)
Davidson College (NC) (m/w)
Defiance College (OH) (m/w)
Delaware State University (DE) (m/w)
Delaware Valley College (PA) (m/w)
Denison University (OH) (m/w)
DePaul University (IL) (m/w)
DePauw University (IN) (m/w)
DeSales University (PA) (m/w)
Dickinson College (PA) (m/w)
Dickinson State University (ND) (m/w)
Doane College (NE) (m/w)
Dordt College (IA) (m/w)
Drake University (IA) (m/w)
Duke University (NC) (m/w)
Duquesne University (PA) (m/w)
Earlham College (IN) (m/w)
East Carolina University (NC) (m/w)
Eastern Connecticut State University (CT) (m/w)
Eastern Illinois University (IL) (m/w)
Eastern Kentucky University (KY) (m/w)
Eastern Mennonite University (VA) (m/w)
Eastern Michigan University (MI) (m/w)
Eastern Oregon University (OR) (m/w)
Eastern Washington University (WA) (m/w)
East Stroudsburg University of Pennsylvania (PA) (m/w)
East Tennessee State University (TN) (m/w)
Edinboro University of Pennsylvania (PA) (m/w)
Edward Waters College (FL) (m/w)
Elizabeth City State University (NC) (w)
Elizabethtown College (PA) (m/w)
Elmhurst College (IL) (m/w)
Elon University (NC) (w)
Emmanuel College (MA) (m/w)
Emory University (GA) (m/w)
Emporia State University (KS) (m/w)
Eureka College (IL) (m/w)
Evangel University (MO) (m/w)

Farmingdale State University of New York (NY) (m/w)
Fayetteville State University (NC) (m/w)
Ferris State University (MI) (m/w)
Fisk University (TN) (m/w)
Fitchburg State College (MA) (m/w)
Florida Agricultural and Mechanical University (FL) (m/w)
Florida Atlantic University (FL) (w)
Florida International University (FL) (m/w)
Florida Memorial College (FL) (m/w)
Florida State University (FL) (m/w)
Fontbonne University (MO) (w)
Fordham University (NY) (m/w)
Fort Hays State University (KS) (m/w)
Fort Valley State University (GA) (m/w)
The Franciscan University (IA) (m/w)
Francis Marion University (SC) (m/w)
Franklin and Marshall College (PA) (m/w)
Franklin College (IN) (m/w)
Fresno Pacific University (CA) (m/w)
Friends University (KS) (m/w)
Frostburg State University (MD) (m/w)
Furman University (SC) (m/w)
Gallaudet University (DC) (m/w)
Gardner-Webb University (NC) (m/w)
Geneva College (PA) (m/w)
George Fox University (OR) (m/w)
George Mason University (VA) (m/w)
Georgetown University (DC) (m/w)
Georgia Institute of Technology (GA) (m/w)
Georgia Southern University (GA) (w)
Georgia State University (GA) (m/w)
Gettysburg College (PA) (m/w)
Glenville State College (WV) (m/w)
Gonzaga University (WA) (m/w)
Goshen College (IN) (m/w)
Goucher College (MD) (m/w)
Grace College (IN) (m/w)
Graceland University (IA) (m/w)
Grambling State University (LA) (m/w)
Grand Valley State University (MI) (m/w)
Greenville College (IL) (m/w)
Grinnell College (IA) (m/w)
Grove City College (PA) (m/w)
Gustavus Adolphus College (MN) (m/w)
Gwynedd-Mercy College (PA) (m/w)
Hamilton College (NY) (m/w)
Hamline University (MN) (m/w)
Hampton University (VA) (m/w)
Hanover College (IN) (m/w)
Harding University (AR) (m/w)
Harris-Stowe State College (MO) (w)
Hartwick College (NY) (m/w)
Harvard University (MA) (m/w)
Haskell Indian Nations University (KS) (m/w)
Hastings College (NE) (m/w)
Haverford College (PA) (m/w)
Heidelberg College (OH) (m/w)
Hendrix College (AR) (m/w)
High Point University (NC) (m/w)
Hillsdale College (MI) (m/w)
Hiram College (OH) (m/w)
Hope College (MI) (m/w)
Houghton College (NY) (m/w)
Howard Payne University (TX) (m/w)
Howard University (DC) (m/w)
Humboldt State University (CA) (m/w)
Hunter College of the City University of New York (NY) (m/w)
Huntington College (IN) (m/w)
Huston-Tillotson College (TX) (m/w)
Idaho State University (ID) (m/w)
Illinois College (IL) (m/w)

Illinois State University (IL) (m/w)
Illinois Wesleyan University (IL) (m/w)
Indiana State University (IN) (m/w)
Indiana University Bloomington (IN) (m/w)
Indiana University of Pennsylvania (PA) (m/w)
Indiana University–Purdue University Fort Wayne (IN) (w)
Indiana Wesleyan University (IN) (m/w)
Iona College (NY) (m/w)
Iowa State University of Science and Technology (IA) (m/w)
Iowa Wesleyan College (IA) (m/w)
Ithaca College (NY) (m/w)
Jackson State University (MS) (m/w)
Jacksonville State University (AL) (w)
Jacksonville University (FL) (w)
James Madison University (VA) (m/w)
Jamestown College (ND) (m/w)
Jarvis Christian College (TX) (m/w)
John Carroll University (OH) (m/w)
The Johns Hopkins University (MD) (m/w)
Johnson C. Smith University (NC) (m/w)
Juniata College (PA) (m/w)
Kansas State University (KS) (m/w)
Kansas Wesleyan University (KS) (m/w)
Kean University (NJ) (m/w)
Keene State College (NH) (m/w)
Kennesaw State University (GA) (m/w)
Kent State University (OH) (m/w)
Kentucky State University (KY) (m/w)
Kenyon College (OH) (m/w)
Knox College (IL) (m/w)
Kutztown University of Pennsylvania (PA) (m/w)
Lafayette College (PA) (m/w)
Lake Superior State University (MI) (m/w)
Lamar University (TX) (m/w)
Lane College (TN) (m/w)
Langston University (OK) (m/w)
La Salle University (PA) (m/w)
Lawrence University (WI) (m/w)
Lebanon Valley College (PA) (m/w)
Lees-McRae College (NC) (m/w/w)
Lehigh University (PA) (m/w)
Lehman College of the City University of New York (NY) (m/w)
Lewis & Clark College (OR) (m/w)
Lewis-Clark State College (ID) (m/w)
Lewis University (IL) (m/w)
Liberty University (VA) (m/w)
Lincoln University (MO) (m/w)
Lincoln University (PA) (m/w)
Lindenwood University (MO) (m/w)
Lindsey Wilson College (KY) (m/w)
Linfield College (OR) (m/w)
Lipscomb University (TN) (w)
Livingstone College (NC) (m/w)
Lock Haven University of Pennsylvania (PA) (m/w)
Long Island University, Brooklyn Campus (NY) (m/w)
Long Island University, C.W. Post Campus (NY) (m/w)
Loras College (IA) (m/w)
Louisiana State University and Agricultural and Mechanical College (LA) (m/w)
Louisiana Tech University (LA) (m/w)
Loyola University Chicago (IL) (m/w)
Loyola University New Orleans (LA) (m/w)
Luther College (IA) (m/w)
Lycoming College (PA) (m/w)
Lynchburg College (VA) (m/w)
Macalester College (MN) (m/w)
Malone College (OH) (m/w)

Manchester College (IN) (m/w)
Manhattan College (NY) (m/w)
Mansfield University of Pennsylvania (PA) (m/w)
Marian College (IN) (m/w)
Marietta College (OH) (m/w)
Marist College (NY) (m/w)
Marquette University (WI) (m/w)
Marshall University (WV) (m/w)
Mars Hill College (NC) (m/w)
Martin Luther College (MN) (m/w)
University of Mary Washington (VA) (m/w)
Massachusetts Institute of Technology (MA) (m/w)
McDaniel College (MD) (m/w)
McKendree College (IL) (m/w)
McMurry University (TX) (m/w)
McNeese State University (LA) (m/w)
McPherson College (KS) (m/w)
Medgar Evers College of the City University of New York (NY) (m/w)
Messiah College (PA) (m/w)
Methodist College (NC) (m/w)
Miami University (OH) (m/w)
Michigan State University (MI) (m/w)
Michigan Technological University (MI) (m/w)
MidAmerica Nazarene University (KS) (m/w)
Middlebury College (VT) (m/w)
Middle Tennessee State University (TN) (m/w)
Midland Lutheran College (NE) (m/w)
Miles College (AL) (m/w)
Millersville University of Pennsylvania (PA) (m/w)
Milligan College (TN) (m)
Millikin University (IL) (m/w)
Milwaukee School of Engineering (WI) (m/w)
Minnesota State University Mankato (MN) (m/w)
Minnesota State University Moorhead (MN) (m/w)
Minot State University (ND) (m/w)
Mississippi College (MS) (m/w)
Mississippi State University (MS) (m/w)
Mississippi Valley State University (MS) (m/w)
Missouri Southern State University (MO) (m/w)
Missouri Valley College (MO) (m/w)
Molloy College (NY) (m/w)
Monmouth College (IL) (m/w)
Monmouth University (NJ) (m/w)
Montana State University–Bozeman (MT) (m/w)
Montclair State University (NJ) (m/w)
Moravian College (PA) (m/w)
Morehead State University (KY) (m/w)
Morehouse College (GA) (m)
Morgan State University (MD) (m/w)
Morningside College (IA) (m/w)
Morris College (SC) (m/w)
Mount Holyoke College (MA) (w)
Mount Marty College (SD) (m/w)
Mount Mercy College (IA) (m/w)
Mount Saint Mary's University (MD) (m/w)
Mount Union College (OH) (m/w)
Muhlenberg College (PA) (m/w)
Murray State University (KY) (m/w)
Muskingum College (OH) (m/w)
Nazareth College of Rochester (NY) (m/w)
Nebraska Wesleyan University (NE) (m/w)
New Jersey City University (NJ) (m/w)
New Mexico State University (NM) (w)

New York City College of Technology of the City University of New York (NY) (m/w)
New York Institute of Technology (NY) (m/w)
New York University (NY) (m/w)
Nicholls State University (LA) (m/w)
Norfolk State University (VA) (m/w)
North Carolina Agricultural and Technical State University (NC) (m/w)
North Carolina Central University (NC) (m/w)
North Carolina State University (NC) (m/w)
North Central College (IL) (m/w)
North Dakota State University (ND) (m/w)
Northeastern University (MA) (m/w)
Northern Arizona University (AZ) (m/w)
Northern Illinois University (IL) (w)
Northern Michigan University (MI) (w)
Northern State University (SD) (m/w)
North Park University (IL) (m/w)
Northwest College (WA) (m/w)
Northwestern College (IA) (m/w)
Northwestern College (MN) (m/w)
Northwestern State University of Louisiana (LA) (m/w)
Northwest Missouri State University (MO) (m/w)
Northwest Nazarene University (ID) (m/w)
Northwood University (MI) (m/w)
Northwood University, Texas Campus (TX) (m/w)
Notre Dame College (OH) (m/w)
Oberlin College (OH) (m/w)
Occidental College (CA) (m/w)
Oglethorpe University (GA) (m/w)
Ohio Northern University (OH) (m/w)
The Ohio State University (OH) (m/w)
Ohio University (OH) (m/w)
Ohio Wesleyan University (OH) (m/w)
Oklahoma Baptist University (OK) (m/w)
Oklahoma Christian University (OK) (m/w)
Oklahoma State University (OK) (m/w)
Olivet College (MI) (m/w)
Olivet Nazarene University (IL) (m/w)
Oral Roberts University (OK) (m/w)
Oregon Institute of Technology (OR) (m/w)
Oregon State University (OR) (w)
Ottawa University (KS) (m/w)
Otterbein College (OH) (m/w)
Pace University (NY) (m/w)
Pacific Lutheran University (WA) (m/w)
Pacific University (OR) (m/w)
Paine College (GA) (m/w)
Park University (MO) (m/w)
Paul Quinn College (TX) (m/w)
The Pennsylvania State University at Erie, The Behrend College (PA) (m/w)
The Pennsylvania State University University Park Campus (PA) (m/w)
Pittsburg State University (KS) (m/w)
Pitzer College (CA) (m/w)
Point Loma Nazarene University (CA) (m/w)
Polytechnic University, Brooklyn Campus (NY) (m/w)
Pomona College (CA) (m/w)
Portland State University (OR) (m/w)
Prairie View A&M University (TX) (m/w)
Princeton University (NJ) (m/w)
Principia College (IL) (m/w)
Providence College (RI) (m/w)
Purdue University (IN) (m/w)
Queens University of Charlotte (NC) (m/w)
Quinnipiac University (CT) (m/w)
Radford University (VA) (m/w)
Ramapo College of New Jersey (NJ) (m/w)

Regis College (MA) (w)
Rensselaer Polytechnic Institute (NY) (m/w)
Rhode Island College (RI) (m/w)
Rhodes College (TN) (m/w)
Rice University (TX) (m/w)
The Richard Stockton College of New Jersey (NJ) (m/w)
Rider University (NJ) (m/w)
Ripon College (WI) (m/w)
Roanoke College (VA) (m/w)
Robert Morris University (PA) (m/w)
Roberts Wesleyan College (NY) (m/w)
Rochester Institute of Technology (NY) (m/w)
Rose-Hulman Institute of Technology (IN) (m/w)
Rowan University (NJ) (m/w)
Rust College (MS) (m/w)
Rutgers, The State University of New Jersey, Camden (NJ) (m/w)
Rutgers, The State University of New Jersey, New Brunswick/Piscataway (NJ) (m/w)
Sacred Heart University (CT) (m/w)
Saginaw Valley State University (MI) (m/w)
St. Ambrose University (IA) (m/w)
Saint Augustine's College (NC) (m/w)
St. Cloud State University (MN) (m/w)
St. Francis College (NY) (m/w)
Saint Francis University (PA) (m/w)
St. Gregory's University (OK) (m/w)
Saint John's University (MN) (m)
St. John's University (NY) (w)
Saint Joseph's College (IN) (m/w)
Saint Joseph's University (PA) (m/w)
St. Lawrence University (NY) (m/w)
Saint Martin's College (WA) (m/w)
Saint Mary's University of Minnesota (MN) (m/w)
St. Norbert College (WI) (m/w)
St. Olaf College (MN) (m/w)
Saint Paul's College (VA) (m/w)
Saint Peter's College (NJ) (m/w)
Salem State College (MA) (m/w)
Salisbury University (MD) (m/w)
Salve Regina University (RI) (w)
Samford University (AL) (m/w)
Sam Houston State University (TX) (m/w)
San Diego State University (CA) (w)
San Francisco State University (CA) (m/w)
Savannah State University (GA) (m/w)
Seattle Pacific University (WA) (m/w)
Seton Hall University (NJ) (m/w)
Shaw University (NC) (m/w)
Shippensburg University of Pennsylvania (PA) (m/w)
Siena Heights University (MI) (m/w)
Simpson College (IA) (m/w)
Si Tanka Huron University (SD) (m/w)
Slippery Rock University of Pennsylvania (PA) (m/w)
Smith College (MA) (w)
Sonoma State University (CA) (w)
South Carolina State University (SC) (m/w)
South Dakota School of Mines and Technology (SD) (m/w)
South Dakota State University (SD) (m/w)
Southeastern Louisiana University (LA) (m/w)
Southeast Missouri State University (MO) (m/w)
Southern Arkansas University–Magnolia (AR) (m/w)
Southern Connecticut State University (CT) (m/w)

Southern Illinois University Carbondale (IL)
(m/w)
Southern Illinois University Edwardsville (IL)
(m/w)
Southern Methodist University (TX) (m/w)
Southern Nazarene University (OK) (m/w)
Southern Oregon University (OR) (m/w)
Southern University and Agricultural and
Mechanical College (LA) (m/w)
Southern University at New Orleans (LA)
(m/w)
Southern Utah University (UT) (m/w)
Southern Vermont College (VT) (m/w)
Southern Virginia University (VA) (m/w)
Southwest Baptist University (MO) (m/w)
Southwestern Assemblies of God University
(TX) (m/w)
Southwestern College (KS) (m/w)
Southwestern University (TX) (m/w)
Southwest Missouri State University (MO)
(m/w)
Spring Arbor University (MI) (m/w)
Springfield College (MA) (m/w)
Stanford University (CA) (m/w)
State University of New York at Binghamton
(NY) (m/w)
State University of New York at New Paltz
(NY) (m/w)
State University of New York at Oswego
(NY) (m/w)
State University of New York at Plattsburgh
(NY) (m/w)
State University of New York College at
Brockport (NY) (m/w)
State University of New York College at
Cortland (NY) (m/w)
State University of New York College at
Fredonia (NY) (m/w)
State University of New York College at
Geneseo (NY) (m/w)
State University of New York College at
Oneonta (NY) (m/w)
State University of New York College of
Technology at Delhi (NY) (m/w)
State University of West Georgia (GA) (m/w)
Stephen F. Austin State University (TX)
(m/w)
Sterling College (KS) (m/w)
Stevens Institute of Technology (NJ) (m/w)
Stillman College (AL) (m/w)
Stonehill College (MA) (m/w)
Stony Brook University, State University of
New York (NY) (m/w)
Sul Ross State University (TX) (m/w)
Susquehanna University (PA) (m/w)
Swarthmore College (PA) (m/w)
Syracuse University (NY) (m/w)
Tabor College (KS) (m/w)
Tarleton State University (TX) (m/w)
Taylor University (IN) (m/w)
Temple University (PA) (m/w)
Tennessee State University (TN) (m/w)
Tennessee Technological University (TN) (w)
Texas A&M University (TX) (m/w)
Texas A&M University–Commerce (TX)
(m/w)
Texas A&M University–Corpus Christi (TX)
(m/w)
Texas A&M University–Kingsville (TX)
(m/w)
Texas Christian University (TX) (m/w)
Texas Lutheran University (TX) (w)
Texas Southern University (TX) (m/w)
Texas State University-San Marcos (TX)
(m/w)

Texas Tech University (TX) (m/w)
Thiel College (PA) (m/w)
Tiffin University (OH) (m/w)
Towson University (MD) (m/w)
Trinity Christian College (IL) (m/w)
Trinity College (CT) (m/w)
Trinity College (DC) (w)
Trinity University (TX) (m/w)
Troy State University (AL) (m/w)
Truman State University (MO) (m/w)
Tufts University (MA) (m/w)
Tulane University (LA) (m/w)
Tuskegee University (AL) (m/w)
Union College (NY) (w)
United States Air Force Academy (CO) (m/w)
United States Coast Guard Academy (CT)
(m/w)
United States Merchant Marine Academy
(NY) (m/w)
United States Military Academy (NY) (m/w)
United States Naval Academy (MD) (m/w)
University at Albany, State University of New
York (NY) (m/w)
University at Buffalo, The State University of
New York (NY) (m/w)
The University of Akron (OH) (m/w)
The University of Alabama (AL) (m/w)
The University of Alabama at Birmingham
(AL) (w)
The University of Alabama in Huntsville
(AL) (w)
University of Alaska Anchorage (AK) (m/w)
The University of Arizona (AZ) (m/w)
University of Arkansas (AR) (m/w)
University of Arkansas at Little Rock (AR)
(m/w)
University of Arkansas at Pine Bluff (AR)
(m/w)
University of California, Berkeley (CA) (m/w)
University of California, Davis (CA) (m/w)
University of California, Irvine (CA) (m/w)
University of California, Los Angeles (CA)
(m/w)
University of California, Riverside (CA)
(m/w)
University of California, San Diego (CA)
(m/w)
University of California, Santa Barbara (CA)
(m/w)
University of Central Florida (FL) (w)
University of Charleston (WV) (m/w)
University of Chicago (IL) (m/w)
University of Cincinnati (OH) (m/w)
University of Colorado at Boulder (CO)
(m/w)
University of Colorado at Colorado Springs
(CO) (m/w)
University of Connecticut (CT) (m/w)
University of Dallas (TX) (m/w)
University of Dayton (OH) (w)
University of Delaware (DE) (m/w)
University of Detroit Mercy (MI) (m/w)
University of Dubuque (IA) (m/w)
The University of Findlay (OH) (m/w)
University of Florida (FL) (m/w)
University of Georgia (GA) (m/w)
University of Hartford (CT) (m/w)
University of Hawaii at Manoa (HI) (w)
University of Houston (TX) (m/w)
University of Idaho (ID) (m/w)
University of Illinois at Chicago (IL) (m/w)
University of Illinois at Urbana–Champaign
(IL) (m/w)
University of Indianapolis (IN) (m/w)
The University of Iowa (IA) (m/w)

University of Kansas (KS) (m/w)
University of Kentucky (KY) (m/w)
University of La Verne (CA) (m/w)
University of Louisiana at Lafayette (LA)
(m/w)
University of Louisiana at Monroe (LA)
(m/w)
University of Louisville (KY) (m/w)
University of Maine (ME) (m/w)
University of Mary (ND) (m/w)
University of Maryland, Baltimore County
(MD) (m/w)
University of Maryland, College Park (MD)
(m/w)
University of Maryland Eastern Shore (MD)
(m/w)
University of Massachusetts Amherst (MA)
(m/w)
University of Massachusetts Dartmouth
(MA) (m/w)
University of Massachusetts Lowell (MA)
(m/w)
The University of Memphis (TN) (m/w)
University of Miami (FL) (m/w)
University of Michigan (MI) (m/w)
University of Minnesota, Duluth (MN) (m/w)
University of Minnesota, Morris (MN) (m/w)
University of Minnesota, Twin Cities
Campus (MN) (m/w)
University of Mississippi (MS) (m/w)
University of Missouri–Columbia (MO)
(m/w)
University of Missouri–Kansas City (MO)
(m/w)
University of Missouri–Rolla (MO) (m/w)
University of Mobile (AL) (m/w)
The University of Montana–Missoula (MT)
(m/w)
University of Nebraska at Kearney (NE)
(m/w)
University of Nebraska at Omaha (NE) (w)
University of Nebraska–Lincoln (NE) (m/w)
University of Nevada, Las Vegas (NV) (w)
University of Nevada, Reno (NV) (w)
University of New Hampshire (NH) (m/w)
University of New Haven (CT) (m/w)
University of New Mexico (NM) (m/w)
University of New Orleans (LA) (m/w)
The University of North Carolina at
Asheville (NC) (m/w)
The University of North Carolina at Chapel
Hill (NC) (m/w)
The University of North Carolina at
Charlotte (NC) (m/w)
The University of North Carolina at
Greensboro (NC) (m/w)
The University of North Carolina at
Pembroke (NC) (m/w)
The University of North Carolina at
Wilmington (NC) (m/w)
University of North Dakota (ND) (m/w)
University of Northern Colorado (CO) (m/w)
University of Northern Iowa (IA) (m/w)
University of North Florida (FL) (m/w)
University of North Texas (TX) (m/w)
University of Notre Dame (IN) (m/w)
University of Oklahoma (OK) (m/w)
University of Oregon (OR) (m/w)
University of Pennsylvania (PA) (m/w)
University of Pittsburgh (PA) (m/w)
University of Pittsburgh at Johnstown (PA)
(w)
University of Portland (OR) (m/w)
University of Puerto Rico at Bayamón (PR)
(m/w)

University of Puerto Rico at Humacao (PR) (m/w)

University of Puerto Rico, Cayey University College (PR) (m/w)

University of Puerto Rico, Mayagüez Campus (PR) (m/w)

University of Puerto Rico, Río Piedras (PR) (m/w)

University of Puget Sound (WA) (m/w)

University of Redlands (CA) (m/w)

University of Rhode Island (RI) (m/w)

University of Richmond (VA) (m/w)

University of Rio Grande (OH) (m/w)

University of Rochester (NY) (m/w)

University of St. Francis (IL) (w)

University of Saint Francis (IN) (m/w)

University of St. Thomas (MN) (m/w)

University of San Francisco (CA) (w)

University of Sioux Falls (SD) (m/w)

University of South Alabama (AL) (m/w)

University of South Carolina (SC) (m/w)

The University of South Dakota (SD) (m/w)

University of Southern California (CA) (m/w)

University of Southern Indiana (IN) (m/w)

University of Southern Maine (ME) (m/w)

University of Southern Mississippi (MS) (m/w)

University of South Florida (FL) (m/w)

The University of Tennessee (TN) (m/w)

The University of Tennessee at Chattanooga (TN) (m/w)

The University of Texas at Arlington (TX) (m/w)

The University of Texas at Austin (TX) (m/w)

The University of Texas at El Paso (TX) (m/w)

The University of Texas at San Antonio (TX) (m/w)

The University of Texas–Pan American (TX) (m/w)

University of the Incarnate Word (TX) (m/w)

University of the South (TN) (m/w)

University of Toledo (OH) (w)

University of Tulsa (OK) (m/w)

University of Utah (UT) (m/w/w)

University of Vermont (VT) (w)

University of Virginia (VA) (m/w)

University of Washington (WA) (m/w)

University of West Florida (FL) (w)

University of Wisconsin–Eau Claire (WI) (m/w)

University of Wisconsin–La Crosse (WI) (m/w)

University of Wisconsin–Madison (WI) (m/w)

University of Wisconsin–Milwaukee (WI) (m/w)

University of Wisconsin–Oshkosh (WI) (m/w)

University of Wisconsin–Parkside (WI) (m/w)

University of Wisconsin–Platteville (WI) (m/w)

University of Wisconsin–River Falls (WI) (m/w)

University of Wisconsin–Stevens Point (WI) (m/w)

University of Wisconsin–Stout (WI) (m/w)

University of Wisconsin–Superior (WI) (m/w)

University of Wisconsin–Whitewater (WI) (m/w)

University of Wyoming (WY) (m/w)

Upper Iowa University (IA) (m/w)

Ursinus College (PA) (m/w)

Utah State University (UT) (m/w)

Valparaiso University (IN) (m/w)

Vanderbilt University (TN) (w)

Vanguard University of Southern California (CA) (m/w)

Villanova University (PA) (m/w)

Virginia Commonwealth University (VA) (m/w)

Virginia Intermont College (VA) (m/w)

Virginia Military Institute (VA) (m/w)

Virginia Polytechnic Institute and State University (VA) (m/w)

Virginia State University (VA) (m/w)

Virginia Union University (VA) (m/w)

Voorhees College (SC) (m/w)

Wabash College (IN) (m)

Wagner College (NY) (m/w)

Wake Forest University (NC) (m/w)

Walsh University (OH) (w/w)

Warner Pacific College (OR) (m/w)

Warner Southern College (FL) (m/w)

Wartburg College (IA) (m/w)

Washington & Jefferson College (PA) (m/w)

Washington and Lee University (VA) (m/w)

Washington State University (WA) (m/w)

Washington University in St. Louis (MO) (m/w)

Wayland Baptist University (TX) (m/w)

Wayne State College (NE) (m/w)

Webber International University (FL) (m/w)

Weber State University (UT) (m/w)

Wellesley College (MA) (w)

Wesleyan University (CT) (m/w)

West Chester University of Pennsylvania (PA) (m/w)

Western Carolina University (NC) (m/w)

Western Illinois University (IL) (m/w)

Western Kentucky University (KY) (m/w)

Western Michigan University (MI) (m/w)

Western Oregon University (OR) (m/w)

Western State College of Colorado (CO) (m/w)

Western Washington University (WA) (m/w)

Westfield State College (MA) (m/w)

West Liberty State College (WV) (m/w)

Westminster College (PA) (m/w)

Westmont College (CA) (m/w)

West Virginia State College (WV) (m/w)

West Virginia University (WV) (w)

West Virginia Wesleyan College (WV) (m/w)

Wheaton College (IL) (m/w)

Wheaton College (MA) (m/w)

Wheeling Jesuit University (WV) (m/w)

Whittier College (CA) (m/w)

Whitworth College (WA) (m/w)

Wichita State University (KS) (m/w)

Widener University (PA) (m/w)

Wiley College (TX) (m/w)

Willamette University (OR) (m/w)

William Jewell College (MO) (m/w)

William Paterson University of New Jersey (NJ) (m/w)

William Penn University (IA) (m/w)

Williams College (MA) (m/w)

Wilmington College (OH) (m/w)

Winona State University (MN) (w)

Winthrop University (SC) (m/w)

Wisconsin Lutheran College (WI) (m/w)

Wittenberg University (OH) (m/w)

Wofford College (SC) (m/w)

Worcester Polytechnic Institute (MA) (m/w)

Worcester State College (MA) (m/w)

Wright State University (OH) (w)

Xavier University of Louisiana (LA) (m/w)

Yale University (CT) (m/w)

York College (NE) (m/w)

York College of Pennsylvania (PA) (m/w)

York College of the City University of New York (NY) (m/w)

Youngstown State University (OH)(m/w)

Volleyball

Abilene Christian University (TX) (w)

Adams State College (CO) (w)

Adelphi University (NY) (w)

Adrian College (MI) (w)

Agnes Scott College (GA) (w)

Alabama Agricultural and Mechanical University (AL) (w)

Alabama State University (AL) (w)

Albany State University (GA) (w)

Albertson College of Idaho (ID) (w)

Albertus Magnus College (CT) (w)

Albion College (MI) (w)

Albright College (PA) (w)

Alcorn State University (MS) (w)

Alderson-Broaddus College (WV) (w)

Alfred University (NY) (w)

Allegheny College (PA) (w)

Allen University (SC) (w)

Alliant International University (CA) (w)

Alma College (MI) (w)

Alvernia College (PA) (w)

Alverno College (WI) (w)

American International College (MA) (w)

American University (DC) (w)

Amherst College (MA) (w)

Anderson College (SC) (w)

Anderson University (IN) (w)

Angelo State University (TX) (w)

Anna Maria College (MA) (w)

Appalachian State University (NC) (w)

Aquinas College (MI) (w)

Arcadia University (PA) (w)

Arizona State University (AZ) (w)

Arkansas State University (AR) (w)

Arkansas Tech University (AR) (w)

Armstrong Atlantic State University (GA) (w)

Asbury College (KY) (w)

Ashland University (OH) (w)

Assumption College (MA) (w)

Auburn University (AL) (w)

Augsburg College (MN) (w)

Augustana College (IL) (w)

Augustana College (SD) (w)

Augusta State University (GA) (w)

Aurora University (IL) (w)

Austin College (TX) (w)

Austin Peay State University (TN) (w)

Averett University (VA) (w)

Avila University (MO) (m/w)

Azusa Pacific University (CA) (w)

Babson College (MA) (w)

Bacone College (OK) (w)

Baldwin-Wallace College (OH) (w)

Ball State University (IN) (m/w)

Baptist Bible College of Pennsylvania (PA) (m/w)

Barber-Scotia College (NC) (w)

Bard College (NY) (m/w)

Barry University (FL) (w)

Barton College (NC) (w)

Bates College (ME) (w)

Baylor University (TX) (w)

Bay Path College (MA) (w)

Belhaven College (MS) (w)

Bellarmine University (KY) (w)

Bellevue University (NE) (w)

Belmont Abbey College (NC) (w)

Belmont University (TN) (w)

Beloit College (WI) (w)

Bemidji State University (MN) (w)
Benedict College (SC) (w)
Benedictine College (KS) (w)
Benedictine University (IL) (w)
Bennett College (NC) (w)
Bentley College (MA) (w)
Berea College (KY) (w)
Bernard M. Baruch College of the City
  University of New York (NY) (m/w)
Bethany College (KS) (w)
Bethany College (WV) (w)
Bethany College of the Assemblies of God
  (CA) (w)
Bethel College (IN) (w)
Bethel College (KS) (w)
Bethel College (TN) (w)
Bethel University (MN) (w)
Bethune-Cookman College (FL) (w)
Biola University (CA) (w)
Birmingham-Southern College (AL) (w)
Blackburn College (IL) (w)
Black Hills State University (SD) (w)
Bloomfield College (NJ) (w)
Bluefield College (VA) (w)
Bluffton College (OH) (w)
Boise State University (ID) (w)
Boston College (MA) (w)
Bowdoin College (ME) (w)
Bowie State University (MD) (w)
Bowling Green State University (OH) (w)
Bradley University (IL) (w)
Brandeis University (MA) (w)
Brenau University (GA) (w)
Brescia University (KY) (w)
Brevard College (NC) (w)
Brewton-Parker College (GA) (w)
Briar Cliff University (IA) (w)
Bridgewater College (VA) (w)
Bridgewater State College (MA) (w)
Brigham Young University (UT) (m/w)
Brigham Young University–Hawaii (HI) (w)
Brooklyn College of the City University of
  New York (NY) (m/w)
Brown University (RI) (w)
Bryan College (TN) (w)
Bryant College (RI) (w)
Bryn Mawr College (PA) (w)
Bucknell University (PA) (w)
Buena Vista University (IA) (w)
Buffalo State College, State University of
  New York (NY) (w)
Butler University (IN) (w)
Cabrini College (PA) (w)
California Baptist University (CA) (m/w)
California Institute of Technology (CA) (w)
California Lutheran University (CA) (w)
California Maritime Academy (CA) (w)
California Polytechnic State University, San
  Luis Obispo (CA) (w)
California State Polytechnic University,
  Pomona (CA) (w)
California State University, Bakersfield (CA)
  (w)
California State University, Chico (CA) (w)
California State University, Dominguez Hills
  (CA) (w)
California State University, Fresno (CA) (w)
California State University, Fullerton (CA)
  (w)
California State University, Hayward (CA)
  (w)
California State University, Long Beach (CA)
  (m/w)
California State University, Los Angeles (CA)
  (w)

California State University, Monterey Bay
  (CA) (w)
California State University, Northridge (CA)
  (m/w)
California State University, Sacramento (CA)
  (w)
California State University, San Bernardino
  (CA) (w)
California State University, Stanislaus (CA)
  (w)
California University of Pennsylvania (PA)
  (w)
Calumet College of Saint Joseph (IN) (m/w)
Calvin College (MI) (w)
Cameron University (OK) (w)
Campbellsville University (KY) (w)
Campbell University (NC) (w)
Canisius College (NY) (w)
Capital University (OH) (w)
Cardinal Stritch University (WI) (m/w)
Carleton College (MN) (w)
Carlow College (PA) (w)
Carnegie Mellon University (PA) (w)
Carroll College (MT) (w)
Carroll College (WI) (w)
Carson-Newman College (TN) (w)
Carthage College (WI) (w)
Cascade College (OR) (w)
Case Western Reserve University (OH) (w)
Catawba College (NC) (w)
The Catholic University of America (DC) (w)
Cazenovia College (NY) (w)
Cedar Crest College (PA) (w)
Cedarville University (OH) (w)
Centenary College (NJ) (w)
Centenary College of Louisiana (LA) (w)
Central Christian College of Kansas (KS) (w)
Central College (IA) (w)
Central Connecticut State University (CT)
  (w)
Central Methodist College (MO) (w)
Central Michigan University (MI) (w)
Central Missouri State University (MO) (w)
Central Washington University (WA) (w)
Centre College (KY) (w)
Chadron State College (NE) (w)
Chaminade University of Honolulu (HI) (w)
Chapman University (CA) (w)
Charleston Southern University (SC) (w)
Chatham College (PA) (w)
Chestnut Hill College (PA) (w)
Cheyney University of Pennsylvania (PA) (w)
Chicago State University (IL) (w)
Chowan College (NC) (w)
Christian Brothers University (TN) (w)
Christian Heritage College (CA) (w)
Christopher Newport University (VA) (w)
The Citadel, The Military College of South
  Carolina (SC) (w)
City College of the City University of New
  York (NY) (m/w)
Claflin University (SC) (w)
Claremont McKenna College (CA) (w)
Clarion University of Pennsylvania (PA) (w)
Clark Atlanta University (GA) (w)
Clarke College (IA) (m/w)
Clarkson University (NY) (w)
Clark University (MA) (w)
Clemson University (SC) (w)
Cleveland State University (OH) (w)
Coastal Carolina University (SC) (w)
Coe College (IA) (w)
Coker College (SC) (w)
Colby College (ME) (w)
Colby-Sawyer College (NH) (w)

Colgate University (NY) (w)
College Misericordia (PA) (w)
College of Charleston (SC) (w)
College of Mount St. Joseph (OH) (w)
College of Mount Saint Vincent (NY) (m/w)
The College of New Rochelle (NY) (w)
College of Notre Dame of Maryland (MD)
  (w)
College of Saint Benedict (MN) (w)
College of St. Catherine (MN) (w)
College of Saint Elizabeth (NJ) (w)
College of Saint Mary (NE) (w)
The College of Saint Rose (NY) (w)
The College of St. Scholastica (MN) (w)
College of Staten Island of the City University
  of New York (NY) (w)
College of the Holy Cross (MA) (w)
College of the Ozarks (MO) (w)
College of the Southwest (NM) (w)
The College of William and Mary (VA) (w)
The College of Wooster (OH) (w)
Colorado Christian University (CO) (w)
The Colorado College (CO) (w)
Colorado School of Mines (CO) (w)
Colorado State University (CO) (w)
Colorado State University-Pueblo (CO) (w)
Columbia College (MO) (w)
Columbia College (NY) (w)
Columbia College (SC) (w)
Concord College (WV) (w)
Concordia College (MN) (w)
Concordia College (NY) (w)
Concordia University (CA) (w)
Concordia University (IL) (w)
Concordia University (MI) (w)
Concordia University (NE) (w)
Concordia University (OR) (w)
Concordia University at Austin (TX) (w)
Concordia University, St. Paul (MN) (w)
Concordia University Wisconsin (WI) (w)
Connecticut College (CT) (w)
Converse College (SC) (w)
Coppin State University (MD) (w)
Cornell College (IA) (w)
Cornell University (NY) (w)
Cornerstone University (MI) (w)
Covenant College (GA) (w)
Creighton University (NE) (w)
Crown College (MN) (w)
Culver-Stockton College (MO) (w)
Cumberland College (KY) (w)
Cumberland University (TN) (w)
Daemen College (NY) (w)
Dakota State University (SD) (w)
Dakota Wesleyan University (SD) (w)
Dallas Baptist University (TX) (m/w)
Dana College (NE) (w)
Daniel Webster College (NH) (w)
Dartmouth College (NH) (w)
Davidson College (NC) (w)
Davis & Elkins College (WV) (w)
Defiance College (OH) (w)
Delaware State University (DE) (w)
Delaware Valley College (PA) (w)
Denison University (OH) (w)
DePaul University (IL) (w)
DePauw University (IN) (w)
DeSales University (PA) (w)
Dickinson College (PA) (w)
Dickinson State University (ND) (w)
Dillard University (LA) (w)
Doane College (NE) (w)
Dominican College (NY) (w)
Dominican University (IL) (w)
Dominican University of California (CA) (w)

Dordt College (IA) (w)
Dowling College (NY) (w)
Drake University (IA) (w)
Drury University (MO) (w)
Duke University (NC) (w)
Duquesne University (PA) (w)
D'Youville College (NY) (m/w)
Earlham College (IN) (w)
East Carolina University (NC) (w)
Eastern Connecticut State University (CT) (w)
Eastern Illinois University (IL) (w)
Eastern Kentucky University (KY) (w)
Eastern Mennonite University (VA) (m/w)
Eastern Michigan University (MI) (w)
Eastern Nazarene College (MA) (w)
Eastern New Mexico University (NM) (w)
Eastern Oregon University (OR) (w)
Eastern University (PA) (w)
Eastern Washington University (WA) (w)
East Stroudsburg University of Pennsylvania (PA) (m/w)
East Tennessee State University (TN) (w)
East Texas Baptist University (TX) (w)
Eckerd College (FL) (w)
Edgewood College (WI) (w)
Edinboro University of Pennsylvania (PA) (w)
Elizabeth City State University (NC) (w)
Elizabethtown College (PA) (w)
Elmhurst College (IL) (w)
Elmira College (NY) (w)
Elms College (MA) (m/w)
Elon University (NC) (w)
Embry-Riddle Aeronautical University (AZ) (w)
Embry-Riddle Aeronautical University (FL) (w)
Emerson College (MA) (w)
Emmanuel College (MA) (m/w)
Emory & Henry College (VA) (w)
Emory University (GA) (w)
Emporia State University (KS) (w)
Endicott College (MA) (m/w)
Eureka College (IL) (w)
Evangel University (MO) (w)
The Evergreen State College (WA) (w)
Fairfield University (CT) (w)
Fairleigh Dickinson University, College at Florham (NJ) (w)
Fairmont State University (WV) (w)
Farmingdale State University of New York (NY) (w)
Faulkner University (AL) (w)
Fayetteville State University (NC) (w)
Felician College (NJ) (w)
Ferris State University (MI) (w)
Ferrum College (VA) (w)
Fisk University (TN) (w)
Flagler College (FL) (w)
Florida Agricultural and Mechanical University (FL) (w)
Florida Atlantic University (FL) (w)
Florida Gulf Coast University (FL) (w)
Florida Institute of Technology (FL) (w)
Florida International University (FL) (w)
Florida Memorial College (FL) (w)
Florida Southern College (FL) (w)
Florida State University (FL) (w)
Fontbonne University (MO) (w)
Fordham University (NY) (w)
Fort Hays State University (KS) (w)
Fort Lewis College (CO) (w)
Fort Valley State University (GA) (w)
Framingham State College (MA) (w)
The Franciscan University (IA) (w)

Francis Marion University (SC) (w)
Franklin and Marshall College (PA) (w)
Franklin College (IN) (w)
Franklin Pierce College (NH) (w)
Freed-Hardeman University (TN) (w)
Fresno Pacific University (CA) (w)
Friends University (KS) (w)
Frostburg State University (MD) (w)
Furman University (SC) (w)
Gallaudet University (DC) (w)
Gannon University (PA) (w)
Gardner-Webb University (NC) (w)
Geneva College (PA) (w)
George Fox University (OR) (w)
George Mason University (VA) (m/w)
Georgetown College (KY) (w)
Georgetown University (DC) (w)
The George Washington University (DC) (w)
Georgia Institute of Technology (GA) (w)
Georgian Court University (NJ) (w)
Georgia Southern University (GA) (w)
Georgia Southwestern State University (GA) (w)
Georgia State University (GA) (w)
Gettysburg College (PA) (w)
Glenville State College (WV) (w)
Goldey-Beacom College (DE) (w)
Gonzaga University (WA) (w)
Gordon College (MA) (w)
Goshen College (IN) (w)
Goucher College (MD) (w)
Grace College (IN) (w)
Graceland University (IA) (m/w)
Grambling State University (LA) (w)
Grand Canyon University (AZ) (w)
Grand Valley State University (MI) (w)
Grand View College (IA) (w)
Green Mountain College (VT) (w)
Greensboro College (NC) (w)
Greenville College (IL) (w)
Grinnell College (IA) (w)
Grove City College (PA) (w)
Guilford College (NC) (w)
Gustavus Adolphus College (MN) (w)
Gwynedd-Mercy College (PA) (w)
Hamilton College (NY) (w)
Hamline University (MN) (w)
Hampton University (VA) (w)
Hannibal-LaGrange College (MO) (w)
Hanover College (IN) (w)
Harding University (AR) (w)
Hardin-Simmons University (TX) (w)
Harris-Stowe State College (MO) (w)
Hartwick College (NY) (w)
Harvard University (MA) (m/w)
Haskell Indian Nations University (KS) (w)
Hastings College (NE) (w)
Haverford College (PA) (w)
Hawai'i Pacific University (HI) (w)
Heidelberg College (OH) (w)
Henderson State University (AR) (w)
Hendrix College (AR) (w)
High Point University (NC) (w)
Hilbert College (NY) (m/w)
Hillsdale College (MI) (w)
Hiram College (OH) (w)
Hofstra University (NY) (w)
Hollins University (VA) (w)
Holy Family University (PA) (w)
Holy Names University (CA) (w)
Hood College (MD) (w)
Hope College (MI) (w)
Hope International University (CA) (m/w)
Houghton College (NY) (w)
Houston Baptist University (TX) (w)

Howard Payne University (TX) (w)
Howard University (DC) (w)
Humboldt State University (CA) (w)
Hunter College of the City University of New York (NY) (m/w)
Huntingdon College (AL) (w)
Huntington College (IN) (w)
Husson College (ME) (w)
Huston-Tillotson College (TX) (w)
Idaho State University (ID) (w)
Illinois College (IL) (w)
Illinois Institute of Technology (IL) (w)
Illinois State University (IL) (w)
Illinois Wesleyan University (IL) (w)
Immaculata University (PA) (w)
Indiana State University (IN) (w)
Indiana University Bloomington (IN) (w)
Indiana University Northwest (IN) (w)
Indiana University of Pennsylvania (PA) (w)
Indiana University–Purdue University Fort Wayne (IN) (m/w)
Indiana University–Purdue University Indianapolis (IN) (w)
Indiana University Southeast (IN) (w)
Indiana Wesleyan University (IN) (w)
Iona College (NY) (w)
Iowa State University of Science and Technology (IA) (w)
Iowa Wesleyan College (IA) (w)
Ithaca College (NY) (w)
Jackson State University (MS) (w)
Jacksonville State University (AL) (w)
Jacksonville University (FL) (w)
James Madison University (VA) (w)
Jamestown College (ND) (w)
Jarvis Christian College (TX) (w)
John Brown University (AR) (w)
John Carroll University (OH) (w)
John Jay College of Criminal Justice of the City University of New York (NY) (w)
The Johns Hopkins University (MD) (w)
Johnson & Wales University (CO) (m/w)
Johnson & Wales University (RI) (m/w)
Johnson C. Smith University (NC) (w)
Judson College (IL) (w)
Juniata College (PA) (m/w)
Kalamazoo College (MI) (w)
Kansas State University (KS) (w)
Kansas Wesleyan University (KS) (w)
Kean University (NJ) (w)
Keene State College (NH) (w)
Kendall College (IL) (m/w)
Kent State University (OH) (w)
Kentucky State University (KY) (w)
Kentucky Wesleyan College (KY) (w)
Kenyon College (OH) (w)
Keuka College (NY) (w)
King College (TN) (w)
King's College (PA) (w)
Knox College (IL) (w)
Kutztown University of Pennsylvania (PA) (w)
Lafayette College (PA) (w)
LaGrange College (GA) (w)
Lake Erie College (OH) (w)
Lake Forest College (IL) (w)
Lakeland College (WI) (w)
Lake Superior State University (MI) (w)
Lamar University (TX) (w)
Lambuth University (TN) (w)
Lander University (SC) (w)
Lane College (TN) (w)
La Roche College (PA) (w)
La Salle University (PA) (w)
Lasell College (MA) (m/w)

Lawrence University (WI) (w)
Lebanon Valley College (PA) (w)
Lees-McRae College (NC) (m/w)
Lee University (TN) (w)
Lehigh University (PA) (w)
Lehman College of the City University of New York (NY) (m/w)
Le Moyne College (NY) (w)
LeMoyne-Owen College (TN) (w)
Lenoir-Rhyne College (NC) (w)
Lesley University (MA) (w)
LeTourneau University (TX) (w)
Lewis & Clark College (OR) (w)
Lewis-Clark State College (ID) (w)
Lewis University (IL) (m/w)
Liberty University (VA) (w)
Limestone College (SC) (w)
Lincoln Memorial University (TN) (w)
Lincoln University (PA) (w)
Lindenwood University (MO) (m/w)
Lindsey Wilson College (KY) (w)
Linfield College (OR) (w)
Lipscomb University (TN) (w)
Livingstone College (NC) (w)
Lock Haven University of Pennsylvania (PA) (w)
Long Island University, Brooklyn Campus (NY) (w)
Long Island University, C.W. Post Campus (NY) (w)
Long Island University, Southampton College (NY) (m/w)
Loras College (IA) (w)
Louisiana State University and Agricultural and Mechanical College (LA) (w)
Louisiana Tech University (LA) (w)
Loyola College in Maryland (MD) (w)
Loyola Marymount University (CA) (w)
Loyola University Chicago (IL) (m/w)
Loyola University New Orleans (LA) (w)
Lubbock Christian University (TX) (w)
Luther College (IA) (w)
Lycoming College (PA) (w)
Lynchburg College (VA) (w)
Lynn University (FL) (w)
Lyon College (AR) (w)
Macalester College (MN) (w)
MacMurray College (IL) (w)
Madonna University (MI) (w)
Malone College (OH) (w)
Manchester College (IN) (w)
Manhattan College (NY) (w)
Maranatha Baptist Bible College (WI) (w)
Marian College (IN) (w)
Marian College of Fond du Lac (WI) (w)
Marietta College (OH) (w)
Marist College (NY) (w)
Marquette University (WI) (w)
Marshall University (WV) (w)
Mars Hill College (NC) (w)
Martin Luther College (MN) (w)
Martin Methodist College (TN) (w)
Mary Baldwin College (VA) (w)
Marymount University (VA) (w)
Maryville College (TN) (w)
Maryville University of Saint Louis (MO) (w)
University of Mary Washington (VA) (w)
Marywood University (PA) (w)
Massachusetts College of Liberal Arts (MA) (w)
Massachusetts Institute of Technology (MA) (m/w)
Massachusetts Maritime Academy (MA) (w)
The Master's College and Seminary (CA) (w)
Mayville State University (ND) (w)

McDaniel College (MD) (w)
McKendree College (IL) (w)
McMurry University (TX) (w)
McNeese State University (LA) (w)
McPherson College (KS) (w)
Medaille College (NY) (m/w)
Medgar Evers College of the City University of New York (NY) (m/w)
Menlo College (CA) (w)
Mercer University (GA) (w)
Mercy College (NY) (w)
Mercyhurst College (PA) (m/w)
Meredith College (NC) (w)
Merrimack College (MA) (w)
Mesa State College (CO) (w)
Messiah College (PA) (w)
Methodist College (NC) (w)
Metropolitan State College of Denver (CO) (w)
Miami University (OH) (w)
Michigan State University (MI) (w)
Michigan Technological University (MI) (w)
MidAmerica Nazarene University (KS) (w)
Mid-Continent College (KY) (w)
Middlebury College (VT) (w)
Middle Tennessee State University (TN) (w)
Midland Lutheran College (NE) (w)
Midwestern State University (TX) (w)
Miles College (AL) (w)
Millersville University of Pennsylvania (PA) (w)
Millikin University (IL) (w)
Millsaps College (MS) (w)
Mills College (CA) (w)
Milwaukee School of Engineering (WI) (m/w)
Minnesota State University Mankato (MN) (w)
Minnesota State University Moorhead (MN) (w)
Minot State University (ND) (w)
Mississippi College (MS) (w)
Mississippi State University (MS) (w)
Mississippi University for Women (MS) (w)
Mississippi Valley State University (MS) (w)
Missouri Baptist University (MO) (m/w)
Missouri Southern State University (MO) (w)
Missouri Valley College (MO) (m/w)
Missouri Western State College (MO) (w)
Molloy College (NY) (w)
Monmouth College (IL) (w)
Montana State University–Billings (MT) (w)
Montana State University–Bozeman (MT) (w)
Montana State University–Northern (MT) (w)
Montana Tech of The University of Montana (MT) (w)
Montclair State University (NJ) (w)
Montreat College (NC) (w)
Moravian College (PA) (w)
Morehead State University (KY) (w)
Morgan State University (MD) (w)
Morningside College (IA) (w)
Morris College (SC) (w)
Mountain State University (WV) (w)
Mount Holyoke College (MA) (w)
Mount Ida College (MA) (m/w)
Mount Marty College (SD) (w)
Mount Mercy College (IA) (w)
Mount Olive College (NC) (m/w)
Mount Saint Mary College (NY) (w)
Mount Union College (OH) (w)
Mount Vernon Nazarene University (OH) (w)
Muhlenberg College (PA) (w)

Murray State University (KY) (w)
Muskingum College (OH) (w)
National American University (SD) (w)
Nazareth College of Rochester (NY) (w)
Nebraska Wesleyan University (NE) (w)
Neumann College (PA) (w)
Newberry College (SC) (w)
Newbury College (MA) (m/w)
New Jersey City University (NJ) (m/w)
New Jersey Institute of Technology (NJ) (m/w)
Newman University (KS) (m/w)
New Mexico Highlands University (NM) (w)
New Mexico State University (NM) (w)
New York City College of Technology of the City University of New York (NY) (m/w)
New York Institute of Technology (NY) (w)
New York University (NY) (m/w)
Niagara University (NY) (w)
Nicholls State University (LA) (w)
Norfolk State University (VA) (w)
North Carolina Agricultural and Technical State University (NC) (w)
North Carolina Central University (NC) (w)
North Carolina State University (NC) (w)
North Carolina Wesleyan College (NC) (w)
North Central College (IL) (w)
North Dakota State University (ND) (w)
Northeastern University (MA) (w)
Northern Arizona University (AZ) (w)
Northern Illinois University (IL) (w)
Northern Kentucky University (KY) (w)
Northern Michigan University (MI) (w)
Northern State University (SD) (w)
North Greenville College (SC) (w)
Northland College (WI) (w)
North Park University (IL) (w)
Northwest College (WA) (w)
Northwestern College (IA) (w)
Northwestern College (MN) (w)
Northwestern State University of Louisiana (LA) (w)
Northwestern University (IL) (w)
Northwest Missouri State University (MO) (w)
Northwest Nazarene University (ID) (w)
Northwood University (MI) (w)
Northwood University, Florida Campus (FL) (w)
Notre Dame College (OH) (w)
Notre Dame de Namur University (CA) (w)
Nova Southeastern University (FL) (w)
Nyack College (NY) (w)
Oakland City University (IN) (w)
Oakland University (MI) (w)
Oberlin College (OH) (w)
Occidental College (CA) (w)
Oglethorpe University (GA) (w)
Ohio Dominican University (OH) (w)
Ohio Northern University (OH) (w)
The Ohio State University (OH) (m/w)
Ohio University (OH) (w)
Ohio Valley College (WV) (w)
Ohio Wesleyan University (OH) (w)
Oklahoma Wesleyan University (OK) (w)
Olivet College (MI) (w)
Olivet Nazarene University (IL) (w)
Oral Roberts University (OK) (w)
Oregon Institute of Technology (OR) (w)
Oregon State University (OR) (w)
Ottawa University (KS) (w)
Otterbein College (OH) (w)
Ouachita Baptist University (AR) (w)
Pace University (NY) (w)
Pacific Lutheran University (WA) (w)

Pacific Union College (CA) (m/w)
Pacific University (OR) (w)
Paine College (GA) (w)
Park University (MO) (m/w)
Paul Quinn College (TX) (w)
Peace College (NC) (w)
The Pennsylvania State University Altoona
    College (PA) (w)
The Pennsylvania State University at Erie,
    The Behrend College (PA) (w)
The Pennsylvania State University University
    Park Campus (PA) (m/w)
Pepperdine University (CA) (m/w)
Peru State College (NE) (m/w)
Pfeiffer University (NC) (w)
Philadelphia Biblical University (PA) (m/w)
Philadelphia University (PA) (w)
Piedmont College (GA) (w)
Pikeville College (KY) (w)
Pine Manor College (MA) (w)
Pittsburg State University (KS) (w)
Pitzer College (CA) (w)
Plymouth State University (NH) (w)
Point Loma Nazarene University (CA) (w)
Point Park University (PA) (w)
Polytechnic University, Brooklyn Campus
    (NY) (m/w)
Pomona College (CA) (w)
Portland State University (OR) (w)
Prairie View A&M University (TX) (w)
Presbyterian College (SC) (w)
Presentation College (SD) (w)
Princeton University (NJ) (m/w)
Principia College (IL) (w)
Providence College (RI) (w)
Purdue University (IN) (w)
Queens College of the City University of
    New York (NY) (m/w)
Queens University of Charlotte (NC) (w)
Quincy University (IL) (m/w)
Quinnipiac University (CT) (w)
Radford University (VA) (w)
Ramapo College of New Jersey (NJ) (m/w)
Randolph-Macon College (VA) (w)
Randolph-Macon Woman's College (VA) (w)
Regis College (MA) (w)
Regis University (CO) (w)
Reinhardt College (GA) (w)
Rhode Island College (RI) (w)
Rhodes College (TN) (w)
Rice University (TX) (w)
The Richard Stockton College of New Jersey
    (NJ) (w)
Rider University (NJ) (w)
Ripon College (WI) (w)
Rivier College (NH) (m/w)
Roanoke College (VA) (w)
Robert Morris College (IL) (w)
Robert Morris University (PA) (w)
Roberts Wesleyan College (NY) (w)
Rochester Institute of Technology (NY) (w)
Rockford College (IL) (w)
Rockhurst University (MO) (w)
Rocky Mountain College (MT) (w)
Roger Williams University (RI) (m/w)
Rollins College (FL) (w)
Rose-Hulman Institute of Technology (IN)
    (w)
Rosemont College (PA) (w)
Rowan University (NJ) (w)
Russell Sage College (NY) (w)
Rust College (MS) (m/w)
Rutgers, The State University of New Jersey,
    Camden (NJ) (w)

Rutgers, The State University of New Jersey,
    Newark (NJ) (m/w)
Rutgers, The State University of New Jersey,
    New Brunswick/Piscataway (NJ) (w)
Sacred Heart University (CT) (m/w)
Saginaw Valley State University (MI) (w)
St. Ambrose University (IA) (m/w)
St. Andrews Presbyterian College (NC) (w)
Saint Anselm College (NH) (w)
Saint Augustine's College (NC) (w)
St. Cloud State University (MN) (w)
St. Edward's University (TX) (w)
St. Francis College (NY) (w)
Saint Francis University (PA) (m/w)
St. John Fisher College (NY) (w)
St. John's University (NY) (w)
Saint Joseph College (CT) (w)
Saint Joseph's College (IN) (w)
Saint Joseph's College of Maine (ME) (w)
St. Joseph's College, Suffolk Campus (NY)
    (w)
St. Lawrence University (NY) (w)
Saint Leo University (FL) (w)
St. Louis College of Pharmacy (MO) (w)
Saint Louis University (MO) (w)
Saint Martin's College (WA) (w)
Saint Mary's College (IN) (w)
Saint Mary's College of California (CA) (w)
St. Mary's College of Maryland (MD) (w)
Saint Mary's University of Minnesota (MN)
    (w)
St. Mary's University of San Antonio (TX)
    (w)
Saint Michael's College (VT) (w)
St. Norbert College (WI) (w)
St. Olaf College (MN) (w)
Saint Paul's College (VA) (w)
Saint Peter's College (NJ) (w)
St. Thomas Aquinas College (NY) (w)
St. Thomas University (FL) (w)
Saint Xavier University (IL) (w)
Salem International University (WV) (w)
Salem State College (MA) (w)
Salisbury University (MD) (w)
Salve Regina University (RI) (w)
Samford University (AL) (w)
Sam Houston State University (TX) (w)
San Diego State University (CA) (w)
San Francisco State University (CA) (w)
San Jose State University (CA) (w)
Santa Clara University (CA) (w)
Savannah College of Art and Design (GA)
    (w)
Savannah State University (GA) (w)
Schreiner University (TX) (w)
Seattle Pacific University (WA) (w)
Seattle University (WA) (w)
Seton Hall University (NJ) (w)
Seton Hill University (PA) (w)
Shawnee State University (OH) (w)
Shaw University (NC) (w)
Shenandoah University (VA) (w)
Shepherd University (WV) (w)
Shippensburg University of Pennsylvania
    (PA) (w)
Shorter College (GA) (w)
Siena Heights University (MI) (w)
Simmons College (MA) (w)
Simpson College (IA) (w/w)
Si Tanka Huron University (SD) (w)
Skidmore College (NY) (w)
Slippery Rock University of Pennsylvania
    (PA) (w)
Smith College (MA) (w)
Sonoma State University (CA) (w)

South Carolina State University (SC) (w)
South Dakota School of Mines and
    Technology (SD) (w)
South Dakota State University (SD) (w)
Southeastern Louisiana University (LA) (w)
Southeastern Oklahoma State University
    (OK) (w)
Southeast Missouri State University (MO)
    (w)
Southern Arkansas University–Magnolia
    (AR) (w)
Southern Connecticut State University (CT)
    (w)
Southern Illinois University Carbondale (IL)
    (w)
Southern Illinois University Edwardsville (IL)
    (w)
Southern Methodist University (TX) (w)
Southern Nazarene University (OK) (w)
Southern New Hampshire University (NH)
    (w)
Southern Oregon University (OR) (w)
Southern University and Agricultural and
    Mechanical College (LA) (w)
Southern Vermont College (VT) (w)
Southern Virginia University (VA) (w)
Southern Wesleyan University (SC) (w)
Southwest Baptist University (MO) (w)
Southwestern Assemblies of God University
    (TX) (w)
Southwestern College (KS) (w)
Southwestern University (TX) (w)
Southwest Minnesota State University (MN)
    (w)
Southwest Missouri State University (MO)
    (w)
Spalding University (KY) (w)
Spelman College (GA) (w)
Spring Arbor University (MI) (w)
Springfield College (MA) (m/w)
Spring Hill College (AL) (w)
Stanford University (CA) (m/w)
State University of New York at Binghamton
    (NY) (w)
State University of New York at New Paltz
    (NY) (m/w)
State University of New York at Oswego
    (NY) (w)
State University of New York at Plattsburgh
    (NY) (w)
State University of New York College at
    Brockport (NY) (w)
State University of New York College at
    Cortland (NY) (w)
State University of New York College at
    Fredonia (NY) (w)
State University of New York College at
    Geneseo (NY) (w)
State University of New York College at Old
    Westbury (NY) (w)
State University of New York College at
    Oneonta (NY) (w)
State University of New York College at
    Potsdam (NY) (w)
State University of New York College of
    Technology at Delhi (NY) (w)
State University of New York Institute of
    Technology (NY) (w)
State University of New York Maritime
    College (NY) (w)
State University of West Georgia (GA) (w)
Stephen F. Austin State University (TX) (w)
Stephens College (MO) (w)
Sterling College (KS) (w)
Stetson University (FL) (w)

Stevens Institute of Technology (NJ) (m/w)

Stillman College (AL) (w)

Stonehill College (MA) (w)

Stony Brook University, State University of New York (NY) (w)

Suffolk University (MA) (w)

Sul Ross State University (TX) (w)

Susquehanna University (PA) (w)

Swarthmore College (PA) (w)

Sweet Briar College (VA) (w)

Syracuse University (NY) (w)

Tabor College (KS) (w)

Tarleton State University (TX) (w)

Taylor University (IN) (w)

Teikyo Post University (CT) (w)

Temple University (PA) (w)

Tennessee State University (TN) (w)

Tennessee Technological University (TN) (w)

Tennessee Wesleyan College (TN) (w)

Texas A&M International University (TX) (w)

Texas A&M University (TX) (w)

Texas A&M University–Commerce (TX) (w)

Texas A&M University–Corpus Christi (TX) (w)

Texas A&M University–Kingsville (TX) (w)

Texas Christian University (TX) (w)

Texas College (TX) (w)

Texas Lutheran University (TX) (w)

Texas Southern University (TX) (w)

Texas State University-San Marcos (TX) (w)

Texas Tech University (TX) (w)

Texas Wesleyan University (TX) (w)

Texas Woman's University (TX) (w)

Thiel College (PA) (w)

Thomas College (ME) (w)

Thomas More College (KY) (w)

Tiffin University (OH) (w)

Towson University (MD) (w)

Transylvania University (KY) (w)

Trevecca Nazarene University (TN) (w)

Trinity Christian College (IL) (m/w)

Trinity College (CT) (w)

Trinity College (DC) (w)

Trinity International University (IL) (w)

Trinity University (TX) (w)

Tri-State University (IN) (w)

Troy State University (AL) (w)

Truman State University (MO) (w)

Tufts University (MA) (w)

Tulane University (LA) (w)

Tusculum College (TN) (w)

Tuskegee University (AL) (w)

Union College (KY) (w)

Union College (NY) (w)

Union University (TN) (w)

United States Air Force Academy (CO) (w)

United States Coast Guard Academy (CT) (w)

United States Merchant Marine Academy (NY) (w)

United States Military Academy (NY) (w)

United States Naval Academy (MD) (w)

University at Albany, State University of New York (NY) (w)

University at Buffalo, The State University of New York (NY) (w)

The University of Akron (OH) (w)

The University of Alabama (AL) (w)

The University of Alabama at Birmingham (AL) (w)

The University of Alabama in Huntsville (AL) (w)

University of Alaska Anchorage (AK) (w)

University of Alaska Fairbanks (AK) (w)

The University of Arizona (AZ) (w)

University of Arkansas (AR) (w)

University of Arkansas at Little Rock (AR) (w)

University of Arkansas at Pine Bluff (AR) (w)

University of Bridgeport (CT) (w)

University of California, Berkeley (CA) (w)

University of California, Davis (CA) (w)

University of California, Irvine (CA) (m/w)

University of California, Los Angeles (CA) (m/w)

University of California, Riverside (CA) (w)

University of California, San Diego (CA) (m/w)

University of California, Santa Barbara (CA) (m/w)

University of California, Santa Cruz (CA) (m/w)

University of Central Arkansas (AR) (w)

University of Central Florida (FL) (w)

University of Central Oklahoma (OK) (w)

University of Charleston (WV) (w)

University of Chicago (IL) (w)

University of Cincinnati (OH) (w)

University of Colorado at Boulder (CO) (w)

University of Colorado at Colorado Springs (CO) (w)

University of Connecticut (CT) (w)

University of Dallas (TX) (w)

University of Dayton (OH) (w)

University of Delaware (DE) (w)

University of Denver (CO) (w)

University of Dubuque (IA) (w)

University of Evansville (IN) (w)

The University of Findlay (OH) (m/w)

University of Florida (FL) (w)

University of Georgia (GA) (w)

University of Great Falls (MT) (w)

University of Hartford (CT) (w)

University of Hawaii at Hilo (HI) (w)

University of Hawaii at Manoa (HI) (m/w)

University of Houston (TX) (w)

University of Idaho (ID) (w)

University of Illinois at Chicago (IL) (w)

University of Illinois at Springfield (IL) (w)

University of Illinois at Urbana–Champaign (IL) (w)

University of Indianapolis (IN) (w)

The University of Iowa (IA) (w)

University of Kansas (KS) (w)

University of Kentucky (KY) (w)

University of La Verne (CA) (m/w)

University of Louisiana at Lafayette (LA) (w)

University of Louisiana at Monroe (LA) (w)

University of Louisville (KY) (w)

University of Maine (ME) (w)

University of Maine at Farmington (ME) (w)

University of Maine at Machias (ME) (w)

University of Maine at Presque Isle (ME) (w)

University of Mary (ND) (w)

University of Mary Hardin-Baylor (TX) (w)

University of Maryland, Baltimore County (MD) (w)

University of Maryland, College Park (MD) (w)

University of Maryland Eastern Shore (MD) (w)

University of Massachusetts Boston (MA) (w)

University of Massachusetts Dartmouth (MA) (w)

University of Massachusetts Lowell (MA) (w)

The University of Memphis (TN) (w)

University of Miami (FL) (w)

University of Michigan (MI) (w)

University of Michigan–Dearborn (MI) (w)

University of Minnesota, Crookston (MN) (w)

University of Minnesota, Duluth (MN) (w)

University of Minnesota, Morris (MN) (w)

University of Minnesota, Twin Cities Campus (MN) (w)

University of Mississippi (MS) (w)

University of Missouri–Columbia (MO) (w)

University of Missouri–Kansas City (MO) (w)

University of Missouri–St. Louis (MO) (w)

The University of Montana–Missoula (MT) (w)

The University of Montana–Western (MT) (w)

University of Montevallo (AL) (w)

University of Nebraska at Kearney (NE) (w)

University of Nebraska at Omaha (NE) (w)

University of Nebraska–Lincoln (NE) (w)

University of Nevada, Las Vegas (NV) (w)

University of Nevada, Reno (NV) (w)

University of New England (ME) (w)

University of New Hampshire (NH) (w)

University of New Haven (CT) (m/w)

University of New Mexico (NM) (w)

University of New Orleans (LA) (w)

University of North Alabama (AL) (w)

The University of North Carolina at Asheville (NC) (w)

The University of North Carolina at Chapel Hill (NC) (w)

The University of North Carolina at Charlotte (NC) (w)

The University of North Carolina at Greensboro (NC) (w)

The University of North Carolina at Pembroke (NC) (w)

The University of North Carolina at Wilmington (NC) (w)

University of North Dakota (ND) (w)

University of Northern Colorado (CO) (w)

University of Northern Iowa (IA) (w)

University of North Florida (FL) (w)

University of North Texas (TX) (w)

University of Notre Dame (IN) (w)

University of Oklahoma (OK) (w)

University of Oregon (OR) (w)

University of Pennsylvania (PA) (w)

University of Pittsburgh (PA) (w)

University of Pittsburgh at Bradford (PA) (w)

University of Pittsburgh at Greensburg (PA) (w)

University of Pittsburgh at Johnstown (PA) (w)

University of Portland (OR) (w)

University of Puerto Rico at Bayamón (PR) (m/w)

University of Puerto Rico at Humacao (PR) (m/w)

University of Puerto Rico, Cayey University College (PR) (m/w)

University of Puerto Rico, Mayagüez Campus (PR) (m/w)

University of Puerto Rico, Río Piedras (PR) (m/w)

University of Puget Sound (WA) (w)

University of Redlands (CA) (w)

University of Rhode Island (RI) (w)

University of Rio Grande (OH) (w)

University of Rochester (NY) (w)

University of St. Francis (IL) (w)

University of Saint Francis (IN) (w)

University of Saint Mary (KS) (w)

University of St. Thomas (MN) (w)

University of San Diego (CA) (w)
University of San Francisco (CA) (w)
The University of Scranton (PA) (w)
University of Sioux Falls (SD) (w)
University of South Alabama (AL) (w)
University of South Carolina (SC) (w)
University of South Carolina Aiken (SC) (w)
University of South Carolina Spartanburg (SC) (w)
The University of South Dakota (SD) (w)
University of Southern California (CA) (m/w)
University of Southern Indiana (IN) (w)
University of Southern Maine (ME) (w)
University of Southern Mississippi (MS) (w)
University of South Florida (FL) (w)
The University of Tampa (FL) (w)
The University of Tennessee (TN) (w)
The University of Tennessee at Chattanooga (TN) (w)
The University of Tennessee at Martin (TN) (w)
The University of Texas at Arlington (TX) (w)
The University of Texas at Austin (TX) (w)
The University of Texas at Dallas (TX) (w)
The University of Texas at El Paso (TX) (w)
The University of Texas at San Antonio (TX) (w)
The University of Texas of the Permian Basin (TX) (w)
The University of Texas–Pan American (TX) (w)
University of the District of Columbia (DC) (w)
University of the Incarnate Word (TX) (w)
University of the Pacific (CA) (m/w)
University of the Sciences in Philadelphia (PA) (w)
University of the South (TN) (w)
University of Toledo (OH) (w)
University of Tulsa (OK) (w)
University of Utah (UT) (w)
University of Virginia (VA) (w)
The University of Virginia's College at Wise (VA) (w)
University of Washington (WA) (w)
The University of West Alabama (AL) (w)
University of West Florida (FL) (w)
University of Wisconsin–Eau Claire (WI) (w)
University of Wisconsin–Green Bay (WI) (w)
University of Wisconsin–La Crosse (WI) (w)
University of Wisconsin–Madison (WI) (w)
University of Wisconsin–Milwaukee (WI) (w)
University of Wisconsin–Oshkosh (WI) (w)
University of Wisconsin–Parkside (WI) (w)
University of Wisconsin–Platteville (WI) (w)
University of Wisconsin–River Falls (WI) (w)
University of Wisconsin–Stevens Point (WI) (w)
University of Wisconsin–Stout (WI) (w)
University of Wisconsin–Superior (WI) (w)
University of Wisconsin–Whitewater (WI) (w)
University of Wyoming (WY) (w)
Upper Iowa University (IA) (w)
Urbana University (OH) (w)
Ursinus College (PA) (w)
Ursuline College (OH) (w)
Utah State University (UT) (w)
Utica College (NY) (w)
Valdosta State University (GA) (w)
Valley City State University (ND) (w)
Valparaiso University (IN) (w)
Vanguard University of Southern California (CA) (w)

Vassar College (NY) (m/w)
Villa Julie College (MD) (m/w)
Villanova University (PA) (w)
Virginia Commonwealth University (VA) (w)
Virginia Intermont College (VA) (w)
Virginia Polytechnic Institute and State University (VA) (w)
Virginia State University (VA) (w)
Virginia Union University (VA) (w)
Virginia Wesleyan College (VA) (w)
Viterbo University (WI) (w)
Voorhees College (SC) (w)
Wagner College (NY) (w)
Wake Forest University (NC) (w)
Waldorf College (IA) (w)
Walsh University (OH) (w)
Warner Pacific College (OR) (w)
Warner Southern College (FL) (w)
Wartburg College (IA) (w)
Washburn University (KS) (w)
Washington & Jefferson College (PA) (w)
Washington and Lee University (VA) (w)
Washington College (MD) (w)
Washington State University (WA) (w)
Washington University in St. Louis (MO) (w)
Wayland Baptist University (TX) (w)
Waynesburg College (PA) (w)
Wayne State College (NE) (w)
Wayne State University (MI) (w)
Webber International University (FL) (w)
Weber State University (UT) (w)
Webster University (MO) (w)
Wellesley College (MA) (w)
Wentworth Institute of Technology (MA) (m/w)
Wesleyan College (GA) (w)
Wesleyan University (CT) (w)
West Chester University of Pennsylvania (PA) (w)
Western Baptist College (OR) (w)
Western Carolina University (NC) (w)
Western Connecticut State University (CT) (w)
Western Illinois University (IL) (w)
Western Kentucky University (KY) (w)
Western Michigan University (MI) (w)
Western New England College (MA) (w)
Western New Mexico University (NM) (w)
Western Oregon University (OR) (w)
Western State College of Colorado (CO) (w)
Western Washington University (WA) (w)
Westfield State College (MA) (w)
West Liberty State College (WV) (w)
Westminster College (UT) (w)
Westminster College (MO) (w)
Westminster College (PA) (w)
Westmont College (CA) (w)
West Texas A&M University (TX) (w)
West Virginia State College (WV) (w)
West Virginia University (WV) (w)
West Virginia University Institute of Technology (WV) (w)
West Virginia Wesleyan College (WV) (w)
Wheaton College (IL) (w)
Wheaton College (MA) (w)
Wheeling Jesuit University (WV) (w)
Whitman College (WA) (w)
Whittier College (CA) (w)
Whitworth College (WA) (w)
Wichita State University (KS) (w)
Widener University (PA) (w)
Wiley College (TX) (w)
Wilkes University (PA) (w)
Willamette University (OR) (w)
William Jewell College (MO) (w)

William Paterson University of New Jersey (NJ) (w)
William Penn University (IA) (w)
Williams Baptist College (AR) (w)
Williams College (MA) (w)
William Woods University (MO) (m/w)
Wilmington College (DE) (w)
Wilmington College (OH) (w)
Wilson College (PA) (w)
Wingate University (NC) (w)
Winona State University (MN) (w)
Winston-Salem State University (NC) (w)
Winthrop University (SC) (w)
Wisconsin Lutheran College (WI) (w)
Wittenberg University (OH) (w)
Wofford College (SC) (w)
Worcester Polytechnic Institute (MA) (w)
Worcester State College (MA) (w)
Wright State University (OH) (w)
Xavier University (OH) (w)
Xavier University of Louisiana (LA) (w)
Yale University (CT) (w)
Yeshiva University (NY) (m)
York College of Pennsylvania (PA) (w)
York College of the City University of New York (NY) (m/w)
Youngstown State University (OH)(w)

Wrestling

Adams State College (CO) (m)
Albright College (PA) (m)
American International College (MA) (m)
American University (DC) (m)
Anderson College (SC) (m)
Appalachian State University (NC) (m)
Arizona State University (AZ) (m)
Ashland University (OH) (m)
Augsburg College (MN) (m)
Augustana College (IL) (m)
Augustana College (SD) (m)
Bacone College (OK) (m)
Baldwin-Wallace College (OH) (m)
Baptist Bible College of Pennsylvania (PA) (m)
Bethel College (IN) (m)
Bloomsburg University of Pennsylvania (PA) (m)
Boise State University (ID) (m)
Boston University (MA) (m)
Briar Cliff University (IA) (m)
Bridgewater State College (MA) (m)
Brown University (RI) (m)
Buena Vista University (IA) (m)
California Polytechnic State University, San Luis Obispo (CA) (m)
California State University, Bakersfield (CA) (m)
California State University, Fresno (CA) (m)
California State University, Fullerton (CA) (m)
Campbell University (NC) (m)
Carson-Newman College (TN) (m)
Case Western Reserve University (OH) (m)
Centenary College (NJ) (m)
Central College (IA) (m)
Central Michigan University (MI) (m)
Central Missouri State University (MO) (m)
Central Washington University (WA) (m)
Chadron State College (NE) (m)
The Citadel, The Military College of South Carolina (SC) (m)
Clarion University of Pennsylvania (PA) (m)
Cleveland State University (OH) (m)
Coe College (IA) (m)

College of Mount St. Joseph (OH) (m)
The College of New Jersey (NJ) (m)
Colorado School of Mines (CO) (m)
Columbia College (NY) (m)
Concordia College (MN) (m)
Concordia University Wisconsin (WI) (m)
Cornell College (IA) (m)
Cornell University (NY) (m)
Cumberland College (KY) (m)
Cumberland University (TN) (m)
Dakota Wesleyan University (SD) (m)
Dana College (NE) (m)
Davidson College (NC) (m)
Delaware State University (DE) (m)
Delaware Valley College (PA) (m)
Dickinson State University (ND) (m)
Drexel University (PA) (m)
Duke University (NC) (m)
Duquesne University (PA) (m)
Eastern Illinois University (IL) (m)
Eastern Michigan University (MI) (m)
East Stroudsburg University of Pennsylvania
    (PA) (m)
Edinboro University of Pennsylvania (PA)
    (m)
Elizabethtown College (PA) (m)
Elmhurst College (IL) (m)
Embry-Riddle Aeronautical University (AZ)
    (m)
Fort Hays State University (KS) (m)
Franklin and Marshall College (PA) (m)
Gallaudet University (DC) (m)
Gannon University (PA) (m)
Gardner-Webb University (NC) (m)
George Mason University (VA) (m)
Gettysburg College (PA) (m)
Harvard University (MA) (m)
Heidelberg College (OH) (m)
Hofstra University (NY) (m)
Hunter College of the City University of New
    York (NY) (m)
Illinois College (IL) (m)
Indiana University Bloomington (IN) (m)
Iowa State University of Science and
    Technology (IA) (m)
Ithaca College (NY) (m)
James Madison University (VA) (m)
Jamestown College (ND) (m)
John Carroll University (OH) (m)
The Johns Hopkins University (MD) (m)
Johnson & Wales University (RI) (m)
Kent State University (OH) (m)
King's College (PA) (m)
Knox College (IL) (m)
Kutztown University of Pennsylvania (PA)
    (m)
Lakeland College (WI) (m)
Lawrence University (WI) (m)
Lehigh University (PA) (m)
Limestone College (SC) (m)
Lindenwood University (MO) (m)
Lock Haven University of Pennsylvania (PA)
    (m)
Loras College (IA) (m)
Luther College (IA) (m)
Lycoming College (PA) (m)
MacMurray College (IL) (m)
Manchester College (IN) (m)
Maranatha Baptist Bible College (WI) (m)
Massachusetts Institute of Technology (MA)
    (m)
McDaniel College (MD) (m)
McKendree College (IL) (m)
Menlo College (CA) (m)
Mercyhurst College (PA) (m)

Messiah College (PA) (m)
Michigan State University (MI) (m)
Millersville University of Pennsylvania (PA)
    (m)
Millikin University (IL) (m)
Milwaukee School of Engineering (WI) (m)
Minnesota State University Mankato (MN)
    (m)
Minnesota State University Moorhead (MN)
    (m)
Missouri Baptist University (MO) (m)
Missouri Valley College (MO) (m)
Montana State University–Northern (MT)
    (m)
Montclair State University (NJ) (m)
Morningside College (IA) (m)
Mount Union College (OH) (m)
Muhlenberg College (PA) (m)
Muskingum College (OH) (m)
New York University (NY) (m)
North Carolina State University (NC) (m)
North Central College (IL) (m)
North Dakota State University (ND) (m)
Northern Illinois University (IL) (m)
Northern State University (SD) (m)
Northwestern College (IA) (m)
Northwestern University (IL) (m)
Norwich University (VT) (m)
Ohio Northern University (OH) (m)
The Ohio State University (OH) (m)
Ohio University (OH) (m)
Oklahoma State University (OK) (m)
Old Dominion University (VA) (m)
Olivet College (MI) (m)
Oregon State University (OR) (m)
Pacific University (OR) (m)
The Pennsylvania State University University
    Park Campus (PA) (m)
Plymouth State University (NH) (m)
Portland State University (OR) (m)
Princeton University (NJ) (m)
Purdue University (IN) (m)
Rhode Island College (RI) (m)
Rider University (NJ) (m)
Rochester Institute of Technology (NY) (m)
Roger Williams University (RI) (m)
Rose-Hulman Institute of Technology (IN)
    (m)
Rutgers, The State University of New Jersey,
    New Brunswick/Piscataway (NJ) (m)
Sacred Heart University (CT) (m)
St. Cloud State University (MN) (m)
Saint John's University (MN) (m)
St. Olaf College (MN) (m)
San Francisco State University (CA) (m)
Shippensburg University of Pennsylvania
    (PA) (m)
Simpson College (IA) (m)
Si Tanka Huron University (SD) (m)
Slippery Rock University of Pennsylvania
    (PA) (m)
South Dakota State University (SD) (m)
Southern Illinois University Edwardsville (IL)
    (m)
Southern Oregon University (OR) (m)
Southern Virginia University (VA) (m)
Southwest Minnesota State University (MN)
    (m)
Springfield College (MA) (m)
Stanford University (CA) (m)
State University of New York at Binghamton
    (NY) (m)
State University of New York at Oswego
    (NY) (m)

State University of New York College at
    Brockport (NY) (m)
State University of New York College at
    Cortland (NY) (m)
State University of New York College at
    Oneonta (NY) (m)
State University of New York Maritime
    College (NY) (m)
Stevens Institute of Technology (NJ) (m)
Thiel College (PA) (m)
Trinity College (CT) (m)
Truman State University (MO) (m)
United States Air Force Academy (CO) (m)
United States Coast Guard Academy (CT)
    (m)
United States Merchant Marine Academy
    (NY) (m)
United States Military Academy (NY) (m)
United States Naval Academy (MD) (m)
University at Buffalo, The State University of
    New York (NY) (m)
University of California, Davis (CA) (m)
University of Central Oklahoma (OK) (m)
University of Chicago (IL) (m)
University of Dubuque (IA) (m)
The University of Findlay (OH) (m)
University of Illinois at Urbana–Champaign
    (IL) (m)
University of Indianapolis (IN) (m)
The University of Iowa (IA) (m)
University of Mary (ND) (m)
University of Maryland, College Park (MD)
    (m)
University of Michigan (MI) (m)
University of Minnesota, Morris (MN) (m)
University of Minnesota, Twin Cities
    Campus (MN) (m)
University of Missouri–Columbia (MO) (m)
University of Nebraska at Kearney (NE) (m)
University of Nebraska at Omaha (NE) (m)
University of Nebraska–Lincoln (NE) (m)
The University of North Carolina at Chapel
    Hill (NC) (m)
The University of North Carolina at
    Greensboro (NC) (m)
The University of North Carolina at
    Pembroke (NC) (m)
University of Northern Colorado (CO) (m)
University of Northern Iowa (IA) (m)
University of Oklahoma (OK) (m)
University of Oregon (OR) (m)
University of Pennsylvania (PA) (m)
University of Pittsburgh (PA) (m)
University of Pittsburgh at Johnstown (PA)
    (m)
University of Puerto Rico at Bayamón (PR)
    (m)
University of Puerto Rico at Humacao (PR)
    (m)
University of Puerto Rico, Cayey University
    College (PR) (m)
University of Puerto Rico, Mayagüez
    Campus (PR) (m)
University of Puerto Rico, Río Piedras (PR)
    (m)
The University of Scranton (PA) (m)
University of Southern Maine (ME) (m)
The University of Tennessee at Chattanooga
    (TN) (m)
University of Virginia (VA) (m)
University of Wisconsin–Eau Claire (WI) (m)
University of Wisconsin–La Crosse (WI) (m)
University of Wisconsin–Madison (WI) (m)
University of Wisconsin–Oshkosh (WI) (m)
University of Wisconsin–Parkside (WI) (m)

University of Wisconsin–Platteville (WI) (m)
University of Wisconsin–Stevens Point (WI) (m)
University of Wisconsin–Whitewater (WI) (m)
University of Wyoming (WY) (m)
Upper Iowa University (IA) (m)
Ursinus College (PA) (m)
Virginia Military Institute (VA) (m)
Virginia Polytechnic Institute and State University (VA) (m)

Wabash College (IN) (m)
Wagner College (NY) (m)
Waldorf College (IA) (m)
Wartburg College (IA) (m)
Washington & Jefferson College (PA) (m)
Washington and Lee University (VA) (m)
Waynesburg College (PA) (m)
Wesleyan University (CT) (m)
Western New England College (MA) (m)
Western State College of Colorado (CO) (m)

West Liberty State College (WV) (m)
West Virginia University (WV) (m)
Wheaton College (IL) (m)
Wilkes University (PA) (m)
William Penn University (IA) (m)
Williams College (MA) (m)
Wilmington College (OH) (m)
Worcester Polytechnic Institute (MA) (m)
Yeshiva University (NY) (m)
York College of Pennsylvania (PA)

College Athletic Programs by Division

NCAA Division I

Alabama Agricultural and Mechanical University (AL)
Alabama State University (AL)
Alcorn State University (MS)
Alderson-Broaddus College (WV)
American International College (MA)
American University (DC)
Appalachian State University (NC)
Arizona State University (AZ)
Arkansas State University (AR)
Auburn University (AL)
Austin Peay State University (TN)
Ball State University (IN)
Baylor University (TX)
Belmont University (TN)
Bentley College (MA)
Bethune-Cookman College (FL)
Birmingham-Southern College (AL)
Boise State University (ID)
Boston College (MA)
Boston University (MA)
Bowling Green State University (OH)
Bradley University (IL)
Brigham Young University (UT)
Brown University (RI)
Bucknell University (PA)
Butler University (IN)
California Polytechnic State University, San Luis Obispo (CA)
California State University, Fresno (CA)
California State University, Fullerton (CA)
California State University, Long Beach (CA)
California State University, Northridge (CA)
California State University, Sacramento (CA)
Campbell University (NC)
Canisius College (NY)
Centenary College of Louisiana (LA)
Central Connecticut State University (CT)
Central Michigan University (MI)
Charleston Southern University (SC)
Chicago State University (IL)
The Citadel, The Military College of South Carolina (SC)
Clarke College (IA)
Clarkson University (NY)
Clemson University (SC)
Cleveland State University (OH)
Coastal Carolina University (SC)
Colgate University (NY)
College of Charleston (SC)
College of the Holy Cross (MA)
The College of William and Mary (VA)
The Colorado College (CO)
Colorado State University (CO)
Columbia College (NY)
Coppin State University (MD)
Cornell University (NY)
Creighton University (NE)

Dartmouth College (NH)
Davidson College (NC)
Delaware State University (DE)
DePaul University (IL)
Drake University (IA)
Drexel University (PA)
Drury University (MO)
Duke University (NC)
Duquesne University (PA)
East Carolina University (NC)
Eastern Illinois University (IL)
Eastern Kentucky University (KY)
Eastern Michigan University (MI)
Eastern Washington University (WA)
East Tennessee State University (TN)
Elon University (NC)
Fairfield University (CT)
Florida Agricultural and Mechanical University (FL)
Florida Atlantic University (FL)
Florida International University (FL)
Florida State University (FL)
Fordham University (NY)
Furman University (SC)
Gardner-Webb University (NC)
George Mason University (VA)
Georgetown University (DC)
The George Washington University (DC)
Georgia Institute of Technology (GA)
Georgia Southern University (GA)
Georgia State University (GA)
Gonzaga University (WA)
Grambling State University (LA)
Hampton University (VA)
Hartwick College (NY)
Harvard University (MA)
High Point University (NC)
Hobart and William Smith Colleges (NY)
Hofstra University (NY)
Howard University (DC)
Idaho State University (ID)
Illinois State University (IL)
Indiana State University (IN)
Indiana University Bloomington (IN)
Indiana University–Purdue University Fort Wayne (IN)
Indiana University–Purdue University Indianapolis (IN)
Iona College (NY)
Iowa State University of Science and Technology (IA)
Jackson State University (MS)
Jacksonville State University (AL)
Jacksonville University (FL)
James Madison University (VA)
The Johns Hopkins University (MD)
Kansas State University (KS)
Kent State University (OH)
Lafayette College (PA)
Lamar University (TX)

La Salle University (PA)
Lehigh University (PA)
Lewis University (IL)
Liberty University (VA)
Lipscomb University (TN)
Long Island University, Brooklyn Campus (NY)
Louisiana State University and Agricultural and Mechanical College (LA)
Louisiana Tech University (LA)
Loyola College in Maryland (MD)
Loyola Marymount University (CA)
Loyola University Chicago (IL)
Manhattan College (NY)
Marist College (NY)
Marquette University (WI)
Marshall University (WV)
McNeese State University (LA)
Mercer University (GA)
Mercyhurst College (PA)
Miami University (OH)
Michigan State University (MI)
Michigan Technological University (MI)
Middle Tennessee State University (TN)
Minnesota State University Mankato (MN)
Mississippi State University (MS)
Mississippi Valley State University (MS)
Monmouth University (NJ)
Montana State University–Bozeman (MT)
Morehead State University (KY)
Morgan State University (MD)
Mount Saint Mary's University (MD)
Murray State University (KY)
New Mexico State University (NM)
Niagara University (NY)
Nicholls State University (LA)
Norfolk State University (VA)
North Carolina Agricultural and Technical State University (NC)
North Carolina State University (NC)
Northeastern University (MA)
Northern Arizona University (AZ)
Northern Illinois University (IL)
Northern Michigan University (MI)
Northwestern State University of Louisiana (LA)
Northwestern University (IL)
Oakland University (MI)
The Ohio State University (OH)
Ohio University (OH)
Oklahoma State University (OK)
Old Dominion University (VA)
Oral Roberts University (OK)
Oregon State University (OR)
The Pennsylvania State University University Park Campus (PA)
Pepperdine University (CA)
Philadelphia University (PA)
Portland State University (OR)
Prairie View A&M University (TX)

Princeton University (NJ)
Providence College (RI)
Purdue University (IN)
Quincy University (IL)
Quinnipiac University (CT)
Radford University (VA)
Rensselaer Polytechnic Institute (NY)
Rice University (TX)
Rider University (NJ)
Robert Morris University (PA)
Rutgers, The State University of New Jersey, Newark (NJ)
Rutgers, The State University of New Jersey, New Brunswick/Piscataway (NJ)
Sacred Heart University (CT)
St. Bonaventure University (NY)
St. Cloud State University (MN)
St. Francis College (NY)
Saint Francis University (PA)
St. John's University (NY)
Saint Joseph's University (PA)
St. Lawrence University (NY)
Saint Louis University (MO)
Saint Mary's College of California (CA)
Saint Peter's College (NJ)
Samford University (AL)
Sam Houston State University (TX)
San Diego State University (CA)
San Jose State University (CA)
Santa Clara University (CA)
Seton Hall University (NJ)
Siena College (NY)
South Carolina State University (SC)
Southeastern Louisiana University (LA)
Southeast Missouri State University (MO)
Southern Illinois University Carbondale (IL)
Southern Methodist University (TX)
Southern University and Agricultural and Mechanical College (LA)
Southern Utah University (UT)
Southwest Missouri State University (MO)
Stanford University (CA)
State University of New York at Binghamton (NY)
State University of New York College at Oneonta (NY)
Stephen F. Austin State University (TX)
Stetson University (FL)
Stony Brook University, State University of New York (NY)
Syracuse University (NY)
Temple University (PA)
Tennessee State University (TN)
Tennessee Technological University (TN)
Texas A&M University (TX)
Texas A&M University–Corpus Christi (TX)
Texas Christian University (TX)
Texas Southern University (TX)
Texas State University-San Marcos (TX)
Texas Tech University (TX)
Towson University (MD)
Troy State University (AL)
Tulane University (LA)
United States Air Force Academy (CO)
United States Military Academy (NY)
United States Naval Academy (MD)
University at Albany, State University of New York (NY)
University at Buffalo, The State University of New York (NY)
The University of Akron (OH)
The University of Alabama (AL)
The University of Alabama at Birmingham (AL)

The University of Alabama in Huntsville (AL)
University of Alaska Anchorage (AK)
University of Alaska Fairbanks (AK)
The University of Arizona (AZ)
University of Arkansas (AR)
University of Arkansas at Little Rock (AR)
University of Arkansas at Pine Bluff (AR)
University of California, Berkeley (CA)
University of California, Irvine (CA)
University of California, Los Angeles (CA)
University of California, Riverside (CA)
University of California, Santa Barbara (CA)
University of Central Florida (FL)
University of Cincinnati (OH)
University of Colorado at Boulder (CO)
University of Connecticut (CT)
University of Dayton (OH)
University of Delaware (DE)
University of Denver (CO)
University of Detroit Mercy (MI)
University of Evansville (IN)
The University of Findlay (OH)
University of Florida (FL)
University of Georgia (GA)
University of Hartford (CT)
University of Hawaii at Manoa (HI)
University of Houston (TX)
University of Idaho (ID)
University of Illinois at Chicago (IL)
University of Illinois at Urbana–Champaign (IL)
The University of Iowa (IA)
University of Kansas (KS)
University of Kentucky (KY)
University of Louisiana at Lafayette (LA)
University of Louisiana at Monroe (LA)
University of Louisville (KY)
University of Maine (ME)
University of Maryland, Baltimore County (MD)
University of Maryland, College Park (MD)
University of Maryland Eastern Shore (MD)
University of Massachusetts Amherst (MA)
University of Massachusetts Lowell (MA)
The University of Memphis (TN)
University of Miami (FL)
University of Michigan (MI)
University of Minnesota, Twin Cities Campus (MN)
University of Mississippi (MS)
University of Missouri–Columbia (MO)
University of Missouri–Kansas City (MO)
The University of Montana–Missoula (MT)
University of Nebraska–Lincoln (NE)
University of Nevada, Las Vegas (NV)
University of Nevada, Reno (NV)
University of New Hampshire (NH)
University of New Mexico (NM)
University of New Orleans (LA)
The University of North Carolina at Asheville (NC)
The University of North Carolina at Chapel Hill (NC)
The University of North Carolina at Charlotte (NC)
The University of North Carolina at Greensboro (NC)
The University of North Carolina at Wilmington (NC)
University of North Dakota (ND)
University of Northern Iowa (IA)
University of North Texas (TX)
University of Notre Dame (IN)
University of Oklahoma (OK)

University of Oregon (OR)
University of Pennsylvania (PA)
University of Pittsburgh (PA)
University of Portland (OR)
University of Rhode Island (RI)
University of Richmond (VA)
University of San Diego (CA)
University of San Francisco (CA)
University of South Alabama (AL)
University of South Carolina (SC)
University of Southern California (CA)
University of Southern Mississippi (MS)
University of South Florida (FL)
The University of Tennessee (TN)
The University of Tennessee at Chattanooga (TN)
The University of Tennessee at Martin (TN)
The University of Texas at Arlington (TX)
The University of Texas at Austin (TX)
The University of Texas at El Paso (TX)
The University of Texas at San Antonio (TX)
The University of Texas–Pan American (TX)
University of the Pacific (CA)
University of Toledo (OH)
University of Tulsa (OK)
University of Utah (UT)
University of Vermont (VT)
University of Virginia (VA)
University of Washington (WA)
University of Wisconsin–Green Bay (WI)
University of Wisconsin–Madison (WI)
University of Wisconsin–Milwaukee (WI)
University of Wyoming (WY)
Utah State University (UT)
Valparaiso University (IN)
Vanderbilt University (TN)
Villanova University (PA)
Virginia Commonwealth University (VA)
Virginia Military Institute (VA)
Virginia Polytechnic Institute and State University (VA)
Wagner College (NY)
Wake Forest University (NC)
Washington State University (WA)
Wayne State University (MI)
Weber State University (UT)
West Chester University of Pennsylvania (PA)
Western Carolina University (NC)
Western Illinois University (IL)
Western Kentucky University (KY)
Western Michigan University (MI)
West Virginia University (WV)
Wichita State University (KS)
Winthrop University (SC)
Wofford College (SC)
Wright State University (OH)
Xavier University (OH)
Yale University (CT)
Youngstown State University (OH)

NCAA Division II

Abilene Christian University (TX)
Adams State College (CO)
Adelphi University (NY)
Albany State University (GA)
Alderson-Broaddus College (WV)
American International College (MA)
Anderson College (SC)
Angelo State University (TX)
Arkansas Tech University (AR)
Armstrong Atlantic State University (GA)
Ashland University (OH)
Assumption College (MA)
Augustana College (SD)

Augusta State University (GA)
Barry University (FL)
Barton College (NC)
Bellarmine University (KY)
Belmont Abbey College (NC)
Bemidji State University (MN)
Benedict College (SC)
Bentley College (MA)
Bloomfield College (NJ)
Bloomsburg University of Pennsylvania (PA)
Bluefield State College (WV)
Bowie State University (MD)
Brigham Young University–Hawaii (HI)
Bryant College (RI)
Caldwell College (NJ)
California State Polytechnic University, Pomona (CA)
California State University, Bakersfield (CA)
California State University, Chico (CA)
California State University, Dominguez Hills (CA)
California State University, Los Angeles (CA)
California State University, San Bernardino (CA)
California State University, Stanislaus (CA)
California University of Pennsylvania (PA)
Cameron University (OK)
Carson-Newman College (TN)
Catawba College (NC)
Central Missouri State University (MO)
Central Washington University (WA)
Chadron State College (NE)
Chaminade University of Honolulu (HI)
Cheyney University of Pennsylvania (PA)
Christian Brothers University (TN)
Clarion University of Pennsylvania (PA)
Clark Atlanta University (GA)
Clayton College & State University (GA)
Coker College (SC)
College of Charleston (SC)
The College of Saint Rose (NY)
Colorado Christian University (CO)
Colorado School of Mines (CO)
Colorado State University-Pueblo (CO)
Columbia Union College (MD)
Columbus State University (GA)
Concord College (WV)
Concordia College (NY)
Concordia University, St. Paul (MN)
Converse College (SC)
Dallas Baptist University (TX)
Davis & Elkins College (WV)
Delta State University (MS)
Dominican College (NY)
Dowling College (NY)
Drury University (MO)
East Central University (OK)
Eastern New Mexico University (NM)
East Stroudsburg University of Pennsylvania (PA)
Eckerd College (FL)
Edinboro University of Pennsylvania (PA)
Elizabeth City State University (NC)
Emerson College (MA)
Emporia State University (KS)
Erskine College (SC)
Fairmont State University (WV)
Fayetteville State University (NC)
Felician College (NJ)
Ferris State University (MI)
Florida Gulf Coast University (FL)
Florida Institute of Technology (FL)
Florida Southern College (FL)
Fort Hays State University (KS)
Fort Lewis College (CO)

Fort Valley State University (GA)
Francis Marion University (SC)
Franklin Pierce College (NH)
Gannon University (PA)
Georgia College & State University (GA)
Georgian Court University (NJ)
Glenville State College (WV)
Goldey-Beacom College (DE)
Grand Canyon University (AZ)
Grand Valley State University (MI)
Green Mountain College (VT)
Harding University (AR)
Haverford College (PA)
Hawai'i Pacific University (HI)
Henderson State University (AR)
Hillsdale College (MI)
Holy Family University (PA)
Humboldt State University (CA)
Indiana University of Pennsylvania (PA)
Indiana University–Purdue University Fort Wayne (IN)
Johnson C. Smith University (NC)
Kennesaw State University (GA)
Kentucky State University (KY)
Kentucky Wesleyan College (KY)
Kutztown University of Pennsylvania (PA)
Lake Superior State University (MI)
Lander University (SC)
Lane College (TN)
Lees-McRae College (NC)
Le Moyne College (NY)
LeMoyne-Owen College (TN)
Lenoir-Rhyne College (NC)
Lewis University (IL)
Limestone College (SC)
Lincoln Memorial University (TN)
Lincoln University (MO)
Livingstone College (NC)
Lock Haven University of Pennsylvania (PA)
Long Island University, C.W. Post Campus (NY)
Long Island University, Southampton College (NY)
Longwood University (VA)
Lynn University (FL)
Mansfield University of Pennsylvania (PA)
Mars Hill College (NC)
Mercy College (NY)
Mercyhurst College (PA)
Merrimack College (MA)
Mesa State College (CO)
Metropolitan State College of Denver (CO)
Michigan Technological University (MI)
Midwestern State University (TX)
Miles College (AL)
Millersville University of Pennsylvania (PA)
Minnesota State University Mankato (MN)
Minnesota State University Moorhead (MN)
Mississippi University for Women (MS)
Missouri Southern State University (MO)
Missouri Western State College (MO)
Molloy College (NY)
Montana State University–Billings (MT)
Morehouse College (GA)
Mount Olive College (NC)
Newberry College (SC)
New Jersey Institute of Technology (NJ)
New Mexico Highlands University (NM)
New York Institute of Technology (NY)
North Carolina Central University (NC)
North Dakota State University (ND)
Northeastern State University (OK)
Northern Kentucky University (KY)
Northern Michigan University (MI)
Northern State University (SD)

North Greenville College (SC)
Northwest Missouri State University (MO)
Northwest Nazarene University (ID)
Northwood University (MI)
Nova Southeastern University (FL)
Nyack College (NY)
Oakland City University (IN)
Ohio Valley College (WV)
Oklahoma Panhandle State University (OK)
Ouachita Baptist University (AR)
Pace University (NY)
Paine College (GA)
Pfeiffer University (NC)
Philadelphia University (PA)
Pittsburg State University (KS)
Presbyterian College (SC)
Queens College of the City University of New York (NY)
Queens University of Charlotte (NC)
Quincy University (IL)
Regis University (CO)
Rockhurst University (MO)
Rollins College (FL)
Saginaw Valley State University (MI)
St. Andrews Presbyterian College (NC)
Saint Anselm College (NH)
Saint Augustine's College (NC)
St. Cloud State University (MN)
St. Edward's University (TX)
Saint Joseph's College (IN)
Saint Leo University (FL)
Saint Martin's College (WA)
St. Mary's University of San Antonio (TX)
Saint Michael's College (VT)
Saint Paul's College (VA)
St. Thomas Aquinas College (NY)
Salem International University (WV)
San Francisco State University (CA)
Savannah State University (GA)
Seattle Pacific University (WA)
Seattle University (WA)
Shaw University (NC)
Shepherd University (WV)
Shippensburg University of Pennsylvania (PA)
Slippery Rock University of Pennsylvania (PA)
Sonoma State University (CA)
South Dakota State University (SD)
Southeastern Oklahoma State University (OK)
Southern Arkansas University–Magnolia (AR)
Southern Connecticut State University (CT)
Southern Illinois University Edwardsville (IL)
Southern New Hampshire University (NH)
Southwest Baptist University (MO)
Southwestern Oklahoma State University (OK)
Southwest Minnesota State University (MN)
State University of West Georgia (GA)
Stonehill College (MA)
Tarleton State University (TX)
Teikyo Post University (CT)
Texas A&M University–Commerce (TX)
Texas A&M University–Kingsville (TX)
Texas Woman's University (TX)
Truman State University (MO)
Tusculum College (TN)
Tuskegee University (AL)
The University of Alabama in Huntsville (AL)
University of Alaska Anchorage (AK)
University of Alaska Fairbanks (AK)
University of Arkansas at Monticello (AR)

University of Bridgeport (CT)
University of California, Davis (CA)
University of California, San Diego (CA)
University of Central Arkansas (AR)
University of Central Oklahoma (OK)
University of Charleston (WV)
University of Colorado at Colorado Springs
  (CO)
The University of Findlay (OH)
University of Hawaii at Hilo (HI)
University of Indianapolis (IN)
University of Massachusetts Lowell (MA)
University of Minnesota, Crookston (MN)
University of Minnesota, Duluth (MN)
University of Minnesota, Morris (MN)
University of Missouri–Rolla (MO)
University of Missouri–St. Louis (MO)
University of Montevallo (AL)
University of Nebraska at Kearney (NE)
University of Nebraska at Omaha (NE)
University of New Haven (CT)
University of North Alabama (AL)
The University of North Carolina at
  Pembroke (NC)
University of North Dakota (ND)
University of Northern Colorado (CO)
University of North Florida (FL)
University of Pittsburgh at Johnstown (PA)
University of Puerto Rico at Bayamón (PR)
University of Puerto Rico at Humacao (PR)
University of Puerto Rico, Cayey University
  College (PR)
University of Puerto Rico, Mayagüez
  Campus (PR)
University of Puerto Rico, Río Piedras (PR)
University of South Carolina Aiken (SC)
University of South Carolina Spartanburg
  (SC)
The University of South Dakota (SD)
University of Southern Indiana (IN)
The University of Tampa (FL)
University of the District of Columbia (DC)
University of the Incarnate Word (TX)
The University of West Alabama (AL)
University of West Florida (FL)
University of Wisconsin–Parkside (WI)
Valdosta State University (GA)
Virginia State University (VA)
Virginia Union University (VA)
Washburn University (KS)
Wayne State College (NE)
Wayne State University (MI)
West Chester University of Pennsylvania (PA)
Western New Mexico University (NM)
Western Oregon University (OR)
Western State College of Colorado (CO)
Western Washington University (WA)
West Liberty State College (WV)
Westminster College (PA)
West Texas A&M University (TX)
West Virginia State College (WV)
West Virginia University Institute of
  Technology (WV)
West Virginia Wesleyan College (WV)
Wheeling Jesuit University (WV)
Wilmington College (DE)
Wingate University (NC)
Winona State University (MN)
Winston-Salem State University (NC)

NCAA Division III
Adrian College (MI)
Agnes Scott College (GA)
Albertus Magnus College (CT)

Albion College (MI)
Albright College (PA)
Alfred University (NY)
Allegheny College (PA)
Alma College (MI)
Alvernia College (PA)
Alverno College (WI)
Amherst College (MA)
Anderson University (IN)
Anna Maria College (MA)
Arcadia University (PA)
Augsburg College (MN)
Augustana College (IL)
Aurora University (IL)
Austin College (TX)
Averett University (VA)
Babson College (MA)
Baldwin-Wallace College (OH)
Baptist Bible College of Pennsylvania (PA)
Bard College (NY)
Bates College (ME)
Bay Path College (MA)
Beloit College (WI)
Benedictine University (IL)
Bennett College (NC)
Bernard M. Baruch College of the City
  University of New York (NY)
Bethany College (WV)
Bethel University (MN)
Blackburn College (IL)
Bluffton College (OH)
Bowdoin College (ME)
Brandeis University (MA)
Bridgewater College (VA)
Bridgewater State College (MA)
Brooklyn College of the City University of
  New York (NY)
Bryn Mawr College (PA)
Buena Vista University (IA)
Buffalo State College, State University of
  New York (NY)
Cabrini College (PA)
California Institute of Technology (CA)
California Lutheran University (CA)
California State University, Hayward (CA)
Calvin College (MI)
Capital University (OH)
Carleton College (MN)
Carnegie Mellon University (PA)
Carroll College (WI)
Carthage College (WI)
Case Western Reserve University (OH)
Castleton State College (VT)
The Catholic University of America (DC)
Cazenovia College (NY)
Cedar Crest College (PA)
Centenary College (NJ)
Central College (IA)
Centre College (KY)
Chapman University (CA)
Chatham College (PA)
Chestnut Hill College (PA)
Chowan College (NC)
Christopher Newport University (VA)
City College of the City University of New
  York (NY)
Claremont McKenna College (CA)
Clarke College (IA)
Clarkson University (NY)
Clark University (MA)
Coe College (IA)
Colby College (ME)
Colby-Sawyer College (NH)
College Misericordia (PA)
College of Mount St. Joseph (OH)

College of Mount Saint Vincent (NY)
The College of New Jersey (NJ)
The College of New Rochelle (NY)
College of Notre Dame of Maryland (MD)
College of Saint Benedict (MN)
College of St. Catherine (MN)
College of Saint Elizabeth (NJ)
The College of St. Scholastica (MN)
College of Staten Island of the City University
  of New York (NY)
The College of Wooster (OH)
The Colorado College (CO)
Concordia College (MN)
Concordia University (IL)
Concordia University at Austin (TX)
Concordia University Wisconsin (WI)
Connecticut College (CT)
Cornell College (IA)
Curry College (MA)
Daniel Webster College (NH)
Defiance College (OH)
Delaware Valley College (PA)
Denison University (OH)
DePauw University (IN)
DeSales University (PA)
Dickinson College (PA)
Dominican University (IL)
Drew University (NJ)
D'Youville College (NY)
Earlham College (IN)
Eastern Connecticut State University (CT)
Eastern Mennonite University (VA)
Eastern Nazarene College (MA)
Eastern University (PA)
East Texas Baptist University (TX)
Edgewood College (WI)
Elizabethtown College (PA)
Elmhurst College (IL)
Elmira College (NY)
Elms College (MA)
Emerson College (MA)
Emmanuel College (MA)
Emory & Henry College (VA)
Emory University (GA)
Endicott College (MA)
Eureka College (IL)
Fairleigh Dickinson University, College at
  Florham (NJ)
Farmingdale State University of New York
  (NY)
Ferrum College (VA)
Fisk University (TN)
Fitchburg State College (MA)
Fontbonne University (MO)
Framingham State College (MA)
Franklin and Marshall College (PA)
Franklin College (IN)
Frostburg State University (MD)
Gallaudet University (DC)
George Fox University (OR)
Gettysburg College (PA)
Gordon College (MA)
Goucher College (MD)
Greensboro College (NC)
Greenville College (IL)
Grinnell College (IA)
Grove City College (PA)
Guilford College (NC)
Gustavus Adolphus College (MN)
Gwynedd-Mercy College (PA)
Hamilton College (NY)
Hamline University (MN)
Hampden-Sydney College (VA)
Hanover College (IN)
Hardin-Simmons University (TX)

Hartwick College (NY)
Heidelberg College (OH)
Hendrix College (AR)
Hilbert College (NY)
Hiram College (OH)
Hobart and William Smith Colleges (NY)
Hollins University (VA)
Hood College (MD)
Hope College (MI)
Howard Payne University (TX)
Hunter College of the City University of New York (NY)
Huntingdon College (AL)
Husson College (ME)
Illinois College (IL)
Illinois Wesleyan University (IL)
Immaculata University (PA)
Ithaca College (NY)
John Carroll University (OH)
John Jay College of Criminal Justice of the City University of New York (NY)
The Johns Hopkins University (MD)
Johnson & Wales University (RI)
Johnson State College (VT)
Juniata College (PA)
Kalamazoo College (MI)
Kean University (NJ)
Keene State College (NH)
Kenyon College (OH)
Keuka College (NY)
King's College (PA)
Knox College (IL)
LaGrange College (GA)
Lake Erie College (OH)
Lake Forest College (IL)
Lakeland College (WI)
La Roche College (PA)
Lasell College (MA)
Lawrence University (WI)
Lebanon Valley College (PA)
Lehman College of the City University of New York (NY)
Le Moyne College (NY)
Lesley University (MA)
LeTourneau University (TX)
Lewis & Clark College (OR)
Lincoln University (PA)
Linfield College (OR)
Loras College (IA)
Louisiana College (LA)
Luther College (IA)
Lycoming College (PA)
Lynchburg College (VA)
Macalester College (MN)
MacMurray College (IL)
Maine Maritime Academy (ME)
Manchester College (IN)
Manhattanville College (NY)
Maranatha Baptist Bible College (WI)
Marian College of Fond du Lac (WI)
Marietta College (OH)
Martin Luther College (MN)
Mary Baldwin College (VA)
Marymount University (VA)
Maryville College (TN)
Maryville University of Saint Louis (MO)
University of Mary Washington (VA)
Marywood University (PA)
Massachusetts College of Liberal Arts (MA)
Massachusetts Institute of Technology (MA)
Massachusetts Maritime Academy (MA)
McDaniel College (MD)
McMurry University (TX)
Medaille College (NY)

Medgar Evers College of the City University of New York (NY)
Menlo College (CA)
Meredith College (NC)
Messiah College (PA)
Methodist College (NC)
Middlebury College (VT)
Millikin University (IL)
Millsaps College (MS)
Mills College (CA)
Milwaukee School of Engineering (WI)
Mississippi College (MS)
Monmouth College (IL)
Montclair State University (NJ)
Moravian College (PA)
Mount Holyoke College (MA)
Mount Ida College (MA)
Mount Saint Mary College (NY)
Mount Union College (OH)
Muhlenberg College (PA)
Muskingum College (OH)
Nazareth College of Rochester (NY)
Nebraska Wesleyan University (NE)
Neumann College (PA)
Newbury College (MA)
New England College (NH)
New Jersey City University (NJ)
New York City College of Technology of the City University of New York (NY)
New York University (NY)
Nichols College (MA)
North Carolina Wesleyan College (NC)
North Central College (IL)
Northland College (WI)
North Park University (IL)
Norwich University (VT)
Oberlin College (OH)
Occidental College (CA)
Oglethorpe University (GA)
Ohio Northern University (OH)
Ohio Wesleyan University (OH)
Olivet College (MI)
Otterbein College (OH)
Pacific Lutheran University (WA)
Pacific University (OR)
Peace College (NC)
The Pennsylvania State University Altoona College (PA)
The Pennsylvania State University at Erie, The Behrend College (PA)
Philadelphia Biblical University (PA)
Piedmont College (GA)
Pine Manor College (MA)
Pitzer College (CA)
Plymouth State University (NH)
Polytechnic University, Brooklyn Campus (NY)
Pomona College (CA)
Principia College (IL)
Ramapo College of New Jersey (NJ)
Randolph-Macon College (VA)
Randolph-Macon Woman's College (VA)
Regis College (MA)
Rensselaer Polytechnic Institute (NY)
Rhode Island College (RI)
Rhodes College (TN)
The Richard Stockton College of New Jersey (NJ)
Ripon College (WI)
Rivier College (NH)
Roanoke College (VA)
Rochester Institute of Technology (NY)
Rockford College (IL)
Roger Williams University (RI)
Rose-Hulman Institute of Technology (IN)

Rosemont College (PA)
Rowan University (NJ)
Russell Sage College (NY)
Rust College (MS)
Rutgers, The State University of New Jersey, Camden (NJ)
Rutgers, The State University of New Jersey, Newark (NJ)
St. John Fisher College (NY)
Saint John's University (MN)
Saint Joseph College (CT)
Saint Joseph's College of Maine (ME)
St. Joseph's College, Suffolk Campus (NY)
St. Lawrence University (NY)
Saint Mary's College (IN)
St. Mary's College of Maryland (MD)
Saint Mary's University of Minnesota (MN)
St. Norbert College (WI)
St. Olaf College (MN)
Salem State College (MA)
Salisbury University (MD)
Salve Regina University (RI)
Schreiner University (TX)
Shenandoah University (VA)
Simmons College (MA)
Simpson College (IA)
Skidmore College (NY)
Smith College (MA)
Southern Vermont College (VT)
Southwestern University (TX)
Spelman College (GA)
Springfield College (MA)
State University of New York at New Paltz (NY)
State University of New York at Oswego (NY)
State University of New York at Plattsburgh (NY)
State University of New York College at Brockport (NY)
State University of New York College at Cortland (NY)
State University of New York College at Fredonia (NY)
State University of New York College at Geneseo (NY)
State University of New York College at Old Westbury (NY)
State University of New York College at Oneonta (NY)
State University of New York College at Potsdam (NY)
State University of New York Institute of Technology (NY)
State University of New York Maritime College (NY)
Stephens College (MO)
Stevens Institute of Technology (NJ)
Stillman College (AL)
Suffolk University (MA)
Sul Ross State University (TX)
Susquehanna University (PA)
Swarthmore College (PA)
Sweet Briar College (VA)
Texas Lutheran University (TX)
Thiel College (PA)
Thomas College (ME)
Thomas More College (KY)
Transylvania University (KY)
Trinity College (CT)
Trinity College (DC)
Trinity University (TX)
Tufts University (MA)
Union College (NY)
United States Coast Guard Academy (CT)

United States Merchant Marine Academy (NY)
University of California, Santa Cruz (CA)
University of Chicago (IL)
University of Dallas (TX)
University of Dubuque (IA)
University of La Verne (CA)
University of Maine at Farmington (ME)
University of Mary Hardin-Baylor (TX)
University of Massachusetts Boston (MA)
University of Massachusetts Dartmouth (MA)
University of New England (ME)
University of Pittsburgh at Bradford (PA)
University of Pittsburgh at Greensburg (PA)
University of Puget Sound (WA)
University of Redlands (CA)
University of Rochester (NY)
University of St. Thomas (MN)
The University of Scranton (PA)
University of Southern Maine (ME)
The University of Texas at Dallas (TX)
University of the Ozarks (AR)
University of the South (TN)
University of Wisconsin–Eau Claire (WI)
University of Wisconsin–La Crosse (WI)
University of Wisconsin–Oshkosh (WI)
University of Wisconsin–Platteville (WI)
University of Wisconsin–River Falls (WI)
University of Wisconsin–Stevens Point (WI)
University of Wisconsin–Stout (WI)
University of Wisconsin–Superior (WI)
University of Wisconsin–Whitewater (WI)
Upper Iowa University (IA)
Ursinus College (PA)
Utica College (NY)
Vassar College (NY)
Villa Julie College (MD)
Virginia Wesleyan College (VA)
Wabash College (IN)
Wartburg College (IA)
Washington & Jefferson College (PA)
Washington and Lee University (VA)
Washington College (MD)
Washington University in St. Louis (MO)
Waynesburg College (PA)
Webster University (MO)
Wellesley College (MA)
Wells College (NY)
Wentworth Institute of Technology (MA)
Wesleyan College (GA)
Wesleyan University (CT)
Wesley College (DE)
Western Connecticut State University (CT)
Western New England College (MA)
Westfield State College (MA)
Westminster College (MO)
Wheaton College (IL)
Wheaton College (MA)
Wheelock College (MA)
Whitman College (WA)
Whittier College (CA)
Whitworth College (WA)
Widener University (PA)
Wilkes University (PA)
Willamette University (OR)
William Paterson University of New Jersey (NJ)
Williams College (MA)
Wilmington College (OH)
Wilson College (PA)
Wisconsin Lutheran College (WI)
Wittenberg University (OH)
Worcester Polytechnic Institute (MA)
Worcester State College (MA)

Yeshiva University (NY)
York College of Pennsylvania (PA)
York College of the City University of New York (NY)

NAIA

Albertson College of Idaho (ID)
Alice Lloyd College (KY)
Allen University (SC)
Alliant International University (CA)
Aquinas College (MI)
Asbury College (KY)
Athens State University (AL)
Atlanta Christian College (GA)
Auburn University Montgomery (AL)
Avila University (MO)
Azusa Pacific University (CA)
Bacone College (OK)
Baker University (KS)
Barber-Scotia College (NC)
Belhaven College (MS)
Bellevue University (NE)
Benedictine College (KS)
Berea College (KY)
Berry College (GA)
Bethany College (KS)
Bethany College of the Assemblies of God (CA)
Bethel College (IN)
Bethel College (KS)
Bethel College (TN)
Biola University (CA)
Black Hills State University (SD)
Bluefield College (VA)
Blue Mountain College (MS)
Brenau University (GA)
Brescia University (KY)
Brevard College (NC)
Brewton-Parker College (GA)
Briar Cliff University (IA)
Bryan College (TN)
California Baptist University (CA)
California Maritime Academy (CA)
California State University, Hayward (CA)
California State University, Monterey Bay (CA)
California State University, San Marcos (CA)
Calumet College of Saint Joseph (IN)
Campbellsville University (KY)
Cardinal Stritch University (WI)
Carlow College (PA)
Carroll College (MT)
Cascade College (OR)
Castleton State College (VT)
Cedarville University (OH)
Central Christian College of Kansas (KS)
Central Methodist College (MO)
Christian Heritage College (CA)
Claflin University (SC)
College of St. Joseph (VT)
College of Saint Mary (NE)
College of Santa Fe (NM)
College of the Ozarks (MO)
College of the Southwest (NM)
Columbia College (MO)
Columbia College (SC)
Concordia University (CA)
Concordia University (MI)
Concordia University (NE)
Concordia University (OR)
Cornerstone University (MI)
Covenant College (GA)
Crown College (MN)
Culver-Stockton College (MO)

Cumberland College (KY)
Cumberland University (TN)
Daemen College (NY)
Dakota State University (SD)
Dakota Wesleyan University (SD)
Dana College (NE)
Davenport University (MI)
Dickinson State University (ND)
Dillard University (LA)
Doane College (NE)
Dominican University of California (CA)
Dordt College (IA)
Eastern Oregon University (OR)
Edward Waters College (FL)
Embry-Riddle Aeronautical University (AZ)
Embry-Riddle Aeronautical University (FL)
Emmanuel College (GA)
Evangel University (MO)
The Evergreen State College (WA)
Faulkner University (AL)
Fisher College (MA)
Flagler College (FL)
Florida Memorial College (FL)
The Franciscan University (IA)
Freed-Hardeman University (TN)
Fresno Pacific University (CA)
Friends University (KS)
Geneva College (PA)
Georgetown College (KY)
Georgia Southwestern State University (GA)
Goshen College (IN)
Grace College (IN)
Graceland University (IA)
Grand View College (IA)
Hannibal-LaGrange College (MO)
Harris-Stowe State College (MO)
Haskell Indian Nations University (KS)
Hastings College (NE)
Holy Names University (CA)
Hope International University (CA)
Houghton College (NY)
Houston Baptist University (TX)
Huntington College (IN)
Husson College (ME)
Huston-Tillotson College (TX)
Illinois Institute of Technology (IL)
Indiana Institute of Technology (IN)
Indiana University Northwest (IN)
Indiana University South Bend (IN)
Indiana University Southeast (IN)
Indiana Wesleyan University (IN)
Iowa Wesleyan College (IA)
Jamestown College (ND)
Jarvis Christian College (TX)
John Brown University (AR)
Johnson & Wales University (CO)
Johnson & Wales University (FL)
Judson College (IL)
Kansas Wesleyan University (KS)
Kendall College (IL)
King College (TN)
Lambuth University (TN)
Langston University (OK)
Lee University (TN)
Lewis-Clark State College (ID)
Lindenwood University (MO)
Lindsey Wilson College (KY)
Louisiana State University in Shreveport (LA)
Loyola University New Orleans (LA)
Lubbock Christian University (TX)
Lyndon State College (VT)
Lyon College (AR)
Madonna University (MI)
Malone College (OH)
Marian College (IN)

Martin Methodist College (TN)
The Master's College and Seminary (CA)
Mayville State University (ND)
McKendree College (IL)
McPherson College (KS)
Menlo College (CA)
MidAmerica Nazarene University (KS)
Mid-Continent College (KY)
Midland Lutheran College (NE)
Midway College (KY)
Milligan College (TN)
Mills College (CA)
Minot State University (ND)
Missouri Baptist University (MO)
Missouri Valley College (MO)
Montana State University–Northern (MT)
Montana Tech of The University of Montana (MT)
Montreat College (NC)
Morningside College (IA)
Morris College (SC)
Mountain State University (WV)
Mount Marty College (SD)
Mount Mercy College (IA)
Mount Vernon Nazarene University (OH)
National American University (SD)
Nebraska Wesleyan University (NE)
Newman University (KS)
North Georgia College & State University (GA)
Northwest College (WA)
Northwestern College (IA)
Northwestern College (MN)
Northwestern Oklahoma State University (OK)
Northwood University, Florida Campus (FL)
Northwood University, Texas Campus (TX)
Notre Dame College (OH)
Notre Dame de Namur University (CA)
Ohio Dominican University (OH)
Oklahoma Baptist University (OK)
Oklahoma Christian University (OK)
Oklahoma City University (OK)
Oklahoma Wesleyan University (OK)
Olivet Nazarene University (IL)
Oregon Institute of Technology (OR)
Ottawa University (KS)
Pacific Union College (CA)
Park University (MO)
Patten University (CA)
Paul Quinn College (TX)
Peru State College (NE)

Pikeville College (KY)
Point Loma Nazarene University (CA)
Point Park University (PA)
Presentation College (SD)
Purdue University Calumet (IN)
Purdue University North Central (IN)
Reinhardt College (GA)
Robert Morris College (IL)
Roberts Wesleyan College (NY)
Rocky Mountain College (MT)
St. Ambrose University (IA)
St. Gregory's University (OK)
St. Louis College of Pharmacy (MO)
St. Thomas University (FL)
Saint Vincent College (PA)
Saint Xavier University (IL)
Savannah College of Art and Design (GA)
Seton Hill University (PA)
Shawnee State University (OH)
Shorter College (GA)
Siena Heights University (MI)
Simpson College (IA)
Si Tanka Huron University (SD)
South Dakota School of Mines and Technology (SD)
Southern Nazarene University (OK)
Southern Oregon University (OR)
Southern Polytechnic State University (GA)
Southern University at New Orleans (LA)
Southern Virginia University (VA)
Southern Wesleyan University (SC)
Southwestern Assemblies of God University (TX)
Southwestern College (KS)
Spalding University (KY)
Spring Arbor University (MI)
Spring Hill College (AL)
State University of New York College of Technology at Delhi (NY)
Sterling College (KS)
Tabor College (KS)
Taylor University (IN)
Tennessee Wesleyan College (TN)
Texas A&M International University (TX)
Texas College (TX)
Texas Wesleyan University (TX)
Thomas University (GA)
Tiffin University (OH)
Tougaloo College (MS)
Trevecca Nazarene University (TN)
Trinity Christian College (IL)
Trinity International University (IL)

Tri-State University (IN)
Union College (KY)
Union University (TN)
University of Great Falls (MT)
University of Illinois at Springfield (IL)
University of Maine at Fort Kent (ME)
University of Maine at Machias (ME)
University of Maine at Presque Isle (ME)
University of Mary (ND)
University of Michigan–Dearborn (MI)
University of Mobile (AL)
The University of Montana–Western (MT)
University of Rio Grande (OH)
University of St. Francis (IL)
University of Saint Francis (IN)
University of Saint Mary (KS)
University of Science and Arts of Oklahoma (OK)
University of Sioux Falls (SD)
The University of Texas of the Permian Basin (TX)
University of the Sciences in Philadelphia (PA)
The University of Virginia's College at Wise (VA)
Urbana University (OH)
Ursuline College (OH)
Valley City State University (ND)
Vanguard University of Southern California (CA)
Virginia Intermont College (VA)
Viterbo University (WI)
Voorhees College (SC)
Waldorf College (IA)
Walsh University (OH)
Warner Pacific College (OR)
Warner Southern College (FL)
Wayland Baptist University (TX)
Webber International University (FL)
Western Baptist College (OR)
Westminster College (UT)
Westmont College (CA)
Wilberforce University (OH)
Wiley College (TX)
William Carey College (MS)
William Jewell College (MO)
William Penn University (IA)
Williams Baptist College (AR)
William Woods University (MO)
Xavier University of Louisiana (LA)
York College (NE)